Routledge Encyclopedia of PHILOSOPHY

General Editor
EDWARD CRAIG

London and New York

First published 1998
by Routledge
11 New Fetter Lane, London EC4P 4EE
Simultaneously published in the USA and Canada
by Routledge
29 West 35th Street, New York, NY 10001

©1998 Routledge

Typeset in Monotype Times New Roman by
Routledge

Printed in England by
T J International Ltd, Padstow, Cornwall, England

Printed on acid-free paper which conforms to ANS1.Z39, 48-1992 and ISO 9706 standards

All rights reserved. No part of this book may be reprinted or
reproduced or utilized in any form or by any electronic,
mechanical, or other means, now known or hereafter
invented, including photocopying and recording, or in any
information storage or retrieval system, without permission in
writing from the publishers.

British Library Cataloguing-in-Publication Data
A catalogue record for this book is available from the British Library

The Library of Congress Cataloguing-in-Publication data is given in volume 10.

ISBN: 0415-07310-3 (10-volume set)
ISBN: 0415-18706-0 (volume 1)
ISBN: 0415-18707-9 (volume 2)
ISBN: 0415-18708-7 (volume 3)
ISBN: 0415-18709-5 (volume 4)
ISBN: 0415-18710-9 (volume 5)
ISBN: 0415-18711-7 (volume 6)
ISBN: 0415-18712-5 (volume 7)
ISBN: 0415-18713-3 (volume 8)
ISBN: 0415-18714-1 (volume 9)
ISBN: 0415-18715-X (volume 10)

ISBN: 0415-16916-X (CD-ROM)
ISBN: 0415-16917-8 (10-volume set and CD-ROM)

Contents

General Editor's preface and acknowledgements
Publisher's acknowledgements
Editorial Board
Routledge team
Using the *Encyclopedia*
List of entries and contributors

Volume 1	A posteriori – Bradwardine, Thomas
Volume 2	Brahman – Derrida, Jacques
Volume 3	Descartes, René – Gender and science
Volume 4	Genealogy – Iqbal, Muhammad
Volume 5	Irigaray, Luce – Lushi chunqiu
Volume 6	Luther, Martin – Nifo, Agostino
Volume 7	Nihilism – Quantum mechanics, interpretation of
Volume 8	Questions – Sociobiology
Volume 9	Sociology of knowledge – Zoroastrianism
Volume 10	List of contributors and entries
	Using the index
	Index
	List of permission acknowledgements

General Editor's preface and acknowledgements

After extensive market research in Britain and the USA involving groups of librarians, students and academics, work on the *Routledge Encyclopedia of Philosophy* began in earnest in April 1991. The first task was the recruitment of Subject Editors, and happily this immediately gave us encouraging signs of the prestige which the project has turned out to enjoy within the profession. In spite of the intensive and long-term commitment implied, it proved gratifyingly easy to assemble an excellent team – fewer than two invitations, on average, led to an acceptance.

The Subject Editors were each asked to submit, within certain guidelines, the list of headwords (and attached word-lengths) which they judged appropriate to cover their area of specialization. These lists were compared with each other and some adjustments made; later, in response to further market research, we extended the coverage, adding two more Subject Editors to the team. Commissioning of the original list was by then in progress; we asked authors to work to a widely staggered set of deadlines so as to generate a reasonably paced flow of editorial work. The first entry to be completed and accepted reached the publisher in December 1992; it was *Belinskii* by Viktor Terras, destined to wait nearly six years for publication. It is sad, but inevitable, that those many authors who dutifully stuck to what they knew to be very early deadlines have been those who have had to wait longest for the final request to update their bibliographies. We are especially grateful to them; they saved us from bottlenecks of nightmarish dimensions in the later stages. Without their conscientiousness, the *Routledge Encyclopedia of Philosophy* would have achieved the rare and dubious distinction of being published a millenium later than planned.

Statistical milestones came and went with a reassuring regularity. We had 10% of the text in by spring 1994, 40% by 1995, over 70% by 1996, and by the beginning of 1997 it was clear that, barring a rash of defections, we were going to get very close indeed to 100% delivery. And so it turned out: by the time the icy rigours of the production schedule closed in on us, all but three of our planned entries had been safely gathered in. Furthermore, we were on schedule, give or take a month. In 1994 I had written, in an article in the *Times Literary Supplement*:

> ...the idea that over twelve hundred authors, thirty subject editors, a chief editor, and a publisher's copy-editing, indexing and production teams, each depending on the others in reverse order, will deliver nearly two thousand entries, five million words of text, plus bibliographies, in a print and electronic version right on time...is bound to produce a twinge of doubt in those given to believing that there is any uniformity in nature.

Reasonable enough, one might think. But in the event the scepticism proved unjustified – and this in spite of my underestimate of the number of entries that would finally be involved. One source of inspiration, beyond doubt, was the evident interest of the numerous librarians who regularly kept us up to the mark with inquiries about our timetable.

The middle years of work on the *Encyclopedia* were not exactly incident-free. There was the case of the draft entry which was eaten by its owner's dog – 'don't get jam on your typescripts' is apparently the lesson we should all learn. There was the contributor who, asked for an entry of 5,000 words, sent in some 18,000 words with the remark that the Subject Editor might like to cut it down a bit – I still wonder from time to time what lesson we should learn from that.

Then there was the gunfight at the San Fernando Valley Post Office. I quote from a contributor's email message to one of our copy-editors:

> Please let me know when you receive the materials. I posted them about 8am at the San Fernando Valley Chandler Post Office. About 9am a couple of gunmen burst into a bank nearby and a major shootout ensued – Ah! Life in the Old West. Though I assume no problems, check the package for bullet holes.

The pioneering spirit, it seems, still lives. We hope and believe that the discerning user will be able to detect some of it in the *Routledge Encyclopedia of Philosophy*.

Meanwhile, intensive work was in progress on the CD-ROM version. It had long been intended that there would be an electronic as well as a traditional print version. In view of the hectic pace of change both in technology and publishing practice, the policy was to delay any irrevocable decision about the details until the very last moment, which turned out to be as late as November 1996. But although the electronic version can be said to have the shorter past, it will probably have the longer future: being relatively simple to update, it could well be the ancestor of a long line of subsequent editions.

* * *

Planning of the *Routledge Encyclopedia of Philosophy* began against the background of a single constraint: the project was to be completable, with available means, within a reasonable time-span. The grounds for this were partly economic, but only partly. Since there was no other reason to offer a successor to the justly famous *Encyclopedia of Philosophy*, edited by Paul Edwards for Macmillan and The Free Press, other than the fact that it had become in a number of respects out of date, it would have made little sense to replace it by a project of such proportions as to go out of date itself during the period of production. We allowed ourselves a maximum of eight years, later reduced to seven-and-a-half, from appointment of the General Editor to publication. This of course suggested advisable constraints on size. It was the firm intention that within these limits our *Encyclopedia* should be as inclusive as possible.

The first thing to be included was full and detailed coverage of philosophy as understood by the Anglo-American academic mainstream. One commercial and one intellectual consideration made this mandatory. First, any project of this size must aim to satisfy its principal market; and second, so much of what belongs to the English-speaking philosophical mainstream belongs to it by well-established right – no encyclopedia of philosophy worthy of the name could possibly fail to cover it extensively. But here the inclusivist policy got off to a good start, for by the 1990s the mainstream itself had become a much broader river than it had been twenty or thirty years before, when a narrowly focused jet might have been a more appropriate image. It was also far less clear where the banks were, and we were glad not to have to concern ourselves with that question. In the 1960s philosophy felt fairly sure of its business and its boundaries; in the 1990s it does not have the same confidence (though it does not lack individual confident voices), and a clear mark of this is a greater tendency to look around, historically and geographically, to see what the others are doing. An editorial policy that was unwilling to reflect the growing pluralism would be widely held to have imposed far too much of itself on the material.

The clearest beneficiary of this policy has been what is increasingly called 'world' philosophy. Chinese, Japanese and Korean, Indian and Tibetan, Jewish, Arabic and Islamic, Russian, Latin American and African philosophy have between them 400 entries. We believe that the user of the *Encyclopedia* can gain a thorough grounding in the philosophy of any of these regions. Someone seeking a firm foothold in Buddhist philosophy will find themselves as well served as those looking for philosophical logic. Readers with an interest in Western metaphysics are invited to pursue their interests to India. Back in Europe, but equally suspect to many mainstreamers: the devotee of later twentieth-century French thought will find their interests well catered for. In all these cases, we believe, we have provided more topics, more detail, and more bibliographical information than any previous general encyclopedia of philosophy.

It is one thing to be inclusive, another to ensure proper treatment for everything one includes. Our strategy was that Subject Editors should provide a perspective on their own area that practitioners within it could at least recognize, and preferably identify with, and therefore that they should have the space, the words and the number of entries to do so. A number of these areas are ones to which the Anglo-American mainstream has assigned little importance. We wanted to minimize the effect of this on the coverage of the outlying areas: the periphery was not to be kept peripheral by being presented as it appears from the centre. By far the main influence on the shaping of each area was to be someone for whom that area was the centre of their academic life. This was one of our reasons for adopting the more complex editorial structure, with a layer of specialist Subject Editors taking decisions about headwords, word-counts and commissioning, though keeping in touch with a General Editor while doing so, rather than having a Chief Editor acting with the help of specialist advisers. Another reason, of course, was the thought that one makes better use of the available expertise by bringing it to bear directly, than by applying it via a less expert intermediary.

One possible disadvantage of the Subject Editor system is the problem of mutual communication. In earlier years it might have been very serious, but email is a wonderful instrument for this kind of work, especially when reinforced by the fax machine. The more serious worry nowadays is that one may divide the subject matter up in ways which, although they have some underlying rationale, also introduce certain arbitrary divisions – worse, they may confirm such divisions by making use of classifications which the academic world has historically blundered into.

Our response to this worry was to see it not so much as a threat as an opportunity. In so far as compartmentalization is a threat, it threatens the whole business of academic philosophy, not just the *Routledge Encyclopedia of Philosophy*. And the production of an encyclopedia is one of the rare opportunities to do something towards breaking the barriers down. The first and most obvious move is to present the results in alphabetical order of headword, rather than in subject-oriented volumes. The second, which we have followed throughout, is to keep Subject Editors aware of related activity in neighbouring sections. Many Subject Editors have been in contact with others on an almost day-to-day basis – nothing could be further from the truth than to think of this *Encyclopedia* as the sum of the separate work of some thirty isolated units, all stirred in together after each had finished. We see no reason to fear that a reader who wishes to pursue some general theme across several of the standard academic boundaries will find the ride a bumpy one. Besides, in our approach to cross-referencing between entries the encouragement of their type of enterprise was always one of our aims.

Certain differences between the work of different Subject Editors may, of course, remain. But those that do are not undesirable, so long as they arise directly out of differences of content. We required all authors to adopt a certain format (which the reader will quickly recognize), and have worked hard to ensure consistency in this respect, as also in more detailed matters of copy-editing; we encouraged continuous lines of thought in connected prose, rather than staccato, telegraphic gobbets of information; we looked for authors who would give us positive and sympathetic, though not necessarily uncritical treatment of their topics. But we judged that, apart from this, meddling would do more harm than good. We made no attempt, for example, to enforce a policy that material should be divided up into more, shorter entries, rather than integrated into fewer, longer ones, let alone to try to make mathematical logicians sound like sinologists.

An encyclopedia cannot replace a library. But it can enable its users to get the most from their library, by providing clear and informative bibliographies with each entry. Thinking in particular of the less experienced reader, we have asked authors to provide a brief comment to accompany each item, indicating such things as its content, its level of difficulty, its position in the debate about the topic of the entry. Where an item itself contains a good and extended bibliography of the topic, we have asked that it be indicated as doing so. Our aim throughout has been to build the most convenient bridge possible between the *Routledge Encyclopedia of Philosophy* and the rest of the vast corpus of philosophical literature.

A further challenge has been to provide a work that will be valuable to a very wide range of users, from beginners making their first acquaintance with philosophy, to professional colleagues doing what one might call routine maintenance work on one of their favourite areas; from a full-time student sitting down to a new topic with two or three clear days ahead of them, to someone wanting a quick outline in five minutes. It was with this variety of use and user in mind that we decided upon the dual structure which users will find in each entry: first a short section giving essential information, written where at all possible in a relatively undemanding way; then the main entry, going into much more detail and expecting a somewhat more experienced reader.

It has been the greatest pleasure to have had Paul Edwards as an adviser and a contributor. His *Encyclopedia of Philosophy* may now be a little out of date, but only, we would stress, in certain respects. Thirty years on, it is still the inevitable first point of comparison, and the most natural question to ask about the present work is: what does it provide that Edwards didn't?

In claiming greater inclusiveness we make no suggestion that Edwards ignored a mass of available material. It may seem an obvious plan for an encyclopedia to cover previously uncovered ground, or to cover thinly sketched-in areas in much greater detail. So it is, but equally obviously an authoritative encyclopedia needs expert authors; it cannot go where nobody has gone, only try to expose to the attention of the many the fact that a few have gone there. So our broadened and deepened coverage of previously 'off-road' countryside is a record of the way in which philosophy itself has changed its outlook over the last thirty years, and could not have been achieved unless that change had preceded it. There has been more intensive historical research, more of the world has appeared on the philosophers' map. One might instance the way in which central thinkers of the nineteenth century, such as Hegel, Marx, Nietzsche and Schopenhauer, Schleiermacher and Peirce are now more seriously and more frequently studied, and an increasing interest in idealism has led to the rediscovery of Schelling, Bradley, Royce and others.

In medieval philosophy, to select just one more instance from several, the discovery and editing of texts has brought about a rapid expansion in range and depth of knowledge. In a few cases results of recent research are published in the *Routledge Encyclopedia of Philosophy* for the first time.

It is not just a matter of new topics; some of the

GENERAL EDITOR'S PREFACE AND ACKNOWLEDGEMENTS

traditional areas of concern have undergone extensive change. The philosophy of mind, for example, has been greatly affected by the rise of 'cognitive science', the investigation of the mind from the point of view of psychology, linguistics, neurophysiology and computer science. Advances in the latter have gone along with, in part emerged out of, the creation of a new annexe to mathematical logic, computability theory. The philosophy of language is almost a new subject, transformed by the effects of the new linguistics on the one hand and on the other by a flood of specialized work on the theory of meaning, semantics and pragmatics, much of it barely in its infancy in the 1960s. A quick way to catch the flavour is to note that the index of the previous encyclopedia (published in 1967) directs the user to just one brief appearance of Kripke, one of Grice (in connection with Quine's attack on the analytic/synthetic distinction), and records no mention of Donald Davidson. Epistemologists may well try to look up 'Gettier'. It isn't there. One easily forgets how recent is so much that we now take for granted – or perhaps we are just slow to realize how long thirty years can be in philosophy.

Neither ethics nor political philosophy was flourishing then. Ethics usually meant meta-ethics in one subjectivist guise or another. The traditional Platonic discussion of how we ought to live was largely in abeyance; the revival of interest in Kantian ethics, or in virtue ethics, lay in the future. 'Applied ethics' was scarcely part of the philosophical vocabulary; yet here we are able to present two dozen separate entries on topics in it, maybe a handful more depending on where one draws the borderlines. Political philosophy has also acquired new momentum. The work of John Rawls attracted attention to theories of justice; more recently, focus has shifted to liberalism and its relation to communitarianism, and also the issues concerning citizenship raised by multiculturalism and feminism. There has been more interchange between Anglo-American and French and German thought, as there has also been in ethics.

The mention of feminism brings us to another of the most prominent developments of the last three decades. In one, perhaps its most important, sense feminism has of course existed for a very long time indeed, but as an academic subject with numerous specialized areas and the internal debate characteristic of a branch of philosophy it is quite recent, as anyone perusing earlier encyclopedias will quickly discover. The *Routledge Encyclopedia of Philosophy* contains numerous entries devoted to feminism, plus entries on a number of writers included for their contribution to feminist thought.

Then there is Postcolonialism, and Post-structuralism, and Deconstruction and Postmodernism; and on top of all those another generation or so of eminent philosophers to be chronicled. But still these are only examples of what is new since Paul Edwards' contributors finished their work; one could go on for some time in the same vein. I have to confess to being surprised at the magnitude of the changes in philosophy since my early acquaintance with it in the sixties. I began as General Editor in the frame of mind that things had changed a bit, enough at any rate to warrant the production of a new encyclopedia. One of the many things I have learnt is how gross an underestimate that was. More inviting now is the other extreme. The great old landmarks are still there, as they presumably always will be; but it has to be admitted that many of them look quite different – consider for instance Hume or Hegel today, and the Hume or Hegel of three decades ago. Around and among them, much of the scene is hardly recognizable.

* * *

It will surprise nobody to hear that acting as General Editor of the *Routledge Encyclopedia of Philosophy* has been hard work. Very occasionally – since, even though General Editors are chosen with this sort of thing in mind, it could hardly be expected that one person would have equal interest in every entry, every bibliography of the 2,054 – it has been a little monotonous. From time to time, and briefly, it has been somewhat irritating. But always, and predominantly, it has been a very great pleasure. When on the point of accepting the post I was warned, by friends with some experience of what they were talking about, that it might prove almost intolerable. They were right – it *might* have done – as I can now clearly see. That it has in fact turned out so enjoyable and rewarding is due to three institutions: the Philosophy Faculty of the University of Cambridge, Churchill College, and the publishers – and any number of individuals within them and without. It is no easy task to thank any of them properly, let alone all. (For if anyone should keep within their word-limit, then surely the General Editor.)

That charity begins at home is unlikely to be true; if it were, it would not be said so often. But gratitude, at least in this case, begins at home: to my wife Gillian, who added her voice to my reasons for taking on the Editorship, and has since supported me, with great patience, through some seven years of only partially foreseeable consequences. Not very far from home (less than ten minutes walk), Churchill College could hardly have been more helpful if its very *raison d'être* had been the promotion of philosophy. In allowing me to lighten my teaching duties at one or two crucial junctures, in providing computing

GENERAL EDITOR'S PREFACE AND ACKNOWLEDGEMENTS

assistance, in its cooperation over secretarial arrangements, in its willingness to tie my occupancy of a large office to my work on the *Encyclopedia* rather than to anything I was doing for the College itself, in all these ways and more it has been as supportive as could well be imagined. I hope it may long be proud to have been the cradle of the *Routledge Encyclopedia of Philosophy*; if so, it has certainly earned the right. The help of four people in particular compels mention: our computer officers Hilary Stobart and Richard Dexter, our librarian Mary Kendall, and most of all Wendy Elner, who so cheerfully and flexibly did the secretarial work, to the very end, from soon after the very beginning. My thanks to the guardians of our Porters' Lodge, who run the College postal service and dealt uncomplainingly with a substantial extra load over several years; also to all those who helped sustain morale by showing interest during casual conversation.

Of the many factors which have made this work rewarding, perhaps the main one is the deepened and broadened contact with other areas of philosophy, and more importantly still with the colleagues who specialize in them. In saying this I am thinking of the Subject Editors, with whom it has been a great privilege to collaborate, of the huge cohort of authors who gave their time and energy to the project, and of the much smaller, unfortunately unnameable, group who acted as referees and did much essential work in the assessment, and from time to time improvement, of entries. All constantly impressed us by the extent of their expertise; the appreciation and encouragement many of them so kindly expressed was a more valuable tonic, one suspects, than they realized.

Finally, there are the staff of Routledge. Their names are listed elsewhere in this volume, but it cannot be said there what talents they brought to the job, nor how hard they worked, nor how much overtime they put in, nor with what goodwill they laboured, nor what excellent colleagues they have been for these past seven years. So let it be said here, clearly and gratefully, that the *Routledge Encyclopedia of Philosophy* is as much their triumph as anyone's.

EDWARD CRAIG

Publisher's acknowledgements

We are deeply indebted to Edward Craig and the team of Subject Editors for their unfailing commitment, enthusiasm and dedication. We could not have hoped for a better, more cooperative team and the *Routledge Encyclopedia of Philosophy* is a testament to its excellence. While all were exceptional colleagues, a special thank you must go to those who helped in difficult times: to Oliver Leaman for his work on Jewish philosophy and to John Worrall for taking over the Philosophy of Science in the vital, final stages.

Approximately thirteen hundred philosophers from six continents contributed to the *Routledge Encyclopedia of Philosophy*. Over 99% of the commissioned authors wrote and delivered their entries; rarely have authors shown such commitment to a reference work, not only in producing the work in a timely way but in the consistently high standard of writing.

The role librarians have played in developing the *Routledge Encyclopedia of Philosophy* cannot be underestimated. Librarians from the UK, the USA and from Europe participated in testing the idea of a new encyclopedia of philosophy, gave feedback on the style and content of sample entries, and commented extensively on electronic media and the needs of libraries. This advice has been central to our plans. We cannot thank everyone by name but we would especially like to thank the librarians – from numerous college, public and specialist libraries – who attended our focus groups in London, Manchester and New York, and at the American Library Association conferences over many fruitful years.

Finally, the *Routledge Encyclopedia of Philosophy* is the product of countless individuals and organizations who have given their time and energy and without whom it would not have been published. We would especially like to acknowledge, and say thank you, to:

Betty Andrews, Robert Audi, Frederick Beiser, Jay M. Bernstein, Ned Block, George Boolos, Ian Boyd, Jordi Cat, Simon Christmas, Churchill College Cambridge, Brendan Cohen, Lorraine Code, Gillian Craig, Anthony S. Cua, Database Publishing Systems Ltd, Michael Devitt, Paul Edwards, Wendy Elner, Daniel Garber, David L. Hall, Nancy Hall Davenport, M.A. Higton, David Hull, Sarah Hutton, Indexing Specialists Ltd, InterMedia Graphic Systems Ltd, P.J. Ivanhoe, Thomas P. Kasulis, Mark Kavanagh, Christine Korsgaard, Thomas Lennon, Jerrold Levinson, Charles Löhr, Ian Maclean, Jonathan Maskit, Brian Marshall, Carl Maycock, David McCarty, Vann McGee, Elizabeth McKenzie, Mulholland Research Associates, Steven Nadler, Karen Neander, Richard Neville, Eileen O'Neill, Alex Oliver, Margaret Osler, Gavin Paisley, John Paler, Joseph Pearson, Michael Potter, Henry Rosemont Jr, William Ruddick, Thomas Scanlon, Jerome B. Schneewind, Malcolm Schofield, Michael Slote, Timothy Smiley, Richard Sorabji, Tom Sorrell, Simon Thompson, Judith Vandervelde, Mary Ellen Waithe, Theo Verbeek, Steve White-Hart and Jan Williams.

Editorial Board

GENERAL EDITOR

Edward Craig
General Editor and Subject Editor for metaphysics
Reader in Modern Philosophy, University of Cambridge, and Fellow of Churchill College, Cambridge, UK

Dr Edward Craig has held visiting appointments at the Universities of Bayreuth, Hamburg, Heidelberg and Melbourne, and a visiting Professorship at the Indian Institute of Advanced Studies. He works on the history of philosophy in the modern period and on the theory of knowledge. His main publications are *David Hume: eine Einführung in seine Philosophie* (Klostermann, 1979), *The Mind of God and the Works of Man* (Oxford University Press, 1987) and *Knowledge and the State of Nature* (Oxford University Press, 1990). He was elected a Fellow of the British Academy in 1993. He is the Knightbridge Professor-elect at the University of Cambridge and will take up his post in October 1998.

SUBJECT EDITORS

Roger T. Ames
Chinese, Japanese and Korean philosophy
Professor of Philosophy and Director of the Center for Chinese Studies at the University of Hawaii, USA

Professor Ames is editor of *Philosophy East and West* and *China Review International*. His recent publications include translations of Chinese classics: *Sun-tzu: The Art of Warfare* (Ballantine, 1993), *Sun Pin: The Art of Warfare* (Ballantine, 1996) and *Tracing Dao to its Source* (1997) (both with D.C. Lau); and the *Confucian Analects* (with H. Rosemont) (1998). He has also written many interpretive studies of Chinese philosophy and culture: *Thinking Through Confucius* (SUNY Press, 1987), *Anticipating China: Thinking Through the Narratives of Chinese and Western Culture* (SUNY Press, 1995) and *Thinking from the Han: Self, Truth, and Transcendence in Chinese and Western Culture* (SUNY Press, 1997) (all with D.L. Hall).

Kwame Anthony Appiah
African philosophy
Professor of Afro-American Studies and Chair of Philosophy, Harvard University, USA

Professor Appiah was raised in Ghana and educated at the University of Cambridge in England. He is the author of *Assertion and Conditionals* (Cambridge University Press, 1985), *For Truth in Semantics* (Blackwell, 1986), *In My Father's House: Africa in the Philosophy of Culture* (Oxford University Press, 1992) and (with Amy Gutmann) of *Color Conscious: The Political Morality of Race* (Princeton University Press, 1996). He is working with his mother, the novelist and folklorist Peggy Appiah, on a translation and interpretation of 7,500 Akan proverbs from Ghana.

E.J. Ashworth
Renaissance philosophy
Professor of Philosophy, University of Waterloo, Canada

Professor Ashworth read history at Girton College, Cambridge, before going to the USA, where she received her Ph.D. in philosophy from Bryn Mawr College. She has taught in Canada since 1964. She is the author of many books and articles on medieval and Renaissance logic and philosophy of language; and she contributed to both the *Cambridge History of Later Medieval Philosophy* (Cambridge University Press, 1982) and the *Cambridge History of Renaissance Philosophy* (Cambridge University Press, 1988).

Michael R. Ayers
Seventeenth-century philosophers
Professor of Philosophy, University of Oxford, and Fellow of Wadham College, Oxford, UK

Professor Ayers was educated at St John's College, Cambridge. His many publications, both interpretive and critical, on the history of philosophy include *Locke: Epistemology and Ontology* (2 vols, Routledge, 1991). He is co-editor of the *Cambridge History of Seventeenth-Century Philosophy* (Cambridge University Press, 1988).

EDITORIAL BOARD

Thomas Baldwin
Twentieth-century philosophers
Professor of Philosophy at the University of York, UK

Until recently Professor Baldwin was a Fellow of Clare College, Cambridge, and a Lecturer in Philosophy at the University of Cambridge. He has also taught at Makerere University in Uganda. His publications include *G.E. Moore* in the 'Arguments of the Philosophers' series (Routledge, 1990) and he has edited new editions of some of Moore's writings, including *Principia Ethica* (Cambridge University Press, 1993). He is also the author of numerous articles in metaphysics and the philosophy of language.

Beverley A. Brown
Philosophy of law
Professor of Legal Theory at the University of East London

Professor Brown was previously a member of the Centre for Law and Society at the University of Edinburgh. She is a leading authority on feminism, gender studies and legal theory.

Malcolm Budd
Aesthetics
Professor of Philosophy at University College London, UK

Professor Budd's publications include *Music and the Emotions* (Routledge, 1985), *Wittgenstein's Philosophy of Psychology* (Routledge, 1989) and *Values of Art* (Allen Lane, 1995). He is a Fellow of the British Academy.

Roger Crisp
Ethics
Fellow and Tutor in Philosophy, St Anne's College, University of Oxford, UK

Dr Crisp is the author of *Mill on Utilitarianism* (Routledge, 1997), and edited the 'Oxford Philosophical Text' of *Utilitarianism* (1998). He has edited two books on virtue ethics: *How Should One Live?* (Clarendon Press, 1996) and *Oxford Readings on the Virtues* (with Michael Slote) (Oxford University Press, 1997). He has written articles in several areas of philosophy, including ethics and political theory, is editor of *Utilitas* and is a member of the *Analysis* committee.

Mark Crimmins
Philosophy of language
Associate Professor of Philosophy, University of Michigan, USA

Professor Crimmins received his Ph.D. from Stanford in 1989, after which he taught at Cornell University. He has published a number of articles in philosophy of language and philosophy of mind, as well as the book *Talk About Beliefs* (MIT Press, 1992).

Michael Detlefsen
Philosophy of mathematics; Formal logic
Professor of Philosophy at the University of Notre Dame, USA

Professor Detlefsen has written extensively on Hilbert's Programme, Gödel's theorems, intuitionism, constructivist philosophies of mathematics and other topics in the philosophy of mathematics and logic. He has been the recipient of various faculty research awards, including fellowships from the Fulbright Foundation, the Alexander von Humboldt Stiftung and the National Endowment for the Humanities. He is co-editor-in-chief (with Anand Pillay) of the *Notre Dame Journal of Formal Logic* and is on the editorial boards of *Philosophica Mathematica* and the *Journal of Universal Computer Science*.

Arthur Fine
Philosophy of science
John Evans Professor of Philosophy, Northwestern University, USA

Professor Fine is a former president of the Philosophy of Science Association and President-elect of the Central Division of the American Philosophical Association. His works include *The Shaky Game: Einstein, Realism and the Quantum Theory* (University of Chicago Press, 1986).

Richard Foley
Epistemology
Professor of Philosophy, Dean of Arts and Sciences, and Dean of the Graduate School, Rutgers University (New Brunswick), USA

Professor Foley received his Ph.D. from Brown University. He has published widely in epistemology, including two books: *Working Without a Net: A Study of Egocentric Epistemology* (Oxford University Press, 1993) and *The Theory of Epistemic Rationality* (Harvard University Press, 1987). He won *American Philosophical Quarterly*'s Prize Essay in 1979 for his essay 'Justified Inconsistent Beliefs'.

EDITORIAL BOARD

Graeme Forbes
Philosophy of logic
Celia Scott Weatherhead Distinguished Professor of Philosophy, Tulane University, USA

Professor Forbes was educated at Glasgow University and Balliol and New College, Oxford. He has held teaching appointments at Merton College, and at the University of California at Santa Barbara and at Riverside. His publications include *The Metaphysics of Modality* (Oxford University Press), *Languages of Possibility* (Blackwell, 1989), *Modern Logic* (Oxford University Press, 1994) and over fifty articles in journals and edited collections.

Lenn E. Goodman
Jewish philosophy
Professor of Philosophy at Vanderbilt University, USA

Professor Goodman specializes in metaphysics, ethics, Jewish and Islamic philosophy. His books include *God of Abraham* (Oxford University Press, 1996), *Avicenna* (Routledge, 1992), *On Justice* (Yale University Press, 1991), *Saadiah Gaon's Commentary on the Book of Job* (Yale University Press, 1988), *Rambam* (Viking, 1976), *Ibn Tufayl: Hayy Ibn Yaqzan* (Gee Tee Bee, 1992) and *The Case of the Animals vs Man* (Gee Tee Bee, 1978).

John Haldane
Eighteenth-century philosophers
Professor of Philosophy and Director of the Centre for Philosophy and Public Affairs at the University of St Andrews, Scotland, UK

Professor Haldane publishes widely on ethics, history of philosophy, philosophy of mind, and social philosophy. He also publishes in art, educational studies and theology. Recent publications include *Atheism and Theism* with J.J.C. Smart (in the 'Great Debates in Philosophy' series, Blackwell, 1996). He is also writing *An Intelligent Person's Guide to Religion* for the Duckworth series of 'Intelligent Guides'.

Richard P. Hayes
Indian and Tibetan philosophy
Associate Professor, Faculty of Religious Studies, McGill University, Canada

Professor Hayes received his Ph.D. in Indian Buddhist philosophy from the department of Sanskrit and Indian Studies at the University of Toronto. His principal interests have been in Nāgārjuna, Vasubandhu, Dignāga and Dharmakīrti. Since 1988 he has taught Sanskrit language and Indian philosophy in the Faculty of Religious Studies and Department of Philosophy at McGill University.

Frank Jackson
Philosophy of mind
Professor of Philosophy, Institute of Advanced Studies, Australian National University, Australia

Professor Jackson has held a number of visiting appointments, including Senior Humanities Council Fellow at Princeton University and John Locke Lecturer at the University of Oxford. He is the author of *Perception* (Cambridge, 1977), *Conditionals* (Blackwell, 1987) and, with David Braddon-Mitchell, *Philosophy of Mind and Cognition* (Blackwell, 1996), and has published articles in philosophy of mind, philosophical logic and ethics.

Aileen Kelly
Russian philosophy
Lecturer in Slavonic Studies, University of Cambridge, and Fellow of King's College, Cambridge

Dr Kelly has published widely on Russian intellectual history. Her main publications include *Mikhail Bakunin: A Study in the Psychology and Politics of Utopianism* (Oxford University Press, 1982) and *Towards Another Shore: Russian Thinkers between Necessity and Chance* (Yale University Press, 1998).

Peter D. Klein
Epistemology
Professor of Philosophy, Rutgers University, USA

Professor Klein received his Ph.D. from Yale in 1966. He is best known as one of the developers of the defeasibility theory of knowledge, in such works as 'A Proposed Definition of Propositional Knowledge (*Journal of Philosophy*, 1971) and *Warrant, Proper Function, Reliabilism and Defeasibility* in *Warrant and Contemporary Epistemology* (Rowman & Littlefield, 1996), and for his work on scepticism in *Certainty* (Minnesota Press, 1981) and 'Skepticism and Closure: Why the Evil Genius Argument Fails' (*Philosophical Topics*, 23.1, Spring 1995).

Norman Kretzmann
Medieval philosophy
Susan Linn Sage Professor Emeritus of Philosophy, Sage School of Philosophy, Cornell University, USA

Professor Kretzmann has written numerous books and articles in medieval philosophy, including *The Metaphysics of Theism: Aquinas's Natural Theology in Summa Contra Gentiles I* (Clarendon Press, 1977). He was Principal Editor of *The Cambridge History of Later Medieval Philosophy* (Cambridge University

Press, 1982), and also edited *Infinity and Continuity in Ancient and Medieval Thought* (Cornell University Press, 1982), *Meaning and Inference in Medieval Philosophy* (Kluwer Academic Books, 1988) and *The Cambridge Companion to Aquinas* (with Eleonore Stump) (Cambridge University Press, 1993).

Oliver Leaman
Islamic philosophy; Jewish philosophy
Professor of Philosophy at Liverpool John Moores University, UK

Professor Leaman taught previously at the University of Khartoum, Sudan. He is the author of *An Introduction to Medieval Islamic Philosophy* (Cambridge University Press, 1985), *Evil and Suffering in Jewish Philosophy* (Cambridge University Press, 1995), *Moses Maimonides* (Curzon, 1997) and *Averroes and his Philosophy* (Curzon, 1997). He is the editor of *Friendship East and West* (Curzon, 1996), *The Future of Philosophy* (Routledge, 1998) and co-editor of the *History of Islamic Philosophy* (Routledge, 1996) and the *History of Jewish Philosophy* (Routledge, 1997).

Neil MacCormick
Philosophy of law
Regius Professor of Public Law and the Law of Nature and Nations at the University of Edinburgh, Scotland, UK

Professor MacCormick is a former president of the Association of Legal and Social Philosophy, and former vice-president of the parent International Association. He is a Fellow of the British Academy and of the Royal Society of Edinburgh. His principal publications are *Legal Reasoning and Legal Theory* (Clarendon Press, 1978), *H.L.A. Hart* (1981), *Legal Right and Social Democracy* (Stanford University Press, 1982), *An Institutional Theory of Law* (with Ota Weinberger) (Kluwer, 1986), *Interpreting Statutes* (edited with R.S. Summers) (Dartmouth, 1991) and *Interpreting Precedents* (edited with R.S. Summers) (Dartmouth, 1997).

John McCumber
Postmodern French philosophy
Koldyke Professor of Philosophy at Northwestern University, USA

Professor McCumber received his Ph.D. in Philosophy and Greek from the University of Toronto and has taught at the University of Michigan–Dearborn, the Graduate Faculty of the New School for Social Research, and the Collegium Phaenomenologicum. He currently teaches both philosophy and German. His publications include *Poetic Interaction* (University of Chicago Press, 1989) and *The Company of Words: Hegel, Language, and Systematic Philosophy* (Northwestern University Press, 1993), as well as numerous articles on Hegel, Heidegger and the history of philosophy.

David Miller
Political philosophy
Official Fellow in Social and Political Theory at Nuffield College, University of Oxford, UK

Dr Miller was educated at Cambridge and Oxford and taught at the Universities of Lancaster and East Anglia before taking up his present post. His publications in political philosophy include *Social Justice* (Clarendon Press, 1976), *Philosophy and Ideology in Hume's Political Thought* (Clarendon Press, 1981), *Market, State, and Community* (Clarendon Press, 1989) and *On Nationality* (Clarendon Press, 1995).

Amy A. Oliver
Latin American philosophy
Associate Professor of Spanish and Latin American Studies and Director of Women's and Gender Studies at American University in Washington, DC, USA

Professor Oliver serves on the editorial boards of *Cuadernos Americanos* and the Social Philosophy Research Institute, and is a past president of the Society for Iberian and Latin American Thought (of the American Philosophical Association) and former chair of the Five College Council on Latin American Studies. She has written about Latin American intellectual history, especially Mexican and Brazilian culture and philosophy, and has recently conducted research in Argentina and Uruguay.

Onora O'Neill
Ethics
The Principal, Newnham College, University of Cambridge, UK

Dr O'Neill is the author of *Faces of Hunger: An Essay on Poverty, Development and Justice* (Allen & Unwin, 1986), *Constructions of Reason: Explorations of Kant's Practical Philosophy* (Cambridge University Press, 1989) and *Toward Justice and Virtue: A Constructive Account of Practical Reasoning* (Cambridge University Press, 1996), as well as numerous articles on practical reason, ethics, political philosophy and the interpretation of Kant.

EDITORIAL BOARD

Georges Rey
Philosophy of psychology
Professor of Philosophy, University of Maryland at College Park, USA

Professor Rey received his Ph.D. from Harvard University in 1978. He has taught at SUNY Purchase and the University of Colorado at Boulder, and has been a visiting Professor at Massachusetts Institute of Technology. He is the author of *Contemporary Philosophy of Mind: A Contentiously Classical Approach* (Blackwell, 1997) and numerous articles on the philosophy of mind.

David-Hillel Ruben
Philosophy of social science
Professor of Philosophy, London School of Economics, UK

Professor Ruben received his Ph.D. from Harvard University in 1971. He has lectured at the Universities of Edinburgh, Glasgow and Essex, and at the City University, London. His publications include *Marxism and Materialism* (1979), *The Metaphysics of the Social World* (Routledge, 1985), *Explaining Explanation* (Routledge, 1990) and *Explanation* (ed.) (Oxford University Press, 1993). He has also edited a number of collections and published numerous articles in journals.

David Sedley
Ancient philosophy
Professor of Ancient Philosophy, University of Cambridge, and Fellow of Christ's College, Cambridge, UK

Professor Sedley has taught classics at Cambridge since 1975 and has held visiting Professorships at Princeton, Berkeley and Yale Universities. He has been editor of the *Classical Quarterly* (1986–1992) and of *Oxford Studies in Ancient Philosophy* (1998–). He is the author of *The Hellenistic Philosophers* (Cambridge, 1987, jointly with A.A. Long), of a recently completed book on Lucretius, and of many articles on ancient philosophy. He was elected a Fellow of the British Academy in 1994.

Robert Stern
Nineteenth-century philosophers
Lecturer, Department of Philosophy, University of Sheffield, UK

Dr Stern came to the University of Sheffield in 1989, having been a graduate and Research Fellow at St John's College, Cambridge. He is the author of *Hegel, Kant and the Structure of the Object* (Routledge, 1990), and editor of *G.W.F. Hegel: Critical Assessments* (Routledge, 1993). He is also editor of the *Bulletin of the Hegel Society of Great Britain*, and has published several papers relating to German and British Idealism.

Eleonore Stump
Philosophy of religion
Robert J. Henle Professor of Philosophy, St Louis University, USA

Professor Stump specializes in philosophy of religion and medieval philosophy. Her publications include *Dialectic and its Place in the Development of Medieval Logic* (Cornell University Press, 1989), *Reasoned Faith* (Cornell University Press, 1993), 'Eternity' (with Norman Kretzmann, *Journal of Philosophy* 78 (1981): 429–58), and 'Sanctification, Hardening of the Heart, and Frankfurt's Concept of Free Will' (*Journal of Philosophy* 85 (1988): 395–420). From 1995 to 1998 she was President of the Society of Christian Philosophers.

John Worrall
Philosophy of science
Professor of Philosophy of Science at the London School of Economics, UK

Professor Worrall is a former editor of *The British Journal for the Philosophy of Science*. He is the author of numerous articles including 'Structural Realism: the Best of Both Worlds' in *Philosophy of Science* (ed. D. Papineau, Oxford University Press, 1996) and is currently completing a book on theory-change.

CONSULTANT EDITOR

Paul Edwards
Professor of Philosophy (Emeritus), Brooklyn College, City University of New York, USA

Professor Edwards was General Editor of *The Encyclopedia of Philosophy* (Macmillan and The Free Press, 1967).

ADVISORY EDITORS

Lorraine Code
Professor of Philosophy, York University, Ontario, Canada

Christine Korsgaard
Professor and Chair of Philosophy, Harvard University, USA

Routledge team

Editorial

Publisher
Anna Hodson

Development Manager, Multivolumes
Tara Montgomery

Managing Editor, REP
Sharon McDuell

Project Manager, Electronic REP
Judith Beare

Editorial Assistant
Hamish Long

Philosophy Editor
Adrian Driscoll

Readers
Simon Christmas, Rowena Gaunt, Morgen Witzel

Electronic advisor
Brad Scott

Copy editing

Editorial Manager
Steve Turrington

Copy-editors
Tarquin Acevedo, Carol Baker, Lisa Blackwell, Owen Burdekin, Simon Coppock, Neville Hawcock, James Pickford, Kevin O'Rourke, Alisa Salamon, Adam Swallow, Emma Touffler, Morgen Witzel

Administration
Leigh Wilson, Kris Wischenkaemper

Thanks are also due to the numerous freelance copy-editors, proofreaders and taggers who contributed to the *Routledge Encyclopedia of Philosophy*.

Pre-press

Phil Gooch, Sean Harrop, Nigel Marsh

Indexing

Indexing Specialists, Hove, UK

Design and manufacturing

David Babb, Michelle Draycott, Jo Hart

Systems

Rob Newall, Matt Kenyon

Marketing

UK/Rest of World
Jane Gardner, Donna Stevens

North America
Rea Christoffersson, David Gilligan, Koren Thomas

Electronic Marketing
Rachel Pritchard

Internet Marketing
Rachel Gibbard

Publicity
Ben Page

Other acknowledgements

Encyclopedias take a long time to write and to publish. Over the seven years since the *Routledge Encyclopedia of Philosophy* was commissioned, many people have made invaluable contributions in their publishing roles. They are: Sue Bilton, Beth Harrison, Chris Hill, Maureen MacGrogan, Jen Mediano, Shân Millie, Wendy Morris, Don O'Connor, Gordon Smith, Helen Sutcliffe, Pippa Sweeney, Judith Watts, Elizabeth White, Julian Zinovieff.

And last but not least, a special acknowledgement of the work of Jonathan Price, who commissioned the *Routledge Encyclopedia of Philosophy*.

Using the *Encyclopedia*

The *Routledge Encyclopedia of Philosophy* is designed for ease of use. The following notes outline its organization and editorial approach and explain the ways of locating material. This will help readers make the most of the *Encyclopedia*.

SEQUENCE OF ENTRIES

The *Encyclopedia* contains 2,054 entries (from 500 to 19,000 words in length) arranged in nine volumes with a tenth volume for the index. Volumes 1–9 are arranged in a single alphabetical sequence, as follows:

Volume 1: A posteriori *to* Bradwardine, Thomas
Volume 2: Brahman *to* Derrida, Jacques
Volume 3: Descartes, René *to* Gender and science
Volume 4: Genealogy *to* Iqbal, Muhammad
Volume 5: Irigaray, Luce *to* Lushi chunqiu
Volume 6: Luther, Martin *to* Nifo, Agostino
Volume 7: Nihilism *to* Quantum mechanics, interpretation of
Volume 8: Questions *to* Sociobiology
Volume 9: Sociology of knowledge *to* Zoroastrianism

Alphabetical order

Entries are listed in alphabetical order by word rather than by letter with all words including *and, in, of* and *the* being given equal status. The exceptions to this rule are as follows:

- biographies: where the forenames and surname of a philosopher are inverted, the entry takes priority in the sequence, for example:

  Alexander, Samuel (1859–1938)
  Alexander of Aphrodisias (*c.* AD 200)
  Alexander of Hales (*c.* 1185–1245)

- names with prefixes, which follow conventional alphabetical placing (see Transliteration and naming conventions below).

A complete alphabetical list of entries is given in each of the Volumes 1 to 9.

Inverted titles

Titles of entries consisting of more than one word are often inverted so that the key term (in a thematic or signpost entry) or the surname (in a biographical entry) determines the place of the entry in the alphabetical sequence, for example:

Law, philosophy of *or*
Market, ethics of the *or*
Hart, Herbert Lionel Adolphus (1907–93)

Conceptual organization

Several concerns have had a bearing on the sequence of entries where there is more than one key term.

In deciding on the sequence of entries we have tried, wherever possible, to integrate philosophy as it is known and studied in the USA and Europe with philosophy from around the world. This means that the reader will frequently find entries from different philosophical traditions or approaches to the same topic close to each other, for example, in the sequence:

Political philosophy [signpost entry]
Political philosophy, history of
Political philosophy in classical Islam
Political philosophy, Indian

Similarly, in entries where a philosophical tradition or approach is surveyed we have tried, whenever appropriate, to keep philosophical traditions from different countries together. An example is the sequence:

Confucian philosophy, Chinese
Confucian philosophy, Japanese
Confucian philosophy, Korean
Confucius (551–479 BC)

Finally, historical entries are usually placed with contemporary entries under the topic rather than the historical period. For example, in the sequence:

Language, ancient philosophy of
Language and gender
Language, conventionality of
Language, early modern philosophy of
Language, Indian theories of
Language, innateness of

Dummy titles

The *Encyclopedia* has been extensively cross-referenced in order to help the reader locate their topic of interest. Dummy titles are placed throughout the alphabetical sequence of entries to direct the reader to the actual title of the entry where a topic is discussed. This may be under a different entry title, a synonym or as part of a larger entry. Wherever useful we have included the numbers of the sections (§§) in which a particular topic or subject is discussed. Examples of this type of cross-reference are:

AFRICAN AESTHETICS *see*
Aesthetics, african

CANGUILHEM, GEORGES *see*
French philosophy of science §§3–4

TAO *see* Dao

Glossary of logical and mathematical terms

A glossary of logical and mathematical terms is provided to help users with terms from formal logic and mathematics. 'See also' cross-references to the glossary are provided at the end of entries where the user might benefit from help with unfamiliar terms. The glossary can be found in Volume 5 under L (Logical and mathematical terms, glossary of).

The Index Volume

Volume 10 is devoted to a comprehensive index of key terms, concepts and names covered in Volumes 1–9, allowing readers to reap maximum benefit from the *Encyclopedia*. A guide to the index can be found at the beginning of the index. The index volume includes a full listing of contributors, their affiliations and the entries they have written. It also includes permission acknowledgements, listed in publisher order.

Structure of entries

The *Routledge Encyclopedia of Philosophy* contains three types of entry:

- 'signpost' entries, for example, Metaphysics; Science, philosophy of; East Asian philosophy. These entries provide an accessible overview of the sub-disciplines or regional coverage within the *Encyclopedia*; they provide a 'map' which directs the reader towards and around the many entries relating to each topic;
- thematic entries, ranging from general entries such as Knowledge, concept of, to specialized topics such as Virtue epistemology;
- biographical entries, devoted to individual philosophers, emphasizing the work rather than the life of the subject and with a list of the subject's major works.

Overview

All thematic and biographical entries begin with an overview which provides a concise and accessible summary of the topic or subject. This can be referred to on its own if the reader does not require the depth and detail of the main part of the entry.

Table of contents

All thematic and biographical entries over 1000 words in length are divided into sections and have a numbered table of contents following the overview. This gives the headings of each of the sections of the entry, enabling the reader to see the scope and structure of the entry at a glance. For example, the table of contents in the entry on Heraclitus:

1 Life and work
2 Methodology
3 Unity of opposites and perspectivism
4 Cosmology
5 Psychology, ethics and religion
6 Influence

Cross-references within an entry

Entries in the *Encyclopedia* have been extensively cross-referenced in order to indicate other entries that may be of interest to the reader. There are two types of cross-reference in the *Encyclopedia*:

1. 'See' cross-references

Cross-references within the text of an entry direct the reader to other entries on or closely related to the topic under discussion. For example, a reader may be directed from a conceptual entry to a biography of the philosopher whose work is under discussion or vice versa. These internal cross-references appear in small capital letters, either in parentheses, for example:

> Opponents of naturalism before and since Wittgenstein have been animated by the notion that the aims of social science are not causal explanation and improving prediction, but uncovering rules that make social life intelligible to its participants (see Explanation in history and social science).

or sometimes, when the reference is to a person who

has a biographical entry, as small capitals in the text itself, for example:

> Thomas NAGEL emphasizes the discrepancy between the objective insignificance of our lives and projects and the seriousness and energy we devote to them.

For entries over 1,000 words in length we have included the numbers of the sections (§) in which a topic is discussed, wherever useful, for example:

> In *Nicomachean Ethics*, Aristotle criticizes Plato's account for not telling us anything about particular kinds of goodness (see ARISTOTLE §§ 21–6).

2. 'See also' cross-references

At the end of the text of each entry, 'See also' cross-references guide the reader to other entries of related interest, such as more specialized entries, biographical entries, historical entries, geographical entries and so on. These cross-references appear in small capitals in alphabetical order.

References

References in the text are given in the Harvard style, for example, Kant (1788), Rawls (1971). Exceptions to this rule are made when presenting works with established conventions, for example, with some major works in ancient philosophy. Full bibliographical details are given in the 'List of works' and 'References and further reading'.

Bibliography

List of works

Biographical entries are followed by a list of works which gives full bibliographical details of the major works of the philosopher. This is in chronological order and includes items cited in the text, significant editions, dates of composition for pre-modern works (where known), preferred English-language translations and English translations for the titles of untranslated foreign-language works.

References and further reading

Both biographical and thematic entries have a list of references and further reading. Items are listed alphabetically by author's name. (Publications with joint authors are listed under the name of the first author and after any individual publications by that author). References cited in the text are preceded by an asterisk (*). Further reading which the reader may find particularly useful is also included.

The authors and editors have attempted to provide the fullest possible bibliographical information for every item.

Annotations

Publications in the 'List of works' and the 'References and further reading' have been annotated with a brief description of the content so that their relevance to readers' interests can be quickly assessed.

EDITORIAL STYLE

Spelling and punctuation in the *Encyclopedia* have been standardized to follow British English usage.

Transliteration and naming conventions

All names and terms from non-roman alphabets have been romanized in the *Encyclopedia*. Foreign names have been given according to the conventions within the particular language.

Arabic

Arabic has been transliterated in a simplified form, that is, without macrons or subscripts. Names of philosophers are given in their Arabic form rather than their Latinate form, for example, IBN RUSHD rather than AVERROES. Arabic names beginning with the prefix 'al-' are alphabetized under the substantive part of the name and not the prefix, for example:

KILWARDBY, ROBERT (d. 1279)
AL-KINDI, ABU YUSUF YAQUB IBN ISHAQ (d. *c*.866–73)
KNOWLEDGE AND JUSTIFICATION, COHERENCE THEORY OF

Arabic names beginning with the prefix 'Ibn' are alphabetized under 'I'.

Chinese, Korean and Japanese

Chinese has been transliterated using the Pinyin system. Dummy titles in the older Wade–Giles system are given for names and key terms; these direct the reader to the Pinyin titles.

Japanese has been transliterated using a modified version of the Hepburn system.

Chinese, Japanese and Korean names are given in Asian form, that is, surname preceding forenames, for example:

WANG FUZHI
NISHITANI KEIJI

The exception is where an author has chosen to present their own name in conventional Western form.

Hebrew

Hebrew has been transliterated in a simplified form, that is, without macrons or subscripts.

USING THE *ENCYCLOPEDIA*

Russian

Cyrillic characters have been transliterated using the Library of Congress system. Russian names are usually given with their patronymic, for example, BAKUNIN, MIKHAIL ALEKSANDROVICH.

Sanskrit

A guide to the pronunciation of Sanskrit can be found in the INDIAN AND TIBETAN PHILOSOPHY signpost entry.

Tibetan

Tibetan has been transliterated using the Wylie system. Dummy titles in the Virginia system are given for names and key terms. A guide to Tibetan pronunciation can be found in the INDIAN AND TIBETAN PHILOSOPHY signpost entry.

European names

Names beginning with the prefixes 'de', 'von' or 'van' are usually alphabetized under the substantive part of the name. For example:

BEAUVOIR, SIMONE DE
HUMBOLDT, WILHELM VON

The exception to this rule is when the person is either a national of or has spent some time living or working in an English-speaking country. For example:

DE MORGAN, AUGUSTUS
VON WRIGHT, GEORG HENRIK

Names beginning with the prefix 'de la' or 'le' are alphabetized under the prefix 'la' or 'le'. For example:

LA FORGE, LOUIS DE
LE DOEUFF, MICHÈLE

Names beginning with 'Mc' or 'Mac' are treated as 'Mac' and appear before Ma.

Historical names

Medieval and Renaissance names where a person is not usually known by a surname are alphabetized under the forename, for example:

GILES OF ROME
JOHN OF SALISBURY

List of entries and contributors

Below is a complete list of entries and contributors in the order in which they appear in the *Routledge Encyclopedia of Philosophy*.

A posteriori
  Paul K. Moser
A priori
  Paul K. Moser
'Abduh, Muhammad
  Neal Robinson
Abelard, Peter
  Martin M. Tweedale
Aberdeen Philosophical Society
  Paul Wood
Abhinavagupta
  Paul E. Muller-Ortega
Abravanel, Isaac
  Oliver Leaman
Abravanel, Judah ben Isaac
  Idit Dobbs-Weinstein
Absolute, the
  T.L.S. Sprigge
Absolutism
  Anthony Pagden
Abstract objects
  Bob Hale
Academy
  Jonathan Barnes
Action
  Jennifer Hornsby
Adorno, Theodor Wiesengrund
  J.M. Bernstein
Adverbs
  James Higginbotham
Aenesidemus
  R.J. Hankinson
Aesthetic attitude
  Malcolm Budd
Aesthetic concepts
  Marcia Eaton
Aesthetics
  Malcolm Budd
Aesthetics, African
  Barry Hallen
Aesthetics and ethics
  Michael Tanner
Aesthetics, Chinese
  Stephen J. Goldberg
Aesthetics in Islamic philosophy
  Deborah L. Black
Aesthetics, Japanese
  Meera Viswanathan
Affirmative action
  Bernard Boxill
al-Afghani, Jamal al-Din
  Elsayed M.H. Omran
  Oliver Leaman
African philosophy
  K. Anthony Appiah
African philosophy, anglophone
  Kwasi Wiredu
African philosophy, francophone
  F. Abiola Irele
African traditional religions
  K. Anthony Appiah
Agnosticism
  William L. Rowe
Agricola, Rudolph
  Peter Mack
Agricultural ethics
  Gary L. Comstock
Agrippa
  R.J. Hankinson
Agrippa von Nettesheim, Henricus Cornelius
  Michael H. Keefer
Ailly, Pierre d'
  Olaf Pluta
Ajdukiewicz, Kazimierz
  Jan Woleński
Akan philosophical psychology
  Kwasi Wiredu
Akrasia
  Helen Steward
Albert of Saxony
  Joël Biard
Albert the Great
  Alain de Libera
Albo, Joseph
  Daniel H. Frank
Alchemy
  Michela Pereira
Alcinous
  John Dillon
Alcmaeon
  Malcolm Schofield
Alemanno, Yohanan ben Isaac
  Abraham Melamed
D'Alembert, Jean Le Rond
  Paul F. Johnson
Alexander, Samuel
  Dorothy Emmet
Alexander of Aphrodisias
  R.W. Sharples
Alexander of Hales
  Gedeon Gál
Alienation
  Allen W. Wood
Alighieri, Dante
  Dominik Perler
Alison, Archibald
  Dabney Townsend
Alterity and identity, postmodern theories of
  Peter Fenves
Althusser, Louis Pierre
  Alex Callinicos
Ambedkar, Bimrao Ramji
  Alan Sponberg
Ambiguity
  Kent Bach
American philosophy in the 18th and 19th centuries
  Russell B. Goodman
  William C. Dowling
al-'Amiri, Abu'l Hasan Muhammad ibn Yusuf
  Tom Gaskill
Ammonius, son of Hermeas
  Christian Wildberg

LIST OF ENTRIES AND CONTRIBUTORS

Amo, Anton Wilhelm
  John S. Wright
Analysis, nonstandard
  Moshé Machover
Analysis, philosophical issues in
  I. Grattan-Guinness
Analytic ethics
  Peter Railton
Analytical philosophy
  Thomas Baldwin
Analytical philosophy in Latin America
  Oscar R. Martí
Analyticity
  George Bealer
Anaphora
  Nicholas Asher
Anarchism
  George Crowder
Anaxagoras
  Malcolm Schofield
Anaxarchus
  Jacques Brunschwig
Anaximander
  Richard McKirahan
Anaximenes
  Richard McKirahan
Ancient philosophy
  David Sedley
Anderson, John
  A.J. Baker
Animal language and thought
  Dale Jamieson
Animals and ethics
  James Rachels
Anomalous monism
  Brian P. McLaughlin
Anscombe, Gertrude Elizabeth Margaret
  Michael Thompson
Anselm of Canterbury
  Jasper Hopkins
Anthropology, philosophy of
  Merrilee H. Salmon
Antiochus
  Jonathan Barnes
Antiphon
  Angela Hobbs
Anti-positivist thought in Latin America
  Michael A. Weinstein
Antirealism in the philosophy of mathematics
  A.W. Moore
Anti-Semitism
  Oliver Leaman
  Clive Nyman
Antisthenes
  Malcolm Schofield
Applied ethics
  Brenda Almond
Apuleius
  John Dillon
Aquinas, Thomas
  Norman Kretzmann
  Eleonore Stump
Arama, Isaac ben Moses
  Josef Stern
Arcesilaus
  Jonathan Barnes
Archaeology, philosophy of
  Alison Wylie
Archē
  Richard McKirahan
Architecture, aesthetics of
  John J. Haldane
Archytas
  Hermann S. Schibli
Arendt, Hannah
  B. Parekh
Aretē
  David Sedley
Argentina, philosophy in
  Juan Carlos Torchia Estrada
Aristippus the Elder
  Voula Tsouna
Ariston of Chios
  David Sedley
Aristotelianism in Islamic philosophy
  Kiki Kennedy-Day
Aristotelianism in the 17th century
  Roger Ariew
Aristotelianism, medieval
  Mark D. Jordan
Aristotelianism, Renaissance
  Edward P. Mahoney
  James South
Aristotle
  T.H. Irwin
Aristotle commentators
  Richard Sorabji
Arithmetic, philosophical issues in
  Michael Potter
Armstrong, David Malet
  Frank Jackson
Arnauld, Antoine
  Steven Nadler
Art, abstract
  John Brown
Art and morality
  Michael Tanner
Art and truth
  Paul Taylor
Art criticism
  Colin Lyas
Art, definition of
  Stephen Davies
Art, performing
  Stephen Davies
Art, understanding of
  Colin Lyas
Art, value of
  Malcolm Budd
Art works, ontology of
  Gregory Currie
Artificial intelligence
  Margaret A. Boden
Artistic expression
  Stephen Davies
Artistic forgery
  Gregory Currie
Artistic interpretation
  Alan H. Goldman
Artistic style
  Jenefer M. Robinson
Artistic taste
  Ted Cohen
Artist's intention
  Paul Taylor
Arya Samaj
  K.S. Kumar
Asceticism
  Philip L. Quinn
Ash'ariyya and Mu'tazila
  Neal Robinson
Asmus, Valentin Ferdinandovich
  David Bakhurst
Astell, Mary
  Eileen O'Neill
Atheism
  William L. Rowe
Atomism, ancient
  David Sedley
Atonement
  Colin Gunton
Augustine
  Gareth B. Matthews
Augustinianism
  Mark D. Jordan
Aureol, Peter
  Robert Pasnau

LIST OF ENTRIES AND CONTRIBUTORS

Aurobindo Ghose
  Stephen H. Phillips
Austin, John
  Robert N. Moles
Austin, John Langshaw
  J.O. Urmson
Australia, philosophy in
  C.A.J. Coady
Authority
  Leslie Green
Autonomy, ethical
  Andrews Reath
Avenarius, Richard
  Augustin Riska
Averroism
  Sten Ebbesen
Averroism, Jewish
  Oliver Leaman
Awakening of Faith in Mahāyāna
  Peter N. Gregory
Awareness in Indian thought
  Stephen H. Phillips
Axiology
  Barry Smith
  Alan Thomas
Axiom of choice
  Gregory H. Moore
Ayer, Alfred Jules
  Graham MacDonald
Bachelard, Gaston
  Mary Tiles
Bacon, Francis
  J.R. Milton
Bacon, Roger
  Georgette Sinkler
al-Baghdadi, Abu'l-Barakat
  Y. Tzvi Langermann
Bakhtin, Mikhail Mikhailovich
  Gary Saul Morson
Bakunin, Mikhail Aleksandrovich
  Aileen Kelly
Báñez, Domingo
  Mauricio Beuchot
Bar Hayya, Abraham
  Geoffrey Wigoder
Barth, Karl
  Jean-Loup Seban
Barthes, Roland
  James Risser
Bartolus of Sassoferrato (or Saxoferrato)
  William M. Gordon
Bataille, Georges
  Jonathan Maskit

Baudrillard, Jean
  Mark Poster
Bauer, Bruno
  Lawrence S. Stepelevich
Baumgardt, David
  Ze'ev Levy
Baumgarten, Alexander Gottlieb
  Dabney Townsend
Bayle, Pierre
  Charles Larmore
Beattie, James
  Paul Wood
Beauty
  John H. Brown
Beauvoir, Simone de
  Eva Lundgren-Gothlin
Beck, Jacob Sigismund
  Eckart Förster
Behaviourism, analytic
  David Braddon-Mitchell
Behaviourism in the social sciences
  Rom Harré
Behaviourism, methodological and scientific
  C.R. Gallistel
Being
  Mark Okrent
Belief
  David Braddon-Mitchell
  Frank Jackson
Belief and knowledge
  Steven Luper
Belinskii, Vissarion Grigorievich
  Victor Terras
Bell's theorem
  Arthur Fine
Benjamin, Walter
  Julian Roberts
Bentham, Jeremy
  Ross Harrison
Bentley, Richard
  Rom Harré
Berdiaev, Nikolai Aleksandrovich
  James P. Scanlan
Bergson, Henri-Louis
  A.R. Lacey
Berkeley, George
  Ian Tipton
Berlin, Isaiah
  Bernard Williams
Bernard of Clairvaux
  Sean Murphy
Bernard of Tours
  Winthrop Wetherbee

Bernier, François
  Thomas M. Lennon
Bernstein, Eduard
  H. Tudor
Beth's theorem and Craig's theorem
  Zeno Swijtink
Bhartṛhari
  Johannes Bronkhorst
Bible, Hebrew
  Dan Cohn-Sherbok
Biel, Gabriel
  John L. Farthing
Bioethics
  R.G. Frey
Bioethics, Jewish
  Noam J. Zohar
Blackstone, William
  N.E. Simmonds
Blair, Hugh
  Richard Sher
Blanchot, Maurice
  Alan Milchman
  Alan Rosenberg
Blasius of Parma
  Graziella Federici Vescovini
Bloch, Ernst Simon
  Vincent Geoghegan
Bobbio, Norberto
  Patrizia Borsellino
Bodily sensations
  M.G.F. Martin
Bodin, Jean
  Julian H. Franklin
Boehme, Jakob
  Jean-Loup Seban
Boethius, Anicius Manlius Severinus
  Henry Chadwick
Boethius of Dacia
  Sten Ebbesen
Bogdanov, Aleksandr Aleksandrovich
  David Joravsky
Bohr, Niels
  Mara Beller
Bold, Samuel
  G.A.J. Rogers
Bolzano, Bernard
  Wolfgang Künne
Bonaventure
  Bonnie Kent
Bonhoeffer, Dietrich
  Jean-Loup Seban
Bonnet, Charles
  F.C.T. Moore

LIST OF ENTRIES AND CONTRIBUTORS

Boole, George
　Theodore Hailperin
Boolean algebra
　J.L. Bell
Bosanquet, Bernard
　Peter P. Nicholson
Bourdieu, Pierre
　Patrick Baert
Boutroux, Emile
　Didier Gil
Bowne, Borden Parker
　Keith E. Yandell
Boyle, Robert
　Rose-Mary Sargent
Bradley, Francis Herbert
　Stewart Candlish
Bradwardine, Thomas
　Edith Dudley Sylla
Brahman
　Stephen H. Phillips
Brahmo Samaj
　K.S. Kumar
Brazil, philosophy in
　Fred Gillette Sturm
Brentano, Franz Clemens
　Roderick M. Chisholm
　Peter Simons
Bridgman, Percy William
　Frederick Suppe
Brinkley, Richard
　Robert Andrews
Brito, Radulphus
　Sten Ebbesen
Broad, Charlie Dunbar
　Peter Smith
Brown, Thomas
　Christopher Bryant
Browne, Peter
　Kenneth P. Winkler
Brunner, Emil
　Jean-Loup Seban
Bruno, Giordano
　E.J. Ashworth
Brunschvicg, Léon
　Maurice Loi
Bryce, James
　Colin Munro
Buber, Martin
　Tamra Wright
Büchner, Friedrich Karl Christian Ludwig (Louis)
　Michael Heidelberger
Buddha
　L.S. Cousins

Buddhism, Ābhidharmika schools of
　Collett Cox
Buddhism, Mādhyamika: India and Tibet
　Leslie S. Kawamura
Buddhism, Yogācāra school of
　Dan Lusthaus
Buddhist concept of emptiness
　Paul Williams
Buddhist philosophy, Chinese
　Dan Lusthaus
Buddhist philosophy, Indian
　Richard P. Hayes
Buddhist philosophy, Japanese
　John C. Maraldo
Buddhist philosophy, Korean
　Sungtaek Cho
Buffier, Claude
　James W. Manns
Buffon, Georges Louis Leclerc, Comte de
　Robert Wokler
Bulgakov, Sergei Nikolaevich
　Bernice Glatzer Rosenthal
Bultmann, Rudolf
　Jean-Loup Seban
Buridan, John
　Jack Zupko
Burke, Edmund
　Iain Hampsher-Monk
Burley, Walter
　Edith Dudley Sylla
Burthogge, Richard
　Michael Ayers
Bushi philosophy
　Paul Varley
Business ethics
　Tom Sorell
Butler, Joseph
　R.G. Frey
Byzantine philosophy
　Phil Linos Benakis
Cabanis, Pierre-Jean
　F.C.T. Moore
Cabral, Amílcar
　K. Anthony Appiah
Cajetan (Thomas de Vio)
　Edward P. Mahoney
Calcidius
　John Dillon
Callicles
　Angela Hobbs
Calvin, John
　Ronald J. Feenstra

Cambridge Platonism
　Frederick Beiser
Campanella, Tommaso
　John M. Headley
Campbell, George
　Jeffrey M. Suderman
Campbell, Norman Robert
　D. H. Mellor
Camus, Albert
　David A. Sprintzen
Cantor, Georg
　Ulrich Majer
Cantor's theorem
　Mary Tiles
Capreolus, Johannes
　Michael Tavuzzi
Cardano, Girolamo
　Eckhard Kessler
Carlyle, Thomas
　A.L. Le Quesne
Carmichael, Gershom
　James Moore
　Michael Silverthorne
Carnap, Rudolf
　Richard Creath
Carneades
　Jonathan Barnes
Carolingian renaissance
　John Marenbon
Cassirer, Ernst
　Donald Phillip Verene
Casuistry
　Martin Stone
Categories
　Robert Wardy
Category theory, applications to the foundations of mathematics
　Colin McLarty
Category theory, introduction to
　Colin McLarty
Cattaneo, Carlo
　Delia Frigessi
Causality and necessity in Islamic thought
　David Burrell
Causation
　Nancy Cartwright
Causation, Indian theories of
　Roy W. Perrett
Cavell, Stanley
　Stephen Mulhall
Cavendish, Margaret Lucas
　Eileen O'Neill
Celsus
　John Dillon

Certainty
  Peter Klein
Certeau, Michel de
  Tom Conley
Chaadaev, Pëtr Iakovlevich
  Andrzej Walicki
Chaldaean Oracles
  Lucas Siorvanes
Change
  Robin Le Poidevin
Chaos theory
  Stephen H. Kellert
Charity
  Bernard Hoose
Charity, principle of
  Richard Feldman
Charleton, Walter
  G.A.J. Rogers
Charron, Pierre
  Richard H. Popkin
Chartres, School of
  John Marenbon
Chatton, Walter
  Stephen F. Brown
Chemistry, philosophical aspects of
  Noretta Koertge
Cheng
  Philip J. Ivanhoe
Cheng Hao
  Hoyt Cleveland Tillman
Cheng Yi
  Hoyt Cleveland Tillman
Chernyshevskii, Nikolai Gavrilovich
  Andrzej Walicki
Chillingworth, William
  J.R. Milton
Chinese classics
  Lisa Raphals
Chinese philosophy
  David L. Hall
  Roger T. Ames
Chinese Room Argument
  Robert Van Gulick
Chinul
  Robert E. Buswell, Jr
Chisholm, Roderick Milton
  David Benfield
Chomsky, Noam
  Norbert Hornstein
Chŏng Yagyong
  Yŏng-ho Ch'oe
Christine de Pizan
  Charity Cannon Willard
Chrysippus
  David Sedley

Church, Alonzo
  Peter Dolník
Church's theorem and the decision problem
  Rohit Parikh
Church's thesis
  Stewart Shapiro
Cicero, Marcus Tullius
  Stephen A. White
Cieszkowski, August von
  Lawrence S. Stepelevich
Citizenship
  Will Kymlicka
Civil disobedience
  Kent Greenawalt
Civil society
  Jean L. Cohen
Cixous, Hélène
  Verena Andermatt Conley
Clandestine literature
  Antony McKenna
Clarembald of Arras
  Stephen F. Brown
Clarke, Samuel
  Stephen Gaukroger
Clauberg, Johannes
  Daniel Garber
Cleanthes
  David Sedley
Clement of Alexandria
  Henry Chadwick
Cleomedes
  Robert B. Todd
Cockburn, Catharine
  Sarah Hutton
Coercion
  Joel Feinberg
Cognition, infant
  Alison Gopnik
  Andrew N. Meltzoff
Cognitive architecture
  Zenon W. Pylyshyn
Cognitive development
  F.C. Keil
  G. Gutheil
Cognitive pluralism
  Stephen P. Stich
Cohen, Hermann
  Michael Zank
Coleridge, Samuel Taylor
  Mary Anne Perkins
Collegium Conimbricense
  John P. Doyle
Collier, Arthur
  Kenneth P. Winkler

Collingwood, Robin George
  Simon Blackburn
Collins, Anthony
  Kenneth P. Winkler
Colour and qualia
  Joseph Levine
Colour, theories of
  David R. Hilbert
Combinatory logic
  David Charles McCarty
Comedy
  John Morreall
Comenius, John Amos
  Josef Zumr
Common Law
  Martin Krygier
Common Sense School
  Edward H. Madden
Common-sense ethics
  Charlotte R. Brown
Common-sense reasoning, theories of
  John Horty
Commonsensism
  Roderick M. Chisholm
Communication and intention
  Simon Blackburn
Communicative rationality
  Peter Dews
Communism
  Lyman Tower Sargent
Community and communitarianism
  Allen Buchanan
Complexity, computational
  Alasdair Urquhart
Compositionality
  Mark Richard
Computability and information
  Cristian S. Calude
Computability theory
  Daniele Mundici
  Wilfried Sieg
Computer science
  John Winnie
Comte, Isidore-Auguste-Marie-François-Xavier
  Angèle Kremer-Marietti
Concepts
  Georges Rey
Conceptual analysis
  Robert Hanna
Condillac, Etienne Bonnot de
  Paul F. Johnson
Condorcet, Marie-Jean-Antoine-Nicolas Caritat de
  David Williams

LIST OF ENTRIES AND CONTRIBUTORS

Confirmation theory
Theo A.F. Kuipers
Confucian philosophy, Chinese
A.S. Cua
Confucian philosophy, Japanese
Peter Nosco
Confucian philosophy, Korean
Michael C. Kalton
Confucius
D. C. Lau
Roger T. Ames
Connectionism
Brian P. McLaughlin
Conscience
Nicholas Dent
Consciousness
Eric Lormand
Consent
A. John Simmons
Consequence, conceptions of
Timothy Smiley
Consequentialism
David McNaughton
Conservation principles
James T. Cushing
Conservatism
Anthony O'Hear
Constant de Rebeque, Henri-Benjamin
Dennis Wood
Constitutionalism
Ulrich K. Preuß
Constructible universe
John P. Burgess
Constructivism
Stephen M. Downes
Constructivism in ethics
Onora O'Neill
Constructivism in mathematics
David Charles McCarty
Content, indexical
Kent Bach
Content, non-conceptual
Tim Crane
Content: wide and narrow
Kent Bach
Contextualism, epistemological
Bruce W. Brower
Contingency
Ralph C.S. Walker
Continuants
Robin Le Poidevin
Continuum hypothesis
Mary Tiles

Contractarianism
Samuel Freeman
Conventionalism
Paul Horwich
Conway, Anne
Sarah Hutton
Copernicus, Nicolaus
Ernan McMullin
Cordemoy, Géraud de
Steven Nadler
Corruption
Mark Philp
Cosmology
Ernan McMullin
Cosmology and cosmogony, Indian theories of
Edeltraud Harzer Clear
Counterfactual conditionals
Frank Döring
Cournot, Antoine Augustin
H. O. Mounce
Cousin, Victor
David Leopold
Crathorn, William
Robert Pasnau
Cratylus
A.A. Long
Creation and conservation, religious doctrine of
William Hasker
Crescas, Hasdai
Seymour Feldman
Crime and punishment
R.A. Duff
Criteria
Marie McGinn
Critical legal studies
Alan Norrie
Critical realism
Andrew Collier
Critical theory
Raymond Geuss
Croce, Benedetto
Richard Bellamy
Crucial experiments
Peter Achinstein
Crusius, Christian August
Michael J. Seidler
Cudworth, Ralph
Sarah Hutton
Cultural identity
John A. Loughney
Culture
Anthony O'Hear

Culverwell, Nathaniel
Frederick Beiser
Cumberland, Richard
Knud Haakonssen
Cynics
R. Bracht Branham
Cyrenaics
Voula Tsouna
Czech Republic, philosophy in
Josef Zumr
Dai Zhen
Yü Ying-shih
Damascius
John Dillon
Damian, Peter
William E. Mann
Dance, aesthetics of
Graham McFee
Dao
David L. Hall
Roger T. Ames
Daodejing
Michael LaFargue
Daoist philosophy
David L. Hall
Roger T. Ames
Darwin, Charles Robert
Peter J. Bowler
David of Dinant
William E. Mann
Davidson, Donald
Ernie Lepore
al-Dawani, Jalal al-Din
John Cooper
Daxue
Tu Weiming
De
David L. Hall
Roger T. Ames
De Man, Paul
Timothy Bahti
De Morgan, Augustus
Daniel D. Merrill
De re/de dicto
André Gallois
Death
Fred Feldman
Decision and game theory
Cristina Bicchieri
Deconstruction
Christopher Norris
Dedekind, Julius Wilhelm Richard
Howard Stein
Deductive closure principle
Anthony Brueckner

Definition
G. Aldo Antonelli
Definition, Indian concepts of
Sibajiban Bhattacharyya
Deism
William L. Rowe
Deleuze, Gilles
Dorothea E. Olkowski
Delmedigo, Elijah
Kalman Bland
Demarcation problem
Peter Achinstein
Democracy
Ross Harrison
Democritus
C.C.W. Taylor
Demonstratives and indexicals
Harry Deutsch
Dennett, Daniel Clement
William G. Lycan
Denys the Carthusian
Kent Emery Jr
Deontic logic
Marvin Belzer
Deontological ethics
David McNaughton
Depiction
R. D. Hopkins
Derrida, Jacques
Andrew Cutrofello
Descartes, René
Daniel Garber
Descriptions
Stephen Neale
Desert and merit
David Miller
Desgabets, Robert
Patricia A. Easton
Desire
Philip Pettit
Determinism and indeterminism
Jeremy Butterfield
Development ethics
David A. Crocker
Dewey, John
James Gouinlock
Dharmakīrti
Ernst Steinkellner
Dialectical materialism
Allen W. Wood
Dialectical school
David Sedley
Dialogical logic
Erik C.W. Krabbe

Dicey, Albert Venn
Martin Loughlin
Diderot, Denis
Robert Wokler
Dietrich of Freiberg
Fiona Somerset
Digby, Kenelm
Christia Mercer
Dignāga
Richard P. Hayes
Dilthey, Wilhelm
Rudolf A. Makkreel
Diodorus Cronus
Nicholas Denyer
Diogenes Laertius
David T. Runia
Diogenes of Apollonia
Malcolm Schofield
Diogenes of Oenoanda
Michael Erler
Diogenes of Sinope
R. Bracht Branham
Discourse semantics
Nicholas Asher
Discovery, logic of
Thomas Nickles
Discrimination
James W. Nickel
Dissoi logoi
M.F. Burnyeat
Dodgson, Charles Lutwidge (Lewis Carroll)
Peter Heath
Dōgen
Thomas P. Kasulis
Dong Zhongshu
Michael Nylan
Dooyeweerd, Herman
John Bolt
Dostoevskii, Fëdor Mikhailovich
Gary Saul Morson
Double effect, principle of
Suzanne Uniacke
Doubt
Michael Williams
Doxography
David T. Runia
Dreaming
Roberto Casati
Du Bois-Reymond, Emil
Daniel N. Robinson
Du Châtelet-Lomont, Gabrielle-Émilie
Robert L. Walters

Dualism
David M. Rosenthal
Ducasse, Curt John
Edward H. Madden
Duhem, Pierre Maurice Marie
Don Howard
Dühring, Eugen Karl
Robin Small
Dummett, Michael Anthony Eardley
Barry Taylor
Duns Scotus, John
Stephen D. Dumont
Duran, Profiat
Menachem Kellner
Oliver Leaman
Duran, Simeon ben Tzemach
Menachem Kellner
Durandus of St Pourçain
Mariateresa Fumagalli Beonio-Brocchieri
Durkheim, Emile
Marco Orrú
Duty
Robert L. Frazier
Duty and virtue, Indian conceptions of
John A. Taber
Dworkin, Ronald
Emilios A. Christodoulidis
Dynamic logics
Ulf Friedrichsdorf
East Asian philosophy
Roger T. Ames
Eberhard, Johann August
Henry E. Allison
Ecological philosophy
Freya Mathews
Ecology
John Beatty
Economics and ethics
Daniel Hausman
Michael S. McPherson
Economics, philosophy of
Daniel Hausman
Education, history of philosophy of
Randall R. Curren
Education, philosophy of
Randall R. Curren
Edwards, Jonathan
William J. Wainwright
Egoism and altruism
Richard Kraut
Egyptian cosmology, ancient
John D. Ray

LIST OF ENTRIES AND CONTRIBUTORS

Egyptian philosophy: influence on ancient Greek thought
Mary Lefkowitz
Einstein, Albert
Arthur Fine
Don Howard
John D. Norton
Electrodynamics
James T. Cushing
Eliade, Mircea
Bryan Stephenson Rennie
Eliminativism
Georges Rey
Eliot, George
John Beer
Elisabeth of Bohemia
Eileen O'Neill
Emerson, Ralph Waldo
Russell B. Goodman
Emotion in response to art
Jerrold Levinson
Emotions, nature of
Robert C. Solomon
Emotions, philosophy of
Robert C. Solomon
Emotive meaning
David Phillips
Emotivism
Michael Smith
Empedocles
Malcolm Schofield
Empiricism
William P. Alston
Encyclopedists, eighteenth-century
John Hope Mason
Encyclopedists, medieval
Samuel Barnish
Engels, Friedrich
Terrell Carver
Engineering and ethics
Michael Davis
Enlightenment, continental
Robert Wokler
Enlightenment, Jewish
Jay M. Harris
Enlightenment, Russian
W. Gareth Jones
Enlightenment, Scottish
Christopher J. Berry
Enthusiasm
Robert Shaver
Environmental ethics
Andrew Brennan
Epicharmus
Glenn W. Most

Epictetus
Brad Inwood
Epicureanism
David Sedley
Epicurus
David Sedley
Epiphenomenalism
Keith Campbell
Nicholas J.J. Smith
Epistemic logic
Jaakko Hintikka
Ilpo Halonen
Epistemic relativism
Stephen P. Stich
Epistemology
Peter D. Klein
Epistemology and ethics
Richard Feldman
Epistemology, history of
George S. Pappas
Epistemology in Islamic philosophy
Shams C. Inati
Epistemology, Indian schools of
Stephen H. Phillips
Equality
Albert Weale
Erasmus, Desiderius
Erika Rummel
Eriugena, Johannes Scottus
Dermot Moran
Erotic art
Jerrold Levinson
Error and illusion, Indian conceptions of
Stephen H. Phillips
Eschatology
Stephen T. Davis
Essentialism
Stephen Yablo
Eternity
Eleonore Stump
Norman Kretzmann
Eternity of the world, medieval views of
J.M.M.H. Thijssen
Ethical systems, African
K. Anthony Appiah
Ethics
Roger Crisp
Ethics in Islamic philosophy
Majid Fakhry
Ethiopia, philosophy in
Claude Sumner

Ethnophilosophy, African
Ivan Karp
D.A. Masolo
Eudaimonia
C.C.W. Taylor
Eudoxus
Liba Taub
Eurasian movement
Nicholas V. Riasanovsky
Eusebius
Christopher Stead
Evans, Gareth
John McDowell
Events
D. H. Mellor
Evil
John Kekes
Evil, problem of
Marilyn McCord Adams
Evolution and ethics
Elliott Sober
Evolution, theory of
Elisabeth A. Lloyd
Evolutionary theory and social science
Elliott Sober
Examples in ethics
Robert B. Louden
Existence
Penelope Mackie
Existentialism
Charles B. Guignon
Existentialist ethics
David E. Cooper
Existentialist theology
C. Stephen Evans
Existentialist thought in Latin America
María Teresa Bertelloni
Experiment
Margaret C. Morrison
Experiments in social science
John A. Hughes
Explanation
Philip Kitcher
Explanation in history and social science
David-Hillel Ruben
Fa
Thomas P. Kasulis
Fackenheim, Emil Ludwig
Michael L. Morgan
Facts
Alex Oliver

Fact/value distinction
  Roger Crisp
Faith
  Nicholas P. Wolterstorff
Fallacies
  Douglas Walton
Fallibilism
  Nicholas Rescher
Family, ethics and the
  William Ruddick
Fanon, Frantz
  K. Anthony Appiah
al-Farabi, Abu Nasr
  Ian Richard Netton
Fardella, Michelangelo
  Luciano Floridi
Farrer, Austin Marsden
  Thomas Williams
Fascism
  Roger Eatwell
Fatalism
  Edward Craig
Fatalism, Indian
  Julian F. Woods
Fazang
  Francis H. Cook
Fechner, Gustav Theodor
  Daniel N. Robinson
Federalism and confederalism
  Wayne Norman
Fëdorov, Nikolai Fëdorovich
  George M. Young
Feminism
  Susan James
Feminism and psychoanalysis
  Margaret Whitford
Feminism and social science
  Alison Wylie
Feminist aesthetics
  Carolyn Korsmeyer
Feminist epistemology
  Lorraine Code
Feminist ethics
  Rosemarie Tong
Feminist jurisprudence
  E.F. Kingdom
Feminist literary criticism
  Gayatri Chakravorty Spivak
Feminist political philosophy
  Susan Mendus
Feminist theology
  Marjorie Suchocki
Feminist thought in Latin America
  Amy A. Oliver

Fénelon, François de Salignac de la Mothe
  Patrick Riley
Ferguson, Adam
  David Kettler
Ferrier, James Frederick
  John J. Haldane
Feuerbach, Ludwig Andreas
  Hans-Martin Sass
Feyerabend, Paul Karl
  Michael Williams
Fichte, Johann Gottlieb
  Daniel Breazeale
Ficino, Marsilio
  James Hankins
Fiction, semantics of
  Robert Howell
Fictional entities
  Peter Lamarque
Fictionalism
  Arthur Fine
Field theory, classical
  Mark Wilson
Field theory, quantum
  Paul Teller
Film, aesthetics of
  Gregory Currie
Filmer, Sir Robert
  Johann P. Sommerville
Florenskii, Pavel Aleksandrovich
  Robert Slesinski
Fludd, Robert
  Stephen Gaukroger
Fodor, Jerry Alan
  Peter Godfrey-Smith
Folk psychology
  Georges Rey
  Stephen P. Stich
Fonseca, Pedro da
  John P. Doyle
Fontenelle, Bernard de
  Martin Schönfeld
Forcing
  John P. Burgess
Forgiveness and mercy
  Jeffrie G. Murphy
Formal and informal logic
  Douglas Walton
Formal languages and systems
  Heinrich Herre
  Peter Schroeder-Heister
Formalism in art
  Malcolm Budd
Foucault, Michel
  Gary Gutting

Foucher, Simon
  Steven Nadler
Foundationalism
  Ernest Sosa
Francis of Meyronnes
  Jeffrey Hause
Frank, Jerome
  Neil Duxbury
  Neil MacCormick
Frank, Semën Liudvigovich
  Philip J. Swoboda
Frankfurt School
  Axel Honneth
Franklin, Benjamin
  Murray G. Murphey
Free logics
  Ermanno Bencivenga
Free logics, philosophical issues in
  Karel Lambert
Free will
  Galen Strawson
Freedom and liberty
  Joel Feinberg
Freedom, divine
  William L. Rowe
Freedom of speech
  Peter Jones
Frege, Gottlob
  Alexander George
  Richard Heck
Frei, Hans
  Nicholas P. Wolterstorff
French philosophy of science
  Gary Gutting
Freud, Sigmund
  James Hopkins
Friendship
  Neera K. Badhwar
Fries, Jacob Friedrich
  Allen W. Wood
Fujiwara Seika
  John Allen Tucker
Fuller, Lon Louvois
  Massimo La Torre
Functional explanation
  Richard N. Manning
Functionalism
  David Papineau
Functionalism in social science
  John Bigelow
Future generations, obligations to
  Avner de-Shalit
Fuzzy logic
  Charles G. Morgan

LIST OF ENTRIES AND CONTRIBUTORS

Gadādhara
Jonardon Ganeri
Gadamer, Hans-Georg
Kathleen Wright
Gaius
Grant McLeod
Galen
R.J. Hankinson
Galilei, Galileo
Ernan McMullin
Gandhi, Mohandas Karamchand
Frank J. Hoffman
Gaṅgeśa
Stephen H. Phillips
Garrigou-Lagrange, Réginald
Ralph McInerny
Gassendi, Pierre
Margaret J. Osler
Gauḍīya Vaiṣṇavism
Jan K. Brzezinski
Gautama, Akṣapāda
Eli Franco
Karin Preisendanz
Gender and science
Sandra G. Harding
Genealogy
R Kevin Hill
General relativity, philosophical responses to
T.A. Ryckman
General will
Peter P. Nicholson
Genetics
Lindley Darden
Genetics and ethics
Ruth Chadwick
Gentile, Giovanni
Richard Bellamy
Gentzen, Gerhard Karl Erich
Volker Peckhaus
Geology, philosophy of
Rachel Laudan
Geometry, philosophical issues in
T.A. Ryckman
George of Trebizond
John Monfasani
Gerard, Alexander
Dabney Townsend
Gerard of Cremona
Mark D. Jordan
Gerard of Odo
Bonnie Kent
Gerbert of Aurillac
Fiona Somerset

Gerdil, Giancinto Sigismondo
Patrick Riley
German idealism
Paul Franks
Gerson, Jean
Mark S. Burrows
Gersonides
Seymour Feldman
Gestalt psychology
Barry Smith
Gettier problems
Robert K. Shope
Geulincx, Arnold
Theo Verbeek
al-Ghazali, Abu Hamid
Kojiro Nakamura
Gilbert of Poitiers
Klaus Jacobi
Giles of Rome
Francesco del Punta
Cecilia Trifogli
Gioberti, Vincenzo
Mario Piccinini
Glanvill, Joseph
G.A.J. Rogers
Gnosticism
Christopher Stead
God, arguments for the existence of
Alvin Plantinga
God, concepts of
Brian Leftow
God, Indian conceptions of
Sibajiban Bhattacharyya
Gödel, Kurt
John W. Dawson, Jr
Gödel's theorems
Michael Detlefsen
Godfrey of Fontaines
John F. Wippel
Godwin, William
Mark Philp
Goethe, Johann Wolfgang von
Nicholas Boyle
Good, theories of the
Christine M. Korsgaard
Goodman, Nelson
Catherine Z. Elgin
Goodness, perfect
Linda Zagzebski
Gorgias
Charles H. Kahn
Grace
David Braine
Gramsci, Antonio
Richard Bellamy

Greek philosophy: impact on Islamic philosophy
Majid Fakhry
Green political philosophy
Terence Ball
Green, Thomas Hill
Richard Bellamy
Gregory of Rimini
Stephen F. Brown
Grice, Herbert Paul
Judith Baker
Grosseteste, Robert
Scott MacDonald
Grote, John
John Gibbins
Bart Schultz
Grotius, Hugo
J.D. Ford
Guanzi
Isabelle Robinet
Gurney, Edmund
Jerrold Levinson
Ahad, Ha'am
Ze'ev Levy
Habermas, Jürgen
Kenneth Baynes
Haeckel, Ernst Heinrich
Paul Weindling
Hägerström, Axel Anders Theodor
Thorild Dahlquist
Ann-Mari Henschen-Dahlquist
Halakhah
Noam J. Zohar
Halevi, Judah
L.E. Goodman
Hamann, Johann Georg
Frederick Beiser
Hamilton, William
H. O. Mounce
Han Feizi
Leo S. Chang
Han Wônjin
Michael C. Kalton
Han Yu
Charles Hartman
Hanslick, Eduard
Peter Kivy
Hanson, Norwood Russell
Edward Mackinnon
Happiness
J.P. Griffin
Hare, Richard Mervyn
A.W. Price
Harrington, James
Mark Goldie

Hart, Herbert Lionel Adolphus
Neil MacCormick
Hartley, David
Roy Porter
Hartmann, Karl Robert Eduard von
Christopher Adair-Toteff
Hartmann, Nicolai
Michael Inwood
Hasidism
Rachel Elior
Hayek, Friedrich August von
Chandran Kukathas
Heaven
Linda Zagzebski
Heaven, Indian conceptions of
Frederick M. Smith
Hedonism
Justin Gosling
Hegel, Georg Wilhelm Friedrich
Rolf-Peter Horstmann
Hegelianism
Robert Stern
Nicholas Walker
Hegelianism, Russian
Andrzej Walicki
Heidegger, Martin
Thomas Sheehan
Heideggerian philosophy of science
Joseph Rouse
Heisenberg, Werner
Mara Beller
Hell
Marilyn McCord Adams
Hellenistic medical epistemology
R.J. Hankinson
Hellenistic philosophy
David Sedley
Helmholtz, Hermann von
Catherine Chevalley
Helmont, Franciscus Mercurius van
Stuart Brown
Help and beneficence
Liam B. Murphy
Helvétius, Claude-Adrien
Mark Hulliung
Hempel, Carl Gustav
R. Jeffrey
Henricus Regius
Daniel Garber
Henry of Ghent
Steven P. Marrone
Henry of Harclay
George Molland
Heraclides of Pontus
H.B. Gottschalk

Heraclitus
A.A. Long
Herbart, Johann Friedrich
Alfred Langewand
Herbert Edward (Baron Herbert of Cherbury)
David A. Pailin
Herbrand's theorem
A.M. Ungar
Herder, Johann Gottfried
Frederick Beiser
Hermeneutics
Michael Inwood
Hermeneutics, Biblical
Anthony C. Thiselton
Hermetism
John Procopé
Herrera, Abraham Cohen de
Nissim Yosha
Hertz, Heinrich Rudolf
Peter Barker
Hervaeus Natalis
Dominik Perler
Herzen, Aleksandr Ivanovich
Aileen Kelly
Heschel, Abraham Joshua
David Novak
Hesiod
Glenn W. Most
Hess, Moses
Shlomo Avineri
Hessen, Sergei Iosifovich
Andrzej Walicki
Heytesbury, William
John Longeway
Hierocles
Brad Inwood
Hilbert's Programme and Formalism
Michael Detlefsen
Hildegard of Bingen
Claudia Eisen Murphy
Hillel ben Samuel of Verona
Caterina Rigo
Hindu philosophy
Edeltraud Harzer Clear
Hippias
Charles H. Kahn
Hippocratic medicine
R.J. Hankinson
Historicism
Christopher Thornhill
History, Chinese theories of
Philip J. Ivanhoe

History, philosophy of
Gordon Graham
Hobbes, Thomas
Tom Sorell
Hohfeld, Wesley Newcomb
Neil MacCormick
Holcot, Robert
Robert Pasnau
Hölderlin, Johann Christian Friedrich
Nicholas Walker
Holism and individualism in history and social science
Rajeev Bhargava
Holism: mental and semantic
Ned Block
Holmes, Oliver Wendell, Jr
Matthew H. Kramer
Holocaust, the
Steven T. Katz
Home, Henry (Lord Kames)
Roger L. Emerson
Homer
Glenn W. Most
Honour
Julian Roberts
Hooker, Richard
A.S. McGrade
Hope
Philip Stratton-Lake
Horkheimer, Max
J.M. Bernstein
Huainanzi
H.D. Roth
Huet, Pierre-Daniel
Luciano Floridi
Hugh of St Victor
Mark D. Jordan
Human nature
Ian Shapiro
Human nature, science of, in the 18th century
Christopher J. Berry
Humanism
John C. Luik
Humanism, Renaissance
John Monfasani
Humboldt, Wilhelm von
Frederick Beiser
Hume, David
Annette Baier
Humour
Jerrold Levinson
Hungary, philosophy in
László Perecz

LIST OF ENTRIES AND CONTRIBUTORS

Hus, Jan
 Curtis V. Bostick
Husserl, Edmund
 Dagfinn Føllesdal
Hutcheson, Francis
 David Fate Norton
Huxley, Thomas Henry
 Mario A. Di Gregorio
Hypatia
 Lucas Siorvanes
Iamblichus
 Lucas Siorvanes
Ibn 'Adi, Yahya
 Shams C. Inati
Ibn al-'Arabi, Muhyi al-Din
 Neal Robinson
Ibn ar-Rawandi
 Shams C. Inati
Ibn Bajja, Abu Bakr Muhammad ibn Yahya ibn as-Say'igh
 Shams C. Inati
Ibn Daud, Abraham
 Norbert M. Samuelson
Ibn Ezra, Abraham
 Raphael Jospe
Ibn Ezra, Moses ben Jacob
 Paul B. Fenton
Ibn Falaquera, Shem Tov
 Raphael Jospe
Ibn Gabirol, Solomon
 Daniel H. Frank
Ibn Hazm, Abu Muhammad 'Ali
 Oliver Leaman
 Salman Albdour
Ibn Kammuna
 Y. Tzvi Langermann
Ibn Khaldun, 'Abd al-Rahman
 Charles Issawi
 Oliver Leaman
Ibn Massara, Muhammad ibn 'Abd Allah
 George N. Atiyeh
Ibn Miskawayh, Ahmad ibn Muhammad
 Oliver Leaman
Ibn Paquda, Bahya
 L.E. Goodman
Ibn Rushd, Abu'l Walid Muhammad
 Oliver Leaman
Ibn Sab'in, Muhammad ibn 'Abd al-Haqq
 Elsayed M.H. Omran
Ibn Sina, Abu 'Ali al-Husayn
 Salim Kemal

Ibn Taymiyya, Taqi al-Din
 James Pavlin
Ibn Tufayl, Abu Bakr Muhammad
 Shams C. Inati
Ibn Tzaddik, Joseph ben Jacob
 Tamar Rudavsky
Idealism
 T.L.S. Sprigge
Idealizations
 Ronald Laymon
Ideals
 Connie S. Rosati
Identity
 Timothy Williamson
Identity of indiscernibles
 Peter Simons
Ideology
 Michael Freeden
Ikhwan Al-Safa'
 Ian Richard Netton
Il'enkov, Eval'd Vasil'evich
 David Bakhurst
Il'in, Ivan Aleksandrovich
 Philip T. Grier
Illuminati
 Margaret C. Jacob
Illumination
 Scott MacDonald
Illuminationist philosophy
 Hossein Ziai
 Oliver Leaman
Imagery
 Michael Tye
Imagination
 J. O'Leary-Hawthorne
Immanuel ben Solomon of Rome
 Caterina Rigo
Immutability
 Brian Leftow
Impartiality
 John Cottingham
Imperative logic
 Mitchell Green
Implicature
 Wayne A. Davis
Incarnation and Christology
 Peter van Inwagen
Incommensurability
 Dudley Shapere
Indian and Tibetan philosophy
 Richard P. Hayes
Indicative conditionals
 Frank Jackson
Indirect discourse
 Gabriel Segal

Induction, epistemic issues in
 Mark Kaplan
Inductive definitions and proofs
 Vann McGee
Inductive inference
 Patrick Maher
Inference, Indian theories of
 Brendan S. Gillon
Inference to the best explanation
 Jonathan Vogel
Infinitary logics
 Bernd Buldt
Infinity
 A.W. Moore
Information technology and ethics
 Helen Nissenbaum
Information theory
 Kenneth M. Sayre
Information theory and epistemology
 Fred Dretske
Ingarden, Roman Witold
 Antoni B. Stepien
Inge, William Ralph
 Keith E. Yandell
Innate knowledge
 Elliott Sober
Innocence
 Bernard Hoose
Institutionalism in law
 Anna Pintore
Intensional entities
 George Bealer
Intensional logics
 James W. Garson
Intensionality
 Simon Christmas
Intention
 Robert Dunn
Intentionality
 Tim Crane
Internalism and externalism in epistemology
 William P. Alston
International relations, philosophy of
 Charles R. Beitz
Interpretation, Indian theories of
 Madhav M. Deshpande
Introspection, epistemology of
 Hilary Kornblith
Introspection, psychology of
 Barbara Von Eckardt
Intuitionism
 David Charles McCarty

Intuitionism in ethics
  Robert L. Frazier
Intuitionistic logic and antirealism
  Peter Pagin
Iqbal, Muhammad
  Riffat Hassan
Irigaray, Luce
  Tina Chanter
Isaac of Stella
  Winthrop Wetherbee
Islam, concept of philosophy in
  Oliver Leaman
Islamic fundamentalism
  Youssef Choueiri
Islamic philosophy
  Oliver Leaman
Islamic philosophy, modern
  Parviz Morewedge
  Oliver Leaman
Islamic philosophy: transmission into Western Europe
  Charles Burnett
Islamic theology
  Abdelwahab El-Affendi
Israeli, Isaac Ben Solomon
  Daniel J. Lasker
Italy, philosophy in
  Gaetano Chiurazzi
Itō Jinsai
  John Allen Tucker
Jacobi, Friedrich Heinrich
  George di Giovanni
Jaina philosophy
  Jayandra Soni
James of Viterbo
  Edward P. Mahoney
James, William
  Ruth Anna Putnam
Japanese philosophy
  Thomas P. Kasulis
Jaspers, Karl
  Kurt Salamun
Jefferson, Thomas
  Murray G. Murphey
Jewish philosophy
  L.E. Goodman
Jewish philosophy, contemporary
  Henry S. Levinson
  Jonathan W. Malino
Jewish philosophy in the early 19th century
  Kenneth Seeskin
Jhering, Rudolf von
  Elspeth Attwooll

Jia Yi
  Michael Nylan
Joachim of Fiore
  Sean Eisen Murphy
John of Damascus
  John Longeway
John of Jandun
  Edward P. Mahoney
John of La Rochelle
  Mark D. Jordan
John of Mirecourt
  Fiona Somerset
John of Paris
  Mark D. Jordan
John of Salisbury
  Mark D. Jordan
John of St Thomas
  John P. Doyle
Johnson, Alexander Bryan
  K.T. Fann
Johnson, Dr Samuel
  Roy Porter
Johnson, Samuel
  Charles J. McCracken
Journalism, ethics of
  Andrew Belsey
Judah ben Moses of Rome
  Caterina Rigo
Jung, Carl Gustav
  George B. Hogenson
Jungius, Joachim
  Ralph Häfner
Jurisprudence, historical
  Peter Stein
Justice
  Brian Barry
  Matt Matravers
Justice, equity and law
  John Tasioulas
Justice, international
  Brian Barry
  Matt Matravers
Justification, epistemic
  Richard Foley
Justification, religious
  Diogenes Allen
Justinian
  Grant McLeod
al-Juwayni, Abu'l Ma'ali
  Oliver Leaman
  Salman Albdour
Kabbalah
  Oliver Leaman
Kaibara Ekken
  Mary Evelyn Tucker

Kant, Immanuel
  Paul Guyer
Kantian ethics
  Onora O'Neill
Kaplan, Mordecai
  David Ellenson
Karaism
  Daniel Frank
Karma and rebirth, Indian conceptions of
  Wilhelm Halbfass
Katharsis
  Glenn W. Most
Kauṭilya
  Purushottama Bilimoria
Kautsky, Karl Johann
  H. Tudor
Keckermann, Bartholomew
  Christia Mercer
Kelsen, Hans
  Zenon Bankowski
Kemp Smith, Norman
  Robert R. Calder
  George Davie
Kepler, Johannes
  Ernan McMullin
Keynes, John Maynard
  Margaret Schabas
Kierkegaard, Søren Aabye
  Patrick Gardiner
Kilvington, Richard
  Norman Kretzmann
Kilwardby, Robert
  Alessandro D. Conti
al-Kindi, Abu Yusuf Ya'qub ibn Ishaq
  Kiki Kennedy-Day
Knowledge and justification, coherence theory of
  Laurence BonJour
Knowledge by acquaintance and description
  Richard Fumerton
Knowledge, causal theory of
  Marshall Swain
Knowledge, concept of
  Peter D. Klein
Knowledge, defeasibility theory of
  Marshall Swain
Knowledge, Indian views of
  Stephen H. Phillips
Knowledge, tacit
  C.F. Delaney
Knutzen, Martin
  A. Laywine

LIST OF ENTRIES AND CONTRIBUTORS

Kojève, Alexandre
　Michael S. Roth
Kokoro
　Meera Viswanathan
Kotarbiński, Tadeusz
　B. Stanosz
Koyré, Alexandre
　Pietro Redondi
Krause, Karl Christian Friedrich
　Teresa Rodriguez de Lecea
Kripke, Saul Aaron
　Michael Jubien
Kristeva, Julia
　Tina Chanter
Krochmal, Nachman
　Jay M. Harris
Kronecker, Leopold
　Ulrich Majer
Kropotkin, Pëtr Alekseevich
　Caroline Cahm
Kuhn, Thomas Samuel
　Paul Hoyningen-Huene
Kūkai
　Thomas P. Kasulis
Kuki Shūzō
　Nagatomo Shigenori
Kumazawa Banzan
　Steven Heine
Kyoto school
　J.W. Heisig
La Forge, Louis de
　Steven Nadler
La Mettrie, Julien Offroy de
　Kathleen Wellman
Labriola, Antonio
　Geoffrey Hunt
Lacan, Jacques
　Thomas Brockelman
Lachelier, Jules
　Michel Piclin
Lacoue-Labarthe, Philippe
　Giovanni Scibilia
Lakatos, Imre
　John Worrall
Lambda calculus
　David Charles McCarty
Lambert, Johann Heinrich
　Günter Zöller
Lange, Friedrich Albert
　George J. Stack
Langer, Susanne Katherina Knauth
　Peg Brand
Language, ancient philosophy of
　Christopher Shields

Language and gender
　Sally McConnell-Ginet
Language, conventionality of
　Barry C. Smith
Language, early modern philosophy of
　Zoltán Gendler Szabó
Language, Indian theories of
　Johannes Bronkhorst
Language, innateness of
　Fiona Cowie
Language, medieval theories of
　Sten Ebbesen
Language of thought
　Georges Rey
Language, philosophy of
　Mark Crimmins
Language, Renaissance philosophy of
　E.J. Ashworth
Language, social nature of
　Barry C. Smith
Lassalle, Ferdinand
　H. Tudor
Latin America, colonial thought in
　Walter B. Redmond
Latin America, philosophy in
　Amy A. Oliver
Latin America, pre-Columbian and indigenous thought in
　Laura Mues de Schrenk
Latitudinarianism
　John Marshall
Lavrov, Pëtr Lavrovich
　Andrzej Walicki
Law and morality
　N.E. Simmonds
Law and ritual in Chinese philosophy
　R.P. Peerenboom
Law, economic approach to
　Jules L. Coleman
Law, Islamic philosophy of
　Norman Calder
Law, limits of
　G.W. Smith
Law, philosophy of
　Neil MacCormick
　Beverley Brown
Law, William
　Paul G. Stanwood
Laws, natural
　C.A. Hooker
Le Clerc, Jean
　Theo Verbeek

Le Doeuff, Michèle
　Max Deutscher
Le Grand, Antoine
　Patricia A. Easton
Le Roy, Edouard Louis Emmanuel Julien
　Don Howard
Learning
　C.R. Gallistel
　Clark Glymour
Lebensphilosophie
　Jason Gaiger
Lefebvre, Henri
　Rob Shields
Legal concepts
　Åke Frändberg
Legal discourse
　Beverley Brown
Legal evidence and inference
　David A. Schum
Legal hermeneutics
　Peter Goodrich
Legal idealism
　Elspeth Attwooll
Legal positivism
　Mario Jori
Legal realism
　Neil Duxbury
Legal reasoning and interpretation
　Neil MacCormick
Legalist philosophy, Chinese
　Leo S. Chang
Legitimacy
　David Beetham
Leibniz, Gottfried Wilhelm
　Daniel Garber
Leibowitz, Yeshayahu
　David Hartman
Lenin, Vladimir Il'ich
　Robert Service
Leont'ev, Konstantin Nikolaevich
　George L. Kline
Leśniewski, Stanisław
　Jan Woleński
Lessing, Gotthold Ephraim
　Dabney Townsend
Leucippus
　C.C.W. Taylor
Levinas, Emmanuel
　Robert Bernasconi
Lévi-Strauss, Claude
　Olivia Harris
Lewis, Clarence Irving
　Sandra B. Rosenthal

LIST OF ENTRIES AND CONTRIBUTORS

Lewis, Clive Staples
  Richard L. Purtill
Lewis, David Kellogg
  Peter van Inwagen
Li
  Philip J. Ivanhoe
Liber de causis
  Hannes Jarka-Sellers
Liberalism
  Jeremy Waldron
Liberalism, Russian
  G.M. Hamburg
Liberation philosophy
  Horacio Cerutti-Guldberg
Liberation theology
  Roger Haight
Libertarianism
  Jonathan Wolff
Libertins
  Ian Maclean
Lichtenberg, Georg Christoph
  Günter Zöller
Life and death
  John Harris
Life, meaning of
  Susan Wolf
Life, origin of
  Lenny Moss
Limbo
  Linda Zagzebski
Linear logic
  G.M. Bierman
Linguistic discrimination
  Naomi Scheman
Linji
  Shigenori Nagatomo
Linnaeus, Carl von
  P.F. Stevens
Lipsius, Justus
  E.J. Ashworth
Literature, philosophy in Latin American
  José Luis Gómez-Martínez
Literature, philosophy in modern Japanese
  Paul Anderer
Llewellyn, Karl Nickerson
  William Twining
  Neil MacCormick
Llull, Ramon
  Mark D. Johnston
Locke, John
  Michael Ayers
Logic, ancient
  Paul Thom
Logic in China
  Chad Hansen
Logic in Islamic philosophy
  Deborah L. Black
Logic in Japan
  Thomas P. Kasulis
Logic in the 17th and 18th centuries
  Mirella Capozzi
Logic in the 19th century
  Randall R. Dipert
Logic in the early 20th century
  Gregory H. Moore
Logic machines and diagrams
  Randall R. Dipert
Logic, medieval
  E.J. Ashworth
Logic of ethical discourse
  Mark Timmons
Logic, philosophy of
  Graeme Forbes
Logic, Renaissance
  E.J. Ashworth
Logical atomism
  Alex Oliver
Logical constants
  Timothy McCarthy
Logical form
  Christopher Menzel
Logical laws
  Greg Restall
Logical positivism
  Michael Friedman
Logical and mathematical terms, glossary of
  Michael Detlefsen
  David Charles McCarty
  John B. Bacon
Logicism
  Howard Stein
Logos
  Christopher Stead
Loisy, Alfred
  Keith E. Yandell
Lombard, Peter
  Marcia L. Colish
Lonergan, Bernard Joseph Francis
  Hugo Meynell
Lorenzen, Paul
  Julian Roberts
Losev, Aleksei Fëdorovich
  George L. Kline
Lossky, Nicholas Onufrievich
  James P. Scanlan
Lotze, Rudolf Hermann
  David Sullivan
Love
  Martha C. Nussbaum
Löwenheim-Skolem theorems and non-standard models
  W.D. Hart
Lu Xiangshan
  Anne D. Birdwhistell
Lucian
  R. Bracht Branham
Lucretius
  Michael Erler
Lukács, Georg
  Alex Callinicos
Łukasiewicz, Jan
  Jan Woleński
Lushi chunqiu
  James D. Sellmann
Luther, Martin
  M.A. Higton
Luxemburg, Rosa
  H. Tudor
Lyotard, Jean-François
  David Carroll
Mach, Ernst
  Andy Hamilton
Machiavelli, Niccolò
  Mary G. Dietz
MacIntyre, Alasdair
  Alan Thomas
McTaggart, John McTaggart Ellis
  Thomas Baldwin
Mādhava
  Edeltraud Harzer Clear
Madhva
  Valerie Stoker
Mahāvīra
  Jayandra Soni
Maimon, Salomon
  Paul Franks
Maimonides, Abraham ben Moses
  Paul B. Fenton
Maimonides, Moses
  L.E. Goodman
Maine de Biran, Pierre-François
  F.C.T. Moore
Major, John
  Joël Biard
Malebranche, Nicolas
  Steven Nadler
Mamardashvili, Merab Konstantinovich
  Caryl Emerson
Mandeville, Bernard
  M.M. Goldsmith

LIST OF ENTRIES AND CONTRIBUTORS

Manicheism
  Christopher Kirwan
Manifoldness, Jaina theory of
  Jayandra Soni
Many-valued logics
  Charles G. Morgan
Many-valued logics, philosophical issues in
  Lloyd Humberstone
Marcel, Gabriel
  David E. Cooper
Marcus Aurelius
  Brad Inwood
Marcuse, Herbert
  Alex Callinicos
Marginality
  Amy A. Oliver
Maritain, Jacques
  Ralph McInerny
Marius Victorinus
  John Peter Kenney
Market, ethics of the
  David Miller
Marsilius of Inghen
  E. P. Bos
Marsilius of Padua
  A.S. McGrade
Marston, Roger
  Girard J. Etzkorn
Martineau, Harriet
  R. K. Webb
Marx, Karl
  Michael Rosen
Marxism, Chinese
  Donald J. Munro
Marxism, Western
  John Torrance
Marxist philosophy of science
  Richard W. Miller
Marxist philosophy, Russian and Soviet
  David Bakhurst
Marxist thought in Latin America
  Ofelia Schutte
Masaryk, Thomáš Garrigue
  Josef Zumr
Masham, Damaris
  Sarah Hutton
Mass terms
  Jeffry Pelletier
Materialism
  George J. Stack
Materialism in the philosophy of mind
  Howard Robinson

Materialism, Indian school of
  Eli Franco
  Karin Preisendanz
Mathematics, foundations of
  Michael Detlefsen
Matter
  Dudley Shapere
Matter, Indian conceptions of
  Paul Schweizer
Matthew of Aquasparta
  Stephen F. Brown
Mauthner, Fritz
  Elizabeth Bredeck
Maxwell, James Clerk
  C.W. F. Everitt
Mead, George Herbert
  Hans Joas
Meaning and communication
  Simon Blackburn
Meaning and rule-following
  Barry C. Smith
Meaning and truth
  Stephen G. Williams
Meaning and understanding
  Ian Rumfitt
Meaning and verification
  W.D. Hart
Meaning in Islamic philosophy
  Oliver Leaman
Meaning, Indian theories of
  Madhav M. Deshpande
Measurement, theory of
  Patrick Suppes
Mechanics, Aristotelian
  Allan Franklin
Mechanics, classical
  Mark Wilson
Medical ethics
  Daniel Wikler
Medicine, philosophy of
  Kenneth F. Schaffner
  H. Tristram Engelhardt, Jr
Medieval philosophy
  Scott MacDonald
  Norman Kretzmann
Medieval philosophy, Russian
  Claire Farrimond
Megarian School
  David Sedley
Meinecke, Friedrich
  Roger Hausheer
Meinong, Alexius
  Peter Simons
Meister Eckhart
  Jan A. Aertsen

Melanchthon, Philipp
  Peter Mack
Melissus
  David Sedley
Memory
  Max Deutscher
Memory, epistemology of
  Earl Conee
Mencius
  Bryan W. Van Norden
Mendelssohn, Moses
  Allan Arkush
Mental causation
  Barry Loewer
Mental illness, concept of
  Karen Neander
Mental states, adverbial theory of
  Michael Tye
Mereology
  Peter Forrest
Merleau-Ponty, Maurice
  Thomas Baldwin
Mersenne, Marin
  Peter Dear
Messer Leon, Judah
  Hava Tirosh-Samuelson
Metaphor
  A.P. Martinich
Metaphysics
  Edward Craig
Methodological individualism
  Gabriel Segal
Mexico, philosophy in
  Horacio Cerutti-Guldberg
Meyerson, Emile
  David A. Sipfle
Mi bskyod rdo rje
  Paul Williams
Midrash
  Philip S. Alexander
Mikhailovskii, Nikolai Konstantinovich
  Andrzej Walicki
Miki Kiyoshi
  J.W. Heisig
Mill, James
  Terence Ball
Mill, John Stuart
  John Skorupski
Millar, John
  Martin Loughlin
Mīmāṃsā
  John A. Taber
Mimēsis
  Glenn W. Most

LIST OF ENTRIES AND CONTRIBUTORS

Mind, bundle theory of
Stewart Candlish
Mind, child's theory of
Alan M. Leslie
Mind, computational theories of
Ned Block
Georges Rey
Mind, identity theory of
Frank Jackson
Mind, Indian philosophy of
Joy Laine
Mind, philosophy of
Frank Jackson
Georges Rey
Mir Damad, Muhammad Baqir
Hamid Dabashi
Miracles
David Basinger
mKhas grub dge legs dpal bzang po
José Ignacio Cabezón
Modal logic
Steven T. Kuhn
Modal logic, philosophical issues in
Thomas J. McKay
Modal operators
Paul Schweizer
Model theory
Wilfrid Hodges
Models
Elisabeth A. Lloyd
Modernism
Thomas Vargish
Modularity of mind
Zenon W. Pylyshyn
Mohist philosophy
Philip J. Ivanhoe
Molecular biology
Michael R. Dietrich
Molina, Luis de
Alfred J. Freddoso
Molinism
Alfred J. Freddoso
Molyneux problem
Menno Lievers
Momentariness, Buddhist doctrine of
Alexander von Rospatt
Monboddo, Lord (James Burnett)
Robert Wokler
Monism
Edward Craig
Monism, Indian
Stephen H. Phillips
Monotheism
George I. Mavrodes

Montague, Richard Merett
Terence Parsons
Montaigne, Michel Eyquem de
Richard H. Popkin
Montesquieu, Charles Louis de Secondat
Mark Hulliung
Moore, George Edward
Thomas Baldwin
Moral agents
Vinit Haksar
Moral development
Owen Flanagan
Moral education
John White
Moral expertise
Brad Hooker
Moral judgment
Garrett Cullity
Moral justification
T.M. Scanlon
Moral knowledge
Geoffrey Sayre-McCord
Moral luck
Daniel Statman
Moral motivation
R. Jay Wallace
Moral particularism
Roger Crisp
Moral pluralism
Daniel M. Weinstock
Moral psychology
Michael Slote
Moral realism
Jonathan Dancy
Moral relativism
David B. Wong
Moral scepticism
Mark T. Nelson
Moral sense theories
Jacqueline Taylor
Moral sentiments
R. Jay Wallace
Moral standing
Arthur Kuflik
Moralistes
Ian Maclean
Morality and emotions
Martha C. Nussbaum
Morality and ethics
John Skorupski
Morality and identity
Ira Singer
More, Henry
Kenneth P. Winkler

Moscow-Tartu School
William Mills Todd III
Motoori Norinaga
Thomas P. Kasulis
Mozi
Robin D.S. Yates
Mujō
Monte S. Hull
Mulla Sadra (Sadr al-Din Muhammad al-Shirazi)
John Cooper
Multiculturalism
Arthur Ripstein
Multiple-conclusion logic
Timothy Smiley
al-Muqammas, Daud
Sarah Stroumsa
Music, aesthetics of
Jerrold Levinson
Musonius Rufus
Brad Inwood
Mystical philosophy in Islam
Seyyed Hossein Nasr
Mysticism, history of
Steven Payne
Mysticism, nature of
Steven Payne
Næss, Arne
Ingemund Gullvåg
Nāgārjuna
Mark Siderits
Nagel, Ernest
Isaac Levi
Nagel, Thomas
Sonia Sedivy
Nahmanides, Moses
Josef Stern
Nancy, Jean-Luc
Peter Fenves
Narrative
Gregory Currie
Nation and nationalism
David Miller
Native American philosophy
Peter M. Whiteley
Nativism
Jerry Samet
Natural deduction, tableau and sequent systems
A.M. Ungar
Natural kinds
Chris Daly
Natural Law
John Finnis

xli

LIST OF ENTRIES AND CONTRIBUTORS

Natural philosophy, medieval
  Edith Dudley Sylla
Natural theology
  Scott MacDonald
Naturalism in ethics
  Nicholas L. Sturgeon
Naturalism in social science
  Ted Benton
Naturalized epistemology
  Steven Luper
Naturalized philosophy of science
  Ronald N. Giere
Nature, aesthetic appreciation of
  Allen Carlson
Nature and convention
  Kate Soper
Naturphilosophie
  Michael Heidelberger
Necessary being
  Brian Leftow
Necessary truth and convention
  Alan Sidelle
Neckham, Alexander
  Mark D. Jordan
Needs and interests
  Albert Weale
Negative facts in classical Indian philosophy
  Brendan S. Gillon
Negative theology
  David Braine
Nemesius
  John Bussanich
Neo-Confucian philosophy
  Philip J. Ivanhoe
Neo-Kantianism
  Hans-Ludwig Ollig
Neo-Kantianism, Russian
  Thomas Nemeth
Neoplatonism
  Lucas Siorvanes
Neoplatonism in Islamic philosophy
  Ian Richard Netton
Neo-Pythagoreanism
  Hermann S. Schibli
Neumann, John von
  Brian Rosmaita
Neurath, Otto
  Nancy Cartwright
  Jordi Cat
Neutral monism
  Nicholas Griffin
Neutrality, political
  Jeremy Waldron
Newman, John Henry
  Ian Ker
Newton, Isaac
  William L. Harper
  George E. Smith
Nichiren
  J.W. Heisig
Nicholas of Autrecourt
  Dominik Perler
Nicholas of Cusa
  Jasper Hopkins
Niebuhr, Helmut Richard
  Martin E. Marty
Niebuhr, Reinhold
  Martin E. Marty
Nietzsche, Friedrich
  Maudemarie Clark
Nietzsche, impact on Russian thought
  Bernice Glatzer Rosenthal
Nifo, Agostino
  Edward P. Mahoney
Nihilism
  Donald A. Crosby
Nihilism, Russian
  Stephen Lovell
Nirvāṇa
  L.S. Cousins
Nishi Amane
  Himi Kiyoshi
Nishida Kitarō
  John C. Maraldo
Nishitani Keiji
  Graham Parkes
Nominalism
  Michael J. Loux
Nominalism, Buddhist doctrine of
  John D. Dunne
Non-constructive rules of inference
  A.P. Hazen
Non-monotonic logic
  André Fuhrmann
Normative epistemology
  Earl Conee
Norms, legal
  Zenon Bańkowski
Norris, John
  Sarah Hutton
Nous
  A.A. Long
Nozick, Robert
  Jonathan Wolff
Numbers
  Graham Priest
Numenius
  John Dillon
Nursing ethics
  Geoffrey Hunt
Nyāya-Vaiśeṣika
  Eli Franco
  Karin Preisendanz
Nygren, Anders
  Diogenes Allen
Oakeshott, Michael Joseph
  Kenneth Minogue
Objectivity
  Alexander Miller
Obligation, political
  A. John Simmons
Observation
  Peter Kosso
Occasionalism
  William Hasker
Ogyū Sorai
  John Allen Tucker
Oken, Lorenz
  Barry Gower
Olivecrona, Karl
  Aleksander Peczenik
Olivi, Peter John
  Robert Pasnau
Oman, John Wood
  Keith E. Yandell
Omnipotence
  Joshua Hoffman
  Gary Rosenkrantz
Omnipresence
  Brian Leftow
Omniscience
  Thomas P. Flint
Ontological commitment
  Michael Jubien
Ontology
  Edward Craig
Ontology in Indian philosophy
  David Ambuel
Opera, aesthetics of
  Michael Tanner
Operationalism
  Frederick Suppe
Optics
  Roger Jones
Ordinal logics
  Solomon Feferman
Ordinary language philosophy
  A.P. Martinich
Ordinary language philosophy, school of
  Geoffrey Warnock

LIST OF ENTRIES AND CONTRIBUTORS

Oresme, Nicole
George Molland
Orientalism and Islamic philosophy
Ubai Nooruddin
Origen
Jeffrey Hause
Orphism
Walter Burkert
Ortega y Gasset, José
N. Orringer
Oswald, James
M.A. Stewart
Other minds
Alec Hyslop
Otto, Rudolf
Keith E. Yandell
Overton, Richard
Udo Thiel
Owen, Gwilym Ellis Lane
John M. Cooper
Oxford Calculators
Edith Dudley Sylla
Paine, Thomas
Bruce Kuklick
Paley, William
Charlotte R. Brown
Panaetius
Stephen A. White
Pan-Africanism
K. Anthony Appiah
Panpsychism
T.L.S. Sprigge
Pan-Slavism
Nicholas V. Riasanovsky
Pantheism
Keith E. Yandell
Paracelsus (Philippus Aureolus Theophrastus Bombastus von Hohenheim)
E.J. Ashworth
Paraconsistent logic
Graham Priest
Paradoxes, epistemic
Jonathan L. Kvanvig
Paradoxes of set and property
Gregory H. Moore
Paranormal phenomena
Stephen E. Braude
Parapsychology
Allen Stairs
Pareto principle
David Miller
Parmenides
David Sedley

Particulars
John Bigelow
Partiinost'
David Joravsky
Pascal, Blaise
Ian Maclean
Passmore, John Arthur
Frank Jackson
Patañjali
Johannes Bronkhorst
Paternalism
Richard J. Arneson
Patočka, Jan
Josef Zumr
Patristic philosophy
John Peter Kenney
Patrizi da Cherso, Francesco
E.J. Ashworth
Paul of Venice
E.J. Ashworth
Pecham, John
Girard J. Etzkorn
Peirce, Charles Sanders
Christopher Hookway
Pelagianism
Christopher Kirwan
Perception
M.G.F. Martin
Perception, epistemic issues in
Brian P. McLaughlin
Perfectionism
Thomas Hurka
Performatives
Kent Bach
Peripatetics
R.W. Sharples
Personal identity
Brian Garrett
Personalism
Keith E. Yandell
Persons
Brian Garrett
Peter of Auvergne
Robert Andrews
Peter of Spain
John L. Longeway
Petrarca, Francesco
John Monfasani
Petrażycki, Leon
Aleksander Peczenik
Phenomenalism
Richard Fumerton
Phenomenological movement
Lester Embree

Phenomenology, epistemic issues in
Jane Howarth
Phenomenology in Latin America
María Teresa Bertelloni
Phenomenology of religion
Merold Westphal
Philip the Chancellor
Scott MacDonald
Philo of Alexandria
David T. Runia
Philo of Larissa
Jonathan Barnes
Philo the Dialectician
Nicholas Denyer
Philodemus
Michael Erler
Philolaus
Hermann S. Schibli
Philoponus
Christian Wildberg
Photography, aesthetics of
Gregory Currie
Physis and nomos
Angela Hobbs
Piaget, Jean
Alison Gopnik
Pico della Mirandola, Giovanni
James Hankins
Pietism
Allen C. Guelzo
Planck, Max Karl Ernst Ludwig
Don Howard
Platform Sutra
John R. McRae
Plato
Malcolm Schofield
Platonism, Early and Middle
John Dillon
Platonism in Islamic philosophy
David Burrell
Platonism, medieval
Dermot Moran
Platonism, Renaissance
James Hankins
Pleasure
Graeme Marshall
Plekhanov, Georgii Valentinovich
James D. White
Plotinus
Eyjólfur Kjalar Emilsson
Pluralism
Edward Craig
Plutarch of Chaeronea
John Dillon

xliii

LIST OF ENTRIES AND CONTRIBUTORS

Pneuma
  Christopher Stead
Poetry
  Richard M. Shusterman
Poincaré, Jules Henri
  David J. Stump
Poland, philosophy in
  Jan Czerkawski
  Antoni B. Stępień
  Stanisław Wielgus
Polanyi, Michael
  R.T. Allen
Polish logic
  Jan Zygmunt
Political philosophy
  David Miller
Political philosophy, history of
  Iain Hampsher-Monk
Political philosophy in classical Islam
  Daniel H. Frank
Political philosophy, Indian
  Sohail Inayatullah
Political philosophy, nature of
  Raymond Plant
Pomponazzi, Pietro
  Martin L. Pine
Popper, Karl Raimund
  Ian C. Jarvie
Population and ethics
  David Heyd
Pornography
  Susan Mendus
Porphyry
  Lucas Siorvanes
Port-Royal
  Antony McKenna
Posidonius
  Keimpe A. Algra
Positivism in the social sciences
  Harold Kincaid
Positivism, Russian
  Andrzej Walicki
Positivist thought in Latin America
  Oscar R. Martí
Possible worlds
  Joseph Melia
Post, Emil Leon
  Michael Scanlan
Postcolonial philosophy of science
  Sandra G. Harding
Postcolonialism
  Ato Quayson
Postmodern theology
  Merold Westphal
Postmodernism
  Elizabeth Deeds Ermarth
Postmodernism and political philosophy
  Stephen K. White
Postmodernism, French critics of
  Reginald Lilly
Post-structuralism
  Gary Gutting
Post-structuralism in the social sciences
  Gary Gutting
Potentiality, Indian theories of
  Richard P. Hayes
Pothier, Robert Joseph
  Neil MacCormick
Pound, Roscoe
  Neil MacCormick
Power
  Leslie Green
Practical reason and ethics
  Onora O'Neill
Pragmatics
  François Recanati
Pragmatism
  Richard Rorty
Pragmatism in ethics
  J.E. Tiles
Praise and blame
  Martha Klein
Praxeology
  Bengt Molander
Prayer
  George I. Mavrodes
Predestination
  George I. Mavrodes
Predicate calculus
  Shaughan Lavine
Predication
  Kevin Mulligan
Prescriptivism
  R.M. Hare
Presocratic philosophy
  David Sedley
Presupposition
  Ian Rumfitt
Price, Richard
  Stephen Darwall
Prichard, Harold Arthur
  Jim MacAdam
Priestley, Joseph
  Robert E. Schofield
Primary-secondary distinction
  A.D. Smith
Prior, Arthur Norman
  C.J.F. Williams
Privacy
  Frances Olsen
Private language argument
  Stewart Candlish
Private states and language
  Edward Craig
Probability, interpretations of
  Paul Humphreys
Probability theory and epistemology
  Barry Loewer
Process philosophy
  David Ray Griffin
Process theism
  David Basinger
Processes
  Dorothy Emmet
Proclus
  Lucas Siorvanes
Prodicus
  Charles H. Kahn
Professional ethics
  Ruth Chadwick
Projectivism
  Simon Blackburn
Promising
  T.M. Scanlon
Proof theory
  Wilfried Sieg
Proper names
  Graeme Forbes
Property
  Stephen R. Munzer
Property theory
  Nino B. Cocchiarella
Prophecy
  David Shatz
Propositional attitude statements
  Kenneth A. Taylor
Propositional attitudes
  Graham Oppy
Propositions, sentences and statements
  Pascal Engel
Protagoras
  Charles H. Kahn
Proudhon, Pierre-Joseph
  Richard Vernon
Provability logic
  Albert Visser
Providence
  William Hasker
Prudence
  Gerard J. Hughes

Pseudo-Dionysius
  Hannes Jarka-Sellers
Pseudo-Grosseteste
  Mark D. Jordan
Psychē
  A.A. Long
Psychoanalysis, methodological issues in
  Patricia Kitcher
Psychoanalysis, post-Freudian
  James Hopkins
Psychology, theories of
  N. E. Wetherick
Ptolemy
  Ferruccio Franco Repellini
Public interest
  Albert Weale
Pufendorf, Samuel
  J.D. Ford
Purgatory
  Linda Zagzebski
Putnam, Hilary
  Yemima Ben-Menahem
Pyrrho
  Jacques Brunschwig
Pyrrhonism
  R.J. Hankinson
Pythagoras
  Hermann S. Schibli
Pythagoreanism
  Hermann S. Schibli
Qi
  David L. Hall
  Roger T. Ames
Qualia
  Janet Levin
Quantification and inference
  Jeffrey C. King
Quantifiers
  Jaakko Hintikka
  Gabriel Sandu
Quantifiers, generalized
  Dag Westerståhl
Quantifiers, substitutional and objectual
  Mark Richard
Quantum logic
  Peter Forrest
Quantum measurement problem
  Jeffrey Bub
Quantum mechanics, interpretation of
  Allen Stairs
Questions
  David Harrah

Quine, Willard Van Orman
  Alex Orenstein
Rabelais, François
  Edwin M. Duval
Race, theories of
  Michael Banton
Radbruch, Gustav
  Massimo La Torre
Radhakrishnan, Sarvepalli
  Robert N. Minor
Radical translation and radical interpretation
  Roger F. Gibson
Rahner, Karl
  Jack A. Bonsor
Ramakrishna movement
  Thomas L. Bryson
Rāmānuja
  Jan K. Brzezinski
Ramsey, Frank Plumpton
  D. H. Mellor
Ramsey, Ian Thomas
  Keith E. Yandell
Ramus, Petrus
  Peter Mack
Rand, Ayn
  Chandran Kukathas
Randomness
  William A. Dembski
Rashdall, Hastings
  Keith E. Yandell
Rational beliefs
  Christopher Cherniak
Rational choice theory
  Russell Hardin
Rationalism
  Peter J. Markie
Rationality and cultural relativism
  Lawrence H. Simon
Rationality of belief
  Jonathan E. Adler
Rationality, practical
  Jean Hampton
Ravaisson-Mollien, Jean-Gaspard Félix Lacher
  Pierrette Bonet
Rawls, John
  Samuel Freeman
al-Razi, Abu Bakr Muhammad ibn Zakariyya'
  Paul E. Walker
al-Razi, Fakhr al-Din
  John Cooper
Realism and antirealism
  Edward Craig

Realism in the philosophy of mathematics
  Patricia A. Blanchette
Reasons and causes
  Michael Smith
Reasons for belief
  Robert Audi
Reciprocity
  Lawrence C. Becker
Recognition
  Axel Honneth
Rectification and remainders
  Claudia Falconer Card
Recursion-theoretic hierarchies
  Harold Hodes
Reduction, problems of
  Jaegwon Kim
Reductionism in the philosophy of mind
  Kim Sterelny
Reference
  Michael Devitt
Régis, Pierre-Sylvain
  Thomas M. Lennon
Reichenbach, Hans
  Wesley C. Salmon
Reid, Thomas
  Roger Gallie
Reinach, Adolf
  Barry Smith
Reincarnation
  Keith E. Yandell
Reinhold, Karl Leonhard
  George di Giovanni
Relativism
  Edward Craig
Relativity theory, philosophical significance of
  Michael Redhead
Relevance logic and entailment
  Stephen Read
Reliabilism
  Alvin I. Goldman
Religion and epistemology
  Alvin Plantinga
Religion and morality
  Richard J. Mouw
Religion and political philosophy
  Paul J. Weithman
Religion and science
  Nancey Murphy
Religion, critique of
  Matthias Lutz-Bachmann
Religion, history of philosophy of
  William P. Alston

LIST OF ENTRIES AND CONTRIBUTORS

Religion, philosophy of
  Eleonore Stump
Religious experience
  William P. Alston
Religious language
  William P. Alston
Religious pluralism
  Philip L. Quinn
Renaissance philosophy
  E.J. Ashworth
Renner, Karl
  Richard Kinsey
  Neil MacCormick
Renouvier, Charles Bernard
  Laurent Fedi
Representation, political
  Andrew Reeve
Reprobation
  Ronald J. Feenstra
Reproduction and ethics
  Rosalind Hursthouse
Republicanism
  Russell L. Hanson
Respect for persons
  Thomas E. Hill, Jr
Responsibilities of scientists and intellectuals
  Alan Montefiore
Responsibility
  R.A. Duff
Resurrection
  Peter van Inwagen
Revelation
  Richard Swinburne
Revolution
  Peter A. Schouls
rGyal tshab dar ma rin chen
  Georges B.J. Dreyfus
Rhetoric
  Eugene Garver
Richard of Middleton
  Stephen F. Brown
Richard of St Victor
  Kent Emery, Jr
Richard Rufus of Cornwall
  Rega Wood
Ricoeur, Paul
  John B. Thompson
Right and good
  Charles Larmore
Rights
  Rex Martin
Risk
  Kristin Shrader-Frechette
Risk assessment
  Kristin Shrader-Frechette
Ritual
  Howard Wettstein
Rohault, Jacques
  Theo Verbeek
Roman law
  P.B.H. Birks
Romanticism, German
  Frederick Beiser
Rorty, Richard McKay
  Michael David Rohr
Roscelin of Compiègne
  Martin M. Tweedale
Rosenzweig, Franz
  Myriam Bienenstock
Rosmini-Serbati, Antonio
  Guido Verucci
Ross, Alf
  Enrico Pattaro
Ross, William David
  David McNaughton
Rousseau, Jean-Jacques
  N.J.H. Dent
Royce, Josiah
  Robert W. Burch
Rozanov, Vasilii Vasil'evich
  Bernice Glatzer Rosenthal
Ruge, Arnold
  Hans-Martin Sass
Rule of law (Rechtsstaat)
  T.R.S. Allan
Russell, Bertrand Arthur William
  Nicholas Griffin
Russian empiriocriticism
  David Joravsky
Russian literary formalism
  Carol Any
Russian Materialism: 'The 1860s'
  James P. Scanlan
Russian philosophy
  Aileen Kelly
Russian religious-philosophical renaissance
  Bernice Glatzer Rosenthal
Ryle, Gilbert
  William Lyons
Sa skya paṇḍita
  Georges B.J. Dreyfus
Saadiah Gaon
  L.E. Goodman
al-Sabzawari, al-Hajj Mulla Hadi
  John Cooper
Sacraments
  David Braine
Saint-Simon, Claude-Henri de Rouvroy, Comte de
  David Leopold
Salvation
  Keith E. Yandell
Sanches, Francisco
  Richard H. Popkin
Sanctification
  Diogenes Allen
Śaṅkara
  Andrew O. Fort
Sāṅkhya
  Dan Lusthaus
Santayana, George
  John Lachs
Sapir-Whorf hypothesis
  John A. Lucy
Sartre, Jean-Paul
  Christina Howells
Saussure, Ferdinand de
  David Holdcroft
Savigny, Friedrich Karl von
  Neil MacCormick
Scandinavia, philosophy in
  Dagfinn Føllesdal
Scepticism
  Stewart Cohen
Scepticism, Renaissance
  Richard H. Popkin
Scheler, Max Ferdinand
  Francis Dunlop
Schelling, Friedrich Wilhelm Joseph von
  Andrew Bowie
Schellingianism
  Victor Terras
Schiller, Ferdinand Canning Scott
  Reuben Abel
Schiller, Johann Christoph Friedrich
  T.J. Reed
Schlegel, Friedrich von
  Frederick Beiser
Schleiermacher, Friedrich Daniel Ernst
  Günter Meckenstock
Schlick, Friedrich Albert Moritz
  Thomas Oberdan
Schmitt, Carl
  David Ludovic Dyzenhaus
Schopenhauer, Arthur
  Christopher Janaway
Schumpeter, Joseph Alois
  Richard Swedberg
Schurman, Anna Maria van
  Eileen O'Neill

LIST OF ENTRIES AND CONTRIBUTORS

Schütz, Alfred
  Finn Collin
Science in Islamic philosophy
  Ziauddin Sardar
Science, 19th century philosophy of
  Robert E. Butts
Science, philosophy of
  John Worrall
Scientific method
  Gary Hatfield
Scientific realism and antirealism
  Arthur Fine
Scientific realism and social science
  Russell Keat
Scope
  Mark Richard
Searle, John
  Ernie Lepore
Second- and higher-order logics
  Shaughan Lavine
Second-order logic, philosophical issues in
  Stewart Shapiro
Secondary qualities
  Colin McGinn
Selden, John
  Peter Goodrich
Self, Indian theories of
  T.S. Rukmani
Self-control
  Philip L. Quinn
Self-cultivation in Chinese philosophy
  Tu Wei-ming
Self-deception
  Alfred R. Mele
Self-deception, ethics of
  Mike W. Martin
Self-realization
  Mark Evans
Self-respect
  Cynthia A. Stark
Sellars, Wilfrid Stalker
  Jay F. Rosenberg
Semantic paradoxes and theories of truth
  Vann McGee
Semantics
  Mark Crimmins
Semantics, conceptual role
  Ned Block
Semantics, game-theoretic
  Michael Hand

Semantics, informational
  Brian P. McLaughlin
  Georges Rey
Semantics, possible worlds
  John R. Perry
Semantics, situation
  John R. Perry
Semantics, teleological
  Peter Godfrey-Smith
Semiotics
  W.C. Watt
Seneca, Lucius Annaeus
  Brad Inwood
Sengzhao
  Thomas P. Kasulis
Sense and reference
  Genoveva Martí
Sense perception, Indian views of
  Stephen H. Phillips
Sense-data
  André Gallois
Sergeant, John
  Beverley Southgate
Set theory
  John P. Burgess
Set theory, different systems of
  Michael Potter
Sextus Empiricus
  R.J. Hankinson
Sexuality, philosophy of
  Alan Soble
Shaftesbury, Third Earl of (Anthony Ashley Cooper)
  David McNaughton
Shah Wali Allah (Qutb al-Din Ahmad al-Rahim)
  Hafiz A. Ghaffar Khan
Shao Yong
  Anne D. Birdwhistell
Shem Tov Family
  Hava Tirosh-Samuelson
Shestov, Lev (Yehuda Leib Shvartsman)
  Bernice Glatzer Rosenthal
Shinran
  Taitetsu Unno
Shintō
  Paul Varley
Shōtoku Constitution
  Yukio Kachi
Shpet, Gustav Gustavovich
  Alexander Haardt
Sidgwick, Henry
  Bart Schultz

Siger of Brabant
  John F. Wippel
Signposts movement
  Aileen Kelly
al-Sijistani, Abu Sulayman Muhammad
  George N. Atiyeh
Silvestri, Francesco
  Michael Tavuzzi
Simmel, Georg
  David Frisby
Simplicity (in scientific theories)
  Elliott Sober
Simplicity, divine
  Brian Leftow
Simplicius
  Christian Wildberg
Sin
  Philip L. Quinn
Sirhak
  Yŏng-ho Ch'oe
Situation ethics
  Gene Outka
Skinner, Burrhus Frederick
  Owen Flanagan
  Georges Rey
Skovoroda, Hryhorii Savych
  Taras D. Zakydalsky
Slavery
  Stephen L. Esquith
  Nicholas D. Smith
Slavophilism
  Andrzej Walicki
Slovakia, philosophy in
  Josef Zumr
Smart, John Jamieson Carswell
  Frank Jackson
Smith, Adam
  Knud Haakonssen
Social action
  Raimo Tuomela
Social choice
  Alan Hamlin
Social democracy
  David Miller
Social epistemology
  Frederick F. Schmitt
Social laws
  Philip Pettit
Social norms
  Margaret Gilbert
Social relativism
  Alan Musgrave

xlvii

Social science, contemporary philosophy of
David Braybrooke
Social science, history of philosophy of
Peter T. Manicas
Social science, methodology of
Alex Rosenberg
Social sciences, philosophy of
David-Hillel Ruben
Social sciences, prediction in
Eerik Lagerspetz
Social theory and law
Roger Cotterrell
Socialism
Russell Keat
John O'Neill
Society, concept of
Angus Ross
Socinianism
John Marshall
Sociobiology
Alex Rosenberg
Sociology of knowledge
David Bloor
Sociology, theories of
Jeffrey C. Alexander
Socrates
John M. Cooper
Socratic dialogues
Charles H. Kahn
Socratic schools
Voula Tsouna
Solidarity
Andrew Mason
Solipsism
Edward Craig
Soloveitchik, Joseph B.
D. Hartman
Solov'ëv, Vladimir Sergeevich
Andrzej Walicki
Sophists
Charles H. Kahn
Sorel, Georges
Jeremy Jennings
Sôsan Hyujông
Sung Bae Park
Soto, Domingo de
John P. Doyle
Soul in Islamic philosophy
Shams C. Inati
Soul, nature and immortality of the
Richard Swinburne

South Slavs, philosophy of
Aleksandar Pavković
Živan Lazović
Sovereignty
J.D. Ford
Space
Roberto Torretti
Spacetime
Roberto Torretti
Spain, philosophy in
José Luis Abellán
Species
Kim Sterelny
Speech acts
Kent Bach
Spencer, Herbert
Tim S. Gray
Speusippus
John Dillon
Spinoza, Benedict de
Henry E. Allison
Split brains
Charles Marks
Sport and ethics
Drew A. Hyland
Sport, philosophy of
Drew A. Hyland
Staël-Holstein, Anne-Louise-Germaine, Mme de
David Leopold
Stair, James Dalrymple, Viscount
Scott C. Styles
State, the
Peter P. Nicholson
Statistics
James Woodward
Statistics and social science
Peter Spirtes
Steiner, Rudolf
Keith E. Yandell
Stevenson, Charles Leslie
James Dreier
Stewart, Dugald
Edward H. Madden
Stirner, Max
David Leopold
Stoicism
David Sedley
Strato
R.W. Sharples
Strauss, David Friedrich
Horton Harris
Strauss, Leo
Shadia B. Drury

Strawson, Peter Frederick
Paul F. Snowdon
Structuralism
Jonathan Culler
Structuralism in linguistics
D. Holdcroft
Structuralism in literary theory
Joseph Margolis
Structuralism in social science
Theodore R. Schatzki
Suárez, Francisco
John P. Doyle
Subject, postmodern critique of the
Laura Hengehold
Sublime, the
Paul Crowther
Substance
Michael Ayers
Suchon, Gabrielle
Michèle Le Doeuff
Suffering
David DeGrazia
Suffering, Buddhist views of origination of
Marek Mejor
al-Suhrawardi, Shihab al-Din Yahya
John Cooper
Suicide, ethics of
Paul Edwards
Sunzi
Roger T. Ames
Supererogation
Gregory Velazco y Trianosky
Supervenience
Simon Blackburn
Supervenience of the mental
B. Loewer
Suso, Henry
John Bussanich
Swedenborg, Emanuel
Alison Laywine
Symbolic interactionism
Arthur Brittan
Syntax
Stephen Neale
Systems theory in social science
Alan Ryan
James Bohman
Tagore, Rabindranath
Robert N. Minor
Taine, Hippolyte-Adolphe
Colin Evans
Tanabe Hajime
Himi Kiyoshi

LIST OF ENTRIES AND CONTRIBUTORS

Tarski, Alfred
  Roman Murawski
Tarski's definition of truth
  Anil Gupta
Tauler, John
  John Bussanich
al-Tawhidi, Abu Hayyan
  Charles Genequand
Taxonomy
  David L. Hull
Taylor, Charles
  Craig Calhoun
Taylor, Harriet
  Candace Vogler
Technology and ethics
  Carl Mitcham
  Helen Nissenbaum
Technology, philosophy of
  Peter Kroes
Teilhard de Chardin, Pierre
  Keith E. Yandell
Tel Quel School
  Stephen Heath
Teleological ethics
  Christine M. Korsgaard
Teleology
  Andrew Woodfield
Telesio, Bernardino
  Eckhard Kessler
Temple, William
  Keith E. Yandell
Tennant, Frederick Robert
  Stephen Maitzen
Tense and temporal logic
  Quentin Smith
Tertullian, Quintus Septimus Florens
  John Peter Kenney
Testimony
  C.A.J. Coady
Testimony in Indian philosophy
  Purushottama Bilimoria
Tetens, Johann Nicolaus
  Günter Zöller
Thales
  Richard McKirahan
Themistius
  John Bussanich
Theological virtues
  William E. Mann
Theology, political
  Matthias Lutz-Bachmann
Theology, Rabbinic
  Aryeh Botwinick
Theophrastus
  Pamela M. Huby
Theoretical (epistemic) virtues
  William G. Lycan
Theories, scientific
  Frederick Suppe
Theory and observation in social sciences
  William Outhwaite
Theory and practice
  John O'Neill
Theory of types
  Nino B. Cocchiarella
Theosophy
  Michael B. Wakoff
Thermodynamics
  Lawrence Sklar
Thielicke, Helmut
  Keith E. Yandell
Thierry of Chartres
  John Marenbon
Thomas à Kempis
  Kent Emery, Jr
Thomas of York
  Fiona Somerset
Thomasius (Thomas), Christian
  Knud Haakonssen
Thomism
  John Haldane
Thoreau, Henry David
  Timothy Gould
Thought experiments
  David C. Gooding
Thrasymachus
  Angela Hobbs
Thucydides
  Paul Woodruff
Ti and yong
  Philip J. Ivanhoe
Tian
  David L. Hall
  Roger T. Ames
Tibetan philosophy
  Tom J.F. Tillemans
Tillich, Paul
  Guyton B. Hammond
Time
  Lawrence Sklar
Time travel
  Paul Horwich
Timon
  Jacques Brunschwig
Tindal, Matthew
  Jean-Loup Seban
Tocqueville, Alexis de
  L.A. Siedentop
Todorov, Tzvetan
  Françoise Lionnet
Toland, John
  J.A.I. Champion
Toleration
  John Horton
Toletus, Franciscus
  John P. Doyle
Tolstoi, Count Lev Nikolaevich
  Gary Saul Morson
Tominaga Nakamoto
  John Allen Tucker
Tonghak
  Yŏng-ho Ch'oe
Totalitarianism
  Margaret Canovan
Tradition and traditionalism
  Anthony O'Hear
Tragedy
  Susan L. Feagin
Transcendental arguments
  Ross Harrison
Translators
  Jozef Brams
Trinity
  Peter van Inwagen
Troeltsch, Ernst Peter Wilhelm
  Jean-Loup Seban
Trotsky, Leon
  Alex Callinicos
Trust
  Karen Jones
Truth, coherence theory of
  Richard L. Kirkham
Truth, correspondence theory of
  Richard L. Kirkham
Truth, deflationary theories of
  Richard L. Kirkham
Truth, pragmatic theory of
  Richard L. Kirkham
Truthfulness
  Sissela Bok
Tschirnhaus, Ehrenfried Walther von
  Martin Schönfeld
Tsong kha pa Blo bzang grags pa
  Tom J.F. Tillemans
Tucker, Abraham
  T. McNair
Turing, Alan Mathison
  James H. Moor
Turing machines
  Guglielmo Tamburrini

xlix

LIST OF ENTRIES AND CONTRIBUTORS

Turing reducibility and Turing degrees
Harold Hodes
Turnbull, George
Paul Wood
al-Tusi, Khwajah Nasir
John Cooper
Twardowski, Kazimierz
Jan Woleński
Type/token distinction
Linda Wetzel
Udayana
Joy Laine
Uddyotakara
Joy Laine
Ûisang
Robert E. Buswell, Jr
Ulrich of Strasbourg
John Bussanich
Unamuno y Jugo, Miguel de
Nelson R. Orringer
Unconscious mental states
Georges Rey
Underdetermination
Larry Laudan
Unity of science
Jordi Cat
Universal language
Donald Rutherford
Universalism in ethics
Onora O'Neill
Universals
John Bigelow
Universals, Indian theories of
John A. Taber
Use/mention distinction and quotation
Corey Washington
Utilitarianism
Tim Chappell
Roger Crisp
Utopianism
Lyman Tower Sargent
Vagueness
Michael Tye
Vaihinger, Hans
Christopher Adair-Toteff
Valla, Lorenzo
John Monfasani
Vallabhācārya
Richard J. Cohen
Value judgements in social science
Tom L. Beauchamp
Value, ontological status of
Alex Oliver

Values
Alan Thomas
Vasubandhu
Richard P. Hayes
Marek Mejor
Vātsyāyana
Joy Laine
Vedānta
Stephen H. Phillips
Venn, John
Daniel D. Merrill
Vernia, Nicoletto
Edward P. Mahoney
Vico, Giambattista
Leon Pompa
Vienna Circle
F. Stadler
Villey, Michel
Neil MacCormick
Violence
C.A.J. Coady
Virtue epistemology
Linda Zagzebski
Virtue ethics
Roger Crisp
Virtues and vices
Bernard Williams
Vision
Frances Egan
Vital du Four
William E. Mann
Vitalism
William Bechtel
Robert C. Richardson
Vitoria, Francisco de
Anthony Pagden
Vives, Juan Luis
Rita Guerlac
Vlastos, Gregory
Daniel W. Graham
Voegelin, Eric
H.M. Höpfl
Voltaire (François-Marie Arouet)
David Williams
Voluntarism
Brian Leftow
Voluntarism, Jewish
Allan Lazaroff
Von Wright, Georg Henrik
Ilkka Niiniluoto
Vulnerability and finitude
Onora O'Neill
Vygotskii, Lev Semënovich
David Joravsky

Vysheslavtsev, Boris Petrovich
James P. Scanlan
Wallace, Alfred Russel
Barbara G. Beddall
Wang Chong
Agnes Chalier
Wang Fuzhi
Alison H. Black
Wang Yangming
Shun Kwong-loi
War and peace, philosophy of
Terry Nardin
Watsuji Tetsurō
Steve Odin
Weber, Max
Stephen P. Turner
Regis A. Factor
Weil, Simone
R. Williams
Weinberger, Ota
Neil MacCormick
Welfare
Albert Weale
Weyl, Hermann
T.A. Ryckman
Weyr, František
Ota Weinberger
Whewell, William
Menachem Fisch
White, Thomas
Beverley Southgate
Whitehead, Alfred North
James Bradley
Will, the
Thomas Pink
William of Auvergne
Steven P. Marrone
William of Auxerre
Scott MacDonald
William of Champeaux
Martin M. Tweedale
William of Conches
John Marenbon
William of Ockham
Claude Panaccio
William of Sherwood
John Longeway
Williams, Bernard Arthur Owen
Ross Harrison
Wisdom
Nicholas D. Smith
Witherspoon, John
R.J. Fechner
Wittgenstein, Ludwig Josef Johann
Jane Heal

LIST OF ENTRIES AND CONTRIBUTORS

Wittgensteinian ethics
Sabina Lovibond
Wodeham, Adam
Rega Wood
Wolff, Christian
Charles A. Corr
Wollaston, William
Charlotte R. Brown
Wollstonecraft, Mary
Susan Khin Zaw
Wônch'ŭk
Shotaro Iida
Wônhyo
Sung Bae Park
Work, philosophy of
Richard Arneson
Wróblewski, Jerzy
Marek Zirk-Sadowski
Wundt, Wilhelm
Jens Brockmeier
Wyclif, John
Jeremy Catto
Xenocrates
John Dillon
Xenophanes
J.H. Lesher
Xenophon
David K. O'Connor
Xin (heart and mind)
David L. Hall
Roger T. Ames

Xin (trustworthiness)
Philip J. Ivanhoe
Xing
David L. Hall
Roger T. Ames
Xunzi
A.S. Cua
Yang Xiong
Michael Nylan
Yangzhu
H.D. Roth
Yi Hwang
Michael C. Kalton
Yi Kan
Michael C. Kalton
Yi Yulgok
Young-chan Ro
Yijing
Richard John Lynn
Yin-yang
Roger T. Ames
Yoruba epistemology
Barry Hallen
You-wu
David L. Hall
Roger T. Ames
Zabarella, Jacopo
Eckhard Kessler
Zeami
Michiko Yusa

Zeno of Citium
David Sedley
Zeno of Elea
Stephen Makin
Zermelo, Ernst
Volker Peckhaus
Zhang Zai
Kirill Ole Thompson
Zheng Xuan
Michael Nylan
Zhi
David L. Hall
Roger T. Ames
Zhi Dun
John R. McRae
Zhiyi
Daniel B. Stevenson
Zhongyong
Tu Wei-ming
Zhou Dunyi
Kirill Ole Thompson
Zhu Xi
Kirill Ole Thompson
Zhuangzi
Roger T. Ames
Zionism
Ze'ev Levy
Zongmi
Peter N. Gregory
Zoroastrianism
Alan Williams

An alphabetical list of contributors, their affiliations and the entries they have written can be found in the index volume (Volume 10).

A POSTERIORI

A prominent term in theory of knowledge since the seventeenth century, 'a posteriori' signifies a kind of knowledge or justification that depends on evidence, or warrant, from sensory experience. A posteriori truth is truth that cannot be known or justified independently of evidence from sensory experience, and a posteriori concepts are concepts that cannot be understood independently of reference to sensory experience. A posteriori knowledge contrasts with a priori knowledge, knowledge that does not require evidence from sensory experience. A posteriori knowledge is empirical, experience-based knowledge, whereas a priori knowledge is non-empirical knowledge. Standard examples of a posteriori truths are the truths of ordinary perceptual experience and the natural sciences; standard examples of a priori truths are the truths of logic and mathematics. The common understanding of the distinction between a posteriori and a priori knowledge as the distinction between empirical and non-empirical knowledge comes from Kant's Critique of Pure Reason *(1781/1787).*

1 Empirical warrant
2 Coherentism about empirical warrant
3 Foundationalism about empirical warrant

1 Empirical warrant

Kant (1781/1787: A2/B3) notes that 'opposed to [a priori knowledge] is empirical knowledge, which is knowledge possible only a posteriori, that is, through experience' (see KANT, I. §4). Empirical knowledge is a posteriori in virtue of the kind of warrant, or justification, it requires for the proposition known: a kind of warrant somehow grounded in sensory experience. The standard approach to knowledge claims that propositional knowledge requires justified true belief. The belief condition for knowledge, according to this approach, must be appropriately related to the satisfaction of the truth condition, thereby excluding true groundless conjectures from the category of knowledge. This requirement involves a justification condition for knowledge, and this condition typically receives most of the attention from contemporary accounts of empirical knowledge.

Contemporary accounts of empirical, or a posteriori, justification ordinarily seek to explain what sorts of processes (vision, memory, introspection, inference and so on) can, and perhaps standardly do, yield empirical justification for beliefs. These accounts typically assume *fallibilism* about empirical justification: an empirically justified contingent belief can be false (see FALLIBILISM). These accounts also typically assume that evidence providing empirical justification for a belief need not logically entail that belief, but can be inductive or probabilistic. Although contemporary epistemologists do not share a single account of the kind of probability appropriate to empirical justification, they largely agree that empirical evidence is *defeasible*, that it can cease to be justifying upon one's acquiring broader evidence. Upon approaching an apparent large pool of water on the road, for example, one might lose one's justification for thinking that there actually is such a pool on the road. An account of empirical justification must, in any case, identify a suitable role for sensory experience in the conferring of justification. Otherwise, the distinction between a posteriori and a priori warrant and knowledge will be unclear.

Contemporary philosophers debate whether any necessarily true proposition is knowable a posteriori. Saul KRIPKE, for instance, has argued that some necessarily true propositions must be known a posteriori if they are to be known at all. His main examples are true identity statements involving names: for example, 'Hesperus is Phosphorus'. Kripke holds that such statements are necessarily true, but that they cannot be known a priori (Kripke 1980). Other philosophers have challenged the view that such identity statements are necessarily true.

2 Coherentism about empirical warrant

Coherentism about empirical justification identifies particular 'coherence relations' among beliefs as constituting empirical justification. Coherence relations can include logical entailment relations, relations of explanation, and various probabilistic, or inductive, relations. Whatever they include, coherentism about empirical justification must identify what makes justification empirical; it must acknowledge a role for sensory experience.

Coherentism about empirical justification faces an objection if empirical evidence can come from a kind of sensory experience that does not require corresponding beliefs descriptive of the relevant sensory experience. Suppose, for instance, that empirical evidence can come from the non-propositional contents (such as visual images) of one's non-belief sensory awareness-states (for example, non-belief visual states). Not all sensory states are, or even require, belief states. One might believe that one has a certain visual image, but this does not entail that the image in question is a proposition one believes; nor does this entail that every visual image requires a corresponding belief descriptive of that image. Coherentism makes justification depend just on coherence relations among propositions one believes. It thus neglects the evidential role of non-belief sensory experiences in empirical justification. In particular, coherentism apparently permits that what is warranted by coherence relations among one's beliefs can be isolated, or divorced, from the perceptual contents of one's non-belief sensory experiences. This would be a serious defect in an account of empirical justification, justification dependent on sensory experience. Proponents of coherentism have not reached agreement on how to treat the previous objection (see KNOWLEDGE AND JUSTIFICATION, COHERENCE THEORY OF).

Coherentism about justification is often called 'epistemic holism'. According to Quine and others, such holism recommends that we dispense with (1) the analytic–synthetic distinction and (2) the view that our beliefs are tested individually against the input of sensory experience (see QUINE, W.V. §3). Our beliefs, given epistemic holism, are confirmed or disconfirmed as a system, collectively rather than individually. In addition, Quine holds, any of our beliefs can be held true come what may, if we make drastic enough changes elsewhere in our system of beliefs; by the same token, none of our beliefs is immune to revision. On this basis, Quine opposes any distinction between the a priori and the a posteriori due to considerations about irrevisability of beliefs. This is not, however, a general argument against the distinction between the a priori and the a posteriori, because some versions of the distinction do not appeal to considerations about irrevisability. Some versions appeal, instead, to considerations about the dependence of relevant evidence on sensory experience.

3 Foundationalism about empirical warrant

The leading alternative to coherentism is *foundationalism* about empirical justification: empirical justification has a two-tier structure in that some instances of such justification are non-inferential, or foundational, and all other instances of such justification are inferential, or non-foundational, owing to their dependence on foundational justification. Bertrand Russell, A.J. Ayer, and C.I. Lewis advanced influential twentieth-century versions of foundationalism about empirical knowledge and justification. Foundationalists differ among themselves on two key matters: the explanation of what precisely constitutes non-inferential, foundational empirical justification, and the explanation of how empirical justification can be transmitted from foundational beliefs to non-foundational beliefs. Opposing the radical foundationalism of Descartes, contemporary foundationalists typically endorse *modest* foundationalism, implying that foundational beliefs need not possess or yield certainty and need not deductively support justified non-foundational beliefs. A foundational belief, minimally characterized, is non-inferentially justified in that its justification does not derive from other beliefs.

Traditionally, empiricist proponents of foundationalism have countenanced foundational justification by non-belief sensory experiences. These empiricists, notably represented by C.I. Lewis, hold that foundational empirical beliefs can be justified by non-belief sensory experiences (for example, your non-belief experience involving your 'seeming to see' a book page) that either make true, are best explained by, or otherwise support those foundational beliefs (for example, the belief that there is, or at least appears to be, a book page here, before you). More recently, proponents of foundational empirical justification by reliable empirical origins have proposed that non-inferential empirical justification derives from a belief's origin in a non-belief empirical belief-forming process (for example, perception, introspection) that is truth-conducive to a certain extent, in virtue of tending to produce true rather than false beliefs. The latter proposal, a species of 'process reliabilism', cites the reliability of a belief's non-belief origin, whereas the previous view invokes, as justifiers, the particular sensory experiences that underlie a foundational belief. Both approaches can, however, accommodate the view that foundational empirical justification is defeasible, or overridable given the acquisition of new evidence (see FOUNDATIONALISM).

A comprehensive account of empirical justification will explain the nature of sensory experience. If sensory experience does not have a non-conceptual component, it will be ill-suited to serve the purposes of traditional foundationalism about empirical justification. In that case, sensory experience will fail to provide a basis for justified empirical beliefs that does not itself require evidential support. If sensory experience is identical to conceptualization, judgment or belief, then it will itself need evidential support if it is to confer justification on some beliefs; and if this needed support is to be genuinely empirical, it will have to involve more than just propositional relations among beliefs. At least, various proponents of traditional foundationalism have, on this basis, sought a non-conceptual foundation for empirical justification in sensory experience, a foundation that yields a straightforward distinction between a posteriori and a priori warrant.

See also: A PRIORI; EMPIRICISM; JUSTIFICATION, EPISTEMIC; KNOWLEDGE, CONCEPT OF; RATIONAL BELIEFS; REASONS FOR BELIEF

References and further reading

Ayer, A.J. (1936) *Language, Truth, and Logic*, New York: Dover, 2nd edn, 1946. (An accessible defence of extreme empiricism about meaning and knowledge.)

BonJour, L. (1985) *The Structure of Empirical Knowledge*, Cambridge, MA: Harvard University Press. (A defence of coherentism about empirical justification; see §2 above.)

Carruthers, P. (1992) *Human Knowledge and Human Nature*, Oxford: Oxford University Press. (An accessible treatment of issues about the sources of empirical knowledge.)

Goldman, A.I. (1986) *Epistemology and Cognition*, Cambridge, MA: Harvard University Press. (Defends an account of justification and knowledge in terms of reliable belief-forming processes, discussed in §3 above.)

* Kant, I. (1781/1787) *Critique of Pure Reason*, trans. N. Kemp Smith, London: Macmillan, 1963. (Classic statement of the a priori–a posteriori and analytic–synthetic distinctions; see especially the introduction, §§I–IV.)

Kripke, S.A. (1980) *Naming and Necessity*, Oxford: Blackwell, and Cambridge, MA: Harvard University Press. (An influential treatment of the a priori–a posteriori distinction.)

Lewis, C.I. (1946) *An Analysis of Knowledge and Valuation*, LaSalle, IL: Open Court. (A classic statement of foundationalism that acknowledges a central role for a 'given' element in empirical justification.)

Moser, P.K. (1989) *Knowledge and Evidence*, Cambridge: Cambridge University Press. (A defence of a foundationalist approach to empirical knowledge that acknowledges empirical justification by non-belief sensory experiences; see §3 above.)

—— (1993) *Philosophy After Objectivity*, New York: Oxford University Press. (An examination of the kinds of warrant available for claims to objective knowledge, knowledge of the external world.)

Moser, P.K. and Vander Nat, A. (eds) (1987) *Human Knowledge: Classical and Contemporary Approaches*, New York: Oxford University Press, 2nd edn, 1995. (Classical and contemporary selections bearing on the conditions for a priori and a posteriori knowledge. Includes selections from Ayer, Kripke, Lewis, Quine and Russell, among others.)

Quine, W.V. (1953) *From a Logical Point of View*, Cambridge, MA: Harvard University Press, 2nd edn, 1961. (Includes 'Two Dogmas of Empiricism', an influential defence of epistemic holism and challenge to the analytic–synthetic distinction.)

Yolton, J. (1984) *Perceptual Acquaintance from Descartes to Reid*, Oxford: Blackwell. (A survey of classical modern approaches to the nature of perceptual experience.)

PAUL K. MOSER

A PRIORI

An important term in epistemology since the seventeenth century, 'a priori' typically connotes a kind of knowledge or justification that does not depend on evidence, or warrant, from sensory experience. Talk of a priori truth is ordinarily shorthand for talk of truth knowable or justifiable independently of evidence from sensory experience; and talk of a priori concepts is usually talk of concepts that can be understood independently of reference to sensory experience. A priori knowledge contrasts with a posteriori knowledge, knowledge requiring evidence from sensory experience. Broadly characterized, a posteriori knowledge is empirical, experience-based knowledge, and a priori knowledge is non-empirical knowledge. Standard examples of a priori truths are the truths of mathematics, whereas standard examples of a posteriori truths are the truths of the natural sciences.

1   Necessity, analyticity and the a priori
2   Innate concepts, certainty and the a priori
3   Prominent explanations of the a priori

1   Necessity, analyticity and the a priori

Contemporary understanding of the distinction between the a posteriori and the a priori, as the distinction between the empirical and the non-empirical, derives mainly from Kant's *Critique of Pure Reason* (1781/1787), although versions of it precede Kant in the writings of Leibniz and Hume (see KANT, I. §4). The epistemological distinction between a priori and a posteriori knowledge differs from the logical or metaphysical distinction between necessary and contingent truth, and from the semantical distinction between analytic and synthetic truth (see ANALYTICITY). In particular, the concept of a priori knowledge is not the same as either the concept of what is (logically or metaphysically) necessarily true or the concept of what is true analytically, just in virtue of the meanings of a proposition's constituent terms. Kant's talk of a priori 'modes of knowledge' suggests an epistemological, knowledge-oriented characterization of what is a priori. As standardly characterized, a priori knowledge is knowledge that does not depend on evidence from sensory experience. The previous considerations do not, however, settle the issue of whether every proposition knowable a priori is either necessarily true or analytically true.

A necessarily true proposition is not possibly false, or in Leibniz's words, is true in 'all possible worlds'. Contingently true propositions are possibly false, that is, false in some possible worlds. Traditionally, many philosophers have assumed that a proposition is knowable a priori only if it is necessarily true, presumably on the ground that if a proposition is possibly false, then it requires for its justification supporting evidence from sensory experience. Contingent truths, according to this traditional view, are not candidates for a priori knowledge.

Saul Kripke (1980) has argued that some contingently true propositions are knowable a priori. He cites the knowledge that stick S is one metre long at a certain time, where stick S is the standard metre-bar in Paris. If one uses stick S to 'fix the reference' of the term 'one metre', then, according to Kripke, one can know a priori that stick S is one metre long. The truth that stick S is one metre long is contingent rather than necessary; for S might not have been one metre long. (Application of sufficient heat to S, for instance, would have changed its length.) It seems arguable, then, that some contingent truths are knowable a priori, contrary to what many philosophers have assumed. This matter has prompted considerable discussion among contemporary philosophers, with some still contending that no contingently true proposition is knowable a priori. Some of the latter philosophers have noted, with regard to Kripke's example, that 'one metre' can be used either as (1) the name of the length of S whatever that length may be, or as (2) the name of a particular length singled out by a speaker. Given option (1), these philosophers hold, the claim that stick S is one metre long will be necessary and knowable a priori, and given option (2), the claim that stick S is one metre long will be contingent and knowable only a posteriori.

Many philosophers have held that a priori knowledge is restricted to such analytic truths as 'All rectangles have four sides' and 'All bodies are extended'. If such truths are analytic, they are true just in virtue of the meanings of their constituent terms. Such truths differ from synthetic truths, which are true in virtue of something other than just the meanings of their constituent terms (for example, in virtue of observable situations in the world). Synthetic judgments, according to Kant, are 'ampliative' in that they 'add to the concept of the subject a predicate which has not been in any wise thought in it, and which no analysis could possibly extract from it' (1781/1787: A7/B11). Some philosophers, notably W.V. Quine, have contested the viability of any philosophically important distinction between analytic and synthetic truths (see QUINE, W.V. §3).

One issue of philosophical controversy is whether any synthetic truth is knowable a priori. Kripke's aforementioned metre example offers, according to some philosophers, a synthetic truth knowable a priori. Kant held that some synthetic truths, for example, those of geometry, have a kind of necessity that cannot be derived from experience, and can be known a priori. Such synthetic truths, Kant argued, can be known independently of evidence from sensory experience. Kant's doctrine of synthetic a priori truths still generates controversy among philosophers, specifically in connection with such apparently synthetic propositions as 'Nothing can be green and red all over' and 'A straight line is the shortest path between two points'. The later Wittgenstein, for example, proposed that propositions of the latter sort are actually conventional 'rules of grammar', or non-synthetic normative standards for representation (see NECESSARY TRUTH AND CONVENTION).

2 Innate concepts, certainty and the a priori

Many philosophers deny that having a priori knowledge requires having innate concepts, concepts that do not derive from, or depend for their being understood on, sensory experience. (Some theorists, in the tradition of Platonism, hold that mathematical concepts, among others, are innate.) Propositions, one might suppose, consist of concepts, perhaps analogously to the way in which sentences consist of terms. Propositions knowable a priori, according to the philosophers in question, need not consist of innate concepts. The notion of a priori knowledge depends on a notion of a priori *warrant*, not on a notion of a non-empirical origin of the concepts constituting the known proposition. A notion involving special conditions for the justification of a believed proposition is not automatically a notion involving special conditions for either the origin or one's understanding of the belief in question.

The notion of a priori knowledge, construed as a notion of non-empirically grounded knowledge, is not the same as a notion of epistemic certainty. Philosophers have understood 'epistemic certainty' in various ways: for instance, as epistemically indubitable belief or as self-evident belief. A belief is epistemically indubitable if and only if it would not be epistemically justifiable to doubt that belief under any circumstance. It is not obvious that a priori warrant for a proposition requires epistemic indubitability of this proposition. A proposition's being warranted a priori for someone seemingly allows for an expansion of their relevant evidence, whereby a proposition justified on the original evidence ceases to be justified on the expanded evidence. (One might, for example, come to appreciate further implications of a proposition that was justified a priori.) A priori justification for a proposition apparently can be subject to 'epistemic defeat' given a change in a priori evidence (see CERTAINTY; DOUBT).

Philosophical talk of 'self-evidence' is often unclear. On a literal construal, a self-evident proposition is justified but does not depend on anything else for its justification. The problem in linking a priori warrant to such self-evidence is that a priori warrant is compatible with *inferential* warrant, wherein a proposition owes its warrant to inferential relations with other propositions, as might a theorem in a mathematical system. (It is a separate issue whether *all* a priori warrant might be inferential.) The notion of a priori knowledge should thus be explained independently of a literal construal of self-evidence. Other construals of self-evidence will contribute here only if they elucidate a notion of non-empirical warrant that differs from notions of necessary truth, analyticity and certainty as epistemic indubitability.

3 Prominent explanations of the a priori

Philosophers have long sought an account of the defining feature of truths that humans can know a priori. One result is a variety of accounts of the a priori in circulation. *Psychologism* about the a priori, advanced initially but later opposed by Husserl, claims that a true proposition is knowable a priori by humans if and only if our psychological constitution precludes our regarding that proposition as false. *Linguisticism* about the a priori, endorsed by A.J. Ayer and various other twentieth-century empiricists, states that a true proposition is knowable a priori if and only if our denying that proposition would violate rules of coherent language-use; this view denies the existence of synthetic a priori truths. *Pragmatism* about the a priori, advanced by C.I. Lewis, claims that a true proposition is knowable a priori by a person if and only if it describes their pragmatically guided intention to use a certain conceptual scheme of classification for the organizing of experiences. Lewis argued that pragmatic considerations regarding what suits one's needs guide the way in which one formulates a conceptual scheme. A different view, supported by Roderick Chisholm and many others, affirms that a true proposition is knowable a priori by us if and only if our understanding that proposition is all the evidence we need to see that the proposition in question is true. Yet another view about the a priori is suggested by the later writings of Wittgenstein: A proposition is knowable a priori by us if and only if our 'forms of life' (that is, human nature as determined by our biology and cultural history) preclude the intelligibility for us of the denial of that proposition. (Wittgenstein did not offer a detailed account of 'forms of life' or of their role in determining what is a priori.) These are the most influential, but not the only, accounts of the a priori in circulation.

A theory of a priori knowledge should identify the strengths and weakness of the aforementioned accounts of the a priori. It should also identify the feature of a priori justification that requires limitation of the set of propositions knowable a priori to the distinctive kind of propositions specified by that theory. Such a theory must avoid confusing the notion of what is a priori with the notions of what is necessarily true, what is analytically true, what is innate, and what is certain. It must also draw a clear distinction between what is a priori and what is a posteriori.

See also: A POSTERIORI; JUSTIFICATION, EPISTEMIC; INNATE KNOWLEDGE; KNOWLEDGE, CONCEPT OF; RATIONAL BELIEFS; RATIONALISM

References and further reading

Carruthers, P. (1992) *Human Knowledge and Human Nature*, Oxford: Oxford University Press. (An accessible treatment of issues about the sources of knowledge, including a priori knowledge.)

Coffa, J.A. (1991) *The Semantic Tradition from Kant to Carnap*, Cambridge: Cambridge University Press. (A history of philosophical reaction to Kant's doctrine of the a priori.)

* Kant, I. (1781/1787) *Critique of Pure Reason*, trans. N. Kemp Smith, London: Macmillan, 1963. (Classic statement of the distinctions a priori–a

posteriori and analytic–synthetic; see especially the introduction, §§I–IV.)
* Kripke, S.A. (1980) *Naming and Necessity*, Cambridge, MA: Harvard University Press. (Referred to in §1 above. Challenges the view that only necessarily true propositions are knowable a priori.)
Moser, P.K. (ed.) (1987) *A Priori Knowledge*, Oxford: Oxford University Press. (Contains ten of the most important recent essays on a priori knowledge and a bibliography of recent work on the topic. The selections in this book treat the positions identified in §3 above.)
Moser, P.K. and Vander Nat, A. (eds) (1987) *Human Knowledge: Classical and Contemporary Approaches*, New York: Oxford University Press, 2nd edn, 1995. (A wide range of classical and contemporary selections bearing on the conditions for a priori and a posteriori knowledge.)
Pap, A. (1958) *Semantics and Necessary Truth*, New Haven, CT: Yale University Press. (A detailed survey and assessment of many prominent seventeenth through twentieth century views on necessity, analyticity and the a priori, including the views of Leibniz, Kant, Locke and Hume.)
Quine, W.V. (1953) *From a Logical Point of View*, Cambridge, MA: Harvard University Press, 2nd edn, 1961. (Includes 'Two Dogmas of Empiricism', an influential challenge to the analytic–synthetic distinction.)
Shanker, S.G. (1987) *Wittgenstein and the Turning-Point in the Philosophy of Mathematics*, London: Croom Helm. (Expounds Wittgenstein's views on mathematical truth and the a priori.)

PAUL K. MOSER

ABDUCTION see DISCOVERY, LOGIC OF; INFERENCE TO THE BEST EXPLANATION; PEIRCE, CHARLES SANDERS

'ABDUH, MUHAMMAD (1849–1905)

The Egyptian reformer and Muslim apologist Muhammad 'Abduh was a pupil and friend of al-Afghani. Although deeply influenced by him, 'Abduh was less inclined to political activism and concentrated on religious, legal and educational reform. His best-known writings are a theological treatise, Risalat al-tawhid *(translated into English as* The Theology of Unity*), and an unfinished Qur'anic commentary,* Tafsir al-manar *(The Manar Commentary), on which he collaborated with Rashid Rida. One of the key themes of these works is that since modernity is based on reason, Islam must be compatible with it. But 'Abduh's 'modernism' went hand in hand with returning to an idealized past, and his 'rationalism' was tempered by a belief in divine transcendence which limits the scope of intellectual inquiry. In ethics as in theology, he regarded the classical debates as arid and divisive, although on the issues of free will and moral law his position was in fact similar to that of the Mu'tazila.*

1 Faith and reason
2 Ethics

1 Faith and reason

'Abduh trained as an *'alim* (religious scholar) at al-Azhar where, under al-Afghani's influence, he developed an interest in Islamic philosophy and a revulsion for traditional teaching methods which encouraged *taqlid*, the unquestioning acceptance of received opinion. The rational liberalism which he imbibed from AL-AFGHANI was, however, only one facet of his thought. In his youth he was drawn to Sufism and, despite his subsequent attacks on popular superstition, he seems never to have lost his respect for those who in some conditions 'have access in part to the ultimate mysteries and true insights into the visionary world' (*Risalat al-tawhid*, in Musa'ad and Cragg 1966: 97) (see MYSTICAL PHILOSOPHY IN ISLAM). A third influence – the one which is dominant in the *Risalat al-tawhid* (The Theology of Unity) and the *Tafsir al-manar* (The Manar Commentary) – is that of the fourteenth-century Hanbalite jurist IBN TAYMIYYA, who fuelled his desire to purify Islam of later accretions and return to the essentials of the faith as practised by the first generations of Muslims.

'Abduh believed that Islam was the one true religion based on reason and revelation, but that in the course of time it had become distorted by various extrinsic factors. For instance, whereas the Qur'an fosters the scientific spirit by directing man to inquire rationally into the workings of the universe, the Islamic philosophers had uncritically accepted the theories of matter and physics propounded by PLATO and ARISTOTLE, with the result that the Islamic world had come to lag behind Europe in science and technology. His rejection of Greek philosophy in favour of modern science was, however, only partial.

He accepted the distinction between necessary being, possible things and impossible things, using it to prove the existence of God. He also accepted the distinction between essences and accidents, arguing that reason gives us knowledge of the latter but not of the former. A corollary of this is that it is pointless for theologians to argue about the divine attributes because we cannot know their nature (see ISLAMIC THEOLOGY).

2 Ethics

On the issue of free will versus predestination, 'Abduh's starting point is the recognition that the man of sound mind is conscious of acts which stem from his volition:

> He weighs them and their consequences in his mind and evaluates them in his will, and then effectuates them by an inward power. To deny any of this would be tantamount to a denial of his existence itself, so opposed would it be to rational evidence.
> (*Risalat al-tawhid*, in Musa'ad and Cragg 1966: 62)

However, 'Abduh is equally insistent that all events in the world are ordered by God in accordance with his knowledge and will. He rejects further inquiry into how human freedom and divine prescience can be reconciled, on the grounds that such speculation is forbidden.

In discussing the moral law, 'Abduh again begins with an appeal to common sense, arguing that we have no difficulty in recognizing our voluntary actions as good or bad in themselves or by reference to their particular or general consequences. If actions are self-evidently good or bad in the absolute way in which 'Abduh alleges, however, it might be thought that religion is unnecessary. On the contrary, in matters of right and wrong, rational proof will not obviate conflict because people differ in intelligence, the vast majority being unable to understand Platonic philosophy or Aristotelian logic. Moreover, because of its stress on God's pleasure and wrath, religion has a greater impact on ordinary folk than the moralist's claim that some acts are beneficial and others harmful. In any case there are some elements of the Qur'anic revelation which could not be known by unaided reason. These include the certainty of the afterlife, and the various ritual prescriptions.

All this is far-removed from the traditional Ash'arite position. It is possible that here 'Abduh was influenced by Mu'tazilism as mediated by al-Afghani's Shi'ism, or less probably that we should detect the influence of Kantian philosophy. There seems little doubt, however, that his ethical thinking was moulded by the needs of apologetics. This is particularly clear in his essay on Islam and Christianity, in which he replied to Hanotaux, a French cabinet minister who had contrasted the Semitic mentality of Islam – with its transcendentalism, predestinarianism and contempt for individuals – with the Aryan humanism of Christianity, which through the Trinity raised human dignity to that of God.

See also: AL-AFGHANI; ISLAMIC PHILOSOPHY, MODERN

List of works

'Abduh, M. (1874) *Risalat al-waridat* (Treatise of Mystical Inspirations), Cairo.
—— (1876) *Hashiyya 'ala sharh al-Dawwani li 'l-'aqa'id al-adudiyya* (Gloss on Dawwani's Commentary on the Sentences of Adud al-Din al-Iji), Cairo.
—— (1897) *Risalat al-tawhid* (The Theology of Unity) Cairo; trans. I. Musa'ad and K. Cragg, *The Theology of Unity*, London: George Allen & Unwin, 1966. (One of 'Abduh's major works on philosophical theology.)
—— (1902) *al-Islam wa-'l-nasraniyya ma'a al-'ilm wa 'l-madaniyya* (Islam and Christianity in Relation to Science and Civilization), Cairo.
'Abduh, M. and Rida, M.R. (1927–36) *Tafsir al-Qur'an al-hakim* (Commentary on the Wise Qur'an), Cairo. (Commentary on the Wise Qur'an usually referred to as *Tafsir al-manar* because it originally appeared in instalments in the journal *al-Manar*).

References and further reading

Abu Rabi, I. (1996) 'The Arab World', in S.H. Nasr and O. Leaman (eds) *History of Islamic Philosophy*, London: Routledge, ch. 64, 1082–1114. (Detailed description of the various ways in which modern Arabic philosophy has responded to the issues of modernity and Westernization.)
Adams, C.C. (1933) *Islam and Modernism in Egypt*, London: Oxford University Press. (Classic work, unsurpassed despite its early date.)
Amin, O. (1944) *Muhammad Abduh essai sur les idées philosophiques et religieuses* (Muhammad 'Abduh, Essay on his Philosophical and Religious Ideas), Washington, DC. (English translation of the standard Arabic biography.)
Badawi, M.A.Z. (1978) *The Reformers of Egypt*, London: Croom Helm. (Critical analysis by an Egyptian scholar of the views of al-Afghani, 'Abduh and Rida.)
Hourani, A. (1983) *Arabic Thought in the Liberal Age*

1798–1939, Cambridge: Cambridge University Press. (Devotes only thirty pages specifically to 'Abduh, but strongly recommended for anyone who wishes to situate his work in its historical context.)

Jomier, J. (1954) *Le commentaire coranique du Manar: tendances modernes de l'exégèse coranique en Égypte* (The Manar Commentary on the Qur'an: Modern Trends in Qur'anic Exegesis in Egypt), Paris: Maisonneuve. (Painstaking thematic analysis of the Qur'anic commentary by a French Dominican; particularly valuable because of the way in which it distinguishes between the views of 'Abduh and Rida.)

NEAL ROBINSON

ABELARD, PETER (1079–1142)

Among the many scholars who promoted the revival of learning in western Europe in the early twelfth century, Abelard stands out as a consummate logician, a formidable polemicist and a champion of the value of ancient pagan wisdom for Christian thought. Although he worked within the Aristotelian tradition, his logic deviates significantly from that of Aristotle, particularly in its emphasis on propositions and what propositions say. According to Abelard, the subject matter of logic, including universals such as genera and species, consists of linguistic expressions, not of the things these expressions talk about. However, the objective grounds for logical relationships lie in what these expressions signify, even though they cannot be said to signify any things. Abelard is, then, one of a number of medieval thinkers, often referred to in later times as 'nominalists', who argued against turning logic and semantics into some sort of science of the 'real', a kind of metaphysics. It was Abelard's view that logic was, along with grammar and rhetoric, one of the sciences of language.

In ethics, Abelard defended a view in which moral merit and moral sin depend entirely on whether one's intentions express respect for the good or contempt for it, and not at all on one's desires, whether the deed is actually carried out, or even whether the deed is in fact something that ought or ought not be done.

Abelard did not believe that the doctrines of Christian faith could be proved by logically compelling arguments, but rational argumentation, he thought, could be used both to refute attacks on Christian doctrine and to provide arguments that would appeal to those who were attracted to high moral ideals. With arguments of this latter sort, he defended the rationalist positions that nothing occurs without a reason and that God cannot do anything other than what he does do.

1 Life
2 Works
3 Pagan wisdom and Christian faith
4 Logic
5 Ontology
6 Psychology of signification
7 Ethics
8 Theodicy

1 Life

In comparison with most other medieval thinkers we know a great deal about Abelard's career, since he left an autobiographical essay entitled *Historia Calamitatum* (The Story of My Misfortunes), which in effect recounts his life up to about 1132. He was born to a noble and very religious family in Le Pallet, near Nantes in Brittany, in 1079. ROSCELIN OF COMPIÈGNE was one of his earliest teachers, and later in Paris he studied under WILLIAM OF CHAMPEAUX. In these years Abelard's main interest was logic, or dialectic as it was then called, which also included metaphysical issues such as the status of universals as well as psychological topics such as the role of images in thought. It was over the subject of universals that Abelard came into acrimonious conflict with William of Champeaux, and eventually he left Paris to set up his own schools nearby, first in Corbeil and later in Melun.

Having achieved a reputation as a subtle logician, Abelard moved on to study theology with Anselm of Laon, but here again he fell into competition with his teacher and even lured away some of his students. The stay at Laon was short, and by 1114 Abelard was back teaching logic in Paris. However, theology was to move more and more to the centre of his interests as his career progressed.

It was at this juncture that Abelard's famous romance with Heloise began. Heloise was only 17 but was well educated, thanks to the devotion of her guardian and uncle, Fulbert. It was by securing from Fulbert the job of teaching her that Abelard was able to pursue his amorous ends. Abelard confesses that during the height of their passion he was more given to writing love poems than studying logic. Heloise became pregnant, and Abelard took her away to his home in Brittany without Fulbert's permission. There she gave birth to their only child, Astrolabe. In order to reconcile himself to Fulbert, Abelard married Heloise and brought her back to Paris where she again lived with her uncle. The marriage was to have been kept secret in order not to endanger Abelard's career as a cleric, but Fulbert broadcast the news, with the result that Abelard had Heloise removed to a convent. Fulbert was so enraged by this that he hired thugs who attacked Abelard and castrated him. Subsequently, Heloise remained a nun for the rest of her life and became herself well known in this vocation. Abelard resumed his scholarly career after first entering the abbey of St Denis.

The next period of Abelard's life was intensely productive. His most important logical works, as well as the first version of his *Theologia* (Theology), were probably produced while he was at St Denis. Some of his enemies, well placed in the church hierarchy, found in the *Theologia* what they took to be errors, and at a church council summoned in April 1121 in Soissons, Abelard's work was condemned (this condemnation was later revoked). However, Abelard thrived on controversy, and from 1122 to 1127 he continued his teaching and work at a retreat in the country near Quincy. His reputation became even greater, and students from all over Europe flocked to his lectures on both logic and theology.

In 1127 Abelard accepted an appointment as the abbot of a monastery in Brittany known for its moral laxity. By this time he had become a strong proponent of church reform, especially in moral matters. His efforts to establish discipline at the monastery only angered the monks there, to the point where they tried several times to murder him. Eventually Abelard was relieved of these duties, and returned to Paris to teach at the school on Mont Ste-Geneviève.

Following the council at Soissons Abelard had revised his *Theologia* several times, but his doctrine of the Trinity as well as his view of sin again angered the church hierarchy, including the now very powerful BERNARD OF CLAIRVAUX. In June of 1140, a council of bishops at Sens condemned several of his positions. Abelard's appeal to the pope was countered by Bernard, but eventually a reconciliation was arranged. Abelard died at Cluny on 21 April 1142.

Although in his own day Abelard was famous and influential, his impact on later generations was less than might have been expected. Peter Lombard's *Sentences*, which became the standard theological textbook in the thirteenth century, owed much to Abelard's *Sic et Non* (Yes and No), and strong realism about universals was never an option after Abelard's attack; but many of Abelard's logical innovations were forgotten once the corpus of Aristotle's logic became available in the West. Abelard was hardly ever referred to after 1200, and a fellow nominalist like WILLIAM OF OCKHAM, writing around 1317, seems totally unaware of his work.

2 Works

In order to understand and assess Abelard as a philosopher, it is important to consider not only his works on logic but also his writings on theology. At risk of considerable over-simplification, his works may be divided into those composed before his stay in the community near Quincy (1122–7) and those written during and after that stay. As C.J. Mews (1985) has pointed out, this break seems to correspond with certain revisions Abelard made in both his logical and theological teachings.

In the earlier group lie his two great logical works, *Dialectica* and the *Logica ingredientibus* (Logic for Beginners). The latter is really four works, consisting of glosses on four earlier and important logical works, Porphyry's *Isagoge*, Aristotle's *Categories*, Aristotle's *Peri hermenias* or *De Interpretatione*, and on Boethius' *De differentiis topicis* (see ARISTOTLE; BOETHIUS, A.M.S.; PORPHYRY). These were interpretative commentaries on what was later called the 'old logic'. The *Dialectica* is an independent treatise roughly covering the same topics treated in the old logic, but without direct commentary. In theology, Abelard produced in the period before Quincy the version of his *Theologia* known as the *Theologia 'Summi Boni'* (Theology of the Highest Good) and the collection of conflicting passages from scriptures and earlier church fathers and doctors known as the *Sic et Non*.

After he moved to Quincy, Abelard's *Theologia* went through several revisions, resulting in a long work divided into five books now referred to as the *Theologia Christiana* (Christian Theology). A final reworking of his theological ideas in shorter form is found in the *Theologia 'Scolarium'* (Theology for Students). Also in the area of theology from the later period is his *Dialogus inter philosophum, Iudaeum et Christianum* (Dialogue of a Philosopher with a Jew and a Christian) and his *Ethica* or *Scito te ipsum* (Ethics, or Know Thyself). Abelard's work in logic seems to have diminished in the post-Quincy period, but he did compose a new and important gloss on Porphyry's *Isagoge* called the *Glossule super Porphyrium* or *Logica 'nostrorum petitioni sociorum'* (Logic in Response to the Request of Our Comrades), probably while at Quincy. Because of this diminishing interest, Abelard never made much use of the 'new logic', that of Aristotle's *Analytics*, *Topics* and *Sophistical Refutations*, which became available in western Europe in the 1130s (see TRANSLATORS).

3 Pagan wisdom and Christian faith

Abelard was, at least in his later life, a devout Christian committed to the moral reform of the church and the defence of traditional orthodox Christian beliefs. However, he was also well read in the literature of pagan Greece and Rome, and was convinced that among the works of the philosophers of the ancient world could be found useful models of moral life and more precise understandings of dogmas such as the Trinity than were to be found even in the Old Testament. His *Theologia* evidences an overriding concern to defend the use of pagan learning in explicating and defending the Christian faith, while at the same time refuting 'pseudo-philosophers' who in his own day were creating difficulties for belief by misusing that most important legacy of the ancients, logic.

Abelard found that the ancient philosophers, although they had lived before the time of Christ, had already taught some of the most important doctrines of the Christian religion, namely the immortality of the soul, the existence of a creator, the supreme importance of living virtuously, the likelihood of retribution in the next life for sins in this one and even, in Plato's case, the doctrine of the Trinity (see PLATO; TRINITY). It was not Abelard's view that the ancient sages came to these insights simply by the use of reason and other natural cognitive faculties; rather, he held that God had given them a certain revelation as a reward for their exemplary lives.

4 Logic

Abelard's actual knowledge of ancient philosophy outside of ethics was very limited and was often reliant on the fragmentary accounts of it given by early Christian thinkers such as AUGUSTINE. In the field of logic he at least had translations of a few primary sources, such as Aristotle's *Categories* and *Peri hermenias* and Porphyry's *Isagoge*. Also in his possession were the commentaries of Boethius on these sources, as well as a few of Boethius' own treatises. The rest of Aristotle's logical works became available only late in Abelard's life, after his own interest in logic had waned. In this legacy Abelard's genius discovered many difficulties and omissions, and his reflection on these led him to develop a quite original logical theory, even though he always presented it as an extension and modification of the traditional Aristotelian framework.

Perhaps the most un-Aristotelian feature of Abelard's logical theory is the central role he gives to sentences and what sentences say, rather than to terms. Any sentence, even a question or an imperative, says or proposes something called a *dictum*, although only assertions commit the speaker to the truth of what is said. These *dicta* are the primary subjects of truth and falsity, with assertions being true or false only insofar as their *dicta* are. Abelard recognizes that the genuine contradictory of an affirmative sentence is one in which the negation operates on the whole *dictum* of the latter, not just on the predicate. His elaborate theory of conditionals rests on the view that a conditional is true only when the truth of the antecedent's *dictum* requires the truth of the consequent's *dictum*. We have here the makings of a genuinely 'propositional' logic akin to that developed in ancient times by the Stoics, that is, a logic in which the basic logical relationships of entailment, opposition and so on are seen as holding between propositions (see STOICISM).

Abelard's appreciation of the saying-function of sentences leads him to a very original analysis of what is involved in verbs, and in the verb 'to be' used as a copula. The tendency of Aristotelian logic is to view simple categorical sentences as having three parts: two noun phrases linked by some form of the copula. Thus 'Socrates is a human' has as its parts the noun phrases 'Socrates' and 'a human', plus the copula 'is'. Abelard, on the other hand, sees such sentences as falling into two parts, a subject noun phrase and a predicate verb phrase. The peculiar function of the verb is thus to provide the saying-force, without which the string of words would be at best a list rather than an assertion. The copula really has no signification on its own, but merely acts to transform a noun phrase into a verb.

Nouns, he thinks, turn out to be implicit verbs, as can be inferred from their covert importation of tense. In 'Some man is a philosopher' 'man' extends over only presently existing men, so that the whole sentence really means 'Something which is now a man is a philosopher', where the verb implicit in the subject is made explicit. Although nouns often have 'appellation' – for example, in many contexts they are taken as applying to or naming certain individual things – these things are nevertheless not what the noun signifies. Signification has both a psychological and more properly a semantic aspect. The former will be discussed later, but as for the latter, Abelard refers to *status* or 'natures' as what is signified by both verbs and nouns. These are apparently referred to by verbal nominalizations such as 'being a man' or 'walking'. Perhaps the best way to view a *status* is as that which, in a *dictum*, corresponds to the predicate of the corresponding sentence, for Abelard talks in much the same way about *status* as he does about *dicta*. Thus a *status* or nature associated with a predicate is what might be said of some thing by using that predicate in a sentence in which the subject noun named that thing.

Status and *dicta* turn out to be important both for Abelard's analysis of modal propositions and for his treatment of conditionals. A modal proposition, such as 'It is possible for this man, who is sitting, to be standing', turns out to have a false sense in which the whole *dictum* of the sentence 'This man, who is standing, is sitting' is the apparent subject of the modality, and another true sense in which what is being asserted is both that standing is compatible with the *status* of being a man and that the man in question is in fact sitting. Conditional propositions are necessarily true only if the *dictum* of the antecedent explicitly or implicitly contains the dictum of the consequent. Necessarily true conditionals such as, 'If there is a rose, there is a flower', the truth of which depends simply on the logical relationship between the natures of being a rose and being a flower, are sometimes called 'laws of nature' by Abelard and are fundamental for science (see LANGUAGE, MEDIEVAL THEORIES OF; NATURAL PHILOSOPHY, MEDIEVAL §§8–9).

5 Ontology

Although Abelard never had a kind word for his old teacher Roscelin and the two quarrelled bitterly over matters of theology, it is clear that the student in large measure took over his master's view that logic is about vocally produced sounds qua signifiers, not about the things those sounds may be used to refer to. Such a view sharply separates logic from sciences such as physics, which talk directly about things without regard to any use of them as signifiers. Instead, physics treats logic as a tool which can be of help in any inquiry that employs language. Abelard conducted a vigorous attack on 'realist' views of logic, such as that held by William of Champeaux. This dispute focused on 'universals', for example, items such as genera and species (that is, the items which Aristotle claimed were each predicated of many subjects by true affirmations), since these were crucial to Aristotelian logic and science. As viewed in Abelard's day, the issue was whether universals were things existing independently of language (realism) or whether they were only the words that referred to things (nominalism). Abelard came down clearly on the latter side (see NOMINALISM; REALISM AND ANTI-REALISM; UNIVERSALS).

William's version of the realist position treated genera and species as something like materials common to many things. The different things they are common to are differentiated by opposed forms which also exist in these materials. Abelard argued that the end result of this view is that one and the same individual thing may have opposed characteristics at the same time. Abelard's own positive view shifted somewhat from that of his *Logica ingredientibus*, where it is simply the vocally produced physical sound (the *vox*) which is a universal, and that of the *Logica 'nostrorum petitioni sociorum'*, where it is words (*sermones*) that are universals and different words might share the same physical sound. However, the basic idea remains: universality results from some thing being used as a sign of many.

Where Abelard's view differs radically from that of his teacher Roscelin is in the role of the *status*. Abelard claims that the *status* 'being a human' is the reason why the term 'human' applies to the many things to which it does apply; but, he says enigmatically, this is 'no thing'. Nevertheless it is that which verbs, and nouns, signify. Do they signify, then, without signifying anything? In the *Logica 'nostrorum petitioni sociorum'*, Abelard explains that through the idea associated with a universal word there does not have to be some particular thing that one thinks of when one uses the word. For example, in just the way that there does not have to be some thing that I want when I want a hood – in other words, I can want a hood without there being any particular thing that I want – similarly I can think of something through the idea associated with 'human' even though there is no particular thing (or human) that I think of.

Dicta, too, turn out not to be things. Abelard thinks it would make the necessity of any conditional proposition incomprehensible if we thought of the *dicta* of the antecedent and consequent as things. Nevertheless, his whole semantic theory is deeply dependent on talk about both *status* and *dicta*. Even in his theory of the Trinity, without *status* he has no grounds on which to defend the objective differentiation of the three divine persons. Apparently Abelard thought it was possible to evade the embarrassing ontological consequences of a 'realist' approach to logic while retaining all the advantages of an approach which bases logic in objective facts, for, as discussed below, he eschews the idea of founding logic on relations between mental entities such as ideas or concepts. Perhaps the chief conundrum for interpreters of Abelard is how this is supposed to be possible.

Abelard also introduces here the concept of 'impersonal' propositions wherever there is a statement of grammatical subject-predicate form but the subject is the nominalization of a verb phrase or a sentence (see above). Since neither verb phrases nor sentences name anything, Abelard thinks it is a mistake to take their nominalizations as nonetheless naming something. It is not just that 'being a human' fails to name a thing; it doesn't name at all. Nouns like *status* and *dictum*, since their use is based in their being predicated of items like being a human and Socrates' being a human, likewise do not really name at all. Is this tantamount on Abelard's part to saying that the language in which we talk about the foundations of logic necessarily escapes the scope of the very logic about which it is designed to talk? A full study of the implications of Abelard's logic has yet to be written.

Another area of ontology in which Abelard was very inventive concerns the doctrine of sameness and distinctions. While defending the doctrine of the Trinity, Abelard was led to develop the idea that items might be the same 'essentially' even though some predicates true of one are not true of the other, because the items are distinct 'in property'. An example is the way that a wax statue is the same 'essentially' as the wax that composes it; but the statue is not the matter for the statue, even though the wax is. This same idea lies behind the distinction of words from the physical sounds in which they are realized. The word is the same 'essentially' as the sound, but nevertheless two words might be the same as one vocal sound and yet not the same as each other.

6 Psychology of signification

Although logic is about words that are realized in sound, Abelard acknowledges that those sounds constitute words and thus have properties significant for the logician only because they express ideas in the mind of the speaker. His views on the mental side of signification are fairly elaborate and reflect his careful reading of Aristotle's *Peri hermenias*.

The fundamental notion here is that of an 'idea' (*intellectus*), which is a genuine mental thing, an act or a disposition toward a mental act. The idea is not the content of such an act, but rather the idea itself always has some content. Only beings with reason can have ideas and thus ideas must be distinguished from both sensings and imaginings. Abelard locates this distinction in the way an idea isolates some property for attention, while sensings and imaginings grasp something without separating out some single property or complex of properties of that thing from its other properties. In other words, any idea reflects a certain abstractive thought process. What is isolated and thought of through the idea is some *dictum* or *status*: in other words, what is signified by the word or words which express the idea in question.

Abelard often talks of linguistic expressions as signifying the ideas they express, but he makes it clear that this sense of 'signification' is not one which permits inferring that language necessarily talks about ideas. He is very insistent that we must avoid a semantic theory which would have all language ultimately be about something in the mind. This applies also to the images which the mind creates in order to give itself something to focus on when it thinks. Abelard does not think that these images are mental things in the way ideas are; indeed, they are not 'things' at all. My image of a four-sided tower is not a four-sided thing which exists, either in my mind or in external reality. Such images cannot be equated with what words signify, since, Abelard claims, we can use exactly the same image when we use words with different meanings. The 'attention' of the mind allows us to focus on one property at one time and another at another time, in both cases using the very same image. The image is not the content of the idea that uses it.

The contents of ideas, then, are the *status* or *dicta* which are the 'things' (as opposed to the ideas) which words signify. Since, as noted above, *status* and *dicta* are not themselves things, Abelard's position here teeters on the brink of self-contradiction. However, he argues vigorously that we need not always find something for our terms to signify. When I am thinking of a man, I need not be thinking of any particular man. In the sentence 'A man is in the house' 'a man' does not signify any particular man, not even the one which happens to be in the house, if such a person exists. Abelard is keenly aware that noun phrases in certain contexts are used 'non appellatively', in other words in such a way that one cannot point to any particular thing and say that it is the referent of the phrase. His observation here clearly dovetails with the view mentioned in §5, that an idea can be of something even though there is no particular thing it is of, and is thus part of Abelard's perhaps dubious way of avoiding the apparent ontological implications of his semantics.

7 Ethics

Abelard's positions on ethical questions were heavily influenced on the one hand by what he knew of Stoic ethics, and on the other hand by the Christian doctrine of rewards and punishments in the next life for righteousness or sinfulness in this one. Stoic ethical doctrines were accessible to Abelard through the writings of CICERO and SENECA, as well as through the detailed accounts of Stoic ethics in the writings of Augustine and other church fathers. His views largely amount to an attempt to take the Stoic doctrine of moral virtue and vice and make it the basis of how God judges souls to be meritorious (deserving of eternal blessedness) or guilty (deserving of damnation). In the course of this effort, however, a number of important notions are drastically redefined.

Whereas in the Stoic view virtues and vices were settled practices of deliberately choosing good and bad courses of action, for Abelard they are inclinations which manifest themselves prior to choice and over which we have little control. In his view, a tendency to get angry too easily is a vice, but having that vice does not of itself make one sinful and deserving of punishment. It is deciding to yield to that tendency that is sinful. In Abelard's view, then, there is no logical inconsistency in supposing that a person has many vices but is in fact a very righteous person deserving of God's rewards. In fact, Abelard says, having vices to fight against is required in order to attain the highest merit. The person who has nothing but virtues easily does the right thing and thus merits reward less.

Neither does Abelard think that sin or righteousness lies merely in willing something. Here his view changed somewhat over time, but in his *Ethica*, probably a late work, he adopts a conception of a will which equates it with a desire, not with any deliberate decision to undertake some course of action nor with a mere faculty for such decisions. On this point Abelard was clearly not in accord with earlier writers such as Augustine and ANSELM. Given such a definition of will, Abelard has no trouble showing that a person can have a will to do something they should not and yet not sin, and also sin while not having any will for doing something they should not. The first case is illustrated by a man who lusts after a married woman but restrains himself and never adopts the intention to seduce her. The second is exemplified by a servant who kills his master in self-defence; he never willed the death of his master but rather only desired his own life, a perfectly legitimate will. And yet (on Abelard's very rigorous moral standard) he sinned in not allowing himself to be killed rather than engage in a killing.

Once the firm intention to do wrong is formed, however, the guilt exists, and it is not increased by the actual performance of the deed. Thus Christ can rightly condemn men for having committed adultery in their hearts even if they have not actually seduced a woman. Sin, in Abelard's view, lies entirely in the consent to do what one knows one should not, or to omit doing what one knows one should. (The men Christ condemned, Abelard believes, had consented to such a seduction; they had not merely lusted after the woman.) This alone makes one guilty and deserving of retribution from God. That sinners must know they are wrong is important for Abelard. One of the theses which the bishops at the council of Sens objected to was Abelard's claim that, because they thought they were doing what they were supposed to do, the men who crucified Christ were not guilty. The consent or intention to do something may be objectively bad – what one consents to may in fact be something one ought not consent to – and yet, because of the ignorance of the person who consents, no guilt be incurred. The consent is sinful when and only when it amounts to contempt for what is good and right, which Abelard often equates with contempt for God. Likewise, a consent is meritorious only when it shows respect and love for what is good, in other words, for God (see SIN).

Although sin is the only thing that makes one deserving of punishment, both divine and human punishment can in certain circumstances be justifiably visited on those who do not deserve it. Abelard describes a case where a woman, who was only trying to keep her baby warm, accidentally smothered it to death. The judge, he says, is justified in punishing her in order to set an example that will remind others to be more careful. Human justice, he claims, is legitimately more concerned with outward deeds than with inner intentions, since it is the former, not the latter, that directly affect the peace and welfare of the community. Similarly, Abelard allows the doctrine that, for obscure reasons of his own, God is justified in condemning to eternal death some unbaptized infants who have never sinned.

8 Theodicy

Abelard argues for God's existence as follows. We recognize that we ourselves are not made by ourselves but by something else; however, we as rational beings are certainly superior to the world of non-rational things. This would not be so if that world were something that caused itself, because anything which relies only on itself for its subsistence is superior to anything that relies on something other than itself. Hence that world is brought into existence by something else, a maker or ruler, and this we call God (see GOD, ARGUMENTS FOR THE EXISTENCE OF).

Abelard recognizes that logically this argument is less than completely compelling, but he thinks that in this area we should accept those arguments which make an appeal to our better sentiments. His attitude here reveals how far Abelard was from developing theology as a branch of rational philosophy or metaphysics in the way that would be attempted later, in the thirteenth century (see AQUINAS, T.).

One conclusion that Abelard reached on the basis of such arguments was that everything that is or occurs has a reason for being or occurring. To allow otherwise would be to claim that there are some things that God either makes occur or allows to occur, without having a full reason for why these rather than other things should occur. This Abelard thinks would detract from the divine goodness. On this basis, Abelard draws the conclusion that God could not do or omit anything other than what he at some time does do or omit. He will not allow that God might be faced with several alternatives which are equally best, so that there could be no reason for him to choose one rather than the other. And, of course, God cannot choose an alternative to which there is a better alternative. From God's point of view, then, all that he does or omits he must do or omit (see OMNIPOTENCE). This view too was among those condemned at Sens, and Abelard admitted that few agreed with him on this subject. Although he cleverly used his theory of modalities to argue otherwise, the position seems clearly headed toward fatalism of the Stoic variety. That Abelard proposed such a view at all shows to what extent he was attracted by the extreme rationalism represented in ancient Stoicism.

See also: ARISTOTELIANISM, MEDIEVAL; BERNARD OF CLAIRVAUX; LANGUAGE, MEDIEVAL THEORIES OF; LOGIC, MEDIEVAL; NOMINALISM; PLATONISM, MEDIEVAL; WILLIAM OF CHAMPEAUX

List of works

Abelard, P. (*c.*1120?) *Logica ingredientibus* (Logic for Beginners), ed. B. Geyer in *Peter Abaelards Philosophische Schriften* (Peter Abelard's Philosophical Writings), Beiträge zur Geschichte der Philosophie des Mittelalters 21, Heft 1–3, Münster: Aschendorffschen Verlagbuchhandlung, 1919–27. (The most important Latin text for Abelard's logic. The *Gloss on Porphyry* has been translated by Paul Spade in *Five Texts on the Medieval Problem of Universals: Porphyry, Boethius, Abelard, Duns Scotus, Ockham*, Indianapolis, IN: Hackett, 1994, pages 26–56.)
—— (*c.*1120?) *Dialectica*, ed. L.M. de Rijk, Assen: Van Gorcum, 1970. (After the previous work, the most significant of Abelard's philosophical writings.)
—— (*c.*1124?) *Logica 'nostrorum petitioni sociorum'* (Logic in Response to the Request of our Comrades), ed. B.Geyer in *Peter Abaelards Philosophische Schriften* (Peter Abelard's Philosophical Writings), Beiträge zur Geschichte der Philosophie des Mittelalters 21, Heft 1–3, Münster: Aschendorffschen Verlagbuchhandlung, 1919–27. (A short piece on Porphyry's *Isagoge*, that reviews the earlier gloss in the *Logica ingredientibus*.)
—— (*c.*1120?) *Theologia 'summi boni'* (Theology of the Highest Good), ed. E.M. Buytaert and C.J. Mews in *Petri Abaelardi Opera Theologica* III, Corpus Christianorum, Continutatio Mediaevalis XIII, Turnholt: Brepols, 1987, 39–201. (The first version of Abelard's *Theologia*.)
—— (*c.*1125?) *Theologia Christiana* (Christian Theology), ed. E.M. Buytaert in *Petri Abaelardi Opera Theologica* II, Corpus Christianorum, Continuatio Mediaevalis XII, Turnholt: Brepols, 1969, 5–372. (The second and most complete version of Abelard's *Theologia*, including his doctrine on the Trinity.)
—— (*c.*1135?) *Theologia Scolarium* (Theology for Students), ed. E.M. Buytaert and C.J. Mews in *Petri Abaelardi Opera Theologica* III, Corpus Christianorum, Continuatio Mediaevalis XIII, Turnholt: Brepols, 1987, 203–613. (The third version of Abelard's *Theologia*.)
—— (*c.*1125?) *Dialogus inter philosophum, Iudaeum et Christianum* (Dialogue of a Philosopher with a Jew and a Christian), ed. R. Thomas, Stuttgart-Bad Cannstatt: Frommann, 1970; trans. P.J. Payer, Toronto, Ont.: Pontifical Institute of Mediaeval Studies, 1979. (Abelard's attempt to view Christianity as much more in line with ancient philosophy than was Judaism.)
—— (*c.*1138?) *Ethica* or *Scito te ipsum* (Ethics, or Know Thyself), ed. and trans. D.E. Luscombe in *Peter Abelard's Ethics*, Oxford: Clarendon Press, 1971. (Contains Abelard's fullest explanation of the doctrine of sin.)

References and further reading

Jolivet, J. (1969) *Arts du language et théologie chez Abailard* (Arts of Language and Theology in Abelard), Études de philosophie médiévale 58, Paris: Vrin. (The most detailed account of how Abelard used his logic in his theology.)
Luscombe, D.E. (1988) 'Peter Abelard', in P. Dronke (ed.) *A History of Twelfth Century Western Philosophy*, Cambridge: Cambridge University Press, 279–307. (A brief survey of Abelard's philosophical views.)
—— (1969) *The School of Peter Abelard*, London: Cambridge University Press. (Describes the influence of Abelard's thought in the early scholastic period.)
Marenbon, J. (1997) *The Philosophy of Peter Abelard*, Cambridge: Cambridge University Press. (The most recent biography of Abelard.)
* Mews, C.J. (1985) 'On dating the works of Peter Abelard', *Archives d'histoire doctrinale et littéraire du moyen âge*, 52: 73–134. (The most thorough attempt so far to order and date all of Abelard's works.)
Mews, C.J. and Jolivet, J. (1990) 'Peter Abelard and His Influence', in G. Floistad (ed.) *Contemporary Philosophy*, Dordrecht: Kluwer, vol. 6, ed. R. Klibansky. (A complete bibliography of recent Abelard studies.)

Tweedale, M.M. (1976) *Abailard on Universals*, Amsterdam: North Holland. (Translates and analyses from a modern perspective the main texts relating to Abelard's ontology.)

MARTIN M. TWEEDALE

ABERDEEN PHILOSOPHICAL SOCIETY

The Aberdeen Philosophical Society (1758–73) played a formative role in the genesis of Scottish common sense philosophy. Its founder members included the philosopher Thomas Reid and the theologian George Campbell. Its discussions favoured the natural and human sciences, particularly the science of the mind, and one of its central concerns was the refutation of the work of David Hume.

Popularly known as the 'Wise Club', the Aberdeen Philosophical Society was founded in January 1758 by a core group of six men that included the philosopher Thomas REID and the theologian George CAMPBELL. The Society initially brought together individuals who were either associated with the two Aberdeen colleges or connected with the local political magnate, Lord Deskford. During the next decade, figures such as Alexander GERARD and James BEATTIE joined the club, and the Society became a respected body within the European republic of letters because of the growing reputation its leading members had achieved through their publications. However, by the late 1760s the Society was in decline, and it finally dissolved in 1773 due to internal divisions caused by college politics.

Unlike other prominent Scottish groups of the period, the Wise Club carefully circumscribed the scope of its proceedings. According to its constitution the Society was to exclude the discussion of the traditional scholarly fields of grammar, philology and history, and limit itself to 'philosophical' subjects. Under this rubric the founding members included reports on matters of fact, inductive generalizations concerning the phenomena of the material and mental realms, disquisitions on false theoretical systems and erroneous methods of philosophizing, and the exploration of the relations between philosophy and the practical arts. Consequently, the Society focused largely on topics drawn from the natural and human sciences, and rarely touched on the literary and artistic questions which interested many of the other polite clubs of the Scottish Enlightenment (see ENLIGHTENMENT, SCOTTISH). The most popular subject for discussion was the anatomy of the mind, particularly as it related to morals. Other areas canvassed at meetings included politics, education, political economy, mathematics, natural philosophy, natural history and agricultural improvement. Thus, like most provincial clubs of the eighteenth century, the Aberdeen Philosophical Society covered a broad spectrum of topics, but the scientistic approach to moral philosophy which it espoused was rooted in the local philosophical tradition initiated by the moralist George TURNBULL.

Although their debates ranged widely, the members of the Society were centrally concerned with the refutation of the writings of David HUME. One of the club's founders, Robert Trail, had earlier criticized Hume in a sermon published in 1755, and his fellow members subsequently took up the charge. Alexander Gerard and George Campbell attacked Hume's critique of religion; while Thomas Reid, John Farquhar and James Beattie among others challenged various aspects of his epistemology. The Society therefore functioned as a forum for the articulation of a common-sense reponse to Humean scepticism, and Thomas Reid did not exaggerate when he wrote to Hume in 1763 that 'If you write no more in morals, politics, or metaphysics, I am afraid we [that is, the Wise Club] shall be at a loss for subjects' (Ulman 1990: 57).

See also: COMMON SENSE SCHOOL

References and further reading

* Ulman, H.L. (ed.) (1990) *The Minutes of the Aberdeen Philosophical Society 1758–1773*, Aberdeen: Aberdeen University Press. (Includes a transcription of the minute books of the Wise Club, along with biographical entries on the members, a detailed analysis of the proceedings and a comprehensive bibliography.)

PAUL WOOD

ABHIDHARMA *see* BUDDHISM, ĀBHIDHARMIKA SCHOOLS OF

ABHINAVAGUPTA (*c*.975–1025)

Abhinavagupta was a Kashmiri philosopher, theologian and early exponent of the Hindu Tantra, often counted as the most illustrious representative of the nondual

ABHINAVAGUPTA

Śaivism of Kashmir. Author of influential Sanskrit works dealing with the philosophy of recognition and the theological interpretation of the Śaivite scriptures, including the encyclopedic Tantrāloka *(Light on the Tantras)*, he also wrote definitively on Indian aesthetic theory. The tradition of the nondual Śaivism of Kashmir gathers up the teachings of several related lineages of northern Śaivite philosophers which developed in Kashmir between the ninth and thirteenth centuries, such as Vasugupta, Kallaṭa, Somānanda and Utpala. Basing his writings on these authors as well as on revealed texts, Abhinavagupta propounds a tantric alternative to the restrictive and orthodox Mīmāṃsā and elaborates a challenge to the later mainline Vedānta. He offers the earliest theoretical bases for a complex and sophisticated Hindu Tantra based on the notion of Śiva as the nondual and all-pervading consciousness. His writings highlight the centrality of the Goddess as the Śakti or power of consciousness. Abhinavagupta elaborates the ritual and meditative methods for the experiential and blissful recognition of Śiva as the intrinsic self-identity of the practitioner.

1 General context and life
2 Śiva's nonduality
3 Philosophy of recognition
4 Tantric metaphysics and mysticism

1 General context and life

Abhinavagupta is considered to be one of the most sophisticated and enduringly definitive theoreticians of the medieval Hindu Tantra. His work as a theoretician of the Hindu Tantra and as an interpreter of the revealed scriptures of Śaivism is intertwined with his life as a devotee of Śiva. Abhinavagupta's contributions to the philosophy of language and as a philosophical interpreter of aesthetic theory remain definitive. His tantric synthesis is termed the Trika-Kaula because it skillfully melds together doctrinal and ritual elements drawn from these two Śaivite preceptorial lineages.

Abhinavagupta (*c.*975–*c.*1025) was born to a rich and noble Brahman family residing in the city of Śrinagar. His mother, Vimalā, died when he was still young and her death affected him greatly. The family were devotees of Śiva and Abhinavagupta matured in an atmosphere charged with religious devotion and dedication to learning. He began his studies with his learned father, Narasimhagupta, but quickly began visiting teachers in Kashmir and elsewhere. While he was studying literature and poetry, he was overcome with an intoxicating devotion to Śiva. After this, he studied everything he could: traditional texts of the dualistic and monistic Śaivism, literature, drama and aesthetic theory, Indian philosophical thought and the various branches of Śaivism. He also studied with Buddhist and Jaina teachers. His love of learning and spiritual search led him to Jālandhara where he encountered the tantric master, Śambhunātha, who initiated him into the practices of the Kaula tradition.

This early period of study and spiritual practice lead to a mature life dedicated to the absorption of knowledge in an atmosphere of extreme religious fervour. He never married, and spent his life living in the homes of his many teachers. At the height of his fame, he was revered as an authoritative and charismatic tantric master whose authority as guru or teacher was enhanced by the fact that he was considered to be a *mahāsiddha* (perfected and accomplished mystic). Twenty-one of his works are extant and there are references to titles of twenty-three others now apparently lost. His primary disciple was Kṣemarāja who wrote works applying his master's teachings. We have no definitive information about Abhinavagupta's death. Local Kashmiri legend has it that the great master walked into a cave with 1,200 of his disciples and simply disappeared.

Given his deep erudition, the intellectual context of Abhinavagupta's writings is very broad, in part due to his relatively late date with regard to the earlier traditions of Indian philosophy and religion. In addition to the revealed Hindu literature and to the texts produced by his predecessors in the Śaivism of Kashmir, Abhinavagupta's work resonates with practically all that precedes him in Indian thought, including the traditional brahmanical or Vedic literature, the debates of the philosophical traditions, the mysticism of the Yogis, the various Bhakti traditions and the varieties of Buddhist and Jaina philosophical discourse.

2 Śiva's nonduality

From a doctrinal point of view, Abhinavagupta's articulation of the nondual Śaivism of Kashmir is to be distinguished philosophically by its assertion that what is termed 'Śiva', the absolute and primordial consciousness, is nondual. Moreover, this nondualism differs in important ways from the Vedāntic *advaita*. For the Kashmiri nondual Śaivites, the nondualism or Śiva does not in any way imply that the world and all who dwell in it are illusory. On the contrary, Abhinavagupta asserts that this world is real precisely because it is only Śiva, the absolute consciousness. However, this assertion of the reality of the world does not fall into a position of naive realism. Rather, it seeks to articulate the enlightened and transformed vision of the mystic for whom the paradoxical omnipresence of Śiva has become a tangible experience. Thus, Śiva's nonduality allows without contradiction for the arising of duality and diversity within it. In addition, Abhinavagupta's expression of nondual Śaivism places emphasis on the ultimate power (*śakti*) that abides inseparably with the absolute consciousness. Although one, this transcendent power of consciousness has many faces: the powers of freedom, of grace or revelation and of manifestation or concealment.

This doctrine resides at the very core of Abhinavagupta's entire intellectual production, which is large in scope and has not been fully explored by scholarship. Often, facets of his intellectual production have been characterized in a piecemeal fashion, text by text, or in terms of the various initiatory lineages (rather than schools), thought to determine the content of individual texts. However, there is another, more general way to approach Abhinavagupta's work. In philosophical terms, we find in it three connected although differentiable intellectual agendas which are best characterized in terms of the mode of knowledge that predominates in each of them: inference, revealed scripture and enlightened knowledge. Each of these agendas articulates an aspect of this core doctrine of Śiva's nonduality.

3 Philosophy of recognition

Abhinavagupta's first intellectual agenda revolves around the philosophical interpretation of the doctrine of recognition. His writings on the 'school' of recognition, primarily in the *Īśvarapratyabhijñāvimarśinī* (Commentary on the Recognition of the Lord), are systematic philosophical exposition and argument. An appeal is made to the authority of good reasoning, and arguments through inference are employed as the primary mode of philosophical discourse. The major audience seems to have been external, for these are primarily polemical works of intellectual debate aimed at philosophical opponents.

Abhinavagupta's writings on the philosophy of recognition are continuous with the debates put forward by the philosophers of Nyāya-Vaiśeṣika, the Mīmāṃsā, the Advaita Vedānta, the schools of Buddhist logic and the traditional Grammarians (see MĪMĀṂSĀ; NYĀYA-VAIŚEṢIKA; VEDĀNTA). Buddhism was a vigorous presence in the Kashmir of Abhinavagupta's time. While his opponents in these texts include proponents of Sāṅkhya, as well as Vaiṣṇavas and Jainas, his primary philosophical arguments were aimed at the Buddhist logicians (see SĀṄKHYA). The Buddhists marshalled arguments against the primary categories of the Śaiva philosophy including the notion of the self, the idea of the Lord, the *śakti* and the manifested universe (see BUDDHIST PHILOSOPHY, INDIAN).

In his works on recognition, Abhinavagupta elaborates closely reasoned arguments to counter the Buddhists' criticisms. He points to the notion of Śiva as the absolute consciousness and posits a reality that is totally free, completely unbounded and blissful in its intrinsic nature. This he says is the reality of consciousness, saturated with power (*śakti*) of at least five different kinds: the powers of consciousness, bliss, will, knowledge and action. It is this absolute consciousness surcharged with power that both dwells within all beings as their true nature and mutates to appear as the forms composing the manifest universe.

Abhinavagupta contends that it is because of doubt that the recognition of this omnipresent consciousness does not take place. Consequently, his philosophy of recognition is meant to present the good reasoning that will remove doubt. This precipitates the process of recognition of what is already the case, namely, that the self is in fact the powerful Lord, filled with *śakti* and creative of the visible universe.

This initial description of an absolute consciousness reveals the shape of a problematic in Abhinavagupta's work that bridges philosophy, theology and mysticism. Ordinary human awareness and perception do not reveal that an absolute consciousness is operative either as the inner reality of the self, or as the underlying reality of the visible and manifest universe. Therefore, Abhinavagupta is concerned to show why this is the case: that is, how and why the obscuring of the absolute takes place and how and why the absolute comes to be revealed. The first of these questions involves Abhinavagupta in descriptions of the nature of bondage and contraction, involving a series of limiting sheaths and impurities. The second leads him to a discussion of tantric metaphysics and mysticism.

4 Tantric metaphysics and mysticism

The second major agenda found in Abhinavagupta's works is what might be called a systematic theology of the Hindu Tantra. This is best exemplified by his *Tantrāloka* (Light on the Tantras) where he interprets the tantric metaphysics and esotericism of the revealed scriptures, particularly the *Mālinīvijayottara Tantra*. In this aspect of his works he writes as an authoritative religious and theological exponent of Śaivism. His appeal is to the authority of revealed scripture, which must be systematically interpreted in the light of reason and spiritual insight so that apparent contradictions may be rationalized. The major audience for this aspect of his work were the varied schools of Śaivism prevalent in the Kashmir of his day. Thus, his mode of discourse is that of religious theology and the systematic exposition of the doctrines of Śaivism.

The themes taken up in the *Tantrāloka* (Light on the Tantras) (and elsewhere in Abhinavagupta's Śaivite theology) are complex and detailed. One strand of discourse explores the contraction of the ultimate consciousness and the manifestation of the world in terms of an emanationist scheme composed of thirty-six progressively more manifest principles of reality (*tattvas*). Another important strand centres on a mysticism of the Word, filled with vibration and dwelling in unity with the absolute consciousness at the transcendent level of reality. This supreme Word of consciousness is termed the supreme mantra *aham* (I am) and it is understood as the perfectly full and blissful egoity.

The third major intellectual agenda in his works might be called a practical theology or mysticism of Śaivism, encountered primarily in his elaboration of Kaula mysticism in his *Parātriṃśikāvivaraṇa* (Longer Commentary on the Thirty Verses on the Supreme). Here, Abhinavagupta advances interpretations of the many Śaivite lineages into which he had been initiated as well as offering interpretations of the meanings of tantric ritual and practice. The appeal is to the authority of his own enlightened experience, and the audience seems to have been primarily his own initiated disciples whom he was addressing in the role of spiritual teacher.

A central concern in this dimension of his work is the elaboration of the meaning of *jīvanmukti* (liberation while still alive) in terms of the mystical experiences of the yogin, who, by penetrating the core of that absolute consciousness, achieves identity with Śiva and experiences the universe as continuously unfolding and being reabsorbed into his own consciousness.

Abhinavagupta's discussion of tantric initiation includes a long clarification of the descent of the energy of Śiva's grace. In addition, he elaborates the intrinsic meanings of the great variety of rituals in the Hindu Tantra linked to an elaborate pantheon of tantric deities. The primary hermeneutical move throughout is one of interiorization and of interpretation in terms of the mechanics of an overarching consciousness. Thus, while the earlier tantric tradition will speak of external goddesses who are to be appeased by a variety of transgressive offerings in the tantric ritual, Abhinavagupta will consistently recast these goddesses as the forces of the absolute consciousness present in the depths of the practitioner's own being.

Abhinavagupta's core statements about Śiva modulate into an ambitious and multivalent intellectual and theological enterprise. This enterprise will also allow him to put forward an innovative interpretation of aesthetic theory that posits an analogy between the absorption of the yogin and the refined aesthete's delectation of the experience of art. Abhinavagupta's work will have manifold direct and indirect influences on all that follows him in the subsequent evolution of the Hindu Tantra.

See also: HINDU PHILOSOPHY; MYSTICISM, HISTORY OF; MYSTICISM, NATURE OF

List of works

Abhinavagupta (*c*.990–*c*.1014) *Īśvarapratyabhijñāvimarśnī* (Commentary on the Recognition of the Lord), ed. M. Rāma, Srinagar: Research Department, Jammu and Kashmir Government, 1918; trans. K.C. Pandey, *Bhāskarī: The Īśvara Pratyabhijñā Vimarśinī*, The Princess of Wales Saraswati Bhavana Texts, Lucknow: Superintendent, Printing and Stationery, 1954. (The *Commentary on the Recognition of the Lord* sets out Abhinavagupta's arguments about the nature of the process of recognition of Śiva.)

—— (*c*.990–*c*.1014) *Srī Mālinīvijayavārtika*, ed. M. Kaul, Srinagar: Research Department, Jammu and Kashmir Government, 1921. (A commentary on the first verse of the *Mālinīvijayottara Tantra* which is considered by Abhinavagupta to be the most authoritative scripture on which his Trika-Kaula synthesis is based.)

—— (*c*.990–*c*.1014) *Paramārthasāra* (Essence of the Highest Truth), Srinagar: Research Department, Jammu and Kashmir State, 1916; French translation by L. Silburn, *Le Paramārthasāra*, Publications de l'Institut de Civilisation Indienne, Paris: Éditions E. de Boccard, 1957. (The *Essence of the Highest Truth* is a summary text of Abhinavagupta's essential teachings.)

—— (*c*.990–*c*.1014) *Parātriṃśikālaghuvṛtti* (The Short Gloss on the Supreme, the Queen of the Three), ed. J. Zādoo, Srinagar: Research Department, Jammu and Kashmir Government, 1947; Italian translation by R. Gnoli, *La Trentina della Suprema*, Turin: Boringhieri, 1978. (*The Short Gloss on the Supreme, the Queen of the Three* is a concise statement on the nature of tantric *sadhana* dealing especially with mantra.)

—— (*c*.990–*c*.1014) *Parātriṃśikāvivaraṇa* (Longer Commentary on the Thirty Verses on the Supreme), ed. M. Rāma, Srinagar: Research Department, Jammu and Kashmir Government, 1918; trans. J. Singh, *A Trident of Wisdom*, Albany, NY: State University of New York Press, 1989. (The *Longer*

Commentary on the Thirty Verses on the Supreme comments on the same āgamic verses as the previous text, but here Abhinavagupta places great emphasis on the emanationist system of the *tattvas*, the theology of the Word and the esoteric mysticism of the Trika-Kaula practices.)
—— (c.990–c.1014) *Tantrāloka* (Light on the Tantras), M. Rāma and M. Kaul (eds), Srinagar: Research Department, Jammu and Kashmir Government, 1918–38. (The *Light on the Tantras* presents Abhinavagupta's major statement of scriptural interpretation and exegesis.)
—— (c.990–c.1014) *Tantrasāra* (Essence of the Tantras), ed. M. Rāma, Srinagar: Research Department, Jammu and Kashmir Government, 1918. (The *Essence of the Tantras* is Abhinavagupta's epitome of his longer *Tantrāloka*.)

References and further reading

Dyczkowski, M. (1992) *The Stanzas on Vibration*, Albany, NY: State University of New York Press. (An excellent introduction to the Spanda lineages of Kashmiri Śaivism.)
Masson, J.L. and Patwardhan, M.V. (1969) *Śāntarasa and Abhinavagupta's Philosophy of Aesthetics*, Bhandarkar Oriental Series 9, Poona: Bhandarkar Oriental Research Institute. (A detailed discussion of aspects of the aesthetic dimension of Abhinavagupta's work.)
Muller-Ortega, P.E. (1989) *The Triadic Heart of Śiva: Kaula Tantricism of Abhinavagupta in the Non-Dual Shaivism of Kashmir*, Albany, NY: State University of New York Press. (An introduction to the Kaula mysticism of the heart as elaborated by Abhinavagupta.)
Padoux, A. (1990) *Vāc: The Concept of the Word in Selected Hindu Tantras*, Albany, NY: State University of New York Press. (Treats in detail the philosophy of language and the topic of mantra.)
Pandey, K.C. (1963) *Abhinavagupta: An Historical and Philosophical Study*, Chowkhamba Sanskrit Studies, vol. 1, Varanasi: Chowkhamba Sanskrit Series Office. (The only existing in-depth study of Abhinavagupta's life and work. Considerably dated but still contains much that is useful.)
Sanderson, A. (1986a) 'Mandala and Agamic Identity in the Trika of Kashmir', in *Mantra et Diagrammes Rituels dans l'Hindouisme*, ed. A. Padoux, Paris: CNRS. (Offers solutions to many historical and interpretive problems surrounding the Śaivism of Kashmir.)
—— (1986b) 'Purity and Power among the Brahmans of Kashmir', *The Category of the Person: Anthropology, Philosophy, History*, M. Carrithers, S. Collins, S. Lukes (eds), Cambridge: Cambridge University Press, 1986, 190–216. (Deals with many historical and interpretive problems surrounding Śaivism.)
Silburn, L. (1970) *Hymnes de Abhinavagupta*, Publications de l'Institut de Civilisation Indienne, Paris: Institut de Civilisation Indienne avec le concours du Centre National de la Recherche Scientifique. (Silburn presents the tantric dimensions of Abhinavagupta's thought.)
—— (1975) *Hymnes aux Kālī: la Roue des Energies Divines* (Hymn to Kālī: the Wheel of Divine Energies), Publications de l'Institut de Civilisation Indienne, Paris: Editions E. de Boccard. (Another dimension of Abhinavagupta's thought.)
Singh, J. (trans. and ed.) (1991) *The Yoga of Delight, Wonder, and Astonishment: A Translation of the Vijñānabhairava*, Albany, NY: State University of New York Press. (A useful translation of one of the definitive tantras often referred to by Abhinavagupta.)

PAUL E. MULLER-ORTEGA

ABORTION see LIFE AND DEATH (§5); REPRODUCTION AND ETHICS

ABRAHAM IBN EZRA see IBN EZRA, ABRAHAM

ABRAVANEL, ISAAC (1437–1509)

Abravanel is often seen as having a unique position in Jewish philosophy, between the end of the Middle Ages and the beginning of the Renaissance. His ideas point both to the past – especially to Maimonides – and to the future, in his approach to the questions of history and of authority in the state. His defence of what he takes to be religious orthodoxy is carried out with serious attention to the arguments of his predecessors. Abravanel takes great pains to understand their reasoning. He even supplies them with additional arguments, before he presents what he takes to be a decisive objection. In particular he expounds Maimonides' thought in considerable detail, defending him from his critics, while also insisting that Maimonides misrepresented the religious notions he analyses.

Abravanel's most original work lies in his view of history as either natural or artificial. Most human history is artificial, since it represents life in rebellion against God. The best form of government is not a monarchy, despite the views of most Jewish philosophers. For a monarchy does not essentially replicate the relationship of God with his subjects, and other forms of government can produce relatively successful societies. The Messiah, who will eventually transform artificial into natural history, is not a king but more a judge and prophet. He will establish the perfect society through a divine miracle. As long as the state is an absolute monarchy, however, its citizens owe absolute obedience to its ruler.

1 Life and works
2 The principles of religion
3 Political philosophy
4 Philosophy of history

1 Life and works

Isaac Abravanel lived a politically active life during a particularly difficult time for the Jews in the Iberian Peninsula. Born in Lisbon, he received an education which was not concerned exclusively with Jewish subjects and from an early age he was writing philosophy and theology. He worked as the treasurer of the ruler of Portugal, and then in Spain, until the expulsion of the Jews in 1492 drove him to Naples. He then moved to Venice, where he did important political work for the authorities. His time in Italy seems to have been his most productive as a writer, and by his death he had composed a large number of works. Many of these are mainly theological, commentaries on the books of the Bible and other Jewish writings, but he also wrote more strictly philosophical works dealing with the thought of MAIMONIDES (§3) and the particular theological and philosophical topics that Maimonides had made so controversial in Jewish philosophy. These include prophecy, providence, the creation of the world and the principles of Judaism. Abravanel is remarkable for his careful descriptions of the arguments of Maimonides and his opponents; indeed he lavishes so much time on exposition it is often difficult to discriminate his own opinion among those of the thinkers he discusses. He tends to argue that both Maimonides and his leading critics are mistaken in their arguments. Powerful though those arguments may appear, they need to be replaced by better arguments which accord more surely with the principles of Judaism.

2 The principles of religion

The cornerstone of Abravanel's critique of Maimonides lies in his response to Maimonides' theory of prophecy (see PROPHECY §4). Maimonides provides what seemed to Abravanel to be an excessively naturalistic account of prophecy in his *Guide to the Perplexed*, and Abravanel was determined to establish that this could not be the Jewish position. Abravanel argued that prophecy is not a natural phenomenon but a miracle established by God. An individual requires no special characteristics, such as the wisdom that Maimonides had supposed was a minimal prerequisite of any authentic prophecy. On the contrary, Abravanel argues, God can make anyone prophesy whom he wishes. It is not true, Abravanel reminds his readers, that only Moses received prophecy at Sinai. On the contrary, Scripture makes it clear that all Israel participated directly in the communication from God. Nor is it the case, as Maimonides supposed, that only Moses could achieve prophecy through his intellect alone. Other prophets too surpass reliance on imagination when prophesying. Nor is prophecy a matter of dreaming; it is a miracle and unique. Abravanel was concerned that the stature of Maimonides as a rabbinic jurist would mislead Jews into thinking that the doctrine of the *Guide to the Perplexed* is an accurate guide to the correct understanding of the Jewish religion. In that book, Maimonides argues that (apart from the vexed question of creation and a few related issues) there is no essential incompatibility between Aristotelian philosophy (of the Neoplatonic variety then widely accepted) and the principles of religion. True, Maimonides had argued that ordinary believers should not have their faith challenged by having to work out how the philosophical and scriptural systems of thought are to be connected. Abravanel seeks to show that the biblical and philosophical theories are incompatible, and that the latter cannot be seen as a valid distillation of the former.

He argues further that the view that prophecy is a miracle is the only view that is compatible with the religious texts of Judaism. The prophet's natural abilities are insufficient to produce prophecy of themselves, and the only necessary condition of being a prophet that human beings can achieve is moral excellence. Since all prophecy is miraculous, there is no essential distinction in this regard between Mosaic and non-Mosaic prophecy. Moses' prophecy is certainly superior to that of the other prophets in degree, but there is no qualitative difference between it and the revelations received by other prophets. The difference is that the prophecy of Moses came from God directly without going through the 'active intellect', the imagination or material apprehensions. Moses, moreover, prophesied while fully conscious. The message he received was entirely conceptual; it was grasped wholly by the intellect. A less perfect form of prophecy, intellectual prophecy, comes from God via the active intellect. It reaches the intellect of the prophet and not his imagination. At a still lesser level, imaginative prophecy consists of images, parables and mysteries. These may seem to resemble dreams, but in fact they are quite different. Imaginative prophecy receives the objective truth from God, albeit in a rather garbled form; dreams are merely subjective ideas produced by the imagination when not under any rational control. The least perfect form of prophecy is that experienced by the Israelites at Sinai through sight and sound, without going through either the intellect or the imagination. The prophet is the passive recipient of what flows from God, and the words and images of the prophecy itself are a direct result of God's will. The real distinction between Mosaic and non-Mosaic prophecy is simply that in that the former is received directly from God. The active intellect, moreover, is not to be understood in the Maimonidean way as a more or less free-standing source of natural events, but rather as a completely determined instrument of the divine will.

Although Abravanel seeks to counter Maimonides' theory of prophecy and to replace it with a theory which in his view more accurately coheres with the religious texts of Judaism, it is noticeable that he stays very close to the Maimonidean methodology in *Perush le-Moreh Nevukhim*, his commentary on the *Guide to the Perplexed*. In *Rosh Amanah* (Principles of Faith), Abravanel takes up the defence of Maimonides' 'Thirteen Principles', which had led to much controversy in medieval Jewish philosophy. Maimonides had identified thirteen principles of belief that form the basis of the immortality promised to all Israel in the Talmud. The singling out of these thirteen beliefs seemed to claim for them a special status as the core expression of the theological essence of Judaism. But that would seem to imply that there are many other aspects of the religion that are not basic dogmas and so may be questioned without offending orthodoxy. Maimonides' approach to formulating a Jewish creed was criticized on this basis, and Abravanel stoutly defends the importance of Maimonides' principles against his critics, especially CRESCAS (§3) and ALBO (§2), while finally arguing that these principles should not be regarded as the axioms of Judaism but just as very important beliefs, among many other doctrines and practices. The point of the principles, he suggests, is to impress upon ordinary believers what they should believe, since they are unlikely to have studied enough of the Torah to have understood the whole breadth of the 613 commandments. Maimonides is seen as presenting his principles as a religious aid for the intellectually unsophisticated. The more sophisticated understand that there are no basic dogmas in Judaism, and that all the commandments constitute the essence of the religion.

3 Political philosophy

The state arises as a necessity only through the expulsion of Adam from Eden. It will survive until the coming of the Messiah. Political life reflects our spiritual exile. It can never be perfect, although some states are more successful than others at fulfilling the spiritual as well as the political needs of citizens. In his commentaries on the Bible, Abravanel provides an account of what he takes to be the best form of society. This proves largely to be a recapitulation of Mosaic society. He sees this ideal state as consisting of lower courts, a high court and a ruler, perhaps a king. The officials of the lower courts are chosen by the people and handle their local affairs for themselves, while the high court or Sanhedrin is appointed by the ruler and establishes the juridical structure of the state as a whole. The members of this court are to be selected from the priests and levites. What is interesting in this notion of a mixed constitution is that it radically reduces the religious role of the king. There had been something of a tradition in Jewish philosophy of emphasizing the role of the king, given biblical passages which seem to suggest that choosing a king was a duty imposed by God.

Abravanel deals with these passages by arguing that what they mean is that choosing a king in Israel was not a duty, but simply a practice that was allowed. If a king is to be chosen, the biblical account tells the Jews what characteristics he is to have. But there is no necessity to select a king for the state to be properly organized. Abravanel gives the examples of republican Rome and Venice to suggest that the desirable features of a monarchy can be easily replicated in a very different form of society. Israel does not require a king, because the judges can do whatever a king could do. Indeed, even judges are not essential, since God and the divine law, the Torah, can organize society correctly. Judges, of course, are required to carry out sanctions for disobedience to divine law. But in a society that is truly regulated by God, there would be no need for sanctions. Gentiles, since they do not have the Torah, do require political organization, and a king might be the right person to carry out this task for them. But from the experience of the Scriptures, there is no reason to think that a monarchy represents the best form of government for Israel. For the nation can rely on divine support and leadership for its welfare.

In states where a king disregards the laws and becomes a tyrant, his subjects have no right of rebellion. As subjects they must obey the monarch unconditionally; otherwise they are not subjects. The king in the state replicates God in the world. He has the right to take action not simply as regulated by the law but as is required by the particular facts of the case. As far as Israel is concerned, the choice of the king is a matter for God, and no one else has the right to remove or challenge him. Gentiles may rebel against monarchs who are not behaving as they ought, but Jews should not. Even a Gentile king should not be overthrown, since even he is in the place of God as far as his Jewish subjects are concerned, carrying out whatever punishment God thinks appropriate for his people. There is no point in Jews actively trying to set up a government which accords with Messianic rule. They must wait for God to bring this about when he decides the time is right. In a sense, then, Gentile rulers rule by divine right and with some degree of arbitrary authority, but Jewish rulers do not; they rule within the context of Jewish law. There are strong religious arguments, Abravanel argues, forbidding rebellion against either type of monarch. Within the context of the perfect society, however, in Messianic times, there is no need for a king. It would be better to be ruled by a group of judges guided by the will of God. It is not unlikely that this somewhat muffled but still perceptible anti-monarchistic line has its origins in Abravanel's knowledge of Christian political thinkers, whose reflections he applies to Jewish political problems (see POLITICAL PHILOSOPHY, HISTORY OF).

4 Philosophy of history

History is the result of God's decisions, and he is entirely free to do whatsoever he wishes, having created the world *ex nihilo* (see HISTORY, PHILOSOPHY OF). Both form and matter are divine creations, so there are no limitations on God's power. God has not set up a natural mechanism which then operates independently of him, as the thinking of Maimonides might seem to suggest. Rather, the events that befall humanity are due either to the direct influence of God, the actions of another supernatural being, or the choices made by the exercise of human freedom. History starts with the creation of the universe. It consists of a divinely organized pattern of events. The end of history is salvation, which will be established by the Messiah and which will see Judaism triumph over its enemies. Adam was a perfect being who could have stayed in the Garden of Eden and developed his spiritual potentialities, but he freely chose to act otherwise. He disobeyed God through eating from the forbidden tree of knowledge, and in consequence he became subject to death and life in a hostile environment. Yet the possibility of salvation remained, and the Jews were established to represent the continuity of salvation. Their role is identical to the role of history itself, to attain final salvation for the whole of humanity. To make this possible God has helped the Jews, providing them with prophecy, which finally led up to the revelation at Sinai. He also took them to the land of Israel, which was entirely appropriate for their spiritual perfection and prophecy. Like Adam, though, they sinned and were punished. The Temple was destroyed, and they were sent into exile, a state which will continue until the coming of the Messiah, when history will come to an end, the Jews will be redeemed and perfect peace will prevail. At that time, humanity will be transformed into a final state of perfection and fulfilment. The sovereignty of the Messiah will be universal, the distortion of humanity since the exile from Eden will be ended, and human beings will once again be in a position to realize their own potentialities. The physical universe will be replaced by a spiritual realm in which human souls become immortal as they contemplate eternally the nature of the deity.

Abravanel's general philosophical approach is entirely coherent, in that he sets out to link what he takes to be orthodox rabbinic Judaism with rational understanding. Where Maimonides goes awry, he argues, is in seeking religious correlates for his philosophical views. The sort of philosophy that attracted Maimonides is completely incompatible with Judaism, something which the extraordinary status of Maimonides in Jewish law tends to disguise. Abravanel has his finger on a vital issue here, in that it is the constant argument of Maimonides that if one looks at scriptural and legal texts in the right sort of way one comes to realize that they are just another way of expressing philosophical truths. Abravanel seeks to establish an understanding of Judaism close to its literal formulation, and he argues that the apparent contradictions which Maimonides highlights between religion and philosophy are in fact real contradictions which show that Aristotelian philosophy cannot do justice to the Jewish religion. The thought of Maimonides is worthy of detailed study, since as a system in itself it represents an impressive attempt at a rational grasp of Judaism. All the same the effort eventually comes to nothing.

While Maimonides is a far more radical thinker than Abravanel when dealing with metaphysics, the position is reversed when it comes to political philosophy. Abravanel is prepared to interpret scriptural passages far more freely than is Maimonides. And he arrives does so quite uninhibitedly in his critique of monarchy as a system of government. His motives here arise from his attempt at establishing the genuine position of rabbinic Judaism as he sees it, but they are also mixed with his experience as a politician serving under a wide variety of rulers. The remarkable nature of his thought has led to its widespread study in both Jewish and Christian contexts.

See also: HISTORY, PHILOSOPHY OF; MAIMONIDES, M.; POLITICAL PHILOSOPHY, HISTORY OF; PROPHECY

List of works

Abravanel, I. (1494) *Rosh Amanah* (Principles of Faith), trans. M. Kellner, London: Associated University Presses, 1982. (A detailed introduction and notes of one of Abravanel's most accessible works.)

—— (1498) *Shamayim Chadashim* (New Skies), Roedelheim, 1829; repr. in *Opera Minora*, London: Gregg International, 1972. (An account of creation, where Abravanel argues that belief in creation is an axiom for Judaism.)

—— (1501) *Mif'alot Elohim* (Works of God), Venice, 1592; repr. in *Opera Minora*, London: Gregg International, 1972. (Another account of his views on the creation of the world.)

—— (before 1509) *Perush le-Moreh Nevukhim* (Commentary on the *Guide to the Perplexed*), trans. A. Reines, *Maimonides and Abrabanel on Prophecy*, Cincinatti, OH: Hebrew Union College, 1970. (His analysis of Maimonides' arguments, critical but always respectful.)

—— (before 1509) *Perush 'al-ha-Torah* (Commentary on the Torah), Jerusalem: Torah we-Da'at, 1969. (An interesting approach to the Bible, in which Abravanel introduces many contemporary political concerns.)

References and further reading

Kellner, M. (1980) 'Rabbi Isaac Abravanel on Maimonides' Principles of Faith', *Tradition* 18: 343–56. (A useful summary of the topic.)

Kimmelman, R. (1995) 'Abravanel and the Jewish Republican Ethics', in D. Frank (ed.) *Commandment and Community: New Essays in Jewish Legal and Political Philosophy*, Albany, NY: State University of New York Press, 195–216. (An excellent analysis of the precise reasons for Abravanel's lukewarm attitude towards monarchy as a form of government.)

Netanyahu, B. (1972) *Don Isaac Abravanel: Statesman and Philosopher*, Philadelphia, PA: Jewish Publication Society. (The standard work on the life and thought of Abravanel.)

Sirat, C. (1985) *A History of Jewish Philosophy in the Middle Ages*, Cambridge: Cambridge University Press, 393–7. (A short but useful summary of his thought.)

Trend, J. and Loewe, R. (eds) (1937) *Isaac Abravanel: Six Lectures*, Cambridge: Cambridge University Press. (Some important contributions to a general understanding of Abravanel.)

Weiler, G. (1988) 'Antipolitics Articulate and Triumphant in Abravanel', in *Jewish Theocracy*, Leiden: Brill, 69–85. (An interesting approach to the understanding of Abravanel's political thought.)

OLIVER LEAMAN

ABRAVANEL, JUDAH BEN ISAAC (*c*.1460/5–*c*.1520/5)

Judah ben Isaac Abravanel was born in Lisbon. After the expulsion of the Jews from Spain in 1492, Leone, as he was known, and his family migrated to Naples, but fled two years later following the French invasion. After brief residences in various Italian cities, Leone returned to Naples where he served as court physician to the Spanish Viceroy. Well-versed in the sciences of his day, including physics, medicine and philosophy, whether Jewish, Islamic or Christian, he composed his major work, Dialoghi d'amore *(Dialogues of Love), in 1501–2. Although the work influenced such important thinkers as Montaigne, Bruno and Spinoza, its main influence was in literature rather than philosophy. Its style resembles that of other Renaissance works in the ambit of Ficino's commentary on Plato's* Symposium *but, unlike these works, it is neither philosophical commentary nor courtly literature. Adopting the idiom of courtly love and drawing on Platonic and Neoplatonic sources, it complements them with mythological, biblical and Aristotelian sources to produce a novel synthesis of Plato and Aristotle with ideas drawn from the pagan and the revealed traditions, aiming to demonstrate that love is the animating principle of the universe and the cause of all existence, divine as well as material.*

The three dialogues between Philo, the poetic lover, and his beloved Sophia address the relations between love and desire, the universality of love and the origin of love. Each discussion pivots on an apparent opposition between Philo's Aristotelian and Sophia's Platonic views. The discussion of the relations between love and desire raises fundamental questions about the relations of soul and body.

1   **Life**
2   **History and structure of *Dialoghi d'amore***
3   **Philosophical significance of *Dialoghi d'amore***

ABRAVANEL, JUDAH BEN ISAAC

1 Life

Son of the well-known Jewish thinker and statesman ISAAC ABRAVANEL, Judah ben Isaac Abravanel, known as Leone Ebreo, was born in Lisbon (the Italian Leone rendering the Hebrew Judah, in accordance with custom). Despite the family's fame, our knowledge of Leone's life is scant and rife with rumour and surmise. The following is restricted to what is relatively certain.

After serving for years as treasurer to the Portuguese King Alfonso V, Don Isaac Abravanel and his family fled Lisbon for Spain in 1483 when, after Alfonso's death, Don Isaac was accused of conspiring against the new king. He was soon summoned to the service of Ferdinand and Isabella and raised funds needed in their consolidation of power. The monarchs none the less decreed the tragic expulsion of the Jews from Spain in 1492. The Abravanel family migrated to Naples but were forced to flee again by the wars following the French invasion of 1494. After brief residences in various Italian cities, including Genoa, Barletta and Venice, Leone returned to Naples and became court physician to the Spanish Viceroy, Don Gonsalvo de Cordoba. The last reliable evidence about him is a document dated 1520 exempting 'Master Leon Abarbanel, the physician' and his family from all tribute in recognition of his services to the Viceroy. He died in Naples at some time between 1520 and 1525.

Leone was well-versed in the sciences of his day, including physics, astronomy, medicine and philosophy from the Presocratics to the Renaissance, spanning the Jewish, Christian and Islamic philosophical traditions. During his sojourns in various Italian cities, he visited the Italian academies, met celebrated Renaissance thinkers and wrote a treatise *De Coeli Harmonia* (On the Harmony of the Heavens), at the request of Pico della Mirandola (probably the elder Pico, Giovanni, rather than his nephew Gianfracesco, who studied Hebrew under another well-known Jewish thinker, Yohanan Alemmano) (see PICO DELLA MIRANDOLA, G.). Leone also composed poetry, including an autobiographical Hebrew poem, *T'lumah 'al ha-Z'man* (A Plaint on Time).

2 History and structure of *Dialoghi d'amore*

Uncertainties and controversies surround Leone's famous work, but by the author's own testimony, it was written in 5262 of the Hebrew calendar, that is, 1501/2. It was published in 1535 at Rome, when Leone's friend Mariano Lenzi 'rescued the work from the shades in which it was buried'. It first appeared in Italian, but the language of its original composition is disputed. Spanish, *Ladino* and Hebrew have their advocates, all more or less nationalistic in their motives and all prepared to argue that so erudite an author as Leone Ebreo should exhibit a more elegant style, even in an acquired language, than the published text presents. The only tangible evidence for a Hispanic original is a single late *Ladino* manuscript extant in the British Museum. Arguments for a Hebrew original are based on the presumed Jewish audience of the work, the long delay in its publication, and the survival of different Italian versions.

The desire to claim Leone extends to his religious affiliation. The title page of the second and third editions of *Dialoghi d'amore*, describes Leone as Hebrew by nation but Christian by faith, prompting claims that he converted late in life. But there is no evidence of such a conversion, and the inscription, published in a period of religious intolerance (1541 and 1545), may well be bogus or wishful.

Ironically, in view of the efforts to claim them, Dialoghi d'amore is often dismissed as derivative of the Renaissance Platonist tradition that began with Marsilio Ficino's commentary on Plato's *Symposium* (see FICINO, M.). Yet the influence of *Dialoghi d'amore* extended far wider than Ficino's work. In the twenty years following its appearance the work had five Italian editions, three Spanish translations, two French translations, and translations into Latin and Hebrew. It influenced thinkers from MONTAIGNE and Burton to BRUNO and SPINOZA, whose library contained a Spanish edition. Its poetic, dialogical style and what may superficially appear as an indiscriminate blending of sources focused its abiding acknowledged influence more in literature than in philosophy.

Dialoghi d'amore comprises three discussions of love as the animating principle of the universe. Philo is the poetic lover; Sophia, his beloved. The first dialogue discusses the relations between love and desire; the second the universality of love; the third the origin of love. The theoretical discussions in each dialogue are framed by a brief preliminary dialogue represented as an actual exchange between lovers, in which Philo voices his desire for Sophia and she critically refuses his seductive attempts to unite with her. The dialogical structure of the text arises from a fundamental difference between two philosophical views about love, broadly stated: (1) that love and desire are essentially the same, since we desire what we love, since love and desire are always for the good, and since genuine desire is based upon knowledge; (2) that love and desire are opposites, since love originates in knowledge of what is and is good, desire in knowledge of what is lacking in being and in goodness. The first opinion is Philo's and can loosely be called Aristotelian; the second is Sophia's and can be identified as Platonic.

The entire exchange, of course, is an allegory of philosophy. Philo's desire for Sophia is the philosopher's quest for wisdom, which is human perfection. The three successive dialogical attempts to resolve an apparently fundamental disagreement between Plato and Aristotle are also attempts to delineate the relations between the human and the divine. The dialogues progress from the more to the less evident, gaining in abstraction and complexity. Each later discussion develops the conclusions of what has gone before. The second discussion is twice as long as the first; the third, over twice as long as the second. No resolution of the question is presented, prompting the received opinion that Leone meant to compose a concluding fourth dialogue. This inference is unwarranted. The twenty years between the completion of *Dialoghi d'amore* and Leone's death suggests that he had ample time to complete the work had he considered it either possible or necessary. Rather, the lack of an explicit resolution mirrors the structure of the Platonic dialogues, especially the *Symposium*, the model for all Renaissance writings on love.

3 Philosophical significance of *Dialoghi d'amore*

The Platonic form that situates *Dialoghi d'amore* among other Renaissance discussions of love unfortunately obscures as much about its philosophical lineage and import as it discloses. Western scholars typically read Renaissance Platonic texts in Christian perspective, ignoring or misconstruing the influence of Islamic and Jewish philosophy, traditions that are seen as predominantly Aristotelian and thus fundamentally at odds with Renaissance Platonism, especially as regards the central issues of the *Dialoghi d'amore*. As a result, the influence here of such thinkers as Maimonides, Avicenna and Averroes tends to be judged rather superficially and on the basis of the few explicit references to them. For example, the possible influence of Avicenna's *Risalah fi'l-'ishq* (Treatise on Love), or of Maimonides' focus on the intellectual love of God are rarely mentioned, and the Jewish aspect of Leone's work is reduced to its biblical allusions, for example Leone's claim that the Platonic ideas have a Mosaic origin (see MAIMONIDES, M.; IBN SINA).

Presuming that the literary genre of *Dialoghi d'amore* reflects sheer Christian Platonism, moreover, occludes the subtlety of Leone's resolution of the tension between the Platonic and Aristotelian approaches and covers over the contributions which the Aristotelian view of the soul can make to an understanding of desire, love and knowledge. Indeed, Leone's literary style may reflect a deliberate intention to occlude the radical thesis of the dialogue, a deistic conclusion that identifies God with the totality of the world.

Rather than contribute further to the obscuring of Leone's subtle and original contribution to Renaissance philosophy by offering an overview of *Dialoghi d'amore*, with its numerous, circuitous, subordinate discussions, lengthy and popularizing disquisitions on ancient mythology, astronomy and astrology, we shall focus on Leone's nuanced resolution of the primary disagreement about the relations between desire and love, that is, the apparent contradiction between the claims that desire and love are the same, and that they are opposites. But we must note at the start that, while the first claim does not require a strict identity, the second assumes that any opposition implies a contradiction.

From the outset, Sophia's resistance to Philo depends on interpreting the Platonic position as requiring a strict division between body and soul. It also requires real divisions within the soul, making its most noble part, the intellect, a distinct entity, absolutely independent of embodiment. Thus Sophia, the personification of wisdom, repeatedly and severely insists that if Philo truly loves her he should desire to satisfy that alone which pleases her, her mind.

There is a poignant irony here in the inverted relation between the male and female personae. Philo the male, or formal principle of the dialogue denies the real distinction between body and soul and, hence, between desire and love, whereas Sophia, the female, traditionally material, principle insists on such distinctions. But the resolution of the apparent contradiction between the Platonic and Aristotelian positions will establish body and soul, desire and love, male and female as natural correlatives: neither could be without the other. The same natural correlation is found between God and the world, as is mentioned briefly in passing, in the philosophical parts of the dialogues, thus protecting its radical theses from 'vulgar' view.

In the third, as in the preceding dialogues, Philo's philosophical analyses (as distinct from the long poetic digressions) are distinctly Aristotelian in form, and often in content. Sophia's objections continuously challenge the Aristotelian position with a Platonic one. In view of Philo's pedagogic role in *Dialoghi d'amore*, the text can be read as the re-education of Sophia, whose Platonism reflects the dogma of Christian Neoplatonism. Thus, before he reverts to the definition of love, Leone makes amply evident his Aristotelian view of the soul:

The soul is in itself one and indivisible, but by distributing its powers throughout the body and permeating even its surface and extremities, it branches out to certain activities pertaining to perception, movement and nutrition among various organs and divides itself among many diverse faculties.

This view of the relationship between body and soul will be reflected in Leone's view of the relationship between the One and the many, that is, God and the world. Again, in the discussion of beauty as the form of the object which originates the motion of desire, Leone 'corrects' the Platonic doctrine of knowledge as recollection with an Aristotelian view of knowledge as arising from sensation. Forms do not exist independently of their corporeal manifestations but are embodied. They are abstracted by the intellect, which is initially mere receptivity to form. The 'correction' here is in fact a reconciliation of Plato with Aristotle, transposing the Platonic myth of anamnesis into a philosophical mode while simultaneously retrieving it from Christian interpretations:

> You must know, therefore, that all forms and Ideas do not spring from bodies into our souls, because to migrate from one subject to another is impossible; but their representation by the senses makes these same forms and essences to shine forth which before were latent in our soul. This enlightenment Aristotle calls the act of understanding and Plato memory, but their meaning is the same, although differently expressed.

Plato's and Aristotle's views are not only compatible, they are interdependent. Their harmony makes evident the insufficiency of either position taken in isolation. Plato's teachings may be divinely inspired, but his mode of presentation lacks philosophical precision and so might lead to error. The resolution of the tension between Plato and Aristotle, fully and finally articulated in the third dialogue, makes clear that the opposition is only apparent and reflects terminological differences and a failure to recall that natural opposites belong to a single motion from potentiality to act.

Returning to the discussion of love in the third dialogue, Philo proceeds in an exemplary Aristotelian manner, pointing out that the questions 'What is love?' and 'What is its first cause or origin?' presuppose that love exists. He repeats the definition of love as desire and answers Sophia's insistent objections that love and desire are not the same, since we love what is and what we actually possess, but desire what we lack and what may or may not exist, by pointing out that reason demonstrates that love and desire are the same, although 'in the vulgar tongue each has its own significance'. Sophia has taken a mere linguistic, conventional distinction for a real one, a confusion that Philo finds to be common among 'certain modern theologians'.

Love and desire are different words denoting a single affection of the soul. Desire is a motion towards a desired object, love, a motion towards the beloved, which is the desired object. The cause of this motion, that is, the origin of love, is the desire for the pleasure of union with the beloved. Furthermore, *pace* Plato, love and desire are found in God. Indeed, God is their origin; in God they are found most eminently, as the desire for the perfection of all that is.

By following Aristotle closely, Philo demonstrates the proximity of truth and desire characteristic of true friendship, especially a friendship oriented by and toward God. Echoing the *Nicomachaean Ethics*, Philo explains to Sophia that he disagrees with Plato 'because, as Aristotle, his disciple, said of him, although I am the friend of Plato, I am a greater friend of truth'. It is in virtue of their common love of truth that philosophers are friends and are also friends of God, a friendship, Philo insists, that cannot be one-sided.

To appreciate the radical force of the definition of love that emerges from the resolution of the tension between the Platonic and Aristotelian positions, we must turn to the cosmology underlying *Dialoghi d'amore*. According to Philo, the universe is a single individual composed of perfectly proportioned parts, all of which, whether eternal or perishable, are constitutive of its perfection. The perfection proper to each part, its final end or good, is the perfection of the whole, not just its own perfection. More precisely, since the final end or good is the perfection that all things by nature desire, all strive in proportion to their capacity to attain the perfection of the universe. Thus the natural perfection desired by each part is simultaneously a desire for perfect harmony or union with the whole. That is why love is the animating principle of the entire universe, of being as well as becoming. As the animating principle of the universe, love is its efficient cause; as the desire for the perfection of the whole, it is its final cause. The universe as a whole is a perfect circle, its final cause identical with its other causes, first, formal and efficient. Conceived as unified, this cause is identical with God.

The identity of God and the whole of nature cautiously alluded to in the philosophical parts of *Dialoghi d'amore* was later developed explicitly and in detail by Spinoza. Nowhere is the kinship between the two Portuguese Jewish thinkers more evident than in

Leone's description of the union between the human and divine intellects:

> The pure intellect which shines forth in us is likewise the copy of the pure divine intellect, and is stamped with the unity of all the Ideas; and this it is which, crowning the discourse of reason, reveals to us those ideal essences in intuitive, single, and abstract knowledge, when our well schooled reason merits such knowledge. So that with its eyes, we may behold in one intuition the highest beauty of the first intellect and of the divine ideas.

See also: ARISTOTLE; ARISTOTELIANISM, RENAISSANCE; LOVE; PLATO; PLATONISM, RENAISSANCE

List of works

Abranavel, Judah ben Isaac (1501/2) *Dialoghi d'amore* (Dialogues of Love), ed. S. Caramella, Bari: Laterza e figli, 1929; ed. C. Gebhardt, *Dialoghi d'Amore: hebraeische Gedichte*, Frankfurt am Main: Curis Societatis Spinozanae, 1929; trans. F. Friedberg-Seeley and J. H. Barnes, *The Philosophy of Love*, London: Soncino Press, 1937; trans. M. Dorman, *Sihot 'al ha-Ahavah*, Jerusalem: Mossad Bialik, 1983. (Comprises three discussions of love as the animating principle of the universe. The three dialogues are between Philo, the poetic lover, whose beliefs about love can can loosely be called Aristotelian, and Sophia, Philo's beloved, whose views can be identified as Platonic. The entire exchange is an allegory of philosophy. Philo's desire for Sophia is the philosopher's quest for wisdom, which is human perfection. The three successive dialogical attempts to resolve an apparently fundamental disagreement between Plato and Aristotle are also attempts to delineate the relations between the human and the divine.)

References and further reading

Cooperman, D. (ed.) (1983) *Jewish Thought in the Sixteenth Century*, Cambridge, MA: Harvard University Press. (Of particular importance are the papers by Herbert Davidson, Alfred Ivry and Shlomo Pines.)

Damiens, S. (1971) *Amour et Intellect chez Leon l'Hebreu*, Toulouse: Privat. (The only recent sustained philosophical study of Leone Ebreo.)

Martins, J.V. de Pina (1989) *Humanisme et Renaissance de l'Italie au Portugal: Les deux regards de Janus*, Lisbon and Paris: Fondation Calouste Gulbenkian, vol. 1, 357–81. (Devoted to the *Dialoghi*.)

Ruderman, D. (ed.) (1992) *Essential Papers on Jewish Culture in Renaissance and Baroque Italy*, New York: New York University Press. (Of special importance is 'The Place of the *Dialoghi d'amore* in Contemporaneous Jewish Thought', by A.M. Lesley.)

—— (1988) 'The Italian Renaissance and Jewish Thought', in A. Rabil (ed.) *Renaissance Humanism: Foundations, Form, and Legacy*, vol. 1, Philadelphia, PA: University of Pennsylvania Press, 382–433. (An essay on the current understanding of the impact of the Italian Renaissance movement on major Jewish thinkers of the time.)

IDIT DOBBS-WEINSTEIN

ABSOLUTE, THE

The expression 'the Absolute' stands for that (supposed) unconditioned reality which is either the spiritual ground of all being or the whole of things considered as a spiritual unity. This use derives especially from F.W.J. Schelling and G.W.F. Hegel, prefigured by J.G. Fichte's talk of an absolute self which lives its life through all finite persons. In English-language philosophy it is associated with the monistic idealism of such thinkers as F.H. Bradley and Josiah Royce, the first distinguishing the Absolute from God, the second identifying them.

1 Theories of the Absolute
2 Bradley and Royce

1 Theories of the Absolute

With Fichte, Kant's transcendental ego (the relation of which to individual persons was somewhat vague) became a single absolute cosmic self which lives its life through each of us and posits the natural world as that through struggle with which it can develop itself morally (see FICHTE, J.G. §3). With Schelling, the absolute self became the Absolute as the mysterious ground of all being, revealing itself in parallel both in *nature* (the creation of our shared unconscious) and in *finite thought*, of which it is somehow the identity-in-difference (see SCHELLING, F.W.J. §1). Later, Schelling held that the ordinary world of finite things springs from their somehow falling away from their proper eternal place within the Absolute in an arrogant attempt at independent existence. With Hegel, the Absolute became the Absolute Idea, somehow both the culmination and the self-differentiating unity of the cosmic dialectical sequence or circle (see HEGEL, G.W.F. §6). This may be most conveniently conceived as starting with the concept of pure being, moving through a series of concepts towards their exhibition in empirical nature, and finally through a series of levels of human life, until it becomes self conscious as Absolute Spirit in the higher forms of this, especially in the civilized nation state and in the philosophic mind. Whether Hegel also ascribes to it a more cosmic self-consciousness is controversial – certainly it is somehow a self-differentiating spiritual unity.

More conspicuous in the English-speaking philosophical world were the conceptions of the Absolute of F.H. BRADLEY, Josiah ROYCE, J.M.E. MCTAGGART and other absolute idealists in a tradition not yet dead (and still representing, arguably, our best grasp of how things really are). For Bradley and Royce, the Absolute was a single spiritual individual of which all finite things are, if not exactly parts, at least part-like aspects. For McTaggart, in contrast, it was the Universe conceived as a system of selves linked directly or indirectly by bonds of affection and appearing to each other much of the (apparent) time as the physical world.

British and US absolutists tended to treat time more bluntly as an illusion than did their German predecessors mentioned above. For the former, the Absolute was a *Nunc Stans* containing all finite experiences which, although they appear to themselves to be in time, are in truth its eternal components. For the German absolutists (at least for Fichte and Schelling) free will, fairly much as it is commonly conceived, was among the most stressed features of the Absolute, and derivatively of humans. Indeed, their chief quarrel with SPINOZA, whose monism they were trying to capture in more Kantian terms, was his determinism. The British and US absolutists were more Spinozistic on this matter, believing frankly in a 'block universe'.

2 Bradley and Royce

Arguably the best case for, and the best characterization of, the Absolute was that of Bradley and Royce. For Bradley, the Absolute was 'a single Experience, superior to relations and containing in the fullest sense everything which is' (Bradley 1914: 246). For Royce it was a universal self whose life is composed of the lives of all conscious beings (there being no others) experienced in unity.

Their argument was somewhat as follows. First comes the well-argued idealist claim that there is no such thing as unexperienced reality – in fact there is nothing other than lived experience itself. Now, on the face of it, experiences occur as aspects or components of finite centres of experience, such as we think of as the consciousness of men and animals, so it seems that the world must be the totality of these. But how are they in any real relation to one another rather than isolated monads, each altogether wrapped up in itself? The common-sense view is that they are variously juxtaposed in a single space and time, just as are the brains which underpin them. But for idealism, space and time and all their contents exist only as presentations within, or constructions wrought within, centres of experience so that it is these that contain them rather than vice versa. There must, then, be some kind of whole other than that of space and time within which finite centres of experience exist, and this can only be some more comprehensive, indeed 'infinite', centre of experience within which they all occur together in a mutually necessitating manner. This will be timeless, yet will contain each centre of experience in every one of its temporal phases, and it will be a state of perfect understanding of, and satisfaction with, itself and all that it contains (for ignorance and dissatisfaction can have no place when nothing from outside can block knowledge or desire).

Royce added his own special twist to the argument by contending that there could not be a relation of *aboutness* between one's thoughts and external objects (and that therefore one's thoughts could only be about the present contents of one's own mind) unless the thoughts and the external objects were all contents of one all-embracing mind which used the former as a correct or incorrect way of characterizing the latter.

One problem with the Absolute, as conceived by Bradley and Royce, was a special version of the problem of evil: How can the whole be perfect when so many of its parts or aspects are so bad? This objection was presented in its most lively form by William JAMES. Royce gave the most elaborate solution. The highest goods consist in the overcoming of evils, so that what is mere evil from a finite point of view is, from the Absolute's point of view, that which is eternally overcome by the good which keeps it down. The true image of the Absolute is Saint George, with the dragon struggling perpetually beneath him, the whole thereby possessing a perfection much greater than the merely saccharine goodness of a world without evil (see EVIL, PROBLEM OF §1).

Many of these absolutists, though decidedly not all, saw the Absolute as the Christian God properly conceived; however, in some respects the Absolute of Western absolute idealism is much closer to Brahman as conceived by Advaita Vedānta though a more active Brahman than the West wrongly supposes to be the Hindu one (see VEDĀNTA).

See also: IDEALISM ; KANT, I.

References and further reading

* Bradley, F.H. (1897) *Appearance and Reality*, Oxford: Oxford University Press, 1930. (Main statement of Bradley's metaphysics, one of the most important original works of metaphysics written in English.)
* —— (1914) *Essays on Truth and Reality*, Oxford: Clarendon. (Major essays containing developments of Bradley's logic and metaphysics. Source of definition cited in §2 above.)
  Fichte, J.G. (1794) *The Science of Knowledge*, trans. P. Heath and J. Lachs with the 1797 introduction, Cambridge: Cambridge University Press, 1982. (This is the main statement of Fichte's extremely difficult philosophy.)
  Findlay, J.N. (1970) *Ascent to the Absolute*, London: George Allen & Unwin. (Argues for a revival of 'absolute theory', that is, the study of the unconditioned basis of all things.)
  Hegel, G.W.F. (1817) *The Encyclopedia of the Philosophical Sciences*, translated in volumes as: Vol. 1 *The Logic of Hegel*, trans. W. Wallace, Oxford: Oxford University Press, 1974; Vol. 2 *Hegel's Philosophy of Nature*, trans. M.J. Petry, Oxford: Oxford University Press, 1970; Vol. 3 *Hegel's Philosophy of Mind*, trans. W. Wallace and A.V. Miller, Oxford: Oxford University Press, 1971. (Vols 1 and 3 are those of most interest to the modern reader. These works give a summary statement of Hegel's view of the world as the gradual growth to self-knowledge, through the human mind, of the Absolute Idea as infinite spirit.)
  McTaggart, J.M.E. (1921, 1927) *The Nature of Existence*, Cambridge: Cambridge University Press, 2 vols. (One of the most closely argued works of constructive metaphysics ever written, though its conclusions are somewhat fantastic.)
  Royce, J. (1885) *The Religious Aspect of Philosophy*, Gloucester, MA: Peter Smith, 1965. (The first and perhaps finest of Royce's philosophical works. As well as arguing for the existence of the Absolute as an all-including consciousness, it is outstanding for its treatment of how *ought* relates to *is*.)
  Schelling, F.W.J. (1797) *System of Transcendental Idealism*, trans. P. Heath, Charlottesville, VA: University Press of Virginia, 1978. (Schelling changes his philosophical position several times. This is the main statement of it in its earliest form.)
  Sprigge, T.L.S. (1983) *The Vindication of Absolute Idealism*, Edinburgh: Edinburgh University Press. (This argues first for the impossibility of an unexperienced reality, deducing therefrom a panpsychic view of nature and the existence of an absolute, all-containing consciousness.)

T.L.S. SPRIGGE

ABSOLUTISM

The term 'absolutism' describes a form of government in which the authority of the ruler is subject to no theoretical or legal constraints. In the language of Roman law – which played a central role in all theories of absolutism – the ruler was legibus solutus, *or 'unfettered legislator'. Absolutism is generally, although not exclusively, used to describe the European monarchies, and in particular those of France, Spain, Russia and Prussia, between the middle of the sixteenth century and the end of the eighteenth. But some form of absolutism existed in nearly every European state until the late eighteenth century. There have also been recognizable forms of absolute rule in both China and Japan.*

As a theory absolutism emerged in Europe, and in particular in France, in the late sixteenth and early seventeenth centuries, in response to the long Civil Wars between the Crown and the nobility known as the Wars of Religion. In the late eighteenth century, as the reform movement associated with the Enlightenment began to influence most European rulers, a form of so-called 'enlightened absolutism' (or sometimes 'enlightened despotism') emerged. In this the absolute authority of the ruler was directed not towards enhancing the power of the state, but was employed instead for advancing the welfare of his subjects.

1   The legal definition
2   Two theories of absolutism
3   Absolutism and the modern state

1   The legal definition

Like most such terms, absolutism is a nineteenth-century coinage. But the term 'royal power absolute' was employed, in one context or another, by nearly all the monarchs of Europe from the late fifteenth to the mid-eighteenth century.

Although it was sustained by, and has become associated with, a number of social and cultural developments – lavish courts, an extensive bureaucracy, standing armies and the creation of a new noble class – absolutism was primarily a theory of legislative authority. This maintained that all rulers possessed exclusive executive and legislative authority, and consequently that the laws they made constituted an expression of their will. In the formula used by the jurist Ulpian, and repeated in one form or another by all would-be absolute monarchs, 'that which pleases the prince has the force of law'. All theories of absolutism claimed, in effect, that modern kings possessed the same authority – frequently described by the term *imperium* – as that once exercised by the Roman emperors. To sustain this claim common law, based as it was upon the legislative will of the community, was gradually replaced throughout Europe during the sixteenth and seventeenth centuries by Roman law. (The sole major exception was England, the ambition of whose monarchs was checked by the execution of Charles I in 1649.) The only theoretical limit to the monarch's legislative authority was the Divine and Natural Laws, which, since there was no one other than God to execute them, provided only the flimsiest of constraints. The kings' positive laws might be interpreted within certain narrowly defined limits (although all absolute rulers from Justinian to Napoleon attempted by codification to eliminate interpretation), but they were mandatory (see ROMAN LAW).

Absolutism was thus a radical attempt by increasingly centralized, increasingly modern, states to overturn the broadly contractual theories of authority which had grown up after the collapse of the Roman Empire. These had maintained that the king derived his authority from a contract with the people, who had been granted power directly by God himself (see CONTRACTARIANISM). The laws were made by the representative assemblies of the people and administered by the king. He was the *servant* of his people, and his role was one of magistrate not judge. And although in practice the people had few means by which they might rid themselves of a ruler, there did exist quite powerful safeguards for their collective rights. Absolutism, in contrast, denied the representative assemblies any legislative or executive power. In Spain, the Cortes had been reduced to little more than a tax-voting body by the mid-sixteenth century. In France, the Estates General fell into disuse after 1612, and in 1673 the Parlement of Paris, a body which modelled itself on the Roman Senate, was deprived of even its hallowed right to remonstrate against royal edicts before registering them.

2 Two theories of absolutism

Despite its essentially legal core, absolutism was by no means a single or unitary theory. In its most extreme form, it maintained that the power of the ruler derived directly from God, as the source of all created things. This, know as Divine Right, found its most powerful exponent in Jacques-Bénigne Bossuet. Bossuet claimed (an argument he derived from Hobbes) that as the people had had no historical sovereign before the institution of kingship, kings must have been the creation of God, and were, therefore, accountable to him alone. Most theories, however, including Hobbes's own, were dependent upon some version of an original contract theory (see HOBBES, T. §7). These fell into two broad categories.

The first maintained that royal authority derived, as the contractualists had maintained, from an agreement between the ruler and his people, but that since this was a contract, it involved an irreversible transference of power. The people might be entitled under certain conditions to resist their rulers, but they no longer possessed the authority to replace him. Perhaps the most persuasive, and certainly the earliest exponent of these claims was Jean BODIN (§3) whose *Les six livres de la république* (The Six Books of a Commonwealth) first appeared in 1576. For Bodin the state was the 'lawful government of many families'. The ruler held the same position *vis-à-vis* society as the father did towards the members of his family. This granted him absolute and undisputed power over them. (Bodin even wished to see the right granted to fathers by Roman law to execute their children reintroduced into France.) Sovereignty, which was to become the key term in all subsequent discussions of royal authority, could thus be defined as 'the giving of laws to their subjects in general without their consent'. Legal authority and the state itself thus became an expression of the king's legislative will (see SOVEREIGNTY).

The second theory, whose most powerful exponent was the Spanish Jesuit theologian and jurist Francisco SUÁREZ (§4), maintained that the authority of all rulers derived from a delegation of power from the people (Suárez 1612). Although, like Divine Right, this granted the ruler absolute legislative and executive authority, it meant that the people could, *in extremis* (or if the throne fell vacant), reclaim that authority. For this reason Suárez, like most Jesuits, accepted that tyrannicide might be an acceptable means of disposing of an unjust ruler, an opinion which led to the public burning of his writings in both London and Paris.

On both accounts, the people retained certain rights as individuals; crucially, that of self-defence and (for Bodin) the right of property. Having surrendered, in Hobbes' formulation, both their will and their judgment to their rulers, they were wholly subject to them, but they remained free agents. Furthermore, although his person and the state became a single entity, the ruler did not have property rights in the state and could not, therefore, alienate any part of it. There therefore existed a distinction, albeit one which subsequent legal theorists such as Montesquieu would reject as illusory, between 'absolutism' and 'despotism'. As even Bossuet was prepared to concede, a king's rule should be absolute, but never (as the Ottoman Sultan's was thought to be) arbitrary. In practical terms this meant that the king should, wherever possible, consult the representatives of his subjects, but he was not obliged to follow their advice. The king should also abide by his own laws, and respect local custom. But all absolutists allowed that such constraints could be set aside in cases of necessity. The concept of 'necessity' as a device whereby the rule of law might be suspended – closely associated as it was with theories of 'reason of state' – thus became a key term in the vocabulary of absolutism.

3   Absolutism and the modern state

For all its archaic trappings, absolutism was essentially a modern theory of state authority. Writers like Bodin, Hobbes, Suárez and Bossuet possessed a recognizably modern conception of legislative authority as the means to protect the interests of the entire society. All, in different idioms, argued that unless such authority was clearly vested in one source, no society could ultimately escape internal conflict of the kind which had afflicted France in the sixteenth and England in the seventeenth century.

Numerous historians have argued that, despite the vast body of theoretical literature endorsing absolute rule, the power of early-modern monarchs was never in fact complete. But no state power ever is. The theory of absolute sovereignty was about *de jure* not *de facto* power. By the end of the seventeenth century, moreover, the rulers of Spain, France, Sweden, Russia and large parts of Germany had gained effective control over all the armed forces and communications within their territories. Their subjects may have defied them, but they never consistently challenged their right to rule.

Absolutism sought to establish in this way the undisputed power of the state over the numerous factional and regional interests which had governed medieval societies. In the sixteenth and seventeenth centuries this power was embodied in kings. But, as Hobbes said, it did not really matter if the ruler was one or many. The final beneficiaries of this insight were the French Revolutionaries. Far from being the end of absolutism, the Revolution was its fulfilment. For it was the Revolutionaries who, by replacing the monarch with an assembly, assured the final transformation of French society into a modern – and absolute – parliamentary state. By the end of the nineteenth century all the major states in Europe, with the exception of Britain and Russia, had followed their example.

See also: FILMER, SIR ROBERT

References and further reading

Anderson, P. (1974) *Lineages of the Absolutist State*, London: Verso. (A wide-ranging (England to Japan) and highly intelligent, if now somewhat dated, Marxist interpretation.)

* Bodin, J. (1576) *Les six livres de la république*, Paris: Jacques du Puy, 1583; repr. Aalen: Scientia, 1961; trans. J. Bodin, *De republica libri sex*, Paris: Jacques du Puy, 1586; trans. R. Knolles, *The Six Books of a Commonwealth*, London: B. Bishop, 1606; repr. ed. K.D. McRae, Cambridge, MA: Harvard University Press, 1962; ed. and partial trans. J.H. Franklin, as *Bodin: On Sovereignty*, Cambridge: Cambridge University Press, 1992.

* Bossuet, J.-B. (1709) *Politique tirée des propres paroles de l'Écriture-Sainte*, ed. J. Le Brun, Geneva, 1967; ed. and trans. P. Riley, *Politics drawn from the very words of Holy Scripture*, Cambridge: Cambridge University Press, 1991.

Franklin, J.H. (1969) *Constitutionalism and Resistance in the Sixteenth Century*, Cambridge: Cambridge University Press. (Provides the background for the early development of absolutism.)

—— (1973) *Jean Bodin and the Rise of Absolutist Theory*, Cambridge: Cambridge University Press. (The best detailed study of Bodin's political writings.)

Fulbrook, M. (1983) *Piety and Politics*, Cambridge: Cambridge University Press. (Mostly concerned with England and Prussia.)

Giesey, R.E. (1961) *The Juristic Basis of Dynastic Right to the French Throne*, Philadelphia, PA. (A detailed account of the legal arguments for sovereignty.)

Gilmore, M. (1941) *Argument from Roman Law in Political Thought 1200–1600*, Cambridge: Cambridge University Press. (Still the only comprehensive study of the role of Roman law in the formation of the absolutist state.)

Harth, E. (1983) *Ideology and Culture in Seventeenth-Century France*, Ithaca, NY: Cornell University Press. (Studies the uses made of culture by the French monarchy to enforce the power of the state.)

Hobbes, T. (1651) *Leviathan*, ed. R. Tuck, Cambridge: Cambridge University Press, 1991.

Keohane, N. (1980) *Philosophy and the State in France from the Renaissance to the Enlightenment*, Princeton, NJ: Princeton University Press. (An outstanding account of the transformation of political thinking in this period.)

MacFarlane, L.J. (1977) 'Absolutism, Tyranny and the Minimum Conditions for Constitutional Rule', *Government and Opposition* XII: 212–33.

Skinner, Q. (1978) *The Foundations of Modern Political Thought*, vol. 2, *The Age of Reformation*, Cambridge: Cambridge University Press. (Provides the most succinct account of the political theory of absolutism.)

Sommerville, J.P. (1991) 'Absolutism and Royalism', in *The Cambridge History of Political Thought 1450–1700*, eds. J.H. Burns and M. Goldie, Cambridge: Cambridge University Press, 347–73. (A useful general survey of the literature.)

* Suárez, F. (1612) *Tractatus de legibus ac deo legislatore* (On Laws), in *Corpus Hispanorum de Pace*, ed. L. Perena, V. Abril and P. Suner, Madrid: Consejo Superior de Investigaciones Cientificas, 1971–81, vols 11–17, 21–2.

ANTHONY PAGDEN

ABSTRACT OBJECTS

The central philosophical question about abstract objects is: Are there any? An affirmative answer – given by Platonists or Realists – draws support from the fact that while much of our talk and thought concerns concrete (roughly, spatiotemporally extended) objects, significant parts of it appear to be about objects which lie outside space and time, and are therefore incapable of figuring in causal relationships. The suggestion that there really are such further non-spatial, atemporal and acausal objects as numbers and sets often strikes Nominalist opponents as contrary to common sense. But precisely because our apparent talk and thought of abstracta encompasses much – including virtually the whole of mathematics – that seems indispensable to our best attempts to make scientific sense of the world, it cannot be simply dismissed as confused gibberish. For this reason Nominalists have commonly adopted a programme of reductive paraphrase, aimed at eliminating all apparent reference to and quantification over abstract objects. In spite of impressively ingenious efforts, the programme appears to run into insuperable obstacles.

The simplicity of our initial question is deceptive. Understanding and progress are unlikely without further clarification of the relations between ontological questions and questions about the logical analysis of language, and of the key distinction between abstract and concrete objects. There are both affinities and, more importantly, contrasts between traditional approaches to ontological questions and more recent discussions shaped by ground-breaking work in the philosophy of language initiated by Frege. The importance of Frege's work lies principally in two insights: first, that questions about what kinds of entity there are cannot sensibly be tackled independently of the logical analysis of language; and second, that the question whether or not certain expressions should be taken to have reference cannot properly be separated from the question whether complete sentences in which those expressions occur are true or false.

1 **Logical and ontological categories**
2 **The abstract–concrete distinction**
3 **Grounds for belief in abstract objects**
4 **Grounds for disbelief**

1 Logical and ontological categories

Although what most obviously needs explaining is the abstract–concrete distinction, the relevant notion of *object* also calls for elucidation. There is a familiar, everyday use of the term 'object' in which we may speak of the objects found in the accused's pockets, for example. There are probably no very precise rules governing this use, but it seems clear that being extended in space and time is at least a necessary – but probably not a sufficient – condition for its application. If 'object' is so understood, the term 'abstract object' is straightforwardly self-contradictory. We should infer, not that Nominalism wins by default, but that some other more general, less restrictive notion of object is in play in philosophical discussions. But if so, how should it be characterized? To avoid begging questions, it might be proposed that anything should be reckoned an object to which we may make reference. Arguably, however, this goes too far the other way – we may as well be said to refer to fiddling as to Nero, when we assert that Nero fiddled, but should be loathe to count fiddling an *object*.

A way forward which preserves this general approach is to take objects to be the referents of expressions of a certain restricted class – what are usually called 'singular terms'. To take this step is to follow FREGE in viewing the ontological categorization of entities as dependent upon a prior logical categorization of expressions. Objects, properties and relations, for example, are essentially the non-linguistic correlates of, respectively, singular terms (for example 'Nero', 'this lake', 'the dome of St. Peter's' and so on), one-place predicates ('...fiddles', '...is deep'), and two- or more-place predicates ('...loves...', '...is taller than...'). An object, on this account, is the referent of an actual or possible singular term.

When *object* is so understood, our opening question is, in an important sense, a distinctively *modern* one. It is not that we can discern no significant common concerns underlying ancient disagreements over the status of Plato's Forms and the great medieval battle between realists and nominalists over the existence of universals on the one hand, and modern ontological disputes on the other. Traditional and modern discussions share a general concern with the relations between language and the world. At bottom, disagreement over abstract entities is disagreement over whether an adequate account of language–world relations can be provided without reference to any such entities. It remains the case that a fundamental shift has taken place in the way very many philosophers conceive and argue about ontological issues in general, and issues about abstract entities especially. Ancient and medieval disputes focused on the existence of universals as opposed to particulars, with the former thought of as abstract entities which both predicates ('is red', 'is wise') and corresponding abstract nouns ('redness', 'wisdom') stand for. But on the Fregean approach, it makes no sense to suppose some one kind of thing to be the common referent of expressions of completely different logical types. This need not mean that there is no significant disagreement between medieval realists and nominalists; but it does mean that they misconceived the issue, or at least ran together questions we should separate. For it is one question whether abstract nouns are to be conceived as genuine singular terms, standing for objects, and a quite distinct question whether the corresponding predicates have reference – if so, then they stand, not for objects, but for properties (concepts, in Frege's sense) (see UNIVERSALS).

2 The abstract–concrete distinction

Abstract objects can be neither seen nor heard, nor can they be tasted, felt or smelled. But for several reasons it would be unsatisfactory to take inaccessibility to sense-perception as the basis of our distinction. Besides importing an unwanted relativity to human sensory faculties, it would fail to draw the distinction clearly, there being room for dispute over what should count as perceiving something. If the range of sense-perception is taken as including only what can be discerned with the naked organ, as it were, the condition for being concrete is clearly too restrictive. The range might be extended to allow for detection via more or less remote effects, but once the criterion is loosened in this way, the proposal slides into taking capacity for involvement in causal interactions as the mark of the concrete. This suggestion avoids the difficulties with a sensory-access criterion but, even if extensionally correct, does not go to the heart of the matter. We expect capacities in general to have some categorical basis. Why are concrete objects capable of causal interaction but abstract objects not? The answer, it would seem, should yield a more illuminating account of the distinction. Partly for this reason, a more promising account of the distinction sees lack of location in space or time as distinctive of the abstract – what cannot be anywhere, anywhen, cannot be a factor in the causal nexus.

Although it is widely endorsed and gives intuitively correct results in the cases to which philosophers have attended, this account is nevertheless flawed. This is because there are candidates for abstract status which, though plainly lacking spatial properties, are not wholly atemporal. In the sense in which two pairs of players at different chessboards may be said to be engaged in one and the same game, the game of chess is plausibly taken to be an abstract object; but while it is not located anywhere, it has not always existed, but was devised at a certain time. Other examples are natural languages, many if not all works of art, and words and letters in the type- as opposed to token-sense (roughly, the sense in which there are just six, not eight, distinct letters in the word 'abstract') (see TYPE/TOKEN DISTINCTION). Thus while the abstract–concrete distinction undoubtedly has much to do with spatiality and temporality, it does not seem straightforwardly identifiable with the distinction between what has spatial or temporal position and what has neither. An alternative proposal of considerable interest is that concrete objects are those which are, in principle, capable of being picked out ostensively, while abstract objects are those to which we can refer only by means of some functional expression (Dummett 1973: ch. 14). Thus we may pick out a particular tree by the words 'That beech', perhaps accompanying our utterance with a pointing gesture; but we cannot, for example, literally point to a certain shape or number – rather, we must refer to them as, say, the shape of such and such a vase or the number of eggs in the carton (Noonan 1976; Hale 1987: ch. 3).

3 Grounds for belief in abstract objects

Many philosophers, appealing to Ockham's Razor – the principle that entities should not be multiplied beyond necessity – deem it mortally sinful to believe in abstract objects unless such belief is unavoidable, but disagree about whether it is actually avoidable. Orthodox nominalists hope to avoid it by carrying through a programme of reductive paraphrase. However, in view of the resistance of various kinds of apparent reference to/quantification over abstract objects to elimination by reductive paraphrase or re-interpretation in concrete terms, this does not appear feasible as a completely general means of escaping commitment to abstract objects (see ONTOLOGICAL COMMITMENT). This has led some philosophers to conclude that reference to and quantification over domains including abstract objects is indispensable to a fully adequate account of the world. There is a strong appearance that this is the case with reference to mathematical entities – numbers of various kinds, functions and more generally, sets. On the face of it, the natural sciences, and physics especially, require substantial use of arithmetic and analysis, and the latter in turn draws fairly heavily on set theory. This argument – known as the Quine–Putnam Indispensability Argument – provides, if accepted, a strong *indirect* reason for believing in numbers and sets at least: scientific theories require acceptance of mathematical theories, so that whatever reasons we have to believe that our best scientific theories are true is reason to accept mathematical theories, and so to believe in the abstract objects of which they speak.

This argument has been vigorously contested, particularly by Field (1980), who argues – in support of a new and highly unorthodox brand of nominalism – that there is, contrary to appearances, no need for mathematical theories to be true for their use in science to be justified. It is enough that such theories should have a certain strong kind of consistency property, which he calls 'conservativeness'. Since a nominalist can accept mathematical theories as having this property without believing them to be true, they have no need to engage in any kind of reductive translation programme of the sort previously mentioned – they can simply use mathematical theories while denying that they are literally true, thereby avoiding commitment to the abstract objects their truth requires. Among the difficulties confronting this approach, one important assumption Field makes is worth highlighting. Field takes the Quine–Putnam argument to offer the only ground worth taking seriously for holding mathematical theories to be true, so that if he is able to undermine it, there remains no pressure to take on the ontological commitments they import. If Field's assessment were correct, the best grounds we could have for believing maths and so on, would be indirect and a posteriori. But this assessment rests upon the challengeable assumption that the only statements we may justifiably accept on other-than-indirect a posteriori grounds are those directly ascertainable as true by observation. Perhaps we should take seriously, as he does not, the possibility that belief in the truth of mathematical statements and acceptance of their ontology may be warranted a priori.

4 Grounds for disbelief

Unquestionably the most important arguments against abstract objects are epistemological. One is that – in view of the presumed causal inertia of abstract objects – to construe statements of some given kind as having their truth-conditions constituted by states of affairs essentially involving such objects, puts those statements irretrievably beyond the reach of our knowledge. Crudely, if mathematical statements have Platonistic truth-conditions, we could not possibly know them to be true; since we do have mathematical knowledge, Platonism is false. In its simplest and earliest versions, this argument relies upon a very exacting form of causal theory of knowledge, which takes it to be an invariably necessary condition for a thinker X to know that p, that X's true belief that p should itself be caused by, or otherwise suitably causally related to, the fact that p (see KNOWLEDGE, CAUSAL THEORY OF). A problem with this argument is that while such a strong condition (just how strong depends on how precisely the vague phrase 'suitable causal relation' is understood) may be satisfied in standard cases of perceptual and memory knowledge, it is very hard to see how it could be quite generally met, even when restricted in scope to ordinary empirical knowledge concerning perfectly concrete matters. Our inductively grounded belief that all aardvarks have bugs is, we may suppose, causally induced by inspection of a large and suitably varied contingent of bug-infested aardvarks – but there is no sort of causal relation, however complicated or attenuated, of which it may with any plausibility be claimed both that it holds between our general belief and the fact that all past, present or future aardvarks have bugs and that its holding is epistemically significant. If knowledge does not demand a suitable causal link in every case, the argument against Platonism collapses, at least in its present form.

A related argument alleges that no satisfactory sense can be made of the idea that we are capable of identifying reference to or thought about abstract objects. And once again, the argument in its simplest form rests upon an eminently challengeable assumption – in this case, that identifying reference or thought about a particular object *always* requires a suitable causal link between the speaker/thinker (or their utterance/thought) and the object in question (see REFERENCE). Opponents of Platonism may hope to fashion more sophisticated causal analyses of knowledge and reference which are strong enough to sustain versions of these objections without being so strong as to be independently objectionable, but none has yet come forth.

A more powerful epistemological objection appeals to the thought that, even if knowledge is not to be analysed in specifically causal terms, we should expect to be able to provide a naturalistic explanation of our tendency to get things right significantly more often than not, in any area where we are disposed to credit ourselves with a capacity for knowledge (see RELIABILISM). In the absence of causal or other natural relations between ourselves and abstract objects, it is hard to see how any such credible explanation might run for any region of discourse whose statements are supposed to carry Platonistic truth-conditions. The argument relies on the assumption that ontological views are tenable only to the extent that they leave space for a credible epistemology. The arguments reviewed here confront Platonism with a strong challenge, even if they could not, by their very nature, tell decisively against it.

See also: NOMINALISM; ONTOLOGY; REALISM AND ANTIREALISM; UNIVERSALS

References and further reading

* Dummett, M. (1973) *Frege: Philosophy of Language*, London: Duckworth. (Hard going, but the best introduction to Frege's approach to the analysis of language. Chapters 2, 4 and 14 are especially relevant.)
* Field, H. (1980) *Science without Numbers*, Oxford: Blackwell. (Introduction and chapter 1 give a clear outline of the approach discussed in §3 above.)
—— (1989) *Realism, Mathematics and Modality*, Oxford: Blackwell. (Occasionally technically difficult, but generally very readable. Chapters 1 and 2 provide an excellent account of Field's overall position; chapter 7.2 develops the epistemological argument against Platonism mentioned in §4 above.)
Frege, G. (1884) *The Foundations of Arithmetic*, trans. J.L. Austin, Oxford: Blackwell, 1953. (Essential reading for anyone wishing to pursue the present subject in depth. See especially §§60–8.)
—— (1892) 'On concept and object' in P. Geach and M. Black (eds) *Translations from the Philosophical Writings of Gottlob Frege*, Oxford: Blackwell, 1970. (Especially relevant to §1 above. Provides a very readable informal elucidation of Frege's contrasted notions of object and concept, indicating their connection with his fundamental distinction, at the level of language, between proper names and predicates.)
Goodman, N. and Quine, W.V.O. (1947) 'Steps towards a constructive nominalism', *Journal of Symbolic Logic* 12: 105–22; repr. in N. Goodman *Problems and Projects*, Indianapolis, In and New York: Bobbs-Merrill, 1972, 173–98. (Classic nominalist manifesto. Technically quite difficult after opening sections.)
* Hale, R. (1987) *Abstract Objects*, Oxford: Blackwell. (Along with Noonan (1976), chapter 3 develops a proposal to base the abstract–concrete distinction on the different kinds of identity criterion appropriate to the different kinds of object. Chapters 1–3 are relevant to §§1–2 above, chapter 5 to §3, and chapters 4, and 7 to §4.)
—— (1994) 'Is Platonism epistemologically bankrupt?', *Philosophical Review* 103 (2): 299–325. (Defends Platonism against arguments discussed in §4 above.)
Hale, R. and Wright, C. (1993) 'Nominalism & the Contingency of Abstract Objects' *Journal of Philosophy* 89 (3): 111–35. (Criticizes Field's version of nominalism.)
Lewis, D. (1987) *On the Plurality of Worlds*, Oxford: Blackwell. (Very readable. Chapter 2 discusses problems with the abstract–concrete distinction.)
* Noonan, H. (1976) 'Dummett on abstract objects', *Analysis* 36 (2): 49–54. (Difficult but rewarding discussion, relevant to §2 above.)
Putnam, H. (1971) 'Philosophy of logic', in *Mathematics, Matter and Method: Philosophical Papers*, vol. 1, Cambridge: Cambridge University Press, 1979, 2nd edn. (Technically difficult in places, but contains important material relevant to §3 above, including presentation of indispensability arguments.)
Quine, W.V.O. (1948) 'On what there is', in *From a Logical Point of View*, New York: Harper Torchbooks, 1961, 1–19. (Classic paper on ontology, with strong nominalist sympathies.)
Wright, C. (1983) *Frege's Conception of Numbers as Objects*, Aberdeen: Aberdeen University Press. (Excellent exposition and vigorous defence of Frege's position. Chapters 1 and 2 are especially relevant.)

BOB HALE

ABUBACER *see* IBN TUFAYL, ABU BAKR MUHAMMAD

ACADEMY

The Academy was a public gymnasium in northwest Athens. Plato taught there, and the Academy remained the centre of Platonic philosophizing until the first century BC. Hence the term 'Academy' came to be used to designate Plato's school; members of the school were called 'Academics'. (And hence, ultimately, the modern use of the words to describe intellectual institutions and their members.)

The word 'Academy' originally had a topographical reference. A mile and a half northwest of the Athenian agora, along the Ceramicus road, there was a public gymnasium and wrestling square set in a spacious park. Like most gymnasia, the Academy contained an exedra – a sort of open-air lecture theatre. Here PLATO talked and taught philosophy. He set up a shrine to the Muses in the park; and he acquired a house, with a little garden, in the neighbourhood, where his friends and pupils congregated. A contemporary comic poet imagines a group of students assembled in the garden earnestly attempting to produce a definition of the pumpkin.

Plato's house was used by his successors until the time of Polemo (in the late fourth century BC), whose pupils lived in huts in the garden; and Platonists continued to teach in the Academy until the beginning of the first century BC. But after that time there seems to have been no special relationship between Platonism and the geographical Academy.

The word 'Academy' was readily transferred from the concrete to the abstract: it came to designate the school or institution which Plato established and which his successors conserved. The nature of the institution is imperfectly known; but it is clear that there was a head, or 'scholarch', who was (at least sometimes) elected to office; that there were senior and junior members; and that there were discussions, lectures and dinners. Yet the Academy was not an embryonic university: there were no degrees and no administration block.

On Plato's death in 347 BC, his nephew SPEUSIPPUS led the school. He was followed by XENOCRATES Polemo and Crates. In about 265 BC ARCESILAUS assumed the scholarchate and turned Platonism down the sceptical path which it followed for almost two centuries. Of later scholarchs the most engaging and the most celebrated was CARNEADES. In 88 BC, when Athens was in the grip of war, the scholarch PHILO OF LARISSA decamped to Rome. It seems likely that Philo was the last Platonist geographically connected to the Academy. But philosophy is above mere geography, and Platonism survived and flourished until the end of the ancient world. Modern authors will refer to later Platonists as Academics: the nomenclature is inaccurate, the inaccuracy venial.

Ancient writers, remarking upon apparent changes in the intellectual drift of the school, would speak of a plurality of Academies. The most generous listed five: the Old Academy, which lasted from Plato to Polemo; the Middle Academy, founded by Arcesilaus; the New Academy, inaugurated by Carneades; a fourth Academy under Philo; and a fifth under ANTIOCHUS. The Academics did not necessarily endorse these divisions. Thus CICERO, himself professing an Academic scepticism, simply distinguished between the Old Academy from Plato to Polemo and the New Academy from Arcesilaus onwards; and Philo notoriously maintained that there had only ever been one Academy.

See also: PLATONISM, EARLY AND MIDDLE §1

References and further reading

Billot, F.-M. (1989) 'Académie', in R. Goulet (ed.) *Dictionnaire des philosophes antiques*, vol. 1, Paris: Éditions du CNRS. (Documents the archaeological and literary evidence.)

Cicero, M.T. (early 45 BC) *Academics*, trans. H. Rackham, Loeb Classical Library, Cambridge, MA: Harvard University Press, and London: Heinemann, 1933. (A philosophical retrospect on the Academy by one of its best-known adherents.)

Glucker, J. (1978) *Antiochus and the Late Academy*, Hypomnemata 56, Göttingen: Vandenhoeck & Ruprecht. (Includes an exhaustive account of all non-philosophical aspects of the Academy.)

Philodemus (c. 50 BC) *History of the Academy*, trans. T. Dorandi, *Filodemo: storia dei filosofi – Platone e l'Academia*, Naples: Bibliopolis, 1991. (A biographical account of the school's history; includes Greek text, and Italian translation and commentary.)

JONATHAN BARNES

ACQUAINTANCE AND DESCRIPTION, KNOWLEDGE BY *see* KNOWLEDGE BY ACQUAINTANCE AND DESCRIPTION

ACRASIA *see* AKRASIA

ACTION

Philosophical study of human action owes its importance to concerns of two sorts. There are concerns addressed in metaphysics and philosophy of mind about the status of reasoning beings who make their impact in the natural causal world, and concerns addressed in ethics and legal philosophy about human freedom and responsibility. 'Action theory' springs from concerns of both sorts; but in the first instance it attempts only to provide a detailed account that may help with answering the metaphysical questions.

Action theorists usually start by asking 'How are actions distinguished from other events?'. For there to be an action, a person has to do something. But the ordinary 'do something' does not capture just the actions, since we can say (for instance) that breathing is something that everyone does, although we don't think that breathing in the ordinary way is an action. It seems that purposiveness has to be introduced – that someone's intentionally *doing something is required.*

People often do the things they intentionally do by moving bits of their bodies. This has led to the idea that 'actions are bodily movements'. The force of the idea may be appreciated by thinking about what is involved in doing one thing by doing another. A man piloting a plane might have shut down the engines by depressing a lever, for example; and there is only one action here if the depressing of the lever was (identical with) the shutting down of the engines. It is when identities of this sort are accepted that an action may be seen as an event of a person's moving their body: the pilot's depressing of the lever was (also) his moving of his arm, because he depressed the lever by moving his arm.

But how do bodies' movings – such events now as his arm's moving – relate to actions? According to one traditional empiricist account, these are caused by *volitions when there are actions, and a volition and a body's moving are* alike parts of the action. *But there are many rival accounts of the causes and parts of actions and of movements. And volitional notions feature not only in a general account of the events surrounding actions, but also in accounts that aim to accommodate the* experience *that is characteristic of agency.*

1   Actions, events and individuation
2   'Basic acts'
3   Volitional theories: actions, parts and causes
4   Agents' experience and knowledge
5   Philosophy of action applied to ethics and law

1   **Actions, events and individuation**

'Action' and 'act' are often used interchangeably. But 'action' is given a definite meaning when actions are taken to be a species of events: it denotes particulars of a certain sort – concrete items in the spatiotemporal world. It is useful then to give a different meaning to 'act': acts are things people do (which are sometimes called act-types). Such things are not particulars, since one person can do the same thing as another. If Mary and John both voted for Smith, for instance, then Mary's act (voting for Smith) was the same as John's; but obviously the event that was Mary's voting for Smith was not the same action as John's voting for Smith.

Is Mary's voting for Smith ever the same action as *Mary's* doing some *other* act? This is a question now about the individuation of actions. Proponents of a fine-grained account (for example Goldman 1970) say that there are as many actions as there are acts exemplified by the agent on occasion, so that, in our pilot example, the man's depressing of the lever is one action and his shutting down of the engines is another action. Proponents of a coarse-grained account, on the other hand (for example Davidson 1971), assert the identity of his depressing of the lever with his closing down of the engine. They think that actions are often described in terms of their effects. When the description 'Paul's depressing of the lever' is used, an event is seen to have resulted in the lever's being depressed; when 'Paul's shutting down the engines' is used, an event is seen to have resulted in the engines' shutting down. But if Paul shut down the engines *by* depressing the lever, then the lever's coming to be down in its turn caused the engines' cutting out, so that in fact an action of Paul's is spoken of twice over here: it is described now in terms of one effect, now in terms of another.

This coarse-grained account can be made plausible by thinking of *Paul's* part in the engines' coming to be shut down as his moving of his arm. The thought is that for the engines to shut down, nothing was required of Paul after his arm had moved. Since he is the only relevant agent, Paul's moving his arm is the only action that there is, and 'his moving of his arm' is just one of its descriptions.

Various objections are made to the coarse-grained account, and these have led some philosophers (for example Ginet 1990) to intermediate accounts of actions' individuation. (An intermediate account might have it that Paul's moving his arm is the same as his moving his arm against the lever (which would be denied by the fine-grained theorist), but is different from his shutting down of the engines (which would be denied by the coarse-grained theorist).) One objection to the coarse-grained account would say about Paul's case that his shutting down of the engines (s) took place later than his moving his arm

(m), so that these have different properties: m occurred at t, s at $t + n$, so that $m \neq s$. A proponent of the coarse-grained account of course maintains that s really did occur at t if m did. They claim that our tendency to suppose otherwise is explained by our confusing s with the effect in terms of which we think of it. (The engines' shutting down is an effect which indeed occurred later than the action, they say.) A related objection relies on intuitions about when tensed sentences such as 'He has shut down the engines' are first true. Here the coarse-grained account's proponent allows the relevant intuition: this sentence is not true until some time later than 'He has moved his arm' is first true. But, they say, the truth of 'He has shut down the engines' requires more than the past occurrence of the event s: it also requires the past occurrence of the engines' shutting down.

The coarse-grained account joins with a definition of 'an action' as 'someone's intentionally doing something' to give intuitively right results. Suppose that Paul's shutting down of the engines was a terrible mistake, and that he was responsible for an accident. We understand how we can think of Paul as an agent in respect of something he did quite unintentionally, when we appreciate that his doing one thing was (the same as) his doing another. One thing he did was to shut down the engines, and he did this accidentally; but his doing this was his depressing of the lever, and depressing the lever was something that he did intentionally. For an event actually to have been an action of some person's according to the definition, it has to be true only that at least one of the things they did was something they intentionally did.

This criterion of actionhood is sometimes put by saying that an action has to be 'intentional under one of its descriptions'. 'Under a description' has wide philosophical currency. But it can be misleading. When 'doing things under descriptions' is employed, it is made to seem as if there were these things people do, and that *they* have various descriptions. Things people do do not have various descriptions, however: people's *actions* have various descriptions, and these descriptions correspond one:one with the things, or acts, that they then do.

2 'Basic acts'

Acts are done by doing other acts. But not every act someone does could be done by doing some different one, or nothing would ever get done. Among the things that a person does on occasion, then, there must be something which is *simply* done – not done by doing something else. This has been called the basic act. Where someone Φs by Ψ-ing, Ψ-ing is said to be *more basic than* Φ-ing; and the basic act is defined as the one than which no other was more basic.

Moving the body (that is, moving a bit of it in one or another way) is usually a basic act. When Mary raises her right arm directly – in order to vote at the meeting – raising the right arm is the basic act. But in the unusual case in which someone raises their right arm by lifting it with their left arm, raising the right arm, although a bodily act, is not the basic one. (What is basic here is moving the left arm.) Such an example shows that in order to say what was basic in a particular case, one has to know not only what bodily movements occurred in that case but also what was actually done by doing what else. Acts, then, are not basic *tout court*. Relative to Mary's action, but not relative to the action that was someone's raising their right arm 'indirectly', raising the right arm is basic.

The need to think about applications of basicness in connection with particular cases has sometimes given rise to talk of basic *actions*. But such talk conflicts with the coarse-grained account of actions' individuation. Where a person's raising their arm is considered to be identical to their voting, it cannot be supposed that their raising their arm is basic and their voting is not. If a notion of a basic act that is not relativized to particular cases is wanted, we have to think about what someone *can* do directly. (The person who used their left arm to raise their right arm might, or might not, have been *able* to simply raise their right arm.) Using a notion of a basic *ability*, we could speak of things as basic for a person with a particular repertoire of motions (not relative to any particular action now).

We encounter relations of dependence when we go through a list of more and more basic acts. Considering Paul's action, and going through his various acts – causing an accident, shutting off the engine, depressing the lever, moving the arm – it is natural to think of what is less basic as depending on what is more basic. We may think of all the dependencies as causal ones in the particular example. But there are different kinds of dependence, and when the different kinds are distinguished, different relations of 'more basic than' can be distinguished. For example if we take it that a convention must obtain for someone's raising their arm to count as their voting, we could say about Mary's action that voting was *conventionally* more basic than raising the arm.

The thought that moving the body is basic seems now to be the thought that moving the body does not usually depend upon anything else – neither causally, nor in any other way. And yet physiologists tell us that, in fact, our bodily movements depend upon our muscles' contractions – that we move our bodies by contracting our muscles. It seems, then, that even where someone simply moved their arm we have a candidate for a more basic act than moving the arm – namely, contracting muscles. In fact, what this shows is that the perspective of an agent is ordinarily assumed in thinking about what is done; when moving the body is taken as basic, the focus is on things that the people might think of themselves as doing. A different notion of *basicness* is needed to accommodate the facts that the shift to a physiologists' perspective reminds us of. To allow for the fact that moving the body depends upon other things being done, a 'purely causal' notion of basicness may be introduced. This is not the intuitive, central notion that recapitulates the idea of what someone 'simply does' or 'does directly'. Philosophers have meant a variety of different things by 'more basic than'.

3 Volitional theories: actions, parts and causes

Events like muscles' contractions, which occur beneath the body's surface, come to notice not only in our thinking about different ideas of basicness: they may be prominent also when we enquire what precise causal story should be told about any action. And it is not only physiological thinking which makes philosophers want a precise causal story: a definition of 'an action' as 'someone's doing something intentionally' belongs with a view which distinguishes actions from other events by reference to a particular sort of psychologically specifiable causal history. On this view, a person who does something intentionally does the thing because they have a reason to. Saying what their reason was requires knowing what their relevant beliefs and desires were (see BELIEF; DESIRE; INTENTION); and it provides a distinctive kind of explanation of why they did the thing (see REASONS AND CAUSES). But it may be asked whether there is not a more immediate causal story to be told about an action than that which shows up in a reason explanation. Do actions have immediate mental antecedents of a certain sort?

It has sometimes seemed that actions must have such antecedents, because wanting, believing and intending all seem inadequate to explain actually doing something. Suppose you want to move your arm. Your arm doesn't move until … what? 'Until there is a volition' was an answer often given in the eighteenth and nineteenth centuries: philosophers often posited volitions, or acts of will (as they are alternatively called), as events which initiate the causal process of acting, bridging the gap between wanting and doing. This was a gap between the mind and the body in the thinking of dualists (see DUALISM; WILL, THE).

Volitions fell out of philosophical favour when Ryle objected to them as spurious (Ryle 1949). Ryle asked why 'the Will' has to be exercised in action at all, thinking that the postulation of volitions was a hangover from the idea of a 'ghost in the machine'. One of his arguments against volitions posed a dilemma: either volitions are themselves 'active', or they are not. If they are 'active', then if a volition really were required for a genuine action, we should always have to posit a new volition as cause of any volition, and we should be led to an infinite regress. If, on the other hand, volitions are not themselves 'active', but are mere causes of actions, it is hard to see why anyone should think that their introduction helps in recording what is special to action.

Some volitional theories rather obviously escape this objection. John Stuart Mill, for instance, thought that an action was 'a series of two things; the state of mind called a volition followed by an effect' (Mill 1843: I 3.5). In its twentieth-century guise, the Millean theory takes an action to be composed from (a) a volition (b) a movement of a bit of the body of the person whose volition it is. On this theory, Ryle's question as to whether a volition itself, or only its effect, is 'active' has no simple answer, since each of these things is a *part* of an action. But Ryle's underlying question may still be pressed: 'Why posit a sort of mental item such that actions are present only when an item of that sort is a cause?'

The account of volitions as parts of actions draws attention to the distinction between *actions*, each one of which is someone's moving a bit of their body, and *bodies' movements*, each one of which is a bit of someone's body's moving. (The thesis which is often used to summarize the coarse-grained view of actions' individuation – that actions are bodily movements – is now seen to be crucially ambiguous at best.) When this distinction is made, there are two other views about bodies' movements, both different from the Millean, componential view. (A) Actions are identical with bodies' movements, so that, for instance, a person's raising their arm is their arm's rising. (B) Bodies' movements are not even parts of actions, so that a person's arm's rising is wholly distinct from their raising it. (A) is implausible inasmuch as it seems to sever the connection between acting and doing something; unless a person's arm's rising is itself the person's doing something, that connection is broken when movements are identified with actions. (B) is a more plausible view – at least for the philosopher who think that actions are described in terms of their effects; for the latter, a person's arm's going up can be the effect of their raising it, just as a flag's going up is the effect of someone's raising the flag.

According as (A) or (B) is accepted, the doctrine that volitions cause bodies' movings turns out differently. When bodies' movings are thought to be actions, volitions are conceived in the manner Ryle found objectionable – they are thought of as the last item in a mental causal chain leading outward to something physical. But when bodies' movings are thought to be *no parts* of actions, the theorist can say that a volition causes a body's movement and is itself an action. When that is said, an item is recognized the status of which is ineluctably *psychophysical*, being both a volition and an action; the theorist may refuse any picture in which the mental can be marked off from the physical on a causal chain. It remains a good question why one should suppose that there is a faculty of the Will the products of which, volitions, have to be brought into an account. But when volitions are identified with actions, we can be certain at least that there is nothing mythical or 'ghostly' about them.

The claim that physical actions are redescribable in recognizably psychological terms is made not only by philosophers who say that actions are volitions, but also by others who have no truck with volitions. Some philosophers argue that anyone who does something intentionally *tries to* do it. (They allow that one need not *think of* oneself as trying to do the things one does intentionally, and they allow that 'They tried to do it' is not usually a natural thing to say about someone who encountered no difficulties and who did not need to make any special effort.) If that is correct, then, given a coarse-grained view of individuation, each action *is* someone's trying to do something. One may arrive at an account in which a person's having a reason to do something leads to their trying to do it; when their trying to do it has the effects they want (as usually it does), it is their doing the thing. To the question 'Your arm doesn't move until … what?', the answer now could just as well be 'Until you move your arm' or 'Until you try to move it' (see MENTAL CAUSATION).

4 Agents' experience and knowledge

When the Will features in accounts of action, it may be thought of, in Cartesian spirit, as something the operations of which are available only to introspection (see INTROSPECTION, PSYCHOLOGY OF; PRIVATE STATES AND LANGUAGE). One of the ideas to which Ryle was objecting in his attack on volitions was the idea that for each visible action of a person there is an inner item accessible to them alone. Now, although we may not wish to describe our experience of agency in Cartesian terms, it seems undeniable that there is consciousness of voluntary agency. If volition is thought of as action's conscious aspect, then it is not an invention of philosophers but a feature of everyone's experience. So it could be correct to suppose that volition is a part of the phenomenon of action, even if it should be denied that *each* action has *a* volition as a part or as a cause.

A person who is doing something intentionally knows what they are doing – or, if they do not know this, they know at least what they are trying to do; and they know this without making observations of themselves of a kind that others can make. The experience of acting, which is the basis of such knowledge, is not just proprioceptive experience (it is not just experience got from information fed back from the body about the body when the body is moved). So the idea of a distinctive conscious state contemporaneous with an action seems correct. There is little agreement about how such an idea should be recorded in an account. Sometimes the content of the experience of acting is spoken of in terms of 'exertion', which can make it seem as though some actual effort were always required to move a bit of the body. But if the idea of experienced exertion is meant only to capture the fact that it would feel very differently to us if we did not move our bodies voluntarily, it is acceptable. Suppose that you were wired up in such a way that your efferent neural pathways could be so stimulated that your muscles would contract and your finger move when some other person determined that this should happen. Of course there would not be an action of your moving your finger in that case; but also, we think, the characteristic experience of agency would be missing.

Such experience, it might be thought, is present in all conscious creatures who do things – whether or not they are rational agents who do things intentionally. If that is right, it may be necessary also to record another kind of experience, which is peculiarly human now, and which may be called the experience of freedom, or the sense of alternative possibilities (see FREE WILL §5). Thinking of agents as conscious subjects can remind us of how narrowly focused the philosophy of action becomes when it is concerned exclusively with questions of actions, events and individuation, basic acts and volitional theories (see CONSCIOUSNESS).

5 Philosophy of action applied to ethics and law

There is another sort of narrowness in accounts of action that confine themselves to a conception of actions as a species of events. In marking out a class of actions, and investigating how these relate to volitions, movements, etc., the philosopher does not start to address many of the conceptual questions that are asked about action by the legal, or moral, philosopher. An ordinary concern with human action is not a concern with which events occur, but is a concern with what people do. (A fine-grained ontology, of 'act tokens' or 'tropes' is sometimes introduced in order to reflect this ordinary concern.)

Arguably 'intentionally' is the only piece of psychological vocabulary needed to characterize the actions, when actions are taken to be a species of events (see above). But resources beyond 'intentionally' are certainly required to make the many distinctions needed to understand lawyers' accounts of *mens rea* and moral philosophers' accounts of responsibility. In considering someone's culpability, it is not enough to consider those of their attitudes which constitute their reason for doing what they do and which connect with what they do *intentionally*. One might need to know, for instance, whether some effect that was not intended by them as a means was or was not one which they *foresaw* as resulting from their choice. (Did Paul know what he was doing when he unintentionally shut down the engines?)

For a person to be praised or blamed as an agent there need not be any event which is an action of theirs. There are cases, for example, where someone intentionally does not do something (Jane intentionally did not answer the question, say), and where although 'intentionally' applies, its application is not to any *event* (there is no *event* which is Jane's not answering the question). There are other cases where an agent is held responsible for some effect in the world, but where none of the things they did or did not do was something they *intentionally* did, or did not, do. Legal conceptions of recklessness, negligence, or strict liability would all introduce examples in this category (see MORAL AGENTS; RESPONSIBILITY).

Questions asked in legal and moral philosophy require a more broadly-based conception of the phenomena of agency than the action/theoretic account on its own can provide.

See also: RATIONALITY, PRACTICAL

References and further reading

Brand, M. and Walton, D. (eds) (1976) *Action Theory*, Dordrecht: Reidel. (Varied collection of accessible articles.)

Danto, A. (1965) 'Basic Actions', *American Philosophical Quarterly* 2: 141–48. (Original source for the idea of basicness: see above §2.)

* Davidson, D. (1971) 'Agency', in R. Binkley *et al.* (eds) *Agent, Action and Reason*, Toronto, Ont.: Toronto University Press; repr. in Davidson (1980). (Defends a coarse-grained account of actions' individuation, working with the idea of actions as a species of events which are 'intentional under some description'.)

—— (1980) *Essays on Actions and Events*, Oxford: Oxford University Press. (The author's ideas in the philosophy of action are presented (in the five essays in part 2) in the context of an account of events (part 1) and an account of the psychological (part 3).)

Donagan, A. (1987) *Choice: The Essential Element in Human Action*, London: Routledge & Kegan Paul. (Readable introduction, introducing more background than many standard works on 'action theory'.)

* Ginet, C. (1990) *On Action*, Cambridge: Cambridge University Press. (Good, elementary, if not easy, introduction, defending a 'medium-grained account of actions' individuation and a phenomenologically-based version of volitionalism. Also addresses some questions about human freedom.)

* Goldman, A. (1970) *A Theory of Human Action*, Princeton, NJ: Princeton University Press. (Defends a fine-grained account of the individuation of act-tokens, or tropes. Considers some issues connected with responsibility.)

Hornsby, J. (1980) *Actions*, London: Routledge & Kegan Paul. (Attends to distinctions between notions of basicness (in chapters 5 and 6), and to different versions of doctrines about actions' parts and causes (in chapters 3 and 4).)

* Mill, J.S. (1843) *A System of Logic*, London: Parker, 8th edn, 1961. (One source of a componential volitionalist view.)

O'Shaughnessy, B. (1980) *The Will*, 2 vols, Cambridge: Cambridge University Press. (Detailed and sustained defence of a psychophysical conception of willed behaviour, paying close attention to phenomenology.)

* Ryle, G. (1949) *The Concept of Mind*, London: Hutchinson, ch.3. (Source of objections to dualistically conceived volitionalism.)

Searle, J. (1983) *Intentionality*, Cambridge: Cambridge University Press. (Chapter 3 explores the relation between intentions and actions using a conceptual apparatus developed for analysing problems of intentionality.)

JENNIFER HORNSBY

ADORNO, THEODOR WIESENGRUND (1903–69)

Philosopher, musicologist and social theorist, Theodor Adorno was the philosophical architect of the first generation of Critical Theory emanating from the Institute for Social Research in Frankfurt, Germany. Departing from the perspective of more orthodox Marxists, Adorno believed the twin dilemmas of modernity – injustice and nihilism – derived from the abstractive character of Enlightenment rationality. In consequence, he argued that the critique of political economy must give way to a critique of Enlightenment, instrumental reason.

Identity thinking, as Adorno termed instrumental rationality, abstracts from the sensory, linguistic and social mediations which connect knowing subjects to objects known. In so doing, it represses what is contingent, sensuous and particular in persons and nature. Adorno's method of negative dialectics was designed to rescue these elements from the claims of instrumental reason. Adorno conceded, however, that all this method could demonstrate was that an abstract concept did not exhaust its object. For a model of an alternative grammar of reason and cognition Adorno turned to the accomplishments of artistic modernism. There, where each new work tests and transforms the very idea of something being a work of art, Adorno saw a model for the kind of dynamic interdependence between mind and its objects that was required for a renewed conception of knowing and acting.

1 **Life**
2 **For and against Marx**
3 **A genealogy of reason**
4 **Nonidentity and negative dialectics**
5 **Aesthetic theory**

1 Life

Theodor Wiesengrund-Adorno (Wiesengrund, his father's name, shrank to the initial W. during his exile in California in 1943) was born in 1903 in Frankfurt. From his mother and sister the young Adorno derived his lifelong passion for music. Near the end of the First World War, Adorno began spending his Saturday afternoons studying Kant's *Critique of Pure Reason* with the social critic and film theorist Siegfried Kracauer. Under Kracauer's guidance, Adorno came to experience the first *Critique* not as mere epistemology, but 'as a kind of coded text from which the historical situation of spirit could be read' (1992: vol. 2, 58). This method of reading and thinking, entwining epistemology with social physiognomy, became the constitutive gesture of Adorno's philosophy.

After completing a dissertation on Edmund HUSSERL's phenomenology, Adorno received his doctorate from the Johann Wolfgang Goethe University in 1924. In the following year, he travelled to Vienna to study composition with Alban Berg and involve himself with the circle of composers and musicians gathered around Arnold Schoenberg. His Vienna interlude was to have a lasting impact; not only did he become a leading advocate of the 'new music', but his philosophical style can be traced to the 'atonal' compositional techniques of Schoenberg and Berg.

Returning to his studies in Frankfurt, Adorno took his habilitation with a thesis published as *Kierkegaard: Konstruktion des Ästhetischen* (Kierkegaard: The Construction of the Aesthetic) (1933). In this difficult work, three themes that were to remain decisive emerge: (1) the criticism of existentialism as betraying its desire for concreteness by transforming existential elements into abstract categories, such as that of subjectivity in KIERKEGAARD (Adorno continued to make an analogous criticism of Heidegger's notion of 'being'); (2) a reading of the social world as reified, that is, a world in which institutions indifferent to the claims of subjectivity dominate over persons; (3) the attempt to provide a historical and materialist concretization of theological ideas.

Adorno fled Hitler's Germany in 1934 to Merton College, Oxford. During his three and a half years in England, Adorno wrote articles for the house journal of the *Institut für Sozialforschung* (Institute for Social Research), which was then under the direction of his friend Max Horkheimer (see FRANKFURT SCHOOL), and worked on a book on Husserl, which was eventually published in 1956. Adorno spent the war years in the USA. During that time he collaborated with Horkheimer on *Dialektik der Aufklärung* (Dialectic of Enlightenment) (1947), often regarded (not altogether accurately) as *the* statement of first-generation critical theory (see CRITICAL THEORY).

After the war, Adorno returned to Frankfurt to help rebuild the Institute. Over the next twenty years he produced a stream of works of musical and literary criticism, social theory and philosophy. His 1957 article 'Sociology and Empirical Research' is now regarded as the initiator of the 'positivist dispute' that raged in Germany in the 1960s, with Adorno and Karl POPPER as the main combatants. Adorno's two major philosophical works, *Negative Dialektik* (Negative Dialectics) (1966) and *Ästhetische Theorie* (Aesthetic Theory) (1970), were written during this period, the latter published a year after Adorno's death.

2 For and against Marx

Adorno's philosophy is a response to his understanding of the social world he inhabited. Adorno never doubted that advanced, Western societies were structured by capitalist relations of production as analysed by MARX. In particular, he accepted Marx's account of commodity fetishism and the domination of use values by exchange value. Adorno also accepted the proposal that the same mechanisms structuring the economy were effective in structuring cultural practices. While domination and poverty (broadly speaking, injustice) are the central consequences of capital's rationalization of the economy, alienation and meaninglessness (broadly speaking, nihilism) are the central consequences of its rationalization of culture (see ALIENATION; NIHILISM).

However, against the background of the rise of fascism in Europe and the dissolution of workers' movements, later augmented by the events of the Holocaust, Adorno came to doubt that there really were significantly progressive tendencies latent in the economic and social fabric of the modern world. On the contrary, he came to believe that the rationalization of modern societies was all but complete, and hence came to view Marx's theory of history, with its commitment to an intrinsically progressive developmental sequence of social formations, as drawing on the same structures of rationality as those governing capitalist processes of production. If it is those structures of reason and rationality that are at the roots of the deepest dilemmas of modernity, then the crisis of modernity is primarily a crisis of reason. What is thus required before all else is a critical diagnosis of modern reason; in criticizing this formation of reason Adorno is simultaneously criticizing the world it engenders and providing the terms for a radical transformation of that world.

3 A genealogy of reason

It is modern scientific rationality, with its commitment to the primacy of method, analysis, subsumption, universality and logical systematicity, that Adorno believes is at the centre of the modern crisis of reason. He contends that knowing and its objects become deformed or distorted when reason is defined in terms radically independent of the objects to which it applies, where by 'objects' Adorno means not just objects known, but equally the sensory images of those objects, the articulation of those images in language, the entanglement of natural languages in social practices and the complex histories of those practices. Each of these items could be regarded as a systematic source of error (and in the course of the emergence of modern, enlightened rationality was so regarded), from sceptical worries about the deliverances of the senses to concern about collective prejudices sedimented in linguistic and social practice (see DESCARTES, R.; BACON, F.). With respect to the theory of rationality, anxieties about these sources of error led to the view that reason must be fully autonomous, and not determined by anything external to it. It is this thought that underlies the primacy of method. In the theory of language, the same project is pursued in the attempt to eliminate opacity, indeterminacy and vagueness from the meaning of concepts; this is the project of positivism and the analytic tradition generally.

Dialectic of Enlightenment aims to provide a genealogy of enlightened rationality. Enlightenment opposes myth, the enchantment of the natural world through the projection onto it of human fears and hopes. The presumed superiority of reason over myth is hence its freedom from anthropomorphic projections; reason depicts the world objectively rather than through subjective projections. Horkheimer and Adorno contend that this flattering self-image of reason is both formally and substantively fallacious. Both myth and reason emerge in the course of humankind's struggle to free itself from bondage to mythic powers (themselves projections of primordial fear of the natural world in which humankind was immersed) and to gain control over the natural world in order to satisfy human needs and desires. Both myth and reason employ the principle of immanence, the explanation of every event as the repetition of a given pattern or law (what Adorno elsewhere calls 'identity thinking'), in order to combat fear of the natural world by bringing it into an explicable order. Repetition, 'the new is the old', originally provides for conceptual control over the natural world by revealing an intelligible order and eventually, through the technological application of modern science, for actual control over the natural world. Hence the formal features which provide for the supposed autonomy of enlightened reason are in fact grounded in the anthropogenesis of human reason in its struggle with nature. Enlightened reason is not objective, but subservient to the human desire to control nature; such reason can be construed as the discursive embodiment of the human drive for self-preservation, and hence as instrumental.

4 Nonidentity and negative dialectics

Enlightened reason is premised on a false inference: because some false beliefs (myths, superstitions and the like) are subjective projections, then the medium of those projections (sensory images, language, social practices and history) must themselves be systematic sources of error. Complete independence from these mediums is thus taken to be a condition for true knowledge. This drive for independence is most fully elaborated in the writings of the German Idealists, above all KANT and FICHTE, where the autonomy of reason and the meaning-independence of concepts become explicitly identified with the spontaneity of the 'transcendental' subject. Unknown to itself, this subject and the philosophical concept of system it subtends are still in the throe of the drive to self-preservation, their abstract conceptuality still harbouring both fear and rage against their objects. The conception of idealism as rationalized rage is Adorno's appropriation and transformation of NIETZSCHE's notion of *ressentiment*. Idealist rage is directed at anything that refuses to fit or, in Adorno's terminology, is nonidentical with the demands of autonomous reason. Because the autonomy of reason is secured through the meaning-independence of concepts from concrete experience and its mediums, then what is incommensurable with this reason is whatever is irredeemably particular and contingent. The goal of Adorno's philosophy is the 'rescue' of nonidentity – the thing in itself in its concrete, historically mediated sensuous particularity.

Adorno's method of rescue is the use of dialectic. The point of dialectical analysis is to demonstrate that the rationalized concept of an object does not exhaust the thing conceived. It attains this end by showing that what were conceived to be extrinsic encumbrances on reason (sensory images and so on) that could be stripped away in its attainment of autonomy are in fact the *necessary mediations* through which knowing subjects come into relation to objects known. Adorno borrowed this conception of dialectic from HEGEL. Adorno construes his dialectic as 'negative', in opposition to Hegel, because, on the one hand, he believes that Hegel's 'system' collapses back into the kind of identity thinking that dialectic opposes; and, on the other hand, because he believes that dialectical analysis only works under conditions in which the mediations it elaborates are systematically, in theory and in practice, denied.

Because an alternative conception of reason is not currently available, despite being a real historical possibility, Adorno's philosophy is utopian. Cognitively and practically, utopia is conceived of by Adorno 'as above identity and above contradiction; it would be a togetherness of diversity' ([1966] 1973: 150). An image of such 'togetherness of diversity' is provided by modernist works of art.

5 Aesthetic theory

Adorno argues that distinctly modernist works of art exemplify the possibility of an alternative grammar of reason and cognition. He focuses on modernist works – atonal music, abstract painting, 'absurdist' literature (particularly Kafka and Beckett) – because these works self-consciously attempt to establish their aesthetic validity, and hence their objectivity, in explicit opposition to all existing norms for artistic production and all established criteria in accordance with which art works have been judged. Existing norms and established criteria are the equivalents in art to the demands of method in science. Enlightened reason has it that such norms and criteria, in science and art, are spontaneous products of reason itself. Success for a modernist work is for it to be compelling, demanding aesthetic attention and assent, in excess of established criteria of aesthetic value and, even more radically, in excess of all criteria which heretofore have constituted what it is for an item to be a work of art.

'The falsehood opposed by art,' Adorno argues, 'is not rationality *per se* but the fixed opposition of rationality to particularity' ([1970] 1997: 144). The binding of rationality to what occurs in particular cases refutes the thesis of the meaning-independence of concepts from their objects and the autonomy of reason, and hence the principle of immanence. That this refutation occurs in art works entails that such binding is only a semblance or image of an alternative grammar of reason, since in modernity art is no longer a rationally legitimated vehicle of representation; art works now are 'meaningful' wholes without external purpose. That what happens in art can none the less matter to rationality generally derives from the hypothesis that the language of art and the discourse of rationality outside the artworld are not mutually indifferent language games. Rather, art picks up the debris of nonidentity left over from rationalization processes outside art; it is the refuge of the nonidentical. Further, art is driven to its modernist extremes of atonality, abstraction and absurdity in order to sustain itself as *art*, unique works of contemplation, in opposition to the recurrent demands of the principle of immanence.

Adorno's philosophical practice explicitly binds itself to the practices and fate of artistic modernism, and in this he is being self-consistent. Adorno aims to expose philosophy, the attempt to ground rationality and cognition, to its nonidentical other, forcing philosophy to surrender its claim to autonomy and meaning-independence. This is an avowedly peculiar terminus for a radical philosopher: defending the claims of the victims of history by forging an alliance between philosophy and high modernist art.

This state of affairs links together with the three dominant lines of criticism of Adorno's thought: (1) it is unduly pessimistic about the emancipatory potential of modern liberal societies; (2) it turns its face against the call for praxis indigenous to the Marxist tradition; (3) it provides only an aesthetic alternative to current problems and conceptions of reason. Although it will remain a matter of dispute, it can be argued that these objections simply bypass Adorno's original insight, namely that the dilemmas of injustice and nihilism have a common root in the abstractive achievements of autonomous reason. Traditional Marxism focuses on the question of injustice, while ignoring the problem of nihilism; conversely, existentialists such as Nietzsche and Heidegger aim to overcome nihilism while they remain insensitive to the claims of justice. If Adorno is correct in maintaining that these dilemmas are interconnected, then his philosophy has something to say to us. The fragile hope of his philosophizing lies in the belief that the claims of justice are best served through the defence of the claims of the rationality inherent in modernist works of art.

See also: ENLIGHTENMENT, CONTINENTAL

List of works

Adorno, T.W. (1933) *Kierkegaard. Konstruktion des Ästhetischen*, Tübingen: J.C.B. Mohr; trans. R. Hullot-Kentor, *Kierkegaard: Construction of the Aesthetic*, Minneapolis, MN: University of Minnesota Press, 1989. (This is Adorno's first major work, and it includes all the major themes – the critique of existentialism as abstract, the role of aesthetics, the thematics of sacrifice – that will come to dominate his thought. The introduction to the translation by Hullot-Kentor is helpful.)

Adorno, T.W. and Horkheimer, M. (1947) *Dialektik der Aufklärung*, Amsterdam: Querido; trans. J. Cumming, *Dialectic of Enlightenment*, London: Allen Lane and New York: Herder & Herder, 1972. (This is the founding document of first-generation Critical Theory in which the critique of instrumental reason comes to displace the critique of political economy. It includes Adorno's famous treatment of Odysseus as already enacting the Enlightenment sacrifice of the particular to the universal, and his analysis of the culture industry.)

Adorno, T.W. (1949) *Philosophie der neuen Musik*, Tübingen: J.C.B. Mohr; trans. A.G. Mitchell and W. Blomster, *Philosophy of Modern Music*, Sheed & Ward, 1973. (Adorno's classic defence of Arnold Schoenberg's twelve-tone system as the high point of musical modernism. Its conception of modern music was the crucial source for Thomas Mann's *Doctor Faustus*.)

—— (1951) *Minima Moralia. Reflexion aus dem Beschädigten Leben*, Frankfurt: Suhrkamp; trans. E.F.N. Jephcott, *Minima Moralia: Reflections from Damaged Life*, London: New Left Books, 1974. (One hundred and fifty-three dazzling aphorisms, in which Adorno reflects on the vanishing of concrete, individual experience in modern, bourgeois society. Its fluent mixture of philosophy and cultural criticism makes it the most accessible of his works.)

—— (1956) *Zur Metakritik der Erkenntnistheorie. Studien über Husserl und die phänomenologischen Antinomien*, Stuttgart: Kohlhammer; trans. W. Domingo, *Against Epistemology: A Metacritique, Studies in Husserl and the Phenomenological Antinomies*, Oxford: Blackwell, 1982. (A dense reading of Husserl's phenomenology, with the emphasis on the inevitable abstractness of the phenomenological method, and hence its loss of the very concreteness it seeks.)

—— (1957) 'Sociology and Empirical Research', in T.W. Adorno *et al.*, *Der Positivismusstreit in der deutschen Soziologie*, Neuwied and Berlin: Luchterhand, 1969; trans. G. Adey and D. Frisby, *The Positivist Dispute in German Sociology*, London: Heinemann, 1970. (Includes essays by Popper, Habermas, Dahrendorf, Harald Pilot and Hans Albert, among others. The translation also includes a review of the original by Popper, and a helpful introduction by David Frisby.)

—— (1963) *Drei Studien zu Hegel*, Frankfurt: Suhrkamp; trans. S.W. Nicholsen, *Hegel: Three Studies*, Cambridge, MA, and London: MIT Press, 1993. (These very essayistic explorations of Hegel elaborate the competing ideals of rationality in dialectical and deductive thinking.)

—— (1964) *Jargon der Eigentlichkeit. zur deutschen Ideologie*, Frankfurt: Suhrkamp; trans. K. Tarnowski and F. Will, *Jargon of Authenticity*, London: Routledge & Kegan Paul, 1973. (Adorno's fiercely critical account of Martin Heidegger's existentialism as abstract and ahistorical.)

—— (1966) *Negative Dialektik*, Frankfurt: Suhrkamp; trans. E.B. Ashton, *Negative Dialectics*, London: Routledge & Kegan Paul, 1973. (This work pursues an immanent critique of the idealism of Kant and Hegel as the vehicle for a critique of modern instrumental reason. It contains Adorno's most sustained arguments concerning the nature of human conceptuality, and his famous reflections on the meaning of philosophy 'after Auschwitz'.)

—— (1970) *Ästhetische Theorie*, Frankfurt: Suhrkamp; trans. R. Hullot-Kentor, *Aesthetic Theory*, London: Athlone Press, and Minneapolis, MN: University of Minnesota Press, 1997. (Arguably this is the premier work of twentieth-century philosophical aesthetics and the philosophy of art. Transforming the central concepts of modern aesthetics accordingly, Adorno contends that the works of high modernism model a suppressed conception of human rationality that challenges that of Enlightenment rationalism.)

—— (1992) 'The Curious Realist: On Siegfried Kracauer', in *Notes to Literature*, trans. S.W. Nicholson, New York: Columbia University Press. (Adorno's account of the thought and influence of his early tutor.)

See also: LOGICAL AND MATHEMATICAL TERMS, GLOSSARY OF

References and further reading

Bernstein, J.M. (1992) *The Fate of Art: Aesthetic Alienation from Kant to Derrida and Adorno*, Oxford: Polity Press and State College, PA: Penn State Press. (Chapters 4 and 5 detail the argument of §5.)
—— (ed.) (1994) *The Frankfurt School, vol. 2: Horkheimer and Adorno*, London: Routledge. (Contains twenty of the best journal articles on the whole range of Adorno's output, including influential pieces by Jürgen Habermas on *Dialectic of Enlightenment* and Albrecht Wellmer on *Aesthetic Theory*.)
—— (1997) *Adorno: Of Ethics and Disenchantment*, Cambridge: Cambridge University Press. (Expounds the analysis of concepts and rationality in §3, and relates it to the ethical vision animating Adorno's philosophy.)
Buck-Morss, S. (1977) *The Origin of Negative Dialectics: Theodor W. Adorno, Walter Benjamin and The Frankfurt Institute*, Hassocks, Sussex: Harvester Press. (An intellectual biography of Adorno that usefully focuses on the deep influence of his friend Walter Benjamin in the formation of several of the key concepts in Adorno's theory.)
Jarvis, S. (1986) *Adorno: A Critical Introduction*, Cambridge: Polity Press. (An illuminating study that tracks Adorno's Hegelianism and his use of the idea of determinate negation through the breadth of his work.)
Jay, M. (1984) *Adorno*, London: Fontana. (A clear introduction for the general reader, but without a sharp, philosophical focus.)
Rose, G. (1978) *The Melancholy Science: An Introduction to the Thought of Theodor W. Adorno*, London: Macmillan. (An advanced introduction, particularly strong on reification and the concept of dialectic.)
Sacks, M. (1990) 'Through a Glass Darkly: Vagueness in the Metaphysics of the Analytic Tradition', in D. Bell and N. Cooper (eds) *The Analytic Tradition: Meaning, Thought and Knowledge*, Oxford: Blackwell. (Elaborates the suggestion about language made in §3 in Wittgensteinian terms.)
Zuidervaart, L. (1991) *Adorno's Aesthetic Theory: The Redemption of Illusion*, Cambridge, MA, and London: MIT Press. (A sound study of Adorno's aesthetics, especially useful on the central terms of Adorno's argument in *Aesthetic Theory*. Zuidervaart is critical of Adorno's strong cognitivist approach to art.)

J.M. BERNSTEIN

ADVERBIAL THEORY

see MENTAL STATES, ADVERBIAL THEORY OF

ADVERBS

Adverbs are so named from their role in modifying verbs and other non-nominal expressions. For example, in 'John ran slowly', the adverb 'slowly' modifies 'ran' by characterizing the manner of John's running. The debate on the semantic contribution of adverbs centres on two approaches. On the first approach, adverbs are understood as predicate operators: for example, in 'John ran slowly', 'ran' would be taken to be a predicate and 'slowly' an operator affecting its meaning. Working this out in detail requires the resources of higher-order logic. On the second approach, adverbs are understood as predicates of 'objects' such as events and states, reference to which is revealed in logical form. For example, 'John ran slowly' would be construed along the lines of 'there was a running by John and it was slow', in which the adverb 'slowly' has become a predicate 'slow' applied to the event that was John's running.

Since adverbs are exclusively modifiers, they are classed among the syncategorematic words of terminist logic, the investigation of which carried the subject forward from Aristotle in the thirteenth century. (The contrasting 'categoremata' – grammatical subjects and predicates – are those words which have meaning independently.) They are of contemporary interest for philosophical logic and semantic theory, because particular accounts of them carry implications for the nature of combinatorial semantics and language understanding, and for ontology.

1 **Syntactic types and semantic combination**
2 **Ambiguities**
3 **Extensionality**

1 Syntactic types and semantic combination

There are several types of adverbial constructions, of

which we distinguish the following classes: (a) 'manner' adverbs, which intuitively function as simple modifiers of verbs; (b) 'thematic' adverbs, of which some and possibly all function as (at least) two-place predicates in their own right; (c) adverbs of quantification, which express generality applying to whole sentences; and (d) discourse particles, whose meaning evidently derives from their role in linking clauses or independent sentences. (These categories are not exhaustive.) 'Adverbs', especially manner 'adverbs', are not in fact confined to single words. The general category is therefore not that of adverbs, but of adverbial phrases or adverbials (for example, 'more quickly than Mary', 'very frequently').

Typical manner adverbials are as in (1) below, thematic adverbs as in (2) and adverbs of quantification as in (3):

(1) John walked slowly/quietly/more quickly than Mary.

(2) Mary apparently/reluctantly went to New York.

(3) Mary occasionally/always walks to work.

Discourse particles, considered briefly below, include 'but', 'anyway' and several others. We discuss these cases in turn.

The essential logical problem of manner adverbials is already apparent in the simplest examples. A verb combines with a manner adverb to form a complex verbal construction of the same type. Thus 'walk' and 'walk slowly' are both predicates, and the syntax of the combination may be depicted as follows:

$[_V[_V\text{walk}][_{Adv}\text{slowly}]]$

If (disregarding tense) we take 'walk' as a one-place predicate, then the semantics of this combination might be given by positing that 'slowly' is interpreted as a predicate operator; that is, as a function that maps one-place predicate interpretations onto other one-place predicate interpretations. Alternatively, it may be suggested that 'slowly' and the other manner adverbials are, logically speaking, predicates in their own right, specifically predicates of actions. The adjectives to which they are related do seem to play this role. Corresponding to (1), for instance, we have the adjectival predications

(4) John's walk was slow/quiet/quicker than Mary's.

If we take the further step of supposing that the verb 'walk' is in fact a two-place predicate, with a position for actions, then the combination 'walk slowly' can be interpreted as

$\text{walk}(x, e)\ \&\ \text{slow}(e),$

where e ranges over actions. Comparing this account with the first alternative,

$(\text{slowly}(\text{walk}))(x),$

we see a trade-off: where predicates are taken to have a simple structure, the adverbial must be understood as an operator; but where extra structure, in the form of a place for actions, is posited, the semantic combination is truth-functional and predicate operators are not required.

The alternatives just sketched each have their defenders in the literature on adverbials. Adverbs are construed as predicate operators in formal theories of linguistic structure, including those of Montague (1974) and Lewis (1975). The predicative alternative was first advanced at length by Davidson (1967), and is elaborated by Parsons (1990). Semantic and metaphysical issues arise for each account; we take up some of these below.

Thematic adverbs are intuitively distinguished from manner adverbs in as much as they yield constructions adverb + verb which cannot be treated simply as new verbs: apparently going to New York is not a way of going to New York; and reluctantly going to New York is not a manner of travel, but an instance of travel whose agent was reluctant to undertake it. For the examples in (2) the following paraphrases suggest themselves:

It was apparent that Mary went to New York.

Mary went to New York and she was reluctant to go to New York.

The discourse particles, traditionally and appropriately called adverbs, have come under relatively formal study only in recent years. The following examples are representative:

(5) He was poor *but* honest.

(6) *Anyway*, I'm going to New York.

They resist analysis in terms of their contribution to truth-conditions, but carry implications for the discourses in which they occur, with (5) involving some presumptive contrast with what might have been expected and (6), as an assertion, functioning to indicate a return to a superordinate topic of conversation. See Levinson (1983) for examples and discussion.

2 Ambiguities

Many adverbs are ambiguous between thematic-adverbial and manner-adverbial interpretation. In an example such as

(7) Mary quickly objected,

we may have either the interpretation 'Mary's objection was delivered in a quick manner' or the interpretation 'Mary's objection came a short time after the enunciation of the proposition to which she objected'. The second, thematic-adverbial interpretation shows up in the corresponding adjective 'quick' in a construction such as

Mary was quick to object.

These examples suggest that grammatical appearance belies logical structure, since the thematic adverbial in (7) functions, logically speaking, as the main predicate of that sentence. Austin (1956) observed that adverbial position often disambiguates, with post-verb adverbs favouring the manner-interpretation, and pre-verb adverbs the thematic, as in the pair

He trod on the snail clumsily.
Clumsily, he trod on the snail.

Adverbs of quantification pick up arguments including, but not restricted to, the temporal. Sentences such as (8) are ambiguous, depending upon whether the quantification is over occasions, or over the subject:

(8) Travel books are seldom worth reading.

Where the adverb quantifies over time, (8) means that the occasions are few when it is worth reading travel books. But there is another salient interpretation:

Few travel books are worth reading.

Where quantification over time would be ridiculous in view of the subject matter, construal of the adverb with the subject is particularly salient, for example:

Quadratic equations seldom have real solutions.

The above reflections have it that thematic adverbs and adverbs of quantification are not modifiers at all, except in a purely grammatical sense. Inversely, there have been suggestions that what appear in language as if they were arguments to a predicate actually function as adverbial modifiers. Perhaps the best known account of this type is Roderick Chisholm's discussion of a certain class of statements about appearances. Chisholm suggests that a man who 'sees spots before his eyes' should be thought of as 'sensing in a spotty manner' or as someone whom things 'appeared to spottily' (1957). This philosophical move is designed to rid the locution of any implication that in sensing spots before his eyes the man is sensing a mysterious object, an appearance, which is before him, his eyes or his mind (see MENTAL STATES, ADVERBIAL THEORY OF). In a similar vein, Goodman ([1968] 1976) construed the locution 'x represents an F', under the condition where there is no implication that such an F exists, as 'is an F-representation', effectively treating the predicate F adverbially.

The suggestions of Chisholm and Goodman, left as they are, become problematic if the project of giving a combinatorial semantics for language is taken seriously (see COMPOSITIONALITY). Suppose x is a picture and (9) is true, with no existential implications:

(9) x represents two unicorns galloping in a field.

If we write, with Goodman,

x is a two-unicorns-galloping-in-a-field representation,

then we have yet to provide a semantic structure to go along with the syntax. But there must be some such structure, since, for example, (9) obviously implies

x represents more than one unicorn in motion.

Similar issues arise for the predicate-operator theory of manner adverbs. For instance, that theory does not immediately deliver the obvious implication

(10) John walked slowly; therefore, John walked.

In Montague (1974) and much subsequent literature, this and similar implications are the consequences of semantic postulates in the sense of Carnap (1956). Even with such postulates, the relation between the adverbial constructions in (1) and their adjectival paraphrases (4) requires clarification. By contrast, the predicative theory proposed by Davidson is specifically designed to capture such implications and paraphrases. The premise of (10) is rendered as

(11) $(\exists e)(\text{walk}(\text{John}, e) \ \& \ \text{slow}(e))$,

that is, 'There was a walk by John and it was slow'; and the conclusion has the form

(12) $(\exists e)\text{walk}(\text{John}, e)$,

'There was a walk by John', a trivial implicate of the premise. For the paraphrase relation between (1) and (4), we have only to note that the complex noun 'John's walk' would be understood as a definite description of an action; that is, as '(the e) walk(John, e)'. 'John's walk was slow' then becomes

(13) slow((the e) walk(John, e)).

Given any standard treatment of the definite description, (13) will imply (11). However, the Davidsonian view is committed to supplying extra, hidden structure in all cases, and to taking events as individuals, a step that has often been considered metaphysically dubious.

Ensembles of adverbs show ambiguity of scope (see

SCOPE). For example, one interpretation of (14) has John being clever in that he made a stupid response:

(14) John cleverly responded stupidly.

Modal adverbs such as 'necessarily' and 'contingently', which modify whole sentences, allow singular terms and quantifiers within their superficial scope to be interpreted as outside it (a point known to the terminist logicians). Tracking the relative scopes of modalities is part of the contemporary application of modal logic. As in the cases of manner and thematic adverbs, there are both operator-theories and predicate-theories of these expressions; that is, the modalities may be developed as one-place modal operators, with the same syntax as negation; or as predicates of sentences in a first-order formulation of the logical syntax of natural language (see MODAL OPERATORS). Montague (1963) argued that the latter was unacceptable since the normal laws of modal logic could not all be maintained, on pain of paradox. The argument has subsequently been developed and discussed by others: see Koons (1992) for a survey and response.

3 Extensionality

Adverbial constructions of both the manner and thematic types, together with others, show a kind of superficial but persistent non-extensionality: superficial, because it may disappear under analysis; and persistent, because it may show up in places that the analysis itself uncovers. Predicate-operator theories can accept non-extensionality as the norm. Supposing, for example, that those who breathe are exactly those who perceive, it is absurd to infer that x perceives rapidly from the premise that x breathes rapidly. The predicate-operator theory, taking all operations to be in intension, has no such consequence. Or supposing that those who went to New York were exactly those who visited Times Square, it does not follow that if Mary reluctantly went to New York she also reluctantly visited Times Square.

For theories of Davidson's type, the constructions

x breathed rapidly

x perceived rapidly

are of the same logical type, but the events on which the adverb is predicated are different. The coextensiveness of 'breathe' and 'perceive' amounts to the coextensiveness of

(for some e) breathe(x, e)

(for some e) perceive(x, e).

Such coextensiveness no more implies the equivalence of 'x breathed rapidly' to 'x perceived rapidly' than the coextensiveness of 'x kicked something' and 'x saw something' would imply the equivalence of 'x saw something red' and 'x kicked something red'.

Non-extensionality is more troublesome when one considers events related as genus and species. For example, 'Mary flew slowly across Spain' does not imply 'Mary travelled slowly across Spain', even though any event of flying is an event of travelling. It follows that it is inadequate to represent 'Mary flew slowly across Spain' simply as

(for some e) (fly(Mary, e) & across Spain(e) & slow(e)).

Rather, we must add that the event e, which was a flying and therefore a travelling, was slow *for a flying*. These examples show at least that manner adverbials are relative to the sets of events against which a given event is evaluated. Other examples may show that it is not merely sets but also properties, not extensionally individuated, that form the background.

In any case, non-extensionality is evident in constructions with thematic adverbs. Davidson, following a suggestion by Hector-Neri Castañeda, considered examples such as that of

Oedipus intentionally married Jocasta,

from which it does not follow that Oedipus intentionally married his mother. In this case, the locus of non-extensionality, although due to the presence of the adverb 'intentionally', is the predicate 'intend', from which the adverb is derived. In this sense, it is independent of any peculiarities of adverbs, as in the Davidsonian paraphrase

Oedipus married Jocasta, and he intended to marry Jocasta.

Higginbotham (1989) explores a number of similar examples.

See also: LOGICAL AND MATHEMATICAL TERMS, GLOSSARY OF; SYNTAX §6

References and further reading

* Austin, J.L. (1956) 'A Plea for Excuses', *Proceedings of the Aristotelian Society*; repr. in *Philosophical Papers*, Oxford: Clarendon Press, 1961, 123–52. (A famous and highly readable paper in which Austin tries to clarify the nature of action from the way in which we use excuses to escape responsibility for the consequences of what we do.)
* Carnap, R. (1956) *Meaning and Necessity*, Chicago, IL: University of Chicago Press. (Develops the idea

that many apparently logical inferences are to be accounted for by semantic postulates that relate the meanings of the words in premises and conclusion; quite technical.)

* Chisholm, R. (1957) *Perceiving: A Philosophical Study*, Ithaca, NY: Cornell University Press, esp. ch. 8. (Proposes an adverbial analysis of perception statements to avoid commitment to such entities as 'sense-data'.)
* Davidson, D. (1967) 'The Logical Form of Action Sentences', in N. Rescher (ed.) *The Logic of Decision and Action*, Pittsburgh, PA: University of Pittsburgh Press; repr. in *Essays on Actions and Events*, Oxford: Clarendon Press, 1980, 105–48. (An analysis of adverbial modification as predication of events; readable and influential.)
* Goodman, N. (1968) *Languages of Art*, Indianapolis, IN: Hackett Publishing Company, 2nd edn, 1976. (Proposes an adverbial analysis of the likes of 'is a picture of an *F*' to prevent the existence of a picture of an *F* entailing the existence of a pictured *F*.)
* Higginbotham, J. (1989) 'Elucidations of Meaning', *Linguistics and Philosophy* 12: 465–517. (§2 defends a Davidsonian analysis in the context of a discussion of how lexical analysis interacts with permissible modes of syntactic composition; quite technical.)
* Koons, R.C. (1992) *Paradoxes of Belief and Strategic Rationality*, Cambridge: Cambridge University Press. (Mainly concerns the role of common knowledge or mutual belief in generating liar-like paradoxes about rational action; very technical.)
  Kretzmann, N. (1968) *William of Sherwood's Treatise on Syncategorematic Words*, Minneapolis, MN: University of Minnesota Press. (Elucidates the categorematic/syncategorematic distinction mentioned in the introduction to this entry.)
* Levinson, S.C. (1983) *Pragmatics*, Cambridge: Cambridge University Press. (Includes discussion of words such as 'but' and 'anyway' which are traditionally regarded as adverbs but whose contribution to meaning is primarily at the level of pragmatics.)
* Lewis, D.K. (1975) 'Adverbs of Quantification', in E. Keenan (ed.) *Formal Semantics of Natural Language*, Cambridge: Cambridge University Press, 3–15. (Semantics for adverbs construed as predicate operators.)
* Montague, R. (1963) 'Syntactical Treatment of Modality, with Corollaries on Reflexion Principles and Finite Axiomatizability', *Acta Philosophica Fennica* 16; repr. in *Formal Philosophy*, ed. R. Thomason, New Haven, CT: Yale University Press, 1974, 286–302. (Shows that straightforward analysis of modal adverbs ('necessarily', 'possibly') as predicates of sentences ('is necessarily true', 'is possibly true') leads to the generation of a paradox similar to Tarski's in his proof of the 'undefinability of truth'; very technical.)
* —— (1974) *Formal Philosophy*, ed. R. Thomason, New Haven, CT: Yale University Press. (Montague's collected papers in natural language semantics; extremely technical. For adverbs, see especially 'English as a Formal Language'.)
* Parsons, T. (1990) *Events in the Semantics of English*, Cambridge, MA: MIT Press. (Extended development and discussion of Davidson's analysis of adverbs; clear and, for the most part, nontechnical; good bibliography.)

JAMES HIGGINBOTHAM

AEGIDIUS ROMANUS *see* GILES OF ROME

AENESIDEMUS (1st century BC)

Aenesidemus was a Greek philosopher of the first century BC who revived Pyrrhonian Scepticism, formulating the basic Ten Modes of Scepticism, or tropoi, *and demonstrating that concepts such as cause, explanation, goodness and the goal of life engendered endemic and undecidable dispute; faced with this the Sceptic suspends judgment – and tranquillity follows.*

Aenesidemus was probably active around the middle of the first century BC. He considered that Academic scepticism under PHILO OF LARISSA had so far abandoned its original, uncompromising attitude to knowledge that he described the dispute between Philo and ANTIOCHUS as 'Stoics fighting with Stoics' (fr. 71C9). In response, he turned to the Scepticism of PYRRHO for sustenance, effectively re-founding Pyrrhonism and determining the broad outlines it was to follow (see PYRRHONISM). The fundamental arguments of the Ten Modes of Scepticism are attributed to him. He wrote an eight volume *Pyrrhonian Discourses*, a summary of which survives in the ninth-century patriarch Photius' library catalogue (frs 71C, 72L), and is said to have composed an *On Inquiry*, an *Against Wisdom* and a *First Introduction*.

The first book of *Pyrrhonian Discourses* argued that the Academics were in fact dogmatists, committed to beliefs both positive ('some things are plausible') and negative ('nothing is apprehensible'). Pyrrhonists, by contrast, 'determine absolutely nothing, not even this claim that nothing is determined' (fr. 71C8). They will not assert dogmatically (that is, with strong commitment to the truth) that something either is or is not the case, saying only that it no more is than is not, or that it sometimes is and sometimes is not, or that it is for one person and not for another (fr. 71C6–7) (see PYRRHONISM §§1, 3). This, according to Aenesidemus, amounts simply to following the appearances, reacting to the way things seem to be; about reality the Pyrrhonist suspends judgment, the result of such suspension being tranquillity (Diogenes Laertius, IX 106–7).

The remainder of *The Pyrrhonian Discourses* cast doubt on the concepts of dogmatist physics (cause, principle, generation, motion, and so on) (see PYRRHONISM §5) and the veridicality of perception, as well as dealing sceptically with signs, the gods, scientific explanation and various topics in ethics, the aim being to emphasize the dubiousness of all dogmatic positions on these topics and the extent of their differences, with a view to promoting suspension of judgment (and hence tranquillity). Some of these arguments are preserved elsewhere: signs should be evident as signs (that is in what they signify) to everybody if they are to function as signs, but they are not (Sextus Empiricus, *Against the Professors* VIII 215); the concept of cause is incoherent (IX 219–26); scientific 'explanations' are underdetermined (Sextus Empiricus, *Outlines of Pyrrhonism* I 180–5). Aenesidemus' Scepticism appears both consistent and complete.

Elsewhere, however, Sextus reports that 'Aenesidemus… says that the Sceptic way is a road leading to Heraclitean philosophy, since saying that opposites appear to hold of the same thing precedes saying that they actually do hold of the same thing' (*Outlines of Pyrrhonism* I 210) (see HERACLITUS §3). Thus, apparently, indeterminacy in appearances is grounds for belief in indeterminacy in the objects, which is unsceptical, involving a commitment to the way things actually are. Perhaps Aenesidemus simply offered such arguments dialectically, to emphasize dogmatic disagreement; perhaps he thought (possibly following Pyrrho – see PYRRHONISM §1, and compare PYRRHO §3) that such statements were coherently Sceptical; or perhaps he simply changed his mind. The evidence is insufficient – and we can only suspend judgment on the issue.

References and further reading

* Aenesidemus (1st century BC) *Fragments*, in A.A. Long and D.N. Sedley, *The Hellenistic Philosophers*, vol. 1, Cambridge: Cambridge University Press, 1987. (Invaluable collection of fragments in translation with philosophical commentary; contains Photius' report of Aenesidemus at §§71–2.)
* Diogenes Laertius (*c*.early 3rd century AD) *Lives of the Philosophers*, trans. R.D. Hicks, *Diogenes Laertius Lives of Eminent Philosophers*, Loeb Classical Library, Cambridge, MA: Harvard University Press and London: Heinemann, 1925, 2 vols. (Greek text with facing translation; IX 61–116 is devoted to Pyrrhonism.)
  Hankinson, R.J. (1995) *The Sceptics*, London: Routledge. (Chapter VII deals with Aenesidemean Scepticism.)
* Sextus Empiricus (*c.* AD 200) *Outlines of Pyrrhonism*, trans. J. Annas and J. Barnes, *Outlines of Scepticism*, Cambridge: Cambridge University Press, 1994. (Fine translation with introduction and notes.)
—— (*c.* AD 200) *Against the Professors*, trans. R.G. Bury, *Against the Logicians, Against the Physicists, Against the Ethicists* and *Against the Professors*, Loeb Classical Library, Cambridge, MA: Harvard University Press and London: Heinemann, 3 vols, 1935, 1936, 1949. (Parallel Greek text with English translation and minimal notes.)
  Woodruff, P. (1988) 'Aporetic Pyrrhonism', *Oxford Studies in Ancient Philosophy* 6: 139–68. (Stimulating if unorthodox treatment of Aenesidemus' Pyrrhonism.)

R.J. HANKINSON

AESTHETIC ATTITUDE

It is undeniable that there are aesthetic and non-aesthetic attitudes. But is there such a thing as the *aesthetic attitude? What is meant by the aesthetic attitude is the particular way in which we regard something when and only when we take an aesthetic interest in it. This assumes that on all occasions of aesthetic interest the object attended to is regarded in an identical fashion, unique to such occasions; and this assumption is problematic. If an attitude's identity is determined by the features it is directed towards; if an aesthetic interest in an object is (by definition) an interest in its aesthetic qualities; and if the notion of aesthetic qualities can be explained in a uniform manner, then there is a unitary aesthetic attitude, namely an interest in an item's aesthetic qualities. But this conception of the aesthetic attitude would be unsuitable for achieving the main aim of those who have posited the aesthetic attitude. This aim is to provide a definition of the aesthetic, but the aesthetic attitude, understood as any attitude focused upon an object's aesthetic qualities, presupposes the idea of the aesthetic, and cannot be used to analyse it. So the question is whether there is a characterization of the aesthetic attitude that describes its nature without explicitly or implicitly relying on the concept of the aesthetic. There is no good reason to suppose so. Accordingly, there is no such thing as the aesthetic attitude, if this is an attitude that is both necessary and sufficient for aesthetic interest and that can be characterized independently of the aesthetic.*

1 **The idea of the aesthetic attitude**
2 **Aesthetic and non-aesthetic attitudes**
3 **Characterizing the aesthetic attitude**
4 **Transitive and intransitive particularity**
5 **Myth or reality?**

1 The idea of the aesthetic attitude

What is meant by the aesthetic attitude? Although it has often been supposed that there is such a thing, its existence has also been denied. Those who believe in the aesthetic attitude embrace one of two conceptions: either a certain conception of the essence of *aesthetic* appreciation or interest, or a certain conception of the essence of *artistic* appreciation or interest, that is, appreciation of or interest in something *as* a work of art. Each maintains that there is a particular attitude we adopt towards an item when and only when our interest in the item is of a certain kind, and each calls this attitude 'the aesthetic attitude'; but whereas the first alternative specifies this interest as appreciation of the item from the aesthetic point of view, the second identifies it as appreciation of the item as a work of art. The first is usually understood as being the wider conception, including the second as a special case. For it is often believed that (1) aesthetic interest can be directed towards either nature or art, and (2) to be interested in a work of art *as* a work of art is to be interested in it aesthetically. But the first conception is not always thought of as wider than the second. Some thinkers deny (2), on the ground that interest in a work of art as a work of art requires more than, or something different from, an aesthetic interest in the item. And some thinkers maintain that the concept of regarding something as a work of art is basic, and that to regard nature aesthetically *is* to regard it as, or as if it were, a work of art. Without prejudging any of the issues, it will simplify exposition to focus on the first conception.

2 Aesthetic and non-aesthetic attitudes

One source of the idea that there is such a thing as the aesthetic attitude is undoubtedly the thought that any item that we can treat or regard aesthetically we can also treat or regard non-aesthetically. It is indeed true that we can adopt towards any item – even something that is a work of art – an attitude that is not concerned with its aesthetic appeal, for there certainly are non-aesthetic or non-artistic attitudes and no item necessarily precludes having an attitude of one of these kinds directed towards it. You can look at a hibiscus, not to delight in the beauty of its form and colours, but merely to see whether it needs water; and even if you are bored by Bach's The Art of Fugue you might listen to it in order to fall asleep. Now from the fact that for any item it is possible to adopt an attitude towards it that is not concerned with its aesthetic or artistic appeal, it is easy to jump to the conclusion that there is an attitude we adopt towards any item when and only when we take an aesthetic interest in it. This would be *the* aesthetic attitude. However, the conclusion makes a much stronger claim than the premise from which it is derived. The premise claims only that whatever you may be taking an interest in, your interest might not be in its aesthetic or artistic appeal. This does not imply the double-barrelled thesis that (1) when your interest in any item is aesthetic or artistic, your attitude towards the item must always be of the same unitary kind, and (2) whenever your attitude towards anything is of this kind, you are taking an aesthetic or artistic interest in the item. So the conclusion follows from the premise only if the premise is supplemented.

The strongest basis for the conclusion would be, first, an exhaustive specification of different kinds of attitude and, second, a demonstration that one of these attitudes is such that (a) if any other attitude is adopted towards an item, but this attitude is not, then the item is not being regarded aesthetically (and so the attitude is necessary for aesthetic appreciation), and (b) if an item is the object of this attitude, then it is being treated aesthetically, no matter what other kinds of attitude may also be directed towards it (and so the attitude is sufficient for aesthetic appreciation). The provision of such a basis is clearly the intention of those who offer, first, a positive characterization of a certain attitude, all other attitudes being defined by contrast with this attitude (thus exhausting the possibilities), and, second, a number of examples for which, supposedly, the adoption of this attitude is both necessary and sufficient for the item to be the object of aesthetic appreciation.

If there is such a thing as the aesthetic attitude, can it be given a positive characterization that specifies its nature? Nearly all adherents of the aesthetic attitude have believed that it is susceptible of a helpful analysis, but it has also been argued that it is not.

The principal interest of the concept of the

aesthetic attitude derives from a concern to define or circumscribe the notion of the aesthetic or (more usually) of art. One leading idea has been that of defining the notion of a work of art in terms of the aesthetic attitude, perhaps in such a fashion as this: a work of art is an artefact solely, mainly or at least partly designed to give satisfaction to the aesthetic attitude. But a definition of art in terms of the aesthetic attitude will be illuminating only if an understanding of the concept of the aesthetic attitude does not presuppose an understanding of the aesthetic. If the aesthetic attitude is identified merely as the attitude of concern for or interest in an item's aesthetic properties or aesthetic value, and if a work's artistic properties or artistic value are constituted (partly or wholly) by its aesthetic properties or value, then the suggested definition will be unhelpfully circular; and an analogous conclusion will follow if the aesthetic attitude is defined as the attitude necessary for or most conducive to the derivation of the aesthetic pleasure an object merits, or that is necessary to ensure that an aesthetic judgment about an object is as well-founded as it can be. So the question arises of whether it is possible to define the aesthetic attitude independently of any idea of the aesthetic.

I shall consider, first, the project of defining the aesthetic attitude independently of any prior concept of the aesthetic; second, the idea that although there is such a thing as the aesthetic attitude, it resists definition; and third, the claim that the aesthetic attitude is a myth.

3 Characterizing the aesthetic attitude

A recognition of truth, beauty and goodness as the principal concerns of the human mind has given rise to the idea that the aesthetic attitude must be distinguished from, on the one hand, cognitive attitudes, and on the other, practical ones. Whereas a cognitive attitude towards an object is concerned with the acquisition of knowledge from it and a practical attitude with its utility, the aesthetic attitude has a different focus. Or so it is claimed. How might this focus be defined?

In fact, only a small number of locutions have been used to characterize the aesthetic attitude. Perhaps the most common has been in terms of the notion of disinterestedness. That your attitude towards an object is disinterested does not mean that you are not interested in it. What does it mean? If 'disinterested' means no more than 'unbiased', this would not serve by itself to mark off the aesthetic attitude from paradigms of cognitive or practical attitudes, which can also be unbiased. If it means that your attitude is not aesthetic if you are interested in determining what the object is, what to do with it or its suitability for some purpose, it is wide of the mark; for, leaving other considerations aside, it rules as unaesthetic those cases in which you consider whether an object is suitable for an *aesthetic* end, such as when you consider whether a vase is the right shape, size and colour for the collection of flowers you propose to arrange.

It is sometimes suggested that something is an object of aesthetic appreciation only if it is being attended to for its own sake. This idea can be understood in stronger and weaker forms. On the one hand, 'for its own sake' might mean 'for no further reason but just for the sake of it'. But this would yield a mistaken account of aesthetic appreciation, for you can have a variety of reasons for attending to something that you are appreciating aesthetically. On the other hand, 'for its own sake' might mean 'not solely as a means to an end', thus allowing for the possibility that an object is being attended to for its own sake, or as an end in itself, even when it is being attended to for ulterior purposes. If this requires a spectator's interest in the object not to be solely concerned with some *non-aesthetic* end, it would render an account of the essence of the aesthetic in terms of the aesthetic attitude viciously circular. But if the requirement is only that the interest should not be solely as a means to *some* end, then even if this were to be a necessary condition it would not be a sufficient one for the interest to be aesthetic. Your interest in a mathematical proof or a game of soccer is not aesthetic simply because you are uninterested in any use to which these might be put.

Another suggestion is that your attitude towards an object is aesthetic if and only if, in interacting with it, you consider just the object itself – its elements and the relations amongst its elements – not any relations in which it stands to anything other than itself. Accordingly, the aesthetic attitude is thought of as being an attitude of contemplative detachment from all considerations of utility, which focuses only on what the object is 'in itself' (its shapes and colours, for example). But, apart from any other considerations, this overlooks the fact that works of art can be designed to serve non-artistic functions and that aesthetic admiration can encompass the appearance that an object presents of its suitability for discharging these functions. This is especially pertinent to works of architecture, for which harmony of form with function is an aesthetic merit.

So none of these suggestions, either in itself or combined with another, provides a definition of an attitude that satisfies the conditions required by the concept of the aesthetic attitude.

4 Transitive and intransitive particularity

Wittgenstein drew a distinction between a 'transitive' and an 'intransitive' use of the word 'particular'. You use the word in the transitive fashion if you use it as a prelude to a description, comparison or specification of the nature of the phenomenon you are referring to – a description that you intend to produce or, perhaps, that you wish to have produced by the person you are addressing. When you use the word intransitively it is not thereby your intention to follow it up with a specification of anything. Rather, you are using it, Wittgenstein says, as what might be called an 'emphasis': either it has some such force as 'strong', 'striking' or 'impressive', or it merely gives expression to the fact that your attention is taken up with the phenomenon you are indicating.

Richard Wollheim (1980) has argued that although there is such a thing as the aesthetic attitude, which he equates with the attitude of treating or regarding something as a work of art, philosophers of art who refer to the aesthetic attitude as a particular attitude are systematically ambiguous about whether they intend a 'particular attitude' in the transitive or the intransitive sense. And he claims that despite the many attempts to give a positive characterization of the aesthetic attitude, it can be conceived of as a particular attitude only in the intransitive sense. It might seem that this is tantamount to denying the existence of the aesthetic attitude or to asserting that there is nothing distinctive of it. But, Wollheim maintains, the point is rather that 'there need not be any comprehensive way of referring to what is distinctive of it other than as the aesthetic attitude'.

But Wollheim's position receives no support from Wittgenstein's distinction. For consider saying 'Jack has a particular way of asking a favour.' If you are using the word 'particular' transitively, then you will continue in some such fashion as 'namely, he drops his eyes and then looks to see how his request has been received.' If you are using the word in the intransitive sense, you will not continue in this fashion, for you are merely expressing the fixity of your attention on the way John asks a favour. However, it does not follow from the fact that your use is intransitive that there is no particular way in the transitive sense in which Jack asks a favour. Clearly, there is: Jack's way of asking a favour can be characterized in other terms. The same holds for the remark that the aesthetic attitude is a particular attitude. The fact that the word 'particular' is here being used intransitively does not preclude a positive characterization of the nature of the attitude. Hence no reason has been given for believing that what is distinctive of the aesthetic attitude cannot be captured other than by referring to it as the aesthetic attitude.

5 Myth or reality?

Is the aesthetic attitude a myth? That depends, first, on the difference between a single attitude and a motley collection of attitudes, and, second, on what work the aesthetic attitude is supposed to do.

An attitude towards an object is a disposition to think and feel about and to behave towards it in characteristic ways. You have a hostile attitude towards someone if you are liable to think hostile thoughts about them, to experience hostility when meeting them, to avoid their company, and, perhaps, to behave in ways that are harmful to them. Now your attitude towards an object can be such that you are disposed to thoughts about its aesthetic character, to feelings aroused by its aesthetic qualities, and to aesthetically relevant behaviour. But there is no hope of circumscribing aesthetically relevant behaviour without using the concept of the aesthetic, as can be easily seen from the fact that it might on occasion consist in nothing more than walking away from an aesthetically uninteresting picture. And neither aesthetic thoughts nor aesthetic feelings have a nature that can be specified independently of the idea of the aesthetic. Accordingly, even if the diversity of aesthetic thoughts, feelings and behaviour does not imply that aesthetic attitudes are irreducibly diverse, their unity is achieved only by bringing them under the concept of the aesthetic. So the idea of the aesthetic attitude explicated in this way – as an attitude that must be thought of as a disposition to aesthetic thoughts, feelings and behaviour – is not suited to play the foundational role it is often assigned. It does not enable a penetrating analysis of the aesthetic, but must be defined in terms of it.

The prospects are bleak indeed for specifying in non-aesthetic terms an attitude that is both necessary and sufficient for aesthetic appreciation, as my critique of the standard definitions indicates; and the idea that there is an attitude that is distinctive of aesthetic interest but that is resistant to analysis is baseless. Hence, the aesthetic attitude is either a myth or of little interest.

See also: AESTHETIC CONCEPTS

References and further reading

Bullough, E. (1912) '"Psychical Distance" as a Factor in Art and an Aesthetic Principle', *British*

Journal of Psychology 5: 87–118, reprinted in E.M. Wilkinson (ed.) *Aesthetics: Lectures and Essays*, London: Bowes & Bowes, 1957. (A celebrated account of the aesthetic attitude in terms of contemplation free from all practical concerns. Criticized by Dickie.)

Dickie, G. (1964) 'The Myth of the Aesthetic Attitude', *American Philosophical Quarterly* 1 (1): 54–65. (Criticizes a number of attempts to characterize the aesthetic attitude and concludes that it is a myth.)

Stolnitz, J. (1961) 'On the Origins of "Aesthetic Disinterestedness"', *Journal of Aesthetics and Art Criticism* 20: 131–43. (An interesting account of how the idea of disinterestedness, mentioned in §3, was introduced into aesthetic theory.)

* Wittgenstein, L. (1960) *The Blue and Brown Books*, Oxford: Blackwell. (On page 158, the source of the distinction referred to in §4 between transitive and intransitive uses of 'particular'.)

* Wollheim, R. (1980) *Art and Its Objects*, 2nd edn, Cambridge: Cambridge University Press, esp. §§40–2. (Presents the argument of §4 for the view that the aesthetic attitude is a particular attitude only in the intransitive sense.)

MALCOLM BUDD

AESTHETIC CONCEPTS

Aesthetic concepts are the concepts associated with the terms that pick out aesthetic properties referred to in descriptions and evaluations of experiences involving artistic and aesthetic objects and events. The questions (epistemological, psychological, logical and metaphysical) that have been raised about these properties are analogous to those raised about the concepts.

In the eighteenth century, philosophers such as Edmund Burke and David Hume attempted to explain aesthetic concepts such as beauty empirically, by connecting them with physical and psychological responses that typify individuals' experiences of different kinds of objects and events. Thus they sought a basis for an objectivity of personal reactions. Immanuel Kant insisted that aesthetic concepts are essentially subjective (rooted in personal feelings of pleasure and pain), but argued that they have a kind of objectivity on the grounds that, at the purely aesthetic level, feelings of pleasure and pain are universal responses.

In the twentieth century, philosophers have sometimes returned to a Humean analysis of aesthetic concepts via the human faculty of taste, and have extended this psychological account to try to establish an epistemological or logical uniqueness for aesthetic concepts. Many have argued that although there are no aesthetic laws (for example, 'All roses are beautiful,' or 'If a symphony has four movements and is constructed according to rules of Baroque harmony, it will be pleasing') aesthetic concepts none the less play a meaningful role in discussion and disputation. Others have argued that aesthetic concepts are not essentially distinguishable from other types of concepts.

Recently theorists have been interested in ways that aesthetic concepts are context-dependent – constructed out of social mores and practices, for example. Their theories often deny that aesthetic concepts can be universal. For example, not only is there no guarantee that the term 'harmony' will have the same meaning in different cultures: it may not be used at all.

1 Eighteenth-century views
2 Frank Sibley and his critics
3 Recent attempts to establish aesthetic realism
4 Aesthetic concepts as contextual constructs

1 Eighteenth-century views

Although questions about the origin and nature of our ideas of the beautiful, the proportionate, the harmonious, etc. can be found in ancient and medieval writings, the seat of aesthetic concepts developed in the eighteenth century was increasingly located primarily in human experience rather than in the objects of those experiences *per se*. Edmund Burke, for example, set out to explain where our ideas (and hence concepts) of the sublime and beautiful come from, and answered that they come not from objects *per se* but from objects as they are experienced (see SUBLIME, THE §2). Thus one and the same object can be described as 'fearful' or 'sublime' depending upon the circumstances of the viewer. A building in flames is frightful if one is in the building and fears for one's life; it is sublime if one is standing across the street from it and has no fear that oneself or one's loved ones are endangered, and one can thus take pleasure (though Burke called it 'relative pleasure') in the shapes, colours and sounds, etc. (see BURKE, E.).

David Hume asserted that the existence of what are now generally referred to as aesthetic concepts depends upon human beings having the requisite psychophysical machinery for experiencing the world in certain ways. The locus of aesthetic experiences and ideas, he argued, is taste (see ARTISTIC TASTE §1). This faculty not only accounts for the fact that one can claim that, say, a flower is beautiful (just as the faculty of sight accounts for the fact that one can claim that the flower is red), it also provides an empirical basis for what he calls the 'standard of taste'. Just as people with adequate colour vision and proper training will correctly apply colour concepts, that is, apply them in such a way that others with adequate vision and training will agree, so people whose taste is sufficiently sensitive and who have been correctly trained will competently apply aesthetic concepts, and will agree with other similarly competent judges.

Hume's approach exemplifies an urge to reconcile two counterintuitive forces that continue to appeal to both theorists and non-theorists in aesthetics. On the one hand there is the belief that aesthetic concepts are somehow subjective – that, as the saying goes, beauty is in the eye of the beholder. There is no guarantee that my concept of beauty will match yours, indeed there is ample evidence that one should not even hope for such agreement. Some like it cold, some like it hot, and any basis for a standard of application for evaluative concepts like 'aesthetically good' or 'aesthetically bad' seems ineluctably illusive. On the other hand, there does at least sometimes seem to be an objective basis for aesthetic concepts. We do seem to mean the same things when we talk about a beautiful sunset or suspenseful movie. If someone denied the grandeur of the Rocky Mountains, we would think less of the person, and not less of the mountains (see HUME, D.).

The drive to account for both subjectivity and objectivity is at the heart of perhaps the most systematic and influential treatment of the nature of aesthetic concepts in the history of western philosophy, namely that of Immanuel Kant. In his *The Critique of Judgment*, he provides a many-faceted definition of 'the beautiful' (as an exemplar of aesthetic concepts) that incorporates metaphysical, epistemological, psychological and logical analyses and which he believes reconciles the attractions of both subjectivity and objectivity (see BEAUTY §4). Kant, like Hume, agrees that aesthetic concepts are 'taste concepts', whose existence depends upon human experience. In particular, he believes that aesthetic concepts are grounded in pleasure and pain. Hence they are subjective, and any agreement between persons cannot be empirically based, as Hume had hoped. But, Kant argues, aesthetic concepts are pure in the sense that they are neither related to nor dependent upon cognitive or ethical concepts. Our feelings of pleasure or pain in the presence of an object have nothing to do with our scientific conception of the object (and are even independent of our belief that the object exists) nor with our belief that it is useful or morally good (see ART AND MORALITY §3). Since aesthetic concepts are not connected to anything special about me (what I as an individual believe about the nature of the object or its relation to my preferences or duties), I must believe that all human beings who similarly respond as human beings, and not as individuals with special histories, will react as I do – that they will similarly feel pleasure or pain in the presence of this object. Thus an aesthetic concept has a universal aspect. If I attribute beauty to a flower, I expect everyone else (to the extent that they respond aesthetically) to do so, too. Thus aesthetic concepts are subjectively located, but universally applicable, according to Kant.

2 Frank Sibley and his critics

In the twentieth century, the role of taste and the Kantian drive to distinguish aesthetic concepts from other kinds of concepts is exemplified in the writings of the influential British aesthetician, Frank Sibley. Taste, according to Sibley, is a special mental faculty that enables some people to have certain perceptions and to form concepts on the basis of those perceptions. This special psychological faculty explains, he further believes, a special logic that characterizes the use of aesthetic concepts in discussion and argument.

If we observe people describing an event or object, according to Sibley, we notice that there are some features that everyone with normal eyes, ears and intelligence perceives – shape or loudness, for example. But there are also features that are perceived only by people with a special sensitivity – balance or unity, for example. These latter people are the ones who have taste. If a vase is gracefully curved, either one sees the gracefulness or one does not.

Sibley believes that this explains why aesthetic concepts are not condition-governed. That is, no list of non-aesthetic features (those perceivable by everyone) is logically sufficient for deducing that an object or event has any particular aesthetic features (those perceivable only by people with taste). Told that a vase is pink, made of glass, and fifty centimetres high, one is unable to conclude that the vase must be gracefully curved. And this is true, Sibley argues, no matter how long a list of non-aesthetic properties is provided.

None the less, Sibley argues, aesthetic concepts are objective; that is, 'The vase is gracefully curved' is either true or false. In this respect, aesthetic concepts are like colour concepts. Only people with adequate colour vision can see pinkness, but nevertheless we believe that the sentence, 'The vase is pink,' is either true or false. This is because people with normal colour vision agree about it. With respect to aesthetic concepts, agreement also provides the foundation of objectivity. People of taste agree that the vase is gracefully curved, and this is all we need to support the claim that aesthetic judgments have truth values.

Sibley's view combines psychological, logical, epistemological and metaphysical components, and it has been criticized in all of these fields. It is often objected that 'taste' is a very unclear notion – certainly not adequate to support a unique logic of aesthetic concepts. Nor is it so easy to distinguish aesthetic from non-aesthetic properties (and hence the corresponding concepts). And many writers have argued that the analogy of aesthetic and colour concepts does not really support the sought-for objectivity of the former; there is nothing like the widespread agreement that can be found for non-aesthetic qualities (on the assumption that they can be distinguished from aesthetic qualities) in the aesthetic realm. Disagreement among recognized experts in discussions of works of art is notorious.

None the less, many theorists agree with Sibley that there is something special about aesthetic concepts and that there are no 'aesthetic laws', that is, that there is no way of defining an aesthetic concept in terms of non-aesthetic concepts. Isabel Hungerland (1968) has described a distinction that she believes marks non-aesthetic concepts from aesthetic concepts: a seeming/being distinction. One can say that a person looks (seems) healthy but is not healthy, or that a house looks pink but is not pink. But this difference is absent in aesthetic attributions, she believes. If a vase looks gracefully curved, it is gracefully curved; if a voice sounds sweet, it is sweet.

Peter Kivy has objected to this way of distinguishing aesthetic from non-aesthetic concepts (1968). 'Unified', he argues, is surely an aesthetic concept; but it fails Hungerland's seeming/being test. A symphony may seem unified but may not really be unified. Kivy is also sceptical that there are no aesthetic concepts that can be reduced to non-aesthetic concepts. A very full description of a piece of music in non-aesthetic terms may lead one to conclude that the piece is unified. Thus there does not seem to be, for Kivy and others, a definitive way to distinguish aesthetic from non-aesthetic concepts.

3 Recent attempts to establish aesthetic realism

The view that there are no aesthetic laws connecting aesthetic and non-aesthetic concepts remains prevalent. Mary Mothersill, for example, argues that there are no principles or laws of taste and that everyone admits this when pressed (1984). None the less, aesthetic judgments are genuine judgments, that is, they have truth values and play a role in inference. They are open to serious question and debate (unlike, say, judgments about whether raw oysters taste good). They can be confirmed or disconfirmed by pointing to features of an object or event that are believed to cause pleasure, not just in the individual making the judgment but in other individuals who similarly investigate the object or event. Discussions that include aesthetic concepts are undertaken with the same hope of eventual agreement among persons of normal intelligence and interest as are discussions about many non-aesthetic concepts. There may be no reason to expect, as Kant believed, that everyone ought to find the same things beautiful; none the less we do expect that when we point to features or objects or events that we find beautiful, at least like-minded individuals will concur, according to Mothersill.

Another way theorists have tried to establish aesthetic realism is by arguing that aesthetic concepts connect to objective features of the world via a relationship known as 'supervenience' (see SUPERVENIENCE). Even if aesthetic concepts may not be definable in terms of non-aesthetic concepts, if one can establish that the properties associated with these aesthetic concepts supervene on physical properties that exist in the world, then there is a foundation for the objectivity of aesthetic judgments. Philosophers have characterized supervenience in various ways; however, the important feature they all try to capture is the connection between a stable set of base properties and some property that seems to depend upon them, even though that dependence cannot be captured via a strict definition. It is possible to imagine two houses that share all base properties except that one house is yellow, the other not. 'Yellow' is not supervenient. But if both houses share all base properties then it is not possible for one to be beautiful, the other not beautiful. 'Beauty' is supervenient. As long as the base properties are stable and the meaning of 'beauty' remains the same, then it will be either true or false that anything with those base properties is beautiful. Thus a vase's graceful curves cannot be defined in terms of its angles, size, colour, material, etc., but its gracefulness does depend upon the particular physical properties that it possesses. If all the physical properties stay the same, so will all of its aesthetic properties, in this view. Thus aesthetic concepts are connected to the real world, and individual attributions of an aesthetic term can be explained or justified in terms of 'real world' properties.

But not everyone agrees that aesthetic concepts are illuminated via the notion of supervenience. For one thing, it is difficult to specify clearly what counts as a base property. Sibley, for example, thinks that colour is not an aesthetic property (for anyone with ordinary perceptive powers can see the colour of an object); others think that colour is obviously an aesthetic property. Furthermore, an essential assumption is that the meaning of 'beauty' be stable – and this is an assumption that has been seriously questioned. A building considered beautiful in one culture may not be considered beautiful elsewhere. Thus it appears that beauty is not supervenient, for it is possible for two houses to have all the same properties except that one is beautiful, the other not beautiful.

4 Aesthetic concepts as contextual constructs

If taste or some similar universal human propensity to have certain sorts of experiences in the presence of some objects or events is the foundation of aesthetic concepts, then one would expect that all people (at least all who share a certain degree of sensitivity) will form similar concepts. Beauty and ugliness, for example, should be concepts formed and sustained by persons across time and space. Just as colour concepts or concepts of heat and cold exist across cultures because human beings are physically and mentally constructed to experience variations in colour and temperature, so aesthetic concepts should exhibit cross-cultural similarity if we are physically and mentally constructed so as to experience variations, say, in proportion or rhythm.

Recently, however, a growing number of theorists have discussed ways in which aesthetic concepts may be socially constructed. The widely shared common-sense attitude that there is no fact of the matter with respect to aesthetic judgments (some people like opera, some rock music), and the relativism that often accompanies this attitude are more systematically articulated in aesthetic theories that ground aesthetic concepts in contextual features of the circumstances in which they arise.

Not only do people from different communities disagree about what is beautiful, moving or harmonious, communities do not universally share the same aesthetic concepts at all. In Japanese poetry, for example, *makoto* is a very important concern. No direct English translation of the word, however, is possible. At best one can give a rough gloss: sincere or genuine expression of an appropriate emotion. The word is most commonly used in discussions about haiku – a poetic form that also lacks a direct equivalent in English literature. We lack the word and hence the concept. R.G. Collingwood warned that we cannot describe African art in English without making it seem like English art and vice versa. Some ethnomusicologists observe that even as basic a concept as rhythm does not travel from Europe to Africa without significant alteration. One's concepts are determined by the language that one speaks – and this language is shaped and determined by interests and attitudes that are culturally specific.

If aesthetic concepts are culturally determined, then understanding any particular concept will demand fluency in the culture in which it is operative. This is exactly what several contemporary theorists urge. Many feminists theoreticians, for example, criticize aestheticians like Kant and Sibley for assuming that they could speak with a 'universal voice'. If Kant did not see a relation between moral and aesthetic concepts, it does not follow that they are separate in the experiences of all human beings. One's gender, class, religion, economic or political status do often affect the way one forms and applies aesthetic concepts, they insist. If a person does not see what Frank Sibley sees, Sibley is not necessarily a more sensitive person.

Aesthetic concepts are learned in contexts where roles of performer, creator, audience, critic, tourist, etc. are learned. These roles are culture-bound; indeed, some of them do not even exist in some communities. Some aesthetic responses may seem 'natural' (for example, all people seem to like watching sunsets), but many are the consequence of social prescription and proscription. Often sharing non-aesthetic values is a prerequisite of sharing aesthetic values, and hence of sharing aesthetic concepts.

See also: AFRICAN AESTHETICS; ART CRITICISM; FEMINIST AESTHETICS

References and further reading

Brand, P. and Korsmeyer, C. (eds) (1990) 'Feminism and Traditional Aesthetics', special issue of *Journal of Aesthetics and Art Criticism* 48: 4. (Examples of feminist approaches to understanding aesthetic concepts; advanced reading.)

* Burke, E. (1756) *A Philosophical Inquiry into the Ideas of the Sublime and the Beautiful*, Oxford: Blackwell, 1987. (Classic historical text.)

Cohen, T. (1973) 'Aesthetic/Nonaesthetic and the Concept of Taste', *Theoria* 39: 113–152. (A response to Sibley, for the advanced reader.)

Collingwood, R.G. (1938) *The Principles of Art*, Oxford: Clarendon Press. (Influential and readable work on the role of expression in explaining aesthetic concepts.)

Eaton, M.M. (1995) 'The Social Construction of Aesthetic Response', *British Journal of Aesthetics* 35 (2): 95–107. (Contextualist approach to aesthetic concepts, for the advanced reader.)

* Hume, D. (1757) *Of the Standard of Taste and Other Essays*, ed. J.W. Lenz, Indianapolis, IN: Bobbs-Merrill, 1965. (A classic and highly readable historical text.)

* Hungerland, I. (1968) 'Once Again, Aesthetic and Non-Aesthetic', *Journal of Aesthetics and Art*

Criticism 27: 285–95. (Written as a response to Sibley; contains advanced material.)
* Kant, I. (1790) *The Critique of Judgment*, trans. J.C. Meredith, Oxford: Clarendon Press, 1973. (A classic historical text.)
* Kivy, P. (1968) 'Aesthetic Aspects and Aesthetic Qualities', *Journal of Philosophy* 65 (4): 85–93. (One response to Sibley's view; an advanced text.)
  Levinson, J. (1990) 'Aesthetic Supervenience', in *Music, Art, and Metaphysics*, Ithaca, NY: Cornell University Press. (An advanced discussion of supervenience of aesthetic properties.)
* Mothersill, M. (1984) *Beauty Restored*, Oxford: Clarendon Press. (This advanced book presents a twentieth-century Kantian view.)
  Petit, P. (1983) 'The Possibility of Aesthetic Realism', in E. Schaper (ed.) *Pleasure, Preference and Value: Studies in Philosophical Aesthetics*, Cambridge: Cambridge University Press, esp. 17–38. (Good discussion of problems in aesthetic realism; an advanced text.)
* Sibley, F. (1959) 'Aesthetic Concepts', *Philosophical Review* 68: 421–50. (An influential and clearly written article shaping twentieth-century discussion of aesthetic concepts.)
  Stahl, G. (1971) 'Sibley's "Aesthetic Concepts": An Ontological Mistake', *Journal of Aesthetics and Art Criticism* 29: 385–90. (A response to Sibley's 1959 article; for the advanced reader.)

MARCIA EATON

AESTHETICS

Aesthetics owes its name to Alexander Baumgarten who derived it from the Greek *aisthanomai*, which means perception by means of the senses (see BAUMGARTEN, A.G.). As the subject is now understood, it consists of two parts: the philosophy of art, and the philosophy of the aesthetic experience and character of objects or phenomena that are not art. Non-art items include both artefacts that possess aspects susceptible of aesthetic appreciation, and phenomena that lack any traces of human design in virtue of being products of nature, not humanity. How are the two sides of the subject related: is one part of aesthetics more fundamental than the other? There are two obvious possibilities. The first is that the philosophy of art is basic, since the aesthetic appreciation of anything that is not art is the appreciation of it as if it were art. The second is that there is a unitary notion of the aesthetic that applies to both art and non-art; this notion defines the idea of aesthetic appreciation as disinterested delight in the immediately perceptible properties of an object for their own sake; and artistic appreciation is just aesthetic appreciation of works of art. But neither of these possibilities is plausible.

The first represents the aesthetic appreciation of nature as essentially informed by ideas intrinsic to the appreciation of art, such as style, reference and the expression of psychological states. But in order for that curious feeling, the experience of the sublime – invoked, perhaps, by the immensity of the universe as disclosed by the magnitude of stars visible in the night sky (see SUBLIME, THE) – to be aesthetic, or for you to delight in the beauty of a flower, it is unnecessary for you to imagine these natural objects as being works of art. In fact, your appreciation of them is determined by their lack of features specific to works of art and perhaps also by their possession of features available only to aspects of nature (see NATURE, AESTHETIC APPRECIATION OF).

The second fails to do justice to the significance for artistic appreciation of various features of works of art that are not immediately perceptible, such as a work's provenance (see ARTISTIC FORGERY) and its position in the artist's oeuvre. A more accurate view represents the two parts of the subject as being related to each other in a looser fashion than either of these positions recognizes, each part exhibiting variety in itself, the two being united by a number of common issues or counterpart problems, but nevertheless manifesting considerable differences in virtue of the topics that are specific to them. In fact, although some issues are common to the two parts, many are specific to the philosophy of art and a few specific to the aesthetics of non-art objects.

Both works of art and other objects can possess specifically aesthetic properties, such as beauty and gracefulness. If they do possess properties of this sort, they will also possess properties that are not specifically aesthetic, such as size and shape. And they will be susceptible of aesthetic and non-aesthetic appreciation, and subject to aesthetic and non-aesthetic judgments. What distinguishes an item's aesthetic from its non-aesthetic properties and what faculties are essential to detecting aesthetic properties (see AESTHETIC CONCEPTS)? What is the nature of aesthetic appreciation? It has often been thought that there is a particular attitude that is distinctive of aesthetic appreciation: you must adopt this attitude in order for the item's aesthetic properties to be manifest to you, and if you are in this attitude you are in a state of aesthetic contemplation (see AESTHETIC ATTITUDE). This suppositious attitude has often been thought of as one of disinterested contemplation focused on an item's intrinsic, non-relational, immediately perceptible properties. But perhaps this view of aesthetic interest as disinterested attention is the product of masculine bias, involving the assumption of a position of power over the observed object, a reflection of masculine privilege, an expression of the 'male gaze' (see FEMINIST AESTHETICS §3). Another idea is that awareness of an object's aesthetic properties is the product of a particular species of perception, an idea which stands in opposition to the claim that this awareness is nothing but the projection of the observer's response onto the object (see ARTISTIC TASTE).

An object's beauty would appear to be a relational, mind-dependent property – a property it possesses in virtue of its capacity to affect observers in a certain manner. But which observers and what manner? And can attributions of beauty, which often aspire to universal interpersonal validity, ever attain that status (see BEAUTY)? The great German philosopher Immanuel Kant presented a conception of an aesthetic judgment as a judgment that must be founded on a feeling of pleasure or displeasure; he insisted that a pure aesthetic judgment about an object is one that is unaffected by any concepts under which the object might be seen; and he tried to show that the implicit claim of such a judgment to be valid for everyone is justified. But how acceptable is his conception of an aesthetic judgment and how successful is his attempted justification of the claims of pure aesthetic judgments (see KANT, I. §12)?

1 Aesthetics of art

Those questions that are specific to the philosophy of art are of three kinds: ones that arise only within a particular art form or set of related arts (perhaps arts addressed to the same sense), ones that arise across a number of arts of heterogeneous natures, and ones that are entirely general, necessarily applying to anything falling under the mantle of art.

Here are some of the most salient facts about art. Not everything is art. Artists create works of art, which reflect the skills, knowledge and personalities of their makers, and succeed or fail in realizing their aims. Works of art can be interpreted in different ways, understood, misunderstood or baffle the mind, subjected to analysis, and praised or criticized. Although there are many kinds of value that works of art may possess, their distinctive value is their value as art. The character of a work of art endows it with a greater or lesser degree of this distinctive value.

Accordingly, the most fundamental general question about art would seem to be: what is art? Is it possible to distinguish art from non-art by means of an account that is definitive of the nature of art, or are the arts too loosely related to one another for them to possess an essence that can be captured in a definition (see ART, DEFINITION OF)? Whatever the answer to this question may be, another entirely general issue follows hard on its heels. It concerns the ontology of art, the kind of thing a work of art is. Do some works of art fall into one ontological category (particulars) and some into another (types) or do they all fall within the same category (see ART WORKS, ONTOLOGY OF)? And a number of other important general questions quickly arise. What is a work's artistic value and which aspects of a work are relevant to or determine this value? Is the value of a work of art, considered as art, an intrinsic or an extrinsic feature of it? Is it determined solely by the work's form or by certain aspects of its content – its truth or its moral sensitivity, for example? Can judgments about a work's artistic value justifiably lay claim to universal agreement or are they merely expressions of subjective preferences? And how is a work's artistic value related to, and how important is it in comparison with, other kinds of value it may possess (see ART, VALUE OF; FORMALISM IN ART; ART AND TRUTH; ART AND MORALITY; SCHILLER, J.C.F.)? What is required to detect the critically relevant properties of artworks, over and above normal perceptual and intellectual powers, and how can judgments that attribute such properties be supported (see ART CRITICISM)? What kinds of understanding are involved in artistic appreciation, and must an acceptable interpretation of a work be compatible with any other acceptable interpretation (see ART, UNDERSTANDING OF; ARTISTIC INTERPRETATION; STRUCTURALISM IN LITERARY THEORY)? In what way, if any, does the artist's intention determine the meaning or their work (see ARTIST'S INTENTION)? What is an artist's style and what is its significance in the appreciation of the artist's work (see ARTISTIC STYLE)?

2 Aesthetics and the arts

One question that arises only for a small set of art forms concerns the nature of depiction. It might be thought that the analysis of the nature of depiction has no special importance within the philosophy of art, for pictorial representation is just as frequent outside as inside art. But this overlooks the fact that real clarity about the ways in which pictures can acquire value as art must be founded on a sophisticated understanding of what a picture is and the psychological resources needed to grasp what it depicts. So what is it for a surface to be or contain a picture of an object or state of affairs? Must the design on the surface be such as to elicit a certain species of visual experience, and must the function of the means by which the pattern was produced, or the intention of the person who created it, be to replicate features of the visible world? Or is a picture a member of a distinctive kind of symbol system, which can be defined without making use of any specifically visual concepts (see DEPICTION; GOODMAN, N. §2)? Another question that has a limited application concerns the distinctive nature and value of a particular artistic genre, the response it encourages from us, and the insight into human life it displays and imparts. For example, whereas a comedy exploits our capacity to find something funny, a tragedy engages our capacity to be moved by the fate of other individuals, and erotic art aims to evoke a sexual reaction; and this difference in the emotional responses at the hearts of the genres goes hand in hand with the different aspects of human life they illuminate (see COMEDY; EMOTION IN RESPONSE TO ART; EROTIC ART; HUMOUR; TRAGEDY).

Questions about the individual natures and possibilities of the various arts include some that are specific to the particular art and some that apply also to other arts. On the one hand, relatively few art forms (architecture and pottery, for example) are directed to the production of works that are intended to perform non-artistic functions, or are of a kind standardly used for utilitarian purposes, and, accordingly, the issue of the relevance to its artistic value of a work's performing, or presenting the appearance of performing, its intended non-artistic function satisfactorily is confined to such arts (see ARCHITECTURE, AESTHETICS OF). Again, only in some arts does a spectator witness a performance of a work, so that issues about a performer's contribution to the interpretation of a work or about the evaluation of different performances of the same work are limited to such arts (see ART, PERFORMING). And since only some works of art (novels, plays and films, for example) tell a story, and only some refer to fictional persons or events, questions about the means by which a story is told or how references to fictional objects should be understood have a restricted application within the arts (see NARRATIVE; FICTIONAL ENTITIES). On the other hand, most, if not all, arts allow of works within their domain being correctly perceived as being expressive of psychological states, and, accordingly, give rise to the question of what it is for a work to be expressive of such a condition (see ARTISTIC EXPRESSION). But the means available within the different arts for the expression of psychological states are various: poetry consists of words, dance exploits the human body, and instrumental music uses nothing other than sounds. And these different artistic media impose different limits on the kinds of state that can be expressed by works of art, the specificity of the states, and the significance within an art of the expressive aspects of its products (see GURNEY, E. §2). Furthermore, it is a general truth about the various arts, rather than one special to expression, that what can be achieved within an art is determined by the nature of the medium the art is based on. Accordingly, an adequate philosophy of art must investigate the variety of such media and elucidate the peculiar advantages they offer and the limitations they impose (see ART, ABSTRACT; DANCE, AESTHETICS OF; FILM, AESTHETICS OF; HANSLICK, E.; LANGER, S.; LESSING, G.E. §2; MUSIC, AESTHETICS OF; OPERA, AESTHETICS OF; PHOTOGRAPHY, AESTHETICS OF; POETRY).

See also: AESTHETICS, AFRICAN; AESTHETICS AND ETHICS; AESTHETICS, CHINESE; AESTHETICS IN ISLAMIC PHILOSOPHY; AESTHETICS, JAPANESE; BELINSKII, V.G.; METAPHOR; RHETORIC; RUSSIAN LITERARY FORMALISM; TOLSTOI, COUNT L.N.

MALCOLM BUDD

Further reading

Hegel, G. (1835) *Aesthetics: Lectures on Fine Art*, trans. T.M. Knox, Oxford: The Clarendon Press, 1975. (Hegel's lectures on aesthetics, delivered in Berlin in the 1820s, are a classic introduction to the subject.)

Kant, I. (1790) *Critique of Aesthetic Judgement*, trans. W.S. Pluhar, Indianapolis, IN and Cambridge: Hackett Publishing Company, 1987.

Wollheim, R. (1980) *Art and Its Objects*, Cambridge: Cambridge University Press. (Essays considering the philosophical issues of works of art.)

AESTHETICS, AFRICAN

The study and analysis of African art and aesthetics have been dominated by Western culture. Initially the aesthetic sensitivities of African cultures were characterized as 'primitive' and of low intellectual calibre. Africans reacted to such negative stereotyping by articulating their own, deliberately non-Western aesthetic theories. The best known of these is négritude.

With its emphasis on learning about a culture by living in it for a period of time, anthropology encouraged scholars to relate African art directly to the aesthetic values of the cultures that produced it. This kind of contextual approach has also become the special concern of African art historians.

One can exemplify the exploration of the aesthetic conceptions of a particular culture in this way by considering the case of the Yoruba peoples of southwestern Nigeria. The Yoruba have a detailed and refined aesthetic vocabulary that has been subjected to extended description and analysis. Where human beings are concerned the highest form of beauty is attributed to a person's good moral character. Where objects are concerned beauty is influenced by their utility or, in the case of figurative carvings, by the intelligence and ability of the artist.

1 Primitive cultures and *négritude*
2 Anthropology and African art history
3 Yoruba moral discourse
4 Yoruba aesthetic discourse

1 Primitive cultures and *négritude*

The history of Western art and aesthetics might have been different if the founding fathers of these disciplines had been natives of a non-Western culture. The artistic genres and aesthetic standards imputed to Western culture by these experts might have been spurned as mistaken, alien, or pejorative. They might be said to have been prime examples of an ethnocentrism which imposes the aesthetic standards of one culture upon others. They might have succeeded in crossing cultures in order to identify some Western aesthetic sensitivities, about which they may have voiced some derogatory remarks and attributed their origins to something like a 'primitive' or 'child-like' mentality.

Each of these possibilities evokes unpleasant memories of scholarly theses that were enunciated when African and Western cultures interacted over the issue of aesthetic sensitivities, in particular those said to inform the genres of artefact that Western art collectors and museums began to define as constituting African art. The bulk of material published in this field is the product of Western scholarship. This scholarship began by denying African intellectual capabilities the same level of aesthetic consciousness that was embraced by the West. African aesthetic sensitivities were said to be primal, inarticulate, collective and instinctive. Africans were thought to be emotional rather than intellectual. As a result the artefacts produced by their cultures were said to express and represent semiconscious hopes and fears about the vaguely understood forces that controlled tribal society and the natural world. 'Primitive' art was conceived of as the product of 'primitive' understanding.

Eventually this emotional and expressive, as opposed to rational and intellectual, characterization of African personality and culture was adapted and reformulated as a positive, lyrical and intellectually refined aesthetic by indigenous African scholars. Termed *négritude*, this school of thought whose most prominent exponent was the sometime president of Senegal Leopold Sédar Senghor, rebuked Western scholarship for failing to assign African aesthetic sensitivities separate but equal status *vis-à-vis* their Western equivalents. It also inspired a renewed sense of black artistic merit that led to a flowering of modern African art in such diverse fields as drama, poetry, fiction, fashion and dance. Theoretical elements of *négritude* have also been adopted by the cultural and intellectual movements identified with Afrocentrism (see AFRICAN PHILOSOPHY, FRANCOPHONE §4).

Nevertheless, as far as the Western-engendered collection and study of African art was concerned, the predominant interest and emphasis remained with mainly figurative, carved sculpture produced prior to the European colonization of Africa during the nineteenth century. Such pieces were viewed as comparatively 'authentic'. However, this term became associated with exaggerated Western notions of the semibarbaric, isolated, expressive tribal cultures that worshipped them, made sacrifices to them and created them out of an imagination that had not distinguished the rational from the emotional, the scientific from the superstitious.

2 Anthropology and African art history

It was modern twentieth-century Western anthropology which renewed interest in the identification, study and appreciation of the intellectual dimension to African aesthetic values. African art objects, whose aesthetic properties had previously been assessed in virtual ignorance of the specific cultures that produced them (as expressions of a generalized, primitivized mentality) began to be culturally recontextualized on the basis of tribal attributions. Even if African art and aesthetics were not anthropological priorities, the general emphasis upon reintegrating objects and beliefs with the social and cultural contexts that originally produced them eventually reignited interest in indigenous artistic traditions and aesthetic values. Such renewed interest was underscored by the importance of doing fieldwork in Africa.

One controversial issue that remained unresolved was the degree to which traditional Africans were capable of articulating whatever aesthetic values informed their cultures. The point was whether Africans themselves could be relied upon to articulate their aesthetic values or whether (usually foreign) anthropologists would have to intuit them on their behalf. Some scholars continued to argue that much of whatever constituted African culture remained at a preverbal level. Whatever aesthetic standards there were implicit in inherited traditions and traditions governed cultures as rules rather than as reasons. Discussion and innovation were not priorities. The forms of figurative sculpture and patterns of textiles were inherited from a tribal past, replicated in the tribal present and passed on unaltered to the tribal future. In this intellectual atmosphere of elementary discursiveness there was no need to articulate or discuss fundamental aesthetic values. Aesthetic standards need not involve more complex considerations than how to polish an object, or colour a textile.

Increased interest in the social and cultural forces responsible for African art and in the aesthetic values that governed its creation has led to the emergence of a separate and specialized discipline known as African art history. In the process of disengaging itself from traditional anthropological interests and methods, this discipline has come to focus on the artistic and aesthetic in African cultures. Further social and cultural research has been encouraged to illuminate different African artistic and aesthetic elements. The scope of African art and aesthetics has been broadened beyond the objects found in private collections and museums so as to include architecture, bodily adornment and jewellery, as well as craftwork and oil and watercolour paintings. The technical aesthetic vocabulary and standards applied by Africans to the artistic elements of their cultures have been detailed. The peoples of Western cultures have been reminded that their aesthetic sensitivities and artistic preferences are products of Western acculturation and may therefore cause them to perceive the aesthetic in a different manner from individuals who are the product of an African culture. In addition, the level of cross-cultural critical appreciation of African art and aesthetics is in the process of being improved so that its technical, formal and intellectual properties may be better interrelated and appreciated. In this way African art history as subject matter can be accorded separate but equal status alongside the aesthetic traditions and heritages of other geographical and art historical groupings.

3 Yoruba moral discourse

To the philosopher of language the extent to which members of African cultures can articulate their aesthetic values is an important consideration. It seems an unnecessarily indirect and complicated strategy to arrive at the exegesis of any African aesthetic vocabulary by approaching it via the eclectic variety of objects that Western collectors and museums have made into African art. It would make better sense to begin the study of the aesthetic of any African culture with the terminology used by people of that culture. Such an approach may not provide information about whatever technical vocabulary might be employed by professional artists and critics in such a society. But it might be an essential foundational exercise preliminary to the identification and analysis of any more technical terminology.

The Yoruba of southwestern Nigeria have a subtle and systematic aesthetic vocabulary evidenced by ordinary discourse (see YORUBA EPISTEMOLOGY). Yoruba aesthetic discourse is intimately related to Yoruba moral discourse. Moral discourse is grounded in epistemological, or cognitive, considerations as one of the fundamental issues is how a person can know the moral character, or *iwa*, of another. The Yoruba argue that since consciousness – *okon* – is private, behaviour – *isesi* – is the only basis on which the moral character of other people can be judged.

The Yoruba define behaviour by the actions, or *ise*, and words, or *oro enu*, of a person. In philosophical terminology this is conventionally referred to as nonverbal and verbal behaviour. Since the Yoruba equate knowledge, or *imo*, with what a person witnesses at first hand, there are severe strictures governing the attribution of either words or actions not experienced in this way.

Such strictures are predictable in an oral culture where literacy cannot be taken for granted. Their point seems to be as epistemic as it is moral. Just as people in Western cultures are concerned with exercising control over the media, members of Yoruba culture wish to exercise control over the mouths constituting the media in oral culture. False claims of knowledge of technical problems, or the moral character of people can endanger lives and destroy reputations.

4 Yoruba aesthetic discourse

Morality is linked with the aesthetic in everyday Yoruba discourse. This is because the Yoruba believe that the purest or highest form of beauty, or *ewa*, in humans is a good moral character, or *iwa rere*. They appreciate that in purely physical terms one person may be more attractive than others. As this is a matter of chance rather than choice, it is of superficial importance when it is a question of a person whose moral character can be relied upon in any situation. This means that a person who happens to be physically unattractive may still be deeply admired and praised for the beauty of their words and actions. Conversely a person of remarkable physical beauty may come to be regarded as viciously immoral on the basis of their words and actions. This preference for a beauty, or *ewa*, that is 'moral' or 'inner' is summed up by the Yoruba aphorism '*Iwa l'ewa*', meaning 'good moral character is beauty'.

Viewing Yoruba aesthetic discourse from this perspective reminds us that the Yoruba, like many other peoples, spend most of their time talking about 'beauty' with regard to humans rather than to the kinds of African art objects of special interest to collectors and museums. The Yoruba also attribute beauty to the natural world and to human artefacts, although different criteria are employed for measuring it.

With reference to the natural world a thing may be appreciated solely for its physical beauty, as might be the case with a glorious sunset. A natural object may be described as having both beauty (*ewa*) and character (*iwa*) if it is also useful to humankind in the sense of an attractive tree that also provides edible fruit, or a splendidly feathered chicken that also provides eggs and the main course for supper. In other words both beauty and character are most importantly assigned to natural objects by measuring their utility and usefulness to humankind.

With reference to human artefacts, the Yoruba may refer to a well-maintained agricultural farm, a new piece of furniture, or an attractive woven textile as possessing beauty. As with natural objects, the human artefacts may also be said to have character arising from their utility in the sense of a new chair that is comfortable and sturdy and the cloth that is durable as well as attractive.

Figurative sculptures, or carvings of human beings, also fall within the category of human artefacts. However, a sculpture of a human is not human. It cannot say or do and does not behave in any conventional human sense. This means that it cannot have moral character as this arises from verbal and nonverbal behaviour, or *isesi*. Yoruba appreciation of this is indicated by the fact that such objects are referred to as having exterior or bodily (*ara*) beauty (*ewa*). Such beauty takes into account factors such as form, polishing and colouring.

In recent years scholars have sought to identify the more specialized vocabulary by means of which professional artists and connoisseurs in Yoruba society articulate the formal principles and values that define and govern art work in the indigenous culture. The main aims are to elaborate whatever indigenous aesthetic consciousness may inform many of the objects the West has come to regard as African art, as well as to illuminate the many other decorative and performative practices, such as fashion, masquerade, poetry and song that are often of greater aesthetic importance and more enduring value to indigenous Yoruba culture. What is most striking about this more specialized vocabulary is the degree to which it replicates values affirmed by the epistemology and morality. Unlike Western culture, where the importance and relevance of aesthetic theory to artistic practice has declined, the relationship between the aesthetic and the artistic in Yoruba culture appears to be fundamental.

There is an emphasis upon the artist being calm, controlled and reasonable (*ifarabale*). The artist must also possess the aptitude for clear observation, understanding and expression (*iluti*). These essential foundational elements of the aesthetic consciousness must be intact in order to show sensitivity to the subjects portrayed and the audience reached. The Yoruba emphasize that the more narrow and conventional (at least in Western terms) 'artistic imaginative insight', or *oju inu*, which enables artists to 'picture' the forms they seek to instantiate, along with design components, or *oju ona*, such as colour, substance, rhythm, outline or harmony, can be exemplified in a superior manner only if based upon these foundational elements.

Previously published accounts of a Yoruba aesthetic by professional art historians do not present it as a single component belonging to an integrated system of epistemic, moral and aesthetic values. This may be attributed to a variety of influences, such as the vested interests of dealers and private collectors of African art whose focus is on the objects, the vestiges of the false stereotype that Africans are less capable of expressing themselves in rational and systematic terms, and the lack of attention paid by academic philosophers to semantic networks of meaning which underlie African discourse.

There is no obvious reason why the methodological approach illustrated by this account of a Yoruba aesthetic could not be applied to the discourse of other African cultures. Relatively few systematic studies of the values underlying, informing and interrelating epistemological, moral and aesthetic priorities and practices in African cultures have so far been undertaken. Even if their discourse embraces different epistemic standards and alternative moral virtues leading to other aesthetic values, the results could be of interest. In addition, such narratives would help to demonstrate that the museum objects which for many constitute African art may only occupy a minor and subsidiary role in the overall aesthetic that defines such cultures.

See also: AESTHETIC CONCEPTS; AESTHETICS, CHINESE; AESTHETICS, JAPANESE

References and further reading

Abiodun, R., Drewal, H. and Pemberton, J. (eds) (1990) *African Art Studies: the State of the Discipline*, Washington, DC: Smithsonian Institution. (A collection of clear assessments by African art historians, detailing the accomplishments and shortcomings of their discipline. The contribution by R. Abiodun on Yoruba aesthetic terminology is noteworthy.)

—— (1994a) *Yoruba Art and Aesthetics*, Zurich: The Centre for African Art and the Reitburg Museum. (A well-illustrated introductory discussion of Yoruba art and aesthetics, with some discussion of their relationships to Yoruba religion.)

—— (1994b) *The Yoruba Artist: New Theoretical Perspectives on African Arts*, Washington, DC and London: Smithsonian Institution Press. (A critical, innovative and multidisciplinary review of the verbal and visual arts as interpreted by academic disciplines.)

Appiah, K.A. (1982) 'The Post-Colonial and the Postmodern', in *In My Father's House: Africa in the Philosophy of Culture*, London: Methuen; 2nd edn, Oxford: Oxford University Press, 1992, 137–57. (A study of the dangers inherent in discussing art as a cross-cultural phenomenon with particular reference to Africa.)

—— (1995) 'Why Africa? Why Art?', in T. Phillips (ed.) *Africa: the Art of a Continent*, Munich and New York: Prestel, 21–6. (This brief discussion makes it apparent why even the most obvious artistic cross-cultural generalizations may be misguided.)

Blier, S.P. (1987) *The Ontology of Architecture: Ontology and Metaphor in Batammaliba Architectural Expression*, Cambridge: Cambridge University Press. (A detailed and well-illustrated study of the aesthetic values operative in a subject area largely ignored by canonical African art history.)

Boone, S.A. (1986) *Radiance from the Waters: Ideals of Feminine Beauty in Mende Art*, New Haven, CT and London: Yale University Press. (A study of the interplay between human and artistic aesthetic priorities and values.)

Clifford, J. (1988) *The Predicament of Culture: Twentieth Century Ethnography, Literature and Art*, Cambridge, MA: Harvard University Press. (A useful critique of Western cultural values and their consequences for the appreciation of African art and aesthetic values.)

Hallen, B. (1997) 'African Meanings, Western Words', *The African Studies Review* 40 (1): 1–11. (Reflections on the difficulties facing African art historians when they translate African aesthetic terminology into Western languages.)

Irele, A. (1990) *The African Experience in Literature and Ideology*, Bloomington, IN: Indiana University Press. (A cultural and historical analysis of *négritude* as an African ideological movement.)

Lawal, B. (1974) 'Some Aspects of Yoruba Aesthetics', *The British Journal of Aesthetics* 14 (3): 239–49. (An introductory synopsis of everyday Yoruba vocabulary and social conventions relevant to aesthetics.)

Roberts, M. and Roberts, A. (eds) (1996) *Memory: Luba Art and the Making of History*, New York: The Museum for African Art; Munich: Prestel. (An innovative collection that stresses the flexible role of the arts in both recording and interpreting the history of an African ethnic group.)

Thompson, R.F. (1983) *Flash of the Spirit: African and Afro-American Art and Philosophy*, New York: Random House. (An exploratory study of African aesthetics and the diaspora.)

Van Damme, W. (1987) *A Comparative Analysis Concerning Beauty and Ugliness in Sub-Saharan Africa*, Ghent: Rijksuniversiteit. (A pioneering first step towards comparing aesthetic priorities from diverse west, central and southern African languages.)

BARRY HALLEN

AESTHETICS AND ETHICS

The contrast between ethical and aesthetic judgments, which has provided a good deal of the subject-matter of aesthetics, stems largely from Immanuel Kant's idiosyncratic view of morality as a series of imperatives issued in accordance with the dictates of practical reason, while for him judgments of taste are based on no principles. This has led even non-Kantians to argue that aesthetic judgments are primarily concerned, as is art itself, with uniqueness, while morality has mainly to do with repeatable actions. This tends to separate art from other human activities, a separation which was encouraged by the collection of useless items by 'connoisseurs', who took over as their vocabulary of appreciation the traditional language of religious contemplation. This viewpoint has been attacked passionately by idealist aestheticians, who claim that art is a heightening of the common human activity of expressing emotions, to the point where they are experienced and rendered lucidly, as they rarely are in everyday life. Marxist aestheticians, whose roots lie in the same tradition as idealists, argue that art is inherently political, and that the realm of 'pure aesthetic experience' is chimerical. Meanwhile the analytic tradition in aesthetics has spent much effort amplifying Kant-style positions, without taking into account their historical conditioning. There is a tendency to contrast the activities of the moralist, prescribing courses of action, with that of the critic, whose only job can be to point to the unrepeatable features which constitute a work of art.

1 Origins of the discussion
2 Development of a contrast
3 Aesthetics and history
4 Aesthetics and ethics in analytic philosophy

1 Origins of the discussion

Ethics is the study of what people ought to do and the concepts employed in giving an account of why they should behave in certain ways; this study includes consideration of such factors as the nature of the judgments made about people's actions (are they objective or subjective?). Aesthetics is the study of a certain way of responding to nature and to some artefacts, pre-eminently works of art, and an investigation of the status of the judgments we make about them. At least, that is roughly how the subjects have been conceived traditionally. It is impossible to give a noncontroversial definition of either of them. That has consequences for the comparisons and contrasts between them which have been a feature of, at least, aesthetic discussion since Kant (see KANT, I. §12). He was the first great philosopher who gave extended and elaborate treatment to the nature of aesthetic judgment, though unfortunately that was as part of his attempt to overcome crippling difficulties in the rest of his system. Despite that, he largely set the agenda for subsequent discussion of aesthetic judgment, both its form and its content.

Though he did not place his thoughts on the subject in a historical context, it aids understanding if we do. Kant was writing in an intellectual climate in which natural science was increasingly taken to be the paradigm of human knowledge, with its picture of a wholly causally determined order (see DETERMINISM AND INDETERMINISM §1). Kant accepted that account of the world of appearances (nature as we normally conceive it, including human nature), but argued that if we are to be moral agents we must be free in some strong (metaphysical) sense. For Kant, to be free is to be subject to a set of universal laws different to the descriptive laws of nature, namely those of practical reason, which are prescriptive. So as inhabitants of the phenomenal world we are intelligible according to the laws which govern everything else in it. As inhabitants of the noumenal world (the world of things-in-themselves) we are answerable to the moral law, alongside all other rational beings (see KANTIAN ETHICS).

This oppressively well-regulated view of things, in which both as objects and as agents we are to be regarded simply as law-governed items, not only has its own difficulties in reconciling the two kinds of being, but also leaves no room for taking an interest in something without seeing it as a member of a class (see UNIVERSALISM IN ETHICS §3). It is at this point that the aesthetic makes its debut, as a kind of interest in certain things, expressed in a kind of judgment, which is concerned with those things quite apart from any use to which they may be put, or even, Kant says, independently of whether they actually exist: an interest which is without, in the appropriate sense, interest.

2 Development of a contrast

It might be felt that, given the importance which Kant attached to the contrast between an aesthetic and any other kind of interest in things, it is surprising that it had not been made before. In fact it had, but in a different context, as we shall see. Furthermore, a set of pressures of a kind quite remote from anything Kant had in mind made such a contrast not only intelligible but urgent. With the growth of a merchant class intent on displaying its wealth, the purchase of useless objects which could be collected and displayed in private exhibitions became a major form of consumption. Taste, in a new and extended sense, was necessary to make fine discriminations between superior and inferior specimens of the same kind of thing, where what made the crucial difference between good and bad became ever more recondite, requiring the activity of people called 'virtuosi' or, in subsequent gallicized form, 'connoisseurs'. They employed a fairly rich evaluative vocabulary, but the justification for its use was to be found not in general rules, but in the possession by individual things of certain perceptual properties, properties discerned through taste. Thus on account of the colours which constitute them, and the balances between those colours, one judges whether paintings are unified, harmonious, and so on. The proper judgment of taste, as Kant was to put it, is always singular: 'This is beautiful'.

The peculiar set of forces which drove Kant's system, especially by the time he came to deal with beauty in the *Kritik der Urteilskraft* (*Critique of Judgment*) (1790), can be ignored. Despite them he managed to exert a huge influence on the young subject of aesthetics, and to establish a contrast or set of contrasts with ethics which is still going strong, though there have been many opposing voices. As much as the welcome stress on the particular which aesthetic contemplation was alleged to certify, there was a vocabulary at hand which had seemed in danger of losing its employment: the vocabulary of theology, or rather that part of it which was concerned to stress the unique value of the object of devotion. Hence the striking similarity between the traditional terminology of worship and the new one of aesthetic absorption. It is no coincidence that for the first time we come across the phrase 'the religion of art'. The phenomenon itself would have been inconceivable at an earlier date.

3 Aesthetics and history

Though philosophers are notoriously prone to self-consciousness about the nature of their subject, they have tended to regard the relationship between it and other disciplines in a less historically aware way than might have been expected. So the Kantian stress on the uniqueness of the aesthetic object has not often been subjected to historical scrutiny. This failure has resulted in a set of contrasts between the aesthetic and the ethical which have been taken as timeless truths about the two areas, rather than as the consequences of the triumphant progress of science and the decline of religion, among other factors. During the nineteenth century the conflicting, rather than complementary, tendencies to see art and aesthetic experience as *sui generis*, or as socially significant and morally and politically committed, simply confronted one another, strongly-worded manifestos appearing on each side, with little recognition of the elaborate background which had led to this polarization of attitudes.

The most striking contributions to aesthetics have, as a consequence, come from, on the one hand, idealist philosophers, such as R.G. Collingwood (1938), who have stressed the relationship between aesthetic and moral experience, and in general the connections between art and life, to the point where we are all seen as potential artists, though we rarely actualize our capacities (see COLLINGWOOD, R.G.; ART AND MORALITY §1). For a school of thinkers which lays great moral stress on self-realization, and sees the artistic enterprise as a matter of clarifying feelings, it is not surprising that morality finally comes to be seen as an art, if not as art (see SELF-REALIZATION). On the other hand, major statements of a quite different hue have come from Marxist-oriented philosophers, above all some members of the Frankfurt School, such as Theodor ADORNO, who have been at pains to point out both 'the ideology of the aesthetic', that is, the extent to which insisting that aesthetic experience is unrelated to other kinds is itself a political statement, and the general pervasiveness of politics, so that a major function of aesthetic theory is to bring to light the hidden ethical and political allegiances of varying aesthetic stances (see FRANKFURT SCHOOL).

Both these opposing schools derive in large measure from the inspiration of HEGEL (§8); that is not surprising, given the stress in his own writings on aesthetics on the primacy of art rather than nature, the historical dimensions of artistic production and understanding, and the different functions which art serves in different societies, or the same society at different stages.

4 Aesthetics and ethics in analytic philosophy

The least rewarding incursions into aesthetic theory and its relationship to ethics have been by Anglo-American philosophers of the last forty years. They have tended to produce, no doubt unwittingly, parodies of Kantianism, in which the contrast between our responses to art and our moral judgments is rendered so extreme that it has been alleged by, for example, Hampshire (1952) and Strawson (1966) that the uniqueness of art-objects is such as to render them ineffable. These philosophers are so filled with abhorrence at the idea of using works of art for any purpose at all that they claim that their glory is their purposelessness, except perhaps for their unique rendering of uniqueness. On this view, morality assimilates, art differentiates. Whereas the moralist has to recommend and to judge, the critic has only to point out the specific features of objects under contemplation. Aesthetics has as a large part of its point the indication of its own limited range: mainly to stress that it is not, at any crucial juncture, comparable to ethics. Unfortunately the tendency of this tradition of aesthetics to refrain from giving examples means that the reader is likely, when encountering a reference to 'moral actions', to think of keeping a promise, or something equally banal; whereas when the reference is to 'a work of art' the natural tendency will be to think of the Sistine Chapel ceiling, or a Shakespeare play. Hence it is not surprising that morality and art, ethics and aesthetics, are thought to be sharply divergent, and that the critic's role is taken to be utterly dissimilar to the moralist's.

Analytic aesthetics has been written almost exclusively from the spectator's viewpoint. The same may be true of Hegel, but it did not influence the way he saw the subject as it has done recent aesthetics. For most of its history, writing in general terms about art (though it was not then called 'aesthetics') in fact consisted of discussions of the rules which, if not sufficient for the production of great art, were thought to be certainly necessary. Equally, a large amount of moralizing did not take the form of giving rules, but of holding up examples of the good life, of preaching ways of being rather than doing. In such a different climate of thought, the comparisons and contrasts to be drawn between the disciplines of aesthetics and ethics would be startlingly unlike those we have grown familiar with in recent thinking.

See also: AESTHETICS, CHINESE; ART AND MORALITY; ART, VALUE OF

References and further reading

Abrams, M.H. (1985) 'Art-As-Such: The Sociology of Modern Aesthetics', *Bulletin of the American Academy of Arts and Sciences* 38: 8–33; repr. in *Doing Things with Texts*, New York: W.W. Norton, 1989. (An invaluable essay for showing the effect of general historical factors on the production of philosophical theory.)

* Collingwood, R.G. (1938) *The Principles of Art*, Oxford: Oxford University Press. (The most impressive, though extreme, statement of an idealist aesthetic.)

Eagleton, T. (1990) *The Ideology of the Aesthetic*, Oxford: Blackwell. (A useful conspectus, from a Marxist standpoint, of the development of the notion of the aesthetic during the last two centuries.)

* Hampshire, S. (1952) 'Logic and Appreciation', *World Review*; repr. in W. Elton (ed.) *Aesthetics and Language*, Oxford: Blackwell, 1959. (A classic statement of the starkest possible opposition between moral and aesthetic judgments.)

* Kant, I. (1790) *Kritik der Urteilskraft*, trans. W.S. Pluhar, *Critique of Judgment*, Indianapolis, IN: Hackett Publishing Company, 1987. (The basic work in the history of aesthetics, which has determined the way in which the issues have been discussed, as well as what they are.)

Mothersill, M. (1984) *Beauty Restored*, Oxford: Oxford University Press. (A full-length Kantian account of aesthetic judgment, full of resourceful and stimulating argument.)

* Strawson, P.F. (1966) 'Aesthetic Appraisal and Works of Art', *Oxford Review* 3; repr. in *Freedom and Resentment*, London: Methuen, 1974. (A position very similar to Hampshire's, with arguments supplied: it raises the question in the reader's mind of why we should take any interest at all in works of art.)

MICHAEL TANNER

AESTHETICS, CHINESE

*In China, poetry, painting and calligraphy are traditionally known as the 'Three Perfections' of the cultivated scholar. They are construed as ethico-aesthetic acts of self-signification and are evaluated as to their efficacy in fostering harmonious relations of social exchange within the concrete circumstances of particular social contexts. In contrast to Western notions of mimesis, the Chinese poetic tradition assumes the existence of fundamental, mutually implicating correlations between the patterns (*wen*) immanent in nature and those of human culture.*

*This gives rise to two traditions of Chinese poetics. First, there is the canonical tradition of Confucian exegesis, in which a poem was assumed to invoke a network of pre-established categorical correlations (*lei*) between poet and world, which enabled the imagery to be read as verbal indices of both personal feeling and the relative stability of the social and natural order. Second, there is the non-canonical tradition of neo-Daoist and Buddhist-inspired poetics which represented a shift from the didactic to the affective power of natural imagery to make reference to the poet's state of mind.*

Calligraphy and painting were adopted by the gentleman-scholar as ethico-aesthetic practices of xiushen *(self-cultivation) and self-expression, and for promotion of social exchange. Early writings describing calligraphy and painting deploy metaphorical imagery that makes reference to both nature and the body. This imagery invoked the indigenous correlative rhetoric that sought consonance between the patterns immanent within the natural order and those of the human realm. The embodiment of tradition, through the practice of making artistic references to the past, was fundamental to the art of the scholar-painter, for it served to establish one's artistic lineage and to sanction or authorize one's own self-presentation within a particular historical situation.*

1   The ethico-aesthetic Way of Chinese art
2   Poetry
3   Calligraphy and painting
4   Literati aesthetics

1   The ethico-aesthetic Way of Chinese art

In China, poetry, painting, and calligraphy are traditionally known as the 'Three Perfections' (*sanjue*) of the cultivated scholar. They were so designated because each of these modes of aesthetic practice came to serve as an important means of 'self-cultivation' (*xiushen*) as well as self-expression, and often appear combined in a single work of the scholar-artist.

According to tradition, poetry, painting and calligraphy originally stem from a common root-metaphor, namely *wen*. In the first Chinese etymological dictionary, Xu Shen's *Shuowen jiezi* (Explanations of Simple and Compound Characters), *c.* AD 100, the character *wen* is said to consist of 'intersecting strokes, representing a criss-cross pattern'. *Wen* is a semantically multivalent term that can refer to physical markings, patterns on coloured woven silk and painted designs of carriages as well as writing, literature and culture. The aesthetic conception of *wen* is given by Liu Xi (early third century AD) in his lexicographic work *Shiming* (Explanations of Names): '*Wen* means assembling various colours to form brocade or embroidery, assembling words to form phrases and meanings like patterned embroidery' (Liu 1975: 101).

The Western word that comes closest in meaning to *wen* is *textus*, Latin for 'woven', from which the words 'text' and 'textile' are derived. However, *textus* does not connote the cosmological, and thus ethical, implications of *wen*. These can be traced back to the legendary accounts of the sage-king Bao Xi or Fu Xi, recorded in the *Dazhuan* (Great Commentary) to the early divination text, the *Yijing* (Book of Changes). Contemplating the images (*xiang*) in the heavens above and the patterns (*wen*) on earth below, Bao Xi invented the *bagua* or eight trigrams, traditionally regarded as the prototypes of the Chinese scripts, the very foundation of Chinese civilization.

It is precisely through a patterning of human relations in correlation with the configurations immanent in natural phenomena that the ethical implications of *wen* are realized: 'Contemplate the configurations [*wen*] of heaven to observe the changes of seasons; contemplate the configurations of man to accomplish the [cultural] transformation of the world' (Liu 1975: 18–19). It is in light of this that we can appreciate the Chinese word for 'civilization', *wenhua*, which is literally 'transformation through patterning'.

2 Poetry

The earliest writings on Chinese poetry can be found in the *Daxue* (Great Preface) and commentaries to the first anthology of poetry, the *Shijing* (Book of Songs) in the sixth century BC, and commentaries to the *Lisao* (Encountering Sorrow), the longest elegy in the *Chuci* (Songs of Chu) anthology, attributed to Qu Yuan (?343–278 BC). These commentaries, written by Confucian scholars of the Han dynasty (206 BC–AD 220), establish a way of construing poetry as an 'ethico-aesthetic practice' that dominated literary exegesis up until the Tang dynasty (618–906).

Chinese poetry does not take its start, as does Western poetry, from the act of positing the subject and object of cognition (that is, the objectification and independent, self-subsistent existence of self and world). In the dualistic thinking predominant in the West, the poetic representation of objective things and events is a mimetic, and hence fictive, representation of the non-subjective things and events in external reality (see POETRY). The Western conception of mimesis is essentially predicated on the dualistic notion of metaphor as 'identity in difference'. This binary logic has led to two fundamentally opposing positions concerning the image (*imago*), be it poetic or pictorial. Classical views of mimesis treat the image as an imitation (*imitatio*) of a pre-existing phenomenal world (see MIMESIS). Advocates of this position tend to embrace a 'perceptualist' theory of art. The romanticist, however, construes the image as the pure artifice (*inventio*) of the artist, representing, yet distinctly different from, the sensible world.

In contradistinction to the mimetic practices and subject–object duality of the West, the Chinese poetic tradition assumes the existence of fundamental, mutually implicating correlations between the patterns (*wen*) immanent in nature and those of human culture. The Chinese poem was thus understood to invoke a network of pre-established categorical correlations (*lei*) between poet and world, which receives systematic formulation in such thinkers as DONG ZHONGSHU, the leading Confucian of the Western Han period.

The correlation between poetic natural imagery and human situations is achieved through three master tropes: *fu* or descriptive 'exposition', *bi* or metonymic 'comparison', and *xing* or metaphoric substitution or 'stimulus'. What differentiates these poetic tropes from their Western rhetorical counterparts is that they were not construed as the invention of the individual poet. Rather, links between poetic imagery, be they metonymic juxtapositions (as in the *Shijing*) or metaphoric substitutions (as in the *Lisao*), were traditionally considered to draw upon shared affiliations in a priori categorical correlations (*lei*) antecedent to the poem. It is an expressive-affective conception of poetry that assumes an internal (emotion, *qing*) and external (nature, *jing*) correlation, based on relations of causality, which enable the imagery to be read as verbal indices of personal feeling and the stability of the political and cosmic order. It is a Confucian notion of poetry which fulfils a crucial function of moral, social and political critique.

Lyric poetry, according to *Lu Ji* (AD 261–303), 'originates in emotion' (*shi yuan qing*), a response of the poet to the stimulus of nature. This is made clear in his *Wen fu* (Exposition on Literature):

He moves with the four seasons, to sigh at transience,
And looks at the myriad objects, contemplating their complexity.
He laments the falling leaves during autumn's vigour,
And delights in the tender branches of fragrant spring.

(*Wen fu*, in Yu 1987: 33)

Nature is thus conceived as the stimulus or semantic evocator and source of poetic imagery.

It is a stimulus/expression/affect conception of *poesis* in which natural images draw forth pre-established categorical correlations (*ganlei*) which stimulate (*ying*) or arouse (*qi*) in the heart-and-mind (*xin*) of the reader a morally didactic and emotionally affective response (*gan*). Then, through a process of contextualization, the poet's work is interpreted as a didactic response to the particular set of circumstances that occasion the poetic response. In this way, Chinese poetry is understood as ultimately addressing an actual historical condition in the world around the poet. This tradition persisted in later years in attempting to read poetry as a political commentary or moralistic purpose, referring, no matter how obliquely, to the life history of the poet.

With the collapse of the Han Confucian order, China entered into a period of political division and social instability that enabled neo-Daoism and eventually Buddhism to exert an influence on the intelligentsia in southern China. It was during this period that Chinese scholars turned away from the discredited affairs of the court and engaged in practices of 'self-cultivation' and spontaneous acts called 'self-so-ing' (*ziran*) within natural settings (see SELF-CULTIVATION, CHINESE THEORIES OF). It is also at this time that we witness the rise of a tradition counter to that of the Confucian exegetes, beginning with the non-canonical landscape-poetry of Tao Qian (AD 365–427) and Xie Lingyun (AD 385–433) of the Six Dynasties Period and culminating in the classical poetry of Wang Wei, Li Bo and Du Fu of the Tang dynasty (AD 618–906). This represents a shift from the didactic to the affective power of natural imagery. Scenic elements of an ostensibly observed natural scene are not only described in vivid detail, but also integrated into the coherent order of the represented scene and establish correlative relationship with the emotional situation of the poet.

Tao Qian is credited with transforming the expectations of an occasional poem so that it reads less as an allusion to the political realm than as a reference to the life of the individual poet (for example, retirement). While he often employs natural images that carry long established conventional associations (such as the pine tree) by embedding them within passages of detailed descriptions, they are naturalized by the reader as integral parts of the visualized world of the poem. The natural images are read not only as a description of an ostensibly perceived scene, but also as making personal reference to the poet's state of mind.

In the landscape poetry of Xie Lingyun, nature is even more precisely described than in the poetry of Tao Qian. However, it is not a detailed description of nature for its own sake, nor is it meant to convey symbolic or philosophical overtones. In the absence of natural images replete with conventional associations, Xie Lingyun's landscape poems are read as autobiographical narratives whose references are largely personal. The detailing of his perceptions and reactions to apparently observed scenery and his engagement with it carry meanings that establish a relation to the poet's state of mind. This is explicitly brought out in summary statements at the end of his poems.

In the Tang dynasty, this led to a significant reformulation of aesthetic theory, one in which the poet adopts a more receptive attitude and responds spontaneously to the world around him. This is a position informed by Daoist and Buddhist ideals, an embodied subjectivity that enables the poet to lodge his mind in the objects of the world in such a way that they can be imbued with emotional and intellectual content.

In the poetry of Wang Wei and Li Bo, informed by Daoist and Buddhist thought, the agency of the poet as authorial or poetic subject yields to the active presence of the objects of the natural world and defers to natural images to suggest emotion. In Du Fu's poetry, images of self and images of the world are so intertwined as to present, at one level, coherent scenes with a vividness and perceptual accuracy and, at another level, imagery that evokes an unstated emotional and/or intellectual 'meaning beyond the words'. *Ershisi shipin* (The Twenty-four Types of Poetry), by the late Tang poet-critic Sikong Tu (837–908), exemplifies the move toward a poetry that employs natural images of the object world 'to suggest something ineffable and intangible'. The description of nature in his poems embodies the notion of going beyond the words of the poem, pointing to that which lies beyond words.

Although Confucian canonical exegetes focused on the moral implications and didactic force of poetic images of nature, and non-canonical critics focused on the way natural images come to embody human feelings, their premises were nevertheless identical. In the words of Fang Hui (1227–96), 'the profound meaning of the comparison and stimulus is to establish the secret links that hold together all things in the universe' (Yu 1987: 217). Lastly, there was an unstated assumption that all poetry, be it canonical or non-canonical, makes ultimate reference to the world of the poet.

3 Calligraphy and painting

The ethico-aesthetic practice of Chinese calligraphy and, by extension, Chinese painting has its genesis in the ancient ritual practices (*li*) of the Zhou dynasty (1122 BC–221 BC), a formative period in Chinese civilization, which 'witnessed a transition from spirit-centred to human-centred ritual, from shaman-counsellors to sage-counsellors, from authority by virtue of one's position to authority of one's person' (Hall and Ames 1987: 87). One of the ways of seeking moral perfection, of becoming an authoritative person (*ren*), is through the practice of art as a means of self-cultivation (*xiushen*) (see CONFUCIAN PHILOSOPHY, CHINESE).

Calligraphy and music, two of the 'Six Arts' (*liuyi*) in classical Confucian thought, emerge from this formative period of Chinese culture as ritual aesthetic practices for the upper class, as disciplines of the body (*ti*) and mind/heart (*xin*), which engage the gentleman-scholar in the cultivation of the self. *Xiushen* ('self-cultivation', literally 'cultivation of the body') speaks to the 'importance of taking care of one's body as a necessary condition for learning to be human' (Tu 1985: 96) (see SELF-CULTIVATION, CHINESE THEORIES OF). In this respect it is interesting to note that, 'Etymologically the character *yi*, which is commonly rendered as "art", signifies the activity of planting of [sic] cultivating fields' (Tu 1983: 60). Noting the cognate relation between the characters for 'ritual action' (*li*) and 'body' (*ti*), it is interesting to observe that '*li* actions are embodiments or formalizations of meaning and value that accumulate to constitute a cultural tradition' (Hall and Ames 1987: 88).

The idea that art can serve as a means of self-cultivation finds its earliest expression in a passage on the meaning of music in the *Liji* (Book of Rites): 'The perfection of virtue is primary, and the perfection of art follows afterward' (*Liji* 17, 3, §5, in Cahill 1966: 122). An affirmation of the practice of art can also be found in the following statement by Confucius: 'The Master said, Set your heart upon the Way, support yourself by its power, lean upon Goodness, seek delight in the arts' (*Lunyu* 7, 6, §§1–4, in Ledderose 1979: 29).

The concept of the Six Arts did not survive the fall of the Han Dynasty. During the Six Dynasties period, under the influence neo-Daoism and Buddhism, the perfection of selfhood came to be conceived as a 'dynamic process of spiritual development' whose internal generative force was often said to be heavenly endowed in nature. It was during this time that members of China's cultured scholarly elite adopted the practice of calligraphy and the playing of the lute (van Gulick 1969) as the specific means to pursue aesthetic self-expression and self-cultivation. As Tu Wei-ming has noted, 'One learns to play the lute or to sing lyric songs in order to communicate with others and, more importantly perhaps, to experience the internal resonance one shares with nature' (Tu 1983: 62).

In neo-Daoist inspired calligraphy of the Eastern Jin dynasty (AD 317–420), for example, the metaphysical principle *ziran* ('naturalness' or 'self-so-ing'), an impersonal creative potential, is cited as one of the most important aesthetic principles. The Northern Song calligrapher/connoisseur Mi Fu (1052–1107) reserved the aesthetic ideal of *tianzhen* (natural perfection) to praise the calligraphy of the Eastern Jin master Wang Xianzhi (AD 344–88). Lothar Ledderose has observed that: 'plain tranquillity (*pingdan*) and natural perfection (*tianzhen*) were not only stylistic and aesthetic concepts which could be used to describe and evaluate works of calligraphy, but these terms also described the ideal state of mind of the artist' (Ledderose 1979: 58). According to Mi Fu: 'the movement of the brush should come swiftly with a natural perfection and emerge unintentionally' (Ledderose 1979: 64). An appeal to an egoistic source of creativity would simply be unthinkable.

One of the distinguishing features of early Chinese aesthetic discourse is a predominance of physiological and nature imagery. The following passage from the *Bizhen tu* (Diagram of the Battle Formation of the Brush), an early text attributed variously to Wei Furen (AD 272–349) and Wang Xizhi (AD 321–379), exemplifies the way in which the aesthetic discourse on Chinese calligraphy is framed in the terminology of human physiology:

> Calligraphy by those good in brush strength has much bone; that by those not good in brush strength has much flesh. Calligraphy that has much bone but slight flesh is called sinew-writing; that with much flesh but slight bone is called ink-pig. Calligraphy with much strength and rich in sinew is of sage-like quality; that with neither strength nor sinew is sick. Every writer proceeds in accordance with the manifestation of their digestion and respiration of energy, *hsiao-hsi* [*xaoxi*].
> (*Bizhen tu*, in Hay 1983: 85)

In another passage in the *Bizhen tu*, images from nature are used to characterize the ideal rendering of the seven strokes that represent the so-called 'diagram of the battle formation of the brush':

> First stroke – like a cloud formation stretching a thousand *li*; indistinct, but not without form.
>
> Second stroke – like a stone falling from a high peak, bouncing and crashing, about to shatter.
>
> Third stroke – the tusk of an elephant or rhinoceros (thrust into and) broken by the ground.
>
> Fourth stroke – fired from a three-thousand pound crossbow.
>
> Fifth stroke – a withered vine, ten thousand years old.
>
> Sixth stroke – crashing waves or rolling thunder.
>
> Seventh stroke – the sinews and joints of a mighty bow.
>
> (*Bizhen tu*, in Barnhart 1964: 16)

The deployment of metaphorical imagery, referencing the human body and nature in Chinese aesthetic theory, is not simply a rhetorical flourish but, in fact, serves a specific epistemological function. It constitutes an indigenous correlative rhetoric stemming from the Chinese view of spiritual development that sought within the ritual aesthetic acts of self-cultivation to embody patterns of behaviour deemed consonant with the immanent patterns perceived within the natural order of things.

The concepts of *lei* ('kind' or 'categorical correlation') and *ganlei* 'responding according to categorical correlation', which were fundamental to early Chinese poetic theory, play a prominent role in Zong Bing's (375–443) essay *Hua shanshui xu* (A Preface to the Painting of Mountains and Rivers), the earliest extant philosophical treatise on painting written in China. This can be illustrated in the following passage:

> Now the Sage, with his spirit realizes the Way; thus the worthy can pass through it. Mountains and rivers (likewise), with their forms, relish the way; thus the virtuous can enjoy it. How similar they are to each other!
>
> (*Hua shanshui xu*, in Munakata 1983: 118)

The reference to 'mountains and rivers' alludes to the Chinese term for landscape painting, *shanshui hua* (literally, 'mountain-water painting'). Zong Bing's categorical correlation of the 'Sage' and 'mountains and rivers' brings to mind a passage from the Confucian *Lunyu* (Analects):

> The Master said, 'The wise [*zhi*] find joy in water [*shui*]; the benevolent [*ren*] find joy in mountains. The wise are active [*dong*]; the benevolent are still [*jing*]. The wise are joyful [*le*]; the benevolent are long-lived [*shou*]'.
>
> (*Lunyu*, in Lau 1992: 53)

The mountains and waters thus come to symbolize, respectively, the dimensions of constancy and change and, by metaphorical extension, tradition and its creative adaptation to the conditions of an ever-changing present.

The correlative rhetoric of *ganlei* was soon eclipsed by such physiological concepts as *qi* (vital force or energy flow) or *qiyun* (resonance of vital force,) and *xue* (blood) or *xuemo* (blood-pulse). *Qi* is variously translated as 'breath', 'spirit' or 'energy': the vital force that animates life (see QI). *Xue* or *xuemo*, when it appears in discussions on calligraphy, refers to the energy functioning through the rhythmic flow of the ink within and between the characters. The quintessential use of *qi* as an aesthetic term appears in the *Liufa* or 'Six Laws' of painting by the portrait painter and theorist Xie He in the early sixth century AD. The first, and thus most important, of Xie He's laws is '*Qiyun shengdong*' which can be translated as 'life-movement [is achieved through] spirit resonance (or resonance of vital force)'. *Xue*, or the energy functioning through the rhythmic flow of the ink, is implied in the second of Xie He's laws of painting, '*Gufa yongbi*' or 'bone-method (that is, inner structure) when wielding the brush'. This can be interpreted as indicating the precise way in which to achieve 'spirit resonance'. Painting and calligraphy are thus conceived as configurations of energy, materializing through the brush into the traces of ink.

Chinese medical treatises have been shown to be another important source for the deployment of metaphorical imagery referencing the human body and nature in Chinese aesthetic theory. Previously, it was noted that ritual aesthetic acts of self-cultivation embody patterns of behaviour deemed consonant with the immanent patterns perceived within the natural order of things. In traditional Chinese medical treatises, the body is conceived as a system or network of patterned energy flow and transformation, that is, as a microcosmic correlative of the macrocosmic world of nature. Painting and calligraphy, conceived as configurations of energy materializing through movements of the brush into the traces of ink, thus came to be seen as ways of capturing the patterns of *shengdong* or 'life movement' of the phenomenal world.

The *Bifaji* (A Note on the Art of the Brush) of Jing Hao in the early tenth century is a reformulation of Xie He's 'Six Laws' for the purpose of representing the landscape. Jing Hao was a Confucian scholar-painter who, during the social and political turmoil of the Five Dynasties Period, retired to the Taihang mountains of Southern Shenxi. The centrepiece of the *Bifaji* is the Six Essentials in painting a landscape, reported to have been conveyed to the author/narrator by a rustic old man whom he came upon while painting in the Stone Drum Cave:

> Spirit (*qi*) is obtained when your mind moves along with the movement of the brush and does not hesitate in delineating images. Resonance (*yun*) is obtained when you establish forms while hiding [obvious] traces of the brush, and perfect them by observing the proprieties and avoiding vulgarity. Thought (*si*) is obtained when you grasp essential forms eliminating unnecessary details [in your observation of nature], and let your ideas crystallize into forms to be represented.
>
> (*Bifaji*, in Munakata 1974: 12)

These first three essentials of landscape painting prescribe artistic norms and conventions for the use of brush and ink that are self-effacing, concealing all traces of the material or formal process of representation and thus, by implication, all traces of personal expression in order to give transparent access to that which is represented. Jing Hao's 'Six Essentials of Painting' exhibits the influence of neo-Confucian values when it emphasizes the disclosure and transmission, through the receptive mind and the responsive hand of the painter, of the immanent patterns of nature in terms of the rhythmic patterned relations of the painted landscape forms.

4 Literati aesthetics

The re-establishment of national unity and order under the Song dynasty (960–1279) ushered in social and political conditions conducive to the formulation of a new literati aesthetic. The feudal aristocracy of landed gentry, prominent during the Tang dynasty, gave way in the Song to an 'aristocracy of merit' (Bush 1971: 4), a 'meritocracy', as civil service examinations provided truly talented scholars with access to high government office. Towards the end of the Northern Song (960–1126), a new and distinctive literati style of painting and calligraphy began to develop among a small circle of scholar-officials. A literati aesthetic theory was also formulated in an attempt to define the artistic and social identity of what the great Song poet and calligrapher Su Shi (1037–1101) referred to as *shiren hua* (scholar's art), in contradistinction to that of the professional painter and calligrapher. Where professional artists were dependent upon and sought the patronage of others for their livelihood, the literatus engaged in the practice of painting and calligraphy as means of self-cultivation, self-expression and social exchange with other, like-minded scholars. To this end, the literati style placed less emphasis on the descriptive depiction of nature, choosing rather to foreground the expressive potentialities of a more 'calligraphic' handling of the brush. A key tenet of literati aesthetics, the claim of equivalence between literati painting and poetry, appears in an inscription written by Su Shi on a painting by the great Tang poet Wang Wei: 'When one savors Mo-chieh's [Mojie's] poems, there are paintings in them, /When one looks at Mo-chieh's pictures, there are poems' (Bush 1971: 25), became one of the defining features of the literati aesthetic.

Song literati aesthetic theory discounted the mere technical skill of the professional painter to represent nature, in favour of what would come to be termed *xieyi*, 'to sketch, or paint ideas'. Terms such as *chu* (mood or flavour) and *pingdan* (plain tranquility) figure prominently in the writings of Mi Fu (1052–1107) and his son, Mi Yuren (1086–1165). These aesthetic terms identify the emotionally nuanced *yi* ('quality', or 'idea') of a scene, which can only come to artistic expression through the cultivated sensibilities of the literatus. For example, in Mi Fu's opinion: 'When Chu-jan [Zhuran] was young, he made many [forms like] 'alum lumps'; when he was older, in his tranquility (*pingdan*) the flavor (*chu*) was lofty' (Bush 1971: 68). *Pingdan* is 'a simplicity with underlying depth' (Bush 1971: 72).

During the succeeding Mongol Yuan dynasty (1260–1368), literati theory consciously stressed the non-professional status of the scholar-painter and the expressive, non-representational style of literati painting. There were two schools of literati aesthetics: classicist and individualist. Zhao Mengfu (1254–1322), a brilliant painter and calligrapher, is identified with the classicist position. A traditionalist, Zhao Mengfu stressed the importance of *guyi*, or the 'sense of antiquity':

> A sense of antiquity is essential in painting. If there is no sense of antiquity, then although a work is skillful, it is without value. Modern painters only know how to use the brush in a detailed manner and apply colours abundantly, and then think that they are competent artists. The fact is that if a sense of antiquity is lacking, all types of faults appear throughout a work, and why should one look at it? What I paint seems to be summary and rough, but connoisseurs realize that it is close to the ancients, and so consider it beautiful.
>
> (Bush 1971: 121–2)

A more individualist position is asserted by such reclusive scholar-painters as Wu Zhen and Ni Zan

(1301–74). Often, as in the following colophon by Ni Can (dated 1368), there is a self-conscious affirmation of the status of literati painting as merely 'ink-play' (*moxi*) in which great liberty is taken in the rendering of motifs in the interest of expressing the artist's mood:

> Chang I-chung [Zhang Yizhong] always likes my bamboo paintings. I do bamboo simply to express the untrammeled spirit (*yiqi*) in my breast. Then how can I judge whether it is like something or not; where its leaves are luxuriant or sparse, its branches slanting or straight? Often when I have daubed and rubbed awhile, others seeing this take it to be hemp or rushes. Since I cannot bring myself to argue that it is truly bamboo, then what of the onlookers? I simply do not know what sort of things I-chung is seeing.
>
> (Bush and Shih 1985: 280)

In the Ming dynasty (1368–1644), China is once again under native rule. Aesthetic theory as well as artistic practice come to take on an art historical dimension, as scholar-painters explicitly re-assert their social and artistic identity within a lineage of literati painters and calligraphers that is traced back through the Yuan and Song to the patriarchs of the tradition, Wang Wei, Dong Yuan and Zhuran. Towards the end of the Ming, this tendency culminates in the formulation of the theory of the 'Northern and Southern Schools' of painting (*nanbei pai*). Attributed to Dong Qichang (1555–1636), this theory systematically establishes the canon of literati painting and calligraphy (the Southern School) as the orthodox tradition for future generations of scholar-painters.

Dong Qichang formulates an aesthetic theory and artistic practice that synthesizes the classicist and individualist tendencies of the preceding Yuan dynasty. For the late Ming master, the proper approach to the canonical art of the past is one of a 'creative imitation' (*fang*) and 'transformation' (*bian*) within one's own personal style in a way that will allow one to speak with authority to the historical and art historical conditions of the present. Dong Qichang writes:

> Chu-jan [Zhuran] followed [imitated] Tung Yuan [Dong Yuan], Mi Fu followed Tung Yuan, Huang Kung-wang [Huang Gongwang] and Ni Tsan [Ni Can] both followed Tung Yuan. It was all the same Tung Yuan, but there several [versions of his style] did not resemble each other. If another kind of painter had done it, it would have been just like a copy. How could anything done that way be transmitted down through the ages?
>
> (Cahill 1982: 123)

It is precisely through an interpretive re-inscription or 'embodiment' of the 'orthodox' tradition within his own body of artistic expression, that the scholar-painter, sanctioned by the past, comes to signify himself in the present. Dong Qichang's notions of *shenhui* (communion of the spirit), *fang* (creative imitation) and *bian* (transformation) established the basis for both the Orthodox and Individualist Schools of literati painting in the Qing dynasty (1645–1912).

See also: AESTHETICS; AESTHETICS, JAPANESE; ART WORKS, ONTOLOGY OF; ARTISTIC EXPRESSION; POETRY

References and further reading

Acker, W.R.B. (1954) *Some T'ang and Pre-T'ang Texts on Chinese Painting*, Leiden: Brill. (A translation of early Chinese texts on painting.)

* Barnhart, R. M. (1964) 'Wei Fu-jen's *Pi Chen T'u* and the Early Texts on Calligraphy', *Archives of the Chinese Art Society of America* 18: 13–25. (Important discussion of early writings on calligraphy.)

* Bush, S. (1971) *The Chinese Literati on Painting: Su Shih (1037–1101) to Tung Ch'i-ch'ang (1555–1636)*, Cambridge, MA: Harvard University Press. (Systematic survey of literati theories of painting.)

* Bush, S. and Shih Hsiao-yen (eds) (1985) *Early Chinese Texts of Painting*, Cambridge, MA: Harvard University Press. (Thematically arranged compilation of translations of Chinese writings on art.)

* Cahill, J. (1966) 'Confucian Elements in the Theory of Painting', in A. Wright (ed.) *The Confucian Persuasion*, Stanford, CA: Stanford University Press, 115–40. (Discussion of Confucian aspects of Chinese painting.)

* —— (1982) *The Distant Mountains: Chinese Painting of the Late Ming Dynasty, 1570–1644*, New York: Weatherhill. (Thorough discussion of late Ming painting.)

Driscoll, L. and Toda, K. (1935) *Chinese Calligraphy*, Chicago, IL: The University of Chicago Press. (The first systematic discussion of Chinese calligraphy in English.)

* Hall, D.L. and Ames R.T. (1987) *Thinking Through Confucius*, Albany, NY: State University of New York. (A most important discussion of Confucian ways of thought.)

* Hay, J. (1983) 'The Human Body as a Microcosmic Source of Macrocosmic Values in Calligraphy', in S. Bush and C. Murck (eds) *Theories of the Arts in China*, Princeton, NJ: Princeton University Press, 74–102. (Important discussion of the relation of

Chinese medical treatises and early theories of calligraphy.)
* Lau, D.C. (trans.) (1992) *The Analects*, Hong Kong: The Chinese University Press. (A standard translation of this Confucian classic.)
* Ledderose, L. (1979) *Mi Fu and the Classical Tradition of Chinese Calligraphy*, Princeton, NJ: Princeton University Press. (A thorough discussion of the formation and transmission of the Classical tradition of Chinese calligraphy.)
* Liu, J.J.Y. (1975) *Chinese Theories of Literature*, Chicago, IL: University of Chicago Press. (A thorough study of the different theories of Chinese literature.)
  Munakata, K. (1974) *Ching Hao's Pi-fa-chi: A Note on the Art of Brush*, Ascona: Artibus Asiae Publishers. (A translation and discussion of an important early treatise on Chinese landscape painting.)
* —— (1983) 'Concepts of Lei and Kan-lei in Early Chinese Art Theory', in S. Bush and C. Murck (eds) *Theories of the Arts in China*, Princeton, NJ: Princeton University Press, 105–31. (A study of the role of the concept of 'categorical correlation' in early Chinese theories of art.)
  Owens, S. (1992) *Readings in Chinese Literary Thought*, Cambridge, MA: Harvard University Press. (A meticulously annotated translation of seven major works in Chinese literary thought.)
* Tu Wei-ming (1983) 'The Idea of the Human in Mencian Thought: An Approach to Chinese Aesthetics', in S. Bush and C. Merck (eds) *Theories of the Arts in China*, Princeton, NJ: Princeton University Press, 57–73. (An informative discussion of key terms in the philosophy of Mencius and their implications for Chinese aesthetics.)
* —— (1985) *Confucian Thought: Selfhood as Creative Transformation*, Albany, NY: State University of New York Press. (An important discussion of the concept of selfhood in Confucian thought.)
* —— (1979) 'Ultimate Self-Transformation as a Communal Act: Comments on Modes of Self-Cultivation in Traditional China', *Journal of Chinese Philosophy* 6: 237–46. (A discussion of the concept of 'self-cultivation' in Confucian thought.)
* van Gulick, R.H. (1969) *The Lore of the Chinese Lute*, 2nd revised edn, Tokyo: Tuttle. (A study of the role of the lute in Chinese culture.)
* Yu, P. (1987) *The Reading of Imagery in Chinese Poetic Tradition*, Princeton, NJ: Princeton University Press. (A thorough study of the role of imagery in Chinese poetry.)

STEPHEN J. GOLDBERG

AESTHETICS, FEMINIST

see FEMINIST AESTHETICS

AESTHETICS IN ISLAMIC PHILOSOPHY

The major Islamic philosophers produced no works dedicated to aesthetics, although their writings do address issues that contemporary philosophers might study under that heading. The nature of beauty was addressed by Islamic philosophers in the course of discussions about God and his attributes in relation to his creation, under the inspiration of Neoplatonic sources such as the pseudo-Aristotelian Theology of Aristotle, *a compilation based upon the* Enneads *of Plotinus. Considerations of artistic beauty and creativity were also addressed in works inspired by Aristotle's* Rhetoric *and* Poetics, *and Islamic philosophers also adapted some of Plato's views on literature and imitation, particularly those expressed in the* Republic.

On the whole, Islamic philosophers did not view artistic and literary creativity as ends in themselves. Rather, their interest was in explaining the relations of these activities to purely intellectual ends. In the case of poetics and rhetoric in particular, the emphasis in Islamic philosophy was pragmatic and political: poetics and rhetoric were viewed as instruments for communicating the demonstrated truths of philosophy to the populace, whose intellectual abilities were presumed to be limited. The medium of such communication was usually, although not necessarily, that of religious discourse. Islamic philosophers also devoted considerable attention to explaining the psychological and cognitive foundations of aesthetic judgment and artistic production within the spectrum of human knowledge. They argued that rhetoric and poetics were in some important respects non-intellectual arts, and that poetics in particular was distinctive in so far as it addressed the imaginative faculties of its audience rather than their intellects.

1 Beauty
2 Rhetoric and poetics
3 Imitation and imagination

1 Beauty

Plotinus' *Ennead* V.8, 'On Intelligible Beauty', was the basis for the fourth chapter of the Arabic compilation known as the *Theology of Aristotle* (see PLOTINUS §§1, 7). Against the background of the discussion of beauty in this text, Islamic philosophers developed the theme of the differences between sensible and intelligible beauty; and the love and pleasure associated with each.

The notion of intelligible beauty is included in the discussion of the names and attributes of God contained in al-Farabi's *al-Madina al-fadila* (The Virtuous City) (see AL-FARABI §2). Among the divine names al-Farabi lists 'beauty' (*al-jamal*), 'brilliance' (*al-baha'*), and 'splendour' (*al-zina*). Although the connotations of these terms are principally visual and hence sensible, al-Farabi argues that beauty in all things is primarily ontological: the more any being attains its final perfection, the more beautiful it is. From this he reasons that God, whose existence is most excellent, is the most beautiful of beings. Moreover, God's beauty surpasses all other beauty because it is essential, not accidental: the source of God's beauty is his own substance as defined by his self-contemplation, whereas created beauty derives from accidental and corporeal qualities that are not one with their own substances. Finally, al-Farabi argues that pleasure and beauty are intimately related, and that consequently God's pleasure, like his beauty, is beyond our comprehension. Pleasure is attendant upon the perception or apprehension (*idrak*) of beauty, and it increases in proportion to the beauty of what is perceived. Since God is the most beautiful of beings, and since his proper activity consists in an act of self-contemplation in which knower and known are completely one, the intensity and certitude of God's perception of his own beauty, al-Farabi reasons, must yield a pleasure of equal intensity. Moreover, since God's perception of his own beauty is the function of an eternal and uninterrupted act of contemplation, his pleasure, unlike ours, is continual rather than intermittent.

While al-Farabi's treatment of beauty in this context is principally an extension of his general account of divine transcendence and perfection along standard Neoplatonic lines, the development of the connection between beauty, perception and pleasure introduces a more properly aesthetic element into his account. Beauty in God, like beauty in the sublunar world, is found principally in things in so far as they achieve their proper perfection; when that beauty, be it sensible or intelligible, becomes an object of contemplation, it becomes in turn a source of pleasure for the one beholding it.

The contrast between sensible and intelligible beauty and the affective pleasures proper to each is developed in more detail in the *Risala fi al-'ishq* (Treatise on Love) by IBN SINA. In the fifth chapter of this work, Ibn Sina discusses the youthful love of external, bodily beauty. He opens his discussion of the love of beauty with a consideration of four principles, three of which pertain to the psychology of the human soul. The first is based upon Ibn Sina's characteristic view of the soul as a single substantial unity comprising a hierarchy of distinct powers. Either these powers can work together in harmony, in which case the lower will be ennobled by their cooperation with the highest faculty, that of reason, or the lower powers can rebel. These two possibilities are especially evident in the relations between reason and imagination (*al-takhayyul*) and the desires attendant upon them. The second principle is an elaboration upon the first: there are some human actions which pertain only to the bodily, 'animal' faculties within this hierarchy, including sensation, imagination, sexual intercourse, desire and aggression. Either these actions can be pursued in a purely animal fashion, or they can be transformed into something uniquely human under the guidance of reason.

Ibn Sina's third principle is that everything ordained by God has its own proper goodness and hence is the object of some legitimate desire; nonetheless, the lower desires can interfere with the higher, and thus their unlimited pursuit is to be avoided. Finally, Ibn Sina's fourth principle presents his definition of beauty in so far as it is the object of love for both the rational and animal souls: beauty (*al-husn*) consists in order (*al-nazm*), composition, (*al-ta'lif*) and symmetry (*al-i'tidal*). In the animal soul, this love of beauty is purely natural, arising either from instinct or from the simple pleasure of sensible perceptions. In the rational soul, however, love of beauty is more reflective, ultimately resting upon the recognition of the proximity of the beloved object to God, the First Beloved.

In applying these principles, Ibn Sina argues that there is what we might call an innate aesthetic sense implanted in every intellectual being (*al-'aqil*) which kindles in it a passionate desire for what is beautiful to behold (*al-manzar al-husn*). Despite the overall orientation of his discussion to the desire for the supra-sensible and purely intelligible beauty of God, Ibn Sina's remark here clearly pertains to the realm of sensible judgments. In fact, Ibn Sina even argues that such a desire for sensible beauty on the part of an intellectual being can be a noble thing, so long as the purely animal aspects of the desire are subordinated and the intelligible allowed to influence the sensible: such a purified aesthetic desire, according to Ibn Sina, results in a partnership (*al-shirka*) between the animal and rational souls. As evidence of this more general claim, Ibn Sina notes that even the most wise of humans can be preoccupied by a 'beautiful human form', and he implies that such a preoccupation is justified not only by the intrinsic aesthetic principles he has outlined, but also on the assumption that internal and external beauty and harmony mirror one another, unless the external beauty has been accidentally harmed or the internal character has been altered (for better or worse) by habituation. Finally, Ibn Sina also defends the desire for some sort of physical union with such a beloved, through kissing and caressing, although the expression of such an aesthetic impulse through sexual union is considered inappropriate except for the purpose of procreation, and where sanctioned by religious law.

2 Rhetoric and poetics

Most discussions of aesthetic themes by Islamic philosophers occur in the context of their considerations of the arts or rhetoric and poetics and the Aristotelian treatises devoted to these topics (see ARISTOTLE §29). Following a practice established by the sixth-century Greek commentators on Aristotle, these treatises were classified by the Islamic philosophers as parts of Aristotle's logical corpus, the Organon (see ARISTOTELIANISM IN ISLAMIC PHILOSOPHY). Thus the approach to these arts was not primarily aesthetic, but was focused on linguistic issues and the cognitive functions of rhetorical and poetic language. Rhetoric and poetics were classified as popular methods of instruction which produced less than certain states of belief in their audiences, who were assumed to be incapable of grasping the finer points of truly philosophical demonstration.

The Islamic philosophers did not explicitly limit the use of rhetoric and poetics to the spheres of religious discourse and political communication, however, and in their commentaries on Aristotle's *Poetics* some effort was spent on explaining the linguistic mechanisms whereby speech becomes figurative and metaphorical. IBN RUSHD in particular attempted to apply his understanding of Aristotle's views on poetics to the interpretation and criticism of Arabic poetry, and his *Talkhis kitab al-shi'r* (Middle Commentary on the *Poetics*) is full of citations of the works of well-known Arabic poets. Nonetheless, most of the interest taken by the Islamic philosophers in the arts of rhetoric and poetics stemmed from the foundations provided by these arts for explaining the relationship between philosophy and religion. The central books of al-Farabi's *Kitab al-huruf* (Book of Letters), along with Ibn Rushd's *Fasl al-maqal* (Decisive Treatise), are devoted to this theme, which is nicely summed up in the following passage from al-Farabi:

> And since religion only teaches theoretical things by evoking imaginings and by persuasion, and its followers are acquainted with these two modes of instruction alone, it is clear that the art of theology which follows religion is not aware of anything that is not persuasive, and it does not verify anything at all except by persuasive methods and statements.
>
> (*Kitab al-huruf*: 132)

The use of the language of 'imaginings' and 'persuasions' indicates a reference to the cognitive aims that the Islamic philosophers traditionally ascribed to the arts of rhetoric and poetics. Religion is a reflection of and handmaiden to philosophy, dependent upon philosophy as a copy is dependent upon its original. In understanding religion as an imitation of philosophy, the Islamic philosophers were consciously evoking the background of Aristotle's *Poetics* and Plato's *Republic* and the aesthetic theories which they developed through a creative blending of the respective views of their two ancient sources on the nature of imitation.

3 Imitation and imagination

Ibn Sina's *Risala fi al-'ishq*, discussed in §1, contains elements of a theory of aesthetic judgment that is also developed, from a somewhat different perspective, in his discussions of the psychological underpinnings of the art of poetics. In these discussions, aesthetic judgments are attributed to the faculty of imagination (*al-mutakhayyila*) and the related internal sense faculties that formed a part of the Islamic Aristotelians' development of the concept of imagination (*phantasia*) found in Aristotle's *On the Soul* and *Parva naturalia*. In turn the notion of imitation or *mimesis*, as found in Plato's *Republic* as well as in Aristotle's *Poetics*, was interpreted in terms of the functions of the imaginative faculty.

Al-Farabi, Ibn Sina and Ibn Rushd all identify the imagination as the faculty by which poets produce the figurative discourses proper to their art, and to which they appeal in their audience. These authors all contrast this use of and appeal to the imagination with the strictly intellectual and rational aim proper to all other modes of discourse and forms of reasoning. Al-Farabi's *Ihsa' al-'ulum* (*Catalogue of the Sciences*) provides one of the most extensive descriptions of the character of poetic imagination. Two aspects of poetic statements are emphasized by al-Farabi: their representation of their subjects in terms 'more noble or more debased' than they actually are, and their ability to bring about an appetitive, as well as a cognitive, movement in the audience. That is, by depicting a subject in terms of images that evoke a loathsome object, the poet is able to make the hearers feel aversion to the thing depicted, 'even if we are certain that it is not in fact as we imagine it to be' (*Ihsa' al-*

'*ulum*: 84). The reason for this aversion is directly linked to the poet's appeal to the imaginative faculty: 'for the actions of a human being frequently follow his imagination, more than they follow his opinion and his knowledge, because often his opinion or his knowledge are contrary to his imagination, whereas his doing of something is proportional to his imagining of it, and not to his knowledge or his opinion about it' (*Ihsa' al-'ulum*: 85).

A similar point is made by Ibn Sina in a number of texts. Ibn Sina frequently contrasts poetics with other modes of discourse by distinguishing the poet's attempt to produce an act of imagination (*takhyil*) in the audience with the more intellectual goal of seeking to produce an act of assent (*tasdiq*) to the truth or falsity of some claim. Ibn Sina, like al-Farabi, emphasizes the fact that such acts of imagination may often be contrary to what we know or believe to be the case, and he has a favourite example to illustrate this point: if someone tells us that 'honey is vomited bile', we are likely to lose our appetite for the honey before us, even if we are quite certain that the metaphor is literally false. Ibn Sina also echoes al-Farabi's claim that this ability of the imagination to affect our action is owing to the close link between the imaginative faculty and the appetitive motions of the soul.

The emphasis upon the imagination's ability to intervene in the soul's intellectual assent appears to have been directly linked by the Islamic philosophers to the theme of imitation. Al-Farabi, for example, appears to have made this connection in his *Ihsa' al-'ulum*, since he concludes his remarks on the poetic statement's ability to influence behaviour with the observation that this is 'what happens when we see likenesses imitative of the thing, or things resembling something else'. By the same token, throughout his *Talkhis kitab al-shi'r*, Ibn Rushd consistently interprets the Arabic term for *mimesis* (*muhaka*) as equivalent to *takhyil*, the evoking of an image. And in several passages, Ibn Sina contrasts imaginative utterances which 'imitate one thing by another' with imaginative utterances that happen to be literally true as well. Generally, then, for the Islamic philosophers 'imitation' appears to refer to those specific acts of imaginative representation in which the object is depicted in terms not proper to it, or more specifically, which portray it as better or worse than its actual state. In this way, imitation is linked not only or even principally to Aristotelian *mimesis*, but rather to Plato's notion of imitation as it relates to the theory of the Forms found in the *Republic* (see MIMESIS; PLATO §14).

This emerges clearly from a discussion in a little treatise by al-Farabi known simply as the *Kitab al-shi'r* (Book on Poetics). In this treatise, al-Farabi identifies imitation, along with metric composition, as constitutive of the very substance of poetry, with imitation the most crucial of the two elements. In order to explain the nature of poetic imitation, which occurs through language, al-Farabi draws heavily upon its similarities to imitation through action, for example, in the making of statues or in performative imitations. Here too imitation is said to have as its end to 'cause an imagining' of the imitated object, either directly or indirectly. The difference between direct and indirect imitation refers to the distance that separates the representation of the object from the reality itself, as illustrated in the example of a statue. For if an artist wished to imitate a person named Zayd:

> ... he might make a statue which resembles him, and along with this make a mirror in which he sees the statue of Zayd. And it might be that we would not see the statue itself, but rather the form of his statue in the mirror. And then we would know him through what imitates an imitation of him, and thus be two degrees removed from him in reality.
> (*Kitab al-shi'r*: 94–95)

The possibility of degrees of removal from the original is highly evocative of Plato's description of the possible states of removal from the Forms in the myth of the cave. Al-Farabi believes this possibility holds not only for artistic imitation, but also for linguistic imitation in poetry. While these associations are sometimes viewed pejoratively by the Islamic philosophers, as one might expect in the light of their Platonic resonances, this attitude is not universal. Al-Farabi himself reports noncommittally that many people consider the more remote imitation to be the more perfect and artistic, and here as in his other works he admits the power of imitative utterances for inciting humans to actions to which intellectual opinion or knowledge fail to move them.

It is IBN SINA (§8), however, who goes furthest in eliminating the negative overtones of these descriptions of poetic speech. In all but his most youthful writings, Ibn Sina emphasizes that the poet's concern with the imagination requires that his work be judged on its own terms and not on the level of intellectual judgments. Strictly speaking, poetic imaginings are neither true nor false; but in so far as poetic statements may imply corresponding intelligible propositions, they may possess a truth-value incidentally and secondarily. For this reason, although many will remain literally false, this need not be universally the case:

> And in general poetic [syllogisms] are composed of

premises which evoke images... be they true or false. Generally they are composed of premises to the extent that they possess a figure and a composition which the soul receives by means of what is in them of imitation and even of truth; for nothing prevents this [that is, their being true].

(*al-Isharat wa'l-tanbihat*: 80–1)

By the same token, Ibn Sina also allows for the use of poetic and imaginative discourse that is ethically neutral, seeking neither to ennoble nor to debase what is imitated, but rather merely aiming to 'provoke wonder through the beauty of the comparison' and thus to fulfil what could be termed a purely aesthetic end.

See also: AESTHETICS; ARISTOTLE §29; BEAUTY; AL-FARABI; IBN RUSHD; IBN SINA; IMAGINATION; MIMESIS; PLATO §14; PLATONISM IN ISLAMIC PHILOSOPHY; POETRY; RHETORIC

References and further reading

Black, D.L. (1990) *Logic and Aristotle's 'Rhetoric' and 'Poetics' in Medieval Arabic Philosophy*, Leiden: Brill. (Discusses the interpretation of these Aristotelian texts as works of logic; includes considerations of the themes of imagination and imitation.)

* al-Farabi (*c.*870–950) *al-Madina al-fadila* (The Virtuous City), ed. and trans. R. Walzer, *Al-Farabi on the Perfect State*, Oxford: Clarendon Press, 1985. (Text with facing translation of *al-Madina al-fadila*; includes detailed notes regarding al-Farabi's Greek sources and antecedents.)

* —— (*c.*870–950) *Kitab al-shi'r* (Book on Poetics), ed. and trans. A.J. Arberry, 'Farabi's Canons of Poetry', *Rivista degli Studi Orientale* 17 (1938): 267–78; ed. M. Mahdi, *Shi'r* 3 (1959): 91–6. (A curious little text presenting al-Farabi's understanding of Greek poetics.)

* —— (*c.*870–950) *Ihsa' al-'ulum* (Enumeration of the Sciences), ed. U. Amin, Cairo: Librairie Anglo-Égyptienne, 3rd edn, 1968. (Al-Farabi's discussion of different kinds of knowledge.)

* —— (*c.*870–950) *Kitab al-huruf* (The Book of Letters), ed. M. Mahdi, Beirut: Dar el-Mashreq, 1969. (Al-Farabi's account of the nature of logic and languages.)

Heath, P. (1992) *Allegory and Philosophy in Avicenna (Ibn Sina)*, Philadelphia, PA: University of Pennsylvania Press. (Ibn Sina's theories on allegory in the context of his philosophy as a whole; aimed at the non-specialist in philosophy and useful for audiences with primarily literary interests.)

* Ibn Rushd (*c.*1174) *Talkhis kitab al-shi'r* (Middle Commentary on the *Poetics*), trans. C.E. Butterworth, *Averroes' Middle Commentary on Aristotle's 'Poetics'*, Princeton, NJ: Princeton University Press, 1986. (A translation of Ibn Rushd's major work on this topic, with a helpful introduction.)

* —— (*c.*1179–80) *Fasl al-maqal* (Decisive Treatise), trans. G.F. Hourani, *Averroes on the Harmony of Religion and Philosophy*, London: Luzac, 1961. (Translation of Ibn Rushd's analysis of the links between religion and philosophy.)

* Ibn Sina (980–1037) *al-Isharat wa-'l-tanbihat* (Remarks and Admonitions), ed. J. Forget, Leiden: Brill, 1892; part translated by S.C. Inati, *Remarks and Admonitions, Part One: Logic*, Toronto, Ont.: Pontifical Institute of Mediaeval Studies, 1984. (The sixth and ninth 'methods' of this text discuss rhetoric and poetics.)

—— (980–1037) *al-Shifa'* (Healing), *Kitab al-shi'r*, trans. I.M. Dahiyat, *Avicenna's Commentary on the 'Poetics' of Aristotle*, Leiden: Brill, 1974. (Translation of the *Poetics* section of Ibn Sina's encyclopedic work, *al-Shifa'*, with excellent introductory essays; aimed at students of literary theory.)

* —— (980–1037) *Risala fi al-'ishq* (Treatise on Love), trans. E. Fackenheim, 'A Treatise on Love by Ibn Sina', *Mediaeval Studies* 7 (1945): 211–28. (A translation of the *Risala fi al-'ishq*.)

Kemal, S. (1991) *The Poetics of Alfarabi and Avicenna*, Leiden: Brill. (Various aspects of these two philosophers' views on poetics.)

—— (1996) 'Aesthetics', in S.H. Nasr and O. Leaman (eds), *History of Islamic Philosophy*, London: Routledge, ch. 56, 969–78. (Account of some of the main concepts of aesthetics, along with the leading controversies of the classical period.)

DEBORAH L. BLACK

AESTHETICS, JAPANESE

While the terms 'aesthetics' and 'philosophy' were only introduced into Japan during the Meiji Period (post 1868), Japanese culture has nevertheless witnessed the proliferation of various arts and theories of art for over a millenium. Given that 'aesthetics' generally connotes a scientific, often taxonomic approach to the inquiry into beauty and art, it may be preferable to consider Japanese art and theories of art from the perspective of different ways of artistry, rather than impose on it alien categories and assumptions. Even our understanding about what constitutes art must alter when we consider such arts as the production of incense, the tea ceremony, the martial arts or flower arrangement, most of which do not have precise analogues in the West; or if they do, are not considered arts alongside poetry, drama, music and painting.

One of the hallmarks of Japanese art is the emphasis on an awareness of nature. Not only is the natural world a rich storehouse of images and metaphors for use as subject matter, but it is also the means whereby the practices, values and aspirations of the art are defined. Significantly, art itself is seen to be catalysed directly by an encounter with the natural world. All living beings, we are told, are given to song. Yet the natural world also came to be a shibboleth in society among the members of the Japanese court, where a finely honed seasonal awareness came to attest to the refinement and sensibility of the individual. Of all the arts, poetry was seen as pre-eminent, in part because of poetry's powers to influence the spirits inherent in the natural world. Even the emphasis on place and place-names in Japanese art may be traced to an understanding of the Japanese landscape and language as sacredly imbued.

Another feature of Japanese art and theories of art is its orientation toward the human. In other words, we may define Japanese art as 'expressive–affective' in its configuration, stressing the experience of the artist as well as the response of the audience in encountering such a work. In fact, the two roles of artist and audience are related through the focus of the work of art, which usually frames a single moment and its quintessential significance, hon-i, which is unchanging. The quality which ideally characterizes both artist and audience is makoto or sincerity, underlining the point that the function of most Japanese art is to make us feel, rather than think.

As in a number of other traditions, Japanese ways of art are bound up inextricably with issues of religion and religious practice. Not only did Shintō animatism have a profound impact on how Japanese viewed their landscape as well as their own lives, but other imported systems of belief also influenced the course of artistic development, especially Buddhism. Buddhism darkened the hues of classical Japanese art by introducing ideas such as mappō (Latter Days of the Law), which saw the present as degraded and corrupt with respect to the past, and mujō (inconstancy), or the awareness of the ephemerality of this phenomenal world. In Mahāyāna Buddhism, art was perceived as a means of religious awakening, both in the case of poetry viewed as a form of intense meditation (shikan) and as parables whereby the truth could be disseminated obliquely (hōben). This paved the way for the pursuit of various forms of art to become a path (michi) to spiritual awareness. The relation of teacher and student in an art form closely resembled the relation of spiritual master to disciple, a feature which is echoed in the various 'secret' artistic treatises whose form, approach and significance suggest esoteric Buddhist manuals setting forth precepts for future generations.

Japanese theories of art also concerned themselves with various aesthetic ideals, distillations of the changing notion of beauty in each era. From aware (the beauty inherent in transience) and miyabi (courtly beauty) during the Heian Period (784–1185), to yūgen (the beauty of mystery and overtones) and sabi (the beauty of desolation and loneliness) in the medieval period, finally to wabi (the beauty of dearth and the humble) and karumi (the beauty of playful lightness) during the Edo Period (1600–1868), to mention only a few of the many ideals, we see an evolution of ideals as a response to cultural and historical change.

What becomes evident in any survey is the assumption of an underlying unity, as in the notions that the impulse toward art is natural and universal; that art functions as a bridge mediating the experience of artist and audience; that sincerity and heart are to be privileged above all other qualities; and that the discipline of art can be a means of spiritual awakening. But we also discover that ideas, such as play, are critical to all forms of art in Japan. Other issues have surfaced periodically in various art forms in the course of Japanese history, such as the struggle between tradition and innovation or the debate about art as spontaneous versus art as the product of careful cultivation (that is, the question of artifice in art), or the question of the singularity of Japanese art.

1 Art, poetry and the natural world
2 Art in its expressive–affective capacity
3 Art and its relation to religion
4 The historical development of traditional aesthetic ideals
5 The unity of the arts and the identity of the nation

1 Art, poetry and the natural world

Any sustained encounter with Japanese art or theories of art reveals the importance of the natural world, in the form of images of seasonal beauty, organic metaphors derived from natural objects and processes, and the identification of the internal psychological landscape with the natural world. Further, within the notion of the natural world lies embedded the importance of specific places within the landscape of Japan, which serve as touchstones to which art frequently alludes.

The twenty-one imperially commissioned anthologies of classical Japanese poetry (chokusenshū), compiled from the tenth to the fifteenth centuries, illustrate well the ubiquity of natural images and topics; each anthology devotes the first six books specifically to seasonal poems (two each for spring and autumn with one for summer and one for winter) and the remaining books, which focus on travel, love, sorrow and miscellaneous topics, are also replete with natural images. Similarly, most visual art focuses on scenes of natural beauty or wonder, ranging from the three classical beauty spots in Japan known as *nihon sankei* (Matsushima, Amanohashidate and Itsukushima) to typical scenes of enduring beauty (such as cranes amidst the pines) or seasonal beauty (brilliant coloured autumn foliage) to a single object, such as a fish, in the natural world. In fact, the Edo period court painter Tosa Mitsuoki in the *Honchō Gahō Taiden* (The Authoritative Summary of the Rules of Japanese Painting) stresses: 'Anyone who wishes to learn the art of painting should first study the way of things in nature' (Ueda 1967: 31).

Other arts, such as flower arrangement or garden design, have as their explicit object the representation in miniature of the natural world. For example, in the *Sakuteiki* (Notes on Garden Design), an eleventh-century manual by the courtier Tachibana no Toshitsuna, we are instructed from the outset:

> You should design each part of the garden tastefully, recalling your memories of how nature presented itself for each feature.... Think over the famous places of scenic beauty throughout the land, and ... design your garden with the mood of harmony, modelling after the general air of such places.
>
> (Slawson 1987: 57)

Even arts which seem somewhat removed from the natural world (music, calligraphy, incense, swordsmanship) view themselves in some measure as representational arts and use natural images and metaphors taken from life to describe elements of their art, especially the epiphanic culmination of beauty in their art, as in the notion of the Flower (*hana*).

Indeed, while it becomes imperative for the student of any art in Japan to begin by studying nature, it is clearly not enough to have a general feel of the natural world. Instead we are commended to study nature precisely and minutely. The greatest *haiku* poet, Matsuo Bashō, according to his disciple Hattori Dohō, once commented, 'If you wish to learn about a pine, go to a pine and if you wish to learn about bamboo, go to bamboo.' This notion was often echoed by later writers such as the modern poet Masaoka Shiki, who advocated a theory of poetry known as *shasei* (sketch from life) as embodied in his statement: 'If you have the time to sit at a desk and read a book on *tanka* [classical poetry], you should instead pick up a cane and go for a leisurely walk along a path in the woods' (Ueda 1983: 19).

In the course of Japanese cultural history, however, the natural world as embodied in art did not simply realistically reflect external reality. Instead, beginning especially in the courtly Heian Period (784–1185), certain elements of the natural world were deemed to be worthy of inclusion into art, such as cherry blossoms, maple leaves, warblers and frogs, while other natural beings and objects, such as mudsnails, onions, the flowers of maple trees and foliage of cherry trees, were either discarded or ignored entirely. These elements obviously do exist in nature, but courtly poetic decorum eliminated them from the vocabulary of art. Not until the radical rejection of canonical poetic vocabulary by the Kyōgoku–Reizei school in the fourteenth century do we see dogs appear in formal poetry, for example, and it is really with the advent of *haikai* (comic linked–verse poetry) that we see such lowly elements as fleas and lice included as a matter of course.

If the study of the natural world, however circumscribed, seems necessary to the production of good art, it is also true that the genesis of art itself traditionally emerges from a direct encounter with the natural world. For example, Ki no Tsurayuki's [Japanese] Preface to the *Kokinwakashū* (The Anthology of Japanese Poetry Ancient and Modern) (*circa* 905), the *locus classicus* of theories of art in Japan, begins:

> Japanese poetry has the human heart for its seed and burgeons forth into myriad words as its leaves. Human beings in this world confront a plethora of experiences, and, hence, they give utterance to the concerns in their hearts through the sights and sounds around them. When hearing the call of the warbler amidst the blossoms, and the cries of the frog dwelling in the waters, among all living beings, is there any who does not burst forth in song? It is poetry that effortlessly moves both heaven and earth, inspires pity in the unseen demons and gods around us, makes tender the connections between men and women, and consoles the hearts of raging warriors.
>
> (*Kokinwakashū*, in Rodd and Henkenius 1984)

For Tsurayuki, it is the natural world that inspires in us the desire to compose verse and in fact the poetic process itself is posited by him in organic terms, utilizing the metaphor of a plant sprouting.

Echoing the Chinese courtly predilection for appreciating the natural world seasonally (emphasizing autumn and spring), in part derived from the Daoist love of the natural world, Japanese poets typically have associated each season with particular flora and fauna (for example, plum blossoms with very early spring, bell crickets with autumn). Further, each season was paradigmatically embodied in a particular time of day as attested by the opening of the well-known *Makura no Sōshi* (Pillow Book) of the court lady Sei Shōnagon, which begins elliptically, 'In spring the dawn, in autumn the dusk...' An appreciation and understanding of seasonality became a kind of shibboleth among the members of the court, in which the truly refined and courtly sensibility could be discriminated from the uncouth and insensitive through the tacit acknowledgement of or subtle allusion to the modalities of the calendar. In *renga* (linked verse) poetry, flora and fauna became catalogued quite strictly according to the months of the year. For example, we are told that in verse associated with the fifth month, one may mention nightingales, early summer showers, orange flowers and irises. In *haiku* (or *hokku*) poetry, which developed out of *renga*, this seasonal association was mandated in the form of *kigo* or seasonal words, in which through allusion to the month, season, flora, fauna, climatic phenomena, or seasonal occurrence such as a festival, one would indicate the season.

In addition to the widespread use of natural images and topics in various forms of art, the natural world also functioned as a kind of dynamic and resonant mirror to the internal landscape of human feeling. While the notion of 'pathetic fallacy', or the according of human emotion to the natural world, has been derided by some in the Western tradition, notably John Ruskin in the nineteenth century, in Japan it has held a place of overarching importance. The 'pathetic fallacy' in the West implies a heavy-handed anthropomorphizing of nature, for example, 'the heavens weeping rain'. In the Japanese tradition, by contrast, we discover that the natural world and human world serve to mirror one another as well as catalyse parallel feeling in one another, in a much more nuanced fashion. Hence, while autumn with its inevitable desolation of life, withered leaves, and cries of insects comes to embody melancholy, as it often has in Western forms of art, it also serves as an externalized psychological mirror for the human heart, as attested in this illustration from *Genji Monogatari* (The Tale of Genji), when we are informed that following the death of the Emperor's beloved and his rejection of any substitute, 'His serving women were plunged into dew-drenched autumn'. It is both literally autumn and metaphorically autumn, and it is less that one catalyses the other than a parallel accord between the internal and external worlds.

The proliferation of natural imagery in Japanese art also incorporates a preoccupation with place – both generic, as in Tsurayuki's opening, and specific, as in Hiroshige Andō's series of woodblock prints (*ukiyo-e*) in the Edo Period (1600–1868) entitled 'Thirty-six Views of Mount Fuji'. Another illustration of the emphasis on specific place names may be found in the classical poetic rhetorical technique of *utamakura* (the citing of one or more traditional place names from the poetic catalogue, such as Mount Yoshino or Tatsuta River).

Beyond the superficial understanding of Japanese culture as intrinsically enamored of natural beauty, commentators have ascribed this concern with the natural world and with place to either spiritual or functionalist causes, in other words, as the result of the claims of the indigenous system of beliefs known as Shintō and its myriad divinities of the natural world (*kami*), or as the outcome of inhabiting a densely populated island nation, insular and keenly aware of land as precious. These surely have had an impact on the emergence of Japanese consciousness, but what remains obscure is what deeper relation art, especially verbal art, has with the natural world and the idea of place.

Of all the arts, poetry emerges as the most valued form, and one whose assumptions underlie each of the other arts. Further, as we consider the various forms of art that emerged – painting, the study and production of different kinds of incense, flower arranging or sculpture – we detect the importance of the textual and verbal components of each of these arts. The supremacy of poetry among the arts derives not only from its influence on and presence in each of the arts, but also from its extraordinary efficacy, as suggested by the far-reaching claims of the quotation from the preface of the *Kokinwakashū* above.

We may of course ascribe the ubiquity of natural imagery and the pre-eminence of poetry among the different arts to the influence of Chinese culture on Japan, and indeed many of the images that Tsurayuki uses are derived from the Great Preface to the Chinese classic the *Shijing* (Book of Songs), but even in the earliest poems as represented in the oldest texts (*Man'yōshū*, *Kojiki*, *Engi Shiki*) which betray relatively little trace of sinification, we may detect a preoccupation with poetry itself and its manifold powers. Tsurayuki notes in his preface the universality of poetry and how the impulse to sing is shared by all life, but alludes only offhandedly to how poetry is able to accomplish these things, as he speaks of poetry moving the hearts of gods and demons.

Apart from the hierarchy among arts in the course of Japanese cultural development to which we have already alluded, it is generally serious art, which demonstrates a concern with public conventions, that is privileged over comic or aberrant art, which is personal or idiosyncratic in nature. The folklorist-literary scholar Orikuchi Shinobu deduces from all of this that the genesis of poetry arose indeed from the intersection between art and nature, though not simply from lyrical rapture amidst the blossoms, but from ancient word-charms and spells, thought to have been bequeathed by the gods to human society to effect certain results in the natural world (prosperous harvests, purification, exorcism).

In support of this view, many have cited the famous passage in the *Kojiki*, which discusses the origin of the performing arts (drama–dance–mime) in the form of *Nō*, as illustrated by the gods themselves. In this episode, the Sun Goddess, Amaterasu Ōmikami, having been perturbed, has shut herself into a cave thereby relegating the world to darkness. The gods having tried various manoeuvres to persuade her to come out to no avail, another divinity, Ama no Uzume, manages to lure her out by means of a song and dance she performs while in a state of abandoned divine possession. This distracts the gods from their predicament, inspires curiosity in the Sun Goddess and causes all to become engrossed in her performance. It is through the clever and beguiling use of art that order is restored to the world and that the gods of the land themselves have been moved and reconciled. But while this narrative illustrates the placative function of verbal art in dealing with *kami* (spirits inhabiting the natural world), in other words its rhetorical ability to persuade the gods to alter their course of action, as well as suggesting song as a medium familiar to the gods, it does not account for the emphasis on place.

According to the literary critic Konishi Jin'ichi (1984), the problem of place may be resolved through an understanding of the idea of *kotodama* or 'word-spirit'. Various utterances, which could only be pronounced in particular contexts and particular places that were called *kotoage*, unleashed the power of the *kotodama* which could be either malign or benevolent. It was not their semantic or rhetorical capacity that produced these effects, but rather simply the utterance of those syllables by a human voice. He argues that the concept of *kotodama* (and hence the construction of such a term), as opposed to the living enactment of it in archaic Japan, only came much later after Japanese poets in their intercourse with the continent became aware of the singularity of their beliefs about language and the natural world. Since *kotodama* were only efficacious when released by the utterance of *kotoage* in purely Japanese language (with no foreign loan-words) and within Japan itself, there comes about a new understanding of the natural world and the places within it, whose names alone can activate the mighty powers inherent in language.

2 Art in its expressive–affective capacity

A number of critics have pointed out that virtually all Japanese art and theories of art betoken an expressive–affective orientation. In other words, rather than privileging the relation of a work to nature (art as representational or mimetic) or as an elaborate structure whose significance inheres principally in its formal properties, Japanese art emphasizes the relationship between the artist and the work of art as well as the relationship between the work of art and its audience.

More often than not, we are told, artists produce works, not because of a desire to assert themselves but because of an inability to restrain themselves. Tsurayuki's female narrator comments in his fictionalized diary *Tosa Nikki* (Tosa Diary):

> I do not set down these words, nor did I compose the poem, out of mere love of writing. Surely both in China and Japan art is that which is created when we are unable to suppress our feelings.
>
> (Miner *et al.* 1985: 7)

We sense an urgency about art: as humans we are filled with emotions generated by experiences in this world, and we must express them in the form of art.

At its base, we may say that Japanese art is lyrical in nature; it highlights the emotional responses of an individual, or the group in the voice or person of an individual, to the natural world around. Hence we see comparatively little in the way of abstract, didactic or gnomic art, other than explicitly religious or heuristic works such as visual representations of Buddhas or neo-Confucian homilies. The principal function of most art is not to instruct directly (though the very cultivation of art may be seen as uplifting to character or, put more precisely, the pursuit of art necessitates the cultivation of a high moral discipline), but rather to allow the individual to manifest an outpouring of feelings in a resonant fashion that serves as gratifying release.

The focus of many works of art is the revelation of a single moment of being, to use Virginia Woolf's phrase, in which the intensity and purity of feeling and experience are transmuted into a thing of beauty. There is a spontaneity and singularity about the artistic moment, which of course is the culmination of much concentrated study of the art form, and which at particular moments of artistic inception allows the artist to produce a masterpiece without hesitation or conscious forethought. What a work of art offers us ideally is not the opportunity to uncover or unearth the mind or personality of the artist but the quintessential distillation of an authentic human experience amidst the natural world. It is not validity but sincerity (*makoto*) that we prize. Analogously, the affective relation between a work and its audience is intended not so much to make us think, but to make us feel. As a result, a tacit connection is effected between artist and audience which is mediated by the work of art.

Some critics and theorists structure their texts specifically towards the production of art such as Ki no Tsurayuki while others, such as ZEAMI, the great playwright and theorist of *Nō* theatre, stress the role of the audience in its appreciation of art as well as the development of the artist. The more cultivated the audience, the greater the inducement for artists to express themselves well. Thus, Zeami insists: 'It is crucial for the actor to perform in such a fashion so as to harmonize with the feelings of the nobility' (Rimer and Yamazaki 1984: 19). What is idealized is the reciprocal relation between the artist of impeccable sensibility and training and the audience, equally trained and possessed of a discriminating awareness, a relation which allows for the intuited sharing of fundamental experience.

While the focus of the artistic work is understood to be expressive–affective in its orientation, this does not preclude the notion of art as imitation (*monomane*). For example, Ōkura Toraakira in his *Warambegusa* (For My Young Successors) articulates the ideals of *kyōgen* theatre (comic interludes performed in between the more serious and weighty *Nō* dramas), asserting: 'More than anything else *kyōgen* is an art of imitation.... It imitates all kinds of things in this world' (Ueda 1967: 102). However, while *monomane* sounds very much like the idea of mimesis, in fact it suggests less a connection with the object as it exists in the world, than the idealized essence of the object as realized in the realm of art. Zeami mentions the principle, 'first truly become the thing you are performing' (Rimer and Yamazaki 1984: 77), but he does not mean a performance along the lines of method-acting. By 'the thing', he means the reified and transmuted kernel of the role, what is sometimes called *hon-i*, or essential character as codified by artistic conventions, not the role as it is embodied in an actual being in society. Though *hon-i*, derived from a Chinese term *pen-i*, originally meant something like 'individual will or aspiration', it came to connote 'poetic intent', and thence 'fundamental character or nature'. As examples, the *hon-i* of cherry blossoms is embodied by beautiful transience, of travel by misery and loneliness; of age by regret and nostalgia. The artist in encountering the outside world does not in fact confront the real world, but rather the world of *hon-i* or codified essences, those very essences recognized as such by the audience. This is what Chikamatsu Monzaemon, the supreme playwright and arbiter of the Edo-period puppet theatre, *ningyō jōruri*, meant when he asserts, 'Art is that which exists in the slender gap between truth and falsehood.'

The notion of *hon-i* of course represents in part the world of accreted tradition against and atop of which artists inscribe their own work, and poses a critical dilemma about how artists can be authentic about their experience even as their vision is filtered through the screen of tradition. However, *hon-i* is understood to be more than just convention; it is what MOTOORI NORINAGA referred to as 'the heart of things' (*koto no kokoro* or *mono no kokoro*), that essential nature that is not subject to the vicissitudes of time (see KOKORO). Nevertheless, throughout the course of Japanese artistic development we may detect a fruitful tension in the form of tradition versus innovation that is crucial to the expressive–affective orientation, given the inevitable changes that each new generation must confront. Tsurayuki notes at the end of his preface to the *Kokinwakashū*, 'Those who know poetry and who understand the heart of things will look up to the old and admire the new as they look up to and admire the moon in the broad sky' (*Kokinwakashū*: 47). The medieval poets and critics, Fujiwara Shunzei and his son Teika, also address this issue in their well-known exhortation 'old words, new heart'. According to Bashō's disciple Kyorai:

> Of the *haiku* there is a style that remains unchanged for thousands of years. There is also a style that prospers only for a time. These are the two poles of the late Master's teaching, and they are really the same in essence. They are the same, because they both resort to a single source, the poetic spirit.
>
> (Ueda 1967: 147)

Another implication of the emphasis on the expressive–affective orientation, the human aspect of the work of art, is the overriding importance placed on process as opposed to telos, goal or end. Almost all treatises on art in Japan discuss in great detail how artists can go about cultivating their art, rather than enumerate precisely the constituent features of a great work of art in the abstract. The twentieth-century philosopher KUKI SHŪZŌ speaks of the traditional Japanese emphasis on process when he discusses the notion of *bitai* (coquetry) as a cultural ideal and how its evocation of *kanōsei* (possibility) makes it endlessly alluring. He speaks of how after the devastating 1923 Kanto earthquake, the Japanese quickly went about rebuilding the subway in the city of Tokyo, knowing of course that it could be destroyed at any point in time, to the amazement of Europeans for whom it seemed a doomed effort. Kuki explains that it is the process of construction and cultivation, not the end result, that sustains the Japanese will. Hence, he argues that from a Japanese perspective, the position of Sisyphus in Greek myth is quite a desirable one, since he will always be in the midst of a task, never having to confront the bleakness of completion or perfection.

3 Art and its relation to religion

The indigenous system of beliefs known as Shintō had a significant impact on the development of the arts in Japan (see SHINTŌ) and, as some believe, literally gave rise to them in the form of the *kotodama*. Other forms of art associated with Shintō animism (which has been described as a pre-animistic system which features belief in spiritual entities with non-human traits) include *kagura* (god's music), *kamiasobi* (god's dances), both of which contributed to the development of Nō theatre, *norito* (poem-like liturgical texts) and *setsuwa*, or short mythic narratives dealing with the deities and various creation themes, often orally related by professional narrators known as *kataribe*.

As an aside, the *kataribe*, who were often female, were thought to represent a transitional phase in verbal art between the stage of oral transmission and the advent of writing. In a world where memory was being displaced by written text, the *kataribe* functioned as a repository of group memories of ancient narratives until finally they were almost entirely displaced by written accounts in the highly literate late ninth century, when their only remaining function was limited to recitation of specific works at ceremonial times. According to Orikuchi Shinobu, these narratives, as well as poetry and proverbs, originated in the incantatory utterances of shamanesses who were possessed by the spirits of the *marebito*, or the visitor gods, who would descend at regular intervals into the human realm from the Land of the Eternal. Eventually, of the incantations divided into *ji* and *kotoba* sections (third-person and first-person assertions by the god respectively), the former developed into narrative art and the latter into poetry and proverbs. The narratives, no longer seen as the actual words of the gods, came to be related by female *kataribe*, presumably the secularized descendents of and successors to shamanesses who left their ancestral villages, and thus was born narrative art from religious beliefs.

Even more important was the impact of Buddhism on the arts of Japan, in terms of form, practice and understanding (see BUDDHIST PHILOSOPHY, JAPANESE). It is noteworthy to remember that Buddhism was also the principal vehicle whereby writing was introduced into and popularized in Japan. Further, both the Tendai and Shingon sects, but especially Shingon with its emphasis on the symbolic understanding of essential truth as conveyed in art, had a formidable impact on the development of courtly arts from the latter part of the ninth century onwards. Various arts were associated specifically with the religious practices of Buddhism, such as carved wooden statues of Buddhas and Bodhisattvas, the *bussokusekika* (the Buddha's Footprint Poems at Yakushiji in Nara), painted *mandaras* (cosmic diagrams of Buddhist figures), *jigoku-hen* (frightening hell screens designed to chasten unbelievers), and the texts of *Gozan bungaku* (the heavily Chinese-influenced literature of the Zen Buddhist monks of Kyoto and Kamakura during the Kamakura–Muromachi Period). While Jōdo (Pure Land) and Nichiren Buddhism held considerable sway over the populace, it was the esoteric sects as well as Zen that had the greatest influence on the practice of poetics and the development of the arts.

The two Buddhist concepts *mappō* and *mujō* substantially altered the outlook of poets and artists in the medieval period. *Mappō* (the Latter Days of the Law), known in Sanskrit as *Kaliyug* (the Dark Age), represents in the cyclical time of Mahāyāna Buddhism the final corrupt, decadent stage of life in which a Buddha is needed to be born on earth to enlighten the misguided and transmit the Law for the cycle to begin anew. In poetry and poetics, this resulted in the glorification of the past as a kind of Golden Age and the dismissal of the present as a barbarous era in a dismal state of decline. Hence, throughout poetic treatises and works of art we see evidence of this idea in the disdain shown for the present state of affairs and the nostalgia and reverence for the past. *Mujō*, the inconstancy of the phenomenal realm, like the earlier notion of *hakanasa* (ephemerality), underscored change as ineluctable in this world, but presented it in a much darker fashion. It no longer functions as an emblem of the beautiful, but that which we as deluded beings refuse to acknowledge, thereby bringing misery and suffering on ourselves (see MUJŌ). Both *mappō* and *mujō* discomfit us with our place in the present world and foreshadow the need for transcendence.

The paradoxical question of how art, itself rooted in the phenomenal world, can help us to transcend the unrelenting realities of this realm, was thought to be resolved through the evocation of the ideal of *hōben* (skill in means or expediency). In the *Hokkekyō* (Lotus Sutra), the central scripture of Tendai Buddhism, Buddha is asked how one goes about teaching the truth to those ignorant of it and hence unable to recognize truth as truth. Buddha responds with the idea of *hōben* or heuristic aids, such as parables. Even though these are fictions, he explains, ironically they can help the ignorant to grasp some notion of truth, which eventually will lead to complete understanding. Thus, writers in the middle ages were fond of quoting the Tang Chinese poet Bo Zhuyi's famous phrase, *kyōgen kigo* (wild words and fancy phrases) as alluding to the possibilities of art as *hōben*: 'For many years have I hoped one thing, that my actions in this world and the sins resulting from my wild words and fancy phrases shall become ever after a means of paying homage to the Law and be allied to the dissemination of Buddha's truth. Let the countless Buddhas of the Three Realms hearken unto this.'

Thus even art, which does not seem to promulgate religious truth explicitly, may be seen to further the teachings of Buddha. Even a genre perceived to be as frivolous as *monogatari* or narrative may at heart be an instrument for Buddha's teachings. Art, though fictive, can serve to guide an audience indirectly to the higher truth and often with greater efficacy than any tract or scripture. This offers an interesting counterpoint to Sir Philip Sidney's *An Apology for Poetry*, in which he defends art against the criticism that as fiction it lies, by pointing out that since fiction avers nothing, it cannot be equated with falsehood.

Beyond its function as a conduit to truth, art may also serve as a direct means of religious awakening as addressed in the idea of poetry as a form of *shikan*, or the Tendai practice of intense and concentrated meditation. According to the *Maka Shikan* (Great Cessation and Insight), one of the three great texts of the Tendai sect, by desisting from the impulse towards discrimination between objects in the world and concentrating on the integrity of each, we can gain insight into our own inner nature. Fujiwara Shunzei applies the insights garnered from this text to the composition of poetry. Poetry in this form of meditation allows us to dissolve polarities and distinctions, recognizing them as having significance only in the illusory phenomenal world, and in so doing, allows for a fundamental unity to be realized between the poet and the object. Thus, the very act of poetic composition as *shikan* enables us to achieve a higher spiritual awareness of self.

Just as Tendai laid the groundwork for Zen, so too did the notion of *shikan* shape the notion of *michi* (path or way) in its implications for the arts. By the fourteenth century, we see a number of arts subscribing to the Zen notion that any vocation, if pursued fervidly and with a purity of heart, can be a means to enlightenment in the form of *satori* or sudden awakening in this life. These include poetry, tea, flower arrangement, *Nō* theatre, martial arts such as the art of the sword, and a host of others. What is significant about a *michi* is that it requires a singular devotion to the art form, the eschewal of base behaviour, a humble, almost monastic lifestyle, and the realization that the purpose of such a pursuit is neither power nor fame, nor any other mere gratification of the senses, but rather a lofty and transcendent goal which requires us to see into ourselves.

Following a *michi*, whether it be the way of *renga* or calligraphy, does not imply a solitary pursuit, but, more often than not, the attaching of oneself as a student to a teacher or master. The organization of most arts in Japan revolves around specific schools or lines of artistic inheritance known as *ie*. In many ways, this is the legacy of esoteric Buddhism with its emphasis on secret transmission of the innermost truths strictly from master to chief disciple. Just as Saichō (Dengyō Daishi) dispensed precepts for spiritual awakening to his chief disciples (*endonkai*), so too are artistic precepts passed through the *ie* system from master to disciple. Thus, we encounter the practice of *hidensho* or secret treatises, which purport to divulge the ultimate truth that can only be understood by those few chosen initiates. These were often written in a dense and elliptical style that precluded the ignorant from understanding the hidden implications. The *hidensho* were not substitutes for the master's teachings, but instead, since they consisted of generalized truths that could only be understood only by those already initiated into the arcane mysteries of the art, were meant to be passed down through the generations ensuring that the art form continued. In addition, they were proof in themselves of one's having received the mantle of authority in the particular art form. Thus, during the decades that followed the death of the great Fujiwara Teika, his descendents continued to dispute fiercely among themselves about the ownership of his writings and documents, which were simultaneously both a poetic and political inheritance.

The relation between teacher and student in the arts represents an almost sacred bond in which students abase themselves before the master as proof of their readiness to learn, paralleling the relation of monk to spiritual master. To belong to an *ie* headed by a lineal master means to subscribe to its rules, its practices, its dicta, and moreover to learn, not by reading or imagining or experimenting, but rather by direct emulation of the master's teachings. This teaching invariably takes the form of *kuden* or oral transmission, which is seen as far superior to anything transmittable in writing. Further, within esoteric traditions, *kuden* referred to those hermetic teachings, secret in nature, which revealed the ultimate truths. Given the importance placed on *kuden*, many traditional treatises in Japan take the form of *mondo* or catechistic question and answer, as if representing as closely as possible the actual oral transmission.

Though evident in certain periods, in certain genres and in the work of particular artists, both Confucianism and Daoism had much less direct influence than did Buddhism on the course of Japanese poetics and the arts. The didactic strain characteristic of Confucianism does surface on occasion, as in Edo Period literati homilies designed to 'praise virtue, castigate vice' (*kanzen choaku*), a phrase deriving from Confucianism that appears as early as Shōtoku Taishi's *Jūshichijō Kempō* (Seventeen Article Constitution) of 604 (see SHŌTOKU CONSTITUTION). Daoist ideas, while especially evident in certain of the writings of the Man'yō poets, become amalgamated with other forms of Japanese thought such as Zen, and thus manifests itself only indirectly in the general esteem for the natural world, and the borrowing of terms, such as the Chinese *feng-liu* as *fūryū*, or elegance (see below).

4 The historical development of traditional aesthetic ideals

When we look at pre-ninth century Japan, although we encounter a great body of art and poetry, we see little in the way of contemporary commentary on aesthetics and poetics. While later eras detect certain ideals implicit in this period, such as *makoto* (sincerity), *masuraoburi* (ideal of virility) or *man'yō-gokoro* (the Man'yō spirit), in fact these ideals are anachronistic and represent an attempt to instill conceptions of art somewhat removed from the period. What the idealization of these elements reveals is an Edo-period nostalgia for an imagined simpler, more straightforward time, which precluded any outside influence and any notion of transcendence.

One of the earliest commentators on art was the Buddhist monk KŪKAI (Kōbō Daishi), who in his *Bunkyō hifuron* (Secret Treasury of Poetic Mirrors) and *Bumpitsu genjinshō* (Essentials of Poetry and Prose) sought to introduce Chinese theories about verbal art into Japan. It is after this point that we detect the emergence of indigenous artistic ideals that, though indebted at some level to Chinese culture, represent singularly Japanese notions about art. The construction of aesthetic ideals arose mainly in the Heian Period as courtiers sought to codify matters of art into a coherent form that both set itself off from the domain of Chinese culture and art (principally of the Six Dynasties) and within Japan delineated the boundary line between those within and those outside the court.

Apart from critical terms, such as *kokoro* (heart), *kotoba* (words) and *sama* (style), one of the earliest ideals evident in Japan is *aware*, a term signifying poignant beauty that recurs a number of times in works such as *Genji monogatari* (a repository in fictional form for Heian responses to and understanding of art) and the imperially commissioned anthologies of poetry. In Heian Period usage, *aware* seems closely aligned with the idea of *hakanasa* or transience, suggesting the truism that what is sad is necessarily beautiful, and what is beautiful is sad. The notion of *kokoro* is central to the ideal of *aware*, since the capacity to be moved is a function of sensibility. In its approbation of *Genji* as the supreme work of fiction, the *Mumyōzōshi* (Nameless Writings), *circa* 1200, a treatise in the form of a dialogue on *monogatari* or narrative, cites numerous instances of *aware* such as Yūgao's death, Genji's exile and Fujitsubo's becoming a nun and taking the tonsure.

Our modern understanding of *aware* depends in large measure on the Edo commentator Motoori Norinaga's conceptualizing of it in the form of *mono no aware* (the pathos of things), often seen as analogous to the expression *lacrimae rerum*. He explains *aware* as originating in two cries of wonderment at the world, 'Ah', and 'Hare'. While he notes that originally *aware* was used of anything that moved the human heart, later it came to be associated exclusively with the miserable or wretched. For Norinaga, *aware* symbolized the sensitivity to temporal beauty that defines the experience of creating or appreciating art.

The overall aesthetic of the court, especially in the Heian period, was referred to as *miyabi* (also read sometimes as *ga* in its Sino-Japanese reading) or courtly beauty, a beauty that was ornate, brilliant, and characterized by elegance. This is the kind of beauty personified by the title character Genji himself: handsome, refined, well-versed in all the arts, graceful in all his actions. It implies what the Renaissance writer Castiglione referred to as *sprezzatura*, an elegant nonchalance, as well as a peerless sensibility. Closely allied with it was the notion of *fūryū*, from the Chinese Daoist term *fengliu*, which originally connoted the elegant world enjoyed by the Immortals consisting of music, poetry, wine, and the world of desire. *Fūryū*, whose characters were read also as *miyabi* in Japanese, emphasized a fashionable chicness, brilliantly realized as well by the figure of Hikaru Genji, the Shining One. *Miyabi*, needless to say, eschewed anything touched by ugliness, poverty, or corroded by age.

In the late Heian and early part of the Kamakura Period, we see a new set of ideals emerge, the most important of these being *sabi* and *yūgen*, as propounded by Fujiwara Shunzei and his son Teika among others. This new era was heralded by active civil strife from 1183–85 in which the imperial family, various noble clans and the major Buddhist monasteries fractured internally and, in the ensuing conflict, many were eventually decimated. Hence the tone of these new ideals was much darker and more tinctured by the Buddhist notion of the inconstancy (*mujō*) of this phenomenal and deluded world. *Sabi*, or the ideal of loneliness or desolation, remains one of the most enduring ideals in the course of Japanese cultural development, playing a significant role in various arts such as the tea ceremony, flower arrangement and brushed ink painting, as well as later forms of poetry such as the *haikai* of Bashō. *Sabi*, in sharp contrast to *miyabi*, is subdued, monochromatic in hue, and melancholic in tone. We see the opposition of these two ideals in this poem by Teika:

Miwataseba
hana mo momiji mo
nakarikeri
ura no tomaya no
aki no yugure

(As I gaze out, both cherry blossoms and maple leaves are absent, instead grass-thatched huts in the autumn gloaming.)

(*Shinkokinwakashū* 4: 363)

Instead of the gorgeous and conventional images of vernal and autumnal beauty, we are presented with an alternate image of isolated, unadorned, and barely discernible beauty. *Sabi* implicitly acknowledges the darkness of life, even as it reconstructs the misery into a thing of quiet beauty. While Shunzei also favored the ideal of *aware*, similar in content if not in tone or affect, the austerity of *sabi* became the hallmark of his work and this period in Japan. In the hands of later poets, such as Matsuo Bashō, *sabi* or loneliness became conflated with *sabi*, a homophonous word for rust, and thus is transformed into the antithesis of *miyabi*, the beauty of the extraordinary giving way to the beauty of the ordinary, the sere, the solitary.

Another ideal developed by Shunzei's son Teika in his early formulations was the notion of *yōen* or ethereal charm. This, like many other concepts, had its origin in Chinese poetics and signified a dreamy, feminine, winsome beauty of a sort associated with the delicacy of a fragrant blossom or the romance and magic of a spring evening. In its emphasis on transcendent possibility and the resonance of *yojō* or overtones, *yōen* is not unrelated to *yūgen*, perhaps the most profound and ineffable of all Japanese aesthetic ideals. *Yūgen*, the style of mysterious beauty or alternately mystery and depth, was originally a Buddhist term meaning 'obscure, dim, or deep', but was elevated by Shunzei into an aesthetic ideal suggesting great subtlety, complexity and reverberation. *Yūgen* portends an otherworldly atmosphere that hints at but never elucidates fully the possibility of transcendent vision.

Zeami also borrows the notion of *yūgen* from poetry and employs it in his discussions on drama, noting: 'Particularly in the *Nō*, *yūgen* can be regarded as the highest principle.' However, his understanding of it suggests more the mastery of elegant beauty and grace than what is suggested by the use of *yūgen* in poetry. Still, even in *Nō*, *yūgen* continues to represent an elusive ideal that is the culmination of artistic endeavour.

The cultural shifts of the fifteenth and sixteenth centuries foreshadowed the aesthetic ideals of the Edo period, with their emphasis on quotidian life amidst the newly urbanized lower social strata as embodied in the townsmen or *chōnin* class. Sen no Rikyū, the acknowledged master of *sadō* (or *chadō*), the tea ceremony, according to his student Nambo Sokei, preferred above all other ideals *wabi* or the beauty of impoverishment. He remarks, 'There should be a dearth of tea implements in the room', and advises that these few objects should be arrayed simply. Among the many revealing anecdotes related about him is the story of his deliberating mutilating a vase to use in tea ceremony as a reminder to us of the beauty inherent in the imperfect and the shabby.

Bashō, the *haiku* master, embraced the ideals of earlier ages, especially the notion of *sabi*, but sought to mitigate *sabi* first through the humanizing notion of *wabi* and then through the ideal of *karumi* (lightness). *Sabi*, with its unrelieved austerity and detachment, was in some ways as alien to the common people as the earlier *miyabi* had been, and hence Bashō sought to include the commonplace, the humble and the destitute, as well as the simple, the playful and the light-hearted, in his work in order to suggest a more encompassing aesthetic for his age. While *wabi* helped to convey a more humanistic and egalitarian ideal, in that by elevating the disfigured and the discarded we attest indirectly to the resilience and beauty of imperfect humanity, the notion of *karumi* or lightness proved to be central to his poetry in relieving the weight and darkness implied by *sabi*. Both *wabi* and *karumi* are evident in a verse such as this excerpted from a *haikai* sequence:

Te no hira ni
shirami hawasuru
hana no kage

(In the palm of my hand, the lice crawl forth, in the shade of cherry blossoms)

The humble image of lice, juxtaposed with the

traditionally exalted cherry blossoms, is framed by the human observer's eye and hand to produce a poem of considerable whimsy and poignancy.

One last major aesthetic ideal known as *iki* (the ideal of the chic or stylish) emerged in the late Edo period among the female entertainers of the cities of Edo. *Iki* paralleled the ideal of *sui* (written with the same character signifying essence), which dominated in western Japan, but was much less constrained, ornate and traditional as a fashion. *Iki* in its casual nonchalance and disdain for convention suited well the character of Edo, unburdened by many centuries of tradition, and came to symbolize the pragmatic surface coolness belying the sentiment welling up within, characteristic of this period dominated by urban, mercantile values.

5 The unity of the arts and the identity of the nation

Far more than the art and aesthetic theories of other cultures and traditions, those of Japan betray a remarkable uniformity in their underlying assumptions regarding the nature of art, its provenance and its aims. For example, one shared quality (not discussed above), the idea of playfulness, appears in virtually every art form from the comic narrative about the plump, middle-aged goddess Ama no Uzume luring the Sun Goddess from her cave by means of a lascivious primordial striptease, to the courtly game competitions known as *monoawase*, which involved the wagering of iris roots, pictures, poetry or virtually any object, to the various kinds of playful poetry including the courtly *oriku* or acrostic, the *darumauta* or nonsense poetry associated with Zen practices in the medieval period, and the satiric, often bawdy poetry known as *senryū* produced in the Edo period. While art is not always ironic or comic, the notion of art as serious play or pastime prevails across the various genres and modalities of artistic expression in Japan. Even the preference shown by the aristocratic elite for the gifted amateur in the arts, as opposed to the professional, while indeed betraying the influence of Chinese literati notions, also demonstrates this principle of play as being central to art in Japan. Play does not stand in opposition to *makoto* (sincerity); if anything, it attests to it.

Many schemas have been proposed for understanding Japanese art as an integrated unity. The literary critic Donald Keene, for example, offers us a formalist grid in which four qualities recapitulate the notion of beauty within the boundaries of Japanese art and aesthetics: suggestion, irregularity, simplicity and perishability. These can be associated with the ideals that arose in specific historic contexts (that is, *yojō* or *yūgen*; *wabi*; *sabi*; and *hakanasa* or *mujō*), but represent as well enduring concepts that characterize the landscape of Japanese art from tea ceremony to calligraphy to garden design to poetry.

By contrast, other schemas that have been proposed imply an ideological difference that functions to distinguish Japanese art from any other. Konishi Jin'ichi invokes a polar struggle in the tension between what he terms the poles of 'consummation' and 'infinity' in the ubiquitous human 'longing for the eternal'. *Ga*, or the aesthetic of the high and the refined which seeks perfection of form in the flowering of ideals already in existence (in other words, tradition), reflects this impulse toward consummation, whereas *zoku*, or the impulse toward infinity, is characterized by a preoccupation with the low, the vulgar and the popular, embracing innovation freely and with energy. During much of Japan's cultural history, *ga* was associated with the legacy, direct and indirect, of Chinese aristocratic culture whereas *zoku* frequently was associated with indigenous notions emerging from the common people. For Konishi, *ga* and *zoku* function not merely as aesthetic ideals but ideological poles, which have been naturalized in the context of Japanese society and thought and whose dynamic interaction in different eras is evident in the forms of cultural production.

The novelist Tanizaki Jun'ichirō, in his essay 'In'el Raisan' (In Praise of Shadows), also argues for a polarity, but in his case this polarity derives not so much from ideological differences within a society as from differences between Western art and Japanese art. In his wide-ranging analysis which discusses various arts from theatre to domestic architecture, with an especially appealing comparative section on bathrooms, he presents Western art as revolving around the worship of light and illumination, and Japanese art around darkness and obscurity as central metaphors. In many ways, what Tanizaki presents is an apology or defence of Japanese culture and art, suggesting that the very terms of Western approbation are inadequate for understanding Japanese notions of beauty. In doing so, he echoes the ideas of other commentators, such as Okakura Kakuzō who in his *Ideals of the East* and *The Book of Tea* sought to define an aesthetic of Japan that stood aloof from Western paradigms.

Lest this be mistaken as a solely modern impulse to see the ethnic or national character embodied in cultural production, such as art and aesthetic theories, it is useful to recall Tsurayuki's Preface in which the very first words suggest his insistence on and preoccupation with Japanese poetry, attesting to what we might term 'the anxiety of influence' resulting from the penumbra cast by China's looming cultural shadows. We see this same preoccupation with

Japanese art and its implications throughout *Genji Monogatari*, where China functions simultaneously as a yardstick and as that cultural monolith which must be transcended. Without a doubt, we see this same urge to identify artistic production with a peculiarly Japanese understanding of the world in the work of the *kokugakusha* of the eighteenth century, including Kamo no Mabuchi, whose work especially on the *Man'yōshū* asserts the centrality of indigenous thinking, and Motoori Norinaga, perhaps the greatest of all Japanese literary critics, who champions a Japanese artistic perspective that stands apart from Chinese notions of didacticism and morality, stressing both the intrinsic essence of things in the natural world as well as their effect on an observer.

One of the resulting tensions produced by these views is the paradoxical irony of asserting on the one hand the ubiquity of art and its universal nature as exemplified by Japanese art, while simultaneously arguing for its singular Japanese composition and tenor. We encounter this tension in the work of a number of modern philosophers who were engaged by questions of aesthetics in the context of phenomenology and hermeneutics, including KUKI SHŪZŌ (in *Iki no kōzō* (The Structure of Iki)) and WATSUJI TETSURŌ (in *Fūdo* (Climate and Environment)). Kuki saw in the Edo ideal of *iki* a configuration, not merely aesthetic or ideological, which quintessentially mapped out Japanese being along the continuum of possibilities. For Watsuji, whose work also pays homage to the thought of Martin HEIDEGGER, the resolution of this irony depends on understanding all cultural production as emanating from a particular geographical context; in short, he argues that place is as key as time in understanding human being. In other words, we are shaped ineluctably by the land into which we are born and by our society, a view clearly in accord with those articulated in the early works of Japanese art.

See also: AESTHETICS; AESTHETICS, CHINESE; KOKORO; NATURE, AESTHETIC APPRECIATION OF

References and further reading

* Brower, R. and Miner, E. (1961) *Japanese Court Poetry*, Stanford, CA: Stanford University Press. (Seminal study of classical poetry approached historically.)
* Keene, D. (1988) *The Pleasures of Japanese Literature*, New York: Columbia University Press, 1–22. (A collection of thoughtful essays based on lectures on Japanese traditional aesthetics and pre-modern poetry, fiction and theatre.)
* Konishi Jin'ichi (1984) *A History of Japanese Literature*, Volume 1: *The Archaic and Ancient Ages*, trans. A. Gatten and N. Teele, Princeton, NJ: Princeton University Press. (Brilliant and provocative literary history of early Japan.)
* —— (1986) *A History of Japanese Literature*, Volume II: *The Early Middle Ages*, trans. A. Gatten, Princeton, NJ: Princeton University Press. (Continuation of Konishi (1984).)
  LaFleur, W.R. (1983) *The Karma of Words: Buddhism and the Literary Arts in Medieval Japan*, Berkeley, CA: University of California Press. (Focuses on Chōmei's *Hōjōki*, *Nō* and *kyōgen* theatre and poetry.)
* Miner, E., Hiroko Odagiri and Morrell, R.E. (1985) *The Princeton Companion to Classical Japanese Literature*, Princeton, NJ: Princeton University Press. (Extremely useful compendium.)
* Okakura Kakuzō (1903) *Ideals of the East*, London: John Murray. (In English, based on Okakura's extensive travels in Asia, deals with traditional Asian art and thought beginning in China and India and reaching its ultimate flowering, he argues, in Japan. Okakura is also commonly known as Tenshin.)
* —— (1906) *The Book of Tea*, London: Penguin. (In English, this is Okakura's most famous work. He begins with a comparative history of tea-drinking and preparation, and goes on to elucidate the philosophy of tea culture as it developed in Japan, which in his view underlies traditional Japanese aesthetics.)
  Rimer, J.T. and Yamazaki Masakazu (1984) *On the Art of the Nō Drama: The Major Treatises of Zeami*, Princeton, NJ: Princeton University Press. (The introduction is a useful guide to Zeami's principal ideas.)
* Slawson, D.A. (1987) *Secret Teachings in the Art of Japanese Gardens*, Tokyo: Kodansha International. (A how-to manual of Japanese garden design philosophy for contemporary readers, derived from a variety of pre-modern treatises including the Heian period *Sakuleiki*.)
  Suzuki, D.T. (1959) *Zen and Japanese Culture*, Princeton, NJ: Bollingen-Princeton University Press. (An imaginative and insightful explanation of how Zen principles permeate Japanese art and thought by one of the great proponents of our century; the section on 'Zen and Swordsmanship' is especially pertinent.)
* Tanizaki Jun'ichirō (1933–4) 'In'ei Raisan' (In Praise of Shadows), *Keizi Orai*; trans. T.J. Harper and E.G. Seidensticker, Rutland, VT, and Tokyo: Charles E. Tuttle, 1984. (A fascinating and highly idiosyncratic essay on the aesthetic polarities of Japan and the West. He argues that whereas the

West prizes light and clarity, Japan privileges darkness, shadows and the elliptical.)
* Tsurayuki, Ki no (ed.) (905) *Kokinwakashū*, ed. Saeki Umetomo, Nihon Koten Bungaku Taikei, Tokyo: Iwanami Shoten, 1958; trans. L.R. Rodd and M.C. Henkenius, *Kokinshū*, Princeton, NJ: Princeton University Press, 1984. (First imperially commissioned anthology of Japanese poetry whose chief compiler was Tsurayuki; his well-known preface raises critical concerns alluded to by later theorists.)
* Ueda Makoto (1967) *Literary and Art Theories in Japan*, Cleveland, OH: Press of Western Reserve University. (Comprehensive overview of the theories of a number of different theorists from a variety of periods and disciplines.)
* —— (1983) *Modern Japanese Poets and the Nature of Literature*, Stanford, CA: Stanford University Press. (Insightful study of eight major poets and their theories of art.)

MEERA VISWANATHAN

AFFIRMATIVE ACTION

The term 'affirmative action' originated in the USA under President Kennedy. Originally it was designed to ensure that employees and applicants for jobs with government contractors did not suffer discrimination. Within a year, however, 'affirmative action' was used to refer to policies aimed at compensating African-Americans for unjust racial discrimination, and at improving their opportunities to gain employment. An important implication of this shift was that affirmative action came to mean preferential treatment.

Preferential treatment was later extended to include women as well as other disadvantaged racial and ethnic groups. The arguments in favour of preferential treatment can be usefully classified as backward-looking and forward-looking. Backward-looking arguments rely on the claim that preferential treatment of women and disadvantaged racial minorities compensates these groups or the members for the discrimination and injustices they have suffered. Forward-looking arguments rely on their claim that preferential treatment of women and disadvantaged racial minorities will help to bring about a better society.

There has been much criticism of both types of argument. The most common accusation is that preferential treatment is reverse discrimination. Other criticisms are based around who exactly should be compensated, by what means and to what extent, and at whose cost. Finally, there is the fear of the unknown consequences of such action. Arguments have been forwarded to try and solve such difficulties, but the future of preferential treatment seems to lie in a combination of the two arguments.

1 **Backward-looking arguments**
2 **Forward-looking arguments**
3 **Criticisms of backward-looking arguments**
4 **Criticisms of forward-looking arguments**
5 **Conclusion**

1 Backward-looking arguments

In the USA, Native Americans and African-Americans are the best examples of disadvantaged racial minorities that have been treated unjustly. One kind of backward-looking argument claims that the members of these groups suffer from ongoing racial discrimination practised by the white majority, and also from the effects of past injustices that the nation practised against their parents and ancestors; that they therefore deserve to be compensated; and that according them some preference over whites in the competition for jobs, promotions and places at universities is an appropriate way to give them the compensation they deserve. A second kind of backward-looking argument adds that preferential treatment of Native Americans and African-Americans is also a way to compensate the groups to which they belong. Both kinds of arguments are extended with somewhat diminished force to justify preferential treatment of women and other racial minorities that have been unjustly discriminated against.

2 Forward-looking arguments

Forward-looking arguments for preferential treatment do not require that preferentially treated individuals be themselves the victims of injustice. They justify treating some individuals preferentially if this will help make society more efficient, and more likely to give equal consideration to the common interests of its members. For example, preferential treatment of women in fields like engineering may make society more efficient by encouraging women with engineering talent to develop and use it. Similarly, preferential admission of African-Americans to medical school may help enable society if African-American doctors are more likely than white doctors to practise medicine in black ghettos where medical care is relatively scarce.

3 Criticisms of backward-looking arguments

The most general criticism of preferential treatment is

that it is reverse discrimination. The implication is that preferential treatment is morally similar to the discrimination it is meant to compensate for. This implication is false. The discrimination preferential treatment is meant to compensate for is based on contempt for the interests or abilities of those discriminated against (see DISCRIMINATION). Preferential treatment is not based on such contempt. More specific criticisms of preferential treatment are directed at the backward-looking and forward-looking arguments.

Since backward-looking arguments for preferential treatment claim that it is required by compensatory justice, they presuppose a view of what compensatory justice requires. The most elementary requirement of compensatory justice is that those that deserve compensation must have been wrongly injured. Some critics of preferential treatment object that it cannot be justified by compensatory justice because this is not usually the case. When directed against preferential treatment of African-Americans this objection is based on two grounds: an underestimation of the effects of racial discrimination and prejudice; and a false inference based on the fact that the black middle-class beneficiaries of preferential treatment are probably less injured than blacks in the lower and under classes to the conclusion that the former are only slightly injured or not injured at all.

A more serious question concerns who should bear the costs of compensating the beneficiaries of preferential treatment. A plausible view is that the costs of compensating the victims of wrongful injury should be borne by those responsible for the wrongful injury. Many critics object that even if practically everyone in the society is at least indirectly responsible for wrongly injuring the beneficiaries of preferential treatment, the policies implemented in its name usually seem to impose the heaviest costs on those least responsible. A similar objection can be raised if compensatory justice allows that the costs of compensating the victims of wrongful injury may have to be borne by the beneficiaries of the wrongful injury. The most troubling difficulty, however, is that we usually cannot know whether the beneficiaries of preferential treatment are getting the compensation they deserve. A plausible view of compensatory justice is that it requires that the wrongly injured persons be brought up to 'the level of wealth and welfare that they would now have if they had not been disadvantaged' (Nickel 1975: 536). On this account, beneficiaries are compensated presumably if compensatory justice secures them jobs and positions roughly similar to those they would have secured in the absence of injury. But preferential treatment does not obviously secure its beneficiaries the jobs and positions they would have recovered in the absense of injury. Consider, for example, the black beneficiaries of preferential treatment. If unjust racial discrimination had never happened, the conditions and prospects for blacks would be very different from what they are. For example, many more blacks, probably including the beneficiaries of preferential treatment, would be better qualified, and certainly many would be chosen for the jobs and places which preferential treatment secures. What is uncertain is that the black beneficiaries of preferential treatment would be the very ones chosen for these jobs and positions.

This difficulty is not insurmountable, but it has moved some advocates of backward-looking arguments of preferential treatment to stress that the larger aim is to compensate unjustly treated groups. On this account, it does not matter that the individuals who get jobs and places as a result of preferential treatment may not be the ones who would get these jobs and places in the absence of injustice directed at the groups they belong to. What matters is that their getting such jobs and places is a way to compensate these groups. This shift in the backward-looking argument raises a number of questions. Even if the typical beneficiaries of preferential treatment have been unjustly treated, it does not follow that the groups to which they belong are owed compensation; not every group of unjustly treated individuals need be owed compensation over and above the compensation owed the individuals that compose it. Indeed, not every group of unjustly treated individuals is the kind of group that can claim compensation. It is widely acknowledged that certain kinds of groups can claim compensation; nation states, firms and families are examples. But it is not obvious that the groups whose members benefit from typical programmes of preferential treatment are those kinds of groups. This difficulty can probably be resolved with respect to groups like African-Americans and Native Americans, groups that most resemble those that theorists acknowledge can meaningfully be owed compensation. Supposing this to be the case, this still leaves the difficulty of establishing the conditions that have to be satisfied to compensate such groups. Some theorists doubt that preferential treatment as standardly practised satisfies these conditions, given that it seems to contribute to the growing gap between the black middle-class and the black underclass (Wilson 1987). Presumably this objection can be met by redesigning present policies of preferential treatment. More general questions have been raised about the level of wealth and wellbeing preferentially treated groups would have to be brought to in order to be compensated. The assumption that this level is the level of flourishing groups in the society has been challenged on the ground that cultural differences between groups may explain most of the inequalities in their levels of wealth and wellbeing. However, even if this challenge is generally sound it does not defeat the claim that some preferentially treated groups deserve compensation.

4 Criticisms of forward-looking arguments

Forward-looking arguments do not have to resolve the difficult counterfactual problems that beset the backward-looking arguments. A common criticism of forward-looking arguments is that since they justify discriminating in favour of minorities and women when doing so maximizes utility, they must be committed to discriminating against women and minorities when doing so maximizes utility. This criticism is, however, largely irrelevant because most advocates of the forward-looking arguments do not rely heavily on the supposition that preferential treatment maximizes utility; their more favoured supposition is that preferential treatment will enable society to give more equal consideration to the common interests of its members. The example given earlier concerning the treatment of women in fields such as engineering suggests the plausibility of this supposition. A frequent objection is that even if this supposition is plausible, preferential treatment is unjustified because it violates colour-blind or gender-blind principles. These principles forbid denying an individual a place, job or promotion on account of their colour or gender. They are plausibly implied by the equal opportunity principle, assuming that individuals have not previously been denied opportunities to acquire qualifications for places, jobs and promotions on account of their colour or gender. That assumption is false where preferential treatment is urged. However, although preferential treatment violates colour-blind and gender-blind principles it need not violate the equal opportunity principle. On the contrary it may help to implement that principle. For example, preferential admission of women in fields such as engineering may help society equalize opportunities by helping to break down stereotypes that falsely suggest that women cannot perform well in such fields. A deeper weakness of the objection is that it falsely assumes that the purpose of providing opportunities for places and jobs is to reward merit. In fact, the purpose of providing opportunities for places and jobs is to satisfy the needs and give equal consideration to the interests of members of the society. Meeting that purpose may require violating the colour-blind and gender-blind principles.

Further objections to the forward-looking arguments focus on the consequences of preferential treatment. One set of objections denies that it will have the good consequences its advocates predict. A crude example of this kind of objection is that we do not equalize the interests of the black poor in medical treatment by certifying unqualified blacks as doctors to treat them. A more serious objection denies that there is any good reason to suppose that black doctors are more likely than white doctors to work among the black poor. Another set of objections maintain that preferential treatment is likely to have some untoward consequences. Favourite arguments are that it will create the stereotype that women and minorities cannot succeed in competition with white males without special help, and that it will undermine the self-esteem and self-respect of those it sets out to benefit. These dangers seem most likely where the beneficiaries of preferential treatment misunderstand its rationale.

5 Conclusion

The case for preferential treatment remains highly controversial. Philosophers disagree about what its consequences are likely to be, and about who has been injured enough to deserve it. More importantly, they also disagree about the requirements of compensatory justice, the demands of equality and the nature of the good society. The case for preferential treatment of such groups can only be strengthened by grounding it explicitly on well-argued answers to these philosophical questions.

See also: EQUALITY; JUSTICE

References and further reading

Boxill, B. (1992) *Blacks and Social Justice*, Lanham, MD: Rowman & Littlefield, revised edn. (Chapters 7 and 11 contain extended defences of affirmative action.)

Cahn, S. (1993) *Affirmative Action and the University*, Philadelphia, PA: Temple University Press. (A collection of recent, mainly critical, discussions of affirmative action in higher education.)

Chapman, J. (ed.) (1991) *Compensatory Justice*, New York: New York University Press. (Contains sophisticated discussions of compensatory justice.)

Dworkin, R. (1978) 'Reverse Discrimination', in *Taking Rights Seriously*, Cambridge, MA: Harvard University Press. (This essay is a famous interpretation of the forward-looking argument for affirmative action.)

Ezorsky, G. (1991) *Racism and Justice*, Ithaca, NY: Cornell University Press. (A recent persuasive defence of affirmative action.)

Hill, E., Jr (1991) 'The Message of Affirmative Action', in E.F. Paul, F.D. Miller and J. Paul (eds) *Reassessing Civil Rights*, Cambridge, MA: Harvard University Press. (Defends affirmative action in the university and argues that it communicates a message to its beneficiaries, acknowledging that they have been wronged and welcoming them into the university.)

Lawson, P. (1992) *The Underclass Question*, Philadelphia, PA: Temple University Press. (In this collection, several African-American philosophers discuss a variety of recent criticisms of affirmative action.)

McGary, H. (1989) 'Reparations, Self-Respect and Public Policy', in D. Goldberg (ed.) *Ethical Theory and Social Issues*, Fort Worth, TX: Holt. (An excellent defence of backward-looking arguments for affirmative action.)

* Nickel, J.W. (1975) 'Preferential Policies in Hiring and Admissions: A Jurisprudential Approach', *Columbia Law Review* 75 (April): 534–58. (Assesses the affirmative action debate from the point of view of the law.)

* Wilson, W.J. (1987) *The Truly Disadvantaged*, Chicago, IL: University of Chicago Press. (Contains arguments that affirmative action rewards African-Americans who are already advantaged, and adds to the isolation of those who are truly disadvantaged.)

BERNARD BOXILL

AL-AFGHANI, JAMAL AL-DIN (1838–97)

Al-Afghani is often described as one of the most prominent Islamic political leaders and philosophers of the nineteenth century. He was concerned with the subjection of the Muslim world by Western colonial powers, and he made the liberation, independence and unity of the Islamic world one of the major aims of his life. He provided a theoretical explanation for the relative decline of the Islamic world, and a philosophical theory of history which sought to establish a form of modernism appropriate to Islam.

1   Life and times
2   Philosophy of history

1   Life and times

Jamal al-Din al-Afghani was born in 1838 about 180 miles from Kabul, of a distinguished family. He received a thorough training in a variety of languages of Islamic countries and the religious sciences. When he was eighteen years old he began the constant travels which were to mark his life. He visited much of the Islamic world as well as Europe, and set up a political organization which called on Muslims to fight injustice and the imposition of imperialism. He had a great impact upon Muhammad 'Abduh and reactions by intellectual Egyptians to the incursion of the Europeans. He eventually sided with the Ottoman empire but soon became disillusioned with the Sultan, and died in suspicious circumstances in Turkey in 1897.

2   Philosophy of history

Al-Afghani's philosophical contributions are to be found in his book *ar-Radd 'alal-dahriyyin* (Refutation of the Materialists). Citing philosophers such as DEMOCRITUS and DARWIN, he criticized the naturalist and materialist philosophers for their denial, either directly or indirectly, of the existence of God. He then went on to elaborate at great length on religion's contribution to civilization and progress. According to al-Afghani, religion has taught humanity three fundamental beliefs: its angelical or spiritual nature, the belief of every religious community in its superiority over other groups, and the assertion that our existence in this world is but a prelude to a higher life in a world entirely free from sorrow and suffering. Our angelic nature urges us to rise above our bestial proclivities and live in peace with our fellow human beings. The feeling of competitive superiority on the part of the various religious groups generates competitiveness, whereby the various communities will strive to improve their lot and persist in their quest for knowledge and progress. Finally, the third truth provides an incentive to be constantly aware of the higher and eternal world that awaits us. This in turn will motivate human beings to refrain from the evil and malice to which they may be tempted, and live a life of love, peace and justice.

Al-Afghani mentions that religion implants in its believers the three traits of honesty, modesty and truthfulness. He further maintains that the greatness of the major nations of the world has always been entailed by their cultivation of these traits. Through these virtues the Greeks were able to confront and destroy the Persian empire. However, when the Greeks adopted the materialism and hedonism of Epicurus, the result was decay and subjection by the Romans. Likewise the ancient Persians, a very noble people, began with the rise of Mazdaism the same downward journey as the Greeks, which resulted in their moral erosion and subjection by the Arabs.

Similarly, the Muslim empire, which rose on the same solid moral and religious foundation as did both the Greeks and Persians, became so weakened that a small band of Franks (that is, the crusaders), was able to score significant victories against them. Subsequently, the hordes of Genghis Khan were able to trample the whole land of Islam, sack its cities and massacre its people.

Al-Afghani bases his philosophy on a theory of history in which religion is portrayed as a catalytic force in the progress of humanity. Interestingly, he stresses that religious beliefs must be founded upon sound demonstration and valid proof without any supernatural aspect. This rationalism manifests an important element of modernity in al-Afghani's thinking. However, such modernity does not diminish his strong belief in religion as an integral component and fundamental force behind humanity's quest for morality, truthfulness and integrity.

Al-Afghani's philosophical views revealed a great deal of faith in the human mind and its capacity for innovations based on knowledge rather than ignorance. He expressed great faith in humanity as being one of the greatest miracles of the universe, and believed that there are no areas which can remain forever closed to the human mind. Surprisingly, he predicted that people would reach the moon as a step in a series of strides by mankind, as he believed that nature and the universe were created so that we could continue the challenge of unravelling their secrets.

In his criticism of Darwin's theory of evolution (see EVOLUTION, THEORY OF), al-Afghani presents a philosophical theory about nature in response to Darwin's theory. He believes in the nature of what he termed 'natural selection', whereby survival in nature will be for the strongest and the fittest. Thus if a number of plants are planted in a single space of earth which does not have food for all these plants, it will be noticed that the plants will compete among themselves for food. In due course, some of the plants will become more developed than the others, which will wither. He applies the same theory to the world of animals, including human beings, where the influence of power is more noticeable than elsewhere. He even goes further than Darwin by applying the theory to the area of ideas, maintaining that ideas are born out of other ideas and may be greater than those ideas; this explains why posterity may sometimes excel and be superior to its ancestry. Al-Afghani believes that these developments are due to the impact of nature's aspects and not necessarily the result of human effort. His criticism of Darwin's theory lessened gradually as he began to express views similar to those of Darwin. He cites earlier Muslim scholars such as Ibn Bashroun who had talked about the evolution from dust of plants and animals. Al-Afghani, however, continued to maintain strong disagreement with Darwin on one fundamental issue, that of the creation of life; this al-Afghani unequivocally ascribes to God.

See also: 'ABDUH, M.; DARWIN, C.R.; EVOLUTION, THEORY OF; ISLAMIC PHILOSOPHY, MODERN

List of works

al-Afghani (1838–97) *ar-Radd 'alal-dahriyyin* (Refutation of the Materialists), Cairo, 1955. (The main philosophical contribution of al-Afghani.)

References and further reading

Keddie, N. (1968) *An Islamic Response to Imperialism: Political and Religious Writings of Sayyid Jamal al-Din al-Afghani*, Berkeley, CA: University of California Press. (An useful series of essays linking al-Afghani's philosophical and political views.)

—— (1972) *Sayyid Jamal ad-Din al-Afghani: A Political Biography*, Berkeley, CA: University of California Press. (An important study of al-Afghani's politics, with useful material on his general philosophical views.)

Kedourie, E. (1966) *Afghani and 'Abduh*, London: Cass. (Deals extensively with Afghani's political philosophy and its influence on 'Abduh.)

ELSAYED OMRAN
OLIVER LEAMAN

AFRICAN PHILOSOPHY

In order to indicate the range of some of the kinds of material that must be included in a discussion of philosophy in Africa, it is as well to begin by recalling some of the history of Western philosophy. It is something of an irony that Socrates, the first major philosopher in the Western tradition, is known to us entirely for oral arguments imputed to him by his student Plato. For the Western philosophical tradition is, above all else, a tradition of texts. While there are some important ancient philosophers, like Socrates, who are largely known to us through the reports of others, the tradition has developed increasingly as one which pays careful attention to written arguments. However, many of those arguments – in ethics and politics, metaphysics and epistemology, aesthetics and the whole host of other major subdivisions of the subject – concern questions about which many people in many cultures have talked and many, although substantially fewer, have written outside of the broad tradition of Western philosophy. The result is that while those methods of philosophy that have developed in the West through thoughtful analysis of texts are not found everywhere, we are likely to find in every human culture opinions about some of the major questions of Western philosophy. On these important questions there have been discussions in most cultures since the earliest human societies. These constitute what has sometimes been called a 'folk-philosophy'. It is hard to say much about those opinions and discussions in places where they have not been written down. However, we are able to find some evidence of the character of these views in such areas as parts of sub-Saharan Africa where writing was introduced into oral cultures over the last few centuries.

As a result, discussions of African philosophy should include both material on some oral cultures and rather more on the philosophical work that has been done in literate traditions on the African continent, including those that have developed since the introduction of Western philosophical training there.

1 Oral cultures

Two areas of folk-philosophy have been the object of extended scholarly investigation in the late twentieth century: the philosophical psychology of people who speak the Akan languages of the west African littoral (now Ghana) (see AKAN PHILOSOPHICAL PSYCHOLOGY) and the epistemological thought of Yoruba-speaking people of western Nigeria (see YORUBA EPISTEMOLOGY). In both cases the folk ideas of the tradition have been addressed by contemporary speakers of the language with Western philosophical training. This is probably the most philosophically sophisticated work that has been carried out in the general field of the philosophical study of folk-philosophy in Africa. It also offers some insight into ways of thinking about both the mind and human cognition that are different from those that are most familiar within the Western tradition.

One can also learn a great deal by looking more generally at ethical and aesthetic thought, since in all parts of the continent, philosophical issues concerning evaluation were discussed and views developed before writing (see AESTHETICS, AFRICAN; ETHICAL SYSTEMS, AFRICAN). Philosophical work on ethics is more developed than in aesthetics and some of the most interesting recent work in African aesthetics also focuses on Yoruba concepts which have been explored in some detail by Western philosophers. The discussion of the status of such work has largely proceeded under the rubric of the debate about ethnophilosophy, a term intended to cover philosophical work that aims to explore folk philosophies in a systematic manner (see ETHNOPHILOSOPHY, AFRICAN). Finally, there has also been an important philosophical debate about the character of traditional religious thought in Africa (see AFRICAN TRADITIONAL RELIGIONS).

2 Older literate traditions

Although these oral traditions represent old forms of thought, the actual traditions under discussion are not as old as the remaining African literate traditions. The earliest of these is in the writings associated with the ancient civilizations of Egypt, which substantially predate the pre-Socratic philosophers who inhabit the earliest official history of Western philosophy (see EGYPTIAN COSMOLOGY, ANCIENT). The relationship between these Egyptian traditions and the beginnings of Western philosophy have been in some dispute and there is much recent scholarship on the influence of Egyptian on classical Greek thought (see EGYPTIAN PHILOSOPHY: INFLUENCE ON ANCIENT GREEK THOUGHT).

Later African philosophy looks more familiar to those who have studied the conventional history of Western philosophy: the literate traditions of Ethiopia, for example, which can be seen in the context of a long (if modest) tradition of philosophical writing in the horn of Africa. The high point of such writing has been the work of the seventeenth-century philosopher, Zar'a Ya'ecob. His work has been compared to that of Descartes (see ETHIOPIA, PHILOSOPHY IN).

It is also worth observing that many of the traditions of Islamic philosophy were either the product of, or were subject to the influence of scholars born or working in the African continent in centres of learning such as Cairo and Timbuktu (see ISLAMIC PHILOSOPHY). Similarly, the work of some of the most important philosophers among the Christian Church Fathers, was the product of scholars born in Africa, like St AUGUSTINE, and some was written in the African provinces of Rome.

In considering African-born philosophers, there is Anton Wilhelm AMO, who was born in what is now Ghana and received, as the result of an extraordinary sequence of events, philosophical training during the period of German Enlightenment, before returning to the Guinea coast to die in the place he was born. Amo's considerable intellectual achievements played an important part in eighteenth- and nineteenth-century polemics relating to the 'capacity of the negro'. Unfortunately, only a portion of his work has survived.

3 Recent philosophy

Most work in African philosophy in the twentieth century has been carried out by African intellectuals (often interacting with scholars outside Africa) under the influence of philosophical traditions from the European countries that colonized Africa and created her modern system of education. As the colonial systems of education were different, it is helpful to think of this work as belonging to two broadly differentiated traditions, one Francophone and the other Anglophone. While it is true that philosophers in the areas influenced by French (and Francophone Belgian) colonization developed separately from those areas under British colonial control, a comparison of their work reveals that there has been a substantial cross-flow between them (as there generally has been between philosophy in the French- and English-speaking worlds). The other important colonial power in Africa was Portugal whose commitment to colonial education was less developed. The sole Portuguese-speaking African intellectual who made a significant philosophical contribution is Amílcar CABRAL, whose leadership in the independence movement of Guinea Bissau and the Cape Verde islands was guided by philosophical training influenced by Portuguese Marxism. Cabral's influence has not been as great as that of Frantz FANON. He was born in the French Antilles, but later became an Algerian. He was a very important figure in the development of political philosophy in Africa (and much of the Third World).

Among the most important political thinkers influenced by philosophy are Kwame Nkrumah, Kenneth Kaunda and Julius Nyerere (see AFRICAN PHILOSOPHY, ANGLOPHONE). Out of all the intellectual movements in Africa in this century, the two most important ones of philosophical interest have been *négritude* and pan-Africanism (see AFRICAN PHILOSOPHY, FRANCOPHONE; PAN-AFRICANISM).

Philosophy in Africa has changed greatly in the decades since the Second World War and, even more, as African states have gained their independence. Given the significance of the colonial legacy in shaping modern philosophical education in Africa it is not surprising that there have been serious debates about the proper understanding of what it is for a philosophy to be African. These lively debates, prevalent in the areas of African epistemology, ethics and aesthetics, are found in both Francophone and Anglophone philosophy (see AESTHETICS, AFRICAN).

See also: MARGINALITY; POSTCOLONIALISM

References and further reading

Abraham, W.E. (1962) *The Mind of Africa*, Chicago: University of Chicago Press. (A classical discussion of the place of philosophical ideas in African life.)

Eze, E. (1997) *Postcolonial African Philosophy: a Critical Reader*, Cambridge, MA: Basil Blackwell. (A useful collection of important work in contemporary African philosophy.)

Hountondji, P.J. (1983) *African Philosophy: Myth and Reality*, London: Hutchinson. (The most important Francophone discussion of the project of modern African philosophy.)

Masolo, D.A. (1994) *African Philosophy in Search of Identity*, Edinburgh: Edinburgh University Press. (A critical history of modern African philosophy.)

K. ANTHONY APPIAH

AFRICAN PHILOSOPHY, ANGLOPHONE

Contemporary African philosophy is in a state of flux, but the flow is not without some watersheds. The chief reason for the flux lies in the fact that Africa, in most part, is in a state of transition from a traditional condition to a modernized one. Philosophically and in other ways, the achievement of independence was the most significant landmark in this transition. Independence from European rule (which began in Libya in 1951, followed by Sudan in 1956, Ghana in 1957 and continued to be won at a rapid pace in other parts of Africa in the 1960s) did not come without a struggle. That struggle was, of necessity, both political and cultural. Colonialism involved not only political subjection but also cultural depersonalization. Accordingly, at independence it was strongly felt that plans for political and economic reconstruction should reflect the needs not only for modernization but also for cultural regeneration. These are desiderata which, while not incompatible in principle, are difficult to harmonize in practice. The philosophical basis of the project had first to be worked out and this was attempted by the first wave of post-independence leaders. The task of devising technical philosophies cognizant of Africa's past and present and oriented to her long-term future has been in the hands of a crop of professional philosophers trained in Western-style educational institutions. Philosophical results have not been as dramatic as in the case of the political, but the process is ongoing.

The political figures that led African states to independence were not all philosophers by original inclination or training. To start with only the best known, such as Leopold Senghor of Senegal, or Kwame Nkrumah of Ghana, were trained philosophers, but others, such as Kenneth Kaunda of Zambia, brought only an educated intelligence and a good sense of their national situations to the enterprise. In all cases they were rulers enthusiastically anointed by their people to chart the new course and lead them to the promised land. An example of how practical urgency can inspire philosophical productivity can be found in the way that all these philosophers propounded blueprints for reconstruction with clearly articulated philosophical underpinnings. Circumstantial necessity, then, rather than Platonic selection made these leaders philosopher-kings. It is significant, also, to note that all the leaders mentioned (and the majority of their peers) argued for a system of socialism deriving from their understandings of African traditional thought and practice, and from their perceptions of the imperatives generated by industrialization, such as it had been. Concern with this latter aspect of the situation led to some flirtation and even outright marriage with Marxism. But, according to the leaders concerned, the outcome of this fertilization of thought had enough African input to be regarded as an African progeny. Accordingly, practically all of them proffered their theories and prescriptions under the rubric of African socialism. No such labelling is possible in the work of African philosophers, but there are some patterns of preoccupation.

1 The epistemological anthropology of *négritude*
2 Metaphysics and African socialism
3 An analysis of socialism and a reflection on violence
4 The question of African philosophy in our time
5 Typology of current trends
6 Indigenous African philosophers
7 The quest for a synthesis

1   The epistemological anthropology of *négritude*

Of all the African leaders under study, Senghor, poet and man of letters, is perhaps the most learned and most remarkable in his views. He is also the most famous champion of *négritude*. This term refers to both a literary movement and its defining outlook. *Négritude* was focused on restoring in black people the pride in their being and culture that had been eclipsed by colonization. The pioneer of *négritude* was Aimé Césaire, the black poet and playwright from Martinique. In the hands of Senghor, *négritude* also became a kind of epistemological anthropology and a political philosophy.

According to Senghor, *négritude* designates 'the whole complex of civilized values – cultural, economic, social and political which characterize the black peoples or, more precisely, the Negro-African world' (Mutiso and Rohio 1975: 83). The character of these values emerges at the social, and more fundamentally, epistemological levels. Socially, the key to these values was held to consist in what Senghor calls the 'communal' characteristic of African society. Countries exhibiting that kind of social formation are ones in which 'the group takes precedence over the individual'; they are 'above all, religious countries where money is not king' (Senghor 1965: 58). Senghor stresses the importance of the institution of the family, which he says is the 'microcosm' of this kind of society. As he points out, 'family' in this context has to be understood in a non-Western sense as referring to a kinship unit including 'all persons, living and dead, who acknowledge a common ancestor' (1965: 48). Senghor suggests that this unit is better called a clan following anthropological usage. In a typical traditional village or town it would be more numerous and at the level of a nation, innumerable. In its smallest proportions, then, a 'family' in this sense is a substantial community and provides, as the immediate context of early socialization, a natural school for the cultivation of a broad sense of social belonging and obligation. 'The African', says Senghor, 'is thus held in a tight network of vertical and horizontal communities which bind and at the same time support him' (1965: 43). More significantly, Senghor adds, 'He is the fullest illustration of the truth, honored in our time by socialism, that man can only live and realise himself in and through society' (1965: 43).

However, Senghor does not suggest that Africans devalue individuality: the African 'claims his autonomy...to affirm himself as a being' (1964: 94). But, the logical point to be noted here is that in the African scheme of things individuality is defined in terms of community, not vice versa. In consequence, the African approach to self-consciousness is non-Cartesian. Instead of 'I think, therefore I am', he or she, according to Senghor, would say (dispensing with 'the logician's conjunction "therefore"' as a mere distraction), 'I feel, I dance the Other; I am' (1964: 73). This axiom of communalist self-consciousness became even better known about a decade later in Mbiti's formulation as 'I am because we are, and since we are, therefore I am' ([1969] 1990: 106). However, Senghor's epistemological reading of this mode of self-affirmation remains uniquely his own. To him it was typical of the 'emotive' and 'participatory' character of African cognition, which he considered to be in marked contrast with Western ways of knowing. He wrote:

Let us consider the negro-African as he faces the object to be known, as he faces the Other: God, man, animal, tree or pebble, natural or social phenomenon. In contrast to the classic European, the African negro does not draw a line between himself and the object; he does not hold it at a distance, nor does he merely look at it and analyse it. More exactly, after having held it at a distance, after having scanned it without analysing it, he takes it vibrant in his hands, careful not to kill or fix it. He touches it, feels it, smells it ... Thus the negro African sympathises, abandons his personality to become identified with the other.

(Senghor 1964: 72)

Senghor actually maintained that these 'modes of knowledge' or 'forms of thought (are) different and linked to the psycho-physiology of each race' (1965: 33).

Senghor attached great importance to this account of African cognition because he thought that it explained 'the cultural values of the Africans...their religion and social structure, their art and literature, above all the genius of their languages' (1965: 35). Thus the communalist cast of African society is a social manifestation of the sense of community which the African feels with the whole of creation. This manifestation traditionally took the form of social arrangements of mutual caring and support which ensured for the individual a reasonable amount of wellbeing. A key feature of this system was the combined individual and clan ownership of the means of production (mainly land) and the products of labour, which, in the opinion of Senghor, made African society 'collectivist' or 'socialist'. To Senghor, the task facing contemporary African political thought was how to capture this pristine socialism in modern social and political institutions. In the event he found little rationale for extensive nationalization, and his prescriptions and their implementation were only remotely analogous to socialism customarily understood.

From a philosophical point of view the most interesting questions relate to Senghor's theory of 'forms of thought'. Recalling his claim that: 'European reasoning is analytical, discursive by utilization; African reasoning is intuitive by participation' (1964: 73), the following questions may be asked: Do these characterizations represent distinctive cognitive categories? Are they, can they be, physiologically ingrained? And is the racial apportionment justified? In response to outcries from some African intellectuals scandalized by this apparent attribution of a constitutional incapacity for analysis to the African psyche, Senghor, notwithstanding protestations to the contrary, changed his position substantially: 'In truth every ethnic group possesses, along with different aspects of Reason, all the virtues of man, but each has stressed only one aspect of Reason, only certain virtues' (1964: 75). He even called for the integration of cognitive methods.

A striking feature of Senghor's discussions of the philosophical bases of his ideological recommendations is his frequent grappling with Marxism. He is highly impressed by the intellectual power of MARX and much taken with Marx's dialectical method, which he somehow believed was in harmony with African ways of thinking: 'Negro African reason is traditionally dialectical, transcending the principles of identity, non-contradiction and the "excluded middle"' (1964: 75). But there is a pronounced ambivalence with regard to certain elements of the Marxist construct. These were the materialistic aspect of dialectical materialism, its atheism and what he perceived to be its determinism, all of which, in themselves, he regarded as objectionable and incompatible with the traditional African worldview. Moreover, he did not think that the class struggle was a necessary factor in the African quest for a contemporary form of socialism.

2 Metaphysics and African socialism

These rejections of Marxist materialism, atheism and determinism generally came to be taken as the marks by which to distinguish the philosophy of African socialism from the Marxist variety. However, these marks of distinction were not always applicable. For example, the philosophy of Kwame Nkrumah of Ghana, the major architect of Africa's victories in her anti-colonial struggles of this century, was an eminent counterexample in at least two respects. First, although Nkrumah was not an atheist, materialism appealed to him. Second, although he was not initially enthusiastic about the necessity for a class struggle in Africa, he later changed his mind. These differences are symptomatic of a deeper difference in philosophical outlook and ideological commitment. Senghor's appreciation of Marx was theoretical rather than ideological. Nkrumah's, on the other hand, was far-reaching in both its theoretical and ideological aspects. Furthermore, Nkrumah had an emphatically neo-Marxist notion, not apparent in Senghor, of the intimate relationship of abstract philosophy with political practice. This is seen in his book *Consciencism: Philosophy and Ideology for De-Colonization* ([1964] 1970) in assertions like 'Idealism favours an oligarchy, materialism favours an egalitarianism' ([1964] 1970: 75), which illustrate the predominant tendency of the interpretations of the history of

Western philosophy with which he prefaced his ideological affirmations. But by far the most philosophically interesting difference between the two philosopher-kings is the fact that, while Senghor believed that materialism (dialectical or otherwise) was incompatible with religion, Nkrumah did not (see DIALECTICAL MATERIALISM).

Thus, very early in his life as an anti-colonial leader in Ghana Nkrumah proclaimed in a public lecture, 'I am a Marxist Socialist and a nondenominational Christian, and I see no contradiction in this'. In view of his claims of African authenticity for his theory, he also might have added, 'Moreover, I believe in the essentials of the African traditional worldview, and I see no contradiction in this either'. The way in which he defended his belief that the dialectical materialism of Marxism is consistent with the theism of Christianity and the metaphysics of the traditional African worldview was to deploy an ingenious distinction between materialism as the theory of the *sole* reality of matter and the *primary* reality of matter. In Nkrumah's view, the first variety of materialism is injudicious as it conflicts with both fact of mind and the spiritual aspects of human experience. On the other hand, a materialism of the second persuasion can accommodate these previously recalcitrant facts, provided it has an intelligible and valid account of the emergence of mind from matter. Dialectical materialism is, according to Nkrumah, of the second type and he invented for it just such an account: 'The key to the solution of the problem', he explained, 'lies in categorial convertibility' ([1964] 1970: 20). Categorial conversion was defined not by direct specification, but almost recursively, by cases: 'By categorial conversion, I mean such a thing as the emergence of self-consciousness from that which is not self-conscious: such a thing as the emergence of mind from matter, of quality from quantity' ([1964] 1970: 20). As an aid to the understanding of these category transitions, *Consciencism: Philosophy and Ideology for De-Colonization* says that philosophy turns to science for 'models' and discovers exemplars in 'the inter-reducibility of matter and energy' and in chemical change wherein 'physical quantities give rise to emergent qualities' . ([1964]1970:21)

For further enlightenment as to the nature of categorial conversion, the reader was directed to the following explanatory comparison: 'The average man belongs to a category distinct from that of the men and women of flesh and blood; but the concept of the average man is obtained by a certain conceptual conversion of information about individual men and women' ([1964] 1970: 22). Here the category of 'living men and women' is primary and that of the average man derivative. Similarly, from the primary category of matter we can arrive at the derivative category of mind by a logical processing of data about 'nervous' matter. Propositions about the mind are then seen to be 'materially equivalent' to propositions about 'a critical organization of matter'. In this way the categorial differences are revealed as *façons de parler*.

The problems afflicting this account are difficult to minimize. For example, in so far as the average-man illustration is germane, the convertibility involved is a logical relationship. Consequently, phenomena such as the emergence of chemical properties from 'physical quantities' held up as a model must fall beyond the pale of categorial conversion. More gravely, the objective of reconciling dialectical materialism with Christianity, however nondenominational, must entail conceiving of the eternal, supreme, spiritual being of that religion as a kind of emergence from matter, which would mean reconceiving that being out of all recognition. Consistency, then, cannot be achieved. However, given Nkrumah's faith in categorial conversion, it is easy to understand this problematic catholicity on his part. The same faith in the idea of categorial convertibility, which he held was to be found among African traditional conceptions, enabled him to combine Marxist materialism with his background in African thought. That some very transformative 'conversion' was necessary is apparent from the fact that he believed that 'man is regarded in Africa as primarily a spiritual being' ([1964] 1970: 68).

This African connection was as important to Nkrumah as it was to Senghor. To Nkrumah it showed that his appropriation of the Marxist philosophy (and in general his explorations of Western philosophy), did not compromise his African authenticity. With the attainment of independence, Nkrumah felt there was need to articulate a philosophy that could harmonize the competing segments that have come to inhabit the African conscience through historical circumstances. These segments derived from the presence in contemporary Africa of influences from African traditional culture and from Islamic and Euro-Christian sources. The synthesis of Marxist philosophy with some Christian and African traditional conceptions, which Nkrumah called philosophical consciencism, was he said, exactly such a philosophy.

Nkrumah gave the following indications of the traditional African ingredients in this philosophical compound: philosophical consciencism 'agrees with the traditional African idea of the absolute and independent existence of matter, the idea of its powers of self-motion . . . the idea of categorial convertibility, and the idea of the grounding of . . . ethics in the nature of man' ([1964] 1970: 97). Also, as far as socialism is concerned, 'the traditional face of Africa includes an attitude towards man which can only be described, in its social manifestations, as being socialist' ([1964] 1970: 68). The implied reference is to the communalism of traditional Africa, which according to *Consciencism: Philosophy and Ideology for De-Colonization*, is 'the sociopolitical ancestor of socialism' ([1964] 1970: 73). On the question of the socialistic complexion of traditional communalism Nkrumah and Senghor are at one. They are also in agreement with Julius Nyerere of Tanzania, one of the most respected of Africa's statesman-thinkers. However, they differ with Nyerere in other ways. Both Senghor and Nkrumah seem to make a veritable conceptual linkage between their metaphysics and their socialist ideology. This is not true of Nyerere: 'There is not the slightest necessity for people to study metaphysics and decide whether there is one God or many Gods or no God before they can be socialists. These questions are important to man, but irrelevant to socialism' (1969: 39).

3 An analysis of socialism and a reflection on violence

There is an absence of metaphysical learning in Nyerere's pages. However, the reader does find a highly philosophical approach to the socialist ideology based on an analysis of the traditional communalism of his society and its contemporary condition. Nyerere traces the idea of socialism to its foundation, which he finds in the principle of equality. 'Socialism', he says, 'is, in fact, the application of the principle of human equality to the social, economic and political organization of society' (1968: 79). Broadly construed, this is an equality of benefits. Consequently, for Nyerere, socialism is a distributive dispensation and not primarily a system of production. But he concedes that certain forms of production can lead to the unequal acquisition of wealth on a scale which makes it possible for some people to gain exploitative dominance over others. Therefore a rationally selective public ownership of the means of production can become a means for achieving the basic aim of socialism. However, social ownership ought to be distinguished from social control as the former can be combined with all kinds of despotisms, while the latter, if genuine, cannot. Furthermore, the latter can conceivably be had without the former. Hence, what socialism requires is the social control of certain means of production. This has important political implications. Social control is not conducive to socialism (as the social embodiment of human equality) unless it is exercised by a citizenry enjoying equality of freedom and participation. Therefore, 'Democracy is another essential characteristic of a socialist society', and the rule of law is a part of it: 'until it prevails socialism does not prevail' (1969: 31, 34). Besides, a socialist society in Nyerere's view must be suffused with an ethos of cooperativeness as opposed to personal competitiveness.

There have been expositions of social and political testaments with significant philosophical components by other African political leaders, such as Sekou Touré of Guinea, Obafemi Awolowo of Nigeria, Felix Houphouët-Boigny of the Ivory Coast, Kenneth Kaunda of Zambia and Amílcar Cabral of Guinea-Bissau. They all, except Houphouët-Boigny, advocated varieties of socialism, but none surpassed the conceptual clarity of Nyerere. Without exception, however, all the socialisms have come under a cloud on account of the uniform failure of the socialist experiments in Africa and elsewhere. Their philosophical components, nevertheless, challenge a properly philosophical evaluation.

Worthy of special mention in connection with the literature produced by Africa's statesman-philosophers is Kaunda's book of meditations on the theme of violence (*Kaunda on Violence* (1980)). The question of the moral legitimacy of violence in the liberation struggles of Africa was the cause of much earnest soul-searching among sensitive people in Africa (Mazrui (1978), Wiredu (1986), Serequeberhan (1991)). The book by Kaunda is an agonized philosophical soliloquy on his personal evolution from an adherent of Gandhian nonviolence to a principal supporter and sustainer of the armed struggle in southern Africa. His considered judgment, after extended reflections articulated with singular lucidity, is that violence is never justifiable morally, but it may be forgiven (by the Lord Almighty) if it is in reaction to the violence of an oppressor. This thoughtful conclusion raises quite subtle issues in moral philosophy of relevance in Africa and everywhere else. But in Africa it also provides a reasoned contrast to the relatively untroubled advocacy of anti-colonial violence in Fanon's *The Wretched of the Earth* (1961), a book which deservedly has a considerable African following (see FANON, F.).

4 The question of African philosophy in our time

If the challenges of independence provided the direct stimuli of the philosophical enterprises of Africa's political leaders, they also provide the indirect cause of the character and present state of academic philosophy in Africa. This brings us to our second watershed. Pre-independence curricula in philosophy in African universities in the British colonial orbit were unmodified importations from the UK, not to say impositions, without any African admixtures. If mention was made of any African philosophical conception bordering on the philosophical inside those universities, it was likely to emanate from a department of anthropology or religion. Naturally, not long after independence, the general movement towards the reclamation of the African identity made itself felt in philosophy departments in the form of a search for an African orientation in teaching and research in philosophy. Two of the subprojects that have received some attention in the pursuit of this objective are the study of the philosophical ideas embedded in African oral traditions and the utilization of insights from that study in combination with insights from other sources in the contemporary world for the construction of philosophies for modern existence.

To take the first project first: although its necessity is widely recognized, its modalities are enveloped in deepest controversy. Debate has raged principally around the criticisms by Paulin Hountondji (1983) of contemporary studies of traditional African thought that construe it as a continental monolith of philosophical unanimity. Hountondji, the Francophone African philosopher who has most influenced contemporary philosophical discussions in Anglophone Africa, has used the term 'ethnophilosophy' to designate studies of this kind, which he regards not as nonphilosophy (as it is sometimes supposed), but rather as bad philosophy. They are apt, he says, to be 'the description of an implicit, unexpressed worldview, which never existed anywhere but in the anthropologist's imagination' (1983: 63). Among the works Hountondji places in this category are *Bantu Philosophy* (1959) by Placide Tempels, a Belgian missionary and *African Religions and Philosophy* (1969) by John Mbiti, an African theologian. African traditional thought itself, however, according to Hountondji, 'possesses a complexity, a richness and a depth with which we have as yet scant acquaintance, and which we must now recover' (1983: 280). Nevertheless, not being articulated in the form of explicit and systematic expositions, traditional African thought cannot be said to contain the discipline of philosophy, even though its ancestral originators may have been philosophers in their own right. At best, we 'can probably recover philosophical fragments from our oral literature' (1976: 106–7), but the forging of a discipline from this material worthy of the name of philosophy remains a challenge to contemporary Africans that can only be met in close alliance with the quest for scientific knowledge (see ETHNOPHILOSOPHY, AFRICAN).

These sentiments have fallen harshly on the sensibilities of the traditionalists among contemporary African philosophers, and the ensuing controversy has seemed interminable to both onlookers and some insiders (Serequeberhan (1991) is an excellent sampling of the exchanges). Nevertheless, some significant work has been done because of that controversy and alongside it, although it is somewhat scattered. Among the most accessible of such work are Gyekye (1987) and Gbadegesin (1991). These books contain detailed interpretative expositions of African traditional philosophy, focusing on the Akan of Ghana and the Yoruba of Nigeria respectively. Both philosophers find in their traditional heritage dualistic but richly stratified conceptions of human personality. They also find, like the philosopher-kings before them, a communalistic ethic and, contrary to a longstanding orthodoxy, a rationalistic, rather than a supernaturalistic ethics. In philosophical theology they call attention to unaided indigenous postulations of a supreme being, although in Gyekye's interpretation, but not in Gbadegesin's, the conception is substantially similar to the God of Christianity. In either case, their interpretations stand in contrast to the account of Luo traditional religion advanced by Okot P'Bitek, the Ugandan poet, novelist and philosopher, in an earlier phase of contemporary African philosophy. In two books of notable conceptual sophistication, *African Religions in Western Scholarship* (1970) and *Religion of the Central Luo* (1971), P'Bitek argued that the conceptual framework of the Luo has no place for the notion of a supreme being or even for the beginning of the world and that the widely received notions of a Luo supreme being are only thanks to a Western missionary superimposition.

Whatever the truth in this matter, it cannot be doubted that the years of Western leadership in the literature on African thought have left encrustations on indigenous conceptual structures that are due for systematic unscrambling. It is arguable, for example, that the dualistic conception of body and mind, which is often attributed to Africans, in fact, presupposes a mode of conceptualization that ill-coheres with African traditional thought habits, which are frequently empirical, as distinct from empiricist (see AKAN PHILOSOPHICAL PSYCHOLOGY). This suggests a need for conceptual decolonization which, although not in itself a touchstone of philosophical truth, is a necessary preliminary to the accomplishment of the historic tasks facing contemporary African philosophy.

5 Typology of current trends

In addition to traditional thought there have been other objects of attention. In his now famous typology of trends in contemporary African philosophy, the Kenyan philosopher Odera Oruka (1990) discriminates four trends which he lists as (1) ethnophilosophy, (2) philosophic sagacity, (3) nationalist-ideological philosophy and (4) professional philosophy. Subsequently in *Sage Philosophy* (1991) he increased the number to six, adding 'hermeneutic philosophy and artistic or literary philosophy'. By 'artistic and literary philosophy' Oruka means not only the explicit philosophical reflections volunteered from time to time by the creative spirits of contemporary Africa, such as in Wole Soyinka's *Myth, Literature and the African World* (1976), but also the philosophies implicit in their poems, plays, novels and other artistic productions. Oruka's act of inclusion betokens a strong sense of the value of intensive interaction between professional philosophy, on the one hand, and art and literature, on the other, a source of intellectual riches in other traditions.

According to Oruka's scheme of classification the work of the statesman-thinkers falls under nationalist-ideological philosophy while the studies of traditional thought may be said to fall under ethnophilosophy, provided this term is divested of any pejorative connotations. But ethnophilosophy is also generally part of the work of the professionals. The same is true of what Oruka calls 'hermeneutical philosophy'. This he defines as consisting of 'philosophical analysis of concepts in a given African language to help clarify meaning and logical implications' (1990: 11). In illustration of the 'hermeneutical category' he cites Gyekye's *An Essay on African Philosophical Thought* (1987), Wiredu's 'The Concept of Mind with Particular Reference to the Language and Thought of the Akans' (1987) and Hallen's and Sodipo's *Knowledge, Belief and Witchcraft: Analytic Experiments in African Philosophy* (1986).

Of special interest is Gyekye's chapter on 'Philosophy, Logic and the Akan Language'. Disavowing any a priori relativization of philosophical theses to particular languages, Gyekye points out how travel across languages can affect the fate of a philosophical thesis or problem. In one of his examples, he argues that in Akan (the language of one of the ethnic groups of Ghana), the expression *wō hō*, by means of which the concept of existence may be translated, has an irreducibly locative component, carried by the particle *hō*, which means 'at some place'. Given this conceptual situation, he explains, something like St Anselm's ontological argument for the existence of God would be unlikely to enjoy an appearance of plausibility in Akan philosophical discourse. Nor could the controversy, historically precipitated by the Saint's argumentation as to whether existence is a predicate, tempt Akan curiosity, for in Akan terms, the question would reduce to 'something like "Is that something is there an attribute?"', which is 'bizarre' (1987: 179–81) (see EXISTENCE). In a similar vein, Kwasi Wiredu in his article, 'The Concept of Mind with Particular Reference to the Language and Thought of the Akans' (1987) argued the point that any conception of mind as some kind of an entity must jar severely on the conceptual framework embedded in Akan thought and talk about things mental. There is no unanimity among contemporary Akan philosophers on these interpretations, but in matters philosophical this should catch no one by surprise. Furthermore, in neither case are the conceptual disparities revealed taken as proof of philosophical wisdom or its opposite. What they might establish is that certain ways of thought and puzzlement entrenched in Western philosophy are not humanly ineluctable. While it would be premature to invest this reflection with a relativistic significance, the need for a serious examination of relativism is certainly collateral to these types of inquiries.

The book by Hallen and Sodipo (1986) represents something of a methodological innovation in contemporary research in African philosophy (see YORUBA EPISTEMOLOGY). The two academic philosophers sought the expertise of a class of Nigerian traditional healers (known as *onisegun*) recognized for their mastery of Yoruba thought and language, by interacting with them on terms of respectful collegiality. They regarded the *onisegun* not as informants, as was customary in academic research, but as fellow philosophers and held long discussions with them on the semantics of certain philosophically-sensitive Yoruba concepts. They then drew upon the results, which they published in faithful transcription, to make comparisons with approximate conceptual counterparts in English. They discovered that the approximations in every case had a significant roughness at their philosophical edges. The best analogy of the knowledge–belief distinction in the Yoruba language is that between *mò* and *gbàgbó*. But *mò* exacts more stringent conditions than knowledge, as the following observation by Hallen and Sodipo indicates:

> *Gbàgbó* that may be verified is *gbàgbó* that may become *mò*. *Gbàgbó* that is not open to verification (testing) and must therefore be evaluated on the basis of justification (*àlàyé*, *papò*, etc.) cannot become *mò* and consequently its *òótó* [truth] must remain indeterminate.
>
> (Hallen and Sodipo 1986: 81)

The contrast with well-known analyses of knowledge in English-speaking philosophy is so striking that Hallen and Sodipo are moved to conclude that 'propositional attitudes are not universal'. As a brief illustration of one implication of the contrast, it is important to consider the following. In contemporary Anglo-American philosophy it is generally agreed that s knows that p if and only if p is true, s believes that p and s is justified in believing that p under some Gettier-chastened condition(s) (see JUSTIFICATION, EPISTEMIC §3). But, however chastened, the justification condition must be too weak for the Yoruba *mò*, since it requires, as is clear from the context, a first-person experiential verification. More interestingly, the belief condition does not survive a Yoruba conversion either. If a person is acknowledged to *mò* p, then to say that they *gbàgbó* p is not just an understatement, but a self-contradictory misstatement, for the use of *gbàgbó* implies that *mò* is unattained. Thus, though *gbàgbó* may ascend to *mò*, the transformation is qualitative and *mò* at the cognitive apex categorically scorns the base degrees by which it did ascend (with apologies to Shakespeare). All this is, of course, on the assumption that Hallen and Sodipo are right in their interpretation, quoted above, of what the *onisegun* say and furthermore that the *onisegun* are right in their account of the conceptual situation in the African vernacular. Without mentioning the complications introduced by the comparative dimension, this already suggests the multifaceted character of the problem of evaluating all 'hermeneutical studies' that have a transcultural effect. Nevertheless, the importance of such investigations in contemporary African philosophy can hardly be exaggerated.

6 Indigenous African philosophers

Equally important are investigations into what Oruka calls 'philosophic sagacity' or, better, 'sage philosophy'. Oruka himself is responsible for the path-breaking publication in this area of research. In his *Sage Philosophy* (1991) he gives extensive exposure to the philosophical views of indigenous thinkers in contemporary Kenyan society practically uninfluenced by Western ideas. Particularly noteworthy about their thinking is the fact that they are aware of the traditional thought of their community, but not overawed by it. They put forward their views, like most philosophic thinkers, as their own, not as the community's. In this they differ from Hallen and Sodipo's *onisegun*. Although those indigenous experts on Yoruba thought may be bright philosophers, they prefer to throw light on the Yoruba conceptual framework rather than on their own in a personal sense. They abjure intellectual individualism, going as far as to forbid the mention of their names in the published text. Both types of thinkers are known in African society.

To return to Oruka's philosophic sages: in sketches of their philosophical positions in response to their academic interlocutors, they express with force and lucidity a variety of views on many subjects, including God, religion, witchcraft, body and mind, virtue, good and evil, truth and falsehood, happiness, life and death, justice, equality, freedom, law, crime, punishment, human suffering, man and woman, ethnicity, and communalism. Perhaps the most intriguing variation of views is to be found in their conceptions of God. Sage Akoko maintains that the nature of God in unknowable, but his existence can be inferred from the uniformity of nature (1991: 37). Chaungo, on the other hand, is convinced that God is the sun. It 'heats the land all day, and its absence cools the land all night. It dries things: plants use it to grow. Surely, it must be the God we talk about' (1991: 115–6). To Kithanje, God is of the nature of a process rather than of an object. His thought about God revolves round 'the mixture of heat and cold'. When these merge 'there comes life...The act of fusion which brings forth life is what we call God. And that is what we mean when we say that God created the universe' (1991: 134). For his part, Oruka Rang'inya contends that it is wrong to personalize God. He is simply 'an idea, the idea which represents goodness itself' (1991: 119). With Njeru wa Kinyenje, outright atheism is finally reached: 'Both religion and witchcraft...have no truths in them' (1991: 38).

In the literature of African thought south of the Sahara such philosophic individuality has, by a long-standing mistake, rarely been ascribed to individual Africans in traditional life. M. Griaule's *Conversations with Ogotemmeli* (1965) is an apparent exception. Ogotemmeli, a Dogon sage from the west African nation of Mali, is clearly shown to be an individual of outstanding speculative abilities. But the intricate web of thought he weaves belongs to his ethnic group, not to him personally. However, since communal thought is a kind of pooling together of the thought of individual thinkers, the Ogotemmeli phenomenon should have given pause to those who were tempted to suppose that traditional Africa was bereft of individuals of philosophic initiative.

With respect to Africa north of the Sahara, it has not been possible for anyone to harbour a like misapprehension. The existence of individual philosophical thinkers in ancient Egypt has never been in doubt, even if their exact racial identity has been the subject of debate. Moreover, the Arab portions of Africa are heir to a time-honoured Islamic tradition of written philosophy. Even further south, it is widely known, through the industry of Claude Sumner of the University of Addis Ababa, that in Ethiopia there is a historical heritage of written philosophy (see ETHIO-

PIA, PHILOSOPHY IN §1). The high point of that heritage is *The Treatise of Zar'a Ya'ecob* (*c*.1599–*c*.1692 [1993]). Living and meditating contemporaneously with Descartes, although independent of him, and initially in seclusion (by reason of Catholic persecution), Zar'a Ya'ecob developed a philosophy which affirmed belief in God, but subordinated religious creeds and their moral prescriptions to the dictates of reason. He held that in the search for truth, especially in religious matters, no one should passively depend on the determinations of other people 'for all men are plaintiffs and defendants between themselves' ([*c*.1599–*c*.1692] 1993: 17). Everyone should be guided by the light of their own intelligence. That intelligence is capable of conceiving of God as 'a creator, greater than all creatures' and of 'seeing him mentally'. Out of 'the abundance of his intelligence' God has created a world of natural law and order and given us the intelligence to grasp it if we would but inquire rationally. Accordingly, in his evaluations of religious teachings he proceeds on the principle that something accords with the will of God only if it accords with the deliverances of reason. With this intellectual weapon he makes short work of Christian 'stories of miracles that they claim had been wrought in Egypt and on Mount Sinai' by Moses. Nor is he any less scathing of certain Mohammedan tenets. For example, he believes that Mohammed's teaching 'that a man could marry many wives' could not possibly come from God as it 'ruins the usefulness of marriage' ([*c*.1599–*c*.1692] 1993: 18–19).

In general Ya'ecob's treatment of morality is uncompromisingly rationalistic. For him the golden rule is a directive of reason. Since the 'prohibitions of killing, stealing, lying, adultery' are derivable from it, he says of them: 'our reason teaches us these and similar ones'. In respect of these, therefore, 'the decalogue of the Pentateuch expresses the will of the creator'. But he makes an exception in the case of the commandment of the Sabbath because 'reason says nothing of the observance of the Sabbath' ([*c*.1599–*c*.1692] 1993: 21). Altogether, Ya'ecob sets up a stringent regime of reason in the face of which Descartes might conceivably have balked. Undoubtedly, the work of Ya'ecob is eminent in what might be called the classical heritage of African philosophy.

7 The quest for a synthesis

The study and evaluation of African traditional philosophy and the classical heritage of African philosophy are two of the more straightforward components of the agenda of contemporary African philosophy. Another, infinitely trickier, is the project of synthesizing any insights that might be had from the study of Western philosophy (and any other philosophical traditions) with those gained from indigenous sources in the construction of African philosophies for contemporary existence (from which open-minded non-Africans might have something to learn). One potent source of ambivalence among some Africans towards this type of effort, as it pertains to Western philosophy, is the fact that it is apt to look like a mindless imitation of the philosophical ways of one's erstwhile colonizers. The best antidote to such qualms is for African researchers to be conscious of their African purposes and always to scrutinize critically the conceptual pertinence – recall the need for conceptual decolonization – and the theoretical soundness of any appropriations of ideas or adaptations of technique. They do not need to approach the enterprise in a spirit of passivity. In principle, they can make original and enriching contributions, at one and the same time, to the given foreign tradition as well as to their own: a fact which is sometimes forgotten. There are, moreover, existential reasons for African interest in Western philosophy. Through the twin historical facts of Western colonization and Christian evangelization, African cultures have been profoundly impregnated with ethical, metaphysical and epistemological ideas of a Western provenance. These ideas cry out for critical examination in Africa as much as in their places of origin. (The principle is applicable, *mutatis mutandis*, to Islamic ideas in Africa.)

Whether in full realization of these considerations or from a semiconscious attunement to the needs and possibilities of the contemporary African situation, many African philosophers have devoted considerable attention to topics that historically have been grist for the Western philosophical mill. The unspoken principle of this practice is that they can be turned to African purposes too. The 1980s and 1990s have seen a great deal of African philosophical output of this sort.

Africans working towards the advancement of African philosophy can ponder the historic precedent of such famous sons of Africa as Tertullian, St Cyprian and St Augustine. These were among the Graeco-Romanized indigenes of colonized North Africa whose thought has influenced Western philosophy, leaving in some cases permanent imprints. They do not seem in their intellectual efforts to have been motivated by the quest for a synthesis of the African and non-African elements in their experience, although it cannot be assumed that their thinking was altogether without African traces. On the contrary, it may well be, as John Ferguson suggests in his essay 'Aspects of Early Christianity in North Africa' (1969), that the character of the Christianity they advocated owed something to their African background. Nevertheless, forging an African tradition of thought does not seem to have been a priority in their concerns. In pursuit of this objective Africans will have to bend any foreign influences to African purposes. These purposes will sometimes be common to humankind, but sometimes contingent upon the distinctive circumstances of African existence.

See also: AESTHETICS, AFRICAN; AFRICAN PHILOSOPHY, FRANCOPHONE; ETHICAL SYSTEMS, AFRICAN §1; ETHNOPHILOSOHY, AFRICAN §5

References and further reading

Appiah, A.K. (1989) *Necessary Questions: An Introduction to Philosophy*, Engelwood Cliffs, NJ: Prentice Hall. (Lucid introduction to most of the principal areas of philosophy with a concluding chapter that is of special African interest.)

—— (1982) *In My Father's House: Africa in the Philosophy of Culture*, London: Methuen; 2nd edn, Oxford: Oxford University Press, 1992. (Significant, among many things, for the interplay between literature and philosophy in the African intellectual milieu.)

* Bonevac, D. and Phillips, S. (eds) (1993) *Understanding Non-Western Philosophy: Introductory Readings*, Mountain View, CA: Mayfield Publishing Company. (An interesting read.)

Danquah, J.B. (1944) *The Akan Doctrine of God: A Fragment of Gold Coast Ethics and Religion*, London: Frank Cass, 1968. (A classic of Akan philosophy expounding an interpretation of Akan perceptions of deity and morality.)

* Fanon, F. (1961) *The Wretched of the Earth*, London: Penguin, 1983. (An articulation of a philosophy of liberation and national reconstruction by an African-descended thinker.)

* Ferguson, J. (1969) 'Aspects of Early Christianity in North Africa', in J. Ferguson and L. Thompson (eds) *Africa in Classical Antiquity*, Nigeria: Ibadan University Press. (Exploration of the indigenous elements in the thought of prominent African Church Fathers, such as Tertullian and St Augustine in Roman north Africa.)

Fløistad, G. (1987) *Contemporary Philosophy*, vol. 5: *African Philosophy*, Boston, MA: Kluwer. (A collection of some samples of current work in African philosophy.)

Forde, D. (ed.) (1954) *African Worlds: Studies in the Cosmological Ideas and Social Values of African Peoples*, Oxford: Oxford University Press. (Anthropological discussions of the religion, ethos and ethics of a wide range of African peoples.)

* Gbadegesin, S. (1991) *African Philosophy: Traditional Yoruba Philosophy and Contemporary African Realities*, New York: Peter Lang. (In addition to a reflective treatment of Yoruba traditional philosophy, there is a philosophical discussion of cultural, ethical and socioeconomic problems of contemporary Nigerian life.)

* Griaule, M. (1965) *Conversations with Ogotemmeli: An Introduction to Dogon Religious Ideas*, London: Oxford University Press. (An historic exposition of the cosmology of the Dogon people of the west African nation of Mali.)

* Gyekye, K. (1987) *An Essay on African Philosophical Thought: The Akan Conceptual Scheme*, New York: Cambridge University Press; 2nd edn, Philadelphia, PA: Temple University Press, 1995. (An expository as well as analytical account of the philosophical thought of the Akans of Ghana with some characterization of African philosophy in general.)

* Hallen, B. and Sodipo, J.O. (1986) *Knowledge, Belief and Witchcraft: Analytic Experiments in African Philosophy*, London: Ethnographica Ltd. (Inquiries into Yoruba conceptions of belief and knowledge together with clarifications of Yoruba ideas about witchcraft in contrast with some Western ones.)

Hountondji, P. (1983) *African Philosophy: Myth and Reality*, Bloomington, IN: Indiana University Press, 2nd edn, 1996. (Frequently the definitive point of departure in contemporary controversies on the right conception of African philosophy. Stresses the necessity of writing in the discipline of philosophy. Also contains an interesting discussion of A.-W. Amo, the eighteenth-century Ghanaian philosophy professor in Germany, plus an analysis and evaluation of the philosophy and ideology in Nkrumah's *Consciencism: Philosophy and Ideology for De-Colonization* (1964).)

Idowu, E.B. (1962) *Olodumare: God in Yoruba Belief*, London: Longman. (Famous study of traditional Yoruba perceptions of God, personhood and morality by a Yoruba academic.)

* —— (1973) *African Traditional Religion: A Definition*, London: SCM Press. (Attempts a definition of religion in general and African traditional religion in particular, confronting various philosophical questions.)

* Kaunda, K.D. (1980) *Kaunda on Violence*, London: Collins. (Rational soul-searching on the question of the moral legitimacy of violence in the African liberation struggle and in human affairs in general.)

* Lienhardt, G. (1961) *Divinity and Experience: The Religion of the Dinka*, Oxford: Oxford University Press. (A conceptually sensitive and philosophically

useful study of the religion of the Dinka people of Sudan.)
* Mazrui, A.A. (1978) 'Mahatma Gandhi and Black Nationalism', in *Political Values and the Educated Class in Africa*, London: Heinemann. (A discussion of the influence of Gandhi's philosophy of non-violence on African liberation leaders, such as Nkrumah and Kaunda.)
* Mbiti, J. (1969) *African Religions and Philosophy*, London: Heinemann, 2nd edn, 1990. (A survey of religious and philosophical ideas from many parts of Africa. Chapter three gives an account of the concept of time in African thought.)
* Mutiso, G.-C.M. and Rohio, S.W. (1975) *Readings in African Political Thought*, London: Heinemann. (A comprehensive and extremely useful anthology of the political thought of Africa's first wave of post-independence leaders.)
* Nkrumah, K. (1964) *Consciencism: Philosophy and Ideology for De-Colonization*, London: Panaf Books, 1970. (The most severely technical of the philosophical writings by African statesmen in support of socialism.)
* Nyerere, J.K. (1968) *Ujamaa: Essays on Socialism*, New York: Oxford University Press. (Prescriptive discussions of socialism as a basis of development in Tanzania.)
* —— (1969) *Nyerere on Socialism*, Dar es Salaam, Tanzania: Oxford University Press. (A combination of the introductions to two previous books on aspects of socialism. Provides abstract analyses of the socialist idea.)
Okere, T. (1983) *African Philosophy: A Historico-Hermeneutical Investigation of the Conditions of its Possibility*, New York: University Press of America. (A hermeneutically-oriented discussion of the nature of philosophy with illustrative explorations of Hegel, Heidegger, Ricoeur and others as a preliminary to hints as to how best African philosophy might be done.)
* Oruka, O.H. (1990) *Trends in Contemporary African Philosophy*, Nairobi: Shirikon Publishers. (Analyses and criticisms of trends in contemporary African philosophy by one of the most active contributors to the discipline.)
* —— (1991) *Sage Philosophy: Indigenous Thinkers and the Modern Debate on African Philosophy*, Nairobi: African Center for Technology Studies. (Presents in translation the personal philosophical views of some thinkers of Kenya traditional society together with discussions of reprinted criticisms of his methodology.)
* P'Bitek, O. (1970) *African Religions in Western Scholarship, Prose and Poetry*, London: Oxford University Press. (Briefer extracts in the prose section from writings dealing with a variety of topics, including the ideological and the philosophical.).
* —— (1971) *Religion of the Central Luo*, east African Literature Bureau. (An account of the Luo religion.)
* Sawyer, H. (1970) *God, Ancestor or Creator?*, London: Longman. (An inquiry into traditional perceptions of God among the Akans of Ghana, the Yoruba of Nigeria and the Mende of Sierra Leone.)
Second Order (1972–1985), Nigeria: University of Ife Press; new series, Nigeria: Obafemi Awolowo University Press, 1985–. (Served as a vehicle for African philosophical output at a historically critical time.)
* Senghor, L.S. (1964) *On African Socialism*, New York: Praeger. (Senghor's ideological prescriptions for Senegal together with their philosophical underpinnings.)
* —— (1965) *Prose and Poetry*, London: Oxford University Press. (Briefer extracts, in the prose section, from writings dealing with a variety of topics, including the ideological and the philosophical.)
* Serequeberhan, T. (1991) *African Philosophy: The Essential Readings*, New York: Paragon House. (Anthology of contributions to the debate on the meaning and method of African philosophy from Bodunrin, Hountondji, Keita, Okolo, Onyewuenyi, Oruka, Owomoyela, Serequeberhan, Towa, Wamba-Dia-Wamba and Wiredu.)
* Soyinka, W. (1976) *Myth, Literature and the African World*, Cambridge: Cambridge University Press. (Literary and philosophical reflections of one of Africa's foremost writers.)
Sumner, C. (1994) *Classical Ethiopian Philosophy*, Los Angeles, CA: Adey. (A discussion of traditional philosophical systems in Ethiopia.)
* Tempels, P. (1959) *Bantu Philosophy*, Paris: Présence Africaine. (Historic study of an African philosophy from the point of view of a Catholic missionary. Subject of heated discussions in contemporary African philosophy.)
* UNESCO (1984) *Teaching and Research in Philosophy: Africa*, Paris: UNESCO. (Report on the role of philosophy in the educational systems of most African nations from secondary school and beyond. It was the first UNESCO survey of teaching and research in philosophy in various parts of the world.)
Wiredu, K. (1980) *Philosophy and An African Culture*, Cambridge: Cambridge University Press. (Considerations on the tasks of African philosophy and on the concepts of truth and existence.)
* —— (1986) 'The Question of Violence in Contem-

porary African Political Thought', *Praxis International* 6 (3). (Study of contemporary African thought regarding violence and nonviolence as options in the anti-colonial struggle.)
—— (1987) 'The Concept of Mind with Particular Reference to the Language and Thought of the Akans', in G. Fløistad (ed.) *Contemporary Philosophy*, vol. 5: *African Philosophy*, Boston, MA: Kluwer, 1987. (Discussion of the concept of mind in general and Akan thought in particular.)
* Ya'ecob, Z. (*c.*1599–*c.*1692) *The Treatise of Zar'a Ya'ecob*, in D. Bonevac and S. Phillips (eds) *Understanding Non-Western Philosophy: Introductory Readings*, Mountain View, CA: Mayfield Publishing Company, 1993. (The definitive English-language editions of the *The Treatise* by Zar'a Ya'ecob, the seventeenth-century indigenous Ethiopian philosopher and other sources of Ethiopian philosophy are those of Professor Claude Sumner.)

KWASI WIREDU

AFRICAN PHILOSOPHY, FRANCOPHONE

The imaginative and intellectual writings that have come out of French-speaking Africa have tended to be associated exclusively with the négritude *movement and its global postulation of a black racial identity founded upon an original African essence. Beyond its polemical stance with regard to colonialism, the movement generated a theoretical discourse which served both as a means of self-validation for the African in particular and the black race in general. This discourse developed further as the elaboration of a new worldview derived from the African cultural inheritance of a new humanism that lays claim to universal significance.*

Despite its prominence in the intellectual history of Francophone Africa and in the black world generally, négritude *does not account for the full range of intellectual activity among the French-speaking African intelligentsia. The terms of its formulation have been challenged since its inception, leading to ongoing controversy. This challenge concerns the validity of the concept itself and its functional significance in contemporary African thought and collective life. It has involved a debate regarding the essential nature of the African, as well as the possibility of constructing a rigorous and coherent structure of ideas (with an indisputable philosophical status) derived from the belief systems and normative concepts implicit in the institutions and cultural practices subsisting from Africa's precolonial past.*

The postcolonial situation has enlarged the terms of this debate in French-speaking Africa. It has come to cover a more diverse range of issues touching upon the African experience of modernity. As an extension of the 'indigenist' theme which is its point of departure, the cultural and philosophical arguments initiated by the adherents of négritude *encompass a critical reappraisal of the Western tradition of philosophy and its historical consequences, as well as a consideration of its transforming potential in the African context. Beyond the essentialism implied by the concept of* négritude *and related theories of Africanism, the problem at the centre of French–African intellectual preoccupations relates to the modalities of African existence in the modern world.*

From this perspective, the movement of ideas of the French-speaking African intelligentsia demonstrates the plurality of African discourse, as shaped by a continuing crisis of African consciousness provoked by the momentous process of transition to modernity. A convergence can be discerned between the themes and styles of philosophical discourse and inquiry in Francophone Africa and some of the significant currents of twentieth-century European philosophy and social thought engaged with the fundamental human issues raised by the impact of modern technological civilization.

Two dominant perspectives frame the evolution of contemporary thought and philosophical discourse in French-speaking Africa: the first is related to the question of identity and involves the reclamation of a cultural and spiritual heritage considered to be imperilled; the second relates to what has been called 'the dilemma of modernity' experienced as a problematic dimension of contemporary African life and consciousness.

1 The French colonial context
2 Intellectual resistance to colonial discourse
3 Placide Tempels's *Bantu Philosophy*
4 *Négritude*
5 Ethnophilosophy
6 Cheikh Anta Diop
7 The critique of *négritude*
8 V.Y. Mudimbe and the critique of Africanist discourses
9 Summary

1 The French colonial context

The development of philosophical discourse as a distinct current of intellectual activity in Francophone Africa has run parallel to that of an innovative imaginative expression. Such development is bound up with the ideological project of an assertive cultural nationalism. The movement of thought that informs the process of self-reflection on the part of French-speaking African intellectuals, culminating in the idea of *négritude*, derives its impulse from an affective response to the colonial situation. It reflects an effort to grapple with the multiple implications of the collective predicament that forms the larger historical context of the colonial experience, namely the violent encounter between Africa and Europe and its concomitant ideological devaluation of the black race. These factors and the inherent discomforts of the immense process of social and cultural change have been determinants in the origin and evolution of what Robert July (1968) has called 'modern African thought'.

If the general circumstances of the historic conflict between Africa and Europe provide the sentimental hinterland from which the energy of intellectual activity in Africa derives, the specific orientation of contemporary thought in Francophone Africa has been further conditioned by the sustained contact of its intellectual elite with the literary and philosophical traditions to which their French education gave them access. It is worthy of note that the cultural tenets of colonial administration in the areas of Africa under French and Belgian rule, and the educational system they inspired, were given coherence as functional elements of what was termed the policy of assimilation. The notion of the civilizing mission of European colonialism central to this policy was premised on the idea of the basic inferiority of African culture, which was in need of the redeeming function of Western civilizing values. Constraints of assimilation account for the centrality in Francophone African literature of the theme of alienation, which was given expression as a sense of dissociation from the moral and psychological security of defining origins. The imaginative exploration of this theme found its parallel in a conceptual engagement on the part of the Francophone black (African and Caribbean) intellectual elite with the question of identity. The force of lived experience lent urgency to the thought-provoking question of existence. For the Francophone African elite who were 'assimilated' but none the less preoccupied with interpreting and coming to terms with the colonial experience, intellectual activity could only proceed as a meditation upon the self in relation to a singular historicity.

Associated with the cultural malaise of assimilation was the negative image of Africa that was constantly projected by the Western texts on which was based much of the education of the Francophone African elite. The ideological thrust of these texts is exemplified by the work of Pierre Loti (1888) and other writers associated with the so-called colonial novel.

Their perspective helped to propagate the idea of Africa as a landscape whose inhospitable nature was reflected in the savage disposition of its indigenous populations (Fanoudh-Siefer 1968). This literature was the symbolic expression of a European ethnocentrism that had been given philosophical respectability by HEGEL, who excluded the African continent from his conception of the world historical process and the unfolding of the universal mind, the foundations of his philosophical system. Arthur de Gobineau's *Essai sur l'inégalité des races humaines* (1884) gave systematic form to the hierarchy of the races established as commonplace to European thought in his time within which African and black races occupied the lowest level. However, it was left to Lucien Lévy-Bruhl to lend the authority of learned discourse to the great divide between the West and the rest of humanity affirmed in de Gobineau's essay. In the series of studies beginning with *Les fonctions mentales dans les sociétés inférieures* (1912) and culminating in *La mentalité primitive* (1922), Lévy-Bruhl undertook to establish the disparity between Western and non-Western cultures at the level of the mental operations by which both were regulated. The term 'prelogical mentality' which he proposed to describe the quality of mind of non-Western peoples was to have resonance beyond the discipline of anthropology. These and other works of the same tenor composed an articulated Western discourse on Africa, which emerged as the antithesis of Europe in the structure of ideas and images by which the colonial ideology was sustained.

2 Intellectual resistance to colonial discourse

The counterdiscourse that was articulated by the Francophone African elite in the 1930s was called into being by the demoralizing effect and egregious nature of this discourse of imperial hegemony. Their response was facilitated by the crisis of European civilization in the early twentieth century after the First World War. The disenchantment with the traditional humanism in Europe reflected in the literature and philosophy of the period provided an appropriate context for the note of dissidence voiced in the ideological writings of the colonized Francophone black intellectual (Kesteloot 1965). Marxism and Surrealism were primary influences, but more pertinent were the formative roles played by French thinkers in the interwar years, which added a particular tone to the expression of some of the leading figures in Francophone African intellectual movements. Of special interest in this respect is the organic nationalism of Maurice Barrès and the anti-intellectualist philosophy of Henri-Louis BERGSON, both of whom bequeathed an ambiguous legacy of attitudes and ideas to the cultural nationalism of France's colonial subjects. While the conflation of race and culture provided an anchor in Barrès (1897) for an exclusive vision of the national community, Bergson promoted a special reverence for those noncognitive modes of experience embodied in forms of artistic expression in reaction against the dominant rationalist tradition. Both laid the foundation for Senghor's later celebration of *négritude* as a black racial endowment and provided the language for its formulation.

Paradoxically, the discipline of anthropology, in which a new spirit of cultural relativism had begun to prevail, provided the immediate source of intellectual armoury of the Francophone African response to colonial ideology. The efforts of French scholars Robert Delavignette and Maurice Delafosse to explicate African forms of social and cultural expression and accord them recognition culminated in Marcel Griaule's *Dieux d'eau: entretiens avec Ogotemmeli* (1948). The articulation in this work of the elaborate cosmology of the Dogon, as related by the African sage Ogotommeli, revealed an evident symbolic architecture and conceptual organization in an African culture that advanced the case for a revaluation of the continent and its peoples.

3   Placide Tempels's *Bantu Philosophy*

Placide Tempels's *Bantu Philosophy* (1945) was decisive in giving a philosophical orientation to the emerging discourse of cultural nationalism in Francophone African. Tempels's objective was to reveal the existence of a reflective disposition among the Luba, an ethnic group in the then Belgian Congo. He ascribed to them a collective philosophy distinguished by an ontology summed up in the following quotation:

> I believe that we should most faithfully render Bantu thought in the European language by saying that the Bantu speak, act, live as if, for them, beings were forces. Force is not for them an adventitious accidental reality. Force is even more than a necessary attribute of beings: Force is the nature of being, force is being, being is force.
> (1945: 35)

The passage makes obvious the derivation of Tempels's work from Bergson: the notion of 'vital force' by which he sought to characterize Bantu thought recalled the French philosopher's *élan vital*. Tempels's reconstruction of mental structure from 'collective representations' dear to Durkheim and his disciples in the French school of anthropology was an application of Lévy-Bruhl's method, although a reversal of its theoretical import and ideological implications. *Bantu Philosophy* provided the model and conceptual framework for the construction of an original African philosophy and has remained a central reference of philosophical debate in Africa.

4   *Négritude*

It is against this historical and intellectual background that the concept of *négritude* took form. It was the eminent French philosopher Jean-Paul SARTRE who was the first to give the concept extended philosophical formulation. His essay 'Orphée noir' (Black Orpheus) (1949) was an expansive reflection on the term which had been coined by the Martinican poet Aimé Césaire in the context of his poem *Cahier d'un retour au pays natal* (Notebook of a Return to my Native Land) (1939) to denote the advent of a liberated black consciousness. In the essay Sartre offered a definition of *négritude* in Heideggerian/Existentialist terms, as 'the-being-in-the-world-of-the-Negro'. Extending this definition by reference to the orthodoxies of Marxism, he situated the racial consciousness designated by *négritude* and the project of collective freedom it proclaimed in an historical perspective as a stage in a dialectic destined to be transcended by the advent of a classless and raceless world society.

Senghor's conception of *négritude* both enlarges upon Sartre's definition and gives it a new orientation. Rather than a contingent factor of black collective existence and consciousness as with Sartre (for Senghor this aspect corresponds to what he calls 'subjective *négritude*'), the concept denotes for Senghor an enduring quality of being constitutive of the black race and exempt from the exigencies of the historical process. The term further signifies a complex of objective factors that shape the African experience, embodied in forms of life on the continent and manifested in the modes of thought and feeling of its people, hence Senghor's definition of *négritude* as 'the sum total of African cultural values' (1970). His theory of *négritude* takes the form of an exposition of the African's distinctive manner of relating to the world. Appropriating Lévy-Bruhl's notion of 'participation', Senghor accords primacy to emotion as distinctive of an African mode of access to the world. Emotion is accorded special signification by Senghor; it is no longer merely a psychological state, but a mode of apprehension, a 'capturing of integral being – body and consciousness – by the indeterminate world' (1962: 15). Senghor's thinking concerns itself with the opposition between both the mystical approach to reality that the developed emotion determines in the African, as well as the pure intellection that is held to be characteristic of the West and historically enshrined in the *cogito* of Descartes. According to Senghor, emotion is governed by intentionality and thus presents itself as a valid mode of cognition.

We have here the epistemological foundation of the African worldview and collective ethos as interpreted by Senghor, who posits in the African a total grasp of reality embracing the continuum from the realm of nature to the supernatural. The informing principle of this *Weltanschauung* and system of social organization emanating from it amounts to a spiritualism that invests all phenomena with a sacred character. Senghor has extended this idea into his theory of African socialism, presented as the social philosophy entailed by the theory of *négritude*. Although commanded by practical considerations, African socialism as enunciated by him is a strategy for reconciling the imperatives of modernity – social and economic development in Western terms –with an African ethos. For Senghor (1961) this socialist ideal is governed by the need to infuse the humanizing values of traditional Africa into the new structures of collective life in the modern dispensation. Therefore, African socialism presents itself less as the construction of a concrete social progamme than as an axiology.

Senghor's theory of *négritude* developed as a function of his poetic vocation. Although in later works (Ndaw 1983) he restated his system of ideas to align it more closely with the classical epistemology codified by Aristotle, the theory bears a close affinity with the various continental forms of Lebensphilosophie that have sprung up as a reaction to the instrumental reason of modern social organization (see LEBENSPHILOSOPHIE). There is a sense in which Senghor's *négritude* may be interpreted as an African version of Bergsonism: a verification in African form of the cultural expression of the idea of intuition as the sign of experience at the most profound level of consciousness.

5 Ethnophilosophy

Senghor's *négritude* represents an effort to provide a comprehensive elucidation of African being. Despite its limitations and disputed status as philosophy, it marks, as D.A. Masolo has observed, 'the legitimate origin of philosophical discussion in Africa' (1994: 10). The movement of self-definition it initiated led to the effort in Francophone Africa to generate an African philosophy from anthropological literature pertaining to the traditional cultures on the continent. The school of thought spawned by this effort, known as ethnophilosophy, is represented by Alexis Kagamé's *La Philosophie bantu-rwandaise de l'être* (Bantu-Rwandan Philosophy of Being) (1956), a work conceived as a verification and reformulation of Tempels's propositions in more rigorous analytical terms. Kagamé appealed to his native Rwandan language to reconstruct the philosophy underlying his people's worldview. From the root stem, *ntu*, signifying essence in general, Kagamé has deduced four fundamental categories of Bantu thought: man, being endowed with intelligence, or *muntu*; being without intelligence, such as animals, plants, minerals, or *kintu*; the space–time continuum, or *hantu* and modality, or *kuntu*. According to Kagamé these terms function both as markers of implicit thought processes and vehicles of an explicit philosophical discourse demonstrable by reference to Rwandan oral tradition.

Kagamé's exposition is not intended as a reconstruction but as a description, *stricto sensu*, of an authentic system of Bantu thought, which corresponds with Aristotle's system for its translation into a non-African language and frame of reference. For this reason the work raises the question of language in African philosophy and the problem that Benveniste has identified as the relation between 'categories of language and categories of thought' (1966). Kagamé's pioneering effort was followed up by explorations of traditional systems of thought in the work of scholars who form what V.Y. Mudimbe has designated (1986) as Tempels's philosophical school. Composed mainly of central Africans and dominated by clerics, the major preoccupation of this school has been to identify those elements of the African personality compatible with Christian doctrine. Their endeavour has fostered the emergence of a theology that reconciles the West and Africa through a shared spirituality.

6 Cheikh Anta Diop

Ethnophilosophy, as a direct tributary of *négritude*, seeks to define African identity in terms of an ontology. Another current of cultural nationalism, the historical school associated with the work and personality of the Senegalese scholar Cheikh Anta Diop, discovers this identity in what may be called an African *longue durée*. Diop is best known for his book *Nations nègres et culture* (Black Nations and Culture) (1956), which advanced the thesis of ancient Egypt as an integral part of a black African civilization. The real significance of Diop's work resides less in the validity of his arguments and conclusions than in the development he gave to the thesis in subsequent works. In *L'Unité culturelle de l'Afrique noire*

(Cultural Unity of Black Africa) (1959), Diop considered Africa as a single, unified cultural area on the basis of the continuity of cultural forms and value systems between ancient Egypt and indigenous civilizations throughout Africa. This argument was summarized in 'Egypte ancienne et Afrique noire' (1962). The philosophical implications of Diop's work emerge from the comprehensive vision of Africa's historical personality by which it is informed and its spirit of confrontation with Hegel's philosophy of history. The erudition and methodological effort he invested in constructing an 'historical sociology' aimed to restore Africa to an honourable place in universal history. As he says, 'Historical science cannot shed all the light one might expect it to cast upon the past until it integrates the African component of humanity, in proportion to the role it has actually played in history, into its synthesis' (1962: 11). Diop's work established a line of historical reflection and research in Francophone Africa, as exemplified in the writings of Joseph Ki-Zerbo (1972) and especially Théophile Obenga, Diop's most accomplished disciple. His *L'Afrique dans l'Antiquité* (1970) represents a summation of the ideas and methods of the school spawned by Diop (see EGYPTIAN PHILOSOPHY: INFLUENCE ON ANCIENT GREEK THOUGHT).

7 The critique of *négritude*

A reaction set in against the theory of a black racial self and the creation of an African collective identity propounded by *négritude* and endorsed by ethnophilosophy. The critique of *négritude*, which began in the 1950s with attacks on Sartre's definition by Albert Franklin (1953) and Gabriel D'Arboussier (1959), developed into controversy that has not subsided. The radical spirit of this critique was embodied in the work of Frantz FANON, beginning with his analysis of the pathology of colonialism in *Black Skin, White Masks* (1952). This analysis took the form of a Hegelian enactment of the black subject's drama of consciousness, that of the struggle for recognition involved in the master/slave dialectic. Fanon's clinical perspective focused on the inward psychological depredations of colonial domination. The ethics of violence elaborated in *The Wretched of the Earth* (1961) springs from his conception of its restorative value for the colonized native. His uncompromising radicalism with its repudiation of mere culturalism endows violence with a transcendent significance: 'African culture will take concrete shape around the struggle of the people, not around songs, poems or folklore' (1961: 164).

The critique of Senghor undertaken by Stanilas Adotevi (1972) owes its force to Fanon's example and to his disposal of identity as an issue worthy of moral concern and theoretical interest. Fanon's influence also accounts for the break with the spirit of cultural nationalism embodied in *négritude* by the philosopher Marcien Towa (1971). His intransigence is displayed in the following terms: 'The transformation of one's present condition signifies at the same time the transformation of one's essence, of what is particular to the self, of what is original and unique about it; it is to enter into a negative relationship with the self' (1971: 41). This growing disaffection towards *négritude* developed into a theoretical attack on ethnophilosophy as its outgrowth, marking a significant phase in the evolution of Francophone African philosophy. Eboussi-Boulaga's initial objection to Tempels, whose philosophy he described as 'an ontological system that is totally unconscious, and given expression in an inadequate and incoherent vocabulary' (1968) extended in Towa's essay into a critical reappraisal of ethnophilosophy, culminating in an effort to demolish its conceptual edifice in Paulin Hountondji's *African Philosophy: Myth or Reality* (1983). Hountondji's focus on the methodological procedures of the ethnophilosophers led him to discern a 'confusion of genres' in their attempts to construct a philosophical discourse from material with an ethnological interest. For him ethnophilosophy was 'a hybrid ideological discipline without a status in the world of theory' (1983: 52). To the unanimism implicit in the conception of philosophy as a collective system of thought immanent in a people's culture, Hountondji opposed the criterion of philosophy as an explicit discourse and its rigorous character as a critical activity. He represented philosophy as a reflection on science considered as a significant component of modern culture and equated the philosophical enterprise with the development of science. The lack of scientific culture in Africa forced him to reach the conclusion that the continent is a long way from fulfilling the conditions necessary for philosophical practice.

Hountondji progressed from a narrow conception of philosophy to a broader view amounting to a form of pragmatism (see PRAGMATISM), involving an interrogation of the possible function of philosophy in the African context. A reappraisal of modes of scientific thought and practice in traditional Africa and a concern for their modernization and expansion in contemporary Africa have come to provide the principal orientation of his reflection, inspired by a sharper sense of the possible relation of philosophy to public policy and social practice. Therefore, the role of philosophy has come to include for Hountondji 'the analysis of the collective experience with a view toward a critique of everyday life' (1992: 359). The political implications of such a critique, suggested by the work of Henri Lefebvre in France after the precedent of the Frankfurt school, are made clear.

The political dimension of Hountondji's critique is fully actualized in Achille Mbembe's 'Provisional Notes on the Postcolony' (1992: 3–37). A phenomenology of political life in contemporary Africa, the essay emphasizes the introspective and critical character of intellectual activity in French-speaking Africa in the postindependence period as a function of the existential problems inherent in the process of transition in contemporary Africa. Beyond what has been called 'the crisis of relevance' in African philosophy (Oladipo 1992), this activity aims to lay the philosophical foundation for social development in Africa in pursuit of a new order of collective life, which Hountondji termed 'the Utopia of another society' (Mudimbe 1992: 360).

8 V.Y. Mudimbe and the critique of Africanist discourses

Valentin Mudimbe's work is significant in terms of the question of the relationship of discourse and constitution of thought with the ambiguous modernity of Africa. He delineated, after FOUCAULT, an 'archaeology of African knowledge' motivated by the ambition to found a new African philosophy with an original register of enunciation, able to underwrite Africa's conceptual autonomy. In *L'autre face du royaume* (1973), he criticizes the discourse of ethnology as an aberrant language.

The Invention of Africa (1988), Mudimbe's best known work, is a development of this judgment and an examination of its implications for African expression in the modern world. In his view the homology between the political and economic imperialism of the West on one hand and its 'epistemological imperialism' on the other, constitutes Africa as a province of a Western epistemological territory. The function of anthropology developed through the nineteenth century was to 'account for the normality, creative dynamism and achievements of the "civilized world" against the abnormality, deviance and primitiveness of the non-literate world' (1988: 24). African studies formed part of this development. It has been so fully integrated into the Western order of discourse that the entry of Africans served to amplify the conceptual scope of this order in what Mudimbe calls a 'discourse of succession'. Mudimbe remarked that 'the main problem concerning the being of African discourse remains one of the transference of methods and their cultural integration in Africa' (1988: 182). His solution was to adapt structuralism to the project of reconstruction in African philosophy (see STRUCTURALISM). The structuralist method permits an escape from the constraints of a systematized rationality while affording an entry into the truth of the world: 'empirical categories can be used as keys to a silent code, leading to universals' (1988: 35). It is unclear how this approach yields the 'absolute' or 'transhistoric discourse' that Mudimbe claims as the alternative to Western rationality. Despite what a commentator has called 'the ambiguous nature of the project suggested by Mudimbe' (Masolo 1991: 109), the interest in Mudimbe's work resides in its account of the African intellectual adventure, which amounts to a vision of the African mind in its encounter with the Western world system.

9 Summary

The themes and positions reviewed provide the main lines of French African thought which have inspired a current of philosophical activity in Africa with its own style of discourse. This has prompted the view that the academic practice of philosophy in Africa is divided between the analytical tradition in Anglophone Africa and the continental tradition in Francophone Africa. Philosophical inquiry in both parts of Africa exhibits the three modes that Richard Rorty has identified in contemporary Western philosophy as 'science, metaphor, politics' (1991: 9–26). Although French-speaking African philosophers do not employ the vocabulary of Anglo-American analytical philosophy, the debate on the epistemological status of traditional thought in Africa has involved them in a sustained reflection on the nature and scope of philosophy itself. Both sides in the debate have been obliged to undertake a clarification of the terms of their discourse, as with Kagamé, whose categories also receive some close technical scrutiny by Hountondji (1983: 188–9). The debate has generated a metaphilosophy concerned with issues such as the relation of myth to metaphysics and the procedural questions touching upon the proper order of terms and concepts as well as the conditions of philosophy as both a discipline and cultural practice. The debate assumes significance by reason of the comparative perspective it projects on the discipline, covering such questions as the meaning of concepts across cultures, leading ultimately to the problem of universalism.

Francophone African thought provides an African perspective on the relation between 'Thought and Change' (Gellner 1965) demonstrated in the West by the progressive imbrication of social science with philosophy since Weber: a development that points to a critical engagement with the whole range of political, social, cultural, moral and aesthetic issues posed to modern awareness by the triumph of rationalism and the scientific revolution. The critical thrust of current debates associated with postmodernism concerning the philosophical legacy of the Enlightenment reflects a sustained effort of internal reassessment in the West, a process in which the reappraisal of Western rationalism by Senghor and other French-speaking African intellectuals is profoundly implicated. As a 'strategy of differentiation' (Irele 1995: 15–34), *négritude* seeks to redefine the terms of the relationship between peoples and cultures within a comprehensive intelligence of the world. The metaphoric allure of a certain style of philosophical discourse identified by Rorty is captured in *négritude*, whose speculative mode offers a challenge to the Western paradigm in rejection of its 'master narratives' (Lyotard 1979).

Beyond this polemical aspect of *négritude*, which also informs Mudimbe's work, Francophone African philosophy assumed a theoretical and historical interest in a global assessment of the dominant trends in modern philosophy and social thought. The commonality between such developments in Western thought exemplified by the Frankfurt school's critique of culture in modern industrial society (see FRANKFURT SCHOOL), the Neo-Marxism of Henri Lefebvre, North American neopragmatism and 'communitarianism' bears witness to a renewed focus on first order questions and on concrete issues of existence in the 'lifeworld' (Habermas 1985). The intersection between these trends in modern Western philosophy and intellectual activity in French-speaking Africa assumes a broad contemporary significance in this light, as under the pressure of historical experience, French-speaking African intellectuals have forced philosophy to confront anew the problems that presided at its origins in the West and which seem to govern its future direction.

See also: AFRICAN PHILOSOPHY, ANGLOPHONE; CULTURAL IDENTITY; MARGINALITY: LATIN AMERICA

References and further reading

* Adotevi, S. (1972) *Négritude et Négrologues*, Paris: Union Générale d'Editions. (A comprehensive critique of Senghor's concept of *négritude* from a sociological and political standpoint.)
* Barrès, M. (1897) *Le Roman de l'energie nationale* (Book of National Energy), vol. 1, *Les Déracinés* (The Uprooted People), Paris: Fasquelle; repr. Paris: Livre de Poche, 1967. (An early fictional expression of French conservative nationalism, this work exerted a significant influence on Senghor's intellectual development.)
* Benveniste, E. (1966) 'Catégories de pensée et catégories de langue' (Categories of Thought and Categories of Language), *Problèmes de Linguistique Générale*, Paris: Gallimard, 63–74. (Analyses the relation between the concept of being in ancient Greek philosophy and the linguistic structure of classical Greek.)
* Carroll, D. (1995) *French Literary Fascism: Nationalism, Anti-Semitism and the Ideology of Culture*, Princeton, NJ: Princeton University Press. (A study of the relationship between literature and rightwing movements in France from the late nineteenth century up to the outbreak of the Second World War.)
* Césaire, A. (1939) *Cahier d'un retour au pays natal*; repr. Paris: Présence Africaine, 1956; trans. M. Rosello with A. Pritchard, *Notebook of a Return to my Native Land*, Newcastle-upon-Tyne: Bloodaxe Press, 1995. (The long poem in Surrealist imagery in which the word *négritude* first appeared in print.)
  D'Arboussier, G. (1959) 'Une dangereuse mystification: la théorie de la Négritude' (A Dangerous Mystification: the Theory of *Négritude*), *Nouvelle Critique* (June): 34–47. (An early attack on *négritude* from a radical Marxist perspective.)
* Diop, C.A. (1956) *Nations nègres et culture* (Black Nations and Culture), Paris: Présence Africaine. (With this major reference of African historiography, Diop initiated the debate on the racial belonging of the ancient Egyptians.)
* —— (1959) *L'Unité culturelle de l'Afrique noire* (Cultural Unity of Black Africa), Paris: Présence Africaine. (Posits an opposition between the nomadic culture and aggressive disposition of the early Europeans and the sedentary civilization that emerged in the Nile valley and spread to the rest of Africa.)
* —— (1962) 'Egypte ancienne et Afrique noire' (Ancient Egypt and Black Africa), *Bulletin de l'Institut Fondamental de l'Afrique Noire* 24 (3–4): 449–574; repr. Dakar: IFAN, 1989. (Argues for the continuity between ancient Egyptian civilization and indigenous cultures in sub-Saharan Africa.)
* Eboussi-Boulaga, F. (1968) 'Le Bantou problématique' (Bantu Problematic), *Présence Africaine* (April–June): 3–40. (A critical appraisal of Placide Tempels's exposition of Bantu philosophy.)
  Fanon, F. (1952) *Black Skin, White Masks*, London: Pluto Press, 1986. (Explores, in the style of French phenomenology, black subjectivity through its complex mode of responses to colonial domination and racism.)

—— (1961) *The Wretched of the Earth*, London: Penguin, 1983. (An examination of the revolutionary consciousness in Africa and the Third World, grounded in an ethics of violence that is counterpoised to the psychological and moral ravages of the colonial situation.)

Fanoudh-Siefer, L. (1968) *Le Mythe du nègre et de l'Afrique noire dans la littérature française de 1800 à la deuxième guerre mondiale* (The Myth of the Negro and of Sub-Saharan Africa in French Literature from 1800 to the Second World War), Paris: Klincksieck. (The most complete study of the construction of the African image in French literature.)

* Franklin, A. (1953) 'La Négritude: réalité ou mystification? Reflections sur "Orphée noir"' (*Négritude: Reality or Mystification? Reflections on 'Black Orpheus'*), *Présence Africaine* 14: 287–303. (The first text to present theoretical and practical objections to Sartre's definition of négritude.)

* Gellner, E. (1965) *Thought and Change*, London: Weidenfeld & Nicholson. (Opposes the analytical school to argue for an engagement of philosophy with the phenomenon of modernity.)

* Gobineau, A. de (1853–5) *Essai sur l'inégalité des races humaines*, Paris: Didot, 3 vols; trans. A. Collins, *The Inequality of Human Races*, Torrance, CA: Noontide Press, 1983. (Elaborates a hierarchy of races based on the supposed genetic traits and endowments of the different branches of humanity; a central text of European ethnocentrism.)

Griaule, M. (1948) *Dieux d'eau: entretiens avec Ogotemmeli*, Paris: Editions du Chêne; 1st edn trans. R. Butler, 2nd edn trans. A.I. Richards and B. Hooke, *Conversations with Ogotemmeli: An Introduction to Dogon Religious Ideas*, London: Oxford University Press, 1965. (An extended account of the cosmology of the Dogon people in west Africa, narrated to a French anthropologist by a traditional sage.)

* Habermas, J. (1985) *The Philosophical Discourse of Modernity: Twelve Lectures*, Cambridge, MA: MIT Press. (A review of the project of modernity as formulated in Western philosophy since Hegel in order to restate the theory of 'communicative reason' developed by Habermas in earlier works.)

Horton, R. (1993) 'African Traditional Thought and Western Science', in *Patterns of Thought in Africa and the West*, Cambridge: Cambridge University Press, 197–258. (Horton's essay proceeds from a reformulation of classical British anthropology to the postulation of a formal correspondence between African systems of thought and Western scientific methods.)

* Hountondji, P. (1983) *African Philosophy: Myth or Reality*, Bloomington, IN: Indiana University Press, 2nd edn, with preface by author, 1996. (A systematic critique of the effort in ethnophilosophy to derive an African philosophical system from the traditional background of belief.)

* —— (1981) 'Que peut la philosophie?' (What Can Philosophy Do?), *Présence Africaine* 119: 47–71. (A discussion of the practical possibilities of philosophy in the African context.)

* —— (1992) 'Daily Life in Black Africa: Elements for a Critique', in V.Y. Mudimbe (ed.) *The Surreptitious Speech*, Chicago, IL: Chicago University Press, 344–64. (An argument for a moral engagement of philosophy with the political and economic crisis in post-independence Africa.)

* —— (1994) 'Démarginaliser' (Demarginalize), intro. to *Les savoirs endogènes* (Endogenous Knowledge), Dakar: CODESRIA, 1–34. (Outlines the possible relation of indigenous forms of scientific thought and technologies to Western theory and practice.)

* Irele, A. (1995) 'Dimensions of African Discourse', in K. Myrsiades and J. McGuire (eds) *Order and Partialities: Theory, Pedagogy and the 'Postcolonial'*, New York: State University of New York Press, 1995: 15–34. (Includes a discussion of négritude as counter-discourse.)

* July, R. (1968) *The Origins of Modern African Thought*, London: Faber & Faber. (An intellectual history of west Africa from the eighteenth century to the era of independence in the early 1960s.)

* Kagamé, A. (1956) *La Philosophie bantu-rwandaise de l'être* (Bantu-Rwandan Philosophy of Being), Brussels: Académie Royale des Sciences Coloniales; repr. New York: Johnson Reprint Corporation, 1966. (An exposition of the conceptual categories of Bantu philosophy based upon terms in the Rwandan language.)

—— (1976) *La philosophie bantu comparée* (Bantu Philosophy Compared), Paris: Présence Africaine. (A comparison of Bantu philosophy.)

* Kesteloot, L. (1965) *Les écrivains noirs de langue française*, Brussels: Institut Solvay; trans. E. Conroy Kennedy, *Black Writers in French: A Literary History of Négritude*, Washington, DC: Howard University Press, 1991. (Provides an exhaustive account of the genesis of French-speaking African and Caribbean literature and thought.)

* Ki-Zerbo, J. (1972) *Histoire de l'Afrique noire* (History of Black Africa), Paris: Hatier. (A celebration of the medieval states of west African empires as part of a revaluation of the precolonial history of Africa.)

* Lévy-Bruhl, L. (1912) *Les fonctions mentales dans les sociétés inférieures*, Paris: F. Alcan; trans. L. Clare, *How Natives Think*, Princeton, NJ: Princeton

University Press, 1985. (The work in which the author first proposed the concept of 'participation' as the dominant mode of experience in non-Western cultures.)

* —— (1922) *La mentalité primitive*, Paris: Presses Universitaires, 4th edn, 1960; trans. L. Clare, *Primitive Mentality*, New York: AMS Press, 1978. (Develops the notion of 'prelogical mentality'.)

* Loti, P. (1888) *Le Roman d'un Spahi*, Paris: Calman-Levy; trans. M.L. Watkins, *The Romance of Spahi*, New York: Rand, McNaly and Co., 1890. (Set in Africa, this work is the outstanding example of the colonial novel in French literature.)

* Lyotard, J.-F. (1979) *La Condition postmoderne*, Paris: Editions de Minuit; trans. G. Bennington and B. Massumi, *The Postmodern Condition*, Manchester: Manchester University Press, 1984. (The classic statement of the postmodern consciousness and sensibility.)

Masolo, D.A. (1987) 'Alexis Kagamé and African socio-linguistics', in G. Fløistad (ed.) *Contemporary Philosophy*: vol. 5, *African Philosophy*, Boston, MA: Kluwer: 181–205. (A critical discussion of Kagamé's use of Rwanda terms in developing Bantu philosophy.)

—— (1991) 'An Archaeology of African Knowledge', *Callaloo* 14 (4). (A critical discussion of the ideas of Mudimbe.)

* —— (1994) *African Philosophy in Search of Identity*, Bloomington, IN: Indiana University Press. (The most comprehensive study of African philosophy published to date.)

* Mbembe, A. (1992) 'Provisional Notes on the Postcolony', *Africa* 62 (1): 3–37. (A trenchant analysis of the social and mortal consequences of authoritarian rule in postcolonial Africa.)

* Mudimbe, V.Y. (1973) *L'autre face du royaume* (The Other Side of the Kingdom), Paris: L'Age d'Homme. (A critique of anthropology as a form of discourse concerned with African 'otherness'.)

—— (1986) 'On the Question of African Philosophy: the Case of French Speaking Africa', in I. Mowoe and R. Bjornson (eds) *Africa and the West: The Legacies of Empire*, Westport, CT: Greenwood Press, 1986: 89–120. (A review of the development of philosophical discourse in French-speaking central Africa.)

* —— (1988) *The Invention of Africa*, Bloomington, IN: Indiana University Press. (An effort to reconstruct an African philosophy as gnosis – a system that is not answerable to the logic of Western rationality.)

Ndaw, A. (1983) *La Pensée africaine: recherche sur les fondements de la pensée négro-africaine* (African Thought: Research into the Basis of Negro-African Thought), with preface by Senghor, Dakar: Nouvelles Editions Africaines. (An attempt to provide a synthesis of the various indigenous systems of thought in Africa; Senghor's preface is a restatement of his position on modes of thought in African philosophy.)

* Obenga, T. (1970) *L'Afrique dans l'Antiquité* (Africa in Ancient times), Paris: Présence Africaine. (Expands upon the historiography of Diop in its investigation of the Egyptian and Middle Eastern component of the African past.)

* Oladipo, O. (1992) *The Idea of African Philosophy*, Ibadan: Molecular Publishers. (A wide-ranging discussion of the situation and role of philosophy in Africa.)

* Rorty, R. (1991) *Essays on Heidegger and Others: Philosophical Papers*, vol. 2, Cambridge: Cambridge University Press, 9–26. (Reviews three conceptions of philosophy in the twentieth century.)

* Sartre, J.-P. (1949) 'Orphée noir' in *Situations III*, Paris: Gallimard; trans. S. Allen, 'Black Orpheus', Paris: Présence Africaine. (Contains Sartre's philosophical formulation of *négritude*.)

Senghor, L.S. (1961) *Nation et voies africaines du socialisme*, Paris: Présence Africaine; trans. M. Cook, *On African Socialism*, New York: Praeger, 1964. (An attempt to derive a social programme in Africa from the tenets of *négritude*.)

* —— (1962) 'De la Négritude: psychologie du Négro-africain' (About *négritude*: the Psychology of the African Negro), *Diogène* 37. (An interesting discussion.)

* —— (1964) *Liberté I: Négritude et humanisme* (Liberty 1: *négritude* and humanism), Paris: Editions de Seuil. (This volume contains Senghor's principal essays on the theory of *négritude*.)

* —— (1970) 'Négritude: A Humanism of the Twentieth Century', in W. Cartey and M. Kilson (eds) *The African Reader: Independent Africa*, New York: Random House, 1970. (Senghor defends the relevance of *négritude* to contemporary concerns in Africa.)

* Tempels, P. (1945) *Bantu Philosophy*, Paris: Présence Africaine, 2nd edn, 1956. (The first systematic exposition of an indigenous African system of philosophical thought, characterized as an ontology of force rather than of being.)

* Towa, M. (1971) *Essai sur la problématique philosophique dans l'Afrique actuelle* (Essay on the Problem of Philosophy in Contemporary Africa), Yaoundé: CLE. (Proceeds from a critique of *négritude* and ethnophilosophy to a statement of the transformative role of philosophy in Africa.)

Wiredu, K. (1996) *Cultural Universals and Particulars: An African Perspective*, Bloomington, IN: Indiana

University Press. (A discussion of the significance of cultural particularities in philosophical discourse and their role in communication between different cultures and peoples.)

F. ABIOLA IRELE

AFRICAN TRADITIONAL RELIGIONS

Religion has been at the centre of recent philosophical debate in Africa for two major reasons. The first is that the answers to many central canonical philosophical questions in precolonial African societies take a religious form. As a result any attempt to construct an African philosophy begs attention to the epistemological and ontological standing of claims of this general sort. The second reason religion has been central to African philosophy is that one of the major issues in modern African philosophy is whether distinctively African modes of thought exist. Within this debate influential positions have been argued by reflecting on the character of traditional religious thought and practice and contrasting it with modes of thought purportedly associated with Western science.

1 Religion
2 'African traditional religion and Western science'
3 Initial criticism
4 Critiques of the analogy between science and traditional religion
5 Critiques of the open–closed dichotomy
6 The devout opposition

1 Religion

Religion is a term whose definition is seen as controversial. Beliefs, institutions and practices can be said to be religious, but the relative importance of belief as opposed to ritual practice, or of ethical belief as opposed to the metaphysical, varies greatly among the belief systems with which Westerners might be familiar – Christianty, Buddhism, Judaism and Islam. Questions of creed, reflecting both the centrality of such questions to Western philosophy and the crucial role of creeds in Christian thinking are at the heart of the literature under discussion in this entry, which derives mainly from philosophers educated in Christian cultures. It will be necessary to draw attention to matters obscured by the focus on matters of propositional belief.

2 'African traditional religion and Western science'

Philosopher-anthropologist Robin Horton (1967) wrote a paper with this title in which he argued that the religious ideas of precolonial Africa maintained by many postcolonial Africans were best understood as constituting a body of theory whose fundamental aim, like that of Western science, was explanation, prediction and control of the phenomena of everyday life. Horton made the claim that traditional African religion is like modern Western science. Horton begins with the idea that anthropology's first task is to provide for one culture, 'the West', an understanding of the concepts of another. Translation is the first step of this task. In the preface of *Patterns of Thought in Africa and the West* (1993) Horton argued that, 'since translation involved finding equivalences of intention and structure between source-language and target-language, it followed that the scholar in quest of the appropriate translation instruments for African religious thought must be prepared to inquire deeply into the intentions and structures embodied in various areas of Western discourse' (1993: 2). At the time of writing, ethnographic studies of African religion were dominated by a sort of Durkheimian consensus which held that religious notions were fundamentally symbolic of social relations. Taken to extremes this led to the 'symbolist' view that religious practices, far from being attempts to mobilize the world of spirits in the pursuit of mortal ends, were, like art, fundamentally expressive with the aim of representing social norms and ideas. Symbolists wanted to deny in particular that religious appeal to spirits presupposes literal belief in them any more than, for example, the function of *Hamlet* as drama requires belief in the literal existence of a Danish prince.

One motive for this view, Horton suggested, was the urge to escape the ethnocentrism of Victorian anthropology with its image of childlike primitives. In their rush to avoid ethnocentrism Horton thought that some symbolists, faced with the irrationality of traditional beliefs, insist that these beliefs are both rational and 'symbolically' true. Horton shares the urge to avoid ethnocentrism, but argues that the assumption underlying this argument that the beliefs are irrational is equally ethnocentric. False beliefs, simply put, do not have to be irrational.

Against the symbolists Horton argued that if any area of discourse in the West provided a model for the central purposes of African religious thought, it was not art but science. He sketched a picture of the role of science in the West as the development of theories which seek to place events in a wider causal context than that provided by common sense. At the heart of this process, in Horton's account, was the development of a structure of belief in invisible entities whose behaviour accounted for the manifest behaviour of the visible world. He felt a key element of theory building was the development of analogies between invisible entities and visible ones. In the natural sciences these invisible entities – atoms and molecules – were modelled on everyday inanimate objects like tiny billiard balls speeding about in the vast spaces of the microcosm, crashing into each other from time to time. (All this at his time of writing amounted to mainstream philosophy of science.) In African religions, invisible entities – gods and spirits – were modelled not on objects but on human beings.

Horton pointed to this difference and offered to explain it, suggesting that it arose from the fundamental nature of explanation as the reduction of the unfamiliar to the familiar. In traditional cultures nature is untamed, alien and a source of puzzlement and fear. Social relations and people, on the contrary, are familiar and well understood. Thus, explaining the behaviour of nature in terms of agency is reducing the unfamiliar forces of the wild to the familiar explanatory categories of personal relations. In the West, on the other hand, 'alienated man' finds social relations puzzling and problematic and the physical world seems stable and familiar.

Horton went on to argue for a further difference. His summary was that African thought, unlike Western science, operated in a 'closed' predicament. His use of language derived from Karl Popper's distinction between 'open' and 'closed' societies (see POPPER, K.R.), but Horton reduced Popper's connected set of oppositions to a simpler contrast: that between closed cultures 'characterized by a lack of awareness of alternatives, sacredness of beliefs, and anxiety about threats to them' (1993: 223) and open cultures, aware of alternatives and less threatened by the possibility of intellectual change.

These arguments have been subjected over the years to a great deal of scrutiny. The most controversial claims presuppose that precolonial African societies have remain unchanged. The stability of social relations implicit in his explanation of why people are appealed to as models, is belied by the turbulent history of many regions of west Africa since the 1700s. The very same wars and migrations must have made people extremely aware of alternative theoretical possibilities. This question of the openness of traditional cultures will be examined later.

3 Initial criticism

The centrality of Horton's argument about religion to the debate in Anglophone African philosophy is evident in the quantity of papers devoted to this question in the leading Anglophone African journal *Second Order*. In the first issue in 1972 Vernon Pratt argued, after Wittgenstein, that Horton had understated the significance of the fact that it was agents not objects that were central to traditional religious theory. Explanations in terms of agency, he argued, differ from causal explanations in two crucial ways. First, agency is intrinsically unpredictable: someone is predictable only if his choice 'has been made for him'. Second, 'it is of the nature of an action to *break in* on a course of events'. Horton (1967) replied that the first of these claims was mistaken and the second claim, although true, did not distinguish agent explanation from the general causal explanation.

A similar debate occurred between Horton and Beattie, the symbolist-anthropologist, in which Beattie (1973) offered a number of arguments in defence of the view that traditional religion does not involve literal belief in spirits. He argued that the reason why spirits are perceived as unobservable is that the practitioners of traditional religion understand that they do not exist. He suggested that religious entities are invoked at the point where a problem cannot be dealt with by 'available empirically-grounded techniques' and that they must therefore be dealt with 'in terms of expressive symbolism' (1993: 4). Horton responded with the view that there is no reason to suppose either that traditional believers are unconvinced of the existence of the spirits to which they refer or that the only possible response to the failure of 'available empirically-grounded techniques' is symbolic, since scientific theory is also a response to such failures.

An interesting philosophical exchange between Horton and John Skorupski (1976) concerned itself with Horton's proposed explanation of the ethnographic observation that in many traditional religions an object is said to belong to a kind to which, as far as an observer is concerned, it obviously does not belong. (Examples are the Nuer identification of twins with birds, reported by Evans-Pritchard in *Nuer Religion* (1956) and the Dinka claim that some men 'are' lions.) Horton proposed that these should be seen as theoretical identifications, such as the famous identification proposed by Eddington (1928) of the 'hard, solid table of common sense thought and action' with the 'largely empty space, peopled by minuscule planetary systems, of theoretical physics' (Horton 1993: 84).

Skorupski argued that Horton misidentified the character of the theoretical identifications of the sciences, believing instead that they are not inherently paradoxical. He went on to suggest that the right Western analogy can be found in certain Christian biblical tales, such as the identification of Christ's body and blood with the bread and wine of the Eucharist.

4 Critiques of the analogy between science and traditional religion

The Ghanaian philosopher Kwasi Wiredu (1980) has indicated that it is *prima facie* very odd to equate traditional religious belief in west Africa with modern Western scientific theory when the obvious analogy is traditional Western religious belief. Kwame Anthony Appiah (1982), beginning with Wiredu's observation, has argued that the reason the parallel between science and religion is misleading is not, as the symbolists held, that religious appeals to spirits are not meant literally. Rather, Appiah suggested that religion has changed a great deal in the modern West over the centuries, particularly the religious life of intellectuals which has turned increasingly towards 'the contemplative, conceived of as spiritual intercourse with God'. Technical questions have 'remained recalcitrant to scientific investigation – questions about one's relations with others – and questions that could not even in principle be addressed by science – questions of value' (1982: 186). This change makes for substantial differences between the religious life of intellectuals in the industrialized world and that of traditional cultures.

There is a further crucial change, Appiah argues, in the nature of contemplative religion in the West. As interpersonal relations have become less ceremonious, so have private religious acts. Since the reformation, Christian prayer has become more like intimate conversation. The ceremoniousness, or ritual character of religious activity in traditional cultures is not analogous in the world or the practice of science. Appiah also argues that there is more of a fundamental reason why the equation of religion and science is misleading, stating that the social organization of inquiry in modern cultures is radically different from its traditional counterparts. Horton had acknowledged this in his initial discussions of the contrast between 'open' and 'closed' cultures. Much attention has been devoted to criticizing Horton's account and trying to alter it.

5 Critiques of the open–closed dichotomy

Barry Hallen (1977) based his work on his experience of philosophical discussions with Yoruba diviners and healers. He argued that there are certainly African religious traditions that show an awareness of other traditions. Hallen takes as his model Karl Popper's characterization of critical reflection on tradition. This is a significant gesture considering the Popperian provenance of the open–closed dichotomy which identifies the tradition as a tradition, displays an awareness of its consequences and is aware of at least one alternative and might choose to affirm or reject it. These tests show that the Yoruba diviners are critically appreciative of their tradition (see YORUBA EPISTEMOLOGY).

In response to Hallen's critique, Horton chose to speak not of the closed nature of traditional belief systems but, borrowing a term from Wole Soyinka (1976), of their being 'accommodative'. He discussed work by students of UK anthropologist E.E. Evans-Pritchard (1937), such as G. Lienhardt's discussion of Dinka religion in *Divinity and Experience* and J. Middleton's *Lugbara Religion*, which not only addressed the kind of static body of belief captured in Evans-Pritchard's picture of the Azande thought world, but also stressed the dynamic and, as Horton came to admit, 'open' way in which they 'devise explanations for novel elements in . . . experience' and 'their capacity to borrow, re-work and integrate alien ideas in the course of elaborating such explanations'. He claims that it is this '"openness" that has given the traditional cosmologies such tremendous durability in the face of the immense changes that the 20th century has brought to the African scene' (Appiah 1987: 226).

Horton contrasted this accommodative style with the 'adversary' style of scientific theory, characterized by the way in which the main stimulus to change of belief is not 'novel experience but rival theory' (Appiah 1987: 226). This change from the Popperian terminology of 'open' and 'closed' allows Horton to reframe the difference between traditional religion and science as not being related to the individual cognitive strategies, but with social ones.

Evans-Pritchard (1937) argued in his classic work that the Azande were not 'experimentally inclined'; that although inclined to scepticism, their scepticism never reached to the level of general theory; that they did not share their experiences and that their beliefs were 'generally vaguely formulated' (1937: 202–4). However, none of this is true of science: it is centrally experimental; scepticism about general theories is one hallmark of great scientists; information is widely disseminated and precision of formulation is regarded as crucial. Each of these differences, as Appiah argued, is central to the social organization of inquiry.

Anthropologist Jack Goody (1977) argued that a key precondition of these forms of social organization of knowledge is the development of distributed literacy. He claimed that oral cultures have been limited by their inability to reaffirm what other theorists have written against experience. It is this fact, Horton went on to argue (1993: 161–93), that accounts for the possibility of the accommodative style. Literacy makes possible the precise formulation of the issues under discussion as being characteristic of scientific theory. Precise formulation allows inconsistencies to be recognized.

6 The devout opposition

Perhaps the least known of Horton's controversies outside Africa is the best known among students of African religion because he has taken on a consensus view of African traditional religion developed by a group he dubbed 'the devout opposition'. This group included many Christian professors working in such places as Nigeria. For these scholars 'the focal object' (1993: 165) of African religion is the Christian God. Other spirits are regarded as his agencies and the attitude of believers towards God is one of awe. The group also thought that the aim of religious life was to achieve communion with God. Horton's views are summarized in the form of a debate with this group in his later work (1993) in which he argued, first, that the ethnographic evidence does not support these claims and that it is the desire not to denigrate traditional belief, combined with Christian theology, that leads the devout opposition to their views. He says that:

> 'It is not surprising that the clearest indications of the ideological character of the "devout" position should come from African rather than Western scholars. After all, it is *their* non-Christian kith and kin whose status is at stake... it is clear that there is a strong link... between establishing that African religions show the essential characteristics of True Religion and establishing the human worth and dignity of Africans'.
>
> (1993: 191).

Horton wanted to argue that scholarly discussion of religion can proceed while suspending the issue of whether monotheism is true. However, Appiah (1993: 7) suggested that if there is a God who makes himself known, albeit obscurely, in African religious experience, then his existence and these experiences may be as relevant to understanding the beliefs of Africans as any other facts about the world in which they live. Horton does not pretend to be a theist, however, his argument with the devout opposition is both anthropological and theological. Appiah felt that Horton was wrong in his contention that the question of God's existence is irrelevant to the philosophical study of religion.

See also: LATIN AMERICA, PRE-COLUMBIAN AND INDIGENOUS THOUGHT IN; RELIGION AND SCIENCE

References and further reading

* Appiah, K.A. (1987) 'Old Gods, New Worlds: Some Recent Work in the Philosophy of African Traditional Religion', in G. Fløistad (ed.) *Contemporary Philosophy*, vol. 5: *African Philosophy*, Boston, MA: Kluwer, 1987: 207–34. (A review of African debates about Horton's work.)
* —— (1982) *In My Father's House: Africa in the Philosophy of Culture*, London: Methuen; 2nd edn, Oxford: Oxford University Press, 1992. (Chapter 6 includes an extended discussion of the character of traditional religious thought.)
* —— (1993) 'Invisible Entities', *Times Literary Supplement*, 17 July: 7. (A review of Horton's *Patterns of Thought in Africa and the West*, 1993.)
* Beattie, J. (1973) 'Understanding traditional African religion: a comment on Horton', *Second Order* 2 (2): 3–11. (A symbolist anthropologist's response to Horton's original claims.)
* Eddington, A. (1928) *The Nature of the Physical World*, Cambridge: Cambridge University Press. (An examination of Eddington's view that everyday objects have duplicates that can be described in the language of physical theory.)
* Evans-Pritchard, E.E. (1937) *Witchcraft, Oracles and Magic among the Azande*, abridged with intro. by E. Gillies, Oxford: Oxford University Press, 1976. (An anthropological classic that has been the focus of much philosophical discussion.)
* —— (1956) *Nuer Religion*, Oxford: Oxford University Press. (This work discusses aspects of Nuer ritual and belief that are closer than Zande magic to what is ordinarily thought of as religion in the West.)
  Gjertsen, D. (1980) 'Closed and open belief systems', *Second Order* 7 (1): 5–69. (A critique of Horton based on more recent history of science.)
* Goody, J. (1977) *The domestication of the savage mind*, Cambridge: Cambridge University Press. (An important discussion of the significance of literacy for intellectual life.)
* Hallen, B. (1977) 'Robin Horton on Critical Philosophy and Traditional Thought', *Second Order* 6 (1): 81–92. (Hallen criticizes Horton's claims about the uncritical character of traditional thought by reference to Yoruba diviners.)
* Horton, R. (1967) 'African traditional religion and Western science', *Africa* 37 (1–2): 50–71; 155–87. (Horton's classic paper.)
  —— (1976) 'Understanding traditional African religion: a reply to Professor Beattie', *Second Order* 3 (1): 3–29. (A response to the Beattie paper, 1973.)
  —— (1987) 'Traditional Thought and the Emerging African Philosophy Department: A Reply to Dr Hallen', in G. Fløistad (ed.) *Contemporary Philo-*

sophy, vol. 5: *African Philosophy*, Boston, MA: Kluwer, 1987: 207–34. (An unpublished paper in which Horton responded to Hallen's discussion of traditionalism. The paper appeared in K.A. Appiah's 'Old Gods, New Worlds: Some Recent Work in the Philosophy of African Traditional Religion'.)

* —— (1993) *Patterns of Thought in Africa and the West*, Cambridge: Cambridge University Press. (Summarizes the most significant debates in African philosophy of religion from the point of view of a leading partisan.)

Horton, R. and Finnegan, R. (eds) (1973) *Modes of Thought*, London: Faber & Faber. (Contains many important articles relevant to evaluating Horton's position.)

Popper, K. (1962) 'Towards a rational theory of tradition', in *Conjectures and Refutations*, New York: Basic Books. (The account of a critical tradition taken up by Hallen in his critique of Horton.)

* Pratt, V. (1972) 'Science and traditional religion. A discussion of some of Robin Horton's views', *Second Order* 1 (1): 7–20.

* Skorupski, J. (1976) *Symbol and theory*, Cambridge: Cambridge University Press. (A philosophical discussion of symbolism, including a review of the debate between Horton and Skorupski about religious and theoretical identifications.)

* Soyinka, W. (1976) *Myth, literature and the African world*, Cambridge: Cambridge University Press. (A major discussion of contemporary African intellectual life, especially as it relates to drama and the novel, in which Soyinka introduces the contrast between accommodative and adverserial intellectual styles.)

Wiredu, K. (1980) *Philosophy and an African Culture*, Cambridge and London: Cambridge University Press. (This book begins with important discussions of the role of philosophy in contemporary Africa and takes up questions raised by Horton in that context.)

K. ANTHONY APPIAH

AFTERLIFE IN ISLAM *see* SOUL IN ISLAMIC PHILOSOPHY

AGAPE *see* CHARITY

AGENTS, MORAL *see* MORAL AGENTS

AGNOSTICISM

In the popular sense, an agnostic is someone who neither believes nor disbelieves in God, whereas an atheist disbelieves in God. In the strict sense, however, agnosticism is the view that human reason is incapable of providing sufficient rational grounds to justify either the belief that God exists or the belief that God does not exist. In so far as one holds that our beliefs are rational only if they are sufficiently supported by human reason, the person who accepts the philosophical position of agnosticism will hold that neither the belief that God exists nor the belief that God does not exist is rational. In the modern period, agnostics have appealed largely to the philosophies of Hume and Kant as providing the justification for agnosticism as a philosophical position.

1 Degrees of agnosticism
2 Justifications for agnosticism

1 Degrees of agnosticism

Although the philosophical position described as 'agnosticism' – scepticism with respect to the existence or nonexistence of a supernatural divine being – has a long history, the term itself was introduced by Thomas H. Huxley in 1869 in order to provide an 'ism' that described his own intellectual outlook on matters of religion. Huxley held that neither belief nor disbelief in the existence of God or some supernatural divine reality is warranted, because in his judgment we are simply unable to discover sufficient rational grounds to support either belief or disbelief. Thus agnosticism as a philosophical position is best understood as the view that it is beyond our cognitive powers to determine the existence or nonexistence of God or some divine reality responsible for the existence of the natural universe.

We can distinguish three sorts of agnostic – weak, moderate and strong:

(1) An agnostic (weak sense) is one who understands the concept of God and/or the concept of a supernatural divine reality, but who neither believes nor disbelieves in the existence of God or in the existence of a divine reality responsible for the existence of the natural universe. This is the popular sense of the term.

(2) An agnostic (moderate sense) is one who is an agnostic in the weak sense, but who also holds

that human beings are unable to discover sufficient reason to believe or disbelieve in the existence of such a God or divine reality.

(3) An agnostic (strong sense) is one who is an agnostic in the moderate sense, but who also holds that it is wrong or in some way improper to believe or disbelieve in the existence of such a God or divine reality unless one has a sufficient reason to believe or disbelieve.

A person may be an agnostic (weak sense) without holding that it is beyond human cognitive abilities to discover sufficient reason to believe in God. For one may make a correct assessment of one's own lack of sufficient reason for belief or disbelief without affirming that no human being is without such reason. An agnostic in the weak sense need not hold the philosophical position of agnosticism, for that position requires that one hold that human cognitive powers are inadequate to justify belief with respect to the existence or nonexistence of God. On the other hand, one can hold the philosophical position of agnosticism without being an agnostic at all, whether weak, moderate or strong. Some religious thinkers (Kierkegaard, for example) have held that it is proper to believe in God by faith even though reason cannot provide sufficient rational grounds for or against the existence of God. Thus a religious believer may accept the philosophical position of agnosticism without being an agnostic in the sense of someone who neither believes nor disbelieves in God.

The moderate agnostic and the strong agnostic hold the philosophical position of agnosticism, although the moderate agnostic need not be critical of the religious believer or disbeliever. For a moderate agnostic may allow that it is not improper to believe or disbelieve without adequate grounds provided by human reason. Only the strong agnostic must be critical of the believer and disbeliever. It is fair to say that most philosophers who have been agnostics have been strong agnostics.

2 Justifications for agnosticism

Justifying agnosticism as a philosophical position requires a careful investigation of the limits of our cognitive powers. Specifically, it must be shown that human reason is simply incapable of reaching either affirmative or negative judgments concerning the existence of the God of traditional theism or any sort of divine reality responsible for the existence of the natural universe. Huxley and other agnostics professed to find support for their view in the philosophies of HUME §6 and KANT §8. Hume had presented devastating critiques of traditional natural theology in his *Enquiry Concerning Human Understanding* (1748) and his *Dialogues Concerning Natural Religion* (1779). And although Kant, in his *Critique of Pure Reason* (1787), sought to counter what he took to be Humean scepticism regarding scientific knowledge, he repudiated all attempts at speculative metaphysics and natural theology, arguing that such efforts exceed the limits of pure reason.

In the nineteenth century the legacy of Hume and Kant flourished in the agnosticism of Sir William Hamilton, Herbert Spencer, Thomas Huxley, Leslie Stephen and John Stuart Mill. In his influential essay 'Theism' (1874), Mill contended that only the argument from design remained as a potential source for rational support for some form of divine reality responsible for the order, if not the existence, of the natural universe (see GOD, ARGUMENTS FOR THE EXISTENCE OF §§4–5). He noted Darwin's competing explanation involving the struggle for survival and natural selection. But since Mill regarded Darwin's theory as a legitimate but unproven hypothesis, he argued that the apparent design in animal life gives some degree of probability to the view that there is an intelligent being which, though finite in power, is responsible for the order in (but not the existence of) the natural world. However, this degree of probability is for Mill apparently insufficient to warrant belief, for he concludes his essay with the judgment that the rational position with respect to the supernatural is agnosticism as distinguished from either belief or disbelief.

In the twentieth century, two philosophical movements gave at least indirect support to agnosticism: logical positivism and naturalism. Logical positivists held that a statement is cognitively meaningful (asserts something true or false) only if it is either analytic or empirically verifiable in principle. They also maintained that statements about the God of traditional theism (or other supernatural entities) are neither analytic nor empirically verifiable in principle. The result is that logical positivism denies the assumption of agnosticism that theism and atheism are intelligible positions, while affirming its conclusion that neither belief nor disbelief in God is rational. Naturalism's basic thesis is that the only things about which reliable knowledge can be obtained are things that can be investigated by the methods of science. This thesis implies agnosticism concerning the supernatural in so far as the supernatural eludes investigation by the methods of science. Since naturalists tend to hold that the only individual things of whose existence we have reliable knowledge are physical things, the conclusion is drawn that the existence or nonexistence of God is unknowable.

(Some naturalists have gone on to argue that we do have sufficient evidence for atheism.)

With the collapse of logical positivism and the resurgence of philosophy of religion as a discipline in the latter half of the twentieth century, significant challenges to agnosticism and naturalism have been advanced by philosophers seeking either to establish the truth of traditional theism or to establish that belief in theism is rational. The effort to establish that belief in God is rational has taken three directions. First, against the legacy of Hume and Kant it has been argued that there are truth-conducive reasons or evidence for belief in God. Second, following William James' classic essay 'The Will to Believe' (1897), it has been argued that pragmatic (but non-truth-conducive) reasons for belief in God are sufficient to render belief rational (see JAMES, WILLIAM §§4–5). Third, some philosophers (such as Plantinga 1981) have argued that belief in God is rational because it is a justified basic belief, rather than a belief justified by evidence. Agnostics, for the most part, have been concerned only with the issue of whether there are sufficient truth-conducive reasons to support belief or disbelief in a supernatural, divine reality.

See also: ATHEISM; NATURAL THEOLOGY; RELIGION, HISTORY OF PHILOSOPHY OF §8; RELIGION AND EPISTEMOLOGY; RELIGIOUS EXPERIENCE §§2–3

References and further reading

* Hume, D. (1748) *Enquiries Concerning Human Understanding and Concerning the Principles of Morals*, ed. L.A. Selby-Bigge and P.H. Nidditch, Oxford: Clarendon Press, 1975. (Presents Hume's mature philosophy concerning human knowledge and conduct. The first of the two Enquiries contains his important essay attacking the rationality of belief in miracles.)
* —— (1779) *Dialogues Concerning Natural Religion*, ed. with intro. by N. Kemp Smith, Indianapolis, IN: Bobbs-Merrill, 1962.(Hume's major critique of the argument from design. The cosmological argument is also criticized.)
  Huxley, T. (1893–95) *Collected Essays*, vol. 5, London: Macmillan. (In 'Agnosticism' and 'Agnosticism and Christianity' Huxley develops his views about agnosticism in relation to belief in religion, particularly Christianity.)
* James, W. (1897) 'The Will to Believe', in *The Will to Believe and Other Essays*, New York: Dover, 1956. (Presents James' famous argument for the right to believe in God in the absence of sufficient evidence to confirm that God exists.)
* Kant, I. (1787) *Critique of Pure Reason*, trans. N. Kemp Smith, London: Macmillan, 2nd edn, 1933. (Kant's major work on the powers and limitations of human reason. Difficult reading.)
  Krikorian, Y. (ed.) (1944) *Naturalism and the Human Spirit*, New York: Columbia University Press. (Contains a number of classic essays by American philosophers in defence of philosophical naturalism.)
* Mill, J.S. (1874) *Three Essays on Religion*, London: Longmans, Green & Co. (Contains Mill's important essays relevant to religion: 'Nature', 'Utility of Religion' and 'Theism'.)
* Plantinga, A. (1981) 'Is Belief in God Properly Basic?', *Nous* 15 (1): 41–51. (Argues that some beliefs are rational in the absence of evidence and suggests that belief in God is one of them.)
  Quinn, P. (1985) 'On Finding the Foundations of Theism', *Faith and Philosophy* 2 (4): 469–86. (Critically discusses the view that belief in theism is rational because it is properly basic.)

WILLIAM L. ROWE

AGRICOLA, RUDOLPH (1444–85)

Rudolph Agricola was one of the leading humanists of northern Europe in the late fifteenth century. His polished Latin style, his Greek learning and his knowledge of classical literature made him a hero to Erasmus, More, Vives, Melanchthon and Ramus. His major work, De inventione dialectica *(On Dialectical Invention) (1479), provides an original account of practical argumentation by combining elements from the established teachings of rhetoric and dialectic with analysis of passages from classical literature. It includes a new version of the topics of invention, based on Cicero's method of devising arguments, outlined in his* Topics. *Agricola's letter* De formando studio *(On Shaping Studies) (1484), which circulated widely in the sixteenth century, outlines a plan of knowledge and discusses methods of study. Although his approach was strongly humanist and the Roman rhetorician Quintilian was his favourite author, his logic remained firmly Aristotelian, unlike that of his predecessor Lorenzo Valla. He remained aware of the achievements of scholasticism, expressing admiration for Duns Scotus and adopting an extreme realist position in metaphysics.*

1 Life
2 *De inventione dialectica*
3 Other works

1 Life

Rudolph Agricola (born Roeloff Huusman, at Baflo, near Groningen in the north east Netherlands) received a scholastic education in Belgium at Louvain (MA 1465) before moving on like many other northerners to study law in Italy at Pavia. He neglected his legal studies to concentrate on reading classical Latin literature and improving his Latin style. In 1475 he transferred to Ferrara in order to improve his knowledge of Greek. He served Duke Ercole I d'Este as organist for a time and made the acquaintance of prominent humanists such as Battista Guarini and Ermolao Barbaro. In 1479 he returned to Germany with his friend Dietrich von Plieningen, pausing in Dillingen to complete *De inventione dialectica* (On Dialectical Invention) (1479), before returning to Groningen. He was *secretarius* of Groningen from 1482–4, undertaking diplomatic missions on behalf of the town. He was able to return to full-time study, and to begin learning Hebrew, in 1484 when he went to Heidelberg to assist his friend Johann von Dalberg, who had recently become Bishop of Worms. He taught on the fringes of the university and twice preached to the clergy of the diocese. He died on 27 October 1485 shortly after returning from a journey to Rome to congratulate the newly elected Pope Innocent VIII.

Agricola was fortunate to have spent almost ten years in Italy studying Latin and Greek. In Pavia and Ferrara, he lived at the centre of a group of northern students whose unofficial humanistic studies he supervised and with whom he shared his discoveries. He looked on himself as a perpetual beginner, always learning languages while others went on to higher studies. He planned to devote his old age to biblical studies. For the generation of Erasmus he was most important as an example, the Frisian who had equalled Italians in humanistic learning, since his major work did not appear in print until 1515 (see Humanism, Renaissance §§5–6).

2 *De inventione dialectica*

Dialectical invention for Agricola involves not only finding persuasive material for a composition, but also putting it into an effective order. The core of his *De inventione dialectica* is the topics, the subject of Book 1. Agricola's new version provides a full and clear account of how the topics are used, a better organized list of topics, and a carefully exemplified account of the variety within each topic and the uses of each.

The topics are a list of headings (for example, definition, genus, cause, and effect) which can be applied to any subject. Agricola explains that while the things in the world and the connections between them are infinite in number, nevertheless there are certain common characteristics in the links between things, which can therefore be divided into classes. These classes of relations are the topics. In other words the topics are a useful way of investigating the things which are connected to particular subjects because they correspond to connections which exist in the world. This fits in with Agricola's realist position in metaphysics, and it provides (as no one had before) an explanation for the effectiveness of the topics, but it evidently suits some topics (genus, cause) better than others (etymology, similars).

None of his predecessors had attempted to explain how the (rather heterogeneous) list of topics works or why it is complete, whereas Agricola divides the topics into seven groups in line with the degree of closeness to the subject, ranging from 'within the substance' to 'opposites'. Although this list improves on previous accounts by Aristotle (§7) (whose conception of the topic is rather different), Cicero (§2) and Boethius (§3), it remains inconsistent in places. Agricola's new topics entries are much longer than those of his predecessors. His approach is practical (showing how a definition is built up), inquiring (thinking about the different relations between causes, intermediate ends and effects) and literary (taking apart a simile by Lucan and exploring the implications of alternative objects of comparison).

In Book 2 Agricola shows how arguments derived from the topics can be used in real argumentative situations, looking at how material can be prepared for topical invention, analysing argumentative and expository writing, discussing the forms of argumentation appropriate in practical use, and providing a number of drills to familiarize the student with the use of the topics. One of these exercises involves analysing the argumentative structures which underlie passages of writing. Agricola himself used this method in his dialectical commentary on Cicero's oration *On the Manilian Law*, which in turn inspired Melanchthon's commentaries (see Melanchthon §§1–2) and the analyses of Ramus (§2) and his followers.

Book 3 shows how the topics can be used to produce material which will move and please an audience as well as teach them. It includes a discussion of emotion which relies on, and refers the reader to, Aristotle's *Rhetoric*. Agricola also revitalizes the rhetorical art of disposition by illustrating the range of possible forms of organization (both overall and local) available to a writer, and by showing how decisions about ordering involve considering subject-matter, audience and the writer's own persona and intention.

Agricola's work has often been linked with Lorenzo Valla's attack on Aristotelian logic in his *Dialectica* (see VALLA, L. §3), but in fact Agricola endorses many Aristotelian doctrines which Valla rejects. The two men share an interest in the topics and the aim of writing a logic suitable for practical arguing in neoclassical Latin.

Manuscripts of *De inventione dialectica* were hard to find in the twenty years after Agricola's death, but after 1515 it became one of the most influential dialectic books of the sixteenth century, with forty-four editions of the (very long) text, and thirty-two editions of various epitomes. Praise of Agricola and details from his work can be found in many Renaissance dialectic books, notably in the works of Erasmus, VIVES (§4), Melanchthon and Ramus.

3 Other works

Agricola produced translations, orations, letters, poems and treatises. Many of his works are pedagogic in their aim, notably his Latin translation of the *Progymnasmata* (short writing exercises) of Aphthonius, a Greek rhetorician of the third century AD, which in its adaptation by Lorichius became one of the most printed school textbooks of the sixteenth century. His minor works also offer two discussions of the nature and organization of philosophy. The *Oratio in laudem philosophiae* (Oration in Praise of Philosophy) was delivered in autumn 1476 to inaugurate the academic year in Ferrara. Agricola praises philosophy because it investigates everything, because it can turn everything to good, because it enables a person to rise above the vicissitudes of fortune and because the soul knows itself happy in self-contemplation.

Philosophy is divided into rational (grammar, dialectic and rhetoric), natural (physics, which includes medicine, mathematical arts and theology) and moral (politics, justice), according to Agricola. The general scheme seems to derive from the division of philosophy found in Isidore of Seville's *Etymologiae* (see ENCYCLOPEDISTS §7), but Agricola's placing of theology within natural philosophy is original. Agricola's letter *De formando studio* (On Shaping Studies) (1484) chooses philosophy as the subject of study for the addressee, the Antwerp musician Jacques Barbiriau, because of his ability and because he does not require that his studies provide him with income. Philosophy in other words is the highest of studies, but is only open to people with some independence. After setting aside the *trivium* (grammar, rhetoric and dialectic) as the entrance to the arts, not the thing itself, he provides a new division of philosophy into two parts, natural and moral, both of which must be studied using the best authors. Natural philosophy, which includes geography, agriculture, medicine, architecture, painting and sculpture, as well as physics and biology, is valuable in forming the mind because it shows the worthlessness of wealth and the fragility of human bodies. Moral philosophy, the more important part, involves the study of poetry, oratory, history, ethics and sacred writings (both the scriptures and Christian authors).

Agricola discusses three methods of study: reading, the compilation of commonplace books, and the sharing and development of knowledge through composition. In a sense, rather in the manner of Augustine's *De doctrina christiana* (On Christian Doctrine), a literary approach, and a choice of classical and Christian authors, have taken over the whole of philosophy (though it should be remembered that the elder Pliny's *Natural History* was one of Agricola's favourite books). Agricola also wrote two small treatises, *Singulares aliquot de universalibus quaestiones* (Some Questions about the Universals) (1539) and the unpublished *De universali singulari et uno* (On the Universal, the Singular and the One), in which he maintains that all universal terms correspond to real things in the world. These treatises await thorough study, as does Agricola's understanding of Ramon Llull, to whom he makes a tantalizing reference in *De inventione dialectica*.

See also: HUMANISM, RENAISSANCE; LOGIC, RENAISSANCE

List of works

See Akkerman and Vanderjagt (1988) in References and further reading, for details of Agricola's works (some of them unpublished) that are not included in the List of works.

Agricola, R. (1476) *Oratio in laudem philosophiae* (Oration in Praise of Philosophy), in Alardus (ed.) Lucubrationes, Cologne, 1539; repr. Nieuwkoop: de Graaf, 1967, 144–59. (Oration outlining Agricola's earlier view of the shape and contents of philosophy.)

—— (1479) *De inventione dialectica* (On Dialectical Invention), ed. Alardus, Cologne, 1539; repr. Nieuwkoop: de Graaf, 1967; ed. and German trans. L. Mundt, Tübingen: Niemeyer, 1992; English trans. J.R. McNally, 'Rudolph Agricola's *De inventione dialectica*: A Translation of Selected Chapters', *Quarterly Journal of Speech* 34: 393–422. (Agricola's major work, describing the discovery of persuasive arguments and the composition of texts.)

—— (1484) *De formando studio* (On Shaping Studies), in Alardus (ed.) *Lucubrationes*, Cologne, 1539; repr. Nieuwkoop: de Graaf, 1967, 193–201. (Agricola's later outline of an idealized system of education.)

References and further reading

Akkerman, F. and Vanderjagt, A.J. (eds) (1988) *Rodolphus Agricola Phrisius (1444–1485)*, Leiden: Brill. (A valuable collection of essays with a full secondary bibliography and a list of Agricola's works.)

Green-Pedersen, N.J. (1984) *The Tradition of the Topics in the Middle Ages*, Munich: Philosophia. (A fine treatment of the classical background and medieval use of the topics.)

Huisman, G.C. (1985) *Rudolph Agricola: A Bibliography of Printed Works and Translations*, Nieuwkoop: de Graaf. (The standard bibliography of early printed editions.)

Mack, P. (1993) *Renaissance Argument: Valla and Agricola in the Traditions of Rhetoric and Dialectic*, Leiden: Brill. (An analysis of *De inventione dialectica* with an account of Agricola's sources and influence.)

Vasoli, C. (1967) *La dialettica e la retorica dell'Umanesimo*, Milan: Feltrinelli. (A good account of humanist rhetoric and dialectic.)

PETER MACK

AGRICULTURAL ETHICS

Agricultural ethics is the study of moral issues raised by farming. These include: human interference with the course of nature; the effects of certain agricultural practices on present social conditions, and on the conditions under which future generations will live; the treatment of animals, especially when its aim is human advantage; and the value of farming as a human activity in itself.

1 Basic justification
2 Social justice
3 Nonhuman animals
4 Virtue

1 Basic justification

Some anti-agriculturalists defend a return to the life of hunting and gathering. Few philosophers have explicitly defended such a view, but it seems a logical consequence of some positions in environmental ethics. (Taylor 1986), for example, holds that all living things including plants have a *telos*, or 'goal', and that we have at least a corresponding *prima facie* duty not to interfere with them. Most humans could survive, and many could flourish, eating only nuts, berries and vegetable products taken from dead or dying plants. If all living things deserve respect then agriculture, the implements and practices of which are expressly designed to kill targeted plants and animals, might be unjustifiable. Callicott (1989) believes it is our duty genuinely to share the earth with other species, an impossibility when farmers plough up wildlife habitat (see ENVIRONMENTAL ETHICS).

Two popular presentations of the anti-agricultural ideal make explicit its practical implications. In Edward Abbey's novel, *Desert Solitaire*, a character laments the oppressive presence of humans in the United States' Southwest, and opines, 'I'd rather shoot a man than a snake.' In Daniel Quinn's novel, *Ishmael*, a gorilla explains that the majority of humans are 'Takers', who have deprived the world of its wildness and diversity. The preferred form of human life from the gorilla's perspective is that of hunting and gathering in which 'Leavers', eschewing the arts of cultivation, ensure the integrity of nonhuman planetary life.

A more anti-humanistic philosophy seems hardly imaginable when, as Callicott puts it, the measure of a truly ecocentric ethic is the extent of its misanthropy. It would seem to be one of our basic duties, commensurate with others' basic moral rights, to endeavour to feed the world's hungry (see DEVELOPMENT ETHICS; JUSTICE, INTERNATIONAL). To abandon the arts of cultivation would result in our failing to meet this duty. The justification of the practice of agriculture is secured by whatever arguments justify the existence of the most basic of duties.

Many Jewish and Christian theologians formulate duties to nature in terms of stewardship, holding that the earth is a gift of God to humans so that we may use but not abuse soil, water, air and animals. Similarly, many secular philosophers believe that we are justified in cultivating the earth and breeding plants and animals selectively, if we do so in a sustainable way: the entitlement to treat plants and animals as things of instrumental value only is circumscribed by duties to future generations, humans who will need adequate natural resources to grow crops (see FUTURE GENERATIONS, OBLIGATIONS TO).

2 Social justice

Concerns about fairness in the distribution of food and farmland have been raised in both developing and developed countries. Most of the world's poor are small tenant farmers. In order to increase the standard of living of these farmers, the governments of many developing countries adopted in the 1970s the policy of 'industrializing' agriculture; urging their farmers to copy the model of large successful farmers in developed countries. During the green revolution of the 1960s and 1970s, countries such as India, Costa Rica and Nigeria increased the efficiency of farmers' yields by borrowing money from international lending agencies such as the World Bank. The funds were used to extend credit to farmers, who were taught to buy high yielding varieties of seeds (such as rice, wheat, and maize) and to use the necessary accompanying technologies: mechanical implements (tractors) and synthetic chemicals (herbicides and pesticides). Many farmers flourished and nations that once imported grain became self-sufficient in certain crops.

Questions were raised, however, about the equity of the strategy. Critics alleged that industrial farming benefited larger farmers unfairly because they had easier access than small farmers to credit and expanded landholding. As crops were grown in greater abundance, the price farmers received for each bushel decreased and producers were forced to try to spread their costs over more acres. Were the poor and hungry actually disadvantaged by the industrialization of agriculture? Were small tenants dispossessed of land unjustly when larger farmers, beneficiaries of the new technologies, bought up their smallholdings? Some argue that they were (Lappe and Collins 1979), others that they were not (Ruttan and Hayami 1984). The debate turns on the resolution not only of important empirical questions (for instance, did industrial agriculture reduce opportunities for labour employment and earnings?) but also of significant philosophical questions (for example, is it obligatory or supererogatory to aid unfortunates in other nations?).

In developed countries debate about social justice in agriculture sometimes takes as a focus the structure of the agricultural industry. In the United States, for example, the question has been expressed in terms of the desirability of 'saving the family farm'. Family farms are medium-sized businesses owned, worked and loved by families, the kind of farm being displaced by smaller hobby farms, on which the majority of income derives from off-farm activities, and by large super farms, often worked by hourly employees who are not stakeholders.

Questions to be addressed here include: Do family farmers practice better stewardship of the land than other farmers? Are rural communities better places to live if they are surrounded by many medium-sized farms rather than a few large farms? Are farm animals treated more humanely on family farms?

Can smaller farms take advantage of economies of scale and produce food as efficiently as larger farms?

Another issue concerns the role of governments in agriculture. Should public policy target benefits and subsidies at medium-sized farms, and not at hobby or super farms? Or are such policies inherently unfair in so far as they do not benefit all farms equally?

Finally there are social justice questions related to pesticides and farmworker and consumer health. It has been argued on deontological grounds, for example, that farmers are morally unjustified in using chemicals that are carcinogenic to consumers (see RISK).

3 Nonhuman animals

Perhaps the most controversial matter in contemporary agricultural ethics concerns the moral standing of nonhuman animals. Some, such as Regan (1983), argue that it is morally wrong to raise and slaughter animals for food because farm animals typically are 'subjects of a life' with intrinsic value and basic moral rights of their own. Others argue that animals lack moral rights because they lack conscious experiences, moral autonomy and a sense of justice, and that it is therefore permissible to use cows and chickens in humane ways (see MORAL STANDING; ANIMALS AND ETHICS). Utilitarians generally believe that animal pain counts morally, but they differ over whether the benefits of using animals in agriculture outweigh the costs. The issue gains urgency with the development of powerful new scientific techniques to manipulate the animal genome (see GENETICS AND ETHICS §7). As subjects of genetic engineering, farm animals have suffered from unintended deleterious effects, while research animals have suffered the consequences of being intentionally bred for propensity to develop debilitating diseases.

4 Virtue

If we believe Xenophon in the Oeconomicus, Socrates once said that 'the best kind of work and the best kind of knowledge is farming, by which human beings supply themselves with necessary things'. While some believe that the past ten thousand years of agriculture has led inevitably to irreversible catastrophic environmental degradation, many affirm with Xenophon's Socrates that there is no better work or knowledge than farming. What did Socrates mean by the idea that farming provides the best kind of knowledge? Perhaps he meant what Wendell Berry meant when he wrote that it is 'a law' that

> land that is in human use must be lovingly used; it requires intimate knowledge, attention, and

care.... A family that has farmed a farm through two or three generations will possess not just the land but a remembered history of its mistakes and of the remedies of those mistakes.

(1987: 349)

Why should such knowledge be 'the best kind'? Perhaps because in it the intellect is uniquely connected with the body, and spirituality to physicality. As Berry puts it, those who farm 'gain the means of life; ...they gain the longevity and dependability of sources of food, both natural and cultural. [On a farm] the proper answer to the spiritual calling becomes, in turn, the proper fulfilment of physical need' (1987: 351).

To farm may be to practice a virtuous calling, an art with its own intrinsic rewards (see VIRTUE ETHICS). For a people to become landless, or to become utterly dissociated from the means by which their most basic physical needs are met, may mean they are destined to become bereft not only of the best kind of work, but of the best kind of knowledge as well.

See also: APPLIED ETHICS; BUSINESS ETHICS; TECHNOLOGY AND ETHICS

References and further reading

* Abbey, E. (1968) *Desert Solitaire*, New York: Ballantine. (A novel, set in the author's home, the American Southwest. Very influential for the ecology movement in the United States.)
* Aiken, W. and LaFollette, H. (eds) (1977) *World Hunger and Moral Obligation*, Englewood Cliffs, NJ: Prentice Hall. (Widely used collection, including seminal essays by G. Hardin, P. Singer, J. Arthur, J. Narveson, W. Frankena, O. O'Neill, and J. Rachels.)
* Berry, W. (1978) *The Unsettling of America: Culture and Agriculture*, New York: Avon. (Very influential book that argues culture in the United States has declined as more and more of its population has moved off the farm.)
* —— (1987) 'A Defense of the Family Farm', in *Home Economics: Fourteen Essays*, San Francisco, CA: North Point Press; repr. in G. Comstock (ed.) *Is There a Moral Obligation to Save the Family Farm?*, Ames, IA: Iowa State University Press, 1987, 347–60. (Berry, a farmer, poet, and essayist, defends family farms on cultural, moral and spiritual grounds.)
* Blatz, C. (1991) *Ethics and Agriculture: An Anthology on Current Issues in World Context*, Moscow, ID: University of Idaho Press. (Sections on agriculture's aims, practitioners, conduct and development. Includes a useful bibliography.)
* Callicott, J.B. (1989) *In Defense of the Land Ethic: Essays in Environmental Philosophy*, Albany, NY: State University of New York Press. (Argues that animal liberation and environmental ethics are incompatible with the land ethic and attempts to develop a non-anthropocentric holistic ethic.)
* Comstock, G. (ed.) (1987) *Is There a Moral Obligation to Save the Family Farm?*, Ames, IA: Iowa State University Press. (A collection of essays from theologians, sociologists, economists and farmers focused on the social, economic, and moral dimensions of the 'farm crisis' in the United States during the 1980s.)
* Lappe, F.M. and Collins, J. (1979) *Food First: Beyond the Myth of Scarcity*, New York: Ballantine. (An early and seminal statement of the case against viewing industrial agriculture as the best way to feed the world's hungry.)
* Quinn, D. (1992) *Ishmael*, New York: Bantam. (A novel in which a gorilla distinguishes between different types of humans – 'Takers', comprising the majority, who have deprived the world of its wildness and diversity, and 'Leavers', who, by hunting and gathering, eschew the arts of cultivation and thus ensure the integrity of nonhuman planetary life. The novel won the Turner Tomorrow Fellowship prize.)
* Regan, T. (1983) *The Case for Animal Rights*, Berkeley, CA: University of California Press. (The first and best account of the case for attributing moral rights to nonhuman animals based on their ability to be what Regan calls 'subjects of a life'.)
* Ruttan, V. and Hayami, Y. (1984) 'The Green Revolution: Inducement and Distribution', *The Pakistan Development Review* 23: 37–63. (Argues that developing countries must develop more productive agricultural technologies to offset growing populations and to achieve both growth and equity.)
* Taylor, P. (1986) *Respect for Nature: A Theory of Environmental Ethics*, Princeton, NJ: Princeton University Press. (Articulates and defends a biocentric theory of environmental ethics in which all living things possess inherent worth.)
* Xenophon (*c*.360s BC) *Oeconomicus*, trans. E.C. Marchant, Cambridge, MA: Harvard University Press, 1925. (Discusses proper management of a household and presents didactic material on agriculture, within a Socratic dialogue.)

GARY L. COMSTOCK

AGRIPPA (1st/2nd century AD)

Agrippa, a Sceptic of the first or second century AD, compiled five general modes of Sceptical argument: the views of positive theorists are subject to endemic disagreement due to the relativity of appearances, and adjudication cannot succeed, since it will either be mere assertion (and hence will not command assent) or appeal to further considerations, which process will either be infinitely regressive or circular, or terminate in unfounded assumption.

Agrippa is mentioned only once in our sources (Diogenes Laertius, IX 88), where no information is given about him beyond the attribution to him (and his associates) of a set of five modes with which to commend Pyrrhonian Scepticism (see PYRRHONISM). Sextus Empiricus ascribes these modes only to 'the more recent Sceptics' (Outlines of Pyrrhonism I 164), with no mention of Agrippa at all; nor does Agrippa's name figure in the list of prominent Pyrrhonians with which Diogenes Laertius closes his life of Pyrrho (IX 115–16).

The basic argument schemata of Pyrrhonism – Aenesidemus' ten modes (see AENESIDEMUS; PYRRHONISM §2) – collect different types of cases of opposing appearances of one sort or another, and move from the relativity of appearances (and the impossibility of favouring one set over another) to suspension of judgment about the natures of things, although they are less clear as to quite how suspension is to be achieved. The Agrippan modes organize the Sceptical material rather differently, and remedy that last deficiency. The first is that 'according to which we find that an undecidable conflict has arisen among both lay people and philosophers concerning the matter in hand as a result of which, being unable either to accept or reject it, we end up suspending judgment' (Outlines of Pyrrhonism I 165). The third asserts that appearances are in general irremediably relative, which is responsible for the dispute in the first place.

By contrast, the remaining modes are general and methodological, designed to undermine the attempts of dogmatists to offer reasoned defences of their positions. The second mode is that of regress: each supposed justification of a position will itself require justification, and so on *ad infinitum*; but such a sequence offers no ultimate justification at all, and again suspension follows. Dogmatists may sometimes simply offer unargued assumptions, or hypotheses, but these are not compelling since in any case we might equally assume the opposite; this forms the basis of the fourth mode (Outlines of Pyrrhonism I 173–4). Finally dogmatists will sometimes attempt, whether wittingly or not, to show that their suppositions are reciprocally supporting; but, as the fifth mode demonstrates, if p rests on q and q upon p, then neither rests upon anything.

These modes may be (and generally are) deployed in combination against any dogmatist's claim to have established a criterion which might distinguish truth from falsity and thus provide foundations for knowledge (see PYRRHONISM §4). Suppose a dogmatist asserts that p. If that is a mere assertion, then the Sceptic produces the fourth mode. If p is in turn supported by q, and q by r, and so on, either that procedure terminates somewhere (in which case the fourth mode again becomes operable); or it does not, committing the dogmatist to regress; or, eventually one of the supporting propositions is itself shown to rest on p, in which case, as the fifth mode has it, the whole structure is built on sand.

The Agrippan modes are weapons of great scope and power; and Sextus' presentation of the Ten Modes of Scepticism was evidently influenced by them. Indeed, the whole subsequent history of the epistemology of justification may be seen as a series of attempts to evade their purportedly all embracing grasp.

References and further reading

Barnes, J. (1990) *The Toils of Scepticism*, Cambridge: Cambridge University Press. (A detailed and subtle philosophical treatment of Agrippa's modes.)

* Diogenes Laertius (c. early 3rd century AD) *Lives of the Philosophers*, trans. R.D. Hicks, *Diogenes Laertius Lives of Eminent Philosophers*, Loeb Classical Library, Cambridge, MA: Harvard University Press and London: Heinemann, 1925, 2 vols. (Greek text with facing translation; IX 61–116 is devoted to Pyrrhonism.)

Hankinson, R.J. (1994) *The Sceptics*, London: Routledge. (Chapter X deals with the Agrippan modes.)

* Sextus Empiricus (c. AD 200) *Outlines of Pyrrhonism*, trans. J. Annas and J. Barnes, *Outlines of Scepticism*, Cambridge: Cambridge University Press, 1994. (Fine translation with introduction and notes.)

R.J. HANKINSON

AGRIPPA VON NETTESHEIM, HENRICUS CORNELIUS (1486–1535)

Famous in the sixteenth century for writings in which he steps forward variously as magician, occultist, evangelical humanist and philosopher, Agrippa shared with other humanist writers a thoroughgoing contempt for the philosophy of the scholastics. In his more evangelical moods Agrippa could be taken for a radical exponent of the philosophia Christi *of his older contemporary Erasmus, or mistaken for a follower of Luther, whose early writings he actively disseminated in humanist circles. However, his deepest affinities are with magically inflected philosophies: the Neoplatonism and Hermetism of Marsilio Ficino, and the syncretic Christian Kabbalah of Giovanni Pico della Mirandola, Johannes Reuchlin and Johannes Trithemius.*

As well as expounding an influential magical view of language, Agrippa contributed to the sixteenth-century revival of scepticism, denounced the 'tyranny' of those who obstructed a free search for truth, criticized the subjection of women and (with a courage unusual in his time) resisted and mocked the instigators of the witch-craze. Finding in Hermetic–Kabbalistic doctrines the inner truth both of religion and of philosophy, Agrippa was also aware of parallels between these magical doctrines and the Gnostic heresies. His heterodoxy made him a target for pious slanders: within several decades of his death he became the protagonist of demonological fictions which were soon absorbed into the legend of Dr Faustus.

1 Life
2 **Verbal magic**
3 **Agrippa as sceptic and free-thinker**
4 **Agrippa as feminist**
5 **Agrippa's philosophical influence**

1 Life

Born to a family of the lesser nobility in Cologne (from whose Latin name, Colonia Agrippina, he drew his humanist cognomen), Agrippa took his first degree at Cologne in 1502; after further studies in Paris and elsewhere, he claimed to have doctorates in canon law, civil law and medicine – and also to have been knighted in recognition of military service.

In 1508 he took part in an unsuccessful military adventure which a secret occultist society, of which he was a member, undertook in Spain, possibly at the behest of Emperor Maximilian I. Members of this society subsequently became prominent in French humanist and court circles, providing Agrippa with a network of supporters upon whom, as his reputation for encyclopedic learning grew, he was able to draw in his searches for patronage. When in 1509 he lectured on Reuchlin's Kabbalist philosophy at the University of Dôle in Franche-Comté and wrote *De nobilitate* (published in 1532), Agrippa had hopes of preferment in the court of Margaret of Austria, Regent of Franche-Comté and the Low Countries. These were dashed when he was denounced at court by a prominent Franciscan as a 'judaizing heretic'. Returning to Germany, in 1510 he completed the first version of *De occulta philosophia* (published in 1533), and in the same year travelled to England, apparently in the service of Maximilian I.

For the first several years of his Italian sojourn, which lasted from 1511 to 1518, Agrippa continued to serve the emperor both as diplomat and soldier. But by 1515 he was lecturing on the *Hermetica* at the University of Pavia – a position which he promptly lost, along with his library and other possessions, after the French victory at Marignano. In 1518 Agrippa moved north again, taking up a position as city orator and advocate in Metz. Intervening there in the case of a woman accused of witchcraft, he secured her freedom, recovered her property, and accused the inquisitor responsible for torturing her of heresy. But this and other instances of resistance to tyranny and obscurantism made him unpopular with the orthodox. He returned to Cologne in 1520, lived from 1521 to 1523 in Geneva (where he was at the centre of a group of reforming tendencies), and then moved to Fribourg (also in Switzerland), where he practised medicine.

In 1524 Agrippa secured a place in the French royal court at Lyons as personal physician to the queen mother, Louise de Savoy. But by 1526 he was in trouble, having rashly revealed his sympathy for the rebellious Duc de Bourbon and Emperor Charles V, who was at war with King Francis I. During the same year Agrippa wrote *De vanitate* (published in 1530), which includes a vehement critique of the corruption and venality of court life. Perhaps as a result, his salary was withheld, while at the same time he was refused permission to leave the court.

Dismissed at last in 1528, Agrippa obtained a place in the court of Margaret of Austria at Antwerp as historiographer to Emperor Charles V. But when Margaret died in late 1530 he was again unable to secure payment for his services. Furthermore, the printing of *De vanitate* in 1530 had earned him condemnation from the theological faculties of Paris and Louvain, which led to difficulties with the imperial privy council. In 1531 the printing of a much expanded version of *De occulta philosophia* in Antwerp was blocked after the first of its three books had been printed; two years later, thanks to the patronage of the reform-minded Archbishop of Cologne, Agrippa was able to see this book and several others, including *De nobilitate* and a commentary on the art of Ramon Llull, through the press.

Returning in 1535 to Lyons, Agrippa was imprisoned by Francis I for having written against Louise de Savoy. Released through the intervention of friends, he died shortly afterwards in Grenoble.

2 Verbal magic

Agrippa derived from the Neoplatonists (and ultimately of course from Plato's *Cratylus*) the view that the power inherent in natural things lives on and is latent in 'the form of the signification' (1533: I.lxx). Because the hidden powers of things proceed in the first place from celestial causes, and because the celestial powers which move the elemental world, acting from circumference to centre, originate with 'the word of God, which word the wise Chaldeans of Babylon call the cause of causes' (1533: II.lx), it follows that the philosopher or magician whose words can draw upon the power of this originary creative Word should be able to intervene powerfully in the natural order. Agrippa's insistence on the purely natural quality of verbal magic cannot disguise the heterodox implication of this view of language, which is that the magician can get in at the top of the hierarchical structure of the cosmos because his 'mysterious words' and 'ingenious speech' draw upon the power contained within God's Word – a term which refers to the canonical scriptures as well as to Christ, the creative Logos (see LANGUAGE, RENAISSANCE PHILOSOPHY OF).

3 Agrippa as sceptic and free-thinker

The main purpose of *De vanitate* (1530) is to bring the reader to a position of Christian fideism (though one in which Christian faith is thoroughly infused with Hermetic and Kabbalistic motifs). To this end Agrippa's chapter on logic makes a brief but effective deployment of sceptical arguments. Aristotle's principles of demonstration (see ARISTOTLE §6), he argues, require an understanding of causes and principles to which we give our assent on the basis either of authority or of sense-based experience (for knowledge is agreed to arise from the senses, and Averroes (Ibn Rushd) makes agreement with sensible things a criterion of truth) (see IBN RUSHD §6). But the senses are often deceived, and furthermore cannot attain the intellectual level at which we encounter the causes of lower things. It is therefore manifest that 'the way of the truth is shut up from the senses', and that sciences rooted in them are 'uncertain, erroneous and deceitful' (1530: cap. 7). Appeals to authority are no more acceptable, since the final recourse of the scholastics against those who deny the first principles of their sciences is to violence, 'so that of philosophers they are made torturers and hangmen, since they will compel us by force to confess that which they should teach by reason' (1530: cap. 1) (see SCEPTICISM, RENAISSANCE §2).

4 Agrippa as feminist

In *De nobilitate* (1532) Agrippa argues that 'between man and woman by the substance of the soul one has no higher pre-eminence of nobility above the other, but both have by nature equal liberty of worthiness. Yet in all other respects, apart from the divine substance of the soul, the excellence and nobility of womankind surpasses beyond limit the rude gross nature of men' (*Opera*: sig. Ii 4v). Some of the examples with which he develops this claim are deliberately frivolous, and yet he does insistently challenge the misogynist legal culture by which women, 'being subdued as it were by force of arms, are constrained to give place to men, and to obey their subduers, not by any natural or divine necessity or reason, but by custom, education, fortune, and a certain tyrannical occasion' (*Opera*: sig. Ll 3v). François Rabelais' portrait of Agrippa as Her Trippa, an occultist who is ready to predict Panurge's cuckoldry by all the magical arts at his disposal, while remaining unaware that the court lackeys are lining up to frolic with his own wife, can be understood as a sardonic response to Agrippa's feminism (see RABELAIS, F. §3). A more positive response is evident in Johannes Wier's *De praestigiis daemonum* (Of Demonic Deceptions) (1563), a book which in some parts of western Europe had a moderating effect upon the witch-hunts of the time: Wier, who had been Agrippa's student, adopted his opinion that the elderly women who were the prime targets of the witch-hunters were suffering from melancholia rather than demonic possession, and that Christians should give them spiritual and material comfort rather than persecuting and torturing them (see FEMINISM §2).

5 Agrippa's philosophical influence

The apparent contradiction between the sceptical fideism of *De vanitate* and the encyclopedic syncretism of *De occulta philosophia* is to some extent dissipated by Agrippa's reliance in both books upon a Hermetic–Kabbalistic doctrine of spiritual rebirth and deification. However, Agrippa is neither a coherent nor in most respects an original thinker. His most strongly voiced opinions are often taken verbatim from the works of Marsilio FICINO, Giovanni PICO DELLA MIRANDOLA and Johannes Reuchlin, and since he typically appears more interested in assembling diverse opinions on a subject than in assessing their relative truth, his own impulses may seem more antiquarian than philosophical. (Given the hostility he encountered from theologians of the mendicant orders from 1509 onwards, one may suspect that he was content to allow the material he had assembled to work within the reader's mind, without himself taking the risk of underlining its heterodox implications.)

Agrippa was widely read for well over a century after his death. He was, on the one hand, denounced by John Calvin in *De scandalis* (On Scandal) (1550) as a mocker of sacred truths in the vein of Lucian of Samosata, by Jean Bodin in *De la démonomanie des sorciers* (On the Devil-mania of Sorcerers) (1581) as the leading sorcerer of his age, and by André Thevet in *Les vrais pourtraits et vies des hommes illustres* (The True Portraits and Lives of Illustrious Men) (1584) as having spawned hordes both of scoffers and magicians. On the other hand, his works were cited and echoed by literary figures ranging from Jean de la Taille to Sir Philip Sidney, Fulke Greville, Christopher Marlowe and Thomas Nashe, as well as by occult philosophers from John Dee and Giordano BRUNO to Thomas Vaughan. Moreover, Michel de Montaigne's scepticism, which represents man as 'naked and empty, acknowledging his natural weakness, apt to receive from above some strange power, disfurnished of human knowledge, and so much the more fit to harbour divine understanding, nullifying his judgment so as to give more place to faith' ([1580] 1962 (1): 562), is clearly indebted to Agrippa's *De vanitate* (see MONTAIGNE, M. DE §3). Perhaps more significantly, it has recently been argued that René Descartes' writings, from the early *Olympica* (Revelation from Olympus) and *Cogitationes privatae* (Private Thoughts) (1619–21) to the *Meditations* (1641), make sustained use of motifs derived from the philosophical *Hermetica*, and that Descartes' understanding of the Hermetic writings was conditioned by his early reading of Agrippa (see Keefer 1996).

See also: HERMETISM; HUMANISM, RENAISSANCE; KABBALAH; PLATONISM, RENAISSANCE §5; SCEPTICISM, RENAISSANCE §2

List of works

Agrippa, H.C. (1486–1535) *Opera* (Works), Lyons, c.1600, 2 vols; facsimile repr., ed. R.H. Popkin, Hildesheim and New York: Olms, 1970. (The most easily accessible collection of Agrippa's writings – though in Latin.)

—— (1530) *De incertitudine et vanitate scientiarum et artium atque excellentia verbi dei declamatio*, Cologne; trans. J. Sanford, *Of the Vanitie and Uncertaintie of Artes and Sciences*, London, 1569; repr., ed. C.M. Dunn, Northridge, CA: California State University Press, 1974. (Agrippa's most sustained piece of satirical and polemical writing, this work was frequently reprinted and widely quoted – by, among others, later sixteenth-century religious radicals.)

—— (1532) *De nobilitate et praecellentia foeminei sexus*, Cologne; repr. in R.H. Popkin (ed.) *Opera*, vol. 2, Hildesheim and New York: Olms, 1970; trans. T. Clapham, *Of the Nobilitie and Excellencie of Womankynde*, London, 1542. (An important early expression of male feminism; the English translation of this book has been described as 'the most explicitly feminist text to be published in England in the first half of the [sixteenth] century' (Jordan 1990: 122).)

—— (1533) *De occulta philosophia libri tres*, Cologne; trans. J. Freake, *Three Books of Occult Philosophy*, London, 1651; repr., ed. D. Tyson, St Paul, MN: Llewellyn Publications, 1993. (The best-known Renaissance encyclopedia of learned magic, this book effectively de-centres orthodox Christianity through its explorations of parallels with Judaic, Muslim and pagan traditions.)

References and further reading

* Hermes Trismegistus (pseud.) (*c.*100–300) *Hermetica*, ed. B.P. Copenhaver, Cambridge: Cambridge University Press, 1992. (The best English translation of writings in which Agrippa was obsessively interested.)

Jordan, C. (1990) *Renaissance Feminism: Literary Texts and Political Models*, Ithaca, NY, and London: Cornell University Press. (Includes an analysis of Agrippa's place on the feminist side of Renaissance debates on the status of women.)

Keefer, M.H. (1988) 'Agrippa's Dilemma: Hermetic "Rebirth" and the Ambivalences of *De vanitate* and *De occulta philosophia*', *Renaissance Quarterly* 41: 614–53. (Explores the commonalities and divergences of Agrippa's two major works in terms of their deployment of motifs derived from the Hermetica and their author's awareness of parallels between Hermetic texts and Gnostic heresies.)

* —— (1996) 'The Dreamer's Path: Descartes and the Sixteenth Century', *Renaissance Quarterly* 49: 30–76. (Referred to in §5, this essay argues that

Agrippa's writings led Descartes to Hermetic texts which were decisive in shaping his philosophical project.)
* Montaigne, M. de (1580) *Essais de Montaigne*, ed. M. Rat, Paris: Éditions Garnier Frères, 1962, 2 vols. (Referred to in §5. Montaigne is both the most engaging and the most influential of sixteenth-century sceptical thinkers; the influence of Agrippa can be detected in the most extended statement of his sceptical philosophy, his 'Apology for Raymond Sebond'. The first edition of Montaigne's essays was published in 1580, although the final, most complete version appeared posthumously in 1595.)
Nauert, C.G., Jr (1965) *Agrippa and the Crisis of Renaissance Thought*, Urbana, IL: University of Illinois Press. (The standard biography and the most detailed study of Agrippa's thought.)
Tomlinson, G. (1993) *Music in Renaissance Magic: Toward a Historiography of Others*, Chicago, IL, and London: University of Chicago Press, 44–66. (The best summary account available of Agrippa's magic.)
Yates, F.A. (1964) *Giordano Bruno and the Hermetic Tradition*, London: Routledge & Kegan Paul. (This compulsively readable account of Renaissance magical traditions includes a rather dismissive account of *De occulta philosophia*.)
—— (1979) *The Occult Philosophy in the Elizabethan Age*, London: Routledge & Kegan Paul. (Gives greater emphasis than Yates' previous books to the influence of Kabbalah on Renaissance occult philosophy.)
Zambelli, P. (1969) 'Cornelio Agrippa, Erasmo e la teologia umanistica' (Agrippa, Erasmus and Humanist Theology), *Rinascimento* 21 (2nd series, 10): 29–88. (See annotation to Zambelli 1985 for details.)
—— (1976) 'Magic and Radical Reformation in Agrippa of Nettesheim', *Journal of the Warburg and Courtauld Institutes* 39: 69–103. (See annotation to Zambelli 1985 for details.)
—— (1985) 'Scholastiker und Humanisten: Agrippa und Trithemius zur Hexerei' (Scholastics and Humanists: Agrippa and Trithemius on Witchcraft), *Archiv für Kulturgeschichte* 67: 41–79. (These and other articles by the leading Agrippa scholar have been crucial in situating his writings in relation to Erasmian humanism, the radical Reformation, and overlapping views of magic and witchcraft.)

MICHAEL H. KEEFER

AILLY, PIERRE D' (1350–1420)

D'Ailly was a prolific writer on a number of subjects. His best known philosophical works concentrate on logic and on faith and reason, with strong influences from Ockham in particular. He also wrote influential works on the nature of the soul. He was one of the most eminent partisans of the late medieval nominalist movement and was numbered among the foremost doctores renovatores by King Louis XI in his decree against the nominalists. His works continued to be highly influential as late as the Reformation period.

Pierre d'Ailly, rector of the Collège de Navarre, chancellor of the University of Paris, bishop of Le Puy and Cambrai, cardinal and papal legate to Germany, was a man of wide interests and inexhaustible energy. He wrote a great number of treatises on the most varied subjects, besides performing the many duties associated with his ecclesiastical and secular posts. He left behind over one hundred and seventy works; those devoted to purely philosophical matters are few in number and were all written in the early years of his academic career, while he was teaching philosophy at the Collège de Navarre. The largest group of his works is devoted to matters relating to the Great Schism (during which there were two, or even three, popes) which endured for almost forty years. After the beginning of the Schism in 1378, d'Ailly concentrated on finding a way to terminate this *horrenda monstruosaque divisio* (abhorrent and monstrous division) and was completely distracted from philosophy.

His influences were widespread and lasting. Martin LUTHER was substantially influenced by d'Ailly's theory of the Eucharist (developed in the fourth book of his *Commentary on the Sentences*, written in 1376–7). In his own treatise *De captivitate Babylonica ecclesiae* (The Babylonian Captivity of the Church), Luther recalls:

Once, during my study of scholastic theology, Pierre d'Ailly gave me occasion to think (while I was reading his fourth book on the Sentences, where he argues most acutely) that it would be much more probable, and one would need fewer of those superfluous miracles, if one would affirm that on the altar there were real bread and real wine, not just their attributes – if the Church had not determined the opposite. When I later realized which Church it was that had determined this – the Thomistic Church, to be sure – I became more courageous.

(*De captivitate Babylonica ecclesiae*)

Christopher Columbus owned d'Ailly's geographical works *Imago mundi* (The Appearance of the World) and *Epilogus mappae mundi* (Epilogue on the Map of the World), both written in 1410. They influenced Columbus in his search for a shorter sea route to India and consequent discovery of America; of the authors Columbus had studied, it was d'Ailly whom he preferred to quote. NICHOLAS OF CUSA used d'Ailly's *Exhortatio super kalendarii correctione* (On Corrections to the Calendar), written in 1411 for Pope John XIII and later publicly read at the Council of Constance, for his own treatise *De correctione kalendarii*. In his *Exhortatio*, d'Ailly advocated – in vain – the reform of the calendar that was later successfully promulgated by Pope Gregory XIII. Johannes KEPLER, himself an apologist for a reformed astrology, explicitly refers to d'Ailly's astrological works in his treatise *De stella nova in pede Serpentarii* (The New Star in the Foot of the Serpent); in one of those works, the *Elucidarium astronomicae concordiae cum theologica et historica veritate* (On the Concordance of Astronomy with Theology and Historical Truth), written in 1414, one finds the first mention of d'Ailly's famous prediction of the French Revolution, which he repeated in his treatise *De persecutionibus ecclesiae* (The Persecutions of the Church).

Much of fourteenth-century thought is characterized by a desire to disengage faith from reason and to build upon empirical facts rather than metaphysical assumptions. Thus, it is not by chance that two of d'Ailly's favourite phrases in his philosophical writings are *docet experientia* (experience teaches) and *patet inductive* (this is clear on the basis of induction). His main sources are WILLIAM OF OCKHAM, Thomas BRADWARDINE, GREGORY OF RIMINI and John BURIDAN, among whom Ockham is clearly the foremost authority: 'a few things said by him I value more highly than many volumes by certain others' (*Tractatus de consolatione philosophiae Boethii*, q.1, art.4: 132).

Pierre d'Ailly's logical writings – *Conceptus* (Concepts), *Insolubilia* (Insolubles), *Exponibilia* (Exponible Propositions) and *Destructiones modorum significandi* (Attacks on the Modes of Signifying) (of dubious attribution) – were very influential in the later Middle Ages and through the fifteenth century. D'Ailly adheres to the Ockhamist tradition in basing his logical theories on the notion of mental language. Concerning paradoxes of self-reference (*insolubilia*), for instance, he holds that there are none in mental language, and that spoken or written paradoxes of this sort are ambiguous sentences in so far as they correspond to two distinct mental sentences, one true and the other false (see LANGUAGE, MEDIEVAL THEORIES OF §§ 2, 3, 14). It is worth noting that the term *vitalis immutatio* (vital change) plays an important role in d'Ailly's definitions of central logical terms such as *conceptus* and *significatio*, which are thus closely connected with his theory of the soul and its powers.

His *Tractatus de anima* (Treatise on the Soul), certainly one of the most important systematic works on philosophical psychology written in the fourteenth century, was widely read throughout the fourteenth, fifteenth and sixteenth centuries. Gabriel BIEL wrote a valuable commentary on it. The first chapter deals with the definition of the soul and its tripartite division, chapters 2–8 deal with the powers of the vegetative, sensitive and intellective soul, while the concluding seven chapters deal with the accidents of the soul: species, the acts of sensation, intellection, volition and passion, and habits. D'Ailly's definition of the soul deviates from Aristotle's formulation: 'The soul is the substantial form of a living body that has within it the capacity to carry out vital activities'. This definition of the soul was adopted by other late medieval authors such as Symphorien Champier (see SOUL, NATURE AND IMMORTALITY OF).

D'Ailly's *Tractatus super De consolatione philosophiae Boethii* (Treatise on Boethius' Consolation of Philosophy) is mainly devoted to the theory of human happiness. Whether a human being can be called 'truly happy in this life' was one of the central ethical questions in the Buridanist school, where the term *homo felicitabilis* (the human being with a capacity for happiness) was coined. In this context, d'Ailly also discusses the question of immortality. In *Tractatus de anima*, he had followed Buridan in affirming that if one follows human reason alone, then Alexander of Aphrodisias' theory of the soul – that the human soul is 'drawn from matter's potentiality' and hence mortal – is the most probable (see ALEXANDER OF APHRODISIAS). But in *Tractatus de anima*, he strongly opposes Alexander and, while relying heavily on arguments taken from ancient authorities like CICERO and SENECA, sides with Nicole ORESME in declaring that even 'in accord with the light of nature', the immortality of the soul is more probable.

See also: NICHOLAS OF CUSA; SOUL, NATURE AND IMMORTALITY OF THE; WILLIAM OF OCKHAM

List of works

D'Ailly, Pierre (1350–1420) *Conceptus* (Concepts), ed. J. Biard, L. Kaczmarek and O. Pluta, forthcoming; trans. P.V. Spade, *Peter of Ailly: Concepts and Insolubles*, Dordrecht: Reidel, 1980. (D'Ailly's writings on logic.)

—— (1350–1420) *Insolubilia* (Insolubles), ed. J. Biard,

F. Del Punta, L. Kaczmarek and O. Pluta, forthcoming; trans. P.V. Spade, *Peter of Ailly: Concepts and Insolubles*, Dordrecht: Reidel, 1980. (D'Ailly's writings on logic.)

—— (1350–1420) *Exponibilia* (Exponible Propositions), ed. J. Biard, L. Kaczmarek and O. Pluta, forthcoming. (D'Ailly's writings on logic.)

—— (1350–1420) *Destructiones modorum significandi* (Attacks on the Modes of Signifying) ed. L. Kaczmarek, Amsterdam: Grüner, 1994. (Dubious attribution.)

—— (1350–1420) *Tractatus de anima* (Treatise on the Soul), in O. Pluta (ed.) *Die philosophische Psychologie des Peter von Ailly*, Amsterdam: Grüner, 1987. (Follows Buridan in supporting the views of Alexander of Aphrodisias.)

—— (1350–1420) *Tractatus super De consolatione philosophiae Boethii*, in M. Chappuis (ed.) *Le Traité de Pierre d'Ailly sur la Consolation de Boéce*, Qu. 1, Amsterdam: Grüner, 1993. (Discusses the theory of human happiness.)

References and further reading

Biard, J. (1992) 'Présence et représentation chez Pierre d'Ailly: Quelques problèmes de théorie de la connaissance au XIVe siècle' (Presence and Representation in the Work of Pierre d'Ailly: Problems of the Theory of Knowledge in the Fourteenth Century), *Dialogue* 31: 459–74. (Expounds and discusses d'Ailly's theory of knowledge as found in his *Commentary on the Sentences* and his philosophical writings.)

Chappuis, M. (1984) 'Notice sur le Traité de Pierre d'Ailly sur la Consolation de Boéce' (Review of Pierre d'Ailly's treatise on the Consolation of Boethius), *Freiburger Zeitschrift für Philosophie und Theologie* 31: 89–107. (Examines all the extant manuscripts of the *Tractatus super De consolatione philosophiae Boethii* and gives a summary of its contents.)

Chappuis, M., Kaczmarek, L. and Pluta, O. (1986) 'Die philosophischen Schriften des Peter von Ailly. Authentizität und Chronologie' (The Philosophical Writings of Pierre d'Ailly: Authenticity and Chronology), *Freiburger Zeitschrift für Philosophie und Theologie* 33: 593–615. (Disputes the authenticity and chronology of d'Ailly's philosophical writings, including the *Destructiones modorum significandi*.)

Kaczmarek, L. (1990) 'Vitalis immutatio. Erkundungen zur erkenntnispsychologischen Terminologie der Spätscholastik' (Lively Changelessness: Explanations of the Epistemological Terminology of Late Scholasticism), in A. Heinekamp, W. Lenzen and M. Schneider (eds) *Festschrift für Heinrich Scheper*, Münster: Nodus, 189–206. (Analyses the use of the term *vitalis immutatio* in John of Ripa's *Commentary on the Sentences* and argues that d'Ailly has adopted this term from him.)

Nuchelmans, G. (1973) *Theories of the Proposition: Ancient and Medieval Conceptions of the Bearers of Truth and Falsity*, Amsterdam: North Holland, 259–65. (Gives an outline of d'Ailly's theory of the proposition in his *Commentary on the Sentences*, *Conceptus*, *Insolubilia* and the (dubious) *Destructiones modorum significandi*.)

Ouy, G. (1975) 'Le Collège de Navarre, berceau de l'humanisme français' (The Collège de Navarre, Cradle of French Humanism), *Actes du 95e Congrès National des Sociétés Savantes de Paris et des Départements*, Sect. de Philologie et d'Histoire, Reims 1970, vol. 1, Paris: Bibliothèque nationale, 275–99. (Shows that the College of Navarre was the cradle of French humanism, its foremost representatives being the 'Navarristes' Pierre d'Ailly and Jean de Montreuil, and later Jean Gerson and Nicolas de Clamanges.)

Pluta, O. (1990) 'Die Diskussion der Frage nach der Unsterblichkeit bei Nikolaus Oresme und Peter von Ailly' (The Discussion of the Question of Immortality in Nicole Oresme and Pierre d'Ailly), *Studia Mediewistyczne* 27 (2): 115–30. (Expounds and discusses the question of immortality as found in Nicole Oresme's *Quaestiones de anima* and d'Ailly's *Tractatus de anima* and *Tractatus super De consolatione philosophiae Boethii*.)

Spade, P.V. (1980) *Peter of Ailly: Concepts and Insolubles, An Annotated Translation*, Dordrecht: Reidel. (The introduction (1–15) presents an introduction to the main topics of *Conceptus* and *Insolubilia* with special emphasis on d'Ailly's sources.)

OLAF PLUTA

AJDUKIEWICZ, KAZIMIERZ (1890–1963)

Ajdukiewicz, like other typical members of the Lwów-Warsaw School, the main Polish analytic movement, was basically interested in logic, philosophy of language, epistemology, and philosophy of science. In the 1930s, he proposed a form of radical conventionalism, an extension of the conventionalism of Duhem and Poincaré. Later, he rejected this radical conventionalism in favour of a semantic epistemology. In the philosophy of science he tried to build a general theory of fallible inferences based on decision theory. Ajdukiewicz's most important contribution to logic is his formal notation for syntactic categories.

1 Life
2 Radical conventionalism
3 Semantic epistemology
4 Philosophy of science
5 Contributions to logic

1 Life

Ajdukiewicz was born on 12 December 1890 in Tarnopol, a town in the Austro-Hungarian Empire (now in Ukraine). In 1908–12 he studied philosophy at the University of Lwów, mainly under Kazimierz TWARDOWSKI. He was also trained by Jan ŁUKASIEWICZ in logic and Wacław Sierpiński in mathematics. In 1912 he obtained his Ph.D.; his dissertation concerned Kant's theory of space. In 1913 Ajdukiewicz studied in Göttingen where he attended courses given by David Hilbert and Edmund HUSSERL. He obtained his *Habilitation* degree from the University of Warsaw with a dissertation on the foundations of mathematics. In 1921–6 he was an associate professor (docent) at the University of Lwów. In 1926 he was appointed as professor of philosophy at the University of Warsaw. In 1928 he returned to Lwów, where he was given a professorship. During the Second World War he lived in Lwów and taught in clandestine Polish schools. In 1945 Ajdukiewicz accepted a professorship at the University of Poznan. In 1955 he moved to the University of Warsaw. He died on 12 April 1963 in Warsaw.

2 Radical conventionalism

Radical conventionalism is closely related to Ajdukiewicz's theory of language and meaning. The meanings of expressions in a language generate rules for accepting sentences of L. Ajdukiewicz singles out three kinds of meaning-rules: axiomatic (they require the unconditional acceptance of certain sentences, for example 'A is A'), deductive (for example, B follows from 'if A then B' and A), and empirical (the sentence 'snow is white' is asserted in a situation in which a person asserting this sentence perceives that snow is white).

It follows from the foregoing explanations that meanings determine meaning-rules. But in general, meaning-rules do not determine the meanings of expressions; this holds, for example, for ordinary language. However, the situation radically changes when we pass to closed and connected languages. Roughly speaking, a language L is open if it can be extended to a new language L' without changes in the meanings of the expressions of L; otherwise, L is closed. A language L is disconnected if there is a non-empty subset X of expressions of L such that no element of X is related by meaning-rules of L to its remaining expressions; otherwise, L is connected. An important consequence of the theory of closed and connected languages is this: if L is a closed and connected language, it is impossible to enrich L by new expressions in such a way that old meanings are preserved.

For Ajdukiewicz, mature, particularly scientific, knowledge is expressed in closed and connected languages. The set of meanings of a closed and connected language L is its conceptual apparatus. From general theorems on closed and connected languages, one can infer that two conceptual apparatuses are either identical or mutually non-translatable. The acceptance or rejection of sentences is always related to a definite language L. If L is closed and connected, empirical situations do not force us either to accept or reject any sentence, because we can always change our conceptual apparatus. This is an essential strengthening of usual conventionalism. For POINCARÉ and DUHEM, we are free to change our theoretical principles, because they are hidden conventions. For Ajdukiewicz, experiential reports are also closely related to conceptual apparatus, and since every conceptual apparatus produces a world-perspective, we can say that theories and observational reports are accepted not absolutely but relative to world-perspectives. This is why Ajdukiewicz called his conventionalism 'radical', contrary to the moderate view of the Frenchmen (see CONVENTIONALISM).

3 Semantic epistemology

In the middle 1930s Ajdukiewicz rejected radical conventionalism, because he came to the view that his idea of connected and closed languages was a 'paper fiction'. The change was also strongly motivated by the work of TARSKI which convinced many philosophers that semantics has important applications in philosophy. When he was a radical conventionalist, Ajdukiewicz did not draw any ontological theses from his epistemological considerations; but his semantic epistemology is an attempt to bring together epistemology and ontology. If we speak about the world, we use an object-language. Since epistemology intends to say something about the world and our knowledge of it, an epistemologist must use a meta-language in order to capture knowledge and its object. Ajdukiewicz, employing metalogic and semantics, gave a rigorous analysis of

Rickert's transcendental idealism and Berkeley's subjective idealism (see BERKELEY, G.). For Ajdukiewicz, both kinds of idealism are incorrect, because they neglect basic results of metalogic and semantics. Ajdukiewicz rejects Rickert's idealism, because truth, contrary to Rickert, cannot be established exclusively by purely deductive procedures; the incompleteness of arithmetic is an essential premise of Ajdukiewicz's argument. Berkeley's thesis that ordinary objects are complexes of our ideas is rejected, because it conflates syntax and semantics. According to Ajdukiewicz, Berkeley uses a language which is very similar to the language of syntax and offers a syntactic-like definition of existence. However, since existence is basically a semantic concept and semantics is not fully definable in syntax, Berkeley's argument fails. Thus, semantic epistemology leads to a realist account of existence.

4 Philosophy of science

In addition to his discussions of radical conventionalism, which implies that there is no absolute gap between theories and experiential reports, Ajdukiewicz also worked on concrete problems in the philosophy of science. In particular, he was interested in the logic of fallible inferences. His approach was based on concepts borrowed from decision theory. In general, acceptances (rejections) of sentences are actions which are associated with profits and losses. Assume that A is a sentence to be accepted and that Z is the minimal acceptable profit for the agent, when A is true, and S is the minimal acceptable loss, when A is false. According to Ajdukiewicz the ratio $S/(S+Z)$ expresses the degree of certainty which an agent accepting A can ascribe to this sentence. This relates degrees of certainty to mathematical probabilities. Having this framework, Ajdukiewicz tried to establish the degree of conclusiveness of a fallible scheme of inference. Assume that K is background knowledge. We are interested in the degree of conclusiveness of a fallible (for example, inductive) inference from premises P to a hypothesis H. This inference is conclusive if the degree of certainty of H does not exceed the ratio of its initial probability to the initial probability of premises, relative to K. Ajdukiewicz's analysis of fallible inferences is a typical example of his pragmatic approach to methodological problems, which consists in relating analysed concepts to attitudes of epistemic agents.

5 Contributions to logic

Ajdukiewicz's notation for syntactic categories is his main contribution to logic. The following example shows how this notation works. We have two basic categories: sentences (s) and terms (n). Now, consider an expression 'is tall'. It forms a sentence together with a term, for example 'Tom'. We ascribe to 'is tall' the symbol s/n which informs us that 'is tall' is a function forming a sentence with a term as an argument. Now we build a sequence of symbols for the sentence 'Tom is tall'. The sequence is this: n, sn. It is obtained by writing the symbols for the categories of all the expressions occurring in the considered sentence. We can simplify the sequence by performing 'arithmetical' operations on symbols by analogy with operations on ratios. Thus, we can 'shorten' $\{n, s/n\}$ by dividing both members by n; we assume that n/n can be cancelled. Thus, we obtain s as the sole member. A general rule is this: if the simplification ends with n or s, the original expression is syntactically correct; otherwise not. This idea gave rise to constructions known as Leśniewski–Ajdukiewicz–Lambek grammar, originated with LEŚNIEWSKI, continued by Ajdukiewicz, and fully developed by Lambek (see SYNTAX).

See also: POLAND, PHILOSOPHY IN

List of works

Ajdukiewicz, K. (1921) *Contributions to the Methodology of Deductive Sciences* (in Polish), Lwów: Polskie Towarzystwo Filozoficzne; partially trans. J. Giedymin (1966), *Studia Logica* 19: 9–46. (Ajdukiewicz's *Habilitation*.)

—— (1934a) 'Sprache und Sinn', *Erkenntnis* 4: 130–8; trans. J. Wilkinson, 'Language and Meaning' in *The Scientific World-Perspective and Other Essays 1931–1963*, Dordrecht: Reidel, 1978: 35–66. (A presentation of the theory of closed and connected languages.)

—— (1934b) 'Das Weltbild und die Begriffsapparatur', *Erkenntnis* 4: 259–87; trans. J. Wilkinson, 'The World-Picture and the Conceptual Apparatus' in *The Scientific World-Perspective and Other Essays 1931–1963*, Dordrecht: Reidel, 1978: 67–89. (A basic paper on radical conventionalism.)

——(1936) 'Die syntaktische Konnexität', *Studia Philosophica* I: 1–276; trans. H. Weber, 'Syntactic Connexion' in *The Scientific World-Perspective and Other Essays 1931–1963*, Dordrecht: Reidel, 1978: 118–39. (Notation for syntactic categories.)

——(1948) 'Epistemologia i semiotyka', *Przeglad Filozoficzny* 44: 336–47; trans. J. Giedymin, 'Epistemology and Semiotics' in *The Scientific World-Perspective and Other Essays 1931–1963*, Dordrecht: Reidel, 1978: 182–91. (Semantic epistemology.)

——(1958) 'Zagadnienie racjonalnosci zawodnych

sposobow wnioskowanis', *Studia Filozoficzne* 4 (7): 14–19; trans. D. Pearce, 'The Problem of Rationality of Non-Deductive Types of Inference' in *The Scientific World-Perspective and Other Essays 1931–1963*, Dordrecht: Reidel, 1978: 239–53. (Ajdukiewicz's analysis of fallible modes of inference.)

—— (1973) *Problems and Theories of Philosophy*, trans. H. Skolimowski and A. Quinton, Cambridge: Cambridge University Press. (An elementary introduction to philosophy; this book was originally published in Polish in 1949.)

——(1974) *Pragmatic Logic*, trans. O. Wojtasiewicz, Dordrecht: Reidel. (An extensive treatise on methodology; this book was originally published in Polish in 1965.)

——(1978) *The Scientific World-Perspective and Other Essays 1931–1963*, Dordrecht: Reidel. (A collection of basic papers by Ajdukiewicz.)

References and further reading

Sinisi, V. and Woleński, J. (eds) (1995) *The Heritage of Kazimierz Ajdukiewicz*, Amsterdam: Rodopi. (A collection of essays on Ajdukiewicz's philosophy; includes the complete bibliography of Ajdukiewicz's writings and a selected bibliography on Ajdukiewicz.)

Woleński, J. (1989) *Logic and Philosophy in the Lvov–Warsaw School*, Dordrecht: Kluwer. (Chapter X gives a presentation of Ajdukiewicz's epistemology.)

JAN WOLEŃSKI

AKAN PHILOSOPHICAL PSYCHOLOGY

The word Akan refers to the Twi-speaking people of southern and central Ghana. Akan traditional philosophy is essentially a philosophy of the person. It has cosmological ramifications, but the basic concepts emerge from the analysis of the human personality. That analysis is extremely sensitive to the complexity of the human psyche and the social dimensions of individual consciousness. These considerations explain and justify the prominent position occupied by the concept of a person in contemporary Akan philosophy.

This emphasis on the person is a time-honoured feature of the written tradition of Akan philosophy and reflects the priorities of the oral tradition, the mainspring of that system of thought. With respect to the nature of personhood, however, there has been a divergence of preoccupation between the oral and the written traditions. The predominant motivation of the written tradition has been metaphysical, as writers have sought to clarify the ontological status of the constituents of human personality, while the main orientation of the oral tradition is social and ethical. Within this tradition, a person is defined by their social relations more crucially than by their ontological essence.

In the Akan tradition the concept of a person has a normative as well as a descriptive component. The word *onipa*, the Akan equivalent of 'person', is often used normatively to designate a person who has largely attained a desirable social standing. To achieve a high degree of personhood is therefore an inherent part of the Akan ethic. To be a person in the fullest sense is to be an adult who works hard, thinks judiciously and is able to support a conjugal household as well as fulfil a range of obligations to an extended group of kinfolk and to the civic community at large. Such an individual, also known as an *obadwenma*, meaning someone of ethical and cerebral maturity, must also listen to and act in accordance with their conscience, known as *tiboa*, or literally, animal in the head (*ti* meaning head and (*a*)*boa* meaning animal).

In Akan circles to talk or act unintelligently is to risk unflattering descriptions of the *adwene* in your head. *Adwene*, or mind, is the noun form of the verb *dwen*, to think. The term denotes mental processes and emotional dispositions. The Akans delight in metaphor and often locate the mind in the head as if it is identical with the brain, or *amene*. Indeed, there is little temptation to identify the mind with the brain or with any other kind of substance, physical, abstract or spiritual.

Because the Akans traditionally do not conceive of the mind as a kind of substance, they do not include it in their ontological inventory of the elements which constitute an *onipa*, or person, in the minimal sense of a human being. Within the oral and written traditions there is near unanimity that a person in Akan traditional thought consists of *ornipadua*, literally the tree of a person, deriving from the *mogya*, or blood of the mother in combination with the *okra*, the animating element which emanates directly from the supreme being. The factor that completes the equation that yields a person is the *sunsum* which originates from the father's input in conception and is held to be responsible for the unique personal presence of every individual. All *akra* (plural of *okra*) are identical in nature in as much as they are all particles of the divine substance, but they are individuated by the unique destinies prenatally assigned to them by the supreme being. In view of this common divine element, all human beings whatever their social achievements or failures, are regarded as children of God each with the gift of immortality. (A famous Akan adage holds that everyone is the child of God; no one is a child of the earth.)

The *okra* and the *sunsum* cannot be identified with the soul or spirit contrary to frequent practice in Akan literature, as in the general cosmology of the Akans, all these entities are conceived in quasi-material terms. However, this and other issues in the interpretation and evaluation of the Akan concept of a person, remain matters of controversy among Akan philosophers.

See also: PERSONS

References and further reading

Abraham, W.E. (1962) *The Mind of Africa*, Chicago, IL: University of Chicago Press. (Chapter 2, especially the section on the Akan 'Theory of Man and Society'.)

Appiah, K.A. (1982) *In My Father's House: Africa in the Philosophy of Culture*, London: Methuen; 2nd edn, Oxford: Oxford University Press, 1992. (Chapter 5: 'Ethnophilosophy and its Critics', especially pages 96–100.)

Busia, K.A. (1954) 'The Ashanti of the Gold Coast', in D. Forde (ed.) *African Worlds: Studies in the Cosmological Ideas and Social Values of African Peoples*, Oxford: Oxford University Press, 1954.

Danquah, J.B. (1944) *The Akan Doctrine of God: A Fragment of Gold Coast Ethics and Religion*, London: Frank Cass, 1968. (Second edition with introduction by K.A. Dickson, 1968. See §§4 and 5.)

Engmann, J. (1992) 'Immortality and the Nature of Man in Ga Thought', in K. Wiredu and K. Gyekye (eds) *Person and Community: Ghanaian Philosophical Studies*, Washington, DC: Council for Research in Values and Philosophy, 1992. (An interesting read.)

Gyekye, K. (1987) *An Essay on African Philosophical Thought: The Akan Conceptual Scheme*, New York: Cambridge University Press. (Chapter 6: 'The Concept of a Person' and pages 163–8, 198–9 contain references to the work of scholars such as Rattray and Meyerowitz on the Akan conception of a person.)

Oguah, B.E. (1984) 'African and Western Philosophy: A Comparative Study', in R.A. Wright (ed.) *African Philosophy: An Introduction*, New York: University Press of America, 1977. (The third edition of this book appeared in 1984.)

Opoku, K.A. (1978) *West African Traditional Religion*, London: FEP International Private Limited. (Chapter 5: 'West African Conception of Man'.)

Parrinder, E.G. (1951) *West African Psychology: A Comparative Study of Psychological and Religious Thought*, London: Lutterworth Press. (Especially interesting are chapters 1–6, pages 1–84.)

Wiredu, K. (1987) 'The Concept of Mind with Particular Reference to the Language and Thought of the Akans', in G. Flöstad (ed.) *Contemporary Philosophy*, vol. 5: *African Philosophy*, Boston, MA: Kluwer, 1987.

KWASI WIREDU

AKRASIA

The Greek word 'akrasia' is usually said to translate literally as 'lack of self-control', but it has come to be used as a general term for the phenomenon known as weakness of will, or incontinence, the disposition to act contrary to one's own considered judgment about what it is best to do. Since one variety of akrasia *is the inability to act as one thinks right,* akrasia *is obviously important to the moral philosopher, but it is also frequently discussed in the context of philosophy of action.* Akrasia *is of interest to philosophers of action because although it seems clear that it does occur – that people often do act in ways which they believe to be contrary to their own best interests, moral principles or long-term goals – it also seems to follow from certain apparently plausible views about intentional action that* akrasia *is simply not possible. A famous version of the suggestion that genuine akrasia cannot exist is found in Socrates, as portrayed by Plato in the* Protagoras. *Socrates argues that it is impossible for a person's knowledge of what is best to be overcome by such things as the desire for pleasure – that one cannot choose a course of action which one knows full well to be less good than some alternative known to be available. Anyone who chooses to do something which is in fact worse than something they know they could have done instead, must, according to Socrates, have wrongly judged the relative values of the actions.*

1 The Socratic view
2 Aristotle on *akrasia*
3 Davidson on weakness of will
4 Moral weakness

1 The Socratic view

The Socratic view that 'no one does wrong willingly' receives its most detailed elaboration in the *Prota-*

goras. The context is a discussion between Socrates and Protagoras about the nature of the virtues. It is in the course of defending the suggestion that the virtues form a kind of unity that Socrates maintains that no one can knowingly choose the worse of two available alternatives.

There is much controversy about how, exactly, Socrates' argument for his conclusion is to be understood. The argument certainly appears to invoke some highly questionable assumptions about the relationship between pleasure and pain and goodness and evil, and between all of these and human motivation; and there has been much debate about whether we ought to regard these assumptions as ones which Socrates himself accepted, or whether he is rather arguing *ad hominem* against those who do accept the hedonistic views on which his argument seems to be based. Protagoras and Socrates declare themselves straightforwardly agreed on the point that knowledge cannot be 'pushed around by all the other affections' (352c1) (that is, that if someone knows which is the best course of action, then nothing can persuade them to act otherwise than as that knowledge dictates). The argument is thus presented as an attempt to convince not Protagoras, but rather those ordinary people who have not realised that there is really no such phenomenon as being induced to act contrary to one's knowledge by the desire for pleasure. This may leave room, therefore, for the view that the premises on which Socrates' argument are based are not ones he himself believed, but rather are assumptions that he attributes to these hypothetical interlocutors.

With this caution in mind, we can say that the structure of the argument is something like this:

(1) The evaluation of actions is always based, ultimately, on judgments about the total amounts of pleasure and pain which will result, overall, from performing them.

(2) Since this is so, the good and the pleasant are (in some sense or other) the same, and similarly for the bad and the painful.

(3) This means that any description of an agent which involves their being said to be 'overcome by pleasure' can be replaced by a description of that agent as 'overcome by the good'. But the good by which the agent is overcome cannot, by hypothesis, outweigh the evil which will result from the action (otherwise the action would be virtuous and the agent would have done nothing wrong).

(4) The agent who is 'overcome by pleasure', therefore, must be described as someone who chooses evil (pain) in exchange for a good (pleasure) which does not adequately compensate for this evil.

(5) But, in weighing pleasures and pains against one another, one must always choose what one believes to be the greater pleasure or the lesser pain – and one must therefore take whichever course of action it is that one believes will result, overall, in the most pleasant or least painful outcome, all things considered.

(6) So, the only possible explanation for someone's choosing an action which will bring more pain, overall, or less pleasure, than some alternative known to be available is that they have misjudged the total amounts of pleasures and pains to be got from the alternative actions.

Obviously, this argument is vulnerable to attack at many points. In particular, the psychological hedonism invoked in premise (5) might be challenged. There may be other reasons for thinking that there is something right about the Socratic view, but it seems fair to say that what we are offered in the *Protagoras* amounts to a less than conclusive case.

2 Aristotle *on akrasia*

Aristotle's views on *akrasia* receive their most extensive airing in Book VII of his *Nicomachean Ethics*, and the bulk of what he says is concentrated in a single chapter of that book, chapter 3. The text of this chapter, however, is dense and complex, and there is considerable disagreement amongst commentators even about the very basic question of whether Aristotle is to be seen as an apologist for the Socratic position or rather as a critic of its over-intellectualized view of the causes of practical error. Some translators (for example Ross 1980) have credited Aristotle with the straightforward assertion, early in his discussion at VII 2, that the Socratic view 'contradicts the plain phenomena' (1145b27), which clearly supports the second hypothesis; but since the Greek word 'phainomena' can also be translated 'common opinions or beliefs', this interpretation is not uncontroversial. And it must be admitted that a good deal of what Aristotle says in VII 3 appears to associate the occurrence of *akrasia* with a special kind of ignorance, an association reminiscent of the Socratic view that if one really knows what is best, one can do nothing else. Furthermore, the chapter ends with the claim that, in the light of what has been said, 'the position that Socrates sought to establish actually seems to result' (1147b14).

On the other hand, there are numerous passages in other of Aristotle's works where Aristotle appears to imply that it is perfectly possible for an agent to pursue an undesirable course of action while knowing full well that it is not the best thing to do. In the *Eudemian Ethics*, for example, it is said that to act incontinently 'is to act through appetite contrary to what the man thinks best' (1223b8–9), and that the *akrates* has 'a pain of expectation, thinking that he is doing ill' (1224b20–21). Then again, in *Magna Moralia*, we have the incontinent agent characterised as one 'who knows indeed from reason that he ought not [to do the wrong thing], but gives in to pleasure and succumbs to it' (1203b5–6). These quotations seem to suggest that Aristotle is perfectly content with the description of *akrasia* that Socrates sought to reject, the condition of one whose knowledge is vanquished, but not necessarily clouded or annihilated, by the desire for pleasure. How, then, are we to square these passages with the appearance that NE VII 3 endorses some version of the Socratic view?

There is not space here to review the many attempts that have been made to resolve the apparent contradiction. Certainly, though, VII 3 does make it seem as though Aristotle is inclined to deny that there can be such a thing as utterly clear-eyed *akrasia* – the calm, deliberate and intentional performance of an action known not to be in one's own best interests. The chapter is largely concerned with the application to the problem of *akrasia* of two distinctions, one rooted in Aristotle's doctrine of the practical syllogism, the other concerned with a contrast between the mere possession of knowledge and its *use* or *exercise*, and it is hard to see how these epistemic considerations are intended if not as qualified support for the Socratic view that knowledge cannot be 'dragged around like a slave'. The suggestion seems to be that passion or desire makes it impossible for the *akrates* to reach full-fledged knowledge of the conclusion of the practical syllogism which would lead him to perform the right action. But if so, Aristotle would seem to be in agreement with Socrates that weakness of will is never really just that – that it is always bound up with some form of self-deception, delusion or other epistemic error (see ARISTOTLE §23).

3 Davidson on weakness of will

In a famous article entitled 'How is Weakness of the Will Possible?' (1970), Donald Davidson locates the problem of *akrasia* firmly within the philosophy of action, discarding its traditional connections with morality and the defeat of moral judgment by passions of various kinds. According to Davidson, an agent acts incontinently if and only if: (a) the agent does x intentionally; (b) the agent believes there is an alternative action y open to them; and (c) the agent judges that, all things considered, it would be better to do y than to do x. It follows that, for Davidson, there is not necessarily anything iniquitous about incontinence. He gives the following example. Suppose that I suddenly remember, having already gone to bed, that I have not brushed my teeth. It is clear to me that missing one night's brushing won't make much difference to my dental health and that getting up may result in my having a disturbed and fitful night's sleep, so I conclude that, all things considered, it would be better for me to stay in bed. Nevertheless, I reluctantly get up and plod to the bathroom. On Davidson's definition, my action counts as incontinent – though it is more plausible to say here that pleasure has been worsted by duty rather than the other way round.

The problem of incontinence is represented by Davidson as an apparent inconsistency between three principles, all of which, according to Davidson, seem 'self-evident', or at any rate can be made so, given suitable interpretation. The three principles (from Davidson [1970] 1980: 23) are the following:

'P1: If an agent wants to do x more than they want to do y and they believe themselves free to do either x or y, then they will intentionally do x if they do either x or y intentionally.

P2: If an agent judges that it would be better to do x than to do y, then they want to do x more than they want to do y.

P3: There are incontinent actions.'

Davidson rejects what he calls 'the most common way of dealing with the problem of incontinence', that is, the abandonment of P2. Though he admits that 'wanting' and 'judging better' can readily be interpreted so as to render P2 false, he insists that there is also a natural reading that makes it true, which leaves the apparent inconsistency intact. 'Judging better', he suggests, cannot be totally divorced both from behaviour and from desire – if one sincerely believes that x is a better course of action, all things considered, than y, then one must, in some sense or other, want to do x more than one wants to do y. And provided one concedes this, the problem about weakness of will will remain.

Davidson's solution to the problem is an attempt to show that P1–P3 are not, after all, inconsistent. The argument turns on a distinction made by Davidson between unconditional evaluative judgments (for example, the straightforward judgment that it is better to do x than to do y) and conditional, or *prima facie*, evaluative judgments, which are relative to some body of evidence or other (such as the judgment that it is better to do x than to do y, given all the relevant factors known to the agent). Davidson offers a treatment of the latter variety of judgment from which it follows that no conditional evaluative judgment can be in any logical conflict with an unconditional one. This enables him to reconcile P1–P3 by saying that the incontinent agent who does x rather than y does indeed want to do x more than y and makes an unconditional judgment that the incontinent course of action, x, is better than y. The awareness that y is better than x, on the other hand, is relative to a body of reasons – the total body of reasons available to the agent – and therefore does not contradict the unconditional judgment in accordance with which the agent acts (see INTENTION §3).

4 Moral weakness

Moral weakness is that particular form of *akrasia* which consists in failing to live up to one's sincerely expressed beliefs about what it would be morally best to do. Nothing is more obvious, one might think, than that people often do things they genuinely consider to be morally wrong; but the existence of this type of weakness has sometimes been thought to present problems for certain moral theories. In particular, any theory which makes action the test or criterion of the sincerity of moral beliefs may have difficulty accounting for moral weakness. For such theories will tend to suggest that those who do not act on the principles they profess cannot really be said to hold those principles at all – thus their failing will turn out to be not *akrasia*, but hypocrisy.

R.M. Hare's ethical prescriptivism is one theory in particular which has been thought to conflict with the existence of moral weakness (see PRESCRIPTIVISM). Hare's view (1963) is that it is part of the meaning of moral judgments that they *prescribe*; that is, they are intended as guides to conduct. The acceptance of some particular moral judgment, then, is the acceptance of a recommendation to act in some particular way in some given circumstance or type of circumstance – but how could one be said sincerely to have accepted such a recommendation if one fails to act in accordance with it? Hare's response, roughly, is to insist that typically, cases of 'moral weakness' are cases where the agents concerned are psychologically incapable of doing what they think they ought. Hare's view is that 'I ought but I can't' is not a contradiction; the agent here is 'prescribing in general terms, but exempting himself because of the impossibility, in his case, of obeying this general prescription' (1963: 53). One might wonder though, whether this is really a satisfactory account of *all* cases of moral weakness. Sometimes, no doubt, moral agents are prevented from acting as they think they ought by compulsions and irresistible forces, but it seems wrong to think of this as the general, or even the typical case.

See also: MORAL AGENTS; MORAL PSYCHOLOGY; REASONING/RATIONALITY: PRACTICAL; SELF-DECEPTION; WILL, THE

References and further reading

* Aristotle (384–322 BC) *Eudemian Ethics*, trans. J. Solomon, in *The Complete Works of Aristotle*, vol. 2, Oxford: Oxford University Press, 1984. (Probably an earlier work than the *Nicomachean Ethics*, with which it has three books in common.)
* —— (384–322 BC) *Nicomachean Ethics*, trans. and notes T. Irwin, Indianapolis, IN: Hackett Publishing Company, 1985; or trans. Sir David Ross, Oxford: Oxford University Press, 1980. (The main discussion of *akrasia* is contained in book VII, chapters 2–4, and is the topic of §2 above.)
* —— (384–322 BC) *Magna Moralia*, trans. St. G. Stock, in *The Complete Works of Aristotle*, vol. 2, Oxford: Oxford University Press, 1984. (No agreed view on date of composition, which may well be a handbook written after Aristotle's time.)
* Davidson, D. (1970) 'How is Weakness of the Will Possible?', in J. Feinberg (ed.) *Moral Concepts*, Oxford: Oxford University Press, repr. in D. Davidson *Essays on Actions and Events*, Oxford: Clarendon Press, 1980. (A classic article, a little technical towards the end; discussed in §3 above.)
Gosling, J. (1990) *Weakness of the Will*, London: Routledge. (A useful overview, which contains a good bibliography.)
* Hare, R.M. (1963) *Freedom and Reason*, Oxford: Oxford University Press. (Chapter 5, 'Backsliding', contains Hare's discussion of moral weakness.)
Lemmon, E.J. (1962) 'Moral Dilemmas', *The Philosophical Review*, 71: 139–58. (Contains a stalwart defence of the existence of moral weakness.)
* Plato (c.386–380 BC) *Protagoras*, trans. and notes C.C.W. Taylor, Oxford: Clarendon, 2nd edn, 1991. (Contains text of the dialogue together with a helpful and detailed commentary. This is discussed in §1 above.)
Santas, G. (1966) 'Plato's Protagoras and Explanations of Weakness', *The Philosophical Review* 75: 3–33. (Good both on the *Protagoras* in particular and on incontinence in general.)

HELEN STEWARD

AKṢAPĀDA GAUTAMA
see GAUTAMA, AKṢAPĀDA

AL- see UNDER NAME OF PERSON (FOR EXAMPLE, AL-FARABI, SEE UNDER FARABI)

ALBERT OF SAXONY (*c*.1316–90)

Albert of Saxony, active in the middle and late fourteenth century, taught at the University of Paris and was later instrumental in founding the University of Vienna. He is best known for his works on logic and natural philosophy. In the latter field he was influenced by John Buridan, but he was also influenced by the English logicians. His thought is rather typical of the sort that followed Buridan, combining critical analysis of language with epistemological realism. He was important in the diffusion of terminist logic in central Europe, and of the new physics in northern Italy.

Albert of Saxony, or Albert of Rickmersdorf (sometimes called Albertus Parvus (Little Albert) to distinguish him from ALBERT THE GREAT) was born in Helmstedt, Germany, around 1316. He studied first in his native region before going on to Erfurt (although this is not known for certain) and then to Paris, where he became Master of Arts in 1351. In 1353, he became rector of the university, and taught in the arts faculty there for a decade; he also studied theology, though apparently without receiving a degree. After a period during which he was involved in diplomatic mediation between the pope and the Duke of Austria, Albert was put in charge of founding the University of Vienna, and in 1365 he became its first rector. In 1366 he was made a canon of Hildesheim and was named bishop of Halberstadt. He remained in the latter position until his death on 8 July 1390.

Since none of his theological writings survives, Albert of Saxony is known especially for his work in logic and natural philosophy. However, he also wrote commentaries on Aristotle's *Ethics* and *Economics*, as well as a few small works on mathematics (*Tractatus proportionum* (Treatise on Proportions), *Quaestio de quadratura circuli* (Question on the Quadrature of the Circle)). In the field of logic, his main work is the summa entitled *Perutilis logica* (Very Useful Logic). He also wrote a voluminous collection of *Sophismata* (examining various difficulties of interpretation due to the presence of syncategorematic words in sentences), a set of *Quaestiones logicales* (Logical Questions) that deal with semantical problems and the status of logic, and commentaries on Aristotle's Organon.

Although BURIDAN was then very popular in the arts faculty at Paris, Albert's work attests also to the influence of English ideas in Paris. The *Perutilis logica*, while developing treatises on obligations, insolubles and consequences, which were becoming more and more important at the time, is organized on the model of William of Ockham's *Summa logicae* (see WILLIAM OF OCKHAM §6). Albert accepts Ockham's conception of the nature of a sign. He believes that signification rests on a referential relation of the sign to the individual thing, and that the spoken sign depends for its signification on the conceptual sign. He follows Ockham again in his conception of universals and, for the most part, in his theory of supposition. In particular, he preserves Ockham's notion of simple supposition, the direct reference of a term to the concept on which it depends when it signifies an extra-mental thing. Finally, Albert follows Ockham in his theory of categories: contrary to Buridan, he refuses to treat quantity as a feature of reality in its own right, but rather reduces it to a disposition of substance and quality.

On a few points, however, Albert distances himself from Ockham. For instance, he denies that in disputation an equivocal proposition must be the object of a distinction through which it is assigned multiple senses: in disputation, even equivocal propositions can only be granted, denied or doubted. In his *Sophismata*, Albert often follows William HEYTESBURY (for example, in the analysis of epistemic verbs or of infinity). He admits that a proposition has its own signification, which is not that of its terms: just like a syncategorematic word, a proposition signifies a 'mode of being'. Albert avoids concretizing such modes of being and, in the final analysis, traces them back to relations among the things to which the terms refer. Nevertheless, he makes use of the idea of the distinguishable signification of the proposition in defining truth and in dealing with 'insolubles' (paradoxes of self-reference). Since every proposition, by its very form, signifies that it is true, an insoluble proposition will turn out to be false because it will signify at once both that it is true and that it is false (see LANGUAGE, MEDIEVAL THEORIES OF).

Albert's analysis of language is combined with an epistemological realism that emerges, for instance, from his analysis of the vacuum. One could imagine that, through divine omnipotence, a vacuum exists. However, no science of nature can countenance the hypothesis of the existence of a vacuum. Albert refuses to extend the reference of the terms of physics to supernatural possibilities; thus in his view, physics cannot be developed through thought experiments or the study of imaginary cases, contrary to what was being done at Oxford at the time. Instead, physics must report on the natural course of things.

Aside from his commentaries on Aristotle's *libri naturales*, Albert wrote a commentary on John of Sacrobosco's *De sphera* (Treatise on the Sphere), and a *Tractatus proportionum* (Treatise on Proportions) inspired by Thomas BRADWARDINE. Following the works of the Oxford Calculators (see OXFORD CALCULATORS), and of Nicole ORESME in Paris, he tried to calculate the acceleration of the fall of bodies, but without succeeding in determining whether it is proportionate to the time elapsed or to the distance covered. He was interested in many natural phenomena and studied the movements of the earth and the phenomena of tides and geology.

It is probably in the field of dynamics, however, that Albert's role is most important. In order to account for the motion of projectiles and for the acceleration in the fall of weights, he adopted Buridan's impetus theory, according to which impetus is a property acquired by bodies. With great clarity, he draws the consequences of extending this theory to celestial movements, and is thus able to reject the traditional notion of intelligences moving the spheres. He studies the motions of terrestrial and celestial bodies according to the same principles. Many of his contributions to the field of dynamics are in his commentary on Aristotle's *On the Heavens*, which was very influential in northern Italy. Albert of Saxony thus took part in the development of a vision of the cosmos which broke with Aristotelian views.

See also: BURIDAN, J.; LANGUAGE, MEDIEVAL THEORIES OF; LOGIC, MEDIEVAL; NATURAL PHILOSOPHY, MEDIEVAL; WILLIAM OF OCKHAM

List of works

Few texts are available in full in modern editions.

Albert of Saxony (before 1390) *Perutilis logica* (Very Useful Logic), ed. and Spanish trans. A. Muñoz de García, Maracaibo: Universidad del Zulia, 1988. (This edition is after the incunable edition, first published in Venice (1522). An edition of the second treatise, *De proprietatibus terminorum* (On the Properties of Terms), was published in C. Kann, *Die Eigenschaften der termini*, Amsterdam: Brill, 1993.)

—— (before 1390) *Quaestiones in artem veterem* (Questions on the Old Logic), ed. A. Muñoz de García, Maracaibo: Universidad del Zulia, 1988. (This is a critical edition.)

References and further reading

Biard, J. (1989) 'Les sophismes du savoir: Albert de Saxe entre Jean Buridan et Guillaume Heytesbury' (The Sophismata on Knowledge: Albert of Saxony between John Buridan and William Heytesbury), *Vivarium* 27: 36–50. (Discussion of one of Albert's sophismata.)

—— (ed.) (1991) *Paris-Vienne au XIVe siècle. Itinéraires d'Albert de Saxe* (From Paris to Vienna in the Fourteenth Century: The Journeys of Albert of Saxony), Actes de la table ronde internationale, Paris, 19–22 juin 1990, Paris: Vrin. (Twenty-one contributions showing the recent state of knowledge about logic and natural philosophy in the fourteenth century.)

—— (1993) 'Albert de Saxe et les sophismes de l'infini' (Albert of Saxony and the Sophismata on Infinity), in S. Read (ed.) *Sophisms in Medieval Logic and Grammar*, Boston: Kluwer, 288–303. (Discussion of Albert's sophismata.)

Gonzales, A. (1958) 'The Theory of Assertoric Consequences in Albert of Saxony', *Franciscan Studies* 18: 290–354, and 19: 13–114. (A formal study of the theory of inferences.)

Braakhuis, H.A.G. (1993) 'Albert of Saxony's *De obligationibus*: Its Place in the Development of Fourteenth Century Obligational Theory', in K. Jacobi (ed.) *Argumentationstheorie: scholastische Forschung zur den logischen und semantischen Regeln korrekten Folgerns*, Leiden: Brill, 323–41. (Discussion of Albert's treatise on obligation.)

Berger, H. (1994) 'Albert von Sachsen (1316[?]–1390). Bibliographie der Sekundärliteratur' (Albert of Saxony: Bibliography of Secondary Literature), *Bulletin de philosophie médiévale* 36: 146–85. (Bibliography of works relevant to Albert.)

Heidingsfelder, G. (1927) *Albert von Sachsen. Sein Lebensgang und sein Kommentar zur Nikomachischen Ethik des Aristoteles* (Albert of Saxony: His Life and Commentary on Aristotle's *Nicomachean Ethics*), Beiträge zur Geschichte der philosophie des Mittelalters XXII, 3–4, Münster: Aschendorff. (The biographical section is now dated, but this remains the only study of Albert's ethics.)

Kann, C. (1993) *Die Eigenschaften der termini. Eine Untersuchung zur 'Perutilis Logica' des Alberts von Sachsen* (The Properties of Terms: A Study of Albert of Saxony's *Perutilis logica*), Amsterdam: Brill. (A study of the theory of the properties of terms, including the theory of supposition, with an edition of the second treatise of the *Perutilis logica*.)

Muñoz García, A. (1990) 'Albert of Saxony, Bibliographie', *Bulletin de philosophie médiévale* 32: 161–98. (Contains lists of manuscripts and editions, most of them in incunabula, of the texts of Albert of Saxony.)

Sarnowsky, J. (1989) *Die aristotelisch-scholastiche Theorie der Bewegung. Studien zum Kommentar Alberts von Sachsen zur Physik des Aristoteles* (The Aristotelian-Scholastic Theory of Motion: Studies on Albert of Saxony's Commentary on Aristotle's *Physics*), Beiträge zur Geschichte der Philosophie und Theologie des Mittelalters XXXII, Münster: Aschendorff. (A complete and documented study of Albert's physics.)

JOËL BIARD

ALBERT THE GREAT (1200–80)

Albert the Great was the first scholastic interpreter of Aristotle's work in its entirety, as well as being a theologian and preacher. He left an encyclopedic body of work covering all areas of medieval knowledge, both in philosophy (logic, ethics, metaphysics, sciences of nature, meteorology, mineralogy, psychology, anthropology, physiology, biology, natural sciences and zoology) and in theology (biblical commentaries, systematic theology, liturgy and sermons). His philosophical work is based on both Arabic sources (including Alfarabi, Avicenna and Averroes) and Greek and Byzantine sources (such as Eustratius of Nicaea and Michael of Ephesus). Its aim is to insure that the Latin world was properly introduced to philosophy by providing a systematic exposition of Aristotelian positions.

Albert's method of exposition (paraphrase in the style of Avicenna rather than literal commentary in the style of Averroes), the relative heterogeneity of his sources and his own avowed general intention 'to list the opinions of the philosophers without asserting anything about the truth' of the opinions listed, all contribute to making his work seem eclectic or even theoretically inconsistent. This was compounded by the nature and number of spurious writings which, beginning in the fourteenth century, were traditionally attributed to him in the fields of alchemy, obstetrics, magic and necromancy, such as The Great and the Little Albert, The Secrets of Women *and* The Secrets of the Egyptians. *This impression fades, however, when one examines the authentic works in the light of the history of medieval Aristotelianism and of the reception of the philosophical sources of late antiquity in the context of the thirteenth-century university.*

1 **Introduction of philosophy to the Latins**
2 **Logic**
3 **Psychology**
4 **Metaphysics**
5 **Ethics**

1 Introduction of philosophy to the Latins

After studying in Padua and Cologne, Albert entered the Dominican order around 1220. He was the first German to become master of theology at the University of Paris (1245–8). He then taught at the Dominican *studium* at Cologne (where his students included Thomas Aquinas (until 1252) and Ulrich of Strasbourg). Between 1254 and 1257 he was the Dominican Provincial of Teutonia (Germany). As bishop of Ratisbon (Regensburg) in 1260, at the express request of Pope Urban IV, he preached the crusade 'in Germany, Bohemia and other Germanic countries'. After various visits to Würzburg (1264) and Strasbourg (1267), he lived in Cologne until his death in 1280.

Albert's teaching in Paris was dominated by his writing the *Summa de creaturis* (Book of the Creatures) before 1246. Despite the censure imposed on the study of ARISTOTLE during the preceding decade, Albert made extensive use of Greek–Arabic Aristotelianism in his theology (see ARISTOTELIANISM, MEDIEVAL). The same tendency can be seen in his commentary on the Sentences, begun in Paris and finished in Cologne in 1249. It was also in Cologne, while at the *studium generale* of the Dominican Order, that Albert wrote most of his works in natural philosophy, including the *Physics*, the commentary on *On the Heavens*, the *Liber de natura locorum* (The Nature of Places) and the *De causis et proprietatibus elementorum* (The Causes and Properties of the Elements). In 1250–2, he presented in lectures his first commentary on the *Nicomachean Ethics* (the *Super Ethica*, a question-commentary). He returned to the *Nicomachean Ethics* in 1262–3, this time producing a paraphrastic commentary, the *Ethica*.

Albert's large-scale paraphrases on the Organon were written between 1252 and 1256, based on Arabic works by Avicenna (see IBN SINA) and Alfarabi (see AL-FARABI) which are for the most part lost today, and also on Latin works (the *Logica modernorum* and commentaries by Robert KILWARDBY, with which Albert became familiar in Paris). The works on botany (*De vegetabilibus et plantis libri VII*) and on mineralogy (*De mineralibus*) were written in 1256–7; the treatises on biology and zoology (*Quaestiones super De animalibus*) are drawn from disputed questions held in 1258. In 1262–3, Albert wrote his commentary on Euclid (*Super Euclidem*). The last years of his life were devoted to metaphysics and theology; his paraphrase of the *Metaphysics* was written in 1263–7. At the same time he wrote the *De causis et processu universitatis* (*The Causes and Development of the Universe*), a general exposition of an Aristotelian natural theology in which Albert brings together all the intellectual themes of late antiquity that were available in the second half of the thirteenth century.

At this time, the mendicant orders vigorously denounced the intrusion of philosophy into theology. For instance, BONAVENTURE in the *Collationes de Decem praeceptis* (Discourses on the Ten Commandments) in 1267 attacked the 'arrogant presumption of philosophical investigation' that 'corrupts all of Holy Scripture' and denounced not only those who 'create' the philosophical 'fictions' but also those who 'sustain and reproduce them'. In that context, Albert's project to 'bring Aristotle to the Latins' constitutes a genuine defence of philosophical endeavour, not only in the medieval university but also in Christian society in general. In Albert's view, the enemies of philosophy who 'killed Socrates, threw Plato out of Athens... and forced Aristotle into exile' (he openly criticizes them in his paraphrase of the *Politics* VIII, 6) are comparable to the 'brute beasts' of his time who 'blaspheme against what they don't know', university 'preachers' who in their sermons 'attack the use of philosophy with all possible means', 'without anyone's being able to answer them' (commentary on the VIIth Letter of Dionysius).

In opposition to these critics, Albert asserts the need to know and assimilate the philosophy of the ancients. His insistence on the need for philosophy might seem ambiguous in so far as it gives rise to a distinction between two disciplines 'distinct in their principles': theology, which is 'founded on revelation and prophecy', and philosophy, which is 'founded on reason' (*Metaphysica* XI, 3, 7). This distinction, however, corresponds to a deeply rooted tendency in the thirteenth century. The condemnations of 1277 at Paris are evidence of its strength and efficacy. *Nihil ad me de Dei miraculis, cum ego de naturalibus disseram* (God's miracles mean nothing to me, since I am discussing natural things and events), the rallying cry of the 'Latin Averroists' popularized by SIGER OF BRABANT (*De anima intellectiva* (The Intellective Soul) III), was originally Albert's (*De generatione et corruptione* I, 1, 22). He borrowed it consciously and simultaneously from two authorities, one philosophical (Averroes (see IBN RUSHD)) and the other theological (BERNARD OF CLAIRVAUX, reformulating a passage from Augustine). Albert wrote all his philosophical paraphrases in order to develop fully the discipline of philosophical research, a discipline that is autonomous in its own domain, the domain of rational argumentation.

The nature of Albert's commentaries might also seem ambiguous, in so far as his avowed Aristotelianism covers a complex mix of Aristotelian and Neoplatonic theses. This ambiguity, however, cannot be blamed on Albert as it is present in his own Arabic 'Aristotelian' sources, which were for the most part permeated with the syncretic view of Aristotle inherited from the Neoplatonic commentators of the fifth and sixth centuries (see ARISTOTELIANISM IN ISLAMIC PHILOSOPHY; NEOPLATONISM IN ISLAMIC PHILOSOPHY). In asserting that 'philosophical perfection' can only be attained with both Aristotle and Plato as its foundation (*Metaphysica* I, 5, 15), Albert, who knows little of Plato, is really taking up the 'harmonizing' reading of the Neoplatonic philosophers of late antiquity (see NEOPLATONISM), which was adopted by the Arabic Aristotelians. If his vision of Aristotle seems more Neoplatonic than Aristotelian, it is precisely because it is based as much on the philosophies of Arabic commentators on Aristotle (Alfarabi, Avicenna, the *Liber de causis* and Averroes) as it is on the philosophy of Aristotle himself.

As the principal engineer of the introduction of philosophy to the Latins, Albert tried to portray as homogeneous a philosophy that is not and cannot be homogeneous in the eyes of the philologist. It is, however, this Arabic–Latin version of Aristotelianism which was successfully installed in the Schools and was opposed to other versions of Aristotle in the fifteenth century, Thomistic Aristotelianism and the Aristotelianism of the school of John BURIDAN, which present Aristotle in a form more recognizable to us (see ARISTOTELIANISM, MEDIEVAL).

2 Logic

Although he paraphrased all of the Organon, in expositions that were used frequently until the end of the fifteenth century, it is not on account of its contribution to the development of the *logica modernorum* that Albert's logical work is most noteworthy. His principal contribution is in connection with the problem of universals (see UNIVERSALS). PORPHYRY, in the *Isagōgē*, had wanted to keep this problem separate from the thought of the logician, and to make it the domain of metaphysics and theology. It was Albert who first systematically formulated the theory of universals that prevailed in scholastic and neoscholastic thought, the doctrine that there are three types of universals (*ante rem, in re* and *post rem*). This doctrine is characteristic of the harmonizing tendency that dominates all of Albert's thought. It is also evidence of the continuity which, thanks to this doctrine, was established between the philosophy of late antiquity and the philosophy of the late Middle Ages.

In answer to Porphyry's problem (whether genera or species exist in themselves or reside in mere concepts alone; whether, if they exist, they are corporeal or incorporeal; and whether they exist apart from or in and dependent on sense objects), Albert does not repeat the arguments and theses of the realists and nominalists of the twelfth century (though he knows them), and he does not choose between realism, conceptualism and nominalism. Instead, he takes up and develops a distinction between types of universals which allows him to give a three-part answer to the problem posed by Porphyry, an answer that is neither realist nor nominalist in the sense of the twelfth century but is meant to transcend the conflict itself. Universals, then, are neither universal extramental 'things' (as the realists believed), nor simple words or concepts (as the nominalists believed). Rather, a universal is one entity with three different aspects, three *modi essendi* (modes of being), which differ depending on whether the universal is considered in itself (in divine thought or the separated Intellects), in natural things or in human thought. Albert draws this three-part distinction from Avicenna's *Logica*, reinforced by certain remarks from Eustratius of Nicaea's *Commentary on the Nicomachean Ethics*. This view of universals makes the Platonic notion of separated Forms compatible with the Aristotelian notions of immanent forms and abstract concepts, and makes it possible to preserve both notions within the same theory.

In reviving this doctrine, Albert unwittingly takes up the Neoplatonic solution to the problem of universals, the distinction between universals that are before particulars (*pro tōn pollōn*), after particulars (*epi tois pollois*) and in particulars (*en tois pollois*), a distinction that was systematized most notably by AMMONIUS, David and Elias (see NEO-PLATONISM). Albert's extensive use of Arabic and Byzantine sources to illuminate Latin knowledge of the twelfth century had at least two clear consequences: the subordination of logic to metaphysics and, in metaphysics itself, the subordination of Aristotle's 'Aristotelianism' to a Greek–Arabic version of Aristotelianism (which became the foundation of early neoscholasticism). Indeed, it is on this structure that Albert's disciples (the 'neo-Albertians') built their school's most characteristic positions as early as the fifteenth century. Jean de Maisonneuve, Albert's principal disciple in Paris in the early 1400s, criticized the nominalist followers of Buridan (the *epicuri litterales*) for reducing the universal to the simple abstract concept, a criticism which Heimeric of Campo levelled against Thomists as well. On the other hand, Heimeric also criticized the *formalizantes* (such as Jerome of Prague) for believing in the existence of separated universals such as Plato's Ideas. In short, Albert's disciples criticized other views of universals for being unilateral philosophies that consider only one aspect of the being of universals.

3 Psychology

In the field of psychology, Albert worked primarily on the exposition of the fundamental concepts of Aristotle's theory of the soul, especially of the theory of the intellect. Albert tried to correct and contribute to the exposition of Aristotle in two areas. He fought against the doctrine of the unity of the intellect (or 'monopsychism' as Leibniz called it), which tradition attributed to Averroes but which Albert attributed to 'all of the Arabs'; and he followed Averroes in criticizing the materialism of ALEXANDER OF APHRODISIAS. In addition to his critical work, Albert also tried to integrate the essence of the Greek–Arabic theory of the intellect, beginning with Averroes' version, from which he 'dissents little' ('*in paucis dissentimus*', *De anima* III, 3, 11). Indeed, it is clear that the monopsychism Albert criticizes is the same as that which Averroes already criticized in his 'Great' commentary on *On the Soul*: Avempace's thesis that there is only one intellect for all men, which is joined to the human soul 'by means of images' (*phantasmata*) (see IBN BAJJA; IBN RUSHD). This view is unacceptable, says Averroes, because it reduces the material intellect to a simple 'faculty of imagination'.

Albert only occasionally extends his criticism of monopsychism to Averroes. There are two reasons for this reticence: first, Albert is too dependent on Averroes to criticize his theory of intellect without making his own theories incoherent; and second, he does not interpret Averroes in the light of the Averroists' extrapolations, as Aquinas does. Far from seeing Averroes as the 'debaser' and the 'corrupter of Aristotelianism', Albert on the contrary wants to show that Averroes is the only one to have successfully opposed Alexander's materialist theory on the grounds that it is a 'very grave error which entails the denial of all the nobility and even of the immortality of the human soul' (*De anima* III, 2,5). Therefore, Albert holds the view that the possible intellect is external to man, not because he understands it as a monopsychist thesis, as Aquinas does, but because, like Averroes, he understands it in the more precise and limited sense that the possible intellect is not the perishable 'form' of a perishable body, nor a 'corporeal power caused by the elements' that constitute the body.

What Albert judges to be fundamental in Averroes, then, is the criticism of Alexander's theory of the 'eduction' of the intellect, not his thesis of the unity of the possible intellect. That is why Albert often asserts his perfect agreement with Averroes who, better than any other, was able to prove the thesis which 'from antiquity, all Aristotelians have held', excepting Alexander, that 'the intellect enters the soul from the outside, it does not arise from the composite or the mix of the elements, and does not preexist in potentiality in them'. To apply the *eductio formarum* (eduction of forms) to the intellect implies denying its 'divinity' and 'depriving man of his nature', and that poses a greater danger than giving an unsatisfactory explanation of the manner in which the possible intellect is united to human beings.

The essence of Albert's criticism of Averroes thus centres on the difficult notion of the 'acquired intellect' (*intellectus adeptus*). Averroes reduces the acquired intellect to a momentary union of the human soul and the separated intellect (each time there is an act of intellection), when instead one should think of it as a real power and part of the soul, emanated in it, which is developed and strengthened by the acquiring of more intelligibles. In Aristotelian language, one should think of the acquired intellect as a stable disposition (*habitus*) and not as a transitory state (*qualitas passibilis*). Thus, Albert does not reject Averroes' view of the union of the soul with the separated intellect: he adapts and perfects it. It is also on the basis of this view that Albert reorganizes the entirety of the Aristotelian doctrine of the intellect; and that he establishes, as early as the *Summa de creaturis*, a correspondence table for the different classifications found in tradition. In this, Albert and AQUINAS are fundamentally opposed. Albert takes Averroes as his guide to reinterpret Aristotelianism, while Aquinas tries to distinguish Averroes from the Arabic sources (Avicenna and AL-GHAZALI) and the 'Greek' sources (Alexander, THEMISTIUS and THEOPHRASTUS) in order to interpret Aristotle anew against him (see AVERROISM).

4 Metaphysics

In the field of metaphysics, Albert's work takes an original direction, again characterized by a certain syncretism. Drawing from Aristotle, Avicenna (see IBN SINA), the *Liber de causis* (see LIBER DE CAUSIS) and PSEUDO-DIONYSIUS, he formulates a system which again places him very much at odds with AQUINAS. Albert's philosophy is set in the context of Aristotelian cosmology, which he claims is valid from the point of view of natural reason. As a consequence, Albert admits in his philosophy the system of Intelligences, which he carefully distinguishes from angels. (He considers that identifying the two is a theological error, though not a specifically Christian one since he denounces it primarily in two Jewish thinkers, Moses of Egypt, also called MAIMONIDES, and Isaac ISRAELI.) This distinction was taken up and made more rigid by Albert's German Dominican followers, including DIETRICH OF FREIBERG and Berthold of Moosburg, together with the distinction between the order of 'natural providence' (the order to which Aristotle, the Arabic philosophers and PROCLUS refer) and the order of 'voluntary providence' (the order to which the Bible and theologians refer). This is a strictly philosophical way of contrasting the world of nature and that of miracles, the world of the natural and that of the supernatural, a contrast which theologians capture by the strictly theological division between the 'ordered' and the 'absolute' power of God.

However, in his formulation of an Aristotelian metaphysics, Albert adds two important corrections to the elements he adopts from the Arabic sources. First, while adopting Avicenna's metaphysics of emanation, he radically modifies the theory of formal emanation (*fluxus* or *influentia*). The *fluxus formae* from which the intelligible and material universe arises does not consist in an 'overflowing' (*infusio, effusio*) of the forms from an emanating Principle (Avicenna's and al-Ghazali's *dator formarum*). Rather, it consists in an anagogical process, the final causality of the 'appeal of the good' (*advocatio boni*), a view Albert draws from Pseudo-Dionysius, John Scottus ERIUGENA and Maximus the Confessor, all of whom he would have read in the Dionysian corpus of the University of Paris. As a partisan of the unity of substantial form, who holds at the same time that the forms of things are contained in matter in an inchoate state ('the inchoation of forms'), Albert views all form-generating processes as ruled by the celestial spheres and their movers by means of a causality of attraction rather than strict emanation. The first principle or 'first Cause' does not infuse forms into matter: form and matter are con-created. The function of the first principle is to call to itself all forms that are contained in matter, to unify them and to assemble them by means of the 'final attraction' that it exerts on everything that is.

This notion of 'attraction' by the Good presupposes an identification of the first Cause of Arabic Aristotelianism with the Platonic Good. Albert makes this identification consciously by showing that the Latins who reduce emanation to a simple metaphysical mechanism corrupt all of philosophy. The true theory of emanation is the one that makes the Good into a principle that is 'diffusive of itself and of being' (*diffusivum sui et esse*), not by overflowing but by attracting. Albert explains that the supreme Good, the first Cause, 'calls all things to be', that is, to 'resemble' it, because the nature of goodness is to call (*bonum* comes from *boo*, *boas*, that is, *voco*, *vocas*, to call), and its diffusion is nothing other than its calling (*diffusio* and *boatus* are synonyms). He supports this view, not without paradox, by appealing to Paul's letter to the Romans 4: 17: 'God calls those things that are not as well as those that are'.

Second, in order to certify that this assimilation of the first cause with the final cause of being qua being is authentically Aristotelian, Albert claims that Aristotle's metaphysics is not the last word of Aristotelianism. Metaphysics must be completed by theology. Albert claims that he finds this theology in the *Liber de causis*. Far from seeing in the *Liber de causis* an Arabic adaptation of Proclus' *Elements of Theology* (as his student Aquinas did), Albert asserts that it is a work compiled by the mysterious 'David the Jew' (possibly IBN DAUD?) on the basis of one of Aristotle's letters *On the Principle of the Universe* (really a work of Alexander of Aphrodisias, which has survived only in Arabic translation) and other elements borrowed from Aristotelian philosophers. Albert's belief in the Aristotelian authenticity of the *Liber* (widely accepted in Paris in the 1250s), allows him to spell out a complete Aristotelian system that comprises metaphysics (the theory of being as being) and theology (the theory of the cause of being) and goes further than the rudiments available in Book XII of Aristotle's *Metaphysics*. The supreme principle is not a mere first mover (*primum movens*), it is also a first producer (*primum agens*) that produces (emanates) all things and draws back (attracts) all things into one.

In his *De causis et processu universitatis*, the height of his speculative philosophy, Albert offers us the most important 'reconstruction' of Aristotelian theology we have received from the middle ages. This complete theology is composed of a theory of the first cause which draws from all the Arabic sources, (in particular AL-GHAZALI), and a theory of emanation drawn from the *Liber de causis*. It is thus clear that, unlike his contemporaries, Albert does not merely contrast revealed theology and rational philosophy, but within philosophy itself he contrasts natural theology and simple metaphysics. Aristotle's metaphysics is therefore completed twice.

Book I of *De causis et processu universitatis*, titled *De proprietatibus primae causae et eorum quae a prima causa procedunt* (On the Properties of the First Cause and of the Beings That Emanate From It), reveals the character of Albert's general inquiry by characterizing the three philosophical positions of antiquity (Epicurean, Stoic and Aristotelian) on the basis of their relation to the fundamental problem of theology: *de primo omnium principio* (the first principle of all things) or *de universi esse principio* (the universal principle of all things). Then comes the analysis of the fundamental themes of Aristotelian theology: *De scientia primi* (the knowledge of the first principle), *De libertate, voluntate et omnipotentia primi* (the freedom, will and omnipotence of the first principle) and *De fluxu causatorum a causa prima et causatorum ordine* (the outpouring of causal things from the first cause and their ordered relationship), all of which are profoundly influenced by al-Ghazali's views. In fact, Treatise IV, which constitutes the transition between Books I and II, corresponds exactly to the programme of metaphysics that al-Ghazali formulates at the beginning of Book I, V, of his own *Metaphysica*: *Quomodo omnia habent esse a primo principio et quomodo omnia perveniunt ad unum qui est causa causarum* (How all things have their being from the first principle, and how all things return to the One that is the cause of causes).

Albert gives his paraphrase of the *Liber de Causis* in Book II, which he devotes to the analysis of the elements of the noetic cosmos (Intelligences and 'noble souls', movers of the heavens), the description of the outpouring of beings (*de fluxu entis*) and the theory of the government of the universe by the First Cause. On almost every point, he holds views opposed to those of Aquinas in the latter's commentary. The strength and appeal of Albert's reading of the completed 'Aristotelian' system is such that it resists Aquinas' philological discovery. Until his death, Albert continued to assert the Aristotelian authenticity of the *Liber de causis*, and the necessity of it for completing the *Metaphysics* with a theology.

The distance between the philosophical positions of Albert and Aquinas can be seen even more clearly in their more specific and detailed theories. In the field of ontology, for example, Albert holds Avicenna's theory of the 'indifference of the essence' (the essence itself is neither universal, in the way empirical abstract concepts are, nor particular, in the way particular beings existing outside the soul are), and he draws a connection between this theory and the theory of the three states of a universal. Thus he provides a picture of the process of abstraction that is entirely different from Aquinas' Aristotelian view. This distance between the two was later reinforced by the neo-Albertians: neither Jean de Maisonneuve nor Heimeric of Campo, for whom 'in its essence, the universal is one, though it can occur in the soul, in the thing and in itself' according to three modes of being, viewed the universal as it is in the soul using nominalist and/or Thomistic models of abstraction. The formation of the universal *in anima* is not the result of abstractive induction on the basis of particulars, but rather the result of a complex illumination of the human soul by the Intelligences, according to the process of mental unification and simplification described in the theory of attractive causality. The formation of the concept called abstract is the result of the fact that the 'human soul is the instrument of the light of the First Intelligence' and that the First Intelligence uses it in order to draw back everything into one.

Similarly, while Albert, like AQUINAS, is a resolute supporter of the analogy of being, his view, described long before that of Aquinas, combines in an original way the 'focal' analogy of Averroes (*analogia attributionis or analogia accidentis*, the coordination of the different ways in which being is accepted by the category of substance), and Pseudo-Dionysius' analogy 'of reception' (*analogia recipientium*, the defining of each being by its 'measure' or 'receptive capacity' which places it in a hierarchy). The problems which Albert's and Aquinas's theories of analogy set out to solve are entirely different. Albert's understanding of analogy is primarily meant to correct the static version of emanationism that dominates the Latin interpretation of the 'Aristotelian' cosmology and noetic. He rejects the Latin analogy between the overflowing of the first cause and the way in which the light of the sun is incorporated into different bodies: God's communication with beings, according to the *analogia recipientium*, is not the simple overflowing of the 'giver of forms' into the universe of beings subordinated to him. For the Latin disciples of Avicenna, the light (*lux*) of the first cause, unique and identical in itself, applies indifferently and uniformly to all beings, shining (*superlucens*) the same light (*lumen*) on all. It gets differentiated within them, according to their receptive capacity, which is determined by their nature or essence. For Albert, the axiom according to which the 'received' (*receptum*) is found in the 'receiver' (*recipiens*) according to its analogy or receptive capacity, is not sufficient to characterize the analogical communication of the Principle (as long as this capacity is conceived as a mere passive reception, and not rather as an active assimilation performed for all beings by the intellectual beings only). The communication of the Principle is fully realized only in the intellectual conversion of the entirety of being. In turn, this conversion occurs through the mediation of those beings that are capable of intellective activity and who insure the anagogical assimilation of the universe to the principle from which it emanates. The diffusion of the Good or the First principle is not a simple 'exit', it is a double movement of exit (*exitus*) and return (*reditus*), of descending and rising, to which all thinking beings contribute.

For Albert, the theory of analogy is thus not primarily meant to answer the problem of the 'multiple meanings of being'. It is not an ontological or semantic theory meant to solve the aporias of the 'problem of being' formulated by Aristotle in Book IV of the *Metaphysics*. Rather, it is a theological doctrine which, under the name of 'Aristotelianism', sets out a peculiar version of the Neoplatonic theory of the intellectual procession of the universe. Despite the fact that Albert and Aquinas share a certain language (indifference of essences, the analogy of being, the analogy of reception), they are answering different problems and their philosophical intentions are not congruent. On all important points of metaphysics, therefore, the historiographical notion of an 'Alberto–Thomist Aristotelianism' seems quite fragile, if not unfounded.

5 Ethics

In moral philosophy, Albert is a resolute supporter of Aristotle's view that the 'contemplative' or 'speculative life' surpasses all other forms of life. Albert describes philosophical contemplation as the height and end of human life. These ideas on 'intellectual happiness' were later taken up both by the Latin Averroists (from JOHN OF JANDUN to Nicoletto VERNIA) and by DANTE in his *Convivio*. Here again, Albert is close to Averroes and far from AQUINAS. Paradoxically, Averroes' claim that the philosophical life is necessary and pre-eminent (see IBN RUSHD §4) finds its clearest exposition in Albert's Aristotelianism. It is in Albert's work that psychology, the science of animate life, manages to grow naturally into a theology, insofar as psychology is in its highest branch a science of human beings, or more precisely in Aristotle's terms, 'a science of the most fundamental and best part of the being of men'.

The achievement of Albert's Aristotelianism, then, is that it naturally links psychology, ethics and philosophical theology. Aristotle's definition of the humanity of man receives an essentially practical interpretation: what defines man is his aspiration to 'live according to the noblest part of himself' (*secundum optimum eorum quae in ipso*). Since this 'noblest' (*principale et melius*) part is the intellect (considered both as a 'divine element present in human beings' and as 'what is in the highest degree man himself') it is by giving a new interpretation of the doctrine of the acquired intellect (*intellectus adeptus*) that Albert builds an ethical system. This ethical system, though it is set 'against the contemplation of love' described by Aquinas and theologians, and despite the condemnations of 1277, imposed itself as a kind of corporate ideal to the masters of arts, both Averroists and others.

The new doctrine of the acquired intellect can be easily summarized. The acquired intellect designates the state of the human soul when it is joined (*conjunctio, connexio*) to the separated agent intellect. This union can be in potentiality – since the agent intellect is naturally joined to us as a power and faculty of the soul – or it can be causal – since the agent intellect is the efficient cause of the actualizing of intelligibles in the soul and since, in the acquired intellect, the agent intellect becomes the form of the soul. Their union produces in the soul the state of contemplative wisdom described by Aristotle as 'the speculative life'. The state of union or speculative life is the state which philosophers define as the 'supreme end' of human life, the object of a specific longing (*fiducia philosophantium*). Thus, there is here on earth a form of life which, while it anticipates the happiness promised to the elect in the next world, is nonetheless self-sufficient (it is in this sense that Alfarabi defines the 'other life' as the union of the philosopher with the separated Intellect, in *De intellectu et intellecto* (see AL-FARABI)). In the most literal sense of the term, this form of life is 'acquired': it is the result of work and implies a progression (*moveri ad continuationem*). The content of this form of life is precisely what Aristotle defined as the object of philosophical theology, the contemplation of the separated beings. The kind of life that is characterized by philosophical contemplation can be called 'intellectual happiness'.

This conception of philosophy as a contemplative form of life is indissolubly speculative and ethical. Albert arrives at it by drawing from diverse sources, not only the Islamic Aristotelians (Alfarabi, Avicenna and Averroes), but also the Byzantine commentators on the *Nicomachean Ethics*, Eustratius of Nicaea and Michael of Ephesus, whom he was one of the first to read (see BYZANTINE PHILOSOPHY). Albert's often repeated identification of the Arabic doctrine of the acquired intellect (*intellectus adeptus*) and the 'Greek' doctrine of the 'possessed intellect' (*intellectus possessus*) is meant to establish the authentically Aristotelian character of Albert's reformulation of the goal of philosophical endeavour. Albert makes his view of this goal an ethical view, by describing philosophy's culmination as a state which he is not afraid to characterize, with Aristotle, as 'divine' (*intellectus divinus*). In comparison with authentic Aristotelianism, however, Albert's position is marked by something remarkably novel: the idea of an ascetic progression of the human soul, rising progressively from the knowledge of the sublunar world to the intellectual intuition of the separated realities.

The central idea in Albert's thought is that here on earth, there is a happiness that rewards a philosophical effort understood as a progressive detachment of the human soul from sensible things and the 'acquisition of the intellect'. Albert's metaphysics, his psychology, his ethics and his natural theology all converge in this central thought. It is this idea that the so-called 'Latin Averroists' in Paris inherited from Albert. It is also, probably, by this aspect of his work that the master of Cologne exerted his most long-lived and varied influence.

See also: ARISTOTLE; ARISTOTELIANISM, MEDIEVAL; AQUINAS, T.; AVERROISM; IBN RUSHD; IBN SINA; ISLAMIC PHILOSOPHY: TRANSMISSION INTO WESTERN EUROPE; LANGUAGE, MEDIEVAL THEORIES OF; LIBER DE CAUSIS; LOGIC, MEDIEVAL; NEOPLATONISM; PLATONISM, MEDIEVAL

List of works

Albert the Great (1200–80) Works, ed. P. Jammy, *Alberti Magni Opera omnia*, Lyon, 1651, 21 vols; ed. A. Borgnet and E. Borgnet, *Alberti Magni Opera omnia*, Paris, 1890–9, 38 vols; *Alberti Magni Opera omnia edenda curavit Institutum Alberti Magni Coloniense Bernhardo Geyer praeside*, Münster: Aschendorff, 1951–. (The latter is a critical edition, publication of which is still underway.)

—— (1200–80) *De anima* (On the Soul), ed. C. Stroik, Opera omnia VII, 1, Münster: Aschendorff, 1968. (Albert's Aristotelian writing on the soul.)

—— (1200–80) *Metaphysica*, ed. B. Geyer, Opera omnia XVI, 1–2, Münster: Aschendorff, 1960–4. (Albert's paraphrase of Aristotle's *Metaphysics*.)

—— (1200–80) *De causis et processu universitatis prima causa* (The Causes and Development of the Universe), ed. W. Fauser, Opera omnia XVII, 2, Münster: Aschendorff, 1993. (Exposition of Aristotelian natural theology.)

References and further reading

Bianchi, L. (1990) *Il Vescovo e i Filosofi. La condanna pariginia del 1277 e l'evoluzione dell'aristotelismo scolastico* (The Bishop and the Philosophers: The Parisian Condemnation of 1277 and the Evolution of Scholastic Aristotelianism), Bergamo: Lubrina. (On the influence of the theory of 'intellectual happiness' on the ethics of the masters of arts.)

D'Ancona Costa, C. (1995) *Recherches sur le Liber de causis* (Research on the *Liber de causis*), Études de philosophie médiévale LXXII, Paris: Vrin. (A precise analysis of the theoretical universe of the *Liber de causis* and of its scholastic reception, with bibliography.)

Hoenen M.J.F.M. and Libera, A. de (1995) *Albertus Magnus und der Albertismus. Deutsche philosophische Kultur des Mittelalters* (Albert the Great and Albertism: German Philosophical Culture of the Middle Ages), Studien und Texte zur Geistesgeschichte des Mittelalters XLVIII, Leiden: Brill. (On the influence of Albert in Germany, and the neo-Albertism of the fifteenth century, particularly Jean de Maisonneuve and Heimeric of Campo.)

Kaluza, Z. (1986) 'Le *De universali reali* de Jean de Maisonneuve et les epicuri litterales' (Jean de Maisonneuve's *De universali reali* and the Followers of Buridan), *Freiburger Zeitschrift für Philosophie und Theologie* 33: 469–516. (Standard exposition of the neo-Albertian doctrine of universals and its criticism of Buridanism.)

Libera, A. de (1990) *Albert le Grand et la Philosophie* (Albert the Great and Philosophy), Paris: Vrin. (A general exposition of the broad themes in Albert's philosophy.)

—— (1994) *La Mystique Rhenane. D'Albert le Grand à Maître Eckhart* (Rhineland Mysticism from Albert the Great to Meister Eckhart), Paris: Éditions du Seuil. (An overview of the German Dominican school beginning with Albert the Great's metaphysics and psychology.)

Weisheipl, J.A. (1980) *Albertus Magnus and the Sciences: Commemorative Essays 1980*, Toronto, Ont.: Pontifical Institute of Mediaeval Studies. (Excellent collective synthesis of Albert's contribution to medieval science.)

Zimmermann, A. (1981) *Albert der Große. Seine Zeit, Sein Werk, Seine Wirkung* (Albert the Great: His Times, His Work and His Influence), Miscellanea Mediaevalia 14, Berlin: de Gruyter. (Collective work covering most of the areas of philosophy to which Albert contributed.)

Translated from the French by
Claudia Eisen Murphy
ALAIN DE LIBERA

ALBERTUS MAGNUS
see ALBERT THE GREAT

ALBO, JOSEPH (*c*.1380–*c*.1444)

Writing in the early fifteenth century, in times of extreme urgency for Spanish Jewry, Joseph Albo presented Judaism as an axiomatic system founded on three primary principles and eight secondary ones. His Sefer ha-'Iqqarim *(Book of Principles), sought to defend Judaism against Christian attacks by laying out the basic presuppositions of the Mosaic law.*

Albo's theology belongs to a tradition of theorizing going back to Maimonides in the twelfth century. But his approach was grounded in a non-Maimonidean moral psychology. Responding to the Aristotelian intellectualism of the Maimonidean philosophy, which held true belief to be essential to human virtue and salvation, Albo focused on practice, fulfilment of the commandments. His act-centred view, grounded in the premise that beliefs cannot be commanded, allowed for a certain latitude in faith, which had both intra-communal and inter-communal advantages. If controversial doctrines such as ex nihilo *creation could be made less prominent, acrimonious internal debates could be avoided, and the community could be somewhat less exposed to external attack.*

1 Life
2 **Thought and action**
3 **Contribution to Jewish philosophy**

1 Life

We know little about Joseph Albo's life. He lived in Christian Spain, in Castile and Aragon, at a particularly troubled time for Spanish Jewry, a time of religious persecution and forced conversion. There were terrible anti-Jewish massacres in 1391 at Barcelona and elsewhere. Albo represented the Jewish community of Daroca (near Saragossa) at the last of the great public disputations, held in 1413–14, in Tortosa. His Christian adversary, Geronimo de Santa Fé, was born a Jew, Joshua Lorki. This *disputatio*, like others held since the mid-thirteenth century, was not a free-ranging debate between disinterested parties, but an occasion staged by the Church for the public humiliation of Jews. In representing the Jewish side, Albo was defending both Judaism and the Jewish people against a prejudiced, or even predetermined, response. Arraying his arguments in what seemed a hopeless cause, he wrote the *Sefer ha-'Iqqarim* (Book of Principles) in four parts, discussing divine law in general and the Mosaic law in particular. The book was hugely popular in Jewish circles and has never been out of print. Translated into Latin, it was highly esteemed by such Christian thinkers as Grotius for its clear differentiation of natural, conventional, and divine law, a distinction Albo probably learned from his study of Aquinas.

2 Thought and action

Albo's contribution to legal theory finds its context in his engagement with the problems of Jewish dogmatics, the quest to define the fundamental principles of Judaism and to lay out the further principles that derive from them. MAIMONIDES was the first thinker in the rabbinic tradition to posit a set of fundamental doctrines or beliefs incumbent upon every Jew. For Maimonides, these beliefs, thirteen in number, included God's existence, unity, incorporeality and ontic primacy, the uniqueness and irreplaceability of the Mosaic revelation, the coming of a messianic redemption, and bodily resurrection. Belief in these ideas defined the Jew and were necessary conditions for the salvation promised to Israel in the world to come. Disbelief in these principles amounted to heresy.

Superficially, Albo may seem to follow Maimonides in outlining a set of necessary beliefs, differing only in that he distinguishes fundamental from derivative principles. But appearances here are deceptive, for Albo does not adopt Maimonides' premise that beliefs are criteria for identifying a Jew or that nonbelief amounts to heresy. This is not to say that Albo thinks an atheist has a place in the community, but for him, like his immediate predecessors Simeon ben Tzemach DURAN and Hasdai CRESCAS, Albo's teacher, the focus is on acts. Acts make us what we are, and acts, unlike beliefs, can be commanded. The point is not that one can believe just anything and still be a member of the community, but that membership is consequent on acts, fulfilment of the commandments. Albo's account of belief is shorn of the normative weighting of Maimonides' account. He does not lay out what must be believed but treats the articles of faith as the presuppositions underpinning the practical life of a professing Jew.

Albo's act-centred theology rests on an original approach to moral psychology. Maimonides, like Aristotle, thought of human virtue as an expression of reason. It requires a rationally attuned disposition and knowledge suitable to one's endeavour. But this account came under fire in the centuries between Maimonides and Albo. Forced to defend themselves in disputations in terms that would have weight with their opponents, Jews in the fourteenth century came under the influence of Christian scholasticism, which was moving increasingly away from its Aristotelian and Averroist moorings. With the condemnation of Averroism in 1277, Aristotelian moral psychology gave way to a greater voluntarism like that found in DUNS SCOTUS and WILLIAM OF OCKHAM. Jewish philosophy mirrored the Christian trend, notably in the case of Crescas. The rejection of intellectualism meant that human felicity was no longer seen as the fruit of intellectual perfection or true belief. As a result, for Albo, as for Crescas, access to salvation takes on a less intellectually elitist cast. A further result of Albo's approach to understanding the principles of Judaism – and indeed of any revealed religion, once these principles are no longer conceived as mandatory dogmas but as necessary presuppositions – is the opening of the way for objective inquiry into revealed religion generally and Judaism in particular.

The *Sefer ha-'Iqqarim* has four parts, an introduction and three books. Its stated purpose is 'to explain those principles which pertain to a divine law in general, the principles without which a divine law cannot be conceived'. Before outlining these principles, Albo explains the need for such a law, relying on arguments as old as Jewish (and Islamic) philosophy itself: 'it is not possible for the human intellect alone to attain a proper knowledge of the true and the good. For human reason is not capable of comprehending things as they are in reality.... There must therefore be something higher than the human intellect by means of which the good can be defined and the truth comprehended so as to leave no doubt. This can be done only through divine guidance. It is incumbent, then, on every person to know that among all laws there is one divine law which gives this guidance' (I.1–2). Only a divine law can take us beyond the objectives of merely utilitarian legislation, which seeks no more than social order and stability, and can open up to us the possibility of our genuine felicity.

All divine law, Albo argues, presupposes three principles: (1) that God exists, (2) that the Torah is divine, and (3) that reward and punishment, both now and in the hereafter, attend our actions. Why does Albo urge that *all* divine legislation presupposes belief in the Torah? Albo's response would be that in fact all monotheistic faiths agree on the divine origin of the Mosaic law, although Christianity and Islam hold that the Mosaic legislation has been superseded. The polemical context that provides the background of Albo's writing is strikingly clear here. But it is important to Albo (partly because of his defensive posture) not to confine his argument suppositiously to parochial assumptions. His intention is to move from the more general to the more particular by specifying the implications of the basic principles. Thus, from his three general or 'root' principles (*'iqqarim*), he derives eight derivative principles, also called roots (*shorashim*). The denial of any one of these latter principles 'is tantamount to a denial of the fundamental principle from which it is derived'. From God's existence, he derives God's (1) unity, (2) incorporeality, (3) atemporality, and (4) perfection. From the divine origins of the Torah, he derives (5) God's wisdom, (6) the possibility of prophecy, and (7) the authenticity of the mission of the historic prophets. From the reality of reward and punishment, he derives (8) divine providence and knowledge of human actions and events.

Even these derivative principles are quite generic. None is distinctive to Judaism. But their derivation from the first tier allows Albo to deny the consistency of Christianity: if God's unity follows from his existence, Catholics should deny the Trinity, lest their view call into question the very existence of God.

A third set of beliefs are called branches (*'anafim*). They are (1) *creatio ex nihilo*, (2) the superiority of the Mosaic prophecy, (3) the irreplaceability of the Torah, (4) the possibility for a human being to attain perfection by fulfilling even a single commandment, (5) resurrection of the body, and (6) messianic redemption. For Albo these six doctrines are not derived from the others but are peculiar to Judaism, traditionally taught and accepted. A divine law can exist without these six 'branches'.

The secondary status of these beliefs seems to allow Albo to defuse the traditionally acrimonious intra-communal debates over such issues as *creatio ex nihilo*. This is not to say that Albo supposes that the tradition does not teach *creatio ex nihilo*, but it does mean that he does not take God's perfection to be inconsistent with the creation of the world from pre-existent matter, as Plato was held to have taught. Those who held to the Platonic doctrine of *formatio mundi* would not, as a result, have to be construed as implying the denial of a fundamental principle – as Trinitarians were. Again, the downplaying of messianism may reflect a reaction against the centrality of that theme in Christianity. Albo's special principles, then, both ground the particularity of Judaism and mitigate the intensity of intra-confessional theological debates.

3 Contribution to Jewish philosophy

Albo comes late in the history of Jewish dogmatics. His contribution lies in the architectonic he constructs for Jewish faith and practice. Maimonides and others present the principles of Judaism on an equal footing. Albo offers a hierarchically graded, logically structured schematization. The structure is designed both for internal strength and for defence against external attack. The scheme allows Albo to contextualize Judaism generically as a divine law but also to render less vexed the internal debates over the niceties of those beliefs that are distinctive to Judaism. Albo's treatment of core beliefs not as axioms but more as themes whose appeal is traditional, but whose nexus to the canonical axioms is not one of entailment, is appreciated by contemporary students of Judaism for fostering a certain openness with respect to belief without departing from the larger axiomatic structure that Albo used in helping to define his faith and to defend it.

See also: ARISTOTELIANISM, MEDIEVAL; AVERROISM, JEWISH; CRESCAS, H.; MAIMONIDES, M.

List of works

Albo, Joseph (*c*.1425) *Sefer ha-'Iqqarim* (Book of Principles), ed. and trans. I. Husik, *Sefer ha-'Iqqarim: Book of Roots*, Philadelphia, PA: Jewish Publications Society, 1946, 5 vols. (The standard critical edition, with an English translation and notes.)

References and further reading

Guttmann, J. (1933) *Die Philosophie des Judentums*, trans. D. Silverman, *Philosophies of Judaism*, New York: Schocken Books, 1973, esp. 275–86. (An account of Albo and his relation to his immediate predecessors, Hasdai Crescas and Simeon ben Tzemach Duran.)

Husik, I. (1916) *A History of Medieval Jewish Philosophy*, New York: Macmillan; repr. New York: Atheneum, 1976, esp. 406–27. (A brief account in a standard history, treating Albo as the last Jewish philosopher, not merely the last medieval Jewish philosopher.)

Hyman, A. (1967) 'Maimonides' "Thirteen Principles"', in A. Altmann (ed.) *Jewish Medieval and Renaissance Studies*, Cambridge, MA: Harvard University Press, 119–44. (A presentation of Maimonides' dogmatics with discussion of various modern accounts of how best to interpret it.)

Kellner, M. (1986) *Dogma in Medieval Jewish Thought: From Maimonides to Abravanel*, Oxford: Oxford University Press, esp. 140–56. (The most recent full-length study of medieval Jewish dogmatics. Philosophically acute.)

Manekin, C. (1997) 'Hebrew Philosophy in the Fourteenth and Fifteenth Centuries: An Overview', in D.H. Frank and O. Leaman (eds) *History of Jewish Philosophy*, London and New York: Routledge, 350–78. (A fairly detailed discussion of major philosophical topics in the post-Maimonidean period.)

Sirat, C. (1985) *A History of Jewish Philosophy in the*

Middle Ages, Cambridge: Cambridge University Press, esp. 374–81. (A brief account of Albo and his work in the context of Jewish–Christian polemics in late fourteenth- and early fifteenth-century Spain.)

DANIEL H. FRANK

ALCHEMY

Alchemy is the quest for an agent of material perfection, produced through a creative activity (opus), in which humans and nature collaborate. It exists in many cultures (China, India, Islam; in the Western world since Hellenistic times) under different specifications: aiming at the production of gold and/or other perfect substances from baser ones, or of the elixir that prolongs life, or even of life itself. Because of its purpose, the alchemists' quest is always strictly linked to the religious doctrine of redemption current in each civilization where alchemy is practised.

In the Western world alchemy presented itself at its advent as a sacred art. But when, after a long detour via Byzantium and Islamic culture, it came back again to Europe in the twelfth century, adepts designated themselves philosophers. Since then alchemy has confronted natural philosophy for several centuries.

In contemporary thought the memory of alchemy was scarcely regarded, save as protochemistry or as a branch of esotericism, until interest in it was revived by C.G. Jung. Recent research is increasingly showing the complexity of alchemy and its multiple relation to Western thought.

1 Name and definition
2 Epistemological structure
3 Features of the alchemical literature
4 Alchemical doctrines
5 Alchemy and Western philosophy
6 Alchemy and the present

1 Name and definition

The name 'alchemy' appeared in Islamic culture, whence it passed to Latin. It evolved (apparently) from the Greek 'chemèia' (art of melting metals) or 'chymos' (juice). An alternative etymology, supported by the Hermetic tradition, indicates 'kemi' (black clay), the ancient name of Egypt, pointing to the mythological link with the god Hermes-Thoth.

Initially alchemy denoted both the art and its product; this latter use, however, is rare in the Western tradition. As a name indicating the art or *opus*, its meaning varies depending on the period referred to: originally it designated the practical and theoretical search for transmutation, whereas in contemporary esotericism it indicates the concrete achievement(s) associated with a pre-eminently spiritual quest.

Accordingly, the decision about what is an alchemical text or an alchemical image may differ: we distinguish a historical, an esoteric and a psychological approach. Historians consider written tradition (manuscript and printed texts and images) the one and only testimony of a doctrine evolving in time. For esotericists, this same tradition is nothing but the surface of a secret, immutable knowledge, often deliberately disguising its truth. For depth psychology alchemy encompasses virtually every kind of symbolic production.

The definition given by H.J. Sheppard (1986), currently the most widely accepted, takes into account all approaches: 'Alchemy is the art of liberating parts of the Cosmos from temporal existence and achieving perfection which, for metals, is gold, and for man, longevity, then immortality and, finally, redemption'.

2 Epistemological structure

The association of practice and theory characterizes alchemy from its very beginning and distinguishes it from other symbolic lore. Archaic metallurgy, in its connection with religious rites, is generally considered the cradle of alchemy: this opinion has accounted for the religious and even mystical elements in alchemy since the work of Zosimus of Panopolis ($c.3$–4 AD). Yet the earliest acknowledged alchemical text (Bolus of Mende, pseud. Democritus, *Physikà kai mystikà* $c.1$ AD) shows that just those metallurgical practices imbued with religious significance were the basis on which a theory of matter was beginning to be built: a theory derived from practice, not the contrary.

Indeed, the dependence of theory on practice marks the whole history of alchemy. For its theoretical content, Western alchemy was called 'the child of Greek philosophy', but we cannot accept such a genealogy without remembering that there was also another 'parent', namely, concrete work on matter. In the Middle Ages, as practical alchemy interacted with the development of techniques and craftmanships (metallurgy, goldsmith, dyeing, pharmacology), it was first considered an 'ars mechanica', but soon its theoretical meaning became clear to philosophers like Albert the Great and Roger Bacon, and the close connection between alchemical practice and religious-philosophical speculation continued with Paracelsus and the Rosicrucians, with Newton and Goethe (see PARACELSUS §3).

Therefore we cannot speak of alchemy proper where we find only a practice, be it metallurgy, distillation or whatever else: the dyeing recipes of medieval painters, or distillation among Renaissance physicians. However, we must be equally careful not to speak of alchemy too readily whenever alchemical symbolism is used for other purposes: for example, by mystics.

The connection between practice and theory accounts for, and delimits, the contribution of alchemy to the birth of chemistry (see CHEMISTRY, PHILOSOPHICAL ASPECTS OF §1). Like ancient artisans, who owned secret techniques transmitted through apprenticeship, alchemists were secretely initiated to the *opus*. The secrecy of alchemy is a major point of divergence from chemistry, which, like all modern sciences, is characterized by public discussion and teaching. Moreover, although alchemists for centuries worked with metals and minerals, invented techniques (for example, distillation), designed and used laboratory apparatus that chemists would inherit, they never relinquished their original religious attitude; as a consequence of this, theoretical developments were radically different from those of modern chemistry. Basically, for alchemists, matter was no inert object but the body of their own Mother Nature. So there is no epistemological continuity between alchemy and chemistry; protochemical features may be disentangled only a posteriori from a doctrinal whole owing its orientation to totally different ideas and purposes.

3 Features of the alchemical literature

The initiatory character of alchemical teaching accounts for the most striking feature of the language of alchemists, that is, the use of a rich symbolism. Metaphorical names for substances and processes were used from the beginning, an attitude reinforced by Arab alchemists and complicated by the obvious difficulties of Latin translators. The use of metaphors met the need for secrecy and facilitated the merging of operative and religious meaning; but it also prevented the creation of a technical vocabulary (another major difference from chemistry) and fostered the transformation of alchemy into an occult art.

This retreat into the occult, accompanied by the development of alchemical imagery, began at the end of the Middle Ages, when metallurgical alchemy was defeated by the denunciation of alchemists as forgers and the idea of the medical elixir began to be associated with the prophetic and visionary mood of the Spirituals. So, while many medieval texts were written in a clear language and even, sometimes, in a truly philosophical style, the number of obscure writings playing with symbols and visions increased steadily from the fourteenth century. Later alchemists went further, explicitly linking their art to ancient mythology and eventually wholly replacing words with images.

Thus the main difference inside alchemical literature is between clear and obscure texts. Various genera belong to the first group: recipes, practical treatises, theory and practice texts, commentaries, veritable summae; rarely does their 'clear' character match our modern demands for clarity. Obscure texts comprise mainly visions, riddles, and poems.

A relevant feature of the alchemical literature, since its very origin, is its pseudoepigraphical character, often connected to the creation of legends concerning the supposed authors of alchemical writings. By means of pseudoepigraphy alchemists clearly attempted to enrol themselves in the philosophical tradition, albeit awkwardly. Texts were attributed to pagan gods, mythological and biblical figures, ancient and medieval philosophers. Such attributions assured secrecy, while raising the prestige of writings of obscure authors; they might even be a subtle indication of affiliation.

4 Alchemical doctrines

The basic idea of alchemy is the identity of nature and first matter as a dynamic unity: elements can pass one into another, in a circular movement that alchemists reproduced in their vessels. No theory of natural *loci* (low and high are interchangeable, according to the *Tabula smaragdina* c.9 AD), no dualism of matter and spirit exists, as first matter is the all-embracing source of change. The alchemist, who can obtain first matter by means of the dissolution of natural bodies, is almost a new creator who makes a new reality come out of the artificially produced chaos 'putting nature into nature', that is, cultivating the seeds of perfection existing in nature (perfect metals) according to natural rules, and 'awaiting nature's time of delivery'. (R. Llull, *Testamentum* c.14 AD).

This structure is first seen as continuity inside the inanimate field of metals, and as analogy between metals and planets: all metals are nothing but imperfect gold (like embryos at various stages), and the alchemist accomplishes nature's work outside the womb of earth in a shortened time, possibly within an astrological framework. Some alchemists viewed the process as a victory over nature and time, foreshadowing the Promethean developments of modern science and technology: there are some hints that medieval theologians rebuked alchemy for this claim. Yet the relation between alchemical art and nature's work was generally considered in a more subtle and complex way, especially in the theoretical attempts made by fourteenth-century alchemists who developed the idea of elixir. Continuity from inanimate matter to human beings was explicitly or implicitly affirmed, and the alchemists were conscious of themselves as a part of the matter/nature that they manipulated in order to perfect, not to dominate. This consciousness preserved their attitude of religious reverence for nature, whose abandonment was a major feature of modern science.

5 Alchemy and Western philosophy

Discussing matter and its transformations, alchemists encountered philosophical themes from the beginning. There have even been attempts to trace back alchemy to Aristotle's idea of change in material substances (see MATTER §1), but actually alchemy (practice plus theory) was not yet born. In later Antiquity an especial relationship existed between alchemy and Hermetic thought (see HERMETISM): the unity of first matter, the principle of sympathy, the doctrine of occult virtues, all are behind Bolus' axiom that 'Nature is charmed by nature, nature prevails over nature, nature rules nature'. The Stoic doctrine of *pneuma* lingers on in the search for material essences through distillation, a practice that goes back to Maria the Jewess (*c.*3 AD) (see STOICISM §4).

Medieval developments were considerable, as Scholastic philosophers and alchemists compared alchemy to the Aristotelian philosophical concepts. According to Albert the Great (*De mineralibus c.*13 AD) alchemy helped to complete the Aristotelian science of metals. Roger Bacon showed a broader concern, viewing alchemy as the general theory of generation and corruption of all natural beings. Some alchemists even tried to translate into Aristotelian language their experience, identifying form with the purest and thinnest substance (quintessence) resulting from sublimation or distillation. How much of Stoic natural philosophy intermingled with Aristotelian ideas in this attempt is unclear. Form was also identified with the soul, so that all material bodies, metals included, were considered endowed with a soul; body and soul were kept united by spirit, an idea which the alchemists could also find in medical literature, and developed into that of the universal 'medium' that gives unity and life to the created world.

The Hermetic elements had never disappeared from Western alchemy, as the central role of the *Tabula smaragdina* shows; during the Renaissance, they became prevalent. Alchemical doctrines were known to virtually every Renaissance philosopher, discussed by most of them, accepted by many. The relation between Renaissance Platonism and alchemical thought might be considered afresh, as alchemy is a project to obtain on earth the stability and perfection that characterize the Platonic world of ideas, manipulating the universal spirit that mediates between matter and the divine world. The most significant development, however, can be found in Paracelsus, whose idea of 'making visible the invisible' rests on the alchemical assumption that the quintessence of material bodies can be revealed through the *opus*. So, Paracelsian alchemy aimed at revealing the secret of life and putting it to work for the spiritual and bodily health of humans. More definitely, the idea of an alchemical remedy or elixir crystallized in that of potable gold, which interested Ficino and Francis Bacon among others.

In the seventeenth century, Francis Mercurius van HELMONT turned the idea of the universal spirit into that of alkahest, the basis for subsequent chemical developments which ultimately led to the discovery of oxygen. Newton's alchemical and cosmological speculation about the creative, non-mechanical spirit animating matter is at the core of the debate about the role of Hermetism in the Scientific Revolution. The re-emergence of Stoic ideas concerning first matter and mixed bodies in seventeenth-century alchemy has recently been considered to establish it as part of the normal science of that epoch. Even after the birth of modern chemistry, alchemy maintained its appeal to speculative spirits: Goethe apart, we have the clear instance of the subsequent development of *Naturphilosophie* in nineteenth-century Germany (see NATURPHILOSOPHIE), with alchemical doctrines flowing into the mainstream of vitalism (see VITALISM). More surprising perhaps is to find alchemy defined in the *Encyclopédie* as chemistry brought to the highest degree of perfection and therefore capable of operating marvellous effects, 'la chimie sublime, la chimie par excellence'.

6 Alchemy and the present

Nineteenth-century scholarly research on protochemistry overlapped with the latest development of esoterical alchemy (hyperchemistry). Historians of chemistry judged alchemy a mix of positive empirical data about chemical matter with obscure mystical speculation. An echo of their attitude is still felt in the consideration of alchemy as an error in the history of science, indeed, according to Bachelard, 'the first error' in the scientific approach to the problem of matter.

Alchemy attracted the attention of C.G. JUNG as a historical testimony of the dynamics of the unconscious. Jung's deep study of alchemy led him first to conceive of it as the projection upon matter of the unconscious tendency to individuation; but he also saw in alchemy the expression of a more complex relation between humanity and nature, where matter is recognized as the feminine counterpart of the divine, and human knowledge is fostered by the very light of nature (a Paracelsian idea), comparable to the light of Revelation. Thus Jung gave a positive value to the link between religious attitude and empirical research in alchemy. On the other hand, the idea of the alchemists as forerunners of the modern ideal of the scientist who overcomes nature and time is at the core of M. Eliade's (1956) view of alchemy as an intermediate stage between archaic metallurgy and modern technology.

Recent proposals from within French esotericism bear on epistemology and aesthetics: A. Faivre's (1971a) conception of the non-dualistic logic of alchemy links it to the most advanced results in the epistemology of physics, while F. Bonardel (1993) defines the alchemist's attitude as taking charge of the created world. She opposes the Promethean–Faustian view of alchemy, and deplores its gradual fall from the original position of the art of Hermes, proposing its identification with poetry. Another contemporary way of stressing the Hermetic meaning of alchemy is that of focusing on its figurative symbolism, not only in the images linked to alchemical texts or in the alchemical interpretation of artists of the past, but even in defining the creative process of contemporary art as alchemy.

References and further reading

* Bachelard, G. (1937) *La formation de l' esprit scientifique*, Paris: Vrin. (Discusses alchemy in the context of scientific epistemology; in his further writings, known as 'quadrilogy of the elements', Bachelard approached alchemy psychologically and poetically.)
* Bonardel, F. (1993) *La philosophie de l'alchimie. Grand Oeuvre et Modernité*, Paris: Presses Universitaires de France. (On alchemy, esotericism and contemporary culture.)
Coudert, A. (1980) *The Philosopher's Stone*, Boulder, CO: Shambala Publications. (A historical survey, not strictly limited to the Western world, paying attention to the religious contents of alchemy.)
Crosland, M.P. (1962) *Historical Studies in the Language of Chemistry*, Cambridge, MA: Harvard University Press. (Discusses the problems of the alchemical language and its relation with chemistry.)
Dobbs, B.J. (1975) *The Hunting of the Green Lion. The Foundation of Newton's Alchemy*, Cambridge: Cambridge University Press. (Connecting alchemical mentality and research to scientific creativity.)
* Eliade, M. (1956) *Forgerons et alchimistes*, Paris: Flammarion. (The origin of alchemy and its relation with ancient metallurgy and religion.)
* Faivre, A. (1971a) 'Alchimie occidentale et logique Aristotélicienne', *Revue d'Histoire des Religions*, new series, XX: 105–10. (The triadic structure of alchemy versus the dualism of matter and form.)
—— (1971b) 'Pour un approche figurative de l'alchimie', *Annales ESC* XXVI: 841–53. (The logical structure of the alchemical *opus*.)
Festugière, A.J. (1942) *La révélation d' Hermès Trismegiste. I. L'Astrologie et les sciences occultes*, Paris: Gabalda. (Reprinted by Les Belles Lettres, 1980; chapter VII presents the texts referring to Hermetic alchemy in the Hellenistic age.)
Halleux, R. (1979) *Les textes alchimiques*, Turnhout: Brepols. (A historical survey of the medieval alchemical literature, with bibliography.)
Hopkins, A.J. (1934) *Alchemy the Child of Greek Philosophy*, New York: Columbia University Press. (A study about the relation of alchemy and classical philosophy.)
Joly, B. (1992) *Rationalité de l'alchimie au XVIIe siècle*, Paris: Vrin. (The Stoic doctrine of matter and the rational ground of the alchemical *opus*.)
Jung, C.G. (1944) *Psychologie und Alchemi*, Olten: Walter Verlag; trans. R. Hull, *The Collected Works of C.G. Jung*, vol. XII, Princeton, NJ: Princeton University Press, and London: Routledge, 1953–91. (Alchemy as historical parallel to psychological individuation.)
—— (1954–6) *Mysterium Coniunctionis*, Olten: Walter Verlag; trans. R. Hull, *The Collected Works of C.G. Jung*, vol. XIV, Princeton, NJ: Princeton University Press, and London: Routledge, 1953–91. (Jung's basic studies give a psychological interpretation of alchemy, and present its historical development as providing a link between ancient Gnosticism and the modern psychology of the unconscious.)
Kren, C. (1990) *Alchemy in Europe. A Guide to Research*, New York and London: Garland Publishing Company. (Bibliographical survey.)
Multhauf, R.P. (1966) *The Origins of Chemistry*, London: Oldbourne. (A history of alchemy as science of matter, with bibliography.)
Newman, W.R. (1989) 'Technology and Alchemical Debate in the Late Middle Ages', *Isis* LXXX: 423–45. (Artificial versus natural in the writings of alchemists and theologians.)
Obrist, B. (1982) *Les débuts de l'imagerie alchimique*, Paris: Le Sycomore. (A historical approach to alchemical iconography.)
* Sheppard, H.J. (1986) 'European Alchemy in the Context of a Universal Definition', in Ch. Meinel (ed.) *Die Alchemie in der europäischen Kultur – und Wissenschaftsgeschichte*, Wiesbaden: Harrassowitz.

(A general definition of alchemy based on comparative research.)

MICHELA PEREIRA

ALCIBIADES see PLATO; SOCRATIC DIALOGUES

ALCINOUS (*c.* 2nd century AD)

Long misidentified with the Middle Platonist philosopher Albinus, Alcinous is author of a 'handbook of Platonism', which gives a good survey of Platonist doctrine as it was understood in the second century AD. The work covers logic, physics and ethics, and shows considerable influence from both Stoicism and Aristotelianism, in both terminology and doctrine, while remaining in all essentials Platonic.

A Middle Platonist philosopher, Alcinous was the author of the *Didaskalikos tōn Platōnos dogmatōn* or 'instruction manual of Platonic doctrine'. He was long identified with the second-century Platonist Albinus, author of an extant introduction to Plato's dialogues, but this identification has been recently abandoned. In consequence, we know strictly nothing of the life or times of this author, nor even whether the name may not be pseudonym. None the less, he seems to fit best within the environment of second-century AD Platonism.

The work *Didaskalikos*, purporting to be a summary of Plato's doctrines, possesses its real value as a summation of the doctrines of at least one school of later Platonists. It presents a concise survey of Platonist doctrine, in thirty-six chapters. After three introductory chapters, concerned respectively with the definitions of philosophy, the laying down of requirements for the successful philosopher and an enumeration of the 'parts' of philosophy (logic, physics and ethics), Alcinous proceeds to take these topics in order, beginning with logic in chapters 4 to 6. Chapters 7 to 26 deal with 'physics', and comprise both an account of first principles, 'matter, form and god' (7–11), and one of the physical world; the latter is very closely based on the *Timaeus* (12–26), although Alcinous holds to a non-literal interpretation of the demiurgic creation myth. The final chapters, 27 to 34 are concerned with ethics.

A good deal of both Peripatetic and Stoic doctrine and formulation is incorporated into the exposition, although normally supported by the adducing of Platonic texts. However, all of Peripatetic logic is claimed for Plato, as well as such Aristotelian ethical principles as the mean, and *metriopatheia* (moderation of the passions). On the other hand, such Stoic concepts as the self-sufficiency of virtue and the concepts of *euphyiai*, or 'good natural dispositions', and *prokopē*, or 'moral progress', are also adopted. Alcinous' position on free will and determinism (ch. 26) also owes a good deal to Stoic theorizing, although Stoic determinism is firmly rejected. On the whole, Alcinous inclines to the Peripatetic rather than to the Stoic wing of Middle Platonism.

Distinctive features of his doctrine are his theology (ch. 10) and his views on the reasons for the embodiment of the soul (ch. 25). In Chapter 10 we find a hierarchy of principles set out, consisting of a supreme god, who is a transcendent intellect, an intellect of the world-soul, and the world-soul itself, which seems to be only rational by participation, after being 'roused up' by the supreme god. This is comparable to other Middle Platonic systems observable in Plutarch and Numenius, but the relationship between the principles is distinctive to Alcinous.

In Chapter 25 we find an interesting list of possible reasons for embodiment, giving evidence of considerable debate on this question, and a theory of three faculties of disembodied souls not found elsewhere. In general, a frustrating aspect of the *Didaskalikos* is the evidence it gives of active philosophical debate within Platonism in this period, while not preserving the actual arguments; but that is inherent in the nature of the work.

See also: PLATONISM, EARLY AND MIDDLE

List of works

Alcinous (*c.* 2nd century AD) *Didaskalikos tōn Platōnos dogmatōn*, in J. Whittaker (ed.) *Alcinoos, Enseignement des Doctrines de Platon* (Alcinous, Teachings on Plato's Doctrines), Paris: Les Belles Lettres, 1990; ed. J. Dillon, *Alcinous, The Handbook of Platonism*, Oxford: Clarendon Press, 1993. (The former offers text, French translation and notes, the latter an English translation, with introduction and philosophical commentary.)

References and further reading

Dillon, J. (1977) *The Middle Platonists*, London: Duckworth, 2nd edn 1996, ch. 6. (Here Alcinous is still identified as Albinus; offers a detailed comparison with the handbook of Apuleius.)

Witt, R.E. (1937) *Albinus and the History of Middle Platonism*, Cambridge: Cambridge University

Press. (Still useful, but with reservations, in that it connects 'Albinus' too closely with Antiochus.)

JOHN DILLON

ALCMAEON (*c.* early to mid 5th century BC)

Alcmaeon of Croton was a Greek thinker with philosophical and medical interests. His work focused on the nature of man. Health was the outcome of 'equal rights' between, for example, hot and cold, moist and dry disease that of the 'monarchy' of one of them. 'Passages' linked the sense organs to the brain, which Alcmaeon took to be the seat of sensation and understanding. Plato followed him in this view, as also in his proof of the immortality of the soul from its continual motion.

Was Alcmaeon a philosopher or a doctor? The interests revealed in our information about his views, some controversial evidence that he practised dissection, and the existence in the southern Italian city of Croton of a medical tradition, famous from the sixth century BC, all suggest a doctor. But Croton was also the centre of Pythagoras' activities; and Aristotle and Theophrastus present Alcmaeon as a philosopher. The book Alcmaeon wrote was probably 'on the nature of man' (as later authors might have titled it). Its opening words survive. They include a dedication to three persons believed in later antiquity to be adherents of Pythagoreanism, although Aristotle implies that, despite some similarities, Alcmaeon was not a Pythagorean himself. In sum, Alcmaeon has the look of an independent thinker who responded creatively to a number of the intellectual currents of his time and place.

The doxographer Aëtius gives a striking exposition of Alcmaeon's theory of health and disease:

Alcmaeon maintains that what sustains health is the 'equal rights' of the powers, moist and dry, cold and hot, bitter and sweet and the rest, while 'monarchy' among them is what causes disease; for the monarchy of either one of a pair is destructive.
(fr. 4)

The use of political metaphor was presumably Alcmaeon's own. Explanatory appeal to opposite powers is a pervasive and fundamental feature of Presocratic thought, but it was here that Aristotle perceived a particular similarity – if also a dissimilarity – with the Pythagoreans' systematic listing of key contrarieties (see PYTHAGOREANISM §2). He ascribes to Alcmaeon the generalizing remark that most things to do with human beings come in twos, yet apparently found in him no attempt to construct a single system of opposites (*Metaphysics* I 5).

Alcmaeon is credited with three notable contributions to the psychology and physiology of the senses. First, humans differ from other animals in that they alone have understanding as well as sense perception (A5). Most Presocratic thinkers treat animals, too, as exercising intelligence. Second, the senses, as Alcmaeon argued case by case, are all connected by 'passages' to the brain, which is conceived of as the seat of sensation (A5). Other Presocratics (for example, Empedocles) identify this seat with the heart. Third, he is said to have been the first person to have performed an *exsectio* (A10). Probably this Latin term means not that he initiated a general medical or scientific practice of dissection, but merely that once he cut out the eyeball of a dead animal in an attempt to verify his theory of 'passages', and thereby revealed the existence of what we call the optic nerve. Some scholars reject the authority of the report. If accepted it confirms the importance Alcmaeon says he attaches to using signs to interpret what is unapparent (fr. 1): which is not however the same as subscribing to a methodology of rigorous empiricism.

What sets Alcmaeon apart from the general run of early medical writers is his willingness to theorize about the soul. Aristotle reports his view in these terms:

He says that the soul is immortal owing to its similarity to the immortals, and that this is true of it because it is always in motion – for everything divine is always in continuous motion: moon, sun, the stars and the whole heaven.
(*On the Soul* I 2)

One testimony suggests in addition that Alcmaeon derived the continual motion of the soul from the capacity of living things for *self*-movement (A12). Another assures us that according to Alcmaeon humans die because they cannot join the beginning to the end (fr. 2). This obscure saying perhaps indicates the way the irreversible process of ageing makes human beings – as opposed to their souls – unlike the heavenly bodies, which continue in motion by everlasting repetition of their revolution in the heavens. This group of texts furnishes evidence of the first attempt we know of to *argue* the Pythagorean doctrine of the soul's immortality.

Alcmaeon's argument for the immortality of the soul is clearly what supplied the inspiration for Plato's proof in the *Phaedrus* (245c). His identification of the brain as the seat of sensation was also accepted by

Plato, after previous development by DIOGENES OF APOLLONIA (§3) and in the Hippocratic treatise *On the Sacred Disease*. Aristotle notoriously took a different view, but even he borrowed from Alcmaeon's ideas; for example, on the cause of sleep. As for Alcmaeon's theory of health and disease, there are reflections of it in various early Hippocratic writings such as *On Ancient Medicine*.

References and further reading

* Alcmaeon (*c.* early to mid 5th century BC) Fragments, in H. Diels and W. Kranz (eds) *Die Fragmente der Vorsokratiker* (Fragments of the Presocratics), Berlin: Weidemann, 1952, 6th edn, vol. 1, 210–16. (The standard collection of the ancient sources, both fragments and testimonia, the latter designated by 'A'; includes Greek texts with translations in German.)
* Aristotle (*c.* mid 4th century BC) *On the Soul* (De Anima), ed. R.D. Hicks, Cambridge: Cambridge University Press, 1907. (Source of Aristotle's views on Alcmaeon quoted above.)
  Guthrie, W.K.C. (1962–78) *A History of Greek Philosophy*, Cambridge: Cambridge University Press. (The most detailed and comprehensive English-language history of early Greek thought; the full treatment of Alcmaeon, in volume 1 pages 341–59, is the best available account of his philosophy in English; translates most of the main texts that are relevant.)
  Lloyd, G.E.R. (1975) 'Alcmaeon and the Early History of Dissection', *Sudhoffs Archiv* 59: 113–47, repr. in *Methods and Problems in Greek Science*, Cambridge: Cambridge University Press, 1991, 164–98. (A full and searching analysis of the problem, including a substantial bibliography; the reprint includes a new introduction.)

MALCOLM SCHOFIELD

ALEMANNO, YOHANAN BEN ISAAC (1433/4–AFTER 1503/4)

An outstanding Jewish thinker of the Italian Renaissance, Alemanno combined an eclectic Jewish philosophic rationalism, steeped in the medieval sources – Maimonidean, Averroist and Kabbalistic – with Renaissance humanism and Neoplatonism. He was an Aristotelian and Maimonidean in ethics, a Platonist and Averroist in political philosophy and a Neoplatonist and Kabbalist in metaphysics. His fusing of Aristotelian rationalism with Platonizing mysticism is striking but not atypical for the period. Influenced by Renaissance thought after he settled in Italy, he was active in Christian as well as Jewish circles in Florence, Padua and Mantua. Pico della Mirandola learned Hebrew under his instruction and relied on him for access to medieval Jewish texts in philosophy and Kabbalah. Both Christian Kabbalah and Renaissance Hebraism were products of the interactions in which Alemanno was a chief participant. His ties to the Florentine Academy of the late 1480s are evident in his adaptations to Jewish thinking of the ideas current among its members as to the unity of truth, the immortality of the soul and the dignity of man.

1 Life and background
2 Writings
3 Philosophy

1 Life and background

Like many of his philosophical contemporaries, Alemanno was an immigrant to Italy. His name is an Italianized rendering of the surname Ashkenazi. He was born in Paris and died probably in Mantua. The work of such immigrants had a profound intellectual impact on the Italian Jewish communities of the latter Middle Ages and the Renaissance. Their influence was also felt on Renaissance culture at large. Like most of his scholarly Jewish contemporaries, Alemanno was a wandering scholar who travelled in search of a livelihood as a private teacher, preacher or secretary, always seeking the patronage of influential Jewish financiers. While wandering among such cities as Florence, Mantua, Padua and Bologna, he met many of the leading Jewish scholars of his time, including Judah MESSER LEON, author of the *Nofet Tzufim* (The Book of the Honeycomb's Flow), an important rhetorical treatise that aimed to integrate biblical rhetoric with the revived Ciceronian tradition of the Renaissance. Messer Leon's work profoundly influenced Alemanno, leading to his discovery of the full gamut of Renaissance humanist and Neoplatonic ideas and to his contacts with such leading exponents of Renaissance humanism as Giovanni PICO DELLA MIRANDOLA, his nephew Alberto Pico and Girolamo Benivieni. These scholars, especially Pico della Mirandola, relied on Jewish scholars like Alemanno, Elijah DELMEDIGO and Abraham Farissol, to learn Hebrew and to gain access to the sources of Jewish philosophy, the fascinating materials of Kabbalah, and the works of such Islamic thinkers as Averroes (see IBN RUSHD), which their Jewish guides translated for them into Latin from the medieval Hebrew and Arabic texts. The collaboration of Jewish with Christian scholars led to the creation of a Christian

Kabbalah and was the foundation of Renaissance Hebraism.

Alemanno and other Jewish scholars cultivated their contacts with the humanists not only as an avenue to patronage, but also for the knowledge it gave them of the latest developments in literature, philosophy, medicine, politics and magic (see HUMANISM, RENAISSANCE). Alemanno was particularly interested in such current learning and in transmitting it to his Jewish students and audiences. While Averroists like DELMEDIGO held suspect the mystical tendencies of Christian Neoplatonism, Alemanno eagerly pursued them. Commissioned by Pico in the late 1480s, the heyday of the Platonic Academy which Marsilio FICINO had established at Florence (see PLATONISM, RENAISSANCE), Alemanno wrote his *Heshek Shelomo* (The Passion of Solomon), an allegory on the Song of Songs and one of the first expressions of the Renaissance ideal of Platonic love, enunciated in Ficino's contemporaneous commentary on Plato's *Symposium*. Jewish exegetes had traditionally read the Song of Songs as an allegory of the spiritual love between God and Israel. That reading was now re-visioned through a Neoplatonic prism, in many ways anticipating the approach of Judah ABRAVANEL (Leone Ebreo) in the *Dialoghi d'Amore* (Dialogues of Love). In the foreword to his long introductory essay, *Shir ha-Ma'alot le-Shlomo* (The Song of Solomon's Ascents), Alemanno describes his contacts with Pico at length, and portrayed Lorenzo di Medici, the patron of the Platonic Academy, as the living embodiment of the Platonic–Averroist philosopher king. In the text itself, King Solomon is made the prototype of the ideal philosophical ruler.

2 Writings

Most of Alemanno's writings survive today only in manuscript. *Shir ha-Ma'alot le-Shlomo* has been printed, but the early editions are partial and inaccurate. Of Alemanno's other writings, only a few extracts have appeared in scholarly papers.

His most important work is *Hai ha-Olamim* (Immortal Life), a work influenced in its construction by Ibn Tufayl's *Hayy Ibn Yaqzan* (The Living Son of the Vigilant) (see IBN TUFAYL). Alemanno in fact wrote a supercommentary on Moses of Narbonne's commentary on this work, most probably for a translation of the work from Hebrew to Latin commissioned by Pico. *Hai ha-Olamim* takes the form of a Platonic dialogue between a plain speaker and a philosopher, which unfolds in painstaking detail the development of the perfect individual, from his creation in the womb, through his physical, moral, political and intellectual development, until he reaches mystical union with God. As the title suggests, the soul of this perfect individual will become an immortal, *Hai ha-Olamim*. The description of his physical and moral perfection follows the Aristotelian tradition; that of his political perfection, mainly the Platonic tradition – all, of course, as seen through the eyes of medieval Muslim and Jewish intermediaries. With the approach to spiritual perfection, the Neoplatonic and Kabbalistic elements intensify, and the discussion ends on a powerful mystical chord.

Alemanno's other major work, *'Enei ha-'Edah* (The Eyes of the Community), is a commentary on the Pentateuch through Genesis 5:1 and was probably linked originally to Pico's *Heptaplus de opere sex dierum Geneseos* (On the Sevenfold Narration of the Six Days of Genesis), which deals with the same text and issues and was composed at the same time, in the late 1480s. His *Liqqutim* (Compendia), comprises notebooks containing early drafts of his mature writings and important data on his life and intellectual background.

3 Philosophy

Rejecting what he saw as a medieval dichotomy between faith and reason, revelation and philosophy, and reacting against the widely bruited Christian Averroist notion of a double truth, Alemanno, like Pico, proclaimed the unity of truth and strove to harmonize philosophy, *halakhah*, Kabbalah, alchemy and astrology (see HALAKHAH; KABBALAH; ALCHEMY; AVERROISM, JEWISH). His synthesis depended on ranking the various disciplines, spheres of existence and virtues in a hierarchy that acknowledged a dynamic relationship of emanation and love between the Creator and creation, and on making frequent analogies between matter and spirit, animal and man, microcosm and macrocosm, the Neoplatonic Intelligences and the Kabbalistic Sefirot (mystic Neopythagorean hypostases that mediate between the Infinite and creation). The heavy reliance on hierarchy and analogy generates a thick amalgam of ideas, in which Alemanno tried, often without success, to validate Neoplatonic theses by way of Aristotelian methods and typologies.

In the face of the esotericism fostered by medieval Jewish philosophers and Kabbalists, and insisted upon by many irate contemporaries, Alemanno addressed his writings to the widest possible audience, as is shown not only by his own declarations but also by his typically humanist attention to style and exposition. His model was the prophetic programme of addressing the entire community, each member in accordance with his highest understanding. For thinkers imbued with the values and practices of medieval Jewish philosophy, such exposure of the higher reaches of tradition to anyone who would listen was palpably subversive, but the aura of revealing long hidden secrets may explain the special interest that Pico and other Christian humanists took in Alemanno.

Central among the mysteries to be made known was the Platonic or Neoplatonic theory of the immortality of the soul, a core topic for the Florentine Academy. Following the teachings of medieval Jewish thought, both philosophical and Kabbalistic, Alemanno identified the soul's immortality with its knowledge of the one eternal truth that puts us in contact with the 'active intellect' and allows us to share the eternity of the Platonic Forms. But unlike many medieval thinkers who tended to limit this possibility to a handful of philosophers, Alemanno strove to widen it to the whole community, giving them access not only to physical resurrection, with the coming of the messiah, but also to spiritual immortality. Alemanno's teaching, preaching and lecturing was not only a quest for a livelihood, but also a vocation, a quest to disseminate knowledge, and so immortality, as widely as possible.

Not surprisingly, Alemanno adopted the Florentine theory of the dignity of man. He dovetailed Ficino's assignment of man to the mid-rank of being, between the bestial and the Divine, with Pico's insistence that while each created being has its proper place in the chain of being, only humans hold all the possibilities of existence. They can choose to descend into bestiality or raise themselves towards the Ideas and God. Alemanno, however, found limits to this freedom in the play of astral influences, and he was less sanguine than Pico as to our ability to make sound choices. In addressing this problem of human moral weakness, which a Christian thinker might have interpreted in terms of original sin, Alemanno fell back on Jewish tradition: following Maimonides, he argued that the Commandments can steady our irresolution. But this meant that only Jews can properly use their freedom to attain the moral perfection that human beings need to achieve intellectual perfection and so be linked to the Sefirot and gain immortality.

See also: AVERROISM, JEWISH; FICINO, M.; HUMANISM, RENAISSANCE; KABBALAH; PICO DELLA MIRANDOLA, G.; PLATONISM, RENAISSANCE

List of works

Alemanno, Yohanan ben Isaac (*c*.1488–92) *Shir ha-Ma'alot le-Shlomo* (The Song of Solomon's Ascents), ed. A.M. Lesley, 'The Song of Solomon's Ascents by Yohanan Alemanno: Love and Human Perfection According to a Jewish Colleague of Giovanni Pico della Mirandola', unpublished Ph.D. dissertation, Berkeley, CA: University of California, 1976, 2 vols. (Lesley's dissertation provides the Hebrew text with English summary and detailed introduction. Alemanno's long introduction to *Heshek Shelomo*, describing the various human virtues embodied by King Solomon.)

—— (*c*.1488–92) *Heshek Shelomo* (The Passion of Solomon), MS Oxford-Bodleian 1535/2 (Laud 103), MS London-Mentefiori 227, MS Berlin 143, and MS Moscow-Ginzburg 140. (An allegorical commentary on the Song of Songs.)

—— (*c*.1470–1503) *Hai ha-Olamim* (Immortal Life). (A detailed description of the various stages of human life, culminating with the metaphysical knowledge of God.)

—— (*c*.1478–1504) *Liqqutim* (Compendia). (An eclectic and fragmentary collection of notes and ideas, accumulated over a long period of time.)

—— (before 1504) *'Enei ha-'Edah* (The Eyes of the Community). (A philosophical commentary on the Torah. We have only the commentary on Genesis 1–5: 31. It is not clear whether it is incomplete or the later parts of the manuscript did not survive.)

References and further reading

Cassuto, U. (1918) *Gli Ebrei in Firenze, Nell' Eta del Rinascimento*, Florence: Tipografia Galletti e cocci, part 3, ch. 3. (Contains a description of Alemanno's life and writings.)

Idel, M. (1983) 'The Magical and Neoplatonic Interpretation of the Kabbalah in the Renaissance', in B.D. Cooperman (ed.) *Jewish Thought in the Sixteenth Century*, Cambridge, MA: Harvard University Press, 186–242. (Examines Alemanno's Kabbalistic ideas and Renaissance Kabbalism.)

Melamed, A. (1988) 'The Hebrew Laudatio of Yohanan Alemanno – In Praise of Lorenzo il Magnifico and the Florentine Constitution', in H. Beinart (ed.) *The Jews in Italy, Studies Dedicated to the Memory of U. Cassuto on the 100th Anniversary of His Birth*, Jerusalem: Magnes. (Discusses Alemanno's political philosophy and Renaissance humanism.)

Novak, B.C. (1982) 'Giovanni Pico della Mirandola and Jochanan Alemanno', *Journal of the Warburg and Courtauld Institutes* 45: 125–47. (A detailed account of their relationship.)

ABRAHAM MELAMED

ALEMBERT, JEAN LE ROND D' (1717–83)

Mathematician, scientist and man of letters, Jean D'Alembert is a central figure of the French Enlightenment. As a young man he made significant contributions to the refinement of mathematical techniques, and later was actively engaged in the theoretical controversies which surrounded the gradual assimilation of Newtonian mechanics into the mainstream of European science. For twelve years (1746–58) he was co-editor, with Denis Diderot, of the Encyclopedia, *the serial publication of which was one of the defining events of the Enlightenment period as a whole. D'Alembert frequented the various Paris salons where much of the intellectual fervour and high-spiritedness of the age was cultivated and given shape. As Secretary of the French Academy he worked assiduously to advance the cause of human knowledge.*

D'Alembert's philosophy is characterized by an abiding commitment to the clarity and precision which attends mathematical abstraction. He believed that in its essence the natural order is internally structured by laws whose operation can be articulated under the principles of geometry. All natural phenomena are to be explained under the terms of those basic mathematical principles that govern the scientific domain in which they are located (chemistry or astronomy for example), and all scientific domains could be brought ultimately to perfect consistency and systematic order within a comprehensive theory. The events and processes which constitute the natural order reflect the reality of the mathematical structure which underlies them. As he says in the Preliminary Discourse *(1751) to the* Encyclopedia *(1751–65), 'The universe would only be one fact and one great truth for whoever knew how to embrace it from a single point of view'.*

1 Life and works
2 Philosophical outlook and the *Preliminary Discourse*
3 Reputation and influence

1 Life and works

D'Alembert was the illegitimate son of Mme de Tencin and the chevalier Louis-Camus Destouches. Shortly after his birth he was left by his mother at the steps of the church St Jean Le Rond in Paris, a circumstance which gave the boy his name. While never formally acknowledging paternity, the father took a devoted interest in his son and provided for his education. Jean was enrolled in the Jansenist Collège des Quatre Nations under the name of Dalemberg, which was later altered to the form by which he is known to history. The boy's intellectual gifts were apparent from the start; he was encouraged to pursue a career in theology, though he never expressed any great interest in it, studied law and medicine for three years, but was increasingly drawn to mathematics. Though his formal instruction in mathematics was limited, by 1739 D'Alembert had attained a sufficient mastery of the subject to submit a paper to the Academy of Sciences in which he pointed out some errors in a popular textbook of the time. On the strength of this and several other mathematical papers he was elected to the Academy of Sciences in 1741.

In 1743 D'Alembert published his *Traité de dynamique* (Treatise on Dynamics), a book which attracted the attention of the leading scientific authorities and helped secure his reputation as a most promising young savant. In this, his first major publication, he attempted to reconstruct the science of motion (mechanics) on a purely formal and mathematical basis, proscribing appeals to any such quasi-metaphysical notions as force or gravity and assigning observation and experiment to the subordinate role of confirming the basic principles of the theory. The axioms of geometry, together with the assumption of the impenetrability of the objects constituting a system, were all that was needed to establish the precision and certainty that should attend the study of motion. By this time Newtonian mechanics was well on its way toward gaining the ascendancy over the vestiges of Cartesian physics, and D'Alembert was in compliance with the best scientific opinion of the day in rejecting Descartes' theory of vortices and his conception of nature as a plenum. In certain fundamental respects, however, D'Alembert retained a decided preference for a rigorous, Cartesian rationalism in his approach to scientific theorizing as opposed to the meticulous empirical observation and data-gathering which characterize Newton's own researches (see EMPIRICISM; RATIONALISM). For D'Alembert priority should always be accorded to the strict logical formulation of the basic principles which grounded any scientific inquiry, and he maintained that such principles could be articulated independently of experience. While many of his contemporaries were impressed by the extent to which D'Alembert had apparently succeeded in preserving and carrying through to completion the best features of the Cartesian approach to physical science, others raised the suspicion that his attempts to mathematicize the foundations of mechanics were based on a confusion regarding the ineluctably empirical dimension of basic mechanical principles. In any case, the *Traité de dynamique* is secure in its place in the history of science for having clarified the central theoretical issues which remained to be addressed in working out the details of the Newtonian programme, preparing the way, in particular, for the later researches of Lagrange (see DESCARTES, R.; NEWTON, I.).

Over the next few years D'Alembert produced a series of scientific monographs in which he applied the principles worked out in the *Traité de dynamique* to specific problems including the behaviour of fluids, the cause of the winds, precise calculations for the incidence of the equinoxes and the vibration of strings, all impressive scientific achievements in their own right. Beginning in 1746, however, D'Alembert's intellectual energies began to move away from such narrowly focused scientific investigations towards a more literary engagement with the broader currents of the Enlightenment movement that were gaining momentum across Europe. This year marks D'Alembert's earliest involvement in the tempestuous history of the publication of the *Encyclopedia* which he was to co-edit with Denis DIDEROT for the next twelve years. In 1751 he produced the *Preliminary Discourse* to the *Encyclopedia*, the work for which he is best known; he would ultimately contribute, or make substantial editorial additions to some 1,500 articles on an enormous range of topics from mathematics and physics (which make up the largest part of his contribution) to music, philosophy and religion. In many of these articles D'Alembert is unabashedly partisan in his support of the philosophical campaign to secure the claims of science and enlightenment against the resistance of the political authorities and the chauvinism of the religious establishment. By his polemical zeal, for example, in his contentions against the unflagging hostility of the Jesuits to the whole *Encyclopedia* project, he makes known his willingness to be counted among the ranks of the *philosophes* who, in turn, were more than happy to have his considerable reputation as a scientist joined to their cause. The depth of D'Alembert's commitment to the cause was challenged, however, when his article 'Genève' appeared in 1757 in the seventh volume of the *Encyclopedia*. He had intended to present a flattering view of the atmosphere of religious tolerance in Geneva at the time by imputing to the authorities there an advocacy of various doctrines associated with SOCINIANISM, such as the denial of the divinity of Christ. The Genevans were neither flattered nor amused. In the firestorm of criticism and vituperation that came down on his head in the months after his article appeared, D'Alembert resigned his position as editor and withdrew from the public controversies altogether, much to the disappointment of his more vociferous comrades including, notably, VOLTAIRE. His further contributions to the *Encyclopedia* would be confined to relatively uncontroversial topics dealing with scientific matters with which he was especially conversant.

In 1754 D'Alembert was elected to the French Academy, and if the high profile and protracted controversies of the *Encyclopedia* project were too much for D'Alembert's tastes, his membership in the Academy provided the ideal setting for his continued advocacy of the natural sciences. For some years prior to his election, the reputation of the Academy had been diminished in the public's estimation by the perception that its members were perhaps too much beholden to the interests of the political establishment. With D'Alembert things changed. By virtue of his own reputation for scholarly achievement and personal integrity he was able to improve contacts with scientific establishments across Europe and cultivate friendly relations with foreign heads of state. Internally, he worked assiduously in the cause of progressive ideas by setting agendas and seeking to advance the careers of like-minded colleagues. In his speeches before the assembly and public addresses he championed the cause of the philosophic spirit and argued the material and moral advantages to a society in which it was permitted to flourish. In ways that were unprecedented he brought the affairs and proceedings of the Academy before the public and thereby enhanced the reputation of the Academy itself while raising at the same time the status and the influence of scientific and philosophic research. In 1772 he acceded to the office of permanent secretary of the Academy in which capacity he continued to serve until his death.

Throughout this period D'Alembert continued to write and publish books and essays on scientific and philosophical topics. In 1759 he published the *Essai sur les éléments de philosophie*; in the aftermath of the Jesuit expulsion from France in 1762 he published the highly polemical essay *Sur la destruction des Jésuites en France* (1765), in which he argued, in effect, that it was the rising tide of enlightenment which precipitated the downfall of this remaining bastion of religious obscurantism. His technical works in mathematics and physics were published in eight volumes as *Opuscules mathématiques* between 1761 and 1780. His voluminous correspondence, his many speeches and elegies were collected and published posthumously.

2 Philosophical outlook and the *Preliminary Discourse*

D'Alembert's philosophy is of decisive importance to anyone who would understand the Enlightenment in its intellectual and theoretical (as distinct from its social and political) dimension because it manifests, more clearly perhaps than any other author's, the delicate combination of French rationalism in the tradition of Descartes and Malebranche and British empiricism as represented by Newton and Locke (see MALEBRANCHE, N.; LOCKE, J.). As a mathematician of the very first rank, D'Alembert was entirely sympathetic to Descartes' insistence upon the clarity and precision of basic principles and the need for rigorous deductive logic in establishing the linkages between one theoretical proposition and any others which might be linked with it. Like virtually all his contemporaries, D'Alembert was hugely impressed by the power of Newtonian mechanics to explain and integrate vast tracts of natural phenomena and predict future events, and by the extent to which observational and experimental data could be incorporated into a system constituted at its core by mathematical principles. To understand D'Alembert himself, and to appreciate his importance as a signal representative of the thought of this watershed period in human history, the relationship between the Cartesian and empirical strands of his work must be made out.

D'Alembert was unequivocal in his rejection of metaphysical principles as constituting an appropriate base for inquiry in the natural sciences. He repudiated the Cartesian doctrine of innate ideas and denied that Descartes' *Cogito* had any value as a starting point in constructing the system of human knowledge. Appeals to divine intervention in the natural order had no place in trying to explain the connection between events or the relation between natural objects and the human perception of them. In this respect, D'Alembert adhered closely to the principles of Lockean epistemology as these were modified and expanded in the works of his friend and colleague, CONDILLAC. With Locke and Condillac, D'Alembert insisted that all knowledge begins by attending to the facts and that the way those facts *appear* to us is as close as we can ever hope to get to their reality. But the facts which present themselves to our experience are only isolated and fragmentary pieces of a greater systematic structure in which they are embedded, and for the full articulation of that structure one must have recourse to the principles of mathematics – specifically those of geometry – in order to represent the orderliness of natural events and processes. The basic principles of any science should consist in perfectly unambiguous and precise mathematical formulas together with whatever basic assumptions are necessary to secure their attachment to the objects which constitute the domain under investigation. The various discrete facts disclosed to our observations can then be expressed as formal propositions which could in turn be fitted into the deductive chain of formulas derivable from the basic principles.

D'Alembert rejected Descartes' notion of the universe as a plenum because it was infected by the unwarranted metaphysical doctrine of substances. In his own conception of the universe, however, D'Alembert maintained that all parts of nature are systematically interrelated in a comprehensive structure of laws which evinces the same integrity, consistency and formal precision as any of the more extended and elegant proofs in geometry. Like Descartes, D'Alembert believed that the methodical and painstaking implementation of human reason would gradually serve to disclose this rational structure, and that, as it came into view, the empirical facts could find their place within it and thereby attain theoretical clarity. By setting his first priority on the articulation of the rational structure which informed all of nature, D'Alembert comports with the most fundamental aspects of Cartesian methodology and reaffirms the optimistic faith of his great precursor in the autonomous power of human reason.

In the *Preliminary Discourse* to the *Encyclopedia* D'Alembert presents an interpretation of the contemporary state of scientific research in which his own rationalistic conception of the structure of human knowledge forms the core. The *Encyclopedia* itself is conceived as a compendium of all the scientific truths so far achieved, but the greater utility and value of the work is found to consist precisely in its capacity to arrange and integrate these results so as to facilitate further research by revealing both the systematic interrelations between seemingly remote domains and the lacunas which remained to be filled in. D'Alembert compares the *Encyclopedia* to a road map: certain areas of the terrain of human knowledge are well understood and laid out in careful detail while the expanses between these areas are marked out only by the most rudimentary traces which might nonetheless provide a researcher with his theoretical bearings as he laboured to extend the boundaries of knowledge ever deeper into the realm of *terra incognita*. All of the articles in the *Encyclopedia* were to be knit together by an extensive network of cross-references so that an arbitrarily selected topic would lead the reader eventually to a comprehensive view of the whole structure in all its intricacies. The *Encyclopedia*, as the systematic embodiment of the whole vast range of human knowledge, would thus reflect the rational structure which constituted the natural order itself.

D'Alembert invokes a second metaphor in the *Discourse*, inspired by the prescient writings of the great English philosopher of science Francis BACON, in which the 'tree of human knowledge', rooted in such fundamental disciplines as mathematics and logic, branches out into the various scientific subregions and extends ever further to include the most narrowly defined and detailed subject matter. Reconfiguring the Baconian conception of knowledge in accordance with the general principles of epistemology worked out by Condillac, D'Alembert recognizes three essential functions of the human mind: memory, reason and imagination. Under these three rubrics all domains of human inquiry, including history (sacred, civil and natural), literature and art, can be systematically interrelated. This second metaphor expresses D'Alembert's view of knowledge as an organic unity, as something which grows from within when all of the various parts derive their sustenance from the flourishing of the others and contribute in turn to the flourishing of the whole.

To D'Alembert's way of thinking there was no area of human inquiry which could not be incorporated into this unified and integrated structure of knowledge, and in this respect the *Preliminary Discourse* gives powerful and eloquent expression to one of the guiding inspirations of the Enlightenment period as a whole. In his own researches he made significant contributions toward bringing the study of language and aesthetics under the purview of science, and believed that ultimately even politics and morality should have to be subsumed under its methodology if there were to be progress. But here, D'Alembert's attachment to rationalistic principles becomes deeply problematic, in that the more inscrutable and ambiguous aspects of human nature seem unamenable to anything like the geometrical precision that he made the hallmark of all true science. If from our historical vantage point his own philosophical commitments should appear somewhat dogmatic and unwarranted, we must at least acknowledge that the issues concerning the relationships between the various domains of human knowledge to which he was so acutely sensitive continue into our own day, reflected in the uneasy division within institutions of higher learning between the humanities and the 'hard sciences'.

3 Reputation and influence

D'Alembert continues to enjoy a rightly prominent role in virtually all historical treatments of the Enlightenment period. He is one of only a few *philosophes* to have achieved the very highest standing as both a scientist and man of letters. His contributions to mathematics and physics stand as significant landmarks in the history of both disciplines. His indefatigable labours as secretary of the French Academy were profoundly efficacious in advancing the cause of enlightenment across Europe. Some of the most important historical figures of the age, including Voltaire, Frederick the Great and David HUME were proud to count him among their friends, a testament to both his high reputation and the warmth and integrity of his personality. His philosophical work was influential in the world of practical affairs as well, for example, in the formation of economic policy under the ministries of Quesnay and Turgot. And it is by no means the least of his contributions to have served as mentor to and helped to advance the careers of some of the brightest young minds of the rising generation such as Laplace, Lagrange and CONDORCET. A close study of D'Alembert's life and works provides an excellent point of entry into the world of the European Enlightenment.

See also: ENCYCLOPEDISTS, EIGHTEENTH CENTURY; ENLIGHTENMENT, CONTINENTAL

List of works

D'Alembert, J. Le R. (1821–2) *Oeuvres*, ed. A. Belin, Paris: Belin, 5 vols.

—— (1799) *Oeuvres posthumes*, ed. C. Pougens, Paris: Pougens, 2 vols.

—— (1743) *Traité de dynamique*, Paris: David.

—— (1744) *Traité de l'équilibre et du mouvement des fluides pour servir de suite au Traité de dynamique*, Paris: David.

—— (1747) *Réflexions sur la cause générale des vents*, Paris: David l'aîné.

—— (1749) *Recherches sur la précession des équinoxes, et sur la nutation de l'axe de la terre dans le système newtonien*, Paris: David.

—— (1751–65) *Encyclopédie, ou, Dictionnaire raisonné des sciences, des arts et de metiers, par une société de gens lettrés*, Paris: Briasson. (Contains the *Discours préliminaire* as a preface to the first volume.)

—— (1751) *Discours préliminaire*, trans. R.N. Schwab, *Preliminary Discourse to the Encyclopedia of Diderot*, Indianapolis, IN: Bobbs-Merrill, 1963.

—— (1759) *Mélanges de littérature, d'histoire et de philosophie*, Paris: David, 4 vols; vol. 5, 1767.

—— (1761–80) *Opuscules mathématiques*, Paris: David, 8 vols.

—— (1765) *Sur la destruction des Jésuites en France, par un auteur désintéressé*, Edinburgh: J. Balfour.

—— (1766) *An account of the destruction of the Jesuits in France*, Glasgow: R. Urie.

References and further reading

Essar, D.F. (1976) 'The language theory, epistemology, and aesthetics of Jean Lerond d'Alembert', *Studies on Voltaire and the Eighteenth Century*, 159.

(Contains an excellent discussion of D'Alembert's researches into the origins and nature of language, and his works on music and the theatre.)

Grimsley, R. (1963) *Jean D'Alembert*, Oxford: Clarendon Press. (Presents a detailed discussion of D'Alembert's engagement with the Encyclopedia and his work in the French Academy; excellent introduction to the life and works of D'Alembert and the French Enlightenment period generally.)

Hankins, T. (1970) *Jean D'Alembert: Science and the Enlightenment*, Oxford: Clarendon Press. (A thorough and more technical examination of D'Alembert's mathematical and scientific works and sets them in the context of the theoretical controversies of the day. Less suitable as an introductory text, but provides a much more comprehensive analysis of the specific contributions that D'Alembert made to mathematics and mechanics. Includes a very useful bibliography.)

Lough, J. (1968) *Essays on the Encyclopédie of Diderot and D'Alembert*, London: Oxford University Press. (Of use to scholars interested in the publication history of the Encyclopedia and the various controversies which attended it. It contains a complete list of the articles that D'Alembert contributed, but on the whole the essays are rather too specialized to be of interest to the general reader.)

Pappas, J.N. (1962) *Voltaire and D'Alembert*, Bloomington, IN: Indiana University Press. (Describes the various ways in which D'Alembert served the cause of the philosophic spirit, with careful discussion of his relations with and influence upon Voltaire.)

PAUL F. JOHNSON

ALEXANDER, SAMUEL (1859–1938)

Alexander propounded a metaphysical system based on a view of Space-Time differentiated into 'motions' from which new qualities emerged at certain levels of organization; matter, life and mind being those qualities so far realized. Space-Time is a process with a 'nisus' (that is, an internal drive) towards a quality, as yet unrealized, called 'Deity'.

1 Space, time and deity
2 Knowledge and values

1 Space, time and deity

Alexander was born in Sydney, Australia, came to Balliol College, Oxford, and was subsequently Fellow of Lincoln College, Oxford, and Professor of Philosophy at the University of Manchester. His metaphysics rested on the concept of a Space-Time continuum ordered in four-dimensional perspectives from 'point-instants', which are not extended events, but limiting cases of 'motions', his term for the actual differentiations within Space-Time. These motions form patterns, the most general of which, notably causation, are all-pervasive categories. As a direct realist, he claimed that these categories were discerned, not imposed, by conceptual schemes. More specific motions in Space-Time displayed patterns in which distinctive qualities emerged at certain levels of organization. 'Matter', with its inertial properties, is the lowest level; certain of its complexes display the new quality 'life', and some of these display a further quality 'mind'. This view is a form of evolutionary naturalism, but not materialism, since 'matter' is the name for certain qualities from which further qualities of life and mind emerge, and these latter are not reducible to the former. Moreover, the basic reality is not matter but Space-Time.

Space-Time is not a closed system within which there can be redistributions of spatiotemporal coefficients. Its temporal aspect makes it an ongoing process in which there is a 'nisus' towards the production of new qualities. Beyond those known to us, there may be one, as yet unrealized, called 'Deity'. 'Deity' is not God as existent, but a quality towards which we can aspire.

2 Knowledge and values

The time dimension of Space-Time gives things an internal aspect as going through a process, while the space dimension sets them in an external relation called 'compresence'. A subject's inner experience of knowing is called 'enjoyment' and its relation of compresence to an object is called 'contemplation'. This is a direct realism, which raises difficulties over questions of error and counterfactual conditions. This realism extends to secondary qualities, such as colours. Besides secondary qualities there are 'tertiary' qualities called values, which arise in situations where one compresent factor is a mind. Chief of these are Truth, Beauty and Goodness. Here Alexander's main interest, expressed in a number of discussions of pieces of prose, poetry, art and architecture, was aesthetics. He held that there is a constructive impulse to manipulate materials which can be disengaged from practical ends and become contemplative, so leading to aesthetic appreciation. In stressing the need for a material medium as the carrier of the value of Beauty, Alexander's aesthetics are of a piece with his view of neurophysiological processes as bearers of non-reducible mental qualities shown in the capacity for conscious enjoyment and contemplation.

See also: AESTHETIC CONCEPTS; BEAUTY; VALUE, ONTOLOGICAL STATUS OF

List of works

Alexander, S. (1889) *Moral Order and Progress: An Analysis of Ethical Concepts*, London: Trüber and Co. (Written from an idealist position that was later abandoned.)

—— (1914) 'The Basis of Realism', *Proceedings of the British Academy* 6: 279–314; republished in R.M. Chisholm (ed.) *Realism and The Basis of Phenomenology*, Glencoe, IL: The Free Press, 1960, 186–222. (This relates Alexander's theory of knowledge to that of other philosophers of the time.)

—— (1920, 1927) *Space, Time and Deity*, London: Macmillan. (The second impression (1927) contains an important new preface. A paperback edition appeared in 1966.)

—— (1933) *Beauty and the Other Forms of Value*, London: Macmillan. (Studies of Valuation, especially of Beauty, where practical impulses become contemplative, and of Goodness, where social impulses become subject to approbation and disapprobation.)

—— (1939) *Philosophical and Literary Pieces*, London: Macmillan. (This is a posthumous collection edited with a memoir by John Laird. It contains a full bibliography of Alexander's writings.)

References and further reading

Broad, C.D. (1921) *Mind* 30: 23–39 and 129–50. (Review articles on *Space, Time and Deity*.)

—— (1929) *The Mind and Its Place in Nature*, London: Routledge & Kegan Paul. (Chapter 2 contains a discussion of the concept of emergence.)

Emmet, D. (1967) 'Alexander, Samuel', *Encyclopedia of Philosophy*, ed. P. Edwards, London and New York: Macmillan, vol. 1, 69–73. (A fuller treatment of Alexander's philosophy.)

—— (1991) 'Whitehead und Alexander' in *Die Gifford Lectures und Ihre Deutung*, ed. M. Hampe and H. Massen, Frankfurt-am-Main: Suhrkamp, 100–20. (Translation by M. Hampe of an article comparing the philosophies of Whitehead and Alexander. This was republished (1992) in its original English version in *Process Studies* 21 (3): 137–48.)

DOROTHY EMMET

ALEXANDER OF APHRODISIAS (*fl. c.* AD 200)

The Peripatetic philosopher Alexander was known to posterity as the commentator on Aristotle, until Averroes took over this title. His commentaries eclipsed most of those of his predecessors, which now survive only in scattered quotations. Used by Plotinus, Alexander's commentaries were the basis for subsequent work on Aristotle by Neoplatonist commentators, and even though some themselves survive only in quotations by these later writers, Alexander's interpretations of particular passages are still helpful and are cited by commentators today.

In addition to Alexander's commentaries we have a number of monographs, and also collections of short discussions which are connected with themes in his writings, though some are probably by pupils rather than by Alexander himself. Alexander's most influential and controversial doctrine has been his interpretation of Aristotle's theory of soul and intellect; regarding the soul as the product of the mixture of the bodily elements, he has been seen as subordinating form to matter and as thereby misinterpreting Aristotle. Certainly his view excludes any immortality for individuals, but even if Aristotle himself allowed this it is arguable that to do so was incompatible with his definition of soul as the form of potentially living body. Alexander himself interpreted Aristotle's 'active intellect' not as an immortal element in each individual, but as god, the unmoved mover, apprehended by our own intellects. Both on the question of soul and on that of the status of universals, Alexander gives a non-Platonizing reading of Aristotle, which accounts for some of the criticism to which he has been subjected by successors both ancient and modern. His treatment of the problem of free will has also been influential, though his criticisms of determinism are more telling than his own positive solution.

Seeing his task as interpreting Aristotle's writings with the aid of one another and explaining apparent inconsistencies, Alexander contributed to the growth of Aristotelianism as a system; he does not criticize nor challenge Aristotle, and regards his own innovations as Aristotelian doctrine, developed in the context of new questions which Aristotle himself had not confronted in the same form. He was better at seeing the details than at comprehending the global picture, and the potential of some of his doctrinal contributions is most apparent in what they suggested to others; but there is still much to interest philosophers in his detailed argumentation on particular points and passages.

1 Life, works and relation to Aristotle
2 Soul and intellect
3 Universals
4 Providence and fate
5 Influence

1 Life, works and relation to Aristotle

Alexander's treatise *On Fate* is dedicated – with some elaborate rhetorical flourishes, and a request to consult him if further clarification is needed – to the emperors Septimius Severus and Caracalla, in gratitude for his appointment as a publicly recognized teacher of Aristotelian philosophy. Since Caracalla was made Augustus as Septimius Severus' colleague in AD 198, and Geta joined them as a third Augustus in AD 209, the date is fixed as between these two points; but we do not know at what stage in Alexander's career the appointment was made. Nor do we know for certain where the post in question was, though it is likely enough that it was the chair at Athens established by MARCUS AURELIUS (§1) in 176; Alexander's use of Aristotle's statue in Athens as an example in *On Aristotle's Metaphysics* (415.29–31) has been seen as supporting this.

Some of the general characteristics of Alexander's writings have been indicated above. His surviving commentaries are those on *Metaphysics* I–V (that on the remainder of the *Metaphysics*, like that on the *Sophistical Refutations*, is not by Alexander but by the twelfth-century Michael of Ephesus), *Prior Analytics* I, the *Topics*, the *Meteorology* and *On Sensation*. They are characterized by the frequent inclusion of alternative explanations, and by an absence of the formal organization, reflecting the programme of teaching in a school context, that is found in the later Neoplatonic commentaries on Aristotle. Alexander also wrote commentaries, now known only from later quotations, on the other logical and physical works of Aristotle. Whether he produced a full-scale commentary on the *Ethics* is debated, and he shows little or no interest in the zoological, political and rhetorical works.

Alexander's monographs include, surviving in Greek, *On the Soul* (as distinct from his commentary, now lost, on Aristotle's *On the Soul*), *On Fate*, *On Mixture*, and, surviving only in Arabic translation, *On the Principles of the Universe* (the authenticity of which has been questioned), *On Providence*, a work on differentiae, and *Refutation of Galen's Attack on Aristotle's Doctrine That Everything That Moves is Set In Motion by a Mover* (the actual connection of this treatise with Galen's views, like much else in the Arabic tradition concerning the relations between Alexander and GALEN, is doubtful). There were other monographs, now lost (see below). In addition, the extant collections of short discussions include, in Greek, the so-called second book of Alexander's *On the Soul*, better known by the name *Mantissa* or 'makeweight' given it by its modern editor, Ivo Bruns; three books of *Quaestiones* (School-Puzzles and Solutions Concerning Nature); and one book of *Ethical Problems*. (Another collection, of *Medical Puzzles and Physical Problems*, has nothing to do with Alexander.) These collections were put together, often ineptly, by editors later than Alexander himself. Other similar material has been preserved in compendia in Greek manuscripts or in Arabic translation. Study of the relative dating of Alexander's works, and on the relation between the commentaries and the short discussions, is still in its infancy.

Both the relationships among Alexander's works and his loyalty to Aristotle can be illustrated by two particular topics. Both in the *Prior Analytics* commentary and in a separate monograph, now lost (see Alexander, *On Aristotle's Prior Analytics* 125.30– 1; Philoponus, *On Aristotle's Prior Analytics* 126.20), Alexander discussed Aristotle's modal logic; Alexander's writings are a major source for the controversy between Aristotle himself and his immediate followers, THEOPHRASTUS (§2) and Eudemus, over the conversion of contingent premises and the modality of the conclusions of syllogisms with 'mixed' premises (for example, one necessary and one assertoric). However, while many would hold that there is more logical elegance in Theophrastus' and Eudemus' view that the conclusion is in every case only as strong as the weakest premise (the medieval rule *peiorem semper conclusio sequitur partem*) Alexander remains loyal to Aristotle (*On Aristotle's Prior Analytics* 125.3–127.16). Second, Alexander answers Aristotle's problem in *Physics* VIII 4 254b33–, 'What is it that causes the natural movement of a falling heavy body?', by an analogy between the soul, as the form of a living creature and cause of its movement, and heaviness, as the form of a heavy body and the internal cause of *its* movement. This analogy – and it is presented only as an analogy – is put forward not only in the *Refutation of Galen on Motion*, but also in *On the Soul* (22.7–) and *On the Principles of the Universe*; and it has been seen by Pines (1961) as a possible ancestor of Philoponus' explanation of the motion of a projectile forced – in Aristotelian terms, rather than natural – by an internal impetus imparted to it by the thrower (see PHILOPONUS §2). Alexander, as quoted by Simplicius, *On Aristotle's Physics* 1346.37–, remains loyal to Aristotle's implausible explanation of the continued motion of a projectile by movement imparted to the air behind the projectile as well as to it.

2 Soul and intellect

Aristotle defines soul as the first actuality of a natural body potentially possessing life, or, more shortly, of an organic body, and regards the soul of a living creature as its form (see ARISTOTLE §17; PSYCHĒ). But it is controversial how this is to be understood. Some have interpreted Aristotle's notion of soul as a functionalist one; but this view has been criticized on the grounds that it does not do justice to the close connection in Aristotle between the performance of a given function and the particular arrangement needed for it. This close connection between form and matter in Aristotle's theory of them has caused major difficulties for interpreters, because it is not clear how soul and body can be logically distinguished, if a lifeless hand or eye is a hand or eye only in name, and only an already living, 'ensouled' body is to count as an organic body. It seems that either body must be defined in terms of soul, which raises the question whether there is any level at which the matter of a living body is specifiable without reference to its soul, or else that soul must be accounted for in terms of the arrangement of the body and its parts.

Interpreters of Aristotle have favoured the former approach. Aristotle himself (in *On the Soul* I 4) rejects – though with some hesitation – the notion that soul can be a 'harmony' or arrangement of the bodily elements, partly because such an arrangement cannot itself be a cause of movement as the soul is. However, Alexander not only defines the soul as the product of the mixture of the bodily elements (*On the Soul* 24.21–3), apparently following Andronicus, but sets out his exposition of the nature of soul by starting with the simple bodies, earth, air, fire and water, and working upwards through progressively more elaborate compounds until he arrives at living creatures and finally at human beings. It is therefore hardly surprising that his account of the soul has often been criticized as materialist, reductivist and un-Aristotelian. However, these criticisms may to some extent reflect the critics' own standpoints, and their own interpretations of Aristotle. It is scarcely un-Aristotelian to suggest that a given form requires a given arrangement of given types of matter, and Alexander's order of exposition need not indicate that he regards more complex forms as posterior to less complex ones so far as explanatory or ontological dependence is concerned. Indeed he derives the substantiality of the form–matter composite from that of the form and the matter (6.2–4), and insists that it is the form of each thing that determines its nature (7.4–8). Moreover, texts attributed to Alexander insist that form is not in matter, or soul in body, in the way that a quality can be in a substrate, because it is by the form and the soul that the matter and the body are characterized in the first place (*Quaestiones* I 8, 17, 26; *Mantissa* 119–122.)

It is true that Alexander's treatment of soul excludes any individual immortality; indeed this was his chief source of popularity in the Renaissance (see §5 below). But Aristotle's view itself arguably encounters difficulties where personal immortality is concerned. Attribution to Aristotle, in his mature period, of belief in personal immortality turns on interpretation of his remarks concerning intellect, and especially the so-called 'active intellect' of his own *On the Soul* III.5 (see ARISTOTLE §19; NOUS). Alexander, however, identifies the active intellect not with an element peculiar to the soul of each individual but with god, the 'unmoved mover' of *Metaphysics* XII. The theory of intellect is discussed both in Alexander's *On the Soul* and in a section of the *Mantissa* which is of doubtful authenticity and seems itself to be a combination of several different texts, but which circulated independently in the Middle Ages first in Arabic translation and then in Latin, and was more influential than Alexander's *On the Soul* itself. Common to both works is the view that the individual human's intellect at birth is purely potential; it is therefore referred to as 'material intellect', by analogy with the potentiality of matter in the ordinary sense of the latter term. Since, however, it must be receptive to all forms, it has no nature of its own (see Aristotle, *On the Soul* III 4, 429b10–22); and indeed in *On the Soul* its state at birth is likened not so much to a blank writing-tablet (Aristotle, *On the Soul* III 4, 429a31–) as to the blankness of the tablet (84.24–7). As a person grows to adulthood the 'material' intellect develops, by the acquisition of concepts through the abstraction of matter from the forms in substances composed of form and matter, until it becomes intellect 'in disposition' (*en hexei*, later Latinized as *in habitu*), capable of independent thought.

What is less clear is the part which the active intellect is supposed to play in this process. Alexander's *On the Soul*, characteristically, simply presents two arguments *that* the unmoved mover, as pure self-thinking intellect and intelligible in its own right, is responsible for our thinking too, without explaining very adequately *how* this comes about. First, as supremely intelligible it must be the cause of other things' intelligibility (88.24–89.8) – an argument which sounds more Platonist than Aristotelian, though it is not indeed being used here to *establish* the existence of intelligible pure form. And second, it is the cause of being for all other things, and thus for all the objects of intellect (89.9–19). This is probably to be understood in terms of the movement of the heavens, caused by the unmoved mover, being the cause of sublunary coming-to-be (see §4 below); but as an explanation of how our intellects become able to think it scarcely seems adequate. In the short text *On Intellect* (107.31–4, 108.19–22), on the other hand, the active intellect appears to act directly upon our intellect, apparently by providing it with a paradigm of pure form and thus enabling it to separate other, 'enmattered' forms from the matter in which they are embodied – which apparently has the rather implausible implication that we must apprehend god, in order to possess this paradigm, before we can think of anything else in general terms. In *On the Soul* 90.11–20 it is argued that, since intellect is identical with its object at any given time, immortality can be present in us when we think of god; but it is not our own 'material' intellect that then becomes immortal. This is the only immortality open to us as individuals (but see below on the eternity of species).

On Intellect (whether itself by Alexander or not) indicates that Alexander's treatment of the topic built upon earlier Peripatetic discussions, and that the identification of the active intellect with god rather than with an element in the individual soul had already been connected with Aristotle's reference to 'intellect from outside' (*Generation of Animals* II 3 736b27–). But that in fact relates to the origin of intellect in the context of the generation of individual human beings, with no explicit identification of the source from which such intellect comes, and no apparent reference to its entering into us through acts of intellectual apprehension, as in Alexander's view.

3   Universals

Aristotle rejects the Platonist view that forms of material objects can exist even in the absence of any material instances, and holds that the form of human being exists only in individual human beings and, in a different way, in the minds that think of them. What is much less clear is Aristotle's view of the ontological status of such forms, and in particular whether they are to be regarded as individual or universal. Alexander regards universals as posterior to individuals. He has therefore been criticized for adopting an un-Aristotelian nominalism; but his position is in fact more subtle. If we accept the evidence of the *Quaestiones* (I 3), Alexander draws a distinction between the nature, as such, of a species, and that nature as a universal. Definition is of what is common to the members of a species, as opposed to the individual accidents due to matter (*On the Soul* 85.15–18, where Alexander seems to adopt a doctrine of numerically distinct forms in different members of the same species; see ARISTOTLE). But the definition of the nature of the species would still be the same even if only one member of the species existed. Definition is thus of what is common, but not of what is common as common, and it is purely accidental to a specific nature whether it is universal, in the sense of having more than one instantiation, or not. However, while the individual is prior to the universal in the sense that an individual can exist without there being a universal, the universal is none the less, in cases where there is more than one instance, prior to any particular individual; the existence of 'human being' does not depend on the existence of Socrates or of any other particular named individual (*On Providence*, Ruland 1976: 89; compare Alexander reported by Dexippus, *On Aristotle's Categories* 45.16 and by Simplicius, *On Aristotle's Physics* 19.5–11). Similarly, the genus is prior to the species (*Quaestiones* I 11–). There can be animals without there being horses, but not horses without there being animals; on the other hand, this horse would still be an animal even if there were no other animals and no other horses at all.

Alexander does say (*On the Soul* 90.2–11) that forms embodied in matter depend for their existence on being intelligized, and that (*Quaestiones* II 28 78.18–20) genus *as genus* – that is, as including several different species – is just a name, its existence depending on its being thought of. But it is not clear that this involves nominalism, if by nominalism is meant the view that common natures are *arbitrary* thought-constructs or that their reality derives purely from our giving a common name to a particular collection of individuals (see NOMINALISM). The point of the statement at *On the Soul* 90.2–11 is to contrast them with pure intelligible forms (the unmoved movers), and, given the part played by specific natures in Alexander's theory of providence (see §4), it seems that, far from being nominalist, Alexander's theory of species is essentialist, involving a rigid distinction between the nature common to the species and individual accidents.

4   Providence and fate

On both providence and fate Alexander adapts Aristotelian materials to the discussion of new issues, presenting the resulting account as 'Aristotelian'. In the case of providence, discussed in the treatise *On Providence* and in several of the *Quaestiones*, especially the unfinished dialogue II 21, he is concerned to mediate between, on the one hand, interpretations of Aristotle (especially but not only by the hostile

Platonist Atticus) as making divine influence on the sublunary world purely accidental and so not providence at all, and, on the other hand, the pantheistic doctrine of the Stoics (see STOICISM §5), which he regards as unworthy of the divine dignity by involving god directly in every detail of the world, however humble, and also as incompatible with the perceived existence of evils. His solution makes use of the Aristotelian theory (*Generation and Corruption* II 10) that the motion of the heavens and especially of the sun on the ecliptic, caused by desire for the unmoved mover, is responsible for the cycle of the seasons and thus for the continuity of coming-to-be and passing-away and the perpetuation of natural kinds. Alexander interprets this as providence, but a providence concerned with the eternity of species rather than with the fortunes of individuals. The charge that providence involves the divine existing for the sake of what is inferior to it was apparently answered by the argument (*Quaestiones* I 23 36.22–3; compare with I 25 41.1–2; *On the Principles of the Universe*, Badawi 1968: 127–8) that the continuation of the sublunary world benefits the heavens by giving them a centre around which to revolve; and Alexander apparently accepted that non-accidental providence must involve some awareness of its objects on the part of what exercises it, the divine presumably being aware of sublunary beings as species but not as individuals. Some of the details remain obscure, especially as concerns the identity of the being or beings exercising providence and the relation here between the divine heavenly spheres on the one hand and the unmoved mover(s) on the other; moreover, Alexander's theory of providence amounts to little more than an upholding of the general ordering of the world, as opposed to the concern with its complex history, and especially with the fortunes of individual human beings, characteristic of both the Stoic and the Judaeo-Christian traditions. At the end of the twelfth century Alexander's treatise *On Providence* was used as a source for ancient Greek theories – and its denial of divine concern for individuals rejected – by Moses MAIMONIDES (*Guide to the Perplexed* III 16–17).

The notion of a general ordering of the universe which is unaffected by variations in detail also appears in Alexander's treatise *On Fate* (ch. 25), where it is used to counter the argument (Stoic, though the determinists attacked in the treatise are never actually named there as Stoics) that a nexus of causes and effects admitting of no exceptions is essential if the unity of the universe is to be preserved (see STOICISM §20). Unfortunately – and characteristically – Alexander in this treatise is more concerned to attack the determinist account of human agency, as conflicting with common experience and detrimental to morality, than to explain how in his own view human agency fits into the world as a whole; this problem is more pressing for him than for Aristotle, because he is concerned to reject determinism while also claiming to avoid the introduction of any 'uncaused motion'. There is a similarity between Alexander's philosophical position here and the way in which Carneades had sought to escape determinism while rejecting the Epicureans' uncaused atomic 'swerve' (see EPICUREANISM §§4, 12; CARNEADES §3; and further below), though the question of possible historical influence of Carneades on Alexander is undecided, and Alexander makes no explicit reference to the atomic swerve or to the problems it involves. An attempt to locate human agency in the context of a general worldview is made by one of the short texts attributed to Alexander (*Mantissa*, Bruns 1887–92: 169–172), which thus reveals the limitations of Alexander's own treatment. However, by linking responsible choice to uncaused motion, contrary to Alexander's own view, it succeeds only in demonstrating the difficulties of a radical indeterminism.

In the absence of any single and systematic account of exceptions to determinism in *On Fate*, we are left with a series of separate claims:

(1) Alexander begins by setting out (chaps 3–6) an anti-determinist doctrine of fate – perhaps taken over, indeed, from earlier Peripatetic sources, basing it on the Aristotelian doctrine of nature as what applies for the most part but not always. Our actions are for the most part in accordance with our individual character, but not inevitably so.

(2) The occurrence of chance events disproves determinism (ch. 8; compare ch. 24). The stock Aristotelian examples of coincidences (finding buried treasure, and the like) which Alexander uses can, however, be accommodated within the Stoic system; true, if everything that happens is part of a single providential plan they will not really be coincidences, but Alexander's claim that they are rests, like much of his anti-Stoic argumentation in *On Fate*, on appeals to a common opinion which turns out to be Aristotelian school doctrine.

(3) Alexander argues (ch. 15) that our action can be free from being predetermined, and yet not be uncaused, because we ourselves, as agents, are the cause, this indeed being what it means to be human. This argument resembles, in general character though not in the details of its expression, that of Carneades on the same issue (Cicero, *On Fate* 25) which Richard Taylor has seen as anticipating modern agent causation theory. It is

not, however, clear that introducing non-physical causes can provide a way out of the dilemma that either everything that occurs is predetermined on the physical level, or else there must be some break in the continuity of such physical causation.

(4) Following Aristotle (*Nicomachean Ethics* III 5), Alexander argues (chaps 27–9) that even if an agent cannot act contrary to a developed character, the development of that character is itself the agent's responsibility. This argument is unsatisfactory in itself – as Alexander apparently realizes; see (5) below – simply pushing the problem back into the past; it also involves a view of the relation between natural endowment, developed character and action which is at least on the face of it different from that in (1). (Other texts attributed to Alexander take up this point, reconciling the two approaches by arguing that, while innate proclivities vary, everyone who is not morally deformed has the capacity to become virtuous: *Mantissa* 175.25–32; *Ethical Problems* 161.15–29.)

(5) To meet the difficulty of reconciling responsible choice, understood as requiring that the agent be able (and 'able' not just in a counterfactual sense) either to perform or not to perform the act in question, with the argument that for any given agent with a given perspective on a given situation only one course of action will be reasonable, Alexander makes three points. First, our actions are aimed not towards one goal but towards three: the noble, the advantageous and the pleasant (ch.15). The identification of these three ends is Aristotelian (*Nicomachean Ethics* II 3, 1104b30–), but not their treatment as equally valid alternatives for a single individual, and in the context of Alexander's argument it raises the question of what account we are to give of an agent's choice between them. Second, there is a certain degree of latitude, more than one possible action expressing a given character-trait or goal (ch. 29). This seems not to capture morally significant choices. Third, we may sometimes act otherwise than we normally would in a given situation, just to prove that we have the capacity to do so, and especially to confound a prophet (ch. 29). (A modern version might put it in terms of confounding a psychologist.) But this is entirely compatible with determinism, the abnormal action itself being a theoretically predictable reaction to an unusual situation.

Although Alexander fails to clarify his position, to such an extent that D. Frede has classified his position as compatibilist rather than libertarian (see FREE WILL §1), the detailed arguments of the treatise *On Fate* anticipate many of the moves made in the free-will debate subsequently, and show considerable ingenuity. Alexander's strongest anti-determinist argument rests on the inability of determinism to make sense of our experiences of choice and deliberation; and, in an argument analogous to Pascal's wager (see PASCAL §6), he claims (ch. 21) that there is less danger in believing our actions are not predetermined when in fact they are, than in believing that they are when in fact they are not.

5 Influence

Alexander's commentaries were read in the school of PLOTINUS, the founder of NEOPLATONISM (Porphyry, *Life of Plotinus* 14). Studies of Alexander's influence on Plotinus have tended to find numerous correspondences in points of detail rather than conclusive evidence of influence on the major features of Plotinus' system. Plotinus used Alexander essentially as a guide to understanding Aristotle; the way in which Plotinus formulates the Aristotelian principle of the identity of intellect and its object shows Alexander's influence, but the doctrine itself had been adopted by Platonism earlier. Some have seen a connection between Alexander's discussion of a plurality of pure forms without matter (the plurality of unmoved movers) and Plotinus' doctrine of the unity of 'forms in intellect'; but Plotinian, and Platonic, forms are related to sensible objects in a different way from the Aristotelian unmoved movers, and in any case Alexander refers to pure forms sometimes in the singular and sometimes in the plural without seeming to attach much significance to the difference between the two. If Alexander's remarks did influence the Plotinian theory, they probably did so because of Plotinus' reflecting upon them rather than because of any awareness by Alexander of their possible significance. Similarly, too, with the suggestion that for Alexander our intellect, by apprehending the divine intellect, also apprehends its eternal objects; such a theory can be seen as a logical extension of Alexander's views, but it goes beyond anything that he actually says.

This point can be generalized. The limitations of Alexander's discussion of the active intellect have already been mentioned; his relatively terse reference to our achieving temporary immortality through contemplation of god is probably to be interpreted in terms not so much of mystical experience as of a desire to develop the logical implications of his account. Nevertheless, Alexander's doctrine of a single suprapersonal active intellect was immensely influential; it was later adopted by Averroes, though he – influenced by Neoplatonism – regarded the 'passive' or potential intellect too as one for all human beings. Aquinas was therefore able to cite Alexander for the individuality of the passive intellect in his controversy with the Averroists (see AQUINAS §7; AVERROISM §1,2), even though differing from him concerning the active intellect and the immortality of the individual. In the sixteenth century Alexander's view, rejecting personal immortality, was advocated notably by Petro POMPONAZZI, in successful defiance of the decree of the Lateran Council in 1513 that 'individual immortality could be demonstrated philosophically and consequently had to be defended by all philosophers' (Kessler 1988: 495, 507), and by Jacopo ZABARELLA.

See also: PERIPATETICS; ARISTOTLE COMMENTATORS

List of works

Apart from *On Fate* (dated between AD 198 and 209; see §1 above), none of Alexander's works can be dated absolutely, and the study even of relative dates is still in its infancy. For texts preserved in Arabic see the listing and bibliography in Sharples (1987), to be corrected in the light of Hasnawi (1994) and Zimmermann (1994); Moraux *et al.* (forthcoming).

Alexander *(fl. c.* AD 200) Commentaries on Aristotle, in H. Diels (ed.) *Commentaria in Aristotelem Graeca* I–III, Berlin: Reimer, 1883–1901. (Greek text; for individual commentaries, see §1 above.)

—— *(fl. c.* AD 200) Other writings, in I. Bruns (ed.) *Supplementum Aristotelicum* II.1–2, Berlin: Reimer, 1887–92. (Greek text; see §1 above.)

—— *(fl. c.* AD 200) Various works, trans. in R. Sorabji (ed.) *The Aristotelian Commentators*, London: Duckworth, 1987–. (Annotated translations of various works.)

—— *(fl. c.* AD 200) *On the Soul* and *On Intellect*, trans. in A.P. Fotinis, *The De Anima of Alexander of Aphrodisias*, Washington, DC: University Press of America, 1979. (English translation, with commentary.)

—— *(fl. c.* AD 200) *On the Soul*, trans. P. Accattino and P.L. Donini, *Alessandro di Afrodisia: L'anima*, Rome and Bari: Laterza, 1996. (Italian translation, with commentary.)

—— *(fl. c.* AD 200) *On Intellect*, trans. in F.M. Schroeder and R.B. Todd, *Two Aristotelian Greek Commentators on the Intellect*, Toronto, Ont.: Pontifical Institute of Medieval Studies, 1990. (English translation, with commentary.)

—— *(fl. c.* AD 200) *On Fate*, in R.W. Sharples, *Alexander of Aphrodisias On Fate*, London: Duckworth, 1983; and in P. Thillet, *Alexandre d'Aphrodise: Traité du Destin*, Paris: Les Belle Lettres, 1984. (Sharples has Greek text reprinted from Bruns (1887–92), with English translation and commentary; Thillet has Greek text with French translation and introduction.)

—— *(fl. c.* AD 200) *On Mixture*, in R.B. Todd, *Alexander of Aphrodisias on Stoic Physics*, Leiden: Brill, 1976. (Greek text, with English translation and commentary.)

—— *(fl. c.* AD 200) *On Providence*, in H.-J. Ruland, *Die arabischen Fassungen zweier Schriften des Alexander von Aphrodisias* (Arabic Versions of Two Texts of Alexander of Aphrodisias), Saarbrücken: dissertation, 1976; and trans. S. Fazzo and M. Zonta, *Alessandro d'Afrodisia, Sulla Provvidenza*, Milan: Rizzoli, 1998. (Ruland has Arabic text, with German translation, introduction and appendices; Fazzo and Zonta, Italian translation with commentary.)

—— *(fl. c.* AD 200) *On the Principles of the Universe* and other works, trans. A. Badawi, in *La transmission de la philosophie grecque au monde arabe* (The Transmission of Greek Philosophy to the Arab World), Paris: Vrin, 1968. (French translations from the Arabic.)

References and further reading

Donini, P.L. (1974) *Tre studi sull' aristotelismo nel II secolo d.C.* (Three Studies of Aristotelianism in the Second Century AD), Turin: Paravia. (Discusses, in part 1, Alexander in relation to Neoplatonism and, in Part 3, Alexander on free will and determinism in the context especially of his psychology.)

* Frede, D. (1984) 'Could Paris (Son of Priam) Have Chosen Otherwise?', *Oxford Studies in Ancient Philosophy* 2: 279–92. (Compatibilist interpretation of Alexander; see §4.)

Hasnawi, A. (1994) 'Alexandre d'Aphrodise vs Jean Philopon: notes sur quelques traités d'Alexandre "perdus" en grec, conservés en arabe' (Alexander of Aphrodisias v. John Philoponus: Notes on Some of Alexander's Treatises, 'Lost' in Greek and Preserved in Arabic), *Arabic Sciences and Philosophy* 4: 53–109. (Corrects misattributions to Alexander.)

* Kessler, E. (1988) 'The Intellective Soul', in C.B. Schmitt and Q. Skinner (eds) *The Cambridge History of Renaissance Philosophy*, Cambridge: Cambridge University Press, 485–534. (Account of the Renaissance controversies referred to in §5.)

Lloyd, A.C. (1976) 'The Principle that the Cause is Greater Than its Effect', *Phronesis* 21: 146–56. (Discusses Alexander's use of this principle in connection with the active intellect; see §2.)

Merlan, P. (1967) 'Greek Philosophy from Plato to Plotinus', in A.H. Armstrong (ed.) *The Cambridge History of Later Greek and Early Medieval Philosophy*, Cambridge: Cambridge University Press, 117–23. (Sees Alexander very much as a precursor of Neoplatonism; see §5.)

Moraux, P. *et al.* (forthcoming) *Der Aristotelismus bei den Griechen* (Aristotelianism among the Greeks), vol. 3, ed. J. Wiesner, Berlin: de Gruyter. (Completed by others after Moraux's death, the definitive treatment of all aspects of Alexander's philosophy.)

* Pines, S. (1961) 'Omne quod movetur necesse est ab aliquo moveri' (Everything that is moved must necessarily be moved by something), *Isis* 52: 21–54; repr. in *Studies in Arabic Versions of Greek Texts and in Medieval Science*, Jerusalem: Magnes Press, and Leiden: Brill, 1986, 218–51. (In English. Definitive treatment of Alexander's contributions to dynamics and possible influence; see §1.)

Robinson, H. (1991) 'Form and the Immateriality of the Intellect from Aristotle to Aquinas', in H. Blumenthal and H. Robinson (eds) *Aristotle and the Later Tradition*, Oxford: Clarendon Press, 207–26. (Forceful criticism of both Alexander and modern scholars for alleged reductivist misinterpretation of Aristotle's theory of soul; see §2.)

Sharples, R.W. (1987) 'Alexander of Aphrodisias: Scholasticism and Innovation', in W. Haase (ed.) *Aufstieg und Niedergang der römischen Welt*, Berlin and New York: de Gruyter, II 36 2: 1, 176–243. (Full list of works attributed to Alexander, and more comprehensive discussion of the topics of the present article, with complete bibliography to 1986.)

—— (1990) 'The School of Alexander', in R. Sorabji (ed.) *Aristotle Transformed: The Ancient Commentators and Their Influence*, London: Duckworth, 83–111. (Discusses Alexander's relation to earlier philosophical tradition, the didactic context of the shorter works and their relation to the commentaries.)

* Taylor, R. (1967) 'Determinism', in P. Edwards (ed.) *Encyclopedia of Philosophy*, New York: Macmillan, vol. 2, 369. (A comprehensive general treatment of the free-will problem in all its aspects.)

Tweedale, M.M. (1984) 'Alexander of Aphrodisias' Views on Universals', *Phronesis* 29: 279–303. (A definitive discussion of the subject.)

Zimmermann, F.W. (1994) 'Proclus Arabus Rides Again', *Arabic Sciences and Philosophy* 4: 9–51. (Corrects misattributions to Alexander, and discusses the methods of the Arabic translators and adaptors.)

R.W. SHARPLES

ALEXANDER OF HALES (*c.*1185–1245)

Alexander's emphasis on speculative theology initiated the golden age of scholasticism. His philosophy was influenced by that of Aristotle, particularly in the field of ethics, and also by Augustine, Boethius and Peter Lombard. He believed that philosophy, based on natural reason, and theology, based on divine revelation, were two different disciplines and that philosophy ought to be independent of theology. He himself was primarily a theologian, and the colossal Summa Halesiana, *most of which was compiled under his direction, constitutes the first complete theological synthesis in the West.*

1 Life and influences
2 Works

1 Life and influences

Alexander of Hales, called *doctor irrefragabilis* (the invincible doctor), was born in the village of Hales in the county of Shropshire (possibly the present Halesowen, now in neighbouring Worcestershire) *circa* 1180–85. The son of a rich rural family, he studied at the University of Paris, where he became regent master first in the faculty of Arts and later in the faculty of Theology. In 1230, he represented the University as procurator at the Papal Curia. In 1231, he returned for a short while to England, where he was made canon of Lichfield and soon after archdeacon of Coventry. In 1235, he was one of King Henry III's deputies, charged with renewing the peace treaty between England and France.

During this period, however, he retained his chair at the University of Paris. In 1236, he renounced honours and riches and entered the Order of St Francis, but he remained a master of theology and continued teaching as regent master in the Franciscan friary in Paris, which was an integral part of the University. Alexander was the first Franciscan Master of Theology and the first to teach theology by lecturing on the *Sentences* of Peter LOMBARD. His most prominent disciples include BONAVENTURE, RICHARD RUFUS OF CORNWALL and JOHN OF LA ROCHELLE, to whom he resigned his chair in theology near the end of his life. Alexander died in Paris on 21 August 1245.

As a master of arts, Alexander was familiar with the logical works of Aristotle, and with Books II and III of the *Nicomachean Ethics*, the so-called *ethica vetus*. He accepted Aristotle's definition of virtue and some of his views on the passions. Again following Aristotle, Alexander distinguished voluntary acts, involuntary acts and acts resulting from ignorance, and held that certain acts are indubitably evil.

By contrast, Alexander's knowledge of the *Metaphysics*, *Physics* and *On the Soul* was scant and superficial. At the time he was studying and teaching in the faculty of Arts, the so-called *libri naturales* were not available in Latin translation, and when they became available their reading and teaching were forbidden in Paris for several years. Philosophically, Alexander is more closely related to AUGUSTINE and BOETHIUS than to Aristotle. He took from Augustine the distinction between natural, rational and moral philosophy, and from Boethius the distinction between nature and person and the view that all creatures are composed of essence (*quod est*) and existence (*quo est*). Most of the philosophical speculations in the *Summa Halesiana* must be attributed to Alexander's younger collaborators, John of La Rochelle, William of Militona and Odo Rigaldi, who had more thorough training in the philosophy of Aristotle.

2 Works

Alexander was, above all, a theologian. Though he believed that all philosophy begins with the principle of non-contradiction, he maintained that we must humble our minds in obedience to Christ and accept what appear to be contradictory statements if that is what faith requires (*Glossa* III d.24 FBS 14: 295). However, Alexander also supported the disciplinary separation of philosophy and theology which was to allow the independence of philosophy. He held that since philosophy is based on natural reason and theology on divine revelation, the two disciplines follow different paths and arrive at different levels of certitude.

Before 1945, none of Alexander's certainly authentic works were known. His fame and reputation rested entirely on the very extensive *Summa theologica* or *Summa Halesiana*, originally called the *Summa Fratris Alexandri*. However, the authenticity of this great work was a matter of debate among medievalists. This is partly because the Franciscan Roger BACON, Alexander's contemporary, suggested that others wrote the *Summa* and attributed it to Alexander out of reverence. Also, different parts seem to be by different redactors; they are not always consistent. Finally, the Summa borrows from the writings of contemporary or earlier authors. Nevertheless, it is now an established fact that the first three books (with the exception of some later additions) were composed before Alexander's death in 1245, very likely under his supervision, and the principal sources used were Alexander's own earlier writings. Therefore, even though the work is not, strictly speaking, a *Summa Fratris Alexandri*, it is correct to call it *Summa Halesiana*. The fourth book was finished after Alexander's death by William of Militona, who incorporated into it his own extensive and influential questions on the sacraments.

Later in his career as a master of theology, Alexander held many disputations on a variety of theological problems. The 68 questions he disputed before he became a Franciscan friar in 1236 have been edited; a further 78 questions, disputed later, still await editing.

Alexander's earliest known work, his commentary (*Glossa*) on books of the *Sentences* of Peter Lombard, was composed between 1223 and 1227. In the first book of the *Glossa*, there is a remarkable analysis of the mystery of the Trinity with subtle distinctions between properties, relations and notions (see TRINITY). In Book II, Alexander teaches how we can see the vestiges of the Creator in the created universe and the image of the Trinity in the rational soul, which is one simple substance endowed with intellect, will, and memory (Fornaro 1985) (see SOUL, NATURE AND IMMORTALITY OF). In Book III, the doctrine of the hypostatic union is impressive for both its range of interest and its originality. It surpasses earlier authors in the variety of topics it treats, the sophistication of its theological method and the profundity of its thought (Principe 1967). In the fourth book, on the seven sacraments of the Church, he reveals himself an accomplished canonist, quoting Gratian and the *Decretals* of Gregory IX hundreds of times.

According to Roger Bacon, Alexander was the first to introduce the four books of the *Sentences* of Peter Lombard as a textbook for the faculty of theology. It was Alexander who divided the books into 'distinctions', according to the principal problems treated. As divided by Alexander, the *Sentences* remained the basis of theological instruction for three centuries; hundreds of commentaries were written on it. Alexander of Hales fully deserves his reputation as one of the greatest theologians of the thirteenth century.

See also: ARISTOTELIANISM, MEDIEVAL; AUGUSTINIANISM; JOHN OF LA ROCHELLE; LOMBARD, P.; TRINITY

List of works

Alexander of Hales (1223–7) *Glossa in Quattuor Libros Sententiarum Petri Lombardi* (Commentary on the Four Books of *Sentences* of Peter Lombard), Bibliotheca Franciscana Scholastica Medii Aevi XII–XV, Quaracchi: Collegii S. Bonaventurae, 1951–57. (V. Doucet's prolegomenon to this edition

(XII: 7–130) contains all the information available about Alexander of Hales and his works.)
—— (before 1236) *Quaestiones disputatae* (Disputed Questions), Bibliotheca Franciscana Scholastica Medii Aevi IXI–XXI, Quaracchi: Collegii S. Bonaventurae, 1960. (Directed by V. Doucet, covers a variety of theological questions.)
—— (1241–42) *Expositio quattuor magistrorum super regulam Fratrum Minorum (1241-2)* (Commentary by Four Masters on the Rule of the Friars Minor), ed. L. Oliger, Rome: Edizione de 'Storia e Letteratura', 1950. (A commentary on the Franciscan Rule, written with others.)
—— (before 1245) *Summa Halesiana*, ed. as *Doctoris Irrefragabilis Alexandri de Hales Ordinis Minorum Summa Theologica*, vols I–III, Quaracchi: Collegii S. Bonaveturae, 1924-48. (The vast prolegomenon in Librum III necnon in Libros I et II *Summae Fratris Alexandri* is a work of extraordinary erudition, a mine of information about scholastic authors in the first half of the thirteenth century.)

References and further reading

Bacon, Roger (1268) *Opus Minus*, ed. J.S. Brewer, Rerum Britannicarum Medii Aevi Scriptores 15, London: Longman, Green, Longman & Roberts, 1859: 325–29. (An important source for Alexander's life and works).
Boehner, P. (1945) 'The System of Metaphysics of Alexander of Hales', *Franciscan Studies* 5: 366–414. (Based on the *Summa Halesiana*.)
Doucet, V. (1947) 'The History of the Problem of the Authenticity of the Summa', *Franciscan Studies* 7: 26–41, 274–312. (See especially pages 310–12. Doucet was the foremost recent authority on Alexander and chief editor of his works.)
* Fornaro, I. (1985) *La Teologia dell'Imagine nella Glossa di Alessandro d'Hales* (The Image of God in Creation According to Alexander of Hales' *Glossa*), Vicenza: Edizione L.I.E.F. (The possibility of learning about God on the basis of creation.)
Gössmann, E. (1964) *Metaphysik und Heilsgeschichte. Eine theologische Untersuchung der Summa Halesiana* (Metaphysics and the Doctrine of Salvation: A Theological Examination of the *Summa Halesiana*), Munich: Max Huber Verlag. (A modern version of Boehner's study, which includes a full bibliography.)
* William of Militona [Guillelmi de Militona] (c.1245–60) *Quaestiones de Sacramentis* (Questions on the Sacraments), ed. C. Piana and G. Gál, Bibliotheca Franciscana Scholastica Medii Aevi XXII–XXIII, Quaracchi: Collegii S. Bonaventurae, 1961. (Militona finished the fourth part of the *Summa Halesiana*, using his own *Quaestiones de Sacramentis*.)
Herscher, I. (1945) 'A Bibliography of Alexander of Hales', *Franciscan Studies* 5: 434–54. (An extensive bibliography of editions, books and articles in different languages.)
Osborne, K.B. (1994) 'Alexander of Hales: Precursor and Promoter of Franciscan Theology', in *The History of Franciscan Theology*, St Bonaventure, NY: The Franciscan Institute, 1–38. (A survey of Alexander's life, works and contribution to the field of theology.)
* Principe, W.H. (1967) *The Theology of Hypostatic Union in the Early Thirteenth Century*, Vol. II, *Alexander of Hales' Theology of Hypostatic Union*, Toronto, Ont.: Pontifical Institute of Mediaeval Studies. (An excellent exposition of Alexander's Christology).

GEDEON GÁL

ALGAZEL see AL-GHAZALI, ABU HAMID

ALHAZEN see IBN HAZM, ABU MUHAMMAD 'ALI

ALIENATION

'Alienation' is a prominent term in twentieth-century social theory and social criticism, referring to any of various social or psychological evils which are characterized by a harmful separation, disruption or fragmentation which sunders things that properly belong together. People are alienated from one another when there is an interruption in their mutual affection or reciprocal understanding; they are alienated from political processes when they feel separated from them and powerless in relation to them. Reflection on your beliefs or values can also alienate you from them by undermining your attachment to them or your identification with them; they remain your beliefs or values faute de mieux, *but are no longer yours in the way they should be. Alienation translates two distinct German terms:* Entfremdung *('estrangement') and* En-Entaußerung *('externalization'). Both terms originated in the philosophy of Hegel, specifically in his* Phenomenology of Spirit *(1807). Their influence, however, has come chiefly from their use by Karl Marx*

in his manuscripts of 1844 (first published in 1930). Marx's fundamental concern was with the alienation of wage labourers from their product, the grounds of which he sought in the alienated form of their labouring activity. In both Hegel and Marx, alienation refers fundamentally to a kind of activity in which the essence of the agent is posited as something external or alien, assuming the form of hostile domination over the agent.

1   Hegel
2   Feuerbach
3   Marx
4   The alienation of labour
5   Alienation in the later Marx
6   Alienation and meaningful life

1   Hegel

Hegel's philosophy regards all reality as *Geist*, or 'spirit' or 'mind'; Hegel's concept of spirit is at the same time a model of the human mind and human agency. It views mind or spirit as an activity which posits a reality or object distinct from itself and then for the first time achieves actuality as spirit by knowing this object as itself. Spirit is therefore a twofold activity, of creation or self-expression and of the reconciling self-interpretation of what it has created. The process through which spirit actualizes itself therefore involves an intermediate moment of 'division' (*Entzweiung*) in which its objectivity has been posited as external to it but has not yet been reconciled or taken back into it. The immediate positing of the object is 'externalization' (*Entaußerung*); the experience of it as an alien reality is 'estrangement' (*Entfremdung*). Thus spirit achieves full actuality only through becoming alienated and then overcoming its alienation. Spirit is this process not only at the level of individual activity but even more so at a social level. Alienation and its overcoming are a process through which whole societies, peoples and historical traditions actualize freedom by expressing themselves in otherness, losing themselves through alienation and then regaining themselves through spiritual reconciliation (see HEGEL, G.W.F. §8).

Hegel's chief use of the theme of alienation in *Phenomenology of Spirit* (1807) is to represent the rise of Christian culture out of classical antiquity as 'spirit in self-alienation' and to portray modernity as the process of overcoming this alienation. For Hegel, the paradigm of alienation is the 'unhappy consciousness', the finite, transitory, individual consciousness which feels itself cut off from its essence, which it posits in a perfect, unchanging deity residing in a 'beyond'. Or in other words, it is a form of misunderstood Christian religiosity which still has not achieved the form of Hegelian speculative pantheism. But the unhappy consciousness is merely the expression at the level of self-consciousness of a social process. 'Spirit in self-alienation' refers primarily to the loss of the social harmony which was present in the Greek *polis*, and its replacement by the supranational despotism of the Roman Empire. Because individuals no longer feel at home in their earthly society, they regard their true home as lying in a 'beyond', a 'kingdom of God'. The positive outcome of this process, however, is a deepening and transformation of individual self-consciousness through the rise of 'subjectivity': the modern conception of each individual as possessing a dignity, and of the social order as having to respect its sacred rights. Modern subjectivity also involves a transformation of the social order. As the religious alienation of the Christian Middle Ages gives way to modern moral consciousness, the right of the individual is reconciled with rational community in the form of the modern state. For Hegel, the decisive event on the spiritual level was the Lutheran Reformation; on the political level it was the French Revolution.

2   Feuerbach

Hegel's concept of alienation (although less often the term itself) is employed in Ludwig Feuerbach's critique of religion (see FEUERBACH, L.A. §2). According to Feuerbach, the idea of God is really no more than the idea of our own human essence or species essence (*Gattungswesen*) projected as a supernatural entity distinct from and opposed to us. Thus for Feuerbach, religion is the 'self-alienation of the human being, the division of the human being from himself'. The real appeal of religion is the appeal of our own self-affirmation, especially our collective or species affirmation, the appeal of a true human community and human love. But in religion this love and affirmation are actually subverted and denied, because they are misdirected toward an imaginary being alien to us. 'To enrich God, man must become poor; that God may be all, man must be nothing.' Feuerbach's critique of religious alienation is also aimed at its harmful moral and social consequences: the devaluation of our earthly wellbeing and of earthly (especially sexual) love in favour of its alienated religious counterpart, and the separation of men and women from each other in the strife of religious sectarianism and the oppressive class divisions in society. The overcoming of religious alienation is for Feuerbach the prerequisite for a transformation of real life.

179

3 Marx

Karl MARX used the concepts of *Entaußerung* and *Entfremdung* to portray the situation of modern individuals – especially modern wage labourers – who are deprived of a fulfilling mode of life because their life activity as socially productive agents is devoid of any sense of communal action or satisfaction and gives them no ownership over their own lives or their products. In modern society, individuals are alienated in so far as their common human essence, the actual cooperative activity which naturally unites them, is powerless in their lives, which are subject to an inhuman power – created by them, but separating and dominating them instead of being subject to their united will. This is the power of the market, which is 'free' in the sense that it is an autonomous power beyond the control of its human creators, enslaving them by separating them from one another, from their activity and from their products.

4 The alienation of labour

In the manuscript *Alienated Labour* (1844), Marx attempts to portray the social existence of human beings found in modern capitalism, and theorized by political economy, as a form of practical alienation. He distinguishes four aspects of this alienation:

(1) alienation of workers from the product of their labour;
(2) alienation of workers from their own labouring activity;
(3) alienation of individual human beings from their species essence;
(4) alienation of one human being from another.

(1) The natural relation between labour and its product is one of appropriation: labour appropriates its product for the labourer. Alienated labour, however, delivers the worker's product over to an alien power, the power of capital, which not only appropriates the worker's product but also turns it into an alien power over him. 'The object which labour produces stands opposed to it as an *alien thing*, as a *power independent* of the producer.' Further, the more workers produce, the larger grows the power of capital over them, and the more value accrues to this inhuman power, the more valueless the worker becomes. 'The worker becomes poorer the more wealth he produces.... The *increase* in the *value* of the world of things is directly proportional to the *decrease in value* of the human world.'

(2) Marx seeks the root of this relationship and locates it in the labouring activity itself. 'How could the worker stand in an alien relationship to the product of his activity if he did not alienate himself from it in the very act of production?... If the product of work is externalization, production itself must be active externalization, externalization of activity, activity of externalization.' This may be seen as the first anticipation of Marx's materialist conception of history: social and economic relationships always depend ultimately on the productive powers people employ, hence on the kind of labour they perform. But for Marx, alienated activity refers also to the fact that modern labour in factories is dehumanizing to workers, not actualizing their humanity but stunting and warping it. The lives of wage labourers are without meaning.

(3) The objective possibility for meaningful life present in all forms of social labour is that individuals confirm their humanity by contributing to the satisfaction of human needs, not only their own but even more the needs of the species. Alienated labour is meaningless labour because its conscious aim takes the egoistic form of satisfying individual needs, which for the worker are reduced to the barest conditions of physical survival. 'Life itself appears only as a *means of life*'; workers labour only to sustain the absurd cycle of their existence. By 'making species life the means of individual life' alienated labour reverses the natural relationship between the two and hence alienates individuals from their own species essence. Since Marx regards the relation of each human being to the human species as its relation to nature, he also includes under this heading the alienation of human beings from nature, 'the inorganic body of the human species'.

(4) Finally, alienated labour alienates human beings from one another by making another human being the owner of their product, hence constituting one human being as an alien power over another human being. At the point where the *Alienated Labour* breaks off, Marx is in the process of comparing this relationship to Hegel's famous 'master–servant' dialectic in *Phenomenology*.

5 Alienation in the later Marx

The 'theory' of alienation sketched in this early fragment is Marx's first recognizable attempt to articulate the complex interconnections he sees between the various ills and irrationalities characteristic of modern industrial society. Like Hegel, the early Marx views alienation as a phase of a developmental process leading to human self-actualization. 'Alienation is founded in the essence of human development.' Yet Marx was already breaking away from Hegel and the entire 'Young Hegelian' movement (represented by Feuerbach and

Marx's teacher Bruno Bauer (see BAUER, B. §1). In his view, they located the essence of alienation in a certain kind of *consciousness*, and believed that a practical reform of the social world must follow a reform in ideas, led by philosophers. In contrast to this, Marx maintained that alienation was fundamentally a matter of social practice, and that alienated forms of consciousness (such as religion) are merely a symptom of alienated activity. They can be abolished only by abolishing the alienation in real life.

Both the term 'alienation' (*Entfremdung*) and the concept (expressed in other terms) continue to play a prominent role in Marx's mature writings, especially in the *Grundrisse* (1857–8) and *Capital* (1867, 1884, 1894). But their function has changed. The philosophical concept of alienation is no longer viewed as fundamental to a systematic explanation of capitalism; it is now employed descriptively or diagnostically to characterize some of the evils and irrationalities of the system.

6 Alienation and meaningful life

The German verbs *entaußern* and *entfremden* are often reflexive, and for Marx, as for Hegel and Feuerbach, alienation is fundamentally *self*-alienation. To be alienated is to be separated from one's own essence or nature; it is to be forced to lead a life in which that nature has no opportunity to be fulfilled or actualized. In this way, the experience of alienation involves a sense of a lack of self-worth and an absence of meaning in one's life.

Alienation in this sense is not fundamentally a matter of whether your conscious desires are satisfied, or how you experience your life, but rather whether your life objectively actualizes your nature, especially your life with others as a social being on the basis of a determinate course of historical development. The view that alienation, so conceived, can nevertheless have historical consequences, and even be a lever for social change, clearly involves some sort of realism about the human good: it makes a difference, psychologically and socially, whether people actualize their nature, and when they do not, this fact explains what they think, feel and do, and can play a decisive role in historical change.

See also: MARXISM, WESTERN §2

References and further reading

Feuerbach, L. (1841) *The Essence of Christianity*, trans. M. Evans, New York: Harper & Row, 1957. (Feuerbach's famous critique of human alienation in the Christian religion.)

—— (1843) *Principles of the Philosophy of the Future*, trans. M. Vogel, Indianapolis, IN: Bobbs-Merrill, 1966. (The chief text of Feuerbach in which the term alienation is explicitly employed.)

Geuss, R. (1981) *The Idea of a Critical Theory*, Cambridge: Cambridge University Press. (An excellent critical discussion of the kind of social theory in which the concept of alienation figures.)

* Hegel, G.W.F. (1807) *Phenomenology of Spirit*, trans. A.V. Miller, Oxford: Oxford University Press, 1977. (Chapters IV, VI B and VII C contain the chief historical sources of the concept of alienation.)

* Marx, K. (1857–8) *Grundrisse der Kritik der politischen Ökonomie*, trans. M. Nicholas, *Grundrisse*, Harmondsworth: Penguin, 1973. (An abandoned draft on political economy – superseded by *Das Kapital*.)

* —— (1867, 1884, 1894) *Capital*, 3 vols, trans. B. Foulkes, Harmondsworth: Penguin, 1977. (Marx's mature masterpiece.)

Marx, K. and Engels, F. (1975–) *Collected Works*, New York: International Publishing Co. (Volume 3 contains the principal texts which discuss alienation.)

Ollman, B. (1976) *Alienation*, Cambridge: Cambridge University Press, 2nd edn. (A widely-known philosophical discussion of Marx's concept of alienation.)

Meszaros, I. (1972) *Marx's Theory of Alienation*, New York: Harper & Row. (An attempt to reconstruct the early Marx's theory of alienation as the foundation of his thought.)

Plamenatz, J. (1975) *Karl Marx's Philosophy of Man*, Oxford: Oxford University Press. (A thoughtful critical appraisal of Marx, emphasizing the theme of alienation.)

Wood, A. (1981) *Karl Marx*, London: Routledge. (Chapters I–IV contain an account of alienation.)

ALLEN W. WOOD

ALIGHIERI, DANTE (1265–1321)

Although Dante never received a systematic training in philosophy, he tackled some of the most controversial philosophical problems of his time. In his theory of science, he asked how we are to explain the fact that science is a unified, strictly ordered system of knowledge. He answered by comparing the scientific disciplines with the celestial spheres, claiming that the system of knowledge mirrors the cosmological order. In his political philosophy, he asked why all humans want to live in a peaceful society. All humans seek full use of their cognitive capacity, was his answer, and they can achieve it only if they interact socially. In his philosophy of nature, Dante asked what brings about the order of the elements, and suggested that the elements obey the laws of a universal nature in a strictly ordered cosmos. He elaborated all his answers in a scholastic framework that made use of both Aristotelian and Neoplatonic traditions.

1 Philosophical works and intellectual background
2 Scope and division of philosophy
3 Political philosophy
4 Natural philosophy

1 Philosophical works and intellectual background

Dante Alighieri, best known as the author of the poetic work *Divina Commedia* (Divine Comedy), was not only one of the most influential Italian poets but was also a scholastic philosopher, perceived and praised by his earliest commentators such as Marsilio FICINO as a 'poetic philosopher'. Three distinctively philosophical works of Dante's have been transmitted: the *Convivio* (The Banquet), a philosophical symposium that addresses all who strive for knowledge but lack higher education; *Monarchia* (The Monarchy), a treatise on political philosophy that aims to prove the need for a universal monarchy; and the *Questio de aqua et terra* (Question on Water and Earth), a short work in natural philosophy that discusses the order among the elements. Since no medieval manuscript of this work is known (it has been preserved in an early printed edition), its authenticity has been disputed. In addition, the first part of his treatise *De vulgari eloquentia* (On Eloquence in the Vernacular), dealing with the origin and function of language, includes important semantic theses, and in a long letter addressed to Cangrande della Scala, Dante expounds his hermeneutic principles.

Unlike the overwhelming majority of medieval philosophers, Dante was never a member of a monastery or a university and never received a systematic training in philosophy. Rather, he was a layman (*laicus*) in the medieval dual sense of the word: neither a clergyman nor a professional intellectual. He acquired his philosophical knowledge, as he confesses in an autobiographical passage (*Convivio* II, xii, 5), by frequenting the 'disputations of the philosophizing people' in Florence (probably in the Franciscan school of Santa Croce and in the Dominican school of Santa Maria Novella) between 1291 and 1295. He may have furthered his education during a stay in Paris (1310). However, his knowledge remained eclectic. He appears to have been more influenced by a reading of anthologies and texts by popular philosophical authors (such as Brunetto Latini) than by a systematic study of ARISTOTLE and contemporary philosophers.

2 Scope and division of philosophy

Dante confesses (*Convivio* II, xii, 1–10) that after the death of Beatrice (the beloved woman who became Dante's guide in the Paradise, the third part of the *Divina Commedia*) in 1290, he could not find consolation until he started reading philosophical books. CICERO, BOETHIUS and other classical authors helped him overcome his grief. He discovered that philosophy is a 'noble lady' (*donna gentile*):

> Only in glancing at her does one acquire human perfection, that is the perfection of reason, on which depends our essence as on its most fundamental part. And all our other activities, such as perceiving and nourishing, are founded upon reason. But reason exists through herself and not through something else. If reason is perfect, she is so perfect that a human being qua human being realizes that his desire is satisfied in her. And so a human is happy.
>
> (*Convivio* III, xv, 4)

This passage is not just a literary *topos* that alludes to Boethius' presentation of Lady Philosophy in the *De consolatione philosophiae* (Consolation of Philosophy). It is also deeply rooted in the Aristotelian dictum that all human beings naturally seek knowledge – Dante opens both the *Convivio* and *Monarchia* with this famous statement – and that humans find happiness only if they satisfy their intellectual needs. Moreover, Dante's praise of intellectual activity betrays his acquaintance with certain late thirteenth-century authors sometimes labelled 'radical Aristotelians', such as BOETHIUS OF DACIA and Aubry of Reims (see AVERROISM). These Parisian masters claimed that philosophy is autonomous and should not be subordinated to any other discipline, in particular not to theology, because it provides humans with all the knowledge required for obtaining happiness. Since humans are essentially rational animals, they fully realize their capacities if they dedicate themselves to the most rational activity, philosophy.

Dante conceives of philosophy – 'philosophy' taken synonymously with 'science' (*scientia*) – as a unified system of knowledge that can be hierarchically divided. He explains the order by comparing these disciplines with the celestial spheres. There are at least three reasons, he claims, for making such a comparison (*Convivio* II, xiii, 3–6). First, every science moves around its subject, just as a celestial sphere turns around its immovable centre. Second, every science makes its subject clear and understandable, just as a celestial sphere illumines the things around which it turns. Third, every science leads to a certain perfection by structuring and explaining things, just as a celestial sphere improves things by keeping them in order and moving them. Not only is there, according to Dante, an analogy between science as a whole and the celestial spheres, but one can even attribute a specific science to each of the nine celestial spheres. There is a correspondence between each of the first seven spheres (Moon, Mercury, Venus, Sun, Mars, Jupiter and Saturn) and each of the seven liberal arts (grammar, logic, rhetoric, arithmetic, music, geometry and astrology). Physics and mathematics, dealing with innumerably many entities, correspond to the eighth sphere that consists of innumerable fixed stars. Finally, moral philosophy (including both ethics and political philosophy) corresponds to the ninth, so-called 'crystalline sphere', because moral philosophy enables humans to study all the other sciences just as this ninth unmoved sphere moves all the other spheres.

Not only does Dante believe, as did many medieval philosophers of science (for example, Robert KILWARDBY), that philosophy (or science) is a unified, strictly ordered system of knowledge, but he also claims that the scientific system mirrors the cosmological system (see NATURAL PHILOSOPHY, MEDIEVAL). Whereas he follows the traditional scheme in his ordering of the seven liberal arts, he deliberately deviates from tradition in his claim that moral philosophy and not metaphysics, usually taken as 'first philosophy', is the highest scientific discipline. Although it is important to know, in the Aristotelian framework of metaphysics, what being *qua* being and its principles are, this is not the highest goal in philosophy. One obtains perfect knowledge, Dante claims, only if one is aware of the principles leading to a good life. That is why 'morality is the beauty of philosophy' (*Convivio* III, xv, 11). When one takes this important claim into account, it becomes clear why Dante emphatically holds that human happiness is to be sought through philosophy. Since moral philosophy, the culmination of every scientific activity, enables humans to recognize the principles governing a good life in a peaceful community, humans must philosophize if they want to attain such a life (see HAPPINESS).

3 Political philosophy

In the *Monarchia*, a treatise that is highly scholastic in both style and content, Dante aims to show first, that a universal monarchy is necessary for a peaceful community of humans, second, that the Roman nation legitimately acquired its hegemony over all other nations, and third, that the power of the Roman emperor is not subordinate to that of the pope. Thus the main purpose of the work is clearly political and has to be understood in the light of the late medieval controversies over mundane and spiritual power (notably those between King Philip the Fair of France and Pope Boniface VIII). Yet in his defence of the Roman emperor, Dante makes a rich use of philosophical arguments, often going beyond the concrete political context. This becomes clear from his discussion of the principle governing human behaviour, a principle that underlies all his political theses, as he explicitly says (*Monarchia*, I, ii, 8).

Dante starts his search for such a principle by asking why humans want to live in a community. Following the Aristotelian tradition, he gives a teleological answer; all humans have certain goals they want to obtain. However, unlike most medieval authors in the Aristotelian tradition, he claims that there is not only a goal for each individual, each household and each city, but also a goal for the entire human species. This goal is to be attained only through an activity of the entire species. Such an activity consists in all realization of the 'possible' intellect (*Monarchia* I, iii, 8), that is, in an exhaustive development of one's cognitive capacity. An isolated person, limited in activity, is never able to achieve such development, which requires one's integration into a peaceful community in which all humans participate.

It is remarkable and original in the medieval context that Dante uses an epistemological argument to justify his political theory. Neither a natural order established by God, nor a need for protection, nor a need for exchanging goods and making contracts is the main reason for which humans want to live in a peaceful community. Rather, the main reason is an intellectual need; humans want to use their cognitive capacity. Following ARISTOTLE, Dante claims that this capacity is nothing other than the possible intellect that is 'realized', or put to active use, when it receives the forms of the cognized things. But, unlike Aristotle, he does not take the use of this intellect to be a mere individual operation; and, contrary to some radical Aristotelians (for example, Boethius of Dacia or SIGER OF BRABANT), he does not hold that every person is an autonomous cognizer, capable of acquiring all possible knowledge through an individual contemplation of the highest principles. Nor does he make the controversial Averroistic claim, as his first critics (such as Guido Vernani) complained, that there is just one possible intellect for all humans, so that every individual would be dependent upon this all-embracing intellect. Rather, Dante holds that every person has an individual possible intellect; but one can make full use of one's own possible intellect only if one is a member of a peaceful community. Thus, social interaction is a *sine qua non* for successful cognitive activity (see POLITICAL PHILOSOPHY, HISTORY OF).

4 Natural philosophy

In the *Questio*, a written record of a scholastic debate, Dante (if indeed the text was written by him) raises the question of how the elements water and earth are related to each other. Which element has a higher location, water or earth? At first sight, this question seems puzzling or even pointless. Is it not obvious that there are some places (such as the mountains) where earth is higher, and others (such as the sea) where water is higher? But considered from a medieval point of view, the question points to a serious problem. According to the geocentric model that was strongly influenced by the Euclidean theory of spheres, the terrestrial world is located in the middle of a spherical cosmos and consists of four spherically ordered elements: earth, water, air and fire. The element water completely surrounds and covers the element earth, located in the middle of all the spheres. Thus we are confronted with a conflict between the common sense view that there is no fixed order among the elements, and the theoretical view that there must be a strict order according to the spherical model.

In light of this conflict, it is not surprising that the question raised by Dante was a prominent puzzle in medieval philosophy of nature (Duhem 1958: 79–235). Dante tried to resolve this dilemma by introducing a distinction between two kinds of nature. The 'universal nature' is present in the celestial spheres and determines the movement of all terrestrial things. The 'particular nature', on the other hand, is present in each terrestrial thing and makes it tend toward the place it is suited for. So, according to the particular nature, inherent in the elements, earth tends toward the middle of all elements and is completely covered by water. However, the universal nature is able to influence and change this tendency so that there can be some dry places (the so-called 'habitable parts') where earth emerges from water and, therefore, has a higher location than water (*Questio* 49). Dante claims that this general nature is to be found in the eighth sphere, the 'crystalline sphere' (*Questio* 69).

This explanation allows Dante to maintain the geocentric spherical model without rejecting the common sense view. It also allows him to avoid the solution suggested by earlier authors such as Andalò del Negro, that the two spheres (earth and water) may not be concentric. Such a solution would threaten the entire cosmological model. If there is no concentricity, neither is there any guarantee that all the spheres – and not just one element – will revolve around the earth. While insisting on the concentric order, Dante introduces a distinction between two kinds of nature that betrays a Neoplatonic background: God, the first cause of everything, created the celestial spheres, which act as secondary causes. Thus the cosmos is taken to be a strictly ordered, closed system in which the place and movement of every singular thing or element can be explained in terms of its dependency on certain causes (see NATURAL PHILOSOPHY, MEDIEVAL).

See also: COSMOLOGY; LANGUAGE, MEDIEVAL THEORIES OF (§17); NATURAL PHILOSOPHY, MEDIEVAL; POLITICAL PHILOSOPHY, HISTORY OF

List of works

Alighieri, Dante (1265–1321) *Opere minori* (Minor Work), ed. C. Vasoli *et al.*, Milan: R. Ricciardi, 1979–84. (Authoritative edition of all Dante's philosophical works with extensive commentaries. *Philosophische Werke*, ed. R. Imbach, Hamburg: F. Meiner, 1993–, is a bilingual edition with extensive commentaries focusing on philosophical aspects.)

—— (1304–7) *Convivio* (The Banquet), ed. C. Vasoli and D. de Robertis, *Opere minori* I.2, Milan: R. Ricciardi, 1988. (Philosophical symposium including an extensive discussion of problems in the theory of science.)

—— (c.1305) *De vulgari eloquentia* (On Eloquence in the Vernacular), ed. P.V. Mengaldo, *Opere minori* II, Milan: R. Ricciardi, 1979, 26–237. (Treatise on the origin and function of natural languages.)

—— (1310–7) *Monarchia* (The Monarchy), ed. B. Nardi, *Opere minori* II, Milan: R. Ricciardi, 1979, 280–503. (Treatise on political philosophy that makes original use of Aristotelian psychology.)

—— (before 1321) *Questio de aqua et terra* (Question on Water and Earth), ed. F. Mazzoni, *Opere minori* II, Milan: R. Ricciardi, 1979, 744–73. (Based on a disputation held in Verona in 1320; short scholastic text that discusses the order among the elements.)

References and further reading

Bosco, U. (1970–8) *Enciclopedia Dantesca* (Dante Encyclopedia), Rome: Istituto della Enciclopedia Italiana, 6 vols. (Most comprehensive presentation, including many articles dealing with philosophical aspects of Dante's work.)

Boyde, P. (1981) *Dante Philomythes and Philosopher, Man in the Cosmos*, Cambridge: Cambridge University Press. (Detailed study of Dante's natural philosophy and cosmology with an extensive analysis of the scholastic background.)

—— (1993) *Perception and Passion in Dante's Comedy*, Cambridge: Cambridge University Press. (Study focusing on Dante's philosophy of mind and epistemology.)

Corti, M. (1983) *La felicità mentale. Nuove prospettive per Cavalcanti e Dante* (Intellectual Happiness: New Perspectives on Cavalcanti and Dante), Turin: Einaudi. (Study focusing on Dante's praise of the philosopher's life; challenging theses about the origin and medieval background of this attitude.)

* Duhem, P. (1958) *Le système du monde. Histoire des doctrines cosmologiques de Platon à Copernic* (The System of the World: A History of Cosmological Doctrines from Plato to Copernicus), vol. 9, Paris: Hermann. (Pioneer study of the ancient and medieval background of the problem discussed in the *Questio*.)

Gilson, E. (1939) *Dante et la philosophie* (Dante and Philosophy), Paris: J. Vrin. (Pioneering study that provides a detailed interpretation of all philosophical works.)

Imbach, R. (1989) *Laien in der Philosophie des Mittelalters* (Laymen in Medieval Philosophy), Amsterdam: B.R. Grüner. (Important study of Dante's social and intellectual context and his definition of philosophy.)

* Ficino, M. (1433–99) *Prohemia sopra la Monarchia* (Commentary on the *Monarchia*), ed. P.A. Shaw in 'La versione ficiniana della "Monarchia"', *Studi danteschi* 51, 1978: 277–408. (Late fifteenth-century commenary on the *Monarchia*, presenting Dante as a 'poetic philosopher'.)

Nardi, B. (1967) *Saggi di filosofia dantesca* (Essays in Medieval Philosophy), Florence: La Nuova Italia. (Provocative essays dealing with a variety of philosophical problems, taking into account both the distinctively philosophical and the literary works.)

—— (1985) *Dante e la cultura medievale* (Dante and Medieval Culture), ed. P. Mazantini, Bari/Rome: Laterza. (A collection of important essays focusing on epistemology, theories of language and the soul.)

DOMINIK PERLER

ALISON, ARCHIBALD (1757–1839)

Archibald Alison was born in Edinburgh but was educated at Balliol and ordained in the Church of England. He returned to Edinburgh in 1800 as an Anglican clergyman and served there until his death. His published works included collections of sermons, but he is best known for his Essays on the Nature and Principles of Taste. *This work was published in 1790, the same year as Immanuel Kant's third Critique; but it became popular only after a second edition appeared in 1811.*

Archibald Alison, Anglican clergyman, born in 1757 in Edinburgh, broke with earlier eighteenth-century theorists of taste in two respects. He denied that taste is a product of an internal sense, and he described the emotion of taste as complex rather than simple. Earlier theorists had developed taste using the analogy of sense perception. The exact nature of this sense varied. In some cases it was taken quite literally; in others, it was little more than a convenient analogy. In general, however, an internal sense was a reflexive, immediate response of the mind to qualities presented by objects. Alison abandoned such a sense altogether. Instead, the emotions of taste are the product of mental operations to which the mind contributes and in which the mind discovers its own qualities. Such emotions are inherently complex. Alison reasoned that if a simple perceptual quality such as colour were the source of an emotion of taste, that emotion would always accompany perceptions of colour. Such is not the case. Only when the mind operates on the perception in a certain way does the emotion of pleasure identified with taste occur.

In place of a simple emotion and an internal sense, Alison introduced expression, imagination, and association as the key aesthetic terms. Imagination is a faculty which acts upon simple emotions. It suggests other images which are not directly present but which share the emotional qualities of the perception. The emotional links themselves are formed by association. So both imagination and association are necessary conditions for emotions of taste. When, in addition, the emotions are expressive of qualities of mind, one has emotions of taste – what Immanuel KANT and later theorists came to call aesthetic emotions. Alison projected the following schema: natural objects are suited to produce simple emotions; those simple emotions are extended by association and take on qualities of mind (for example tenderness); the imagination is the faculty which accomplishes this extension. When the imaginative associations are unified throughout an occasion, the result will be a special emotion of taste – either beauty or sublimity, depending on the emotion. Pleasure always accompanies this extension.

Alison went substantially beyond earlier theorists in the way that he developed expressiveness as a quality of mind and in the way that he used association. Earlier eighteenth-century theorists, including Joseph PRIESTLEY, Alexander GERARD, and Thomas REID, all spoke of a certain kind of mental exertion as intrinsically pleasurable and thus as a key element in taste. They were thinking of a physiological phenomenon, however. Strong, violent mental exertion could not produce the calm passions of beauty, but neither could a too languid mental operation. The emotions of taste were conceived of as belonging to the middle range – neither too strong, nor too mild. Alison, on the other hand, thought not of the exertion of the mind, but of qualities which, through association, became expressive of the mind's own powers. A natural quality becomes beautiful by acquiring mental associations.

Alison's theory of association is also substantially different as a consequence. Earlier theories of association, particularly that of David HARTLEY, sought to account for how the mind could produce ideas in the absence of immediate experience. The function of association was thus to extend experience and to provide a mechanism for the recall and production of mental images. Hartley's account is strongly mechanistic, for example. Alison used association differently. By itself, a colour would produce no emotion, he reasoned. But association connects perception with other experiences so that the emotional qualities of the complex are produced by the perception as well. So red can be exciting, white pure, and so forth. Association brings together disparate images and ideas into a complex which has emotional consequences. Its faculty is imagination, and its consequence is expression. Beauty is the complex result of a kind of associative network. These associations give rise to a multitude of predicates, and Alison made extensive use of language as an indicator of what emotional associations a particular kind of perception had acquired.

Alison distinguished natural from relative beauty. Natural beauty arises from the associations the mind forms in its direct encounters with the world. Alison's paradigms for natural beauty are scenery and gardens. Relative beauty depends on associations which suggest a fitness and utility; it includes design, skill, and art. Thus Alison established an implicit hierarchy, in which art is secondary to nature as an aesthetic source. Design, fitness, and utility presuppose a mental order and a mind, so they are expressive and beautiful. But their expressiveness depends on complex emotions such as tenderness, grandeur, and majesty, which are first inspired by the imagination acting on natural scenes. The common feature is that both produce a special form of pleasure, which Alison, like Kant, called delight.

Alison continued a century-old tradition of speculation about taste and beauty along empiricist lines. He shared with that tradition a reliance on experience and an attempt to classify and codify elements of experience into a theory of beauty. Alison extended that empiricism in a significant way, however. His analysis relies on language, particularly emotive predicates. Association is based on similarity – which may be perceptual or metaphorical, but is always created by the mind itself. The imagination becomes a creative faculty, and aesthetic theory is less concerned with standards and epistemological questions than with the production of emotion. Alison remained a moralist. Nature, not art, is the source of emotion, and nature is God's handiwork, not ours. But it is a short step from Alison's forms of imagination and expressiveness to that of the Romantics who use many of the same terms. The aesthetic ground has shifted substantially.

See also: EMOTION IN RESPONSE TO ART; TASTE, ARTISTIC

List of works

Alison, A. (1790) *Essays on the Nature and Principles of Taste*, London. (Alison's principal work went through a number of editions in the nineteenth century, but there is no modern reprint.)

References and further reading

Dickie, G. (1974) *Art and the Aesthetic: An Institutional Analysis*, Ithaca, NY: Cornell University Press. (In the first part of his theory, Dickie traces the rise of the concept of aesthetic experience and rejects Stolnitz's interpretation of Alison.)

Hipple, W. (1957) *The Beautiful, the Sublime, and the Picturesque in Eighteenth-century British Aesthetic Theory*, Carbondale, IL: Southern Illinois University Press.

Kant, I. (1790) *Kritik der Urteilskraft*, Berlin: Lagarde; trans. J.C. Meredith, as *Critique of Aesthetic Judgement*, Oxford: Clarendon Press, 1911; repr. as *Kant's Critique of Judgement*, trans. J.C. Meredith, Oxford: Clarendon Press, 1952. (Kant's *Critique of Judgement* is his primary critical treatment of aesthetic issues. It is the third and final of Kant's

Critiques, in which he integrates the realms of theory and value, both aesthetic and moral.)

Kivy, P. (1976) *The Seventh Sense*, New York: Franklin. (Traces the concept of internal sense through eighteenth-century aesthetics.)

McCosh, J. (1875) *The Scottish Philosophy* New York: Carter; repr. Bristol: Thoemmes, 1990; New York: AMS Press, 1980. (Brief biographical sketch and commentary.)

Stolnitz, J. (1961) 'On the Origins of Aesthetic Disinterestedness', *Journal of Aesthetics and Art Criticism* 20: 131–43. (Stolnitz identifies Alison as the first aesthetic attitude theorist.)

Townsend, D. (1988) 'Archibald Alison: Aesthetic Experience and Emotion', *British Journal of Aesthetics* 28: 132–44. (Places Alison's theory in the context of shifting empiricist problems.)

DABNEY TOWNSEND

ALTERITY AND IDENTITY, POSTMODERN THEORIES OF

Theories of alterity and identity can be said to be 'postmodern' if they challenge at least two key features of modern philosophy: (1) the Cartesian attempt to secure the legitimacy of knowledge on the basis of a subject that immediately knows itself and (2) the Hegelian attempt to secure self-knowledge and self-recognition by showing that knowledge and recognition are mediated by the whole. Postmodern thought does not necessarily champion a wholly other, but it generally conceives of self-identity in terms of a radical alterity.

1 Features of postmodern thought
2 The dialectics of desire
3 The experience of alterity
4 Aporias of the wholly other

1 Features of postmodern thought

Postmodern theories of identity and alterity refer to the use of these terms in modern philosophy. But the relation between modernity and postmodernity is not a simple matter, for much of what has come to be known as postmodern thought seeks to discover a 'postmodern moment' at the inception of modernity. According to Jean-François LYOTARD, whose *Postmodern Condition* (1984) ignited many of the philosophical debates concerning the status of postmodernity, the various manifestations of modernity – in architecture, literature, art and philosophy – can be seen as retreats from these postmodern moments, and one of the tasks of postmodern thought is to retrieve the gestures and motifs that modernity has been compelled to erase in order to institute itself as an ever renewable project or method. Postmodernity appears in its own right once these projects and methods can no longer *guarantee* their own legitimacy.

In order to understand the 'postmodern condition' it is therefore necessary to pay attention to the breakdown of the various 'meta-narratives' by which modernity has tried to legitimize itself. To the extent that modern philosophy from its inception in Descartes' *Meditations* sets out to secure the validity of knowledge, postmodern thought can be understood as a wide-ranging effort to come to terms with – and not simply denounce or repair – the failure of all philosophical attempts to secure the legitimacy of knowledge. The concepts of identity and alterity are of particular importance for this effort because the Cartesian attempt to secure the legitimacy of knowledge finds its principle point of reference in the identity of the self-conscious subject. This subject can serve as the source of legitimation to the extent that it can immediately identify itself and can treat its act of self-identification as knowledge. Postmodern theories of identity and alterity are concerned for the most part with the nature of self-identity and with the relation between the self and whatever presents itself as other than the self. The following discussion does not seek to cover all of the writers who have been classified as postmodern but first defines one version of postmodern philosophy and then considers certain exemplary thinkers for whom the nature of self-identity and the relation of the self to the other are of paramount importance.

If modern philosophy rests on the principle of self-consciousness, then one criterion for a postmodern philosophy would be its contesting of this principle. Yet postmodern philosophy cannot simply demonstrate that the self-conscious subject is unable to secure the legitimacy of knowledge by an act of immediate self-identification: not only are such demonstrations part and parcel of many modern philosophical projects, Hegel's attempt to complete modern philosophy begins by pointing out the abstract character of the Cartesian ego. In order for postmodern thought to distinguish itself from its modern counterparts it cannot simply assert that the identity of the self is derived from – or, in the Hegelian version, mediated by – something else; the other that allows the self to identify itself cannot be, as for Hegelians, the whole; it must be the *wholly* other, not the other *of* the self but an other that no longer pertains to the self. Even if this other grants the subject its identity, it must retreat from all attempts on the part of philosophical methods or systems to grasp it *as* something, even as something 'other'. The importance of Nietzsche and Freud for the development of postmodern thought can be seen from this perspective, for they provide intricate analyses of consciousness as a secondary process and also propose something – the will, the unconscious – that withdraws from consciousness but cannot then be reinterpreted in terms of a metaphysical substance (as can Schopenhauer's will or Hartmann's unconscious). Postmodern thought does not necessarily champion a 'wholly other', but it declines the Hegelian proposal that the legitimacy of knowledge, including self-knowledge and self-consciousness, should be sought in the concept of a self-mediating whole.

2 The dialectics of desire

The rejection of Hegelian accounts of the relation between the self and the other can be counted among the criteria of postmodern thought. A decisive moment in the development of such thought – and a reason it has developed most conspicuously in France – is found in Alexandre Kojève's striking interpretation of Hegel's 'master-slave dialectic' as a logic of human desire (see KOJÈVE, A.). According to Kojève, the object of desire is never a tangible thing; every desire is a desire for recognition by the other. The slave wants to be recognized by the master; but since the master cannot be recognized by the slave without ceasing to be a master, he must look toward the 'absolute master' – death – to secure recognition. Self-negating (suicidal) desire propels history toward its completion, at which point everyone recognizes everyone else; but this stage of satisfied desire, 'the Sunday of History', is itself deeply problematic because all the categories by which someone can be recognized as something have been exhausted. By taking seriously Hegel's talk of the end of history and the end of philosophy, Kojève set the stage not only for postmodern thought but also for a host of 'post-philosophical' and 'post-historical' pronouncements.

Some of those who heard Kojève's lectures on Hegel, especially Georges BATAILLE and Jacques LACAN, developed new concepts of the subject from his dialectics of desire. Bataille (1985) wrote extensively of a sovereign subject which is always other than itself precisely because it never recognizes itself in any other, and Lacan found in Freudian psychoanalysis a subject of dreams and slips of the tongue, a subject which is therefore no longer in control of, or even present to, itself. According to Lacan's famous theory of the 'mirror stage', the self does not constitute itself by recognizing itself in its other but by identifying itself with its specular image: its identity is thus based on misrecognition (*méconnaissance*). The Other, who is not to be confused with another self or an *alter ego*, 'mediates' between the self and its specular counterpart. According to Lacan, Freud discovers a 'radical heteronomy... gaping within man' and responds to the question 'who, then, is this other to whom I am more attached than to myself, since at the heart of my assent to my identity it is still he who agitates me?' ('Agency of the Letter', in Lacan 1977) by conceiving of the other side of consciousness in a radically new way. Without 'the discourse of the Other' – which is one of Lacan's names for the unconscious – there would be neither the desire for recognition nor recognition of desire, for no object is adequate to desire. The locus of such inadequation is language, more exactly, 'the signifier' understood as that which forever slips away from signification. Lacan then defines desire as 'the desire of the Other', but this definition does not mean that the ego wants what an *alter ego* desires; rather, it indicates that the self desires only *as* the Other and thus cannot recognize the object of its desire. The self is, as it were, a detour in the trajectory of the desire of the Other.

Lacan's theory of desire arrives at a conundrum: how can we understand the fact that subjects desire very specific objects? He invented the term 'object a' (where the 'a' stands for *autre*, 'other') in response to this question. Such objects are distinguished by the fact that 'they have no specular image, or, in other words, alterity' ('Subversion of the Subject', in Lacan 1977). When Lacan counts the subject of consciousness among these 'other objects', he makes the question of self-identity considerably more complicated, for, on the one hand, the self is constituted by misidentifying itself with its specular image, and, on the other, it has no specular image but is only, as Lacan says, a 'shadow'. One trenchant response to the complications generated by Lacan's attempt to understand the specificity of objects of desire can be found in the work of Julia KRISTEVA, especially in her *Powers of Horror* (1982). Kristeva articulates the Lacanian analysis of alterity into three distinct moments – the Other, the *alter ego*, and the 'other' as object of desire – by concentrating on what cannot be captured by a dialectics of desire: the utterly undesirable or 'abject'. The self experiences abjection when it senses an undefinable 'something' that precedes, inhabits, and threatens to engulf it. For this reason, the abject is violently – but also only incompletely – expelled:

> I experience abjection only if an Other has settled in place and stead of what will be 'me'. Not at all an other with whom I can identify and incorporate,

but an Other who precedes and possesses me, and through such possession causes me to be.

(Kristeva 1982: 10)

Certain categories of religious discourse such as defilement, abomination and purification can be understood, according to Kristeva, in terms of abjection. Once the abject is excluded, it serves as the foundation of an always precarious culture within which objects of desire can be separated from one another.

3   The experience of alterity

The writings of Lacan and Kristeva are as much contributions to psychoanalytic practice as independent theoretical exercises. Yet the questions to which they are addressed – the dialectics of desire, the experience of the alterity of the self – have also been posed by Emmanuel LEVINAS from a very different perspective. While studying the work of Husserl and Heidegger, Levinas came to realize that the phenomenology of the other cannot be accomplished in the same manner as the phenomenology of consciousness or the hermeneutics of existence. Levinas opens his most extensive work, *Totality and Infinity* (1969), by defining desire as 'desire for the absolutely other'. Because every object is inadequate to desire, its meaning must lie in the 'alterity of the Other [*autrui*]'. The phenomenological elucidation of the *autrui* (the 'personal' other) cannot simply be a matter of theoretical attitudes and descriptions because the *autrui* is never a definable theme. Instead of grounding philosophy on the *cogito*, Levinas returns to Descartes' discussion of 'the idea of infinity' as that which 'overflows' every intentional state. *Totality and Infinity* then presents subjectivity 'as welcoming the Other, as hospitality; in it the idea of infinity is consummated' (1969). Not only is the totality of entities to be distinguished from the totally other, so too is the phenomenon from the face: in the naked face of the *autrui* the idea of infinity overflows consciousness and its objects. The other can never be reduced to the same – not to the identity of the *cogito* (epistemology) nor to the sameness of being (ontology) – and so ethics becomes, for Levinas, 'first philosophy'.

In his second major work, *Otherwise than Being* (1981), Levinas no longer speaks of subjectivity as hospitality but as hostage: the self is not only held hostage by the other, but, as a hostage, it also 'substitutes' – and thus takes responsibility – for the other who holds it hostage. This paradoxical responsibility cannot be represented in terms of a self-positing subject, for, as the term 'hostage' indicates, the self is from the start sheer passivity:

The uniqueness of the ego, overwhelmed by the other in proximity, is the other in the same, the psyche. But it is I, I and no one else, who am hostage for the others. In substitution my being that belongs to me and not to another is undone, and it is through this substitution that I am not 'another', but me.

(1981: 116)

It is only because the self is assigned to the other before it acts on its own that it can be itself, that is, singular. Throughout his writing Levinas discovers an unmediated alterity in every identity: the vulnerability, susceptibility and 'nudity' of the self is evidence of such alterity. For philosophy to come to terms with evidence of this kind it must abandon idealism as well as empiricism and revise its notions of experience and sensibility. Experience does not consist in subsuming mental representations under general terms but in taking responsibility for the other and exposing oneself to one's own alterity.

Although the work of Gilles DELEUZE could hardly be more different in tone and texture than that of Levinas, he too seeks to revise philosophical concepts of experience and sensibility, and, like Levinas, his programme takes its point of departure from a critique of all claims to identity. But unlike Levinas, he does not undertake this critique as an advocate, so to speak, of the transcendence of the other but as a champion of entirely immanent 'differential forces'. Whereas Kant treats identity and difference as concepts of reflection, Deleuze tries to develop a concept of difference in which it is no longer a term of reflection and can no longer be seen as the opposite of identity. Difference, for Deleuze, always implies a multiplicity of relations among positive forces, each of which expresses itself but none of which opposes any other. According to the terms set forth in *Difference and Repetition* (1981), every 'philosophy of representation' rests on a principle of identity. The reduction of difference to opposition serves to make singularities – and, for Deleuze, everything is a singularity – into representations of generic types. Every philosophy of representation denies difference in favour of identity and thus turns into a philosophy of negation. Difference must be negated in order to save the self-identical subject, even if – as in the case of Hegelianism – this negation is doubled, and the subject appears only as the negation of everything that opposes it.

All of Deleuze's writings emphasize the positivity of difference. *Anti-Oedipus* (Deleuze and Guattari 1977), perhaps his best-known book, not only attacks psychoanalysis for conceiving of desire in terms of castration (lack of the phallus) but seeks to undermine every conception of desire as absence or negativity. The question then arises: how can one account for alterity without using concepts such as lack, absence or negativity? The concluding sections of *Difference and Repetition* respond to this question. Sensible differences, according to Deleuze, are always differences of intensity: 'Intensity is the form of difference in so far as this is the reason of the sensible' (1994: 222). In order for an intensity to be experienced, it must first be developed or 'explicated'. But an intensity (a *quale*) cannot be explicated unless it is transformed into an extension (a quantity) in accordance with a specific principle of identity. The 'psychic system I-Self' is one particularly complicated version of explication. The other enters into Deleuze's philosophical scenario as the site of still unexplicated intensities. Instead of using words like 'negativity' or 'absence' to conceive of alterity, Deleuze employs a modal version of these terms – possibility – and he, like Levinas, finds in the human face the exemplary experience of alterity: 'Consider a terrified face.... This face expresses a possible world: the terrifying world.... In every psychic system there is a swarm of possibilities around reality, but our possibles are always Others' (1994: 260). The self, in sum, is the explication of implied intensities in accordance with a principle of identity, whereas the other, as an expression of a possible world, 'represents' the otherwise inaccessible intensities on which the 'psychic system' is founded.

4 Aporias of the wholly other

Jacques DERRIDA, like Deleuze, has developed a philosophy of difference, but unlike Deleuze, he does not present it as an alternative to the philosophy of identity. Derrida's philosophical enquiries respond to a double exigency: they seek to show, on the one hand, that the operation of the principle of identity always rests on an unacknowledged play of difference and, on the other, that neither difference nor alterity can serve as principles on which a new philosophical project can be built. Derrida begins one of his earliest writings, 'Descartes and the History of Madness', by showing that the project Foucault undertakes in *Madness and Civilization* (1965) cannot be accomplished: it is not only impossible to let madness 'itself' speak, but it is also impossible to write an 'archaeology' of the silence into which the mad are driven without relying on the resources of reason (*logos*). Derrida then interrogates the very opposition between madness and reason by pointing toward a madness (or being *aliéné*) at the heart of modernity's first philosophical manifesto, Descartes' *Meditations*: in the process of constituting itself, according to Derrida's reading, the self-reflective subject exposes itself to a doubt so hyperbolic that it exceeds every effort on the part of the self-reflective subject to bring it under control.

Because it is impossible to find a position from which to criticize the principle of identity without defining this position in terms of self-identity, Derrida refrains from describing his work as a 'critique' and prefers the word 'deconstruction' (see DECONSTRUCTION). The deconstruction of the principle of identity not only demonstrates the impossibility of any critique of identity in the name of alterity but welcomes this impossibility, for it implies that the self can never be entirely separated from the other. Philosophy cannot disclose a pure self or a pure other, but this impossibility cannot be resolved in a Hegelian manner by representing the subject as the process of self-mediation in the other. Yet it is *also* impossible, according to Derrida, simply to refuse this Hegelian move and once again presuppose, posit or postulate a wholly other. There is, for Derrida, such an other, but it does not exist, if 'existence' is defined by self-identity and presence-to-oneself. A philosophical enquiry cannot set out from or arrive at the wholly other; it *comes* – without being destined and without destination. Insofar as the future (*avenir*) is opened up by this coming (*venir*), it is the venue of alterity, and insofar as justice (in contrast to legal norms) always implies a singular relation to a singularity, according to Derrida, this future is also the site of justice.

All of the aporias surrounding the idea of a radical alterity are captured in one of Derrida's most suggestive sentences: *tout autre est tout autre*, 'every other is wholly other' (1994: 82). This assertion of the radical and irreducible alterity of every other is at the same time a radical assertion of identity, for the sentence can also be understood as a tautology: 'every other is every other'. In a single sentence Derrida thus captures one of the great challenges of all postmodern thought: by championing a radical alterity, it runs the risk of turning into a tautological affirmation of identity. Derrida emphasized the impossibility of safeguarding any thought of the wholly other from this risk, but he also insists that thought can never run away from such risks.

See also: POSTMODERNISM; SUBJECT, POSTMODERN CRITIQUE OF

References and further reading

* Bataille, G. (1985) *Visions of Excess*, trans. A. Stoekl, Minneapolis, MN: University of Minnesota Press. (Important, difficult, but often readable essays on many of the topics that have come to occupy postmodern thought.)

Baudrillard, J. (1988) *Selected Writings*, ed. M. Poster, Stanford, CA: Stanford University Press. (A good, very accessible introduction to an influential postmodern sociologist.)

Bertens, J. (1995) *The Idea of the Postmodern*, New York: Routledge. (A readable introduction to the history of postmodernism.)

Borch-Jacobsen, M. (1991) *Lacan: The Absolute Master*, trans. D. Brick, Stanford, CA: Stanford University Press. (An advanced introduction to Lacan and the philosophical atmosphere in which he developed his version of psychoanalysis; an excellent, well-written, although at times difficult book.)

* Deleuze, G. (1994) *Difference and Repetition*, trans. P. Patton, New York: Columbia University Press. (A major philosophical statement; the most accessible of Deleuze's independent philosophical works.)

* Deleuze, G. and Guattari, F. (1977) *Anti-Oedipus*, trans. R. Hurley, M. Seem and H. Lane, New York: Viking. (One of the principal points of reference for postmodern philosophy.)

Derrida, J. (1978) *Writing and Difference*, trans. A. Bass, Chicago, IL: University of Chicago Press. (Important, often difficult essays in which Derrida works out his relation to contemporary attempts to rethink the relation of the self to other; especially significant are the essays on Foucault, Levinas, Bataille, and Freud.)

—— (1993) *Aporias*, trans. T. Dutoit, Stanford, CA: Stanford University Press. (A good introduction to Derrida's thought, especially his way of coming to terms with the paradoxes of alterity.)

* —— (1994) *The Gift of Death*, trans. D. Wills, Chicago, IL: University of Chicago Press. (A highly readable exploration of the relation between giving, dying, sacrificing and secrecy.)

Descombes, V. (1980) *Modern French Philosophy*, trans. L. Scott-Fox and J. Harding, Cambridge: Cambridge University Press. (Originally titled 'The Same and the Other', this is a good, critical introduction to many of the debates surrounding postmodern philosophy.)

* Foucault, M. (1965) *Madness and Civilization*, trans. R. Howard, New York: Pantheon. (One of Foucault's most accessible books. As an 'archaeology' of the silence to which the mad were condemned in the 'age of reason', it is the point of departure for many re-evaluations of modern rationality.)

Habermas, J. (1987) *The Philosophical Discourse of Modernity*, trans. F. Lawrence, Cambridge, MA: MIT Press. (Important and influential essays attacking postmodern thought as a retreat from the unending project of modernity and enlightenment. Important for understanding all of the philosophical debates around the significance and validity of postmodern theory.)

Jameson, F. (1991) *Postmodernism, or, The Cultural Logic of Late Capitalism*, Durham, NC: Duke University Press. (A wide-ranging, easily accessible description and evaluation of various versions of postmodernism from a Marxist perspective.)

Hoesterey, I. (1991) *Zeitgeist in Babel: The Postmodernist Controversy*, Bloomington, IN: Indiana University Press. (A collection of essays on postmodernism in a variety of fields with an informative section on the political and social stakes of postmodern theory.)

* Kojève, A. (1969) *Introduction to the Reading of Hegel*, trans. J. Nichols, Ithaca, NY: Cornell University Press. (One of the seminal books of twentieth century French thought. Familiarity with Hegel and Marx is indispensable for understanding this book.)

* Kristeva, J. (1982) *Powers of Horror*, trans. L. Roudiez, New York: Columbia University Press. (A series of essays on abjection, selfhood, religious discourses and practices; includes a lengthy confrontation with abjection and horror in the writings of Céline.)

* Lacan, J. (1977) *Écrits*, trans. A. Sheridan. New York: W.W. Norton. (Very difficult essays, but indispensable for an understanding of postmodern discourse on identity and alterity.)

* Levinas, E. (1969) *Totality and Infinity*, trans. A. Lingis, Pittsburgh, PA: Duquesne University Press. (Levinas's most extensive treatise; it is generally quite readable, and it is important for all subsequent attempts to conceive of radical alterity.)

* ——(1981) *Otherwise than Being, or, Beyond Essence*, trans. A. Lingis, The Hague: Martinus Nijhoff, 1981. (One of Levinas's most important philosophical statements. Familiarity with phenomenological discourse helpful but not indispensable.)

* ——(1989) 'Substitution', in S. Hand (ed.) *The Levinas Reader*, Oxford: Blackwell. (One of the preliminary drafts of *Otherwise than Being*, this essay argues for the idea of a responsibility that is justified by no prior commitment.)

* Lyotard, J.-F. (1984) *The Postmodern Condition: A Report on Knowledge*, trans. G. Bennington and B. Massumi, Minneapolis, MN: University of Minnesota Press. (A very readable book that is the starting points for many of the debates about postmodern thought and culture.)

—— (1988) *The Differend*, trans. G. van den Abbeele, Minneapolis, MN: University of Minnesota Press. (Lyotard's most thorough philosophical work; often difficult, with allusions to a wide variety of philosophical theories.)

Norris, C. (1990) *What's Wrong with Postmodernism: Critical Theory and the Ends of Philosophy*, Baltimore, MD: Johns Hopkins University Press. (A series of essays that attempt to stake out a version of postmodern philosophy and criticism that are heirs to enlightenment thought. Polemical and generally accessible.)

Pefanis, J. (1991) *Heterology and the Postmodern: Bataille, Baudrillard, and Lyotard*, Durham, NC: Duke University Press. (A readable introduction to postmodern theory which pays particular attention to the question of alterity.)

Rorty, R. (1989) *Irony, Contingency, Solidarity*, Cambridge: Cambridge University Press. (A collection of essays that have served as reference points for defining an influential version of postmodern thought.)

Vattimo, G. (1988) *The End of Modernity: Nihilism and Hermeneutics in Postmodern Culture*, trans. J. Snyder, Baltimore, MD: Johns Hopkins University Press. (Accessible meditations on both the general problem of postmodernity and the nature of postmodern philosophy.)

PETER FENVES

ALTHUSSER, LOUIS PIERRE (1918–90)

Louis Althusser was the most influential philosopher to emerge in the revival of Marxist theory occasioned by the radical movements of the 1960s. His influence is, on the face of it, surprising, since Althusser's Marx is not the theorist of revolutionary self-emancipation celebrated by the early Lukács. According to Althusser, Marx, along with Freud, was responsible for a 'decentring' of the human subject. History is 'a process without a subject'. Its movement is beyond the comprehension of individual or collective subjects, and can only be grasped by a scientific 'theoretical practice' which keeps its distance from everyday experience. This austere version of Marxism nevertheless captured the imagination of many young intellectuals by calling for a 'return to Marx', with the implication that his writings had been distorted by the official communist movement. In fact, Althusser later conceded, his was an 'imaginary Marxism', a reconstruction of historical materialism reflecting the same philosophical climate that produced the post-structuralist appropriations of Nietzsche and Heidegger by Deleuze, Derrida and Foucault. Most of the philosophical difficulties in which Althusser found himself can be traced back to the impossibility of fusing Marx's and Nietzsche's thought into a new synthesis.

1 Life
2 Rereading Marx
3 Conclusion

1 Life

On a pessimistic view of his influence, Althusser may be chiefly remembered for strangling his wife, Helene Rytman, on 16 November 1980, in their flat at the École Normale Superieure in Paris. Deemed unfit to stand trial for the murder, Althusser spent the last decade of his life in and out of mental hospitals. His attempt to explain this disaster – in *L'Avenir dure longtemps* (The Future Lasts A Long Time) (1992), an extraordinary confessional autobiography, posthumously published, which traced the manic depressive outbursts which dogged his adult life back to a Freudian family drama which began even before his birth in Algeria – has been shown by Yann Moulier Boutang (1992) to be as much fiction as fact.

Thanks, however, to his own memoirs and Moulier Boutang's biography, the outline of Althusser's public life is now becoming clear. From his Lyons schooldays in the 1930s until the early 1950s he was active in Catholic political circles. But, whereas before the Second World War Althusser was associated with the anti-republican right ('We were more or less... royalists then', he later wrote), the four years he spent in a German prisoner-of-war camp after France's defeat in 1940 pushed him to the left. Like many young French intellectuals of his generation, he rallied to the communist party after the war, joining in 1948. Until the Church's suppression of the worker-priest movement in the early 1950s Althusser sought to reconcile Marxism and Catholicism. In these years he espoused a messianic Hegelian Marxism, in some ways reminiscent of the early Georg Lukács (see LUKÁCS, G. §2). The thesis for which Althusser was to become famous in the 1960s – that MARX had had to break with his own youthful Hegelian past – therefore recapitulated his own personal development.

In July 1948 Althusser was appointed *caïman* at the École Normale Superieure, a post he was to hold until the tragedy of November 1980. He was responsible for preparing philosophy students for the *agrégation*, or final examination. Althusser was an outstanding teacher, and the central role which the École Normale played in the teaching of philosophy in France (virtually every major twentieth-century French philosopher has been a *normalien*) meant that he had an exceptional influence on French intellectuals for a generation. But it was his writings of the 1960s – notably those in *Pour Marx* (For Marx) and *Lire le Capital* (Reading Capital), both published in 1965 – which made Althusser a major figure on the intellectual scene. His reinterpretation of Marx, developed in collaboration with an exceptionally talented group of pupils, served to articulate young left-wing intellectuals' impatience with the caution and conservatism (as they saw it) of the communist party leadership. Unlike many of his followers, Althusser did not break with the party, even after what he regarded as its failure to seize the revolutionary opportunity presented by the events of May–June 1968. He found himself, however, increasingly at odds with the official apparatus. His last major public act was 'What Must Change in the Party', a root-and-branch denunciation of the leadership published in *Le Monde* in April 1978. By then, however, the Parisian intelligentsia had fallen out of love with Marxism, and Althusser's last years were spent in intellectual as well as personal isolation.

2 Rereading Marx

Althusser's reinterpretation of Marx involves, in the first place, a theory of interpretation. 'There is no such thing as an innocent reading', he says. Every approach to a text brings with it certain theoretical presuppositions. Therefore 'a new theory of "reading"' is required, one that is concerned to identify the theoretical framework implicit in the text itself, or what Althusser calls its 'problematic'. The problematic, he claims, is typically concealed within the text rather than visible on its surface. It can be detected, rather like the repressed desires which psychoanalysis supposes it uncovers, in the text's silences, gaps, ambiguities and inconsistencies. Texts are thus complex, and this complexity is, as we shall see, one aspect of the complexity of history itself.

When applied to Marx, this theory of reading reveals a discontinuity. Marx's writings up to and including the *Economic and Philosophic Manuscripts of 1844* belong to one problematic which Althusser regards as ideological. Their leading characteristic is their humanism: history is depicted as the unfolding of a human essence which, alienated under capitalism, will find fulfilment under communism. These early works of Marx are separated from his later writings, above all *Capital*, by an 'epistemological break' marking the formation of a new science of history. The mature Marx is a 'theoretical anti-humanist', for whom history is 'a process without a subject or goal'. It is not the development of the productive forces, or the self-realization of the working class conceived (as it was by the early Lukács) as the 'identical subject–object' of history, nor is socialist revolution the inevitable culmination of the historical process. Althusser liked to say that 'the materialist...is a man who catches a moving train without knowing where it has come from or where it is going' (1992: 210). Human beings are the 'bearers' of a process they neither create nor control.

The break from which Althusser's scientific, antihumanist Marx emerged was above all one with HEGEL. Althusser's most celebrated essay, 'Contradiction and Overdetermination' (1962; repr. in *For Marx*), was a direct attack on the idea, hitherto basic to Marxist orthodoxy, that Marx, while rejecting Hegel's idealist system, had taken over his dialectical method. Althusser pointed out that this contrast between method and system involved a separation of form and content that was itself 'pre-dialectical', contradicting Hegel's own account of his method. The formulation of a materialist dialectic required not the application of Hegel's method to a different object but 'the transformation of its structures'. Althusser sought to bring out the difference between Marx and Hegel by contrasting their conceptions of totality. As Lukács had argued, both might view society as an integrated whole, but the way in which they conceived this whole was very different. Hegel's was an 'expressive totality', in which all the different aspects of social life reflected a single informing centre. Taken over in a Marxist framework, this totality leads to economic reductionism; everything becomes an expression of the fundamental economic contradiction, in the way that, according to Lukács, reification pervades the whole of capitalist society (see MARXISM, WESTERN §2).

For Marx, by contrast, each social formation is a complex, structured totality composed of a plurality of practices irreducible to one another. The economy is 'determinant in the last instance', that is, its primacy consists not so much in its directly shaping the course of historical development, as in its selecting some particular 'instance' (or practice) to play the dominant role (politics, for example, in feudal society). Economic causality thus operates indirectly, and always in combination with non-economic practices. As Althusser famously put it, 'the lonely hour of the "last instance" never comes' ([1965] 1969: 113). What Marx called the superstructure – politics, law and ideology – is 'relatively autonomous': each practice develops according to its own specific laws, within the limits set for it by the economy. Thus major historical events, for example, the Russian Revolution of February 1917, are 'overdetermined': they are not simply expressions of an underlying contradiction between the forces and relations of production, but involve a combination of heterogeneous factors – economic, political, ideological – which accumulate until they produce a rupture.

This complexity of the social whole is one reason why Althusser does not believe that individuals can understand the history in which they are caught up. Ideology, he believes, is a necessary feature of any society, including the classless communism of the future. It serves as a factor of social cohesion, adapting human beings to the roles required of them as bearers of the prevailing relations of production. The very form of subjectivity – individuals' conception of themselves as coherent and autonomous persons – is the means through which they are subsumed under ideological social relations. The only way out of this imaginary relationship lies in scientific theory. The formation of a scientific problematic – for example, Marx's epistemological break – allows an escape from the repetition of a few stereotyped ideological themes into a potentially infinite process of theoretical self-development. Here too, however, individuals figure only as the bearers of an impersonal social process, since each science develops according to the conceptual patterns specific to it.

3 Conclusion

Though carried out under the slogan of a 'return to Marx', his rescue from the misinterpretations perpetrated both by orthodox Communists and by Hegelians such as the early Lukács, Althusser's reading of Marx was on his own admission a 'guilty' one, reflecting a variety of influences. He himself paid explicit tribute to Spinoza and Freud in particular, and the debt his philosophy of science owed to his teacher Bachelard is evident. More generally, Althusser's anti-humanism bears a strong resemblance to the attack on the subject as a unified and sovereign entity which, initiated in the 1950s by Lacan and Levi-Strauss, was to be radicalized in the late 1960s by Deleuze, Derrida and Foucault (see POST-STRUCTURALISM §§2–4). But post-structuralism derives ultimately from Nietzsche's critique of modernity, with its tendency (never fully realized in Nietzsche himself, but taken much further in his own way by Heidegger) to reject the Enlightenment *tout court*. How could Marxism, deeply embedded in which are preoccupations with progress and emancipation, place itself in the camp of the counter-Enlightenment? More specifically, in rejecting economically reductionist versions of Marxism, was not Althusser in danger of developing a pluralist conception of the social whole in which the economy had lost any causal primacy? Again, if each 'theoretical practice' developed autonomously according to its own internal norms, how could Althusser maintain a distinction between science and ideology and thereby resist Foucault's Nietzschean reduction of all knowledge to expressions of the will to power? Althusser's philosophical enterprise ultimately ran aground on these and similar difficulties. Nevertheless, his insistence on a careful conceptual analysis of Marx's writings as the basis of a reconstruction of historical materialism, his demonstration of the methodological gulf separating Marx and Hegel, and his sensitivity to developments in the philosophy of science that were ignored by the Frankfurt School, for example, make his work of lasting value.

See also: DIALECTICAL MATERIALISM §2

List of works

Althusser, L. (1959) *Montesquieu, La politique et l'historie*, Paris: Presses Universitaires de France; trans. B. Brewster in *Politics and History*, later renamed *Montesquieu, Rousseau, Marx*, London: New Left Books, 1972. (A stimulating interpretation of Montesquieu as both a theorist of absolutism and one of the first historical sociologists; the English edition contains important essays on Rousseau's *Social Contract*, and on Marx's relationship with Hegel.)

—— (1965) *Pour Marx*, Paris: Maspero; trans. B. Brewster, *For Marx*, London: Allen Lane, 1969. (Althusser's most famous book, a collection of essays that outline his theory of overdetermination and his account of the 'epistemological break' separating the young Marx from the old.)

Althusser, L., Balibar, E., Establet, R., Macherey, P. and Ranciere, J. (1965) *Lire le Capital*, Paris: Maspero; partly trans. B. Brewster in Althusser, L. and Balibar, E., *Reading Capital*, London: New Left Books, 1970. (The most sustained attempt by Althusser and his pupils to characterize what distinguishes Marx's method from the Hegelian dialectic; it helped to stimulate close philosophical scrutiny of the conceptual structure of *Capital*.)

Althusser, L. (1969) *Lénine et La philosophie*, Paris: Maspero; trans. B. Brewster in *Lenin and Philosophy and Other Essays*, London: New Left Books, 1972. (Advances the notorious thesis that 'philosophy is, in the last instance, the class struggle in theory'; the English edition also includes two of Althusser's most influential essays: 'Freud and Lacan' and 'Ideology and the Ideological State Apparatuses'.)

—— (1970) 'Sur le Rapport de Marx à Hegel', in J. D'Hondt (ed.) *Hegel et la pensée moderne*, Paris: Presses Universitaires de France; trans. B. Brewster, 'Marx's Relation to Hegel', in *Politics and History*,

London: New Left Books, and New York: Verso, 1972. (Argues that Marx understood Hegel's dialectic in terms of process.)

—— (1973) *Réponse à John Lewis*, Paris: Maspero; trans. G. Locke in *Essays in Self-Criticism*, London: New Left Books, 1976. (Althusser's polemical defence of his 'theoretical anti-humanism' at the height of his Maoist phase.)

—— (1974a) *Éléments d'autocritique*, Paris: Hachette; trans. G. Locke in *Essays in Self-Criticism*, London: New Left Books, 1976. (A self-criticism which takes *For Marx* and *Reading Capital* to task for 'theoreticism' and 'flirting with strucuralism'.)

—— (1974b) *Philosophie et philosophie spontanée des savants*, Paris: Maspero; trans. W. Montag in *Philosophy and the Spontaneous Philosophy of the Scientists and Other Essays*, London: Verso, 1990. (Althusser's main discussion of the relationship between philosophy and the sciences; the English edition also reprints 'Lenin and Philosophy' and other important texts of the 1960s and 1970s.)

—— (1978) *Ce qui ne peut pas plus durer dans le parti communiste*, Paris: Maspero; trans. P. Camiller, 'What Must Change in the Party', *New Left Review* 109: 19–45. (First published in *Le Monde*, 24–7 April 1978, in the wake of the left's defeat in the French legislative elections; a fierce indictment of the communist party's Stalinist internal regime.)

—— (1988) 'Machiavelli's Solitude', trans. T. O'Hagan, *Economy and Society* 17 (4): 468–79. (A lecture on Machiavelli, a thinker who was a major influence on Althusser.)

—— (1992) *L'avenir dure longtemps suivi de les faits*, Paris: Stock/IMEC; trans. R. Veasey, *The Future Lasts a Long Time*, London: Chatto & Windus, 1993. (Two autobiographical texts; the first and longer one, written after Althusser's disgrace, is a remarkable human document, and contains important reflections on his philosophical and political career. The second edition, published by Stock/IMEC in 1994, contains some important additional material, including a text in which Althusser discusses Machiavelli and Spinoza as materialist precursors of Marx.)

—— (1993) *Ecrits sur la psychoanalyse* (Writings on Psychoanalysis), Paris: Stock/IMEC. (Brings together all Althusser's writings on Freud, thereby helping to clarify the significant influence that Jacques Lacan had on him.)

—— (1994) *Sur la philosophie* (On Philosophy), Paris: Gallimard. (An interview and correspondence with Latin American admirers, dating from the mid-1980s, and chiefly notable as an instance of the late Althusser's stress on 'the true materialist tradition' (Macchiavelli, Spinoza and Rousseau) that antedated Marx.)

—— (1994, 1995) *Ecrits philosophiques et politiques*, Paris: Stock/IMEC, 2 vols. (Volume 1 contains Althusser's previously unpublished early Hegelian writings; Volume 2 offers a wealth of hitherto unpublished texts from Althusser's middle and late periods.)

References and further reading

Anderson, P. (1980) *Arguments within English Marxism*, London: Verso. (A measured assessment of Althusser's contribution to Marxism.)

Benton, T. (1984) *The Rise and Fall of Structural Marxism*, London: Macmillan. (A sympathetic critical assessment of Althusser and some of those influenced by him.)

Callinicos, A. (1976) *Althusser's Marxism*, London: Pluto. (Concentrates on the tensions internal to Althusser's philosophical project.)

Elliott, G. (1987) *Althusser – the Detour of Theory*, London: Verso. (A meticulous historical reconstruction of Althusser's political and intellectual thought, with the best available bibliography of his writings.)

—— (ed.) (1994) *Althusser: A Critical Reader*, Oxford: Blackwell. (Includes contemporary critical reactions to Althusser by Eric Hobsbawm, Axel Honneth, Paul Ricoeur and Pierre Vilar, and a discussion by the editor of the autobiographical writings.)

Geras, N. (1972) 'Althusser's Marxism', *New Left Review* 71: 57–86. (A careful and probing critique, written from the standpoint of classical Marxism.)

Glucksmann, A. (1972) 'A Ventriloquist Structuralism', *New Left Review* 72: 68–92. (Virtuoso exposition of the conceptual flaws in *For Marx* and *Reading Capital*.)

Lazarus, S. (ed.) (1993) *Politique et philosophie dans l'oeuvre de Louis Althusser* (Politics and Philosophy in the Work of Louis Althusser), Paris: Presses Universitaires de France. (Collection of essays, many by some of Althusser's leading pupils.)

Moulier Boutang, Y. (1992) *Louis Althusser: Une biographie: la formation du mythe (1918–1956), tome I*, Paris: Bernard Grasset. (Indispensable corrective to Althusser's myth-making in his autobiography; of great value on Althusser's early political and philosophical development.)

Sprinker, M. (ed.) (1993) *The Althusserian Legacy*, London: Verso. (Collection of essays perhaps most notable for a lengthy interview with Derrida on Althusser and Marxism, and for the speech he delivered at Althusser's graveside.)

Thompson, E.P. (1978) *The Poverty of Theory and Other Essays*, London: Merlin. (A great historian's brilliantly written damnation of Althusser and all his works.)

ALEX CALLINICOS

ALTRUISM *see* EGOISM AND ALTRUISM; MORAL MOTIVATION

AMBEDKAR, BHIMRAO RAMJI (1891–1956)

Bhimrao Ramji Ambedkar was a statesman, scholar, human rights advocate, educator, barrister, first law minister of the Republic of India and architect of its constitution. Born into the untouchable Mahar sub-caste, he became the widely revered leader of India's more than 100 million hereditary outcastes, the social and psychological emancipation of whom remained his lifelong objective. Strongly influenced by Anglo-American liberalism and pragmatism, Ambedkar was a staunch constitutionalist and social democrat. Locating the source of untouchability within the caste system itself, he became a militant critic of Hinduism, eventually affirming Buddhism as the universal ethical teaching that he felt could lead all of India into modernity.

Sponsored by a socially progressive Indian mahārāja, Ambedkar became the first of his outcaste background to complete a full course of postgraduate study, receiving a Ph.D. from Columbia University and a D.Sc. from the University of London in addition to qualifying for the bar from Gray's Inn, London.

Ambedkar drew on both Indian and Western sources to formulate his social philosophy. Early in life he identified the Buddha, Kabīr and Jyotibā Phule as his principal preceptors: the Buddha (sixth–fifth century BC) because of his programme of ethical and spiritual cultivation including an explicit critique of the caste system; the radical poet-saint and mystic Kabīr (fifteenth century) for his anti-Brahmanic, egalitarian spirituality; and the militant educationalist Phule (1828–90) as the Shudra founder of the nineteenth-century non-Brahman movement in Maharashtra that first coupled Western rationalism and liberalism with more traditional social and spiritual critiques of casteism and untouchability. Ambedkar was widely read in the modern classics of Western social and political theory and he was especially influenced by the faculty at Columbia University during his graduate period there from 1913–16. Through his contact with John DEWEY, James Shotwell, Edwin Seligman, James Harvey Robinson, Franklin Giddings and Alexander Goldenweiser in particular, he acquired a pragmatic, even optimistic, conviction in the potential of democratic institutions to bring about social equality. Given Ambedkar's consequent commitment to constitutional democracy, it was inevitable that he would clash with GANDHI, rejecting both the latter's willingness to move outside the bounds of the legal process and also his patriarchal belief that emancipation of the Untouchables would result from a change of heart on the part of caste Hindus rather than from the political and ethical transformation of the Untouchables themselves (see POLITICAL PHILOSOPHY, INDIAN).

A jurist and statesman more than a political philosopher, Ambedkar's chief intellectual contributions lay in the realm of social theory. His MA thesis revised prevailing sociological views regarding the origins of caste in India. It argued that caste discrimination arose not from race, colour, or occupation, but rather from the Brahmanic concept of endogamy-based ritual purity and pollution, a worldview subsequently adopted by other caste communities in imitation of the Brahmans. Later in his life he expanded this position with the provocative thesis linking the development of untouchability to Brahmanic oppression of Buddhist minorities beginning in the fifth century.

In assessing Ambedkar's social philosophy and his career as a statesman one must recognize three distinct but interlinked spheres of concern. He felt that India would not be fully liberated until its outcastes were emancipated and he further asserted that this emancipation must be legal, material and spiritual. Each of these three dimensions became the focus of successive, overlapping phases of his activities. His first object was to secure the legal status of equal rights for Untouchables and the illegality of traditional practices of caste discrimination that restricted access to water sources and other public facilities. This phase began with his early efforts in the 1920s and 1930s to organize *satyagraha* demonstrations and legal suits and culminated with his decisive role in bringing the new Indian constitution to ratification in 1949.

As an economist and sociologist he recognized that legal protection alone was not sufficient. Thus, his second sphere of concern focused on the material improvement of the Untouchables. Efforts to establish legally mandated reservations guaranteeing Untouchables access to the political and educational systems, the civil service and many public sector professions were crucial to this phase of Ambedkar's activity, but at its heart lay his recognition that change would come only when the Untouchables were able to take full advantage of these opportunities. This realization led him in 1945 to establish the People's Education Society. Its success has led to the introduction of over thirty institutions of higher education open to all castes, but was especially intended to help the ex-Untouchables gain the education necessary for social advancement. In retrospect Ambedkar appears more successful as an educator than a politician: a fact evidenced by the recent emergence of a strong ex-Untouchable urban middle class and the flourishing of a vigorous and nationally influential *Dalit* (oppressed) literature movement in Marathi, Gujarati and other Indian languages.

The third concern that Ambedkar thought should be addressed went beyond his efforts to secure legal and material advancement for his people. He believed that educational economic advancement would be meaningless unless it was coupled with ethical and spiritual development. It was in Buddhism that he found an indigenous Indian source for completing his vision of emancipation, a source he felt was compatible with his Western rationalism and egalitarianism. The importance of this third element in his thought has been minimized by the more politically minded of his successors, some of whom feel that renouncing Hinduism is sufficient to break the stigma of caste. This was not Ambedkar's view. Attracted to the Buddha's compassionate injunction to work for the welfare of the many as early as 1908, Ambedkar swore in 1935 that although he had been born a Hindu he would not die a Hindu. By 1950 he had come to believe that it was only through Buddhism that the Untouchables would gain the self-respect and self-reliance necessary to realize fully their own advancement. In 1956 just weeks before his untimely death, he inaugurated a mass conversion movement that has subsequently attracted more than 10 million new Indian Buddhists.

See also: POLITICAL PHILOSOPHY

List of works

Ambedkar, B.R. (1919–57) *Dr. Babasaheb Ambedkar Writings and Speeches*, ed. V. Moon, Bombay: Education Department, Government of Maharashtra, 1979, 13 vols. (The most complete collection of Ambedkar's works available, including the three important works listed separately below.)
—— (1945) *What Congress and Gandhi Have Done to the Untouchables*, Bombay: Thacker, 2nd edn, 1946. (Ambedkar's critique of the Gandhian solution to untouchability as both insufficient in scope and paternalistic in attitude.)
—— (1948) *The Untouchables*, New Delhi: Amrit Book Co. (A historical and sociological monograph developing Ambedkar's thesis that the Untouchables were the remnants of India's original Buddhist population, the broken men oppressed and marginalized after a resurgence of Brahmanic Hinduism beginning in the fifth century.)
—— (1957) *The Buddha and His Dhamma*, Bombay: People's Education Society. (Ambedkar's critical assessment of the Buddha's teaching, considered especially with regard to the contemporary needs of the ex-Untouchables.)

References and further reading

Keer, D. (1954) *Dr Ambedkar: Life and Mission*, Bombay: Popular Prakashan; revised 3rd edn, 1971. (The most popular and complete biography of Ambedkar.)
Sangharakshita (1986) *Ambedkar and Buddhism*, Glasgow: Windhorse Publications. (The best critical monograph available on Ambedkar to date, written by an English-born Buddhist monk who has worked with the Ambedkarite Buddhist movement since 1952.)
Zelliot, E. (1992) *From Untouchable to Dalit: Essays on the Ambedkar Movement*, New Delhi: Manohar. (An excellent collection of essays comprehensively covering many aspects of Ambedkar and the ex-Untouchable Buddhist movement he initiated. The volume includes Zelliot's especially seminal essay on Gandhi and Ambedkar and also extensive bibliographic references.)

ALAN SPONBERG

AMBIGUITY

A word, phrase or sentence is ambiguous if it has more than one meaning. The word 'light', for example, can mean not very heavy or not very dark. Words like 'light', 'note', 'bear' and 'over' are lexically ambiguous. They induce ambiguity in phrases or sentences in which they occur, such as 'light suit' and 'The duchess can't bear children'. However, phrases and sentences can be ambiguous even if none of their constituents is. The phrase 'porcelain egg container' is structurally ambiguous, as is the sentence 'The police shot the rioters with guns'. Ambiguity can have both a lexical and a structural basis, as with sentences like 'I left her behind for you' and 'He saw her duck'.

The notion of ambiguity has philosophical applications. For example, identifying an ambiguity can aid in solving a philosophical problem. Suppose one wonders how two people can have the same idea, say of a unicorn. This can seem puzzling until one distinguishes 'idea' in the sense of a particular psychological occurrence, a mental representation, from 'idea' in the sense of an abstract, shareable concept. On the other hand, gratuitous claims of ambiguity can make for overly simple solutions. Accordingly, the question arises of how genuine ambiguities can be distinguished from spurious ones. Part of the answer consists in identifying phenomena with which ambiguity may be confused, such as vagueness, unclarity, inexplicitness and indexicality.

1 Types of ambiguity
2 Ambiguity contrasted
3 Philosophical relevance

1 Types of ambiguity

Ambiguity is a property of linguistic expressions. A word, phrase or sentence is ambiguous if it has more than one meaning. Obviously this definition does not say what meanings are or what it is for an expression to have one (or more than one). For a particular language, this information is provided by a grammar, which systematically pairs forms with meanings, ambiguous forms with more than one meaning (see SEMANTICS).

There are two types of ambiguity, *lexical* and *structural*. Lexical ambiguity is by far the more common. Everyday examples include nouns like 'chip', 'pen' and 'suit', verbs like 'call', 'draw' and 'run' and adjectives like 'deep', 'dry' and 'hard'. There are various tests for lexical ambiguity. One test is having two unrelated antonyms, as with 'hard', which has both 'soft' and 'easy' as opposites. Another is the conjunction reduction test. Consider the sentence, 'The tailor pressed one suit in his shop and one in the municipal court'. Evidence that the word 'suit' (not to mention 'press') is ambiguous is provided by the anomaly of the 'crossed interpretation' of the sentence, on which 'suit' is used to refer to an article of clothing and 'one' to a legal action.

The above examples of ambiguity are each a case of one word with more than one meaning. However, it is not always clear when we have only one word. The verb 'desert' and the noun 'dessert', which sound the same but are spelled differently, count as distinct words (they are homonyms). So do the noun 'bear' and the verb 'bear', even though they not only sound

the same but are spelled the same. These examples may be clear cases of homonymy, but what about the noun 'respect' and the verb 'respect' or the preposition 'over' and the adjective 'over'? Are the members of these pairs homonyms or different forms of the same word? There is no general consensus on how to draw the line between cases of one ambiguous word and cases of two homonymous words. Perhaps the difference is ultimately arbitrary.

Sometimes one meaning of a word is derived from another. For example, the cognitive sense of 'see' (to see that something is so) seems derived from its visual sense. The sense of 'weigh' in 'He weighed the package' is derived from its sense in 'The package weighed two pounds'. Similarly, the transitive senses of 'burn', 'fly' and 'walk' are derived from their intransitive senses. Now it could be argued that in each of these cases the derived sense does not really qualify as a second meaning of the word but is actually the result of a lexical operation on the underived sense. This argument is plausible to the extent that the phenomenon is systematic and general, rather than peculiar to particular words. Lexical semantics has the task of identifying and characterizing such systematic phenomena. It is also concerned to explain the rich and subtle semantic behaviour of common and highly flexible words like the verbs 'do' and 'put' and the prepositions 'at', 'in' and 'to'. Each of these words has uses which are so numerous yet so closely related that they are often described as 'polysemous' rather than ambiguous.

Structural ambiguity occurs when a phrase or sentence has more than one underlying structure, such as the phrases 'Tibetan history teacher', 'a student of high moral principles' and 'short men and women', and the sentences 'The girl hit the boy with a book' and 'Visiting relatives can be boring'. These ambiguities are said to be structural because each such phrase can be represented in two structurally different ways, for example '[Tibetan history] teacher' and 'Tibetan [history teacher]'. Indeed, the existence of such ambiguities provides strong evidence for a level of underlying syntactic structure (see SYNTAX). Consider the structurally ambiguous sentence, 'The chicken is ready to eat', which could be used to describe either a hungry chicken or a cooked chicken. It is arguable that the operative reading depends on whether or not the implicit subject of the infinitive clause 'to eat' is tied anaphorically to the subject ('the chicken') of the main clause.

It is not always clear when we have a case of structural ambiguity. Consider the elliptical sentence, 'Perot knows a richer man than Trump'. It has two meanings, that Perot knows a man who is richer than Trump and that Perot knows a man who is richer than any man Trump knows, and is therefore ambiguous. But what about the sentence 'John loves his mother and so does Bill'? It can be used to say either that John loves John's mother and Bill loves Bill's mother or that John loves John's mother and Bill loves John's mother. But is it really ambiguous? One might argue that the clause 'so does Bill' is unambiguous and may be read unequivocally as saying in the context that Bill does the same thing that John does, and although there are two different possibilities for what counts as doing the same thing, these alternatives are not fixed semantically. Hence the ambiguity is merely apparent and better described as semantic underdetermination.

Although ambiguity is fundamentally a property of linguistic expressions, people are also said to be ambiguous on occasion in how they use language. This can occur if, even when their words are unambiguous, their words do not make what they mean uniquely determinable. Strictly speaking, however, ambiguity is a semantic phenomenon, involving linguistic meaning rather than speaker meaning (see MEANING AND COMMUNICATION). Generally when one uses ambiguous words or sentences, one does not consciously entertain their unintended meanings, although there is psycholinguistic evidence that when one hears ambiguous words one momentarily accesses and then rules out their irrelevant senses. When people use ambiguous language, generally its ambiguity is not intended. Occasionally, however, ambiguity is deliberate, as with an utterance of 'I'd like to see more of you' when intended to be taken in more than one way in the very same context of utterance.

2 Ambiguity contrasted

It is a platitude that what your words convey 'depends on what you mean'. This suggests that one can mean different things by what one says, but it says nothing about the variety of ways in which this is possible. Semantic ambiguity is one such way, but there are others: homonymy (mentioned in §1), vagueness, relativity, indexicality, nonliterality, indirection and inexplicitness. All these other phenomena illustrate something distinct from multiplicity of linguistic meaning.

An expression is vague if it admits of borderline cases (see VAGUENESS). Terms like 'bald', 'heavy' and 'old' are obvious examples, and their vagueness is explained by the fact that they apply to items on fuzzy regions of a scale. Terms that express cluster concepts, like 'intelligent', 'athletic' and 'just', are vague because their instances are determined by the application of several criteria, no one of which is decisive.

Relativity is illustrated by the words 'heavy' and 'old' (these are vague as well). Heavy people are lighter than nonheavy elephants, and old cats can be younger than some young people. A different sort of relativity occurs with sentences like 'Jane is finished' and 'John will be late'. Obviously one cannot be finished or late *simpliciter* but only finished with something or late for something. This does not show that the words 'finished' and 'late' are ambiguous (if they were, they would be ambiguous in as many ways as there are things one can be finished with or things one can be late for), but only that such a sentence is semantically underdeterminate – it must be used to mean more than what the sentence means.

Indexical terms, like 'you', 'here' and 'tomorrow', have fixed meaning but variable reference. For example, the meaning of the word 'tomorrow' does not change from one day to the next, though of course its reference does (see DEMONSTRATIVES AND INDEXICALS).

Nonliterality, indirection and inexplicitness are further ways in which what a speaker means is not uniquely determined by what their words mean (see SPEECH ACTS §4). They can give rise to unclarity in communication, as might happen with utterances of 'You're the icing on my cake', 'I wish you could sing longer and louder', and 'Nothing is on television tonight'. These are not cases of linguistic ambiguity but can be confused with it because speakers are often said to be ambiguous.

3 Philosophical relevance

Philosophical distinctions can be obscured by unnoticed ambiguities. So it is important to identify terms that do double duty. For example, there is a kind of ambiguity, often described as the 'act/object' or the 'process/product' ambiguity, exhibited by everyday terms like 'building', 'shot' and 'writing'. Confusions in philosophy of language and mind can result from overlooking this ambiguity in terms like 'inference', 'statement' and 'thought'. Another common philosophical ambiguity is the type/token distinction. Everyday terms like 'animal', 'book' and 'car' apply both to types and to instances (tokens) of those types. The same is true of linguistic terms like 'sentence', 'word' and 'letter' and of philosophically important terms like 'concept', 'event' and 'mental state' (see TYPE/TOKEN DISTINCTION).

Although unnoticed ambiguities can create philosophical problems, ambiguity is philosophically important also because philosophers often make spurious claims of it. Indeed, the linguist Charles Ruhl (1989) has argued that certain ostensible ambiguities, including act/object and type/token, are really cases of lexical underdetermination. KRIPKE

(1977) laments the common stratagem, which he calls 'the lazy man's approach in philosophy', of appealing to ambiguity to escape from a philosophical quandary, and GRICE (1967) urges philosophers to hone 'Modified Occam's Razor: senses are not to be multiplied beyond necessity'. He illustrates its value by shaving a sense off the logical connective 'or', often thought to have both an inclusive and exclusive sense. Grice argues that, given its inclusive meaning, its exclusive use can be explained entirely on pragmatic grounds (see IMPLICATURE §6; PRAGMATICS §12). Another example, prominent in modern philosophy of language, is the ambiguity alleged to arise from the distinction between referential and attributive uses of definite descriptions (see DESCRIPTIONS §5). Less prominent but not uncommon is the suggestion that pronouns are ambiguous as between their anaphoric and deictic use. So, for example, it is suggested that a sentence like 'Oedipus loves his mother' has two 'readings' – that is, it is ambiguous – because it can be used to mean either that Oedipus loves his own mother or that Oedipus loves the mother of some contextually specified male. However, this seems to be an insufficient basis for the claim of ambiguity. After all, being previously mentioned is just another way of being contextually specified. Accordingly, there is nothing semantically special in this example about the use of 'his' to refer to Oedipus.

Claims of structural ambiguity can also be controversial. Of particular importance are claims of scope ambiguity, which are commonly made but rarely defended (see SCOPE). A sentence like 'Everybody loves somebody' is said to exhibit a scope ambiguity because it can be used to mean either that for each person, there is somebody that that person loves or (however unlikely) that there is somebody that everybody loves. These uses may be represented, respectively, by the logical formulas '$(\forall x)(\exists y)(Lxy)$' and '$(\exists y)(\forall x)(Lxy)$'. It is generally assumed that, because different logical formulas are needed to represent the different ways in which an utterance of such a sentence can be taken, the sentence itself has two distinct logical forms (see LOGICAL FORM). Sustaining this claim of ambiguity requires identifying a level of linguistic description at which the sentence can be assigned two distinct structures. Some grammarians have posited a level of LF, corresponding to what philosophers call logical form, at which relative scope of quantified noun phrases may be represented. However, LF of this kind does not explain scope ambiguities that philosophers attribute to sentences containing modal operators and psychological verbs, such as 'The next president might be a woman' and 'Ralph wants a sloop'. An utterance of such a sentence can be taken in either of two ways, but it is arguable that the sentence is not ambiguous but merely semantically underdeterminate with respect to its two alleged 'readings'.

Notwithstanding the frequency in philosophy of unwarranted and often arbitrary claims of ambiguity, it cannot be denied that some terms really are ambiguous. The nouns 'bank' and 'suit' are clear examples and so are the verbs 'bank' and 'file'. Philosophers sometimes lament the prevalence of ambiguity in natural languages and yearn for an ideal language in which it is absent. But ambiguity is a fact of linguistic life. Despite the potentially endless supply of words, many words do double duty or more. And despite the unlimited number of sentences, many have several meanings and their utterance must be disambiguated in the light of the speaker's likely intentions.

See also: LANGUAGE, PHILOSOPHY OF; SEMANTICS

References and further reading

Atlas, J.D. (1989) *Philosophy Without Ambiguity: A Logico-Linguistic Essay*, Oxford: Oxford University Press. (Examines ambiguity tests and questions certain philosophical appeals to ambiguity.)

Bach, K. (1994) 'Conversational Implicature', *Mind and Language* 9: 124–62. (Identifies ways, distinct from those identified by Grice, in which linguistic meaning can underdetermine speaker meaning and, in particular, contrasts semantic underdetermination with ambiguity.)

Cruse, D.A. (1986) *Lexical Semantics*, Cambridge: Cambridge University Press. (Chapter 3 discusses linguistic features of ambiguity and examines tests for it.)

* Grice, H.P. (1967) 'Logic and Conversation', *Studies in the Way of Words*, Cambridge, MA: Harvard University Press, 1989. (Chapter 2 of this collection explains how multiple uses of an expression can often be explained without appealing to ambiguity.)

* Kripke, S.A. (1977) 'Speaker's Reference and Semantic Reference', *Midwest Studies in Philosophy* 2: 255–76. (A case study, focusing on the distinction between referential and attributive uses of definite descriptions, in how to expose a gratuitous philosophical claim of ambiguity.)

May, R. (1985) *Logical Form: Its Structure and Derivation*, Cambridge, MA: MIT Press. (Investigates the hypothesis within generative grammar that there is a level of representation, Logical Form.)

* Ruhl, C. (1989) *On Monosemy: A Study in Linguistic Semantics*, Albany, NY: State University of New York Press. (Argues for the presumption that a

word has a single, though highly abstract, meaning rather than the multiplicity of meanings commonly attributed, as by the list of definitions in its dictionary entry.)

Zwicky, A. and Sadock, J. (1975) 'Ambiguity Tests and How to Fail Them', in J. Kimball (ed.) *Syntax and Semantics*, vol. 4, New York: Academic Press. (Presents and assesses various linguistic tests of ambiguity.)

KENT BACH

AMERICAN INDIAN PHILOSOPHY see NATIVE AMERICAN PHILOSOPHY

AMERICAN PHILOSOPHY IN THE 18TH AND 19TH CENTURIES

Jonathan Edwards, the first great American philosopher, interpreted Calvinist theology within the newer framework of Newtonian physics and Lockean empiricism in his Freedom of the Will *(1754). However, he was all but forgotten by the end of the eighteenth century, when political rather than theological issues held centre stage. In the years leading up to the American Revolution, the moral sense theory of Shaftesbury and Hutcheson, Lockean liberalism and classical republican theory all contributed to the thought of Thomas Jefferson, James Madison and others who saw themselves as parties to a contract with a monarch, defenders of the rights of humans, and members of a new and virtuous republic.*

In the early nineteenth century, Scottish common sense realism prevailed in the universities, but the most original and influential philosophical writing came from the communities of the transcendentalists. Emerson and Thoreau developed philosophies of life, language, knowledge and being in writings drawing on the Greek and Roman classics, English and German Romanticism, Christianity, and non-Western thought. After the Civil War (1861–5), a series of clubs in the East and Midwest, and the new Journal of Speculative Philosophy made Hegel more accessible to Americans; while in Cambridge, Massachusetts, the 'Metaphysical Club' of William James, Charles Peirce, Chauncey Wright and Oliver Wendell Holmes Jr became the birthplace of pragmatism.

The last quarter of the nineteenth century saw the professionalization of American philosophy: new graduate departments at Harvard and Johns Hopkins, professional journals, and state-supported universities in the Midwest building non-denominational departments of philosophy. By the end of the century, James had published his vast Principles of Psychology *(1890) and enunciated a version of pragmatism; Peirce had produced an outpouring of writing on pragmatism, scientific method, logic, semiotics and metaphysics; and Josiah Royce and John Dewey were launched on influential academic careers.*

1   Colonial America
2   19th century philosophy
3   Classical American philosophy

1   Colonial America

The early Puritan communities were sustained by an intense and continuous involvement with abstract ideas. To the Harvard undergraduate studying Ramus' *Dialectica*, as to the townsman poring over Calvin's *Institutes*, questions concerning conversion and sanctification were understood to lie at the heart of New England covenant theology, and these in turn were inseparable from a set of problems in what we now call epistemology, ontology and ethics or moral psychology.

In the immediate background of New England Puritan divinity lay an unstable synthesis of medieval scholasticism and Calvinist theology, with what Calvin himself called the 'awful decree' of predestination at its centre. This synthesis would be exploded by Newton's *Principia* and Locke's *Essay Concerning the Human Understanding*, the two works together regarded in England's American colonies, as in England and Europe, as heralding the advent of a New Science and a new philosophical empiricism.

The great monument of the encounter between covenant theology and the new empiricism is Jonathan Edwards' *Freedom of the Will* (1754), deservedly famous for its apparently effortless reinterpretation of Calvinist doctrine within the newer framework of Newtonian physics – especially the new atomic or 'corpuscular' theory of matter – and Lockean sensationalism. This was the first significant work of philosophy produced in America, and the first American work in any category to have an important influence on European thought. Yet, although certain elements of his metaphysics were absorbed into Concord Transcendentalism, Edwards' influence on American philosophy was otherwise virtually extinct by the end of the eighteenth century (see EDWARDS, J.).

After Edwards, 'abstract' discourse in America – that is, discourse concerned with ideas and principles – shifted from a theological to a political register, as it did also in Europe (for example, in Montesquieu's *Lettres Persanes* and Voltaire's *Lettres Philosophiques*). In European political theory, a new sense of cultural relativity or 'climate of contingency' is reflected in the contract theories of Hobbes, Locke and Rousseau: consent is the necessary basis for the polity, and the particular form of a society may vary according to cultural and historical contingencies. According to 'Lockean liberal' interpretations of the political philosophy of the Founders (Hartz, Boorstin), the Continental Congress applied the principles of Locke's Two Treatises on Civil Government to their own case in declaring their independence from Britain: the monarch had violated his contract with the people, so the arrangement between them was dissolved.

The Federalist Papers (1787–8) of John Madison and Alexander Hamilton (with some assistance from John Jay) constitute an extraordinary intervention of philosophy in the historical process, as they were written for a New York newspaper in the period when the Constitution was being voted on in the state legislatures. In the background of this and other American political documents of the late eighteenth century lies a sea of European ideas and their American inflections, including not just Lockean liberalism, but the moral sense theory of SHAFTESBURY and HUTCHESON, and classical republican theory (deriving ultimately from Aristotle and Polybius via Machiavelli, Montesquieu and the English 'Country party' of Bailyn, Pocock and Dowling). Classical republican theory, with its vocabulary of 'luxury' and 'corruption' as opposed to 'virtue', allowed the American colonists to think of themselves as returning to something like the 'virtuous' state of ancient Rome. Moral sense theory provided an idea central to many revolutionary documents: that all human beings are possessed of a 'moral sense' that discerns right from wrong in the same way as the ear hears a dissonance in music (see MORAL SENSE THEORIES).

It was in fact the transmutation of moral sense theory into the common sense epistemology of Thomas REID, Dugald STEWART and Sir William HAMILTON that became the dominant philosophy taught at American universities from the late eighteenth century and through much of the nineteenth century. These writers offered a defence of direct perception against the scepticism of Hume that, in the hands of such teachers as John Witherspoon of Princeton (appointed in 1766), or Levi Hedge, the first professor of philosophy at Harvard (1792), could be seen as 'deist' or 'Christian'. God created a material world, these writers held, which we by our ingenuity and careful observation can know and improve. WITHERSPOON, a conservative Scottish Presbyterian who became a signatory of the Declaration of Independence, taught that moral questions could be investigated scientifically, and argued against radical scepticism on the ground that we know our experiential errors by means of other experiences. His *Lectures on Moral Philosophy and Eloquence* (1800) became a standard college text. Scots common sense theory helped make empiricism and science orthodox within the universities, while in its realism and insistence that relations are perceived, it anticipated doctrines of Peirce and James (see COMMON-SENSE ETHICS; COMMON-SENSE SCHOOL).

2 19th century philosophy

The most original and influential early nineteenth century philosophical writers arose not in the universities, however, but among the Concord Transcendentalists. This group included Amos Bronson Alcott (1799–1888), Frederick Henry Hedge (1805–90), George Ripley (1802–80), Ralph Waldo Emerson (1803–82), Margaret Fuller (1810–50) and Henry David Thoreau (1817–62). Among these, Emerson and Thoreau stand out for their power as writers, and for their influence on such subsequent philosophers as James, Dewey, Nietzsche, and Ghandi.

EMERSON enjoyed a highly visible career as a lecturer and writer. His sources include the classical philosophy he studied at Harvard, English and German Romantic poetry and philosophy, Hinduism and other non-Western philosophies and, of course, Christianity. Emerson's first book, *Nature* calls for a new 'original relation to the universe' (Emerson 1836). His controversial *'Divinity School Address'* (1838) condemns the 'Monster' of historical Christianity and urges the divinity graduates to find their own original natures, without which they can offer nothing to others. One makes the most sense to others, Emerson holds, by diving deeply into one's own heart. Emerson's *First Series* (1841) and *Second Series* (1844) of essays offer striking aphorisms and powerful paragraphs advocating a life of 'self-reliance', expanding 'circles', deep-seeing 'intellect', and balanced 'experience'. *Representative Men* (1850) and *The Conduct of Life* (1860) are important later works.

THOREAU thought of philosophy as a practice: a life of 'simplicity, independence, magnanimity, and trust' (Thoreau 1854). *Walden* is a record of that practice, based on two years spent living in the woods near Concord, Massachusetts, and offers a series of reflections on nature and human life. Thoreau finds the mass of men and women living 'lives of quiet desperation', driving themselves like slaves. In *Walden*'s long opening chapter on Economy, Thoreau construes his life at Walden as an 'experiment' to show how little is really necessary for life and, by contrast, how needlessly complex most people's lives happen to be. Later chapters blend descriptions of Walden Pond with reflections on the peculiar power of literature – 'the work of art nearest to life itself' (Thoreau 1854), on reading, vegetarianism, spring, ice, living in the present and neighbourliness. Thoreau's other works include his essays 'Walking' (1862), and the influential 'Civil Disobedience' (1849).

After the Civil War (1861–5), two of the many philosophical clubs scattered throughout the East and Midwest played a special role in the development of American philosophy. The 'St. Louis Hegelians' were led by William Torrey Harris (1835–1909) and Hans Conrad Brokmeyer (1826–1906). Brokmeyer emigrated to the US from Prussia in 1844, practised law, and eventually became lieutenant governor of Missouri. A leader in the German community, he worked on a translation of Hegel's *Logic*, which circulated in manuscript. Harris, a native of Connecticut who left Yale in his junior year, taught school in St. Louis and eventually became United States Commissioner of Education. He studied Bronson Alcott and Emerson, Goethe and Victor Cousin; with Brokmeyer, he founded the St. Louis Philosophical Club in 1866 and *The Journal of Speculative Philosophy* in 1867. The latter was the first technical philosophical journal in the USA or England, and published papers not only by US and English Hegelians such as Harris and Edward Caird, but by Peirce, Dewey, and William James (parts of *The Principles of Psychology* were first published in the journal). A few weeks of joint philosophical efforts among the Midwest and Eastern 'idealists' and the university professors of philosophy occurred during the summers of 1879–83, when the Concord School, founded by Emerson and Alcott, enlisted Harris, William James, Benjamin Peirce (Charles' father, a Harvard professor of mathematics), James McCosh (last of the Princeton Scottish realists), George Sylvester Morris (the Hegelian teacher of Dewey and Royce at Hopkins), and Emerson himself as lecturers.

The Cambridge Metaphysical Club had its origins in James' 1868 proposal to Oliver Wendell Holmes Jr (1841–1935) that they should establish 'a philosophical society to have regular meetings and discuss none but the very tallest and broadest questions' (Kuklick 1977: 47). By 1871 the club centred around six men, all with Harvard degrees: James and Holmes, Charles Peirce, Chauncey Wright, Nicholas St. John Green, and Joseph Bangs Warner. Green, a Boston attorney, introduced the thought of the British psychologist and philosopher Alexander Bain (1818–1903), particularly his definition of belief as 'that upon which a man is prepared to act'. Wright was a mathematician employed by the *Nautical Almanac* as a 'calculator', and an occasional lecturer in psychology and physics at Harvard. He applied Darwin's evolutionary theory to the development of consciousness in such publications as 'Evolution of Consciousness' (1873), maintaining that consciousness comes about not from any new capacity but from using an old capacity – forming images – in a new way (see EVOLUTION, THEORY OF).

3 Classical American philosophy

Although Wright was regarded as the leader of the Metaphysical Club, Peirce and then James proved to be its most significant members. PEIRCE seemed destined for intellectual achievement from an early age, and he began publishing papers on logic and semiotics in the 1860s. 'Some Consequences of Four Incapacities' (1868) contains the first published statement of his view that all thought is in signs, and 'On a New List of Categories' (1867) a first statement of his categorial scheme. Peirce presented what came to be called 'the pragmatic maxim' to the Metaphysical Club in an 1872 version of his paper 'How to Make Our Ideas Clear' (1878): 'Consider what effects, which might conceivably have practical bearing, we conceive the object of our conception to have. Then our conception of these effects is the whole of our conception of the object'. In 'The Fixation of Belief' (1877) Peirce considers four ways in which we come to form beliefs: by authority, tenacity (holding on to the beliefs one already has), rationality, or science. Only science, Peirce argues, has the integrity that comes from allowing itself to be determined by 'some external permanency—by something upon which our thinking has no effect' (Peirce 1877).

Peirce worked at the US Coast and Geodetic Survey in the 1860s and 1870s, and was appointed to a lectureship in logic in the new Graduate School at Johns Hopkins in 1879; but he was dismissed in 1884 and, despite occasional lectures at Harvard arranged by William James, never taught regularly again. In a series of papers in *The Monist* in the early 1890s he developed a system of metaphysics according to which absolute chance operates in the universe, but so does 'evolutionary love'; and matter is 'effete mind'. Central to Peirce's many writings was the idea of three categories, Firstness, Secondness, and Thirdness. He held that all signs are 'thirds': besides a purely linguistic element and an object of reference, they contain an irreducible element of interpretation.

William JAMES studied chemistry in the Lawrence Scientific School at Harvard in the 1860s, and biology with Louis Agassiz (including fifteen months in Brazil), receiving his degree in medicine in 1869. He began teaching anatomy and physiology in 1872, and became an assistant professor of psychology in 1875, when he established the first psychological laboratory in America. James' earliest publications did not report research in physiology or the new psychophysics, however, but were a series of critiques of books on science, philosophy and culture. He argues in 'The Sentiment of Rationality' (1879), for example, that reason is a passion, and at the end of 'Remarks on Spencer's Definition of Mind as Correspondence' (1878) he anticipates the voluntaristic pragmatism of his later works:

> The knower is not simply a mirror floating with no foot-hold anywhere, and passively reflecting an order that he comes upon and finds simply existing. The knower is an actor, and co-efficient of the truth on one side, whilst on the other he registers the truth which he helps to create.
>
> (James 1878: 21)

James' masterpiece, *The Principles of Psychology* (1890) gathers and integrates his writings of the 1870s and 1880s in a one-thousand-page work of physiology, psychology, and philosophy. The book became a standard text in newly established psychology programmes (especially in its shortened form), and influenced philosophers as diverse as Edmund Husserl (by its phenomenological description) and Bertrand Russell (by its distinction between knowledge by acquaintance and by description – see KNOWLEDGE BY ACQUAINTANCE AND DESCRIPTION). James introduces the ideas of the stream of thought and the 'vague' or 'fringe' areas of consciousness, in opposition to the discrete atomic sensations of traditional British empiricism. He stresses the importance of attention and habit in our mental life, and offers a theory of the emotions as responses to, rather than causes of, emotional behaviour. James' moral outlook appears throughout the *Principles* and indeed throughout his philosophy, but is particularly explicit and prominent in the collections of papers, some from as early as the 1870s, that he published as *The Will to Believe and Other Essays in Popular Philosophy* (1896).

Although he credited Peirce with originating pragmatism, a lecture James gave at the University of California at Berkeley in 1898 entitled 'Philosophical Conceptions and Practical Results', contains the first published use of the term. Pragmatism, for James, is the view that 'the effective meaning of any philosophic proposition can always be brought down to some particular consequence, in our future practical experience, whether active or passive'. He credits 'English-speaking philosophers' such as Locke and Berkeley with introducing the pragmatic 'custom of interpreting the meaning of conceptions by asking what difference they make for life', as Berkeley did when he found the 'cash-value' of matter to lie solely in our sensations.

Josiah ROYCE was brought up in the California goldrush town of Grass Mountain, studied English at Berkeley and philosophy in Germany. At Johns Hopkins from 1876 to 1878, he studied with George Sylvester Morris, a scholar of German philosophy and a proponent of T.H. Green. Receiving his Ph.D. in 1878, Royce taught English at Berkeley, then philosophy at Harvard, where he became a mainstay of the department. Royce introduced formal logic into the curriculum, and was a respected idealist opponent of James' more naturalistic, open-ended pragmatism.

Royce's early philosophical writing is in accord with his lifelong interests both in the history of philosophy, and in developing his own version of metaphysical idealism. His first book, *The Religious Aspect of Philosophy* (1885) argues for an Absolute Mind that contains all thoughts and their objects. In *The Spirit of Modern Philosophy: An Essay in the Form of Lectures* (1892), Royce traces 'the rediscovery of the inner life' from Spinoza to Kant, with special emphasis on Fichte – praised for his 'beautiful waywardness', the Romantic School, including Goethe, Novalis and Schelling, and Hegel. Royce argues, however, that the inner life is essentially public: that we live in our coherence or relationships with other people.

The third great pragmatist to emerge in the late nineteenth century, John DEWEY, had neither the scientific background of Peirce and James, nor their association with Harvard. Dewey attended the University of Vermont in his home town of Burlington from 1875 to 1879. He studied not only the Scottish school but Kant and Hegel with the university's philosophy professor, H.A.P. Torrey (1837–1902). According to his own testimony, Dewey found in Hegel's philosophy 'an immense release, a liberation' from a sense of divisions between self and world, soul and body, nature and God. Enrolling in the new graduate school at Johns Hopkins in 1882, he studied Hegel and Green with Morris, logic with Charles Peirce, and the newly emerging experimental psychology with G. Stanley Hall (1844–1924). Appointed to a post at the University of Michigan in 1884, he taught there, with the exception of a year at

Minnesota, till 1894 when he began teaching at the University of Chicago.

Dewey's early papers argue for a reconciliation of Darwinism, Hegelian idealism and religion. Intelligence, Dewey asserts, is latent in evolving matter. In the 1890s Dewey called his synthesis of Hegelianism and science 'experimental idealism', but he gradually moved – as he says in the title of his autobiography – 'from absolutism to experimentalism'. His paper 'The Reflex Arc Concept in Psychology' (1896), presages his future instrumentalism and pragmatism in its attacks on the prevailing stimulus–response theory, which Dewey sees as preserving a sharp metaphysical and epistemological distinction between sensory stimulation and motor response. Stimulus and response are, Dewey argues, aspects of a basic 'sensorimotor coordination', a 'circuit' or 'continual reconstitution'. The sensorimotor coordination, like Dewey's later 'problem situation', shares with Hegelian logic the idea of a progression of temporally evolving wholes.

Dewey's educational philosophy also took shape in the 1890s, when he was a professor not only of philosophy but also of psychology and pedagogy. He worked with high school faculty in Michigan, and with the Laboratory School at Chicago. In 'Interest in Relation to the Training of the Will' (1896), Dewey argues that because interest is a complex of felt worth and incipient action, when we are genuinely interested in something, we do not have to will to do it. Only through such genuine interest, which 'marks the annihilation of the distance between the person and the materials and results of his action', can the will be effectively trained (Dewey 1896). In 'My Pedagogic Creed' (1897), Dewey maintains that education is 'a process of living and not a preparation for future living', and that therefore it must seek 'forms of life that are worth living for their own sake' (Dewey 1897).

See also: HEGELIANISM §5

References and further reading

Works and English translations of philosophers mentioned in the text and not included here can be found in the individual biographical entries throughout the Encyclopedia.

Appleby, J. (1984) *Capitalism and a New Social Order: The Republican Vision of the 1790s*, New York: New York University Press. (Argues that Jeffersonian democracy was the triumph in America of an economic individualism rooted in the political thought of John Locke.)

Bailyn, B. (1973) *The Ideological Origins of the American Revolution*, Cambridge, MA: Belknap Press of Harvard University Press. (The book that discovered the roots of Revolutionary thought in 'country ideology' – the local variant of classical republicanism that the colonists imported from England.)

Boorstin, D. (1964) *The Americans: The Colonial Experience*, New York: Vintage Books. (The American Revolution as the ideological triumph of Lockean liberal individualism.)

Cameron, S. (1985) *Writing Nature: Henry Thoreau's Journal*, New York and Oxford: Oxford University Press. (A fine literary study, discussing the relation of Thoreau's immense journal to nature, to his audience and to Walden.)

Cavell, S. (1980) *The Senses of Walden, An Expanded Edition*, Chicago, IL: University of Chicago Press. (A pioneering study of Thoreau as a philosopher of language and knowledge. The essays 'Thinking of Emerson' and 'An Emerson Mood' explore Emerson's epistemology and his relation to Heidegger.)

—— (1988) *In Quest of the Ordinary: Lines of Skepticism and Romanticism*, Chicago, IL: University of Chicago Press. (Contains 'Being Odd, Getting Even,' an existentialist reading of Emerson's 'Self-Reliance', and 'The Philosopher in American Life', discussing the 'repression' of Emerson and Thoreau in accounts of American philosophy and culture.)

—— (1990) *Conditions Handsome and Unhandsome: The Constitution of Emersonian Perfectionism*, Chicago, IL: University of Chicago Press. (Moral and political aspects of Emerson's thought.)

Clebsch, W. (1973) *American Religious Thought*, Chicago, IL: University of Chicago Press. (Readable and sympathetic account, emphasizing continuities among Edwards, Emerson and James.)

Conkin, P.K. (1968) *Puritans and Pragmatists: Eight Eminent American Thinkers*, Bloomington, IN: Indiana University Press. (Fine study of Edwards, Franklin, Adams, Emerson, Peirce, James, Dewey and Santayana by a distinguished historian.)

Coughlan, N. (1975) *Young John Dewey*, Chicago, IL: University of Chicago Press. (Superb short account of Dewey's development and career to 1894, when he began teaching at the University of Chicago.)

* Dewey, J. (1897) 'My Pedagogic Creed', *School Journal* 54: 77–80; repr. in *The Early Works of John Dewey*, ed. J.A. Boydston, Carbondale, IL: Southern Illinois University Press, 1969–90, vol. 5, 84–95. (Dewey maintains that education must proceed through 'forms of life' that are 'worth living for their own sake'.)

Dowling, W.C. (1990) *Poetry and Ideology in Revolutionary Connecticut*, Athens, GA and London:

University of Georgia Press. (Excellent survey of relations between classical republican political theory and poetry during the Revolution and early republic.)

Dunn, J. (1969) 'The Politics of Locke in England and America in the Eighteenth Century', in J.W. Yolton (ed.) *John Locke: Problems and Perspectives*, Cambridge: Cambridge University Press, 45–80. (First important allegation of Locke's non-importance in eighteenth-century political theory in both England and America.)

Fiering, N. (1981) *Moral Philosophy at Seventeenth-Century Harvard*, Chapel Hill, NC: University of North Carolina Press. (Discusses the yielding of scholastic premises to Hutchesonian moral sense theory between 1650 and 1725.)

Flower, E. and Murphey, M.G. (1977) *A History of Philosophy in America*, New York: Capricorn Books, 2 vols. (Volume 1 contains important chapters on Jonathan Edwards and the development of Scottish common sense philosophy in the American context. Volume 2 discusses the St. Louis Hegelians, Peirce, James, Royce, Santayana and Dewey.)

Goodman, R.B. (1990a) *American Philosophy and the Romantic Tradition*, Cambridge and New York: Cambridge University Press. (Challenges the view that American philosophy originates with the Puritans by considering the influence of Romantic poetry and philosophy on Emerson, James and Dewey.)

—— (1990b) 'East-West Philosophy in Nineteenth Century America: Emerson and Hinduism', *Journal of the History of Ideas* 1990: 625–45. (Discussion of Emerson's interest in and use of Hindu texts in such essays as 'Plato, or the Philosopher'.)

Guelzo, A.C. (1989) *Edwards on the Will: A Century of American Theological Debate*, Middletown, CT: Wesleyan University Press. (Summary account of Edwards' New Divinity and its Historiography.)

* Hamilton, A. (and Madison, J.) (1787–8) *The Federalist Papers*, ed. C. Rossiter, New York: New American Library, 1961. (A defence of the new United States Constitution and the federal government it represents.)

Hartz, L. (1955) *The Liberal Tradition in American History: An Interpretation of American Political Thought Since the Revolution*, New York: Harcourt Brace. (The *locus classicus* of the 'Lockean liberal' interpretation of the American Revolution.)

* James, W. (1878) 'Remarks on Spencer's Definition of Mind as Correspondence'; repr. in *The Will to Believe and Other Essays in Popular Philosophy*, Cambridge, MA: Harvard University Press, 1979.

* —— (1879) 'The Sentiment of Rationality', *Mind* 4: 317–46; repr. in *The Will to Believe and Other Essays in Popular Philosophy*, Cambridge, MA: Harvard University Press, 1979. (Characterizes the sentiment of rationality as a feeling of ease, peace and rest, the result of a transition from a state of perplexity to one of lively relief and pleasure.)

* Kuklick, B. (1977) *The Rise of American Philosophy: Cambridge, Massachusetts, 1860–1930*, New Haven, CT: Yale University Press. (A history of the great Harvard department of James, Royce and others; excellent bibliography.)

—— (1985) *Churchmen and Philosophers*, New Haven, CT: Yale University Press. (Traces continuing religious strains in American thought from Edwards through Dewey; contains a bibliographic essay.)

McCoy, D. (1980) *The Elusive Republic: Political Economy in Jeffersonian America*, Chapel Hill, NC: University of North Carolina Press. (Traces the influence of Rousseau and classical republican political theory on Jefferson's idealized agrarianism.)

Marsh, J. (1976) *Selected Works of James Marsh*, intro. P.C. Carafiol, Delmar, NY: Scholars Facsimiles and Reprints, 3 vols. (Volume 1 contains the 1829 edition of S.T. Coleridge's *Aids to Reflection*, with Marsh's preliminary essay – an important source for Emerson and Dewey.)

Miller, P. (1939) *The New England Mind*, New York: Macmillan. (Classic account of Covenant theology as it developed in New England between the first and second Puritan generations.)

Perry, R.B. (1935) *The Thought and Character of William James*, Boston, MA: Little Brown & Company; repr. Nashville, TN: Vanderbilt University Press, 1995. (Affectionate and philosophically sophisticated account of James and his work).

Pocock, J.G.A. (1975) *The Machiavellian Moment: Florentine Political Thought and the Atlantic Republican Tradition*, Princeton, NJ: Princeton University Press. (Magisterial summary of the classical republic political tradition from Aristotle to Jefferson. Claims that English Opposition thought – Bolingbroke, Trenchard and Gordon – rather than Locke, was the real source of revolutionary theory in the colonies.)

Rockefeller, S.C. (1991) *John Dewey: Religious Faith and Democratic Humanism*, New York and Oxford: Columbia University Press. (Contains an account of Dewey's early development as a Hegelian idealist and Christian social activist.)

Schneider, H. (1963) *A History of American Philosophy*, New York: Columbia University Press, 2nd edn. (Classic study, containing a good bibliography of primary sources.)

West, C. (1989) *The American Evasion of Philosophy: A Genealogy of Pragmatism*, Madison, WI: University of Wisconsin Press. (Political and prophetic interpretation of American philosophy, beginning with Emerson.)

Wills, G. (1978) *Inventing America: Jefferson's Declaration of Independence*, Garden City, NY: Doubleday. (Scottish moral sense theory as the origin of the language of rights in the American constitution.)

Wright, C. (1877) *Philosophical Discussions*, ed. C.E. Norton; repr. New York: Burt Franklin, 1971. (Contains 'Evolution of Consciousness' (199–266) and other writings on Darwinian theory.)

Zuckert, M. (1994) *Natural Rights and the New Republicanism*, Princeton, NJ: Princeton University Press. (Reasserts the importance of Locke's influence on American political thought.)

RUSSELL B. GOODMAN
WILLIAM C. DOWLING

AL-'AMIRI, ABU'L HASAN MUHAMMAD IBN YUSUF (d. 992)

Although al-'Amiri had only a limited long-term impact, his extant works provide useful insights into an extremely creative period in Islamic philosophy in the tenth century AD. He attempted to reconcile philosophy with religion by showing that the genuine conclusions of philosophy could not contradict the revealed truths of Islam, and attempted to build consensus within Islam. He argued for the individual immortality and the punishment or reward of the soul. His analysis of the soul is largely Neoplatonic. The reward of the afterlife is determined by the actualization of the intellect in this life, aided primarily by right actions which moderate the physical faculties and turn the intellect toward the Divine.

Abu'l Hasan Muhammad ibn Yusuf al-'Amiri was born in Khurasan (in modern Iran) in the early fourth century AH (tenth century AD) and died in Nishapur in AH 381/AD 992. He began his career in Khurasan, where he studied under Abu Zayd al-Balkhi, and moved to Rayy and Baghdad, where he met and was discussed by such substantial intellectuals as AL-TAWHIDI and IBN MISKAWAYH. He ended his career in Bukhara, where he had access to the Samani library (in which IBN SINA studied shortly thereafter), and in Nishapur.

Al-'Amiri's main concern was the rational defence of Islam against a form of philosophy regarded as independent of revelation, and against competing religious traditions. In the tradition of AL-KINDI, he attempted to reconcile philosophy with religion by showing that the real conclusions of philosophy could not contradict the revealed truths of Islam. Unlike his contemporary AL-FARABI, however, al-'Amiri argued that revealed truth must be superior to philosophy, since revelation was necessary for the completion of the human intellect and as the indubitable guide to right action. The Greeks possessed useful wisdom, but they could not be considered final authorities because they lacked a prophet.

In spite of his attacks on, for example, the Mu'tazila and the Batiniya esotericists, al-'Amiri's approach was generally conciliatory toward philosophy, the *mutakallimun* (theologians) and a wide variety of Islamic sects. His respected treatise on Sufism, for example, provided both a rational, Aristotelian interpretation of Sufism and a reconciliation of Sufism with more conventional Islam. He preferred to emphasize areas of agreement between philosophers and Islamic sects, perhaps because he perceived the dangers of sectarianism in the diverse environment of Khurasan and perhaps also because Islam had not fully consolidated its position relative to pre-Islamic traditions. He had a marked preference for religious, rather than philosophical, terminology (for example, *ruh* rather than *nafs* for the soul), indicating that his probable primary audience was the Islamic religious elite.

In *al-I'lam bi manaqib al-Islam* (An Exposition on the Merits of Islam) and *Inqadh albashar min al jahr wa'l-qadar* (Deliverance of Mankind from the Problem of Predestination and Free Will), al-'Amiri attempted a rational justification of the moral superiority of Islam to other religions, especially to Zoroastrianism and Manicheism. In the latter work, he also attempted a resolution of the theological problem of free will by the application of Aristotelian principles, a project which he repeated with greater philosophical subtlety in his *al-Taqrir li-awjuh al-taqdir* (The Determination of the Various Aspects of Predestination).

His resolution of the problem of predestination required a distinction between necessary, contingent and possible beings. Only God is necessary existence (*wajib al-wujud*), whose essence is identical with his existence. Human use of multiple terms for divine attributes is thus figurative, since God is essentially a unity. All other existents are contingent and, in so far as they require the support of necessary existence, are preordained. The relations of contingent things to each other, however, are of a different order, in which individual responsibility is possible. Significantly, al-'Amiri's use of the term *wajib al-wujud* is one of only two extant examples (the other is Ibn Miskawayh) of the use of this term prior to Ibn Sina, who adopted the term into the very heart of his thought. Al-'Amiri's interpretation of EMPEDOCLES suggests the possible existence of a pseudo-Empedoclean text or tradition extant in his time which might have been a significant precursor of some important Avicennan arguments.

Al-'Amiri's list of the five 'sages' of Greek philosophy is unusual, since Empedocles is first in a line which progresses through PYTHAGORAS, SOCRATES, PLATO and ARISTOTLE. In keeping with al-'Amiri's conciliatory method, each was given a means of contact with a prophetic tradition, even though each spoke from the perspective of reason alone. Empedocles was said to have studied with Luqman in Syria, and Pythagoras with the companions of Solomon in Egypt. Socrates, Plato and Aristotle then preserved and developed the wisdom of Pythagoras. Al-'Amiri's sources for philosophical history are primarily Neoplatonic, especially pseudo-Ammonius (see NEOPLATONISM).

One or more fragmented translations of the *Phaedo* were especially important for al-'Amiri's *Kitab al-amad 'ala'l-abad* (On the Afterlife), in which he argued for the individual immortality and punishment or reward of the soul. His analysis of the soul is largely Neoplatonic, and the reward of the afterlife is determined by the actualization of the intellect in this life, aided primarily by right actions which moderate the physical faculties and turn the intellect toward the Divine.

Al-'Amiri's work was soon eclipsed by the philosophical revolution brought about by Ibn Sina. Nevertheless, his work provides a window into the philosophical and religious debates which formed the background of that revolution and into the sources upon which the participants in those debates drew. Although partisans of various schools may find his interpretations problematic, his emphasis on the importance of good action over particulars of doctrine and his synthesizing interpretations represent an important attempt to build consensus within Islam during a turbulent, fractious, creative period in its history.

See also: IBN SINA; ISLAMIC THEOLOGY; NEOPLATONISM IN ISLAMIC PHILOSOPHY; PREDESTINATION; SOUL IN ISLAMIC PHILOSOPHY

List of works

Al-'Amiri (before 992) *al-I'lam bi manaqib al-Islam* (An Exposition on the Merits of Islam). (A translation of most of Chapter 1, 'The Quiddity of Knowledge and the Appurtenances of its Species', can be found in F. Rosenthal, *The Classical Heritage of Islam*, Berkeley, CA: University of California Press, 1973, 63–70. A translation by F. Rosenthal of Chapter 7, 'The Excellences of Islam in Relation to Royal Authority', appears in 'State and Religion According to Abu l-Hasan al-'Amiri', *Islamic Quarterly* 3: 42–52.)

—— (before 992) *Inqadh albashar min al jahr wa'l-qadar* (Deliverance of Mankind from the Problem of Predestination and Free Will). (There is at present no modern edition of this work.)

—— (before 992) *al-Taqrir li-awjuh al-taqdir* (The Determination of the Various Aspects of Predestination). (There is at present no modern edition of this work.)

—— (before 992) *Kitab al-amad 'ala'l-abad* (On the Afterlife), ed. and trans. E.K. Rowson, *A Muslim Philosopher on the Soul and Its Fate: Al-'Amiri's Kitab al Amad 'ala l-abad*, New Haven, CT: American Oriental Society, 1988. (Rowson contains a critical edition and translation with a commentary on al-'Amiri's most influential work, with thorough background and bibliographic material.)

References and further reading

Biesterfeldt, H.H. (1977) 'Abu'l-Hasan al-'Amiri und die Wissenschaften' (Abu'l Hasan al-'Amiri and the Sciences), *Zeitschrift der Deutschen Morgenländischen Gesellschaft*, Supplement III (1), Wiesbaden. (A useful discussion of the division of the sciences in the *I'lam*.)

Rowson, E.K. (1996) 'Al-'Amiri', in S.H. Nasr and O. Leaman (eds) *History of Islamic Philosophy*, London: Routledge, ch. 14, 216–21. (Concise evaluation of the career of this influential thinker.)

Vadet, J.C. (1974–5) 'Une Défense philosophique de la sunna: les *Manaqib al-islam* d'al-'Amiri', *Revue des études islamiques* 42: 245–76 and 43: 77–96. (An overview of the *I'lam*.)

TOM GASKILL

AMMONIUS, SON OF HERMEAS (*c.* AD 440–521)

The Greek philosopher Ammonius, 'son of Hermeas' was an Alexandrian Neoplatonist. Educated by Proclus in Athens, he succeeded his father as head of the school in Alexandria, where he cultivated the tradition of

learned commentary on Aristotle. Simplicius, Philoponus, Asclepius, Damascius and Olympiodorus ranked among his pupils.

Ammonius' calibre is hard to assess: important works like commentaries on Aristotle's *On the Heavens* and *Meteorology* and on Plato's *Gorgias*, as well as monographs on logic and theology, are lost. Moreover, with the exception of the commentary on Aristotle's *De interpretatione*, Ammonius left the task of writing out his lectures in full to his students. The case of PHILOPONUS (§1) teaches us that they were not always entirely faithful to their master's ideas. Ancient sources praise Ammonius' abilities as a commentator, mathematician and astronomer. The extant works bearing his name suggest that he dedicated himself to sober, instructive and learned exegeses of Aristotelian treatises. Ammonius held strong views on the order in which these had to be studied, starting with logic, followed by ethics, physics, mathematics and finally theology (On Aristotle's Categories 5.31–6.8). In preparation for Aristotle's *Categories*, freshmen were exposed to Porphyry's *Introduction (Isagōgē)* to Aristotle's *Categories*, a logical treatise in which Porphyry discusses the five predicables (genus, species, differentia, property, and accident). Ammonius begins by telling his class what philosophy means to a Neoplatonist (On Porphyry's Introduction 2.22–5.27), emphasizing that philosophy assimilates the soul to the godhead, separates it from the body, and turns it towards the source and highest Neoplatonic principle, the One.

Ammonius accepts the common Neoplatonist contention that Plato and Aristotle substantially agree with one another. The *Categories* commentary begins with ten questions on Aristotle's philosophy, concerning the division and order of his works, their format and purpose, and, finally, the requisite character of a commentator. According to Ammonius, a commentator ought to adopt a position of critical independence: the truth must be preferred to what Aristotle says (8. 15–18).

In his commentary on Aristotle's *De interpretatione* Ammonius dedicates an excursus on Chapter 9 to the problem of future contingents. Although he upholds God's full knowledge of events past, present and future, he nevertheless rejects determinism. God sees all things in the way appropriate to him, that is, at once in a single, eternal now, but this does not entail that future events are determined. The whole commentary seems to owe much to Proclus' lectures.

In a lost theological treatise Ammonius argued that Aristotle's prime mover is both the final and the efficient cause of the universe. The suggestion that the ideas put forward in the treatise were motivated by the influence of Christianity and amounted to a substantial deviation from orthodox Neoplatonism has been plausibly rejected.

The *Metaphysics* commentary of Asclepius of Tralles as well as the early commentaries of Philoponus are greatly indebted to Ammonius, while the *De interpretatione* commentary influenced Aquinas by way of a Latin translation.

See also: AQUINAS, T.; ARISTOTLE COMMENTATORS; NEOPLATONISM §1; SIMPLICIUS §1

List of works

It is impossible to date Ammonius' works with any accuracy, although it is likely that they were composed after the death of Proclus in 485 and before Philoponus assumed responsibility for publication in the decade beginning 510. Below they are listed in the order in which Ammonius intended them to be read.

Ammonius Hermeae (c.485–510) *On Porphyry's Introduction*, ed. A. Busse, *Commentaria in Aristotelem Graeca* IV 3, Berlin: Reimer, 1891. (A commentary on Porphyry's immensely influential introductory treatise on Aristotle's *Categories*.)

— (c.485–510) *On Aristotle's Categories*, ed. A. Busse, *Commentaria in Aristotelem Graeca* IV 4, Berlin: Reimer, 1895; trans. S.M. Cohen and G.B. Matthews, *Ammonius On Aristotle's Categories*, London: Duckworth, 1991. (The latter contains a concise introduction to Ammonius by Richard Sorabji.)

— (c.485–510) *On Aristotle's De interpretatione*, ed. A. Busse, *Commentaria in Aristotelem Graeca* IV 5, Berlin: Reimer, 1897; partial trans. by D. Blank, *Ammonius' Commentary on On Interpretation*, London: Duckworth, 1995. (The commentary contains, on pages 129–39, an excursus on the divine knowledge of future contingents.)

— (c.485–510) *On Aristotle's Prior Analytics I*, ed. M. Wallies, *Commentaria in Aristotelem Graeca* IV 6, Berlin: Reimer, 1899. (Ammonius' lectures on Aristotle's theory of the syllogism.)

References and further reading

Barnes, J. (1991) 'Ammonius and Adverbs', *Oxford Studies in Ancient Philosophy*, suppl. vol.: 145–63. (An ideosyncratic discussion of aspects of Ammonius' modal logic.)

Merlan, P. (1968) 'Ammonius Hermiae, Zacharias Scholasticus and Boethius', *Greek, Roman and Byzantine Studies* 9: 193–203. (A brief discussion of the Ammonius, a dialogue written by the Christian Zacharias Scholasticus and focusing on the pagan/Christian controversy about the eternity of the world.)

Obertello, L. (1981) 'Proclus, Ammonius and Boethius on Divine Knowledge', *Dionysius* V: 127–64. (This article includes a lucid outline of Ammonius' solution to the problem of future contingents and divine foreknowledge.)

Verrycken, K. (1990) 'The Metaphysics of Ammonius Son of Hermeias', in R.R.K. Sorabji (ed.) *Aristotle Transformed*, London: Duckworth, 199–231. (A rejection of the notion that Ammonius substantially modified the Neoplatonist metaphysical scheme.)

Westerink, L.G. (1990) 'The Alexandrian Commentators and the Introductions to their Commentaries', in R.R.K. Sorabji (ed.) *Aristotle Transformed*, London: Duckworth, 325–48. (This whole volume is an excellent guide to philosophy in late antiquity, offering an extensive bibliography.)

CHRISTIAN WILDBERG

AMO, ANTON WILHELM (*c.*1703–56)

The first European-trained African philosopher, Amo pursued a scholarly career in jurisprudence and then in rationalist psychology, logic, and metaphysics. He trained at Halle, Wittenberg and Jena universities, and was influenced by the systems of Gottfried Wilhelm Leibniz and Christian von Wolff. While at Halle university, he wrote a pioneering legal dissertation on the application of Roman laws of slavery to Africans in Europe. Subsequently drawn to classical, biblical, and hermetic traditions that apotheosized a cultural continuity with ancient Africa, Amo focused his theoretical and practical concerns on the exterior world of international law and the interior world of deliberative intellectual acts.

The first African philosopher to study and teach in European universities, Anton Wilhelm Amo was born at Axim in Ghana to Nzima parents who were converted to Christianity by Dutch missionaries. Sent to The Netherlands at the age of four for a religious education, Amo was then transferred by representatives of the Dutch West India Company to the service of Anton Ulrich, Duke of Brunswick-Wolfenbüttel, whose Hapsburg court was the intellectual centre of early Enlightenment Germany. Through the Duke's patronage, which also supported G.W. LEIBNIZ, Amo became proficient in Dutch, Hebrew, Greek, Latin, French and German and subsequently trained at the universities of Halle, Wittenberg and Jena in philosophy and jurisprudence.

As a student at Halle of Johann Peter von Ludewig, the Prussian diplomat and legal scholar, Amo prepared a dissertation, *De Jure Maurorum in Europa* (On the Rights of Moors in Europe) (1729), which utilized Roman law, hermeneutical and historiographical traditions to assert ancient prohibitions against enslaving Africans in Europe. He based his argument on legal rights ostensibly inherited from the early Christian era compacts between the Emperor Justinian and the indigenous kings of Roman north Africa. Amo's dissertation, extant only in digest form, represents one of the earliest scholarly responses to the growing legal dispute over slavery and the status of Africans as aliens in Europe during a period of expanding overseas slave colonies. It reflected the impact of rising African populations in metropolitan Europe and the Holy Roman Empire's disintegrating hegemony. The natural law principles and imperial precedents he employed paralleled those developed in Spain by the legal philosopher and theologian, FRANCISCO DE VITORIA, to oppose the 'Astral Empire' that Charles V planned to build, through slavery, at the outset of the New World conquest.

In philosophy, where Amo's interests inclined towards the Enlightenment rationalism of Leibniz and the related system of CHRISTIAN WOLFF, he specialized in pneumatology (rational psychology), logic and metaphysics. In rational psychology, he attempted to reconcile the tensions between Thomistic faculty psychology (see AQUINAS, T. §1; THOMISM §1) as it focused on the 'free' operations of intellect or will, and the more deterministic empirical psychology rooted in Lockean sensationalism (see LOCKE, J.) and medical physiology. In logic, he explored the nature of intellective acts such as contemplation, deliberation and reflection. Applying the mathematico-deductive method, Amo adopted precepts from the PORT ROYAL semioticians, from modal logic and syllogistic methods, and from Christian Thomasius's 'practical logic' (see THOMASIUS, C.). In metaphysics, a religious attraction to the Cistercian, Carmelite and Franciscan spiritual orders immersed him in the study of Aristotle's *On the Soul* and the church fathers TERTULLIAN and St AUGUSTINE, all of whom Amo traced through such modern thinkers as P. Melanchthon, R. Descartes, G.W. Leibniz, J. Le Clerc, and C. Wolff.

As a professor at Halle, Wittenberg and Jena, Amo lectured on topics that included Leibniz's principle of sufficient reason, the political thought of C. Wolff, J. Lorenz Fleischer's theories of the law of nature and the law of nations, and the decimal system. However, his interests were not confined to the formal university curriculum: as a private tutor, he conducted classes on several of the *ars hermetica* (the occult arts and sciences), including physiognomy, chiromancy, geomancy, natural astrology and decipherment. In 1738 as a member of various learned societies in Europe, including the academy of Flushing in The Netherlands, he published in Latin a compendium of his selected university lectures known as *Tractatus de Arte Sobrie et Accurate Philosophandi* (A Treatise on the Art of Philosophizing Soberly and Accurately).

After the death of his academic patron, von Ludewig, Amo found his position in German academic and social circles increasingly tenuous and himself subject to racial rebuff. In 1747 he returned to Ghana and changed his profession to the honoured Ashanti vocations of goldsmith and seer. He died there in 1756. Since his philosophical writings remained largely inaccessible until their recovery and dissemination in the twentieth century, Amo's historical influence lies primarily in his posthumous role in the international antislavery movement, where his example served to vindicate African moral and intellectual capacities. He is also known as a moral and intellectual vindicationist.

See also: SLAVERY

List of works

Amo, A.W. (*c*.1703–56) *Antonius Guilielmus Amo Afer of Axim in Ghana: Translation of his Works*, ed. D. Siegmund-Schultze; trans. L.A. Jones and W.E. Abraham, Halle: Martin Luther University Halle-Wittenberg, 1968. (A collection of all of Amo's works.)

—— (1729) *De Jure Maurorum in Europa* (On the Rights of Moors in Europe), unpublished. (Amo's dissertation against the enslavement of Africans in Europe.)

—— (1738) *Tractatus de Arte Sobrie et Accurate Philosophandi* (A Treatise on the Art of Philosophizing Soberly and Accurately), unpublished. (A compendium of Amo's university lectures.)

References and further reading

Abraham, W.E. (1964) 'The Life and Times of Anton Wilhelm Amo', *Transactions of the Historical Society of Ghana* 7: 60–81. (Accessible biographical discussion.)

Brentjes, B. (1977) 'Anton Wilhelm Amo in Halle, Wittenberg and Jena', *Universitas* 6 (1): 39–55. (Accessible discussion of Amo's period in these three universities.)

Hountondji, P.J. (1983) 'An African Philosopher in Germany in the Eighteenth Century: Anton Wilhelm Amo', *African Philosophy: Myth and Reality*, Bloomington, IN: Indiana University Press, 111–30. (Reflections on Amo by a major contemporary African philosopher.)

Lochner, N. (1958) 'Anton Wilhelm Amo: a Ghana Scholar in Eighteenth Century Germany', *Transactions of the Historical Society of Ghana* 3: 169–79. (First significant modern discussion of Amo's life.)

JOHN S. WRIGHT

ANALECTS *see* CONFUCIUS

ANALOGIES IN SCIENCE
see INDUCTIVE INFERENCE; MODELS

ANALYSIS, CONCEPTUAL
see CONCEPTUAL ANALYSIS

ANALYSIS, NONSTANDARD

Nonstandard analysis is an important application of mathematical logic to the rest of mathematics. Invented in 1960, it provided a long-sought-for rigorous justification for the use of infinitely large and infinitely small (infinitesimal) quantities in the differential and integral calculus, and the first sound canon for manipulating such quantities.

Consider the structure $\Re$ of real numbers, that is, the set of real numbers together with operations and relations on them. We specify a formal language $\mathcal{L}$, which has names for all individual real numbers as well as for the operations and relations of $\Re$. We can then obtain an enlargement (a special kind of extension) $^*\Re$ ('pseudo-$\Re$') of $\Re$ such that $^*\Re$ and $\Re$ have exactly the same formal properties: that is, properties expressible in $\mathcal{L}$. But, far from being merely a copy of $\Re$, $^*\Re$ has convenient properties not expressible in $\mathcal{L}$, which are not shared by $\Re$. In particular, $^*\Re$ has additional 'nonstandard' objects (which have no names in $\mathcal{L}$), some of which behave as infinite or infinitesimal quantities. If, using these novel objects and properties of $^*\Re$, we prove a proposition about $^*\Re$ that can be expressed in $\mathcal{L}$, then this proposition holds automatically also for $\Re$. Such 'nonstandard' proofs of results about $\mathfrak{R}$ are often easier and more intuitive than conventional proofs, which operate wholly within $\mathfrak{R}$.

More generally, this method is applied to other structures, in virtually every branch of mathematics – including algebraic number theory, various branches of classical and modern analysis, probability theory and mathematical physics, to yield highly intuitive characterizations of various infinitary concepts, to simplify proofs and to provide new, efficient ways of generating mathematical constructs.

1 Historical background
2 Enlargements
3 Higher-order and special enlargements
4 Range of applications
5 Status of NSA

1 Historical background

The lineage of nonstandard analysis (NSA) goes back to Leibniz in two ways: first, his advocacy of the use of infinite and infinitesimal quantities in analysis was remarkably sophisticated for his time (see ANALYSIS, PHILOSOPHICAL ISSUES IN §1); and second, his vision of *lingua characteristica* and *calculus ratiocinator* foreshadowed the invention of mathematical logic, which was to provide the means for a rigorous justification of the use of those quantities.

Leibniz regarded infinite and infinitesimal quantities as 'useful fictions'; ideal (rather than metaphysically real) entities, whose status was similar to that of imaginary roots such as $\sqrt{-2}$, and whose adjunction to the standard real numbers serves to shorten proofs and aid mathematical invention in problems involving continuity.

Like complex (and, in particular, imaginary) numbers, infinite and infinitesimal quantities were freely used by mathematicians during the eighteenth century, despite known inconsistencies apparently inherent in this practice, which provoked protests by philosophical critics such as Berkeley.

During the nineteenth century, with the development of a more critical attitude to the foundations of analysis, the notions of the real and complex number structures were greatly clarified, and consistent canons were established for operating with these entities (see NUMBERS). However, no rigorous canon was found for the use of infinite and infinitesimal quantities. (Cantor, the inventor of set theory, thought that he could actually *prove* that no such canon was possible, and his view was accepted by Peano and others.) Instead, work on the foundations of analysis – by Bolzano, Weierstrass, Dedekind and others – followed a different route (whose viability had also been asserted by Leibniz): the 'delta–epsilon' method, whereby 'instead of the infinite or infinitely small, one takes [standard] quantities as large or as small as required to make the error smaller than [any] given error' (see ANALYSIS, PHILOSOPHICAL ISSUES IN §2).

By the twentieth century, the success of this method (in effect, an extension of Archimedes' method of exhaustion) had been so spectacular and its domination in pure mathematics so total, that Russell was merely expressing received opinion when he asserted that 'infinitesimals as explaining continuity must be regarded as unnecessary, erroneous, and self-contradictory' ([1903] 1937: 345). Nevertheless, the older, now officially discredited, method survived in 'lowbrow' (mainly applied) mathematics and – as a powerfully creative heuristic aid – in the 'underground' private deliberations of 'highbrow' mathematicians.

Before the advent of NSA, some isolated attempts were still made, in the face of received opinion, to provide a rigorous justification for the use of infinite and infinitesimal quantities in analysis. None of these was fully successful, although Schmieden and Laugwitz (1958) came quite close. The successful solution of this problem, achieved by NSA, was to use tools produced by mathematical logic during the first half of the twentieth century, in particular, the notion of a nonstandard model. Skolem showed the existence of nonstandard models of axiomatic set theory (1923) and of arithmetic (1934), but for a long time such models were regarded by logicians as pathological 'monsters' rather than a serious object of study – let alone a useful tool. This attitude began to change in about 1949, and during the 1950s there was a growing body of research into the properties and inner make-up of nonstandard models of arithmetic. This set the stage for Abraham Robinson's invention, in the autumn of 1960, of NSA, which uses nonstandard models as an instrument.

2 Enlargements

The method consists in systematically exploiting the peculiar properties of an enlargement (a special kind of nonstandard extension) *$\mathfrak{U}$ (pronounced 'pseudo-$\mathfrak{U}$') of a mathematical structure $\mathfrak{U}$, in order to study $\mathfrak{U}$ itself.

As a paradigmatic example, consider the structure $\mathfrak{R}$ whose domain of individuals is the set $\mathbb{R}$ of real numbers. Apart from the domain $\mathbb{R}$, $\mathfrak{R}$ has as constituents all relations and operations on this domain. Let $\mathcal{L}$ be a first-order formal language which can be interpreted in $\mathfrak{R}$: so that the domain $\mathbb{R}$ can be taken as the range of the variables of $\mathcal{L}$, and for each entity of $\mathfrak{R}$ – an individual real, or a relation among reals, or an operation on reals – $\mathcal{L}$ has a symbol intended as a name for that entity.

Using the 'compactness theorem', we can prove the existence of a structure *$\mathfrak{R}$, satisfying two conditions. First, *$\mathfrak{R}$ is an 'elementary extension' of $\mathfrak{R}$. Second ('weak saturation condition'), if Φ is any family of $\mathcal{L}$-formulas having one free variable **x**, which is finitely satisfiable in $\mathfrak{R}$ (that is, every finite subset of Φ is satisfied by some individual real), then Φ as a whole is satisfiable in *$\mathfrak{R}$.

The elementary extension condition is tantamount to the following 'transfer principle': any $\mathcal{L}$-sentence is true (when interpreted) in $\mathfrak{R}$ if and only if it is true (when re-interpreted) in *$\mathfrak{R}$.

Thus any property of $\mathfrak{R}$ that can be formalized by means of an $\mathcal{L}$-sentence is true also of *$\mathfrak{R}$, and conversely. For example, many well-known arithmetical laws (such as the fact that $x+y=y+x$ for any reals x and y) are automatically transferred to the extended domain *$\mathbb{R}$ of the structure *$\mathfrak{R}$. Similarly, the fact that the relation denoted by ' $<$ ' is a total (that is, linear) ordering of $\mathbb{R}$ also transfers to *$\mathbb{R}$. In this sense, $\mathfrak{R}$ and *$\mathfrak{R}$ have exactly the same formal properties.

The members of *$\mathbb{R}$ are called '*reals' ('pseudoreals'). Note that every (standard) real (that is, member of $\mathbb{R}$) is also a *real, but not conversely. A *real which does not belong to $\mathbb{R}$ is said to be 'nonstandard'.

As an illustration of the (weak) saturation condition, consider the family of all $\mathcal{L}$-formulas of the form **r** < **x**, where **x** is a variable (common to all these formulas) and **r** is any $\mathcal{L}$-constant denoting a real r. Clearly, this family of formulas is finitely satisfiable in $\mathbb{R}$, because for any finitely many reals $r_1, r_2, \ldots, r_n$ there is always another real greater than all of them. Hence by saturation there exists some – necessarily nonstandard – *real s such that $r<s$ for every real r. Such an s, being greater than all reals, is to be regarded as a 'positive infinite' quantity. Similarly, there are nonstandard 'negative infinite' *reals. The reciprocals of infinite *reals, as well as the real 0, are 'infinitesimals', which are smaller than all positive reals and greater than all negative ones.

If s and t are *reals such that $s-t$ is infinitesimal, we write '$s \approx t$' and say that s and t are 'infinitely close' to each other. In whimsical homage to Leibniz, the collection $\mu(r)$ of all *reals infinitely close to a given real r was termed by Robinson the 'monad' of r.

By referring to the entities of an enlargement *$\mathfrak{R}$, many standard concepts of analysis receive intuitively appealing characterizations which, while being rigorous, are often strikingly similar to the definitions used (without rigorous justification) before the advent of the 'delta–epsilon' method. For example, let f be a real-valued function defined in the neighbourhood of a real r. Then f is continuous at r if and only if $f(s) \approx f(r)$ whenever $s \approx r$. Also, f is differentiable at r if and only if there is a unique real d such that

$$\frac{f(r+\delta)-f(r)}{\delta} \approx d$$

for every non-zero infinitesimal δ. This d is then the derivative of f at r.

Such nonstandard characterizations of standard concepts can be used to obtain nonstandard proofs of standard results concerning $\mathfrak{R}$ itself. NSA is 'conservative', in the sense that any standard result that can be proved using NSA can, at least in principle, be proved also by purely standard means. However, the nonstandard proof is often considerably shorter and more transparent – and therefore easier to construct – than a conventional standard proof. Moreover, as shown by Henson and Keisler (1986), NSA is essentially more powerful than traditional standard analysis. (See also Keisler 1994.)

The ideas outlined so far in connection with the first-order structure $\mathfrak{R}$ of reals apply quite generally to any first-order mathematical structure $\mathfrak{U}$. Any such $\mathfrak{U}$ can be taken as the 'ground' structure: we can prove the existence of an enlargement *$\mathfrak{U}$ of $\mathfrak{U}$ satisfying the same two conditions (elementary extension and weak saturation).

3 Higher-order and special enlargements

Modern analysis is largely concerned with higher-order entities such as arbitrary sets of reals, sets of real-valued functions, sets of sets of functions, sets of sets of reals, functions from sets of reals to sets of reals, and so on.

To apply NSA in this wider context, Robinson used (from 1962) a type-theoretic approach: he considered a 'layered' type-theoretic structure which, in addition to the ground-level individuals, say, the reals, also contains all entities of finite orders obtainable from these individuals (such as those mentioned in the preceding paragraph). By a well-known procedure, a layered type-theoretic structure can be replaced by a first-order structure. Essentially, this amounts to considering the higher-order entities as ground-level individuals of different sorts. The membership relation between entities of different orders now becomes a first-order relation connecting individuals of different sorts. This many-sorted first-order structure can be taken as the ground structure $\mathfrak{U}$ whose enlargements are obtained as outlined in §2 above.

An equivalent but technically simpler approach, first proposed by Machover (1967), is to embed the original set of individuals in a model of Zermelo's set theory – a sufficiently large part of the so-called 'cumulative hierarchy of sets' (see SET THEORY §1). This constitutes a first-order structure in which all the entities of analysis are present as individuals (of the same sort). The basic relations in such a Zermelo structure are the first-order relations of equality ($=$) and set membership ($\in$). Zermelo structures can be enlarged in the usual way.

Another set-theoretic approach, invented by E. Nelson (1977), proceeds axiomatically. Nelson's internal set theory is a conservative extension of Zermelo–Fraenkel set theory with the axiom of choice (see SET THEORY §1). Its universe of discourse contains all standard sets as well as nonstandard *sets. Using a special formal primitive predicate, 'is standard', counterparts of the transfer principle and saturation conditions are decreed as additional postulates.

For many applications of NSA it is irrelevant which of the infinitely many enlargements of a given ground structure is used. But special enlargements are sometimes singled out either for convenience of exposition or because their special properties are needed for a particular application.

One special kind of enlargement is obtained by taking an 'ultrapower' of the ground structure – an infinitary construction foreshadowed by Skolem in 1934 for the natural numbers and Hewitt (1948) for the reals. Luxemburg used an ultrapower enlargement of $\Re$ in one of the earliest broad expositions of NSA (1962). The advantage of this lucid presentation is that it does not presuppose acquaintance with logical technicalities, and was therefore particularly suited for an audience of mathematicians unfamiliar with them. However, it paid for this convenience by having to prove separately each instance of the transfer principle.

Some applications of NSA need enlargements that satisfy certain stronger saturation conditions. Notably, the extremely useful procedure for obtaining a Loeb measure (see below) requires the enlargement to satisfy a condition known as '$\aleph_1$-saturation'.

4 Range of applications

Robinson himself initiated a formidable array of applications of NSA in a wide spectrum of mathematical topics, ranging from algebraic number theory, through various branches of classical and modern analysis and probability theory, to mathematical physics. Here we can mention only a few applications.

Generally speaking, NSA is a particularly powerful tool in problems involving the topological notion of compactness, because the nonstandard characterization of compactness is extremely simple and transparent compared with the standard definition.

Indeed, one of the earliest impressive successes of NSA was the solution by Robinson (1966) with A.R. Bernstein of an open problem concerning Hilbert spaces, which involved topological compactness in an essential way. Since then there have been many important applications to linear spaces and functional analysis.

NSA also provides illuminating insights into structures in which continuity or analyticity and algebraic notions interact; for example, in topological and analytic groups, whose nonstandard study was initiated by Robinson. In such structures, the whole of the continuous or analytic aspect is 'algebraicized' and encapsulated in a single group of infinitesimal *members. Exploiting these ideas, Hirschfeld (1990) was able to simplify very significantly the solution of one of Hilbert's celebrated problems.

Some of the most spectacular achievements of NSA are in probability theory. In this connection, E. Nelson's work (1987) is noteworthy in providing a far-reaching simplification of difficult parts of the theory. Arguably the most important breakthrough in NSA published after Robinson's death was the invention by Loeb (1975) of a powerful nonstandard procedure for obtaining standard probability measures (as well as more general unbounded measures) with prescribed desirable properties.

Robinson himself was – unusually for a logician – an expert in applied mathematics and mathematical physics (particularly in fluid dynamics). Applications of NSA in these areas, initiated by him and continued by others, have been of very great importance.

5 Status of NSA

If revolutions have ever occurred in mathematics, then NSA may be described as one of them (Dauben 1992). Logicians have in general welcomed it, in some notable cases with great enthusiasm. Thus, in Gödel's view, 'there are good reasons to believe that nonstandard analysis, in some version or other, will be the analysis of the future' (see Robinson [1966] 1974). Some logicians have written elementary calculus textbooks for beginners using NSA (for example, Keisler 1976).

Among working mathematicians generally, the spread of NSA techniques has been relatively slow. As pointed out in §2, any nonstandard proof of a standard theorem can theoretically be replaced by a standard proof. Although nonstandard techniques are often significantly more efficient, they require familiarity with logic, which many mathematicians do not possess. However, the acceptance of NSA among mathematicians has been boosted by the successes of its practitioners. In this respect the results initiated by Loeb's work (see §4) have played a pivotal role.

But the view that NSA is destined to supersede standard analysis altogether should be taken with a grain of salt. This is because a given structure has infinitely many enlargements, none of which can be singled out as in any way canonical or 'best', and a standard definition is needed in order to verify that a nonstandard characterization of a concept is independent of the choice of enlargement (see Machover 1993).

See also: LOGICAL AND MATHEMATICAL TERMS, GLOSSARY OF

References and further reading

Capiński, M. and Cutland, N. (1992) 'Stochastic Navier–Stokes Equations', *Acta Applicanda Mathematicae* 25: 59–85. (Powerful use of Loeb measure and other NSA tools to solve a long-standing existence problem in applied mathematics.)

Cutland, N. (ed.) (1988) *Nonstandard Analysis and its Applications*, Cambridge: Cambridge University Press. (Collection of papers on NSA, including a wide range of applications to pure and applied mathematics. See especially S. Albeverio, 'Applications of Nonstandard Analysis in Mathematical Physics', and C.W. Henson, 'Infinitesimals in Functional Analysis'.)

* Dauben, J.W. (1992) 'Revolutions Revisited', appendix to 'Conceptual Revolutions and the History of Mathematics: Two Studies in the Growth of Knowledge', in D. Gillies (ed.) *Revolutions in Mathematics*, Oxford: Clarendon Press. (Assessment of NSA as 'a contemporary revolution in mathematics'; mentioned in §5.)

—— (1994) *Abraham Robinson: The Creation of Nonstandard Analysis, a Personal and Mathematical Odyssey*, Princeton, NJ: Princeton University Press. (An authoritative scientific biography.)

* Henson, C.W. and Keisler, H.J. (1986) 'The Strength of Nonstandard Analysis', *Journal of Symbolic Logic* 51: 377–86. (Explores the strength of NSA compared to conventional analysis; mentioned in §2.)

* Hewitt, E. (1948) 'Rings of Real-Valued Continuous Functions I', *Transactions of the American Mathematical Society* 64: 54–99. (Construction of a structure that, in retrospect, is seen to be essentially an ultrapower enlargement of $\Re$; mentioned in §3.)

* Hirschfeld, J. (1990) 'The Nonstandard Treatment of Hilbert's Fifth Problem', *Transactions of the American Mathematical Society* 321: 379–400. (Great simplification compared to the original 1955 solution by D. Montgomery and L. Zippin; mentioned in §4.)

* Keisler, H.J. (1976) *Elementary Calculus*, Boston, MA: Prindle, Weber & Schmidt. (A beginner's calculus course using NSA; mentioned in §5.)

* —— (1994) 'The Hyperreal Line', in P. Ehrlich (ed.) *Real Numbers, Generalizations of the Reals, and Theories of Continua*, Dordrecht: Kluwer. (A masterly survey of NSA as applied to the real line. Discusses the philosophical status of the *reals. Mentioned in §2.)

Lindstrøm, T. (1988) 'An Invitation to Nonstandard Analysis', in N. Cutland (ed.) *Nonstandard Analysis and its Applications*, Cambridge: Cambridge University Press. (A very user-friendly introduction to NSA. Extensive bibliography up to the late 1980s.)

* Loeb, P.A. (1975) 'Conversion from Nonstandard to Standard Measure and Applications in Probability Theory', *Transactions of the American Mathematical Society* 211: 113–22. (Construction of the Loeb measure. Pivotal advance in NSA. Mentioned in §4.)

* Luxemburg, W.A.J. (1962) *Non-Standard Analysis: Lectures on A. Robinson's Theory of Infinitesimals and Infinitely Large Numbers*, Pasadena, CA: California Institute of Technology. (Early extensive presentation of NSA; uses ultrapower construction of enlargement but no formal logic; mentioned in §3.)

* Machover, M. (1967) *Nonstandard Analysis Without Tears: An Easy Introduction to A. Robinson's Theory of Infinitesimals*, Technical Report no. 27, US Office of Naval Research, Jerusalem: The Hebrew University. (Introduces a set-theoretic framework for applying NSA to higher-order entities; mentioned in §3.)

* —— (1993) 'The Place of Nonstandard Analysis in Mathematics and in Mathematics Teaching', *British Journal for the Philosophy of Science* 44: 205–12. (Expands on §5.)

* Nelson, E. (1977) 'Internal Set Theory: A New Approach to Nonstandard Analysis', *Bulletin of the American Mathematical Society* 83: 1,165–98. (Elegant axiomatic framework for NSA; mentioned in §3.)

* —— (1987) *Radically Elementary Probability Theory*, Annals of Mathematics Studies 117, Princeton, NJ: Princeton University Press. (Tour de force of simplification: advanced probability theory brilliantly made easy by NSA; mentioned in §4.)

Robinson, A. (1961) 'Non-Standard Analysis', *Proceedings of the Royal Academy of Sciences, Amsterdam*, series A, 64: 432–40. (The first publication on NSA.)

* —— (1962) *Complex Function Theory over Non-*

Archimedean Fields, Technical-Scientific Note no. 30, US Air Force Office of Scientific Research, Jerusalem: The Hebrew University. (NSA applied for the first time extensively to higher-order entities, using a type-theoretic framework, to prove new results on the zeros of complex polynomials and on the behaviour of an analytic function near an essential singularity; mentioned in §3.)

* —— (1966) *Non-Standard Analysis*, Amsterdam: North Holland; 2nd revised edn, 1974. (Uses a type-theoretic framework for higher-order entities; includes a wealth of applications; and presents the result on Hilbert spaces, mentioned in §4, proved with A.R. Bernstein. A historical chapter discusses in some detail topics touched upon in §1 and quotes extensively from Leibniz and others. Gödel's preface to the 1974 edition gives his assessment of NSA quoted in §5.)

—— (1979) *Selected Papers of Abraham Robinson*, vol. 2, *Nonstandard Analysis and Philosophy*, ed. H.J. Keisler, W.A.J. Luxemburg and S. Körner, New Haven, CT: Yale University Press. (Includes Robinson's papers on NSA, including seminal applications in diverse fields.)

* Russell, B.A.W. (1903) 'Philosophical Arguments concerning the Infinitesimal', in *The Principles of Mathematics*, London: Cambridge University Press, 2nd edn, 1937; repr. London: Routledge, 1992. (Quoted in §1.)

* Schmieden, C. and Laugwitz, D. (1958) 'Eine Erweiterung der Infinitesimalrechnung' (An Extension of the Infinitesimal Calculus), *Mathematische Zeitschrift* 69: 1–39. (The last, partly successful, pre-NSA attempt to justify infinitesimals.)

* Skolem, T. (1923) 'Einige Bemerkungen zur axiomatischen Begründung der Mengenlehre', in *Matematikerkongressen i Helsingfors den 4–7 Juli 1922, Den femte skandinaviska matematikerkongressen, Redogörelse*, Helsinki: Akademiska Bokhandeln, 217–32; trans. S. Bauer-Mengelberg, 'Some Remarks on Axiomatized Set Theory', in J. van Heijenoort (ed.) *From Frege to Gödel: A Source Book in Mathematical Logic, 1879–1931*, Cambridge, MA: Harvard University Press, 1967, 291–301. (Proves the existence of nonstandard models of axiomatic set theory and hints at the existence of nonstandard models of arithmetic; mentioned in §1.)

* —— (1934) 'Über die nicht-charakterisierbarkeit der Zahlenreihe mittels endlich oder abzählbar unendlich vieler Aussagen mit ausschliesslich Zahlenvariablen' (On the Non-Characterizability of the Number Sequence by Finitely or Denumerably Many Statements with Number Variables Only), *Fundamenta Mathematicae* 23: 150–61. (Existence of nonstandard models of arithmetic proved using a construction foreshadowing ultrapowers.)

MOSHÉ MACHOVER

ANALYSIS, PHILOSOPHICAL ISSUES IN

The term 'mathematical analysis' refers to the major branch of mathematics which is concerned with the theory of functions and includes the differential and integral calculus. Analysis and the calculus began as the study of curves, calculus being concerned with tangents to and areas under curves. The focus was shifted to functions following the insight, due to Leibniz and Isaac Newton in the second half of the seventeenth century, that a curve is the graph of a function. Algebraic foundations were proposed by Lagrange in the late eighteenth century; assuming that any function always took an expansion in a power series, he defined the derivatives from the coefficients of the terms. In the 1820s his assumption was refuted by Cauchy, who had already launched a fourth approach, like Newton's based on limits, but formulated much more carefully. It was refined further by Weierstrass, by means which helped to create set theory. Analysis also encompasses the theory of limits and of the convergence and divergence of infinite series; modern versions also use point set topology. It has taken various forms over the centuries, of which the older ones are still represented in some notations and terms. Philosophical issues include the status of infinitesimals, the place of logic in the articulation of proofs, types of definition, and the (non-)relationship to analytic proof methods.

1   The calculus: Newton, Leibniz and Lagrange
2   Mathematical analysis: Cauchy and Weierstrass
3   Some philosophical issues

1 The calculus: Newton, Leibniz and Lagrange

To begin in geometric terms, the differential calculus provides methods of determining the slope of a tangent to a curve, while the integral calculus finds the area between the curve and the x-axis. The study of tangents and areas goes back to ancient times, but prior to Isaac Newton and G.W. Leibniz tangents were determined at specific points and areas were always definite ones, that is, taken between a specific starting point and end point on the x-axis. Their new insight – treating a curve as being the graph of a function $f(x)$ – was to determine the tangents and areas as new *functions*. Thus the derivative function f' gives the rate of change of the function f, and the indefinite integral $\int f$ is a function showing how the area under f (taken from some arbitrary starting point) varies with the end point. The two calculi are inverse: the 'fundamental theorem' states that

(1) $\quad (\int f)' = f$ and also $\int (f') = f$ (+ constant).

In Newton's version (created 1660s, published 1700s; see Newton (1967–81); NEWTON, I. §6) the differential was a 'fluxion', the rate of change of a variable quantity relative to time (understood conventionally); conversely, that variable was the 'fluent' of its fluxion. His definitions involved changes in dimension: a point as the limit of a sequence of lines of decreasing length, and so on. He defined his functions in terms of limits, but in a very naïve way.

Leibniz formed his differential and integral calculus in the 1670s (published 1680s; see LEIBNIZ, G.W. §§1, 10) independently of Newton, and in a quite different form. It was based on the idea that a 'differential' dx could be created as an infinitesimal increment on x, with the same dimension as x; the slope of the tangent to the curve corresponding to $f(x)$ was $df(x)/dx$. For linear variables x and $f(x)$ the 'integral' $\int f(x)dx$ was the sum of the areas of rectangles $f(x)$ high and dx wide. Thus his version of the principal relationship (1) is

(2) $\quad d(\int f(x)dx)/dx = \int (df(x)/dx)dx = f(x)$.

Another point of superiority of these theories over their predecessors was that the defined functions were themselves variable; thus they admitted of higher-order fluxions (differentials) and fluents (integrals). Physical phenomena of certain kinds could be expressed as 'differential' (or 'fluxional') equations of some order; finding their solution(s) became a major concern in mathematics, with many important applications in mechanics and geometry.

Of the two forms, Leibniz's gradually gained a considerable ascendancy during the eighteenth century. In one respect his use of the word 'function' was misleading, in that often no functional dependence obtained: variables could vary together. But during the 1750s Leonhard Euler realized the advantage of systematically specifying one variable (x, say) as a basis in a problem, relative to which the others were functionally dependent. His criterion was that dx be constant, so that further derivatives $ddx, \ldots$ were all zero; then the differentials of other variables (y, say) were related to dx via 'differential coefficients' $p(x), q(x), \ldots$ of $f(x)$ with respect to x:

(3) $\quad df(x) = p(x)dx,$
$\quad\quad ddf(x) = q(x)(dx)^2, \ldots.$

Another major extension due then to Euler and others was to allow several variables in a problem to be independent; this move greatly increased the range of phenomena which could be represented, in 'partial differential equations'.

During the late eighteenth century J.L. Lagrange proposed, as an alternative to limits and infinitesimals, that the differential calculus was obtainable from the so-called 'Taylor series', the expansion of a function f about any value of x with $h > 0$:

(4) $\quad f(x+h) = f(x) + hf'(x) + h^2 f''(x)/2! + \ldots.$

(This important result had been named after Brook Taylor, although it had already been found by his master Newton and by Leibniz.) The 'derived functions' $f'(x), f''(x), \ldots$ (to use Lagrange's name and notation for them) were *defined* as the coefficients of powers of h in the expansion (4); in his opinion they could be determined solely from (4) and algebraic manipulations. The integral calculus was based on reversing the operations; from f'' to f', and so on.

Lagrange's approach became most widely circulated through the textbook *Théorie des fonctions analytiques* (1797), which was based upon his teaching at the recently founded École Polytechnique in Paris. He also extended his approach and associated with it an allied subject, the calculus of variations, which produced from a given function neighbouring functions which varied slightly from it. This theory, which became of major importance in applications, is also of philosophical interest, in that it requires possible worlds in which, for example, a particle may move along curves defined by functions varying slightly from the function whose curve it actually followed and which the theory was intended to determine.

Lagrange's approach also came to have profitable influences on algebra in the early nineteenth century; in particular, some of its consequences provided powerful analogies for Boole and De Morgan in their contributions to algebraic logic. But the assumptions behind (4) seemed too good to be true; and in fact (4) was refuted by means of counter-examples, in the 1820s.

2 Mathematical analysis: Cauchy and Weierstrass

These torpedoes came from A.L. Cauchy, who had already begun to develop a fourth approach – 'mathematical analysis' (his name) – as part of his own teaching at the École Polytechnique. As with Newton's calculus, the theory of limits served as his basis, but he treated them in a far more careful way, with general definitions and an exploration of properties. In addition, the theory of functions and the convergence of infinite series joined the calculus under limit theory. He raised the level of rigour in various ways, of which some involved points of logic. He gave independent definitions of the derivative and the integral:

$$f'(x) := \lim[(f(x+h)-f(x))/h] \text{ as } h \to 0;$$

$$\int f(x)\mathrm{d}x := \lim_r \sum[(x_r - x_{r-1})f(x_{r-1})]$$

with, $x_0 \leqslant x_{r-1} < x_r$

and $x_0 \leqslant x \leqslant \lim_{r\to\infty} x_r$, as $\max_r |x_r - x_{r-1}| \to 0$.

Cauchy retained Lagrange's notation and name for $f'(x)$, but otherwise things were quite different. In particular, for the first time, (1) became the fundamental *theorem* of the calculus, concerning the inverse relationship between differentiation and integration under the sufficient conditions that $f(x)$ was continuous (in his sense); previously the switch between the two calculi had been more or less automatic. He showed the merit of systematically specifying necessary and/or sufficient conditions under which theorems were held to be true, and of enhancing theory by seeking weaker versions of the former and stronger versions of the latter. He even pioneered the methodical numbering of expressions in a paper or book.

Although Cauchy's theory is not very intuitive (his students and colleagues hated it), it gradually became accepted, especially after its adoption and refinement by Karl Weierstrass (at his widely influential lecture courses at Berlin from the 1860s) as the now standard 'epsilon-delta' treatment of limits. He stressed the need for extra care when several variables were moving towards their respective limits simultaneously, for example, in distinguishing between the following:

(5) $\lim_{x\to a, r\to\infty} \sum_r u_r(x),$

$\lim_{x\to a} \lim_{r\to\infty} \sum_r u_r(x),$

$\lim_{r\to\infty} \lim_{x\to a} \sum_r u_r(x),$

where in the first case the two limits move together. Weierstrass and his followers also realized the importance of distinguishing the least upper bound of a collection of values from its upper limit. For example, the upper limit of the sequence 5, 7, -4, $\frac{3}{2}$, $\frac{5}{3}$, $\frac{7}{4}$,...$(2n-1)/n$,... is 2, but the least upper bound is 7.

Among related developments, Georg Cantor was inspired from the early 1870s to create both his point set theory and transfinite arithmetic from solving certain technical questions in analysis by Weierstras-

sian methods. The further refinement of conditions on theorems such as (1) included the need to define irrational numbers in terms of rationals in order to prove theorems on their existence without begging the question posed. Cantor and Weierstrass had versions, but the best remembered is the 'cut' definition of Richard Dedekind in 1872. Associate each rational number with a point on the continuous straight line by natural order. Cut the line at any point, then the numbers are divided into two classes: to left (L) and to right (R). If L has no greatest member and R no smallest, then the cut does not correspond to any rational number, and thereby defines an irrational one (see NUMBERS §6).

The generally rising levels of rigour in proof – especially the increasing numbers of variables in problems, with ever more intricate functional relationships between them – inspired Giuseppe Peano in the late 1880s to create elements of 'mathematical logic' (his phrase), in order that the language itself of mathematical analysis would be made more rigorous, by relying less on prose. He formulated the propositional calculus in quite an axiomatic manner (not a common way of doing mathematics at that time), and introduced 'propositional functions' and quantification over their argument places. The latter technique was especially significant in clarifying the order of quantifiers for several variables; distinguishing the expressions in (5) is an important example.

The Weierstrassian tradition, together with Cantorian set theory, became standard fare in pure mathematics and some (but by no means all) applications by the beginning of the twentieth century. Cauchy's theory of the integral was extended into the measure theory of Henri Lebesgue and others in the 1900s. At the same time various forms of the axiom of choice were found, revealing unexpected gaps and assumptions in proof methods; but gradually their place in analysis (and set theory) was evaluated and (for most figures) their non-constructive character was tolerated. Various generalizations were made: for example, defining the calculus over groups of some kind rather than over real numbers. In addition, the mathematical analysis of complex variables, which Cauchy had initiated along with his creation of the real-variable theory, rose to major status in mathematics – in his version and in alternatives due to Bernhard Riemann and to Weierstrass.

In one respect, reaction to Cauchy was negative. He had declared that divergent series were normally illegitimate for mathematical use; however, in the late nineteenth century, it became understood that the sum of a series could only be defined relative to a manner of summing its terms, and that the normal method (first term + second term +...) was not the only one. Thus a sum such as

(6) $1 - 1 + 1 - 1 + \ldots = \tfrac{1}{2}$

was true under certain methods of summation, although the series had no sum under the usual method of adding term by term. This discovery rendered still more complicated the relationship between series and functions, which had already suffered a jolt from Cauchy's refutation of Lagrange's assumption (4).

3 Some philosophical issues

Several points of philosophical interest have already arisen. A few others will be made here.

Various types of infinitesimal had been used in the calculus and analysis over the centuries. The three main kinds, not always clearly distinguished, were: (a) the 'infinitely small', a variable quantity with limiting value zero (Cauchy proposed a new form of this kind); (b) 'nulls', such as the dx in (2), which are smaller than normal quantities; and (c) 'pseudo-infinitesimals' – quantities different from zero and yet smaller than any assignable quantity (Berkeley's criticism of the foundations of the calculus in 1734 were based upon this view). They all became unacceptable in Weierstrass' reign; but even then they gained some adherents, and since the 1960s theories have been produced which vindicate their use. The best known is the 'nonstandard analysis' of Abraham Robinson (see ANALYSIS, NONSTANDARD).

One aspect which splits limit theory apart from infinitesimals is that of dimensions. For Leibniz, if x is a line, dx is a very short line, dd$x$ is a very, very short line, and so on; thus dimensions are preserved under the operations of differentiation and integration. By contrast, a theory which uses limits changes dimensions; for example, the limit of a sequence of lines is a point. Intellectually this difference is vast, with profound consequences for applications; it is one source of the non-intuitiveness of mathematical analysis, and applied mathematicians have often preferred to work with differentials, which allow the geometry of a given problem, controlled by dimensions, to be represented and manipulated with incomparable clarity and flexibility.

Once Euler had introduced the differential coefficient (alongside infinitesimals) with (3) above, the notion of function was at centre stage. A major philosophical consideration was that of *generality* of the notion of function. Euler himself had said that variables x and y may be related 'in any way' by a function, but he had in mind only the kinds of functions normally used in his day. The same remark applies to successors in the nineteenth century, such as J.P.G. Dirichlet, though with a somewhat wider realm in mind. Only in the era of measure theory do we find the set-theoretic version which is now standard; that x and y are functionally related without assuming any details about the means. A striking example is the 'characteristic function of the rationals', a type of totally discontinuous function which takes one constant value when x is rational and a different one when x is irrational. Dirichlet had held it to be pathological, as it had no integral in any sense that he could imagine; by contrast, it played a central role in Lebesgue's formulation of measure theory.

It followed from Cauchy's theory of functions that a continuous function may be without a derivative at certain points. Riemann extended this aspect by producing an exotic range of functions with corners and/or discontinuities; and Weierstrass capped it in 1872, with an example of a continuous function which never had a derivative. Results of this kind raised new questions in the traditional discourse of continuity and discontinuity (see INTUITIONISM).

The axiomatic treatment of analysis is often based on the completeness axiom – every non-empty bounded set of real numbers has a least upper bound (equivalent to Dedekind's cut principle mentioned in §2 above). The completeness axiom is impredicative and therefore violates Russell's vicious circle principle (see CONSTRUCTIVISM IN MATHEMATICS).

Cauchy's rigour was based in part upon broad definitions of basic concepts; definabilty and modes of definitions remained an important topic. In particular, Peano treated them as a central part of his logico-analysis: rules for forming them correctly, and the role in theories of definition under hypothesis. In addition, Cauchy had insisted that a mathematical function always be single-valued (so that, for example, $\sqrt{x}$ would have to be split into $+\sqrt{x}$ and $-\sqrt{x}$); in expressing this feature Peano came in 1897 to formulate the criteria for the existence of a referent to a definite description in mathematics that Bertrand Russell was to propose in 1905 for natural language in his famous paper 'On Denoting' (see DESCRIPTIONS; RUSSELL, B.A.W. §9).

The long-suffering word 'analysis' was forced to fulfil still more duties by this subject. The traditional link with algebra was already becoming tenuous by the late eighteenth century, and was weakened further by Cauchy's refutation of (4) as a foundation. In addition, proofs in mathematical analysis from Cauchy onwards are usually synthetic, in that they start out from definitions of basic notions (continuity of a function, say) and/or proven results and finish with the theorem required.

Weierstrass introduced a methodology, with particular bearing upon mathematical analysis: examine all the exceptional and special cases, and do not be content with theorems about 'in general...'. Cantor was led to his set theory by obeying such a stricture (see CANTOR, G. §1).

Do foundations have foundations of their own? Mathematical analysis shows beautiful examples to illustrate this question: Weierstrass underpinned the foundations which Cauchy had provided by refining single-limit theory into multiple-limit theory and the other aspects mentioned above, which Cauchy and his contemporaries had handled freely; but he and his generation took for granted making an infinite selection of members from a set, which was recognized in the axiom of choice to be an additional question.

See also: AXIOM OF CHOICE; CONTINUUM HYPOTHESIS; LOGICAL AND MATHEMATICAL TERMS, GLOSSARY OF

References and further reading

Bos, H.J.M. (1974) 'Differentials, Higher-Order Differentials and the Derivative in the Leibnizian Calculus', *Archive for History of Exact Sciences* 14: 1–90. (On Leibniz and Euler.)

Bottazzini, U. (1986) *The Higher Calculus*, Heidelberg: Springer. (Covers both real and complex analysis, 1750–1900.)

Cohen, H. (1883) *Das Princip der Infinitesimalmethode und seine Geschichte* (The Principle of the Infinitesimal Method and its History), Berlin: Dummler. (A fine historico-philosophical survey.)

Grattan-Guinness, I. (ed.) (1980) *From the Calculus to Set Theory, 1630–1910*, London: Duckworth. (Covers only real-variable analysis.)

Hardy, G.H. (1949) *Divergent Series*, Oxford: Clarendon Press. (Fine coverage, with historical notes.)

Hawkins, T.W. (1970) *Lebesgue's Theory of Integration: Its Origins and Development*, Madison, WI: University of Wisconsin Press; repr. New York: Chelsea, 1975. (On measure theory.)

Landau, L. (1930) *Grundlagen der Analysis* (Foundations of Analysis), Leipzig: Teubner; repr. and trans. New York: Chelsea, 1951. (Classic introductory text.)

* Newton, I. (1967–81) *The Mathematical Papers of Isaac Newton*, ed. D.T. Whiteside, Cambridge: Cambridge University Press, 8 vols. (Extensive selection of manuscripts and editorial commentary.)

Yushkevich, A.P. (1976) 'The Concept of Function up to the Middle of the 19th Century', *Archive for History of Exact Sciences* 16: 37–85. (On the development of functions and real variables.)

I. GRATTAN-GUINNESS

ANALYTIC ETHICS

*Moral philosophy has traditionally been divided into normative ethics and meta-ethics. Normative ethics concerns judgments about what is good and how we should act. Meta-ethics, with which 'analytic ethics' is typically identified, seeks to understand such judgments. Are they factual statements capable of being literally true or false (*cognitivism*)? Or are they commands or expressions of attitude, capable only of greater or lesser appropriateness or efficacy (*noncognitivism*)? Cognitivists focus on whether the facts to which they claim moral judgments correspond are discovered from experience, or whether they occupy a different realm, as do mathematical facts. Noncognitivists, in contrast, arguing that moral judgments are not fact-stating, ask if they signal our feelings or commitments, or are imperatives of conduct.*

Other questions concerning moral judgments include whether they are subjective or objective, and how they are connected to motivation. Analytic ethics therefore not only concerns the meaning of moral terms, but ranges over such areas as epistemology, metaphysics and the theory of action. As a field it remains full of controversy. It has developed approaches that afford specific insights into morality, and contributed to our understanding of the functions of thought and language.

1 From intuitionism to noncognitivism
2 Challenges to noncognitivism
3 Leading issues

1 From intuitionism to noncognitivism

Prior to the twentieth century, questions about the nature of moral judgment were framed primarily in substantive terms: Which 'faculties' are involved? What sorts of acts or traits of character are morally good or bad, right or wrong? Some philosophers (such as Hutcheson and Hume) emphasized the role of sentiment, while others (such as Kant) stressed reason (see KANTIAN ETHICS; MORAL SENSE THEORIES). Some (Hume, Kant) took ordinary moral practice as a touchstone, while others (Bentham, Mill) attempted to defend an 'external standard' that could reform moral opinion.

In the twentieth century, G.E. MOORE succeeded in founding a new tradition that came to insist upon a rigorous separation of questions of meaning from substantive questions. In *Principia Ethica* (1903), he introduced the 'open question' argument: for any purported analysis *A* of a moral concept in nonmoral terms (for example, 'Good' = 'Conducive to happiness'), consider the question, 'Yes, I see that *x* is *A* (for instance, *x* conduces to happiness), but is *x* good?'; if this question is intelligible, and not as trivial as, 'Is *x*, which is *A*, also *A*?', then even if we come to agree that *A* is good, *A* cannot simply be what we *mean* in calling something 'good'. Moore used this argument to advance his claim that 'good' names a *sui generis*, non-natural property, known by a kind of rational intuition (see INTUITIONISM IN ETHICS). Moore also believed that this property supervenes on natural properties: any two things with just the same natural properties would necessarily be equally good (or bad) (see SUPERVENIENCE). Natural properties were thus seen as 'good-making', but Moore thought it a 'naturalistic fallacy' to equate good with them.

Subsequent philosophers tended to agree that good cannot be analytically reduced to a natural property, but rejected Moore's rational intuition. Logical positivists, for example, divided cognitively significant propositions into two categories, the analytic, knowable a priori because tautological, and the synthetic, knowable a posteriori by empirical means (see LOGICAL POSITIVISM §3; ANALYTICITY). Intuitionist claims of synthetic a priori moral knowledge fit neither category: the open question argument showed that substantive moral theories are not analytic, but the lack of any empirical procedure for resolving fundamental moral disputes showed that they could not be synthetic either. Loyal to the positivist bifurcation, A.J. Ayer (1936) concluded that moral judgments expressed not cognitively significant propositions, but emotions (see AYER, A.J.).

C.L. Stevenson (1944) endorsed this conclusion, though not for positivistic reasons, and moreover showed how emotivism could explain something intuitionism had made very mysterious – the seeming 'magnetism' or 'action-guidingness' of moral judgments. Intuitionists see moral judgments as descriptions of a special realm of abstract qualities, such as moral rightness. But description seems motivationally neutral. Why then is it odd for someone to say, 'This is the right thing to do, but I'm in no way for it'? (Contrast this with the remark, 'This is the tidiest thing to do, but I'm in no way for it.') Emotivists, on the other hand, see judgments of moral rightness as expressions of one's approval of a course of action, establishing a necessary or 'internal' connection to the speaker's motivations. Moral disagreement among speakers is seen as conflict in attitudes or commitments among speakers, given its special interest by the need for resolving the question, 'How should I (or we) act?' (see EMOTIVISM; MORAL MOTIVATION §§1–2).

Emotivism is one form of noncognitivism, which interprets moral judgments as expressions or imperatives, not as descriptions of 'objective reality'. Must noncognitivists therefore see moral judgments as 'merely subjective', immune to rational argument and liable to revision whenever the mood strikes? Stevenson, R.M. Hare (1952) and others have argued that nothing in noncognitivism prevented speakers from seeing their attitudes as based upon straightforwardly cognitive, objective considerations, so long as this relation is not seen as an analytic derivation (see HARE, R.M.). Perhaps it is part of what makes an attitude moral that one is committed to universalizing the judgments it supports or giving certain kinds of impersonal reasons in its defence. By the 1950s, noncognitivism's combination of explanatory power with freedom from metaphysical baggage enabled it thoroughly to supplant intuitionism as the dominant position in analytic ethics.

2 Challenges to noncognitivism

Not everyone was convinced that noncognitivism could adequately accommodate the cognitive aspects of moral thought and language. Peter Geach (1965) pointed out that noncognitivists failed to show how moral claims, construed as essentially non-propositional, could display the full logic and grammar of propositions, as actual moral judgments unquestionably do. If, for example, 'Stealing is wrong' expresses one's attitude of disapproval of stealing, then how are we to understand the conditional, 'If stealing is wrong, then stealing without being caught is still wrong', which could be asserted sincerely by someone who does not disapprove of stealing at all? Recent noncognitivists, notably Simon Blackburn and Allan Gibbard, have taken up Geach's challenge, but it is fair to say that no fully satisfactory solution has yet been given.

Critics like Philippa Foot (1978) and Geoffrey Warnock followed a different strategy against noncognitivism, in part by noting that the open question argument has narrower scope than previously supposed. Understanding moral language, they argued, involves grasping certain contentful relations of relevance as well as knowing how to use its expressive force. Consider the remark, 'This new petrochemical project is an ethical marvel; it will make our firm famous throughout the world! Of course, it will cause human dislocation and suffering – but what could that possibly have to do with ethics?' Such a remark would betray a very imperfect understanding of moral language, even on the part of someone indifferent to human suffering who nevertheless cared unconditionally about the fame of his company. A plausible noncognitivism must at least allow that substantive norms of relevance govern moral discourse and that descriptive content can thereby accrue to moral language in a secondary way. But once substantive content has been admitted, the challenge can be pushed further. Why say that content is secondary and expressive force primary? Noncognitivists will point to the success of their 'internalist' account of the relation of moral judgment and motivation. But Foot challenges this. If a person calls their project an ethical marvel because it publicizes their company, we do not know what they are talking about. But someone who says, 'Sure, a progressive tax on incomes would be more just, and that is fine if you care about justice for its own sake, but what is it to people like me?', will strike us as more antipathetic than linguistically confused. Perhaps, as Foot and William Frankena have suggested, it would accord better with actual use to see the connection between moral judgment and motivation as a matter of what is typical rather than essential. Typically we care very much, individually and socially, about the kinds of things morality is concerned with – such as wellbeing and even-handedness – and we tend to dislike and distrust those who show no interest in such matters. Moreover, we tend to think they ought to show more interest. But we can understand this 'ought' as signalling the unconditional character of moral norms, without seeing it as marking a special realm of rational or motivational necessity. After all, we apply norms of etiquette even to the obdurately rude.

Critics have also questioned some of the contrasts upon which noncognitivism has been based. Some have followed Quine in challenging the logical positivist's version of the analytic/synthetic distinction (see QUINE, W.V. §§3, 8). Thomas Nagel (1970) and John McDowell (1985) have considered alternatives to the Humean thesis that cognitive states cannot suffice for action except when combined with desires. McDowell and David Wiggins (1987) have challenged us to rethink the subjective/objective distinction, by exploring a possible analogy between value and secondary qualities such as colour, which seem both to involve a human response and to be objective (see SECONDARY QUALITIES). Hilary Putnam (1981) has argued that philosophy of science no longer supports the fact/value contrast as traditionally drawn, since rationally optional norms suffuse the process of scientific 'fact-finding' (see PUTNAM, H. §8).

At the same time, various philosophers have sought to develop a positive conception of the factual status of moral judgments. Some have done so 'on the cheap', by urging a minimalist conception of truth according to which a discourse is apt for truth or falsity merely if it displays the full grammar and logic of assertion, as moral discourse uncontroversially does. Others have retained a substantive notion of truth, but have claimed that moral statements can earn truth-evaluabilty in this more robust sense. For example, one group of nonreductionist moral realists, including Richard Boyd and Nicholas Sturgeon, have argued that moral predicates can meet naturalistic criteria of property-attribution by playing a role in the best explanatory theories of empirical science. Other philosophers who take naturalistic concerns seriously, such as Richard Brandt, Gilbert Harman and David Lewis, have sought to provide reductions or reforming definitions of moral notions in terms of idealizations of psychological properties. Yet another group, partly inspired by a non-naturalist Kantian tradition, have argued that the objectivity of moral judgment cannot be impugned by invidious comparisons with empirical science. Morality's subject matter, they argue, is a realm of practical reasons – reasons for action, not belief – and whether this domain can be a source of truth and knowledge depends not upon vindicating an ontology of 'moral facts', but upon the existence of objective reasons for agents. Kurt Baier, Thomas Nagel and John Rawls, among others, have attempted to show how we might understand the possibility of such reasons.

Other critics of the dialectic set in motion by noncognitivism have taken a more radically questioning stance. Bernard Williams (1985), Alasdair MacIntyre and various feminist philosophers have in different ways asked where the demand for objective or rational validation in ethics comes from in the first place, and whether, on reflection, it has sufficient credibility or interest to sustain the project of analytic ethics or 'moral theory' (see WILLIAMS, B.A.O.; FEMINIST ETHICS).

3 Leading issues

Although noncognitivism has been widely criticized, no cognitivist explanation of moral phenomena has yet been developed with anything like the systematic power found in the work of Stevenson, Hare or Gibbard. Nor have those who call for an end to ethical theorizing managed to show how we could do without it. The main questions one might expect to figure in continuing debates include: In what sense is it a substantial achievement for a discourse to be truth-evaluable, or is this the modest and inevitable outcome of an assertoric grammar? If the former, then what does that achievement require? If the latter, then what notions, if any, of objectivity and factuality remain to distinguish among assertoric practices, and how does ethics stand with these? Is motivation necessarily related to making or being subject to moral judgment? Is a noncognitivist approach to moral discourse ultimately self-destabilizing, since it construes normativity in non-factualist terms and yet appears to presuppose for its own purposes facts of meaning, arguably a normative domain? Should historicist and feminist criticism of analytic ethics be understood as offering an alternative, or as showing how a more genuinely objective and worthwhile analysis of ethics might be possible?

See also: MORAL JUDGMENT; MORAL KNOWLEDGE; MORAL REALISM; MORAL SCEPTICISM; MORALITY AND ETHICS; NATURALISM IN ETHICS

References and further reading

* Ayer, A.J. (1936) *Language, Truth and Logic*, London: Gollancz; 2nd edn, 1946, esp. ch. 6. (Groundbreaking discussion of the status of moral judgments within the logical empiricist programme.)
Brandt, R.B. (1979) *A Theory of the Good and the Right*, New York: Oxford University Press. (Systematic presentation of a contemporary naturalism based upon 'reforming definitions' and psychological theory.)
Darwall, S., Gibbard, A. and Railton, P. (1997) *Moral Discourse and Practice*, New York: Oxford University Press. (Anthology containing a selection of papers by authors discussed in this entry. Also contains an introductory overview of twentieth-century analytic ethics and bibliography.)
* Foot, P. (1978) *Virtues and Vices*, Berkeley, CA: University of California Press. (A collection of essays that traces the evolution of Foot's discontent with noncognitivist accounts of moral language, and with categorical conceptions of moral imperatives. Her views have since evolved yet further.)
* Geach, P. (1965) 'Assertion', *Philosophical Review* 74: 449–65. (Seminal criticism of noncognitivism; Geach attributes the basic insight to Frege.)
* Gibbard, A. (1990) *Wise Choices, Apt Feelings*, Cambridge, MA: Harvard University Press. (Powerful presentation of a norm-expressivist analysis of our discourse about rationality, with extensions to ethics.)
* Hare, R.M. (1952) *The Language of Morals*, Oxford: Oxford University Press. (The first of Hare's series of highly influential books developing and defending his 'non-descriptivist' interpretation of moral language – he rejects the term 'noncognitivism' because it fails to reflect how his account makes moral judgment reason-giving.)
* McDowell. J. (1985) 'Values and Secondary Qualities', in T. Honderich (ed.) *Morality and Objectivity*, London: Routledge & Kegan Paul. (Influential revival of the analogy between values and secondary qualities, such as colour.)
* Moore, G.E. (1903) *Principia Ethica*, Cambridge: Cambridge University Press. (Original presentation of the 'open question' argument; set the terms for much of twentieth-century analytic ethics.)
* Nagel, T. (1970) *The Possibility of Altruism*, Oxford: Clarendon Press. (Powerful revival of the Kantian idea that moral objectivity consists in rational requirements on action.)
Pojman, L. (ed.) (1989) *Ethical Theory: Classical and Contemporary Readings*, Belmont, CA: Wadsworth. (Useful anthology containing many influential writings in analytic ethics.)
* Putnam, H. (1981) *Reason, Truth, and History*, New York: Cambridge University Press. (Critical re-examination of orthodox assumptions about the fact/value distinction and the notion of rationality.)
Rawls, J. (1971) *A Theory of Justice*, Cambridge, MA: Harvard University Press. (Highly influential discussion not only of the concept of justice but also of coherence and contractarian methods of justification in ethics.)
Sayre-McCord, G. (ed.) (1988) *Moral Realism*, Ithaca, NY: Cornell University Press. (Anthology containing relevant essays by Boyd, McDowell, Sturgeon and others.)
* Stevenson, C.L. (1944) *Ethics and Language*, New Haven, CT: Yale University Press. (Seminal work in developing noncognitivism.)
* Wiggins, D. (1987) *Needs, Values, Truth*, Oxford: Blackwell. (Contains several important essays discussing truth in ethics and the possibility of a sensible, cognitivist subjectivism.)
* Williams, B. (1985) *Ethics and the Limits of Philosophy*, Cambridge, MA: Harvard University Press and London: Fontana. (Influential criticism of various trends in moral theory.)

PETER RAILTON

ANALYTICAL PHILOSOPHY

Philosophical analysis is a method of inquiry in which one seeks to assess complex systems of thought by 'analysing' them into simpler elements whose relationships are thereby brought into focus. This method has a long history, but became especially prominent at the start of the twentieth century and, by becoming integrated into Russell's development of logical theory, acquired a greater degree of sophistication than before. The logical positivists developed the method further during the 1930s and, in the context of their anti-metaphysical programme, held that analysis was the only legitimate philosophical inquiry. Thus for them philosophy could only be 'analytical philosophy'.

After 1945 those philosophers who wanted to expand philosophical inquiries beyond the limits prescribed by the positivists extended the understanding of analysis to include accounts of the general structures of language and thought without the earlier commitment to the identification of 'simple' elements of thought. Hence there developed a more relaxed conception of 'linguistic analysis' and the understanding of 'analytical philosophy' was modified in such a way that a critical concern with language and meaning was taken to be central to it, leading, indeed, to a retrospective re-evaluation of the role of Frege as a founder of analytical philosophy. At the same time, however, Quine propounded influential arguments which suggest that methods of analysis can have no deep significance because there is no determinate structure to systems of thought or language for the analytical philosopher to analyse and assess. Hence some contemporary philosophers proclaim that we have now reached 'the end of analytical philosophy'. But others, who find Quine's arguments unpersuasive, hold that analytical philosophy has virtues quite sufficient to ensure it a role as a central philosophical method for the foreseeable future.

1 The method of analysis
2 From philosophical analysis to analytical philosophy
3 Linguistic analysis
4 The end of analytical philosophy?

1 The method of analysis

The term 'analysis' has its origins in a classical Greek word denoting the activity of taking something apart; and the thought that such an activity might be a model for explanations of complex structures by reference to their simpler parts is itself a Greek thought, exemplified by Socrates' dream in Plato's *Theaetetus* (see PLATO §15). In the early modern period, the idea of analysis reappears in Descartes' injunction that one should identify the 'simple natures' characteristic of one's subject-matter, which Arnauld explicitly describes in *La logique, ou l'art de penser* (The Art of Thinking) (1662) as the adoption of a 'method of analysis' (see ARNAULD, A.; DESCARTES, R.). This method then can be found in much of the philosophy of the period, as in Locke's account of 'complex ideas' in his *Essay Concerning Human Understanding* (1689), which is conducted in terms of an analysis of them into their constituent 'simple ideas' (see LOCKE, J. §4).

Kant's 'Transcendental Analytic' in his *Critique of Pure Reason* moves away from the Cartesian analysis of 'ideas' to the analysis of our capacities for understanding and judgment (see KANT, I. §§6–7); and as the idealist tradition develops, especially in the work of HEGEL, there is a further shift away from the method of analysis to the 'method of dialectic'. Hence one aspect of the break with idealism initiated by G.E MOORE (§2) is a call for a return to the method of analysis: thus in the course of arguing against idealist accounts of judgment, he maintained that 'a thing becomes intelligible first when it is analysed into its constituent concepts' (Moore 1899: 182). As RUSSELL always acknowledged, it was this Moorean conception of analysis which initially inspired his own analytical programme, although in also accepting that there is a sense in which 'analysis is falsification' (Russell 1903: 141), he equally recognized its limitations.

Although Russell had a decisive role in the emergence of the self-consciously 'analytical' conception of philosophy, many other philosophers at the end of the nineteenth century sought to return to a method of analysis. Brentano's approach to psychology was explicitly analytical, and there is a direct route from Brentano's analytical psychology to Husserl's programme of phenomenological analysis (see BRENTANO, F.; HUSSERL, E.; PHENOMENOLOGY, EPISTEMIC ISSUES IN). Similarly, from among the American pragmatists, C.S. PEIRCE wrote that that 'the only thing I have striven to do in philosophy has been to analyse sundry concepts with exactitude' (Passmore [1957] 1968: 104).

2 From philosophical analysis to analytical philosophy

The core thought behind this conception of analysis is that of the explanation of a whole by reference to its parts. But since philosophical analysis involves no physical decomposition of a whole into its parts, it needs to be made clear how this talk of 'analysis' makes sense.

In the case of logical analysis the basic idea is that one can explain the inferential significance of a statement through an account of its 'logical form', which, by identifying the presence of certain simple 'logical constants' in the statement, enables one to fit it into a general logical theory that shows how to argue for it and from it. In Russell's writings the scope of this idea was much extended by allowing that the logical analysis of a statement can lead one to an account of its logical form which discerns the presence of logical constants that were certainly not apparent in the surface structure of the statement. His theory of descriptions, which assigns to the statement 'The present King of France is bald' the logical form '$(\exists x)(Fx \,\&\, (\forall y)(Fy \to y = x) \,\&\, Bx)$' is a classic case of a logical analysis of this kind (see DESCRIPTIONS). Russell further enhanced the significance of logical analysis by taking it that a statement's logical analysis revealed the 'constituents' of the proposition expressed by the statement. Thus he took it that his theory of descriptions showed that it was a mistake to regard the phrase 'The present King of France' as identifying a constituent of the propositions expressed by statements in which it occurs, even when they are true, since the description is eliminated by the logical analysis (see LOGICAL CONSTANTS; LOGICAL FORM).

In the case of epistemological analysis, the guiding assumption is that complex claims to knowledge are justified by reference to simpler items of evidence, typically observations concerning which a high degree of certainty can be accepted. Hence the classic context for epistemological analysis is the empiricist theory that all evidence is, in one way or another, perceptual evidence and many empiricists have held that, in so far as beliefs about the world are warranted at all, it should be possible to provide an epistemological analysis of them which shows just how they can be supported by perceptual evidence (see EMPIRICISM).

Both logical and epistemological analyses are normative, and for this reason can also be subversive. Russell develops his theory of descriptions into a theory of 'logical fictions' which implies that our ontological commitments are less extensive than we might at first suppose. Likewise, epistemological analyses imply that where a putative belief (a belief in immortality, perhaps) is one for which analysis reveals no satisfactory evidence, the credentials of the belief are called into question. This normativity is an aspect of all properly philosophical analyses: phenomenological analyses, properly understood, are not just introspective descriptions of appearances; they are supposed to elucidate the priorities within different modes of consciousness.

I shall not attempt to characterize here all the different kinds of analysis that are properly philosophical. For 'analytical philosophy' can be provisionally defined by the priority it assigns to logical and epistemological analysis. I have already mentioned the work of Moore and Russell, though neither of them held that philosophy is just analysis. Their most famous pupil was WITTGENSTEIN, whose *Tractatus Logico-Philosophicus* (1922) is a paradigmatic exercise in logical analysis, resting on the assumption that 'A proposition has one and only one complete analysis' (1922: 3.25) (see LOGICAL ATOMISM). A little later, the members of the Vienna Circle sought to develop the analyses of Russell and Wittgenstein within the context of their positivist programme (see VIENNA CIRCLE). Despite their many disagreements, one common feature of their programme was the belief that 'what is left over for *philosophy*... is only a *method*: the method of logical analysis' (Carnap 1932: 77). They held that the only proper task for the philosopher is to engage in logico-epistemological analysis which clarifies the sense of questions about the world in such a way that they can be answered on the basis of scientific observation and experiment. It is, then, in the explicitly anti-metaphysical context of logical positivism that there occurs the transition from 'philosophical analysis', conceived of as *an* important method of inquiry, to 'analytical philosophy', which restricts genuine philosophy to analysis (as in Bergmann (1945: 194), which is, I think, the first explicit use of the term 'analytical philosophy').

3 Linguistic analysis

In the early post-1945 period this positivist conception of analytical philosophy was regarded as unnecessarily restrictive by many philosophers, especially those not enamoured of the scientific context of the positivist programme. Not wanting to return directly to old-fashioned metaphysics, they sought instead to extend the range of analytical techniques to cover a general concern with the normative aspects of language, while shedding a commitment to the identification of simple meanings or basic certainties. In Wittgenstein's writings of this period the underlying hope was the 'therapeutic' aspiration that philosophical perplexities would thereby be set to rest; whereas in the writings of RYLE, AUSTIN, STRAWSON and other 'ordinary language' philosophers there was still the presumption that answers to old metaphysical questions such as those concerning the status of the mind (Ryle), appearances (Austin) and universals (Strawson) could be extracted from these inquiries (see ORDINARY LANGUAGE PHILOSOPHY, SCHOOL OF).

This broader conception of 'analytical philosophy' came to self-consciousness in the 1961 Anglo-French conference at Royaumont (Montefiore and Williams 1966), and it is, I think, only after this conference that use of the term 'analytical philosophy' became widespread (as in the title of the characteristic collections *Analytical Philosophy*, edited by R.J. Butler – Butler 1962, 1965). The sense of the term was, therefore, no longer confined to the logico-epistemological analyses of Russell and the logical positivists; instead it embraced a much broader critical concern with language, still resting on the presumption that this concern could somehow be put to work to solve, or dissolve, important philosophical problems.

This conception of analytical philosophy has been further refined by Michael DUMMETT, who has maintained that its distinctive feature is the priority it assigns within philosophy to the philosophy of language and that the founder of analytical philosophy, so conceived, is not Russell, but FREGE (Dummett 1993). Both these claims, however, need some qualification.

As Dummett acknowledges, his emphasis on Frege's work is in part a retrospective re-evaluation. For although familiarity with Frege's work in logic and mathematics played an essential part in the development of Russell's work, Russell took his basic philosophical assumptions from Moore. Doubtless it would have been better if Russell had appreciated the significance of Frege's sense/reference distinction, but in fact he famously thought that his theory of descriptions rendered it unnecessary (Russell 1905). However, Rudolf CARNAP – who, as we have seen, is one of the first to propound the thesis that philosophy can only be analytical – explicitly acknowledges his indebtedness to Frege, whose lectures he had attended (Carnap 1937: xvi); and it was, therefore, through Carnap's writings that Frege's philosophy of language was brought into the mainstream of analytical philosophy. Carnap also here acknowledges his debt to the great Polish logicians AJDUKIEWICZ, Leśniewski, Łukasiewicz and TARSKI, whose works constitute in their own right major contributions to analytical philosophy, though ones that there is no space to describe here in detail (a full account should also include an account of the work of HÄGERSTRÖM and the other members of the early Swedish school of analytical philosophers) (see POLISH LOGIC; SCANDINAVIA, PHILOSOPHY IN).

Although Dummett's claim that the distinctive feature of analytical philosophy is the priority it assigns to the philosophy of language fits well the conception of analytical philosophy that emerged from the early work of Wittgenstein and Carnap, it is certainly not a feature of Russell's early work nor, in fact, a self-conscious feature of Frege's writings, which famously include instead the thesis that sentences are true only in virtue of the nonlinguistic thoughts they express. Further, although Dummett's explanation of this priority in terms of the basic role within philosophy of a 'theory of meaning' fits his own writings and some of those of Donald DAVIDSON, one has only to think of the hostility to 'theorizing' that is characteristic of Wittgenstein's later writings to see that Dummett's account is distinctly tendentious.

Indeed, recent work in the philosophy of language and of mind increasingly calls into doubt Dummett's priority thesis (Stalnaker 1984) (see EVANS, G.). Yet since those who argue for the alternative priority of mind over language employ the methods of logical and epistemological analysis characteristic of previous analytical philosophers – though applied now to the structure of mental, rather than just linguistic, representations – it would be quite inappropriate to locate here a movement that threatens to bring about the 'end of analytical philosophy'. That threat certainly exists, but it comes from another direction.

4 The end of analytical philosophy?

Just when analytical philosophy was coming to self-consciousness in the early post-war period, two of the assumptions of traditional methods of logical and epistemological analysis were called into question by W.V. QUINE: (1) the assumption that there is a clear distinction (the 'analytic/synthetic' distinction) between logic and other disciplines which enables one to conduct the logical analysis of a statement without reference to these other disciplines; (2) the assumption that there is a single chain of justification from observation to more speculative claims about the world which enables one to construct an epistemological analysis of the latter in terms of the former (Quine 1953). In both cases Quine argued that in fact we find only a complex network of interdependent relationships which undermines the prospect of establishing definitive logical or epistemological analyses. Further, he argued later (Quine 1960), our understanding of each other, and in particular of each other's utterances, is generally underdetermined by our observations of each other, and, as a consequence, the meaning of most of our utterances must be intrinsically indeterminate since there cannot be anything more to their meaning than is available to an intelligent observer (see ANALYTICITY; RADICAL TRANSLATION AND RADICAL INTERPRETATION).

Despite the fact that Quine's writings employ the standard techniques of logical analysis, some hold that his conclusions signal the end of analytical philosophy (Rorty (1980) gives an influential statement of this thesis). In thinking about this, however, one must bear in mind that already by 1945 most analytical philosophers had abandoned any commitment to simple meanings and basic certainties, and that the positivist thesis that philosophy could only be analytical philosophy was also soon rejected. Instead, the practice of analytical philosophers rested only on the assumption that methods of analysis can clarify conceptual and epistemological relationships in a way which contributes to the resolution or dissipation of philosophical problems. Do Quine's claims show that this assumption is unfounded? His indeterminacy thesis implies that the results of analytic inquiries can only be relative to one of an indefinite number of alternative systems of 'analytical hypotheses' between which there is nothing to choose (Quine 1960: 68), and thus that little of intrinsic significance can be detached from them. But Quine's arguments for the indeterminacy thesis are problematic since he allows only a narrow, behaviourist characterization of the evidence that is admissible to determine questions about the meaning of utterances. In order to question this restriction one need only invoke his own criticisms of 'foundationalist' approaches to questions of justification which imply that no such restriction on admissable evidence is legitimate. Quine's earlier arguments, by contrast, point to the holistic structure of our language and beliefs, and few analytical philosophers would want to dispute this (though there are exceptions, such as Dummett). But they will argue that indeterminacy does not follow from holism; on the contrary, talk of holism implies a system of normative relationships that is itself a legitimate subject for analytical inquiry. Admittedly, if there is no absolute analytic/synthetic distinction, the significance of these inquiries must itself remain open to question in the light of the broader theoretical concerns that influence one's choice of logic and epistemology. But this, so far from being the end of analytical philosophy, just reiterates the anti-positivist thesis that philosophy is not just analysis.

Analytical philosophy can, therefore, survive the contemporary prophets of doom by retreating to the pre-positivist thesis of the merits of philosophical analysis as an ingredient of philosophical inquiry, with a core commitment to the *explicit* articulation of the normative relationships, involving inference and justification, that connect concepts, beliefs and statements. This may seem too minimal a commitment to be worth a distinctive characterization as a kind of philosophy, but one has only to sample contemporary philosophical writings that do not share this commitment to recognize its value. To say this is not to say, however, that the methods of philosophical analysis are equally valuable in all areas of philosophy. There are those, such as Bernard WILLIAMS, who hold that in ethics and aesthetics the characteristic virtues of philosophical analysis may actually obstruct the proper exercise of a philosophical inquiry that aims to be truthful or imaginative (Williams 1995).

None the less, the robustness of analytical philosophy thus understood is best seen in the remarkable expansion in the acceptance and use of its methods that has taken place during the last half-century. This expansion has been both geographical and disciplinary. There has been an explosion of interest in analytical philosophy within non-anglophone countries, both in Europe and elsewhere (for instance, South America), leading to new dialogues between philosophers who had previously remained isolated in their own traditions. At the same time the ideas and methods of analytical philosophy have been applied to advance debates in areas of philosophy which had previously appeared remote from analytic concerns, such as the study of ancient philosophy (see OWEN, G.E.L.; VLASTOS, G.) and Marxism (Cohen 1978). By putting down roots around the globe and throughout the academy, analytical philosophy has shown that it is far too early to write its obituary (see ANALYTIC ETHICS; ANALYTICAL PHILOSOPHY IN LATIN AMERICA).

See also: LOGICAL POSITIVISM

References and further reading

Analysis (1933–) (A journal founded to promote analytical philosophy, whose style remains a characteristic expression of this kind of philosophy.)

* Arnauld A. (1662) *La logique, ou l'art de penser*, Paris; trans. J. Dickoff and P. James, *The Art of Thinking*, Indianapolis, IN: Bobbs-Merrill, 1964. (In chapter 4 Arnauld commends Descartes' method of inquiry as the 'method of analysis'.)

Austin, J.L. (1962) *Sense and Sensibilia*, ed. G. Warnock, Oxford: Oxford University Press. (Austin uses his analysis of the language of perception to criticize sense-datum theories of perception.)

Ayer, A.J. (1936) *Language, Truth and Logic*, London: Gollancz. (A classic statement of logical positivism: chapter 2 proclaims that philosophy can only be analysis).

—— (ed.) (1959) *Logical Positivism*, Glencoe, IL: Free Press. (A useful collection of writings from the logical positivists.)

Baldwin, T.R. (1990) *G.E. Moore*, London: Routledge. (Chapters 1 and 2 discuss Moore's break with idealism and early conception of analysis; in chapter 7 his later conception of philosophical analysis is discussed critically.)

* Bergmann, G. (1945) 'A Positivistic Metaphysics of Consciousness', *Mind* new series 54: 193–226. (While criticizing the logical positivist account of the intentionality of consciousness, Bergmann describes the positivists as 'analytical philosophers'.)

* Butler, R.J. (ed.) (1962, 1965) *Analytical Philosophy*, Oxford: Blackwell, 2 vols. (A characteristic expres-

sion of the kind of linguistic analysis that was practised in Oxford in the early 1960s.)

* Carnap, R. (1932) 'Überwindung der Metaphysik durch logische Analyse der Sprache', *Erkenntnis* 2: 219–41; trans. A. Pap, 'The Elimination of Metaphysics through Logical Analysis of Language', in Ayer 1959, 60–81. (Carnap's statement of the logical positivist thesis that philosophy can only be the logical analysis of language.)

* —— (1937) *The Logical Syntax of Language*, trans. A. Smeaton, London: Routledge & Kegan Paul. (Carnap's further development of his logical positivist programme for the analysis of language.)

* Cohen, G.A. (1978) *Karl Marx's Theory of History: A Defence*, Oxford: Clarendon Press. (An application of the methods of analytical philosophy to the study of Marxism; the starting-point of 'Analytical Marxism'.)

Descartes, R. (1701) *Rules for the Direction of the Mind*, Amsterdam: P. & J. Blaeu; trans. J. Cottingham, R. Stoothof and D. Murdoch, in *The Philosophical Writings of Descartes*, vol. 1, Cambridge: Cambridge University Press, 1985. (Rules 6 and 12 prescribe the discerning intuition of 'simple natures'.)

Davidson, D. (1984) *Inquiries into Truth and Interpretation*, Oxford: Clarendon Press. (A collection of Davidson's papers in which he develops his conception of a 'theory of meaning' and its place in philosophy.)

—— (1986) 'A Nice Derangement of Epitaphs', in E. LePore (ed.) *Truth and Interpretation*, Oxford: Blackwell. (A paper in which Davidson substantially qualifies the conception of a theory of meaning advanced in Davidson 1984.)

* Dummett, M.A.E. (1993) *The Origins of Analytical Philosophy*, London: Duckworth. (Dummett's most extended discussion of his theses that the mark of analytical philosophy is the priority it assigns to the philosophy of language, and that Frege is the founder of analytical philosophy so conceived.)

—— (1976) 'What is a Theory of Meaning? II' in G. Evans and J. McDowell (eds) *Truth and Meaning*, Oxford: Clarendon Press, 67–115. (Dummett's fullest statement of his conception of a 'theory of meaning' which, for him, is the core of a philosophy of language.)

Evans, G. (1982) *The Varieties of Reference*, Oxford: Clarendon Press. (Evans here argues that the theory of reference for language needs to be situated within a broader understanding of mental content, thus challenging Dummett's 'priority of language' thesis.)

Frege, G. (1892) 'Über Sinn und Bedeutung', Zeitschrift fur Philosophie und philosophische Kritik 100: 25–50; trans. M. Black as 'On Sense and Reference', in *Translations from the Philosophical Writings of Gottlob Frege*, ed. M. Black and P. Geach, Blackwell: Oxford, 1952. (Frege's classic statement of his sense/reference distinction which has become a central feature of analytical philosophy.)

Gibson R. (1988) *Enlightened Empiricism*, Tampa, FL: University of Southern Florida Press. (A robust defence of Quine's sceptical arguments.)

Hacking, I. (1975) *Why Does Language Matter to Philosophy?*, Cambridge: Cambridge University Press. (A discussion of the idea of linguistic analysis and its development in the period 1950–75; the 1992 edition of Rorty (1967) contains as an afterword a critical discussion ('Ten Years After') of this book by Rorty.)

Hylton, P. (1990) *Russell, Idealism and the Emergence of Analytical Philosophy*, Oxford: Clarendon Press. (An account of the development of Russell's philosophy over the period 1900–12.)

* Kant, I. (1781/1787) *Critique of Pure Reason*, trans. N. Kemp Smith, London: Macmillan, 2nd edn, 1933. (The standard translation of the *Critique*.)

* Locke, J. (1689) *An Essay Concerning Human Understanding*, ed. P. Nidditch, Oxford: Oxford University Press, 1975. (A classic application of the method of analysis in the context of an empiricist theory of ideas.)

* Montefiore, A. and Williams, B. (1966) *British Analytical Philosophy*, London: Routledge. (An influential collection of papers in which the postwar Oxford conception of linguistic analysis is propounded and discussed.)

* Moore G.E. (1899) 'The Nature of Judgment', *Mind* new series 8: 176–93. (Moore's critique of the idealist theory of judgment, in which he propounds his analytic programme.)

—— (1903) *Principia Ethica*, Cambridge: Cambridge University Press. (Moore's presentation of analytical ethics, resting on the thesis that the concept of intrinsic value is 'unanalysable'.)

—— (1925) '*A Defence of Common Sense*', in J.H. Muirhead (ed.) *Contemporary British Philosophy* (second series), London: Allen & Unwin, 193–223; repr. in T. Baldwin (ed.) *G.E. Moore: Selected Writings*, London: Routledge, 1993, 106–33. (Contains Moore's later view that the difficult task for philosophy is not to defend common sense, but to analyse it.)

Passmore, J. (1957) *A Hundred Years of Philosophy*, London: Duckworth; 2nd edn repr. Harmondsworth: Penguin, 1968. (Much of the second half of the book provides a survey of the development of

analytical philosophy, which is carried further in the 1966 Penguin edition.)
* Plato (*c.*380–367 BC) *Theaetetus*, trans. J.H. McDowell, Oxford: Clarendon Press, 1973. (Socrates' dream (201d–202c) marks the first appearance of the method of analysis.)
* Quine, W.V. (1953) *From a Logical Point of View*, Cambridge, MA: Harvard University Press. (A collection of Quine's early papers including 'Two Dogmas of Empiricism' in which he launches his radical critique of the analytic/synthetic distinction.)
* —— (1960) *Word and Object*, Cambridge, MA: MIT Press. (In chapter 2 Quine launches his notorious thesis of the indeterminacy of translation.)
—— (1990) *Pursuit of Truth*, Cambridge, MA: Harvard University Press. (A lucid recent statement by Quine of his views about meaning and evidence.)
Rorty, R.M. (1967) *The Linguistic Turn*, Chicago, IL: University of Chicago Press. (A collection of essays, expository and critical, on philosophy as 'linguistic analysis' with an excellent bibliography; the 1992 edition has two retrospective essays by Rorty in which he looks back critically at the pretensions of linguistic analysis.)
—— (1980) *Philosophy and the Mirror of Nature*, Princeton, NJ: Princeton University Press. (In chapter 6 Rorty argues that the time has come to move beyond analytical philosophy, and in chapter 8 he describes post-analytical philosophy as the 'conversation of mankind'.)
* Russell, B.A.W. (1903) *The Principles of Mathematics*, London: Allen & Unwin (Russell's first systematic attempt at a programme of logical analysis.)
* —— (1905) 'On Denoting', *Mind* 14: 479–93; repr. in *Logic and Knowledge*, ed. R. Marsh, London: Allen & Unwin, 1956, 41–56. (Russell's presentation of his theory of descriptions.)
—— (1921) *The Analysis of Mind*, London: Allen & Unwin. (A characteristic expression of Russell's mature analytic programme in philosophy, especially notable for the priority given to the philosophy of mind over the philosophy of language.)
* Ryle, G. (1949) *The Concept of Mind*, London: Hutchinson. (Ryle uses the techniques of linguistic analysis to criticize Descartes' 'Myth of the Mind'.)
Stalnaker, R. (1984) *Inquiry*, Cambridge, MA: MIT Press. (Chapters 1 and 2 are an excellent critical discussion of the 'priority of language' thesis.)
* Strawson, P.F. (1959) *Individuals*, London: Methuen. (An account of universals and particulars by reference to an account of the roles of subject and predicate in language; but other chapters, especially chapter 2 on 'Sounds', show Strawson venturing well beyond analytic inquiries.)
Urmson, J.O. (1956) *Philosophical Analysis*, Oxford: Clarendon Press. (A description of the development of twentieth-century philosophical analysis from the perspective of Oxford philosophy of the 1950s.)
* Williams, B.A.O. (1995) 'Contemporary Philosophy: A Second Look', in N. Bunnin and E.P. Tsui-James (eds) *The Blackwell Companion to Philosophy*, Oxford: Blackwell, 25–37. (A sceptical discussion of the limited virtues of the methods of analytical philosophy especially as applied within ethics.)
* Wittgenstein, L.J.J. (1922) *Tractatus Logico-Philosophicus*, trans. C.K. Ogden and F.P. Ramsey, London: Routledge & Kegan Paul. (Wittgenstein's classic statement of the logical atomist position.)

THOMAS BALDWIN

ANALYTICAL PHILOSOPHY IN LATIN AMERICA

In Latin America, philosophical analysis has been portrayed as an intellectual revolution. Its avowed goal has been to replace the abstruseness and obscurantism of scholastic and metaphysical jargon perceived as typical of much of Latin American philosophy with the clarity and rigour of mathematical and scientific discourse. Arriving around the mid-1940s analytic philosophy at first met with little interest because of a shortage of its classics in translation, cultural obstacles and opposition from the more traditional, entrenched philosophies. By the 1960s it had overcome many obstacles and stimulated considerable philosophical activity, mainly in Mexico and Argentina. By the 1980s, in spite of political opposition, analysis had created an international forum for the discussion of philosophical problems. It attracted to its ranks several distinguished philosophers and scientists with philosophical interests, among them Mario Bunge (Argentina and Canada), Héctor-Neri Castañeda (Guatemala and the USA) and Francisco Miró Quesada (Peru). An ambitious translation effort was launched and several important journals were founded, such as Análisis filosófico *(Philosophical Analysis),* Revista latinoamericana de filosofía *(Latin American Journal of Philosophy) (Argentina),* Crítica. Revista hispanoamericana de filosofía *(Criticism. Hispanoamerican Journal of Philosophy) (Mexico),* Manuscrito *(Manuscript) (Brazil) and* Diálogos *(Dialogues) (Puerto Rico).*

1 **Early development**
2 **Mexico**
3 **Argentina**
4 **Elsewhere in Latin America**

ANALYTICAL PHILOSOPHY IN LATIN AMERICA

1 Early development

Broadly understood, philosophical analysis is a collection of methods for uncovering the presuppositions, implicit meanings and logical implications of statements in philosophical, scientific, or ordinary language. Some Latin American contemporaries, such as Rabossi (1977), have portrayed analysis as a set of common concerns, an attitude of caution towards metaphysics, a demand for logical rigour and conceptual clarity and an interest in scientific and linguistic problems. Others, such as Salmerón (1992) considered it to be a collective task of philosophical reconstruction which leaves little space for local or personal peculiarities and makes international life and communications easier. Still others viewed it as 'an intellectual revolution... It's object is relatively clear: to steer philosophy in the direction of a coherent and scientific investigation' (Nuño 1965). The inspiration for analysis was the historical movement that emerged from the philosophical activities of FREGE, RUSSELL, MOORE, and the Vienna Circle (see ORDINARY LANGUAGE PHILOSOPHY, SCHOOL OF; VIENNA CIRCLE).

In Latin America, analysis did not receive much attention until the mid-1940s. A lack of translations accounts for this late start. Prior to 1945 only two works on analysis were available in Spanish: *Ethics* (Moore 1912) and *Problems of Philosophy* (Russell 1912), both of which were published in Buenos Aires in 1929, with a Portuguese edition of the latter at São Paulo in 1939. From 1945 a stream of translations began to appear of the work of such philosophers as Wittgenstein, Carnap, Ayer and Max Black. Another reason for the late start of analysis was a lack of awareness in Latin America of modern logical techniques so important to analytic work. Up to the 1940s most logic studies were about syllogisms (Romero and Pucciarelli 1939), or fallacies (Vaz Ferreira 1910). After the 1940s the modern logic texts of Ferreira da Silva (1940), Quine (1944) and Miró Quesada (1963) stand out. Later, the texts of Ferrater Mora and Leblanc (1955) and Hegenberg (1966) were prominent.

Other factors impeded the diffusion of analysis. Links to logical positivism brought to mind the outdated views of Comte, Spencer and the nineteenth-century Latin American positivists (see ANTI-POSITIVIST THOUGHT IN LATIN AMERICA). The popularity of opposing approaches, such as well-entrenched idealism, Marxism, with its careful socio-economic analysis of reality, or neo-Thomism, with its rigorous criticisms of science and modern formalism, hindered the growth of analysis. As a further hindrance, Gaos and other refugees from the Spanish Civil War brought with them well-articulated forms of existentialism and phenomenology. Several other Latin American philosophers expressed reservations about analysis, including Caso (1939; 1941) and Bunge (1944), both of whom were critical of logical positivism, and Frondizi (1945).

Some early support for analysis came from personal contacts with visiting scholars, such as Quine, Strawson and von Wright and from local philosophers who had direct acquaintance with logical positivists, such as Schajowicz (1964) and Lindemann (1946). It was not until the 1950s that analysis began to flourish, particularly in Mexico and Argentina.

2 Mexico

In Mexico, the earliest discussion of analysis can be found in Caso's works (1939; 1941). Caso, an opponent of nineteenth-century positivism, formulated a phenomenalist critique of what he called neopositivism. Philosophical analysis remained taboo until it was defended by Molina Flores (1954). However, it took six years for the Centro de Estudios Filosóficos, renamed in 1964 the Instituto de Investigaciones Filosóficas, to publish his translations of Moore (1912), Carnap and Ayer in its series *Cuadernos*.

With a growing body of translations and an increase in interest, the centre became a hub of analytic work and sponsored the journal *Crítica. Revista hispanoamericana de filosofía* (Criticism. Hispanoamerican Journal of Philosophy), under the editorial supervision of Villoro, Salmerón and Rossi. The journal's policy was to display a critical attitude towards metaphysical speculation, traditional philosophical systems and problems, *Weltanschauung* philosophies and cultural or anthropological reflections on Latin American cultures. Committed to establishing a body of rigorous professional and technical materials, *Crítica. Revista hispanoamericana de filosofía* (Criticism. Hispanoamerican Journal of Philosophy)'s editors expressed a preference for verifiable explanations which referred to description and analysis, linked philosophy with methodological and scientific problems in the physical or social sciences, and which required rigour, precision and clarity instead of oratory or literary elegance. *Crítica. Revista hispanoamericana de filosofía* (Criticism. Hispanoamerican Journal of Philosophy)'s editors had originally trained in phenomenology under Gaos, but shifted towards analysis over a twenty-year period.

During the 1970s and 1980s, analysis became well established and a generation of students who grew up from there began to work at the institute, for instance, Trejo (1977), Margain (1978) and Olivé (1985a, 1985b). The institute brought to Mexico many well-known analytic philosophers. It also drew from the growing ranks of Latin American philosophers doing analysis, such as Bunge (1980) and Moulines (1982), as well as Castañeda, Coffa, Gracia and Sosa (see MEXICO, PHILOSOPHY IN).

3 Argentina

One of the first Argentinian philosophers to be identified with analysis was Mario Bunge. A graduate from the University de la Plata, with a doctorate in physics from Simon Fraser University, Bunge was attracted to analysis after his initial rejection of it. In 1944 he became editor of the short-lived Minerva: Revista continental de filosofía (Minerva: Continental Magazine of Philosophy) (1944–5), the first Latin American journal dedicated exclusively to philosophy. Opting for an open, pluralistic approach, the journal published several early discussions on logical positivism, including Lindemann's, 'El "Círculo de Viena" y la filosofía crítica' (The Vienna Circle and Critical Philosophy) (1944).

In 1945 the members of the Grupo Argentino de la Academia Internacional de la Historia y Filosofía de la Ciencia began to meet periodically to examine the works of Russell and Moore. By 1952 the number of philosophers interested in analysis was large enough to found the Círculo Filosófico de Buenos Aires, with Bunge as its first chair. It was at the Círculo in 1954 that a draft of Bunge's important analysis of causality was first discussed (Bunge 1959). In 1956 the Agrupación Rioplatense de Lógica y Filosofía Científica was founded as a forum for Argentinian and Uruguayan philosophers and scientists interested in logic and the philosophy of science. Greater interest and specialization led in 1957 to the formation of two complementary groups. One, led by Gioja, the new director of the Instituto de Filosofía del Derecho y Sociología at the University of Buenos Aires, focused on problems in the philosophy of law, ethics, society and politics. The institute became a gathering place for international figures like Strawson, von Wright, Castañeda and younger Argentinian philosophers of law with an analytic orientation, among them Carrió (1965; 1970) and Rabossi (1977). The institute also sponsored Notas de filosofía del derecho (Notes on Legal Philosophy) (1964–9), a journal which published essays with an analytic orientation. The other, a more informal group, was interested in problems related to the philosophy of science, logic and language. It was led by Klimovsky and García, both of whom had joined Bunge in 1957 at the University of Buenos Aires. Of this group, Simpson distinguished himself with Formas lógicas, realidad y significado (Logical Forms, Reality and Significance) (1964), one of the earliest books in Spanish that dealt with such philosophers as Russell and Frege from an analytic perspective (see ARGENTINA, PHILOSOPHY IN).

Between 1966 and 1983 political events decimated Argentinian intellectual life and many, including several analytic philosophers, were forced into exile – some permanently (Bunge went to Canada, Coffa and Gómez to the USA).

4 Elsewhere in Latin America

In Brazil, the reaction against nineteenth-century positivism shifted attention to other approaches, such as Marxism and existentialism at the expense of the philosophies of science and logic. However, in São Paulo two of the earliest works in formal logic to appear in Latin America were published: Ferreira da Silva's Elementos (Foundations of Mathematical Logic) (1940) and Quine's O Sentido da Nova Lógica (The Meaning of Modern Logic) (1944). Quine's presence at the University of São Paulo in the early 1940s helped to make formal logic part of the philosophy curriculum and allowed Granger (1955), French philosopher of science, to teach logic and philosophy of science there from 1947 onwards. However, the 1964 military coup, in an effort to purge progressive elements at the University of São Paulo, eliminated logic and philosophical analysis from the curriculum. Philosophers found themselves without a livelihood or means of disseminating their knowledge until the late 1970s, when J.P. Monteiro, a specialist in Hume and contemporary epistemology, founded Ciência e Filosofia (1979–86), an interdisciplinary journal which published some analytic works. In 1975 Porchat Pereira, an Aristotelian scholar and logician, left the University of São Paulo to found the Centro de Lógica, Epistemología e História da Ciência at the University of Campinas. This new centre attracted many philosophers concerned with analysis, among them, da Costa, a specialist in nonstandard logic, and Dascal. It began to publish its journal, Manuscrito in 1977 (see BRAZIL, PHILOSOPHY IN).

In Peru two figures are important, Salazar Bondy, who died young and Miró Quesada, both members of the editorial board of Crítica. Revista hispanoamericana de filosofía (Criticism. Hispanoamerican Journal of Philosophy). Salazar Bondy's essays were published in Para una filosofía del valor (Towards a Philosophy of value) (1971), a book on the analysis of the language of values in which he blends logical positivism and critical idealism to form a normative axiology. Miró Quesada, aware of the shortcomings of the traditional views of logic and science, found that formal logic and conceptual analysis provide both a critical attitude and a superior methodology, as they study the foundations of philosophy, or metatheory: 'a theory of theories.... Its subject matter encompasses the study of principles, the analysis of points of departure, and the possibilities of deriving consequences of their fundamental presuppositions' (1963).

In Chile, where phenomenalism and neo-Thomism were popular, Rivano's translation of Ayer (1926) and Stahl's work on formal logic (1956; 1964) provided a theoretical base for later works by such philosophers as Torretti (1967), who made a study of Kant and later (1983) turned to problems of the history of science and Gómez-Lobo (1989), who translated Frege and applied the methods of analysis to ancient philosophy.

In Venezuela, Nuño turned to analysis after becoming interested in contemporary semantics. A polemical writer, his *Sentido de la filosofí contemporánea* (Directions in Contemporary Philosophy) (1965) is a general view of contemporary philosophy, especially logical empiricism and analytic philosophy. Elsewhere in Latin America, there has been little analytic activity. However, the wide dissemination of journals and books on analysis (Cuba being the exception) and the large number of international congresses and visiting philosophers make the scope of analysis (and of other Latin American philosophic movements as well) intercontinental. Contributing to that dissemination are the many philosophers who have migrated to the USA and Canada, such as Frondizi, Bunge, Castañeda, Gómez, Gómez-Lobo, Torretti, Sosa and Gracia. Of these, some, like Castañeda and Sosa, identify themselves with the English-speaking tradition: others, like Frondizi, with Latin America. While others, like Gracia, have succeeded in bridging the two continents.

See also: ANALYTICAL PHILOSOPHY

References and further reading

* *Análisis filosófico* (Philosophical Analysis) (1981–), Buenos Aires, Sociedad Argentina de Análisis Filosófico. (Argentinian journal dedicated to philosophical analysis.)
* Ayer, A. (1926) 'Eliminación de la metafísica' (Elimination of metaphysics), trans. J. Rivano and C. Narvarte, *Revista de filosofía* 4 (2–3): 55–69, 1957. (One of many translations that appeared in this Chilean journal deriving from the department of philosophy in at the University of Chile.)
* Bunge, M. (1944) '¿Qué es la epistemología?' (What is Epistemology?), *Minerva* 1: 27–43. (An early criticism of logical positivism.)
* —— (1959) *Causality*, Cambridge, MA: Harvard University Press. (An important analysis of causality in the physical sciences.)
* —— (1980) *Epistemología* (Epistemology), Barcelona: Ariel. (An essay on epistemology and the philosophy of science.)
* Carnap, R. (1932) 'Überwindung der Metaphysik durch logische Analyse der Sprache', *Erkenntnis* 2; trans. A. Pap, 'The Elimination of Metaphysics Through the Logical Analysis of Language', in A.J. Ayer (ed.) *Logical Positivism*, Glencoe, IL: Free Press, 1959, 60–81. (This essay was translated into Spanish by C.N. Molina Flores and appeared in *Cuadernos* 10, 1961.)
* Carrió, G.R. (1965) *Notas sobre derecho y lenguaje* (Notes on Rights and Language), Buenos Aires: Abeledo-Perrot. (An ordinary language analysis of rights.)
* —— (1970) *Principos jurídicos y positivismo* (Legal Principles and Legal Positivism), Buenos Aires: Abeledo-Perrot. (An essay on legal positivism.)
* Caso, A. (1939) *Meyerson y la física moderna* (Meyerson and Modern Physics), Mexico: La Casa de España en Mexico. (A negative assessment of logical positivism.)
* —— (1941) *Positivismo, neopositivismo y fenomenología* (Positivism, Neopositivism and Phenomenology), Mexico: Centro de Estudios Filosóficos de la Facultad de Filosofía y Letras. (A comparison of nineteenth-century and logical positivisms.)
* *Crítica. Revista hispanoamericana de filosofía* (Criticism. Hispanoamerican Journal of Philosophy) (1967–), Mexico, Instituto de Investigaciones Filosóficas, Universidad Nacional Autónoma de México. (Mexican journal dedicated to philosophical analysis.)
* *Diálogos* (Dialogues) (1961–), Puerto Rico, Departamento de Filosofía de la Facultad de Humanidades de la Universidad de Puerto Rico. (Puerto Rican journal which publishes articles on analysis.)
* Ferrater Mora, J. and Leblanc, H. (1955) *Lógica matemática* (Mathematical Logic), Mexico: Fondo de Cultura Económica. (A textbook of mathematical logic.)
* Ferreira da Silva, V. (1940) *Elementos da lógica matemática* (Foundations of Mathematical Logic), São Paulo. (A basic logic textbook.)
* Frondizi, R. (1945) *El punto de partida del filosofar*

(The Starting Point in Philosophy), Buenos Aires: Losada. (A critical assessment of logical positivism.)
* Gómez-Lobo, A. (1989) *La ética de Socrates* (Socratic Ethics), Mexico: Fondo de Cultura Económica. (A discussion of Socratic ethics.)
Gracia, J.J.E (1984) 'Philosophical Analysis in Latin America', *History of Philosophy Quarterly* 1 (1): 111–12. (An overview of philosophical analysis in Latin America.)
Gracia, J.J.E., Rabossi, E., Villanueva, E. and Dascal, M. (eds) (1984) *Philosophical Analysis in Latin America*, Synthese Library, Studies in Epistemology, Logic, Methodology and Philosophy of Science 172, Dordrecht: D. Reidel. (The best collection in English of contemporary Latin American analytic philosophers.)
* Granger, G.G. (1955) *Lógica e filosofia das ciências* (Logic and Philosophy of Science), São Paulo: Edições Malhoramentos. (An introduction to logic and the philosophy of science.)
* Hegenberg, L. (1966) *Lógica simbólica* (Symbolic Logic), São Paulo: Editora Herder. (A text on symbolic logic.)
* Lindemann, H. (1944) 'El "Círculo de Viena" y la filosofía crítica' (The Vienna Circle and Critical Philosophy), *Minerva* 1: 123–51. (An early sketch in Latin America of logical positivism and of the Vienna Circle by a participant.)
* —— (1946) *Lenguaje y filosofía* (Language and Philosophy), Buenos Aires: Edición Problemas de América. (An analysis of contemporary language by a participant in the Vienna Circle.)
* *Manuscrito* (Manuscript) (1977–), Brazil, Universidade Estadual de Campinas, Centro de Lógica, Epistemólogia e História da Ciência. (Brazilian journal on logic, epistemology and the history of science.)
* Margain, H. (1978) *Racionalidad, lenguaje y filosofía* (Rationality, Language and Philosophy), Mexico: Fondo de Cultura Económica. (An analysis of metaphysical and epistemological problems.)
Martí, O.R. (1986) 'Review of Philosophical Analysis in Latin America', in J. Gracia, E. Rabossi, E. Villanueva and M. Dascal (eds) *Metaphilosophy* 17: 351–7. (A critical review of the first major English anthology of Latin American analytic philosophers.)
—— (1992) 'Gigantes y Cabezudos: la querella entre los historicistas y los analíticos' (Giants and Headstrong: The Quarrel Between Historicists and Analytic Philosophers), in *América Latina, historia y destino. Homenaje a Leopoldo Zea* (Latin America, History and Destiny: Homage to Leopoldo Zea) 2: 161–8. (A critical appraisal of the debate between analytical philosophers and historians of philosophy.)
* Miró Quesada, F. (1963) *Apuntes para una teoría de la razón* (Notes Towards a Theory of Reason), Lima: Universidad Nacional Mayor de San Marcos, Facultad de Letras. (A logical analysis of reasoning, logic and classical epistemological problems.)
* —— (1980) *Filosofía de las matemáticas* (Philosophy of Mathematics), Lima: I. Prado Pastor. (A discussion of the logical foundations of mathematics.)
* Molina Flores, C. (1954) *Matemática y filosofía* (Mathematics and Philosophy), Mexico. (An essay on the demarcation between mathematics and philosophy.)
* Moore, G.E. (1912) *Ethics*, London: Williams & Norgate. (A translation of Moore's book by C. Molina Flores appeared in 1959.)
* Moulines, C.U. (1982) *Exploraciones metacientíficas* (Metascientific Explorations), Madrid: Alianza Editorial. (An essay on methodology and the philosophy of science.)
* Nuño, J.A. (1965) *Sentido de la filosofía contemporánea* (Directions in Contemporary Philosophy), Caracas: Universidad Central de Venezuela. (A discussion of logical empiricism and analytical philosophy.)
* Olivé, L. (1985a) *Estado, legitimación y crisis* (The State, Legitimization and Crisis), Mexico: Siglo XXI. (An analysis of the epistemological presuppositions of capitalism.)
* —— (1985b) *La explicación social del conocimiento* (The Social Explanation of Knowledge), Mexico: Universidad Nacional Autónoma de México, Instituto de Investigaciones Filosóficas. (A study of the sociology of knowledge.)
* Quine, W.V. (1944) *O Sentido da Nova Lógica* (The Meaning of Modern Logic), São Paulo: Livraria Martins Editora. (An essay on trends in modern logic.)
* Rabossi, E. (1977) *Análisis filosófico, lenguaje y metafísica* (Philosophical Analysis, Language and Metaphysics), Caracas: Monte Ávila. (Essays on analytical philosophy.)
* *Revista latinoamericana de filosofía* (Latin American Journal of Philosophy) (1975–), Centro de Investigaciones Filosóficas. (Argentinian philosophy journal with an analytical perspective.)
* Romero, F. and Pucciarelli, E. (1939) *Lógica y nociones de teoría del conocimiento* (Logic and Foundations of a Theory of Knowledge), Buenos Aires: Espasa-Calpé Argentina, 2nd edn. (A basic logic text.)
* Russell, B. (1912) *The Problems of Philosophy*, Oxford: Oxford University Press, 1974. (An intro-

duction to philosophy, with an emphasis on epistemology.)

* Salazar Bondy, A. (1971) *Para una filosofía del valor* (Towards a Philosophy of Value), Santiago: Editorial Universitaria. (A discussion on axiology.)
* Salmerón, F. (1992) 'Nota sobre la recepción del análisis filosófico en América Latina' (Notes on the Reception of Philosophical Analysis in Latin America), in *América Latina, historia y destino. Homenaje a Leopoldo Zea* (Latin America, History and Destiny: Homage to Leopoldo Zea) 2: 305–22, Mexico: Universidad Nacional Autónoma de México. (A recollection of the development of analysis in Latin America.)
* Schajowicz, L. (1964) *La filosofía y el mundo contemporáneo* (Philosophy and the Contemporary World), Rio Piedras: Editorial Universities, Universidad de Puerto Rico. (An analysis of contemporary philosophical problems.)
* Simpson, T.M. (1964) *Formas lógicas, realidad y significado* (Logical Forms, Reality and Significance), Buenos Aires: Editorial Universitaria de Buenos Aires. (With a prologue by Gregorio Klimovsky, this is one of the earliest Latin American books to approach philosophy from an analytic perspective.)
* Stahl, G. (1956) *Introducción a la lógica simbólica* (Introduction to Symbolic Logic), Santiago de Chile: Ediciones de la Universidad de Chile. (An introductory textbook to symbolic logic.)
* —— (1964) *Elementos de la metalógica y metamatemática* (Elements of Metalogic and Metamathematics), Santiago de Chile: Editorial Universitaria. (A text on logical theory.)
* Torretti, R. (1967) *Manuel Kant* (Immanuel Kant), Santiago de Chile: Ediciones de la Universidad de Chile. (A study of Kant's philosophy.)
* —— (1983) *Relativity and Geometry*, New York: Pergamon Press. (A study of the problems of relativity and geometry.)
* Trejo, W. (1977) *Fenomenalismo y realismo* (Phenomenalism and Realism), Mexico: Universidad Nacional Autónoma de México. (A logical analysis of realism and phenomenology.)
* Vaz Ferreira, C. (1910) *Lógica viva* (Living Logic), Montevideo: Talleres Gráficos A. Barreiro y Ramos. (An examination of fallacies.)

OSCAR R. MARTÍ

ANALYTICITY

In Critique of Pure Reason *Kant introduced the term 'analytic' for judgments whose truth is guaranteed by a certain relation of 'containment' between the constituent concepts, and 'synthetic' for judgments which are not like this. Closely related terms were found in earlier writings of Locke, Hume and Leibniz. In Kant's definition, an analytic judgment is one in which 'the predicate B belongs to the subject A, as something which is (covertly) contained in this concept A' ([1781/ 1787] 1965: 48). Kant called such judgments 'explicative', contrasting them with synthetic judgments which are 'ampliative'. A paradigmatic analyticity would be: bachelors are unmarried. Kant assumed that knowledge of analytic necessities has a uniquely transparent sort of explanation. In the succeeding two centuries the terms 'analytic' and 'synthetic' have been used in a variety of closely related but not strictly equivalent ways. In the early 1950s Morton White (1950) and W.V. Quine (1951) argued that the terms were fundamentally unclear and should be eschewed. Although a number of prominent philosophers have rejected their arguments, there prevails a scepticism about 'analytic' and the idea that there is an associated category of necessary truths having privileged epistemic status.*

1 The attack on 'analytic'
2 Extending the attack to 'necessary' and 'a priori'
3 Defending 'analytic' against Quine
4 More damaging problems with 'analytic'
5 Epistemological problems with 'analytic'
6 Whither 'analytic'?

1 The attack on 'analytic'

'Analytic' has been used in a wide variety of ways: truth by conceptual containment and truth whose denial is contradictory (Kant 1781/1787); logical truth (Bolzano 1837; Feigl 1949); truth by definition and logical derivation (Frege 1884; Pap 1958); truth in virtue of form (Schlick 1930–1); truth by definition and logical truth (Carnap 1937, 1947); truth by definition (Ayer 1936); truth based on meaning (Ayer 1936; C.I. Lewis 1944); truth by semantical rule (Carnap 1947); truth in all possible worlds (C.I. Lewis 1944; D.K. Lewis 1969); convertibility into logical truth by substitution of synonyms (Quine 1951); truth by implicit convention (Putnam 1962); and so on. Although related, not all of these uses are equivalent. For example, logical truths are not true by definition (in the sense of explicit definition), but they are trivially true by definition *plus* logic. Furthermore, Gödel's incompleteness result shows that logical derivability and logical truth are not equivalent (see GÖDEL'S THEOREMS §3). Likewise various principles (for example, supervenience principles; see SUPERVENIENCE) which are true in all possible worlds seem not to be true by definition plus logic (if 'definition' does not include 'implicit definitions'; see DEFINITION). Similarly, it may be doubted that correct definitions provide exact synonyms (see §4). Little care has been taken to distinguish these disparate uses and needless confusions have resulted. But, as Strawson and Grice (1956) note, observations of this sort 'would scarcely amount to a rejection of the distinction [as Quine urges]. They would, rather, be a prelude to clarification'.

In 'Two Dogmas of Empiricism' (1951), Quine went far beyond the call for clarification; he argued that there simply was no distinction between analytic and synthetic truths. Quine's argument is an enthymeme with roughly the following form: there is no non-circular, purely *empiricist* clarification of the distinction, and therefore there is no distinction at all: 'That there is such a distinction to be drawn at all is an unempirical dogma of empiricists, a metaphysical article of faith' (see QUINE, W.V. §8).

2 Extending the attack to 'necessary' and 'a priori'

Quine's attack did not stop with 'analytic'. Following the lead of logical positivists, he (wrongly) held that, if there were any such distinctions, the analytic/synthetic distinction would be the same as the necessary/contingent distinction, which in turn would be the same as the a priori/a posteriori distinction. So, on his view, since there is no analytic/synthetic distinction, there is no necessary/contingent distinction and no a priori/a posteriori distinction either. It is an error, however, to equate these distinctions, so these further conclusions do not follow.

Quine's attack on the necessary/contingent distinction has not convinced many. Most philosophers accept the distinction and invoke it in their work; modal logic and modal metaphysics are thriving subjects (see MODAL LOGIC; MODAL LOGIC, PHILOSOPHICAL ISSUES IN). Do modal notions have non-circular definitions? Although definitions have been suggested, such as Church (1951) and Bealer (1982), there would be nothing unreasonable in holding them to be primitive (Prior and Fine 1977). After all, everyone must take *some* notions to be primitive.

What *epistemic justification* do we have for the necessary/contingent distinction? No doubt Quine was right that it cannot be justified on purely empirical grounds (that is, using only phenomenal experience and/or observation). But justification is not always purely empirical: logicians, mathematicians, linguists and philosophers rely heavily on *intuitions* in the justification of their theories. (Quine himself relies on intuition in defending his formulations of set theory over others.) And there are no convincing arguments that such use of intuitions is illegitimate. Once one acknowledges intuitive evidence, the necessary/contingent distinction has a straightforward justification: we have a very wide range of robust modal intuitions (for example, the intuition that it is contingent that the number of planets is greater than seven – there could have been fewer), and when such intuitions are taken as evidence, the best theory is one which accepts the distinction at face value.

The necessary/contingent distinction is a metaphysical distinction. The a priori/a posteriori distinction, by contrast, is epistemological. Indeed, Kripke and Putnam have convincingly argued that there are necessary truths (Hesperus is Phosphorus, water is H_2O, and so on) which are impossible to justify a priori (see KRIPKE, S.A. §3; PUTNAM, H. §3). While the former distinction might well lack a non-circular analysis, the latter certainly has one: p is a piece of a posteriori evidence if and only if p is the content of an experience (a phenomenal experience, observation, memory or testimony); p is a piece of a priori evidence if and only if p is a piece of evidence which is not the content of an experience in the relevant sense. (On the assumption that one's intuitions are evidence, the contents of those intuitions would constitute one's a priori evidence.) A theory has an a posteriori justification if and only if the evidence on which that justification is based is a posteriori; a theory has an a priori justification if and only if the evidence on which that justification is based is a priori. Note that this sort of analysis does not presuppose that any theory has an a priori justification; one could deny that there is any a priori evidence. The point is that, contrary to Quine's allegation, the *notion* of a priori justification has a straightforward analysis (see A POSTERIORI; A PRIORI).

Quine seems to assume that a priori judgments would need to be infallible and unrevisable. But this is mistaken, as is evident from our ongoing a priori theorizing about the logical paradoxes. One of the main traditional lines of thought on the a priori – from Plato to Gödel – recognizes that a priori justification is fallible and holistic, relying on dialectic and/or a priori theory construction.

3 Defending 'analytic' against Quine

Unlike 'necessary', 'analytic' is a technical term. Accordingly, it is legitimate to demand, as Quine (1951) does, that its use be explained. This could be done with examples, but none of the (nonequivalent) notions listed above fits the standard examples perfectly, nor does any stand out as *the* most salient. This leaves the alternative of giving a definition. Quine's view is that *not one* of the historically prominent uses of 'analytic' (except the 'logical truth' use) has a satisfactory definition. But this radical scepticism is unwarranted.

Consider the following definition: a necessarily true sentence is analytic if and only if it may be converted into a logically true sentence by replacing its syntactically simple predicates with predicates which mean exactly the same thing. This seems to respect the idea that analytic truths are a priori and moreover are justifiable in a specially simple way. Quine (1960) would object to this definition by appeal to his thesis of the indeterminacy of translation – the thesis that 'there is no fact of the matter' concerning claims about identity of meaning (see RADICAL TRANSLATION AND RADICAL INTERPRETATION §§1–3). His arguments for this thesis have not convinced many philosophers, however, for they depend on quasi-verificationist or behaviourist premises. Most philosophers reject Quine's scepticism about meaning, realism having become the dominant view. One reason for this is the advent of the broadly Gricean picture (Grice 1989) according to which meaning is analysable in terms of the propositional attitudes. Accordingly, if there is a fact of the matter about the latter, there is about the former (see COMMUNICATION AND INTENTION). And, since the cognitivist revolution in psychology and philosophy of mind, nearly everyone is a realist about propositional attitudes. Thus, at least one use of 'analytic sentence' ought to be acceptable to these realist philosophers.

The same moral holds for at least certain uses of 'analytic' as it applies to propositions. Despite Quine's scepticism, most philosophers have become convinced that in logic, psychology and semantics there is need for structured propositions, that is, propositions which have a logical form (or sense structure). This makes possible a definition of 'analytic' in another one of its standard uses (Katz 1986; Bealer 1982): p is analytic iff$_{def}$ every proposition having the same form (structure) as p is necessary.

4 More damaging problems with 'analytic'

Although the above definition of 'analytic' is cogent, the term so-defined fails to apply to a number of examples which traditionally would have been deemed 'analytic'; the definition is too narrow. For example, the defined use does not cover Kant's paradigm example of an analyticity, namely, that bodies are extended. To accommodate this and a wide array of other examples (that circles are curves and so forth; see below), one must turn to a wider definition of 'analytic' – one relying on some philosophically robust notion such as definition, conceptual analysis, or the kind of meaning relations which hold between a definiendum and a definiens or between an analysandum and an analysans. For example, it is at least credible that there is a definition of 'body' in one of its senses according to which 'Bodies are extended' would be true by definition. Unfortunately, these wider accounts of 'analytic' give rise to a complementary problem: they let in too much.

The following familiar definitions illustrate the problem: x is a circle if and only if x is a closed plane figure every point on which is equidistant from a common point; x is a circle if and only if x is a closed plane figure every arc of which has equal curvature. There seems to be nothing to recommend one over the other; if either is a correct definition, both are. In that case it seems that the following would be true by definition plus logic: x is a closed plane figure every point on which is equidistant from a common point if and only if every arc of x has equal curvature. But Kant would deem this biconditional 'ampliative': in any standard axiomatic formulation of geometry, the proof of it would require axioms and axioms – as opposed to definitions – are supposed to be synthetic. Evidently, this argument can be adapted to many other a priori necessities traditionally thought to be paradigmatically synthetic.

A related kind of problem arises in connection with conceptual analysis. One of the most celebrated conceptual analyses in mathematical philosophy is the classical analysis of effective calculability, or computability. On Church's version, a function is effectively calculable if and only if it is lambda-calculable. On Turing's version, a function is effectively calculable if and only if it is Turing computable (see CHURCH'S THESIS). Most philosophers deem each version to be a successful conceptual analysis. But when the two analyses are combined, it follows immediately that a function is recursive if and only if it is Turing computable. But this biconditional – which is an important 'ampliative' theorem of formal number theory – would then turn out to be analytic (in the sense of being true by conceptual analysis plus logic) even in the event that logicism is false.

These problems suggest that there is no coherent way to draw an analytic/synthetic distinction along the lines Kant thought. One response is to settle for a severely restricted use of 'analytic' which concerns only concepts with unique structures (that is, unique 'decompositions'). The price of this move, however, is high: the vast majority of our concepts – including nearly all of the concepts philosophers have sought to define or analyse (good, true, valid, number, meaning, knowledge, and so on) – are in this sense unstructured and so would not give rise to new analyticities. At best, rather uninteresting concepts (such as bachelor) are of this sort. In consequence, even if knowledge of analyticities (in the narrow sense) had a transparent epistemic explanation as Kant assumed, the sort of knowledge one seeks in typical philosophical definitions or analyses would need quite another sort of explanation.

5 Epistemological problems with 'analytic'

Kant and his successors simply assumed that knowledge of analyticities has a transparent sort of explanation (often linked to a simplistic 'pictorial' or 'mereological' view of concepts). Just what that explanation is supposed to be has never been satisfactorily stated. It cannot be that analytic propositions are those whose truth is recognized just by virtue of possessing the constituent concepts, for *no* proposition is like this. For example, it is in principle possible that someone who possesses the relevant concepts but who is in sufficiently defective cognitive conditions (deficient intelligence, attentiveness, and so on) might fail to recognize that all and only bachelors are unmarried men. It does no good to relax this account by holding that analytic propositions are those whose truth would be recognized by anyone in sufficiently good cognitive conditions just by virtue of possessing the constituent concepts, for this lets in too much: anyone in sufficiently good cognitive conditions could not fail to recognize, say, that figure A is congruent with figure B if and only if B is congruent with A. But such propositions are the very paradigms of what Kant would have deemed synthetic a priori and requiring a different sort of explanation. (For these same reasons, purely epistemic definitions of 'analytic' are problematic.)

Another line of explanation is to liken our knowledge, say, that bachelors are men to our knowledge that unmarried men are men, or more generally, that ABs are Bs – that is, to liken this knowledge to our knowledge of a certain kind of *logical* truth. But how do we know the logical truth that ABs are Bs? Is the explanation fundamentally different from the explanation of our knowledge of other kinds of logical truths – for example, that Bs are As or Bs? It is hard to see why it should be. This raises the question of how we know logical truths generally. For instance, is the explanation of our (logical) knowledge that identity is a symmetric relation ($A = B$ iff $B = A$) really different from the explanation of our (nonlogical) knowledge that congruence is a symmetric relation? From a phenomenological point of view, both instances of knowing (logical and nonlogical) arise from a priori intuitions and these intuitions, phenomenologically, are not relevantly different. On this score, therefore, there is no reason to think that our a priori knowledge divides neatly into two kinds having quite different explanations.

On the contrary, there is a promising unified explanation of a priori knowledge generally, which goes roughly as follows. In every case a priori knowledge is based evidentially on a priori intuition. The evidential force of a priori intuition is to be explained in terms of a general analysis of concept possession: it is constitutive of concept possession that in suitably good cognitive conditions intuitions regarding the behaviour of the concept need to be largely correct. If in suitably good cognitive conditions one did not have such intuitions, one would not be said to possess the concept. If something like this is right, then, although they mark cogent logical and metaphysical distinctions, all the listed uses of 'analytic' – even the narrow uses – fail to mark an epistemically significant category of knowledge.

The picture that results is complicated somewhat by Kripke and Putnam's doctrine that there are essentially a posteriori necessities – for example, water = H_2O. Among these are some which may plausibly be deemed *scientific definitions*. If 'analytic' is used in the sense of truth by definition plus logic, where 'definition' is understood to include scientific definitions, then there would be necessities which would be both analytic and essentially a posteriori. Evidently the Kripke–Putnam doctrine applies only to 'semantically unstable' expressions – that is, expressions ('water', 'gold', 'heat', and so on) whose meaning could be different in some population of speakers whose epistemic situation is qualitatively identical to ours. These are expressions to whose meaning the external environment makes some contribution (see CONTENT: WIDE AND NARROW). The above picture, however, holds straightforwardly for semantically stable expressions ('conscious', 'know', 'good', and so on) which loom large in philosophical analysis.

6 Whither 'analytic'?

At this stage, one may reasonably ask whether continued use of 'analytic' serves any purpose in philosophy. Although the term evidently lacks the epistemological significance once attributed to it, the wider use of 'analytic' in the sense of true by definition plus logic still has utility, namely, in posing an important question: Are there necessary truths (supervenience principles, the incompatibility of colours, and so on) which are not analytic in this sense? The answer appears to be affirmative if 'definition' is understood straightforwardly as ordinary explicit definition. But if, as some have proposed, 'definition' is understood to include 'implicit definitions', the answer is controversial and depends on what information may legitimately be loaded into 'implicit definitions'. On pain of trivializing significant traditional questions, however, surely not everything is admissible. Plainly there still are unanswered questions here. But they are really about the nature of definitions; 'analytic' does no work.

See also: CARNAP, R.; CONCEPTS; CONCEPTUAL ANALYSIS; INTENSIONAL ENTITIES; KANT, I.; LOGICAL AND MATHEMATICAL TERMS, GLOSSARY OF; LOGICAL POSITIVISM; NECESSARY TRUTH AND CONVENTION

References and further reading

* Ayer, A.J. (1936) *Language, Truth and Logic*, London: Gollancz. (Uses of 'analytic' mentioned in §1.)
* Bealer, G. (1982) *Quality and Concept*, Oxford: Clarendon Press. (Definition of 'analytic' in terms of propositions and concepts discussed in §3.)
—— (1996) 'A Priori Knowledge and the Scope of Philosophy', *Philosophical Studies* 81: 121–42. (Account of a priori justification and knowledge in terms of intuition and concept possession described in §§2 and 5.)
Boghossian, P. (1997, forthcoming) 'Analyticity', in C. Wright and B. Hale (eds) *A Companion to the Philosophy of Language*, Oxford: Blackwell. (Epistemic account of analyticity.)
* Bolzano, B. (1837) *Wissenschaftslehre*, Sulzbach: Seidel, 4 vols; trans. and ed. R. George, in *Theory of Science*, Oxford: Blackwell, 1972; trans. B. Terrell, ed. J. Berg, in *Theory of Science*, Dordrecht: Reidel, 1973. (Use of 'analytic' mentioned in §1. The George and Terrell translations provide selections from Bolzano's work.)
* Carnap, R. (1937) *Logical Syntax of Language*, London: Routledge. (Uses of 'analytic' mentioned in §1.)
* —— (1947) *Meaning and Necessity*, Chicago, IL: University of Chicago Press. (Uses of 'analytic' mentioned in §1.)
* Church, A. (1951) 'A Formulation of the Logic of Sense and Denotation', in P. Henle, H.H. Kallen and S.K. Langer (eds) *Structure, Method and Meaning: Essays in Honor of Henry M. Scheffer*, New York: Liberal Arts Press, 3–24. (Offers noncircular definitions of modal notions.)
* Feigl, H. (1949) 'Logical Empiricism', in H. Feigl and W. Sellars (eds) *Readings in Philosophical Analysis*, New York: Appleton-Century-Crofts, 3–26. (Use of 'analytic' mentioned in §1.)
Fine, K. (1994) 'Essence and Modality', *Philosophical Perspectives* 8: 1–16. (Account of analyticity and definition in terms of the notion of essence.)
* Frege, G. (1884) *Die Grundlagen der Arithmetik: eine logisch-mathematische Untersuchung über den Begriff der Zahl*, Breslau: Koebner; trans. J.L. Austin, *The Foundations of Arithmetic: A Logico-Mathematical Enquiry into the Concept of Number*, Oxford: Blackwell, 2nd edn, 1980. (Use of 'analytic' mentioned in §1.)
* Grice, H.P. (1989) *Studies in the Way of Words*, Cambridge, MA: Harvard University Press. (Analysis of meaning in terms of propositional attitudes discussed in §3.)
* Kant, I. (1781/1787) *Critique of Pure Reason*, trans. N. Kemp Smith, New York: St Martin's Press, 1965. (Provides the original definition of 'analytic' and 'synthetic' and an account of the possibility of synthetic a priori knowledge.)
* Katz, J.J. (1986) *Cogitations*, Oxford: Oxford University Press. (Account of analyticity in terms of sense structure mentioned in §§3 and 5.)
* Lewis, C.I. (1944) 'The Modes of Meaning', *Philosophy and Phenomenological Research* 4: 236–49; repr. L. Linsky (ed.) *Semantics and the Philosophy of Language*, Urbana, IL: University if Illinois Press, 1952, 50–63. (Uses of 'analytic' cited in §1.)
* Lewis, D.K. (1969) *Convention*, Cambridge, MA: Harvard University Press. (Use of 'analytic' mentioned in §1.)
* Pap, A. (1958) *Semantics and Necessary Truth*, New Haven, CT: Yale University Press. (Use of 'analytic' mentioned in §1 and extended discussion of analyticity and related issues.)
Parsons, C. (1997, forthcoming) *Quine and Gödel on Analyticity*, in P. Leonardi and M. Santambrogio (eds) *On Quine*, Cambridge: Cambridge University Press. (Discussion of Gödel's uses of 'analytic' in relation to Quine.)
* Prior, A.N. and Fine, K. (1977) *Worlds, Times and Selves*, London: Duckworth. (Defends thesis that modal notions are primitive.)
* Putnam, H. (1962) 'The Analytic and the Synthetic', in H. Feigl and G. Maxwell (eds) *Minnesota Studies in the Philosophy of Science*, vol. 3, Minneapolis, MN: University of Minnesota Press; repr. H. Putnam, *Mind, Language and Reality: Philosophical Papers*, vol. 2, Cambridge: Cambridge University Press, 1975, 33–69. (Use of 'analytic' mentioned in §1.)
* Quine, W.V. (1951) 'Two Dogmas of Empiricism', *Philosophical Review* 60: 20–43; repr. in *From a Logical Point of View*, Cambridge, MA: Harvard

University Press, 1953, 20–46. (Classic attack on the analytic/synthetic distinction.)
* —— (1960) *Word and Object*, Cambridge, MA: MIT Press. (Defence of indeterminacy of translation and attack on the ontology of propositions discussed in §3.)
—— (1970) *Philosophy of Logic*, Englewood Cliffs, NJ: Prentice Hall. (Attack on the ontology of propositions discussed in §3.)
* Schlick, M. (1930–1) *Wissenschftlicher Jahresbericht der Philosophischen Gesellschaft an der Universität zu Wein für das Vereinsjahr 1930/1*, repr. as 'Is There a Factual A Priori?', in H. Feigl and W. Sellars (eds) *Readings in Philosophical Analysis*, New York: Appleton-Century-Crofts, 1949, 277–94. (Use of 'analytic' mentioned in §1.)
* Strawson, P.F. and Grice, H.P. (1956) 'In Defense of a Dogma', *Philosophical Review* 65:141–58; repr. in H.P. Grice, *Studies in the Way of Words*, Cambridge, MA: Harvard University Press, 1989, 196–212. (Early response to Quine mentioned in §1.)
* White, M. (1950) *The Analytic and the Synthetic: An Untenable Dualism*, in S. Hook (ed.) *John Dewey: Philosopher of Science and Freedom*, New York: The Dial Press, 316–30; repr. in L. Linsky (ed.) *Semantics and the Philosophy of Language*, Urbana, IL: University of Illinois Press, 1951, 272–86. (Classic attack on the analytic/synthetic distinction.)

GEORGE BEALER

ANAPHORA

Anaphora describes a dependence of the interpretation of one natural language expression on the interpretation of another natural language expression. For example, the pronoun 'her' in (1) below is anaphorically dependent for its interpretation on the interpretation of the noun phrase 'Sally' because 'her' refers to the same person 'Sally' refers to:

(1) Sally likes her car.

As (2) below illustrates, anaphoric dependencies also occur across sentences, making anaphora a 'discourse phenomenon':

(2) A farmer owned a donkey. He beat it.

The analysis of anaphoric dependence has been the focus of a great deal of study in linguistics and philosophy. Anaphoric dependencies are difficult to accommodate within the traditional conception of compositional semantics of Tarski and Montague precisely because the meaning of anaphoric elements is dependent on other elements of the discourse.

Many expressions can be used anaphorically. For instance, anaphoric dependencies hold between the expression 'one' and the indefinite noun phrase 'a labrador' in (3) below; between the verb phrase 'loves his mother' and a 'null' anaphor (or verbal auxiliary) in (4); between the prepositional phrase 'to Paris' and the lexical item 'there' in (5); and between a segment of text and the pronoun 'it' in (6).

(3) Susan has a labrador. I want one too.
(4) John loves his mother. Fred does too.
(5) I didn't go to Paris last year. I don't go there very often.
(6) One plaintiff was passed over for promotion. Another didn't get a pay increase for five years. A third received a lower wage than men doing the same work. But the jury didn't believe any of it.

Some philosophers and linguists have also argued that verb tenses generate anaphoric dependencies.

1   Syntactic and static semantic approaches
2–3   Dynamic semantics

1   Syntactic and static semantic approaches

An expression is 'anaphoric' if it depends for its interpretation on the interpretation of another expression. For example, the pronoun 'her' in (1) below is anaphorically dependent on the noun phrase 'Sally'.

(1)   Sally likes her car.

Anaphoric dependencies also occur across sentences, making anaphora a discourse phenomenon:

(2)   A farmer owned a donkey. He beat it.

Though anaphoric dependencies are a semantic phenomenon, syntax has a very important role to play in their analysis. In the early sixties, syntacticians noticed that anaphoric dependencies were subject to peculiar constraints that syntax could explain. For instance, consider (3) and (3'):

(3)   John hit himself.
(3') John hit him.

In (3) 'John' and 'himself' must refer to the same thing (they must be 'coreferential'), while in (3') 'John' and 'him' cannot do so. Such observations prompted Chomsky (1981) to devise a theory of binding for anaphoric expressions, whereby all noun phrases in the syntactic representation are assigned an index. Reflexive pronouns are subject to a constraint that forces 'himself' in (3) to be co-indexed with and so bound to some noun phrase (NP) that occurs within the same clause, while nonreflexive pronouns obey another constraint that implies that 'him' in (3′) cannot be bound by an NP within the same clause in which it occurred.

While Chomsky and other syntacticians recognized that there is a semantic component to anaphora, they never clearly articulated the semantic interpretation of co-indexed and non-co-indexed NPs. Semantics furnishes a translation of a syntactic structure into a logical representation, a 'logical form', that can then be assigned a model-theoretic interpretation using the formal semantics for the logical representation language, typically the language of first-order or higher-order logic (see MODEL THEORY). The syntactically generated indices on NPs are interpreted as indices on variables. Pronouns introduce an indexed variable in the logical form, while noun phrases introduce a generalized quantifier, which in turn introduces a bound variable with the index of the NP. The quantifier binds all occurrences of the same variable in its scope. So a sentence such as (1) can be represented as follows:

(1′) $\exists x_j \exists x_i (x_i = \text{Sally} \& \text{car}(x_j) \& \text{owns}(x_i, x_j) \& \text{likes}(x_i, x_j))$.

This approach works well enough for the simple cases of intra-sentential anaphora. But anaphoric links between pronouns and their antecedents also occur across sentences. For example, in giving the logical form of (2) above, anaphoric pronouns cause a problem. Formally, the first sentence yields (ignoring tense):

(2a) $\exists x (\text{farmer}(x) \& \exists y (\text{donkey}(y) \& \text{owns}(x, y)))$.

We now tackle the second sentence. The pronouns in the second sentence are anaphorically bound to the noun phrases in the first sentence, and so we should translate the pronouns as variables that are to be bound by the quantifiers introduced by the noun phrases in the first sentence. But we have already finished the translation of the first sentence and so closed off the rightward scope of the quantifiers. Conjoining the translation of the second sentence does not produce a bound variable reading of the variables introduced by the pronouns. It produces an open sentence:

(2′) $\exists x (\text{farmer}(x) \& \exists y (\text{donkey}(y) \& \text{owns}(x, y))) \& \text{beats}(x, y)$.

Montague Grammar (see MONTAGUE, R.M.) seems to solve this problem with the procedure of 'quantifying in' (Gamut 1991). We first postulate a syntactic rule on which the noun phrase is replaced in the syntactic tree by a pronoun with an appropriate index, and the original noun phrase is adjoined with the sentence. We then apply the Montague Grammar translation procedure. Now if we interpret a sequence of two sentences as a conjunction, we can then use the quantifying-in procedure to interpret (2). First, we quantify in the two noun phrases 'a farmer' and 'a donkey'. The syntactic rule for quantifying in produces the following structure for (2):

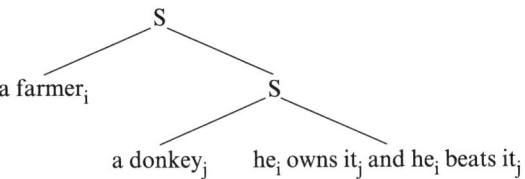

This tree now yields in Montague Grammar the correct logical form for (2):

(2*) $\exists x_j \exists x_i (\text{farmer}(x_i) \& \text{donkey}(x_j) \& \text{owns}(x_i, x_j) \& \text{beats}(x_i, x_j))$.

However, if we wish to continue to use the procedure of quantifying in to deal with discourses in which anaphoric linkage to an antecedent occurring noun phrase exists over multiple sentences as in (4), then we must suppose a complete syntactic analysis of the discourse prior to the interpretation of any of its constituent sentences.

(4) A farmer owned a donkey. He beat it. It ran away.

This conclusion is not cognitively plausible and suggests that the Montague approach to anaphora is wrong. There are other difficulties too. Anaphoric dependencies across attitude contexts such as that between 'a witch' and 'she' in (5) below are also difficult to treat for Montague Grammar without assuming a *de re* reading of the attitude reports (see further Geach 1963).

(5) Hob believes that a witch blighted his mare. Nob believes she killed his cow.

2 Dynamic semantics

Kamp (1981) and Heim (1982) independently proposed a formal and rigorous solution to the problem of anaphoric pronoun interpretation that has come to be called 'dynamic semantics'. The solution redefines the semantic contribution of a sentence to the content of a discourse. In Montague Grammar, the contribution of a sentence is a proposition – formally, a set of possible worlds in which the sentence is true (see SEMANTICS, POSSIBLE WORLDS). Such a proposition contributes to the content of a discourse in a simple way: the meaning of a discourse is just those possible worlds that are in the intersection of all the propositions that are the meanings of the discourse's constituent sentences. In dynamic semantics, the interpretation of a sentence S is a function from a discourse context to another discourse context. Such contexts may be understood in different ways (see Barwise 1987, Groenendijk and Stokhof 1991, Webber 1978). Sketched below is Kamp's approach to discourse semantics, 'Discourse Representation Theory' or DRT.

A discourse context in DRT contains a set of discourse entities or 'discourse referents' to which elements of subsequent discourse may refer. DRT assigns a truth-conditional meaning to a natural language discourse in two steps. First, we construct a representation of the content of the discourse known as a 'discourse representation structure' or DRS. Second, we embed a DRS in a Tarskian model of the sort familiar from first-order logic to provide truth-conditions. A DRS is naturally construed as a partial model and conceptual representation of the discourse. It consists of a pair of sets: a set of discourse referents, or universe; and a set of conditions. The universe of a DRS is analogous to the domain of a partial model; it contains the objects (discourse referents) talked about in the discourse. Conditions are property ascriptions to these discourse referents (Asher 1993). DRSs as partial models should be distinguished from the language used to describe them. The DRS language uses a box notation – the upper part of the box lists the discourse referents in the universe of the DRS, while the lower part of the box describes the conditions. For instance, the DRS for 'a farmer owns a donkey' is given below. It tells us that the discourse speaks of two entities, one a farmer (x), the other a donkey (y), and that the farmer owns the donkey.

(K2a)

x y
farmer(x)
donkey(y)
owns(x,y)

(Wada and Asher (1986), Zeevat (1989) and Asher (1993) develop a construction procedure whereby each lexical element contributes some sort of DR-theoretic structure. These then combine together compositionally following the syntactic structure of the sentence to produce a DRS for the sentence.) A noun phrase such as 'a farmer' introduces a novel discourse referent into the DRS as well as a condition on that discourse referent, while verbs introduce conditions on the discourse referents introduced by the noun phrases that constitute their syntactic arguments. Anaphoric pronouns, following the original Kamp treatment of DRT in 1981, are treated analogously to bound variables; they introduce occurrences of discourse referents that have been introduced previously by the processing of noun phrases in prior discourse.

The construction of a DRS for a discourse proceeds incrementally, exploiting the syntactic parse of each sentence. If $\mathbf{K}^-$ is the DRS derived from the first n sentences and K_{n+1} is the DRS derived from the sentence $n+1$, then the DRS for the $n+1$ sentence discourse is just the DRS that combines the universes of $\mathbf{K}^-$ and K_{n+1} and their condition sets:

$$\langle (U_{\mathbf{K}^-} \cup U_{K_{n+1}}), (\mathrm{Con}_{\mathbf{K}^-} \cup \mathrm{Con}_{K_{n+1}}) \rangle$$

So in constructing a DRS for (4), for example, we would add to the DRS K2a above the conditions 'beats(x, y)' and 'runs away(y)' to get a DRS for (4):

(K4)

x y
farmer(x)
donkey(y)
owns(x,y)
beats(x,y)
runs away(x,y)

DRT solves another problem for Montague Grammar, having to do with indefinites, pronouns and conditionals. In Montague Grammar (as for Frege), the noun phrase 'a man' contributes a property of properties – that is, the property of some property P that there is some man that has P or, in symbols, $\lambda P \exists x (\mathrm{man}(x) \& P(x))$. But then how do we account for the contribution of 'a farmer' in (6)?

(6) If a farmer owns a donkey, he beats it.

If we translate 'a farmer' with the existential quantifier, we must assign it wide scope over the conditional in order to bind the variable introduced by 'he' which is intuitively linked to 'a farmer'. But this gives (6) incorrect truth-conditions. (6) requires the following translation for 'a farmer':

$$\lambda P \forall x (\mathrm{farmer}(x) \rightarrow P(x)).$$

Montague Grammar has no uniform translation of the indefinite determiner that yields a correct treatment of (2) and (6), and also fails to explain why its translation of indefinites is context sensitive in this way. DRT, however, has a uniform translation. DRT uses its analysis of indefinite noun phrases and pronouns, together with construction procedures for conditionals and universally quantified NPs. Both constructions introduce what is known as a 'complex condition' in a DRS; complex conditions consist of DRSs as arguments to some operator. For instance, the grammatical conjunction 'If..., then...' introduces the following relation on DRSs:

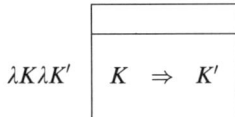

When we have two clauses linked by 'If..., then...', the first clause gives us a DRS replacing the variable K, while the second gives us a DRS replacing K'. For example, if we choose the right discourse referents for the pronouns 'he' and 'it', we translate (6) as in the DRS below, using a uniform treatment of indefinites, conditionals and pronouns.

(K6)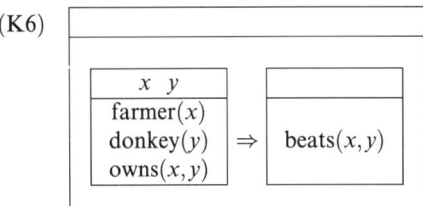

As K6 shows, DRSs can occur within DRSs. DRT postulates a constraint on anaphora called 'accessibility' which exploits these complex structures. A discourse referent 'α' is accessible from a condition 'β' if and only if 'α' is declared in the universe of a DRS that either contains 'β' or a DRS containing 'β', or is the antecedent of a conditional '$\Rightarrow$' of which the DRS containing 'β' is the consequent. We may translate a pronoun with the discourse referent 'α' only if 'α' is accessible to the conditions of which the pronoun is the argument. This means that DRT predicts some anaphoric connections to be semantically incoherent – for example, as in 'If a farmer$_i$ owns a donkey, he$_i$ beats it. *He$_i$ is fined'.

3 Dynamic semantics (cont.)

Let us now briefly discuss the correctness definition for DRSs. The correctness definition tells us what conditions must obtain in order for a DRS to be properly embedded in a 'DRS model'. These are the truth-conditions for the discourse the DRS represents. A DRS model is a pair $\langle D, I \rangle$, where D is a non-empty set (a domain of individuals) and I is a function that assigns to atomic n-ary conditions of DRSs n-tuples from D^n. Atomic conditions are those conditions that are derived from natural language nouns, verbs and some adjectives – the sort that are contained in the DRSs for (2) and (6). A DRS K is properly embedded in a DRS model M if and only if there is a function from U_K into the universe of M such that all the conditions of K are satisfied in M. What we have to do now is to define satisfaction of a condition in K. For atomic DRS conditions, the definition of satisfaction is completely analogous to the satisfaction of an atomic formula of first-order logic relative to a model and an assignment to free variables. The recursive definition for, for example, complex conditions of the form $K \Rightarrow K'$, however, is novel, reflecting the quantificational force of '$\Rightarrow$'. $K \Rightarrow K'$ is satisfied in a DRS model M relative to an embedding function f if and only if for every function g that extends f to a proper embedding of K in M there is an extension h of g that is a proper embedding of K' in M.

In applying the correctness definition to K4, we get the intuitively right truth-conditions for the sentence. The function f is a proper embedding of K4 just in case there is an object a and an object b such that a is a farmer, b is a donkey, a owns b, a beats b, and b runs away. The correctness definition also captures the truth-conditions of a conditional sentence such as (6) – for more details see Kamp and Reyle (1993).

Since its introduction, DRT and other theories of dynamic semantics have been used to analyse various anaphoric phenomena – for example, plural anaphora (Kamp and Reyle 1993), anaphora across attitude contexts (Asher 1987), temporal anaphora (Kamp and Rohrer 1983, Kamp and Reyle 1993) and verb phrase (VP) ellipsis (Klein 1986).

DRT makes an important contribution to our understanding of anaphora. But there are problems. DRT's approach to anaphors and quantification sometimes fails to get the right readings in examples such as the following:

(12) If I have a dime in my pocket, I'll put it in the meter.

DRT predicts that every dime I have in my pocket will be put in the meter, a prediction that must somehow be blocked. Sentences involving pronouns and other quantifiers yield similar difficulties. (13) casts doubt on a basic principle of both Montague Grammar and DRT; the 'it' in (13) does not seem to function as a bound variable but rather as a definite description (Evans 1980).

(13) Either there's no bathroom in this house, or it's in a funny place.

Yet another difficulty for the DRT account of anaphora is that it cannot handle many cases of propositional anaphora. DRT does not offer for (14), for instance, any entities of the appropriate type to which 'it' can refer.

(14) One plaintiff was passed over for promotion. Another didn't get a pay increase for five years. A third received a lower wage than men doing the same work. But the jury didn't believe any of it.

One approach to propositional anaphora such as that in (14) has been to analyse in greater detail the discourse structure of a text. Interpreters naturally understand a text as divided into meaningful segments related in various ways. Some parts give a narrative; others furnish a background for a narrative; still others may elaborate or explain other parts. Such discourse structure is completely missing from DRT, but Asher (1993) and Webber (1991) argue that these parts of the text can serve as referents to anaphoric pronouns. Notions of discourse structure have been incorporated into a dynamic-semantic framework (Asher 1993) to analyse propositional anaphora, VP ellipsis and temporal anaphora (Lascarides and Asher 1993).

See also: DISCOURSE; LOGICAL AND MATHEMATICAL TERMS, GLOSSARY OF

References and further reading

* Asher, N. (1987) 'A Typology for Attitude Verbs and their Anaphoric Properties', *Linguistics and Philosophy* 10: 125–97. (This research paper gives a detailed study of anaphora across attitude contexts within DRT.)
* —— (1993) *Reference to Abstract Objects in Discourse*, Dordrecht: Kluwer. (This book offers an extension of DRT for the purpose of analysing anaphoric reference to propositions and other abstract objects.)
* Barwise, J. (1987) 'Noun Phrases, Generalized Quantifiers, and Anaphora', in E. Engdahl and P. Gärdenfors (eds), *Generalized Quantifiers: Linguistic and Logical Approaches*, Dordrecht: Reidel. (This article offers an alternative formulation of dynamic semantics. It does not use semantic representations such as DRSs.)
* Chomsky, N. (1981) *Lectures on Government and Binding: The Pisa Lectures*, Dordrecht: Foris. (This is one of the central works on syntactic constraints on anaphora.)
* Evans, G. (1980) 'Pronouns', *Linguistic Inquiry* 11: 337–62. (This is one of the classic articles in the philosophy of language on anaphora. It introduces an alternative to the bound variable approach.)
* Gamut, L.T.F. (1991) *Logic, Language and Meaning*, esp. vol. 2, *Intensional Logic and Logical Grammar*, Chicago, IL: University of Chicago Press. (This book is a very good introduction to semantics. Dynamic semantics is presented in volume 2.)
* Geach, P.T. (1963) *Reference and Generality*, Ithaca, NY: Cornell University Press. (This classic text includes many puzzles for semantics.)
* Groenendijk, J. and Stokhof, M. (1991) 'Dynamic Predicate Logic', *Linguistics and Philosophy* 14: 39–100. (This article presents an alternative to DRT's treatment of dynamic semantics. It is similar to Barwise's approach but better worked out.)
* Heim, I. (1982) *The Semantics of Indefinite and Definite Noun Phrases* (Ph.D. thesis), Amherst, MA: University of Massachusetts Press. (Besides Kamp's 1981 paper, this is the principal source for dynamic semantics. It is devoted to the study of indefinite and definite noun phrases and their behaviour as anaphoric referents.)
* Kamp, H. (1981) 'A Theory of Truth and Semantic Representation', in J. Groenendijk, T. Janssen and M. Stokhof (eds) *Formal Methods in the Study of Language*, Amsterdam: Mathematisch Centrum Tracts, 277–322; repr. in J. Groenendijk *et al.* (eds) *Truth, Interpretation and Information*, Dordrecht: Foris, 1984, 1–41. (This is Kamp's first paper on DRT. It is difficult to read but is the principal source for many if not most of the developments in dynamic semantics.)
* Kamp, H. and Reyle, U. (1993) *From Discourse to Logic: Introduction to Model-Theoretic Semantics of Natural Language, Formal Logic and Discourse Representation Theory*, Dordrecht: Kluwer. (This book is a lengthy but readable introduction to DRT. It is written for the non-specialist but also includes valuable material for the specialist.)
* Kamp, H. and Rohrer, C. (1983) 'Tense in Texts', in R. Bäuerle, C. Schwarze and A. von Stechow (eds) *Meaning, Use and Interpretation of Language*, Berlin: de Gruyter, 250–69. (This article describes a dynamic-semantic approach to tense and temporal anaphora. The study is carried out in DRT.)
* Klein, E. (1986) 'VP Ellipsis in DR Theory', in J. Groenendijk (ed.) *Studies in Discourse Representation Theory and the Theory of Generalized Quantifiers*, Dordrecht: Foris. (This paper shows how dynamic semantics can be used to analyse VP ellipsis.)
* Lascarides, A. and Asher, N. (1993) 'Temporal Interpretation, Discourse Relations, and Commonsense Entailment', *Linguistics and Philosophy* 16:

437–93. (This article criticizes the dynamic-semantic treatment of tense and temporal anaphora.)
* Wada, H. and Asher, N. (1986) 'BLDRS: A Prolog Implementation of LFG and DR Theory', *Proceedings of the 11th International Conference on Computational Linguistics*, Bonn, 540–5. (This was one early implementation of DRT and suggested a compositional treatment of dynamic semantics. Some other such implementations are mentioned in the bibliography.)
* Webber, B.L. (1978) *A Formal Approach to Discourse Anaphora*, report 3761, Boston, MA: Bolt, Beranek & Newman Research. (This is a computational approach to anaphora. It has some similarities to dynamic semantics.)
* —— (1991) 'Structure and Ostension in the Interpretation of Discourse Deixis', *Language and Cognitive Processes* 6: 107–36. (This article investigates a variety of anaphoric phenomena in discourse.)
* Zeevat, H. (1989) 'A Compositional Approach to Discourse Representations', *Linguistics and Philosophy* 12: 95–131. (This article gives the first compositional treatment of DRT that brings out the similarities with dynamic predicate logic.)

NICHOLAS ASHER

ANARCHISM

Anarchism is the view that a society without the state, or government, is both possible and desirable. Although there have been intimations of the anarchist outlook throughout history, anarchist ideas emerged in their modern form in the late eighteenth and early nineteenth centuries in the wake of the French and Industrial Revolutions.

All anarchists support some version of each of the following broad claims: (1) people have no general obligation to obey the commands of the state; (2) the state ought to be abolished; (3) some kind of stateless society is possible and desirable; (4) the transition from state to anarchy is a realistic prospect

Within this broad framework there is a rich variety of anarchist thought. The main political division is between the 'classical' or socialist school, which tends to reject or restrict private property, and the 'individualist' or libertarian tradition, which defends private acquisition and looks to free market exchange as a model for the desirable society. Philosophical differences follow this division to some extent, the classical school appealing principally to natural law and perfectionist ethics, and the individualists to natural rights and egoism. Another possible distinction is between the 'old' anarchism of the nineteenth century (including both the classical and individualist traditions) and the 'new' anarchist thought that has developed since the Second World War, which applies the insights of such recent ethical currents as feminism, ecology and postmodernism.

Anarchists have produced powerful arguments denying any general obligation to obey the state and pointing out the ill effects of state power. More open to question are their claims that states ought to be abolished, that social order is possible without the state and that a transition to anarchy is a realistic possibility.

1 **Philosophical anarchism**
2 **Abolition of the state**
3 **Types of anarchy**
4 **Theories of transition**
5 **The 'new' anarchism**

1 Philosophical anarchism

A common starting point for anarchists is 'philosophical anarchism', the denial of any general duty in the individual to obey the laws of the state. The best-known formulation of this view is that of R.P. Wolff (1970), who argues that any such claim of duty comes into conflict with the individual's moral autonomy (see AUTONOMY, ETHICAL). People who accept a duty to act merely because the state has so commanded thereby surrender their capacity to judge the rightness of actions for themselves. Assuming that moral autonomy should never be surrendered, a general duty to obey the state (regardless of the content of its command) is inadmissible. This argument is a strong one, but from a genuinely anarchist point of view its implications are limited. Even if one should not act merely because the action has been commanded by the state, there may be good reason, acceptable to an autonomous agent, to comply with the state's command in particular cases. Philosophical anarchism is consistent with accepting the state's continued existence. It is at best a necessary, not a sufficient, element of a full anarchist case.

2 Abolition of the state

Full-blooded anarchism involves the claim that the state should be abolished. Anarchists have advanced several lines of argument to this end.

First, a utilitarian case might be made, in the manner of Godwin, the earliest systematic writer in the 'classical' anarchist tradition (Crowder 1991) (see GODWIN, W. §3). For Godwin, the disutility of government results, first, from its support for 'the established administration of property', which diminishes the sum of human happiness by dividing society into unequal and antagonistic classes; second, from its tendency to overreach the limits of its competence (Godwin 1798). Utility requires that goods be distributed so as to bring about the greatest happiness, and that people's affairs be left to those most familiar with them, namely the individuals themselves (see UTILITARIANISM).

A second line of argument is also found in Godwin: perfectionism (see PERFECTIONISM). Anticipating J.S. Mill, Godwin sees 'the perfection of which human nature is capable' as involving the development of a robustly autonomous personality. Government, however, by its very nature tends to crush or undermine this kind of autonomy, either by coercion, or by encouraging an attitude of servile obedience or by upholding relations of economic inequality that place one class at the mercy of another. Government must thus be abolished, as an obstacle to the realization of true humanity. A similar element of perfectionism is present in all the classical anarchists. In BAKUNIN, KROPOTKIN and others, the influence of the romantic movement is apparent in their insistence that perfection requires the development of individual uniqueness. This is an emphasis popular among contemporary anarchists, but in the classical texts the promotion of personal idiosyncrasy is usually circumscribed by a prior commitment to some conception of a universal moral law.

This latter insistence suggests a third ground of opposition to the state, the assumption, again characteristic of the classical anarchists, that there is an objective moral law somehow immanent in or deducible from nature. This group thus subscribes to the notion of natural law (see NATURAL LAW §3). As to the precise form and content of natural law they offer different accounts, but all agree that it is violated by the state. Closest to the traditional Thomistic notion of natural law as the command of God is the view found put forward by Lev TOLSTOI (Tolstoi 1936). For Tolstoi, the content of the moral law is Christian, centring upon the idea of universal brotherhood and the command to love one's neighbour. These imperatives, Tolstoi believes, are incompatible with the existence of states, since states set up barriers of enmity between people by creating false national identities and shoring up class distinctions.

Tolstoi is the only major anarchist thinker to adopt an explicitly theistic and Christian foundation; the general self-image of the anarchists is militantly antireligious, an outlook exemplified by Bakunin's (1882). The most fully worked out account of natural law along these secular lines is found in the work of Kropotkin, who takes his cue from Darwinian evolution. In opposition to 'social Darwinists' like Herbert Spencer, Kropotkin (1902) argues that the dominant factor of evolutionary development is not competition but 'mutual aid' within species (see EVOLUTION AND ETHICS). The state must be abolished because, divisive and hierarchical, it constitutes an obstacle to humanity's conforming with this law of nature. Once government is removed, nature can be expected to take its course, ushering in a new era of universal cooperation and brotherhood.

In the individualist tradition, the natural law style of argument against the state takes the form of claims to natural rights. Murray Rothbard (1973), for example, argues that the kind of rights defended by John Locke – rights, rooted in human nature, to security of person and possessions – are incompatible with the state. Government, by its very nature, violates people's rights by coercing them in various ways, including the taxation of their property. Although it might be replied that government is also capable of protecting the individual's rights, the individualist anarchist response is that such protection is provided only at the cost of invading rights in other respects. This is impermissible, since natural rights are absolute. (A similar argument is made by 'minimal state' liberals like Robert Nozick (see LIBERTARIANISM §3; NOZICK, R.).)

Another line of individualist argument appeals to self-interest. Ethical egoism, the view that people ought to prefer their own self-interest to any other principle of conduct, was first developed in an anarchist direction by the Young Hegelian STIRNER. Extending Feuerbach's argument against religion to strike at all notions of 'the sacred', Stirner (1845) argues that people's potential for self-realization is impeded by the very idea of ethical obligation. Among the various 'spooks' that restrict our lives at present, the state, with its demand for obedience, is one of the most oppressive. The state is not the sacred institution we suppose it to be, but merely an especially pervasive agency of violence and coercion. Self-interest demands that we dismantle it.

These arguments may be challenged on many points. For example, the anarchist arguments based on natural law and natural rights may be thought to illustrate some familiar problems with those doctrines, such as the apparent arbitrariness of the content attributed to them (see NATURAL LAW §5). Kropotkin does not adequately justify his emphasis on mutual aid rather than competition; Rothbard's natural rights are narrowly defined to exclude the possibility of 'positive' rights to welfare assistance of the kind historically associated with government intervention. More generally, all these anarchist arguments may be accused of a certain one-sidedness. Taken by themselves, the anarchists' criticisms of the state are often powerful, but their attacks are seldom balanced by any fair consideration of points in government's favour. The tendency is to set out a vivid catalogue of the evils of which the state is capable, and to leave the argument at that.

3 Types of anarchy

After the attack on the state, the next step in the anarchist case is the presentation of some account of the stateless society as a desirable alternative. The general picture anarchists present varies from case to case; their different grounds of opposition to government imply different values to be promoted in anarchy. At one extreme is Kropotkin's vision of a society characterized by voluntary mutual aid, at the other Stirner's conception of a 'union of egoists' in which the only constraints on people's conduct will be the limits of their personal power.

A major source of contrast between different anarchies is the issue of how goods should be distributed. Roughly speaking, the classical tradition argues for the rejection or restriction of private property; the individualist school defends it, looking to market exchange as its central model of social relations. The dominant view in the classical tradition is Kropotkin's 'communist' anarchism, which requires distribution according to need (see COMMUNISM). At the other end of the spectrum, contemporary individualists like Rothbard reject virtually all restrictions on the operation of the market, and are happy to accept the label 'anarcho-capitalist'. On this view, even services traditionally performed by governments, such as law enforcement and defence, should be voluntarily purchased from private suppliers. An intermediate position is occupied by Proudhon's 'mutualism' (see PROUDHON, P.-J.), under which goods are to be distributed by free contract, with the strong qualification that prices be fixed according to units of labour-time. The good society would thus be one in which all would work, and each (assuming roughly equal abilities and industry) would receive roughly similar rewards (Proudhon 1923).

The many difficulties faced by all of these schemes lead to a general problem with conceptions of anarchy, that of how to ensure social order in the absence of the familiar enforcement machinery of the state. Here again there are several different proposals. Confronted by the problem of crime, most classical anarchists first suggest that there will be very much less crime in the absence of private property and its associated inequalities. But assuming the likelihood of at least occasional criminal acts and, more generally, interpersonal disputes, they part company over the best response. For some, such problems will be solved by an eventual universal convergence of ethical judgment brought about by either or both of the following: (1) the release (especially through revolutionary comradeship) of natural feelings of solidarity hitherto suppressed by artificial state-imposed divisions; (2) an improvement in rational understanding of ethical obligations resulting from advances in the natural and social sciences. A second response to the problem of order is the device of public censure, under which people will be brought into line by the pressure of public opinion. Third, some individualists are happy to endorse a system of courts and coercive enforcement, as long as this is maintained by voluntarily paid subscription.

4 Theories of transition

A perennial difficulty in anarchist thought is the question of how society can pass from the existing state system, apparently well entrenched, to the future stateless order. It was principally on this point that the anarchist and Marxist streams of nineteenth-century socialism eventually diverged (see SOCIALISM). Anarchists like Bakunin rejected the Marxist notions of a vanguard party and a transitional period of revolutionary government on the ground that these devices are incipiently authoritarian, and in this they may appear prescient. But the price of their consistency is that they are left to formulate a plausible alternative.

Some anarchists insist on strictly nonviolent means, relying on rational enlightenment (Godwin) or religious reawakening (Tolstoi). Bakunin and Kropotkin emphasize the role of science in promoting progress through rational agreement. Individualists like Tucker (1972) are generally committed to nonviolence, allowing at most passive forms of civil disobedience such as refusing to serve in the armed forces or to pay taxes.

Alongside these irenic views, and sometimes awkwardly combined with them, there is also a strong commitment in some anarchists (Proudhon, Bakunin, Kropotkin) to revolutionary action (see REVOLUTION). All these thinkers agree in principle that the anarchist revolution must be spontaneous or 'bottom-up' rather than subject to any kind of leadership that could evolve into a government. There are, however, various proposals for ways of stimulating the revolution without actually leading it. 'Anarcho-syndicalists' believe that the revolution is to be advanced by direct industrial action culminating in a general strike (Rocker 1938). The school of 'propaganda by deed' urges that the insurrection be inspired by sudden, symbolic acts of anti-bourgeois terrorism. The resulting popular association of anarchism with arbitrary violence is, however, unfair and misleading. It is true that some anarchists, like Bakunin, place an emphasis on the violent destruction of the existing order that sometimes goes beyond the recommendation of a necessary means to an end and becomes a form of self-affirmation held to be valuable in itself. But this tendency is not distinctively anarchist, and neither follows from nor fits comfortably with the most fundamental anarchist principles, which give priority to autonomous judgment and ethical restraint.

5 The 'new' anarchism

The anarchists' principled repudiation of governmental organization even for the purposes of revolution is one of several factors that contributed to the eclipse of anarchism as a political force after the Second World War. Against a background of expanded welfare states in the West and state socialist hegemony in the East, the inheritors of the classical tradition in particular were challenged to revise their thinking. The results have been described as a 'new' generation of anarchist thought (Runkle 1972).

Not surprisingly, some post-war anarchists (see, for example, Ward 1973) have retreated from theories of comprehensive social transformation, concentrating instead on developing spheres of individual and small-group autonomy in the interstices of existing state structures. In this connection, existentialist approaches to anarchism have been developed (see, for example, Read 1954). More ambitious claims continue to be advanced, however. In the 1960s some anarchists were attracted to the apparently revolutionary potential of the 'situationist' ethic that emerged from the amorphous New Left movement (Debord 1983). However, current interest is for the most part focused on three main lines of thought: feminism, ecology and postmodernism.

Feminist anarchism, pioneered by Emma Goldman (1917), is the view that the state is a typical institution of patriarchy, an expression of the characteristic male ethic of impersonal 'justice' backed by violence. Women, in contrast, are said to be anarchists by nature, since female instincts and ideals – of sexuality and motherhood, for example – are non-hierarchical and anti-authoritarian. This claim is vulnerable to the same objections that attach to any 'essentialist' form of feminism, namely that evidence for distinctively male and female 'natures', and hence male and female ethics, is inconclusive (see FEMINIST POLITICAL PHILOSOPHY §5). That is not to rule out the more moderate claim that the historical experience of women gives them an interest in dismantling the state over and above the interest in doing so possessed by men.

The leading ecological anarchist, Murray Bookchin (1982), argues that the state expresses and reinforces a principle of hierarchy which, when applied to people's dealings with nature, encourages the view that humanity's proper relation to the natural world is one of control and conquest. The result is the devastation of our environment. The solution is the 'ecological society', which will be an anarchist society, since in repudiating the hierarchical values that threaten nature it will abandon the hierarchies that have oppressed human beings. To this it might be replied that it is far from obvious that a society that considers itself an equal partner with nature must be internally egalitarian; ecological goals might well be achieved – perhaps more easily achieved – through non-democratic institutions (see GREEN POLITICAL PHILOSOPHY §§1, 3).

Finally, the loosely defined tendency in contemporary thought known as 'postmodernism' may be thought suggestive from an anarchist point of view (May 1994). Michel Foucault's technique of undermining dominant value systems by laying bare the contingent and power-seeking genealogies underlying them implies a kind of liberation for those people previously controlled or marginalized by such systems. It is easy to see that notions of government, state and authority could be dismantled in this way. Less obvious is the possibility of passing from here to a positive recommendation of anarchism, since this too could be undermined by the same genealogical method. An anarchism based on postmodernism is conceivable, but it would probably be negative or destructive in tone (see POSTMODERNISM AND POLITICAL PHILOSOPHY).

Short of massive and unforeseeable changes in world political and economic conditions, it is hard to see any of these more recent developments leading to a revival of anarchist influence at the level it enjoyed in the late nineteenth century. The present power of states, the pervasive influence of international capitalism and the widespread demand for the goods and services these institutions provide, all combine to make anarchism an unlikely political option. The new formulations testify, nevertheless, to the resilience of anarchist ideas and to their continuing role as correctives or counterweights to more conventional views.

References and further reading

Bakunin, M. (1961–80) *Archives Bakounines*, ed. A. Lehning, Leiden: Brill, 7 vols in 8. (The best scholarly edition, although not yet complete.

Another standard edition is the *Oeuvres de Bakounine*, ed. J. Guillaume, Paris: Stock, 6 vols, 1895–1914.)

—— (1973) *Selected Writings*, trans. S. Cox and O. Stevens, ed. A. Lehning, London: Jonathan Cape. (The best selection of Bakunin's writings available in English.)

* —— *God and the State*, trans. B. Tucker, New York: Dover, 1970. (The best known work by Bakunin available in English. Contains a characteristic anarchist attack on religion as an ally of government; see §2.)

—— (1990) *Bakunin: Statism and Anarchy*, ed. M. Shatz, Cambridge: Cambridge University Press. (The leading anarchist critique of Marxism: see §4.)

* Bookchin, M. (1982) *The Ecology of Freedom*, Palo Alto, CA: Cheshire. (Argues for a link between anarchist and ecological ideas; see §5.)

* Crowder, G. (1991) *Classical Anarchism: The Political Thought of Godwin, Proudhon, Bakunin, and Kropotkin*, Oxford: Oxford University Press. (A critical study, arguing that the 'classical' tradition of anarchism is more coherent and persuasive, in historical context, than usually believed.)

* Debord, G. (1983) *Society of the Spectacle*, Detroit, MI: Black & Red. (A manifesto of New Left 'situationism'; see §5.)

* Godwin, W. (1798) *Enquiry Concerning Political Justice*, ed. I. Kramnick, Harmondsworth: Penguin, 1976. (The 1976 edition is the most accessible but there is also the standard modern edition (ed. F.E.L. Priestley, Toronto: University of Toronto Press, 3 vols, 1946) which includes a facsimile of the 3rd edition (London: Robinson, 3 vols) and variant readings among the three editions.)

—— (1993) *Political and Philosophical Writings of William Godwin*, ed. M. Philp, M. Fitzpatrick and W. St Clair, London: Pickering & Chatto. (A selection of the most significant of Godwin's writings in politics and philosophy.)

* Goldman, E. (1917) *Anarchism and Other Essays*, New York: Mother Earth Publishing Association, 3rd edn; repr. New York: Dover, 1969. (A collection of essays combining anarchist and feminist insights.)

* Kropotkin, P. (1902) *Mutual Aid*, London: Heinemann. (Argues that the 'dominant factor' of evolution is cooperation rather than competition.)

* —— (1912) *Modern Science and Anarchism*, London: Freedom Press. (Sees anarchist principles as demonstrable by the methods of the natural sciences.)

—— (1927) *Revolutionary Pamphlets*, ed. R. Baldwin, New York: Vanguard. (A collection of influential essays, including Kropotkin's 1905 article on anarchism for the *Encyclopedia Brittanica*.)

* May, T. (1994) *The Political Philosophy of Poststructuralist Anarchism*, University Park, PA: Pennsylvania State University Press. (Explores the affinities between anarchism and postmodernism.)

Miller, D. (1984) *Anarchism*, London: Dent. (The best analytical and critical introduction.)

* Proudhon, P.-J. (1851) *General Idea of the Revolution in the Nineteenth Century*, trans. J.B. Robinson, London: Freedom Press, 1923. (Includes the idea of contract as 'mutualist' exchange; see §3.)

—— (1923–59) *Oeuvres complètes*, ed. C.C.A. Bouglé and H. Moysset, Paris: Rivière, 15 vols in 19. (The standard scholarly edition.)

—— (1840) *What is Property?*, ed. and trans. D. Kelley and B. Smith, Cambridge: Cambridge University Press, 1994. (The famous answer is 'theft'.)

* Read, H. (1954) *Anarchy and Order*, London: Faber. (A collection of essays drawing connections between anarchism and existentialism; see §5.)

Ritter, A. (1980) *Anarchism: A Theoretical Analysis*, Cambridge: Cambridge University Press. (Argues that 'communal individuality' rather than freedom is the paramount value for anarchists.)

* Rocker, R. (1938) *Anarcho-Syndicalism*, London: Secker & Warburg. (Anarchist goals can be pursued through the trade union movement; see §4.)

* Rothbard, M. (1973) *For a New Liberty*, New York: Macmillan. (A defence of 'individualist' anarchism in its anarcho-capitalist form; see §2.)

* Runkle, G. (1972) *Anarchism: Old and New*, New York: Delta. (A useful survey, proposing a distinction between two phases of anarchism; see §5.)

* Stirner, M. (1845) *The Ego and its Own*, trans. S. Byington, London: Rebel, 1982. (An 'egoist' critique of the state; see §2.)

* Tolstoi, L. (1936) *The Kingdom of God and Peace Essays*, trans. A. Maude, London: Oxford University Press. (Anarchist conclusions reached from a Christian point of view; see §2.)

* Tucker, B. (1972) *Instead of a Book*, New York: Arno. (Essays by a leading US individualist anarchist of the nineteenth century, influenced by Bakunin, Proudhon and Stirner.)

* Ward, C. (1973) *Anarchy in Action*, London: Freedom Press. (A pragmatic from of anarchism, operating alongside the modern state; see §5.)

* Wolff, R.P. (1970) *In Defense of Anarchism*, New York: Harper Torchbooks. (An argument for philosophical anarchism; see §1.)

Woodcock, G. (1963) *Anarchism*, Harmondsworth: Penguin. (The classic general introduction.)

GEORGE CROWDER

ANAXAGORAS (500–428 BC)

Anaxagoras of Clazomenae was a major Greek philosopher of the Presocratic period, who worked in the Ionian tradition of inquiry into nature. While his cosmology largely recasts the sixth-century system of Anaximenes, the focus of the surviving fragments is on ontological questions. The often quoted opening of his book – 'all things were together' – echoes the Eleatic Parmenides' characterization of true being, but signals recognition of time, change and plurality. Even so, Anaxagoras is deeply committed to the Eleatic notions that, strictly speaking, there can be no coming into being or going out of existence, nor any separation of one part of reality from any other. His main object is to show how the variety of the world about us is somehow already contained in the primordial mixture, and is explicable only on the assumption that latent within each substance are portions of every other. Whether or not he owed his conception of unlimited smallness to Zeno of Elea, he held that there could be no such thing as a magnitude of least size; and he claimed that there was accordingly no difference in complexity between the large and the small.

Mind, however, is a distinct principle; unlimited, autonomous, free from the admixture of any other substance. Hence Anaxagoras' decision to make it the first cause of the ordered universe we now inhabit. Mind initiates and controls a vortex, which from small beginnings sucks in an ever-increasing expanse of the surrounding envelope. The vortex brings about an incomplete separation of the ingredients of the original mixture: hot from cold, dry from wet, bright from dark, and so on, with a flat earth compacted at the centre and surrounded by misty air and clearer ether above and below. Contemporaries were scandalized by Anaxagoras' claim that sun, moon and stars were nothing but incandescent stones caught up in the revolving ether.

Later fifth-century physicists – notably Archelaus and Diogenes of Apollonia – developed revised versions of Anaxagoras' system, but abandoned his dualism. His conception of mind excited but disappointed Socrates, and exercised a profound influence on Plato's cosmology and Aristotle's psychology. Aristotle was also fascinated by the complexities of the remarkable theory of 'everything in everything'. Anaxagoras' philosophy was never subsequently revived, but he was remembered as the mentor of the statesman Pericles and the poet Euripides. His reputation as a rationalist critic of religion persisted throughout antiquity.

1 Life and work
2 The original condition
3 In everything a portion of everything
4 Mind
5 Conclusion

1 Life and work

Anaxagoras, son of Hegesibulus, was a native of Clazomenae (a coastal town in what is now Turkey). He was the first major philosopher to spend time in Athens, where he was an associate of the statesman Pericles. The evidence for his residence there is confused although quite extensive. He is said to have arrived in Athens in the archonship of Callias (456/5 BC). Knowledge of his ideas probably preceded his arrival, to judge from echoes of his explanation of physical phenomena in Aeschylus' tragedies *Supplices* (*c.*463 BC) and *Eumenides* (458 BC). He was believed to have predicted the fall of a large meteorite in Thrace that is dated *c.*467 BC. Anaxagoras' stay in Athens may have lasted for about twenty years (so Mansfeld 1779–80), until his prosecution and trial on a charge of impiety (dated by Mansfeld to 437/6 BC). He died in Lampsacus on the Hellespont, where the funeral honours accorded to him suggest a high reputation.

Diogenes Laertius (I 16) counts Anaxagoras among those philosophers who wrote only one work. But some of his views, for example those on perspective and geometry, may have been the subjects of separate memoranda (A38–40). The surviving fragments all appear to come from a general work on the nature and origins of the physical world. The fact of their survival makes for a more direct impression of Anaxagoras' style of thought and his major theses than is possible in the case of Presocratics such as Anaximenes. However, there remain considerable problems of interpretation. One reason is that Anaxagoras' prose, while capable of striking and elevated effect, is too dense and imprecise to allow determinate formulation of the subtle and ingenious distinctions which scholarship has seen as fundamental to his system. Another is that the Aristotelian commentator Simplicius, who is responsible for preserving most of the fragments, quotes them not in the course of a straightforward exposition of Anaxagoras' philosophy, but in order to illustrate various points in either Aristotle's account of Anaxagorean ontology or his own Neoplatonist interpretation of the cosmogony. So while possession of actual extracts from Anaxagoras' book is a huge

249

bonus, their function in his argumentative or expository strategy often eludes us.

2 The original condition

The first few sentences of Anaxagoras' book ran as follows:

> All things were together, unlimited both in quantity and in smallness. For the small was indeed unlimited. And with all things being together nothing was manifest on account of smallness. For air and ether contained all things, both being unlimited. For these are the greatest present among the totality of things, both in quantity and in magnitude.
>
> (fr. 1)

Much in this speculative story is mysterious. What range or category of items count as 'things' (*chrēmata*)? How is their 'smallness' to be understood? In what sense did air and ether 'contain' everything? What is the difference intended between their greatness in quantity and their greatness in magnitude? It was a characteristic trait of Presocratic writing first to grab the reader's attention with a memorable opening, and then to whet the appetite with a pregnant development whose full meaning and justification would emerge only gradually. Anaxagoras provides a copybook example of the technique.

Only one other fragment describes the original condition:

> Before these things were separated off, when all things were together, not even any colour was manifest. For the mingling together of all things prevented it – of the wet and the dry and the hot and the cold and the bright and the dark, much earth being present there also and seeds unlimited in quantity, in no way like each other. For of the others no one is at all like another. Since this is so, one must suppose that all things were present in the totality.
>
> (fr. 4, second part)

Putting the two passages together, we get the following lists of ingredients of the mixture: (1) air and ether (the predominant constituents), a lot of earth and seeds unlimited in number; (2) the wet and the dry, the hot and the cold, and so on. The relation of lists (1) and (2) is obscure. It may be that the wet and the dry and so on, simply *are* earth, air, ether, and so on, under another description, one particularly important for understanding the process of separation which initiates cosmogony. There is also the question of which form of description Anaxagoras conceived as the more fundamental for ontology.

The major items listed in (1) are presumably the actual quantities of the material stuffs which dominate the universe as it is now. The identity and ontological status of Anaxagoras' seeds has been much debated. The final sentences of fragment 4 suggest that he is once again extrapolating from what the universe at present contains to what it must be supposed to have contained originally. A best guess is that from the irreducible present variety of an unlimited number of living species (plants as well as animals), he infers unlimited numbers of biological seeds in the original condition. These he may have conceived as small particles – that would make sense of the explanation in fragment 1 that nothing was manifest 'on account of smallness'. So interpreted, Anaxagoras is making the general assumption that instances of whatever clearly differentiated species of living things now exist must also have existed at least in seminal form before cosmogony.

The thesis in fragment 1 – that there is no lower limit on how small something could be in the original condition – has as its counterpart the thesis that there is no upper limit on how large things can be. From fragment 2, which speaks of what surrounds our differentiated universe as unlimited in quantity, we can infer that the totality was and is infinite in size. Anaxagoras appears to argue the point about largeness by parity of reasoning:

> For of the small there is no least but always a lesser (for what is cannot not be) – but also there is always a larger than the large. And it is equal in quantity to the small. But with respect to itself each thing is both large and small.
>
> (fr. 3)

Readers of fragment 3 have often been reminded of Zeno's paradoxes (see ZENO OF ELEA §§4–6), although it is not known which philosopher wrote first. Anaxagoras evidently differs from Zeno in finding the notion of infinite divisibility basically unproblematic. The similarity lies not just in the denial that there is a least, but in the metaphysical status of that claim, sustained as it is not by physical considerations but by reflection on our conceptions of magnitude, and here particularly the logic of 'large' and 'small'.

3 In everything a portion of everything

The evidence suggests that Anaxagoras next introduced the theme of the separation of the ingredients of the primordial mixture. It looks as though this section of the book emphasized not the process itself nor its outcome in cosmic order, but a very general feature of reality as it is in its separated state: in everything there is a portion of everything. Despite separation, there is a sense in which mixture remains the general condition of things.

This paradoxical theory dominates the presentation of Anaxagoras' views in Aristotle and in what we can recover of other ancient writers who report them. Anaxagoras apparently appealed to several different lines of argument, perhaps designated 'signs' (*sēmeia*) or 'evidences' (*tekmēria*), in recommending the theory to his readers. For one of these we have his own statement (fr. 6). Others are mentioned by Aristotle and the subsequent tradition; here only one sentence attributable to Anaxagoras himself survives (fr. 10).

Most weight was accorded to an argument from growth (for example, A46). Bread and water must contain hair, flesh, nails, bone, and so on. Otherwise the ingestion of food would not make them grow: 'how could hair come from non-hair or flesh from non-flesh?' (fr. 10). As Aristotle puts it, Anaxagoras said that everything is in everything because he saw everything coming to be from everything (*Physics* I 4). A subsidiary argument developed a parallel story about opposites. White has black in it: otherwise the brilliance of snow could not turn into the darkness of water (A97). Anaxagoras made a similar point (details unknown) about heavy and light. Finally, only if there were indivisible minima would it be possible for microscopic pure stuffs to be isolated (fr. 6). But as it is there is no lower limit on smallness (fr. 3), and indeed the small (that is, the latent) must be regarded as no less complex than the large (that is, the manifest):

> And since, too, there are portions equal in number of both the large and the small, in this way too all things will be in everything; nor can they exist separately, but all participate in a portion of everything. Since the least cannot be, none of them could be separated, nor come to be on its own, but as in the beginning so too now all things must be together. And in all things there are many even of those that are separating off, equal in number in both the larger and the smaller.
>
> (fr. 6)

Ancient and modern interpreters alike have been intrigued by the doctrine that there is something of everything in everything. It has accordingly been subject to post-Anaxagorean theoretical refinement and elaboration. Aristotle, followed by the doxographical tradition, inferred from Anaxagoras' arguments for it that the basic building blocks of his ontology were 'homoeomerous', that is, things whose parts were all the same in character as the whole (fr. 6). And he identified these building blocks as the bone, flesh and so on, introduced in the main argument (see, for example, A43, 46). On two occasions he went so far as to claim that air and fire are not themselves elements but composites of 'these and all the other seeds' (see, for example, A43).

These interpretative moves are probably all mistaken. Seeds certainly look to be fundamental items in Anaxagoras' system. But if it is right to suppose that they are conceived in biological terms, as containing what we would call the genetic code for the various living forms which will emerge from them, none like any other, then they cannot be identified with homoeomerous substances such as bone. Indeed, in containing something of everything they will have bone, flesh and so on, as actual or potential ingredients. Whether biological seeds are themselves homoeomerous seems irrelevant to their role in Anaxagoras' system. Again, while Anaxagoras undoubtedly treated bone, flesh and so on, as ingredients also of bread and water, it is unlikely that he regarded them as more fundamental than the animal seeds from which ultimately they emerge. Lastly, to treat air and ether as composites of other more elemental items is to reverse the whole direction of Anaxagoras' explanatory enterprise, which insists on the irreducibility of the variety of the world, and is guided by the maxim: 'The appearances are a sight of what is not manifest' (fr. 21a).

Although Aristotle gave pride of place to homoeomerous stuffs in his account of Anaxagoras' ontology, he also acknowledged the elemental role of opposites. Some modern scholarship has argued that this relative emphasis should be reversed. In the surviving fragments it is certainly the opposites dry and wet, hot and cold, dark and bright and so on, which figure most prominently in Anaxagoras' most general statements about ingredients of mixtures and separation from mixtures. They also recur as the key factors in his explanation of perception (see §5): we discern the cold by the hot, the drinkable by the brackish, the sweet by the pungent. This evidence has suggested that the claim that there is a portion of everything in everything is to be understood primarily as the thesis that every substance or seed of an organism contains opposite powers of every sort – as fragment 4 puts it: 'forms and colours and savours of every kind'. On this view, Anaxagoras may well have conceived such powers as more fundamental than air, ether, earth and living species, at least to the extent of holding that such things derive their distinctive characters and causal properties from the particular combinations of opposite powers which are inherent in them as portions.

The word 'portion' (*moira*) looks as if it may be an Anaxagorean technical term. Modern scholarship has argued that it should be interpreted as equivalent to '*pro*portion'. On this view the point of its introduction can be elucidated by confronting an objection to Anaxagoras' thesis that 'each thing is or was most manifestly the things it contains or contained most of' (fr. 12, end). Take the convenient if probably non-Anaxagorean example of gold. If to count as gold a substance has to contain a predominance of gold, even though it has in it something of everything, must not the predominant gold itself contain a predominance of gold, and so *ad infinitum*? This potentially vicious regress succumbs to a distinction between the discrete substances apparent in the world about us, which contain portions of all things, and the unmixed elements that in different proportions make up these discrete substances. Gold is most manifestly gold because it contains a predominant proportion of *pure* gold. So construed, participation (*metechein*) in portions begins to look like an anticipation of Plato's notion of participation in Forms.

Some distinction of this kind is undoubtedly needed if Anaxagoras' doctrine of a portion of everything in everything is to sustain a claim to intelligibility. And the proposal that the expression 'portion' is its vehicle is unquestionably attractive. But it is not without difficulties. Consider for example the beginning of fragment 4: 'These things being so, it is right to think that in all the things that were being put together there were many things of all kinds, and seeds of all things – having forms and colours and savours of every kind'.

This statement is clearly a version of the doctrine. The words 'these things being so' might even be a reference to the *tekmēria* we have just been reviewing. In any event, Anaxagoras is here applying the theory to emerging compounds, and highlighting the omnipresence of seeds within them. But are ingredient seeds pure elemental portions? Not if as argued above they are complex particles, which mention of forms, colours and so on, tends to confirm. Perhaps seeds are ingredients which are themselves made up of elemental portions; or perhaps there is a degree of indeterminacy in the notion of a portion.

4 Mind

At least once in his exposition of the doctrine of 'everything in everything' Anaxagoras announced an exception to the general rule: 'In everything there is a portion of everything except mind, but there are some things in which there is mind too' (fr. 11). Fragment 12 issues a symmetrical disclaimer: just as there are things whose ingredients do not include mind, so mind is something which itself has no ingredients. This is less obviously true, so Anaxagoras argues out the proposition at some length:

The other things participate in a portion of everything, but mind is unlimited and self-controlling and is not mixed with any thing, but exists alone itself by itself. For if it were not by itself but had been mixed with something else, it would participate in all things, if it had been mixed with any (for in everything there is a portion of everything, as I have said earlier); and the things mixed together with it would be preventing it, so that it would not control any thing in the same way as it actually does being alone by itself. For it is finest of all things and purest; moreover it has all knowledge about everything and harbours greatest strength; moreover all the things that have soul, both the larger and the smaller, all of them mind controls.

(fr.12)

This passage establishes Anaxagoras as a dualist. It is an open question whether in predicating fineness and purity of mind he means to characterize it as incorporeal, or as a uniquely pure body unlike any other material substance – or perhaps simply as something with no specific features of its own other than the capacity for knowledge and control, as seems to be Aristotle's interpretation. Some scholars, noting the hymnic quality of some of the prose in fragment 12, write 'Mind', not 'mind'. But Anaxagoras is talking in general terms, even though the agent of the cosmogony he is about to describe must be a supreme mind. In seeking to identify a cause adequate to account for an ordered universe, he hits on two properties of mind which qualify it alone for the role: its freedom from the (unspecified) limitations which inhibit all other substances, and its power of controlling movement (presumably other things are subject to the forces exercised upon them by other bodies). No earlier thinker enunciated either the concept of a first cause or its identity as mind with anything approximating Anaxagoras' explicitness.

Having established mind's aptness for the task, Anaxagoras went on to sketch his hypothesis about how the world was formed. He writes as though there *is* only one world, and the ancient doxographers confirm that this was his view, despite some now obscure discussion by him of a separation 'elsewhere' (fr. 4, first part). The account runs as follows:

And mind controlled the whole rotation, so that it began to rotate at the beginning. And first it began to rotate in a small way, but it is rotating more, and it will rotate more. And the things which were being mixed together and separated off and distinguished, mind knew them all. And whatever things were to be – both those which were and those which are now and those which will be – all these mind ordered, and also this rotation in which now rotate the stars and the sun and the moon and the air and the ether which are being separated off. And the rotation itself caused them to be separated off. And the dense is separated off from the rare, and the hot from the cold, and the clear from the murky, and the dry from the wet.

(fr. 12, continued)

Aristotle echoed the Platonic Socrates' disappointment with this account (A47). Anaxagoras' introduction of mind as principal cause seemed to them to promise a demonstration of how things were ordered for the best. But its actual role in his cosmogony seemed like a mere device to trigger the vortex, which is what does all the real explanatory work. It is indeed quite unclear how mind exercises any 'control' over the process. Should we suppose that, like a design engineer, it could have designed a different mechanistic system from the one it actually produced? Another complaint was that in accounting for particular phenomena Anaxagoras seldom invoked mind, but appealed to 'airs and ethers and waters and many other absurdities' (Plato, *Phaedo* 98c). Post-Newtonian and post-Darwinian readers may think this a point in his favour.

The principal function of the vortex is clearly to 'separate off' (*apokrinein*) concentrations of air and ether, or again of heavier matter; for example, in the form of the earth and the heavenly bodies. But something else mind achieves is 'dispersal' (*diakrinein*):

And when mind had begun to cause motion, it was separated off from everything moved by it. And whatever mind set in motion, all this was dispersed. But once such things were being moved and dispersed the rotation caused them to be dispersed much more.

(fr. 13)

The idea of dispersal is less clear than that of separation. Perhaps it is the process whereby 'seeds' are disentangled from one another, in contrast with what is necessary for stuffs like air and ether. 'Mixture' (*symmisgesthai*), the other main process referred to in fragment 12 and elsewhere, is not attributed to mind's activity. Doubtless it is the mechanism by which humans and animals and plants are 'compounded' (fr. 4): fragment 17 asserts that what the Greeks call coming into being is really mixture. The extant fragments say nothing about how mixture works. Do seeds somehow control a process whereby portions of the appropriate stuffs are absorbed from the earth and elsewhere into the growing organism? On this view they would exercise one of the key functions carried out in Empedocles' system by Love, with mind playing a role analogous to his Strife (see EMPEDOCLES §5).

5 Conclusion

Anaxagoras evidently included in his book discussion of the full range of particular physical problems that had become mandatory topics for a treatise on nature. These include details of the formation of the earth and the heavenly bodies, accounts of meteorological phenomena, a treatment of the origins of animal life and an exploration of the fundamentals of human physiology and psychology. By comparison with his ontology, Anaxagoras' views on these issues are mostly less original. None the less some specific points deserve a mention.

Anaxagoras knows, for example, that the moon has plains and ravines, borrows its light from the sun and is eclipsed when screened by the earth. His explanation of the rising of the Nile in summer, as due to snows melting to the south, is eminently reasonable, albeit probably wholly speculative (A42). His most interesting remark about humans is the claim that 'it is the possession of hands which makes them the wisest of living things' (A102). Theophrastus tells us at some length about Anaxagoras' theory of sensation. The main idea is that like is not affected by like: something that is as warm or cold as us does not warm or cool us. We are aware of warmth because we are cold, or rather because the warmth in us is deficient relative to the cold (A92).

Anaxagoras' physical system, like the atomism of Leucippus and Democritus, is developed within a framework that is at once Eleatic and Ionian. But he offers an opposite approach to most of the problems he attacks. He is what would nowadays be described as a mind–matter dualist: they are materialists. In place of discrete atoms in eternal motion through a void, he thinks of matter as intrinsically inert, and constituting an infinitely divisible continuum. And the powers inherent in matter are without effect unless triggered by the purposive decision of mind.

References and further reading

* Anaxagoras (500–428 BC) Fragments in H. Diels and W. Kranz (eds) *Die Fragmente der Vorsokratiker* (Fragments of the Presocratics), Berlin: Weidemann, 6th edn, 1952, vol. 2, 5–44. (The standard collection of the ancient sources, including fragments and testimonia, the latter designated by 'A'; includes Greek texts with translations in German.)

Furth, M. (1991) 'A "Philosophical Hero"? Anaxagoras and the Eleatics', *Oxford Studies in Ancient*

Philosophy 9: 95–129. (One of a sequence of excellent philosophical articles on Anaxagoras' theory of matter; comments on many of the earlier classic essays on this subject.)

Guthrie, W.K.C. (1962–78) *A History of Greek Philosophy*, Cambridge: Cambridge University Press, 6 vols. (The most detailed and comprehensive English-language history of early Greek thought; a serviceable treatment of Anaxagoras, in vol. 2 pages 266–338, which includes a useful appendix offering translations of selected passages on his theory of matter.)

Kirk, G.S., Raven, J.E. and Schofield, M. (1983) *The Presocratic Philosophers*, Cambridge: Cambridge University Press, 2nd edn. (A valuable survey of Presocratic philosophy, including texts and translations; contains a useful study of Anaxagoras.)

Lanza, D. (1966) *Anassagora: Testimonianze e frammenti*, Florence: La Nuova Italia. (Reproduces the fragments and testimonia as in Diels and Kranz (1952), with Italian translation and commentary.)

* Mansfeld, J. (1979–80) 'The Chronology of Anaxagoras' Athenian Period and the Date of his Trial', *Mnemosyne* 32: 39–60 and 33: 17–95; repr. in part in *Studies in the Historiography of Greek Philosophy*, Assen and Maastricht: Van Gorcum, 1990, 264–306. (The most complete study of Anaxagoras' chronology.)

Schofield, M. (1980) *An Essay on Anaxagoras*, Cambridge: Cambridge University Press. (A monograph on Anaxagoras' theories of mind and matter based on detailed study of the principal fragments.)

Sider, D. (1981) *The Fragments of Anaxagoras*, Meisenheim am Glan: Verlag Anton Hain. (A useful edition of the Greek text of the fragments, with translation and commentary.)

MALCOLM SCHOFIELD

ANAXARCHUS
(*c*.380–*c*.330 BC)

The Greek philosopher Anaxarchus of Abdera was a friend of Alexander the Great, teacher and friend of Pyrrho, and heroic victim of a tyrant. More a court philosopher than a school one, and an ambiguous personality, he seems to have mixed a highly original philosophical cocktail: a primarily ethical, cynically inclined outlook, combined with certain elements of Democritean ethics, epistemology and physics. His only attested work was a treatise On Kingship, *his dominant interest perhaps being the theory and practice of relations between intellectual and ruler.*

Little is known of Anaxarchus' early life before meeting Alexander. His background lay in the writings of DEMOCRITUS, like him a native of Abdera, and in the teaching of the obscure Diogenes of Smyrna, a pupil of the sceptical Democritean, Metrodorus of Chios. The ancient writers of philosophical 'successions' placed Anaxarchus in a chain running from the Eleatics and Democritus to PYRRHO, to give Pyrrhonian scepticism a distinguished ancestry. That chain underlies the life of Anaxarchus recounted by Diogenes Laertius (Book IX).

After somehow joining Alexander's inner circle, Anaxarchus followed him on his eastern campaign, and brought Pyrrho with him. Alexander's biographers frequently cite his witticisms and sayings. He comes over mainly as caustic and arrogant – strongly enough placed to have no fear of making enemies, notably Nicocreon, who later took cruel vengeance on him, and Callisthenes, a relative of Aristotle who was eventually put to death by Alexander. This feud with Callisthenes explains the striking hostility of the Peripatetic tradition towards Anaxarchus, described in it as a voluptuary and an odious flatterer of Alexander (A4, A9). His attitude towards the king seems actually to have been the much more complex one of a sort of philosopher-jester. Boldly exercising his 'freedom of speech' (*parrhēsia*) in sometimes risky jokes, he pretends to encourage Alexander's ambitions of conquering the world, of being hailed in the oriental fashion (*proskynēsis*), or of being acknowledged as a god, using doubled-edged arguments which are implicitly derisive. He mocks the tears which Alexander sheds after killing his friend Clitus, with the put-down remark that 'everything done by those in power is just and lawful'. In these different situations, Anaxarchus 'skilfully mixes sweetness and acidity' (A7), and perhaps shows how we may interpret his ambition of 'bringing people back to their senses in the easiest way' (A1). The two preserved fragments of his treatise *On Kingship* happen to bear on the two areas in which the relations between the intellectual and power can pose thorny problems: the spoken word (fr. 1) and money (fr. 2). In these areas, one should show the kind of wisdom which Anaxarchus (fr. 1) defines as 'knowledge of the measures of *kairos* [the right moment]'.

The tales of Anaxarchus' death, however, confirm that he was not merely an opportunistic courtier. Having accidentally fallen into the hands of his old enemy, the Cypriot tyrant Nicocreon, he was thrown into a mortar and crushed with iron pestles. Retaining his calm and his irony even under torture, he said: 'Crush, crush Anaxarchus' container; Anaxarchus himself you will not crush.' This heroic death, like

Socrates', long remained a paradigm of philosophical martyrdom.

According to Plutarch, Anaxarchus 'from the beginning beat an original path in philosophy'. This frustratingly brief statement is hard to flesh out. On the basis of his nickname, 'the happiness man' (*eudaimonikos*), earned by 'his impassivity and his even temper in life' (A1), late sources (A14) implausibly make him the founder of a 'happiness school'. In reality, 'impassivity' was a Cynic trait and 'even temper' a Democritean one. Both passed, in time, into Pyrrhonism (see PYRRHONISM §6).

According to Sextus Empiricus (A16), many ranked Anaxarchus with the philosophers who 'abolished the criterion of truth'. However, it is unlikely that he maintained a very sophisticated scepticism. In one of his preserved fragments (fr. 1) he presents himself implicitly as a 'polymath', someone of multiple knowledge, and one anecdote (A11) has him, in conversation with Alexander, preaching the Democritean doctrine of infinite worlds. If there is any scepticism in him, it is rather a practical, lived scepticism, albeit influenced by Democritus' famous assault on the reality of the sensible world (see DEMOCRITUS §3). It is expressed in the ironic yet despairing saying attributed to Anaxarchus, as also to the Cynic Monimus: 'They compared existing things to a stage-painting (*skēnographia*), and thought that they resembled the images seen in dreaming or insanity' (A16).

Just as an old world was vanishing and a new one being born amidst the din, the blood and the fury, Anaxarchus knew how to give striking expression to that feeling of unreality which accompanies such turnings in the tide of history. In that troubled age, which lost its bearings without finding new ones, Anaxarchus remained happy both in pleasure and under torture. He won and kept the friendship of people like Alexander and Pyrrho, and aroused the lasting hatred and resentment of someone like Nicocreon. No doubt he was, as Timon suggests (A10), an ambiguous man. Certainly he was no ordinary man.

References and further reading

* Anaxarchus (*c.*380–*c.*330 BC) Fragments and testimonia in H. Diels and W. Kranz (eds) *Die Fragmente der Vorsokratiker*, Berlin: Weidemann, 6th edn, 1952, vol. 2, 235–40. (Standard collection of the ancient sources, both fragments and testimonia, the latter designated by 'A'; includes Greek texts with translations in German; now superseded by Dorandi (1994).)

* —— (*c.*380–*c.*330 BC) Fragments and testimonia in T. Dorandi, 'Anaxarchi Democritei Fragmenta', *Atti e Memorie dell'Accademia Toscana di Scienze e Lettere 'La Colombaria'* 59, 1994, 9–59. (More complete and accurate than Diels and Kranz; with Italian translation.)

Bernard, P. (1984) 'Le philosophe Anaxarque et le roi Nicocréon de Salamine', *Journal des Savants*: 3–49. (Searching analysis of Anaxarchus' jokes and of the material circumstances of his death.)

Brunschwig, J. (1993) 'The Anaxarchus Case: An Essay on Survival', *Proceedings of the British Academy* 82: 59–88. (General portrayal of the person and his ambiguities as an intellectual in the face of absolute power; comparison with Curzio Malaparte.)

* Diogenes Laertius (*c.* early 3rd century AD) *Lives of the Philosophers*, trans. R.D. Hicks, *Diogenes Laertius Lives of Eminent Philosophers*, Loeb Classical Library, Cambridge, MA: Harvard University Press and London: Heinemann, 1925, 2 vols. (Book IX, 58–60 is a life of Anaxarchus.)

Goulet, R. and Queyrel, F. (1989) 'Anaxarque d'Abdère', in R. Goulet (ed.) *Dictionnaire des philosophes antiques*, Paris: Éditions du CNRS, vol. 1, 188–91. (General portrayal, bibliography and iconography.)

JACQUES BRUNSCHWIG

ANAXIMANDER (*c.*610–after 546 BC)

The Greek philosopher Anaximander of Miletus followed Thales in his philosophical and scientific interests. He wrote a book, of which one fragment survives, and is the first Presocratic philosopher about whom we have enough information to reconstruct his theories in any detail. He was principally concerned with the origin, structure and workings of the world, and attempted to account for them consistently, through a small number of principles and mechanisms. Like other thinkers of his tradition, he gave the Olympian gods no role in creating the world or controlling events. Instead, he held that the world originated from a vast, eternal, moving material of no definite nature, which he called apeiron *('boundless' or 'unlimited'). From this, through obscure processes including one called 'separation off', arose the world as we know it. Anaximander described the* kosmos *(world) and stated the distances of the celestial bodies from the earth. He accounted for the origin of animal life and explained how humans first emerged. He pictured the world as a battleground in which opposite natures, such as hot and cold, constantly encroach upon one another, and described this process as taking place with order and regularity.*

1 Life and work
2 The *apeiron*
3 The *kosmos*
4 Anaximander's fragment

1 Life and work

Very little is known of Anaximander's life. His dates (*c.*610 BC–shortly after 546 BC) are not certain, but make him a generation younger than Thales, whose pupil, successor and associate he is variously called. Like Thales he was a Milesian. He is said to have travelled to Sparta, where he predicted an earthquake and set up a *gnōmōn* (a Babylonian invention for marking the length of the sun's shadow, which he is credited with discovering) on the sundials there to mark solstices, equinoxes and the hours of the day. He is also said to have led a Milesian colony to Apollonia on the Black Sea and, it is reported, made the first map and the first 'sphere' or celestial globe. He wrote at least one work, known as *On Nature* (the title the Alexandrian scholars later gave to the works of most of the Presocratics; it is not Anaximander's title) in which he presented his views on the *kosmos*. (We hear of several other works – *Circuit of the Earth*, *On the Fixed Stars*, *Celestial Globe* – but these are dubious.)

As with other reported discoveries of the Presocratics, this evidence demands cautious treatment. The map is possible, although it will have been extremely crude and founded more on principles of symmetry than on measurement. (See Herodotus, IV 36 for a critical assessment of early maps.) And, since Anaximander had views about the size and shape of the *kosmos*, he may have constructed a model of it. If he foretold an earthquake however, it was just a lucky guess. Alternatively, later authors could have invented the prediction to give Anaximander something comparable to Thales' prediction of an eclipse. The report about the *gnōmōn* is usually accepted as likely, as it agrees with Anaximander's undoubted interest in astronomy.

2 The *apeiron*

Anaximander is best known for his physical theory, which described the original material of the universe as *apeiron*: 'boundless' or 'unlimited' or, possibly, 'indefinite' (the word later acquired the more technical meaning of 'infinite'). What this material is like, how it is related to the *kosmos* around us, and how Anaximander justified his view are basic and controversial issues in understanding his thought. To begin with, what kinds of bounds or limits does it lack? The description 'eternal and unageing' indicates that it is unlimited in time, and since it 'surrounds all the *kosmoi* [plural of *kosmos*]' (Hippolytus, *Refutation* I 6.1, A11) it is vast in extent, and if not infinite, at least unlimited in that there is nothing outside it that limits or determines its size. Furthermore, since it is 'neither water nor any other of the things called elements, but some different *apeiron* nature' (Simplicius, *On Aristotle's Physics* 24.16, A9), it is without any definite character or qualities. Hence some argue that it was called unlimited because it lacks internal boundaries or distinctions. It is not clear that the word *apeiron* can bear this meaning, but Anaximander's original substance is nevertheless indefinite in this way too. The original substance was also the originative substance 'out of which came to be all the heavens and the *kosmoi* in them' (*On Aristotle's Physics* 24.17, A9). Anaximander presented a cosmogony in which the *kosmos* arose from the *apeiron* in a series of developmental stages. Thus, the *apeiron* is the ancestor of all that exists.

Aristotle and his followers present another view: the *apeiron* is the element or substance out of which everything is composed, an Aristotelian material cause (see ARISTOTLE §9). Thus, everything is made of *apeiron* in the way coal and diamonds are made of carbon. Aristotle occasionally identifies the *apeiron* instead as a mixture of the four elements that he recognized, and also as a substance intermediate between fire and air or between air and water. These 'mixture' and 'intermediate' interpretations must be discarded as guesswork, and the idea that it is a material cause must be rejected as Aristotelian invention too, since it does not fit the rest of the evidence on the role of the *apeiron* in Anaximander's system.

Not only is the *apeiron* our ancestor, it is divine. Anything that is 'eternal and ageless' and also 'in motion' (*On Aristotle's Physics* 24.13, A9), which is 'immortal and imperishable' and which 'surrounds all and steers all' counts, for the Greeks, as a divine being (Aristotle, *Physics* 203b11–13, A15). It is disputed how many of these words were Anaximander's, but the ideas they represent seem authentic. Just what 'divine' means in this context is of critical importance. In some sense the *apeiron* is the Creator, but it is remote from the Greeks' anthropomorphic conception of the Olympian gods, who demand worship, intervene in human affairs and are motivated by pride, anger and favouritism. Like Xenophanes' god, the *apeiron* is 'not similar to mortals in form or thought' (Xenophanes, fr. 23) (see XENOPHANES §3). Unlike Xenophanes' god, the *apeiron* lacks perceptive and cognitive capacities (Xenophanes, fr. 24). It seems to have generated the *kosmos* not through any conscious purpose, but somehow as the result of its eternal motion, and the sense in which it 'steers all' seems to be simply that the way the *kosmos* was generated guarantees that the events that take place in it are governed by an immutable, impersonal, universal law.

Why make the originative substance *apeiron*? The sources attribute two arguments for this thesis to Anaximander (although other ancient arguments are sometimes thought to go back to him as well). The first, which argues that it must be *apeiron* in the sense of 'unlimited in extent', goes as follows: 'it must be unlimited lest generation fail' (Aristotle, *Physics* 208a8, A14; Aëtius, I 3.3, A14). Aristotle criticizes the argument on the grounds that 'the destruction of one thing can be the origin of another, the total being limited'. If Anaximander is assumed to be referring either to our own finite *kosmos* or to a succession of finite *kosmoi*, one after another (see §3), it is indeed a bad argument. But if he held that there are an unlimited number of *kosmoi* at the same time, as Aëtius' text suggests, the argument succeeds as far as the vagueness of the term 'unlimited' permits.

The second argument concludes that the *apeiron* is qualitatively indefinite: 'The elements have opposite qualities. Air is cold, water wet, fire hot. If any of them were infinite, the others would have been destroyed. Therefore, the elements arise from something different' (Aristotle, *Physics* 204b26, A16). As it stands, the argument is laden with Aristotelian terminology, and does not prove that the *apeiron* is qualitatively indefinite, only that it is different from the four Aristotelian elements. Its authenticity has been questioned, but it probably has an Anaximandrian kernel, attacking Thales' conception of water as the basic material of the universe using the argument: 'If everything were made of, or originated from, water, then everything would be wet; but some things are wet, others dry (the opposite of wet); therefore, the basic substance cannot be wet, or dry either' (see THALES §2). The argument can be generalized to show that the basic substance is unlike any definite substance and lacks all perceptible qualities.

3 The *kosmos*

The point of having an indeterminate originative substance is to allow to arise the wide variety of things (including opposites) that we find in the world around us. Anaximander's account of the origin of the *kosmos* confirms this interpretation. From the eternal *apeiron*, 'something capable of producing hot and cold' separated off. This gave rise to hot in the form of a sphere of flame, which surrounded cold, in the form of dark mist, 'like bark around a tree'. The sphere of flame subsequently broke up to form the sun, moon and stars, while the mist afterwards became earth and sea.

This is not a creation myth where a divinity creates or acts on matter separate from itself, but an essentially biological account of generation or development which takes place because of the nature of the material that generates the *kosmos*. On this account, the *apeiron* plays no active role after the obscure initial process, which is described as 'separation off'. Once started, the world goes its own way. Anaximander speaks of other events that involve 'separation off', and to judge by them the process does not require purposeful activity or the intervention of an agent. It need not involve any more than some part or amount of an existing thing coming together and being isolated from the rest in such a way as to take on a distinct identity from the rest and behave differently.

Several details of Anaximander's astronomy deserve mention. The heavenly bodies are rings of fire enclosed in tubes of mist pierced with holes for the fire to shine through. Eclipses and the phases of the moon are caused when the holes are blocked. The sun is the same size as the earth. The sun is farthest from the earth, followed by the moon, with the stars nearest. The earth is a cylinder, 'like a column drum', whose depth is one-third its breadth. Anaximander gave the distances of the heavenly bodies from the earth, and although the evidence is untidy, most scholars agree that he made the distances of the stars, moon and sun respectively nine, eighteen and twenty-seven times the size (?breadth) of the earth. The earth is in the centre of the *kosmos* and remains there without support.

The absence of the *apeiron* and of the Olympian gods is notable, as is the boldness of Anaximander's ideas. His figures for the size of the *kosmos* are fanciful, but his conviction that the *kosmos* is symmetrical and based on proportion, and the tenet that important facts about the physical world can be expressed numerically, are a priori principles worthy of a scientist. The odd picture of the celestial bodies as rings rather than points of fire is doubtless the answer to the question where all the fire in the cosmogonic sphere of flame went to. Anaximander may (although this is speculation) have located the stars nearest the earth through the following reasoning: their light is dimmest and they give the least heat because the fire they are made of is less pure than that of the sun; celestial fire is purer the less affected it is – and therefore the more remote it is – from the cool region of the earth; therefore the stars are nearest the earth and the sun farthest.

Anaximander believed the earth stays in the centre

without support 'because it stays put on account of its similar distance from all things' (Hippolytus, *Refutation* I 6.3, A11). Also, 'it is no more appropriate for what is located in the middle and similarly related to the extremes to move up, down or sideways; and it is impossible to move in opposite directions simultaneously; and so by necessity it is at rest' (Aristotle, *On the Heaven* 295b12, A26). Although not all scholars accept this reasoning as Anaximander's, there is no reason why he could not have said something similar to the former of these reports. Aristotle could then have supplied the missing steps in the argument, which amounts to the first recorded use of the Principle of Sufficient Reason. The picture of the earth hanging free in the middle of the *kosmos* contrasts with Greek mythology and with Thales' belief that the earth rests on water, as well as with that of Anaximander's successor, ANAXIMENES (§2), who believed that it is supported by a column of air. It is based on our experience that the earth does not seem to move, along with Anaximander's theory of the origin and structure of the *kosmos*, which leaves no room for a prop.

Like other Presocratics, Anaximander gave accounts of meteorological phenomena agreeing with his cosmogony and cosmology. Fire and dark mist are again prominent, as is 'separation off', this time caused by the sun's heat, which accounts for wind, clouds and (if 'separation off' of dry from wet involves 'exhalation' and 'drying') rain, as well as other effects, including the eventual desiccation of the earth. Wind in turn is the cause of thunder, lightning, thunderbolts, waterspouts and hurricanes.

Anaximander took the same approach to the problem of the origin of life. 'The first animals were born in moisture, surrounded by thorny barks, and when they grew older they went forth onto drier regions, and when the bark broke off they lived a different life for a brief time' (Aëtius, V 19.4, A30). Animals have a similar origin to the *kosmos* (the repetition of the image of a tree's bark is hardly coincidental) and one linked to the progressive drying out of the sea. Regarding the beginning of human life, 'from water and earth that had been heated arose fishes or animals very similar to fishes; humans grew in these and remained inside until puberty; then at last they burst and men and women came forth already able to feed themselves' (Censorinus, 4.7, A30). Although this is not an anticipation of the theory of evolution (as some have thought), it gives a typically bold solution to the problem of how the first generation of humans could have survived until they could take care of themselves and reproduce.

Two other issues are whether our *kosmos* will last forever and whether it is unique. Regarding the first, Anaximander's fragment can be taken to imply that the inconclusive war between opposites will continue forever, so that our *kosmos* has a beginning but no end. However, there is no trace of such a view in the sources and, since later Greek philosophers strongly rejected such asymmetries, the silence indicates that Anaximander did not maintain the view explicitly. On the other hand, since it is unclear how the *kosmos* would come to an end, it is likely that he did not discuss the matter in any detail.

Regarding the second issue, most scholars hold either that Anaximander considered the *kosmos* unique or that he posited an infinite succession of *kosmoi*, one after another. However, several sources mention a limitless number of coexistent *kosmoi*. The evidence is not unanimous and can be taken in different ways, but it would arguably be consistent with Anaximander's system and with his use of the Principle of Sufficient Reason for him to maintain that the process which formed our world need not occur only at one time or in one place.

4 Anaximander's fragment

Aside from a few words in the doxography which may be original, we possess one fragment less than a sentence long. Even here it is disputed which words are original and which are paraphrase. The passage reads as follows (the material in italics is widely thought to be genuine): 'Things that are perish into the things from which they arise, *according to necessity. For they pay penalty and retribution to one another for their injustice, according to the ordinance of time*'. Simplicius, who quotes the fragment in his text *On Aristotle's Physics* (24.18, fr.1), says it describes the relation between things in the world and the *apeiron*, but on grammatical as well as systematic grounds most scholars think it gives Anaximander's view of events in the world without reference to the *apeiron*. Day and night, summer and winter, and many other phenomena involve the regular alternation of the preponderance of one opposite over another. The opposites here are hot and cold, wet and dry, light and dark, etc, conceived not as properties of substances but as 'powers' (*dynameis*) which are capable of affecting things and are embodied or contained in the substances characterized by them. The *kosmos*, then, is a battleground in a war between opposites, a dynamic equilibrium in which one invades the other's territory but is repulsed and loses some of its own ground in turn. On this interpretation the fragment accords with the view favoured above, that the *apeiron* plays no part in the ongoing functioning of the *kosmos*; it was needed at the beginning of the *kosmos*, but, because of the way the *kosmos* was generated, things go on without further need of it.

Noteworthy is the legal language, which Anaximander probably meant literally, since he and other Presocratics did not contemplate any radical difference between humans and the rest of the *kosmos* that would make certain concepts and vocabulary appropriate to one but not the other. Also significant is the idea that events in the world are governed by necessity and occur in an inevitable sequence – a revision of traditional beliefs about the powers of the Olympian gods.

Anaximander brilliantly extended Thales' approach to the understanding of the world to explain a wide range of phenomena. He saw the *kosmos* as a place of order, balance and symmetry; also of change and conflict, subordinated to larger-scale patterns of stability. The testimonia reveal him as a pioneer in several fields of science, but at least as important is his unprecedented use of abstract and general considerations in his reasoning, together with his observations of the world, to articulate a largely unified and coherent understanding of it. His most striking theories were too bold for his immediate successors, but his goal of constructing an intelligible account of the history and workings of the *kosmos* remained as his legacy to philosophy and science.

See also: ARCHĒ; PRESOCRATIC PHILOSOPHY

References and further reading

* Anaximander (c.610–after 546 BC) Fragments, in H. Diels and W. Kranz (eds) *Die Fragmente der Vorsokratiker* (Fragments of the Presocratics), Berlin: Weidemann, 6th edn, 1952, vol. 1, 67–81. (The standard collection of the ancient sources, both fragments and testimonia, the latter designated by 'A'; includes Greek texts with translations in German.)
Barnes, J. (1979) *The Presocratic Philosophers*, London: Routledge & Kegan Paul. (Chapter 2 contains an examination of Anaximander's arguments; good bibliography.)
Classen, C.J. (1965) 'Anaximander', in A. Pauly, G. Wissowa and W. Kroll (eds) *Realencyclopädie der Altertumswissenschaft*, Stuttgart: Druckenmueller, suppl. vol. 12, cols 30–69. (Detailed and exhaustive discussion of the evidence; German text.)
Furley, D.J. (1987) *The Greek Cosmologists* vol. 1, Cambridge: Cambridge University Press. (Pages 16–30 give a general treatment of Milesian cosmology with special reference to Anaximander; argues for some non-traditional interpretations.)
Guthrie, W.K.C. (1962–78) *A History of Greek Philosophy*, Cambridge: Cambridge University Press, 6 vols. (Volume 1 pages 72–115 offer a thorough discussion of Anaximander; good bibliography.)
Hölscher, U. (1953) 'Anaximander und die Anfänge der Philosophie', Hermes 81: 257–77 and 385–418; trans. D.J. Furley and R.E. Allen, 'Anaximander and the Beginnings of Greek Philosophy', in D.J. Furley and R.E. Allen (eds) *Studies in Presocratic Philosophy*, 1970, vol. 1, 281–323. (Considers the source materials on Anaximander and locates him in relation to Hesiod and to the other Milesians.)
Kahn, C.H. (1960) *Anaximander and the Origins of Greek Cosmology*, New York: Columbia University Press; repr. Indianapolis, IN: Hackett, 1994. (The best book on the Milesians.)
Kirk, G.S., Raven, J.E. and Schofield, M. (1982) *The Presocratic Philosophers*, Cambridge: Cambridge University Press, 2nd edn. (Chapter 3 presents a general treatment of Anaximander, based on texts which are given in the original and in English translation.)
McKirahan, R.D. (1994) *Philosophy before Socrates*, Indianapolis, IN: Hackett. (Translation and discussion of source materials; Chapter 5 covers Anaximander.)

RICHARD McKIRAHAN

ANAXIMENES (6th century BC)

The Greek philosopher Anaximenes of Miletus followed Anaximander in his philosophical and scientific interests. Only a few words survive from his book, but there is enough other information to give us a picture of his most important theories. Like the other early Presocratic philosophers he was interested in the origin, structure and composition of the universe, as well as the principles on which it operates. Anaximenes held that the primary substance – both the source of everything else and the material out of which it is made – is air. When rarefied and condensed it becomes other materials, such as fire, water and earth. The primordial air is infinite in extent and without beginning or end. It is in motion and divine. Air generated the universe through its motion, and continues to govern it. The human soul is composed of air and it is likely that Anaximenes believed the entire kosmos *(world) to be alive, with air functioning as its soul. Like other Presocratics, he proposed theories of the nature of the heavenly bodies and their motions, and of meteorological and other natural phenomena.*

ANAXIMENES

1 Air, the cosmic principle
2 The *kosmos*

1 Air, the cosmic principle

Practically nothing is known of Anaximenes' life. He is called the associate and the pupil of Anaximander, on which inadequate basis the ancient testimony makes him a generation younger than his teacher. He wrote a book in 'plain and simple Ionian dialect', but like the works of the other Presocratics it has not survived, although it must be the source of the few words the sources assign to Anaximenes.

From Aristotle onwards, Thales, Anaximander and Anaximenes have been accepted as working within a single tradition: they tackled a single set of problems and used the same methods to solve them (see THALES; ANAXIMANDER). These three Milesian philosophers initiated the Greek philosophical tradition by investigating the origin, structure and workings of the *kosmos* by rational means, abandoning traditional religious and mythological accounts in favour of observation and reason. It is commonly accepted that Anaximander designed important elements of his system to avoid objections he found to Thales' views, and that Anaximenes returned to a theory closer to Thales' but one that both avoided Anaximander's objections and did not suffer from faults that can be found in Anaximander's theory. On this standard view, Milesian philosophy made progress from philosopher to philosopher, and the progress was due to the use of rational criticism. While this line of interpretation is plausible for certain central elements in the thought of these three thinkers, most obviously for their views on the nature of the basic substance, it does not give an adequate picture of other facets of their wide-ranging theories. Also, it is an interpretative construct, not one based on original texts. The sources tell to some extent what the three men's theories were, but not why they adopted them.

Where Anaximander postulated a substance of indeterminate nature, unlike anything found in the world around us, as the ultimate source of the diversity of materials found in the *kosmos*, Anaximenes returned to Thales' idea of basing the *kosmos* on a single familiar substance. However, where Thales selected water, Anaximenes chose air. According to the standard interpretation, Anaximander rejected water because there are materials in the world, such as fire, that lack the properties of water (indeed, they have opposite properties), and so could not have arisen from or be made of water. Thus, the basic material must lack all perceptible properties. Anaximenes objected to Anaximander's idea of founding the world on something imperceptible, indefinite and unfamiliar, and returned to a form of material monism, but one not open to Anaximander's objection. Anaximenes held that air in its most 'even' state (as on a clear, dry, windless day when the air seems neither hot nor cold) is imperceptible, but when it becomes more rare or more dense it turns into other kinds of materials. 'When thinned out it becomes fire, and when thickened it becomes wind, then cloud, and when thickened still more, water, then earth, then stones, and the rest come from these' (Theophrastus, quoted by Simplicius, *On Aristotle's Physics* 24.29–31, A5). The mechanisms of rarefaction and condensation engender a more sophisticated monism, according to which fire, for example, is not really different from air, but *is* air in a certain condition, just as ice is not really different from water, but is water in a certain state. 'And the rest come from these' suggests (although this issue is disputed) that air occurs in certain basic forms (the ones listed above), and that other substances, such as wood or wheat, arise through some combination of them. If Anaximenes held this 'proto-chemical' view of the composition of entities, the absence of further discussion in the sources makes it unlikely that he developed the idea through analysis of particular kinds of materials or illustrative examples of other sorts.

Anaximenes was the first reductionist. From the familiar phenomenon that when we exhale through pursed lips our breath feels cold, but when we exhale with the mouth wide open it feels warm, he concluded generally that compression is the cause of cooling and rarefaction the cause of heating, so that hot and cold depend on rare and dense (Plutarch, *The Principle of Cold* 947F, fr.1). The observation on which this conclusion is based is hardly a scientific experiment (although it has sometimes been called the first one), but there are many elements of scientific reasoning in the way Anaximenes begins from a repeatable result and generalizes it to an explanatory principle related to a larger theory, and also in the way he accounts for one range of phenomena in terms of another which he considers more basic. The fact that his conclusion is exactly wrong is less important than these other considerations.

Density and rarity are quantitative concepts – more or less of something in a given volume – while hot and cold are qualities. Anaximenes is thus credited with being the first to subscribe to the scientific objective (also pursued shortly afterwards by the Pythagoreans) of reducing qualities to quantities (see PYTHAGOREANISM §2). This is probably a misinterpretation however. For although we define density in quantitative terms, Anaximenes need not have seen it this way. There is no reason to suppose he thought there were fixed proportions governing the changes of air, so that, for example, so much fire contains the same amount of air as so much water. He held that ice is denser than water (Aëtius, III 4.1, fr. 3), but is there more water in a cup full of ice than in a cup full of water? (Indeed, water at 4° Celsius is denser than ice, but Anaximenes was unaware of this fact.) The evidence suggests that he did not take a quantitative view of these matters, but considered air, clouds, rain, etc. as more or less dense, as if rarity and density were qualities apparent to the senses and not dependent on measurement.

Like Anaximander's originative substance, Anaximenes' air is described as eternally in motion and also as *apeiron* ('boundless' or 'unlimited'; the word later meant 'infinite', but in Anaximenes' time did not yet have any precise mathematical sense), meaning that it has no limits in space or time. Not that all air is in motion all the time, since air in motion is wind, and wind is denser than air in its most 'even' state. Thus, air is mobile, and at any given time, much of it is in motion. Moving through its own nature, it is alive, and being everlasting, it is divine. (These were also Anaximander's reasons for regarding his basic substance as divine.)

2 The *kosmos*

Like other Presocratic philosophers, Anaximenes proposed a cosmogony and a cosmology that fitted his basic principles. Little information on these topics survives and some of it seems to be inconsistent. Our *kosmos* originated out of the self-moving air which became so dense in one region that it was 'felted' (the word may be Anaximenes' own), or compressed, to form earth. The earth is a flat 'table-like' disc and so rides on the air beneath it like a leaf. There are different accounts of the heavenly bodies. According to the most plausible one, as the earth grew more dense there arose from it moisture that became rarefied and turned into fire; the fire went aloft and became the heavenly bodies. The stars do not give heat because of their great distance from the earth. Like the earth, these fiery bodies stay aloft because of their flatness. There are also earthen bodies in the heavens, which may be posited to account for eclipses. The heavenly bodies do not move underneath the earth, but around it, as when a felt cap (shaped like a yarmulke) is turned about its centre while on someone's head. The geometry of this model is difficult to work out, but the simple and homespun analogy is characteristic of Anaximenes.

Also typical of the Presocratics is Anaximenes' interest in meteorological phenomena. Wind, clouds, rain, etc. are condensed air. When rain freezes as it falls it becomes hail, and it becomes snow when 'something of the nature of breath' is combined with the moisture. Anaximenes explains the rainbow, traditionally the goddess Iris, as the effect of the sun's rays striking condensed air, and offers an account of why it has different colours. Lightning and earthquakes (the work of Zeus and Poseidon) likewise receive naturalistic explanations.

To our knowledge, Anaximenes did not discuss the origin and conditions of animal life, although this may be due to the meagre evidence we possess about his ideas. Certainly these issues were prominent with Anaximander. Anaximenes did declare that the gods are made of air, thus decisively subordinating the Olympian religion to physics. A purported quotation bears on the nature of the soul, a topic which as far as we know Anaximander did not discuss: 'As our soul, being air, holds us together and controls us, also breath and air surrounds the whole *kosmos*' (fr. 2). This fascinating statement (some of whose language is almost certainly a rewording of the original) starts from the traditional, non-philosophical idea that the soul, or principle of life, is the breath. The soul maintains us in existence ('holds us together') as living beings and governs our activities ('controls'), although how it governs and what activities it controls are unclear. (So, for example, we cannot tell whether the soul has cognitive or moral aspects, or whether creatures other than humans possess souls.) The point of the analogy must be that 'breath and air' has (note the singular verb, as in the Greek of the fragment; 'breath and air' is a single idea, perhaps equivalent to 'breath in the form of air') similar functions in the *kosmos*. As it stands, the fragment is not an argument. It is an analogy, which despite its lack of probative force may reveal one of the insights that led Anaximenes to choose air as his basic substance or one that confirmed his choice. The fragment contains the first explicit use of the microcosm-macrocosm analogy in Greek thought. It suggests (although it is not certain that Anaximenes held this view) that air is the soul of the *kosmos*, and therefore that the entire universe is alive. This idea resembles the view attributed to Thales that all things possess soul through their connection with the divine originative substance water. Anaximenes, then, may have found air a more plausible basic substance than water because of the animating functions it possesses according to the traditional conception of the 'breath-soul'.

The last of the great Milesian thinkers, Anaximenes shared with his predecessors an interest in the natural world and the goal of explaining its principal features acceptably to human reason. His cosmology influenced many of the later Presocratics. More conservative than Anaximander in some ways, he devised a theory of the *kosmos* that was intellectually justifiable by the standards of his time and also closer to common experience.

See also: ARCHĒ ; DOXOGRAPHY

References and further reading

* Anaximenes (6th century BC) Fragments, in H. Diels and W. Kranz (eds) *Die Fragmente der Vorsokratiker* (Fragments of the Presocratics), Berlin: Weidemann, 6th edn, 1952, vol. 1, 90–6. (The standard collection of the ancient sources; includes Greek texts with translations in German.)

Barnes, J. (1979) *The Presocratic Philosophers*, London: Routledge & Kegan Paul. (Chapter 3 contains an examination of Anaximenes' arguments; good bibliography.)

Guthrie, W.K.C. (1962–78) *A History of Greek Philosophy*, Cambridge: Cambridge University Press, 6 vols. (Volume 1 pages 115–40 offers a thorough discussion of Anaximenes; good bibliography.)

Kahn, C.H. (1960) *Anaximander and the Origins of Greek Cosmology*, New York: Columbia University Press; repr. Indianapolis, IN: Hackett, 1994. (The best book on the Milesians.)

Kirk, G.S., Raven, J.E. and Schofield, M. (1982) *The Presocratic Philosophers*, Cambridge: Cambridge University Press, 2nd edn. (Chapter 4 offers a general treatment of Anaximenes based on texts which are given in the original and in English translation.)

McKirahan, R.D. (1994) *Philosophy before Socrates*, Indianapolis, IN: Hackett. (Translation and discussion of source materials; Chapter 6 covers Anaximenes.)

RICHARD McKIRAHAN

ANCIENT PHILOSOPHY

The philosophy of the Greco-Roman world from the sixth century BC to the sixth century AD laid the foundations for all subsequent Western philosophy. Its greatest figures are Socrates (fifth century BC) and Plato and Aristotle (fourth century BC). But the enormously diverse range of further important thinkers who populated the period includes the Presocratics and Sophists of the sixth and fifth centuries BC; the Stoics, Epicureans and sceptics of the Hellenistic age; and the many Aristotelian and (especially) Platonist philosophers who wrote under the Roman Empire, including the great Neoplatonist Plotinus. Ancient philosophy was principally pagan, and was finally eclipsed by Christianity in the sixth century AD, but it was so comprehensively annexed by its conqueror that it came, through Christianity, to dominate medieval and Renaissance philosophy. This eventual symbiosis between ancient philosophy and Christianity may reflect the fact that philosophical creeds in late antiquity fulfilled much the same role as religious movements, with which they shared many of their aims and practices.

Only a small fraction of ancient philosophical writings have come down to us intact. The remainder can be recovered, to a greater or lesser extent, by piecing together fragmentary evidence from sources which refer to them.

1 Main features

'Ancient' philosophy is that of classical antiquity, which not only inaugurated the entire European philosophical tradition but has exercised an unparalleled influence on its style and content. It is conventionally considered to start with THALES in the mid sixth century BC, although the Greeks themselves frequently made HOMER (*c.* 700 BC) its true originator. Officially it is often regarded as ending in 529 AD, when the Christian emperor Justinian is believed to have banned the teaching of pagan philosophy at Athens. However, this was no abrupt termination, and the work of Platonist philosophers continued for some time in self-imposed exile (see ARISTOTLE COMMENTATORS; NEOPLATONISM §1; SIMPLICIUS §1).

Down to and including Plato (in the first half of the fourth century BC), philosophy did not develop a significant technical terminology of its own – unlike such contemporary disciplines as mathematics and medicine. It was Plato's pupil Aristotle, and after him the Stoics (see STOICISM), who made truly decisive contributions to the philosophical vocabulary of the ancient world.

Ancient philosophy was above all a product of Greece and the Greek-speaking parts of the Mediterranean, which came to include southern Italy, Sicily, western Asia, and large parts of North Africa, notably Egypt. From the first century BC, a number of Romans became actively engaged in one or other of the Greek philosophical systems, and some of them wrote their own works in Latin (see LUCRETIUS; CICERO; SENECA; APULEIUS). But Greek remained the *lingua franca* of philosophy. Although much modern philosophical terminology derives from Latinized versions of Greek technical concepts, most of these stem from the Latin vocabulary of medieval

Aristotelianism, not directly from ancient Roman philosophical writers.

2 The sixth and fifth centuries BC

The first phase, occupying most of the sixth and fifth centuries BC, is generally known as Presocratic philosophy (see PRESOCRATIC PHILOSOPHY). Its earliest practitioners (THALES; ANAXIMANDER; ANAXIMENES) came from Miletus, on the west coast of modern Turkey. The dominant concern of the Presocratic thinkers was to explain the origin and regularities of the physical world and the place of the human soul within it (see especially PYTHAGOREANISM; HERACLITUS; ANAXAGORAS; EMPEDOCLES; DEMOCRITUS), although the period also produced such rebels as the Eleatic philosophers (PARMENIDES; ZENO OF ELEA; MELISSUS), whose radical monism sought to undermine the very basis of cosmology by reliance on a priori reasoning.

The label 'Presocratic' acknowledges the traditional view that SOCRATES (469–399 BC) was the first philosopher to shift the focus away from the natural world to human values. In fact, however, this shift to a large extent coincides with the concerns of his contemporaries the Sophists, who professed to teach the fundamentals of political and social success and consequently were also much concerned with moral issues (see SOPHISTS). But the persona of Socrates became, and has remained ever since, so powerful an icon for the life of moral scrutiny that it is his name that is used to mark this watershed in the history of philosophy. In the century or so following his death, many schools looked back to him as the living embodiment of philosophy and sought the principles of his life and thought in philosophical theory (see especially SOCRATIC SCHOOLS).

3 The fourth century BC

Socrates and the Sophists helped to make Athens the philosophical centre of the Greek world, and it was there, in the fourth century, that the two greatest philosophers of antiquity lived and taught, namely Plato and Aristotle. PLATO, Socrates' pupil, set up his school the Academy in Athens (see ACADEMY). Plato's published dialogues are literary masterpieces as well as philosophical classics, and develop, albeit unsystematically, a global philosophy which embraces ethics, politics, physics, metaphysics, epistemology, aesthetics and psychology.

The Academy's most eminent alumnus was ARISTOTLE, whose own school the Lyceum came for a time to rival its importance as an educational centre. Aristotle's highly technical but also often provisional and exploratory school treatises may not have been intended for publication; at all events, they did not become widely disseminated and discussed until the late first century BC. The main philosophical treatises (leaving aside his important zoological works) include seminal studies in all the areas covered by Plato, plus logic, a branch of philosophy which Aristotle pioneered. These treatises are, like Plato's, among the leading classics of Western philosophy.

Platonism and Aristotelianism were to become the dominant philosophies of the Western tradition from the second century AD at least until the end of the Renaissance, and the legacy of both remains central to Western philosophy today.

4 Hellenistic philosophy

Down to the late fourth century BC, philosophy was widely seen as a search for universal understanding, so that in the major schools its activities could comfortably include, for example, biological and historical research. In the ensuing era of Hellenistic philosophy, however, a geographical split helped to demarcate philosophy more sharply as a self-contained discipline (see HELLENISTIC PHILOSOPHY). Alexandria, with its magnificent library and royal patronage, became the new centre of scientific, literary and historical research, while the philosophical schools at Athens concentrated on those areas which correspond more closely to philosophy as it has since come to be understood. The following features were to characterize philosophy not only in the Hellenistic age but also for the remainder of antiquity.

The three main parts of philosophy were most commonly labelled 'physics' (a primarily speculative discipline, concerned with such concepts as causation, change, god and matter, and virtually devoid of empirical research), 'logic' (which sometimes included epistemology), and 'ethics'. Ethics was agreed to be the ultimate focus of philosophy, which was thus in essence a systematized route to personal virtue (see ARETĒ) and happiness (see EUDAIMONIA). There was also a strong spiritual dimension. One's religious beliefs – that is, the way one rationalized and elaborated one's own (normally pagan) beliefs and practices concerning the divine – were themselves an integral part of both physics and ethics, never a mere adjunct of philosophy.

The dominant philosophical creeds of the Hellenistic age (officially 323–31 BC) were Stoicism (founded by ZENO OF CITIUM) and Epicureanism (founded by EPICURUS) (see STOICISM; EPICUREANISM). Scepticism was also a powerful force, largely through the Academy (see ARCESILAUS; CARNEADES), which in this period functioned as a critical rather than a doctrinal school, and also, starting from the last decades of the era, through Pyrrhonism (see PYRRHONISM)

5 The imperial era

The crucial watershed belongs, however, not at the very end of the Hellenistic age (31 BC, when the Roman empire officially begins), but half a century earlier in the 80s BC. Political and military upheavals at Athens drove most of the philosophers out of the city, to cultural havens such as Alexandria and Rome. The philosophical institutions of Athens never fully recovered, so that this decentralization amounted to a permanent redrawing of philosophical map. (The chairs of Platonism, Aristotelianism, Stoicism and Epicureanism which the philosopher-emperor MARCUS AURELIUS (§1) established at Athens in AD 176 were a significant gesture, but did not fully restore Athens' former philosophical pre-eminence.) Philosophy was no longer, for most of its adherents, a living activity within the Athenian school founded by Plato, Aristotle, Zeno or Epicurus. Instead it was a subject pursued in small study groups led by professional teachers all over the Greco-Roman world. To a large extent, it was felt that the history of philosophy had now come to an end, and that the job was to seek the correct interpretation of the 'ancients' by close study of their texts. One symptom of this feeling is that doxography – the systematic cataloguing of philosophical and scientific opinions (see DOXOGRAPHY) – concentrated largely on the period down to about 80 BC, as did the biographical history of philosophy written *circa* AD 300 by DIOGENES LAERTIUS.

Another such symptom is that a huge part of the philosophical activity of late antiquity went into the composition of commentaries on classic philosophical texts. In this final phase of ancient philosophy, conveniently called 'imperial' because it more or less coincides with the era of the Roman empire, the Hellenistic creeds were gradually eclipsed by the revival of doctrinal Platonism, based on the close study of Plato's texts, out of which it developed a massively elaborate metaphysical scheme. Aristotle was usually regarded as an ally by these Platonists, and became therefore himself the focus of many commentaries (see PLATONISM, EARLY AND MIDDLE; PERIPATETICS; NEOPLATONISM; ARISTOTLE COMMENTATORS). Despite its formal concern with recovering the wisdom of the ancients, however, this age produced many powerfully original thinkers, of whom the greatest is PLOTINUS.

6 Schools and movements

The early Pythagoreans constituted the first philosophical group that can be called even approximately a 'school'. They acquired a reputation for secrecy, as well as for virtually religious devotion to the word of their founder PYTHAGORAS. 'He himself said it' (best known in its Latin form '*ipse dixit*') was alleged to be their watchword. In some ways it is more accurate to consider them a sect than a school, and their beliefs and practices were certainly intimately bound up in religious teachings about the soul's purification.

It is no longer accepted, as it long was, that the Athenian philosophical schools had the status of formal religious institutions for the worship of the muses. Their legal and institutional standing is in fact quite obscure. Both the Academy and the Lyceum were so named after public groves just outside the walls of Athens, in which their public activities were held. The Stoics too got their name from the public portico, or 'stoa', in which they met, alongside the Athenian agora. Although these schools undoubtedly also conducted classes and discussions on private premises too, it was their public profile that was crucial to their identity as schools. In the last four centuries BC, prospective philosophy students flocked to Athens from all over the Greek world, and the high public visibility of the schools there was undoubtedly cultivated partly with an eye to recruitment. Only the Epicurean school kept its activities out of the public gaze, in line with Epicurus' policy of minimal civic involvement.

A school normally started as an informal grouping of philosophers with a shared set of interests and commitments, under the nominal leadership of some individual, but without a strong party line to which all members owed unquestioning allegiance. In the first generation of the Academy, for example, many of Plato's own leading colleagues dissented from his views on central issues. The same openness is discernible in the first generations of the other schools, even (if to a much lesser extent) the Epicurean. However, after the death of the founder the picture usually changed. His word thereafter became largely beyond challenge, and further progress was presented as the supplementation or reinterpretation of the founder's pronouncements, rather than as their replacement.

To this extent, the allegiance which in the long term bound a school together usually depended on a virtually religious reverence for the movement's foundational texts, which provided the framework within which its discussions were conducted. The resemblance to the structure of religious sects is no accident. In later antiquity, philosophical and religious movements constituted in effect a single cultural phenomenon, and competed for the same spiritual and intellectual high ground. This includes Christianity, which became a serious rival to pagan philosophy (primarily Platonism) from the third century onwards, and eventually triumphed over it. In seeking to understand such spiritual movements of late antiquity as Hermetism, Gnosticism, Neo-Pythagoreanism, Cynicism and even Neoplatonism itself, and their concern with such values as asceticism, self-purificaton and self-divinization, it is inappropriate to insist on a sharp division between philosophy and religion (see HERMETISM; GNOSTICISM; NEO-PYTHAGOREANISM; CYNICS §4; NEOPLATONISM).

'Ancient philosophy' is traditionally understood as pagan and distinguished from the Christian Patristic philosophy of late antiquity (see PATRISTIC PHILOSOPHY). But it was possible to put pagan philosophy at the service of Judaism (see PHILO OF ALEXANDRIA), or Christianity (see for example CLEMENT OF ALEXANDRIA; ORIGEN; AUGUSTINE; BOETHIUS; PHILOPONUS), and it was indeed largely in this latter capacity that the major systems of ancient philosophy eventually became incorporated into medieval philosophy and Renaissance philosophy, which they proceeded to dominate (see MEDIEVAL PHILOSOPHY; RENAISSANCE PHILOSOPHY).

This extensive overlap between philosophy and religion also reflects to some extent the pervasive influence of philosophy on the entire culture of the ancient world. Rarely regarded as a detached academic discipline, philosophy frequently carried high political prestige, and its modes of discourse came to infect disciplines as diverse as medicine, rhetoric, astrology, history, grammar and law. The work of two of the greatest scientists of the ancient world, the doctor GALEN and the astronomer PTOLEMY, was deeply indebted to their respective philosophical backgrounds.

7 Survival

A very substantial body of works by ancient philosophical writers has survived in manuscript. These are somewhat weighted towards those philosophers – above all Plato, Aristotle and the Neoplatonists – who were of most immediate interest to the Christian culture which preserved them throughout the Middle Ages, mainly in the monasteries, where manuscripts were assiduously copied and stored. Some further ancient philosophical writings have been recovered through translations into Arabic and other languages, or on excavated scraps of papyrus. The task of reconstituting the original texts of these works has been a major preoccupation of modern scholarship.

For the vast majority of ancient philosophers, however, our knowledge of them depends on secondary reports of their words and ideas in other writers, of whom some are genuinely interested in recording the history of philosophy, but others bent on discrediting the views they attribute to them. In such cases of secondary attestation, strictly a 'fragment' is a verbatim quotation, while indirect reports are called 'testimonia'. However, this distinction is not always rigidly maintained, and indeed the sources on which we rely rarely operate with any explicit distinction between quotation and paraphrase.

It is a tribute to the philosophical genius of the ancient world that, despite the suppression and distortion which its contributions have suffered over two millennia, they remain central to any modern conspectus of what philosophy is and can be.

See also: EGYPTIAN PHILOSOPHY: INFLUENCE ON GREEK THOUGHT; ATOMISM, ANCIENT; ARCHĒ; GREEK PHILOSOPHY: IMPACT ON ISLAMIC PHILOSOPHY; LANGUAGE, ANCIENT PHILOSOPHY OF; LOGIC, ANCIENT; OWEN, G.E.L.; VLASTOS, G.; LOGOS; NOUS; PNEUMA; PSYCHE.

References and further reading

Algra, K., Barnes, J., Mansfeld, J. and Schofield, M. (eds) (1998) *The Cambridge History of Hellenistic Philosophy*, Cambridge: Cambridge University Press. (Bridges the gap between Guthrie (1962–81) and Armstrong (1967).)

Armstrong, A.H. (ed.) (1967) *The Cambridge History of Later Greek and Early Medieval Philosophy*, Cambridge: Cambridge University Press. (Continuation of Guthrie (1962–81), but skipping Hellenistic philosophy.)

Guthrie, W.K.C. (1962–81) *A History of Greek Philosophy*, Cambridge: Cambridge University Press, 6 vols. (The major work of its kind in English, but does not go beyond Aristotle.)

Zeyl, D. (1997) *Encyclopedia of Ancient Philosophy*, Westport, CT: Greenwood Press. (An comprehensive guide to the Greek and Roman philosophers.)

DAVID SEDLEY

ANCIENT PHILOSOPHY OF LANGUAGE *see* LANGUAGE, ANCIENT PHILOSOPHY OF

ANDERSON, JOHN (1893–1962)

Arguing against metaphysical 'ultimates' (that is, supposed unconditioned conditions of things), relative truth, appeals to subjective experience, and opposing some of the main tendencies of twentieth-century philosophy, Anderson developed a wide-ranging realist and empiricist philosophy. Highly critical of religion, he was much concerned with other cultural values and advanced views (influential in Australia) on freedom of thought, education, ethics and aesthetics. In ethics, for example, his view is that objective good is not good because it is approved of by certain people; rather those who approve of good (or have other relations to it) do so because it is *good. He carefully distinguished questions about the intrinsic character of good from those about relations social groups may have to it, and goes on to develop an account of intrinsic goods as certain socio-mental activities: enterprise or freedom, objective inquiry, artistic production and appreciation, love and courage.*

Similarly, in aesthetics he distinguishes characteristics of works of art from possible relations between artists, works, appreciators and critics, such as a work's relation to a writer's intentions. In Anderson's view the character and structure of the work itself alone provides an aesthetic criterion for assessing the merit of works of art.

1 Life
2 Systematic realism
3 Logic, categories
4 Theory of mind, determinism
5 Social thought

1 Life

John Anderson, Scottish-born philosopher, studied at Glasgow University and lectured there and in Cardiff and Edinburgh before becoming professor of philosophy at Sydney University (1927–58) where he became the leading Australian philosopher of his time, and also a leading controversialist. He was twice censured by the New South Wales Parliament, but was also named as one of the official 200 Australian 'Greats' at the 1988 Bicentenary.

Anderson was influenced by idealist teachers at Glasgow and subsequently in realist ways by William James, G.E. Moore, the New Realists, Kemp Smith, and above all Samuel Alexander. He was also influenced by Heraclitus, Plato, Sorel, Freud, Marx, Vico and Croce, and on wider issues by *The New Age*, a journal of critical thought, during its editorship by A.R. Orage.

A charismatic teacher, Anderson influenced people in a remarkable number of fields, including about thirty who became professional philosophers. These varied in the extent to which they used or agreed with his views. For example, J.A. PASSMORE, J.L. Mackie and D.M. ARMSTRONG produced well-known work of their own (although Mackie did expand Anderson's views on causes and on hypotheticals), while others, such as A.R. Walker, T.A. Rose, A.J. Anderson and W.V. Doniela, taught and developed views more in the Andersonian tradition. In Britain, Anderson influenced Rush Rhees at Edinburgh and through him his students at Swansea.

Anderson's political orientations, though not his main social theory, changed over the years. At first a communist sympathizer (he mistakenly believed Soviet workers were exhibiting Sorel's 'ethic of the producer'), he was then a Trotskyist between 1933 and 1937, and finally a critical oppositionist concerned to defend pluralist values and 'expose illusions' wherever they are found. In the 1950s he criticized communism and the welfare 'servile state' while tenaciously defending learning and thinking values in education against practicalist and supposedly 'egalitarian' ones.

2 Systematic realism

In Anderson's view there is a certain dogmatism about advancing any philosophic position; nevertheless, support can be offered by showing confusions and inconsistencies in rival views and, as Socrates suggested, by using a hypothetical method to reveal the consequences of your position. Criticism is integral to Anderson's philosophizing; not someone who relies on announcing his 'intuitions', he is one of the leading philosophical 'arguers'.

For brevity, Anderson's position is best stated in terms of the '-isms' he sometimes employed. It is mainly one of realism, objectivism, empiricism and pluralism – interlocking views which may be summed up as 'systematic realism'. Conceptions of relative truth are rejected. There may be much illusory thinking, but attempts to deny the absolute or objective truth of *all* propositions are self-refuting – 'If I say "X is true for me", then I am saying that X's being true for me is an absolute fact' (1962: 294). Anderson likewise rejects, for instance, antirealist claims that unverified propositions about the past which are unverifiable today are not true or false.

Contrary to idealists and phenomenalists, he holds that the knower and the known have independent status. Opposing views, as in conceptions of 'dependent existences' such as ideas, perceptions or sense-data, involve confusions of qualities with relations, and Anderson calls such views 'relativist'. In a relational situation in which A has r to B, neither A nor r nor B ontologically constitutes any of the others, even when, say, B depends on A for its origin or continued existence. But in the case of knowledge, relativist confusions are common and are facilitated by cognate accusatives, talk of intentional objects and other ambiguities in the use of such words as 'perception' and 'experience'. Confusions about qualities and relations are also notably rife in ethics and aesthetics (see PHENOMENALISM AND IDEALISM; REALISM AND ANTIREALISM; RELATIVISM).

Anderson's realism and empiricism (which differs from traditional empiricism) rejects overt and covert rationalistic attempts to set up 'levels of reality' in the shape of philosophical 'ultimates' such as necessary or divine beings, monism's one, dualism's two, or the units of atomistic philosophers (for example, HUME's perceptions and the simples of RUSSELL and the early WITTGENSTEIN). Arguing against such views – that 'monism explodes into dualism', though dualism cannot account for the relations between its two sides, and that atomism fails to reduce complexity to unitary elements – Anderson is an ontological egalitarian: whatever exists is on *the same level of existence* as anything else, and is open to objective, empirical investigation, but there are no underlying ultimate, final or purposive explanations.

In Anderson's empiricism all knowledge is obtained by observation (and experiment), including introspection, but observation is not indubitable. In any field there is the possibility of discovery and also of error, which arises because of the 'pluralist complexity' both of mind and of non-mental things. Mind is a network of varied and conflicting tendencies: because of this and because of Freudian mechanisms we are prone to *mis*observe as well as observe. He sums up his pluralism thus: 'There is not only an unlimited multiplicity of things to which the single logic of events applies but anything whatever is infinitely complex so that we can never cover its characters in a single formula or say that we know "all about it"' (1958: 55) (see PLURALISM).

3 Logic, categories

Although the different parts of his position are separably arguable for or against, Anderson places special emphasis on a realist 'logic of events', including a realist formal logic. While his broad conception of logic is of the conditions of existence, his formal logic is traditional logic developed and made consistently realist. It deals with AEIO propositional forms, their implications and other logical relations. Just as there is one level of existence, there is one level of discourse and nothing is above or below the proposition whose copula is the 'is' of occurrence coupling two terms, one of which, the subject, locates an actual or possible situation, and the other of which, the predicate, characterizes it. Identity, existential and hypothetical statements are analysed in AEIO ways, any term is a 'real term' – or presupposed to exist in Strawson's sense – and more precisely is a 'complex place-character' which is the subject of some true propositions and predicate of others. The force of the last point – in regard to the problem of universals – is that there are not separate entities, particular or universal; every situation has both particularity and universality (see ANCIENT LOGIC §3; STRAWSON, P.F. §§2–3; UNIVERSALS §3).

Anderson's acceptance of subject-predicate logic thus puts him at variance with the assumptions of modern logic. But Anderson considers that modern logic and its refinements are derivative from realist logic, in that without prior recognition of the truths of that logic, modern logic would have no objective basis. In any case his logic provides a thoroughgoing realist version of syllogistic logic by requiring all propositions to be contingent and all terms, including their 'logical opposites', to be non-empty, and by paying considerable attention to complex terms and to arguments other than syllogistic ones.

The logic is also closely connected with Anderson's theory of space, time and the categories, which is a revised version of Alexander's theory, and ties in the categories with the form of the proposition as a kind of realistic parallel to Kant's 'metaphysical deduction' of the categories (see ALEXANDER, S.). In Anderson's theory, the categories – particularity, universality, causality and so on – are not compartmentalized, but as pervasive conditions of existence they are all present in all situations.

4 Theory of mind, determinism

Anderson takes a materialist view of mind, maintaining that mental phenomena have spatial, temporal, chemical and suchlike properties. He disagrees, however, with the identification of mind and brain (as made, for instance, by Armstrong 1968) on the grounds that this position is excessively physicalist. His own view is that there is a qualitative difference between mental and non-mental brain processes, consisting in the fact that mind is feeling or emotion.

Mental occurrences, he argues, are all caused, but we can distinguish certain *free* mental activities – ones which have a spontaneous, unstrained way of working – from activities which have a forced or compulsive character. Anderson is a 'pluralist determinist', criticizing conceptions of a single transitive chain of causes and the like. There are, he holds, separate, complex series of causal factors, interacting in various ways, as a result of which complete prediction is impossible. That is why his social theory is critical of social planners and would-be social engineers. Though every social occurrence has causal conditions, we cannot often predict what is going to happen, let alone bring it about; and furthermore social planning very often has undesired, unanticipated consequences.

One of his original conceptions concerns the causal 'field' – what the cause acts on to produce the effect, as when a virus causes a person to have influenza. Attention to the field helps clear up problems about necessary and sufficient conditions, causal series, and 'immediate', 'underlying', 'principal' causes and so on, since differing fields are involved.

5 Social thought

Anderson is a pluralist both in holding that society's way of working is pluralist and in espousing pluralist values. Against the claims of social voluntarism and atomism ('methodological individualism') that unitary individuals and subordinate relations between them are the main determinants of social affairs, he argues that 'forms of association are the primary social fact' (Baker 1979: 17) (see INDIVIDUALISM, METHODOLOGICAL). These associations, such as movements and institutions, involve 'forms of psycho-social activity' passing through individuals: that is, these are forms of activity that exist in their own right. He likewise argues that solidarist or totalistic conceptions are falsified by the variety of factors which are present, including conflicts of group interests, some of which are irreconcilable. Appeals to the 'good of all', for example, disguise actual conflicts and have the covert effect of confusing issues and furthering certain special interests at the expense of other special interests. Social unity and harmony theorists, in Anderson's view, would be wise to heed what Heraclitus said long ago: 'Homer was wrong in saying: "Would that strife might perish from among gods and men!" He did not see that he was praying for the destruction of the universe; for if his prayer were heard, all things would pass away' (Burnet 1908: Fr. 43, 150).

In the case of MARX and Marxists, Anderson rejects their main totalistic conception of society and history and its associated 'philanthropic, servile and salvationist' ethic, but argues that there is a different, scientific and pluralistic strain in Marx's though which lays the foundation of a 'materialism of a non-totalistic kind' with its 'doctrine of social struggles throughout history'. With regard to freedom and democracy, Anderson argues that for people to be more than 'mere voting machines' what is needed is their active concern with the affairs of society at large and with those institutions to which they belong. Such activity is rarely widespread – all the less so with increasing government bureaucratization – but has enough strength to keep alive a permanent struggle of positive freedom against servility, which has its ups and downs (he here agrees with VICO and CROCE) and is gauged by 'the extent of opposition to the ruling order, or criticism of ruling ideas' as carried on by resistant social groups (see DEMOCRACY).

Partly because Anderson was little known outside Australia and partly because of the range of his thought, much of his position was neither subjected to informed criticism, nor refined or worked out in detail.

See also: AUSTRALIA, PHILOSOPHY IN §3

List of works

Anderson, J. (1958) 'Realism', *The Australian Highway* September: 53–6. (An inaccessible journal, but a good short summation of Anderson's position.)

—— (1962) *Studies in Empirical Philosophy*, Sydney: Angus & Robertson. (Contains most of Anderson's philosophical articles.)

—— (1980) *John Anderson, Education and Inquiry*, ed. D.Z. Phillips, Oxford: Blackwell. (Articles and lecture notes on education.)

—— (1982) *John Anderson, Art and Reality*, ed. Janet Anderson *et al.*, Sydney: Hale & Iremonger. (Writings on aesthetics and literature.)

References and further reading

Anderson, A.J. (1987) 'Following John Anderson', *Dialectic* (University of Newcastle Philosophy Club) 30: 129–43. (Deals especially with ethics.)

Armstrong, D.M. (1963) 'Is Introspective Knowledge Incorrigible?', *The Philosophical Review* 72: 417–32. (Defends empiricism of Anderson's kind.)

—— (1968) *A Materialist Theory of the Mind*, London: Routledge & Kegan Paul. (Argues for the identification of brain and mind.)

Baker, A.J. (1966) 'Non-empty Complex Terms', *Notre Dame Journal of Formal Logic* 7: 48–56. (Develops Anderson's logic in regard to these terms.)

—— (1977) 'Classical Logical Relations', *Notre Dame Journal of Formal Logic* 18: 164–8. (Presents a consistent, Andersonian analysis.)

—— (1979) *Anderson's Social Philosophy: The Social Thought and Political Life of Professor John*

Anderson, Sydney: Angus & Robertson. (As the sub-title indicates, the book elucidates Anderson's social (and ethical) theory, and his political history and public controversies.)

—— (1986) *Australian Realism, The Systematic Philosophy of John Anderson*, Cambridge: Cambridge University Press. (Analyses the main features of Anderson's overall philosophy.)

* Burnet, J. (1908) *Early Greek Philosophy*, London: Adam & Charles Black, especially 143–91. (Anderson was much influenced by Burnet's treatment of Heraclitus.)

Mackie, J.L. (1962) 'Counterfactuals and Causal Laws', in R.J. Butler (ed.) *Analytical Philosophy*, Oxford: Blackwell, 66–80. (Develops Anderson's views on hypotheticals.)

—— (1963) 'Are There Any Incorrigible Empirical Statements?', *Australasian Journal of Philosophy* 41: 12–28. (Defends empiricism of Anderson's kind.)

—— (1965) 'Causes and Conditions', *American Philosophical Quarterly* 2: 245–64. (Develops views on causation of Anderson's kind.)

McMullen, T. (1996) 'John Anderson on Mind as Feeling', *Theory and Psychology* 6 (1): 153–68. (Defends and develops Anderson's view that feeling or emotion is the distinctive quality of mind.)

Rhees, R. (1947) 'Social Engineering', *Mind* 56: 317–31. (Endorses Anderson's social theory.)

Rybak, J. and Rybak, J. (1984) 'Mechanizing Logic', *Notre Dame Journal of Formal Logic* 25: 250–82. (Shows in an extended Andersonian way how complex and relational arguments can be dealt with by map logic and computer.)

Ryle, G. (1950) 'Logic and Professor Anderson', *Australasian Journal of Philosophy* 28: 137–53. (Gives a lively assessment of Anderson's philosophy, although parts of it are misunderstood.)

A.J. BAKER

ANEKĀNTAVĀDA

see MANIFOLDNESS, JAINA THEORY OF

ANIMAL LANGUAGE AND THOUGHT

The question of animal language and thought has been debated since ancient times. Some have held that humans are exceptional in these respects, others that humans and animals are continuous with respect to language and thought. The issue is important because our self-image as a species is at stake.

Arguments for human exceptionalism can be classified as Cartesian, Wittgensteinian and behaviourist. What these arguments have in common is the view that language and thought are closely associated, and animals do not have language. The ape language experiments of the 1960s and 1970s were especially important against this background: if apes could learn language then even the advocates of human exceptionalism would have to admit that they have thoughts. It is now generally believed that whatever linguistic abilities apes have shown have been quite rudimentary. Yet many sceptics are willing to grant that in some cases apes did develop linguistic skills to some extent, and clearly evidenced thought. Studies of other animals in captivity and various animals in the wild have provided evidence of highly sophisticated communicative behaviour. Cognitive ethology and comparative psychology have emerged as the fields that study animal thought. While there are conceptual difficulties in grounding these fields, it appears plausible that many animals have thoughts and these can be scientifically investigated.

1   **Human exceptionalism versus continuity across species**
2   **Arguments for human exceptionalism**
3   **The ape language controversy**
4   **Animal communication**
5   **Thought without language**

1   Human exceptionalism versus continuity across species

Richard Sorabji (1993) has argued that debates about animal language and mind go to the core of the western philosophical tradition. Aristotelians and Stoics argued that only humans have reason or belief; some Platonists and Pythagoreans argued that these are shared by many kinds of animal. Indeed, Plato himself challenged the very framework presupposed by the debate. He thought that it was just as sensible to divide the world into cranes and non-cranes as humans and non-humans (see *Statesman* 263d).

Both human exceptionalism (HE) and continuity across species (CAS) have had strong supporters. HE was defended by Aquinas, Descartes and many twentieth-century linguistic philosophers, CAS by Voltaire, Hume and Darwin.

Although it is easy to characterize HE and CAS generally, it is difficult to do so precisely. Roughly, those who espouse HE believe that humans are unique in having language and sophisticated thought, and that there is a deep chasm between these human capacities and whatever thoughts and communication systems other animals may have. Those who embrace CAS hold that humans share the capacity for language or thought with at least some other animals and that the differences with respect to these capacities between humans and other animals are gradual and incremental.

However advocates of HE need not hold that humans are exceptional with respect to every capacity and every animal. They may contemplate honorary humanhood for dolphins (for example), or grant that a few other animals have thoughts but insist that these thoughts are always first-order or nonconscious, and thus very different from the thoughts that humans are capable of having. Defenders of HE may allow that many animals have communication systems, but then go on to claim that these are vastly weaker and less sophisticated than human language.

Supporters of CAS may grant that humans are capable of having some thoughts that no other animal can have. But they will generally see this as an evolutionary fact about humans that is not importantly different from other evolutionary facts about other animals. Perhaps only humans can ponder the neurophysiology of the wildebeest, but lions can think thoughts about wildebeests that humans cannot conceive. Defenders of CAS sometimes grant that only humans use language, but they often see this as a matter of definition or otherwise trivial. They are inclined to see complex communication systems as similar to languages or as sophisticated and important. Although the difference between HE and CAS may be vague, proponents of HE assert that there are enormous differences between humans and animals that centre on language and thought while advocates of CAS deny this.

The dispute between HE and CAS is important for several reasons. If animals lack central features of language and thought that humans have, then a profound gulf separates us from them. The existence of this gulf may have implications about the relations between the natural sciences and the human sciences. It may also justify discontinuous moralities with respect to humans and animals (see ANIMALS AND ETHICS; MORAL STANDING). If HE is correct, then we may be justified in seeing ourselves as special – perhaps even as 'the crown of creation'. On the other hand, if CAS is correct, this may mean that action theory and philosophy of language should be seen as branches of ethology, and that our treatment of animals is a moral scandal. We may have to give up the view of ourselves as morally and metaphysically privileged, and instead see ourselves as one animal species among many. What is potentially at stake in arguments about animal language and thought is our human self-image – who we are, what we are like and what constitutes our proper relations with the rest of nature.

2 Arguments for human exceptionalism

Many philosophers have defended HE. Any attempt to collect these views into categories and to develop generic arguments involves regimentation. With these caveats in mind, it is useful to divide the arguments for HE into three categories: Cartesian, Wittgensteinian and behaviourist.

Cartesian views about animal language and thought have been influential on philosophers and linguists such as Vendler (1972) and Chomsky (1966). Although there is controversy about the exact nature of Descartes' views about animals, the broad outlines are clear.

Chomsky credits Descartes with recognizing that language use is 'creative': it is both unbounded in scope and stimulus-free. Descartes wrote that while 'magpies and parrots are able to utter words just like ourselves' this is mechanical, 'a movement of mere nature' rather than a sign of thought (*Discourse on Method*, 1637: Part V). Having established to his satisfaction that animals do not have language, Descartes infers that they do not have thought, 'for the word is the sole sign and the only certain mark of the presence of thought hidden and wrapped up in the body' (letter to Henry More, 1649). Although Descartes is ambivalent about whether it can be proved that animals do not have thoughts, clearly he believes that they do not. Since animals do not have thoughts they do not have 'real feeling', for 'real feeling' involves propositional content and animals are incapable of propositional content because they do not have language.

Wittgensteinian accounts of animal language and thought have been given by Malcolm (1972–3) and Leahy (1991). Wittgenstein's own views are characteristically difficult to unravel. In *Philosophical Investigations* (1953) he claims that animals 'do not use language – if we except the most primitive form of language', but appears to think that animals have sensations, emotions, intentions and first-order beliefs. However, Wittgenstein denies that animals have the power to simulate pain, to talk to themselves, or have attitudes about future events.

According to Malcolm, animals think but do not have thoughts. Having thoughts involves formulating and entertaining propositions, and he believes that animals are incapable of this. Although Malcolm (1972–3) does not identify thought with language, he claims that the relationship is 'so close that it is really senseless to conjecture that people may *not* have thoughts, and also really senseless to conjecture that animals *may* have thoughts'. However, we know that animals think because 'in real life we commonly employ the verb "think" in respect to animals'. Clearly Malcolm believes that animal thinking does not involve having thoughts, but says very little about how we are to understand it.

Behaviourists in both science and philosophy have denied animal language and thought (see BEHAVIOURISM, ANALYTIC; BEHAVIOURISM, METHODOLOGICAL AND SCIENTIFIC). Although some behaviourists deny thought to humans as well, most reserve their deepest scepticism for animals. Quine (1960) takes it as obvious that animals do not have language, and that ascribing thoughts to animals is an 'essentially dramatic idiom' – we imagine ourselves in the animal's place and say what thoughts we would have were we the animal.

Davidson (1975) has produced the following argument for supposing that animals do not have thoughts: if an animal has a thought, then this thought must occur in a network of beliefs. This follows from Davidson's holism which he takes from Quine: thoughts or beliefs come in 'webs', they cannot occur singly. In order to have a network of beliefs, an animal must have the concept of belief. This is because having a network of beliefs requires the ability to distinguish between someone holding a sentence to be true and the sentence actually being true. But having the concept of belief requires having language, for Davidson believes that this concept only arises in the context of linguistic interpretation. Since no animals have language they do not have the concept of belief. Since they do not have the concept of belief they do not have networks of beliefs. Hence, they do not have beliefs at all (see DAVIDSON, D. §8).

What is striking about the arguments for HE, taken together, is that they turn on supposing a very close connection between language and thought. All of the arguments that we have reviewed suppose that having language is a necessary condition for having thoughts (although Malcolm grants that some kind of thinking may occur in the absence of language and thought). Moreover, some of these philosophers (for example, Malcolm) think that having language is sufficient for having thoughts.

It is against this background that the ape language experiments of the 1960s and 1970s caught the attention of philosophers. If it could be shown that apes could learn language then many philosophers would be convinced that apes are capable of having thoughts. Indeed, some philosophers would be convinced by nothing short of this.

3 The ape language controversy

Since the beginning of the twentieth century there have been at least half a dozen attempts to teach spoken language to an ape. In 1966 Beatrice and R. Allen Gardner began teaching American Sign Language to a chimpanzee named Washoe, and throughout the late 1960s and 1970s studies employing animals of different species using different communication systems were undertaken by David Premack, Duane Rumbaugh, Roger Fouts, Francine Patterson and others. In some cases extravagant claims were made about the linguistic abilities of these apes. These claims were deflated by Herbert Terrace in the late 1970s.

From 1973 to 1977 Terrace studied a chimpanzee named Nim Chimpsky. He concluded (1980) that there is no unequivocal evidence for supposing that apes can master syntactic, semantic or pragmatic aspects of language. Terrace's results were devastating to the credibility and funding base of the ape language projects. The projects of Patterson and Fouts continue, funded primarily by private donations. The Rumbaugh project, now headed by Sue Savage-Rumbaugh, is one of the few that continues to produce significant scientific publications.

Beginning in 1981 Savage-Rumbaugh turned her attention to bonobos (so-called 'pygmy chimpanzees'). Using a specially designed keyboard connected to a speech synthesizer one bonobo, Kanzi, has shown a surprising understanding of spoken English. He has a large vocabulary, is capable of communicating novel information and clearly follows simple syntactic rules. In a comparative study (1994) Savage-Rumbaugh concluded that the eight-year-old Kanzi's linguistic skills were superior to those of a normal human two-year-old.

The ape language studies have been controversial from the beginning and continue to be so today. Terrace and other critics accuse most researchers of inaccurate observation and analysis, overinterpretation and cuing desired behaviour. Terrace has been faulted for failing to obtain results because of a lack of rapport with his subject and an impersonal training regime.

Animal behaviour, like human behaviour, is indeterminate, description-relative and open to interpretation. John Dupré (1991) has argued that the dispute over the ape language experiments primarily involves conflicts about the goals and methods of scientific research. The critics demand that claims about the linguistic abilities of apes be backed by compelling evidence that conforms to the most rigorous canons of scientific methodology. However, in the case of humans, language develops in a highly complex and emotive context and the application of principles of charity is an important part of the language-learning process (see CHARITY, PRINCIPLE OF §4). It may be that there is an intrinsic conflict between teaching apes language in the most effective way possible and doing so in a way that will satisfy the scientific scruples of the sceptics.

It is clear that the ape language experiments have not convinced philosophers that at least some animals have language and therefore thoughts. However, one point is worth considering. Even sceptics may admit that some apes have demonstrated linguistic capacities to some degree or in some respect. But a similar view with respect to having thoughts is difficult to even understand. Having a thought appears to be an all or nothing matter. This may provide some evidence against the view that language and thought are as closely tied as some philosophers have claimed.

4 Animal communication

Even some scientists and philosophers friendly to the idea that animals have thoughts have been sceptical of the ape language experiments. For these experiments have focused on very few individuals from an even smaller number of species. They have been directed towards eliciting a variety of behaviours that these animals do not manifest under natural conditions.

In addition to the ape language experiments there have been other interesting studies of the communication abilities of other captive animals (see Bekoff and Jamieson 1995; Ristau 1991). Louis Herman has claimed that bottle-nosed dolphins are capable of semantic and syntactic processing that 'utilize a rich network of mental representations when responding to language-mediated tasks', although they are less able to produce semantically and syntactically dense utterances. Irene Pepperberg has trained an African grey parrot to respond accurately to questions about the colour, shape, name and category of a variety of objects.

Under natural conditions many animals engage in highly sophisticated communicative activities. Cheney and Seyfarth have shown that vervet monkeys distinguish several different kinds of alarm call and behave appropriately with respect to each. Carolyn Ristau suggests that the broken wing displays in various species of plovers may be intended to lead intruders away from their nests. Deception has been claimed for a variety of animals including chimpanzees and elephants.

5 Thought without language

As we have come to know more about animals, the possibility that they may have thoughts without language has become increasingly plausible to many people. Even Joel Wallman (1992), one of the most thorough-going critics of the ape language experiments, holds that apes are 'highly intelligent', 'reflexive' and capable of 'impressively abstract mentation'. Cognitive ethology and comparative psychology have emerged as the scientific fields that study the cognitive capacities of animals that may underlie some of their behaviour.

The dominant view in cognitive ethology, as well as among some philosophers who have written about cognitive ethology, is that an animal's cognitive states must be inferred from its behaviour. Since an animal's mental states are never observed but only inferred, the claim that an animal has a particular mental state or cognitive capacity can only be more or less probable. Often it is said even by cognitive ethologists that we can never really know that animals have thoughts.

In my view, this way of approaching the question of animal thought is fundamentally flawed. If by hypothesis the existence of animal thoughts can only be known by inference from behaviour, then it will always be an open question whether or not animals have thoughts. But if there are no convincing conceptual arguments for supposing that they do not, then we are justified in approaching the question of animal thoughts in the way that we approach the question of human thoughts. For there is no behaviour that an animal can engage in that will ineluctably drive us to the conclusion that it has thoughts. But if we were to view the claim that humans have thoughts as an inference from human behaviour, a sceptic could consistently deny the conclusion (see OTHER MINDS). As a matter of fact, however, we learn to view other humans as having thoughts in the process of psychological and social development. In many cases it is true to say that we see their thought in action. We can be wrong about the content of a particular thought, and indeed some versions of solipsism and scepticism may be logically possible or even defensible in a philosophy journal or seminar. But we do not confuse this with the practices of everyday life. Similarly, it seems that viewing some animals as sometimes having thoughts is part of our cultural practice. While we can take a sceptical stance and it may be useful to do so for certain methodological purposes, there is little reason to do so when it comes to fixing our beliefs. The idea that we are continuous with animals, unless it can be shown otherwise, appears to be a plausible naturalistic hypothesis.

Some philosophers may still be bothered by the fact that animals do not have full-blown human languages. But many animals may have powerful enough, nonlinguistic, representational systems to make their thoughts a significant possibility. For that matter, philosophers such as Ryle who deny that thinking necessarily involves manipulating representations may well be correct. At this stage in the investigation, the possibility that animals may have thoughts without language does not appear to be blocked by any convincing philosophical argument.

References and further reading

* Bekoff, M. and Jamieson, D. (eds) (1995) *Readings in Animal Cognition*, Cambridge, MA: MIT Press. (This is a collection of articles on animal cognition by leading philosophers, psychologists and biologists, including Cheney and Seyfarth, Herman, Ristau and Savage-Rumbaugh.)
* Chomsky, N. (1966) *Cartesian Linguistics*, New York: Harper & Row. (A defence of the Cartesian foundations of Chomsky's linguistic theory.)
* Davidson, D. (1975) 'Thought and Talk', repr. in *Truth and Interpretation*, Oxford: Oxford University Press, 1984, 155–70. (This is the most influential recent article that denies that animals have thoughts.)
* Dupré, J. (1991) 'Conversations with Apes: Reflections on the Scientific Study of Language', in J. Hyman (ed.) *Investigating Psychology: Sciences of the Mind After Wittgenstein*, London: Routledge, 95–116. (This is an especially interesting philosophical assessment of the ape language studies.)
  Jamieson, D. (1998, forthcoming) 'Science, Knowledge, and Animal Minds', *Proceedings of the Aristotelian Society*. (Discussion of the 'other minds' problem as applied to animals.)
* Leahy, M.P.T. (1991) *Against Liberation*, London: Routledge. (This attack on animal liberation argues that talk about animal thought and language is largely anthropomorphic.)
* Malcolm, N. (1972–3) 'Thoughtless Brutes', repr. in D.M. Rosenthal (ed.) *The Nature of Mind*, New York: Oxford University Press, 1991, 454–61. (A Wittgensteinian defence of the view that animals think but do not have thoughts.)
* Quine, W.V. (1960) *Word and Object*, Cambridge, MA: MIT Press. (Foundational work in behaviourist philosophy of language.)
* Ristau, C. (ed.) (1991) *Cognitive Ethology*, Hillsdale, MI: Lawrence Erlbaum Associates. (A collection of essays including the work of Ristau, Cheney and Seyfarth, and Pepperberg.)
* Savage-Rumbaugh, E.S. and Lewin, R. (1994) *Kanzi: The Ape at the Brink of the Human Mind*, New York: Wiley. (The popular exposition of Savage-Rumbaugh's work.)

Savage-Rumbaugh, E.S. *et al.* (1993) 'Language Comprehension in Ape and Child', *Monographs of the Society for Research in Child Development* 233 (58). (The technical exposition of Savage-Rumbaugh's work. Co-authors are Jeanine Murphy, Rose Sevcik, Karen Brakke, Shelly Williams and Duane Rumbaugh, with commentary by Elizabeth Bates.)
* Sorabji, R. (1993) *Animal Minds and Human Morals*, Ithaca, NY: Cornell University Press. (The best discussion of the ancient debate over animal minds.)
* Terrace, H.S. (1980) *Nim*, London: Methuen. (A critique of the ape language experiments and the report of a failed attempt to teach language to a chimpanzee.)
* Vendler, Z. (1972) *Res Cogitans*, Ithaca, NY: Cornell University Press. (A contemporary defence of a Cartesian theory of mind.)
* Wallman, J. (1992) *Aping Language*, New York: Cambridge University Press. (A systematic, sceptical discussion of the ape language controversy.)
* Wittgenstein, L. (1953) *Philosophical Investigations*, ed. G.E.M. Anscombe and R. Rhees, trans. G.E.M. Anscombe, Oxford: Blackwell. (Profoundly influential discussion of language and mind.)

DALE JAMIESON

ANIMALS AND ETHICS

Does morality require that we respect the lives and interests of nonhuman animals? The traditional doctrine was that animals were made for human use, and so we may dispose of them as we please. It has been argued, however, that this is a mere 'speciesist' prejudice and that animals should be given more or less the same moral consideration as humans. If this is right, we may be morally required to be vegetarians; and it may turn out that laboratory research using animals, and many other such practices, are more problematic than has been realized.

1 The traditional view
2 Challenges to the traditional view
3 The contemporary debate

1 The traditional view

In some Eastern systems of thought, animals are accorded great respect. The Jains of India hold that all life is sacred, drawing no sharp distinction between human and nonhuman life. They are therefore vegetarians, as are Buddhists, whose sacred writings forbid all needless killing. In the West, however, it was traditionally believed that animals were made for human use. This idea, familiar from the Old Testament book of Genesis and elaborated by a long line of Jewish and Christian thinkers, also formed part of Aristotle's worldview. Aristotle taught that 'nature does everything for a purpose', and so, just as plants exist to provide food for animals, animals exist to provide food and other 'aids in life' for humans (see Regan and Singer (eds) 1989).

This was cosmology with a moral point. Aquinas, who emphasized that it was God himself who provided the animals for human use, made the point explicit: 'Therefore,' he said, 'it is not wrong for man to make use of them, by killing or in any other way whatever' (Summa contra gentiles). Are there, then, no limits on how animals may be treated? One might think we have a duty to be kind to them out of simple charity. But Aquinas insisted that this is not so. 'Charity,' he said, 'does not extend to irrational creatures.'

There was, however, one way in which animals could gain a degree of protection. They might be the incidental beneficiaries of obligations owed to humans. If someone has promised to look after your dog, he is obliged to care for it. But the obligation is owed to you, not to the dog. There might even be a general duty not to torment animals, because, as Kant put it, 'He who is cruel to animals becomes hard also in his dealings with men' (1780–81: 240). But once again, the point was to protect the men, not the animals. (This has sometimes been called the 'indirect duty view' – that we can have duties to animals, but only indirect ones.)

This view might seem extreme in its near total disregard for nonhumans. Nevertheless, the idea that animals are essentially resources for human use was accepted by almost every important thinker in the Western tradition – including such figures as St Francis, who is popularly but wrongly believed to have advocated a more charitable stance. For this view to be defensible, however, there must be some difference between humans and other animals that would explain why humans have a privileged moral status. Traditional thought cited two such differences. For Aristotle, the difference was that humans alone are rational. Religious figures added that man alone was made in the image of God. These explanations seemed sufficient until 1859, when Darwin's *On the Origin of Species* (1859) transformed our understanding of man's relation to the rest of nature (see DARWIN, C.).

2 Challenges to the traditional view

Darwin demonstrated that humans are not 'set apart' from other animals, but are related to them by evolutionary descent (see EVOLUTION, THEORY OF). It is no accident that we bear such a startling resemblance to the apes. Our bones and muscles are but modified versions of the ape's bones and muscles – they are similar because we inherited them from the same ancestors. The same is true of our rational faculties. Man is not *the* rational animal, for other animals also possess a degree of rationality. How could it be otherwise, when our brains developed from a common source? Darwin went so far as to declare, 'There is no fundamental difference between man and the higher mammals in their mental faculties' (1859: 35). Such differences as do exist, he said, are matters of degree, not kind.

Today it is widely accepted that Darwin was right, at least in the main outlines of his view, and this poses an obvious ethical dilemma: if humans are similar in so many ways to other animals, and humans merit moral protection, then why should other animals not merit protection too? As Asa Gray, Darwin's friend in America, put it, 'Human beings may be more humane when they realize that, as their dependent associates live a life in which man has a share, so they have rights which man is bound to respect' (1880: 54). Darwin himself regarded cruelty to animals, along with slavery, as one of the two great human moral failings.

Another nineteenth-century development also cast doubt on the traditional exclusion of animals from the range of moral concern. The utilitarians, led by Jeremy Bentham and John Stuart Mill, argued that morality is fundamentally a matter of seeking to promote happiness and prevent suffering (see UTILITARIANISM). But Bentham saw no reason to limit moral concern to human suffering. In fact, he suggested that disregard for animals was a form of discrimination analogous to racism:

> The day may come when the rest of the animal creation may acquire the rights which never could have been withholden from them but by the hand of tyranny. The French have already discovered that the blackness of the skin is no reason why a human being should be abandoned without redress to the caprice of a tormentor. It may one day come to be recognized that the number of the legs, the villosity of the skin, or the termination of the os *sacrum* are reasons equally insufficient for abandoning a sensitive being to the same fate.... The question is not, Can they *reason*? nor, Can they *talk*? but, Can they *suffer*?
>
> (1789: 311; original emphasis)

It must be noted, however, that for most of Western history the moral status of animals did not seem to be much of an issue, and philosophers did not write very extensively about it (Bentham's discussion, for example, is confined to a footnote). The subject began to be widely discussed among philosophers only after the publication of Peter Singer's *Animal Liberation* in 1975.

3 The contemporary debate

One of the striking things about the debate concerning animals is that it is possible to reach radical ethical conclusions by invoking only the most common moral principles. The idea that it is wrong to cause suffering, unless there is a sufficient justification, is one of the most basic moral principles, shared by virtually everyone. Yet the consistent application of this principle seems to lead straight to vegetarianism or at least to the avoidance of factory-farmed meat. The argument is disarmingly simple. In modern factory farms, animals who are raised and slaughtered for food suffer considerable pain. Since we could easily nourish ourselves without eating them, our only reason for eating them seems to be our enjoyment of how they taste. So, unless one thinks our gustatory pleasure is a sufficient justification for causing torment, the obvious conclusion is that we are wrong to produce and consume such products.

Other arguments appeal to less commonplace notions. The word 'speciesism' was coined by Richard Ryder, a British psychologist who ceased experimenting on animals after becoming convinced it was immoral, and popularized by Singer in *Animal Liberation*. Speciesism is said to be analogous to racism. Just as racists unjustifiably give greater weight to the interests of the members of their own race, speciesists unjustifiably give greater weight to the interests of the members of their own species (see DISCRIMINATION §1).

Consider, for example, the very different standards we have for using humans and nonhumans in laboratory research. Why do we think it permissible to perform a painful and destructive experiment on, say, a rhesus monkey, when we would not perform the same experiment on a human? Someone might suggest that, say, humans are more intelligent than monkeys, or that their social relationships are more complex. But consider mentally retarded persons whose cognitive and social capacities are no greater than those of the animal. Would it be permissible to perform the same experiment on them? Many people think that, simply because they are human, it would not. This is speciesism laid bare: there is no difference between the human and the nonhuman in their abilities to think, feel or suffer, and yet the human's welfare is counted for more.

This line of thought suggests that animals may be treated differently from humans when, and only when, there are morally relevant differences between them. It may be permissible to admit humans, but not other animals, to universities, because humans can read and other animals cannot. But in cases where there are no relevant differences, they must be treated alike. This is the sense in which humans and nonhumans can be said to be morally 'equal': the bare fact that one is human never itself counts for anything, just as the bare fact that one has one skin colour or another never itself counts for anything. So we may not treat an animal in any way in which we would not be willing to treat a human with the same intellectual and emotional capacities.

Such arguments have, of course, provoked lively opposition. Many philosophers find it difficult to believe that mere animals could have such powerful claims on us. Morality, they say, is fundamentally a human institution established to protect human rights and human interests (see MORALITY AND ETHICS). Contractarianism, which has emerged in the latter half of the twentieth century as the principal rival to utilitarianism, makes this point most clearly. According to this view, morality rests on agreements of mutual benefit. Morality arises within a community when each person agrees to 'play the social game', respecting other people's rights and interests, provided others will do so as well. This agreement makes social living possible, and everyone benefits from it (see CONTRACTARIANISM IN ETHICS AND POLITICAL PHILOSOPHY). But animals are unable to participate in such agreements, so they do not come within the sphere of moral protection.

In addition to initiating a philosophical debate, Peter Singer's book is perhaps the most conspicuous example of a philosophical work triggering a social movement. The animal rights movement, with its principled opposition to such practices as factory farming, the use of animals in commercial and scientific research, and the fur trade, has become a familiar part of contemporary life. Rarely, if ever, have philosophical thinking and social activism been linked so closely.

See also: AGRICULTURAL ETHICS §3; ENVIRONMENTAL ETHICS; EVOLUTION AND ETHICS; RIGHTS

References and further reading

* Aquinas, T. (*c*.1259–65) *Summa contra gentiles*

(Synopsis [of Christian Doctrine] Directed Against Unbelievers), trans. English Dominican Fathers, Chicago, IL: Benziger Brothers, 1928, III.2, c.112. (Argues that animals are made by God for human use.)

* Bentham, J. (1789) *An Introduction to the Principles of Morals and Legislation*, New York: Hafner, 1948. (Argues on utilitarian grounds that the suffering of animals counts equally with the suffering of human beings.)

* Darwin, C. (1859) *On the Origin of Species*, London: John Murray; repr. Cambridge, MA: Harvard University Press, 1975. (The classic source of the theory of evolution by natural selection.)

Finsen, L. and Finsen, S. (1994) *The Animal Rights Movement*, New York: Twayne Publishers. (An overall view of the movement, covering its history and the philosophical and religious arguments on which it is based.)

Frey, R.G. (1983) *Rights, Killing, and Suffering: Moral Vegetarianism and Applied Ethics*, Oxford: Blackwell. (Argues that the various pro-animal arguments do not succeed.)

* Gray, A. (1880) *Natural Science and Religion: Two Lectures Delivered to the Theological School of Yale College*, New York: Charles Scribner's Sons. (Argues that we must acknowledge that animals have rights because we share common traits with them.)

* Kant, I. (1780–81) *Lectures on Ethics*, trans. L. Infield, New York: Harper & Row, 1963. (Holds that humans have no duties to animals because animals are not self-conscious.)

Regan, T. (1983) *The Case for Animal Rights*, Berkeley, CA: University of California Press. (Defends the view that nonhuman animals have moral rights comparable to the rights of humans. One of the most important philosophical defences of animals.)

* Regan, T. and Singer, P. (eds) (1989) *Animal Rights and Human Obligations*, Englewood Cliffs, NJ: Prentice Hall, 2nd edn. (A collection of readings on all sides of the issue. Includes a selection from Aristotle, which illustrates his view that because humans have a privileged moral status, on the grounds that they alone are rational, animals exist to provide food and other 'aids in life' for humans.)

* Singer, P. (1975) *Animal Liberation*, New York: New York Review Books; 2nd edn, 1990. (A clear and well-written book, arguing that the same moral principles that govern how people should be treated also apply to animals.)

JAMES RACHELS

ANNICERIS *see* CYRENAICS

ANOMALOUS MONISM

Anomalous monism, proposed by Donald Davidson in 1970, implies that all events are of one fundamental kind, namely physical. But it does not deny that there are mental events; rather, it implies that every mental event is some physical event or other. The idea is that someone's thinking at a certain time that the earth is round, for example, might be a certain pattern of neural firing in their brain at that time, an event which is both a thinking that the earth is round (a type of mental event) and a pattern of neural firing (a type of physical event). There is just one event, that can be characterized both in mental terms and in physical terms. If mental events are physical events, they can, like all physical events, be explained and predicted (at least in principle) on the basis of laws of nature cited in physical science. However, according to anomalous monism, events cannot be so explained or predicted as described in mental terms (such as 'thinking', 'desiring', 'itching' and so on), but only as described in physical terms. The distinctive feature of anomalous monism as a brand of physical monism is that it implies that mental events as such (that is, as described in mental terms) are anomalous – they cannot be explained or predicted on the basis of strict scientific laws.

1 Psychophysical identity and strict laws
2 Psychological anomalism
3 Psychophysical anomalism
4 Psychophysical anomalism and supervenience

1 Psychophysical identity and strict laws

Davidson proposed the following argument for a psychophysical identity thesis: let m be any arbitrary mental event that causally interacts with some physical event p. Events related as cause and effect fall under strict laws. But if m and p fall under a strict law, that strict law is a physical law as all strict laws are physical laws. If an event falls under a strict physical law, then it is a physical event. Hence, m is a physical event. As Davidson points out, if one makes the plausible assumption that every mental event causally interacts with some physical event, one can arrive by the same reasoning at the more general conclusion that every mental event is a physical event.

Although questions can be raised about various steps in this argument, its conclusion is fairly widely accepted (see MIND, IDENTITY THEORY OF). The focus of attention has been on his claim that although mental events are physical events, there are no strict psychological laws (psychological anomalism) and there are no strict psychophysical laws (psychophysical anomalism) – the doctrines that make his version of monism count as a version of *anomalous* monism. Before discussing the anomalism theses, let us turn to the notion of a strict law itself.

According to Davidson, laws are true general statements that support counterfactuals and other subjunctive conditionals (see COUNTERFACTUALS), and which are confirmable by their positive instances. *Strict* laws are sometimes claimed to be laws that contain no escape clauses such as 'other things being equal', or 'typically', or 'for the most part', or the like. However, Davidson appears to have a stricter notion of law in mind than that. For the statement 'All sentient beings are mortal' contains no explicit escape clauses and expresses as exceptionless a law as one can hope to find, yet it appears that Davidson would not count it. His notion of a strict law is one that is as explicit, precise, and exceptionless as nature permits, or that can be refined into such a law by the addition of further explicit provisos and conditions stated in the same theoretical vocabulary as the original law statement. In contrast, nonstrict laws can be made exceptionless only by explicitly citing probabilities in the law itself, or, at the cost of explicitness and precision, by adding *ceteris paribus* clauses or hedges, or else by employing predicates (like 'sentient' and 'mortal') whose analyses require appeal to *ceteris paribus* clauses or hedges that cannot be fully spelled out in the same theoretical vocabulary as the original law statement. This difference between strict and nonstrict laws, according to Davidson, is due to the fact that strict laws, unlike nonstrict ones, are couched in the vocabulary of a closed, comprehensive theory. A theory *T* is closed if and only if events within the domain of *T* causally interact only with other events within the domain of *T*. A theory *T* is comprehensive if and only if every event within its domain satisfies a unique *T*-description under which it is subsumed by one of *T*'s laws. Davidson allows that while strict laws are, or can be refined into, laws as exceptionless as nature permits, a strict law, even fully refined, may prove to be probabilistic; but if it does, there will be no law covering exactly the same causal transactions it covers that is more explicit, precise, and has fewer exceptions. Nonstrict laws, Davidson says, can support causal claims concerning individual events. But they do so, he maintains, by providing evidence that there is a strict law at work that is free of either explicit or implicit escape clauses, and that precisely states all the causal factors at work in the particular causal transactions in question.

Davidson's notion of a strict law remains a subject of interpretation. The following is textually defensible. A strict law is a law that is couched solely in a basic vocabulary of a closed, comprehensive theory, or in terms that can be defined by terms logically constructible from such a basic vocabulary, or be reduced by bridge laws to terms so constructible; a nonstrict law is a law not couched in such terms, or solely in such terms. A set of terms is a basic vocabulary of a closed comprehensive theory if and only if it is a set of terms sufficient for the formulation of a closed comprehensive theory, and no proper subset of it is.

2 Psychological anomalism

Davidson argues as follows for psychological anomalism. Psychology is not a closed theory; and, further, psychological terms cannot be incorporated by reductive bridge law or definition into the vocabulary of a closed, comprehensive theory. Therefore, there are no strict psychological laws.

Psychology is indeed not closed; there is overwhelming empirical reason to believe that there are nonmental events that causally interact with mental events. To be sure, biology is not a closed theory either; indeed, none of the special sciences is closed. Davidson tells us that most of science employs only nonstrict laws. He holds, however, that strict laws can be found in physics, either in current physics, or, if it falls short of what it promises to be (that is, closed and comprehensive), then in some (as yet unstated, perhaps never to be stated) improved version of current physics. All strict laws are either laws of physics or laws that can be refined to laws of physics by appeal to reductive laws and/or definitions, and (if necessary) adding physical provisos.

Some philosophers maintain, on the following grounds, that special science laws, including even chemistry, are typically not strict since they cannot be so refined: the event and state types cited in special science laws are, typically, widely and multiply realized by the event and state types cited in physics, and hence the former cannot be reduced to the latter. Davidson has, however, marshalled reasons for holding that certain mental predicates, in particular, cannot possibly be reduced to physical predicates, reasons which make no appeal to the notion of realization. The predicates in question are ones that contain essential occurrences of propositional attitude verbs such as 'believes', 'desires' and the like (see PROPOSITIONAL ATTITUDES). Davidson maintains that propositional attitude concepts are such that predicates that express them could not possibly be reduced to physical predicates. His reasons are discussed in the following section. (Hereafter, 'mental event' will be used in a restricted sense to mean acquiring or losing a propositional attitude.)

3 Psychophysical anomalism

One way that psychophysical anomalism could fail is if there is a basic vocabulary for a closed, comprehensive theory that includes both mental and physical terms. A Cartesian interactionist (see DUALISM) might argue that any basic vocabulary for a closed, comprehensive theory true of our world would have to contain both mental and physical terms; for the mental properties expressed by at least some mental terms are fundamental force-generating properties. However, this position is empirically implausible: mechanics seems to have no need of the hypothesis that there are mental events.

There is another way that psychophysical anomalism could fail, namely if mental terms can be defined by terms constructible from the basic vocabulary of a closed, comprehensive theory or be reducible to such terms by reductive bridge laws. Davidson offers reasons that appeal to the nature of mental concepts for holding that no mental predicate (more specifically, no propositional attitude predicate) could be reduced to any physical predicate, no matter how complex, in either of these two ways. If definitional psychophysical reduction were possible, then a physical predicate could express an unhedged sufficient condition of application for a mental predicate – one unqualified by any escape clauses. That, Davidson argues, is impossible: no physical predicate could express such an unhedged sufficient condition of application. Hence, definitional reduction is impossible. The same consideration arguably shows that reduction via bridge laws is impossible. For if a psychophysical bridge law were a reductive law, rather than an emergent law, the law would have to be a derivative law, rather than a fundamental law. The law would have to be implied by laws of the reducing theory, physical theory, together with physical conditions, and only analytical principles, and perhaps other necessary truths. Otherwise, the truths of physical theory itself would not imply the psychophysical truths in question. It is arguable that if the truths of physical theory itself imply such psychophysical truths, then unhedged analytical generalizations with physical (and logical) predicates in their antecedents and mental predicates in their consequents would be possible. But such generalizations are impossible if mental predicates could not have unhedged physical conditions of application. Davidson does not consider the possibility, however, that there are metaphysically necessary truths that are not analytical truths, and that enable psychophysical reduction; of that consideration, more in §4.

There are, in Davidson's work, several lines of argument for the claim that mental predicates cannot have unhedged physical sufficient conditions of application; and other proponents of psychophysical anomalism have contributed to the development of some of these lines of argument. Much of the interest in anomalous monism has centred on whether a sound argument for the claim can be found.

Every line of argument appeals to what Davidson calls 'the holism of the mental' – (roughly) the view that propositional attitude types, identified by their intentional mode (for example belief) and their content (for example that the earth is round), are individuated holistically by their place in a network of other propositional attitude types. The place of a propositional attitude state type in such a network is partly determined by logical and semantical relationships between its content and the contents of a vast range of other state types in the network. For networks of propositional attitude types must, Davidson argues, exhibit a large degree of rational coherence. Irrationality is possible, obviously, but only against a background of largely rational coherence. To make coherent propositional attitude attributions, our attributions must conform to standards of rational coherence, standards concerning what it would make sense to believe given certain other beliefs, what it would make sense to value given certain beliefs and desires, and what courses of action would make best sense given a certain pattern of beliefs, desires, values, and so on.

One line of argument is that if unhedged physical conditions of application were possible, propositional attitude attributions could be made solely on the basis of such conditions, and thus without reliance on rational assessment. But that, it is claimed, would amount to changing the subject, since principles of rational assessment are constitutive of the very meaning of such mental predicates. This line of argument is, however, inconclusive. If there are constitutive principles of rational assessment that implicitly define mental predicates, then, indeed, unhedged sufficient physical conditions of application cannot permit attributions that contravene the principles without changing the subject. Nevertheless, so long as those principles would not be contravened by attributions made solely on the basis of unhedged physical conditions, there would be no change of subject. It thus remains to be seen why such attributions would have to contravene principles of rational coherence.

It has also been argued, however, that there is no complete set of impersonal, objective principles of rational coherence. This idea has been put by saying that there is no complete set of codifiable principles of rationality that can supply a common, objective standard in attributing mental states to others. We must rely on our own standards of assessment in understanding others; there is no single objective standard to which we can appeal. The claim that there are no codifiable objective standards of rationality is contentious. Decision theory and confirmation theory, for instance, attempt to formulate such standards (see CONFIRMATION THEORY; DECISION AND GAME THEORY). Perhaps they cannot succeed, but if they cannot, it remains to be seen why they cannot. Suppose, however, that there is indeed no single set of codifiable objective standards of rationality, that there are at best rules of thumb, and that we must invariably rely to some extent on our subjective sense of what makes rational sense – what it makes sense to believe given other beliefs, and so on – in making mental attributions. The question arises, then: would this imply that unhedged physical conditions of application for propositional attitudes would invariably contravene our assessments of rational coherence?

If there is a set of codifiable principles of rational assessment for each attributor at a time, then such contravention might be avoidable. When two individuals' propositional attitude attributions are governed by somewhat different sets of principles, there would arguably be some difference in the meanings of the propositional attitude predicates they employ. Similarly, the meanings of propositional attitude predicates a given individual employs would arguably change somewhat over time as somewhat different sets govern the individual's attributions at different times. Propositional attitude predicates could be, in principle, rendered unambiguous by relativizing them to such sets of principles. Unhedged physical sufficient conditions of attribution for mental predicates understood as governed by a particular set of principles of rationality would, then, have to be such that they do not contravene the principles. However, if they did not, there would be no change of subject.

It might be responded that there will be no set of codifiable principles of rational assessment even for an attributor at a time. But a case for that remains to be made. In any event, for present purposes, suffice it to note that the reasoning in favour of psychophysical anomalism remains a topic of controversy.

4 Psychophysical anomalism and supervenience

While Davidson denies that mental characteristics reduce to physical characteristics, he maintains that they are supervenient on physical characteristics in this sense: there cannot be two events alike in every physical respect but differing in some mental respect.

Various kinds of supervenience relations have been distinguished (see SUPERVENIENCE; SUPERVENIENCE OF THE MENTAL). The kind Davidson appeals to appears to be a particularly weak kind. While he eschews talk of possible worlds, it can, nevertheless, be stated by quantifying over them: for any possible world, w, if any event x in w differs in any mental respect from event y in w, then x differs in some physical respect from y. This weak psychophysical supervenience thesis implies neither strict nor non-strict psychophysical laws, and is thus compatible with psychophysical anomalism.

Many philosophers hold, however, that mental characteristics must supervene on physical characteristics in the following stronger sense, if mental characteristics indeed make a difference to causal relations: for any possible worlds w and w^*, and any event x in w and any event y in w^*, if x and y differ in some mental respect, then they differ in some physical respect. This strong supervenience thesis, in conjunction with the assumption that physical conditions are closed under complementation (negation will be part of the basic vocabulary of physical theory), implies that for any propositional attitude type, there is some unhedged, metaphysically sufficient physical condition for its occurrence. Strong psychophysical supervenience is thus incompatible with the thesis that mental predicates cannot have such physical conditions of application.

Strong psychophysical supervenience is, however, arguably compatible with psychophysical anomalism itself. For, laws, according to Davidson, must be confirmable by their positive instances, and that there are such metaphysically sufficient unhedged, physical conditions does not imply that there are true, unhedged psychophysical generalizations that are confirmable by their positive instances. Moreover, psychophysical anomalism remains a deeply interesting doctrine, even if it is compatible with the possibility of unhedged metaphysically sufficient physical conditions of application for propositional attitude predicates. For it is deeply interesting whether our propositional attitude concepts are such that generalizations purporting to state such conditions of application could be confirmable by their positive instances.

See also: LAWS, NATURAL ; REDUCTIONISM IN THE PHILOSOPHY OF MIND; REDUCTION, PROBLEMS OF

References and further reading

Child, W. (1993) 'Anomalism, Uncodifiability, and Psychophysical Relations', *Philosophical Review* 102: 215–45. (Argues that Davidson's reasoning for anomalism can be reconstructed employing the idea that there is no complete set of codifiable principles of rationality.)

* Davidson, D. (1970) 'Mental Events', in *Actions and Events*, Oxford: Clarendon Press, 1980. (The seminal paper on anomalous monism.)

—— (1973) 'The Material Mind', in *Actions and Events*, Oxford: Clarendon Press, 1980. (Includes a detailed discussion of anomalous monism.)

—— (1974) 'Psychology as Philosophy', in *Actions and Events*, Oxford: Clarendon Press, 1980. (Contains an elaboration and defence of anomalism monism along with some replies to objections to the doctrine.)

—— (1980) *Actions and Events*, Oxford: Clarendon Press. (Collection of some of Davidson's papers on actions, events, causation, and anomalous monism.)

—— (1993) 'Thinking Causes', in J. Heil and A. Mele (eds) *Mental Causation*, Oxford: Clarendon Press. (Davidson argues that anomalous monism and the principle of the nomological character of causality do not commit him to the view that mental types and properties make no difference to causal relations.)

—— (1995) 'Donald Davidson', in S. Guttenplan (ed.) *A Companion to the Philosophy of Mind*, Oxford: Blackwell. (Davidson's latest statement on anomalous monism.)

Heil, J. and Mele, A. (eds) (1993) *Mental Causation*, Oxford: Clarendon Press. (Contains essays discussing whether anomalous monism implies epiphenomenalism.)

Honderich, T. (1981) 'Psychophysical Lawlike Connections and their Problem', *Inquiry* 24: 277–303. (An attempt to show that anomalous monism is committed to property epiphenomenalism.)

Kim, J. (1985) 'Psychophysical Laws', in E. LePore and B.P. McLaughlin (eds) *Actions and Events: Perspectives on the Philosophy of Donald Davidson*, Oxford: Blackwell. (Attempts to spell out Davidson's reasons for denying the existence of psychological laws and psychophysical laws.)

LePore, E. and McLaughlin, B.P. (1985) *Actions and Events: Perspectives on the Philosophy of Donald Davidson*, Oxford: Blackwell. (Contains essays on anomalous monism.)

McLaughlin, B.P. (1985) 'Anomalous Monism and the Irreducibility of the Mental', in E. LePore and B.P. McLaughlin (eds) *Actions and Events: Perspectives on the Philosophy of Donald Davidson*, Oxford: Blackwell. (Contains a discussion of Davidson's central arguments for psychophysical identity, and for psychological and psychophysical anomalism.)

Stanton, W.L. (1983) 'Supervenience and Psychological Law in Anomalous Monism', *Pacific Philosophical Quarterly* 64: 72–9. (Contains an examination of Davidson's argument for the identity thesis, a discussion of whether psychophysical supervenience is consistent with the anomalism of the mental, and offers the explication of a strict law presented in §1.)

BRIAN P. McLAUGHLIN

ANSCOMBE, GERTRUDE ELIZABETH MARGARET (1919–)

Elizabeth Anscombe has contributed to all principal areas of philosophy, most influentially to ethics and the philosophy of mind. She is the founder of contemporary action theory, and an important source of the revival of interest in virtue ethics. The chief influences on her thought are the work of her teacher, Ludwig Wittgenstein, much of which she has translated and of which she is an important interpreter, and the classical and medieval traditions, as found in Aristotle and Aquinas. She has also made a number of contributions to the defence of Roman Catholic religious belief.

1 *Intention*
2 *Other works*

1 *Intention*

Anscombe's most important work, *Intention* (1957a), is the founding document of contemporary philosophy of action. Much of her later thought may be said to move out from this essay in three main directions: towards ethics; general problems of explanation or 'causality'; and associated problems in the philosophy of mind.

The concept of intention is employed, she says, in three main connections: we speak of 'events in a man's history' as *intentional actions*, of the *intention with which* an action is performed, and of the *expression of intention*, or of the corresponding 'pure' intention for the future, which may exist though no action has yet been done with that intention. Taking the notion of intentional action as prior, she argues that an action is intentional when it is subject to a certain form of explanation: that is, when, as she puts it, 'a certain sense of the question "Why?" has application' to it. Her task is then to isolate this particular form of explanation. It is without application, she argues, if the agent is unaware of doing the thing; or if the agent knows that he or she is, but only by having noticed it – that is, 'by observation', or where, though the agent knows that the thing is going on without observation, he or she can give no account of it, or none without observation, conjecture and so forth. If a piece of behaviour passes these tests, it is an intentional action, unless perhaps it is a case of 'mental causality', like a gasp that is given at the hissing of a snake. These latter cases she excludes by a series of more complex tests (see ACTION §1; INTENTION §5).

Like Oedipus, I may *strike a person* intentionally, and *strike my father* unintentionally, though these are not two distinct events or two distinct actions of mine. Actions are thus intentional only 'under a description'. What is given in answer to the question 'Why?' is in fact often a further description of the same action. A series of such questions will thus reveal an order among many of the descriptions true of an action: 'Why are you moving your arm up and down?' –'Because I'm pumping water' – 'But why pump water?' – 'Because I'm replenishing the house water supply'. This chain of questions 'Why?' may often be pressed into the future, and thus beyond any description of what is now happening; the responses will then merely express the *intention with which* the action mentioned earlier is performed. In general, if the question 'Why?' has application to a first-person future-tense description of action, then the description is an *expression of intention* and not a mere prediction.

The idea that 'practical knowledge' (the knowledge one has of one's intentional action) does not spring from observation leads to some of the more striking claims of the work. She famously compares the relation that practical thought bears to action with the relation a shopping list bears to the contents of the shopper's basket. The corresponding model of non-practical or 'speculative' thought is given by the relationship between the same basket and the list of its contents constructed by the detective who follows its owner. The difference is in 'direction of fit', as it is now called: the detective amends a mismatch between list and basket by altering his list, the shopper by altering the contents of the basket. These matters are elucidated by an extended discussion of Aristotle's notion of a 'practical syllogism'. It is argued, among other things, that the order of descriptions of an action which we elicit with the question 'Why?' is the reverse of the order of descriptions articulated by the agent in reasoning from end to means (see PRACTICAL REASON AND ETHICS §3).

2 Other works

Much of Anscombe's ethical work also concerns the notion of intention and the relationship of thought to action. In 'Modern Moral Philosophy' (1958) she argues that contemporary thought on these matters is so wide of the mark that there is no point in practising moral philosophy at all. A naïve philosophy of mind and action has led, for example, to what she calls 'consequentialism' – the view that whether a person intends something or not is irrelevant to the question whether he is responsible for it (see CONSEQUENTIALISM §1). (In 'Mr. Truman's Degree' (1957b) she claims that the familiar justifications for the bombing of Hiroshima and Nagasaki, which she argues was murderous, presuppose just such thinking.) She also maintains that the programme of attempting to elucidate the 'moral sense of "ought"' must be jettisoned: it presupposes a theory of ethics as founded in divine law. Only an Aristotelian ethical theory, she thinks, can be given an intelligible secular development. But this would require clarification of such concepts as 'virtue', 'human nature' and 'human flourishing', and thus renewed inquiry into philosophy of mind and action (see VIRTUE ETHICS §2).

In 'Causality and Determination' (1971), Anscombe attacks the notion that 'if an effect occurs in one case and a similar effect does not occur in an apparently similar case, there must be a relevant further difference' (1971: 133). Having attacked this view, she attempts to show how freedom of the will, which she argues is incompatible with it, is to be understood in the light of its rejection. An event not explicable in terms of prior determining physical causes may yet, she argues, be subject to other forms of explanation.

Much of Anscombe's work on the general philosophy of mind attempts to extend and clarify the teachings of WITTGENSTEIN (§13). Her boldest claims are found in 'The First Person' (1974). There she argues that the word 'I' is not a referring term, that self-consciousness is not awareness of an object (a 'person' or 'self'), and that if either of these things were the case then the object of reference and awareness would have the character of a Cartesian ego.

See also: CAUSATION §6; FREE WILL §2; REASONS AND CAUSES §2

List of works

Anscombe, G.E.M. (1981) *Collected Philosophical Papers*, Minneapolis, MN: University of Minnesota

Press, 3 vols. (The definitive edition of Anscombe's works.)
—— (1957a) *Intention*, Oxford: Blackwell; 2nd edn, 1963. (On the concepts of action, intention and a reason for action.)
—— (1957b) 'Mr. Truman's Degree', privately published pamphlet; repr. in Anscombe (1981), vol. 3, 62–71. (A popular work attacking President Truman's use of the atomic bomb and defending an 'absolutist' account of the prohibition of murder.)
—— (1958) 'Modern Moral Philosophy', *Philosophy* 33; repr. in Anscombe (1981), vol. 3, 26–42. (Counselling a revival of ancient forms of ethical theory especially that of Aristotle; defines and attacks 'consequentialism'.)
—— (1959) *An Introduction to Wittgenstein's 'Tractatus'*, Philadelphia, PA: University of Pennsylvania Press; 2nd edn, 1971. (An introduction to some aspects of the teachings of Frege, Russell and the early Wittgenstein.)
Anscombe, G.E.M. and Geach, P. (1961) *Three Philosophers*, Ithaca, NY: Cornell University Press. (The first essay, an interpretation of Aristotle's doctrine of substance, is by Anscombe.)
Anscombe, G.E.M. (1963) 'The Two Kinds of Error in Action', *Journal of Philosophy* 60, 393–401; repr. in Anscombe (1981), vol. 3, 3–9. (On the role of knowledge and intention in morals and in criminal law.)
—— (1965a) 'The Intentionality of Sensation', in R.J. Butler (ed.) *Analytical Philosophy*, second series, New York: Barnes & Noble, 143–58; repr. in Anscombe (1981), vol. 2, 3–20. (On the concept of 'an object of perception'.)
—— (1965b) 'Thought and Action in Aristotle', in R. Bambrough (ed.) *New Essays on Plato and Aristotle*, London: Routledge & Kegan Paul, 158–80; repr. in Anscombe (1981), vol. 1, 66–80. (An interpretation and critique of Aristotle's conception of deliberation.)
—— (1971) 'Causality and Determination', inaugural lecture, Cambridge University; repr. in Anscombe (1981), vol. 2, 133–47. (Defends a much looser account of the notion of a cause than is prevalent in contemporary philosophy; the essay ends with a very difficult discussion of freedom of the will.)
—— (1974) 'The First Person', in S. Guttenplan (ed.) *Mind and Language*, Oxford: Oxford University Press, 45–65; repr. in Anscombe (1981), vol. 2, 21–36. (On the first person and self-conscious thought.)
—— (1978) 'Rules, Rights and Promises', *Midwest Studies in Philosophy* 3, 318–23; repr. in Anscombe (1981), vol. 3, 97–106. (On the genesis of the concepts of a rule and of a right.)
—— (1979) 'Under a Description', *Nous* 13, 219–33; repr. in Anscombe (1981), vol. 2, 208–19. (A response to critics of *Intention*, which clarifies some of its teachings.)
—— (1982a) 'Action, Intention and Double Effect', *Proceedings of the American Catholic Philosophical Association* 56, 12–25. (A defence, from a modern point of view, of some aspects of the moral philosophy of Thomas Aquinas.)
—— (1982b) 'Murder and the Morality of Euthanasia', in *Euthanasia: A Clinical Perspective*, London: Linacre Centre, 23–36; repr. in L. Gormally (ed.) *Euthanasia, Clinical Practice and the Law*, Indianapolis, IN: Hackett, 1994, 37–50. (A semi-popular attempt at a definition of murder as a moral category.)
—— (1989) 'Von Wright on Practical Reason', in L. Hahn and P. Schilpp (eds) *The Philosophy of Georg Heinrik von Wright*, La Salle, IL: Open Court, 376–404; repr, in R. Hursthouse, G. Lawrence and W. Quinn (eds) *Virtues and Reasons*, Oxford: Oxford University Press, 1995, 1–34. (An important revision of the doctrine of *Intention* concerning practical reason.)

References and further reading

Bennett, J. (1966) 'Whatever the Consequences', *Analysis* 26, 83–102. (A spirited attack on the 'absolutism' of Anscombe (1957) and (1958).)
Davidson, D. (1963) 'Actions, Reasons and Causes', *Journal of Philosophy* 60, 685–700; repr. in Davidson, 1980, 83–102. (An influential attack on the notion, apparently present in Anscombe's *Intention*, that the reason why an action was performed is in no sense a cause of it.)
—— (1978) 'Intending', in Y. Yovel (ed.) *Philosophy of History and Action*, Dordrecht: Reidel, 41–60; repr. in Davidson, 1980, 83–102. (Attacking Anscombe's methodological claim in *Intention* that the notion of *intentional action* should be treated in advance of that of *intention*.)
—— (1980) *Essays on Actions and Events*, Oxford: Oxford University Press. (The first six essays in this volume present the most influential alternative to Anscombe's philosophy of action; despite the doctrinal divergence, they have contributed greatly to the currency of her central concepts and distinctions.)
Diamond, C. and Teichmann, J. (1979) *Intention and Intentionality*, Ithaca, NY: Cornell University Press. (A volume honouring Anscombe and containing many important criticisms of her work.)
Foot, P. (1967) 'Abortion and the Doctrine of Double Effect', *Oxford Review* 5, 5–15; repr. in P. Foot,

Virtues and Vices, Berkeley, CA: University of California Press, 1978, 5–15. (An attack, friendlier than that of Bennett (1966), on Anscombe's 'absolutism'; Foot's method of relating abstract principles to her picturesque examples was of great influence in later moral philosophy.)

MICHAEL THOMPSON

ANSELM OF CANTERBURY (1033–1109)

Anselm of Canterbury, also known as Anselm of Aosta and Anselm of Bec or Saint Anselm, was first a student, then a monk, later prior and finally abbot of the monastery of Bec in Normandy, before being elected Archbishop of Canterbury in 1093. He remains one of the best-known and most readily engaging philosophers and theologians of medieval Europe. His literary corpus consists of eleven treatises or dialogues, the most important of which are the philosophical works Monologion and Proslogion and the magnificent theological work Cur deus homo (*Why God Became a Man*). He also left three meditations, nineteen prayers, 374 extant letters including Epistolae de Sacramentis (*Letters on the Sacraments*) and a collection of philosophical fragments, together with a compilation of his sayings (Dicta Anselmi) by Alexander, a monk of Canterbury, and a compilation of his reflections on virtue, De morum qualitate per exemplorum coaptationem (*On Virtues and Vices as Illustrated by a Collage of Examples*), possibly also by a monk at Canterbury.

At Bec Anselm wrote his first philosophical treatise, the Monologion, *a title signifying a soliloquy. This work was followed by the* Proslogion, *the title meaning an address (of the soul to God). At Bec he also completed the philosophical dialogues* De grammatico (*On (an) Expert in Grammar*), De veritate (*On Truth*), De libertate arbitrii (*Freedom of Choice*) and De casu diaboli (*The Fall of the Devil*). Near the end of his time at Bec, he turned his attention to themes more theological, drafting a first version of De incarnatione Verbi (*The Incarnation of the Word*) before September 1092 and completing the final revision around the beginning of 1094. During his time in office at Canterbury, which included two long exiles from England (1097–1100 and 1103–6), he wrote the Cur deus homo, *followed by the concisely reasoned treatises* De conceptu virginali et originali peccati (*The Virgin Conception and Original Sin*), De processione Spiritus Sancti (*The Procession of the Holy Spirit*) *and* De concordia praescientiae et praedestinationis et gratiae dei cum libero arbitrio (*The Harmony of the Foreknowledge, the Predestination and the Grace of God with Free Choice*).

Though his principal writings at Bec were more philosophical while his foremost writings as archbishop were more theological, still we must remember that Anselm himself made no express distinction between philosophy and theology, that at Bec he also wrote two meditations and sixteen prayers, and that his Cur deus homo *and* De concordia, *in dealing with the weighty theological doctrines of atonement, predestination and grace, incorporate philosophical concepts such as* necessitas praecedens (*preceding necessity*) *and* necessitas sequens (*subsequent necessity*).

Anselm's most famous philosophical work is certainly the Proslogion, *while his most influential theological work is undoubtedly the* Cur deus homo. *The style of the* Proslogion *imitates that of Augustine in the* Confessiones, *where the soul invokes God as it prayerfully reflects and meditates. By contrast, the* Cur deus homo *is cast in dialogue form because, as Anselm states in I.1, 'issues which are examined by the method of question and answer are clearer, and so more acceptable, to many minds – especially to minds that are slower.' About his aims in the* Proslogion *there is no scholarly consensus. The traditional view holds that he is undertaking the twofold task of demonstrating the existence of God and demonstrating certain truths regarding God's attributes. In carrying out this task, he has recourse to a single consideration (*unum argumentum*), namely, that God is* aliquid quo nihil maius cogitari potest (*something than which nothing greater can be thought*). *This single consideration gives rise to a single argument form; the logical structure of the reasoning which purports to establish that* quo nihil maius *is actually existent is also the structure of the arguments which conclude that* quo nihil maius *is so existent that it cannot be thought not to exist, is alone existent* per se, *is omnipotent, merciful yet impassable, is supremely just and good, is greater than can be thought, and so on. According to this interpretation, the* Proslogion *seeks to establish most of the same conclusions that were reached in the earlier* Monologion, *but to establish them more directly, simply and tersely.*

The central thrust of the Cur deus homo *may be discerned from the title: namely, to explain why it was necessary for God, in the person of the Son, to become a man (that is, to become incarnate as a human being (*homo*)). Anselm uses the Latin word* homo *generically and not in the sense of male (*vir*). This fact is seen clearly in* Cur deus homo II, 8: 'nil convenientius, quam ut de femina sine viro assumat [deus] illum hominem quem quaerimus' (*nothing is more fitting than that God assume from a woman without a male that man [human being] about whom we are inquiring*). *Though the sense of* homo *varies in accordance* *with whether Anselm is speaking about a human being or about a human nature, there is no doubt about the meaning of the title: the Son of God assumed a human nature, thereby becoming a man; he did not assume another man (in other words, assume a human person together with a human nature) as the heretical Nestorians had taught, nor did he become man (in other words, become universal man, by assuming unindividuated human nature as such).*

Anselm's detailed theory of satisfaction for sin was in large measure a putative theoretical justification of the institutionalized practices of the confessional and the penitential system as found in the medieval Christian church, which understood every sin to constitute a punishable demerit and to require both the imploring of God's forgiveness and the making of amends for having dishonoured him. Throughout the intricate and sustained reasoning of the Cur deus homo, *Anselm seeks to show one central truth: 'because only God can make this satisfaction and only a man ought to make it, it is necessary that a God-man make it' (*Cur deus homo *II, 6).*

As in the Cur deus homo, *so also in his other treatises Anselm proceeds insofar as he deems possible,* sola ratione *(by recourse to rational considerations alone). Accordingly, he is rightly called the 'Father of Scholasticism'. He understands* ratio *in a broad sense, broad enough to encompass appeals to experience as well as to conceptual intelligibility. Although the main intellectual influence upon him was Augustine, he is less platonistic than the latter, and the influence of Aristotle's* De interpretatione *and* Categories *(from Boethius' Latin translations) is clearly discernible in his philosophical works.*

1   Biography
2   Philosophical method
3–6 Philosophical works
7–9 Theological works
10 Conclusion

1   Biography

Major details of Anselm's life come down to us through his contemporary secretary and biographer, Eadmer, an English monk at Canterbury and author of the *Vita Anselmi* (Life of Anselm) and *Historia Novorum in Anglia* (History of Recent Events in England). Eadmer knew little of, and reported meagrely on, Anselm's childhood and youth. It is known that Anselm was born of noble lineage in the Burgundian town of Aosta, near the border with the Kingdom of Lombardy (now in Italy). In 1056, however, several years after his mother's death and as a result of his father's hostility, Anselm left home. Some three years later, following intermittent studies, he arrived at the Benedictine Abbey of Bec in Normandy, having journeyed there to place himself under the tutelage of the Abbey's prior and schoolmaster, Lanfranc of Pavia. He was then twenty-six years old.

After his father's death (presumably in 1060), Anselm chose to enter the monastic order at Bec rather than return to the family estate. In 1063 he was elected prior of Bec, succeeding Lanfranc, who had been called to the abbey of St.-Etienne in Caen; in 1078 he was chosen abbot, in spite of his disinclination to assume the office. He showed even more reluctance and protestation when selected as archbishop of Canterbury in 1093, again in succession to Lanfranc. Eadmer tells of Anselm's vigorous and poignantly futile efforts to resist election, first to the abbacy at Bec and later to the archepiscopacy at Canterbury. When the monks of Bec besought Anselm to dispense with the customary protests and agree to become abbot, he threw himself prostrate on the floor, begging them not to weigh him down with so burdensome an office. A similar scene took place in England: when King William II, fearing that his sudden sickness was mortal, named Anselm archbishop and when the bishops carried him forcibly to William's bedside to receive from him the episcopal staff, Anselm kept his fist clenched, thus refusing the staff. Nonetheless, the staff was pressed against his hand by the bishops, the *Te deum* was chanted and he was proclaimed archbishop-elect on 6 March 1093. His consecration followed on 4 December.

Anselm's subsequent quarrels with William II (son of William the Conqueror) and with his brother and successor Henry I are well known. He contested William's exercise of jurisdiction over the church, in particular William's claim that he alone, as king, was entitled to convoke future reform synods and had the right to decide which rival for the papacy – Urban II or Clement III – to recognize. Relations became so tense that Anselm, acting on his own initiative, chose to leave England for three years (November 1097–September 1100) to consult with Urban II in Rome. Upon his return to England after William's death, he then quarrelled with Henry I over Urban's injunction against any bishop doing homage to a king or being invested with his bishop's office by a king or any other layman. Anselm, at Henry's behest, once again departed from England for three years (April 1103–August 1106), this time to consult with Pope Paschal II. The investiture controversy was settled only in 1107, twenty months before Anselm's death, when King Henry formally forswore the right of investiture at the Concordat of London.

Two conflicting portraits of Anselm's mature life

and of his attitude towards his roles as theologian and prelate have emerged. The standard portrayal, that of R.W. Southern, who agrees in general with Eadmer, shows Anselm as a devout monk who was committed to the ideals of monasticism and who aspired to a life of scholarly study and spiritual meditation. Dreading to trade the tranquillity of Bec for the combative milieu of Canterbury, he experienced his elevation to the archbishopric as 'his nearest approach to hell' (Southern 1988: 187). In his preface to the *Cur deus homo* (Why God Became a Man), Anselm spoke of his tribulation of heart and his great suffering, presumably because of his clashes with King William over the extent of regal power. Anselm seemed most content when he could withdraw from the public arena, as he did in the Italian mountain village of Liberi while finishing the *Cur deus homo*, during his first exile.

A contrary portrait of Anselm is that of S.N. Vaughn (1987), who dismisses much of Eadmer's report as tendentious and too intent upon depicting Anselm as a saint. Anselm, says Vaughn, was a man politically astute and personally calculating, manipulative enough to enlist the support of his friends against his enemies and clever enough actively to fashion a positive historical image of himself by omitting from his collection of letters those that would have cast him in a less favourable light. Moreover, his very remonstrations and protestations when assuming high office were not only a formality – the expected and requisite display of humility – but also a test of the intensity of his electors' support. In fact, Vaughn claims, Anselm adroitly schemed to become selected as archbishop once he became convinced that God had destined him for this office. He did not desire the office and its burdens; but, despite this disinclination, he manoeuvred cleverly to obtain it in compliance with the perceived will of God. Once in the office he executed it with talent, protecting against regal confiscation the holdings and preserving from regal encroachment the prerogatives of the previously weakened English church.

Both these mutually incompatible pictures of the historical Anselm seem extreme. Neither is likely to be shown conclusively wrong by future scholarly debate, except in the unlikely event that new evidence is forthcoming. Scholarly caution must be exercised, however, in attempting radically to reshape Eadmer's testimony that Anselm neither sought nor desired to become archbishop – testimony corroborated by Anselm's own letters and not clearly contradicted by circumstantial evidence.

2 Philosophical method

Anselm did not write his first philosophical treatise, the *Monologion*, until he was forty-three. Even his earliest letters, prayers and meditations do not antedate 1070. Thus his entire corpus of writings arises from his mature years, after he had already been a monk at Bec for at least ten to sixteen years. Not surprisingly, his works show a consistency that cannot be found in a more prolific writer such as Augustine, who in later years felt obliged to write *retractationes* (reconsiderations) of his earlier work.

Stylistically, Anselm often uses streamlined Latin sentences that are set out in simple vocabulary. However, his concise style and his well-focused treatment of topics do not ensure that his ideas are easy to understand. On the contrary, understanding is frequently impeded by his failure to introduce more elaborate distinctions and to explore the metaphysical complexities that underlie his ostensibly straightforward assertions. More like Aristotle than like Augustine, he introduces into his argumentation appeals to common linguistic parlance, as when he explains that our saying 'Nothing caused it' ordinarily means that it is not the case that anything caused it. Similarly, when we say that God is unable to sin (an expression that seems to convey the idea of imperfection because of powerlessness), we usually mean that God has the ability always to keep from sinning (and to have this ability is to have a perfection).

Anselm is called the 'Father of Scholasticism' because he endeavours to show that revealed truths can be established on an independent rational basis. In the *Monologion*, where he professes to proceed *sola ratione* (by recourse to rational considerations alone), he regards himself as having demonstrated not only that God exists but also that God is triune and that the human soul is immortal. Similarly, in the concluding chapter of the *Cur deus homo*, he claims unhesitatingly that 'whatever is contained in the Old and in the New Testament has been proved, by the solution of the single problem which we have set forth.' Thus he goes further than his predecessor Augustine and his successor Aquinas, neither of whom supposed that either the doctrine of the Trinity or the doctrine of the inerrancy of Scripture is rationally demonstrable.

An example of Anselm's reasoning as a Scholastic may be drawn from *De casu diaboli (The Fall of the Devil)* 21, which asks the question of whether Satan was able to foreknow that he would fall. Anselm begins by stating that either Satan did know this or he did not. On the assumption that he foreknew, he either was willing that the fall should occur, or he was unwilling. Were he willing, however, then he did not foreknow a future fall, since he was already fallen by virtue of that evil consent; and if he were unwilling, then he who because of his sinlessness deserved to be happy would because of his foreknowledge have been filled with grief, a theological inconsistency. Hence, concludes Anselm, Satan was not able to foreknow that he would fall. In reaching this conclusion, he extends theological truth beyond what is overtly taught in Scripture.

The scholastic method of *sola ratione* characterizes most of Anselm's philosophical and theological works, ranging from the *Proslogion* (whose original title was *Fides quaerens intellectum* (Faith Seeking Understanding)) to the *Cur deus homo*, which appears to be tacitly oriented toward Scripture in spite of its purporting to presuppose nothing about Christ. In *De incarnatione Verbi* (The Incarnation of the Word) 6, Anselm explicitly links the method of the *Proslogion* with that of the *Monologion*, when he states that both of these works show that 'what we hold by faith regarding the divine nature and its persons – excluding the topic of incarnation – can be proven by compelling reasons (*necessariis rationibus*) apart from appeal to the authority of Scripture.' In this context, to proceed *necessariis rationibus*, as do both the *Monologion* and the *Proslogion*, is to proceed *sola ratione*. Moreover, in the *Cur deus homo* he elaborates upon the notion of *rationes necessariae* but does so without this notion's being at odds with that of *remoto Christo* (arguing without recourse to any knowledge of Christ derived from Scripture or from history). Furthermore, in the terminal chapter of the *Cur deus homo*, the interlocutor Boso summarizes: 'You prove the necessity of God's becoming a man, and you do so in such a way that even if the few things you have introduced from our books are removed (for example, what you mentioned about the three persons of God and about Adam), you would satisfy not only the Jews but also the pagans *sola ratione*.' Finally, in *De incarnatione Verbi* 6, Anselm intimates that even the *Monologion* can be characterized as *fides quaerens intellectum*. The same is true of the *Cur deus homo*, as is attested by Boso's last speech in I, 25.

The distinction that Anselm makes in the Cur deus homo between *rationes necessariae* and *rationes convenientes* (fitting reasons) is the following: necessary reasons are reasons that by themselves are compelling, while fitting reasons are weaker reasons that, nonetheless, are compelling in the absence of more powerful contrary considerations. With regard to fitting reasons and their compelling power, Anselm's proposal to Boso in the *Cur deus homo* is crucial:

I would like for us to agree to accept, in the case of God, nothing that is in even the least degree unfitting and to reject nothing that is in even the slightest degree reasonable unless something more reasonable opposes it. For in the case of God, just as an impossibility results from any unfittingness, however slight, so necessity accompanies any degree of reasonableness, however small, provided it is not overridden by some other more weighty reason.

(*Cur deus homo* I, 10)

The fact that an overall consistency of method characterizes Anselm's treatises does not mean that he never relied upon Scripture to furnish a premise needed for a given argument. However, he sought to avoid doing so, and it is interesting to note that he did not write a single commentary on any book of Scripture.

All of the foregoing serve to distinguish Anselm from AUGUSTINE, to whom he is nevertheless deeply indebted. The *Proslogion*'s very description of God as *aliquid quo nihil maius cogitari potest* (something than which nothing greater can be thought) seems to be drawn from *Confessiones* 7.4, and its theme *fides quaerens intellectum* is taken from Augustine's *Sermon* 44.6.7 (and ultimately from Isaiah 7: 9), just as in the *Monologion* the main ideas regarding the Trinity are appropriated from Augustine's *De trinitate* (On the Trinity). Likewise, Anselm's analysis of free choice in terms of the distinction between having an ability and exercising it, together with his reasoning about the impossibility of an upright human will's being overpowered by the force of temptation, harks back to Augustine. Yet, Anselm is no mere reiterator of Augustine's points. Just as his *Proslogion* argument advances well beyond any cognate systematic reasoning found in Augustine, so his theory of atonement lays a foundation different from Augustine's Devil-ransom theory, though a summary of that theory is incorporated into the *Cur deus homo*. Likewise, his definition of free choice has no parallel in Augustine's writings, even though his concept of 'free choice' is allied with that of Augustine.

3 Philosophical works: *Monologion*

The *Monologion* and the *Proslogion* should be studied together, since each in certain respects elucidates the other. Anselm himself never thought of the *Proslogion* as replacing the *Monologion*. Although the more creditable (and traditional) view maintains that chapters 1–4 of the *Monologion* aim at proving the existence of God, this view has been challenged by F.S. Schmitt and others. Schmitt (1969) regards

Anselm as striving to demonstrate something not about the existence of God but about God's essence: Anselm does not undertake to show that a Supreme Being exists as the cause of the universe, but endeavours instead to prove that the cause of the universe, a cause that is presupposed to exist, is a supreme being (*Analecta Anselmiana* vol. I: 45). Furthermore, Schmitt contends that in these chapters Anselm self-consciously deplatonizes Augustine, from whose *De trinitate* 8.3 he is borrowing. Anselm, he says, leaves aside three Neoplatonistic tenets found in Augustine's discussion: (1) that the concept of the good is impressed (by God) upon the human mind; (2) that the mind beholds both good things and the Good itself; and (3) that good things participate in the Good itself. Critics of Schmitt, however, question whether Anselm is actually borrowing from *De trinitate* 8.3 anything more than Augustine's topic; and if he is not borrowing, then he cannot be said to be deliberately leaving some particular doctrines aside (see AUGUSTINIANISM).

There is a clear strand of Neoplatonism that runs throughout the *Monologion*. In *Monologion* 9 Anselm teaches the doctrine of exemplarism, although he goes on to maintain that there is only a single Form, or Exemplar, of creation: namely, the second member of the Trinity, or the Eternal Word of God (*Monologion* 30-3). He also accepts a doctrine of degrees of existing, whereby a plant exists more than does a stone, whereas a horse exists more than does a plant (*Monologion* 31). Moreover, he implies that existence is a perfection:

> No one doubts that created substances exist in themselves very differently from the way they exist in our knowledge. For in themselves they exist in virtue of their own being; but in our knowledge their likenesses exist, not their own being. It follows, then, that the more truly they exist anywhere by virtue of their own being than by virtue of their likenesses, the more truly they exist in themselves than in our knowledge.
>
> (*Monologion* 36)

Since Anselm correlates existing truly with existing greatly (*Monologion* 31; *Proslogion* 3), he regards something as existing more greatly (in other words, more perfectly) if it exists 'in its own being' in addition to existing in someone's knowledge. In contrast to the Neoplatonists, however, Anselm holds to a doctrine of analogy on the basis of which some of our predicative discourse about God bears some real but very remote likeness to the Divine Nature (*Monologion* 65; *Responsio* 8). He links our conceiving of God with our conceiving of ourselves:

> The mind, then, can very fittingly be called its own mirror, as it were, in which it beholds, so to speak, the image of this Being which it cannot see face to face. For if of all created things the mind alone can remember itself, understand, and love, then I do not see why we should deny that there is in it the true image of this Being, which exists as an ineffable trinity of self-remembrance, understanding and love.
>
> (*Monologion* 67)

Speaking more generally, Anselm states that 'every being in the degree to which it exists is in that degree similar to the Supreme Being' (*Monologion* 66). These resemblances, though very distant, serve as the foundation for analogical predications (see EXISTENCE; GOD, CONCEPTS OF; TRINITY).

4 Philosophical works: *Proslogion*

No portion of Anselm's literary corpus has evoked as much controversy as has his *Proslogion*. Interpretation of this 'pious breathing', as one translator calls it, is beset by a maze of criss-crossing textual and conceptual problems. Textually, a number of questions are raised. Does Anselm here aim to set forth a proof or proofs of God's existence, and if so, in what chapter(s) is the proof located? Does Anselm's use of the description *id quo maius cogitari nequit* and its variants differ from his use of the description *aliquid quo nihil maius cogitari potest* and its variants; are these really descriptions, or are they definitions? If they are descriptions, are they interchangeable with the description 'greatest conceivable being'? What is meant by *maius*, by *cogitari*, by *intellectus*? If *cogitari posse* means 'to be conceivable', can it be equivalently replaced by 'to be logically possible'? In the opening sentence of *Proslogion* 2, is Anselm asking to be granted to understand *quia es sicut credimus*, or *quia es, sicut credimus*? Does *Proslogion* 2 presuppose that existence is a perfection (an attribute or a property)? In *Proslogion* 4, what is the proper English rendering of *Qui ergo intelligit sic esse deum*? When Anselm writes in *Proslogion* 15, *es quiddam maius quam cogitari possit*, is he claiming that God is inconceivable?

Such textual problems cannot be resolved simply by re-examining the Latin passages, for the proper construal of the respective texts requires the elimination of ambiguities. Invariably, all such translations will be interpretative. Some translators, for example, construe the opening sentence of *Proslogion* 2 as Anselm's request to be granted to understand 'that You exist, even as we believe [You to exist]', so that *sicut credimus* is parenthetical. Others have taken *sicut* to mean 'in the manner that' and have dropped the editorial comma that precedes it, so that Anselm is seen as asking to understand 'that You exist in the manner that we believe [You to exist]'. According to this latter rendering, Anselm is not aiming to prove the existence of God; rather, he wants to show that God, whom he believes to exist, exists in a manner different from the mode of existence of all finite beings: that is, he exists so truly and eternally and immutably that he cannot even conceivably not exist. In comparison with this mode of existence, finite beings are as nothing. In this interpretation, first advanced by Stolz (1933) and subsequently repeated in modified form by many others, the *Proslogion* is primarily an exercise in mystical theology.

By contrast, Malcolm (1960) maintains that *Proslogion* 3 contains the elements of a second version of Anselm's argument, which Malcolm takes to be aiming at demonstration (as does also the first). This second version is supposed to be superior to the reasoning in Chapter 2, inasmuch as it does not require the dubious presupposition that mere existence is a perfection. Instead, it acceptably presupposes that necessary existence is more excellent than is contingent existence. Disagreeing with Malcolm and with almost everyone else, Anscombe (1985) views Anselm as proposing a decidedly different argument. She punctuates a key sentence in *Proslogion* 2 as *Si enim vel in solo intellectu est, potest cogitari esse et in re quod maius est*, and interprets this as: 'For if it [*quo nihil maius*] is only in the intellect, what is greater can be thought to be in reality as well.' Campbell, in turn, perceives Anselm as engaged in the analysis of a speech-act: Anselm's argument 'shows that if one speaks of something-than-which-a-greater-cannot-be-thought one is committed to asserting that such a thing exists' (Campbell 1976: 193–4), but nothing prevents an atheist from refusing to speak of something-than-which-a-greater-cannot-be-thought.

Even one of Anselm's earliest interpreters, Gaunilo, a monk from Marmoutier, had difficulty with Anselm's text. He misinterpreted Anselm to be saying that if *quo nihil maius* 'existed solely in the understanding, then whatever existed also in reality would be greater than it'. He also failed to see that his own counter-argument about an island that excelled in perfection above all other lands did not have a logical structure parallel to the structure of Anselm's argument. For he speaks of something than which no other actually existing land is more perfect; but Anselm speaks of something than which nothing conceivable is perfect. In other respects, Anselm himself also partly misapprehended Gaunilo's critique. He did not recognize that Gaunilo's phrase *maius omnibus* is shorthand for *illud maius omnibus quae cogitari possunt* and not for *illud maius omnibus quae sunt*. Moreover, he incorrectly accused Gaunilo of contradicting himself, an accusation resulting from a misreading of Gaunilo's words *non [posse] hoc aliter cogitare, nisi intelligendo, id est scientia comprehendo, re ipsa illud existere*. Anselm wrongly takes Gaunilo to be defining 'understanding x' as 'apprehending with certainty that x really exists', whereas Gaunilo is merely defining 'understanding' as 'apprehending with certainty'.

Going beyond the many textual issues, contemporary philosophers have also noted a variety of conceptual problems with the *Proslogion* 2 argument. First, does it confuse two different domains, *de dicto* and *de re*; that is, from something's inconceivable nonexistence, does it follow that that thing exists in reality? Second, does the argument beg the question by assuming that the existence of God is possible? Third, does it beg the question inasmuch as the proposition 'that than which a greater cannot be thought is not that than which a greater cannot be thought' is not self-contradictory unless the existence of that than which a greater cannot be thought is presupposed? This question involves a theory about the logic of definite descriptions: for example, 'the prime number between 3 and 5 is not between 3 and 5' is self-contradictory only if 'the prime number between 3 and 5 is between 3 and 5' is true; and it is true only if there is a prime number between 3 and 5.

Does the argument successfully establish the compossibility of the various perfections that it ascribes to *quo nihil maius*, and does it successfully demonstrate that *quo nihil maius* is indeed a unique being? Is the very concept of *quo nihil maius* intelligible, or is it like the concept of an integer than which none greater can be thought? Can a being that is maximally and absolutely perfect be intelligibly said to be comparatively greater than all existing things, things that are subject to degrees of perfection (greatness)? These and other questions have perpetuated continuing disagreement about just where and how Anselm's argument goes wrong. Among philosophers, the strong feeling that the argument is unsound has contributed to a tendency to regard the entire *Proslogion* as a meditation on the majesty and greatness of God rather than as an attempted, and failed, set of proofs. However, the fact remains that Anselm, at the end of his reply to Gaunilo, spoke of himself as having engaged in proving:

> I have now showed, I believe, that in the aforementioned treatise I proved – not by inconclusive reasoning but by very compelling reasoning – that something than which a greater cannot be thought exists in reality.... For the signification of

this utterance ['something than which a greater cannot be thought'] contains so much force that what is spoken of is, by the very fact that it is understood or thought, necessarily proved to exist in reality and to be whatever ought to be believed about the Divine Substance.

(*Responsio* 10)

Anselm is not a mystic, as some have claimed him to be. Nor should his meditative reflections in the *Proslogion* misleadingly be called confessions, even though their style is reminiscent of Augustine's *Confessiones* (see GOD, ARGUMENTS FOR THE EXISTENCE OF).

5 Philosophical works: *De grammatico*

This dialogue reflects the emphasis at Bec on studying the trivium (dialectic, grammar and rhetoric, as opposed to the quadrivium: arithmetic, geometry, astronomy and music); moreover, it bears witness to the esteem in which Aristotle and his *Categories* were held within the School of Bec. The Latin word *grammatica* indicates not only the subject matter that we today call grammar but also the subject matter that we call literature. Anselm himself expresses a disaffection for teaching the former (*Epistola* 64). Contemporary interest in *De grammatico* is due largely to D.P. Henry (1964), who insightfully recognised it as a serious study in paronymy. Paronyms are words (such as *grammaticus*, meaning 'expert in grammar') that derive from other words from which they differ only in case ending (such as *grammatica*, meaning 'expertise in grammar') and that function as both adjectives and nouns (for example, we can say both that someone is expert in grammar and that someone is *an* expert in grammar). Accordingly, the title *De grammatico* is properly translated not as 'On the Grammarian' but as 'On (an) Expert in Grammar', where the parentheses around the indefinite article 'an' serve to signal that it is operative in English when 'expert in grammar' functions as a noun, but is dispensed with when 'expert in grammar' functions as an adjective. (Latin has neither a definite nor an indefinite article.)

In this light, the central question raised within the dialogue is *utrum grammaticus sit substantia an qualitas* (whether (an) expert-in-grammar is a substance or a quality)? Aristotle and medieval textbooks cited grammaticus as an example of quality because the word itself signifies a quality (namely, *grammatica*). However, in the work, Anselm's fictional interlocutor, the Student, points out that in customary parlance *grammaticus* is spoken of as a substance and not as either a quality or an accident. Anselm resolves the question by showing the Student that *grammaticus* signifies both a quality and a substance, for it signifies both expertise in grammar and man, in different ways. Principally and *per se* and substantially it signifies expertise in grammar; and because expertise in grammar is a quality, being expert in grammar is also a quality. Improperly and *per aliud* and accidentally it signifies man; and because man is a substance, being an expert in grammar is also a substance.

Anselm understands a word to have signification insofar as that word calls something to mind. 'Expert in grammar' calls to mind both expertise in grammar and man, though it does so in different ways. A word which signifies *per aliud* (that is, which does not in and of itself call something to mind but instead calls that thing to mind on the basis of something else and accidentally) is said by Anselm to be appellative of the thing that is thus signified *per aliud*. At this point Anselm tightens his terminology, reserving the word 'signifying' for properly signifying, that is, signifying *per se*: 'expert in grammar' signifies, but is not appellative of, expertise in grammar, while it is appellative of, but does not signify, man. Indeed, only man is called (an) expert in grammar because only man has the accident (the quality) of expertise in grammar. A term is appellative of a thing, says Anselm, 'if this thing is called by this name in the customary course of speaking'. Names signify things, not concepts (though there might be second-order names, which signify other names).

In interpreting *De grammatico*, we must beware of two traps: first, that of supposing that *significatio per se* has to do exclusively with meaning and that *significatio per aliud* (that is, *appellatio*) has to do exclusively with reference; and second, that of supposing that Anselm considers *grammaticus est grammatica* to state a logical truth (Henry 1974: 183). With regard to the first misconception, Anselm regards a speaker as at times able to refer to an object either by using the word that *per se* signifies that object, or by using a word that is an appellative of that object. In a proffered example, he notes that someone might refer to a horse by using the word 'horse', which *per se* signifies a horse, that is, which in and of itself calls (the thought of) a horse to mind. Or he might refer to a horse by using the appellative *albus* ('the white one'), in a situation where a white horse is standing next to a black ox. The hearer would know – not purely on the basis of the signification of the word 'white', but also and additionally on the basis of his knowledge that of the two animals, only the horse is white – that the horse was being referred to. Concerning the second misconception, neither Anselm nor the Student regards the phrase *grammaticus est grammatica* as stating a logical truth (while trespassing against *usus loquendi* (ordinary usage)). Rather, both agree that *grammaticus* signifies *grammatica* because it signifies *sciens grammaticam* (having expertise in grammar). Since *grammaticus* is an accident only of man, we say *grammaticus est sciens grammaticam*, rather than saying *grammaticus est grammatica*. This latter sentence is no more a logical truth than it is meaningful. By contrast, the former sentence (*grammaticus est sciens grammaticam*) has a double meaning which results from the fact that *grammaticus* is a paronym: 'being (an) expert in grammar is having expertise in grammar'.

The real importance of *De grammatico* for Anselm lay in its pedagogical usage as an exercise in dialectic. Its contemporary importance lies in the fact that it attests to Anselm's awareness of the need to be clear about the elusive relationship between signifier and signified; and it witnesses, further, to his desire to do so by recourse to *rationes necessariae* (*De grammatico* 1) (see LANGUAGE, MEDIEVAL PHILOSOPHY OF; LANGUAGE, PHILOSOPHY OF).

6 Philosophical works: *De veritate, De libertate arbitrii, De casu diaboli*

These three dialogues centre around the notion of *rectitudo* (rectitude, rightness, uprightness). 'Truth', says Anselm, is definable as 'rectitude perceptible to the mind alone'. Justice is rectitude kept for its own sake, and freedom is, also by definition, rectitude of will kept for its own sake. In eliciting his definition of 'truth', Anselm examines truth insofar as it is found in statements, thoughts, acts of will, actions, the senses and in the very being of things. A statement is true when it signifies what it ought to, that is, when it signifies correctly; and it signifies correctly when it either signifies to be the case that which actually is the case, or signifies not to be the case that which really is not the case. Thus, a statement's truth is its rightness, correctness or rectitude.

However, a statement does not always do what it is designed to do (namely, signify correctly what is, or is not, the case), for the statement is also capable of being used to signify falsely (that is, to signify that what-is is not, or that what-is-not is). Even when the statement signifies falsely, it retains the capability to signify truly, because it remains a meaningful set of words. Indeed, such a statement never loses its capability to be used to signify truly and correctly. Insofar as the statement retains this capability, we may also say of it that it is as it ought to be, that it is correct and has correctness, or rightness, or truth.

Thus, reasons Anselm, a true statement has two truths: the truth that accords with its signifying what it is designed to signify, and the truth that accords with its being capable of signifying what it is designed to signify. This latter truth belongs to the statement naturally, inasmuch as it is retained even when the statement signifies otherwise than it is designed to (that is, even when it signifies that what-is is not or signifies that what-is-not is). The former truth belongs to the statement accidentally and only at such time as the statement signifies a correct state of affairs. Anselm follows Aristotle in regarding the statement 'Socrates is sitting' as true so long as Socrates is seated but as becoming false when Socrates stands up.

Anselm goes on to point out that the foregoing distinction between two truths applies to thoughts, acts of will, actions, the senses and the very being of things insofar as they all both do what they ought to do and are capable of doing what they ought to do, whether they actually succeed or not. He develops a sense in which thoughts, acts of will and so on may be said to signify, in a twofold way. For example, truth (which is a form of rightness) is said to be in the being of things when these things are as they ought to be (that is, when they conform to what God designed for things of their kind to be); in another sense they 'signify' by their very existence that what they are is what they ought to be, whether or not they are defective specimens. For example, a misbegotten animal is not what it ought to be, as measured by the perfection of its species; but it is what it ought to be insofar as it is an existent thing (because otherwise God would not have allowed it to be).

Since a natural rightness belongs to statements, thoughts, acts of will and so on (even when they do not do what they are designed to do, or are not what they are designed to be), this rightness through which they are right continues to exist when the different statements, thoughts, beings and so on signify falsely. Indeed, this rightness accords with a Rightness that is one and the same in them all, and that continues to exist even when the things themselves and their natural rightness perish. Anselm (borrowing from his own *Monologion* 18) infers that this Rightness, which is perceptible by the mind alone, is eternal. The statement 'something was going to exist' was always true in the past, and the statement 'something has existed' will always remain true in the future; and since each of them can be true only if there is truth, truth is eternal. Like Augustine in *De libero arbitrio* (On Free Choice of the Will), and like Scripture itself in John 14: 6, Anselm identifies Eternal Truth with God.

In *De libertate arbitrii* (Freedom of Choice), Anselm searches for a definition of 'free choice' that will elucidate the essential freedom of God, unfallen angels, fallen angels, pre-fallen Adam, post-fallen Adam, Adam's earthly descendants and redeemed

Adamic human beings in their sanctified, heavenly state. He concludes that 'freedom of choice' is unexceptionably definable as 'the ability to keep uprightness-of-will for its own sake', an ability which every rational being always possesses. This definition has both philosophical and theological aspects. Philosophically, the definition is meant to exclude the view that having freedom of choice consists essentially in having the power of alternative choice: the ability to choose either that which is morally right or that which is morally wrong. Neither God, the good angels, nor human beings in the heavenly state have this power; and yet Anselm considers them all to have free will. Even regarding cases where agents do have the power of alternative choice, their freedom does not consist therein. For example, when Satan and Adam first sinned (although they were under no necessity to do so), each sinned 'by his own choice, which was free'; but neither did so 'by means of that in virtue of which his choice was free', the ability to maintain a righteous will. Instead, each used another ability, namely, the ability to abandon uprightness of will. Anselm's distinction between having an ability and using that ability – a distinction appropriated from Augustine – allows him to assert, paradoxically, that evil acts of will and evil actions are done freely even though they are not done by means of that ability whose possession is essential to freedom (see FREE WILL; FREEDOM, DIVINE).

In further expounding his theory of freedom, Anselm encounters a second paradox. He distinguishes ability not only from use but also from motivation; in other words, he distinguishes being *able* to will from being *motivated* to will. However, in some contexts he proceeds to talk as if certain intense motivations were so disenabling that they deprived one's will of freedom:

> If the faithful were immediately transformed at baptism or at martyrdom into the state of incorruption, then merit would perish and men would be saved without merit.... For since men would see those who would be converted to Christ pass over immediately into the state of incorruptibility, there would be no one who would be able even to will to turn away from this very great happiness which he would behold.
> (*De concordia* III, 9)

This point of view is reinforced by Anselm's notion that in the future life, redeemed human beings will be like the good angels: they will be unable to sin because they will no longer see anything more to will than that which they shall already have (*De casu diaboli* 6). Anselm also closely links motivation and ability/inability when he states that if Satan had known that he would actually be punished if he sinned, rather than knowing simply that he could deservedly be punished, then 'he would not have been able freely to will what would have caused him to be unhappy' (*De casu diaboli* 23). In other words, he would not have been able to sin. However, if certain patterns of intense motivation are disenabling, how is it plausible that the will of a rational creature is really always free?

On the more centrally theological plane, a third paradox arises. Although Anselm teaches that each human being always retains the ability to keep uprightness of will, he also teaches that no human being has the ability, by his own efforts, to regain uprightness of will once it has been abandoned. Only God can restore this uprightness; but God does so only with respect to those who repent. This doctrine leaves Anselm in the awkward position of maintaining that if someone's will lacks uprightness, then he cannot will uprightly, even though he is still free by virtue of his having the ability to keep uprightness of will if uprightness of will were restored to him. In having an ability that cannot be used, such a man is said by Anselm to resemble someone who has the power of sight but who cannot use this power because he is located in a totally darkened room; still, he could actually see if light were restored to the room. There is something strange about Anselm's calling someone's will free when it is not free actually to will uprightly. Recognizing this point, Anselm refers to a man as both a servant and free. This paradox reaches its most concise expression in *De concordia* III, 13: 'without justice the will is never free, because without justice the natural freedom of choice is futile'.

A fourth paradox emerges in conjunction with the third. If one's will is no longer upright by virtue of one's having willed evilly, and if God restores uprightness only to the will of those who repent, how can one be willing to repent unless one's will is to some extent already upright prior to the restoration of uprightness? Anselm expresses this paradox in terms of conversion (though it applies, as well, after conversion): 'Those who say "Convert us, O God" are already to some extent converted, because in willing to be converted they have an upright will' (*De concordia* III, 6). By prevenient grace, maintains Anselm, God guides toward repentance those whom he has foreordained.

A fifth paradox surfaces when Anselm contends that the force of temptation can never overpower an upright will. The force of temptation, if it were to succeed, would have to compel an individual to accede; but, philosophizes Anselm, again following Augustine, no one can be constrained to will. A soldier, for example, can be tortured or even killed against his will; however, he cannot be made to will against his will, for anyone who wills consents to will, that is, wills willingly. Anselm construes 'being constrained to will' as 'being made to will unwillingly'; and this latter expression he regards as incoherent, on the grounds that if one were unwilling to will, then there would be no actual willing. However, a critic could contend that Anselm's analysis of 'constrained to will' is tendentious and oversimplified.

A sixth paradox has to do with Anselm's view that Satan's will to persevere in justice both failed him and did not fail him. It failed him because, although he was created with a preponderant, supernatural inclination-for-justice, he nonetheless willed unjustly. On the other hand, it did not fail him because the supernatural inclination for justice, with which he was created, did not wane. In attempting to dissolve the paradox of how Satan, who was created with a strong inclination for justice and who was placed in an environment with reinforcing incentives, would have been motivated to will evilly, Anselm introduces a 'Scholastic-like' distinction: it is not the case that Satan's willingness to desert justice was caused by an antecedent waning of the willingness to keep justice but, rather, the willingness to desert caused the not-willingness to keep. Satan willed to desert justice in order to secure a desired benefit that it was unjust for him to have at that time. The deeper paradox now becomes one of why Satan, a rational creature, would irrationally and knowingly choose to have a benefit the choosing of which would risk the loss of all happiness? Anselm's answer, 'only because he willed to', transforms the paradox into a mystery.

A final paradox relates to Anselm's statement that:

> God causes all the things which are done by a just or an unjust will, viz., all good and evil deeds. Indeed, in the case of good deeds he causes what they are [essentially] and the fact that they are good; but in the case of evil deeds he causes what they are [essentially] but not the fact that they are evil.
>
> (*De concordia* I, 7)

These paradoxes Anselm himself regards as only apparent. Yet, whatever be one's own final appraisal of Anselm's theory of freedom, one must bear in mind that Anselm is a determinist and a compatibilist: only Satan's initial choice of evil was done simply because Satan willed thus to choose. All other reflective choices are such that they are 'caused' by factors that, in principle, are subject to investigation and description (and that do not deprive the agent of free choice):

> Even as every will wills something, so it also wills for the sake of something. And just as we must consider what it wills, so we must also notice why it wills. For a will ought to be upright in willing what it ought and, no less, in willing for the reason it ought. Therefore, every will has both a what and a why. Indeed, whatsoever we will, we will for a reason.
>
> (*De veritate* 12)

Having in *De veritate* (On Truth) defined 'justice' as 'uprightness of will kept for its own sake', and having indicated that he means 'kept for its own sake only', Anselm in *De casu diaboli* (The Fall of the Devil) interprets the evil of injustice to be the absence of justice from a will in which justice ought to be present. Accordingly, injustice is a privation; and a privation, he thinks, is a kind of not-being. However, if the evil that is injustice is a kind of not-being, how can the word 'evil' be significative, wonders the Student interlocutor. The Teacher, Anselm, gives three replies. First, 'evil', 'injustice' and 'nothing' signify, respectively, a removal of good, justice and something. Since a removal can be signified only by also signifying that which is to be removed, expressions such as 'not good', 'not just' and 'not something' obliquely signify good, just and something, without signifying them by positing them. Second, 'evil' and 'injustice' do not signify anything *secundum rem* (according to fact) but they are significative *secundum formam* (according to linguistic form), for we use these terms to speak of evil and injustice as if these latter were something – as when we say 'evil caused it' or 'injustice caused it'. Third, 'evil' is sometimes used to signify *incommodum* (detriment) rather than to signify injustice or an absence; in this respect it signifies something and not merely as-if-something (*quasi aliquid*).

In *De casu diaboli*, Anselm seeks to remind us that 'we ought not to cling to the verbal impropriety concealing the truth as much as we ought to attend to the true propriety hidden beneath the many types of expression'. In the process of heeding his own injunction, he there appeals to many of the same distinctions that are also found in his *Philosophical Fragments*.

7 Theological works: *De incarnatione Verbi* and *De processione Spiritus Sancti*

De incarnatione Verbi (The Incarnation of the Word) contains Anselm's defence of the doctrine of God's triunity. This defence is mounted against ROSCELIN OF COMPIÈGNE, a French cleric who maintained that if the three persons of God were only one thing and not three separate things, then the incarnation of the Son would, untowardly, have necessitated the incarnation of the Father and the Holy Spirit as well.

Anselm examines the meaning of 'thing' (*res*) and explains that the three persons are three distinct (but not separate) things with respect to their distinguishing properties, but are one thing with respect to the nature that they have in common. Exhibiting masterly skill as a dialectician, he contends that Roscelin's view leads either to tritheism or to Sabellianism, both of which doctrines are objectionable to Roscelin himself. He further contends that Roscelin's own articulation of his own claim is such that it entails the very same untoward consequence from which Roscelin is attempting to escape: namely, the incarnation of the Father and the Holy Spirit along with that of the Son. After advancing an argument to show that there can be no more than one God, Anselm explains why this one God became incarnate in the person of the Son rather than in the person of the Father or of the Holy Spirit. To complete his dialectical strategy, he provides a symbolic illustration to lend credence to the very notion of trinity: the Nile, while being one body of water, is also a three-ness of spring, river and lake.

The divine trinity and oneness is explored more fully in *De processione Spiritus Sancti* (The Procession of the Holy Spirit), where the Augustinian emphasis upon relatio looms larger. The three persons of God are three relations, three ways in which the one Divine Nature relates itself to itself. These relations are irreducible, inasmuch as the Father would not be a father unless he had a son, but the Father himself cannot be his own son; the Son would not be a son unless he had a father, but the Son himself cannot be his own father; and the Holy Spirit would not be a common spirit unless he proceeded from both the Father and the Son, but he himself cannot be either of the two from whom he proceeds. In line with the Nicene-Constantinople creed, Anselm defends the *filioque* doctrine against the Greek Orthodox teaching that the Holy Spirit proceeds from the Father alone. No other medieval treatises so concisely, clearly and vigorously display the rationale of orthodox trinitarianism as do these two Anselmian works (see TRINITY).

8 Theological works: *Cur deus homo* and *De conceptu virginali*

Desirous to explain the reasons for the Incarnation, Anselm undertakes in the *Cur deus homo* an elaborate demonstration of his view that only by means of incarnation could God have made provision for human salvation. Adam's sinful fall, as well as the ensuing sins of all his natural descendants, could not simply be overlooked by God, since doing so would do violence to God's justice. Hence, every sinner is under obligation to make payment for his sins, sins which rob God of honour by detracting from the splendour of creatures and therefore from God's own accomplishment as Creator. Payment must involve both restitution of what has been stolen and compensation for the injury done. Now, every rational creature, even if sinless, owes to the Creator perfect and voluntary obedience – indeed, owes itself and all that it is. A sinner, who has stolen honour from God by stealing from God the obedience due to him, is obliged to resume rendering the requisite obedience and, in addition to make compensation, or satisfaction, for the perpetrated wrong. In this twofold way the sinner would fully restore God's honour.

However, once having sinned, the sinner's will is deprived of uprightness, which by its own efforts it cannot recover; and hence no sinner can attain perfect obedience. Moreover, the sinner has nothing with which to compensate God. Compensation must be equal to the gravity of the wrong that was done; but any disobedience to God's command is so grave, teaches Anselm, that it ought not to be done even if one could thereby save an infinite number of worlds from perishing. Since the sinner is obliged to offer as satisfaction, or compensation, something greater than is that for whose sake he is obliged not to dishonour God, and given that he is not to dishonour God even in order to save an infinite number of worlds from perishing, he must render to God something of greater value than are an infinite number of worlds. But only God can make such a payment, whereas only a human being of Adam's race ought to. Hence, if payment is to be made, it must be made by a God-man.

Yet, queries Anselm, what payment could a God-man make in addition to perfect and voluntary obedience? What is it that he would not already owe to God and that would count as satisfaction? The God-man, reasons Anselm, would make satisfaction by choosing righteousness in preference to life. Being sinless, and in this respect unlike all other human beings, he alone would not be under the penalty-of-death, which resulted from the Fall. He would yield up his life to the honour of God by allowing himself to be put to death for righteousness' sake – that is, to be put to death for refusing, when accused of blasphemy, to profess the untruth that he was not God. Since the evil of sinning against the person of God is the greatest conceivable evil, the goodness of the God-man's life must be the greatest conceivable goodness. Thus in choosing righteousness even in the face of death, the God-man restored honour to God by rendering a service more valuable than the value of the totality of things that are not God. Such a service deserves to be rewarded. And because the God-man needs nothing, he may admissibly transfer this reward to cancel the debt incurred by Adam and his natural descendants (see ATONEMENT; SALVATION; SIN).

In the course of his argument, Anselm explains once again why it was most fitting for the Son of God and not for either of the other two members of the Trinity to become incarnate. He hastens to point out that those who actually put to death the Jesus of history were guilty of only a venial sin, having acted in ignorance of his Messianic identity. In *De conceptu virginali et originali peccato* (The Virgin Conception and Original Sin), he distinguishes between Adam's person and his nature. When Adam sinned personally, his sinful person contaminated his nature. As a result, his descendants are born with an individuated Adamic nature whose will lacks justice. This unjust nature contaminates their persons, predisposing them to sin personally when they reach the age of accountability. Anselm offers an explanation of how Jesus, who was of Adam's nature, was nonetheless able to remain free of original sin – that is, remain free of contracting the necessity–of–sinning upon attaining the age of reason. He insists that Adam's descendants are not condemned for Adam's sin but only for their own, even though Adam's sin is a cause of their own fallen nature. Anselm does not teach the doctrine of Mary's own immaculate conception (see INCARNATION AND CHRISTOLOGY).

9 Theological works: *De concordia*

Oriented around the topics of grace, foreknowledge and predestination, *De concordia praescientiae et praedestinationis et gratiae dei cum libero arbitrio* (The Harmony of the Foreknowledge, the Predestination and the Grace of God with Free Choice) not only extends the views previously advanced in *De libertate arbitrii* and *De casu diaboli* but also places them squarely within a theological context. Predestination is a theological doctrine that relates primarily to the attendant doctrine of salvation. The New Testament seems to teach that some individuals are foreordained to salvation, whereas others are not. Anselm follows Augustine both in accepting this doctrine and in acknowledging that he has no explanation for why God singles out some and not others. As early as *Proslogion* 11 he prayed: 'But if we can somehow grasp why You can will to save those who are evil, surely we cannot at all comprehend why from among those who are similarly evil You save some and not others because of Your supreme goodness, and condemn some and not others because of Your supreme justice.' Yet predestination and enabling grace do not violate human freedom, believes Anselm, because inducing someone's assent and trust is not identical with compelling assent and trust.

Three considerations reassure Anselm that divine foreknowledge, like predestination, is not incompatible with human free will. First of all, God foreknows not only what a given individual will do but knows also *how* the individual will do it, whether freely or by necessity. Assume that the individual will act freely: then, if it is necessary that what-God-foreknows come to pass, it is necessary that the individual do freely what will be done. This necessity which guarantees one's freedom cannot at the same time be a necessity that deprives one of freedom. Anselm believes that the expression 'it is necessary that...' is misleading because it tends to suggest that the event in question happens by necessity, whereas in the present context it means only 'it is certain that...'. Second, something may be certain to occur either because God efficaciously wills that it occur, or because he foreknowingly wills to permit its occurrence. In the latter case, his foreknowledge does not efficiently cause the action or the event to happen. In fact, Anselm reminds us as early as *De casu diaboli* 21, God is improperly said to foreknow the future, since his eternal knowledge is knowledge of things as present. The present knowledge of something's happening does not necessarily make it happen. Third, God's will must be (conceived of as) free, because otherwise God could be thought to be more perfect – something which is impossible. By the same token, he must be regarded as knowing his own will. If his knowledge of his own will does not deprive it of freedom, then *prima facie* there is no reason to infer that his knowledge of the human will deprives it of freedom (see ETERNITY; FREE WILL; GRACE; OMNISCIENCE; PREDESTINATION; SALVATION).

10 Conclusion

Anselm's paramount publications, though only eleven in number, have had a significant (though never major) impact upon the history of Western philosophy. Peter ABELARD, Thomas AQUINAS, John DUNS SCOTUS, WILLIAM OF OCKHAM, NICHOLAS OF CUSA and others found it helpful to quote from them, sometimes approvingly, sometimes disapprovingly. Anselm's learned command of Aristotle's *logica vetus*, his insightful appeal to the Latin community's *usus loquendi* and his bold utilization of the method of *sola ratione* bear ample witness to his gifted philosophical mind. Yet, like any good philosopher, he knew when to be tentative, as evidenced by his conclusion to *De conceptu virginali*:

> In accordance with the capacity of my understanding I have briefly made these statements about original sin – not so much by way of

asserting them as by way of provisionally inferring them – until God shall somehow reveal to me something better. But if someone has a different view, I do not reject anyone's opinion provided it can be proved to be true.

(*De conceptu virginali* 29)

In spite of his emphasis upon *rationes necessariae*, he sensed a danger in trusting bloated, over-confident and self-confident reason. Consequently, he was not averse to declaring with respect to deep theological mysteries: 'if someone thinks he knows something, he does not yet know it as he ought to know it' (*De incarnatione Verbi* 1). Because he regarded such knowledge and understanding as a grace, he was willing to continue to believe – in the hope of one day better comprehending.

See also: AUGUSTINIANISM; FREE WILL; GOD, CONCEPTS OF; LANGUAGE, MEDIEVAL THEORIES OF; LOGIC, MEDIEVAL; MEDIEVAL PHILOSOPHY; OMNISCIENCE; PLATONISM, MEDIEVAL; SALVATION; TRINITY

List of works

Anselm of Canterbury (1033–1109) *S. Anselmi Opera Omnia* (Complete Works of Saint Anselm), ed. F.S. Schmitt, Stuttgart: Frommann. (This edition is a reprint, consisting of six volumes in two tomes, of Schmitt's earlier edition of Anselm's works, published by Thomas Nelson.)

—— (1033–1109) Philosophical Fragments, ed. F.S. Schmitt, *Ein neues unvollendetes Werk des hl. Anselm von Canterbury*, Beiträge zur Geschichte der Philosophie und Theologie des Mittelalters 33. 3, 1936; ed. R.W. Southern and F.S. Schmitt, *Memorials of St. Anselm*, London: British Academy, 1969. (Southern and Schmitt includes the philosophical fragments as well as the compilations *Dicta Anselmi* and *De morum qualitate per exemplorum coaptationem*.)

—— (1033–1109) *Fragmenta Philosophica* (Philosophical Fragments), trans. J. Hopkins and H. Richardson, *Anselm of Canterbury*, vol. 2, New York: Mellen, 1976. (A translation of philosophical fragments.)

—— (1070–1109) *Epistolae* (Letters), trans. W. Fröhlich, *The Letters of Saint Anselm of Canterbury*, Kalamazoo, MI: Cistercian Publications, 1990–4, 3 vols. (Anselm's collected letters in translation.)

—— (1072–1103) *Orationes sive meditationes* (Prayers and Meditations), trans. B. Ward, *The Prayers and Meditations of Saint Anselm*, Baltimore, MD: Penguin, 1973. (Collected theological writings.)

—— (1076) *Monologion*, trans. J. Hopkins, *A New Interpretive Translation of St. Anselm's Monologion and Proslogion*, Minneapolis: Banning, 1986. (Anselm's first major philosophical work, showing the influence of Neoplatonism.)

—— (1077–8) *Proslogion*, trans. J. Hopkins, *A New Interpretive Translation of St. Anselm's Monologion and Proslogion*, Minneapolis: Banning, 1986. (Includes Gaunilo's *Pro insipiente* (On Behalf of the Fool) and Anselm's *Responsio* (Reply to Gaunilo).)

—— (*c.*1080–5?) *De grammatico*, trans. J. Hopkins and H. Richardson, *Anselm of Canterbury*, vol. 2, New York: Mellen, 1976. (Grammatical work, notable for its emphasis on signification.)

—— (*c.*1080–5) *De veritate* (On Truth), trans. J. Hopkins and H. Richardson, *Anselm of Canterbury*, vol. 2, New York: Mellen, 1976. (Contains Anselm's definition of truth, identifying eternal truth with God.)

—— (*c.*1080–5) *De libertate arbitrii* (Freedom of Choice), trans. J. Hopkins and H. Richardson, *Anselm of Canterbury*, vol. 2, New York: Mellen, 1976. (Searches for a definition of 'free choice'.)

—— (*c.*1085–90) *De casu diaboli* (The Fall of the Devil), trans. J. Hopkins and H. Richardson, *Anselm of Canterbury*, vol. 2, New York: Mellen, 1976. (Anselm's work on the relationship between sin and free will.)

—— (1092–4) *De incarnatione Verbi* (The Incarnation of the Word), trans. J. Hopkins and H. Richardson, *Anselm of Canterbury*, vol. 3, New York: Mellen, 1976. (Anselm's defence of the doctrine of God's triunity.)

—— (completed 1098) *Cur deus homo* (Why God Became a Man), trans. J. Hopkins and H. Richardson, *Anselm of Canterbury*, vol. 3, New York: Mellen, 1976. (Demonstrates Anselm's view that only through incarnation could God have made provision for human salvation.)

—— (1099–1100) *De conceptu virginali et originali peccato* (The Virgin Conception and Original Sin), trans. J. Hopkins and H. Richardson, *Anselm of Canterbury*, vol. 3, New York: Mellen, 1976. (Discussion of the nature of sin, including original sin.)

—— (1102) *De processione Spiritus Sancti* (The Procession of the Holy Spirit), trans. J. Hopkins and H. Richardson, *Anselm of Canterbury*, vol. 3, New York: Mellen, 1976. (A further exploration of Trinity and oneness, showing Augustinian influences.)

—— (1106–7) *Epistolae de sacramentis* (Letters on the Sacraments), trans. J. Hopkins and H. Richardson,

Anselm of Canterbury, vol. 3, New York: Mellen, 1976. (Anselm's views on the sacraments.)

—— (1107–8) *De concordia praescientiae et praedestinationis et gratiae dei cum libero arbitrio* (The Harmony of the Foreknowledge, the Predestination and the Grace of God with Free Choice), trans. J. Hopkins and H. Richardson, *Anselm of Canterbury*, vol. 3, New York: Mellen, 1976. (Expands the views previously advanced in *De libertate arbitrii* and *De casu diaboli*.)

References and further reading

Adams, M. (1992) '*Fides Quaerens Intellectum*: St. Anselm's Method in Philosophical Theology', *Faith and Philosophy* 9: 409–35. (Relates Anselm's methodology to his station in life.)

* Anscombe, G.E.M. (1985) 'Why Anselm's Proof in the *Proslogion* is not an Ontological Argument', *Thoreau Quarterly* 17: 32–40. (An extreme, but extremely intriguing, interpretation.)

* Campbell, R. (1976) *From Belief to Understanding: A Study of Anselm's Proslogion Argument on the Existence of God*, Canberra: Australian National University. (More important for the major philosophical issues it insightfully develops than for the controversial conclusions about Anselm that it reaches.)

* Eadmer (1093–1125) *Vita Anselmi* (The Life of St Anselm, Archbishop of Canterbury), ed. and trans. R.W. Southern, London: Thomas Nelson, 1962. (Appears to have been written in two stages, roughly, between 1093 and 1100, and between 1109 and 1125.)

* —— (1109–14) *Historia Novorum in Anglia*, ed. M. Rule, London: Longmans, 1884. (Later edition trans. G. Bosanquet as part of *Eadmer's History of Recent Events in England*, London: Cresset, 1964. A record of Anselm's public life during his tenure at Canterbury, completed between 1109 and 1114.)

Evans, G. (ed.) (1984) *A Concordance To the Works of St. Anselm*, Millwood, NY: Kraus. (A valuable tool, in spite of containing too many trivial entries.)

Fröhlich, W. (1984) 'The Letters Omitted from Anselm's Collection of Letters', *Anglo-Norman Studies 6: Proceedings of the Battle Conference, 1983*, Woodbridge: Boydell, 58–71. (Assesses Anselm's motivation in not having certain letters copied for posterity and indicates the extent to which this 'suppression' occurred.)

Gombocz, W. (1980) 'Anselm von Canterbury. Ein Forschungsbericht über die Anselm-Renaissance seit 1960' (Anselm of Canterbury: A Research Report on the Anselm Renaissance since 1960), *Philosophisches Jahrbuch* 87: 109–34. (Contains a wealth of bibliography.)

* Henry, D.P. (1964) *The De Grammatico of St. Anselm: The Theory of Paronymy*, Notre Dame, IN: Notre Dame University Press. (Provides a translation and an analysis.)

—— (1967) *The Logic of Saint Anselm*, Oxford: Clarendon. (Skillfully covers the principal aspects).

* —— (1974) *Commentary on De Grammatico: The Historical–Logical Dimensions of a Dialogue of St. Anselm's*, Dordrecht: Reidel. (A painstakingly detailed further scrutiny of Anselm's views on paronymy.)

McIntyre, J. (1954) *St Anselm and his Critics: A Reinterpretation of the Cur Deus Homo*, London: Oliver & Boyd. (An older but penetrating examination of Anselm's theory of atonement.)

* Malcolm, N. (1960) 'Anselm's Ontological Arguments', *Philosophical Review* 69: 41–62. (Claims that Anselm had two different ontological arguments in Proslogion 2 and 3, respectively.)

Rowe, W. (1976) 'The Ontological Argument and Question-Begging', *International Journal for Philosophy of Religion* 7: 425–32. (Makes a strong case for regarding the argument of *Proslogion* 2 as question-begging.)

Schmitt, F.S. (1968) 'Prolegomena seu Ratio editionis', *S. Anselmi Opera Omnia*, Stuttgart: Frommann, Tome 1, 1*–244*. (A cluster of critical considerations regarding the chronology, authenticity and manuscript tradition of Anselm's works.)

* —— (1969) 'Anselm und der (Neu-)Platonismus' (Anselm and (Neo-) Platonism), *Analecta Anselmiana* I: 39–71. (Looks at Neoplatonic elements in Anselm's writings.)

Serene, E. (1981) 'Anselm's Modal Conceptions', in S. Knuuttila (ed.) *Reforging the Great Chain of Being: Studies in the History of Modal Theories*, Dordrecht: Reidel, 117–62. (Explores Anselm's *Philosophical Fragments*, which are not dealt with in this entry.)

* Southern, R.W. (1988) 'Sally Vaughn's Anselm: An Examination of the Foundations', *Albion* 20: 181–204. (Sharpens the issues that separate the two conflicting interpretations of Anselm's life.)

—— (1990) *Saint Anselm: A Portrait in a Landscape*, Cambridge: Cambridge University Press. (Replaces his older work *Saint Anselm and his Biographer*, 1963.)

* Stolz, A. (1933) 'Zur Theologie Anselms im Proslogion' (Anselm's Theology in the *Proslogion*), *Catholica* 2: 1–24. (Argues that the *Proslogion* is an exercise in mystical theology.)

* Vaughn, S.N. (1987) *Anselm of Bec and Robert of Meulan: The Innocence of the Dove and the Wisdom*

of the Serpent, Berkeley, CA: University of California Press. (Suggests that Anselm was a more gifted and scheming statesman than Eadmer makes him out to be.)

—— (1988) 'Anselm: Saint and Statesman', *Albion* 20: 205–20. (A response to Southern's critique of her historical portrait of Anselm.)

Vuillemin, J. (1971) *Le Dieu d'Anselme et les apparences de la raison* (The God of Anselm and the Semblances of Reason), Paris: Montaigne. (A clear appraisal of Anselm's concept of God as it functions in the *Monologion* and the *Proslogion*.)

JASPER HOPKINS

ANTHROPOLOGY, PHILOSOPHY OF

Anthropology, like philosophy, is multifaceted. It studies humans' physical, social, cultural and linguistic development, as well as their material culture, from prehistoric times up to the present, in all parts of the world. Some anthropological sub-fields have strong ties with the physical and biological sciences; others identify more closely with the social sciences or humanities. Within cultural and social anthropology differing theoretical approaches disagree about whether anthropology can be a science. The question of how it is possible to understand cultures different from one's own, and to transmit that knowledge to others is central to anthropology because its answer determines the nature of the discipline. Philosophy of anthropology examines the definitions of basic anthropological concepts, the objectivity of anthropological claims and the nature of anthropological confirmation and explanation. It also examines the problems in value theory that arise when anthropologists confront cultures that do not share their own society's standards.

1 Epistemological problems
2 Ethical problems

1 Epistemological problems

Despite a shared commitment to fieldwork and to the role of anthropologists as participant-observers, different theoretical schools of anthropology disagree sharply about how it all works, and in particular about whether anthropology is or can be a science. According to one prominent school – cognitive anthropology – culture consists of a set of rules in the minds of its members (Frake 1969). To understand another culture, anthropologists must internalize those rules well enough to respond to new situations in a culturally appropriate way. In its approach to cultural behaviour as rule-governed, and in its broad interpretation of rules, cognitive anthropology accords with Winch's (1958) Wittgensteinian account of the nature of human social life (see SOCIAL NORMS). Winch, however, does not share cognitive anthropology's view that anthropology is a science. Linguistic rules – primary examples of cultural rules – offer an entry into the rest of the culture. To begin to learn a new set of cultural rules, cognitive anthropologists question informants about how they would classify various observable phenomena. The point is not merely to discover the names that others give to the objects and categories familiar to the anthropologist, but to grasp the other culture's own, possibly different, way of structuring the stream of experience into categories. To this end, cognitive anthropologists – who are also called 'ethnoscientists' – elicit indigenous classifications of features of the natural world (for example, colours, birds, fish, plants). They test their grasp of the rules by observing whether their own efforts at extending classifications gain the approval of their informants. When the anthropologists have mastered the new system, they compare and contrast it with their own (Western, scientific) system. The results of such investigations are usually put forth as evidence against radical forms of cognitive relativism (see SOCIAL RELATIVISM §3; RELATIVISM).

Cognitive anthropology offers a clear answer to the first part of the central question raised above: one comes to understand another culture by becoming proficient in its rules through interaction with members of the culture. How that knowledge is transmitted to those not initiated into the culture remains problematic, however, for it is not clear that one system of rules can be translated into another. Although cognitive anthropologists view themselves as engaging in scientific studies of culture, and are concerned with the objectivity and predictive success of their claims, their account of the nature of cultural knowledge and how it is acquired works against its dispersal in the usual scientific channels, such as journal articles.

An opposing approach, symbolic anthropology, maintains that anthropology is ethnography. The business of anthropology is to write accounts of human culture that can be read, analysed, discussed and challenged by students and peers, now and in the future. Doing anthropology does not require one to internalize some set of rules, as cognitive anthropologists suppose, but instead to figure out what people are up to when they say and do certain things. Culture is not a set of rules located in anyone's mind, it is symbolic behaviour. Culture is thus a 'public document' that anthropologists are trained to 'read', just as literary critics read (interpret) poems and novels.

Comparing anthropology with literary interpretation highlights the issue of objectivity. Do standards exist for 'correct' interpretations of cultures or do anthropologists have the same latitude as literary critics to offer alternative, and perhaps incompatible, accounts? Geertz (1975), borrowing Ryle's terminology, notes that ethnography at its most basic level involves 'thick descriptions' rather than the reporting of 'raw' data. That is to say, any description of human behaviour (as opposed to mere bodily movement) imputes an intention to it, and thus, at least partially, explains the behaviour. Collingwood in *The Idea of History* (1946) had already stressed the same point, using it to argue for a fundamental difference between interpretive explanations of human behaviour and causal explanations of 'mere' physical events (see COLLINGWOOD, R.G.). Nevertheless, he insisted that hypotheses about intentional descriptions could be subjected to rigorous examination, and accepted or rejected objectively, on the basis of evidence. Latter-day interpretivists, however, regard the impossibility of peeling away all layers of interpretation to get at 'the fact of the matter' as support for relativism (see SOCIAL SCIENCE, CONTEMPORARY PHILOSOPHY OF §3). One interpretation may be preferred to another because it is more coherent, richer, more subtle or relevant to contemporary concerns, but not because one is true and the other false. The latter terms are not applicable, at least in their usual sense, to interpretations. Because symbolic anthropologists emphasize the importance of interpretation over causal explanation and prediction, they see a significant gap between anthropology and science. While cognitive anthropology and symbolic anthropology are dominant theoretical approaches and loom large in philosophical discussions, many anthropologists, particularly those whose training was completed when earlier schools (for example, functionalism, historical particularism) flourished would not identify themselves with either school.

2 Ethical problems

Respect for the beliefs, practices and values of other cultures, no matter how different from one's own, is a hallmark of anthropological wisdom. Franz Boas (1940), whose name is inevitably linked with cultural relativism, rejected invidious comparisons between the 'high culture' of northern Europeans and the art forms, languages, myths and religious practices of indigenous Americans, just as he rejected 'progressive' evolutionary accounts, offered by physical anthropologists early in the twentieth century, that put the former at a more advanced stage of physical development than the latter. He insisted that the culture of each group should be studied in terms of its own historical development and appreciated in that context rather than judged by the standards of another culture.

Since moral beliefs and practices, like other beliefs and practices, depend on the cultural context, many anthropologists regard ethical relativism as an easy consequence of cultural relativism. Some moral philosophers have challenged this slide into relativism by claiming that while societies differ in their derivative moral judgments (for example, the propriety of cross-cousin marriage), they agree in their more fundamental moral judgments (for example, the immorality of incest). Whether universal agreement exists on any basic moral judgment is at least in part an empirical question – one to which Turnbull's studies of the Ik (1972) suggest a negative answer. A different attack on relativism maintains that establishing genuine relativism requires showing that people's basic ethical judgments would conflict even if they shared all the same factual beliefs and were fully enlightened as to the consequences of their views. On this view, the mere absence of universally accepted principles is not sufficient to prove relativism. By the same token, finding universally accepted moral principles would not disprove their dependence on particular cultures. The agreement could be accidental.

Despite such philosophical attacks on ethical relativism, most practising anthropologists continue to embrace it, for they equate ethical relativism with tolerance for the moral codes of others. Teachers of anthropology present relativism as the received view, usually also admonishing students to distinguish objective factual claims from subjective and relative value judgments. The student's ability to reserve judgment on the moral codes and practices of others is regarded as a prerequisite for anthropological fieldwork and for acceptance into the discipline.

Anthropologists' alleged commitment to relativism, however, is undermined by their own professional code of behaviour, as stated, for example, in the guidelines of the Society for Applied Anthropology (Bernard 1988). The dominant theme of these guidelines is Kantian: treat the people whom you study as ends not as means. Respect their right to self-determination, to arrange their lives as they see fit according to their standards. Anthropologists who are accused of violating this code must defend themselves satisfactorily or face professional sanctions.

Most field anthropologists believe that relativism

permits or even requires them to defend 'their people' against interference from governments, missionaries, or other agents of so-called advanced civilizations. The common justification for such defences, however, is the society's right of self-determination. Anthropologists also take up the cause of oppressed minorities within the societies that they study. For example, feminist anthropologists work to improve the status of women in many cultures. Thus even when denying absolute moral values, anthropologists embrace moral guidelines that are supposed to hold across cultures. They unilaterally condemn behaviour that infringes on the rights of others.

See also: UNIVERSALISM IN ETHICS; VALUE JUDGMENTS IN SOCIAL SCIENCE

References and further reading

* Bernard, H. (1988) *Research Methods in Cultural Anthropology*, Newbury Park, CA: Sage Publications. (See Appendix A for 'Statement on professional and ethical responsibilities. Society for Applied Anthropology'.)
* Boas, F. (1940) *Race, Language and Culture*, New York: Free Press. (Presents Boas' historical-particularist account of culture.)
* Collingwood, R. (1946) *The Idea of History*, Oxford: Oxford University Press. (States the classic interpretivist position.)
* Frake, C. (1969) 'The ethnographic study of cognitive systems', in S. Tyler (ed.) *Cognitive Anthropology*, New York: Holt, Rinehart and Winston, 28–41. (A brief introduction to cognitive anthropology.)
* Geertz, C. (1975) *The Interpretation of Cultures*, London: Hutchinson. (See Introduction for modern interpretivist view by a prominent symbolic anthropologist.)
  Hollis, M. and Lukes, S. (eds) (1982) *Rationality and Relativism*, Cambridge, MA: MIT Press. (Essays by contemporary philosophers and anthropologists.)
  Salmon, M. (1992) 'Philosophy of the social sciences' in M. Salmon, J. Earman, *et al.*, *Introduction to the Philosophy of Science*, Englewood Cliffs, NJ: Prentice Hall, 404–25. (Discusses the senses in which social sciences can be scientific.)
  Sperber, D. (1993) 'Remarques anthropologiques sur le relativisme moral' (Anthropological remarks on moral relativism), in J.-P. Changeux (ed.), *Fondements Naturels de l'Ethique* (Natural Foundations of Ethics), Paris: Editions Odile Jacob, 319–34. (A critical account of ethical relativism.)
* Turnbull, C. (1972) *The Mountain People*, New York: Simon & Schuster. (An account of the Ik.)
* Winch, P. (1958) *The Idea of a Social Science and its Relation to Philosophy*, London: Routledge & Kegan Paul. (Wittgensteinian account of social science.)

MERRILEE H. SALMON

ANTIOCHUS (*c.*130–68 BC)

For most of his career the Greek philosopher Antiochus of Ascalon, a pupil of Philo of Larissa, was an orthodox 'sceptical' Academic. He then changed his philosophy: some called him a Stoic, but he himself claimed to be returning to the Old Academy of Plato and his immediate successors. He took a generous view of his new home, urging that the Peripatetics and the Stoics were not new schools of thought but mere modifications of Platonism, and the philosophical position which he advocated was a 'syncretism' – an amalgam of ideas and doctrines and arguments taken from several sources. To philosophy itself he contributed little, but he was a figure of considerable importance in the larger world, where he presented Greek philosophy to an educated Roman public.

1 Life
2 Thought
3 Influence

1 Life

Antiochus came from Ascalon in Syria. Circumstantial evidence places his birth *c.*130 BC. At some point he went to Athens, where he studied philosophy with Philo of Larissa and perhaps also with the Stoic Mnesarchus. The Academy won his heart (see ACADEMY): he remained under Philo's wing for an unusually long period and wrote books in defence of Academic scepticism. After years of fidelity he defected – perhaps in the 90s BC. He abandoned scepticism, claiming to restore the true Academy of Plato. The autumn of 87 BC found him in Alexandria in the entourage of the Roman statesman Lucullus. There he was scandalized by Philo's 'Roman books' (see PHILO OF LARISSA §2) and wrote his own version of the story. He may have stayed in Lucullus' company for some years. By 79 BC he was back in Athens, where CICERO (§1,3) listened to his lectures for six months. A few years later he returned to the East, again in the company of Lucullus. He died, in Mesopotamia, in 68 BC.

Antiochus is referred to as head of a school, perhaps the Academy or perhaps a school of his own.

Academic scholarch or not, he was a popular and an influential figure. He had a gentle and attractive personality, and a beguiling eloquence. He charmed Cicero, whom he did not convince, but who described him as 'the most accomplished and the most acute of all the philosophers I have known' (*Academics* II 113). He charmed – and convinced – the scholar Varro. He was the house-philosopher of Lucullus. He also had other friends among the eminent of Rome.

He wrote copiously: we know of certain sceptical books (written before 95 BC); of the *Sosus*, written against Philo in 86 BC; of a work on the agreement between the Stoics and the Peripatetics, dating from c. 80 BC; of a late essay *On the Gods*; and of a work on epistemology called *Canonics*, the date of which is uncertain. All of these writings are lost; but the speech which Cicero attributes to Lucullus in *Academics* II is described by him as 'Antiochean', and the account of Academico-Peripatetic ethics in Cicero's *On Ends* is said to represent the views of Antiochus and of the Peripatetic Staseas. From these two Ciceronian works we can thus gain an idea of some of the general lines of Antiochus' thought. But Cicero is not translating, or even paraphrasing, Antiochus. Some scholars have supposed that Antiochus ghosted many or most of Cicero's philosophical works, and that he lies behind various other later philosophical texts. There is nothing to be said for these suppositions.

2 Thought

When, in 87 BC, Philo gave up scepticism and the Stoic definition of knowledge (see PHILO OF LARISSA §2; STOICISM §12), Antiochus was upset. Not because Philo had become a dogmatist, but because he had rejected the definition:

> when Philo weakens and destroys this, he does away with any criterion for what is known and unknown; hence it follows that nothing can be apprehended and he foolishly finds himself in the position he least wished.
>
> (Cicero, *Academics* II 18)

The criticism of Philo is weak, but Antiochus' own position emerges with clarity: he is a dogmatist, not a sceptic; and he believes that the Stoic definition of knowledge must be upheld.

Antiochus himself had converted from scepticism to dogmatism some ten years earlier. (Since Cicero did not know why he changed his opinion, we will never uncover his reasons.) In his own view, he removed from the New Academy to the Old. Others seemed to see matters differently:

> Antiochus led the Stoa into the Academy, so that it was actually said of him that he practised Stoic philosophy in the Academy for he tried to show that the Stoic doctrines are found in Plato.
>
> (Sextus Empiricus, *Outlines of Pyrrhonism* I 235)

The accusation of Stoicism is not a Sextan absurdity: Cicero remarks that 'although he called himself an Academic, he was – if you changed a few items – a full-blooded Stoic' (*Academics* II 132). How so? And if so, why did not Antiochus simply convert to Stoicism (as Cicero himself pertinently asked)?

Cicero observes that the Old Academy and Zeno the Stoic 'disagree on one point only and agree wonderfully in everything else' (*Laws* I 53–4) – and he ascribes the observation to Antiochus. According to Antiochus, the Stoics were at one with the Old Academy; and in addition, 'the Stoics agree with Peripatetics in substance and dispute only over terminology' (Cicero, *On the Nature of the Gods* I 16). Thus Stoicism and Peripateticism are essentially forms of Platonism, so that a move to the Old Academy was by that very token an acceptance of Stoic and Peripatetic philosophy.

Granted this conglomerative or syncretistic account of Old Academic philosophy, Antiochus' 'Stoicism' ceases to amaze. But the syncretism itself may seem bizarre. None the less, it was not a crude fantasy: Antiochus knew something about the history of philosophy and based his syncretic claim on putative historical fact; nor did he pretend that Zeno and Aristotle swallowed Platonism whole and agreed perfectly with one another. Moreover, certain features which to us seem essential to Platonism – notably the theory of Forms – had no place in Antiochus' scheme of things; and other early Platonists had made a contribution to the philosophy of the Old Academy – Antiochus 'especially approved of Polemo' (Cicero, *Academics* II 131).

In any event, the syncretism is far from idiotic. One dogmatic school is omitted from it: Epicureanism. Antiochus realized that the cleft in dogmatic philosophy divided the Epicureans from everyone else. On the main questions, Old Academics, Peripatetics and Stoics were indeed in broad agreement: they were for knowledge and against scepticism, for virtue and against voluptuarism, for teleology and against mechanism, they were for continuity and against atomism.

Antiochus' syncretistic philosophy dealt with all three of the traditional 'parts' of the subject (logic, physics and ethics); but he urged that

> there are two things of the greatest importance in philosophy: the judgment of truth and the determination of the good. For no-one can be wise

unless he is aware both of the beginning of knowledge and of the end of desire, unless he knows whence he is to begin and whither he is to journey.

(Cicero, *Academics* II 29)

For the beginnings of knowledge, Antiochus sketched a standard empiricist account of the development of science from sense-perception; he defended the Stoic definition of knowledge; and he argued that attacks by sceptics all failed. For 'the end of desire', Antiochus used the 'Carneadean division' (see CARNEADES §2) and urged that the 'end' or *telos* consists in the primary goods of nature together with virtue. He managed to marry this rudely Stoic thought to the Aristotelian idea that the *telos* is intellectual activity or *theōria*. He was also exercised by the question of whether 'external' goods such as riches and beauty are necessary for happiness (see EUDAMONIA). He answered with engaging good sense that you can be happy if you are poor and ugly but that to be *very* happy you need to be wealthy and handsome.

3 Influence

Antiochus had some professional pupils, but most of them deserted his doctrines. His syncretism was not welcomed by the Stoa. Indeed, there is no evidence that his new version of the Old Academy was taken seriously by any of his colleagues. (There is nothing in the old theory that it was Antiochus who inaugurated what we now call 'Middle Platonism' (see PLATONISM, EARLY AND MIDDLE).) But he was not an insignificant figure. He was writing primarily for a lay public – a public of educated and intelligent Romans. For such a public, technical treatises and professional pedantries were inappropriate, and the rough syncretism which Antiochus offered made sound sense. Antiochus succeeded in impressing Cicero, and Cicero was no slouch in philosophy.

References and further reading

Barnes, J. (1989) 'Antiochus of Ascalon', in M. Griffin and J. Barnes (eds) *Philosophia Togata I*, Oxford: Clarendon Press. (Contains everything one needs to know, and more, about Antiochus.)
* Cicero, M.T. (early 45 BC) *Academics*, trans. H. Rackham, Loeb Classical Library, Cambridge, MA: Harvard University Press and London: Heinemann, 1933. (Varro in book I and Lucullus in book II represent Antiochus' views.)
* —— (mid 45 BC) *On Ends*, trans. H. Rackham, Loeb Classical Library, Cambridge, MA: Harvard University Press and London: Heinemann, 1914. (Book V is largely Antiochean in inspiration.)
Glucker, J. (1978) *Antiochus and the Late Academy (Hypomnemata 56)* Göttingen: Vandenhoeck & Ruprecht. (Includes a detailed discussion of Antiochus and his relation to the Academy.)
Mette, H.-J. (1986/7) 'Philon von Larisa und Antiochus von Askalon' (Philo of Larissa and Antiochus of Ascalon), *Lustrum* 28/9: 9–63. (Collects the ancient testimonies on Antiochus.)
* Sextus Empiricus (c. AD 200) *Outlines of Pyrrhonism*, trans. J. Annas and J. Barnes, *Outlines of Scepticism*, Cambridge: Cambridge University Press, 1994. (Fine translation with introduction and notes.)

JONATHAN BARNES

ANTIPHON (late 5th century BC)

Antiphon was a Greek Sophist. His most famous work, On Truth, *partially survives in two substantial papyrus fragments, plus a number of purported quotations. It sets up a bold antithesis between the claims of* physis *(nature) and* nomos *(law/convention), arguing that it is more advantageous to follow nature when one can do so without detection. The antithesis suggests several important questions about the meaning of 'nature' and its role in ethics, the origin of social laws and their authority and the meaning and value of justice. It is disputed whether he is to be identified with the orator Antiphon of Rhamnus.*

1 Life and works.
2 *On Truth*
3 The claims of nature
4 Practical implications and influence.

1 Life and works

Nothing is known of Antiphon's life. Doubts over his identity with Antiphon the Orator rest on the apparent tension between the conservative views of the Orator's *Tetralogies*, in which obedience to law is highly praised, and the seemingly radical arguments of *On Truth*. For similar reasons some have doubted whether the same man could have written *On Truth* and the conventional gnomic utterances of *On Concord*. In defence of a single identity it has been urged that: (1) *On Truth* is not as radical as it appears, but simply a plea for legal reform; (2) its doctrines, although radical, are not endorsed by Antiphon himself; and (3) Antiphon changed his mind. Antiphon is also credited – although this too is disputed – with a *Politicus* (Statesman) and *On the Interpretation of Dreams*, but these attributions too are disputed.

2 On Truth

In *On Truth* Antiphon argues that 'justice' consists of not transgressing the laws and customs (the *nomoi*) of the state in which you are a citizen. Consequently, to treat justice in the way that is most advantageous to yourself you should respect the *nomoi* in the presence of witnesses, but follow the claims of nature when witnesses are absent. Disobedience to nature will always harm you; disobedience to the *nomoi* will harm you only if you are detected. Furthermore, most *nomoi* are hostile to nature and act as shackles, whereas those things laid down by nature as advantageous promote freedom and pleasure.

Nor can the law provide the protection it promises: it cannot prevent aggression, nor guarantee that aggressors will be found guilty. Laws and customs are also based on false distinctions of class and race: we all possess the same intrinsic needs and faculties. Finally, the *nomoi* that we call 'justice' are internally contradictory: they require an individual not to harm anyone except in retaliation, yet if called upon as witness a person is required to give potentially harmful evidence in court against someone who has never harmed them. Giving such testimony may also prove dangerous: the witness may have made an enemy for life.

3 The claims of nature

What precisely is meant by 'nature'? Internal evidence suggests Antiphon means 'human nature', but the opposition he draws between this and culture prompts the fundamental question whether such a thing as 'raw' unsocialized human nature exists, and how we could know about it even if it did.

Even if we grant that Antiphon's stark distinction between nature and culture is sustainable, why does he rank the claims of nature above those of society? His first argument appeals to the automaticity of nature's reprisals if flouted, as opposed to the uncertain outcome of a flouted law or convention. Antiphon is ascribing to nature the inevitability which Greek thought had traditionally ascribed to the anthropomorphic deities or fate; in this he may have been influenced by the mechanical physical systems of LEUCIPPUS and DEMOCRITUS.

The inevitability of nature's workings would nevertheless be irrelevant without Antiphon's further claim of a systematic hostility between *nomos* and nature, with an individual's advantage tied to following the latter. In Greek 'advantageous' has medical connotations, and apparently Antiphon is primarily arguing that only by following the claims of nature can we safeguard our physical wellbeing, and indeed survival. His examples of social constraints, however, suggest that he is thinking not only in physiological terms but also of desire-satisfaction in general.

What are these constraints on our natural inclinations? Antiphon certainly holds (1) that the *nomoi* discourage us from attacking a potential aggressor, and encourage us to honour our parents, even if they have maltreated us: in both instances our natural tendency towards self-protection is thwarted. He may, however, also be claiming (2) that society restrains us from aggressive behaviour in general, and from satisfying whatever desires we happen to have. If this is his position (the text is too fragmentary to allow certainty), then underlying his argument is a view of 'raw' human nature as comprised of fierce egoistic drives antithetical to social harmony.

This choice between readings substantially affects the tenability of Antiphon's position. On reading (1) it seems reasonable for him to argue that social conventions which hinder our ability to defend ourselves are injurious to the individual. On reading (2), however, one may question whether social restrictions on aggressive behaviour in general are in fact ultimately to the individual's disadvantage. Clearly such constraints aim to frustrate the immediate desire, but one may argue that in the long run all individuals are better served if certain aggressive and egoistic aspects of human nature are curbed wholesale: what Antiphon regards as fetters could also be regarded as the bonds which keep society together. One might have expected Antiphon's own words to prompt him in this direction. He does after all admit that death is natural yet disadvantageous; why then does he not concede that a considerable number of the *nomoi* are aimed at protecting the individual from premature death? It is true that he nowhere recommends discarding the *nomoi* altogether, but he still does not consider the general undermining effect on security that repeated disregard for the *nomoi* might have. Possibly his argument is intended only to apply to those who can take care of themselves in all eventualities.

Furthermore, if the *nomoi* are generally disadvantageous, how did they come to exist at all? Antiphon gestures towards a social contract theory: there are opaque references to the *nomoi* being 'agreed' and to 'those who made the agreement' (it is unclear whether this is intended to represent a historical event). This supposed agreement is used by Antiphon as a reason for disobeying the *nomoi* – 'agreed' is interpreted as 'artificial' – but it is equally possible to reach the opposite conclusion: the *nomoi* were agreed because they were perceived to be beneficial and this is a good reason for obeying them. PROTAGORAS (§2) maintained precisely such a position, and it may be that *On Truth* is partly directed against him. Again, the question is raised whether Antiphon's argument is intended to apply to everyone or only to those who think they have sufficient resources to ignore the benefits of a social contract.

Antiphon's attack on the *nomoi* continues by claiming that they give unmerited preferential treatment to the high-born and Greeks (and given that most Greeks justified their practice of enslaving other races by appeal to the racial superiority which they claimed, he is probably criticizing the institution of slavery as well). Such criticisms suggest a reason why Antiphon called his work *On Truth*: he wishes to oppose the false ontological divisions of *nomos* to the true divisions of *physis*. In a separate fragment he also deplores the ambiguity of language; his criticisms in the papyrus fragments of the internal contradictions in the notion of 'justice' may be an example of this (Caizzi 1989).

4 Practical implications and influence

What, if anything, is Antiphon proposing that we actually do? On one view he is not recommending any course of action: he is not speaking *in propria persona* but simply setting up a debate. That would still leave the question whether the words in the text, even if not endorsed by Antiphon, are saying that we *ought* to follow nature when witnesses are absent; and if they are, whether this is an example of the 'naturalistic fallacy', the (allegedly) illegitimate inference of a prescription for action from a simple description of how things are (see NATURALISM IN ETHICS §3). The most plausible interpretation is that the text commends following nature as advantageous, but does not set it up as a moral imperative; it certainly does not propose an alternative description of 'justice'.

Another possibility is that Antiphon's real concern is with legal reform: he wishes to remodel the *nomoi* to harmonize with nature. The key issue here is again Antiphon's underlying view of humanity: if he thinks our natural inclinations tend towards unprovoked aggression rather than mere self-defence, then it is unclear how the *nomoi* could be remodelled accordingly yet still retain their social character. Nevertheless, his criticisms unquestionably force us to reconsider the origin and purpose of our own laws and customs and the nature and function of legal punishment.

Perhaps Antiphon's most important contribution to philosophy is his insistence that human physiology and psychology be included in ethical and political thought: our basic needs and desires cannot be ignored. The tensions he perceived between these natural desires and the claims of society were taken up in Plato's *Republic*, he was thus the first to lay down what Plato saw as the fundamental ethical challenge.

See also: CALLICLES; PHYSIS AND NOMOS; SOPHISTS

References and further reading

* Antiphon (5th century BC) Fragments, in H. Diels and W. Kranz (eds) *Die Fragmente der Vorsokratiker* (Fragments of the Presocratics), Berlin: Weidemann, 6th edn, 1952, vol. 2, 334–70. (The standard collection of the ancient sources; includes Greek texts with translations in German.)

Barnes, J. (1979) *The Presocratic Philosophers*, London: Routledge & Kegan Paul. (Chapter 23 includes an English translation and a crisp appraisal.)

* Caizzi, F.D. (1989) 'Antipho' in *Corpus dei papiri filosofici greci e latini* (Corpus of Greek and Latin Philosophical Papyri), Part I *, Florence: Olschki, 176–236. (Contains the most complete reconstruction in Greek of the papyrus fragments of *On Truth*, together with a sound and scholarly commentary in Italian and a very detailed bibliography.)

Furley, D. (1981) 'Antiphon's Case against Justice', in G.B. Kerferd (ed.) *The Sophists and their Legacy*, Wiesbaden: Steiner, 81–91; repr. in D. Furley, *Cosmic Problems*, Cambridge: Cambridge University Press, 1989. (Lucid and incisive; includes translation in English of some passages.)

Guthrie, W.K.C. (1969) *A History of Greek Philosophy*, vol. 3, Cambridge: Cambridge University Press; part of vol. 3 repr. as *The Sophists*, Cambridge: Cambridge University Press, 1971. (Interesting and scholarly discussions of Antiphon; see especially pages 107–13 and 285–94.)

Kerferd, G.B. (1981) *The Sophistic Movement*, Cambridge: Cambridge University Press. (The best introductory handbook to the Sophists in general.)

Sprague, R.K. (ed.) (1992) *The Older Sophists*, Columbia, SC: University of South Carolina Press, 106–240. (Full English translation of the fragments and testimonia from Diels and Kranz (1952) plus the speeches of Antiphon of Rhamnus.)

ANGELA HOBBS

ANTI-POSITIVIST THOUGHT IN LATIN AMERICA

Anti-positivist philosophy arose in Latin America at the turn of the twentieth century in response to the dominance of closed positivistic systems of historical development in the climate of intellectual opinion. Argentina, Mexico and Uruguay were all centres of anti-positivist theorizing. Philosophers such as Mexicans Antonio Caso and José Vasconcelos, the Argentinian Alejandro Korn and the Uruguayan Carlos Vaz Ferreira attacked Auguste Comte's positivism, as well as deterministic forms of scientific Marxism and Herbert Spencer's social Darwinism for their denials of creative freedom and spiritual values. Latin American anti-positivism is characterized as a form of modernism although it incorporates elements of traditionalism. It is self-consciously critical of the limitations of modern progressivism and willing to supplement the modern paradigm with premodern discourses. Anti-positivist philosophy is also firmly committed to the modern embrace of process over fixed form.

Latin American anti-positivism is founded in a comprehensive interpretation of experience that embraces phenomena such as creative freedom, tentative and experimental thinking, imaginative coordination and charitable love. These aspects are excluded from the purview of what positivists allow to be objects of scientific knowledge. Anti-positivists interpret experience as a bi-polar struggle in which the free side of life battles to prevail over the forces of necessity, system, abstraction and egoism.

South American anti-positivists concentrated on issues of knowledge and the structure of thought and experience, whereas Mexican anti-positivists, who were products of a formal education modelled on Comte's prescriptions, undertook a more total revolt. This revolt had metaphysical, moral and political dimensions.

For the most part anti-positivists did not fully escape the doctrines they criticized. They took from these doctrines descriptions of unredeemed, degraded and mechanized life which they opposed to redemptive practices of struggle.

1 Motivation
2 Major figures
3 The Ateneo
4 Ramos, Zea

1 Motivation

At the turn of the twentieth century, positivism was the dominant tendency of thought, philosophy and ideology in Latin America. In the strongest and most specific sense, the Mexican dictatorship of Porfirio Díaz attempted to legitimate itself as the applier of Auguste Comte's positivistic philosophy to national development, which included basing the educational system on a Comtian curriculum (see COMTE, A.). In a more general sense, evolutionary philosophies with naturalistic foundations, such as Comte's positivism, *fin-de-siècle* scientific Marxism and Herbert Spencer's social Darwinism, shaped the major component of educated opinion throughout Latin America, especially in Argentina and Uruguay (see SPENCER, H.; MARX, K.). Anti-positivism is the intellectual response to the positivist milieu of the generation that came of age in the first two decades of the twentieth century.

Latin American anti-positivism is determined by a sense of intellectual suffocation from positivistic systems. Late nineteenth-century positivism was naturalistic, deterministic, evolutionary, rationalist and scientific. The generation that came of age in that climate of opinion rebelled against confinement in prisons of thought which justified and even glorified inadequate social conditions, reduced human beings to egoists and had already mapped out the future. Drawing upon the emerging vitalistic philosophies in Europe, such as Friedrich Nietzsche's life philosophy (see NIETZSCHE, F.) and Henri-Louis Bergson's vitalism (see BERGSON, H.-L.; VITALISM) both of which opposed monistic nineteenth-century systems, the Latin American anti-positivists explored and advanced dimensions of human existence that had been neglected or silenced by positivism.

Latin American anti-positivism is a proclamation of the liberty to break out of the confines of nineteenth-century opinion and be open to a wealth of new experiences. As a variant of modernism, it is self-conscious of its own modernity and affirming of it, although, perhaps critical of it.

2 Major figures

The major Latin American anti-positivist philosophers include José Vasconcelos, Antonio Caso, and two generations later Leopoldo Zea in Mexico, Alejandro Korn in Argentina and Carlos Vaz Ferreira in Uruguay. The South Americans carried on their anti-positivist projects in the areas of epistemology and philosophy of experience, whereas the Mexicans took a more complete approach that included metaphysics, ethics, depth psychology, sociology of knowledge and social philosophy, as well as reflections on knowledge and experience. Also, the South Americans based their modernism on an extension of the modern fixation on the category of development to an affirmation of the pure process of creative freedom. Whereas the Mexicans, while also insisting on creative freedom, brought to bear pre-modern thought (with its normative content) on their ethical and socio-political positions. The South Americans could be considered to be progressive modernists, kindred to William JAMES in the USA, who reveal the intuition of continuous change which grounds and simultaneously deconstructs any evolutionary system of development. The Mexicans, in contrast, are complex figures who resemble Anglo-American traditional modernists, such as T.S. Eliot, Irving Babbitt and George Grant, in their return to pre-modern discourses, despite the utopian humanism rather than conservatism evident in their social philosophy.

As epistemology and philosophy of experience, Latin American anti-positivism has a basic structure which distinguishes it from other vitalist and existentialist tendencies (see EXISTENTIALISM; EPISTEMOLOGY, HISTORY OF). The anti-positivists share a commitment to an expanded empiricism which comprehends all aspects of human experience, including those that do not seem amenable to the methods of natural science (see EMPIRICISM). They also subscribe to a dualistic philosophy of experience in which they set up irreducible polarities in human experience and then describe and prescribe a continuous struggle to overcome one side of those dualisms.

The substance of the dualisms developed by Latin American philosophers pits creative liberty, aesthetic synthesis, disinterested commitment to ideals, charity and the flux of fermentative thought, against mechanistic determinism, material entropy, utilitarianism and fixed and absolute systems (see UTILITARIANISM). Underlying this content is a deeper philosophical structure which involves uncompromising commitment to describe clearly the highest human ideals joined with the equally intense commitment to describe realistically the limitations, failings, frustrations and coercions of human existence. It is within the tension set up between uncompromising idealism and intense realism that human beings struggle to realize their provisional victories over physical and spiritual death.

Korn constructed his philosophy of creative liberty from a Kantian background, arguing that Kant's dualisms can be made empirical by interpreting the split between subject and object as the experienced opposition between liberty and necessity (see KANT, I). For Korn (1963), the field of experience is a dynamic process in which subject and object are reciprocal functions. Necessity is objective in that it comprehends the succession of facts linked by the principle of physical causality into mathematical laws and excludes personal will. Liberty is definitive of subjects, constituting them as a process of valuation presupposed by the plurality of ideals acknowledged by Korn, such as wellbeing, happiness, love, power, justice, sanctity, goodness, truth and beauty. According to Korn, epistemology and axiology are inseparable: as a process of valuation, the founding act of the subject is the valuation that there be a valuing process, that is, the affirmation of creative liberty raised against economic coercion, the more intimate coercion of the passions and the tyranny of necessitarian doctrines such as nineteenth-century positivism (see AXIOLOGY).

Vaz Ferreira, more strict an empiricist and more sceptical than Korn, based his dualistic philosophy of experience on what he called the greatest revolution in intellectual history which was taking place in his own time – the liberation of thought from words. Vaz Ferreira (1961) distinguished between thought which draws from its datum a system meant to be applied to every case, and thought which reserves and elaborates its datum so that it becomes available to enlighten deliberation on concrete problems. The latter, known as fermentative thinking, operates according to a 'living logic' that is personal and intransferable and reaches its fruition in 'hyper-logical good sense' (1961: 197). This is a process of balancing opposed arguments and facilitating the interplay of diverse ideas so as to prevent any single idea from dominating thought and protect against systematization. Like Korn, Vaz Ferreira prescribes a philosophy of struggle, a life of 'superquixotism' (1961: 274) in which the individual, on the one hand, renounces adherence to any single ideal or value theory as that would bind life to a system, and on the other, embraces an effort to appreciate a multitude of diverse and sometimes contradictory ideals. To Vaz Ferreira, struggle is defined with particular clarity because he challenges individuals to engage the mechanistic aspects of their own thought.

3 The Ateneo

Mexican anti-positivism was far more intricate, historically-based and comprehensive than its South American counterpart. The initiators of anti-positivist philosophy in Mexico were part of a larger group of rebels representing different branches of the humanities. They were the privileged products of the positivistic curriculum which had been set up during the long rule of Díaz. In the first decade of the twentieth century, these young dissidents created a counter-educational institution of their own which they called the Ateneo de la Juventud (Athenaeum of Youth). The institution was partly devoted to fostering extensive study of the ancient Greek classics in order to liberate the mind from the confines of positivistic doctrine. Positivism in Mexico was a totalistic ideology that called for economic modernization, scientific education and administration of the country by technocrats, or *cientÚficos*, who claimed they were above politics. Given the anti-metaphysical bias of positivism, the initial project of the Ateneists was the rehabilitation of metaphysics. However, they were not traditionalists or reactionaries, but modernists, who questioned the deprivation of modern values while maintaining the primacy of action and process over contemplation and form.

The aims of the Ateneists were not confined to educational reform, but touched on political morality. Caso, the only member of the Ateneo who supported Díaz, was still able to summarize his generation's criticism of the positivistic polity for making economic development the supreme goal of the society, believing that wealth was the sole basis of strong government and suppressing democracy in the name of national welfare. This is not to say that the members of the Ateneo were primarily concerned with political issues, or that they were direct forebears of the Mexican Revolution of 1910, but rather that their cultural politics, like that of the French philosophers of the eighteenth century, helped to undermine the legitimacy of established authority.

The two leading philosophers of the Ateneo, Caso and Vasconcelos, went on to write bodies of work that touched on most of the major branches of philosophy. The basic structure of their thought was the same as that of their South American counterparts. It was a comprehensive empiricism constituted by a polarized struggle. For Vasconcelos (1961), the struggle was between the ascending and erotic tendency of conscious experience as a process of coordinating heterogeneous contents into moving totalities, or aesthetic wholes, and the counter-tendency towards entropy, the dispersion of things into flat homogeneity. Like Vaz Ferreira, Vasconcelos advanced an informal logic to describe the coordinative process he identified. Vasconcelos (1961) opposed his 'organic logic', based on the categories of melody and counterpoint, to conceptual logic, which analyses things as components and then reconstitutes them through systems of abstraction. For Vasconcelos, life should be a ceaseless struggle to overcome entropy in favour of coordination.

Caso's (1943) dualism is moral as it puts into play opposing attitudes to existence. At one pole of experience is 'existence as economy', the principle of the positivistic polity which prescribes maximum advantage with minimum effort. At the other pole is 'existence as disinterest', or aesthetic contemplation and 'existence as charity', or the pure act of self-giving love, which transcend the economy of selfishness by prescribing, respectively, maximum effort with indifference to advantage and maximum effort with minimum advantage. For Caso (1943) life is a heroic struggle to overcome and reverse the normal selfish tendencies of the organism.

In their revolt against positivism both Vasconcelos and Caso retained its stamp: Vasconcelos by using the physical science of his time as a metaphor for the structure of experience and Caso by accepting as true the positivistic model of the individual as a selfish competitor. Their prime concern was not restrictive speculative systems parading as scientific, but forces in human nature that impede the fulfilment of spiritual value, which they understood as non-natural, not extra-experiential. In their later work, Vasconcelos and Caso, having witnessed the rise of Communist and fascist regimes in Europe, like many intellectuals throughout the Western world, turned to the Christian faith as a bulwark to protect the values they had sought to redeem from positivistic neglect and disparagement. Indeed, they recognized in twentieth-century totalitarianism the same phenomenon against which they had battled in their youth (see TOTALITARIANISM).

4 Ramos, Zea

In the generation following the Ateneo, one major philosopher rose up as an organic critic of the anti-positivists. Samuel Ramos, a former student of Caso, broke with his master over the issue of basing philosophical reflection on intuition, which all the anti-positivists had done in some way, following Bergson. According to Ramos anti-positivism had erred from attention both by degrading reason and diverting thought to private states, to coming to terms with and improving objective conditions. Although he was a realist opposed to according primacy to imagination and introspection, Ramos's reaction did not represent a return to positivism. Rather, it represented an exploration of self-critical diagnosis of national character which culminated in his classic *El perfil del hombre y la cultura en México* (Profile of Man and Culture in Mexico) (1934). The book had many imitators in the decades following its publication. Later in his career, Ramos grew closer to anti-positivism, drawing on Max Scheler's anti-naturalistic axiology to ground a new humanism that would save civilization from totalitarian threats (see SCHELER, M.F. §8).

The cycle of Mexican anti-positivism reached completion in the next generation in Leopoldo Zea's *El positivismo en México* (Positivism in Mexico)

(1968), which applied Karl Mannheim's sociology of knowledge to positivism as an ideology. Zea argued that behind the facade of scientific administration were the particular interests of a small segment of the middle class who reaped their rewards by representing foreign economic interests. For Zea, the decline of positivism in Mexico was due to the increasing exploitation of the rest of the middle class by the positivistic elite and by the inability of positivism to preserve its claims to political neutrality against the attacks of liberals and Catholics. This led to the revolution of 1910. By the time the Ateneo arose, positivistic ideology and educational practice had become so diluted that the governing elite no longer had any clear legitimating principle.

From the viewpoint of sociology of knowledge, the anti-positivist generation in Mexico represented the middle class that had been marginalized by the positivistic elite. Their appeal to spiritual values sublimated the democratic demands that would be expressed in the revolution. Their subsequent fusion of utopian, often religious humanism and pre-modern discourses reflected the equivocal role of the post-revolutionary middle class as both essential to and alienated from the corporative structures that developed to integrate workers and peasants into the post-revolutionary regime.

See also: POSITIVIST THOUGHT IN LATIN AMERICA; TRADITION AND TRADITIONALISM

References and further reading

* Caso, A. (1943) *La existencia como economía, como desinterés, y como caridad* (Existence as Economy, as Disinterest and as Charity), Mexico: Ediciones de la Secretaría de Educación Pública. (A founding work of Mexican anti-positivism that counterposes a moral ontology of aesthetic contemplation and charity to the positivistic celebration of self-interest.)
* Korn, A. (1963) *La libertad creadora* (Creative Liberty), Buenos Aires: Editorial Claridad. (An anti-postivist defence of the creative liberty of the human subject against doctrines of metaphysical necessity.)
* Ramos, S. (1934) *El perfil del hombre y la cultura en México*, Buenos Aires: Espasa-Calpe, 2nd edn, 1951; trans. P.G. Earle, *Profile of Man and Culture*, Austin, TX: University of Texas Press, 1962. (A critique of Mexican social character employing the perspective of Alfred Adler's psychology.)
  Stabb, M.S. (1967) *Latin America in Quest of Identity*, Chapel Hill, NC: University of North Carolina Press. (A general background of the historical conditions for the development of anti-positivism in Latin America.)
* Vasconcelos, J. (1961) *Obras completas* (Complete Works), Mexico: Libreros Mexicanos Unidos. (Comprehensive empiricism constituted by a polarized struggle.)
* Vaz Ferreira, C. (1961) *Estudios filosóficos* (Philosophical Studies), Buenos Aires: Aguilar. (A description of the informal processes of thought that underlie formal logical systematizations.)
  Weinstein, M.A. (1976) *The Polarity of Mexican Thought: Instrumentalism and Finalism*, University Park, PA: Pennsylvania State University Press. (An account of the dimensions of anti-positivist philosophy in Mexico through its successive generations.)
* Zea, L. (1968) *El positivismo en México*, Mexico: Fondo de Cultura Económica; trans. J. Schulte, *Positivism in Mexico*, Austin, TX: University of Texas Press, 1974. (An account of the history of positivism in Mexico using the perspective of sociology of knowledge.)

MICHAEL A. WEINSTEIN

ANTIREALISM

see INTUITIONISTIC LOGIC AND ANTIREALISM; REALISM AND ANTIREALISM; SCIENTIFIC REALISM AND ANTIREALISM

ANTIREALISM IN THE PHILOSOPHY OF MATHEMATICS

Realism in the philosophy of mathematics is the position that takes mathematics at face value. According to realists, mathematics is the science of mathematical objects (numbers, sets, lines and so on); mathematicians, to use the old metaphor, are discoverers, not inventors. Moreover, just as there may be truths about physical reality which we can never know, so too, realists say, there may be truths about mathematical reality which we can never know.

It is this claim in particular which antirealists find unacceptable. Equating what can be known in mathematics with what can be proved, they insist that only what can be proved is true. (Only what can *be proved: different accounts of what this 'can' means, facing*

different difficulties, generate different positions.) This leads antirealists to recoil not only from realism but also from the practice of mathematicians themselves. For the orthodox assumption that every mathematical statement is either true or false would be invalidated, on the antirealist view, by a statement that was neither provable nor disprovable. Not that antirealists themselves can see it in these terms. For if a statement were neither provable nor disprovable, that would itself be an unprovable truth about mathematical reality. Antirealists must learn how to be circumspect even in defence of their own circumspection.

1 Realism and its rivals
2 The antirealist challenge
3 What kind of possibility does antirealism involve?
4 Implications for mathematical practice

1 Realism and its rivals

Consider the following view. Any mathematical statement such as '$7+5=12$' or '$7+5=13$' or 'Every even number greater than 2 is the sum of two primes' is straightforwardly true or false. If mathematical reality is as the statement says it is, then the statement is true. Otherwise, it is false. How the statement connects with mathematical reality is indicated by its grammatical structure. To each singular term there corresponds an object, to each sortal noun a kind of object, to each quantifier a range of objects, and so on. Which grammatical category an expression belongs to depends solely on how it functions. Thus '7', which functions as a singular term, *is* a singular term: it stands for a particular mathematical object. 'Prime', which functions as a sortal noun, *is* a sortal noun: it picks out a particular kind of mathematical object. 'Every even number', which functions as a quantifier, *is* a quantifier: it ranges over a particular domain of mathematical objects. These objects, which exist outside space and time, are mind-independent. How they stand in relation to one another is not determined by how we think they stand in relation to one another. In some cases how they stand in relation to one another is completely unknown. It may even be unknowable.

This is, in its most extreme form, 'realism' (see REALISM IN THE PHILOSOPHY OF MATHEMATICS). It is also known as 'Platonism' (see PLATO §10). But if this is realism, then any number of things might reasonably be meant by 'antirealism'. Each part of this view can be challenged, and has been. Thus there are those who have claimed:

(1) That no mathematical statement is strictly true or false: mathematics consists in the manipulation of meaningless symbols in accordance with certain formal rules.
(2) That this is true of certain auxiliary parts of mathematics: not *all* mathematical statements are strictly true or false (see HILBERT'S PROGRAMME AND FORMALISM).
(3) That all mathematical statements are strictly true or false, but not straightforwardly so: '$7+5=12$', for example, is like 'Hamlet was the prince of Denmark' – a fictional truth that is literally false.
(4) That the apparent grammatical structure of mathematical statements is misleading: '7' is no more a singular term than 'John's sake' in 'She did it for John's sake'.
(5) That the apparent grammatical structure is not misleading, but does not determine in the standard way how mathematical statements connect with mathematical reality: '7' does not stand for a particular object, but rather indicates part of a structure which any objects whatsoever could instantiate.
(6) That there are particular mathematical objects in just the way that the grammatical structure suggests, but they are mind-dependent creations of ours: how they stand in relation to one another is not totally independent of how we think they stand in relation to one another (see INTUITIONISM; CONSTRUCTIVISM IN MATHEMATICS). This allows for the possibility that there are certain mathematical statements, rather like 'Father Christmas is left-handed', whose truth or falsity has never been settled (see CANTOR'S THEOREM; CONTINUUM HYPOTHESIS; EXISTENCE).
(7) Finally, that how things are in mathematical reality, though it is sometimes unknown, is never unknowable. This brings us full circle, for, as we shall see, this last challenge in turn becomes a challenge to the idea that every mathematical statement is true or false.

2 The antirealist challenge

The term 'antirealism' is most frequently reserved for the last of the above challenges, and that is what this entry will focus on. Not that only one view about the nature of mathematical truth is in question. On the contrary, as we shall see, there are radically opposed views which issue in this particular challenge: that is, there are radically opposed reasons for thinking that mathematical truth can never outstrip knowability.

Knowability in a mathematical context can be regarded as provability. The idea of a proof must then be suitably construed. For instance, a self-evident axiom must be allowed to count as a one-line proof of itself: otherwise it would be unprovable, and hence, *ex hypothesi*, unknowable. On the other hand, clearly not every mathematical statement can count as a one-line proof of itself. Let us assume that a satisfactory account of proof can be given. The question now is: can there be unprovable mathematical truths?

One reason for denying that there can be was mentioned in the previous section. If mathematical objects are mind-dependent creations of ours, then there is nothing to them beyond what is invested in the various principles of proof that constitute the creation. The best-known exponent of such a view was L.E.J. Brouwer (1913). He held further that the raw material for the creation is provided by something essentially private and incommunicable: our experience of time. This is the position known as 'intuitionism'.

It is a consequence of intuitionism that the meaning of a mathematical statement is itself something essentially private and incommunicable. A diametrically opposed outlook is canvassed in the writings of Michael Dummett. According to this outlook, the meaning of a mathematical statement is something essentially public and communicable. So there can be nothing more to that meaning, ultimately, than how the statement and its constituents are used in actual mathematical practice: nothing else of potential relevance can be communicated. But this too leads to a denial of the possibility of unprovable mathematical truths. For if a mathematical statement were unprovably true, then its meaning would be something that went beyond how the statement and its constituents were used, or indeed could be used.

This second brand of antirealism, which I shall refer to as 'Dummettian' antirealism (though Dummett has never actually endorsed it; see Dummett 1973; DUMMETT, M.A.E. §3), depends on broadly Wittgensteinian considerations about the nature of meaning (see WITTGENSTEIN, L. §12). Such considerations could just as well be applied in a non-mathematical context. Nevertheless, there are reasons for thinking that they are peculiarly suited to mathematics. For whether or not mathematical objects are mind-dependent creations of ours, there is surely something in the idea that they are nothing apart from the techniques and proof-procedures of mathematical practice. They lack the 'solidity' of physical objects. So even if there is some prospect that we can capture such 'solidity' in our use of language, and thereby express inaccessible truths about physical objects, there is no prospect that we can do anything similar in the case of mathematical objects.

A third brand of antirealism takes off from the observation that mathematics makes essential use of infinite domains. On one very attractive view, an infinite domain is unlike a finite domain in that its members cannot be given 'all at once'. Somewhat less metaphorically, they cannot all have a separate involvement in any one state of affairs, or make a separate contribution to any one truth. For a statement about them all to be true, there has to be a single principle which determines its truth. That is, there has to be a proof.

All these brands of antirealism have a revisionary impact on standard mathematical practice. Consider a statement that has never been proved or disproved. At the time of writing, Goldbach's conjecture – that every even number greater than 2 is the sum of two primes – is an example. It is part of standard mathematical practice to assume that the statement is either true or false. (This is an application of the law of the excluded middle.) Antirealists cannot share this assumption. To make the assumption is to register indifference about whether the statement can be proved or disproved. It is to allow that the statement may be true without proof, a kind of 'infinite coincidence'. This is precisely what antirealists cannot allow.

3 What kind of possibility does antirealism involve?

The antirealist view is that only what can be proved is true. A much more radical view (not without adherents) is that only what *has been* proved is true. By holding back from this more radical view, antirealists inevitably draw attention to the 'can'. But what sense of 'can' is intended? Certainly, it is what can be proved *by us* that counts, and not, for example, by an infinite being existing outside space and time. But that does not answer the question.

Basically, antirealists need to decide whether they mean 'can in principle' or 'can in practice'. Not that a simple one-or-other verdict will do. Both 'can in principle' and 'can in practice' require further elucidation. (How and where do scientific limitations figure? Or technological limitations? Or medical limitations?) But the broad distinction remains. And it is clear that if antirealists mean 'can in practice', then the revisionary impact on standard mathematics is going to be enormous. There are some numbers which are so big that we cannot, in practice, tell whether or not they are prime. So given such a number, we shall not be entitled to assume that the number is either prime or not. More generally, since mathematics cannot be extended to the unmanageably big, we shall not be entitled to assume that mathematical reality is infinite.

The resultant version of antirealism is known as 'strict finitism'. Many antirealists think that strict finitism is incoherent. Call such antirealists 'moderates'. For them, the 'can' must mean 'can in principle'. But they need to explain why, given that their arguments would break down if the 'can' did not mean that, the arguments are not to be distrusted anyway. Dummettian moderates in particular are likely to experience some difficulty here. Others, whose very starting point is that mathematical reality is infinite, experience no difficulty at all.

A quite different problem for moderate antirealists is to explain why their own version of antirealism is not just a terminological variant of realism. For cannot any statement be proved or disproved *in principle*? Reconsider Goldbach's conjecture. What is wrong with the following recipe for either proving it or disproving it? 'Check successive even numbers greater than 2. In each case, ascertain whether or not it is the sum of two primes. Keep going until either every such number has been checked or a counterexample to the conjecture has been found.' It is of no avail to reply simply that this process might never end. Something needs to be said to forestall the objection that if we spend half a minute checking 4, a quarter of a minute checking 6, an eighth of a minute checking 8, and so on, then the process will end in a minute – at most. Of course, we cannot in practice do this. But that is beside the point.

It is by no means clear that moderate antirealists have nothing to say here. But they may have nothing to say which is not question-begging. For instance, they may be forced to deploy a conception of what is possible in principle which itself incorporates an antirealist understanding of what it is to do infinitely many different things. If so, that is not an objection to moderate antirealism. But it does raise the spectre of realists and moderate antirealists operating with two quite different, incommensurable, individually coherent conceptions of what is possible in principle, together with two correspondingly different conceptions of how to do mathematics. Ultimately, perhaps, the realist is prepared to make certain assumptions in mathematics which the moderate antirealist is not prepared to make, and, to the extent that they are incapable of finding any independent leverage to settle their differences, they are talking past each other.

4 Implications for mathematical practice

The sheer fact that realists are willing to endorse standard mathematical practice might be thought to count in their favour. For, arguably, reversing Marx's dictum, it is not the business of philosophers of mathematics to *change* mathematics, only to interpret it. (Wittgenstein famously wrote that 'philosophy leaves mathematics as it is'.) Here, as before, there is a particular difficulty for Dummettian antirealists. For they are only too keen to cast actual mathematical practice in the role of a datum. Dummett's own reaction to this difficulty is to argue that, even if actual mathematical practice is a datum, it is not an indissoluble datum: nothing in the view he canvasses precludes criticizing some parts of that practice for failing to harmonize with other parts.

Suppose there *is* room for a non-conservative philosophy of mathematics. Antirealists face a further difficulty. They have no satisfactory answer to the question 'When exactly does standard mathematical practice lead us astray?'. They cannot answer, 'Whenever a statement is neither provable nor disprovable'. For if a statement were neither provable nor disprovable, that would itself be an unprovable truth about mathematical reality. (To prove that a statement was not provable would already be to disprove it.) Likewise, if, say, there were no proof of Goldbach's conjecture, nor, as it happened, a counterexample, that would itself be an 'infinite coincidence' of the very kind that antirealists disavow. Antirealists have no option, then, but to adopt a kind of stoic silence. Whenever others make assumptions in mathematics which they are not themselves prepared to make, they must withhold assent, but they have no satisfactory way of saying what is holding them back. As far as anything they can say is concerned, their restraint may be a result, not of nonconformity, but of sheer reticence.

Antirealism remains of the utmost importance, despite this very real difficulty. Indeed, part of its importance may be in drawing the difficulty to our attention. For if antirealists are right, then it may be that their knowledge of correct mathematical practice is a prime example of a fundamental and neglected philosophical category: knowledge that is essentially ineffable.

See also: LOGICAL AND MATHEMATICAL TERMS, GLOSSARY OF

References and further reading

Benacerraf, P. and Putnam, H. (eds) (1964) Introduction to *Philosophy of Mathematics: Selected Readings*, Cambridge: Cambridge University Press, 2nd edn, 1983, 1–37. (Useful survey of the basic issues in the philosophy of mathematics, touching helpfully on both realism and antirealism.)

Bernays, P. (1935) 'Sur le Platonisme dans les mathématiques', *L'enseignement mathématique*, 1st series, 34: 52–69; trans. C.D. Parsons, 'On Platonism in Mathematics', in P. Benacerraf and H. Putnam (eds) *Philosophy of Mathematics: Selected Readings*, Cambridge: Cambridge University Press, 2nd edn, 1983, 258–71. (Classic survey of Platonism/realism and standard antirealist reactions.)

* Brouwer, L.E.J. (1912) *Intuitionisme et Formalisme*,

Groningen: Noordhoff; trans. A. Dresden, 'Intuitionism and Formalism', *Bulletin of the American Mathematical Society* 20: 81–96, 1913; repr. in P. Benacerraf and H. Putnam (eds) *Philosophy of Mathematics: Selected Readings*, Cambridge: Cambridge University Press, 2nd edn, 1983, 77–89. (Classic statement of some of the fundamental tenets of intuitionism.)

* Dummett, M.A.E. (1973) 'The Philosophical Basis of Intuitionist Logic', in H.E. Rose and J.C. Shepherdson (eds) *Proceedings of the Logic Colloquium, Bristol, July 1973*, Amsterdam: North Holland, 1975, 5–40; repr. in *Truth and Other Enigmas*, London: Duckworth, 1978, 215–47; and in P. Benacerraf and H. Putnam (eds) *Philosophy of Mathematics: Selected Readings*, Cambridge: Cambridge University Press, 2nd edn, 1983, 97–129. (Expounds the argument sketched in §2 for 'Dummettian' antirealism.)

—— (1977) *Elements of Intuitionism*, Oxford: Clarendon Press, 1990. (A very thorough account of intuitionistic revisions to mathematics, together with a full discussion of antirealist reasons for adopting them.)

George, A. (1993) 'How Not to Refute Realism', *Journal of Philosophy* 90 (2): 53–72. (Identifies question begging in certain antirealist arguments, and lends support to the suggestion of §3 that realism and antirealism may be two equally acceptable but incommensurable alternatives.)

Lear, J. (1977) 'Sets and Semantics', *Journal of Philosophy* 74 (2): 86–102. (Argues that even realists have reasons for adopting intuitionistic revisions to mathematics.)

McDowell, J. (1989) 'Mathematical Platonism and Dummettian Anti-Realism', *Dialectica* 43 (1/2): 173–92. (Endorses the suggestion of §2 that the basic considerations in favour of 'Dummettian' antirealism apply only in a mathematical context, where the objects of investigation lack 'solidity'.)

Prawitz, D. (1977) 'Meaning and Proofs: On the Conflict Between Classical and Intuitionistic Logic', *Theoria* 43 (1): 2–40. (Good general account of the argument expounded in Dummett (1973) and sketched in §2).

Putnam, H. (1980) 'Models and Reality', *Journal of Symbolic Logic* 45 (3): 464–82; repr. in P. Benacerraf and H. Putnam (eds) *Philosophy of Mathematics: Selected Readings*, Cambridge: Cambridge University Press, 2nd edn, 1983, 421–44. (Uses the Löwenheim–Skolem theorem to attack extreme realism.)

Rotman, B. (1993) *Ad Infinitum… The Ghost in Turing's Machine*, Stanford, CA: Stanford University Press. (Defends a version of strict finitism.)

Wittgenstein, L.J.J. (1956) *Remarks on the Foundations of Mathematics*, ed. G.H. von Wright, R. Rhees and G.E.M. Anscombe, trans. G.E.M. Anscombe, Oxford: Blackwell, 2nd edn, 1967; 3rd edn, 1978. (*Locus classicus* of Wittgenstein's later philosophy of mathematics, with its own distinctive brand of antirealism.)

Wright, C. (1980) *Wittgenstein on the Foundations of Mathematics*, London: Duckworth. (Very thorough discussion of antirealism in Wittgenstein's later philosophy of mathematics.)

—— (1982) 'Strict Finitism', *Synthese* 51: 203–82; repr. in *Realism, Meaning and Truth*, Oxford: Blackwell, 1986; and in A.W. Moore (ed.) *Infinity*, Aldershot: Dartmouth, 1993, 251–330. (Sympathetic discussion of strict finitism and its revisionary impact on mathematics.)

A.W. MOORE

ANTI-SEMITISM

Anti-Semitism is a form of racism which sees Jews as a dangerous and despicable group in society. It has solid philosophical sources in the work of German Idealism which emphasized the distinctiveness of Judaism and how it has been superseded by Christianity. Both Kant and Hegel made a sharp distinction between Judaism and what they regarded as more rational religions, and they questioned the capability of the Jewish people for playing an integral role in the state. Sartre used the notion of anti-Semitism to show how a sense of self-identity is created by the attitudes of others towards the individual and the group. That is, what makes Jews Jews is the fact that there is anti-Semitism, and there is nothing that Jews can do about anti-Semitism. Anti-Semitism is a problem for the anti-Semites themselves; anti-Semitism, by Sartre's account, is in fact an attempted solution to the difficulties of taking free and authentic decisions. Anti-Semitism has played an important role in Jews' self-definition, in attitudes to the State of Israel and to the religion of Judaism itself.

1   Kant
2   Hegel
3   Sartre
4   **Anti-Semitism as a philosophical notion**
5   **Anti-Semitism and Jewish self-understanding**

1   Kant

KANT presents generally critical views of Judaism. He argues that Judaism is primarily a religion of statutes, a system of positive law, and that it is also largely based on revelation. These characteristics lead him to deny its moral character, since the will of a supreme authority cannot be properly considered a source of morality. In Kantian philosophy, the essence of morality is the ability of subjects to place themselves under entirely general and rational laws, so a faith which is limited to a particular people and which is based on a particular form of revelation, does not fit his notion of morality. Kant even criticizes the laws themselves, regarding them as crude imperatives which demand a certain standard of conduct but do not insist on appropriate attitudes. This leads Kant even to deny that Judaism is a stage of religious development in the direction of Christianity, since Judaism has, by his account, so little genuinely religious content. Judaism makes worship of God primary and virtue subsidiary, and so is really just a form of belief limited to a particular group of people.

The emphasis Kant finds in Judaism on obedience to God leads it, he argues, to a form of legalism which he regards as far from a rational faith. Revelation and messianism are problematic from a rational point of view, since they relate to a particular relationship with a particular group of people, and can hardly be seen in universal terms (see REVELATION). Also, the laws of the religion seem to be both pedantic and rigid, based more on the necessity to achieve isolation rather than on any quest to establish general forms of behaviour applicable to any human being. The empty legalism of Judaism plays no part in improving the human moral disposition, KANT argues, and so cannot be considered as a genuine expression of rational religion.

2 Hegel

Hegel's views on religions and their interrelationships are far more developed than those of Kant, but they are also quite negative with respect to Judaism (see HEGEL, G.W.F.). The trouble with Judaism, says Hegel, is that it is a religion that emphasizes fear, a religion that stresses the object. Hegel has a view of the development of history as a movement of self-consciousness through different historical and religious epochs. In this movement, the ideal is to be approached through an ever-increasing perfection of that self-consciousness. Judaism has an important, but essentially limited, role on the route to perfection. Judaism regards religious law as an independent entity, embodying the self-alienation of human society. This means that Judaism obeys a legal system without the capacity to master society itself. This domination of life by law is total in Judaism, Hegel asserts, and the religion itself is a compulsory faith, with a notion of God that is represented as a command and not as a truth. There is no scope for the notion of individual rights, but a type of divine despotism that bases itself on the family as the ultimate social unit.

Judaism sees the important relationship with God as essentially external, where God is the subject and his creatures the object. This results in alienation from the universe, the effect of which on individual Jews is that they do not regard their lives as belonging properly to them. They instead belong to God; Jews, as a result, are entirely passive in their attitudes to the creator. This is hardly surprising, Hegel reasons, since the nature of Judaism is to deny the possibility of raising human existence to the realm of spirit; that is, Judaism makes such a huge distinction between the divine and the finite that it cannot conceive of transcending that gap. God is regarded as spirit, but to the extent that he entirely transcends the world, which makes it impossible for humanity to be reconciled with God. Judaism is a constant struggle against idolatry. This struggle is represented by Abraham's leaving his family in Ur to become a wanderer. Jews cannot see the things in the world as embodying the divine. As a result, the ordinary world is literally emptied of the divine. Unlike both Christianity and the religion of classical Greece, Judaism does not offer a dialectical relationship with what is invisible and infinite. Judaism can only serve as an antithesis in the progress of the self-realization of the spirit. That is, it is a stage along the path of increasing self-consciousness and serves to reveal how unsatisfactory a particular way of understanding our links with the divine are. Judaism, concludes Hegel, is a way of thinking which is primitive and needs to be superseded.

3 Sartre

By far the most interesting and original use of anti-Semitism as a philosophical vehicle was created by the existentialist Jean-Paul SARTRE. He reverses the traditional way of understanding racism, which was to look at the particular group selected as a target of hatred and to ask what it was about it which made that targeting feasible. Sartre argues, by contrast, that we need to wonder what it is that racism provides for the racist. Furthermore we also should examine the role of racism in creating the despised group itself. The racist, according to Sartre, chooses hatred as a way of avoiding confronting problems rationally. Racism is an attempted escape from the need to think for oneself and to make free decisions. It is essentially a way of trying to escape from the human condition. In his accounts of anti-Semitism, Sartre points out how natural it is for particular people to adopt this way of thinking, since it saves them from the necessity of distinguishing themselves from their social role.

Sartre sees anti-Semitism as a failure of rationality; anti-Semites fail to use rationality to understand that their lowly role in life may be due to their lack of talent, or to an unjust social system. The Jew is the person whom the anti-Semite thinks is a Jew, incorrectly or otherwise. This can result in Jews trying to deny their Jewishness in order to avoid persecution. Sartre criticizes this strategy by Jews, arguing that it is as inauthentic an attitude as the adoption of anti-Semitism itself. The important point is that racism is primarily a problem for the racists. There is nothing the despised group can do to change that attitude.

4 Anti-Semitism as a philosophical notion

It is wrong to see anti-Semitism as a specifically Christian movement, or as having anything particularly to do with Germany. From the very first times that Jews lived among Gentiles, in Greece and the Roman Empire, prejudice against them was often commonplace. The construction of philosophical theories to justify this prejudice did take place for the first time within Christianity. It stems from early Christian polemics against the rival faith and from claims as to the original responsibility of Jews for the crucifixion of Jesus. Embedded in a variety of doctrinal and institutional structures, anti-Semitism was intensified by those structures themselves; for example, by the mercantile the role that Jews were compelled to play in the medieval society.

The theories that bolstered Christian anti-Jewish and anti-Judaic attitudes were followed up in the nineteenth and twentieth centuries by theories that sought to place racism on a scientific footing, arguing that racial differences define human possibilities (see RACE, THEORIES OF). There were also theories that tried to establish the existence of a Jewish conspiracy against the Gentile world. Such ideas, although largely bereft of evidentiary support, form the theoretical underpinnings of modern anti-Semitism.

It would be quite mistaken to draw a direct linkage between the views of Kant and Hegel on Judaism and the development of the systematic anti-Semitism which has played such an important role in Europe in the last two centuries. For one thing, both Kant and Hegel had many Jewish followers. Those followers saw the ideas of German Idealism as entirely compatible with the principles of Judaism (see GERMAN IDEALISM). Hermann COHEN, for example, was a fervent Kantian and Emil FACKENHEIM a Hegel enthusiast. On the other hand, the radical distinction which Kant and Hegel both made between Judaism and other systems of religion, which they took to be more rational, was echoed by many lesser thinkers to imply the radical inferiority of the Jewish people or its culture and religion. The idea that Judaism is a morally limited and outmoded religion fosters the notion that Jews are legalistic and are wedded to an archaic way of life and thought, incapable, for that reason of being proper constituents of civil society. Indeed, these modern versions of ancient canards are used, ultimately, in behalf of the claim that Jews are the enemies of society. Such ideas reached an extreme in the thinking that gave rise to the Holocaust (see HOLOCAUST, THE).

Some thinkers such as Karl POPPER see Hegel as being vastly influential in the development of totalitarian forms of thought, and it is true that Hegel's views on Jews and Judaism do appear congruent with some aspects of later German anti-Semitism. But we need to make a distinction between theories which regard Jews as playing a distinctive or even outmoded role in society, as with Kant and Hegel, and theories which explicitly justify treating Jews in discriminatory or even murderous ways. It may be that there is a psychological, political or rhetorical link between the two types of theories, but there is need not be a logical link between the two types of theories, but there is certainly not a logical link between them.

5 Anti-Semitism and Jewish self-understanding

The significance of anti-Semitism for Jewish self-understanding has been considerable. It played an important part in the construction of theories of Zionism, since at least one rationale for a Jewish state is the difficulty that Jews face as a minority in states dominated by Gentiles (see ZIONISM). Had anti-Semitism not been so prevalent, the motivation for statehood would not have been so powerful. Also, there is a tendency for some Jews to see themselves as defined through anti-Semitism, as Sartre pointed out, so that they are either victims or defiant resisters of persecution. Some critics of this form of self-definition have argued that it perverts the nature of Judaism. Judaism, they argue, is a religion based on belief in God and the covenant (Goldberg 1995). Its message should not be deflected persistent (if necessary) attention to the need constantly to repel the hostility of actual and potential persecutors. Many Jews find the most potent source of their emotional relationship to Judaism to be their commitment to the State of Israel. But this attachment itself reflects in part the phenomenon of anti-Semitism. For the enthusiasm is directed to the survival of the State and of the Jewish people in the face of threats to the survival of both.

See also: FASCISM; HOLOCAUST, THE; JEWISH PHILOSOPHY, CONTEMPORARY; RACE, THEORIES OF

References and further reading

* Goldberg, M. (1995) *Why Should Jews Survive? Looking Past the Holocaust Toward a Jewish Future*, New York: Oxford University Press. (A sustained critique of Jewish self-definition through the Holocaust and anti-Semitism.)
Hegel, G. (1807) *Phänomenologie des Geistes* (The Phenomenology of Mind), trans. J. Baillie, London: Allen & Unwin, 1931. (Hegel's mature views on the development of religions as spirit tries to understand itself as spirit.)
Kant, I. (1783) *Die Religion innerhalb der Grenzen der blossen Vernunft* (Religion Within the Limits of Reason Alone), trans. T. Greene and H. Hudson, New York: Harper & Row, 1960. (Kant's mature work in which he discusses religious institutions and compares faiths.)
Kaufmann, W. (1960) 'The Hegel Myth and its Method', in W. Kaufmann, *From Shakespeare to Existentialism*, New York: Anchor, 95–128. (A powerful critique of Popper's attack on Hegel as a source for Naziism.)
Popper, K. (1945) *The Open Society and its Enemies*, London: Routledge & Kegan Paul. (Analysis of thinkers whom Popper argues are the intellectual founders of racism and totalitarianism.)
Rose, P. (1990) *Revolutionary Anti-Semitism in Germany from Kant to Wagner*, Princeton, NJ: Princeton University Press. (Interesting argument that most German Idealists were anti-Semitic, with useful references to personal quotations about their attitudes to the Jews.)
Rotenstreich, N. (1963) *The Recurring Pattern: Studies in Anti-Judaism in Modern Thought*, London: Weidenfeld & Nicolson. (Interesting discussion of Kant, Hegel and Toynbee and their uniformly negative views on Judaism.)
Sartre, J-P. (1946) *Réflexions sur la question juive* (Reflections on the Jewish Question), trans. E. de Mauny, *Portrait of an Anti-Semite*, London: Secker & Warburg, 1948. (The best formulation of Sartre's approach to the significance of anti-Semitism.)

OLIVER LEAMAN
CLIVE NYMAN

ANTISTHENES (*c*.445–*c*.365 BC)

Antisthenes was one of the most devoted followers of Socrates. As a young man he was heavily influenced by the display speeches of Gorgias the rhetorician and the interpretation of Homer practised by the Sophists. He himself wrote much in the same vein, although almost all has been lost.

Antisthenes' influence can be recognized most in the writer Xenophon. Although it is likely that he succeeded in annoying Plato and Isocrates, his influence on Cynicism has been greatly exaggerated.

Little survives of his moral philosophy, but what there is is Socratic in conception, and indeed Socrates' own courage and tenacity are its avowed inspiration. Antisthenes focuses on virtue, conceived as inner strength, a fortress founded on wisdom and its unassailable reasonings. Virtue is acquired and maintained by 'exertions', a term deliberately recalling the labours of Heracles: these consist of the struggle to overcome the difficulties of, for example, poverty or unpopularity, by understanding how they can be viewed as good things – provided the riches of the soul are intact. Pleasure and sex are accordingly seen as threats to virtue's integrity. Antisthenes enjoins us to redraw our moral categories: the good and just are our true friends and kin.

In theory of language Antisthenes defended the paradox that contradiction is impossible, deriving his argument from the idea that there can be no successful reference to anything except by its own 'account', revealing what it is.

1 Life and work
2 Antisthenes and the Cynics
3 Ethics
4 Language and *logos*

1 Life and work

Of all Socrates' followers none was perceived as closer to him than the Athenian Antisthenes (Xenophon, *Memorabilia* III 11.17). His origins were apparently humble, and his circumstances not affluent. Calculation of his dates depends on scanty and doubtful evidence. What is clear is that Antisthenes successively inhabited the world of the fifth-century SOPHISTS familiar from Plato's early dialogues and the no-less-competitive intellectual scene of the early fourth century, where Socrates' philosophical heirs jostled among themselves as well as with Sophists and rhetoricians.

Xenophon's Socrates suggests that it was in fact

Antisthenes who introduced Prodicus and Hippias to their patron Callias (*Symposium* 4.62). A report by Diogenes Laertius makes him a pupil initially of Gorgias the rhetorician. Much of Antisthenes' literary output reflects his immersion in this milieu: 'He brings the rhetorical style into his dialogues, especially Truth and Exhortations' (Diogenes Laertius, VI 1). Like the Sophists he wrote numerous works on Homeric interpretation. How early in life he became attracted to Socrates is not clear: Diogenes Laertius suggests middle age; Xenophon's *Symposium* (dramatic date 421 BC) may imply sooner. It is uncertain therefore whether Antisthenes' Sophistic writings belong to a period of his life separate from those recommending Socratic ethics. The Socratic dialogues he is credited with must be assumed to postdate Socrates' death; and his thesis that a person who has attained discretion would do better not to study literature is hard to square with an approach to truth through study of the poets.

The only items surviving intact from a huge body of work are a complementary pair of speeches, quite possibly authentic, entitled *Ajax* and *Odysseus*, in which the two heroes contend for the arms of Achilles. Also preserved is a fragment of a dialogue debating the meaning of Homer's description of Odysseus as a man of 'many ways' (fr. 51), in a manner reminiscent of Plato's *Hippias Minor*. A certain amount can be gleaned from Xenophon's *Symposium* and from the list of book titles found in Diogenes Laertius, (VI 15–18). For further information about Antisthenes' thought we are dependent on doxographical summaries (notably Diogenes Laertius, VI 10–11), occasional quotations or mentions of his views, and – for what they are worth – anecdotes: for example, his notorious anti-Platonic remark 'I see a horse, but I do not see horseness' (fr. 50). These ancient reports are dominated by preoccupation with his Socratic conception of ethics, but Aristotle in particular has some tantalizing references to logical doctrines (see §4).

Xenophon sketches a playful portrait of Antisthenes in his *Symposium*. In contrast with the urbane Socrates he is presented as an abrupt, sarcastic and pedantic interlocutor. But as the work unfolds his fierce attachment to Socrates becomes ever more apparent. This is not simply a matter of his practising a form of Socratic *elenchos* (cross-examination). Antisthenes develops in Socratic style the doctrine that true riches are found in the storehouse of the soul. And before the end he shows and avows his love for Socrates.

2 Antisthenes and the Cynics

An ancient tradition makes Antisthenes the originator of the Cynic philosophy and teacher of DIOGENES OF SINOPE. It shapes not only the account of Antisthenes but the whole presentation of Cynicism and Stoicism in Diogenes Laertius (see especially VI 2, 15, 21, 103–5), and it is assumed in writers of the imperial period like Epictetus and Dio Chrysostom. Many modern discussions of Antisthenes accept the tradition, or suppose him a principal influence on Diogenes. However, the verdict of the best critical scholarship (for example, Dudley) is that the story is a fabrication.

Although Diogenes' chronology is a good deal more obscure than that of Antisthenes', it is at least doubtful whether the two *could* have met. None of the fragments of early Cynic writers mentions Antisthenes. The distinctive Cynic garb of cloak doubled up, staff and wallet is ascribed to him only in late sources. If Diogenes had a precedent for adopting it, contemporary Pythagoreans like Diodorus of Aspendos seem likelier models. Although Diogenes earned himself the nickname 'dog' – and 'Cynic' means 'Dog-philosopher' – the attempt to derive the expression from the Cynosarges gymnasium where Antisthenes is alleged to have taught seems a desperate measure.

The idea that Diogenes was in some sense Antisthenes' 'successor' could build on Antisthenes' ethics of frugality and inner resilience. What explains the promotion of that idea in the ancient sources is the need of later philosophy, and more particularly Stoicism, to rewrite its own history. The Stoics could not easily deny the impact of Cynicism on their founder Zeno. Opponents represented this as disreputable. Construction of a pedigree for Stoicism through Cynicism via Antisthenes and back to Socrates was to prove an effective way of recovering the moral high ground for Stoics.

3 Ethics

The principal account of Antisthenes' ethical teaching in Diogenes Laertius reflects the preoccupations of Stoicism outlined in §2, certainly in its emphases (VI 10–13, 104–5). Fortunately enough specific items of information are recorded in his pages and elsewhere for a reader to get a sense of Antisthenes' key ideas. The figures of Heracles and Cyrus of Persia, each the subject of more than one of Antisthenes' writings, were evidently presented as exemplars of the proper acquisition of virtue. To achieve it 'nothing was needed but the strength of a Socrates' (VI 11). And Antisthenes famously taught that exertion or *ponos* (as in the 'labours' of Heracles) is a good (VI 2). Deeds, not words, are what matter (VI 11; fr. 86).

This was not conceived as an anti-intellectualist position: 'Get understanding – or a noose', said

Antisthenes (fr. 67). The exertions of the good are pictured as a campaign waged from a stronghold of wisdom (*phronēsis*), which has to be constructed by unassailable reasonings. The weapon no one can rob the good of is virtue, and their allies are those who are just as well as brave. The most indispensable item of knowledge Cyrus of Persia acquires is to *un*learn what is evil (fr. 21). Few specific examples of appropriate exertions survive. A bad reputation is said to be good and 'equal to exertion' (Diogenes Laertius, VI 11).

The sayings ascribed to Antisthenes indicate a strong tendency (congenial to Stoicism) to redraw concepts like kinship and friendship in terms of moral notions such as justice and goodness, or to prefer the candour of an enemy to the blandishments of flatterers. Similarly, the law of virtue displaces the established laws of the city as the imperative the wise person will obey. Antisthenes represents wisdom as what enables people to make everything work for them, so that nothing is any longer 'alien'. This philosophy of life is interpreted in terms of the Stoic doctrine that virtue is self-sufficient in Diogenes Laertius' doxography (VI 11).

Antisthenes' views on pleasure attracted quotation by later authors. Most popular was: 'I would rather be mad than feel pleasure' (Diogenes Laertius, VI 3; fr. 108). Other texts reveal a more nuanced position: pleasure is a good if it does not require subsequent repentance (fr. 110); 'there is no pleasure in a symposium without concord or in riches without virtue' (fr. 93); 'we should prefer the pleasure after, not before, exertions' (fr. 113). The power of sex provoked the comment: '*I would shoot down Aphrodite if I could apprehend her, because she has corrupted many of our fine and good women*' (fr. 109). But his most notorious remark on the subject sounds thoroughly Cynic: one should sleep with 'those women who will be grateful' (VI 3), interpreted by Xenophon (*Symposium* 4.38) as recommending as entirely sufficient immediate satisfaction of physical desire with women who have nobody else to want them. When the doxography in Diogenes Laertius reports that for the sake of having children the wise man will marry, 'sleeping with the women whose nature is best suited' (VI 11), the plural gives cause for suspicion that Antisthenes' amoral advice has been bowdlerized in the interests of moral propriety.

Scholars have harboured hopes of recovering from Xenophon more substantial tracts of Antisthenian moral argument than these brief maxims and summaries. A long speech on the sufficiency of a frugal life provided we possess riches in the soul is put in his mouth in the *Symposium* (4.34–44). This is very likely a free reworking of genuine Antisthenian ideas. But other attempts to identify specific Antisthenian material in the *Memorabilia*, even if it derives inspiration from his view of Socrates and of philosophy, have gone unproven.

4 Language and *logos*

Several texts credit Antisthenes with advancing the claim that contradiction is an impossibility (frs 47–9). One story makes controversy with Plato about the claim the occasion for Antisthenes' composition of his dialogue *Satho* (Diogenes Laertius, III 25, VI 16): the title was intended as a satirical play on the name 'Plato' (fr. 37) – it means 'prick'.

The argument that no one can contradict anyone else carries resonances of the Sophists. For PROTAGORAS(§3) it was a consequence of the relativity of truth. Plato has the Sophist Dionysodorus derive it from the premise that the *logos* or account of each thing must say that thing as it is. So if I succeed in saying the *logos* of some particular thing, you cannot be referring to that same thing at all if you attempt to contradict. According to Aristotle Antisthenes followed Dionysodorus' line of reasoning: 'nothing could be said except by its own (Greek *oikeios*) *logos*, one to one – from which it followed that contradiction is impossible, and one might almost say falsehood in general' (*Metaphysics* 1024b32–4; fr. 49).

It is tempting to connect Antisthenes' premise about 'its own *logos*' with Diogenes Laertius' information that 'he was the first to define *logos*, saying: "*logos* is what reveals the *what it is or was*"' (VI 3). Scholars have disputed whether *logos* here should be taken as 'statement' or 'definition'. Statement has been thought to be too weak a notion to capture something that reveals the *what it is or was*. But if the connection just proposed is correct, any statement that succeeds in being about some particular thing will be a true account of that thing as it is and as nothing else is, and such a statement will therefore satisfy the terms of Antisthenes' definition (or statement). His position on *logos* resembles the view of names ascribed to CRATYLUS in Plato's *Cratylus*. Similarities with the 'dream' theory of names in Plato's *Theaetetus*, which actually speaks of *oikeios logos* (202a), have also been canvassed in the past, but not much illumination either of the dialogue or of Antisthenes' views has been achieved by the comparison.

Despite affinities between this Antisthenian material and positions argued by Sophists and others in Plato's dialogues, it may well be that Antisthenes conceived of himself as explicating the philosophy of Socrates in logic as he did for ethics. Epictetus attributes to Antisthenes the dictum: 'The starting-point for education is the examination of *onomata* (words or names)' (*Discourses*, I 17.12) and follows it with a very similar remark ascribed to Xenophon's Socrates. Since Socrates was constantly asking the question: 'What is *X*?', it would be natural for Antisthenes to want to clarify what kind of answer would in principle meet the inquiry. There is evidence that he specifically attacked Plato's assumption that what Socrates wanted was a *definition*. Aristotle, discussing the requirements of a good definition, says at one point:

> There is a certain timeliness in the difficulty raised by the Antisthenians and similarly uneducated persons, namely, that it is impossible to define what a thing is (because, it is claimed, a definition is a long *logos*), whereas it can be explained what sort of thing it is, for example it can be explained that silver is like tin, but not what silver is.
>
> (Metaphysics 1043b23–8)

(A 'long *logos*' refers to an evasive rigmarole told, for example, by a slave to conceal the truth.) It is obviously difficult to reconcile Antisthenes' doctrine of *logos* with the proposal that the most an attempt at saying what something is can achieve is explanation of what it is like. Perhaps Antisthenes was arguing *ad hominem*: given Plato's wrong assumption that one can reveal the nature of things in terms not special to such things but common to other things, a comparison is the best one can do – brief and to the point, if not a proper *logos*.

Some have concluded that the only statement that could qualify as a *logos* under Antisthenian rules would be a tautology. It is hard to believe this was his intention, not least because of evidence of exploitation of the idea of *oikeios logos* in his rhetorical theory (fr. 51). But further progress in interpretation is crippled by the complete absence in our sources of any explicit examples of an Antisthenian *logos*, except for his *logos* of *logos* itself.

See also: CYNICS; SOCRATIC DIALOGUES; SOCRATIC SCHOOLS

References and further reading

* Antisthenes (*c.* 445–*c.* 365 AD) Fragments, ed. F. Decleva Caizzi, *Antisthenis Fragmenta*, Varese and Milano: Istituto Editoriale Cisalpino, 1966. (A pocket-sized edition, with good brief notes and bibliography; no translations are supplied. Fragments are cited in this entry according to this edition.)
* Aristotle (*c.* mid 4th century) *Metaphysics*, ed. H. Tredenrick, Loeb Classical Library, Cambridge, MA: Harvard University Press and London: Heinemann, 1933–5, 2 vols; trans. in J. Barnes (ed.), *The Complete Works of Aristotle*, Princeton, NJ: Princeton University Press, 1984.(Tredenrick contains Greek text and English translation. Passages in Books VI and VII constitute the principal evidence for Antisthenes' logic.)
* Diogenes Laertius (early 3rd century AD) *Lives of the Eminent Philosophers*, trans. R.D. Hicks, Loeb Classical Library, Cambridge, MA: Harvard University Press and London: Heinemann, 1925, 2 vols. (Book VI, sections 1–19 contain his life of Antisthenes.)
* Dudley, D.R. (1937) *A History of Cynicism*, London: Methuen. (Chapter 1 remains an excellent introduction to the problem of Antisthenes' relationship to Cynicism.)
* Epictetus (late 1st– early 2nd century AD) *Discourses*, trans. W.A. Oldfather, Loeb Classical Library, Cambridge, MA: Harvard University Press and London: Heinemann, 1925–1928. (Greek text and English translation: mentions Antisthenes occasionally.)

Giannantoni, G. (1990) *Socratis et Socraticorum Reliquiae* (Surviving Fragments of Socrates and the Socratics), Naples: Bibliopolis, 4 vols. (Volume 2 section VA contains fragments and other evidence about Antisthenes, without translation; volume 3 has a full bibliography and indexes; volume 4 notes 21–40 (195–411) contains a magisterial scholarly review of all major and most minor questions of fact and interpretation relating to Antisthenes.)

Guthrie, W.K.C. (1969) *A History of Greek Philosophy*, vol. 3, Cambridge: Cambridge University Press. (Pages 209–16 and 304–11 contain the best account of Antisthenes in English, judicious and attractively written, with much useful comment on bibliography.)

* Xenophon (*c.* 370s BC and *c.* 385 BC) *Symposium*, trans. O.J. Todd, Loeb Classical Library, Cambridge, MA: Harvard University Press and London: Heinemann, 1923. (Contains a convincing portrait of Antisthenes.)
* —— (*c.* 360s BC) *Memorabilia*, trans. E.C. Marchant, Loeb Classical Library, Cambridge, MA: Harvard University Press and London: Heinemann, 1923. (Antisthenes appears in *Memorabilia*, whose presentation of Socrates may owe something to Antisthenes' understanding of Socratic ethics.)

MALCOLM SCHOFIELD

APPLIED ETHICS

Applied ethics is marked out from ethics in general by its special focus on issues of practical concern. It therefore includes medical ethics, environmental ethics, and evaluation of the social implications of scientific and technological change, as well as matters of policy in such areas as health care, business or journalism. It is also concerned with professional codes and responsibilities in such areas.

Typical of the issues discussed are abortion, euthanasia, personal relationships, the treatment of nonhuman animals, and matters of race and gender. Although sometimes treated in isolation, these issues are best discussed in the context of some more general questions which have been perennial preoccupations of philosophers, such as: How should we see the world and our place in it? What is the good life for the individual? What is the good society? In relation to these questions, applied ethics involves discussion of fundamental ethical theory, including utilitarianism, liberal rights theory and virtue ethics.

'Applied ethics' and 'applied philosophy' are sometimes used as synonyms, but applied philosophy is in fact broader, covering also such fields as law, education and art, and theoretical issues in artificial intelligence. These areas include philosophical problems – metaphysical and epistemological – that are not strictly ethical. Applied ethics may therefore be understood as focusing more closely on ethical questions. Nevertheless, many of the issues it treats do in fact involve other aspects of philosophy, medical ethics, for example, including such metaphysical themes as the nature of 'personhood', or the definition of death.

1 Definitions
2 Theory and practice
3 Method
4 Critics and opponents
5 Historical context
6 Professional ethics
7 Are there ethical experts?
8 Research in applied ethics
9 Institutions

1 Definitions

While the name 'applied ethics' is comparatively new, the idea is not. Philosophy has traditionally concerned itself with questions both of personal morality (what should I do?) and public morality (what is the good society?), but while these questions are fundamental to applied ethics, they could also be said to characterize ethics in general. Applied ethics is therefore distinguished commonly as that part of ethics that gives particular and direct attention to practical issues and controversies.

In the private sphere, ethical issues include, for example, matters relating to the family (see FAMILY, ETHICS AND THE), or to close personal relationships (see FRIENDSHIP), the care of the old or disabled, the raising of the young, particularly where matters of morality are concerned, or personal ethical problems arising for the individual in the work-place. In the public sphere, applied ethics may involve assessing policy in the light of the impact of advances in biomedical technology (see LIFE AND DEATH; RISK; TECHNOLOGY AND ETHICS), or assessing international obligations and duties to future generations in the light of environmental problems (see FUTURE GENERATIONS, OBLIGATIONS TO; POPULATION AND ETHICS). The public arena includes, too, a range of issues for the plural society, such as ethnicity or gender in relation to discrimination, cultural understanding and toleration; more widely still, it may extend to issues of interest also to political philosophy, such as terrorism and the ethics of war. In all these matters, the concern of applied ethics is not only to supply a personal ethical perspective, but also to provide guidelines for public policy.

Applied ethics includes, as well, the area of professional ethics; it examines the ethical dilemmas and challenges met with by workers in the health care field – doctors, nurses, counsellors, psychiatrists, dentists – and by a wide range of workers in other professions including lawyers, accountants, managers and administrators, people in business, police and law enforcement officers. Specific ethical issues such as confidentiality, truth-telling, or conflicts of interest may arise in all or any of these areas, and most professions seek to codify their approaches and provide guidance for their members.

2 Theory and practice

Underlying all such issues are questions about justice, rights, utility, virtue and community. The practice of distinguishing between theoretical and applied ethics must, therefore, be treated with some caution. Indeed, some have regarded the term 'applied' as redundant, on the grounds that there cannot be an 'ethics' which is not applied: on the one hand, they argue, theoretical concepts such as rights and justice should not be viewed as mere abstractions; and, on the other, applied ethics should not be detached from its roots in traditional morality. But while it is important to stress this continuity, there are certain characteristic features of applied ethics which mark it out in practice from theoretical ethics. These are (a) its greater attention to context and detail and (b) its more holistic approach – its willingness to link ethical ideals to a conception of human nature and human needs (see HUMAN NATURE; NEEDS AND INTERESTS). Thus practitioners of applied ethics may be more willing than proponents of traditional academic moral philosophy to recognize that psychology and sociology, a knowledge of culture and history, the insights of good literature, and even an understanding of humans as biological entities, are all relevant to the determination of moral issues in personal and public life.

The demarcation line between applied and theoretical ethics which this suggests may be drawn at that point on the spectrum of ethics where ethical theory stops short of normative recommendations and confines itself to the analysis of moral concepts such as 'right', 'good', 'responsibility', 'blame' and 'virtue' and to discussion of what might be called the epistemology of ethics – such theories as ethical realism, subjectivism and relativism (see ANALYTIC ETHICS; MORAL KNOWLEDGE; MORAL REALISM; LOGIC OF ETHICAL DISCOURSE). This is the area sometimes described as 'meta-ethics'. Drawing the line at this point may be useful so long as it is not allowed to obscure the truth that applied and theoretical ethics are not discrete but lie on a continuum from the particular to the general, the concrete to the abstract.

The ultimate focus of applied ethics may well be entirely particular: the individual case-study. And it is this that gives rise to a further characteristic feature of applied ethics: its concern with dilemmas – not necessarily in the hard logical sense of situations in which it is impossible to act rightly because each of two opposite courses of action is either judged to be mandatory or judged to be wrong; but in the looser sense of cases in which a choice between courses of action may be extremely difficult, the arguments on both sides being compelling, and the person who must act being strongly influenced in opposing directions (for example, to sanction drastic medical intervention to save a severely disabled baby which would otherwise die, or to allow nature to take its course). It should be said, though, that choosing between options which are not morally equal is not, strictly speaking, a dilemma, although it is admittedly likely to be emotionally traumatizing, while choosing between moral obligations that are indisputably of equal weight is not a *moral* problem. The question for applied ethics in such cases may well be whether or not the available options are indeed morally equal.

Because it focuses on individual dilemmas, applied ethics must confront the question of universalization, which may also be seen as a 'free rider' problem: many things are judged to be wrong as a result of asking the question, 'What if everyone did that?', even though, in a particular case, it might seem harmless and more convenient for an individual to ignore the rule, while benefiting from the fact that everyone else is following it (see UNIVERSALISM IN ETHICS). The applied ethicist, like the theoretical moral philosopher, must find a way to deal with this problem, but for the applied ethicist, the problem is bound up with the need to employ what is sometimes called moral casuistry. This ancient science is not necessarily to be despised, for while a secondary meaning of the term 'casuist' is indeed 'sophist' or 'quibbler', it was not originally a term of abuse, but simply meant accepting in a theological context people's desire to work out the 'right answer' to a difficult issue of conscience in a particular set of circumstances (see CASUISTRY).

3 Method

One method of reasoning employed in applied ethics may be compared to that of a designer who starts with a blueprint, but has to adapt it to the materials to hand and to the situations in which it is required. There is some resemblance in this case to the Hegelian method of dialectical reasoning, as well as to the method of reflective equilibrium favoured by such contemporary writers as Rawls (1971), in which intuitions in response to particular cases are measured against principles, causing them to be revised and their implications for particular cases again reappraised (see MORAL JUSTIFICATION §2). According to this view of the subject, the method of applied ethics is neither purely deductive nor purely inductive. For others, however, the deductive model is more powerful, and the question to be answered in any particular case is simply *which* (inviolable) principle it falls under. Others again would favour the inductive model, according to which, by clearly seeing what is right in particular cases, it becomes possible to formulate a general principle encompassing these and other particular judgments (see UNIVERSALISM IN ETHICS §3).

In general, discussion of ethical theories in applied ethics aims to pursue, in the direction of the highest degree of generality and abstraction, the question of what humans should do. In practice, discussion of theories is often confined to their implications for the resolution of particular problems, since applied ethics characteristically seeks to answer the broad question with a much greater degree of particularity.

4 Critics and opponents

In seeking answers to practical problems, applied

ethics runs counter to much recent philosophy. For the view that prevailed during the dominance of empiricism and positivism (the greater part of the twentieth century) is that philosophy can have nothing to say about pressing practical problems.

This view is grounded in two important philosophical arguments: (a) Hume's objection to arguments that seek to derive an 'ought' from an 'is' (see HUME, D. §4; LOGIC OF ETHICAL DISCOURSE §2–4); and (b) Moore's argument that to identify moral characteristics with 'natural' or empirical ones is to commit a 'naturalistic fallacy' (see MOORE, G.E. §1; NATURALISM IN ETHICS §3). Both of these arguments must be resisted if applied ethics is to succeed in closing the gap between factual descriptions of situations and moral judgments, and both may partially at least be answered by insisting that some facts 'speak for themselves' – torture, child-murder, genocide, for example.

The argument that facts and values are to be kept apart is, however, less of an obstacle to philosophers outside the English-speaking world; the notion of praxis, for example, is familiar from various continental traditions, including Marxism, the Frankfurt School, and the philosophy of Habermas (see THEORY AND PRACTICE §3); while the idea of the philosopher as *engagé* – as concerned with playing a part in the world – is an important part of French existentialist thought, made familiar in the works of Sartre. These sources have, however, produced a different kind of challenge to the notion of applied ethics as an impartial and essentially reason-based approach to ethical issues in society. Objections to the conception of universal moral norms and to foundationalist procedures in reasoning (the 'postmodernist' challenge) are associated with recent developments in Marxist theory, certain feminist approaches to ethics and epistemology, and the deconstructionist movement – schools of thought which may also adopt an analysis of power-structures in society incompatible with belief in individual freedom of action (see FEMINISM AND PSYCHOANALYSIS; DECONSTRUCTION). Supporters of these theoretical positions often make strong claims for the recognition of rights, but this is probably better seen as exploitation of the preconceptions of their opponents, rather than as recognition of universal ethical concepts and human freedom.

Other critiques of traditional ethics may, however, be more sympathetic to applied ethics. On the basis of research revealing the contextuality of many women's responses to ethical dilemmas, some feminist writers, most prominently Carol Gilligan (1982), have argued that women in general are likely to adopt an ethic of care and responsibility to particular others rather than an abstract morality of principles, rights or justice (see FEMINIST ETHICS §1). Such an approach may well seem better adapted to the resolution of 'hard cases' in, for example, health care or social work (see NURSING ETHICS).

Similarly, the approach known as 'virtue ethics', with its emphasis on seeking the good in particular situations, may seem well adapted to applied ethics, even if its proponents sometimes appear to view it in opposition, regarding their own stand as more objective, and wrongly equating applied ethics with subjectivism and relativism (see VIRTUE ETHICS).

Other stereotypes to be rejected are political: applied ethics has typically been associated with vegetarianism, pacifism, feminism and environmentalism. It should be noted, however, that it also includes criticism and evaluation of these positions: defences of meat-eating or animal experiments, scepticism about feminism, and resistance to new 'ecological ethics' are to be found alongside more orthodox publications on library shelves. There is nothing wrong with variety of opinion so long as this is within a broad ethical framework, for it is of the essence of applied philosophy in general to approach individual issues in their own right and not as part of an ideological package-deal.

Applied ethics, then, is part of a whole view of the human condition and takes a broad view of ethical decision-making. Essentially, this is ethical decision-making seen as practical policy that consciously recognizes the constraints of moral norms, rights and ethical principles capable of commanding universal respect. Where this is accepted, the object of applied ethics is plain: it is to gain clearer perceptions of right and wrong, with a view to embodying these insights in manners and institutions.

5 Historical context

The inception of applied philosophy could well be said to coincide with that of the Western philosophical tradition as a whole, for the first of the early Greek philosophers, Thales (c.585 BC), is recorded as having combined his speculative philosophical interests with economic acumen and an interest in legal and political reform. Later schools of philosophy in ancient times – Pythagoreans, Epicureans, Stoics – offered their followers principles for living and even indeed distinctive codes of practice.

For both Plato and Aristotle, ethical and political questions were posed in terms of such notions as the good for man, the ultimate good, or what is good in itself and for its own sake (see PLATO §16; ARISTOTLE §21). Their assumption was that this inquiry led both to a way of life for the individual, and to a conception of the good society. They disagreed about whether this would lead an individual necessarily to live according to the ethical insight thus gained, Aristotle, unlike Plato in his earlier writings, allowing for the intervention of weakness of will to divert the person who has recognized the good from pursuing it (see AKRASIA).

Subsequent philosophers frequently applied their ethical assumptions to particular cases, and saw this, not as a way of fractionizing moral philosophy – making it the science of the particular – but as a route to formulating guiding principles. Aquinas treated a range of practical issues including marriage and the family in Summa theologiae, and this tradition was developed further by Suárez (1612–21) and Grotius (1625). Locke (1689) wrote on the issue of toleration, Kant (1785; 1797) on suicide and on the question of whether it is ever right to tell a lie from benevolent motives (see LOCKE, J. §7; TOLERATION §1; SUICIDE, ETHICS OF §5). Bentham (1789) put forward a complex theory of punishment, even formulating plans for a new type of prison, to be called the 'panopticon'. He also wrote on legal and political reform. Hegel's philosophy included views on the family and on punishment. J.S. Mill's writings on toleration, paternalism and feminism (1859) continue to be of interest in the present day, as the controversies involved in these areas remain subjects of disagreement and debate (see FEMINISM; PATERNALISM), and Dewey's theories of education (1916) exercised enormous practical influence on education systems in the USA and Britain (see EDUCATION, HISTORY OF PHILOSOPHY OF).

The tradition in moral philosophy unsympathetic to applied ethics is in fact of fairly recent origin. It was associated with the dominance of positivism and empiricism in the philosophy of science, and the vogue for linguistic analysis in epistemology. This is a twentieth-century phenomenon and, right up to the closing years of the nineteenth century, a more generous conception of ethics flourished. If a certain myopia on applied issues is recognized amongst philosophers in the English-speaking world, coinciding roughly with the first half of the twentieth century, various explanations may be offered for the gradual return of visual focus. For those with an interest in medical ethics, a research project in Tuskegee in the USA in which a control group with syphilis remained untreated for decades after safe treatment was known to be possible is often cited as a trigger generating widespread discussion of issues such as autonomy, beneficence and nonmaleficence, medical confidentiality, and the ethics of experiments on human subjects (see MEDICAL ETHICS §§1–3). This case may have been, however, a symptom rather than a cause, for in general medicine moved during those decades from being a practice with little power to influence the natural course of disease, to being a powerful interventionist tool. Whatever the specific cause, then, from roughly this period medical ethics became an arena of critical and controversial discussion.

Again in the USA, the Vietnam War and the protests which it generated are cited as having promoted discussion of a different range of applied issues (civil disobedience, duty to conscience versus duty to society) and as having led in a fairly direct way to the setting up of the Society for Philosophy and Public Affairs and the journal *Philosophy and Public Affairs* (see CIVIL DISOBEDIENCE; CONSCIENCE).

Others, focusing on the applied philosopher's interest in animal welfare, cite the publication of the volume Animal Liberation (1975) by Peter Singer as ushering in a new conception of ethics as a practical and possibly even campaigning area (see ANIMALS AND ETHICS §3). Already, too, Rachel Carson's *Silent Spring* (1962) had alerted the general public to many environmental hazards and thus opened the way to an enlarged philosophical perspective in which developments in science and technology and the way in which these were applied by firms and governments to the environment were seen as matters of ethical concern. It was a decade or so later that the internal operations of businesses became matters for ethical scrutiny, prompted by scandals connected with sharp practices such as insider trading.

Finally, it must be said that philosophy itself no doubt provided a spur to the growth of applied ethics. The preoccupation of academic moral philosophy with entirely minor moral issues in a century which had witnessed two world wars and many accompanying gross violations of human rights, was too remarkable to pass for long, particularly with wider access to higher education and hence to the hitherto elite and somewhat esoteric pursuit of philosophy.

This account of the rise of contemporary applied ethics raises the question of what kind of study applied ethics is. Is it merely another kind of academic study, or is it committed to the promotion of change in the world? Is it conservative or radical? Reactionary or revolutionary? The answer to this last question is that it can be either. Reflection may make one seek to promote change for the better, but it may also cause one to recoil from change and seek to preserve what is best from the past. The controversial nature of most of the issues involved is itself a spur to their philosophical study, for it is probably true to say that until recently, despite differences of religious or ideological background, a common moral approach could in general be assumed, and accepted norms of moral behaviour could be taken as a starting-point for ethical reasoning. Such moral consensus cannot now be presupposed, and, while absolutist approaches are by no means inconsistent with mainstream philosophical ethics, in practice the defence of an absolute conception of morality against relativistic, subjective and utilitarian approaches is often associated with a religious perspective.

Many writers on applied ethics, however, adopt a secular utilitarian stance. These include the Australian philosopher Peter Singer, and the Oxford philosopher Jonathan Glover, who has written especially in the area of medical ethics (see UTILITARIANISM). R.M. HARE, in *Moral Thinking* (1981), puts forward a prescriptivist theory which combines utilitarianism with Kantian universalizability (see PRESCRIPTIVISM). Also influential is the ethic of care mentioned above, which is often linked to gender differences. Other views include those of the Australian philosopher John PASSMORE, who defends a liberal moral perspective, especially in relation to environmental ethics, and John RAWLS, whose notion of reflective equilibrium combines intuitionism with contract theory (see MORAL JUSTIFICATION §2). Rawls' *A Theory of Justice* (1971) inaugurated a new more practical approach in ethics, which had implications for economics, law and political theory. Sissela Bok has written on the fine texture of issues in public life in *Lying: Moral Choices in Public and Private Life* (1978) and *Secrets* (1984) (see TRUTHFULNESS); Mary Midgley, in *Beast and Man* (1978) and elsewhere, has discussed the relations between humans and other species; and Onora O'Neill (1986) has brought a Kantian ethic to bear on the issues of famine and poverty (see DEVELOPMENT ETHICS). The debate between communitarians and libertarians about the ethics of capitalism and the role of welfare can also be seen as a part of applied ethics (see COMMUNITY AND COMMUNITARIANISM; MARKET, ETHICS OF THE). The German philosopher, Jürgen HABERMAS, an influential figure both in continental Europe and the English-speaking world, has put forward a notion of consensus as the object of theory expressed in practice.

6 Professional ethics

Similar divisions may reveal themselves in professional ethics, although the idea that there should be special codes of ethics peculiar to particular professions has been current since ancient times, when the Hippocratic oath was required of those engaging in medical practice. Many modern groups, including engineers, nurses and lawyers, have adopted formal codes setting standards of ethical practice for their profession (see PROFESSIONAL ETHICS).

Ethics also plays an increasing role in the training of professionals. Often the preferred approach is through the use of case studies, sometimes fictional, sometimes using videos of actual cases. One problem with the case study approach is its possible negative effect. In stressing that there are at least two sides to many ethical problems, and in presenting ethical theories as giving conflicting outcomes, they may risk generating a facile moral or cultural relativism – the view that there are only opinions, not answers. The use of case studies and discussion based on situational ethics may also tacitly undermine principles (see SITUATION ETHICS). In contrast, some courses aim simply to increase the moral sensitivity of trainees, on the assumption that if this is successful they will go on to make good professional decisions (see EXAMPLES IN ETHICS).

7 Are there ethical experts?

Applied ethics does not involve a claim of moral expertise, but often involves collaboration with specialists in practical areas in order to arrive at policy decisions that allow ethical considerations a determining role.

There is now wide acceptance of the principle of ensuring that a philosophical or ethical viewpoint is represented in certain kinds of forums, such as public enquiries, the reports of legislative committees or commissions of inquiry, and hospital ethics committees. The USA has a President's Commission to report directly on bioethical issues to the US President, the UK has a National Bioethics Committee funded independently of government, while in France there is a French National Committee on Ethical Affairs in Public Debate. In 1985, the Council of Europe created a multidisciplinary body with experts appointed by each member country, now called the Comité Directeur de Bioethique (CDBI). Canada set up a Royal Commission on New Reproductive Technologies, and the European Parliament commissions advice on scientific and technological policy options. Other countries are following a similar pattern. In addition, the Council of Europe in 1990 began working on a European Convention on biomedical ethics, which would be a legally binding instrument on all countries signing it, the object being ultimately to harmonize European legislation.

Individuals are also used as consultants on public policy issues. In Europe, Jonathan Glover, in collaboration with nationals of other European countries, produced a report on fertility and the family for the European Commission (1989), while Will Kymlicka has advised on this topic as a member of the Canadian Royal Commission and, in the USA, Arthur Caplan was a member of the President's Task Force on National Health Care Reform. In Britain, the philosopher Mary Warnock (1985) was responsible for official reports on the educational needs of children with disabilities and learning difficulties, and on new developments in reproductive medicine and embryology; Bernard Williams (1979) played a similar role in relation to pornography and censorship. The debate about euthanasia in the Netherlands has engaged philosophers, lawyers, and social theorists. Less happily, a visit by Peter Singer to Germany provoked widespread protest related to the debate on euthanasia and has led to the unpopularity of bioethics in some circles, and a general and unjustified rejection of applied ethics.

Some achievements in these areas may also be recorded; examination of the ethics of clinical trials, for example, particularly in relation to AIDS, led to a total reconceptualization of what clinical trials require, and to a multi-choice system being devised which is both scientifically acceptable and also allows a more acceptable level of choice to patients and physicians.

8 Research in applied ethics

In general, those who fund research regard the gathering of facts, often called the 'generation of new knowledge', as crucial; philosophy, in contrast, appears to involve reflection on facts, while normative philosophy generates proposals for action or policy. Applied ethics offers at its best an opportunity to combine these approaches: for facts to be made the fruitful object of analytic and morally sensitive reflection, and for philosophical inquiry to accept the discipline of the need to take account of the practical framework within which speculation is cast.

Research in applied ethics, then, ideally starts from a perceived problem and is motivated to find a solution to that problem. It is frequently interdisciplinary. A research programme is often inspired by technological progress, for it is this that has placed ethical considerations at the heart of many areas of public debate. Typical of these are the controversies already mentioned surrounding the new technologies of reproduction: embryo research, donation of gametes, surrogate motherhood, which raise questions about the status of the human embryo and the definition of parenthood (see REPRODUCTION AND ETHICS).

Other appropriate areas where ethics impinges on practical inquiry include, for example, the ethical implications of the Human Genome Project, the ethics of confidentiality, insurance in relation to AIDS or inherited disease, the care of the elderly, homelessness, and mental illness (see GENETICS AND ETHICS; MEDICAL ETHICS §§4–5; NURSING ETHICS). One caveat to be noted here, however, is that simply gathering data about what people think is right is sociology, not ethics, applied or otherwise.

9 Institutions

Many research centres have been created in recent decades. Their function is usually to conduct research, to produce publications and to arrange lectures, seminars and conferences on practical issues of ethical concern.

North America has the best-established institutional network. First in the field was the Hastings Center, New York (1969), then the Center for Philosophy and Public Affairs, University of Maryland and the Center for the Study of Ethics in the Professions at the Illinois Institute of Technology (1976), the Center for the Study of Values, University of Delaware (1977), and the Social Philosophy and Policy Center, Bowling Green State University, Ohio (1981). There are now many other centres in universities in the USA and elsewhere, including, in the UK, the Centre for Philosophy and Public Affairs at the University of St Andrews, the Centre for Medical Law and Ethics at King's College London, and the Social Values Research Centre at the University of Hull. The Netherlands has Bioethics Centres in Utrecht and Maastricht and work in applied ethics in the Scandinavian countries is increasing, with a strong interest in reproductive ethics in Aarhus, Denmark and in animal welfare issues in Copenhagen. The European Business Ethics Network (EBEN) began with an initiative from Switzerland, and business ethics is also well-established in Spain and Germany. Apart from university-based units, the Society for Applied Philosophy (1982) has general interests in most areas of applied ethics and has a broad membership not confined to professional philosophers.

Australia has been a pioneer in many fields of applied ethics: Peter Singer, together with Helga Kuhse, founded the Centre for Human Bioethics (1980) at Monash University, and there are now several other applied ethics centres in Australasia; it is worth noting the particular degree of interest there in environmental ethics, where the issues of species preservation, wilderness, and ecological threats such as damage to the ozone layer are of direct concern to residents.

The creation of a Chair of Environmental Ethics at Warsaw University represents the strong interest, partly political in origin, in environmental ethics in the former communist countries of Eastern Europe. Other countries where applied ethics is of growing interest are parts of Southeast Asia, including Thailand and Hong Kong, India, and several African countries.

See also: AGRICULTURAL ETHICS; BIOETHICS; BUSINESS ETHICS; ENGINEERING AND ETHICS; ENVIRONMENTAL ETHICS; JOURNALISM, ETHICS OF; INFORMATION TECHNOLOGY AND ETHICS; RESPONSIBILITIES OF SCIENTISTS AND INTELLECTUALS; SEXUALITY, PHILOSOPHY OF

References and further reading

* Aquinas, T. (1266–73) *Summa theologiae* (Synopsis of Theology), ed. T. Gilby, London: Eyre & Spottiswoode, 1963–, 60 vols. (A theological work, which provides a place for the Aristotelian virtues, conscience and natural law, and also deals with practical ethical issues including marriage and the family.)
* Bentham, J. (1789) *An Introduction to the Principles of Morals and Legislation*, ed. J.H. Burns and H.L.A. Hart, revised F. Rosen, Oxford: Clarendon Press, 1996. (Sets out the foundations of a utilitarian theory of ethics, law and punishment.)
* Bok, S. (1978) *Lying: Moral Choices in Public and Private Life*, New York: Pantheon. (Practical discussions of ethical considerations raised by practice of lying in connection with many professional areas.)
* —— (1984) *Secrets*, New York: Random House. (Practical discussion of issues of confidentiality and secrecy in public life.)
* Carson, R. (1962) *Silent Spring*, London: Hamish Hamilton. (Although not itself a work in applied ethics, this was instrumental in drawing public attention to the threat to the environment poaed by the use of pesticides in agriculture.)
  Clark, S.R.L. (1977) *The Moral Status of Animals*, Oxford: Oxford University Press. (A philosophical and ethical examination of the status of animals in their relations to human beings.)
  Dewey, J. (1916) *Democracy and Education*, New York: The Free Press, 1966. (Sets out an approach to the education of young children, which includes the use of discovery methods and the arrangement of the classroom as wookroom for cooperative projects.)
* Gilligan, C. (1982) *In a Different Voice: Psychological Theory and Women's Development*, Cambridge, MA: Harvard University Press; 2nd edn, 1993. (Account of research which first suggested that women might be articulating a different view of morality, contextual and personal rather than universal and abstract.)
  Glover, J. (1977) *Causing Death and Saving Lives*, Harmondsworth: Penguin. (Comprehensive and wide-ranging discussion from a utilitarian standpoint of issues in medical ethics.)
* Glover, J. et al. (1989) *Fertility and the Family: The Glover Report on Reproductive Technologies to the European Commission*, London: Fourth Estate Ltd. (A cooperative international report for the European Commission.)
* Grotius (1625) *De iure belli ac pacis*, trans. F. Kelsey, *The Law of War and Peace*, Oxford: Oxford University Press, 1925. (Sets out the conditions for the conduct of a just war, and reasons which would justify going to war.)
* Hare, R.M. (1981) *Moral Thinking*, Oxford: Oxford University Press. (Important statement of a distinctive philosophical approach to practical ethics: universal prescriptivism.)
  Hursthouse, R. (1987) *Beginning Lives*, Oxford: Blackwell. (A discussion of the ethical aspects of abortion.)
* Kant, I. (1785) *Grundlegung zur Metaphysik der Sitten*, trans. H.J. Paton, *Groundwork of the Metaphysics of Morals* (originally *The Moral Law*), London: Hutchinson, 1948; repr. New York: Harper & Row, 1964. (Provides the fundamentals of Kant's moral theory according to which actions have moral worth if they are done from the motive of duty and fit with the principle of universalizability.)
* —— (1797) 'On a Supposed Right to Lie from Altruistic Motives', in *The Philosophy of Immanuel Kant*, trans. L.W. Beck, Chicago, IL: University of Chicago Press, 346–9. (Argues, contrary to the usual opinion, that it is never right to tell a lie, even to achieve some good.)
* Locke, J. (1689) *A Letter concerning Toleration*, ed. J.W. Gough and R. Kilbansky, Oxford: Oxford University Press, 1968. (Discusses political authority and its limits, and sets out the fundamental rights of individuals.)
* Midgley, M. (1978) *Beast and Man*, Ithaca, NY: Cornell University Press. (Philosophical discussion of issues in sociobiology.)
* Mill, J.S. (1859) *On Liberty*, Harmondsworth: Penguin, 1982. (Classic defence of liberty and toleration; includes practical examples of the way on which these principles are to be applied.)
* O'Neill, O. (1986) *Faces of Hunger*, London: Allen & Unwin. (Kantian approach to the issues of famine and Third World poverty.)
  Passmore, J. (1974) *Man's Responsibility for Nature:*

ecological problems and Western traditiions, London: Duckworth; 2nd edn, 1980. (Comprehensive discussion by a leading Australian philosopher of ethical issues concerned with the environment.)

Rachels, J. (ed.) (1971) *Moral Problems*, New York: Harper & Row; 3rd edn, 1979. (Usefully representative collection of articles on applied ethics, including discussion of racism, discrimination, obligations to poorer countries.)

—— (1986) *The End of Life: Euthanasia and Morality*, Oxford and New York: Oxford University Press. (Discusses ethical issues concerning the end of life and the issue of euthanasia.)

* Rawls, J. (1971) *A Theory of Justice*, Oxford: Oxford University Press. (Seminal work which initiated a new era of practical philosophy; aims to establish universal principles for social living on rational grounds.)

* Singer, P. (1975) *Animal Liberation*, New York: New York Review of Books Press; repr. London: Jonathan Cape, and New York: Random House, 1990. (Presents Singer's arguments for ethical treatment of animals as contrasted with current practise in food production and laboratory research.)

—— (1979) *Practical Ethics*, Cambridge: Cambridge University Press; 2nd edn, 1993. (Utilitarian perspective on applied ethics; includes reading guides and bibliographies on specific topics.)

—— (ed.) (1986) *Applied Ethics*, Oxford: Oxford University Press. (Classic articles, including Hume on suicide and Mill on the death penalty.)

Suárez, F. (1612–21) Selections from Three Works of Francisco Suárez, S.J., trans. G.L. Williams *et al.*, in J.B. Scott (ed.) *Classics of International Law* 20, vol. 2, Oxford: Clarendon Press, 1944. (Discusses the nature of law, largely following Aquinas, and also the concept of obligation.)

Walzer, M. (1977) *Just and Unjust Wars*, New York: Basic Books. (An examination of arguments concerning war and morality.)

* Warnock, M. (1985) *A Question of Life: The Warnock Report on Fertilisation and Embryology*, Oxford: Blackwell. (Based on a report on the ethics and law of reproductive medicine prepared for the British government, with recommendations for policy.)

* Williams, B. *et al.* (1979) *Report of the Committee on Obscenity and Film Censorship ('The Williams Report') Cmnd 7772*, London: Her Majesty's Stationery Office; abridged version repr. as B. Williams (ed.) *Obscenity and Film Censorship*, Cambridge: Cambridge University Press, 1981. (A report prepared for the British government advising on the issue of censorship and the law.)

Ethics (1890–) (A journal which publishes articles in all areas of ethics.)

Philosophy (1925–) Cambridge: Cambridge University Press. (A journal which publishes articles in all areas of philosophy, usually of a non-technical area.)

Social Theory and Practice (1970–) (An interdisciplinary journal of social philosophy.)

Philosophy and Public Affairs (1971–) (A journal dedicated to the philosophical study of issues of public concern, including legal, social and political problems.)

Journal of Applied Philosophy (1984–) (A journal contributing to discussion of ethical and philosophical issues in many areas of practical debate.)

Public Affairs Quarterly (1987–) (A journal of philosophical studies of public policy issues.)

BRENDA ALMOND

APULEIUS (*c.* AD 125–80)

The Latin writer Apuleius of Madaura was a professional rhetorician, a novelist and an amateur Platonist. His handbook of Platonism and his essay on the guardian spirit of Socrates are valuable sources on Middle Platonism. The handbook is comparable to that of his probable contemporary Alcinous, but covers only physics (including metaphysics) and ethics.

Apuleius was born in Madaura in North Africa, of respectable provincial family. He received the best rhetorical education available in Carthage and then, around AD 150, set out for Athens to study philosophy. It is possible that, when there, he studied with the Platonist Calvenus Taurus, whose lectures Aulus Gellius also attended, but we cannot be certain. None the less, Apuleius acquired in Athens a good working knowledge of Platonism, which he puts to various uses.

After more time in North Africa, he returned to practise as a lawyer and rhetorician in Carthage, where he was celebrated in an inscription of *c.* AD 161 as a rhetorician, poet and Platonic philosopher. At some time after this he composed his chief contribution to philosophy, a basic handbook, *On Plato and his Doctrine*, of a similar nature to that of the more-or-less contemporary text of ALCINOUS. This is written in a flat, scholastic style, very unlike that of his rhetorical compositions, so much so that its authenticity has been questioned, but without adequate grounds. Another philosophical treatise, probably also from this period, is his essay *On the Daemon of Socrates*; in florid, rhetorical style, it does however contain useful Middle Platonist doctrine on daemons.

On Plato is in two books, the first dealing with 'physics' (including metaphysics), the second with ethics and politics. A third section, devoted to logic, is envisaged in the preface, but there is no sign of it; instead, we have the (possibly spurious) *De interpretatione*. *On Plato* begins with four chapters on the life of Plato, which constitute valuable evidence for the state of the Plato myth in Apuleius' time. Thereafter, Apuleius embarks on a systematic survey of Platonic philosophy, beginning with the first principles God, Matter and the Ideas (chs 5–6), and continuing through the topics of the formation of the elements and of the world, the soul of the world, time, the heavenly bodies, classification of animate beings, gods and daemons, and fate and free will. This is followed by an anthropological section, on the parts of the soul and the body, the senses and bodily health and disease. All of this, as with the parallel treatise of Alcinous, is heavily dependent on Plato's *Timaeus* (see PLATO §16). Most distinctive, perhaps, is his doctrine of fate and providence (ch. 12), postulating three levels of providence, in which he shows interesting affinities with the pseudo-Plutarchan treatise *On Fate*.

Book II of *On Plato* covers the various main topics of ethical theory, followed by a discussion of the nature of the perfect sage, and a short disquisition on politics, again not differing greatly from Alcinous, and identifying Apuleius as an adherent of the Peripateticizing wing of Middle Platonism. As for the work *De interpretatione*, it gives a summary account of Aristotelian logic, reflecting later developments in the Peripatetic school

Apuleius was a man of many parts. He is best known today for his novel *The Golden Ass*. As a philosopher, he would make no great claim to originality, but he provides useful evidence for the state of Platonism in the mid second century AD.

See also: PLATONISM, EARLY AND MIDDLE §§1, 4, 7–9

List of works

Apuleius (AD 158/9) *Apology*, ed. P. Vallette, Paris: Les Belles Lettres, 2nd edn, 1960. (With French translation.)

—— (between AD 140 and 180) *On the Daemon of Socrates, On Plato and his Doctrine, On the World*, in J. Beaujeu (ed.) *Apulée, Opuscules philosophiques et fragments* (Apuleius, Philosophical Minor Works and Fragments), Paris: Les Belles Lettres, 1973. (With French translation.)

—— (between AD 140 and 180) *De interpretatione*, in D. Londrey and C. Johanson (eds) *The Logic of Apuleius*, Leiden: Brill, 1987. (In English translation with a useful logical commentary.)

—— (between AD 140 and 180) *The Golden Ass* (or Metamorphoses), trans. J.A. Hanson, Cambridge, MA: Harvard University Press, 1989. (Of little interest philosophically, but notable as the only surviving novel in Latin.)

References and further reading

Dillon, J. (1977) *The Middle Platonists*, London: Duckworth. (Chapter 6 offers an introductory account of Apuleius.)

Hijmans, B.J. (1987) *Apuleius Philosophus Platonicus* (Apuleius, Platonic Philosopher), in W. Haase (ed.) *Aufstieg und Niedergang der römischen Welt*, Berlin: de Gruyter, II 36: 1, 395–475. (A rather idiosyncratic account, concentrating more on Apuleius' style than on his content.)

Moreschini, C. (1978) *Apuleio e il Platonismo* (Apuleius and Platonism), Florence: Olschki. (Essays in Italian on various aspects of Apuleius.)

Sullivan, M.W. (1967) *Apuleian Logic*, Amsterdam: Hakkert. (A good discussion of sources and influence.)

JOHN DILLON

AQUINAS, THOMAS (1224/6–74)

Aquinas lived an active, demanding academic and ecclesiastical life that ended while he was still in his forties. He nonetheless produced many works, varying in length from a few pages to a few volumes. Because his writings grew out of his activities as a teacher in the Dominican order and a member of the theology faculty of the University of Paris, most are concerned with what he and his contemporaries thought of as theology. However, much of academic theology in the Middle Ages consisted in a rational investigation of the most fundamental aspects of reality in general and of human nature and behaviour in particular. That vast domain obviously includes much of what is now considered to be philosophy, and is reflected in the broad subject matter of Aquinas' theological writings.

The scope and philosophical character of medieval theology as practised by Aquinas can be easily seen in his two most important works, Summa contra gentiles *(Synopsis [of Christian Doctrine] Directed Against Unbelievers) and* Summa theologiae *(Synopsis of Theology).*

However, many of the hundreds of topics covered in those two large works are also investigated in more detail in the smaller works resulting from Aquinas' numerous academic disputations (something like a cross between formal debates and twentieth-century graduate seminars), which he conducted in his various academic posts. Some of those topics are taken up differently again in his commentaries on works by Aristotle and other authors. Although Aquinas is remarkably consistent in his several discussions of the same topic, it is often helpful to examine parallel passages in his writings when fully assessing his views on any issue.

Aquinas' most obvious philosophical connection is with Aristotle. Besides producing commentaries on Aristotle's works, he often cites Aristotle in support of a thesis he is defending, even when commenting on Scripture. There are also in Aquinas' writings many implicit Aristotelian elements, which he had thoroughly absorbed into his own thought. As a convinced Aristotelian, he often adopts Aristotle's critical attitude toward theories associated with Plato, especially the account of ordinary substantial forms as separately existing entities. However, although Aquinas, like other medieval scholars of western Europe, had almost no access to Plato's works, he was influenced by the writings of Augustine and the pseudo-Dionysius. Through them he absorbed a good deal of Platonism as well, more than he was in a position to recognize as such.

*On the other hand, Aquinas is the paradigmatic Christian philosopher-theologian, fully aware of his intellectual debt to religious doctrine. He was convinced, however, that Christian thinkers should be ready to dispute rationally on any topic, especially theological issues, not only among themselves but also with non-Christians of all sorts. Since in his view Jews accept the Old Testament and heretics the New Testament, he thought Christians could argue some issues with both groups on the basis of commonly accepted religious authority. However, because other non-Christians, 'for instance, Mohammedans and pagans – do not agree with us about the authority of any scripture on the basis of which they can be convinced... it is necessary to have recourse to natural reason, to which everyone is compelled to assent – although where theological issues are concerned it cannot do the whole job', since some of the data of theology are initially accessible only in Scripture (*Summa contra gentiles *I.2.11). Moreover, Aquinas differed from most of his thirteenth-century Christian colleagues in the breadth and depth of his respect for Islamic and Jewish philosopher–theologians, especially Avicenna and Maimonides. He saw them as valued co-workers in the vast project of philosophical theology, clarifying and supporting doctrine by philosophical analysis and argumentation. His own commitment to that project involved him in contributing to almost all the areas of philosophy recognized since antiquity, omitting only natural philosophy (the precursor of natural science).*

A line of thought with such strong connections to powerful antecedents might have resulted in no more than a pious amalgam. However, Aquinas' philosophy avoids eclecticism because of his own innovative approach to organizing and reasoning about all the topics included under the overarching medieval conception of philosophical Christian theology, and because of his special talents for systematic synthesis and for identifying and skilfully defending, on almost every issue he considers, the most sensible available position.

1 **Early years**
2 **First Paris regency**
3 **Naples and Orvieto:** ***Summa contra gentiles*** **and biblical commentary**
4 **Rome: disputed questions, Dionysius and the** ***Compendium***
5 **Rome: Aristotelian commentary**
6 **Rome:** ***Summa theologiae***
7 **Second Paris regency**
8 **Last days**
9 **Metaphysics**
10 **Philosophy of mind**
11 **Theory of knowledge**
12 **Will and action**
13 **Ethics, law and politics**
14 **Theology: natural, revealed and philosophical**

1 Early years

Thomas Aquinas was born at Roccasecca, near Naples, the youngest son of a large Italian aristocratic family. As is generally true of even prominent medieval people, it is hard to determine exactly when he was born; plausible arguments have been offered for 1224, 1225 and 1226. He began his schooling in the great Benedictine abbey at Monte Cassino (1231–9), and from 1239–44 he was a student at the University of Naples. In 1244 he joined the Dominican friars, a relatively new religious order devoted to study and preaching; by doing so he antagonized his family, who seem to have been counting on his becoming abbot of Monte Cassino. When the Dominicans ordered Aquinas to go to Paris for further study, his family had him abducted en route and brought home, where he was kept for almost two years. Near the end of that time his brothers hired a prostitute to try to seduce him, but Aquinas angrily chased her from his room. Having impressed his family with his high-minded determination, in 1245 Aquinas was allowed to return to the

Dominicans, who again sent him to Paris, this time successfully.

At the University of Paris, Aquinas first encountered ALBERT THE GREAT, who quickly became his most influential teacher and eventually his friend and supporter. When Albert moved on to the University of Cologne in 1248, Aquinas followed him there, having declined Pope Innocent IV's extraordinary offer to appoint him abbot of Monte Cassino while allowing him to remain a Dominican.

Aquinas seems to have been unusually large, and extremely modest and quiet. When during his four years at Cologne his special gifts began to be apparent, despite his reticence and humility, Albert assigned the still-reluctant Aquinas his first active part in an academic disputation. Having failed in his efforts to shake his best student's arguments on this occasion, Albert declared, 'We call him the dumb ox, but in his teaching he will one day produce such a bellowing that it will be heard throughout the world'.

In 1252 Aquinas returned to Paris for the course of study leading to the degree of master in theology, roughly the equivalent of a twentieth-century PhD. During the first academic year he studied and lectured on the Bible; the final three years were devoted to delivering in lecture form his commentary on Peter Lombard's *Sentences*, a standard requirement for the degree at that time (see LOMBARD, P.). Produced in 1253–6, Aquinas' massive commentary (often referred to as the *Scriptum super libros Sententiarum* (Commentary on the Sentences) is the first of his four theological syntheses. It contains much valuable material, but because it is superseded in many respects by his great *Summa contra gentiles* (Synopsis [of Christian Doctrine] Directed Against Unbelievers) and *Summa theologiae* (Synopsis of Theology) the *Scriptum* has not yet been studied as much as it should be.

During that same four-year period, Aquinas produced *De ente et essentia* (On Being and Essence), a short philosophical treatise written for his fellow Dominicans at Paris. Although it owes something to Avicenna's *Metaphysics*, *De ente* is distinctively Aquinas' own, expounding many of the concepts and theses that remained fundamental to his thought throughout his career (see §9 below).

2 First Paris regency

In the spring of 1256, Aquinas was appointed regent master (professor) in theology at Paris, a position he held until the end of the academic year 1258–9. *Quaestiones disputatae de veritate* (Disputed Questions on Truth) is the first of his sets of disputed questions and the most important work he produced during those three years. It grew out of his professorship, which obliged him to conduct several formal public disputations each year. *Quaestiones disputatae de veritate* consists of twenty-nine widely ranging Questions, each devoted to some general topic such as conscience, God's knowledge, faith, goodness, free will, human emotions and truth (the first Question, from which the treatise gets its name). Each Question is divided into several Articles, and the 253 articles are the work's topically specific units: for example, q. 1, a. 9 is 'Is there truth in sense perception?'

The elaborate structure of each of those articles, like much of Aquinas' writing, reflects the 'scholastic method', which, like medieval disputations in the classroom, had its ultimate source in Aristotle's recommendations in his *Topics* regarding cooperative dialectical inquiry. Aquinas' philosophical discussions in that form typically begin with a yes/no question. Each article then develops as a kind of debate. It begins with arguments for the answer opposed to Aquinas' own position; these are commonly, if somewhat misleadingly, called 'objections'. Next come the arguments *sed contra* (but, on the other hand), which are in later works often reduced to a single citation of some generally accepted authority on Aquinas' side of the issue. The *sed contra* is followed by Aquinas' reasoned presentation and defence of his position. This is the master's 'determination' of the question, sometimes called the 'body' of the article (indicated by 'c' in references). An article normally concludes with Aquinas' rejoinders to each of the objections (indicated by 'ad 1', and so on, in references).

Conducting 'disputed questions' was one of the duties of a regent master in theology, but the theology faculty also provided regular opportunities for 'quodlibetal questions', occasions on which a master could, if he wished, undertake to provide replies to any and all questions proposed by members of the academic audience. These occasions were scheduled, for the master's own good, during the two penitential seasons of the church year. Aquinas seems to have accepted this challenge on at least five of the six such occasions occurring during his first regency at Paris, producing *Quaestiones quodlibetales* (Quodlibetal Questions) in which he offers his considered judgment on issues ranging from whether the soul is to be identified with its powers to whether the damned behold the saints in glory.

Aquinas' commentaries on Boethius' *De trinitate* (On the Trinity) and *De hebdomadibus* (sometimes referred to as 'How Substances are Good') are his other philosophically important writings from this period of his first regency. Although several philosophers had commented on those Boethian treatises in the twelfth century, the subsequent influx of Aristotelian works had left them almost universally disregarded by the time Aquinas wrote his commentaries (see ARISTOTELIANISM, MEDIEVAL; BOETHIUS, A.M.S.). No one knows why or for whom he wrote them, but he might well have undertaken these studies for his own edification on topics that were then becoming important to his thought. The *De trinitate* commentary (*Expositio super librum Boethii De trinitate*) presents Aquinas' views on the relationship of faith and reason and on the methods and interrelations of all the recognized bodies of organized knowledge, or 'sciences'. Boethius' *De hebdomadibus* is the *locus classicus* for the medieval consideration of the relation between being and goodness. Dealing with this topic in his commentary on that treatise, Aquinas also produced his first systematic account of metaphysical participation, one of the important Platonist elements in his thought. Participation, he claims, obtains when the metaphysical composition of something includes, as one of the thing's metaphysical components, X, which also belongs, to something else that is X in its own right in a way that is presupposed by the first thing's having X. In this way a running man participates in running, human being participates in animal, and an effect participates in its cause (see also §9 below) (see PLATONISM, MEDIEVAL).

3 Naples and Orvieto: *Summa contra gentiles* and biblical commentary

Aquinas' activities between 1259 and 1265 are not well documented, but he seems definitely to have left his professorship at Paris at the end of the academic year 1258–9. He probably spent the next two years at a Dominican priory in Naples, working on the *Summa contra gentiles*, which he had begun in Paris and which he subsequently finished in Orvieto where, as lector, he was in charge of studies at the Dominican priory until 1265.

Summa contra gentiles is unlike Aquinas' three other theological syntheses in more than one respect. Stylistically, it is unlike the earlier *Scriptum* and the later *Summa theologiae* in not following the scholastic method; instead, it is written in ordinary prose divided into chapters, like his *Compendium theologiae* (Compendium of Theology) which he seems to have written immediately afterwards (1265–7). More importantly, the *Scriptum*, *Summa theologiae* and the *Compendium* are all contributions to revealed theology, which essentially includes the data of revelation among the starting points of its theorizing. In *Summa contra gentiles*, on the other hand, Aquinas postpones revealed theology to the last (fourth) book, in which he deals with the 'mysteries', the few doctrinal propositions that cannot be arrived at by natural reason alone and that have their sources in revelation only; and he takes these up with the aim of showing that even those propositions 'are not opposed to natural reason' (*Summa contra gentiles* IV.1.3348). He devotes the first three books to fully developing a natural theology, dependent on natural reason of course, but independent of revelation. As developed in Books I–III, this natural theology is able to accomplish a very large part of theology's job, from establishing the existence of God through working out details of human morality (see also §13 below).

Discussions important for understanding Aquinas' positions in many areas of philosophy are also scattered, not always predictably, among interpretations of the text in his biblical commentaries. During Aquinas' stay in Orvieto and around the time he was writing Book III of *Summa contra gentiles*, on providence and God's relations with human beings, he also produced his *Expositio super Iob ad litteram* (Literal Commentary on Job), one of the most fully developed and philosophical of his biblical commentaries, rivalled in those respects only by his later commentary on Romans. The body of the Book of Job consists mainly of the speeches of Job and his 'comforters'. Aquinas sees those speeches as constituting a genuine debate, almost a medieval academic disputation (determined in the end by God himself), in which the thought develops subtly, advanced by arguments. His construal of the argumentation is ingenious, the more so because twentieth-century readers have tended to devalue the speeches as tedious reiterations of misconceived accusations countered by Job's slight variations on the theme of his innocence.

Aquinas' interpretation of the book's subject is also unlike the modern view, which supposes it to be the biblical presentation of the problem of evil, raised by a good God's permitting horrible suffering to be inflicted on an innocent person. Aquinas seems scarcely to recognize that Job's story raises doubts about God's goodness. As he interprets it, the book explains the nature and operations of divine providence, which he understands as compatible with permitting bad things to happen to good people. As Aquinas sees it:

> If in this life people are rewarded by God for good deeds and punished for bad, as Eliphaz [one of the comforters] was trying to establish, it apparently follows that the ultimate goal for human beings is in this life. But Job means to rebut this opinion, and he wants to show that the present life of human beings does not contain the ultimate goal, but is related to it as motion is related to rest, and a road to its destination.
>
> (*Expositio super Iob ad litteram* 7: 1–4)

The things that happen to a person in this life can be explained in terms of divine providence only by reference to the possibility of that person's achieving the ultimate goal of perfect happiness, the enjoyment of union with God in the afterlife.

In discussing Job's lament that God doesn't hear his prayers, Aquinas says that Job has that impression because God sometimes 'attends not to a person's pleas but rather to his advantage. A doctor does not attend to the pleas of the invalid who asks that the bitter medicine be taken away (supposing that the doctor doesn't take it away because he knows that it contributes to health). Instead, he attends to the patient's advantage; for by doing so he produces health, which the sick person wants most of all.' In the same way, God sometimes permits a person to suffer despite prayers for deliverance, because he knows that those sufferings are helping that person achieve what he or she wants most of all (*Expositio super Iob ad litteram* 9:16).

4 Rome: disputed questions, Dionysius and the *Compendium*

In 1265 Aquinas went from Orvieto to Rome, having been appointed to establish a Dominican *studium* (something like a twentieth-century college) and to serve as regent master there. This Roman period of his career, which lasted until 1268, was particularly productive. Some of his major works dating from 1265–8 are just what would have been expected of a regent master in theology, in particular, three sets of disputed questions, *Quaestiones disputatae de potentia* (Disputed Questions on [God's] Power), *Quaestio disputata de anima* (Disputed Question on the Soul) and *Quaestio disputata de spiritualibus creaturis* (Disputed Question on Spiritual Creatures). In the earliest of these, *De potentia*, there are eighty-three Articles grouped under ten Questions; the first six questions are on divine power, while the final four are on problems associated with combining the doctrine of Trinity with God's absolute simplicity. The much shorter *De anima* is concerned mainly with metaphysical aspects of the soul, concluding with some special problems associated with the nature and capacities of souls separated from bodies (Articles 14–21). The eleven articles of *De spiritualibus creaturis* again address many of those same concerns but also go on to some consideration of angels as another order of spiritual creatures besides human beings, whose natures are only partly spiritual.

During this same period, or perhaps while he was still at Orvieto, Aquinas wrote a commentary on the pseudo-Dionysian treatise *De divinis nominibus* (On the Divine Attributes), a deeply Neoplatonist account of Christian theology dating probably from the sixth century. Aquinas, like everyone else at the time, believed that it had been written in the apostolic period by the Dionysius who had been converted by St Paul. For that reason, and perhaps also because he had first studied the book under Albert at Cologne, it had a powerful influence on Aquinas' thought. Very early in his career, while he was writing his *Scriptum*, he thought Dionysius was an Aristotelian (*Scriptum* II, d.14, q.1, a.2), but while writing the commentary on this text he realized that its author must have been a Platonist (*Expositio super librum Dionysii De divinis nominibus*, prooemium; *Quaestiones disputatae de malo* 16.1, ad 3). His commentary, which makes clear sense of a text that is often obscure, may, like his commentaries on Boethius, have been written for his own purposes rather than growing out of a course of lectures. In any case, his study of Dionysius is one of the most important routes by which Platonism became an essential ingredient in his own thought (see also PSEUDO-DIONYSIUS).

The *Compendium theologiae* (Compendium of Theology), already mentioned in connection with *Summa contra gentiles*, was once thought to have been written much later and to have been left incomplete because of Aquinas' death. However, its similarity to *Summa contra gentiles* not only in style but also in content has lately led many scholars to assign it to 1265–7. Among Aquinas' four theological syntheses, the *Compendium theologiae* is unique in the brevity of its discussions and in having been organized around the 'theological virtues' of faith, hope and charity. Had it been completed, it might have provided a novel reorientation of the vast subject matter of medieval theology, but Aquinas wrote only ten short chapters of the second section, on Hope, and none at all of the third section, on Charity. He did complete the first section on Faith, but since most of the 246 chapters in the section simply provide much briefer treatments of almost all the theological topics Aquinas had already dealt with in *Summa contra gentiles*, the *Compendium* as he left it seems important mainly as a precis of material that is developed more fully in the other work (and in *Summa theologiae*).

5 Rome: Aristotelian commentary

While some of Aquinas' prodigious output in Rome from 1265–8 is, broadly speaking, similar to work he had already done, it also includes two important innovations, one of which is the first of his twelve commentaries on works of Aristotle. At the beginning of this commentary on *De anima* (*Sententia super De anima*), his approach is still a little tentative and (for Aquinas) unusually concerned with technical details.

These features of the work once led scholars to describe the commentary on the first book of *De anima* as a *reportatio* (an unedited set of notes taken at his lectures), or even to ascribe this first third of Aquinas' commentary to another author. However, Gauthier (1984: *275–82) has argued persuasively that the difference between the commentary's treatments of Book I and of Books II and III of *De anima* is explained by differences between the books themselves, and that in fact none of Aquinas' commentaries on Aristotle resulted from lectures he gave on those books. Discrepancies within this work, the first of Aquinas' Aristotelian commentaries, are likely to be at least in part a consequence of the fact that he was finding his way into this new sort of enterprise, at which he quickly became very adept. In a recent volume of essays on Aristotle's *De anima*, Martha Nussbaum describes Aquinas' work as 'one of the very greatest commentaries on the work' and 'very insightful' (Nussbaum 1992: 3–4). T.H. Irwin, a leading interpreter of Aristotle, acknowledges that at one point in the *Sententia libri Ethicorum* (Commentary on Aristotle's *Nicomachean Ethics*) Aquinas 'actually explains Aristotle's intention more clearly than Aristotle explains it himself' (Irwin 1992: 467). Such judgments apply pretty generally to Aquinas' Aristotelian commentaries, all of which are marked by his extraordinary ability as a philosophical commentator to discern a logical structure in almost every passage he examines in every sort of text: not only Aristotle's but also those of others, from Boethius to St Paul.

Since commenting on Aristotle was a regular feature of life for a member of a medieval arts faculty but never part of the duties of an academic theologian, Aquinas' many Aristotelian commentaries were technically extra-curricular and therefore an especially impressive accomplishment for someone who was already extremely busy. Some scholars, admiring Aquinas' achievements in general but focusing on the fact that his professional career was entirely in the theology faculty, have insisted on classifying only the Aristotelian commentaries as philosophical works. Certainly these commentaries are philosophical, as purely philosophical as the Aristotelian works they elucidate. However, Aquinas wrote these commentaries not only to make good philosophical sense of Aristotle's very difficult texts but also, and more importantly, to enhance his own understanding of the topics Aristotle had dealt with. As he remarks in his commentary on *De caelo*, 'the study of philosophy has as its purpose to know not what people have thought, but rather the truth about the way things are' (*Sententia super libros De caelo et mundo* I.22.228), and he believed that the theologian's attempt to understand God and everything else in relation to God was the fundamental instance of the universal human drive to know the truth about the way things are. Moreover, his view of the best way of making intellectual progress in general looks very much like the age-old method of philosophy: 'But if any people want to write back against what I have said, I will be very gratified, because there is no better way of uncovering the truth and keeping falsity in check than by arguing with people who disagree with you' (*De perfectione spiritualis vitae* 26) (see ARISTOTELIANISM, MEDIEVAL; ARISTOTLE; ARISTOTLE COMMENTATORS).

6 Rome: *Summa theologiae*

The other important innovation from Aquinas' three-year regency in Rome is *Summa theologiae*, his greatest and most characteristic work, begun in Rome and continued through the rest of his life. *Summa theologiae*, left incomplete at his death, consists of three large Parts. The First Part (Ia) is concerned with the existence and nature of God (Questions 1–43), creation (44–9), angels (50–64), the six days of creation (65–74), human nature (75–102) and divine government (103–19). The Second Part deals with morality, and in such detail that it is itself divided into two parts. The first part of the Second Part (IaIIae) takes up human happiness (Questions 1–5), human action (6–17), the goodness and badness of human acts (18–21), passions (22–48) and the sources of human acts: intrinsic (49–89) and extrinsic (90–114). The second part of the Second Part (IIaIIae) begins with the three theological virtues and corresponding vices (Questions 1–46), goes on through the four 'cardinal virtues' and corresponding vices (47–170) and ends with special issues associated with the religious life (171–89). In the Third Part, Aquinas deals with the incarnation (Questions 1–59) and the sacraments (60–90), breaking off in the middle of his discussion of penance.

Aquinas thought of *Summa theologiae* as a new kind of textbook of theology, and its most important pedagogical innovation, as he sees it, is in its organization. He says he has noticed that students new to theology have been held back in their studies by several features of the standard teaching materials, especially 'because the things they have to know are not imparted in an order appropriate to a method of teaching': an order he proposes to introduce. It may well have been his enthusiasm for this new approach that led him to abandon work on his quite differently organized *Compendium theologiae*, and his natural preoccupation during this period with the writing of *Summa theologiae* Ia may also help to account for the

7 Second Paris regency

In 1268 the Dominican Order again assigned Aquinas to the University of Paris, where he was regent master for a second time until, in the spring of 1272, all lectures at the university were canceled because of a dispute with the bishop of Paris. The Dominicans then ordered Aquinas to return to Italy.

Among the astounding number of works Aquinas produced in those four years is the huge Second Part of *Summa theologiae* (IaIIae and IIaIIae), nine Aristotelian commentaries, a commentary on the pseudo-Aristotelian *Liber de causis* (which, as Aquinas was the first to realize, is actually a compilation of Neoplatonic material drawn from Proclus), sixteen biblical commentaries and seven sets of disputed questions (including the set of sixteen *Quaestiones disputatae de malo* (Disputed Questions On Evil), the sixth of which provides his fullest discussion of free choice). His literary productivity during this second regency is the more amazing because he was at the same time embroiled in various controversies.

Sending Aquinas back to Paris in 1268 seems to have been, at least in part, his order's response to the worrisome movement of 'Latin Averroism' or 'radical Aristotelianism', then gaining ground among members of the arts faculty who were attracted to interpretations of Aristotle found in the commentaries of Averroes (see AVERROISM). However, only two of his many writings from these years seem to have obvious connections with the Averroist controversy. One of these, his treatise *De unitate intellectus, contra Averroistas* (On [the Theory of] the Unicity of Intellect, against the Averroists) is an explicit critique and rejection of a doctrine distinctive of the movement; the theory, as Aquinas describes it, that the aspect of the human mind 'that Aristotle calls the possible intellect... is some sort of substance separate in its being from the body and not united to it in any way as its form; and, what is more, that this possible intellect is one for all human beings' (*De unitate intellectus*, prooemium). After briefly noting that this view's incompatibility with Christian doctrine is too obvious to warrant discussion at any length, Aquinas devotes the entire treatise to showing that 'this position is no less contrary to the principles of philosophy than it is to the teachings of the Faith', and that it is even 'entirely incompatible with the words and views' of Aristotle himself (*De unitate intellectus*, prooemium).

Besides the unicity of intellect, the other controversial theory most often associated with thirteenth-century Averroism is the beginninglessness of the universe. In many of his works Aquinas had already considered the possibility that the world had always existed, skilfully developing and defending the bold position that revelation alone provides the basis for believing that the world began to exist, that one cannot prove either that the universe must or that it could not have begun, and that a world both beginningless and created is possible (although, of course, not actual). The second of Aquinas' Parisian treatises that is plainly relevant to Averroism is *De aeternitate mundi, contra murmurantes* (On the Eternity of the World, against Grumblers), a very short, uncharacteristically indignant summary of his position. Aquinas could not complain that Aristotle had been misinterpreted regarding the eternity of the world; after initially supposing this to be the case, he had become convinced that Aristotle really did think he had proved that the world must have existed forever. Aquinas' position on this issue did not distance him enough from the Averroists in the view of their contemporary 'Augustinian' opponents, most notably the Franciscans BONAVENTURE and PECHAM. In fact, the 'Grumblers' against whom Aquinas directed this treatise were probably not so much the Averroists in the arts faculty as those Franciscan theologians who maintained that they had demonstrated the impossibility of a beginningless world (see AUGUSTINIANISM; ETERNITY OF THE WORLD, MEDIEVAL VIEWS OF).

Aquinas' principled dissociation from some important Franciscans on this point must have helped to make his second Paris regency much more troubled than his first. In disputations conducted in Paris in 1266–7, the Franciscan master William of Baglione implicated Aquinas' views in the propositions he attacked, claiming that things Aquinas was saying encouraged the two heretical Averroist theses denounced by Bonaventure, namely the eternity of the world and the unicity of the intellect. 'The "blind leaders of the blind" decried by William evidently include Thomas as their chief' (Tugwell 1988: 226). It has also been persuasively argued that Aquinas' *De aeternitate mundi* was directed in particular against his Franciscan colleague in theology, John Pecham (Brady 1974). It seems, then, that Aquinas' development of a distinctly philosophical theology – which, like Albert's, was more Aristotelian than Augustinian – was dividing him from his colleagues in the Paris faculty of theology during these years. It may also have been bringing him closer to the philosophers in the arts faculty.

8 Last days

In June 1272 the Dominicans ordered Aquinas to leave Paris and go to Naples, where he was to establish another studium for the order and to serve as its regent master. Except for some interesting collections of sermons (originally preached in his native Italian dialect), the works dating from this period – two Aristotelian commentaries and the Third Part of *Summa theologiae* – were left unfinished. On or about 6 December 1273, while he was saying mass, something happened to Aquinas that left him weak and unable to go on writing or dictating. He himself saw the occasion as a special revelation. When Reginald of Piperno, his principal secretary and longtime friend, tried to persuade him to return to work on the Third Part of *Summa theologiae*, he said, 'Reginald, I can't.' And when Reginald persisted, Aquinas finally said, 'Everything I've written seems like straw by comparison with what I have seen and what has been revealed to me'. He believed that he had at last clearly seen what he had devoted his life to figuring out and, by comparison, all he had written seemed pale and dry. Now that he could no longer write, he told Reginald, he wanted to die. Soon afterwards he did die, on 7 March 1274 at Fossanuova, Italy, on his way to the Council of Lyons, which he had been ordered to attend.

9 Metaphysics

Every part of Aquinas' philosophy is imbued with metaphysical principles, many of which are recognizably Aristotelian. Consequently, concepts such as potentiality and actuality, matter and form, substance, essence, accident and the four causes – all of which are fundamental in Aquinas' metaphysics – should be considered in their original Aristotelian context (see ARISTOTLE §11). He invokes such principles often, and he employs them implicitly even more often. Two of his earliest writings – *De principiis naturae* (On the Principles of Nature) and especially *De ente et essentia* (On Being and Essence) – outline much of his metaphysics, almost as if they had been designed to provide guidelines for the development of his philosophy. Perhaps the most important thesis argued in De ente is the one that became known as 'the real distinction', Aquinas' view that the essence of any created thing is really, not just conceptually, distinct from its existence. Metaphysically speaking, corporeal beings are composites of form and matter, but all creatures, even incorporeal ones, are composites of essence and existence. Only the first, uncreated cause, God, whose essence is existence, is absolutely simple.

Except for his commentary on Aristotle's *Metaphysics*, Aquinas devoted no mature treatise to metaphysics itself. However, since he considers metaphysics to be the science of being considered generally (*ens commune*), and since he argues that being itself is first of all God himself and that all being depends on God, his philosophy does begin with metaphysics insofar as the most systematic presentations of his thought (in *Summa contra gentiles* and *Summa theologiae*) start with the investigation of God-in-himself considered as the foundation of the nature and existence of everything (see for example, *Summa contra gentiles* III.25; *Expositio super librum Boethii De trinitate* V.4, VI.1; §14 below).

Being, Aquinas says, is intellect's most fundamental conception, 'inherently its most intelligible object and the one in which it finds the basis of all conceptions.... Consequently all of intellect's other conceptions must be arrived at by adding to being... insofar as they express a mode of being which is not expressed by the term "being" itself' (*Quaestiones disputatae de veritate* 1.1c). There are, he claims, just two legitimate ways of making such additions. The first results in the ten Aristotelian Categories, each of which is a 'specified [or specific] mode of being' – substance, quantity, quality and the rest. The results of 'adding to being' in the second way are less familiar. Aquinas takes them to be five modes of being that are entirely general, characterizing absolutely every being. That is, being, wherever and however instantiated, exhibits these five modes, which transcend the Categories because they are necessary modes of all specified being: thing (*res*), one, something (*aliquid*), good, true. These five, together with being itself, are the 'transcendentals', predicable correctly (if sometimes a little oddly) of absolutely anything that is. 'Good' and 'true' are the philosophically interesting cases, because some beings are obviously not good and because 'true' seems applicable only to propositions.

The claim that all beings are true depends on taking 'true' in the sense of 'genuine', as in 'true friend', a sense that had been explored in detail by ANSELM OF CANTERBURY. In Anselm's view, any being is true in this sense to the extent to which it agrees with the divine idea of such a thing (and is otherwise false, but only to some extent). Absolutely every thing that is agrees to some extent with the divine idea that is an ingredient in its causal explanation. Propositions are true if they correspond to the way things are in the world; things in the world are true if they correspond to what is in the mind, God's mind first, ours derivatively. So, Aquinas says, 'in the soul there is a cognitive and an appetitive power. The word "good", then, expresses the conformity of a being to appetite (as is said at the beginning of the *Ethics*: "The good is what all desire"). The word "true", however, expresses the conformity of a being to intellect' (*Quaestiones disputatae de veritate* 1.1c).

The central thesis of Aquinas' meta-ethics grows out of this theory of the transcendentals. The thesis is the metaphysical principle that the terms 'being' and 'good' are the same in reference, differing only in sense (*Summa theologiae* Ia.5.1). What all desire is what they take to be the good, and what is desired is at least perceived as desirable (see for example, *Summa contra gentiles* I.37; III.3). Desirability is thus an essential aspect of goodness. If a thing of a certain kind is genuinely desirable as a thing of that kind, it is desirable to the extent to which it is perfect of that kind: a complete specimen, free from relevant defect. But a thing is perfect of its kind to the extent to which it has actualized its specifying potentialities, the potentialities that differentiate its species from other species in the same genus. So, Aquinas says, a thing is desirable as a thing of its kind and hence good of that kind to the extent to which it is actualized and in being (*Summa theologiae* Ia.5.1). Generally, then, 'being' and 'goodness' have the same referent: the actualization of specifying potentialities. The actualization of a thing's specifying potentialities to at least some extent is on the one hand its existence as such a thing; it is in this sense that the thing is said to have being. However on the other hand, the actualization of a thing's specifying potentialities is, to the extent of the actualization, that thing's being whole, complete, free from defect: the state all things are naturally aimed at. It is in this sense that the thing is said to have goodness (see for example *Summa theologiae* IaIIae.1.5; 94.2; *Summa contra gentiles* III.3; *Quaestiones disputatae de veritate* 21.1–2.)

Aquinas' concept of analogy is important to his thought, though perhaps not so important as it has sometimes been made to seem. It is often presented, correctly, in terms of analogical predication. However, his concept of analogy can be explained at a more fundamental level in connection with causation. Setting aside 'accidental' causation – for example, a gardener's uncovering buried treasure – Aquinas thinks that efficient causation always involves an agent (A), a patient (P), and a form (f). In non-accidental efficient causation, A antecedently has f, somehow. A's exercising causal power on P brings about f in P, *somehow*. Thus the efficient cause is A's acting (or exercising a power it has), and the effect is P's having f. The fact that A and P can have f in several different ways is what is brought out in '*somehow*'. The paradigm – straightforward efficient causation – is the kind Aquinas calls *univocal*: cases in which first A and then P have f in just the same way, and in which f can therefore be predicated truly of each in just the same sense. The metal hotplate and the metal kettle bottom resting on it are both called hot univocally: the form heat in these two causally related objects is the same specifically and differs only numerically.

However, Aquinas also recognizes two kinds of non-univocal efficient causation. The first, *equivocal* causation, characterizes cases in which there is no obvious respect in which to say that the f effected in P is found antecedently in A, and yet there is a natural causal connection (as there standardly is an etymological explanation for equivocal predication). If A is solar power and its effect is the hardening (f) of some clay (P), then obviously the sun's power is not itself hard, as the clay is. To say what it is about solar power that hardens clay will not be as easy as explaining the heating of the kettle, and yet the hardening of the clay must, somehow, be brought about by that power. In such a case, A has f only in the sense that A has the power to bring about f in P.

Second, *analogical* causation occurs when, for instance, a blood sample (P) is correctly labelled 'anaemic', although of course the blood itself doesn't have anaemia and cannot literally be anaemic. The physiology of the sample's donor (A) brings about a condition (f) in the sample that is an unmistakeable sign of anaemia in A, thus justifying that (analogical) labeling of the sample. For theological purposes, Aquinas is interested not in natural analogical causation but rather in the artificial kind: the kind that involves ideas and volitions, the artisan's kind. 'In other agents [the form of what is to be brought about occurs antecedently] in keeping with *intelligible* being, as in those agents that act through intellect – the way a likeness of the house exists antecedently in the builder's mind' (*Summa theologiae* Ia.15.1c). Since the status of entirely univocal causation depends on there being a merely numerical difference between the f in A and the f in P, an intellective agent effecting its ideas is obviously not a univocal cause. But neither is this difference between the antecedent f and the consequent f so wide as to constitute equivocal causation. In fact, the kind of association between the idea and its external manifestation is closer than the kind found in natural analogical causation; and since, in Aquinas' view, 'the world was brought about not by chance but by God acting through intellect... it is necessary that there be a form in the divine mind, a form in the likeness of which the world was made' (*Summa theologiae* Ia.15.1c). God, then, is the non-univocal, non-equivocal, intellectively analogical efficient cause of the world (see CAUSATION; GOD, CONCEPTS OF).

10 Philosophy of mind

Aquinas' philosophy of mind is part of his more general theory of soul, which naturally makes use of his metaphysics. Obviously he is not a materialist – most obviously because God, the absolutely fundamental element of his metaphysics, is in no way material. Aquinas classifies everything other than God as either corporeal or incorporeal (spiritual); he sometimes calls purely spiritual creatures – such as angels – 'separated substances' because of their essential detachment from body of any sort. However, this exhaustive division is not perfectly exclusive because human beings, simply by virtue of the human soul, must be classified not as simply corporeal but also as spiritual in a certain respect.

Merely having a soul of some sort is not enough to give a creature a spiritual component, however. Every animate creature has a soul (*anima*) – 'soul is what we call the first principle of life in things that live among us' (*Summa theologiae* Ia.75.1c) – but neither plants nor nonhuman animals are in any respect spiritual. Aquinas holds that even the merely nutritive soul of a plant, or the nutritive + sensory soul of a beast, is like the soul of a human being in being the *form* of a body. No soul, no first principle of life, can be *matter*. On the other hand, any vegetable or animal body has the life it has only in virtue of being a body whose special organization confers on it natural potentialities: that is, in virtue of the substantial form that makes it actually be such a body. Therefore, the first principle of life in a living non-human body, its soul, is no bodily part of that body but is rather its form, one of the two metaphysical components of the composite of matter and form that every body is. For plants and beasts, unlike humans, the form that is the soul goes out of existence when the composite dies, and it is in that sense that the souls of plants and beasts are not spiritual.

Only the soul of a human being is analyzed as nutritive + sensory + *rational*. Aquinas thinks of this soul not as three nested, cooperating forms, but as the single substantial form that gives a human being its specifically human mode of existence. (In defending this thesis of 'the unicity of substantial form', Aquinas differed from most of his contemporaries.) He often designates this entire substantial form by its distinctively human aspect of rationality. He also thinks that the human soul, unlike the souls of plants and beasts, is subsistent: that is, it continues to exist after separating from the body in death. He says, for example: 'It is necessary to say that that which is the principle of intellective activity, what we call the soul of a human being, is an incorporeal, subsistent principle' (*Summa theologiae* Ia.75.2c). The human soul, just because it is distinctively mind (the principle of intellective activity), must therefore be described not only as incorporeal but also as subsistent.

It may seem impossible for Aquinas' account to accommodate the claim that souls persist and engage in mental acts after the death of the body. If the separated soul is a form, what is it a form of? Aquinas is not a universal hylomorphist; unlike some of his contemporaries, he does not think that there is 'spiritual matter' that angels or disembodied souls have as one of their components, but rather that they are separated forms that configure no matter at all. Thus when he claims that the soul exists apart from the body, he seems to be holding the view that there can be a form with nothing of which it is the form. Moreover, Aquinas thinks that an angel or the soul separated from the body engages in mental activity. However, a form seems not to be the sort of thing that enages in acts of any sort, and so it appears that even if there were some way to explain the existence of the soul apart from the body, its acting could not be explained.

In this connection, it is helpful to examine Aquinas' broader view of form. The world is ordered metaphysically in such a way that at the top of the universal hierarchy there are forms – God and angels – that are not forms *of* anything. Near the bottom of the hierarchy are forms that configure matter but cannot exist in their own right, apart from the corporeal composites they inform. The forms of inanimate things and of animate, non-rational things are of that sort. Those forms inform matter, but when the resultant composites cease to exist, those forms also cease to exist. In the middle – 'on the borderline between corporeal and separated [that is, purely spiritual] substances' – are human souls, the metaphysical amphibians (*Quaestio disputata de anima* 1c). Like angels, human souls are subsistent, able to exist on their own; but, like the forms of inanimate things, human souls configure matter.

Seeing the soul in this light helps to explain some of what is initially puzzling in Aquinas' account. The human soul has a double character. On the one hand, unlike the forms of other material things, it is created by God as an individual entity in its own right, able to exist by itself as do purely immaterial angels. On the other hand, like the form of any corporeal thing, it exists in the composite it configures, and it comes into existence only with that composite, not before it (see SOUL, NATURE AND IMMORTALITY OF THE).

11 Theory of knowledge

Nature, Aquinas thinks, must be arranged so as to enable human beings in general to satisfy their natural desire to know (*Sententia super Metaphysicam* I.1.3–4). His view of the arrangement actually provided seems at first too tight to be true, involving some sort of formal identity between the extra-mental object (*O*) and the cognizing faculty (*F*) in its actually cognizing *O*. However, Aquinas takes that (Aristotelian) identity-claim to mean only that the form of *O* is somehow *in F* (*Summa theologiae* Ia.85.2, ad 1). *O*'s form comes to be in *F* when *F* receives species, either sensory or intellective, of *O*. These species may be thought of as encodings of *O*'s form. If *O* is a particular corporeal object – an iron hoop, for instance – then in *O* itself *O*'s form informs matter to produce an iron hoop of just those dimensions at just that spatio-temporal location. (In Aquinas' account of individuation, it is matter that is 'designated' or 'determinate' in this way that individuates *O*'s form: see for example *De ente et essentia* 2.) But when the appropriately encoded form is received in an external sense faculty *F* (which uses a bodily organ), then, even though it is received *materially* in *F*'s matter, it is nonetheless received differently from its reception in the matter of the hoop. The imposition of the form on the matter of the sense organ constitutes an 'intentional' or 'spiritual' reception of the form, contributing to a cognition of the hoop rather than metaphysically constituting a new, individuated matter–form composite.

Sensory species received in external senses are standardly transmitted to 'internal senses', the organs for which, Aquinas thought, must be located in the brain. Among the most important of these for purposes of cognition are 'phantasia' and 'imagination' (although Aquinas usually treats imagination as part of the power of phantasia). Phantasia and imagination produce and preserve 'phantasms', the sensory data that are necessary preconditions for intellective cognition. Imagination and phantasia are also indispensable to conscious sensory cognition. In Aquinas' view, sensible species themselves are not the objects of cognition, and what he says about phantasia suggests that having sensible species isn't sufficient for having sensory cognition. *O* itself, currently having a natural effect on the external senses, is consciously sensed because phantasia has processed *O*'s sensible species into phantasms.

The form presented in a phantasm has of course been stripped of its original, individuating matter, but a phantasm of *O* remains particularized as a phantasm in virtue of having been received in the *different* matter of phantasia's organ, while remaining recognizably the form of *O* because of the details of *O* that are preserved in it. However, cognition of *O* as an iron hoop is conceptual, intellective cognition, for which phantasms are only the raw material.

In intellect itself, Aquinas distinguishes two Aristotelian 'powers'. The first is *agent intellect*, the essentially active or productive aspect of intellect, which acts on phantasms in a way that produces 'intelligible species'. These constitute the primary contents of intellect, stored in *possible intellect*, intellect's essentially receptive aspect. 'Through intellect it is natural for us to have cognition of natures. Of course, [as universals] natures do not have existence except in individuating matter. It is natural for us to have cognition of them, however, not as they are in individuating matter but as they are abstracted from it by intellect's consideration', the work of agent intellect, producing intelligible species (*Summa theologiae* Ia.12.4c). The intelligible species of *O* are unlike sensory species of it in that they are only universals, which occur as such only in possible intellect: for example, round, metallic, iron hoop. These 'universal natures' are not only received in the intellective faculty *F*, the possible intellect, but are also of course used regularly as the devices indispensable for intellective cognition of corporeal reality: 'Our intellect both abstracts intelligible species from phantasms, insofar as it considers the natures of things universally, and yet also has intellective cognition of them [the things] in the phantasms, since without attending to phantasms it cannot have intellective cognition of even those things whose [intelligible] species it abstracts' (*Summa theologiae* Ia.85.1, ad 5). It is in this way that 'in intellection we can have cognition of such [particular, corporeal, composite] things in universality, which is beyond the faculty of sense' (*Summa theologiae* Ia.12.4c).

Thus both sense and intellect have cognition of *O*, a particular corporeal thing. However, sense has cognition of *O* only in its particularity (*Sententia super Posteriora analytica* II.20.14). Further, an individual intellect that happened to have the concept 'iron hoop' would have cognition only of a universal nature that happened to be instantiated in *O*, and not also of any instantiation of that nature – unless that intellect were also attending to phantasms of *O*. It is as a result of this attending that intellect also cognizes *O* itself, but as exemplifying a universal, for example, as an iron hoop (*Summa theologiae* Ia.85.5c; *Sententia super De anima* II.12.377).

Although intellect regularly has cognition of a corporeal particular in the way described, its proper object, Aquinas says, is that particular's universal nature, or 'quiddity'. Intellect's 'first operation', then, is its cognition of a universal, its proper object (although as we have seen, agent intellect's abstracting of intelligible species is a necessary step on the way to the cognition of the quiddities of things). Aquinas sometimes calls this first operation 'understanding'.

However, *scientia*, which is one of the last operations of intellect, a pinnacle of intellective cognition, also has the natures of things as its objects (see below). Universal natures, the proper objects of intellect's first operation and the objects of the culminating theoretical knowledge of nature, must then be thought of as proper objects of both the beginning and the culmination of intellective cognition. What is cognised in an unanalysed way in the first operation of the intellect – for example, *animal* – is in scientific cognition analysed into the essential parts of its nature – *sensitive animate corporeality* – which are themselves comprehended in terms of all their characters and capacities. In theory, in potentiality, the culminating cognitive state is all that could be hoped for: 'if the human intellect comprehends the substance of any thing – a rock, for example, or a triangle – *none* of the intelligible aspects of that thing exceeds the capacity of human reason' (*Summa contra gentiles* I.3.16).

Intellect's 'second operation' is the making of judgments, affirming by propositionally 'compounding' with one another concepts acquired in the first operation, or denying by 'dividing' them from one another. At every stage past initial acquisition, the cognition of quiddities will partially depend on this second operation, and on reasoning as well: 'the human intellect does not immediately, in its first apprehension, acquire a complete cognition of the thing. Instead, it first apprehends *something* about it – that is, its quiddity, which is a first and proper object of intellect; and *then* it acquires intellective cognition of the properties, accidents, and dispositions associated with the thing's essence. In doing so it has to compound one apprehended aspect with another, or divide one from another, and proceed from one composition or division to another, which is reasoning.' This is sometimes called intellect's third operation (*Summa theologiae* Ia.85.5c).

The framing of propositions and the construction of inferences involving them are necessary preconditions of the culminating intellective cognition Aquinas recognizes as *scientia*, which he discusses in greatest detail in his *Sententia super Posteriora analytica* (Commentary on Aristotle's *Posterior Analytics*). The interpretation of his account of *scientia* is controversial, but one helpful way to view it is as follows. To cognize a proposition with *scientia* is, strictly speaking, to accept it as the conclusion of a 'demonstration'. Of course, many premises in demonstrations may themselves be conclusions of other demonstrations; some, however, must be accepted not on the basis of demonstration but *per se* (*Sententia super Posteriora analytica* I.7.5–8). Such propositions, knowable *per se* (although not always *per se* knowable by us) are Aquinas' first principles. Like Aristotle, he calls them immediate propositions; that is, they cannot themselves be the conclusions of demonstrations, and their truth is evident to anyone who fully understands their terms, who not merely grasps their ordinary meaning but also comprehends the real nature of their referents. The predicate of an immediate proposition belongs to the *ratio* of the proposition's subject, and the *ratio* is the formulation of the subject's real nature (*Sententia super Posteriora analytica* I.10; 33). Thus for example, Aquinas considers 'God exists' to be self-evident, since according to the doctrine of simplicity God's nature is God's existence. 'God exists' is a good example of a proposition knowable *per se* but, as Aquinas insists in rejecting Anselm's ontological argument, not knowable *per se* by us. It is for that reason that he develops a number of *a posteriori* arguments for God's existence, among which the most famous are the 'Five Ways', found in *Summa theologiae* Ia.2.3c (see GOD, ARGUMENTS FOR THE EXISTENCE OF).

Anyone who has a developed concept of the subject's real nature is certain of the truth of such an immediate proposition, 'but there are some immediate propositions the terms of which not everyone knows. That is why although the predicate of such a proposition does belong to the ratio of its subject, the proposition need not be granted by everyone, just because its subject's [metaphysical] definition is not known to everyone' (*Sententia super Posteriora analytica* I.5.7). Because proper demonstrations are isomorphic with metaphysical reality, the facts expressed in their premises are regularly to be construed as causes of the facts in their conclusions (*Sententia super Posteriora analytica* I.2.9), although in some cases demonstrative reasoning goes the other way, from effects to causes. So, having *scientia* with respect to some proposition is the fullest possible human cognition, by which one situates the fact expressed by a conclusion in an explanatory theory that accurately maps metaphysical or physical reality.

According to Aquinas, then, what demonstration provides is not so much knowledge as it has been conceived of by foundationalists (for example, DESCARTES) as it is depth of understanding and explanatory insight. In general, Aquinas does not begin with self-evident principles and derive conclusions from them deductively; 'rather [he begins] with a statement to be justified (it will become the "conclusion" only in a formal restatement of the argument) and "reduce[s]" it back to its ultimate explanatory principles' (Durbin 1968: 82). When Aquinas himself describes his project generally, he says that there are two different processes in which human reason engages: *discovery* (or invention) and *judgment*. When we engage in discovery, we proceed from first principles, reasoning from them to other things; in judgment we reason to first principles on the basis of a kind of analysis. In his view, it is judgment's reasoning process, not that of discovery, that leads to *scientia*, and judgment is the subject of the *Posterior Analytics*: 'Judgment goes with the certitude of *scientia*. And it is because we cannot have certain judgment about effects except by analysis leading to first principles that this part of human reasoning is called "analytics"' (*Sententia super Posteriora analytica*, prooemium).

Sceptical worries seldom intrude on Aquinas' scattered development of his systematically unified theory of knowledge, largely because it is based on a metaphysics in which the first principle of existence is an omniscient, omnipotent, perfectly good God, whose rational creatures could not have been made so as to be standardly mistaken about the rest of creation (see GOD, CONCEPTS OF; KNOWLEDGE, CONCEPT OF).

12 Will and action

Philosophy of mind is obviously relevant to epistemology in its account of the mechanisms of cognition, especially of intellect. In its account of will it is just as obviously relevant to action theory and to ethics. Aquinas' concern with moral issues is even greater than his considerable interest in epistemological issues, and his ethics is so fully developed that he integrates his systematic treatment of acts of will into it rather than including such a treatment in his philosophy of mind.

As intellect is the cognitive faculty of the distinctively human rational soul, so will is its appetitive faculty. Will's metaphysical provenance is more primitive than intellect's; it is merely the most subtle terrestrial instantiation of an utterly universal aspect of creation. Not only every sort of soul but absolutely every form, Aquinas maintains, has some sort of inclination essentially associated with it; and so every hylomorphic thing, even if inanimate, has at least one natural inclination: 'on the basis of its form, fire, for instance, is inclined toward a higher place, and toward generating its like' (*Summa theologiae* Ia.80.1c). Inclination is the genus of appetite, and appetite is the genus of will. The human soul of course involves *natural appetites* – for example, for food – but its sensory and intellective modes of cognition bring with them *sensory appetites*, or passions – for example, for seafood – and *rational appetite*, or volition – for example, for food low in fat content.

In human beings, sensory appetite, or 'sensuality', is a cluster of inclinations (passions) to which we are subject (passive) by animal nature. Following an Aristotelian line, Aquinas thinks of sensuality as sorted into two complementary powers: the *concupiscible* – pursuit/avoidance instincts – and the *irascible* – competition/aggression/defense instincts. With the former are associated the emotions of joy and sadness, love and hate, desire and repugnance; with the latter, daring and fear, hope and despair, anger.

For philosophy of mind and for ethics, one important issue is the manner and extent of the rational faculties' control of sensuality, a control without which the harmony of the human soul is threatened and morality is impossible – especially in Aquinas' reason-centered ethics with its focus on virtues and vices. A human being who is not aberrantly behaving like a non-rational animal 'is not immediately moved in accordance with the irascible and concupiscible appetite but waits for the command of will, which is the higher appetite' (*Summa theologiae* Ia.81.3c). But the kind of control exercised by a cognitive rational faculty (standardly identified in this role as 'practical reason' rather than the broader 'intellect') is less obvious, and is particularly interesting in view of Aquinas' account of intellective cognition. The rational faculties can direct the attention of the external senses and compensate to some extent for their malfunctioning, but they cannot directly control what the external senses initially perceive on any occasion. On the other hand, sensuality and the internal senses are not directly related to mind-independent external things, and so to some extent 'they are subject to reason's command', although they too can fight against reason (*Summa theologiae* Ia.81.3, ad 3). Elaborating an Aristotelian theme (*Politics* I, 2), Aquinas observes that the soul's rule over the body is 'despotic': in a normal body, any bodily part that can be moved by an act of will will be moved immediately when and as will commands. But the rational faculties rule sensuality 'politically', because the powers and passions that are the intended subjects of this rational governance are also moved by imagination and sense, and so are no slaves to reason. 'That is why we experience the irascible or the concupiscible fighting against reason when we sense or imagine something pleasant that reason forbids, or something unpleasant that reason commands' (*Summa theologiae* Ia.81.3, ad 2).

According to Aquinas, the volition for happiness in general is an ineluctable part of human nature (see §13 below). Nonetheless, 'the movement of a creature's will is not determined in particular to seeking happiness in this, or in that' (*Quaestiones disputatae de veritate* 24.7, ad 6). This sort of freedom of will is freedom of specification or 'freedom as regards the object', freedom in the 'determining' aspect of volition. It is distinguished from freedom of exercise or 'freedom as regards the act', freedom associated with will's 'executive' capacity, for either acting or not acting to achieve something apprehended as good.

The interpretation of Aquinas' account of freedom of will is controversial. The very phrase 'freedom of will' is part of the difficulty, because it imports a concept from a later tradition. Aquinas conceives of freedom as *liberum arbitrium* (free decision or judgment), which cannot be attributed to will alone. It is a property that inheres in the system of intellect and will as a whole, that emerges from their interaction. However, it is perhaps safe to say that, since Aquinas emphatically denies that any volition caused by something extrinsic to the agent can be free, his account of freedom of will is not a version of compatibilism (see for example *Summa theologiae* IaIIae.6.4). The one apparent exception has to do with God's acting on a human will. Aquinas holds that among extrinsic forces, God alone can act directly on some other person's will without violating the will's nature, that is, without undermining its freedom (see for example *Summa theologiae* IaIIae.9.6). On this basis, some interpreters characterize Aquinas as a theological compatibilist; however, the subtle complexities of his account of God's action on human wills leads others to claim that a full appreciation of those complexities would show that Aquinas is not in any sense a compatibilist (see DETERMINISM AND INDETERMINISM; FREE WILL).

Aquinas' analysis of human action, built on his account of will and intellect, is complicated and not readily summarized. Generally speaking, he finds elaborately ordered mental components in even simple acts. For instance, in a case of raising one's hand to attract attention we are likely to suppose that the mental antecedents of the bodily movement are just the agent's combined beliefs and desires, whether or not the agent is fully conscious of them. Aquinas would of course agree that the agent need not be completely aware of the overt action's mental antecedents, but he sees them as having a complex, hierarchical structure.

On his analysis, the action begins when (I1) the agent's intellect apprehends a certain end – attracting attention – as a good to be achieved in these particular circumstances. (I1) thus gives rise to a second component: (W1) the agent's will forms a simple volition for that end. Then, (I2) the agent's intellect considers whether the end can be achieved at that time. If the result of (I2) is affirmative, then on that basis (W2) the agent's will forms an intention to achieve the end by some means or other. Next, (I3) the agent's intellect surveys the available means and settles on one or more that would be suitable to achieve the end and acceptable to the agent, and (W3) the agent's will accepts the means. If intellect has found more than one suitable and acceptable means, then (I4) intellect compares them and determines which is best in the circumstances, and (W4) will opts for that means. The process comes to its natural end when (W5) the agent's will exercises its control over the agent's arm, and the arm goes up. This ordered series looks deterministic, but as Aquinas views the interaction between intellect and will, the process could go otherwise at almost any point because will could direct intellect to reconsider, to direct attention in some other way, or even just to stop thinking about the issue (*Summa theologiae* IaIIae.6–17).

13 Ethics, law and politics

Aquinas' moral theory is developed most extensively and systematically in the Second Part of *Summa theologiae*. (Broadly speaking, the general theory is in IaIIae and the detailed consideration of particular issues is in IIaIIae.) Like almost all his predecessors, medieval and ancient, Aquinas sees ethics as having two principal topics: first, the ultimate goal of human existence, and second, how that goal is to be won, or lost. Of the 303 Questions making up *Summa theologiae*'s Second Part, 298 are concerned in one way or another with the second topic, and only the first 5 are concerned directly with the first (although in *Summa contra gentiles* III he devotes chapters 25–40 to a detailed examination of it).

Summa theologiae IaIIae.1–5, sometimes called the Treatise on Happiness, develops an argument to establish the existence and nature of a single ultimate end for all human action, or, more strictly, the kind of behaviour over which a person has 'control'. First, 'all actions that proceed from a power are caused by that power in accordance with the nature of its object. But the object of will is an end and a good', that is, an end perceived as good by the willer's intellect (*Summa theologiae* IaIIae.1.1c). From this starting point Aquinas develops an argument designed to show that a human being necessarily (though not always consciously) seeks everything it seeks for its own ultimate end, happiness.

Aquinas argues that the often unrecognized genuine ultimate end for which human beings exist (their 'object') is God, perfect goodness personified; and perfect happiness, the ultimate end with which they may exist (their 'use' of that object), is the enjoyment of the end for which they exist. That enjoyment is fully achieved only in the beatific vision, which Aquinas conceives of as an activity. Since the beatific vision involves the contemplation of the ultimate (first) cause of everything, it is, whatever else it may be, also the perfection of all knowledge and understanding (*Summa theologiae* IaIIae.1.8; 3.8).

Aquinas devotes just four questions of *Summa theologiae* IaIIae (18–21) to 'the goodness and badness of human acts in general'. Although considerations of rightness and wrongness occupy only a little more than ten per cent of the discussion in Questions 18–21, Aquinas nonetheless appears to think of rightness and wrongness as the practical, distinctively moral evaluations of actions. His emphasis on the broader notions of goodness and badness reveals the root of his moral evaluation of actions in his metaphysical identification of being and goodness (see §9 above).

What makes an action morally bad is its moving the agent not toward, but away from, the agent's ultimate goal. Such a deviation is patently irrational, and Aquinas' analysis of the moral badness of human action identifies it as fundamentally irrationality, since irrationality is an obstacle to the actualization of a human being's specifying potentialities, those that make *rational* the differentia of the human species. In this as in every other respect, Aquinas' ethics is reason-centred:

> In connection with human acts the words 'good' and 'bad' are applied on the basis of a comparison to reason, because... a human being's good is existing in accordance with reason, while what is bad for a human being is whatever is contrary to reason. For what is good for any thing is what goes together with it in keeping with its form, and what is bad for it is whatever is contrary to the order associated with its form.
>
> (*Summa theologiae* IaIIae.18.5c)

It would be a mistake, however, to suppose that Aquinas takes moral evil to consist in intellective error. Because of the very close relationship he sees between intellect and will, the irrationality of moral wrongdoing will be a function of will as well, not just of intellect. In Aquinas' view, the moral evaluation of a human action attaches primarily to the 'internal act', the volition from which the external act derives. Since 'will is inclined toward reason's good [the good presented to will by intellect] by the very nature of the power of will', bad volition stems from defective deliberation (*Summa theologiae* IaIIae.50.5, ad 3). As intellect and will continually influence each other, so bad deliberation can also be an effect of bad volition. Moreover, practical intellect's mistakes in identifying the best available course of action may also have the passions of the sensory soul as sources.

Furthermore, 'because the good [presented by intellect] is varied in many ways, it is necessary that will be inclined through some habit toward some determinate good presented by reason so that [will's determining] activity may follow more promptly' (*Summa theologiae* IaIIae.50.5, ad 3). Habits of will are conditions necessary for our carrying out our volitions in particularly good or particularly bad ways, as regards both the 'executive' and the 'determining' aspects of volition; and the habits that play these crucial roles in Aquinas' moral theory are the virtues and the vices.

The four 'cardinal virtues' can be understood as habits of this sort. Reason's habit of good governance generally is *prudence*; reason's restraint of self-serving concupiscence is *temperance*; reason's persevering despite self-serving 'irascible' passions such as fear is *courage*; reason's governance of one's relations with others despite one's tendencies toward selfishness is *justice*. Aquinas' normative ethics is based not on rules but on virtues; it is concerned with dispositions first and only then with actions. In addition to the moral virtues in all their various manifestations, Aquinas also recognizes intellectual virtues that, like the moral virtues, can be acquired by human effort. On the other hand, the supreme theological virtues of faith, hope and charity cannot be acquired but must be directly 'infused' by God. Aquinas introduces these virtues and others in *Summa theologiae* IaIIae 49–88 and examines them in detail throughout IIaIIae (see VIRTUE ETHICS).

Passions, virtues and vices are all intrinsic principles, or sources, of human acts. However, there are extrinsic principles as well, among which is law in all its varieties. Consequently, Aquinas moves on in *Summa theologiae* IaIIae.90–108 to his Treatise on Law, a famous and original treatment of the subject. The best-known feature of the treatise is Aquinas' concept of natural law. Law in general is 'a kind of rational ordering for the common good, promulgated by the one who takes care of the community' (*Summa theologiae* IaIIae.90.4c), and 'the precepts of natural law are to practical reasoning what the first principles of demonstrations are to theoretical reasoning.... All things to be done or to be avoided pertain to the precepts of natural law, which practical reasoning apprehends naturally as being human goods' (IaIIae.94.2c). Human laws of all kinds derive, or should derive, from natural law, which might be construed as the naturally knowable rational principles underlying morality in general: 'From the precepts of natural law, as from general, indemonstrable principles, it is necessary that human reason proceed to making more particular arrangements... [which] are called human laws, *provided that* they pertain to the definition (*rationem*) of law already stated' (IaIIae.91.3c). As a consequence of this hierarchy of laws, Aquinas unhesitatingly rejects some kinds and some particular instances of human law, for example: 'A tyrannical law, since it is not in accord with reason, is not unconditionally a law but is, rather, a perversion of law' (IaIIae.92.1, ad 4). Even natural law rests on the more fundamental 'eternal law', which Aquinas identifies as divine providence, 'the very nature of the governance of things on the part of God as ruler of the universe' (IaIIae.91.1c) (see NATURAL LAW).

In *De regimine principum* (The Governance of Rulers), his most important political work, Aquinas begins by sounding the familiar medieval theme: monarchy is the best form of government. However, he realizes that a single ruler is easily corrupted and that monarchy therefore has a tendency to turn into tyranny. He seems not to countenance revolution against a legitimate ruler who has become tyrannical (*De regimine principium* 6), but he maintains that radical means, including tyrannicide, may be justified against a usurper. Perhaps because he came to appreciate the dangers in monarchy, he gradually works republican elements into his theory of good government. His later commentary on Aristotle's *Politics* seems to erode the dominant monarchical model further in its treatment of the notions of the commonwealth (*res publica*) and of the citizen as one who rules and is ruled in turn (see POLITICAL PHILOSOPHY, HISTORY OF).

14 Theology: natural, revealed and philosophical

Because Aquinas developed most of his thought within the formal confines of thirteenth-century theology, and because this has in turn affected his place in the history of philosophy and the assessment of his work, some attention must be paid to the ways in which much of what we recognize as philosophy was an essential component of what he thought of as theology.

Aquinas devotes the first three books of *Summa contra gentiles* to a systematic development of natural theology, which he saw as part of philosophy (*Summa theologiae* Ia.1.1, ad 2) (see NATURAL THEOLOGY). As part of philosophy, natural theology must of course be based entirely on 'principles known by the natural light of intellect' (*Summa theologiae* Ia.1.2c), principles of the sort that underlie Aristotle's metaphysics, which Aristotle himself thought of as culminating in 'theology' (see Aquinas' interpretation of that thought in the prooemium to his *Sententia super Metaphysicam* (Commentary on Aristotle's *Metaphysics*). In fact, the way Aquinas works in *Summa contra gentiles* I–III strongly suggests that he may have thought of natural theology as a science subordinate to metaphysics, somewhat as he would have understood optics to be subordinate to geometry.

However, there is something odd about that project of his. By Aquinas' day the churchmen governing universities had overcome most of their initial misgivings about the recently recovered works of the pagan Aristotle, and had acknowledged officially that the study of Aristotelian physics and metaphysics (with their integrated minor component of natural theology) was compatible with the then universally recognized availability of revealed truths about God. Medieval Christians had come to appreciate the ancient philosophers' attempts to uncover truths about God on the basis of observation and reasoning alone as having been justified, even commendable, given their total ignorance of revelation. However, no philosopher in Aquinas' circumstances could have justifiably undertaken a new project of natural theology heuristically.

Still, no opprobrium would attach to natural theology taken up expositionally. The aim of such an enterprise would be not to develop theology from scratch but rather to show, in the spirit of Romans 1: 20, the extent to which what had been supernaturally revealed could, in theory, have been naturally discovered. Such an enterprise is what *Summa contra gentiles* I–III seems to represent.

Evidence from a chronicle written about seventy years after Aquinas began *Summa contra gentiles* once led scholars to suppose that he had written it as a manual for the use of Dominican missionaries to Muslims and Jews. If that were so, then the work's presentation of natural instead of revealed theology in its first three books would have been dictated by the practical purpose of rationally deriving the truth about God, and about God's relation to everything else, for people who would not have acknowledged the revealed texts Aquinas would otherwise have cited as the source of that truth. But nobody, and certainly not Aquinas, could have supposed that Muslims or Jews needed to be argued into perfect-being monotheism of the sort developed in those first three books, which contain nothing that he would have taken to be contrary to Judaism or Islam. If Aquinas had intended *Summa contra gentiles* as a manual for missionaries to educated Muslims, Jews or Christian heretics, he would have wasted the enormous effort represented in the 366 copiously argued chapters of Books I–III (see Gauthier 1961, 1993, for a persuasive rejection of the earlier account).

What Aquinas himself says about his purpose in writing *Summa contra gentiles* suggests that what he wrote had at least its formal cause not in an attempt to aid missionary activities, but instead in his consideration of the interrelation of philosophy and

Christianity. He begins by writing about the concerns of a wise person, one of those 'who give things an appropriate order and direction and govern them well' (*Summa contra gentiles* I.1.2). Obviously, such a person has to be concerned with goals and sources, and so the wisest person will be 'one whose attention is turned toward the universal goal, which is also the universal source', which Aquinas takes to be God (I.1.3). Because this natural theology is oriented as it is, 'it must be called the greatest wisdom itself, as considering the absolutely highest cause of all' (II.4.874). Therefore, the highest, most universal explanatory truth must be wisdom's concern. Anyone aspiring to wisdom will attend to metaphysics, since, Aquinas reports, Aristotle rightly identified metaphysics as 'the science of truth – not of just any truth, but of the truth that is the origin of all truth, the truth that pertains to the first principle of being for all things' (I.1.5). And, as he says in an observation that suits his own enterprise, 'sometimes divine wisdom proceeds from human philosophy's starting points' (II.4.875). However, since it is the business of one and the same science 'to pursue one of two contraries and to repel the other... the role of the wise person is to meditate on the truth, especially the truth regarding the first principle, and to discuss it with others, but also to fight against the falsity that is its contrary' (I.1.6). The truth regarding the first principle will be the truth about God, supposing natural theology can show that God exists; and so the explanatory truth associated here with metaphysics is the truth associated also with theology.

No one knows what title, if any, Aquinas himself gave to this work. In some of its medieval manuscripts, it is entitled *Liber de veritate catholicae fidei contra errores* (A Book About the Truth of the Catholic Faith, Directed Against Mistakes), a title that comes closer to accurately representing the book's aim and contents than the more pugnacious, traditional *Summa contra gentiles* (Synopsis [of Christian Doctrine] Directed Against Unbelievers). During the nineteenth century, when *Summa theologiae* (Synopsis of Theology) was instead normally referred to as *Summa theologica* (Theological Synopsis), *Summa contra gentiles* was sometimes published under the deliberately contrasting title *Summa philosophica* (Philosophical Synopsis). That contrast, although potentially misleading, has some truth in it, as may be seen in Aquinas' plan for *Summa contra gentiles* I–III: 'Since we intend to pursue by way of reason the things about God that human reason can investigate, the first consideration is of matters associated with God considered in himself [Book I]; second, of the emergence of created things from him [Book II]; third, of the ordering and directing of created things toward him as their goal [Book III]' (I.9.57).

In this pursuit by way of reason, Aquinas must and does shun 'authoritative arguments' of any sort, but he shows good sense in not restricting himself to 'demonstrative arguments' in developing natural theology. He does, of course, use demonstrative arguments when he thinks he has them, but, like almost all philosophers of any period, he recognizes philosophy's need for 'probable aguments' as well. A demonstrative argument takes as its premises propositions that explain the fact in the argument's conclusion by elucidating its causes (or, sometimes, its effects), and so it produces, or presents, scientific understanding. A probable argument – the sort that has always been most prevalent and most appropriate in philosophy – is one based on premises of any sort that are accepted widely or by experts in the relevant field, and so one group may be convinced by a probable argument that another group rejects. Of course, Aquinas has to make use of authoritative arguments in the fourth (and last) book, where he turns from natural to revealed theology, and his tolerance of them there is part of what distinguishes Book IV's argumentation from the sort that characterizes Books I–III.

In *Summa contra gentiles* IV, Aquinas engages in what has come to be called *philosophical theology*, the application of reason to revelation. Philosophical theology shares the methods of natural theology broadly conceived – in other words, analysis and argumentation of all the sorts accepted in philosophy – but it lifts natural theology's restriction on premises, accepting as assumptions revealed propositions. This includes those that are initially inaccessible to unaided reason, such as the 'mysteries' of Christian doctrine. In his many works of philosophical theology, Aquinas tests the coherence of doctrinal propositions (including the mysteries), attempts explanations of them, uncovers their logical connections with other doctrinal propositions and so on, in order to bear out his conviction that the doctrines themselves are eminently understandable and acceptable, and that the apparent incoherence of some of them is only a feature of our initial, superficial view of them.

Summa theologiae is the paradigm of philosophical theology. The very first Article of the very first Question makes it clear at once that it is not natural theology that *Summa theologiae* is a summa of, since it begins by asking whether we need any 'other teaching, besides philosophical studies'; which in Aquinas' usage means the studies that medieval beginners in theology would have just completed in the arts faculty. The question arises because philosophical studies are characterized not only as dealing with 'the things that are subject to reason', but also as encompassing 'all beings, including God', as a consequence of which 'part of philosophy is called theology'.

Although Aquinas accepts this characterization of philosophy's subject matter as universal and as including a part that is properly called theology, he offers several arguments to support his claim that revealed theology is nonetheless not superfluous. In one of those arguments, he claims that a thing's 'capacity for being cognized in various ways brings about a difference between sciences'. By this he means that different sciences can reason to some of the same conclusions on the basis of different premises or evidence. In his example, he points out that in order to support the proposition that the earth is round a naturalist uses empirical observations, while a cosmologist might support that same conclusion on a strictly formal basis. 'And for that reason', he concludes, 'nothing prevents the same things from being treated by philosophical studies insofar as they can be cognized by the light of natural reason, and also by another science insofar as they are cognized by the light of divine revelation. That is why the theology that pertains to *sacra doctrina* [in other words, revealed theology] differs in kind from the theology that is considered a part of philosophy' (ad 2).

In this argument, Aquinas might appear willing to concede that revealed and natural theology differ only in this methodological respect, that they simply constitute two radically different ways of approaching the very same propositions about God and everything else. However, he would not actually concede this. There are propositions that belong uniquely to revealed theology's subject matter, simply because the different premises with which revealed theology begins can also lead to conclusions not available to unaided reason. And, of course, no doctrinal proposition that is initially available to human beings only in virtue of having been revealed by God can be part of natural theology's subject matter.

On the other hand, no propositions appropriate to natural theology are excluded from *Summa theologiae*'s subject matter. The propositions that belong to natural theology form a proper subset of those that belong to revealed theology:

> It was necessary that human beings be instructed by divine revelation even as regards the things about God that human reason can explore. For the truth about God investigated by a few on the basis of reason [without relying on revelation] would emerge for people [only] after a long time and tainted with many mistakes. And yet all human well-being, which has to do with God, depends on the cognition of that truth. Therefore, it was necessary for human beings to be instructed about divine matters through divine revelation so that [the nature of human] well-being might emerge for people more conveniently and with greater certainty.
>
> (*Summa theologiae* Ia.1.1c)

When he sums up his examination of *sacra doctrina*, or revealed theology, Aquinas says that its 'main aim ... is to transmit a cognition of God, and not only as he is in himself, but also as he is the source of things, and their goal – especially of the rational creature' (*Summa theologiae* Ia.2, intro.). Thus the subject matter of *sacra doctrina*, the theology presented in this summa of theology, is the most basic truths about *everything*, with two provisos: first, it is about God and about things other than God as they relate to God as their source and goal; second, among things other than God it deals with, it is especially about human beings, whose study of theology should be motivated by the fact that their well-being depends specially on their grasp of certain theological truths. And, Aquinas insists, universal scope is just what one would expect in a rational investigation of the truth about God: 'All things are considered in *sacra doctrina* under the concept of God, either because they *are* God, or because they have an ordered relationship *to* God as to their source and goal. It follows from this that the subject of this science is really God', even though the intended explanatory scope of the science is universal (*Summa theologiae* Ia.1.7c).

In referring to *sacra doctrina* as a 'science', Aquinas means to characterize it as a systematic, reasoned presentation of an organized body of knowledge consisting of general truths about some reasonably unified subject matter. In that broadly Aristotelian sense, it is not obviously wrong to think of theology as a science (as it would be in the narrower, twentieth-century sense of 'science'). It is in that sense that the science of theology as Aquinas develops it in *Summa theologiae* would now be called philosophical theology, the enterprise of employing the techniques and devices of philosophy in clarifying, supporting and extending the propositions that are supposed to have been revealed for theology's starting points. Thus, some of the work of philosophical theology is an attempt to explain revealed propositions and systematically work out their implications.

Like natural theology, which is subordinate to metaphysics, philosophical theology is a subordinate science. However, because it begins its work on divinely revealed propositions, Aquinas identifies the 'science' to which it is subordinate as God's knowledge of himself and everything else, available to human beings directly only in the afterlife (*Summa theologiae* Ia.1.2c). As he says earlier, 'For us, the goal of faith is to arrive at an understanding of what we believe – [which is] as if a practitioner of a subordinate science were to acquire in addition the knowledge possessed by a practitioner of the higher science. In that case the things that were only believed before would come to be known, or understood' (*Expositio super librum Boethii De trinitate* 2.2, ad.7).

Not even the doctrinal mysteries are impervious to rational investigation, although unaided reason could never have discovered them. Regarding one central mystery, for example, Aquinas says: 'It is impossible to arrive at a cognition of the Trinity of the divine persons by means of natural reason' (*Summa theologiae* Ia.32.1c). However, he says this in the twenty-second of a series of seventy-seven articles of *Summa theologiae* devoted to analysing and arguing about the details of Trinity, in other words, in the midst of subjecting this mystery to philosophical theology. As he explains in the very Article in which he rules out the possibility of rationally discovering that there are three divine persons:

> There are two ways in which reason is employed regarding any matter... in one way to provide sufficient proof of something fundamental... in the other way to show that consequent effects are suited to something fundamental that has already been posited.... It is in the first way, then, that reason can be employed to prove that God is one, and things of that sort. But it is in the second way that reason is employed in a clarification of Trinity. For once Trinity has been posited, reasonings of that sort are suitable, although not so as to provide a sufficient proof of the Trinity of persons by those reasonings.
>
> (*Summa theologiae* Ia.32.1c)

Aquinas is also careful to point out that it isn't mere intellectual curiosity or even a defence of the faith that is served by a rational clarification of Trinity. In his view, this application of philosophical theology – confirming faith by reason, showing that Trinity is not after all irrational, exposing the intricate connections between these and other doctrinal propositions – aids one's understanding of creation and salvation (see TRINITY).

See also: ALBERT THE GREAT; ARISTOTELIANISM, MEDIEVAL; AUGUSTINIANISM; AVERROISM; DUNS SCOTUS, J.; DURANDUS OF ST POURÇAIN; GILES OF ROME; GOD, CONCEPTS OF; GODFREY OF FONTAINES; HERVAEUS NATALIS; JOHN OF PARIS; KILWARDBY, R.; KNOWLEDGE, CONCEPT OF; LOGIC, MEDIEVAL; MEDIEVAL PHILOSOPHY; NATURAL PHILOSOPHY, MEDIEVAL (§7); NATURAL THEOLOGY; PECHAM, J.; PETER OF AUVERGNE; RICHARD OF MIDDLETON; SIGER OF BRABANT; THOMISM

List of works

Not all of Aquinas' works exist in critical editions, but the many volumes of the Leonine Edition ordinarily provide the best available Latin texts. Most volumes of the Marietti Editions reproduce the Leonine text in handier form with useful aids to research. There are many translations into English and other modern languages, but by no means all the works have been translated. For detailed lists of editions and translations of each work see Torrell (1993), Weisheipl (1983) or Gilson (1956). Ingardia (1993) is an indispensable bibliography. Deferrari and Barry (1948) is an indispensable lexicon. Busa (1974–80) provides an exhaustive but somewhat unwieldy resource for research in Aquinas. The following is an approximately chronological list of works, excluding letters and liturgies. Places of composition are given after each work.

Aquinas, Thomas (1248–73) *Opera omnia* (Complete Works), ed. Leonine Commission, *S. Thomae Aquinatis Doctoris Angelici. Opera Omnia. Iussu Leonis XIII, P.M. edita*, Rome: Vatican Polyglot Press, 1882–. (Many of the editions in this series are repeated in the Marietti Editions.)

—— (1248–52, or 1252–6) *De principiis naturae, ad fratrem Sylvestrum* (On the Principles of Nature, for Brother Sylvester). (Written either at Cologne, 1248–52, or Paris, 1252–6).

—— (1251/2) *Expositio super Isaiam ad litteram* (Literal Commentary on Isaiah). (Written at Cologne.)

—— (1251/2) *Postilla super Ieremiam* (Commentary on Jeremiah). (Written at Cologne.)

—— (1251/2) *Postilla super Threnos* (Commentary on Lamentations). (Written at Cologne.)

—— (1252/3? or 1273?) *Postilla super Psalmos* (Commentary on Psalms). (Written either at Paris, 1252/3, or Naples, 1273. Incomplete, covers Psalms 1–54.)

—— (1252–6) *De ente et essentia, ad fratres et socios suos* (On Being and Essence, For His Brothers and Companions). (Written at Paris.)

—— (1253–6) *Scriptum super libros Sententiarum* (Commentary on the Sentences). (Written at Paris.)

—— (1256) *Principia:'Hic est liber mandatorum Dei' et 'Rigans montes de superioribus suis'* (Inaugural Lectures: 'This Is the Book of God's Commandments' and 'Watering the Hills from His Places Above'). (Written at Paris.)

—— (1256) *Contra impugnantes Dei cultum et religionem* (Against Those Who Assail the Worship of God and Religion). (Written at Paris, a refutation of William of Saint-Amour's *De periculis novissimorum temporum*.)

—— (1256–9) *Quaestiones disputatae de veritate* (Disputed Questions on Truth). (Written at Paris.)

—— (1256–9) *Quaestiones quodlibetales VII–XI* (Quodlibetal Questions VII–XII). (Written at Paris.)

—— (1257/8) *Expositio super librum Boethii De trinitate* (Commentary on Boethius' *De trinitate*). (Written at Paris; incomplete.)

—— (1259?) *Expositio super librum Boethii De hebdomadibus* (Commentary on Boethius' *De hebdomadibus*). (Written at Paris; incomplete.)

—— (1259–65) *Summa contra gentiles* (Synopsis [of Christian Doctrine] Directed Against Unbelievers). (Written at Paris, Naples and Orvieto.)

—— (1261–5) *Expositio super Iob ad litteram* (Literal Commentary on Job). (Written at Orvieto.)

—— (1261–5, or 1265–8) *Expositio super librum Dionysii De divinis nominibus* (Commentary on Dionysius' *De divinis nominibus*). (Written at Orvieto, 1261–5, or Rome, 1265–8.)

—— (1262–8) *Glossa continua super Evangelia (Catena aurea)* (A Continuous Gloss on the Four Gospels (The Golden Chain)). (Written at Orvieto and Rome.)

—— (1263/4) *Contra errores Graecorum, ad Urbanem IV Pontificem Maximum* (Against Mistakes of the Greek [Fathers of the Church], for Pope Urban IV). (Written at Orvieto, on an anonymous treatise, *De fide sanctae trinitatis contra errores Graecorum*.)

—— (1264) *De rationibus fidei contra Saracenos, Graecos, et Armenos, ad cantorem Antiochiae* (On Arguments for the Faith Directed against Mohammedans, Greek Orthodox Christians and Armenians, for the Cantor of Antioch).

—— (1265–6) *Quaestiones disputatae de potentia* (Disputed Questions on Power). (Written at Rome.)

—— (1265–6) *Quaestio disputata de anima* (Disputed Question on the Soul). (Twenty-one articles, written at Rome.)

—— (1265–7) *Responsio ad fr. Ioannem Vercellensem de articulis 108 sumptis ex opere Petri de Tarentasia* (Reply to Brother John of Vercelli Regarding 108 Articles Drawn from the Work of Peter of Tarentaise [on the Sentences]). (Written at Rome.)

—— (1265–7) *Compendium theologiae, ad fratrem Reginaldum socium suum* (A Compendium of Theology, for Brother Reginald, his Companion). (Written at Rome, incomplete.)

—— (1266–72) *Quaestiones disputatae de malo* (Disputed Questions on Evil). (Written at Rome and Paris.)

—— (1266–68) *Summa theologiae Ia* (Synopsis of Theology, First Part). (Written at Rome. See below for IaIIae, IIaIIae and IIIa. The whole of the *Summa theologiae* can be found in the Leonine edition, vols 4–12.)

—— (1267) *De regno [or De regimine principum], ad regem Cypri* (On Kingship [or On the Governance of Rulers], for the King of Cyprus). (Written at Rome. Authentic only through Book II, c. 4.)

—— (1267–8) *Sententia super De anima* (Commentary on Aristotle's *On the Soul*). (Written at Rome.)

—— (1267–8) *Quaestio disputata de spiritualibus creaturis* (Disputed Question on Spiritual Creatures [Angels]). (Eleven articles, written at Rome.)

—— (1268–9) *Sententia super Physicam* (Commentary on Aristotle's *Physics*). (Written at Paris.)

—— (1268–9) *Sententia super Meteora* (Commentary on Aristotle's *Meteora*). (Written at Paris, incomplete.)

—— (1268–70) *Sententia super De sensu et sensato* (Commentary on Aristotle's *De sensu et sensato*). (Written at Paris.)

—— (1268–71) *Summa theologiae IaIIae* (Synopsis of Theology, First Part of the Second Part). (Written at Rome and Paris.)

—— (1268–72) *Quaestiones quodlibetales I–VI, XII* (Quodlibetal Questions I–VI, XII). (Written at Paris.)

—— (1269) *De forma absolutionis sacramentalis, ad generalem magistrum Ordinis* (On the Form of Sacramental Absolution, for the Master General of the Order [John Vercelli]). (Written at Paris.)

—— (1269) *De secreto* (On Secret Testimony). (Written at Paris. A committee report in which Aquinas is the lone dissenter, supporting the right of a religious superior to compel a subject to reveal a secret even under the seal of confession.)

—— (1269–70) *Lectura super Matthaeum* (Lectures on the Gospel of Matthew). (Written at Paris.)

—— (1269–70) *De perfectione spiritualis vitae* (On the Perfecting of the Spiritual Life). (Written at Paris, directed against Gérard d'Abbeville's *Contra adversarium perfectionis christianae*.)

—— (1269–72) *Sententia libri Politicorum* (Commentary on Aristotle's *Politics*). (Written probably at Paris; incomplete.)

—— (1270?) *Sententia super De memoria et reminiscentia* (Commentary on Aristotle's *De memoria et reminiscentia*). (Written probably at Paris.)

—— (1270) *Tabula libri Ethicorum* (An Analytical Table of Aristotle's *Ethics*). (Written at Paris, incomplete.)

—— (1270) *De unitate intellectus, contra Averroistas* (On the Unicity of Intellect, Against the Averroists). (Written at Paris.)

—— (1270–1) *Sententia super Peri hermenias* (Commentary on Aristotle's *De interpretatione*). (Written at Paris, incomplete.)

—— (1270–2) *Lectura super Ioannem* (Lectures on the Gospel of John). (Written at Paris.)

—— (1270–3) *Sententia super Metaphysicam* (Commentary on Aristotle's *Metaphysics*). (Written at Paris and Naples.)

—— (1270–3) *Expositio et lectura super Epistolas Pauli Apostoli* (Commentary and Lectures on the Epistles of Paul the Apostle). (Written at Paris and Naples.)

—— (1271) *De aeternitate mundi, contra murmurantes* (On the Eternity of the World, Against Grumblers). (Written at Paris.)

—— (1271) *Responsio ad magistrum Ioannem de Vercellis de articulis 42* (Reply to Master John Vercelli Regarding Forty-Two Articles). (Written at Paris. Aquinas' answers to doctrinal questions which Vercelli submitted also to Albert the Great and Robert Kilwardby.)

—— (1271–2) *Summa theologiae IIaIIae* (Synopsis of Theology, Second Part of the Second Part). (Written at Paris.)

—— (1271–2) *Contra doctrinam retrahentium a religione* (Against the Teaching of Those Who Dissuade [Boys] from Entering the Religious Life). (Written at Paris, opposing the work of Gérard d'Abbeville.)

—— (1271–2) *Sententia libri Ethicorum* (Commentary on Aristotle's *Nicomachean Ethics*). (Written at Paris.)

—— (1271–2) *Sententia super Posteriora analytica* (Commentary on Aristotle's *Posterior Analytics*). (Written at Paris.)

—— (1271–2) *Quaestio disputata de virtutibus in communi* (Disputed Question on the Virtues in General). (Thirteen articles, written at Paris.)

—— (1271–2) *Quaestio disputata de caritate* (Disputed Question on Charity). (Thirteen articles, written at Paris.)

—— (1271–2) *Quaestio disputata de correctione fraterna* (Disputed Question on Fraternal Correction). (Two articles, written at Paris.)

—— (1271–2) *Quaestio disputata de spe* (Disputed Question on Hope). (Four articles, written at Paris.)

—— (1271–2) *Quaestio disputata de virtutibus cardinalibus* (Disputed Question on the Cardinal Virtues). (Four articles, written at Paris.)

—— (1271–3) *De substantiis separatis, ad fratrem Reginaldum socium suum* (On Separated Substances [Angels], for Brother Reginald, his Companion). (Written at Paris or Naples, incomplete.)

—— (1272) *Quaestio disputata de unione verbi incarnati* (Disputed Question on the Unity of the Incarnate Word). (Five articles, written at Paris.)

—— (1272) *Expositio super librum De causis* (Commentary on the *Liber de causis*). (Written at Paris.)

—— (1272–3) *Summa theologiae IIIa* (Synopsis of Theology, Third Part). (Written at Paris and Naples, incomplete.)

—— (1272–3) *Sententia super libros De caelo et mundo* (Commentary on Aristotle's *On Heaven and Earth*). (Written at Naples, incomplete.)

—— (1272–3) *Sententia super libros De generatione et corruptione* (Commentary on Aristotle's *On Generation and Corruption*). (Written at Naples, incomplete.)

—— (1273, or 1261–8?) *Collationes in decem praecepta* (Sermon Commentaries on the Ten Commandments). (Written at Naples, 1273, or possibly at Orvieto and Rome, 1261–8.)

—— (1273, or 1268–72?) *Collationes super Ave Maria* (Sermon Commentaries on the *Ave Maria*). (Written at Naples, 1273, or possibly at Paris, 1268–72.)

—— (1273) *Collationes super Credo in Deum* (Sermon Commentaries on the Apostles' Creed). (Written at Naples, 1273.)

—— (1273) *Collationes super Pater Noster* (Sermon Commentaries on the Lord's Prayer). (Written at Naples, 1273.)

References and further reading

Aertsen, J.A. (1988) *Nature and Creature: Thomas Aquinas' Way of Thought*, Leiden: Brill. (Novel approaches to establishing the inner coherence and identifying the direction of Aquinas' philosophy and theology.)

—— (1993) 'Aquinas' Philosophy in its Historical Setting', in N. Kretzmann and E. Stump (eds) *The Cambridge Companion to Aquinas*, Cambridge: Cambridge University Press, 12–37. (A concise presentation of the development of Aquinas' thought.)

Ashworth, E.J. (1991) 'Signification and Modes of Signifying in Thirteenth-Century Logic: A Preface to Aquinas on Analogy', *Medieval Philosophy and Theology* 1: 39–67. (The best introduction to the topic and the recent literature.)

Bigongiari, D. (ed.) (1953) *The Political Ideas of St. Thomas Aquinas*, New York: Hafner. (A useful survey.)

* Brady, I. (1974) 'John Pecham and the Background of Aquinas' *De Aeternitate Mundi*', in A.A. Maurer (ed.) *St. Thomas Aquinas 1274–1974: Commemorative Studies*, Toronto, Ont.: Pontifical Institute of Mediaeval Studies, vol. II, 141–78. (A well-

informed, persuasive presentation of the treatise's Augustinian background.)

Burrell, D.B. (1986) *Knowing the Unknowable God: Ibn Sina, Maimonides, Aquinas*, Notre Dame, IN: University of Notre Dame Press. (A knowledgeable exploration of Aquinas' intellectual relations with Islamic and Jewish thinkers.)

—— (1993) 'Aquinas and Islamic and Jewish Thinkers', in N. Kretzmann and E. Stump (eds) *The Cambridge Companion to Aquinas*, Cambridge: Cambridge University Press, 60–84. (An updated synopsis of material in Burrell (1986).)

Busa, R. (1974–80) *Index Thomisticus*, Stuttgart–Bad Cannstatt: Fromann-Holzboog. (Incomparably the most complete, multi-faceted research tool devised for the works of any medieval philosopher, accompanied by a complete but not readily usable edition of Aquinas' works.)

Chenu, M.D. (1964) *Toward Understanding St Thomas*, Chicago, IL: Regnery. (A classic interpretation.)

Copleston, F.C. (1955) *Aquinas*, Baltimore, MD: Penguin. (A philosophically and historically well-informed complete study; still useful.)

Davies, B. (1992) *The Thought of Thomas Aquinas*, Oxford: Clarendon Press. (An impressive attempt to present a complete picture of Aquinas' thought, following the schema of *Summa theologiae*.)

Deferrari, R.J. and Barry, Sister M. Inviolata (eds) (1948) *A Lexicon of St. Thomas Aquinas*, Washington, DC: Catholic University of America Press. (Still useful, and handier than Busa.)

Doig, J. (1972) *Aquinas on Metaphysics: A Historico-Doctrinal Study of the Commentary on the Metaphysics*, The Hague: Martinus Nijhoff. (Historically useful.)

Donagan, A. (1977) *The Theory of Morality*, Chicago, IL: University of Chicago Press. (A philosophically sophisticated development of Aquinas' moral theory.)

—— (1982) 'Thomas Aquinas on Human Action', in N. Kretzmann, A. Kenny and J. Pinborg (eds) *The Cambridge History of Later Medieval Philosophy*, Cambridge: Cambridge University Press, 642–54. (A good short analysis of Aquinas' complex action theory.)

* Durbin, P.T. (1968) *St Thomas Aquinas: Summa Theologiae*, Blackfriars edition and translation, vol. XII, New York: McGraw-Hill. (Useful notes and appendices on Aquinas' theory of the nature and activity of intellect.)

Fabro, C. (1961) *Participation et causalité selon Saint Thomas d'Aquin* (Participation and Causality in the Work of Saint Thomas Aquinas), Louvain: Publications Universitaires de Louvain. (An influential study bringing out Platonist elements in Aquinas' metaphysics.)

Finnis, J. (1980) *Natural Law and Natural Rights*, New York: Oxford University Press. (A magisterial presentation of these notions and their place in Aquinas' thought.)

Foster, K. (1959) *The Life of Saint Thomas Aquinas, Biographical Documents*, London: Longmans, Green. (A translation of the oldest biographies and other documents used in the canonization proceedings, 1317–23.)

* Gauthier, R.-A. (1961) 'Introduction', in *Saint Thomas d'Aquin: Contra Gentiles, Livre premier*, Lyon: P. Lethielleux. (A ground-breaking study of the background and purposes of *Summa contra gentiles*, persuasively rejecting the 'missionary' account.)

* —— (ed.) (1984) *Sancti Thomae de Aquino: Opera Omnia iussu Leonis XIII P.M. edita, Tomus XLV, 1: Sentencia libri de anima*, Rome: Commissio Leonina. (A particularly impressive volume of the Leonine edition, with a very thorough scholarly introduction based on original research.)

* —— (1993) *Saint Thomas d'Aquin: Somme contre les gentils. Introduction*, Collection Philosophie Européene, dirigée par H. Hude, Paris: Éditions universitaires. (A magisterial survey of historical and textual evidence.)

Gilby, T. (1955) *The Political Thought of Thomas Aquinas*, Chicago, IL: University of Chicago Press. (A general introduction that is still useful.)

Gilson, E. (1956) *The Christian Philosophy of St. Thomas Aquinas*, trans. L.K. Shook, New York: Random House. (A classic; originally published in French in 1948, but still worth consulting.)

Henle, R.J. (1956) *Saint Thomas and Platonism*, The Hague: Martinus Nijhoff. (One of the best known studies of neo-Platonist influences on Aquinas.)

Ingardia, R. (1993) *Thomas Aquinas: International Bibliography 1977–1990*, Bowling Green, KY: The Philosophy Documentation Center. (A well-organized, well-indexed list in which many entries are accompanied by synopses.)

* Irwin, T.H. (1992) 'Who Discovered the Will?', in J.E. Tomberlin (ed.) *Philosophical Perspectives 6: Ethics*, Atascadero, CA: Ridgeview. (Uses Aquinas' interpretation in a convincing argument for attributing the concept of will to Aristotle.)

Jaffa, H.V. (1952) *Thomism and Aristotelianism*, Chicago, IL: University of Chicago Press. (A controversial study of Aquinas' Commentary on the *Nicomachean Ethics*.)

Jordan, M.D. (1986) *Ordering Wisdom: The Hierarchy of Philosophical Discourses in Aquinas*, Notre Dame, IN: University of Notre Dame Press. (A study of Aquinas' thought in terms of the 'discourses' of physics, metaphysics, and theology; good bibliography.)

—— (1993) 'Theology and Philosophy', in N. Kretzmann and E. Stump (eds) *The Cambridge Companion to Aquinas*, Cambridge: Cambridge University Press, 232–51. (A well-argued presentation of the sort of interpretation that identifies Aquinas as a theologian rather than a philosopher.)

Kenny, A. (1980a) *Aquinas*, New York: Hill & Wang. (A philosophically sophisticated, critical introductory study, focusing on metaphysics and philosophy of mind.)

—— (1980b) *The Five Ways: St Thomas Aquinas' Proofs of God's Existence*, Notre Dame, IN: University of Notre Dame Press. (An untraditional critical analysis.)

—— (1993) *Aquinas on Mind*, London: Routledge. (Stimulating studies, occasionally too ready to reject parts of the account that need further investigation.)

—— (ed.) (1969) *Aquinas: A Collection of Critical Essays*, Garden City, NY: Doubleday. (A somewhat dated but still stimulating set of papers on all aspects of Aquinas' philosophy.)

Kremer, K. (1971) *Die neuplatonische Seinsphilosophie und ihre Wirkung auf Thomas von Aquin* (Neoplatonist Metaphysics and Their Effect on Thomas Aquinas), Leiden: Brill. (A study of Neoplatonist elements in Aquinas' metaphysics.)

Kretzmann, N. (1988) '*Lex iniusta non est lex*: Laws on Trial in Aquinas' Court of Conscience', *The American Journal of Jurisprudence* 33: 99–122. (The moral assessment of law in Aquinas' theory.)

—— (1992) 'Infallibility, Error, and Ignorance', *Canadian Journal of Philosophy*, supp. vol. 17: 159–94. (An attempt to explain puzzling features of Aquinas' account of intellective cognition.)

—— (1993) 'Philosophy of Mind', in N. Kretzmann and E. Stump (eds) *The Cambridge Companion to Aquinas*, Cambridge: Cambridge University Press, 128–59. (A concise critical account.)

—— (1997) *The Metaphysics of Theism: Aquinas's Natural Theology in Summa Contra Gentiles I*, Oxford: Clarendon Press. (An examination of the philosophical account of 'God considered in himself'.)

Kretzmann, N. and Stump, E. (eds) (1993) *The Cambridge Companion to Aquinas*, Cambridge: Cambridge University Press. (Ten studies specifically designed to introduce all the important aspects of Aquinas' thought; includes bibliography.)

Lonergan, B. (1946) *Grace and Freedom: Operative Grace in the Thought of St. Thomas Aquinas*, ed. J.P. Burns, New York: Herder & Herder. (A sophisticated, learned account, still worthwhile.)

—— (1967) *Verbum: Word and Idea in Aquinas*, ed. D.B. Burrell, Notre Dame, IN: University of Notre Dame Press. (An original treatment of the metaphysical side of Aquinas' theory of cognition.)

MacDonald, S. (1984) 'The *Esse/Essentia* Argument in Aquinas' *De ente et essentia*', *Journal of the History of Philosophy* 22: 157–72. (A well-argued assessment and resolution of the crucial difficulty in *De ente*.)

—— (ed.) (1991) *Being and Goodness: The Concept of the Good in Metaphysics and Philosophical Theology*, Ithaca, NY: Cornell University Press. (Twelve essays, most of them not published elsewhere, on the most important relationship among the 'transcendentals'.)

—— (1991) 'Ultimate Ends in Practical Reasoning: Aquinas' Aristotelian Moral Psychology and Anscombe's Fallacy', *The Philosophical Review* 100: 31–66. (A careful analysis and defense of the central argument in Aquinas' 'Treatise on Happiness'.)

—— (1993) 'Theory of Knowledge', in N. Kretzmann and E. Stump (eds) *The Cambridge Companion to Aquinas*, Cambridge: Cambridge University Press, 160–95. (An examination of all aspects of the theory of cognition, but especially the notion of *scientia*.)

Maritain, J. (1951) *Man and the State*, Chicago, IL: University of Chicago Press. (A classic application of Aquinas' political theory.)

McInerny, R. (1990) *Boethius and Aquinas*, Washington, DC: Catholic University of America Press. (The best available study of the important influence of Boethius on Aquinas.)

—— (1992) *Aquinas on Human Action*, Washington: Catholic University of America Press. (The fullest study of Aquinas' action theory.)

—— (1993) 'Ethics', in N. Kretzmann and E. Stump (eds) *The Cambridge Companion to Aquinas*, Cambridge: Cambridge University Press, 196–216. (An engaging survey of the elements of Aquinas' moral theory.)

* Nussbaum, M.C. (1992) 'The Text of Aristotle's *De anima*', in M.C. Nussbaum and A.O. Rorty (eds) *Essays on Aristotle's De anima*, Oxford: Clarendon Press, 1–6. (Appreciation of Aquinas as an Aristotelian interpreter is also found elsewhere in this volume of essays by various authors.)

Owens, J. (1980) *St. Thomas Aquinas on the Existence of God: Collected papers of Joseph Owens*, ed. J. Catan, Albany, NY: State University of New York Press. (Eleven important articles by a renowned student of Aquinas, the first five on topics other than the existence of God.)

—— (1986) 'Aquinas' Distinction at *De ente et essentia* 4.119–123', *Mediaeval Studies* 48: 264–87. (An important contribution to the debate represented in MacDonald (1984).)

—— (1993) 'Aristotle and Aquinas', in N. Kretzmann and E. Stump (eds) *The Cambridge Companion to Aquinas*, Cambridge: Cambridge University Press, 38–59. (A survey, distilling a lifetime's study of this intellectual relationship.)

Pegis, A.C. (1934) *St Thomas and the Problem of the Soul in the Thirteenth Century*, Toronto, Ont.: Pontifical Institute of Mediaeval Studies. (A helpful introduction to Aquinas' philosophical psychology in its historical setting.)

Ross, J.F. (1985) 'Aquinas on Belief and Knowledge', in G. Etzkorn (ed.) *Essays Honoring Allan B. Wolter*, St Bonaventure, NY: Franciscan Institute. (A philosophically sophisticated, somewhat idiosyncratic interpretation.)

Sigmund, P.E. (1993) 'Law and Politics', in N. Kretzmann and E. Stump (eds) *The Cambridge Companion to Aquinas*, Cambridge: Cambridge University Press, 217–31. (A survey bringing out connections to twentieth-century institutions and events.)

Stump, E. (1990) 'Intellect, Will and the Principle of Alternate Possibilities', in M. Beaty (ed.) *Christian Theism and the Problems of Philosophy*, Notre Dame, IN: University of Notre Dame Press. (An attempt to show that Aquinas' libertarian account of human freedom does not need the principle.)

—— (1992) 'Aquinas on the Foundations of Knowledge', *Canadian Journal of Philosophy*, supp. vol. 17: 125–58. (Rejects the traditional account of Aquinas as a foundationalist.)

—— (1993) 'Aquinas on the Sufferings of Job', in E. Stump (ed.) *Reasoned Faith*, Ithaca, NY: Cornell University Press, 328–57. (Aquinas' account of providence and the problem of evil as shown in biblical commentary.)

—— (1993) 'Biblical Commentary and Philosophy', in N. Kretzmann and E. Stump (eds) *The Cambridge Companion to Aquinas*, Cambridge: Cambridge University Press, 252–68. (Shows the philosophical significance of Aquinas' biblical commentaries.)

Stump, E. and Kretzmann, N. (1988) 'Being and Goodness', in T.V. Morris (ed.) *Divine and Human Action*, Ithaca, NY: Cornell University Press, 281–312; reprinted in MacDonald (1991). (An analysis of the interrelation of these transcendentals in Aquinas, especially in his metaethics.)

Torrell, J.-P. (1993) *Initiation à Saint Thomas d'Aquin: Sa Personne et Son Oeuvre* (Introduction to Saint Thomas Aquinas: His Character and His Work), Fribourg and Paris: Éditions universitaires and Éditions du Cerf. (Supersedes Weisheipl and Tugwell on the life and works, offering persuasive evidence for new hypotheses.)

* Tugwell, S. (1988) *Albert and Thomas: Selected Writings*, The Classics of Western Spirituality, Mahwah, NJ: Paulist Press. (In the scholarly but eminently readable introduction to the Aquinas translations, Tugwell supersedes Weisheipl on the life and works.)

Van Steenberghen, F. (1980) *Le problème de l'existence de Dieu dans les écrits de S. Thomas d'Aquin*, Louvain-la-Neuve: Editions de l'Institut Superieur de Philosophie. (The most complete critical study of Aquinas' many arguments for the existence of God.)

—— (1980) *Thomas Aquinas and Radical Aristotelianism*, Washington, DC: Catholic University of America Press. (An analysis of the role played by Latin Averroism in Aquinas' second Paris regency.)

Vollert, C., Kendzierski, L. and Byrne, P. (eds) (1984) *On the Eternity of the World*, Milwaukee, WI: Marquette University Press. (A collection of medieval texts in translation, including Aquinas, with a helpful introductory study.)

Weisheipl, J. (1983) *Friar Thomas D'Aquino: His Life, Thought, and Works*, Washington, DC: Catholic University of America Press. (A revised edition of the classic biography, updated in some respects; superseded by Tugwell (1988) and Torrell (1993).)

Westberg, D. (1994) *Right Practical Reason: Aristotle, Action, and Prudence in Aquinas*, Oxford: Clarendon Press. (A wide-ranging historical and theological discussion of practical reason in Aquinas' thought.)

Wippel, J.F. (1984) *Metaphysical Themes in Thomas Aquinas*, Washington, DC: Catholic University of America Press. (A valuable collection of the author's articles on Aquinas' metaphysics, with some attention to Henry of Ghent; excellent bibliography.)

—— (1987) 'Thomas Aquinas and Participation', in J.F. Wippel (ed.) *Studies in Medieval Philosophy*, Washington, DC: Catholic University of America Press. (The best discussion of this important, difficult topic.)

—— (1989) 'Truth in Thomas Aquinas (part I)', *Review of Metaphysics* 43 (2): 295–326. (The first of a pair of articles, which together constitute a very well-informed study of the topic.)

—— (1990) 'Truth in Thomas Aquinas (part II)', *Review of Metaphysics* 43 (3): 543–567. (The second of the pair of articles referred to above.)

—— (1993) 'Metaphysics', in N. Kretzmann and E. Stump (eds) *The Cambridge Companion to Aquinas*,

Cambridge: Cambridge University Press, 85–127. (A magisterial survey, including a discussion of the close connection between philosophy and theology in Aquinas' thought.)

Zimmermann, A. (1965) *Ontologie oder Metaphysik? Die Diskussion über den Gegenstand der Metaphysik im 13. und 14. Jahrhundert* (Ontology or Metaphysics? The Discussion of the Object of Metaphysics in the Thirteenth and Fourteenth Centuries), Leiden: Brill. (A useful historical introduction.)

NORMAN KRETZMANN
ELEONORE STUMP

AR-RAWINDI *see* IBN AR-RAWANDI

ARABIC PHILOSOPHY
see ISLAM, CONCEPT OF PHILOSOPHY IN; ISLAMIC PHILOSOPHY

ARAMA, ISAAC BEN MOSES (*c*.1420–94)

Like many of his fifteenth-century Spanish contemporaries, Arama opposed the Aristotelianism of Maimonides. His philosophical sermons and biblical commentaries attack Jewish Aristotelians on charges of subordinating revelation to reasoning, upholding an eternal universe whose necessity limits God's power, and excluding miracles and individual providence. Yet while stressing the fallibility of human reason, Arama is no fideist. An eclectic, he values reason and philosophy as ways of deepening the understanding of Scripture through allegorical interpretation. He also develops striking philosophical theories of miracles, providence and the fundamentals of faith.

A leading rabbi of the generation that underwent expulsion from Spain in 1492, Isaac ben Moses Arama is best known for the philosophical sermons he composed to counter the conversionist Christian sermons which his congregants were compelled to attend. Preserved in the chapters of his popular and influential biblical commentary, *'Aqedat Yitzhaq* (The Binding of Isaac), each of these discourses has two parts, one addressing a philosophical or theological problem, the other, like the scholastic *quaestiones* and *dubitationes*, raising issues in the exegesis of a biblical passage, which is then interpreted in light of the earlier philosophical account.

Arama is most influenced by HALEVI and CRESCAS among Jewish thinkers; and, among the Muslims, by AL-GHAZALI. The essential beliefs of Judaism, he argues, transcend or contradict reason and must be accepted on faith. Even beliefs that lie within the scope of reason should be accepted on faith and only then verified by reason. Just as Abraham overcomes his reason when he determines to sacrifice his son, so the ideal religious person must seek out irresolvable paradoxes of reason, learning to subordinate intellect to faith, philosophy to revelation.

Arama harshly criticizes fourteenth-century Maimonists like Moses of Narbonne (Narboni) and Joseph ibn Caspi (see AVERROISM, JEWISH §§3–4), charging that they favour philosophy over revelation. He is especially sensitive to their use of allegorical exegesis. He himself did much to revive and develop the allegorical method, which had fallen into decline after the 'Maimonidean controversy'; but he also defends the validity of the literal meaning, which is enriched by philosophical interpretation. The Maimonists, by contrast, are charged with seeking to replace the literal sense with the Greek philosophical ideas which they claim to discover as the true meaning of Scripture.

Arama's position in the fifteenth-century debate over the foundational beliefs of Judaism shows the subtlety of his approach to the relations of philosophy and revelation. His articles of faith are the principles essential not just to the idea of a divine law generically but to Judaism uniquely. Connecting these principles with the Mosaic commandments, he argues with Halevi and against Maimonides that one achieves immortality not through intellectual perfection but by performance of the commandments, the one feature that truly distinguishes Judaism from other religions and from the generic theism of a philosopher. The commandments are not themselves articles of faith. Rather, Arama identifies the true principles as those that are embodied in and derived from specific commandments, as belief in creation is embedded in the Sabbath laws.

Creation is the most important of Arama's principles. All the rest are derivable from it. Like Moses MAIMONIDES, he locates the problem of the origin of universe beyond rational demonstration. But creation for him is typical in this respect of all the essential truths of Judaism. Nonetheless, perhaps influenced by NAHMANIDES, he offers a quasi-Platonic account of the world's origin from pre-existent matter, itself created *ex nihilo* by God. Essential here is the commitment to God's unconstrained will: only if the world was created freely can there be providence, miracles, or divine omnipotence. As evidence against eternity, Arama appeals not only to the diverse and irregular motions of the spheres (as Maimonides did) but also to the occurrence of miracles as, attested in Scripture.

Despite the centrality of miracles and omnipotence in his scheme, Arama does not wish to reject the idea of natural laws. He therefore distinguishes between two coexisting natures: an unintelligent 'natural nature', whose laws apply without regard to human merit, and a 'supernatural nature' directed purposefully by an intelligence sensitive to human deserts. Miracles violate natural nature; but, as instances of supernatural nature, they are fully natural. Besides the observed violations of natural nature that we call miracles, Arama (recalling Nahmanides) argues that 'hidden' miracles occur constantly. Their miraculousness usually goes unnoticed, but their true explanation lies in supernatural nature. All miracles therefore fall under *a* nature. Analogously, there is a 'natural' governance that does not attend to the moral perfection of individuals but only to preservation of species, and a second, 'providential', governance that is sensitive to the moral perfection of individuals. In general the latter is limited to Israel.

Philosophers deny supernatural nature and providential governance, Arama reasons, only because they rank humanity beneath the celestial spheres and cannot understand why God would violate a higher order for a lower one. Following Saadiah's premise that humankind is the final act of creation (see SAADIAH GAON), Arama argues that the spheres themselves were created for mankind's sake and can therefore be manipulated in our behalf. Part of the original creation, moreover, gave man a special power over nature. When the soul rules, establishing the 'divine image' in the microcosm of the human body, harmony results in the macrocosm as well; when sin disrupts the microcosmic harmony, the macrocosmic harmony is ruptured too, causing universal evils. Human beings can ensure cosmic harmony only by living in harmony with nature – following the natural law, which is most fully realized in the Mosaic Torah. Its commandments instill all moral and intellectual virtues, including those unknown to reason. Only a life according to this revealed law brings the highest, spiritual happiness, the ultimate goal of philosophy.

See also: MAIMONIDES, M.

List of works

Arama, I. (1522) *'Aqedat Yitzhaq* (The Binding of Isaac), ed. H. Pollack, Pressburg, 1849; English trans. E. Munk, *Aqaydat Yitzchaq*, Jerusalem: Feldheim, 1986, 2 vols. (Arama's classic commentary on the Pentateuch; this standard edition in Hebrew also includes Arama's commentaries on the Five Scrolls – Song of Songs, Ruth, Lamentations, Ecclesiastes and Esther – and his *Hazut Kashah* (Grievous Vision), a polemic on the relations of philosophy and religion. The English translation is the only extended selection of Arama's writings available in a language other than the Hebrew original; but it must be used with great caution.)

References and further reading

Bettan, I. (1939) *Studies in Jewish Preaching: Middle Ages*, Cincinnati, OH: Hebrew Union College Press, 130–91. (The classic study of Arama's homiletics.)
Heller Wilensky, S.O. (1953) 'Isaac Arama on the Creation and Structure of the World', *Proceedings of the American Academy for Jewish Research* 22: 131–50. (An English translation of chapter 4 of Heller Wilensky (1956).)
—— (1956) *R. Yitzhaq Arama Umishnato* (Isaac Arama and his Philosophical System), Jerusalem and Tel Aviv: Bialik/Dvir Publishing House. (A systematic reconstruction of the philosophy scattered through Arama's sermons.)
Kellner, M. (1986) *Dogma in Medieval Jewish Thought*, New York: Littman Library and Oxford: Oxford University Press, 159–61. (Contains a good but brief discussion of Arama's views on the articles of faith.)
Pearl, C. (1971) *The Medieval Mind*, London: Vallentine, Mitchell. (An accessible, thorough exposition of Arama's philosophy.)

JOSEF STERN

ARCESILAUS (*c*.316–*c*.240 BC)

Arcesilaus of Pitane came to Athens as a young man, and was seduced by Platonic philosophy. Around 265 he became head of the Academy. He turned the school in a sceptical direction, urging that Plato himself had been of a sceptical bent. He revived the Socratic practice of dialectical argument, in which he displayed remarkable logical skill and honeyed oratorical talent. His dialectical prowess led him to 'suspend judgment about everything'; but the main target of his arguments was Stoicism, and in particular Stoic epistemology, which he claimed to reduce to incoherence. Recognizing that a sceptic must live and act, he introduced the notion of 'the reasonable' as a criterion of sceptical action.

ARCESILAUS

1 Life and thought
2 Scepticism

1 Life and thought

Arcesilaus was born in Pitane, in north-west Asia Minor. As a youth he was a pupil of the mathematician Autolycus, whom he followed to Sardis. He then travelled to Athens where he studied with THEOPHRASTUS. He was destined for a rhetorical career; but his head lay for philosophy. When he removed to the ACADEMY and heard Polemo and Crantor and Crates, he deemed that they were 'either gods or else remnants of those men of old who were formed from the golden generation' (Philodemus, *History of the Academy* XV 5–10). The rest of his life he spent in the Academy. On the death of Crates in *c.*265 BC he became scholarch, a position he held until his death some twenty-five years later.

He was a celebrated figure, known for caustic wit and also for kindness, for oratorical skill and for the rigour of his argumentation. He wrote epigrams, he enjoyed dalliance and dinner parties – and he was regarded as one of the leading philosophers of the age. But he produced no philosophical writings, and what we learn of his views derives from hearsay: perhaps from first-hand hearsay, for we are told that one of his pupils, Pythodorus, took notes of his lectures.

The Stoic ARISTON OF CHIOS, his contemporary, parodied a Homeric verse in describing him as 'Plato in front, at the back Pyrrho, Diodorus between them'. Homer was describing the chimera, and Ariston insinuates that Arcesilaus was a philosophical monster, a three-fold hybrid.

Arcesilaus began his philosophical life as an orthodox Platonist (see PLATO; PLATONISM, EARLY AND MIDDLE) – we are told that he acquired a copy of Plato's works as a boy, and that 'at first when he stated a thesis he argued in accordance with the tradition from Plato and Speusippus up to Polemo' (Philodemus, *History of the Academy* XVIII 7–12). He taught a dogmatic Platonism and then became a sceptic.

Later authors spoke of the foundation of a New Academy. But by his own lights Arcesilaus was no innovator – rather, he turned the Academy back to pure Platonism. Not (as some alleged) because he dissembled, secretly teaching unsceptical doctrine, but because (as he argued) Plato himself had been a sceptic. 'From several of Plato's books and Socratic dialogues he took the idea that nothing is certain' (Cicero, *The Orator* III 67). There are indeed sceptical touches in some of Plato's works – notably in the early dialogues, which generally end in puzzlement, and in the *Theaetetus*, which raises and conspicuously fails to answer the question, 'What is knowledge?' Yet Arcesilaus could read the Platonic corpus and say that 'in his books nothing is asserted, many issues are argued on both sides, everything is a matter of investigation, nothing certain is said' (Cicero, *Academics* I 46).

DIODORUS CRONUS was celebrated for 'dialectic': his philosophical interests were absorbed by logical problems and puzzles. Arcesilaus did not himself engage in logical study – indeed, anecdote has him dismiss dialectic. He took after Diodorus in his practice, inasmuch as he too was renowned for his argumentative ingenuity. He excelled at arguing 'on both sides of the question': a proposition (no matter what) is put forward, and first you argue for it and then you argue against it, 'the arguments on each side being equally powerful' (Eusebius, *Preparation of the Gospel* XIV 4.15). The technique finds antecedents in Aristotle's dialectic. Arcesilaus also harked back to SOCRATES (§3) and the Socratic *elenchos* or method of refutation: a thesis (no matter what) is proposed, and you show by arguments which the proposer must accept that it is untenable.

Each of these two techniques demands logical versatility or sophistical sleight of hand. The ancient sources often link them, for if you can argue for and against any proposition then *a fortiori* you can argue against any thesis, and if you can argue against any thesis whatsoever then you can argue for and against any proposition.

2 Scepticism

It is Arcesilaus' affinities with PYRRHO, the archetypal sceptic of the ancient world, which give him his philosophical bite. 'He created a new philosophy of non-philosophizing' (Lactantius, *Divine Institutions* IV 11), and introduced suspension of judgment and scepticism into the Academy. But even in antiquity, the nature of Arcesilaus' scepticism was a matter of dispute. According to NUMENIUS (§1), Arcesilaus 'was a Pyrrhonist in all but the name' (Eusebius, *Preparation of the Gospel* XIV 6.6); and a half dozen texts, independent of one another and drawing on early sources, agree that Arcesilaus 'suspended judgment about everything': that is to say, he held no beliefs on any subject, and the end of his philosophizing was the eradication of all belief and the introduction of universal suspension of judgment.

Arcesilaus' logical techniques open a direct route to Pyrrhonism (see PYRRHONISM). If you can produce equally powerful arguments on each side of a proposition, then you will neither believe nor disbelieve that proposition, and if you can produce equally powerful arguments on each side of every proposition, then you will believe no proposition at all. And Arcesilaus had a second route to Pyrrhonism, for he championed *akatalēpsia* or 'inapprehensibility': 'he denied that there is anything which can be known – not even the one thing which Socrates allowed himself, that he knew that he knew nothing' (Cicero, *Academics* I 45). Hence if you have any beliefs, they will be mere opinions. But no one of any sense embraces what he takes to be a mere opinion. Hence no one of any sense will hold any beliefs.

Arcesilaus was a polemicist. He attacked all-comers and exploded any thesis anyone might propose, 'affirming nothing himself but merely refuting other positions' (Philodemus, *History of the Academy* XX 1–4). Such a polemical scepticism is the natural child of the Socratic *elenchos*, and some scholars have urged that Arcesilaus' philosophy was essentially a negative and a destructive thing. But polemical scepticism easily fades into Pyrrhonism. For if I refute a thesis which you propound, then I shall not uphold the thesis myself; if I can refute any thesis which is propounded to me, then I shall believe no thesis; and so I shall end up as a Pyrrhonist.

It is sometimes supposed that Arcesilaus always argued *ad hominem*: if you maintain a certain thesis, then Arcesilaus will show not that *the thesis* is untenable but that *you* have no good grounds for maintaining it. It is consistent with a successful *ad hominem* argument that *there are* good grounds for holding the thesis, and that Arcesilaus himself holds it on such grounds. Yet the *ad hominem* approach, universally applied, again fades into Pyrrhonism, for if Arcesilaus can argue *ad hominem* against all-comers, then in effect he can argue against any thesis.

Much of Arcesilaus' philosophical activity was directed against the Stoics. Thus he took the Stoic thesis that two stuffs may completely blend or interpenetrate and, relying wholly on ideas which the Stoics themselves maintained, reduced it to absurdity. (He chose a grotesque example: amputate your leg, grind it up, and blend it into the Aegean sea. By the thesis of interpenetration, the leg will blend with every part of the sea and the fleet of King Antigonus will sail through your leg.)

The Stoics held that if you know something, you must have 'apprehended' it; that apprehension is assent to an 'apprehensive appearance' (*phantasia kataleptikē*); and that an appearance of something is apprehensive if it is true of that thing, if it was caused by that thing, and if it could not have been produced by anything else (see STOICISM §12). Arcesilaus urged that the third of these conditions could never be met and hence that there are no apprehensive appearances. Hence 'everything being inapprehensible, it will follow that, for the Stoics too, the Sage suspends judgment' (Sextus Empiricus, *Against the Mathematicians* VII 155).

But if Arcesilaus was at his most vigorous against the Stoics, no ancient text suggests that anti-Stoicism exhausted his intellectual parts. The evidence suggests rather that the quarrel with the Stoics was one glamorous episode in his campaign to restore peace and scepticism to the land: the Stoics were the leading 'dogmatic' philosophers in town, and any sceptic would feel bound to have a confrontation with them. In any event, the arguments which Arcesilaus used against the Stoics could readily be adapted for use against others: a clever philosopher would not ignore and a combative philosopher would not decline these tempting possibilities. Anti-Stoicism, in other words, soon leaches into a more general *ad hominem* scepticism and hence, in the end, into Pyrrhonism.

It has often been wondered if Pyrrhonian scepticism is a serious or an interesting philosophical option. One argument which ancient dogmatists deployed against their sceptical colleagues was the following. Human actions are characteristically explained in terms of the beliefs (and the desires) of their agents. But sceptics have no beliefs. Hence sceptics cannot act. Hence sceptics cannot live – the only good sceptic is a dead sceptic.

Arcesilaus was aware of this argument, and had an answer. The argument, he claimed, supposes that three things are necessary for action: before you sink your teeth into the succulent flesh, you must have received an appearance ('That apple looks ripe'), you must have given your 'assent' and formed a belief ('That apple is ripe'), and you must have had an impulse or desire (you wanted to eat a ripe apple). Arcesilaus demurred:

> *Two* things are necessary for action, an appearance of something appropriate and an impulse towards the appropriate item which has appeared – and neither of these conflicts with suspension of judgement. It is belief, and not appearance or impulse, from which argument separates us.
> (Plutarch, *Against Colotes* 1122C–D)

The apple looks juicy and Arcesilaus wants an apple – so he eats it. No belief intervenes, and none is needed. It is enough to 'follow the appearances'.

In addition Arcesilaus observed that 'anyone who suspends judgment about everything will measure his choices and aversions, and in general his actions, by what is reasonable (*to eulogon*); and if he proceeds in accordance with this standard (*kritērion*) he will be successful' (Sextus Empiricus, *Against the Mathematicians* VII 158). A sceptic will choose to perform those actions which, were they done, could be reasonably defended. Is Arcesilaus here telling us what *dogmatists* – what *Stoics* – will be obliged to do, once his arguments have reduced them to scepticism? Or is he reflecting more generally on the way in which any sceptics will make their way through the world? And in the latter case, are his reflections compatible with scepticism – can a sceptic consistently appeal to 'the reasonable'? To such teasing questions our texts yield no safe answers.

See also: CARNEADES; SOCRATES §8

References and further reading

Annas, J. (1992) 'Plato the Sceptic', in J. Klagge and N. Smith (eds) *Methods of Interpreting Plato and his Dialogues*, Oxford Studies in Ancient Philosophy supplementary vol., Oxford: Clarendon Press. (A discussion of the sceptical interpretation of Plato.)

* Cicero (45 BC) *Academics*, trans. H. Rackham, Loeb Classical Library, Cambridge, MA: Harvard University Press and London: Heinemann, 1933. (A main source for Academic scepticism.)

Couissin, P. (1929) 'The Stoicism of the New Academy', in M.F. Burnyeat (ed.) *The Skeptical Tradition*, Berkeley, CA: University of California Press, 1983. (Argues that Arcesilaus' scepticism was purely anti-Stoic.)

Long, A.A. (1986) 'Diogenes Laertius, Life of Arcesilaus', *Elenchos* 7: 429–49. (Primarily biographical.)

Maconi, H. (1988) 'Nova non philosophandi philosophia' (A new philosophy of not philosophizing), *Oxford Studies in Ancient Philosophy* 6: 231–53. (On the nature of Arcesilaus' scepticism.)

Mette, H.-J. (1984) 'Zwei Akademiker heute: Krantor von Soloi und Arkesilaos von Pitane'(Two Academics: Crantor and Arcesilaos), *Lustrum* 26: 7–94. (Collects the ancient texts bearing on Arcesilaus.)

* Philodemus (*c*.80–40 BC) *History of the Academy*, trans. T. Dorandi, *Filodemo. Storia dei filosofi. Platone e l'Academia*, Naples: Bibliopolis, 1991. (Greek text, with Italian translation and commentary; a biographical history.)

Striker, G. (1980) 'Sceptical Strategies', in M. Schofield, M.F. Burnyeat and J. Barnes (eds) *Doubt and Dogmatism*, Oxford: Clarendon Press. (An account of the aims and methods of Academic scepticism.)

JONATHAN BARNES

ARCHAEOLOGY, PHILOSOPHY OF

Questions about the scientific status of archaeology have been central to field-defining debates since the late nineteenth century and have frequently involved appeals to philosophical sources. With the possible exception of Collingwood, however, there was little systematic exploration of the bearing of philosophical literature on these questions until the advent, in the 1960s and 1970s, of the New Archaeology, a self-consciously positivist research programme. The New Archaeology originated in North America but has been widely influential, especially in giving prominence to philosophical and theoretical issues. The New Archaeologists' advocacy of a positivist (Hempelian) conception of scientific goals and practice provoked intense debate which involved philosophers of science as well as archaeologists from the early 1970s. Although the positivist commitments of the programme were widely repudiated a decade later, philosophical exchange has continued and expanded to include consideration of a range of post-positivist models of scientific inference that emphasize the theory-ladenness of archaeological evidence, as well as hermeneutic and post-structuralist models of archaeological interpretation. The analysis of epistemological issues is also closely tied to foundational questions about how the cultural subject of archaeological inquiry should be conceptualized and has led, increasingly, to a consideration of normative questions about the values and interests that shape archaeological research and the ethical responsibilities of practitioners. In 1992 Embree argued that work in this area had achieved sufficient maturity to be recognized as a subfield which he designated 'meta-archaeology'.

1   The emergence of meta-archaeology
2   Explanation
3   Inference
4   Evidence
5   Contextualism, ideals of objectivity and professional ethics

1   The emergence of meta-archaeology

As advocates of an explicitly scientific research programme, the New Archaeologists rejected what they described as traditional 'inductive' practice; they insisted that law-governed, deductive-nomological explanation should be their primary goal, and that interpretive hypotheses should be rigorously tested following a hypothetico-deductive model of confirmation (see EXPLANATION §2). When these commitments were made explicit in the early 1970s they generated debate within archaeology about philosophical theories of science which drew the attention of several philosophers. R.A. Watson consistently defended the positivist orientation of the New Archaeology against its critics. Most others objected that internal, philosophical critiques had substantially undermined Hempelian models by the 1970s (see EXPLANATION §3), when they were taken up by archaeologists, and cautioned against treating philosophical models as authoritative recipes for scientific practice; these are properly 'theses to be argued', not 'established truths' (Nickles 1977: 164). Despite the contentious tone of some of these exchanges, a number of philosophers and archaeologists persisted in discussion across disciplinary boundaries, and have produced an increasingly sophisticated, diverse and resolutely interdisciplinary literature on philosophical issues raised by and about archaeological practice.

Contributors to this jointly archaeological and philosophical literature frequently address questions about how the project of meta-archaeology should be defined and situated. Some insist that there are irreducible differences between the interests of philosophers and archaeologists, even where similar questions seem to be at issue. Typically, however, the case is made for establishing meta-archaeology as an interdisciplinary venture that includes a range of science study disciplines. As such, philosophy of archaeology may exemplify a pattern of development within post-positivist philosophy of science which has led philosophers in many areas to establish increasingly close ties with the sciences they study.

2 Explanation

The New Archaeologists attempted to fit the explanatory goals of their discipline to a particularly narrow philosophical template. After an initial round of debate which focused on standard philosophical objections to covering-law models, attention turned to questions about explanation that arise from archaeological practice. At one end of a continuum of views are arguments that explanation should not be treated as the central objective of scientific inquiry, however conceptualized. Morgan (1973) took this position in debate with Watson *et al.* (1971). Kelley and Hanen (1988) have since argued that an antirealist, pragmatist view of explanation makes best sense of archaeological practice; on this account explanations are simply answers to 'why-questions' which deploy whatever scientifically credible information will satisfy a specific inquirer (see SCIENTIFIC REALISM AND ANTIREALISM). Although this suggests that explanation is a byproduct of scientific inquiry, not its goal, Kelley and Hanen also treat explanatory power as a key consideration in the evaluation of competing hypotheses, so explanatory goals, reconceptualized, remain central to their account. A robustly realist alternative has been proposed by Gibbon (1989), and causalist models have been developed by Salmon (1982), who recommends a 'causally supplemented' statistical-relevance model of explanation, and by Wylie (1996a), who uses archaeological examples as the basis for a critique of unificationist accounts of explanation. As in these last cases, close consideration of archaeological practice frequently leads to the reassessment of philosophical models. For example, Nickles (1977) uses archaeological examples to establish a case for recognizing forms of 'singular causal' explanation which do not depend on laws, and Salmon (1982) argues that any adequate account of explanation must make sense of forms of functional explanation which are ubiquitous in archaeology (see CAUSATION; EXPLANATION; FUNCTIONAL EXPLANATION).

Analyses of explanation in archaeology are closely connected to foundational questions about the nature of the cultural subject matter. The New Archaeologists conceptualized their subject domain in terms that could support a search for laws; cultures were understood to be ecologically adaptive systems, and the New Archaeologists' ambition was to understand, not just the specific events and conditions that produced the archaeological record but, through them, larger scale processes shaping cultural systems in adaptation to their external environments. Archaeological critics insisted, on ethnographic and archaeological grounds, that this view is untenable; dynamics internal to the ethnographic life-world of cultural subjects can substantially shape the large scale, long term development of cultural systems. Likewise, most parties to the philosophical debate about explanation in archaeology insist that questions of content cannot be settled in advance; models of explanation must be flexible enough to accommodate reconstructions of beliefs, intentions, cultural conventions, social institutions, and various 'cognitive' dimensions of human life, even though some of these are unlikely to be law-governed (Nickles 1977) or accessible to material-causal analysis (Salmon 1982). Some urge recognition that, in practice, the 'archaeological record' is treated ambiguously, both as a fossil record which requires scientific modes of explanation and as a textual record of intentional, meaningful action, for which interpretive approaches are appropriate (Patrik 1985) (see EXPLANATION IN HISTORY AND SOCIAL SCIENCE). The advocates of interpretivist approaches are influenced by COLLINGWOOD's argument that historians must grasp the 'insides of actions' (Hodder 1991); by symbolic and structuralist trends in anthropology (Hodder 1982); by hermeneutics, phenomenology and critical theory (Leone 1982; Preucel 1991) (see STRUCTURALISM IN SOCIAL SCIENCE; HERMENEUTICS; PHENOMENOLOGY, EPISTEMIC ISSUES IN; CRITICAL THEORY). Increasingly, those who endorse scientific modes of inquiry also insist on the importance of considering 'cognitive' dimensions of the cultural past (Gardin and Peebles 1992; Bell 1994).

As discussion of the goals of archaeology has expanded, it has become clear that archaeologists 'explain' in many different senses and at different levels. Frequently they explain archaeological data in quite localized terms, as the products of specific events, conditions of life, intentional actions, and the various 'formation processes' responsible for the surviving archaeological record. The more ambitious goal of understanding large scale cultural processes both depends upon and is continuous with these more modest explanations.

3 Inference

A second major theme in the philosophical literature on archaeology is the concern to explicate the forms of inference by which archaeological data are systematized, and hypotheses about the cultural past are generated and evaluated in light of these data. Reacting to the deductivism of the New Archaeology, philosophical analysts have explored a range of models which more adequately capture the inductive complexity of archaeological practice. Salmon (1982) proposes a modified Bayesian account as a framework for understanding the nuanced judgements archaeologists make about the significance of archaeological evidence; for example, where the confirming or disconfirming import of specific evidential outcomes is assessed in light of the prior plausibility of a test hypothesis and the likelihood that the evidence in question uniquely confirms this hypothesis (see CONFIRMATION THEORY; PROBABILITY THEORY AND EPISTEMOLOGY). The comparative nature of hypothesis evaluation is emphasized by Kelley and Hanen (1988) who also argue that, in addition to considerations of empirical adequacy, explanatory power and consistency with established 'core beliefs' play a crucial role in hypothesis evaluation. They conclude that archaeological practice is best understood as a matter of 'inference to the best explanation' which proceeds through 'eliminative induction'; assessments of evidential support serve as grounds for eliminating implausible hypotheses as much as for accepting those that seem relatively well confirmed (see INFERENCE TO THE BEST EXPLANATION). Gibbon (1989) holds a similar position but, as a realist, can argue that 'best explanations' are those which afford the most comprehensive and plausible causal explanation of the available data. In 1994, Bell renewed the argument against 'inductivism' and formulated a set of guidelines for archaeological inquiry that translate, into practical terms, the central philosophical insights of Popperian refutationism (see POPPER, K.R. §2). Bell urged archaeologists to treat hypothesis evaluation as a matter of endangering bold conjectures rather than of building evidential support for hypotheses.

A condition for evaluating claims about the cultural past, on any of these models, is the formulation of typologies and other tools of analysis which allow archaeologists to systematize their data. Since the 1930s, typological constructs have been the subject of ongoing debate within archaeology. The central questions are whether useful, perspicuous typologies are nothing more than problem-specific 'tools' for manipulating data or have greater significance, capturing structures inherent in archaeological assemblages and, perhaps, underlying cultural norms and categories (see TAXONOMY). A sophisticated argument for 'typological instrumentalism' is developed by Adams and Adams (1991), and an account of the inferential processes underlying all forms of 'archaeological constructs' is proposed by Gardin (1980) using a 'logicist' approach. Both draw attention to the selective, interpretive dimensions of the process by which archaeologists describe and systematize their data.

4 Evidence

Since the mid-1980s the most pressing epistemological problem raised by archaeology is that of explaining how, and under what conditions, archaeological data may be taken as evidence of the cultural past. Early analysis focused on the role of analogical inference in establishing the evidential significance of archaeological data. Despite the New Archaeologists' categorical rejection of analogical inference as a form of speculative induction – a projection of the present onto the past – several philosophical commentators argued that ampliative inference of this sort is inescapable, and that it can be closely controlled (Salmon 1982; Wylie 1985). Shelley (1996) has since developed a sophisticated account of abductive reasoning in archaeology that considers the role of visual mental imagery in generating hypotheses about the cultural significance of archaeological material.

By the early 1980s, both critics and proponents of archaeological positivism had accepted the point that archaeological data are necessarily 'theory-laden' (see OBSERVATION §§3–4). These data stand as evidence of the cultural past only under interpretation, and their interpretation depends on a wide array of auxiliary assumptions ('middle-range theory') which establish causal, functional, symbolic and other connections between elements of material culture and the conditions responsible for their production and survival in archaeological contexts. While many archaeologists have made it a priority to develop the necessary linking principles through experimental and ethnographic research, others insist that such principles can never stabilize 'ascriptions of meaning' to archaeological data: interpretively constituted evidence cannot provide an 'independent' test for explanatory or interpretive hypotheses. In a discussion of 'bootstrapping' models of confirmation, Wylie (1986) has argued that the reliance on auxiliaries need not entail vicious circularity: it is not necessarily the case that the linking principles required to establish evidential significance will ensure support for a favoured hypothesis even if both derive from a common theory. This strategy is further developed in analyses of various kinds and degrees of independence that may be realized between hypotheses and supporting or test evidence by Wylie (1996b; Pinsky and Wylie 1989), and by Kosso (1991, 1992, 1993) in an important series of articles on 'observation of the past'.

5 Contextualism, ideals of objectivity and professional ethics

Challenges to ideals of objectivity, which have dominated archaeological debate since the early 1980s, arise not only from concerns about the instability of evidence but from reflection on the results of detailed empirical studies of the 'sociopolitics' of archaeology. These have been undertaken largely by archaeologists and document the influence on archaeology of its colonial, nationalist and imperialist entanglements (Trigger 1989); its relationship to intra-national and international elites; its class structure (Patterson 1986, 1995); its assimilation of racist and sexist presuppositions (Trigger 1980; Gero and Conkey 1991); and myriad features of its funding base, internal communication patterns, institutionalization, recruiting and training, and reward structures (Gero, Lacey and Blakey 1983; Kelley and Hanen 1988; Gibbon 1989). Although these analyses undermine objectivist ideals which make a primary virtue of neutrality and value freedom, most who urge attention to 'contextual' factors resist relativist conclusions. Their hope is that critical analysis will make archaeology more accountable for its presuppositions and will yield better informed judgments about the credibility and likely limitations of archaeological knowledge.

The pressure to engage normative issues has been mounting since the early 1970s when it became clear that the future of archaeology was threatened by accelerated destruction of archaeological resources and an unprecedented expansion of the international antiquities market. In addition, descendent populations and other national and public interest groups have challenged archaeologists' rights of access to archaeological sites and material, often on grounds that scientific investigation does not serve their interests in what they regard as their cultural heritage. Such changes in the contexts of archaeological practice raise ethical questions about whether archaeologists are ever justified in making professional use of looted or illegally traded material; whether they should consider the preservation of archaeological resources as important a goal as that of exploiting them for scientific purposes; what responsibilities they have to communities affected by their research; and how the goals of scientific investigation are to be weighed against heritage interests when these conflict (see, for example, Salmon 1997; Wylie 1996c).

See also: POSTCOLONIAL PHILOSOPHY OF SCIENCE

References and further reading

* Adams, W.Y. and Adams, E.W. (1991) *Archaeological Typology and Practical Reality: A Dialectical Approach to Artifact Classification and Sorting*, Cambridge: Cambridge University Press. (The product of collaboration between an archaeologist and a philosopher, this is an analysis of typological construction that is grounded in close consideration of archaeological practice.)
* Bell, J.A. (1994) *Reconstructing Prehistory: Scientific Method in Archaeology*, Philadelphia, PA: Temple University Press. (Bell advocates Popperian refutationism as a model and source of guidelines for archaeological practice.)
* Embree, L. (ed.) (1992) *Metaarchaeology: Reflections by Archaeologists and Philosophers*, Boston Studies in the Philosophy of Science, Boston, MA: Clair. (Embree provides a detailed survey of jointly philosophical and archaeological analyses which he designates 'meta-archaeology' and assembles representative essays by most of those he discusses in his introduction.)
* Gardin, J.-C. (1980) *Archaeological Constructs*, Cambridge: Cambridge University Press. (A distinctively French, 'logicist' analysis of the conceptual categories and forms of reasoning that structure archaeological writing.)
* Gardin, J.-C. and Peebles, C.S. (eds) (1992) *Representation in Archaeology*, Bloomington, IN:

Indiana University Press. (The editors provide useful surveys of 'semiotic trends' in archaeology and of the prospects for scientific investigation of the cognitive aspects of human evolution.)
* Gero, J.M. and Conkey, M.W. (eds) (1991) *Engendering Archaeology: Women and Prehistory*, Oxford: Blackwell. (The first collection of essays to appear in archaeology which made questions about women and gender their central concern.)
* Gero, J.M., Lacy, D.M. and Blakey, M.L. (eds) (1983) *The Socio-Politics of Archaeology*, Research Report Number 23, Amherst, MA: Department of Anthropology, University of Massachusetts. (The first major collection of essays on the sociological conditions of archaeological practice.)
* Gibbon, G. (1989) *Explanation in Archaeology*, New York: Blackwell. (An analysis of philosophical issues raised by the New Archaeology, undertaken by an archaeologist, which provides a survey of debates about the positivist commitments of the New Archaeology and an assessment of alternative philosophical models of science.)
* Hodder, I. (ed.) (1982) *Symbolic and Structural Archaeology*, Cambridge: Cambridge University Press. (Hodder was one of the most influential critics of the New Archaeology and has been a primary exponent of symbolic and structuralist alternatives. In this collection of essays he assembled a range of theoretical and empirical studies that illustrate the potential of what came to be known as post-processualism.)
* —— (1991) 'Interpretive Archaeology and its Role', *American Antiquity* 56: 7–18. (Here Hodder argues the case for a hermeneutic approach to interpretation of the archaeological record, extending and reframing his earlier recommendations for post-processual archaeology.)
* Kelley, J. and Hanen, M. (1988) *Archaeology and the Methodology of Science*, Albuquerque, NM: University of New Mexico Press. (A collaboration between an archaeologist and a philosopher which provides a review of the history of philosophical interest within archaeology and a model of archaeological practice based on the analysis of a wide range of case studies.)
* Kosso, P. (1991) 'Method in Archaeology: Middle-range Theory as Hermeneutics', *American Antiquity* 56 (4): 621–7. (Kosso argues that, despite the antipathy between scientific, processual archaeologists and interpretive post-processualists, both make essentially the same use of linking principles – 'middle-range theory' – to interpret archaeological data as evidence.)
* —— (1992) 'Observation of the Past', *History and Theory* 31 (1): 21–36. (A view recognizing the independence of archaeological evidence from the reconstructive hypotheses it is used to support, despite reliance on interpretive principles.)
* —— (1993) 'Middle-range Theory in Historical Archaeology', *Studies in the History and Philosophy of Science* 24 (2): 163–84. (A sophisticated account, by a philosopher, of how archaeological data are constituted as evidence of the cultural past.)
* Leone, M.P. (1982) 'Some Opinions about Recovering Mind', *American Antiquity* 47 (4): 742–60. (An influential argument for attending both to intentional ideational dimensions of the cultural subject and to ideological-political factors that shape archaeological practice.)
* Morgan, C.G. (1973) 'Archaeology and Explanation', *World Archaeology* 4: 259–76. (A sharply critical commentary, by a philosopher, on the New Archaeologists' appeals to positivist models of science; Morgan focuses on Watson, Leblanc and Redman's Explanation in Archaeology.)
* Nickles, T. (1977) 'On the Independence of Singular Causal Explanation in Social Science: Archaeology', *Philosophy of Social Science* 7: 163–87. (Examples of archaeological explanation serve as the basis for an argument against the Hempelian requirement that explanations presuppose covering laws.)
* Patrik, L.E. (1985) 'Is there an Archaeological Record?', in M.B. Schiffer (ed.) *Advances in Archaeology*, vol. 8, New York: Academic Press. (Patrik argues that archaeologists conceptualize the 'archaeological record' in two fundamentally different senses, both as 'fossil' record and as textual record.)
* Patterson, T.C. (1986) 'The Last Sixty Years: Toward a Social History of Americanist Archaeology in the United States', *American Anthropologist* 88: 7–22. (Patterson identifies several distinct traditions of archaeological practice which he argues are aligned with the political economy of regional elites in the USA.)
* —— (1995) *Toward a Social History of Archaeology in the United States*, Orlando, FL: Harcourt Brace. (An examination of the history of professional archaeology in the USA, especially its class structure, which sets the development of the New Archaeology and associated philosophical debates in a larger socio-political context.)
* Pinsky, V. and Wylie, A. (1989) *Critical Traditions in Contemporary Archaeology: Essays in the Philosophy, History and Socio-politics of Archaeology*, Cambridge: Cambridge University Press. (A collection of essays that provides an overview of philosophical debate in archaeology, and a selection of

empirical studies of the historical formation of the discipline and its contemporary soco-political dynamics.)

* Preucel, R.W. (ed.) (1991) *Processual and Postprocessual Archaeologies: Multiple Ways of Knowing the Past*, Carbondale, IL: Southern Illinois University Press, 17–29. (Preucel's essay, 'The Philosophy of Archaeology', provides a useful survey of competing philosophical positions in archaeology through the 1980s.)

* Salmon, M.H. (1982) *Philosophy and Archaeology*, New York: Academic Press. (Through the 1970s Salmon, a philosopher, published several essays for an archaeological audience on philosophical issues raised by the New Archaeology and then this monograph, the first sustained analysis of philosophical models for archaeological practice.)

* —— (1997) 'Ethical Considerations in Anthropology and Archaeology, or Relativism and Justice for All', *Journal for Anthropological Research* 53: 47–63. (An analysis of ethical issues that arise for anthropologists generally; Salmon argues a commitment to the codes of ethics developed by a number of anthropological associations.)

* Shelley, C. (1996) 'Visual Abductive Reasoning in Archaeology', *Philosophy of Science* 63: 278–301. (A sophisticated account of the role of visual imagery in archaeology that is addressed to a philosophical audience.)

* Trigger, B.G. (1980) 'Archaeology and the Image of the American Indian', *American Antiquity* 45: 662–76. (An early critical analysis of racist presuppositions inherent in archaeological interpretation.)

* —— (1989) *A History of Archaeological Thought*, Cambridge: Cambridge University Press. (A comprehensive historical account that traces the emergence of distinct national traditions of archaeological practice.)

* Watson, P.J., Leblanc, S.A. and Redman, C.L. (1971) *Explanation in Archaeology: An Explicitly Scientific Approach*, New York: Columbia University Press. (The most explicit and widely influential statement of the positivist commitments of the New Archaeology.)

* Wylie, A. (1985) 'The Reaction Against Analogy', in M.B. Schiffer (ed.) *Advances in Archaeological Method and Theory*, New York: Academic Press, vol. 8, 63–111. (A model of analogical reasoning that counters the claim, associated with the New Archaeology, that archaeological uses of analogy are inevitably speculative.)

* —— (1986) 'Bootstrapping in Un-Natural Sciences: An Archaeological Case', in A. Fine and P. Machamer (eds) *PSA 1986*, East Lansing, MI: Philosophy of Science Association, vol. 1, 314–22. (Glymour's bootstrapping model provides the framework for showing how a limited independence of evidence from hypotheses can be realized even when both the test hypothesis and interpretive principles derive from common encompassing theory.)

* —— (1996a) 'Unification and Convergence in Archaeological Explanation: The Agricultural 'Wave of Advance' and the Origins of Indo-European Languages', in D.K. Henderson (ed.) *The Southern Journal of Philosophy*, Supplement Explanation in the Human Sciences 34: 1–30, 1996. (The adequacy of Kitcher's unificationist model of explanation is assessed in light of an archaeological debate over the credibility of explanatory appeals to the unifying power.)

* (1996b) 'The Constitution of Archaeological Evidence', in P. Galison and D.J. Stump(eds) *The Disunity of Science: Boundaries, Contexts, and Power*, Stanford, CA: Stanford University Press, 311–43. (A model is proposed for understanding how archaeologists stabilize evidential claims, exploiting local independence between lines of evidence, and between evidence and test hypotheses.)

* —— (1996c) 'Ethical Dilemmas in Archaeological Practice: Looting, Repatriation, Stewardship, and the (Trans)Formation of Disciplinary Identity', *Perspectives on Science* 4 (2): 154–94. (An overview of the history of debate about ethical issues within North American archaeology, and an assessment of epistemic and normative issues that underlie these debates.)

ALISON WYLIE

ARCHĒ

*Archē, or 'principle', is an ancient Greek philosophical term. Building on earlier uses, Aristotle established it as a technical term with a number of related meanings, including 'originating source', 'cause', 'principle of knowledge' and 'basic entity'. Accordingly, it acquired importance in metaphysics, epistemology and philosophy of science, and also in the particular sciences. According to Aristotle's doctrine of scientific principles, all sciences and all scientific knowledge are founded on principles (*archai*) of a limited number of determinate kinds.*

Archē is an ancient Greek term meaning 'rule' (in a political sense) and 'beginning'. The latter sense was developed in philosophical contexts to mean 'origin', 'starting point', and 'principle' or 'first principle'. It derives from the verb *archō*, 'to begin', 'to rule'. Both verbal meanings are found in Homer, although he does not use the noun '*archē*' to mean 'rule'. In historical and political writings archē means 'sovereignty', 'realm', 'political office', and, in the plural, 'authorities', 'magistrates'. The history of the noun as a philosophical term is controversial. Passages like Simplicius, *On Aristotle's Physics* 24.15 and 150.23 have led many to believe that ANAXIMANDER (§2) was the first to use *archē* in a philosophical sense, while according to others these passages simply mean that he was the first to refer to the first principle of his system (in Simplicius' vocabulary, the *archē*) as *apeiron*. Depending on the view taken, the history of *archē* as a philosophical term begins either in the sixth century BC or much later.

The latter view is probably correct. *Archē* is not used in a distinctively philosophical way in the authentic fragments of any Presocratic philosopher before PHILOLAUS and although it carries philosophical weight in his writings (fragments 6, 8, 13) as well as in the Hippocratic medical writings, in Plato (especially *Phaedo* 101, *Phaedrus* 245 and *Republic* 510–11, 533), and possibly in early Greek mathematics, we must look to Aristotle for systematic discussion and use of the term (see ARISTOTLE §6).

In *Metaphysics* V 1 Aristotle says the term *archē* is used in six ways, including the following: 'that from which (as an immanent part) a thing first arises, for example, the foundation of a house'; 'that from which (not as an immanent part) a thing first arises, and from which the movement or the change naturally first proceeds, as a child comes from the father and the mother'; 'that by whose choice that which is moved is moved and that which changes changes, for example, the magistracies in cities, and the arts'; and 'that from which a thing can first be known; for example, the hypotheses are the origins of demonstrations'. Aristotle points out that all causes (*aitia*) are *archai*, as are the nature (*physis*) of a thing, the elements, thought, choice, substance, and 'that for the sake of which'.

In accordance with some of these conceptions of *archē*, Aristotle and his Peripatetic successors refer to the basic principles of the Presocratics (whether they were conceived of as originative substances or as fundamental entities) as *archai*. In *Physics* I, Aristotle develops a more abstract account of physical *archai*, identifying them as two (matter and form) or three (matter, form and privation) (see ARISTOTLE §8). The Stoics, who were material monists, believed in two *archai* – a passive principle, matter, and an active principle, god, which like Aristotle's physical *archai* are best understood as inseparable aspects of substance (see STOICISM §3).

It is unclear how, why or in what field the Greeks first conceived of basing proofs on unprovable principles (the fundamental step in axiomatics). By the late fifth century BC mathematics had made progress in this direction. In discussing mathematical method in the *Republic*, Plato emphasizes the way geometry establishes conclusions on the basis of unproved 'hypotheses' which are considered obvious, but which are not, strictly speaking, known. (Unfortunately, Plato does not make clear what these 'hypotheses' are.) By contrast, dialectic proceeds from hypotheses to an 'unhypothetical' *archē* which is the basis of certain knowledge.

Influenced to some extent by mathematics, Aristotle asserts in the *Posterior Analytics* that every science is based on three kinds of *archai*: definitions (*horismoi*), hypotheses, which seem to posit the existence of the basic entities which the science studies, and common principles (*koina*) or axioms (*axiōmata*) such as the Law of Non-Contradiction, used in more than one science. These kinds of principles correspond approximately, but not perfectly, to the principles on which the geometry of Euclid's *Elements* is based: definitions (*horoi*), construction postulates (*aitēmata*) and 'common notions' (*koinai ennoiai*).

The *Posterior Analytics* develops a general doctrine of scientific *archai*. Every science (*epistēmē*) consists of demonstrations of conclusions from *archai*. Aristotle argues that the *archai* cannot themselves be demonstrated. The *archai* must satisfy several strict conditions: they must be true, primary, immediate, and prior to the conclusions that follow from them. Moreover, they must be better known than and causes (that is, *aitia*: 'grounds', 'explanations') of these conclusions. 'Primary' and 'immediate' here mean 'unprovable' or 'basic'. By 'better known' and 'prior' Aristotle means better known and prior 'in nature' to the conclusions; that is, more intelligible. By 'causes', Aristotle indicates that scientific *archai* are causally prior to the facts that follow from them; he is thus committed to believing in a real ordering of facts in which some are more causally basic than others, and to holding that scientific knowledge is a matter of knowing the basic facts, knowing that they are basic, and knowing how the derivative facts follow from them. It follows that scientific *archai* are basic both ontologically and epistemologically; an *archē* is an *archē* within the context of a single science. In general, an *archē* of one science has no status either as *archē* or as conclusion in another science. In one sense *archē* is a relative term: an *archē* is an *archē* of or for certain other facts or propositions (Aristotle did not always distinguish these from one another). In another sense an *archē* is absolute: a fact is basic whether or not anyone happens to recognize it as such.

References and further reading

* Aristotle (*c.* mid 4th century BC) *Posterior Analytics*, trans. J. Barnes, Oxford: Clarendon Press, 2nd edn, 1994. (Includes notes.)
* —— (*c.* mid 4th century BC) *Metaphysics*, books IV, V, VI, trans. C. Kirwan, Oxford: Clarendon Press, 1971. (Includes notes.)
  Fritz, K. von (1955) 'Die *Archai* in der griechischen Mathematik' (*Archai* in Greek Mathematics), *Archiv für Begriffsgeschichte* 1: 13–103; repr. in *Grundprobleme der Geschichte der antiken Wissenschaft* (Fundamental Problems in the History of Classical Science), Berlin: de Gruyter, 1971, 335–429. (Discusses the kinds of principles Aristotle prescribes, and their relations with Greek mathematics.)
  Huffman, C. (1993) *Philolaus of Croton, Pythagorean and Presocratic*, Cambridge: Cambridge University Press. (See pages 78–92 for the meaning of the term *archē* in Presocratic philosophy, the Hippocratic writings and early Greek mathematics.)
  Lapidge, M. (1973) '*Archai* and *Stoicheia*: A Problem in Stoic Cosmology', *Phronesis* 18: 240–78. (Important study of these concepts in Stoic physics.)
  McKirahan, R.D. (1992) *Principles and Proofs. Aristotle's Theory of Demonstrative Science*, Princeton, NJ: Princeton University Press. (Discusses the nature of science according to Aristotle, including the kinds of scientific principles and their roles in demonstrations.)
* Plato (*c.* 380–367 BC) *Republic*, trans. P. Shorey, Loeb Classical Library, Cambridge, MA: Harvard University Press and London: Heinemann, 1930; repr. in *Plato, The Collected Dialogues including Letters*, ed. E. Hamilton and H. Cairns, Princeton, NJ: Princeton University Press, 1961. (Parallel Greek text and English translation; see books 6–7 for Plato's notion of *archē*.)

RICHARD McKIRAHAN

ARCHITECTURE, AESTHETICS OF

The philosophy of architecture is a branch of philosophical aesthetics concerned with various issues arising from the theory and practice of building design.

The oldest writings on architecture date from antiquity and link architectural principles to more general, metaphysical elements of form and order. This tradition persisted into and beyond the Renaissance, but in the eighteenth century it began to give way to new philosophies of mind and value, according to which the determining factors of aesthetic experience are the interests and attitudes of informed subjects. Thereby architecture came within the sphere of the theory of taste.

Nineteenth-century revivals of classical and Gothic styles produced renewed interest in the nature of architecture, its place within the scheme of arts and sciences, and its role in society. Following this, twentieth-century modernism offered various accounts of the rational basis of architectural form and combined these with utopian political philosophies. As it had been in antiquity and during the Renaissance, architecture was again viewed as central to and partly definitive of a culture. More recently, however, attention has returned to analytical questions such as 'What is the nature of the aesthetic experience of architecture?' and, relatedly, 'How is it possible for there to be reasoned, critical judgments about the meaning and value of buildings?'

In order to deal with such issues philosophers in different traditions have begun to develop accounts of the social aspects of architecture, recognizing that critical judgments presuppose the capacity to identify buildings as being of various types: public, domestic, formal, informal and so on. The nature of architecture is in part, therefore, a matter of social convention or more generally 'forms of life', and this limits the scope for abstract ahistorical theorizing. None the less, the resources of metaphysics, the theories of mind, action, meaning and value are all utilized in contemporary philosophy of architecture.

1 The subject and its central themes
2 Pre-Kantian traditions
3 Post-Kantian perspectives
4 Postmodern prospects

1 The subject and its central themes

Two works have influenced Western architectural theory throughout most of its history: Vitruvius' *De architectura libri X* (*Ten Books on Architecture*); and Alberti's *De re aedificatoria* (*On Architecture*). The first bears a dedication to Augustus Caesar, and the second, which derives from it, is a product of the Italian Renaissance. Ironically, although written 1,500 years apart, they were first published in printed form within a year of each other – Alberti in 1485 and Vitruvius in 1486 – and have stood side by side as foundational texts ever since.

Like most writers of treatises on architecture, Vitruvius and Alberti are largely concerned with practical questions of design and construction, but they also address aesthetic aspects of the subject. Commenting on the 'departments of architecture', Vitruvius writes

> all of these must be built with due reference to durability (*utilitas*) and beauty (*venustas*)...[and beauty will be assured] when the appearance of the work is pleasing and in good taste, and when its members are in due proportion according to correct principles of symmetry.
>
> (*De architectura libri X*, I, iii, 2)

Earlier he explains that symmetry consists in 'a proper agreement between the members of the work itself, and relation between the different parts and the whole general scheme, in accordance with a certain part selected as standard'. (*De architectura libri X*, I, ii, 4)

The classical idea that architectural beauty rests upon compositional unity is taken up by Alberti and developed in a direction that raises a further philosophical issue, namely, that of the proper object of aesthetic assessment. At the outset of *De re aedificatoria* he writes

> It is the property and business of the design to appoint to the edifice and all its parts their proper places, determinate number, just proportion and beautiful order; so that the whole form of the structure be proportionable. Nor has this design anything that makes it in its nature inseparable from matter.... Which being granted, we shall call the design a firm and graceful pre-ordering of the lines and angles conceived in the mind, and contrived by an ingenious artist.
>
> (1452, I, i)

Subsequent authors have returned to these ideas of the nature and of the true bearer of architectural beauty; mostly to endorse them, but also to develop or reject them. In the seventeenth century, for example, the English theorist Sir Henry Wotton coined a much quoted formula that derives (via Palladio and Alberti) from Vitruvius, when he wrote that architecture must aim to provide 'commodity, firmness and delight'. In the following century the French architect and theorist Étienne-Louis Boullée echoed Alberti's claim that architecture should be identified with abstract design rather than with material construction:

> What is architecture? Shall I join Vitruvius in defining it as the art of building? Indeed, no, for there is a flagrant error in this definition. Vitruvius mistakes the effect for the cause. In order to execute it is first necessary to conceive...it is this product of the mind, this process of creation, that constitutes architecture.
>
> (Boullée 1790)

Although none of these writers is a philosopher, the issues they raise are instances of central topics in aesthetic theory, namely, the basis of value and the objects of appreciation. Reflection on architecture gives rise to further questions concerning its status in respect of the fine arts, the character of our experience of designs and buildings, and the relation of the built environment to other aspects of human existence, for example, religion, morality and politics. The systematic exploration of these and similar issues constitutes the philosophy of architecture.

Conceived in these terms the subject is a modern one, for although the roots of architectural theorizing run deep into the foundations of Western culture, the writings so far cited contain, at best, incidental reflections on normative and ontological issues. It is only with the development of aesthetics as a distinct branch of academic philosophy, a process begun in the eighteenth century, that conceptual resources were fashioned for constructing comprehensive philosophical accounts of architecture. Indeed, it can even be argued that the existence of the subject dates from the publication of Roger Scruton's *The Aesthetics of Architecture* in 1979. For until then philosophical discussions were partial and generally ill-informed. What Scruton offers, by contrast, is a sustained investigation of the aesthetic experience of architecture which draws upon several parts of analytical philosophy, most prominently the philosophy of mind and action, and the theory of meaning.

One way of reading Scruton's work is as an attempt to answer the question of how there can be a critical experience of architecture. This follows the Kantian approach, according to which the general form of a philosophical question is 'How is such-and-such possible? Scruton is an avowed admirer of Kant and particularly values the account of aesthetic experience set out in *Critique of Judgment*, even though his own view departs significantly from Kant's. It is therefore unsurprising that the perspective developed in *The Aesthetics of Architecture* is broadly Kantian in nature. Before coming to this, however, and in order to ensure a proper appreciation of his work and its point of departure from a purely Kantian aesthetic, it is necessary to return to antiquity and to examine some of the central ideas that informed pre-Kantian thought.

2 Pre-Kantian traditions

In Book IX, Vitruvius discusses the wisdom of the ancients, illustrating this with accounts of the geometrical discoveries of Plato and Pythagoras. He cites the latter's famous triangle theorem and adds, 'When Pythagoras discovered this fact, he had no doubt that the Muses had guided him... and it is said that he very gratefully offered sacrifice' (1914, 253). Although Vitruvius is concerned with the practical applications of the theorem, mention of Pythagoras and the occult nature of his discovery expressed the common view that perceptible forms are underwritten by an abstract, numerically expressible, transcendental order.

Thus when, Vitruvius, Alberti, Palladio, Wotton and others write of the importance of proportion they are drawing upon a metaphysical theory of regularity. On this account beauty is obtained by designing compositions in which symmetry (*symmetria*) and due proportion (*eurythmia*) are realized, these being determined by relevant units or modules, and various operations ('modulations') performed upon them. The central Pythagorean idea see (PYTHAGOREANISM §2), refashioned by Plato and subsequent Neoplatonists, is that empirical order results from the imposition or expression of abstract principles upon or through a medium, in this case matter. In some accounts the units and modes of combination are few and underlie all compositions; in others the modules differ according to the nature of the thing in question. Thus, one might hold that human anatomy expresses the same basic order as the relative positions and movements of the planets, or that each system is based upon its own units and modulations. Such differences, however, are less important than the extent and duration of the consensus that beauty attends correct composition and that correct composition is a matter of cosmically legitimated proportion.

Although Vitruvius was not printed until the fifteenth century, many manuscript versions survive from the medieval period, and it is clear from this and other evidence that the Graeco-Roman metaphysics of architecture informed the theory and practice of design throughout antiquity and the Middle Ages. This raises the question of what philosophical difference, if any, underlay the development of European architecture from Greek to Romanesque and later to 'Gothic'.

At the philosophical level the difference was one of addition and interpretation rather than of replacement. For medieval builders, Platonism was maintained in a Christianized version that included the ideas of divinely ordained symmetry and proportion. Additionally these notions came to be associated with elements from scripture, and architecture came to be seen as an enduring medium for the symbolic representation of a transcendent reality. As before, the application of geometry to part and whole dominated the practice of design but a growing interest in natural forms and their variety led to an enrichment of architectural forms.

In *Gothic Architecture and Scholasticism* (1951), Erwin Panofsky proposed an interesting, though contestable, general parallelism between High Gothic cathedrals and High Scholastic philosophical and theological treatises (such as Aquinas' *Summa Theologiae*), arguing that each aspires to 'totality', 'articulation' and 'coherence'. As far as architecture is concerned, this involves an integration of theology, morality, nature and history in the plan, elevation and furnishings of the great cathedral churches; in consequence their interpretation and appreciation calls for more than (but not less than) an ability to discern and enjoy geometrical proportion.

Given their shared assumptions about the proper sources of architectural form it is unsurprising that people of the ancient and medieval worlds thought of its beauty as objective, and of aesthetic experience as an encounter with properties whose nature is independent of our experience of them. Aquinas' definition of beauty (*Summa Theologiae*, Ia.39.8.), involving integrity (*integritas*), proper proportion (*proportio sive consonantia*) and clarity (*claritas*) is an important post-Platonist statement of this idea, though its last condition introduces an element of relativity inasmuch as being 'clearly manifest' is a relational property requiring a possible knower.

Once introduced, this relational element was bound to give rise to a question of the degree to which the nature of the knower conditions the experience of beauty – and indeed of the extent to which the grounds of beauty are themselves relative. In the seventeenth century a famous dispute concerning just these matters took place between two French classical architects: Claude Perrault and François Blondel. Beginning with his edition of Vitruvius (published in 1673), Perrault (1674) contested the standard view that the object of aesthetic experience is harmonious unity established by true order and proportion. Instead he distinguished 'convincing' (*convaincantes*) and 'arbitrary' (*arbitraires*) types of beauty, the first being universally pleasing, the second depending on subjective factors such as convention, familiarity and contingent associations. On this basis he reasoned that proportion and its beauty are arbitrary, that is, not fixed by an independent reality but determined by intersubjective agreement. In reply, Blondel (1675) argued for the importance of architecture as a bridging art between painting and sculpture, and upheld the objectivity of the harmonious unity of proportionate orders. In this latter he was subsequently and emphatically supported by Boullée who insisted upon the certainty that proportion derives from natural symmetry: 'The basic rule and the one that governs the principles of architecture, originates in regularity' (Boullée 1790).

To some extent the debate was misconceived since, like Aquinas, Blondel acknowledged human relational elements in the analysis of beauty (as did Boullée and Perrault conceded the objectivity of certain kinds of aesthetic properties. None the less, it marked the beginning of a period in which philosophers and others turned towards nonobjectivist aesthetic theories. In his *Philosophical Inquiry into the Origin of our Ideas of the Sublime and the Beautiful* (1757), for example, Edmund BURKE gives various psychological explanations of architectural features and of our approval of them, including the claim that Stonehenge is judged 'grand' because of the idea it induces of the difficulty of its creation (II, §12)

3 Post-Kantian perspectives

Like all such generalizations, the claim that philosophical aesthetics began with Kant is open to contention. It is undisputed, however, that his *Critique of Judgment* (1790), like his other major works, represents one of the points of definition of modern philosophy (see KANT, I. §12). In aesthetics, as in theoretical and moral thought, Kant's principal innovation was to convert the relationship between subject and object, and to argue that sceptical doubts were answered by the consideration that since the structure of the human mind conditions the realm of its experience and understanding there is no general possibility that facts should elude the power of the mind to grasp them. The conditions of something being the case include its being a possible object of experience.

In the realm of aesthetics Kant's aim was to show how judgments of beauty could be subjective and yet assessable as correct or incorrect. When I say, 'This arched gateway is beautiful', I am not simply saying that I like it, but rather that my liking it arises from my judgment of its quality. For Kant an explanation of this involves the free play of the imagination engaged by something possessing form. Since form in this sense is a function of the mind's organizing tendency, and this tendency and the imagination are powers common to all rational subjects, if I regard the gateway as a formal object and view it apart from any practical or scientific interest then the experience I have and the pleasure that this involves will be similar for anyone else in an equivalent condition. In other words, aesthetic judgment admits the possibility of intersubjective validity.

From the perspective of the older metaphysical rationalism of Vitruvius, intersubjectivity is still subjectivity and thus falls short of what, on that account, a recognition of architectural beauty implies; but whether the Kantian view is incompatible with the kind of formal objectivism advanced by Aquinas and Blondel is another more subtle question. Concerning aesthetic experience in general and specifically that of architecture, even a supporter of Kant's general perspective may, however, take issue with his distinction between 'free' and 'dependent' beauty.

The experience of sensible forms such as a rainbow or a curling plume of rising smoke, attended to for their own sake and without any concern for their scientific nature or practical function, is the occasion of pure judgments of free beauty. Contrasted with these, and very much secondary to them, are applied judgments of dependent beauty. In the case of the latter, the experience and judgment is conditional upon a conception of the nature of the thing in question. Thus if in judging that a chapel is beautiful I take account of its religious function and relate its aesthetic qualities to this, judging it to be 'a beautiful chapel', then the beauty is dependent and the judgment is applied.

It is clear, however, that a theory of aesthetic experiences of architecture must accommodate the fact that buildings are functional objects. Someone whose judgments always abstracted from the fact that what they were looking at was an occupiable structure designed as such – a house, a church or an airport, for example – would rightly be held to be missing the whole point of these things. Architecture is not abstract sculpture and any theory of its nature and of our experience of it that seeks to give it this status is on the wrong track.

Scruton's appropriation of Kant takes the form of an acceptance of much of his general theoretical and practical philosophy, and the adoption of the structure of his aesthetic theory, with the major qualification that what was secondary and derivative in the *Critique of Judgment* becomes paradigmatic in *The Aesthetics of Architecture*. The experience of architecture is typically a judgment of feeling of something recognized to be a building and found to be pleasing as such. With this foundation in place, Scruton is able to build a theory that incorporates elements from idealist and other anti-empiricist sources. From Hegel and Wittgenstein, for example, he takes the idea that the conditions of individual subjectivity and hence of creative imagination include the pre-existence of a community within which relevant forms of practice are operative. The ability to design and to appreciate design, and the experience of occupying built designs, are constituents of given forms of life.

4 Postmodern prospects

While Scruton's book and subsequent articles comprise the most systematic and extensive conceptual study of the subject, the most active sources of writings now catalogued as philosophy of architecture lie within what is generally described as 'continental' philosophy, that is, those branches of speculative and political thought that derive from existential phenomenology and structuralism, and which include post- and neo-structuralism, deconstruction and postmodernism. Following the example of essays such as Heidegger's 'Building, Dwelling, Thinking' (1975), some writers have tried to construct a reflective phenomenology of the experience of place and of physical containment. Even when these are effective, however, they stand in need of some more general framework such as Scruton provides. It may therefore be useful to think of the two approaches as complementary, rather than as opposed to one another.

The question of how, if at all, buildings convey meaning is a recurrent theme of both analytical and continental writings, as is the issue of the connection between architecture and aspects of the wider culture. Writers of the left, such as Habermas, and those of the right, principally Scruton and Watkin, both find reasons to follow Ruskin in relating aspects of architectural theory and practice to political ideas. A common target of much recent criticism is the utopian character of the Modern Movement as expressed in the writings and work of its leading figures, such as Gropius and Le Corbusier. To some extent the latter's theories of the nature of architecture and the basis of its aesthetic values recall the earlier, pre-modern, Neoplatonic traditions; but they also embody a notion of the architect as Messiah, bringing to a heedless world the redemptive truths of a revolutionary social message – a creed the advent of which has been determined by the logic of history. As Le Corbusier expressed it:

> A great epoch has begun. There exists a new spirit …. If we challenge the past, we shall learn that styles no longer exist for us, that a style belonging to our own period has come about; and that there has been a revolution.
>
> (1923)

Any plausibility such views might once have had was long ago undermined by the conspicuous failures of modernist architecture; but the philosophical attack upon them has been directed against their historicist and totalitarian assumptions. The collapse of Marxism-Leninism and the rise of radical relativism among thinkers of the left have produced less ambitious, more provisional and contextual ideas about the role of architecture as an element in social policy.

This last trend also contributes to one important strand of postmodernist thought. The term 'postmodernism', though since deployed very widely, had some of its earliest uses in the context of architectural criticism; and it was within this context that a distinction came to be drawn between two reactions to modernism. First there is that associated with Derrida and Rorty, the defining characteristic of which has been the claim that rational legitimation is impossible. On this account, metaphysical theism and the foundationalist projects of Cartesian and Kantian rationalism have all failed and no other 'metanarrative' is available. Appeals to reason are usually veiled exercises of power, and all that remains is the ironic affirmation of ideas and images that are without any means of validation.

The second postmodern reaction is characterized by Kenneth Frampton (1985) as 'critical regionalism'. Like its radical counterpart it rejects universal doctrines and policies, but not as part of a general attack on reason as such. Instead it favours local customs and practices and looks for vernacular solutions to contextually defined problems. This way of thinking about architecture has certain parallels with the style of moral and social philosophy advocated by Alasdair MacIntyre in a series of works beginning with *After Virtue* (1985).

Finally, thinking about the nature of the built environment cannot proceed for long without taking account of the natural one. The distinction between nature and artifice is indeed a philosophical question, but however this is defined it can hardly be denied that there are differences of kind or of degree between what has been built and the landscape within which it is set. As the continental and analytical traditions come into closer contact, and moral philosophers and aestheticians within each tradition learn about each other's concerns, it seems very likely that interest in the philosophy of architecture will grow and that it will become part of a larger philosophy of environment; at which point the metaphysics of symmetry can be expected to make a reappearance.

See also: HABERMAS, J.; MODERNISM

References and further reading

* Alberti, L.B. (1452) *De re aedificatoria*; ed. J.

Rykwert, trans. J. Leoni (1726), *Ten Books on Architecture*, London: Tirantif, 1955. (The first and most influential architectural treatise of the Renaissance, first printed in 1485.)

* Blondel, F. (1675, 1698) *Cours d'architecture*, Paris; selections, with accompanying translations, appear in W. Tatarkiewicz, *History of Aesthetics*, vol. 3, *Modern Aesthetics*, ed. D. Petsch, The Hague: Mouton, 1974. (A defence, against Perrault, of the objectivity of correct proportion as the basis of architectural beauty.)

* Boullée, É.-L. (1790) 'Architecture, essai sur l'art', trans. S. de Vallée (1953) in H. Rosenau, *Boullée and Visionary Architecture*, London: Academy Editions, 1976. (Unpublished until 1953, this is an engaging defence of the assumptions and values of neoclassicism.)

* Burke, E. (1757) *A Philosophical Enquiry into the Origin of our Ideas of: the Sublime and the Beautiful*, ed. A. Phillips, Oxford: Oxford University Press, 1990. (A youthful study of the connections between aesthetic qualities and psychological phenomena, in particular emotions.)

* Frampton, K. (1985) 'Towards a Critical Regionalism: Six Points for an Architecture of Resistance', in H. Foster (ed.) *Postmodern Culture*, London: Pluto Press. (Written in a popular style, this argues against the universalism and rationalism of modernist architectural theory.)

* Goodman, N. (1985) 'How Buildings Mean', *Critical Inquiry* 11: 642–53. (One of the major figures of analytical aesthetics examines the possibility of architecture having a symbolic function.)

* Habermas, J. (1989) 'Modern and Postmodern Architecture', in S.W. Nicholson (trans. and ed.) *The New Conservatism*, Oxford: Polity Press. (An account of modernism and of possible alternatives to it by the leading advocate of post-Marxist critical theory.)

* Heidegger, M. (1975) 'Building, Dwelling, Thinking', trans. and ed. A. Hofstader, in *Poetry, Language, Thought*, New York: Harper & Row. (A phenomenological-cum-existentialist exploration of spatial aspects of the experience of being-in-the-world.)

Horden, P. (1983) 'The Function of Forms: Recent Architectural Aesthetics', *Oxford Art Journal* 5: 39–45. (A useful discussion of psychological and philosophical approaches, focusing on Scruton as seen against the background of Neo-Kantian idealism.)

* Kant, I. (1790) *Critique of Judgment*, trans. W. Pluhar, Indianapolis, IN: Hackett Publishing Company, 1987. (Notwithstanding its obscurity and difficulty this is generally held to be the classic work of philosophical aesthetics.)

* Le Corbusier (1923) *Vers une architecture*, trans. F. Etchells, *Towards a New Architecture*, London: Architectural Press, 1927. (A typically extravagant statement of the revolutionary aims of utopian modernism.)

* MacIntyre, A. (1985) *After Virtue*, London: Duckworth, 2nd (corrected) edn. (Very influential presentation of the claim that contemporary liberal societies are in a state of moral chaos resulting from the fragmentation of traditions.)

* Panofsky, E. (1951) *Gothic Architecture and Scholasticism*, London: Thames & Hudson, 1957. (A lively exploration of the idea that thirteenth-century architecture and philosophy exhibit significant parallels.)

* Perrault, C. (1674) *Abrégé des dix livres d'architecture de Vitruve*, Paris. Selections, with accompanying translations, appear in W. Tatarkiewicz, *History of Aesthetics*, vol. 3, *Modern Aesthetics*, ed. D. Petsch, The Hague: Mouton, 1974. (The work that opened the seventeenth-century debate about the objectivity of architectural beauty.)

Scott, G. (1914) *The Architecture of Humanism*, London: Methuen, 1961. (A defence of the values of classicism and of the autonomy of architectural aesthetics against several explanatory theories.)

* Scruton, R. (1979) *The Aesthetics of Architecture*, London: Methuen. (The *locus classicus* of philosophical architectural aesthetics, written from a neo-Kantian and conservative perspective.)

—— (1994) *Classical Vernacular: Architectural Principles*, Manchester: Carcanet. (A further collection of essays in which Scruton develops his case against various aspects of modernism in architecture and defends the superiority of the classical understanding.)

* Vitruvius (c.30 BC) *De architectura libri X*, trans. M. Morgan, *Ten Books on Architecture*, Cambridge, MA: Harvard University Press, 1914. (The primary text in the canon of architectural writings and the only such work to have survived from antiquity.)

Watkin, D. (1975) *Morality and Architecture*, Chicago, IL: University of Chicago Press. (A study of the historicist and utopian assumptions of modernist writings, particularly those of Pevsner.)

JOHN J. HALDANE

ARCHYTAS (early to mid 4th century BC)

Archytas of Tarentum (modern Taranto in southern Italy) was a contemporary and personal acquaintance of Plato, and the last of the famous Pythagoreans in antiquity. An ancient source (Proclus) chytas with those mathematicians 'who increased the number of theorems and progressed towards a more scientific arrangement of them' and ranks him among the predecessors of Euclid. His chief contribution in mathematics was to find a solution for the doubling of the cube. As a Pythagorean philosopher, Archytas gave mathematics universal scope: he viewed the four cardinal branches of Greek scientific knowledge – arithmetic, geometry, astronomy and music – as 'sister sciences' since they could be formulated mathematically. In both mathematics and music he emphasized the study of mean proportionals. He also conducted empirical investigations in acoustics and invented simple technical devices by which to illustrate the application of mathematical principles to mechanics. Archytas was able to combine his philosophical-scientific interests with an active political career; he was a leading statesman of Tarentum and served as a successful general.

1 Life
2 Mathematics and music
3 Miscellanea

1 Life

When Plato, on his third trip to Sicily, was forcibly detained in Syracuse by Dionysius II, he requested the help of Archytas and other friends in Tarentum, who sent a ship to rescue him. This took place in 361/360 BC, which locates Archytas' activity in the first half of the fourth century BC. (The label 'Presocratic', often used of him, describes Archytas' intellectual, rather than his strictly chronological, position.) Tarentum had continued as a stronghold of PYTHAGOREANISM (§1) after the general dispersal of the Pythagoreans and their emigration from southern Italy. Archytas, who supposedly studied with Philolaus, devoted his interests chiefly to mathematics, musical theory and mechanics. His stature as a leading Pythagorean thinker was such that Aristotle wrote three separate treatises about him. In addition to his philosophical-scientific enterprises, Archytas achieved renown as a military commander of Tarentum, earning continual reappointments beyond the usual terms of office.

2 Mathematics and music

Archytas is famous for his geometrical solution to the problem of doubling the cube. This long-standing problem, which may originally have arisen among the Greeks from architectural consideration of how to double a solid body while retaining its shape, had been reduced by Hippocrates of Chios to that of finding the two mean proportionals. Building on Hippocrates' insight, Archytas solved the problem by means of moving, three-dimensional constructions (half-cylinders and cones), thus also introducing the concept of movement into geometry (previous Pythagoreans had not concerned themselves with motion). This has earned him a place in the annals of mathematics. But Archytas is of no less significance to historians of philosophy for at least two reasons: first, because he makes evident the high degree of sophistication that mathematics had attained by the fourth century BC, against which background the mathematical activities of Plato and his associates in the Academy must be understood; second, and more generally, because although his mathematics far surpasses in complexity the number speculation of early Pythagoreanism, Archytas none the less gives the clearest expression of the Pythagorean view that mathematics provides the philosophical key for the understanding of all of nature. The cosmic application of mathematics appears more pronounced in Archytas than in his fellow, non-Pythagorean Greek mathematicians (for example, Hippocrates of Chios, EUDOXUS and, later, Euclid). The following fragment reveals the universal importance that Archytas assigned to mathematical insight:

> Mathematicians seem to me to have excellent discernment, and it is not at all strange that they should think correctly about the particulars that are; for inasmuch as they can discern excellently about the nature (*physis*) of the universe, they are also likely to have an excellent perspective on the particulars that are. Indeed, they have transmitted to us a keen discernment about the velocities of the stars and their risings and settings, and about geometry, numbers [arithmetic], sphericity [astronomy], and, not least of all, music. These seem to be sister sciences, for they concern themselves with the first two related forms of being [that is, number and magnitude].
>
> (fr. 1)

Mathematics is thus foundational for correct thinking about being. The view of number as an all-powerful explanatory concept for the orderly arrangement of the universe originated from the Pythagoreans' discovery of the numerical ratios governing musical harmony and seemed to them to be corroborated by the observation that figures and shapes could be expressed arithmetically: for example, the line by two, the triangle by three, the pyramid by four points (see PYTHAGOREANISM §2). That even three-dimensional bodies could in one way be accounted for by an aggregate of points led to a certain fusion of mathematical and physical properties in Pythagorean philosophy, allowing Aristotle to say of the Pythagoreans that 'they construct the whole universe out of numbers – only not numbers consisting of abstract units; they suppose the units to have spatial magnitude' (Metaphysics 1080b18–20). Archytas reports of another Pythagorean, Eurytus, that he arranged a number of pebbles to represent the figures of man or horse, and after counting the pebbles declared that such was the number of man and such of horse. Pythagorean number theory, even in the crude form it assumed in the pebble arithmetic of Eurytus, comes to a legitimate fruition with Archytas. He viewed geometry, arithmetic, astronomy and music – the classic quadrivium of medieval authors – collectively as 'sister sciences' (as later Plato would call astronomy and harmonics, expressly citing Pythagorean precedent (Republic 530d)), since they all have to do with number or numerical relations: geometry and arithmetic for obvious reasons, astronomy because it was treated mathematically, notably when the properties of the sphere were studied as a geometrical model to explain the movements of the celestial sphere, and music because it involved numerically expressed harmonic proportions. His high regard for these sciences was governed by the conviction – still held in modern science, whose theses often take the form of equations and formulas – that number supplies the precise, quantitative measures by which to comprehend the world.

Fragment 1, which concerns the universality of mathematical insight, forms the introduction to a work that is variously entitled *On Mathematics* or *On Harmonics*. Indeed, Archytas immediately continues to discuss the relation between pitch and frequency, citing a series of examples to show that swift movements produce high notes and slow movements low notes (for example, a stick moved at different speeds produces variations in the pitch of the sound, or the air emitted from the upper holes of a pipe yields higher notes than that from the lower holes). While Archytas' account also contains some inaccurate conclusions from his observations (the speed of the motion that produces a sound was confused with the speed of the sound itself), his acoustic theories are none the less informative about the type of rudimentary empirical investigation that characterized Presocratic science. Moreover, Archytas' acoustics provide an interesting footnote to Plato: discussing physical sense-experience in the *Timaeus* (67b, 80a), Plato appears to rely on Archytas to explain hearing and sound (where again the speed of the propagation of sound is confused with frequency: higher notes are said to reach the ear more quickly than lower notes).

In his treatment of harmonics proper, Archytas further developed Pythagorean musical theory (see PHILOLAUS §5). He calculated the numerical ratios of the intervals in all three scales of the tetrachord (diatonic, chromatic and enharmonic) and specified a doctrine of 'means' to elucidate the connection of proportion and music. The three basic means are the arithmetic (in 6, 9, 12, the difference between the first and the second number equals that between the second and the third), the geometric (in 2, 4, 8, the ratio of the first to the second corresponds to that of the second to the third) and the subcontrary or the harmonic (in 6, 8, 12, the proportion of the first by which the second, the harmonic mean, exceeds the first ($\frac{1}{3}$) is the same as the proportion of the third ($\frac{1}{3}$) by which the third exceeds the second). The knowledge of the means is presupposed by Plato when in the *Timaeus* (35b–36b) he divides the world-soul into harmonic intervals.

However, Archytas' emphasis on means, as evidenced both in his drawing upon the mean proportionals to explain the doubling of the cube and in his determining the means of the musical proportions, goes beyond the confines of geometry and musicology. A single fragment that preserves Archytas' thoughts on political-ethical matters indicates that he regarded a just society as one ruled by equality in something like the mathematical sense of proportion:

> When calculation has been found, it checks political faction and increases concord, for there is no unfair advantage in its presence, and equality reigns. With calculation we smooth out differences in our dealings with each other. Through it the poor take from the powerful, and the rich give to the needy, both trusting in it to obtain an equal share...
>
> (fr. 3)

Archytas envisions here a society whose equilibrium depends upon right 'calculation' (*logismos*), a word that in Greek also means 'reasoning', but whose root meaning of 'counting' or 'calculating' was never wholly lost to sight (the plural *logismoi* can in fact be translated as 'arithmetic') and such a form would especially be favoured by the mathematical mind of Archytas. Calculation, in its political application, leads (ideally) to figuring out the right proportion between rich and poor, establishing the means, as it were, between them, and thus ensuring political equality (*isotēs*, a term which also refers to mathematical proportion). That Archytas engaged in political reflections with mathematical overtones is not surprising, given that he was both a pre-eminent statesman and a mathematician. His stress on finding the right proportions in both domains make him what may be called 'the philosopher of means'.

3 Miscellanea

The extent to which Archytas dedicated himself to specific problems of cosmology is not known, although fragment 1 allows the assumption that he brought mathematical insights to bear on physics and astronomy. It was most probably in the course of such pursuits that he took up the question of infinite space. Archytas posed to himself the question as to whether or not, standing at the heaven of the fixed stars (that is, the edge of the world) he could extend his hand or a staff (A24). The implication being that he could, it appears Archytas was trying to lend support to the Pythagorean idea of the 'unlimited' outside the heavens (see PHILOLAUS §3).

Besides the theoretical concerns of Archytas, we are further informed of certain practical inventions. He is said to have constructed a wooden dove that could fly and a popular rattle for children to keep them amused and from breaking things in the house. These inventions, the technical details of which are not known, were probably devised in part to illustrate Archytas' scientific theories, since he was noted for making mechanics systematic by applying mathematical principles.

In sum, although our knowledge of Archytas is comparatively meagre, it reveals one of the most versatile and creative thinkers of the fourth century BC – philosopher, statesman, mathematician and musical theorist combined in one person. Certainly, his indebtedness to previous Pythagoreans, Presocratics and contemporary Greek philosophers cannot be discounted, but despite this he evinces considerable originality. The original cast of his mind is well typified in the following fragment in which he presents, somewhat paradoxically, the philosophical craft as a process of independent discovery:

> To become knowledgeable about things one does not know one must either learn from others or find out for oneself. Now learning derives from someone else and is foreign, whereas finding out is of and by oneself. Finding out without seeking is difficult and rare, but with seeking it is manageable and easy, though someone who does not know how to seek cannot find.
>
> (fr. 3)

References and further reading

Archytas (early to mid 4th century BC) Fragments, in H. Diels and W. Kranz (eds) *Die Fragmente der Vorsokratiker* (Fragments of the Presocratics), Berlin: Weidmann, 6th edn, 1952 vol. 1: 421–39. (The standard collection of the ancient sources, both fragments and testimonia, the latter designated by 'A'; includes Greek texts with German translations.)

Burkert, W. (1972) *Lore and Science in Ancient Pythagoreanism*, trans. E.L. Minar, Jr, Cambridge, MA: Harvard University Press. (Discusses *passim* the science and philosophy of Archytas; in particular, pages 379–83 consider Archytas' acoustics in the context of Presocratic science, pages 384–9 examine his musical theory and pages 442–7 his number theory.)

Freeman, K. (1947) *Ancilla to the Pre-Socratic Philosophers*, Oxford: Blackwell, 6th edn, 1971. (Includes, at pages 78–80, an English translation of the major fragments of Archytas.)

Heath, T. (1921) *A History of Greek Mathematics*, Oxford: Oxford University Press; repr. New York: Dover, 1981. (Volume 1 pages 213–16 give a general introduction to the achievements of Archytas, followed by an account of his proof that there can be no number (the geometric mean) between two numbers of a superparticular proportion; pages 247–9 explain in detail Archytas' duplication of the cube.)

Lloyd, G.E.R. (1990) 'Plato and Archytas in the seventh latter', *Phronesis* 35.2: 159–73. (Examines the evidence for the relationship of Plato and Archytas as given in Plato's Seventh Letter.)

* Plato (*c*.366–360 BC) Timaeus, trans. F.M. Cornford, *Plato's Cosmology*, London: Routledge & Kegan Paul, 1937.

Portnoy, J. (1954) *The Philosopher and Music*, New York: Humanities Press. (A readable survey of the relationship of philosophers to music in Western civilization; Chapter 1 provides a useful discussion of the significance of music for Greek philosophers and includes a short section on Archytas.)

HERMANN S. SCHIBLI

ARENDT, HANNAH (1906–75)

Hannah Arendt was one of the leading political thinkers of the twentieth century. She observed Nazi totalitarianism at close quarters and devoted much of her life to making sense of it. In her view it mobilized the atomized masses around a simple-minded ideology, and devised a form of rule in which bureaucratically minded officials performed murderous deeds with a clear conscience. For Arendt the only way to avoid totalitarianism was to establish a well-ordered political community that encouraged public participation and institutionalized political freedom. She considered politics to be one of the highest human activities because it enabled citizens to reflect on their collective life, to give meaning to their personal lives and to develop a creative and cohesive community. She was deeply worried that the economically obsessed modern age discouraged political activity, and created morally superficial people susceptible to the appeal of mindless adventurism.

1   Life
2   *The Origins of Totalitarianism*
3   *The Human Condition*
4   Later works

1   Life

Born into a Jewish family in Königsburg, Arendt went on to study philosophy, first under Heidegger and Bultmann at Marburg and then under Husserl and Jaspers respectively at Freiburg and Heidelberg. The Nazi rise to power put paid to her academic ambitions and she became active in Jewish politics. She was arrested and detained in 1933, but was soon able to escape to France. She was briefly interned in a French prison camp, from where she escaped to the USA in 1941. She held various academic positions there, the last at the New Centre for Social Research. She regularly wrote on public issues but was not otherwise politically active.

2   *The Origins of Totalitarianism*

Arendt made her name with *The Origins of Totalitarianism* (1951), a somewhat misleading title for a book that was concerned not only with totalitarianism but also with the rise of anti-Semitism, imperialism and racism, the 'three elements of shame' in the modern age as she called them. She argued that Nazi and Stalinist totalitarianism represented a wholly new form of rule based on ideology and its twin terror. Ideology, the *logos* of an idea, centred around a specific idea, be it race, class or nation. It teased out the logical implications of the idea, built a tightly knit system around them, and sought to reconstruct a polity on that basis. This necessarily involved terror, by which Arendt meant a systematic, institutionalized, carefully planned and legally unrestrained use of physical and psychological violence. In Arendt's view totalitarianism found a fertile soil in an environment in which society had been dissolved into loose and rootless masses and the hollowed out state had been reduced to an unrestrained coercive apparatus. For her, totalitarianism, born out of the rejection of the ordinary world as we know it, had its paradigmatic expression in concentration camps – a mechanical, impersonal and unworldly 'world' utterly devoid of thinking, feeling, judgment, personal identity, privacy and all else that distinguishes human existence (see IDEOLOGY §1; TOTALITARIANISM §2).

The Origins of Totalitarianism was an important work. It offered brilliant insights into the nature and role of political institutions, the inner contradictions of the modern nation-state, and the human need for rootedness. But it also had its weaknesses. Arendt treated totalitarianism as an independent and self-subsisting phenomenon relentlessly unfolding its inner logic and subject to no human constraints. She uncritically equated the Nazi and Stalinist 'forms' of totalitarianism, and her analysis was underpinned by theories of man and society that were nowhere clearly stated and defended. In her subsequent writings Arendt often returned to the large philosophical questions raised by the Nazi experience but inadequately explored in *The Origins of Totalitarianism*. She asked such questions as what it meant to be human, how we should live both individually and collectively, in what kind of world it was possible to lead a meaningful life, why human beings committed evil, how thinking was related to action, and what future modernity held in store for humankind.

3   *The Human Condition*

Arendt first dealt systematically with some of these questions in *The Human Condition* (1958). She distinguished two kinds of life, the *vita activa* and the *vita contemplativa*, and concentrated on the former. For her, humans are a part of nature and subject to its necessity, but are also able to transcend it and act in a truly free and gratuitous manner. She divided human activities into labour, work and action, each presupposing but going beyond and hence higher than the preceding one. Labour referred to the familiar daily round of activities centred around the production and reproduction of life. Work referred to activities in which human beings controlled nature and interposed a durable and distinctively human world between themselves and nature. It included such things as building houses, crafts, writing books, painting pictures and composing music. Action was uniquely interpersonal and referred to activities in which human beings transcended nature, interacted with others, began something new, and made a distinct mark on the world. Action, the unique expression of the human capacities for freedom and transcendence, was a distinctively human achievement; it included such things as speaking, arguing, persuading, taking initiatives, standing up for a cause and protesting against an evil.

Although action occurred in all areas of life, Arendt argued that politics was its ideal home. The political life provided such necessary preconditions of action as a plurality of participants, publicity, public space, shared interests, the inspiring tradition of action and the possibility of immortal fame. By challenging people to 'dare the extraordinary' and leave behind an inspiring story that gave meaning to their existence and raised the level of communal life, the political community, a community living together in the mode of acting and speaking, realized the full potential of human existence. For Arendt this was why man was by nature a political 'animal'.

For Arendt the classical world of Athens and Rome respected the hierarchy of the *vita activa* and nurtured a climate conducive to action, freedom and meaningfulness. The late middle and early modern ages gave the pride of place to work, and admired the craftsman. Modernity reversed the hierarchy and was centred around labour. It was distinguished by such features as an excessive preoccupation with life and its endless wants, a subjectivist morality, the loss of stable structures, the deterministic and process-like character of human existence and the reduction of government to administration. Since modernity did not nurture the necessary climate for action, people in the modern world lacked the opportunity to give meaning to their lives, and either led meaningless lives or sought a pseudo-meaning in following the allegedly objective laws of history.

4 Later works

After *The Human Condition* Arendt wrote several books, all containing stimulating insights but lacking in philosophical rigour and penetration and none matching its imaginative power. In 1961 she published *Between Past and Future*, a collection of six essays of varying quality. She explored the nature of political authority, freedom, political judgment and culture in greater detail than before, and showed her growing sympathy for Kant. She insisted that political thinking was public and representative in character and involved looking at a subject from a variety of different standpoints. The greater its range and imaginative sympathy, the more representative and valid was the resulting opinion or judgment.

In 1963 Arendt published *On Revolution*, bubbling with suggestive but sketchily explored ideas and showing signs of hurry. She argued that revolution, one of the highest forms of political action, was modern in origin and aimed to establish a secure framework of freedom. Since it was political in character, it succeeded in the USA where it did not overstep its limits, and failed in France where the revolution of 1789 was subverted by concern over the problem of poverty. In her view even the American Revolution was only a partial success. By failing to give a constitutional status to local assemblies and town hall meetings, it discouraged active political participation and the development of public spirit. Thanks to several factors, including the enormous influence of Karl Marx, the greatest theorist of revolution, it was not the American but the French Revolution that became the model of all subsequent revolutions, including the Russian revolution of 1917. For Arendt, they were all doomed from the start. She pleaded for a fuller appreciation of the 'lost treasures' of the revolutionary tradition, especially its concern to set up a participatory polity constructed from the bottom upwards (see REVOLUTION §2).

In 1963 Arendt also published *Eichmann in Jerusalem* based on the Israeli trial of a prominent Nazi. Eichmann was a Nazi officer who dutifully carried out his superior's orders and murdered several thousand Jews in one of the German concentration camps. Modifying some of her views in the *Origins of Totalitarianism*, she argued that Eichmann's enormous crimes proceeded not so much from wickedness as from sheer thoughtlessness. He did not personally hate the Jews, nor was he a sadist or an evil man. All he did was mechanically to carry out his bureaucratic duties out of a blind sense of loyalty to the *Führer*, without once pausing to reflect on the enormity of what he was doing. His evil had neither moral depth nor deep roots in his psyche, and lacked the power to fascinate. He was a boring, banal and morally superficial man whose evil deeds, although not done inadvertently, had no deeper meaning for him and were incidental to his murderous job. Arendt's book aroused heated controversy and made her a pariah in several Jewish and even non-Jewish circles. Her analysis was not wrong but partial. It took no account of the passionate and fiercely moralized anti-Semitism of Nazism, did not explain why Eichmann did not think about what he was doing, and failed to explore the deeper nature and sources of evil (see HOLOCAUST).

In the late 1960s, Arendt increasingly returned to an exploration of the *vita contemplativa* to which she had hitherto paid only cursory attention. The result was her posthumously published *The Life of the Mind* (1978). The work was intended to be in three volumes, devoted respectively to the analyses of the nature of and interrelations between the three basic human capacities to think, will and judge, but she managed to finish only the first two. For her the *vita contemplativa* took two forms, namely thinking and knowing, paradigmatically expressed in philosophy and science respectively. Thinking is concerned with a quest for meaning or significance, knowing with a search for truth. Science inquires into 'what is', and is motivated by a passionate love of truth, while philosophy inquires into 'what it means for it to be' and is motivated by an equally passionate love of wisdom. Science is analytical and investigative, philosophy reflective and meditative. Science offers hard conclusions, whereas philosophy is tentative and endlessly exploratory and, like Penelope's web, begins the day by unscrambling the certainties of the previous night. Science remains confined to the world, while philosophy transcends it and is a unique expression of human freedom.

Given her view of thinking, Arendt had some difficulty relating it to both willing and action. Willing was a worldly faculty involving other people, a wish to change the world, and a measure of moral certainty; by contrast, thinking was solitary, tentative and inconclusive. Arendt neither satisfactorily resolved their tension nor showed how the two were mediated. She faced a similar difficulty in relating thinking and action to philosophy and politics. She was puzzled as to why many philosophers displayed a great hostility to the politics of a free society and supported authoritarian rule. Sometimes she explained this in terms of the philosopher's inappropriate ambition to discover the truth about the world and to 'coerce' people into accepting it by the 'force' of logic. For the most part she stressed philosophy's solitary and unworldly nature which made it impatient of the plurality, unpredictability and the apparent chaos of political life. The latter view implied that the philosopher and the political community could never be at peace with each other, and that political philosophy was impossible. Arendt found the conclusion unpalatable, but could not see an alternative.

Arendt was a highly original thinker, who made substantial contributions to political philosophy. She offered a body of profound insights into the nature, structure and role of political life, developed a wholly new vocabulary, explored long-neglected dimensions of political experience, and highlighted some of the seductive but dangerous aspects of modernity. She helped sustain the tradition of political philosophy at a time when it was in a state of decline by asking new questions, offering new ways of answering old ones, and showing that a systematic political philosophy did not have to result in an elaborate system.

List of works

Arendt, H. (1951) *The Origins of Totalitarianism*, New York: Harcourt Brace; 2nd edn, enlarged, 1958. (A study of the development and operation of the Nazi and Communist systems of government.)

—— (1958) *The Human Condition*, Chicago, IL: University of Chicago Press. (An examination of the nature of modernity in the light of Arendt's discussion of labour, work and action.)

—— (1961) *Between Past and Future*, New York: Viking Press; 2nd edn, enlarged, 1968. (A collection of essays on such subjects as freedom, authority and culture.)

—— (1963a) *On Revolution*, New York: Viking Press. (A critical examination of French and American revolutions.)

—— (1963b) *Eichmann in Jerusalem*, New York: Viking Press. (A critical analysis of the Israeli trial of Eichmann.)

—— (1972) *Crises of the Republic*, New York: Harcourt Brace. (A collection of essays on subjects of current political interest.)

—— (1978) *The Life of the Mind*, New York: Harcourt Brace. (Investigations into the nature of thinking and willing.)

—— (1982) *Lectures on Kant's Political Philosophy*, ed. R. Beiner, Chicago, IL: Chicago University Press. (An incomplete study of the nature and basis of judgment.)

References and further reading

Canovan, M. (1992) *Hannah Arendt: A Reinterpretation of her Political Thought*, Cambridge: Cambridge University Press. (A sympathetic and comprehensive study of Arendt's political thought, with an excellent bibliography. Stresses the centrality of the totalitarian experience to Arendt's thought.)

D'Entreves, M.P. (1994) *The Political Philosophy of Hannah Arendt*, London: Routledge. (A generally sympathetic study of Arendt's political thought against the background of her critique of modernity.)

Kateb, G. (1984) *Hannah Arendt: Politics, Conscience, Evil*, Oxford: Martin Robertson. (A critical study of Arendt's moral thought stressing the limitations of her account of evil.)

Parekh, B. (1981) *Hannah Arendt and the Search for a New Political Philosophy*, London: Macmillan. (A detailed examination of Arendt's critique of traditional political philosophy and her attempt to construct an alternative.)

Young-Bruehl, E. (1982) *Hannah Arendt: For the Love*

of the World, New Haven, CT: Yale University Press. (A good biography of Arendt.)

B. PAREKH

ARETĒ

A pivotal term of ancient Greek ethics, aretē *is conventionally translated 'virtue', but is more properly 'goodness' – the quality of being a good human being. Philosophy came, largely through Plato, to recognize four cardinal* aretai*: wisdom (*phronēsis*), moderation (*sōphrosynē*), courage (*andreia*) and justice (*dikaiodikaiosynē*). Others, considered either coordinate with these or their sub-species, included piety, liberality and magnanimity. The term generated many controversies. For example, is* aretē *a state of intellect, character or both? Does it possess intrinsic or only instrumental value? Is it teachable, god-given or otherwise acquired? Is it one thing or many? If many, how are they differentiated, and can you have one without having all?*

In ordinary Greek, *aretē* functions as the abstract noun correlated with *agathos*, meaning 'good', and 'goodness' is in most contexts a correct translation. However, 'goodness', unlike *aretē*, lacks a plural, and so requires awkward periphrases such as 'kinds of goodness' or 'ways of being good'. Hence 'virtue(s)' (sometimes 'excellence(s)') is usually preferred. Similarly, 'vice(s)' is favoured for its opposite, *kakia*, more correctly rendered 'badness'. In early Greek, *aretē* has no narrowly moral use, but is contextualized to mean prowess in any field – athletic, military, political, and so on. Given the predominance of male values, it often approximates to 'valour'. This is reflected in its eventual Latinization as *virtus*, literally 'manliness', which has made 'virtue' the almost inevitable modern rendering.

A specifically moral use of *aretē* emerged gradually in the fifth and fourth centuries BC. The centrality of civic obligations in the Greek (especially the Athenian) value system gave cooperative virtues such as justice and courage a special standing, even before philosophers like SOCRATES and PLATO began to scrutinize them. Many of the Sophists professed to teach *aretē* to the young (see SOPHISTS §4). How if at all it could be acquired was a much-debated issue: would it be by teaching, practice, nature, divine favour or sheer luck?

Whereas modern virtue ethics tends to stress the culture-specific character of virtue implicit in such a background (see VIRTUE ETHICS), Greek thought rarely acknowledged this, and sometimes explicitly denied it. The dominant concern was to investigate goodness as a universal human property or ideal.

Aretē is above all functional goodness. In Plato, *Republic* I, Socrates investigates the 'goodness' of a soul by direct analogy with that of an eye: just as the *aretē* of an eye is what enables it successfully to perform its function, seeing, so the *aretē* of a soul is what enables it successfully to perform its own function, living. Aristotle's conception of *aretē* is founded on the analogous idea that there is a distinctively human function, which can be performed better or worse (see ARISTOTLE §21). All this points to the intimate link between *aretē* and 'living well', a regular equivalent of 'happiness' (see EUDAIMONIA).

One recurring issue is the nature of that link. Socratic thought tended to make *aretē* and happiness extensionally equivalent. Aristotle's modification was to locate happiness in the active use of virtue, not its mere possession. A third tradition, sketched in Plato's *Protagoras* and later fully developed in Epicureanism, gives *aretē* purely instrumental value, as the prudential skill of maximizing the one intrinsic good, pleasure (see EPICUREANISM §10).

Socrates, on Plato's usual portrayal of him, has little sympathy with this instrumentalist account, but does favour one feature of it, the identification of *aretē* with some sort of knowledge or wisdom. Nothing is valuable unless used wisely; hence wisdom is the only underivatively valuable thing.

In Plato's *Protagoras*, Protagoras himself considers the political *aretai* – justice, courage and so on – to be innate human potentialities which can be realized by training. He sees them as separate capacities, so that someone might become, for example, brave but not wise. This separability assumption may well have been widespread, but philosophers in the wake of Socrates formed a united front against it. In the *Protagoras*, Socrates treats *aretē* as a single thing, never using the plural, and argues that justice, moderation and so on are not its 'parts' (perhaps meaning species?) but coreferential terms for it. This strong thesis of the Unit of Virtue was developed in the later Socratic tradition, especially by the Stoic, ARISTON OF CHIOS (§3), who maintained that 'justice', 'courage' and so on are all names for a single state of psychic health, differentiated purely by the contexts to which its possessor responds (apportionment, danger...). A version of the same thesis – in effect, that there is just one way of being a good person – is applied by Socrates in Plato's *Meno* to gender and class distinctions: the *aretē* of men and women, free and slaves, is one and the same; they are all good in the same way.

Others considered the several *aretai* to be essentially distinct states of the person, but still inseparable.

For mainstream Stoicism, this arose from the analysis of them as exact sciences, each with its own defining concerns, but made interdependent by their shared stock of theorems (see STOICISM §16). In the case of Plato and Aristotle, it was arrived at by concluding, *contra* Socrates, that the soul has emotive components as well as reason, and that moral *aretai* consist in a properly balanced relation between emotion and reason. Consequently the various *aretai* admit of complex analyses which enable them to be more clearly differentiated. For Plato in *Republic* IV, there are three psychic components – one rational, one spirited or competitive, one appetitive – and each of the cardinal *aretai* consists in a different relation between them. For Aristotle, each *aretē* is an educated disposition to make choices which strike a mean between excess and deficiency, especially in the relevant emotions; the rational component lies in the 'practical wisdom' (*phronēsis*) with which the choices must be informed (see ARISTOTLE §§22–4).

The conception of *aretē* varied with the conception of human good. In his more other-worldly moods, especially in the *Phaedo*, Plato located true *aretē* in the soul's purification from bodily concerns and return to its natural discarnate state of purity and wisdom. This emphasis on intellectual (as distinct from moral) *aretē*, later taken up in earnest by Neoplatonism (see NEOPLATONISM) is also reflected in Aristotle. To *aretai* of character ('ethical' *aretai*) Aristotle adds intellectual *aretai*, including not just practical wisdom but also pure wisdom (*sophia*). The highest form of happiness, the life of contemplation, is achieved by concentration on the latter.

See also: VIRTUES AND VICES

References and further reading

See also the entries on Socrates, Plato, Aristotle, Stoicism and Epicureanism for the further reading recommended on ethics.

Adkins, A.W.H. (1962) *Merit and Responsibility*, Oxford: Oxford University Press. (Useful guide to the early Greek background.)

* Aristotle (*c.* mid 4th century BC) *Nicomachean Ethics*, trans. T.H. Irwin, Indianapolis, IN: Hackett, 1985. (Books II-V cover the ethical *aretai*, VI the intellectual ones.)

* Plato (*c.*380s BC) *Protagoras*, trans. C.C.W. Taylor, Oxford: Clarendon Press, 2nd edn, 1991. (Debates the relation of *aretē* to knowledge.)

* —— (*c.*380s BC) *Meno*, trans. W.K.C. Guthrie, Harmondsworth: Penguin, 1956; repr. in *The Collected Dialogues of Plato including the Letters*, ed. E. Hamilton and H. Cairns, Oxford: Oxford University Press, 1975. (On the theme 'is *aretē* teachable?')

* —— (*c.*380s BC) *Phaedo*, trans. D. Gallop, Oxford: Clarendon Press, 1975, 68–9. (On the soul's detachment from the body.)

* —— (*c.*370s BC) *Republic*, trans. P. Shorey, Loeb Classical Library, Cambridge, MA: Harvard University Press and London: Heinemann, 1930; repr. in *The Collected Dialogues of Plato including the Letters*, ed. E. Hamilton and H. Cairns, Oxford: Oxford University Press, 1975. (The former contains the Greek text too; Plato's most influential work on moral and political philosophy.)

Plotinus (*c.* AD 250–66) *Enneads* I 2, trans. A.H. Armstrong, Loeb Classical Library, Cambridge, MA: Harvard University Press and London: Heinemann, 1966. (Parallel Greek text and English translation; a characteristic Neoplatonist account.)

Prior, W.J. (1991) *Virtue and Knowledge: An Introduction to Ancient Greek Ethics*, London: Routledge. (An elementary history from Homer to Stoicism.)

DAVID SEDLEY

ARGENTINA, PHILOSOPHY IN

Philosophy has been present throughout Argentine cultural life since the beginning of Spanish colonization. Despite institutional ups and downs, the teaching of philosophy was a practically constant component of higher and even secondary education. The principal currents that shaped that teaching for more than three centuries were Scholasticism, French ideology, eclectic spiritualism, positivism and in the twentieth century, all of the contemporary manifestations, such as, Husserlian phenomenology, existentialism, analytical philosophy and structuralism. A permanent characteristic, nevertheless, has been that the political vicissitudes of the country affected educational institutions.

In the nineteenth century, during the period of national independence and organization, public figures used philosophical ideas to analyse the problems of society and to make the political and institutional contributions that a country in formation required. Juan Bautista Alberdi and Domingo Sarmiento are, in this respect, two representative examples.

In the twentieth century, the figure of the professional philosopher, one who is interested in philosophical research for itself, emerged and expanded. However, thought that reflected direct interest in the problems of the community and in the ethical demands of praxis did not disappear during this era. This can be seen in such thinkers as José Ingenieros and Alejandro Korn and more recently in what has been called liberation philosophy.

Academic philosophy has made considerable progress. In the second half of the twentieth century, it has attained a high level of professional quality. In some cases, even original contributions have been made which go beyond assimilation or commentary about external philosophical influences.

In Argentina, as in the rest of Latin America, philosophy began as a pure transplant brought by those who conquered the continent. Upon creating centres of higher education (either as part of the religious orders or with the character of universities), the philosophical teaching being practised in the Spanish universities of Salamanca and Alcalá was reproduced in the Spanish colonies.

Argentine philosophy shares the same general characteristics and historical periods with the philosophies developed in other Latin American countries. In general terms, philosophy can be divided into three periods: the colonial period, the nineteenth century, or national period and the twentieth century.

1   The colonial period
2   The nineteenth century
3   The twentieth century

1   The colonial period

Philosophical activity during the colonial period was exclusively didactic. The subject matter taught was Scholastic philosophy, which had predominated in Europe during the Middle Ages and continued to exist in Spain in a renewed form well beyond the Renaissance period. Those who transmitted this knowledge were members of the Church.

The teaching of philosophy began at the University of Córdoba in the seventeenth century. However, the first indications that allow us a better idea of its content come from the eighteenth century.

Following medieval tradition, the teaching of philosophy was imparted in the College of Arts where 'grammar' students who had studied Latin, the language of instruction, were admitted. The subjects taught were logic, physics, metaphysics and ethics. The study of the arts was necessary to enter into the course of study of the highest distinction, theology, law or medicine, where these were available.

Although scholastic philosophy in the River Plate lasted until the dawn of the nineteenth century, in the eighteenth century there was a perception of the advance of modern natural science and its consequences for the worldview of the time which was based on the science of Aristotle. Thus, there were attempts to accommodate traditional teaching to the new modalities. Some Jesuit professors at the University of Córdoba (before the expulsion of the order in 1767) were up-to-date on the 'new physics' without this altering the institution of scholastic metaphysics. In the Franciscan era (from the expulsion of the the Jesuits until 1808) at the same university, modern figures such as Descartes were discussed, but not always with the approval of their doctrines. Meanwhile, in Buenos Aires education at the San Carlos School was kept on a more traditional level.

2   The nineteenth century

Generally, in all Latin American countries after their declaration of independence, there was a long period of political instability often accompanied by bloody civil wars. Argentina was no exception. However, philosophy was not absent in the fifty years that followed the separation from Spain; that is, before the country was unified and began its march towards modernization and material progress, around 1860.

At the beginning of the nineteenth century there were calls to introduce the new philosophical and scientific currents into the curriculum. To begin with more practical studies linked to scientific progress were being requested. Such was the case of a new plan of studies prepared in 1813 by Gregorio Funes, rector of the University of Córdoba. Funes proposed limiting the duration of courses in logic and metaphysics to provide for an entire year dedicated to the study of mathematics, signalling a great innovation.

In 1819 at the School of the Union of the South (a continuation of the San Carlos School) Juan Crisóstomo Lafinur initiated a new era of teaching philosophy in Argentina. The content of that teaching was French ideology and classes began to be taught in Spanish. Juan Manuel Fernández de Agüero and Diego Alcorta continued the same trend until 1842 at the University of Buenos Aires. The philosophy taught was the sensualism of Etienne Bonnot de CONDILLAC and the ideas of the French ideologues, especially Pierre-Jean CABANIS and Destutt de Tracy.

In the nineteenth century the first manifestation of a personal philosophical expression which was not derived from university teaching was the work of Juan Bautista Alberdi (1810–84), a public figure known for his contribution to the drafting of the Argentine constitution of 1853. Alberdi found ideology inadequate and was open to the influences of COUSIN, Jouffroy, Lerminier and Leroux. He had a pragmatic view of philosophy in the sense of considering that philosophical studies in Latin American countries should be applicable to concrete problems of those countries: their art, laws, politics and industry. This provides the basis for a possible Spanish American philosophy in which a certain line of current Latin American thought finds an antecedent. The most important philosophical writing of Alberdi is his *Fragmento preliminar al estudio del derecho* (Prologue to the Study of Law) (1837). In this work he maintains that each society should address its own reality: the course of history has its own defined periods and each people should know the one in which they find themselves to apply authentic rather than imitative solutions to their problems. *Fragmento preliminar al estudio del derecho* (Prologue to the Study of Law) is also a philosophy of law that deals with natural and positive law and the theory of jurisprudence. The theoretical framework is borrowed primarily from Jouffroy and Lerminer.

In the nineteenth century other European currents were also present, like French eclecticism and Krausism. Eclectic spiritualism was represented in the secondary teaching of philosophy by French manuals from that school. Krausism, whose presence became notable around 1870, was adopted in the fields of pedagogy and law (see KRAUSE, K.C.F.).

3 The twentieth century

The first Argentine philosophical movement which was widely disseminated and involved various major figures was positivism. In the Argentine case, this term implied that which was understood in Europe under that name (the doctrines of COMTE and SPENCER), but also the influence of Darwinian biological evolutionism and a high regard for the type of explanation provided by the natural sciences. The combination is more of a positivist or scientific naturalism than a positivism in the strict sense (see POSITIVIST THOUGHT IN LATIN AMERICA).

There were positivist followers of Comte in Argentina, such as Alfredo Ferreira (1836–1938), who founded the Argentine Positivist Committee in 1924. Ferreira was principally an educator and despite adhering to the religion of humanity, his association with Comte was not dogmatic.

Darwinism was represented principally by the paleontologist Florentino Ameghino (1845–1911), who culminated vast scientific work in a brief text, 'Mi credo' (My Creed) (1915), in which he expressed his materialist and scientistic *Weltanschauung*.

The greatest individual figures of Argentine positivism are Carlos Octavio Bunge (1875–1918) and José Ingenieros (1877–1925), especially the latter. Bunge is not easily categorized in a particular positivist orientation. He applied his points of view to three principal themes: psychology, ethics and law. The ultimate tenets of his position in the three cases are biological. Ingenieros was a psychologist and psychiatrist of international renown besides being a philosopher. He defended a moral idealism in his works, widely read throughout Latin America, such as *El hombre mediocre* (Mediocre Man) (1913a) and *Las fuerzas morales* (Moral Forces) (1925). His two principal philosophical works are *Principios de psicología* (Principles of Psychology) (1913b) and *Proposiciones relativas al porvenir de la filosofía* (Propositions Relative to the Future of Philosophy) (1918). The psychology of Ingenieros is of a naturalist nature and specifically biological, with clear application of Darwinian theory. In his work biology is explained in terms of energy, following Wilhelm Ostwald (1853–1932). This position did not prevent Ingenieros from considering that authentic philosophical problems were outside the field of science. In this sense, in his aforementioned *Proposiciones relativas al porvenir de la filosofía* (Propositions Relative to the Future of Philosophy), he identifies philosophy with metaphysics, understanding philosophy as the realm of hypotheses that go beyond experience, but depart from it and cannot contradict it. This thesis represents one of the first expressions of the transition towards the next phase of the surpassing of positivism, which developed in the warm glow of new European philosophical trends, through forms of transition represented by Fouillé and Guyau, for example, and later through the enormous prestige of BERGSON and CROCE. In this transition two factors were pivotal: the founding of the School of Philosophy and Humanities of the University of Buenos Aires in 1896 and the first visit of José Ortega y Gasset to Argentina in 1916, with his prestige and the dissemination of the new European currents.

Following the example of Rodolfo Rivarola in the newly founded School of Philosophy and Humanities, who was interested in the thought of Kant, the two primary figures who were influential in the change of philosophical atmosphere were Coriolano Albernini (1886–1960) and Alejandro Korn (1860–1936). The first had a decisive influence on university life; the second has become a classic of Latin American philosophy. The criticism by Albernini of positivism was caustic and effective. Korn constructed his philosophy on the basis of the freedom of ethical conduct and rejected in that field the determinism of positivist naturalism (see ANTI-POSITIVIST THOUGHT IN LATIN AMERICA). For Korn, freedom makes possible the moral voluntarism that facilitates human excellence. In addition to Albernini and Korn, Alberto Rougès (1880–1947), from the interior of the country, wrote *Las jeraquías del ser y la eternidad*

(Hierarchies of Being and Eternity) (1943), one of the most important works of Argentine philosophy in the first half of the century.

Around 1940 when positivism had clearly been left behind, a new phase of Argentine philosophy began that has lasted despite its lack of uniformity over the course of its development. Its principal characteristics amount to a considerable increase in philosophical activity, especially in the number of people engaged in philosophy, the number of university professorships and the number of journals and publications; philosophical activity being carried out primarily in universities; an increase in the quality of professional training of philosophical practitioners and an openness to all the currents and problems of Western thought.

The first part of this phase witnessed the influence of German philosophy from the first decades of the century: HUSSERL and his direct disciples of the phenomenological school, along with SCHELER, HARTMANN and HEIDEGGER. Such was the case of Francisco Romero (1891–1962), who developed his own philosophical position stemming from Scheler and Hartmann. In his day, Romero was considered one of the major Spanish-speaking philosophers. His position culminated in the publication of his principal work, *Teoría del hombre* (Theory of Man) (1952), which is a philosophical anthropology based on the concept of intentionality. He also outlined the fundamentals of axiology, a theory of culture and a metaphysics of transcendence. Various figures can be linked to Romero: Risieri Frondizi (1910–83), one of the few members of this group who was influenced by English-language philosophy and whose principal work is a theory of values; Aníbal Sánchez Reulet, who examined philosophy as a problem in *Raíz y destino de la filosofía* (The Root and Destiny of Philosophy) (1942) and Eugenio Pucciarelli (1907–95), who investigated the problems of reason, time and technique.

Carlos Astrada (1894–1970) and Luis Juan Guerrero (1896–1956) also moved into the realm of German philosophy. Astrada developed an extensive body of work influenced by Heidegger and concluding in Marxism. Guerrero developed a detailed aesthetics. For his part, Carlos Cossio (1903–87) developed his 'egological theory of law' in *La teoría egológica del derecho y el concepto jurídico de libertad* (The Egological Theory of Law and the Juridical Concept of Freedom) (1944) derived from Husserl, Heidegger and KELSEN.

Close to existentialism one finds Vicente Fatone (1903–62) and Miguel Angel Virasoro (1900–66). Fatone was one of the most outstanding expositors of existentialist philosophy, but also dealt in Hindu doctrines and philosophy of religion. Oriental thought as well as philosophy of religion have also been studied by subsequent researchers. Virasoro combines the influence of Hegel and that of existentialism. In addition, Angel Vassallo developed themes that came from the great Western metaphysicians and from Blondel and Marcel (see EXISTENTIALIST THOUGHT IN LATIN AMERICA).

The work of Juan Adolfo Vázquez is characterized by a high degree of interest in metaphysics and an affinity for the mystical. Following Fatone, Víctor Massuh continued the study of philosophy of religion, while Adolfo Carpio of Romero's group, authored a work of Heideggerian bent about the significance of the history of philosophy.

With respect to Catholic thought, the Thomist thinker of the most substantive work and the greatest renown is Octavio Derisi. An important Thomist figure in Córdoba was Nimio de Anquín, who wrote about ancient and medieval philosophy as well as contemporary thought. Two Jesuits who came later and who produced considerable bodies of work are Juan Sepich and Ismael Quiles. In the context of the great dissemination of existentialist philosophy, the latter developed his theory of 'in-sistentialism'. Similar to Nimio de Anquín, although a generation later, is Alberto Caturelli, who developed a metaphysics opposed to modern and contemporary immanentism. One should also note Diego Pró, who has worked with Aristotelian thought, and like Caturelli is the author of numerous studies about philosophy in Argentina.

Moving away from the predominance of French and German influences, a group of followers of English-speaking analytic philosophy was formed in the early 1970s. In 1972 the Argentine Society of Philosophical Analysis was founded, which brought together philosophers of varying thematic interests but with great *esprit de corps* and keen awareness of their difference from representatives of other movements. This group is in close contact with its counterpart in Mexico, which publishes the journal *Crítica*. This movement is characterized by a distrust of metaphysics, an interest in the accomplishments of science and in linguistic problems and an attempt to produce rigorous conceptual analyses. Similarly opposed to the majority of other currents in Argentina, but a thinker who is an independent figure of considerable international prestige, is the philosopher of science, Mario Bunge, who settled in Canada (see ANALYTICAL PHILOSOPHY IN LATIN AMERICA).

At the beginning of the 1970s the philosophy of liberation movement began in Argentina and later spread throughout Latin America. It was considered by many to be the most authentic expression of Latin

American thought. This style of philosophy sought to be distinguished from traditional academic forms, to hold that philosophy is justified only by immediate engagement with praxis and to maintain as its principal focus the question of the dependence of Latin America. This philosophy promotes the liberation of the region and that of its most overlooked sectors (the masses, the oppressed, the poor). It has natural affinities with theology of liberation. The first synthesizing overview of the movement was the work of Horacio Cerutti Guldberg, *Filosofía de la liberación latinoamericana* (Latin American Philosophy of Liberation) (1983). The criticism that the book contains about other members of the movement and the responses of the latter to the criticisms, illustrate the internal differences in the movement. However, aside from those differences, philosophy of liberation taken as a whole has a well-defined profile at the forefront of Argentine and Latin American thought (see LIBERATION PHILOSOPHY; LIBERATION THEOLOGY).

Dialectical materialism did not produce theoretical works of consequence in Argentina, but the founder of the Argentine Socialist Party and translator of Marx, Juan Justo (1865–1928) combined Marxism with biology and Darwinism in his work. Aníbal Ponce (1898–1938), who was a disciple of Ingenieros, moved from the biological orientation of his teacher to a Marxist position.

Recent philosophical activity is characterized by an intensification of the themes indicated as belonging to the post-1940 era. The international philosophical movement is experienced with first-hand immediacy and many philosophers are in a position to participate fully in international philosophical dialogue. In some cases, affinities of ideas and philosophical positions are reflected in institutional groupings or in publications that represent them. For example, the journal *Análisis Filosófico* (Philosophical Analysis) is for the analytic group, the Centre for Philosophical Studies is affiliated with the *Revista latinoamericana de filosofía* (Latin American Journal of Philosophy), the National Academy of Sciences with *Escritos de filosofía* (Philosophical Writings). This philosophical activity is not carried out solely in Buenos Aires, but also in various state and private universities in the rest of the country.

Part of the historical-philosophical task is devoted to Argentine and Latin American thought. The two classics of the history of ideas in Argentina are *La evolución de las ideas argentinas* (Evolution of Argentine Ideas) (1918–20) by José Ingenieros and *Influencias filosóficas en la evolución nacional* (Philosophical Influences on National Evolution) (1936) by Alejandro Korn. The most recent and complete panorama of the development of philosophy in the country is contained in the work of Francisco Leocata, *Las ideas filosóficas en Argentina* (Philosophical Ideas in Argentina) (1992, 1993). Among the outstanding authors who specialize in Argentine and Latin American thought are Gregorio Weinberg (1995) (history of education and science) and Arturo Roig (1981). The work of the latter, in addition to its historiographic importance, is considered a major contribution to the philosophical interpretation of Latin America. There are professorships of Argentine thought at the universities of Buenos Aires, La Plata, Córdoba, Tucumán and Mendoza where the journal *Cuyo: Anuario de historia de la filosofía argentina y americana* (Cuyo: Journal of the History of Argentine and Latin American Philosophy) has been published since 1965.

Since the beginning of the century, various foreign professors have contributed to the formation of contemporary Argentine philosophy. Perhaps the most notable is the Italian historian of philosophy Rodolfo Mondolfo.

References and further reading

* Alberdi, J.B. (1837) *Fragmento preliminar al estudio del derecho* (Prologue to the Study of Law), Buenos Aires: Facultad de Derecho y Ciencias Sociales, Universidad de Buenos Aires, 1942. (Alberdi maintains that each society should address its own reality.)
* Ameghino, F. (1915) 'Mi Credo' (My Creed), in *Doctrinas y descubrimientos* (Doctrines and Discoveries), Buenos Aires: La Cultura Argentina. (Written in 1906, but published posthumously.)
  Biagini, H. (ed.) (1985) *El movimiento positivista argentino* (The Positivist Movement of Argentina), Buenos Aires: Editorial de Belgrano. (Collective work which includes numerous aspects of the positivist movement.)
  Cappelletti, A.J. (1995) *Filosofía argentina del siglo XX* (Argentinian Philosophy of the Twentieth Century), Rosario: Facultad de Humanidades y Artes, Universidad Nacional de Rosario. (Provides a survey of twentieth-century philosophy and contains good essays on Alejandro Korn, Alberto Rougès, Alfredo Franceschi, Francisco Romero, Risieri Frondizi and others.)
* Cerutti Guldberg, H. (1983) *Filosofía de la liberación latinoamericana* (Latin American Philosophy of Liberation), Mexico: Fondo de Cultura. (The first work to synthesize the philosophy of liberation.)
* Cossio, C. (1944) *La teoría egológica del derecho y el concepto jurídico de libertad* (The Egological Theory of Law and the Juridical Concept of Freedom), Buenos Aires: Editorial Losada. (The

egological theory of law, the author's own theory, is first propounded in this book.)

Gracia, J.J.E. (ed.) (1986) *Latin American Philosophy in the Twentieth Century*, Buffalo, NY: Prometheus Books. (An anthology including the works of Francisco Romero, Risieri Frondizi, Carlos Astrada, Alejandro Korn and Arturo Roig.)

* Ingenieros, J. (1913a) *El hombre mediocre* (Mediocre Man), Madrid: Editorial Renacimiento. (Moral idealism is defended in this work.)
* —— (1913b) *Principios de psicología* (Principles of Psychology), Madrid: Jorro. (One of the author's main philosophical works.)
* —— (1918) *Proposiciones relativas al porvenir de la filosofía* (Propositions Relative to the Future of Philosophy), Buenos Aires: Talleres L.J. Rosso. (Philosophy is identified with metaphysics.)
* —— (1918–20) *La evolución de las ideas argentinas* (Evolution of Argentine Ideas), Buenos Aires: Losada. (One of the classic books on the history of ideas.)
* —— (1925) *Las fuerzas morales* (Moral Forces), Buenos Aires: Talleres L.J. Rosso. (Widely read throughout Latin America.)
* Korn, A. (1936) *Influencias filosóficas en la evolución nacional* (Philosophical Influences on National Evolution), Buenos Aires: Editorial Claridad. (A classic in the area of the history of ideas.)
* Leocata, F. (1992, 1993) *Las ideas filosóficas en Argentina* (Philosophical Ideas in Argentina), Buenos Aires: Centro Salesiano de Estudios, vols 1 and 2. (Covers the colonial period to the twentieth century. Although volumes of this work are still forthcoming, this is the most complete panorama to date.)
* Roig, A. (1981) *Teoría y crítica del pensamiento latinoamericano* (Theory and Critique of Latin American Thought), Mexico: Fondo de Cultura. (A major contribution to the philosophical interpretation of Latin America.)
* Romero, F. (1952) *Teoría del hombre* (Theory of Man), Buenos Aires: Losada. (The outline of metaphysics is developed.)
* Rougès, A. (1943) *Las jerarquías del ser y la eternidad* (Hierarchies of Being and Eternity), Tucumán: Facultad de Filosofía y Letras, Universidad Nacional de Tucumán. (One of the most important works of Argentine philosophy.)
* Sánchez Reulet, A. (1942) *Raíz y destino de la filosofía* (The Root and Destiny of Philosophy), Tucumán: Facultad de Filosofía y Letras, Universidad Nacional de Tucumán. (The problematics of philosophy are examined.)
—— (1954) *Contemporary Latin American Philosophy*, Albuquerque, NM: University of New Mexico Press. (Selections of texts with useful introductions to authors, such as, Korn, Ingenieros and Romero.)

Torchia Estrada, J.C. (1961) *La filosofía en la Argentina* (Philosophy in Argentina), Washington, DC: Pan American Union. (The sections on ideology, Alberdi and Ingenieros and the antipositivist revolt are still relevant.)

* Weinberg, G. (1995) *Modelos educativos en la historia de América Latina* (Educational Patterns in the History of Latin America), Buenos Aires: Editora AZ. (An historical study of the Latin American education system.)

JUAN CARLOS TORCHIA ESTRADA

ARISTIPPUS THE ELDER (*c*.435–*c*.355 BC)

Aristippus of Cyrene was a member of Socrates' entourage who after Socrates' death (399 BC) founded the Cyrenaic school. He was primarily interested in practical ethics. He focused on the concepts of pleasure and pain, and classed them as bodily motions of which we are conscious. He considered pleasure a major component of happiness, but also attributed intrinsic value to virtue and emphasized the importance of study and exercise as means to self-control.

Aristippus, son of Aritades, was born at Cyrene. He moved to Athens at a young age, where he became an associate of SOCRATES and also frequented Sophistic circles (see SOPHISTS). After Socrates' death, he taught philosophy during his numerous travels to Syracuse, Asia Minor, Corinth, Megara and Aegina, and probably returned to Cyrene towards the end of his life. It may have been there that he founded the Cyrenaic school (see CYRENAICS) and that he trained his daughter, Arete, in philosophy. He must be distinguished from his grandson and second successor as head of the school, Aristippus the Younger (born *c*.380 BC), with whom he is occasionally confused.

Some sources maintain that he wrote nothing at all, perhaps in deliberate imitation of Socrates. But our most reliable informants report that he wrote several dialogues and a history of Libya in three books. The titles attest a vivid interest in practical ethics, but also a concern for rhetoric, history, literature, linguistic morphology and semantics. His argument establishing that no morally neutral object exists may be taken to indicate an additional interest in theoretical ethics. He disallowed the study of mathematics and of physics, but recognized that logic may be useful in so far as it sharpens our dialectical capacities.

Few tenets can be ascribed to Aristippus with confidence. It seems that he had no detailed epistemological views; the Cyrenaic theory of knowledge was probably formulated by his grandson. However, he focused on the notions of pleasure and pain which he classed as *pathē*, ways of being affected, and described them in terms of smooth and rough motions of the flesh which result in sensation. These *pathē* are short-lived due to their kinetic nature: the motions associated with them expire with time. To this extent, Aristippus foreshadows Cyrenaic subjectivism, which equated the *pathē* experienced in the present moment with bodily motions detected by 'internal touch', self-evident and incorrigibly known.

Regarding Aristippus' ethics, the evidence is divided. According to one tradition, he was a hedonist who defined bodily pleasure experienced in the present moment as the moral end, and thus formulated the core of the ethical doctrine held by his grandson and by the orthodox branch of the Cyrenaic school (see HEDONISM). However, according to a second group of sources, he never defended a particular moral doctrine but only gave the impression of being a hedonist on account of his numerous lectures on pleasure and of his voluptuous life. There are good reasons for accepting this latter testimony: Aristippus attributed intrinsic value to virtue, and this is incompatible with a straightforward hedonism positing the short-lived pleasures of the present moment as the only intrinsic good; he emphasized the importance of study, exercise and self-control, all of which have non-pleasurable aspects; he recommended the enjoyment of bodily pleasures only if they do not endanger one's control over oneself; and he tended to look at his life as a single whole, not as a series of discrete pleasurable episodes, as is exemplified by his assertion that he aimed 'at the easiest and pleasantest life'. Such evidence indicates that Aristippus was a eudaemonist who considered pleasure the major component of happiness and spoke of happiness in terms of a pleasurable condition extending over one's lifetime (see EUDAIMONIA).

This conception of happiness influenced his social and political attitudes, which are marked by a strict individualism. He claimed for himself a freedom which entailed the rejection of the political condition of citizenship and abstention from duties and obligations to any particular city. In his view, part of the happiest life is 'to live as a foreigner in every land'.

References and further reading

Classen, C.J. (1958) 'Aristippos', *Hermes* 86: 182–92. (Standard reference article in German.)

Doering, K. (1988) *Der Sokratesschüler Aristipp und die Kyrenaiker* (Socrates' Pupil Aristippus and the Cyrenaics), Wiesbaden and Stuttgart: Akademie Verlag. (The most recent book-length study on Aristippus and the Cyrenaic school.)

Giannantoni, G. (1990) *Socratis et Socraticorum Reliquiae* (The Fragments of Socrates and the Socratics), Naples: Bibliopolis. (Volume 2 includes the fullest available collection of Greek and Latin testimonies on Aristippus.)

Xenophon (*c.* 360s BC) *Memoirs of Socrates*, trans. H. Tredennick (1970), revised R. Waterfield, Harmondsworth: Penguin, 1990. (Aristippus appears as one of Socrates' interlocutors in II 1 and III 8.)

VOULA TSOUNA

ARISTON OF CHIOS (early to mid 3rd century BC)

The Greek philosopher Ariston (alternatively Aristo), from the Aegean island of Chios, was an exceptionally independent-minded member of the early Stoic school. A pupil of the founder Zeno of Citium, he was among the most prominent philosophers working at Athens in the mid-third century BC. He concentrated on ethics, dismissing logic and physics as irrelevant.

Like many contemporary philosophers, including Zeno, Ariston undoubtedly saw his own views as the ones most authentically capturing those of Socrates. Virtue he considered a unitary intellectual state, its conventional fragmentation into kinds being misleading at best. He resisted Zeno's doctrine that nonmoral desiderata like health, although indifferent, were naturally 'preferable'. Total indifference to them, rather than rationally choosing between them, was the true goal of life. He rejected rules of conduct – much favoured by Zeno – as founded on the same mistake of treating indifferent things as if they could be ranked in terms of intrinsic values.

1 Life and work
2 Indifference
3 Virtue

1 Life and work

Ariston of Chios was, during much of the third century BC, as important a figure in the Stoic school at Athens as ZENO OF CITIUM, its official founder and his own teacher. But very little is known about Ariston's life. Probably he was Zeno's pupil in the early years of the third century, outliving him by a substantial period and perhaps well into the second half of the century.

Ariston's interests were almost entirely ethical, although there is some evidence of an interest in poetics, and possibly even in grammar. He stayed much closer to Cynic ethics (see CYNICS) than Zeno himself did, and in the long run it was the differences between the two that were most noticed. The later Stoic tradition chose to revere Zeno but not Ariston, and, because history is written by the winners, Ariston has come to be seen with hindsight as a marginal and heretical figure. This was certainly not so in his own day, when his impact at Athens was enormous. For example, ARCESILAUS, who had led the Academy into its sceptical phase (see ACADEMY), appears to have engaged in debate with Ariston at least as much as with Zeno. Ariston's own pupils included a leading Stoic Apollophanes, and the celebrated scientist Eratosthenes. Ariston was an acute observer of contemporary philosophy, and his mock-Homeric line of verse about Arcesilaus as a philosophical chimera ('Plato in front, Pyrrho behind, Diodorus in the middle') became famous (see ARCESILAUS §1).

What is harder to know is how far the later tradition may have exaggerated or even invented doctrinal differences between Ariston and Zeno. But there seems little doubt that some of these were real. During Zeno's lifetime, open disagreement with him was apparently acceptable in the school. After Zeno's death (262), however, his thought became canonized: Ariston's independence now began to look like heresy. It was probably at this stage that he set up his own school, said to have been in the Cynosarges gymnasium outside the city walls of Athens.

Ariston is reported to have written a number of works. The titles of fourteen are listed by Diogenes Laertius in a short biography of him. Some later Stoics disputed the authenticity of most of these, attributing them instead to the Peripatetic Ariston of Ceos, with whom Ariston of Chios certainly is sometimes confused in ancient sources. However, there is a good chance that all or most are genuine. They include *Chreiai* (a typically Cynic collection of moral anecdotes), *Dialogues*, *On Zeno's Doctrines*, *Against the Orators* and *Against the Dialecticians*. A further work, *Comparisons*, was a collection of Ariston's graphic philosophical similes (look out for some below).

Ariston objected to Zeno's tripartite philosophical curriculum, consisting of logic, physics and ethics. Echoing SOCRATES (Plato, *Apology* 19b–c), he dismissed physics as 'above us'. Dialectic, the formal study of argument, and hence a mainstay of the branch called 'logic', Ariston likened to cobwebs (technically complex, but useless), to quicksand, and to eating crabs (lots of bones, little nutriment). He judged these parts of philosophy – as also much of the traditional Greek educational curriculum – an irrelevance to what really mattered in life: moral knowledge. Consistently with this, his own important contributions were in ethics.

2 Indifference

Socrates had argued that most things conventionally judged good or bad, such as health and illness, are in themselves neither, since they only get their value from the way they are used. Health and sickness wisely used are great goods, while unwisely used they are great evils. The consequence, that only virtue or wisdom is good, only vice or folly bad, while everything else is morally 'indifferent', was widely endorsed in the fourth-century BC Socratic tradition, including Cynicism. Zeno's innovation (see STOICISM §15) was to rank the indifferents on a scale of natural preferability, while continuing to call them indifferent. He also, in consequence, attached enormous importance to rules or 'precepts', as offering indispensable guidelines to a proper choice among the indifferents, and thus a start towards the goal of 'living in accordance with nature'.

Ariston fought a rearguard action against this dilution of Socratic/Cynic values: indifferents really are just that, indifferent. He denied rules any moral value. And in place of Zeno's formulation of the goal, he described it as 'living with a disposition of indifference towards what is intermediate between vice and virtue, not retaining any difference at all within that class of things, but being equally disposed towards them all'. He is said to have formed his view when, during Zeno's illness, he attended the lectures of Zeno's old Platonist teacher Polemo (see PLATONISM, EARLY AND MIDDLE §1). Paradoxically, Polemo himself was attacking Zeno from the other direction, for refusing to call such items as health and illness 'good' and 'bad'. No doubt Polemo argued for a straight choice: either such items are good and bad, or they cannot be valued relatively to each other at all. While Polemo took the former option, Ariston was persuaded by the latter.

Ariston's fundamental objection to rules of conduct seems to have been as follows. Typical precepts ('Don't get drunk', 'Look after your health', 'Avoid enslavement' and so on) misleadingly attach preferential value to items such as sobriety, health and freedom, which are in themselves totally indifferent and are worthy of choice purely according to circumstances. It was as if in spelling one were to favour some letters as intrinsically preferable to others. Rules of conduct, he concluded, have no place outside the kindergarten.

Ariston's rejection of rules has led some to call him an 'intuitionist'; and he is indeed reported as saying the sage will do 'whatever comes to mind' (Cicero, *On Ends* IV 43). But we also know that, as a Socratic, he held that virtue is an intellectual state – knowledge of good and bad (although also called 'health', that is, of the soul) – and that in place of rules he recommended reliance on 'doctrine'. He therefore must have thought correct moral decisions were arrived at by reasoning, not intuition. The serious problem that confronted him was, rather, how non-moral decisions should be made. If public image, comfort and so on are literally indifferent, how can we make such trivial decisions as which clothes to wear or which food to eat? Yet if we could not choose, we would wear and eat nothing. It was almost certainly to answer this that Ariston's appeal to intuition came in. If the objection was that the Aristonian sage will, like Buridan's ass, starve to death through inability to choose between indifferents, Ariston's answer was that in such situations it is rational simply to do the first thing that comes into your head.

3 Virtue

Since virtue is simply a matter of knowing good and bad, it becomes hard to see how it can have distinct parts, species or branches. In the wake of Socrates (see especially Plato's *Protagoras* and SOCRATES §5), every Socratic philosopher defended some version of his thesis of the unity of the virtues. To some (for example, Chrysippus: see STOICISM §16) this meant no more than their inseparability, but Ariston was one of those who took them to be literally one and the same thing. Why then do they have different names? His answer was that the very same state of mind was named differently according to the circumstances in which it was located. In situations of danger, for example, knowledge of good and bad was called 'courage'; in situations involving appetite, 'self-discipline' (*sōphrosynē*), and so on. It was, he said, as if one were to vary between calling the power of eyesight 'white-seeing' and 'black-seeing', according to the objects it happened to be confronted with. Chrysippus devoted a treatise to refuting Ariston on this issue.

The clear implication is that the different species names of virtue are superficial and accidental, misleadingly fragmenting what is in reality a unitary intellectual power. This disdain for conventional distinctions was characteristic of Ariston, and did much to give his pronouncements their strongly Cynic flavour. Consider his striking assertion of cosmopolitanism: 'A native land does not exist by nature, any more than does a house, a field, a smithy or a doctor's surgery. Each one of these comes to be so, or rather is so named and called, always in relation to the occupant and user.'

References and further reading

Arnim, H. von (1903–5) *Stoicorum Veterum Fragmenta* (Fragments of the Early Stoics), Leipzig: Teubner, with vol. 4, indexes, by M. Adler, 1924. (The standard collection of early Stoic fragments, in Greek and Latin, commonly abbreviated as *SVF*; Ariston is in volume 1, 75–90.)

Boys-Stones, G. (1996) 'The *epeleustikē dynamis* in Aristo's Psychology of Action', *Phronesis* 41: 75–94. (Defends a partly different view on Ariston's 'intuitionism' from that in §2 of the entry on him.)

* Diogenes Laertius (early 3rd century AD) *Lives of the Philosophers*, trans. R.D. Hicks, *Diogenes Laertius Lives of Eminent Philosophers*, Loeb Classical Library, Cambridge, MA: Harvard University Press and London: Heinemann, 1925, 2 vols. (VII 160–4 in volume 2, is his life of Ariston.)

Ioppolo, A.M. (1980) *Aristone di Chio e lo stoicismo antico* (Ariston of Chios and Early Stoicism), Naples: Bibliopolis. (The classic study, in Italian, of Ariston's work and his place in Stoicism.)

Long, A.A. (1988) 'Socrates in Hellenistic Philosophy', *Classical Quarterly* 38: 150–71; repr. in A.A. Long, *Stoic Studies*, Cambridge: Cambridge University Press, 1996, 1–34. (Important on Zeno's and Ariston's rival interpretations of Socrates on moral indifferents.)

Schofield, M. (1984) 'Ariston of Chios and the Unity of Virtue', *Ancient Philosophy* 4: 83–96. (Subtle evaluation of Ariston's place in this debate.)

Seneca (*c*. AD early 60s) *Letters to Lucilius*, trans. R.M. Gummere, Loeb Classical Library, Cambridge, MA: Harvard University Press and London: Heinemann, 1917–25. (Latin text with English translation. Letters 94–5 place Ariston on one side of an extended debate about moral rules; but there is less genuinely Aristonian material here than is usually assumed.)

DAVID SEDLEY

ARISTOTELIANISM IN ISLAMIC PHILOSOPHY

In Arabic, Aristotle was referred to by name as Aristutalis or, more frequently, Aristu, although when quoted he was often referred to by a sobriquet such as 'the wise man'. Aristotle was also generally known as the First Teacher. Following the initial reception of Hellenistic texts into Islamic thought in al-Kindi's time, al-Farabi rediscovered a 'purer' version in the tenth century. In an allusion to his dependence on Aristotle, al-Farabi was called the Second Teacher. Ibn Rushd, known in the West as Averroes, was the last great Arabophone commentator on Aristotle, writing numerous treatises on his works. A careful examination of the Aristotelian works received by the Arabs indicates they were generally aware of the true Aristotle. Later, transmission of these works to Christian Europe allowed Aristotelianism to flourish in the scholastic period.

We should not take at face value the Islamic philosophers' claims that they were simply following Aristotle. The convention in Islamic philosophy is to state that one is repeating the wisdom of the past, thus covering over such originality as may exist. There was a tendency among Islamic philosophers to cite Aristotle as an authority in order to validate their own claims and ideas.

1 Early influence
2 Middle stage: Ibn Sina and al-Farabi
3 Late period: the legacy of Aristotelianism

1 Early influence

Among the major differences between the Islamic philosophers and ARISTOTLE are the questions of the eternity or creation of the world, the nature of Being and a real-world distinction between essence and existence. The ninth-century philosopher AL-KINDI used Aristotle, in Arabic translations, as a base for his own philosophical works. Among other works, al-Kindi wrote one treatise specifically dealing with Aristotle, *Fi kammiya kutub Aristutalis wa ma yahtaj ilahi fi tahsil al-falsafa* (The Quantity of the Books of Aristotle and What is Required for the Acquisition of Philosophy). The early part of this treatise gives an accurate summary of various logical works by Aristotle, such as *Categories* and *De Interpretatione*, before diverging into a decidedly non-Aristotelian précis on questions found in the physical treatises. Though he owed a large debt to Aristotelian thought, al-Kindi parted company with Aristotle in espousing the idea of creation from nothing by a Creator. Furthermore, in writing about creation al-Kindi does not ascribe the idea to Aristotle in the text of his treatises. Debate still continues over whether al-Kindi should be considered more 'Platonic' or 'Aristotelian'.

An inventory of those works attributed to Aristotle which were available to early Islamic philosophers appears in the *Fihrist* of the tenth-century bibliographer Ibn al-Nadim. The work known as the *Theology of Aristotle* appears in the *Fihrist*, although it is mentioned only in passing. Greater attention is paid to other correctly attributed works of philosophy and logic by Aristotle, including such detailed information as the translator, the number of sections and the work's Arabic commentators, suggesting the relative importance of these works to Ibn al-Nadim and his audience. Judging from the list available in the *Fihrist*, the Islamic philosophers would have been able to appreciate Aristotle's logic, physics and metaphysics. However, since the *Theology of Aristotle* was really a Neoplatonic work (see NEOPLATONISM IN ISLAMIC PHILOSOPHY §1), based on the *Enneads* of PLOTINUS, accepting this attribution would have obscured understanding of Aristotle. Whatever the influence of Aristotle on Islamic philosophy, the Muslims were nonetheless obliged to work out for themselves certain underlying issues, such as conceptualizing ideas in their own language. In particular, they had to implement a philosophical terminology, as there was a lack of abstract nouns in Arabic.

2 Middle stage: Ibn Sina and al-Farabi

The Islamic philosophers picked and chose from Aristotle's texts, using him as an authority when it suited their purposes, and knowing that philosophy was a 'foreign science' in need of an external authority as it lacked an indigenous authority. While aspects of Avicennan philosophy continue the Aristotelian tradition in broad terms, Ibn Sina's ideas about the Necessary Existent and the Possible Existent do not have their antecedents in Aristotle's philosophy (see IBN SINA). However, as Ibn Sina himself hailed from Khurasan, one cannot dismiss the possible influences of Buddhism, Zoroastrianism and Hinduism on his philosophy. The differences with Aristotle go back to the fact that the philosophers are writing in an Islamic milieu, and certain changes had to take place to correlate with the religious ideology. Seen in some lights, these changes may be considered peripheral; the philosophers continued to hold a solidly Aristotelian view of such basic ideas as the relationship of form and matter.

Among the scholars of the Middle Period – the fourth and fifth centuries AH (tenth and eleventh centuries AD) – AL-FARABI is considered the foremost Aristotelian, and was indeed known as the Second Teacher (Aristotle himself being the First Teacher). Some scholars have divided his works into those which admit Aristotelian influence, such as *Kitab al-huruf* (The Book of Letters), and more popular works, such as *Kitab fi mabadi' ara' ahl al-madina al-fadila* (The Book of the Principles of the Opinions of the People of the Virtuous City), usually known simply as *al-Madina al-fadila* (The Virtuous City), a utopian treatise which espouses Neoplatonic theories such as emanation, in which everything is said to flow from the One. His internalization of Aristotle is apparent in his treatment of the four causes in *Tahsil al-sa'ada* (The Attainment of Happiness), echoing those found in *al-Tabi'a* (The Physics). Here he shows a complete familiarity with the Aristotelian idea of the four causes, but is equally willing to propound his own interpretation, preferring the word *mabadi'* (literally, principles) rather than *asbab* (causes), which was the translator Ibn Ishaq's choice.

On another important point, however, al-Farabi is not conceptually Aristotelian. In *al-Madina al-fadila*, we do not find the long discourses on the inherent weakness of women, children and slaves, which are found in Aristotle; rather, he distinguishes the inhabitants of the virtuous city from those of the ignorant cities by their moral character.

Al-Farabi considered his *Kitab al-huruf*, which takes its title from the Greek letters which entitle Aristotle's chapters, to be a commentary on Aristotle's *Metaphysics*. While *al-Huruf* is inspired by Aristotle's concerns, and deals with many of the same subjects, it does not slavishly imitate or even follow the order of the *Metaphysics*. Al-Farabi also believed in the ultimate harmony of the opinions of Plato and Aristotle, a difficult notion for many philosophers today to accept.

One might ask why Ibn Sina (Avicenna) would be taken in by a false treatise, the *Theology of Aristotle*, when he had such a good command of Aristotelian concepts that he could quote accurately from memory. In his 'Letter to Kiya', Ibn Sina expresses doubt about the authorship of the *Theology of Aristotle*, remarking that the text is 'somewhat suspect' (Gutas 1988). The tone of his discussion indicates that while he included this work with other Aristotelian treatises, he has by no means concluded it is genuinely an Aristotelian text. On the other hand, in the *Danashnama-i 'ala'i* (The Book of Knowledge for 'Ala'), his account of metaphysics, Ibn Sina derives a quotation from Aristotle where he claims that Aristotle describes the First Being as having complete happiness in itself. It is uncertain to which part of the *Metaphysics* Ibn Sina is referring, as such a passage does not appear to exist.

Elsewhere, Ibn Sina claims to quote Aristotle from memory when discussing the theory of definition for his treatise on Definitions, when he suggests that in the *Topics*, Aristotle defines definition as 'a statement indicating the quiddity of a thing'. This is an exact quotation. It is remarkable that Ibn Sina appears to remember Aristotle's important ideas word for word after having, he says, read the books only once and thereafter being unable to refer to them. Given his life as a wanderer, this statement is credible.

3 Late period: the legacy of Aristotelianism

Unlike the Islamic east, where a Hellenistic tradition of philosophy flourished from the ninth century, philosophy reached al-Andalus later. IBN BAJJA, known as Avempace in Latin, was one of its first practitioners, active in the early part of the twelfth century. His heavily Aristotelian commentaries on the logical works of al-Farabi still survive. The sociohistorian IBN KHALDUN ranked him with Ibn Rushd, and Ibn Bajja no doubt influenced this, the most famous, philosopher of Muslim Spain.

IBN RUSHD, better known in the West as Averroes, is considered not nearly as influential in the Islamic world as he was in medieval Europe. Here, either because he lived on the Western periphery of the Islamic world or because he wrote such extensive commentaries on Aristotle, he became renowned (see AVERROISM §1). Latin translations of Ibn Rushd's texts were available in Europe within a century of his death. Coming from a family of eminent jurists, Ibn Rushd had legal as well as philosophical training. He wrote commentaries on a wide range of Aristotle's works, including his *Physics, Metaphysics, Book of the Soul, On the Heavens* and *Posterior Analytics*, the last dating from 1170. In both long and intermediate commentaries as well as short paraphrases, Ibn Rushd tried to analyse the extent of his Islamic predecessors' deviation from Aristotle. He also exerted himself in reconciling religion and philosophy in his *Fasl al-maqal* (Decisive Treatise On the Harmony of Religion and Philosophy). He discovers a duty to reflect with the intellect on existing beings and to seek knowledge in the Qur'anic injunction found at Surah 49: 2: 'Consider, you who have vision.'

There is good reason to consider another of Ibn Rushd's works, the *Tahafut al-tahafut (The Incoherence of the Incoherence)* to be an attack on Neoplatonism and a defence of true Aristotelianism. On the question of the origin of the world, Ibn Rushd promulgated eternal creation but did not accept emanation. While he wrote the *Tahafut* primarily as a rebuttal of al-Ghazali's attack on the philosophers, he also disagreed with Ibn Sina's ideas about necessity.

Ibn Rushd was also to be the last in the line of Islamic Aristotelians. Throughout the classical period of Islamic thought, there were always some thinkers who distrusted rationalism and logic, certain that the study of philosophy results in a loss of faith. AL-GHAZALI and IBN TAYMIYYA are the two best known examples. Al-Ghazali studied philosophy to be able to rebut it; he suggested that knowledge is inferior to faith, as knowledge could not overcome doubts. His *Tahafut al-falasifa* (The Incoherence of the Philosophers) had a lasting influence. Here al-Ghazali attacked Aristotle and his followers, al-Farabi and Ibn Sina, particularly objecting to the Aristotelian notion of the eternity of the world, which he found irreconcilable with the Qur'anic description of God's creation of the world from nothing. Al-Ghazali also saw this as an idea which limited God in a totally unacceptable manner. Two centuries later, Ibn Taymiyya wrote *al-Radd 'ala al-mantiqiyyin* (Against the Logicians) as an attack on the method of definition and demonstration used by the philosophers who were influenced by Aristotle. He argued that logic is based on the faculty of human reason, which is necessarily inferior to divine revelation.

Despite the efforts of Ibn Rushd to rehabilitate philosophy, many scholars believe that Islamic philosophy never completely recovered from al-Ghazali's massive and brutal assault on it. In the Latin West, Islamic Aristotelianism was reincarnated as Averroism, that is, Aristotle's works as taught by Ibn Rushd and translated into Latin (see ARISTOTELIANISM, MEDIEVAL §4; AVERROISM §1). His works also came to have great influence in Jewish philosophy, and for many years led to a strong strain of Aristotelianism among Jewish philosophers (see AVERROISM, JEWISH). Aristotelianism continued to have an effect on Islamic philosophy through opposition to it from Illuminationist philosophy (see ILLUMINATIONIST PHILOSOPHY), and in particular thinkers such as AL-SUHRAWARDI, al-Shahrazuri, IBN KAMMUNA and others, often based in Persia. The latter sought to attack what they took to be the principles of Aristotelianism, especially its logical and ontological axioms, and produced critiques of Aristotelian essentialism which are sometimes quite similar to that of WILLIAM OF OCKHAM. It is accurate to say, however, that Aristotelianism as a school of philosophy in the Islamic world found no Muslim successors after the death of Ibn Rushd.

See also: ARISTOTELIANISM, MEDIEVAL; ARISTOTLE; ARISTOTLE COMMENTATORS; AL-FARABI; GREEK PHILOSOPHY: IMPACT ON ISLAMIC PHILOSOPHY; IBN RUSHD; IBN SINA; ISLAM, CONCEPT OF PHILOSOPHY IN; LOGIC IN ISLAMIC PHILOSOPHY; PLATONISM IN ISLAMIC PHILOSOPHY

References and further reading

Abed, S. (1991) *Aristotelian Logic and the Arabic Language in Alfarabi*, Albany, NY: State University of New York Press. (A study on al-Farabi's use of Aristotle's works.)

Burrell, D.B. (1986) 'Essence and Existence: Avicenna and Greek Philosophy', *Mélanges de l'Institut dominicain d'études orientales du Caire* 17: 53–66. (An interesting discussion of Ibn Sina's distinction and his Greek forbears.)

El-Ehwany, A.F. (1963) 'Ibn Rushd', in M.M. Sharif (ed.) *History of Muslim Philosophy*, Wiesbaden: Harrasowitz, ch. 28: 540–64. (Summary of Ibn Rushd's philosophy.)

* al-Farabi (c.870–950) *Kitab al-huruf* (The Book of Letters), ed. M. Mahdi, Beirut: Dar al-Mashreq. (A new edition and translation is in progress, but no date has been set for its appearance.)

—— (c.870–950) *Alfarabi's Philosophy of Plato and Aristotle*, trans. M. Mahdi, New York: Free Press of Glencoe, 1962. (A reliable translation of three Farabian treatises: *Tahsil al-sa'ada* (The Attainment of Happiness), *Falsafa Aflatun* (Philosophy of Plato) and *Falsafa Aristutalis* (Philosophy of Aristotle).)

—— (c.870–950) *Sharh al-Farabi li-kitab Aristutalis fi al-'ibara*, ed. W. Kutch and S. Marrow, Beirut, 1960; trans F.W. Zimmerman, *Al-Farabi's Commentary and Short Treatise on Aristotle's De interpretatione*, Oxford: Oxford University Press, 1981. (Commentaries by al-Farabi on Aristotle.)

* al-Ghazali (1058–1111) *Tahafut al-falasifa* (The Incoherence of the Philosophers), ed. M. Bouyges and M. Fakhry, Beirut: Dar al-Mashreq, 4th edn, 1990; trans. S.A. Kamali, *Tahafut al-falasifah (Incoherence of the Philosophers)*, Lahore: Pakistan Philosophical Congress, 1963. (Al-Ghazali's attack on the philosophers.)

* Gutas, D. (1988) *Avicenna and the Aristotelian Tradition*, Leiden: Brill. (A new interpretation of Ibn Sina's development as a philosopher.)

* Ibn al-Nadim (before c.995) *Kitab al-fihrist*, ed. G. Flügel, Beirut: Khayyat, 1964; trans. B. Dodge, *The Fihrist of al-Nadim*, New York: Columbia University Press, 1970. (Early inventory of the works of Aristotle.)

Ibn Rushd (c.1170) *Averroes' Middle Commentaries on Aristotle's Categories and De Interpretatione*, trans. C.E. Butterworth, Princeton, NJ: Princeton University Press, 1983. (Contains the *Talkhis kitab al-maqulat* (Middle Commentary on the *Categories*) and *Talkhis kitab al-'ibara* (Middle Commentary on *De interpretatione*). A detailed account of the approach by Ibn Rushd to these texts.)

* —— (*c.*1179–80) *Kitab fasl al-maqal* (Decisive Treatise on the Harmony of Religion and Philosophy), trans. G. Hourani, *On the Harmony of Religion and Philosophy*, London: Luzac, 1961. (Ibn Rushd's attempt to reconcile philosophy and religion.)
* —— (*c.*1180) *Tahafut al-tahafut* (The Incoherence of the Incoherence), ed. S. Dunya, Cairo: Dar al-Ma'aref, 1950, 2 vols; trans. S. Van Den Bergh, *Averroes' Tahafut al-tahafut (The Incoherence of the Incoherence)*, London: Oxford University Press, 1954, 2 vols. (Ibn Rushd's attack on al-Ghazali.)
* Ibn Sina (980–1037) *Danishnama-i 'ala'i, ilahiyyat* (Book of Knowledge for 'Ala'), ed. M. Mu'in, Tehran, 1952; trans. P. Morewedge, *The Metaphysics of Avicenna (Ibn Sina)*, New York: Columbia University Press, 1973. (The metaphysical portion of the *Danashnama*.)
* Ibn Taymiyya (1309–10) *al-Radd 'ala al-mantiqiyyin*, trans. W.B. Hallaq, *Ibn Taymiyya Against the Greek Logicians*, Oxford: Clarendon Press, 1993. (Translation with an introduction discussing in detail Ibn Taymiyya's objections to Aristotelian logic.)
* al-Kindi (*c.*873) *Rasa'il al-Kindi al-falsafiyya* (The Philosophical Treatises of al-Kindi), ed. M.A.H. Abu Ridah, Cairo: Dar al-fikr al-'arabi, 2 vols in 1, 1953. (The early edition is better than the recent reprint, but is hard to find. Many of the treatises have not been edited into European languages.)

Leaman, O. (1988) *Averroes and His Philosophy*, Oxford: Clarendon Press; repr. Richmond: Curzon, 1997. (A basic introduction to Ibn Rushd.)

Mahdi, M. (1990) 'Al-Farabi's Imperfect State', *Journal of the American Oriental Society* 110 (4): 691–726. (A review article that lays out many of the questions in the study of Islamic philosophy and its Greek origins.)

Peters, F. (1968) *Aristoteles Arabus*, Leiden: Brill. (Very much the standard work on Aristotle as understood in Arabic.)

—— (1996) 'The Greek and Syriac Background', in S.H. Nasr and O. Leaman (eds) *History of Islamic Philosophy*, London: Routledge, ch. 3, 40–51. (Discussion of some of the important features of Greek and Syriac culture as sources of Islamic philosophy.)

Shayegan, Y. (1996) 'The Transmission of Greek Philosophy into the Islamic World', in S.H. Nasr and O. Leaman (eds) *History of Islamic Philosophy*, London: Routledge, ch. 6, 98–104. (Detailed account of how the transmission took place, paying particular attention to the Persian background.)

Urvoy, D. (1996) 'Ibn Rushd', in S.H. Nasr and O. Leaman (eds) *History of Islamic Philosophy*, London: Routledge, ch. 23, 330–45. (Detailed analysis of Ibn Rushd's thought and career.)

Walzer, R. (1962) *Greek into Arabic*, Cambridge, MA: Harvard University Press. (A traditional approach to Hellenistic influences on Islamic philosophy.)

KIKI KENNEDY-DAY

ARISTOTELIANISM IN THE 17TH CENTURY

Aristotelians in the seventeenth century comprised a group of mostly anonymous textbook writers whose chief claim to fame is that their philosophy was opposed by such as Descartes and Galileo. In line with the characterization of them by their opponents, their philosophy has generally been depicted as extremely conservative, monolithic and moribund. However, it is difficult to ratify such judgments. As Aristotelians, these philosophers do not seem particularly conservative; they appear to have assimilated many of the scientific developments of the seventeenth century, and the diversity and range of their views is quite broad. Some of the doctrines peculiar to them, or their particular developments of older views, can be seen as the background against which modern philosophy developed.

1 **Some notable doctrines**
2 **Textbooks and notions of order**
3 **Matter and form**
4 **The concept of place**
5 **The origins of the modern concept of** *idea*
6 **Late seventeenth-century scholastics**

1 Some notable doctrines

What was taught in the schools during the seventeenth century was Aristotelian, but remains difficult to describe: probably not one of Aristotle's doctrines was held by all early modern scholastics. Some central Aristotelian theses were discarded. For example, Théophraste Bouju, in a work whose title page announces that all of it has the authority of Aristotle, rejected the Aristotelian four elements, discarding the sphere of fire and, as a consequence, argued against the radical heterogeneity of the sub-lunary and supra-lunary spheres (Bouju 1614). However, he safeguarded the *de facto* immutability of the heavens. Many of the theses that became canonical with later Aristotelians, such as the doctrine of substantial forms, also found early modern critics (Maignan 1653; Fabri 1686); there were even textbook writers who proclaimed the compatibility of peripatetic philosophy and atomism (Sennert 1618; Casimir of Toulouse 1674). Thus, it would be difficult to justify the epithet 'monolithic', although such pejorative labels have been applied to late scholasticism from the beginning. René DESCARTES wrote in a letter to Mersenne dated 11 November 1640 that there is nothing that seems as improbable to him than the philosophy of the schools: he does not think it difficult to refute, 'for one can easily upset all the foundations to which they agree and, once this is achieved, their particular disputes would appear inept'.

In fact, many Aristotelians of the seventeenth century were forward-looking, accepting the latest scientific developments including Galileo's celestial observations (Crassot 1618; du Chevreul 1623; du Moulin 1644, and others). Their philosophy of science can be characterized as probabilistic (Eustachius 1609 III.1: 1–3; and others), and some of their doctrines provide a background against which modern philosophy developed (see §§2, 5 of this entry). With the exception of the most noted (including Franciscus SUÁREZ and, possibly, Eustachius a Sancto Paulo, studied at least for his significance for Descartes) these thinkers are now generally neglected. In the Protestant world, such scholastic writers as Franco Burgersdijk at Leiden and Bartholomaeus KECKERMANN at Heidelberg were widely read, gaining fame primarily as logicians. In England, philosophers such as Thomas WHITE and Kenelm DIGBY demonstrated flexibility in their attempts to graft the new philosophy on to Aristotelian roots.

2 Textbooks and notions of order

Eustachius a Sancto Paulo studied at the Sorbonne, receiving his doctorate in 1604. The following year he entered the Cistercian congregation of the Feuillants where he held various prominent positions, and became very influential in the French Catholic revival. He wrote two popular textbooks, a *Philosophy* (1609) and a *Theology* (1613–16), as well as two manuals of spiritual exercises.

Eustachius' *Philosophy* was considered by Descartes to be the best textbook in philosophy – Descartes even considered publishing it, together with his notes, other opinions, and his own philosophy. To understand the genre and its popularity, it must be contrasted with other such texts. Among the widely-read authors at the end of the sixteenth and the beginning of the seventeenth century were the Coimbrans and Franciscus Toletus. The Coimbrans (the Conimbricenses) were professors at the Jesuit Colègio das Artes, Coimbra (Portugal), who published a series of encyclopedic commentaries on Aristotle's works (see COLLEGIUM CONIMBRICENSE). The principal Coimbran was Petrus FONSECA, who separately published his own commentary on Aristotle's *Metaphysics*. Franciscus TOLETUS, a professor at the Jesuit Collegio Romano, similarly published commentaries on Aristotle's works, including an important *Logic* (1572), *Physics* (1573) and *On the Soul* (1574). (Other noted Jesuits who published textbooks for the collegiate curriculum included Rodericus Arriaga, Christopher Clavius and Antonius Rubius). In France, non-Jesuit philosophy texts from the same period included those by doctors associated with the University of Paris, such as Eustachius and Charles d'Abra de Raconis (whose *Philosophy* was published in 1617), Jean Crassot (1618), Jean-Cécile Frey (1633) and François Le Rées. Judging from the number of editions, the texts of Eustachius and de Raconis were the most widely read Latin-language philosophies of the first half of the seventeenth century, Eustachius' *Philosophy* taking first place.

The seventeenth century also saw an enormous growth of philosophy textbooks in French, written by the tutors of the nobility (themselves often nobles). The movement began in the 1560s with the first French translations of Aristotle's works, but took off in the 1590s with the first French-language commentaries on Aristotle's *Physics*. Works in this genre include the 1614 textbook by Henry IV's almoner, Théophraste Bouju, and the 1643 volume by René de Ceriziers, a Jesuit who became a secular almoner of the Duc d'Orléans and later counsellor to the King. The most frequently reprinted work in the genre was the *Philosophy* (1627) by Scipion Dupleix, Cardinal Richelieu's favourite historian. This work alone seems to have exceeded Eustachius' in popularity.

The proliferation of textbooks in philosophy was a response to important changes taking place in pedagogy. The Jesuits, following the example of the University of Paris, had reorganized and standardized their curriculum. Textbooks, both Jesuit and non-Jesuit, were consequently modified. For example, the Coimbrans wrote volumes by committee, presenting the works of Aristotle that were taught in the curriculum; they followed the model of the great medieval commentaries, each volume treating a specific text (*Physics, On the Soul, On the Heavens* and so on), but with an elaborate (post-Renaissance) scholarly apparatus, giving both Aristotle's Greek text and its Latin translation, as well as Latin paraphrases (*explanationes*) and *quaestiones*, the analysis of standard problems relevant to the text being discussed. This pattern was generally followed by other textbook writers, although later editions of the Coimbran commentaries and textbooks such as those of Toletus omitted the Greek versions of Aristotle. Ultimately, Eustachius' *Philosophy* even omitted Aristotle's text itself. Eustachius simply arranged the *quaestiones* in the order in which the curriculum would have presented them, doing so for all the Aristotelian sciences within the frame of the whole philosophy curriculum – ethics and logic, physics and metaphysics – in a single volume. Dupleix followed the same pattern, as did de Raconis who also gave paraphrases along with the *quaestiones*. As their names generally indicated, the latter works were usually divided into four parts, following the collegiate curriculum. However, the *Philosophy* (1644) by the Protestant, Pierre du Moulin (whose logic text was also translated into English), was a three-part textbook (metaphysics having been omitted), and the *Philosophy* (1642) of Léonard Marandé added theology as a fifth part.

Underlying the format of these textbooks was a Renaissance concern with order or method. In one of the preliminary questions on the *Physics* Eustachius asked whether there is an order in the different parts of philosophy. He affirmed that there is one, appropriate both for the nature of things and for doctrine: namely, that which goes from the simplest to the more complex, from the principles to that of which they are constituted, and at the same time proceeding from the most universal things to the less universal, to the genera and species. Eustachius also asserted that Aristotle used such an 'order or method' in his writings on the various parts of philosophy. According to Eustachius, Aristotle in the *Physics* began with the principles, causes and general properties of natural things, then proceeded 'in part according to an analytic order and in part according to a synthetic order', from the most universal principles to the particular species of natural bodies. Eustachius consequently ordered his own presentation of natural philosophy into three parts: (1) natural bodies in general, from the principles of natural things to their causes and common properties, from matter and form, to causes, to place, infinity, void, time and motion; (2) inanimate natural bodies, from the world to the heavens and from elements to heterogeneous bodies; and (3) animate natural bodies, from soul in general to vegetative, sensible and rational soul. In fact, Eustachius reorganized Aristotle's topics and even reordered the *Physics* itself in keeping with his notion of order.

A general characterization of the doctrines of the first half of the seventeenth century is that the Jesuit textbooks (Coimbrans and Toletus, for example) usually propounded Thomist interpretations of Aristotle, while those associated with the University of Paris (Eustachius and de Raconis) did not, often preferring Scotist doctrines (see AQUINAS; DUNS SCOTUS, J.). The French-language authors varied in outlook: Bouju was a Thomist in many respects; Dupleix was vociferously anti-Thomist, resembling greatly the non-Jesuit Paris philosophers; and de Ceriziers seems to have supported a later, hybrid version of Thomism, answering many of the charges levelled against Thomism. By 1665 even the Jesuits, as evidenced by Pierre Galtruche's textbook (a work approved by the Order), seem to have rejected the Thomist positions in philosophy. However, the debate about Thomism and Scotism continued into the seventeenth century. (To illustrate these generalizations, §§3 and 4 of this entry offer two examples from the foundations of natural philosophy.)

3 Matter and form

There was a debate in school texts about whether matter can exist without form. A positive resolution of this esoteric topic might lead one towards a dualistic, as opposed to a hylomorphic, conception of substance. Toletus (1589 I.13) discussed whether prime matter is a substance and detailed Aquinas' negative answer. According to Aquinas, prime matter is pure potency or has only potential being, so prime matter cannot be brought into being without form and cannot subsist without form. Toletus also explained Scotus' affirmative reply, that matter is a positive entity really different from the reality of form and can subsist in its own right distinct from form. Toletus shared Aquinas' view, his own doctrine being that prime matter is imperfect in itself (Toletus 1589 I.13: fol. 34 *verso*). Bouju also followed the Thomist line (Bouju 1614 I: 315–31). In contrast, Eustachius supported a variant of Scotus' doctrine: 'Though matter cannot be produced nor annihilated by any natural agent, God can create or annihilate it... God can strip naked all forms, substantial and accidental, from matter, or create it naked, without form, *ex nihilo*, and allow it to subsist by its own power in such a state' (1609 III.1.2.4: 16–17). Abra de Raconis agreed; quoting both Aquinas and Scotus, he said that matter is an incomplete substance, but maintained that God can create matter without substantial form ([1617] 1651 *Tractatus de Principiis* 4: 35–9). Scipion Dupleix threw into relief the disagreement between Thomists and Scotists:

> Thus matter deserves the name of substance because it subsists by itself and is not in any subject. This reply is based on the Philosopher's doctrine, but it does not satisfy everyone, particularly Saint Thomas Aquinas and his followers, who hold that such matter is not in nature, and cannot

be in it, and even that this is so repugnant to nature that God himself cannot make it subsist thus stripped of all form. But this opinion is too bold, too mistaken, and it has been rejected by Scotus the Subtle [Doctor] and by several others.

(Dupleix [1603] 1990: 131)

It is interesting to note that Dupleix argued against Aquinas' doctrine of prime matter by analogy to the sacrament of the Eucharist requiring real qualities and substantial forms, a difficulty that would haunt Cartesians and atomists later in the century. Some textbook writers got around the accusation by accepting the reality of matter as a miracle – for example, de Ceriziers argued that there can be no form without matter and no matter without form naturally, but added 'however, one must not deny that God can conserve matter without any form, since these are two beings that can be distinguished, that no more depend upon one another than accident from substance, the former being separated from the latter in the Eucharist' (1643 III: 51–2). The solution seems to have been unstable, so that by 1665 (II: 27) Gaultruche argued against the Thomists (*contra Thomistas*) about prime matter.

Not everyone gave up the Thomist doctrine of matter. Although Scotists such as Frassen seem to have had the best of the argument, and Thomists and Jesuits such as Barbay and Vincent needed to opt for middle ground, some Thomists resolutely maintained their position (Frassen 1686: 36–41; Barbay 1676b: 64–72; Vincent 1660: 2.74–7). For example, the Dominican Antoine Goudin wrote:

it can be asked whether God by means of his omnipotence could create matter without it having a form. Scotus asserts it, as do some authors outside of Saint Thomas' school; Saint Thomas and all the Thomists deny it. . . . It seems that matter cannot exist without form even by means of God's absolute power. That is what Saint Thomas states (III quodlib. art 1). God himself cannot make it that something exist and not exist. He cannot make something that implies a contradiction and, consequently, he cannot make matter be without form.

(Goudin [1668] 1864 II: 131)

4 The concept of place

Seventeenth-century school philosophy debated whether place itself is mobile or not – which is to say, whether there is a fixed reference for motion. Thomists distinguished between material place and formal place (where formal place is the real ground or *ratio* of place, in Aquinas' vocabulary). Place is then movable accidentally (as material place) and immovable *per se* (as formal place, defined as the place of a body with respect to the universe as a whole). Thus a ship is formally immobile with respect to the universe as a whole when the waters flow around it. Scotists rejected the distinction between material and formal place, arguing instead that place is a relation of the containing body with respect to the contained body. Place is then a relative attribute of these bodies. (They also made use of the term *ubi*, sometimes referred to as inner place, to denote the symmetric relation of the contained body with respect to the containing body.) Since the relation changes with any change of either the contained body or the containing body, the place of a body does not remain the same when the matter around changes, even though the body in question might remain immobile. When a body is in a variable medium, the body is in one place at an instant and in another at an other instant; to capture what is meant by the immobility of place, Scotists said that the two places are distinct but *equivalent places* from the view of local motion.

Toletus took Aquinas' side against Scotus (Toletus 1589 IV.5: fol. 120 recto–121 recto). So did Bouju who also kept some Averroist elements. Bouju asserted that place is movable *per se* in what he called 'lieu de situation' and *per accidens* in what he called 'lieu environnant':

The earth . . . is in a *lieu environnant* and can also be said to be in a *lieu de situation* with respect to the poles of the world. But it cannot change place with respect to its totality; thus it is immobile in that respect and mobile only with respect to some parts that can be separated from the totality and moved into others. The firmament is also in a *lieu de situation* with respect to the earth, but it cannot change except with respect to its parts and not in its totality, in the fashion of the earth.

(Bouju 1614 I: 458–9; see also I: 460)

Eustachius, on the other hand, used Scotus' vocabulary: place and *ubi* being relations between the containing and contained bodies, and places being the same *by equivalence* (Eustachius 1609 III.3.2.1: 56–8). Abra de Raconis held a similar doctrine. De Raconis discussed two kinds of place, external and internal, external being the surface of the concave ambient body, and internal being the space occupied by the body. According to de Raconis, the ultimate heaven is in place internally, or occupies a space of three dimensions (Raconis [1617] 1651 *Physics* IV.2.1–2: 204–5). The distinction between external and internal place (or space) can also be found in Toletus and the Coimbrans; but they did not use the distinction in their resolution of issue of the mobility of place.

As was often the case, it was Scipion Dupleix who put the greatest contrast on the situation. He held that place was immobile in itself, while bodies change places. He took it that Aquinas had a different opinion, interpreting Aquinas' doctrine of formal place as the view that one can imagine a distance from each place to certain parts of the world with respect to which a given place, though changeable, may be said to be immobile. Scipion raged against the doctrine: 'But since all this consists only in useless imaginations, I am surprised that this opinion was received in several schools of philosophy; however, there are so many weak though opinionated brains who follow so closely the doctrine of certain persons that they would follow them right or wrong, and forget the golden sentence of the Philosopher: *I am a friend of Socrates, a friend of Plato, but rather more a friend of truth*' (Dupleix [1603] 1990: 149–50). On the subject of the place of the universe, Dupleix also rejected Aquinas' opinion, preferring a doctrine he attributed to Philoponus and Averroes, that when air is blowing around a house, one says that the place of the house changes accidentally. The house is in the same place *by equivalence* (that is, of the successive, distinct accidental places). Finally even Gaultruche rejected the Thomist doctrine of place, including the Thomist doctrine that the universe cannot move as a whole (Gaultruche 1655 II: 331). As with matter and form, the debate about the concept of place was not completely settled by the second half of the seventeenth century, overlapping similar disputes among the new philosophers (Frassen 1686: 357; Barbay 1676b: 261–72; Vincent 1660 II: 847–925; Goudin [1668] 1864 II: 504–6).

5 The origins of the modern concept of *idea*

Not all early modern scholastic debates took the form of Thomism versus Scotism. Some developments might have been equally at home in either camp. An interesting case, in view of the later philosophy of history, is a development of the Platonic and Neoplatonic theory of ideas within an Aristotelian context in the first few decades of the seventeenth century (see NEOPLATONISM). The discussion of ideas in Bouju's *Philosophy* is fairly standard. Enumerating the four Aristotelian causes, Bouju adds an account of 'exemplary causation'. Ideas are routinely identified with exemplars, either Platonic ideas or ideas in God's mind, and the question discussed is, whether in serving as models for creation, ideas as exemplars *cause* the things that imitate them in some fifth way. Further, the physician has an idea of health, the architect in building a house tries to make it like the one 'he has in his mind', and so on. Bouju is echoing a well-established Scholastic-Aristotelian tradition, in which ideas are either the forms in God's mind according to which he makes things, or the exemplars in artificers' minds when they make their artefacts. Ideas as exemplars, however, are not strictly psychological. They are forms which are general, not particular, patterns to be followed in this or that case, rather than particular mental events (Bouju 1614 I: 297–8).

Possibly the first instance of a new, psychological usage of 'idea' in the philosophical literature seems to occur in the first part of the *Physics* of Eustachius. Again the question is whether exemplary causes constitute a fifth class in addition to the canonical four. Eustachius' answer is that in the case of natural causation exemplary cause may be taken to be a kind of efficient cause, but in the case of an artificer it is, rather, the formal cause:

> What the Greeks call Idea the Latins call Exemplar, which is nothing else but the explicit [*expressa*] image or species of the thing to be made in the mind of the artificer. Thus the idea or exemplar is in this case some image [*phantasma*] or work of imagination [*phantasiae*] in the artificer to which the external work conforms. And so in the artificer in so far as he is an artificer there are two internal principles of operation, namely the art in his mind or reason and the idea or exemplar in his imagination [*phantasia*]. Art is a certain disposition, but idea is a certain act or concept represented by the mind. So, the mind first represents a copy of the thing to be made through art, then it contemplates what it has represented, and directs the external work to its likeness.
>
> (Eustachius 1609 III.1.3: 36.)

Here the idea is an image and (particularly crucial for the Cartesian reading) it is 'an act' or 'concept expressed by the mind'. In this brief passage, then, we have the contemporary meaning that Descartes will exploit; idea is, as it were, an image, expressive of something, something which the mind contemplates. It is both something I do as well as something I 'see'.

One finds a similar account in Abra de Raconis ([1617] 1651: 94). Clearly, Descartes would not have to look far to find the term 'idea' used with the kind of ambiguity that he assigned to it in the Meditations.

6 Late seventeenth-century scholastics

By the end of the seventeenth century, Cartesianism and other versions of the new philosophy began to take hold and scholastics ranked themselves pro and con – mostly con. Many of them wrote critiques of

Descartes (Huet 1689; La Grange 1692; Jean Duhamel 1692) or inserted critiques of Descartes into their textbooks (Frassen 1686; Barbay 1675–6; Vincent 1660, 1667; Goudin 1668; Jean Duhamel 1705); some even wrote satire of Cartesianism (Huet 1692; Daniel 1690, 1693) (see HUET, P.D.). And some attempted reconciliations between what they took to be Aristotelianism and Cartesianism (Jean-Baptiste Duhamel 1677; Le Bossu 1674). A few became Cartesians (Pourchot 1695). In England, Edward Stillingfleet and the 'Blackloist' John SERGEANT were important critics of John LOCKE from an Aristotelian point of view.

See also: ARISTOTLE; ARISTOTELIANISM, MEDIEVAL; ARISTOTELIANISM, RENAISSANCE; SUAREZ, F.

List of works

Arriaga, R. (1632) *Cursus philosophicus* (Philosophy course). (A complete philosophy course by a Jesuit professor.)

Barbay, P. (1675) *Commentarius in Aristotelis logicam* (Commentary on Aristotle's Logic), Paris. (The first portion of the philosophy course by a professor at the University of Paris. Barbay's texts were recommended by both Jesuits and Oratorians.)

—— (1675b) *Commentarius in Aristotelis metaphysicam* (Commentary on Aristotle's Metaphysics), Paris. (The third portion of Barbay's course.)

—— (1676) *Commentarius in Aristotelis moralem* (Commentary on Aristotle's Ethics), Paris. (The fourth portion of Barbay's course.)

—— (1676b) *Commentarius in Aristotelis physicam* (Commentary on Aristotle's Physics), 2nd edn, Paris. (The second portion of Barbay's course.)

Bossu, R. le (1674) *Parallele des principes de la physique d'Aristote, et de celle de René Des Cartes* (Parallel between the Principles of Physics of Aristotle and Descartes), Paris. (An attempt to reconcile the philosophies of Aristotle and Descartes.)

Bouju, T. (1614) *Corps de toute la Philosophie* (The whole of philosophy), Paris. (An early French-language complete philosophy course.)

Casimir de Toulouse (1674) *Atomi peripateticae, sive tum veterum tum recentiorum atomistarum placita ad neotericae scholae methodum redacta,* (Peripatetic atomism...), Toulouse. (An attempt to reconcile atomism and Aristotelianism.)

Ceriziers, R. de (1643) *Le philosophe français* (The French philosopher), Paris. (A complete French-language philosophy course by a Jesuit.)

Chevreul, J. du (1623) *Sphaera* (The Sphere), Paris. (A standard mathematics textbook teaching the rudiments of scholastic astronomy but taking Galileo's observations into account.)

Clavius, C. (1611–12) *Opera mathematica* (Mathematical works), Rome. (The mathematical texts of the Collegio Romano Jesuit professor most responsible for the training of Jesuits who went on to teach in the colleges of the order.)

Conimbricenses (Jesuits of the University of Coimbra) (1592) *Commentarii in octo libros physicorum Aristotelis* (Commentaries on the eight books of Aristotle's Physics), Coimbra. (The commentary of the Jesuits of the University of Coimbra dealing with bodies, motion, and their metaphysical foundations, that is, the beginning of the physics course.)

—— (1598) *Commentarii in tres libros de anima* (Commentaries on the three books on the soul), Coimbra. (The commentary of the Jesuits of the University of Coimbra dealing with animate creatures, usually the end of the physics course.)

—— (1606) *Commentarii in universam dialecticam Aristotelis* (Commentaries on the whole of Aristotle's logic), Coimbra. (The logic textbook of the Jesuits of the University of Coimbra.)

Crassot, J. (1618) *Physica* (Physics), Paris. (A physics textbook from a professor at the University of Paris.)

Daniel, G. (1690) *Voyage du monde de Descartes*, Paris; trans. as *A Voyage to the World of Cartesius*, London, 1692. (A satire of Cartesian philosophy by a Jesuit.)

—— (1693) *Nouvelles difficultés proposées par un péripatéticien à l'auteur du 'Voyage du monde de Descartes'* (New difficulties proposed by a peripatetic to the author of 'Voyage to the World of Descartes'), Paris. (The continuation of Daniel's satire of Cartesian philosophy.)

Duhamel, J. (1692) *Reflexions critiques sur le système cartesien de la philosophie de mr. Régis* (Critical reflections on the Cartesian system of philosophy of Mr Régis), Paris. (A critical examination of the Cartesian textbook of Pierre-Sylvain Régis by a professor at the University of Paris.)

—— (1705) *Philosophia universalis sive commentarius in universam Aristotelis philosophiam ad usum scholarum comparatam* (The whole of philosophy...), Paris. (The philosophy course of Duhamel, a professor at the University of Paris, containing many critical references to Descartes' philosophy, including a listing of condemnations by various authorities.)

Duhamel, J.-B. (1677) *Philosophia vetus et nova* (Philosophy old and new). (An attempt to reconcile old (mostly Aristotelian) and new (mostly Cartesian and Gassendist) philosophies.)

ARISTOTELIANISM IN THE 17TH CENTURY

Dupleix, S. (1603a) *La logique ou art de discourir et raisonner* (Logic...), Paris: Fayard, 1984. (The first portion of Dupleix's course.)

—— (1603b) *La physique* (Physics), Paris: Fayard, 1990. (The second portion of Dupleix's course.)

—— (1610a) *La métaphysique* (Metaphysics), Paris: Fayard, 1992. (The third portion of Dupleix's course.)

—— (1610b) *L'ethique ou philosophie morale* (Ethics), Paris: Fayard, 1994. (The fourth portion of Dupleix's course.)

—— (1627) *Corps de philosophie* (Collection of philosophy), Geneva. (A popular complete French-language philosophy course, including the separately published *Logic*, *Physics*, *Metaphysics* and *Ethics*.)

Eustachius a Sancto Paulo (Asseline) (1609) *Summa philosophica quadripartita de rebus dialecticis, moralibus, physicis, et metaphysicis* (Sum of philosophy in four parts...), Paris. (A popular Latin-language complete philosophy course, which Descartes wanted to publish together with his philosophy to enable readers to contrast the two.)

Fabri, H. (1666) *De plantis et de generatione animalium, de homine* (On plants and on the generation of animals, on man), Lyons. (A physics text by a late seventeenth-century French Jesuit with atomist tendencies.)

Frassen, C. (1686) *Philosophia Academica* (Academic philosophy), 3rd edn. (A philosophy textbook that defends Scotist school doctrines.)

Frey, J.-C. (1628) *Cribrum philosophorum qui Aristotelem superiore & hac aetate oppugnarunt* (The sieve of the philosophers...), Paris. (An attack on anti-Aristotelians by a professor at the University of Paris.)

—— (1633) *Universae philosophiae compendium* (Compendium of the whole of philosophy), Paris. (The philosophy course by Frey, professor at the University of Paris.)

Gaultruche, P. (1665) *Philosophiae ac mathematicae totius clara, brevis, et accurata institutio* (Instruction on all of philosophy and mathematics...), Caen, 5 vols. (The philosophy and mathematics courses by a Jesuit professor at Clermont, the main Jesuit college in Paris.)

Goclenius, R. (1613) *Lexicon Philosophicum* (Philosophical dictionary), Frankfurt. (A comprehensive dictionary of late scholastic philosophical terms.)

Goudin, A. (1668) *Philosophie suivant les principes de Saint Thomas* (Philosophy following the Principles of Saint Thomas), trans. T. Bourard, Paris, 1864. (A philosophy textbook that defends Thomist school doctrines.)

Grange, J.-B. de la (1682) *Les principes de la philosophie contre les nouveaux philosophes, Descartes, Rohault, Regius, Gassendi, le P. Maignan, etc.* (The principles of philosophy against the new philosophers...). (A critique of Cartesian and other new philosophies by an Oratorian.)

Huet, P.D. (1689) *Censura philosophiae cartesianae* (Judgment on Cartesian philosophy), Paris. (A critique of Cartesian philosophies by Huet, who was a Cartesian in his youth.)

—— [M.G. de L'A.] (1692) *Nouveaux mémoires pour servir à l'histoire du cartésianisme* (New memoirs for the history of Cartesianism). (A satire of Cartesian philosophy, anonymously by Huet.)

Maignan, E. (1653) *Cursus philosophicus* (Philosophical course), Toulouse. (A philosophy course by a Minim, which was thought too much a departure from Aristotelianism by some.)

Marandé, L. (1642) *Abrégé curieux de toute la philosophie* (Curious summary of all of philosophy), Paris. (A summary of what is generally contained in philosophy courses, including a section on theology.)

Moulin, P. du (1644) *Philosophie mise en francois et divisee en trois parties, scavoir, elements de la logique, la physique ou science naturelle, l'ethyque ou science morale* (Philosophy translated into French...). (A philosophy course, minus metaphysics, by a French Protestant.)

Pourchot, E. (1695) *Institutio philosophica* (Philosophical instruction), Paris. (The first philosophy course by a professor of philosophy at the University of Paris who was sympathetic to Cartesianism.)

Raconis, C.F.d'A. de (1617) *Summa totius philosophiae* (Sum of all philosophy), Paris, 1651. (A complete philosophy course by a professor at the University of Paris.)

Sennert, D. (1618) *Epitome naturalis scientiae*, Wittenberg; trans. as *Thirteen books of natural philosophy*, London, 1659. (A physics textbook by a physician who attempts to reconcile Aristotelianism and atomism.)

Toletus, F. (1572) *Commentaria una cum quaestionibus in universam Aristotelis logicam* (Commentary on the totality of logic), Venice. (The logic text of a Jesuit *Collegio Romano* professor.)

—— (1574) *Commentaria una cum quaestionibus in tres libros Aristotelis de amina* (Commentary on the three books on the soul), Venice. (The commentary of a Jesuit Collegio Romano professor dealing with animate creatures, usually the end of the physics course.)

—— (1589) *Commentaria una cum quaestionibus in octo libros de physica auscultatione* (Commentary on the physics), Venice. (First edition published in

1573, this is the commentary of a Jesuit *Collegio Romano* professor dealing with the beginnings of the physics course.)

Vincent, J. (1660) *Cursus philosophicus* (Philosophy course), Toulouse. (A complete Philosophy course by a Jesuit professor.)

—— (1677) *Discussio peripatetica in qua philosophiae cartesianae principia* (Peripatetic discussion regarding the principles of Cartesian philosophy), Toulouse. (A critical examination of Cartesian philosophy by a Jesuit.)

References and further reading

Blair, A. (1993) 'The Teaching of Natural Philosophy in Early Seventeenth-Century Paris: The Case of Jean-Cecile Frey', *History of Universities* 1993: 95–158. (Gives an account of the life and works of a seventeenth-century professor of philosophy.)

Bouillier, F. (1868) *Histoire de la Philosophie cartésienne* (History of Cartesian philosophy), 2 vols. (Concerns the reception of Cartesianism, pro and con, including accounts of the 'persecution' of Cartesianism by scholastics and Jesuits.)

Brockliss, L.W.B. (1987) *French Higher Education in the Seventeenth and Eighteenth Centuries: A Cultural History*, Oxford: Oxford University Press. (Details the curriculum in French colleges and universities in the humanities, philosophy, theology, law and medicine.)

Dear, P. (1987) *Mersenne and the Learning of the Schools*, Ithaca, NY: Cornell University Press. (Includes an account of the scholastic, mostly Augustinian sources used by Descartes' mentor, Marin Mersenne, in his advocacy of mathematical physics.)

Des Chene, D. (1995) *Physiologia: Philosophy of Nature in Descartes and the Aristotelians*, Ithaca, NY: Cornell University Press. (Compares late scholastics and Descartes on such topics as motion, principles of change, the essence of matter, mechanism and final cause.)

Gilson, E. (1976) *Études sur le rôle de la pensée médiévale dans la formation du système cartésien* (Studies on the role of medieval thought in the formation of the Cartesian system), 2nd edn, Paris: Vrin. (Consists of a collection of essays which trace the roots of Cartesianism in late scholasticism.)

Lohr, C. (1988) *Latin Aristotle Commentaries, II: Renaissance Authors*, Florence: Olschki, 1995. (The most complete bibliography of Latin language late-scholastic texts, includes bibliographic and biographic references to Arriaga, Burgersdijk, Conimbricenses, Crassot, Eustachius, Frey, Goclenius, Keckermann, de Raconis, Sennert and Toletus, among others.)

Reif, P. (1962) *Natural Philosophy in Some Early Seventeenth Century Scholastic Textbooks*, unpublished dissertation, Saint Louis University. (Still the only comparative full-scale study of the contents of seventeenth century textbooks.)

Sortais, G. (1924) *Histoire de la Philosophie moderne depuis Bacon jusqu'à Leibniz* (History of modern philosophy from Bacon to Leibniz), Paris: Beauchesne. (Imparts a history of seventeenth century philosophy that does not neglect minor figures, including scholastics.)

Verbeek, T. (1992) *Descartes and the Dutch*, Carbondale, IL: University of Southern Illinois Press. (Concerns the reception of Cartesianism at Utrecht and Leiden.)

Wallace, W. (1984) *Galileo and His Sources*, Princeton, NJ: Princeton University Press. (Includes an account of the natural philosophy, logic, and mathematics taught at the Collegio Romano, the Jesuits' main college in Rome.)

ROGER ARIEW

ARISTOTELIANISM, MEDIEVAL

Although there are many possible definitions, 'medieval Aristotelianism' is here taken to mean explicit receptions of Aristotle's texts or teachings by Latin-speaking writers from about AD 500 to about AD 1450. This roundabout, material definition avoids several common mistakes. First, it does not assert that there was a unified Aristotelian doctrine across the centuries. There was no such unity, and much of the engagement with Aristotle during the Middle Ages took the form of controversies over what was and was not Aristotelian. Second, the definition does not attempt to distinguish beforehand between philosophical and theological receptions of Aristotle. If it is important to pay attention to the varying and sometimes difficult relations of Aristotelian thought to Christian theology, it is just as important not to project an autonomous discipline of philosophy along contemporary lines back into medieval texts.

The most important fact about the medieval reception of Aristotle is in many ways the most elementary: Aristotle wrote in Greek, a language unavailable to most educated Europeans from 500 to 1450. Aristotle's fate in medieval Europe was largely determined by his fate in Latin. Early on, Boethius undertook to translate Aristotle and to write Latin commentaries upon him in order to show the agreement of Aristotle with Plato, and also presumably to make Aristotle available to readers increasingly unable to construe Greek. He was able to finish translations only of the logical works, and to write commentaries on a few of them and some related treatises. Even this small selection from Aristotle was not received entire in the early Middle Ages. Of the surviving pieces, only the translations of the Categories and De interpretatione were widely studied before the twelfth century, though not in the same way or for the same purposes. Before the twelfth century, Aristotelian teaching meant what could be reconstructed or imagined from a slim selection of the Organon and paraphrases or mentions by other authors.

The cultural reinvigoration of the twelfth century was due in large part to new translations of Greek and Arabic works, including works of Aristotle. Some translators worked directly from the Greek, among whom the best known is James of Venice. Other translators based themselves on intermediary Arabic translations; the best known of these is Gerard of Cremona. Although the translations from Greek were often the more fluent, translations from the Arabic predominated because they were accompanied by expositions and applications of the Aristotelian texts. To have a Latin Aristotle was not enough; Latin readers also needed help in understanding him and in connecting him with other authors or bodies of knowledge. Hence they relied on explanations or uses of Aristotle in Islamic authors, chiefly Avicenna.

The thirteenth century witnesses some of the most important and energetic efforts at understanding Aristotle, together with reactions against him. The reactions begin early in the century and continue throughout it. The teaching of Aristotelian books was condemned or restricted at Paris in 1210, 1215 and 1231, and lists of propositions inspired by certain interpretations of Aristotle were condemned at Paris and Oxford in 1270 and 1277. However, interest in Aristotle continued to grow, fuelled first by the translation of Averroes' detailed commentaries, then by new translations from Greek. At the same time, some of the most powerful Christian theologians were engaged in large-scale efforts to appropriate Aristotle in ways that would be both intelligible and congenial to Christian readers. Albert the Great composed comprehensive paraphrases of the whole Aristotelian corpus, while his pupil Thomas Aquinas undertook to expound central Aristotelian texts so as to make them clear, coherent, and mostly concordant with Christianity.

Very different projects predominate in the fourteenth century. For John Duns Scotus and William of Ockham, the texts of Aristotle serve as distant ground against which to elaborate philosophical and theological teachings often radically anti-Peripatetic. If they are fully conversant with Aristotle, if they speak technical languages indebted to him, they are in no way constrained by what they take his teaching to be. Other fourteenth-century projects include the application of procedures of mathematical reasoning to problems outstanding in Aristotelian physics, the elaboration of Averroistic positions, and the rehabilitation of Albert's Peripateticism as both faithful and true to reality. By the end of the Middle Ages, then, there is anything but consensus about how Aristotle is to be interpreted or judged. There is instead the active rivalry of a number of schools, each dependent in some way on Aristotle and some claiming to be his unique interpreters.

1 Scope
2 **Boethius and the earlier Middle Ages**
3 **The twelfth century**
4 **The thirteenth century**
5 **The fourteenth and fifteenth centuries**

1 Scope

Before it can be defined, the phrase 'medieval Aristotelianism' has to be stripped of a modern presupposition and restricted in its extension. 'Aristotelianism' and similar philosophical terms are neither ancient nor medieval, but modern. When these were popularized in the eighteenth century, they were not proposed neutrally. 'Aristotelianism' was coined with the meaning that the historical fate of Aristotle's texts and teachings could be reduced to a pure position, an unhistorical set of propositions that could be analysed or criticized. By contrast, ancient historians of philosophy tended to think of Aristotle's legacy as a school in some stronger sense, that is, as a succession of communities arising from his writings and attempting to practice the way of life they proposed as best (see ARISTOTLE). Medieval Christians, who thought that their faith prevented them from claiming membership in pagan communities without qualification, often thought of philosophical teaching as an inheritance of human wisdom passed down through lines of authoritative texts and their recognized interpreters. On neither of these ancient or medieval views is the teaching of Aristotle understood or judged apart from one or another of its actual genealogies. This entry is aligned with the earlier views, and so understands 'Aristotelianism' as referring to historical engagements with the texts and teachings of Aristotle rather than to some abstract arrangement of 'Aristotelian' tenets.

Removing the modern presupposition makes the ambiguities of extension for 'medieval Aristotelianism' more difficult. There are, first, ambiguities of appropriation. Aristotelian teachings, texts and methods run through medieval learning from early to late, in almost every discipline and at every level. Many of these appearances are implicit or anonymous: Aristotle's terminologies or procedures became common learning, no longer considered the property of an Aristotelian school. Clusters of terms such as 'form/matter', 'act/potency', 'substance/accident' or 'formal/material/efficient/final' appear in biblical commentaries, legal codifications, pharmaceutical handbooks and guides for composing poetry. Even explicit mentions of Aristotle come in half a dozen forms. Sometimes Aristotle figures merely as an ornament, in much the way that bits of Shakespeare or the Authorized Version of the Bible were once used by English speakers. At other times Aristotle is invoked merely to secure a general principle in no way specific to him. Explicit theoretical engagements with Aristotle themselves range from deployments of single phrases or sentences, through sustained amplification or criticism of arguments, to the detailed interpretation of whole texts. A single writer may show all of these relations to Aristotle over works in different genres or, indeed, in a single work.

Other ambiguities in extension are introduced by the interaction of Aristotle with Jewish, Christian and Islamic religious thinking. The Christian ambiguities are perhaps the most familiar. Almost all of the Christian Aristotelians in the Latin West were members of the clergy. Most spent their professional lives teaching and writing, not the liberal arts or philosophy, but Christian theology. It remains controversial whether or to what extent we can find an autonomous or even a textually distinguishable Aristotelian philosophy among them. Similar difficulties arise in trying to distinguish philosophy from other learned disciplines. Medieval students of Aristotle followed him through the host of topics that he broaches in his writings, from logic to poetics, from the physics of moving bodies through the species of fish to the motions of celestial spheres. We tend to divide these topics according to modern disciplinary divisions, but historically it is all 'Aristotelianism' and, in many ways important to medieval writers, all equally 'philosophy'.

A final set of ambiguities lies around the term 'medieval'. It is notorious that the 'Middle Ages' cannot be cut off neatly, either at their beginning or their end. Many learned medieval people considered themselves direct heirs and successors to pagan antiquity and the early centuries of the Christian churches. They admitted no chronological divide. At the other end, the 'Renaissance' is a slogan as much as a fact; there are as many continuities as discontinuities between philosophical thinkers of the thirteenth and fifteenth centuries (see ARISTOTELIANISM, RENAISSANCE). Similar uncertainties affect geographical or cultural boundaries. Any span of time appropriately called medieval will include, in territories we now consider European, segments of both the Byzantine and Islamic traditions of Aristotle. Although these traditions figure prominently in any retelling of Latin receptions of Aristotle, they are separate and quite complex traditions that would require separate and substantial treatment (see BYZANTINE PHILOSOPHY; ARISTOTELIANISM IN ISLAMIC PHILOSOPHY).

Faced with these difficulties of matter, discipline, chronology and geography, the most prudent position is the most modest. Within this article, 'medieval Aristotelianism' will be restricted to explicit receptions and examinations of Aristotle's texts or teachings by Latin-speaking writers from about AD 500 to about 1450. The emphasis throughout will be on explicit relations to Aristotle rather than on diffuse transformations or absorptions of him. No attempt will be made to distinguish beforehand between philosophers and theologians, though much attention will be paid to the varying and sometimes difficult relations of Aristotelian thought to Christian theology. The arrangement will be according to traditional chronological divisions, though the chronological order is not mean to suggest that the topics or figures discussed can be subsumed under a single history. What follows are not incidents in a single narrative plot, but examples of the diversity of explicit receptions of Aristotle.

2 Boethius and the earlier Middle Ages

As Aristotle wrote in Greek, a language unknown to most educated Europeans from AD 500 to 1450, knowledge of his works in medieval Europe is largely determined by the extent to which they had been translated into Latin. The first important translator was BOETHIUS in the sixth century. Before him, Aristotle seems not to have been translated into Latin in any systematic way. There certainly were Latin summaries of Aristotelian doctrine: one of these, a fourth-century outline of basic logic called *Categoriae decem* (Ten Categories), was widely studied in the earlier Middle Ages on the assumption that it had been written by AUGUSTINE. There were also paraphrases or criticisms of Aristotelian doctrine in Latin works, both pagan and Christian. However, these traces are slight, and for good reason. Well into the fifth century, the Roman empire conducted its philosophy in Greek. Citizens even of the westernmost provinces were taught Greek as the language not only of philosophy but also of medicine, natural science and, to some extent, of *belles lettres*.

Boethius may have suspected that this erudite bilingualism would not continue past his own lifetime. More importantly, he himself may have suffered from the increasing inaccessibility of Greek learning. His references to Aristotelian texts outside the Organon appear to derive from notations in the manuscripts he used or from Greek commentators on the logical works (see ARISTOTLE COMMENTATORS). It may be that Boethius translated only the logical works of Aristotle because these were the only works he had at hand in Italy.

Whatever the problems of decline in the Latin West, Boethius' stated reasons for undertaking the translations would have been recognized by any Greek-speaking student of philosophy. Boethius translated Aristotle and wrote Latin commentaries on him in order to show the agreement of Aristotle with Plato. The project of reconciliation was already an old one, with multiple sources. Latin philosophy had been eclectic in its borrowing from Greek since CICERO. It was part of Cicero's philosophic identity to take what was best from every philosophic school. This tendency was reinforced and given grander theoretical justification in Neoplatonism from PORPHYRY on. If there was disagreement among Neoplatonists about the extent to which Aristotle had dissented from Plato, there was unanimity in thinking that Aristotle had accepted much from his teacher and that he had gone on to treat certain subjects with richer detail. Thus almost all of the Neoplatonists, beginning with Porphyry, wrote commentaries on Aristotle (see NEOPLATONISM). The appearance of these commentaries in Latin during the later Middle Ages influenced scholastic discussions at many points, but they also show that Boethius' project of translation and commentary had a long pedigree. The reconciliation of Aristotle and Plato, which meant most often the subordination of Aristotle to Plato, was a familiar programme by which Boethius could justify his project of translation and commentary.

In the end, Boethius translated the *Categories*, *De interpretatione*, *Prior* and *Posterior Analytics*, *Topics* and *Sophistical Refutations* – in short, all of the logical works of the Organon. He certainly wrote both rudimentary and advanced commentaries for *De interpretatione* and Porphyry's *Isagōgē* (Introduction) to the *Categories* and single commentaries on the *Categories* and *Topics*, as well as the *Topics* of Cicero. Even this small selection from Aristotle was not received entire in the early Middle Ages. The translation of the *Posterior Analytics* was lost early, as was the commentary on the *Topics*. Of the surviving pieces, only the translations of the *Categories* and *De interpretatione* were widely studied before the twelfth century, though not in the same way or for the same purposes. For example, Boethius' first commentary on *De interpretatione*, the more rudimentary one, predominated in the ninth and tenth centuries while the second commentary received much more attention in the eleventh century. With Boethius as in so many later cases, the rule is evident: translation is not the same as reception. Something can exist and even circulate in translation, but not yet be appropriated for speculative use. The reception can be limited for any number of reasons: because copies are scarce, because the work is too difficult, or because learned taste has turned to other topics.

The Aristotelian logic that Boethius had made available passed down to later readers in company with other works, among them the anonymous *Categoriae decem*. Together, these works constituted the curriculum not only in logic but also in philosophy in general. They provided the instruments and the occasions for reflection on any number of topics, including theological ones. Indeed, the most striking early medieval appearances of Aristotle are in theological debate, for example in Carolingian debates about the Trinity (see CAROLINGIAN RENAISSANCE). There is also the solitary figure of Johannes Scottus ERIUGENA, whose *Periphyseon* enacts yet another appropriation of Aristotelian categorical logic into a Neoplatonic metaphysics. Some of Eriugena's readers later reversed the circle by copying bits of his teachings into texts of Aristotelian logical works as explanatory glosses. In the tenth and eleventh centuries, however, attention swung back to the *Categories* and *De interpretatione* with their Boethian commentaries. These were utilized regularly not only for the basic teaching of logic but also for theological debates (about the Eucharist, for example) and for scriptural exegesis (on passages such as Paul's doctrine of salvation in the letter to the Romans).

3 The twelfth century

The cultural reinvigoration of the twelfth century was due in large part to new translations of Greek and Arabic works in philosophy, the natural sciences and medicine. Prominent among these translations were works of Aristotle. It is important to distinguish the various routes by which the new Aristotle arrived in the West, especially as translations were often accompanied by strong interpretations – and not just in the sense that every translation is itself an interpretation.

The first stage in the recovery of Aristotle was neither translation nor interpretation, but the finding and using of manuscripts of Boethius' translations of works other than the *Categories* and *De interpretatione*. It was not that these manuscripts had been lost or hidden away; they simply were not read, taught, annotated or widely copied until a revived interest in logic made them pertinent. The turn back to these Boethian translations was already evident in the 1120s.

By the 1130s, translators had begun to work directly from Aristotle's Greek editions. These first translators worked in northern Italy, chiefly in cities such as Pisa and Venice that had active trading relations with Greek-speaking Byzantium (see TRANSLATORS). The principal Aristotelian translator is James of Venice, who translated *Posterior Analytics* and *Sophistical Refutations* once again, as well as *Physics*, *On the Soul*, five of the seven so-called *Parva naturalia* (Smaller Natural Works) and *Metaphysics* 1–4.4. James also translated at least some parts of late Imperial Greek commentaries on Aristotle, but these translations did not circulate widely.

James wrote his own commentary, using Byzantine models, on the *Sophistical Refutations*, making him one of the earliest Latin writers to comment on the so-called 'new logic'. This 'new logic' contained segments of the Organon that were either unstudied or untranslated before the twelfth century. It provided not only any number of technical teachings, but also the doctrine of the *Posterior Analytics* on the nature of demonstratively organized bodies of knowledge. This doctrine made it possible to construct a comprehensive account of 'science' within which physical, mathematical, metaphysical and even theological doctrines could be ordered and criticized (see LOGIC, MEDIEVAL). However, even with the recovery of Boethian versions and the new translations of James and his colleagues, something less than one-third of what we today consider the Aristotelian corpus was then available in Latin. Notably lacking were the foundational works in physical science.

Some of these gaps were soon filled by another species of translation, translations into Latin of Arabic versions of Greek works (see ISLAMIC PHILOSOPHY: TRANSMISSION INTO WESTERN EUROPE). These translations were made in areas of greatest contact with Arabic civilization, principally in Spain. Although these translators followed the translators in northern Italy by three decades, their versions of Aristotle taken from Arabic were to become more important than those made directly from the Greek. The reason is not to be found in the clarity of translation: the Greek versions are generally more fluent, not so say more accurate. Rather, what was needed was not so much texts as textbooks. Confronted with the bald text of Aristotle, many readers were at a loss. They needed tutors, and they had in their Arabic sources more powerful pedagogical aids than they had yet found in Greek. The Arabic texts of AL-FARABI or Avicenna (see IBN SINA) showed how Aristotle could be applied to questions of interest to Latin readers. They also offered more immediately attractive forms of specialized or technical knowledge. Some idea of the allure of this knowledge can be seen in the biographies of the translators: they came from all parts of northern Europe, including England and the Low Countries, to work in Toledo, Barcelona, Tarazona, Segovia, Leon, Pamplona and southern France (see TRANSLATORS). The most prominent of the translators working in Spain was an Italian, GERARD OF CREMONA.

Gerard's work as a translator spans about forty years (c.1150–87), during which time he translated at least seventy works and perhaps as many as a dozen more. His translations of Aristotle include *Posterior Analytics* (with the commentary of THEMISTIUS), *Physics*, *On the Heavens*, *On Generation and Corruption* and *Meteorology* 1–3. Two of these works had, of course, already been translated by James of Venice from the Greek, but that was either not known or did not matter to Gerard. The separation of the Italian and Spanish translations can also be seen as Gerard began translating Aristotelian commentaries from the Arabic. Some of these commentaries were originally Greek (for example, Themistius on the *Physics*), though Gerard translated them from Arabic. Other commentaries and expository treatises had been written in Arabic as part of the Arabic culture's own appropriation of Greek learning (as in the case of al-Farabi's commentary on the *Physics*).

Two related facts provide important context for Gerard's Aristotelian translations. The first is that the Aristotelian translations were only a small part of his labour; he translated many more works on medical, astronomical and mathematical subjects. Gerard's Aristotle came into Latin surrounded by a small library of natural science. The second fact is that Gerard translated a number of works as part of the Aristotelian corpus that were not at all Aristotelian. The most important of these is the so-called *Liber de causis* (Book of Causes), a compilation of material mostly from PROCLUS (see LIBER DE CAUSIS). This treatise on the cosmic participation of such transcendental features as goodness or unity was read for about a century after Gerard's translation as if it had been written by Aristotle, and so guided interpretations of the whole Aristotelian corpus. Other pseudonymous Aristotelian works circulating by the end of the twelfth century included treatises on the properties of elements, on how the soul causes basic bodily operations, on health and on alchemy. The presence of such heterogeneous works within the Aristotelian corpus would complicate the reading of Aristotle beyond the end of the Middle Ages.

The most dramatic effects of the Arabic and

Neoplatonic Aristotle on Latin-speaking thought did not occur until well into the thirteenth century, but it is important to suggest how the new texts were already being received in the twelfth century. The most thorough reception was that of the logical works, which began to be appropriated in the schools of liberal arts as early as the 1130s. There are traces of the 'new logic' in the later works of Peter ABELARD, but the impact is felt primarily in the next generation of writers, especially after the middle of the century, in the works of Adam of Balsham 'Parvipontanus', Alberic of Paris and Geoffrey of St Victor, with their colleagues and followers. The impact is not what one might expect. The first works of the 'new logic' to have an impact were the *Sophistical Refutations* and the *Topics*, which were read for what they could contribute to the analysis of procedure in disputation and to an understanding of signification and fallacies. The *Prior Analytics* was much slower in displacing Boethius' teaching on syllogism, and the *Posterior Analytics*, which might seem the most important work, was the last to make its teaching felt. Equally interesting is the fact that the new Aristotelian texts were not received through the writing of detailed, literal commentaries; these did not appear until the next century. The new logic was received rather as an aid or instigation to projects of logical research that had begun before these texts were known. The effects also vary by topic or tradition of inquiry. For example, Peter Helias' *Summa* on Priscian, written *circa* 1150, contains half as many references to Aristotle as to Boethius (see LANGUAGE, MEDIEVAL THEORIES OF).

The physical works had an even more patchy reception. Traces of the early translations from the Greek can be found in the writers associated with the cathedral school at Chartres (see CHARTRES, SCHOOL OF, and especially WILLIAM OF CONCHES). At the same time, if not earlier, bits of Aristotelian natural science began to figure in the teaching texts of the medical school at Salerno. By the end of the century, Urso of Salerno had written a treatise *On the Mixture of the Elements*, which was an attempt to resolve a vexed question in Aristotelian physics: what kind of virtual existence do the properties of individual elements have when those elements enter into compounds actualized by another substantial form? The whole of natural philosophy and medicine had hardly become Aristotelian, however. It could not, since so much of the scientific corpus remained untranslated. At century's end, the sum of translations available in Latin came to just half of the Aristotelian writings. There were, for example, no Latin versions of the bulky books on animals: together, these zoological treatises make up one-quarter of the whole corpus, and they contain the longest single Aristotelian book, *History of Animals* (see NATURAL PHILOSOPHY, MEDIEVAL). Nor had translators yet gone far into the ethical, political or literary parts of the corpus. There is an anonymous twelfth-century translation of *Nicomachean Ethics* II and III, but that is the only piece attested; there is nothing from *Politics*, *Rhetoric* or *Poetics*.

4 The thirteenth century

At the beginning of the thirteenth century, in scattered places and among diverse writers, there was a growing uneasiness about the Aristotelian and Islamic works entering Latin at such a rapid rate. This unease was evident particularly among theologians, who saw the possibility that the Aristotelian natural philosophy would contradict or displace views on the natural world considered essential for Christianity. One early official reaction came in 1210, at a provincial synod of the archdiocese of Sens, the ecclesiastical authority responsible for Paris and its schools. The archbishop was Peter of Corbeil, master of theology and of canon law at Paris from 1190–98. He knew and endorsed the view of his former colleagues that there were heresies in theology (linked to the works of Amaury of Bène and DAVID OF DINANT) and dangerous teaching in the faculty of liberal arts, sparked by the newly translated books. The heresies are difficult to reconstruct, in part because they were so effectively suppressed. The measures taken against the teaching of Aristotle and his interpreters, certainly Avicenna and possibly ALEXANDER OF APHRODISIAS, were relatively milder. The assembled bishops ordered that no books of Aristotle on natural philosophy or their commentaries were to be lectured on at Paris, in public or in private, under penalty of excommunication. The prohibition seems to have been ineffective: a weaker prohibition is reiterated five years later, in the statutes of the papal legate, Robert of Courçon. His statues only prohibit public lecturing on 'the books of Aristotle on metaphysics or on summaries of them' within the faculty of arts. Even this prohibition was barely effective; it was reiterated in a papal letter of 1228, but softened to compromise three years later. Pope Gregory IX then ordered that the theologians should confine themselves to questions that could be settled from theological authorities, while the masters of liberal arts were to refrain from lecturing on the prohibited books until they had been examined and expurgated by an expert committee. A committee was indeed appointed, but seems never to have done its work. From 1235 on, Aristotelian works were studied with increasing diligence and attention in their original, unexpurgated versions. By the end of the 1240s, at the latest, their study was not only permitted but required in arts faculties and they were in constant use by the most eminent theologians, despite the fact that Gregory's prohibitions were reiterated pro forma in 1245 and 1263.

It is difficult to say how much expert acquaintance informed the reaction against Aristotle. Aristotelian books were regularly confused with works translated alongside them or purporting to be drawn from them. Hence the decrees of 1210 or 1215 can be regarded as uninformed protests against a poorly known physicalism in which Aristotle was implicated. Even two or three decades later, theological authors at Paris who cited Aristotle frequently continued to judge harshly the materialism they thought latent in him, and which they found expressed by some of his commentators or disciples. WILLIAM OF AUVERGNE for example, rails against Alexander of Aphrodisias' doctrine and heresies related to it, and against physicalist biases in Avicebron (see IBN GABIROL) and Avicenna. The entangling of Aristotle with his interpreters was only made worse by the appearance in Latin of the works of Averroes (see IBN RUSHD).

Latin versions of many of the commentaries of Averroes began to circulate early in the second quarter of the thirteenth century. The most important group of these was produced by Michael Scotus in the 1220s and 1230s. Averroes had written three kinds of commentaries: epitomes, 'middle' commentaries, and 'great' or 'large' commentaries. These three genres represent increasing levels of attention to the letter of Aristotle's texts, with the 'great' commentaries being by far the most detailed. Michael Scotus had a preference for these: he translated the 'great' commentaries on *Physics*, *On the Heavens*, *On Generation and Corruption*, *Meteorology*, *On the Soul* and *Metaphysics*. Other translators rendered Averroes' middle commentaries on most of the Organon and on the *Nicomachean Ethics*. If these expositions helped Latin readers to interpret Aristotle and to avoid the difficulties or controversies that had trapped earlier readers, they also created many difficulties for Christians. These difficulties lay not so much in the differences between Christianity and Islam as in those between Christianity and Aristotle's paganism, since Averroes was often painfully clear about Aristotelian teachings that contradicted the revelations of both the Bible and the Qur'an.

The story of condemnation and appropriation at Paris should not be taken as the only story about the reception of Aristotle. There are others elsewhere, including some at schools that had steady traffic with Paris. John Blund, for example, seems to have taught at both Paris and Oxford early in the thirteenth century. His *On the Soul*, which probably derives from a course of lectures given at Oxford in Arts, draws heavily from Avicenna in the interpretation of Aristotle. More important but more obscure is the career of Robert GROSSETESTE. Grosseteste may have studied and taught at both Oxford and Paris before 1214; by the 1220s he was a theologian of reputation at Oxford. Before or around this time, he was engaged in writing commentaries on a range of Aristotelian works. After he was made bishop of Lincoln in 1235, Grosseteste organized a team of translators that produced a Latin version of the *Nicomachean Ethics* and Greek commentaries on it. Another example can be found in RICHARD RUFUS OF CORNWALL, who like many of his brethren was a mature scholar when he joined the Franciscans at Paris in 1238. He had already composed commentaries on both *Metaphysics* and *Physics*. However, the influence of these works would be felt most at Oxford after he began teaching theology there in 1250. Both commentaries show an acquaintance with Averroes and such parts of earlier commentary traditions as Averroes records. Rufus' work also shows his concern to resolve the contradictions between Aristotle and Christian revelation by holding Aristotle to the highest Aristotelian standards.

Aristotle was widely read by the middle of the century, but the work of receiving him was hardly finished. It was now up to Latin readers to construct coherent and defensible readings for an expanded and much controverted corpus. One response was to make Aristotle accessible by systematizing him with available bodies of knowledge. Around 1250, ALBERT THE GREAT undertook to write paraphrases of the entire corpus in order to make Aristotle 'intelligible for the Latins'. The project stretched out over twenty years and required that Albert fill gaps in the corpus with what he thought Aristotle had taught. The concern throughout was to make whatever was true in Aristotle cohere with the rest of speculative knowledge, which in Albert's case meant to cohere both with a Neoplatonic metaphysics and with specialized sciences not discussed by Aristotle or not known to him.

Another interpretative project was more concerned with finding a coherent teaching across the Aristotelian texts. Around 1266, Thomas AQUINAS inaugurated a series of line-by-line expositions of Aristotle. Their form depended partly on that of Averroes' 'great' commentaries, but more exactly on models that Thomas had learned in the arts faculty at Paris twenty years earlier. More importantly, Thomas was borrowing the modified Averroistic format to show that it was possible to read Aristotle against Averroes on disputed points such as the demonstrability of the eternity of the world (see ETERNITY OF THE WORLD, MEDIEVAL VIEWS OF), the individuality of human intellects or the substantial union of human soul and body. Thomas undertook to expound only some of the most important Aristotelian books or parts of books, and his expositions limit themselves at most points to giving the briefest reading consistent with clarity and coherence. They do not rehearse many controversies or tease out many subtleties, and they rarely bring in alternate accounts of the things discussed. The simplicity of Thomas' commentaries made them influential even among readers not otherwise favourable to him.

Thomas was aided in his work of exposition by yet another effort of translation. A fellow Dominican, William of Moerbeke, had begun around 1260 to retranslate from the Greek most of the principal works of the Aristotelian corpus. More importantly, he translated for the first time some of the principal ancient commentaries on Aristotle, including that of Alexander of Aphrodisias on *Metaphysics*, AMMONIUS on *De interpretatione*, and both PHILOPONUS and THEMISTIUS on *On the Soul*. These texts were acquired avidly by Thomas Aquinas and others as witnesses to the authentic meaning of Aristotle, a meaning different from that thought to have been imposed by Averroes. The Averroistic Aristotle was being confronted with an arguably Greek Aristotle, who was on many points made more congenial to Christian teaching.

The question of how far Albert and Thomas were Aristotelians in their own thinking has been debated for centuries without resolution. On the one hand, it is certainly the case that neither Albert nor Thomas called themselves Aristotelian. Albert several time reminds his readers that he is expounding Aristotle, not endorsing him. Thomas will not even use the word 'philosopher' when speaking of Christians, much less of theologians. On the other hand, many of their contemporaries in the faculties of theology thought that they were all too ready to accept Peripatetic doctrines uncritically. In 1273, for example, BONAVENTURE gave a series of lectures at Paris in which he excoriated those who based philosophy or theology on Aristotelian doctrines. Bonaventure identifies the principal Aristotelian errors in physics, ethics and metaphysics, thus showing his own technical mastery of the Aristotelian corpus. If much of Bonaventure's anger is directed at teachers of arts, some of it at least is reserved for theologians who embrace the same errors.

The controversies occasioned by the teaching of Aristotle in the arts faculty were not confined to the writing of alternate commentaries and counter-attacks. They resulted in two sets of ecclesiastical condemnations at Paris, one in 1270 and a second, much larger and more important, in 1277. A prominent target of the first condemnations was SIGER OF BRABANT. Around 1265, when Siger was a master of arts, the controversy over the radical reading of Aristotle began to build between the faculty of theology and the faculty of arts at Paris. This has often been described, rather inaccurately, as a quarrel between 'Augustinians' and 'Latin Averroists' (see AUGUSTINIANISM; AVERROISM). The 'Augustinian' theologians were in fact, if unknowingly, indebted to PLOTINUS and Avicenna as well as Augustine, and they often engaged in the constructive interpretation of Aristotle. The 'Latin Averroists' were so described not just because they took up Averroes' commentaries, but because they were thought to teach a number of Averroes' controversial doctrines, including the subordination of religion to philosophy (a doctrine misleadingly described as 'double truth'). Behind these labels, the quarrel was clearly a fight over claims for autonomy not only on behalf of philosophical speculation, but also of a philosophical way of life. The arts were repeatedly attacked for asserting not just that they could demonstrate conclusions while keeping out of view the articles of Christian faith, but that the study of philosophy or the practice of natural contemplation could lead to happiness.

Many of the accused denied the charges, and it is difficult to know how much the teachings of the 'artists' were distorted in polemic and in the ensuing legal proceedings. Siger himself was already in trouble with ecclesiastical authorities as early as 1266. A first set of general condemnations came in December, 1270. Etienne Tempier, Bishop of Paris, condemned thirteen propositions drawn from Siger's writings. Fifteen months later, masters in the arts faculty were prohibited from disputing theological matters or from determining philosophical questions in a way contrary to the faith. Finally, in 1276, Siger and two other masters from Brabant were summoned before the inquisitor of France to answer charges of heresy. It is not clear what happened to Siger afterwards. Finally, some 219 propositions were condemned by Tempier in Paris on 7 March 1277. The list was hastily composed by a mostly anonymous committee, and even its defenders would later admit that it contained inconsistencies and points which were not clear. A much shorter and better organized list was condemned at Oxford eleven days later. The Oxford list proscribed thirty propositions divided under the headings of logic, grammar and natural philosophy.

The 219 condemned propositions cannot be summarized: they are too imprecise and heterogeneous. Some of the propositions declared false evidently contradict the Christian faith. Others, however, seem to have been rejected because they relied on argumentative procedures or presuppositions that troubled the theological censors. Among these are some procedures that would figure prominently in speculative thought during the next two centuries: the distinction between God's power as unrestricted and as exercised (*potentia absoluta, potentia ordinata*), or the analysis of physical problems by conceiving alternate worlds or by transposing them to an imagined vacuum. In these ways, the list of propositions shows not just the topics of controversy between theologians and teachers of arts, but the budget of topics considered worthy of investigation by students of Aristotle.

There has been considerable contemporary dispute over the importance of the condemnations of 1277. Some have held that they were a local aberration forgotten after a few decades, others that they had a chilling effect on theological speculation for a century or more. In either case, it is worth remembering that the condemnations were not seen as a rejection of Aristotle, but rather of a certain sort of Aristotelianism. HENRY OF GHENT, for example, who authored some of the condemnations, placed himself as a theologian in the tradition of Augustine, but knew Aristotle well and used his knowledge frequently in exploring or defending theological points. Indeed, Aristotelian terms, principles, examples and arguments had so permeated theological learning by the end of the thirteenth century that no theologian, no matter how critical of certain points in Aristotle, could be anything less than fluent as an Aristotelian.

5 The fourteenth and fifteenth centuries

Two figures dominate the reception of Aristotle at the beginning of the fourteenth century: John DUNS SCOTUS and WILLIAM OF OCKHAM. They would determine the reading of Aristotle not only by their own efforts, but by the prominence of their disciples over the next two centuries.

No brief description of the engagement of either Duns Scotus or Ockham with Aristotle can fail to be misleading. The thought of each is not only difficult, but continues to occasion strikingly different interpretations, let alone evaluations. Duns Scotus' writings are brutally original in manner of expression and teaching. Ockham writes more conventionally, but in the service of a critique of prevailing views no less sharp. Neither hesitated to reject central Aristotelian teachings: Duns Scotus denies Aristotle's accounts of intellection and substantial individuation, Ockham the accounts of linguistic foundations and ethical truth. Again, neither was to provide literal expositions of Aristotle's works or other rudimentary exegetical works, genres in which they might have expressed general positions on Aristotle.

Both Duns Scotus and Ockham did write what are sometimes called commentaries on Aristotle. Duns Scotus wrote an early treatise in connection with *Metaphysics*, as well as multiple treatments of issues in *Categories*, *De interpretatione*, *Sophistical Refutations* and Porphyry's *Isagōgē*. These 'commentaries' engage prevailing disputes attached to the Aristotelian texts by only the frailest threads: Duns Scotus uses his writing to declare and defend positions on these disputes rather than to set out a simple reading of Aristotle. Ockham also wrote on the four logical works, with the aim of showing that none of them required a realist view of language or conception. He wrote in three different genres on *Physics*: in an exposition, a *summulae* (summary) and a set of disputed questions. The balance of exegesis and dispute varies in these three, but some indication of Ockham's authorial position may be given by the *summulae*; he begins that work with the assertion of a number of his characteristic positions, such as the non-existence of universals and the strictness of the criteria for scientific demonstration. Neither Duns Scotus nor Ockham was concerned to present a comprehensive interpretation of the Aristotelian corpus after the different styles of Averroes, Albert or Aquinas.

Still, it would be inaccurate and unjust to suggest that Duns Scotus and Ockham were incapable of close exegesis, just as it would be unjust to conclude that Scotistic or Ockhamistic views somehow precluded engagement with Aristotle. One of the most systematic commentators on Aristotle in the fourteenth century was John BURIDAN, a near contemporary of Ockham who shared many of the latter's concerns for linguistic and conceptual criticism. In the 1320s, Buridan began writing a mixture of expositions and disputed questions on Aristotle's books, frequently writing in both genres on a single book. Eventually he covered almost the entire corpus, with the exception of the *History of Animals* and the *Poetics*, doing so with careful attention to Aristotle's purposes and meanings. If Buridan's 'nominalism' was anti-Aristotelian, it certainly did not prevent him from being a tenacious expositor of Aristotle.

Scotistic or Ockhamistic views entered into combination with several other projects for explaining, extending and correcting Aristotle. One of these projects found an institutional home in Merton College, Oxford, with a group active from the 1320s onwards (see OXFORD CALCULATORS). The principal figures among these 'calculators' were Thomas

Bradwardine, Richard Kilvington, William Heytesbury, Richard Swineshead and John Dumbleton. There are numerous differences among them, as there are numerous similarities linking them to their colleagues working in the established logical genre of sophisms. What the Mertonians share are procedures of mathematical reasoning as applied to the resolution of problems outstanding in Aristotelian physics. One central problem concerned the intensification and remissions of accidental forms, while another concerned the motion of projectiles. These problems in Aristotelian physics were not discovered in the fourteenth century; they had been known to late Roman and Islamic commentators, as well as to readers in the prior two centuries. What distinguishes the treatment of these problems among the calculators is not so much the statement of the problem or even its doctrinal resolution, but the sophistication of its mathematical development. In the case of projectile motion, for example, members of the groups posited an inner force or *impetus*, which they then proceeded to describe through accelerations and decelerations (though this doctrine too may derive from previous commentaries on Aristotle).

The methods of the Mertonians were to have considerable consequences for the reading of Aristotle's *Physics*. The theologian Nicole Oresme, a student of Buridan, having learned a basic reading of the principal texts of Aristotle and a nominalist critique of them, went on to take up the methods of mathematical analysis. He wrote sets of questions on a number of Aristotelian texts, as well as vernacular commentaries on the *Nicomachean Ethics* and the *Politics*. His masterwork is a dialectical response to Aristotle's *On the Heavens*. Here, Oresme first expounds the literal sense, next extracts the principal theses, then produces arguments for their negations and finally affirms either the thesis or its negation depending on his judgment of the matter at hand.

A second approach to the relation of Duns Scotus or Ockham to Aristotle was a frank rehabilitation of Averroes. The principal figures of this movement were John of Jandun, Thaddeus of Parma and Angel of Arezzo. John of Jandun was a master of arts at Paris in the first decade of the fourteenth century, and wrote disputed questions on the central works of Aristotelian physics and metaphysics. In these questions, John frequently rehearses the readings of his predecessors, including Thomas Aquinas (whom he calls 'old expositor'), but then asserts quite plainly the views of Averroes, which agree with those of Aristotle. John confronts contradictions between an Averroistic Aristotle and Christian doctrine with a simple and unexplained profession of faith.

A third aspect of the fourteenth-century reception of Aristotle, widespread in faculties of theology across northern Europe, took the form of a perceived recovery of essential Aristotelian truths, against all rivals. Jean Gerson, who became chancellor of the university of Paris in 1395, describes three contending schools of thought: 'formalizers', 'nominalists' and 'Peripatetics'. Each of the three groups claimed medieval proponents: the formalizers claimed Duns Scotus, the nominalists claimed Ockham and Buridan, and the Peripatetics claimed Albert and Thomas. Each group was also held to reflect or descend from an ancient source: the formalizers from Plato, the nominalists from Epicurus and the Peripatetics, obviously, from Aristotle. The Aristotelian tradition invoked here is that of a specific line of thinkers. One writer traces it from Alexander of Aphrodisias and Themistius, through Boethius and John Philoponus, Avicenna and Averroes, to Albert the Great and Thomas Aquinas. The tradition is also characterized by a set of conclusions that emanate from the view (very roughly) that the human mind knows fixed, universal truths by abstracting universals from singulars, which it does without the need of any special divine assistance. This was taken to be the foundation of Aristotle's teaching and, by its proponents, the foundation of sound philosophy or theology.

This school called itself Peripatetic and also, perhaps surprisingly, Albertist. The preference for Albert over Thomas is evident in a group of writers which included John of Maisonneuve and his student, Heimeric de Campo. John taught as master of arts in Paris from 1400 onwards, while Heimeric was master of theology at Cologne and Louvain from 1428 onwards. John wanted to defend against both nominalists and formalizers a cognitive realism grounded in appeals to the divine ideas. Heimeric extended this Albertist project into a sustained critique of Thomas Aquinas. If both John and Heimeric seem at times to attribute certain views to Albert unreflectively, they are equally capable of careful readings in which they argue for Albert's Aristotle as the most accurate and the truest. Albert's work is presented as the completion of Aristotelian inquiry.

There is obviously no final medieval consensus about the reception of Aristotle, as there is no end to the traditions of 'medieval Aristotelianism'. The main medieval appropriations of Aristotle propounded around 1450, whether Albertist, Thomist, Scotist or Ockhamist, would continue to find advocates up into the twentieth century, especially in Roman Catholic schools and universities. Particular parts of the medieval Aristotle would also survive in general philosophical learning. The most obvious survival was of the logical doctrines, which attracted readers as astute as KANT, despite repeated attacks. Medieval versions of Aristotle on intellection would influence the development of modern epistemology at many points, saliently in the terminology of DESCARTES, WOLFF and their various followers. Even medieval receptions of Aristotelian physics would have a long afterlife: Galileo's critique of Aristotle owes much to late medieval debates over objections against Aristotelian texts in the ancient commentary tradition (see GALILEI, GALILEO).

See also: ALBERT THE GREAT; AQUINAS, T.; ARISTOTELIANISM IN ISLAMIC PHILOSOPHY; ARISTOTELIANISM IN THE 17TH CENTURY; ARISTOTELIANISM, RENAISSANCE; ARISTOTLE; ARISTOTLE COMMENTATORS; AVERROISM; DUNS SCOTUS, J.; HENRY OF GHENT; ISLAMIC PHILOSOPHY: TRANSMISSION INTO WESTERN EUROPE; LANGUAGE, MEDIEVAL THEORIES OF; LOGIC, MEDIEVAL; MEDIEVAL PHILOSOPHY; NATURAL PHILOSOPHY, MEDIEVAL; OXFORD CALCULATORS; TRANSLATORS; WILLIAM OF OCKHAM

References and further reading

Aristoteles Latinus (1957–), individual publication details as follows:
VII.2, *Physica: Translatio Vaticana*, ed. A. Mansion, Paris: Desclée de Brouwer, 1957;
I.1–5, *Categoriae vel Praedicamenta*, ed. L. Minio-Paluello, Paris: Desclée de Brouwer, 1961;
XXIX.1, *Politica: Translatio imperfecta*, ed. P. Michaud-Quantin, Paris: Desclée de Brouwer, 1961;
III.1–4, *Analytica priora*, ed. L. Minio-Paluello, Paris: Desclée de Brouwer, 1962;
II.1–2, *De interpretatione vel Periermenias*, ed. L. Minio-Paluello and G. Verbeke, Paris: Desclée de Brouwer, 1965;
XI.1–2, *De mundo*, ed. W.L. Lorimer, revised L. Minio-Paluello, Paris: Desclée de Brouwer, 1965;
I.6–7. *Categorium supplementa: Porphyrii Isagoge et Liber sex principorum*, ed. L. Minio-Paluello, Paris: Desclée de Brouwer, 1966;
XVII.2, *De generatione animalium*, ed. H.J. Drossaart-Lulofs, Paris: Desclée de Brouwer, 1966;
IV.1–4, *Analytica posteriora*, ed. L. Minio-Paluello and B.G. Dod, Paris: Desclée de Brouwer, 1968;
XXXIII.1–2, *De arte poetica*, ed. L. Minio-Paluello, Paris: Desclée de Brouwer, 1968;
V.1–3, *Topica*, ed. L. Minio-Paluello, Paris: Desclée de Brouwer, 1969;
XXV.1–1a, *Metaphysica: Translatio Iacobi ('Vetustissima') et Translatio composita ('Vetus')*, ed. G. Vuillemin-Diem, Paris: Desclée de Brouwer, 1970;
XXXVI.1–3, *Ethica Nicomachea*, ed. R.A. Gauthier, Leiden: Brill and Paris: Desclée de Brouwer, 1972–4;
VI.1–3, *De sophisticis elenchis*, ed. B.G. Dod, Leiden: Brill and Paris: Desclée de Brouwer, 1975;
XXV.2, *Metaphysica: Translatio anonyma ('Media')*, ed. G. Vuillemin-Diem, Leiden: Brill, 1976;
IX.1, *De generatione et corruptione*, ed. J. Judycka, Leiden: Brill, 1986;
VII.1, *Physica*, ed F. Bossier and J. Brams, Leiden: Brill, 1990;
XXV.3, *Metaphysica*, ed. G. Vuillemin-Diem, Leiden: Brill, 1995.
(Editions of surviving medieval translations of Aristotle into Latin, in progress. The texts and prefatory material are mostly in Latin. Three volumes of a survey of manuscripts have also been published; these are *Codices: pars prior*, ed. G. Lacombe *et al.*, La Libreria dell Stato, 1939; *Codices: pars posterior*, ed. G. Lacombe *et al.*, Cambridge: Cambridge University Press, 1955; and *Codices: supplementa altera*, ed. L. Minio-Paluello, Paris: Desclée de Brouwer, 1961.)

* Blund, John (*c.*1200) *Tractatus de anima* (Treatise on the Soul), ed. D.A. Callus and R.W. Hunt, Auctores Britannici Medii Aevi 2, London: British Academy, 1970. (An excellent, fully annotated edition.)

Corpus Latinum Commentariorum in Aristotelem Graecorum (1961–), Leiden: Brill. (Editions of medieval Latin translations of Greek commentaries on Aristotle, including Themistius and Philoponus on *On the Soul*, Ammonius on the *Peri hermeneias*, Alexander of Aphrodisias on the *Meteorology*, Simplicius on *Categories*, and various commentators on the *Nicomachean Ethics* and *Sophistical Refutations*. Texts are in Latin, prefatory material is in French or English.)

Dod, B.G. (1982) 'Aristoteles latinus', in N. Kretzmann, A. Kenny and J. Pinborg (eds) *The Cambridge History of Later Medieval Philosophy*, Cambridge: Cambridge University Press, 45–79. (Includes a very helpful chart summarizing medieval Latin translations of Aristotle.)

* Heimeric of Campo (1428) *Tractatus problematicus* (Treatise of Problems), published as *Problemata inter Albertum Magnum et Sanctum Thomam ad utriusque opinionis intelligentiam*, Cologne, 1496. (This remains the only printing of Heimeric's treatise.)

* Helias, Peter (1140s) *Summa super Priscianum* (Summa on Priscian), ed. J.E. Tolson, *Cahiers de l'Institut du Moyen-âge Grec et Latin* 27–8, 1978: 1–210. (A careful edition, with a helpful preface by Margaret Gibson.)

* John of Maisonneuve (1406–18) *De universali reali* (On the Universal Considered as Real), in A.G. Weiler, 'Un traité de Jean de Novo Domo sur les universaux', *Vivarium* 6, 1968: 108–54. (The edition itself is on pages 126–52. Weiler provides a useful introduction to the edition.)

Lohr, C.H. (1967–74) 'Medieval Latin Aristotle Commentaries', *Traditio* 23–30 (in installments). (A comprehensive listing of commentators, with details of the commentaries and a bibliography of pertinent scholarship.)

—— (1988) *Commentateurs d'Aristote au moyen-âge latin: Bibliographie de la littérature secondaire récente* (Medieval Latin Aristotle Commentators: A Bibliography of Recent Secondary Literature), Paris: Éditions du Cerf. (A supplement to Lohr 1967–74, bringing the scholarly bibliography up through 1987.)

* Robert of Courçon (1215) Statutes, in H. Denifle and É. Chatelain (eds) *Chartularium Universitatis Parisiensis*, Paris: Delalain, 1889–97, vol. 1, no. 20. (Includes one of the prohibitions on certain teachings of Aristotle.)

Schmitt, C.B. (1983) *Aristotle and the Renaissance*, Martin Classical Lectures 27, Cambridge, MA: Harvard University Press. (Chapter 1 contains an interesting and partly retrospective discussion of Renaissance Aristotelians.)

—— (1986) 'Pseudo-Aristotle in the Latin Middle Ages', in J. Kraye, W.F. Ryan, and C.B. Schmitt (eds) *Pseudo-Aristotle in the Middle Ages: The Theology and Other Texts*, London: Warburg Institute/University of London. (A very useful survey of texts passing under the name of Aristotle.)

Sorabji, R. (ed.) (1987) *Philoponus and the Rejection of Aristotelian Science*, London: Duckworth, and Ithaca, NY: Cornell University Press. (A collection of essays that treats in part the recovery of Philoponus in the medieval West.)

—— (ed.) (1990) *Aristotle Transformed: The Ancient Commentators and Their Influence*, London: Duckworth, and Ithaca, NY: Cornell University Press. (Chapters 15–16 treat Boethius, and Chapter 19 considers the sources of medieval logic.)

Thijssen, J.M.M.H. (1991) 'Some Reflections on Continuity and Transformation of Aristotelianism in Medieval (and Renaissance) Natural Philosophy', *Documenti e studi sulla tradizione filosofica medievale* 2 (2): 503–8. (Discusses especially some varieties of Aristotelianism from the later Middle Ages.)

* Urso of Salerno (*c.*1180?) *De commixtionibus elementorum* (On the Mixture of the Elements), ed W. Stürner, Stuttgart: Klett, 1976. (A critical edition of an important text, it suffers from the lack of study of Urso's predecessors at Salerno.)

Van Steenberghen, F. (1955) *Aristotle in the West: The Origins of Latin Aristotelianism*, trans. L. Johnston, Louvain: E. Nauwelaerts. (A narrative survey of the reception of Aristotle in Paris and Oxford to 1277; somewhat dated.)

—— (1980) *Thomas Aquinas and Radical Aristotelianism*, Washington, DC: Catholic University of America Press. (A retelling of some of the central incidents treated in Van Steenberghen (1955).)

MARK D. JORDAN

ARISTOTELIANISM, RADICAL see AVERROISM

ARISTOTELIANISM, RENAISSANCE

By the Renaissance here is meant the period of the fifteenth and sixteenth centuries during which there was a deliberate attempt, especially in Italy, to pattern cultural activities on models drawn from antiquity. However, Aristotelianism during that period was not cut off from medieval developments, since earlier interests and topics of discussion still held the attention of philosophers, theologians and non-academic intellectuals. Moreover, given that Aristotelianism was embedded in the university curriculum, the approach and activities of Renaissance Aristotelians often reflected earlier institutional developments. The educational reforms of the German Lutheran Philipp Melanchthon and of the newly-founded Society of Jesus (the Jesuits) ensured that Aristotle remained central to the curriculum. On the other hand, deliberate attempts to divorce themselves from earlier structures and approaches can be discerned in some Renaissance Aristotelians. Owing to the influence of humanism, professors of philosophy whose loyalty was to Aristotle came to study Greek and explicate Aristotle from the Greek text, to imitate the style of classical models, and to prefer the Greek commentators over the medieval Latins because their language was Greek.

Renaissance Aristotelianism did not constitute a uniform, coherent school of thought with a clearly defined body of doctrines shared by all adherents. A careful reading of the many commentaries, paraphrases, textbooks and treatises based on Aristotle's works reveals a surprisingly wide variation in interpretation and a strong tendency to modify or supplement the Stagirite's teachings with tenets derived from other philosophical or scientific sources or from contemporary interests and discoveries. It is perhaps wise to speak of a variety of Aristotelianisms rather than to perpetuate the long-standing caricature of 'modern' philosophy and science arising by throwing off the shackles of a monolithic Peripatetic orthodoxy. The various Aristotelianisms included Albertism, Thomism, Scotism and Averroism, but as a result of the new translations of the Greek commentators on Aristotle there were also Renaissance Aristotelians who approached Aristotle by way of Alexander of Aphrodisias, Themistius, Simplicius and John Philoponus. Another current is best described as 'eclectic Aristotelianism'. Some Aristotelians adopted a 'philological' approach, approaching Aristotle simply through analysis of the Greek text and not as a philosophical challenge. This approach made Aristotelianism irrelevant to the enterprise of philosophy, but fortunately did not predominate.

1   Aristotle, the Greek text and the Greek commentators
2   Logic and method
3   Natural philosophy
4   Psychology
5   The debate over immortality
6   Metaphysics
7   Ethics and political philosophy

1   Aristotle, the Greek text and the Greek commentators

Although Aristotle was accorded the honorific title of 'The Philosopher' by most philosopher-theologians of the high Middle Ages (see ARISTOTELIANISM, MEDIEVAL), there were also some who viewed him far less favourably. The fourteenth-century Franciscans FRANCIS OF MEYRONNES, Antonius Andreas and John Canonicus carried Bonaventure's critique of Aristotle to its ultimate conclusion (see BONAVENTURE). The first called Aristotle 'the worst metaphysician', and both Andreas and Canonicus viewed him as a poor natural philosopher. Their critical views were known to Renaissance Aristotelians like Nicoletto VERNIA, Agostino NIFO and Marcantonio Zimara (c.1475–1532). Nevertheless, Aristotle's influence on philosophy and science during the Renaissance was profound. Both his own works and those of his many late ancient and medieval interpreters attracted a wide audience. His writings on logic and natural philosophy formed the centrepiece of university studies in the arts and provided essential preparation for a career in medicine, law or theology, while his works on ethics, poetics and politics were widely read and discussed by a learned public increasingly educated in the schools of the humanists.

Despite the emphasis given to Renaissance Platonism in general histories of culture, a survey of the philosophical and scientific literature actually produced during the period from 1400 to 1600 clearly establishes the Renaissance as a golden age in the history of Aristotelianism. Since Renaissance philosophers trained in the arts faculties of major European universities had normally received a thorough grounding in Aristotle, those who became professors in their own right for the most part continued to base their instruction on the Aristotelian corpus. Their writings often reflected this, taking the form of commentaries on Aristotle, though works devoted to the systematic exposition of a particular topic – such as Pietro Pomponazzi's famous treatise *De immortalitate animae* (On the Immortality of the Soul) (1516) or Jacopo Zabarella's *De naturalis scientiae constitutione* (On the Nature of Natural Science) (published in 1586) – were not infrequent, particularly when aimed at a general learned audience rather than at other scholars (see POMPONAZZI, P. §2; ZABARELLA, J. §6). Aristotle's dominance among university professors withstood the challenge mounted by the handful of appointments of chairs of Platonic philosophy in Italy (see PLATONISM, RENAISSANCE §5).

Much of the continued predominance of Aristotle was due to the work of humanists, their knowledge of Greek, and the new critical techniques they developed. The Greek text of Aristotle's works was published, notably in the edition of 1495–8 printed by Aldo Manuzio. New translations were done, and from the 1530s onward, bilingual editions were produced. From 1499 onward, but especially in the 1520s and 1530s, editions of the Greek commentators on Aristotle were printed, and these in turn were translated, many for the first time. Nor was attention paid only to the Greek commentators, for in 1483 Nicoletto Vernia edited an important Aristotle-Averroes edition, and 1550–2 saw the great Giunta Aristotle–Averroes edition containing many works not previously included. The Aristotle commentaries of such medieval Latin authors as ALBERT THE GREAT and Thomas AQUINAS were also printed. At the same time, attention was paid to the canon of Aristotle's work. Many dubious and spurious works had been excluded by 1600. On the other hand, the *Poetics*, which had been little read during the Middle Ages, came to have a great influence on literary criticism, and the pseudo-Aristotelian *Mechanics* also attracted a good deal of attention.

2 Logic and method

Renaissance Aristotelians developed an account of scientific methodology that built on insights put forward by ARISTOTLE (§6) in his *Posterior Analytics* and *Physics*. In a well-known passage in the *Posterior Analytics* Aristotle distinguishes between two types of demonstration. The first he calls demonstration of the fact (*to hoti*) or demonstration *quia*. Its primary characteristic is that the middle terms of such demonstrations tell us only the fact that something is the case and not why this is the case. The second type of demonstration has a middle term that tells us the reason why (*to dioti*). Medieval thinkers inspired by this analysis connected Aristotle's remarks on demonstration with his remarks at the beginning of the *Physics* concerning the proper method for establishing the principles of nature. There Aristotle claims that one should start with those things that are more knowable to us and proceed to those things more knowable or intelligible by nature, though not to us. In addition, some later thinkers equated two methods set forth by GALEN (§§3–4) with the two sorts of demonstration. In his *Art of Medicine*, Galen distinguishes between what he calls the method of resolution, in which an object is broken down into its component parts, and the method of composition, in which the components used in the resolution are put into their proper order. Late medieval Aristotelians, like Pietro d'Abano (1257–1315) in his *Conciliator differentiarum philosophorum et praecipue medicorum* (Conciliator of the Differences between Philosophers and Especially Physicians) (composed around 1300), conflated demonstration *quia* and *propter quid* with resolution and composition, and were thus able to offer a sophisticated account of both the method of scientific discovery and the proper way to order such knowledge.

PAUL OF VENICE, a member of the Augustinian Order who studied at Oxford before returning to teach at Padua, sets forth the procedure of going from effect to cause and back to the effect, and defends it against the charge of circularity. He is also careful to note that demonstration in natural science does not yield the necessity and certitude of mathematics, since it deals with what happens for the most part. Natural science is thus a demonstrative science, but is only a science of what usually occurs. Two contemporaries of Paul, Hugo of Siena and Jacopo da Forli, also discuss the resolutive method. However, it is Nicoletto VERNIA (§3) who examines in greater depth questions regarding demonstration and the resolutive method in his Paduan lectures on the *Posterior Analytics*. Vernia also takes up the question whether demonstration is circular. He points out that there must first be a movement from an effect by way of demonstration *quia* but thereafter there must be a return back to the effect if natural science is to be perfect. That is to say, after the resolution (*resolutio*) of an 'effect' – that is, what is experienced through the senses – into an initial universal knowledge, we still lack demonstration *propter quid*, which is knowledge based on the essential principles of the thing. Vernia therefore postulates a movement of the intellect (*negotiatio intellectus*) enabling it somehow to discern the true cause of the effect and the necessary causal connection of that cause to its effect. A genuine apodictic demonstration *propter quid* is the result.

The topic of resolutive or regressive method (*regressus*) was also treated by Agostino NIFO (§2), Vernia's former student. In his youth he too postulated a movement of the intellect (*negotiatio intellectus*) enabling it to discern the true cause of an effect so that a strict demonstration was possible. However, later in his career, after studying the Greek commentators, namely ALEXANDER OF APHRODISIAS, THEMISTIUS, SIMPLICIUS and PHILOPONUS, he denied the need for such a special movement of the intellect and held that the most that could be achieved in natural science was a hypothetical syllogism and a hypothetical demonstration.

Discussions regarding these methodological issues are also to be found in such contemporaries as Marcantonio Zimara and Bernardinus Tomitanus (d. 1576). But it is Jacopo ZABARELLA (§5), a student of Tomitanus, who stands at the end of this long line of development. In his treatise *De regressu* (On the Regress), Zabarella sets forth a systematic discussion of the nature of scientific investigation in which he assumes like the earlier theorists a basic continuity between Aristotle and Galen. He argues that demonstration *quia* provides us with a method of reasoning from effect to cause, but does not tell us the proper reason for the effect. Nevertheless, from the cause to which our initial knowledge of the effect leads, we can eventually achieve a full account of the proximate cause of the effect. That is, we can arrive at an argument that fully reveals the cause by giving a *propter quid* demonstration that states the reason why. What keeps this regressive method from being purely formal is the positing of the intermediate step of the movement (*negotiatio*) of the intellect, going from an initially confused and improper knowledge of the cause to a distinct and proper knowledge of it (see GALILEI, GALILEO).

3 Natural philosophy

One of the issues discussed by medieval Aristotelians that continued to concern Aristotelian philosophers during the Renaissance was the identification of the subject of natural philosophy. This issue was thought to be important because it concerned not only the relationship between metaphysics (the science of being *qua* being) and natural philosophy, but also the place of immaterial created beings, such as angels, within Aristotelian science. Thomas AQUINAS (§9) had argued that mobile or changeable being (*ens mobile*), which seems to include all beings liable to change (that is, everything other than God), was the subject of natural philosophy, whereas his teacher ALBERT THE GREAT (§4) took it to be mobile or changeable body (*corpus mobile*). Later, PAUL OF VENICE states that the subject matter is natural body (*corpus naturale*), while his student, Cajetan of Thiene (Gaetano da Thiene) (1387–1485), maintained that it is sensible substance (*substantia sensibilis*). Subsequently the whole issue was approached in a systematic fashion by Cajetan's student, Nicoletto VERNIA (§3), who composed a separate question on whether mobile being is the subject of all natural philosophy. In it he reviews and compares a wide range of authors including Antonius Andreas and John Canonicus, whom he attacks for judging Aristotle to have erred in natural philosophy. Vernia accuses them of not speaking naturally but rather introducing theological considerations into the discussion, namely the question of the motion of angels. Vernia himself upholds and defends mobile being as the subject, which he took to be the position of Averroes. Thereafter Vernia's student Agostino NIFO (§2) took up the question of the subject matter of natural philosophy in his commentary on the *Physics*. He rejects the respective positions of Albert and Aquinas but then attempts to conciliate them, arguing that mobile being can be considered the subject of natural science if by subject is meant the genus or most general predicate applying to the things considered in natural science, whereas mobile body can also be considered the subject if by that is meant the most general species to which all and only the things considered in natural science belong. He presents Averroes as holding that the total subject of natural science is a sensible thing (*res sensibilis*) in so far as it moves, that is, in so far as it contains the principle of motion.

Jacopo ZABARELLA (§6) who, like Vernia, wrote a systematic work on the question of the subject of natural philosophy, echoes the earlier discussions. He declares the common subject of all natural science to be body taken universally (embracing both the earthly bodies and also the bodies in the heavens), but in so far as body has within it a nature (that is, the principle of motion). He insists that this is the position of ARISTOTLE (§10) in the *Physics* and *On the Heavens*.

As to the subject of Aristotle's *On the Soul*, he takes it to be animate body (*corpus animatum*). Further echoes of the discussion are still found in the seventeenth century (see JOHN OF ST THOMAS §3).

Another issue in the area of natural philosophy that merits mention is the challenge of Richard Swineshead and the fourteenth-century Oxford Calculators' tradition of interest in physics (see OXFORD CALCULATORS). Central was their doctrine of measuring the intension and remission of forms, that is, physical properties, and stating this measurement in mathematical language. Paul of Venice was one of those who brought this manner of doing natural philosophy to Italy, and he promoted it in his teaching and writings. But it was also taught and fostered at Pavia in the teaching and writings of Giovanni Marliani (d. 1483). Nicoletto Vernia, who spent a year at Pavia, and studied Swineshead's major work as well as other works in the tradition of the Oxford Calculators, emphatically rejected such an approach to natural philosophy as untrue to Aristotle and Averroes. Agostino Nifo also rejected the approach of the Calculators, insisting that their principles were those of mathematics and were therefore incapable of providing the basis of a true natural science.

4 Psychology

The background for the discussion of psychology was provided by Aristotle's doctrine in his *On the Soul* of three types of soul, the vegetative, sensitive and intellective, and by his division of the intellect into an active element and passive or receptive element. The Aristotelian tradition would call these two elements the agent intellect and the potential or possible intellect respectively (see ARISTOTLE §19). Some of the Latin medievals also saw Aristotle as maintaining a psychological power of the human soul, identified as the will (*voluntas*). These divisions raised such questions as whether the three souls were separate within the human being, whether the powers of intellect and will were distinct, and whether the agent and possible intellects were distinct either from each other or from the human being. Alexander of Aphrodisias had identified God as the agent intellect. Avicenna held that there was one agent intellect for all human beings, namely the lowest Intelligence, though each had an individual potential intellect (see ALEXANDER OF APHRODISIAS §2; IBN SINA §6). In the work on the soul known to the Latin medievals, Averroes held that there was just one separate intellect, but it was composed of both the agent and the potential intellects (see IBN RUSHD §3; SOUL IN ISLAMIC PHILOSOPHY, THE).

Two particular problems about human cognition

deserve mention. The first regards the nature of sensation as presented by the theory of the agent sense, proposed as an analogue of the agent intellect. Inspired by remarks of Averroes, JOHN OF JANDUN had held that the object of sensation had to be spiritualized by an active power, an agent sense (*sensus agens*), if sensation was to take place. He thought that this agent sense was internal to and multiplied in each human being, though others like GILES OF ROME (§3) held it to be a separate substance, that is, an Intelligence. The agent sense was discussed during the fourteenth century by such philosophers as John BURIDAN (§3), Nicole Oresme, MARSILIUS OF INGHEN (§1), and Taddeo of Parma (fl. early fourteenth century). It is also discussed by Blasius (see BLASIUS OF PARMA §3), Paul of Venice and Cajetan of Thiene. The latter proposes in a special question on the agent sense that a separate Intelligence provides the spirituality required for the act of sensation to occur. In like fashion, Agostino NIFO (§3) proposes in his own special treatise on the agent sense that God provides the spirituality required for sensation to take place. Cardinal Cajetan, Pietro Pomponazzi, Francesco Silvestri, and later the Jesuit scholastics also take up the question. In his own *Liber de sensu agente* (Book on the Agent Sense) (published 1590), Zabarella pays particular attention to Nifo's theory.

The second particular problem regards the need for intelligible species in the process of intellectual cognition. This need had already been proposed by medievals like Albert the Great, Thomas Aquinas and DUNS SCOTUS (§13). What is involved is a universal representative image (*imago*) or likeness (*similitudo*) that is distinct from the act of intellection itself, yet needed to explain how humans can be united cognitively to external objects. In his explication of the cognitive psychology of Averroes, John of Jandun argued that Averroes had postulated intelligible species in the single possible or potential intellect. This interpretation of Averroes was heatedly debated during the Renaissance by philosophers like Antonio Trombetta (1436–1517) and Marcantonio Zimara, who agreed with Jandun, as well as by Alessandro Achillini (1463–1512) and Agostino NIFO (§3), who denied that Averroes had maintained intelligible species. In an early treatise on intelligible species, Pomponazzi maintained that Averroes had in fact held to such species; he accused Achillini and Nifo of having simply revived an old opinion, namely that of Walter BURLEY. Pomponazzi considers their opinion stupid and bestial. In fact, although Nifo maintained that neither Aristotle nor Averroes held to intelligible species, he himself takes as true that the human being does need intelligible species in order to think. This he maintains both in his early *De intellectu* (On the Intellect) (1503) and also in his later *De immortalitate animae* (On the Immortality of the Soul) (1518). The doctrine of intelligible species better enabled him to explain the knowledge enjoyed by the disembodied soul after death. In his own treatise on the topic, ZABARELLA (§§5–6) maintains that the intelligible species is the same thing as the act of thinking and does not remain after death. It is called an intellection if it is related to the intellect in which it exists, but it is called a species or image when it is related to the external thing known.

That intelligible species differ from the act of thinking and are images and likenesses necessary for human thinking was the common doctrine of Jesuit scholasticism. However, concepts as well as intelligible species were postulated, in line with Aquinas' distinction between the intelligible species and the inner word (see AQUINAS §10). The need for such intelligible species and concepts was maintained by Franciscus TOLETUS (§5), the authors of the Coimbra commentaries (see COLLEGIUM CONIMBRICENSE), and Francisco SUÁREZ (§3). But both Toletus and Suárez also maintained, in clear opposition to Aquinas, that there are intelligible species and concepts of individuals as opposed to common natures.

The most important question about the intellective soul concerned its relation to the human body. The variously nuanced definitions of the soul that the Renaissance Aristotelians formulated took as their starting point Aristotle's statement in his *On the Soul* that the soul is the first actuality of a body that has life potentially in it (see ARISTOTLE §17). What had been an issue in earlier discussions and continued to be an issue was whether this definition could be read in such a way as to allow a dualistic interpretation. The striking dualism to be found in the thought of Avicenna and the modified dualism that was to be found in the thought of Thomas Aquinas were of course not unknown. But what made the discussions somewhat more complicated was the availability by the end of the fifteenth century of translations of Alexander of Aphrodisias' own *On the Soul*, Themistius' paraphrases of Aristotle's *On the Soul* and the commentary on the same work that was traditionally attributed to Simplicius. Alexander's work presented a view of the soul as resulting from the harmony of bodily parts, while the commentary attributed to Simplicius presented a strikingly dualistic conception of the relation of the soul to the body (see ALEXANDER OF APHRODISIAS §2).

While those who read Alexander and Simplicius would have found the human soul to be many, that is, one soul for each human being, the interpretation of

Averroes was quite different. The theory of the human soul that emerged from Averroes' *Long Commentary on Aristotle's 'On the Soul'* was that each human being had an individual sensitive soul and a set of internal senses that were numerically distinct in each human being. On the other hand, there was numerically only one intellect for the entire human race, and that intellect served as the 'intellective soul' for each human being (see IBN RUSHD §3). Renaissance Aristotelians like Paul of Venice, Apollinaris Offredi (fl. fifteenth century), Johannes Argyropoulos (c.1415–87), Nicoletto Vernia, Agostino Nifo, Alessandro Achillini, Marcantonio Zimara, Pietro Trapolin (1451–1506), Marcantonio Genua (d. 1563) and Jacopo Zabarella, expended much of their philosophical and academic energies on explicating the text of Averroes and facing the serious problems that lurk in such a theory of the soul and intellect. In doing so they were in fact following in the footsteps of medievals like Thomas Aquinas, Siger of Brabant, GILES OF ROME (§3), JOHN OF JANDUN and John Baconthorpe among others. It bears noting that in his early thought Pomponazzi took Averroes to present the correct interpretation of Aristotle concerning the human soul. Only later did he attack Averroes, using Aquinas' arguments against Averroes' doctrine of the unity of the intellect.

5 The debate over immortality

The question of whether the personal immortality of the human soul could be demonstrated had already been answered in the negative by such medieval thinkers as SIGER OF BRABANT (§2) (at least in his earlier works), John Duns Scotus, JOHN OF JANDUN and John Buridan. Soon afterwards, BLASIUS OF PARMA (§2) denied the demonstrability of personal immortality. His position reflected the thought of Buridan and Alexander of Aphrodisias. Blasius, who had already stated in questions on Aristotle's *On the Soul* that human cognition has a material basis and is simply a grade of perfection of living matter, reasoned that inasmuch as the human soul has no operation independent from the body, there are no grounds for arguing that the human soul can survive the death of the body. He was reprimanded in 1396 by the Bishop of Pavia for remarks against the Catholic faith and the Church.

A little later, PAUL OF VENICE in his commentary on Aristotle's *On the Soul* stresses, in opposition to Alexander of Aphrodisias, the intellect's ability to reflect upon itself and to know universals. The doctrine of the unity of the intellect that he ascribes to Aristotle he rejects as being counter to moral philosophy, since all rewards for those who are good and all punishments for those who are evil would thereby be destroyed. The view that virtue is its own reward and vice its own punishment he rejects as inadequate. And in his commentary on Aristotle's *On Generation and Corruption* he argues for personal immortality on the grounds that there is a natural desire in each human to enjoy a perpetual beatitude. Subsequently Agostino NIFO (§3) presented similar moral arguments for personal immortality in his early work *De intellectu* (On the Intellect) (1503).

Cajetan of Thiene, who succeeded Paul of Venice as the major professor at Padua, believed that Averroes' doctrine of the unity of the intellect could in fact be disproven by human reason and that probative arguments for personal immortality could be given. Johannes Argyropoulos, who had studied with Cajetan of Thiene, also offered arguments for personal immortality. In contrast, Nicoletto VERNIA (§4), who succeeded to Cajetan of Thiene's chair at Padua, was a strict follower of Averroes regarding the unity of the intellect in an early treatise on the intellective soul; in it, he denied that personal immortality could be demonstrated. In like fashion, Vernia's student, Agostino Nifo, stated in his earliest works that Averroes was the correct interpreter of Aristotle regarding the soul and intellect, and that personal immortality could not be demonstrated. However, a new set of factors dramatically changed the course of discussions regarding immortality, and both Vernia and Nifo came to hold that personal immortality could be demonstrated. These factors were the publication in 1481 of Ermolao Barbaro's Latin translation of Themistius' paraphrases on Aristotle's *On the Soul*, the publication in 1495 of Girolamo Donato's translation of Alexander of Aphrodisias' *On the Soul*, and the circulation of a now lost translation of the commentary on Aristotle's *On the Soul* attributed to Simplicius. These works, made available by the humanists, allowed philosophers to study the conflicting conceptions of the soul as subsistent and independent of the body and of the soul as the product of the harmony of the body. Vernia and Nifo fought over the correct interpretation of Alexander, since Vernia seemed unwilling to admit that Alexander denied personal immortality. Others like Giovanni Pico della Mirandola would also maintain the same mistaken interpretation of Alexander.

Both Vernia and Nifo later turned away from Averroes as the true interpreter of Aristotle regarding the soul and intellect and came to accept Themistius and Simplicius as truer guides. Pomponazzi too followed a similar path. He regarded Averroes as the true interpreter of Aristotle in his early questions on the soul and intellect, though he does also cite

Alexander from Donato's translation. Eventually in his *De immortalitate animae* (1516) POMPONAZZI (§2) uses arguments from Thomas Aquinas to discredit Averroes and his doctrine of the unity of the intellect, though he goes on to marshal arguments from Alexander to discredit Aquinas' attempt to demonstrate the intellective soul's independence of the body. He rejects moral arguments for immortality and retorts that virtue and vice are their own reward and punishment. It is noteworthy that there was a similar shift in the thought of the Dominican Cardinal CAJETAN (§4) from acceptance of the demonstrability of personal immortality to a denial that such arguments have probative force. By this denial he was of course breaking with Thomas Aquinas, his intellectual master. Oddly enough, Antonio Trombetta, the major Franciscan theologian at Padua towards the end of the fifteenth century, did not follow his own master, Duns Scotus, on the question but held that immortality could be demonstrated.

Throughout the sixteenth century the possibility of demonstrating the immortality of the human soul continued to be debated. Simone Porzio (1496–1554), in his *De humana mente disputatio* (On the Human Mind) (first published in 1551), taught that the coming-to-be and passing-away of humans is not different from that of the animals. The intellect is inseparable from the body and can be considered to be material. Jacopo Zabarella clearly states in his commentary on Aristotle's *On the Soul* that according to true philosophy the human soul is a form giving existence to matter and yet separable and immortal, since it is not educed from the potency of matter but created by God. This view agrees with the Christian religion and with truth, but it is not the position of the philosophy of Aristotle. Indeed Zabarella notes in his own *Liber de mente humana* (On the Human Mind) (published in 1590) that it is doubtful that Aristotle knew of such a creation. Although he judges Pomponazzi to have come closest to the mind of Aristotle, he criticizes his views on what Aristotle meant by stating that the intellect comes from outside. On the other hand, Francesco Piccolomini (1520–1604) maintained that Aristotle considered the human soul to be immortal despite the contrary interpretation of others like Pomponazzi and Cardinal Cajetan. He takes Aristotle to have held that the human soul is not the form of the body but is related to the body as its actuality in the manner in which a sailor is the actuality of a ship. Finally it should be emphasized that Jesuit scholastics like Franciscus TOLETUS (§5) and Francisco SUÁREZ (§3) offered rational arguments for the immortality of the soul (see SOUL, NATURE AND IMMORTALITY OF THE).

6 Metaphysics

Various metaphysical topics debated during the Middle Ages continued to be of interest during the Renaissance. The nature of the distinction between essence and existence that divided AQUINAS (§10) and DUNS SCOTUS (§6) was studied by their Renaissance followers (see BÁÑEZ, D.; CAJETAN §5; FONSECA, P. DA §3; NIFO, A. §4; SUÁREZ, F. §2), and whether being involved a univocal or an analogous concept was also debated (see LANGUAGE, RENAISSANCE PHILOSOPHY OF §4; CAPREOLUS, J.; CAJETAN §2; FONSECA, P. DA §3; SILVESTRI, F.). The Dominican Paolo Barbo Soncinas (d. 1494) discussed analogy and the distinction of essence and existence. Trombetta and Maurice O'Fihely (1463–1514), both Franciscans, defended Scotus' views on the formal distinction and the univocal concept of being (see DUNS SCOTUS §5). Cardinal Cajetan wrote a commentary on Aquinas' treatise *De ente et essentia* (On Being and Essence) and also claimed to set forth Aquinas' views in his own treatise *De Nominum Analogia* (On the Analogy of Names) (1498). How close his thought is to Aquinas himself has been questioned. Achillini and Nifo both discussed the transcendentals, as did the Dominican Crisostomo Javelli (1470–1538) who defended Aquinas' views. Various Aristotelian thinkers like Elijah DELMEDIGO, Cajetan, Trombetta and Nifo all debated whether human reason could prove God's power to be infinite. Zimara, Delmedigo and Nifo also attempted to establish the mode of causality enjoyed by God and the Intelligences according to Aristotle and Averroes. Yet another topic of interest was whether according to reason and philosophy there could be a direct cognitive 'conjunction' of the human being with God and the Intelligences. This topic was inspired by Averroes and had already been discussed by medievals like Albert, Aquinas and John of Jandun. Nifo treated it seriously; Pomponazzi mocked it.

One of the most interesting developments to take place in Renaissance Aristotelianism concerned a conceptual scheme of metaphysical hierarchy first elaborated at the end of the thirteenth century. Albert the Great and Thomas Aquinas had spelled out this scheme, basing themselves on PROCLUS and PSEUDO-DIONYSIUS the Areopagite. God and nothingness (or matter) serve as two measures for the hierarchy of being. As a being 'approaches' God and 'recedes' from nonbeing, it holds an accordingly higher grade in the hierarchy. The scheme was also adopted with variations by SIGER OF BRABANT (§4), GILES OF ROME (§2), HENRY OF GHENT (§2), GODFREY OF FONTAINES (§3) and JAMES OF VITERBO. However, during the fourteenth century and thereafter it was challenged on the grounds that if God always remains at an 'infinite distance' from all creatures then no creature would be any closer to God than any other, and there would be no hierarchy of being.

One solution to this dilemma was to borrow from Richard Swineshead and the Oxford Calculators, who measured physical qualities like heat only from the lowest or zero grade (see OXFORD CALCULATORS). This route was pursued by PAUL OF VENICE, who appears to be the target of Marsilio Ficino's attack on 'barbarians' (*barbari*) who do not take God as a measure of the hierarchy of being and settle on nonbeing alone (see FICINO, M.). A similar attack was mounted by Pomponazzi, who dismisses Swineshead's views and insists that the Aristotelian position is to measure things by the highest grade. On this topic Pomponazzi is anything but a 'radical philosopher'.

A major statement of the conceptual scheme of hierarchy as elaborated by Albert and Aquinas was given by Agostino Nifo, who attributed both the scheme and also a metaphysics of participation to Averroes. Marcantonio Zimara also attributed the scheme and a metaphysics of participation to Averroes. Other contemporaries who interested themselves in the scheme include Gabriele Zerbo (1435–1535), Trombetta, Cardinal Domenico Grimani (1461–1523), Achillini, the young Thomas de Vio (who was to become Cardinal Cajetan), Crisostomo Javelli and Gaspare Contarini (1483–1542). Later philosophers who examined and accepted the scheme include Francesco Buonamici (*c.*1540–1603) and Iacopo Mazzoni (1548–98). They were respectively the teacher and the colleague of Galileo Galilei at Pisa. Galileo himself presented arguments in his *juvenilia* against taking God as a measure of things (see GALILEI, GALILEO). The scheme was also rejected by Cesare Cremonini (1550–1631), Galileo's contemporary at Padua. One solution to the problem of how an infinite God could serve as a measure was to take God as finite. Achillini, Contarini and Buonamici accepted this solution.

7 Ethics and political philosophy

Aristotle's ethical writings interested and influenced a wide range of thinkers throughout the fifteenth and sixteenth centuries, from humanist authors such as Leonardo Bruni (1370–1444) to scholastic writers such as Francisco Suárez. Indeed the fifteenth century saw the diffusion of Aristotle's ethical thought to a new audience that was characterized by the concerns that cluster under the term 'humanism'. Bruni's approval of Aristotle marked the beginning of a new view, one that stressed Aristotle as a guide in rhetoric and moral philosophy and showed little interest in his views on logical, physical, psychological or metaphysical questions. Bruni thereby provided the inspiration for intellectuals who were not professional philosophers to use Aristotle as a guide to practical life and avoid more technical philosophical issues (see HUMANISM, RENAISSANCE §§5, 7; PLATONISM, RENAISSANCE §§1, 4).

At the beginning of the fifteenth century, the extant translations of Aristotle's *Nicomachean Ethics* were literal, technical and frequently relied on transliteration. To those taught according to humanist ideals, such translations were uninviting. Under the influence of Cicero and his own teacher Manuel Chrysoloras, Bruni developed a theory of translation unlike the typical medieval method. The sense of the Greek passage had to be understood and then translated according to the best models of Latin prose. Bruni claimed the translations used by scholastic philosophers led them to misunderstand Aristotle even on minor points. He himself completed translations of the *Nicomachean Ethics* and the *Politics*, as well as the pseudo-Aristotelian *Economics*. His translation of the *Nicomachean Ethics* was hugely successful. He also wrote two works that reflect Aristotelian influence, namely an *Isagogicon moralis philosophiae* (Introduction to Moral Philosophy) (published between 1424 and 1426) and a *Vita Aristotelis* (Life of Aristotle) (published in 1428 or 1429). In the latter, Bruni takes Plato to task on several fronts, notably for his faulty methodology and for his views on such matters as the holding of wives and property in common.

The medieval Aristotelian tradition of political thought that was of Thomistic inspiration was passed on to Italy through two Florentine Dominicans who studied in Paris, namely Ptolemy of Lucca (*c.*1236–1327) and Remigio de'Girolami (1235–1319). Ptolemy had studied with Aquinas and wrote the continuation of Aquinas' *De regno* (On Kingship), known also as *De regimine principum* (On the Rule of Princes). Although Aquinas accorded primacy to monarchy, Ptolemy took Aristotle to prefer republican or elective rule regulated by law. Political rule is simply rule in accordance with written laws, while royal or despotic rule ignores law. Since the stars influence humans, some provinces are fit for liberty and others for servitude. The city-states of Northern Italy are suitable for political rule, since men there are self-confident and virile, like the ancient Romans. In contrast, the inhabitants of Sicily, Sardinia and Corsica are servile and therefore should have royal rule. Remigio attempted to conciliate Aristotle and Augustine, and also favoured Cicero as an authority and Ancient Rome as a model. In his *De bono communi* (On the Common Good) (written in 1302 or 1303), he discerned inordinate self-love as the cause of widespread discord; in his *De bono pacis* (On the Good of Peace) (written in 1304) he justified the ruler confiscating some individual's possessions for the greater good of the city.

Two Renaissance Dominicans need to be mentioned. Girolamo Savonarola (1452–98) wrote an early compendium of philosophy based on Aristotle and Aquinas that also reflects the thought of Ptolemy of Lucca (see SCEPTICISM, RENAISSANCE §3). Indeed his later treatise on governing Florence is a defence of republicanism dependent on Ptolemy's ideas in *De regimine principum*. He argues that since Florentines are vital and intelligent, their habit is to have civil rule. In the republicanism that he sets forth, he stresses the central role of a Great Council patterned on that of Venice. Another famed Dominican, Tommaso CAMPANELLA (§3), had a less favourable view of Aristotle. He noted that Aristotle denied that artisans, farmers and merchants could be citizens, since they lacked the virtues necessary to be either citizens or rulers. This would mean that only the nobles in Venice could be citizens: in fact they are tyrants, since other humans are thereby made their slaves and enemies. Consequently Aristotle's state is contrary to nature.

A more positive evaluation of Aristotle and the Venetian republic emerges from Francesco Piccolomini's *Universa philosophia de moribus* (Universal Philosophy Concerning Ethical Matters) (completed and published in 1583). He praises individual Venetians for their virtue and also the education offered young Venetian nobles at the University of Padua preparing them for service to Venice; nobles are more suited to be led to virtue. He also discusses at length how Venice is a mixed constitution and boldly claims that of all republics it approximates most closely to the republic that is ruled by God: the City of God.

Following Aristotle, Piccolomini takes ethics and political philosophy to be parts of one science. Whereas the subject of the *Nicomachean Ethics* involves human actions as they render humans good, the subject of the *Politics* is human actions as public good arises from them, namely the forming and the preserving of republics. The five grades of virtue are the natural, moral or civil, rational, heroic, and divine. Each represents a step towards becoming like God, the purpose of virtue. For Aristotle, human happiness is found primarily in contemplation and secondarily in moral goodness, while human virtue is found primarily in wisdom and only secondarily in moral virtue. Piccolomini rejects as against Aristotle the view of Averroes and Avicenna that the highest good in this life is a cognitive union with a separate intellect.

Piccolomini emphasizes the limits of Aristotle's ethics, noting that he knew neither another life nor union with God. Theologians know from divine revelation that the highest good of such a union is available only in the next life, but it is open to humans of every age and social class. In contrast, the highest good of Aristotle is available only in this life, and is not open to children, slaves, women and the poor. Aristotle's moral virtue forms one into an upright human being, citizen and ruler, but the theologian's infused or divine virtues of faith, hope and charity form one into a Christian and a citizen of heaven. And yet Piccolomini declares the Love Command of the Gospels to be demanded by natural law.

See also: ARISTOTLE; ARISTOTLE COMMENTATORS; ARISTOTELIANISM IN THE 17TH CENTURY; ARISTOTELIANISM, MEDIEVAL; AVERROISM; DELMEDIGO, E.; HUMANISM, RENAISSANCE; LANGUAGE, RENAISSANCE PHILOSOPHY OF; LOGIC, RENAISSANCE; MELANCHTHON, P.; NIFO, A.; RENAISSANCE PHILOSOPHY; VERNIA, N.

References and further reading

Copenhaver, B.P. and Schmitt, C.B. (1992) *Renaissance Philosophy*, Oxford and New York: Oxford University Press. (A readable general account that pays only limited attention to the scholastic tradition. Good bibliography.)

Garin, E. (1966) *Storia della filosofia italiana* (History of Italian Philosophy), Turin: Piccola Biblioteca Einaudi, 499–580. (A detailed and insightful overview of Renaissance Aristotelianism by a master historian of philosophy.)

Kessler, E. (1988) 'The Intellective Soul', in C.B. Schmitt (ed.) *The Cambridge History of Renaissance Philosophy*, Cambridge: Cambridge University Press, 485–534. (An informative account of the cognitive theories of leading Renaissance Aristotelians.)

Kraye, J. (1993) 'The Philosophy of the Italian Renaissance', in G.H.R. Parkinson (ed.) *The Renaissance and Seventeenth-Century Rationalism*, London and New York: Routledge. (A brief introductory discussion with a topically-organized bibliography.)

Kristeller, P.O. (1974) 'Thomism and the Italian Thought of the Renaissance', ed. and trans. E.P. Mahoney, *Medieval Aspects of Renaissance Learning*, New York: Columbia University Press, 2nd edn; repr. 1992, 29–91. (A pioneering study of Aquinas' influence on Renaissance philosophy by a celebrated scholar.)

—— (1979) *Renaissance Thought and its Sources*, ed. M. Mooney, New York: Columbia University Press.

(A model overview of Renaissance philosophy that discusses the different interpretations of Aristotle and the development of scholasticism.)

Lohr, C.H. (1988) *Latin Aristotle Commentaries: II, Renaissance Authors*, Florence: Olschki. (Alphabetically organized list of Renaissance Aristotelians, with biographies and bibliographies of primary and secondary sources.)

Mahoney, E.P. (1980) 'Albert the Great and the *Studio Patavino* in the Late Fifteenth and Early Sixteenth Centuries', in J.A. Weisheipl (ed.) *Albertus Magnus and the Sciences. Commemorative Essays 1980*, Toronto, Ont.: Pontifical Institute of Mediaeval Studies. (Shows the important authority granted to Albert by major Renaissance Aristotelians.)

—— (1982a) 'Neoplatonism, the Greek Commentators, and Renaissance Aristotelianism', in D.J. O'Meara (ed.) *Neoplatonism and Christian Thought*, Albany, NY: State University of New York Press, 169–77, 264–82. (Demonstrates the impact of the Greek commentators and Ficino's translation of Plotinus on Renaissance Aristotelians.)

—— (1982b) 'Metaphysical Foundations of the Hierarchy of Being according to some Late Medieval and Renaissance Philosophers', in P. Morewedge (ed.) *Philosophies of Existence: Ancient and Medieval*, New York: Fordham University Press, 165–257. (A seminal article on the concept of the Great Chain of Being from Albert the Great to Cremonini and Galileo and early modern thought.)

—— (1988) 'Aristotle as "The Worst Natural Philosopher" (*pessimus naturalis*) and "The Worst Metaphysician" (*pessimus metaphysicus*): His Reputation among Some Franciscan Philosophers (Bonaventure, Francis of Meyronnes, Antonius Andreas, and Joannes Canonicus) and Later Reactions', in O. Pluta (ed.) *Die Philosophie im 14. und 15. Jahrhundert*, Amsterdam: B. Grüner, 261–73. (Some medieval attacks on Aristotle, and how they were received by Vernia and Nifo among others.)

—— (1995) 'From the Medievals to the Early Moderns: Themes and Problems in Renaissance Political Thought', in B. Carlos Bazán, E. Andújar and L.G. Sbrocchi (eds) *Les philosophies morales et politiques au Moyen Age/Moral and Political Philosophies in the Middle Ages*, Proceedings of the Ninth International Congress of Medieval Philosophy Ottawa (17–22 August 1992), Ottawa, Ont.: Legas, vol. 1, 193–225. (Pays particular attention to the influence of Plato and Aristotle as variously interpreted by Renaissance figures.)

Nardi, B. (1958) *Saggi sull'aristotelismo padovano dal secolo XIV al XVI* (Essays on Paduan Aristotelianism from the 14th to the 16th Century), Università degli Studi di Padova: Studi sulla tradizione aristotelica nel Veneto 1, Florence: Sansoni. (Classic statement of Aristotelian tradition as found in Padua: old but still very useful.)

Olivieri, L. (ed.) (1983) *Aristotelismo veneto e scienza moderna. Atti del 25° anno accademico del Centro per la Storia della Tradizione Aristotelica nel Veneto* (Venetian Aristotelianism and Modern Science), Padua: Antenore, 2 vols. (Rich collection of studies in several languages on a wide range of Aristotelian philosophers during the Renaissance.)

Poppi, A. (1966) *Causalità e infinità nella scuola padovana dal 1480 al 1513* (Causality and Infinity in the Paduan School from 1480 to 1513), Padua: Antenore. (Discusses issues such as God's intensive infinity and how this is related to God's efficient causality.)

—— (ed.) (1983) *Scienza e filosofia all'Università di Padova nel quattrocento* (Science and Philosophy at the University of Padua in the 15th Century), Contributi alla storia dell'Università di Padova 15, Padua: Edizioni Lint. (Studies on the philosophical and scientific ideas of fifteenth- and sixteenth-century thinkers including Copernicus and Pomponazzi.)

Schmitt, C.B. (1981) *Studies in Renaissance Philosophy and Science*, London: Variorum. (An important collection of informative studies by a distinguished Renaissance scholar.)

—— (1983) *Aristotle and the Renaissance*, Cambridge, MA, and London: Harvard University Press. (A very clear introduction to the subject that delineates the different types of Renaissance Aristotelianism.)

Skinner, Q. (1978) *The Foundations of Modern Political Thought*, Cambridge: Cambridge University Press, 2 vols. (A masterful account of late medieval, Renaissance and Reformation thought.)

Spruit, L. (1995) *Species Intelligibilis: From Perception to Knowledge. Vol. 2. Renaissance Controversies, Later Scholasticism, and the Elimination of the Intelligible Species in Modern Philosophy*, Brill's Studies in Intellectual History 49, Leiden: Brill. (Chronicles a large number of Italian and Spanish Aristotelians on the question of the representative nature of intellectual cognition.)

Wallace, W.A. (1972) *Causality and Scientific Explanation. Volume 1: Medieval and Early Classical Science*, Ann Arbor, MI: The University of Michigan Press. (Situates methodological doctrines of Renaissance Aristotelians in a tradition developing from Aristotle and his medieval commentators.)

EDWARD P. MAHONEY
JAMES SOUTH

ARISTOTLE (384–322 BC)

Aristotle of Stagira is one of the two most important philosophers of the ancient world, and one of the four or five most important of any time or place. He was not an Athenian, but he spent most of his life as a student and teacher of philosophy in Athens. For twenty years he was a member of Plato's Academy; later he set up his own philosophical school, the Lyceum. During his lifetime he published philosophical dialogues, of which only fragments now survive. The 'Aristotelian corpus' (1462 pages of Greek text, including some spurious works) is probably derived from the lectures that he gave in the Lyceum.

Aristotle is the founder not only of philosophy as a discipline with distinct areas or branches, but, still more generally, of the conception of intellectual inquiry as falling into distinct disciplines. He insists, for instance, that the standards of proof and evidence for deductive logic and mathematics should not be applied to the study of nature, and that neither of these disciplines should be taken as a proper model for moral and political inquiry. He distinguishes philosophical reflection on a discipline from the practice of the discipline itself. The corpus contains contributions to many different disciplines, not only to philosophy.

Some areas of inquiry in which Aristotle makes a fundamental contribution are these:

(1) Logic. Aristotle's Prior Analytics *constitutes the first attempt to formulate a system of deductive formal logic, based on the theory of the 'syllogism'. The* Posterior Analytics *uses this system to formulate an account of rigorous scientific knowledge. 'Logic', as Aristotle conceives it, also includes the study of language, meaning and their relation to non-linguistic reality; hence it includes many topics that might now be assigned to philosophy of language or philosophical logic (*Categories, De Interpretatione, Topics*).*

(2) The study of nature. About a quarter of the corpus (see especially the History of Animals, Parts of Animals, *and* Generation of Animals; *also* Movement of Animals, Progression of Animals*) consists of works concerned with biology. Some of these contain collections of detailed observations. (The* Meteorology *contains a similar collection on inanimate nature.) Others try to explain these observations in the light of the explanatory scheme that Aristotle defends in his more theoretical reflections on the study of nature. These reflections (especially in the* Physics *and in* Generation and Corruption*) develop an account of nature, form, matter, cause and change that expresses Aristotle's views about the understanding and explanation of natural organisms and their behaviour. Natural philosophy and cosmology are combined in* On the Heavens.

(3) Metaphysics. In his reflections on the foundations and presuppositions of other disciplines, Aristotle describes a universal 'science of being qua *being', the concern of the* Metaphysics. *Part of this universal science examines the foundations of inquiry into nature. Aristotle formulates his doctrine of substance, which he explains through the connected contrasts between form and matter, and between potentiality and actuality. One of his aims is to describe the distinctive and irreducible character of living organisms. Another aim of the universal science is to use his examination of substance to give an account of divine substance, the ultimate principle of the cosmic order.*

(4) Philosophy of mind. The doctrine of form and matter is used to explain the relation of soul and body, and the different types of soul found in different types of living creatures. In Aristotle's view, the soul is the form of a living body. He examines the different aspects of this form in plants, non-rational animals and human beings, by describing nutrition, perception, thought and desire. His discussion (in On the Soul, *and also in the* Parva Naturalia*) ranges over topics in philosophy of mind, psychology, physiology, epistemology and theory of action.*

*(5) Ethics and politics (*Nicomachean Ethics, Eudemian Ethics, Magna Moralia*). In Aristotle's view, the understanding of the natural and essential aims of human agents is the right basis for a grasp of principles guiding moral and political practice. These principles are expressed in his account of human wellbeing, and of the different virtues that constitute a good person and promote wellbeing. The description of a society that embodies these virtues in individual and social life is a task for the* Politics, *which also examines the virtues and vices of actual states and societies, measuring them against the principles derived from ethical theory.*

*(6) Literary criticism and rhetorical theory (*Poetics, Rhetoric*). These works are closely connected both to Aristotle's logic and to his ethical and political theory.*

1 Life
2 **Order of Aristotle's works**
3 **Appearances**
4 **Thought and language**
5 **Deduction**
6 **Knowledge, science and demonstration**
7 **Categories and beings**
8 **Change and substance**
9 **Causes**
10 **Change**
11 **Metaphysics**
12 **From being to substance**
13 **Why is form substance?**

14 What are substantial forms
15 Universals, Platonic Forms, mathematics
16 Metaphysics: God
17 Soul and body
18 Perception
19 Appearance and thought
20 Desire and voluntary action
21 The human good
22 Virtue of character
23 Virtue, practical reason and incontinence
24 Choice, virtue and pleasure
25 Virtue, friendship and the good of others
26 Two conceptions of happiness?
27 Politics: ideal states
28 Politics: imperfect states
29 Rhetoric and poetics
30 Influence

1 Life

Aristotle was born in 384 BC, in the Macedonian city of Stagira, now part of northern Greece. In his lifetime the kingdom of Macedon, first under Philip and then under Philip's son Alexander ('the Great'), conquered both the Greek cities of Europe and Asia and the Persian Empire. Although Aristotle spent much of his adult life in Athens, he was not an Athenian citizen. He was closely linked to the kings of Macedon, whom many Greeks regarded as foreign invaders; hence, he was affected by the volatile relations between Macedon and the Greek cities, especially Athens.

Aristotle was the son of Nicomachus, a doctor attached to the Macedonian court. In 367 BC Aristotle came to Athens. He belonged to Plato's Academy until the death of Plato in 347; during these years Plato wrote his important later dialogues (including the *Sophist*, *Timaeus*, *Philebus*, *Statesman*, and *Laws*), which reconsider many of the doctrines of his earlier dialogues and pursue new lines of thought. Since there was no dogmatic system of 'Platonism', Aristotle was neither a disciple of such a system nor a rebel against it. The exploratory and critical outlook of the Academy probably encouraged Aristotle's own philosophical growth.

In 347 BC Aristotle left Athens, for Assos in Asia Minor. Later he moved to Lesbos, in the eastern Aegean, and then to Macedon, where he was a tutor of Alexander. In 334 he returned to Athens and founded his own school, the Lyceum. In 323 Alexander died; in the resulting outbreak of anti-Macedonian feeling in Athens Aristotle left for Chalcis, on the island of Euboea, where he died in 322.

Aristotle married Pythias, a niece of Hermeias, the ruler of Assos. They had a daughter, also called Pythias. After the death of his wife, Aristotle formed an attachment to Herpyllis, and they had a son Nicomachus.

2 Order of Aristotle's works

By the end of Aristotle's life the Lyceum must have become a well-established school. It lasted after Aristotle's death; his successor as head of the school was his pupil THEOPHRASTUS. Many of the works in the Aristotelian corpus appear to be closely related to Aristotle's lectures in the Lyceum. The polished character of some passages suggests preparation for publication (for example, *Parts of Animals* I 5), but many passages contain incomplete sentences and compressed allusions, suggesting notes that a lecturer might expand (for example, *Metaphysics* VII 13). We cannot tell how many of his treatises Aristotle regarded as 'finished' (see §11 on the *Metaphysics* and §21 on the *Ethics*).

It may be wrong, therefore, to ask about the 'date' of a particular treatise. If Aristotle neither published nor intended to publish the treatises, a given treatise may easily contain contributions from different dates. For similar reasons, we cannot plausibly take cross-references from one work to another as evidence of the order of the works. External, biographical considerations are unhelpful, since we lack the evidence to support any detailed intellectual biography of Aristotle.

A few points, however, may suggest a partial chronology.

(1) Some of Aristotle's frequent critical discussions of Plato and other Academics may have been written (in some version) during Aristotle's years in the Academy. The *Topics* may reflect the character of dialectical debates in the Academy.

(2) It is easier to understand the relation of the doctrine of substance in the *Categories* and *Physics* I–II to the doctrine and argument of *Metaphysics* VII if we suppose that *Metaphysics* VII is later.

(3) The Organon (see §4) does not mention matter, perhaps because (a) Aristotle had not yet thought of it, or because (b) he regarded it as irrelevant to the topics considered in the Organon. If (a) is correct, the Organon precedes the works on natural philosophy.

(4) Some of the observations used in Aristotle's biological works probably came from the eastern Aegean. Hence, Aristotle probably pursued his biological research during his years away from Athens. We might trace his biological interests to the Academy (see Plato's *Timaeus*); he may also have acquired them from his father Nicomachus, who was a doctor. Probably, then, at least some of the

biological works (or versions of them) are not the latest works in the corpus.

(5) The *Magna Moralia* (if it is genuine) and the *Eudemian Ethics* probably precede the *Nicomachean Ethics* (see §21).

The order in which Aristotle's works appear in the Greek manuscripts goes back to early editors and commentators (from the first century BC to the sixth century AD); it reflects their view not about the order in which the works were written, but about the order in which they should be studied. This entry generally follows the order of the corpus, except that it discusses *On the Soul* after the *Metaphysics* (see §17), not among the works on natural philosophy (where it appears in the manuscripts).

3 Appearances

The general aim of rational inquiry, according to Aristotle, is to advance from what is 'better known to us' to what is 'better known by nature' (see *Physics* I 1; *Posterior* Analytics 71b33; *Metaphysics* 1029b3). We achieve this aim if: (1) we replace propositions that we thought we knew with propositions that we really know because they are true and we understand them; (2) we find general principles that explain and justify the more specific truths that we began from; (3) we find those aspects of reality that explain the aspects that are more familiar to us.

The things better known to us in a particular area are the relevant 'appearances' (*phainomena*). Aristotle presents them through detailed collections of empirical data, reached as a result of 'inquiry' (*historia*; for example, *Parts of Animals* 646a8). Empirical inquiry proceeds from particular observations, by means of generalizations through induction (*epagōgē*) from these particular cases, until we reach experience (*empeiria*). Experience leads us to principles that are better known by nature (*Prior Analytics* 46a17); we also rely on it to test principles we have found (*Generation of Animals* 760b28).

Philosophical inquiry also relies on 'appearances'. However, the appearances that concern it are not empirical observations, but common beliefs, assumptions widely shared by 'the many and the wise'. The critical and constructive study of these common beliefs is 'dialectic'. Aristotle's method is basically Socratic. He raises puzzles in the common beliefs, looking for an account that will do them justice as a whole. Among common beliefs Aristotle considers the views of his predecessors (for example, *Metaphysics* I; *On the Soul* I; *Politics* II), because the puzzles raised by their views help us to find better solutions than they found.

Inquiry leads us to causes and to universals. Aristotle has a realist conception of inquiry and knowledge; beliefs and theories are true in so far as they grasp the reality that we inquire into (see REALISM AND ANTIREALISM §2). Universals and causes are 'prior by nature'; they are not created by, or dependent on, any theory, but a true theory must fit them.

If we attended only to Aristotle's remarks on what is better known to us and on the process of inquiry, we might regard his position as a form of empiricism (see EMPIRICISM). But in his remarks on what is better known by nature, he insists on the reality of universals and on the importance of non-sensory forms of knowledge (see §15 on universals, §19 on thought).

4 Thought and language

One means of access to appearances, and especially to common beliefs, is the study of what words and sentences 'signify' (*sēmainein*). This is part of 'logic' (*logikē*, derived from *logos*, which may be translated 'word', 'speech', 'statement', 'argument' or 'reason': see LOGOS), which is discussed in the first section of Aristotle's works (*Categories, De Interpretatione, Prior Analytics, Posterior Analytics, Topics*). This section of the corpus came to be called the 'Organon' ('instrument'), because logic, as Aristotle conceives it, concerns statements and arguments in general, without restriction to any specific subject matter; it is therefore an instrument of philosophical inquiry in general, rather than a branch of philosophy coordinate with natural philosophy or ethics. The Organon includes some elements of philosophy of language, as well as formal logic (syllogistic; see §5) and epistemology (see §6).

According to Aristotle's account of signification (see especially *De Interpretatione* 1–4), as commonly understood, the word 'horse' signifies horse by signifying the thought of horse; in using the word, we communicate thoughts about horses. When the thoughts about horses we communicate are true, we communicate truths about the universal horse; even when our thoughts are not completely true, we may signify the same universal horse.

To understand the signification of a name '*F*', we look for the corresponding definition (*logos, horismos*) of *F*. Aristotle distinguishes nominal definitions, stating the beliefs associated with the name, from real definitions, giving a true account of the universal that underlies the beliefs embodied in the nominal definition (see *Posterior Analytics* II 8–10. Aristotle himself does not use the labels 'nominal definition' and 'real definition'.).

Not every name corresponds to one nominal and one real definition. Some names correspond to no genuine universal; 'goatstag' signifies (in one way) animals that are both goats and stags, but it does not signify a genuine universal, since there is no natural kind of goatstag. Other names correspond to more than one universal, as 'chest' signifies both a container and a part of an animal. Chests are 'homonymous' (*homōnyma*) or 'multivocal' (*pollachōs legomena*; 'spoken of in many ways'); more than one definition is needed to capture the signification of the name. By contrast, since only one definition corresponds to the name 'horse', horses are 'synonymous' (*Categories* 1).

Other philosophers make serious errors, Aristotle believes, because they suppose they can give a single account of things or properties that are really multivocal. Once we see that different *F*s are *F* in different ways, we see that different, although (in many cases) connected, accounts of what it is to be *F* must be given. Some philosophically important cases of multivocity are cause (Aristotle's doctrine of the four causes; see §9), being (the doctrine of the categories; see §7) and good (the criticism of Plato's belief in a Form of the Good; *Nicomachean Ethics* I 6).

5 Deduction

Part of logic, as Aristotle conceives it, is the study of good and bad arguments. In the *Topics* Aristotle treats dialectical arguments in general. In the *Prior Analytics* he examines one type of argument, a 'deduction' (*syllogismos*; literally, 'reasoning', hence the standard term 'syllogism'). This is an argument in which, if propositions *p* and *q* are assumed, something else *r*, different from *p* and *q*, follows necessarily because of the truth of *p* and *q* (*Prior Analytics* 24b18–20, paraphrased). Aristotle insists that it is not possible for the premises of a deduction to be true and the conclusion false ('follows necessarily'); that a deduction must have more than one premise ('if *p* and *q* are assumed'); that the conclusion cannot be identical to any premise ('different from *p* and *q*'); and that no redundant premises are allowed ('because of the truth of *p* and *q*'). He takes deductions to express affirmative or negative relations between universals, taken either universally ('Animal belongs to every (no) man') or not universally ('Animal belongs (does not belong) to some man'). He takes the affirmative and negative claims to imply existence (so that 'Biped belongs to some dodo' follows from 'Biped belongs to every dodo'; the latter affirmation is not equivalent, therefore, to 'If anything is a dodo, it is biped').

These different features of an Aristotelian deduction differentiate Aristotle's account of a deduction from a more familiar account of deductively valid arguments. An argument may be valid even if it is redundant, or a premise is identical to the conclusion, or it has only one premise, or it is about particulars, or it contains neither 'some' nor 'every' nor 'belongs'; but no such argument is an Aristotelian deduction. Aristotle's theory of the different forms of deduction (often called 'the moods of the syllogism') examines the various forms of argument that necessarily preserve the truth of their premises. He begins from 'complete' (or 'perfect') deductions whose validity is evident, and classifies the different types of arguments that can be derived from (shown to be equivalent to) the complete deductions. He also explores the logical relations between propositions involving modalities ('Necessarily (possibly) animal belongs to every man' and so on). Since Aristotle accepts this relatively narrow account of a deduction, his exploration of the different forms of deduction is not a theory of valid arguments in general; the Stoics come much closer to offering such a theory (see STOICISM §11; LOGIC, ANCIENT).

Aristotle's theory of deduction is developed for its own sake, but it also has two main philosophical applications. (1) Deduction is one type of argument appropriate to dialectic (and, with modifications, to rhetoric; see §29). Aristotle contrasts it with inductive argument (also used in dialectic), in which the conclusion does not follow necessarily from the premises, but is made plausible by them. (2) It is essential for demonstration (*apodeixis*), which Aristotle takes to be the appropriate form for exhibiting scientific knowledge.

6 Knowledge, science and demonstration

The progress from what is known to us to what is known by nature aims at *epistēmē*, the scientific knowledge whose structure is exhibited in the demonstrative pattern described in the *Posterior Analytics*. A demonstration is a deduction in which the premises are necessarily true, prior to and better known than the conclusions, and explanatory of the conclusions derived from them. Aristotle assumes that if I know that *p*, then I can cite some justification *q*, to justify my belief that *p*, and I also know why *q* justifies *p* (*Posterior Analytics* I 2). The right sort of justification relies on things better known by nature – the general laws and principles that explain the truth of *p*. Since these are embodied in demonstrations, grasp of a demonstration of *p* expresses knowledge of *p*. Aristotle's theory of demonstration, then, is not intended to describe a procedure of scientific inquiry that begins from appearances; it is an account of the knowledge that is achieved by successful inquiry.

To show that a deduction is a demonstration, we

417

must show that its premises are better known than the conclusion. Sometimes we can show this by demonstrating them from higher premises that are even better known. This process of justification, Aristotle claims, must be linear and finite. A circular 'justification' must eventually 'justify' a given belief by appeal to itself, and an infinite regress imposes on us a task that we can never complete. Since, therefore, neither a circle nor an infinite regress can really justify, a proper justification must ultimately appeal to primary principles of a science.

These primary principles are 'assumptions' (*hypotheseis*); we must see that they are better known and prior to other truths of a science, without being derived from any further principles. Since they are the basis of all demonstration, they cannot themselves be demonstrated; Aristotle claims that we have non-demonstrative understanding (*nous*: *Posterior Analytics* II 19) of the ultimate principles of each science (see Nous).

How are we entitled to claim understanding of an ultimate principle? Aristotle believes that the principles of a science are reached from appearances (perceptual or dialectical or both), which are the starting points known to us. He may believe that this relation of the principles to appearances justifies us in accepting them as first principles and in claiming to have understanding of them. This explanation, however, does not easily fit Aristotle's demand for linear and finite chains of justification. That demand suggests that the assumptions of a science must be self-evident (seen to be true without any inferential justification), so that his conception of knowledge expresses a foundationalist position (see Foundationalism §3). (On difficulties in foundationalism see Agrippa.)

Although Aristotle's aim of reaching a demonstrative science reveals some of his epistemological doctrines and assumptions, it does not evidently influence most of the structure or content of most of the surviving treatises. In his main philosophical works, the influence of dialectical methods and aims is more apparent.

7 Categories and beings

Part of the task of logic is to explain the nature of predication ('*A* is *B*', analysed by Aristotle as '*B* is predicated of *A*' or '*B* belongs to *A*', as in 'Animal belongs to every man'), which is presupposed by complex *logoi* (statements and arguments). In the *Categories* (*katēgoriai*; predications), Aristotle introduces ten 'categories' (usually called *schēmata tēs katēgorias*, 'figures (that is, types) of predication'). The categories correspond to different sorts of words (for example, count-nouns, adjectives, verbs) and to different grammatical functions (for example, subject, predicate), but they primarily classify the different non-linguistic items introduced in predications. The sentences 'Socrates is a man' and 'Socrates is a musician' are grammatically similar, but they introduce different sorts of things; the first predicates a second substance of a first substance, whereas the second predicates a non-substance of a first substance.

The first category is called *ousia* (literally, 'being'), which is translated into Latin as 'substantia', and hence usually called 'substance' (see Substance §1). The nine non-substance categories include quality, quantity and relative (the only ones that Aristotle refers to often; the categories are listed in *Categories* 4, *Topics* I 9). Each category contains both particulars and universals. The statement that this individual man is an animal predicates a second substance (that is, a universal in the category of substance) of a first substance (that is, a particular in the category of substance). 'White is a colour' predicates one universal quality of another.

The categories display the multivocity of beings (see §4). Whereas animals constitute an ordinary univocal genus with a single definition, beings do not constitute an ordinary genus; hence there is no single account of what it is for something to be a being. Aristotle believes Plato mistakenly pursued a single account of beings; the theory of categories is meant to avoid Platonic errors.

In marking categorial divisions, Aristotle is influenced by grammar and syntax, but also by his ontology – his classification of beings. This classification rests on his view of nature and change, which clarifies his analysis of predication.

8 Change and substance

Aristotle's *Physics* discusses nature, *physis*. The nature of *x* is a principle (or 'source'; *archē*), internal to *x*, of change and stability in *x*; hence the inquiry into nature leads to a discussion of change in natural substances (the elements, plants and animals). Aristotle proceeds dialectically, raising and solving puzzles involved in the understanding of natural change. In solving the puzzles, he introduces the different types of beings that are presupposed by a coherent account of natural change.

In *Physics* I 7–8, Aristotle analyses a simple example of change – Socrates changing from being pale to being tanned. This change involves a subject (or 'underlying thing'; *hypokeimenon*), Socrates, who loses one contrary (his pale colour) and acquires another contrary (his tan). Neither of the contraries persists, but the subject persists (otherwise there would not be a change in Socrates). This particular subject that persists through change is what the *Categories* calls a first substance. First substances differ both from second substances and from non-substances by being capable of undergoing change; they persist while receiving opposites (as Socrates is first pale and then tanned). They cannot, however, remain in existence irrespective of any properties gained or lost; Socrates' ceasing to be a man is not a change in Socrates, but the perishing of Socrates.

The properties that a first substance cannot lose without perishing constitute (approximately) the essence of that first substance (see ESSENTIALISM). These essential properties define a kind to which the first substance belongs. A kind may be a species (*eidos*), for example, man or horse, or a genus (*genos*), for example, animal. In predicating a second substance of a first substance (as in 'Socrates is a man'), we place the first substance in the kind it belongs to. If we predicate one of the contraries that the first substance can lose without perishing, we introduce an item (Socrates' pale colour, his particular height, his ignorance, his being the husband of Xanthippe) in one of the non-substance categories (quality, quantity, relative, and so on). The kinds to which these non-substantial items belong are non-substantial universals.

Aristotle also examines the coming to be and perishing of a first substance. Here again, he distinguishes a persisting subject and two contraries. If we make a statue from bronze, the lump of bronze (the subject) acquires the shape of the statue, and loses the shapelessness it had, and so changes between contraries. But although the lump remains in existence, a new subject, the statue, has come into being. In this case, the subject of the change is the matter (*hylē*), and what it acquires is the form (*eidos*, also rendered 'species').

This analysis of change suggests an argument (*Physics* II 1) to show that the genuine subject, and hence the genuine substance, is the matter, whereas the apparent substance (for example, the statue) is simply matter with a certain shape. Socrates does not become another subject if he changes shape; hence (we may argue) the lump of bronze does not become another subject simply by acquiring the shape of a statue. Similarly, then, a natural organism might be understood as a piece of matter shaped in a certain way so as to embody Socrates. Natural organic 'substances', such as Socrates and this tree, turn out to be not genuine subjects, but mere configurations of the matter that is the real substance.

Aristotle does not endorse this eliminative attitude to natural organic substances. He uses the argument to raise a puzzle about whether matter or form is substance. He discusses this puzzle in *Metaphysics* VII (see §12–14). This discussion relies on his account of causation and explanation.

9 Causes

When we correctly answer questions such as 'Why does this event happen?', or 'Why is this object as it is?', we state the cause (or explanation; *aition*) of the event or object. Aristotle believes that causes are multivocal (see *Physics* II 3; *Metaphysics* I 3). Different accounts of a cause correspond to different answers to why-questions about (for example) a statue. (1) 'It is made of bronze' states the material cause. (2) 'It is a statue representing Pericles' states the formal cause, by stating the definition that says what the thing is. (3) 'A sculptor made it' states the 'source of change', by mentioning the source of the process that brought the statue into being; later writers call this the 'moving cause' or 'efficient cause'. (4) 'It is made to represent Pericles' states 'that for the sake of which', since it mentions the goal or end for the sake of which the statue was made; this is often called the 'final' (Latin *finis*; 'end') cause.

Each of the four causes answers a why-question. Sometimes (as in our example) a complete answer requires all four causes. Not all four, however, are always appropriate; the (universal) triangle, for example, has a formal cause, stating its definition, but no efficient cause, since it does not come into being, and no final cause, since it is not made to promote any goal or end.

Some have claimed that Aristotle's 'four causes' are not really causes at all, pointing out that he takes an *aition* to be available even in cases where the why-question (for example, 'Why do the interior angles of this figure add up to two right angles?') does not seek what we would call a cause (in Aristotle's division, an efficient cause). When explanations of changes are being sought, however, Aristotle seems to provide recognizably causal explanations. Even the *aitia* (material, formal, final) that do not initially seem to be causes turn out to play an important role in causal explanation; for this reason, the label 'four causes' gives a reasonably accurate impression of Aristotle's doctrine.

His comparison between artefacts and natural organisms clarifies his claims about formal and final causes. The definition of an artefact requires reference to the goal and the intended function. A hammer's form and essence is a capacity to hammer nails into wood. The hammer was designed to have this capacity for performing this function; and if this had not been its function, it would not have been made in the way it was, to have the properties it has. The form includes the final cause, by specifying the functions that explain why the hammer is made as it is.

Similarly, Aristotle claims, a natural organism has a formal cause specifying the function that is the final cause of the organism. The parts of an organism seem to perform functions that benefit the whole (the heart pumps blood, the senses convey useful information). Aristotle claims that organs have final causes; they exist in order to carry out the beneficial functions they actually carry out. The form of an organism is determined by the pattern of activity that contains the final causes of its different vital processes. Hence Aristotle believes that form as well as matter plays a causal role in natural organisms.

To claim that a heart is for pumping blood to benefit the organism is to claim that there is some causal connection between the benefit to the organism and the processes that constitute the heart's pumping blood. Aristotle makes this causal claim without saying why it is true. He does not say, for instance, either (1) that organisms are the products of intelligent design (as Plato and the Stoics believe), or (2) that they are the outcome of a process of evolution.

Aristotle's account of causation and explanation is expressed in the content and argument of many of his biological works (including those connected with psychology). In the *Parts of Animals* and *Generation of Animals* for instance, he examines the behaviour and structure of organisms and their parts both to find the final causes and to describe the material and efficient basis of the goal-direction that he finds in nature (*Parts of Animals* I 1). He often argues that different physiological processes in different animals have the same final cause.

Some ascribe to Aristotle an 'incompatibilist' view of the relation between final causes and the underlying material and efficient causes. Incompatibilists concede that every goal-directed process (state, event) requires some material process (as nutrition, for example, requires the various processes involved in digesting food), but they argue that the goal-directed process cannot be wholly constituted by any material process or processes; any process wholly constituted by material processes is (according to the incompatibilist) fully explicable in material-efficient terms, and therefore has no final cause.

Probably, however, Aristotle takes a 'compatibilist' view. He seems to believe that even if every goal-directed process were wholly constituted by material processes, each of which can be explained in material-efficient terms, the final-causal explanation would still be the only adequate explanation of the process as a whole. According to this view, final causes are irreducible to material-efficient causes, because the explanations given by final causes cannot be replaced by equally good explanations referring only to these other causes. This irreducibility, however, does not require the denial of material constitution.

10 Change

Aristotle studies nature as an internal principle of change and stability; and so he examines the different types of change (or 'motion'; *kinēsis*) that are found in the natural elements and in the natural organisms composed of them. In *Physics* III 1 he defines change as 'the actuality of the potential *qua* potential'. His definition marks the importance of his views on potentiality (or 'capacity'; *dynamis*) and actuality (or 'realization'; *energeia* or *entelecheia*) (see *Metaphysics* IX 1–9).

The primary type of potentiality is a principle (*archē*) of change and stability. If x has the potentiality F for G, then (1) G is the actuality of F, and (2) x has F because G is the actuality of F. Marathon runners, for instance, have the potentiality to run 26 miles because they have been trained to run this distance; hearts have the capacity to pump blood because this is the function that explains the character of hearts. In these cases, potentialities correspond to final causes.

Potentiality and possibility do not, therefore, imply each other. (1) Not everything that is possible for x realizes a potentiality of x. Perhaps it is possible for us to speak words of Italian (because we recall them from an opera) without having a potentiality to speak Italian (if we have not learnt Italian). (2) Not everything that x is capable of is possible for x; some creatures would still have a potentiality to swim even if their environment lost all its water.

These points about potentiality help to clarify Aristotle's definition of change. The building of a house is a change because it is the actuality of what is potentially built in so far as it is potentially built. 'What is potentially built' refers to the bricks (and so on). The completed house is their complete actuality, and when it is reached, their potentiality to be built is lost. The process of building is their actuality in so far as they are potentially built. 'In so far...' picks out the incomplete actuality that is present only as long as the potentiality to be built (lost in the completed house) is still present. Aristotle's definition picks out the kind of actuality that is to be identified with change, by appealing to some prior understanding of potentiality and actuality, which in turn rests on an understanding of final causation.

In the rest of the *Physics*, Aristotle explores different properties of change in relation to place and time. He discusses infinity and continuity at length, arguing that both change and time are infinitely divisible. He tries to show that the relevant type of infinity can be defined by reference to potentiality, so as to avoid self-contradiction, paradox or metaphysical extravagance. In his view, infinite divisibility requires a series that can always be continued, but does not require the actual existence of an infinitely long series. Once again, the reference to potentiality (in 'can always...') has a crucial explanatory role.

11 Metaphysics

Some of the basic concepts of the *Categories* and *Physics* – including substance, particular, universal, form, matter, cause and potentiality – are discussed more fully in the *Metaphysics*. This is a collection of fourteen books, some of them loosely connected. Aristotle probably did not deliver a course of lectures in the order of the present treatise. Parts of book I are almost repeated in book XIII. Book V is a 'philosophical dictionary' that seems to interrupt the argument of books IV and VI. Book XI summarizes parts of book IV. Books II and XI were probably not written entirely by Aristotle.

Still, whatever their literary origins, all these books have a common subject matter, since they all contribute to the universal science that studies the common presuppositions of the other sciences. This universal science has four names. (1) 'First philosophy': it studies the 'first principles' and 'highest causes' (including the four causes of the *Physics*) presupposed by the other sciences. (2) 'The science of being': every science presupposes that it studies some sort of being, and the science of being examines and defends this presupposition. (3) 'Theology': first philosophy is not only first in so far it is most universal, but also in so far as it deals with the primary sort of being, the sort on which all other beings depend. The primary sort of being is substance, and the primary sort of substance is divine substance; hence the science of being must study divine substance. (4) 'Metaphysics' (*ta meta ta physika*; 'the things after the natural things'): it is 'after' or 'beyond' the study of nature because (a) as theology, it studies entities outside the natural order, and (b) as first philosophy, it starts from the study of nature (which is prior and better known 'to us') and goes beyond it to its foundations and presuppositions (which are prior and better known 'by nature'; see §3).

The first three of these names are used by Aristotle himself (*Metaphysics* IV 1–3, VI 1). The fourth was given to the treatise in antiquity (at an uncertain date); its use of 'after' captures Aristotle's different claims about the relation of the universal science to other sciences.

The universal science is the science of being *qua* being – that is, being in so far as it is being – just as mathematics is the science of some beings *qua* mathematical objects (see §16) and physics is the science of some beings *qua* changeable. The science of being studies the beings that are also studied by other sciences, but it isolates the relevant properties of beings by a different level of abstraction; it does not rely on the fact that they have the properties of mathematical or natural objects, but simply on the fact that they are beings studied by a science (*Metaphysics* IV 1–2).

A special science assumes that it begins with a subject that has properties. The universal science is the science of being because it studies the sort of subject that is presupposed by the other sciences; and it is primarily the science of substance because substance is the primary sort of being. Aristotle's analysis of change in *Physics* I introduces substances as subjects; the *Metaphysics* asks what sorts of subjects and substances must be recognized by special sciences.

Aristotle argues that if we are to signify a subject, it is impossible for each of its properties both to belong and not to belong to it. This principle is often called the 'Principle of Non-Contradiction' (*Metaphysics* IV 3–4). To defend the principle, Aristotle considers an opponent who is willing to assert that a single subject, man, is both a bipedal animal and not a biped animal. If the opponent really says this about a single subject, then, when he uses 'man', he must signify one and the same subject, man. If he agrees that in using 'man' he signifies a biped animal, then he cannot also deny that man is a biped animal; for if he denies this, he can no longer say what 'man' signifies, and hence he cannot say what subject it is that he takes to be both a biped animal and not a biped animal. This property (which one cannot also deny of a subject) is an essential property. Hence, the attempt to reject subjects with essential properties is self-undermining.

Subjects of change must also, according to Aristotle, have objective properties (that is, properties that they have whether or not they appear to have them). An argument against Protagoras seeks to show that any attempt to reject objective properties undermines itself (*Metaphysics* IV 5). PROTAGORAS denies that there are any objective properties, because he claims that how things appear to someone is how they are. If he is to maintain the infallibility of appearances against any possibility of correction, then, Aristotle argues, he must claim that it is possible for the same subject to change in every respect at every time (to match different appearances). This is possible, however, only if the same subject can remain in being, but change in all respects. Aristotle replies that if the same subject persists, it must keep the same essential property (the 'form'); hence it cannot change in every respect (IV 5).

12 From being to substance

In *Metaphysics* IV 2 and VII 1 Aristotle argues that, since substance is the primary type of being and other beings are in some way dependent on substances, the science of being must primarily be concerned with substance. The arguments of IV 4–5 describe some features of substances; they must be subjects with stable, objective, essential properties. Books VII–IX describe these subjects more fully, by re-examining the conception of substance that is presented in the *Categories* and *Physics* (see §§7–8).

Aristotle observes that we regard substance both as 'a this' and as 'essence' (or 'what it is'). We might assume that these two descriptions pick out two sorts of substances – a particular subject ('this') and a universal ('what it is'), corresponding to the first and second substances of the *Categories*. Aristotle, however, insists that his question 'What is substance?' will be satisfactorily answered only when we have found the one thing that best satisfies the conditions for being both a subject (a 'this') and an essence ('what it is'). Whatever best satisfies these conditions is primary substance.

The different candidates that Aristotle considers for this role are matter, form and the compound of the two. He argues against the first and third candidates, and defends the second. He regards matter and compound as types of substance, but argues that they are secondary to form because they do not meet the relevant conditions to the same degree. To show that form is primary substance, he argues that a form is both a subject and an essence of the right sort. In books VIII–IX he clarifies his answer by identifying form with the actuality for which the matter is the potentiality.

13 Why is form substance?

In claiming that form is substance, Aristotle relies on the connections between form, cause, essence and identity. He rejects the eliminative view (§8) that the so-called 'coming-to-be' or 'perishing' of an artefact or organism is simply an alteration of the matter. According to the eliminative view, this alteration does not involve the existence or non-existence of a distinct substance, any more than Socrates' coming to be musical involves the existence of a distinct substance, musical Socrates. Aristotle replies that the production of an artefact and the generation of an organism introduce a new subject, a substance that is neither identical to nor wholly dependent on the matter that constitutes it at a time (see IDENTITY §2). Although this statue of Pericles has come into being from a particular piece of bronze, we may repair the statue by replacing damaged bits; we preserve the same statue but we cause a different bit of bronze to constitute it. Similarly, an organism remains in existence as long as it replaces its matter with new matter: it persists as long as its form persists (*Generation and Corruption* I 5).

When Aristotle speaks of the relation of form to matter, he may refer to either of two kinds of matter: (1) the proximate, organic matter (for example, the organs and limbs making up the organic body); and (2) the remote, non-organic matter (for example, blood, earth, water) of which the organic body is made. Remote matter can exist without the form of the organism, but the organism can persist without any particular piece of remote matter. Proximate matter cannot exist without the form (since it is the function of an arm or heart that makes it the limb or organ it is); the form is the actuality of which the proximate matter is the potentiality (*On the Soul* 412a10; *Metaphysics* 1038b6, 1042b10).

The role of the form in determining the persistence of an organism results from its role as the source of unity. The form, including the organism's vital functions, makes a heap of material constituents into a single organism (*Metaphysics* VII 16). A collection of flesh and bones constitutes a single living organism in so far as it has the form of a man or a horse; the vital functions of the single organism are the final cause of the movements of the different parts. The organism remains in being through changes of matter, as long as it retains its formal, functional properties. Since the structure, behaviour and persistence of the organism must be understood by reference to its form, the form is irreducible to matter (see §9); the organism, defined by its form, must be treated as a subject in its own right, not simply as a heap of matter.

These facts about organisms explain why Aristotle sees a close connection between primary substance and form. Organisms are substances primarily because of their formal properties, not because of their material composition; hence we cannot identify all the basic subjects there are unless we recognize the reality of formal properties and of subjects that are essentially formal.

14 What are substantial forms?

The conclusion that primary substance and form are

closely connected, however, explains only why some substances are essentially formal; it does not explain why form itself is substance. To explain this further claim, we need to decide whether Aristotle regards a substantial form as (1) a species form (shared by all members of a given species, for example, the form of man or horse), normally taken to be a universal, or as (2) a particular form, proprietary to (for example) Socrates. (See *Metaphysics* VII 10–16, XII 5, XIII 10, *Generation of Animals* IV 3 for important evidence.)

Some points favouring the 'universal solution' are the following. (1) Aristotle often contrasts the form with the compound of form and matter, and describes particulars as compounds; hence he apparently does not regard particulars as forms. (2) Similarly, he says that a particular differs from a universal in having both form and matter; hence no particular seems to be simply a form. (3) He says the form is what is specified in a definition, but there is no definition of a particular; hence a particular apparently cannot be a form. (4) He says that substance is prior in knowledge to non-substance, but scientific knowledge of particulars is impossible; hence they apparently cannot be substances, and only a universal can be a substance.

In favour of the 'particular solution' it may be argued: (1) a substance must be a subject, whereas all universals are said of subjects; (2) a substance must be a 'this', as opposed to a 'such', and hence, apparently, some sort of particular; (3) Aristotle argues at length that no universal can be a substance.

We might be tempted to conclude that Aristotle's position is inconsistent. His conviction that substance as 'this' and substance as 'what is it' must be the same thing leads him to insist that the successful candidate for substance must satisfy the criteria for being both a this (a subject, and hence a particular) and an essence (a property, and hence a universal). If one and the same thing cannot satisfy both criteria, then no one thing can satisfy all Aristotle's conditions for being a substance.

We need not draw this conclusion, however. We can maintain that Aristotle consistently favours the universal solution, if we can show: (1) a 'this' need not be a particular; (2) some universals are subjects; (3) a species form is not the sort of universal that cannot be a substance.

We can maintain that he consistently favours the particular solution, if we can show the following. (1) The contrast between form and matter does not imply that they are always mutually exclusive; some forms may be constituted by, or embodied in, particular bits of matter. Sometimes, indeed, Aristotle speaks as though a form is a subject that can persist and perish and can exchange its matter. (2) The sense in which particulars do not allow definition and scientific knowledge does not prevent them from also being, in an appropriate sense, prior in definition and knowledge to universals (*Metaphysics* XIII 10 may attribute the relevant priority to particular substances).

These two solutions are different ways of expressing Aristotle's belief that substances are basic. Both his metaphysics and his natural philosophy express and defend the conviction that natural organisms and their kinds are substances because they are fundamental; they are fundamental because they are irreducible to their constituent matter. It is more difficult to decide whether the individuals or their kinds are more fundamental. Perhaps, indeed, we ought not to decide; different things may be fundamental or irreducible in different ways.

15 Universals, Platonic Forms, mathematics

These disputes partly concern Aristotle's attitude to the reality of universals. One-sided concentration on some of his remarks may encourage a nominalist or conceptualist interpretation (see NOMINALISM §§1,2). (1) He rejects Plato's belief (as he understands it) in separated universal Forms (see PLATO §§10, 12–16), claiming that only particulars are separable. (2) In *Metaphysics* VII 13–16 he appears to argue that no universal can be a substance. (3) He claims that the universal as object of knowledge is – in a way – identical to the knowledge of it (*On the Soul* 417b23).

Other remarks, however, suggest realism about universals. (4) He claims they are better known by nature; this status seems to belong only to things that really exist. (5) He believes that if there is knowledge, then there must be universals to be objects of it; for our knowledge is about external nature, not about the contents of our own minds.

Aristotle's position is consistent if (1)–(3) are consistent with the realist tendency of (4)–(5). The denial of separation in (1) allows the reality of universals. Similarly, (2) may simply say that no universals are primary substances (which are his main concern in *Metaphysics* VII). And (3) may simply mean (depending on how we take 'in a way') that the mind's conception of the extra-mental universal has some of the features of the universal (as a map has some of the features of the area that it maps). While Aristotle denies that universals can exist without sensible particulars to embody them, he believes they are real properties of these sensible particulars.

He offers a rather similar defence of the reality, without separability, of mathematical objects (*Physics* II 2; *Metaphysics* XIII 3). While agreeing with the Platonist view that there are truths about, for example, numbers or triangles that do not describe the sensible properties of sensible objects, he denies that these truths have to be about independently-existing mathematical objects. He claims that they are truths about certain properties of sensible objects, which we can grasp when we 'take away' (or 'abstract') the irrelevant properties (for example, the fact that this triangular object is made of bronze). Even though there are no separate objects that have simply mathematical properties, there are real mathematical properties of sensible objects.

16 Metaphysics: God

When Aristotle claims that first philosophy is also theology (see §11), he implies that the general discussion of being and substance is the basis for the special discussion of divine substance. (Hence later writers distinguish 'special metaphysics', dealing with God, from 'general metaphysics', dealing with being in general.) The different features of substance explained in *Metaphysics* VII–IX are included in the divine substance of XII. (1) Primary substance is to be identified in some way with form rather than with matter or with the compound of form and matter; divine substance is pure form without matter. (2) Primary substance is in some way numerically one, a 'this' rather than a 'such'; divine substance is completely one and indivisible. (3) Primary substance is in some way actuality rather than potentiality; divine substance is pure actuality with no potentiality. (4) Primary substance is soul rather than body (see §17); divine substance is pure intellect without sense or body.

In each case the properties of primary substance are found in a sensible substance (an animal or a plant) only in so far as they belong to an object that also has other properties; hence primary substance in sensible reality is the form and actuality of an object (a horse, for example) that also has matter and potentiality. In divine substance, however, each feature is found in separation from these other properties; that is why a divine substance lacks matter, multiplicity, parts or potentiality. Aristotle argues that a substance with these pure substantial properties must exist if any sensible substances are to exist; for the existence of potentialities that can be actualized presupposes the existence of an actuality that does not itself include any potentiality (to avoid an infinite regress).

Since this primary type of substance is divine, it is what traditional belief in the Olympian gods was about, what the Presocratics were talking about when they spoke of 'the divine', and what Plato was talking about in speaking of a supreme god. Aristotle mentions the traditional Olympian gods without committing himself to acceptance of the traditional conception of them. He rejects anthropomorphic views of the gods, but he speaks of the divine nature as a kind of mind. He believes that there is something divine about the order and workings of nature, and still more divine in the heavenly substances (*Parts of Animals* I 5). Although he continues to speak of gods in the plural, he also speaks of one divine mind as the ultimate cause of the whole universe; these remarks help to justify the later interpreters who take him to speak of the one God who is the subject of (for example) Aquinas' 'Five Ways' (*Summa Theologiae* 1a q.2 a.3) (see AQUINAS, T. §11).

Aristotle's God is the ultimate cause of the physical universe, but not its creator (as Plato's demiurge is), since Aristotle believes the universe is eternal. Nor does Aristotle suggest that God has providence or foreknowledge concerned with future contingent events. But he believes that the physical universe is dependent on God. In *Physics* VIII he argues that the explanation of motion requires recognition of a first cause of motion, and in *Metaphysics* XII this first cause is identified with divine, immaterial, substance. This first mover is itself unmoved; it initiates motion only as an object of love initiates motion by attraction. It is the ultimate final cause of the various movements in the universe.

In treating the divine substance as a god, and hence as a being with a soul and an intellect, Aristotle attributes some mental life to it. But since it would be imperfect if it thought of objects outside itself (because it would not be self-sufficient), it thinks only of its own thinking. This restriction, however, is not as severe as it may seem, since Aristotle believes that the various objects of thought are in some way identical to the mind that thinks them (see §15). In so far as God thinks of his own mind, he thereby also contemplates the order of the universe as a whole; this is the order that the different movements in the universe seek to embody.

Sometimes (as in *Physics* VIII) Aristotle argues for a single first mover. In *Metaphysics* XII, however, he argues that an unmoved mover must be postulated for each of the distinct movements of the heavenly bodies. This astronomical interpretation of his theological doctrine is difficult to reconcile with his belief, reaffirmed in *Metaphysics* XII 10, that in some way the universe is unified by a single first unmoved mover.

17 Soul and body

Aristotle's treatise *On the Soul* is placed among the works on natural philosophy, but should be read with *Metaphysics* VII–IX. In Aristotle's view, disputes about soul and body are simply a special case of the more general disputes about form and matter. He rejects both the Presocratic materialist assumption that the soul is simply non-organic matter, and the Platonic dualist claim that it must be something entirely non-bodily. He argues that soul is substance because it is the form of a natural body, and that the body is the matter informed by the soul. Although the soul is a substance distinct from the non-organic body (the collection of non-organic matter belonging to a living organism; see §13), it is not immaterial (if being immaterial excludes being composed of matter), nor is it independent of some non-organic body or other.

Aristotle assumes that the soul is the primary principle of life, and hence that it distinguishes the living from the non-living. A living organism is nourished, grows and diminishes, through itself – from a causal origin within itself rather than from the action of external agents. A living organism must, therefore, be teleologically ordered, since (for Aristotle) nutrition and growth cannot be understood without appeal to final causation (see TELEOLOGY).

If life must be conceived teleologically, and the soul is the *primary* principle of life, then the soul is form rather than matter. For the primary principle is whatever explains our vital activities; since these are goal-directed activities, their explanation must refer to the goal-directed features of the subject, and so to the form rather than the matter. If the soul is what we live by primarily, it must be the final cause of the body, and so a formal, not a material, aspect of the subject. Soul must, therefore, be substance as form.

Aristotle attributes to the soul the features of substantial form (see §13). (1) It is a substance that is irreducible to a material non-organic body (remote matter); to that extent the soul is incorporeal, and not just some ordinary material stuff. (2) It is the source of unity that makes a heap of material constituents into a single organism. For a collection of flesh and bones constitutes a single living organism in so far as it is teleologically organized; the activities of the single organism are the final cause of the movements of the different parts. Since a single organism has a single final cause, it has a single soul and a single body. (3) The identity and persistence of the soul determine the identity and persistence of the creature that has it. If something has a soul in so far as it has life, then Socrates perishes if and only if his soul does. The truth of this Platonic claim (*Phaedo* 115c–e) does not imply Platonic dualism. (4) The definition of a soul must mention the proximate material subject (the organic body and its parts) whose capacities are actualized in the functions of the organism (*Metaphysics* 1036b28–30). A soul must be non-coincidentally connected to a specific sort of organic body (*On the Soul* 407b20–4).

Some of the puzzles in Aristotle's doctrine of substantial form arise in his doctrine of soul and body. If, for instance, he recognizes particular substantial forms, then he also recognizes (as the previous paragraph assumes) the individual souls of Socrates and Callias; if, however, he recognizes only one substantial form for each species, then he recognizes only one soul for human beings, another for horses, and so on.

Since the soul is the form of the living body, an account of the different 'parts' or 'capacities' (or 'faculties'; *dynameis*) of the soul does not describe the different physiological processes underlying the different activities of a living organism, but describes their formal and goal-directed aspects. Aristotle describes the capacities that distinguish the different types of souls: nutrition (characteristic of plants), perception and appearance (characteristic of animals) and rational thought (characteristic of rational animals) (see PSYCHĒ). He describes some of the physiological basis of these psychic capacities in the shorter treatises on natural philosophy, including the *Parva Naturalia*, the *Movement of Animals*, and the *Progression of Animals*.

18 Perception

To define perception, Aristotle returns to his contrast between form and matter. Perception happens in so far as (1) the perceiver becomes like the object (*On the Soul* 417a18); (2) the perceiver that was potentially F (for example, white) becomes actually F when it perceives the actually F object (418a3); (3) the perceiver acquires the form, but not the matter, of the object (424a18–24). These descriptions express a realist view of perception and its objects; Aristotle assumes in (2) that an object is actually white, square, and so on in its own right, before we perceive it.

He is sometimes taken to imply in (1) that perception requires physical similarity; but (3) counts against this interpretation. A sense receives the form without the matter in the way in which a house without matter is in the soul of the architect before the house is built. In the latter case, nothing that looks like a house is in the builder, but features of the house correspond to features of the builder's design. Similarly, when we hear a tune, our ears do not necessarily sound like the tune, but a state of us systematically corresponds to the tune (as features of a map correspond to features of the area it maps).

A 'common sense' perceives common properties of sensible objects, such as size, shape and number, which are all perceived through the perception of motion (*On the Soul* 425a14–20). This is not a sixth sense independent of the other five, but the result of the cooperation of the five senses. Aristotle argues that we can explain our grasp of these common properties without supposing that they are objects of intellect rather than sense (contrast Plato, *Theaetetus* 184–6).

19 Appearance and thought

Appearance (or 'imagination'; *phantasia*) links perception to goal-directed movement. A lion sees or smells a deer; it takes pleasure in the prospect of eating the deer, and so wants to catch the deer. To connect perception with pleasure and desire, we need to say how the deer appears to the lion (as prey); this is what Aristotle calls the lion's appearance of the deer (*On the Soul* III 3, 7).

Aristotle denies that this appearance constitutes a belief (*doxa*). He argues that belief requires reason and inference, which non-human animals lack; in his view, they lack any grasp of a universal, and have only appearances and memory of particulars (*Nicomachean Ethics* 1147b4–5). The operations of sense, memory and experience are necessary, but not sufficient, for the grasp of a universal that is expressed in concepts and beliefs (*Posterior Analytics* II 19; *Metaphysics* I 1).

Concepts and beliefs require intellect (*nous*) actualized in 'understanding' or 'thinking' (*noein*; *On the Soul* III 4)(see Nous). Thought differs from perception in so far as it grasps universal essences – for example, what flesh is, as opposed to flesh. Perception does not include grasp of the universal as such; in grasping the universal, we recognize some feature of our experience as a ground for attributing the universal to a particular that we experience.

To explain how the mind is capable of grasping universals when we interact causally with particular perceptible objects, Aristotle distinguishes two aspects of intellect – passive and 'productive' (or 'active' or 'agent') – claiming that these two aspects must combine to produce thought of universals (*On the Soul* III 5). He does not say how productive intellect contributes to our grasp of universals. Later interpreters suggest that productive intellect abstracts the aspects relevant to the universal from the other features of particulars that are combined with them in perception (Aquinas, *Summa Theologiae* 1a q.79 a.3).

Aristotle takes the presence of this productive intellect to be necessary for any thinking at all. Moreover, he believes that productive intellect is capable of existing without a body. He still maintains his belief in the inseparability of soul from body; for since productive intellect is not a type of soul, its separate existence is not the separate existence of a soul.

20 Desire and voluntary action

Perception, appearance and thought are connected to goal-directed movement by means of desire. The appearance of something as desirable is the source of an animal's tendency to pursue one sort of thing rather than another. External objects, however, appear desirable to different agents in different ways. Aristotle distinguishes the appetite (*epithymia*) that animals have from the wish (rational desire; *boulēsis*) that only rational agents have; appetite is for the pleasant and wish is for the good (*On the Soul* 414b2–6, 432b5–7, *Politics* 1253a15–18).

A rational agent's wish differs from appetite in so far as it is guided by deliberation resting on one's conception of one's good. Such a conception extends beyond one's present inclinations both at a particular time and over time. Rational agents are aware of themselves as extending into past and future. Deliberation that is guided by reference to these broader aspects of one's aims and nature results in the rational choice that Aristotle calls 'decision' (*prohairesis*; *Nicomachean Ethics* III 3).

Agents who act on desire and appearance also act voluntarily (*hekousiōs*), in so far as they act on some internal principle (*archē*). While voluntary action is not confined to rational agents, their voluntary action has special significance, because it is an appropriate basis for praise and blame. Since it has an internal principle, it is in our control as rational agents, and therefore we are justly praised and blamed for it. We are held responsible for our actions in so far as they reflect our character and decisions (*Nicomachean Ethics* III 1–5).

Aristotle's defence of his belief that we are appropriately responsible agents does not confront the questions later raised by Epicurus' claim that responsibility is incompatible with the complete causal determination of our actions (see EPICUREANISM §12). An incompatibilist position is ascribed to Aristotle by Alexander in *On Fate* (see ALEXANDER OF APHRODISIAS §4.) Aristotle neither explicitly presents an incompatibilist position nor explicitly endorses a compatibilist position of the sort later defended by the Stoics.

A discussion of time, truth and necessity (the 'Sea Battle'; *De Interpretatione* 9) has suggested to some interpreters that Aristotle is an indeterminist. His opponent is a fatalist, who assumes that (1) future-tensed statements about human actions (for example, 'There will be a sea battle tomorrow') were true in the past, and infers that (2) the future is necessarily determined, independently of what we choose. Aristotle certainly rejects (2). If he accepts the validity of the fatalist's argument, and rejects (1), then he accepts indeterminism.

An alternative reply to the fatalist would be to accept (1) and to deny the validity of the argument. We might argue that the past truth of statements about my actions does not imply that my actions are determined independently of my choices. If on Friday Socrates decides to walk, and he acts on his decision on Friday, then it was true on Thursday that Socrates would walk on Friday, and also true that on Friday he would act on his decision to walk, but it was not true on Thursday that he would walk whether or not he decided to (see STOICISM §21). Probably Aristotle accepts this alternative reply to the fatalist, and hence does not endorse indeterminism.

21 The human good

Aristotle's account of rational agents, choice, deliberation and action is an appropriate starting point for his ethical theory. Ethics is concerned with the praiseworthy and blameworthy actions and states of character of rational agents; that is why it concerns virtues (praiseworthy states) and vices (blameworthy states) (see ARETĒ).

Aristotle's ethical theory is mostly contained in three treatises: the *Magna Moralia*, the *Eudemian Ethics* and the *Nicomachean Ethics*. The titles of the last two works may reflect a tradition that Eudemus (a member of the Lyceum) and Nicomachus (the son of Aristotle and Herpyllis) edited Aristotle's lectures. The *Magna Moralia* is widely agreed not to have been written by Aristotle; some believe, with good reason, that it contains a student's notes on an early course of lectures by Aristotle. The *Eudemian Ethics* is now widely agreed to be authentic, and generally (not universally) and reasonably taken to be earlier than the *Nicomachean Ethics*. Three books (*Nicomachean Ethics* V–VII = *Eudemian Ethics* IV–VI) are assigned by the manuscripts to both the *Eudemian Ethics* and the *Nicomachean Ethics*.

Aristotle conceives 'ethics' (*Magna Moralia* 1181a24) as a part of political science; he treats the *Nicomachean Ethics* and the *Politics* as parts of a single inquiry (*Nicomachean Ethics* X 9). Ethics seeks to discover the good for an individual and a community (*Nicomachean Ethics* I 2), and so it begins with an examination of happiness, (*eudaimonia*). ('Wellbeing' and 'welfare' are alternative renderings of *eudaimonia* that may avoid some of the misleading associations carried by 'happiness'; see EUDAIMONIA.) Happiness is the right starting point for an ethical theory because, in Aristotle's view, rational agents necessarily choose and deliberate with a view to their ultimate good, which is happiness; it is the end that we want for its own sake, and for the sake of which we want other things (so that it is the ultimate non-instrumental good). If it is to be an ultimate end, happiness must be complete (or 'final'; *teleion*) and self-sufficient (*Nicomachean Ethics* I 1–5, 7).

To find a more definite account of the nature of this ultimate and complete end, Aristotle argues from the human function (*ergon*), the characteristic activity that is essential to a human being in the same way that a purely nutritive life is essential to a plant and a life guided by sense perception and desire is essential to an animal (*Nicomachean Ethics* I 7). Since a human being is essentially a rational agent, the essential activity of a human being is a life guided by practical reason. The good life for a human being must be good for a being with the essential activity of a human being; hence it must be a good life guided by practical reason, and hence it must be a life in accordance with the virtue (*aretē*) that is needed for achieving one's good. The human good, therefore, is an actualization of the soul in accordance with complete virtue in a complete life. This 'complete virtue' appears to include the various virtues described in the following books of the *Nicomachean Ethics*; this appearance, however, may be challenged by *Nicomachean Ethics* X (see §26).

22 Virtue of character

From the general conception of happiness Aristotle infers the general features of a virtue of character (*ēthikē aretē*; *Nicomachean Ethics* I 13). He agrees with Plato in recognizing both rational and non-rational desires (see PLATO §14). One's soul is in a virtuous condition in so far as the non-rational elements cooperate with reason; in this condition human beings fulfil their function well. The argument from the human function does not make it clear what states of a rational agent count as fulfilling the human function. Aristotle seeks to make this clearer, first through his general account of virtue of character, and then through his sketches of the individual virtues.

A virtue of character must be a 'mean' or 'intermediate' state, since it must achieve the appropriate cooperation between rational and non-rational desires; such a state is intermediate between complete indulgence of non-rational desires and complete suppression of them. (Aristotle is not recommending 'moderation' – for example, a moderate degree of anger or pleasure – in all circumstances.) The demand for cooperation between desires implies that virtue is more than simply control over desires; mere control is 'continence' (*enkrateia*) rather than genuine virtue.

The task of moral education, therefore, is to

harmonize non-rational desires with practical reason. Virtuous people allow reasonable satisfaction to their appetites; they do not suppress all their fears; they do not disregard all their feelings of pride or shame or resentment (*Nicomachean Ethics* 1126a3–8), or their desire for other people's good opinion. Aristotle's sketches of the different virtues show how different non-rational desires can cooperate with practical reason.

23 Virtue, practical reason and incontinence

A virtuous person makes a decision (*prohairesis*) to do the virtuous action for its own sake. The correct decision requires deliberation; the virtue of intellect that ensures good deliberation is prudence (or 'wisdom', *phronēsis*; *Nicomachean Ethics* VI 4–5); hence the mean in which a virtue lies must be determined by the sort of reason by which the prudent person would determine it (1107a1–2). Virtue of character is, therefore, inseparable from prudence. Each virtue is subject to the direction of prudence because each virtue aims at what is best, as identified by prudence.

In claiming that prudence involves deliberation, Aristotle also emphasizes the importance of its grasping the relevant features of a particular situation; we need to grasp the right particulars if deliberation is to result in a correct decision about what to do here and now. The right moral choice requires experience of particular situations, since general rules cannot be applied mechanically. Aristotle describes the relevant aspect of prudence as a sort of perception or intuitive understanding of the right aspects of particular situations (*Nicomachean Ethics* VI 8, 11).

These aspects of prudence distinguish the virtuous person from 'continent' and 'incontinent' people (*Nicomachean Ethics* VII 1–10). Aristotle accepts the reality of incontinent action (*akrasia*), rejecting Socrates' view that only ignorance of what is better and worse underlies apparent incontinence (see SOCRATES §6; AKRASIA §1). He argues that incontinents make the right decision, but act contrary to it. Their failure to stick to their decision is the result of strong non-rational desires, not simply of cognitive error. Still, Aristotle agrees with Socrates in believing that ignorance is an important component of a correct explanation of incontinence, because no one can act contrary to a correct decision fully accepted at the very moment of incontinent action.

The error of incontinents lies in their failure to harmonize the demands of their appetites with the requirements of virtue; their strong appetites cause them to lose part of the reasoning that formed their decision. When they act, they fail to see clearly how their general principles apply to their present situation. If their failure results from an error in deliberation, it is clear why Aristotle insists that incontinent people lack prudence.

24 Choice, virtue, and pleasure

It is initially puzzling that virtuous people decide to act virtuously for its own sake as a result of deliberation. If they decide on virtuous action for its own sake, then their deliberation causes them to choose it as an end in itself, not simply as a means. Decision and deliberation, however, are not about ends but about 'the things promoting ends' (*ta pros ta telē*, often rendered 'means to ends'). Aristotle's description of the virtuous person, then, seems to attribute to decision a role that is excluded by his explicit account of decision.

This puzzle is less severe once we recognize that Aristotle regards different sorts of things as 'promoting' an end. Sometimes he means (1) that the action is external and purely instrumental to the end; in this way buying food 'promotes' eating dinner. Sometimes, however, he means (2) that the action is a part or component of the end, or that performing the action partly constitutes the achieving of the end; in this way eating the main course 'promotes' eating dinner. Deliberation about this second sort of 'promotion' shows that an action is worth choosing for its own sake, in so far as it partly constitutes our end.

This role for deliberation explains how virtuous people can decide, as a result of deliberation, on virtuous action for its own sake; they choose it as a part of happiness, not as a merely instrumental means. Prudence finds the actions that promote happiness in so far as they are parts of the happy life. Such actions are to be chosen for their own sake, as being their own end; they are not simply instrumental means to some further end. The virtuous person's decision results from deliberation about the composition of happiness; virtuous people decide on the actions that, by being non-instrumentally good, are components of happiness in their own right.

Aristotle's demand for the virtuous person to decide on the virtuous action for its own sake is connected with two further claims: (1) the virtuous person must take pleasure in virtuous action as such; (2) in doing so, the virtuous person has the pleasantest life. In these claims Aristotle relies on his views about the nature of pleasure and its role in happiness (*Nicomachean Ethics* VII 11–14, X 1–5).

He denies that pleasure is some uniform sensation to which different kinds of pleasant action are connected only causally (in the way that the reading of many boring books on different subjects might induce the same feeling of boredom). Instead he argues that the specific pleasure taken in x rather than y is internally related to doing x rather than y, and essentially depends on pursuing x for x's own sake. Pleasure is a 'supervenient end' (1174b31–3) resulting from an activity that one pursues as an activity (*praxis* or *energeia*) rather than a mere process or production (*kinēsis* or *poiēsis*).

Aristotle insists, following Plato's *Philebus*, that the value of the pleasure depends on the value of the activity on which the pleasure supervenes (1176a3–29). The virtuous person has the pleasantest life, but the pleasantest life cannot aim exclusively at pleasure.

25 Virtue, friendship and the good of others

The virtuous person's deliberation, identifying the mean in relation to different desires and different situations, is articulated in the different virtues of character (described in *Nicomachean Ethics* III–V). The different virtues are concerned with the regulation of non-rational desires (for example, bravery, temperance, good temper), external goods (for example, magnificence, magnanimity) and social situations (for example, truthfulness, wit). Some concern the good of others to some degree (bravery, good temper, generosity).

Aristotle's Greek for virtue of character, *ēthikē aretē*, is rendered into Latin as 'virtus moralis'. The English rendering 'moral virtue' is defensible, since the virtues of character as a whole display the impartial concern for others that is often ascribed to morality. They are unified by the aim of the virtuous person, who decides on the virtuous action because it is 'fine' (*kalon*). Fine action systematically promotes the good of others; we must aim at it if we are to find the mean that is characteristic of a virtue (1122b6–7).

A second unifying element in the virtues, inseparable from concern for the fine, is their connection to justice (V 1–2). Aristotle takes justice to be multivocal (see §4), and distinguishes general justice from the specific virtue concerned with the prevention and rectification of certain specific types of injustices. General justice is the virtue of character that aims specifically at the common good of a community. Since it is not a different state of character from the other virtues, they must incorporate concern for the common good.

To explain why concern for the good of others, and for a common good, is part of the life that aims at one's own happiness, Aristotle examines friendship (*philia*; *Nicomachean Ethics* VIII–IX). All three of the main types of friendship (for pleasure, for advantage and for the good) seek the good of the other person. Only the best type – friendship for the good between virtuous people – includes A's concern for B's good for B's own sake and because of B's essential character (*Nicomachean Ethics* VIII 1–4).

In the best sort of friendship, the friend is 'another self'; A takes the sorts of attitudes to B that A also takes to A. Aristotle infers that friendship is part of a complete and self-sufficient life (IX 9–11). Friendship involves sharing the activities one counts as especially important in one's life, and especially the sharing of reasoning and thinking. Friends cooperate in deliberation, decision and action; and the thoughts and actions of each provide reasons for the future thoughts and actions of the other. The cooperative aspects of friendship more fully realize each person's own capacities as a rational agent, and so promote each person's happiness. Hence the full development of a human being requires concern for the good of others.

26 Two conceptions of happiness?

Although Aristotle emphasizes the other-regarding, social aspects of happiness, he also advocates pure intellectual activity (or 'study', *theōria*) – the contemplation of scientific and philosophical truths, apart from any attempt to apply them to practice (*Nicomachean Ethics* X 6–8). The connection between the human function and human happiness (see §21) implies that contemplation is a supremely important element in happiness. For contemplation is the highest fulfilment of our nature as rational beings; it is the sort of rational activity that we share with the gods, who are rational beings with no need to apply reason to practice. Aristotle infers that contemplation is the happiest life available to us, in so far as we have the rational intellects we share with gods (see §16).

According to one interpretation, Aristotle actually identifies contemplation with happiness: contemplation is the only non-instrumental good that is part of happiness, and the moral virtues are to be valued – from the point of view of happiness – simply as means to contemplation. If this is Aristotle's view, it is difficult to see how the virtues of character are even the best instrumental means to happiness. Even if some virtuous actions are instrumental means to contemplation, it is difficult to see how the motives demanded of the virtuous person (see §§24–5) are always useful, rather than distracting, for those who aim at contemplation.

Probably, however, Aristotle means that contemplation is the best component of happiness. If we were pure intellects with no other desires and no bodies, contemplation would be the whole of our good. Since,

429

however, we are not in fact merely intellects (*Nicomachean Ethics* 1178b3–7), Aristotle recognizes that the good must be the good of the whole human being. Contemplation is not the complete good for a human being.

If this is Aristotle's view, then contemplation fits the conception of happiness that is upheld in the rest of the *Nicomachean Ethics* and in the other ethical works. The virtues of character, and the actions expressing them, deserve to be chosen for their own sakes as components of happiness. In the virtuous person, they regulate one's choice of other goods, and so they also regulate one's choices about contemplation. The *Politics* may be taken to develop this conception of happiness, since (in book VII) it sets contemplation in the context of a social order regulated by the moral virtues.

27 Politics: ideal states

The *Politics* pursues three connected aims: (1) it completes the discussion of happiness, by showing what kind of political community achieves the human good (mainly books I, II and VII); (2) it sets out moral and political principles that allow us to understand and to criticize the different sorts of actual states and their constitutions (mainly books III and IV); (3) it offers some proposals for improving actual states (mainly books V and VI). The order of the books probably reflects Aristotle's aim of describing an ideal state after examining the strengths and weaknesses of actual states.

An individual's desire for happiness leads eventually to the city. A human being is a 'political animal', because essential human capacities and aims are completely fulfilled only in a political community; hence (given the connection between the human function and the human good) the individual's happiness must involve the good of fellow members of a community. The relevant sort of community is a *polis* ('city' or 'state') – a self-governing community whose proper function (not completely fulfilled by every actual political community) is to aim at the common good of its citizens, who (normally) share in ruling and in being ruled. The city is the all-inclusive community, of which the other communities are parts, since it aims at advantage not merely for some present concern but for the whole of life (*Nicomachean Ethics* 1160a9–30). Since happiness is complete and self-sufficient, the city is a complete and self-sufficient community (*Politics* 1252b28), aiming at a complete and self-sufficient life that includes all the goods needed for a happy life.

The connection between human nature, human good and the political community is most easily understood from Aristotle's account of friendship. Complete friendship, which requires living together and sharing rational discourse and thought, is restricted to individuals with virtuous characters, but this is not the only type of friendship that achieves self-realization in cooperation; a similar defence can be given for the friendship of citizens. Collective deliberation about questions of justice and benefit contributes to the virtuous person's self-realization because it extends the scope of one's practical reason and deliberation beyond one's own life and activities. Since the city is comprehensive, seeking to plan for everything that is needed for the complete good, a rational agent has good reason to want to share in its deliberations.

Since, then, Aristotle believes that political activity contributes in its own right to the human good, he argues against a 'social contract' theory that assigns a restricted instrumental function to the state (safety, or mutual protection, or the safeguarding of what justly belongs to each person; *Politics* III 9). Political life is to be valued for itself, apart from any instrumental benefit; the best city aims at the development of the moral virtues and at the political participation of all who are capable of them.

In the light of these aims, Aristotle describes the best city. It has to assume favourable external conditions (geographical and economic) to allow the development of political life. Its criteria for citizenship are restricted, since they exclude everyone (including women and manual labourers) whom Aristotle regards as incapable of developing the virtues of character. Within the class of citizens, however, Aristotle is concerned to avoid gross inequality of wealth. and to ensure that everyone shares both in ruling and in being ruled. The institutions of the best state provide the political, social, economic and educational basis for the practice of the moral virtues and for contemplation.

28 Politics: imperfect states

Just as a correct conception of happiness is the basis of the ideal city, various incorrect conceptions of happiness define mistaken aims for different cities. These mistaken aims underlie the different conceptions of justice that are embodied in the constitutions of different cities. Partisans of oligarchy, for instance, take happiness to consist in wealth; they treat the city as a business partnership (*Politics* 1280a25–31). Partisans of democracy take happiness to consist simply in the satisfaction of desire; they assume that if people are equal in the one respect of being free rather than slaves, they are equal altogether, and should have an equal share in ruling (1280a24–5). Neither view is completely mistaken, since neither wealth nor freedom is irrelevant to questions of justice, but each is one-sided.

These one-sided views cause errors about the just distribution of political power or other goods. The proper basis for assigning worth in distribution will be whatever is relevant for the common good, since that is the aim of general justice. Since a correct conception of the common good requires a correct conception of happiness, a correct answer to the question about distribution must appeal to a true conception of happiness.

The criticism of existing constitutions seeks to show both how they fall short of the norms that are met by the ideal state, and how they can be improved. Aristotle wants to describe not only the ideal state, but also the best organization of each political system. In some circumstances, he believes, economic, social, and demographic facts may make (for example) democracy or oligarchy difficult to avoid. Still, an imperfect constitution can be improved, by attention to the aspects of justice, and hence the aspects of happiness, that this constitution tends to ignore. Even when Aristotle may appear to be engaged in empirical political sociology, or to be offering hints for the survival of a particular regime, he is guided by the moral and political principles that he defends in the more theoretical parts of the *Politics*.

29 Rhetoric and poetics

In Aristotle's classification, rhetoric and poetics (*poiētikē*; literally 'productive') count as 'productive' rather than 'practical' disciplines; they are concerned with 'production' (*poiēsis*) – purely instrumental action aiming at some external end – rather than with 'action' (*praxis*) – action that is also an end in itself. Rhetoric is a productive discipline in so far as it aims at persuasion in public speaking, and seeks the arguments, diction, language, metaphor, appeals to emotion and so on, that are most likely to persuade different types of audiences. Hence Aristotle's treatise on rhetoric contains sections on these different topics. Dialectic and logic are useful to a student of rhetoric, even though rhetoric does not aim at the truth; for true or plausible claims tend to be persuasive. *Rhetoric* II deals with another aspect of rhetorical persuasion, by describing the different emotions; the student of rhetoric must know how to arouse emotions in an audience.

Aristotle also takes his moral and political theory to be relevant to rhetoric, for two main reasons. (1) Rhetoric is concerned with the moral and political issues discussed in public assemblies or in courts, and the orator needs to be familiar with the convictions of a given audience. (2) Even more important, the orator should be guided by correct moral and political convictions (without necessarily grasping their philosophical basis). Aristotle does not endorse the conception of oratory as a technique of persuasion that is indifferent to the moral and political aims that it serves. This conception of oratory arouses Plato's criticism in the *Gorgias* (see Plato §7) Aristotle replies to such criticism by arguing that the orator should learn, and should be guided by, correct principles. He sets out some of these in the *Rhetoric*.

Moral and political principles are also relevant to Aristotle's treatment of literary criticism in the *Poetics*. The surviving part of this treatise deals mainly with tragedy. Some of it is similar to the *Rhetoric*, in so far as it discusses matters of technique and psychology; Aristotle describes the various sorts of plots, characters, and dramatic devices that affect the audience in different ways. He is also concerned, however, about the moral aspects of tragedy; in this he may be responding to the criticisms of tragedy in book X of Plato's *Republic*. He argues that tragedy achieves its appropriate effect when it directs pity, fear, sympathy and revulsion at the appropriate sorts of people and situations; and he examines the plots and characters of various tragedies from this point of view (see Katharsis; Mimesis).

30 Influence

Some aspects of Aristotle's philosophy have become so familiar that we do not even attribute them to him. When we say that an event was a mere 'coincidence', or that an ignorant person is 'ill-informed', or that someone's behaviour is forming good or bad 'habits', our vocabulary expresses Aristotelian assumptions, transmitted through Latin translations and interpretations.

The explicit influence of Aristotle's philosophical works and theories has been variable. In Hellenistic philosophy, he is not prominently cited or discussed (see Hellenistic Philosophy); some have even doubted whether the major Stoics knew his works. From the first century BC, however, the study of Aristotle revived. This revival produced philosophers defending an Aristotelian position, often incorporating Stoic or Platonist elements, but sometimes sharpening contrasts between Aristotle and the Hellenistic schools (see Alexander of Aphrodisias; Peripatetics). These Aristotelians began a long series of Greek commentaries (lasting until the sixth century AD). Many of the later commentators were Neoplatonists; some of whom tried to reconcile Aristotelian with Platonic doctrines (see Aristotle

COMMENTATORS; PLATONISM, EARLY AND MIDDLE §§8–9; NEOPLATONISM §1; PORPHYRY §2).

Between the sixth and the thirteenth centuries, most of Aristotle's works were unavailable in western Europe, although he was still studied in the Byzantine empire and the Islamic world (see ARISTOTELIANISM IN ISLAMIC PHILOSOPHY). Two leading figures in the revival of Aristotelian studies and of Aristotelian philosophy in medieval Europe were the translator William of Moerbeke and Thomas Aquinas (see ARISTOTELIANISM, MEDIEVAL). Aquinas' attempt to combine Aristotelian philosophy with orthodox Christian theology was at first rejected by ecclesiastical authority, but then came to be accepted (see AQUINAS, T.).

The 'scholastic' philosophy of Aquinas and his successors is often opposed, but often presupposed, by Descartes, Locke, Hobbes and many of their successors, who often do not distinguish it from Aristotle's own philosophy. The reader who compares their representation of the scholastic position with Aristotle's own works (or with Aquinas) will often be surprised by the sharp differences between Aristotle's (and Aquinas') own positions and the positions that are attributed to him by the seventeenth-century philosophers who reject his authority (see ARISTOTELIANISM IN THE 17TH CENTURY).

Modern historical study of Aristotle begins in the early nineteenth century. It has led to philosophical reassessment, and his works have once again become a source of philosophical insight and argument. Many of the themes of Aristotelian philosophy – the nature of substance, the relation of form to matter, the relation of mind to body, the nature of human action, the role of virtues and actions in morality – have reappeared as issues in philosophical debates, and Aristotle's contributions to these debates have influenced the course of philosophical discussion.

In some ways, Aristotle has suffered from his success. At different times he has been regarded as the indisputable authority in astronomy, biology, logic and ethics; hence he has represented the traditional position against which reformers have revolted. If he is regarded neither as the indisputable authority nor as a repository of antiquated and discarded doctrines, his permanent philosophical value can be more justly appreciated.

See also: ARCHĒ; ARISTOTELIANISM, RENAISSANCE; AVERROISM; BEING; CHANGE; DUALISM; FRIENDSHIP; METAPHYSICS; PNEUMA; PRUDENCE; STRATO; TELEOLOGICAL ETHICS; TENSE AND TEMPORAL LOGIC; VIRTUE ETHICS; VIRTUES AND VICES

List of works

The works of Aristotle are usually cited by conventional Latin titles, or by English translations of these titles (often mere Anglicizations rather than proper translations). This list omits: works preserved in the Aristotelian corpus, but now generally agreed to be spurious; lost works; and the *Constitution of Athens* (probably not by Aristotle himself; discovered after the standard arrangement of Aristotle's works was established).

Neither the absolute nor the relative dates of individual treatises can be established (see §2). The list below follows the thematic order outlined in the entry.

Recommended editions (Greek text with commentary) and translations of individual works are listed below. The standard text of most treatises appears in the Oxford Classical Texts (Oxford: Oxford University Press, various editors and dates), or, when these are lacking, in the Teubner texts (Leipzig: Teubner, various editors and dates). The Greek text, with facing English translation (not always reliable) appears in the Loeb Classical Library (Cambridge, MA: Harvard University Press and London: Heinemann, various editors and dates).

The date for all of Aristotle's works cited in this bibliography is *c.* mid 4th century BC.

Aristotelis Opera, ed. I. Bekker, Berlin: Reimer, 1831–70, 5 vols. (The first modern edition of the Greek text and the source of the page and line references normally used.)

The Works of Aristotle, ed. W.D. Ross and J.A. Smith, Oxford: Oxford University Press, 1908–54, 12 vols. (The Oxford Translation.)

The Complete Works of Aristotle, ed. J. Barnes, Princeton, NJ: Princeton University Press, 1984, 2 vols. (The standard English translation of the whole corpus; contains the revised Oxford Translation.)

The Basic Works of Aristotle, ed. R. McKeon, New York: Random House, 1941. (A selection from the Oxford Translation.)

A New Aristotle Reader, ed. J.L. Ackrill, Oxford: Oxford University Press, 1984. (Selections from existing translations.)

Aristotle: Selections, trans. G. Fine and T. Irwin, Indianapolis, IN: Hackett Publishing Company, 1995. (New translations with notes.).

Logic

Categories (*Categoriae*), trans. J.L. Ackrill, Clarendon

Aristotle Series, Oxford: Oxford University Press, 1963. (Outline of the theory of categories.)

On Interpretation (*De Interpretatione*), trans. J.L. Ackrill, Clarendon Aristotle Series, Oxford: Oxford University Press, 1963. (Thought, language and logic.)

Prior Analytics (*Analytica Priora*), trans. R. Smith, Indianapolis: Hackett, 1989. (Deductive logic: the theory of the syllogism.)

Posterior Analytics (*Analytica Posteriora*), trans. J. Barnes, Clarendon Aristotle Series, Oxford: Oxford University Press, 2nd edn, 1993. (The theory of demonstration: the structure of knowledge.)

Topics (*Topica*) trans. A.W. Pickard-Cambridge in *The Complete Works of Aristotle*, ed. J. Barnes, Princeton, NJ: Princeton University Press, 1984, 2 vols, 167–314. (The theory, strategy and tactics of dialectical argument.)

Natural philosophy

Physics (*Physica*), ed. W.D. Ross, in *The Works of Aristotle*, Oxford: Oxford University Press, 1949; Books I–II, trans. W. Charlton, Clarendon Aristotle Series, Oxford: Oxford University Press, 1970; Books III–IV trans. E.L. Hussey, Clarendon Aristotle Series, Oxford: Oxford University Press, 1983. (General principles of natural philosophy – form, matter, explanation – and their application to motion, infinity, place and time.)

On the Heavens (*De caelo*), Books I–II trans. S. Leggett, Warminster: Aris & Phillips, 1995. (Cosmology: application of Aristotle's theory of motion to the four elements and their interaction in the universe.)

Generation and Corruption (*De generatione et corruptione*), ed. H.H. Joachim, Oxford: Oxford University Press, 1922; trans. C.J.F. Williams, Clarendon Aristotle Series, Oxford: Oxford University Press, 1982. (Account of change in natural substances; alteration, growth, coming-to-be and perishing; matter and the four elements.)

Meteorology (*Meteorologica*), trans. H.D.P. Lee, Loeb Classical Library, Cambridge, MA: Harvard University Press and London: Heinemann, 1952. (Collection of observations on winds, tides and other aspects of inanimate nature.)

History of Animals (*Historia animalium*) trans. A.L.Peck, Loeb Classical Library, Cambridge, MA: Harvard University Press and London: Heinemann, 1965–91, 3 vols. (Collection of observations on different kinds of animals and their behaviour, providing a basis for Aristotle's biological explanations.)

Parts of Animals (*De partibus animalium*), Book I, trans. D.M. Balme, Clarendon Aristotle Series, Oxford: Oxford University Press, 1972. (Introduction to the study of animals; explanation of physiology, organs and behaviour, in light of Aristotle's explanatory scheme.)

Generation of Animals (*De generatione animalium*), trans. A.L.Peck, Loeb Classical Library, Cambridge, MA: Harvard University Press and London: Heinemann, 1942. (Application of Aristotle's explanatory scheme to reproduction and heredity.)

On the Movement of Animals (*De motu animalium*), ed. and trans. M.C. Nussbaum. Princeton, NJ: Princeton University Press, 1978. (Physiology and psychological explanation of animal movement.)

On the Progression of Animals (*De incessu animalium*), trans. E.S. Foster, Loeb Classical Library, Cambridge, MA: Harvard University Press and London: Heinemann, 1937. (Physiology of animal movement.)

Metaphysics

Metaphysics (*Metaphysica*), ed. W.D. Ross, Oxford: Oxford University Press, 1924, 2 vols; books IV–VI, trans. C.A. Kirwan, Clarendon Aristotle Series, Oxford: Oxford University Press, 1971; Books VII–VIII trans. D. Bostock, Clarendon Aristotle Series, Oxford: Oxford University Press, 1994; Books XIII–XIV trans. J. Annas, Clarendon Aristotle Series, Oxford: Oxford University Press, 1976. (Collection of treatises centred on the 'science of being', especially substance, form and matter, potentiality and actuality, culminating in theology.)

Psychology

On the Soul (*De anima*), ed. R.D. Hicks, Cambridge: Cambridge University Press, 1907; Books II–III trans. D.W. Hamlyn, Clarendon Aristotle Series, Oxford: Oxford University Press, 1968. (Application of theory of form and matter to questions about soul and body; perceptio, thought and action.)

Short Natural Treatises (*Parva naturalia*), ed. W.D. Ross, Oxford: Oxford University Press, 1955. (Short essays, physiological and psychological, on themes connected with *On the Soul*.)

Ethics

Nicomachean Ethics (*Ethica Nicomachea*) commentary by J.A. Stewart, Oxford: Oxford University

Press, 1892, 2 vols; trans. T.H. Irwin, Indianapolis, IN: Hackett Publishing Company, 1985. (Normally regarded as Aristotle's most important contribution to moral philosophy.)

Eudemian Ethics (*Ethica Eudemia*), Books I–II trans. M.J. Woods, Clarendon Aristotle Series, Oxford: Oxford University Press, 1982. (Similar in content to the *Nicomachean Ethics*, though different in important details. Normally regarded as an earlier version of Aristotle's ethical theory.)

Great Ethics (*Magna moralia*), trans. G. Stock, in *The Complete Works of Aristotle*, revised Oxford Translation, ed. J. Barnes, Princeton, NJ: Princeton University Press, 1984, 2 vols, 1868–1991. (The standard English translation of the whole corpus; contains the revised Oxford Translation.)

Politics

Politics (*Politica*), ed. W.L. Newman, Oxford: Oxford University Press, 1887–1902, 4 vols; Books I–II trans. T.J. Saunders, Clarendon Aristotle Series, Oxford: Oxford University Press, 1995. (Aristotle's major work in political theory, including ethics, history and sociology; examines the imperfections of actual states and proposes an ideal state.)

Rhetoric and Poetics

Rhetoric (*Rhetorica*), ed. E.M. Cope, Cambridge: Cambridge University Press, 1877, 3 vols; trans. G. Kennedy, *Aristotle on Rhetoric: A Theory of Civic Discourse*, New York: Oxford University Press. (The theory and practice of public speaking, based on Aristotle's logic, dialectic, psychology, ethics and political theory.)

Poetics (*De arte poetica*), ed. D.W. Lucas, Oxford: Oxford University Press, 1968; trans. R. Janko, Indianapolis, IN: Hackett Publishing Company, 1987. (Analysis of poetry (in the surviving part of the treatise, tragic drama) from linguistic, stylistic, psychological, and moral points of view.)

References and further reading

Ackrill, J.L. (1981) *Aristotle the Philosopher*, Oxford: Oxford University Press. (This and Barnes (1982) are the best short introductions.)

Barnes, J. (1982) *Aristotle*, Oxford: Oxford University Press. (Along with Ackrill (1981), one of the best short introductions to Aristotle.)

—— (ed.) (1994) *The Cambridge Companion to Aristotle*, Cambridge: Cambridge University Press. (Good bibliography.)

Barnes, J., Schofield, M. and Sorabji, R. (eds) (1975–9) *Articles on Aristotle*, London: Duckworth, 4 vols. (Good collections of essays, including translated selections from non-English works; full bibliographies.)

Bonitz, H. (1870) *Index Aristotelicus*, Berlin: Reimer. (Outstandingly useful guide to Aristotle's vocabulary.)

Broadie, S.W. (1991) *Ethics with Aristotle*, Oxford: Oxford University Press. (This and Hardie (1980) are the best general guides to the *Ethics*; Hardie is more accessible to a beginner.)

Charles, D. (1984) *Aristotle's Philosophy of Action*, London: Duckworth. (Detailed and sophisticated discussion, focusing on *Physics* and *Ethics*.)

Fine, G. (1993) *On Ideas*, Oxford: Oxford University Press. (On Aristotle's criticism of Plato.)

Furley, D.J. and Nehamas, A. (eds) (1994) *Philosophical Essays on Aristotle's Rhetoric*, Princeton, NJ: Princeton University Press. (Collection of essays; this and Rorty (1995) provide a survey of recent work on the *Rhetoric*.)

Furth, M. (1988) *Substance, Form, and Psyche*, Cambridge: Cambridge University Press. (Furth, Lewis (1991), Loux (1991) and Witt (1989) provide a guide to debates about the *Metaphysics*, especially Books VII–IX.)

Gotthelf, A. and Lennox, J. (eds) (1987) *Philosophical issues in Aristotle's Biology*, Cambridge: Cambridge University Press, 1987. (Collection of essays.)

Hardie, W.F.R. (1980) *Aristotle's Ethical Theory*, Oxford: Oxford University Press, 2nd edn. (Alongside Broadie (1991), one of the best general guides to the *Ethics*.)

Irwin, T.H. (1988) *Aristotle's First Principles*, Oxford: Oxford University Press. (This and Lear (1988) explore themes connecting several aspects of Aristotle's philosophy.)

—— (ed.) (1995) *Classical Philosophy*, vols 5–7, New York: Garland. (Collection of essays on Aristotle.)

Jaeger, W. (1923) *Aristoteles: Grundlegung einer Geschichte seiner Entwicklung*, Berlin: Weidmann; trans. R. Robinson, *Aristotle: Fundamentals of the History of his Development*, Oxford: Oxford University Press, 2nd edn, 1948. (English translation; formerly influential account of Aristotle's intellectual development.)

Judson, L. (ed.) (1991) *Aristotle's Physics*, Oxford: Oxford University Press. (Collection of essays.)

Keyt, D. and Miller, F.D. (eds) (1991) *A Companion to Aristotle's Politics*. Oxford: Blackwell. (Collection of essays.)

Kraut, R. (1989) *Aristotle on the Human Good*, Princeton, NJ: Princeton University Press. (Clear

and full discussion of happiness in *Nicomachean Ethics* I, X.)
Lear, J. (1988) *Aristotle: The Desire to Understand*, Cambridge: Cambridge University Press. (Explores themes connecting several aspects of Aristotle's philosophy; see also Irwin (1988).)
Lewis, F.A. (1991) *Substance and Predication in Aristotle*, Cambridge: Cambridge University Press. (Provides the most detailed guide to debates about the *Metaphysics*, especially books VII–IX; see also Furth (1988), Loux (1991) and Witt (1989).)
Loux, M.J. (1991) *Primary Ousia*, Ithaca, NY: Cornell University Press. (Provides a guide to debates about the *Metaphysics*, especially Books VII–IX; see also Furth (1988), Lewis (1991) and Witt (1989).)
Miller, F.D. (1995) *Nature, Justice, and Rights in Aristotle's Politics*, Oxford: Oxford University Press. (Discussion of major issues in Aristotle's political theory.)
Nussbaum, M.C. and Rorty, A.O. (eds) (1992) *Essays on Aristotle's De Anima*, Oxford: Oxford University Press. (Collection of essays, mostly recent.)
Organ, T.W. (1949) *An Index to Aristotle*, Princeton, NJ: Princeton University Press. (Moderately useful attempt to construct an index to the Oxford translation.)
Owen, G.E.L. (1986) *Logic, Science, and Dialectic*, Ithaca, NY: Cornell University Press. (Includes several seminal papers on Aristotle's logic and metaphysics.)
Rorty, A.O. (ed.) (1980) *Essays on Aristotle's Ethics*, Berkeley, CA: University of California Press. (Collection of essays, covering the main themes of the *Ethics* in order.)
—— (ed.) (1992) *Essays on Aristotle's Poetics*, Princeton, NJ: Princeton University Press. (Collection of essays.)
—— (ed.) (1995) *Essays on Aristotle's Rhetoric*, Berkeley, CA: University of California Press. (Alongside Furley and Nehamas (1994), provides a survey of recent work on the *Rhetoric*.)
Ross, W.D. (1923) *Aristotle*, London: Methuen. (Extremely useful summary of all of Aristotle's works.)
Sorabji, R. (1980) *Necessity, Cause, and Blame*, London: Duckworth. (Covers central areas in natural philosophy, metaphysics, and ethics in accessible style.)
Waterlow, S. (1982) *Nature, Change, and Agency*, Oxford: Oxford University Press. (Thought-provoking discussion of themes in *Physics*.)
Witt, C. (1989) *Substance and Essence in Aristotle*, Ithaca, NY: Cornell University Press. (Provides the most accessible guide to debates about the *Metaphysics*, especially Books VII–IX; see also Furth (1988), Lewis (1991) and Loux (1991).)

T.H. IRWIN

ARISTOTLE COMMENTATORS

Aristotle's school treatises were given renewed prominence by Andronicus of Rhodes in the first century BC, and from then on numerous commentaries were written on them. The main modern edition runs to 15,000 pages. They are not just commentaries, but represent the thought and classroom teaching on philosophy quite generally first of the Peripatetic (that is, Aristotelian) school, and then of the Neoplatonists between AD 200 and 600, with further activity from the ninth century in the Islamic world and from the eleventh in the Byzantine.

The commentary movement followed and is commonly thought to have been inspired by the work of Andronicus of Rhodes, who, perhaps around 60 BC, began a massive study of Aristotle's writings (see ARISTOTLE). Of the extant commentaries, the earliest come from Peripatetics of the first half of the second century AD, Adrastus and Aspasius. The early commentaries culminate in the work of the greatest Peripatetic elaborator of Aristotle, ALEXANDER OF APHRODISIAS (second to third century; see PERIPATETICS). But the later commentaries by Themistius (fourth century), though presented as mere paraphrases, and though informed by certain Neoplatonist developments, are similar in content to those of Alexander.

Outside the Peripatetic school, the chief interest in the first century BC and the first two centuries AD focused on Aristotle's *Categories* (see CATEGORIES §1; ARISTOTLE §7). Under the influence of the Neoplatonist PORPHYRY (third century), who rejected the complaint of his teacher PLOTINUS Aristotle's *Categories* ignores the Platonic Forms, Aristotle's logic and a wide selection of his other texts became a standard prerequisite for studying Plato in the Neoplatonist schools, Neoplatonism being by then the dominant philosophy (see NEOPLATONISM).

Porphyry's insistence on the harmony of Plato and Aristotle inaugurated a Neoplatonist tradition. His pupil IAMBLICHUS (third to fourth century) and Iamblichus' pupil Dexippus further defended the compatibility of Aristotle's *Categories* with Plato's theory of Forms, and Iamblichus is even said to have denied that Aristotle contradicted the theory of

Forms at all. In fifth-century Alexandria, first Hierocles and then AMMONIUS, SON OF HERMEAS represented Plato and Aristotle as agreeing that god was the artificer of a beginningless universe. This harmonization, though historically untenable, proved philosophically fruitful, producing a new amalgamation of the ideas of Plato and Aristotle.

After Iamblichus, the study of Aristotle as a propaedeutic to Plato acquired a new significance, because the study of Plato himself was seen as leading to the Neoplatonist ideal of ascent to god. In Iamblichus' Platonic curriculum, Plato's *Timaeus* and *Parmenides* were put last, and seen as theological treatises describing the supreme divinities. From Ammonius onwards formalized introductions were prefixed to commentaries on Aristotle's *Categories*, the first Aristotelian work in the curriculum. The introductions covered ten points which, we are told, had been made standard by Ammonius' teacher PROCLUS (fifth century), one of them being that the eventual aim of studying Aristotle is ascent to god through the theological works of Plato. Even before the *Categories*, the curriculum included Porphyry's introduction to the *Categories*, known as the *Isagōgē* or *Quinque Voces*. Commentaries on that work were prefaced by a description of the nature of philosophy.

The commentaries of the Alexandrian Neoplatonist school after Ammonius are sometimes divided into portions which would have taken an hour to deliver as lectures. Often there is a double discussion, a *protheōria* or treatment of Aristotle's doctrine in a passage, followed by an exegesis of the exact wording of the text (*exēgēsis tēs lexeōs*).

In Alexandria, the Christian Platonist PHILOPONUS (490–570s) worked out a complete alternative to the Aristotelian physics which the Neoplatonists had accepted, and thus went on to influence the development of Islamic and Western physics. Many of his unorthodox ideas were included in his attack *Against Proclus*, published in 529, but he also began to introduce them into his commentaries on Aristotle. Meanwhile SIMPLICIUS, a pious devotee of Neoplatonist religion, had left Athens for Persia as one of the seven displaced Athenian philosophers after the Christian emperor Justinian closed the Athenian Neoplatonist school in 529. He wrote bitterly about Philoponus' Christianity and about the unorthodox interpolations in his commentaries. He emphasizes the harmony of virtually all Greek thought, partly in order to rebut Christian charges of contradictions. It has been suggested that Simplicius finished up in Ḥarrān, just within the borders of modern Turkey, and wrote his Aristotelian commentaries there after 532. It was from Ḥarrān that Thābit ibn Qurra later went, to found the Platonizing school in Baghdad.

This school became the driving force behind the translation into Arabic of Aristotle and his commentators in the ninth century, which was to inspire new philosophizing in the Islamic world.

Meanwhile commentaries were made available in Latin by BOETHIUS (died *c.*525), but only on two logical works of Aristotle and on Porphyry's introduction (*Isagōgē*) to that logic. The Alexandrian School may have survived until the Arab capture of the city in 642, and a tradition continued in Constantinople. There in the twelfth century the princess Anna Comnena organized a circle that included the commentators Eustratius and Michael of Ephesus, whose commentaries were completed in 1138 or later. It may have been from Michael's workshops that James of Venice was able, around 1130, to collect Greek commentaries for translation into Latin. In the same century, Gerard of Cremona was translating Aristotelian commentaries into Latin from the Arabic versions. During the next century, the process of transmission from both languages to the Latin-speaking world turned from a trickle into a flood, and Thomas AQUINAS was a beneficiary of this development. He was thus responding not just to Aristotle, but to Aristotle transformed by the ancient commentators.

The commentaries embed fragments from all 1,150 years of ancient philosophy from 550 BC to AD 600, notably those of the PRESOCRATICS. And many ideas which were previously thought to date from later times can actually be traced back to the commentators. In dynamics, the idea of an impetus, which in its medieval context has been hailed as a scientific revolution, can be seen to have travelled by an Arabic route from the sixth-century commentator Philoponus. Galileo in his early works mentions Philoponus more often than he mentions Plato. And BRENTANO in the nineteenth century got from the commentary tradition, and not from Aristotle himself, his idea that all activity of the mind is directed towards intentional objects.

See also: ARISTOTELIANISM IN ISLAMIC PHILOSOPHY; ARISTOTELIANISM, MEDIEVAL; DAMASCIUS; NEOPLATONISM IN ISLAMIC PHILOSOPHY; TRANSLATORS; GREEK PHILOSOPHY: IMPACT ON ISLAMIC PHILOSOPHY

References and further reading

* Boethius (*c.* AD 510) Commentary on Aristotle's *Categories*, in J.-P. Migne (ed.) *Patrologia Latina*, vol. 64, Paris, 1860. (The primary surviving ancient Latin commentator.)
* —— (*c.* AD 510s) Two Commentaries on Aristotle's *De*

interpretatione, ed. R. Meiser, Leipzig: Teubner, 1877–80, 2 vols.

Diels, H. (ed.) (1882–1909) *Commentaria in Aristotelem Graeca*, Berlin: Reimer, 23 vols, with 3 supplementary vols. (Includes text of most of the ancient Greek commentaries. The commentators included are, in chronological order: Adrastus, Aspasius, Alexander of Aphrodisias, Porphyry, Dexippus, Themistius, Syrianus, Ammonius, Priscian of Lydia, Asclepius, Philoponus, Simplicius, Olympiodorus, Elias, David, Stephanus, Eustratius, Michael of Ephesus, Sophonias.)

Sorabji, R. (ed.) (1987–) *Ancient Commentators on Aristotle*, London: Duckworth and Ithaca, NY: Cornell University Press. (English translations, with introduction and notes, to be supplemented by a sourcebook.)

—— (ed.) (1990) *Aristotle Transformed: The Ancient Commentators and their Influence*, London: Duckworth and Ithaca, NY: Cornell University Press. (A comprehensive survey of the present state of knowledge, with extensive bibliography.)

RICHARD SORABJI

ARISTUPPUS THE YOUNGER
see CYRENAICS

ARITHMETIC HIERARCHY
see RECURSION-THEORETIC HIERARCHIES

ARITHMETIC, PHILOSOPHICAL ISSUES IN

The philosophy of arithmetic gains its special character from issues arising out of the status of the principle of mathematical induction. Indeed, it is just at the point where proof by induction enters that arithmetic stops being trivial. The propositions of elementary arithmetic – quantifier-free sentences such as '$7 + 5 = 12$' – can be decided mechanically: once we know the rules for calculating, it is hard to see what mathematical interest can remain. As soon as we allow sentences with one universal quantifier, however – sentences of the form '$(\forall x) f(x) = 0$' – we have no decision procedure either in principle or in practice, and can state some of the most profound and difficult problems in mathematics. (Goldbach's conjecture that every even number greater than 2 is the sum of two primes, formulated in 1742 and still unsolved, is of this type.)

It seems natural to regard as part of what we mean by natural numbers that they should obey the principle of induction. But this exhibits a form of circularity known as 'impredicativity': the statement of the principle involves quantification over properties of numbers, but to understand this quantification we must assume a prior grasp of the number concept, which it was our intention to define. It is nowadays a commonplace to draw a distinction between impredicative definitions, which are illegitimate, and impredicative specifications, which are not. The conclusion we should draw in this case is that the principle of induction on its own does not provide a non-circular route to an understanding of the natural number concept. We therefore need an independent argument. Four broad strategies have been attempted, which we shall consider in turn.

1 Formalism
2 Empiricism
3 Intuitionism
4 Logicism

1 Formalism

Although the problem of accounting for both the objects apparently spoken of and the knowledge we appear to have about them in a way that explains both the apparent necessity and the apparent applicability of this knowledge is one which arises for all areas of mathematics, arithmetic has features which make some answers to the question seem especially plausible. In the language we use to express arithmetic every number has a canonical name (called a 'numeral'). This fact has made formalism a persistently attractive option in the case of arithmetic: since every number has a numeral to represent it, we can restrict our attention to the symbols and let numbers themselves drop out of the account entirely. It is not clear that this move helps very much with the epistemological part of the problem, since if the account is to license the whole of arithmetic, numerals will have to be abstract entities our knowledge about which demands explanation. But in any case formalism as just described is untenable, since it leaves the applicability of arithmetic wholly unexplained: we cannot rest content with the claim that arithmetic is just a game with symbols and not demand an account of why it should be *this* game that we play rather than any other.

If the fault in formalism is that it does not allow arithmetical statements to be meaningful, it might be thought an improvement to regard the terms occurring in our formal theory as being given their meaning by the role they play in the axioms of the theory. This variant of formalism has been advanced as an account not just of Peano's axiomatization of arithmetic but of the axiomatic method generally (most famously by Hilbert in his correspondence with Frege; see Frege 1980). It is far from clear, however, that the terms of a formal language can be invested with meaning this easily. In the 1920s and 1930s the members of the Vienna Circle (most notably their 'logician-in-chief', Rudolf Carnap) regarded arithmetic as true only 'by convention'. But if we were to adopt an inconsistent convention our language would be incapable of saying anything about the world. The general point, then, is that formalism cannot explain applicability without assuming consistency, and the most obvious sort of proof of the consistency of arithmetic appeals to our prior grasp of an infinite model, thus facing again the very difficulty formalism was intended to solve.

In his later work Hilbert had the idea of partitioning arithmetic into a real part, for which he gave a finitistic justification (see §3 below), and an ideal part, to be treated formally and justified instrumentally as a method of providing shorter or more comprehensible proofs of results in the real part. The consistency problem arises once more, of course, but Hilbert hoped to be able to solve it without supplying a model, by a combinatorial analysis of the syntax of the formal language. Such an analysis could, he thought, be carried out using the conceptual resources of the finitistically justified real part. Gödel's incompleteness theorems coupled with Turing's analysis of the notion of computability killed Hilbert's programme in the grand form originally envisaged. However, mathematicians hardly ever exploit the full strength of the classical system and not everyone has given up hope of an instrumental justification on Hilbertian lines of the parts they actually use (see GÖDEL'S THEOREMS §6; HILBERT'S PROGRAMME AND FORMALISM §4; TURING, A.M.).

2 Empiricism

If objections to formalism lead us to believe that arithmetical statements really are *true*, we might try Mill's strategy, which treats numbers as empirical and arithmetical statements as empirical generalizations (see MILL, J.S. §3). This strategy has not been popular – our conviction that the hardness of the logical 'must' applies in arithmetic too seems difficult to dispel – but it is quite difficult to refute decisively. Frege objected to it on the grounds that if numbers were empirical, only what is empirical could be counted, whereas number, in Locke's phrase, 'applies itself to men, angels, actions, thoughts – everything that either doth exist or can be imagined' (1689: II.xvi.1). This is not, however, a decisive objection, since the empiricist may be prepared to accept that 'everything that doth exist or can be imagined' is ultimately explicable in empirical terms. A better objection is that empiricism seems ill-equipped to ground our knowledge about large numbers (for example, those larger than the number of atoms in the observable universe). Even though such numbers are practically useless (which is precisely why empirical evidence provides no confirmation for assertions about them), the revision to arithmetic which would be needed if we did not admit them is radical and the resulting system would be awkward to use. The most persuasive objection of all, however, is the difficulty the arithmetical empiricist has in justifying the principle of mathematical induction. It is very hard to see what would count as empirical evidence either for or against this principle.

3 Intuitionism

A third broad strategy is to appeal to intuition to explain how arithmetical knowledge is possible. This approach is due to Kant, whose account of arithmetic parallels quite closely his account of geometry. A geometric proof typically begins with a construction (of a triangle, for instance), on which various operations are then performed. Since I construct the triangle in intuition, Kant held that it will be subject to just the spatial structure which sensibility imposes on all my experience. As a consequence, the geometric theorem I prove by this means is applicable a priori to experience. Similarly, in order to prove that $7+5=12$ I must first construct the concept 'seven' in intuition and then perform on my construction various operations. What is less clear in the arithmetical case than in the geometric one is how the structure imposed by sensibility – what Kant calls the 'form' of intuition – constrains the construction. Kant admits that we do not depend on sensibility for the *concepts* of arithmetic, which are therefore purely intellectual in contrast to those of geometry, but he holds that constructing the concepts depends on counting, which is a process apparently subject to the forms of space and time. It was common in the nineteenth century to read Kant as advocating a neat parallelism – that arithmetic is the science of time just as geometry is that of space – but this is at best a simplification. It is in any case far from clear that counting depends on time. Notice, though, that if we abandon this dependence we thereby give up just what Kant saw as the principal advantage of his account, namely its explanation of the applicability of arithmetic. The moral is quite general: the appeal to intuition beyond the limits of logic, which is characteristic of Platonism, does nothing to explain the applicability of mathematics when it is removed from the Kantian framework (see KANT, I. §5).

If I assert an arithmetical proposition, I am, according to Kant, reporting the result of a mental construction which I have performed or could in principle perform. But as Frege said, 'another man's idea is another idea'. Kant's account makes '$7+5=12$' express a different statement on each person's lips. It is therefore unavoidably solipsistic.

A further difficulty is caused by Kant's insistence that sensibility is passive and that the intuitions it supplies are immediate representations: it is hard to believe that I can have in my mind an *immediate* representation of a very large number, such as 10^{100}. The notion (denied by Kant) that humans are capable not only of passive intuition through the faculty of sensibility but also of creative – Kant calls them 'intellectual' – intuitions is a theme of German romanticism in the nineteenth century. In application to arithmetic it was used by Brouwer to provide an account on which our experience of time unfolding gives us an intuition of succession – what Brouwer calls the bare two-oneness – which we can repeat for ourselves at will as creative subjects. On this view the law of the excluded middle is not justified: if numbers are mind-dependent and have no existence outside of our constructions, then, for example, there is no reason to believe that Goldbach's conjecture (that every even number greater than 2 is the sum of two primes) must be either true or false in advance of constructing either a proof or a counterexample.

Hilbert's justification for the real part of his real/ideal partition mentioned in §1 above proceeds on similar lines to Brouwer's, although the intuitions on which numbers are based are for Hilbert those of finite arrangements of concrete objects. For this reason Hilbert's account seems less likely than Brouwer's to descend into solipsism. But the principal difference between their conceptions is that Brouwer regarded arithmetical statements and proofs as mental constructions available within arithmetic in the same way as numbers themselves. For Hilbert, on the other hand, any application of arithmetic to proofs is a matter for the metatheory. The result is that Hilbert's finitism can justify directly only a fragment of arithmetic with a limited induction principle (so-called primitive recursive arithmetic), whereas Brouwer's intuitionism has a much stronger induction principle available to it.

There is a persistent worry, however, as to whether either Hilbert or Brouwer overcame the problem Kant's account faced with large numbers. Both were ready to accept arguments on the basis of what humans can do in principle: these arguments seem to turn on a distinction between finite and infinite which is not available from their perspective without independent justification. If so, their position collapses into 'strict finitism', the view that we cannot have a general grasp of the notion of arbitrarily large finite numbers.

4 Logicism

The last strategy, the formulation of which is due to Frege, is to show that arithmetical truths are logical. One way of doing this is to postpone the attempt to explain the substantival use of number-words and to explain instead their adjectival use. This can be done by defining not the numbers themselves but the numerically definite quantifiers:

$$\exists^0 xFx \equiv_{Df} \sim\exists xFx$$
$$\exists^{n+1} xFx \equiv_{Df} \exists x(Fx \wedge \exists^n y(Fy \wedge y \neq x)).$$

From these definitions we can prove logically that, for example,

$$\exists^7 xFx \wedge \exists^5 xGx \wedge \exists^0 x(Fx \wedge Gx) \supset \exists^{12} x(Fx \vee Gx),$$

which we can interpret as being what is meant by '$7+5=12$'. By the same means we can generate the whole of the positive part of elementary arithmetic, that is, the true quantifier-free equalities. What we cannot generate is the negative part, that is, the true inequalities. For this we would need a guarantee, which logic alone cannot supply, that there is no finite bound to the number of objects that there are. (WITTGENSTEIN in the *Tractatus* (1922) proposed a rather more general variant of the same strategy, but it seems to be susceptible, in the context of Wittgenstein's system, to just the same difficulty over proving inequalities.)

Frege considered the introduction of numbers via numerically definite quantifiers in his *Grundlagen* (1884). What led him to reject it was not the difficulty of deriving inequalities but a problem facing not just this but any strategy involving implicit definitions, namely that such definitions do not fully determine the identity conditions of the objects they attempt to introduce. This is nowadays known as the Julius Caesar problem because Frege posed it by asking how one could tell from the implicit definitions whether or not Julius Caesar is a number. In the present context this question creates a problem not for the project of explaining the adjectival use of number-words but for the strategy of explaining their substantival use in *terms* of their adjectival use. The problem bites, therefore, only when we attempt to move beyond elementary arithmetic and quantify over numbers.

Another logicist strategy considered and rejected by Frege, but the subject of renewed attention at the end of the twentieth century, is to derive arithmetic from the 'numerical equivalence', that is, the contextual principle (sometimes called 'Hume's principle' or 'N=') that the number of Fs is the same as the number of Gs if and only if the Fs and the Gs can be correlated one-to-one. As a technical programme this is perfectly feasible, as Frege was the first to realize. He sketched in the *Grundlagen* a construction of the natural numbers and a proof that they satisfy Peano's axioms, assuming only second-order logic and the numerical equivalence. He nevertheless rejected the strategy of basing arithmetic on this equivalence because the Julius Caesar problem applies to it as much as to the previous contextual strategy. Interest in the strategy has been revived by Crispin Wright, who argued (1983) that the Julius Caesar problem can be solved by appeal to an independently plausible 'sortal inclusion principle' to the effect that objects must be of different sorts if the content of their identity conditions is sufficiently different.

The proposal Frege settled on instead was to define the number of Fs explicitly as the class of all concepts equinumerous with F. He showed in *Grundgesetze der Arithmetik* (1893–1903) that on this definition of number arithmetic can be deduced from what he took to be logical principles. (One of his allegedly logical principles was inconsistent, however, and subsequent attempts – most notably by Whitehead and RUSSELL – to repair Frege's system have had to appeal to principles even their advocates have baulked at calling logical.)

Frege's solution to the Julius Caesar problem (the underdetermination of the objects of arithmetic by the principles about them to which we are committed) is in any case under threat from the opposite problem: any non-arithmetical determination of the objects which solves the Julius Caesar problem will give numbers extra properties which, since they do not flow from the principles governing numbers, must be arbitrary and hence spurious. This problem was mentioned by Dedekind (in a letter to Weber dated 24 January 1888; see Ewald 1996), but it has come to prominence more recently through a much-cited paper by Benacerraf (1965). Two ways of dealing with it have been advanced under the generic label of 'structuralism'. Dedekind's way – that we are capable, once we have given a logical construction of one model of Peano's axioms, of abstracting away from its particular features to gain a conception of a model without those features – appeals to a mental process (abstraction) that many have found mysterious.

Benacerraf's way – that arithmetic should be seen as the study not of one particular model of Peano's axioms but of the structure which all such models have in common – is in danger of relapsing into the axiomatic formalism we considered earlier.

What Russell's paradox has suggested to Michael Dummett is that the concept 'set' is what he calls 'indefinitely extensible' (see Dummett 1991; DUMMETT, M.A.E. §3). This means that any attempt to regard the objects falling under the concept as forming a definite totality leads inevitably to the realization that there are other objects not in the totality which we are nevertheless forced to admit as falling under the concept. Dummett holds that the presence of 'indefinitely extensible' concepts is a characteristic feature of mathematics which should lead us to espouse for it the anti-realism which his more general meaning-theoretic arguments make room for. He recommends that we abandon the law of the excluded middle and espouse the mathematics of intuitionism but not Brouwer's solipsistic conception of its objects. Dummett thinks that in this way we can retain Frege's logicist insight that numbers are abstract objects truths about which embody deductive subroutines whose application to the world is validated by logic alone.

Just as Brouwerian intuitionism has been accused of an instability which reduces it to strict finitism, not everyone is persuaded that Dummett's position does not collapse into the ultra-intuitionism of middle-period Wittgenstein, according to which the meaning of an arithmetical generalization is identical with its proof. On this view Goldbach's conjecture does not in the present state of knowledge have any meaning at all.

See also: FREGE, G.; HUSSERL, E.; LOGICAL AND MATHEMATICAL TERMS, GLOSSARY OF

References and further reading

* Benacerraf, P. (1965) 'What Numbers Could Not Be', *Philosophical Review* 74: 47–73; repr. in P. Benacerraf and H. Putnam (eds) *Philosophy of Mathematics: Selected Readings*, Cambridge: Cambridge University Press, 2nd edn, 1983. (Referred to in §4. The impetus for much recent work on the philosophy of arithmetic.)
Benacerraf, P. and Putnam, H. (eds) (1964) *Philosophy of Mathematics: Selected Readings*, Cambridge: Cambridge University Press, 2nd edn, 1983. (Includes work by Hilbert and Benacerraf referred to in this entry, as well as several other relevant articles.)
Carnap, R. (1934) *Logische Syntax der Sprache*, Vienna: Springer; trans. A. Smeaton, *The Logical*

Syntax of Language, London: Kegan Paul, 1937. (The most developed expression of the Vienna Circle's view of mathematics as being true by convention.)

Dedekind, R. (1888) *Was sind und was sollen die Zahlen?*, Braunschweig: Vieweg; trans. 'What are Numbers and What Should They Be?', in W.B. Ewald (ed.) *From Kant to Hilbert: A Source Book in the Foundations of Mathematics*, Oxford: Clarendon Press, 1996. (A beautiful presentation of arithmetic as the study of 'simply infinite' systems, that is, models of what are now known as Peano's axioms.)

* Dummett, M.A.E. (1991) *Frege: Philosophy of Mathematics*, London: Duckworth. (A lucid critique of Frege's logicism and a brief account of Dummett's own views on indefinitely extensible concepts.)

* Ewald, W.B. (ed.) (1996) *From Kant to Hilbert: A Source Book in the Foundations of Mathematics*, Oxford: Clarendon Press. (Includes the letter from Dedekind to Weber referred to in §4, as well as much relevant material by Kant, Hilbert, Brouwer and others.)

* Frege, G. (1884) *Die Grundlagen der Arithmetik: eine logisch-mathematische Untersuchung über den Begriff der Zahl*, Jena: Pohle; trans. J.L. Austin, *The Foundations of Arithmetic: A Logico-Mathematical Enquiry into the Concept of Number*, Oxford: Blackwell, 2nd edn, 1980. (Referred to in §4. An accessible, entertaining classic.)

* —— (1893–1903) *Grundgesetze der Arithmetik*, Jena: Pohle, 2 vols; Part 1 of vol. 1 trans. M. Furth, *Basic Laws of Arithmetic*, Berkeley, CA: University of California Press, 1964. (Referred to in §4. Despite the contradiction at its core, includes much that is still of interest.)

* —— (1980) *Philosophical and Mathematical Correspondence*, trans. H. Kaal, ed. G. Gabriel *et al*, Oxford: Blackwell. (Includes the correspondence between Frege and Hilbert referred to in §1.)

Hilbert, D. (1926) 'Über das Unendliche', *Mathematische Annalen* 95: 161–90; trans. 'On the Infinite', in P. Benacerraf and H. Putnam (eds) *Philosophy of Mathematics: Selected Readings*, Cambridge: Cambridge University Press, 2nd edn, 1983. (A statement of Hilbert's programme.)

* Locke, J. (1689) *An Essay concerning Human Understanding*, ed. P.H. Nidditch, Oxford: Clarendon Press, 1979. (Referred to in §2. Includes an account of arithmetic that presages some aspects of Kant's.)

* Wittgenstein, L. (1922) *Tractatus Logico-Philosophicus*, trans. D.F. Pears and B.F. McGuiness, London: Routledge, 1961. (Referred to in §4. The treatment of arithmetic is to be found in the 6.1s and 6.3s.)

—— (1929–30) *Philosophical Remarks*, ed. R. Rhees, trans. R. Hargreaves and R. White, Oxford: Blackwell, 1978; repr. Chicago, IL: University of Chicago Press, 1980. (The source for the ultra-intuitionistic conception of Wittgenstein's middle period.)

* Wright, C. (1983) *Frege's Conception of Numbers as Objects*, Aberdeen: Aberdeen University Press. (Referred to in §4. A fascinating defence of the contextual strategy Frege rejected.)

—— (1986) 'Strict Finitism', in *Realism, Meaning and Truth*, Oxford: Blackwell. (A rare recent example of a philosopher taking strict finitism seriously.)

MICHAEL POTTER

ARMSTRONG, DAVID MALET (1926–)

David Armstrong was born in Melbourne, and studied philosophy at the Universities of Sydney and Oxford. He returned to Australia to teach at the University of Melbourne and later moved to the chair at Sydney. He has made many major contributions to central topics in epistemology and metaphysics, including perception, laws, universals, the mind, belief and knowledge, and possibility. His overall programme has been the articulation of a naturalistic metaphysics, understood as the doctrine that nothing at all exists except the single world of space and time.

A notable feature of his work in these contentious areas has been its directness and clarity, and the central importance he attaches to squaring what the philosopher says with what science, especially physical science, teaches us. In both these respects he is like another important Australian philosopher, J.J.C. Smart, and together they have influenced the way a generation of philosophers in Australia do philosophy, as well as influencing the doctrines they espouse.

1 Biography
2 Central state theory of mind
3 Perception, belief, knowledge
4 Universals, laws and possibility

1 Biography

David Armstrong was born in 1926 in Melbourne, Australia. He studied philosophy at the University of Sydney under John ANDERSON, a major figure in the history of Australian philosophy. He went to Oxford and took the recently established B. Phil. degree in 1954, taught briefly at Birkbeck College, London, before returning to Australia to teach at the

University of Melbourne. He succeeded J.L. Mackie in Anderson's chair at Sydney in 1964. Although he studied at Oxford during the heyday of linguistic philosophy (see ORDINARY LANGUAGE PHILOSOPHY, SCHOOL OF), his work has always been very much in the tradition of the systematic metaphysicians who saw their business as the articulation of a comprehensive picture of what there is, what it is like, and how we know about it.

2 Central state theory of mind

Armstrong is probably best known for his influential *A Materialist Theory of the Mind*. He was originally a Rylean behaviourist but became converted to the identity theory of mind, the theory that mental states are brain states, by John Jamieson Carswell SMART (see IDENTITY THEORY OF MIND). The book is a defence of a central state version of the identity theory.

Armstrong argues that the concept of a mental state is the concept of a state that plays a distinctive, causally intermediate role between stimuli, other mental states and behavioural responses. Thus, to give the rough idea, pain is the state that is typically caused by bodily damage, and typically causes a desire that the state cease, a desire that in turn causes a behavioural response that is believed will tend to satisfy this desire and minimize the damage. This account makes good evolutionary sense of why we feel pain by making transparent the survival value of pain. This claim, and the corresponding claims for the other mental states, are put forward as conceptual analyses, and constitute the central state theory of mind. Most of the book is devoted to defending central state analyses of various mental concepts.

On the central state theory, the question of the identity of a given mental state M is the empirical question of what plays the distinctive, causally intermediate role assigned to M by the central state theory. Armstrong observed that in each case it will most likely turn out to be some state or other of the brain that plays the distinctive role, so deriving the identity theory from his central state theory.

Armstrong's central state theory gave a central place to causal connections between mental states as well as to those between stimuli, mental state and response. His theory was thus one of the first versions of functionalism (see FUNCTIONALISM) though it was not marketed as such.

3 Perception, belief, knowledge

In the early- to mid-twentieth century, the view that perceptual experience is most directly an acquaintance with something mental, and the view that physical objects are some kind of logical construction out of perceptual experiences, were widely entertained (see PERCEPTION; SENSE DATA). Armstrong's *Perception and the Physical World*, published in 1961, defends direct realism – the view that we are directly acquainted with physical reality in perception, and that physical objects exist independently of our experiences. The most distinctive feature of his defence is his analysis of perception in terms of the acquisition of belief. Previous discussion of perception by philosophers had made perception implausibly distinct from what is after all its central function – the acquisition of belief.

Armstrong's treatment of belief follows a suggestion of F.P. Ramsey's that belief is like a map by which we steer (see RAMSEY, F.P.). Inside our heads is a master map that moves us through the world in such a way that what we desire is achieved to the extent that the map is correct, and individual beliefs are thought of as sub-maps of the master map. This approach to belief is now the standard alternative to the internal sentence theory of belief (see BELIEF).

His treatment of knowledge is a version of reliabilism. It is widely accepted that knowledge necessarily involves true belief: if S knows that P, then S believes that P, and it is true that P. But not all true belief is knowledge – the truth of a belief may be a fluke, and flukiness is incompatible with knowledge. Armstrong's suggestion, roughly, is that S's true belief that P is knowledge if it is an empirically reliable sign that P.

4 Universals, laws and possibility

The role of a truth maker plays a central role in Armstrong's metaphysics. If some sentence or proposition is true, there must be something that makes it true; if some predicate applies to something, there must be something that makes it true that the predicate applies. You cannot say that the word 'red' applies to X, and that that is all there is to say. There must be something about X, maybe a relational something, that makes it true that 'red' applies to it.

Armstrong's answer to what makes it true that predicates apply to particulars is a species of realism about universals or properties and relations (see UNIVERSALS). There are universals, and a predicate applies to X because of the universals that X instantiates. These universals have the following features. They exist independently of the classifications that we find natural; his theory is thus a version of realism, not of conceptualism. Second, they are not to be reduced to sets, or to resemblances between particulars; his theory is not a sort of nominalism.

Third, there are no uninstantiated universals. Every universal is possessed by at least one thing; thus his theory is not a platonic realism. Fourth, there is not a distinct universal for each semantically distinct predicate. One and the same universal may, and typically does, make many different predicates true of a particular. His theory is thus a sparse theory of universals. Finally, which universals there are is an a posteriori matter to be settled by total science. Armstrong's theory is thus a version of scientific realism. This highly original theory has established itself as a major position in the debate over universals.

Armstrong's account of laws of nature and of possibility draws on his realism about universals. A long-standing challenge in philosophy has been to distinguish universal statements of the form 'Every F is G' that express laws of nature, are nomic universals, from those that express accidental regularities. 'Every massive body attracts every other massive body' is a law of nature. 'Everyone in this room speaks English' is an accidental regularity (in the sense of not being a law, not in the sense of being a fluke) (see LAWS, NATURAL). Armstrong's theory, roughly, is that the laws are the universal statements that correspond to relations of nomic necessitation between universals: 'Every F is G' is a law if being F necessitates being G.

Armstrong's account of possibility is a combinatorial one, drawing on his realism about universals. We can think of how things are as a huge arrangement of particulars and universals. The various possibilities can then be thought of as all the combinations and recombinations of these particulars and universals according to various rules for combining particulars and universals. Thus, to give the barest bones of the idea, suppose that there is in fact mass M at point p, and mass N at point q. What makes it possible that there be mass M at q, and mass N at p? The fact that putting being M with being at q, and putting being N with being at p, do not violate the rules of combination.

See also: AUSTRALIA, PHILOSOPHY IN; PERCEPTION; RELIABILISM

List of works

Armstrong, D.M. (1960) *Berkeley's Theory of Vision*, Melbourne: Melbourne University Press. (Critical discussion of George Berkeley's *A New Theory of Vision*.)
—— (1961) *Perception and the Physical World*, London: Routledge & Kegan Paul. (Discussed in §3.)
—— (1962) *Bodily Sensations*, London: Routledge & Kegan Paul. (An account of bodily sensations in terms of the perception of happenings inside the body.)
—— (1968) *A Materialist Theory of the Mind*, London: Routledge & Kegan Paul. (Discussed in §3. A paperback edition with a new preface and bibliography appeared in 1993.)
—— (1973) *Belief, Truth and Knowledge*, Cambridge: Cambridge University Press. (Discussed in §3.)
—— (1978) *Universals and Scientific Realism*, Cambridge: Cambridge University Press, 2 vols. (Discussed in §4.)
—— (1983) *What is a Law of Nature?*, Cambridge: Cambridge University Press. (Discussed in §4.)
—— (with N. Malcolm) (1984) *Consciousness and Causality: a Debate on the Nature of Mind*, Oxford: Blackwell. (A debate between Armstrong and Norman Malcolm.)
—— (1989a) *Universals: an Opinionated Introduction*, Boulder, CO: Westview Press. (Introduction to the problem of universals from his general perspective on the problem.)
—— (1989b) *A Combinatorial Theory of Possibility*, Cambridge: Cambridge University Press. (Discussed in §4.)
—— (1997) *A World of States of Affairs*, Cambridge: Cambridge University Press.

References and further reading

Bacon, J., Campbell, K. and Reinhardt, L. (1993) *Ontology, Causality and Mind*, Cambridge: Cambridge University Press. (Good collection of papers on Armstrong's work with replies by Armstrong. Also contains a bibliography of his writings up to 1992.)
Bogdan, R. (ed.) (1984) *D.M. Armstrong*, vol. 4, *Profiles*, Dordrecht: Reidel. (Good collection of papers on Armstrong's work with replies by him and an intellectual autobiography. Also contains an annotated bibliography of his writings up to 1984.)

FRANK JACKSON

ARNAULD, ANTOINE (1612–94)

Antoine Arnauld, a leading theologian and Cartesian philosopher, was one of the most important and interesting figures of the seventeenth century. As the most prominent spokesperson and defender of the Jansenist community based at Port-Royal, almost all Arnauld's efforts were devoted to theological matters. But early on, with his largely constructive objections to

Descartes' Meditations *in 1641, he established a reputation as an analytically rigorous and insightful philosophical thinker. He went on to become perhaps Descartes' most faithful and vociferous defender. He found Cartesian metaphysics, particularly mind-body dualism, to be of great value for the Christian religion. In a celebrated debate with Nicolas Malebranche, Arnauld advanced something like a direct realist account of perceptual acquaintance by arguing that the representative ideas that mediate human knowledge and perception are not immaterial objects distinct from the mind's perceptions, but are just those perceptions themselves. His criticisms of Leibniz gave rise to another important debate. He also co-authored the so-called 'Port-Royal Logic', the most famous and successful logic of the early modern period. The underlying motives in all Arnauld's philosophical writings were, however, theological, and his greatest concern was to safeguard God's omnipotence and to defend what he took to be the proper Catholic view on questions of grace and divine providence*

1 Life and works
2 Arnauld and Descartes
3 The Arnauld–Malebranche debate
4 Correspondence with Leibniz

1 Life and works

Antoine Arnauld was born in Paris on 6 February 1612, one of the many children of an established and well-connected family. He intended to become a lawyer, but the Abbé St Cyran who was spiritual director of Port-Royal (where Arnauld's sister was abbess) convinced him to follow the ecclesiastical life (see PORT-ROYAL). He was ordained and received his doctorate in theology in 1641, and was admitted to the faculty of the Sorbonne in 1643. Most of Arnauld's work throughout his life was theological, devoted to, among other things, an explanation and defence of what he took to be the orthodox Augustinian doctrine of grace and a strict contritionism (see AUGUSTINE §5, 7). But he was also responsible for a significant and influential philosophical output, mostly polemical. In 1640, Arnauld was asked by Mersenne to comment upon Descartes' *Meditations*, and his objections were published, with Descartes' responses, as the fourth set in the first edition of the work (1641) (see DESCARTES, R. §1, 7). The most important of Arnauld's religious works, *De la fréquent communion*, appeared in 1643. This was a defence of the ethical principles of St Cyran and an indictment of what he saw as the indulgent morals of the Jesuits. In the early 1660s, Arnauld co-authored two important works on language and method: the *Grammaire générale et raisonnée* (1660, with Claude Lancelot) and *La Logique, ou l'art de penser* (1662, written with Pierre Nicole, adopting some ideas of PASCAL). Better known as the 'Port-Royal Logic', the latter was a treatise on method and reasoning that drew heavily on Descartes' epistemological and methodological doctrines, particularly those found in the *Rules for the Direction of the Mind*.

Meanwhile, Arnauld, as the most prominent representative of the Jansenist movement centred at Port-Royal, continued to be persecuted for his religious views and, like all Jansenists, was suspected of Protestant persuasions and of harbouring politically subversive opinions. In 1656 he was excluded from the Sorbonne for his refusal to submit to the Church on the issue of whether or not Jansenius' *Augustinus* contained heretical propositions. After years of harassment and fearing for his safety, Arnauld left France for the Netherlands in 1679. From there he continued his theological and philosophical polemics. In 1683 he composed *Des vraies et des fausses idées* (On True and False Ideas), a philosophical attack upon Nicolas Malebranche's *De la recherche de la vérité* (The Search After Truth). This was followed two years later by his *Réflexions philosophiques et théologiques sur le nouveau système de la nature et de la grace* (Philosophical and theological reflection on the new system of nature and grace), in which he addressed Malebranche's theodicy and views on providence and grace. The debate with Malebranche, one of the great intellectual events of its day, continued until the end of Arnauld's life, often in harsh and highly personal terms. He also began a brief but philosophically rich correspondence with Leibniz in 1686 over Leibniz's metaphysical views. Arnauld died in exile in 1694.

2 Arnauld and Descartes

Arnauld's attraction to Descartes' philosophy began early. His objections to the *Meditations* are clearly offered in a constructive spirit by an ally who hopes to see the system move towards greater consistency. Descartes, in fact, found Arnauld's comments to be the most reasonable and serious of all. Arnauld divided his objections into three parts: the first two dealing with 'philosophical' issues, the third concentrating on 'points which may cause difficulty for theologians'. In the first part, 'The Nature of the Human Mind', he questions Descartes' claim that, since it is possible to form a concept of oneself embodying nothing but the certain knowledge that one is a thinking thing, thought alone constitutes one's essence. The most that can be concluded with certainty from such a premise, Arnauld insists, is 'that

I can obtain some knowledge of myself without knowledge of the body'; not, however, that there is a 'real distinction in existence between mind and body'. In the second part, 'Concerning God', Arnauld raises his famous objection to the circularity of Descartes' attempts to draw epistemic warrant from demonstrations of God's existence: 'I have one further worry, namely, how the author avoids reasoning in a circle when he says that we are sure that what we clearly and distinctly perceive is true only because God exists. But we can be sure that God exists only because we clearly and distinctly perceive this. Hence, before we can be sure that God exists, we ought to be able to be sure that whatever we perceive clearly and evidently is true' (Arnauld 1641: 32).

In the final part, Arnauld's most important remark concerns the consequences of Descartes' metaphysics for the Catholic doctrine of Eucharistic transubstantiation. Descartes has emptied the material world of sensible qualities (colour, taste, smell and so on), leaving behind only extension and its properties, modes which necessarily inhere in a substance. His ontology thus appears to Arnauld to be inconsistent with faith, which has traditionally been aligned with the view that the substance of the bread of the Eucharist is either converted into, or annihilated and replaced by, Christ's body, and only the accidents of the bread (colour, taste, smell) remain. Such a real existence of accidents, independent of any underlying substance, is ruled out on Cartesian principles. Descartes responded with one of his tentative reinterpretations of transubstantiation. Ironically, it would be on just this issue of the compatibility of Cartesian metaphysics with the Catholic dogma of the Eucharist that Arnauld would become Descartes' most loyal and vociferous defender over the next fifty years. He generally approved of Cartesianism not just because it seemed closer to the truth than any other system – especially the Aristotelian – but also because its doctrines were the most supportive of Christian piety. Arnauld believed that Descartes 'has demonstrated the existence of God better than anyone else', and that his mind–body dualism has laid the surest foundation for the immortality of the soul.

3 The Arnauld–Malebranche debate

In 1680, Arnauld came across the manuscript of Malebranche's *Traité de la nature et de la grace* (Treatise on Nature and Grace), which was in the process of being printed. He was so astounded by what he read there that, unable to halt its publication, he decided to publicly refute Malebranche's entire system. His ultimate target was Malebranche's views on grace and on God's general *modus operandi*. But he chose to begin his attack by undermining what he took to be the philosophical foundations of Malebranche's theology. Thus, in 1683 he published *Des vraies et des fausses idées*, an attack on Malebranche's theory of ideas as presented in his most important philosophical work, *De la recherche de la vérité* (1674–5) (see MALEBRANCHE, N. §§2, 3, 6).

Malebranche had argued that ideas, the immaterial representations present to the mind in perception and knowledge, are not themselves modes of our thought, as sensations are, but are the very archetypes or essences of things in God's mind, to which we have access through a kind of divine illumination or union with God.

Like most seventeenth-century philosophers, Arnauld believed that representative ideas play an essential role in human cognition. His objection was to thinking of ideas as image-objects in their own right, independent of the mind and mediating its access to the external world. Malebranche's view, he alleged, is a result of the same confusions that gave rise to the Aristotelians' 'sensible species'. As children, we wrongly assume that the images or reflections through which we sometimes see things not actually before the eyes are themselves objects, and later come to suppose that it is through similar image-objects that the mind thinks of things in their absence. But philosophers have realized that even in ordinary sense-perception the material bodies before the eyes are not immediately present to the soul. They conclude that in sense-perception what is directly perceived are representative beings rather than bodies themselves. This line of reasoning, Arnauld argues, treats the soul as if it were material, assuming that the way the senses work and the way the mind works are analogous. More importantly, a theory that makes ideas into mind-independent entities mediating cognition of the world has the absurd consequence that we never know or perceive that world: all we ever perceive are ideas. The mind is surrounded by a 'palace of ideas' that keeps it from the world of things that God intended it to know. Malebranche 'transports us to unknown lands...where a man sees, instead of the men toward whom he turns his eyes, only intelligible men; instead of the sun and the stars which God has created, only an intelligible sun and intelligible stars' (Arnauld 1683: 227–8). Even Malebranche must reject such extreme Pyrrhonism (see PYRRHO; PYRRHONISM).

Arnauld goes on to argue that the ideas that function in human perception and knowledge are not 'representative beings distinct from the mind's perceptions', but just *are* those perceptions: 'I take the idea of an object and the perception of an object to be the same thing' (1683: 198). To have an idea of a thing just is to perceive or think of that thing; it is not to have some proxy object standing before the mind. The idea is a mental act or operation which, through its 'form' (a term borrowed from Descartes, who defines an idea as the *forma cogitationis*), is directed at some object but which is not itself the object of perception. One can thus characterize a thought through its object (for example, as the idea of the sun) by attending to its form, or one can consider it simply as an act or mode of the mind:

> I have said that I take the perception and the idea to be the same thing. Nevertheless, it must be remarked that this thing, although single, stands in two relations: one to the soul which it modifies, the other to the thing perceived, in so far as it exists objectively in the soul. The word *perception* more directly indicates the first relation; the word *idea*, the latter.
>
> (Arnauld 1683: 198)

There is still a sense in which we perceive material objects only mediately or indirectly, since we perceive a thing through the form of the perceptual act (that is, through the idea of the thing). But it does not follow from this that we perceive things indirectly in the strong and unacceptable sense of 'indirect' entailed by Malebranche's account.

In Arnauld's eyes, then, his debate with Malebranche over the nature of ideas pitted something like a direct realist account of perceptual acquaintance with Malebranche's representationalist or indirect realist account. But the debate is also a rich source for early modern theories of intentionality (see INTENTIONALITY). Arnauld claims that it is not his intention to do away with all representative beings, since he grants that the mind's modifications are themselves representative of objects. This, in fact, is how his act-ideas achieve their relatedness to objects (the second relation in which every idea stands). Every perception is the perception *of* something because it has a representational content (what Arnauld, again following Descartes, calls its 'objective reality') and thus is representative of some object: 'The perceptions that our soul has of objects are necessarily representative of these objects' (Arnauld 1684: 381). This representative character is an intrinsic feature of the perceptual act and is what gives the act its intentionality, or directedness-towards-an-object. And for Arnauld this is true for every mental event – not just clear and distinct perceptions, but also sensations and passions. Malebranche, by contrast, claims that only intellections have intentionality, and their intentionality is explained by the real presence to the mind of some distinct object which the mind apprehends – that is, a divine idea – and not by some features intrinsic to the mental operation itself.

Arnauld also directed his considerable critical skills to the doctrine of the vision in God. Much of his concern was focused on Malebranche's claim that our ideas of extended beings, or the idea of extension itself (what Malebranche calls the 'infinite intelligible extension') are in God. He suspected that this was tantamount to placing extension itself really or 'formally' in God and thus making God extended or material, and that Malebranche's doctrine harboured a latent Spinozism or Gassendism (see SPINOZA, B. DE §4; GASSENDI, P. §4). Arnauld accused Malebranche of distorting the thought of both Descartes and Augustine – whom Arnauld and Malebranche alike took as their mentors – and even of propounding anti-Cartesian, anti-Augustinian and anti-Christian views.

The clash over representative ideas – which continued until Arnauld's death – was only supposed to be a preliminary, however, for the real issue: God's manner of acting in the realms of nature and grace. Malebranche, in his theodicy, had argued that evil and sin occur because God acts only by what he calls 'general volitions' – volitions that carry out general and simple laws. God would like to forestall evil and to save every human being, but actually to do so would require a great number of *ad hoc*, particular volitions and would demand that God should violate the principles of his own nature, which determines him to carry out his plans by the wisest and most simple means. So God must *allow* imperfections in the world and the damnation of many (see MALEBRANCHE, N. §5).

Arnauld objected strongly to this model of God's activity. He accused Malebranche of undermining God's omnipotence and of treating God's agency no differently from human agency. He insists that, on Malebranche's account, God is like some distant king who only issues general edicts and has no concern over how his kingdom is run in its details. Such a picture threatens the true Catholic system of divine providence and removes God from direct governance of the world. Moreover, Arnauld rejects any attempt to limit God's absolute power, even if that limit comes from God's own nature. God's absolute freedom is the freedom of a will that determines itself and wills with a complete indifference.

Many of Arnauld's criticisms of Malebranche are rooted in his Jansenism. For it is clear that what really bothers Arnauld is the notion that God could will something (for example, that all humans should be saved or that the world should be without evil) and the object of his will not obtain, that is, that a divine volition might not be efficacious. For Arnauld, all

God's volitions are necessarily efficacious, and if God had willed that all humans should be saved – and this claim is, by itself, unacceptable to Arnauld – then all humans would have been saved.

4 Correspondence with Leibniz

This same concern for safeguarding God's omnipotence and freedom is also apparent in Arnauld's critical remarks on Leibniz's metaphysics. In 1686, seeking to enlist Arnauld's support for his ecumenical project of bringing about a reconciliation of the Catholic and Protestant faiths, Leibniz sent a summary of his *Discours de la métaphysique* to Arnauld. Among the propositions upon which Arnauld focused was one related to Leibniz's notion of substance: that the individual concept of every person involves, once and for all, everything that will ever happen to them. Arnauld responded by saying that if that is so, then 'God was free to create or not to create Adam, but supposing he decided to create him, all that has since happened to the human race or which will ever happen to it has occurred and will occur by a necessity more than fatal' (Montgomery 1980: 73). God, having chosen to create Adam, therefore has no freedom or control over the course of events that constitutes the history of the world, since it all apparently follows necessarily from the concept of the first human. Arnauld suggested that Leibniz should cease such metaphysical speculations and think seriously of the condition of his soul and of entering the fold of the Catholic Church. Fortunately their correspondence continued, and Arnauld's objections and queries – concerning necessity, divine providence, causality, the being of possibles, the nature of individual essences and the distinction between essential and accidental properties – led Leibniz to think more deeply about many of his doctrines, and were certainly of great importance in the development of Leibniz's mature metaphysics (see LEIBNIZ, G.W. §I, 4, 6–7).

See also: DUALISM; FREEDOM, DIVINE; PERCEPTION

List of works

Arnauld, A. (1775–83) *Oeuvres de Messire Antoine Arnauld, Docteur de la Maison et Société de Sorbonne* (Collected works), Paris: Sigismond D'Arnay, 43 vols. (This authoritative collection contains all works by Arnauld listed below.)

—— (1641) *Quartae objectiones*, in *Oeuvres*, vol. 38; trans. J. Cottingham, D. Murdoch and R. Stoothoff as 'Fourth Objections', *The Philosophical Writings of Descartes*, vol. 2, Cambridge: Cambridge University Press, 1984. (Arnauld's objections to Descartes' *Meditations*.)

—— (1643) *De la fréquent communion*, in *Oeuvres*, vol. 27. (A critique of Jesuit morality and a defence of Jansenist penitential discipline.)

—— (1660) *Grammaire générale et raisonnée*, in *Oeuvres*, vol. 41; trans. J. Rieux and B.E. Rollin as *General and Rational Grammar: the Port-Royal grammar*, The Hague: Mouton, 1975. (Treatise on language and grammar, co-authored with C. Lancelot. The translation contains a preface by A.C. Danto and a critical essay by N. Kretzmann.)

—— (1662) *La Logique, ou l'art de penser* (Logic or the art of thinking), in *Oeuvres*, vol. 41; trans. J. Buroker, Manchester: Manchester University Press, (forthcoming). (Treatise on language, reasoning, and method, co-authored with P. Nicole.)

—— (1683) *Des vraies et des fausses idées*, in *Oeuvres*, vol. 38; trans. E. Kremer as *On True and False Ideas*, Lewiston, NY: Edwin Mellon Press, 1990; also trans. S. Gaukroger, Manchester: Manchester University Press, 1990. (Arnauld's attack on Malebranche's theory of ideas and doctrine of the vision in God.)

—— (1684) *Défense de M. Arnauld contre la réponse au livre des vraies et des fausses idées* (Monsieur Arnauld's defence against the response to the book on true and false ideas) in *Oeuvres*, vol. 38. (Arnauld's response to Malebranche's initial counterattack.)

—— (1685) *Réflexions philosophiques et théologiques sur le nouveau système de la nature et de la grace* (Philosophical and theological reflection on the new system of nature and grace) in *Oeuvres*, vol. 39. (Arnauld's critique of Malebranche's theodicy and account of God's causal agency.)

References and further reading

Descartes, R. (1620–c.28) *Rules for the Direction of the Mind* in *The Philosophical Writings of Descartes*, vol. 1, trans. J. Cottingham, D. Murdoch and R. Stoothoff, Cambridge: Cambridge University Press, 1984. (Descartes' early methodological treatise.)

Dominicy, M. (1985) *La naissance de la grammaire moderne* (The birth of modern grammar), Brussels: Pierre Mardaga. (An examination of the emergence of linguistics as a specific discipline from the work of Arnauld, Nicole and Lancelot.)

Jansenius, C. (1640) *Augustinus*. (The Bishop of Ypres' monumental work of Augustinian theology.)

Kremer, E.J. (ed.) (1994) *The Great Arnauld and Some of his Philosophical Correspondents*, Toronto, Ont.:University of Toronto Press. (A collection of

important essays by leading scholars on Arnauld's philosophy and philosophical theology.)
— (1996) *Interpreting Arnauld*, Toronto, Ont.: Univerity of Toronto Press. (Another collection of important essays by leading scholars on Arnauld's philosophy and philosophical theology.)
Laporte, J. (1923) *Exposition de la doctrine* (d'aprés Arnauld), in vol. 2 of *La Doctrine de Port-Royal*, Paris: Presses Universitaires de France. (Part 1, 'Les vérités de la Grâce', provides a masterly study of Arnauld's views on grace, divine agency and freedom.)
Leibniz, G.W. *Discours de la méthode*, trans. G.R. Montgomery as *Discourse on Metaphysics/Correspondence with Arnauld*, La Salle II: Open Court, 1980. (Leibniz's metaphysics; Arnauld's critique, 1686–7.)
* Malebranche, N. (1674–5) *De la recherche de la vérité*, trans. T. Lennon and P.J. Olscamp as *The Search After Truth/Elucidations of the Search After Truth*, Columbus, OH: Ohio State University Press, 1980. (Malebranche's major philosophical work.)
— (1680) *Traité de la nature et de la grace*, in *Oeuvres* vol. 5; trans. P. Riley as *Treatise on Nature and Grace*, Oxford: Oxford University Press, 1992. (Malebranche's solution to the theodicy problem with respect to natural evils and to the distribution of grace.)
Nadler, S. (1988) 'Arnauld, Descartes, and Transubstantiation', *Journal of the History of Ideas* 49 (2): 229–46. (Discusses Arnauld's initial objections regarding the Eucharist and his later defence of Descartes on this issue.)
— (1989) *Arnauld and the Cartesian Philosophy of Ideas*, Princeton, NJ: Princeton University Press. (An analysis of Arnauld's theory of ideas and his account of perception and intentionality.)
Ndiaye, A.R. (1991) *La philosophie d'Antoine Arnauld* (The philosophy of Antoine Arnauld), Paris: J. Vrin. (A general analysis of Arnauld's philosophical opinions.)
Sleigh, R.C., Jr (1990) *Leibniz and Arnauld: A Commentary on Their Correspondence*, New Haven, CT: Yale University Press. (A rigorous and enlightening analysis of various philosophical themes from the correspondence.)

STEVEN NADLER

ART AND EMOTION

see EMOTION IN RESPONSE TO ART

ART, ABSTRACT

The use of the term 'abstract' as a category of visual art dates from the second decade of the twentieth century, when painters and sculptors had turned away from verisimilitude and launched such modes of abstraction as Cubism, Orphism, Futurism, Rayonism, and Suprematism. Two subcategories may be distinguished: first, varieties of figurative representation that strongly schematize, and second, completely nonfigurative or nonobjective modes of design (in the widest sense of that term). Both stand opposed to classic representationalism (realism, naturalism, illusionism, mimeticism) understood as the commitment to a relatively full depiction of the subject matter and construed broadly enough to cover the traditional 'high art' canon through to Post-Impressionism. Analytic and Synthetic Cubism are model cases of the first subcategory while Mondrian's neoplasticism and Pollock's classic drip works are paradigms of the second. Though the effect was revolutionary, the positive motivations for this degree of abstraction in visual art were not wholly new. What was new was the elevation of previously subordinate aims to the front rank and the pursuit of certain principal aims in isolation from the full pictorial package. Thus abstract art variously celebrates structural and colour properties of objects, scenes and patterns; effects of motion, light and atmosphere; aspects of perceptual process, whether normal or expressively loaded; and forms expressing cosmic conceptions, visionary states or utopian ambitions. With a few exceptions (for example, the Futurists) the founders of abstract art were far from lucid or forthcoming about the significance of their work, and viewers have found successive waves of abstraction initially baffling and even offensive. But abstract art now forms a secure part of the 'high art' canon, though generally its appeal is less well understood than that of the classic modes of representation. Criticisms of abstract art have also become more lucid.

The chief philosophical issues affecting abstract art concern the definition of the term and the delineation of subordinate types; the relation between abstraction and other modes of avant-garde art that superficially resemble it; the magnitude of the artistic values so far achieved by the various forms; and finally the theoretical limits of significance attainable by abstraction as compared with the limits encountered in figurative art.

1 **The history of the category**
2 **Basic distinctions**
3 **Schematizing abstraction**
4 **Nonfigurative or nonobjective abstraction**
5 **Intellectual and expressive values in abstract art**
6 **The limits of abstract art**

ART, ABSTRACT

1 The history of the category

The nearest precedent of the category and its label is the use, from about 1870, of the term 'abstract music' for music without lyrics or programme. Until late in the nineteenth century, use of the vocabulary of abstraction in relation to the visual arts was rare and predominantly pejorative. For example, Gustave Courbet in 1861 claimed that abstraction, by which he meant undue emphasis on any partial aspect of art, puts the true end of art beyond reach. Purity was a more common metaphor in early writings about the new art, as it had been in relation to music. The positive implications of 'abstraction' were first exploited in a major way by Willhelm Worringer (1908) and Wassily Kandinsky (1911), though the two had quite different art in mind. They argued persuasively that the 'urge to abstraction' is a 'primal artistic impulse' (Worringer's phrases). The term gained additional currency from the proclamation by Apollinaire and other champions of the new trends in France of a new art of 'pure painting' which drew more on 'conceived reality' than on the data of everyday vision (and not coincidentally evaded rivalry with photography). The category and label remained problematic for decades. Some artists (Braque and Mirò, for example) objected to any of their works being called abstract although the present consensus favours taking many of them that way.

2 Basic distinctions

'Schematizing abstraction' covers here certain forms of depiction which severely curtail the extent to which the visible properties of their subjects are made manifest. The outcome might have been produced by beginning from a natural motif seen from a single point of view and then, for ends quite removed from verisimilitude, reducing its descriptive content as well as adding pattern that is either not descriptive or deviantly so, relative to traditional standards. In contrast, nonfigurative or nonobjective abstraction eliminates all literally descriptive references in order to free expressive or intellectual content from all encumbrance. The work might be produced by beginning from lines, forms, textures, and colours, which are then worked up into aesthetically self-sufficient totalities. Neither category has a sharp boundary, and claims for the superiority of one over the other are doubtful. But the distinction deserves respect since it denotes a significant difference of interest of both the artist and the appropriately responsive viewer.

3 Schematizing abstraction

The schematic rendering of figures, appearances and space of an appropriate sort, carried to the required degree, allows seemingly endless variations, for which no systematic classification has yet been devised. Analytic Cubism, a prime instance, geometricizes contours, evacuates or etherealizes solids, and expunges much other detail. On the constructive side, it repeats edges at different eye-levels, imports contours from quite different points of view, and fractures objects and regions of empty space into overlapping facets or shards, as if an eccentric crystalline structure were being revealed. Since many of the interpolations and displacements are depictively cryptic or altogether nonfunctional, the perceptible nature of the motif tends to be obscured or confused. In classic cases (for example, Picasso's Portrait of Kahnweiler, 1911) the central motif (a man dressed in a neat wool suit over a ribbed shirt, embellished by necktie and watch chain, with his hands folded, and a bottle on a table to his right, light coming in from his left, etc.) emerges against the odds from a farrago of translucent angular clutter. Carried to an extreme the process renders the motif unidentifiable. The appeal of this sort of abstraction has been explained in terms of its power to convey the intricacy, instability or illusoriness of perception or of the material world, or alternatively the inner vitality of objects – a power deemed beyond the range of any traditional mode of representation.

Synthetic Cubism revises the schematizing process in two directions. Aspects that are curtailed further include atmosphere and depth. Compositions are dominated by template-like forms, often closely stacked, blocking recession, and with it, atmosphere. Media motifs, printed materials and other inherently flat elements are deployed to similar effect. Suggestions of ambient lighting and perceptual process, typical of Analytic Cubism, are also generally reduced or entirely banished. All this, together with the evident arbitrariness of many of the forms, creates the impression of the composition having been built up (synthesized) from invented components rather than derived by analytic decomposition of a natural motif. Contrarily, descriptive content is in certain respects enhanced compared with the norm in Analytic Cubism. Some forms signify sizeable sections of recognizable objects (a guitar, a table, for instance).

Synthetic Cubist figures may be invested with an uncanny presence, as they are in Picasso's Three Musicians, 1921 (The Museum of Modern Art version). Having assumed some of the properties of the flattened planes of which they are composed, yet being represented in full view without any optical interference, the figures have become enigmatic new realities inhabiting an equally unnatural space. This contrasts with the effect in Analytic Cubism of normal objects seen through a radically fractured lens.

Another of the many currents of schematic abstraction is generally known as lyrical or expressionist and is represented by various works of Kandinsky, Franz Marc, Paul Klee and others. Objects and space are dematerialized by blurred and calligraphically naive transforms of the Cubist schemata just cited, and by a dispersal of emphasis over the entire picture plane. Colour is typically dramatic or evocative.

4 Nonfigurative or nonobjective abstraction

Preliminary steps towards nonfigurative abstraction are discernible in forms of schematizing abstraction, notably in the works of Kandinsky, Malevich and Mondrian, but it seems best to define the category independently of this lineage and of the implication of a higher aspiration that may cling to it. (For the same reason 'pure' is best avoided, as is 'impure' for schematizing abstraction.) The key concept is that of a design which conveys no implication of actual (physical or 'tactile') space, though it is optional how strictly one applies this criterion. In no case are figure–ground distinctions excluded, any more than they are in abstract decorative designs. It is enough that depth cues be too faint, too fragmentary, too flagrantly inconsistent, or too dispersed for the image as a whole to convey the sense of any conceivable three-dimensional space. 'Figures' in the weak sense are woven or soaked into the ground, or fused to its surface like letters on a page; or the ground may press so closely upon the figures or switch relations with them so extensively that the continuity, uniformity and ubiquity necessary to accommodate physical contents is implicitly denied. The depth relations suggested by the parts of the design taken in isolation thereby collapse into mere appearances, though they remain vital to the aesthetic effect. This accords with the description by Greenberg and Fried of the pictorial space in nonfigurative abstractions as not tactile, but optical, indeterminate, or virtual – in a sense doubly illusionistic.

Kendall Walton (1990) proposed an alternative explanation of the figurative–nonfigurative distinction. On this view a nonfigurative Suprematist composition by Malevich represents the coloured patches that are part of the design itself fictionally standing in three-dimensional relations to each other. Were the design figurative, the patches would represent fictive three-dimensional forms, for example, ordinary physical objects, as standing in comparable relations.

Whatever the proper analysis, it seems plain that the appeal of most nonfigurative abstractions depends significantly on the viewer's susceptibility to spatial and more specifically pictorial ways of seeing. Under normal (if not always optimal) viewing conditions Mondrian's grids evoke lattices, windows, partitions or street patterns as if, or almost as if, 'seen' in the sense proper to representations. Similarly Helen Frankenthaler's works often evoke cloud and landscape forms. Even the Arthur Danto 'push-pull' tensions in works by Hans Hofmann and the titanic dimensions of Franz Kline's motifs capitalize on the involuntary exertion of the perceptual energies typically brought to bear on ordinary spatial presentations. The mystery felt to inhere in the more potent nonfigurative abstractions derives largely from the profusion of such subliminal underground connections, which trigger responses even when viewers are discouraged from making a literally representational reading. Possibly even the appeal of Ellsworth Kelly's hard-edged colour-blocks and Agnes Martin's misty stripes devolves in part from the challenge they pose to the space-obsessed visual system.

Closely related to the preceding is the dialectic of image and support stressed by formalist analysts such as Greenberg and Fried. For instance, recognizing that traditional art often seeks to make the support 'disappear' in favour of the illusory image (whereas in the ordinary, nonpictorial experience of a surface the percipient seeks to resolve perceptual flux and obtain a firm grasp of the objective reality) abstract artists have often sought to reverse priorities or play with tensions. Thus drips and slashing brushstrokes are intended to bring the surface to the fore, leaving only fleeting suggestions of images; and colour is poured directly on to unsized, unprimed canvas to bond image to fabric and evade the normal dichotomy of drawn edge and coloured area. Likewise solid 'op art' designs dissolve into fluctuating afterimages or visual squirm in the viewer's perceptual field, even when one attempts to see the surface merely as surface. Formalists regard the exploration of such paradoxes and inversions as a prime aim of nonfigurative abstraction. Others place greater weight upon the externally referential intellectual and expressive content which supposedly becomes available through the unsettling of normal perceptual expectations.

5 Intellectual and expressive values in abstract art

Writers such as Arthur Danto (1981) have demonstrated how much of a worldview may be teased out of seemingly inarticulate art. Thus the brushstroke paintings of De Kooning or their effigies in Lichtenstein are shown to have, in context, a wondrous depth of implication. Arguably the effect results from otherwise inexpressive elements acquiring magnified significance given an initial limitation to minimal means, a long tradition of thought and feeling conveyed by figurative means, and the conviction that authenticity demands zero excess, in the 'less is more' tradition. Where these conditions are met the sparest of patterns can express Zen simplicity, as in the late works of Ad Reinhardt; and Eva Hesse's crumpled cylinders, ragged sheets of plastic and wires wrapped in lumps can balance finely between a buoyant absurdity and pathos. Construed in this way, the game of viewing art can become one of sensitizing oneself to the merest or most idiosyncratic of signifiers.

From its inception the literature of abstraction has made much of abstract works of art conveying, reflecting, exploring, questioning or commenting upon scientific, semantical, aesthetic, or metaphysical concepts and theories. Abstract compositions are said to be creative responses to atomic or other physical theories, mathematical relationships, musical forms, laws of perception and other cognitive processes, unconscious psychological structures, conceptual or categorial truths, or to ideas and issues relating to art itself. Artists are said to engage in research in these domains. Difficulties arise, however, whenever works are presumed to do more than allude in an unspecific way to such referents and projects. To date, the specific content supposedly conveyed or the specific question posed has rarely been divulged. Mondrian, for example, repeatedly declares that art reveals and expresses 'laws of pure plastics' but he never enlightens us as to what these laws are or how we are to derive them from works of art. Nor do propounders of such interpretations ever raise the crucial question of whether a work misconceives or misrepresents its referent. Such reticence obviously casts a shadow over the credibility of these claims. Also, when explicit reference to intellectual content is implied by title, as it is in Georges Vantongerloo's paintings of the 1920s and 1930s (for example, Composition 15 derived from the equation $Y = ax^2 + bx + 18$, 1930), doubts arise as to what aesthetic sustenance the viewer can derive from the connection between design and content. Similarly, Josef Alber's Homage to the Square series is tied to his research into colour-interaction phenomena, but the paintings themselves would be ill-served by viewers ascribing artistic merit to them because they exemplify the principles governing such phenomena.

6 The limits of abstract art

The category of abstract art is defined in part by opposition to what is here called classic representationalism. But there is reason to think it should not embrace all nonrepresentational modes. A case in point is art which is 'concrete' in the sense of presenting material objects as such, including, for instance, Marcel Duchamp's unassisted ready-mades. Related examples occur here and there in the multifarious category of conceptual art: Joseph Kosuth's Titled [Art as Idea as Idea], [water], 1966, which consists of an enlarged photocopy of a dictionary definition of 'water'. These works undeniably abstract from representation in that they disavow all fictive appearances, even purely 'optical' ones. But their obtrusive and calculated ordinariness seems to close off all connection to the accepted paradigms of abstract art.

This breach results in significant part from the fact that the ordinariness of the works, taken in context, rebuffs aesthetic contemplation or freely imaginative engagement. Instead of offering a feast for the visual system, the work purports to deliver a message concerning art, the art world or society at large, and one that typically excoriates commodity fetishism, elitism and reverence for art. The mode of signification, on which the work's standing as art depends, resembles that of a rebus or emblem, whose decipherment is most efficaciously accomplished by limiting one's attention to the properties that convey the meaning – convey it, that is, given a detailed context which may include statements or even lectures by the artist. The work cooperates by offering scant aesthetic distraction. Much the same syndrome is found in Robert Morris' quasi-minimalist sculpture. For example, the erect and fallen shafts comprising Columns (1961/73) forswear almost all of the modernist sources of sculptural appeal: refined finish, defiance of gravity, balance, precise placement, and so forth.

Perhaps from this analysis a criterion may be devised for distinguishing between minimalist or conceptual works that count as abstract art and those that are best placed elsewhere. Qualifying works would be those inviting fairly comprehensive and sustained aesthetic contemplation. A work that aims mainly at blocking or deflecting such engagement in favour of other ends would fall into one or another adjacent category. Naturally, delicate distinctions are required to apply the criterion. For example, Christo's wrappings may straddle the boundary, since they purport to offer variable but generally quite limited contemplation-worthy fare.

Another boundary question arises over pre-modern works that radically schematize: Cycladic figures,

Sepik masks, and countless other 'primitive' images. Accepting such works into the category might seem justified inasmuch as they exemplify the 'urge to abstraction'. On the other hand, the works were certainly not inspired by a conscious rejection of classic representationalism. Further, nothing resembling the play with space fundamental to most twentieth-century abstraction can be plausibly ascribed to them. Thus including them would risk diluting the common ground on which the category was initially based. This issue is rarely discussed in the literature, but obviously deserves attention.

See also: DEPICTION; EXPRESSION, ARTISTIC

References and further reading

Barr, A.H., Jr (1936) *Cubism and Abstract Art*, New York: The Museum of Modern Art, 1966. (A classic account of varieties of Cubism.)

Cheetham, M. (1991) *The Rhetoric of Purity: Essentialist Theory and the Advent of Abstract Painting*, Cambridge: Cambridge University Press. (Detailed analysis of philosophical theories influencing Gauguin, Kandinsky and Mondrian.)

* Courbet, G. (1861) 'Letter in the *Courrier du dimanche*, December 25 1861', in L. Nochlin (ed.) *Realism and Tradition in Art, 1848–1900: Sources and Documents*, Englewood Cliffs, NJ: Prentice Hall, 1966, 34–6. (Gives Courbet's criticism of abstraction in visual art referred to in §1.)

* Danto, A.C. (1981) *The Transfiguration of the Commonplace*, Cambridge, MA: Harvard University Press. (Contains ambitious interpretations of works by abstraction expressionists and their successors, among others; relevant to §5.)

* Fried, M. (1965) *Three American Painters*, Boston: Garland Publishing Company. (Impressive formalist analysis of spatial effects in nonfigurative abstraction; relevant to §4.)

* Greenberg, C. (1973) *Art and Culture*, London: Thames & Hudson. ('Collage' and 'Abstract, Representational, and so forth' deal with the relation of image to surface discussed in §4.)

* Kandinsky, W. (1911) *Concerning the Spiritual in Art*, trans. and with intro. by M.T.H. Sadler, New York: Dover, 1977. (An early, highly speculative attempt to provide a theoretical basis for abstraction by one of its principal creators.)

Museum of Modern Art (1984) *The Museum of Modern Art, New York: the History and the Collection*, New York: Harry N. Abrams and The Museum of Modern Art. (Especially useful compendium of illustrations of cited works.)

Osborne, H. (1979) *Abstraction and Artifice in Twentieth-Century Art*, Oxford: Clarendon Press. (The only comprehensive treatment of the subject by a philosopher available in English. Generally sound, provided that one abstracts from the information-theoretic concepts by substituting 'schematic' for 'semantic' and 'nonfigurative' for 'syntactic' [abstraction].)

Pohribny, A. (1979) *Abstract Art*, Oxford: Phaidon. (Rich in illustrations of cited works; also contains a useful historical summary of modes of abstraction through the mid-1970s, except for Cubism.)

Rosenberg, C.M. (1971) 'Cubist Object Treatment: a Perceptual Analysis', *Artforum* 9 (8): 30–36. (An insightful, though somewhat technical analysis of Cubist pictorial devices.)

Schapiro, M. (1978) *Modern Art: 19th and 20th Centuries, Selected Essays*, New York: George Braziller. ('Abstract Art' and 'Mondrian' give probing analyses of the relation of abstract art to its antecedents and social context.)

* Walton, K.L. (1990) *Mimesis as Make-Believe: On the Foundations of the Representational Arts*, Cambridge, MA and London: Harvard University Press. (Major study of representation and fictional worlds.)

Whitford, F. (1984) *Understanding Abstract Art*, New York: E.P. Dutton. (A wide-ranging introduction to abstract painting.)

* Worringer, W. (1908) *Abstraction and Empathy: A Contribution to the Psychology of Style*, trans. Michael Bullock, Cleveland, OH: World Publishing Company, 1967. (A seminal study of abstraction in traditional art, both fine and decorative.)

JOHN BROWN

ART AND MORALITY

A complex set of questions is raised by an examination of the relationship between art and morality. First there is a set of empirical considerations about the effect that works of art have on us – one obviously contentious case is that of pornography. Many would argue that the artistic merits of a work are independent of any attitudes or actions it may lead us to adopt or perform. This claim does not survive scrutiny, however, though there is a distinction to be drawn between artistic value and the value of art as a whole. Though there are no coercive arguments to show that we have to take into account the moral qualities of works of art, it is in practice very difficult to ignore them, especially when the point of the work is insistently moral, or when the work is conspicuously depraved.

There is a long tradition, dating back to Plato, of regarding art with suspicion for its power over our emotions, and much of Western aesthetic theorizing has been a response to Plato's challenge. The longest-lasting defence justified art in terms of a combination of pleasure and instruction, though the two never hit it off as well as was hoped. In the early nineteenth century a new, more complex account of art was offered, notably by Hegel, in the form of a historicized view in which art is one of the modes by which we come to self-awareness; the emphasis altered from truth to an independently existing reality to truthfulness to our own natures, as we explore them by creating art. Taken into the social sphere, this became a doctrine of the importance of art as an agent of political consciousness, operating in subtle ways to undermine the view of reality imposed on us by the ideologies that hold us captive.

1   The range of issues
2   The empirical issue
3   Artistic value and the value of art
4   Art and the self; art and society
5   Conclusion

1   The range of issues

The relationship between art and morality is the most fraught and complex in the philosophy of art. One reason for this is that, from Plato onwards, several key issues have not been adequately distinguished. For instance, one important question concerns the effect of works of art on the audience, which is an empirical matter. Does pornography, for example, inflame sexual drives or does it provide substitute gratification? Or does it have different effects on different people (the most plausible answer)? Philosophers, and many others, tend to argue about this question on the basis of nothing more than perfunctory introspection. A separate question is whether works of art should be designed to have moral effects, and if so, how best that can be achieved. The major tradition of Western criticism, from Aristotle to the end of the eighteenth century, has been that literary works should at least aim to instruct as well as delight, and a great deal of debate has been occupied with the relationship between the two goals. This discussion has been complicated, if not bedevilled, by Plato's postulation of the supreme trinity of forms: truth, beauty and goodness. If everything is to be allotted to one of these categories, it would seem that the object of art is beauty. But is it the case that all successful works of art are beautiful? It would seem that, unless one made it a matter of definition that they are, many clearly are not, including some of the greatest. This is especially the case with tragedies, where pain, evil and death predominate. Many artists have evidently felt it their duty to portray reality as vividly as possible, feeling an allegiance to truth rather than beauty. The characteristically philosophical hope that the three categories ultimately coincide seems to be more a case of wishful thinking than of rigorous argument. Nietzsche, in a late unpublished note, put the counter-position with typical incisiveness: 'For a philosopher to say, "the good and the beautiful are one", is infamy; if he goes on to add, "also the true", one ought to thrash him. Truth is ugly.'

It is already clear that profound and very difficult questions proliferate in this area. It is tempting to hold them in check by postulating a kind of experience that is 'purely aesthetic', then to consider further matters, especially that of the relationship of art to morality, as separable issues. But examples of purely aesthetic experience are less common, it turns out, than might be hoped. And it is unclear what a purely aesthetic experience of, say, *King Lear* would be. Would it be a concentration on the form of the play without regard to its content? But what would that mean? It is unclear that in any of the cases which really bother us a distinction of that kind can be made. A related question asks whether there can be works of art that express strikingly uncouth world-views. For example, is it a contingent matter that no great Nazi art was produced? And if it is not, how much light does that cast on the relationship between art and morality? And what of works that have an admirable moral content or message, but are of low aesthetic merit, such as Harriet Beecher Stowe's *Uncle Tom's Cabin*? Does that indicate something about the moral content itself, as some have held, or only about the author's lack of talent?

If art is not to be divorced from all other human activity – such a position is known as 'aestheticism', but has never been clearly stated – then the question of its place in the economy of human concerns is clearly crucial. After the effective demise of the classical tradition, the most striking series of attempts to relate art to our other endeavours has been that of the Idealist philosophers. These attempts begin with Hegel and continue at least as far as R.G. COLLINGWOOD (§3), and include the politically motivated theorists who stand in a complicated relationship to those earlier philosophers, and who have seen art as a mode of articulating our responses to a reality which we are at least in part responsible for creating. The stress has moved, consequently, from imitation to expression; from the registration of the way we find the world to the expression of our attitude towards it; and thus to sincerity, a term that connects truth and genuineness, and in assorted ways puts art at the centre of our moral experience, and vice versa.

2 The empirical issue

It is often plausibly said that totalitarian regimes take art more seriously than democratic ones. Whatever one's attitude to censorship, it shows at the least that art is felt to have an influence on people's behaviour. And in practice there are virtually no societies in which some form of censorship is not operated. Democracies pride themselves on not prohibiting art, but only various objectionable forms of entertainment or propaganda. It is not clear, however, that the definitions drawn here are more than terminological. 'Art' often has an honorific connotation, so that anything sufficiently degraded is allotted a separate category, such as 'pornography'; 'erotic art' is then claimed to be that which has sexual content but is not arousing (see EROTIC ART). This is all very suspicious. What it seems to show is that everyone agrees that there are artefacts with a *prima facie* claim to artistic status which can also be arousing, or can incite racial hatred, etc. If one simply decrees that in so far as they have effects on attitudes and behaviour they are not art, or that these effects are irrelevant to their artistic status or stature, this seems an easy way with a hard question. That some works of art have drastic practical effects seems undeniable: a notorious case was Goethe's *The Sorrows of Young Werther*, which led to a wave of romantically inspired suicides. That fact is not used to discredit the book now, though if a contemporary work were to have the same effect it undoubtedly would.

What remain perennial sources of dispute are those works which have a strong emotional effect, but which make it difficult for us to decide, on account of their complexity, how they influence our outlook and thus our conduct. This lies at the centre of the long-lasting debate about the effect of tragedy (see TRAGEDY). It seems strange that we should be unable to decide whether tragedies of great power, such as *Oedipus the King*, exalt, devastate, bewilder, affirm or question basic values, and so on. Yet all these positions are held and argued about with passion. That the issue remains so contentious is no doubt partly due to the fact that there is often a discrepancy between how they make us feel and what we think they ought to make us feel, and that it is difficult to keep in focus, after the immediate experience of such works, what we actually did feel. As any experience of great complexity recedes, we are apt to simplify its effect on us, especially if we are in the grip of a gratifying theory. The only thing that can be confidently asserted in this area is that there is no doubt that some works of art have moral (and of course political) effects.

3 Artistic value and the value of art

Although works of art do have moral effects, it has been argued that it is not part of their value that they do. It was largely in reaction to the oppressive moralism of Victorian criticism that Wilde remarked that there are no such things as moral or immoral works of art. And it is widely agreed (though not universally) that art which, in Keats' words, 'has palpable designs upon us' is inferior. But that does not mean that the moral effects of art are irrelevant to its value as art, only that it is less likely to achieve them if they are crudely manifest. Nor does the oft-cited fact that those who frequent art are not conspicuously better than those who do not have any cogency. It is very difficult to improve people and failure to do so may reflect more on people than on the attempt. Further, to claim that art in some cases derives its value from its moral qualities is not to claim that they are invariably relevant. It is not easy to envisage a plausible argument to show that much instrumental music or painting has moral properties or effects; and the same is true of a considerable amount of literature. The claim, made by Tolstoy, that art is only valuable in so far as it has a beneficial influence on people's behaviour, cannot be refuted, but equally cannot be established. It is an attitude one might choose to adopt, but it would certainly eliminate a great deal of what is normally called art. It might be claimed that any interesting aesthetic theory will do this, and that what matters is how radical we are prepared to allow an aesthetic theory to be. Any theory that rules out much of what is widely valued, either on the ground that it is not art at all, or that it is bad art, risks appearing ridiculous.

There is a certain amount of art (not a great deal, but a significant amount) which takes the form of something approaching a parable. Tolstoy's great short story 'How much land does a man need?' is a good example. In such cases it is hard to say that someone could appreciate it without grasping its moral point. To confine oneself to admiration for its economy, tension, verve, but not to recognize the end those qualities serve would be to fail to recognize a realized intention. Similarly, in a rather more complex case, to see or listen to Beethoven's Fidelio without taking into account its concern with injustice, heroism and freedom (and that not surprisingly it favours the last two and opposes the first) would be so strange that we would normally say that anyone who claimed to be indifferent to its political and moral qualities was simply not responding to the work. If such a person said that they were only moved by the music, and regarded the drama as too crude to take any interest in, we would wonder how they could be moved appropriately by the music without acknowledging that it was articulating the dramatic action. Of course one could listen to the music in a purely abstract way, regarding the voices simply as instruments, but that would not be listening to Fidelio, but only to an aspect of it, somewhat as if one were to enjoy the sound of a poem in a language that one did not understand. Of course one need not agree with the morality that one takes a work to be propounding or embodying in order to value it. But once more it does not follow from this that one ignores its morality or regards it as irrelevant, nor does it follow that one thinks less well of the work. One may welcome art which puts a moral position that one can't share in a plausible light. The phenomenology of responses to art is itself a highly complex matter, but it seems to be the case that in imaginatively entering the world of a work one is enabled to test one's reactions to people who hold sets of moral views very different from one's own, and that this is one of the reasons that we value the experience of novels, dramas, etc. Though it is notoriously hard to say precisely what effect a powerful work of art has on us, there is wide agreement that we do sometimes feel changed by such works, which is a cause both for valuing them and also for feeling anxious about them. The latter tends to have dominated Western speculation on the subject, because many philosophers, Plato being the first and most influential, have taken it that art typically works on 'the passions', of which they have harboured deep suspicions, because they are thought of as hard to govern, irrational, selfish and destructive. And the greater the work of art in terms of its power to affect us, the more dangerous it may be.

This raises the issue of internal and external reasons for valuing art. Might it not be the case that the reasons we have for valuing a work as art are, at least sometimes, equally reasons for disapproving of it morally? An analogy with sport might make the point more clearly. Within such a sport as soccer one may behave in a way that is beneficial to the side one is playing on, in that it helps to score a goal; but the whole activity might be frowned on for fostering a spirit of competitiveness, if that is thought to be a bad thing. Victorian schoolmasters were very keen on competitive sports for a range of reasons which might need examining. But it would be possible to disapprove of the whole set of sporting activities that they promoted while being able to make judgments about how well someone was playing a specific game. Similarly, the reasons we give for putting a high value on a work of art might, in the context of our complete set of standards, be reasons for thinking that art itself is deplorable; or that most of what is highly esteemed is deplorable. In practice it turns out to be difficult to maintain this distinction, so that we often find people making what appear to be artistic judgments when they are really making judgments about the whole institution. Conversely, an overenthusiastic application of the distinction leads people to adopt a very narrow set of terms or concepts which they take to be appropriate for judging individual works, and many considerations which might be considered relevant are claimed to be external, that is, to be dealing with a different question – the nature and value of art itself.

4 Art and the self; art and society

Continuing this line of thought, we can deal briefly with two other lines of thought about art and its relation to other enterprises, both of which derive more or less directly from HEGEL (§8). It was characteristic of him to take a historical perspective on art, valuing the art of different ages and cultures in terms of its connections with their other concerns. For us, living in a culture decisively formed in all its aspects by Christianity, art takes on a 'romantic' aspect, in his idiosyncratic use of that term. Hegel sees the tension in all kinds of art as the relationship between the medium, which is sensuous, and the content, which is spiritual. Operating along these lines, but without subscribing to Hegel's often bizarre views, Idealist aestheticians have seen artistic activity (which is by no means confined to artists) as the attempt to achieve a perfect congruence between the inner and the outer. Thus the emphasis shifts to art as self-expression; it is seen as a demanding and ultimately moral activity, since one finds out who one is in the process of its creation. Nietzsche, hostile to Idealism in general, none the less took over this element and in his middle period advocated that we should make our lives into works of art, thus effecting a synthesis of the moral and the aesthetic.

Deviating much further from Hegel, but inconceivable without him, is the tradition of thought loosely called 'Marxist'. Marx himself contributed little on the subject of art, but many theorists working within his general framework have produced general theories of the nature and purpose of art and many specific judgments on works of art, both of which construe it as a crucial contribution to the class struggle. The most crass versions of such a line of thought were perpetrated in the Soviet Union and its satellites, where art was esteemed for bolstering the workers' spirits as they battled against the bourgeois and fascist enemies. The result, in terms of both the kind of art encouraged and endorsed and the fate of artists who failed to conform, is an eloquent testimony to the necessity for a large degree of freedom of expression. 'Socialist realism', which was the approved art of the Soviet bloc, like Fascist art, did not succeed even ephemerally. In the case of Marxism, however, there has been an immense and impressive body of theory in which it is clearly seen that if radical political goals are to be effectively furthered by art, they will not be achieved with slogans and propaganda, but involves the transformation of consciousness – a point that could have been taken from Hegel in the first place. The leading group of theorists has been the Frankfurt School, of which the salient figure was Theodor W. ADORNO (§5), a man of immensely rich culture and a modernist in his artistic affiliations. His views on the function of art as critique of society, and the consequent particular value judgments he made on a vast range of works of art, especially music, represent what may be the most impressive single body of work in the field. He expounds the complex relations between the moral and social on the one hand and the artistic on the other with a detailed force that breaks through the obscurity with which they are expressed.

5 Conclusion

As is the case with many profound conceptual issues, it can confidently be predicted that the nature of the relationship between art and morality will never be settled. What does seem to have been established, though, is that the discussion must always take account of historical considerations. The appearance on the scene of new art-forms, such as the realistic novel and large-scale instrumental music, alone makes it unlikely that a theory produced at a given time will ever be adequate for later times. And the more art we have to ponder upon, the more intimate will be the relationship between our theorizing and what we are theorizing about. Hegel may have been exaggerating when he said that writing about art would finally take the place of art itself, but the element of truth in this claim means that the range of moral views available to us and their engagement with the vast body of art guarantees an indefinite future for meditation on the connections between them.

See also: ARISTOTLE ; CROCE, B. §2 ; EMOTION, IN RESPONSE TO ART; JOHNSON, S. ; KANT, I. §12 ; POETRY §§1–3; PORNOGRAPHY; SCHILLER, J.C.F. ; TOLSTOY, L. §4

References and further reading

Adorno, T.W. (1991) *The Culture Industry*, London: Routledge. (The most accessible introduction to Adorno's Marxist attack on mass culture, and a defence of the social role of art.)

Aristotle (perhaps *c.*330BC) *Poetics*, trans. R. Janko, Indianapolis, IN: Hackett Publishing Company, 1987, chaps 6, 9, 11, 13, 14. (A defence of art, and of tragedy in p articular, in terms of its moral effects in purging our emotions.)

Collingwood, R.G. (1938) *The Principles of Art*, Oxford: Clarendon Press. (The introduction and first book provide a sophisticated exposition of art in terms of expression, and launch a vehement attack on all other theories).

Hegel, G.W.F. (1835) *Lectures on Aesthetics*, trans. T.M. Knox, Oxford: Clarendon Press, 1975. (The introduction gives Hegel's most succinct account of his general theory of the development of art, and its varying role in the progression of self-consciousness.)

Johnson, S. (1765) 'Preface to Shakespeare', in H.R. Wouhuysen (ed.) *Samuel Johnson on Shakespeare*, London: Penguin, 1989. (The culminating statement of the classical tradition, defending art when it shows us the good prospering and the bad coming to grief.)

Pater, W. (1858) *The Renaissance*, Berkeley, CA: University of California Press, 1980. (The conclusion offers the classic statement of the irrelevance to art of all but 'purely aesthetic' properties – though Pater adds an important concession.)

* Plato (*c.*380s–370s BC) *Republic*, trans. P. Shorey, Cambridge, MA: Loeb Classical Library, Harvard University Press, 1930, 602c–608b. (The first and most famous denunciation of art on moral grounds.)

* Tolstoy, L. (1896) *What is Art?*, trans. A. Maude, New York: Bobbs-Merrill, 1962. (An attack on almost all art, except that which unites all people in fellow-feeling and that which brings us closer to God.)

MICHAEL TANNER

ART AND TRUTH

Some things are true within the world of a literary work. It is true, in the world evoked by Madame Bovary, *that Emma Rouault married Charles Bovary. In this entry, however, we are not concerned with truth in fiction but rather with what it is for a work of art to be true of, or true to, the actual world. Representational works represent states of affairs, or objects portrayed in a certain way. The concept of truth naturally gets a grip here, because we can ask whether the represented state of affairs actually exists in the world, or whether a represented object exists and really is the way it is represented to be, or whether a representation of a kind* of thing offers a genuinely representative example of that kind. If so, we could call the work true, or true in the given respect.

A work will often get us to respond to what is portrayed in a way similar to what our response would have been to the real thing – we are moved to fear and pity by objects we know are merely fictions. But a work could also portray characters responding in certain ways to the imaginary situations it conjures, often with the implication that the response is a likely human emotional or practical response to that situation, or a response to be expected of a character of the given type, and we could reasonably call the work true if we believed the portrayed reaction was a likely one.

Arguably, if we judge a work to be in some respect true to life, we must already have known that life was like that in order to make the judgment. But, interestingly, works of art appear to be able to portray situations that we have not experienced, in which the portrayal seems to warrant our saying that the work has shown (that is, taught) us a likely or plausible unfolding of the portrayed situation, or shown us what it would have been like to experience the situation. It is also said, especially of narrative fiction, that, because of its power to show us what various alternative imaginary situations would be like, it can enlighten us about how we ought to live.

So we may consider how a work of art might be a vehicle of truths about the actual world. This gives rise to a further question – sometimes called the problem of belief – of whether the value of a work of art as a piece of art is related to its truth. If a work implies or suggests that something is the case, ought I to value it more highly as art if I accept what it implies as the truth? Alternatively, should I take it as an aesthetic shortcoming if I do not?

1 **Literature as a vehicle of truth: the *Poetics***
2 **Literature and moral insight**
3 **Other arts**
4 **The artistic relevance of truth**

1 **Literature as a vehicle of truth: the Poetics**

Aristotle's *Poetics* provides a good starting point for considering the claim that art informs us about or illuminates the actual world. Discussing tragedy (which in Aristotle's terms is a form of poetry) he makes the following claims: (1) that plot is the most important aspect of a tragedy, which is a depiction of actions which form a unity, and (2) that tragedy (along with other forms of poetry) is more philosophical and more important than history, because it makes universal statements rather than statements about particular events.

Here is a suggestion that connects claims (1) and (2). Taking up the point in (1) that plot is a depiction of actions, we can assume that Aristotle means the actions of the characters in the story. A plot, we can now say, is unified to the extent that its depicted actions follow upon one another in a natural or plausible way. What we find plausible depends, of course, on our assumptions about human behaviour. Aristotle suggests that a good plot is able to bring an audience together in its responses to events and hence that some responses are practically universal, resting on truths about human conduct that are 'necessary or probable' – a phrase he uses repeatedly in the *Poetics*. This provides a connection with (2). By structuring itself around these 'universal' assumptions, a good tragedy can be said to be more like philosophy than history, in that it is biased away from the accidental, towards generality. History simply records events as they happen. It is a matter of indifference to the faithful recorder of history whether historical events are the product of accident or agency, or whether recorded actions are sane or mad, intelligible or whimsical. By contrast, a tragic plot, according to Aristotle, is spoilt if it is interspersed with accidents of nature or with actions that we cannot readily understand through our first-hand familiarity with ourselves and other people. Such a plot is 'episodic' in Aristotle's terms – his word for a narrative sequence whose elements are not, as in a properly unified plot, linked by what is 'necessary or probable'.

Consider *Madame Bovary* as our 'tragedy'. Might it be said to depict actions as forming a unity? To begin with, Flaubert's readers are carried along by the narrative because of the way the depicted actions are motivated and connected by familiar human impulses. His characters behave in ways that are accessible and plausible given their different temperaments, histories and circumstances. The function of Flaubert's narrative is to draw us into the developing story in a way that depends on our tacit assent to the successive links in the plot, so that we become involved in the fates of its characters as if they were part of our own lives. This suggests the following way in which narratives can be informative. Out of the 'necessities and probabilities' that drive the plot, eliciting our implicit consent along the way, Flaubert develops a complex situation with a dramatic outcome that lies outside our experience and would normally beg an explanation. But his plot and characterization enable us to experience this world from within, so that we get to know what the fictional situation would have felt like if real. At the same time we come to understand how Emma feels, and hence why she does what she does. So we increase the range of our experience and advance our understanding, because a piece of human behaviour that may otherwise have seemed strange or impenetrable has been placed within the range of what is intelligibly human. Where a brief report of Emma's gruesome and tragic demise might have met with incomprehension or prompted a shallow and moralistic banality, the narrative elicits instead a response closer to Flaubert's: 'Madame Bovary, c'est moi!'

2 Literature and moral insight

Since literature seems able to provide an impression of what a possible situation would feel like to us if actual, it suggests itself as a useful tool for exploring the merits of various imagined alternatives to existing lifestyles or kinds of society. Hilary Putnam (1978) has claimed that since the choice between styles of living involves a full human response, including the capacity to feel, it is not an appropriate subject for science, which is essentially propositional in character. (Putnam surmises that we store certain kinds of information in the form of images rather than propositions.) The choice of lifestyles requires practical rather than theoretical reasoning, the former, as much as the latter, being a process subject to rational criticism. The search for better ways of living suggests a significant role for the imagination – and for imaginative literature. Putnam's idea is not that literature should present ideal lifestyles as 'solutions' to the question of how we ought to live, but that it should play a critical role. For example, by showing us what it would be like to live as a certain kind of person in a society organized in a specific way or having various imagined features, it can present us with 'perplexities' which enable us to refine our thinking about the desirability of the way of life represented.

The most substantial explication of the idea that literature can illuminate how we ought to live has come from Martha Nussbaum. Her detailed analyses of literary works – the novels of Henry James in particular – set out to show that literature provides a means of extending our moral awareness beyond the limits to which traditional moral philosophy can take us. 'Schematic philosophers' examples', Nussbaum says, 'almost always lack the particularity, the emotive appeal, the absorbing plottedness, the variety and indeterminacy, of good fiction; they lack, too, good fiction's way of making the reader a participant and a friend' (1990: 46). Only once its many aspects are adequately represented can a complex ethical question become the subject of clear reflection, and then it is easier to see the various and sometimes conflicting values that are at stake. For example, by taking us into the lives of its characters, Henry James' *The Golden Bowl* is able to show us how Maggie Verver's aspirations to a certain kind of moral perfection stand in the way of the full flourishing of her marriage; her love for the prince, fully acknowledged, calls for a more complex moral stance in which she must relinquish the hope of guiltless moral perfection. Thus, she must confront the fact that the full expression of her love may require 'a tragically necessary blindness' (*ibid.*: 144) – it may require her sometimes to turn away from or even wound others who are close to her.

3 Other arts

It is natural that representational art, especially literature, should offer the clearest examples of works that are in some way true of the world. But it may not offer the only examples. Turning to nonrepresentational art, Jerrold Levinson has argued (1990) that there are various ways in which music, a mainly nonrepresentational art form, can aptly be described as true. Suppose we accept (as seems reasonable) that anger is a destructive emotion. Passages in the fourth movement of Beethoven's Pastoral symphony express anger, Levinson suggests, and the anger is presented as destructive. In this case it seems natural to describe the passages as true. A different kind of example occurs where a transition in a piece of music from one emotional quality to another carries the implicit suggestion that that transition is psychologically plausible in human terms; and we judge the music true if we think it plausible in this way.

Nelson GOODMAN (§2) holds that all the arts, representational and nonrepresentational, serve a cognitive function (1972). Thus it is a mistake to associate science alone with the cognitive and to limit the concerns of art to the evocation or expression of feeling. For him, inventiveness in both art and science consists in the development or modification of elements in a symbol system. Successful symbols illuminate the world through the aptness with which they fit their subject-matter, rewarding those who engage with them with enlightening new ways of seeing the world.

Goodman's ideas can fruitfully be read in conjunction with Ernst Gombrich's work on the visual arts (1951). Gombrich starts by attacking the 'myth of the innocent eye'. The recognition of what lies in our field of view when we perceive, he argues, requires the organization of visual input: what we see is structured by what we expect to see. Just as scientific discovery is preceded by the invention of successful hypotheses, the development of our awareness of the visual world requires inspired modifications to the 'schemas' we bring to bear upon it. The history of painting,

Gombrich suggests, can be seen as an experimental process by which our actual visual capacities are gradually enhanced by painters' corrective modifications to the existing schemas available for representing the visible world. Rather than simply assuming that our visual awareness reflects the world in an unproblematic way, providing the touchstone by which the accuracy of a picture can be judged, Gombrich's account construes painting as a means by which that awareness is developed.

The view, shared by Goodman and Gombrich, that art is an instrument of perception, is not unproblematic. But it is an important development in twentieth-century aesthetics, and its exposition in the work of these philosophers provides some of the best reading the subject has to offer.

4 The artistic relevance of truth

If a work of art implies the accuracy or correctness of a certain claim, representation, perspective or attitude, can it or should it increase our estimation of the artistic worth of the work if we take the claim or representation to be true or the attitude or perspective to be accurate or correct? A negative answer is implied by I.A. Richards when he writes of our response to literature:

> the question of belief or disbelief, in the intellectual sense, never arises when we are reading well. If unfortunately it does arise....we have for the moment ceased to be reading poetry and have become astronomers, or theologians, or moralists, persons engaged in quite a different type of activity.
> (1929: 277)

Support for Richards's claim might come from the idea that art is a distinct category of human activity, with its own purposes and hence its own criteria of merit. On this view, just as we judge the merits of, say, the binding of a book by the standards of bookbinding, so we should judge poetry (remaining with the case of literature) by the special qualities that set poetry apart as an activity: the aptness of verbal choices, the displayed command of metre and rhythm, the elegance and unity of the poem as a whole, and so on. But it is unclear that poetry (or any other art form) comprises a self-contained activity with a fixed purpose that defines it as poetry, and dogmatic to suppose that its 'purpose' necessarily excludes the accurate representation of how things stand in the world. Furthermore, a view like Richards's is hard to reconcile with past and current critical practice. Henry James is widely admired for his moral subtlety, and critics generally assume (and it would seem bizarre to deny) that this quality adds to his stature *as* a serious novelist.

Malcolm Budd (1983) has produced an important argument that bears on this issue. He makes the point that the value of a work of art as art is always intrinsic to the experience it offers. It therefore does not include the beneficial effects the work may have upon our lives. For example, if a novel contains an insight that could illuminate our lives, its insightfulness may accrue to its value as art, but only in so far as the insight informs the reading experience itself, and not in virtue of the work's educative effects. This seems right, for someone could value and enjoy a work as art even though, due to complacency, forgetfulness or some other idiosyncracy, they failed to respond to it in such a way that it benefited or informed their life. But to say this is not to drive a wedge between artistic or aesthetic value, on the one hand, and moral or intellectual value, on the other. These values are not in opposition. It may be its intellectual or moral character that accounts for much of a work's impact as an object of experience; if it displays intellectual or moral shortcomings – philosophical immaturity, for example, or racist attitudes – then that is likely to diminish the value we place on the experience it offers. So, regarding the artistic relevance of truth, we may indeed value a work less as art if we fail to be persuaded about the truth of a claim it implicitly makes about the world – provided its failure to persuade lessens its value as an object of experience.

See also: ART AND MORALITY; ART, VALUE OF; FICTIONAL ENTITIES; NARRATIVE

References and further reading

All the articles listed are untechnical and should be accessible to someone with only a limited knowledge of philosophy.

* Aristotle (perhaps *c*.330 BC) *Poetics*, trans. R. Janko, Indianapolis, IN: Hackett Publishing Company, 1987. (Aristotle's famous examination of the nature of poetry and tragedy.)
* Budd, M. (1983) 'Belief and Sincerity in Poetry', in E. Schaper (ed.) *Pleasure, Preference and Value*, Cambridge: Cambridge University Press, 137–57. (A clear and careful discussion of the parallel issues of sincerity in literature and the problem of belief.)
* Gombrich, E.H. (1951) 'Meditations on a Hobby Horse or the Roots of Artistic Form', repr. in *Meditations on a Hobby Horse and other essays on the theory of art*, London: Phaidon, 1–11, 1963. (A good entry point into Gombrich's philosophy of fine art.)

* Goodman, N. (1972) 'Art and Inquiry', in *Problems and Projects*, New York: Bobbs-Merrill, 103–19. (A good introduction to Goodman's important and influential philosophy of art.)

Gulley, N. (1979) 'Aristotle on the Purposes of Literature', in J. Barnes, N. Schofield and R. Sorabji (eds) *Articles on Aristotle, 4: Psychology and Aesthetics*, London: Duckworth, 166–76. (A brief, authoritative and readable introduction to the Poetics.)

* Levinson, J. (1990) 'Truth in Music', in *Music, Art and Metaphysics*, Ithaca, NY: Cornell University Press, 279–305. (This is a clear and fertile discussion of the topic of its title.)

* Nussbaum, M.C. (1990) *Love's Knowledge: Essays on Philosophy and Literature*, New York: Oxford University Press, 3–53 and 125–47. (The fullest available treatment of the way literature illuminates morality.)

* Putnam, H. (1978) *Meaning and the Moral Sciences, Part Two*, London: Routledge & Kegan Paul, 83–94. (A relatively lucid discussion of the capacity of literary works to give us knowledge; compares the cognitive function of literature with that of science.)

* Richards, I.A. (1929) *Practical Criticism*, London: Routledge & Kegan Paul, 271–91. (Referred to in §4.)

PAUL TAYLOR

ART CRITICISM

To criticize a work of art is to make a judgment of its overall merit or demerit and to support that judgment by reference to features it possesses. This activity is of great antiquity; we find Aristotle, for example, relating the excellence of Sophocles' Oedipus Rex *to the excellence of its plot construction. Criticism became a topic in philosophy because reflection on the kinds of things said by critics generated various perplexities and in some cases encouraged a general scepticism about the possibility of criticism. Two general and related problems in particular have taxed philosophers. The first is the question of whether criticism is a rational activity, that is to say, whether critics can give reasons for their judgments that would persuade potential dissenters of the rightness of those judgments. The second, a matter to which Kant and Hume made notable contributions, is the problem of the objectivity of critical judgments, it being widely believed that critical appraisals are wholly subjective or just 'a matter of taste'. Arguments that use deductive or inductive reasoning to demonstrate the possibility of proofs of critical judgments are generally agreed to have failed. Another approach redescribes the critic altogether, not as someone who uses argument to prove their judgments to an audience, but as someone who aims to help the audience perceive features of the work of art and understand their role in the work. This entry will concentrate on the issues of the rationality and objectivity of art criticism.*

1 A case for subjectivism
2 The impossibility of deduction and induction
3 Generality
4 An alternative model
5 Final remarks

1 A case for subjectivism

Disagreements in art criticism are widespread and frequently intractable. Subjectivists, wishing to demonstrate the impossibility of objective judgment in art, often begin with this apparently indubitable fact – though this tactic suffers from the fact that an observer is as likely to notice the widespread agreement in critical judgments over the pre-eminence of such figures as Sophocles, Mozart, Tolstoy, Beethoven, Rembrandt and Shakespeare. Nevertheless, the existence of often intense disagreement cannot be denied, but to concede this is not as yet enough to establish a subjectivist case. For while there are vehement and intractable disagreements in, say, mathematical theory and in physics, these disagreements do not entail the subjectivity of physics or mathematics.

Apart from the fact that disagreements occur in it, there must then be some aspect of criticism that underlies the claim that it is subjective in a way that physics and mathematics are not. It is tempting to think that while mathematics and physics possess proof or decision procedures, agreed on by practitioners of those subjects, in terms of which enquiries in those subjects proceed and disputes in them are in principle resolvable, there are no such agreed procedures in criticism. There, in lieu of argument and proofs, we have only unsupportable opinion. The denial that criticism is a rational activity (one in which reasons can be given for judgments) becomes a principal ground for asserting that critical judgments are subjective.

2 The impossibility of induction and deduction

The above section sketches the claim that there are no proof procedures in art criticism, as there are in physics and mathematics. But what proof is offered for such a claim? One way to argue that proof procedures have no place in criticism would be to take the two most commonly accepted forms of proof – deduction and induction – and show that these cannot be invoked in support of critical judgments.

For induction, one might argue that since all pictures by Rembrandt that have been hitherto examined have been found to be great paintings, any hitherto unexamined Rembrandt is probably a great painting. This use of induction has two weaknesses. First, on what basis was it asserted that the first Rembrandt ever examined was a great painting? Since it was the first Rembrandt, the assertion cannot have been based on inductive proof. Instead, an appreciator probably looked at the picture and simply pronounced that it was a great painting; here the sceptic merely repeats the question of whether that judgment can be proved by reasons. Second, the inductive judgment I have sketched has a peculiar uselessness for the would-be appreciator. Induction might indeed lead the appreciator to conclude that an unexamined Rembrandt was probably a great one. But the appreciator wants not merely to *know indirectly* that the picture is a great one: they wish to see and experience its greatness directly.

Various attempts have been made to introduce inductive procedures into criticism in order to underpin its status as a rational proof procedure. One of the most famous uses the notion of the Golden Section. The claim is that a certain ratio is to be found in all pictures that are the subject of favourable judgments. Hence the presence of that ratio in a picture constitutes a reason to believe that it is admirable. The claim that any picture exhibiting the Golden Section is admirable is not a self-evident truth, since it seems possible to imagine cases in which a picture that is admirable fails to exhibit the requisite ratio, or cases in which the ratio is exhibited in a picture that is a failure. Hence the claim must be an inductively based and probabilistic one: since admirable pictures have been found to exemplify the Golden Section, and since this picture exemplifies the Golden Section, we conclude that this picture is probably admirable. But, again, one wishes to know how the correlation between being an admirable picture and exemplifying the Golden Section was established in the first place. Presumably, someone asserted that a picture was admirable, then noticed that it exemplified a certain ratio and made a generalization from this. Then, however, the original judgment that the picture is admirable is not justified by induction, but rather underpins subsequent inductive arguments. Again, the sceptic can ask what, if anything, underpins the original judgment that the picture is admirable.

Deduction fares little better in justifying critical judgments. In deductive argument, one offers statements in support of one's judgment, and these statements, if accepted, absolutely force the interlocutor to accept the judgment. It is difficult to see how such a process could work with judgments of art criticism. If I say that a painting is superb and support this statement with the assertion that its composition is admirable, its drawing excellent and its colours radiant, one of two things may happen. First, you may agree that the composition, the drawing and the colour are as I say they are and yet not be forced to concede that the picture is superb. You might, for instance, claim that the composition, drawing and colour, though individually excellent, do not work together. Alternatively, you may deny that the colour, the drawing or the composition are as I say they are. How then am I to convince you that they are? I may go on to claim that what gives the picture its compositional quality is the presence of a patch of colour in a certain position. The problem is that, while you may agree that the patch of colour is in this position, you may not see the contribution that it makes to the composition, and thus not yet be forced to conclude that the location of the patch of colour entails the presence of the compositional quality to which I referred.

3 Generality

The conclusion that neither inductive nor deductive reasoning can be used to prove, and thus justify, critical judgments may be reinforced by another, related set of considerations. A reason has to have a generality. If your doing a certain action in certain circumstances is a reason for praising you, it is reason for praising anyone who does that action in those circumstances. Some thinkers (Stuart Hampshire (1953), for example) have argued that reasoning in criticism is impossible because of the impossibility of this sort of generality in that context. Thus, it is claimed, the fact that a painting has a patch of colour in a certain position may be the explanation for its admirable compositional features. But the existence of that patch in that location cannot be cited as a reason for concluding that the painting is admirably composed. For precisely that shade of colour in the same position in another picture may be the cause of that picture's bad composition. And if exactly the same feature can sometimes count for a conclusion and sometimes against it, it cannot be cited as a reason for believing that conclusion.

Care needs to be exercised here, however. Sibley has remarked that we can make a distinction between what he calls the 'neutral' features of a work of art and the 'merit' features. A neutral feature would be a feature such as the possession of iambic pentameter, an alliteration or a colour patch in a certain position. The feature is neutral with respect to merit conclusions because it is possible without any unnaturalness to say, for example, 'it is the alliteration that spoils this line', and, in the case of another poem, 'it is the (self-same) alliteration that makes this poem.' Statements about neutral features cannot, indeed, be used as reasons in support of critical judgments. However, as Sibley observes, other terms do not have the neutrality of those just cited. If we take terms such as 'witty', 'radiantly coloured', 'elegantly composed', 'subtle in its harmonic variations', 'ham-fisted' or 'ponderously executed', then these terms seem to have a positive (or negative) merit force. Though there would be nothing unusual about saying 'What makes it so good is its wit', it would be odd to say, 'What makes it bad is the subtlety of its harmonic variations.' These terms do then seem to have a general positive or negative force and are generally (and so genuinely) reasons for thinking something good or bad. However, as Sibley also pointed out, this positive or negative force is at best *prima facie*. That is to say, although the possession of wit is a *prima facie* reason for saying that something is good, we cannot argue that because something possesses wit, it is for that reason good or has something good about it; for the wit might be out of place, as, for example, it is sometimes said to be in the Porter scene in *Macbeth*. For that reason we cannot deduce a work's value from the fact that it has wit in it. Once again the critic's judgments seem not demonstrable by reason, a fact that, again, may appear to support subjectivism.

4 An alternative model

Hypnotized by the successes of the physical sciences and mathematics, many who thought about criticism – including, notably, the Russian Formalists – sought to remodel it along the lines of these activities and to look for inductive and deductive ways of proving critical judgments, the impossibility of such proofs being evidence of the unscientific subjectivity of criticism. In view of arguments already given no programme of this sort could succeed. Observable features, such as onomatopoeia, alliteration, patterns of plots, no less than sound patterns in music or colour areas in paintings are neutral features, as likely to count for merit as against it, and cannot support critical judgments in any deductive way.

In fact the model of the sciences and mathematics provides the wrong model for the procedures of critical judgment. What is required in criticism is not inductive and deductive argument but an ability to *see* the qualities of visual works of art, *hear* the qualities of music and *notice* the features of literature. The model that best fits the practices of criticism appears to be the model of getting someone to perceive something rather than arguing someone into something. This is not, as it is with the colours of traffic lights, simply a matter of pointing the gaze of a colour-sighted person in the right direction. Like wine-tasting, aesthetic perception may require practice and experience. The critic, in helping one to see, hear or notice, can use a variety of devices, ranging from simply pointing out the features believed to be present to the use of analogies, metaphors, comparisons and gestures, in the way in which a conductor may help a choir to sing a phrase in a certain way by hand movements.

If this kind of model is adopted – and, given that we use our eyes and ears in artistic appreciation, what more appropriate one suggests itself? – then the questions of rationality and objectivity assume a different aspect. First, the scope of reasoning in artistic judgment is immediately narrowed. What the critic wishes to do is to help the reader, viewer or listener to see or hear what is there to be seen and heard. And although critics can give reasons for looking and listening ('because the object will reward your contemplation'), and although they can give reasons, possibly of a deductive or inductive kind, for believing that something has merit or demerit ('most people think this is good, so try it'), they cannot give reasons that will make people see or hear something. The case is analogous to that of ordinary perception: I can give you reasons to look at the traffic light but not to see that it is red.

Although critical judgments are thus not objective in the sense that reasons can be given to prove them, this is not the only way in which objectivity is possible. We need to ask, then, what kind of objectivity is appropriate to critical judgments. Given that these are perceptual judgments, the kind of objectivity they will have, if any, will be the kind that can be possessed by perceptual judgments. We do have an inclination to believe that statements about the colours of traffic lights and the sounds of fog horns can be true and false, right or wrong. That possibility depends upon there being some kind of agreement in visual response among human beings in the presence of such things as grass and tomatoes. Some, notably Sibley, have suggested that this kind of agreement is found in cases of art appreciation, and hence that this activity, too, has some claim to objectivity. That this objectivity is dependent upon human responses does not, as Hume argued (1757), prevent there being standards in terms of which we might adversely judge the adequacies of certain responses: for example, the response of someone who thought Barry Manilow superior to Bach.

5 Final remarks

To assert that Bach is superior to Barry Manilow is not to rule out anyone's right to prefer Manilow to Bach. As Kant remarked in one of the most important treatises in aesthetics (1790), if all one wishes to say is that one likes a thing, then, at least in aesthetics, who is to deny one that right? But if one wishes to say that the thing is good, great or awful, one is making a claim that goes beyond any statement of one's personal preferences, a claim that, as I have suggested above, may invoke an appeal to a shared sentiment.

Next, it needs to be noted that discussions of subjectivity and objectivity are bedevilled by assertions that judgments must be either one or the other. Better perhaps to think of the subjective and the objective as poles of a spectrum; to think of the judgments we make, affected as they will almost certainly be by our life histories and our distinctive human personalities, as lying somewhere along this spectrum; and to be characterized, at most, as tending towards one or other of its poles according to the perhaps excusable degree of idiosyncrasy they display.

Finally, we may sum up art criticism as the activity of detecting and of helping others to detect the perceptual value and devaluing features of works of art. In understanding that activity we need to distinguish two uses of the term 'reason': the justificatory sense, when, for instance, we say, 'A reason for believing that it is good is that most competent critics say that it is so', which is of doubtful use in art criticism; and the explanatory sense, when we say, 'The reason it is balanced is the patch of red in the left-hand corner.' Acute critics are often good at offering such explanations, and this is indeed one of the ways in which we might be helped to see the qualities to which our attention is being directed.

See also: AESTHETIC CONCEPTS

References and further reading

Beardsley, M. (1981) *Aesthetics*, 2nd edn, Indianapolis, IN, and Cambridge: Hackett Publishing Company. (Denies the relevance of critical references to sincerity. Chapter 10 contains a striking account of critical evaluation, vigorously debated in Sibley (1983). The postscript to the second edition contains important remarks on criticism.)

Bell, C. (1914) *Art*, London: Chatto & Windus. (Queries references to representation in criticism.)

Erlich, V. (1955) *Russian Formalism*, New Haven, CT: Yale University Press. (Informative and very accessible account of the Russian Formalist attempts, referred to in §4, to make criticism scientific.)

* Hampshire, S. (1954) 'Logic and Appreciation', in W. Elton (ed.) *Aesthetics and Language*, Oxford: Blackwell. (Referred to in §3 as denying the possibility of generality of reasoning in critical appraisal.)

* Hume, D. (1757) 'Of The Standard of Taste', in *Philosophical Works*, London: Longman Green, 1875. (Referred to in §4 as combining a commitment to subjectivism and a belief in standards of taste. A justly famous, elegant and enormously influential piece of writing.)

* Kant, I. (1790) *The Critique of Judgment*, trans. J.C. Meredith, Oxford: Oxford University Press, 1928. (Part I, *The Critique of Aesthetic Judgment*, makes an important contribution to the analysis of aesthetic judgment in an extraordinarily demanding but essential work.)

Lyas, C. (1992) 'The Evaluation of Art', in O. Hanfling (ed.) *Philosophical Aesthetics*, Oxford: Blackwell. (A much expanded version of many of the arguments in this entry.)

* Sibley, F.N. (1965) 'Aesthetic and Non-Aesthetic', *Philosophical Review* 74. (Clear and accessible statement of the claim, in §4, that aesthetic judgment is perceptual, and of the claim, in §5, that reason in judgment needs to distinguished from reason in explanation.)

* —— (1968) 'Aesthetics and Objectivity', in *Proceedings of the Aristotelian Society* Supplementary vol. 42. (Referred to in §4 as offering a clearly presented account of the analogy between colour and aesthetic judgments and of the case for treating the latter as having a degree of objectivity.)

* —— (1983) 'General Criteria in Aesthetics', in J. Fisher (ed.) *Essays in Aesthetics*, Philadelphia, PA: Temple. (Presents the distinction between merit and neutral terms referred to in §4 and argues the case for some area of generality in critical reasoning. Contains also a lucid and powerful account of the theory of critical judgment offered by Monroe Beardsley (1981).)

Strawson, P.F. (1974) 'Aesthetic Appraisal', in *Freedom and Resentment*, London: Methuen. (Relevant to the discussion of the generality of critical reasoning.)

With the exception of the Kant essay, all of these are clearly and non-technically presented.

COLIN LYAS

ART, DEFINITION OF

Many of the earliest definitions of art were probably intended to emphasize salient or important features for an audience already familiar with the concept, rather than to analyse the essence possessed by all art works and only by them. Indeed, it has been argued that art could not be defined any more rigorously, since no immutable essence is observable in its instances. But, on the one hand, this view faces difficulties in explaining the unity of the concept – similarities between them, for example, are insufficient to distinguish works of art from other things. And, on the other, it overlooks the attractive possibility that art is to be defined in terms of a relation between the activities of artists, the products that result and the audiences that receive them.

Two types of definition have come to prominence since the 1970s: the functional and procedural. The former regards something as art only if it serves the function for which we have art, usually said to be that of providing aesthetic experience. The latter regards something as art only if it has been baptized as such through an agent's application of the appropriate procedures. In the version where the agent takes their authority from their location within an informal institution, the 'artworld', proceduralism is known as the institutional theory. These definitional strategies are opposed in practice, if not in theory, because the relevant procedures are sometimes used apart from, or to oppose, the alleged function of art; obviously these theories disagree then about whether the outcome is art.

To take account of art's historically changing character a definition might take a recursive form, holding that something is art if it stands in an appropriate relation to previous art works: it is the location of an item within accepted art-making traditions that makes it a work of art. Theories developed in the 1980s have often taken this form. They variously see the crucial relation between the piece and the corpus of accepted works as, for example, a matter of the manner in which it is intended to be regarded, or of a shared style, or of its being forged by a particular kind of narrative.

1 Definitions
2 Early definitions of art
3 Functionalism and proceduralism
4 Recursive definitions

1 Definitions

If the purpose of a definition of art is to facilitate the unequivocal identification of items as art works, then it should characterize a property, or some combination of properties, displayed by each and every art work and belonging exclusively to art works, that is, a feature or set of features marking all art works and only them. Such a definition is called 'real' or 'essential' (see DEFINITION); it specifies one or more necessary conditions which in the combination indicated are together sufficient for anything to be of the kind in question.

Definitions can serve goals other than that of unequivocal identification and they need be no more rigorous than is required by the chosen purpose. We might look to a definition simply for the sake of knowledge; for instance, in seeking a precise and systematic catalogue of things. We might aim, alternatively, to teach the meaning of a term and will use such definitional methods as are adequate to achieving that end – ostension, enumeration, dictionary meanings, reference to paradigms. We could wish to prescribe a new meaning or use for a term by an act of stipulation, either for a special purpose (in which case the definition is sometimes called 'operational') or in order to change its meaning altogether (as in revisionist definitions). We might be concerned, instead, to characterize a thing's typical features, or the properties that are significant in our use of that thing; these emphases might result in partial definitions drawing attention to non-essential features. As is apparent from this list, sometimes the task of definition is purely descriptive and at others it is regulative; sometimes it is concerned with the way the world is and at others with linguistic practices; sometimes it is controlled by our interests and at others is largely independent of them.

2 Early definitions of art

Many of the famous theories of art offered in the past – Plato's conception of art as *mimesis* (imitation or representation), Tolstoy's view of art as the communication of feeling, Clive Bell's account of art as significant form – fail very obviously when treated as real definitions. If the key notions are construed so broadly that all art works cannot help falling under them, these notions are also bound to cover many things that are not art works. If the central terms are read narrowly, then, they still seem certain to apply to some things that are not art, as well as not applying to some pieces that generally are agreed to be art. It is best to treat these views as recommending fruitful approaches to art's interpretation, or indicating art's more salient or valuable features, rather than as real definitions. Indeed, this is the spirit in which most were offered. These theories are addressed to an audience already skilled in the identification of art, and take that common understanding for granted.

Is a more rigorous approach to a definition of art

possible? Morris Weitz (1956) has famously and influentially argued that art has no fixed essence and, hence, that no real definition of art can be successful. He notes that when we look, we find no property common to all works of art. Art-making is creative and, hence, inevitably defeats the definer's attempt to congeal what is a fluid process. Weitz explains the unity of the concept of art with the idea of a network of 'family resemblances', a notion he adopts from Wittgenstein's *Philosophical Investigations* (see WITTGENSTEIN, L. §§9–11). Works of art are appropriately grouped together in terms of similarities that link them, though there is no single feature or set of qualities shared by all.

Weitz's positive view faces serious difficulties. Similarity could not provide a basis for recognizing the first works of art, since these had no artistic forebears that they might resemble. Nor does the appeal to similarity explain the status of more recent art works. Some art works, such as ready-mades or representational works, more closely resemble things that are not art than they resemble art works; for instance, art films are more like TV 'soaps' and home videos than sculptures. A counter to this objection might insist that only relevant numbers, kinds, or degrees of similarity are significant in establishing the classification of things as art. To enumerate and clarify the types of resemblance that count towards something's being a work of art is to return to art's definition, however, for one would have to specify the set of similarities that are necessary and sufficient for something to count as art. Weitz's reliance on the notion of resemblance does not replace the need for definitions of the type he declared to be impossible.

On the face of it there is no significant property perceptible in all art works. If so, this counts against the kinds of theories Weitz was keen to attack, namely, those proposing that art might be defined in terms of shared aesthetic properties, these being conceived as qualities revealed directly to the senses. But it is not clear that Weitz has demonstrated the impossibility of defining art, for the relevant properties might be imperceptible. (One cannot distinguish uncles from other males merely by examining their appearances, but this does not show that the idea of an uncle is indefinable.) It is plausible to expect that some complex, imperceptible relation between creators, the things they make and the audience that receives them will lie behind a definition of art. Hence, even if Weitz is correct in claiming that we do not see a property common to all art works, this does not show art to be indefinable.

What of Weitz's further claim – that a real definition of art will be refuted and repudiated by artists' creativity? Again, the claim appears plausible only when directed against definitions holding that art works must possess aesthetic qualities (given a limited set of these). A definition relating artists, their products and audiences might easily accommodate innovative kinds of art, because it emphasizes the context of creation and reception rather than the constitution of the piece involved in this transaction.

I have suggested that neither Weitz's arguments nor the fact that most adults have a secure grasp of the concept shows the irrelevance or impossibility of defining art. Moreover, there is an obvious need for such a definition, since the claim to art-status of many pieces created in the twentieth century is hotly debated. Some artists have deliberately produced works that challenge the border between art and non-art, provoking the question 'But is it art?' If we could define art we would have a means of resolving disputes about 'hard cases' of this sort. And even if the attempt to formulate a correct definition is likely to remain controversial, we might come to a deeper understanding of art and its context through the pursuit of such a definition. While Weitz's arguments have been influential and the impossibility of defining art is still asserted, the number of publications presenting new definitions indicates that reports of the death of the enterprise have been greatly exaggerated.

It might be said that it is not so much for us to *discover* whether things are works of art as a result of applying to them an independent standard captured in a definition but, rather, to *decide* whether they are art. I regard this response as misguided. As an aspect of culture, the nature of art is socially constructed and historically malleable, depending on human interests and judgments. If the nature of art is relative to, and affected by, human concerns and practices, this will be mentioned in an adequate definition; such a definition could play a role in settling the appropriateness of our deciding a particular hard case in one way or another. Even if it is for us to decide whether something is art, it does not follow that that decision can be entirely arbitrary, for there must be a difference between our coining an additional meaning for an old term and our resolving that some controversial case is to be properly grouped with undisputed paradigms under the same conceptual umbrella.

3 Functionalism and proceduralism

Many definitions offered in recent decades can be classed as functional or procedural. Functional definitions give centrality to the necessary condition that works of art serve a purpose or purposes distinctive to art, whereas procedural definitions stress that they are created according to certain conventions and social practices. A composite definition mentioning both of these necessary conditions, as well as others, is possible. In practice, though, these two kinds of definition oppose each other, because the procedures by which the status of art is usually conferred have been used to create pieces that fail to serve functions traditionally met by art. Indeed, items may be presented as art, though they have as their point the goal of opposing the attempt to appreciate them in the orthodox fashion. Some functionalists offer their definitions with the goal of excluding such pieces from the realm of art, whereas proceduralists aim to include them. These approaches also differ concerning the connection between something counting as art and its having artistic value. Functionalists see the possession of a degree of aesthetic value, measured in terms of an item's success in fulfilling one or more of the functions of art, as essential to its qualifying as art, while proceduralists regard the artistic evaluation of a thing as separable from the determination of its status as art. The proceduralist's definition is purely descriptive, having little to say about the significance of art or about the reasons that might lead someone so authorized to confer art-status on one thing rather than another. By contrast, the functionalist's definition is normative.

Monroe C. Beardsley (1982), a functionalist, characterizes an art work as either an arrangement of conditions intended to be capable of affording an aesthetic experience valuable for its marked aesthetic character, or (incidentally) an arrangement belonging to a class or type of arrangement that is typically intended to have this capacity. A more recent version of functionalism is given by Robert Stecker (1994), according to which an item is a work of art at time t if and only if either (a) it is in one of the central art forms at t and is intended to fulfil a standard or correctly recognized function within the set of central art forms at t or (b) it is an artefact that achieves excellence in fulfilling a function belonging to the set of functions for central art forms (whether or not it is in a central art form and whether or not it was intended to fulfil such a function).

Among the tasks and difficulties faced by functionalist accounts are as follows. (1) Specifying the functions of art. For Beardsley, the main purpose is that of providing an aesthetic experience. (2) Acknowledging both that the point of art might alter through time and that the art-historical context of creation affects the aesthetic character of the work and, thereby, its functionality. The historicism introduced by Stecker's time-indexing is designed to cover such considerations. (3) Explaining the dysfunctionality of very poor works of art. Both Beardsley and Stecker do so by allowing that something intended to serve the point or points of art might become an art work even if that intention is unsuccessful. (4) Resolving the status of the hard cases mentioned previously. Beardsley denies that Duchamp's pieces are works of art, whereas Stecker argues that, within their art-historical setting, they serve accepted functions of art (reference to and rebellion against former artistic types and practices). He notes that they could not have served equivalent functions in earlier times.

The most detailed version of a procedural account is the institutional theory developed by George Dickie. His most recent definition (1984) runs: (a) an artist is a person who participates with understanding in the making of an art work; (b) a work of art is an artefact of a kind created to be presented to an artworld public; (c) a public is a set of persons the members of which are prepared in some degree to understand an object which is presented to them; (d) the artworld is the totality of all artworld systems; (e) an artworld system is a framework for the presentation of a work of art by an artist to an artworld public. The 'artworld' is the historical and social setting constituted by the changing practices and conventions of art, the heritage of works, the intentions of artists, the writings of critics, and so forth.

Among the difficulties faced by the proceduralist are as follows. (1) Showing that the relevant procedures are established (and, in its institutional version, demonstrating that they mark an informal institution distinguishable from similar institutions with different goals). (2) Accounting for the art-status of works never presented to, or intended for, a public, including the products of isolated artists, of the earliest artists in history and of those working outside the officially recognized boundaries of the artworld, such as embroiderers. Dickie's definition requires not that the piece be presented, but that it be of a kind suitable for presentation; also, he could allow that some pieces are enfranchised as art from within the institution after their creation. (3) Avoiding a vicious circularity in characterizing the procedures, or the institution in which they are applied, without assuming their products to be art works. Dickie claims that the circularity in his own account is benign. (4) Resolving the status of the hard cases mentioned previously. Dickie sees it as an advantage of his theory that it accommodates Duchamp's ready-mades, but one might wonder if the procedural account is able to explain what makes such cases hard.

4 Recursive definitions

Weitz's suggestion that something is a work of art in virtue of its resemblance to other (prior) works of art indirectly acknowledges the historicist character of art-making. Artists frequently draw on, refer to or react against their predecessors. Moreover, what constitutes art and what can be done within art depends on what has been art and what has been done within art in the past; the art of the distant past of a culture might differ in many respects from the art of its present, despite the continuity of the process that links one to the other. The historicist character of art has received growing recognition within philosophical aesthetics since the 1950s; more recent attempts at a definition reflect this.

In crude outline, a historicist definition of art has two parts. The first explains how the first works in history came to be art – perhaps by stipulation, or because they served an appropriate function. The second, recursive part states that 'Something is an art work if it stands in an appropriate relation to art that predates it.' The 'appropriate relation' is characterized in various ways. A suitably historicized functionalist definition, for example, would construe the relation as holding between the (intended, central, significant) function of the present candidate and the (intended, central, significant) functions of past works. A suitably historicized proceduralist definition would construe the relation as holding between the procedures applied to the present candidate and the procedures used successfully in conferring art-status on prior works. (I have already noted the historicist aspect given to functionalism by Stecker. The institutional theory is ripe for and would be improved by a similar treatment.)

Some recent historicist definitions conceive the defining relation neither in terms of function nor procedure. Jerrold Levinson (1979) sees the defining relation in the intended treatment of the candidate – a work of art is a thing that has been 'seriously intended for regard-as-a-work-of-art'; that is, regard (meaning treatment, taking, engagement with or approach) in any way pre-existing works of art are or were correctly regarded. James Carney (1991) characterizes the defining relation as a shared style: an object is a work of art if and only if it can be linked by those suitably informed, along one or more various specific dimensions, to a past or present general style or styles exhibited by prior works of art. Noël Carroll (1993) takes the unifying relation to be that of narrative continuity, though he denies offering this as a definition. In his view, something is an art work if it can be linked to preceding art-making practices and contexts by a narrative committed to historical accuracy that reveals the piece as an intelligible outcome of recognizable modes of thinking and making of a sort already commonly adjudged to be artistic. If there is dispute about the artistic nature of the context from which the candidate work arose, then this is to be settled by appeal to a meta-narrative that links that context with acknowledged artworld practices, procedures and processes.

The detail of each of these theories might be examined critically. For instance, one might ask if Levinson can distinguish the art-making intention from other intentions that similarly invite a regard of something as if it were art without aiming, directly or indirectly, at making that thing art; and one might consider whether Carney could analyse the notion of artistic style, or Carroll could develop the relevant notion of continuity in narrative, without begging the definitional question. (Of course, a theorist might avoid such queries by further generalizing the recursive part of the definition – something is a work of art if and only if it stands in the appropriate art-creating relation to previous works. This approach meets these objections, though, only by emptying the definition of content.)

Instead of pursuing such matters here I will mention one concern about the general strategy. It seems that there is more than one tradition of art-making and appreciation; also, what is possible at a given time within one tradition might not be possible at the same time, or at any time, in others. Recursive definitions explain how something is art by relating it in the appropriate way to a given tradition. Such definitions will be at best incomplete, because so much of the explanatory burden is carried by the implicit, undefined notion of an artistic tradition. If something is a work of art within only one of many possible traditions, then the notion of art is not fully explicated until a basis is provided for distinguishing traditions of art from other historically continuous, cultural processes or practices and, also, for individuating one artistic tradition from another.

Two ways of attempting to dismiss this point fail, I think. First, it would be both false and offensive to confine art to a single cultural tradition, such as that arising from western Europe, and to dismiss other traditions merely as generating non-art that serves functions similar to those of art. And even if we allow for the many human artistic traditions, it might be implausible to reject the possibility of non-human, non-terrestrial art. Second, it would be an error to suggest that the proposed definition allows that something is a work of art if it relates appropriately to any pieces in *any* tradition of art-making, for the work then becomes decontextualized. This is unconvincing because it implies that, if something could become art within one tradition, it could become art in any; if Duchamp could make a work of art of a urinal in USA, a Chinese artist might have done the same in China. Rather than emphasizing that the art status of a piece depends on the piece's historico-cultural location, this approach treats the place of the piece in its given tradition as irrelevant to its status as art.

See also: ARTIST'S INTENTION; COLLINGWOOD, R.G. §3; CROCE, B. §2 ; TOLSTOY, L. §4

References and further reading

These readings are not introductory in style, though none is forbiddingly technical or formal.

* Beardsley, M.C. (1982) 'Redefining Art', in M.J. Wreen and D.M. Callen (eds) *The Aesthetic Point of View*, Ithaca, NY, and London: Cornell University Press, 298–315. (A functionalist definition according to which art provides aesthetic experience.)
* Carney, J.D. (1991) 'Style Theory of Art', *The Pacific Philosophical Quarterly* 72: 272–89. (A recursive definition identifying style as the crucial relation.)
* Carroll, N. (1993) 'Historical Narratives and the Philosophy of Art', *Journal of Aesthetics and Art Criticism* 51: 313–26. (Elaborates and refines a theory first introduced in 1988 according to which the continuity of a narrative charts the course of art.)
—— (1994) 'Identifying Art', in R.J. Yanal (ed.) *Institutions of Art*, University Park, PA: Penn State Press, 3–39. (Advances the theory of 1993 while criticizing alternative views.)
Davies, S. (1991) *Definitions of Art*, Ithaca, NY, and London: Cornell University Press. (Detailed review of philosophical treatments of the topic since the 1950s; contains a bibliography.)
Dickie, G. (1974) *Art and the Aesthetic: An Institutional Analysis*, Ithaca, NY, and London: Cornell University Press. (The first developed account of an institutional theory.)
* —— (1984) *The Art Circle: A Theory of Art*, New York: Haven. (The institutional theory revised and refined.)
Diffey, T.J. (1969) 'The Republic of Art', *British Journal of Aesthetics* 9: 145–56. (The most sophisticated of the first articulations of the institutional theory.)
* Levinson, J. (1979) 'Defining Art Historically', *British Journal of Aesthetics* 19: 232–50. (First version of his recursive definition.)
—— (1989) 'Refining Art Historically', *Journal of Aesthetics and Art Criticism* 47: 21–33. (Revises and defends Levinson (1979).)
—— (1993) 'Extending Art Historically', *Journal of Aesthetics and Art Criticism* 51: 411–23. (Revises and defends Levinson (1979) and (1989).)
Sparshott, F. (1982) *The Theory of the Arts*, Princeton, NJ: Princeton University Press. (Detailed coverage of the arts, including their definition.)
* Stecker, R. (1994) 'Historical Functionalism or the Four Factor Theory', *British Journal of Aesthetics* 34: 255–65. (A historicist, sophisticated version of functionalism.)
* Weitz, M. (1956) 'The Role of Theory in Aesthetics', *Journal of Aesthetics and Art Criticism* 15: 27–35. (A famous attempt to show that art has no definable essence.)

STEPHEN DAVIES

ART, EROTIC *see* EROTIC ART

ART, FORMALISM IN
see FORMALISM IN ART

ART, PERFORMING

Some works, such as plays and pieces of classical music, are created as instructions (either notated or implicit in an exemplar) for performers; performances of such pieces arise from the appropriate execution of those instructions. Because the instructions do not specify all features possessed by an accurate performance, performers inevitably contribute something to the performance; even ideally accurate performances differ in the interpretations they offer. Some such works serve primarily to highlight the performer's talents. Even where this is not so, some awareness of what is involved in rendering a piece is necessary to appreciate a work written for performance, since the skills and techniques of performance are the artistic media through which the work's contents are presented. Performances are evaluated for the life, integrity and interest of their interpretations, as well as for their accuracy. The desirability of one performance over another relates partly to the knowledge and experience of the intended audience.

Other works, such as films, involve performance in their creation rather than in their transmission. If these works are multiple, they are so because copies are cloned from a master. When completed, such pieces are not performed or interpreted; they are shown or displayed.

Free improvisation might stand as performance in its own right, being neither the creation of a work nor an instance of one. The criteria in terms of which improvisations are evaluated differ from those involved in the creation or transmission of works, taking into account the fact that the improviser's efforts involve the risks, as well as the delights, of spontaneity.

1 Arts involving performance
2 Works for performance
3 The centrality of the performer
4 Works made through performance
5 Performance in the absence of works

1 Arts involving performance

The performing arts include theatre, dance and other forms of movement, opera, film and television, as well as instrumental and vocal music. Some performing arts are now lost – sagas, narrative poetry and storytelling, for instance; others are marginal as performing arts – poetry, for example. Some activities that include performance are not counted among the arts, such as circus, striptease and televised advertisements.

2 Works for performance

In the case of works created for performance, artists (such as playwrights, composers, choreographers and authors) produce either instructions (in oral form, or in the form of a script or score) that performers execute or a model instance that they emulate in delivering instances of the works. A work for performance is complete when its score, script or model is complete. Such pieces are instantiated in their various performances. The works are distinct from their performances; they have been variously characterized as universals, types, kinds or classes (see ART WORKS, ONTOLOGY OF §2). Pieces represented by a score or script might never be performed; that is, they might have no instances. Theorists sometimes distinguish performance for an audience from rehearsal, practising or private enactments. What should be acknowledged is that the activity takes its point from generating and publicly transmitting instances of given works.

In the case of works for performance, artists' instructions should be interpreted in light of the relevant performance practices; what can be presupposed might not be mentioned or notated, despite its being required, and not all that is mentioned or notated will be mandatory. To perform a work, performers typically produce an instance of the work by following the artist's instructions or model, or by copying other performances derived from those. (If a gust of wind by chance produces a sound acoustically indistinguishable from some performance of a Beethoven symphony, that sound-event would neither be a performance nor would it otherwise instantiate Beethoven's work.) A performance of a given work that contains some departures from the artist's instructions might still be regarded as a performance of that work, provided the work remains recognizable in the performance. To the extent that it diverges (whether this is intended by the performer or not) from the artist's determinative instructions, a performance is inaccurate or unauthentic as an account of the artist's work.

The relevant conventions and artists' notations underspecify or do not determine many of the features displayed in a performance of the work, and where performers emulate a model instance, the realization of many details is by convention left at their discretion. Where performers are left free, they are constrained only by the wider conventions of style or genre. The level of the performer's creative autonomy varies within and between the performing arts; jazz dancers have more liberty in their actions than do ballerinas. But, even in those performing arts that provide highly detailed instructions, many crucial choices are left to performers; for instance, many aspects of speech delivery and gesture are not indicated by the playwright. It is by their treatment of those matters on which performers are free that equally faithful (but different) interpretations are distinguished. A single interpretation or production might receive more than one performance.

Though the work is distinct from the score, script or model instance produced by the artist, I hold that the identity of the work derives from the instructions notated or implicit in the model. These, in turn, are identified in relation to the artist and the period of creation. In that case, one cannot perform the work except by performing it as its creator's, and doing this requires faithfulness in the relevant respects (as determined by artistic conventions of the genre at the time) to the instructions produced by the artist. A performance can instantiate a given work only if it is faithful or authentic to the appropriate degree. I claim that we are interested in performances primarily as performances of artists' works and that this is how they are advertised and represented. (This is not to say, though, that we shun works from unknown provenances; a speculative account of a work consistent with the conventions of its time usually provides something worth considering, if not definitively its artist's work.)

The history of its performances and the constitution of the intended audience also are relevant in assessing the degree of faithfulness appropriate for a performance, as Jerrold Levinson has argued (1987). The first performance of a work should aim at a high degree of faithfulness, as should a performance directed at novices. Where works are well known, as are Shakespeare's plays in the West, much of the performer's duty of faithfulness has been discharged already; other desiderata, such as contemporary relevance, novelty and verve, become more prominent. Performances are evaluated in terms of the life, coherence, variety and interest they bring to the work, and these features are relative to the audience's prior experience of that work or similar ones, as well as to the materials furnished by the work's creator.

Stan Godlovitch (1993) specifies the following conditions for the integrity of live performances: only one work is performed at a time; its proper sequence is respected, as is the indicated rate of delivery; the performance is continuous, without unjustified breaks; performers comply with the appropriate roles (and do not, for example, swap parts midway through the work). Also, the audience should be in a position to receive the entire performance in every detail. Note that such conditions are required by the view presented earlier: the primary aim of performance is to deliver the artist's work, as specified, to an audience.

3 The centrality of the performer

That artists need the services of performers in instancing their work is not to say merely that performers are means for the work's transmission. The foundry workers who follow the sculptor's instructions and the film's projectionist help to create or transmit the work, but theirs is not the pivotal role of the performer. They might be replaced by technologically superior alternatives without thereby altering the artistic character of the statue or film, whereas the performer's task is ineliminably part of works created for performance.

Artists work with media; the appreciation of art requires the audience to be aware of the limits and possibilities of the media employed. In the performing arts, the requirements of performance are part of the medium in which artists operate. Artists do not create works that happen to be performed; rather, they write *for* performance, taking into account what will be involved for performers when they produce the outcome. (So it is that a new, though derivative, piece results when a musical work is transcribed for instruments different from those specified for the original.) Just as the viewers of a painting consider not only what it represents, but also its surface and the manner of its representation, so audiences in the performing arts consider the artist's use of the performers and their props or tools. They should be aware, for instance, that a dance depicts the death of a swan, that a given actor is playing the parts of several characters and that organists use their feet as well as their hands.

Many works for performance employ the performer's skills in order to achieve narrative, expressive, formal or other effects. These, rather than the performer's activity, are the proper focus of appreciative concern, even if that concern involves an awareness of the connection between the artist's instructions, the performer's efforts and the artistic result. In other pieces, though, the artistic point of the work is to highlight the expertise and techniques of the performer. This is the case with works providing virtuosic roles for one or two performers; some genres, such as the concerto and étude, are of this kind. As Thomas Carson Mark suggests (1980), such pieces are about the talents required to perform them; the audience's fullest appreciation requires a recognition of the difficulties overcome by the performer in making the rendition seem effortless.

Combining the points just made with the earlier emphasis on the relation between the work's identity and its means of performance, it is possible to see why the tools, techniques and skills of the performer come to be valued and preserved in their own right, sometimes despite the availability of simpler alternatives. If a new ballet shoe were capable of doubling the height of a dancer's leap, it would not be appropriate for dancers to wear the new shoes for performances of nineteenth-century ballets; even if exaggerated elevation is a desirable feature in such works, the difficulty of achieving that elevation is also part of those works. Similarly, the programmed synthesizer is no substitute for the violin when it comes to performing Bach's Partitas, even if it exactly reproduces the sound of a violin. It is not surprising, then, that musicians, dancers and actors of the past formed guilds, not only to train novices but also to keep secret the tricks of their crafts. Contemporary performers are expected to maintain the required standards.

The central place of artistic skill and creativity in performances helps to explain the distinction between, on the one hand, the disc jockey or ink-printer and, on the other, the performer. The former might be involved in delivering a work of art to an audience, but their roles lack the particular skills for which artists plan the shapes of their works. Tragedies are written for actors and concertos are written for pianists, but films are not made for projectionists and bronzes are not made for casters. Thus it is sometimes said that performers are artists' collaborators, not their servants.

4 Works made through performance

By contrast with pieces created for performance, some kinds of art involve performance not in instantiating the work but, rather, as an essential element in its creation. This is typically the case in cinema. Unlike a play, a movie is not completed as a work when it is scripted; movies must be made, and performers contribute to this process. Once finished, the cinematic work is screened, not performed. The cinematic art work is the master print, which is multiply instantiated by prints cloned from it. The same is also true for some kinds of music, such as electronic pieces that use tapes of the voice or instruments as their source material; the work is the finished master tape and the copies made from it.

An interesting puzzle is raised by popular music, in which discs derived from the master have a dominant status and 'performances' frequently involve 'lip- and hand-synching' to recordings. (Multi-tracking might preclude genuine live performance.) Is the importance of these recordings a sign that they are definitive of the work? If so, artists' rerecordings of their own compositions result in new works, not merely in new performances. Alternatively, is it that the recording is a model instance that may be performed live? In that case, the recording is the more important, not because it is that work's only instance, but because it sets the standard for the work's subsequent performances. (Or are these questions redundant, because the piece has become the music video, which has superseded the audio tape?)

5 Performance in the absence of works

So far I have concentrated on the connection between performances and art works, but performances might take place in the absence of works, as is sometimes the case with street theatre. Dancers might dance without making an instance of any work, or thespians might act without performing a play or making a film. Where there is no work to be followed, the content of the performance is improvised. While there is much to appreciate that is common to both improvised performances and performances of works, there also are differences to be recognized, as Philip Alperson has noted (1984). Obviously one cannot criticize free improvisers for lack of faithfulness to artists' specifications, since they follow none. (There can be mistakes in improvisation, however, when, for example, conventions of the adopted style are violated.) Spontaneity and inventiveness are valued in improvisation; meanwhile, some looseness of structure and lack of polish are less blameworthy in an improvised performance than in one in which such factors are produced by the artist or result after hours of rehearsal. And where there is common ground for appreciation the basis for evaluations can differ. Both improvisations and works for performance might be enjoyed for their narrative or formal structures, inner harmony or overall beauty, but it is relevant that, in the case of the former, responsibility for the achievement lies solely with the performers, who act freely and do so at the moment of performance.

Why not say that improvisation results in a work created by someone who acts both as performer and artist, even if the piece that is the outcome is not itself *for* performance? The difference between improvisation and the creation of a work through performance does not depend on the number of instances, because an improvisation might be taped and, thereby, duplicated, just as a film might have many prints. The results of improvisation are not more ephemeral in principle than are works created with the help of performers. The basis for the distinction, I suggest, is a matter of convention – we talk of films as works, yet we do not describe sessions of free improvisation by this term. This way of talking implicitly acknowledges differences in the goals of improvising and of creating permanent works through performance.

Why not allow that improvisation results in a model of a work for performance? The answer is as before: improvisation is not conventionally approached as providing a work recipe for others to realize through emulation. An artist might recall and notate a piece that was originally improvised, as J.S. Bach is thought to have done with his Musical Offering, but this shows not that all acts of improvisation simultaneously involve the creation of works for performance but only that a work for performance might be composed through improvisation. It matters that the artist supplies a notation or specifies that the original improvisation be taken as a model performance, for without such indications there is no warrant for regarding the result as the creation or performance of a work.

See also: DANCE, AESTHETICS OF §§4, 6; MUSIC, AESTHETICS OF §3

References and further reading

* Alperson, P. (1984) 'On Musical Improvisation', *Journal of Aesthetics and Art Criticism* 43: 17–30. (Argues, as in §5, that the goals of improvisation differ from those relevant to the performance of works but departs from the above in regarding improvisations as works.)

Carlson, M. (1984) *Theories of the Theatre: A Historical and Critical Survey from the Greeks to the Present*, Ithaca, NY, and London: Cornell University Press. (A detailed survey of the methods, aims, functions and characteristics of Western theatre from the Greeks to the present.)

Davies, S. (1991) 'The Ontology of Musical Works and the Authenticity of their Performances', *Nous* 25: 21–41. (Covers prevailing views on the ontology of musical works and on the relevance of authenticity in performance; argues for the connectedness of these issues; and includes a bibliography.)

Godlovitch, S. (1990) 'Music Performance and the Tools of the Trade', *IYYUN, The Jerusalem Philosophical Quarterly* 39: 321–38. (Argues, as in §3, that the difficulties of performing on musical instruments sometimes are essential, not incidental, features of the works that employ them.)

* —— (1993) 'The Integrity of Musical Performance', *Journal of Aesthetics and Art Criticism* 51: 573–87. (Characterizes conditions for the integrity of musical performances as listed in §2.)

* Levinson, J. (1987) 'Evaluating Musical Performance', *The Journal of Aesthetic Education* 21 (1): 75–88. (Emphasizes, as in §2, that the features desirable in a performance are relative to, among other things, the audience's context and knowledge.)

—— (1990) 'Authentic Performance and Performance Means', in *Music, Art, and Metaphysics*, Ithaca, NY, and London: Cornell University Press, 393–408. (Argues, as in §2, that the means of performance are criterial for the identity of works for performance, because the use of the means generates some of the work's artistically important properties.)

McFee, G. (1992) *Understanding Dance*, New York: Routledge. (Introductory text on the philosophy of dance.)

* Mark, T.C. (1980) 'On Works of Virtuosity', *The Journal of Philosophy* 77: 28–45. (Argues, as in §3, that virtuosic works are about the virtuosity they display and that performances themselves can be works of art.)

Saltz, D. (1991) 'How To Do Things On Stage', *Journal of Aesthetics and Art Criticism* 49: 31–45. (Considers the extent to which an actor's actions could be the actions of the character portrayed by the actor, with discussion of different models.)

Sparshott, F. (1988) *Off the Ground: First Steps to a Philosophical Consideration of the Dance*, Princeton, NJ: Princeton University Press. (Detailed discussion of the metatheory of dance.)

Thom, P. (1993) *For an Audience: A Philosophy of the Performing Arts*, Philadelphia, PA: Temple University Press. (Attempts to define the performing arts, distinguishing them from nonperformance arts and from nonartistic performance.)

STEPHEN DAVIES

ART, UNDERSTANDING OF

Art engages the understanding in many ways. Thus, confronted with an allegorical painting such as Van Eyk's The Marriage of Arnolfini, *one might want to understand the significance of the objects it depicts. Similarly, confronted with an obscure poem, such as Eliot's* The Waste Land, *one might seek to understand what it means. Sometimes, too, we claim not to understand a work of art, a piece of music, say, when we are unable to derive enjoyment from it because we cannot see how it is organized or hangs together. Sometimes what challenges the understanding goes deeper, as when we ask why some things, including such notorious productions of the avant garde as the urinal exhibited by Marcel Duchamp, are called art at all. Some have also claimed that to understand a work of art we must understand its context. Sometimes the context referred to is that of the particular problems and aims of the individual artist in a certain tradition, as when the church of St Martin-in-the-Fields is understood as a contribution by its architect to the vexing problem of combining a tower with a classical façade. Sometimes the context is social, as when some Marxists argue that works of art can best be understood as reflections of the more or less inadequate economic organizations of the societies that gave rise to them. The understanding of art becomes a philosophical problem because, first, it is sometimes thought that one of the central tasks of interpretation is to understand the meaning of a work. However, recent writers, notably Derrida (1972), query the notion of the meaning of a work as something to be definitively deciphered, and offer the alternative view of interpretation as an unending play with the infinitely varied meanings of the text. Second, a controversial issue has been the extent to which the judgment of works of art can be divorced from an understanding of the circumstances, both individual and cultural, of their making. Thus Clive Bell argued that to appreciate a work of art we need nothing more than a knowledge of its colours, shapes and spatial arrangements. Others, ranging from Wittgenstein to Marxists, have for a variety of different reasons argued that a work of art cannot be properly understood and appreciated without some understanding of its relation to the context of its creation, a view famously characterized by Beardsley and Wimsatt as the 'genetic fallacy'.*

1 Minimal understanding
2 Categories
3 Evaluation and explanation
4 Understanding, truth and morality
5 Criticism as retrieval

1 Minimal understanding

Some, notably Clive Bell (1914), have argued that in order to appreciate a work of art we need a very minimal understanding of it. We do not need to understand what, say, an allegorical picture represents, or when, how and why it was painted. All we need is knowledge of its form as revealed in its colours, shapes and spatial arrangements. Apart from the unfortunate way in which this encourages appreciators to treat representations of suffering, grief and loss as exercises in aesthetic pleasure-seeking, and apart from the cavalier dismissal of the delight that we take in representation and expression, this theory fails even as an account of the appreciation of form. Sometimes it is only when we understand what is depicted that we can appreciate the formal composition of a work. In Stubbs's painting *The Duke of Richmond's Racehorses at Exercise*, it is only because we recognize a pointing hand leading our eyes in a certain direction that we understand the composition of the painting.

Wollheim (1980) has argued that the very possibility of representational painting entails a reference to the pictorial intentions of artists. Hence, granted that representation is a relevant concern to the appreciator of art, understanding is, on Wollheim's view, related to intention. For seeing a canvas as a representational painting differs from seeing, by an exercise of one's fancy, pictures in a moss-covered wall; the difference, Wollheim claims, being a matter of there being a standard of correctness for representation. We correctly understand a representation when there is a match between what we impute to the canvas and what the artist intended to represent. Both to understand that something is a representation and to understand what it represents we need a reference to intentional activity.

2 Categories

Some, including Kendall Walton (1970), have argued that evaluation and understanding are related, since in order to make a proper evaluation of a work of art it is sometimes necessary to understand to which category of art it belongs, a view also argued by Richard Wollheim, and vehemently denied by Croce in his attack on the notion of artistic genres. This view has some affinity with a discussion in moral philosophy initiated by Peter Geach in his distinction between predicative and attributive terms (1956). Consider the difference between 'grey' (predicative) and 'big' (attributive). 'This is a grey mouse' divides with no oddity into 'This is grey' and 'This is a mouse'. This being so, we could know that a thing is grey without knowing to what category it belongs. But 'This is a big mouse' does not appear so easily to divide into 'This is big' and 'This is a mouse'. The truth of assertions about bigness (unlike those for greyness) seems to be related to different standards of normal size for different categories of things. Similarly some have argued that judgments of merit in aesthetics are relative to categories. What is beautiful as the neck of a horse might not be beautiful as the neck of a Vice Chancellor, and the excellences of sonnets are not those of haiku. A clear case of a need to know the category of a work is the case in which we need to know that a work is ironic or a parody in order to appreciate it properly.

It is not, however, entirely clear that critical as opposed to classificatory judgments of works of art do require understanding of categories. It is legitimate to ask whether what is a good sonnet in the sense in which it meets the requirements of membership of that category is also a good literary work of art – a question that seems to invoke non-specific categories of appraisal in use across the arts.

3 Evaluation and explanation

Many have argued that it is one thing to evaluate a work of art and another to seek an understanding or explanation of its genesis. Beardsley and Wimsatt (1954), for example, claimed that understanding a poem as a prelude to critically appraising it requires only such knowledge of the public language as could be obtained from dictionaries or from any competent speaker. It does not require knowledge of the intentions of the poet to mean something, for the words of the poem belong not to the poet but to the language. This does not rule out historical studies. In the case of a work of some antiquity, as the critical apparatus of most Shakespeare plays will demonstrate, in order to secure understanding we might have to do considerable research to find out what the public meanings of the words were at the time of publication. According to Beardsley and Wimsatt, this does not license biographical enquiries, however, since what we are interested in are the public words of a public text, not the private meanings of an author.

To investigate the genesis of the work would indeed be to understand more about it and how it came to be as it is, but this, Beardsley and Wimsatt claim, would not be relevant or necessary to its assessment. A similar line was taken by Trotsky, who argued that a work of art is to be judged by its own laws (1923). That done, a Marxist could explain, as Marxists can for any human product, valuable or not, how that artistic product had ultimately arisen from a certain economic sub-structure of a society (see MARX, K.). The understanding of the work that this would yield would not, however, be relevant to judgments of artistic merit. In the next two sections we shall look more closely at such attempts to separate understanding and evaluation.

4 Understanding, truth and morality

Much of the debate about art and understanding is a debate about how much of what might rightly be called an understanding of art is relevant to questions of the evaluation of art. Bell, for example, would not have denied that it is a fact about Frith's Victorian narrative painting *Paddington Station* that it is a representational painting. To understand that is to understand something about the painting. What Bell would have denied was that this understanding had anything to do with the appreciation or value of the work. Bell's denial of the relevance of an understanding of the representational aspects of a painting, however, seems merely by fiat to eliminate aspects of paintings which people unhesitatingly enjoy and which, as Wollheim and others have argued, are highly relevant to aesthetic effects.

We may take as a more promising example of the debates about the relevance of certain sorts of understanding the vigorously controversial issue of the relevance to evaluation of an understanding of the truth and morality of a work of art. Some, including Wilde, have denied that works of art can be true or moral at all. But among those who concede that a work of art might contain truths (as Kafka is said sometimes to have captured a truth about the human condition) and might articulate a moral stance (as Jane Austen is often said to do) there are those who deny that an understanding that a work truly has these aspects has any bearing on its evaluation. As to morality, there is a perfectly good sense in which anyone who missed the fact that a certain moral outlook pervades a novel by Jane Austen has not understood that novel. The question is whether that understanding is involved in the assessment of the work, a question to which F.R. Leavis categorically gave an affirmative answer and to which Croce gave an equally categorical negative reply (see ART AND MORALITY §3).

When we come to relevance of an understanding that a work of art articulates a view of life, including a view that can be characterized as morally correct, matters are initially muddier because of the complexities involved in assessing views of life. (How is pessimism to be weighed against optimism? Fielding against Kafka? Jane Austen against Sartre?)

One very important approach, adopted by certain Marxists, relates understanding the point of view of a work intrinsically to its evaluation. Suppose we allow that a work of art can articulate a view of life, and that to understand that work is, in part at least, to understand the view of life that it articulates. But, on one reading, Marxist theory claims to possess a privileged understanding of the objective laws of historical progress. In terms of those laws it is possible for a Marxist to say that such and such a state of society is a defective stage of human organization, to be surpassed in the forward march of history, and, further, to say that anyone endorsing that state of society shows a defective understanding of history. Then the way is open for a Marxist to say that a worldview articulated in a work of art can display a defective understanding of social relations (as some alleged was the case with Dickens's *Hard Times*). It would seem narrowly prescriptive to say, without further argument, that this judgment is irrelevant to an assessment of a work of art. For it attributes to a work a lack of understanding, perceptiveness, and possibly imagination. It certainly treats it as the expression of an inadequate state of social consciousness. But then, it seems that there is at least one account that links understanding a work of art with its evaluative judgment. For to understand the work of art is to understand it as the articulation of a worldview, and to understand that aspect is to open the possibility of assessing the work in terms of the adequacy of the worldview it articulates as well as the adequacy of its articulation of it.

Whether such an account can ever be made to work depends on the truth of the Marxist claim – vigorously contested – that they have a privileged access to the objective laws of history. Even if such a claim were false, it should not be forgotten that part of our understanding of a work may involve an understanding of the view of life articulated in it, and, further, that our reaction to a work is often very much bound up with our feelings, not merely about the quality of the way in which that view is expressed, but also about the view itself (see ART AND TRUTH §4). Hence Wittgenstein's frequent comment that he could not understand and engage with some works of art, for example the music of Mahler, as opposed to the works of Brahms, because he could not see the world from that viewpoint (1966).

5 Criticism as retrieval

Many have spoken as if the central task of all our dealings with art is evaluation, and other activities, such as the understanding of the whole context of a work, are irrelevant to criticism and appreciation. The element of truth in this is that we tend to embark upon enquiries into genesis and context after we have made the decision that the work is worth it. We study the origins of *The Waste Land* because, prior to any such study, we found *The Waste Land* rewarding. However, we cannot conclude from the fact that we are prompted to learn more about the circumstances of a work after it has impressed us favourably that information discovered about it subsequently is irrelevant to our assessment. Things that emerge on further enquiry might produce radical alterations in assessments (as when we discover that we were taken in by the excellence of a parody).

Second, on reading a work, we may find things in it that puzzle us. Beardsley and others are right that it is a fact about some works that they are puzzling. It is possible, however, not merely to settle for the knowledge *that* a work is puzzling. That leaves a gap in our understanding which we can plug by seeking reasons for why the work is as it is. The positioning of the figures in Picasso's *Les Demoiselles d'Avignon* will not change when we examine its very many drafts and sketches. But puzzlement as to why they are as they are will be replaced by a better understanding.

Finally, it is too easy to talk as if evaluation in some narrow sense were all there is to the appreciation of art. There is also such a thing as a love of a work of art, which, as is often the case with love, wishes to know all there is to know about the object of love and ultimately to understand it as fully as possible. To the lover of the work nothing about it is ultimately irrelevant. And this is related to the view that Richard Wollheim has defended of criticism as 'retrieval', where that involves:

> the reconstruction of the creative process, where the creative process must in turn be thought of as something not stopping short of, but terminating on, the work of art itself. The creative process reconstructed, or retrieval complete, the work is then open to understanding.
>
> (1980: 204)

Understanding and appreciation cannot be divorced, if for no other reason than that to understand a work of art may just be to hear, read or look at it with a certain kind of appreciative enjoyment. As Wittgenstein remarks, understanding that a Brahms rhythm has a certain queer quality is inseparable from experiencing that quality in it (1966: 20).

See also: ARTIST'S INTENTION; ARTISTIC INTERPRETATION

References and further reading

* Bell, C. (1914) *Art*, London: Chatto & Windus. (A classic statement of the case that only a minimal understanding of art is needed as a precondition for appreciation.)
* Beardsley, M.C. and Wimsatt, W.K. (1954) 'The Intentional Fallacy', in Wimsatt, W.K. (ed.) *The Verbal Icon*, New York: Noonday. (Seminal statement of the view that the understanding of the work deriving from studies of its genesis is irrelevant to its evaluation.)
* Croce, B. (1902) *Estetica come scienza dell'espressione e linguistica generale*, trans. C. Lyas, *The Aesthetic as the Science of Expression and of the Linguistic in General*, Cambridge: Cambridge University Press, 1992. (Referred to in §2 for its trenchant statement of the irrelevance of genre criticism and in §4 for its rejection of moralism in art.)
* Derrida, J. (1972) *Margins*, trans. A. Bass, Brighton: Harvester Wheatsheaf, 1982. (Referred to in the introductory remarks as denying that the task of the interpreter is to understand a text by deciphering its meaning. Notoriously obscure writer, though the text cited is one of the more accessible, see esp. 316ff.)
  Elliott, R.K. (1972) 'The Critic and the Lover of Art', in Mays, W. and Brown, S.C. (eds) *Linguistic Analysis and Phenomenology*, London: Macmillan. (Highly relevant and beautifully written contribution to the discussion of the love of art.)
* Geach, P.T. (1956) 'Good and Evil', *Analysis* 17: 33–42. (The early discussion of the predicative/attributive distinction.)
  Scruton, R. (1974) *Art and Imagination*, London: Methuen. (Argues that understanding might just be having the right sort of experience of a work. Ch. 12 discusses detailed examples.)
* Trotsky, L. (1924) *Literature and Revolution*, trans. R. Stransky, London: Redwords, 1991. (Denies the relevance of Marxist understandings of art to its evaluation. Further details on the various Marxist positions mentioned in §4 can be found in the essay by S. Sim 'Marxism and Aesthetics', in O. Hanfling (ed.) *Philosophical Aesthetics*, Oxford: Blackwell, 1992.)
* Walton, K. (1970) 'Categories of Art', *Philosophical Review* 79: 334–67. (Proposes the view that an understanding of the category of a work of art bears on its evaluation.)
* Wittgenstein, L. (1966) *Lectures and Conversations on Aesthetics, Psychology and Religious Belief*, ed. C.

Barrett, Oxford: Blackwell. (Highly relevant to discussions of the relevance of understanding to appreciation, as are the remarks on various artists: for example, on Shakespeare and Mahler, in L. Wittgenstein (1977), *Culture and Value*, Oxford: Blackwell.)

* Wollheim, R. (1980) 'Criticism as Retrieval' and 'Seeing-as, Seeing-in, and Pictorial Representation', in *Art and Its Objects*, 2nd edn, Cambridge: Cambridge University Press. (*Art and its Objects*, although sometimes difficult, bears importantly on questions of the place of understanding in art appreciation.)

COLIN LYAS

ART, VALUE OF

Art has as many kinds of value as there are points of view from which it can be evaluated. Moreover, the benefits of art vary with the role of the participant, for there are benefits that are specific to the creation, the performance and the mere appreciation of art. But in the philosophy of art one value is basic, namely the distinctive value of a work of art, its value as a work of art, which can be called its 'artistic value'. This value is intrinsic to a work in that it is determined by the intrinsic, rather than the instrumental, value of an informed experience of it, an experience of it in which it is understood. Artistic value is a matter of degree, but it is not a measurable quantity, and whether one work is better than another may be an indeterminate issue. A judgment about a work's artistic value claims validity, rightly or wrongly, not merely for the person who makes the judgment but for everyone. Both David Hume and Immanuel Kant tried to show how such a claim could be well-founded, but their attempts are usually considered failures, and there is no accepted solution to the problem they addressed. Many philosophers have been concerned with the relation between artistic value and other values. The most famous attack on art, founded on its supposed relation to other values, was made by Plato, who claimed that nearly all art has undesirable social consequences and so should be excluded from a decent society. Plato overlooked many possibilities, however, and the question of art's beneficial or harmful influence is a much more complex issue than he recognized.

1 A multitude of values
2 Artistic value
3 Incommensurability
4 Hume and Kant
5 Non-artistic values
6 Plato's critique of art

1 A multitude of values

There is no such thing as *the* value of art. For works of art can be evaluated from many different points of view and, corresponding to these points of view, they have many different kinds of value: moral, political, social, historical, religious, sentimental or therapeutic, for example. Moreover, for a particular kind of value, whether a work possesses that value, and the degree to which it does so, will often be a relative matter, depending on the kinds of people whose involvement with the work is in question. Furthermore, for any given person this value will be relative to the role they occupy in the creation, performance and appreciation of the work – the contribution of any one of these roles to the value in question being unlikely to coincide with the contribution of any of the others.

2 Artistic value

But although art has many kinds of value, within the theory of art one particular value is fundamental, namely the value that is distinctive of art, a work of art's distinctive value, the value of a work of art *as* a work of art, or, as I shall call it, its artistic value. Just as moral value is the kind of value that moral judgment is concerned with, so artistic value is the concern of artistic judgment. This value is fundamental in an account of the value of art; for whatever other kind of value a work of art may possess, the important question is how this other kind of value is related to its artistic value.

Perhaps it will be thought that there is no such thing as a work's artistic value, or that the identification of such a value must be the expression of a moral or political ideology, rather than the acknowledgement of what should be recognized from any position as the distinctive value of art. I believe that this view is mistaken. Although the identification of a certain value as the distinctive value of art must, given what has happened to the concept of art in this century, be to a certain extent stipulative, the identification should not and does not need to be the product of an ideology. It is a mistake to think that the identification of artistic value must have built into it a commitment to some other kind of value, of which the identification is a mere reflection, or a claim to the supremacy of artistic value over other values. Rather, artistic value can and should be identified in such a way that its own worth, as measured by some other standard, is left entirely open, as a matter for further investigation.

What is needed is the specification of a value that all great works of art possess to a high degree and that an artist, in their role as artist, attempts to endow their work with. Such a value exists and can be specified without prejudging any questions about how important it is or what its relations to other kinds of value may be. Clearly, a work's artistic value is simply how good a work of art it is. Accordingly, artistic value is a matter of degree: works are not just better or worse than other works, but they can be much better or worse, or perhaps only slightly better or worse. The question, therefore, is what kind of value is credited to a work of art when it is valued as a work of art, and what value is withheld if the work is thought not to be a good work of art?

A plausible way of conceiving of artistic value emerges from two considerations, the first concerning the importance of understanding a work for the viability of a verdict on its artistic value that rests on that understanding, the second concerning the way in which works of art matter to us when we value them as art.

The first consideration is that whether there is just one correct and complete understanding of a work or many, a verdict on a work's artistic value is insecure unless it is based on a correct understanding of the work. In other words, the fact that you do not properly understand a work undermines the authority of your evaluation. The second consideration is that when we value a work of art as a work of art we value it on account of what it provides us with *in* the experience of it, rather than for something it achieves *by means of* our interaction with it. Artistic value thereby contrasts with medicinal value, for example. The medicinal value of a drug is determined not by the nature of the experience of taking it but by the beneficial or harmful effects that it has on our health. But a work's artistic value is dependent on nothing other than the nature of the experience involved in the appreciation of it.

Putting these two thoughts together, the natural way to think of the artistic value of a work of art is as the intrinsic value of the kind of experience someone has when they experience the work with understanding. A work is valuable as art to the degree that the experience it offers is valuable, not in virtue of any beneficial effects it might bring about, but in itself. What directly determines the artistic value of a work is not the values that are realised in the various *effects* of the experience, but those that are realised in the experience. A fine work of art is its own reward – it rewards in the very experience of it. The suitability of a work, when experienced with understanding, to reward the reader, spectator or audience, and the nature of the rewards on offer, determine the artistic value of the work. If the work is such that it merits being found intrinsically rewarding to experience with understanding, then the experience it offers is intrinsically valuable and, accordingly, the work is valuable as art.

3 Incommensurability

It does not follow from the fact that artistic value is a matter of degree that each work of art possesses artistic value to a *precise* degree, enabling the construction of an order of rank in which each work is either a precise amount above or below, or at exactly the same level as, any other work. In fact, if one work is better than another, it is never better by a definite amount. Moreover, artistic value does not impose even a unique ordering on works of art, for issues of comparative artistic value are sometimes indeterminate: it is not true that, for any pair of works, either one must be better than the other or they must be exactly as good as each other. Sometimes, but not always, the most that can be said about the comparative ranking of two works, whether of the same art form or of different art forms, is that they are of roughly the same order of merit. For example, Vermeer's *Head of a Girl* is undoubtedly a better work than Murillo's *The Young Beggar*, and Mozart's *Symphony in G Minor* (KV 550) is better than Schubert's *Symphony in C Minor*; but if it is conceded that neither the Vermeer nor the Mozart can be said to be superior to the other, the insistence that they must be precisely equal in value imposes an unreal precision on the concept of artistic value. This is not because the works of Vermeer and Mozart belong to different arts, for the Mozart is better than the Murillo and the Vermeer better than the Schubert. Rather, the incommensurability of artistic value and the indeterminacy of many issues of the comparative rank of works of art arises from the fact that there are many different kinds of quality that can endow a work with artistic value; there is no common unit that would allow the contribution of different kinds of quality to a work's artistic value to be measured; and even if there were, a quality that in one context constitutes an artistic merit can in other contexts detract from a work's artistic value by being combined in an incongruous manner with other qualities of the work, so that the contribution of a quality to a work's artistic value is not an individual matter but holistic.

4 Hume and Kant

A difficult problem arises concerning the implicit claim of a judgment of artistic value to interpersonal validity. How, if at all, might such a claim be well-founded? Both David Hume and Immanuel Kant attempted to answer this question. Each sought to identify a point of view, the adoption of which is definitive of artistic value. The chosen point of view defines this not merely by imposing on any individual a criterion that determines how *they* should judge, but by introducing a condition that determines how *everyone* should judge. The condition secures this result because, it is claimed, the achievement of this condition is – in virtue of the identical operation in each relevant person of the human faculties involved in the appreciation of artistic value – open to all, or to all relevant persons, by the adoption of the indicated point of view: from this point of view human emotional response to a particular work is uniform.

Hume thought to reconcile the fact that a work's artistic value ('beauty') is not a mind-independent quality but the projection onto things of the pleasure they induce with the intersubjective character of judgments of artistic value, by the exploitation of a supposed parallel between artistic value and secondary qualities – colour, for instance. Just as, he believed, though colour lies in the eye of the beholder, there is such a thing as an object's true colour, namely the colour it appears in daylight to a normal human being; so, though artistic value is based in the human mind, a work has a single, true artistic value, determined by the pleasurable or unpleasurable response of a human being of a certain kind (a 'true judge'), someone of superior discriminatory powers, who interacts with the work in the right way and in the right conditions.

Kant's fundamental thought was that interpersonal validity of a judgment of artistic value is warranted only if such a judgment is not based on anything that might be idiosyncratic or not common to all other persons. By defining such a judgment as the product of a disinterested pleasure in a work's form; by construing this pleasure as the experience of the free and harmonious play of the faculties of imagination and understanding, the two faculties that yield perceptual knowledge; and by maintaining the essential uniformity of the operation of these faculties for all people; Kant believed that he had established the validity of the claim to intersubjective agreement demanded by a judgment of artistic value (see KANT, I. §12).

So whereas Hume bases his account on the idea of a person of exceptional powers of discrimination, Kant relies upon what he takes to be common to our powers of perception. But neither Hume's nor Kant's solution commands assent. Apart from any other considerations, the reasons that each provides for believing in the (supposedly definitive) uniformity of response postulated by their theories are not compelling; and their attempts to capture the idea of a correct judgment of artistic value in terms of the pleasure that would be experienced by someone who interacts with a work in a certain manner under certain conditions appear not to do justice to the normativeness that is integral to the judgment.

The issue of the intersubjective validity of a judgment of artistic value – whether such a judgment can be valid for all people, and, if so, what validates it – has still not been adequately resolved.

5 Non-artistic values

There are many interesting questions about the relations between artistic value and other kinds of value, especially cognitive value and ethical value. For example: Is there an inherent link between the kind and degree of artistic value of a work and values of other kinds? Do certain other kinds of value *determine* artistic value in the sense that they are essential conditions of it? Are works (or works of a certain kind) with a high degree of artistic value naturally suited to support or enhance certain other kinds of value? Some thinkers have attempted to establish a particularly close connection between artistic value and certain other kinds of value, especially ethical value. For example, Tolstoy defined the activity of art as the transmission of a feeling from artist to audience by means of the artist's creation of a suitable public vehicle, and he drew the conclusion that the better the feeling transmitted – the most valuable feelings being moral–religious ones – the better the work of art that transmits it. His attempt to moralize artistic value, however, like other such attempts, proceeds by way of a tendentious characterization of the nature of art.

6 Plato's critique of art

Plato proceeded in an entirely different manner. Rather than offering a definition of art from which a favoured criterion of artistic value can be extracted, he merely held up against various artistic practices and accepted paradigms of good or great art *other* values, by which standards these practices and works were, he claimed, found wanting. This was not an unreasonable procedure. For a justification of the importance of art in human life would be best founded on an account of the importance of works that are good *as art*, and a critique of the value of art must undermine the claims of good and great art to a valuable role in our lives.

But is Plato's famous dismissal of most forms of art from his ideal state, the Republic, well-founded? His attack on art is directed at all three of the central artistic roles, the artist, the performer and the audience or spectator, and it is based on a number of grounds. I shall sketch just one or two of the principal claims. A central allegation is that the works of such representational artists as the painter and the poet are twice removed from Platonic Reality, for they are mere representations of things that are only specimens of what is truly real – namely, the archetypes (Plato's Ideas or Forms) of what is represented, which are timeless entities more real than any specimens of them and the objects of the highest knowledge. Furthermore, a picture is only an imitation of the visual appearance of what it depicts – it is designed to present to the beholder an appearance similar to that of its subject – and, accordingly, the painter, as such, is not an expert about the reality whose appearance art imitates: the painter knows only how things look, not how they really are or whether they are well-suited to their natural or intended function. Likewise, poets lack the expertise to perform well in the occupations or roles of the characters they represent in their works. So artists can produce only more or less plausible images of the natural and human world: they possess only the art of imitation, not real knowledge; their works do not express or encourage knowledge of the highest Reality, nor do they display any other knowledge worth having. Hence works of art are cognitively worthless. Now this would not matter so much if works of art were harmless, both cognitively and otherwise. Plato's most serious charge is that they are not. On the contrary, they stimulate and foster the inferior part of the soul at the expense of the superior. Pictures, being mere imitations of visual appearances, can appeal only to the nonrational element of the soul, and an indulgence of an appetite for pictures weakens the superior, rational element by strengthening the inferior. Thus although pictures are delightful, they are not beneficial, but are indeed harmful. Likewise, the other main form of mimetic art, poetry, and especially the art of tragedy, encourages socially undesirable feelings and attitudes in people. It corrupts even the better kind of person by eliciting powerful emotional responses to characters who are not really present but only artistically represented as being present, and in unleashing these emotions threatens to usurp the governing power of reason in the life of the person outside art. Accordingly, the appeal of poetry should be resisted; the ideal state will proscribe it, allowing only models of human excellence, hymns to the gods and praises of good men.

It is clear that Plato's fundamental concern in considering whether art should be welcomed or even admitted into a just society is the social value of works of art, that is to say, their value in promoting or hindering the development of socially desirable characteristics in members of a society. This is underscored by his advocacy of the censorship of poetic misrepresentation of the nature of gods and heroes. For it is not so much falsehood that he objects to, but rather the power of poetry to engender beliefs and attitudes that are not beneficial to society. He is willing even to suppress the poetic expression of the truth if this is necessary to preserve a well-governed society.

Plato's specific criticisms of the social value of representational art are unconvincing. I believe that his misgivings about the effects of the powerful arousal of emotions in response to the thoughts, feelings, actions and fates of dramatic characters were effectively answered by Aristotle in his *Poetics*, and that his other charges have little force (see ARISTOTLE §29). But whatever the truth of this, it is clear that Plato's critique suffers from the generality of his claims about the effects of works of art, which he was in no position to verify. We should in fact reject altogether the question, 'What is the social value of art?' For there are different social values – qualities that it is desirable for members of a society to possess and value in others – and works of art have different social values, not only by being variously beneficial or harmful with respect to the same social value, but by enhancing or weakening different social values, which themselves are of greater or lesser importance to society, to a type of society, or to a specific society. Moreover, whether a work produces a certain social effect – one that it produces in some people, say – and the degree to which it does so, depends on the nature of the individual who responds to it, understands or fails to understand it, is moved or unmoved by it, and how often and in what conditions they interact with it. And what holds for social value holds, *mutatis mutandis*, for other kinds of value in so far as these values are determined by the actual effects of works of art on people, in the short- or long-term. The great variety of works of art, the different ways in which they achieve artistic value, the different temperaments, personalities, histories and capacities of individuals, make any global connections between artistic value and any values not intrinsic to the experience of works unlikely. A more convincing account than Plato gives of art's tendency or capacity to further or hinder non-artistic values must therefore be more exploratory, less partisan, more various and founded upon both a deeper understanding of human nature and a recognition of individual intellectual and emotional differences that affect the influence of works of art on people.

See also: ART AND MORALITY; ART, UNDERSTANDING OF; ARTISTIC TASTE

References and further reading

* Aristotle (c.360s–320s BC) *The Poetics of Aristotle*, trans. and commentary by S. Halliwell, Chapel Hill, NC: University of North Carolina Press, 1987. (Referred to in §6. Primarily an account of the nature of tragedy, and in part a response to Plato's hostile view of tragedy.)

Budd, M. (1995) *Values of Art*, London: Allen Lane, The Penguin Press. (Part 1 contains an account of artistic value and a consideration of the views of Hume and Kant referred to in §4.)

Goldman, A.H. (1995) *Aesthetic Value*, Oxford: Westview Press. (A wide-ranging account of judgments about artistic value advocating a nonrealist view of evaluative aesthetic properties.)

Hegel, G.W.F. (1835) *Aesthetics: Lectures on Fine Art*, trans. T.M. Knox, Oxford: Clarendon Press. (In parts extremely obscure, but an impressive and influential compilation that evaluates works of art by reference to what is claimed to be the highest function of art – the expression in a sensuous medium of the self-awareness of humanity's deepest interests.)

* Hume, D. (1757) 'Of the Standard of Taste', in E.F. Miller (ed.) *David Hume, Essays: Moral, Political, and Literary*, Indianapolis, IN: Liberty Classics, 1987. (Referred to in §4. A classic attempt to explain the status of artistic value.)

Janaway, C. (1995) *Images of Excellence: Plato's Critique of the Arts*, Oxford: Clarendon Press. (A comprehensive and penetrating examination of Plato's views about the value of art.)

* Kant, I. (1790) *Critique of Aesthetic Judgment*, trans. J.C. Meredith, Oxford: Clarendon Press, 1957. (Referred to in §4. Perhaps the most important attempt to elucidate the nature of a judgment of artistic value. Also tries to establish an intrinsic connection between artistic value and morality.)

* Plato (c.375 BC) *Republic*, trans. P. Shorey, Cambridge, MA: Loeb Classical Library, Harvard University Press, 1930. (Books 2, 3 and 10 contain Plato's famous critique of the arts, referred to in §6.)

Schiller, J.C.F. (1795) *On the Aesthetic Education of Man: In a Series of Letters*, ed. and trans. E.M. Wilkinson and L.A. Willoughby, Oxford: Clarendon Press, 1982. (Schiller's celebrated argument that the ideal, harmonious human life, perfection of moral character, and a stable society that respects each person's inalienable freedom is achievable only through the aesthetic education offered by art.)

* Tolstoy, L. (1898) 'What is Art?', trans. A. Maude, in *Leo Tolstoy, What is Art? and Essays on Art*, London: Oxford University Press, 1959. (Referred to in §5. A famous attempt to define the nature of art and to explain its importance in terms of the quality of the feelings it transmits.)

MALCOLM BUDD

ART WORKS, ONTOLOGY OF

In trying to decide what kinds of thing art works are, the most natural starting point is the hypothesis that they are physical objects. This is plausible only for certain works, such as paintings and sculptures; in such cases we say that the work is a certain marked canvas or piece of stone. Even for these apparently favourable cases, though, there is a metaphysical objection to this proposal: that works and the physical objects identified with them do not possess the same properties and so cannot be identical. There is also an aesthetic objection: that the plausibility of the thesis for painting and sculpture rests on the false view that the authentic object made by the artist possesses aesthetically relevant features which no copy could possibly exemplify. Once it is acknowledged that paintings and sculptures are, in principle, reproducible in the way that novels and musical scores are, the motivation for thinking of the authentic canvas or stone as the work itself collapses.

For literary and musical works, the standard view is that they are structures: structures of word-types in the literary case and of sound-types in the musical case. This structuralist view is opposed by contextualism, which asserts that the identity conditions for works must take into account historical features involving their origin and modes of production. Contextualists claim that works with the same structure might have different historical features and ought, therefore, to count as distinct works.

Nelson Goodman has proposed that we divide works into autographic and allographic kinds; for autographic works, such as paintings, genuineness is determined partly by history of production: for allographic works, such as novels, it is determined in some other way. Our examination of the hypothesis that certain works are physical objects and our discussion of the structuralist/contextualist controversy will indicate grounds for thinking that Goodman's distinction does not provide an acceptable categorization of works.

A wholly successful ontology of art works would tell us what things are art works and what things are not; failing that, it would give us identity conditions for them, enabling us to say under what conditions this work and that are the same work. Since the complexity of the issues to be discussed quickly ramifies, it will be appropriate after a certain point to consider only the question of identity conditions. For simplicity, this entry concentrates on works of art that exemplify written literature, scored music and the plastic and pictorial arts.

1 **Works as physical objects**
2 **Works as types**
3 **Works and their histories**
4 **Autographic and allographic**

1 **Works as physical objects**

As in other parts of metaphysics, a theory of what art works are should seek to provide as simple and economical an account as possible, consistent with robust intuition about sameness and difference between works. We shall begin with maximum simplicity, introducing complications as required by consideration of particular cases, some of them real and some of them highly artificial constructs. By the end we shall have arrived at a position of some complexity, but one which has the virtue of treating all works of the kind we shall consider here in a uniform manner.

It seems relatively easy to say what a painting or a sculpture is: a canvas on a gallery wall, a piece of stone shaped in a certain way. In that case, these works are just physical objects. Three objections to this proposal have been made. The first is that art works have properties that a physical object could not have: aesthetic, expressive and representational properties, for example. This objection relies on the assumption that a physical object can have only physical properties. But a physical object might become, say, valued without ceasing to be physical, and being valued is not a physical property.

The second objection is this. If Michaelangelo's statue *David*, D, is identical with a certain block of stone, B, then D and B must have the same properties. But B existed prior to D, which came into existence only when Michaelangelo set to work. So 'existing prior to D' is a property B possesses and D lacks. One response to this objection is to say that physical objects are four-dimensional, extended in time as well as in space, and therefore possessed of temporal parts that are themselves physical objects. In that case we can say that D is identical with a physical object B*, which consists of that temporal part of B that began when *David* was fashioned from the stone and ends when the degraded condition of the stone no longer warrants our saying that *David* exists. But now the distinct-properties argument can be used again to show that D and B* are different. It is true of D that, if Michaelangelo had not lived, it would not have existed; the same is not true of B*. Substantial deformation would destroy D but not B*.

An alternative and less ambitious proposal would be that art works (of the kinds we are currently considering) are not identical with physical objects; instead they are embodied in or constituted by physical objects. I shall not pursue this line of thought further here. Many of the arguments about identity and constitution apply equally to art works and to other kinds of things (for example, tools), and so belong to general metaphysics, as do the arguments we have considered so far. The only specifically aesthetic argument that has been developed in connection with this is an argument against both the idea that art works are physical objects and the idea that art works are constituted by physical objects. To this argument we now turn.

The claim that certain works are physical objects or are constituted by them depends on an intuitive contrast between singular and multiple works. Among works of the former kind are paintings and sculptures, where the object fashioned by the artist (the 'authentic' object) seems to have a unique status – a proper appreciation of the work requires that the viewer sees that object rather than any copy of it, however good. With novels, plays and poems, on the other hand, the original inscription of the work by the author (the autograph) has no special significance for appreciation of the work; any word-for-word copy of the autograph will do. But the significance placed on authenticity in painting and sculpture is due to the fact that aesthetically adequate copies of these works are very hard to achieve. Every visible feature of the work is potentially relevant to the proper appreciation of it, and so an aesthetically adequate copy of the work would have to look exactly like the original. With literature, mere sameness of spelling with the autograph is all that is required of a copy for it to allow us to appreciate the work fully. But this difference between painting and literature is a merely technical one and cannot be the basis for treating these two forms as fundamentally distinct. It is possible (though by no means easy) to produce copies of paintings and sculptures indistinguishable from their originals by the modes of perceptual access appropriate for those works. If this were frequently done, the aura of indispensability that surrounds originals would dissipate. They would be regarded as no more essential to the existence of the work than autographs of novels currently are. (Originals might continue to command high prices on grounds of their personal and historical interest, much as autographs of novels and poems do.) In that case, the claim that in painting and sculpture the work is the authentic object is only as plausible as the comparable claim that the novel is the autograph copy, and this is untenable, as we shall now see.

2 Works as types

Let us consider works of literary and musical art. There are physical objects significantly associated with both genres and these are analogous to authentic objects in painting and sculpture: autograph copies of the text or score. But neither Austen's autograph nor any other copy of the text can be regarded as identical with the work *Emma*, since no particular copy need survive in order for the work to survive. (Word processing makes the ontological irrelevance of an autograph particularly obvious.) Nor can the work be identified with the class of copies of its text or score. Classes are so defined that a class could not have had members different from those it does have. But there could have been more or fewer or different copies of *Emma* than there are, without the identity of the novel being threatened. With music, drama and other 'performance' works, there are performances to consider as well as copies of the score. But a sonata cannot be identified with its original performance by the composer – there may be no such performance – nor with the class of its performances: a symphony might have had different performances from the ones it did, or might never have been performed, without being a different or non-existent work.

For these reasons we may choose to identify literary and musical works with 'types', of which copies of their text or score are 'tokens'. It is common to make a distinction between word- (or letter-) types and tokens, since the same word (or letter) may be inscribed many times; these inscriptions are tokens of the type. The same distinction applies to items of musical notation; we say there are a number of D^+ semiquavers on the page. Sentence-types are sequences of word-types (which are sequences of letter-types), and texts are sequences of sentence-types. On the view we are now considering, literary works are texts. The closest parallel to this idea for musical works is that they are scores, which are similarly defined as sequences of note-types, the tokens of which are particular inscriptions of notes. Since texts and scores as defined here are abstract structures, we may call an approach of the kind just described a version of structuralism.

One objection to this proposal is that it does not allow us to say that works are created by their authors or composers, since types are abstract objects not capable of being affected by human action; instead, what we normally think of as the act of composition would, according to the structuralist, be an act of discovery. This objection is not decisive. The structuralist need not deny any of the evident facts about composition: that hard work and talent are required for the composition of significant works; that without that talent and effort these works would not be available to us. We admire those who prove difficult and important mathematical theorems, and our admiration does not dissipate with the thought that these theorems are not created by the people that prove them. Whether the work of the artist is to be described as creation or as discovery can be counted as spoils to the victor in this debate.

Another, more serious objection, but one answerable within a generally structuralist outlook, is that the proposal does not make any provision for the obvious difference between 'performance' and 'non-performance' works, since it treats plays, symphonies and novels alike as having tokens which are particular inscriptions. We can rectify this by saying that musical works are sequences of sound-types rather than note-types. While note-types have as their tokens particular inscriptions, sound-types have as their tokens particular sounds. A sound-type might be identified by specifying a pitch, a duration and a degree of loudness. (To conform with our ordinary ways of individuating sounds we would need to preserve some vagueness in these specifications.) Thus defined, an instance of the work would consist in the actual production of tokens of the sound-types constitutive of the work; it would be a performance of the work. A comparable stipulation can be made for plays and other non-musical performance works.

There are facts in addition to mere performability which seem equally to demand reflection in our theory of the work. Musical works, at least typically, are intended to be performed *on certain instruments*, and the specification of the work in terms of sound-types alone fails to accommodate this: a sound-type can be produced in ways that would be inappropriate for many works. We could meet the performance-means objection by specifying that the work is a sequence of sound-types-as-performed-on-certain-instruments. But we must go further still. A person who produces the appropriate sequence of sounds on the appropriate instruments by accident, or while improvising, is not, strictly speaking, performing the work. We need to specify further that the work is a sequence of sound-types-as-performed-on-certain-instruments-as-a-result-of-intentionally-following-a-certain-score.

3 Works and their histories

What if our performer, Jones, was following the score of an existing work – the *Hammerklavier* sonata, for instance – but was doing so as a result of having hit upon that score himself by an act of composition undertaken in ignorance of Beethoven's previous efforts? Would he be performing Beethoven's *Hammerklavier* sonata? Structuralists say yes, assuming Jones was playing the instrument specified by Beethoven. Some writers have argued that the correct answer is that he is not playing Beethoven's work, and that consequently the structuralist approach elaborated above is wrong; he is playing a distinct work composed by Jones himself. The argument for this is another version of the distinct properties argument of §1. For the well-informed listener, much of what is interesting and valuable in a musical work derives from the work's art-historical features. Works are variously describable as stunningly original, fresh, deliberately anachronistic, shamelessly plundered from better composers. We notice and enjoy or deplore their quotation from and commentary on other works. If such features are features of the works themselves, we cannot say that Beethoven's and Jones's works are identical just because they are correctly performed on the same instruments in accordance with the same score. Jones's twentieth-century work may reflect the influence of Brahms, express outrage at the practice of atonality and consciously submit itself to the discipline of an earlier age; Beethoven's does none of these things. So these works have distinct properties and cannot be the same work. Structuralism's identity conditions are ahistorical and fail to locate this vital divergence on historical properties, so they falsely identify distinct works.

Three responses to contextualism have been voiced. The first agrees that works do have the kinds of historically determined features just mentioned, but says that their having them is an objection to the structuralist account of work-identity only as long as we think of these historical features as essential features of works. This response is best clarified in terms of possible worlds. The contextualist is interpreted as saying that in the actual world Beethoven's work, B, has a certain historically determined feature, F, while in some merely possible world Jones composes an identically scored work, J, which lacks F. But it is agreed that objects have properties in one world that they lack in another; such properties are accidental rather than essential. If we think that historical properties of the kind just described are accidental, we can therefore continue to assert the identity of B and J. This response misunderstands the contextualist's position. The world the contextualist imagines as a counterexample to structuralism is one in which Beethoven's composition of B is just as it is in the actual world *and* in which Jones also composes J. If it is agreed that in this (merely possible) world, B possesses F and J does not, then certainly B and J are distinct, since an object cannot possess and lack a property in a single world. Contextualism does not depend on any controversial assumption about what properties of works are essential.

The second response claims that historical features such as those described above are not properties of works at all. Instead they are properties of acts of composition. So there is no barrier to identifying B and J, and we may say that there is in this case one work and two acts of composition. The problem for someone who advocates this response is to find a principled way of distinguishing properties of the work from properties of the act of composition. An appeal to common speech or practice will not do, since we commonly speak of works themselves as original or conventional. We might say that, in the musical case, the properties of the work itself are just those that determine how it sounds; the historical properties just mentioned do not do this, since it is agreed that B and J sound the same (in the sense that one could not tell, by attending to sound alone, that something was a performance of B rather than of J). This would have the uncomfortable consequence of driving us back to the original structuralist position, according to which the correctness of a performance of a work depends only on how it sounds and not on the choice of instruments for performing it.

The third response to contextualism says that the historical features described above are features of the work, but insists that they are incompletely specified by expressions like 'is original'. Rather, they are all properties that need to be relativized to contexts of composition, much as velocity needs to be relativized to a frame of reference. On this interpretation, what looks like the paradox of saying 'B is F, while J, identical with B, is not' emerges as the consistent avowal that B is F-in-the-Beethoven-context while J is not-F-in-the-Jones-context. This position faces the same difficulty as the previous one: it must be supported by a principled distinction between relativized and unrelativized properties if it is not to be judged *ad hoc*. If such a distinction can be made, a version of structuralism may be defensible.

4 Autographic and allographic

In the previous section we focused on the question, 'Under what conditions is this work identical with that one?' We now turn to a different but related question: 'What makes an object an instance of this work rather than of that one?' The canvas painted by Leonardo is a genuine instance of *The Madonna of the Rocks*; it is also an authentic instance deriving from the hand of the artist, and those who think painting a singular art say that, for that reason, it is the only instance. The prints pulled from Rembrandt's plate by the artist himself (or authorized by him) are genuine instances of the etching *Tobit Blind*; they are also authentic instances. Are they the only instances? Those who think the artist's canvas is the only instance of a painting will presumably say yes, on the grounds that printmaking is like painting in that only authentic items are instances of the work. In line with this idea, Goodman classifies paintings, sculptures, prints and moulded figures as 'autographic'. Something is an instance of an autographic work only if it has a certain history of production; these arts are all autographic, then, because to be an instance of a work in any of these forms, the thing in question must issue from the hand of the artist, or by their instructions. Autographic arts can be singular, as with painting, or multiple, as with prints.

What, on the other hand, makes something an instance of the novel *Emma*? For Goodman, the criterion is that it should have the same spelling as Austen's autograph; in this and like cases we identify objects as instances of particular works by their structural features and not in terms of their histories of production. A typing monkey could produce something which is, in Goodman's sense, an instance of *Emma*, and a monkey with the luck to strike the right piano keys will produce a performance of the *Hammerklavier* sonata. Novels, poems, plays and musical works are all 'allographic' because of the irrelevance of history to the identification of work-instances. Allographic works are all multiple.

If we accept the argument of §1 according to which authentic instances of paintings, sculptures, prints and moulded figures have no privileged status, we shall deny Goodman's claim that, for works of these kinds, the only instances are the authentic ones. We shall say that indiscernible copies of authentic instances are also instances. Still, we would remain broadly in agreement with Goodman, for the condition of being a copy of an authentic instance is one that appeals to history of production, and so these arts remain autographic. A more radical disagreement with Goodman emerges when we consider the contextualist's argument of §3 which claims that literary and musical works need to be identified historically. If that argument is right, and two distinct novels or sonatas could have the same structure, then, before we can know whether this performance is a performance of B or of J, we need to know whether the performers' knowledge of the score is traceable through a causal chain back to B's act of scoring or to J's. That way, being an instance of a literary or musical work is partly a matter of history of production, and so all works are to be categorized as autographic. Something which looks exactly like Leonardo's *Madonna of the Rocks* might not be an instance of that work because it is copied from another, independently produced, canvas of identical appearance. And this bundle of pages is a copy of *Emma* rather than of the same-spelled but independently produced *Schemma* because it derives causally from Austen's act of composition and not from that of her lesser-known rival Schmausten. We now have a uniform theory of identity conditions for art works of all the kinds considered here.

See also: ARTISTIC FORGERY; TYPE/TOKEN DISTINCTION

References and further reading

Currie, G. (1989) *An Ontology of Art*, London: Macmillan. (Emphasizes the requirement that an ontology of art incorporate an historical dimension.)

—— (1991) 'Work and Text', *Mind* 100: 325–40. (Applies antistructuralist arguments to the case of literary works.)

Elgin, C.Z. and Goodman, N. (1988) 'Interpretations and Identity: Can the Work Survive the World?', in *Reconceptions in Philosophy*, London: Routledge. (Argues for the identification of the literary work with its text.)

* Goodman, N. (1981) *Languages of Art*, 2nd edn, Brighton: Harvester Wheatsheaf. (A classic work containing, along with a great deal else, an account of the autographic/allographic distinction.)

Kivy, P. (1983) 'Platonism in Music: A Kind of Defence', *Grazer Philosophische Studien* 19: 109–29. (Defends the view that musical works are discovered.)

Levinson, J. (1990) *Music, Art, and Metaphysics*, Ithaca, NY, and London: Cornell University Press. (An important collection of essays giving arguments and examples which favour contextualism.)

Walton, K. (1970) 'Categories of Art', *Philosophical Review* 79: 334–67. (Argues that the aesthetic qualities of works depend on the genres to which they belong.)

Wollheim, R. (1978) 'Are the Criteria of Identity that Hold for a Work of Art in the Different Arts Aesthetically Relevant?', *Ratio* 20: 29–48. (Argues that questions about work identity must be settled by reference to the artist's theory of work identity.)

—— (1980) *Art and Its Objects*, 2nd edn, Cambridge: Cambridge University Press. (A clear statement of both the physical object and the structuralist hypotheses.)

Wolterstorff, N. (1980) *Worlds and Worlds of Art*,

Oxford: Clarendon Press. (An influential approach somewhat different from those discussed here.)

GREGORY CURRIE

ARTHA see MEANING, INDIAN THEORIES OF

ARTIFICIAL INTELLIGENCE

Artificial intelligence (AI) tries to make computer systems (of various kinds) do what minds can do: interpreting a photograph as depicting a face; offering medical diagnoses; using and translating language; learning to do better next time.

AI has two main aims. One is technological: to build useful tools, which can help humans in activities of various kinds, or perform the activities for them. The other is psychological: to help us understand human (and animal) minds, or even intelligence in general.

Computational psychology uses AI concepts and AI methods in formulating and testing its theories. Mental structures and processes are described in computational terms. Usually, the theories are clarified, and their predictions tested, by running them on a computer program. Whether people perform the equivalent task in the same way is another question, which psychological experiments may help to answer. AI has shown that the human mind is more complex than psychologists had previously assumed, and that introspectively 'simple' achievements – many shared with animals – are even more difficult to mimic artificially than are 'higher' functions such as logic and mathematics.

There are deep theoretical disputes within AI about how best to model intelligence. Classical (symbolic) AI programs consist of formal rules for manipulating formal symbols; these are carried out sequentially, one after the other. Connectionist systems, also called neural networks, perform many simple processes in parallel (simultaneously); most work in a way described not by lists of rules, but by differential equations. Hybrid systems combine aspects of classical and connectionist AI. More recent approaches seek to construct adaptive autonomous agents, whose behaviour is self-directed rather than imposed from outside and which adjust to environmental conditions. Situated robotics builds robots that react directly to environmental cues, instead of following complex internal plans as classical robots do. The programs, neural networks and robots of evolutionary AI are produced not by detailed human design, but by automatic evolution (variation and selection). Artificial life studies the emergence of order and adaptive behaviour in general and is closely related to AI.

Philosophical problems central to AI include the following. Can classical or connectionist AI explain conceptualization and thinking? Can meaning be explained by AI? What sorts of mental representations are there (if any)? Can computers, or non-linguistic animals, have beliefs and desires? Could AI explain consciousness? Might intelligence be better explained by less intellectualistic approaches, based on the model of skills and know-how rather than explicit representation?

1 Historical beginnings
2 Classical AI
3 Classical AI and human thinking
4 Connectionism and hybrid systems
5 Situated robotics and anti-representationalism
6 The neo-Heideggerian challenge

1 Historical beginnings

Artificial intelligence (AI) researchers make two assumptions. The first is that intelligent processes can be described by algorithms (sometimes called 'effective procedures'), which are rules where each step is so clear and simple that it can be done automatically, without intelligence. This is an empirical hypothesis, which some critics of AI accept (Searle, in Boden 1990: ch. 3) and others reject (Penrose 1989). The second is that all algorithms can be implemented on some general-purpose computer. This assumption is generally accepted. It is based on the Church–Turing thesis, which states that a universal Turing machine, to which general-purpose computers are approximations, can compute any algorithmically computable function (see CHURCH'S THESIS; TURING MACHINES).

The best-known types of AI – classical AI and connectionism – share these two assumptions. But they differ in other ways (see §§2–4). Classical AI involves serial, or one-by-one, processing of (sometimes complex) formal instructions, whereas connectionism involves parallel, or simultaneous, processing among many simple units. Classical computation uses programs made up of formal rules to generate, compare and alter explicit symbol structures (see MIND, COMPUTATIONAL THEORIES OF; LANGUAGE OF THOUGHT). Connectionist computation typically uses numerical (statistical) rules to determine the activation within networks of locally interacting units and, in systems that can learn, to alter the firing thresholds of individual units and the (excitatory or inhibitory) 'weights' on their interconnections. The system's 'knowledge' is contained implicitly in the constellation of connection weights (see CONNECTIONISM). Some philosophers use 'computation' to apply only to the classical type, first defined by Turing in 1936. AI researchers themselves normally use the term to cover both kinds of information processing.

Despite their differences, both these types of AI started from the same source: a seminal article written in 1943 by McCulloch and Pitts (Boden 1990: ch. 1). This discussion of 'A Logical Calculus of the Ideas Immanent in Nervous Activity' integrated three powerful ideas of the early twentieth century: propositional logic, the neuron theory of Charles Sherrington, and Turing computability.

The authors showed that simple combinations of (highly idealized) neurons could act as 'logic gates'. For instance, a McCulloch–Pitts neuron with two inputs could fire if and only if both inputs were firing (an 'and'-gate), or if only one input were firing (an 'or'-gate), or if some specific input were not firing (a 'not'-gate). Since every truth-function can be expressed with 'not' and 'or' alone, McCulloch and Pitts were able to show that every function of the propositional calculus is realizable by some neural net; that every net computes a function that is computable by a Turing machine; and that every computable function can be computed by some net. Their work inspired early efforts in both classical and connectionist AI because they appealed to logic and Turing computability, but described the implementation of these notions as a network of abstractly defined 'neurons' passing messages to their neighbours.

The neural networks discussed in this entry were extremely simple. For example, any link always had the same amount of influence, whereas most modern connectionist systems allow for continuous changes in the weight of each connection. But the authors' theoretical ambitions were vast. Perception, reasoning, learning, introspection, motivation, psychopathology and value judgments: all, said McCulloch and Pitts, could in principle be understood in their terms. The whole of psychology would in future consist of the definition of various kinds of nets capable of doing the things minds do – that is, capable of computing the sorts of things which minds compute. Neurophysiology and neuroanatomy would show how networks are implemented in the brain, but psychology would define their logical-computational properties. Their views on the relation between psychology and physiology (or mind and body) anticipated later developments in the philosophy of mind (see FUNCTIONALISM).

McCulloch and Pitts' 1943 paper made AI possible in three ways. It influenced von Neumann, in designing the digital computer, to use binary arithmetic and binary logic (see NEUMANN, J. VON). It gave both psychologists and technologists the confidence to model propositional (symbolic) reasoning, as opposed to only arithmetical calculation, on logic-based computers. And it inspired people to start studying the computational properties of various types of neural network. Although classical and connectionist AI are often described as utterly distinct paradigms, research in both these approaches commenced because of this paper.

Early connectionist work was further encouraged by McCulloch and Pitts in a paper of 1947. They pointed out that the brain is a parallel-processing device, not a sequential one. Moreover, it can function acceptably even when some cells misfire or die, or when the input signal is 'noisy'. The perfect input data assumed within their first paper are, in real life, neither necessary nor often available. The question arises, then, how we (and animals) manage without them. McCulloch and Pitts described a statistical technique, based on differential equations like those of thermodynamics, whereby a parallel-processing system could compute (learn to distinguish) various patterns despite slight variations in the input. These (statistical) ideas were less biologically unrealistic than their earlier (logic-based) discussion. Nevertheless, the 1947 paper was less influential over the next three decades than their earlier work. Only in the 1980s did statistical, parallel-processing models achieve prominence (see §3 below).

2 Classical AI

Classical AI is the best-known type of AI, and is sometimes called traditional AI. It uses sequential programming (do this, then do that), and employs internal representations of lists, semantic networks, arrays and other information-processing structures. These representational structures and their components are interpreted as symbolic representations of propositions and concepts (or beliefs and ideas). Accordingly, this approach is also called symbolic AI.

Most internal representations in classical AI are language-like, being constructed from components each of which has some distinct causal-semantic role (though just which role may vary according to context). Some philosophers, such as Jerry Fodor, explain human mental states, or propositional attitudes, in terms of a hypothetical 'language of thought' having logical properties (compositionality, productivity, systematicity) like those exploited in classical AI (see FODOR, J.A.; LANGUAGE OF THOUGHT). A 'toy' example of one simple type of classical AI program (a production system) might look something like this:

If thirsty
then set goal to drink.
If current goal is drink *and* weather is cool
then set goal to seek kettle.
If current goal is seek kettle *and* not in kitchen
then go to kitchen *and* locate kettle.
If kettle is empty
then fill kettle with water.
If kettle is full
then put kettle on hob *and* heat hob *and* locate teapot.
(and so on)

As this toy example suggests, every action, and every condition for action, has to be explicitly specified. Actions that undo previous actions (such as emptying the kettle you just filled) must be avoided. Some unintended consequences of actions have to be anticipated and tidied up (turn off the hob). Default steps must be specified in case any precondition is not satisfied (hot weather, not thirsty). Goal–subgoal structure must be recognized, and the program must be able to 'pop up' to the top goal-level when the lowest sub-goals have been achieved or abandoned. Moreover (what the toy program does not show), procedures must be provided for carrying out the tests (is it cool, and is the kettle full?) and for executing the lowest-level actions (going to the kitchen, locating and filling the kettle) (see RATIONALITY, PRACTICAL).

Classical AI modelling is widespread in computational research. It is used to study, for example, problem solving, planning, vision, robotics, learning, natural-language understanding, analogy and the perception and performance of music (Boden 1987, 1988, 1990; Rich and Knight 1991). It is applied also to phenomena often assumed to be intractable for a computational (or even scientific) explanation, such as motivation, emotion and creativity.

Among the advantages of classical AI are its ability to represent hierarchical structure and to provide relatively transparent models (whose workings can be well understood by inspecting the program). A further advantage is that it can define 'strong' (exceptionless) problem constraints. It is sometimes forgotten, especially by proponents of connectionism, that strong problem constraints are often needed. For instance, every sentence must have a noun phrase and a verb phrase; and waltz time in music demands that each bar have exactly three beats. Admittedly, a composer may produce some anomalous bars (for example, having only two beats in the upper voice along with three in the lower); but one cannot keep doing this, or break out into march time, without abandoning the goal of composing a waltz. Nor can one communicate intelligibly if one omits most noun phrases. Given that certain rules are mandatory, an AI system should respect them, not approximate them by blurring them with others.

Although it began no earlier than connectionism, classical AI achieved visible success before parallel-processing models did. The first major successes occurred in the 1950s. The logic theorist and general problem-solver of Newell and Simon introduced 'means-end analysis', wherein a program analyses the problem as a hierarchy of goals and sub-goals (on indefinitely many levels) and chooses the action most likely to reduce the difference between the current state and the desired state (the goal). This method was widely adopted in theorem proving, problem solving and planning. Another early landmark was Samuels' draughts (checkers) player, which played well and even learned to adapt to its opponent's individual style. And early language-using programs used stored English word strings and simple linguistic schemata to conduct 'conversations' in which the human interlocutors were occasionally (if briefly) persuaded that they were interacting with another person. (See Feigenbaum and Feldman 1963.)

By the early 1970s there had been considerable advance. For instance, natural-language processing could now be sensitive to highly complex syntactic structure or to the unspoken assumptions hidden in the semantics underlying the actual words – so that programs could 'answer' questions about things not explicitly mentioned. Machine learning was sometimes achieved through the program's having a model not only of the task domain but also of its own action strategies – which, with experience, it modified. Other advances followed. Various high-level AI programming languages were developed, such as LISP ('list-processing language') and PROLOG ('programming in logic'). And Newell and Simon developed 'production systems', a programming method based on if-then (condition-action) rules: if the condition is satisfied, then the action is taken. The condition may be a complex conjunction or disjunction, including (sometimes) a statement of the system's current goal; similarly, the action may be complex and/or internal (see the toy AI program above). These developments affected both technological and psychological AI. Production systems, for instance, are the core of most 'expert systems', but were originally proposed as a model of human thinking. (An expert system is an AI program consisting of a set of 'If...then' rules, which can be used to aid human beings in solving specialist problems such as locating oil, planning a travel itinerary or diagnosing a disease.)

3 Classical AI and human thinking

Traditional AI began with the assumption that symbolic logic is a normative model for both human and automated reasoning (see COMMON-SENSE REASONING, THEORIES OF). This assumption sits well with some forms of reasoning, such as theorem-proving (although even there, human beings sometimes employ non-logical methods, such as imagery and analogy). But most human reasoning is approximate and qualitative. We can understand speech even when it is ungrammatical, heavily accented and partly obscured by noise; and we can recognize imperfect handwriting, shadowy scenes, and perceptual or linguistic analogies of many kinds. Also, we can use world knowledge in solving logical problems and in deciding whether strictly logical reasoning, as opposed to fallible heuristics based on experience, is appropriate in a given case. For example, even teachers of logic can solve a problem concerning rules of postage (reversing a minimum number of envelopes to inspect the postage stamps) more easily than a problem of identical logical form posed in abstract terms. In short, we have common sense (see RATIONALITY OF BELIEF; COMMON-SENSE REASONING, THEORIES OF).

Work in AI has increasingly focused on common-sense reasoning, not least because classical AI systems tend to be 'brittle'. If data are missing or corrupted, a classical AI program may give an absurd answer, or none at all. For example, a story-writing program may allow a character to drown a few feet away from a potential rescuer on the river bank, because the programmer did not explicitly include the information that one is normally able to see whatever is going on in front of one's eyes. Similarly, an expert system might ask whether a particular three-year-old girl has any children, not knowing that pre-pubertal girls cannot conceive. People know many such facts about the world and often give something near the right answer (a good guess) even when they lack some relevant information. So AI research has studied probabilistic reasoning, non-monotonic logic (where not-p may turn out to be true even though p had been proved earlier), case-based or analogical explanation, deep (causal) reasoning, and common-sense semantic networks and belief systems (see NON-MONOTONIC LOGIC). As these new methods are incorporated into classical AI programs, the brittleness typical of first-generation AI models (for example, the rule-based 'expert systems' used by many commercial and public institutions) should be reduced.

To reduce brittleness, however, is not to avoid it entirely. Some critics believe that classical AI methods will never model everyday human thinking. A leading AI logicist has recently recanted (McDermott, in Boden 1990: ch. 9). Classical AI has been criticized also by philosophers who reject the Platonist assumption that all truths are analysable in terms of formalizable elements (Dreyfus 1979). Some philosophers see connectionism as immune to philosophical critiques of classical AI (see §3 below), while others regard it as acceptable only up to a point (Dreyfus and Dreyfus, in Boden 1990: ch. 13).

For AI to be deeply relevant to theoretical psychology and the philosophy of mind, it need not promise actual replication of all human behaviour. So someone (such as Fodor) who propounds a computational philosophy of mind may, without contradiction, doubt whether AI systems could ever in practice achieve more than a tiny fraction of human behaviour. Nor need AI researchers themselves believe in this possibility. They may allow that certain behaviour cannot, in principle or in practice, be replicated by AI (of any type). Moods, for instance, may be unreplicable in principle, and superb novel-writing may be unachievable in practice.

Even AI workers who do believe that full replication is possible need not accept the Turing test (see TURING, A.M. §3) as their criterion of intelligence. They all allow that a non-mental thing could sometimes fool us into thinking it intelligent; indeed, this happened so often with ELIZA, an early language-using program, that this user illusion is called the 'ELIZA effect'. And some, for example, argue that mere replication of behaviour, without evolutionary descent of the underlying causal mechanisms, would not suffice for true understanding.

One well-known philosophical critic of AI, especially (though not exclusively) in its classical form, is John Searle (see Boden 1990: ch. 3; CHINESE ROOM ARGUMENT). Searle argues that even if an AI model passed the Turing test (which he thinks is in principle possible), it would not really be thinking, or understanding, anything. Correlatively, a computational psychology could not explain how we can understand: at best, it could explain what we do with meanings once we have them. He argues that programs are defined purely syntactically (by formal rules defined over formal constituents), whereas intentionality – or meaning – involves more than mere syntax. Searle's argument has been challenged in many ways by philosophers and AI scientists, and remains controversial. Most opponents accept his assumption that computation is purely syntactic, disagreeing with him on other grounds. However, this assumption is also controversial (see Boden 1990: ch. 4). The nature of computation – and its connection with meaning – is less clear, and less universally agreed, than Searle supposes (see LANGUAGE OF THOUGHT).

More generally, many philosophical critiques – and defences – of AI turn on issues of semantics (not behavioural replication). But philosophical semantics is itself disputed. To speak of 'information processing' is problematic, because the nature of information is controversial (see SEMANTICS, INFORMATIONAL). Similar remarks apply to symbol manipulation. Other connected issues include whether meanings are 'in the head' (semantic internalism) or partly constituted by the things to which they refer (externalism) (see CONTENT: WIDE AND NARROW), and the relevance (if any) of evolution in establishing meaning (see SEMANTICS, TELEOLOGICAL). Even within AI, researchers give differing accounts of semantics (and not all AI workers subscribe to 'strong AI' as Searle defines it). Some, for example, accept a procedural semantics wherein the execution of particular computations, or mini-programs, suffices for particular meanings (see SEMANTICS, CONCEPTUAL ROLE). Others see causal interaction with the external world (and even evolutionary history) as necessary for meaning. In short, the semantics of AI are controversial both within and outside the field.

4 Connectionism and hybrid systems

Connectionist models are parallel-processing systems, involving mutually interactive computations grounded in local interactions between connected units (see CONNECTIONISM). Each individual computation is much simpler than a typical instruction in a classical AI program. Even so, connectionist units and computations (and learning rules, if any) vary significantly.

For instance, the semantic interpretation given to connectionist units by AI researchers differs. (This is true irrespective of philosophers' theories about semantics, and the relation of AI and meaning.) Some connectionist units are described as computing the truth-values of entire propositions; others are intended to code familiar concepts. The representational role of these units is thus comparable to the rules and rule components in the toy AI program in §2 (however, connectionist systems cannot specify action hierarchies, like that outlined above for quenching thirst). Yet other connectionist units stand for detailed subsymbolic micro-features, which are not always expressible in terms of everyday concepts or symbols. Thus an input unit might code for a tiny patch of a highly specific (unnamed) shade of purple.

The symbolic/subsymbolic distinction, so defined, is sometimes thought to distinguish (all) connectionist from (all) classical AI. This is a mistake. The distinction is vague: just which concepts count as everyday concepts? Moreover, not all connectionist systems employ subsymbolic processing, and many classical AI programs, especially in vision and natural-language processing, code for subsymbolic microfeatures. The distinction is better defined in terms of the presence or absence of causally efficacious and semantically evaluable logical constituents. Such (symbolic) constituents typify classical AI. Subsymbolic units (in this sense) have no fixed, context-free interpretation, since their effect on processing varies according to the simultaneous activation of the other units.

In the late 1950s and the 1960s, classical AI progressed faster than connectionism. None the less, some researchers persevered with early forms of connectionist modelling. But in 1969 Minsky – widely acknowledged as a father of classical AI, but also the first person to build a connectionist learning machine – proved surprising limitations on what very simple networks ('perceptrons') could compute (see Minsky and Papert 1969). Although he stated that more complex networks might be more powerful, there was a marked drop in interest in connectionist research.

A few individuals within AI, and some in psychology and physics, worked on connectionist systems during the 1970s and early 1980s. But not until 1986 did connectionism attract substantial attention. In the late 1980s it hit the headlines and attracted attention from philosophers, being widely hailed as a new, all-powerful computing methodology. More accurately, one specific type of connectionism attracted attention (others being largely ignored): 'parallel distributed processing' (PDP). In a distributed connectionist system, a concept is not stored by a single unit (as in localist connectionism). Rather, it is represented by a global pattern of activation spread across the entire network, many different units making some contribution. It may be impossible to assign a specific, context-free interpretation to a given unit. Moreover, no individual unit is either necessary or sufficient for the whole network to represent some particular concept (recognize some particular pattern).

PDP models themselves vary in important ways. Not all employ subsymbolic processing, though most do. Some allow only for on–off variation in the activity of each unit, while others allow for continuous weights defining the unit's influence. Not all PDP models can learn, though most can. Those which can learn employ various learning rules. The number of units can vary, with significant implications for the type of learning achievable. And although most PDP systems have only 'feed-forward' connections, passing from units nearer the input to units nearer the output, some have backward links also (called 'back-propagation'). In general, PDP systems work by adjusting the simultaneous activity of the constituent units until some global equilibrium is reached (different concepts are represented by different equilibria within the same PDP system). This is achieved not by a sequence of symbolic rules, but by numerically described statistical processes like those of thermodynamics. The changing states of the system are described not as symbol structures (such as lists), but as numerical vectors.

Because of their statistical design, PDP systems are better able than classical models to perform well despite noisy input, and to retrieve an entire memory given only a fragment. Some classical AI programs can do this too, up to a point, if specifically pre-programmed to do so. PDP models, by contrast, 'naturally' achieve a plausible end-state given partially conflicting evidence, weighing both strong and weak constraints (and the extent of their mutual coherence). That is, they perform multiple constraint satisfaction, where the information may be partially conflicting and/or missing. And PDP systems with learning rules (which change the activation weights on the connections with experience) can learn –as people can – from being shown a range of examples.

PDP models are unlike real brains in many ways. For instance, the widely used back-propagation algorithm learns in a very un-biological fashion. Less neurophysiologically unrealistic forms of connectionism have been developed, but even these fall far short of neural networks in the brain.

Another drawback of first-generation PDP systems is that, unlike classical AI programs, they cannot model hierarchical structure or sequential processing. Some types of human thinking – many aspects of language and problem-solving, for example – require both these features. Most AI researchers use only classical, or only connectionist, models. This sociological fact has encouraged some philosophers to exaggerate the differences, and the supposed superiority of one approach over the other. However, these AI methods have complementary strengths and weaknesses. Accordingly, there is growing interest in hybrid models, which try to get the best of both worlds.

Various philosophers use connectionist ideas in addressing important philosophical problems. These include symbol grounding, the problem of how words and concepts acquire meaning (Cussins, in Boden 1990: ch. 15); the role of folk psychology in cognitive science (Clark 1989); family likenesses, paradigm cases, and prototypes of concepts (Clark 1993); eliminative materialism (Churchland, in Boden 1990: ch. 14); and scientific explanation (Churchland 1990). Many philosophers see affinities between connectionism and Wittgensteinian views of language, because connectionist representations are not cut and dried like those used in classical AI but allow for borderline cases and for varying degrees of similarity.

5 Situated robotics and anti-representationalism

Classical and connectionist AI share a commitment to internal representation as integral to intelligence. Both these approaches (and most cognitive scientists) posit identifiable data structures 'in the head' that are distinguishable from the system's processing (which is done 'on' or 'with' them), and that stand for things in the world. This commitment has been (controversially) abandoned by AI work in situated robotics (Boden 1996; Maes 1991). Situated robotics is sometimes termed *'nouvelle* AI' (in contrast to traditional AI), or 'behaviour-based AI' (in contrast to AI based on abstract task decomposition). It claims to be more biologically realistic than classical AI. It emphasizes 'autonomous' systems specifically adapted to their environment, not general-purpose computers controllable by many different programs. And it builds whole (sensory-motor) systems, rather than decomposing intelligence into distinct tasks (vision, planning, motor action) which then have to be integrated to provide a functioning robot.

Situated robotics avoids using internal representations of the external (objective) world, although some systems use temporary representations of their own (subjective) place in or actions on their immediate environment. And it uses a bottom-up approach to generate complex behaviour. Because the environment is assumed to be noisy, dynamic and inconvenient, the detailed world-modelling and top-down planning typical of classical AI are rejected. No complex program is involved to decide on, monitor and control the creature's activities. Instead, the control of behaviour flows from the nature of the system itself, in the sense that the system is engineered (not programmed) to respond to environmental triggers in certain ways. By these means, researchers in situated robotics seek to avoid the notorious 'frame problem' (Boden 1990: chaps 7–9). This problem bedevils AI work on robot planning, language understanding and common-sense reasoning. It concerns foresight of the many intended and unintended consequences of action. For instance, if a box is moved across the floor then all its contents move also, whereas the chairs (and table and curtains) do not. A formal representation of action must explicitly allow for *all* the intended effects, or some may not happen. And the action's many unintended effects will be wholly irrelevant only if the agent is very lucky, or very thorough in explicitly anticipating potentially relevant outcomes.

Classical robots rely on planning, done within an

internal world model. To avoid the frame problem, they must explicitly anticipate a host of intended consequences and unintended side-effects. Although this exhaustive listing of consequences is feasible in artificially impoverished environments, it is impractical in the real world (the thirst-quenching program in §2 would often lead to disappointment, because of unexpected facts about the house concerned). Moreover, because the real world cannot be relied on to remain unchanged, detailed anticipatory plans may fail on execution. Instead of manipulating complex internal representations of the world, situated robots deal directly with it. Situated roboticists eschew the abstract functional task-decomposition employed by classical AI. Instead, they analyse intelligence in terms of 'behaviours'. Their robots engage in simple, hardwired behaviour triggered by specific, ecologically relevant, environmental cues.

The anti-representationalist stance of *nouvelle* AI is controversial. Some situated robots use temporary representations that are not objective but 'deictic' (subject-centred), being closely bound to the robot's behaviour in *this* place on *this* occasion (see CONTENT, INDEXICAL). Admittedly, some situated robots – including some of those which show apparently 'cooperative' behaviour, like that of some social insects – do not employ representations even in this sense. Instead, they are engineered to respond directly to certain conditions, without the central world-models favoured by classical AI. Nevertheless, whether human, or even much animal, intelligence can be modelled without internal representations of any kind is unclear.

Evolutionary AI uses genetic algorithms (GAs) to improve programs by artificial evolution. Evolution involves replication, random variation, and selection. GAs make random changes within a program, and (at each generation) identify the most efficient of the resulting rules. These rules are then assigned a high probability of 'breeding' the next generation. Eventually, a system evolves which is efficient, perhaps even optimal. This technique is widely used within classical AI, for inductive problem-solving and classification (Holland *et al.* 1986) and for evolutionary art – GA-directed computer graphics, or music – where the selection at each generation can be done by the human user (Todd and Latham 1992). GAs are used also for evolutionary robotics (in which the robot's design is automatically evolved), and for other work in artificial life, which studies self-organizing, self-replicating adaptive systems (Boden 1996).

6 The neo-Heideggerian challenge

Most AI researchers presuppose the Cartesian distinction between the mind as psychological subject and the real world as object of the mind's (representational) thinking (see DESCARTES, R.; DUALISM). On this view, intelligence is located in the brain, for perceptual input from the world is followed by inner thinking, which in turn causes motor action. Organisms (and artefacts) are assumed to be located within, and adapted to, an environment whose properties are independent of any perceptions of it. Different creatures perceive and affect different world properties. But those properties are objectively there, independent of creatures' relations to them.

These neo-Cartesian assumptions have been questioned by philosophers drawing on WITTGENSTEIN, HEIDEGGER and phenomenology (see Dreyfus 1979; van Gelder 1995). Similar questions have been raised within AI and cognitive science. For instance, some work in situated robotics and artificial life offers an anti-Cartesian critique of mainstream (classical and connectionist) AI. Such critics reject the subject–object distinction, theories positing internal representations, and the notion of intelligence as a causal series (perception, then thought, then action). Instead, they see organisms as dynamic systems closely coupled with their environment, which (so they argue) cannot be independently defined (see Port and van Gelder 1995; van Gelder 1995; Varela *et al.* 1991; Wheeler, in Boden 1996; CONTENT: WIDE AND NARROW). 'Coupling' is a relation of simultaneous mutual causation whereby two systems constantly interact and interpenetrate, each causing changes not only in the other's superficial behaviour but also in its background parameters. If this interpenetration were wholly chaotic, we could not identify two systems. We can (approximately) distinguish systems, and subsystems, only when certain states are relatively stable through time.

Intelligence, on this view, is a function not of the brain but of the whole system constituted by nervous system, body and environment. Likewise, depth vision is a function not of a tiny region of cells, but of the whole visual cortex – indeed, of the entire brain. Computationalism, though not computer modelling, is rejected. It is replaced by dynamic systems theory drawn from physics, which employs differential equations rather than discrete algorithms, and focuses on intrinsic physical states (described by numerical vectors) rather than symbolic representations. (Strictly, since a dynamic system is one whose changes of state can be described by some rule, classical AI programs are a special case; however, real time and/or continuous variables do not feature in classical – or most connectionist – AI, whereas they do feature in the dynamic theories of physics.)

This anti-Cartesian challenge is highly controversial, both scientifically and philosophically. In scientific terms, dynamic systems theory (like first-generation connectionism) is largely a promissory note. Certainly, organisms are dynamic systems – but we need to know how this explains the specific phenomena of human and animal intelligence. Such explanations will require concepts at a higher level than dynamic systems in general.

References and further reading

* Boden, M.A. (1987) *Artificial Intelligence and Natural Man*, London: MIT Press, 2nd edn, expanded. (A non-technical introduction to AI, including its philosophical, psychological and social implications; extensive bibliography.)
* —— (1988) *Computer Models of Mind: Computational Approaches in Theoretical Psychology*, Cambridge: Cambridge University Press. (A textbook on computational psychology; extensive bibliography.)
* —— (ed.) (1990) *The Philosophy of Artificial Intelligence*, Oxford: Oxford University Press. (Papers on the main philosophical–methodological disputes within AI, with a bibliography.)
* —— (ed.) (1996) *The Philosophy of Artificial Life*, Oxford: Oxford University Press. (Papers on the philosophy of artificial life, with a bibliography.)
* Churchland, P.M. (1990) *A Neurocomputational Perspective: The Nature of Mind and the Structure of Science*, Cambridge, MA: MIT Press. (A defence of Churchland's approach to connectionism, with applications to various philosophical problems including the philosophy of science.)
* Clark, A.J. (1989) *Microcognition: Philosophy, Cognitive Science, and Parallel Distributed Processing*, Cambridge, MA: MIT Press. (An accessible introduction to connectionism with a discussion of its relation to classical AI and of the role of folk psychology in cognitive science.)
* —— (1993) *Associative Engines: Connectionism, Concepts, and Representational Change*, Cambridge, MA: MIT Press. (A more advanced discussion of connectionism and its application to various problems in philosophy and psychology; many references.)
* Cliff, D., Harvey, I. and Husbands, P. (1993) 'Explorations in Evolutionary Robotics', *Adaptive Behavior* 2: 73–110. (A survey of work in evolutionary robotics discussed in §5 above.)
* Dreyfus, H.L. (1979) *What Computers Can't Do: The Limits of Artificial Intelligence*, New York: Harper & Row, 2nd edn. (A philosophical critique of the foundations of classical AI, in relation to Platonic, Cartesian and Continental philosophy.)
* Feigenbaum, E.A. and Feldman, J. (eds) (1963) *Computers and Thought*, New York: McGraw-Hill. (A collection of classic papers in AI, with an extensive bibliography.)
* Gelder, T. van (1995) 'What is Cognition, if not Computation?', *Journal of Philosophy* 91. (A defence of dynamical systems, as opposed to computation, as the basis of mental processing.)
* Holland, J.H., Holyoak, K.J., Nisbet, R.E. and Thagard, P.R. (1986) *Induction: Processes of Inference, Learning, and Discovery*, Cambridge, MA: MIT Press. (Describes how genetic algorithms work, and how they have been applied to various problems, including some of philosophical interest. Fairly difficult.)
* Maes, P. (ed.) (1991) *Designing Autonomous Agents*, Cambridge, MA: MIT Press. (A collection of articles on situated robotics, with many references.)
* Minsky, M.L. and Papert, S. (1969) *Perceptrons: An Introduction to Computational Geometry*, Cambridge, MA: MIT Press. (Limitations on what very simple networks ('perceptrons') can compute.)
* Penrose, R. (1989) *The Emperor's New Mind*, Oxford: Oxford University Press. (An attack on the notion that all human thought can be described by algorithms.)
* Port, R. and Gelder, T. van (eds) (1995) *Mind as Motion: Dynamics, Behavior and Cognition*, Cambridge, MA: MIT Press. (A collection of papers illustrating the dynamic-systems approach in cognitive science, and its critique of representation.)
* Rich, E. and Knight, K. (1991) *Artificial Intelligence*, New York: McGraw-Hill, 2nd edn. (A comprehensive textbook of AI, including detailed descriptions of various AI methods; good bibliography.)
* Todd, S. and Latham, W. (1992) *Evolutionary Art and Computers*, London: Academic Press. (A detailed description of the use of genetic algorithms by a professional artist to produce 'families' of three-dimensional computer sculptures.)
* Varela, F.J., Thompson, E. and Rosch, E. (1991) *The Embodied Mind: Cognitive Science and Human Experience*, Cambridge, MA: MIT Press. (A defence of 'embodiment' and 'embeddedness' in anti-Cartesian cognitive science.)

MARGARET A. BODEN

ARTISTIC EXPRESSION

Many kinds of psychological state can be expressed in or by works of art. But it is the artistic expression of emotion that has figured most prominently in philosophical discussions of art. Emotion is expressed in pictorial, literary and other representational works of art by the characters who are depicted or in other ways presented in the works. We often identify the emotions of such characters in much the same way as we ordinarily identify the emotions of others, but we might also have special knowledge of a character's emotional state, through direct access to their thoughts, for instance.

A central case of the expression of emotion by works of art is the expression of emotion by a purely musical work. What is the source of the emotion expressed by a piece of music? While art engages its audience, often calling forth an emotional response, its expressiveness does not consist in this power. It is not because an art work tends to make us feel sad, for instance, that we call it sad; rather, we react as we do because sadness is present in it. And while artists usually contrive the expressiveness of their art works, sometimes expressing their own emotions in doing so, their success in the former activity does not depend on their doing the latter. Moreover, the expressiveness achieved has an immediacy and transparency, like that of genuine tears, apparently at odds with this sophisticated, controlled form of self-expression. It is because art presents emotion with simple directness that it can be a vehicle for self-expression, not vice versa. But if emotions are the experiences of sentient beings, to whom do those expressed in art belong if not to the artist or audience? Perhaps they are those of a fictional persona. We may imagine personae who undergo the emotions expressed in art, but it is not plain that we must do so to become aware of that expressiveness, for it is arguable that art works present appearances of emotions, as do masks, willow trees and the like, rather than outward signs of occurrent feelings. Expressiveness is valuable because it helps us to understand emotions in general while contributing to the formation of an aesthetically satisfying whole.

1 The expression of emotion
2 Characters in works
3 Arousal theory
4 Expression theory
5 Fictional authors and personae
6 Expressiveness as a property of art works
7 The value of artistic expressiveness

1   The expression of emotion

Thoughts and attitudes can be expressed. My concern here, though, is with artistic expressions of emotions, feelings and moods. I shall consider what and whose emotions are communicated in art, and the nature of expressiveness in art works.

Sometimes a person's expressions are distinguished from their dispassionate reports of their emotions (because the emotion is not directly present in the utterance). Also, expressions might be separated from uncontrolled ventings of emotions, these latter being regarded as symptoms, like the spots of measles, that betray or symptomize the condition without expressing it. My own approach is more liberal. I count as an expression any behaviour or display that communicates the agent's emotion, feeling or mood. Such instances of behaviour might be unintended and unthinking, or deliberate and self-conscious. (Indeed, their expressive character might depend on their being the one rather than the other. If my weeping is deliberate and controlled, this suggests pretence rather than expression; if my behaviour is unintended, then it cannot involve the use of social conventions for expression, even if it seems to match these.)

Typically, emotions depend on causal circumstances, take intentional objects and involve beliefs and desires (or make-beliefs and make-desires) concerning that object. For example, I hope for peace at a time of conflict because a treaty has been signed and because I believe treaties lead to the cessation of hostilities, which is what I desire. A person's emotion might be apparent to another who possesses knowledge of any suitable combination of these elements.

In some cases, a person's nonverbal actions alone will indicate that they feel an emotion. In fewer cases – those in which an emotion has an unambiguous mode of nonverbal expression – actions alone might indicate that a particular emotion is experienced. (Perhaps only the broadest categories for happiness and sadness have patterns of behavioural expression sufficiently distinctive for this to be the case; cognitively complex emotions, such as hope or jealousy, have many behavioural expressions none of which is distinctive.) More often, behaviour expresses the agent's emotions only where the wider context is known.

There are further possibilities for the communication of emotion: one can learn of a person's emotions from true descriptions of them given by knowledgable third parties, or from their own sincere reports. If emotions can be individuated solely by their sensational character and the dynamic structure of their phenomenology, one's knowledge of the detail of a person's 'internal' experience could communicate their emotions. Finally, note that the expression of emotion has a social, arbitrarily conventional dimension. In some cultures, for instance, the wearing of black clothes and veils is an expression of grief or respect for the dead. The relevant conventions must be followed deliberately and sincerely if the resulting actions are to express an emotion the person feels.

2 Characters in works

If the work contains characters (for example, through depiction or description), then these characters might experience emotions to which their behaviour or circumstances give expression. Unless the audience is given reason in the work's contents, its genre, or the context of presentation to make-believe otherwise, it is to assume that the beliefs, behaviour, bodily attitudes and causal circumstances of the work's world correspond to those of the actual world. Accordingly, the audience can learn what emotions the work's characters experience in the same manner as it recognizes the emotions communicated by others in the ordinary world, except that the audience's relation to the world of the work depends on make-believe rather than belief.

Some differences are worth noting, however. In the case of narratives written in the first person, the audience might come to know 'from the inside' what a character experiences or believes, and hence what they feel, even if that feeling is not outwardly indicated. Second, the protagonists might be non-human or unreal concoctions, such as elephants or intelligent ants. In considering the emotions of such creations, information about their point of view will be relevant – their cognitive commitments and values, their vulnerabilities and aspirations, their intellect, physiology and the like. In addition, artists create expressive contexts that do not or could not arise in the actual world. For instance, the use of leitmotiv in opera to recall actions or words might reveal that a character's passion is meant for X despite being directed at Y. Quotation and reference, both within and between works, might establish an expressive ambience one would not normally find or look for.

In addition to the emotions of their characters, art works seem to embody and express emotions of their own. This applies to all kinds of works but is perhaps most striking in abstract pieces, including pure music, where expressiveness is present in the absence of a narrated or depicted content. Whose emotions are expressed thereby and how are they expressed?

3 Arousal theory

One suggested answer to the above question is that we ascribe emotions to art works just because those emotions are awakened in us. This is the theory of emotivism or arousalism. Two cases need to be distinguished. In the first, the art work or some aspect of it is the emotional object of a response in the standard way. As a result of realizing that a character in a work is dying unloved one feels sadness for and pity towards that character. Or, believing that the dramatic potential of the last act was botched by the playwright, one feels disappointed by the play. Or one is delighted by the felicity of a turn in the melody. In the second case, one tends to respond with sadness to works called sad, or with happiness to works said to express happiness. Something in the work calls forth the reaction that mirrors the work's expressive character. One does not then feel sad or happy *about* the work; indeed, the response seems to lack an emotional object, though the work is its perceptual object and cause.

Arousalism refers to this second kind of response in analysing artistic expressiveness: an art work expresses an emotion if and only if it has the power to arouse or tends to arouse that emotion without an object in an appropriate audience. In this view the sadness of the art work is like the greenness of grass; some property of the thing in question disposes it to affect the experience of those perceiving it. The sadness is attributable to the art work, not to the person in whom the feeling is aroused, because the work has the power to awaken the same feelings in a variety of suitably qualified perceivers. Similarly, we say it is the grass that is green, not the perceiving of it, just because its effect on perceivers is largely indifferent to their individuality and idiosyncrasies.

The arousal theory faces two main lines of objection. The first, pursued by Peter Kivy (1989), denies that there are any objectless responses of the kind described – sad music, for instance, never leads listeners to feel sad. A more plausible objection denies the match (postulated by arousalism) between artistic expressiveness and the audience's tendency to respond. The audience might be unmoved, or might not feel what the work expresses, despite their correctly recognizing its expressive character. In reply to this, the arousalist points out that a tendency to respond can be blocked or inhibited – for example, where one is distracted from or overexposed to the given piece, and so on. In some cases contemporary values and sentiments might permanently block the tendency that would have triggered a response at the time of the work's creation. Though it might deal with some counterexamples, I am doubtful that arousalism successfully accounts for all the mismatches between artistic expressiveness and audience's reactive tendencies, where these threaten its plausibility.

One can reject the arousalist account of artistic expressiveness while accepting that sad works sometimes evoke sad reactions. One might explain the echoing response as occasioned by the work's expressiveness. Whereas arousalism holds that art works are sad because they make us feel sad, one might instead maintain that it is because they are sad that we respond as we do. We find the emotional moods of others contagious, even if we are not aware of having anything to be happy or sad about; perhaps we react to art works similarly. And perhaps we are open to this mode of response because we approach art as human communication.

4 Expression theory

In creating their works, do artists express feelings? Surely this is often so. In that case, are the emotions expressed in art works those of their artists? We approach many works, including abstract ones, as dealing not merely with the affective side of life but with personal feelings. One view, the expression theory, asserts that expressiveness can be attributed to art works only where there is this discharge of feeling, and because of it: art works are expressive because they stand in relation to artists' occurrent emotions as do tears to sadness, as both arising from and revealing the feeling. Just as emotions are presented immediately and transparently in genuine tears, so that no inference from crying to sadness is required, we experience the expressiveness of art as residing in it. Also, we find the expressiveness of art works highly evocative of sharing or empathic reactions and this is how we respond to open, primary displays of emotion.

Despite its attractions, the expression theory seems to fail by entailing that when an art work expresses an emotion, the artist experienced that emotion. This generalization is patently false. The process in which art works have their genesis allows little scope for unthinking expression or for undergoing emotions powerful enough to produce the outcome as described. Moreover, some artists turn to creation to escape their traumatic circumstances and, in doing so, produce works that do not reveal the emotions dominating their lives at the time. The expressiveness of art works is usually achieved by their artists, but this happens typically by design. So structured and conventionalized is art, and so practical is the knowledge brought to its creation, that the making of art, even of an expressive variety, cannot continue long or far without reflection, including attention to technique, detail, the nature of the medium and overall structure. Besides, art works are not the kinds of things that arise causally or naturally as immediate, transparent expressions of occurrent emotions. A tendency to create art, unlike a tendency to tears, is not an essential part of sadness, so art works should not be the kind of thing from which sadness can be read directly. In a few cases an artistic action transfers its character to the product that results – violently produced brushstrokes often display the energy that went into their making. But in general, artists' creative acts, even where these are impelled by emotions, are not such as to transfer that expressive character directly to the resulting piece.

The theory fares no better if performers (should the work have them) are substituted for artists, or where the approach is counterfactual in suggesting that a piece expresses such and such if it is the kind of art work that a person feeling such and such would create. The first alternative encounters objections like those confronting the original theory. The second presupposes art's expressiveness, without analysing it; one could recognize the work's aptness for expression only if it already independently displays the appropriate character.

Now, how could it be that art works display expressive directness while expressing the artist's feeling if they do not relate to that feeling as tears relate to sadness? One way this could be achieved would be by the appropriation of something that itself possesses or simulates the immediate, primary presentation of feeling. For instance, a grieving person might employ professional mourners to weep on their behalf, or might show how they feel by deliberately putting on a sad face or by pointing to a mask of tragedy. Artists, in a similar fashion, might express their feeling through those of characters in the work or by matching the expressive tone of the work to their feelings. But in either case, the expressiveness present in the work has its character independently of the artist's use of it, so expressions of artists' feelings through the works they create presuppose, rather than explain, the expressiveness of those art works.

One version of the expression theory that has been influential in the recent history of aesthetics is that propounded by Benedetto CROCE §2 and R.G. COLLINGWOOD §3. In outline, their account is this: the process of artistic creation is one in which, through the articulation of inchoate feelings and impulses, the artist comes to express a particular, unique emotion, thereby bringing it to their conscious awareness. The emotion is constituted through the act of expression, having no prior identity; that is, the emotion achieves its particular character through the manner of its expression. Collingwood regards art as expression at the level of imagination; for Croce, art is intuitive expression. Both tend to dismiss creation that does not satisfy this model as not truly artistic.

The impression that this view offers an account of the psychology of the creative process and not of the nature of the art work is misleading, for the work is regarded as primarily mental, as existing in the artist's mind and inseparable from the act of expression. The artist might work in a physical medium on a public object as they create the work, but this is not necessary, and a work can be created without being 'externalized'. Externalization is crucial, though, if the artist wishes to communicate the work to others. The object then created is not strictly the work, but the vehicle by which an awareness of the work can be transmitted. Communication is successful when the audience comes, through contemplation of the public object, to recognize or share the mental condition that is the work's existence. Collingwood denies, however, that it is the function of art to arouse emotion. Artists could pursue that goal only if they knew what emotion they wanted to arouse, and such knowledge comes only with successful expression and, hence, after the work's completion. Accordingly, art is primarily concerned with the self-awareness accomplished by the artist through their act of self-expression.

As an account of the creative process, which is much more variable than is specified, the theory is too narrow, and in so far as it applies to activities not normally regarded as issuing in art works, such as formulating and clarifying one's thoughts in language, it is also too broad. Second, in according primacy to the private, mental dimension of affective experience and in treating public expressions of emotion as dispensable ancillaries, the theory's account of expression is questionable. In addition, it leaves underexplained the process by which an audience comes to know the work and its expressive character. How do we map elements of the work's externalization to mental states and processes, thereby recreating those of the artist? Finally, in its account of the response appropriate to the appreciation of works of art, the theory seems at odds with the widespread view that most works admit a variety of interpretations and responses.

To the extent that it downplays the public context of presentation and appreciation, as well as the social determination and significance of artistic conventions, practices and genres, the account is committed to an uncomfortably idealist ontology for art works. It disregards the close identification we make in the case of singular pieces, such as oil paintings, between the work and the physical object in which it is realized. We speak of the properties and fate of such a work in terms of the qualities possessed and the vicissitudes undergone by that physical object. Art works are not deprived of their existence by the death of the artist, and their properties do not fade along with the artist's memories of its creation. Also, the theory cannot readily acknowledge the importance we accord to the artistic contribution of the performer in art forms such as drama, music and ballet. In general, the theory underplays the way in which the physical properties of a medium affect a work's artistic character by presenting distinctive possibilities and problems for the artist; or, to the extent that it admits such considerations, the account undermines the distinction it emphasizes between the (mental) act of creation and the (dispensable) activity of providing a public externalization of the work.

5 Fictional authors and personae

In the case of narrative or depictive works, it might be appropriate to regard the work as a communication from a fictional narrator or viewer, rather than from its artist. In line with critical practice, such an approach more readily tolerates the multiplicity of legitimate interpretations and the attribution of ideas and meanings to the work that were not held or intended by its artist. This fictional person, who stands outside the work and is distinct from its characters (including its internal narrator, should it have one), is constructed by the audience on the basis of the work's contents and conventions relating to what can be known and assumed in interpreting a work of the relevant time and place (see NARRATIVE §2).

Once this strategy has been adopted, it will be natural to attribute to the fictional narrator or viewer attitudes and emotions expressed in the manner of the work's presentation, as well as beliefs and desires. For instance, we might learn from the story that a character feels pride, but from the tone in which this is described also that the fictional narrator regards this pride as disappointing and contemptible. In that case it could be said that the fictional narrator is disappointed in the character's behaviour, even if there is not sufficient warrant for extending this reaction to the work's artist – indeed, even if there is reason to think the actual author might have had a more detached or ironic view.

The interpretive procedure outlined above might be extended to works that are neither narrations nor depictions, so that the expressiveness of such pieces is attributed to a fictional persona (whose thoughts and beliefs are largely absent from the expressive context). The work is approached, if not as a story, then as dealing piecemeal with the emotional experiences of a person about whom one knows little except that they undergo an emotion or sequence of feelings, the course of which is revealed in the work's contents and structure.

One might hear, say, a symphony as conveying the feelings of a fictional persona, but is this necessary for one to be aware of the work's expressiveness? If words for emotions always name the experiences of sentient beings, it might be thought that some such make-believing is involved, unconsciously if not consciously, where the work's expressiveness is not attributed to its artist, performer or audience, or to a character within it. Alternatively, if expressiveness can be present in the absence of occurrent emotions, this approach might be gratuitous.

6 Expressiveness as a property of art works

Several attempts to divorce the expressiveness of art works from expressions of occurrent feelings are unconvincing. We do sometimes say that art is expressive without indicating what it is expressive of. But, unlike Scruton (1983), I do not think that art deals with a kind of expression that is not the expression of an emotion or the like; rather, it reveals our concern (sometimes) to highlight the manner of a thing's being expressive, or the subtlety of its expressive nuance, above identifying or classifying the content of that expressiveness. Also unsatisfactory is the suggestion that art expresses emotions that are *sui generis* in being unfelt and non-cognitive, for this view, in divorcing artistic expressiveness from the world of human feeling, makes inexplicable art's power to move us as it does. And the supporting claim that art's expressiveness is ineffable is misplaced (in confusing description with duplication) and exaggerated (because it is only at a rather general level of expressiveness that there is sufficient interpersonal agreement to suggest that it is the work, rather than the responder, that is described). Nor does it help to call artistic expressiveness metaphorical. Metaphors take many forms and serve many purposes, so the suggestion is no substitute for an analysis of the phenomenon; analyses of literary metaphor seem not to be readily generalized to painterly or musical expressiveness; and many words for emotions seem no more lively as metaphors when predicated of art works than does talk of the necks of bottles.

Here is one argument for the view that art works are expressive without giving expression to occurrent emotions. We experience resemblances between art works and humanly expressive behaviour (voices, faces, deportment, actions). We do not notice similarities and infer a connection. (This is false to the phenomenology of the experience and, anyway, explains neither the direction of the inference nor our failure to connect art to many other things it might be seen as resembling.) Instead, as Kivy would have it, we are 'wired' to animate our experiences if we can.

We see cars with faces, dolphins with smiles and willows with gloomy demeanours. The similarity resides, as I said, in the *experiences* we have of human and artistic expressiveness; basic resemblances that might underpin this experience, those between elements of human expressive behaviour and features of art works, are located, if at all, after the fact. In art, this potential for resemblance is frequently modified and structured by conventions, so it will be apparent only to those familiar with the appropriate artistic practices.

Why, though, should this experience of resemblance justify the attribution of expressiveness to art, since we know the analogy cannot be carried through because works of art cannot embody occurrent experiences? Sometimes attributions of expressiveness concern the character of an appearance (of a body, or face) without regard to feelings. We might identify a person's bearing as sad without meaning that they feel sad, or entertaining that thought, or regarding them as prone to the feeling, but merely as a description of their deportment. (Obviously this secondary use of terms of emotion follows on the primary one in which we are interested in expressive appearances for the feelings they display or convey. The behaviour that betrays a feeling in one context is likely, in the absence of feeling, to produce an appearance with a corresponding expressive characteristic.) It is arguable that when we say, for example, that a musical piece is sad, our use concerns not occurrent emotions but emotional characteristics presented in the sound of the music as we experience it. Such appearances are more compelling in art than in nature, where they also occur, because we know them to have been deliberately employed by the artist.

Such a view meets several of the desiderata of an account of the expressiveness attributed to art works themselves. It locates the expressiveness in the work, explains the immediacy and directness with which this is experienced, and connects ascriptions of expressiveness to art with, if not the primary uses of those terms in connection with occurrent emotions, then with secondary uses of a familiar kind. Moreover, it fortunately does not describe the audience's experience as involving conscious inference or fanciful imaginings, since these seem to be absent from the reactions of many.

7 The value of artistic expressiveness

Expressiveness in art is usually thought to be value-conferring. Sometimes its value is described as instrumental – art is a source of knowledge about and mastery of the emotions, and is the more useful for presenting or arousing these in contexts that lack 'life implications', thereby permitting us to contemplate and savour their natures. The value of artistic expressiveness is also intrinsic in that it contributes to and is an aspect of narrative, depictive, formal and sensuous elements that together provide an integrated entity, the appreciation and understanding of which is pleasurable. Art's expressiveness is an invitation to engagement; a person's recognition of and response to its expressiveness can be as revealing of their understanding as would be their dispassionate description of the piece. In its expressiveness, art might best be regarded not as a mirror of life, a lesson on it or a preparation for it, but as a celebration of its affective side.

See also: EMOTIONS, PHILOSOPHY OF; EMOTION IN RESPONSE TO ART; HANSLICK, E.

References and further reading

These works are not introductory in style, though none is forbiddingly technical or formal.

Bouwsma, O.K. (1950) 'The Expression Theory of Art', in M. Black (ed.) *Philosophical Analysis*, Englewood Cliffs, NJ: Prentice Hall, 71–96. (Widely reprinted. Classic discussion of a spread of relevant issues. See §3–6 of this entry.)

Budd, M. (1985) *Music and the Emotions: The Philosophical Theories*, London: Routledge & Kegan Paul. (Fine discussion of theories of music's expressiveness and of Hanslick's denial of such expressiveness; includes a chapter on the nature of the emotions.)

—— (1995) *The Values of Art: Pictures, Poetry and Music*, London: Allen Lane, The Penguin Press. (Includes discussions of the nature and value of expressiveness in art with special attention to music.)

Davies, S. (1986) 'The Expression Theory Again', *Theoria* 52: 146–67. (Criticizes the expression theory and distinguishes modes of expressive behaviour.)

—— (1994) *Musical Meaning and Expression*, Ithaca, NY, and London: Cornell University Press. (Presents a detailed critique of theories of expressiveness in the arts, especially music; defends the account of artistic expressiveness outlined in §4; discusses the value of expressiveness; contains extensive bibliography.)

Elliott, R.K. (1966–7) 'Aesthetic Theory and the Experience of Art', *Proceedings of the Aristotelian Society* 67: 111–26. (Art is to be experienced imaginatively from within, and objectively from without.)

Gombrich, E.H. (1962) 'Art and the Language of the Emotions', *Proceedings of the Aristotelian Society* Supplement 36: 215–34. (Argues that, in art, the natural dimension of expressiveness is structured by conventions.)

* Kivy, P. (1989) *Sound Sentiment*, Philadelphia, PA: Temple University Press. (Includes The 'Corded Shell' (1980), in which he argues that music expresses emotion mainly by resembling expressive behaviour, and additional papers on the topic. See §§3, 6.)

Osborne, H. (1982) 'Expressiveness in the Arts', *Journal of Aesthetics and Art Criticism*, 41: 19–26. (Outlines the difficulties of attributing expressive properties to art works and argues that music expresses moods, not emotions.)

Robinson, J. (1983) 'Art as Expression', in H. Curtler (ed.) *What Is Art?*, New York: Haven, 93–121. (Emphasizes that artistic expressiveness is treated as a communication from the artist, though not as a direct expression of occurrent feelings.)

* Scruton, R. (1983) 'The Nature of Musical Expression', in *The Aesthetic Understanding*, London: Methuen, 49–61. (Regards musical expressiveness as gestural and metaphoric, and distinguishes 'transitive' from 'intransitive' expressiveness. See §6.)

Speck, S. (1988) '"Arousal Theory" Reconsidered', *British Journal of Aesthetics* 28: 40–7. (A defence of arousal theory.)

Stecker, R. (1984) 'Expression of Emotion in (Some of) the Arts', *Journal of Aesthetics and Art Criticism* 42: 409–18. (Holds that the arts differ in the manner of their expressiveness, depending on whether they possess a semantic, representational or other content.)

Tormey, A. (1971) *The Concept of Expression*, Princeton, NJ: Princeton University Press. (A detailed and sophisticated account of the notion of expressiveness in art; includes extended criticism of the expression theory.)

Vermazen, B. (1986) 'Expression as Expression', *The Pacific Philosophical Quarterly* 67: 196–224. (Holds that, in ascribing expressiveness to art works, including nonrepresentational ones, we are talking of the emotions of a fictional persona that we locate in the work.)

Wollheim, R. (1968) 'Expression', *Royal Institute of Philosophy Lectures* 1: 227–44. (Discusses expressiveness in painting, the artist's expression of emotion, and the conventions involved in this. See §4.)

STEPHEN DAVIES

ARTISTIC FORGERY

Forgery in art occurs when something is presented as a work of art with a history it does not actually have. Typically this involves a false claim about the producer's identity. Forgeries are most usually works in the style of the artist whose work they falsely claim to be, while a forgery that is a copy of an existing work is a fake. Forgery is most common in the visual arts, but is also possible in other arts, such as literature and music.

The main aesthetic problem that forgery poses is that typically no deception is practised concerning what we might call the appearance of the forged object (generalizing from the pictorial case). Thus the forger does not deceive us about the disposition of colours on the canvas, the sequence of musical notes in the score, or the sequence of words in the text. If we adopt the widely held view that aesthetic value is a function of appearance alone, we shall conclude that something's being a forgery is irrelevant to its aesthetic worth; whatever false beliefs the viewer might be induced to have about the work, those beliefs could not affect an honest judgment of its aesthetic value. But in the art world it is universal practice to condemn forgery. If that practice is to be justified as anything other than artistic snobbery and the protection of prices in the art market, it must be shown that the aesthetic interest of a work is not exhausted by its appearance alone. In fact it can be shown that the aesthetic features of a work often depend on its historical features as well as on its appearance, and that these historical features are likely to be obscured by the deception that forgery involves.

1   Forgery and fakery
2   The aesthetic significance of forgery

1   Forgery and fakery

The most common type of artistic forgery is that of painting in the style of another, more valued artist; as, for example, when the failed Dutch artist van Meegeren painted and sold a series of 'Vermeers'. But forgery is possible in other arts, and poems, novels and musical works have had their origins intentionally misrepresented. Fakery also occurs, as when, for instance, a faked *Mona Lisa* was left in the Louvre to conceal the theft of the original. Fakery is less common than forgery, because the normally well-established facts of a painting's whereabouts make the deception involved in fakery hard to effect. The boundary between fakery and other kinds of forgery is hazy: Suppose A is a work, now lost, about whose appearance we have little information. I create B, without copying any work, and present it as A. Is B a fake of A, or merely an unfaked forgery? There are also works presented as the products of someone whose very identity is fabricated, such as the sixteen-poem oeuvre of the fictitious Ern Malley, composed as a trap for modernist enthusiasms by two poets in the Australian army.

Fakery and non-faked forgery, while different, pose questions for the aesthetician that can be given rather similar formulations. With a case of fakery (a case that is successful from the point of view of reproducing the given work's appearance) we ask, 'Is there an aesthetic difference between A, the original, and B, the fake, even though there is no difference in appearance between them?' In the case of non-faked forgery we ask, 'Is there a difference between A as it actually is, namely as something with a given appearance falsely purporting to be the work of X, and A as it might have been, namely as something with that same appearance but now genuinely the work of X?' In the case of fakery we are comparing objects within a single possible world; in the case of non-faked forgery we are comparing objects across possible worlds. In this brief survey we shall proceed informally, not making explicit this modal difference when arguing for the aesthetic relevance of forgery in general and fakery in particular. In this section we consider the varieties of forgery and fakery that are possible, and in the next section we shall tackle the aesthetic issue.

Forgery is possible in any art form, but Nelson Goodman has argued that fakery is not possible in music, literature and other 'allographic' arts, but only in 'autographic' arts such as painting and printmaking. (See ART WORKS, ONTOLOGY OF §4 for critical discussion of this and other distinctions employed in this entry; here it is assumed that the autographic/allographic distinction divides the arts as Goodman claims, and that painting and printmaking are autographic while literature and music are allographic.) In autographic arts, a work's genuineness is a matter of its having the right history of production; in allographic arts it is not. Any sheaf of pages on which are inscribed the correct word sequence for *Northanger Abbey* is genuinely an instance of that work, irrespective of how, when or by whom it was produced. It is not possible to make a false claim that such a sheaf is genuine, because it is genuine. But it is possible to make a false claim that something which looks just like the authentic painting *Lucretia* by Rembrandt is an instance (in fact the unique instance) of that work, or that something with the appropriate appearance is an authentic instance of his etching *Tobit Blind*.

There is a difference between the painting case and the printmaking case. With painting, the unique instance of the work is identical to or constitutive of the work itself; with printmaking, where many authentic instances can be pulled from the same plate, no single instance, however authentic, is the work itself. So falsely presenting something as the painter's canvas amounts to falsely presenting something as the work itself; it is fakery of the work. Falsely presenting something as a print originating, in an authorized way, from the artist's block, amounts only to falsely presenting something as an instance of the work; it is not fakery of the work.

There is also a difference between autographic and allographic arts in the possibility of non-faked forgery: one can forge (but not fake) a work in the allographic arts without presenting anything that purports to be from the hand of the artist; this is not possible in the autographic arts. I might claim to be in possession of a poem by another hand, and produce as evidence for this a page of writing which I present as a mere copy of the alleged poet's autograph rather than as the autograph itself. This would be forgery. I can also falsely present something as a copy of a painting that is now lost. I could even present my copy as a perfect copy, and thus as a reliable guide to the appearance of that supposed work – how readily this would be believed is another matter. But it is doubtful whether this performance in the painting case constitutes forgery of any kind. Forgery is the activity of fraudulently claiming to present an instance of the work, and what counts as presenting an instance varies between the autographic and the allographic cases. In literature, an allographic art, any lexically correct copy of the original autograph is an instance of the work, and so the non-faking forger need claim only that what they present as an instance is lexically correct. For an autographic art form, the instances are just those with the requisite history, and the activity of presenting a copy not claimed to possess that history cannot count as presenting an instance of the work, and so cannot count as forgery.

2 The aesthetic significance of forgery

In this section we consider the potential impact that the discovery that an object is a forgery might have on our judgment of its merit as a work of art. It will not be argued that forgeries are automatically devoid of artistic worth, nor even that the fact of forgery is itself grounds for aesthetic reappraisal, though these claims have sometimes been made. It will be argued merely that the misrepresentation involved in a forgery is likely to have resulted in some other fact about the work being obscured, where the discovery of this other fact would justifiably lead to an aesthetic reappraisal.

The forger, in art and elsewhere, typically presents an object with a certain appearance, and hopes that we will make a plausible but erroneous inference from this appearance to certain other properties – its having been made by a certain person at a certain time and place, for example. If the aesthetic features of a work depend entirely on the appearance the forgery really has, and not on those inferred properties the forger hopes we will believe it has, forgery would have no aesthetic significance. Thus the visual appearance of van Meegeren's *Emmaus*, the word-sequence of the Malley poems, the ordering of musical notes in a Kreisler 'Mozart' piece, are evident features of these works. If they alone determine the aesthetic value of the work, the forger will not have practised any aesthetic deception. It seems we must say either that forgery is aesthetically irrelevant, or that the aesthetic qualities of the work depend on more than its evident features alone.

Someone unwilling to say either might appeal to an argument of Goodman's. Goodman claims that the best account we can give of the idea of two pictures looking exactly alike is one restricted to occasions of observation, that is, 'A and B are indistinguishable *for me now*'. So the fact that B is a forgery, though currently indistinguishable by me from A, may still be an aesthetically relevant fact for me now, because that fact will contribute to my future looking, and may result in my being able to see a difference between them. Even accepting Goodman's restriction of the notion of sameness of appearance, this argument is doubtful. To claim that the fact that one item is a forgery and the other is not constitutes an aesthetic difference because it *may* lead to the discovery of a difference of appearance seems to conflate possible and actual differences. If knowing that B is a forgery does lead me to notice a difference in appearance between A and B I may conclude that A and B differ aesthetically. If I do not find such a difference, then I have no reason to say that A and B differ aesthetically, whatever skills and knowledge I acquire in the process of examining them – so long, that is, as appearance is all that matters aesthetically.

If we are to establish the aesthetic significance of forgery we must abandon the idea that appearance alone determines a work's aesthetic value. A number of thought experiments have been suggested in which nonperceptible factors can be seen to make a difference to the value, *qua* works of art, of perceptually indistinguishable objects. To consider just the pictorial case: our judgment about this work's aesthetic success may crucially depend on whom we think it depicts. It may seem to capture the appearance and character of person X very successfully; when we learn that it is a picture of Y, our view may change. Its being a picture of Y rather than of X is not a feature of its appearance but of its history, and in particular of the history of its causal relations to X and to Y. Part of the impact of a work may consist in our recognition that it constitutes a strikingly original development of style or genre; a picture identical in appearance but produced much later would seem not original, but nostalgic or dull. Features of the work we would describe as elegant or delicate, which we thought had been produced by hand, would have little impact if we knew they were the product of a machine capable of producing lines of arbitrary thinness and complexity. There is little one can say about the appearance of an object that would be immune to these revisions based on a reassessment of the work's history. A description of the particular colours occurring at particular places on the surface might be the only claim immune to such revisions.

One response to the sorts of examples just cited is to say that they show simply that, when we judge a work according to representational, art-historical or technical criteria, we are not adopting a properly aesthetic standpoint. But it is unlikely that this narrowly aesthetic standpoint corresponds to the ways in which art works have traditionally been judged *qua* works of art, and its adoption would greatly impoverish our aesthetic discourse. The natural geometric partition of a picture, which we can describe in terms of abstract lines and planes, often depends on representational features, like the joined parts of a human body, that give salience to certain shapes. To ignore the representational features of the picture is to be no longer able to see what is natural about the geometric description. Apparently aesthetic predicates, such as 'is dynamic', when used for a painting, would not be aesthetic in this narrow sense; as Ernst Gombrich has emphasized (1977), a work like Mondrian's *Broadway Boogie-Woogie* can seem dynamic because works in the class to which it is naturally compared, namely Mondrian's other works, are rather static. Imagine *Broadway Boogie-Woogie* to have a different history, and it might be less appropriate to call it dynamic.

It is sometimes said that the upshot of our acquiring knowledge of the referential, art-historical and technical features of a work is that the object *looks different* to us from the way it had looked before we acquired that knowledge. And so, the objection goes, the examples described above are not really counterexamples to the thesis that there is no aesthetic difference without a difference of appearance. Rather, they are examples of the ways in which the work's appearance itself depends on extrinsic factors. If the objection were right, we should be able to answer the charge that forgery is aesthetically irrelevant immediately and without difficulty, saying simply that, since objects with different histories look different, there can be no objection to re-evaluating a work when we come to know that its history has been falsified, because that will change its appearance. However, the objection misses the point. To say that two objects are indistinguishable in appearance is not to say that how they look to the viewer is independent of the viewer's beliefs about their histories. A single object may look different to the viewer on two occasions of looking if they learn something about its history between the times of looking, but there is still a sense in which its appearance is unchanged. The sense in which objects can look the same despite differences between them in respect of facts about reference, history and technique is this: there could be a copy of the *Mona Lisa* so similar to the original that no one would be able to tell, on the basis of merely looking, whether the copy had been substituted for the original. The fact that, were the substitution pointed out, the copy would now look different to you from the way it had looked before (and different from the way the original had looked) is no objection to the claim that copy and original look exactly the same. It is in this sense of 'look the same' – being an indiscernible substitute for – that there can be an aesthetic difference between works that look the same.

We may conclude, then, that objects with the same appearance may yet have distinct aesthetic properties, and that therefore the aesthetic properties of the work are not fully determined by its appearance. In that case, the deception involved in forgery may result in the audience being misinformed about historical properties of the object potentially relevant to the determination of its aesthetic properties. Forgery is to that extent an aesthetically relevant fact.

See also: ARTIST'S INTENTION

References and further reading

Currie, G. (1989) *An Ontology of Art*, London: Macmillan. (Discusses forgery within a framework that rejects the usefulness of the autographic/allographic distinction.)

Danto, A.C. (1981) *The Transfiguration of the Commonplace: A Philosophy of Art*, Cambridge, MA: Harvard University Press. (Argues that works identical in appearance may have distinct aesthetic properties.)

Dutton, D. (1983) *The Forger's Art*, Berkeley, CA, and Los Angeles, CA: University of California Press. (An anthology of work by art historians, critics and philosophers.)

* Gombrich, E. (1977) *Art and Illusion: A Study in the*

Psychology of Pictorial Representation, London: Phaidon, 5th edn. (An important historical work which, though it is not directly concerned with forgery, vividly illustrates some of the ways in which our perception of pictures depends on assumptions about their histories.)

* Goodman, N. (1981) *Languages of Art*, 2nd edn, Brighton: Harvester Wheatsheaf. (A classic work that includes an account of the autographic/allographic distinction and its application. Sometimes intricate, but Part 3 on 'art and authenticity' is quite accessible.)

Sagoff, M. (1978) 'On Restoring and Reproducing Art', *Journal of Philosophy* 75: 453–70. (Argues for the aesthetic worthlessness of forgeries.)

GREGORY CURRIE

ARTISTIC INTERPRETATION

Interpretation aims to advance understanding by providing explanations of various kinds. In art, it should aim to maximize our understanding and appreciation of a work, and enable us to grasp its artistic values. When we interpret an art work we may explain why its elements are placed in their contexts, for example, to convey a certain meaning or express a certain feeling. In the case of literature we explain why words and passages are placed where they are, why characters and events are described as they are, and so on. When we interpret whole works, we explain how they fit into broader explanatory frameworks (for instance, Freudian or Marxist) or how they relate to various traditions so as to serve (or reject) the values emphasized in those traditions.

The distinction between description, or the presentation of the fundamental data constituting a work of art, and interpretation, which involves explaining why those elements exist in a work, what values they serve, may be used to justify claims that interpretations can never be known to be true, while descriptions are obviously true or false. While this is reinforced by the fact that a work may generate conflicting interpretations, the distinction does not imply that interpretations cannot be known to be correct.

In a related debate, many see the artist's intention in creating their work as the key to a valid interpretation. Since, however, many people find value in works in ways unintended by the artist, the onus is on the intentionalist to demonstrate the primacy of the value that the artist intended the work to have.

Ultimately, contending interpretations may not present as great a problem to a theory of interpretation as at first seems inevitable. Interpretations give priority in different ways to different artistic values; the choice of these values is simply a matter of artistic taste, not truth, and may not threaten the validity of any reasonably grounded interpretation.

1 **Interpretation and description**
2 **Meaning**
3 **Intention**
4 **Incompatible interpretations**

1 Interpretation and description

Based on the fact that there is often more conflict among interpretations than among non-interpretive descriptions of works, many philosophers claim that interpretation is always on weaker epistemic ground than description. They claim that interpreters cannot know, or cannot know that they know, that their interpretations are correct. This epistemic weakness is supposed in itself to mark the distinction between interpretation and description of art works. But examples doom this attempt at distinguishing interpretation. Lady Macbeth can be known to be ambitious and manipulative, and this is an interpretation, albeit an obvious one, of her character. The distinction instead lies in the fact that interpretations are inferred, as explanations for what can be described without being interpreted. We non-interpretively describe what we directly perceive (as opposed to infer) in works; and such descriptions elicit universal agreement from audiences knowledgeable about the media in question, while interpretations need not elicit such agreement.

All artistic media present us with elements that can be described without being interpreted. Such elements constrain acceptable interpretations of the works that contain them, in that interpreters must explain why those elements exist as they do in the works. In painting and music the existence of such elements is obvious. Included among them are coloured shapes or notes and their formal relations. These make up the data or evidence for acceptable interpretations, which cannot be incompatible with their agreed descriptions. The counterparts in literature are not simply physical marks on paper, but words and sentences with their standard meanings. We do not perceive ink marks and infer that they are there to represent meaningful words. Instead, we directly perceive words and sentences, and, if we understand the language being used, agree on their standard meanings. Such elements make up texts, which should be defined in terms of standard lexical meanings at the times the texts are written. Even when we interpret such elements as metaphor or irony, we infer such interpretations as the best explanations for words with those standard or literal meanings being placed in those contexts. We make such inferences when doing so makes for more interesting readings or valuable literary experiences.

Some contemporary theorists of literary criticism deny that texts constrain acceptable interpretations. They see readers or critics as joining in the production of texts through their interpretive readings. To see pre-existing texts as constraints is, according to these theorists, to underestimate the degree of freedom that critics have in specifying their meanings and significance. Poetry is so notoriously open to radically different readings that it is empty to claim that poetic texts, as opposed to critical communities, constrain what is acceptable as interpretation. But these theorists exaggerate. Even a poem such as William Blake's 'The Tyger', which is notorious for eliciting diverse interpretations, shows otherwise. For acceptable interpretations, no matter how divergent, must explain, for example, why Blake centrally used a term that ordinarily refers to tigers.

Others deny the distinction between description and interpretation by pointing out that what we take to be fictional facts in a work can depend on our interpretation of it. There are ghosts in *The Turn of the Screw* only if we interpret it as a ghost story. There is an egg in Piero della Francesca's Brera altarpiece only if we interpret a certain mysterious object in that way. But whenever interpretations are needed to determine what is (fictionally) true in a work, there remains a level of description of painted shapes or words used that cannot be placed in doubt. We may similarly grant that interpretations guide what we attend to or perceive in a work. The painted shapes to which we attend on a canvas will be those we take to contribute to the artistic value of the painting, and this will vary according to whether we interpret it as an allegory, a formal structure, and so on. But the shapes can nevertheless be described without being interpreted.

Finally, we may admit that the line between interpretation and description must sometimes be drawn finely, while maintaining that the distinction is crucial for understanding the constraints on acceptable interpretations. To point out, for example, that a musical passage leads back to the tonic key is to describe it non-interpretively, but to explain it simply as a bridge passage is to interpret it, however obviously.

2   Meaning

Most theorists of literary criticism agree that the interpretation of literature aims to disclose meanings in texts. They disagree about the ground of such meaning, whether it is simply the semantic conventions of the language, the intentions of authors, or the interpretive activities of readers or critics. But it should be clear that interpretation does not always consist in disclosing meanings (unless we think of meaning in the broad sense of significance, and of significance as the value of a work or the place of its parts in its broader structure); and disclosing meaning is not always interpreting. Trivially, in musical works and paintings there is not always semantic content to be revealed. In literature, if revelation of meaning were always interpretation, then every obvious paraphrase of every section of text would count as literary interpretation. But we need not interpret every simple sentence in a novel, and stating the ordinary dictionary meanings of the words in such sentences does not count as literary interpretation. As noted above, we simply grasp the meanings of such sentences as we read them, much as we see trees in a true-to-life landscape painting without having to interpret the painted shapes as trees.

One way of avoiding this objection is to view interpreting as determining the meaning of a whole text or a large segment of it from the lexical meanings of its words and sentences. But this view ignores the fact that phrases and even words in texts can be interpreted as well. Stating the meaning of some obscure phrase or line in a poem constitutes an interpretation when there is an implicit claim that the phrase is there to convey that meaning, and that its literary value lies at least partially in its doing so. Statements of meanings will rarely be complete interpretations of texts, since in literature the ways in which meanings are presented are relevant to the values of the works. Hence form and not merely content must be explained in complete interpretations. But certainly words often have value in a text largely because of the meanings they convey.

The idea that interpretation consists in determining the meaning of a whole text also implies that a simple paraphrase of a whole work is the paradigm interpretation of it. According to the explanatory account, it is most unlikely to be an interpretation at all. Simply to paraphrase a work is not normally to indicate the ways that its passages contribute to its overall artistic value. Conveying certain meanings is normally only part of that value, and paraphrase is needed to explain that part only when the text itself is ambiguous or obscure. Explanation of metaphorical, symbolic or ironic meaning is more often a part of genuine literary interpretation.

3 Intention

Much debate on this topic has centred on the relevance of artists' intentions. According to one side of this debate, if there is to be a standard of correct interpretation, it must lie in uncovering the intentions of artists regarding the meanings and expressive properties in their works, since otherwise these matters remain indeterminate and open to conflicting construals. According to this view, art is a form of communication, and the aim of the recipient, as in all communication, is the discovery of the speaker's intentions. According to the other side, artists' intentions are inaccessible or irrelevant, since, if they are successfully realized, the results will be apparent in the works themselves; and if they are unsuccessful, they cannot determine how a work should be interpreted.

Viewing interpretation as value-enhancing explanation provides a different perspective on this issue. From this viewpoint there is certainly some value to be derived from seeing the world of an art work (and perhaps the real world as well) as its creator saw it and intended it to be seen. Seeing through another's eyes, or imagining through another's creative genius, so as to alter one's own imaginative vision, is a major benefit to be derived from the appreciation of art. This benefit requires fidelity to artists' intentions, where these are recoverable.

On the other side, to accept recoverable intentions as constraints on correct interpretations, to insist that there is always only one correct interpretation of any work of art and that this is the one intended by its artist, may be to rob contemporary audiences of valuable experiences they might have of the work. A Freudian reading of *Hamlet* may afford illuminating insights into its characters, whether or not such an interpretation was or could have been intended by Shakespeare. It is commonplace in the domain of music for conductors and performers not to be limited to conveying expressive properties specifically intended by composers. (It might be objected here that the performative interpretations of musicians do not fit the definition of interpretation given above, since they are not explanations. But they are informed by critical interpretations that are not constrained by composers' explicit intentions.)

The intentionalist can also be accused of confusing speakers' (artists') meanings, or what speakers intend to say, with utterance (text) meanings, or what their language conveys according to its semantic conventions. If an utterance or text is unclear or ambiguous, then a speaker's intentions cannot in themselves make it less so. In ordinary communicative contexts, we do not use speakers' intentions to clarify the meanings of their utterances; instead, we use the semantic conventions governing their utterances as guides to recovering their linguistic intentions.

Thus, the best argument for intentionalism – the claim that interpretation aims only to disclose artists' intentions – must be that art is a form of communication and, as such, shares this aim. This is partially correct in that, as indicated above, it points to one major value in the experience of art. But there are others. Since certain art works may be more interesting or expressive if not limited by their creators' specific intentions, the intentionalist must argue that the value indicated by the communicative model trumps all other values to be derived from the experience of art.

It should be noted finally here that we may ascribe intentions to artists on different levels of specificity. They may intend, for example, not only to convey specific meanings, but for their works to have certain dramatic or expressive effects, or, most broadly, for their works to be appreciated to the fullest extent possible. The realization of this broadest (and perhaps most common) intention may require creative acts of interpretation on the part of audiences. The problem with the orthodox intentionalist view is not (as some critics claim) that it forces us to search outside the work itself for its proper interpretation. We must in any case locate a work correctly in its broader artistic context and tradition to interpret and evaluate it correctly. The problem is rather that it focuses only on one sort of intention and one sort of value at the expense of others.

4 Incompatible interpretations

If acceptable interpretations guide perceptions or experiences of works towards enhanced appreciation of their values, and if art works have potential values that cannot be realized simultaneously in experiences of them, then incompatible interpretations might be equally acceptable. The second antecedent is true of many works and their parts. Iago's 'Credo' aria in Verdi's *Otello*, for example, can be interpreted as boisterously defiant or as broodingly sinister, and these different readings of the score and text will lead to different understandings of the character and his relations to other characters and to the dramatic events, and to different experiences of the work's expressive qualities. We cannot simply combine these interpretations by viewing the aria as ambiguous, since a reading or performance of it as ambiguous would differ from both these interpretations. It would be probably less satisfying, if more subtle, than either of the single interpretations, each of which could be equally satisfying or acceptable.

Interpretations are incompatible when they ascribe properties to a work (or its parts) that it cannot simultaneously possess. They are acceptable when they produce understanding and experience of works that enhances the appreciation of central values in those works. Since great works of art are often multidimensional, it is rare that all their artistic values can be appreciated under single interpretations. When there are at least two incompatible but equally acceptable interpretations of a work, we cannot simply equate acceptability with truth. Inconsistent ascriptions cannot all be true, at least not absolutely. Talk of plausibility will not do here either, since plausibility must be defined in terms of probable truth. In such cases we can speak only of either acceptability or of truth relative to an acceptable interpretive scheme. When there is only one acceptable interpretation of some part of a work, we can continue to speak simply of truth.

That many works of art are intended to be susceptible to a variety of interpretations is indicated by their frequent use of metaphor and symbol, and by the incompleteness of their notations (especially in music). A theory of interpretation must explain why many apparent critical disagreements seem irresolvable. The theory presented above explains such disagreements as symptoms of incompatible but equally acceptable interpretations, and it explains the latter as resulting ultimately from differences in taste. If different interpretations enhance different artistic values by explaining elements within works as serving those values, then preference for one interpretation of a work over another will reflect a preference for particular kinds of experience that can be derived from the work. That is, it will reflect a particular taste in art.

Thus, interpretive disputes will mirror disagreements in evaluations of various works. Only realists or absolutists about the latter should be realists or absolutists about the former. Nevertheless, the acceptance of incompatible interpretations of the same works does not imply a lack of standards. Iago's aria may be interpreted in either of the irreconcilable ways mentioned above, but a reading or performance of it as light-heartedly humorous would be clearly inappropriate. An acceptable interpretation must adequately explain the work of art as it can be non-interpretively described.

See also: Art criticism; Art, understanding of; Artist's intention; Barthes, R.; Derrida, J.; Structuralism in literary theory §§2–3

References and further reading

Barnes, A. (1988) *On Interpretation*, Oxford: Blackwell. (Distinguishes interpretation on epistemic grounds.)

Beardsley, M. (1970) *The Possibility of Criticism*, Detroit, MI: Wayne State University Press. (Argues the anti-intentionalist position.)

Eco, U. (1990) *The Limits of Interpretation*, Bloomington, IN: Indiana University Press. (Reasserts limits to the freedom of interpreters.)

Fish, S. (1980) *Is There a Text in This Class?*, Cambridge, MA: Harvard University Press. (Argues that communities of critics produce texts, which do not exist without them.)

Gill, N.S. (ed.) (1982) *Structuralism and Literary Criticism*, Atlantic Highlands, NJ: Humanities Press. (A collection of French structuralist interpretation.)

Hirsch, E.D. (1967) *Validity in Interpretation*, New Haven, CT: Yale University Press. (Argues the intentionalist position.)

Young, R. (ed.) (1981) *Untying the Text*, Boston, MA: Routledge & Kegan Paul. (A collection of post-structuralist interpretation.)

ALAN H. GOLDMAN

ARTISTIC STYLE

Artistic style is a problematic notion in several ways. Sometimes the term refers to style in general, as it does in 'Good style requires good diction'. Sometimes it refers to style as a particular, as in 'Van Gogh's style' or 'the Baroque style'. In antiquity, style was a rhetorical concept referring to diction and syntax; consequently style is very often identified with the formal elements of a work of art as opposed to the content. However, the kind of subject matter an artist chooses may itself be a significant feature of style. One way of thinking about style is as a set of recurrent features of works of art that identify them as the product of a particular person, period or place. This may be adequate for some purposes, but it ignores the fact that a style has a unified 'physiognomy' or expressive character. The relation between style and expression is complex. A period style is often thought to express the cultural attitudes of the period, but it cannot do so in a very direct way. What a style expresses is a function of where it occurs in the history of style. Similarly, a work of art in an artist's individual style will be expressive only in the context of the possibilities of that style. According to the Romantic tradition, individual style is a genuine expression of the artist's self. But according to others, style is simply a construction by readers, viewers and listeners.

1 Historical background
2 Style and form
3 Style and signature
4 Style and expression
5 Style and personality

1 Historical background

The concept of style in the arts was first elaborated in Ancient Greek and Roman treatises on rhetoric – the art of public speaking. The ancients distinguished style from invention (subject matter) and organization (the arrangement of subject matter into parts). Style is diction, or word use, and composition, or the way in which words are combined into sentences. It is form rather than content: not what you say, but how you say it. Good style consists in correctness, clarity, ornamentation and decorum (appropriateness). However, since all good speech should be grammatically correct and clear, what chiefly makes the difference between one style and another is the use of ornamentation or rhetorical 'figures' and tropes. The principle of decorum stipulates that the style of a speech be appropriate to the total situation in which it is delivered, including who the speaker is, what they are talking about and what audience they are addressing. The ancients distinguished three kinds of style – plain, middle and grand – and each was appropriate to different occasions and purposes. It was very important to know how to adapt your style so as to secure the desired intellectual and emotional effect in your audience. Finally, style is sometimes thought of as an image of the speaker: Cicero's style to some extent reflects Cicero himself.

The rhetorical concept of style endured largely unaltered through the Enlightenment, and extended its area of application to music and the visual arts. The same 'subject', such as a portico or a representation of the Crucifixion, could be presented in different styles to achieve different effects. Different styles were individuated and organized into hierarchies. Decorum remained important: just as the epic poem demanded a more elevated style than the lyric, so in painting the grand style was suited to history painting as opposed to still life. Critics such as John Dryden took issue with Shakespeare because he mixed the grand style of tragedy with the low style of comedy in such works as *Hamlet* and *King Lear*, and the music theorist Johann Joseph Fux insisted that the styles of church music should not be confused with those of theatre and dance.

The advent of Romanticism and German Idealism radically altered the way in which style was conceived. The Romantics rejected the hierarchy of genres and the idea that a particular subject demanded a particular appropriate style. They argued that style and subject are not independent and that style cannot be defined in terms of a list of rhetorical ornaments. Coleridge, for example, celebrates the poem as a living, organic whole in which style and content are fused. To the Romantics a work of art was an emotional expression by an artist with a unique sensibility, whose emotional responses to a subject were embodied in both the style and content of their work. Individual style was the expression of all the peculiarities of the artist's qualities of mind and feeling.

On an altogether more grand scale, Hegel argued that different period styles are expressions of culture in general. For Hegel, art is a sensuous manifestation of Spirit, and the successive phases of art correspond to the inevitable movement of Spirit towards self-realization (see HEGEL, G.W.F. §8). Each phase corresponds to a style – the Symbolic, the Classical and the Romantic (post-Classical or Christian) – and each is expressive of a different culture – the Ancient Egyptian, Ancient Greek and modern. Shorn of some of their metaphysical underpinnings, these ideas re-emerge in the theories of period style and style change developed by the great nineteenth-century German art historians, Heinrich Wölfflin, Alois Riegl, Paul Frankl and others. For example, Wölfflin identified five contrasting style qualities – the most famous being 'linear' versus 'painterly' – through which he defined the contrast between the art of the High Renaissance and that of the Baroque period. He argued that there was a necessary evolution from the first set of qualities to the second, that this pattern of development recurred in most historical periods, and that it was due to principles internal to the history of art.

2 Style and form

The ancient rhetoricians discussed style in terms of rhetorical figures, both semantic (such as metaphor and personification) and syntactic (such as asyndeton and antithesis). Contemporary stylisticians and discourse analysts have used modern linguistic techniques to identify particular stylistic features of poems, plays and ordinary discourse. Style in this sense is identified as how something is said rather than what is said: with form rather than content. Very different things can be said in the same style, so style would appear to be independent of content. And the same content can be expressed in different styles: 'The cat is on the mat' is in plain style, in contrast to 'The feline animal is situated upon the rug', which is (inappropriately) in grand style, but they mean much the same thing. Style would therefore seem to involve choice of words and syntax – the 'formal' elements of the discourse rather than the content.

Are all formal elements part of style? Monroe Beardsley (Lang 1987) has tried to mark off stylistic from non-stylistic features of a discourse as those linguistic features which carry connotative or secondary meaning or which enable it to 'reflect a subordinate illocutionary action'. So Caesar's famous assertion, 'Veni, vidi, vici', primarily means that he came, he saw and he conquered, but in leaving out 'and' the utterance also implicitly asserts that Caesar operated quickly and decisively. The trouble is that any linguistic feature can have connotative or secondary meaning. Even when I say 'The cat is on the mat', I am implying that what I say is plain and straightforward. Indeed, any attempt to distinguish stylistic from non-stylistic linguistic features may well fail, since any word or grammatical construction in an appropriate context can contribute to style. The same is true of formal elements in the other arts, such as a particular sequence of chords or colours. The attempt to define a set of uniquely stylistic formal features seems to be hopeless.

3 Style and signature

In contemporary debates in aesthetics what is at issue is not normally style or stylistic features in general, but rather what is the nature of 'a style'. Since a style is what picks out the work of a particular artist, period or place, perhaps a style can be thought of as the recurrent formal elements that identify a work as belonging to that artist, period or place.

The most important problem with the formalistic approach to style is that a style consists of more than just a set of formal elements. Styles have particular expressive qualities: they are plain, ornate, pompous, diffuse, sweet, euphonious, Miltonic, energetic, Latinate, abstract or flabby. Very often, subject matter is stylistically important: a penchant for subjects from Roman myth and legend together with fanciful Roman landscapes is arguably a feature of Poussin's style, just as a tendency to domestic pastoral landscape is a feature of the Barbizon school style. A particular kind of iconography or conventional symbolism may also be important. Sometimes the use of certain materials – a preference for oil over watercolour or for bronze over marble – can be a feature of style, as can the use of certain techniques. In recognition of these multiple possibilities, Nelson Goodman has defined a style as 'a complex characteristic that serves somewhat as an individual or group signature…in general stylistic properties help answer the questions: who? when? where?' (1975).

The problem with this proposal is that not all identifying features are stylistic; the actual signature on a painting, for example, might not be part of the painter's style. What, then, is distinctive about style regarded as signature? One answer is that it is only aesthetically salient qualities that count as stylistic. But on the one hand, some aspects of a work of art, such as its size and subject matter, are always aesthetically salient whether or not they are part of style; on the other hand, style features are not always particularly salient: often only a very careful study will unearth them.

One of the important facts about a style is that it comes across as an expressive unity. A set of recurrent features is not a style unless the features themselves combine to form a certain 'physiognomy': the style is pompous or sentimental or Ciceronian. Hence style qualities do not just identify an artist, school or period; they also contribute to the expression of a particular 'character'. One plausible suggestion, therefore, is to count as stylistic all those features of subject matter, form, expression, symbolism, materials and so on which contribute towards the expression of the overall character of the individual or period in question.

4 Style and expression

The Hegelian idea that a period style expresses the collective spirit of an epoch or country and that the style of a particular work of art is a symptom of that spirit has been roundly criticized by twentieth-century art historians. Meyer Schapiro (1994) has urged that we should not extrapolate from a single painting to cultural attitudes in general: one-to-one correlations usually hold only between single aspects of a painting and the culture from which it originates. Erwin Panofsky (1955) has shown how we cannot tell what general attitudes are expressed by a painting unless we can place the picture in the history of style and the history of iconography. We can interpret what Tintoretto's *Last Supper* expresses only if we know the history of renderings of the Last Supper. The picture has to be seen as a response to and a rejection of previous *Last Suppers*, such as Giotto's and Leonardo's. Ernst Gombrich (1960) has made a similar point with respect to works within a painter's individual style: what a painting expresses is a function of its place within the artist's 'language' or repertoire. Van Gogh's painting of his room at Arles is relatively serene in the context of Van Gogh's oeuvre, whereas if it were (*per impossibile*) by Cézanne it would express much greater turbulence and distress.

Deterministic theories of style change have also been criticized. All such theories treat style as inevitably moving towards some goal, but artists cannot be striving to achieve a perfection that has not yet come about and of which they cannot be cognizant. Style change is the result of individual artists responding to many influences, including the challenges posed by the art of the past, and should be thought of, says James Ackerman, not as 'a succession of steps towards a solution to a given problem, but as a succession of steps away from one or more original statements of a problem' (1963). Nevertheless, certain patterns of development do recur in the history of art, for example in the development of sculpture in Ancient Greece and the Renaissance. Ackerman suggests that this is due to a similarity in the way that the problems facing sculptors were conceived, as well as a similarity in the solutions they found. Thus both ancient and Renaissance sculptors were struggling with the same problem of how to create beautiful human forms out of blocks of stone, and there is the same development from a 'blocky' archaic style to the ideal Classical solution, and from that to the development of a freer, more dynamic style.

If style change and the expressiveness of style can only be understood as the result of individual artists responding to the art of the past and implicitly either accepting or rejecting specific alternatives, then it might seem as if style entails choice: in developing a style an artist chooses one particular form of words or configuration of lines in preference to others, depending upon what they want to express. Leonard Meyer, for example, defines style in music as a 'replication of patterning...that results from a series of choices made within some set of constraints' (1989). For example, given the constraints on the style of the classical sonata, Beethoven's decision to begin his piano sonata, 'Les Adieux', with a deceptive cadence is an unexpected stylistic choice that permits the opening phrase to express an uncertain, plaintive quality. On the other hand, the word 'choice' may be misleading if it implies deliberation and conscious decision-making.

5 Style and personality

Most of the theories of style discussed so far have considered style from the historian's point of view. It is, for example, a third-person viewpoint which treats Beethoven as working within certain constraints and as making certain choices. A different approach has been taken by Richard Wollheim (Lang 1987), who argues that there is an important theoretical distinction between the individual style of a particular artist and such general style categories as school style (the style of the school of Giotto), period style (Baroque concerto-grosso style, Augustan poetic style) and universal style (the geometric style, the heroic-epic style). General style categories are the invention of historians, who try to organize a body of knowledge according to their own interests and purposes. By contrast, an artist's individual style has 'psychological reality' and can be captured only by a 'generative' conception of style that picks out and groups together elements of the artist's work which are 'dependent upon processes or operations' characteristic of the artist's acting as an artist. Wollheim restricts his theory to pictorial style, since he is thinking of style processes not only as psychologically dependent on the artist but also as physically embodied in motor habits and motor memory. However, the theory can be generalized to the other arts if style is thought of as a way of doing or making something which is expressive of the artist's character, qualities of mind, attitudes and sensibility.

This way of thinking about style is reflected in Arthur Danto's maxim that style is 'what is done without art or knowledge' (1981). On this view, artists, in developing their individual styles, do not literally 'choose' among alternatives. Being of a certain character, the artist is able to paint or write only in accordance with that character. By the same token, a forgery of a painting, even one that cannot be distinguished from the original, cannot have style. It is a deliberate imitation of an already existent work or style, whereas the original is a genuine expression of the artist's self. For the same reason a forgery has no genuine aesthetic significance, for having a formed style is a precondition of expressiveness and hence of aesthetic interest (see ARTISTIC FORGERY).

The theory that style is a way of doing something that expresses the artist's unique personality, character and ways of thinking and feeling explains many of the puzzles surrounding the concept of style. It explains why not all formal features of a work or oeuvre are stylistic, why subject matter can but need not be a feature of style, and why a feature can be a stylistic feature in one work or oeuvre and not in another: in every case it depends on whether the feature is expressive of the artist's character or personality. Similarly, the theory explains the unity of style in terms of the unity of the personality expressed and it explains the difference between style and signature: a recurrent feature of an artist's oeuvre is not stylistic unless it contributes to the expression of the artist's character. Thus a literal signature is not usually a feature of style.

However, the theory is unattractive to those who think of style as irremediably conventional, as the result of operations performed by readers. Some writers have argued that style is a function of the operations performed by the 'implied author' of the work, as constructed by the reader or viewer. Michel FOUCAULT takes a more extreme position (1979). He argues that the notion of a unified style is simply one of the principles that identify the 'author-function' of a work, this function being characteristic of works which have a certain status and are designed to be received in a certain way. On this view style has no reality at all; it is just a social construction.

See also:; AESTHETIC CONCEPTS §4; FORMALISM IN ART

References and further reading

Abrams, M.H. (1953) *The Mirror and the Lamp*, Oxford: Oxford University Press. (Still perhaps the best introduction to the history of ideas in the Romantic movement in literature.)

* Ackerman, J. (1963) 'Style', in J. Ackerman and R. Carpenter (eds), *Art and Archeology*, Englewood Cliffs, NJ: Prentice Hall, 174–86. (A theory of style in the visual arts by an art historian.)

Carter R. and Simpson, R. (1989) *Language, Discourse and Literature*, London: Unwin Hyman. (An introduction to stylistics and discourse analysis.)

Cooper, L. (1912) *Theories of Style*, New York: Macmillan. (Contains theories of literary style by many great writers, including Aristotle, Longinus and Coleridge.)

* Danto, A.C. (1981) *The Transfiguration of the Commonplace*, Cambridge, MA: Harvard University Press, esp. ch. 7. (Application of Danto's general philosophy of art to style and expression.)

* Foucault, M. (1979) 'What is an Author?', in J.V. Harari (ed.), *Textual Strategies*, Ithaca, NY: Cornell University Press, 141–60. (Translation of a 1969 essay by the French philosopher.)

* Gombrich, E.H. (1960) *Art and Illusion*, London: Phaidon, esp. ch. 11. (Fascinating discussion of the development of style in Western 'realistic' painting and the relation between style and expression.)

* —— (1968–79) 'Style', in D. Sills (ed.), *International Encyclopedia of the Social Sciences*, New York: Macmillan, 18 vols, 15: 352–61. (A summary of Gombrich's views on style.)

* Goodman, N. (1975) 'The Status of Style', *Critical Inquiry* 1: 799–811. (A theory of style by a philosopher, which complements the views developed in his *Languages of Art*.)

Kennedy, G. (1994) *A New History of Classical Rhetoric*, Princeton, NJ: Princeton University Press. (Gives a good account of the treatment of style in Ancient Greece and Rome.)

* Lang, B. (1987) *The Concept of Style*, Ithaca, NY: Cornell University Press. (First edition 1979. Contains a number of important essays on style by philosophers, art historians and others, including several mentioned in this entry: Leonard Meyer, 'Toward a Theory of Style', Richard Wollheim, 'Pictorial Style: Two Views', and Monroe Beardsley, 'Verbal Style and Illocutionary Action'.)

* Meyer, L. (1989) *Style and Music*, Philadelphia, PA: University of Pennsylvania Press. (An expansion of the essay in Lang (1987) by a music theorist.)

Minor, V.H. (1994) *Art History's History*, Englewood Cliffs, NJ: Prentice-Hall. (Useful if brief introduction to the major figures in Western art history.)

* Panofsky, E. (1955) *Meaning in the Visual Arts*, Garden City, NY: Doubleday, 26–54. (First published in 1939, this essay explains Panofsky's principles of art historical interpretation. Page reference marks 'Iconography and Iconology: An Introduction to the Study of Renaissance Art'.)

Podro, M. (1982) *The Critical Historians of Art*, London: Yale University Press. (The theories of post-Hegelian art historians.)

Robinson, J.M. (1985) 'Style and Personality in the Literary Work', *Philosophical Review*, 94: 227–47. (Development of some of the ideas in §5.)

* Schapiro, M. (1994) *Selected Papers, Volume 4: Theory and Philosophy of Art: Style, Artist and Society*, New York: George Braziller, 51–102. (A seminal essay on style, originally published in 1962; contains a useful bibliography.)

Van Eck, C., McAllister, J. and Van de Vall, R. (1995) *The Question of Style in Philosophy and the Arts*, Cambridge: Cambridge University Press. (A collection of essays on style.)

Wölfflin, H. (1950) *Principles of Art History*, New York: Dover. (First published in 1915, this book explains the five principles which are said to distinguish Renaissance from Baroque style.)

JENEFER M. ROBINSON

ARTISTIC TASTE

Taste has been variously understood as (1) the capacity to take pleasure in certain artistic and natural objects, (2) the capacity to identify the constituent elements in such objects, and (3) the capacity to discern certain special properties. Taste in sense (1) has been a topic since the early eighteenth century, culminating in the work of Hume and Kant. This conception of taste is annexed to the idea that 'beauty' or 'artistic excellence' is not itself an objective property of things, but that it is recorded in judgments of beauty as a report of a certain kind of pleasure felt by the judge in the presence of these things. Taste in sense (2), which is an analogue of the notion of taste as the ability to discriminate with the tongue and taste buds, has also been a topic since the eighteenth century, articulated perhaps most clearly by Hume. A connection between sense (1) and sense (2) is intended by eighteenth-century authors, but the connection has not been formulated clearly. Taste in sense (3) is a conception originating in the mid-twentieth century, notably in the work of Frank Sibley. It is primarily the idea that beauty, elegance, gracefulness and other properties – collectively called 'aesthetic properties' – require a special capacity for their discernment, although these are truly objective properties located in the objects being judged.

1   Hume
2   Kant
3   Sibley
4   Further issues

1   Hume

The idea of taste was given a central position in the philosophy of art in the eighteenth century, and though, after Kant, it ceased to be an especially lively topic, it has returned in the twentieth century and continues to receive considerable attention.

For more than two centuries taste has been thought of, roughly, as the human capacity to respond to beauty, and in early theories – David Hume's, in particular – the capacity to elicit certain responses of taste was taken to be the mark of beauty. Thus Hume understands the 'standard of taste and beauty' to be located in judges of particularly qualified taste.

In the eighteenth century, taste is characterized in two ways, whose relation is not obvious. (1) Taste is thought of as the capacity to respond with affirmative and negative feelings to items of beauty and ugliness. (2) Taste is thought of as the ability to discriminate the elements present in some item. The term 'discriminating', as in the expression 'a person of discriminating taste', tends to meld senses (1) and (2), sometimes without regard to an apparent logical difference between them. In one sense, a person of taste is said to be someone whose personal preferences attach to objects of merit: the person is someone who likes good things and dislikes poor things. In the other sense, a person of taste is said to be someone who can distinguish and identify the objects they deal with. People with taste in wine, for instance, are thought of both as people who truly enjoy better wines and are put off by poor wines, and as people who can identify and describe the qualities of any wine they happen to taste, and can, perhaps, identify the vintage. Both these senses of 'taste' are present in Hume's texts:

> There is a *delicacy* of *taste* observable in some men, which very much resembles this *delicacy* of *passion*, and produces the same sensibility to beauty and deformity of every kind, as that does to prosperity and adversity, obligations and injuries.
>
> (1741: 4)

> Where the organs are so fine, as to allow nothing to escape them; and at the same time so exact as to perceive every ingredient in the composition: This we call delicacy of taste, whether we employ these terms in the literal or metaphorical sense.
>
> (1757: 235)

When taste is thought of as a basis for normative judgments of beauty or artistic excellence, then the two senses of taste can be set in a kind of pragmatic relation. The determination of the aesthetic quality of something (its beauty, ugliness, artistic excellence, artistic failure, etc.) is formulated in terms of how someone of adequate taste feels about the thing. The determination that this judge has adequate taste is in turn formulated in terms of the judge's ability to distinguish the components of the thing. This relation threatens to be circular unless either the merit of the thing or the qualifications of the judge can be independently established. Because those interested in the idea of taste have customarily hoped to define beauty in terms of the responses of judges of taste, their best recourse seems to be an attempt to show that the qualifications of the judge can be established independently of all considerations of beauty. Thus Hume says:

> But if we consider the matter aright, these [questions of whether someone has adequate taste] are questions of fact, not of sentiment. Whether any particular person be endowed with good sense and a delicate imagination, free from prejudice, may often be the subject of dispute, and be liable to great discussion and enquiry... Where these doubts occur, men can do no more than in other disputable questions, which are submitted to the understanding: They must produce the best arguments, that their invention suggests to them; they must acknowledge a true and decisive standard to exist somewhere, to wit, real existence and matter of fact.... It is sufficient for our present purpose, if

we have proved, that the taste of all individuals is not upon an equal footing.

(1757: 242)

This suggests a thesis that, in general, holds an object to be beautiful because it elicits pleasure in someone possessing the requisite capacity to respond, and it takes this requisite capacity to be identifiable in a person through the use of empirical, verifiable tests. Beauty is essentially a matter of human response, and is in this sense subjective, but since it is possible to authenticate the legitimacy of responses, the possession of taste is in this sense an objective fact; the attribution of beauty is thus a matter for empirical investigation (see HUME, D.).

2 Kant

Kant denies this possibility. He agrees that beauty is experienced essentially and solely in the exercise of taste, but denies that there is any empirical test that might determine whether taste is being properly exercised. Thus Kant supposes that someone making what they take to be 'a pure judgment of taste' is justified in supposing that the object being judged is indeed beautiful, but that neither they nor anyone else can in principle *prove* that the judgment is correct. Despite his insistence that the judgment of taste is not an objective judgment, Kant argues that it is a unique and essential illustration of the general human capacity to make judgments of any kind, including those which are not 'aesthetical' and hence 'subjective', but are genuinely what Kant calls 'logical', 'objective' judgments.

One peculiarity of Kant's work is that he initially develops his theory of taste exclusively in terms of objects of nature. Later he turns to the consideration of the exercise of taste in judgments of works of art, developing an elaborate theory of such judgments, but declaring that judgments of beauty made about works of art are inevitably 'impure', because the judge is implicitly aware that the object was *made*. Kant's argument for the impurity of such judgments is elliptical. It turns on his conviction that a pure judgment of taste does not involve the application of a predicate concept, while the recognition that an object was made involves a recognition that some concept was instrumental in the making of the object, this concept then inevitably figuring in one's taste-judgment of the object (see KANT, I. §12).

3 Sibley

In the mid-twentieth century the idea of taste was reconceived, notably in the work of Frank Sibley and the many commentators on his work. Whereas eighteenth-century theorists conceived taste either as the capacity to feel pleasure in the presence of certain objects or as the capacity to discern the properties of objects, Sibley conceives it as the ability to detect various special properties he calls 'aesthetic properties'. Although it is not clear whether these properties are distinguished by requiring taste for their perception, or whether taste itself is understood as the ability to perceive them, Sibley gives them an uncircular, working characterization by enumerating some of them: they are the properties named by 'graceful', 'elegant' and 'delicate', for instance, and he calls these words 'aesthetic terms'. He is content to identify aesthetic terms, in general, as terms similar to those that he enumerates. Taste thus becomes the ability to apply aesthetic terms, presumably by virtue of one's possession of the associated 'aesthetic concepts'. He also characterizes the exercise of taste independently of any considerations of feeling. Sibley's conception of taste is thus similar to the eighteenth-century idea of taste as an ability to detect properties, but unlike eighteenth-century authors, he regards the relevant properties as members of a special class, and again, unlike those authors, he does not treat the capacity for feeling as an essential aspect of the exercise of taste, while not denying that feelings might be attendant upon the exercise of taste. The success of Sibley's conception is a matter of current debate. Two questions deserve particular attention: (1) Can the ideas of taste and aesthetic properties be characterized independently of each other, or at least characterized in a manner that is not viciously circular? (2) Is there an adequate criterion for distinguishing aesthetic properties from non-aesthetic properties?

4 Further issues

It may be thought that the only point of interest in the topic of taste arises from an epistemological conviction that judgments in aesthetics must be grounded in feelings, and, therefore, that the status of these feelings is implicated in any possibility of the objectivity of aesthetic judgments. This is not so. The question of one's personal taste retains philosophical interest even if there is an objective, independent standard of beauty, or if there can be no standard even in terms of taste.

In the first case, we imagine that there is some impersonal, objective measure of beauty. We will then think of a person of good taste as someone who has positive feelings about objects of merit (and, perhaps, negative feelings about meritless things). The question arises, should one like the objects of merit and dislike the inferior ones? What kind of obligation is this?

Contemporary moral theorists have tended to separate questions of normative assessments of actions from questions of motivation. That is, the question of which action should be carried out is kept independent of the question of whether an agent is moved to do that action. One might think of a morally perfect person – a saint, for example – as someone who is always moved to do, and feels like doing the right thing. Analogously, one might think of an aesthetically perfect person as someone who always likes beautiful things, and only likes beautiful things. The relation of moral judgment to moral motivation is far from clear, but there is no doubt that a remark like this is sensible: 'I knew that it was the right thing to do, but I could not bring myself to do it.' Is there a parallel in the aesthetic case? In other words, is it sensible to say, 'I know that it is a beautiful thing, but I cannot bring myself to care for it'?

If a person making judgments about beauty distinguishes between judging something to be beautiful and merely having a positive feeling for the object, then in what way, if any, are such judgments and feelings related? Could one have positive feelings without being inclined to judge the object beautiful? Could one judge the object beautiful in the absence of any positive feelings of one's own? An explanation of the relation between feeling and judgment – in a single person – seems to be required, even if individual feeling were not a factor in the formulation of a standard of beauty.

In the second case, we imagine that there is no objective measure of beauty, that people making such judgments are only expressing their own feelings and preferences. It may still be wondered whether individual people, exercising their taste in expressions of liking, disliking and preferences, display self-consistency. If these people like something, say, a work of art, and believe that they like it on account of some property the work possesses, then what if they fail to like some other work that possesses the same property? Besides this question of an individual's aesthetic consistency, there is also a question of how to understand the totality of one's taste. It is, after all, the same person that likes one thing, dislikes another, prefers one thing to another, etc. Since these exercises of taste exhibit and define a person's aesthetical self, it is necessary to ask how one would characterize the 'logic' of that self.

However taste is conceived, and however we are to understand its constitution and expression in a single person, there remains this question: is it better to have good taste? Why? Because it leads one to a life of greater pleasure? Surely that is but a hope, contingent on the objects one might encounter, and threatened by the fact that pleasures of taste are only some of the pleasures available to a person – they might be outweighed by other pleasures, the pursuit of which is blocked by the development and exercise of one's taste. Perhaps the possession of good or delicate taste makes for an improvement in one's well-being, and is necessary for enjoying a better life; it remains to explain why.

See also: AESTHETIC CONCEPTS; BEAUTY

References and further reading

Cohen, T. and Guyer, P. (eds) (1982) *Essays in Kant's Aesthetics*, Chicago, IL: University of Chicago. (Essays on various aspects of Kant's theory, with an editors' introduction which gives a brief description of the theory.)

Dickie, G. (1995) *The Century of Taste: Five Philosophers*, New York: Oxford University Press. (A critical history of the development of the theory of taste in Hutcheson, Gerard, Alison, Kant and Hume, which argues that Hume's version of the theory is the most defensible.)

Dickie, G., Sclafani, R. and Roblin, R. (eds) (1989) *Aesthetics: A Critical Anthology*, 2nd edn, New York: St Martin's Press. (A useful reprinting of Sibley's original essay, along with some criticism and an excellent guide to the literature. It also contains remarks offered by Sibley for this edition of the anthology.)

Guyer, P. (1993) 'The Standard of Taste and the "Most Ardent Desire of Society"', in T. Cohen, P. Guyer and H. Putnam (eds) *Pursuits of Reason: Essays in Honor of Stanley Cavell*, Lubbock, TX: Texas Tech University Press. (An excellent analysis of Hume's theory, relating it to his other work.)

—— (1979) *Kant and the Claims of Taste*, Cambridge, MA: Harvard University Press. (A difficult book, but the best one-volume discussion of Kant's theory of taste.)

* Hume, D. (1741) 'Of the Delicacy of Taste and Passion' and (1757) 'Of the Standard of Taste', both reprinted in Miller, E.F. (ed.) *David Hume, Essays: Moral, Political, and Literary*, Indianapolis, IN: Liberty Classics, revised edn 1987. (Also contains an excellent bibliographical account of the original publication of these essays in the eighteenth century.)

* Kant, I. (1790) *Kritik der Urtheilskraft*, Berlin: Lagarde & Friederich; trans. W.S. Pluhar, *Critique of Judgment*, Indianapolis, IN: Hackett Publishing Company, 1987. (The most reliable translation of Kant's text, with a somewhat contentious commentary.)

Kivy, P. (1976) *The Seventh Sense*, New York: Burt

Franklin. (A very readable history of Hutcheson's aesthetics and its influence in Britain.)
* Sibley, F. (1959) 'Aesthetic Concepts', *Philosophical Review* 68: 421–50. (The first exposition of Sibley's thesis.)
* —— (1963) 'Aesthetics Concepts: A Rejoinder', *Philosophical Review* 72: 79–83. (A clarification of Sibley's thesis by way of a response to early criticism.)
* —— (1965) 'Aesthetic and Nonaesthetic', *Philosophical Review* 74: 135–59. (An extension of the thesis.)

TED COHEN

ARTIST'S INTENTION

W.K. Wimsatt and Monroe C. Beardsley's famous paper 'The Intentional Fallacy' (1946) began one of the central debates in aesthetics and literary theory of the last half-century. By describing as a fallacy the belief that critics should take into account the author's intentions when interpreting or evaluating a piece of literature, they were rejecting an entrenched assumption of traditional criticism – and a natural one, since we normally take it for granted that understanding actions, including acts of speech and writing, requires a grasp of the intentions of the agent. But they were expressing an idea that has been greatly influential; it was a central claim of the 'new criticism', while the marginalization of the author is also a marked feature of structuralist and poststructuralist literary theory. Most of the debate over the artist's intentions – 'artist' here being used as a general word for writer, composer, painter, etc. – has centred on their relevance for interpreting art works. More particularly, the question has been whether external evidence about the artist's intentions – evidence not presented by the work itself – is relevant to determining the work's meaning.

1 Some arguments against the relevance of intention
2 Privacy and the mind
3 Art and experience
4 Meaning and use

1 Some arguments against the relevance of intention

(1) Wimsatt and Beardsley (1946) argue that the intention of the author is not available to the interpreter of a literary work. More recently, Jacques DERRIDA has claimed that writing remains essentially readable even when its original context is forgotten, inviting the conclusion that writing is able to fulfil its function without the reader needing to consider the intentions of the writer. In partial support of these claims, it seems reasonable to say, at least, that for many art works (those of Homer, say) we know little about any of the day-to-day thoughts their authors had about them at the time of their composition. Since this seems to present no serious impediment to the process of interpretation and criticism, some theorists conclude that questions of intention are irrelevant to interpretation.

(2) It seems uncontentious that the critic's basic task is to interpret and assess the work, for its own sake and not as a means of discovering something about the author. That the author had a certain intention is a fact about the author, not the work, and an intention with regard to the work is merely a seed in the author's mind, until the intention is carried out. If it is successfully carried out, say Wimsatt and Beardsley, the feature is now visible in the work and it is not necessary to consider the author's intentions, and if not, the feature has not been realized in the work, and so any concern with it is irrelevant to criticism.

(3) It is generally agreed that a work may have 'personal' features: it may be cheerful, sentimental, ironic, patriotic. However, Wimsatt and Beardsley say that the work is merely a dramatized response of an implied speaker to some situation. They rightly point out that there is no reason to identify the narrative voice with that of the author, but also suggest, more contentiously, that the tone of the work or any pervasive attitude to be found in it – cheerfulness, irony – are to be imputed to a purely literary or imaginary figure conjured up by the work and, if to the author at all, only by an act of biographical inference. Such an inference, by which we might try to pin down the author's intentions, would take critics beyond the task of criticism; as critics, their concern is solely with the attitudes portrayed in the work.

(4) Few would dispute that, without generally observed rules of grammar and usage, no particular use of language could be understood. Certainly, the work of an author who uses a private code of 'intended meanings' would be entirely opaque. But literature is accessible. Beardsley and Wimsatt conclude that (with the exception of certain 'private and semi-private' meanings that may have become part of a word's history) it is the public rules of syntax and semantics that determine a work's meaning, and not the intentions of the author. A similar argument has been used by structuralists, for whom meaning depends on the system of 'differences' established by words in relation to one another, and on 'codes' governing their usage. It is held that a necessary and sufficient condition of interpretation is a knowledge of the system of inter-related words and the applica-

tion of the codes, and that the author's intentions are therefore irrelevant.

2 Privacy and the mind

Argument (1) needs to be assessed in the context of recent developments in the philosophy of mind, and especially of the way these have helped advance the debate on other minds. In at least some versions, the argument appears to presuppose a dualistic conception of the mind by suggesting that a difficulty with intention-based criticism is that it could only work in those cases where authors have left detailed accounts of their intentions regarding their writing. But a widely preferred alternative to dualism – which we shall call the 'explanation' view – holds that we do not form our impressions of the mental states of others solely on the basis of their own reports, but according to the evidence of what they do more generally. We assume that their intentional activities are carried out in accordance with their beliefs and desires, and, starting from our available knowledge of their character and projects, construe those activities in the light of whatever motivational states best explain them. On this view any of their activities can reveal their intentions. Once it is accepted that, in general, someone's mental states show through in what they do, the question arises of why there should be any special difficulty about determining writers' intentions given the evidence of their writing itself. Those wishing to defend argument (1) have to show that the compositional activities of writers lack the evidential character of behaviour in general. They must establish this against the plausible claim that, among the various products of human effort, works of art are, if anything, unusually rich with the signs of their maker's cogitations and interests and so provide a wealth of evidence of the artist's intentions. (This reply to argument (1) can concede for the purpose of argument that no external evidence is available, though it is worth noting that even in the most challenging cases we are more than likely to have some general information about the historical and social circumstances of the artist, while more usually we also have a fair amount of biographical information.)

Opponents of intention-based criticism often point out that critics seldom feel bound by an artist's *avowals* of intention, and override them when they fail to make the best sense of what we find in the work. But this, while true, does not show that intentions are irrelevant to criticism. Proponents of the explanation view will want to point out that one kind of evidence for the presence of an intention can be overridden by another. Depending on the merits of the case, the artist's avowals (and other forms of external evidence) can sometimes be ignored in favour of indications of intention suggested by the configuration in the work itself.

3 Art and experience

Argument (2) rightly assumes that the critic's task is to understand the work itself, and that for a claim about the artist (for example, one concerning the artist's intentions) to be relevant to criticism, the claim must potentially make a difference to the way we experience the work. But this only tells us that the critic's interest in the artist should be for the sake of understanding the work and not vice versa. (An analogy: to inquire whether someone's hand gesture was intended as a greeting, not an insult, is in a sense to look past the gesture to the agent; but the answer would also help the inquirer to see the gesture itself more clearly.)

Argument (2) also seems to assume that a realized intention will automatically make its presence felt in the work, whereas an unrealized one can have no bearing on the experience of the work. These assumptions are called into question by a commonplace of the philosophy of perception, namely, that the way we experience an object is in part a product of our mental orientation towards it. In that case, even if an intention is realized we may sometimes not see that the work is the outcome of that intention unless alerted to the fact by external evidence. And if it is not realized, external evidence about the unrealized intention could conceivably modify and enrich the way the work is experienced. It is worth noting, finally, that the very idea of a straightforward distinction between internal and external evidence is called into question once it is conceded that what is visible in a work is modified by what is known about it.

Turning to argument (3), it must be conceded in its favour that in calling a piece of fiction or a poem cheerful we are not usually saying or implying that the writer felt cheerful at the time of writing it. But in the case of some personal qualities, the presence of the quality in the writing does seem to depend on whether the writer wrote the piece in an appropriate state of mind. Nor does it always seem possible to reconstrue the apparent viewpoint of the writer as a merely notional viewpoint within the work. Perhaps the underlying principle of argument (3) is that in aesthetic matters what counts is whether the work presents an *impression* of a certain attitude, while it is irrelevant whether that happens to coincide with what the artist felt. One difficulty with this is that the impression is likely to vary with what we take the underlying attitude of the artist to have been. A defender of the principle might now say that in that case the work is ambiguous, and that we should always apply the most charitable reading, again disregarding what the artist's actual attitude might have been. But this may be simplistic. Suppose that according to the charitable reading a poem expresses sympathy for the victims of a war, but that external evidence shows that rather than (a) expressing an actually felt sympathy, the poet had (b) perfectly contrived the mere impression of sympathy in order cynically to exploit a general climate of concern for the victims. Someone tempted by the 'impression' principle should carefully consider whether it really is critically irrelevant that we have a case of (a) or (b). Another difficulty with the 'impression' principle is that some of the features we ascribe to writing cannot *but* be features of the writer. We cannot ascribe virtues like intelligence, perceptiveness or wit to a piece of writing without being prepared to ascribe these to the writer. And similarly, it is hard to avoid the implication that, when we attribute certain shortcomings to writing – pretentiousness, sentimentality, narcissism – we are implicitly criticizing the writer.

4 Meaning and use

Argument (4) turns on the claim that literary works are composed in a public medium. Certainly, poets and novelists do not choose the meanings they give to words but work within the constraints of general usage. But defenders of (4) need more than this to make their case. They need to establish that a knowledge of syntax, semantics and general usage is not merely necessary but also *sufficient* for interpretation. Counting against this is a commonplace of linguistic theory, namely, that when a sentence is encountered in isolation, the semantics and syntax of the language will enable native speakers to grasp only its propositional content, and that until the particular circumstances of its use have shown the user's specific intentions, it has been understood only in an attenuated sense. But perhaps a defender of (4) will argue that *literary* interpretation is not concerned with those aspects of meaning which are associated with intention. This, however, seems implausible, because it threatens to exclude tonal features of writing like irony and sarcasm, as well as the import of metaphors, allusions and the like, all of which depend on the intentions with which words are used. Alternatively, the claim might be that a work of art can be said to have whatever features of meaning most enhance the resulting aesthetic impression, provided that, given its syntactic and semantic character, the work can plausibly be seen or imagined *as* the outcome of intentions associated with that meaning. But this is also an extreme claim. Consider a painting that is a portrait of A. You could treat it as though it were intended as a portrait of B (the effect could be as satisfying as you like) but this would not make it a portrait of B. Returning to literature, a well-known problem case is Blake's use of the phrase 'dark satanic mills' in his poem Jerusalem. The phrase has often been interpreted as a reference to the factories of the Industrial Revolution, but it is now commonly accepted that this reading is historically impossible. Suppose, then, that Blake was not indeed referring to factories, but that the impossible reading is, none the less, more satisfying than more plausible ones. One reason for ruling it out, despite its appeal, would be that it is not, strictly speaking, an interpretation of Blake's poem, since we know that Blake's poem does not refer to factories. Someone might attempt to legitimate the unintended but supposedly more attractive reading of the poem by saying that it is a valid critical activity to view a poem simply as a timeless verbal configuration, ignoring constitutive features it acquired through the context in which it was written. However, there appears to be only a difference of degree between a case like this and, say, the case of a free adaptation of *Macbeth* which transposes the play into a present day political setting with familiar contemporary politicians in leading roles – surely a case of a new play created out of the old. We may still call this an 'interpretation' of *Macbeth*, but then we are talking about a special activity, whose existence, however welcome, is no threat or rival to interpretation as exegesis.

See also: ART, UNDERSTANDING OF; ARTISTIC EXPRESSION; ARTISTIC INTERPRETATION§3; ARTISTIC STYLE §4; BARTHES, R.; INTENTION; STRUCTURALISM IN LITERARY THEORY

References and further reading

Armstrong, D.M. (1970) 'The Nature of Mind', in C.V. Borst (ed.) *The Mind/Brain Identity Theory*, London: Macmillan, 67–79. (A clear exposition and defence of what is referred to, in the discussion of argument (1), as the explanation view of the mind.)

Cioffi, F. (1963) 'Intention and Interpretation in Criticism', reprinted in D. Newton-De Molina (ed.) *On Literary Intention*, Edinburgh: Edinburgh University Press, 1974, 55–73. (A famous response to Beardsley and Wimsatt; particularly relevant to the issues raised by argument (1).)

Davies, S. (1982) 'The Aesthetic Relevance of Authors' and Painters' Intentions', *Journal of Aesthetics and Art Criticism* 41 (1): 65–76. (A good discussion of issues bearing on argument (4).)

Fish, S.E. (1982) 'With the Compliments of the

Author: Reflections on Austin and Derrida', *Critical Inquiry* 8 (4): 693–721. (Discusses, with references, Derrida's version of argument (1) mentioned in §2, and offers a relatively lucid interpretation and defence of a deconstructionist view of literary interpretation.)

Lyas, C. (1983) 'The Relevance of the Author's Sincerity', in P. Lamarque (ed.) *Philosophy and Fiction*, Aberdeen: Aberdeen University Press, 17–37. (Especially helpful for coming to grips with arguments (3) and (4).)

Mele, A.R. and Livingston, P. (1992) 'Intentions and Interpretations', *Modern Language Notes* 107: 931–49. (Well informed on relevant work in the philosophy of mind and especially illuminating on argument (1).)

Sturrock, J. (1986) *Structuralism*, London: Paladin, ch. 4, 103–35. (A brief and clear introduction to structuralism as a critical movement. Shows the structuralist version of argument (4).)

* Wimsatt, W.K. and Beardsley, M.C. (1946) 'The Intentional Fallacy', reprinted in D. Newton-De Molina (ed.) *On Literary Intention*, Edinburgh: Edinburgh University Press, 1974, 1–13. (The *locus classicus* of the 'intentional fallacy' debate; presents versions of all the arguments discussed in this entry.)

Wollheim, R. (1980) 'Criticism as Retrieval', in *Art and Its Objects*, 2nd edn, Cambridge: Cambridge University Press, 185–204. (Especially insightful on the issues raised by argument (2).)

PAUL TAYLOR

ARYA SAMAJ

The Arya Samaj (ārya-samāj, 'The Association of Nobles') is a Hindu reform movement founded in 1875 by Swami Dayanand Saraswati (1824–83). Based on the supposition that the true religion of India was put forth in the ancient Vedas, rather than in later epics and cycles of myths, the principal aim of the Arya Samaj is to purge modern Hinduism of beliefs and practices associated with the devotional and mythic literature of India. Condemning the hereditary caste system and dismissing the practice of using icons and idols in worship, the society favoured a more rationalistic, humanistic and nationalistic form of Hinduism as India entered the modern era.

The Arya Samaj, a prominent Hindu reform movement, was founded in the nineteenth century by Swami Dayanand Saraswati. Also known as Mul Shankar and nicknamed 'the Luther of India', Dayanand was born in 1824 into a Brahmanical family of Gujarat. As a boy he always doubted the divinity of idols of Hindu gods. The death of his sister turned him to pondering the problems of life and death. Consequently, he ran away from home and wandered for many years in search of a guru. At last in Mathura he found a blind teacher named Swami Brijanand, who taught him the philosophical interpretations of the Vedas, the most ancient collection of sacred writings in India.

Through his study of the Vedas, Swami Dayanand became convinced that selfish and ignorant priests had pervaded the Hindu religion during the post-Vedic period. Part of the reason for this corruption, he believed, were the Purāṇas, the eighteen collections of myths and legends of gods and heroes that form the basis of most devotional forms of Hinduism in the medieval and modern periods. These texts, which had informally acquired the status of sacred scripture and the contents of which had become much more familiar to most Hindus than the Vedas, were, Dayanand believed, full of false teachings. Linking priestly corruption with these (for him, apocryphal) Purāṇas, and seeing both priestly and textual corruption as the source of contemporary social problems, Dayanand began in 1863 to preach his doctrines publicly. Twelve years later, in 1875, he established the Arya Samaj (*ārya-samāj*, 'The Association of Nobles') in Bombay.

Dayanand regarded the Vedas as eternal and infallible and laid down his own interpretations of them in a book entitled *Satyārth Prakāś*. He considered the Vedas to be the inspired word of God and the fount of all knowledge. He rejected all later religious thought on the grounds of its conflict with the Vedas. Thus, unlike most traditional Hindu thinkers, Dayanand repudiated the authority of the post-Vedic texts, such as the Purāṇas, and regarded the epics, the *Rāmāyaṇa* and the *Mahābhārata*, as literary treasures and nothing more. His total dependence on the Vedas and their infallibility gives his teachings an orthodox colouring, for in orthodox Hindu thought, scriptural infallibility means that human reason is subordinate to sacred texts. Despite this appearance of orthodoxy, Dayanand's approach in fact has rationalistic and humanistic leanings, because the Vedas, though revealed, are to be interpreted by himself and other human beings. Thus, in the final analysis, Dayanand insisted that individual reason is the deciding factor in arriving at religious knowledge.

In keeping with his rejection of the mythology of the Purāṇas, Dayanand condemned the idolatry associated with their mythology. He also rejected the hereditary system of caste, giving it instead an ethical and occupational interpretation, somewhat as the Buddha had done. He questioned the authority and social superiority of Brahmans, and was against animal sacrifices and long pilgrimages. A confirmed nationalist, Dayanand believed that 'Aryans were the chosen people, the Vedas the chosen gospel and India the chosen land'. So the Arya Samaj looked upon the Vedas as India's 'rock of ages' and coined the slogan 'go back to the Vedas'.

The Arya Samaj, like the Brahmo Samaj, worked courageously to eliminate the social evils that it believed had crept into Hindu society. It was more a social reform movement than a strictly religious or philosophical school. In the area of social reform, the Arya Samaj struggled against child marriage and campaigned to fix the minimum age of marriage for boys and girls at 25 and 16 respectively. It advocated a status for women equal to that of men. Intercaste marriage was encouraged, as was the remarriage of widows. In addition to advocating progressive reforms, the Arya Samaj undertook charitable works during national disasters such as earthquakes, famines and floods, and it opened orphanages and homes for widows, thereby giving a new lease of life to the distressed.

The leaders of the Arya Samaj were aware of the supreme importance of education, but sharp differences arose within the movement over the question of the best system. One faction favoured the ancient system of Hindu education. One of its leaders, Swami Shardhanand, started the 'Gurukul' near Haridwar in 1902 to propagate the more traditional ideas. Another faction recognized the value of British education and established a network of 'Dayanand Anglo-Vedic Schools and Colleges' for both boys and girls throughout the country. Lala Hansraj played a leading part in this effort.

In order to counter Christian and Muslim missionary activities, the Arya Samaj started the *śuddhi* (purity) movement for the reconversion of those Hindus who had been unwillingly or forcibly converted to Islam or Christianity. They could now be readmitted to Hinduism after passing through a ceremony of purification. While the Arya Samaj's work in social reforms tended to unite people, its religious work tended, though perhaps unconsciously, to work against the growing sense of national unity arising among the Hindus, Muslims, Parsis, Sikhs and Christians of India.

Though founded in Bombay, the Arya Samaj found its true home in Punjab, and it later spread far and wide over the whole of northern India. After Dayanand's death in 1883, the work he had begun was continued by a band of followers. Even today, the spirit of the Samaj is active in the towns and villages of India, as well as in communities of Indians who have emigrated to other parts of the world.

See also: BRAHMO SAMAJ

References and further reading

* Dayanand Saraswati, Swami *Satyārth Prakāś*, trans. C. Bharadwaja, *Light of Truht* [sic], New Delhi: Saradeshik Arya Pratinidhi, 1975. (An introduction to the Vedas and their interpretation.)
—— *Ṛgvedādibhāṣyabhūmikā*, trans. Paramanand, *An Introduction to the Four Vedas*, New Delhi: Meharchand Lachhmandas Publications, 1981. (An introduction to the Vedas and their interpretation.)
Lajpat Rai, L. (1967) *A History of the Arya Samaj: An Account of its Origin, Doctrines and Activities, with a Biographical Sketch of the Founder*, Bombay: Orient Longman. (A very good book for the beginner, giving the historical development and basic principles of Arya Samaj, along with a biography of its founder, Swami Dayanand Saraswati.)
Sen, N.B. (1964) *Wit and Wisdom of Swami Dayanand*, New Delhi: New Book Society of India. (Sayings of Dayanand Saraswati classified under 250 subjects.)
Sharma, S.K. (1985) *Social Movements and Social Change: A Study of Arya Samaj and Untouchables in Punjab*, Delhi: B.R. Publishing Corporation. (A monograph describing the impact of the Arya Samaj movement on the untouchables in the northern Indian province of Punjab.)

K.S. KUMAR

ĀRYADEVA *see* BUDDHISM, MĀDHYAMIKA: INDIA AND TIBET

ASCETICISM

The term 'asceticism' is derived from the Greek word askēsis, *which referred originally to the sort of exercise, practice or training in which athletes engage. Asceticism may be characterized as a voluntary, sustained and systematic programme of self-discipline and self-denial in which immediate sensual gratifications are renounced in order to attain some valued spiritual or mental state. Ascetic practices are to be found in all the major religious traditions of the world, yet they have often been criticized by philosophers. Some argue that the religious doctrines that they presuppose are false or unreasonable. Others contend that they express a preference for pain that humans cannot consistently act upon.*

The chief ascetic practices are fasting, sexual continence, living in seclusion, living in voluntary poverty, and inflicting pain upon oneself. Such practices are elements in all the major religious traditions, and at least some of them are found in most of the religions of non-literate people that anthropologists have studied. Some philosophical movements, such as Stoicism, which is not ordinarily classified as a religion, also endorse certain ascetic practices (see STOICISM §19). Ascetic practices are relatively common in Jainism, Tibetan Buddhism, early Christianity and various branches of Hinduism (see JAINA PHILOSOPHY §3; BUDDHIST PHILOSOPHY, INDIAN §2; SANCTIFICATION §1; HINDU PHILOSOPHY §5); they are relatively uncommon in Confucianism, Zoroastrianism and Judaism. All the major religions condemn extreme forms of asceticism, but pathological excesses have appeared in every tradition.

Some forms of asceticism involve an attitude of detachment from worldly things. This is expressed in the scriptural injunction to be in the world but not of it and in the *Bhagavad Gītā*'s recommendation of renunciation in action but not of action. Max Weber described the disciplined, methodical and controlled pursuit of one's vocation in the world, as service to God that is characteristic of certain kinds of Protestant Christianity, as 'inner-worldly asceticism', because worldly success is valued not for its own sake but only as a confirmation of one's salvation.

In theistic religions the ultimate aim of ascetic practices is to promote union with the deity. Many Christian ascetics take self-inflicted pain to further their identification with the suffering Jesus who is God the Son. In Christianity, ascetic practices also have other functions. One is penitential. Self-denial is considered an appropriate way to make reparation for past misdeeds that have offended God. Another is disciplinary. Unruly bodily appetites are, in the fallen human condition, the source of much wrongdoing, and asceticism can serve to check and subdue or even to extirpate them.

Non-theistic religions propose various ends for ascetic practices. In Hindu traditions, awareness is fostered of one's true self (*ātman*), which is identical with the ground of all being (*Brahman*). Theravāda Buddhism promotes the extinction of desire, which in turn leads to freedom from suffering and the illusions of the phenomenal world and to ultimate liberation (*nirvāṇa*) (see NIRVĀṆA). In such traditions, ascetic practices, particularly the self-infliction of pain, also function as penance for past evil deeds in this life or in previous incarnations.

The rationale for a particular ascetic practice varies from one religious tradition to another. Christianity, for example, recommends fasting on the grounds that it produces discomfort which can function either penitentially or as a means to identification with the suffering deity, while Yoga recommends it on the ground that it alleviates discomfort by eventually rendering one oblivious to the body and thus better able to direct energy to meditation (see BUDDHISM, YOGĀCĀRA SCHOOL OF). There are also differences concerning who should engage in the more severe forms of ascetic discipline. Often they are reserved for people with special religious vocations, such as monks or nuns. Ordinary believers are frequently told that the extreme asceticism of saints such as Simeon Stylites, who lived atop a pillar for nearly forty years, is to be admired but not imitated.

It is not surprising that asceticism has not found favour with most of those who subscribe to the worldview of secular modernity. It has been criticized by some important modern philosophers. Bentham (1789) argued that humans cannot consistently practise asceticism because they are by nature motivated to seek pleasure and to avoid pain (see BENTHAM, J. §2). Typically, however, ascetics do not seek pain for its own sake but rather as a means to something they take to be a great good such as union with God. That humans seek painful medical treatment for the sake of their health suffices to show that they can practise asceticism, including the infliction of pain on themselves, if they perceive doing so as a means to some good end. Nietzsche represented ascetics as weak people who, being unable to exercise power over the strong, express their will to power by turning it on themselves and exercising power over their own appetites (see NIETZSCHE, F. §6). He also portrayed asceticism as a means by which religious leaders exercise power over their followers. It seems clear that such things are true in some cases, but history also provides examples of strong ascetics who, like Ignatius Loyola, were capable of exercising power over others yet chose instead to devote themselves to ascetic practices at certain stages of their lives.

Some critics are prepared to concede that moderate asceticism makes sense within religious contexts, but argue that it should be rejected because the religious assumptions offered to justify it are false or unreasonable. For example, it is sometimes alleged that asceticism presupposes an untenable dualism of mind and body or of matter and spirit (see DUALISM). There are, however, non-dualistic forms of asceticism, and dualism, though it faces philosophical difficulties, has not been shown to be untenable. It is also alleged that belief in the existence of God or of Brahman is false or, at least, irrational belief (see GOD, ARGUMENTS FOR THE EXISTENCE OF).

See also: RELIGION AND MORALITY; SELF-CONTROL; SEXUALITY, PHILOSOPHY OF; SUFFERING; SUFFERING, BUDDHIST VIEWS OF ORIGINATION OF

References and further reading

* *Bhagavad Gītā* (*c*.400–100 BC), trans. E. Deutsch, *The Bhagavad Gītā*, Lanham, MD: University Press of America, 1982. (Presents an ideal of asceticism that has influenced Hindu traditions.)
* Bentham, J. (1789) *An Introduction to the Principles of Morals and Legislation*, ed. J.H. Burns and H.L.A. Hart, revised F. Rosen, Oxford: Clarendon Press, 1996. (Contains Bentham's argument against asceticism.)
  Hardman, O. (1924) *The Ideals of Asceticism: An Essay in the Comparative Study of Religion*, New York: Macmillan. (A readable but somewhat dated overview, written from an explicitly Christian perspective.)
  Kaelber, W.O. (1987) 'Asceticism', in M. Eliade (ed.) *The Encyclopedia of Religion*, New York: Macmillan. (A brief and up-to-date overview of religious asceticism.)
* Nietzsche, F. (1887) *Zur Genealogie der Moral*, trans. W. Kaufmann and R.J. Hollingdale, *On the Genealogy of Morals*, New York: Random House, 1989. (The third essay presents Nietzsche's most fully developed critique of ascetic ideals.)
  Oman, J.C. (1903) *The Mystics, Ascetics and Saints of India*; repr. New Delhi: Cosmo Publications, 1984. (A classic collection of information about Hindu and Muslim ascetics in India that is very readable if not always credible.)
* Weber, M. (1904–05) *Die protestantischen Sekten und der Geist des Kapitalismus*, trans. T. Parsons, *The Protestant Ethic and the Spirit of Capitalism*, London: Routledge, 1985. (Discusses 'innerworldly asceticism'.)
  Wellman, C. (1967) 'Asceticism', in P. Edwards (ed.) *The Encyclopedia of Philosophy*, New York: Macmillan. (Contains a brief survey of philosophical arguments for and against asceticism.)

PHILIP L. QUINN

ASCLEPIADES *see* HELLENISTIC MEDICAL EPISTEMOLOGY

ASH'ARIYYA AND MU'TAZILA

The Mu'tazila – literally 'those who withdraw themselves' – movement was founded by Wasil bin 'Ata' in the second century AH (eighth century AD). Its members were united in their conviction that it was necessary to give a rationally coherent account of Islamic beliefs. In addition to having an atomistic view of the universe, they generally held to five theological principles, of which the two most important were the unity of God and divine justice. The former led them to deny that the attributes of God were distinct entities or that the Qur'an was eternal, while the latter led them to assert the existence of free will.

Ash'ariyya – named after its founding thinker, al-Ash'ari – was the foremost theological school in Sunni Islam. It had its origin in the reaction against the excessive rationalism of the Mu'tazila. Its members insisted that reason must be subordinate to revelation. They accepted the cosmology of the Mu'tazilites but put forward a nuanced rejection of their theological principles.

1   **Historical survey**
2   **Cosmology**
3   **The five principles**
4   **The unity of God**
5   **Divine justice and human destiny**

1   Historical survey

The Mu'tazila originated in Basra at the beginning of the second century AH (eighth century AD). In the following century it became, for a period of some thirty years, the official doctrine of the caliphate in Baghdad. This patronage ceased in AH 238/AD 848 when al-Mutawakkil reversed the edict of al-Ma'mun, which had required officials to publicly profess that the Qur'an was the created word of God. By this time, however, Mu'tazilites were well established in many other centres of Islamic learning, especially in Persia, and had split into two rival factions, the Basran School and the Baghdad School. Although their links with these two cities became increasingly tenuous, both schools flourished until the middle of the fifth century AH (eleventh century AD), and the Basran School only finally disappeared with the Mongol invasions at the beginning of the seventh century AH (thirteenth century AD). After the demise of the Mu'tazila as a distinct movement, Mu'tazilite doctrine – by now regarded as heretical by Sunnis – continued to be influential amongst the Shi'ites in Persia and the Zaydis in the Yemen.

Al-Ash'ari (d. AH 324/AD 935) was a pupil of Abu 'Ali al-Jubba'i (d. AH 303/AD 915), the head of the Basran School. A few years before his master's death, al-Ash'ari announced dramatically that he repented of having been a Mu'tazilite and pledged himself to oppose the Mu'tazila. In taking this step he capitalized on popular discontent with the excessive rationalism of the Mu'tazilites, which had been steadily gaining ground since their loss of official patronage half a century earlier. After his conversion, al-Ash'ari continued to use the dialectic method in theology but insisted that reason must be subservient to revelation. It is not possible to discuss al-Ash'ari's successors in detail here, but it should be noted that from the second half of the sixth century AH (twelfth century AD) onwards, the movement adopted the language and concepts of the Islamic philosophers whose views they sought to refute. The most significant thinkers among these later Ash'arites were AL-GHAZALI and Fakhr al-Din AL-RAZI.

2 Cosmology

Popular accounts of the teaching of the Mu'tazilites usually concentrate on their distinctive theological doctrines. To the philosopher, however, their cosmology, which was accepted by the Ash'ariyya and other theological schools, is a more appropriate starting point.

To the Mu'tazila, the universe appears to consist of bodies with different qualities: some are living while others are inanimate, some are mobile while others are stationary, some are hot and some are cold, and so on. Moreover, one and the same body may take on different qualities at different times. For instance, a stone may be mobile when rolling down a hill but stationary when it reaches the bottom, or hot when left in the sun but cold after a long night. Yet there are some qualities which some bodies cannot acquire; for example, stones are invariably inanimate, never living. How are the differences between bodies, and between one and the same body at different times, to be explained?

The answer given by the Mu'tazilites is that all bodies are composed of identical material substances (*jawahir*) or atoms (*ajza'*), on which God bestows various incorporeal accidents (*a'rad*). This view was first propounded by Dirar ibn 'Amr (d. *c.*AH 200/AD 815) and elaborated by Abu al-Hudhayl (d. AH 227/AD 841 or later), both of whom were early members of the Basran School. Abu al-Hudhayl held that isolated atoms are invisible mathematical points. The only accidents which they can be given are those which affect their ability to combine with other atoms, such as composition or separation, motion or rest. Conglomerates of atoms, on the other hand, can be given many other accidents such as colours, tastes, odours, sounds, warmth and coldness, which is why we perceive them as different bodies. Some of these accidents are indispensable, hence the differences between bodies, whereas others can be bestowed or withdrawn, thus explaining the differences between one and the same body at different times.

This account of the world gained rapid acceptance amongst Islamic theologians, although to begin with it was rejected by two Mu'tazilites of the Basran School, al-Nazzam (d. AH 221/AD 836) and Abu Bakr al-Asamm (d. AH 201/AD 816?). The former, who was Abu al-Hudhayl's nephew, argued that atoms which were mere mathematical points would not be able to combine with one another and that, rather than being composed of atoms, bodies must therefore be infinitely divisible. Abu al-Hudhayl replied that God's bestowal of the accident of composition on an isolated atom made it three-dimensional and hence capable of combining (see ATOMISM, ANCIENT). Al-Asamm, on the other hand, objected to the notion of accidents, arguing that since only bodies are visible their qualities cannot have an independent existence. Abu al-Hudhayl retorted that such a view was contrary to divine laws because the legal obligations and penalties for their infringement were not directed at the whole person but at one of his 'accidents', such as his prostration in prayer or his flagellation for adultery.

3 The five principles

According to the Muslim heresiographers, who are our main source of information about the Mu'tazila, members of the movement adhered to five principles, which were clearly enunciated for the first time by Abu al-Hudhayl. These were: (1) the unity of God; (2) divine justice; (3) the promise and the threat; (4) the intermediate position; and (5) the commanding of good and forbidding of evil.

The first and second principles are of major importance and will be discussed in detail below. The third principle is really only an adjunct of the second, and is here treated as such. The fourth principle is a relatively unimportant doctrine which probably only figures in the list because it was thought to have been the reason for the Mu'tazila's emergence as a distinct movement; it is said that when Hasan al-Basri was questioned about the position of the

Muslim who committed a grave sin, his pupil Wasil bin 'Ata' said that such a person was neither a believer nor an unbeliever, but occupied an intermediate position. Hasan was displeased and remarked, 'He has withdrawn from us (*i'tazila 'anna*)', at which Wasil withdrew from his circle and began to propagate his own teaching. The historicity of this story has been questioned on the ground that there are several variants: according to one version the person who withdrew was Wasil's associate 'Amr ibn 'Ubayd (d. AH 141/AD 761), and according to another the decisive break came in the time of Hasan's successor Qatada. Moreover it is noteworthy that at least one influential member of the Basran school, Abu Bakr al-Asamm, rejected the notion of an intermediate position and argued that the grave sinner remained a believer because of his testimony of faith and his previous good deeds. This was also the view of the Ash'arites.

The fifth principle, which is derived from several passages in the Qur'an (for example, Surah 9: 71), and which the Mu'tazilites understood as an obligation incumbent on all Muslims to intervene in the affairs of state, was rarely put into practice. For the Ash'arites, the commanding of good and forbidding of evil was the prerogative of the head of state, who acted on behalf of the Muslim community.

4 The unity of God

The first half of the *shahada*, the Muslim declaration of faith, is the testimony that there is no god besides Allah. Thus the numerical unity of God is axiomatic for all Muslims. Nevertheless, although the Qur'an explicitly asserts that God is one, and equally explicitly rejects polytheism and the Christian doctrine of the Trinity, it speaks of God's 'hands' (Surah 38: 75), 'eyes' (Surah 54: 14) and 'face' (Surah 55: 27), and of his seating himself on his throne (Surah 20: 5), thus apparently implying that he has a body. Moreover, in describing the radiant faces of believers 'looking towards their Lord' on the Day of Resurrection (Surah 75: 23), it suggests the possibility of a beatific vision.

However, the Mu'tazilites emphatically rejected such notions, insisting that God is not merely numerically one but also that he is a simple essence. This led them to deny that he has a body or any of the characteristics of bodies such as colour, form, movement and localization in space; hence he cannot be seen, in this world or the next. The Mu'tazila therefore interpreted the Qur'anic anthropomorphisms as metaphors – God's 'hands' are his blessing, God's 'eyes' are his knowledge, his 'face' is his essence and his seating himself on his throne is his omnipotence – and argued that, since the Qur'an elsewhere asserts that 'sight cannot reach Him' (Surah 6: 103), the phrase *ila rabbiha nazira* means 'waiting for their Lord' rather than looking towards him.

Some of the later Ash'arites accepted the Mu'tazilite position on the Qur'anic anthropomorphisms. In al-Ash'ari's own view, however, they are neither to be dismissed in this way nor understood to imply that God has a body like human beings. They are 'revealed attributes', whose existence must be affirmed without seeking to understand how (*bi-la kayfa*). Furthermore, the possibility of beatific vision depends not on God's embodiment, but on his existence. God can show us everything which exists. Since he exists, he can therefore show us himself. Hence the statement that 'sight cannot reach Him' must apply only to this world, where he impedes our vision.

Much more problematic than the Qur'an's anthropomorphisms are the adjectives which it employs to describe God. He is said, for instance, to be 'living', 'knowing', 'powerful' and 'eternal'. If we deny these qualities to God, we must then attribute to him their opposites, which are imperfections. But God is by definition free from imperfections; therefore God must always have had these qualities. But does this mean that he possesses the attributes of 'life', 'knowledge', 'power' and 'eternity' and that they are distinct from his essence? The Mu'tazilites reasoned that this was impossible because it would imply plurality in the Godhead. When we speak of God as 'living', 'knowing', 'powerful' and 'eternal', we are, in their opinion, merely considering him from different points of view. God's 'attributes of essence' (*sifat al-dhat*), as they are generally called, are a product of the limitations and the plurality of our own intellectual faculties; in reality, they are identical with God's essence. Thus, according to al-Ash'ari (*Maqalat*: 484), Abu al-Hudhayl maintained that 'God is knowing by virtue of a knowledge which is His own essence' and that he is likewise powerful, living and eternal by a power, a life and an eternity which are none other than his own essence. Al-Nazzam expressed this even more forcefully when he said, 'If I say that God is knowing, I merely confirm the divine essence and deny in it all ignorance. If I say that God is powerful, living and so forth, I am only confirming the divine essence and denying in it all powerlessness, mortality and so forth' (*Maqalat*: 484).

Al-Ash'ari himself rejected this reductionist account of the 'attributes of essence' which made them artefacts of human reason, but his arguments for doing so are far from compelling. He alleged that since in the case of human beings knowing implies possessing knowledge as an entity distinct from the knower, the situation with God must be analogous. Hardly more cogent is the claim that if God knew by his essence, he would be knowledge. Finally, al-Ash'ari's assertion that the 'attributes of essence' are neither other than God nor identical with him is simply a retreat into paradox. However, al-Ash'ari was not alone in wishing neither to affirm the independent existence of these attributes nor to deny it outright. Al-Jubba'i's son Abu Hashim (d. AH 321/ AD 933) attempted to resolve the problem by introducing the idea of 'state' (*hal*). A state is not something which exists or which does not exist; it is not a thing and it cannot be known in itself, only with an essence. Nevertheless it has an ontological reality. According to Abu Hashim, there are in God permanent states such as 'his mode of being knowing' (*kawnuhu 'aliman*), 'his mode of being powerful' and so forth, which give rise to distinct qualicatives. This compromise was accepted by many of Abu Hashim's fellow Mu'tazilites of the Basran school, but was unanimously rejected by those of Baghdad.

In addition to the attributes of essence, the Qur'an employs a whole series of adjectives such as 'providing' and 'forgiving', which describe God in relation to his creatures. It is easy to imagine a time when God did not have these attributes. The Mu'tazilites called these 'attributes of action' (*sifat al-fi'l*) because they deemed them to come into being when God acts. In their reckoning, God's 'speech' belongs to this category of attributes, for it does not make sense to think of his commandments as existing before the creation of the beings to whom they are addressed. Thus the Qur'an itself, although the Word of God, is temporal and not eternal. It was created initially in the 'guarded tablet' (Surah 85: 22) and subsequently recreated in the hearts of those who memorize it, on the tongues of those who recite it and on the written page. Although not denying the existence of attributes of action, al-Ash'ari insisted that 'speech' – along with 'hearing' and 'vision' – was an attribute of essence. He argued that if God's word were not eternal, it would have had to have been brought into being. Furthermore, since it is an attribute, it could not have been brought into being other than in an essence in which it resides. In which case either God brought it into being in himself, or he brought it into being in another. But if he had brought it into being in himself, he would be the locus of things which come into being, which is impossible. If, on the contrary, he had brought it into being in another, it is the other, and not God, who would have spoken by the word.

5 Divine justice and human destiny

In addition to championing the unity of God, the Mu'tazilites stressed his justice. They held that good and evil are objective and that the moral values of actions are intrinsic to them and can be discerned by human reason. Hence God's justice obliges him to act in accordance with the moral law. For instance, he is thus bound to stand by his promise to reward the righteous with paradise and his threat to punish the wicked with hellfire. More importantly, the reward and punishment which he metes out must be merited by creatures endowed with free will (see FREE WILL). Thus although the Qur'an says that God guides and leads astray those whom he wills (Surah 14: 4), it cannot mean that he predestines them. This and similar texts refer rather to what will happen after the judgement, when the righteous will be guided to paradise and the wicked will be caused to stray far from it. With regard to our acts in this world, God creates in us the power to perform an act but we are free to choose whether or not to perform it.

Many of the Mu'tazilites held that the principle of justice made it requisite for God always to do for people what was to their greatest advantage. Al-Jubba'i went as far as to claim that God is bound to prolong the life of an unbeliever if he knows that the latter will eventually repent. In view of this, al-Ash'ari is alleged to have asked him about the likely fate of three brothers: a believer, an unbeliever and one who died as a child. Al-Jubba'i answered that the first would be rewarded, the second punished and the third neither rewarded nor punished. To the objection that God should have allowed the third to live so that he might have gained paradise, al-Jubba'i replied that God knew that had the child lived he would have become an unbeliever. Al-Ash'ari then silenced him by asking why in that case God did not make the second brother die as a child in order to save him from hellfire!

For al-Ash'ari, divine justice is a matter of faith. We know the difference between good and evil solely because of God's revelation, and not by the exercise of our own reason. God makes the rules and whatever he decrees is just, yet God himself is under no obligation: if he wished, he could punish the righteous and admit the wicked to paradise (see VOLUNTARISM). Moreover, to suppose as the Mu'tazilites did that human beings had free will would be to restrict the sovereign freedom of the creator. On the contrary, God creates in his creature both the power and the choice; then he creates in us the actions which correspond to these. Nevertheless, we are conscious of a difference between some actions, such as the rushing of the blood through our veins, which are involuntary, and others, such as standing up or sitting down, which are in accordance with our own will. Al-Ash'ari argues that by approving of these latter actions, which God created in us, we 'acquire' them and are thus held responsible for them.

See also: CAUSALITY AND NECESSITY IN ISLAMIC THOUGHT; FREE WILL; ISLAM, CONCEPT OF PHILOSOPHY IN; ISLAMIC THEOLOGY; KARAISM

References and further reading

* al-Ash'ari (before 935) *Maqalat al-islamiyyin* (Islamic Dogmas), ed. H. Ritter, Wiesbaden, 2nd edn, 1963. (Valuable source of information about earlier thinkers.)

Gimaret, D. (1990) *La doctrine d'al-Ash'ari* (The Doctrine of al-Ash'ari), Paris: Éditions du Cerf. (A systematic and comprehensive treatment of the subject.)

—— (1992) 'Mu'tazila', in *Encyclopaedia of Islam*, New Edition, Vol. VII, fasc. 127–8: 783–93. (Short survey of the topic.)

Hourani, G. (1985) *Reason and Tradition in Islamic Ethics*, Cambridge: Cambridge University Press. (Excellent defence of the Mu'tazilite position.)

Leaman, O. (1985) 'Are the Ethics of Religion Objective or Subjective?', in *Introduction to Medieval Islamic Philosophy*, Cambridge: Cambridge University Press, ch. 4, 123–65. (Critique of the Mu'tazilite interpretation.)

Nader, A.N. (1984) *Le système philosophique des Mu'tazila* (The Philosophical System of the Mu'tazila), 2nd edn, Beirut: Dar el-Machreq. (Somewhat outdated; apparently a simple reprint of the first edition of 1956.)

Van Ess, J. (1984) *Une lecture à rebours de l'histoire du Mu'tazilisme* (A Controversial Reading of the History of Mu'tazilism), Paris: Geuthner. (Brief and lively discussion of the early period.)

NEAL ROBINSON

ASMUS, VALENTIN FERDINANDOVICH (1894–1975)

One of the most accomplished thinkers in the Soviet Marxist tradition, Asmus wrote extensively in many areas of philosophy, and was widely regarded as the Soviet Union's principal Kant scholar. Early in his career, he became associated with the influential school of 'dialecticians' led by A.M. Deborin and produced a number of significant writings in the history of philosophy. When Deborin and his followers were condemned as 'Menshevizing idealists' in 1931, Asmus shifted the principal focus of his work to aesthetics and logic. His 1947 textbook of formal logic subsequently became the principal text for logic instruction in the USSR.

Throughout his long career, Asmus experienced a number of political difficulties. Nevertheless, he avoided imprisonment and published consistently, though he was never permitted to go abroad. His importance in Russian philosophy derives not so much from the significance of his theories, but from his role in preserving philosophical culture in Russia through the Stalin period. He aspired to high standards of scholarship and worked hard to foster the study of logic and the history of philosophy. The breadth of his interests and his excellence as a teacher made him an inspirational figure to the young scholars striving to revive Soviet philosophy in the 1960s.

1 Life
2 Ideology, culture and explanation
3 Philosophy and its past
4 Logic and aesthetics
5 Asmus' legacy

1 Life

V.F. Asmus was born in Kiev. In 1919, he graduated from Kiev University, where he studied with V.V. Zenkovsky and A.N. Giliarov. Asmus taught philosophy and aesthetics in Kiev for a number of years, until he was appointed to Moscow's Institute of Red Professors in 1927. There his expert appreciation of the history of philosophy made him an ally of the school of 'dialecticians' led by Abram Deborin, which dominated the Soviet philosophical institutions at that time. Asmus participated in the dialecticians' controversies with Soviet positivists, or 'mechanists', and in the later conflicts with Party activists 'on the philosophical front' that led in 1931 to the dissolution of Deborin's school. Although condemned as a 'Menshevizing idealist' and temporarily denied the right to teach, Asmus was spared the fate that befell many Deborinites in the purges, probably because of his 'non-Party' status.

As Soviet philosophy increasingly became an instrument for the propagation of Party ideology, so Asmus shifted the focus of his work to aesthetics and the philosophy of literature, becoming a member of the Writer's Union in 1935 and completing his doctoral dissertation on 'Aesthetics in Classical Greece' in 1940, the first thesis to be defended at Moscow's Institute of Philosophy. Asmus could not, however, elude political controversy altogether. In 1938, he was endangered by his former association with Bukharin, though he fortuitously escaped arrest. And in 1944, Asmus was among the authors of the third volume of the *Istoriia filosofii* (History of

Philosophy), edited by G.F. Aleksandrov *et al.*, which the Central Committee withdrew from publication because its sympathetic treatment of German idealism was deemed inappropriate in the climate of anti-German feeling provoked by the Great Patriotic War. It was fortunate for the contributors that they had earlier received the Stalin prize for an earlier volume. Thereafter Asmus, who had been a professor at Moscow University since 1939, sought refuge in its Department of Logic where he made an important contribution to the development of formal logic in Russia. He returned to the history of philosophy only after the Stalin period. A close friend of Boris Pasternak's, Asmus is reputed to have influenced the philosophical content of *Doctor Zhivago*. In 1960, he was once again embroiled in controversy when he gave a eulogy at Pasternak's graveside. Asmus continued to work actively in philosophy until his death.

2 Ideology, culture and explanation

Among the works which brought Asmus into the limelight was his debate with the mechanist A. (Sandor) Var'iash, published in *Pod znamenem marksizma* (Under the Banner of Marxism) (in 1926-7). In his *Istoriia novoi filosofii* (History of Modern Philosophy) (1926), Var'iash argues that if Marxism is to provide a consistently monist account of reality, it must explain how all forms of ideological activity, including literature, science and philosophy, arise from specific socioeconomic relations. By this, Var'iash means not just that philosophical or scientific theories cannot be understood without reference to the historical circumstances of their emergence, but that both the content and the logical structure of theories are ultimately causally determined by the forces of production. Var'iash's work examines how such causal relations can be traced. In reply, Asmus maintains that Var'iash succeeds in demonstrating only that, for any era, a correspondence exists between the social needs defined by the relations and forces of production and the general themes of scientific research. Asmus argues that it is in principle impossible to derive the logical characteristics of a theory from considerations about the sociohistorical conditions of its production, and that Var'iash's position must ultimately collapse into a disastrous relativism, for unless we distinguish between the 'genetic' analysis of a theory's origins and the logical analysis of its content, the concepts of proof and truth will be undermined. In addition, Asmus rejects Var'iash's view that the causal determination between 'economic base' and 'ideological superstructure' proceeds only in one direction.

The controversy is sometimes portrayed as a conflict between Var'iash's 'vulgar sociological' approach and Asmus' cultured historicism. This is misleading, for Var'iash was aware of his position's counter-intuitive aspects and developed his case with considerable ingenuity, while Asmus was sometimes overconfident in his arguments, no doubt because he knew they would find favour with the Deborinite orthodoxy. Nevertheless, the debate is testimony to the vigour and seriousness of Soviet philosophy in the 1920s, and illustrates Asmus defending the irreducibility of cultural phenomena against positivist or crude Marxist conceptions, a position which became a leitmotif of his work.

3 Philosophy and its past

One theme prominent in Asmus' dispute with Var'iash is the nature of philosophy's relation to its past. For Asmus, Marxism represents the outgrowth of a long historical development and incorporates insights from many philosophical positions. The history of philosophy is not simply a history of previous error. Accordingly, Asmus sought throughout his career to uphold standards of historical scholarship in philosophy, both in his own writings on ancient, early modern and nineteenth-century Russian philosophy, and in the many collaborative projects in which he was engaged. He was particularly well known for his studies of Kant, for whose thought he had a special affection.

Asmus' approach to the history of philosophy is exemplified by his *Ocherki istorii dialektiki v novoi filosofii* (Essays on the History of Dialectics in Modern Philosophy) (1930). Here he argues that dialectic represents a method of cognition, designed to capture how development occurs through the resolution of contradiction. Asmus traces the origins of Marx's conception of dialectic in the work of Descartes, Spinoza, Kant, Schelling, Fichte and Hegel. He argues that it was Kant who first grasped the significance of dialectical contradiction, though he mistakenly confined its influence to the realm of thought. Hegel, in contrast, correctly discerned that the development of being itself is dialectical, but his account is belied by his idealist metaphysics and teleological conception of history. It was Marx and Engels, Asmus argues, who identified the true empirical content of Hegel's system and turned dialectic into a method for the analysis of real human history.

Though Asmus' exposition conforms to the standard Soviet vision of philosophy's history, it contains many subtleties, both in the detailed accounts of particular philosophers and in his appreciation of the complexities of Marx's method. Though Asmus invokes familiar dialectical materialist formulas (such as the triad of thesis–antithesis–synthesis) to characterize the structure of dialectical development, he is adamant that all such schema represent crude simplifications. The central feature of Marx's dialectical method, he argues, is its sensitivity to the specific logic of development of particular objects of cognition, a sensitivity which cannot be captured in principles or schema. Thus no substantive content-neutral specification of dialectical method is possible. This view, undeveloped in the Stalin period, was later explored by Soviet thinkers in the 1960s.

For Asmus, the history of philosophy culminates in the final emancipation of humanity: Marxism renders transparent the laws of historical development and permits human beings to harness the forces which have hitherto shaped their lives. The relation of freedom and necessity is thus a pervasive theme in Asmus' historical writings. Like many of his Soviet colleagues, he follows Engels and Plekhanov in maintaining that freedom and necessity are not irreconcilable; we are free when we act consciously in full appreciation of the laws which govern our deeds. The proletariat, the first class to understand the circumstances of its own agency, thus reconciles freedom and necessity in its very practice.

As will be evident, Asmus presents a view of philosophy's development hardly less teleological than Hegel's, and in his more encyclopedic writings he is inclined to represent each pre-Marxist philosopher's contribution as a combination of 'progressive' and 'reactionary' elements, the former contributing to the eventual emergence of Marxism, the latter the result of constraints imposed by the socioeconomic climate in which the philosopher worked. For example, his entry on Kant in the Soviet *Filosofskaia èntsiklopediia* (Philosophical Encyclopedia) (1962) concludes by chiding Kant for his 'agnostic' denial that we can have knowledge of things-in-themselves, his 'subjective idealist' view of cognition as the imposition of a priori categories on the deliverances of experience, and his 'formalistic' approach to ethics and aesthetics. At the same time Asmus praises Kant's insights about dialectical contradiction, his concern with the justification of scientific knowledge, and his view of aesthetics as transcending the conflict between theoretical and practical reason. Asmus' scholarly writings, in contrast, provide a more nuanced (though no less linear) account of philosophy's development and transcend the Manichean vision that dominates so much Soviet philosophical writing.

4 Logic and aesthetics

Asmus had an important influence on the study of logic in the USSR. In the 1930s and 1940s, it was widely held that formal logic's allegiance to the law of non-contradiction made it ill-suited to represent dialectical thinking; formal logic must be supplanted by a higher 'dialectical logic'. As a result, the study of formal logic was almost totally neglected. Alarmed by this, the Central Committee invited Asmus to write an elementary logic text. The work, published in 1947, was widely used and logic was gradually rehabilitated (though controversies about the relation of formal and dialectical logic continued into the 1970s). Though Asmus felt himself ill-equipped to pursue studies in mathematical logic, he did much to encourage its development at Moscow University. He also continued to write on broadly logical topics, particularly on the concept of proof (1954). In this work, Asmus denies that there is a sharp distinction between logical and empirical argument, and maintains that all axioms and definitions have empirical content and derive their justification ultimately from their role in human practice.

Asmus also made significant contributions to Soviet aesthetics. In addition to studies in classical aesthetics, he produced erudite and insightful pieces on Goethe, Lermontov, Tolstoi and Schiller.

5 Asmus' legacy

Asmus will be remembered not so much for the novelty of his philosophical ideas as for his contribution to the survival of philosophical culture in Russia during the most oppressive periods of Soviet history. Though his work cannot be compared to that of LOSEV (who reputedly felt that Asmus had squandered his philosophical talents) and BAKHTIN, there is no denying the extent of his influence on his peers and students, particularly the younger generation of philosophers who sought to reanimate Soviet philosophy in the late 1950s and early 1960s. For them, Asmus was an inspiring teacher who represented a living connection with the traditions of the pre-Stalin period and a writer whose breadth of interests and scholarly integrity were unparalleled among Soviet Marxists.

See also: MARXIST PHILOSOPHY, RUSSIAN AND SOVIET

List of works

Asmus, V.F. (1924) *Dialekticheskii materializm i logika* (Dialectical Materialism and Logic), Kiev.

(Asmus' first major work and one which brought him to the attention of Deborin and his followers in Moscow.)

—— (1926) 'Spornye voprosy istorii filosofii' (Controversial Questions in the History of Philosophy), in *Pod znamenem marksizma* (Under the Banner of Marxism) 7–8: 206–25. (Asmus' critique of Var'iash (1926).)

—— (1927) 'K spornym voprosam istorii filosofii' (On Controversial Questions in the History of Philosophy), in *Pod znamenem marksizma* (Under the Banner of Marxism), 1: 165–94. (Asmus' rebuttal of Var'iash's (1927) reply to Asmus (1926).)

—— (1929) *Dialektika Kanta* (Kant's Dialectic), Moscow; repr. as *Immanuil Kant*, Moscow, 1973. (An assessment of Kant's thought. Asmus later claimed that Kant's philosophy was 'the foundation of his worldview'. The 1973 edition is reworked and expanded.)

—— (1930) *Ocherki istorii dialektiki v novoi filosofii* (Essays on the History of Dialectics in Modern Philosophy), Moscow and Leningrad. (A presentation of Marx's 'synthetic' dialectic in contrast to the views of Descartes, Spinoza, Kant, Fichte, Schelling and Hegel.)

—— (1933) *Marks i burzhuaznyi istorizm* (Marx and Bourgeois Historicism), Moscow and Leningrad. (Asmus traces the origins of Marx's view of history in Bacon, Herder, Kant, Fichte, Schelling and Hegel, and contrasts it with the irrationalism of Schopenhauer and Spengler.)

—— (1940s) 'V.S. Solov'ëv: Opyt filosofskoi biografii' (V.S. Solov'ëv: A Philosophical Biography), in *Voprosy filosofii* (Questions of Philosophy), (1988) 6: 70–89; 'V.S. Solov'ëv: An Attempt at Philosophical Biography', in *Soviet Studies in Philosophy* 28 (1989), 2: 66–93. (The first chapter of an unfinished book on Solov'ëv, written in the 1940s. Asmus stresses the distinctiveness of Solov'ëv's thought, arguing that it represents a new stage in Russian idealism.)

—— (1947) *Logika* (Logic), Moscow. (Asmus' influential logic text.)

—— (1954) *Uchenie logiki o dokazatel'stve i oproverzhenii* (The Logic of Proof and Refutation), Moscow. (A broad discussion of issues in the philosophy of logic.)

—— (1956) *Dekart* (Descartes), Moscow. (An account of Descartes' philosophy.)

—— (1960) *Demokrit* (Democritus), Moscow. (A discussion of Democritus' atomism as a precursor of modern materialism.)

—— (1962) 'Kant', in *Filosofskaia èntsiklopediia* (Philosophical Encyclopedia), vol. 2: 418–27. (A systematic presentation of Kant's philosophy, though significantly less sophisticated than Asmus' books on Kant.)

—— (1963) *Nemetskaia èstetika XVIII veka* (German Aesthetics in the 18th Century), Moscow: Iskusstvo. (A scholarly discussion of the aesthetics of Baumgarten, Lessing, Kant and Schiller.)

—— (1968a) *Voprosy teorii i istorii èstetiki* (Questions in the Theory and History of Aesthetics), Moscow: Istussvo. (A collection of essays on Aristotle, Schiller, Pushkin, Tolstoi, Stanislavskii and others; includes the influential 'Krug idei Lermontova' (Lermontov's Circle of Ideas).)

—— (1968b) *Antichnaia filosofiia* (Ancient Philosophy), Moscow, 2 vols; 2nd edn 1976. (A widely used textbook on classical philosophy.)

—— (1969–71) *Izbrannye filosofskie trudy* (Selected Philosophical Works), Moscow, 2 vols. (A representative selection of Asmus' works with an introduction by the author.)

—— (1973) *Immanuil Kant* (Immanuel Kant), Moscow. (A reworking and expansion of Asmus (1929).)

—— (1975) *Platon* (Plato), Moscow. (An account of Plato's thought.)

—— (1988) 'V.S. Solov'ëv: Opyt filosofskoi biografii', in *Voprosy filosofii* (Questions of Philosophy) 6: 70–89; trans. 'V.S. Solov'ëv: An Attempt at a Philosophical Biography', in *Soviet Studies in Philosophy* 28 (1989) 2: 66–93. (The first chapter of an unfinished book on Solov'ëv, written in the 1940s. Asmus stressed the distinctiveness of Solov'ëv's thought, arguing that it represents a new stage in Russian Idealism.)

—— (1995) 'Dialektika neobkhodimosti i svobody v filosofii istorii Gegelia' (The Dialectic of Necessity and Freedom in Hegel's Philosophy of History), in *Voprosy filosofii* (Questions of Philosophy) 1: 52–69. (A sympathetic discussion of Hegel's reconciliation of freedom and necessity; surveys conceptions of freedom in ancient, early modern and classical German philosophy.)

References and further reading

* Aleksandrov, G.F., Bykhovskii, B.E., Mitin, M.B. and Iudin, P.F. (eds) (1941–3) *Istoriia filosofii* (History of Philosophy), Moscow: Gospolitizdat, 3 vols. (A collective history of philosophy, to which Asmus was a significant contributor. Although the project had earlier won the Stalin prize, the third volume was denounced by the Central Committee for its sympathetic treatment of Western philosophy.)

Sadovskii, V.N. (1993) 'Filosofiia v Moskve v 50-e i 60-e gody' (Philosophy in Moscow in the 1950s and 1960s), in *Voprosy filosofii* (Questions of Philo-

sophy) 7: 147–64. (A valuable account of the climate within Soviet philosophy after the Stalin period, including a discussion of Asmus' contribution.)
* Var'iash, A. (1926) *Istoriia novoi filosofii* (History of Modern Philosophy), Moscow and Leningrad. (The book which provoked the controversy between Asmus and Var'iash in 1926–7.)
* —— (1927) 'Monisticheskii vzgliad na istoriiu filosofii i eë spornye voprosy' (The Monist View of the History of Philosophy and its Controversial Questions), in *Pod znamenem marksizma* (Under the Banner of Marxism) 1: 142–64. (Var'iash's reply to Asmus (1926).)
'V.F. Asmus – pedagog i myslitel' (V.F. Asmus – teacher and thinker) (1995), in *Voprosy filosofii* (Questions of Philosophy) 1: 31–51. (Insightful reminiscences of Asmus' life and work by former students and colleagues commemorating the hundredth anniversary of his birth.)

DAVID BAKHURST

ASSERTION see SPEECH ACTS

ASTELL, MARY (1666–1731)

Best known for her proposal to establish a women's college, Astell published on a variety of other topics: religious dissent, the social contract, the marriage contract, epistemic issues, mind–body dualism, immortality, proofs for God's existence, reason and revelation, and Locke's views on 'thinking matter'. Her correspondence with John Norris treated the pure love of God and occasionalism. On marriage she drew a shrewd contrast between the treatment of political tyranny by contractarians (such as Locke), and their failure to deal with domestic tyranny. Some of her reactions to the views of major philosophers anticipated later debates.

1 Philosophical influences on life and works
2 Social and political thought
3 The rejection of occasionalism
4 Other metaphysical topics

1 Philosophical influences on life and works

Mary Astell gained notoriety in her native England and beyond for *A Serious Proposal to the Ladies...* (1694), which advocated the founding of an Anglican academy for women. *Letters Concerning the Love of God* (1695) followed – her side of this correspondence with Cambridge Platonist John NORRIS was praised by Leibniz. Having failed to get support for her educational institution, Astell offered women a manual for improving their understanding: *A Serious Proposal to the Ladies, Part II* (1697) drew on Lockean views, Cartesian 'method', and the Port Royal *Logic* (see PORT-ROYAL). After examining the marriage contract in *Some Reflections Upon Marriage* (1700), Astell became a pamphleteer on religious and political topics, criticizing Defoe, Swift, SHAFTESBURY and LOCKE. (Swift retaliated by satirizing her in the *Tatler*.) *The Christian Religion...* (1705) responded to Locke, Damaris MASHAM and Archbishop Tillotson. Her circle of friends included Lady Mary Wortley Montagu, for whose posthumously published letters she wrote a preface, and the Anglo-Saxon scholar Elizabeth Elstob.

2 Social and political thought

According to Springborg (1996), the real focus of Astell's *Reflections Upon Marriage* is the 'absurdity of contractarian voluntarism'. Here, and in her pamphlets, Astell wants to show that contractarians such as Locke are reluctant to accept arguments against domestic tyranny on the basis of consent, while they press these arguments against the state. Indeed, Springborg suggests that Astell may be the first systematic commentator on Locke's *Two Treatises of Government*.

In *Moderation Truly Stated...* (1704a) and *An Impartial Enquiry into the Causes of Rebellion and Civil War in This Kingdom* (1704c), Astell defended the royalist cause and the Established Church, while challenging the work of James Owen and Charles Davenant; *A Fair Way with the Dissenters...* (1704b) attacked Defoe; *Bart'lemy Fair or an Enquiry after Wit* (1709) criticized Shaftesbury's *Letter Concerning Enthusiasm* and charged Swift with irreligion.

3 The rejection of occasionalism

In *Letters Concerning the Love of God*, Norris had argued that God should be the sole object of our love and that Malebranche's occasionalism ensures this conclusion (see OCCASIONALISM): all our perceptions and sensations, all our sources of pleasure, are caused solely by God. Astell had reservations about this view and, before allowing the correspondence to be published, appended a letter arguing specifically against occasionalism. Her criticisms are prefigured in medieval debates on secondary causation. The first is that 'it seems more agreeable to the Majesty of God, and that Order he has established in the World, to say that he produces our Sensations mediately by his Servant Nature, than to affirm that he does it immediately by his own Almighty Power' (1695: 281–2). Although Aquinas' *Summa Contra Gentiles* and Molina's *Concordia* had advanced similar arguments, this objection is not conclusive (see AQUINAS §3; MOLINA, L. DE). For occasionalists, to hold that God concurs with secondary causes is to hold that God's own causal role in natural change is not sufficient to determine effects in all their specificity. They can therefore claim that their doctrine is more consistent with God's majesty than that of concurrence.

Astell's other objection is more powerful: if bodies contain 'nothing in their own Nature to qualify them to be instrumental to the Production of... sensations' (1695: 279), and if God is sufficient to cause these natural changes, then it seems God has created bodies in vain – which would be contrary to God's perfection. Aquinas had stated a like objection in *Summa Contra Gentiles*.

In place of occasionalism, Astell maintains that sensation is directly caused by mind–body interaction, and mediately caused by God. She goes beyond this Cartesian account to suggest that something like More's Neoplatonic 'plastic part of the soul' might explain the agreement between external objects and sensations (see MORE, H.).

4 Other metaphysical topics

The Christian Religion... attempts (1) to show how religious belief can and should be grounded in reason, (2) to determine the roles of reason and revelation, (3) to encourage women to examine Christian doctrines rationally, and (4) to examine the obligations that determine Christian practice. Towards these ends, Astell critically evaluates Archbishop Tillotson's sermons, Locke's *The Reasonableness of Christianity*, Masham's *A Discourse Concerning the Love of God*, and the anonymous *Ladies' Religion*. In place of the Socinianism and scepticism she finds there, she offers her own rational accounts of revelation and Christian practice, which frequently rely on substantive metaphysical arguments (see SOCINIANISM). For example, in addition to an ontological argument for God's existence, Astell offers a cosmological argument that turns on a 'causal likeness principle' different from that of Descartes. Her argument is vulnerable, none the less, to the well-known criticisms of Descartes' version.

She also offers a two-part argument for the immortality of the human mind: first she argues for the immortality of immaterial things, and then offers a 'real distinction' argument to prove that the mind contains none of the properties of extended matter.

Her Platonic first argument bears a striking resemblance to that of Leibniz for the 'natural indestructibility' of monads:

> A Being is Mortal and Corruptible, or ceases to Be, when those Parts of which it consists... are no longer thus or thus United.... Hence it follows, That a Being which is Uncompounded, which has no Parts, and which is therefore incapable of Division and Dissolution, is in its own Nature Incorruptible.... If then the Mind be Immaterial, it must in its own Nature be Immortal.
> (Astell 1705: 248–9, §§257–8)

In response to the possibility of divine annihilation, she adds: 'He does nothing in vain, and can't be suppos'd to Make a Creature with a design to Destroy or Unmake it'. In addition to depending upon speculation about the 'purposes of God', this response also does not address an issue which also remained for Leibniz: the possibility of instantaneous *natural* annihilation.

Astell's version of the real distinction argument is especially of interest in light of twentieth-century interpretations of Descartes' argument as an epistemic one (Wilson 1978). She reasons:

> When two Complete Ideas... have different Properties and Affections, and can be consider'd without any Relation to, or Dependance on each other, so that we can be sure of the Existence of the one, even at the same time we can suppose that the other does not Exist, as is indeed the case of a Thinking and of an Extended Being, or of Mind and Body; here these two Ideas, and consequently the things they represent, are truly Distinct and of Different Natures.
> (Astell 1705: 248–9, §§257–8)

Astell regarded the foregoing arguments and their theological consequences as threatened by the possibility of Locke's 'thinking matter'. She notes that according to Locke's *Essay*:

> it is impossible for *a Solid Substance to have Qualities, Perfections, and Powers, which have no Natural or Visible Connexion with Solidity and Extension*; and since there is no Visible Connexion between Matter and Thought, it is *impossible for Matter*, or *any Parcels of Matter to Think*.
> (Astell 1705: 259, §267)

This view parallels what Margaret Wilson has called Locke's 'official position': all properties and powers of an object 'stand in comprehensible or conceivable relations to its Boylean "primary qualities"' (1979: 144). Like Wilson, Astell argues that this position is inconsistent with Locke's view in his third letter to

Stillingfleet: *'Some Parcels of Matter be so order'd by Omnipotence as to be endued with a Faculty of Thinking'* (Astell 1705: 259, §267). Astell concludes that God's superaddition of thought to matter could only create an 'Arbitrary Union' between matter and the faculty of thought, so that 'it is not Body that Thinks, but the mind that is United to it, Body being still as incapable of Thought as it ever was' (1705: 261, §269).

List of works

Astell, M. (1694) *A Serious Proposal to the Ladies, For the Advancement of their true and greatest Interest. By a lover of Her Sex*, London; repr. in *A Serious Proposal to the Ladies Parts I and II, by Mary Astell*, ed. P. Springborg, Brookfield, VT: Pickering & Chatto, 1996. (An important early English text concerning women's education, which advocates the founding of an Anglican academy for women.)

—— (1695) *Letters Concerning the Love of God, Between the Author of the Proposal to the Ladies and Mr. John Norris: Wherein his late Discourse, shewing That it ought to be intire and exclusive of all other Loves, is further cleared and justified. Published by J. Norris, M.A. Rector of Bemerton near Sarum*, London. (Astell's correspondence with the Cambridge Platonist who defends Malebranche's occasionalism; her appended letter makes clear her reasons for rejecting occasionalism.)

—— (1697) *A Serious Proposal to the Ladies, Part II. Wherein a Method is offer'd for the Improvement of their Minds*, London; repr. in *A Serious Proposal to the Ladies Parts I and II, by Mary Astell*, ed. P. Springborg, Brookfield, VT: Pickering & Chatto, 1996. (A manual for improving the understanding, designed for women; it draws on the views of Locke, Descartes and the Port-Royal logicians.)

—— (1700) *Some Reflections Upon Marriage, Occasion'd by the Duke and Duchess of Mazarine's Case; which is also consider'd*, London; *Reflections Upon Marriage. The Third Edition. To which is Added A Preface, in Answer to some Objections*, London, 1706. (An examination of women's position in the 'estate of marriage'; it argues that contractarians use arguments from political tyranny against the state, but are reluctant to deal with domestic tyranny.)

—— (1704a) *Moderation truly Stated: Or, A Review Of A Late Pamphlet Entitul'd, Moderation a Vertue. With a Prefatory Discourse To Dr. D'Aveanant, Concerning His late Essays on Peace and War*, London. (An examination of the relation between church and state, by way of a detailed rebuttal of the defence of 'occasional conformity' to the Church of England; Astell argues for strict conformity.)

—— (1704b) *A Fair Way With The Dissenters and Their Patrons. Not Writ by Mr. L[esle]y, or any other Furious Jacobite whether Clergyman or Layman; but by a very Moderate Person and Dutiful Subject to the Queen*, London. (An attack against Defoe's satirical defence of religious toleration.)

—— (1704c) *An Impartial Enquiry Into The Causes of Rebellion and Civil War In This Kingdom: In an Examination of Dr. Kennett's Sermon, Jan. 31. 1703/4. And Vindication of the Royal Martyr*, London. (A royalist defence, arguing that Whigs and religious dissenters erode the authority of the state by placing supreme power in the people.)

—— (1705) *The Christian Religion, As Profess'd by a Daughter Of The Church of England*, London. (A response to Locke and Masham.)

—— (1709) *Bart'lemy Fair: Or An Enquiry after Wit in which due Respect is had to a Letter Concerning Enthusiasm, To my Lord * * *. By Mr. Wotton*, London. (An attack on Shaftesbury's argument that the application of good sense and pointed ridicule, rather than the elimination of liberty of conscience, are the best ways to deal with religious fanaticism.)

—— (1996) *Astell: Political Writings*, ed. P. Springborg, Cambridge: Cambridge University Press. (This contains a useful introduction and bibliography, as well as the best modern editions of *Reflections upon Marriage*, *A Fair Way with the Dissenters and their Patrons*, and *An Impartial Enquiry into the Causes of Rebellion*.)

References and further reading

Ballard, G. (1752) *Memoirs of several Ladies of Great Britain...*, Oxford: W. Jackson; repr. ed. R. Perry, Detroit, MI: Wayne State University Press, 1985. (The only source of biographical data from someone roughly contemporary to Astell.)

Ferguson, M. (ed.) (1985) *First Feminists: British Women Writers 1578–1799*, Bloomington, IN: Indiana University Press, 1985. (Places Astell's social philosophy about women in its historical context; includes excerpts from *A Serious Proposal* and *Some Reflections Upon Marriage*.)

Kinnaird, J. (1979) 'Mary Astell and the Conservative Contribution to English Feminism', *The Journal of British Studies* 19 (1): 53–75. (An introduction to Astell's social and political views.)

Perry, R. (1986) *The Celebrated Mary Astell: An Early English Feminist*, Chicago, IL: University of Chicago Press. (A detailed social and intellectual history of Astell and her times; appendices include some of Astell's letters and poems.)

Smith, F. (1916) *Mary Astell*, New York: Columbia University Press. (The first major study of Astell; it provides a good survey of her thought.)

Smith, H. (1982) *Reason's Disciples: Seventeenth-Century English Feminists*, Urbana, IL: University of Illinois Press. (An examination of seventeenth-century social and political philosophy, and the women writers of that period who, like Astell, foreshadowed the feminism of Wollstonecraft.)

Squadrito, K.M. (1991) 'Mary Astell', *A History of Women Philosophers*, vol. 3, ed. M.E. Waithe, Dordrecht: Kluwer Academic Publishers. (A survey of Astell's philosophical contributions.)

* Wilson, M.D. (1978) *Descartes*, London: Routledge & Kegan Paul. (Offers an epistemic reading of Descartes' real distinction argument which parallels that of Astell.)

* —— (1979) 'Superadded Properties: The Limits of Mechanism in Locke', *American Philosophical Quarterly* 16 (2): 143–50. (As in *The Christian Religion*, this piece charges Locke with inconsistent views regarding thinking matter.)

EILEEN O'NEILL

ATHEISM

Atheism is the position that affirms the nonexistence of God. It proposes positive disbelief rather than mere suspension of belief. Since many different gods have been objects of belief, one might be an atheist with respect to one god while believing in the existence of some other god. In the religions of the west – Judaism, Christianity and Islam – the dominant idea of God is of a purely spiritual, supernatural being who is the perfectly good, all-powerful, all-knowing creator of everything other than himself. As used in this entry, in the narrow sense of the term an atheist is anyone who disbelieves in the existence of this being, while in the broader sense an atheist is someone who denies the existence of any sort of divine reality. The justification of atheism in the narrow sense requires showing that the traditional arguments for the existence of God are inadequate as well as providing some positive reasons for thinking that there is no such being. Atheists have criticized the traditional arguments for belief and have tried to justify positive disbelief by arguing that the properties ascribed to this being are incoherent, and that the amount and severity of evils in the world make it quite likely that there is no such all-powerful, perfectly good being in control.

1 The meaning of 'atheism'
2 Historical sketch of Western atheism
3 Justification of atheism: insufficiency of proofs of the existence of God
4 Justification of atheism: disproving the existence of God

1 The meaning of 'atheism'

As commonly understood, atheism is the position that affirms the nonexistence of God. So an atheist is someone who disbelieves in God, whereas a theist is someone who believes in God. Another meaning of 'atheism' is simply nonbelief in the existence of God, rather than positive belief in the nonexistence of God. These two different meanings are sometimes characterized as positive atheism (belief in the nonexistence of God) and negative atheism (lack of belief in the existence of God). Barring inconsistent beliefs, a positive atheist is also a negative atheist, but a negative atheist need not be a positive atheist. One advantage of using 'atheism' in these two different senses is that negative atheism, but not positive atheism, characterizes the position of the logical positivists, who hold that statements purportedly about God, including the statement 'God does not exist', are cognitively meaningless. If one holds that the statements 'God exists' and 'God does not exist' are cognitively meaningless, and therefore neither true nor false, one cannot consistently believe that it is true that God does not exist or that it is true that God does exist. So the logical positivist cannot espouse positive atheism, but can be characterized as espousing negative atheism. Nevertheless, since the common use of 'atheism' to mean disbelief in God is so thoroughly entrenched, we will follow it. We may use the term 'non-theist' to characterize the position of the negative atheist. So instead of saying that the logical positivist is a negative but not a positive atheist, we shall say that the logical positivist is a non-theist but not an atheist.

Since human beings have worshipped many different gods, what god or gods is it whose existence, if denied, makes one an atheist? Generally, it is the dominant or official god of one's country or culture that plays that role. (Early Christians were called atheists because they rejected belief in the official gods of the Roman state.) But given that there are a number of different conceptions of the divine in a given culture, it is best to distinguish a restricted or narrow sense of 'atheism' and 'theism' from a broader sense. In the major religions of the West – Judaism, Christianity and Islam – the traditional conception of God is of a purely spiritual, supernatural being who is the perfectly good, all-powerful, all-knowing creator of everything other than himself. As used in this entry, an atheist in the narrow sense of the term is anyone who disbelieves in the existence of this being, just as a theist in the narrow sense is anyone who believes in the existence of this being. In the broader sense, a theist is someone who believes in the existence of any divine being or divine reality, even if it is quite different from the idea of God just described. Similarly, an atheist, in the broader sense of the term, is someone who disbelieves in every form of deity, not just the God of traditional Western theology.

To avoid confusion, it is important to keep in mind both the narrow and the broader senses of these terms. In the narrow sense, the Protestant theologian Paul TILLICH (§2) was an atheist, for he disbelieved in the existence of the God of traditional theism. But in the broader sense he was a theist, since he believed that there is a divine reality, being-itself (the God beyond the traditionalistic theistic God). The chief concern of this entry will be an investigation of the reasons supporting atheism in the narrow sense. While someone may readily undertake to give reasons for thinking that the God of traditional Western theology does not exist, it would be a vastly larger task to review all the ideas of the divine that human beings have generated over time and then undertake to justify belief in the nonexistence of each divine being or divine reality.

2 Historical sketch of Western atheism

Perhaps the best way to understand the struggle between atheism and theism is to note theism's insistence on an agent explanation of various natural phenomena, including the existence of the universe. We typically explain our actions and their results in terms of our purposes and our power as agents to make things happen. When the idea that the sun, moon and stars are themselves agents was abandoned, it seemed reasonable to explain their movements, and other natural happenings in the world, as the result of powerful agents (gods) acting upon inert material bodies. Thus the gods served to explain events in nature for which no other explanation was then available, particularly events directly affecting human welfare. And by worshipping and beseeching the gods, human beings undoubtedly hoped to influence the course of natural events in their favour.

The seeds of atheism in Western society were sown with the beginning of science. For the trend of science over the centuries has been to replace explanations of natural events by the activity of divine agents with explanations by means of other natural phenomena (see RELIGION AND SCIENCE §§1–3). As early as Epicurus, one finds an explicit attempt to rule out any explanation of natural phenomena by reference to the activity of supernatural agents (see EPICUREANISM §§8–9). But while it is one thing to observe the steady retreat of the gods from a significant place in explanations of phenomena within nature, it is quite another thing to discredit the view that the natural universe itself owes its existence to the creative activity of a supernatural deity. Moreover, the appearance of design in plants and animals made it difficult to find a plausible explanation in something other than the activity of an intelligent being. So, although the growth of the natural sciences did much to remove human dependence on the gods to explain events within nature, a foothold in ultimate explanations still remained; and certain phenomena in nature, particularly the apparent design in plants and animals, continued to suggest an intelligent being exercising a causal influence within nature. An attack on the need and possibility of ultimate explanations was left to philosophers, particularly to HUME (§6) and KANT (§8), although the argument from design received its most devastating blow from the work of Darwin and Wallace in the nineteenth century. It is not surprising, therefore, that atheism has flourished in the nineteenth and twentieth centuries, being advocated by such influential thinkers as Feuerbach, Nietzsche, Marx, Freud, Russell and Sartre.

3 Justification of atheism: insufficiency of proofs of the existence of God

As noted above, this entry will focus primarily on the reasons given in support of atheism in the narrow sense, the view that the God of traditional Western theology does not exist. If atheism in the narrow sense is to be established or shown to be probably true, two different sorts of reasons need to be given. First, one must give reasons that would be sufficient to justify disbelief in God if they constituted the only reasons we have that bear on the question of God's existence. Second, one must refute or show the insufficiency of reasons that have been given to justify belief in God. The necessity of the second undertaking is due to the possibility that reasons in support of a claim may outweigh reasons against the claim. The necessity of the first undertaking is due to the general principle that in the absence of good reasons in support of a claim the proper response is suspension of belief rather than disbelief. However, if we were to have sufficient reason to believe that the God of traditional Western theology (if he existed) would make available to us clear evidence of his existence, we would be entitled to adopt atheism once it had been shown that the reasons given in support of theism are inadequate. But it has been argued that if God made it altogether

531

clear that he exists we would not be cognitively free in relation to him – that is, we would not be independent autonomous persons free to make our way in the world with or without God. Since it is difficult to know that this is not so, and difficult to know that God's purpose for us would not involve our being cognitively free in relation to him, we cannot be confident that the absence of sufficient reasons to believe in God warrants disbelief in God rather than suspension of belief. Thus the justification of atheism requires reasons in support of atheism as well as refutation of purported sufficient reasons in support of theism.

One popular argument for theism relies on the claim that belief in some sort of deity is universal among humans. What better explanation of this fact than that theism is true and God has implanted some recognition of himself, however poorly grasped, in the peoples of the world? Against this argument there are two decisive objections. First, if the argument supports anything, it more directly supports polytheism than theism, for the peoples of the world tend to believe in many distinct deities rather than the single supernatural, perfectly good, all-powerful, all-knowing being of traditional theism. Second, there are plausible naturalistic explanations of the near universal belief in some deity or other. For example, it has been argued that before our ancestors gained any significant control over nature – or at least an understanding of its workings – they personified the forces of nature, made gods of them, and thus sought to control nature by praying to the gods. Such naturalistic explanations of the near universal belief in gods add to the implausibility of using this belief as support for the existence of the theistic god. In addition to such popular arguments, there are the more serious arguments advanced by philosophers and theologians. The most important of these are the argument from the idea of God, the argument from the existence of the world, the argument from the existence of a world supportive of life and consciousness, the argument from objective moral values and the argument from religious experience.

The argument from the idea of God as a being exhibiting every perfection in the highest possible degree (the ontological argument) has been found wanting by most philosophers. In its place, a modal version has been advanced that rests on the premise that it is logically possible that a being having all perfections in the highest degree exists in every possible world. But if it is logically possible that there is at least one possible world in which every being has some minor defect, the premise of the modal version is false. So although the argument is valid, there is no good reason to think it is sound.

The argument from the existence of the world (the cosmological argument) reasons that the world is contingent; it either might or might not have existed. Since whatever exists but might not have existed must owe its existence to some being that brought it into existence, the world owes its existence to a being that produced it. If the being who produced the world were itself contingent, then it would be part of the world and could not be the cause of the world. Therefore, the being who produced the world does not owe its existence to anything else; it exists necessarily. This argument faces two difficulties. First, if it is correct, it establishes only a necessary cause of the contingent world. It does not establish that the necessary cause of the world has the properties definitive of the theistic God. Attempts to carry out this further task have not been particularly successful. Second, the argument rests on a rather strong but unsubstantiated causal principle: every contingent thing (or collection of such things) has a cause of its existence.

The argument from the existence of a world supportive of life and consciousness is the successor to an earlier argument from apparent design in plants and animals (the design argument), an argument that has been seriously weakened, if not damaged beyond repair, by the naturalistic explanation based on Darwin's theory of evolution through natural selection. According to the new argument, we know that a universe with initial conditions and laws permitting the emergence of life and consciousness is only one of vastly many ways the universe might have been. Had it been slightly different in any one of ever so many ways, life and consciousness would not have been possible. For example, had the rate of expansion after the Big Bang been slightly slower or slightly faster, life could not have occurred. Thus, it is extremely improbable that life should have emerged, given the vast number of alternative ways things could have gone. Of course, the initial conditions and order necessary for the emergence of life could have occurred randomly, but on the hypothesis of theism it is much more likely that these conditions and this order would occur. So, given that they have occurred, theism is more likely than any purely naturalistic account. This argument has merit provided we assume that our universe is a one-time affair. But if the present universe is only one of vastly many universes that have emerged and disappeared, it would not be so improbable that at least one such universe should contain the initial conditions and laws permitting the emergence of life and consciousness. And that it is our universe that contains these conditions and laws is, of course, not unlikely at all. For if it did not, we would not be here to ask why it does (see RELIGION AND SCIENCE §6).

The moral argument is generally presented in three steps. First, it is argued that there are objective moral truths. By this it is meant that independent of what we may feel or think, some acts just are morally wrong, others morally right (see MORAL REALISM). Second, it is argued that these moral truths about right and wrong depend on an ultimate superhuman moral lawgiver who establishes these truths. Finally, it is argued that without some being who brings it about that human happiness is proportioned to our obedience to the demands of morality, we would lack sufficient incentive to be moral (see RELIGION, HISTORY OF PHILOSOPHY OF §5). While this argument has always had some appeal, it has been severely criticized. It is argued that even the will of an omnipotent, perfectly good being cannot be the ultimate source of morality. For something is not morally right because an omnipotent, perfectly good being commands it; rather such a being would command it because it is morally right. Also, it is argued that there is no inconsistency in happiness being disproportionate to the moral life. For all we know, morality may be its own reward.

The argument from religious experience rests on the principle that if a person has an experience that seems to be of a particular object, they are justified in thinking that the object exists unless there is some reason for thinking otherwise. The application of this principle to experiences that seem to be of God gives grounds for thinking that God exists (see Swinburne 1979). Against this argument we should note three points. First, we know in advance roughly what an object such as a dog or a cat would look like were we to have a perception of it. Few people have any idea how the theistic God would appear if they were to perceive him. Second, in the case of physical objects we have some reasonably clear idea of how to discover reasons for thinking our perceptual experience was not a genuine perception of a physical object. Examples of such reasons might be finding that others who were in a position to see or hear it report seeing or hearing nothing, or determining that the supposed object is of a sort (a fire-breathing dragon, for instance) that we have good reason to think does not exist. Because we are not in such a position with regard to the supposed object of religious experience, the fact that it is difficult to discover reasons for thinking such experiences are not genuine perceptions provides little or no reason to think they are genuine. Third, religious experience seems incapable of establishing that the object of the experience has some of the properties (being creator of the world, being infinitely powerful, being eternal, and so on) essential to the God of traditional theism. Thus, many philosophers believe that the argument from religious experience provides little support for the view that the God of traditional theism exists (see RELIGIOUS EXPERIENCE).

It is generally conceded that none of these arguments constitutes a proof of the existence of the God of traditional theism. Nor does any one of them appear to make the existence of this being so probable as to warrant belief. Some philosophers contend that considered together they provide sufficient grounds to warrant belief in theism. But critics insist that even this judgment is too strong. Some critics suggest that at best the arguments make it likely that some sort of divine intelligence had something to do with the ordering of the universe, but point out that this is a far cry from having grounds to believe that there is an omnipotent, omniscient, perfectly good creator. They claim that unless we have something else to go on we simply lack sufficient reason to believe in the God of traditional Western theology.

4 Justification of atheism: disproving the existence of God

What of the other side? Are there reasons to think that this being does not exist? Supporters of atheism typically focus on two issues: conceptual difficulties in the perfections ascribed to the God of traditional theism, and the problem of evil. With respect to the former, there are serious difficulties in formulating adequate accounts of omniscience and omnipotence. There are also formidable arguments to the effect that divine omniscience is inconsistent with immutability (an attribute long considered essential to the theistic God), and that God's essential moral perfection is incompatible with any significant divine freedom with respect to whether to create and what world to create (see OMNISCIENCE §2; FREEDOM, DIVINE). Finally, there is the general problem of whether those divine perfections that vary in degrees (knowledge, power, goodness) have an upper limit. But while these difficulties raise genuine doubts as to whether the traditional theistic conception of God is coherent, many philosophers believe that they fall short of a proof of incoherence.

The fundamental issue in the problem of evil is this. Do we have good reason to think that evils occur in the world that an omnipotent, omniscient and perfectly good being would not be justified in permitting? In so far as we do have good reason to believe this, we have a good reason to believe that atheism is true. When we consider horrendous evils or the sheer magnitude of human and animal suffering, the idea that an omnipotent, omniscient, perfectly good being is in control of the world may strike us as absolutely astonishing, something almost beyond belief (see Rowe 1979). What could possibly justify his permitting such monstrous evils? Theists generally accept the view that there must be some good or goods whose realization justifies his permission of these monstrous evils. Some theists propose theodicies that purport to tell us what these goods may be. Other theists say that we do not understand what these goods might be and, furthermore, we should not expect to understand. After all, God's mind is infinite and the goods in question are likely to be very complex and thus beyond our comprehension. Critics respond that God could at least make his presence known and provide some direct assurance, for example, to the mother whose child has been raped, tortured and brutally murdered, assuring her that all this serves some good purpose. Would that not go some way towards comforting the mother in her suffering? Yes, some theists reply, but the mother's sense of the absence or silence of God is just one more evil that God permits in order to realize some justifying goods. But what are these goods and why must God permit such evils in order to realize them? After all, he is omnipotent. Theists reply that with our finite minds we should not expect to understand.

Although the proponent of the argument from evil may be able to show that it is quite likely, if not certain, that no goods we know of justify God in permitting all these horrendous evils, no one can provide a proof that there are no goods realizable in some future state of the world – an afterlife – that would be sufficient to justify the theistic God in permitting the monstrous evils that occur in this life. But the proponent of the argument from evil does argue that it is rational to believe that there are no such goods as these. Indeed, the atheist typically thinks that the argument from evil is of sufficient strength to justify belief in atheism (in the narrow sense) provided the case for theism is itself inadequate. But few theists share this judgment.

See also: AGNOSTICISM; EVIL, PROBLEM OF; GOD, ARGUMENTS FOR THE EXISTENCE OF; GOD, CONCEPTS OF

References and further reading

Flew, A. (1976) *The Presumption of Atheism*, London: Pemberton Publishing Co. (Argues that the burden of proof is on the theist in the debate between theism and atheism.)

Gale, R. (1991) *On the Nature and Existence of God*, Cambridge: Cambridge University Press. (Sophisticated critique of the consistency of the divine attributes and of the major arguments for the existence of God. Includes a discussion of prudential arguments for belief in God.)

Mackie, J.L. (1982) *The Miracle of Theism*, Oxford: Oxford University Press. (A sophisticated study of the arguments for and against the existence of God. An important critique of theism.)

Martin, M. (1990) *Atheism: A Philosophical Justification*, Philadelphia, PA: Temple University Press. (A comprehensive critique of the major arguments for theism and a defence of various arguments in support of atheism.)

* Rowe, W.L. (1979) 'The Problem of Evil and Some Varieties of Atheism', *American Philosophical Quarterly* 16 (3): 335–41. (Presents a version of the evidential argument from evil in support of atheism.)

* Swinburne, R. (1979) *The Existence of God*, Oxford: Oxford University Press. (A careful, sympathetic presentation of most of the major arguments for the existence of God. Also works out a theodicy in answer to the problem of evil.)

Thrower, J. (1971) *A Short History of Western Atheism*, London: Pemberton Publishing Co. (A very readable summary of the development of Western atheism.)

WILLIAM L. ROWE

ĀTMAN *see* SELF, INDIAN THEORIES OF

ATOMISM, ANCIENT

Ancient Greek atomism, starting with Leucippus and Democritus in the fifth century BC, arose as a response to problems of the continuum raised by Eleatic philosophers. In time a distinction emerged, especially in Epicurean atomism (early third century BC), between physically indivisible particles called 'atoms' and absolutely indivisible or 'partless' magnitudes.

The term 'atom' (*atomon*), literally 'uncuttable', was coined in the fifth century BC by the first atomists, LEUCIPPUS (§2) and DEMOCRITUS (§2). As the name suggests, its primary sense is an unbreakable particle, and their theory was certainly a physical one about the ultimate constituents of phenomenal bodies. Later theorists, in the late fourth century BC and after, sometimes spoke of 'partless' or 'minimal' magnitudes or bodies, terms which focus more on the mathematical aspects of the entities in question. The

Platonist XENOCRATES (§2) and the Dialectician DIODORUS CRONUS (§2) developed such theories, although it is unclear whether, and if so how far, these were also applied to the problems of physics. In the early third century BC, EPICUREANISM (§§2–3) combined the physical and mathematical approaches, positing atomic physical particles which were themselves further analysable into absolute 'conceived as altogether', irreducibly small magnitudes.

Despite the above crude distinction between physical and mathematical indivisiblity, it is unlikely that the two concepts were originally distinct. The origins of atomism lay in the conceptual arguments of the Eleatic philosophers. PARMENIDES (§5) had argued that that-which-is is indivisible because it is 'all alike'. Some took this to mean that if a thing were divisible anywhere it would have to be divisible everywhere; hence it would consist of infinitely many parts of zero size, making the whole either infinitely large or sizeless. Zeno's puzzles about plurality and motion (ZENO OF ELEA §§4–6) were thought to raise similar problems. The atomist solution was that body is divisible in some places but not others: divisible in the void interstices between portions of body, but nowhere else. This is a metaphysical and mathematical thesis, but the resultant discrete portions of body easily became the basic particles of physics. Atoms, although themselves unchangeable, were held to come in varying shapes and sizes. By the motion of infinitely many of them in an infinite void, worlds and all their contents could be formed.

The emergence, especially with Diodorus and Epicurus, of a thesis of mathematical or absolute minima may reflect the feeling that atoms of varying shapes and sizes could not adequately answer the Eleatic puzzles. Such atoms must have parts, and, whether or not they could be physically fragmented into them, the same problems about measuring and counting the parts threatened to recur. Hence minima were conceived as altogether partless portions of body, and the same concept spread to the analysis of time and space. Thus all magnitudes came to be seen as granular in structure.

Opponents, whether sceptics (like Sextus Empiricus) or champions of the continuum (including Aristotle and the Stoics), could point out many conceptual difficulties, although whether these outnumbered the paradoxes of the continuum is debatable. Perhaps the toughest was: what would happen to two bodies approaching each other at equal speed across a distance consisting of an odd number of minima?

Ancient physical atomism won numerous adherents in the Renaissance and among early modern philosophers and scientists. Its most powerful exponent, GASSENDI (§§2, 4), studied his Epicurean sources minutely. From him an unbroken line of influence runs to modern atomic physics.

See also: MATTER, INDIAN CONCEPTIONS OF; STOICISM §4

References and further reading

* Aristotle (*c.* mid 4th century BC) *Generation and Corruption*, trans. C.J.F. Williams, Oxford: Oxford University Press, 1982. (Book I chapter 2 offers a particularly illuminating report and critique of Democritus' atomism; includes commentary.)
Barnes, J. (1979) *The Presocratic Philosophers*, London: Routledge & Kegan Paul. (Includes an excellent chapter on Democritus' 'corpuscularian hypothesis'.)
Furley, D.J. (1967) *Two Studies in the Greek Atomists*, Princeton, NJ: Princeton University Press. (Seminal study of atomism in Democritus and Epicurus.)
Kretzmann, N. (ed.) (1982) *Infinity and Continuity in Ancient and Medieval Thought*, Ithaca, NY: Cornell University Press. (Wide-ranging and important collection.)
Makin, S. (1989) 'The Indivisibility of the Atom', *Archiv für Geschichte der Philosophie* 71: 125–49. (Helpful analysis of the reasoning behind Democritean atomism.)
* Sextus Empiricus (2nd century AD) *Against the Professors*, ed. and trans. R.G. Bury, Loeb Classical Library, Cambridge, MA: Harvard University Press and London: Heinemann, 1936. (Greek text of Books IX–XI with English translation; Book X, which is also called *Against the Physicists* Book II, is an invaluable guide to ancient arguments on both sides of the debate about divisibility.)
Sorabji, R. (1983) *Time, Creation and the Continuum*, London: Duckworth. (Includes a magisterial study of the debate between atomicity and continuity, from the fifth century BC to the fourteenth century AD.)
White, M. J. (1992) *The Continuous and the Discrete: Ancient Physical Theories from a Contemporary Perspective*, Oxford: Oxford University Press. (Conceptually sophisticated reconstruction.)

DAVID SEDLEY

ATOMISM IN THE 17TH CENTURY *see* GASSENDI, PIERRE

ATONEMENT

As a theological concept, atonement articulates the acts by which relations between God and creatures, disrupted by human offence, can be restored. Although other cultures show an awareness of the need for atonement, the Christian tradition understands it as provided by God's particular historical action in Jesus Christ. At its centre is the notion of reconciliation between God and his alienated creatures, which is achieved particularly by the death of Jesus. The distinctive philosophical and other problems of atonement theology derive from two features in particular: its claiming of universal significance for the historical life and death of Jesus of Nazareth (the problem of universality); and the moral difficulties, especially in the realm of human freedom and responsibility, which arise from the claim that he is the vehicle of atonement with God (the problem of human autonomy).

Although there were many theologies of atonement before Anselm of Canterbury's, his systematic treatment is the fountainhead of much modern discussion, both Roman Catholic and Protestant. Centring on the concept of satisfaction, it understands Christ as the God-man, satisfying both divine justice and human need by a free gift of his life. Criticisms of the formulation have centred on its understanding of sin and its tendency to understand atonement in external, transactional terms. Subsequent discussion of the concept has also raised questions about Christ's substitutionary and representative roles and about the relation between the justice and the love of God. A significant proportion of modern thinkers have rejected the need for any concept of atonement at all. They have preferred instead to understand Jesus as an example to be followed ('exemplarism') or to concentrate upon the effect his behaviour and example have on the believer ('subjectivism') – or to adopt a combination of both.

1 Atonement as moral necessity
2 The Bible and the Fathers
3 The doctrine of satisfaction
4 After Anselm
5 Theological and philosophical theses

1 Atonement as moral necessity

The word 'atonement' is a Christian theological coinage, supposedly the only one made by an English theologian ('at-one-ment'). Along with many of the words found in its conceptual field – such as 'sacrifice' – its everyday uses are wide and general. Thus criminals are sometimes said to suffer punishment 'to atone' for their crime. This entry, however, will focus on the technical sense of the term, which applies primarily to relations between moral agents and the God to whom they are conceived to be responsible. In atonement theology, God is supposed to be in varying ways the active agent and passive recipient of atoning action. Most of the conceptual complications surrounding the topic derive from the various ways of construing this relation.

The concept of atonement, though developed in the Christian theological tradition in a number of related ways, is arguably of much broader provenance with respect to the moral and theological realities with which it purports to deal. Its underlying insight is that moral offences bring about an objective disruption of patterns of interpersonal life – indeed, in some accounts, of universal order also – of such a kind that some form of reparation or restoration is necessary if the resulting imbalance is to be corrected. To atone for one's offence is to act in such a way that the imbalance is corrected or reparation made to the offended. The specifically Christian understanding is that the impact of cumulative human offence is such that atonement must in some way be provided by God himself, the agents of moral offence having been rendered impotent by the weight of evil. Much ensuing discussion, particularly philosophical discussion, is centred on whether this can be conceived to take place without some violation of moral reality or human autonomy.

Classical Greek sources show that a need for atonement for wrong done is evidenced in cultures not directly affected by biblical categories. In Presocratic philosophy (EMPEDOCLES (§2), for instance) and Athenian drama there is a clear sense that moral agents are so bound up with both social and universal order that offence requires some form of atoning or purifying action. The Oedipus cycle makes clear the relation between moral impurity – particularly that deriving from the spilling of blood – and social disorder. The anthropologist René Girard (1977) has demonstrated the essentially rational way in which primitive religion understands and deals with violence as socially disruptive. Of particular importance for an understanding of substitutionary or vicarious aspects of atonement thought is his treatment of the fact that purificatory or avenging violence is often inflicted on someone or something other than the offender in order to break a cycle of revenge. Girard's is important evidence for the claim that matters of universal import underlie the particular forms of atonement theory in the Western Christian tradition.

In the Bible it is possible to discern a generally fourfold matrix within which atonement is understood. The moral offence which must be atoned for takes place in a network of relations between God, the offender, society and the cosmic order. Despite a range of interpretations of the opening chapters of Genesis the general pattern is clear. The disruption of a due relation to God (Genesis 3) has consequences for both social order (for example, the story of Cain and Abel) and the human relation to nature (Genesis 3: 17–19). It is for the sake of a restored social order based on a renewed relation to God that the cultic and legal order of Israel, with its inextricably related atoning and juridical institutions, is described in succeeding books. It is in the light of such considerations that the New Testament and later theological discussion of the death of Jesus and its atoning significance should be understood.

2 The Bible and the Fathers

The New Testament, drawing as it does on a world of imagery deriving from the Old Testament as well as on non-biblical sources from the surrounding culture, contains the bases of the later, more systematically articulated theologies of atonement. Different writers centre their thought on the development of particular families of metaphor without drawing on one exclusively. St Paul developed metaphors derived from the law in expounding the atoning significance of Jesus of Nazareth. In the Letter to the Romans, his development of the theology of justification expounds the claim that the death and resurrection of Jesus are the way by which God is able to forgive and renew while remaining true to moral reality. It is noteworthy, however, that at a crucial stage of his argument he draws also on the imagery of the altar. The Authorized Version of the Bible controversially translates his word describing the atoning work of Jesus Christ as 'propitiation'; later translations, fearing suggestions of substitutionary placation of an angry deity, tend to prefer 'expiation', implying more neutrally a means of taking away fault or pollution. All versions, however, draw on metaphors from the altar of sacrifice.

The author of the Letter to the Hebrews develops a theology of atonement drawing largely on such imagery. According to him, the eternal Son of God become man is at once human priest and victim, who perfects and replaces the Old Testament institutions of animal sacrifice. The author takes seriously the (atoning) purpose of those replaced institutions, and, while expounding the moral inadequacy of animal sacrifice (a view anticipated in the Old Testament prophets), theologizes the doctrine by centring atonement on the representative human achievement of the saviour. The effect of this metaphorical transformation of the language of the cult was recognized by later Christian writers who argued that Christ's death as a universal sacrifice renders all animal sacrifice obsolete. The Johannine tradition likewise assimilates various aspects of the sacrificial tradition to Jesus ('the lamb of God who takes away the sin of the world' (John 1: 29)), but also fuses it with the military language of victory (see particularly Revelation 5).

For the purposes of this entry, the military imagery will be left to one side because the characteristic philosophical problems associated with atonement theology centre on legal and sacrificial notions, particularly those of representation, substitution and the forgiveness of sins. The notion of substitution encapsulates the claim made in some theologies that Jesus suffers *in place of* the human sinner in relation to God; that of representation the claim that Jesus acts *on behalf of* either the human race or (in some traditions) those elect for whom he is said to have died.

However these are to be understood, it can be argued that the New Testament concepts, which in different ways encourage both interpretations, come together in the expression often translated as 'reconciliation' (*katallage* and cognates). God in Christ is primarily the active subject of this verb (2 Corinthians 5: 18–20); believers are claimed (factually) to have been reconciled to God (Romans 5: 10–), but are also urged to 'be reconciled to God' (2 Corinthians 5: 20). The chief reference appears to be to a past, completed divine act which both determines the status of believers (and, possibly, everyone) and requires an appropriate religious and ethical response; in the Letter to the Ephesians, this is the reconciliation in one church of the once estranged Jews and Gentiles.

While the notion of substitution has little prominence in early theology, the notion of exchange (suggested by the primary meaning of *katallage*, which in turn is deeply indebted to the Old Testament – see Isaiah 52–3) prepares the way for later discussion. The anonymous (probably second-century) *Letter to Diognetus* celebrates the matter with no suggestion of the theological and moral difficulties that are later to arise: 'O sweetest exchange! O unfathomable work of God!.... The sinfulness of many is hidden in the Righteous One, while the righteousness of the One justifies the many that are sinners' (9.5). The foundations of the classical doctrine of the atonement were later laid by the patristic writers, for example Athanasius, who in *On the Incarnation* (*c*.316–18) employed forensic, sacrificial and military imagery in his account of the saving significance of Jesus. But, although this is manifestly a theology of atonement, there was little systematic articulation of the problems in the early period.

Three generalizations are useful for an understanding of the later debates. First, the early writers, and the Eastern Orthodox tradition until today, tend to speak of redemption by Christ's self-sacrifice rather than atonement, and exposition is rather in terms of a wealth of images than of a systematic working out of a theology. Second, Orthodox theology tends to speak more of an ontological change brought about in the believer as a result of the self-giving sacrifice of Christ and the life of the church than of a moral or legal reconciliation concentrating on Christ's death. Third, theology in the West until the Middle Ages was very much shaped by Gregory of Nyssa's celebrated image of redemption: on the cross, Jesus cheats the devil of his human prey, deceiving him into thinking that here is but a man. The devil swallows his victim, only to be caught on the hook of his hidden divinity. Gregory's way of speaking was the catalyst for the critique of Christian theology which drew a definitive response from Anselm of Canterbury.

3 The doctrine of satisfaction

The doctrine of satisfaction has its origins in the rather juridical conception of the human relation to God developed in the West. In the first instance, it was used of the human response to God, with few overtones of atonement theology. For Tertullian, the human calling was conceived in terms of satisfying the just demands of God, the sovereign of the moral order. The concept was adopted and developed as a metaphor to express the atoning act of the Son of God by ANSELM OF CANTERBURY (§8) in his *Cur Deus homo* (Why God Became a Man) (completed in 1098). In response to criticisms of the irrationality of Christian atonement teaching made by opponents (probably Jewish and Muslim thinkers), he rejected the then reigning theology of atonement, which was heavily influenced by Gregory of Nyssa and according to which the death of Jesus on the cross had freed humankind from the legal power of the devil. Anselm's rejection was based on a conception of the sovereignty of God whereby God has no need to bargain with one who is his own creature. His own theory attempted to establish the necessity of the atonement understood in terms of satisfaction.

The assumption underlying Anselm's argument – and it is probably a necessary assumption for Christian theologies of atonement – is a belief in universal moral order and God's responsibility for upholding it. The human breach of this moral order has led, on the one hand, to human moral incapacity to atone, because of the infinite weight of accumulated offence; on the other, it has led to a situation in which God must either punish or provide some alternative (such as satisfaction) if his purposes in creation are not to be frustrated. Anything else (for example, the mere remission of sins) would involve an offence against universal order, and so be unjust, even (or especially) for God. Punishment would consist in annihilating the human race and so would involve an abandonment of God's purposes in creation; satisfaction requires a counterbalancing act of restitution which maintains that order.

Satisfaction is provided by the gift to God the Father of the God-man's life, offered by means of his free human obedience; as the life of God it outweighs even the infinity of human offence. This notion of satisfaction provides the basis of all claims for the universal significance of the particular historical act of Jesus. Because it is the act of God in the context of universal human fallenness – at one level, a gift by God to God; at another, an act of human reparation – it is of universal significance. Recent commentators (such as Steindl), in line with a long tradition of biblical theology of salvation, have emphasized that satisfaction, as an alternative to punishment, represents not the infliction of a penalty on a human Jesus in place of the actual offenders, but a creative act whereby God, by a new initiative, overcomes evil by good.

Anselm's aim was the limited one of establishing the rationality and necessity of the God-man, so there is a measure of injustice in insisting that he should have done things that he never set out to do. But subsequent theology has criticized him for omissions as well as commissions in his treatment of the atonement. Objectors have identified the excessively legal and mathematical terms of the conception, with its transactional rather than relational or personal emphasis, and the failure of the theology to give some account of the appropriation of salvation by the believer. Both criticisms observe a tendency to see the atonement as external to the human recipient of salvation and so inadequate as an account of reconciliation, which concerns relationships.

4 After Anselm

Important variations on Anselm's theme were produced by Thomas Aquinas and John Calvin, both of whom strengthened it where it appeared weak, but remained broadly within his tradition. Aquinas broadened the terms in which the atonement was to be understood, balancing and expanding talk of a debt paid with that of a stain erased. Some of the external features are mitigated when the legal metaphor of satisfaction is enriched with sacrificial imagery which suggests cleansing rather than remission of penalty.

Calvin's treatment of the atonement is the fountainhead of many recent disputes. The context is Luther's reassertion and reshaping of the Pauline and

Augustinian doctrine of justification by faith in terms of personal and relational categories (see JUSTIFICATION, RELIGIOUS §4; LUTHER, M.). Justification for Calvin is a metaphor of legality and therefore still within the Anselmian penumbra, but because his account centres on the subjective appropriation of the act of atonement by God in Christ, it helps to obviate the externalism of the Anselmian view. He buttressed his teaching of justification 'by faith through grace' with a theology of the objective atoning act of Christ. This act derives from the love of God (a note strangely absent from Anselm, who prefers to speak of God's mercy). The wrath from which it saves us is, according to Calvin, the necessary means by which we are made aware of our need for salvation. Christ saves us by both a propitiatory sacrifice, which Calvin understands similarly to Anselm, and by a representative obedience. Another central aspect of Calvin's teaching is the *participation* of the believer in the achievement of Christ, another blow against externalism (see CALVIN, J. §4).

Differences over justification led to a parting of the ways between the two main streams of Western Christianity. Over against the Reformers, with their teaching of the complete forgiveness of sin, the sixteenth-century Council of Trent, building on Anselm and Aquinas in a very different way, stressed the merit earned by Christ on the cross and communicable to believers especially through the mass. The Roman Catholic church taught until recent times that sinners must continue to atone for their sins in this world and after death in purgatory (see PURGATORY). In the teaching of the Second Vatican Council, juridical conceptions have given way to the view that by the death and resurrection of Jesus, God overcame evil and made humanity a new creation. However, because the chief intellectual battles since the Reformation have been between the orthodox and liberal wings of Protestantism, we shall concentrate on these developments.

Although Calvin did not say, any more than Anselm, that Jesus is punished instead of us, some of his successors were less careful in their expression of the doctrine. The neglect of his participatory language had two important consequences. First, the doctrine was again taken as teaching some external 'transaction', sometimes construed as a 'penal substitution' in which Christ was seen as suffering an equivalent penalty to that to which the guilty were liable. Second, and more important for the later history of the doctrine, it became liable to criticisms of varying degrees of severity.

On the one hand are the more radical critiques based on doctrines of moral autonomy. The source of this approach is the medieval philosopher Peter Abelard. While there is disagreement about the interpretation of his theology, it appears to make its chief appeal not to the reconciliation of those who are in some way at odds, but to a definitive act in which God shows his love to sinners. Those successors of Abelard who move in the direction of theories that are called subjective (because they deny an objective reconciling act) or exemplarist (because they see the work of Christ as essentially an example to be followed) can scarcely be said to produce theologies of atonement at all, because they have no place for a historic act of reconciliation of opposed or estranged parties. Their arguments are of interest here for their objections to forms of atonement theology proper.

The Socinians, the first influential opponents of a theology of atonement, taught the non-transferability of penalty and a strongly individualist conception of moral responsibility, and thus provide the strongest possible challenge to traditional conceptions (see SOCINIANISM §§2–3). Their approach has its paradigmatic modern treatment in Kant's *Religion within the Limits of Reason Alone* (1793) (see KANT, I. §11). Kant accepts two features of the orthodox teaching: a doctrine of the fallenness of the human race ('radical evil'), and the requirement for some form of atonement. But the atonement cannot be anything other than a kind of individual philosophical and inner conversion. In describing this conversion, Kant uses all kinds of traditional atonement language, but transfers its reference from the historical cross to the individual's soul.

On the other hand, the doctrine of atonement has been revised from within by a number of theologians who wished to remain true to its insight that Jesus Christ, and particularly his cross, is definitive for human salvation. Their criticism centred on the doctrine of a limited atonement taught by some Calvinists, that Christ died only for the elect. Many have held this limitation on the universality of atonement to be inconsistent with the justice of God. Influential in the development of more universal theologies was John McLeod Campbell. Early in the twentieth century, the Scottish Congregationalist P.T. Forsyth, while accepting aspects of liberal criticism, yet felt it necessary to stress the holiness of God, in the light of which conception he argued for the need for the historic act of God in the substitutionary cross of Jesus. Similarly, Karl BARTH (§§2–3) attempted to combine the elements of truth in substitutionary and representative theologies, while seeing the atonement as the historical outworking of God's universal electing and covenant love.

5 Theological and philosophical theses

Substitution and representation. There is a strong case for holding that Christian atonement theology requires some element of substitution if it is to give an adequate account of the teaching that human fallenness required the death of the saviour who on the cross took our place before God. Biblical teaching is, however, unanimous that there is no breach between the actions of God the Father and God the Son. The Son dies as a result of the love of God the Father, even though he also undergoes the effects of divine judgment on human sin. Here a distinction should be drawn between substitutionary atonement and substitutionary punishment. One cannot be punished for the offences of others, but one can make substitutionary atonement for them by taking their place in a transformative act of love. On this account, the Son of God, as representative of the human race, freely enters that relation to God which is the universal fate of those who reject God's love. His death is not so much a punishment as a sharing of the *relationlessness* which is the just fate of those who would deny their nature as existing in relation to God and others.

Justice and love. The classical Pauline view of the cross is that it expresses at once the love and justice of God. The cross and resurrection of Jesus show that he is at once just and justifies. That is to say, the reconstitution of human life by means of atonement establishes rather than undermines morality. Christian theology's claim is that God himself has provided the solution to the problem of moral evil by himself bearing its consequences, as a way of overcoming evil with good. This has encountered opposite objections from left and right: that God should be able to forgive simply by an exercise of power, and that morality is undermined by forgiveness. But the first objection fails to uphold the reality of the moral law, while the second ignores the transformative effects of atonement, the overcoming of evil by good.

Moral responsibility. A conception of atonement of this kind also requires a relational view of humanity. While I am responsible for my sins, what I am is also inextricable from my relation to God and to others. Modern objections, particularly those expressed in Kantian theories of autonomy, mistake the human condition in two important respects. They are individualist, and they assume a false or non-theological conception of human freedom. The participatory dimensions of atonement theology show that by participating in the (representative) achievement of Christ – particularly in those sacraments constitutive of the new community of forgiveness (baptism and the Lord's Supper) – the believer shares a form of community within which reconciled forms of life are realized.

The particular and the universal. As we have seen, Anselm's concept of universality derived from a particular conception of the divine act in Christ. Any attempt to show that a particular historical event or person is of universal moment depends on two features: its determination in divine intention to be what it is, and its answering to the needs of the human condition, particularly fallenness. If the human race does not have within itself the capacity for moral regeneration, there is a case for arguing that it is to be found in the reconstitutive acts of the life, death and resurrection of Jesus.

See also: GRACE; SIN

References and further reading

* Anon. (2nd or early 3rd century) *Letter to Diognetus*, in C.C. Richardson (ed.) *The Early Christian Fathers*, The Library of Christian Classics 1, London: SCM Press, 1953, 213–24. (An early summary of the Christian faith containing a notion of exchange.)
* Anselm of Canterbury (completed 1098) *Cur Deus homo* (Why God Became a Man), in E.R. Fairweather (ed.) *A Scholastic Miscellany: Anselm to Ockham*, The Library of Christian Classics 10, London: SCM Press, 1956, 100–83. (The medieval source of all modern discussion of atonement theology.)
Aquinas, T. (1266–73) *Summa theologiae* IIIa, qq.46–9, trans. with intro. by R.T.A. Murphy, London: Eyre & Spottiswoode, 1965, 2–115. (Important revisions of Anselm's theology of atonement.)
* Athanasius (c.316–18) *On the Incarnation*, in E.R. Hardy (ed.) *Christology of the Later Fathers*, The Library of Christian Classics 3, London: SCM Press, 1954, 55–110. (Classic early statement of a theology of redemption.)
Barth, K. (1956) *Church Dogmatics*, vol. 4/1: *The Doctrine of Reconciliation*, trans. G.W. Bromiley, Edinburgh: T. & T. Clark. (A major twentieth-century treatment of the doctrine.)
Calvin, J. (1559) *Institutes of the Christian Religion*, trans. J.T. McNeil and F.L. Battles, The Library of Christian Classics 20, London: SCM Press, 1960. (With Anselm, the fountainhead of modern debate about atonement.)
Campbell, J.M. (1878) *The Nature of the Atonement*, London: Macmillan. (A modern attempt to stress representative rather than substitutionary aspects of atonement.)

Cassirer, H. (1988) *Grace and Law: St Paul, Kant and the Hebrew Prophets*, Edinburgh: Handsel Press. (Argues that Paul's account of the human condition is philosophically superior to Kant's.)

Douglas, M. (1984) *Purity and Danger: An Analysis of the Concepts of Pollution and Taboo*, London: Ark Books. (A pointer to universal concerns underlying atonement theology.)

Feenstra, R. and Plantinga, C. (eds) (1989) *Trinity, Incarnation, and Atonement*, Notre Dame, IN: University of Notre Dame Press. (Contains essays discussing philosophical problems of atonement theology.)

Forsyth, P.T. (1965) *The Work of Christ*, London: Collins. (An important modern statement of a substitutionary theology of atonement.)

* Girard, R. (1977) *Violence and the Sacred*, trans. P. Gregory, Baltimore, MD: Johns Hopkins University Press. (An anthropological study with discussion of the meaning of substitutionary sacrifice.)

Gregory of Nyssa (c.383) *An Address on Religious Instruction*, in E.R. Hardy (ed.) *Christology of the Later Fathers*, The Library of Christian Classics 3, London: SCM Press, 1954, 268–325. (An influential early theology.)

Gunton, C. (1988) *The Actuality of Atonement: A Study of Metaphor, Rationality and the Christian Tradition*, Edinburgh: T. & T. Clark. (An attempt to state a theology of atonement with the aid of recent philosophy of language.)

* Kant, I. (1793) *Religion within the Limits of Reason Alone*, trans. T.M. Greene and H.H. Hudson, New York: Harper & Row, 1960. (The most important restatement of atonement as a philosophy of individual self-realization.)

McIntyre, J. (1954) *St Anselm and his Critics: A Reinterpretation of the Cur Deus Homo*, Edinburgh: Oliver & Boyd. (An important study of Anselm's philosophy and theology.)

Steindl, H. (1989) *Genugtuung: Biblisches Versöhnungsdenken – eine Quelle für Anselms Satisfaktionstheorie?* (Satisfaction: Biblical Thought about Reconciliation – a Source for Anselm's Theory of Satisfaction?), Freiburg: Universitätsverlag. (An important recent study of Anselm's background and theology.)

Stump, E. (1988) 'Atonement According to Aquinas', in T.V. Morris (ed.) *Philosophy and Christian Faith*, Notre Dame, IN: University of Notre Dame Press, 61–91. (A discussion of Aquinas in the context of modern problems.)

Swinburne, R. (1989) *Responsibility and Atonement*, Oxford: Clarendon Press. (A modern philosopher's Anselmian reflections on the Christian understanding of atonement.)

Taylor, V. (1941) *Forgiveness and Reconciliation: A Study in New Testament Theology*, London: Macmillan. (A summary of the main biblical teaching.)

Weingart, R.E. (1970) *The Logic of Divine Love: A Critical Analysis of the Soteriology of Peter Abailard*, Oxford: Clarendon Press. (A study of the source of modern exemplarist theories.)

White, V. (1991) *Atonement and Incarnation: An Essay in Universalism and Particularity*, Cambridge: Cambridge University Press. (A philosophically sophisticated discussion of claims of universality.)

COLIN GUNTON

AUGUSTINE (AD 354–430)

Augustine was the first of the great Christian philosophers. For well over eight centuries following his death, in fact until the ascendancy of Thomas Aquinas at the end of the thirteenth century, he was also the single most influential Christian philosopher. As a theologian and Church Father, Augustine was the person who did the most to define Christian heresy and so, by implication, to formulate Christian orthodoxy. Of the three most prominent heresies defined by Augustine – Donatism, Pelagianism and Manicheism – the latter two also have especially important philosophical implications. In rejecting Pelagianism and its thesis of human perfectibility, Augustine rejected one form of the principle, often associated with Kant, that 'ought' implies 'can', and in rejecting Manicheism, with its doctrine that good and evil are equally basic metaphysical realities, Augustine rejected one solution to the philosophical problem of evil.

The Categories *may have been the only work of Aristotle that Augustine actually read. Plato he knew somewhat better. He seems to have been familiar with several Platonic dialogues and he clearly felt a special affinity for Plato and the Platonists, which is particularly evident in* De civitate Dei *(The City of God) and* De vera religione *(On True Religion). Although he could be said to have responded to classical Greek philosophy in consequential ways, it must be added that what he responded to had been filtered through Neoplatonism, Hellenistic scepticism and Stoicism. It was principally through the writings of Cicero that Augustine became schooled in the opinions of his philosophical predecessors, and it was through the works of the Neoplatonists that he developed his deep appreciation for Plato.*

Augustine's philosophy thus draws significantly on the philosophy of late antiquity as well as on Christian revelation. Its originality lies partly in its synthesis of Greek and Christian thought, and partly in its development of a novel ego-centred approach to philosophy that anticipates modern thought, especially as exemplified in the philosophy of Descartes. In his De trinitate *(The Trinity)* and De civitate Dei, Augustine presents a line of thinking that foreshadows Descartes' famous cogito, ergo sum. Through his Confessionum libri tredecim *(Confessions, more usually known as Confessiones)*, the first significant autobiography in Western literature, and also through his Soliloquia *(Soliloquies)*, which is a dialogue between himself and Reason, Augustine introduced a first-person perspective to Western philosophy.

Early in his career, Augustine found himself attracted to philosophical scepticism. In his earliest extant work he offers his most extensive response to the main sceptical arguments of his day, including those that raise the possibility one might only be dreaming. His later responses to scepticism, though less extensive, are better focused; they concentrate on the self-knowledge he considers directly available to each knowing subject, including the knowledge that one exists. Taking the first-person perspective one can also develop, he tries to show, in his De trinitate, a convincing argument for mind–body dualism. But supposing, as he does, that each of us knows from our own case what a mind is raises, as Augustine is perhaps the first philosopher to realize, a problem about how one can ever know that there are minds in addition to one's own.

Augustine's account of language and meaning influenced the development of 'terminist' logic in the high middle ages. His thoughts on language acquisition in Confessiones provide a foil for Wittgenstein in the latter's Philosophical Investigations. Yet, some of Augustine's own reflections on ostensive definition in his dialogue De magistro *(The Teacher)* anticipate Wittgenstein's own views on language learning.

Augustine develops what is described as an 'active' theory of sense perception, according to which rays of vision touch objects whose consequent action on the body is 'noticed' by the mind or soul. Although his ideas on sense perception are interesting, his most influential epistemological conception is certainly his 'theory of illumination'. Instead of supposing that what we know can be abstracted from sensible particulars that instantiate such knowledge, he insists that our mind is so constituted as to see 'intelligible realities' directly by an inner illumination.

The modern concept of the will is often said to originate with Augustine. Certainly the idea of will is central to his philosophy of mind, as well as to his account of sin and the origin of evil. Strikingly, he uses psychological 'trinities', including the trinity of memory, understanding and will, to illuminate the doctrine of the Divine Trinity, where there is also a baffling unity in plurality. The theological warrant for this analogy Augustine finds in the biblical idea that God created human beings, and specifically the human mind, in his own image.

Augustine's attempts to achieve a philosophical understanding of theology and religious belief set the framework for much later medieval and early modern philosophy. On the issue of how reason should bear on religious faith, Augustine develops the idea that reason should work out an understanding of what we must first accept on faith. Yet he also displays a keen sensitivity to those issues most likely to challenge one's religious faith. Prominent among his concerns is the philosophical problem of evil, to which he offers what has proved to be perhaps the most influential type of solution.

Particularly striking is Augustine's virtually lifelong preoccupation with human freedom and how the fact that human beings are free to make their own choices can be reconciled with the Christian doctrines of God's foreknowledge, predestination and grace. Almost every important medieval philosopher in the Christian West would later contribute to the continuing effort to achieve a satisfactory reconciliation of these issues. It is significant that Leibniz, who gave the problem of freedom, foreknowledge, predestination and grace one of its most sophisticated treatments, also gave much of his philosophical attention to the equally Augustinian problem of evil.

Although Augustine did present an argument for the existence of God, it is his understanding of the divine attributes, and especially his insistence on divine 'simplicity', that is, on the idea that God is not distinct from his attributes, that has been especially influential on later thinkers. Also influential are his various attempts to understand the created world. Augustine made several important efforts, perhaps most notably in the last books of his Confessiones and in his De genesi ad litteram *(The Literal Meaning of Genesis)* to give a philosophically sophisticated account of the creation story in the biblical book of Genesis. His contrast between God's eternity and human temporality set the stage for later medieval and modern discussions of these issues, and his discussion of the nature of time in Book XI of his Confessiones is sometimes taken to epitomize philosophy.

Augustine's descriptions of mystical experience are among the most eloquent in Western literature; they belong among the classic texts of mysticism. However, Augustine's attempts to understand ritual are perhaps more remarkable for the directness with which he identifies and confronts difficult issues than for the success of his efforts to solve them. Those efforts seem to be hobbled by his version of mind–body dualism.

Augustine is a thoroughgoing intentionalist in ethics. This feature of his thought, as well as his unflinching insistence that one can do what one knows one ought not to be doing, mark him off from ethicists of the classical Greek period. Yet Augustine also preserves in his own thinking important strands of ancient Greek thought. Thus, for example, his development of the doctrine of the Christian virtues includes an echo of Plato's idea of the unity of the virtues. His insistence that 'ought' does not, in any straightforward way, imply 'can', distinguishes him, not only from his contemporary Pelagius, whom he helped brand as a Christian heretic, but also from most modern ethicists as well.

The philosophy of history Augustine develops in De civitate Dei *initiates a branch of philosophy that came into full flower in the nineteenth century. Also in that same work Augustine makes an influential contribution to what has come to be called 'just war theory', an applied ethical theory that has continued to develop even into the latter half of the twentieth century.*

1 Life
2 Scepticism
3 Philosophy of language
4 Epistemology
5–6 Philosophy of mind
7–8 Metaphysics
9–11 Philosophy of religion
12–14 Ethics
15 Philosophy of history

1 Life

Augustine was born Aurelius Augustinus, in the North African town of Tagaste (modern Souk Ahras in eastern Algeria), in the Roman Province of Numidia in the waning years of the Roman Empire. Except for a five-year stay in Italy, he spent his entire life in North Africa. Ordained a priest in AD 391 and made a bishop four years later, he lived out the remaining thirty-five years of his life, first as a coadjutor and then as the diocesan Bishop of Hippo (later Bône, now Annaba, Algeria), which was at the time the second most important port city in Africa.

Augustine's mother, Monica, was a devout Christian; his father, Patricius, a man of modest means, was not given a Christian baptism until he was on his death bed. Augustine received a classical education, first in the local grammar school, then in a higher school in nearby Madaura and finally, under the patronage of a local nobleman named Romanianus, at the university in Carthage. It was in Carthage as a student of rhetoric that he read Cicero's now lost dialogue, *Hortensius*, which, as he later wrote in *Confessionum libri tredecim* (Confessions, more usually known as *Confessiones*) altered his sensibility and brought him under the spell of philosophy.

After a brief period as a teacher of rhetoric in his home town, Augustine returned to Carthage and then, in AD 383, sailed for Rome. The five years he spent in Italy included a period as professor of rhetoric at Milan. Also in Milan, Augustine joined a circle of Neoplatonists and turned away from the Manicheism he had embraced in Carthage. In Book VII of *Confessiones* he explains how profoundly the Neoplatonic works he read in that Milanese circle helped him think about the nature of God and the problem of evil.

It was also in Milan, after he had immersed himself in Neoplatonism, that Augustine finally became a Christian convert, under the tutelage of Ambrose, Bishop of Milan, and through the continuing influence of his mother, who had followed him to Milan. The year before his baptism in AD 387 Augustine withdrew with several philosophically-minded relatives and associates to a villa at Cassiciacum, perhaps near Lake Como, where he wrote four of his earliest works, including an extremely interesting dialogue critical of the scepticism of the New Academy, *Contra academicos* (Against the Academicians), as well as the *Soliloquia* (Soliloquies).

Shortly after Augustine's baptism, his mother died. Following a brief stay in Rome, Augustine returned to Carthage in AD 388 and never left North Africa again. When he became first a priest and then a bishop, he sought to combine his pastoral duties with extensive excursions into philosophy and theology. It was in response to the spread of Donatism, Pelagianism and Manicheism in North Africa that Augustine wrote great treatises to expose those trends as heretical (see MANICHEISM; PELAGIANISM). It was in further response to the decline and fall of the Roman Empire, blamed by critics of Christianity on the Christianization of Rome, that Augustine wrote *De civitate Dei*. Rome had already been sacked in AD 410; Hippo itself was under siege as Augustine died twenty years later.

Augustine's literary output, produced with the help of scribes, is enormous. Chadwick (1986) claims that what survives of his work is the largest body of writing left by any ancient author. In addition to approximately one hundred books and treatises there are some two hundred letters and over five hundred sermons. Three years before his death, Augustine went through all his works and listed and commented on them in a great compendium, the *Retractationes*, or reviews. In some cases he retracts claims made in the works he reviews, or expresses regret at having made them. However, most of what he had written he lets stand. On the basis of these reviews, we may conclude that at least 90 per cent of Augustine's writings have survived.

After Augustine became a priest in AD 391, he wrote no single work that could be said to be entirely philosophical. On the other hand, hardly anything he wrote at any time in his life was entirely devoid of philosophy. Philosophical reflections, analyses and explorations turn up, often quite unexpectedly, in his sermons and letters and, of course, in the great theological, exegetical and doctrinal treatises. By the time Augustine came to write *De civitate Dei*, his lingering admiration for the grand ambitions of speculative philosophy and natural theology had become tempered with an acute awareness of how the human mind on its own is too crippled by old vices to be able to 'enjoy and abide in the changeless light' (*De civitate Dei* XI.2). Be that as it may, the philosophical light in his own eye burned brightly until the very end of his long and singularly productive life.

2   Scepticism

In Rome at the beginning of his stay in Italy Augustine grew increasingly dissatisfied with Manicheism, to which he had provisionally given his allegiance in Carthage. He found himself attracted to the sceptical viewpoint of the Academics, the followers of ARCESILAUS and the New Academy, who 'held that everything was a matter of doubt and asserted that we can know nothing for certain' (*Confessiones* V.10.19). Augustine seems to have learned of ancient scepticism, and of the debate between Arcesilaus and the stoic ZENO OF CITIUM from Cicero's *Academica* (see CICERO).

Augustine's most extensive discussion of scepticism is to be found in his earliest surviving work, the dialogue *Contra academicos*, written at Cassiciacum just months before his baptism. The Academics, according to him, base their claim that nothing can be known on the application of a strict criterion for knowledge put forward by Zeno. Although Augustine formulates Zeno's criterion in several ways and it is difficult to be certain exactly how he wants it to be understood, the point seems to be that, according to this criterion, something can be known just in case it cannot even seem to be false. Indubitability would then be both necessary and sufficient for knowledge. Against accepting such a criterion, Augustine proposes a dilemma: either the criterion is known to be true, or it is not. If it is known to be true, then the sceptics are wrong, since something is known. If it is not known to be true, then the sceptics have given us no adequate reason to become sceptics.

Augustine is not satisfied, however, with merely demonstrating the self-defeating character of the Academic position; he goes on to offer sample knowledge claims that he dares the sceptic to challenge. These sample claims fall naturally into three groups: *logical truths* (for example, 'There is one world or there is not'), *mathematical truths* (for example, 'Three times three is nine'), and *reports of immediate experiences* (for example, 'That tastes pleasant to me'). Of special interest is Augustine's response to the sceptical challenge, 'How do you know that this world exists if the senses are deceptive?' (*Contra academicos* III.11.24). Augustine answers: 'I call this entire thing, whatever it is, which surrounds and nourishes us, this object, I say, which appears before my eyes and which I perceive is made up of earth and sky, or what appears to be earth and sky, the world.' His idea is that, even if he is asleep and dreaming, he can know that 'the world' exists in the stipulated sense that there is for him at least a phenomenal world.

Although Augustine never goes on, in the fashion of DESCARTES (§9) to offer an argument for the existence of a world that is independent of him and his sense-impressions – what came later to be called 'the external world' – he does at least entertain the thought that there might not be such a world. As we know from later philosophy, that supposition is of great philosophical moment. Furthermore, his idea of an apparent world that fills our phenomenal space, whether or not there is an independent external world that resembles it, suggests a very Cartesian concept of mind.

Augustine never again devoted a whole treatise to the refutation of scepticism, but he did respond, again and again, to the challenge of Academic scepticism. Among the most interesting of these anti-sceptical passages are two in which he presents reasoning remarkably like Descartes' *cogito, ergo sum*:

> In respect of those truths I have no fear of the arguments of the Academics. They say, 'What if you are mistaken?' If I am mistaken, I am [*Si fallor, sum*]. Whoever does not exist cannot be mistaken; therefore I exist, if I am mistaken. Because, then, I exist if I am mistaken, how am I mistaken in thinking that I exist, when it is certain to me that I am if I am mistaken?
>
> (*De civitate Dei* XI.26)

Similar reasoning is to be found in *De trinitate* (On The Trinity), except that there Augustine defends the 'inner' knowledge by which we each know, in our own case, that we are alive. (Presumably 'alive' must be understood here not in a specifically biological sense, but rather in the sense in which we may ask if there is life after death.)

Although Augustine's way of certifying his claim to know that he exists is indeed very similar to the reasoning of Descartes, the similarities should not obscure the equally important differences. Perhaps the crucial difference is that, unlike Descartes, Augustine does not use 'I exist' as a foundation stone in a rational reconstruction of knowledge. Indeed, although there are passages in Augustine in works such as *De libero arbitrio* (On Free Choice of the Will) that suggest a foundationalist approach to knowledge, he never really offers anything that could be called a systematic reconstruction of what one can be said to know. His defence of 'I know I exist', in particular, is meant simply to defeat universal scepticism, of the sort that occupied his attention in *Contra academicos*. His idea is that, if universal scepticism can be defeated by an unassailable knowledge claim, then the Academics are not after all 'wiser than the rest' and not everything is 'a matter of doubt', as he had earlier been tempted to think.

An important weapon in the attacks of the Academic sceptics on putative knowledge claims was always the question, 'What if you are dreaming?' In a passage from Book XV of *De trinitate* that parallels the *si fallor, sum* passage from *De civitate Dei* just discussed, Augustine considers the Academic's taunt: 'Perhaps you are sleeping, and you do not know, and you see in your dreams.' Augustine replies: 'He who is certain about the knowledge of his own life does not say in it: "I know that I am awake," but "I know that I live".... He cannot be deceived in his knowledge of this even by dreams, because both to sleep and to see in dreams belong to one who lives' (*De trinitate* XV.12.21). In *Contra academicos*, Augustine rejects in a similar way the idea that not knowing whether one is dreaming might be a threat to one's claim to know logical and mathematical truths, or truths about one's immediate experiences.

However, Augustine never questions the assumption that we are sometimes awake and having veridical sense experiences, as well as sometimes dreaming. (He asserts that he sometimes knows, while he is dreaming, that he is dreaming, but he does not explain how he can know this.) Thus Augustine seems never to have considered the ultimate Cartesian challenge that perhaps no thought that has ever entered one's mind is any more nearly true than the illusions of one's dream: in effect, all life might be simply one's dream.

3 Philosophy of language

In Book I of *Confessiones*, Augustine presents a classic view of language acquisition through ostension: 'When [my elders] named some object, and accordingly moved towards something, I saw this and I grasped that the thing was called by the sound they uttered when they meant to point it out' (*Confessiones* I.8.13). This passage, made famous by WITTGENSTEIN in his *Philosophical Investigations*, may seem to most readers of the work to be little more than an aside. Yet, reflections on language appear throughout Augustine's writings, and language acquisition is a special concern of a relatively early work, the dialogue *De magistro* (The Teacher), a dialogue between Augustine and his young son Adeodatus (who died at age 16, shortly after the dialogue was written).

In *De magistro*, Augustine clearly poses the problem of the ambiguity of ostension, and indeed does so in a most memorable way. First, the issue is raised as to how one can point to the colour of a body as distinct from the body itself. Then, there are more general worries:

Augustine: Come now, tell me; if I, knowing absolutely nothing of the meaning of the word, should ask you while you are walking what walking is, how would you teach me?

Adeodatus: I should walk somewhat more quickly...

Augustine: Don't you know that walking is one thing and hurrying is something else?

(*De magistro* 3.6)

This last worry is surprisingly Wittgensteinian; as is Augustine's response. Although Augustine admits there is no way to eliminate all conceivable ambiguity in ostension, an intelligent learner, he thinks, will eventually catch on.

In *De magistro*, Augustine seems to want to account for meaning solely by appeal to what terms refer to. However, he does point out that for some pairs of words, each signifies 'as much' (*tantundem*) as the other; that is, the terms are co-referential, even though they do not signify 'the same' (*idem*) in that they do not have the same meaning or sense. Thus 'word' (*verbum*) and 'name' (*nomen*) are said to be co-referential, though not identical in meaning. Here Augustine relies on blurring the distinction, made in later medieval philosophy, between the personal and the material supposition of a term, or, we might say today, between *using* a term and *mentioning* it by quoting it (see LANGUAGE, MEDIEVAL THEORIES OF).

The discussion in later writings such as Book XV of *De trinitate* of the 'inner word' that is in no natural language seems to be, in part at least, an attempt to allow that a sense or concept mediates between a general term in a natural language and its extension:

For the thought formed from that thing which we know is the word which we speak in our heart, and it is neither Greek, nor Latin, nor of any other [natural] language; but when we have to bring it to the knowledge of those to whom we are speaking, then some sign is adopted by which it may be made known. And generally this is a sound, but at times also a nod; the former is exhibited to the ears, the latter to the eyes, in order that that word which we bear in our mind may also become known by bodily signs to the senses of the body.

(*De trinitate* XV.10.19)

Although the idea that thinking might be inner talking is as old as Plato's *Theaetetus*, it is to Book XV of *De trinitate* that WILLIAM OF OCKHAM, for example, makes reference in the *Summa logicae* (I.1) when he wants backing for the idea of there being a mental language, as well as spoken and written languages.

Augustine begins *De magistro* with an inquiry into the purpose of using language. His son's first suggestion, that we speak either to teach or to learn, encourages us to accept the common assumption that we use language, either mainly or solely, to pass on information. Although Augustine and his son quickly come to include singing and praying among the language activities they discuss, the dialogue never gives proper consideration in the manner of, for example, Wittgenstein or J.L. AUSTIN, to the full range of activities that make use of language or to the variety of roles individual utterances may play in our lives. On the contrary, Augustine concludes his dialogue with the suggestion, backed by an intriguing but somewhat elusive line of reasoning, that language only reminds us of what we already know.

Other important discussions of language are to be found in Augustine's *De doctrina Christiana* (On Christian Doctrine), especially at the beginning of Book II, as well as in the early treatise *De dialectica* (On Dialectic) (the authenticity of which, though contested, seems now to be quite generally accepted).

4 Epistemology

Augustine is said to have an 'active' theory of sense perception. The term 'active' in this context includes the idea that in vision the eyes emit rays that touch the object of vision. This is an idea that can be found in Plato's *Timaeus*, for example, as well as in other ancient sources (see PERCEPTION; PLATO). More generally, it is Augustine's contention that, although bodily sense organs undergo change during perception, perception is not something undergone by the soul. 'Perception', he writes in a famous passage, 'is something undergone by the body *per se* that is not hidden from the soul [*non latens animam*]' (*De quantitate animae* 48). The soul takes note of what the body undergoes: 'For it is not the body that perceives, but the soul through the body, which messenger, as it were, the soul uses to form in itself the very thing which is announced from the outside' (*De genesi ad litteram* XII.24.51).

In Book XII of *De genesi ad litteram*, Augustine departs altogether from commenting on the biblical book of Genesis and offers instead a somewhat independent treatise on three kinds of vision: bodily vision, spiritual vision and intellectual vision. What Augustine calls *bodily vision* is in fact sense perception; *spiritual vision* is the entertaining of mental imagery, whether in memory or imagination; and *intellectual vision* is the non-imaginal perception of universal objects, structures and truths. This work includes Augustine's most serious attempt to account for error in sense perception. It also includes one of his most beautiful descriptions of mystical vision, and in fact this work took on great significance for the discussion of mysticism in the later Middle Ages (see MYSTICISM, HISTORY OF).

Augustine's theory of sense perception seems not to be representational in the sense of making an image or sense-datum the direct object of perception. Thus in his discussion of vision in *De trinitate*, he claims that in seeing a body, we immediately form an image of it in our sense; yet we cannot discriminate between the form of the body seen and the form of the image we produce in our sense. He offers analogies and arguments to convince his readers that sight does have an image of the body seen, as soon and as long as it is seen, an image we may retain in memory after the perception. However, he seems to consider the formation of this inner image to be part of the process of seeing the *body*, not the production of something that could properly be said to be the direct object of perception.

Augustine's account of knowing, for example, what is virtue or what is a square, is not based on the idea of abstraction, as the accounts of AQUINAS and sometimes even ARISTOTLE are said to be. Rather, he espouses what is called 'the theory of illumination'. Augustine's talk of illumination is, in part, simply the deployment of an apt and traditional metaphor, that of light. He often uses this metaphor in discussions of cognition, as in the *Soliloquia*:

> So, whoever apprehends what is transmitted in the sciences, admits without any hesitation that this is absolutely true; and it must be believed that it could not be apprehended, if it were not illuminated by another sun, as it were, of its own.
>
> (*Soliloquia* I.5)

Platonic resonances in this passage are obvious. What exactly is meant by 'illumination' in this context is, however, less immediately obvious. What is the cash value of this light metaphor? Why does Augustine insist that whatever is apprehended through the sciences could not be apprehended if it were not appropriately 'illuminated'?

Perhaps the basic idea in Augustinian illumination is a generalization of the problem of learning by ostention. No group of instances of F-ness will display F-ness unambiguously as the single feature those items have in common; thus, if we ever come to understand what F-ness is, it will be only by an inner illumination that reveals something that cannot be unambiguously pointed to or displayed. In *De magistro*, Augustine concludes that no 'outward' teacher can teach us what anything is by asking or telling us something. At most, the 'outward' teacher can admonish or remind us to look 'within', where Christ the inner teacher dwells. Christ is identified as 'the unchangeable excellence of God and the everlasting wisdom that every rational soul does indeed consult' (*De magistro* 11.38) (see ILLUMINATION).

More generally, Augustine, like Plato before him, insists that 'intelligible realities', presumably including what we might think of as a priori truths, cannot be learned or even confirmed in sense experience. However, Augustine explicitly rejects Plato's idea that the soul might have been introduced to the intelligible realm before birth; instead he espouses innatism. Referring to the Socratic interrogation of the slave boy in Plato's *Meno*, which is meant to demonstrate that there is latent knowledge of geometry even among the untutored, Augustine protests that not all would have been geometricians in their previous life, 'since there are so few of them in the human race that one can hardly be found.' He goes on:

> We ought rather to believe that the nature of the intellectual mind is so formed as to see those things which, according to the disposition of the Creator, are subjoined to intelligible things in the natural order, in a sort of incorporeal light of its own kind.
> (*De trinitate* XII.15.24)

5 Philosophy of mind: dualism and memory

Although arguments for soul–body, or mind–body, dualism are almost as old as Western philosophy, all such reasoning before Augustine seems to have started from an externalist or third-person perspective. Thus when Plato in the *Phaedo*, for example, has Socrates claim that we have knowledge we could not have acquired in this life and therefore our souls must have existed before they took on this bodily form, he is reasoning from a perfectly impersonal point of view.

By contrast, Augustine's approach is ego-centred, or first-personal. In Book VIII of *De trinitate*, he claims that we, from our own individual first-person perspective, 'know what a soul is, since we have a soul'. In the next book he adds, 'When the mind knows itself, it alone is the parent of its own knowledge' (*De trinitate* IX.12.18). In the following book he surveys philosophical theories about what the mind is (for example, that it is blood, that it is the brain, that it is a collection of atoms, that it is air, that it is fire, that it is some 'fifth body' or that it is a harmony). Reflection on this divergence of philosophical views suggests that the mind does not really know what it is. Yet if, as Augustine has maintained, the mind knows what a mind is from its own case, then it knows and is certain what a mind is. Therefore if the mind is uncertain whether it is blood, or the brain, or fire, or air, or indeed anything corporeal, it is really none of these things; if it is in fact uncertain as to whether it is any of these corporeal things, then it is none of them (*De trinitate* X.10.16).

Of course, the idea that the mind can know what a mind is only from its own case raises the problem of other minds. How do I know that there are minds to go with other human or animal bodies, if all I can ever observe are the motions of those bodies? Augustine's response is the earliest statement of the notorious argument from analogy. 'Just as we move our body in living', Augustine writes, 'so, we notice, those bodies are moved'. We come to think that there is something present in another body 'such as is present in us to move our mass in a similar way' (*De trinitate* VIII.6.9).

Recently, philosophers such as Norman Malcolm (1963) have argued that it is a mistake to suppose that one could come to know from one's own case what a mind is, or what thinking or feeling or having a pain is. They argue that we need a criterion to determine whether x is in pain or whether y even has a mind. Since one does not use a criterion in one's own case, they continue, either the argument from analogy could never get started (because we lack the needed criterion) or it is otiose (because we have such a criterion). Argumentation of this sort is often taken to be directed at Descartes' philosophy of mind; but in fact it is Augustine, rather than Descartes, who offers the argument from analogy and who maintains that each of us knows what a mind is from our own case, and can know what a mind is only from our own case (see DESCARTES, R. §§7–8).

Although Augustine's theory of sense perception seems not to be representational in the sense of making an image or sense-datum the object, or at least the direct object, of perception, his account of memory does seem to be representational. He is inclined to think of what is remembered, or perhaps what is remembered directly, as an image rather than as what the memory image portrays. Indeed, in *De magistro* he asserts flatly, 'When a question arises not about what we sense before us, but about what we have sensed in the past, then we do not speak of the things themselves, but of images impressed from them on the mind and committed to memory' (*De magistro* 12.39). Augustine concludes, incorrectly, from the fact that we have no direct access to absent persons and things, or past events, that there is no way one can make claims about *them*, as distinct from their images, and hence there is no way we can, either falsely or truly, remember those past or absent things themselves.

Although Augustine sometimes uses *memoria* in ways that suggest that it means simply 'memory', he also uses the term much more broadly. Thus Book X of the *Confessiones* is a treatise on *memoria* as mind. In that book, Augustine tells us that the storehouse of his *memoria* includes not only images of objects and of past events but also feelings and experiences, certain facts, himself (!), and principles and laws of various sorts.

About feelings, Augustine asks how one could know what the terms for them mean unless on hearing, for example, the term 'pain', one had in one's *memoria* what that term means. However, if one had pain itself in one's *memoria*, he reasons, it would hurt just to think about the meaning of the word. Yet surely, he goes on, one can think about what 'pain' means, or what a pain is, without being in pain. But how? Augustine is not able to say. Although this apparently original criticism of imagist accounts of meaning seems quite devastating, it did not lead Augustine himself to turn away from his effort to appeal to images in explaining how words for feelings, or moods (such as 'happy' and 'sad') have the meaning they do.

6 Philosophy of mind: will

As Albrecht Dihle (1982) and others have argued, the concept of the will, important in much medieval and modern philosophy including the idea of a volition as an act of will, can be said to originate with Augustine. Plato's division of the self in his *Republic* into reason, spirit and appetite, by contrast, seems to make no room for the will as a distinct faculty or power, and Aristotle's subtle discussion of the voluntary in Book III of his *Nicomachean Ethics* seems not to presuppose the idea of any such force or power as the will.

In *De trinitate*, Augustine presents among other putative analogies to the divine Trinity the mental trinity of memory, understanding and will. His suggestion is that just as each of the three divine persons, Father, Son and Holy Spirit, is distinct from the other two – though each is also God and not just part of God – so memory, understanding and will are each distinct from each other, though each is also mind and not just part of mind. Yet Augustine also recognizes that the human mind, with its various trinities, is only an imperfect image of the divine Trinity. The mind-as-will may well operate in opposition to the mind-as-understanding; indeed, a will that is evil does just that. The idea of there being such a thing as what the Greeks called *akrasia* – doing what one knows one ought not to be doing – is thus not a conundrum for Augustine, in the way that it is for SOCRATES and Plato, or even for Aristotle in *Nicomachean Ethics* VII 3 (see AKRASIA).

Sometimes Augustine suggests that what he terms 'the first cause of sin', namely the will, is itself uncaused. 'What cause of the will could there be', he asks rhetorically in *De libero arbitrio* (III.17), 'except the will itself?' This point is important to Augustine since, as he claims in this passage, there would be no such thing as sin if the acts of one's will were caused by something extraneous to the will. The idea of the will as a first, uncaused cause, should be coupled with Augustine's claim that the will is 'in our power'. Since it is in our power, he writes, it is free for us (*De libero arbitrio* III.3).

There is also, however, a competing suggestion also to be found in Augustine, to the effect that God, through his knowledge, is the cause of all that he foreknows, including free choices of the will (see §7). Since Augustine defines 'will' (*voluntas*) as 'a movement of the soul, under no compulsion, either toward getting or not losing something' (*De duabis animabus contra Manichaeos* (On the Two Souls) 10.14), it follows that the will is free from compulsion. In discussing this definition Augustine makes clear that ignorance, though it may excuse an action that would otherwise count as sinful, does not render the will unfree (*Retractationes* 14.3).

In his efforts to define and reject Pelagianism as a heresy, however, Augustine has to explain how the grace of God can work on the human will without destroying its freedom. 'Do we then by grace make free will void?' is how he puts the challenge to himself in *De spiritu et littera* (On The Spirit and the Letter) XXX.52. His answer is that, no, 'free will is not made void through grace, but is established, since grace cures the will whereby righteousness is freely loved.' This is the doctrine of 'prevenient' grace, which Augustine distinguishes from various other kinds of grace. The concept of the will is thus a point of intersection for several characteristic Augustinian doctrines. First, human wills are depraved as a result of Adam's original sin. Second, a human will is able to act rightly only through the grace of God. Third, if our wills were not free, we could not be justly punished for choosing wrongly. Fourth, God foreknew who among human creatures would choose rightly and become saints, and he also predestined them, or foreordained that they would do so. It seems that Augustine's emphasis on the efficacy and importance of God's grace must inevitably qualify his defense of free will. Nevertheless, the anti-Pelagian writings Augustine composed in the last two decades of his life are eloquent testimony to the ingenuity with which he sought to reconcile the doctrine of divine grace with his insistence that human beings are free to make their own choices (see GRACE).

Augustine's efforts to establish the compatibility of God's foreknowledge with human free will were almost as extensive as his attempts to show that God's grace is also compatible with free will. However, Augustine paid much less attention to the worry that predestination also poses a threat to the possibility of free will. Thus in his *De praedestinatione sanctorum* (On the Predestination of Saints) 37, he insists that God chose the elect 'before the foundation of the world', not simply because they were in fact going to be 'holy and immaculate' but that they might become so. Clearly he thinks of predestination as something additional to mere foreknowledge. So, even if we understand how it can be that God's foreknowledge does not render our choices unfree, we will still need to deal with the additional threat to our freedom that seems to be posed by predestination (see PREDESTINATION).

Knowing, as already noted, can be thought of as a sort of seeing; and we are not usually tempted to think of seeing as determining the nature of what is seen. However, predestination is a form of predetermination, and how predetermination can be compatible with human freedom is much more difficult to understand. Augustine, though he certainly does not ignore this problem, is less helpful in showing how it can be dealt with than he is with the problem of foreknowledge and free will.

7 Metaphysics: God and divine attributes

In *De libero arbitrio* (II.15.39), Augustine offers an argument for the existence of God. He first gets his interlocutor to admit that (1) x is God if and only if x is more excellent than our minds and nothing is more excellent than x. He then tries to establish that (2) truth exists and is more excellent than our minds. From these two premises he concludes that (3) something is God (in other words, God exists). His idea is that either nothing is more excellent than truth, so that, since truth is more excellent than our minds,

truth itself is God; or else something is more excellent even than truth, in which case it (or, we could add, something even more excellent than it) is God.

In fact, Augustine has the idea that God is not only something more excellent than our minds, but is also something than which our minds can conceive nothing more excellent. Thus he writes that 'God is the supreme good, and that than which nothing can be nor can be conceived to be better.' This formula is remarkably close to the one ANSELM uses in formulating the ontological argument: 'For we believe that you are something than which nothing greater can be conceived' (*Proslogion* 2) (see GOD, CONCEPTS OF).

Augustine made important contributions toward the project of giving a philosophical analysis of the divine attributes, or divine 'names', as philosophers of the high Middle Ages sometimes called them. Thus he made clear that, although God is omnipotent, he is unable to do certain things, such as sin, die or make a mistake. According to Augustine, 'x is omnipotent' means that 'x does whatever x wills'. However, Augustine does not deal with seeming difficulties posed by this account, for example, whether 'if God wills to sin, God sins' can be true even if its antecedent is necessarily false, or what to say about an agent with only minimal power whose wants, because they are also minimal, never outrun the agent's power to satisfy them (see OMNIPOTENCE).

Augustine is perhaps the first in a long line of philosophers to maintain that God is perfectly simple, that is, that God is identical with his attributes (*De civitate Dei* XI.10; *De trinitate* VI.7.8). Thus God is his goodness, he is his wisdom, and so forth. Later philosophers who made this claim central to their philosophical theologies include Anselm and Aquinas (see IMMUTABILITY; SIMPLICITY, DIVINE).

Augustine links divine simplicity to God's immutability. Sometimes he even explains simplicity in terms of immutability. 'The reason why a nature is called simple', he writes, 'is that it cannot lose any attribute it possesses, that there is no difference between what it is and what it has' (*De civitate Dei* XI.10). He goes on to add that even the incorruptible body we shall receive in the resurrection is neither simple nor unchangeable. That body will not be simple, he maintains, because the substance 'in virtue of which it is called a body is other than the quality from which it derives the epithet incorruptible.' Even the human soul, he continues, is other than its wisdom. Only God *is* his wisdom.

In his effort to clarify the divine attributes, Augustine sometimes admits defeat. Thus, in Book I of *De doctrina Christiana*, he concedes that his efforts to clarify the doctrine of the Trinity have been unworthy of God and suggests that God is ineffable.

He then notes that to say God is ineffable is to describe God and therefore to show, by saying it, that what one says is false.

8 Metaphysics: creation, time and eternity

Plato, in his *Timaeus*, pictures creation as the action of a divine craftsman who looks at eternal paradigms to form instances in an also pre-existent 'receptacle'. Augustine, interpreting Genesis 1: 1 to mean that God created the heavens and the earth out of nothing (*ex nihilo*), insists that God created unformed matter, as well as what he formed from it. His rejection of the Platonic alternative is explicit: 'You did not hold anything in your hand, of which you made this heaven and earth; for how could you come by what you had not made, to make something? For what is there that exists, except because you exist?' (*Confessiones* XI.5.7). Augustine's assumption is that nothing exists, except because God exists. Moreover, because everything changeable has a beginning, and the heavens and the earth are certainly changeable, God created them.

Not only did God create the world, and create it out of nothing, according to Augustine, he also conserves or sustains it, lest it disappear into nothing. If God's power 'ever ceased to govern creatures', he writes:

> their essences would pass away and all nature would perish. When a builder puts up a house and departs, his work remains in spite of the fact that he is no longer there. But the universe will pass away in the twinkling of an eye if God withdraws his ruling hand.
>
> (*De genesi ad litteram* IV.12.22)

Here is the precursor of Descartes' idea that 'the same power and action are needed to preserve anything at each individual moment of its duration as would be required to create that thing anew if it were not yet in existence' (*Meditation* III) (see CREATION AND CONSERVATION, RELIGIOUS DOCTRINE OF).

If the idea that God created matter is philosophically troublesome, even more puzzling is the contention, which Augustine affirms, that God created time. To make sense of that claim, one must study what Augustine says about time. In a much cited passage, Augustine asks, 'What then is time?' and responds: 'If nobody asks me, I know; but if I am asked what it is and want to explain, I don't know how to' (*Confessiones* XI.14). Wittgenstein (1958a: 26) thought this question epitomized philosophy as a misguided search for definitions (see WITTGENSTEIN, L. §§15–17). By contrast, Bertrand Russell praised Augustine's theory of time as 'a very able theory, deserving to be seriously considered', and 'a great advance on anything to be found on the subject in Greek philosophy' (Russell 1945: 354).

In his discussion, Augustine appeals to the fact that we speak of 'a long time' and 'a short time'. He then develops a perplexity that Aristotle had raised in a highly condensed form in Book IV of his *Physics* but never resolved. 'How can anything that does not exist', Augustine asks, 'be either long or short?' (*Confessiones* XI.15.18). But the past is no more and the future is not yet, he continues; only the present exists. 'Can present time be long?' he asks. For any present period of time, he notes – the present century, the present year, the present day, or whatever – part of it is no more and part is not yet. All that is ever really present is the instantaneous divider between what is not yet and what is no more. As a simple divider between the past and the future, the present, the 'now', has no duration at all and so cannot be either long or short. Therefore, how can times be either long or short? Augustine concludes that it is in his own mind that he measures time. It is mental impressions that one measures, he says, and therefore time is the measure of something mental.

Early on in Book XI, Augustine had sought to deal with the sceptical question, 'What was God doing before he made heaven and earth?' (*Confessiones* XI.10.12). His answer is to say that 'there cannot possibly be time without a creature [*sine creatura*]' (*Confessiones* XI. 30), presumably because the mind of God is timeless, as time is a measure of created minds.

In Book XI of *De civitate Dei*, Augustine seems to revert to a more Platonic theory of time, according to which time is the motion of bodies, perhaps especially the motion of the heavenly bodies. The explicit question up for discussion is why God made the world at one time rather than another. Augustine may have derived this sceptical question, and the earlier one in *Confessiones* introducing the discussion of time, from Cicero's *De natura deorum*, although Cicero was himself passing on discussions that have their roots in Presocratic philosophy.

It would have been odd for Augustine to conclude that time is the measure of bodily motion, since he explicitly rejects such a theory in *Confessiones* with the apt objection that time may equally be the measure of a body's rest. In Book XII of *De civitate Dei*, however, Augustine makes it clear that he considers the movements of the angels to be sufficient for there to be time. Angels have always existed, he claims, in the sense that there is no time at which they failed to exist. Nevertheless, they are created beings; indeed time was created with them.

In supposing that God creates time, Augustine does

not of course suppose that this creation took place in time. 'There can be no doubt', he writes, 'that the world was not created *in* time but *with* time' (*De civitate Dei* XI.6). Augustine's idea is that God timelessly creates time; indeed, God's own being is immutable and timeless. In supposing that God timelessly creates time, Augustine avoids a paradox in the idea of time having been created. One might otherwise suppose that the idea of time having been created must somehow involve a contrast between a time when there was no time and the temporal period that began with time's creation. The absurdity of that idea seems to have led Aristotle to reason that time, like the universe, is eternal. But Aristotle did not consider the Augustinian idea that God timelessly creates time, perhaps even a first time (see TIME).

Though Augustine often uses temporal words to talk about God and God's actions, those words are to be understood in a special sense. Sometimes Augustine warns his readers of this need. Thus he writes in *Confessiones* (XI.13.16), addressing God: 'It is not in time that you are before times; otherwise you would not be before all times; you precede all past times in the loftiness of your ever-present eternity.' He adds, 'Your years, because they abide, all abide at once.'

One might suppose that, if God is eternal in the sense of being 'before' or 'outside' all time, God could have no causal efficacy *in* time. With similar reasoning, Aristotle complained that Plato's Forms, being eternal and unchanging, could not be the cause of something's happening now rather than earlier or later. With Aristotle's criticism in mind, a Christian believer might complain that Augustine's depiction of God as being out of time means that God could not act in history. Augustine is, however, in a rather different position from Plato, since he supposes God to have created time. Though we may speak of God's actions *in* history, God in Augustine's view brings it about timelessly; there is time in which the entities of creation can act and be acted on by him. In the dialogue *De libero arbitrio* (II.3), the character Evodius maintains that 'God has decided once and for all how the order of the universe he created is to be carried out, and does not arrange anything by a new act of will' (see ETERNITY).

Following in the Platonic and Neoplatonic tradition, Augustine supposes there are different senses of 'exist', or ways in which something may be said to exist. He assigns the highest way, or the strictest sense, to the existence of God: 'Being is in the highest and truest sense of the term, proper to Him from whom being derives its name' (*De trinitate* V.2.3). Here Augustine links Platonic metaphysics with God's saying to Moses in Exodus 3:14, 'I am who am.' God truly is, Augustine writes in *De natura boni* 19, because he is immutable. 'For every change', Augustine goes on, 'makes what was, not to be; therefore he truly is who is unchangeable.'

9 Philosophy of religion: problem of evil

Although the author of the biblical book of Job questioned how it can be that unjust suffering is compatible with the nature of God, he seems not to have had a problem with the mere existence of evil. It may be that EPICURUS was the first thinker to ask how the existence of evil could be compatible with the nature of God (Lactantius, *De ira Dei* (The Wrath of God) 13).

In *Confessiones* (VII.5.7), Augustine raises this compatibility problem in a particularly persistent way. Put in a somewhat more modern way, the problem is how the statements (1) God is all-good and (2) God is all-powerful, can be consistent with (3) there is evil. Although the conjunction of these three statements is not logically inconsistent, it is natural to assume that (4) if there existed some being both all-good and all-powerful, evil would not exist. The conjunction of (1), (2), (3) and (4) is indeed logically inconsistent (see EVIL, PROBLEM OF; LEIBNIZ, G.W. §3).

When Augustine was a Manichean, he rejected (2) and, insofar as for Manicheans the principle of evil was coequal with the principle of good, there is a way in which he could also be said to have rejected (1). However, as Augustine moved toward Christianity, those options became closed. In *Confessiones* (VII.5.7), Augustine considers rejecting (3). 'Can it be', he asks, 'that there simply is no evil?' But if there really is no evil, he reasons, our fear of evil is unfounded; however, an unfounded fear of evil would itself be evil. If there is no evil, therefore, there is evil; so, there is evil. Augustine returns a few sections later in the same work to embrace the Neoplatonic idea that evil is not a reality but a mere privation and so, in a way, does not exist. Yet the fear of something nonexistent can itself be evil.

In *De civitate Dei* (XII.8), Augustine finds the root cause of evil in human free will. 'A will could not become evil', he writes, 'if it were unwilling to become so; and therefore its shortcomings are justly punished, being not necessary but voluntary.' In insisting that the existence of free but evil choices of human agents is compatible with the all-goodness and all-power of God, Augustine thus rejects (4) above. Since the problem of evil, conceived as a problem about the apparent inconsistency among (1), (2) and (3), is a purely *a priori* problem, all one would need to do to solve it would be to show that (4) is not a necessary or conceptual truth. Augustine, however, tries to do more; he tries to show that (4) is actually false.

When Augustine uses what has recently come to be called the 'free-will defence' to solve the problem of evil, he does not reject the logical possibility that human beings might have been created to have free will, yet never sin. For example, he supposes that the saints in heaven will have free will, yet they will sin no more. 'Now the fact that they will be unable to take pleasure in sin', he writes in *De civitate Dei* (XXII.30), 'does not entail that they will have no free choice. In fact, the will will be the freer in that it is freed from taking pleasure in sin and immovably fixed in the pleasure of not sinning.' Adam's freedom, Augustine goes on in the same passage, was an ability not to sin, combined with the possibility of sinning. The freedom the saints will enjoy in heaven will bring with it, he says, the impossibility of sinning. Lest we protest, in the manner of philosophers who have discussed this issue in our own time, that the impossibility of sinning would destroy free will, Augustine adds that God cannot sin, yet surely God has free will.

Thus Augustine's rejection of (4) does not rest on a rejection of the logical possibility that God might have created a sinless world in which agents exercise their free will. Rather, it rests on Augustine's belief that the impossibility of sinning, when it finally comes to the saints in heaven, is a free gift of God's grace, not anything God is constrained to bestow on creatures, not even by his all-goodness. Another way that Augustine tries to show (4) is false is to suggest that evil, or sin, is like a dark colour in a beautiful painting: in itself, ugly, but in context something that contributes to the beauty and goodness of the whole (*De civitate Dei* XI.23).

10 Philosophy of religion: divine foreknowledge and free will

The problem of how God's foreknowledge of what an agent will do is compatible with that agent's acting freely seems to be a specific version of the problem Aristotle discusses in *De interpretatione* about how the prior truth of a statement about a future event is compatible with that event's being contingent. Aristotle's discussion and the commentaries on it by BOETHIUS, as well as the latter's own discussion of the problem of foreknowledge in Book V of his *De consolatione philosophiae* (The Consolation of Philosophy), were influential on later medieval discussions. Also influential, however, was Augustine's discussion in Book III of his *De libero arbitrio*, and perhaps even more so in Book V of the *De civitate Dei*.

In *De civitate Dei*, Augustine takes Cicero as his target. As represented by Augustine, Cicero argues that (1) if God foreknows all events, then all events happen according to a fixed, causal order, and (2) if all events happen according to a fixed, causal order, then nothing depends on us and there is no such thing as free will. If we can then add (3) God foreknows all events, as Augustine insists we can, we can conclude that (4) nothing depends on us and there is no such thing as free will. Augustine attempts to defeat this argument by insisting that 'our wills themselves are in the order of causes' (*De civitate Dei* V.9), and adds it is necessary that, 'when we will, we will by free choice' (V.10). Moreover, among the things that God foreknows are the things that we will to do of our own free choice. Thus premise (2) is false and God's foreknowledge, rather than being a threat to free will, is in a way its guarantor.

Talk of God's foreknowledge, as Augustine himself realizes and points out, is somewhat misleading. God, as an eternal being, is outside time. However, for any event that to us temporal creatures is still in the future, it is true to say of God that God knows, as we should say from our own point of view, 'already' what will happen. Augustine's explicit discussion of the problem of foreknowledge and free will proceeds as though God's knowledge perfectly reflects the causal order in which human wills operate freely, without itself causing that order. Thus he insists in *De civitate Dei* (V.10), for example, that 'it is not that one sins because God foreknew that one would sin'. But in fact, Augustine, like AQUINAS after him, seems to hold the view that God's knowledge actually causes to happen what God knows will happen.

The context for Augustine's assertion that God causes what he knows is a discussion of how God can know the material world without himself having a body or any sense organs. Rejecting the suggestion that God might need messengers of any sort, whether sense organs or angelic witnesses, Augustine boldly denies that God's knowledge is in any way dependent on what he knows. God does not know creatures because they are, he writes in *De trinitate* (XV.13.22); rather, they are because God knows them. Indeed, Augustine adds in the same passage, God learns nothing about creatures from the creatures themselves. If then we are unable to surprise God with any of our free choices, and God's perfect and immutable knowledge not merely reflects but actually causes us to be the (to God) unsurprising creatures we are, how is there any metaphysical room for human free will? And how can it not be the case that we sin because God foreknows we will?

It seems to be Augustine's view that God's foreknowledge that, for example, Peter would deny Christ three times somehow causes Peter's denial without making it unfree and, therefore, without detracting from Peter's responsibility for it. Indeed, the view seems to be that God's foreknowledge of a free choice can cause there to be the very free choice that there is. Moreover, even though the choice is caused by God, it is the agent, not God, who makes the choice. Since the free choice is voluntary, the agent is responsible for it.

Of course, the problem mentioned earlier as to how predestination is consistent with free will is directly relevant here. If Augustine's account of God's grace can make clear how it is possible for God to foreordain and predestinate human choices without rendering those choices unfree, then perhaps it will also make clear how God can cause them without making them unfree. On the face of it, however, the claim that (1) God causes everything he foreknows, including the free choices human beings make, seems simply to contradict the assurance that (2) 'it is not that one sins because God foreknew that one would sin' (*De civitate Dei* V.10). If there should be no satisfactory way of reconciling (1) and (2), (1) should be qualified or rejected as a true reflection of Augustine's view, since it is far less prominent in Augustine's writings than the repeated insistence on (2) (see FREE WILL; OMNISCIENCE; PREDESTINATION).

11 Philosophy of religion: faith, reason and mysticism

When discussing the relationship of faith and reason, Augustine characteristically insists that faith must precede understanding. 'For understanding is the reward of faith', he writes in his *In Ioannis evangelium tractatum* (Homilies on the Gospel of John), adding: 'Therefore do not seek to understand in order to believe, but believe that you may understand' (29.6).

The comment of Augustine's interlocutor, Evodius, in the dialogue *De libero arbitrio* (II.2), 'But we want to know and understand what we believe', is apt, not only for much of Augustine's own writing but for much of medieval philosophy as well. The *Proslogion*, the treatise in which ANSELM develops his famous ontological argument, carries the Augustinian subtitle, 'Faith in Search of Understanding'.

In Question 48 of *De diversis quaestionibus LXXXIII* (Eighty-Three Different Questions), Augustine divides the classes of things to be believed into three. In the first class, ranging over the temporal dealings of human beings, are things that are 'always believed and never understood'. In the second group, which are 'understood as soon as they are believed', are 'human reasonings'. It is the third group, which concern divine dealings, that are first believed and afterward understood. However, even if 'I believe in order that I may understand' applies only to theological questions, there is still a problem. How can one believe something before one even understands it? As Augustine himself points out in his sermons, his hearers need to understand what he is saying before they are in position to believe what he says. How can one believe, for example, the biblical claim that the earth was once invisible and without form before one even understands what that claim means? In *Confessiones* (XII.23), Augustine makes a distinction between questions about truth and those about meaning. He seems to suppose one can accept that, for example, the biblical account of creation in Genesis 1 is true without knowing what each of the statements that make it up means. Of course one would need to have some general idea of what those statements might mean in order for one's faith in the truth of the account to have any real content, but even a minimal understanding might be enough to give one's faith some purchase.

How, though, did Augustine think one is to choose among rival authorities in coming to accept, for example, some biblical or creedal statement, or some commentary on the Bible or the creed, as true? He seems to have allowed for both prior and subsequent constraints on what should be believed. As for prior constraints, he writes in *De moribus ecclesiae catholicae* (Morals of the Catholic Church) 7.11: 'We must have recourse to the teachings of those who were in all probability wise'. As for subsequent constraints, he looked for predictions that are not borne out as discrediting a putative authority. Thus he discredited astrologers in *Confessiones* (VII.6) by pointing out that it sometimes happens that a slave in misery has a twin brother who prospers as a freeman, though the twins were born under precisely the same astrological sign.

Later in *Confessiones* (VII.17), Augustine describes an early attempt at mystical ascent. Though 'in an instant of awe', his mind, he says, caught sight of God, he had not the strength to continue the vision; the memory remained with him as something he longed for. In the same work, he describes a more prolonged ascent that grew out of conversation with his mother:

> As the flame of love burned stronger in us and raised us higher towards the Selfsame, we passed through all corporeal things, and the heavens themselves, from which the sun and the moon and the stars shine down upon the earth.... At length we came to our own minds and passed beyond them to that place of everlasting plenty, where you feed Israel forever with the food of truth. There life is the Wisdom by which all things are made.
>
> (*Confessiones* IX.10)

Shortly thereafter Augustine's mother died.

Augustine wonders whether the moment when he

and his mother 'reached out in thought and touched the eternal Wisdom' prefigured life in heaven. In perhaps his most eloquent description of the beatific vision, Augustine suggests that such an experience may help one live a more moral life on earth:

> There the virtues of the soul are not laborious and wearisome. For there desire is not bridled by the work of temperance, or adversities borne by the work of fortitude, or iniquities punished by the work of justice, or evils shunned by the work of prudence. There the one virtue and the whole of virtue is to love what you see and the greatest happiness is to have what you love. For there the heavenly life is drunk at its source, from which a little is splashed over onto this human life so that it is lived among the temptations of this world with temperance, with fortitude, with justice, and with prudence.
>
> (*De genesi ad litteram* XII.26.54)

In Chapter 7 of the treatise *De cura pro mortuis* (On the Care of the Dead), Augustine raises a problem for the understanding of religious ritual. He wonders what can be the point of bending one's knees, holding out one's hands or prostrating oneself in supplication to God when the prayer we have in our hearts is already known to God. Augustine's problem is really two problems. First, why should we go through a prayer, whether inwardly or outwardly, when God already knows what we want to say? Second, why should we give outward expression to a prayer, since God, the intended recipient, knows already what we say inwardly in our hearts? He then gives an answer which is intended to apply to both problems: 'Although these motions of the body cannot come to be without a motion of the mind preceding them, when they have been made, visibly and externally, that invisible inner motion which caused them is itself strengthened' (*De cura pro mortuis* 5.7). The idea is that going through a prayer intensifies the thoughts and feelings that the prayer expresses, which answers the first problem. Moreover, doing this outwardly, with appropriate bodily motions, strengthens the inner feelings that such bodily motions express, thus answering the second problem. Augustine must have known as well as we do today that ritual sometimes actually gets in the way of our thinking the thoughts and having the feelings that the ritual is supposed to express. However, it would be enough for him if religious ritual regularly, or even just often, had the effect of nurturing and strengthening religious feelings and attitudes.

An odd thing about Augustine's response to his problem is that, according to his own metaphysical principles, the response is inappropriate, or even false. The reason is that, in Augustine's view, the soul or mind is superior to the body and what is superior cannot be affected by what is inferior to it (*De genesi ad litteram* XII.16.33). So, neither the physical productions of sound in saying a prayer nor the physical movements of kneeling or stretching out one's hands can possibly have the effect of intensifying thoughts or feelings.

No doubt what Augustine should have concentrated on is not the bodily motions of tongue, hand or knee in prayer, but rather the importance to a relationship, whether it is a relationship with God or with another human being, of giving expression to one's feelings of gratitude, remorse or whatever else might be appropriate. Thus God's omniscience is really inessential to the issues Augustine is raising. Because some person, A, knows another person, B, very well, it might be the case that A knows that B is sorry for having wronged A, even though B has not yet apologized or asked for forgiveness. In that case, for A to apologize or ask for forgiveness would not have the purpose of passing on information to A; nevertheless, it might be important to their relationship. This might also be true of a relationship between a human being and God. This alternative response to the problems Augustine raises about ritual should remind us of Augustine's tendency, noted in the discussion of *De magistro* above, to try to reduce the role of language as well as that of gesture to one of passing on information, or even to merely reminding us of what we already know.

12 Ethics: sin, vice and virtue

For Socrates, Plato and Aristotle, there existed the problem of how we can ever do what we know we ought not to be doing. This is the problem of *akrasia* (see AKRASIA). From this ancient perspective, perhaps the most striking thing about Augustinian ethics is its easy acceptance of *akrasia*. In *Confessiones* II, Augustine tells of stealing pears as a boy of sixteen. He spends two chapters ruminating on what might have motivated his theft. It was not the pears themselves, he says, for he had better ones at home. He concludes that it was the flavour of sinning that motivated him.

In *De libero arbitrio* (I. 2), Augustine admits that the question of why we do evil disturbed him greatly when he was young and moved him toward Manicheism. Once he accepted the idea of original sin, however, he found nothing paradoxical in saying of someone: 'He hates the thing itself because he knows that it is evil; and yet he does it because he is bent on doing it' (*De nuptiis et concupiscentia* (On Marriage and Concupiscence) I.28.31).

Augustine was an extreme intentionalist in ethics. In *De sermone Domini in monte* (Commentary on the Lord's Sermon on the Mount) I.12.34, he identifies three necessary and sufficient conditions for committing a sin: receiving an evil suggestion, taking pleasure in the thought of performing the act suggested and consenting to perform the act. Thus in Augustine's view, whether one commits a sin is in no way dependent on whether the contemplated action is actually carried out. Even when the action is carried out, it is the intention (understood as suggestion, pleasure and consent), rather than the action itself, or its consequences, that is sinful.

Augustine also devoted two treatises to the topic of lying. In the first of these, *De mendacio* (On Lying), he first suggests that a person S lies in saying p if, and only if (1) p is false, (2) S believes that p is false and (3) S says p with the intention of deceiving someone. He then considers three cases: first, that of someone with a false belief who wants to deceive another by saying something that is, unknown to them, quite true; second, the case of someone who expects to be disbelieved and so knowingly says what is false in order to instill a true belief; and third, the case of someone who, also expecting to be disbelieved, knowingly speaks the truth in order to instill a falsehood. Augustine seems not to know what to do about these problem cases. He contents himself with insisting that the conditions (1)–(3) are jointly sufficient, without taking a stand on whether each is singly necessary (*De mendacio* 4.5).

Discussing virtue and vice, Augustine contrasts those things that are desirable in themselves with those that are desirable for the sake of something else. He says that things of the first sort are to be enjoyed (*frui*) whereas those of the second sort are to be used (*uti*). Vice, he adds, is wanting to use what is meant to be enjoyed or wanting to enjoy what is meant to be used (*De diversis quaestionibus LXXXIII* 30).

Ambrose had already added the Pauline virtues of faith, hope and love to the classical virtues of temperance, courage, wisdom and justice. Augustine follows Ambrose in this, and he follows St Paul in assigning first importance to love; in fact, he offers an interpretation of each of the seven virtues that makes it an expression of the love of God. Thus temperance is love 'keeping itself whole and incorrupt for God'; fortitude, or courage, is love 'bearing everything readily for the sake of God', and so on (*De moribus ecclesiae catholicae* (On the Morals of the Catholic Church) 15.25). Virtue, he says, is nothing but the perfect love of God. In this way Augustine provides a Christian analogue to Plato's idea of the unity of the virtues (see VIRTUES AND VICES).

13 Ethics: 'ought' and 'can'

Augustine also attacked the Pelagians for their views on the avoidance of sin, focusing on the question of 'ought' and 'can'. Two of his contemporaries, the British monk Pelagius and his disciple Coelestius, had made the principle that 'ought' implies 'can' a central tenet of their religious and ethical teaching. As already noted, Augustine was the person primarily responsible for defining their teaching, Pelagianism, as a Christian heresy (see PELAGIANISM). In his treatise *De perfectione justicia hominis* (On Man's Perfection in Righteousness), subtitled 'In opposition to those who assert that it is possible for one to become righteous by one's own strength alone', Augustine describes the chief thesis of Coelestius as the contention that if something is unavoidable, then it is not a sin; there is simply no such thing as an unavoidable sin. Augustine responds to Pelagius and his disciple by rejecting the simple disjunction that either something is not a sin or it can be avoided. 'Sin can be avoided', he writes, 'if our corrupted nature be healed by God's grace.' Thus in a way, Augustine agrees that 'ought' does imply 'can', but only with a crucial qualification. 'Ought' implies 'can with the gratuitous assistance of God', but it does not imply 'can without any outside help' (see KANT, I.).

Augustine's response to dreaming as a possible threat to knowledge claims fits together with his intentionalism in ethics and his anti-Pelagianism to produce an interesting problem as to whether one is morally responsible for the acts of one's dream self. He agonizes over this problem in *Confessiones* (X.30). Three ways of justifying a claim of no responsibility suggest themselves. I could say I am not responsible (1) because I am not my dream self, or (2) because what happens in a dream does not really happen, or (3) because I am powerless to avoid doing what my dream self does, and 'ought' implies 'can'.

Augustine's philosophical and theological commitments seem to undercut each of these three responses. Thus (1) is undercut, it seems, by his somewhat concessive response to scepticism. I can know that something tastes sweet to me, Augustine insists in *Contra academicos* (III.11.26), whether or not I am dreaming. It seems to be a consequence of this insistence that, if I am dreaming, I am my dream self. As for (2), it seems to be undercut by Augustine's strong intentionalism in ethics. Thus when I commit adultery in my dreams, even if no 'outward' adultery takes place, still I entertain the evil suggestion, take pleasure in the evil suggested and give consent; so there is wrongdoing. As for (3), as noted above, Augustine rejects the Pelagian insistence that 'ought' implies 'can'. or rather, he accepts it only with an important qualification. Although 'I ought to refrain from consenting to fornicate' does, in Augustine's view, entail that I can so refrain with the help of God's grace, it does not entail that I can refrain strictly on my own, that is, without any divine grace. Yet if I receive no grace and consent to fornicate, I sin, according to Augustine, and it is just for God to punish me.

14 Ethics: on killing

Although Augustine's thoughts on suicide are not particularly original, they have been extremely influential. His position became Christian orthodoxy, which in turn influenced decisively the legal thinking in predominantly Christian countries. Augustine's position is that, with certain specifiable exceptions (primarily, lawful executions and killings in battle by soldiers fighting just wars (see below), anyone who kills a human being, whether himself or anyone else, is guilty of murder (*De civitate Dei* I.21), and murder is prohibited by divine commandment (see DEATH; SUICIDE, ETHICS OF).

Augustine did not invent the idea that certain requirements must be satisfied if a war is to count as just. The theory of just warfare – both the conditions that must be satisfied if a war is to be entered into justly (*jus ad bellum*) as well as the requirements of justice in the waging of war (*jus in bello*) – are already well developed by CICERO in his *On the Republic*. Nor was Augustine the first Christian thinker to develop a theory of just warfare; Ambrose had already done so (Christopher 1994). Nevertheless, Augustine is usually considered the father of the modern theory of the just war. Such deference is appropriate in that it is in Augustine, more than in Cicero or Ambrose or anyone else in the ancient world, that later theorists have found their earliest inspiration.

Although Augustine accepts the commandment, 'Thou shalt not kill', he interprets it in such a way that not everyone who brings about the death of another can be properly said to kill. Thus, he writes in *De civitate Dei* (I.21), 'One who owes a duty of obedience to the giver of the command does not himself kill; he is an instrument, a sword in its user's hand.' Thus an executioner may bring about the death of a convict without killing, and so may a soldier end another's life without killing, especially when war is being waged 'on the authority of God'.

In general, Augustine takes over the Roman principles of just war as set forth by Cicero and adds his own emphasis on the intention with which the acts of war are performed. This following passage is characteristic:

What is the evil in war? Is it the death of some who will soon die in any case, that others may live in peaceful subjection? This is merely cowardly dislike, not any religious feeling. The real evils in war are love of violence, revengeful cruelty, fierce and implacable enmity, wild resistance, the lust of power, and such like; and it is generally to punish these things, when force is required to inflict the punishment, that, in obedience to God or some lawful authority, good men undertake wars.

(*Contra Faustum manichaeum* 22.74)

Beyond such insistence that war should not be fought from love of violence, revengeful cruelty or lust for power, Augustine did not work out specific principles for the just conduct of war. Still, in making it plausible to many Christians that killing in war need not fall under the divine commandment not to kill, Augustine freed others to develop principles for what might be considered the just declaration of war, as well as the just conduct of war, once it has been justly entered into (see WAR AND PEACE, PHILOSOPHY OF).

15 Philosophy of history

In the *Poetics*, Aristotle remarks that poetry is more philosophical than history. He seems to have thought of the historian as the mere chronicler of events, whereas the tragedian tells us what sort of person would, probably or necessarily, do or say what sorts of things. Augustine was the first important philosopher to treat the writing of history in a more philosophical way. In *De civitate Dei*, he rejects the idea of eternal recurrence, later associated with NIETZSCHE, according to which:

just as Plato, for example, taught his disciples at Athens in the fourth century, in the school called the Academy, so in innumerable centuries of the past, separated by immensely wide and yet finite intervals, the same Plato, the same city, the same school, the same disciples have appeared time after time, and are to reappear time after time in innumerable centuries in the future.

(*De civitate Dei* XII.14)

Although Augustine does not offer philosophical arguments for his own 'linear' view of history, he does offer a variety of criticisms of what he takes to be the main philosophical argumentation in support of the cyclical theories (*De civitate Dei* XII.18).

The account of history Augustine offers is meant to be a universal history, that is, a history of the world. It divides the history of the world into seven ages, analogous to the seven days of creation. The discussion proceeds, however, more as a gloss on scripture than by appeal to rational considerations or nontheological evidence. Although he does not try to establish the nature of 'God's universal providence' by general considerations or evidence that is independent of Christian revelation, he does seek to establish that divine providence, like divine foreknowledge and divine predestination, is compatible with human free will. On a more general level he tries to establish that history can have a meaning, in fact the meaning God foreordains it to have, even though human agents are perfectly free; and indeed, are foreordained to be free (see HISTORY, PHILOSOPHY OF).

See also: AUGUSTINIANISM; BOETHIUS, A.M.S.; ENCYCLOPEDISTS §2; ANCIENT PHILOSOPHY; MANICHEISM; NEOPLATONISM; PATRISTIC PHILOSOPHY; PELAGIANISM; PLATONISM, MEDIEVAL; RELIGION, HISTORY OF PHILOSOPHY OF; SCEPTICISM

List of works

Augustine (386–429) Collected Works. (The seventeenth-century Maurist edition of Augustine's works is to be found in J.P. Migne (ed.) *Patrologia Latina*, Paris, 1844–6, vols 32–47. Critical editions of many of his works are to be found scattered through the Corpus Scriptorum Ecclesiasticorum, Vienna: Tempsky, 1866–, as well as in the Corpus Christianorum, Series Latina, Turnholt: Brepols, and The Hague: Nijhoff, 1953–. English translations of Augustine's major works are to be found in P. Schaff (ed.) *A Select Library of the Nicene and Post-Nicene Fathers of the Christian Church*, First Series, Edinburgh: T. & T. Clark, 1886–8, repr: Grand Rapids, MI: Eerdmans, 1971–74. A smaller selection is found in W. Oates (ed.) *Basic Writings of Saint Augustine*, New York: Random House, 1948, 2 vols. Individual works are also to be found scattered through the series Fathers of the Church, Washington, DC: Catholic University of America, 1947–, and in the series Ancient Christian Writers: The Works of the Fathers in Translation, New York: Newman, 1946–. The first English translation of Augustine's complete works is currently being published in 46 vols, edited by J.E. Rotelle, Hyde Park, NY: New City Press, in conjunction with the Augustinian Heritage Institute.)

—— (386) *Soliloquia* (Soliloquies), trans. C.C. Starbuck, in W. Oates (ed.) *Basic Writings of Saint Augustine*, New York: Random House, 1948, vol. 1, 257–97. (A dialogue between Augustine and Reason, this work assumes the first-person persepctive that marks one of Augustine's special contributions to philosophy.)

—— (386) *Contra academicos* (Against the Academicians), trans. P. King (along with *The Teacher*), Indianapolis, IN: Hackett, 1995. (Augustine's most sustained effort to refute the scepticism of the New Academy.)

—— (387) *De dialectica* (On Dialectic), trans. B.D. Jackson, Dordrecht: Reidel, 1975. (The first book in a planned but later abandoned series on the liberal arts.)

—— (387/8) *De quantitate animae* (The Magnitude of the Soul), trans. J.J. McMahon, Fathers of the Church vol. 4, Washington, DC: Catholic University of America, 1947, 49–149. (Augustine's early philosophy of mind.)

—— (387–9) *De moribus ecclesiae catholicae* (Morals of the Catholic Church), trans. R. Stothert in P. Schaff (ed.) *A Select Library of the Nicene and Post-Nicene Fathers of the Christian Church*, First Series, 1886–8, vol. 4, 37–63. (Includes a Christian definition of the classical virtues.)

—— (388–95) *De diversis quaestionibus LXXXIII* (Eighty-three Different Questions), trans D.L. Mosher, Fathers of the Church vol. 70, Washington, DC: Catholic University of America, 1977. (Short discussions of a variety of metaphysical, epistemological and theological topics.)

—— (388–95) *De libero arbitrio* (On Free Choice of the Will), trans. T. Williams, Indianapolis, IN: Hackett, 1993. (The first philosophically important treatment of how to reconcile human free will with divine foreknowledge.)

—— (389) *De magistro* (The Teacher), trans. J.M. Colleran, *The Teacher* (along with *The Greatness of the Soul*), New York: Newman, 1950; trans. P. King, *The Teacher* (along with *Against the Academicians*), Indianapolis, IN: Hackett, 1995. (An important attempt to consider whether the meanings of words can be learned by ostension.)

—— (389/91) *De vera religione* (On True Religion), trans. J.H.S. Burleigh, *Augstine: Earlier Writings*, London: SCM Press, 1953, 218–83. (Augustine here finds truth even in doubting.)

—— (392/3) *De duabus animabus contra Manichaeos* (On the Two Souls), trans. A.H. Newman in P. Schaff (ed.) *A Select Library of the Nicene and Post-Nicene Fathers of the Christian Church*, First Series, 1886–8, vol. 4, 91–124. (A spirited rejection of the Manichean idea that each person has both a good and an evil soul.)

—— (394) *De mendacio* (On Lying), trans. M.S. Muldowney, Fathers of the Church vol. 14, Washington, DC: Catholic University of America, 1952, 45–120. (The earlier of two treatises devoted to an analysis of the sin of lying.)

—— (394) *De sermone Domini in monte* (Commentary on the Lord's Sermon on the Mount), trans. J.J.

Jepson, New York: Newman Press, 1948. (Perhaps the most important statement of Augustine's intentionalist ethics.)

—— (396–426) *De doctrina christiana* (On Christian Instruction), trans. J.J. Gavigan, Washington, DC: Catholic University of America, 1947. (Augustine's handbook of biblical exegesis.)

—— (397–401) *Confessionum libri tredecim* (Confessions), trans. F.J. Sheed, Indianapolis, IN: Hackett, 1993; trans. R.S. Pine-Coffin, Harmondsworth: Penguin, 1961; trans. H. Chadwick, Oxford: Oxford University Press, 1991. (This is no doubt the most widely and frequently translated of Augustine's works. The above are the English translations deserving of special mention.)

—— (399) *De natura boni contra manichaeos* (The Nature of the Good), trans. A.H. Newman in W. Oates (ed.) *Basic Writings of Saint Augustine*, New York: Random House, 1948, vol. 1, 429–57. (An attempt to make plausible the idea that evil is a privation.)

—— (400) *Contra Faustum manichaeum* (Reply to Faustus), trans. R. Stothert in P. Schaff (ed.) *A Select Library of the Nicene and Post-Nicene Fathers of the Christian Church*, First Series, 1886–8, vol. 4, 151–345. (A major polemic against the leading Manichee of Augustine's time.)

—— (400–16) *De trinitate* (The Trinity), trans. S. McKenna, Washington, DC: Catholic University of America, 1962. (The last eight of this work's fifteen books constitute Augustine's most fully stated philosophy of mind.)

—— (401–14) *De genesi ad litteram* (The Literal Meaning of Genesis), trans. J.H. Taylor, New York: Newman, 1982, 2 vols. (Augustine's commentary on Genesis includes important discussions of metaphysics and philosophical theology; the last treatise is a separate treatise on vision, including mystical vision.)

—— (412) *De spiritu et littera* (On the Spirit and the Letter), trans. P. Holmes in W. Oates (ed.) *Basic Writings of Saint Augustine*, New York: Random House, 1948, vol. 1, 561–20. (An attempt to argue that God's grace does not void free will, but rather grounds it.)

—— (413–27) *De civitate Dei* (The City of God), trans. J. O'Meara, Harmondsworth: Penguin, 1972. (Several good English translations exist, of which the above is the most notable.)

—— (415–16) *De perfectione justicia hominis* (On Man's Perfection in Righteousness), trans. P. Holmes and R.E. Wallis in P. Schaff (ed.) *A Select Library of the Nicene and Post-Nicene Fathers of the Christian Church*, First Series, 1886–8, vol. 5, 177–212. (A treatise on the accusations against Pelagius.)

—— (416) *In ioannis evangelium tractatus* (Homilies on the Gospel of John), trans. J.W. Rettig, Fathers of the Church vols 78–9, 88, 92, Washington, DC: Catholic University of America, 1988–95. (Sermons on St John's Gospel arranged systematically so as to constitute a complete commentary on that gospel.)

—— (419–21) *De nuptiis et concupiscentia* (On Marriage and Concupiscence), trans. P. Holmes and R.E. Wallis in P. Schaff (ed.) *A Select Library of the Nicene and Post-Nicene Fathers of the Christian Church*, First Series, 1886–8, vol. 5, 257–308. (A somewhat qualified defence of the good of marriage in response to the Pelagians.)

—— (421) *De cura pro mortuis* (On the Care of the Dead), trans. J.A. Lacey, Fathers of the Church vol. 27, Washington, DC: Catholic University of America, 1955, 347–84. (A defence of burial services that raises interesting questions about ritual.)

—— (426/7) *Retractationes* (Retractations), trans. M.I. Bogan, Fathers of the Church vol. 60, Washington, DC: Catholic University of America, 1968. (Augustine's efforts to review, in order of composition, all of his earlier works and, where he thinks it necessary, correct his earlier views.)

—— (429) *De praedestinatione sanctorum* (On the Predestination of Saints), trans. R.E. Wallis in W. Oates (ed.) *Basic Writings of Saint Augustine*, New York: Random House, 1948, vol. 1, 775–817. (A final effort to insist that even the beginning of a believer's faith is God's predestined gift, though God does not act in human sin.)

References and further reading

Brown, P. (1967) *Augustine of Hippo*, Berkeley, CA: University of California. (The best general biography in English.)

Bubacz, B. (1981) *St. Augustine's Theory of Knowledge: A Contemporary Analysis*, New York: Mellen. (A good review of central passages on perception, memory and illumination.)

* Chadwick, H. (1986) *Augustine*, New York: Oxford University Press. (A first introduction to Augustine.)

* Christopher, P. (1994) *The Ethics of War and Peace*, Englewood Cliffs, NJ: Prentice Hall. (Chapter 3, 'Saint Augustine and the Tradition of Just War', describes Augustine's theory.)

* Dihle, A. (1982) *The Theory of Will in Classical Antiquity*, Berkeley, CA: University of California. (One chapter is devoted to Augustine's theory.)

Gilson, E. (1960) *The Christian Philosophy of Saint*

Augustine, New York: Random House. (A learned Thomist's best attempt to understand Augustine's philosophy.)

Holmes, R.L. (1989) *On War and Morality*, Princeton, NJ: Princeton University Press. (Judiciously places Augustine in the just war tradition.)

Kirwan, C. (1989) *Augustine*, London: Routledge. (The best treatment of Augustine's philosophy from a contemporary analytic point of view.)

* Malcolm, N. (1963) 'Knowledge of Other Minds', in N. Malcolm, *Knowledge and Certainty*, Englewood Cliffs, NJ: Prentice Hall, 130–40. (A classic Wittgensteinian critique of the appropriateness and efficacy of the argument from analogy for the existence of other minds.)

Markus, R.A. (1967) 'Marius Victorinus and Augustine', in A.H. Armstrong (ed.) *The Cambridge History of Later Greek and Early Medieval Philosophy*, Cambridge: Cambridge University Press, 331–419. (A learned by accessible summary of Augustine's philosophical views.)

Matthews, G.B. (1992) *Thought's Ego in Augustine and Descartes*, Ithaca, NY: Cornell University Press. (A discussion of the *cogito*, various dream problems, the problem of other minds and other issues that arise from the attempt to pursue philosophy from a first-person point of view.)

O'Daly, G. (1987) *Augustine's Philosophy of Mind*, London: Duckworth. (A detailed treatment of Augustine's views on sense perception, imagination, memory and knowledge.)

Portalie, E. (1960) *A Guide to the Thought of Saint Augustine*, Chicago, IL: Regnery. (Still valuable as a guide to the interrelations between Augustine's various views in philosophical theology and theological ethics.)

* Russell, B. (1945) *A History of Western Philosophy*, New York: Simon & Schuster. (A bold and always stimulating attempt to state succinctly and assess the contribution of each of the major Western philosophers.)

Sorabji, R. (1983) *Time, Creation and the Continuum*, London: Duckworth. (Puts Augustine's views on time, creation and mysticism into the context of ancient and early medieval thought.)

Wetzel, J. (1992) *Augustine and the Limits of Virtue*, Cambridge: Cambridge University Press. (Focuses on the moral relevance of Augustine's concept of will, and also on the idea that virtue is invulnerable to misfortune.)

* Wittgenstein, L. (1958a) *The Blue and Brown Books*, Oxford: Blackwell. (Early formulations of views characteristic of Wittgenstein's later period.)

* —— (1958b) *The Philosophical Investigations*, trans. G.E.M. Anscombe, Oxford: Blackwell. (The most important later work of Wittgenstein.)

GARETH B. MATTHEWS

AUGUSTINIANISM

The influence of Augustine on Western philosophy is exceeded in duration, extent and variety only by that of Plato and Aristotle. Augustine was an authority not just for the early Middle Ages, when he was often the lone authority, but well into modern times. He was in many ways the principal author in contention during the Reformation and Counter-Reformation, and in France alone he was variously received by authors as diverse as Montaigne, Descartes, Malebranche, Arnauld and Pascal. The breadth of Augustine's influence makes it difficult to give precise sense to the term 'Augustinianism', even when considering only a single period.

Historians of medieval philosophy use the term 'Augustinianism' to describe three rather different relations to the thought of Augustine. The first relation is a comprehensive dependence on Augustine both for philosophical principles or arguments, and for instruction in the topics and procedures of ancient philosophy. Augustine serves as the trustworthy guide to philosophy as a whole. The second kind of relation is a defence of specific Augustinian teachings in the face of rival teachings, most especially those of Aristotle. These Augustinian teachings include the function of divine ideas in knowledge, the unity of the human soul's essential powers, and the unfolding of potential intelligibilities in material substances. The third relation is the reappropriation of Augustinian principles, especially those of his later writings, to address quandaries newly formulated with the tools of nominalist semantics and the mathematics of continuities. Among these quandaries are the contingency of future human actions and the certainty of human cognition.

These three relations to Augustine can be found in texts throughout the medieval period. They are not neatly correlated with particular centuries, but one or another does tend to be predominant at different times. Thus the first relation, of comprehensive dependence, is seen in the great majority of Latin writers on philosophic topics through the twelfth century. The second relation, of topical defence, appears prominently during the thirteenth-century contest between so-called 'Augustianians' and 'Aristotelians'. The third relation, of reappropriation in reaction to newly formulated quandaries, is found particularly in writings of the fourteenth century and beyond.

AUGUSTINIANISM

1 Scope
2 The reception of Augustine through the twelfth century
3 The thirteenth century
4 The fourteenth century

1 Scope

At face value, 'Augustinianism' would seem to refer generally to the teaching of AUGUSTINE or to one of the many adaptations of it. To use the term in this sense is to rob it of usefulness. The influence of Augustine on Western philosophy is exceeded in duration, extent and variety only by that of Plato and Aristotle. Augustine's writings served as authoritative works in the early Middle Ages, when he was often the sole philosophical authority referred to; the influence of Augustine is so pervasive in Latin Christian thought that any medieval Latin author on philosophic topics will show some borrowings from Augustine, and most of the best-known authors can be seen to engage him in sustained ways. Augustine was traditionally counted one of four 'Fathers' or 'Teachers' of the Latin-speaking Church, along with Jerome, Ambrose and Gregory the Great (see PATRISTIC PHILOSOPHY). His influence exceeded that of the other three in most theological areas and in all philosophical ones except for ethics, where Gregory's *Moral Readings on Job* provided more detailed if less systematic teaching about virtues. Further, the influence of Augustine can be seen well beyond the medieval period. During the Reformation and Counter-Reformation in the sixteenth century he was one of the principal authors referred to by both contending parties, and he was variously received by modern philosophic authors as diverse as MONTAIGNE, DESCARTES, MALEBRANCHE, ARNAULD and PASCAL.

The term 'Augustinianism' can be made useful only by being applied to specific relations to Augustine. Three rather different relations have been used by historians of medieval philosophy. The first is a *comprehensive dependence* on Augustine, both for philosophical principles or arguments and for instruction in the topics and procedures of ancient philosophy. Second, there was a *defence* of specific Augustinian teachings in the face of rival teachings, in particular those of Aristotle (see ARISTOTELIANISM, MEDIEVAL). Third, there was a *reappropriation* of Augustinian principles, especially those from Augustine's later works, in order to address quandaries newly formulated in the languages of nominalist semantics and the mathematics of continuities (see NOMINALISM; OXFORD CALCULATORS).

All three relations can seem to be progressively narrower or more restricted; indeed, it is tempting to understand them as a sequence of comprehensive Augustinianism, disputed Augustinianism and adapted or revivified Augustinianism. This conception of a sequence would be false in two important ways. First, it would ignore Augustine's permanent and unsurpassed authority in Christian theology, which provides so much of the context for medieval philosophy and, indeed, for modern European philosophy. Second, it would mislead one into thinking that philosophical interest in Augustine was at a low ebb at the end of the Middle Ages, whereas in fact Renaissance and early modern philosophy shows a striking resurgence of interest in Augustine. Any narrowing in the application of the term 'Augustinianism' should be imputed as much to the optical illusions of historiography as to the facts of reception. Contemporary historians of philosophy know more of philosophical writing before the thirteenth century than of what was written during or after that period, in large measure because there is so much more of the latter to know. Hence any narrative of medieval thought tends to become much more selective as it proceeds.

From the very beginning, Augustine's work was not easy to appropriate for philosophical uses. His body of writings is enormous and topical, not to mention contradictory in some of its details. Although there were early attempts to make his work both more accessible and more systematic, the interpretations of Augustine's writings depended very much on which works were being read. There was not always a choice in what to read. The reception of any author in the earlier Middle Ages depended on the hard facts of manuscript survival and distribution. In the cultural disarray that destroyed books and the means of producing them, Augustine was relatively fortunate; his works were copied steadily and widely. But to say that Augustine was frequently copied is not to say that he was uniformly copied. Not all parts of the Augustinian corpus were equally well known, and even in the thirteenth and fourteenth centuries certain Augustinian texts were much more rare than others. Thomas AQUINAS revised a number of his opinions in mid-career, after coming into possession of texts of Augustine that he had not known before. The period 1325–35 in England also saw a sharp increase in commentaries on Augustine's knottiest writings, especially those of his later years.

Beyond problems of access there was also, and from early on, the problem of spurious works. Given Augustine's immense authority and his reputation for universal genius, it is not surprising that pious readers would attribute to him any number of works they admired. To extract the authentic works from this mass has been the labour of many centuries, a labour still unfinished with regard to some sorts of works, such as the homilies. These variations and uncertainties in the availability of Augustine's texts should be kept in mind through all that follows.

2 The reception of Augustine through the twelfth century

The first sense of 'Augustinianism' distinguished above refers to comprehensive influence exerted by Augustine on philosophic writers from his own time through the twelfth century. The most popular of his works not only set the terms and starting points for addressing many theological questions that were to vex early medieval authors, they also passed down precious information about ancient pagan philosophy and provided much-needed introductions to its teachings. Even after the conditions of learning had improved significantly in western Europe, Augustine continued to be followed as a sure guide through the confusing thicket of ancient philosophical debates.

Three examples can show the variety of relations to Augustine. The first is John Scotus ERIUGENA, who is best known for his technical command of late Greek Neoplatonism (see NEOPLATONISM). Some find in his work a turning away from the eclectic philosophy of Augustine, but it is just as possible to read Eriugena's *Periphyseon* as the incorporation of newer Neoplatonic elements within a framework that is deliberately and thoroughly Augustinian. Certainly Eriugena knew Augustine's work well, and just as certainly he engages the latter even when he disagrees with him.

The second, more obvious example is that of ANSELM OF CANTERBURY. In the prologue of his *Monologion*, Anselm explicitly submits his works to the test of conformity with Augustine. He advises readers to take Augustine's *De trinitate* (On the Trinity) as the measure of his own 'little work'. There is no irony or duplicity here. If Anselm goes on in his treatises to argue by reasoning alone, without frequent appeal to authorities, his arguments are still just so many variations on Augustinian themes. The famous definition of God used in the *Proslogion* to begin what came to be called the 'ontological argument' is Augustinian, and the argument's procedure follows closely several of Augustine's hierarchical arguments for the existence of God. Again, Anselm's analysis of truth as 'rightness' (*rectitudo*), however much it depends on more recent logical techniques such as the substitution of equipollent propositions, remains in its premises an Augustinian teaching about the communicative intention in language.

A final example of the comprehensive reception of Augustine in philosophy can be found in the work of HUGH OF ST VICTOR. Hugh is principally and formally a writer of theology, and he understands highest 'philosophy' to be the monk's prayerful contemplation of God. Hugh's works also rehearse a number of doctrines that are philosophic in a less exalted sense. These doctrines are drawn from many sources, but they are given shape after Augustinian patterns. In the survey of philosophical topics in the *Didascalicon*, Hugh quotes from a number of authors, including BOETHIUS and his commentators, CICERO, Macrobius (see ENCYCLOPEDISTS §3), CALCIDIUS and Augustine. The judgments on the right ordering of philosophy, as on particular philosophic doctrines, are taken for the most part from Augustine. If Augustine is invoked at times to supply some bit of learning about ancient philosophy, he is relied upon throughout in subordinating philosophy to Christian theology.

These two examples only begin to suggest the various relations between Augustine and later writers on philosophy. It should also be remembered that in the twelfth century, Augustine was the chief authority on theology. His works are given pride of place in Peter Lombard's influential theological codification, the *Sententiae in IV libris distinctae* (Four Books of Sentences), and many of the topics under debate there are ones that Augustine would have recognized. Roughly the same is true in philosophy, despite the influx of newly translated Aristotelian works. A century later, however, Augustine's work was being increasingly challenged (see LOMBARD, P.).

3 The thirteenth century

The second sense of 'Augustinianism' distinguished above refers to the defence of particular Augustinian tenets against increasingly attractive Aristotelian alternatives. Indeed, some historians of medieval philosophy describe the principal philosophical developments from the middle of the thirteenth century onwards as a protracted contest between 'Augustinians' and 'Aristotelians'. They find evidence of the contest in a number of struggles within the universities of Paris and Oxford, and they see an important triumph for the Augustinian party in the condemnations pronounced at Paris and Oxford in 1270 and 1277. The 'Aristotelians', in this account, were not just the teachers of extreme positions in the Faculty of Arts but also, perhaps especially, Dominican theologians such as ALBERT THE GREAT and Thomas AQUINAS who approved some Aristotelian doctrines in philosophy and appropriated them integrally for theological use. By contrast, the 'Augustinians' were not just conservative masters of theology, but theologians who found the growing use of Aristotle damaging both to faith and to philosophy. Among the 'Augustinians' are usually accounted the Franciscans ALEXANDER OF HALES, BONAVENTURE and John PECHAM. Because these controversies seem to have divided Dominicans from Franciscans, the quarrel of 'Aristotelians' and 'Augustinians' is often made into a quarrel between the two religious orders.

This way of describing the controversies makes caricatures of them. Augustine and Aristotle were in fact studied, quoted and defended by controversialists on both sides. Some of the best known 'Augustinians' spent considerable time explicating the text of Aristotle precisely in order to resist attempts to Christianize him, offering instead exacting interpretations of his original sense. More generally, Aristotelian terminology was used as the lingua franca by all members of the universities. On the other side, some of the leading 'Aristotelians' argued that the Augustine of their opponents was not the authentic Augustine at all, but a hyper-Platonist drawn largely from Islamic sources. As a result, great care should be taken when using the terms 'Augustianian' and 'Aristotelian' as designations for groups of medieval authors.

What is clear is that some of the Franciscan controversialists described themselves as defenders of Augustinian tenets in philosophy. They were quite willing to specify at least some of tenets they meant. In a letter of 1285, John Pecham wrote that he was not attacking the 'study of philosophers' so much as the 'profane novelties' of the 'Aristotelians'. These novelties are opposed to 'whatever Augustine teaches on the eternal rules and the unchangeable [intellectual] light, the powers of the soul, on the seed-like intelligibilities inserted into matter, and on innumerable other things like these' (Pecham, Letter of 1 January 1285). The three doctrines that Pecham mentions were indeed at the centre of the thirteenth-century disputes; they are known to historians of philosophy as doctrines of divine illumination, psychic essentialism and seminal reasons.

Augustine was understood to have taught that all knowledge worthy of the name was made possible only by the 'illumination', that is, by the intelligible presence of the 'divine rules' or 'divine reasons', God's own patterns for making creatures (see AUGUSTINE §10). On most readings, this did not mean that a human mind in the present life could see the divine essence or could know something just by relying on divine illumination. BONAVENTURE, for example, is explicit that the presence of the divine ideas is ordinarily a necessary but not sufficient cause for cognition. By contrast, Thomas AQUINAS argues that no 'special' illumination is required; the mind's 'participation' in the divine light given at its creation is sufficient for ordinary cognition.

The second doctrine singled out by Pecham concerns the relation of a soul to its powers, such as reason and will. Some authors, claiming to follow Augustine, held that the soul's powers were nothing more than its relations to various acts. Hence there could be no essential distinctions among the powers, which were all referred to the soul's single essence. Other authors, following Aristotle, held that the soul's powers inhered in the soul as accidents in a substance. In this view, the powers were essentially distinct. A third group attempted to split the difference; they held that the soul's powers were only derivatively or analogically located in the category of substance. They should be considered as really different, not as essences are different, but as powers of a single essence can still be essentially different. Proponents of this third view, such as Bonaventure, thought that this was Augustine's most careful teaching on the matter. Bonaventure also remarks that the debate is more curious than useful; none of the positions, he says, is opposed to faith or good morals.

The third disputed doctrine, that of seminal reasons, is adapted by Augustine from Stoic physics (see STOICISM §3). Knowing little of the genealogy, medieval readers held this doctrine as an affirmation of the completeness of divine creation and as an alternative to Aristotelian accounts of the pure potency of matter. They understood Augustine to teach that God had inserted into matter, at the moment of creation, intelligible patterns that could be actualized over time. So, for example, Bonaventure holds that the souls of non-rational animals and of plants were created not out of nothing nor simply out of some pre-existing matter, but rather 'in the manner of a seed'. They were created, in other words, by actualizing an active potency in matter, which serves as a 'seed bed' of such potencies. After the moment of creation, animal souls are reproduced without divine intervention by the natural actualization of such 'seed-like reasons'. These 'reasons' also contain the latent forms of certain lower-order substances which are produced by the corruption or commingling of other specific forms. In this way, every kind of form that would sometime attain actuality was put into the created world at the beginning.

Pecham's letter also alludes to other doctrines disputed between the followers of Augustine and their adversaries. Principal among these were two, the plurality of forms and the universality of the form–matter distinction. The teaching on the plurality of forms, to which Pecham was particularly attached, held that multiple forms could exist in a single substance without having to be reduced to accidents of a single substantial form. This teaching was particularly important in analysing the relation of human souls and bodies. Pecham thought it nonsensical to say that the separable, immortal soul was the single substantial form of the body–soul composite. As to the other point, defenders of Augustine taught that something properly called a form–matter distinction could be found in all creatures, including the incorporeal substances known to theology as angels. If this 'spiritual matter' was not identical with ordinary matter, it was nonetheless a material principle.

Pecham's version of Augustine can be found in other writers, if not so emphatically articulated. His Augustinian programme is in some ways more retrospective than prospective. Already by Pecham's time, Augustine was being appropriated in more subtle and novel ways by a new group of authors, most notably HENRY OF GHENT. From Henry through John DUNS SCOTUS and WILLIAM OF OCKHAM, one can trace profoundly original transformations of Augustinian principles and problems. Indeed, Scotus and Ockham have been counted, in their very different ways, as a second 'school' of Franciscan Augustinians. Here, however, the term 'Augustinianism' begins to become much too diffuse to be useful.

A more specific 'Augustinianism' is sometimes claimed for the writers of the religious order of Augustinian friars. The order was organized out of existing communities between 1244 and 1256, and its constitutions were ratified in 1290. Some historians have wanted to see in this order an institutional home for an 'Augustinian' school of philosophy and theology, but the matter is not so simple. GILES OF ROME, first Parisian master from the order and later its Prior General, was a student of Thomas Aquinas. He often appears in narrative histories as an ardent if somewhat inexact Thomist. In fact, he differs from Thomas on a number of points, such as the nature of the essence/existence distinction and the plurality of substantial forms. For these reasons among others, Giles was claimed by later members of the Augustinian order as founder of a 'school' of thought (the *schola Aegidiana*) which those members understood themselves to be continuing. But Giles was hardly a programmatic Augustinian in philosophy, and the most interesting philosophical adaptations of Augustine at the end of the thirteenth century were happening outside the Augustinian order.

4 The fourteenth century

The third relation to Augustine distinguished above is the most difficult to characterize. It combines motives of textual fidelity with motives of reappropriation. Textual fidelity led to an intensive re-reading of Augustine, culminating in Oxford during the second quarter of the fourteenth century. Reappropriation stemmed from the desire to respond to the sea-change in philosophy marked by Scotus and Ockham. The most prominent fourteenth-century Augustinians wanted to understand and to rehabilitate Augustine's central teachings in response to the quandaries produced by the 'modern way' in philosophy; some of these writers, notably Thomas BRADWARDINE, are distinguished by their willingness to restate difficult Augustinian principles against accepted conclusions of the latest semantics and the mathematical analysis of nature. Other writers are marked out by their fidelity to Augustine across a range of topics and in the face of the increasingly popular alternative ways of thinking; the most famous of these is GREGORY OF RIMINI.

Bradwardine was prominent among the Oxford 'Calculators', a group of Masters of Arts centred in Merton College, Oxford, during the 1320s and 1330s (see OXFORD CALCULATORS). He wrote important works on logical quandaries and on proportions. While at Oxford, Bradwardine also wrote what is counted a centrepiece of fourteenth-century Augustinianism, *Summa de causa Dei contra Pelagium et de virtute causarum* (On God's Cause against Pelagius and on the Power of Causes). The work is, as its title proclaims, a polemical one, written against certain 'new Pelagians' (see PELAGIANISM). Bradwardine seems to refer by this epithet to some of his Oxford contemporaries, perhaps especially Richard Fitzralph, Robert HOLCOT, Adam WODEHAM and Thomas Buckingham. He accuses them of denying all of God's providence, cooperation, conservation and predestination with respect to creaturely activity. Denying these things, Bradwardine's Pelagians effectively deny the existence of God, because they deny that God is God. Against them, Bradwardine offers 'the grace of God, which precedes all good merits with a priority of both time and nature; I mean the gracious will of God, prior in both these ways, which wills to save the one who merits it, and naturally produces merit in him even before he does, just as He is the first mover in all motions.' This Augustinian doctrine came to Bradwardine in a moment of intellectual conversion, which he explicitly links to Augustine's narrative in the *Confessiones*.

Though Bradwardine confronts the Pelagians on a number of fronts, his sharpest and most technical attack comes in considering the problem of future contingents. This problem had been much debated in Oxford for several decades. Bradwardine considered it the crucial case for the Pelagians – and the one that revealed the depth of their error. According to

Bradwardine, the new Pelagians held that while singular propositions about future contingents always possessed a determinate truth, the contingents were themselves not determined. A truth about them could become false. By contrast, the truth of propositions about present events was fixed, and the truth of propositions about past events was necessary. It might seem a long way from Bradwardine's Augustinian conversion to these logical issues, but the way is in fact quite short. Views on the truth of future contingents had immediate consequences for the question of divine foreknowledge and, indeed, on such specific topics as the truth of prophetic revelations about future events. For Bradwardine, the Pelagians' doctrines concerning the mutability of future contingents denied both the immutability of divine knowledge and the honesty of divine revelation. If the truth of propositions about the future is different from the truth of propositions about the past, then the character of God's knowledge must change with time; and if the truth of a specific proposition about a future event is contingent, then a prophecy of that event can be falsified. Bradwardine finds both conclusions monstrous. The first makes God into a creature; the second, into a deceiver. Bradwardine teaches, on the contrary, that all future events are necessitated in respect to higher causes, though some of them may be understood to be free in present time with respect to lower causes. This position is, on Bradwardine's reading, precisely that of AUGUSTINE.

With GREGORY OF RIMINI, one may begin to speak of an Augustinian school within the order of Augustinian friars. He was elected Prior General of the order in 1357 after a distinguished teaching career in Paris and Italy. Gregory's appropriation of Augustine is wider and more nuanced than Bradwardine's. A sample can be had in Gregory's discrimination among the types of human knowledge. He agrees with Ockham in criticizing the pretensions of empirical knowledge, and he is equally firm in advancing the claims of introspection, which he describes by citation from Augustine's *De trinitate*. More strikingly, Gregory claims that intelligible knowledge depends upon certain innate ideas that direct the soul to its cognitive and moral end. His explicit source here is Augustine's *De libero arbitrio* (On Free Choice of the Will). In these and other instances, Gregory aligns problems or models from the most recent philosophy with principles retrieved from Augustine.

It is difficult to assess the immediate influence of Thomas Bradwardine or Gregory of Rimini without deciding how far they contributed to the heterodox reform movements that would eventually lead into the Reformation. A case in point is John WYCLIF, who invokes Bradwardine as one of his intellectual masters. Indeed, the study of Augustinianism shows with particular clarity how arbitrary is the division between late medieval and early modern philosophy. The culmination of the medieval relations to Augustine's philosophical texts is not to be found in the Middle Ages; the conclusion comes in the sixteenth and seventeenth centuries, in the Reformation and in the genesis of several of the most important philosophical movements of early modernity, including Cartesianism and the philosophy of the Jansenists.

See also: ARISTOTELIANISM, MEDIEVAL; AUGUSTINE; BONAVENTURE; BRADWARDINE, T.; GREGORY OF RIMINI; HENRY OF GHENT; MEDIEVAL PHILOSOPHY; PECHAM, J.; RELIGION, HISTORY OF PHILOSOPHY OF

References and further reading

Courtenay, W.J. (1980) 'Augustinianism at Oxford in the Fourteenth Century', *Augustiniana* 30: 58–70. (A well-documented introduction to the reappropriation of Augustine.)

Crouse, R.D. (1987) 'Anselm of Canterbury and Medieval Augustinianisms', *Toronto Journal of Theology* 3 (1): 60–8. (A brief but very helpful introduction to the varieties of Augustinianism through the twelfth century; richly annotated.)

Genest, J.-F. (1992) *Prédétermination et liberé créé à Oxford au XIVe siècle: Buckingham contre Bradwardine* (Predetermination and Free Will at Oxford in the Fourteenth Century: Buckingham versus Bradwardine), Paris: Vrin. (Detailed introduction to the debates over contingency; contains an edition of Buckingham's *Determinatio de contingentia futurorum* (Determination Concerning the Contingency of Future Things).)

King, E.B., and Schaefer, J.T. (1988) *Saint Augustine and His Influence in the Middle Ages*, Sewanee, TN: Press of the University of the South. (Anthology of conference papers; the contributions by Chadwick and Evans are particularly pertinent.)

Marrou, H.I. (1959) *Saint Augustin et l'Augustinisme*, Paris: Éditions du Seuil. (There is also an English translation from an earlier edition by P. Hepburne Scott and E. Hill, *St. Augustine and His Influence through the Ages*, New York: Harper Torchbooks and London: Longmans, 1957. General and now somewhat dated.)

Oberman, H.A., and James III, F.A. (eds) (1991) *Via Augustini: Augustine in the Later Middle Ages, Renaissance, and Reformation: Essays in Honor of Damasus Trapp*, Leiden/New York: Brill. (Anthology of rather narrowly focused essays.)

O'Donnell, J.J. (1991) 'The Authority of Augustine',

Augustinian Studies 22: 7–35. (Reflections on Augustine's influence and authority from the fifth century onwards.)
* Pecham, John (1285) Letter of 1 January 1285, number 625 in C.T. Martin (ed.) *Registrum epistolarum Fratris Johannis Peckham, archiepiscopi Cantuariensis*, Rolls Series 77, London, 1885, vol. 3, 870–72. (Pecham's description of doctrines disputed between followers of Augustine and Aristotle.)
Wippel, J.F. (1977) 'The Condemnations of 1270 and 1277 at Paris', *Journal of Medieval and Renaissance Studies* 7: 169–201. (Richly annotated introduction to the motives and contexts of the two sets of condemnations.)

MARK D. JORDAN

AUREOL, PETER (c.1280–1322)

A master of theology at the University of Paris and a member of the Franciscan order, Peter Aureol helped shape the philosophical agenda of the fourteenth century. His original and provocative views were widely discussed during the later Middle Ages, but his influence was rather indirect since his views almost always met with hostility. Although Aureol wrote extensively on a wide range of philosophical and theological issues, his most-discussed contributions to philosophy, in epistemology and metaphysics, centre on his theory of esse apparens *(apparent existence).*

Aureol, known as the *Doctor facundus* (Fluent Doctor), was born near Gourdon in the south of France. He seems to have joined the Franciscan order in his teens, and to have studied at Paris, perhaps in 1304. There has been speculation that he was a student of John DUNS SCOTUS at that time, but there is little evidence for the claim. Aureol's magnum opus, his *In quatuor libros Sententiarum* (Commentary on Peter Lombard's Sentences), began taking shape in his lectures at Franciscan houses of study in Bologna (beginning in 1312) and Toulouse (in 1314). In 1316 he was sent to Paris to continue his lectures, and he remained there until 1320, becoming regent master in 1318, lecturing on the Bible, and completing a single quodlibetal question. He became an archbishop in 1321, and died shortly thereafter.

Aureol thoroughly edited the first book of his *Sentences* commentary, and this so-called *Scriptum*, together with the other parts of his commentary (the less polished *Reportationes*), constitute Aureol's most significant philosophical work. In it, he ranges widely over the theological and philosophical problems of his day, making interesting and original suggestions about the relationship between soul and body, the nature of grace and justification, and the status of future contingents and divine foreknowledge, among many other topics. However, the issues that have drawn most attention are those that surround his theory of *esse apparens* (apparent existence), a kind of non-real, merely apparent existence that is the key to Aureol's theories of universals, perception and conceptual thought.

Aureol first alludes to this *esse apparens* when he takes up Duns Scotus' distinction between intuitive and abstractive cognition (*Scriptum* pro. s.2). This distinction applies at both the intellectual and sensory levels, and is most easily described by examples: imagination (in the absence of the imagined object) counts as abstractive cognition, for instance, whereas ordinary sense perception is one kind of intuitive cognition. But although the extension of these categories was relatively uncontroversial, it proved much more difficult to give a general account of what distinguishes intuitive from abstractive cognition. Duns Scotus claimed that intuitive cognition takes as its object something that is present to the cognitive agent. Aureol objects to this claim by describing various cases of non-veridical perception, such as after-images and double-vision, where there is no object corresponding to what is being perceived. These should all be counted as instances of intuitive cognition, Aureol argues, and he goes on to claim that this sort of empirical evidence should be taken more seriously than any logical argument that might be put forward. In opposition to Scotus' proposal, Aureol suggests that intuitive cognition, at both the sensory and intellectual levels, be defined as cognition that is direct (not inferential), and that makes the object appear present, actual and existent.

These claims naturally lead Aureol to raise more general questions about perception, and in particular to ask how perception is able to make an object appear present, whether or not it is actually present. His answer is that the senses give the object apparent existence. (He also speaks of this as *intentional* existence.) When a stick is swung rapidly in a circle, something circular appears. There is nothing circular that really exists, because the appearance is there only for as long as someone is watching. However, Aureol insists that the appearance, this apparent entity, exists in the very place where it appears to exist. It is not in the eye or the brain, nor anywhere in the intervening air. (Aureol does incorporate sensible and intelligible *species* into his account, but he attributes real existence to them, not apparent or intentional existence, and he takes them to be pure intermediaries which are never themselves the objects of cognition.) Aureol uses these illusory cases to establish a general theory of perception: all perception involves the formation of *esse apparens*, but it is illusions that point to the true nature of perception, because ordinarily we can't distinguish *esse apparens* from *esse reale*: 'In the case of true vision they occur together' (*Scriptum* d.3 s.14 a.1).

Aureol gives a similar account at the intellectual level. Indeed, he explicitly defines cognition, sensory and intellectual, as 'having something present as an appearance'. Thus if a picture of Caesar on a wall were to make Caesar appear to that wall, then 'the wall would be said to be cognizing Caesar' (*Scriptum* d.35 a.1). At the intellectual level, an apparent entity exists within the intellect, and is in fact the focus of intellect's attention (*Scriptum* d.9 a.1; d.27 a.2). Aureol thinks that he can make this claim without epistemological difficulties, for he stresses in many places that it is the object itself that has apparent existence within intellect. One's concept of a rose is not distinct from the thing itself in the external world. It just is that rose, in *esse apparens*: thus 'the objects are cognized directly' (*Scriptum* d.3 s.14 a.3).

These considerations form the basis for Aureol's conceptualist theory of universals (*II Reportationes* d.3 q.2; d.9 q.2). Nothing outside mind is universal; mental concepts are universal only in the sense that some concepts have a less determinate content than others. Indeed for Aureol, 'everything, inasmuch as it is, is singular'. Individuation is a primitive feature of reality, and so 'to seek that through which a thing outside the intellect is singular, is to seek nothing' (*II Reportationes* d.9 q.2). However, Aureol's position seems readily distinguishable from nominalism because he rejects the view that mental concepts might merely denote objects in a certain indefinite and universal way (see NOMINALISM §§1–2). Mental concepts, as universals, are more than mere representations, because they *are* the objects, in *esse apparens*.

See also: CHATTON, W.; DUNS SCOTUS, J.; PERCEPTION

List of works

Note: There are no published translations of Aureol's work.

Aureol, Peter (1312–20) *In quatuor libros Sententiarum* (Commentary on Peter Lombard's *Sentences*), Rome, 1596–1605. (This early edition is not widely available, but is currently the only printed source for most of the *Sentences* commentary, as well as for his *Quodlibet*.)

—— (1317) *Scriptum super primum Sententiarum*, ed. E.M. Buytaert, St Bonaventure, NY: Franciscan Institute, 1956, 2 vols. (Covers only the first eight of 48 distinctions.)

References and further reading

Boehner, P. (1948) '*Notitia intuitiva* of non-existents according to Peter Aureoli O.F.M. (1322)', *Franciscan Studies* 8: 388–416. (A good introduction to Aureol's disagreement with Scotus over intuitive cognition.)

Dreiling, R. (1913) *Der Konzeptualismus in der Universalienlehre des Franziskanererzbischofs Petrus Aureoli* (Conceptualism in the Theory of Univerals of the Franciscan Archbishop Peter Aureol), Beiträge zur Geschichte der Philosophie des Mittelalters 11, 6, Münster: Aschendorff. (The best source for information on Aureol's theory of universals, although Dreiling judges Aureol quite harshly.)

Henninger, M. (1989) *Relations: Medieval Theories 1250–1325*, Oxford: Clarendon Press. (Devotes a chapter to Aureol's interesting claim that relations have no extramental existence.)

Normore, C. (1993) 'Petrus Aureoli and His Contemporaries on Future Contingents and Excluded Middle', *Synthese* 96: 83–92. (Discusses Aureol's claim that some future contingent propositions are neither true nor false.)

Perler, D. (1994a) 'What Am I Thinking About? John Duns Scotus and Peter Aureol on Intentional Objects', *Vivarium* 32: 72–89. (Compares the views of Aureol and Scotus.)

—— (1994b) 'Peter Aureol vs. Hervaeus Natalis on Intentionality', *Archives d'Histoire Doctrinale et Littéraire du Moyen Age* 61: 227–62. (Edits and supplies a useful introduction to part of *Scriptum* d.23, concerning so-called 'second intentions'.)

Tachau, K. (1988) *Vision and Certitude in the Age of Ockham: Optics, Epistemology and the Foundations of Semantics, 1250–1345*, Leiden: Brill. (Contains a detailed discussion of Aureol's theory of *esse apparens*.)

Teetaert, A. (1935) 'Pierre Auriol ou Oriol', *Dictionnaire de Théologie catholique* XII (2), Paris, 1810–81. (This book-length article provides the most complete treatment of Aureol's life and work.)

Vignaux, P. (1934) *Justification et prédestination au XIVe siècle: Duns Scot, Pierre d'Auriole, Guillaume d'Occam, Grégoire de Rimini* (Justification and Predestination in the Fourteenth Century: Duns Scotus, Peter Aureol, William of Ockham, Gregory of Rimini), Paris: E. Leroux. (The most detailed study of Aureol's thought in these areas.)

ROBERT PASNAU

AUROBINDO GHOSE (1872–1950)

Aurobindo Ghose was a leading Indian nationalist at the beginning of the twentieth century who became a yogin and spiritual leader as well as a prolific writer (in English) on mysticism, crafting a mystic philosophy of Brahman (the Absolute or God). Aurobindo fashioned an entire worldview, a system intended to reflect both science and religion and to integrate several concerns of philosophy – epistemology, ontology, psychology, ethics – into a single vision. Of particular importance to his cosmological thinking was evolutionary biology. But Aurobindo also understood the fundamental nature of matter to include – for metaphysical reasons – an 'evolutionary nisus' that ensures the emergence of individuals capable of mystical experience in which the supreme reality, Brahman, is revealed.

1 Life
2 Metaphysics
3 Views on evil
4 Relation to classical Vedānta

1 Life

Commonly referred to as Aurobindo, or, by followers, as Sri Aurobindo ('Sri' is honorific), Aurobindo Ghose was born in Calcutta. He spent fourteen years in England from the age of seven until graduating from King's College, Cambridge University. He died surrounded by disciples in the French colony of Pondicherry in South India.

Aurobindo's politics were not of the passivist variety later endorsed by Gandhi. He used the editorial columns of the nationalist newspaper *Bande Mataram* (Hail to Mother India) to call rather openly for open rebellion. Arrested on charges of sedition and then 'waging war', he spent a year in prison before being acquitted in 1909. Still harassed by the British authorities, he retreated to Pondicherry, retired from politics and wrote voluminously while practising meditation and yoga. In addition to his metaphysical writings, Aurobindo wrote an epic poem (*Savitri*, one of the longest in English) and works on psychology, political philosophy, ethics, culture and yoga.

2 Metaphysics

Aurobindo puts forth in *The Life Divine*, his principal work of philosophy, a thoroughly realist metaphysics: there is an essential God or Brahman (the two terms are with Aurobindo roughly interchangeable) and real physical objects – transcendent in the sense of existing independently of our experience – with much intermediate to these two 'poles of being'. He couples his realism with an empiricist epistemology that brooks no illusory element. Illusions and misperceptions are analysed as false combinations of presentations of realities. Objects stand in causal relations to perceivers, though causal media vary. Aurobindo defends an epistemic parallelism between the indications of sensory and mystical experiences, with the latter carrying most of the weight regarding the existence and nature of Brahman – although variations on teleological, cosmological and other arguments of rational theology are presented too. Aurobindo's realism is not unreflective; he considers and rejects several varieties of phenomenalism, including Buddhist and Vedāntic theories that use a phenomenalist understanding of sensory objects to defend the possibility of enlightenment experiences held to be a supreme personal good. Aurobindo endorses such possibilities of enlightenment (*nirvāṇa*, for example), but proposes that his realist views provide better explanations both of mystical experiences and of our everyday world. There is tension, in Aurobindo's metaphysical writings, between a mystical foundationalism, Aurobindo's sense of the veridicality of yogic experiences, and a speculative theology, a sense that Brahman as the Absolute cannot be perfectly known.

Throughout *The Life Divine*, Aurobindo weaves a view of a 'self-manifesting Brahman' with close attention to an overall coherence of theory. Brahman – in essence perfect Being, Consciousness-Will and Bliss or Value (so Aurobindo renders a traditional characterization of Brahman as *saccidānanda*) – involutes aspects of itself – that is, contracts – so that certain finite possibilities can emerge, a process that has an outer limit in the 'inconscient' energies of matter. But such apparent inconscience cannot remain because it is nothing but Brahman. Conceivable universes that are incompatible with Brahman's essential nature are strictly impossible. Thus conscious beings are destined to evolve. In other words, God (that is, Brahman) works within limits, and could not, for example, make $2 + 2 = 5$. God cannot create an entirely insentient world since God is constrained by the metaphysical law *ex nihilo nihil fit* ('nothing from nothing') to create out of God's own nature of Consciousness and Bliss. Thus this world is destined to evolve sentient material beings and

567

eventually a divine life conceived as a society where many have experience of Brahman.

3 Views on evil

Evil, which is rooted in the insentience of matter and the limitations it imposes on life (the converse of valuable possibilities it secures), is fated to diminish and even disappear as evolution proceeds – possibly past the human species. The future evolution that Aurobindo envisages is the working out of a divine intention in which human effort, however, has a crucial role. Humans have developed a sufficient measure of freedom and self-determination to further the evolutionary progression, as divine delegates as it were. In a second, revised and expanded, edition of *The Life Divine* (1943-4), Aurobindo elaborates his theory of individual progress, amplifying a mystical psychology and enlarging on a theory of rebirth. Brahman's self-manifestation includes other 'worlds', or 'planes of being', said to be accessible to us in a mystic trance and which the developing divine individual ('psychic being' or 'soul') is said to enter upon the death of the body. The material universe does not exhaust the manifestation of Brahman, but it is, Aurobindo claims, the only evolutionary world. The others are 'typal', with no evolutionary emergence. In this world, the soul, profiting from all its experience, develops an increasingly refined and finely etched personality in terms of body, life and mind. The value of this development discounts, Aurobindo reasons, the evil made possible and even necessary by the insentience of matter inasmuch as matter makes possible such an evolutionary world.

4 Relation to classical Vedānta

Aurobindo manages an extraordinary consistency; critics have tended to fault him not for tensions among his many claims but for wrongly weighing 'mystical data'. Though little known in the West, his system enjoys in India significant influence both among professional philosophers and a larger intellectual community.

The speculative originality evident in Aurobindo's intricate theodicy and theory of evolutionary progress sets his system apart from classical Vedānta, the traditional Hindu philosophy based on sacred texts (principally Upaniṣads and the *Bhagavad Gītā*). But Aurobindo also relies heavily on these works. He says he understands them as records of mystical experiences similar to his own, not as mainstays of a revealed tradition. Critics, particularly in India, have often misunderstood Aurobindo's approach to traditionally sacred texts, viewing his philosophy as Neo-Vedānta and fuelling worries that Aurobindo, like all mystics perhaps, is ethnocentric in his claims. But despite the distancing from traditional Hinduism, such worries about cultural shaping remain (see MYSTICISM, NATURE OF §3).

Western influences on Aurobindo's thought have not been adequately studied. Platonic and Neoplatonic reverberations abound, and there are echoes of Hegel and Nietzsche. Aurobindo read widely in Western literature (he won prizes in Classics at Cambridge) as well as in Sanskrit, which he learned through English, in effect his mother tongue. A hero of the Indian nationalist movement could be expected to cast his thought in the rich philosophical terminology of the classical Sanskrit tradition (consider also the case of Gandhi). But Aurobindo's inspirations were arguably as much Western as Indian. There is also with Aurobindo, as with all great thinkers, an element of creativity that transcends cultural precedent.

See also: BRAHMAN; VEDĀNTA

List of works

Aurobindo Ghose (1973) *Sri Aurobindo Birth Centenary Library*, Pondicherry: Sri Aurobindo Ashram Trust, 30 vols. (Aurobindo's collected works.)

—— (1914–21) *The Life Divine*, Pondicherry: Sri Aurobindo Ashram Trust, revised edn, 1943–4, 2 vols. (Aurobindo's major work of philosophy, written in dozens of chapters, with much repetition of the principal themes.)

—— (1914–21) *The Synthesis of Yoga*, Pondicherry: Sri Aurobindo Ashram Trust, revised edn, 1959. (Aurobindo's teaching of yoga, that is, of 'self-discipline' and mystical technique.)

—— (1918–21) *The Foundations of Indian Culture*, Pondicherry: Sri Aurobindo Ashram Trust, 1973. (An early work of an incensed Aurobindo defending Indian culture against European belittlement.)

—— (1950–1) *Savitri*, Pondicherry: Sri Aurobindo Ashram Trust. (The *Mahābhārata* story of Sāvitrī, who by debate wins back into life the soul of her husband from Yama, Death, is used by Aurobindo to express mystical experiences and a worldview in a massive English epic.)

References and further reading

Bolle, K.W. (1965) *The Persistence of Religion*, Leiden: Brill. (Debunks religion sociologically with special reference to Aurobindo's mystic views.)

Heehs, P. (1989) *Sri Aurobindo: A Brief Biography*, Delhi: Oxford University Press. (Contains useful summaries of the various areas of Aurobindo's writing as well as a lively account of Aurobindo's political life.)

Maitra, S.K. (1941) *An Introduction to the Philosophy of Sri Aurobindo*, Calcutta: Culture, 2nd edn, 1965. (A sympathetic and highly readable overview.)

Phillips, S.H. (1986) *Aurobindo's Philosophy of Brahman*, Leiden: Brill. (An inquiry into Aurobindo's metaphysics and mystic epistemology.)

Singh, S.P. (1972) *Sri Aurobindo and Whitehead on the Nature of God*, Aligarh: Vigyan Prakashan. (Perhaps the best of many comparative studies that have appeared in India.)

STEPHEN H. PHILLIPS

AUSTIN, JOHN (1790–1859)

Although written in the early nineteenth century, Austin's is probably the most coherent and sustained account of the theory of legal positivism. The complex relationships between legal positivism and the concepts of morality and politics are explored by him but are often neglected or misunderstood in modern commentaries.

John Austin became in 1829 the first Professor of Jurisprudence at the newly established University of London, having previously spent a brief spell in the army, followed by a somewhat longer period of work in barristers' chambers as an equity draftsman. In preparation to take up his chair, he spent two years studying in Bonn, acquainting himself with classical Romano-German legal science. A neighbour of James MILL and Jeremy BENTHAM, he was much of their intellectual circle, and had John Stuart MILL as a student. His main work was a systematic explanation of some basic social concepts in terms which have been received as the classical statement of 'legal positivism', according to which law is dependent on the will of superior(s) over inferior(s) (see LEGAL POSITIVISM §2).

Austin wanted all lawyers to commence their studies with the cognitive sciences, logic and ethics. Politics and the study of law were seen by him as subcategories of ethics. More than half of his introductory series of lectures was given over to an exposition of the principle of utility – seen either as the index to the laws of God, or as the rational basis of ethics (see UTILITARIANISM).

He said that all laws (apart from scientific laws) were set to intelligent beings by intelligent beings, having power over them. There are two basic types of laws – those set by God for people and those set by people for others. Of the laws set by God, Austin said that he would normally call these 'natural' laws, but as this word is likely to be confused with aspects of sociology, he would instead call them 'divine' laws. He recognized that 'non-believers' would prefer the word 'ethics'. On either view, these provide the standard by which all other laws should be judged. Many modern positivist scholars think that positivism and natural law are opposed to each other – not so for Austin.

Austin said that of laws set by people there can also be two types – those set by them as political superiors (positive law) and those set by them in other capacities (positive morality). Having set out the basic categories of ethics, positive law and positive morality, Austin went on to explain their common and distinctive features. They have in common the concepts of 'commands', 'duties' and 'sanctions'. The intelligent being or person lays down some *general* rule for the guidance of human conduct. If it is not complied with, the maker of the rule can exact some *detriment* for non-compliance.

The distinctive features of 'positive law' (the law of the state) are that it comprises rules made by 'sovereigns' addressed to 'subjects' within an 'independent political society'. While these ideas are scorned by most contemporary legal theorists, they remain fundamental in international politics and foreign affairs policy. Austin made it clear that the study of politics is logically and socially prior to the study of state law. Without political stability there is no state, and without the state no law of the state. The most contentious aspects of Austin's views were his claims that 'sovereigns' cannot be *bound* by state laws, and that the 'laws' operating between states would be better viewed as 'international positive morality'. Both points relate to the role of coercion, assuming that the author of a coercive law cannot, logically, also be subject to it, and that state boundaries limit the enforceability of state laws, but not necessarily their range of application (see SOVEREIGNTY §§2, 3).

Some suggest that his separation of the concepts of positive (state) law, positive (existing or customary) morality, and ethics (the critical base), entails that the positive law can be understood or implemented without understanding its relationship to the other factors. This is plainly wrong.

There has been much debate about this 'separation of law and morality'. Most writers on the topic forget that Austin said – 'Positive law (or *jus*), positive morality (or *mos*) together with the principles which form the test of both, are the inseparably connected parts of a vast organic whole' (1861–3: 17). An unfulfilled project of his was to write a book on *The Principles and Relations of Jurisprudence and Ethics*. It follows from Austin's analysis that as we are dealing with three types of rules there are also three types of duties as well as three types of commands and sanctions. Austin said that if there should be any conflict between the duties of positive law and the duties of ethics or divine law, then because the sanctions which God could impose would greatly outweigh those which could be imposed by the human makers of positive law, it would accord with the principles of utility to act in accordance with the natural or divine law and not the law of the state.

The law of the state, he said, had its basis in the positive morality of the wider community, and should be guided in its development by the positive morality of the legal and international communities.

Austin had no time for 'the childish fiction employed by our judges, that judiciary law or common law is not made by them, but is a miraculous something made by nobody, existing, I suppose from eternity, and merely declared from time to time by the judges' (1861–3: 634). He explains at some length how it is that judges *make* the law rather than just find it, and entitles chapters 35–9 of his *Lectures* 'Judicial Legislation'. In its conceptual aspects, Austin's approach influenced the work of people such as W.N. Hohfeld, and in its social aspects has much in common with the writing of the later legal realists (see HOHFELD, W.N.; LEGAL REALISM).

Austin's strongest supporter was his wife Sarah, who was accomplished and well known in the intellectual circles of London and Paris, and with a number of important translations to her credit. As a teacher, Austin was not conspicuously successful, and his periods of formal academic employment were quite brief, at the University of London (1829–33) and at the Inns of Court in London (1834). He also worked with the British Criminal Law Commission (1833) and for a short period as a Commissioner to the Royal Commission on Malta (1836–8).

See also: LAW, PHILOSOPHY OF; NORMS, LEGAL §2

List of works

Austin, J. (1832) *The Province of Jurisprudence Determined*, London: John Murray; with intro. by H.L.A. Hart, London: Weidenfeld and Nicolson, 1954; with intro. by W.E. Rumble, Cambridge: Cambridge University Press, 1995. (The only book to be published by Austin in his lifetime, being a series of six lectures originally delivered as ten. It states his central tenets in clear terms, and has remained a focus of controversy, and of frequent attempts at refutation, more or less since its first publication. The 1995 edition includes a good bibliography.)

—— (1859) *A Plea for the Constitution*, London: John Murray. (This is the best known and most significant of Austin's later pamphlets; it is a forceful statement of opposition to radical reform of the franchise, based on the idea that habitual or customary acceptance of a constitutional order is the foundation of a stable polity and thus of law.)

—— (1861–3) *Lectures on Jurisprudence or the Philosophy of Positive Law*, ed. R. Campbell, London: John Murray, 5th edn, 1885. (This is the complete statement of Austin's views and of his legal-conceptual analyses, based on his London lectures. The two volumes were first published from his working papers as edited by Sarah Austin. First and subsequent editions contain the most moving piece about Austin's life, in the Preface written by Sarah.)

References and further reading

Anon. (1861) 'English Jurisprudence', *The Edinburgh Review* 114: 463. (This early review of Austin's *Province* exemplifies the nineteenth-century response thereto.)

Anon. (1863) 'Austin on *Jurisprudence*', *The Edinburgh Review* 118: 439. (A contemporary reviewer's response to the *Lectures*.)

Hamburger, L. and Hamburger, J. (1985) *Troubled Lives: John and Sarah Austin*, Toronto: University of Toronto Press. (A biographical account of a remarkable marriage, showing that behind a staid exterior storms may rage.)

Hart, H.L.A. (1961) *The Concept of Law*, Oxford: Clarendon Press, 2nd edn, 1994. (This exceptionally influential work contains a sustained critique of Austin's work, and an attempt to replace it with a different version of legal positivism.)

Hohfeld, W.N. (1919) *Fundamental Legal Conceptions as Applied in Judicial Reasoning*, New Haven, CT: Yale University Press. (An influential account of such basic concepts as 'duty', 'right' and 'power' in a way that develops some of the ideas originally deployed in Austin's *Lectures*.)

Moles, R.N. (1987) *Definition and Rule in Legal Theory*, Oxford: Blackwell. (This presents a reasoned rejection of most conventionally accepted critiques of Austin's work, especially that of H.L.A. Hart, which it claims rests on a serious misunderstanding of Austin.)

Morison, W.L. (1982) *John Austin*, London: Edward Arnold. (A readable, but in places polemical, account of Austin's life, work, and jurisprudential doctrines, arguing for the substantial correctness of Austin's views. Good bibliography.)

Rumble, W.E. (1985) *The Thought of John Austin*, London: Athlone Press. (This is a good scholarly account of Austin's work; good bibliography, and comprehensive survey of the works.)

ROBERT N. MOLES

AUSTIN, JOHN LANGSHAW (1911–60)

J.L. Austin was a leading figure in analytic philosophy in the fifteen years following the Second World War. He developed a method of close examination of nonphilosophical language designed to illuminate the distinctions we make in ordinary life. Professional philosophers tended to obscure these important and subtle distinctions with undesirable jargon which was too far removed from everyday usage. Austin thought that a problem should therefore be tackled by an examination of the way in which its vocabulary is used in ordinary situations. Such an approach would then expose the misuses of language on which many philosophical claims were based.

In 'Other Minds' ([1946] 1961), Austin attacked the simplistic division of utterances into the 'descriptive' and 'evaluative' using his notion of a performatory, or performative utterances. His notion was that certain utterances, in the appropriate circumstances, are neither descriptive nor evaluative, but count as actions. Thus to say 'I promise' is to make a promise, not to talk about one. Later, he was to develop the concepts of locutionary force (what an utterance says or refers to), illocutionary force (what is intended by saying it) and perlocutionary force (what effects it has on others).

1 Life and early period
2 Analysis of ordinary language
3 Philosophical linguistics

1 Life and early period

John Langshaw Austin, a graduate of Balliol College, Oxford, was successively a Fellow of All Souls' (1933) and Magdalen Colleges (1935) at Oxford until appointed White's Professor of Moral Philosophy in 1952. He was a distinguished Intelligence Officer in the Second World War, latterly at Supreme Headquarters, Allied Expeditionary Force, being awarded the OBE, the Croix de Guerre and made an Officer of the Legion of Merit.

In the pre-war period Austin worked mainly on the history of philosophy, particularly on Aristotle and Leibniz, though publishing nothing on them. He was a caustic observer of the contemporary scene, as is clear from his only pre-war publication, the devastating, amusing and wholly negative paper 'Are There A Priori Concepts?' ([1939] 1961), but as yet he spoke with no clear voice of his own. He himself regarded his later work as quite different from anything he had done before the war.

2 Analysis of ordinary language

During his five years absence on military service Austin's thought matured, and on returning to Oxford in 1945 he immediately became a leading force in philosophy there and, soon after, in analytic philosophy throughout the world. His work was based on three convictions.

(1) Ordinary language, by which is meant language other than that of philosophy, as the tool of communication, contains all the distinctions about the world that people have found it necessary to make – not, of course, all that can be made. As such, he thought, while it was not perfect, it was a much more powerful and subtle tool of thought than philosophers had traditionally recognized. What, for example, philosophers have hastily treated as synonyms, would usually be found on careful examination to mark distinctions that might be important. Where synonyms arose, the daily use of language would usually lead either to the abandonment of one or the development of a distinction in their employment.

(2) Philosophers consistently misused and abused ordinary language, blurring and perverting the distinctions it made. When they abandoned ordinary language in favour of a technical vocabulary of their own it was usually confused and imprecise, creating confusion and darkness rather than shedding light. Thus they neglected and damaged the powerful tool available to them in ordinary language in favour of a less efficient one; no wonder that little headway was made in answering the problems they tried to solve.

(3) While holding that much philosophical work was full of confusion, Austin did not, however, share the view that the sole task of the philosopher was to expose these confusions and to 'show the fly the way out of the fly-bottle' (see WITTGENSTEIN, L. §17). He thought that progress could be made, and that philosophy could shed light as well as clear away fog. But this required slow and careful labour, especially including a thorough examination of the vocabulary available and used in the area where the problem arose, long before asking the huge and assault-defying major questions.

Some have wrongly thought that Austin believed that his way of working in accordance with these convictions was the be-all and end-all of philosophy;

this he denied, though he said that it might be the begin-all. But he once gave the title 'One way of possibly doing one part of philosophy' to an unpublished talk, and he ascribed his lack of use of more formal procedures to ignorance.

Most of Austin's work based on these convictions was carried out in discussion and in lectures. He believed that his sort of work on language was best done by groups working together. He himself published only a handful of papers, never spontaneously, but almost always at the request of the Aristotelian Society and for symposia, the subjects of which were often not of his choosing. But from these, together with posthumous publications, it is possible to illustrate how his fundamental ideas were employed.

In his posthumously published lectures entitled *Sense and Sensibilia* (1962a) (Austin parodying Austen), he is mainly concerned to illustrate the second conviction above. He looks closely, very closely, at the invented philosophical terminology for discussing the problems of perception – terms such as 'sensum', 'sensibile' and 'sense-datum' – and also at the use (or, as he thought, abuse) by philosophers of such existing terms as 'illusion', 'delusion', 'look', 'seem', 'appear' and 'veridical' (see PERCEPTION §1). Thus, for example, philosophers had tended to treat 'look', 'seem' and 'appear' as synonyms, which, he tries to show, they are not. The argument from illusion, he said, gained virtually all its force from misuse of words. That, for example, the fact that a penny looks elliptical from certain angles is part of our evidence that it is round, not an illusion that suggests that it is not round. He uses A.J. Ayer's book *The Foundations of Empirical Knowledge* (1940) as his main illustrative text, attempting to show that Ayer's problems are largely of his own making and result from abuse of language (see AYER, A.J. §3). In his paper 'Other Minds' ([1946] 1961) he similarly seeks to show that much scepticism about the possibility of knowledge was based on continuing to use the word 'know', but with impossibly stringent criteria of application quite different from those of ordinary speech. If we cannot know according to criteria we never use, what then? In this paper Austin also insists that if, having made a claim to knowledge in circumstances which would normally be considered to provide complete justification for the claim, some freak circumstance arises (in Austin's example, what the experts agree to be a goldfinch explodes or quotes Virginia Woolf), we should not naturally agree that the experts were wrong, but rather admit that words fail us. Language makes no provision for circumstances which do not in fact arise.

His more constructive work in this field is to be found in some of his papers. Thus there is the traditional problem of the nature of action. Austin was sure that to plunge in at the deep end by asking 'What is an action?' was mere folly. The way to start was by a close examination of the language ordinarily used for discussing action; a sub-area of this vocabulary is that which is concerned with the defects that actions may exhibit; they may, for example, be unintended, mistakes, inadvertences, involuntary or clumsy (see ACTION §5). As a deliberate illustration of his general ideas, he set out to examine some of these terms in a paper called 'A Plea for Excuses' ([1956a] 1961). His technique, as usual, was to take a real or imaginary situation and ask what we should say about it. Thus, take a situation in which you and I keep a donkey each in the same field and I, wishing to shoot mine, instead shoot yours. If I (a) fire accurately at your donkey, thinking it is mine, or (b) fire at mine, but the bullet ricochets and hits yours, which, if either, would you call a mistake or an accident? Or are the terms interchangeable? Austin had an unusual facility for bringing out differences which we implicitly observe in our daily use of language, but which we do not ordinarily make explicit and which we may fail to notice in philosophical discussion. 'A Plea for Excuses' also contains a short but illuminating account of his methods of work at a more general level.

Another important illustration of this aspect of Austin's work is the paper 'Ifs and Cans' ([1956b] 1961). Here he typically approaches the problem of the freedom of the will by a careful examination of such expressions as 'I could have...' and, especially, 'I could have if I had chosen...', rather than by an immediate attempt on the big question (see FREE WILL §§1–2). He brings out defects in the account given by G.E. MOORE in his *Ethics* (1912), and by others, of the way such expressions are used in real life. Notably he brings out the inadequacy of the traditional accounts of hypotheticals. In the sentence, 'There are biscuits on the sideboard if you want some', for example, the truth of the conseqent should not be taken to follow from the truth of the antecedent. What is the force of 'if I choose'? Does it give a necessary or sufficient condition of one's being able to act, or does it function in some way more similar to that of 'if you want some' in the example above?

3 Philosophical linguistics

Austin thought that ordinary language did not provide us with ready-made distinctions for use in discussing the nature of language, and that many of the technical terms already existing in philosophy were ill-suited to this purpose. Here was an area in which he thought that technical terms were necessary, not as a substitute for existing linguistic resources, but as a supplement to them. One of his most disliked targets was the distinction commonly made between the descriptive and evaluative uses of language, which he thought to blur a host of more effective distinctions that needed to be made. He started to remedy the situation by drawing attention to what he first called the performatory, later the performative, use of language. It was introduced in the paper 'Other Minds' with great brevity; a performative utterance is typically couched in an indicative sentence but is neither a description nor an evaluation, nor is it true or false; rather, one utters a formula or performs a ritual in appropriate circumstances which itself counts as the performance of an act which would not be naturally regarded as a linguistic act, provided that the utterer is in a position to make the utterance. Thus to say 'I promise' is to make a promise, not to talk about one, and to say 'I name this ship "Generalissimo Stalin"' is, if one is a duly authorized person, to give a ship a name. There are many types of action that can be best performed by such specified formulas, such as making contracts, making appointments and christening. Making a promise, for example, is more like shaking hands over a bargain in a recognized context, than describing anything whatsoever (see PERFORMATIVES).

In his posthumously published William James Lectures, *How to Do Things with Words* (1962b), based on earlier lectures given at Oxford over a series of years with the title 'Words and Deeds', Austin set out to provide an ambitious classification of types of force of linguistic utterances on a far wider scale. Thus at a higher level he distinguished between different types of force, such as locutionary, illocutionary and perlocutionary force. The locutionary force is roughly the sense and reference of the utterance, the illocutionary force is what one is doing in making an utterance with a given locutionary force, and the perlocutionary force is the effect that is intended to be achieved by an utterance with a given illocutionary force. Thus the locutionary force of 'The bull is charging' is simply the predication of something of an animal; the illocutionary force may be that of a warning, a comment on the scenery or an exclamation; and if the illocutionary force is that of warning, the perlocutionary effect intended may well be to make somebody run for it. Not all these forces are always present; I may utter a sentence without even locutionary force merely to test a microphone or to give an example in a philosophical paper. So Austin further distinguishes the merely phonetic act of making a noise vocally and the phatic act of uttering an intelligible sentence (as when I say 'The bull is charging' merely to test a microphone) from each other and from the other forces (see SPEECH ACTS §1).

These and other distinctions have been widely used, sometimes with modifications, and also, needless to say, widely criticized (for example, Searle 1969). Their influence is apparent in theoretical linguistics as well as in philosophy. What is certain is that this work has had profound effects on philosophical linguistics. One notable feature is the way that Austin chose to present his classification of utterances as arising from a criticism and, eventually, the abandonment of the performative as a special type of utterance and its subsumption under the doctrine of illocutionary forces. Thus what had been counted as the action performed by the utterance of a performative now becomes the illocutionary force of that utterance, and the performative is no longer treated as importantly different from other speech acts having an illocutionary force. This may accurately reflect the historical development of Austin's views, but it appears to some to involve a denaturing of the performative (Warnock 1973; Urmson 1977). In particular Austin now includes as performatives utterances which seem to lack the formulaic or ritual character early ascribed to performatives.

See also: ORDINARY LANGUAGE PHILOSOPHY, SCHOOL OF

List of works

Austin, J.L. (1961) *Philosophical Papers*, Oxford: Clarendon Press; 3rd edn, enlarged, 1979. (Contains 'Are There A Priori Concepts?' (1939), 'Other Minds' (1946), 'A Plea For Excuses' (1956a), and 'Ifs and Cans' (1956b), and all Austin's writings except two or three reviews and the books listed below.)

—— (1962a) *Sense and Sensibilia*, reconstructed from the manuscript notes by G.J. Warnock, Oxford: Clarendon Press. (Attacks all sense-datum theories of perception, but principally phenomenalism as developed by A.J. Ayer. It is urged that these theories stem from a perverted interpretation of the main terms which are used with reference to sense perception. Originally delivered as lectures at Oxford.)

—— (1962b) *How to Do Things with Words*, Oxford: Clarendon Press; revised edn by J.O. Urmson and M. Sbisà, 1975. (Develops a theory of speech acts based on a critique of Austin's own theory of performative sentences that we utter and the acts, such as stating, promising, condemning, that we perform in uttering them. The William James

Lectures given at Harvard in 1955, based on lectures delivered at Oxford previously.)

References and further reading

* Ayer, A.J. (1940) *The Foundations of Empirical Knowledge*, London: Macmillan. (A phenomenalist theory of perception.)
—— (1973) 'Has Austin Refuted Sense-Data?', in *Essays on J.L. Austin*, Oxford: Clarendon Press. (Answers Austin's criticism of the above in *Sense and Sensibilia*.)
Berlin, I. et al. (1973) *Essays on J.L. Austin*, Oxford: Clarendon Press. (Essays discussing both the man and his work.)
Fann, K.T. (ed.) (1969) *Symposium on J.L. Austin*, London: Routledge & Kegan Paul. (Contains many relevant papers.)
* Moore, G.E. (1912) *Ethics*, London: Williams & Norgate. (A utilitarian theory based on the idea of 'good' as an a priori concept.)
* Searle, J. (1969) *Speech Acts*, Cambridge: Cambridge University Press. (A development and criticism of Austin's *How To Do Things With Words*.)
* Urmson, J.O. (1977) 'Performative Utterances', in *Midwest Studies in Philosophy 2*. (Criticizes Austin's later treatment of performatives.)
* Warnock, G.J. (1973) 'Some Types of Performative Utterance', in *Essays on J.L. Austin*, Oxford: Clarendon Press. (Criticizes Austin's later views on performatives.)
—— (1980) *J.L. Austin*, London: Routledge. (A general critical account of Austin's philosophy.)

J.O. URMSON

AUSTRALIA, PHILOSOPHY IN

Australian academic philosophy has made an international impact disproportionate to the country's small population, though its beginnings contain little that might have suggested such influence. The first Philosophy Chair was established at the University of Melbourne in 1886 and its occupant Henry Laurie was more notable for extravagant shyness than public impact or academic achievement. Until the 1920s, the dominant philosophical outlook was idealism. After the arrival from Glasgow of the charismatic John Anderson to the Chair in Sydney in 1927, this outlook was challenged by his vigorous, distinctive, highly metaphysical and somewhat dogmatic version of realism. Anderson had little international recognition during his working life, but he had a powerful effect upon Australian cultural life and upon students who themselves achieved a significant international presence. Thinkers like David Armstrong, John Mackie and John Passmore diverged in many ways from Andersonianism but the indelible mark of the Sydney baptism remained with them even when they had accommodated to the international profile.

For twenty-five years or so, there was a strong contrast and rivalry between the style of philosophy done in Sydney and that done in Melbourne. Idealist influences persisted longer in Melbourne due to the two Boyce Gibsons (father and son) who occupied the Melbourne Chair successively, but the significant contrasts really began when Melbourne came under the sway of Wittgenstein's philosophy in the 1940s. This was due principally to the presence during the war years of G.A. Paul, one of Wittgenstein's pupils, and later Paul's friend Douglas Gasking, who had studied under Wittgenstein in Cambridge, and another pupil of Wittgenstein, A.C. ('Camo') Jackson. Where Anderson's orientation was systematic, metaphysical and provincial, the Melbournians were piecemeal, anti-metaphysical and (relatively) cosmopolitan. As a direct force in academic philosophy, Anderson's system died with him in 1962, as did the striking contrast in style between Melbourne and Sydney philosophy. With the expansion of universities and philosophy departments, the metaphysical emphasis of Sydney and the analytical professionalism of Melbourne merged in a technique that had no particular regional significance, even when some of its concerns were distinctive. Among these was the phenomenon known as Australian Materialism, associated principally with J.J.C. Smart and David Armstrong. This continued the metaphysical orientation of so much Australian philosophy, though deploying the analytical and argumentative skills by then common to English-speaking philosophy anywhere. Much of the passion surrounding the materialism debates of the 1960s and 1970s, involving the pros and cons of 'the scientific world view' and its reductionist enthusiasms, dissipated into broader metaphysical and psychological interests such as the discussion of universals and laws, realism versus antirealism, the ontology of space and time, and the status and pretensions of cognitive science.

There remains important work that is somewhat independent, even occasionally sceptical, of these metaphysical directions: work in epistemology, philosophical psychology, history of philosophy, and value theory. In pure value theory, there has been little homegrown work that is highly original though there have been many solid contributions by Australian philosophers to international debates, and Peter Singer is famous beyond philosophical circles for his theorizing of 'animal liberation' and opposition to 'sanctity of human life' outlooks in bioethics. The general tenor of Australian philosophy remains resolutely 'analytical' though there is a significant minority interest in 'continental' philosophy and some efforts to reach a modus vivendi between the two. Until late in the twentieth century, women played no prominent role, but women philosophers and feminist philosophy have become increasingly significant and, although many find the 'continental' mode congenial to their approach, there is strong representation of the more 'analytic' tradition. Another prominent emphasis has been environmental philosophy which incorporates the traditional interest in metaphysics but with a less reductive touch than has been characteristic of the mainstream.

1 **Beginnings**
2 **Early influences**
3 **Anderson**
4 **The Melbourne flavour**
5 **Australian materialism**
6 **Besides metaphysics**
7 **Feminism and other tendencies**

1 Beginnings

Academic philosophy, the home for almost all contemporary philosophy, effectively began its Australian life in Melbourne where the first lecturer in logic was appointed at the University of Melbourne in 1881. The appointee was the Scottish-born journalist, Henry Laurie, who shortly afterwards (1886) became the country's first philosophy Professor. Prior to Laurie, some logic and political theory had been taught at Melbourne by the redoubtable W.E. Hearn, an extraordinary polymath with an international scholarly reputation, who also taught at various times English, Ancient and Modern History, Political Economy and Classical Literature, before becoming the University's first Dean of Law. In Sydney, some logic had been taught along with classics since the University's foundation in 1850, but a lectureship in philosophy was not established until 1888. There had been a compendious Chair in English Language and Literature and Mental and Moral Philosophy established earlier at the University of Adelaide, but its first occupants had no philosophical claims. The professing of philosophy there really began in 1894 with the appointment of the gifted, if often obscure, William Mitchell who gave the prestigious Gifford Lectures in Aberdeen in 1924–6, later published as *The Place of Minds in the World*. Mitchell (later Sir William) was a great public figure in South Australia where he was Vice-Chancellor of the university for twenty-six years and Chancellor for a further six. He died in 1962 at the age of 101 and, in his nineties, was capable of vigorous exchanges with one of his young successors in the philosophy Chair, J.J.C. Smart.

Both Laurie and Mitchell were Scots and the Scottish influence on the formative years of Australian philosophy is even more remarkable than its notable influence upon Australian universities generally. In Sydney, the Scottish influence was if anything even more emphatic and enduring – it was Glasgow University that produced the first lecturer in philosophy (1888) and then the Challis Professor of Mental and Moral Philosophy (1890) in the (same) person of Francis Anderson. Like Mitchell, Francis Anderson was later knighted, but more for his services to education than philosophy. Some thirty-seven years after Anderson's appointment to the Chair, another (unrelated) Anderson came from Glasgow (via Cardiff and Edinburgh) as the third and most famous occupant of the Chair, though there was never any question of his being given, or accepting, Royal honours.

Philosophy in Australia in the late nineteenth century made little impact on the rest of the world and not much impact on the country's intellectual or social life. The US idealist philosopher, Josiah Royce, took leave from Harvard to sail to the Antipodes in 1887, seeking recovery from a bout of depression. The visit cured him, and much that he observed filled him with admiration for Australia and New Zealand. Upon his return to the USA, he wrote extensively of his impressions, but made no comment upon the fledgling state of academic philosophy or, indeed, of university life at all. In political philosophy, Royce was what would now be called a 'communitarian', and he was taken with what he thought was the more community-oriented nature of Australian attitudes compared to the individualism of the USA. If he made no contact with academic philosophers, he did become acquainted with some influential politicians and was greatly impressed by the philosophical outlook and statesmanship of the Victorian politician Alfred Deakin, who was to be one of the 'founding fathers' of the Federated Commonwealth, and eventually Australia's second Prime Minister. Royce described Deakin as 'a lover of metaphysics' and continued to correspond with him after returning to the US. Deakin seems to have drawn his own philosophical inspiration from overseas and, in any event, no Australian philosophers contributed significantly to theoretical debates about Federation or the form of the Australian Constitution as it was drawn up in 1900. Whether because of this, or because so few of its drafters had the philosophical and cultural leanings of a Deakin, the document is notably prosaic, legal, and uninspiring. This is in striking contrast to the highly philosophically oriented US constitution, but that was of course the product of a revolution of arms and of thought, whereas it was Australia's fate to achieve a peaceful evolution to independence.

2 Early influences

Well into the twentieth century, Australian philosophy was predominantly idealistic in orientation, eclectic in shape and inspired by foreign models. Its Scottish origins ensured the influence of Scots thought, but the great days of the Scottish School of Common Sense were past by the time philosophy began to be taught seriously in Australia, so it was Sir William HAMILTON's rather windy, Neo-Kantian 'corrections' of Thomas REID, and A.S. Pringle Pattison's idealism that prevailed, rather than Reid's own vigorous, realistic, somewhat Aristotelian elaboration of a common-sense philosophy (see COMMONSENSISM). Earlier in the century, Reid had had a powerful influence upon the development of US philosophy, an influence which contributed to the growth of a distinctively national style of philosophy in the form of pragmatism. In Australia, however, the initial Scottish influences gave rise to no native school. Mitchell, it is true, made many shrewd philosophical observations and developed an original and, to some degree, internationally recognized version of idealism, but the opacity of his thought virtually prohibited its development by others. Laurie was a capable teacher, but he had no distinctive philosophy to impart and was, in addition, painfully shy. Francis Anderson, though more expansive, was notable for educational reforms rather than philosophical innovation.

Besides the Scottish influence, there were also sources from Continental Europe – HEGEL, of course, but subsequently BERGSON, HUSSERL and Eucken, these latter notably present in Laurie's successor at Melbourne, W.R. Boyce Gibson. The older Gibson assumed the Chair in 1911 and his son Alexander followed him in 1935. The Gibson reign thus lasted fifty-four years, from 1911 to 1965. Gibson senior studied in Europe and, at Jena, came under the spell of Rudolf Eucken. Later, he attended Husserl's seminars and translated one of his books. It is a curiosity of the history of thought that Eucken (now almost utterly forgotten) should have so influenced the older Boyce Gibson in Jena when there was in that same university at the time a philosopher at the height of his powers, destined to exert a massive influence upon modern analytical philosophy. Of course, Gottlob FREGE was in the mathematics department and unacknowledged in his own time and his own university, but what a difference it might have made to the development of Australian philosophy had Gibson brought Frege rather than Eucken to Melbourne! Although Gibson had a mathematics background and was to co-author a logic text-book, he seems to have known nothing of Frege and would have found Frege's realism nowhere near as sympathetic as Eucken's personal idealism.

Idealism was thought to support certain forms of religion, indeed of Christianity, and there is much emphasis upon the significance of religious belief among the early Australian philosophers. This emphasis is both metaphysical and moral. It engages with the Victorian era's anxieties about whether faith can survive the encounter with science and, even more urgently, whether morality can survive the demise of religion. The response is heavily, if sometimes inflatedly, metaphysical and the metaphysical interest will later survive the disappearance of the original question and the attempt to bolster religion. It is arguable that this metaphysical cast of mind is one of the most distinctive features of the Australian philosophical tradition, and it early received one of its most striking manifestations in the work of an expatriate Australian, Samuel Alexander.

Alexander was born in Sydney in 1859, but pursued undergraduate studies at the University of Melbourne before leaving Australia to study at Oxford. He was made Professor of Philosophy at Manchester in 1893, having earlier had the distinction of being the first Jew appointed to a Fellowship at either Oxford or Cambridge. During the First World War he gave the Gifford lectures in Glasgow, published as *Space, Time and Deity* in 1920. Alexander's work is a fascinating blend of old and new. It has a traditional commitment to large-scale metaphysical vision, a commitment that would soon begin to appear outmoded, but it was determinedly realistic in a way that placed Alexander with the burgeoning revolt against idealism. He gave a primary emphasis to experience and science, but insisted on finding a role for religion and God. His moral philosophy was also markedly metaphysical and unusual. In spite of his birth and upbringing, Alexander can only be considered an Australian philosopher in a peripheral sense since his philosophical career was spent entirely in Britain, but his mode of thinking had a powerful influence in his birthplace through its impact upon John Anderson and, to a lesser degree, its very different effect on the second Boyce Gibson. Anderson took from him the opposition to idealism in any form, the resolute realism, the emphasis upon space-time and categories of reality, and the dedication to systematic thought. Gibson was impressed by the emphasis on the significance of religious experience. Interestingly,

Alexander's influence on Australian philosophy was not only abstractly intellectual – he was on the selection committees that appointed both of the Boyce Gibsons and seems also to have had a hand in Anderson's appointment.

3 Anderson

When he was a lecturer at Glasgow, John Anderson had heard Alexander's Gifford lectures, and when appointed to the Sydney Chair in 1927 Anderson had already begun to develop the highly individual outlook on philosophy that was to have such a powerful influence in his adopted country. It was an outlook that gave a distinctive cast to much of the philosophy done in Australia during his thirty-one years in the Chair.

The really remarkable features of Anderson's work were less its realism and argumentativeness (aspects of a mood gathering force throughout much of the philosophical world during Anderson's working life) than its commitment to systematic metaphysics and the eclecticism of its sources. These qualities set Anderson's thought apart from the styles of philosophy that came increasingly to dominate Oxford and Cambridge from the 1920s to the 1950s, for these were mostly hostile to systematic, constructive metaphysics. To be educated by Anderson was to be inducted into a different world, though there was a similar commitment to close, often deflationary, examination and criticism of argument: the term 'criticism' had a mantra-like quality in Andersonian circles that sometimes consorted comically with the deferential use of the system.

Students found that there was not only an Andersonian position on everything from logic to love, from copula to community, from hypotheticals to Hegel, from reason to religion, but that these positions had an (at least apparent) interconnection that could be intoxicating. In addition, the system provided a comprehensive tool for the demolition of the conventional wisdoms of the day, whether religious, political, moral or institutional. Additional edge was provided by a special vocabulary which often employed familiar philosophical jargon in an unfamiliar sense. It was important to be 'empiricist' but not to believe in sense-data or ideas; 'dualist' errors abounded well beyond the philosophy of mind and were committed by believing in God or in any sort of ultimates. From within the system, the misguided were shot down in flames with monotonous regularity, though they were seldom persuaded since they rarely understood the terms of the debate. As the poet James McAuley put it: 'Anderson had an answer to every conceivable question. It was "No"'. In Anderson's case, as in many others, there was a sort of religious, even sectarian quality about his authoritarian presence, his campaigns and many of his followers, which may help explain the combination of liberation and enslavement that Anderson's influence could produce.

David Stove, who absorbed Anderson's influence, but rejected Andersonianism, and developed his own independent, highly polemical philosophical position, once remarked: 'Anderson's powers of dismissal were simply boundless.... Einstein scored just one two-line reference in print from Anderson: it said that his theory was "utterly illogical"' (Grave 1984: 47). The conviction behind such sentiment owed nothing to the developments of modern mathematical logic which Anderson viewed with similar scorn. His logic was based on the traditional syllogistic, ingeniously adapted to try to deal with its apparent deficiencies, and had an almost mystically metaphysical solidity about it. The propositions it dealt with were not ideas or linguistic items or mathematical formulae, not anything representing or picturing other realities or states of affairs, but real states of affairs themselves. To suppose otherwise was to commit the cardinal sin against Anderson's rigorous realism by proposing intermediaries between thinkers and the realities they were considering. For Anderson, the questions which greatly exercise many contemporary philosophers about the role of conceptual schemes in our understanding of reality would have been non-questions. Things, situations, processes existed in space-time and discussion should attend to determining the truth of such matters.

Anderson professed little concern for worldly success or academic advancement, and denounced the cosy certainties of consumerism and progressivism; indeed one of the few things he admired about religion was its potential for opposing such idols. Early on, he was involved with the Australian Communist Party, but became more and more critical of Marxism and moved to a strongly anti-communist position by the late 1930s. He wrote quite a lot but published little in major international journals, and some of his most important writings appeared in obscure places. Gilbert Ryle invited him to contribute to *Mind*, but he saw no point. He drew inspiration from the ancient Greeks, though selectively. He admired the objective attitude of the Presocratics which he contrasted unfavourably with the anthropocentric, subjective concerns of post-Cartesian philosophy, and he had a special admiration for HERACLITUS. Hegel was respected, partly for his opposition to individualism and for the scope of his thought, and MOORE, RUSSELL and Alexander were considered significant enough to be critically adapted, but modern influences on his thought tended to come as much from outside the orthodox philosophical canon as from within: MARX and FREUD, James Joyce and Sorel, Hilaire Belloc and James Burnham.

Some of his students pursued academic philosophy as rather imitative disciples, others became important contributors to philosophy on the Australian and the world scene. John Passmore, David Armstrong, John Mackie and Eugene Kamenka have all expressed a sense of indebtedness to Anderson and, although his system virtually died with him, its influence can be seen in some of their characteristic views. In other areas of the academy, and in the arts and the professions, people profoundly influenced by Anderson had a striking impact on Australian life, especially in New South Wales and Canberra. Two of Australia's finest poets, James McAuley and Alec Hope, were students of Anderson and, as a young man, Hope engaged in print in respectful philosophical controversy about moral philosophy with his mentor. In mature life, neither could be regarded as Andersonians – indeed, McAuley converted to a very conservative version of Roman Catholicism – but typical Andersonian concerns remained with them, as with many journalists, senior lawyers, judges and public servants.

4 The Melbourne flavour

In Melbourne, Anderson's influence was minimal during his heyday, for not only did idealism linger with the influence of Gibson in the 1930s, but Melbourne became an outpost of the new philosophical revolution associated partly with logical positivism and more significantly with the later WITTGENSTEIN. A primary influence in this development was the arrival of G.A. Paul in 1939, fresh from Wittgenstein's Cambridge. Stranded in Australia by the outbreak of the Second World War, Paul was another Scots-born philosopher to exert a great influence upon Australian philosophy. When he returned to England at the end of the war, he was replaced by his friend Douglas Gasking, whom he had earlier encouraged to migrate to a lectureship in Brisbane. Paul and Gasking had both studied under Wittgenstein as did A.C. ('Camo') Jackson, who went from Melbourne to Cambridge for Ph.D. studies in 1946 and returned to a lectureship in the Melbourne department in 1948. Paul not only brought the new philosophy to Australia, but had an immense influence upon the development of other disciplines at the University of Melbourne, most notably History. In one year, all the full-time members of the History department attended Paul's lectures on logic. Like Anderson's, Paul's impact could be partly explained by his being a big fish in a small pond (an especially small pond, in Paul's case, because of the drainage of intellectual talent caused by the war in the period of his greatest influence) but unlike Anderson, Paul was not an original thinker, and the power of his ideas came largely from afar even if he (like Jackson) clearly was a remarkable teacher. He published very little, and the best of that before he arrived in Australia; his paper 'Is there a Problem about Sense-Data?' was his most influential contribution.

The Wittgensteinian tradition thus established in Melbourne began with a somewhat positivist flavour, but later broadened under the impact of Oxford philosophy and the arrival of refugee intellectuals from continental Europe, many of whom had been absurdly deported from Great Britain and interned in Australia during much of the war. During the 1950s, the Melbourne department was host to a number of philosophers, both foreign-born and locally educated, who later left to pursue philosophy overseas. These included such well-known names as W.D. Falk, Kurt Baier (his New Zealand wife Annette also worked in Australia), Alan Donagan, Brian O'Shaughnessy, Paul Edwards, Michael Scriven and George Schlesinger. This established a trend for a later export industry – John Mackie, Jenny Teichman, Michael Devitt, Mark Johnston, to name a few – and the import-export aspect has continued with people like Michael Stocker and Michael Tooley coming to Australia from North America for long stays and then returning. Whereas Andersonian Sydney into the 1950s was confidently parochial and mostly contemptuous of recent developments in international philosophy, Melbourne stood for a more cosmopolitan and contemporary approach. It also hosted a diversity of outlooks and a professional, problem-oriented approach to the subject that Anderson dismissed as 'eclecticism'. The influence of Wittgenstein was strong, but not overwhelming, and indeed many of the best-known products of the department from that period, such as McCloskey, Baier, Donagan and Charlesworth were not in any sense Wittgensteinians. Douglas Gasking succeeded Boyce Gibson in the Melbourne Chair in 1966 and the Melbourne Department remained less metaphysically oriented than other departments in the country or indeed the new departments in the city of Melbourne. The rapid expansion of university education in Australia from the 1960s eliminated the dominance and the opposition of Melbourne and Sydney philosophy; what remains is mostly a Hegelian synthesis of the metaphysical interest derived from Sydney and the internationalist 'analytic' professionalism drawn from Melbourne.

5 Australian materialism

Since the late 1950s, the metaphysical stream in Australian philosophy has been in flood, first in the theory known as central state (or 'Australian') materialism, and then in a particularly forceful version of metaphysical realism. There has also been a persistent interest in the ontology of space and time. J.J.C. Smart, introduced to philosophy in Glasgow and continuing his studies in Oxford, was converted by U.T. Place from the influence of Ryle. In Adelaide he developed a version of materialism about the mind which was taken up and further developed by D.M. Armstrong, first in Melbourne and later when he moved to the Chair in Sydney in 1964. Armstrong's book, *A Materialist Theory of the Mind* (1968), became something of a bible for the materialist school. It propounded the view that 'the mind is the brain' and defended it against a variety of objections. There were differences of emphasis and formulation among the Australian materialists and there were similarities between their approaches and those of several physicalist and materialist philosophers in Britain and the USA.

The background to the movement was an increasing emphasis on the need to locate philosophy within the perspective of the physical sciences. The relation of philosophy to the developing modern sciences had posed a constant puzzle to philosophers since Descartes, but it became an abiding preoccupation once the 1960s saw the development of a dominance by the USA in academic philosophy. Much philosophy in the USA in the twentieth century has had a strong orientation to the physical (and sometimes social) sciences and, since Quine, the idea that philosophy is at best a part of science has achieved a certain orthodoxy. Two aspects of the modern physical sciences particularly impressed the Australian materialists – comprehensiveness and reductionism. Armstrong writes with persistent admiration of 'the scientific world view' as something to which philosophy must not only be accommodated but subject, and the basic concept of the material is elucidated deferentially in terms of whatever may be the basic explanatory concepts of contemporary physics. The success of reductive strategies in chemistry and biology encouraged the idea that all manner of philosophically intractable realities would be more manageably understood in terms of scientific items. Much room remained for debate about the nature of the reduction. The identity theory that underpinned the approach generated worries about the respective merits of type identity and token identity, the precise role of functional explanations of mental concepts within the materialists' framework, and the relation of central-state materialism to eliminative materialism. Eliminativists treat the mental as rather like the magical, a category to be superseded by the march of science. Australian materialism, by and large, resisted eliminativism; its stand on mind–brain identities compared them with identities such as that of water with H_2O, and materialists thought that many of our 'folk' understandings of beliefs, pains, feelings and so on were, in their way, as valid and useful as much of our pre-theoretical thinking about water. Revision in the light of science was certainly possible, but elimination was a defiance of common sense.

The materialist mood was dominant for many years, but not all-conquering. Those more influenced by Wittgenstein or Oxford tended to think of the mental in linguistic or social terms; they were suspicious of ontology, especially a radically simplifying ontology, though some were attracted to the ambiguous physicalism of Donald DAVIDSON. Epistemology, philosophy of language and 'moral psychology' were seen as more important than ontology, though the first two topics, at least, were also of concern to some of the materialists, as of course was the philosophy of science. (The Melbourne History and Philosophy of Science department was the second to be established anywhere, and produced such philosophers as Gerd Buchdahl, George Schlesinger, Hugh Lacey and Brian Ellis.) There were also critics of materialism, more sympathetic to the ontologizing mood, who held out for some residual dualism, often centred on the recalcitrance of 'qualia' to the materialist reduction (see QUALIA). C.B. Martin in Adelaide was a significant influence here, and both Frank Jackson and Keith Campbell defended the ontological significance and irreducibility of the experiential, of what it is (and is 'like') to be aware of one's surroundings. Jackson even went so far as to support an unfashionable sense-data representational theory of perception in his book *Perception*. Campbell, a migrant from New Zealand, succeeded Armstrong in the Chair at Sydney, and Jackson (the son of A.C. Jackson) is a product of the University of Melbourne who was Professor at Monash University in Melbourne and then followed Jack Smart as Professor at the Australian National University. In a curious repetition of the Gibson dynastic tradition, Jackson succeeded his father in the Chair at Monash, and in 1995 became only the second Australian to give the prestigious John Locke Lectures at Oxford (his father was the first). The sympathies of Jackson and Campbell with the scientistic mood of their materialist colleagues, however, lead them to favour an epiphenomenalist account of 'qualia' so that the reality of the mental items they hope to reinstate is somewhat pallid and causally ineffectual (see EPIPHENOMENALISM).

The expatriate Australian, Brian O'Shaughnessy, developed a more positive and original, if sometimes more elusive, double aspect theory of the mind in *The Will* (1980).

More broadly, many critics and defenders of materialism in Australia tended to share a resolute realism in ontology that some believe to have climatic and geographical roots. One external influence has, however, been significant: regular visits since the 1970s of the eminent US philosopher David LEWIS, himself an ultra-realist and something of an 'honorary Australian'. Some feel that Lewis' impact has been excessive; if so, it has merely reinforced a homegrown tendency. A sturdy realism is apparent even in some of the work on space and time; Graham Nerlich defends the view that space is not only absolute but a thing. What antirealism exists tends to be associated with the influence of Oxford's Michael DUMMETT and Harvard's Hilary PUTNAM (especially through the former's sometime pupil Barry Taylor) though there is a certain antirealist flavour about another interesting antipodean development, the work on alternative logics associated mostly with logicians at or connected with the Australian National University from the 1970s onwards. This was not indeed unique to Australia, but its development was vigorous and its interest in formalizing relevance and contextual relations and in allowing for 'good contradictions' was antiphonal to both the traditional Melbourne indifference to formal logic and the Andersonian scepticism about all its modern developments. It is perhaps significant that many of the practitioners of such arcana were migrants, notably Len Goddard and Graham Priest (from the UK), Bob Meyer (from the USA), and Richard Sylvan, formerly Routley (from New Zealand).

6 Besides metaphysics

Compared with achievements in philosophy of mind and metaphysics, Australians have produced little of originality in 'pure' value theory, though there have been some notable performances in applied ethics. Kurt Baier's *The Moral Point of View* (1958) and Alan Donagan's *The Theory of Morality* (1977) had genuine impact in moral theory, but both philosophers spent the major part of their careers in the USA. Similarly, J.L. Mackie's 'error theory' in his book *Ethics: Inventing Right and Wrong* has been much discussed, if seldom endorsed, but it was published long after he had migrated to the UK. D.H. Monro and H.J. McCloskey published books discussing fundamental moral theory, but they were basically intelligent refurbishings of, respectively, subjectivism and intuitionism. McCloskey's most influential work is found in his stern critiques of liberal political theory and his trenchant criticisms of utilitarianism. One notable feature of Australian moral philosophy in the latter part of the twentieth century has been the prevalence of utilitarianism. This parallels the dominance of materialism and the yearning after a 'scientific world view', although most of the materialists were indifferent to ethics, one of them famously sneering that 'ethics is for girls' – a delicious combination of sexism and philistinism. The materialist Jack Smart has, however, been a strong advocate of a rather traditional utilitarianism, and the theory fits the no-nonsense mood of much Australian metaphysics. In political philosophy, Philip Pettit and Robert Goodin also keep consequentialist and utilitarian flags flying (though C.L. Ten and Robert Young are notable non-utilitarians). In addition, Australia's best known moral philosopher, Peter Singer, has been an enthusiastic utilitarian and has deployed the theory in his various writings and activities in applied ethics. Singer's books, especially *Animal Liberation* and *Practical Ethics*, are among the few by professional philosophers in the latter part of the twentieth century to be widely read well beyond academic circles.

Singer has dedicated much of his work to an attack upon the pre-eminence traditionally given to human interests and values in moral thinking. Developing strands present in classical utilitarianism, especially in BENTHAM, and drawing on aspects of the thought of R.M. HARE, Singer has denounced any predominant ethical attachment to the value of human concerns as 'speciesist' on analogy with the sins of racism and sexism. Critics have found the analogy unpersuasive, and the Singer programme allows, in any event, that greater significance can be given the human where it can be shown that particular humans have endowments that deserve better treatment than particular animals or other living organisms. None the less, Singer's denunciation of speciesism has a radical and disturbing bite when it comes to the treatment of the very young, the very old and the seriously incapacitated, since many of these currently lack the endowments that differentiate most humans from animals. Such endowments (predominantly associated with the exercise of rationality) are those that Singer, along with many other philosophers, treat as definitive of a species-transcendent category of 'person'. Since only such persons are allowed a 'right to life' (though other beings should not be treated cruelly or callously without good reason) it follows that there is nothing even presumptively wrong with infanticide, and many other non-voluntary homicides. Consistent with this outlook, Singer has attacked any commitment to 'the sanctity of human life' as the outmoded vestige of religion and superstition.

If philosophy in Australia was marked until the 1920s, and to some degree beyond this, by a desire to reconcile religion with the rise of science and to show the continued relevance to ethics of a religious sense of life, there remains less sign of such concern at the end of the twentieth century. Not only is the mood of 'scientistic' metaphysics and the tenor of utilitarian thought generally hostile, or at best indifferent, to religious outlooks, but there has been little substantial positive work in the philosophy of religion. Several prominent Australian philosophers in the last quarter of the century have been committed Christians, and there is a burgeoning interest in certain Asian philosophies with strong religious components. But, apart from Max Charlesworth's founding of a journal in the philosophy of religion, *Sophia*, there has been little to indicate a revival of this project. Indeed, most of the contributions to *Sophia* come from overseas. Atheists have been more evident. C.B. Martin's *Religious Belief* (1959) accompanied a flurry of local interest in the 1950s in the problem of evil, mainly produced by atheists such as Mackie and McCloskey, but despite the high levels of religious attachment in the wider community (as attested by numerous surveys) academic philosophers in Australia have shown little recent interest in defending the religious outlook. There are some signs that this may be changing.

Something like the religious impulse does have a presence in philosophical engagement with problems of the environment, another area of applied philosophy which has had notable currency in Australia. A good deal of writing in this area invokes utilitarian or other more traditional considerations, but that which appeals to the intrinsic value of the natural order often honours an ideal of respect and even reverence for nature that has distinct religious echoes. The metaphysical impulses of Australian philosophy are well to the fore in much writing on the environment, and appeals to scientific understanding are common enough, but the scientific models invoked are different from those beloved of the materialists. Freya Mathews' *The Ecological Self* (1991), for instance, presents a holistic metaphysics as the basis for appropriate environmental attitudes. There are points of connection between contemporary Australian environmental philosophy and attitudes to nature characteristic of the aboriginal inhabitants of the continent. Whether the aboriginal peoples had a philosophy of the environment is a moot point, but their religious cosmologies and ethical practices foreshadow some of the values and outlooks that many 'green' environmental philosophers seek to defend and systematize (see ECOLOGICAL PHILOSOPHY).

7 Feminism and other tendencies

Environmental and bioethical philosophers alike have an engaged dimension to their work, as do other Australian philosophers who work on questions that connect with different areas of public policy. But one of the most interesting developments of a style of philosophy allied to an activist programme has been the energetic expansion of feminist approaches to philosophy in the last quarter of the twentieth century. Genevieve Lloyd's *The Man of Reason* had a key role in this, and was also influential well beyond Australia. Lloyd, who became the first woman philosophy professor in Australia when appointed to the Chair at the University of New South Wales in 1987, has gone on to explore philosophical interests that are unusual in Australia. Like John Passmore, but in a different way, she works on the history of philosophical ideas and the connections between philosophy and literature. Partly because of the influence of feminism there are significant numbers of women in academic philosophy in Australia at the end of the twentieth century, where for most of its history there were very few. Virtually all women doing philosophy in Australia think of themselves as feminists, and most see their work in philosophy as having feminist aspects. There are complex questions here, not of course restricted to the Australian scene, about the sense in which there can be such a thing as a feminist philosophy (or a Catholic philosophy or a black philosophy) since there are constraints internal to any form of inquiry, whether it be mathematics, physics or philosophy, that rightly resist merely external 'doctrinal' imposition. This complexity, and debate about it, is complemented by another: the way in which feminist thinking is informed and often divided by different philosophical traditions, particularly those rather clumsily characterized as analytic and continental.

It is worth remarking in this connection, that most Australian philosophy departments approaching the twenty-first century are heavily 'analytic' in orientation, though there is usually some continental presence. The small Deakin University department and the General Philosophy department at Sydney University have long been much more continental in orientation, and the Faculties department at the Australian National University has been unique in forging an equal and amicable partnership between the traditions. The General department at Sydney resulted from an acrimonious division in the Sydney Department in 1973. The causes of the split were political and personal rather than philosophical: the Vietnam war and the upsurge of radicalism generated throughout the world in the late 1960s, plus a good deal of personal antagonism. The smaller half of the split, the Traditional and Modern department, included the Professor and Head, David Armstrong and his friend, David Stove, both tough-minded philosophers and dedicated anti-communists who supported the war and much else that the majority of the department opposed. The General Department initially had an assortment of radical feminists, Marxists and 'continentalists', but also contained several mainstream philosophers. Over the years, the General department became less political, and evolved into one specializing in continental philosophy, with a strongly historical approach to philosophy. But although continental philosophy had more presence in Australia at the end of the twentieth century, and there have been useful writings in a commentary style, there has been little distinguished creative philosophy produced. Of course, the terms 'analytic' and 'continental' can be distorting – a very interesting book in mixed mode is Max Deutscher's *Subjecting and Objecting* (1983) which acknowledges an equal debt to Gilbert RYLE and Jean Paul SARTRE, and contains some pungent criticisms of materialism as a form of totalitarianism.

Some of the most distinctive features of Australian philosophy may have been partly a product of the country's isolation and its small academic population. Intellectual fashions were slow to arrive from overseas and, once transplanted, had plenty of time to develop their peculiar, local shapes. Schools like Andersonianism, Melbourne Wittgensteinianism and Australian Materialism flourished in a climate where you did not need to convert many people to have a dominant school. More recently, technology has considerably reduced the isolation, especially in the world of ideas, and the philosophical community in Australia has greatly expanded from the small elite of the 1950s. Contemporary Australian work in philosophy remains very impressive, but it is much less distinctive than it once was; like philosophy elsewhere in the English-speaking world, it has acquired the polished professionalism that is part of a relatively homogenized international product. There remain some specifics of style that set it apart to some degree: on the positive side, a penchant for the direct and argumentative, and a widespread preference for a *modus vivendi* between the plain and the elaborately technical; more negatively, a certain tendency towards conformism, a sense that there are 'respectable' views behind which ranks should be closed to the exclusion of outsiders. This tendency was present in the old days and has curiously survived their passing. Maybe it reflects something in the complex national psyche. Australians romanticize rebels and outsiders, exalt egalitarianism, practice tolerance, and praise straight talking, but we have a strong need to belong and we find oddballs and deviants disturbing. A distinguished British philosopher visiting Australia in the late 1960s is said to have remarked of Australian philosophers (perhaps under the pressure of not being treated as deferentially as he had expected): 'They're either mad or boring.' If we read 'competent' for 'boring' and 'visionary' or 'unusual' for 'mad', then perhaps Australians should hope for more madness into the twenty-first century.

See also: ALEXANDER, S.; ANDERSON, J.; ARMSTRONG, D.M.; PASSMORE, J.; SMART, J.J.C.; IDENTITY THEORY OF MIND; MATERIALISM IN THE PHILOSOPHY OF MIND; SCIENTIFIC REALISM AND ANTIREALISM

References and further reading

* Alexander, S. (1920) *Space, Time and Deity*, London: Macmillan, 2 vols. (Gifford lectures by Australian expatriate philosopher with considerable impact on the development of Australian philosophy.)

Anderson, J. (1962) *Studies in Empirical Philosophy*, Sydney: Angus & Robertson. (A collection of Anderson's major articles and the primary source for understanding his thought.)

* Armstrong, D. (1968) *A Materialist Theory of the Mind*, London: Routledge & Kegan Paul. (A crucial document for the development of 'Australian' materialism.)

—— (1984) 'Self-Profile', in R.J. Bogdan (ed.) *David Armstrong*, Dordrecht: Reidel. (An often amusing and elegantly presented short account of his own philosophical and intellectual development and the Australian and international influences upon it.)

* Baier, K. (1958) *The Moral Point of View*, Ithaca, NY: Cornell University Press. (Vigorously defends an objective approach to ethics that treats moral rules as those that are for the good of everyone alike and would be apparent from the point of view of 'an independent, unbiased, impartial, objective, dispassionate, disinterested observer'.)

Baker, A.J. (1986) *Australian Realism: the Systematic Realism of John Anderson*, Cambridge: Cambridge University Press. (A thorough exposition and defence of Anderson's philosophy by a former student and colleague. It also contains an introduction by the Oxford philosopher, Anthony Quinton, placing Anderson in a broader context and speculating on the nature of his achievements.)

Brown, R. (1988) 'Recent Australian Work in Philosophy', *Canadian Journal of Philosophy* 18 (3): 545–78. (Challenges Sylvan's claims – see below – about the existence and need for a regional philosophy, and gives a review of the contemporary scene in Australian philosophy.)

Brown, R. and Rollins, C.D. (1969) *Contemporary Philosophy in Australia*, London: Allen & Unwin. (Articles on sundry philosophical topics by Australians, with an introduction by Alan Donagan on the state of Australian philosophy and its background.)

* Deutscher, M. (1983) *Subjecting and Objecting*, St Lucia: Queensland University Press. (Interesting and unusual employment of analytic and continental resources to discuss traditional philosophical problems.)

* Donagan, A. (1977) *The Theory of Morality*, Chicago, IL: University of Chicago Press. (An ambitious attempt to give a classical rational account of morality drawing upon essential elements in the Judaeo-Christian tradition.)

Donagan, B. (1993) 'Alan Donagan: A Memoir', *Ethics* 104 (1): 148–53. (A historian wife's reflections on her distinguished husband's philosophical career. It includes perceptive comments on the Melbourne department's influences on Donagan and others.)

Eddy, W.C.H. (1961) *Orr*, Brisbane: Jacaranda Press. (A dedicated Orr supporter's account of the dismissal of Sydney Sparkes Orr as Professor of Philosophy at the University of Tasmania in 1956 and his subsequent tribulations. In what was probably the most lurid public scandal involving a philosopher anywhere, Orr was dismissed in controversial circumstances for sexual misconduct with a student. The Orr case divided Australian intellectuals while titillating the public, produced an eight-year staff association 'black ban' on filling the Chair, and culminated in Orr accepting a settlement from the University on his deathbed in 1966.)

* Grave, S.A. (1984) *A History of Philosophy in Australia*, St Lucia: University of Queensland Press. (The definitive work on this subject by a former Professor of Philosophy at the University of Western Australia, Grave's finely researched book is comprehensive, thoughtful, and particularly valuable on the period up to 1970 or so.)

* Jackson, F. (1977) *Perception: A Representative Theory*, Cambridge: Cambridge University Press. (Aims to defend a sophisticated 'sense-data' theory against standard objections.)

* Lloyd, G. (1984) *The Man of Reason*, London: Methuen, 2nd edn, 1993. (Reviews the ways in which the idea of reason has developed in the philosophical tradition so as to make it appear the peculiar province of men.)

* Mackie, J.L. (1977) *Ethics: Inventing Right and Wrong*, Harmondsworth: Penguin. (Deflationary account of the status of ethics, claiming that moral language incorporates a pervasive mistake about the objectivity of moral discourse.)

* Martin, C.B. (1959) *Religious Belief*, Ithaca, NY: Cornell University Press. (A wide-ranging and subtle critique of the philosophical underpinnings of religious belief. Historically important as one of the earliest comprehensive attempts to apply the new analytical techniques to philosophical theology.)

* Mathews, F. (1991) *The Ecological Self*, London: Routledge. (Highly metaphysical treatment of environmental issues.)

* Mitchell, W. (1933) *The Place of Minds in the World*, London: Macmillan. (Originally given as the Gifford Lectures at the Unversity of Aberdeen, 1924–6.)

* O'Shaughnessy, B. (1980) *The Will: A Dual Aspect Theory*, Cambridge: Cambridge University Press, 2 vols. (Subtle and complex defence of a double-aspect theory of volition.)

* Paul, G.A. (1936) 'Is there a Problem about Sense-Data?', *Proceedings of the Aristotelian Society*, supplementary vol. 25: 61–77. (One of Paul's few publications, but a very influential piece which argues that central questions about sense-data should be construed linguistically rather than ontologically. The Wittgenstein influence is clear, but Paul's style foreshadows the Oxford philosophy of ordinary language.)

Pybus, C. (1993) *Gross Moral Turpitude: The Orr Case Reconsidered*, Port Melbourne: William Heinemann Australia. (An absorbing revisionist account of the Orr case, described in Eddy (1961), from a feminist – and somewhat patriotically Tasmanian – perspective that casts severe doubts upon the pro-Orr stance of most of the Australian philosophical community. Pybus has unearthed much new material – including information about how the undistinguished Orr was appointed in 1952 ahead of J.L. Mackie, Kurt Baier and H.P. Grice – and raises interesting questions about the professional ethic appropriate to sexual relations between university academic staff and students.)

* Singer, P. (1976) *Animal Liberation: A New Ethics for our Treatment of Animals*, London: Cape, 2nd edn, 1990. (The bible of animal liberation, this book contains Singer's arguments against the outlook of 'speciesism', and more specifically attacks a variety of abuses of animals that should be repugnant even to many who do not accept his view that there is no moral basis for any preferential treatment of one's own species.)

* —— (1979) *Practical Ethics*, Cambridge: Cambridge University Press, 2nd edn, 1993. (A more directly

philosophical book, and something of a best-seller in those terms. Singer presents, with fluency and directness, an uncompromising case for a utilitarian solution to a range of issues in applied ethics.)

Sylvan, R. (1985) 'Prospects for Regional Philosophies in Australasia', *Australasian Journal of Philosophy* 63 (2): 188–204. (Sylvan argues that a distinctively regional philosophy is emerging in Australia and that this should be encouraged. He cites naturalism, especially its materialist version, and Australian environmentalism as especially distinctive.)

Toulmin, S. (1993) 'Alan Donagan and Melbourne Philosophy', *Ethics* 104 (1): 143–7. (Toulmin reflects, partly from personal experience, on the philosophical climate at the University of Melbourne in the 1940s, with special reference to the influence of Wittgenstein.)

C.A.J. COADY

AUTHORITY

The notion of authority has two main senses: expertise and the right to rule. To have authority in matters of belief (to be 'an authority') is to have theoretical *authority; to have authority over action (to be 'in authority') is to have* practical *authority. Both senses involve the subordination of an individual's judgment or will to that of another person in a way that is binding, independent of the particular content of what that person says or requires. If a person's authority is recognized then it is effective or* de facto *authority; if it is justified then it is* de jure *authority. The latter is the primary notion, for* de jure *authority is what* de facto *authorities claim and what they are believed to have. Authority thus differs from effective power, but also from justified power, which may involve no subordination of judgment. In many cases, however, practical authority is justified only if it is also effective.*

Political authority involves a claim to the obedience of its subjects. Attempts to justify it have always been at the core of political philosophy. These include both instrumental arguments appealing to the expertise of rulers or to their capacity to promote social cooperation, and non-instrumental arguments resting on ideas such as consent or communal feeling. Whether any of these succeed in justifying the comprehensive authority that modern states claim is greatly disputed..

1 The nature and forms of authority
2 Political authority
3 Justifications

1 The nature and forms of authority

What do theoretical and practical authority have in common? George Cornwall Lewis aptly defined the acceptance of theoretical authority as: 'the principle of adopting the belief of others, on a matter of opinion, without reference to the particular grounds on which that belief may rest' (1849). Authority over action shares this feature. HOBBES (§7) put it this way: 'command is where a man saith, *Doe this* or *Doe not this*, without expecting any other reason than the Will of him that sayes it' (1651). Authority thus offers what H.L.A. Hart (1982) calls 'content-independent' reasons for belief or action: the opinion of an expert or the directive of a ruler, parent, manager and so on is itself meant to be taken as a reason, irrespective of the grounds on which that opinion or directive is based.

A second feature of authority is that its requirements bind its alleged subjects: authority has an exigency that advice or requests lack. Some political realists offer a reductionist account of this, claiming that the exigency ultimately amounts to the credible threat of force. Others suggest it is the justification for force. Neither, however, is plausible, for force is necessary only as a backup when authority fails in its primary aim of directing behaviour. A better view is suggested in John Locke's remark: 'All private judgment of every particular member being excluded, the community comes to be umpire, by settled standing rules; indifferent and the same to all parties' (1690). The key here is neither force nor its justifications but rather the exclusion of private judgment (see LOCKE, J. §10). Joseph Raz (1986) has influentially argued that authoritative reasons pre-empt or exclude other reasons the subject might have. Authoritative reasons are thus 'exclusionary': they do not outweigh competing considerations but instead make them irrelevant. (It is, however, unclear how sharp a distinction between outweighing and excluding may be sustained.)

The normative character of authority as content-independent and binding has misled some into thinking that genuine authority must always be justified and that 'illegitimate authority' is a contradiction in terms, but this is wrong. 'Illegitimate authority' is on a par with 'invalid proof': while it purports to be or is accepted as valid, in fact it is not. While 'legitimate authority' is thus not superfluous as a term, it is still the sense generally implicit in the term 'authority': authorities are believed to be legitimate. This is fully compatible with a sociological analysis of the structure and origins of such beliefs, like Weber's three ideal types of rational–bureaucratic, traditional or customary, and charismatic legitimacy (the latter resting on the personal virtue or knowledge of an extraordinary leader) (Weber 1922).

2 Political authority

Three important features distinguish the authority of the state. First, the state claims and enforces compulsory jurisdiction over everyone within its territory. Some, such as the English jurist John AUSTIN, consider that the authority of a sovereign state must also be legally absolute (Austin 1832). In fact, however, while the authority of most states is supreme – that is, binding on all other authorities in its territory – it is normally subject to constitutional limits, although these may consist of the absence of a power to legislate in a certain manner or field rather than the presence of an enforceable duty not to do so.

Second, even when limited the authority of the state is always serious, and it regulates the most vital interests of everyone within its territory. Political authority, as Locke (1690) states, includes the power to regulate life, liberty and property, and to impose any penalties up to and including death.

Finally, political authority claims to impose obligations of obedience. Hobbes doubted this, maintaining that political authority consists only of a liberty to coerce. Friedrich Hayek goes further and states: 'The ideal type of law...provides merely additional information to be taken into account in the decision of the actor' (1960). However, neither of these views can explain the nature of political authority as it is seen by state officials and by many subjects. The state is not indifferent to its citizens either obeying its directives or disobeying while suffering the prescribed penalty; it prefers obedience. It is true that not all authoritative government action purports to create obligations – the state also grants permissions, makes declarations of status, and so on – but creating obligations is central to its other activities.

3 Justifications

Anarchists deny that political authority is justifiable at all (see ANARCHISM §§1-2). Some of their arguments hold that governments are inherently unjust. Others focus on the subordination that is at the heart of authority relations. William GODWIN (§3) and, recently, Robert Paul Wolff argue that there is a deep conflict between personal autonomy and the authority of the state, for the subordination of judgment always violates our most urgent duty, namely, to do what we at that moment think right (Godwin 1793; Wolff 1976). This is, however, an odd view of autonomy, for we regularly subject ourselves to the will of others, for example by making plans and promises without which we would have even less control over our own lives. The real issue is thus not the subordination of judgment as such, but its subordination to the state.

Some religions claim that all political authority is ordained by God. Divine right theories, however, merely defer the problem: what justifies the authority of scripture or of divine commands? Humanistic theories, on the other hand, begin on the footing that practical authorities must in some way benefit people, especially their putative subjects. These benefits may be instrumental or non-instrumental.

Joseph Raz (1986) argues that if authorities are to serve their subjects then justifications for authority must normally show that the alleged subjects are likely to comply with the relevant ultimate reasons if they take the directives as binding and attempt to follow them. They must be more likely to do so than they would if they tried to follow the ultimate reasons directly by relying on their own judgment. On this view, all instrumental justifications for authority are indirect.

Arguments of this form underlie a variety of theories, including consequentialist, natural duty and hypothetical contract arguments, all of which purport to establish a need for authority (see LEGITIMACY §1; OBLIGATION, POLITICAL §1). Two main considerations are offered. The first appeals to the expertise of the rulers; they have knowledge or wisdom that their subjects lack. The second rests on the purported capacity of the state to sustain valuable forms of social cooperation.

The force of these arguments, however, is limited. It is doubtful whether there is relevant expertise in all moral matters (for example, about distributive justice); nor is there any prospect of agreement about who has it, and no a priori reason to suppose it always lies with the government. Moreover, considerations of equality and democracy argue against rule by platonic guardians.

The argument stemming from social cooperation is more plausible. Owing to short-sightedness, limited information and self-defeating motives, we often fail to coordinate action for the common good. By marking certain actions as obligatory and by providing incentives for compliance the state helps overcome this, solving coordination problems, providing public goods and so on. Objections to such arguments are twofold. First, authority systems are themselves the product of social cooperation, so necessarily there is a problem getting them started. Second, there is risk of overkill; even if authority is sometimes needed to secure cooperation, the comprehensive authority of a state may not be. This marks a general difficulty with all indirect, instrumental arguments. It is not sufficient to show that some set of binding rules would be better than individuals following their own judgment; it needs to be shown that the actual set of state-sponsored rules is better than the feasible alternative rules. Moreover, as anarchists argue, to rely generally on the state may weaken the capacity to find better modes of cooperation.

Non-instrumental justifications attempt instead to show that authority relations have an inherent value or are constituent parts or logical results of other valued relations. This may hold if authority is consented to, or if the acceptance of authority expresses gratitude to the state or feelings of communal solidarity. However, actual consent is rarely given and does not always bind, and while obedience may be one way of expressing those attitudes and relations, it is not the only way nor always the best way. In a multicultural world of identity politics, it is not even clear that the state is an appropriate locus of these feelings. Perhaps Harold Laski (1919) and the pluralists were right to state that we are each the nodal point of many competing allegiances, none with inherent priority.

References and further reading

* Austin, J. (1832) *The Province of Jurisprudence Determined*, ed. H.L.A. Hart, London: Weidenfeld & Nicolson, 1954. (See §2.)
* Godwin, W. (1793) *Enquiry Concerning Political Justice*, ed. I. Kramnick, Harmondsworth: Penguin, 1976. (See §3.)
  Green, L. (1988) *The Authority of the State*, Oxford: Oxford University Press. (An examination of the nature of and purported justifications for political authority.)
* Hart, H.L.A. (1982) 'Commands and Authoritative Legal Reasons', in *Essays on Bentham*, Oxford: Oxford University Press. (See §1.)
* Hayek, F.A. (1960) *The Constitution of Liberty*, Chicago, IL: University of Chicago Press, 148–61. (See §2.)
* Hobbes, T. (1651) *Leviathan*, ed. C.B. Macpherson, Harmondsworth: Penguin, 1968. (See §§1–2.)
* Laski, H.J. (1919) *Authority in the Modern State*, New Haven, CT: Yale University Press. (See §3.)
* Lewis, G.C. (1849) *An Essay on the Influence of Authority in Matters of Opinion*, London: John W. Parker. (A rare volume but with a good treatment of theoretical authority and the connections between this and political authority; see §1.)
* Locke, J. (1690) *Two Treatises of Government*, ed. P. Laslett, Cambridge: Cambridge University Press, 3rd edn, 1988. (See §1.)

Lukes, S. (1979) 'Power and Authority', in T. Bottomore and R. Nisbet (eds) *A History of Sociological Analysis*, London: Heinemann, 633–76. (A blend of historical and conceptual analysis.)
McMahon, C. (1994) *Authority and Democracy: A General Theory of Government and Management*, Princeton, NJ: Princeton University Press. (A careful examination of managerial authority in non-governmental organizations, situating it in broader democratic theory.)
* Raz, J. (1986) *The Morality of Freedom*, Oxford: Oxford University Press, 21–105. (One of the most influential accounts of authority; see §§1, 3.)
—— (ed.) (1990) *Authority*, Oxford: Blackwell. (A collection of essays providing a good survey of the issues, with a helpful introduction.)
Simmons, A.J. (1979) *Moral Principles and Political Obligations*, Princeton, NJ: Princeton University Press. (A clear introduction to, and criticism of, theories of the duty to obey the law.)
* Weber, M. (1922) *Economy and Society*, vol. 1, ed. G. Roth and C. Wittich, New York: Bedminster Press, 1968. (See §1.)
* Wolff, R.P. (1976) *In Defense of Anarchism*, New York: Harper & Row, 2nd edn. (See §3.)

LESLIE GREEN

AUTONOMY, ETHICAL

The core idea of autonomy is that of sovereignty over oneself, self-governance or self-determination: an agent or political entity is autonomous if it is self-governing or self-determining. The ancient Greeks applied the term to city-states. In the modern period, the concept was extended to persons, in particular by Kant, who gave autonomy a central place in philosophical discourse. Kant argued for the autonomy of rational agents by arguing that moral principles, which authoritatively limit how we may act, originate in the exercise of reason. They are thus laws that we give to ourselves, and Kant thought that rational agents are bound only to self-given laws. Much contemporary discussion has focused on the somewhat different topic of personal autonomy, and autonomy continues to be an important value in contemporary liberalism and in ethical theory.

It is important to distinguish different senses of autonomy because of variation in how the concept is used. Self-governance or self-determination appears to require some control over the desires and values that move one to action, and some such control is provided by the capacity to subject them to rational scrutiny.

Thus, autonomy is often understood as the capacity to critically assess one's basic desires and values, and to act on those that one endorses on reflection. In other contexts, autonomy is understood as a right, for example as the right to act on one's own judgment about matters affecting one's life, without interference by others. The term is also sometimes used in connection with ethics itself, to refer to the thesis that ethical claims cannot be reduced to nonethical claims.

1 Autonomy in the early modern period
2 Kant's conception of the autonomy of rational agents
3 Contemporary accounts of the nature of personal autonomy
4 Normative dimensions of autonomy
5 The autonomy of ethics

1 Autonomy in the early modern period

Central to autonomy is the notion of self-governance. The earliest use of the term was by ancient Greek writers [*autonomia* (n.), *autonomos* (adj.) from *autos* – self, and *nomos* – law], for whom it was a political concept. A city-state had autonomy if it had authority to enact its own laws and to manage its own affairs, independently of any foreign power. Moral and political philosophy of the early modern period allowed autonomy to be a basic feature of persons, even where the term was not used explicitly. Many seventeenth- and eighteenth-century rationalists held that our moral capacities create the capacity for self-governance. They believed that reason or conscience gives all individuals the ability to discover objective truths either about duty, or about the good, without external guidance through revelation, the church or political authority (see MORAL KNOWLEDGE §3). In addition, they held that agents could be motivated to act simply by their knowledge of moral norms, without the imposition of rewards or punishment (see MORAL MOTIVATION). Since the content of such norms is desire-independent, the capacity to be motivated by one's moral knowledge gives one control over one's desires. On the assumption that reason or conscience occupies an authoritative role within the self, action guided by one's moral knowledge is self-determined.

Social contract theories of this period conceived of human beings as autonomous in a somewhat different sense, by attributing to them an 'original sovereignty' over themselves. The social contract theorists regarded individuals as by nature free, equal and independent, with authority to regulate their own conduct. It follows that one individual can become subject to the authority of another only through an act of consent or agreement, and that legitimate state powers are those it would be rational to agree to. In Locke's view (1690), individuals in the state of nature are bound by a law of nature requiring them both to preserve themselves, and others in so far as they are able. But all individuals in the state of nature have equal authority to judge and to punish violations of the law of nature. This is the basis of political authority. Locke argues that rational individuals in the state of nature would agree among themselves to entrust this authority to enforce the law of nature to a central power, for the limited purposes of preserving one's own life and liberty. Thus, his theory derives political authority from one's original sovereignty over oneself, which in addition limits the legitimate uses of state power (see CONTRACTARIANISM IN ETHICS AND POLITICAL PHILOSOPHY; LOCKE, J. §10).

Rousseau takes the idea of self-governance a step further, claiming that sovereignty – the power to enact laws – resides in the collective body of all citizens, and that legitimate laws must be self-imposed: 'the people that is subject to the laws ought to be their author' (1762: 67) (see ROUSSEAU, J.-J. §3). Rousseau argued that the freedom and independence of each citizen could be preserved only when individuals agree to submit to the 'general will' – the will of society as a whole concerning matters of common interest. The general will is expressed in laws which preserve freedom and equality, and which are, accordingly, enacted by a political process in which all citizens participate (see GENERAL WILL). Thus his political ideal is a participatory democracy preserving the autonomy of each citizen, in which individuals are bound only to laws which they have a role in making, and which express each individual's will. Rousseau's famous remark that 'freedom is obedience to the law one has prescribed for oneself' (1762: 56) provided a model of autonomy for later theorists, in particular for Kant.

2 Kant's conception of the autonomy of rational agents

Two different senses of autonomy emerge in the above theories. One is the capacity to guide one's conduct by one's grasp of moral norms. The other is 'sovereignty over oneself' – a basic right to self-governance, which is the basis of further rights and standards of justification. These aspects of autonomy come together in Kant's moral theory. Kant takes the autonomy of rational agents to be the fact that they have the ability to legislate universally valid principles (the principles of morality) through their will, and are bound only by principles that originate in their own reason. This is a capacity for self-determination because action guided by such principles follows self-given laws. Finally, the autonomy of agents is the basis of specific duties, which are requirements of respect for autonomy (see KANTIAN ETHICS; KANT, I. §9).

Kant writes: 'Autonomy of the will is the property that the will has of being a law to itself (independently of any property of the objects of volition)' ([1785] 1903: 440). One implication of this claim is 'that man [humanity] is subject only to his own, yet universal, legislation and that he is bound only to act in accordance with his own will' ([1785] 1903: 432). Autonomy has both a negative and a positive aspect. Rational agents are not bound by any principles that do not originate in the exercise of reason, or by any sources of authority external to reason. That is, considerations such as desire, convention, the will of God, or uncritically accepted authorities are not inherently reason-giving; they provide reasons for action only if the agent takes them to. Positively, rational agency is the source of authoritative normative principles. A deliberative process expressing the basic features of rational agency generates authoritative principles of action, in particular, the basic principles of morality (see PRACTICAL REASON §§2–3). Kant's conception of autonomy reflects the political origin of the concept in that he regards rational agents as a kind of sovereign authority who can give universal law through their willing. So understood, autonomy presupposes certain deliberative and motivational capacities: the capacities to assess critically any proposed reason for action and to be motivated by reasons that are independent of one's desires and presently held values.

Comparisons with earlier moral theories bring out the full dimensions of Kant's conception. In contrast to empiricists, Kant recognized reasons and principles that are not desire-based. Like rationalist theorists, Kant thought that morality consists of necessary desire-independent principles. But he did not think that such principles represent an objective order of values existing independently of rational volition. Rational deliberation is not the discovery of objective principles, but rather the process by which they are generated. Thus, Kant held that agents who act on moral principles act from self-given laws, since these are principles that originate in the use of one's reason. Kant argued that earlier attempts to ground obligation in, for example, the will of God, an objective order of values or obligations, or features of human psychology, all lead to 'heteronomy of the will', because such theories would subject rational agents to an authority external to reason.

Kant thought that the autonomy of rational agents is consistent with moral objectivity. The categorical imperative is the basic principle to which any agent with autonomy is committed, and generates universally valid principles of action. Agents express their autonomy by deliberating and acting from the categorical imperative because it is a rational procedure through which any agent can arrive at principles that other agents can acknowledge as authoritative; that is, it enables one to give law through one's will. Though Kant conceived of autonomy primarily as a feature of persons, individual actions guided by the categorical imperative are autonomous in a derivative sense, since they are guided by self-given principles. By contrast, actions determined by desires or uncritically accepted values are guided by principles external to reason.

Kant's conception of agents as having autonomy determines the content of his normative theory. Kant held that the capacity to give moral principles through one's will is the basis of human dignity, and that all agents are committed to valuing the exercise of their rational capacities. These assumptions underlie his general principle that rational nature should be treated as an end, and never as a means only (see RESPECT FOR PERSONS §2). The application of this principle leads to requirements not to undermine the exercise of rational agency through, for example, coercion, deception, paternalistic interference, or contempt and ridicule, as well as positive duties to support the exercise of rational agency through mutual aid and perfection of one's talents. Thus, the autonomy of rational agents is the basis of specific duties to respect the exercise of rational agency.

3 Contemporary accounts of the nature of personal autonomy

Some contemporary writers concerned with the nature of personal autonomy have distinguished between autonomy as a capacity for self-governance or self-determination, as the actual condition of self-governance, as a personal ideal, and as a right or a social value. (see Feinberg 1986; Hill 1991). Though these notions are defined and related in differing ways, the capacity for self-governance may be viewed as the basis of the other notions. An agent who exercises this capacity effectively is in the condition of autonomy. The personal ideal or virtue of autonomy would be the set of character traits associated with the complete development of the capacity, viewed as a component of the admirable or fulfilling life (see EUDAIMONIA; VIRTUES AND VICES §3). Autonomy viewed as a right is the general right to the unimpeded exercise of this capacity in matters concerning one's own life. The next two sections will focus on contemporary accounts of the capacity for autonomy, and on autonomy as a value.

Self-governance intuitively requires that one have control over the psychological states that determine one's actions, and that the desires and values that guide one's choices be 'truly one's own'. One might hold that one's desires and values are one's own when one identifies with or endorses them as a result of critical reflection. Thus, autonomy may be defined as the capacity to assess critically one's basic desires and values, to revise them if one judges that there is reason to, and to act on those that one identifies with or endorses upon critical reflection. This capacity enables one to take responsibility for one's basic desires and values, and to shape the direction of one's life.

This definition relies on a distinction between first-order desires (desires for certain objects or activities) and higher-order reflection about one's first-order desires, and makes the capacity for higher-order critical reflection central to autonomy. Higher-order values may be viewed as judgments about which of one's first-order desires and values one wants to be moved by; or alternatively, as evaluative judgments as to whether goals or activities towards which one is inclined are really worth pursuing, whether certain of one's values or character traits are good, and so on. Take, for example, a person who cares greatly about material goods. Agents with autonomy can ask whether they want to be moved by materialistic desires to the extent they currently are, or whether it is good to care about material goods to that extent. Moreover, such agents can modify their values and conduct if they see reason to. Note that autonomy should not be interpreted as a capacity to create one's desires and values *ex nihilo*. That would imply, implausibly, that no one possesses autonomy, since individuals are deeply influenced by social and cultural factors. Autonomy need not require that one be the ultimate source of one's desires and values, but only that one have the capacity to assess them critically.

The capacity for critical higher-order reflection is a normal feature of rational agency which may be developed to differing degrees by different agents, and which can be interfered with by such factors as psychological disorder, external manipulation of an agent's deliberative processes, and social conditioning. A full treatment of personal autonomy must spell out the kinds of influence that undermine autonomy. It must also provide some account of the process of critical reflection. Here several questions arise. What guides the formation of one's higher-order values? While autonomy would seem to require some control over one's higher-order values, even they are unavoidably shaped by upbringing, culture, and other factors beyond one's control. Which forms of social and cultural influence at this level are consistent with autonomy? Some of these problems are illustrated by the following example. Imagine a woman who has been socialized to believe that women ought to be subordinate to men and who has internalized this social role. On conscious reflection she judges that she is leading a good life, identifying with her subservient social role and endorsing the character traits of submissiveness that enable her to fulfil the expectations imposed upon women in her society. This sort of example suggests that a capacity to apply critical reflection to one's higher-order values – which appears lacking in this person – is necessary for autonomy. The question of when one's values are 'truly one's own' arises for higher-order values, just as it does for first-order desires and values. Should we then conclude that the higher-order values leading to endorsement of one's first-order desires and values should themselves be accepted or endorsed through critical reflection? If so, how do we avoid ascending levels of higher-order evaluation continuing *ad infinitum*? The worry is that either critical reflection must continue indefinitely, or the point at which it terminates is arbitrary.

Most theorists would agree that a capacity for ongoing critical reflection about one's higher-order values is necessary for autonomy; that there are empirical limitations on the level to which individuals can carry higher-order reflection, and that contingency is inevitable in the higher-order values that determine one's first order identifications; and that higher-order reflection can be terminated in non-arbitrary ways. But there are different views about the resolution of higher-order reflection, which represent different views about the critical reflection needed for autonomy. One might hold that critical higher-order reflection, in principle, permits individuals to call into question any deeply held value. While never totally free of social and cultural influence, individuals can, either on their own or in dialogue with others, achieve sufficient distance from their basic values to view them critically. Eventually, one must decide which values to accept. But such a decision is not arbitrary when underwritten by the judgment that further reflection will confirm one's present decision.

Other theorists have argued that the process of critical reflection must principally satisfy 'conditions of procedural independence': it must be free from such obstructions as internal obstacles (such as psychological disturbance), manipulation, coercion, and unacceptable social conditioning (Dworkin 1988). The burden on such a theory is to spell out these conditions of procedural independence. This approach places no constraints on the substantive values that an autonomous agent could accept. Any values are consistent with autonomy, as long as one accepts them on one's own. A different approach holds that autonomy requires the capacity to modify one's values in the light of objective or fully reasonable values. This theorist would take the failure of an agent's reflective values to satisfy certain objective standards (for example, if one's values are clearly detrimental to individual fulfilment, or are morally flawed) as indicating a lack of autonomy.

4 Normative dimensions of autonomy

In much contemporary ethical and political theory, autonomy plays both a foundational and a normative role, as illustrated by the structure of Kant's ethical theory. The capacity for autonomy, as described in the previous section, is so central to agency that respect for persons is plausibly construed as respect for the exercise of this capacity. Thus in much contemporary ethical theory, a view of persons as having autonomy is the basis of a general right to act on one's own judgment of what one has most reason to do, from which one can derive more specific principles, such as duties not to interfere with a person's freedom, duties to refrain from coercion, manipulation, paternalistic interference, and so on, as well as positive duties to support autonomy. Many theorists hold that the wrongness of certain kinds of actions may be explained by noting how they interfere with, or deprive individuals of their autonomy. It is important to note that what autonomy-centred theories value is the opportunity to guide one's actions by one's exercise of the capacity for critical reflection. This is considerably more complex than simply acting on one's own desires.

Similarly, autonomy is a central value in modern liberalism and democratic theory (see LIBERALISM §3). A conception of persons as having autonomy figures in liberal conceptions of justice, the liberal principle that the state should not promote any particular conception of the good, and in arguments against state paternalism (see JUSTICE §5; PATERNALISM §3). It is the basis of those rights and liberties that are the institutional means necessary for individuals to exercise autonomy – including liberty of conscience, rights of free expression, liberty to develop one's own plan of life (within the limits of justice), and rights of political participation. While autonomy is more prominent in the Kantian and social contract traditions, it can also play a role in utilitarian theories (see UTILITARIANISM). Mill, for example, argues in *On Liberty* (1859) that the exercise of judgment, choice and responsibility, and the development of individuality are essential to individual fulfilment. This conception of happiness permits him to argue on utilitarian grounds against state paternalism and for a set of civil liberties that allow individuals to exercise autonomy. His view, in short, is that institutionalized liberties protecting individual autonomy will promote general happiness (see MILL, J.S. §§11–12).

The importance of autonomy to contemporary liberalism is illustrated by features of Rawls' theory of justice (1993). One of the organizing ideas of Rawls' theory is a conception of persons as possessing two 'moral powers', which they have a fundamental interest in exercising. These are a capacity to develop, revise and pursue a conception of the good and a capacity for a sense of justice. Possession of these moral powers is the basis of moral equality, entitling individuals to equal consideration. The principles of justice which Rawls derives set out the political and social conditions that guarantee to each individual opportunity to exercise these moral powers effectively, with the principle of equal liberty listing basic individual liberties, and the principle of equal opportunity together with the difference principle (that inequalities should benefit the least advantaged) spelling out further social and material conditions. In this way, a conception of persons as having autonomy plays a role in determining the content of a conception of justice. A further aspect of Rawls' theory directly parallels Kant's conception of autonomy. Kant held that rational agents are bound only by principles that originate in their own will. Similarly, in Rawls' theory, the final standards of justice are those that persons would autonomously choose for themselves. Rawls supports his conception of justice by arguing that the two principles would be chosen in the 'original position' – a conceptual device representing a fair choice by free and equal persons, with an interest in securing the exercise of their two moral powers. This particular aspect of autonomy is seen in the fact that the agents in the original position are not bound by any antecedently given moral principles. They are free to choose whatever conception of justice will best advance their basic interest in the exercise of their moral powers, and whatever would result from such a choice determines what is just (see RAWLS, J.).

The value placed on autonomy is not unchallenged. Many theorists have argued that the emphasis on autonomy ignores or fails to leave room for other important values, such as the value of ties and attachments to others, loyalty to groups, respect for tradition, or the value of community. Versions of this objection hold that within autonomy-centred theories, personal commitments and attachments and obligations to others become purely voluntary, and thus cannot be definitive of the self. But surely, the objection continues, we can have commitments, attachments and obligations that are essential to our identity (see MORALITY AND IDENTITY §4). In reply, it is sufficient to say that autonomy need not be conceived in a way that makes it inconsistent with such values, and that viewing autonomy as central does not entail viewing it as the sole value (see MORAL PLURALISM). Nothing in the conceptions of autonomy surveyed above precludes agents from deciding as a result of critical reflection to take on binding obligations or to affirm attachments to others, or from concluding that certain commitments and ties are inescapable because constitutive of who they are. We may conclude that autonomy is deeply embedded in the modern notion of the person and is an important modern value.

5 The autonomy of ethics

The autonomy of ethics uses 'autonomy' in a sense not directly related to the autonomy of agents. It is the thesis that ethical principles or claims cannot be reduced to, or explained in terms of, statements containing no normative terms (see LOGIC OF ETHICAL DISCOURSE §§2–4). 'Normative terms', such as 'ought', 'good' and 'bad', 'right' and 'wrong', 'just' and 'unjust', are those which state the intrinsic value of, approve or recommend an action or state of affairs, or state that there is reason to perform certain actions or pursue certain ends. (They contrast with 'descriptive terms', which describe or report purely factual states of affairs.) The autonomy of ethics, for example, can allow claims about what is right to be explained in terms of the good (or vice versa), but holds that any such explanation of an ethical claim must use some normative language. Theorists who accept the autonomy of ethics can include intuitionists, for whom ethical statements are claims about mind-independent ethical properties, such as rightness or goodness (see INTUITIONISM IN ETHICS); noncognitivists, who take ethical claims to express attitudes of approval or recommendation (see ANALYTIC ETHICS); or practical reason theorists, who hold that ethical claims are based on principles of practical reason – principles which we accept in virtue of being rational (see PRACTICAL REASON). Common to these theories is the view that the normative aspect of ethical discourse is not capturable in language devoid of normative terms.

More broadly, the autonomy of ethics includes the independence of ethical theory both from other areas of philosophy and from the natural and behavioural sciences. This does not mean that ethical theory can ignore these fields. Rather, it means that questions about the content and validity of fundamental moral principles do not depend on answers to questions of, for example, metaphysics, epistemology, or philosophy of mind, and that they are not dictated by the results of empirical inquiry. Ethical theory, as concerned with normative questions, has its own distinctive subject matter and tools of inquiry. To give one example, modern Kantians have thought that the moral principles that we accept should not be restricted by a picture of motivation derived solely from empirical inquiry, rejecting the idea that our motivational capacities can be described without any reference to normative principles. If we can be motivated by our acceptance of moral principles, then certain motivational states can be described only by reference to the reasoning that underlies them. Moral theory is then required for insight into certain of our motivational capacities (see Rawls 1975, 1993; Nagel 1970).

See also: FREEDOM AND LIBERTY; FREE WILL; SELF-CONTROL

References and further reading

Christman, J. (ed.) (1989) *The Inner Citadel: Essays on Individual Autonomy*, Oxford: Oxford University Press. (A collection of contemporary essays. Good introduction to contemporary discussions of personal autonomy, with an extensive bibliography.)

* Dworkin, G. (1988) *The Theory and Practice of Autonomy*, Cambridge: Cambridge University Press. (Accessible treatment of the nature and value of autonomy.)

* Feinberg, J. (1986) 'Autonomy', in *Harm to Self*, Oxford and New York: Oxford University Press, ch. 18; repr. in J. Christman (ed.) *The Inner Citadel: Essays on Individual Autonomy*, Oxford: Oxford University Press, 1989. (A clear analysis of different meanings of autonomy.)

Frankfurt, H. (1988) *The Importance of What We Care About*, Cambridge: Cambridge University Press. (Contains influential essays on freedom of the will of importance to the nature of personal autonomy.)

* Hill, T.E., Jr (1991) *Autonomy and Self-Respect*, Cambridge: Cambridge University Press, chaps 3, 4, 7. (Develops an accessible account of autonomy and of its normative significance.)

—— (1992) *Dignity and Self-Respect*, Ithaca, NY: Cornell University Press, chaps 1, 5–7. (Develops an accessible account of Kant's views about autonomy.)

* Kant, I. (1785) *Grundlegung zur Metaphysik der Sitten*, in *Kants gesammelte Schriften*, ed. Königlichen Preußischen Akademie der Wissenschaften,

Berlin: Reimer, vol. 4, 1903; trans. J.W. Ellington, *Grounding for the Metaphysics of Morals*, Indianapolis, IN: Hackett Publishing Company, 1993. (References made to this work in the entry give the page number from the 1903 Berlin Akademie volume; these page numbers are included in the Ellington translation. A classic work of moral theory which bases morality on autonomy.)

Korsgaard, C. (1996) *Creating the Kingdom of Ends*, Cambridge: Cambridge University Press. (Essays on Kant's moral theory and on contemporary moral theory relevant to several aspects of autonomy.)

* Locke, J. (1690) 'The Second Treatise of Government', in *Two Treatises on Government*, ed. P. Laslett, Cambridge: Cambridge University Press, 1988, 269–78, 323–33. (Classic social contract theory which bases the legitimacy of political authority on the consent of citizens.)

* Mill, J.S. (1859) *On Liberty*, ed. E. Rappaport, Indianapolis, IN: Hackett Publishing Company, 1978, esp. 53–71. (Classic account of individual civil liberties developed within a utilitarian framework.)

* Nagel, T. (1970) *The Possibility of Altruism*, Princeton, NJ: Princeton University Press. (Develops a contemporary Kantian view of motivation.)

Rawls, J. (1971) *A Theory of Justice*, Cambridge, MA: Harvard University Press. (Seminal contemporary work arguing that principles of justice can be viewed as the result of an autonomous choice of free and equal persons.)

* —— (1975) 'The Independence of Moral Theory', *Proceedings and Addresses of the American Philosophical Association* 48: 5–22. (Argues for the independence of moral theory from other areas of philosophy.)

* —— (1993) *Political Liberalism*, New York: Columbia University Press, paperback edition with new material, 1996. (Lecture II discusses the role of autonomy in the theory of justice.)

Reath, A. (1994) 'Legislating the Moral Law', *Nous* 28: 435–64. (Scholarly account of Kant's concept of autonomy.)

* Rousseau, J.-J. (1762) *Du Contrat social*, trans. J.R. Masters, ed. R.D. Masters, *On the Social Contract*, New York: St Martin's Press, 1978. (Classic social contract theory that gives a central role to the notions of autonomy and self-legislation.)

Scanlon, T.M. (1972) 'A Theory of Freedom of Expression', *Philosophy and Public Affairs* 1: 204–06. (Develops a theory of free expression based on a conception of autonomy.)

Schneewind, J.B. (1986) 'The Use of Autonomy in Ethical Theory', in T.C. Heller, M. Sosna and D.E. Wellbery (eds) *Reconstructing Individualism*, Stanford, CA: Stanford University Press, 64–75. (Discussion of autonomy in Butler, Kant and Rawls.)

—— (1991) 'Natural Law, Skepticism and Methods of Ethics', *Journal of the History of Ideas* (52): 289–308. (Shows how eighteenth-century empiricist moral theories developed a morality of autonomy that dispenses with the need for moral authorities of various sorts.)

—— (1993) 'Modern Moral Philosophy: From Beginning to End?', in P. Cook (ed.) *Philosophical Imagination and Cultural Memory*, Durham, NC: Duke University Press. (Accessible overview of the history of early modern ethics, stressing the emergence of autonomy as a central notion.)

ANDREWS REATH

AVEMPACE see IBN BAJJA, ABU BAKR MUHAMMAD IBN YAHYA IBN AS-SA'IGH

AVENARIUS, RICHARD (1843–96)

Richard Avenarius, a German philosopher, is known as a proponent of 'empiriocriticism' and the principle of economy of thinking. Empiriocriticism is a modern version of empiricism which attempts to restore the concept of the natural world and 'pure experience' through the elimination of 'introjection', understood as an insertion of redundant or distorted ideas and images into the objects of our knowledge. Avenarius traced back the origin of introjection to the cultural stages dominated by magic and mythology, yet his criticism applied also to traditional philosophy and science. His position is usually classified as a version of positivism, closely resembling the empiricist doctrine of Ernst Mach. Although his influence on some members of the Vienna Circle, especially Moritz Schlick, was considerable, the impact of his contribution has been hampered by his idiosyncratic use of language, especially in his masterpiece Kritik der reinen Erfahrung *(The Critique of Pure Experience) (1888–90).*

Avenarius was born in Paris, where his father owned a German publishing house. However, he spent his formative years in Leipzig and Berlin and received his Ph.D. in 1868 for a dissertation concerned with aspects of Spinoza's philosophy. Avenarius' *Habilita-*

tionsschrift, presented in Leipzig under the title *Philosophie als Denken der Welt gemäss dem Prinzip des kleinsten Kraftmasses* (Philosophy as Thinking of the World in Accordance with the Principle of the Least Amount of Energy Expenditure) (1876), contributed to his fame and facilitated his appointment as Professor for Inductive Philosophy in Zurich, Switzerland. Avenarius held this position until his untimely death in 1896. During this period he published his significant works: *Kritik der reinen Erfahrung* (The Critique of Pure Experience) (1888–90) and *Der menschliche Weltbegriff* (The Human Concept of the World) (1891). In 1877 Avenarius founded an important philosophical journal, *Vierteljahrsschrift für wissenschaftliche Philosophie* (A Quarterly for Scientific Philosophy), which he edited until his death. Perhaps the most famous of his disciples is Joseph Petzoldt, who edited posthumous editions of Avenarius' works.

Avenarius combines his version of empiriocriticism with the concept of the natural world which he wanted to restore. His method comes very close to Husserl's phenomenological technique of pure description (see HUSSERL, E.). 'Findings' (phenomena) are the point of departure for such pure description, and they encompass environmental components including the bodies of other persons. To distinguish human persons from other environmental components, Avenarius employs a linguistically founded hypothesis amounting to the interpretation of certain movements and sounds of fellow humans as statements. Accordingly, the endorsement of the natural concept of the world assumes that fellow human beings are not mere thoughtless and emotionless mechanisms. This principle offers then an opportunity to treat the empirical (verifiable) content of human knowledge through an appropriate analysis of meaningful statement-components – a very modern method indeed. Avenarius underscores another basic interpretative principle of empiriocriticism: the 'democratic' supposition of 'human equality'. This principle enables him to make short-cut inferences (by analogy) to similar experiences in other persons, as long as their statement-contents are meaningfully interpreted by the observer. It is through the contents of statements made by other persons that the so-called E-values are recognized; the E-values are then divided into 'elements' (for example, 'green', 'warm' and so on) and 'characters' (such as 'pleasant', 'ugly' and so on). It seems that Avenarius anticipates here the distinction between cognitive and noncognitive (emotive) constituents of statements, so dear to the later positivists. The E-values ultimately depend on the environmental components – on the so-called R-values (for example, trees, rivers, the sun). These are the things within the natural environment which a person (called M) finds as 'given' – the 'independent factors' of the first kind. Among the environmental components one must further distinguish the physical bodies of other persons, for whom Avenarius reserves the symbol T. His empiriocritical triad MRT symbolizes the presence and relationship between these three factors. The dependence of the E-values on the R-values is mediated by the brain and the entire central nervous system of the person in question. This empirical system C is then regarded as the 'independent factor' of the second kind. Impressed by the optimistic results of neurophysiology in his time, Avenarius strongly emphasizes this system C. He assumes that there is an obvious dependence relation between an E-value (say, of the person M) and some change in the person's system C, symbolized by ΔC. The complete account of these dependencies yields the following:

$$R \rightarrow M \rightarrow C_M \rightarrow E_M$$

We read this: a certain environmental component R is affecting the body of the person M and further, through the proper nervous channels, the brain of the person M who then produces the respective E-value (expressed in statements). In *Kritik der reinen Erfahrung* Avenarius offers the following explanation: 'In every case, in which E is regarded as dependent upon R, E is taken as immediately dependent upon a *change* of C' (1888–90: 1, 80). Yet the indirect dependence relation of E_M upon R is treated by Avenarius as a purely logical functional relation, in accord with his positivistic rejection of causality. Avenarius undertook a grandiose programme of biological reductionism, supported by his principle of economy of energy expenditure: the limited amount of energy possessed by human organisms should not be wasted beyond necessity. Actively or passively, the human organism (governed by its system C) participates in a multitude of processes which are arranged into time-dependent 'vital series' of two basic types: independent and dependent. Avenarius characterizes the vital preservation maximum of an organism as the equality of its partial systematic factors:

$$\Sigma f(R) + \Sigma f(S) = 0$$

In this equation, the sum of environmental factors R equals the (negatively prefixed) sum of the bodily factors S. Variations in these interactions are responsible for a variety of 'vital differences' expressed in inequalities. The organism tends to reduce or eliminate such differences if they weaken its preservation value. Allegedly, the system C of the organism is setting up an idealized goal of perfect vital series and it affects variations of the actual vital series in this direction.

This biologically founded teleological doctrine is related to Avenarius' rejection of 'introjection' as an unwarranted insertion of something which distorts the purity of the original experience. Avenarius believed that the elimination of introjection will lead to restoration or 'restitution' of the natural concept of the world, with beneficial results for human knowledge and action. His ideals of 'pure experience' demanded the rejection of any philosophical dualism and a positivistic revision of traditional metaphysical beliefs. Thus he got close to the 'neutral monism' of Ernst MACH (§4), William JAMES (§6) or the early Bertrand RUSSELL (§13) (see NEUTRAL MONISM). In the Preface to *Kritik der reinen Erfahrung*, Avenarius programmatically declared his intention to go directly to things as such ('*an die Sachen anzuknüpfen*'), thus foreshadowing the later goals of Husserl and Heidegger.

See also: EMPIRICISM; PHENOMENALISM

List of works

Avenarius, R. (1868) *Über die beiden ersten Phasen des Spinozischen Pantheismus und das Verhältniss des zweiten zur dritten Phase* (On Both First Phases of Spinoza's Pantheism and the Relationship between the Second and the Third Phase), Leipzig: E. Avenarius; repr. 1980. (Avenarius' Ph.D. dissertation, concerned with the order and publication time of Spinoza's earlier writings.)

—— (1876) *Philosophie als Denken der Welt gemäss dem Prinzip des kleinsten Kraftmasses: Prolegomena zu einer Kritik der reinen Erfahrung* (Philosophy as Thinking of the World in Accordance with the Principle of the Least Amount of Energy Expenditure), Leipzig: O.R. Reisland; Berlin: J. Guttentag, 1903, 1917. (A short book, yet widely read and cited.)

—— (1888–90) *Kritik der reinen Erfahrung* (The Critique of Pure Experience), Leipzig: O.R. Reisland; 2nd, 3rd edn, ed. J. Petzoldt; repr. 1980, University Microfilms International, Ann Arbor, MI, 2 vols. (Avenarius' masterpiece, almost 800 pages long, very difficult to read. Volume 1 deals with the independent vital series, while volume 2 treats dependent vital series.)

—— (1891) *Der menschliche Weltbegriff* (The Human Concept of the World), Leipzig: O.R. Reisland; 2nd edn, 1905, ed. J. Petzoldt; later editions 1912, 1917. (English translation in progress by A. Riska; much more accessible presentation of Avenarius' 'metaphysics', as he himself called this relatively short work.)

—— (1913) *Zeitschrift für positivistische Philosophie* (Journal of Positivist Philosophy) 1 (4): 34–54. (Avenarius' own summary of his four major works. These summaries were originally published in *Vierteljahrsschrift für wissenschaftliche Philosophie* (A Quarterly for Scientific Philosophy) between 1888 and 1892.)

References and further reading

Numerous references to Avenarius' philosophy can be found in the literature relevant to Ernst Mach and logical positivism as well as to Malinowski's functional anthropology. A contemporary systematic treatment of Avenarius' work is sorely lacking.

Arens, K. (1989) *Structures of Knowing: Psychologies of the Nineteenth Century*, Dordrecht: Kluwer. (Avenarius is here treated as one among the German conceptual psychologists of the nineteenth century.)

Bush, U.T. (1905) *Avenarius and the Standpoint of Pure Experience*, New York: Science Press. (Based on a Ph.D. thesis at Columbia University, New York; one of very few English publications on Avenarius' work.)

Carstanjen, F. (1896) 'Nachruf an Richard Avenarius' (In Memory of Richard Avenarius), *Vierteljahrsschrift für wissenschaftliche Philosophie* 20 (4): 361–91. (An obituary; a comprehensive biography and assessment of Avenarius' philosophical contribution.)

Lenin, V.I. (1909) *Materialism and Empirio-Criticism*, Moscow: Zveno Publishing House; trans. Foreign Language Publishing House, Moscow 1952. (While attacking his political opponents, Lenin criticized Mach's and Avenarius' empiriocriticism.)

Mach, E. (1900) *Die Analyse der Empfindungen und das Verhältniss des Physischen zum Psychischen*, 2nd expanded edn, Jena: Fischer; 35–42, 'Mein Verhältniss zu R. Avenarius' (My Relationship to R. Avenarius); trans. *The Analysis of Sensations*, New York: Dover, 1959. (An interesting section which clarifies Mach's critical appreciation of Avenarius' positions.)

Raab, F. (1912) *Die Philosophie von R. Avenarius: systematische Darstellung und immanente Kritik* (The Philosophy of R. Avenarius), Leipzig: F. Meiner. (A systematic exposition and an immanent criticism; a typical, dated attempt to provide a wider view of Avenarius' philosophy.)

Schlick, M. (1925) *Allgemeine Erkenntnislehre*, 2nd edn, Berlin: Springer; trans. A.E. Blumberg, *Gen-*

eral Theory of Knowledge, New York: Springer, 1974. (Many references to Avenarius show Schlick's indebtedness to Avenarius' ideas.)

Swoboda, W. and Hobek, F. (1975) 'Richard Avenarius: mit einer Bibliographie' (Richard Avenarius: with a bibliography), *Conceptus* 9 (26): 25–39. (A useful bibliographical source.)

AUGUSTIN RISKA

AVERROES *see* IBN RUSHD, ABU'L WALID MUHAMMAD

AVERROISM

'Averroism', 'radical Aristotelianism' and 'heterodox Aristotelianism' are nineteenth- and twentieth-century labels for a late thirteenth-century movement among Parisian philosophers whose views were not easily reconcilable with Christian doctrine. The three most important points of difference were the individual immortality of human intellectual souls, the attainability of happiness in this life and the eternity of the world. An 'Averroist' or 'Radical Aristotelian' would hold that philosophy leads to the conclusions that there is only one intellect shared by all humans, that happiness is attainable in earthly life and that the world has no temporal beginning or end. Averroists have generally been credited with a 'theory of double truth', according to which there is an irreconcilable clash between truths of faith and truths arrived at by means of reason. Averroism has often been assigned the role of a dangerous line of thought, against which Thomas Aquinas opposed his synthesis of faith and reason. The term 'Averroism' is also used more broadly to characterize Western thought from the thirteenth through sixteenth centuries which was influenced by Averroes, and/or some philosophers' self-proclaimed allegiance to Averroes.

1 Rise of the terminology
2 'Averroist' doctrine

1 Rise of the terminology

Averroes, the twelfth-century Muslim commentator on Aristotle, exercised a strong influence on Latin scholastics from about 1230 onwards (see IBN RUSHD). Around 1270, the derogatory term *Averroistae* ([too ardent] followers of Averroes) began to be used, principally to characterize adherents of the view that there is only one shared human intellect. In 1277 the Bishop of Paris, Etienne Tempier, accused unnamed masters of arts of the University of Paris of paying more attention to heathen philosophers than to Christian revelation, and of behaving as if there were two truths, one of philosophy and another of faith. The theory of one shared intellect was among the 219 theses the bishop condemned. A generation later, Ramon LLULL launched a series of attacks on university philosophers whom he saw as continuators of the lines of thought condemned in 1277, and used the term *Averroistae* to describe these philosophers.

Based on this medieval use of *Averroistae*, the term 'Averroism' was introduced in nineteenth-century historiography of philosophy. Averroism was conceived of as a movement of thirteenth-century thinkers faithful to Averroes, proclaiming that the same proposition could have different truth values in philosophy and theology, so that there was an unbridgeable inconsistency between philosophy and faith. Averroism was cast as a sinister force (a precursor of modern atheism), valiantly combatted by ALBERT THE GREAT and Thomas AQUINAS, notably in the latter's *De unitate* intellectus (On the Unicity of Intellect) and *De aeternitate mundi* (On the Eternity of the World). Twentieth-century historiography came to identify three main currents in late thirteenth century philosophy: first, Augustinianism, mainly represented by Franciscan thinkers, which combatted the growing influence of Aristotelian philosophy (see AUGUSTINIANISM); second, Averroism, which took a radically Aristotelian approach to philosophical problems, even though this must lead to conflict with Christian faith; and third, the current led by Albert the Great and Aquinas, who produced a synthesis of Aristotle and Christian faith (see ARISTOTELIANISM, MEDIEVAL).

Early in the twentieth century, it was commonly assumed by historians that almost all the 219 theses condemned in 1277 were of Averroist provenance, and since there is medieval evidence that the main targets of the condemnation were BOETHIUS OF DACIA and SIGER OF BRABANT, they were thought to have embraced most of the 'heterodox' opinions. Siger, who is known to have engaged in university politics, began to be seen as the leader of an Averroist party at the University of Paris in the 1260s and 1270s.

Subsequent research has undermined the foundations for the historiographical scheme in which a thirteenth-century 'Averroism' belongs. First, the majority of the theses condemned in 1277 were not inspired by Averroes. Moreover, scholars often apply the label 'Averroist' also to later philosophers who were influenced by Averroes or continued the views of writers such as Siger of Brabant: examples include the

Parisian masters Ferrandus Hispanus in the late thirteenth century and JOHN OF JANDUN in the early fourteenth century, and to a long list of Italian writers from Gentile da Cingoli in the 1290s and Angelo d'Arrezzo in the early fourteenth century to Agustino NIFO in the early sixteenth century. Some of these writers did indeed defend Averroes' views whenever possible, but such loyalty towards Averroes had not been a characteristic of the men who were condemned in 1277.

When these facts became apparent to historians of philosophy, they began to replace 'Averroism' with 'radical Aristotelianism' or 'heterodox Aristotelianism' as the name of this supposed thirteenth-century school of thought. However, so many historical misunderstandings and ideologically motivated judgments cling to all these labels that they are, in the 1990s, being abandoned. Yet, there are some interesting problems that these labels were meant to help explain, and which still have an important place in medieval philosophy.

2 'Averroist' doctrine

In the later half of the thirteenth century, there was a common conviction that some philosophical tenets were inconsistent with Christian doctrine as standardly understood. 'Philosophical' in this connection means Aristotelian on the then standard interpretation of Aristotle, which leaned heavily on Arabic works including the writings of Avicenna and Averroes, and the *Liber de causis* (see ARISTOTELIANISM, MEDIEVAL; LIBER DE CAUSIS).

Three issues stood in the foreground in the conflict between reason and faith: first, whether all humans share a common intellect (monopsychism); second, whether happiness is attainable in this life; and third, whether the world had a temporal beginning.

Monopsychism: It was generally accepted that the intellect (that is, the intellective soul) has both an active component, 'the agent intellect', which forms universal concepts on the basis of particular pieces of information provided by the senses, and a passive component, usually called the 'possible intellect', which is the initially blank wax tablet on which the active component leaves its imprints in the form of concepts and knowledge acquired. The question was, are the agent and possible intellects genuinely different, and if not, does each human being have its own intellect, or is there only one for all to share?

There was a tradition of considering only the agent intellect to be an extra-human separate substance, responsible for humans' shared conceptual apparatus; in this view, the individuality of each person's possible intellect explains why we do not share all our thoughts. One version of this view was held by Roger BACON. By the 1260s, however, this radical separation of the agent and possible intellects had become rather old-fashioned. The main disputants of the time agreed that the two intellects are one substance, but they disagreed about whether that substance is extra-human. Averroes, as he was commonly understood after about 1250, taught that the intellect is a single impersonal substance with which individual souls enter into contact via their mental representations (phantasms) of extramental things; the intellect uses the phantasms as a basis for abstraction. Modern historiography has applied the term 'monopsychism' to this doctrine, which was attacked by Aquinas in his *De unitate intellectus*.

Monopsychism allows for the irrational part of a human soul to be destroyed on death without this affecting the intellect. Like the old assumption of a separate agent intellect, it also accounts for the ability of human beings to share knowledge; but it offers no convincing answer to the objection that if this is the case, then no thought belongs to one individual rather than another. During at least one phase of his career, SIGER OF BRABANT accepted monopsychism, but believed that it was possible to save some private thought for the individual by making the operation of the intellect in a particular human depend on representations (*intentiones imaginatae*) with an origin in sensation unaided by intellect. In his somewhat obscure attempts to explain how the individual 'plugs into' (*continuatur*) the supra-individual intellect, Siger relied heavily on Averroes.

Contemporaries were alert to the Averroistic theory's inability to explain how all humans can share an intellect without sharing all thoughts. However, to medieval thinkers the gravest objection against monopsychism was that it left no individual rational soul to carry responsibility for a deceased person's acts. Nor was it easy to see how an immaterial intellect could fail to be eternal, which was contrary to Christian doctrine that God creates new souls every day and that they are in principle perishable (God could annihilate a soul if he wished). Nonetheless, for the next couple of centuries most philosophers seem to have held that monopsychism was one of the few rationally defensible views about the nature of the intellect, while standard Church doctrine continued to require the intellect to be both the form of the body and capable of separate, individual, existence. The issue was still very much alive in 1513 when the Fifth Lateran Council explicitly condemned the view that the intellective soul is either mortal or only one for all people, and explicitly asserted that it is the form of the human body, immortal, and as many in number as are the bodies into which it is infused.

Happiness in this life: Around 1260–70, masters from the Faculty of Arts at the University of Paris often expressed a great optimism about the attainability of happiness in this life. Their views strongly resemble those of ancient Neoplatonism, but the strongest impetus came from Arabic philosophy rather than directly from ancient sources (see NEOPLATONISM; NEOPLATONISM IN ISLAMIC PHILOSOPHY). The way to happiness was thought to consist in an intellectual ascent to the contemplation of ever higher beings, culminating in contemplation of the First Cause and the (temporary) union of one's possible intellect with the source of intellectual understanding, the agent intellect; In this tradition, the agent intellect was thought to be a separate substance and not identical with God. Such a state of intellectual bliss was held to be the fullest actualization of a person *qua* human, that is, a rational being.

This line of thought would seem to permit the construction of a naturalistic ethics with no need for either divine revelation or an individual life after death in order that human beings may reach their ultimate goal and happiness. BOETHIUS OF DACIA did indeed hold that a natural philosopher must deny the resurrection of the dead, and this was to be a common view for a long time. However, there is little evidence that anyone really wanted to abolish the belief in a second life. The philosophers' point was simply that while it is known through revelation that supranaturally there will be such a life, a claim to that effect cannot be incorporated into a consistent theory of nature (see NATURAL PHILOSOPHY, MEDIEVAL).

Eternity of the world: Before the 1260s there had been some attempts to interpret Aristotle as if he accepted a temporal beginning of the world. Perhaps the first such attempt was made by WILLIAM OF CONCHES in the twelfth century. However, as Robert GROSSETESTE noted in the 1230s, such attempts had failed and the common assumption became that Aristotelian philosophy did in fact require the world to have existed for an unlimited time, partly because creation out of nothing could not be subsumed under any of the Aristotelian modes of change. Change implies the prior existence of something to be the subject of change, and so creation cannot be a species of change. By the 1270s, it was commonly recognized that the concept of creation out of nothing was consistent if not confused with change, but it also became a common conviction that this would wreak havoc on the natural sciences if incorporated among their concepts. The supposed Averroists were thought to have simply denied the temporal beginning of the world (see ETERNITY OF THE WORLD, MEDIEVAL VIEWS OF).

Double truth: Averroists have been credited with a theory of double truth, occasioned by the fact that when medieval thinkers saw a conflict between philosophy (science) and the teaching of the church, they could not simply reject Church doctrine. Instead, they could hold that philosophers had misinterpreted some of the information obtained by natural means (as Aquinas held, for example), or they could hold that there was no way to detect any error in the derivation of the philosophical thesis, so that the only way out of the impasse consisted in rejecting the thesis on the authority of faith (as did Siger). Alternatively, they could try to explain how the assumption of a first cause makes it reasonable to expect that there are truths which no scientific theory can possibly account for; Boethius of Dacia, who distinguished the conditional truth of a scientific theorem from absolute truth, took that line. A fourth way, asserting that the same proposition can be absolutely true philosophically and also absolutely true theologically, had very few followers, if any at all, but has sometimes been imputed to the 'Averroists'.

To understand how this misconception should arise, one should remember that most philosophers of the thirteenth to sixteenth centuries were masters of arts; it was their job to teach a non-Christian (Aristotelian) philosophy in a Christian society, and so they were caught in the contradiction between reason and faith. Guidelines on how to deal with this dilemma were given in a decision by the Faculty of Arts at Paris in 1272: henceforward, any master dealing with a problem that touched both philosophy and faith was bound by oath to solve it a way that was not contrary to faith. The result was a widespread use of the technique of first providing a philosophical solution and then adding one 'according to the truth of faith'. For some twentieth-century scholars use of this technique has sufficed to stamp a philosopher as an adherent of a theory of double truth.

See also: ARISTOTELIANISM, MEDIEVAL; BOETHIUS OF DACIA; IBN RUSHD; ISLAMIC PHILOSOPHY: TRANSMISSION INTO WESTERN EUROPE; NATURAL PHILOSOPHY, MEDIEVAL §9; SIGER OF BRABANT

References and further reading

Boethius of Dacia [Boethus Dacus] (*c*.1275) *Opera* (Works) ed. H. Roos *et al.* in Corpus Philosophorum Danicorum Medii Aevi IV–IX, Copenhagen: DSL/Gad, 1969–. (Critical edition of the extant works, in Latin. Volume IX, *Sophismata*, has not yet appeared.)

—— (c.1275) *On the Supreme Good, On the Eternity of the World, On Dreams*, trans. J.F. Wippel, Medieval Sources in Translation 30, Toronto, Ont.: Pontifical Institute of Mediaeval Studies, 1987. (Small philosophical treatises which forcefully present Boethius' views.)

Fioravanti, G. (1966) 'Boezio di Dacia e la storiografia sull'Averroismo', *Studi Medievali* 3a, serie 7: 283–322. (Excellent survey of the use of the term 'Averroism' in modern times, with pertinent criticism.)

Gauthier, R.A. (1983–4) 'Notes sur Siger de Brabant (I–II)' (Notes on Siger of Brabant), *Revue des sciences philosophiques et théologiques* 67: 201–32; 68: 3–49. (Rectifies a number of myths about Siger and Averroism; downplays the importance of Siger.)

Gorce, M.M. (1931) 'Averroïsme', in *Dictionnaire d'histoire et de géographie ecclésiastiques*, Paris: Letouzey et Ane, vol. 6: 1032–92. (Outdated, but representative of its time.)

Hisette, R. (1977) *Enquête sur les 219 articles condamnés à Paris le 7 mars 1277* (An Investigation of the 219 Articles Condemned at Paris, 7 March 1277), Philosophes Médiévaux 22, Louvain: Publications Universitaires de Louvain. (Contains the text of the condemned theses as well as a detailed study of the origin of each of them.)

Kuksiewicz, Z. (1965) *Averroisme bolonais au XIVe siècle* (Bolognese Averroism in the Fourteenth Century), Wroclaw: Ossolineum. (Study of Averroism in Italy.)

—— (1968) *De Siger de Brabant à Jacques de Plaisance. La théorie de l'intellect chez les averroistes latins des XIIIe et XIV siècles* (From Siger of Brabant to James of Piacenza: The Theory of Intellect in the Work of the Latin Averroists in the Thirteenth and Fourteenth Centuries), Wroclaw: Ossolineum. (Valuable as a presentation of texts.)

—— (1982) 'Sense, Intellect, and Imagination in Albert, Thomas and Siger', in N. Kretzmann, A. Kenny and J. Pinborg (eds) *Cambridge History of Later Medieval Philosophy*, Cambridge: Cambridge University Press, 602–22. (Survey of the debate about the intellect.)

Libera, A. de (1991) *Averroès et l'Averroïsme. Que sais-je?* (Averroes and Averroism: Survey), Paris: Presses Universitaires de France. (Good overview of the subject.)

Ramon Llull [Raimundus Lullus] (1263–1316) *Disputatio Raimundi et Averroistae*, in H. Harada (ed.) *Opera latina VII*, Corpus Christianorum Continuatio Mediaevalis 32, Turnholt: Brepols, 1975. (One of Llull's anti-Averroist treatises.)

Mandonnet, P. (1899) *Siger de Brabant et l'Averroïsme au XIIIe siècle* (Siger of Brabant and Thirteenth-Century Averroism), Fribourg: Librairie de l'Université. (Mandonnet's understanding of 'Averroism' was to dominate the historiography for a century.)

Renan, E. (1852) *Averroès et l'Averroïsme*, Paris: A. Durand. (Initiated the use of 'Averroism' in the historiography of philosophy.)

Siger of Brabant (c.1240–84) *Collected Works*, various editors, in *Philosophes Médiévaux* vols 12–14, 24, 25, Louvain: Publications Universitaires de Louvain, 1972–. (Works of Siger, who is often identified strongly with Averroism.)

Van Steenberghen, F. (1966a) *La philosophie au XIIIe siècle* (Thirteenth-Century Philosophy), Philosophes Médiévaux 9, Louvain: Publications Universitaires de Louvain. (An influential defender of the 'radical/heterodox Aristotelianism' label.)

—— (1966b) 'L'Averroïsme latin' (Latin Averroism), *Philosophia Conimbricensia* 1: 1–32. (Claims that full-fledged Averroism only appears with John of Jandun.)

STEN EBBESEN

AVERROISM, JEWISH

Averroism was enthusiastically taken up by many Jewish philosophers and adapted in a number of ways that extended its scope beyond mere repetition of Averroes' own arguments. Jewish Averroists were particularly drawn by the potential they found in Averroism for resolving the delicate questions they faced about the relationship between philosophy and religion. The idea that both philosophy and religion are true even when they appear to produce different answers to the same question. Fascinated by the Averroistic idea that religious claims can be interpreted as popular expressions of philosophical truths, the Jewish Averroists followed up with vigour the programme of showing how to translate traditional religious statements into philosophical statements.

Many Jewish philosophers found themselves in a difficulty which they took great pains to resolve, namely, how to reconcile what they believed through faith with what they believed through reason. Averroism seems to be the solution to this problem, since it embodies a theory that explains how faith and reason are connected and makes it possible to be both religious and rational at the same time. It is not surprising, then, that many Jewish thinkers were attracted to this philosophical doctrine.

1 Averroes in the Jewish milieu
2 Isaac Albalag
3 Joseph ibn Caspi
4 Moses Narboni
5 Further consequences

1 Averroes in the Jewish world

Averroes (see IBN RUSHD) came to have a significance in both Christian and Jewish settings that far exceeded his influence in the Islamic lands. There are many reasons for this. Jewish philosophers were impressed with the depth of Ibn Rushd's arguments and with his understanding of ARISTOTLE, who was typically regarded as the paradigmatic philosophical thinker. They were undoubtedly also fascinated by the radical implications of his views. There were many translations of his works into Hebrew and transliterations of Arabic texts of his work into Hebrew script, and these extended far beyond Spain and the intellectual world of the Iberian Peninsula. Many Jewish philosophers wrote commentaries on his works and were influenced by him, in particular CRESCAS and GERSONIDES, and he set the agenda for much of Jewish philosophy. The positive references that MAIMONIDES had made to him obviously helped his reception in the Jewish world, and his thought is often linked with that of Maimonides, since on some important topics they are clearly not far apart.

It would be wrong to think of all the Jewish philosophers who were influenced by Averroes as Averroists. Many often argued with his central ideas and criticized his conclusions, and there is no clear category of thinkers who are 'Averroists' in the sense that they accepted everything that Averroes argued. The philosophers discussed below are those who came closest to sharing Averroes' main principles and who tried to adapt them to Jewish intellectual life.

2 Isaac Albalag

Isaac Albalag came from the Pyrenees region during the second half of the thirteenth century. He was in no doubt at all concerning the merits of Averroes over his Islamic predecessors, or even over Maimonides. He translated al-Ghazali's *Maqasid al-falasifah* (Intentions of the Philosophers) into Hebrew, and argued that this book represented al-Ghazali's real views – a thesis that would have horrified the original author (see al-Ghazali §3). Albalag does accept al-Ghazali's argument that there are certain doctrines that must be accepted by religion. These are the existence of reward and punishment for our actions, the survival of the soul after the death of the body and the fact of providence whereby God watches over our actions. In his *Sefer Tikkun ha-De'ot* (Setting Doctrines Right), he recognizes that philosophy in its Averroistic form does not think much of these religious ideas, and suggests that they are to be accepted by ordinary people who are not capable of philosophy. These ideas will enable them to achieve the highest level of well-being of which they are capable; but that must be contrasted with the sort of felicity that philosophers can achieve, since philosophers can understand far more about the nature of reality than can ordinary believers. The vital tool of understanding here is demonstrative argument, which Albalag, like Averroes, saw as the paradigmatic method of philosophy. Only philosophers are really capable of this sort of thought, and as a consequence, only philosophers can really be allowed to say that they know what is the case.

But what about all those religious texts which it is not possible to verify demonstratively, and which are based on prophecy? Albalag argues that these can be known but not necessarily demonstratively, and that this is no criticism of them. Here Albalag deviates from Averroes, since the latter criticized the claims of *kalam* (dialectical theology) to understand religious texts, especially difficult religious texts (see ISLAMIC THEOLOGY §2). There is no point in thinking that theology can help us with such texts, Averroes argued, since it possesses no methodology that can derive a valid conclusion from premises. Albalag tends to place the interpretations of those in the Jewish mystical tradition of the Kabbalah (see KABBALAH) in the same position as Averroes' *kalam* theologians. He holds that they are capable only of providing dubious and weak readings of Scripture. Indeed, he tends to separate philosophical and religious explanations more radically than Averroes allows. Such a separation is a common feature of Christian and Jewish Averroists (see AVERROISM). In Albalag's case, what we find is acceptance of both views, but the treatment of one is much less vigorous and intellectually satisfying than the other: when the literal sense of a text cannot be reconciled with a philosophical understanding of the topic, both the literal sense and the philosophical understanding have to be accepted, but in different ways. The literal sense is accepted as something which one would understand completely if one were in the position of the prophets who had originally transmitted the text. One must assume, even though one cannot see how, that this meaning is reconcilable with the philosophical meaning.

A crucial example in Jewish philosophy is the creation of the world. According to the philosophers, on Albalag's account, this doctrine must be understood to cohere with the eternity of the world. What results is a theory according to which God creates the world eternally (see ETERNITY OF THE WORLD, MEDIEVAL VIEWS OF). Albalag criticizes MAIMONIDES for claiming that Aristotle did not claim to know with certainty whether the world is eternal. In fact, Albalag believes, Aristotle had no doubts concerning the eternity of the world; Maimonides agreed with Aristotle, but did not wish to threaten the faith of the ordinary believers in Judaism. That is the reason for what Albalag sees as Maimonides' ambivalence about the demonstrability of the origins of the world. However, Maimonides should not have suggested that the eternity of the world cannot be established by reason. It can, and philosophers have no choice but to acknowledge that eternity, although they need not broadcast their views widely if they think hearing such things would upset the beliefs and practices of the naive. It is possible to accept the eternity of the world through reason and its createdness through faith, and there is no need to work out how to reconcile these two diverse positions. Albalag does not say why not; but he seems to go further than Averroes, who argues that there is one truth expressible in two different ways, whereas Albalag appears to argue that there are two truths. This takes him closer to the so-called doctrine of double truth often ascribed to the Christian Averroists in their more radical moments.

3 Joseph ibn Caspi

Joseph ibn Caspi was born in 1279 in Provence, and wrote a variety of theological and philosophical works. He was heavily influenced by Maimonides, Averroes and Abraham ibn Ezra, especially by the latter's construction of a philosophical grammar of the Hebrew language (see IBN EZRA, A.). Caspi defended the literal sense of many passages in Scripture as accurate accounts of past events, and criticized as misleading many of Maimonides' attempts at explaining many of them as prophetic allegories. On the other hand, he shares Averroes' rather ambivalent attitude towards miracles, suggesting that there is a natural explanation for miracles, were we able to understand all aspects of the events in question. To understand a report of a miracle, it seems, we need to understand the point of view and knowledge of those actually present at the time. Prophecy also has to be interpreted in terms of the audience it is designed to impress, and if there are aspects of the event which we do not now entirely grasp, we should put this down to our distance from its occurrence and to our relative lack of knowledge of how the event was regarded at that time. Prophets are able to tell what is going to happen in the future because they are able to understand how the things they observe in the present link with what is to come. The role of the deity in this process is quite limited. Many religious statements are not capable of a truth value; their function is to move people to action and to teach them how to behave. Where philosophy and prophecy diverge, we should remember that they are different and it is hardly surprising that they do not always agree. If we really knew why prophets said what they say and why miracles take the forms they do, then we should understand how they might be reconciled; indeed, we might understand how prophecies are merely more popularly accessible expressions of philosophical truth. Since we are limited in our understanding of religious statements by our distance from their original formulation, we have to accept them as aspects of faith. We can remain confident nonetheless that such statements are in principle equivalent to philosophical truths. Unlike Maimonides and Averroes, Caspi had little sympathy with the idea that the secrets of interpretation should be restricted to the intellectual elite. His point was that they have to remain secrets, since there is no possibility now of finding out precisely what the ancient statements originally meant, given the differences in audience, language and context (see PROPHECY).

4 Moses Narboni

Moses Narboni was born in Perpignan around 1300 and died approximately sixty-two years later. He wrote many commentaries on theological and religious texts, together with some original works and several commentaries on the works of Averroes. He wrote extensively on Maimonides, and tended to criticize Maimonides using arguments drawn from Averroes, as he was one of the few philosophers of the time to recognize that Averroes was seeking to challenge the Neoplatonic metaphysics of IBN SINA (Avicenna) which formed so important a part of Maimonides' thinking. Narboni also developed Averroes' theory of the 'active intellect' in such a way as to make it relevant to Jewish philosophy.

As human thinking becomes progressively better perfected it moves from being imaginative to becoming intellectual. Ultimately it fuses with the active intellect itself, which is the very principle of intellectual thought. As a result, the material part of us comes under the control of our thought. Using this theory, Narboni is in a position to explain miracles and prophecy as resulting from a certain sort of thinking that produces appropriate material effects, that optimally illustrate the ideas in the consciousness of the prophets but which adapt those ideas to the level of understanding of the audience the prophet has in mind. Here a kind of Neoplatonism creeps back in, for Narboni's language is clearly based on the idea of a hierarchy of intellects where each intellect is connected with an existent (see NEOPLATONISM IN ISLAMIC PHILOSOPHY §2).

The parallelism between intellects and existents usefully echoes a similar parallelism between doctrines and acts. The idea of what is to be done results in the creation of that state of affairs, and similarly a religious doctrine has as its material aspect a particular form of practice. All of this accords nicely with the unified approach that Averroes takes to the relationship between such diverse phenomena as body and mind, the material and the spiritual, and the theoretical and the practical. The Torah, which is perfect, consists of doctrines which are true and accord with practices designed to bring about a desirable end in line with those true beliefs. Of course, it takes a remarkable individual to understand all aspects of the Torah, and only Moses fulfils that role, a role very similar to that which Averroes ascribes to Muhammad.

Narboni, like Averroes, upholds the principle of plenitude, according to which something is possible only if it is (at some time) actual; and he uses this principle to argue that in an eternal universe, if there can be a most perfect created being then (at some time) there will be. Moses fits the bill exactly. Lesser mortals will not be able to grasp perspicuously the reasons for all the doctrines in the Torah, and will have to accept these doctrines on the basis of faith alone. Narboni thinks it is bad policy to encourage ordinary believers to trouble themselves excessively with finding out the reasons for the commandments. Most people would not understand these reasons even if they were presented with them, and a fruitless search would only frustrate and undermine the faith of the seekers. The prophets are provided precisely for such people, since they are capable of representing philosophical truths in imaginative language which will impress the masses and keep them on the right path. Only those capable of philosophy will understand precisely what is actually intended, and only they should seek such understanding. We see here a reformulation of a genuine doctrine of Averroes, that there is one truth that is expressed in at least two different ways, one intellectually respectable and the other practical and effective.

5 Further consequences

Clearly, there are aspects of Jewish Averroism which are very different both from the philosophy of Averroes himself and from Christian Averroism. In the Jewish milieu, Averroes was commonly linked with Maimonides and, more surprisingly perhaps, with Abraham ibn Ezra. Some thinkers such as Narboni were interested in introducing Kabbalistic doctrines in their explication of the thought of Averroes. Narboni's discussion of providence in terms of astrological causation would have surprised Averroes and horrified Maimonides, but this is by no means a criticism of the approach of the Jewish Averroists to Averroes himself. They employed his thought, and what they considered could be derived from his thought, creatively and combined it with other relevant philosophical and theological theses to produce a novel account of the issues then of concern to the philosophical community.

There were a large number of other thinkers whose work is largely based upon Averroes but who have not been discussed here in detail. The work of Joseph ibn Waqar and Moses ibn Crispin, for example, provides evidence of considerable discussion on Averroistic themes within the Jewish community. It is only with the onset of the Renaissance and the last major Averroist thinker in the community, Elijah DELMEDIGO, that the passionate interest in Averroes started to decline. Averroes was long seen as the first commentator on Aristotle, and the relative decline in interest in Aristotle was matched with decreasing concern for the thought of Averroes.

One of the contributions of Jewish Averroism is its way of tackling the distinction between religious and philosophical truths. The argument that the pursuit of philosophy is not only permitted by religion but is even necessary for the intelligent adherent comes straight from Averroes himself in his *Fasl al-maqal* (Decisive Treatise). The warning against trying to prove the truth of religion through philosophy was taken very seriously by the Jewish Averroists, for two reasons. It is a category mistake to try to explain through philosophy what is capable only of religious explanation. Also, the discovery that the truths of Judaism cannot be established philosophically might lead to disbelief or scepticism. This gives rise to an interesting question. If it is inappropriate to refer to the rational basis of a religion as the justification of that religion, what reason is there to prefer one religion to another? This was a lively issue during the Middle Ages, since there were strenuous efforts by Islam and Christianity to convert Jews, and equally strenuous efforts by Jewish thinkers to resist such pressure. The Jewish Averroists had no doubt of the superiority of their religion over its competitors, and they argued that Christianity in particular involves the acceptance of self-contradictory notions.

We must distinguish between those ideas which are in themselves possible and can be actualized through the miraculous intervention of the deity, and those ideas which even God could not bring about, since they are impossible and only an imperfect deity could wish to bring them about. This was the approach which Jewish philosophers took to the notion of God becoming man, the Incarnation, which they regarded as obviously an imperfection, along with a whole range of other crucial Christian doctrines such as the Trinity, transubstantiation and the Virgin Birth (see INCARNATION AND CHRISTOLOGY; TRINITY). A whole range of logical problems were discovered in these doctrines and contrasted with the bases of Judaism which, it was argued, is an acceptably rational faith. At least Judaism does not involve the acceptance of self-contradictory notions, although it is true that some of the stories of miracles offend against our understanding of natural necessity. As Aristotelians, the Jewish Averroists might have been expected to have been more wary of allowing for miraculous interventions in nature, since Averroes seems to have regarded such events as just as impossible as logical self contradictions. This is where the use of Maimonides and Abraham ibn Ezra in combination with Averroes proves so useful. Maimonides was used to suggest that the accounts of miracles need not be taken to be literally true (by philosophical readers), and Ibn Ezra was used to show that we are so distant from the time of the miraculous events that we do not really know precisely what the narratives about them are supposed to mean. We do not even know what the language used then really meant, nor how astrological forces brought about change in the sublunar world.

Jewish Averroism should not, then, be seen as a slavish adaptation of Averroes to issues of interest in Jewish philosophy. Some of Averroes' main theses were combined with the opinions of quite disparate philosophers and out of this heady mixture a rich variety of arguments emerges. These arguments are generally more than merely eclectic and they involve a sustained treatment of the logic of the relationship between religious and philosophical language.

See also: ARISTOTELIANISM, MEDIEVAL; ARISTOTELIANISM IN ISLAMIC PHILOSOPHY; AVERROISM; IBN RUSHD

References and further reading

Bland, K. (1981) *The Epistle on the Possibility of Conjunction with the Active Intellect by Ibn Rushd with the Commentary of Moses Narboni*, New York: The Jewish Theological Seminary of America. (An edition and translation of an important commentary.)

Golb, M. (1956–7) 'The Hebrew Translation of Averroes' Fasl al-Maqal', *Proceedings of the American Academy for Jewish Research* 25: 91–113; 26: 41–64. (Useful exploration of the popularity of the text in the Jewish world.)

Hayoun, M.-R. (1982) 'L'épitre du libre-arbitre de Moise de Narbonne' (Moses Narboni's Letter on Free Will), *Revue des études juives* 141: 139–67. (An edition and translation of Narboni's *Ma'amar ha-Behira* (Treatise on Free Will).)

—— (1986) *Moshe Narboni*, Tübingen: Mohr. (Edition and translation of Part 1 of Narboni's commentary on Maimonides' *Guide to the Perplexed*.)

Lasker, D. (1980) 'Averroistic trends in Jewish–Christian Polemics in the Late Middle Ages', *Speculum* 55: 294–304. (The relevance of Averroes for interreligious debate.)

Leaman, O. (1988) *Averroes and His Philosophy*, Oxford: Clarendon Press. (A general survey of Averroes and Averroism.)

—— (1996) 'Jewish Averroism', in S.H. Nasr and O. Leaman (eds) *History of Islamic Philosophy*, London: Routledge, 769–80. (Good introductory article.)

Mesch, B. (1982) 'Principles of Judaism in Maimonides and Joseph ibn Caspi', in J. Reinharz and D. Schwetschinski (eds) *Mystics, Philosophers and Politicians*, Durham, NC: Duke University Press, 85–98. (Useful account of the relationship between these thinkers.)

Sirat, C. (1985) *A History of Jewish Philosophy in the Middle Ages*, Cambridge: Cambridge University Press. (Extensive bibliography of Jewish Averroists.)

Steinschneider, M. (1956) *Die hebräischen Übersetzungen des Mittelalters und die Juden als Dolmetscher* (The Hebrew Translations of the Middle Ages and the Jews as Interpreters), Graz: Akademische Druck- under Verlagsanstalt. (Reprint of the celebrated 1893 bibliography.)

Vajda, G. (1952) 'A propos de l'Averroïsme juif' (On Jewish Averroism), *Sefarad* XII: 3– 29. (A useful general survey of the area with interesting remarks on, in particular, the thought of Moses ibn Crispin.)

—— (1960) *Isaac Albalag – Averroiste juif, traducteur et commentateur d'Al-Ghazali* (Isaac Albalag – Jewish Averroist, Translator and Commentator on al-Ghazali), Paris: Vrin. (Translation and study of the *Tikkun ha-De'ot*.)

OLIVER LEAMAN

AVICEBROL/AVICEBRON

see IBN GABIROL, SOLOMON

AVICENNA *see* IBN SINA, ABU 'ALI AL-HUSAYN

AWAKENING OF FAITH IN MAHĀYĀNA

The Awakening of Faith in Mahāyāna *(Dasheng qixinlun) is one of the most influential philosophical texts in East Asian Buddhism. It is most important for developing the Indian Buddhist doctrine of an inherent potentiality for Buddhahood (*tathāgatagarbha*) into a monistic ontology based on the mind as the ultimate ground of all experience. Its most significant contribution to East Asian Buddhist thought is its formulation of the idea of original enlightenment (*benjue*, or in Japanese,* hongaku*).*

Although attributed to Aśvaghoṣa and supposedly translated into Chinese by Paramārtha, there is general consensus among modern scholars that the *Awakening of Faith in Mahāhāyana* (*Dasheng qixunlun*) was most likely composed in China during the third quarter of the sixth century. Apocryphal texts such as the *Awakening of Faith* played a crucial role in justifying innovations in practice and belief that helped give shape to a uniquely East Asian form of Buddhism.

The *Awakening of Faith* was valued as a concise compendium of essential Mahāyāna doctrines. Its style is terse, often to the point of being cryptic. It thus allows for a range of different interpretations, so much so that some of the commentaries on the work sometimes seem to have been written on different texts.

It would be difficult to exaggerate the importance of this text on the development of East Asian Buddhist thought. Beginning with the influential commentary of FAZANG (643–712), for example, it played an increasingly central role within the Huayan tradition, sometimes even eclipsing in importance the *Avataṃsaka (Huayan) Sūtra* on which the tradition based its authority. Its influence permeated early Chan texts in the Tang dynasty (618–907) as well. During the Song dynasty (960–1279), it was at the centre of the doctrinal debates that raged within the Tiantai tradition, as well as to a lesser extent those between the Tiantai and Chan (see BUDDHIST PHILOSOPHY, CHINESE). It also occupied a central place in the thought of CHINUL (1158–1210), whose grand synthesis of Huayan (Hwaŏm) and Chan (Sŏn) was formative in defining the course of Korean Buddhism (see BUDDHIST PHILOSOPHY, KOREAN). In Japan, it provided the cornerstone for the articulation of the so-called 'theory of original enlightenment' (*hongaku shisō*), which provided the doctrinal matrix out of which emerged the great medieval reform movements of Pure Land, Nichiren and Zen (see BUDDHIST PHILOSOPHY, JAPANESE).

The *Awakening of Faith* developed the doctrine of *tathāgatagarbha* (embryo or womb of the Tathāgata) that had been introduced to China in such Indian Mahāyāna scriptures as the *Lion's Roar of Queen Śrīmālā* and the *Laṅkāvatāra Sūtra*. This doctrine had proclaimed the inherent potentiality of enlightenment in all sentient beings. Whereas this doctrine seems to have been of relatively minor importance in Indian Buddhism, it became the underlying premise on which the most distinctively East Asian Buddhist beliefs and practices were built. It was particularly valued because it guaranteed the universal accessibility of enlightenment and because it qualified the radical suspicion of language found in the Madhyamaka tradition by ascribing a series of positive predicates to the absolute (see BUDDHISM, MĀDHYAMIKA: INDIA AND TIBET).

The *Awakening of Faith* addressed a fundamental philosophical problem in the *tathāgatagarbha* tradition having to do with the relationship between enlightenment and ignorance. This problem was even more acute for *Awakening of Faith*'s ontologized understanding of mind. If the fundamental ground of all phenomena is the intrinsically enlightened mind, then how can ignorance be accounted for? The text tries to answer this question by linking the *tathāgatagarbha* with the *ālayavijñāna* (store consciousness), which explained the process of mental conditioning.

The *Awakening of Faith* begins by positing the one mind as the ultimate source of all phenomena. This mind has two aspects, which together totally comprehend all *dharmas*. The first is the mind as suchness (*xin zhenru men*), which the text defines as that which neither is born nor dies. The mind as suchness is the *tathāgatagarbha* in its true guise as the all-pervading, undifferentiated absolute reality (*dharmakāya*). Even though this mind is unborn and imperishable, differentiations come into being because of deluded thinking. Nevertheless, the true nature of the mind is beyond all predication and thought.

The second aspect of the one mind is referred to as the mind subject to birth-and-death (*xin shengmie men*). Founded on the *tathāgatagarbha*, this aspect of the one mind is identified with the *ālayavijñāna*, which the *Awakening of Faith* defines as 'the interfusion of that which is not subject to birth-and-death [that is, the mind as suchness] and that which is subject to birth-and-death in such a way that they are neither one nor different.'

The *ālayavijñāna* also has two modes, which embrace and give rise to all *dharmas*. The first is enlightened (*jue*), and the second is unenlightened (*bujue*). 'Enlightened' is explained as meaning that the essence of the mind is free from thoughts. The characteristic of being free from thoughts is likened to the realm of empty space that pervades everywhere and is equal to the undifferentiated absolute body (*dharmakāya*) of the Buddha. Since the essence of mind is based on the *dharmakāya*, it is said to be intrinsically enlightened.

The *Awakening of Faith* goes on to distinguish intrinsic enlightenment (*benjue*) from experiential enlightenment (*shijue*). Experiential enlightenment, moreover, is contrasted with unenlightenment. In fact, the text states that experiential enlightenment can only be spoken of in the context of unenlightenment. Experiential enlightenment refers to the process by which one awakens to the ultimate source of the mind. Intrinsic enlightenment is at once the ontological ground that makes experiential enlightenment possible, and that which experiential enlightenment realizes.

At this point the *Awakening of Faith* introduces a famous metaphor to explain the relationship between ignorance and enlightenment: just as the originally tranquil ocean is stirred into waves by the wind, so the intrinsically enlightened mind is stirred into thoughts by ignorance. Under the heading of the unenlightened mode of the *ālayavijñāna*, the text then enumerates a series of nine stages that, like the classical twelve-link chain of interdependent origination (*pratītyasamutpāda*), explains how the process of karmic bondage develops. The process begins with the first subtle movement of thought. Based on the unenlightened mode of the *ālayavijñāna*, thought stirs the originally tranquil consciousness, which then manifests itself in terms of subject and object. This bifurcation of consciousness leads to the discrimation of likes and dislikes, and the awareness of pleasure and pain gives rise to associative patterns, which produce attachments, which lead to the generation of karma, which leads to becoming bound within the continuous process of birth and death (see KARMA AND REBIRTH, INDIAN CONCEPTIONS OF).

The theory of mind developed in the *Awakening of Faith* can be seen as an attempt to address the problem of ignorance. The relationship between the absolute and conditioned aspects of the one mind, or the *tathāgatagarbha* and the *ālayavijñāna*, traces back to a paradox at the core of the *tathāgatagarbha* doctrine: the *tathāgatagarbha* is at once intrinsically pure and identical with the *dharmakāya* and yet appears to be defiled. The two aspects of the one mind thus seem to be a matter of perspective, and their difference can be seen as corresponding to the point of view of ultimate and conventional truth. The *tathāgatagarbha* as seen from the enlightened perspective of a Buddha is perfectly pure and undefiled. It is only due to the deluded thinking of unenlightened beings that it appears to be otherwise.

The relationship between these two aspects of the one mind brings into focus the central philosophical problem for the *tathāgatagarbha* tradition: the origin of ignorance. If the mind is intrinsically enlightened, how can it become deluded? The problem arises because it is the consistent position of *tathāgatagarbha* theory that ignorance is only adventitious. The *Awakening of Faith*'s metaphor of the water and waves is thus an unsatisfactory resolution of the problem insofar as the comparison of the wind to ignorance posits a separate origin for ignorance. If ignorance had a separate origin, it would have its own autonomous ontological status placing it on an equal footing with enlightenment. The resulting dualistic ontology would undermine the axial premise of the *tathāgatagarbha* tradition that enlightenment is universally accessible to all beings.

In identifying the *ālayavijñāna* with the *tathāgatagarbha*, the *Awakening of Faith* grounds the process of conditioned origination on an intrinsically pure ontological foundation. This means that the defilements that appear to obscure the intrinsically enlightened mind of suchness are merely the manifestation of that mind as it adapts conditions and have no independent basis of their own.

See also: BUDDHIST PHILOSOPHY, CHINESE; BUDDHIST PHILOSOPHY IN INDIA; BUDDHISM, MĀDHYAMIKA: INDIA AND TIBET; MIND, PHILOSOPHY OF; ONTOLOGY IN INDIAN PHILOSOPHY

References and further reading

Gregory, P.N. (1986) 'The Problem of Theodicy in the *Awakening of Faith*', *Religious Studies* 22: 63–78. (This article explores the problem of theodicy in the *Awakening of Faith*.)

Hakeda Yoshito (1967) *The Awakening of Faith*, New York: Columbia University Press. (Although not always satisfactory, this book offers the best translation of the *Awakening of Faith* into English.)

PETER N. GREGORY

AWARENESS IN INDIAN THOUGHT

Classical Indian schools all stake out positions on awareness, its intrinsic nature, its place in the causal processes crucial to human accomplishment, its relations to objects in the world, and the possibilities, according to certain religious or spiritual theories, of mystical transformation. In several prominent instances, stances taken on awareness may be said to constitute the most salient differentiation among schools, so central to a school's overall outlook is its view on the topic. Classical epistemological conceptions, for example, are in large part shaped by positions on awareness, and the spiritual philosophies for which Indian thought is best known present theories of awareness to guide meditation and mystical practice. Yogic, Vedāntic and Buddhist mysticism all came to be supported by views of the true nature of awareness or its native state.

In the professionalized debates that fill the immense proliferation of philosophical texts in the classical period (from approximately AD 100 to the eighteenth century and later), key issues are whether awarenesses have forms of their own or assume content only with reference to objects, and the precise nature of the relation, or relations, of awarenesses to objects in the world, including the role of awareness in human activity. Some important positions are shared across schools, and apart from the anti-theoretic polemics of Mādhyamaka Buddhists and others, a phenomenalist and idealist stance, a representationalism, and a direct or causal realism are the major theories concerning the content of awarenesses.

The world-oriented philosophies of Logic (Nyāya) and Exegesis (Mīmāṃsā) engage spiritual or mystical views (principally, Buddhist Yogācāra and Advaita Vedānta) on the issue of self-awareness or awareness of awareness. The exchange between upholders of Nyāya and Advaita Vedānta (Vedāntic Monism) on this score is, in particular, an admirable philosophical achievement.

1 Spiritual theories of awareness
2 Representationalism, idealism and direct realism
3 Self-awareness

1 Spiritual theories of awareness

According to preclassical texts called Upaniṣads ('secret doctrines'), human awareness offers a latent possibility of world-transcendence, of 'liberation' (*mukti*) of consciousness from embodiment and finite experience. The classical schools of Vedānta, Sāṅkhya and Yoga develop views centred on such a mystical possibility, as do the socially revolutionary movements of Buddhism and Jainism (though the latter reject Upaniṣadic authority). In Advaita Vedānta, which of the Vedāntic (or Upaniṣadic) subschools is the most emphatic about the world-transcendent nature of awareness, the only veridical content of awareness is self-aware awareness itself. Awareness is by nature *kūṭastha*, 'stationed at the tip', at the far extreme, remote from the world; at least, it is so in its true nature or native state. In fact, awareness' worldly content is viewed as an illusion and a deformation, a falling away from what awareness is in itself. In this way, apparently, discoveries in meditation would be emphasized (see MONISM, INDIAN §§1-2).

A dualistic view of awareness and the world can be teased out of the Advaita position: the world is contrary to the true nature of awareness, albeit the cosmic illusion depends on awareness, which is its substratum. In the schools of Sāṅkhya and Yoga, in contrast, dualism is explicitly maintained: nature and awareness are separate realities, and it is problematic how they are related at all. As in Advaita, the only true content of awareness is awareness itself. With regard to the world, uninvolved witnessing – though, again, problematic (since the witness and the witnessed are unrelated in reality) – is upheld as the state the least estranged from what awareness is in itself (see SĀṄKHYA §§1-2, 6). (The similarities, by the way, among Advaita, Sāṅkhya and Yoga on awareness hold despite the contrast between Advaita's claim that there is in reality only a single self, *ātman* – the appearance of multiple persons belongs to the cosmic illusion – and Yoga's and Sāṅkhya's view that there are an infinite number of true persons, *puruṣa*, who are aware.)

The motivations for all three spiritual philosophies appear to be to show intellectually the possibility of a meditative state of self-absorption as well as to maintain its supreme value and desirability. By viewing awareness in its native state as without content other than self-aware awareness itself, the schools avoid having to explain the possibility of meditative self-absorption; rather, it is deviation from that state that is the mystery.

Taking a different angle on the three schools, we find that with respect to the everyday sort of awareness – perceptual awareness, in particular – intricate and carefully formulated theories emerge. According to Sāṅkhya and Yoga, nature ranges without break from luminous and malleable mentality to gross material elements, with the mind viewed as capable of presenting to the witnessing person or self representations of things that are continuous with the things represented both substantially and causally. In

605

the *Yogasūtra*, which is the Yoga school's foundational text, this view is interwoven with a theory of personal transformation through yogic practice. That is, through psychophysical exercises centring on the ability to focus on and identify with any object whatsoever without distraction, there are, according to Yoga philosophy, practically unlimited possibilities of knowledge by extension of personal identity, a knowing of something ordinarily foreign to the self in the direct manner in which one knows oneself. According to Advaita Vedānta, modifications of a malleable 'internal organ' (*antaḥkaraṇa*) account for perceptions psychologically, although it is continually insisted that awareness itself belongs to another realm of reality. In Advaita's long history, a variety of cosmological theories are presented about how awareness comes to be associated with the internal organ, or mind.

Within Indian Buddhism, distinct views of awareness are constrained by the core teaching of an experiential *nirvāṇa* as the supreme good. Disidentification with the body, emotions, sensory presentations and thought is promoted by a 'no-self' doctrine (Sanskrit: *anātman*), a doctrine central to most Buddhist teachings about the way or path to *nirvāṇa*. Thus the real possibility of *nirvāṇa* experience, along with various prerequisites, is thought to demand a view of awareness as free-floating, unmoored by any enduring self or substratum, as well as a view of the apparent self as a bundle of awarenesses (see BUDDHIST PHILOSOPHY, INDIAN §1; NIRVĀṆA). Within this common frame, different schools of Buddhist philosophy uphold views of awareness that command attention in a host of classical texts that are less, or only peripherally, concerned with mystical possibilities. We shall take up the more refined Buddhist theories of awareness within that broader context.

2 Representationalism, idealism and direct realism

According to a view that appears in schools of early Buddhist philosophy (as well as in Sāṅkhya and, arguably, Advaita Vedānta), awarenesses are of mental figures that represent objects external to awareness. External objects stand in causal relation to their representations, but are not what awarenesses are directly of. Such representationalism is attacked from two sides, from the perspective of phenomenalism and idealism (or at least scepticism about objects' independence of awareness) championed in the Yogācāra Buddhist school, and from the point of view of direct realism formulated in the sister schools of Nyāya (Logic) and Vaiśeṣika (Atomism), as well as in the traditionalist school of Brāhmanism known as Mīmāṃsā (Exegesis). The comparative advantages of representationalism are, first, that different types of awareness – perceptions, memories, imaginings, and so on – can be understood as all of the same type of object, namely, of mental objects, and, second, that the common intuition is affirmed of the independence from awareness of the pots and trees of the world as variously perceived, imagined, and so on, by different perceivers and by the same perceiver at different times. Direct realism has to assume that illusions have ontologically distinct objects from veridical awarenesses (the unreal and the real, respectively), although on any given occasion these cannot be differentiated from a first-person perspective: an illusion can seem to present a real object no less than a veridical awareness. And idealism embraces the counterintuitive position of putting the world in the head (or in the 'warehouse consciousness', *ālaya-vijñāna*; see below).

The Buddhist representationalists (sometimes known as Sautrāntikas) distinguish between the phenomenally existent (*saṃvṛti-sat*) and the substantially real (*dravya-sat*). Substantial existents are ultimate particulars (*svalakṣaṇa*), or atoms, which give rise to, for example, the phenomenon of a pot. Composites are not substantially real – the representation of a particular grouping of atoms, such as a pot, is mind-dependent – and particulars, that is, the substantially real atoms, while causally effective for appearances (though not for wholes *qua* wholes), do not themselves appear, at least not as atoms. The appearance of a pot represents a cluster of atoms, but the particular configuration is determined by human purposes and desires.

DIGNĀGA (b. *c.* 480), a Yogācārin and an innovative logician (studied by philosophers of all schools), voices empiricist criticism of this position. The assumption that atoms cause the content of awareness although awareness does not represent the specific image of atoms means that a pot or a cup or anything might be perceived as anything else. The attributes of the atoms are not perceived, and everything that is perceived is considered, with respect to the atoms, to be like a double moon. 'It [the truly substantial objective support of awareness] is the object which exists internally to knowledge itself as knowable aspect and which appears to us as if it exists externally' (*Ālambanaparīkṣā*, 1942: 48). Whether things really exist externally cannot be known.

According to Yogācāra, an awareness manifests a form internal to itself; it is *sākāra*, 'with form'. Yogācārins earlier than Dignāga maintained that a common 'warehouse consciousness' (*ālaya-vijñāna*) accounts for the intersubjectivity of objects among different subjects, and a beginningless psychological impulsion (*anādi-vāsanā*) for the ineluctable error of taking things to be external. Scholars have also supposed that the idealism here is motivated by a cosmological understanding of *nirvāṇa* or by a sense of a need to explain how *nirvāṇa* is an interactive possibility embracing everyone. Yogācāra is a Mahāyāna Buddhist school, and at the core of Mahāyāna is the teaching that we and everything are all interconnected, and that through the efforts of the Bodhisattvas (those of superlative wisdom and compassion) we shall eventually all arrive together at the supreme felicity (see BUDDHISM, YOGACĀRĀ SCHOOL OF).

But whether Dignāga (or his equally illustrious follower, Dharmakīrti) himself embraced such an idealism has come to be disputed. What is clear is that the later Yogācāra philosophers work out a conceptual logic and a pragmatic epistemology that are supposed to be independent of such metaphysical questions as whether objects of awareness are merely internal to awareness or whether they also reflect external causes (see EPISTEMOLOGY, INDIAN SCHOOLS OF §1). Awareness guides action, and the touchstone of veridicality is success in action as shown by the coherence of the propositional content of one awareness with that of other awarenesses. The main criticism of representationalism is that it is otiose – as is also the direct realism of the Brāhmanical schools.

The direct realists, for their part, ably defend a contrary view of awareness, and voice criticisms of Yogācāra – including the pragmatism and scepticism of the late Yogācāra logicians and epistemologists – as well as of the earlier representationalism. We here focus on Nyāya (the 'Logic' school), although, especially with respect to attacks on Buddhist philosophy, Nyāya reasoners learned much from Mīmāṃsā (the 'Exegesis' school) (see NYĀYA-VAIŚEṢIKA §6; MĪMĀṂSĀ §2).

Awarenesses, according to Buddhists and Nyāya realists alike, are fleeting psychological episodes. So if they do not have extra-mental facts as content, then, since each awareness is itself a unique particular, linguistic practice (*vyavahāra*) could not be based on awarenesses. This is an unhappy ramification of the Buddhist theory. Communicable verbalization of awareness requires generalities or class characters as the content of awareness, because communication requires commonality in the experience of conversers (to talk to oneself would similarly require commonality among one's own experiential episodes). If each awareness has to itself content that is only an internal form, then each awareness, as itself a unique particular, will remain unverbalizable. According to Nyāya, awareness is *nirākāra*, 'without intrinsic form'; its content, including characters shared by things of the same type, is imparted to it by causal processes commencing with contact between sense organ and object.

The Buddhist representationalists, who, to their credit, saw the need for extra-mental causes of awareness content, still made two important mistakes, Nyāya advocates claim. First, generalities have to obtain in nature; neither awareness nor mentality can create the characters shared among things that we are aware of and that make communication possible (this thing as exhibiting the pothood that you from other experiences are acquainted with). Second, there is no need to postulate a third realm of mental figures, for to understand an awareness, itself a mental or internal event (properly, an episodic quality of the self or soul), as directly indicating facts, not mediated by mental figures, is the simpler hypothesis (*lāghavatva*). The occurrence of illusion does not establish such a third realm, because illusion can be explained on realist suppositions: due to an abnormality in a perceptual process, there is projection of a general character with which the subject is acquainted through prior experience and which is stored (associatively) in the subject's memory bank, projection on a particular that is being immediately experienced (see ERROR AND ILLUSION, INDIAN CONCEPTIONS OF §3).

The realist view is plainly vulnerable with respect to the role of memory it finds in illusion; the generality imparted to an awareness thereby is apparently better captured by a Yogācāra theory of a two-stage perceptual process, the first sensory and nonconceptual (involving only individuals or particulars), the second mental and conceptual (where salient groupings, or class characters, are imparted by the mind, in part based on human purposes). Philosophers of early Nyāya, in fact, struggled much with this, and tried, often confusedly, to concoct a similar two-stage realist theory. But the fourteenth-century 'New Logician' (*navya-naiyāyika*) GAṄGEŚA (§2) managed to formulate a much clearer view of a pre-verbalizable stage of sensory awareness in which there is direct grasping of naturally obtaining generalities (and not only, as in the Yogācāra theory, particulars), followed by a verbalizable stage in which these are attributed to particulars (see SENSE PERCEPTION, INDIAN VIEWS OF §6).

3 Self-awareness

According to Nyāya, again in opposition to Yogācāra and also to Advaita Vedānta, self-awareness is not intrinsic to awareness, but is a matter of apperception (*anuvyavasāya*, literally 'after-cognition'), an awareness whose object is a previous awareness (that is, a 'scoped awareness', to use B.K. Matilal's happy phrase). Advaitins, such as the brilliant polemicist

Śrīharṣa (c. 1150), charge that the Nyāya view would make self-awareness impossible, in that as soon as one became aware of an awareness, A_1, the grasping awareness, A_2, not itself self-aware, would require an A_3 to be known, *ad infinitum*. The Advaita view, in contrast, is that every awareness is intrinsically self-aware (Yogcārins also defend this position). Moreover, awarenesses are infallibly known. Śrīharṣa argues, echoing the renowned Śaṅkara (c. 700, usually regarded as the greatest classical Advaitin), that if an awareness *qua* awareness could be doubted, then no resolution of any dispute would be possible. If anything is known, it must be awareness of awareness; awareness is self-luminous (see ŚAṄKARA §2).

Gaṅgeśa and other Nyāya philosophers respond by admitting the potential for a regress; it is simply that we normally have no call to make explicit in further apperception a lower-order apperception. We could do so, however, for as long as we wished to play that game. Normally we have no call to introspect, involved as we are in action and getting things done. Not every fact in the world is cognized by a human being. Similarly, not every awareness is apperceived. As the *Nyāyasūtra* indicates, however, some doubt does result from conflicts of theory, from the opposed positions of different schools, especially concerning the nature of awareness. Thus in philosophy we have special occasion to consult apperception to resolve higher-order doubts and disputes.

According to Gaṅgeśa, in apperception, unlike in first-order awarenesses, the content of the scoped awareness is infallibly cognized as awareness content; that is to say, the scoped awareness is, *qua* awareness, known precisely as the phenomenon it is. Nyāya philosophers are generally fallibilists, taking the position that just about any bit of awareness content could prove to be erroneous. The exception is apperception, where the content of a previous awareness is infallibly known as awareness content. For example, the apperception verbalized as 'I took myself to be seeing a snake' will be veridical whether the scoped awareness' content (namely that something is a snake) obtains in fact. By taking this stance, Gaṅgeśa is able to undercut the criticism of some of his opponents that Nyāya's realism about objects in the external world makes it blind to the infallible presentation of awareness to itself: Nyāya in fact holds that, *qua* subjective phenomenon, an awareness can be infallibly known. The view is also vital to Nyāya philosophers' being able to talk so discriminatingly about awarenesses, despite their direct realism.

See also: KNOWLEDGE, INDIAN VIEWS OF; SELF, INDIAN THEORIES OF

References and further reading

Bhattacharyya, S. (1993) *Gaṅgeśa's Theory of Indeterminate Perception*, New Delhi: Indian Council of Philosophical Research. (Contains a translation of an important section from Gaṅgeśa's philosophic masterpiece, and lucid explanation of the general Nyāya understanding of awareness.)

Dasgupta, S. (1922) *A History of Indian Philosophy*, vol. 1, Cambridge: Cambridge University Press, repr. 1969. (Remains probably the best overall introduction to classical Indian systems, although it is out of date concerning Buddhist views.)

* Dignāga (c. 500) *Ālambanaparīkṣa* (Examination of the Object of Awareness), trans. N.A. Sastri, *Dignāga's Ālambanaparīkṣā*, Madras: The Adyar Library, 1942. (Sastri reconstructs the original Sanskrit, which is lost, from a Tibetan translation, as well as translating the text and much of a commentary by Vinītadeva into lucid English.)

Hayes, R.P. (1988) *Dignāga on the Interpretation of Signs*, Dordrecht: Kluwer. (Includes an annotated translation of two chapters of Dignāga's *Pramāṇasamuccaya* (Collected Writings on the Acquisition of Knowledge); provides detailed contextualization.)

Matilal, B.K. (1986) *Perception: An Essay on Classical Indian Theories of Knowledge*, Oxford: Oxford University Press. (A modern classic by a premier scholar and philosopher intent on defending Nyāya.)

* *Nyāyasūtra* (c. AD 150), trans. M. Gangopadhyay, *Nyāya-Sūtra with Vātsyāyana's Commentary*, Calcutta: Indian Studies, 1982. (A readable and accurate translation.)

Phillips, S.H. (1995) *Classical Indian Metaphysics: Refutations of Realism and the Emergence of 'New Logic'*, La Salle, IL: Open Court. (Contains elaboration of, in particular, what is discussed in §3.)

STEPHEN H. PHILLIPS

AXIOLOGY

Axiology is the branch of practical philosophy which studies the nature of value. Axiologists study value in general rather than moral values in particular and frequently emphasize the plurality and heterogeneity of values while at the same time adopting different forms of realism about values. Historically, three groups of philosophers can be described as axiologists: the original Austrian and German schools of value phenomenologists; American theorists of value who offered an account of value which reduces it to human interests; *and an English school, influenced by Austro-German phenomenology, which included such diverse figures as G.E. Moore, Hastings Rashdall and W.D. Ross. Recent philosophy has seen a resurgence of interest in value realism in the broadly axiological tradition.*

1 Introduction
2 The Austro-German school of phenomenology
3 The British axiological tradition
4 The eclipse of value theory
5 The revival of value theory in recent moral philosophy

1 Introduction

'Axiology' is a translation of the German *Axiologie*, which simply means 'theory of value'. Axiology is the branch of practical philosophy which seeks to provide a theoretical account of the nature of values, whether moral, prudential or aesthetic (see VALUES). Values are understood in their tradition to be the proper objects of practical attitudes, analogous to the way truth is the proper object of our theoretical judgments. Historically, there have been three important groups of philosophers whose work can be described under the heading of 'axiology'. One of these is the American school of John DEWEY and C.I. LEWIS (see PRAGMATISM IN ETHICS). The American school was subjectivist; values were viewed as created by subjective interests, in the form of desires. The Austro-German and British traditions, in contrast, were primarily realist or objectivist (see MORAL REALISM §1).

2 The Austro-German school of phenomenology

Historically the earliest group are the value theorists of nineteenth-century Austria and Germany, a group which includes Franz BRENTANO, Alexius MEINONG, Max SCHELER, and Nicolai HARTMANN. Their work has been neglected, not least because of a perceived distinction between 'analytic' and 'continental' philosophy, which came to dominate post-war analytical philosophy to the detriment of both traditions. These philosophers based their approach to practical philosophy on a 'psychological' or 'phenomenological' method which involves giving a precise description of one's experience, freed as far as possible from all presuppositions and all theoretical interpretation, and paying special attention to the objects of experience precisely as they are experienced (see PHENOMENOLOGICAL MOVEMENT). They aimed to give an account of the contents and objects of evaluative acts which paralleled the move towards the investigation of the contents and objects of theoretical judgments on the part of HUSSERL, FREGE and other logical realists at the turn of the century.

The work on value of Brentano (1889) and Meinong (1917) was grounded in Brentano's revision of the medieval concept of intentionality, which he and his successors took to mean the directedness of thought upon its objects (see INTENTIONALITY). Mental acts, for Brentano, are built up out of three elements: the presentation of an object, for example a sense datum; a dimension of positive or negative belief in the existence of the object of the belief; and finally a third dimension called a 'phenomenon of interest'. Just as judgments may be positive or negative, so also phenomena of interest are divided into positive interest phenomena, or 'love', and negative interest phenomena, or 'hate'. Just as some judgments are 'correct' or 'incorrect' according to whether they are marked by a special quality of clear and distinct evidence, so acts of love and hate, too, may be correct or incorrect. Brentano sees the origin of all ethical knowledge as lying in our experience of correct love and hate. At the same time, with his student Christian von Ehrenfels, he emphasized the role of organic unity in constituting valued objects.

Meinong's theory is a refinement of Brentano's doctrine. Meinong, however, objectified Brentano's phenomena of interest, conceiving of the corresponding acts as having special objects of their own in the realms of value and 'oughtness'.

Complementing the Austrian emphasis on the psychological complexities of valuing, the German contributions of Scheler (1913, 1916) and Hartmann (1926) focus on describing the structures of valuable objects. However, both theories also contain a doctrine of the 'emotional a priori' in which emotion serves as an a priori principle of practical thinking, a view influenced by Lotze and by Brentano's theory of correct and incorrect emotions (see LOTZE, R.H.). The phenomenological investigations of Scheler and Hartmann focus on the classification of the objects of practical judgments into classes such as the 'higher' and the 'lower', on the basis of such criteria as permanence, fundamentality, universality and so on. Hartmann's version of the theory has the merit of emphasizing the possibility of tension and conflict amidst this experienced plurality of values (see MORAL PLURALISM). Scheler sought to provide a 'material' ethics doing justice to the vast plethora of different types of things that different agents in different cultures value. He also emphasized the religious aspects of the value pantheon.

3 The British axiological tradition

In the analytical tradition axiological theses are to be found above all in Moore's *Principia Ethica* (1903), and in the writings of Rashdall and Ross (see MOORE, G.E.). Both Moore and Rashdall were 'ideal consequentialists', whose account of right action sees rightness as consisting in the production of goodness (see CONSEQUENTIALISM). Moore's axiological theses in *Principia* reflect to some degree the influence of the Austrian school which Moore admired: Moore's much criticized account of the faculty of moral intuition includes a reference to feeling and the will (see INTUITIONISM IN ETHICS); his account of goodness and beauty is indebted to Brentano, as is his account of 'organic unities' in value; Moore even offers an account of the structure of the value realm, although it is perhaps rather too committed to the idiosyncratic values of the Bloomsbury group to be entirely convincing.

Hastings Rashdall's now neglected *Theory of Good and Evil* (1912) offers an account similar to that of Moore, with the emphasis falling not on organic wholes, but on states of consciousness as the ultimately valuable objects of our judgment. Interestingly, Rashdall also believes that all values are ultimately commensurable (see RASHDALL, H.).

W.D. Ross (1930) was the third great mid-century English axiologist. While his historical reputation rests largely on his neo-Aristotelian account of duty, axiological themes nevertheless run throughout his work, not least because he exploited the principle of Moore's argument against the definability of 'good' to argue that the term 'right' was similarly undefinable. Ross saw the term 'good' as attaching to states of affairs, whereas 'rightness' is predicated of acts. Ross offers a three-fold classification of values, combined with a thesis of value incommensurability that marked his divergence from Rashdall's otherwise similar position (see ROSS, W.D.; RIGHT AND GOOD).

4 The eclipse of value theory

Value theory has been eclipsed in recent Anglo-American analytical philosophy for several reasons: first, the rise of evolutionary psychology; second, the dominance of rational decision theory; third, the dominance of meta-ethical scepticism about the place of values in the world; fourth, the problem of motivational internalism; and finally certain key changes in the modern view of morality itself.

Evolutionary psychology seems to offer an account of the evolution of our 'moral sense' that dispenses with any reference to objective values. Its apparent elimination of objective values on the grounds of their explanatory dispensability has offered a new impetus to ethical scepticism, as illustrated above all in the work of J.L. Mackie and Michael Ruse, although this interpretation of evolutionary theory has been strongly contested, for example by Robert NOZICK. Nozick (1981) argues that an evolutionary account of the moral sense can no more dispense with values than an evolutionary account of perception can dispense with perceptual objects objectively present in the world.

Decision theory seems to be evaluatively neutral, formulating simply the rules a rational agent must employ to determine the means to established ends; it therefore seems to suggest that values are theoretically eliminable, replaceable by subjective preferences (see DECISION AND GAME THEORY §2). Susan Hurley (1989) and Henry S. Richardson (1994), among others, have argued that the theory of practical reasoning cannot be an autonomous theory which can dispense with reference to values. A central line of argument is that decision theory rests on an insufficiently realistic model of the psychology of practical agents and that a more realistic theory must necessarily refer to values. Hurley argues that the theory of practical reasoning embodied in contemporary decision theory cannot be an empirical theory, applicable to real world agents, unless supplemented by assumptions about what agents value.

Moral scepticism questions how values could be part of the world as described by natural science (see NATURALISM IN ETHICS §1); the sceptic cannot see the justification for postulating values as real entities. On this point David Wiggins (1987) and John McDowell concur with the naturalistic realists known as the 'Cornell school', such as Richard Boyd and David Brink (1989). Evaluative properties are postulated just like any other kind of properties: they are theoretical entities which must earn their keep, ontologically, by playing a role in explaining the responses of a rational agent. However, the Cornell school add the further insistence that such properties must ultimately be naturalistically reducible. This claim is resisted by Wiggins and McDowell; the insight of their much misunderstood secondary property model for evaluative properties is that values may be subjective, in the sense of tied to anthropocentric interests of ours, but nevertheless real in the only way any property is real – by pulling its weight in successful explanations (see MORAL REALISM §§4–5).

The problem of motivational internalism marks a major point of divergence between the British and American versions of moral realism. If one accepts the intuition expressed by internalism to the effect that moral judgments necessarily have an impact on action, how can a perception of objective properties explain such a connection? The Cornell realists simply dispense with the intuition and claim that the link between judgment and motivation is contingent – the thesis of externalism (see MORAL MOTIVATION §1). Wiggins and McDowell argue that the connection is secured via a model of the ideal agent, the virtuous person, who is both equipped to perceive moral properties and disposed to assign these perceptions authority in their practical deliberation. Such a model, in their view, offers a defensible version of internalism.

The last reason for the decline in axiology turns on the fact that objective values seem dispensable to a modern conception of the self as autonomous, a spontaneous creator of value, which values freedom and autonomy above all else (see AUTONOMY, ETHICAL). The value theorist can, however, argue that those features of this modern view of morality that seem to make reference to values dispensable in fact rest on suppressed commitments to certain specific evaluative frameworks – frameworks within which our commitment to such values as autonomy and freedom make sense. This is the central argument of Charles Taylor's *Sources of the Self* (1989), which seeks to overcome the philosophical basis of what he correctly calls an 'ethics of inarticulacy', which is based on the modern values of procedural rationality and freedom, but which is, by its own lights, unable to articulate the ways in which our moral commitments are ultimately based in the theory of value.

5 The revival of value theory in recent moral philosophy

Powerful forces, both outside and inside moral philosophy, have conspired to marginalize value theory in contemporary moral philosophy. Yet the foregoing demonstrates that value theory has undergone a considerable revival in recent moral philosophy.

A strong influence on recent developments was the work of the émigré moral phenomenologist Aurel Kolnai; other 'transmitters' of the Austro-German tradition to Anglo-American moral philosophy were J.N. Findlay (1963), R.M. CHISHOLM and Maurice Mandelbaum. Kolnai's work has in turn influenced the account of moral knowledge found in the work of Wiggins and McDowell.

Quite independent 'theorists of value' in contemporary ethics are Platonists such as Iris Murdoch and Neo-Kantian theorists such as John RAWLS and Robert Nozick. Nozick in particular has looked back to the Austrian and German schools of axiology as inspiration for his work, which even includes a delineation of the valuable 'facets of being', including such categories as 'richness', 'completeness' and 'amplitude', in the manner of Scheler and Hartmann.

See also: GOOD, THEORIES OF THE; VALUE, ONTOLOGICAL STATUS OF; VALUES

References and further reading

* Brentano, F. (1889) *Vom Ursprung sittlicher Erkenntnis*, Leipzig: Duncker & Humblot; 4th edn, ed. O. Kraus, Hamburg: Meiner, 1955; trans. R.M. Chisholm and E.H. Schneewind, *The Origin of our Knowledge of Right and Wrong*, London: Routledge, 1969. (Classic presentation of Brentano's views, in English translation.)
* Brink, D. (1989) *Moral Realism and the Foundations of Ethics*, Cambridge: Cambridge University Press. (Representative of the naturalistic moral realism of the 'Cornell school'.)
* Chisholm, R.M. (1986) *Brentano and Intrinsic Value*, Cambridge: Cambridge University Press. (Important and pioneering study of Brentano's theory of value.)
* Findlay, J.N. (1963) *Meinong's Theory of Objects and Values*, Oxford: Clarendon Press. (General study of Meinong's approach to the contents of thoughts.)
  Grice, H.P. (1991) *The Conception of Value*, Oxford: Oxford University Press. (A recent work of value theory which looks to both Aristotle and Kant for an account of the 'construction' of value.)
* Hartmann, N. (1926) *Ethik*, Berlin: de Gruyter; trans. S. Coit, *Ethics*, London: Macmillan, 1932, 3 vols. (Hartmann's comprehensive system in English translation.)
* Hurley, S. (1989) *Natural Reasons*, Oxford: Oxford University Press. (Wide-ranging study, developing a theory of value in the context of the philosophy of mind more generally conceived. Contains an interesting critique of theories of practical reasoning that do not make assumptions about what agents value.)
  Korsgaard, C. (1996) *The Sources of Normativity*, Cambridge: Cambridge University Press. (Presents an account of values from the point of view of the Kantian rationalist tradition.)
* Meinong, A. (1917) *Über emotionale Präsentation*, Vienna: Holder; repr. 'Über emotionale Präsentation' *Sitzungsberichte der Akademie der Wissenschaften in Wien, philosophisch-historische Klasse* 183, 1924; trans. and ed. M.-L. Schubert Kalsi, *On Emotional Presentation*, Evanston, IL: Northwestern University Press, 1972. (Meinong's central work in value theory.)
* Moore, G.E. (1903) *Principia Ethica*, ed. T. Baldwin, Cambridge: Cambridge University Press, revised

edn, 1993. (One of the classic texts of modern moral philosophy and the origin of the modern British tradition in value theory. This revised edition has a valuable introduction by Thomas Baldwin and includes a reprint of 'The Conception of Intrinsic Value'.)

* Nozick, R. (1981) *Philosophical Explanations*, Cambridge, MA: Harvard University Press, part V, chaps 1–6. (The work of contemporary value theory which stands closes to the Austro-German tradition; contains a comprehensive value theory of its own.)
* Rashdall, H. (1912) *The Theory of Good and Evil*, London: Oxford University Press. (Rashdall's central work in value theory, much discussed by other mid-century British moral philosophers).
* Richardson, H. (1994) *Practical Reasoning About Final Ends*, Cambridge: Cambridge University Press. (A recent work which argues that references to values are indispensable to a correct account of practical reasoning.)
* Ross, W.D. (1930) *The Right and the Good*, Oxford: Clarendon Press. (Classic work, cited here for its contribution to value theory in addition to its more well-known account of *prima facie* duties.)
* Scheler, M. (1913, 1916) *Der Formalismus in der Ethik und die materiale Wertethik*, Halle: Max Niemeyer; trans. M.S. Frings and R.L. Funk, *Formalism in Ethics and Non-Formal Ethics of Values*, Evanston, IL: Northwestern University Press, 1973. (Scheler's central work in translation.)
  Smith, B. (1994) *Austrian Philosophy: The Legacy of Franz Brentano*, Chicago, IL: Open Court. (Historical study of Austrian philosophy which offers a comprehensive background account to the Austrian theory of value, especially Brentano's work.)
* Taylor, C. (1989) *Sources of the Self*, Cambridge: Cambridge University Press. (Historically informed history of the modern view of morality, grounded in a value theoretic perspective.)
* Wiggins, D. (1987) *Needs, Values, Truth*, Oxford: Blackwell; revised edn, 1991. (Collected papers of an important contemporary value theorist who defends a view of moral properties as anthropocentrically conditioned, but none the less indispensable to moral explanations and hence real.)

BARRY SMITH
ALAN THOMAS

AXIOM OF CHOICE

The axiom of choice is a mathematical postulate about sets: for each family of non-empty sets, there exists a function selecting one member from each set in the family. If those sets have no member in common, it postulates that there is a set having exactly one element in common with each set in the family. First formulated in 1904, the axiom of choice was highly controversial among mathematicians and philosophers, because it epitomized 'non-constructive' mathematics. Nevertheless, as time passed, it had an increasingly broad range of consequences in many branches of mathematics.

1 History of the axiom
2 Philosophical questions surrounding the axiom
3 Mathematical theorems that need the axiom

1 History of the axiom

Consider a whimsical example, due to Bertrand Russell, illustrating the need for an axiom of choice (stated above). Suppose a millionaire buys as many pairs of socks as pairs of boots and suppose that at last he has infinitely many pairs of each. Then (1) he has exactly as many boots as he does pairs of boots, and (2) he has exactly as many socks as he does pairs of socks. To show (1), we make use of the fact that there is a rule to pick a boot from each pair (for example, the left one). To establish (2) we must be able to pick a sock from each pair. Leaving aside artificial devices, such as the position of socks in space, there is no way to distinguish a sock in each pair and hence no way to prove (2). The axiom of choice implies the existence of such a choice from each pair, even when no rule is available to make the choice.

Thus the axiom involves infinitely many choices from sets. Despite misunderstandings by some philosophers, it has nothing to do with a single choice from a set or even with a finite number of choices, since these are already validated by first-order logic. Nor does the axiom concern the empirical possibility of actually doing the choosing, although this red herring was once taken seriously.

When first formulated by Ernst ZERMELO in 1904, the axiom of choice was highly controversial. It led a number of British, French and German mathematicians to consider the philosophical side of mathematics, and induced several of them, especially in France, to adopt various constructivist philosophies of mathematics (see CONSTRUCTIVISM IN MATHEMATICS). At issue was the question of what is meant by 'existence' in mathematics.

The axiom of choice also motivated the axiomatization of set theory. Concerned primarily to defend this axiom against its numerous critics and secondarily to avoid the contradictions recently discovered (see PARADOXES OF SET AND PROPERTY), Zermelo axiomatized set theory in 1908. The axiom of choice figured prominently in his axiomatization. It turned out that many mathematical theorems required the axiom, and quite a few were actually equivalent to it (see §3 below).

The axiom is intimately involved with the emergence of important techniques for constructing models of set theory in first-order logic. The first such technique (1938) was Kurt Gödel's constructible sets (see CONSTRUCTIBLE UNIVERSE). The second (1963) was Paul Cohen's method of forcing. These techniques established that the axiom of choice is consistent with the usual axioms of set theory, but also independent from them.

2 Philosophical questions surrounding the axiom

Today almost all mathematicians accept the axiom of choice, although many still remark when they use it. Earlier, Zermelo defended the axiom against its critics on two grounds: its usefulness and its self-evidence. He remarked that it had already been widely used, without being formulated explicitly. Such widespread use, he argued, could only be explained by the axiom's self-evidence.

Opponents of the axiom had various views. Some, such as Emile Borel, accepted the axiom when applied to a denumerable family of sets, but rejected it when applied to a family of larger cardinality, such as the set of all real numbers. Others, including René Baire, tentatively accepted the real numbers but argued against the existence of the set of all subsets of the real numbers, from which subsets Zermelo's choices were made. Many opponents rejected the axiom because it provided no rule for making the choices. Apparently thinking of axioms in the traditional way as self-evident truths, they often failed to understand that the axiom is needed precisely when no rule is available.

Opponents were encouraged by the axiom's counter-intuitive consequences. The most vivid of these was the Banach–Tarski paradox, whereby a sphere S can be decomposed into a finite number of pieces and reassembled into two spheres each of the same size as S. The three-dimensionality is important here, since such a decomposition cannot be done with a two-dimensional figure such as a circle. Euclidean geometry also plays a role, since hyperbolic geometry (in which the parallel postulate is false) allows the various counter-intuitive decompositions without using the axiom.

The irony for the axiom's opponents was that if set theory is understood in a sufficiently constructivist way, then the axiom is true. In the extreme case, when all sets are finite, the axiom is true but trivial. If set theory is restricted to Gödel's constructible sets, then again the axiom is true but now distinctly non-trivial. It is only when set theory is taken in a non-constructive way that the axiom might be false. Even in intuitionism, various restricted forms of the axiom are true, but their meaning is changed since the underlying logic is not first-order logic (see INTUITIONISM).

3 Mathematical theorems that need the axiom

Zermelo introduced the axiom of choice to prove the well-ordering theorem: every set can be well-ordered (see SET THEORY). Previously Georg Cantor had assumed this well-ordering theorem as a 'law of thought', but mathematicians had been sceptical. Zermelo showed that the well-ordering theorem follows from an axiom that is conceptually much simpler: the axiom of choice.

The axiom of choice is vital to the arithmetic of infinite cardinal numbers. In particular, it is equivalent to the proposition that if two cardinals are unequal, then one is greater than the other. It is needed in order to define the addition or multiplication of infinitely many cardinals.

Various definitions of the finiteness of a set involve the axiom. The usual definition says that a set M is finite if it is empty or if there is some counting number n such that M can be put into one-one correspondence with $\{1,2,\ldots,n\}$; otherwise M is infinite. Richard Dedekind formulated the first definition that made no use of numbers. A set M is said to be 'Dedekind-infinite' if there is a one-one function from M to a proper subset of itself; otherwise, M is 'Dedekind-finite'. The philosophical significance of this definition is not only that it dispensed with numbers but also that the infinite is defined positively, rather than as the absence of some property. Intuitively, a set should be finite if and only if it is Dedekind-finite, but this equivalence requires a weak form of the axiom of choice. Moreover, there are definitions of finiteness whose equivalence to the usual definition is itself equivalent to the axiom.

The axiom permeates most branches of mathematics, except geometry. Without the axiom, much of algebra, analysis and topology would not exist. A typical algebraic theorem equivalent to the axiom is that every vector space has a basis. In topology, an equivalent theorem is the proposition that the product of compact topological spaces is compact. In analysis, we rarely need the full strength of the axiom but can get along with a weaker assumption: the principle of dependent choices. This principle asserts the existence of a sequence of choices, each depending on the finitely many choices previously made.

In logic, the axiom of choice also plays an essential role in many important results. It is needed to prove the completeness theorem for first-order logic, as well as the compactness theorem and the completeness theorem for propositional logic, provided that the set of primitive symbols of the logic may have any infinite cardinality. With such a language, the downward Löwenheim–Skolem theorem is also equivalent to the axiom: every model of an infinite set M of sentences has a model whose cardinal is at most that of M (see LÖWENHEIM–SKOLEM THEOREMS AND NON-STANDARD MODELS; MODEL THEORY). It is ironic, and of philosophical significance, that the axiom must be used to prove, via forcing, that there exists a model of set theory in which the axiom is false.

The axiom of choice is implied by various stronger propositions in set theory, such as the axiom of constructibility and the generalized continuum hypothesis (see CONSTRUCTIBLE UNIVERSE; CONTINUUM HYPOTHESIS). Another such proposition, which, unlike those two, is very intuitive, was discovered by John von Neumann: a class M is a proper class (that is, not a set) if and only if M can be put into one-one correspondence with the class of all sets. This beautiful proposition turns Burali-Forti's paradox (see PARADOXES OF SET AND PROPERTY) into an argument that the universe of all sets is well-ordered, and illustrates how paradoxical results, if viewed correctly, can often be transformed into useful theorems.

See also: LOGICAL AND MATHEMATICAL TERMS, GLOSSARY OF

References and further reading

Jech, T.J. (1973) *The Axiom of Choice*, Amsterdam: North Holland. (A careful study of the independence results surrounding the axiom.)

Moore, G.H. (1982) *Zermelo's Axiom of Choice: Its Origins, Development, and Influence*, New York: Springer. (A detailed historical treatment of the axiom from its prehistory to the independence proofs. An appendix gives a translation of the most important document by the French opponents of the axiom.)

Rubin, H. and Rubin, J.E. (1985) *Equivalents to the Axiom of Choice II*, Amsterdam: North Holland. (Statements of many propositions equivalent to the axiom, with proofs.)

Russell, B.A.W. (1919) 'Selections and the Multiplicative Axiom', in *Introduction to Mathematical Philosophy*, London: Allen & Unwin; repr. London: Routledge, 1993. (An introductory discussion of the axiom of choice, which Russell calls the multiplicative axiom, by one of its most prominent philosophical opponents.)

GREGORY MOORE

AYER, ALFRED JULES (1910–89)

A.J. Ayer made his name as a philosopher with the publication of Language, Truth and Logic *in 1936, a book which established him as the leading English representative of logical positivism, a doctrine put forward by a group of philosophers known as members of the Vienna Circle. The major thesis of logical positivism defended by Ayer was that all literally meaningful propositions were either analytic (true or false in virtue of the meaning of the proposition alone) or verifiable by experience. This, the verificationist theory of meaning, was used by Ayer to deny the literal significance of any metaphysical propositions, including those that affirmed or denied the existence of God. Statements about physical objects were said to be translatable into sentences about our sensory experiences (the doctrine known as phenomenalism). Ayer further claimed that the propositions of logic and mathematics were analytic truths and that there was no natural necessity, necessity being a purely logical notion. Finally the assertion of an ethical proposition, such as 'Stealing is wrong', was analysed as an expression of emotion or attitude to an action, in this case the expression of a negative attitude to the act of stealing.*

During the rest of his philosophical career Ayer remained faithful to most of these theses, but came to reject his early phenomenalism in favour of a sophisticated realism about physical objects. This still gives priority to our experiences, now called percepts, but the existence of physical objects is postulated to explain the coherence and consistency of our percepts. Ayer continued to deny that there were any natural necessities, analysing causation as consisting in lawlike regularities. He used this analysis to defend a compatibilist position about free action, claiming that a free action is to be contrasted with one done under constraint or compulsion. Causation involves mere regularity, and so neither constrains nor compels.

1 Life
2 Verificationism
3 Perception
4 Knowledge
5 Ethics

1 Life

A.J. Ayer was educated at Eton and Christ Church, Oxford. As an undergraduate he formed an interest in philosophy and was encouraged by Gilbert RYLE to spend some time in Vienna in 1932. It was at this time that he attended meetings of the Vienna Circle and was converted to logical positivism (see LOGICAL POSITIVISM §4; VIENNA CIRCLE §2). During the Second World War he spent most of his time in military intelligence. After the war he became Grote Professor of Philosophy of Mind and Logic at University College, London, leaving London in 1959 to become the Wykeham Professor of Logic at New College, Oxford. During this time Ayer became a well-known public figure, appearing in radio and television programmes, and he was knighted in 1970. Ayer took a special interest in encouraging younger philosophers, to whom he was always known as 'Freddie'; and well after his retirement in 1978 he continued to enliven the annual British philosophical meetings (the 'Joint Sessions'). He married four times, including one remarriage, and wrote two autobiographies (1977; 1984).

Philosophically Ayer saw himself as being part of the tradition of British empiricism started by Locke and Hume and continued by Russell. He was a prolific writer, contributing especially to epistemology, but also producing many articles in the philosophy of science and philosophy of mind. In addition he wrote books on Hume, Russell and Moore, Wittgenstein, and the American pragmatists, Peirce and James.

2 Verificationism

The anti-metaphysical doctrines of logical positivism attracted Ayer at least partly because of his adverse reaction to the British idealists F.H. Bradley and McTaggart, who denied the reality of matter, space and time (see BRADLEY, F.H. §5; McTAGGART, J.M.E. §3). Positivism provided Ayer with the weapon he needed to denounce such claims as metaphysical nonsense. That weapon was the verificationist theory of meaning, which divided meaningful sentences into those that were analytically true (or false) and so known a priori, and those that expressed propositions that were empirically verifiable. Sentences purporting to express the traditional metaphysical views were deemed to be either disguised analytic statements, reflecting a decision to use words in a certain way, or nonsensical. Ayer's first book, *Language, Truth and Logic* (1936), formulated the verificationist criterion of meaning and pursued its consequences for various philosophical controversies. The book became notorious partly because of its confident and aggressive style, and partly because of the distinctive theses endorsed concerning the nonsensical nature of assertions of God's existence and the analysis of ethical statements as expressive of our emotions, with no cognitive significance. Given the controversial nature of these claims, much rested on a satisfactory formulation of the positivist criterion of meaning, the verification principle.

In the first edition of *Language, Truth and Logic*, Ayer stipulated that a proposition is strongly verifiable if and only if its truth can be conclusively established by experience, and that a proposition is weakly verifiable if and only if it is made probable by experience. Ayer sharpened this definition of weak verifiability to the following: a proposition is weakly verifiable if and only if an observation statement is deducible from it in conjunction with other premises, and not deducible from those other premises alone. This definition proved too permissive: take *any* sentence 'S' and observation statement 'O'; the latter will follow from 'S' and 'if S then O', without following from 'If S then O' alone. To remedy this defect Ayer reformulated the criterion in the introduction to the second edition of *Language, Truth and Logic* (1946). Here he calls a statement 'directly verifiable' if it is either itself an observation statement, or, in conjunction with other observation statements, it entails at least one observation statement not deducible from these other observation statements alone. And a statement is 'indirectly verifiable' if, in conjunction with other premises, it entails a directly verifiable statement which is not deducible from these other premises alone, and provided that these premises are themselves either analytic, or directly verifiable, or independently established as indirectly verifiable. A statement was meaningful if and only if it was either directly or indirectly verifiable in the above sense.

Unfortunately for Ayer this reformulated criterion of meaning was shown to be too permissive as well. Alonzo Church (1949) showed that one can again render *any* statement meaningful according to the reformulated criterion. Let O_1, O_2 and O_3 be logically independent observation statements and S be any statement.

(1) $(\sim O_1 \,\&\, O_2) \vee (O_3 \,\&\, \sim S)$

is then directly verifiable ((1) in conjunction with O_1 entails O_3). As long as O_2 does not follow from (1) alone, S is then indirectly verifiable, as O_2 follows from S and (1), and (1) is directly verifiable. Furthermore, if O_2 follows from (1) alone then O_2 follows from $O_3 \,\&\, \sim S$, which implies that $\sim S$ is directly verifiable, since O_2 and $O_3 \,\&\, \sim S$ are logically independent. Ayer acknowledged the force of this argument, but retained his belief that verifiability was crucial to meaning. He thought that once the theory of confirmation had been worked out in detail it would be possible to overcome the problems posed by Church.

Most of *Language, Truth and Logic* drew out the consequences of Ayer's verificationist theory of meaning. Material objects were construed as being constituted by actual and possible sense-data. Statements about other minds were meaningful on the basis of their verification by behaviour, whereas statements about one's own mind were not analysed as having a behaviourist basis. As a consequence mental predicates had different meanings, depending on whether they were used in judgments about others or oneself. Past-tense statements were originally thought to be rules for the prediction of the experiences which would verify them, a view which made them translatable into propositions about present and future experience. Ayer retracted this in the introduction to the second edition, where he asserted that the present unobservability of such events was accidental, so past-tense statements could be interpreted as analogous to statements about spatially distant events which we could not see. He proposed that they be analysed as being verifiable by those experiences we would have if we were to 'travel' to the historical event being described (see MEANING AND VERIFICATION §§2–4).

Two categories of expression were given fairly extended treatment in *Language, Truth and Logic*: those of logic and mathematics, and those of morality. The truths of logic and mathematics were too important to be declared meaningless, but Ayer resisted the thought that they were empirically verified. Instead such necessary truths were classified as analytic truths, and as such their truth depended solely on facts about how we used certain terms. For example, given that '$\rightarrow$' had been given a meaning in Russell and Whitehead's system of logic, the a priori proposition '$(q \rightarrow (p \rightarrow q))$' was analytically true. The merits of such an account were famously called into question by Quine (1936, 1951) (see NECESSARY TRUTH AND CONVENTION §1; QUINE, W.V. §8). The category of moral statements was approached differently, and will be discussed later.

3 Perception

Verification of sentences proceeded by singling out a favoured class of sentences – 'observation statements' or 'basic sentences', which were the principal verifiers. There was a great deal of controversy among the positivists as to the nature of these sentences. Given the role they are assigned, they cannot themselves be verified by another set of sentences, so they have to be either self-verifiers or chosen independently of a verification criterion. The latter strategy – conventionalism – was favoured by Otto von Neurath, who persuaded Carnap of its virtues (see CONVENTIONALISM §1). Ayer consistently opposed it, arguing that the use of any independent criterion, such as choosing those basic statements agreed upon by scientists, would require the exercise of some judgment as to what had been agreed (Ayer 1937). This judgment would itself require support; so the proposed independent criterion was accused of presupposing verification by experience. The self-verification option was the only one available.

Ayer's own thought about the nature of basic statements changed after his initial statement of it in *Language, Truth and Logic*, but he never gave up on the idea that the foundations of empirical knowledge were to be found in our sensory experience, in sense data or qualia. Sense-datum statements (or observation statements) formed the foundation because they were minimally committal: their function was simply to record what appeared to us without implying anything further about what may be true. Ayer vacillated as to whether such statements were infallible, but decided that the possibility of their fallibility did not make them unsuitable for their role as basic statements. What was essential was that they could not be false in one of the ways in which statements about physical objects could be false, through the person making the statement being misled by appearances. The beauty of sense-data was that their reality coincided with their appearance. Ayer's account of sense-data was criticized by J.L. AUSTIN (1962), to which Ayer responded vigorously in 'Has Austin Refuted the Sense-Datum Theory?' (1967).

What of our knowledge of physical objects? In *Language, Truth and Logic* and *The Foundations of Empirical Knowledge* (1940) Ayer defended phenomenalism, the view that anything said about ordinary physical objects was translatable into a series of statements about sense-data. After the war he rejected phenomenalism on the grounds that no set of sense-datum statements could entail the truth of a statement about a physical object. In *The Central Questions of Philosophy* (1973) Ayer eventually settled for a form of realism which he called 'sophisticated realism' and which he differentiated from naïve realism, which holds that we directly perceive physical objects. For Ayer, our perceptual judgments about physical objects are always dependent upon an inference, usually implicit, from some more secure base. He claimed that it was possible to describe this base in ways which did not commit one to the existence of any physical objects, and named this epistemological basis the primary system. It consisted of neutral (that is, neither public nor private) qualia, such as loudness or greenness. These qualia form patterns in places and times, from which we postulate the more elaborate secondary system, a theory of 'visuo-tactual continuants'. Once this has been done the experiential basis is reinterpreted as consisting of states of the perceiver which are caused by the postulated physical objects. Critics have held that this view of perception is untrue to the facts of perceptual experience, which they claim is more likely to be veridically characterized as consisting in our awareness of the objects we are looking at, rather than these being postulated to exist on the basis of some more primitive sensory experience (see PERCEPTION §§1–2; PHENOMENALISM §1; QUALIA §1; SENSE-DATA §1).

4 Knowledge

In *The Problem of Knowledge* (1956) Ayer claimed that person a's knowledge that p could be analysed into: (1) p being true; (2) a being sure that p; and (3) a having the right to be sure that p. Clause (1) is deemed necessary because we withdraw attributions of knowledge if we discover that the belief is false. Clause (2) is thought to be more or less obvious. Counterclaims trade on the fact that we often act on the basis of knowledge which we do not consciously admit. Clause (3) is inserted in order to avoid attributing knowledge to the lucky guesser – one who believes that p, and p happens to be true, but where the believer had no right to the belief. Ayer claimed that these three clauses were necessary and sufficient for knowledge.

Most of the subsequent discussion has concentrated on the sufficiency claim. Edmund Gettier (1963) produced examples which appeared to satisfy the three clauses but which did not seem to be a case of knowledge. One such example is that of a man, Smith, who has strong evidence for the belief (1) that Jones owns a Ford. On the sole basis of this evidence Smith forms the further belief (2) that Jones owns a Ford, or Brown is in Barcelona. Jones, as it happens, does not own a Ford, but Brown is in Barcelona. The evidence justifies Smith in believing (1), so justifies his belief in (2), and (2) is true. But, Gettier alleges, Smith does not *know* (2), so Ayer's analysis is wrong. Ayer thought that this type of example did not show that his analysis of knowledge was wrong, but simply that the notion of justification was trickier than initially thought. Once this had been sorted out, the counterexamples would be seen to involve unjustified beliefs (see KNOWLEDGE, CONCEPT OF §4).

5 Ethics

One of the most controversial of the theses advocated by the early Ayer was that moral judgments lacked cognitive significance – they were not verifiable by any distinctive 'moral' facts or experience. They functioned, Ayer claimed, to express our emotions or attitudes. When we say 'Killing people is wrong', we are simply expressing a negative attitude to the actions of killing people. Analogously, when we say 'John is a good person' we are just evincing a positive attitude to John. This became known as the 'boo/hurrah' theory of ethics, as Ayer suggested that negative and positive moral judgments had the same cognitive status as saying 'boo!' or 'hurrah!'. Ayer continued to hold the emotivist theory, as it became known, with the slight emendation that the expression of attitude had a prescriptive element built into it. A positive moral judgment both expressed a 'pro-attitude' and enjoined others to have the same attitude. Ayer also made it clear that the attitude expressed was towards a *class* of acts, so when killing was condemned it was not a particular killing, but all killings, which were condemned.

Emotivism, and more generally the non-cognitivism about ethics which it espoused, has been widely discussed in the subsequent literature. One of the most difficult problems any such theory faces is to account for the status of moral expressions when they clearly do not have the force of expressing an emotion, as when they appear in conditionals. If somebody says, 'If stealing is wrong, then nobody ought to steal', there is no straightforward way of construing the meaning of the component sentence 'Stealing is wrong' as consisting just in the expression of emotion, since the person uttering the conditional may not have any negative attitude towards stealing. It is still a matter of some discussion as to whether this problem destroys the emotivist theory. An additional problem is whether the emotivist theory is accurate in its description of another facet of moral discourse, and that is moral argument. We seem to have moral disputes with one another about the correctness of our moral actions and judgments. On the emotivist theory these arguments are not about moral facts, so they were interpreted by Ayer as either being genuine arguments about nonmoral facts or not being genuine arguments (see EMOTIVISM).

Ayer was puzzled as to whether we were morally responsible for our actions or not. It appears as though determinism, the thesis that all our actions are caused, destroys moral responsibility. We should not be held responsible for what we cannot help doing. On the other hand denying determinism did not seem to provide much support for responsibility either –

making our actions independent of causal control made them independent of control by our minds, so again holding anybody morally responsible for what they cannot control seems misplaced. Ayer sought refuge in compatibilism, the thesis that determinism and freedom are reconcilable. He claimed that the mistake made by incompatibilists was to think that actions being caused entailed that they were compelled or constrained. For Ayer, causation was simply correlation of events, not involving any necessary connection between the events, and so an action could be caused without being compelled. Compulsion and free action were to be distinguished by the type of causation of involved. Ayer remained puzzled about whether this was sufficient for our ordinary concept of moral responsibility to have application (see FREE WILL §1).

List of works

Ayer, A.J. (1936) *Language, Truth and Logic*, London: Gollancz; 2nd edn, 1946. (The first classic statement of Ayer's positivist philosophy. The second edition contains an important new introduction amending the verification principle.)

—— (1937) 'Verification and Experience', *Proceedings of the Aristotelian Society* 46: 137–56. (An attack on conventionalist approaches to basic statements.)

—— (1940) *The Foundations of Empirical Knowledge*, London: Macmillan. (Contains Ayer's most fully worked-out phenomenalism.)

—— (1954) *Philosophical Essays*, London: Macmillan. (Essays on freedom, phenomenalism, basic propositions, utilitarianism, other minds, the past and ontology.)

—— (1956) *The Problem of Knowledge*, London: Macmillan. (Formulates and defends Ayer's account of knowledge, with a discussion of scepticism.)

—— (1963) *The Concept of a Person and Other Essays*, London: Macmillan. (Contains essays on truth, privacy and private languages, laws of nature, the concept of a person, and probability.)

—— (1968) *The Origins of Pragmatism*, London: Macmillan. (On the American pragmatists Peirce, James and Dewey.)

—— (1969) *Metaphysics and Common-Sense*, London: Macmillan. (Essays on knowledge, man as a subject for science, chance, philosophy and politics, existentialism, metaphysics, and Austin on the sense-datum theory.)

—— (1971) *Russell and Moore: The Analytical Heritage*, London: Macmillan. (An extended essay on the origins of analytical philosophy.)

—— (1972a) *Probability and Evidence*, London: Macmillan. (A concise presentation of Ayer's seminal work on the theory of probability and confirmation.)

—— (1972b) *Bertrand Russell*, London: Fontana. (An introduction to Russell's philosophy.)

—— (1973) *The Central Questions of Philosophy*, London: Weidenfeld. (An advanced introduction to major philosophical issues, such as perception, knowledge, freedom and morality.)

—— (1977) *Part of my Life*, London: Collins. (An autobiographical account of Ayer's life up to his appointment to the Wykeham Chair of Logic at Oxford University.)

—— (1980) *Hume*, Oxford: Oxford University Press. (A brief introduction to the philosophy of David Hume.)

—— (1982) *Philosophy in the Twentieth Century*, London: Weidenfeld. (Ayer's views on the major developments in twentieth-century philosophy.)

—— (1984) *More of My Life*, London: Collins. (The second and final part of Ayer's autobiography.)

References and further reading

* Austin, J.L. (1962) *Sense and Sensibilia*, London: Oxford University Press. (Includes Austin's critique of Ayer's account of sense-data.)

* Church, A. (1949) 'Review of *Language, Truth and Logic*', *Journal of Symbolic Logic*, 14: 52–3. (Includes Church's famous criticism of Ayer's criterion of meaningfulness.)

Foster, J. (1985) *A.J. Ayer*, London: Routledge & Kegan Paul. (An excellent book-length study of Ayer's philosophy, concentrating on verificationism and knowledge. Fairly rigorous.)

* Gettier, E. (1963) 'Is Justified True Belief Knowledge?', *Analysis* 23: 121–3. (Classic criticism of Ayer's account of knowledge.)

Honderich, T. (1991) *Essays on A.J. Ayer*, Cambridge, Cambridge University Press. (A set of Royal Institute of Philosophy Lectures on aspects of the philosophy of Ayer.)

Lewis, D.K. (1988) 'Statements Partly About Observation', *Philosophical Papers* 17: 1–31. (A further attempt to resuscitate verificationism about meaning, including a response to Wright 1986.)

Macdonald, G. (ed.) (1979) *Perception and Identity*, London: Macmillan. (Essays presented to A.J. Ayer on his retirement from the Wykeham Chair of Logic, covering most of the topics discussed by Ayer. Includes Ayer's replies to the contributors.)

Macdonald, G. and Wright, C. (eds) (1986) *Fact, Science and Morality*, Oxford: Blackwell. (Essays commemorating the publication of *Language, Truth and Logic*.)

* Quine, W.V. (1936) 'Truth by Convention', in O.H. Lee (ed.) *Philosophical Essays for A.N. Whitehead*, New York: Longmans. (An attack on the proposal that logical truth could be explained by reference to linguistic conventions.)
* —— (1951) 'Two Dogmas of Empiricism', *Philosophical Review* 60: 20–43. (A challenge to the idea that distinguishing between analytic and synthetic truth could be philosophically rewarding.)

Wright, C. (1986) 'Scientific Realism, Observation and the Verification Principle', in G. Macdonald and C. Wright (eds) *Fact, Science and Morality*, Oxford: Blackwell, 1986, 247–74. (A sophisticated attempt to revive Ayer's verificationist criterion of meaningfulness.)

—— (1989) 'The Verification Principle: Another Puncture – Another Patch', *Mind* 98: 611–22. (A response to Lewis 1988.)

GRAHAM MacDONALD

B

BACHELARD, GASTON (1884–1962)

One indication of the originality of Bachelard's work is that he was famous for his writings both in the philosophy of science and on the poetic imagination. His work demonstrates his belief that the life of the masculine, work-day consciousness (animus), striving towards scientific objectivity through reasoning and the rectification of concepts, must be complemented by the life of a nocturnal, feminine consciousness (anima), seeking an expanded poetic subjectivity, as, in reverie, it creates the imaginary.

In common with other scientist-philosophers writing in the first half of the twentieth century, Bachelard reflected on the upheavals wrought by the introduction of relativity theory and quantum mechanics. The views at which he arrived were, however, unlike those of his contemporaries; he argued that the new science required a new, non-Cartesian epistemology, one which accommodated discontinuities (epistemological breaks) in the development of science. It was only after he had established himself as one of France's leading philosophers of science, by succeeding Abel Rey in the chair of history and philosophy of science at the Sorbonne, that Bachelard began to publish works on the poetic imagination. Here his trenchantly anti-theoretical stance was provocative. He rejected the role of literary critic and criticized literary criticism, focusing instead on reading images and on the creative imagination.

1   An unconventional philosopher
2   The new scientific spirit
3   Dreamers and thinkers, images and concepts

1   An unconventional philosopher

Gaston Bachelard did not enter philosophy through the standard French academic channels. Perhaps because of this, his work is unconventional, both in style and in range of subject matter. Bachelard was born and spent his childhood in Bar-sur-Aube, Champagne. From 1903 until the outbreak of the First World War he worked for the postal service and pursued scientific studies, receiving his *licence* in mathematics in 1912. He was drafted in 1914 and served in the army for the duration of the war. In 1919 he returned to Bar-sur-Aube to teach physics and chemistry at the local college. He had become interested in philosophy and received his *licence* in 1920, his *agrégation* in 1922 and his doctorate, written under the direction of Abel Rey and Léon Brunschvicg, in 1927. From 1930 until he moved to the Sorbonne in 1940 to succeed Rey in the chair of history and philosophy of science, he taught philosophy at the University of Dijon.

Bachelard's influence on philosophy in France has been much greater than accounts of contemporary French philosophy might suggest. He published twelve books on the philosophy of modern science, two on time and consciousness and nine on poetic imagination. These have been widely read, not least because they became an established part of the French university philosophy syllabus. When Bachelard retired from the Sorbonne in 1954, Georges Canghuilhem succeeded him in the chair of history and philosophy of science, and built on Bachelard's approach in his own work in the life sciences. Between them, Bachelard and Canghuilhem recast the disciplines of epistemology, history and philosophy of science in a way which, as FOUCAULT has insisted, is essential to understanding not only his own work, but also that of ALTHUSSER and the followers of LACAN. In France, Bachelard has been criticized by postmodernists for remaining faithful to some of the methods of critical philosophy, and by Marxists for his humanism. His works on poetics inspired many of the French New Critics (see FRENCH PHILOSOPHY OF SCIENCE §§1–2).

2   The new scientific spirit

To have taught science in the early part of the twentieth century is to have experienced dramatic changes in the character of physics and chemistry. Relativity theory and quantum mechanics did not represent simple additions to, or corrections of, existing science; their acceptance entailed the disruption of the whole framework of classical physics, requiring modifications in the concepts of space, time, causality and substance. These are the concepts which, according to KANT, are constitutive not merely of the framework of classical physics, but of our conception of the physical world. As such they are vital to the way in which the distinction is drawn between inner and outer, subject and object. Bachelard's epistemology is the result of absorbing the radical implications of these developments.

The fact that physics has reworked the very categories which Kant took to be a priori, grounded in the nature of the rational subject, invalidates any philosophy which starts from the presumption of a fixed rational framework, whether found in formal logic, the structures of discourse or the rational subject. Similarly, Bachelard argues, science has reworked its empirical base. Sensory observation of given, natural objects has been replaced by the technologically mediated preparation of laboratory objects and phenomena. The objects of scientific investigation are made, not found; they are defined via their method of preparation or technical detection. We have passed from phenomenology to phenomeno-technique. Modern science thus requires us to put aside any epistemology erected on the foundation of the empirically given, whether sense-data or naturally occurring phenomena.

The epistemology of modern science cannot, therefore, be accommodated within a foundational epistemology, whether rationalist or empiricist; it is necessary to move to the open rationality of a non-Cartesian epistemology. As Bachelard reaches this conclusion he is led to introduce new concepts expressed in unfamiliar terminology: 'epistemological break' ('rupture'), 'epistemological value', 'epistemological obstacle', 'recurrent history' and the distinction between 'lapsed' and 'sanctioned' knowledge (see INCOMMENSURABILITY §1; KUHN, T.S. §2–3).

Bachelard finds the clearest examples of what he calls 'dialectical reasoning' in mathematics. This is the reasoning characteristic of the open rationality of the new scientific spirit, which must reject the closed rationality of classical science as it moves beyond it and is aware of its own transitions. Bachelard's sense of dialectic is very much his own, and is not to be confused either with Hegelian or Marxist dialectic. A dialectical move, such as that from Euclidean to non-Euclidean geometry, takes one from a limited system, a framework which is closed in a certain respect, to one which is more general by being open in this respect. A dialectical development constitutes an 'epistemological break' because it introduces cognitive discontinuities, forcing far-reaching conceptual innovations on the one hand and reorganization and re-evaluation of cognitive fields on the other. In the case of geometry, the terms 'straight line' and 'space' continue to be used, but current concepts stand in no simple logical relation to their Euclidean/Newtonian predecessors. Although a straight line may still be the shortest distance between two points, the characteristics of lines with this property are now systematically related to the character of the space in which they occur. Moreover, a clear distinction is made between mathematical spaces and physical space, where previously there had been what, with hindsight, we judge to have been a complex but unclarified relation, presumed to be unproblematic only because it was taken for granted. In this sense the concept of space has been 'rectified' or 'corrected'.

The discontinuity involved in this epistemological break is not merely a disruption of logical relations; it requires a re-evaluation both of what was taken in the past to be geometrical knowledge, and of the relation between physics and mathematics. The 'epistemological value' attached to past proofs changes. The deductions are not discarded, but Euclid's theorems can no longer be treated as demonstrations of the properties of physical space. A dialectically advancing science will thus engage in periodic reassessments of the epistemological value to be attached to past science, or to what was in the past thought to be science, giving rise to what Bachelard calls 'recurrent history' of science. This history is evaluative; it evaluates the past of science from the standpoint of the present, distinguishing between those parts of past science which are 'sanctioned' (as having constituted progress) and those which are ignored because they are no longer valued ('lapsed science').

'Epistemological obstacles' are those (subjective) factors which contributed to the conviction that, for example, the parallel postulate was a necessary truth, something not open to questioning. They can only be identified with hindsight, after a break has been made and accepted as constituting a progressive move (a move towards greater objectivity). The factors which made the move difficult, which contributed to the closure of thought, then appear as factors which had to be overcome if progress was to be possible. These factors are necessarily hidden to consciousness while they are operative, since they result in the perception of something as self-evident, as beyond question. Epistemological obstacles thus have to be sought not in the cognitive foundations of a discipline, but among the various factors which play a role in shaping thought without our being aware of their operation. So epistemology has to concern itself with factors which condition and limit thought but which operate on a non-conscious, noncognitive level; it cannot restrict itself to considering only logical relations between concepts. Objective knowledge is progressively acquired by overcoming epistemological obstacles; this takes place on the borders of the conscious and the unconscious, between reflective theory and unreflective practice, between subject and object, and involves a continual redrawing of the line between them.

3 Dreamers and thinkers, images and concepts

To move beyond the boundaries set by current concepts, even the scientist must dream or engage in reveries. In Bachelard's opinion, mathematics provides the space within which modern scientists dream. The two aspects of Bachelard's work come together in the figure of the creative thinker who must also be a dreamer and they do so in a way which gives a pivotal role to his highly original philosophy of mathematics, an aspect of his work which has received too little attention.

The axes of poetry and science are, Bachelard says, opposed in the sense that the very law of poetry is to go beyond thought, to take a voyage into the infinite, into an inner realm in which the unreal becomes real, in which images are forged and projected onto the external world. It is in this sense that mathematics is the poetry of science, and this is possible because, and to the extent that, here, as for Kant, there is a special relation between pure formal imagination and the construction of concepts. But even as scientists need to dream to go beyond, and ultimately extend, the boundaries of thought, so too their reveries may take them back to primordial themes, resistant to the teachings of scientific experiment, setting up resistances (epistemological obstacles) to psychological evolution. Drawing on elements of Jung's psychoanalytic theory, Bachelard wants to remind us of the power of elemental images and of the alchemist behind every engineer.

The life of concepts is essentially public. Within scientific communities conceptual boundaries are set by their logical interrelationships. These may be implicitly embedded in reasoning practices and rational standards, or explicitly codified in axioms, law, principles and definitions. The public role of concepts in the quest for objective knowledge is itself open to critical conceptual investigation. The life of images is, however, subjective and private (nocturnal). This is why Bachelard insists that the intellectual criticism of poetry can never lead to the centre where poetic images are formed, hence the image can only be studied through the image, by allowing images to gather in a state of reverie. Bachelard's own writing brilliantly evokes such gatherings of images. It is a form of writing which one cannot respect if one attempts to summarize its content. Bachelard concludes his *La poétique de la rêverie* (Poetics of Reverie) (1960) by saying, 'Since it was written in anima, we would wish that this simple book be read in anima'. And, as he explained at the beginning:

> It is *Anima* who dreams and sings. Dreaming and singing, that is the work of its solitude. Reverie – not the dream [*rêve*] – is the free expansion of all *anima*. It is doubtless with the reveries of his *anima* that the poet manages to give his *animus* ideas the structure of a song, the force of a song.
>
> From that point on, how can we read what the poet has written in an *anima* reverie without *anima* reverie? And that is how I justify not being able to read poets except by dreaming.
>
> ([1960] 1971: 67)

List of works

Bachelard, G. (1928a) *Essai sur la connaissance approchée* (Essay on Approximate Knowledge), Paris: Vrin. (Gives Bachelard's views on mathematics; these shaped his philosophy of science. He also indicates an approach to induction which differs significantly from anything developed in the analytic philosophy of science tradition.)

—— (1928b) *Etude sur l'évolution d'un problème de physique: la propagation thermique dans les solides* (Study of the Evolution of a Problem in Physics: The Propogation of Heat in Solids), Paris: Vrin. (This gives a sense of Bachelard's early views as they emerge in the context of a study in the history of physics.)

—— (1929) *La valeur inductive de la relativité* (The Indicative Value of Relativity), Paris: Vrin. (Here we find the first full exposition of the 'epistemological break (or rupture)'. Bachelard insists on the newness of the theory of relativity and on the way in which it breaks with past thought.)

—— (1932a) *Le pluralisme cohérent de la chimie moderne* (The Coherent Pluralism of Modern Chemistry), Paris: Vrin. (An essay in historical epistemology.)

—— (1932b) *L'intuition de l'instant: étude sur la 'Siloë' de Gaston Roupnel* (Intuition of the Insistent: A Study of Gaston Roupnel's 'Siloë'), Paris: Gonthier. (Bachelard argues against Bergson's isolation of the subject from its world, rejecting his conception of pure consciousness and pure duration.)

—— (1933) *Les intuitions atomistiques: essai de classification* (Atomisitic Intuitions: A Classification), Paris: Vrin. (Another example of the way in which Bachelard uses the history of science as a vehicle for exploring its epistemology.)

—— (1934) *Le nouvel esprit scientifique*, Paris: Presses Universitaires de France; trans. A. Goldhammer, *The New Scientific Spirit*, Boston, MA: Beacon Press, 1985. (A useful introduction to Bachelard's philosophy of science. It is a forceful expression of the idea that scientific reality is dialectically related to scientific reason.)

—— (1936) *La dialectique de la durée* (The Dialectic of Duration), Paris: Presses Universitaires de

France. (In a further move in his polemic against Bergson, Bachelard turns to the adventures of consciousness. The self-proclaimed aim of the work is to present a propaedeutics for a philosophy of space.)

—— (1937) *L'experience de l'espace dans la physique contemporaine* (The Experience of Space in Contemporary Physics), Paris: Presses Universitaires de France. (Critically examines the role of space in substantiating realist views of science.)

—— (1938a) *La psychanalyse du feu*, Paris: Gallimard; trans. A.C.M. Ross, *The Psychoanalysis of Fire*, Boston, MA: Beacon Press, and London: Routledge & Kegan Paul, 1964. (Intended as a companion to 1938b. This marks a turning point in Bachelard's work; he begins to develop a theory of poetic imagination and at the same time discusses fire as an example of an epistemological obstacle.)

—— (1938b) *La formation de l'esprit scientifique: contribution à une psychanalyse de la connaissance objective* (The Formation of the Scientific Spirit: A Contribution to a Psychoanalysis of Objective Knowledge), Paris: Vrin. (A pivotal work, dealing with the boundaries between subjective and objective in the construction of scientific knowledge. Here Bachelard introduces and develops the concept of an epistemological obstacle.)

—— (1939) *Lautréamont*, Paris: José Corti; trans. R. Duprée, *Lautréamont*, Dallas, TX: The Dallas Institute of Humanities and Culture Publications, 1984. (An exploration of analogies between the activities of scientists and poets. Mathematics and poetry are explicitly compared in the context of a discussion of Lautréamont's dynamic imagination.)

—— (1940) *La philosophie du non: essai d'une philosophie du nouvel esprit scientifique*, Paris: Presses Universitaires de France; trans. G.C. Waterston, *The Philosophy of No: A Philosophy of the New Scientific Mind*, New York: Orion Press, 1968. (Contains probably the clearest account of what Bachelard means by dialiectic and the dialectical development of modern science.)

—— (1942) *L'eau et les rêves: essai sur l'imagination de la matière*, Paris: José Corti; trans. E. Farrell, *Water and Dreams: An Essay on the Imagination of Matter*, Dallas, TX: The Dallas Institute of Humanities and Culture Publications, 1983. (A discussion of the relation between form and matter but not in the reasoned language of philosophical theory, rather in the subjective dream life which is shaped by the experience of handling liquids and materials. This leads Bachelard to the concept of the dynamic hand.)

—— (1943) *L'air et les songes: essai sur l'imagination du mouvement*, Paris: José Corti; trans. E. Farrell and F. Farrell, *Air and Dreams: An Essay on the Imagination of Movement*, Dallas, TX: The Dallas Institute of Humanities and Culture Publications, 1988. (Contains a discussion of Shelley's 'Prometheus Unbound' and of the metaphoric link between aspirations to greatness and the idea of taking wing, of soaring into the firmament.)

—— (1948a) *La terre et les rêveries du repos: essai sur les images de l'intimité* (Earth and Reveries of Repose: An Essay on Images of Intimacy), Paris: José Corti. (In many ways this is a continuation and counterpoint to Bachelard 1942, but here the focus is on the matter which is imagined to underlie all form. This leads Bachelard to the notion of material repose.)

—— (1948b) *La terre et les rêveries de la volonté: essai sur l'imagination des forces* (Earth and Reveries of Will: An Essay on the Imagination of Forces), Paris: José Corti. (An exploration focusing on the technically creative impulse and its origin in oneiric hypotheses.)

—— (1949) *Le rationalisme appliqué* (Applied Rationalism), Paris: Presses Universitaires de France. (This work should be read in conjunction with Bachelard 1953. Together they give a sense of the power and originality and fruitfulness of Bachelard's mature philosophy of science.)

—— (1951) *L'activité rationaliste de la physique contemporaine* (The Rationalist Activity of Contemporary Physics), Paris: Presses Universitaires de France. (An illustration of the concept of 'regional rationalism', first worked out in 1949.)

—— (1953) *Le matérialisme rationnel* (Rational Materialism), Paris: Presses Universitaires de France. (Together with 1949 this work constitutes a sustained attack on idealism, Husserlian phenomenology and existentialism.)

—— (1957) *La poétique de l'espace*, Paris: Presses Universitaires de France; trans. M. Jolas, *The Poetics of Space*, New York: Orion Press, and Boston, MA: Beacon Press, 1969. (A counterpart to the earlier explorations of space in the scientific context. Follows up the insights of Bachelard 1929.)

—— (1960) *La poétique de la rêverie*, Paris: Press Universitaires de France; trans. D. Russell, *The Poetics of Reverie*, New York: Orion Press, and Boston, MA: Beacon Press, 1971. (Exploration of the reverie – something that played an increasing role in Bachelard's later works.)

—— (1961) *La flamme d'une chandelle*, Paris: Presses Universitaires de France; trans. J. Caldwell, *The Flame of a Candle*, Dallas, TX: The Dallas Institute of Humanities and Culture Publications, 1988. (A discussion of the relations between humans and things, subjects and objects which rests on uncompromising values concerning the nature of those relations that make us more fully human.)

References and further reading

Lecourt, D. (1975) *Marxism and Epistemology: Bachelard, Canguilhem and Foucault*, trans. B. Brewster, London: New Left Books. (Articulates Marxist criticisms of aspects of Bachelard's epistemology.)

McAllester, M. (ed.) (1989) *The Philosophy and Poetics of Gaston Bachelard*, Washington, DC: Center for Advanced Research in Phenomenology and University Press of America. (Useful collections of papers covering Bachelard's epistemology, his poetics and the relation between them.)

Roy, J.-P. (1977) *Bachelard ou le concept contre l'image*, Montreal, Que.: Les Presses de l'Université de Montréal. (Discusses the relation between Bachelard's epistemology and his poetics.)

Tiles, M. (1985) *Bachelard: Science and Objectivity*, Cambridge and New York: Cambridge University Press. (An introduction to Bachelard's philosophy of science, which compares his approach to that of analytic philosophy of science.)

MARY TILES

BACON, FRANCIS (1561–1626)

Along with Descartes, Bacon was the most original and most profound of the intellectual reformers of the sixteenth and seventeenth centuries. He had little respect for the work of his predecessors, which he saw as having been vitiated by a misplaced reverence for authority, and a consequent neglect of experience. Bacon's dream was one of power over nature, based on experiment, embodied in appropriate institutions and used for the amelioration of human life; this could be achieved only if the rational speculations of philosophers were united with the craft-skills employed in the practical arts.

The route to success lay in a new method, one based not on deductive logic or mathematics, but on eliminative induction. This method would draw on data extracted from extensive and elaborately constructed natural histories. Unlike the old induction by simple enumeration of the logic textbooks, it would be able to make use of negative as well as positive instances, allowing conclusions to be established with certainty, and thus enabling a firm and lasting structure of knowledge to be built.

Bacon never completed his project, and even the account of the new method in the Novum Organum *(1620) remained unfinished. His writings nevertheless had an immense influence on later seventeenth-century thinkers, above all in stimulating the belief that natural philosophy ought to be founded on a systematic programme of experiment. Perhaps his most enduring legacy, however, has been the modern concept of technology – the union of rational theory and empirical practice – and its application to human welfare.*

1 Life
2 Works
3 The division of learning
4 The new logic
5 The idols of the mind
6 Induction
7 Natural philosophy
8 Bacon's influence

1 Life

Francis Bacon was born into the political elite of Elizabethan England. His father, Nicholas, was Lord Keeper; his mother, Anne, sister-in-law to Lord Burghley, the Lord Treasurer. Much of Bacon's career and even some aspects of his philosophy can best be understood as resulting from an upbringing which made him familiar with the exercise of power, and the wealth that came with it. His perspective is always that of an insider, but of one who experienced considerable difficulty in establishing his own position as such.

In 1573 Bacon was admitted to Trinity College, Cambridge. In later recollection at least, he found little to admire in the Aristotelian philosophy to which he was introduced, and still less in the writings of such authors as Peter Ramus, who were becoming fashionable alternatives (see ARISTOTLE; ARISTOTELIANISM, RENAISSANCE; RAMUS, P.). As was usual with undergraduates of his social rank, he did not take a degree. In 1576 he returned to London to train as a barrister at Gray's Inn, an institution with which he was to maintain a much more enduring connection. His father died in 1579, leaving him with only a modest inheritance. Throughout his life Bacon spent freely and lived beyond his income; quite apart from considerable personal ambition, much of his pursuit of office can be seen as an attempt to repair chronic indebtedness.

Though he was elected to successive parliaments from 1581 onwards, Bacon's career did not flourish under Queen Elizabeth, who recognized his abilities but seems to have found his personality unappealing. Burghley was more concerned to advance the career of his own son Robert, later Earl of Salisbury, and Bacon attached himself to Elizabeth's last favourite, the brilliant but insubstantial Earl of Essex. Essex's attempt in 1601 to restore his fortunes by staging an insurrection proved a complete fiasco, and made him liable to prosecution for treason. Bacon adroitly changed sides and prosecuted his former patron with a skill and vigour which provided ample confirmation both of his remarkable talents and of a fundamental coldness of character.

The accession of James I in 1603 presented the prospect – initially unfulfilled – of professional advancement. Bacon was knighted soon after the King's arrival in London, but he had to wait until 1607 before being given his first important office, that of Solicitor General. It was only after the death of Salisbury in 1612 that promotion became truly rapid: in 1613 he was appointed Attorney General, in 1617 Lord Keeper, and in 1618 Lord Chancellor. This last office brought admission to the peerage, first as Baron Verulam (1618) and then as Viscount St Albans (1621).

Bacon's fall was precipitous and catastrophic, though not entirely unpredictable. He had supplemented the income from his office by taking payments from those whose cases he heard, and though this was far from unprecedented it did make him vulnerable to attack. He was also important enough to be a substantial sacrifice to an angry House of Commons, without being so close to James that he could not be dispensed with. At the beginning of May 1621 Bacon was deprived of office, imprisoned – albeit for only a few days – in the Tower of London, fined £40,000, barred from court and prevented from taking his place in the House of Lords.

Despite his best efforts, Bacon never returned to favour. He spent his last five years in retirement, writing incessantly – at first with the hope of regaining office, or at least influence, and then merely to leave a testament to posterity. He died on Easter Day 1626, according to John Aubrey (who had the story from Hobbes) from a cold contracted after an experiment of stuffing a chicken with snow. As has often been remarked, it was a fitting end for so fervent an advocate of experimental science.

2 Works

During the first two decades of his adult life Bacon wrote little, or at least little that survives; it was however in this period that his outlook and basic ideas were formed – certainly by the early 1590s, and probably earlier still; in 1625 he mentioned to a correspondent that forty years earlier he had advocated the reform of learning in a work (now lost) entitled *Temporis Partus Maximus* (The Greatest Birth of Time). The direction of Bacon's interests is apparent in a letter of 1592, written to Lord Burghley, in which he (rather disingenuously) disclaimed any political ambition while simultaneously indicating the scope of his intellectual projects:

> I confess that I have as vast contemplative ends, as I have moderate civil ends: for I have taken all knowledge to be my province; and if I could purge it of two sorts of rovers, whereof the one with frivolous disputations, confutations, and verbosities, the other with blind experiments and auricular traditions and impostures, hath committed so many spoils, I hope I should bring in industrious observations, grounded conclusions, and profitable inventions and discoveries; the best state of that province.
>
> (1857–74 VIII: 109)

These themes, developed and articulated, were to preoccupy Bacon for the remainder of his life. No echo of them was however to appear in print for several years. Apart from some political tracts, the only one of Bacon's writings to be published during Elizabeth's reign was the first edition of the *Essays* (1597); the only portion of this volume of any philosophical significance is a short tract on 'The Colours of Good and Evil', which provides early evidence of Bacon's lifelong interest in fallacies and the pathology of the intellect.

The accession of James I stimulated a new burst of literary activity, of which the most visible result was *The Advancement of Learning* (1605), dedicated to the King and evidently written in the (unfulfilled) hope of munificent royal patronage. This was not the only project to have occupied Bacon's attention during the first years of the new reign. A large number of fragmentary treatises have survived, some in English, some in Latin. Several have strange, enigmatic titles: *Temporis Partus Masculus* (The Masculine Birth of Time), *Valerius Terminus of the Interpretation of Nature with the Annotations of Hermes Stella*, *Filum Labyrinthi* (The Thread of the Labyrinth). Others are more prosaic: *Redargutio Philosophiarum* (The Refutation of Philosophies), *Cogitata et Visa de Interpretatione Naturae* (Thoughts and Conclusions on the Interpretation of Nature). The diversity of the literary form displayed by these works is as striking as their unity of message: Bacon knew at least in outline what he wanted to say, but was undecided as to the most appropriate form in which to say it.

The last of these fragments probably dates from around 1608. For the next twelve years Bacon was increasingly busy with his official duties, and much of the time that remained was spent drafting and redrafting the *Novum Organum*. He did however find time to publish a second expanded edition of the *Essays* (1612) and one new work, *De Sapientia Veterum* (On the Wisdom of the Ancients) (1609), an interpretation of ancient myths as allegories of political and physical doctrine. The same pattern of thought can be found in the unpublished *De Principiis atque Originibus* (On Principles and Origins) (*c*.1610–12?), which also shows the considerable influence of Bernardino TELESIO on Bacon's physical doctrines, as do two other works written around 1612, *Descriptio Globi Intellectualis* (A Description of the Intellectual Globe) and *Thema Coeli* (Theory of the Heavens), both left unfinished and unpublished.

The first instalment of Bacon's chief work, the *Instauratio Magna*, was eventually published with appropriate magnificence in 1620, when Bacon was at the pinnacle of his success. The whole work was to contain six parts, but all that appeared at this stage were a general preface, an outline of the project as a whole (the *Distributio Operis*), an incomplete section of the second part (the *Novum Organum*), and a short *Parasceve ad Historiam Naturalem et Experimentalem* (Preparative towards a Natural and Experimental History).

In the years that followed, Bacon went some way towards filling the lacunae in his original plan. The missing first part was supplied in 1623 by *De Dignitate et Augmentis Scientarum*, a revised and greatly extended translation of *The Advancement of Learning*. Despite its evident incompleteness, nothing more was added to the *Novum Organum*; most of Bacon's efforts went into the natural histories intended to fill Part III, which he rather optimistically planned to produce at the rate of one per month. In the event only two were published before his death: on winds (*Historia Ventorum* 1622) and on life and death (*Historia Vitae et Mortis* 1623), although a work on the condensation and rarefaction of materials (*Historia Densi et Rari*) was also completed in 1623. Bacon's executors ignored this – it eventually appeared in 1658 – but did publish the *Sylva Sylvarum* (1627), a natural history in English filled with some very dubious material, which proved very popular during the remainder of the century, but which provided much material for Bacon's nineteenth-century detractors.

The final three parts of *Instauratio Magna* were never written apart from short prefaces to parts four and five (*Works* II: 687–92). The first of these, *Ladder of the Intellect*, was to contain actual examples of the new method in operation – something closer to perfection than the mere sketches provided in the *Novum Organum*. Part V, *Forerunners, or Anticipations of the Second Philosophy*, would, by contrast, exhibit discoveries made independently of the method, by the ordinary workings of the understanding. The content of the final part, the *Second Philosophy or Active Science*, can only be conjectured; one may suspect that Bacon himself had no very precise idea of what it would contain.

Perhaps the best picture of Bacon's final vision can be found in a work of a very different kind, published in the volume containing the *Sylva Sylvarum* but of uncertain date. *The New Atlantis* is an account of an imaginary voyage to an island in the Pacific Ocean, and of the scientific institution, Salomon's House, found there. Like most utopian narratives, this is deeply revealing of its author and provides the fullest picture we have of Bacon's vision of a reformed, active science, and of the kind of institution that he saw as necessary to its flourishing. It also had a profound influence both on the millennialist, visionary Baconianism of the 1640s and on the founders and early practice of the Royal Society.

3 The division of learning

The Advancement of Learning contains two books, the first on the dignity of learning and the reasons for the discredit with which it was often regarded, the second and much longer on the classification of its various branches; in the 1623 translation this latter was expanded further, and divided into eight books.

The primary division of the branches of learning reflects the faculties of the human mind: history corresponds to memory, poetry to imagination, and philosophy to reason. Philosophy itself has three subdivisions: divine philosophy or natural theology, natural philosophy, and human philosophy, this last including the doctrine of the soul, logic, rhetoric, ethics and politics). Metaphysics is a branch of natural philosophy, concerned with formal and final causes, in contrast with physics which studies the material and the efficient. Metaphysics is a more general and more abstract discipline than physics, and rests on it, just as physics in turn rests on a foundation of natural history. The image is that of a pyramid whose vertex is the summary law of nature, known to God but perhaps beyond the bounds of human enquiry.

Rather unusually, Bacon made a distinction between metaphysics and *philosophia prima* – primitive or summary philosophy. The three main subdivisions of philosophy are not like lines meeting at a point, but like branches of a tree that join in a common stem. Arboreal metaphors of this kind may appear to suggest the Cartesian picture of science, in which the trunk of physics grows out of and is sustained by the roots of an a priori metaphysical system, but the reality is quite different. Bacon's *philosophia prima* is a mere receptacle for such miscellaneous principles as have applications in several different disciplines – for example, that the force of an agent is increased by the reaction of a contrary, a rule with applications in both physics and politics.

Bacon's most important innovation was, however, the close linking of theoretical and practical disciplines. In the Aristotelian tradition these had been kept quite separate, but now (within natural philosophy at least) each speculative discipline was to have its operative counterpart: corresponding to physics there would be mechanics; corresponding to metaphysics, natural magic. Bacon had no illusions about the pervasive fraudulence of the magical tradition, but – as in the parallel case of astrology – he sought reform, not abolition (see ALCHEMY).

This close association of theory and practice was of the utmost importance: Bacon saw the dismal record of earlier natural philosophy as stemming very largely from their divorce. The practitioners of the applied arts had made what progress they had in a purely empirical way, unaided by any method, while the philosophers – especially, although not exclusively, the schoolmen in the universities – had disdained experience and, like spiders, had spun metaphysical cobwebs out of their own insides. The only hope of progress lay in uniting the two approaches.

4 The new logic

The *Novum Organum* has had far fewer readers than either the *Essays* or *The Advancement of Learning*, partly because of its more difficult subject matter, and partly because it was written in Latin; it is, however, Bacon's most remarkable achievement, and the one which he himself regarded most highly. It cost him considerable trouble – William Rawley, his chaplain, described having seen no fewer than a dozen drafts revised year by year in the decade preceding publication. Bacon's chosen form is the aphorism: initially these are short and highly compressed, but as the work proceeds they grow longer. In the second book, clearly less thoroughly revised, Bacon's grip slackens and then loosens altogether, and the aphoristic form is abandoned except in appearance.

As its title makes plain, the *Novum Organum* was intended as an account of a new logic, designed to replace the Aristotelian syllogistic which Bacon saw as having hampered and indeed corrupted the investigation of nature. The full exposition of this is found in Book II; Book I contains a survey of the task and its difficulties.

The basic themes of the *Novum Organum* are set out in the first three aphorisms:

> Man, being the servant and interpreter of nature, can only do and understand so much...as he has observed in fact or in thought of the order of nature: beyond this he neither knows anything nor can do anything.
>
> Neither the naked hand nor the understanding left to itself can effect much. It is by instruments and helps that the work is done, which are as much wanted for the understanding as for the hand. And as the instruments of the hand either give motion or guide it, so the instruments of the mind supply either suggestions for the understanding or cautions.
>
> Human knowledge and human power meet in one, for where the cause is not known the effect cannot be produced. Nature to be commanded must be obeyed; and that which in contemplation is as the cause is in operation as the rule.
>
> (Bacon 1620: i.1–3)

Natural philosophy needs to begin with observation. Though Bacon sharply separated himself from those whom he classed as 'empirics', his objection to them lay in their lack of method and consequent recourse to unsystematic experimentation, not in their reliance on experience itself. Method is absolutely essential: unmethodical experimentation is mere groping in the dark, and is no more likely to produce results than digging for buried treasure on a purely random basis.

It is an essential feature of the new method that it can be openly described, explained and taught. The new reformed science is seen as an essentially collective activity; though undoubtedly presupposing a certain minimum of intelligence in its operatives, such an enterprise does not require, and is therefore not dependent on, the appearance of individual genius:

> But the course I propose for the discovery of sciences is such as leaves but little to the acuteness and strength of wits, but places all wits and understandings nearly on a level. For as in the drawing of a straight line or perfect circle, much depends on the steadiness and practice of the hand, if it be done by aim of hand only, but with the aid of rule or compass, little or nothing; so it is exactly with my plan.
>
> (Bacon 1620: i.61)

There is therefore nothing intuitionistic about Bacon's approach, nothing at all resembling the Cartesian reliance on clear and distinct ideas. Bacon distrusted any appeal to the supposedly self-evident at the outset of any enquiry. Validation could only be retrospective:

it was the ability of a theory to endow its holders with power over nature that provided the best, and indeed the only genuinely satisfactory, evidence for its truth.

Previous attempts at discovery had failed because men had either complacently supposed the mind already to be adequately equipped for the task, or else had despaired altogether. Nature is comprehensible, but its subtlety far exceeds that of the human mind. In order for anything to be achieved, a new logic based not on the *anticipation* but on the *interpretation* of nature needs to be brought into use.

This contrast between anticipation and interpretation is central to Bacon's conception of his project. Anticipations are not hypotheses, but rather 'the voluntary collections that the mind maketh of knowledge; which is every man's reason' ([c.1603] 1857–74 III: 244). The root idea is one of superficiality: these are the notions of 'folk physics' – popular ordinary-language concepts such as arise in the ordinary conduct of life, sometimes refined and made more abstract by the labours of philosophers, but not fundamentally altered. 'There is no stronger or truer reason why the philosophy we have is barren of effects than this, that it has caught at the subtlety of common [*vulgarium*] words and notions, and has not attempted to pursue or investigate the subtlety of nature' ([c.1607] 1857–74 V: 421).

It was the all-pervasive unsoundness of the concepts used that made the old logic useless as a tool for the investigation of nature. Syllogisms incorporating confused and badly abstracted terms merely propagate error without supplying any means of correcting it; more generally, the teaching of deductive logic encourages the natural tendency of the mind to ascend hurriedly and without due examination to propositions of great generality, and then to regard these as securely established when investigating further. Bacon's method requires not the liberation but the regulation of the intellect, which *'must not... be supplied with wings, but rather hung with weights, to keep it from leaping and flying'* (1620: i.104).

Just as syllogisms are useless for any enquiry into nature, so too is the induction by simple enumeration described in logic textbooks. Bacon consistently regarded this with contempt – 'childish' was his favourite term of abuse. It operated on the surface of things, employing 'popular' notions, and was for that reason incapable of delivering certainty. Bacon was no fallibilist, prepared to settle for a natural philosophy of conjectures and merely provisional conclusions. Certainty was quite as important for him as it would be for Descartes, but what he was looking for was certainty of a very different kind – not immunity from sceptical doubt, but complete reliability. This could be furnished by induction, but it would have to be induction of a new and much more elaborate kind, one that could make use of negative as well as positive instances.

5 The idols of the mind

Before the new logic could be put to use, the weaknesses of the human mind which it was designed to correct or evade needed to be analysed. The central section of Book I is a counterpart to the analyses of sophistical reasoning provided in the logic textbooks. What emerged, however, was not merely a list of inductive fallacies, but rather one of the most memorable and original parts of Bacon's system.

Bacon distinguished four classes of idols. The 'Idols of the Tribe' arise from the limitations of human nature; they can be allowed for and guarded against, but not removed entirely. Bacon had in mind such weaknesses as the tendency to suppose more regularity than actually exists, to be over-influenced by the imagination, and even more by hopes and desires. A very different kind of limitation arises from the dullness of the senses. Bacon had no sympathy with radical sceptical doubts of the kind that were to preoccupy Descartes, but he was acutely aware of the weakness of the human senses, and of their complete incapacity to discern the secret workings of nature. The problem was not one to be abandoned to sceptical despair or solved by metaphysical validation. Some assistance could be gained from the use of instruments, but the real solution lay in experimental design. Hidden processes would be linked with observable consequences, and an experimental determination of the latter would reveal the nature of the former.

The 'Idols of the Cave' arise from the idiosyncrasies of individuals, either natural or implanted by education. Some minds are good at seeing distant resemblances, others at making fine distinctions; some are attracted to ancient wisdom, or what might pass for it, others only to novelty; almost everyone is influenced by those disciplines which they know well, and even more by those to which they have contributed.

The 'Idols of the Forum' (or 'Idols of the Market Place') arise from the deficiencies of human speech. Bacon had no respect for the categories of ordinary language, or the habitual thought-patterns of the uneducated; 'popular' is in his lexicon almost invariably a term of disparagement. Words devised for the ordinary purposes of life cannot provide a satisfactory vocabulary for natural philosophy, and attempts to remedy the situation by making definitions achieve nothing: words are defined by other words, which themselves share the same defects.

These three classes of idols can be guarded against and to some extent allowed for, but never extirpated entirely. The fourth class is in this respect different. This consists of the 'Idols of the Theatre' – the point of the name was that rival philosophies were like stage-plays, with different casts and different plots, but all equally fictitious. The potential variety of such systems is clearly unlimited, but Bacon distinguished three main types. The natural philosophy of Aristotle and his followers was corrupted partly by logic, and partly by a reliance on common notions – popular conceptions quite unsuited to the task in hand. The empirical school (exemplified by the alchemists, but also including William Gilbert who investigated magnetism) was misled by too narrow a line of experimental enquiry: restricted ranges of data fill the imagination and lead to one-sided accounts of the world in chemical or magnetic terms. Platonism (Bacon had in mind not so much the doctrines of Plato himself – whom he generally treats with respect – as the Platonism of his own era) (see PLATONISM, RENAISSANCE) was worst affected of all, being corrupted by theology and superstition. Bacon's own religious views are by no means easy to discern and have been very diversely interpreted, but one thing that is abundantly clear is that he was wholly opposed to the intrusion of religious doctrines, Christian or non-Christian, into natural philosophy; the result of allowing this to happen was a corruption of both, into a superstitious philosophy and a heretical religion.

6 Induction

Bacon's methodological proposals occupy Book II of the *Novum Organum*. The first stage in any investigation is the gathering together of a natural and experimental history. This might be quite broad in scope – for example, the history of heat in aphorisms 11–18 – but it could be much more narrowly focused: Bacon's own examples include histories of the rainbow, of honey and of wax. The idea of a natural history was an old one, going back through numerous Renaissance and medieval encyclopedias to Pliny, and ultimately to Aristotle's *Historia Animalium*. Bacon, however, made an innovation of crucial importance. His histories would record not only material gathered from the ordinary workings of nature, but also novel phenomena generated by human activity. In the Aristotelian tradition such artefacts would have been discounted as inappropriate material for investigation; Bacon, however, saw them not merely as legitimate subjects of enquiry, but as especially valuable: 'by the help and ministry of man a new face of bodies, another universe or theatre of things, comes into view' (1857–74 IV: 253). Nature was to be put to the question – a contemporary euphemism for torture.

Histories of this kind could not be assembled quickly, and the whole project would clearly absorb a very large amount of labour and money. Bacon was acutely aware of this, but could see no alternative. The human understanding needed to be purged and cleansed, and this had to be done not by any Platonic (or Cartesian) detachment from the data of the senses, but by an immersion into the world of experience in its full individuality and variety. Bacon was a good nominalist in the English tradition: for him, individuals alone are real and our most reliable cognitions are our direct sensory awareness of them. Withdrawal to a world of abstract objects supposedly accessible to reason leads merely to illusion and the enunciation of empty generalities; for Bacon the word 'abstract' – like 'popular' – almost invariably carries negative connotations.

We have to begin, therefore, with particulars; we have also to begin with as full a range of particulars as possible. Bacon did not require all this data to be correct, though manifestly false material ought to be kept out where possible, and dubious reports marked as such. Some falsehoods were bound to creep in, but these could be dealt with; what could not be dealt with were biases which affected the whole history. Initial attempts to impose criteria of relevance had therefore to be outlawed altogether.

Most histories would contain an immense quantity of data – far too much for any individual human mind to grasp as a whole – and an ordering of this material into some kind of structure was essential. Bacon proposed the use of three tables: first a 'Table of Essence and Presence', listing all the situations in which the nature under investigation is present; then a 'Table of Deviation or Absence in Proximity', describing all those situations which are as close as possible to those in the first table but where the nature under investigation is absent; and finally a 'Table of Degrees or Comparison', a list of those situations where the nature in question varies in intensity, together with details of the circumstances accompanying that variation.

When first drawn up, the second and third tables would both, in general, be incomplete in that they would contain gaps corresponding to entries in the first. One of the chief functions of experiment was to remedy these defects: for example, given that the rays of the sun can be concentrated by a convex lens, a trial should be made to see whether such lenses can produce heat by focusing the rays of the moon, or any rays proceeding from heated stones or vessels containing boiling water.

When the tables have been drawn up it is possible to begin the inductive process itself:

> The first work therefore of true induction...is the rejection or exclusion of the several natures which are not found in some instance when the given nature is present, or are found in some instance where the given nature is absent, or are found to increase in some instance where the given nature decreases, or to decrease where the given nature increases.
>
> (1620: ii.16)

Only when this process of exclusion has been completed will it be possible to grasp the true essence (or form, to use Bacon's own term) of the nature in question.

This method clearly rests on several presuppositions, of which the most fundamental is a principle of limited variety. Though the world as we experience it appears unendingly varied, all this complexity arises from the combination of a finite, and indeed quite small, number of simple natures. There is an alphabet of nature, which cannot be guessed or discovered by speculation, but which will start to be revealed once the correct investigatory procedures are employed. The time needed is indeed not merely finite but quite short: once the natural histories are complete, the unearthing of all the secrets of nature will require no more than a few years.

Bacon also assumed there to be a direct one-to-one correlation between natures and the forms from which they arise. He was aware that critics might deny this and maintain (for example) that the heat of the heavenly bodies and of fire, or the red in a rose and in a rainbow, are only apparently similar, having quite different causes in reality. Bacon firmly denied this – however apparently heterogeneous, these things agree in the forms or laws which govern heat and redness; indeed even such diverse modes of death as by drowning, by hanging and by stabbing agree in the form or law which governs death.

This way of thinking reinforces a tendency already present in the alchemical tradition of considering bodies as collections of simple natures, each explicable (and therefore reproducible) in isolation. Bacon certainly did think in this way: gold is yellow, heavy, ductile, fixed (that is, unaffected chemically by fire) and so on. Whoever knows the forms of these natures can attempt to join them together in a single body, and thereby transform that body into gold. At other times, however, Bacon seems to have recognized that forms are seldom independent: 'since every body contains in itself many forms of natures united together in a concrete state, the result is that they severally crush, depress, break, and enthrall one another, and thus the individual forms are obscured' (1620: ii.24). They are not, however, hidden altogether: since expansion is part of the form of heat, all heated bodies must expand; but while the expansion of air is easily noticed, that of iron is less manifest to the senses.

The justification of the principles of limited variety and of the direct correlation of forms and natures could always be postponed; another problem, however, had to be faced at the outset. Exclusion involves the rejection of simple natures, 'and if we do not yet possess sound and true notions of simple natures, how can the process of Exclusion be made accurate?' (1620: ii.19). The old logic had proved inadequate because of this deficiency; what grounds are there for supposing that the replacement would fare any better?

Bacon was acutely aware of this problem and of the difficulty it posed for his project. His solution was to propose a series of supports of induction: the account of these occupies the last part of Book II of the *Novum Organum* and is (characteristically) lengthy, elaborate and unfinished; indeed all he managed to describe was the first of his nine kinds of support, the 'Prerogatives of Instances', of which he distinguished no fewer than twenty-seven different varieties. Bacon's account of these exhibits, perhaps more clearly than any other passage in his writings, the distinctive strengths and weaknesses of his mind. The discussion is often shrewd and sometimes much more – the *instantia crucis* has passed into modern science, under the name of a crucial experiment – but Bacon's addiction to elaborate systems of classification and portentous schemes of nomenclature is frequently apparent, above all in the nineteen species of motion described in aphorism 48. The immensity of his intellectual distance from such contemporaries as GALILEO is nowhere more apparent than it is here.

7 Natural philosophy

Bacon's intellectual gifts were remarkable, but they were not those of a scientist. He was a lawyer, and it was here, as well as with human affairs in general, that his real area of expertise can be found. He was widely read in natural philosophy, but his approach remained that of an outsider, albeit a shrewd and exceedingly intelligent one. These limitations become particularly apparent when Bacon turned to astronomy, the most highly developed of all contemporary scientific disciplines. He rejected Copernicanism and, although he saw many of the weaknesses of the inherited astronomical tradition, unlike Kepler he had only vague and quite unhelpful ideas about how it might be reformed.

Bacon's own physics was fundamentally non-mechanistic. Bodies contain two types of matter – tangible and spiritual – and the operation of the latter, although never explained clearly, is certainly not conceived in mechanistic terms. Bacon did, however, employ several ideas that were to be taken over by the mechanical philosophers who followed him, in particular that the observable qualities of bodies are to be explained by the constitution of their internal parts. Glass can be made white by being crushed into tiny fragments, and water white by being beaten into foam; heat is not a scholastic real quality but a kind of motion. Later Baconians such as BOYLE and Hooke were able to take over these ideas and express them in more unambiguously mechanistic terms.

8 Bacon's influence

Bacon's philosophical writings met with little appreciation in England during the 1620s and 1630s. Admirers of the older learning, from James I downwards, were for the most part uncomprehending, and the one major scientist then practising, William Harvey, was brutally dismissive. Bacon had more impact in France, where he was carefully read by MERSENNE, GASSENDI and DESCARTES, but even they only responded to selected parts of the system, notably the 'Idols' and the appeal to experiment.

The political turmoil in Britain in the 1640s stimulated a new interest in Bacon's thought, both among the advocates of universal reform like Samuel Hartlib, and among such natural philosophers as Robert Boyle and Robert Hooke. Baconianism indeed became the official philosophy of the Royal Society, celebrated in Thomas Sprat's semi-official *History* (1667). The hopes thus stimulated, however, proved difficult to satisfy. NEWTON paid little attention to Bacon, and the *Principia* was an achievement utterly unlike anything projected in the *Novum Organum*. Locke's debt was rather greater, especially in *The Conduct of the Understanding*, but by the early eighteenth century interest in Baconianism had started to decline.

Following the example of Voltaire, the French encyclopedists treated Bacon with great respect as an empirical, essentially secular thinker, to be contrasted favourably with Descartes who was now seen as scientifically discredited and too deferential to the Church. In Britain Bacon was ignored by HUME, but admired by REID who helped create a widely influential methodological synthesis of Baconian and Newtonian ideas.

The Baconian revival reached its climax in the second quarter of the nineteenth century. Sir John Herschel's *Preliminary Discourse on the Study of Natural Philosophy* (1830) was a thorough attempt to recast Baconianism in a form compatible with contemporary science. John Stuart MILL and William WHEWELL, though disagreeing about almost everything, both acknowledged a deep debt to Bacon, and to the inductive method of science. The most accessible introduction to early-Victorian attitudes towards Bacon is however provided by Macaulay's essay 'Lord Bacon' (1837). Though respectful towards Bacon's thought, Macaulay took a less favourable view of his character, and it was in response to his account that James Spedding undertook the labours that led to his *Life and Letters* (1857-74: vols VIII-XIV), and to the critical edition of Bacon's works produced jointly with R.L. Ellis and D.D. Heath.

In the latter part of the nineteenth century, Bacon's reputation as a methodologist began to decline. The trend continued after 1900, Bacon's reputation reaching its nadir in the mid-century when Karl POPPER proposed a method for science that eschewed induction altogether, and historians such as Alexandre KOYRÉ offered accounts of the scientific revolution that made Bacon's contribution utterly marginal. Since then there has been a modest revival, but Bacon has still not recovered an assured place in the philosophical canon.

See also: INDUCTION, EPISTEMIC ISSUES IN; INDUCTIVE INFERENCE; TECHNOLOGY, PHILOSOPHY OF

List of Works

Bacon, F. (1857-74) *The Works of Francis Bacon*, ed. J. Spedding, R.L. Ellis and D.D. Heath, London: Longmans, 14 vols. (The standard edition, with prefaces that remain of great value. Volumes I-V contain the *Philosophical Works*, VI-VII the *Literary and Professional Works*, and VIII-XIV the *Life and Letters*.)

—— (1903) *The Philosophical Works of Francis Bacon*, ed. J. M. Robertson, London: George Routledge & Sons. (A convenient one-volume abridgement of the Ellis and Spedding edition.)

—— (1996–) *The Oxford Francis Bacon*, Oxford: Clarendon Press. (Of the twelve planned volumes, volume 6 has appeared – *Philosophical Studies, c.1611-1619*, ed. G. Rees. This contains Latin texts and English translations of a group of works on natural philosophy: *Phaenomena Universi, De Fluxu et Refluxu Maris, Descriptio Globi Intellectualis, Thema Coeli* and *De Viis Mortis*.)

—— (1597) *Essayes or Counsell, Civill and Morall*, London; repr. Oxford: Clarendon Press, 1985. (Later considerably expanded editions were published in 1612 and 1625.)

—— (1605) *The Advancement of Learning*; repr. London: Dent, 1973. (A greatly expanded Latin translation was published in 1623 as *De Dignate et Augmentis Scientarum*.)

—— (1609) *De Sapientia Veterum* (Wisdom of the Ancients), London; Kila, MT: Kessinger Publishing, 1992. (An exposition of ancient myths, taken as allegories of philosophical doctrines.)

—— (c.1612) *De Principiis atque Originibus* (On Principles and Origins); repr. in *Philosophical Studies, c.1611–1619*, ed. G. Rees, Oxford: Clarendon Press. (An exposition of Bacon's natural philosophy.)

—— (1620) *Novum Organum*; repr. ed. T. Fowler as *Bacon's Novum Organum*, Oxford: Clarendon Press, 1888; trans. P. Urbach and J. Gibson, La Salle, IL: Open Court, 1994. (Bacon's most important philosophical work, containing a detailed though still important account of his work. Fowler reproduces the original Latin text with very useful notes; Urbach and Gibson offer a good modern translation.)

—— (1627) *New Atlantis*, London; Kila, MT: Kessinger Publishing, 1992. (Incomplete description of a scientific utopia.)

References and further reading

Abbott, E.A. (1885) *Francis Bacon: An Account of his Life and Writings*, London: Macmillan. (Though now very old, perhaps still the most detailed and balanced one-volume biography.)

Coquillette, D.R. (1992) *Francis Bacon*, Edinburgh: Edinburgh University Press. (Deals primarily with Bacon's legal thought, but also his philosophy; good bibliography.)

Farrington, B. (1964) *The Philosophy of Francis Bacon*, Liverpool: Liverpool University Press. (Bacon from a Marxist perspective; contains English translations of *Temporis Partus Masculus* (The Masculine Birth of Time), *Redargutio Philosophiarum* (The Refutation of Philosophies) and *Cogitata et Visa de Interpretatione Naturae* (Thoughts and Conclusions on the Interpretation of Nature), left untranslated by Ellis and Spedding.)

* Herschel, Sir J. (1830) *A Preliminary Discourse on the Study of Natural Philosophy*, London: Longmans. (Discussed in §8 above.)

Jardine, L. (1974) *Francis Bacon: Discovery and the Art of Discourse*, Cambridge: Cambridge University Press. (Links Bacon with debates among his predecessors and contemporaries about the use of rhetoric and dialectic.)

Leary, J.E., Jr (1994) *Francis Bacon and the Politics of Science*, Ames, IA: Iowa State University Press. (Argues for close connection between Bacon's scientific and legal/political projects, but against interpreters who see his work as politically 'progressive'.)

* Locke, J. (1823) *The Works of John Locke*, London: T. Tegg et al., 11th edn, 10 vols; repr. Aalen: Scientia, 1963. (*The Conduct of the Understanding*, a short manuscript posthumously published in 1706, can be found in volume 2.)

* Macaulay, T. (1837) 'Lord Bacon', *Edinburgh Review* (July); repr. in *Critical and Historical Essays*, London: Longmans, 1993. (The most accessible introduction to early-Victorian attitudes towards Bacon.)

Pérez-Ramos, A. (1988) *Francis Bacon's Idea of Science and the Maker's Knowledge Tradition*, Oxford: Clarendon Press. (A detailed and fairly technical discussion of Bacon's theory of induction. Good on Bacon's influence.)

Pentonen, M. (ed.) (1996) *The Cambridge Companion to Bacon*, Cambridge: Cambridge University Press. (A collection of up-to-date surveys, with a full bibliography.)

Quinton, A. (1980) *Francis Bacon*, Oxford: Oxford University Press. (A useful short introduction.)

Rossi, P. (1968) *Francis Bacon: from Magic to Science*, London: Routledge & Kegan Paul. (An important work, stressing Bacon's relation to the magical tradition.)

* Sprat, T. (1667) *The History of the Royal Society of London*, London: J. Martin; facsimile repr. ed. J.I. Cope and H. Whitworth Jones, London: Routledge, 1959. (Mentioned in §8 above.)

Urbach, P. (1987) *Francis Bacon's Philosophy of Science*, Chicago, IL: Open Court. (A sophisticated though sometimes idiosyncratic account.)

Webster, C. (1975) *The Great Instauration: Science, Medicine, and Reform, 1626–1660*, London: Duckworth. (An immensely detailed account of Baconianism in England.)

J. R. MILTON

BACON, ROGER (c.1214–1292/4)

Associated with both the University of Paris and Oxford University, Roger Bacon was one of the first in the Latin West to lecture and comment on Aristotle's writings on subjects other than logic. After he came to know Robert Grosseteste's work in natural philosophy, he became the advocate of a curricular reform that emphasized scientific experiment and the study of languages. His views were often unpopular, and he constantly belittled all who disagreed with him.

Bacon's work in logic and semantic theory had some influence during his lifetime and immediately after his death. His work in science, however, had little impact. His renown in the history of science is due in part to his being viewed as a precursor of the Oxford Calculators, who in turn anticipated certain important developments in seventeenth-century science.

1   Life
2   Views on education
3   Work in science
4   Linguistic work

1   Life

Bacon was born into the minor nobility in Somerset, England. By the time of his death, he had earned the honorific title *Doctor mirabilis* (the Marvellous Doctor) for his prodigious learning in every area of philosophy. He had trained in the Latin classics before attending Oxford University and the University of Paris, and he was Master of Arts at Paris by 1237. At Paris between 1237 and 1247, Bacon wrote his *Sumule dialectices* (Brief Summaries of Dialectic) and *Summa grammatica* (Synopsis of Grammar), and lectured on Aristotelian works, including the *Metaphysics* and *Physics* as well as the pseudo-Aristotelian *De plantis* and *Liber de causis* (see LIBER DE CAUSIS).

During this period, Bacon became intensely interested in another pseudo-Aristotelian text, *Secretum secretorum* (Secret of Secrets), which was thought to have been written by Aristotle for his pupil Alexander the Great. In addition to instruction on kingship, the text contained occult lore ranging from astrology and numerology to the magical medicinal properties of plants, and an account of a unified science supposedly transmitted to Aristotle by God through the Hebrews and Egyptians. According to the treatise, this unified science could be recovered only by those intellectually and morally fit for it.

Bacon was so moved by the vision of knowledge revealed in the *Secretum secretorum* that in 1247 he left his teaching position at Paris, moved back to Oxford and spent the next ten years attempting to realize that vision. His efforts were concentrated on language, mathematics and experimentation because he believed that one could decipher Aristotelian texts only if one understood the nature and nuances of the language in which the texts had been written, or into which they had been translated. He also believed that the study of mathematics (including geometry and astronomy), along with experimentation, provided the key to the sciences. His efforts proved to be physically, emotionally and financially draining.

In 1257 Bacon entered the Franciscan order, hoping to find respect for his work and funds for his scientific instruments. Finding neither, he became embittered, and at every opportunity he railed against those of his contemporaries (such as ALBERT THE GREAT and Thomas AQUINAS) who were taking a more traditional approach to philosophical study. By the early 1260s Bacon had become unpopular among the Franciscans, and was apparently sent to their convent in Paris under an injunction to neither lecture nor circulate his writings outside the Order without approval.

Undaunted, Bacon set about communicating his controversial views to Cardinal Guy le Gos de Foulques. The latter, upon becoming Pope Clement IV in 1265, asked to see the writings in which these views were presented in detail. Although Bacon had not yet actually composed these writings, he managed to do so without his Order's knowledge and to have his work delivered to Clement in 1267. The result, the *Opus maius*, was an encyclopedia of the sciences and a proposal for educational reform. It was followed within the year by synopses, additions and corrections in the *Opus minus* and the *Opus tertium*.

Despite Clement's death during the time these additions were being written, Bacon continued for the next ten years to write on his favourite topics. He produced a Greek grammar, a Hebrew grammar and the *Compendium studii philosophiae* (Compendium of the Study of Philosophy) around 1272. The *Communia naturalium* (General Principles of Natural Philosophy) and *Communia mathematica* (General Mathematical Principles), two surviving sections of a second encyclopedic work begun but never completed, are considered Bacon's most mature work.

Between 1277 and 1279, Bacon's teachings were condemned by the Minister General of the Franciscan Order, Jerome of Ascoli (the future Pope Nicholas IV), and Bacon himself was imprisoned. Why this happened is unclear. Although the official account is that his teachings contained 'suspect novelties' (perhaps some of the propositions condemned in 1277 by Etienne Tempier, the Bishop of Paris), it is possible that his imprisonment came as a response to his refusal to stop verbally abusing everyone whose views he did not share. The targets of this abuse included many of his Franciscan brothers. It is also possible that his imprisonment was the result of the controversial Joachimite views he had embraced (see JOACHIM OF FIORE). Despite these serious problems, Bacon managed before his death some thirteen to fifteen years later to compose at least one more work, *the Compendium studii theologiae* (Compendium of

2 Views on education

In the mid-1260s, Bacon began to insist that the current educational system needed to be completely revised, and that he himself knew exactly what was required. He shared his contemporaries' belief that God is man's ultimate end but, unlike most of them, believed that the pursuit of science should be instrumental in the study of God (and thus in one's pursuit of moral perfection). By understanding the nature of things, one would come to understand the nature of God who made them. Mathematics also figures in this scheme insofar as Bacon considered geometry to be the key to knowing the efficient and generating causes in nature. He believed that mathematics could be used to verify scriptural claims about creation, such as its chronology and geography.

Bacon was also unusual in believing that the study of texts in natural philosophy should be pursued in conjunction with the study of the languages in which the original texts were written, such as Hebrew, Greek and Arabic. He believed that one could also improve one's understanding of Latin with such study, as many Latin words could not be fully understood without a knowledge of Greek. In general, Bacon believed that all study was subordinate to theology and morality, and that the traditionally valued subjects of study such as metaphysics should be ranked below experimental science, mathematics and languages in the hierarchy of academic study. The ecclesiastical authorities in charge of education, he urged, ought to take account of these facts and revise the curriculum accordingly.

These ideas are expressed in detail in the *Opus maius*, along with a general account of why people are in their present predicament with respect to knowledge. Because of sin and humanity's fallen state, truth is difficult for us to discover. We cannot trust reason to provide us with demonstrative proof of anything; but we can use reason to help us formulate hypotheses which can then be confirmed by sense-perception, understood either as ordinary experience or as experience aided by instruments. Reason, according to Bacon, is part of an inner experience which is provided when God illuminates our mind (his debt to AUGUSTINE is evident in this view). However, sin affects our ability to reason in four specific ways. First, we submit to untrustworthy authority; that is, we mistakenly believe sources other than God (in the form of Scripture) or the Church Fathers (who were reliable interpreters of Scripture). Second, we are unduly influenced by long-standing custom, believing that what is traditional must therefore be right. Thus, we give more weight than we should to popular opinion. Fourth, we try to conceal our ignorance with a technical show of wisdom. In this connection Bacon condemned the current practice in the universities of using Peter Lombard's *Sentences* rather than the Bible as a basis for lecturing in theology.

That Bacon was altogether serious about the importance of educational reform is evident not only in his strident disapproval of great men of his day who did not embody the ideals he deemed appropriate – men such as ALEXANDER OF HALES, BONAVENTURE, Albert the Great and Thomas Aquinas – but also in his dedication to the study of optics, the making of experimental instruments and a firm understanding of languages (although he seemed to rely mostly on Latin translations of the treatises he used in his research).

3 Work in science

As already noted, Bacon emphasized the practical objectives of studying both philosophy in general and natural philosophy, or science, in particular. It was his view that science had to do with natural laws that could be expressed or elucidated mathematically, and that true science therefore had nothing to do with magic, which he characterized as a false mathematics based on superstition and the presumption that everything is causally necessitated. His view of mathematics as the key to the sciences seems to have had two sources. First, he accepted Grosseteste's view that everything in the terrestrial and celestial realms is a manifestation of light, the diffusion of which takes place in accordance with laws of geometry (see GROSSETESTE, R.). Second, he believed that mathematical knowledge is certain knowledge insofar as all the other Aristotelian categories depend on a knowledge of quantity, the subject matter of mathematics, and insofar as things known to us and things in nature are absolutely the same only from a mathematical point of view. Given these reasons, it is not surprising that Bacon gave optics (*perspectiva*, or the theory of vision) pride of place among the sciences. He stood apart from his contemporaries in that instead of simply giving an account of optics, he tried to show how it fit into the whole of knowledge and to synthesize what was known about optics up to that time in the work of writers such as Euclid, PTOLEMY and Alhazen.

Bacon also differed from his contemporaries in insisting that science, or a complete account of nature, must include an experimental as well as a theoretical component; without experience, he says, nothing can be known sufficiently. Aristotle's claim that 'a demonstration is a syllogism that makes us know' is to be understood not of the bare demonstration but of the case in which experience of the subject matter accompanies the demonstration. According to Bacon, by means of experiments one could (a) confirm hypotheses formulated on the basis of reason, (b) gain knowledge of that which is inaccessible to proof by deductive arguments, and (c) develop products to aid in everyday life. Examples of such experiments as carried out by Bacon include research into rainbows, the properties of magnets and gunpowder. In the traditional approach to education taken by Bacon's contemporaries, however, this aspect of knowledge was usually not even acknowledged, much less advocated.

Bacon himself did not make the kind of progress in empirical science that might have been expected, given the enthusiasm with which he advocated it, and given the accounts of his scientific prowess made popular during the seventeenth century, after his work had been rediscovered. He did make some advances; for example, he provided models for plane surfaces and for convex refracting surfaces, thereby advancing understanding of the nature of vision and the usefulness of lenses in aiding vision. On the whole, however, he appears not to have been a good scientist or mathematician. He produced no mathematical proofs or theorems, he held alchemy in high regard and he believed that by reading the stars one could come to know about the future. Because he had no disciples, his work was quickly forgotten after his death.

4 Linguistic work

As noted, Bacon's plan for curricular reform included a plea for the study of languages, which he represented as the vehicle of knowledge. He himself took the study of language seriously. Not only did he write grammars for both Greek and Hebrew, but he also devoted part of Part III of the *Opus maius* (called *De signis* (On Signs)) and part of the *Compendium studii theologiae* to discussions of signification in language, and wrote an analysis of the nature of ambiguity in his *Sumule dialectices*.

Bacon's comprehensive approach to the study of natural philosophy was replicated in his study of language. His interest in language was part of a wider interest in the nature of all signs, vocal and otherwise. 'Man', for instance, is a sign of an actually existing universal instantiated in all individual men, and smoke is a sign of fire. This approach was not typical in Bacon's day (see LANGUAGE, MEDIEVAL THEORIES OF).

Bacon's views on how words functions as signs were also unusual, and were developed in opposition to the views of people such as WILLIAM OF SHERWOOD, Lambert of Auxerre, SIGER OF BRABANT and BOETHIUS OF DACIA. For example, it was Bacon's view that all words are equivocal. The basis of this view was his belief that (a) words signify conventionally (*ad placitum*) as a result of meaning being imposed on them, either expressly or tacitly, by an individual or group of individuals, and that (b) any semantic theory must explain how words can signify not only present but also past and future individuals as well as never-existent things. Bacon believed that he could provide such a theory if it were presupposed that first, each act of imposition makes a word signify exactly one thing (where 'thing' is broadly construed as a word or a non-word, particular or universal, existing or imaginary), and second, each imposition lasts only as long as does the signified thing. Thus, if the word 'man' is imposed by someone to signify an individual man, it would acquire another sense in addition to its standard sense (signifying the common nature or universal humanity). In this case, the word 'man' has two senses and is thus equivocal. When the man signified by 'man' in virtue of the special imposition dies, 'man' would not signify him any longer, although one could impose a third meaning on the word 'man' to use it as a sign of the physical remains of what once was a man. There is no determinable limit to the various senses that can be imposed on a word, either consciously or unconsciously. With such a theory of signification, Bacon thought he could solve many of the linguistic puzzles of the day. For example, could Jesus be called a man during his three-day entombment? Can man be said to be an animal when no man exists? Is the sophisma-sentence 'This is a dead man, therefore this is a man' true? His questions, his grand schemes, his idiosyncratic pursuits, even his animosities and his mistakes, show him to have been very much ahead of his time.

See also: GROSSETESTE, R.; LANGUAGE, MEDIEVAL THEORIES OF; NATURAL PHILOSOPHY, MEDIEVAL; OXFORD CALCULATORS

List of works

Bacon, Roger (*c.*1250) *Sumule dialectices* (Brief Summaries of Dialectic), ed. R. Steele, Opera hactenus inedita Rogeri Bacon fasc.15, Oxford: Clarendon Press, 1940; Books I–II ed. A. de Libera, 'Les *Summulae dialectices* de Roger Bacon: I–II *De termino, De Enuntiatione*', Archives d'Histoire Doctrinale et Littéraire du Moyen Âge 61, 1986: 139–289; Book III ed. A. de Libera, 'Les *Summulae* *dialectices* de Roger Bacon: III *De argumentatione*', *Archives d'Histoire Doctrinale et Littéraire du Moyen Âge* 62, 1987: 171–278. (Bacon's writings on language, including an analysis of the nature of ambiguity.)

—— (1267) *Opus maius*, ed. J.H. Bridges, *The 'Opus maius' of Roger Bacon*, Oxford, 1879–90, 3 vols; repr. 1964; Part III, *De signis* (On Signs), ed. K.M. Fredborg, L. Nielsen and J. Pinborg, 'An Unedited Part of Roger Bacon's "*Opus Maius: De Signis*"', *Traditio* 34: 75–136, 1978. (Bacon's encyclopedia of the sciences and proposal for educational reform.)

—— (1267–8) *Opus minus*, ed. J.S. Brewer in *Fr. Rogeri Bacon Opera quaedam hactenus inedita*, London: Longman, Green, Longman & Roberts, 1859; repr. 1965. (Contains synopses, additions and corrections to the *Opus maius*.)

—— (1267–8) *Opus tertium*, ed. J.S. Brewer in *Fr. Rogeri Bacon Opera quaedam hactenus inedita*, London: Longman, Green, Longman & Roberts, 1859; repr. 1965. (Contains further synopses, additions and corrections to the *Opus maius*.)

—— (after 1268) Greek and Hebrew Grammars, ed. E. Nolan and S.A. Hirsch, *The Greek Grammar of Roger Bacon and a Fragment of His Hebrew Grammar*, Cambridge: Cambridge University Press, 1902. (Grammars, produced after finishing the *Opus maius*.)

—— (after 1268) *Communia naturalium* (General Principles of Natural Philosophy), ed. R. Steele, *Opera hactenus inedita Rogeri Bacon*, Oxford: Clarendon Press, fascs 2–4, 1905?–13. (Surviving section of a second, uncompleted encyclopedic work.)

—— (after 1268) *Communia mathematica* (General Mathematical Principles), ed. R. Steele, *Opera hactenus inedita Rogeri Bacon*, Oxford: Clarendon Press, fasc. 16, 1940. (Surviving section of a second, uncompleted encyclopedic work.)

—— (*c.*1271–2) *Compendium studii philosophiae* (Compendiusm of the Study of Philosophy), ed. J.S. Brewer, *Fr. Rogeri Bacon Opera quaedam hactenus inedita*, London, Longman, Green, Longman & Roberts, 1859; repr. 1965. (Intended as an introduction to Bacon's own philosophical writings.)

—— (*c.*1292) *Compendium studii theologiae* (Compendium of the Study of Theology), ed. H. Rashdall, *Fratris Rogeri Bacon Compendium studii theologiae*, Aberdeen: University Press, 1911; repr. 1966; ed. and trans. T.S. Mahoney, *Compendium of the Study of Theology*, Leiden: Brill, 1988. (Bacon's final work, dealing with education and the moral vices of Christendom.)

References and further reading

Crombie, A.C. (1969) *Robert Grosseteste and the Origins of Experimental Science 1100–1700*, Oxford: Clarendon Press. (Discusses the ways Bacon is dependent on Grosseteste in optics; see especially pages 139–62.)

Crowley, T. (1950) *Roger Bacon: The Problem of the Soul in His Philosophical Commentaries*, Louvain: Institut Superieur de Philosophie. (Good study of Bacon's life.)

Hackett, J.M.G., and Mahoney, T.S. (1987) 'Roger Bacon Bibliography (1957–1985)', *The New Scholasticism* 61 (2): 184–207. (This bibliography is continued in *Roger Bacon Essays*, ed. J.M.D. Hackett, Leiden: Brill, forthcoming 1997. The volume contains studies of Bacon's views on science, philosophy of language and ethics.)

Pinborg, J. (1981) 'Roger Bacon on Signs: A Newly Recovered Part of the Opus Maius', *Miscellanea Mediaevalis* 13: 403–12. (Preliminary investigation into Bacon's importance as a philosopher of language.)

GEORGETTE SINKLER

AL-BAGHDADI, ABU 'L-BARAKAT (*fl. c.*1200–50)

A maverick philosopher, respected medical authority, and seemingly somewhat tempestuous individual, Abu 'l-Barakat al-Baghdadi produced one voluminous work (the Kitab al-mu'tabar*) in which the philosophical views current in his day – principally associated with the name of Ibn Sina – were subjected to a penetrating analysis, and many interesting alternatives suggested. His most provocative ideas concern self-awareness, the physics of motion and the idea of time.*

Hibat Allah 'Ali ibn Malka Abu 'l-Barakat al-Baghdadi was an idiosyncratic, highly original philosopher who flourished in the first half of the twelfth century. Precise biographical information is unavailable. We know that he was born into a Jewish family (his Hebrew name was Nathanel) and, as a Jew, was refused entry to the lectures of Abu 'l-Hasan ibn Hibat Allah, a famous physician. Other slights, real or imagined, that he suffered on account of his faith seem to have contributed to his decision, very late in life, to convert to Islam. The appellation *awhad al-zaman*, 'the singular [personage] of his time', probably reflects his medical rather than philosophical achievements. His formal teaching seems to have been limited to medicine, in which he had a number of students. Ibn Khalliqan's biographical dictionary describes him as 'very presumptuous', his haughteur being revealed in his many disputes with the humbler physician Ibn al-Talmidh, which display the 'jealousy and rivalry that typically prevail between men who are eminent in the same profession'. His involvement in philosophy seems to have been informal (even by the standards of the time) and tentative. He had one notable disciple in the polymath Fakhr al-Din AL-RAZI.

Al-Baghdadi's mature views are found in his comprehensive *Kitab al-mu'tabar*, the title of which should be translated, according to Shlomo Pines (1979), 'the book of what has been established by personal reflection'. Al-Baghdadi characteristically begins his investigations with a pellucid statement of each problem he considers. He then surveys earlier opinions in detail, rarely naming his sources. He takes great pains to ferret out the reasoning underlying each claim, following closely the development of the theory, the objections raised against it and the adjustments made by its proponents. Each issue is approached freely and independently, without much reliance on any over-arching methodological or philosophical commitments. The interplay between words and concepts is given particular attention. For example, al-Baghdadi developed his strikingly innovative theory of time after reaching the conclusion that the word 'time' as used in everyday speech stands for a very fundamental concept, the true nature of which has been obscured by scholastic analysis. Again, he lambasts aspects of the sulphur–mercury theory of metals as 'words that denote unreal fancies'.

Perhaps most interesting among al-Baghdadi's achievements is his reappraisal of the idea of time (Pines 1979). Dissatisfied with the regnant approach, which treated time as an accident of the cosmos, al-Baghdadi drew the conclusion that time is an entity whose conception (*ma'qul al-zaman*) is *a priori* and almost as general as that of being, encompassing the sensible and the non-sensible, that which moves and that which is at rest. Our idea of time results not from abstraction, stripping accidents from perceived objects, but from a mental representation based on an innate idea. Al-Baghdadi stops short of offering a precise definition of time, stating only that 'were it to be said that time is the measure of being (*miqdar al-wujud*), that would be better than saying [as Aristotle does] that it is the measure of motion'. His reclassification of time as a subject for metaphysics rather than for physics represents a major conceptual shift, not a mere formalistic correction. It also breaks the traditional linkage between time and space. Concerning space, al-Baghdadi held unconventional views as well, but he did not remove its investigation from the domain of physics (see SPACE; TIME).

Al-Baghdadi's most significant departure in psychology concerns human self-awareness. IBN SINA had raised the issue of our consciousness of our own psychic activities, but he had not fully pursued the implications for Aristotelian psychology of his approach. Al-Baghdadi took the matter much further, dispensing with the traditional psycholgical faculties and pressing his investigations in the direction of what we would call the unconscious.

Al-Baghdadi had many new ideas concerning the physics of motion. He seems to have adumbrated the notion of acceleration as an increase in the velocity of a moving body attributable to the application to it of a constant force. He also seems to suggest that motion is relative, that is, that there is motion only if the relative positions of the bodies in question change. These ideas are highlighted here because of their resemblance to modern thoughts on the same subjects. The *Kitab al-mu'tabar* contains many other, no less innovative ideas that have no modern counterpart; for example, the claim that each type of body has a characteristic velocity that reaches its maximum when its motion encounters no resistance. Although *al-Mu'tabar* is not a systematic work, comprising instead notes on various subjects that al-Baghdadi wrote for himself over the years, Pines showed that the paramountcy of *a priori* knowledge underlies many of the work's criticisms and innovations.

The impact of *al-Mu'tabar* on Islamic thought seems to have been limited to the Ishraqi (illuminationist) tradition, broadly defined (see ILLUMINATIONIST PHILOSOPHY). Indeed, the work's tripartite structure (logic, physics, metaphysics), the pride of place given to *a priori* knowledge, and the consequent primacy given to the author's own speculations, are the distinguishing features of Ibn Sina's *Isharat wa-'l-tanbihat*, the earliest prototype of the genre, and of al-Suhrawardi's *al-Talwihat*, its most important representative. However, the spiritual tone of the latter two books is far less prominent in al-Baghdadi's work, although perhaps not entirely absent. As Pines showed, the Ibn Sina of *al-Shifa'* (Healing) is the target of many of al-Baghdadi's criticisms, strictures often pursued in Fakhr al-Din al-Razi's commentary on *al-Isharat*, and answered in Nasir al-Din al-Tusi's glosses to the same work. AL-TUSI usually refers to 'al-Baghdadi and the other later [philosophers],' giving the impression that al-Baghdadi was the outstanding representative, or even founder, of a whole school of thinkers who challenged some of Ibn Sina's views. Al-Suhrawardi's *al-Talwihat* refers to al-Baghdadi obliquely as 'one of the Jewish philosophers'. The target of that reference is made clear by

IBN KAMMŪNA, whose commentary on *al-Talwihat* cites al-Baghdadi several times. Al-Baghdadi's views were known to al-Shahrazuri, and he is mentioned some half-dozen times in Sadr al-Din al-Shirazi's *al-Asfar al-arba'a*.

Despite his conversion to Islam, al-Baghdadi's works continued to be studied at the *yeshivah* of Baghdad, then the centre of Jewish conservatism, into the thirteenth century. Al-Baghdadi's commentary to the Book of Ecclesiastes continued to be copied at the same *yeshivah*, with full acknowledgement of its authorship. Shmu'el ben Eli, head of the *yeshivah* and archrival of Moses MAIMONIDES, cites the *Mu'tabar* in support of his contention that even 'the philosophers' are forced to admit the possibility of bodily resurrection. Ben Eli does not reveal his source; it appears to have been Maimonides' disciple, Yosef ben Yehudah, who tracked down the reference.

Ibn Khalliqan reports that al-Baghdadi had a high reputation in the field of medicine, and al-Suhrawardi refers to him as 'a physician who sought to do philosophy'. He attended some of the Seljuq sultans and their families and is reported to have cured himself of leprosy, in the process causing himself a period of blindness. Ibn Abi Usaybi'a's biographical compendium relates some anecdotes and sayings and lists several of al-Baghdadi's medical works. However, few if any of these survive, and none have been studied. Al-Baghdadi also wrote a short treatise 'On the Reason that the Stars appear at Night but are invisible during the Day', and another small tract on the intellect.

See also: IBN SINA; ILLUMINATIONIST PHILOSOPHY

List of works

al-Baghdadi (early 12th century) *Kitab al-Mu'tabar*, Hyderabad: Osmania Publication Bureau, 1938–9, 3 vols. (A usable edition, one of the better of the Hyderabad printings.)

—— (early 12th century) Commentaries on Ecclesiastes, ed. S. Pines, 'Towards the Study of Abu al-Barakat's Commentary to Ecclesiastes: Four Texts', *Tarbiz* 33, 1964: 198–213; repr. in *Bein Mahshevet Yisrael li-Mahshevet ha-'Amim*, Jerusalem, 1977. (Four selected passages with translation and analysis, in Hebrew.)

References and further reading

Davidson, H.A. (1992) *Alfarabi, Avicenna, and Averroes, on Intellect*, New York: Oxford University Press, 154–61. (Includes a critical appraisal of Abu 'l-Barakat's ideas on the intellect.)

* Pines, S. (1979) *Studies in Abu'l-Barakat al-Baghdadi: Physics and Metaphysics*, The Collected Works of Shlomo Pines, vol. 1, Jerusalem and Leiden: Magnes & Brill. (A collection of Pines' most important studies on al-Baghdadi, some not published elsewhere.)

Stroumsa, S. (1993) 'On the Maimonidean Controversy in the East: the Role of Abu 'l-Barakat al-Baghdadi', in H. Ben-Shammai (ed.) *Hebrew and Arabic Studies in Honour of Joshua Blau*, Tel Aviv and Jerusalem. (On the role of Abu 'l-Barakat's writings in the resurrection controversy of the twelfth century; in Hebrew.)

Y. TZVI LANGERMANN

BAKHTIN, MIKHAIL MIKHAILOVICH (1895–1975)

Bakhtin is generally regarded as the most influential twentieth-century Russian literary theorist. His writings on literature, language, ethics, authorship, carnival, time and the theory of culture have shaped thinking in criticism and the social sciences. His name is identified with the concept of dialogue, which he applied to language and numerous other aspects of culture and the psyche.

Bakhtin viewed literary genres as implicit worldviews, concrete renditions of a sense of experience. Strongly objecting to the idea that novelists simply weave narratives around received philosophical ideas, he argued that very often significant discoveries are made first by writers and are then 'transcribed', often with considerable loss, into abstract philosophy. For example, he regarded the novelists of the eighteenth century as explorers of a modern concept of historicity long before philosophers took up the topic. He argued that considerable wisdom could be achieved by probing the form, as well as the explicit content, of literary works. In literature as in life, however, much wisdom is never fully formalizable, although we may approximate some of it and gesture towards more. Such partial recuperation was, in Bakhtin's view, the principal task of literary criticism.

Bakhtin's favourite genre was the realist novel. In his view, novels contain the richest sense of language, psychology, temporality and ethics in Western thought. He revolutionized the study of novels by arguing that traditional poetics, which employed categories suitable to poetry and to drama, had been unable to appreciate just what is novelistic and especially valuable about novels. Seeking the essence of 'prosaic intelligence', he therefore formulated an alternative to poetics, which critics have called 'prosaics'. This term also designates an important part of his worldview in approaching many other topics, especially language. Bakhtin stressed the prosaic, ordinary, unsystematic, events of the world as primary. In culture, order can never be presumed, but is always a 'task', the result of work that is never completed and always upset by everyday contingent events. Better than any other form of thought, great prose, especially realistic novels, captures this prosaic sense of life.

Believing in contingency and human freedom, Bakhtin described individual people, and cultural entities generally, as 'unfinalizable'. Human beings always manifest 'surprisingness' and can never be reduced to a fully comprehensible system. Paraphrasing the implications of Dostoevskii's novels, Bakhtin located humanness in the capacity of people 'to render untrue *any externalizing and finalizing definition of them. As long as a person is alive he lives by the fact that he is not yet finalized, that he has not uttered his ultimate word' ([1929] 1984: 59; original emphasis). Ethically, the worst act is to treat people as if some 'secondhand' truth about them were exhaustible. Psychologically,*

> *A man never coincides with himself. One cannot apply to him the formula of identity $A \equiv A$... the genuine life of the personality takes place at the point of non-coincidence between a man and himself... beyond the limits of all that he is as a material being... that can be spied upon, defined, predicted apart from its own will, 'at second hand.'*
>
> ([1929] 1984: 59)

Bakhtin therefore opposed all deterministic philosophies and all cultural theories that understate the messiness of things and the openness of time. He rigorously opposed Marxism and semiotics, although, strangely enough, in the West his work has been appropriated by both schools. Stating his own thought as a paraphrase of Dostoevskii, he wrote:

> *nothing conclusive has yet taken place in the world, the ultimate word of the world and about the world has not yet been spoken, the world is open and free, everything is still in the future and will always be in the future.*
>
> ([1929] 1984: 166)

1 Life
2 Language as dialogic
3 Heteroglossia
4 Double-voicing
5 Psychology and ethics
6 Authorship and polyphony
7 Theories of the novel

1 Life

The son of a bank manager, Bakhtin studied classics and philology at the University of Petrograd (1913–18). His meticulous knowledge of obscure ancient writers is reflected throughout his work. Most of his subsequent life can be seen as a series of escapes into obscurity. During the Russian Civil War, he moved to the small towns of Nevel and Vitebsk, where he worked as a schoolteacher, discussed philosophy and acquired his two best-known disciples, Valentin Voloshinov and Pavel Medvedev. Interested in Neo-Kantianism, Bakhtin worked on a comprehensive treatise about ethics, authorship and the relation of the self to others (see NEO-KANTIANISM). In the 1920s, he also encountered the most influential non-Marxist school of criticism, Russian Formalism, learned from their ideas, and rejected their fundamental approach, which he saw as scientistic in its pursuit of laws at the expense of contingency and individual agency (see RUSSIAN LITERARY FORMALISM). Their reduction of content to form ran counter to his view that literature and language are repositories of wisdom acquired by human experience over 'great time'. In 1924, he moved to Leningrad, where he failed to find stable employment, perhaps because of a bone disease eventually leading to the amputation of his right leg in 1938. In 1929, he published his book on Dostoevskii, which was recognized as a classic.

Nevertheless, his bourgeois background, his interest in religion and his non-Marxist approach made him suspect in the Soviet Union, and in 1929 he was arrested. A sentence that would have meant his death in a harsh labour camp was commuted to six years of internal exile in Kazakhstan. During the 1930s he worked at odd jobs, including bookkeeper on a collective farm. During these years he wrote his classic essays on language and the novel. Out of step with the times, these essays were not published until 1975. He also worked on a study of Rabelais and the institution of carnival, which he described in terms of systematic parody by inversion of social norms. The Rabelais thesis was submitted for a doctorate, but only a lesser degree was awarded, and the book did not appear in print until 1965. Later, it became the first of his works to be widely known in the West.

In 1936 he became a professor at the remote Mordovia State Teachers College, but soon resigned so as to remain less visible during the years of mass arrests. He returned to his professorship at the end of the Second World War. During the 1950s, intellectuals in Moscow were again inspired by Bakhtin's book on Dostoevskii and were surprised to discover that the author (unlike Voloshinov, Medvedev and so many others) had not perished during the years of purges and privation. Celebrated, sometimes worshipped as a secular saint, he inspired reminiscences of dubious accuracy. He continued to write essays on general problems of culture from the perspective of dialogue.

For a time, the rumour circulated that Bakhtin had written some of Voloshinov's and Medvedev's works, and publishers reissued their books under his name. But the weight of argument and evidence indicates that Bakhtin influenced but did not write these books.

2 Language as dialogic

In his book on Dostoevskii, in 'Slovo v romane' (Discourse in the Novel) (1934–5), in 'Problemy rechevykh zhanrov' (Problems of Speech Genres) (1952–3) and elsewhere, Bakhtin offers an alternative to the linguistic theories of SAUSSURE and movements indebted to him, including formalism, structuralism and semiotics (see SEMIOTICS; STRUCTURALISM IN LINGUISTICS). His critique, and that of Voloshinov in *Marksizm i filosofiia iazyka* (Marxism and the Philosophy of Language) (1929), would also apply to the Chomskyite tradition (see CHOMSKY, N.).

For Bakhtin, the fundamental unit of language is not the sentence but the utterance. Whereas sentences are repeatable, utterances occur in a specific situation. Still more important, they are formulated as part of a dialogic exchange. Utterances are not only responded to, but are shaped in anticipation of a response. In a sense, they belong to both speaker and listener. Bakhtin finds simplistic the telegraphic model of communication, in which response (or decoding) simply follows the utterance; the same reasoning would apply to what literary critics think of as reader reception theory.

Bakhtin uses his key term 'dialogue' in three distinct senses: as a worldview or sense of truth, as a particular use of language and as a defining quality of language itself. When taken as a defining quality of language, the term indicates that all utterances are dialogic: they are constituted by their 'addressivity'. Dialogic relations are (from the standpoint of Saussurean linguistics) metalinguistic. Metalinguistic relations are not reducible to logical or linguistic ones. Two sentences may contradict each other, but when they are 'embodied' (spoken by particular people on a particular occasion), new kinds of relations are established. Thus, if two people say, one after another, 'Life is good', from the standpoint of linguistics we have a repetition of the same sentence, from the standpoint of logic we have the relation of identity, but from a dialogic perspective, we have agreement. But agreement is never full, and the second utterance, necessarily embodied by a different person, carries with it a different experience that leads to different implications, which we all keenly sense. Tone, an 'emotional–volitional' stance, is crucial to its meaning, and tone does not appear in the sentence but in the utterance. Indeed, some utterances (hm!) are spoken entirely as carriers of tone, something like verbal gestures. A mapping of dialogic relations (Bakhtin offers an incomplete typology) would necessarily involve complex relations outside the purview of either linguistics or logic. In life, we understand these relations, and if the study of language is to comprehend how language is used, it must describe them.

This approach differs from one focusing on the abstract system of language, which is in any case not as systematic as linguists suppose. Linguists typically avoid the issues on which Bakhtin focuses by 'smuggling' into a sentence features properly belonging to an utterance when convenient.

If one views utterances dialogically, other features not present in sentences come into view. For example, everything we speak about is 'already spoken about' and our utterances orient themselves dialogically not only to potential listeners but also to earlier utterances on the topic. No one is the 'biblical Adam' uttering the first word on a topic, and complexities of meaning, which are reflected in style, arise from the diversity of orientations to previous utterances. Traditional stylistics, which views choice of words simply as the expression of the author, misses the shaping role of both listener and previous speakers. Bakhtin compares 'the word' (utterance) to a ray of light entering a tension-filled, social 'atmosphere filled with alien words, value judgments and accents through which the ray passes on its way to the object' (1934–5: 277).

Thus, some elements of reported speech are present in every utterance. Bakhtin (and Voloshinov) offer detailed analyses of the various forms of reported speech in part because all speech is, obviously or surreptitiously, reported. The obvious forms of reported speech vary from culture to culture, depending on attitudes towards discourse, authority and the relation of self to other. The concept of the 'already-spoken-about' illustrates what Bakhtin means by saying that in calling language dialogic he is referring not only to 'compositionally expressed dialogue', as in play scripts, but also to 'the internal dialogism' of each utterance.

3 Heteroglossia

Because order is always a 'task', Bakhtin argues that 'a unitary language is not something given but is always in essence posited' (1934–5: 270). Language, like the rest of culture, is constantly subject to 'centrifugal' forces disrupting it in unsystematic ways; cultures often respond with 'centripetal' efforts to restore a minimum of unity by writing dictionaries and grammars. What we call *the* English language is in part the effect of nonlinguistic social pressures.

But other ways of speaking exist, and these cannot be adequately understood by referring to dialects. Instead, Bakhtin calls attention to the fact that groups speak differently because they conceive of experience differently. Each profession, generation, locale, ethnic group or any of countless other shifting identities, all have their own characteristic vocabularies, ways of addressing others, styles and intonations because they think and understand the world in their own way. Language is always languages; it manifests 'heteroglossia'. There is no single formal principle for identifying each of these 'languages' because what distinguishes them is conceptualizations of experience, which may be expressed in countless ways, each of which is 'the sclerotic deposit' of specific social activity.

All of us in fact know more than one language of heteroglossia because we function in diverse environments. We often approach one field of experience in one language and with the attitudes of another, and so languages of heteroglossia may enter into dialogue. This process not only changes our sense of experience but also, when repeated by many people, affects the development of language. Bakhtin preferred such messy and unsystematic accounts of language change to notions like those of the Formalists, who saw language as an abstract system developing by principles that were themselves abstract and systematic, so that, as Roman Jakobson and Iurii Tynianov observed, the history of a system is itself a system.

4 Double-voicing

All utterances are dialogic in one sense, but not in another. For utterances have different 'tasks'. Although all utterances can be shown to be cited or reported from other contexts, sometimes we do not want such allusiveness to be perceived; we just want to get our point across. At other times, for example when we engage in parody, perception of 'quotation marks' is necessary to our purposes. Thus, some utterances are monologic, others dialogic; some 'single-voiced' and others 'double-voiced'. In double-voiced utterances we have two speech acts and are meant to perceive both sets of intentions.

Double-voiced utterances may in turn be divided into passive and active. The distinction lies in the relation of the two utterances to each other. The utterance cited or alluded to may be subservient (passive) to the first. In parody, for example, the target utterance clearly enjoys lower semantic authority than the parodying utterance. The two disagree, and we know with whom we are expected to side. In another form of passive double-voiced word, stylization, we distinctly hear two utterances – say, one from another era and style and one currently spoken – that remain in qualified agreement. (One must not forget that agreement is also a dialogic relation.)

Sometimes the second utterance actively resists appropriation by the first. 'In such discourse, the author's thought no longer oppressively dominates the other's thought, discourse loses its composure and confidence, becomes agitated, internally undecided and two-faced' ([1929] 1984: 198). Sometimes, speech seems to take a 'sideward glance' at a possible hostile answer and responds to it in advance; the word has a 'double orientation', towards its topic and towards an expected response so active that it may utterly dominate the utterance. This sort of speech is rather common in everyday life, where it appears in various barbed words, overblown discourse repudiating itself in advance or the speech of deeply agitated people. It is especially well represented in literature. Dostoevskii's *Zapiski iz podpol'ia* (*Notes From Underground*) contains actively double-voiced 'words with a loophole', in which speakers retain the right to reverse their position if they get the wrong response. One may sense a loophole in a tone of potential (but not definitive) self-mockery or in agitated exaggeration.

5 Psychology and ethics

Throughout his life, Bakhtin battled against what he initially called 'theoretism' and (after studying language) named 'monologism': the idea that the world is fundamentally orderly and that experience is in principle fully capturable in abstract theories. What theories that reason down to experience, instead of up from it, usually produce is bloodless 'transcriptions' of events. For example, the heritage of rationalism views events as utterly explicable in terms of underlying laws. Any such approach necessarily reads out of events their 'eventness', that which makes them and the present moment 'momentous' in the face of multiple future possibilities. When applied to language, theoretism leads to the Saussurean division between *langue*, the abstract system of language, and *parole*, the particular speech act, viewed as a mere instantiation of rules. Applied to people, it makes them entirely 'coincident' with themselves, a mere bundle or system of qualities without 'unfinalizability'.

When ethics proceeds in this way, it grossly oversimplifies situations by fitting them into pregiven categories, whereas the most ethically relevant facts may turn out to be entirely unpredictable in advance. In stressing the importance of particulars, Bakhtin revives casuistry's reasoning by cases (see CASUISTRY; MORAL PARTICULARISM). Also, the essence of ethical choice, its 'oughtness', depends on the 'eventness' of the event, which is lost in top-down reasoning. Morality involves taking into account a particular person, not a generalized agent, in a specific, unrepeatable situation: 'What can be accomplished by me cannot be accomplished by anyone else, ever' ([c. early 1920s] 1986: 129). For Bakhtin, the highest value is a human being, and the subordinated value is 'the good', and not the other way around. In the Soviet context, Bakhtin understandably opposed the sort of ideological thinking that displaces responsibility to an abstract authority or set of rules, which we are obliged to follow mechanically (the state of mind he calls 'pretendership'). Rules and many other psychological mechanisms offer us an illegitimate 'alibi' whereas the essence of ethical life is our perpetual state of 'non-alibi'. (This position is loosely comparable to existentialist analyses of authenticity and 'bad faith': see EXISTENTIALIST ETHICS §3.)

Bakhtin's early writings situate ethics within a larger discussion of the phenomenology of self. We see other people as they cannot see themselves. You cannot see the back of your head or the expression of your face when it is unselfconscious; your tears are framed for me by the blue sky behind and your own act of looking cannot appear in your field of vision. That is, I enjoy a 'surplus of vision' with respect to you; people exist in a state of 'outsideness' with respect to each other. For me you are part of the world, whereas your 'I-for-myself' experiences itself as entering into the world. Thus, we never see ourselves in our dreams as a finished presence, as we see others; but when we narrate our dreams later, we make ourselves into a character. In that case, the I-for-myself enters into the world by narrating.

Our selves consist in part of the 'finalized', almost artistically rendered images of ourselves that we receive from others. Bakhtin calls this sense of self received from others the 'soul', which is a 'gift' from outside. For the I-for-myself, the soul is something that we are always transcending, rendering partly untrue; the self is always 'yet-to-be'. Ethically, outsideness and the surplus indicate that empathy, in the sense of merging, is the wrong way to respond to another's suffering. For if merging were successful, no help could be given. Instead, what is needed is 'living into' another in which we put ourselves in the other's position while also retaining our 'surplus', an outside position from which something new and helpful can be offered.

Bakhtin's theories of language led him to the idea that, once a person acquires language, consciousness and selfhood are primarily linguistic in nature, so long as one understands language dialogically. We learn language by internalizing dialogic exchanges, and when we think we enact dialogues (often highly abbreviated) in our heads. Significant people in our lives become the repeated addressees of our inner speech; in effect, we are the voices that inhabit us. Thus, the full range of dialogic phenomena that appear in Bakhtin's theories of language can be reinterpreted psychologically; Bakhtin also adds some new types of internal dialogic relations. In opposition to FREUD, who viewed the self as something that must be socialized, Bakhtin saw the self as essentially social because it is dialogic.

6 Authorship and polyphony

Bakhtin's early works contend that characters in a literary work cannot be truly free. After all, the author knows in advance their ultimate destiny and the significance of everything they do. Because they are part of a larger whole, they are themselves given 'whole', with no room for genuine surprisingness. Readers are always aware that the author is in full control, has planned everything in advance, and so no event is truly 'eventful'. It would appear that narrative art excludes the possibility of representing anything but a pale image of human freedom.

In Bakhtin's view, DOSTOEVSKII discovered how to overcome the tendency of art to impose a destiny on characters. What they say and do is surprising to the author and truly eventful. Critics have plausibly discerned in the idea of polyphony a theological agenda, which could not be expressed directly in the Soviet Union. If we allow that the relation of God to people is analogous to that of an author to heroes, then if a polyphonic author could create characters capable of genuine surprise, God may have created people polyphonically as well. He may have deliberately created the world as a genuinely open process, where he cannot foresee what happens because human freedom genuinely exists.

To create the polyphonic novel, Dostoevskii surrendered an author's 'essential surplus' with respect to his characters. This 'essential surplus' (which is stronger than the ordinary surplus each person enjoys with respect to others) consists in having a plan of the whole. Our knowledge that the author enjoys this surplus means that in a literary work the author must be the 'ultimate semantic authority': the meaning of any character's utterances cannot be taken directly but must be mediated through the work as a whole. But in Dostoevskii's novels, each major character enjoys semantic authority equivalent to the author's. The author (not just the narrator) becomes simply another character. The result is that characters may surprise the author and the work becomes an open-ended, unfinalizable dialogue among distinct points of view.

To create such a work, Dostoevskii does not predetermine a plot, but, through a complicated process, concretely imagines fully realized voices, each expressing a whole sense of existence. He then creates a situation that will provoke the characters into dialogic confrontation; he records, in turn, what each one says, without knowing in advance where the conversation is leading. If a given character or narrator expresses Dostoevskii's own opinions, that voice is just another in the dialogue, and, indeed, may lose the argument or wind up saying things the author has not imagined he could say. The results of each exchange are then allowed to lead to another, and the overall novel is simply the succession of thrilling dialogues. Plot is whatever happens to occur and ceases to be essential; it is no longer the 'clamps' holding the work together. The essence of the work lies in its 'great dialogues'.

In addition to freedom, surprisingness and eventness, polyphony's very form expresses another key idea: 'monologism', 'theoretism' and 'rationalism' are mistaken in recognizing only one kind of truth. Monologism's truth is composed of abstract propositions that 'gravitate' to a system (an 'ideology'), in which the particular voice speaking each proposition does not affect its truth value. But truth may also be dialogic, that is, may require many voices:

> It is quite possible to imagine and postulate a unified truth that requires a plurality of consciousnesses, one that in principle cannot be fitted within the bounds of a single consciousness, one that is, so to speak, by its very nature *full of event potential* [eventness] and is born of a contact among various consciousnesses.
>
> ([1929] 1984: 81)

Any attempt to 'transcribe' or 'monologize' this truth into a proposition will inevitably reduce it to a shadow of itself.

7 Theories of the novel

As we have seen, genres, like languages of heteroglossia, each express a view of experience. Because, according to Bakhtin, novels offer the richest view of life, his elucidation of their hidden wisdom in effect states his own views.

Bakhtin offers three distinct accounts of this genre's 'form-shaping idea'. The first follows from his theory of language. Keenly aware of the vast diversity of social beliefs implicitly carried by each 'language of heteroglossia', novels orchestrate an intense dialogue of those languages. Social values come into unexpected interaction as we see the 'image' of one language from the perspective of another. Novels may exaggerate actually existing dialogues of languages or create new dialogues among languages that have still not encountered each other in real life. The result is to deprive a given language and way of thinking of its naïveté: it can no longer present itself as the unchallenged best way to talk about its central topics. It is now 'contested, contestable, and contesting'. No longer able to regard itself as the unchallenged centre of things, a language ceases to move in a 'Ptolemaic' universe. The novel expresses a 'Galilean language consciousness'.

Poetics and stylistics, which rely on an examination of tropes, miss this essential activity of novels. They look for a style, whereas the novel manifests a peculiar style of styles, an 'interillumination of languages', each approaching others from various angles. Languages hybridize. Bakhtin offers a catalogue of how languages 'reaccentuate' each other. Because novels intensify hybridization always around us in daily life, they become a subtle sociological form. And because our inner speech also consists of such dialogues, novels are revealing about our mental processes in a way otherwise unavailable.

It is important to recognize that when Bakhtin speaks of such dialogues, he is not talking about the exchanges between characters. He has in mind the complex play of languages in the voice of narrators. The novel is distinguished from other genres precisely by its intense orchestration of voices and languages in this way. For example, a given character's particular way of speaking, which reflects a complex of social attitudes, infiltrates the narrator's speech and so may be felt even when the character is not present; the narrator's language is affected by this 'character zone'. Or the 'common language' of some group may be ironically reaccentuated in the narrator's speech, which weaves in and out of various languages. Bakhtin offers a number of examples as he develops a theoretical framework.

Bakhtin's second theory of the novel focuses on its temporality. He offers a catalogue and a history of literary genres, from antiquity to the nineteenth century, each of which embodies implicit assumptions about causality, agency, biography, the social environment's effect on action, a sense of historicity, fate or freedom and countless other topics concerned with our status as actors in a spatiotemporal, sociohistorical world. These assumptions are rarely made explicit, but they may be detected in the characteristic ways a plot is constructed in each genre. For example, action that is plausible in one genre (last-minute escapes in an adventure story) may be completely implausible in another. Bakhtin calls a specific way of conceptualizing human action in time and space a 'chronotope'.

For Bakhtin, GOETHE was the key figure in establishing the chronotope of the modern novel, and so he joins RABELAIS and Dostoevskii as Bakhtin's favourite authors. The novel displays the most sophisticated chronotope for several reasons. It displays a sense of open time: 'Reality as we have it in the novel is only one of many possible realities... it bears within itself other possibilities'. Novels are also 'heterochronous': they display a social world in which many different chronotopes operate and interact. Novels understand how people change. Whereas in picaresque, the order of incidents could be changed because the hero or heroine remains essentially the same, novels show a gradual process of 'becoming'. Moreover, character change is not conceived as a mere 'unfolding' or revealing of inherent qualities, but as a complex process of interaction among social forces, individual initiative and contingent events. Whereas in romances and other genres, the social world is mere background that does not significantly affect the characters, in novels the social world itself partially shapes their development. That is one reason why it has proven easy to transpose romances across centuries or national boundaries, whereas novelistic action is typically located precisely in time and place and would be almost impossible to relocate elsewhere. The novel recognizes both social constraints and individual choice and subtly shows their interaction. Moreover, social forces are themselves seen as in flux – a process of change that is often the key theme of novels. Above all, novels show their main characters as possessing what Bakhtin calls a 'surplus of humanness'. In contrast to Soviet Marxism and other ideologies describing people as, in principle, fully knowable, the novel understands a person as transcending any conceivable 'secondhand' definitions: 'There is no mere form that would be able to incarnate once and forever all of his human possibilities and needs, no form in which he could exhaust himself down to the last word'. For the novelistic hero 'there always remains a need for the future, and a place for this future must be found'.

Deeply suspicious of Soviet and all other 'theoretist' dogmatisms, Bakhtin appropriated the novel as a counter-weapon. This appropriation is most evident in his third theory of the novel as a 'carnivalized' genre, that is, as a form embodying the spirit of various social rituals (especially the ancient Saturnalia and medieval carnival) that subject all received social norms to parody. Whereas theorists conventionally traced the novel to ancient epic, Bakhtin stressed its debt to menippean satire, a literary form beginning in antiquity that mixed philosophy and various kinds of parody in a highly idiosyncratic form. In the Renaissance, Rabelais combined menippean satire with the spirit of carnival to produce a distinctive amalgam leading, by way of Laurence Sterne and others, to the realist novel with its deep suspicion of all dogmatisms. Bakhtin recognized that it is possible to write long prose narratives without this menippean spirit, without the novelistic chronotope and without 'dialogized heteroglossia', but such works (which would include socialist realist fiction) are merely 'unnovelistic novels'. Where 'prosaic intelligence', 'unfinalizability' and the spirit of open-ended dialogue join, as they do in the novel, we reach the most profound human vision – yet.

List of works

Bakhtin, H.M. (written 1919) 'Iskusstvo i otvetstvennost'', trans. V. Liapunov, 'Art and Answerability', in *Art and Answerability: Early Philosophical Essays by M.M. Bakhtin*, Austin, TX: University of Texas Press, 1990, 1–3. (Bakhtin's first published work, a short essay on ethics and literature.)

—— (written c. early 1920s) *K filosofii iskusstva* (Towards a Philosophy of the Act), in *Filosofiia i sotsiologiia nauki i tekhniki 1984–5*, Moscow: Nauka, 1986, 80–160; Austin, TX: University of Texas Press, 1993. (This early work is Bakhtin's key statement on ethics.)

—— (written c.1920–3) 'Author and Hero in Aesthetic Activity', in M. Holoquist and V. Liapunov (eds) *Art and Answerability*, Austin, TX: University of Texas Press, 1990. (A meditation on the relation of selves to others, in life and literature.)

—— (1924) 'The Problem of Content, Material, and Form in Verbal Art' in M. Holoquist and V. Liapunov (eds), *Art and Answerability*, Austin, TX: University of Texas Press, 1990. (Bakhtin's critique of Russian Formalism.)

—— (1929) *Problemy poetiki Dostoevskogo*; expanded 2nd edn 1963; ed. and trans. C. Emerson, *Problems of Dostoevsky's Poetics*, Minneapolis, MN: University of Minnesota Press, 1984. (This is a translation of the expanded 1963 edition. Perhaps his single most important work, it discusses genres, ethics, the novel and the theory of language with Dostoevskii as constant illustration.)

—— (written 1934–5) 'Slovo v romane', trans. C. Emerson and M. Holquist, 'Discourse in the Novel', in *The Dialogic Imagination*, Austin, TX: University of Texas Press, 1981, 259–422. (His theory of language and defence of a specifically prosaic approach to prose.)

—— (written 1936–8) *Roman vospitaniia i ego znachenie v istorii realizma*, trans. V. McGee, 'The Bildungsroman and its Significance in the History of Realism', in *Speech Genres and Other Late Essays*, Austin, TX: University of Texas Press, 1986, 10–59. (These are surviving fragments from Bakhtin's lost book on Goethe and the novel of education.)

—— (written 1937–8) 'Formy vremeni i khronotopa v romane', trans. C. Emerson and M. Holoquist, 'Forms of Time and of the Chronotope in the Novel', in *The Dialogic Imagination*, Austin, TX: University of Texas Press, 1981, 84–258. (The key statement of his philosophy of time. Concluding remarks written 1973.)

—— (written 1940) 'Iz predystorii romannogo slova', trans. C. Emerson and M. Holoquist, 'From the Prehistory of Novelistic Discourse', in *The Dialogic Imagination*, Austin, TX: University of Texas Press, 1981, 41–83. (Like 'Discourse in the Novel' this discusses the theory of novelistic prose.)

—— (written 1941a) 'Epic and Novel', in *The Dialogic Imagination*, Austin, TX: University of Texas Press, 1981, 3–40. (A synthesis of Bakhtin's various theories on the novel.)

—— (written 1941b) *Tvorchestvo Fransua Rable i narodnaia kul'tura*, trans. H. Iswolsky, *Rabelais and His World*, Cambridge, MA: MIT Press, 1968. (This thesis, unsuccessfully submitted for a doctorate, was not published in Russia until 1965.)

—— (written 1952–3) 'Problemy rechevykh zhanrov', trans. V.W. McGee, 'The Problem of Speech Genres', in *Speech Genres and Other Late Essays*, Austin, TX: University of Texas Press, 1986, 60–102. (The importance of genres of daily speech in understanding dialogue.)

—— (1970) 'Otvet na vopros redaktsii Novogo mira', trans. V.W. McGee, 'Reply to a Question from the Novy mir Editorial Staff', in *Speech Genres and Other Late Essays*, Austin, TX: University of Texas Press, 1986, 1–9. (A key statement on the theory of interpretation of texts from remote times and cultures.)

—— (1970–1) 'Iz zapisei 1970–1', trans. V.W. McGee, 'From Notes Made in 1970–71', in *Speech Genres and Other Late Essays*, Austin, TX: University of Texas Press, 1986, 132–58. (A series of jottings on various topics.)

—— (1975a) 'K metodologii gumanitarnykh nauk', trans. V.W. McGee, 'Toward a Methodology for the Human Sciences', in *Speech Genres and Other Late Essays*, Austin, TX: University of Texas Press, 1986, 159–72. (Stresses a dialogic approach.)

—— (1975b) *Voprosy literatury i ėstetiki: Issledovaniia raznykh let* (Questions of Literature and Aesthetics: Research of Various Years), Moscow: Khudozhestvennaia Literatura. (Inlcudes the first publication of some important articles.)

—— (1979) *Ėstetika slovesnogo tvorchestva* (The Aesthetics of Verbal Art), ed. S. Bocharov, Moscow: Iskusstvo. (Collection containing several key texts.)

—— (1986) *Literaturno-kriticheskie stat'i* (Literary-critical Articles), ed. S. Bocharov and V. Kozhinov, Moscow: Khudozhestvennaia literatura. (A comprehensive anthology.)

References and further reading

Bernstein, M.A. (1992) *Bitter Carnival: 'Ressentiment' and the Abject Hero*, Princeton, NJ: Princeton University Press. (Contains a subtle application and moral critique of Bakhtin's ideas on narrative, psychology and carnival.)

Clark, K. and Holquist, M. (1984) *Mikhail Bakhtin*, Cambridge, MA: Harvard University Press. (The first biography of Bakhtin.)

Mandelker, A. (ed.) (1995) *Bakhtin in Contexts: Across the Disciplines*, Evanston, IL: Northwestern University Press. (An anthology demonstrating how Bakhtin's ideas have been used in the humanities and social sciences.)

Morson, G.S. and Emerson, C. (1990) *Rethinking Bakhtin: Extensions and Challenges*, Evanston, IL: Northwestern University Press. (An anthology containing a range of views, including critiques; the introduction offers a detailed summary of *Towards a Philosophy of the Act*.)

—— (1990) *Mikhail Bakhtin: Creation of a Prosaics*, Stanford, CA: Stanford University Press. (Offers a detailed account of all Bakhtin's significant works.)

GARY SAUL MORSON

BAKUNIN, MIKHAIL ALEKSANDROVICH (1814–76)

Bakunin was the leading proponent in the second half of the nineteenth century of a variety of anarchism rooted in a Romantic cult of primitive spontaneity, and one of the principal ideologists of Russian populism. But along with his public defence of the principle of 'absolute liberty' he attempted to set up networks of secret societies which were to direct the revolution and subsequently assume dictatorial powers. The contradiction between these two aspects of his activities has puzzled historians, many of whom have sought the answer in his personality, in which the urge to dominate was as strong as the urge to rebel.

1 Life
2 Thought

1 Life

Born into a gentry family in the Russian province of Tver, Mikhail Aleksandrovich Bakunin became a leading figure in the Moscow intellectual circles of the 1830s as an exponent first of the idealism of Fichte, and subsequently of a conservative interpretation of Hegel. In Germany, where he went to study philosophy in 1840, he was converted to radicalism in philosophy and politics by the Young Hegelians (see HEGELIANISM; HEGELIANISM, RUSSIAN). In France he met PROUDHON, who would have an important influence on his later thought. During the upheavals of 1848–9 he preached a revolutionary Pan-Slavism, calling for a democratic federation of all Slavic nations (see PAN-SLAVISM §3). Arrested in 1849 for revolutionary activities in Dresden, he was handed over first to the Austrian and then to the Russian government, which condemned him to prison followed by exile in Siberia. In 1861 he escaped to London, to collaborate with Aleksandr Herzen's émigré press (see HERZEN, A.I.) on revolutionary propaganda directed at the Russian Empire. After the suppression of the Polish uprising of 1863 he turned his revolutionary hopes to Western Europe and began to expound an anarchist philosophy (see ANARCHISM). He founded his own international organization, the Alliance of Socialist Democracy, which he sought to have affiliated to the First International. He disbanded it as a tactical measure when his request was rejected, and joined the International with his supporters in order to challenge its domination by Marx's faction, which the Bakuninists accused of dictatorial centralism. Expelled from the International in 1872, he devoted his last years to revolutionary projects (including a rising in Lyon during the Franco-Prussian War) which all ended in failure.

2 Thought

Like many of his generation in Russia, Bakunin found in German Idealism a source of compensating fantasies which helped him sublimate his sense of alienation and achieve a foretaste of the wholeness which he craved. He was particularly attracted to Fichte's vision of absolute liberty as an earthly ideal to be attained through a protean feat of will (see FICHTE, J.G. §5). Fantasies of self-affirmation alternated in the young Bakunin's thought with dreams of self-surrender through communion with the Absolute in religious or aesthetic contemplation, or through idealized platonic relationships with others of his circle (the cult of the 'beautiful soul').

Bakunin believed that his arrival in Europe had transformed him from a dreamer into a man of action; but his often-expressed contempt for 'theorizers' was based on the Romantic theory of the regenerative power of primitive spontaneity. He interpreted the unrest among the peoples of the Russian and Austro-Hungarian empires in the 1840s as the expression of elemental forces which were destined to sweep away all the artificial systems and institutions that sought to suppress them. This spirit of instinctive revolt, 'the sole creative force in history', was to be found at its purest in the most primitive, and thereby the least corrupt, of the common people: the peasantry. He placed high hopes on the Russian peasants who had a tradition of revolt, and whom he represents in his *Vozzvanie k Slavianam* (Appeal to the Slavs) of 1846 as a 'fiery ocean' which will engulf Moscow in blood and flame, and bury all the slavery in Europe beneath its own ruins. This faith was based on his version of the revolutionary dialectic of the Left Hegelians. In 'Die Reaktion in Deutschland' (Reaction in Germany) (printed in Arnold Ruge's *Deutsche Jahrbücher* in 1842 under the pseudonym 'Jules Elysard') he proclaims that the total destruction of the 'positive' (the existing order) by the forces of 'negation' will lead to 'a new heaven and a new earth...in which all the discords of our time will be resolved in harmonious unity'. This essay, which gave him his entrée into radical circles in Europe, ended with the famous line: *'Die Lust der Zerstörung ist auch eine schaffende Lust!'* ('The urge for destruction is also a creative urge!')

The anarchism which became his creed in the 1860s was a logical consequence of his cult of spontaneity. He now declared all states to be oppressive by their nature as institutionalizations of the rule of systems over life. The infallible instincts of the masses were the only source of freedom and virtue. These instincts had created the peasant commune which still survived in Russia: a form of self-government which could become universal once the masses were freed from the tutelage of political and intellectual elites who could teach them nothing and who sought to prolong the tyranny of theory over life: as a prime offender in this respect he pointed to the scientific socialism of Marx, although Marx's economic materialism was an important influence on his thought, along with Comtian positivism and Feuerbach's critique of religion (see COMTE, A.; FEUERBACH, L.A.).

He considered himself a materialist, atheist and positivist, but the theoretical basis of his anarchism was flimsy and shot through with contradictions. In particular, his two principal theoretical works, *L'Empire Knouto-Germanique et la révolution sociale* (The Knouto-Germanic Empire and the Social Revolution) (1871) and *Gosudarstvennost' i anarkhiia* (Statism and Anarchy) (1873) belie his self-image as the champion of 'life' against scientific and metaphysical abstraction. In these works he argues that all contemporary conflicts can be traced to the opposition between 'two polarities': the state (equated with reaction), and revolution (identified with his brand of anarchism). He defines the primary characteristic of the masses as their spirit of rebellion: this forces him to exclude from the category of the 'true' people all those not inclined to rebel. Those who were so inclined are much idealized in Bakunin's anarchist writings, along with the revolutionary secret societies for which he tirelessly recruited, but which existed more in his imagination than in fact.

His conspiratorial writings expound the notion of an 'invisible dictatorship' which, by ensuring the unhindered expression of the people's will, would bring about 'absolute liberty', a state of being that Bakunin interprets collectivistically. He reverts to the mystical exaltation of his early idealism in passages in which he invites the revolutionary intellectual to 'drown' in the purifying stream of popular revolt, thereby exchanging the 'appearance' of power for its reality. His plans for dictatorship have been seen as attempts to act out idealist fantasies of spiritual self-fulfilment; they had disastrous consequences in his association with the notorious Jacobin Sergei Nechaev, whose *Catechism of a Revolutionary* justified all methods that furthered the cause of revolution, and who illustrated this theory in a murder that inspired Dostoevskii's *Besy* (The Possessed). Bakunin idealized Nechaev's violent personality and methods as the embodiment of a purifying force of destruction, and in 1869–70 collaborated with him on the production of pamphlets designed to foment a peasant rising in Russia. Bakunin's attempt to justify Nechaev's crime to his fellow revolutionaries was a shameful episode in his career, exemplifying his reluctance to confront the contradiction between his goal of anarchist liberty and the authoritarian means to which, in his millenarian impatience, he was prepared to resort.

List of works

Bakunin, M.A. (1961–) *Archives Bakounine*, ed. A. Lehning, Leiden: Brill. (The first complete edition, still in progress, of Bakunin's works, including previously unpublished manuscripts.)

—— (1873) *Gosudarstvennost' i anarkhiia*, trans. and ed. M.S. Shatz, *Statism and Anarchy*, Cambridge: Cambridge University Press, 1990. (One of his most important theoretical works.)

—— (1973) *Selected Writings*, ed. and introduced by A. Lehning, trans. S. Cox and O. Stevens, New York: Grove Press. (Selections from letters and works from 1836–73, including 'Reaction in Germany'.)

—— (1985) *From Out of the Dustbin: Bakunin's Basic Writings 1869–1871*, trans. and ed. R.C. Cutler, Ann Arbor, MI: Ardis. (Propaganda writings as a member of the International.)

References and further reading

Carr, E.H. (1975) *Michael Bakunin*, London: Macmillan, 2nd edn. (Still the best biography of Bakunin.)

Kelly, A. (1982) *Mikhail Bakunin. A Study in the Psychology and Politics of Utopianism*, Oxford: Clarendon Press. (Focuses on the influence of idealist philosophy on his thought.)

Mendel, A.P. (1981) *Michael Bakunin. Roots of Apocalypse*, New York: Praeger Publishers. (A psychoanalytic approach to the contradictions between Bakunin's authoritarianism and defence of freedom.)

AILEEN KELLY

BÁÑEZ, DOMINGO (1528–1604)

Domingo Báñez, once spiritual advisor to St Teresa of Avila, was a prominent Spanish theologian. In his commentaries on the Summa theologiae *of Thomas Aquinas, he challenged an essentialist reading of Aquinas, and insisted that* esse *(being) was an act. He is best known for his opposition to Molina's attempt to reconcile human free choice with divine foreknowledge, providence and grace. He also wrote on logic, and commented on Aristotle's* On Generation and Corruption.

Báñez studied at Salamanca, where he entered the Dominican Order in 1546. He held a series of teaching and administrative posts in Avila, Alcalá, Valladolid and Toro. In 1577 he returned to the University of Salamanca where he taught theology until he retired in 1600.

In logic, his *Summulae* (1599) stands out for its organization and its moderate use of nominalism (see NOMINALISM §1). Some of Báñez's points were original. For instance, in his section on signs, he rejected formal signs, reducing them to concepts and images, and taking away their character of mental language. As a result, he only accepted instrumental signs. He maintained the traditional division into natural and conventional signs, but explained that linguistic signs (especially onomatopoeia) were not so fully conventional that they had no relation with what is natural (see LANGUAGE, RENAISSANCE PHILOSOPHY OF §1). He restricted the scope of the section on consequences or inferences, and subordinated this material to syllogistic logic. His *Summulae* was very influential in Spain.

In metaphysics, he expounded an existential Thomism in his commentary on the first part of the *Summa theologiae* of Thomas AQUINAS (§§6, 9). He argued that *esse* (being) cannot be seen as a categorial accident. Nor does it enter reductively into the categories, as CAJETAN (§5) and CAPREOLUS held, except in so far as what is participated in is that which realizes *esse*. Nor is *esse* an essence or something arising from essential principles. Rather, it is an act or actuality, and not just the last act, as Cajetan held, but both the first and the last. That is, *esse* not only completes a being, but makes it possible for there to be a being at all. All actuality comes from *esse*, for by it an essence is actualized. This is so in the ideal order as well as the real, for we can only think of something as existent, yet there is still no implication that being should be viewed as quiddity or essence. Being is limited by potentiality and essence, but it also gives content to things, not essential content, but that of existence or actuality. Although *esse* must suffer some imperfection in order to be received in created beings, it perfects essence without being perfected by it, and as a result *esse* is more perfect than essence (see RENAISSANCE PHILOSOPHY §4; ARISTOTELIANISM, RENAISSANCE §2).

Báñez is best known for his work on human free choice. He replied to Luis de Molina's *Concordia* (first edition 1588) in a short work *De vera et legitima concordia liberi arbitrii* (On the True and Legitimate Reconciliation of Free Choice) (1600) (see MOLINA, L. DE §2). Following Aquinas, Báñez argued that the primacy in any action belongs to God's efficacious grace, and that no reconciliation can remove this primacy. There is a physical premotion on God's part which does not affect human freedom, for God moves all things in this way, and humans are able to choose. Moreover, God sees humans as free without his omniscience being affected. In fact, Molina had sought to defend human freedom, but he thought it was enough that there should be a general or simultaneous concurrence of God, as primary cause, and human beings, as secondary causes, in the production of a determinate act. For Báñez this was not enough: a stronger concurrence, including physical premotion on the part of God, was also required. Molina also appealed to God's solicited grace which aided humans to do supernatural works without thereby necessitating their will, and to middle knowledge (*scientia media*) through which God knows what may be brought about with or without secondary causes. God can thus see future contingents (*futuribilia*) in his essence without having to establish predetermined decrees concerning them. Báñez, on the other hand, argued that God's grace must be efficacious, and he believed that God does not need any middle knowledge in order to preserve the purity of human free action. God sees everything at once, and so he sees what is determined as determined, and what is free as free. Báñez showed that Molina's doctrines could not be reconciled with those of Aquinas.

See also: LANGUAGE, RENAISSANCE PHILOSOPHY OF; MOLINA, L. DE §2; MOLINISM

List of works

Báñez, D. (1571–1600) *Commentarios inéditos a la Tercera Parte de Santo Tomás* (Unpublished Commentaries on the Third Part of Aquinas' *Summa theologiae*), ed. V. Beltrán de Heredia, Madrid: Instituto Francisco Suárez, 1951–3, 2 vols.

—— (1583–1600) *Commentarios inéditos a la Prima Secundae de Santo Tomás* (Unpublished Commentaries on the First Part of the Second Part of Aquinas' *Summa theologiae*), ed. V. Beltrán de Heredia, Madrid: Instituto Francisco Suárez, 1942–8, 3 vols.

—— (1584) *The Primacy of Existence in Thomas Aquinas*, trans. B.S. Llamzon, Chicago, IL: Henry Regnery Company, 1966. (Translation of Báñez's commentary on *Summa theologiae* Ia.3.4.)

—— (1584–8) *Scholastica commentaria in primam partem Summae Theologiae S. Thomae Aquinatis* (Scholastic Commentary on the First Part of Aquinas' *Summa theologiae*), ed. L. Urbano, Madrid and Valencia: Editorial F.E.D.A., 1934; repr. Dubuque, IA: W.E. Brown Reprint Library, [1964?]. (The Brown reprint only includes up to question 26.)

References and further reading

Gutiérrez Vega, L. (1954) 'Domingo Báñez, filósofo existencial' (Domingo Báñez: An Existential

Philosopher), *Estudios Filosóficos* 3: 83–114. (On the emphasis that Báñez placed on *esse* within Thomistic metaphysics.)

Llamzon, B.S. (1964) 'The Specification of *Esse*: A Study in Báñez', *The Modern Schoolman* 41: 123–43. (A useful study of being and essence.)

—— (1965) 'Suppositional and Accidental *Esse*: A Study in Báñez', *New Scholasticism* 39: 170–88. (On the ways in which the being of substances and accidents differ.)

Muñoz Delgado, V. (1965) 'Domingo Báñez y las súmulas en Salamanca a fines del siglo XVI' (Domingo Báñez and the Summulae in Salamanca at the end of the 16th century), *Estudios* 21: 3–20. (On Báñez's reforms in logic and the great influence of his work.)

Translated by E.J. Ashworth

MAURICIO BEUCHOT

BAR HAYYA, ABRAHAM (*c*.1016–*c*.1136)

Abraham bar Hayya (also called bar Hiyya) sought to reconcile Jewish tradition with contemporary philosophical thought, in his case that received from Arabic sources. Generally considered to be a Neoplatonist whose philosophy is enriched with Aristotelian accretions, he has also been called the first Jewish Aristotelian. He pioneered the writing of philosophy in Hebrew, and his work influenced later Jewish philosophers and the Kabbalah.

1 Life and works
2 Metaphysics
3 Humility and eschatology
4 Significance

1 Life and works

Little is known of bar Hayya's life. Even the familiar form of his name, bar Hiyya, appears to be mistaken; there is clear evidence, including a rhyme in which he uses his name, that his patronymic was bar Hayya. He is known to have lived in Barcelona, but there is evidence that he visited France, probably Provence. He held high office, probably judicial, in the Jewish community and apparently also in the general community.

A polymath, bar Hayya wrote on astronomy and astrology, mathematics, geography, optics and music as well as philosophy. Some of his works, translated into Latin, became important sources in medieval European science. He himself was a translator from Arabic to Latin, collaborating on a number of scientific translations with the Christian scholar Plato of Tivoli, who transmitted the Ptolemaic system to the Latin world.

Bar Hayya's philosophy is found in two works, *Hegyon ha-Nefesh ha-Azuvah* (The Meditation of the Sad Soul), an ethical work based largely on homiletical expositions of biblical texts, and *Megillat ha-Megalleh* (The Scroll of the Revealer), written to fix an eschatological timetable according to which the Messiah will appear after 1136 and the dead will be resurrected in 1448, but also incorporating philosophical sections.

2 Metaphysics

Unlike many other medieval Jewish philosophers, bar Hayya omits proofs for God's existence and attributes, which he regards as self-evident. The structure of the universe clearly shows the unity of God and reveals him as its creator. Creation *ex nihilo* is assumed. The forms of all things and the archetypes of all species were first created in potentiality during the six days of creation, after which God brought them into actuality to endure throughout time. In potentiality things consist of form, matter and non-being. To bring them to actuality, God removed non-being and joined form to matter. Form and matter, the basic constituents of all that is, exist separately in God's pure thought, until conjoined by the divine will. Both are subdivided: matter into pure matter and sediment; form into closed and open forms. Creation results from the emanation of a light from the closed form (which itself is too pure to combine with matter and is identified with the light created on the first day in the biblical account) (see CREATION AND CONSERVATION, RELIGIOUS DOCTRINE OF). The upper world above the firmament (that is, the heavens) is divided into five worlds of light, the highest of which corresponds to the divine throne. The light emanating from within the closed form shines on the open form, enabling it to combine with matter. From this results the creation of the firmament and the four elements of which the world is composed. The human soul is a form temporarily attached to matter but ultimately destined to return to pure form. Expressed in traditional Jewish terms, the light can exist in this world and the world to come; the firmament and luminaries, in this world but not the next; and the lower creatures, in neither. Human beings are distinguished from other animals by their rational faculty, and those who act appropriately have their real existence in the next world, not this one.

3 Humility and eschatology

Humanity, the summit of creation, has three souls: vegetative, animal and rational (see SOUL, NATURE AND IMMORTALITY OF THE). The goal of human life is to subdue the lower two souls to the rule of the rational. If the rational soul rules, one is righteous; if the others dominate, one is wicked. At death, one retains only the rational soul, and its state determines one's subsequent fate. The highest reward goes to the saint, aloof from affairs of the world, whose whole life is devoted to the hereafter, in fear and worship of God. Such an individual separates himself from this world and is not moved by its desires or lusts. The ascetic ideal bar Hayya expresses here is rare in Jewish contexts, but it is found in his contemporary Bahya IBN PAKUDA. The guiding virtue for bar Hayya is humility, and he despises worldly possessions; but only one in a thousand is perfect and merits the full rewards of the world to come, the world of pure form, in which the saint is completely emancipated from matter. Those who have sinned have the freedom, while still alive, to repent, and the reward of sincere repentance is eternal bliss. The suffering of the righteous serves to test them in this world, so as to enhance their reward in the world to come. Evil, like good, emanates from God. It comes to the world not only to test the righteous but also to requite the wicked (see EVIL, PROBLEM OF). Free will ends with death; there is no subsequent repentance, and the actions of descendants cannot affect the fate of the dead (see FREE WILL).

Things acquired in this world have no permanence. The righteous live in this world only to establish merits that will sustain them in the next. We gain life in the world to come through belief in God and his Torah and by acting only for the sake of God. The wicked have no future after death; their disembodied souls mingle, leaving none distinguishable from its fellow. Obliteration is the fate of all non-Jews; for, even if they repent, it is not for God's sake. The world to come is unalloyed bliss, 'life without death, being without non-being'.

Just as man is superior to other animals, so Israel is superior to the other nations. However, this superiority is not exclusive; it is open to all who are willing to accept the Torah. In the messianic era, all evil will end and enmity will be abolished. All the wicked and most of the nations on earth will perish. Only Israel and true proselytes to the Torah will survive. All the sufferings of Israel will be requited at the time of salvation by punishments exacted upon the other nations of the world. Salvation will be followed by the resurrection of the dead, but only of Israel, the souls of the righteous reunited with their bodies.

4 Significance

Bar Hayya is usually classed within the Neoplatonic tradition because of his emanationism and his doctrine of light (see NEOPLATONISM). However, his ideas of form and matter, potentiality and actuality show the impact of Aristotelian thinking. He imbibes ideas from both traditions. Stitskin (1960) classed him firmly as an Aristotelian, a pioneer of Jewish Aristotelianism and of the reconciliation of biblical with Peripatetic thought, but bar Hayya was well acquainted with the various schools of Greek thought known in his time in Arabic adaptations and abridgments, and he sometimes also reflects Arab mystical thought and the ideas of the Ikhwan al-Safa' (see IKHWAN AL-SAFA'). He was also familiar with Christian thought. His sources were eclectic, and his emphases often motivated by Jewish concerns. He cannot be tied exclusively to a single system.

Like other Jewish philosophers, bar Hayya sought to reconcile Jewish tradition with the rationalism of his day. All his philosophical work has a biblical or rabbinic basis, and it often uses exegetical methodology to link his philosophical reflections to scriptural tradition. Indeed two of the four chapters of the *Hegyon ha-Nefesh* take the form of homilies on the prophetic portions (Isaiah 57: 14–58: 14 and Jonah) read in the synagogue on the morning and afternoon of the Day of Atonement. His treatments of sin, repentance, and eschatology follow rabbinic tradition.

Along with his contemporary fellow-townsman Judah ben Barzillai, bar Hayya was the first Jewish philosopher to write in Hebrew, and as a result he had to coin many of the terms he used (Efros 1926–7). His predecessors had written in Arabic (in Hebrew letters) for an audience of Jews in Islamic countries. Bar Hayya's use of Hebrew in philosophic and scientific works indicates that he was writing for other Jews as well, perhaps in southern France. For them, philosophical thought would have been a novelty, and bar Hayya is at pains to stress that his ideas could be inferred from biblical sources. The influence of his writings can be traced in later Jewish philosophical thinkers, as well as in Kabbalistic thought, including the Book of Bahir and the German pietists.

See also: BIBLE, HEBREW; ESCHATOLOGY; NEOPLATONISM

List of works

Bar Hayya, Abraham (c.1016–c.1136) *Megillat ha-Megalleh* (The Scroll of the Revealer), ed. A. Poznanski, Berlin: Mekitzei Nirdamim, 1924.

(Account of bar Hayya's eschatological views, with their theoretical implications.)

—— (c.1016–c.1136) *Hegyon ha-Nefesh ha-Azuvah* (The Meditation of the Sad Soul), ed. G. Wigoder, Jersualem: Mosad Bialik, 1971; trans. G. Wigoder, *The Meditation of the Sad Soul*, London: Routledge & Kegan Paul, 1969. (Very important text detailing bar Hayya's main philosophical principles.)

References and further reading

* Efros, I. (1926–7) 'Studies in pre-Tibbonian Philosophical Terminology', *Jewish Quarterly Review* 17: 129–64, 323–68, and 20: 113–38. (Discussion of early Jewish philosophical terminology.)
Husik, I. (1942) *History of Medieval Jewish Philosophy*, Philadelphia, PA: Jewish Publications Society of America. (General history of Jewish philosophy.)
* Stitskin, L. (1960) *Judaism as a Philosophy: The Philosophy of Abraham bar Hiyya*, New York: Bloch. (Full-length study of bar Hayya.)
Vajda, G. (1946) 'Les idees théologiques et philosophiques d'Abraham bar Hiyya' (The Theological and Philosophical Ideas of Abraham bar Hayya), *Archives d'Histoire doctrinal et littéraire du moyen âge* 15: 193–223. (Study of bar Hayya's philosophy.)

GEOFFREY WIGODER

BAR HIYYA, ABRAHAM *see* BAR HAYYA, ABRAHAM

BARTH, KARL (1886–1968)

Karl Barth was the most prominent Protestant theologian of a generation shaken by the traumatic experience of the First World War and concerned with giving Christian theology a new grounding. He took a creative part in the struggle of the German Church against National Socialism, and, after the Second World War, exerted a worldwide influence that reached beyond the bounds of Protestantism. Although influenced at first by Christian socialism, Barth came to repudiate such 'hyphenated' versions of Christianity, which, he felt, underemphasize or ignore the otherness of God. There is an infinite qualitative distinction between the divine and the human; the Enlightenment attempt to historicize and secularize revelation was profoundly mistaken. This 'dialectical theology' attracted a number of leading theologians in the 1920s.

Later, however, Barth felt compelled to close the gap with the divine, and developed a 'theology of the Word' to this end. Central to this approach is the concept of the knowledge conferred by faith, which makes theological understanding and rationality possible. It was on the basis of this that Barth constructed his massive Die Kirchliche Dogmatik *(Church Dogmatics) (1932–70). In this, he emphasizes the self-expounding nature of Scripture (by contrast with nineteenth-century biblical scholarship, which stressed the need for a historical approach to the text) and the importance of Christ in the understanding of theology and human nature. He was a determined opponent of natural theology, and was critical of the idea that philosophy could complement theology.*

1 Life
2 Dialectical theology
3 Theology of the Word
4 Philosophy

1 Life

Karl Barth, a German-speaking Swiss theologian, was born in Basle, the son of Fritz Barth and Anna Sartorius. In 1889, his father, a minister and theologian of the liberal school, succeeded Adolf Schlatter at Bern University. Hence Barth was raised in Bern, where he attended the Free Gymnasium. Under his father's influence he read theology at the local divinity school. He completed his theological education in Germany, in Berlin, Tübingen and Marburg. In Berlin, he attended the lectures of the prominent liberal Church historian Adolf von Harnack. In Marburg, he fell under the influence of the Christocentric dogmatician Wilhelm Herrmann, Albrecht Ritschl's most prominent disciple. Barth's career began as assistant pastor in Geneva in 1909 and culminated as professor of theology at Basle University. Meanwhile he had played a crucial role in the German Church's struggle against National Socialism and had become, in Eberhard Jüngel's words, 'the most significant Protestant theologian since Schleiermacher'.

Barth served as a pastor in Safenwil in Aargau from 1911 to 1921. In 1913, he married Nelly Hoffmann, with whom he had five children. A liberal theologian by training, Barth was faced at Safenwil with the predicament of the working class for the first time in his life. To help the workers in his congregation he began to study law. He frequented the 'religious socialists', led by Hermann Kutter and Leonard Ragaz. In December 1911, he delivered a speech to Safenwil's Workers' Union, 'Jesus Christus und der soziale Bewegung' ('Jesus Christ and the

Movement for Social Justice'), which identified Christianity with socialism. Barth claimed that 'Jesus is the social movement and that the social movement is Jesus today'. The start of the First World War broke the spell. His confidence in Culture-Protestantism was shattered. Liberal theologians had failed to prevent a resurgence of barbarism, in spite of their repeated emphasis on the religious, moral and social commitments of the Christian. The open support given by leading German theologians to the Kaiser shocked him deeply.

In September 1919, Barth delivered an epochal lecture, 'Der Christ in der Gesellschaft' ('The Christian in Society'), at a religious socialist conference in Thuringia. Won over to Christoph Blumhardt's millenarian eschatology, Barth deprecated altogether Adolf Stöcker's Christian-social movement, Friedrich Naumann's Protestant-social era, and Ragaz's religious-social programme. All these ventures, charged Barth, result in a 'hyphenated Christianity' that merges religion with socialism at the expense of revelation and the Beyond. Instead, he demanded that the otherworldliness of God be truly respected. Barth's speech marked a return to the theological paradigms of sixteenth- and seventeenth-century Protestantism. The same year, Barth published *Der Römerbrief* (*The Epistle to the Romans*), which heralded a new era in Protestant theology. A revised edition appeared in 1922 and an English translation in 1935. Emil Brunner, a Swiss colleague, praised Barth's commentary as the first victory over the platitudes of nineteenth-century Protestantism, while a dismayed Harnack saw it as part of the sickness of the age.

Barth's *The Epistle to the Romans*, which signalled the end of modernity for Protestantism, established his reputation, and he was called to the chair of Reformed theology at Göttingen in 1922. It also gave rise to the 'theology of crisis' school, the movement baptized by Bultmann as 'dialectical theology'. Eduard Thurneysen, Friedrich Gogarten, Emil BRUNNER (§1) and Rudolf BULTMANN (§2) were among the school's most outstanding advocates. In 1923, the dialectical theologians started the journal *Between the Times*, under the editorship of George Merz, which lasted until the school's disruption in 1933. By the time of Hitler's accession to power, however, the dialectical theologians had gone separate ways. In 1925, Barth assumed the chair of systematic theology at Münster. He moved to the University of Bonn in 1930 and was dismissed in 1935 for refusing to take the oath of allegiance to Hitler. Meanwhile, he had taken part in the struggle against the German Christian movement. The 'Barmen Confession' (1934a), a rallying statement by a collection of evangelical ministers and teachers, was based on preparatory work by Barth. This confessional document spoke against the German Christians' nationalist, racist and anti-Semitic teachings, and affirmed Jesus Christ to be the one Word of God. It gave rise to the Confessing Church.

Barth returned to Switzerland to take a chair of systematic theology in Basel, a position he held until he retired at the age of 75. From there he continued his opposition to the Nazi regime, publishing polemical articles in *Between the Times* and in *Evangelical Theology*, as well as numerous pamphlets. He also pursued the writing of his major work, *Die Kirchliche Dogmatik* (*Church Dogmatics*), which he had begun in 1932. Through the years the work grew to thirteen volumes of over nine thousand pages. The *Church Dogmatics* is more than a systematic theology; it abounds with exegetical, historical, theological, practical and philosophical ideas, and is widely regarded as a classic.

During the Second World War, Barth championed the cause of the Allies. However, he was among the first to plead for reconciliation with defeated Germany. He went back to Bonn in the academic year 1946–7 and lectured at his former university. During the East–West conflict, he refused on moral grounds to view communism as on a level with National Socialism. He delivered the opening address at the first meeting of the World Council of Churches in Amsterdam in 1948, and lectured in many European countries and the USA. In 1966, he visited Rome at the invitation of Pope Paul VI and upon his return published *Ad limina apostolorum* (1967).

2 Dialectical theology

The 'theology of crisis' differs from the theological systems of neo-Protestantism (eighteenth- and nineteenth-century Protestantism) in its task and its method. What Barth proclaims in his *The Epistle to the Romans* is the otherness of God. Contrary to liberal theology, God is neither the sum of subjectivity and objectivity, nor a result of personal experience in either consciousness or history, but the Lord (*Gott der Herr*), the wholly other (*totaliter aliter*). Postulating the identity of God (*Gott ist Gott*) – a tautological axiom – Barth further predicates, under Kierkegaard's influence, an infinite qualitative distinction between time and eternity (see KIERKEGAARD, S.A. §§4–5). He postulates a radical separation between the divine and the human, and understands the relationship between transcendence and immanence as one of absolute apartness. In restoring the sixteenth-century Reformers' supernaturalism, he overturned the nineteenth-century account of the connection between revelation and history and repudiated the cultural objectives of later Protestantism. Barth accused the Enlightenment of having given rise to a way of thinking that psychologized, historicized, moralized and secularized revelation, the eternal and the Beyond. He thus rejected any form of relation between theology and philosophy, the former being the proclamation of God's sovereign grace. Barth put an end to the post-Kantian synthesis of neo-Protestantism, substituting a principle of separation for one of unity, causality and identity.

But if God is uncompromisingly transcendent, how can human beings speak about God? Wilhelm Herrmann's answer was that this is possible because God has revealed himself – we can speak of God because of the Incarnation. The way to God originates from God. Since for Barth human beings are finite, lacking the capacity for the infinite, all human ways are bound to end in failure. Thus faith is a crisis and grace a pure miracle. Barth thus stressed two of the Reformation's fundamental doctrines: the imputed justification by faith and the absent God. Justification comes from beyond us. The resurrection reveals the One who lives in the inaccessible light, the incognito of God.

Concerning the method of theology, Barth discarded the idea of a 'scientific' theology, much valued by the liberals, and instead proposed a theologizing process which starts from the object itself, the Beyond. He inverted the traditional noetic process, which, since Descartes, had proceeded from the thinking subject. On the contrary, claimed Barth, the human knowledge of God originates from God's knowledge. This is a Hegelian legacy. Barth propounded the dialectical method in 1922 in 'Das Wort Gottes als Aufgabe der Theologie' (The Word of God as the Task of Theology). The divine Word is the source of theological knowledge, the foundation of Christian dogmatics and the guiding principle of every theological doctrine. What the dialectical method stresses is the paradoxical nature of the revelation. Barth later realized that the dialectical method hindered theological production and devised a new method.

3 Theology of the Word

The introduction of the Trinity in Barth's structuring of theology in 1924 marked a transition from 'dialectical theology' to the 'theology of the Word'. To bridge the divide between the divine and the human was essential to Barth. Besides Hegel, he followed Peter LOMBARD and BONAVENTURE (§4). In 1927 he published a dogmatics (*Die christliche Dogmatik in Entwurf*, Christian Dogmatics in Outline), and in 1931 a study of Anselm (*Fides quaerens intellectum*, Faith Seeking Understanding) in which he defended a fiducial interpretation of the ontological argument (see ANSELM OF CANTERBURY §§3-4). The Anselmian proof presupposes the fiducial knowledge of the God whose existence it claims to prove rationally. Understanding presupposes belief. The discovery of Anselm made possible what the dialectical method had rendered impossible. Owing to the centrality of the knowledge of faith in the noetic process, understanding and rationality – both indispensable in order to write a dogmatics – were possible. Fiducial knowledge is proper to theology; it becomes rational knowledge through analysis of the content of revelation, which communicates God's Word. And, again following HEGEL (§4), revelation is a self-revelation. Faith and rationality are united in the understanding of faith. Fiducial knowledge is intrinsically rational because its essence, the Word of God, is rational.

From this perspective, Barth undertook the construction of the *Church Dogmatics*, a systematic theology which can best be characterized as biblical, Christocentric and ecclesiastical. The Scripture is the authoritative witness to God's revelation in Jesus Christ. It is the written Word, which points to the Word revealed and grounds the Word preached. The meaning of Scripture can only be obtained by allowing Scripture to be its own interpreter. This idea stems from the sixteenth-century Reformers. Calvin's doctrine of Scripture emphasizes two main ideas: clarity and sacred Scripture as its own interpreter. Like CALVIN (§2), Barth asserts the self-expounding clarity of Scripture. Any prior understanding of God, a philosophical presupposition or anything else, is thus excluded from Barth's hermeneutics. God's self-revelation in Jesus Christ can only be known and confessed as it is attested and expounded by the direct witnesses. Against nineteenth-century biblical scholarship, Barth denied the ability of the historical-critical method to go behind the text. Hearing God's Word comprises three stages: explanation, reflection and appropriation.

Jesus Christ is the ground, content and object of Christian religion. Christian doctrines must therefore be interpreted in the light of the Incarnation. Barth acknowledged the Chalcedonian doctrine of two natures and asserted that the person of Jesus Christ is the union of true deity and true humanity (see INCARNATION AND CHRISTOLOGY §1). The cross and the resurrection clear the way for human justification and sanctification. God's self-revelation, Jesus Christ, is at the same time the true human being. Jesus Christ discloses for us the essential truth about human nature; he is the source of knowledge for anthropology as well as for theology. Barth's Christocentric interpretation of the Bible involved a return to the traditional relationship between creation and redemption, as well as to the Lutheran dialectic of Law and Gospel. As creation must be seen in the light of redemption, so the Law must be understood in the light of the Gospel.

Barth's dogmatics is a systematic theology written within the Church for the Church. The ministry of the Church is threefold: it consists of the declaration, explication and application of God's Gospel. Such ministry may take the form of speech or action. Although salvation primarily concerns human existence, it is essentially eschatological. Hence the Church anticipates the *eschaton*, the fulfilment of redemption.

4 Philosophy

The relationship of Barthian theology to philosophy is ambiguous. Barth made ample use of philosophical structures and concepts, while at the same time claiming the independence of theology from philosophy. He ruled out any possible alliance, even one that would result in philosophy being construed as the handmaid of theology.

Barth discarded any philosophical preconditions for faith. The tautological axiom ('God is God') and the Christocentric principle preclude any knowledge of God from other sources. In Barth's thought, unlike Calvin's, there is no room for a general revelation of God, be it in human consciousness, in nature or in history. Thus he declared war against natural theology, a stance exemplified in the notorious dispute with Emil BRUNNER (§§2, 4) (Barth 1934b). For Barth, natural theology was closely associated with Roman Catholicism and particularly with the Thomist doctrine of the analogy of being. He objected on three major grounds: first, the thinking process starts from below, from finite human understanding; second, it sunders God's essence, which is naturally knowable, from God's action, which is known supernaturally by means of revelation; third, it jeopardizes the exclusiveness of God's revelation in Jesus Christ. Instead, Barth proposed an analogy of faith, or of relation. A faith relationship to God is the prerequisite for any discourse about God. And any true faith relationship exclusively depends on God's self-revelation in Jesus Christ. Furthermore, God's relationship to humanity depends on God's self-relationship, on the interrelatedness of the Trinity as revealer, revelation and revealed (*Offenbarer*, *Offenbarung* and *Offenbarsein*).

In 'Philosophie und Theologie' (1960), Barth appraises the possibility of philosophy and theology coexisting. He observes that philosophers may choose their starting-points whereas theologians are bound to start with the Incarnation. Starting from below, philosophizing is an ascending process. It moves upwards from the phenomenon to the idea, from reason to being. By contrast, theologizing is a retracing of God's condescending movement. Therefore the philosopher and the theologian are separated by a matter of order and priority. They may share a common objective, but their methods are incompatible.

List of works

Barth, K. (1971–) *Gesamtausgabe* (Complete Edition), Zurich: Theologischer Verlag. (Only a few volumes of this massive collection have been published so far.)

—— (1911) 'Jesus Christus und der soziale Bewegung', trans. G. Hunsinger, 'Jesus Christ and the Movement for Social Justice', in G. Hunsinger (ed.) *Karl Barth and Radical Politics*, Philadelphia, PA: Westminster Press, 1976. (In this lecture, delivered on 17 December 1911 in Safenwil, Barth sets out his early view of religious socialism as it relates to faith in Jesus Christ.)

—— (1919a) 'Der Christ in der Gesellschaft', in *Das Wort Gottes und die Theologie* (The Word of God and Theology), Munich: Chr. Kaiser Verlag, 1924; trans. D. Horton, 'The Christian in Society', in *The Word of God and the Word of Man*, London: Hodder & Stoughton, 1928. (In this lecture, delivered on 25 September 1919, Barth distinguishes himself from various forms of religious socialism which do not do justice to God's otherness.)

—— (1919b) *Der Römerbrief*, Bern: Bäschlin; 2nd edn, much changed, Munich: Chr. Kaiser Verlag, 1922; 6th edn trans. E.C. Hoskyns, *The Epistle to the Romans*, Oxford: Oxford University Press, 1968. (A proclamation of the otherness and judgment of God, who nevertheless saves; this book had an incalculable impact on European theology.)

—— (1922) 'Das Wort Gottes als Aufgabe der Theologie' (The Word of God as the Task of Theology), in *Das Wort Gottes und die Theologie* (The Word of God and Theology), Munich: Chr. Kaiser Verlag, 1924; trans. D. Horton, 'The Word of God and the Task of the Ministry', in *The Word of God and the Word of Man*, London: Hodder & Stoughton, 1928. (Barth expanded on his postliberal, dialectical vision of theology in this lecture given on 3 October 1922 in Elgersberg.)

—— (1927) *Die christliche Dogmatik in Entwurf, 1: Die Lehre vom Worte Gottes* (Christian Dogmatics in Outline, 1: The Doctrine of the Word of God),

Munich: Chr. Kaiser Verlag. (An abandoned attempt at a full dogmatics.)

—— (1931) *Fides quaerens intellectum: Anselms Beweis der Existenz Gottes in Zusammenhang seines theologischen Programmes* (Faith Seeking Understanding: Anselm's Proof of the Existence of God in Relation to his Theological Programme), Munich: Chr. Kaiser Verlag; trans. I.W. Robertson, *Anselm: Fides quaerens intellectum*, London: SCM Press, 1960. (Held by some to mark the transition from Barth's dialectical theology to a more expansive, substantive theology of the Word.)

—— (1932–70) *Die Kirchliche Dogmatik* 1 – 4, with index vol., Munich: Chr. Kaiser Verlag, and Zurich: Evangelischer Verlag; trans. G.W. Bromiley *et al.*, ed. G.W. Bromiley and T.F. Torrance, *Church Dogmatics*, Edinburgh: T. & T. Clark, 1956–77. (Barth's greatest, and longest, work: a sadly unfinished interpretation of all the major Christian doctrines.)

—— (1934a) 'Theologische Erklärung zur gegenwärtigen Lage in der Deutschen Evangelischen Kirche' (Theological Declaration on the Present Situation in the German Evangelical Church), in *Junge Kirche* 2, Göttingen; trans. R. McAfee Brown, 'The Barmen Confession', in G. Cassalis, *Portrait of Karl Barth*, New York: Doubleday, 1963. (Barth was heavily involved in drafting this declaration directed against the capitulation of German Christians to Hitler.)

—— (1934b) 'Nein! Antwort an Emil Brunner', *Theological Existenz heute* 14; trans. P. Fraenkel, 'No! Answer to Emil Brunner', in K. Barth and E. Brunner, *Natural Theology*, London: Geoffrey Bles, 1946. (A famous and blunt rejection of natural theology.)

—— (1947a) *Dogmatik im Grundriss*, Zollikon-Zurich: Evangelischer Verlag; trans. G.T. Thomson, *Dogmatics in Outline*, London: SCM Press, 1949. (Not to be confused with Barth 1927 above, this is a beautifully clear introduction to Barth's later work.)

—— (1947b) *Die Protestantische Theologie im 19. Jahrhundert*, Zollikon-Zurich: Evangelischer Verlag; trans. B. Cozens and J. Bowden, *Protestant Theology in the Nineteenth Century*, London: SCM Press, 1972. (Barth's history of the century of theology after Schleiermacher, against which he reacted.)

—— (1954) *Against the Stream: Shorter Post-War Writings 1946–52*, trans. E.M. Delacour and S. Godman, London: SCM Press, 1954. (Political and theological talks and articles.)

—— (1960) 'Philosophie und Theologie', in G. Huber (ed.) *Philosophie und christliche Existenz: Festschrift für Heinrich Barth zum 70 Geburtstag am 3.2.1960*, Basle and Stuttgart: Helbing & Lichtenhahn. (Sets out Barth's understanding of the relationship between these two human enterprises.)

—— (1961) *The Humanity of God*, trans. J. Newton Thomas, Richmond, VA: John Knox Press. (Several shorter pieces; in the title essay, Barth describes how and why his position has modified over the years.)

—— (1967) *Ad limina apostolorum*, Zurich-Zollikon: Evangelischer Verlag; trans. K.R. Crim, *Ad limina apostolorum: An Appraisal of Vatican II*, Richmond, VA: John Knox Press, 1968. (As this work shows, although Barth remained wary of Roman Catholicism, he had great sympathy for much that he found, particularly in Vatican II.)

References and further reading

Balthasar, H.U. von (1976) *Karl Barth: Darstellung und Deutung seiner Theologie*, Einsiedeln: Johannes Verlag, 4th edn; trans. E.T. Oakes, *The Theology of Karl Barth: Exposition and Interpretation*, San Fransisco, CA: Communio Books, 1992. (One of the most influential commentaries on Barth, now a little dated but still important.)

Busch, E. (1976) *Karl Barth: His Life from Letters and Autobiographical Texts*, Philadelphia, PA: Fortress Press. (The standard biographical source.)

Ford, D. (1981) *Barth and God's Story: Biblical Narrative and the Theological Method of Karl Barth in the 'Church Dogmatics'*, Frankfurt am Main and Bern: Verlag Peter Lang. (The best introduction to Barth's hermeneutics, drawing on P. Stern's work on realism.)

Frei, H. (1992) *Types of Christian Theology*, ed. G. Hunsinger and W. Placher, New Haven, CT: Yale University Press. (Contains several sections on Barth, and, in particular, on the relationship of theology and philosophy in his work; argues that there is an *ad hoc* correlation between the two in Barth.)

Hunsinger, G. (1991) *How to Read Karl Barth: The Shape of his Theology*, Oxford: Oxford University Press. (An introduction to reading the *Church Dogmatics*, and a study of Barth's treatment of truth and freedom.)

Jüngel. E. (1986) *Karl Barth: A Theological Legacy*, trans. G.E. Paul, Philadelphia, PA: Westminster Press. (Various essays by perhaps the greatest theological interpreter and follower of Barth.)

McCormack, B. (1995) *Karl Barth's Critically Realistic Dialectical Theology: Its Genesis and Development 1909–1936*, Oxford: Clarendon Press. (The most detailed and lucid survey in English of Barth's development, challenging many received understandings.)

Sykes, S. (ed.) (1989) *Karl Barth: Centenary Essays*, Cambridge: Cambridge University Press. (Several fine essays, including Ingolf Daflerth on Barth and Kantianism.)

Webster, J. (1995) *Barth's Ethics of Reconciliation*, Cambridge: Cambridge University Press. (A clear, volume-by-volume survey of the *Dogmatics*, particularly ethical issues, and an investigation of 'moral ontology' in Barth's work.)

Wildi, H.M. (1984–92) *Bibliographie Karl Barths*, Zurich: Theologischer Verlag, 3 vols. (A complete bibliography of many thousands of primary and secondary items, with comprehensive indices.)

JEAN-LOUP SEBAN

BARTHES, ROLAND (1915–80)

In the field of contemporary literary studies, the French essayist and cultural critic Roland Barthes cannot be easily classified. His early work on language and culture was strongly influenced by the intellectual currents of existentialism and Marxism that were dominant in French intellectual life in the mid-twentieth century. Gradually his work turned more to semiology (a general theory of signs), which had a close association with the structuralist tradition in literary criticism. In his later work, Barthes wrote more as a post-structuralist than as a structuralist in an attempt to define the nature and authority of a text. Throughout his writings Barthes rejected the 'naturalist' view of language, which takes the sign as a representation of reality. He maintained that language is a dynamic activity that dramatically affects literary and cultural practices.

1 Early writings
2 Post-structuralist criticism

1 Early writings

Roland Barthes was born in Cherbourg, France and studied French literature and Classics at the University of Paris. After a long illness that caused him to spend time in sanatoria during the war years, he taught French at the Universities of Bucharest and Alexandria, and began further studies in sociology. In 1947 he published a number of articles in *Combat* on literary criticism that formed the basis of his first book, *Le Degré zéro de l'écriture* (1953) (*Writing Degree Zero*, 1968). In 1960 he began teaching at the École Pratique des Hautes Études, and in 1976 he became Professor of Literary Semiology at the Collège de France. Barthes died after being struck by a van outside the Collège de France.

In *Writing Degree Zero* Barthes formulated a theory of writing on the basis of an account of language as a 'social object' and a 'field of action' in which the writer communicates. This account has much in common with the existentialist writer Jean-Paul SARTRE, who, like Barthes, sought to break free of the orthodox view of literature as a-historical and considered it ideological in its unquestioned acceptance of the bourgeois universe. Against this view the writer is to be a liberator. Unlike Sartre, however, Barthes came to the conclusion that the writer can do little directly to effect social change and that the writer does not write exclusively for the sake of society. The writer also writes for the sake of writing. Barthes uses the special term 'writing' (*écriture*) to capture this double aspect of the writer. Writing is the middle ground between language, as that which resides in history (the material of writing), and style, as that which is indifferent to history and society (personal contribution to writing). Accordingly, writing is neither strictly historical nor strictly personal; it is an ambiguous reality arising as a confrontation of the writer with society and at the same time referring the writer back to the instruments of creation.

Increasingly Barthes came to adopt a more complex view of language, which enabled him further to develop his critique of the status quo. In general this view followed the linguistic structuralism of the Swiss linguist Ferdinand de SAUSSURE, for whom language as a whole was composed of *langue*, the system of signs that allows for the construction of words in an oppositional phonological play, and *parole*, the actual experience of speaking. From the point of view of semiological analysis (analysis of signs) Barthes opposed the prevailing literary ideology that took the sign as a natural representation of reality rather than an arbitrary convention. This criticism was not limited to literature, which he regarded as only one among many signifying systems. Food, clothing, film, advertising and fashion were also viewed as signifying systems. In this broadened universe of signs Barthes directed his criticism at the bourgeois myths that naturalized objects and events so as to exempt them from political change. In *Mythologies* (1957), for example, Barthes showed how something as simple as a photograph appearing on the cover of the magazine *Paris-Match* can signify bourgeois myth. The photograph depicts a black soldier saluting the flag, signifying that France is a great empire without regard to race. Barthes, however, decoded this sign as an implicit defence of French colonialism. In both literary studies and cultural criticism Barthes's goal was to demythologize the sign

2 Post-structuralist criticism

Along with other French intellectuals in the late 1960s, Barthes began to distance himself from the possibility of a science of signs and expanded his critique of writing by adhering to a post-structuralist notion of the text (see POST-STRUCTURALISM). In his critical analysis of a novella of Balzac, *S/Z* (1970), Barthes insisted that the literary text must be explored in terms of the way the text outplays the literary codes which structuralism relies upon to make the text intelligible. The theoretical basis for this changed position is laid out in the brief essay 'The Death of the Author' (1968, in Barthes 1977a). Barthes pointed out that the author is a modern figure, the product of a society that has discovered the prestige of the individual. The author is regarded as the father and owner of the text, as the final signified, which preserves the unity of the text and to which all reading is directed. But Barthes insisted that what is written cannot be reduced to the authority of the author any more than language can be viewed as an unambiguous instrument of communication. Drawing from such literary writers as Joyce and Mallarmé, Barthes claimed that to write is to reach the point where it is not the subject who acts, but language. Writing destroys every point of origin so that the author is never more than the instance writing, 'just as I is nothing other than the instance saying *I*' (Barthes 1977a: 145).

With the death of the author the modern text is in the hands of the new 'scriptor' who practises a different kind of writing, one that no longer imposes a limit on the proliferation of signification. Rather than working from a given meaning, the modern scriptor works towards meaning by writing 'intransitively', infinitely deferring the signified and thereby producing a plurality of meaning. Such writing is viewed as a form of liberation, an anti-theological activity refusing God and his hypostases – reason, science, law. In this new mode of writing, traditional criticism, whether biographical, historical or formalist, is undermined. The role of the critic is not to decipher the meaning, looking for the secret of the text, but to disentangle the plurality of meaning, even transposing meaning from the text into different discourses.

Because of the work of the modern 'scriptor', the reader now assumes the important role of providing the unity of the text. This reader, though, unlike the author, is not personal since the reader is without history, biography or psychology. The reader is simply 'that someone who holds together in a single field all the traces by which the written text is constituted' (Barthes 1977a: 148) In holding the text together in this way, the reader no longer regards the text as an object of consumption, but as an activity of production. The reader becomes a collaborator in the very execution of the text, setting the text free towards meaning.

During the 1970s Barthes continued to develop ways to express his scepticism of normative notions in textual criticism. In *Le Plaisir du texte* (1973) (*Pleasure of the Text*, 1975), which theoretically draws loosely on the framework of psychoanalysis, he described reading as a form of pleasure or bliss (*jouissance*) that allows for a free play of meaning from the text. Reading is not unlike a sexual act with the erotic body of language; it is unpredictable, fleeting, and culminates, like orgasm, in its disappearance. The result of this approach to texts was the espousal of discourse as fragment. Stylistically Barthes's own writing became purposefully fragmentary. His autobiography *Roland Barthes par Roland Barthes* (1975) is a classic illustration of a text without unity. In place of an account of a subject with a coherent identity, Barthes writes, in the third person, on the experience of writing and on the distinctive themes that marked his own literary production.

See also: DECONSTRUCTION

List of works

Barthes, R. (1953) *Le Degré zéro de l'écriture*, trans. A. Lavers and C. Smith, *Writing Degree Zero*, New York: Hill & Wang, 1968.

—— (1957) *Mythologies*, trans. A. Lavers, *Mythologies*, London: Paladin, 1972.

—— (1964) *Essais critiques*, trans. R. Howard, *Critical Essays*, Evanston, IL: Northwestern University Press, 1972.

—— (1966) *Critique et vérité*, trans. K. Keuneman, *Criticism and Truth*, Minneapolis, MN: University of Minnesota Press, 1987.

—— (1970) *S/Z*, trans. R. Miller, *S/Z*, New York: Hill & Wang, 1974.

—— (1973) *Le Plaisir du texte*, trans. R. Miller, *The Pleasure of the Text*, New York: Hill & Wang, 1975.

—— (1975) *Roland Barthes par Roland Barthes*, trans. R. Howard, *Roland Barthes by Roland Barthes*, New York: Hill & Wang, 1977.

—— (1977a) *Image-Music-Text*, trans. S. Heath, New York: Hill & Wang. (A selection of Barthes's uncollected essays, including 'The Death of the Author' and 'From Work to Text'.)

—— (1977b) *Fragments d'un discours amoureux*, trans. R. Howard, *A Lover's Discourse: fragments*, New York: Hill & Wang, 1978.

References and further reading

Culler, J. (1983) *Barthes*, New York: Oxford University Press. (A good introduction to Barthes's work.)

Lavers, A. (1982) *Roland Barthes: Structuralism and After*, Cambridge, MA: Harvard University Press. (A detailed account of Barthes's philosophy concentrating mainly on Barthes's earlier writing.)

Lombardo, P. (1989) *The Three Paradoxes of Roland Barthes*, Athens, GA: University of Georgia Press. (A highly nuanced reading of Barthes's writing, considered thematically.)

JAMES RISSER

BARTOLUS OF SASSOFERRATO (OR SAXOFERRATO) (1313/14–57)

The Bartolist school of civil lawyers or 'commentators' dominated university law teaching from the fourteenth century. Challenged by the humanists in the sixteenth century, they remained influential in practice. Bartolus excelled among them in the ability to devise solutions to practical problems and provide clear and workable doctrines applying the civil law texts to legal and political problems.

Born in Sassoferrato, Bartolus studied civil law under Cinus of Pistoia at Perugia from 1328 but his baccalaureate in 1333 and doctorate in 1334 were at Bologna. He practised for a period and was a legal assessor at Todi, then probably at Cagli and finally at Pisa in 1339. In 1339 he became professor at Pisa. In 1342–3 he moved to Perugia, remaining there until his death in 1357. Baldus was his pupil and, from about 1351, his colleague there.

The older name for the 'commentators' is 'postglossators' because they worked from texts of the *Corpus iuris civilis* (body of the civil law) provided in the thirteenth century with a massive apparatus of glosses, the Accursian or great Gloss, which in effect sums up the work of the preceding school of civilians, the glossators. Their commentaries, a product of their teaching, form a major part of their literary output and give them their name. There and in their other works, using the Aristotelian 'new logic', they draw out from text and gloss ideas which they use to solve current problems. The original context of the texts used is scarcely relevant. From civil (and canon) law texts they thus created a living common law to which appeal could be made where local sources were inadequate.

Bartolus was pre-eminent in authority, noted for his practical sense and his ability to get to the heart of a problem and expound it clearly, for example, in conflict of laws, where more than one legal system is potentially applicable to a legal dispute, and in the issue of sovereignty. His views were constantly referred to and commonly deferred to. Like all medieval lawyers he drew on his predecessors, using especially the ultramontane (French) writers of the later thirteenth century who strongly influenced his first teacher, Cinus. Sometimes, therefore, he is given credit for originating ideas to which he rather gave currency, for example, the distinction between 'real' statutes, applying to things (*res*) and so territorial in operation, and 'personal' statutes, applying to those subject to them everywhere. Where he did adopt ideas he nevertheless gave them his own stamp, and by adopting them he ensured their lasting influence.

Bartolus left a huge body of writing, but both manuscripts and prints contain false attributions. His main works were his commentaries (or *lecturae*, literally, readings) on the various parts of the *Corpus iuris civilis*, along with special lectures (*repetitiones*) some of which are preserved separately, advisory opinions to parties or judges (*consilia*), academic discussions of problem cases (*quaestiones*) and treatises (*tractatus*) on individual topics, legal and political.

See also: LAW, PHILOSOPHY OF; ROMAN LAW

List of works

(The dates of publication given are mainly the dates of first printing. There are numerous later editions up to the seventeenth century.)

Bartolus (1333–57) *Quaestiones* (Academic Disputations), Venice, 1471. (Eighteen disputations; four more in Venice, 1521 edition.)

—— (1339–52) *Lecturae (Commentaria)*, 1st edns from 1470–5 at various locations; facsimile repr. of edn Venice, 1526–9, by and with notes of T. Diplovatatius, 9 vols, Rome: Il Cigno Galileo Galilei. (Commentaries on the texts of the *Corpus iuris civilis*.)

—— (1473) *Consilia* (Advisory Opinions), Rome. (Both manuscripts and prints contain opinions by others; 244 opinions, 117 more published Venice 1521, a further 38 in later editions.)

—— (1477) *Lectura super Authenticis* (Commentaries on the *Authenticae* [Latin versions of the Justinianic *Novels*]), Milan. (Authenticity doubted by Diplovatatius.)

—— (1481–2) *Opera* or *Opera omnia* (Works or Complete Works), Lyon. (Collected editions appear from Lyon, 1481–2, through to the early seventeenth century. Some, like the first, contain only the commentaries.)

—— (1504) *Lectura Institutionum* (Commentaries on the Institutes), Pavia. (False attribution; true author may well be Jacques de Révigny.)

—— (1983) *Tractatus de Guelphis et Gebellinis; de regimine civitatis; de tyranno*, ed. D. Quaglioni, Politica e diritto nel trecento italiano, Florence: Il pensiero politico, biblioteca, vol. 11. (Treatises on Guelphs and Ghibellines; the government of a city; the tyrant.)

References and further reading

Bellomo, M. (1995) *The Common Legal Past of Europe, 1000–1800*, trans. L.G. Cochrane, Studies in Medieval and Early Modern Canon Law, vol. 4, Washington, DC: Catholic University of America Press, esp. 190–95. (Places Bartolus and the commentators in context.)

Canning, J. (1987) *The Political Thought of Baldus de Ubaldis*, Cambridge Studies in Medieval Life and Thought, vol. 6, Cambridge: Cambridge University Press. (Refers back to the seminal work of Bartolus; useful short biographies of major medieval civilians and canonists.)

Clarence Smith, J.A. (1970) 'Bartolo on the Conflict of Laws', *American Journal of Legal History* 14: 157–74, 247–75. (A translation of the sections of Bartolus' commentaries on the *Digest* and *Codex* dealing with conflict of laws, with a brief introduction on Bartolus and the background to his work.)

Segoloni, D. (ed.) (1962) *Bartolo da Sassoferrato. Studi e documenti per il VI centenario*, Milan: Giuffrè. (An invaluable multilingual collection of articles on the work and influence of Bartolus.)

Ullmann, W. (1980) *Jurisprudence in the Middle Ages: Collected Studies*, London: Variorum Reprints. (Useful general background and includes a study of Bartolus' views on customary law.)

Woolf, C.N.S. (1913) *Bartolus of Sassoferrato: His Position in the History of Medieval Political Thought*, Cambridge: Cambridge University Press. (A standard work, with somewhat dated biography; numerous quotations, mainly in Latin, from Bartolus and other sources; gives the gist of quotations but no translation.)

WILLIAM M. GORDON

BASSO, SEBASTIANO *see* ARISTOTELIANISM IN THE 17TH CENTURY

BATAILLE, GEORGES (1897–1962)

Georges Bataille was born in Billom, France, raised in Reims, and spent much of his adult life in Paris. Never formally trained as a philosopher, he worked from 1922 to 1942 as a librarian at the Bibliothèque Nationale. In addition to his philosophical works, Bataille also wrote on the history of art as well as a number of critical works and novels.

Owing to his position outside academic philosophy, Bataille was able to treat diverse topics in ways which might have been unacceptable otherwise. His work addresses the importance of sacrifice, eroticism and death, as well as the kinds of 'expenditure' evidenced by what he called the general economy. *It draws on diverse sources (Hegel, Nietzsche, Marcel Mauss, anthropological research, and the history of religion, among others) and treats a wide range of topics: the role of art in human life, the practice of sacrifice in ancient and modern cultures, the role of death in our understanding of subjectivity, and the limits of knowledge.*

Bataille's major works include: *L'Expérience intérieure* (1943) (*Inner Experience*, 1988; composed 1941–2; materials from 1924 on), *La Part maudite* (1949) (*The Accursed Share*, vol. 1 1949, vols 2–3 1976; written 1946–9; planned as early as 1930), *L'Érotisme* (1957) (*Erotism, Death and Sensuality*, 1986; planned from 1930), *Sur Nietzsche* (1945) (*On Nietzsche*, 1992; written mid-1940s) and *Théorie de religion* (1974) (*Theory of Religion*, 1989; composed late 1940s). He is known largely for his connections with Surrealism, although his alliance with the movement was often strained. He is also considered an important forerunner of 'postmodernism', although he died before the word was coined. Much of his work manifests a resistance to systematicity and a desire to produce texts (which he called *heterologies*) which escape unitary interpretations. Such heterologies concern what is entirely other, and thus resist being reduced to the identities necessary for thought and language. The attempt to think the heterologous means to think that which is outside, and thus to transgress the bounds of thought (which remains, in an important way, an impossible undertaking). Bataille names that which transcends the bounds of science, the everyday, and time the *Sacred*. His work on general economy, however, owing to the influence of Mauss, shows certain systematic and structuralist tendencies.

Many of Bataille's most important texts comprise what he called *La Somme athéologique*, which analyses the Sacred at both individual and societal levels. At the most individual level (that of *inner experience*), Bataille investigates the possibility of transcending our everyday understanding of individuality without losing all notions of subjectivity. These investigations are oriented towards no particular goal or knowledge, but begin with a 'phenomenological' account of experience itself. Drawing on NIETZSCHE, Bataille insists that experiences and sensations take place before there is a subject to experience them; the subject is only established in and through experience. Moreover, if one chooses the right sorts of experience (those of intense suffering), a point is reached where pain ceases to be felt and one's own subjectivity is transcended. Since this experience is often followed by death, research into this kind of transcendence is both dangerous and difficult to replicate. It was these dangers, at least in part, which led Bataille to develop alternative accounts of the move towards the Sacred. What remains constant, however, is the important place he gave to the notion of death.

Later, Bataille developed the important systematic notion of *general economy* with its emphasis on *expenditure*. Focusing on surplus and expenditure as the primary notions of economics (rather than on scarcity, as standard economic models do) allows Bataille to link his work on political economy with his work on inner experience, eroticism and religion, all of which he characterizes as displays of excess or surplus. Here the Sacred is expressed in social practices rather than individual experiences. By focusing on social behaviour which exceeds the limits of (instrumental) rational explanation (such as Amerindian *potlatch* ceremonies), Bataille highlights the myriad ways in which human life and practice resists rational description.

The concept of a general economy of energy flows allows one to analyse not only economic phenomena but social, anthropological, biological and physical ones as well. The fundamental problem with which the general economy must deal is that of excess. The earth has a constant supply of new solar energy which must be either taken up or dispersed in some way. Societies, which draw on this energy, quickly reach a point where production exceeds necessity. The process by which this excess is dealt with is expenditure, which often takes place in a way which expresses the Sacred: through sacrifice or warfare. Such sacrifice may take a literal form (as in Aztec society) or a more figural one as in the modern culture of conspicuous consumption.

Practices such as sacrifice and warfare serve the Sacred by elevating those who are destroyed, together with that in whose name the destruction occurs, above the realm of mere things. Even the victim is elevated; for the destruction that sacrifice is intended to bring about is not annihilation (Bataille 1974: 43).

The Sacred in general removes things from the realm of mere usefulness and thus elevates them above time and its laws of necessity and causality. It not only leaves the realm of reason and discourse behind (which is part of what makes it so difficult for Bataille to discuss it), but actually destroys them (at least temporarily) as well. The human move towards the Sacred is thus beset with a major difficulty. On the one hand, the Sacred allows humans to separate themselves off from the realm of necessity by moving towards transcendence. But if such transcendence leaves the realm of necessity entirely behind, it results in death. Bataille's proposed solution to this problem is to limit moments of sacrifice so that their transcendence *of* time is still caught up *in* time. The first example of this is the festival; the second is war (which still results in death for many of its participants).

Bataille also treats the problem of transcendence through investigations of eroticism. Eroticism is simultaneously the most potent form of embodied experience and one which, like a Dionysian festival, transcends (at least for a time) bodily and temporal limits. And, like the festival, such experiences risk absolute annihilation but usually end with a return to the everyday (although not the same everyday).

See also: POSTMODERNISM; STRUCTURALISM

List of works

Bataille, G. (1927–39) *Visions of Excess: Selected Writings, 1927–1939*, ed. A. Stoekl, trans. A. Stoekl, C.R. Lovitt and D.M. Leslie, Jr, Minneapolis, MN: University of Minnesota Press, 1985. (A good selection of some of Bataille's early, shorter works on a variety of topics.)

—— (1943) *L'Expérience intérieure*, Paris: Gallimard; trans. L.A. Boldt, *Inner Experience*, Albany, NY: State University of New York Press, 1988. (The most important work in *La Somme athéologique*. Treats the problem of transcendence from an individual perspective.)

—— (1945) *Sur Nietzsche*, trans. B. Boone, *On Nietzsche*, New York: Paragon House, 1992. (Part of *La Somme*. Far more an investigation of Bataille's Nietzscheanism than of Nietzsche.)

—— (1945-51) *The Absence of Myth: Writings on Surrealism*, ed. and trans. M. Richardson, London: Verso, 1994. (Together with *Visions of Excess*, a good selection of Bataille's shorter pieces. These treat not only Surrealism but also the notion of the Sacred.)

—— (1949) *La Part maudite*, vol. 1, *La Consommation*, Paris: Éditions de Minuit; trans. R. Hurley, *The Accursed Share*, vol. 1, New York: Zone Books, 1991. (Bataille's definitive text on general economy. The most important work in the later part of the *Somme*. Volume 1 treats historical sources and the importance of sacrifice.)

—— (1957) *L'Érotisme*, Paris: Éditions de Minuit; trans. M. Dalwood, *Erotism, Death and Sensuality*, San Francisco, CA: City Lights, 1986. (Very similar to what would be published in English as volume 2 of *The Accursed Share*. Treats eroticism in connection with death and transcendence.)

—— (1962) *Les Larmes d'Éros*, Paris: Éditions Pauvert; trans. P. Connor, *The Tears of Eros*, San Francisco, CA: City Lights, 1989. (Discusses the importance of the Sacred in art.)

—— (1970-88) *Œuvres complètes*, Paris: Gallimard. (The standard French language edition of Bataille's complete works. Much of this material is unavailable in English.)

—— (1974) *Théorie de religion*, Paris: Gallimard; trans. R. Hurley, *Theory of Religion*, New York: Zone Books, 1989. (More a theory of sacrifice and transcendence than a conventional theological text. A shorter treatment of many of the topics addressed in *The Accursed Share*.)

—— (1976) *The Accursed Share*, vols 2 and 3, trans. R. Hurley, New York: Zone Books, 1993. (Compiled for the *Œuvres complètes* from (mostly) unpublished materials. Volume 2 is a history of eroticism, volume 3 treats the notion of sovereignty and the development of the Soviet economy.)

References and further reading

Bergfleth, G. (1975) *Theorie der Verschwendung* (Theory of Extravagance), Munich: Matthes & Seitz, 1985. (A very good treatment of the distinction between restricted and general economy, but also of the notions of heterology and sovereignty.

Also includes a chapter on the relevance of Bataille's thought for environmentalist philosophy.)

Boldt-Irons, L.A. (ed.) (1995) *On Bataille: Critical Essays*, Albany, NY: State University of New York Press. (A good collection of recent scholarship on Bataille, offering clear treatments of several important issues: heterology, inner experience, expenditure, and Bataille's relation to the history of philosophy.)

Cordier, S. (ed.) (1962) *Bataille*, special issue of *L'Arc* 44, Aix-en-Provence. (Published the year of Bataille's death. Contributions from his colleagues. An interesting collection.)

Derrida, J. (1972) 'From Restricted to General Economy: A Hegelianism without Reserve', trans. A. Bass, in *Writing and Difference*, Chicago, IL: University of Chicago Press, 1978. (Treats the importance of Hegel in Bataille's work on general economy, thus arguing against more Nietzschean interpretations.)

Fourny, J.-F. (1988) *Introduction à la lecture de Georges Bataille* (An Introduction to Reading Georges Bataille), New York: Peter Lang. (A good introduction to Bataille's work as a whole.)

Habermas, J. (1985) 'Between Eroticism and General Economics: Georges Bataille', trans. F. Lawrence, in *The Philosophical Discourse of Modernity*, Cambridge, MA: MIT Press, 1987. (A very clear treatment of the concept of general economy, stressing Bataille's Marxist leanings.)

Hollier, D. (1974) *Against Architecture*, trans. B. Wing, Cambridge, MA: MIT Press, 1990. (Treats the importance of architectural metaphors in Bataille as a way of understanding his resistance to systematicity. Often obscures as much as it clarifies.)

Richardson, M. (1994) *Georges Bataille*, London: Routledge. (A clear but somewhat misleading introduction. Seeks to show that Bataille is not, *pace* many other commentators, a postmodernist.)

Richman, M. (1982) *Beyond the Gift: Reading Georges Bataille*, Baltimore, MD: Johns Hopkins University Press. (A very good introduction to Bataille focusing on the importance of expenditure and general economy. Probably the clearest book on Bataille in English.)

Wiechens, P. (1995) *Bataille: zur Einführung* (Bataille: An Introduction), Hamburg: Junius Verlag. (A good general introduction to all of Bataille's work. Clearer than anything available in English.)

JONATHAN MASKIT

BAUDRILLARD, JEAN (1929–)

Jean Baudrillard taught for most of his career at the Nanterre campus of the University of Paris in the department of sociology. He began writing as a neo-Marxist in the tradition of Henri Lefebvre and Herbert Marcuse but very quickly developed his distinctive style of social and cultural criticism. He may be understood generally as a post-structuralist who focused on the importance of language in society and invented novel concepts and terms to understand the most advanced features of electronic communications. He has been hailed as the guru of postmodernity and berated as faddish trend follower. He has written polemical pieces like Oublier Foucault *(1977) (*Forget Foucault, *1987) and controversial ones such as* La Guerre du Golfe n'a pas eu lieu *(1991b) (*The Gulf War Did Not Take Place, *1995).*

Baudrillard's significance for social philosophy rests with his effort to theorize aspects of popular culture that were generally regarded with disdain (by the FRANKFURT SCHOOL and many others) or uncritically celebrated (by Marshall McLuhan in particular). Baudrillard brought an unprecedented seriousness of theoretical purpose to the questions of the media and consumer culture. It is important to recall this fact because recently he has been denigrated as an unserious intellectual 'star'. From his earliest works, *Le Système des objets* (1968) (*The System of Objects*, 1996) and *La Société de consommation* (1970), Baudrillard attempted to account for the increased prominence of the media in society and the rising significance of consumerism in daily life. In these works he deployed Marxist categories but added semiological and psychoanalytic dimensions to his analysis. Consumption, he argued, must be approached as a system of signs with its own internal quality of articulation, not explained away by categories geared to the process of production or by liberal political complaints. Already in these early writings he employed a post-structuralist method to make intelligible a newly emerging social/cultural sphere. This was so because Baudrillard aimed his theorizing of consumer culture against the liberal logic of *homo economicus* as well as the productivist emphasis in Marxism. In order to theorize the world of consumption, he argues, one must abandon the 'modernist' theoretical fiction of the autonomous rational individual, one who always calculates their utilities for happiness, and abandon as well the socialist view of the worker as a resisting agent upon whom capitalism imposes structures of domination. Baudrillard's early theory of consumer culture was post-structuralist in the double sense that it understood the subject as historically constituted and it recognized the salient role of language in that process of constitution. By bringing these interpretive strategies to the domain of everyday life Baudrillard revolutionized our understanding of them.

Baudrillard definitively broke with Marxism in his works of the mid-1970s: *Pour une critique de l'économie du signe* (1972) (*For a Critique of the Political Economy of the Sign*, 1981), *Le Miroir de la production* (1973) (*The Mirror of Production*, 1975) and *L'Échange symbolique et la mort* (1976) (*Symbolic Exchange and Death*, 1993). In these books Baudrillard specified how media culture and advertising in particular constituted a 'code' which had great influence on individuals. The 'code' was the essence of consumption. People consumed not so much objects but images, ideals, fantasies, styles – all of which were structured through advertising and presented in the electronic media, a strange new dimension of social life which altered forever the older 'bourgeois' culture of modern society. Individuals, Baudrillard argued, construct themselves, or better, their identities in and through their response to advertising and the media. It was pointless to bewail the quality of television shows or consumerism as many liberals and Marxists did because 'vulgarity' and 'exploitation' were irrelevant to the new consumer world. In the malls and shopping centres, in radio and TV ads, a culture was constructed that was capturing the attention and the imagination not only of the masses in the industrialized societies but in the Communist societies of Eastern Europe and in much of the 'Third World' as well. The problem for social theory was to understand how this new world of signification worked, not simply to condemn it in a futile gesture of snobbery. Baudrillard turned to semiology to analyse the structure of advertising and he demonstrated how ads restructured language in such a way that the word 'Coca Cola' would refer not so much to a brown bubbly liquid, its 'referent', but to the images of youth, sexuality and fun that were presented in ads for the product. In the 1970s Baudrillard went so far as to argue in *À l'ombre des majorités silencieuses* (1978) (*In the Shadow of the Silent Majorities*, 1993) that the masses' apparent apathy and lack of revolutionary fervour was in actuality a new form of resistance against the system.

In a series of works in the 1980s and 1990s Baudrillard developed his analysis of media advertising into a general understanding of postmodern culture. From *Simulacres et simulations* (1981) (*Simulacra and Simulations*, 1994) to *L'Illusion de la fin* (1991a) Baudrillard presented an important argument that reality itself was changing as a consequence of the new consumer culture. As people spent more and more time with electronic communications (tuned into the radio, glued to TVs, jacked into computers, turned on to walkmen and ghetto blasters, conversing on telephones, sending faxes, receiving e-mail), more time exchanging symbols through the mediation of increasingly smart machines, the world of face-to-face was becoming the world of the 'interface'. Baudrillard called this emerging culture 'the hyperreal'. Hyperreality was built upon new cultural principles. Symbolic constructions were no longer rooted in an original reference such as a spoken conversation or a written letter. Now language was increasingly 'simulational' in the sense that the presentation is always both an original and a copy. The TV news does not really report about something in an 'external' world: it makes important what it states, creating news as it 'reports' about it. This difficult logic, 'Hyperreality', increasingly dominates the exchanges of words and images, gradually forming a new and very strange culture. If Baudrillard's importance rests on the attention he paid to new cultural formations, his limitations are an overly pessimistic assessment of them, a failure to recognize their limitations, and an inability to take into account new assemblages of humans and machines.

See also: POSTMODERNISM; POST-STRUCTURALISM

List of works

Baudrillard, J. (1968) *Le Système des objets*, Paris: Gallimard; trans J. Benedict, *The System of Objects*, New York: Verso, 1996. (In this ground-breaking study of consumer culture, Baudrillard throws some light on the vexed question of the language of commodities.)
—— (1970) *La Société de consommation*, Paris: Gallimard. (A systematic portrait of the twentieth-century consumer culture.)
—— (1972) *Pour une critique de l'économie du signe*, Paris: Gallimard; trans. C. Levin, *For a Critique of the Political Economy*, St Louis, MN: Telos Press, 1981. (Perhaps Baudrillard's theoretical masterpiece – a comparison of the mode of production to the mode of consumption.)
—— (1973) *Le Miroir de la production*, Paris: Casterman; trans. M. Poster, *The Mirror of Production*, St Louis, MN: Telos Press, 1975. (Baudrillard's critique of, and farewell to, Marxism.)
—— (1976) *L'Échange symbolique et la mort*, Paris: Gallimard; trans. I. Hamilton Grant, *Symbolic Exchange and Death*, London: Sage, 1993. (Baudrillard's theory of an alternative semiotic society, based on the model of the desert.)
—— (1977) *Oublier Foucault*, Paris: Éditions Galilée; trans. S. Lotringer, *Forget Foucault*, New York: Semiotext(e), 1987.
—— (1978) *À l'ombre des majorités silencieuses, ou la fin de la social*, Paris: Utopie; trans. P. Foss, P. Patton and J. Johnston, *In the Shadow of the Silent Majorities – or, The End of the Social and Other Essays*, New York: Semiotext(e), 1983.
—— (1979) *De la séduction*, Paris: Éditions Galilée; trans. B. Singer, *Seduction*, Montreal: New World Perspectives, 1990.
—— (1981) *Simulacres et simulations*, Paris: Éditions Galilée; trans. S. Faria Glaser, *Simulacra and Simulations*, Ann Arbor, MI: University of Michigan Press, 1994. (Baudrillard's most influential work; includes his theory of media effects as a new form of reality, the hyperreal.)
—— (1983) *Les Stratégies fatales*, Paris: Bernard Grasset; trans. P. Beitchman and W.G.J. Niesluchowski, *Fatal Strategies*, New York: Semiotext(e), 1990. (A tragi-comedy of objects.)
—— (1990) *La Transparence du mal: essai sur les phénomènes extrêmes*, Paris: Éditions Galilée; trans. J. Benedict, *The Transparency of Evil: Essays on Extreme Phenomena*, London: Verso, 1993.
—— (1991a) *L'Illusion de la fin*, Paris: Éditions Galilée.
—— (1991b) *La Guerre du Golfe n'a pas eu lieu*, Paris: Éditions Galilée; trans. P. Patton, *The Gulf War Did Not Take Place*, Bloomington, IN: Indiana University Press, 1995.
—— (1995) *Le Crime parfait*, Paris: Éditions Galilée; trans. C. Turner, *The Perfect Crime*, London: Verso, 1996.

References and further reading

Kellner, D. (1989) *Jean Baudrillard: From Marxism to Postmodernism and Beyond*, Stanford, CA: Stanford University Press. (A comprehensive, critical review of Baudrillard's ideas in relation to social theory.)
Kellner, D. (ed.) (1994) *Baudrillard: A Critical Reader*, New York: Blackwell. (Various views and evaluations of Baudrillard's work and standing.)
Poster, M. (ed.) (1988) *Jean Baudrillard: Selected Writings*, Stanford, CA: Stanford University Press. (A sample of Baudrillard's writings, with an introduction by the editor.)

MARK POSTER

BAUER, BRUNO (1809–82)

The career of the Hegelian theologian Bruno Bauer is marked by his sudden turn from a reasoned defender of Christianity into one of its most extreme critics. His radical interpretation of Hegel's philosophy, which he first used to defend orthodox biblical hermeneutics, ultimately led him to become, as one of his admirers said, the 'Robespierre of theology'. As the leader of the so-called 'Young Hegelian' school, Bauer was one of Hegel's most gifted students. However, his condemnation of theology in general and his thesis that the New Testament was merely the fictional product of an unknown author contributed to the general distrust of Hegelianism among religious thinkers. Although his many theological and historical writings now remain largely unread, his 'Critical Philosophy' and his radical atheism exerted a strong influence upon Marx, who was his student and friend, and is still evident in such contemporaries as Jürgen Habermas.

1 The Young Hegelian
2 Later years

1 The Young Hegelian

Bauer entered the University of Berlin in 1828, and gave himself completely over to Hegelianism. From the earliest period of his career until his death, Bauer was concerned with the 'reconciliation' of Hegelianism and orthodox religion – the theme of his doctoral dissertation and final works (see HEGEL, G.W.F. §8; HEGELIANISM §2). However, as his thought developed, Bauer took 'reconciliation' to mean that the religious mind, which had created a history of God out of its own unconsciousness, could only cure itself by coming into a full and critical self-consciousness towards its own unconscious fantasies.

In his first years as a lecturer, Bauer published forty-three articles and reviews. In these first writings, it was his intention to elevate theological consciousness to a speculative level which would resolve the debates between faith and critical reason, a resolution which would occur in the higher synthesis of Hegelian speculation.

In 1835, David F. Strauss's *Das Leben Jesu* (*Life of Jesus*) was published (see STRAUSS, D.F. §1). For Strauss, the New Testament was fundamentally a literary creation generated out of the Messianic expectations of the Jewish people, having little or no historical foundation. The miracle stories were merely pre-Christian 'myths'. The orthodox Hegelians, whose careers were threatened by Strauss's claim that his work was inspired by Hegel, asked Bauer to refute Strauss. Bauer's reply to Strauss, which appeared in a series of articles, attempted to demonstrate that such gospel miracles as the Virgin Birth were the necessary consequences of the historical development of human self-consciousness. Bauer's refutation contained the seed of Bauer's own radical view of the Gospels: that they were merely the fictional creations unconsciously designed to satisfy the needs of the religious mind for some external salvation.

In 1838, Bauer first formulated his own view of the relationship between philosophy and religion in a two-volume work: *Die Religion des Alten Testaments in der geschichtlichen Entwicklung ihrer Principien dargestellt* (The Religion of the Old Testament Presented in its Historical Development and Principles). This work continued Bauer's efforts to treat the Gospel stories as the unconscious expressions of the religious mind, and to trace their historical development. By 1840, he had written a number of multi-volume studies devoted to explaining that biblical history was fundamentally an imaginative exercise of the religious mind, with little or no actual basis in fact. This thesis was set forth in his *Kritik der evangelischen Geschichte des Johannes* (Critique of the Gospel of John). From this point on, Bauer would identify his own position as that of 'critic' and would term his philosophy 'criticism'.

By the end of June 1840, Bauer began another major study of the gospels, the three-volume *Kritik der evangelischen Geschichte der Synoptiker* (Critique of the Synoptic Gospels). In this work the problem of whether or not Jesus was in fact a historical figure was finally resolved: 'To the question of whether Jesus was an authentic historical figure we replied that everything relating to the historical Jesus, all that we know of him, relates to the world of fancy, to be more exact – to Christian fancies. This has no connection with any man who lived in the real world'. In the autumn of 1840, Bauer concluded the writing of *Die Posaune des jüngsten Gerichts über Hegel den Atheisten und Antichristen: Ein Ultimatum* (*The Trumpet of the Last Judgement Against Hegel the Atheist and Antichrist: An Ultimatum*). This anonymous work was to rally all the various interpreters of Hegel into one camp from which they could enter into what he termed 'The Campaign of Pure Criticism'. It asserted that the prudent 'Old Hegelians' associated with German academic life had consciously concealed the total incompatibility of Hegelian philosophy with traditional Christian belief and conservative political order.

In the early 1840s Bauer was the leader of Berlin's notorious club, 'The Free Ones'. This group was the focal point of the radical 'Young Hegelians' – a forum for the discussion of atheism and radical politics. Among the participants were his own brother Edgar, the young Friedrich Engels, and a new friend, the radical individualist Max STIRNER. However, by 1844, Bauer's theoretical and theological concerns were rapidly losing their importance among the radical Hegelians, as they were becoming more concerned with applying their theory towards the practical overthrow of the reactionary forces controlling German political life. Concerned with revolutionary deeds, and preparing for the establishment of a new democratic order, the new generation of radicals rejected Bauer's speculative 'Terrorism of Pure Theory'. Within a few years, Bauer's influence upon such revolutionary Hegelians as Marx and Engels came to a end.

2 Later years

In 1843, Bauer wrote *Das Entdeckte Christentum* (Christianity Exposed), a work intended to bring about a general appreciation of atheism through a rough dissection of Christian attitudes. His belief that the Enlightenment and its 'Age of Reason' embodied his Hegelian trust in the rationality of the real occasioned his next project, the four-volume *Geschichte der Politik, Cultur und Aufklärung des achtzehnten Jahrhunderts* (History of the Politics, Culture and Enlightenment of the Eighteenth Century). In 1846, having concluded his final volume, he continued his historical studies with the issue of the two-volume *Geschichte Deutschlands und der Französischen Revolution* (History of Germany and the French Revolution). These works constituted a complete cultural and political history of the Enlightenment. Given Bauer's scorn of pietistic Christianity and his admiration for the atheists of the Enlightenment, it is not surprising that he considered it to be mankind's greatest age.

In 1847, Bauer, with his usual energy, wrote a three-volume study looking back upon the political events of his own lifetime: *Vollständige Geschichte der Parteikämpfe in Deutschland 1842–1846* (The Complete History of Party Struggles in Germany During the Years 1842–1846). Contrary to its title, the third volume covered only the events up to 1844; a fourth volume was to extend the time frame to 1847. But the Revolution of 1848 intervened, and the final volume was never completed. The volumes are a chronicle of disappointments, from the first deceptively liberal appearance of King Friedrich Wilhelm IV, to the increasingly oppressive measures taken by both state and church throughout the 1840s to stifle democracy. They are bitter works, angry at the passivity of the people, and their temper was reflected in shorter articles of the same period, such as 'Die Gattung und die Masse' ('The Genus and the Crowd') .

In 1852, Bauer returned to theological subjects, and composed *Die theologische Erklärung der Evangelien* (The Theological Explanation of the Gospels) – intended to be the fourth and final volume of his earlier series, *Kritik der evangelischen Geschichte der Synoptiker*. This particular volume brought to a close his criticism of Strauss's 'Tradition Hypothesis' and Bauer developed his theory of the *Urevangelist* – the actual writer who composed the original fictional life of Jesus.

In the next year, with the Crimean War imminent, Bauer wrote a series of studies dealing with the relationship of Russia to the rest of Europe. The first, in 1853, was *Rußland und das Germanentum* (Russia and the Germanic World). It warned of the growing power of Russia, and was followed by other studies focused upon the same issue, such as his 1854 *Deutschland und das Russentum* (Germany and the Russian World). This work was a model for later German nationalistic philosophies of history, in which Germany was seen as the destined, yet scorned, leader of the West.

In 1859, after a few years in various insignificant editorial posts, Bauer became the associate of Hermann Wagener, the editor of such ultra-conservative papers as the *Staats-und-Gesellschaftslexikon*, *Kreuzzeitung*, and *Berliner Revue*. Wagener was not only scornful of the weak democratic forces in Prussia, but virulently anti-Semitic. However, Bauer's anti-Semitism, as his early essay on the 'Jewish Question' indicates, was not an expression of Prussian nationalism, but concerned the nature of the Jewish religion itself. He condemned Judaism as the source and support of Christianity – the prime obstacle to human progress. Bauer wrote no anti-Semitic articles for Wagener.

In his last works, which he produced sporadically until his death in 1882, Bauer fully developed the theory which he had first proposed in the early 1840s – that it was not Jesus or Paul, but Seneca and Philo who were the spiritual creators of the basic gospel story. Today, Bauer's biblical studies are almost totally forgotten, and perhaps rightly. However, his reading of Hegelianism as a revolutionary and atheistic humanism not only set the general course of Young Hegelianism, but remains a viable perspective.

See also: RELIGION AND EPISTEMOLOGY; HERMENEUTICS, BIBLICAL

List of works

Bauer, B. (1838) *Kritik der Geschichte der Offenbarung. I, vol. 1–2: Die Religion des Alten Testaments in der geschichtlichen Entwicklung ihrer Prinzipien dargestellt* (The Religion of the Old Testament Presented in its Historical Development and Principles), Berlin: F. Dümmler; reprinted, Aalen: Scientia, 1983. (Initiates Bauer's lifelong theory that the biblical narratives of both Jews and Christians were largely fictional.)

—— (1840) *Kritik der evangelischen Geschichte des Johannes* (Critique of the Gospel of John), Bremen: Carl Schünemann. (A reduction of St John's Gospel into a pure work of fiction.)

—— (1841, 1842) *Kritik der evangelischen Geschichte der Synoptiker* (Critique of the Synoptic Gospels), Leipzig: Otto Wiegand, 3 vols; reprinted, Hildesheim: Georg Olms, 1974. (A further refinement of Bauer's thesis regarding the fictional nature of Jesus Christ. Volume 3 was published in 1842.)

—— (1841a) *Die Posaune des jüngsten Gerichts über Hegel den Atheisten und Antichristen: Ein Ultimatum*, Leipzig: Otto Wiegand; reprinted, Aalen: Scientia, 1969; trans. L.S. Stepelevich *The Trumpet of the Last Judgement Against Hegel the Atheist and Antichrist: An Ultimatum*, Lewiston, MA: Edward Mellen Press, 1989. (This analysis of Hegel's views on religion and politics, treating them as radical in the extreme, expressed the basic premises of Young Hegelianism.)

—— (1841b) 'Theologische Schamlosigkeiten' (Theological Shamelessness), *Deutsche Jahrbücher* 117–20 (15 November–18 November): 465–79; reprinted in *Feldzüge der Reinen Kritik* (The Campaign of Pure Criticism), ed. and with intro. by H.M. Sass, Frankfurt: Suhrkamp, 1968. (A bitter criticism of pietistic theologians.)

—— (1843a) *Die Judenfrage*, Braunschweig: Friedrich Otto; trans. H. Lederer, *The Jewish Problem*, Cincinnati, OH: Hebrew Union College, 1958. (Karl Marx's review of this work marks his transformation from being mainly concerned with philosophic and religious questions into a radical critic of capitalism.)

—— (1843b) *Das entdeckte Christentum. Eine Erinnerung an das achtzehnte Jahrhundert und ein Beitrag zur Krisis des neunzehnten* (Christianity Exposed), Zürich: Verlag des literarischen Comptoirs; reprinted, Aalen: Scientia, 1989. (This is Bauer's first and clearest statement of his atheism.)

—— (1843, 1844, 1845) *Geschichte der Politik, Cultur und Aufklärung des achtzehnten Jahrhunderts* (History of the Politics, Culture and Enlightenment of the Eighteenth Century), Charlottenburg: Egbert Bauer, 4 vols; reprinted, Aalen: Scientia, 1965. (A positive assessment of Enlightenment rationalism. Volume 1 was published in 1843, volume 2 in 1844 and the last two volumes in 1845.)

—— (1844a) *Briefwechsel zwischen Bruno Bauer und Edgar Bauer während der Jahre 1839–1842 aus Bonn und Berlin* (Letters between Bruno Bauer and Edgar Bauer out of Bonn and Berlin from 1839 to 1842), Charlottenburg: Egbert Bauer; reprinted, Aalen: Scientia Verlag, 1969. (A primary biographical source, and an insight into how Bauer's reading of Hegel antagonized the conservative theological faculty at Bonn University.)

—— (1844b) 'Was ist jetzt der Gegenstand der Kritik?' (What is Now the Object of Criticism?), *Allgemeine Literaturzeitung* 8: 18–26; reprinted in *Feldzüge der Reinen Kritik* (The Campaign of Pure Criticism), ed. and with intro. by H.M. Sass, Frankfurt: Suhrkamp, 1968. (Traces the influence of critical philosophy from the French Revolution to German reform movements.)

—— (1844c) 'Die Gattung und die Masse', *Allgemeine Literaturzeitung* 10 (Sept): 42–8; trans. L.S. Stepelevich, 'The Genus and the Crowd', in *The Young Hegelians: An Anthology*, Cambridge: Cambridge University Press, 1983, 198–205. (A criticism of the public indifference to philosophic progress.)

—— (1846) *Geschichte Deutschlands und der Französischen Revolution unter der Herrschaft Napoleons* (History of Germany and the French Revolution During Napoleon's Rule), Charlottenburg: Egbert Bauer, 2 vols; vol. 1 reprinted, Aalen: Scientia, 1979. (A positive evaluation of the effects of Napoleonic reforms on German society.)

—— (1847) *Vollständige Geschichte der Parteikämpfe in Deutschland während der Jahre 1842–1846* (The Complete History of Party Struggles in Germany during the Years 1842–1846), Charlottenburg: Egbert Bauer; reprinted, Aalen: Scientia, 1964. (A survey of the largely frustrated efforts of German political reformers anticipating the 1848 revolution.)

—— (1851–2) *Kritik der Evangelien und Geschichte ihres Ursprungs* (Critique of the Gospels and History of their Origin), Berlin: Gustav Hempel, 4 vols; reprinted, Aalen: Scientia, 1983. (The final and most coherent statement of Bauer's reading of the Gospel narratives as an example of religious fiction.)

—— (1852) *Rußland und das Germanentum* (Russia and the Germanic World), Charlottenburg: Egbert Bauer; reprinted, Aalen: Scientia, 1972. (An exercise in prophetic history, stressing the future role of Russia in European history.)

—— (1854–5) *Deutschland und das Russentum* (Germany and the Russian World), Charlottenburg: Egbert Bauer. (A continuation of the thesis that Russia represents a threat to Germany. An early nationalistic treatise.)

—— (1874) *Philo, Renan und das Urchristentum*

(Philo, Renan and Primitive Christianity), Berlin: Gustav Hempel; reprinted, Aalen: Scientia, 1972. (Bauer's argument that the Gospel Narratives were, in principle, composed by Philo.)
—— (1877) *Christus und die Cäsaren: Der Ursprung des Christentums aus dem römischen Griechentum*, Berlin: Eugen Grosser. (Continues the argument that either Philo or Seneca composed the Gospel narratives.)
—— (1880) *Jesus und die Cäsaren* (Jesus and the Caesars), Berlin: Eugen Grosser. (A further focusing on the fictional nature of the Christian gospels.)
Schläger, E. (ed.) 'Bruno Bauer und seine Werke' (Bruno Bauer and his Work), *Internationale Monatsschrift. Zeitschrift für allgemeine und nationale Kultur und deren Literatur*, vol. 1, 1882, 377–400; A. Zanardo (ed.) 'Bruno Bauer hegeliano e giovanne hegeliano', *Revista Critica di Storia della Filosofia*, Florence, 1965. (These contain the most comprehensive, yet still incomplete, listing of Bauer's periodical publications.)
Barnikol, E. (1972) *Bruno Bauer: Studien und Materialien*, ed. P. Reimer and H.-M. Sass, Assen: Van Gorcum. (This work provides the most comprehensive listing of Bauer's unpublished works.)

References and further reading

Barnikol, E. (1972) *Bruno Bauer: Studien und Materialien*, ed. P. Reimer and H.-M. Sass, Assen: Van Gorcum. (A 572-page gathering of some of Ernst Barnikol's posthumous papers and research materials dealing with Bauer. An invaluable source, well-edited, but unavoidably uneven in both form and content.)
Brazill, W.J. (1970) 'Bauer, Stirner, and the Terrorism of Pure Theory', in *The Young Hegelians*, New Haven, CT: Yale University Press, 175–225. (A lucid survey of the main figures within the Young Hegelian movement.)
Mah, H. (1987) 'Bruno Bauer and the Crisis in Religious Theory', in *The End of Philosophy, the Origin of 'Ideology'*, Berkeley, CA: University of California Press, Part 2: 45–86. (A readable survey directed towards the political, mainly Marxian, outcome of Young Hegelianism.)
Moggach, D. (1996) 'Bruno Bauer's Political Critique, 1840–1841', *The Owl of Minerva* 27 (2): 137–54. (A detailed study of recent interpretations of Bauer's political thought during the period in which the Young Hegelian school turned its attention from philosophical speculation to political action.)
Rosen, Z. (1977) *Bruno Bauer and Karl Marx*, The Hague: Martinus Nijhoff. (The most detailed study in any language dealing with the six-year relationship between Bauer and Marx.)
Stepelevich, L.S. (1983) 'Bruno Bauer', in *The Young Hegelians: An Anthology*, Cambridge: Cambridge University Press, 173–205. (A brief introduction followed by translations of part of Bauer's *The Jewish Question* and *The Trumpet of the Last Judgment* and 'The Genus and the Crowd'.)
—— (1989) 'Translator's Introduction', to Bauer, B., *Trumpet of the Last Judgement Against Hegel the Atheist and Anti-Christ: An Ultimatum*, Lewiston, MA: Edward Mellen Press, 1–56. (The most extensive biography of Bauer yet written.)
* Strauss, D.F. (1835–6) *Das Leben Jesu*, Tübingen: Osiander; trans. M.A. Evans (George Eliot), *Life of Jesus*, Philadelphia, PA: Fortress, 1972. (Argues that the messianic Christ was merely a mythic figure.)
Towes, J.E. (1980) 'Bruno Bauer and the reduction of absolute spirit to human self-consciousness', in *Hegelianism: The Path Toward Dialectical Humanism, 1805–1841*, Cambridge: Cambridge University Press, 288–326. (A detailed study of the Young Hegelian movement drawn from the perspective of cultural history.)

LAWRENCE S. STEPELEVICH

BAUMGARDT, DAVID (1890–1963)

Baumgardt's early works dealt with the problem of modalities in the philosophies of Kant, Husserl and Meinong and with German philosophical romanticism, especially in the mystic Franz von Baader. Although he never engaged in systematic inquiry into Judaism or Jewish philosophy, he was fascinated by the Jewish religious legacy, and his philosophical reflections on Jewish issues were integral to his philosophical work. A secular Jew, he associated himself with the liberal trends within Judaism. The Jewish philosophers he most highly prized were Maimonides, Spinoza and Mendelssohn. The chief goal of his Jewish studies was to promote those beliefs in Judaism that are of ethical significance and to draw out the import of the moral demands found scattered throughout the ancient Jewish Scriptures. Baumgardt's concern with ethics grew with his increasingly critical stance towards traditional religion. In that vein, he laid great stress on the distinction between knowledge and belief and on that between Jewish rituals and their underlying meaning.

Baumgardt's work did not receive the attention it

deserved, because his career at the University of Berlin (1924–1935) came to an abrupt end with Hitler's rise to power. He was a visiting professor at the University of Birmingham, England from 1935 to 1938 and at Pendle Hill, Pennsylvania from 1939 to 1941. From 1941 to 1954 he served as a consultant on philosophy for the Library of Congress. He thus remained a kind of an outsider, publishing relatively little during his lifetime.

Refusing to draw any clear cut line between Jewish religious problems and general philosophical ones, Baumgardt was much attracted by ethical quandaries like that posed in the biblical story of the Akedah or binding of Isaac (Genesis 22), where the matter was not of choosing between two rights but between two wrongs: that of disobeying God's command and that of killing one's son. Finding no comfort in the many traditional responses to the ancient story, Baumgardt saw its outcome as a sheer aporia and turned increasingly to a form of ethical hedonism as the foundation of his moral philosophy. Some types of hedonism, he argued, must frame the 'supreme rational command'. But even such a philosophy, he argued, 'leaves to us the risk and responsibility of applying the command properly'.

Baumgardt's main contribution to philosophy was in the field of ethics. In 1933 he published *Der Kampf um den Lebenssinn unter den Vorlaeufern der modernen Ethik* (The Struggle for the Meaning of Life among the Precursors of Modern Ethics). Because of the rise of the Nazis the work passed almost unnoticed. In it Baumgardt investigated and criticized the ethical ideas of Kant, whose formalism aroused his resentment, of Herder, Hemsterhuis and Jacobi, all of whom he presented as precursors of modern ethics. As a foil to the shortcomings of their ethical conceptions, he called attention to the ethical ideas to be found in the Bible and the Talmud. But these allusions to Jewish ideas, although they reflect Baumgardt's frame of mind and commitment to his Jewish legacy, did not play any important theoretical role in his ethical investigations.

In his unpublished *History of Modern Ethics* Baumgardt essayed a synoptic view of the ethical theories of the past two hundred and fifty years. He was especially drawn to the utilitarianism of Bentham, which he came to know well in England. His book *Bentham and the Ethics of Today* (1952) included hitherto unpublished writings of Bentham, and Bentham's utilitarianism provided the point of departure for his own ethical hedonism. Seeking to rehabilitate a philosophical tradition stigmatized since antiquity as advocating mere pleasure-seeking, Baumgardt drew inspiration from two sharply opposed philosophical orientations: Bentham's empiricist utilitarianism and Kant's metaphysical morals. What he admired in both was the attempt to lay rational and critical foundations for a secular and autonomous ethics. By creating a synthesis between the two, he hoped to deliver his 'critical hedonism' from the pragmatic bent of traditional utilitarianism. This project came to its fullest expression in his posthumous *Jenseits von Machtmoral und Masochismus* (Beyond the Morality of Power and Masochism) (1977), whose subtitle reads *Hedonistische Ethik als kritische Alternative* (Hedonist Ethics as a Critical Alternative). Despite the work's many interesting ideas, it remains questionable whether it can forge the hoped-for alternative. It does not refer to any works on ethics later than Sartre's writings of the 1940s, and pays almost no attention to analytic philosophy or to Wittgenstein, whose impact on ethical theory cannot be ignored.

Kant and Bentham were contemporaries of one another, and for Baumgardt they remained our contemporaries as well. As regards Kant, Baumgardt was only one among many scholars who investigated his philosophy, but with regard to Bentham he was one of the most insightful.

In chapters 5 and 6 of *Jenseits von Machtmoral und Masochismus*, Baumgardt asks whether the idea of pleasure can be made a basis for the maximization of happiness and the overcoming of meaningless suffering. This, he argues, requires a 'Copernican revolution' in ethics: while egoistic hedonism is concerned exclusively with the pleasure of the self and is indifferent to the suffering of others, a consistent hedonism will strive for the maximization of happiness. This much is little more than the undergirding of Bentham's move from egoism to the greatest happiness principle. But Baumgardt goes on to argue, in more Kantian vein, that appeals to happiness can be deemed morally valid only if they corroborate the principle of greatest happiness by creating a harmonious coherence among all concerned. The point, however, is not to praise or blame human motives but, rather, to evaluate the outcomes of human action.

Although Baumgardt, like most hedonists, grounded his ethics in naturalism, he did not offer any convincing proof of the chief argument of ethical hedonism, the claim that human pursuit of pleasure entails the ethical value of that pursuit. That is, he offered no convincing argument against the objection that in moving from is to ought one commits a naturalistic fallacy.

Although Baumgardt's ethical work, scattered in his articles and notebooks, and in part published posthumously, was not brought to a systematic conclusion, his rehabilitation of hedonism as a legitimate ethical option is a worthy achievement.

The achievement is marred by his lack of a systematic meta-ethics and a weakness in the account of pleasure that he shares with Bentham: individual pleasure is subjective and context-dependent, while pleasure in his more general sense that is most relevant to the greatest happiness principle is linked to interests, ideals, aspirations and goals that can be shared by many. Baumgardt's critical hedonism, a typically reductionist theory, tries to reduce all these to a single measure, Bentham's pleasure/pain principle. And, like earlier hedonist theories, Baumgardt's account has not paid sufficient attention to the cognitive status of deontological assertions. It does, however, represent an important challenge, by a philosophically adept outsider, to modern ethical theory.

List of works

Baumgardt, D. (1927) *Franz von Baader und die philosophische Romantik* (Franz von Baader and Philosophical Romanticism), Halle/Saale: Max Niemeyer. (Unearthing and revitalizing Baader's thought and his critique of Kant.)

—— (1933) *Der Kampf um den Lebenssinn unter den Vorlaeufern der modernen Ethik* (The Struggle for the Meaning of Life among the Precursors of Modern Ethics), Leipzig: Felix Meiner. (A critical confrontation of Kant with his contemporaries, pointing out their continuous relevance to modern ethics.)

—— (1952) *Bentham and the Ethics of Today*, Princeton, NJ: Princeton University Press. (A critical reexamination of Bentham's utilitarianism and first publication of various Bentham manuscripts.)

—— (1961) *Great Western Mystics: Their Lasting Significance*, New York: Columbia University Press. (Has the same content as *Mystik und Wissenschaft*.)

—— (before 1963) *History of Modern Ethics*, ed. A. Figen, unpublished manuscript, New York: Leo Baeck Institute. (Synopsis of ethical theories from the time of Kant and his contemporaries until Sartre. Due to the author's death, it is disorganized and chronologically inconsistent.)

—— (1963) *Mystik und Wissenschaft. Ihr Ort im abendlaendischen Denken* (Mysticism and Science: Their Place in Western Thought), Witten: Luther. (On the essence of mysticism, in particular mysticism of interiority, nature and history.)

—— (1977) *Jenseits von Machtmoral und Masochismus. Hedonistische Ethik als kritische Alternative* (Beyond Masochism and the Morality of Power: Hedonistic Ethics as a Critical Alternative), Meisenheim am Glan: Anton Hain. (Deals with the pluralism of moral, ethical, aesthetic and historio-philosophical positions and the ethics of critical hedonism, as well as a hedonistic critique of the criteria of ethical conduct.)

References and further reading

Frank, J., Minkowski, H. and Sternglass, E.J. (eds) (1963) *Horizons of a Philosopher: Essays in Honor of David Baumgardt*, Leiden: Brill. (Festschrift, including essays on Jewish and ethical issues.)

Levy, Z. (1989) *David Baumgardt and Ethical Hedonism*, Hoboken, NJ: Ktav Publishing House. (An analysis of Baumgardt's Jewish writings and of his ethical theory and a critical inquiry into ethical hedonism.)

Schlodder, H. (1980) *Der kritische Hedonismus David Baumgardts*, Magister-Hausarbeit, Mainz: Johannes-Gutenberg-Universität. (On hedonistic ethics as a means to overcome power morality.)

ZE'EV LEVY

BAUMGARTEN, ALEXANDER GOTTLIEB (1714–62)

The German philosopher Baumgarten is known primarily for his introduction of the word 'aesthetics' to describe the affects of art and nature, which in the course of the seventeenth century replaced the older theory of beauty. Baumgarten derived the term from the Greek aisthanomai, *which he equated with the Latin* sentio *(1739: 79). He understood it to designate the outer, external or bodily sense, as opposed to the inner sense of consciousness. Thus aesthetics is the realm of the sensate, of sense perception and sensible objects. Baumgarten understood his usage to be consistent with classical sources, but he was aware also that he was extending logic and science into a new realm. Baumgarten's importance lay in adapting the rationalism of Leibniz for both the study of art and what came to be known after Kant as the aesthetic.*

1 The aesthetic as a 'confused' concept
2 Aesthetic implications
3 Tensions within Baumgarten's system

1 The aesthetic as a 'confused' concept

Baumgarten accepted the fundamental rationalist, epistemological division between what is clearly and distinctly known, on the one hand, according to concepts and reason and what is known, on the other, by sense. The latter apprehension is 'confused' in a sense that can be traced back to medieval discussions of the problem of universals. According to medieval realism and conceptualism, only the universal deserves the definite article and provides clear, distinct apprehension. So 'the rose' refers not to some existing rose but to the universal type. To refer to a specific rose, one must individuate it either as 'this rose' when dealing with an existential application (cf. *Metaphysica*, para. 151) or as 'a rose' when dealing with an individual which may or may not actually exist. Both the individuation and its indefinite extension are dependent on sense in a way that the universal is not. Both can be said to 'confusedly' represent, therefore, because their referents are present only in limited perceptible and temporal forms, all of which lack some essential distinctness. In this sense, a confused presentation is not faulty or unclear; it is simply lacking in the kind of clarity which only the universal can provide. Its sensate forms limit it. Baumgarten adopted this distinction in describing aesthetic discourse. The aesthetic is sensate and confused or indistinct in this specialized sense.

It does not follow, however, that the aesthetic cannot be clear within its own cognitive sphere. Obscurity and clarity are matters of content. Something is clearer if a higher number of its sensate representations are available. So if one sees an object from all sides, for example, one sees it clearly. If one sees it only from one perspective at a distance, it is seen obscurely. The aesthetic permits an extensively clear form of representation which is determinate and individual. From the standpoint of promoting art, therefore, greater extensive clarity and determinateness are positive features, which enhance the aesthetic effect.

Baumgarten took discourse as the primary form of the aesthetic. Discourse can be construed broadly here, since Baumgarten acceded to Horace's equation of poetry and painting (1735: 52). Representations themselves include both images derived from sense and direct sense-perception. They are combined into thematic wholes on the basis of the connection of the images and resemblance between images. Such wholes are simple or complex, but since complexity is understood as having many themes, not parts, simplicity is an aesthetic virtue. Perceptions and images (which are secondary perceptions) are confused representations because they are not abstract, intelligible forms, which alone would be conceptually distinct. But while they lack intensional clarity, they may have great extensional clarity, and may form thematic wholes based on resemblance, the connection of the images, and ordering of the sensate elements. Baumgarten applied this scheme to poetry and poetic language in his *Meditationes philosophicae de nonnullis ad poema pertinentibus* (1735, translated as *Reflections on Poetry*), and he suggested ways in which it would also apply to painting, sculpture and music. His goal was a science of the perceptual realm that would parallel the more precise sciences of metaphysics and logic.

2 Aesthetic implications

A number of points in Baumgarten's aesthetics bear on later developments in aesthetics. He focused on the affective side of perception. Sensate representations are 'marked degrees of pleasure or pain' (1735: 47). Stronger impressions are more poetic because their impressions are extensively clearer (1735: 27). On the other hand, Baumgarten distinguished aesthetic effects quantitatively, not qualitatively. It is not that feelings of pleasure are intrinsically valuable, but that more effects contribute to a greater perfection of the discourse. The closest that Baumgarten came to a qualitative aesthetic is in his discussion of 'the wonderful', which he characterized as an intuitive grasp of the inconceivable that is not present in perception (1735: 53). He was obviously trying to account for the sense of awe or wonder that is one of the classical marks of the sublime, yet he still explained it in essentially quantitative terms. The wonderful is an intuition of something that is not present. Hence it is an added element in the aesthetic. It depends on a mixture of the unfamiliar and the familiar, and since it cannot be traced to sense impressions, gives a scope to the imagination it would not otherwise have. However, it provides little justification for promoting feeling directly to prominence. Baumgarten is at the opposite extreme from Friedrich SCHLEIERMACHER in his regard for intuitive feeling.

Baumgarten also gave scope to the imagination in a way that reveals a contrast with later exaltations of imagination as the aesthetic faculty. The imagination is productive of fictions. But fictions are categorized in terms of possible worlds. True fictions are possible in this world. The imagination may go beyond what is actually perceived to what may very well be the case. When a painter poses figures to construct a tableau, his painting is a fiction, but a possible representation of an actual event. There could be such an event, and for all we know, this is how it may have looked. Fictions *per se*, however, are impossible in this world. They may be divided into those which are impossible in all worlds, called utopian fictions, and those which are impossible in this world but possible in some world, called heterocosmic fictions. There are no centaurs, and such combinations are biologically impossible. But they are nevertheless possible in some world, whereas a round square is not possible at all. Since utopian fictions cannot be represented, they cannot be aesthetically significant. But heterocosmic fictions can be represented, and in fact art depends on such fictions for its greater extensive clarity and determinateness. Baumgarten arrived at an implicit defence of fictions quite different from the earlier Aristotelian and subsequent Romantic defences, which are based on the positive emotional effects of the imagination. For Baumgarten, fictions and the imagination are needed because they extend the aesthetic beyond the reach of mere sense, without converting it into rational concepts.

Baumgarten thus remained firmly within the rationalist camp. The aesthetic is clearly a lower faculty: 'Therefore *things known* are to be known by the superior faculty as the object of logic; *things perceived* [are to be known by the inferior faculty as the object] of the science of perception, or aesthetic' (1735: 78). But Baumgarten expanded the scope of knowledge in interesting ways. He expected the aesthetic to be a science with its own logic, and in the final, fragmentary 'Kollegium über die Ästhetik', he acknowledged that sensate knowledge is the foundation of clarity and that the aesthetic must come to the aid of logic. The aesthetic is limited by its sensate representations and the imagination must be restricted in order to avoid licence, but within these limits the aesthetic is a legitimate source of a kind of knowledge. The standard remains rational distinctness, but while it is possible to mix distinct, conceptual elements with confused, perceptual elements in complex representations, the aesthetic is independent of the distinct conceptual forms. When conceptual forms dominate, one loses the aesthetic effects. The aesthetic may still be a lower form, but it is legitimate within its own realm, and Baumgarten came close to acknowledging that the aesthetic could be a clearer and more effective form of knowledge than a priori rational concepts for all but the most accomplished metaphysicians.

3 Tensions within Baumgarten's system

The value that Baumgarten assigned to the aesthetic produced some tensions within his system. His ideal was knowledge, and the goal of knowledge is to build a science. So Baumgarten set out to create a science of the sensate. But he also recognized that the rational, conceptual distinctness which he took to characterize knowledge is antithetical to the confused, indistinct, sensible impressions and images on which the aesthetic depends. So the more scientific aesthetics becomes, the more it is in danger of ceasing to be aesthetic. The incompatibility of the rational and aesthetic realms (1735: 42) exposes the inconsistency between Baumgarten's goal of pure knowledge and his defence of sensate discourse. The classical way to resolve this inconsistency was to leave the aesthetic behind as one progressed up the ladder of consciousness. Baumgarten continued to adhere to that classical model in which aesthetics is the product of a lower faculty and is limited to a helping role, but he also separated and gave independence to sensate representations, which suggests that there are simply two different forms of knowledge.

Two themes in Baumgarten's work illustrate how the tension between reason and sensibility arose and how he tried, unsuccessfully, to resolve them. First, Baumgarten's appeals to sensation are essentially quantitative. Consider an instance of sensate discourse. It will be more or less aesthetic depending on its extensive clarity, determinateness and specificity. All of these characteristics are consistent with, and in fact require, confused or indistinct representations, since the discourse would cease to be sensate if it became distinct. The standard of judgment is aesthetic perfection. The aim of the aesthetic is the perfection of sensitive cognition as such; that is also what is meant by beauty (1750: 14). Baumgarten was led to this quantitative standard because it was consistent with his rational epistemology, which was based on completeness. (Quantity in this sense is not inconsistent with simplicity as long as the quantitative impressions are united by a single theme or object.) But while his aesthetics is based on sensibility, it is not based on feeling. So while Baumgarten recognized the close connection between sensate impressions and pleasure or pain, he had no way of incorporating those qualitative impressions into his epistemological scheme.

A second theme in Baumgarten's aesthetics is the requirement for thematic unity and order. The basis for order is the connection of impressions and images (1735: 62ff). The operative principle of connection is sufficient reason, and connections are themselves part of the observable order of indistinct representations. So despite his defence of the sensible realm, Baumgarten was still the disciple of LEIBNIZ in holding that what gave order to sense data was a principle of reason which on Baumgarten's system was external to the data itself. He could forge a unity only by appealing to connections recognized by the mind but present between the sensate impressions. In spite of his desire to found a new science of aesthetics, Baumgarten could only appeal to a priori principles and try to find them reflected in his new aesthetic realm. He thus failed to resolve the tension between his rationalist epistemology and the new realm of science he had defined.

See also: SUBLIME, THE

List of works

Baumgarten, A.G. (1735) *Meditationes philosophicae de nonnullis ad poema pertinentibus*, trans. K. Aschenbrenner and W.B. Holther as *Reflections on Poetry*, Berkeley, CA: University of California Press, 1954. (English translation of Baumgarten's dissertation with a useful introduction.)

—— (1739, 1758) *Texte zur Grundlegung der Ästhetik*, trans. H.R. Schweizer, Hamburg: Felix Meiner Verlag, 1983. (Four key aesthetic texts, including a Latin text with parallel German translation of key sections of Baumgarten's *Metaphysica* of 1739.)

—— (1750, 1758) *Theoretische Ästhetik*, trans. H.R. Schweizer, Hamburg: Felix Meiner Verlag, 1983. (Latin text with parallel German translation of selected sections of Baumgarten's *Aesthetica*.)

References and further reading

Croce, B. (1909) *Aesthetic*, trans. D. Ainslie, New York: Farrar, Straus & Giroux, 1968, 212–19. (An essentially negative evaluation of Baumgarten's contribution to the history of aesthetics.)

Cassirer, E. (1951) *The Philosophy of the Enlightenment*, trans. F.C.A. Koelln and J.P. Pettegrove, Princeton, NJ: Princeton University Press. (In contrast to Croce, Cassirer credits Baumgarten with being the founder of modern aesthetics.)

Gregor, M.J. (1983) 'Baumgarten's *Aesthetica*', *Review of Metaphysics* 37 (2): 357–85. (Argues that while there is a change in perspective, Baumgarten's definitions of the aesthetic remain consistently rationalist.)

Wessell, L.P., Jr (1972) 'Alexander Baumgarten's Contribution to the Development of Aesthetics', *Journal of Aesthetics and Art Criticism* 30 (3): 333–42. (Contends that Baumgarten did free aesthetics from rationalism, but only at the cost of consistency.)

DABNEY TOWNSEND

BAYESIANISM see CONFIRMATION THEORY; INDUCTIVE INFERENCE; PROBABILITY, INTERPRETATION OF; PROBABILITY THEORY AND EPISTEMOLOGY; RAMSEY, FRANK PLUMPTON; STATISTICS

BAYLE, PIERRE (1647–1706)

Bayle was one of the most profound sceptical thinkers of all time. He was also a champion of religious toleration, and an important moral philosopher. The fundamental aim of his scepticism was to curb the pretensions of reason in order to make room for faith. Human reason, he believed, suffers from two fundamental weaknesses: it has a limited capacity to motivate our actions, and it is more a negative than a positive faculty, better at uncovering the defects of various philosophical positions than at justifying any one of them. This conception of reason led Bayle to see, with an uncommon clarity, that the nature of the sceptic's arguments must be to proceed by internal demolition, showing how claims to knowledge undermine themselves in their own terms.

Bayle's moral thought is to be found essentially in his critique of attempts (such as that of Malebranche) to show how God, all-powerful and good, could have created a world in which there is evil. Such theodicies, he argued, rely on unacceptable models of moral rationality. Bayle's arguments reveal a view of moral reasoning that is of considerable interest in its own right. Like Malebranche (and contrary to Leibniz, who attacked Bayle's critique of theodicy), he believed that there are duties superior to that of bringing about the most good overall. But unlike Malebranche, Bayle saw these duties as lying not in what the rational agent owes himself but in what he owes to the inviolable individuality of others. This outlook had its psychological roots, no doubt, in Bayle's own experience as a Huguenot victim of religious persecution.

1 Scepticism
2 Epistemology and metaphysics
3 Theodicy and ethics: Bayle versus Malebranche
4 Bayle and Leibniz

1 Scepticism

Pierre Bayle was one of the most important sceptical thinkers of all time, as well as a notable moral philosopher and advocate of religious toleration. The fundamental motivation of his scepticism was religious: his aim was to curb the pretensions of reason in order to make room for faith. Born into a Calvinist family in Carla in southern France, he became a professor of philosophy in the Protestant academy at Sedan. After its abolition (1681) and the revocation of the Edict of Nantes (1685), which ended Protestant toleration in France, Bayle fled to Holland and spent the rest of his life in Rotterdam. His Calvinist conviction that God is rationally inscrutable spurred his wide-ranging attack on the power of reason to shape our conduct and to make sense of the world. As he wrote in the article on 'Paulicians' in his most important work, the *Dictionnaire historique et critique* (Historical and Critical Dictionary) (1696: 'Paulicians', note E), 'The ways of God are not our ways... [We must accept] the elevation of faith and the abasement of reason'.

Bayle believed that human reason suffers from two fundamental weaknesses. The first is that reason is quite limited in its capacity to motivate our actions. Human beings act more often in virtue of their dominant passions than on the basis of their professed principles. In his first important work, *Pensées diverses sur la comète* (Miscellaneous Reflections on the Comet) (1682), Bayle made use of this observation to argue that, contrary to the accepted opinion of his time, atheists would be able to live together peacefully in society. Were they to follow through on all the consequences of God's nonexistence, they would indeed plunge into a life of vice without remorse. For though convinced that we can know the principles of morality without relying upon belief in God, Bayle thought that without such a belief we would have no reason to subordinate our self-interest to them. Still, the atheist would be unlikely to take up the life of crime, Bayle insisted, because the rational calculation of advantage is a less powerful motive than the concern for honour. The vanity of wishing to be well regarded by others, combined with an interest in using moral principles to blame or approve their actions (if not one's own), would steer the atheist toward mutual cooperation with others.

For Bayle, this argument was not merely a philosophical curiosity. It formed part of his continuing campaign in favour of a society based on religious toleration. The expression of heterodox opinion need not by itself imperil social order. The motivational weakness of reason played a further role in the central argument of Bayle's principal treatise on religious toleration, *Commentaire philosophique sur ces paroles de Jésus-Christ, 'Contrains-les d'entrer'* (Philosophical Commentary on the Following Words of Jesus Christ, 'Compel Them to Enter') (1686). Just as our actions stem less from our reason than from our passions and feelings, so belief itself, Bayle argues here, is not directly under our rational control, but arises involuntarily from inner conviction. As a result, the use of force to impose religious belief must be a futile enterprise. Individual conscience ought to be respected, since sincere belief can have no other source.

The second fundamental weakness of human reason for Bayle was that it is more a negative than a positive faculty. It lends itself better to the refutation of opposing views than to the justification of one's own position. As he wrote in *Réponse aux questions d'un provincial* (Reply to the Questions of a Provincial) (1703–7: II.137), reason 'is better able to demolish than to build, it knows better what things are not than what they are'. When reason is instead put to the use of defending some particular position, it tends naturally to undermine itself. Reason is essentially destructive because it excels in uncovering the self-contradiction into which its positive employment inevitably falls.

This diagnosis underlies two other significant features of Bayle's thought. It allowed him, first of all, to see clearly how sceptical argumentation must proceed in general. The sceptic may not appeal to principles that are not admitted by the position under attack, since such an argument would be irrelevant to the partisans of that position and contrary to the sceptic's own professed lack of knowledge. Instead, Bayle observed, the sceptic must show how the position undermines itself, involving views which are mutually inconsistent or conflicting with opinions every reasonable person holds. The sceptic must work by internal demolition, attacking his adversaries 'on their very own dungheap', as he wrote in the preface to his *Pensées diverses* (see also the 'Second Clarification' in 'Spinoza', *Dictionnaire historique et critique*).

The idea that in its positive employment reason is ultimately self-destructive also shaped Bayle's attitude towards the fundamental conflicts between reason and faith which he doggedly uncovered (see §3). 'If reason were in agreement with itself', he wrote (1703–7: II.137), 'we should be more worried that it agrees so poorly with some of our articles of religion'. Many of Bayle's Enlightenment readers (such as Diderot, in the article 'Pyrrhonian or Sceptic' of the *Encyclopédie*) claimed him for one of their own. But they were wrong to suppose that his attack on rational theology was aimed at the rejection of religious dogma. On the contrary, Bayle's scepticism took the form of a fideism, intended to confirm his Calvinist belief in the radical disparity between God's ways and our own. Indeed, so far was Bayle from being a founding father of the Enlightenment that he was one of the first to express concern about what in the twentieth century has come to be called 'the dialectic of the Enlightenment'. If we follow reason alone, proportioning all our beliefs to the available evidence, we will end up by doing away, he once wrote, not only with superstition and barbarism, but eventually with every sort of conviction: 'Man's fate is so bad that the knowledge that delivers him from one evil throws him into another' (1696: 'Takiddin' Note A).

2 Epistemology and metaphysics

In arguing against the capacity of human reason to acquire knowledge of the world, Bayle focused chiefly on foundational matters. We cannot demonstrate the real existence of the external world, he maintained, nor grasp its fundamental principles. But he appears to have had no serious doubt that straightforwardly empirical questions admit of rational solutions. Indeed, Bayle frequently urged, against the authority of DESCARTES, that philosophy should recognize the validity and importance of historical knowledge, and his own scholarship in the history of philosophy and theology was significant. Bayle's scepticism was therefore restricted to speculative questions of principle. In his *Dictionnaire* article on Pyrrho, he described Pyrrhonism simply as the view that we have no knowledge of the underlying nature of things (see PYRRHONISM).

Such an outlook would seem to place Bayle within the important seventeenth-century current of thought generally called 'mitigated scepticism', the most important exemplars of which were GASSENDI and LOCKE. Like them he believed that, unlike our beliefs about the observable features of the world, ultimate physical explanations can be at most probable, never certain (1696: 'Pyrrho' Note B), and that such explanations refer to what we cannot fully understand. For example, he endorsed Locke's view that we know too little about the nature of matter to rule out the possibility that God might have 'superadded' to it the power of thought (1696: 'Dicaearchus' Note M) (see LOCKE, J. §5).

None the less, Bayle's scepticism ran deeper than that of Gassendi and Locke, for he also believed that ultimate physical principles turn out, upon reflection, to be self-contradictory. This was, for instance, the verdict of his famous discussion of space in the *Dictionnaire* article on ZENO OF ELEA (1696: 'Zeno' Note G). The idea of space, he argued, is incoherent on any of the interpretations one might give of it. Space cannot consist ultimately of mathematical points since the addition of extensionless entities to one another cannot produce extension. Nor can it consist of extended but indivisible physical points, since anything extended is divisible. Nor can it be infinitely divisible, since this would preclude the immediate contiguity of its parts, or would permit the interpenetration of any two contiguous bodies, and in any case would succumb to the well-known paradoxes of the infinite. Here we find a perfect specimen of Bayle's theme that reason tends inevitably to undermine itself. His discussion of space had an important influence on Hume's *Treatise of Human Nature* (1739–41).

3 Theodicy and ethics: Bayle versus Malebranche

Bayle's moral thought is best approached by way of his critique of philosophical *theodicy*. That critique is important, if for no other reason than the fact that Leibniz took it as his main target in his 1710 *Essais de théodicée* (Theodicy). But it also embodies a view of morality that is of genuine interest in its own right.

A theodicy aims to justify the ways of God to humans, showing how God, all-powerful and good, could have created a world in which there is evil. It must therefore make use of a model of moral rationality that lays out the principles according to which one should choose among actions, where each action may involve bad consequences. In this light, theodicies retain a philosophical value even for those who today may find very foreign the idea of justifying the ways of God. Theodicies give vivid expression to models of moral rationality. Accordingly, in seeing why Bayle thought the two leading theodicies of his day were morally unacceptable, we bring into focus his own very interesting conception of moral rationality.

The first of these theodicies was presented by Malebranche in his 1680 *Traité de la nature et de la grâce* (Treatise on Nature and Grace). Malebranche's guiding principle was that God, in creating the world, had to show his wisdom and goodness not only in the result he achieved but also in the means he used. Consequently, God could act to maximize the resulting good in the world only to the extent that at the same time he employed a 'simplicity' of means – that is, a system of universal and immutable laws. As he could foresee, these laws would sometimes result in evil that could have been avoided, had he set about single-mindedly to bring about the greatest good possible. God knew, for example, of the evil that men would do because of the freedom he had given them, when they made use of the laws he set up. This evil, though foreseeable, was not intended, however, since God aimed only to respect his own nature as wise and good. The model of moral rationality that Malebranche assigned to God is therefore one we would call 'deontological': right conduct is that which respects certain principles independently of the bad consequences that the action can foreseeably produce (see MALEBRANCHE, N. §6).

In his first writings, Bayle presented himself as an adherent of Malebranche's theodicy. Thus, in the *Pensées diverses*, he sought to show that sensational phenomena such as comets and monsters, and even sin, represent neither a failure of providence nor God's particular will, but are instead the unintended result of the simple laws by which God rules the world (1682: §§208, 230, 231, 234). It is important to note that, like Malebranche, Bayle did not draw this model of moral rationality from revelation or scripture. We must judge God's rationality, he wrote, by reference to our own (1682: §223). He was convinced that the first principles of morals are open to our reason even 'without knowledge of God' (1682: §178).

This 'autonomy of morality' with respect to religion forms one of the constants of Bayle's thought. It is the principal basis on which later (beginning with the *Dictionnaire* in 1696) he rejected Malebranche's theodicy. He had come to believe that Malebranche's underlying model of moral rationality is incompatible with what we can see to be the first principles of morality. It is in precisely these terms that, in one of his last writings, he explained his change of mind (1703–7: II.91, 155). Bayle's fideism was therefore not the result of any wholesale scepticism about the possibility of knowledge in general. Indeed, as noted in §2 above, Bayle regularly limited his scepticism to speculative questions – he did not question our ability to acquire knowledge of more straightforward matters. And so, in the case of theodicy, he denied that we can ever justify the ways of God because, continuing to consider Malebranche's theory the best conception possible, he found that it conflicted with moral truths we know already.

What exactly did Bayle find morally unacceptable in Malebranche's theodicy? To Bayle it was evident that 'those who permit an evil which it is easy for them to prevent are culpable' and that 'those who let perish a person that they could easily save are guilty of his death'. How, then, could God have let the whole human race fall into crime and misery? He could easily have prevented the disobedience of Adam and Eve or at least have stopped the consequences of their fall. Malebranche's own response, of course, was that God let these things happen because the pursuit of the good must yield to respect for certain general principles. Bayle was not opposed to the idea that there exist duties superior to maximizing the good. But he insisted that such duties consist in securing an urgent good for the agent or someone other, or in saving them from a disastrous evil. These are not, however, considerations which could have moved God in the present case. No other parties but himself and humanity were involved and since, being perfect, he himself had need of nothing, nothing could therefore weigh more heavily than his benevolence toward humanity, his creation (1703–7: II.91, 150, 155).

It could be said that underlying this difference between Malebranche and Bayle were not only two models of moral rationality but also two opposing conceptions of love. On the one hand, there is the idea of love as merited, according to which if one is perfect, one must love oneself above all; on the other hand, there is the idea of love as a gift, which implies that the more perfect one is, the fewer obstacles there must be to the love one bears others. Thus, just as Malebranche wrote that 'one cannot love anything except in proportion to how much one believes it lovable' (Malebranche [1715] 1974 XVI: 96), so Bayle affirmed that 'nothing fits better with true grandeur and supreme perfection than to put one's power and knowledge in the service of others' happiness' ([1707] 1964–8 IV: 63).

In response to Bayle's objection one could imagine Malebranche, like many deontologists, invoking the classic principle of 'double effect', according to which actions are to be judged morally by their intended effects, not by all their foreseeable effects. Is it not true that Adam and Eve were themselves free to prevent the evil, that the responsibility for it was their own, and that it was a paramount duty to respect their freedom of action, even at the price of not doing what one knew would produce the greatest good? Indeed, in a letter of 11 December 1706 to the Père André, Malebranche formally embraced the principle of double effect. But Bayle anticipated this reply, claiming that it is an evident principle that one ought not to give someone a good (such as freedom of action) that one knows the person will abuse (1703–7: II.81).

In the *Dictionnaire* Bayle presents a remarkable example to illustrate this point (1696: 'Paulicians' Remark E). A mother who sent her daughters to a ball knowing that they would succumb to temptation, but being content simply to encourage them to be virtuous and to threaten to disown them if they did not return home virgins, would not count, he observed, as loving either her daughters or chastity. Bayle did recognize duties of 'strict obligation', involving respect for the freedom of others which ordinarily take precedence over the maximization of the good. But he believed that such duties must be suspended in emergency cases, where a catastrophic evil is to be avoided (1696: 'Paulicians' Remark M). There, we must choose the lesser evil (See MALEBRANCHE, N. §§4–5).

4 Bayle and Leibniz

Bayle's critique of Malebranche might suggest that he held a 'consequentialist' conception of moral rationality, according to which we should always seek the greatest net good overall, even at the price of using means that in themselves are bad. This conception underlies, in fact, the theodicy which Leibniz laid out in the *Essais de théodicée*. There he argued that God reasons according to the 'règle du meilleur' ('the rule of the better'), so that what is evil in itself should be chosen if it forms the indispensable means to bringing about the greatest good overall (Leibniz 1710: §§22, 209). The general and immutable laws according to which God created the world constitute not limits (as Malebranche believed) but, rather, means to the maximization of the good.

Leibniz directed the *Essais* primarily against Bayle himself and his claim that theodicy is impossible. In his view, Bayle had sold theodicy short by failing to consider a version which makes rigorous use of 'la règle du meilleur'. Leibniz's position seems to look all the stronger if Bayle's arguments against Malebranche are themselves consequentialist in spirit. However, the argumentative situation is more complex. Bayle's conception of morality was not really consequentialist. And though Bayle died four years before the publication of Leibniz's book, he was familiar with a theodicy of that form and rejected it as morally unacceptable (see LEIBNIZ, G.W. §3).

The consequentialist theodicy with which Bayle was acquainted was one outlined by Isaac Jaquelot in his 1705 book, *La conformité de la raison et de la foi* (The Conformity of Reason and Faith). Jaquelot himself rather closely followed the Malebranchian position. But he claimed that Bayle's objections to Malebranche relied on the principle that one ought always to do that action which will bring about the most good overall. Suppose, he wrote (treating the question of theodicy once again through the story about the mother and her daughters), the mother was sending her daughters to the ball so that, in virtue of all the foreseeable consequences of that decision, a 'great, noble, and comprehensive plan' for the reformation of the kingdom would be realized. If Bayle required that the welfare of the daughters should count for more than the duty of respecting their freedom, he ought also to admit, so Jaquelot argued, that the still greater good of accomplishing that plan should outweigh their welfare. They ought to be sent to the ball. God's decision not to prevent Adam and Eve's disobedience would thus be justified on the same basis – namely, by the greater good which his overall plan of eventual redemption would bring about.

Bayle took up Jaquelot's challenge in his *Réponse aux questions d'un provincial* (1703–7: II.153). Such a mother, he replied, would be even more wicked than the one first imagined. Agreeing that, taken absolutely, the good of the kingdom is greater than the good of the daughters, Bayle maintained that there are some things we should never do to another person, even at the cost of foregoing a tremendous good. This rejoinder to Jaquelot was, no doubt, the objection Bayle would have made to Leibniz had he lived to see Leibniz's *Essais de théodicée*. Once again we find him rejecting a theodicy on the basis of moral principles which he claims we know to be true.

An important question, however, is whether Bayle's moral thought, taken as a whole, is coherent. How can we harmonize his criticism of Malebranche, according to which the prevention of a significant evil must weigh more than the duties of strict obligation, with his objection to Jaquelot (and by anticipation to Leibniz) that the maximization of the good must yield to certain prohibitions on the treatment of others? How, we might say, can Bayle apparently reject both deontological and consequentialist conceptions of moral reasoning? In fact, Bayle was perfectly consistent. In his rejection of Malebranche, the operative principle was that we may suspend a strict duty with regard to an individual if we wish to avoid a very great evil to *this same individual*. Such a principle is clearly compatible with the principle Bayle invoked in his response to Jaquelot, namely that we must never cause a great evil to an individual in order to procure a great good *for others*.

Bayle was no doubt a deontological thinker, since he believed that there are duties superior to that of bringing about the most good overall. The fundamental coherence of Bayle's thought emerges once we recognize that a deontological ethic can take two different forms. Malebranche's version limits the maximization of the good by the demands of what a rational agent owes himself. Bayle's version limits it by the demands of what one owes to the inviolable individuality of others. The core conviction of Bayle's ethics was the refusal to sacrifice individuals to a greater whole. No doubt, it had its psychological roots in his own experience as a Huguenot refugee from religious persecution. Bayle's skill in giving it philosophical articulation shows him to be, despite his scepticism, one of the great moral thinkers.

See also: SPINOZA, B. DE

List of works

Bayle, P. (1682) *Pensées diverses sur la comète*

(Miscellaneous reflections on the comet), critical ed. A. Prat and P. Rétat, Paris: Nizet, 1984. (Best presentation of Bayle's moral psychology.)

—— (1686) *Commentaire philosophique sur ces paroles de Jésus-Christ, 'Contrains-les d'entrer'* (Philosophical Commentary on the following words of Jesus Christ, 'Compel them to enter'), in *Oeuvres Diverses*, Hildesheim: Olms, 1964–8. (Bayle's defence of religious toleration.)

—— (1696) *Dictionnaire historique et critique*; selective trans. R. Popkin and C. Brush, *Historical and Critical Dictionnary*, Indianapolis, IN: Bobbs-Merrill, 1965. (Bayle's most important philosophical work.)

—— (1703–7) *Réponse aux questions d'un provincial* (Reply to the questions of a provincial), in *Oeuvres Diverses*, Hildesheim: Olms, 1964–8. (Contains important clarifications of many of Bayle's views.)

—— (1707) *Entretiens de Maxime et de Thémiste* (Conversations between Maximus and Themistus), in *Oeuvres Diverses*, Hildesheim: Olms, 1964–8. (Devoted to the issue of theodicy.)

—— (1727) *Oeuvres diverses*, The Hague, 4 vols; repr. Hildesheim: Olms, 1964–8. (Contains, with the exception of the *Dictionnaire*, most of Bayle's writings.)

References and further reading

Brush, C. (1966) *Montaigne and Bayle. Variations on the Theme of Scepticism*, The Hague: Martinus Nijhoff. (Very useful study of Bayle's scepticism.)

Delvolvé, J. (1906) *Essai sur Pierre Bayle. Religion critique et philosophie positive* (Essay on Pierre Bayle. Critical religion and positive philosophy.) Paris: Félix Alcan. (Comprehensive philosophical study which underestimates, however, the importance of Bayle's religious faith.)

* Hume, D. (1739–41) *A Treatise of Human Nature*, ed. L.A. Selby-Bigge and P.H. Nidditch, Oxford: Clarendon Press, 1975. (Hume's classic. Bayle's influence on his treatment of space is evident in Book I, section 2.)

* Jaquelot, I. (1705) *La conformité de la raison et de la foi* (The Conformity of Reason and Faith), Amsterdam: Desbordes. (Bayle's example of a consequentialist theodicy.)

Labrousse, E. (1983) *Bayle*, Oxford: Oxford University Press. (The best short introduction by the leading contemporary Bayle scholar; includes bibliography.)

Larmore, C. (1993) 'Théodicée et rationalité morale' (Theodicy and moral rationality), in *Modernité et morale*, Paris: Presses Universitaires de France, 121–38. (Extended treatment of material in §3 and §4 above.)

* Leibniz, G.W. (1710) *Essais de théodicée*; trans. E.M. Huggard as *Theodicy*, La Salle, IL: Open Court, 1985. (Referred to in §4; particularly in its introductory 'Discourse', it contains an important critique of Bayle.)

* Malebranche, N. (1680) *Traité de la nature et de la grâce* (Treatise on nature and grace), in *Oeuvres complètes* vol. 5, Paris: Vrin, 1976. (Referred to in §3; presents the version of theodicy which Bayle considered the strongest possible.)

* —— (1715) *Réflexions sur la prémotion physique* (Reflections on physical premotion), in *Oeuvres complètes*, vol. 16, Paris: Vrin, 1974. (Referred to in §3.)

CHARLES LARMORE

BEATTIE, JAMES (1735–1803)

James Beattie was famed as a moralist and poet in the late eighteenth century, and helped to popularize Scottish common-sense philosophy. At Marischal College, Aberdeen, Beattie cultivated a lecturing style which differed significantly from that of his Aberdonian predecessors. Because he believed that the form of abstract analysis characteristic of the science of the mind in his day often led students into the morass of Humean scepticism, Beattie endeavoured to inculcate sound moral and religious principles through the study of ancient and modern literature. Consequently his version of common-sense philosophy diverged from that developed by Thomas Reid. Beattie was more of a practical moralist than an anatomist of the mind, and his treatment of common-sense epistemology lacked the philosophical range and rigour of Reid's.

1 Life
2 **Professing moral philosophy**
3 **Beattie, Reid and common-sense philosophy**

1 Life

Equally renowned in his day as a poet, the moralist James Beattie was born on 25 October 1735 in Laurencekirk, Scotland. He attended Marischal College, Aberdeen, from 1749 to 1753, when he took his M.A. Beattie shone as a student, and was a favourite of the principal of the college, the noted classicist Thomas Blackwell. After graduating, Beattie became a parish schoolmaster in the village of Fordoun near his home, and he also began to work towards a divinity degree. While at Fordoun, Beattie published occasional poems in the periodical press, and he later consolidated his literary reputation with *The Minstrel* (1771–4). Thanks to the influence of Blackwell and his colleagues, Beattie was appointed to teach at the Aberdeen Grammar School in 1758, and succeeded Alexander GERARD to the Chair of Moral Philosophy and Logic at Marischal in 1760.

Once installed as professor, Beattie became a prominent figure in the ABERDEEN PHILOSOPHICAL SOCIETY (to which he was admitted on 10 February 1761) and the Aberdeen Musical Society. Because of his poetical works Beattie was also increasingly known outside of Aberdeen, and became the darling of the London literati in the early 1770s when he published *The Minstrel* along with his widely read attack on David HUME, *An Essay on the Nature and Immutability of Truth* (1770). For his part, Hume thought the *Essay* a splenetic performance, and his sentiments were echoed by Beattie's most combative critic, Joseph PRIESTLEY. However, the work was applauded by George III and, during a highly successful visit to London, Beattie was rewarded with a royal pension and given an honorary Doctor of Laws degree by Oxford University on 9 July 1773. Among the many friends he made on this trip was the painter Sir Joshua Reynolds, and while he was in the metropolis he sat for the allegorical portrait 'The Triumph of Truth', in which Beattie is juxtaposed with the figure of truth victorious over her opponents. On the Continent Beattie was similarly applauded as a champion of orthodoxy. In 1774 he was elected to the Zealand Society of Arts and Sciences in Holland, and the enthusiastic reception of the *Essay* prompted translations into Dutch, French, German and Italian.

The early 1770s can be seen as marking the high point of Beattie's career. Yet the promise of this period was never completely fulfilled, largely because his already fragile health declined markedly and his wife gradually became mentally unstable. Capitalizing on the popularity of the *Essay*, in 1773 he solicited subscriptions for a new edition which would include additional essays on other topics, and, after delays caused by illness, he saw this enlarged version through the press in 1776. Eventually his deteriorioating condition and that of his wife forced him to abandon any hope of completing a systematic work on moral philosophy. He turned instead to revising segments of his lectures in the winter of 1780–1, and these eventually appeared in 1783 as his *Dissertations Moral and Critical*. The following year Beattie found some consolation in further public recognition, for he was appointed a fellow of the newly founded Royal Society of Edinburgh and elected an honorary member of both the Manchester Literary and Philosophical Society and the American Philosophical Society.

Beattie finally realized his long-standing ambition to publish an accessible defence of Christianity in 1786 when he completed his *Evidences of the Christian Religion*, modelled on an earlier apologetic work by Joseph Addison, whom he greatly admired. Like many of his previous writings the *Evidences* had its origins in the classroom, and he recycled his lectures one last time as the basis for *The Elements of Moral Science* (1790–3). The subsequent popularity of the *Elements* as a textbook attests to Beattie's standing as a pedagogue, but his ill health had somewhat compromised his teaching career. One of his major preoccupations during the 1780s was to find a suitable successor, and in 1787 his Marischal colleagues agreed to nominate his son, James Hay Beattie, as joint professor. However, his son died tragically in 1790, and the issue of succession was not settled until 1796, when George Glennie's appointment as his assistant enabled him to retire from lecturing.

2 Professing moral philosophy

Prior to Beattie's election to the chair, the teaching of moral philosophy at Marischal College can be seen as a volatile mixture of moral exhortation with the rigorous study of the intellectual and active powers of the mind. George TURNBULL was the first pedagogue at Marischal to argue that the lessons of practical morality must be rooted in the empirical investigation of human nature, and his call for a methodological reform in the science of morals was taken up at the college by David Fordyce and Alexander Gerard. Beattie, however, broke with this tradition. When he began lecturing in 1760, his course was virtually the same as that given by his teacher Gerard, but during the next two decades Beattie reoriented the moral philosophy curriculum. Whereas Gerard surveyed the various faculties of the mind in a comprehensive manner, over the years Beattie reduced the number of classes spent on pneumatology to make room for lectures on literary criticism, as well as greatly expanded treatments of language, rhetoric, composition and the writings of Cicero. Along with this literary turn went an increased interest in dreaming, taste and the workings of the imagination and memory; Beattie evidently valued his lectures on these topics in so far as he revised them for inclusion in his *Dissertations Moral and Critical* (1783). Beattie also enlarged the time spent on natural theology and, in the 1770s, his discussion of the rational grounds for Christianity took on a new polemical tone due to his growing obsession with the supposed threat posed by the fashionable scepticism of Hume.

Moreover, Beattie was more emphatic about the prerogatives of practical moralizing than Gerard had been. Whereas Gerard had espoused the view that the pursuit of virtue had to be based on a knowledge of the first principles of morality, Beattie virtually severed the connection between theory and practice by arguing that matters of conduct took priority over metaphysics (by which he meant the abstract study of the mind). Consequently, he eschewed any detailed discussion of the substantive issues debated in the science of the mind as being of little concrete application, and focused instead on the inculcation of sound moral, religious and political attitudes. Indeed, he explicitly warned his students against being seduced by purely speculative metaphysical problems, and urged them to attend to the fulfilment of their various practical duties. Beattie thus endeavoured to disentangle the role of the metaphysician from that of the practical moralist, and in so doing distanced himself from the style of philosophizing cultivated by most of his Scottish contemporaries.

Beattie's change of direction was largely prompted by his animus against David Hume. In Beattie's view, Scottish academic philosophy was far too preoccupied with the epistemological issues raised by Humean scepticism and had lost sight of the primacy of moral preaching. Fearing the dominance of Hume's supposed 'party' of sceptics in Edinburgh, he turned south of the border for inspiration, and cultivated both the teaching practices and the form of polite culture which he associated with the ancient English universities.

3 Beattie, Reid and common-sense philosophy

Joseph Priestley was the first to bracket together the works of Beattie and Thomas REID in his critique of common sense philosophy, and most commentators have subsequently followed his lead. Priestley's elision of their writings, however, conceals as much as it reveals. Beattie was introduced to the elements of common-sense epistemology by Gerard, and this largely accounts for the differences between his exposition of the notion of common sense and that found in the works of Reid. Moreover, Beattie himself lamented Reid's generous public treatment of Hume, which for him showed that Reid was too much of a metaphysician and lacked warmth in the cause of virtue. Beattie's dislike of metaphysics also accounts for the fact that, unlike Reid, he did not engage in a systematic refutation of the theory of ideas as it had evolved in the works of Descartes, Locke, Berkeley and Hume. Given that Reid's painstaking analysis of the mechanisms of human perception was the cornerstone of his response to scepticism, Beattie's lack of interest in this topic serves to underline the contrasts between them. Beattie was much more of a moral preacher and polemicist than Reid, and their divergent styles suggest that Beattie's place in the development of Scottish common-sense philosophy requires reassessment (see COMMON SENSE SCHOOL).

See also: OSWALD, J.

List of works

(Much of Beattie's unpublished correspondence, along with related manuscripts and student lecture notes, is held in Aberdeen University Library. Other important archival materials are to be found in the Scottish Record Office and Edinburgh University Library.)

Beattie, J. (1996) *The Collected Works of James Beattie*, ed. R. Robinson, London: Routledge; Bristol: Thoemmes Press, 10 vols. (Facsimile reprints of all of Beattie's works, plus hitherto uncollected miscellaneous writings and manuscript materials, along with Forbes' biography (1806).)

—— (1760) *Original Poems and Translations*, London: Millar. (A collection of Beattie's earliest poems and translations of selections from Anacreon, Horace, Lucretius, and Virgil.)

—— (1770) *An Essay on the Nature and Immutability of Truth, in Opposition to Sophistry and Scepticism*, Edinburgh: Kincaid & Bell; London: Dilly; repr., intro. F.O. Wolf, Stuttgart-Bad Cannstatt: Frommann, 1973. (Established Beattie's reputation as a moralist, and popularized common-sense philosophy.)

—— (1771–4) *The Minstrel: or, the Progress of Genius*, London: Dilly; Edinburgh: Kincaid & Bell. (Rooted in debates over the nature of poetry, *The Minstrel* consolidated Beattie's standing as a writer.)

—— (1776) *Essays*, Edinburgh: Creech; repr. New York: Garland Press, 1971; Hildesheim: Olms, 1974. (An expanded text of the *Essay*, plus essays on our psychological response to poetry and music, humour, and the usefulness of classical learning.)

—— (1783) *Dissertations Moral and Critical*, London: Strahan & Cadell; repr. New York: Garland Press, 1971; Hildesheim: Olms, 1974. (Six lengthy essays on philosophical, psychological, linguistic, moral, aesthetic, and literary topics derived from his lectures.)

—— (1786) *Evidences of the Christian Religion, Briefly and Plainly Stated*, Edinburgh: Creech; London: Strahan & Cadell, 2 vols. (Popular exposition of the rational case for the truth of Christianity.

—— (1790–3) *The Elements of Moral Science*,

London: Cadell; Edinburgh: Creech, 2 vols; repr. Hildesheim: Olms, 1974. (Influential textbook comprised of revised versions of Beattie's lectures on psychology, natural theology, ethics, economics, politics, and logic.)
—— (1820) *The Letters of James Beattie, LL.D. Chronologically Arranged from Sir W. Forbes's Collection*, London: Sharpe, 2 vols. (The largest published collection of Beattie's letters.)
—— (1908) *James Beattie 'The Minstrel': Some Unpublished Letters*, ed. A. Mackie, Aberdeen: Aberdeen Daily Journal Office. (Twenty-five letters of primarily biographical interest.)
—— (1946) *James Beattie's London Diary 1773*, ed. R.S. Walker, Aberdeen: Aberdeen University Press. (Beattie's detailed chronicle of his extended trip to London in the summer of 1773.)
—— (1948) *James Beattie's Day Book 1773–1798*, ed. R.S. Walker, Aberdeen: The Third Spalding Club. (A selection from Beattie's personal accounts which sheds light on his dealings with his publishers and a number of other topics.)

References and further reading

Bevilacqua, V.M. (1967) 'James Beattie's Theory of Rhetoric', *Speech Monographs* 34: 109–24. (A thorough treatment of Beattie's approach to rhetoric.)
Bower, A. (1804) *An Account of the Life of James Beattie, LL.D. Professor of Moral Philosophy and Logic, Aberdeen*, London: Baldwin. (The earliest biography, which has interesting material on Beattie's Aberdeen context.)
Fabian, B. and Kloth, K. (1967–70) 'The Manuscript Background of James Beattie's *Elements of Moral Science*', *Bibliotheck* 5: 181–9. (Contains a useful list of sets of student notes from Beattie's lectures.)
Forbes, M. (1904) *James Beattie and His Friends*, London: Constable; repr. Bristol: Thoemmes, 1990. (A biography which contains some information and additional letters not found in Forbes (1806).)
Forbes, W. (1806) *An Account of the Life and Writings of James Beattie, LL.D.*, Edinburgh: Constable & Creech, 2 vols. (A detailed biography by one of Beattie's close associates which incorporates a large number of Beattie's letters.)
Grave, S.A. (1960) *The Scottish Philosophy of Common Sense*, Oxford: Clarendon Press. (The standard modern work on the philosophy of Beattie, Reid, and James Oswald.)
Hewitt, D. (1987) 'James Beattie and the Languages of Scotland', in J.J. Carter and J.H. Pittock (eds) *Aberdeen and the Enlightenment*, Aberdeen: Aberdeen University Press, 251–60. (A suggestive essay on Beattie and the politics of language in eighteenth-century Scotland.)
King, E.H. (1977) *James Beattie*, Boston: Twayne. (An introduction to Beattie's career as a man of letters.)
Phillipson, N. (1978) 'James Beattie and the Defence of Common Sense', in B. Fabian (ed.) *Festschrift für Rainer Gruenter*, Heidelberg: Winter, 145–54. (An insightful exploration of the psychological dynamics of Beattie's reaction to Humean scepticism.)
Wood, P.B. (1993) *The Aberdeen Enlightenment: The Arts Curriculum in the Eighteenth Century*, Aberdeen: Aberdeen University Press. (A detailed discussion of matters outlined in §2, which contains further references.)

PAUL WOOD

BEAUTY

On the subject of beauty, theorists generally agree only on rudimentary points about the term: that it commends on aesthetic grounds, has absolute and comparative forms, and so forth. Beyond this, dispute prevails. Realists hold that judgments of beauty ascribe to their subjects either a nonrelational property inherent in things or a capacity of things to affect respondents in a way that preserves objectivity. In both cases acute problems arise in defining the property and in explaining how it can be known. Classical Platonism holds that beauty exists as an ideal supersensible Form, while eighteenth-century theorists view it as a quasi-sensory property. Kant's transcendental philosophy anchors the experience of beauty to the basic requirements of cognition, conferring on it 'subjective universality and necessity'. Sceptics complain that the alleged property is merely a reflection of aesthetic pleasure and hence lacks objective standing. Partly due to its preoccupation with weightier matters, the philosophic tradition has never developed any theory of beauty as fully and deeply as it has, say, theories in the domain of morality. Comparative neglect of the subject has been encouraged by the generally subjectivistic and relativistic bent of the social sciences and humanities, as well as by avant-gardism in the arts. However, several recent and ambitious studies have given new impetus to theorizing about beauty.

1 Areas of general agreement about beauty
2 Specimen issues concerning beauty
3 Beauty as an intrinsic property
4 Response-related realist conceptions of beauty
5 Restoration of beauty as a theoretical subject
6 Subjectivism and relativism regarding beauty

1 Areas of general agreement about beauty

Almost all theorists concerned with the concept of beauty accept the following propositions. The reflective use of terms of beauty standardly expresses not a mere effusion but a favourable aesthetic judgment of a thing as a whole or in part. The commendation is normally associated with the capacity of the thing to yield pleasure, and presupposes a basis of beauty-making properties, on which beauty is said to supervene. The commendation is relative to (a) a threshold which varies widely with speakers, below which lie grades of lesser aesthetic value without a determinable minimum and above which rise grades of eminence also without a fixed limit, and (b) a comparison-class, which in different contexts ranges from the highly restricted ('a beautiful daisy') to the virtually universal ('a beautiful thing'), or a grade of competition ('a beautiful drawing for a beginner'). It seems we need go only a small step beyond these truisms to conclude that all normative disagreements about beauty reduce to differences of comparative rankings (more, less, or equally beautiful or unbeautiful) and that differences regarding threshold or terminology have no theoretical importance. Beyond these elements of the 'logic' of beauty, there is scant agreement.

2 Specimen issues concerning beauty

Perhaps the most fundamental issue is whether beauty exists in any substantial sense. The common saying that beauty is in the eye of the beholder, taken straightforwardly, amounts to a denial that beauty is a property of anything or that anything is genuinely worthy of being aesthetically admired. This denial is a first principle of aesthetic subjectivism (or nihilism), which, if consistent, confines its theorizing to the analysis of aesthetic preference as a socio-psychological phenomenon and as a variably rational or nonrational part of life. Generally, subjectivists in aesthetics, like those in ethics, retain the usual value terms but reinterpret them as avowing, expressing or soliciting preferences. In contrast, aesthetic realists seek to identify the property or state of affairs that beauty consists in and to explain how it can be known.

Many issues are common to aesthetic realism and subjectivism. For instance: (1) What is the range of things to which terms of beauty can be meaningfully applied? Some take beauty to be a transcendental, in the medieval sense of being a category that is applicable to everything. Others deny that it applies to certain classes. Flavours, scents, bodily sensations, thoughts, theories, abstractions, virtues and even natural objects are excluded by one thinker or another. Some allege that the proper referent of terms of beauty is never a physical object but an appearance or 'semblance'. (2) To what extent can aesthetic value be subsumed under the beautiful? Are the sublime, the pretty, the cute, the witty and the tragic species or degree-ranges of beauty, or are they distinct values? (3) To what extent may things of different types be meaningfully compared in respect of beauty? Parrots of a given species may be judged beautiful relative to one other, but can they be ranked against horses or houses? If not, can the beautiful be a single category of appraisal? (4) How determinate can judgments of beauty be when many factors enter into the case? On the face of it we stand on firmer ground in judging that a musical work is beautifully tender or sprightly than when we pass a summative judgment on the total ensemble of its qualities. This has an obvious impact on comparisons: Beethoven's Fifth and Sixth symphonies are replete with beautiful aspects and moments, but can we sum these so exactly as to say which work is more beautiful?

3 Beauty as an intrinsic property

The simplest form of realism about beauty takes it to be an intrinsic or nonrelational property with strong *de facto* and *de jure* ties to love. For Plato and Plotinus it is a supersensible abstract Form, better exemplified by abstractions than by concrete particulars, and supremely exemplified by itself. Acquaintance with beauty begins in commerce with particulars, but only pure thought, on the model of mathematical and moral intuition and demonstration, can elevate the opinions gained through acquaintance to the level of knowledge. Though their theoretical framework does not by itself entail particular normative principles, Platonically-minded thinkers usually favour Apollonian values of order, clarity, harmony and balance as opposed to Dionysian values of profusion, sensuality and vehemence.

A basic question left unanswered by theories of this type concerns the nature of the property of beauty. Neither Plato nor Plotinus offer to identify the property of beauty, and in their writings it tends to acquire a mystical air, due to the obscure nature of its purer exemplars (the Forms) and the extreme breadth of its range. The latter makes it difficult to imagine how any nonrelational property could account for all the indicated sorts of beauty, and the difficulty is compounded by suggestions of a single, universal rank-ordering. Answers to such questions are hampered by the vagueness of theorists' accounts of the relation between properties and their instances, which is especially acute if one takes literally Plato's claim that the property of beauty is supremely self-exemplifying. Platonic ontology aside, citations of primary values such as the medieval triad of clarity, splendour and proportionality invariably omit to supply a working criterion of any of the three, or a summation rule to decide between things which differ in more than one of them.

4 Response-related realist conceptions of beauty

A second sort of realism takes beauty to be essentially related to human response. The manner of relatedness varies. For example, G.E. Moore's definition of beauty as 'that of which the admiring contemplation is good in itself' avoids any reference to actual effects on human feeling. It speaks only of effects which, should they occur, would contribute to the intrinsic value of a state of mind. This allows things to be beautiful even if they are never experienced, or if experienced never admiringly contemplated. At the same time it ties beauty conceptually to human experience. At first sight such a theory has no difficulty explaining the diversity of beautiful things, for why should not endlessly diverse constellations of material and mental properties be intrinsically good to contemplate admiringly? But doubts arise when one asks how to determine which ones qualify. Obviously it will not do to answer, 'the beautiful ones'. And in the end the answer seems irretrievably buried in the nature of intrinsic goodness, since on Moore's view that property is not only simple and therefore unanalysable, but non-natural and consequently inaccessible to empirical observation. One must reach such results as one can by an intuition which, if rational, is inexplicably so.

British eighteenth-century theorists (Hutcheson and Hume, for example) advanced a naturalistic conception of beauty as a relational property, sufficiently similar to a sensory colour or sound to be known by a faculty called the sense of beauty. The sense is internal, in that it responds directly to mental representations, not to external stimuli. A considerably sanitized and amplified development of the central idea might go as follows. The surface colour of a red object is definable as a power (now more commonly called a disposition) to excite a red appearance in optimally colour-sighted percipients under optimal conditions; likewise the beauty of a sensible object is its power to produce, via impressions of the external senses, a beauty-datum (an 'idea' of beauty, in eighteenth-century parlance) in optimally beauty-receptive observers under optimal conditions. (Deviations are explained by non-optimality affecting some part of the sensory process.) The beauty-datum of choice is disinterested pleasure, defined (for instance, by Shaftesbury) as pleasure taken wholly in the object and not at all in the self, or more exactly not in the self's pleasure. Since disinterested pleasure is arguably also a mark of moral discernment (sometimes ascribed to a companion moral sense), an additional qualification is required if beauty is not to be identified with the moral good. (See the proposal by Kant, below.) To cover things of abstract beauty, the theory must assume that the sense also yields a beauty-datum in response to the mental representation of theorems, proofs and so forth, under appropriate conditions of optimality.

Discussions of erroneous judgments of beauty occur in the works of all the major British theorists, Hume's perhaps being most often cited. Pooling the suggestions therein, one might obtain an honestly empirical criterion of accuracy of the sense of beauty by requiring a consensus among maximal beauty-discriminators under optimal beauty-discriminating conditions. Failing that, beauty would not exist. To complete the analogy with sensory properties, the consensus would also have to correlate with a basis in the object comparable to wavelengths, reflectance and the like for sensory properties. Uniformity and variety 'in compound ratio' is Hutcheson's all-purpose candidate for this role. An appropriate brain structure for the sense must also be assumed. None of the theorists acknowledges the full set of necessary components or the theoretical and practical difficulties of establishing that all of them actually exist.

Immanuel Kant's theory of beauty introduces important new ideas, though in such a way as to provoke endless controversy over their precise content and validity (see KANT, I. §12). Aesthetic pleasure is distinguished from its moral counterpart by its freedom from concern with the actual existence or nonexistence of the object of pleasure. Kant circumvents the need to rely on actual agreement among qualified judges by an ingenious but cryptic account of the deep source of pleasure. This is, he says, the harmonious free play of the cognitive powers, the imagination and understanding – free in the sense of not being directed towards actual knowledge. In ordinary cognition the imagination supplements the received sensory data so as to fit them to a concept supplied by the understanding. The result is an objective judgment. In aesthetic contemplation the imagination is free to seek out relations of form without concern for cognitive relevance to the scene which contains them; and the understanding is free to accept the yield and set new pattern-finding tasks for the imagination. Since the routines of this play are indispensable staples of ordinary cognitive processing, they belong to the repertoire of all humans beings, and the pleasurable harmony of the faculties can be presumed universal and necessary – a pleasure we have a right to expect everyone to feel. Because the play is not controlled by definite concepts, the judgment of free beauty is irremediably singular and incapable of being generalized into a rule of beauty.

Kant also recognizes judgments of 'dependent' beauty, where a concept imposes a limitation. For example, to judge the beauty of a human body, one must take account of whether the properties of the body (for example, its proportions) are such as to facilitate the functions of a human being. Only such free beauty as fulfils this condition affects the overall assessment. Though less purely aesthetic than free beauty, dependent beauty is of far greater human significance. Artistic beauty falls under this head, since all art is to some extent constrained by a purpose.

5 Restoration of beauty as a theoretical subject

Twentieth-century philosophies of beauty are comparatively rare, due to a general shift of interest towards the aesthetic. An exception to the rule is a searching, broad-gauge theory by Guy Sircello, which construes virtually all aesthetic values as species of beauty and explains beauty in terms of non-defective and non-defective-seeming 'properties of qualitative degree'. As these properties are highly context-dependent both for their existence and for their status as non-defective and non-defective-seeming, it is hard to be sure of their ontological or, to an extent, their epistemological standing. Moreover, Sircello does not hazard a sufficient condition for the overall beauty of things as opposed to their beauty in respect of a property of the sort mentioned. Another effort was made to revive the theory of beauty by Mary Mothersill, after reflection on Kant's aesthetics, and especially on his dictum that there can be no laws of taste. On her view 'Any individual is beautiful if and only if it is such as to be a cause of pleasure in virtue of its aesthetic properties'. The latter are understood in a new way, namely as properties so sensitive to their context as to be incapable of being possessed by two individuals unless the latter are perceptually indistinguishable under standard conditions of observation. For example, the distinctive wavelike contour running through El Greco's *Burial of Count Orgaz*, when taken in the full context provided by the painting, is qualified by the totality of perceptible relationships between it and all other features of the design. In this way she supports Kant's idea of the judgment of beauty being logically singular, since such radically contextualized properties cannot figure in non-trivial laws or principles. Mothersill's theory, developed with skill and panache, raises daunting problems but, like Sircello's, opens up possibly profitable lines of research.

6 Subjectivism and relativism regarding beauty

Subjectivist theories of beauty, while relieved of the commitment to the identity and 'knowability' of beauty, raise important problems involving the rationality of aesthetic preference. If a judgment of beauty, taken as avowing or expressing an aesthetic pro-attitude, can be counted unjustified if based on error or ignorance regarding its object, then aesthetic subjectivism can impute fault without implying that beauty is a property of anything. Is it amenable to principles of rationality beyond that point? Can it justify favouring consistency in aesthetic attitudes over time or the subsumption of particular attitudes under attitudes of wide scope? If people generally concur in an error-free aesthetic attitude regarding a thing, does that fact give one a reason for suspicion about one's own dissenting but equally error-free attitude?

Relativism holds that beauty varies with cultures or 'taste-publics' without collapsing into personal preference. A version close to the dispositional account in §4 could be obtained by relativizing the beauty-disposition to the maximal discrimination-capacities attainable in distinct cultures, especially if some neural explanation of the difference could be found – following the analogy of sensory colour, which is vulnerable to the same relativization if different cultures are found to have different but equally acute colour-sensibilities. Typically, however, relativists tend towards a notion of aesthetic taste so malleable as to leave no chance of a quasi-realist account – without, it must be observed, offering anything like compelling evidence. An alternative explanation of cultural difference as a specialization-phenomenon is at least as plausible. On this (realist) view, cultures develop special competences in distinct ranges of beauty, without there being any incompatibility among the values most reliably assessed by the respective cultures.

See also: AESTHETIC CONCEPTS; HUME, D.; PLOTINUS §3; ARTISTIC TASTE

References and further reading

Brink, D.O. (1989) *Moral Realism and the Foundations of Ethics*, Cambridge: Cambridge University Press, ch. 2. (Clearer and more detailed explanation of varieties of realism and antirealism with reference

to values than can be found in the aesthetic literature.)
* Hume, D. (1757) 'Of the Standard of Taste', in *Of the Standard of Taste and Other Essays*, ed. J. Lenz, New York: Macmillan, 1965. (Admirably clear discussion of criteria of accuracy of the supposed sense of beauty.)
* Hutcheson, F. (1725) *An Inquiry concerning Beauty, Order, Harmony, Design*, ed., with intro. and notes by P. Kivy, The Hague: Martinus Nijhoff, 1993. (The fullest formulation of the eighteenth-century sense of beauty theory.)
* Kant, I. (1790) *Critique of Judgment*, trans. J.H. Bernard, New York: Macmillan, 1951. (The first part, 'Critique of Aesthetic Judgment', contains Kant's theory of beauty and sublimity.)
  Margolis, J. (1976) 'Robust Relativism', *Journal of Aesthetics and Art Criticism* 35: 37–46, reprinted in J. Margolis, *Philosophy Looks at the Arts*, Philadelphia, PA: Temple University Press, 1978, esp. 387–401. (Brief exposition and defence of aesthetic relativism regarding aesthetic judgments and critical interpretations.)
* Moore, G.E. (1903, 1959) *Principia Ethica*, Cambridge: Cambridge University Press, ch. 4, 'The Ideal'. (A classic statement of the intuitionist position regarding moral and aesthetic value.)
* Mothersill, M. (1984) *Beauty Restored*, Oxford: Oxford University Press. (Contains Mothersill's theory and discussions of historical positions regarding beauty; useful bibliography.)
* Plato (*c*.380s BC) *Phaedrus*, trans. R. Hackford, in *The Collected Dialogues of Plato*, ed. E. Hamilton and H. Cairns, Princeton, NJ: Princeton University Press, 1963, 244–257. (Plato's ideas about love and beauty are presented mythopoeically in Socrates' speech to the god of love.)
* —— (*c*.380s BC) *Symposium*, trans. M. Joyce, in *The Collected Dialogues of Plato*, ed. E. Hamilton and H. Cairns, Princeton, NJ: Princeton University Press, 1963, 209d–212a. (The classic account of the ascent of the soul to the vision of absolute beauty.)
* Plotinus (*c*. AD 260) *Enneads*, trans. S. McKenna, ed. J. Dillon, New York: Viking Penguin, 1991. (See Ennead I, 6th tractate, 'Beauty'; and Ennead V, 8th tractate, 'On the Intellectual Beauty'.)
* Shaftesbury, A. (1711) *Characteristics of Men, Manners, Opinions, Times*, ed. J.M. Robertson, Indianapolis, IN: Bobbs-Merrill, 1964. (Shaftesbury's idea of disinterested pleasure is set forth in Treatise IV, Book 2, Part 2, section 1.)
* Sircello, G. (1975) *A New Theory of Beauty*, Princeton, NJ: Princeton University Press. (A mostly non-technical exposition of the theory discussed in §5.)
* —— (1989) *Love and Beauty*, Princeton, NJ: Princeton University Press. (Links the author's theory of beauty to an equally ambitious theory of love.)

JOHN H. BROWN

BEAUVOIR, SIMONE DE (1908–86)

Simone de Beauvoir, a French novelist and philosopher belonging to the existentialist-phenomenological tradition, elaborated an anthropology and ethics inspired by Kierkegaard, Husserl, Heidegger and Sartre in Pyrrhus et Cinéas *(1944) and* Pour une morale de l'ambiguïté *(The Ethics of Ambiguity) (1947). In her comprehensive study of the situation of women,* Le deuxième sexe *(The Second Sex) (1949), this anthropology and ethics was developed and combined with a philosophy of history inspired by Hegel and Marx. The most prominent feature of Beauvoir's philosophy is its ethical orientation, together with an analysis of the subordination of women. Her concept of woman as the Other is central to twentieth-century feminist theory.*

1 Life
2 *The Ethics of Ambiguity*
3 *The Second Sex*

1 Life

Simone de Beauvoir was born on 9 January 1908 in Paris and lived there almost all her life. Her parents belonged to the bourgeoisie and provided her with a traditional Catholic education. After studies at the Sorbonne, Beauvoir took an *agrégation* in philosophy in 1929 (that is, a higher teaching exam) at the prestigious École Normale Supérieure. There she met Jean-Paul SARTRE, with whom she entered a lifelong bond of intellectual companionship. They never married, nor had any children, but stayed together in a free liaison, allowing intimate relations with others.

In the 1930s, they both studied the phenomenology of HUSSERL and HEIDEGGER, and the existential philosophy of KIERKEGAARD. During and after the war, Beauvoir developed an interest in HEGEL and MARX, especially in the philosophy of the young Marx. In 1945 Beauvoir, Sartre and Maurice MERLEAU-PONTY founded *Les Temps Modernes*, a literary, philosophical and political journal. The same year, Sartre and Beauvoir became known as 'existentialists', a label they reluctantly accepted. Both became leading intellectuals of their generation, politically engaged but non-affiliated leftists. Beauvoir, for her part, also inspired and participated in the feminist movement of the 1970s and 1980s.

Generally, Beauvoir is better known as a novelist than as a philosopher. Still, during the 1940s she produced a number of philosophical essays, the most important being *Pyrrhus et Cinéas* (1944) and *Pour une morale de l'ambiguïté* (The Ethics of Ambiguity) (1947). This was followed by *Le deuxième sexe* (The Second Sex) (1949), labelled one of the most influential books of the twentieth century; its underlying philosophical structure reveals her thought in its mature phase. Novels like *L'Invitée* (She Came to Stay) (1943) and *Tous les hommes sont mortels* (All Men are Mortal) (1946), are also organized around philosophical questions.

2 *The Ethics of Ambiguity*

In *Pyrrhus et Cinéas*, Beauvoir, like Kierkegaard and Sartre, defines the human being as an existent that, lacking an inherent essence, has to form its life and give it meaning. This ethos is repeated in *The Ethics of Ambiguity*, where Beauvoir radically transforms Sartre's view of the human being as a 'useless passion'. According to Sartre, the human is characterized by both the lack of being and an unrealizable passion, the 'desire of being' (*désir d'être*), that is, to attain a fixed identity or essence. Beauvoir adds to this the Heideggerian notion of *Erschlossenheit* (disclosure; in French, *dévoilement*), therewith pointing also to the positive side of existence. According to her, the human being not only lacks and desires being, but also wants to 'disclose being'. Or, through the human's vain desire, the world is disclosed, that is, appears and is given meaning.

Affirmation of this positive side of existence is identified with authenticity: to 'deny the lack as lack', to go through a 'conversion', is to set the 'will to be "in parentheses"'; and further, a recognition of both oneself and the other as free – 'to will man free... is to will the disclosure of being in the joy of existence' ([1947] 1948: 135). Beauvoir thus affirms freedom as a fundamental human characteristic. At the same time she is careful to distinguish the freedom of human consiousness – a free spontaneity, a nothingness without given structures – from freedom as a social and political reality. Central to her ethics is the idea that freedom ought to be founded and defended by the individual. On the other hand, society has to facilitate conditions for the positive fulfilment of this freedom. There are thus objective differences between situations, a theme which is further developed in *The Second Sex* by the aid of such Hegelian-Marxist distinctions as that between 'abstract' and 'concrete' freedom and between 'positive' and 'negative' freedom.

Another central theme introduced in *Pyrrhus et Cinéas* and developed in *The Ethics of Ambiguity* concerns the interdependence of humans. In the latter work she states, 'The me–others relationship is as indissoluble as the subject–object relationship' ([1947] 1948: 72). In *The Second Sex* this interdependence is conceptualized in Heideggerian terms as *Mitsein* (Being-with). Human reality is a being-with-others, and the subject 'achieves freedom only through a continual reaching out towards other freedoms' ([1949] 1953: 27), a theme which points to the ethical orientation of her thought. Unlike Sartre in *Being and Nothingness*, Beauvoir does not see conflict as inevitable, nor intersubjectivity as impossible (see EXISTENTIALISM; EXISTENTIALIST ETHICS).

3 *The Second Sex*

If a prominent feature of Simone de Beauvoir's philosophy is its ethical orientation, another is the analysis of oppression. In *The Second Sex*, the existential anthropology and ethics is transformed under the influence of Hegel and Marx, to be combined with a philosophy of history. Consequently, consciousness is conceptualized as historically mediated and human beings as socially situated. Beauvoir declares, with Merleau-Ponty, that 'man... is a historical idea'. Following Hegel and KOJÈVE, she understands the origins of humanity as characterized by a struggle for recognition between men, which led to the genesis of inequalities and oppression. This Hegelian master–slave dialectic is combined with a Marxist insistence on the importance of productive activity, or work, as key to the development of both the human being and society. Since women, owing to their reproductive function and their lesser physical strength, stood outside both the struggle for recognition and productive activity, and therefore outside the basic dialectic, they were defined by the males as the absolute Other (*l'Autre*). They were cast in the role of the object that never became the subject in relation to men, a situation that with the advent of private property and the state became institutionalized into patriarchal society.

The concept of woman as the Other is probably Beauvoir's most important contribution to philosophy and feminist theory. Accepting the existentialist credo 'essence does not precede existence', Beauvoir rejects any idea of an inherent femininity and asserts 'One is not born, but rather becomes, a woman' ([1949] 1953: 273). Gender is therefore conceptualized as simultaneously socially produced and self-created within the confines of the socio-historical situation. Beauvoir emphasizes that because women have historically been the subordinate sex, the Other from the dominant male point of view, they have also been defined as having a determinate nature, be it evil or good. Women have thus not been seen as subjects in their own right, something which Beauvoir criticizes as inauthentic.

The subordination of women is explained in *The Second Sex* not only as a social and historical phenomenon, but also from an existentialist perspective. If the 'desire of being', in Sartrean terms, is equated with an inauthentic flight from freedom and responsibility, it is equally for Beauvoir an explanation of oppression and submission. Man has sought to fulfil his desire by taking possession of a woman; yet the attempt is as ever vain, and ends only in the man's alienation of himself in the woman. Similarly, woman has tried to fulfil her desire by alienating herself in man as if he were an absolute subject and could take responsibility for her life. The existentialist 'desire of being' is combined in *The Second Sex* with a concept of alienation, influenced by that of the young Marx. This implies a distinction between alienation, which is synonymous with a search for being through the other, or through what one has, and authentic self-fulfilment through objectifying oneself in what one does, through conscious, freely chosen, object-creating activity. This authentic self-fulfilment is also related in *The Second Sex* to a 'conversion', which implies a renunciation of the oppressive 'possession' of others and a recognition of the other as a subject.

In *The Second Sex*, Beauvoir sought to combine an ethics with a theory of oppression and an existentialist phenomenology with a philosophy of history, the latter a combination not unusual in Paris in the 1940s, but none the less fraught with problems. The theory of authenticity, which is developed from Sartre's ahistorical, dualistic ontology, tends to collide with the dialectical and historical ontology inspired by Hegel and Marx. Even though Beauvoir is a forerunner for modern feminist theory, her philosophy has been criticized by feminists. The central concept of transcendence, which implies being a free, self-determining subject that can realize itself in self-chosen activities, is problematic since it tends not only to be conflated with authenticity, but also to be equated with men's traditional way of life and activities. For women to leave immanence, the confined animal-like existence that they have been assigned, they have to transcend the traditional female life-world, which is accordingly denigrated in Beauvoir's philosophy. Bearing and rearing children is not defined as transcendence. Simone de Beauvoir does not question the apparent androcentricity in this, but uses the concept to criticize the exclusion of women from the public sphere and from the arts (see

FEMINISM; FEMINIST ETHICS; FEMINIST POLITICAL PHILOSOPHY).

See also: PHENOMENOLOGICAL MOVEMENT §4

List of works

Beauvoir, S. de (1943) *L'invitée*, Paris: Gallimard; trans. Y. Moyse and R. Senhouse, *She Came to Stay*, London: Secker & Warburg, L. Drummond, 1949. (Beauvoir's debut, a novel which is an account of a triangular relationship between one man and two women. Its philosophical theme is the conflictual relation between human beings, considering the fact that one exists for and is judged by the other.)

—— (1944) *Pyrrhus et Cinéas*, Paris: Gallimard. (Beauvoir's first philosophical essay, which analyses the human being as transcendence and human interdependence. It is also her first inquiry into existentialist ethics.)

—— (1946) *Tous les hommes sont mortels*, Paris: Gallimard; trans. L.M. Friedman, *All Men Are Mortal*, Cleveland, OH: World Publishing Company, 1955. (Through the story of an immortal man whose experiences reach over the centuries, Beauvoir investigates in this novel the importance of human mortality for the meaning of human life.)

—— (1947) *Pour une morale de l'ambiguïté*, Paris: Gallimard; trans. B. Frechtman, *The Ethics of Ambiguity*, New York: Philosophical Library, Citadel, 1948. (Simone de Beauvoir's existentialist ethics, centred around the concepts of ambiguity. Authenticity, freedom and the relation between ethics and politics are essential themes.)

—— (1948) *L'existentialisme et la sagesse des nations*, Paris: Nagel. (Contains four essays previously published in *Les temps modernes*, whose themes are the metaphysical novel, ethics and politics, revenge and justice, and whether existentialism is a philosophy of despair.)

—— (1949) *Le deuxième sexe, tome I, Les faits et les mythes, tome II, L'expérience vécue*, Paris: Gallimard; trans. and ed. H.M. Parshley, *The Second Sex*, London: Jonathan Cape, 1953. (A comprehensive study of the situation of women from prehistory to the 1940s, which shows Beauvoir's philosophy in its maturity. Introduces the important notion of woman as the Other. Note that the English translation is neither complete nor wholly correct philosophically.)

—— (1951–2) 'Faut-il brûler Sade', *Les temps modernes*, Dec. 1951, Jan. 1952; also in *Privilèges*, Paris: Gallimard, 1955; trans. A. Michelson, 'Must We Burn de Sade?', in *The Marquis de Sade: An*

Essay by Simone de Beauvoir, with Selections from his Writings, New York: Grove Press, 1953. ('Faut-il brûler Sade', an essay on Marquis de Sade's philosophy, also shows important aspects of Beauvoir's ethics. Republished in the essay collection *Privilèges* along with 'La pensée de droite aujourd'hui', which treats right-wing ideology, and 'Merleau-Ponty et le pseudosartrisme', a defence of Sartre's philosophy against Maurice Merleau-Ponty's critique in *Les aventures de la dialectique*.)

References and further reading

Butler, J. (1986) 'Sex and Gender in Simone de Beauvoir's Second Sex', in *Simone de Beauvoir: Witness to a Century, Yale French Studies* 72: 35–49, ed. H.V. Wenzel. (A critical account of *The Second Sex* from a feminist perspective.)

Heinämaa, S. (1997) 'What is a woman? Butler and Beauvoir on the Foundations of the Sexual Difference', *Hypatia* 12 (1). (Relevant critique of the usual interpretation of Beauvoir's *The Second Sex* as a theory of gender. Maintains instead that her book should be seen as a phenomenological description of the sexual difference.)

Kruks, S. (1990) *Situation and Human Existence: Freedom, Subjectivity and Society*, London: Unwin Hyman. (An important study of Beauvoir's concepts of freedom and situation and the philosophical relationship between Beauvoir, Sartre and Merleau-Ponty.)

Le Dœuff, M. (1989) *L'étude et le rouet: des femmes, de la philosophie, etc.*, Paris: Seuil; trans. T. Selous, *Hipparchias's Choice: An Essay Concerning Women, Philosophy, etc.*, Oxford: Blackwell, 1991. (Discusses the difficulties women face in gaining recognition as philosophers, with Beauvoir as a case study. Analyses the androcentric aspects of Sartre's philosophy and illustrates the differing approaches to existentialism taken by Sartre and Beauvoir.)

Lundgren-Gothlin, E. (1996) *Sex and Existence: Simone de Beauvoir's 'The Second Sex'*, London: Athlone, and New England: Wesleyan University Press. (An analysis of the philosophical foundations and structure of *The Second Sex*. Expansion of the material of §§2–3 of this entry. Originally published in 1991 in Swedish.)

Moi, T. (1994) *Simone de Beauvoir, The Making of an Intellectual Woman*, Oxford: Blackwell. (A comprehensive study of her life and work from a combined socio-historical, psychoanalytic and feminist perspective.)

Seigfried, C.H. (1984) 'Gender-Specific Values', *Philosophical Forum* 15 (4): 425–42. (A feminist critique of Beauvoir's concepts of transcendence and immanence.)

Simons, M.A. (1983) 'The Silencing of Simone de Beauvoir: Guess What's Missing from The Second Sex', *Women's Studies International Forum* 6 (5): 559–64. (Gives an account of the omissions and of the mistranslations of philosophical terms in the English edition of *The Second Sex*. Essential for readers of the English edition.)

—— (1986) 'Beauvoir and Sartre: The Philosophical Relationship', in *Simone de Beauvoir: Witness to a Century, Yale French Studies* 72: 165–79, ed. H.V. Wenzel. (An account of the complex, two-way, philosophical relationship between Beauvoir and Sartre.)

—— (ed.) (1995) *Feminist Interpretations of Simone de Beauvoir*, Pennsylvania, PA: Pennsylvania State University Press. (A collection of essays treating various aspects of Beauvoir's philosophy, her ethics, her views on the body and sexuality, her concept of freedom, and the relationship between her philosophy and Sartre's. For the most part not difficult reading.)

Singer, L. (1985) 'Interpretation and Retrieval: Rereading Beauvoir', *Women's Studies International Forum* 8 (3): 231–8. (An analysis of Beauvoir's concept of freedom and its relation to her ethics.)

Vintges, K. (1996) *Philosophy as Passion: The Thinking of Simone de Beauvoir*, Bloomington and Indianapolis, IN: Indiana University Press. (An easily comprehensible summary of Beauvoir's philosophy and its relation to her life. Argues that Beauvoir's ethics is an 'art of living', which she formulated through her autobiography and fiction.)

EVA LUNDGREN-GOTHLIN

BECK, JACOB SIGISMUND (1761–1840)

Beck played a brief but important role in the development of post-Kantian philosophy. A former student of Kant, he published at his teacher's instigation three volumes of 'Explanatory Abstracts' of Kant's major writings. In the third volume Beck presented what he regarded as the 'Only Possible Standpoint' from which Critical Philosophy had to be judged if misunderstandings of Kant's work were to be avoided. His 'Doctrine of the Standpoint' involved a 'reversal' of the method of the Critique of Pure Reason *and the elimination of the 'thing-in-itself' from Kant's theoretical philosophy.*

Beck was born in West Prussia in 1761. As a young man he went to Königsberg to study philosophy with Kant, and mathematics with C.J. Kraus and J. Schultz. In 1791 he habilitated at the University of Halle with a thesis in mathematics. In the same year, he accepted an offer from KANT to write *Erläuternde Auszüge* (explanatory abstracts) of Kant's major writings. Kant's hope was that Beck would make his philosophy more accessible to the general reader and answer some of the criticisms that had been levelled against it.

Over the next few years, a highly instructive correspondence ensued between them in which Beck elicited often detailed comments from his teacher. For example, in response to an enquiry about the dynamical theory of matter, Kant admitted that the explanation of the difference in density in matter that he had given in his *Metaphysical Foundations of Natural Science* was circular. As a result, Kant later significantly revised his theory of matter in his *Opus postumum*.

In 1793 the first volume of Beck's *Auszug* appeared, explicating Kant's *Critique of Pure Reason* and *Critique of Practical Reason*. The second volume, addressing Kant's *Metaphysical Foundations of Natural Science* and *Critique of Judgment*, came out in the following year. This volume also made available for the first time the original introduction to the *Critique of Judgment*, which Kant had discarded in favour of a slightly shorter one and later entrusted to Beck.

Most important, however, is the third volume of the *Auszug* (1796), which Beck called the 'Only Possible Standpoint from which Critical Philosophy Must Be Judged'. From the start Beck had planned to respond to critics of the Kantian philosophy in a separate volume. As his work progressed, however, he became convinced that the presentation of transcendental philosophy in the first *Critique* leads the reader astray on several accounts. If it is the function of the categories to make originally possible the reference of our representations to an object, he wrote to Kant (letter of 11 November 1791), one cannot define 'intuition' in the manner of the *Critique* as a representation which immediately relates to an object. Nor is it appropriate to define the categories simply as concepts: reference to objects is not the result of, but is presupposed by, the application of concepts. Transcendental philosophy must thus elucidate the fundamental act through which we represent to ourselves an object originally. For in all thought, Beck argued, we first of all fix for ourselves a point of reference to which we then attribute (*beylegen*) determinations. Concepts are the results of this operation, which Beck calls 'original representing'.

Beck's 'Standpoint' consequently 'reverses' the method of the first *Critique*. Whereas Kant had led the reader gradually to the highest point of transcendental philosophy, or the synthetic unity of consciousness, Beck commences with it: with the postulate to represent originally. He then argues that the categories are but different modes of this original activity. Space emerges in original representing; it is the original synthesis of the homogeneous: 'Before this synthesis there is no space; we generate it, rather, in the synthesis'. When the synthesis is fixated in an 'original recognition', there first arises the notion of a determinate figure: 'Together with original recognition, original synthesis generates the objective unity of consciousness... that is, it generates the original concept of an object' (1793–6: 144). Beck thus undermines the sharp distinction, so crucial to Kant's thinking, between intuition and concept, between what is given and what is thought. Since all objective reference is the result of original representing, he regards as meaningless the notion of a 'bond' or connection between representation and object. Indeed, the concept of such a bond, Beck argues, 'is the source of all errors of speculative philosophy'. The concept of a thing-in-itself is an aberration of critical philosophy. As he later wrote to Kant, 'My intention was to bar the concept of the thing-in-itself from theoretical philosophy' (Letter of 20 June 1797).

Beck's 'Standpoint' met with mixed reactions. The orthodox Kantians regarded it as heresy, but others were more positive: J.G. FICHTE, for example, acknowledged its merits in both introductions to his *Science of Knowledge*. Beck himself, however, sought his teacher's approval; when his efforts to convince Kant of the importance of his 'Standpoint' seemed to fail, his disappointment grew proportionally. In 1797 Kant named not Beck but his colleague Johann Schultz when challenged to state publicly who best understood his philosophy ('Declaration against Schlettwein'), and when, two years later, he included Beck in his notorious 'Open Letter on Fichte's *Wissenschaftslehre*', Beck's alienation from his former mentor was complete. However, unbeknown to Beck, Kant's own reflections at the time began to make him more appreciative of some of Beck's ideas. In correspondence with J.H. Tieftrunk, Kant admitted that Beck's method of beginning with the categories was possible, and in the *Opus postumum* he eventually experimented himself with what could be described as a reversal of the method in Beck's sense: 'that we have insight into nothing except what we can make ourselves. First, however, we must make ourselves. Beck's original representing' (1936–8: 114).

In 1799 Beck was appointed to a chair at the university of Rostock, where he soon became rector. Although he published several books over the next few decades, they were of little philosophical consequence. Beck died in Rostock in 1840.

See also: GERMAN IDEALISM

List of works

Beck, J.S. (1793–6) *Erläuternder Auszug aus den critischen Schriften des Herrn Prof. Kant, auf Anrathen desselben* (Explanatory Abstracts of Prof. Kant's Critical Writings, at the Latter's Instigation), Riga: Hartknoch, 3 vols; vol. 3 is subtitled *Einzigmöglicher Standpunct, aus welchem die critische Philosophie beurtheilt werden muß* (Only Possible Standpoint from which Critical Philosophy Must Be Judged); partly trans. in *Between Kant and Hegel*, ed. G. di Giovanni and H.S. Harris, Albany, NY: State University of New York Press, 1985. (This is Beck's principal text.)

—— (1796) *Grundriß der critischen Philosophie*, Halle: Renger, trans. J. Richardson, *The Principles of Critical Philosophy*, London, 1797 (Another exposition of Kant's philosophy from Beck's standpoint.)

—— (1798) *Commentar über Kants Metaphysik der Sitten* (Commentary on Kant's *Metaphysics of Morals*), Halle: Renger. (Beck's moral philosophy.)

References and further reading

* Fichte, J.G. (1797) 'Erste und zweite Einleitung in die *Wissenschaftslehre*' (First and Second Introductions to the *Science of Knowledge*), trans. and ed. P. Heath and J. Lachs, in *Science of Knowledge*, Cambridge: Cambridge University Press, 1982. (Fichte's subsequent 'introductions' to his main work.)
* Kant, I. (1781) *Kritik der reinen Vernunft*, trans. N. Kemp Smith, *Critique of Pure Reason*, London: Macmillan, 1929. (Kant's principal work.)
* —— (1936–8) *Opus postumum*, partly trans. E. Förster and M. Rosen in *Kant's Opus postumum*, ed. E. Förster, Cambridge and New York: Cambridge University Press, 1993. (Kant's last, unfinished *magnum opus*.)
* —— (1900–2) *Kant's Briefwechsel*, partly trans. A. Zweig in *Kant: Philosophical Correspondence 1759–99*, Chicago, IL: Chicago University Press, 1967. (A selection of letters to and from Kant.)

Meyer, T.L. (1991) *Das Problem des höchsten Grundsatzes der Philosophie bei Jacob Sigismund Beck* (The Problem of a Highest Principle of Philosophy in Jacob Sigismund Beck), Amsterdam: Rudolphi. (A useful introduction with an extended bibliography.)

Schmucker-Hartmann, J. (1976) *Der Widerspruch von Vorstellung und Gegenstand. Zum Kantverständnis von Jakob Sigismund Beck* (The Opposition of Representation and Object. On Jacob Sigismund Beck's Interpretation of Kant), Meisenheim am Glan: Anton Hain. (Thorough but more difficult.)

Wallner, I.M. (1984) 'A New Look at J.S. Beck's "Doctrine of the Standpoint"', *Kant-Studien* 75: 294–316. (A phenomenological interpretation of Beck's main text.)

ECKART FÖRSTER

BEHAVIOURISM, ANALYTIC

Analytical behaviourism is the doctrine that talk about mental phenomena is really talk about behaviour, or tendencies to behave. For an analytical behaviourist, to say that Janet desires ice cream is to say that, all things being equal, she tends to seek it out. To say that Brad is now feeling jealous is to say no more than that he is now behaving in a way characteristic of jealousy, or perhaps that he would do so under appropriate provocation. Analytical behaviourism differs from methodological behaviourism in insisting that our ordinary use of mental language really is, in some sense, already about behaviour. The methodological version claims either that in doing psychology we should restrict ourselves to notions which can be defined behaviourally, or, sometimes, that our general psychological language, even if not already definable in this way, should be reformed in this general direction.

The most telling objection to this account of the mind is that it is inconsistent with the requirement that mental states are causes of behaviour. Ordinarily we might note that Brad has a tendency to display jealous behaviour with little provocation, and conjecture that this is caused by his feeling jealous (rather than, say, practising for his forthcoming part in a Jacobean tragedy). But according to analytical behaviourism his feeling jealous just is his tendency to the behaviour, and since nothing causes itself, his jealousy cannot be the cause of the pattern of behaviour.

1 Introduction
2 Influences and arguments
3 Objections
4 The legacy of behaviourism

1 Introduction

Analytical behaviourists hold that there is a conceptual connection between behaviour and mental states. Talk about mental states just is talk about behaviour and dispositions to behaviour. This can be discovered, the doctrine insists, by proper conceptual analysis of the mental language we use. In its strongest versions the idea is that there can be translations between mental language and behavioural language; for example they might have held that 'Janet desires ice cream' – apparently postulating something about her internal states – can be translated without loss of meaning as 'Janet is likely to eat ice cream'. Sometimes analytical behaviourists admitted that the translations might be difficult or impossible to provide, but contended that there was, nevertheless, some unspecified sort of analytical entailment between mental talk and behavioural talk. Another issue, essentially terminological, is whether the analytical behaviourist claims to eliminate mental states. On one way of saying it, the behaviourist discovers that there are no mental states as such – but mental language is perfectly fine because it is about behaviour. The other way has it that mental states exist but are not internal, occult entities; rather they are to be identified with behaviour or behavioural dispositions. I will use the latter way throughout.

I will start with a few words about the doctrine's roots, and why it seemed so appealing, and in addition explain the usual arguments for it. Then I will discuss the standard objections and assess the important contribution that the doctrine has made to the philosophical treatment of the mind.

2 Influences and arguments

A first, important influence on analytical behaviourism was the doctrine of verificationism (see MEANING AND VERIFICATION; OPERATIONALISM). According to one version of this view, the meanings of statements are given by the procedures used to find out if they are true. This was supposed to eliminate meanings as occult entities, and put the subject on a scientific footing. Anyone attracted by that view would have seen considerable merit in behaviourism. For we typically verify statements about other people's mental states by looking at their current behaviour (including verbal behaviour), or their behaviour over time, drawing conclusions about the dispositional patterns that emerge.

A related influence was that of the success of methodological behaviourism (sometimes known as scientific behaviourism). This somewhat weaker doctrine stipulates that for the purposes of psychology we use terms for mental states which are defined in terms of behaviour (see BEHAVIOURISM, METHODOLOGICAL AND SCIENTIFIC). This was perhaps good advice in the early part of the century; in any case behavioural evidence was the only access then available to psychological information, and the advice yielded reasonable results. The dominance of this idea left philosophers in a difficult position. What scientific psychology talked about was defined in terms of behaviour. The denial of analytical behaviourism would therefore entail that ordinary discourse about the mind is simply not about the same things as scientific discourse – bad news, indeed, for scientifically-minded philosophers. Rather than risk accepting that consequence, it seemed better to insist that everyone really was talking about the same thing, and thus that analytical behaviourism was true.

Another approach to this problem can be found among the methodological behaviourists. We might call it revisionary behaviourism – the view that, to the extent that ordinary talk is not about behaviour, it is defective and should be revised in line with scientific talk. This was never popular amongst philosophers, perhaps because of its consequence that all ordinary talk about psychology before behaviourism was seen as deeply defective. It is hard to believe that Aristotle was not saying something true when he attributed beliefs to Plato.

A crucial influence, especially in the British tradition, was Wittgenstein's scepticism about the possibility of private states contributing to the meaning of expressions in public language (see PRIVATE STATES AND LANGUAGE). If you think that private states can have no role in fixing meaning, then behaviour is the only game in town.

The most attractive thing about analytical behaviourism is that it undoubtedly got some things right. While it might be strange to think that the meaning of mental language is exhausted by talk of behaviour, there surely is some kind of analytic link between behaviour and mental states. If you don't know that someone who desires something will, other things being equal, behave so as to seek it out, then something is wrong with your concept of a desire. If I believe that Janet truly does desire ice cream, and that her desire isn't overruled by another, then there is something deficient in my concept of desire if I am not remotely puzzled when she blithely ignores a convenient ice cream stall.

Behaviour can trump introspective evidence; we are familiar with people who sincerely claim to have desires which they make no attempt to fulfil, even when they claim to have no countervailing desires and believe that the means to their fulfilment are available to them. In such cases you might say that the person doesn't *really* have the desires they say they have, whatever they believe about their desires. If we are tempted by that idea, it might be because it follows from what we mean by desire: that someone who truly desires something behaves so as to fulfil that desire.

3 Objections

There are very few analytical behaviourists left. A range of objections has culled their number over the years, and has led to newer views in the philosophy of mind. I will discuss objections – again not entirely independent ones – in order of increasing severity.

A first objection is that some mental states could have no behavioural consequences. Simple examples of this may merely show that sometimes one mental state outranks another. Suppose that I love ice cream, but am so embarrassed by this that I resolve never to touch it, and succeed in never manifesting in any way whatsoever the difficulty this causes me. Have we not a counterexample to behaviourism?

The behaviourist has two options. One is to say that if this alleged desire has no impact at all – say in exciting my salivary glands when I see photographs of cool, creamy ice cream, and so on – then I indeed do not have any such desire. Another is to point out that there is a case of a resolved conflict of desires here: what I desire over all – to avoid embarrassment – is manifested in behaviour; and the analytic connection between all-things-considered desires and behaviour is maintained.

A stronger version of this objection involves mental states the expression of which is somehow blocked. Perhaps someone could be in pain but, because they are controlled in various ways, cannot express it. A disembodied brain might be an extreme case. Here the analytical behaviourist must resort to the disposition's being there, but being blocked. The dispositions are dispositions to behave in normal circumstances. Although one might worry about how to specify these normal circumstances, these sorts of objections do not seem too troubling.

Behaviourists have more trouble than most in accounting for consciousness. Whilst they can without conceptual difficulty accept that individuals know more about their own mental states than those of others – analysed as having behavioural dispositions which are themselves foreknowledge of their future behaviour – they are hard pressed to explain why this should be so, since the usual behavioural evidence is not available to them.

There is, moreover, no real account of the *nature* of consciousness. Perhaps no one has a satisfactory account, but behaviourists are by their very own doctrine committed to refusing to countenance internal mental states. This leaves them with three options. They can accept conscious states but say they are not mental – but this is a terminological trick that leaves them with an ontology far from the spirit of behaviourism. They can deny that consciousness exists at all – which might be philosophically comforting for some but rather hard to do while keeping a straight face. Finally they can identify consciousness with behaviour or behavioural dispositions. The second, po-faced, option seems to have been most common; none is without difficulty.

The promise of behaviourism was that it would provide an analysis of the meaning of mental language in terms of behaviour. It rapidly became obvious that actually providing such an analysis was not easy: even a flawed one, and even for the simplest cases. The formulation that became popular was that mental states pick out a vague class of behaviour, and this is why the analysis cannot be done in practice. So mental language cannot be dispensed with, since the vagueness is useful to us in tying together the groups of behaviour-patterns, and is ineliminable. This mental language, nevertheless, has nothing but behaviour and behavioural dispositions to be about.

There was, however, a deeper reason for the difficulty than just vagueness. The problem is that there simply is no class of behaviour-patterns associated with individual mental states. Suppose I believe there is a dagger before me. Do I act as if nothing is there, thinking weapons in very poor taste and best ignored? Do I grab it, believing that the gods have put it there to assist in fulfilling my desire to take revenge on my enemies? Do I book in for analysis, thinking this is a hallucination brought on by feelings of remorse and guilt for what happened at a recent departmental committee meeting? Clearly it depends on my other beliefs and desires. This is very different from the sorts of worries mentioned above when we were considering ways in which the normal responses allegedly associated with mental states might be blocked. Here we see that there are, in fact, no normal responses associated with individual mental states.

So talk of 'vague' connections between individual mental states and behaviours misses the point. The point is that, to the extent that there are analytic connections, they are between complexes of mental states and complexes of behaviour.

The final objection, and perhaps the most telling, is that analytical behaviourists must deny that mental states ever cause behaviour. It is central to the idea of a mental state that they sometimes are the cause of our actions. Janet's desire for ice cream actually causes Janet's arm to go up and her legs to move her body towards the ice cream van. For the analytical behaviourist, however, desire for ice cream never *causes* ice cream-seeking behaviour, even when all the attendant beliefs and desires are in place. Since analytical behaviourists are typically physicalists, they admit that there are internal causes of behaviour, but say that these are not mental states. The mental states are the very behaviour caused by the internal states. Further, the behaviour cannot cause itself. The case of dispositions is even harder. The analytical behaviourist has to come up with something to say about the relationship between internal states and the behavioural dispositions. But the causes of the dispositions cannot be the dispositions themselves. So, to the extent that we think that behavioural tendencies like Brad's tendency to jealous behaviour are caused by some mental state rather than another, we cannot accept analytical behaviourism.

While analytical behaviourists were on to something in seeing that there were analytic connections between behaviour and the mental, they drew too strong a connection. What is analytic, they thought, cannot be contingent. But whatever causes Janet's legs to move is some physical system of neurones, nerves and muscles. And it is contingent that that system of neurones, nerves and muscles does the work. She could have had different neurones, used different muscles, or perhaps even had a prosthetic brain. The connection between the behaviour and the mental language, however, is necessary; it is impossible that she, Janet, could desire ice cream without having the appropriate dispositions. The connection is also graspable, in some sense, just through understanding the meaning of the mentalistic language involved.

What has gone wrong here is that the kind of analytic connection they are looking for was too direct. We are now more familiar with analysis proceeding indirectly via how some contingent matter actually is. Imagine a town that has had its water poisoned. The townsfolk coin the phrase 'death potion' to name whatever it is that is actually doing the killing. 'Death potion' is whatever is actually having a certain causal influence on the townsfolk; killing them, in this instance. As it happens, the poison is cyanide. Eventually the townsfolk find this out. They find out that 'death potion' is cyanide; and analysis played a key role in this, via the meaning of 'death potion'. Nevertheless it is quite contingent that the poisoners used cyanide – they could easily have chosen something else.

4 The legacy of behaviourism

The last objection to analytical behaviourism is the starting point for the families of views that have come to replace it. Once we see that analysis gives us indirect linguistic access to unknown internal things – such as whatever it is inside people's bodies that is killing them off – we can accept what is right about analytical behaviourism and yet embrace internal states.

In the example above, the analytic connection was between 'death potion' and whatever it was that (typically) played a certain causal role (the role of causing the sudden spate of deaths). So we sometimes use causal properties to identify states inside systems we do not know much about. It is a move like this that can meet the requirement that mental states cause behaviour while respecting the analytic insight. Janet's desire for ice-cream might be understood not as the ice cream seeking behaviour, but as whatever causes the behaviour. Instead of mental states being behaviour or clusters of behaviour, they might be analysed as states which are typically caused in various ways, and which typically cause the clusters of behaviour. Views of this kind are called functionalism (see FUNCTIONALISM).

See also: RYLE, G.

References and further reading

Armstrong, D.M. (1968) *A Materialist Theory of the Mind*, London: Routledge & Kegan Paul. (First book-length treatment which combines the grains of truth in the behaviourist analysis with an analysis of mental states in causal terms.)

Block, N. (1981) 'Psychologism and Behaviourism', *The Philosophical Review* 90: 5–43. (Advances a range of objections to tying mental states too closely to behaviour.)

Campbell, K. (1984) *Body and Mind*, Notre Dame, IN: University of Notre Dame Press: 2nd edn. (Chapter 4 of this book contains a very accessible discussion of behaviourism.)

Geach, P. (1957) *Mental Acts*, London: Routledge & Kegan Paul. (Contains an early articulation of something like the concerns expressed in §3 about the difficulties of analysing mental discourse in terms of behaviour.)

Putnam, H. (1963) 'Brains and Behaviour', in *Mind, Language and Reality: Philosophical Papers Volume 2*, Cambridge: Cambridge University Press. (An important paper, which advances arguments of the type discussed in §3, to the effect that some mental states have no behavioural consequences, and presaged the development of views of the type discussed in §4.)

Ryle, G. (1949) *The Concept of Mind*, London: Hutchinson. (The central exposition of analytical behaviourism.)

Strawson, P.F. (1959) *Individuals*, London: Methuen. (An influential piece of analytical philosophy in the era of behaviourism. It includes attempts to make sense of the unsatisfactory 'vagueness' account of the difficulty of providing analyses of mental discourse in terms of behaviour.)

Skinner, B.F. (1974) *About Behaviourism*, London: Jonathan Cape. (A full-scale defence of behaviourism. Although he defends methodological behaviourism, it is clear that his view was of the reforming variety: to the extent to which analytic behaviourism is not true of ordinary discourse, ordinary discourse is deficient and should be revised.)

Watson, J.B. (1925) *Behaviourism*, London: Kegan Paul. (The *locus classicus* of a behaviourism of a methodological kind; but like Skinner after him, he believed that if ordinary talk was not about behaviour, it should be revised in line with scentific talk.)

Wittgenstein, L. (1953) *Philosophical Investigations*, trans. G.E.M. Anscombe, Oxford: Blackwell. (The source of Wittgenstein's influence on behaviourists.)

DAVID BRADDON-MITCHELL

BEHAVIOURISM IN THE SOCIAL SCIENCES

Classical behaviourism has had almost no direct reflection in the social sciences, in that there has never been a behaviourist social psychology or sociology. However, various features of the cluster of behaviourist doctrines have been widespread in the human sciences. Behaviourism as it developed from its roots in the proposals of Watson, and in its transformation by Skinner, had two influential aspects, one metaphysical and the other methodological. The metaphysics of behaviourism was positivistic. It was hostile to theory, favouring a psychology the subject matter of which was limited to stimuli and responses. It was hospitable to the conception of causation as regular concomitance of events, rejecting any generative or agent causal concepts. The methodology of behaviourism was hospitable to simple experimental techniques of inquiry, seeking statistical relations between independent and dependent variables. It was hostile to descriptions of human action that incorporated the intentions of the actor, favouring a laconic vocabulary of neologisms. Metaphysically and methodologically behaviourism favoured the individual as the locus of psychological phenomena. But, in practice, the use of statistical analyses of data abstracted psychological processes from real human beings leaving only simplified automata in their place.

1 The behaviourist legacy in social psychology
2 The critique of behaviourism
3 The behaviourist legacy in sociology
4 Summary

1 The behaviourist legacy in social psychology

Despite the influence of aspects of behaviourism on mainstream psychology, in one important respect experimental (or 'old paradigm') social psychology was anti-behaviourist, in that it was in some ways anti-positivist. For example Tajfel's (1982) theory of intergroup relations proposed a cognitive mechanism of social comparison to explain observed correlations. Festinger's (1957) cognitive dissonance theory was based upon the alleged existence of cognitive discomfort in the presence of contradiction between expressed beliefs and actions. Yet the methodological influence of behaviourism is very clear in that both Tajfel and Festinger, and indeed many social psychologists of the post-war generation employed an experimental methodology that was a direct descendent of the methods of inquiry of behaviourism. Only the statistical trends which could be discerned in objectively described experimental manipulations of independent variables were to be admitted into an alleged 'truly' scientific social psychology as data. In this respect 'new paradigm' social psychology, particularly the role-rule model of Harré and Secord (1972), differed considerably in that a methodology of account analysis was recommended instead of simple experimentation. The history of social psychology can be seen in two stages: first the rejection of the metaphysics of behaviourism and only much later the abandonment of its methodology.

Behaviourism was both a learning theory according to which all human behaviour consisted in conditioned responses to types of environmental contingencies and a method of investigation in which the study of mature organisms simply consisted in the attempt to manipulate stimuli so as to discover which responses had indeed been installed in them. Even after the abandonment of behaviourism as general theory of human conduct (Danziger 1990) the use of the 'experimental' method persisted in social psychology. It was assumed that the complex situations in which human beings found themselves could be split up into simple states of the environment which could be treated as values of variables. Responses too were partitioned in a similar manner. Neither the role of the actor's interpretation of the stimulus conditions nor the actor's intention in responding were admitted as relevant, or as competing with the interpretations imposed by experiments (Milgram 1974). By an elementary application of Mill's Canons of Induction, that an effect which was always found to follow a certain phenomenon and which, in the absence of the phenomenon, did not appear, statistical trends in the relationship between stimuli and responses were offered as psychological laws. From the point of view

693

of the social sciences the most important and most paradoxical applications of the experimental method were in social psychology.

The application of the methodological part of the behaviourist paradigm in social psychology led to the setting up of a number of experimental programmes centred around a variety of human social phenomena (Lindzey and Aronson 1968). For example the investigation of interpersonal liking (Zajonc 1968); of the fact that when they were with groups people tended to follow majority opinion (Asch 1956); of the conditions under which people behaved aggressively (Berkowitz 1962), all used the 'experimental' method. Paradoxically this approach to social behaviour in which the role of the individual human actor as agent undertaking various projects, alone or with others, was swept away and replaced by the idea of an automaton reacting with exactly those responses to which it had been conditioned, was dominant in that home of the ethos of the individual, the USA. This poses a fascinating problem for the sociology of science.

2 The critique of behaviourism

It was the acceptance of a Cartesian metaphysics of mind that had led to scepticism about the possibility of public knowledge of mental states and processes from which the original impetus to a behaviourist treatment of problems in the human sciences had come. The most influential criticism of behaviourism was directed not at its Cartesian metaphysics, but at the limitations that it imposed on the possibility of obtaining scientific knowledge of other minds. This line of criticism developed into the 'first cognitive revolution' initiated by J.S. Bruner (1973) and G.A. Miller (Miller and Johnson-Laird 1976). Adopting the hypothetico-deductive conception of scientific method the new cognitivists saw the experiment as playing the role of a test for a hypothesis about publicly unobservable mental processes, rather than as a datum to be used in an induction to a correlative law of stimulus and response. The 'cognitive science' movement developed out of the insights of Bruner and Miller by the adoption of the computer analogy, as a way of systematically formulating hypotheses about mental processes. The computer is to the brain as the running of a programme is to the mental activity of that brain.

A more realistic approach to the study of social psychology, that developed in the 1970s, led to a growing emphasis on language as the main medium of human interaction (Harré 1977). In the behaviourist and immediately post-behaviourist eras, language appeared only in various so-called 'instruments', such as questionnaires, rating scales and so on. Many 'experiments' consisted in asking people to read stories and then to answer questions about their opinions of these stories. Why not, it was asked (for example by Shotter 1993), just abandon misleading talk of experiments, and turn to an analytical study of the many forms of human communication?

3 The behaviourist legacy in sociology

In sociology something akin to behaviourism developed under the influence of the three key factors identified above in the origins of behaviourism in psychology – a positivist philosophy of science, a search for statistical correlations between publicly observable phenomena and a 'regularity' conception of causality. The most influential proponent of positivistic sociology was Émile DURKHEIM. In his famous work on suicide (1908) he correlated local suicide rates with the values of broad social variables. Durkheim also offered to posterity another, non-statistical sociological method, in which publicly observable social phenomena, such as religious ceremonies, were subject to hermeneutical reinterpretation as covert symbolizations of social structure. The history of the debates over sociological method could be presented as a dispute between Durkheim and his *alter ego*.

Ethnomethodology was developed by Harold Garfinkel and his co-workers explicitly in opposition to Durkheimian social fact methodology. Garfinkel (1967) looked at the way social facts, such as suicide statistics, were produced. He found that they were the product of very complex conversational interactions, in the course of which people with various rights and standings took part in a complex and often quite long-running negotiation. This led Garfinkel to a very close analysis of the (conversational) procedures by which everyday reality was constituted as something normal and unattended. At this point we are a long way from positivism. However by a strange shift in focus the very method by which Garfinkel proposed to unveil the methods by which ordinary folk created their worlds turned into a kind of positivistic empiricism. In CA ('conversation analysis'), elementary conversational acts (as identified by the analyst) are sorted into statistical patterns, independent of all contextual features whatever. This development has been subjected to much the same kind of criticism as was classical behaviourism, namely that as a positivistic reduction of the phenomena that define a field of interest of a science it eliminates the thing that it should be attempting to discover by means of a context sensitive methodology, namely the cultural conventions by reference to which the micro-orderliness of social life is maintained.

4 Summary

The behaviourist paradigm has left its traces everywhere in the human sciences and particularly in social psychology. Despite paying lip-service to the idea that human beings in social interaction are active agents engaged in jointly realizing certain projects, plans and intentions and sometimes antagonistically attempting to force their projects on others, we have a view of human social actors as mindless automatons, mere spectators of processes over which they, as individuals, could have no control. This metaphysical position is still implicit in much of the work of US social psychologists (Wrightsman and Dew 1980) and to a much lesser extent in Europe (Farr and Moscovici 1987). The metaphysical foundations of microsociology and social psychology have been strongly criticized. But to treat formalized discussions between psychologists and their subjects as experiments is, according to the critics, to do little more than offer a rhetorical re-description of something which is utterly unlike an experiment in the natural sciences. Instead it is argued that an acknowledgement of the fact that what are treated as experiments are really conversational interactions and should be analysed as such, is the way forward (Potter and Wetherell 1987). All that a psychological experiment can do, if seen in its true light as a kind of conversation, is to enable us to discover the local conventions of social discourse. Once this is achieved we can ask whether some such conventions can be identified in all human communities of which we have any knowledge.

See also: BEHAVIOURISM, ANALYTIC; BEHAVIOURISM, METHODOLOGICAL AND SCIENTIFIC; POSITIVISM IN THE SOCIAL SCIENCES; SKINNER, B.F.

References and further reading

* Asch, S. (1956) 'Studies of Independence and Conformity', *Psychological monographs* 70: 416. (Study of the fact that when in groups people tend to follow the majority opinion.)
* Berkowitz, L. (1962) *Aggression: A Social Psychological Analysis*, New York: McGraw-Hill. (Study of the conditions under which people behave aggressively.)
* Bruner, J.S. (1973) *Beyond the Information Given: Studies in the Psychology of Knowing*, New York: W.W. Norton. (Initiated, with G.A. Miller, the 'first cognitive revolution'.)
* Danziger, K. (1990) *Constructing the Subject*, Cambridge: Cambridge University Press. (Selective history of modern psychology that sees psychology, not so much as a body of facts or theories, but as a special set of social activities intended to produce something that counts as psychological knowledge under certain historical conditions.)
* Durkheim, É. (1908) *Suicide: A Study in Sociology*, trans. J.A. Spaulding and G. Simpson, London: Routledge & Kegan Paul. (Durkheim's famous work in which he correlated local suicide rates with the values of broad social variables.)
* Farr, R. and Moscovici, S. (1987) *Social Representations*, Cambridge: Cambridge University Press. (European work on the metaphysical foundations of social psychology.)
* Festinger, L. (1957) *A Theory of Cognitive Dissonance*, Stanford, CA: Stanford University Press. (Cognitive dissonance theory based upon the alleged existence of cognitive discomfort in the presence of contradiction between expressed beliefs and actions.)
* Garfinkel, H. (1967) *Studies in Ethnometholodogy*, Englewood Cliffs, NJ: Prentice Hall. (Develops ethnomethodology in opposition to Durkheimian social fact methodology.)
* Harré, R. (1977) *Social Being*, Oxford: Blackwell, 2nd edn, 1993. (Emphasizes language as the main medium of human interaction.)
* Harré, R. and Secord, P.F. (1972) *The Explanation of Social Behaviour*, Oxford: Blackwell. (Develops the 'role-rule' model which recommends a methodology of account analysis instead of simple experimentation.)
* Lindzey, G. and Aronson, E. (1968) *Handbook of Social Psychology*, Reading, MA: Addison-Wesley. (Looks at the setting up of a number of experimental programmes centred around a variety of human social phenomena.)
* Milgram, S. (1974) *Obedience to Authority*, New York: Harper & Row. (Study of experiments in social psychology and their interpretations.)
* Miller, G.A. and Johnson-Laird, P.N. (1976) *Language and Perception*, Cambridge: Cambridge University Press. (Initiated, with J.S. Bruner, the 'first cognitive revolution'.)
* Potter, J. and Wetherell, M. (1987) *Discourse and Social Psychology*, London: Sage. (Argues that what are treated as experiments in social psychology are really conversational interactions and should be analysed as such.)
* Shotter, J. (1993) *Conversational Realities: Constructing Life Through Language*, London: Sage. (Claims that naturally occurring psychological and sociological 'realities' are both socially constructed and sustained within everyday conversation.)
* Tajfel, H. (1982) *Social Identity and Intergroup Relativism*, Cambridge: Cambridge University

Press. (Theory of intergroup relations that proposes a cognitive mechanism of social comparison to explain observed correlations.)
* Wrightsman, L.S. and Dew, K. (1980) *Social Psychology in the Eighties*, Monterey, CA: Brooks Cole. (Integrated introduction to social psychology.)
* Zajonc, R.B. (1968) 'Attitudinal Effects of Mere Exposure', *Journal of Personality and Social Psychology*, monograph supplement, 9 (2): 1–27. (Investigation of interpersonal liking.)

ROM HARRÉ

BEHAVIOURISM, METHODOLOGICAL AND SCIENTIFIC

Methodological *behaviourism is the doctrine that the data on which a psychological science must rest are behavioural data – or, at the very least, publicly observable data – not the private data provided to introspection by the contents of an observer's consciousness.* Scientific*, or, as it was sometimes called, 'radical', behaviourism contends that scientific psychology ought to be concerned only with the formulation of laws relating observables such as stimuli and responses; not with unobservable mental processes and mechanisms such as attention, intention, memory and motivation. Methodological behaviourism is all but universally embraced by contemporary experimental psychologists, whereas scientific behaviourism is widely viewed as a doctrine in decline. Both forms of behaviourism were articulated by J.B. Watson in 1913. B.F. Skinner was the most prominent radical behaviourist.*

In addition to its empiricist strictures against inferred mental mechanisms, radical behaviourism was also empiricist in its assumptions about learning, assuming that: (1) organisms have no innate principles that guide their learning; (2) learning is the result of a general-purpose process, not of a collection of mechanisms tailored to the demands of different kinds of problems; and (3) learning is a change in the relation between responses and the stimuli that control or elicit them. Many of these ideas continue to be influential, for example, in connectionism.

1 Methodological behaviourism and scientific behaviourism
2 The two schools of scientific behaviourism
3 Critique of scientific behaviourism

1 Methodological behaviourism and scientific behaviourism

Methodological behaviourism emerged as a reaction to introspectionism, which was the doctrine that psychology was the science of conscious states (see INTROSPECTION, PSYCHOLOGY OF §4). This latter doctrine placed the psychological scientist in a uniquely favourable epistemological position, because knowledge of the contents of consciousness seems direct, unmediated by sensory systems of questionable trustworthiness. However, it had two fatal weaknesses. (1) Because the data (the contents of consciousness) were not publicly observable, there was no way of settling disputes about whether the observer was reporting them accurately. (2) Because there was no way of securing reports from animals, psychology was confined to the study of human consciousness, a profoundly abiological state of affairs. These difficulties were obviated by the emergence of the doctrine that the data of psychology were behavioural. If you doubted the accuracy of someone's report about how their subjects behaved, you could come to their laboratory and see for yourself. And the behaviour of many nonhuman animals was as observable as human behaviour, so it was possible to approach psychology from an evolutionary perspective, dispensing with the pre-Darwinian notion that man was uniquely different from a scientific standpoint.

The doctrine that psychological theory must rest on behavioural (or, in any event, publicly observable) data in no way implies that psychological theory should eschew discussion of inferred mental processes and mechanisms, which was the essence of *scientific* behaviourism. If there were any such implication, then physics could not concern itself with such inferred entities as quarks; nor could classical genetics concern itself with genes, and so on. Cognitive psychology is thoroughly behaviourist in its methodology, but it is anti-behaviourist in its theorizing, which focuses on attention, perception and memory. Scientific or (as it was often called) 'radical' behaviourism is an eliminativist doctrine; it claims that traditional mental phenomena such as these have no place in a scientific psychology (see ELIMINATIVISM).

B.F. SKINNER, the best-known radical behaviourist, argued that concepts such as memory, motivation, emotion, attention, intention and perception should not be part of scientific psychology. He argued that a scientific psychology should be concerned only with physical observables. This was the general position of logical positivism, which flourished for the first half of the twentieth century (see LOGICAL POSITIVISM), but has vanished from contemporary physics, which routinely discusses unobservable entities such as quarks. Similarly, radical scientific behaviourism, which enjoyed a considerable vogue for several decades near the middle of the twentieth century, has diminished in significance with the rise of cognitive psychology.

2 The two schools of scientific behaviourism

At the peak of its popularity in the middle of the twentieth century, there were two principal schools of scientific behaviourism, one identified with J.B. Watson and B.F. Skinner, the other with Ivan Pavlov and Clark Hull. (The latter are sometimes called neo-behaviourists.) Both schools were principally concerned with learning. Both took for granted the traditional empiricist assumption that the organism was initially a blank slate. That is, they assumed that learning was not constrained and directed by innate problem-specific information-acquisition mechanisms whose problem-specific structure made implicit a priori commitments to the structure of the information to be acquired. Such commitments, popular among Rationalists such as Descartes and Leibniz, involve innate principles of the mind (see NATIVISM), and behaviourists rejected the idea that innate principles guided learning. On the contrary, the learning process was thought to be a general-purpose process, applicable regardless of the substance of what was learned. The essence of the process was thought to be the bringing of a response the animal made in the presence of a stimulus under the control of that stimulus. This last assumption gave rise to the term 'stimulus–response' (or 'S–R') psychology.

The two schools had contrasting views on whether any kind of 'theoretical construct' was admissible. A theoretical construct was an entity (for example, a memory or an associative bond) or process (for example, attention) or state (for example, a motivational state) that played a role in explaining observed behaviour but was not directly observed (see OBSERVATION). The Skinnerian school thought that all such constructs should be rejected; even such traditional constructs as the associative bond. The Hull–Pavlov school, on the other hand, thought that a modest number of constructs were essential, but should be closely based on behavioural observation and should have plausible physiological embodiments. When a rat learned to press a lever to obtain food, Skinnerians explained this simply by an appeal to the 'law of effect', which says that when a response is emitted in the presence of a stimulus and followed by a reinforcer, the probability of that response in the presence of that stimulus increases. They thought this kind of Baconian explanation – subsuming observations under generalizations about lawful regularities – was all that psychology should aim for (see BACON, F.). The Hullians, by contrast, aimed for a physiologically plausible conception of the unobserved mechanisms. They imagined that the food reduced a drive (defined as a state of high nervous arousal), which strengthened synaptic connections between sensory and motor neurons – the sensory neurons sensitive to the stimulus and the motor neurons that controlled the response in question. The drive and the change in synaptic connectivity (or associative strength) were the kinds of physiologically plausible theoretical constructs that Hullians thought should play a central role in psychological explanation. The proffered physiological interpretation of these constructs made it reasonable to suppose that one might someday actually observe them.

In short, the Skinnerians were opposed to inferred entities of any kind in psychological explanation, while Hullians wanted to restrict the inferred entities to those with a ready physiological interpretation. Both schools were sceptical of the explanatory value of the mental concepts and mechanisms that have traditionally played a central role in more cognitively oriented psychological theories – attention, perception, intention, memory, motivation (see EXPLANATION).

Behaviourist ideas continue to be influential in contemporary psychology. The assumption of a general-purpose learning process, the assumption that the building blocks of psychological theories should be neurobiologically plausible, and the assumption that learning is fundamentally about changes in synaptic connectivity (associative strengths) are still points of departure for much contemporary work in psychology – both work on animal learning and work on human learning and perception done under the heading of connectionist or neural-net modelling (see CONNECTIONISM; LEARNING §1).

3 Critique of scientific behaviourism

The assumptions of scientific behaviourism may be challenged on a number of fronts. As a perfectly general proposition, the blank-slate assumption is demonstrably false. Fledglings of some species of song bird (for example, white-crowned sparrows) must hear an adult male song of their own species during a critical period if they are to develop normal song. It does not matter what other songs they hear. Even when those other songs are more numerous than that of their own species, the song-learning mechanism picks out the correct song, implying that it is innately tuned to aspects of the song to be learned that distinguish that song from those of other species. The mechanism that mediates song learning has been termed an instinct to learn. Like all instincts, it is a solution to one particular problem, obviously unsuited to many other learning problems. Some contemporary learning theorists argue that the problem-specific structure seen in this and many other examples from the zoological literature is characteristic of all learning mechanisms. Thus, it is open to question whether there is such a thing as a general-purpose learning process (see INNATE KNOWLEDGE; LANGUAGE, INNATENESS OF).

Also demonstrably false is the assumption that an animal must respond during learning. The juvenile white-crowned sparrow is incapable of singing during the critical learning period; all it does is listen. Similarly, nestling buntings, when they are too young to fly, learn the centre of rotation of the night sky by watching the stars rotate about it. Months later, they use this knowledge to keep oriented during the night-time portions of their migratory flights. These examples of purely passive observational learning cannot be conceptualized in S-R terms. Ironically, the phenomenon most studied by Skinnerians has proven to be passive in just this way. To get the pigeon to peck the key, it suffices to arrange for it to observe that soon after the key is illuminated the food hopper opens. If it observes this sequence several times, it begins to peck the key, even if its pecking has no effect on food delivery; indeed, even if its pecking forestalls food delivery! Most learning depends on the perception over time of a systematic stimulus relationship; whatever response the animal may or may not make during the period when the relationship is perceived is of little relevance to the learning that occurs.

There are also many examples of learning that cannot readily be conceptualized as the formation of an association. One example is the learning of one's position by 'dead reckoning', which has been found in animals ranging from insects to humans. Dead reckoning is the integration of one's velocity with respect to time to obtain net displacement: computing where you are from how fast you have moved in which direction for how long. This method of determining where you are relative to where you started is so unlike the traditional conception of learning by association that people when first hearing of it often reject it as an instance of learning. However, if the pre-theoretical definition of learning is the process or processes by which we acquire knowledge from experience, then dead reckoning is demonstrably a principal means by which mobile animals acquire knowledge of their current position in the world from their experience of the direction and rate at which they have moved through it. This example points towards learning as computationally derived knowledge of the world rather than as associated experiences (see LEARNING §2).

Finally, the desirability of constraining the theoretical constructs of psychology to be neurobiologically plausible is debatable. Constraining psychological theory in this way presupposes that neurobiologists have *already* identified those aspects of neural functioning that are relevant to understanding processes such as memory, attention, and thought-processes whose existence we infer from their behavioural manifestations. If the aspects of cellular and molecular neurobiology that are centrally relevant to our understanding of these processes remain to be discovered or identified, then attempts to ground psychological theorizing in well-established supposedly relevant neurobiological mechanisms are certain to lead us astray in that they make us build on what will turn out to be the wrong neurobiological foundations. For the first several decades of the twentieth century, classical geneticists did not attempt to ground their genetic theorizing in biochemistry. It is a good thing that they did not, because the discovery of the biochemical identity of the gene in 1954 revolutionized biochemistry. The biochemistry of the gene in the 1990s rests on concepts and mechanisms undreamed of in the biochemistry of the 1940s.

See also: COGNITIVE DEVELOPMENT

References and further reading

Blumberg, M.S. and Wasserman, E.A. (1995) 'Animal Mind and the Argument from Design', *American Psychologist* 50: 133–44. (A recent discussion of the continuing relevance of behaviourism in psychology.)

Boring, E.G. (1950) *A History of Experimental Psychology*, Englewood Cliffs, NJ: Prentice Hall. (Important early history of behaviourism.)

Catania, A.C. (1992) 'B.F. Skinner, Organism', *American Psychologist* 49: 1,521–30. (An appreciation of Skinner and his thought.)

Chomsky, N. (1959) 'Review of *Verbal Behavior* (by B.F. Skinner)', *Language* 35: 26–58. (An influential critique of behaviourism.)

Dennett, D. (1978) 'Skinner Skinned', in *Brainstorms*, Cambridge, MA: MIT Press. (An engaging discussion of some of the important philosophical issues surrounding behaviourism.)

Fodor, J. (1968) *Psychological Explanation*, New York: Random House. (A philosophical critique of behaviourism.)

Gallistel, C.R. (1990) *The Organization of Learning*, Cambridge, MA: Bradford Books/MIT Press. (A cognitive analysis of learning, the antithesis of the behaviourist analysis.)

Kendler, H.H. (1987) *Historical Foundations of Modern Psychology*, Philadelphia, PA: Temple University Press. (A good historical discussion of behaviourism.)

O'Donnell, M. (1985) *The Origins of Behaviorism: American Psychology 1870–1920*, New York: New York University Press. (Discussions of the background and consequences of Watson's formulation.)

Schultz, D.P. and Schultz, S.E. (1992) *A History of Modern Psychology*, Fort Worth, TX: Harcourt Brace Jovanovich, 5th edn. (A good historical discussion of behaviourism.)

Skinner, B.F. (1990) 'Can Psychology be a Science of Mind?', *American Psychologist* 45: 1,206–10. (Skinner's view of cognitive psychology.)

Watson, J.B. (1913) 'Psychology as the Behaviorist Views It', *Psychological Review* 20: 158–77. (Historically the most important statement of both scientific and methodological behaviourism.)

Zuriff, G.E. (1985) *Behaviorism: A Conceptual Reconstruction*, New York: Columbia University Press. (A philosophically oriented discussion of both aspects of behaviourism.)

C.R. GALLISTEL

BEING

Although 'being' has frequently been treated as a name for a property or special sort of entity, it is generally recognized that it is neither. Therefore, questions concerning being should not be understood as asking about the nature of some object or the character of some property. Rather, such questions raise a variety of problems concerning which sorts of entities there are, what one is saying when one says that some entity is, and the necessary conditions on thinking of an entity as something which is.

At least four distinct questions concerning being have emerged in the history of philosophy: (1) Which things are there? (2) What is it to be? (3) Is it ever appropriate to treat 'is' as a predicate, and, if not, how should it be understood? (alternatively, is existence a property?) (4) How is it possible to intend that something is? Twentieth-century discussions of being in the analytic tradition have focused on the first and third questions. Work in the German tradition, especially that of Martin Heidegger, has emphasized the fourth.

1. **Which things are there?**
2. **What is it to be?**
3. **Is existence a property?**
4. **How is an understanding of being possible?**

1 Which things are there?

Which sorts of things are there? This question asks for an inventory of the population of the world. It is natural to assume that there are middle-sized physical objects, such as organisms and artefacts, but reflection reveals a variety of puzzles. Given that middle-sized objects are composed of simpler material, should our inventory include only the objects, or only the material, or both? Given that objects have properties, and that different objects can have the same property, should our list include those properties, or merely the objects which have them? What about events, or numbers, or times?

It is not immediately clear what kinds of consideration are relevant to answering the population question. How does one decide just which entities there are? One possibility is to think of the question 'What things are there?' as analogous to 'What things are humans?' Ordinarily we think that we can answer the question regarding the population of humans if we know what conditions must be met for a thing to count as human. So, perhaps, we can know which things there are if we know what conditions must be met for a thing to count as something which is. But to know this is to know what it is we are saying when we say that something is. It is to have an answer to the question which Aristotle says 'was raised of old and is raised now and always, and is always the subject of doubt, viz. what being is'.

2 What is it to be?

The form of the question 'What is being?' initially suggests that we should think of 'being' either as a name for an entity or as picking out some property, but both views have proved problematic. When one asks a question of the form 'What is Patagonia?' one is requesting information regarding which entity is picked out by the word 'Patagonia'. So it is perhaps natural to think that the question 'What is being?' is similarly raising an issue regarding the object which is referred to by the word 'being'. But, unlike 'Patagonia', 'being' is not a noun: it is the present participle of the verb 'to be'. This suggests a different analogy. When one asks 'What is running?' (and is not asking which thing is running) one is asking about the character a thing must have in order to count as running. By analogy one might expect that the

699

question 'What is being?' raises the issue of which character or property being is.

The notion that 'being' names an entity was the first possibility explored. PARMENIDES reaches the extraordinary conclusion that there is only one unchanging item in the world inventory – being. He argues in two ways. First, anything which is not being, or is different from being, is not, since it *is not being*, so at most one being is, and that being is being itself. Parmenides is here treating 'being' as a name for a special sort of entity, call it 'being itself', and suggesting that it is correct to say that A *is* just in case A is identical with being itself. Parmenides' second line of argument assumes that all words, including 'being', are meaningful just in case they stand for some thing which is. He suggests that it is impossible truly to say or think that something, A, is not, for if A is not then 'A' stands for nothing. This has suggested to some that words which apparently refer to non-existent entities really do refer to entities which are, even though they do not exist.

Ancient philosophers found Parmenides' conclusions troubling. In response, Plato and Aristotle clarified the distinction between properties and the entities which possess those properties, and recognized that an entity can have some property without being identical to that property. So the fact that A is, does not imply that A is identical to is (or being), and the fact that 'is' is meaningful need not imply that 'is' is the name of an entity. In particular, Aristotle held that those entities which are in the primary sense are those self-subsistent individuals which have properties, the substances. And whatever else 'being' might signify, it does not stand for a self-subsistent individual substance, being-itself (see ARISTOTLE §12).

These distinctions leave open the possibility that 'A is' should be understood as asserting that A has a property, being. And there are strains in Aristotle's thought which attracted the tradition he established to this possibility, as well as strains which undercut this option. On the one hand, Aristotle thinks that it is wrong to see 'being' as picking out a class of thing, as 'human' does. In the 'human' case we assume that we already have a list of the things which are; we ask merely which characteristics distinguish the humans on that list from the nonhumans. For 'human' to serve this function it must be possible for some items on the list to qualify as humans and possible for some to fail to qualify. In the case of 'being' it is precisely the contents of that initial list which are in question, and 'being' cannot differentiate among the items on the list, as all of those items *must* qualify as things which are.

On the other hand, Aristotle hoped to discover which entities are substances by examining those predications in which we specify *what* a thing is, as opposed to merely specifying that some individual has some property. But it is sometimes possible to specify what a thing is without committing oneself to the claim *that* it is: 'Hamlet is a man'. This suggested to later philosophers that a name, such as Hamlet, stands for a possible entity, and that those possible entities which exist have an additional property, actual being, or existence. In that case, the 'is' in 'A is' would serve to distinguish two classes of entities – the actual and the merely possible.

3 Is existence a property?

It is possible to understand what a thing is without asserting that it exists. Kant uses this fact to criticize the view that existence is a property (see KANT, I. §2). Consider a disagreement concerning whether or not some entity, say God, exists. Even though there may be disagreement concerning details, the two disputants agree on a general description of God as omnipotent, omniscient and so on. This description constitutes the concept of God. If there were not such agreement concerning the concept there would be no real dispute. The disagreement concerns only whether there is something which has those properties which, if someone had them, they would be God. Now, if existence were a genuine property there would not be agreement on the concept of God. For in that case the believer's concept of God would differ from the atheist's concept of God in so far as the first would include the property of existence and the second would not. So existence cannot be part of the concept of God, it is not part of a description of the entity which is God, or any other entity, and is no property.

If existence is not a property, there must be something misleading about the grammatical form of the sentence 'God is'. The surface grammar suggests that the function of 'is' is to assert the property of existence of God. Kant suggests we handle this problem by reading 'God is' as 'Something existing is God'. This has the effect of removing 'is' from the predicate position and thus removing the appearance that existence is a property. It also moves 'God' from the subject to the predicate of the sentence, which has further consequences for our understanding of 'being'. Parmenides had argued that words are meaningful just in case they stand for something which is. And many had argued that entities which are merely possible are, even if they are not actual. But if apparently referring expressions such as 'God' are really parts of the predicate, they can be treated as descriptions, rather than as names for things that are, possible or otherwise.

These suggestions have been systematically developed in the twentieth century by RUSSELL and QUINE. Quine's work in particular has important implications for reflections on being. Since antiquity it has been thought that the answer to the population question depends upon the answer to the question regarding what it is to be. Just as A being human involves A satisfying some description which specifies what it is to be human, for A to exist involves A satisfying some description. But if the existential use of 'to be' expresses no property, this model cannot be right. In the assertion 'A is', A can be seen as having descriptive content, while the existential assertion says that there is *something* which satisfies *this* description. Since 'something' serves as a pronoun, this amounts to saying that 'to be is to be in the range of reference of a pronoun', or, 'to be is to be the value of a variable'. The sorts of things we say there are are the sorts of things which can satisfy our descriptions. If we say that there are primes greater than five, we are saying that there is something such that it is a prime and it is greater than five. Since only numbers can be prime, this sentence commits us to the existence of numbers. And numbers *are* just in case some sentences of this type *are true*. Our ordinary assertions commit us to the existence of various types of entities. To know which types of entities exist we need to know only which of those ordinary assertions are true.

Quine's work also has important implications for the relationship between possible and actual existence. Since names need carry no ontological commitment, asserting that some entity is not does not imply that there is some sense in which that entity, though not actual, is. Quine (1953) uses this to argue that there is no warrant for 'expanding our universe to include so-called possible entities' (see ONTOLOGICAL COMMITMENT).

Several philosophers have criticized aspects of Quine's views regarding being. David Lewis (1986) has argued that Quine's own criterion of ontological commitment commits us to the existence of possible entities, and Alvin Plantinga (1974) and Peter van Inwagen (1993) have argued that necessary existence, at least, is a property. These developments point to a reawakening of interest in the issues of what it is for something to be and how we should understand possible and actual being.

4 How is an understanding of being possible?

The twentieth-century philosopher Martin HEIDEGGER attempted to renew interest in the question of being. For Heidegger 'being' is not a name for anything, and he carefully distinguishes among the various questions concerning being. But he follows a distinctive strategy in discussing these questions. He hopes to answer the population question by first answering the question of what it is to be, and to answer this question by answering the question of how it is possible to intend things that are as things that are. He thinks we can answer this question if we come to see how any understanding of being is possible.

Heidegger holds that the recognition that being is not a property leaves an unresolved problem: on what should we base decisions regarding which entities are candidates for descriptions? Quine thinks that this question must be answered pragmatically, holding that there are no general a priori conditions which restrict the range of reference of our pronouns. Heidegger disagrees, holding that there are such conditions which are grounded in necessary conditions for intending anything at all.

We can put Heidegger's strategy in context by returning to Kant. Kant thinks that the recognition that existence is not a property leaves a serious issue unresolved: What are the necessary conditions on the possibility of the objects of experience? What are the a priori constraints on the range of possible entities which we can come to know? He answers by appealing to the necessary conditions on possible experience. For Kant, our sentences can be true of a physical object only if that object is a possible object of experience, and it is possible to experience an object only if it is possible to perceive it. So the range of reference of our pronouns for physical objects is restricted by the condition of perceivability (and its extension in causality). 'The perception which supplies the content of the concept [of actuality] is the sole mark of actuality' (Kant 1781: A225/B273).

Heidegger thought that Kant's strategy had been developed by Edmund HUSSERL. Husserl asked how it is possible for a subject to intend something distinct from its own mental states. We intend a variety of such entities, including physical objects, numbers and norms, and it is puzzling how a subject can intend such independent entities. In order to solve this puzzle, Husserl generalized the notion of linguistic meaning. Each conscious act involves a meaning which is distinct from the act itself, and it is through this meaning that the act is related to its object. The meaning of an act depends upon its being placed within a temporal 'horizon' of past and possible future apprehensions. My current apprehension, for example, has the meaning of 'perception of a rock from this angle'. The act of rock perception has this meaning in virtue of its involving the retention of past apprehensions of the rock from different angles and the 'protention' that, were I to move, additional specific rock perceptions would occur. Intentions directed towards different classes of entities are characterized by different structures of relatedness among current apprehensions, retentions, and protentions, and what it is for an entity of some type to be varies as a function of the structure of the intentions directed towards entities of that type.

Heidegger has serious disagreements with Husserl regarding intentionality. In particular, he holds that intentionality is primarily a matter of action rather than consciousness. For Heidegger the primary way in which we intend a hammer as a tool, for example, is in an overt act of hammering, rather than in an internal conscious act, and the conditions on intending a hammer have more to do with the conditions under which an act can count as hammering than with how we think of a hammer (see INTENTIONALITY).

Nevertheless, Heidegger follows a strategy which is similar to Husserl's. The early Heidegger seizes upon the temporal character of Husserl's understanding of intentionality: 'intentionality... has the condition of its possibility in temporality and temporality's ecstatic horizontal character' (1975 (1982): 268). And, since one can understand what it is for a class of entities to be through determining the conditions necessary for intending that class of entities, Heidegger concludes that 'the central problematic of all ontology is rooted in the phenomenon of time' (1926 (1962): 40). Concretely, such an investigation involves fixing the range of reference for various classes of pronouns by determining the necessary temporal features of intentions directed at entities of that type. To intend a tool as a tool involves intending it as usable in various ways, and to be a tool involves serviceability. To intend a being as *Dasein*, or a being like us, on the other hand, is to intend it as itself capable of intentionality. Given the above, this implies that we are entities who are open to the dimensions of past and future, and Heidegger concludes that 'temporality [is] the meaning of the being which we call "Dasein"' (1926 (1962): 38).

Later, Heidegger came increasingly to concentrate on the contrast between the presence of an entity and the temporal horizon in which it becomes present. He concluded that philosophers have always answered the question regarding what it is to be with variations on the claim that being is constant presence, or being always available for interaction, but had failed to investigate the distinctive character of the horizon which makes an encounter with presence possible. Much of the work of the French philosopher Jacques Derrida, who has been heavily influenced by Heidegger, also focuses on the relationship between an object and the horizon in which it is encountered.

See also: EXISTENCE; ONTOLOGY

References and further reading

Aristotle (*c.*330 BC) *Metaphysics*, trans. W.D. Ross in *The Complete Works of Aristotle*, ed. J. Barnes, Princeton, NJ: Princeton University Press, 1984. (Important discussions of being and substance appear in bks III, IV, and especially bks VII–IX.)

* Heidegger, M. (1975) *Die Grundprobleme der Phänomenologie*, trans. A. Hofstadter as *The Basic Problems of Phenomenology*, Bloomington, IN: Indiana University Press, 1982. (Text of lecture course of 1927; the basic problems all concern being.)

* —— (1926) *Sein und Zeit*, trans. J. Macquarrie and E. Robinson as *Being and Time*, New York: Harper & Row, 1962. (Heidegger's early masterpiece.)

—— (1969) *Zur Sache des Denkens*, trans. J. Stambaugh as *On Time and Being*, New York: Harper & Row, 1972. (Lectures which summarize Heidegger's later views on being, time and philosophy.)

Husserl, E. (1931) *Cartesian Meditations*, trans. D. Cairns, The Hague: Nijhoff, 1960. (Based on 1929 lectures; meditations 2 and 3 contain phenomenological discussions of being.)

—— (1900) *Logische Untersuchungen*, trans. J.N. Findlay as *Logical Investigations*, New York: Humanities Press, 1970. (Meaning is discussed in Investigation I, being in Investigation VI.)

* Inwagen, P. van (1993) *Metaphysics*, Boulder, CO: Westview Press. (Excellent introduction to metaphysics.)

* Kant, I. (1781) *Critique of Pure Reason*, trans. N.K. Smith, London: Macmillan, 1933. (Crucial passages include A154–8, A219–26, A592–602.)

* Lewis, D. (1986) *On the Plurality of Worlds*, Oxford: Blackwell. (Forceful defence of modal realism.)

Parmenides (*c.*500 BC) 'Fragments', trans. and ed. G.S. Kirk, J.E. Raven, and M. Schofield in *The Presocratic Philosophers*, Cambridge, Cambridge University Press, 1983. (Among the first discussions of being.)

* Plantinga, A. (1974) *God, Freedom, and Evil*, New York: Harper & Row. (Discusses necessary existence in the context of a defence of the ontological argument for the existence of God.)

* Quine, W.V.O. (1953) 'On What There Is' in *From a Logical Point of View*, Cambridge, MA: Harvard University Press. (A succinct statement of Quine's views.)

Russell, B. (1918) *The Philosophy of Logical Atomism*, La Salle, IL: Open Court Publishing, 1985. (Sect. V treats existence and general propositions.)

MARK OKRENT

BELIEF

We believe that there is coffee over there; we believe the special theory of relativity; we believe the Vice-Chancellor; and some of us believe in God. But plausibly what is fundamental is believing that *something is the case – believing a proposition, as it is usually put. To believe a theory is to believe the propositions that make up the theory, to believe a person is to believe some proposition advanced by them; and to believe in God is to believe the proposition that God exists. Thus belief is said to be a propositional attitude or intentional state: to believe is to take the attitude of belief to some proposition. It is about what its propositional object is about (God, coffee, or whatever). We can think of the propositional object of a belief as the way the belief represents things as being – its content, as it is often called.*

We state what we believe with indicative sentences in 'that'-clauses, as in 'Mary believes that the Democrats will win the next election'. *But belief in the absence of language is possible. A dog may believe that there is food in the bowl in front of it. Accordingly philosophers have sought accounts of belief that allow a central role to sentences – it cannot be an accident that finding the right sentence* is *the way to capture what someone believes – while allowing that creatures without a language can have beliefs. One way of doing this is to construe beliefs as relations to inner sentences somehow inscribed in the brain. On this view although dogs do not have a public language, to the extent that they have beliefs they have something sentence-like in their heads.*

An alternative tradition focuses on the way belief when combined with desire leads to behaviour, and analyses belief in terms of behavioural dispositions or more recently as the internal state that is, in combination with other mental states, responsible for the appropriate behavioural dispositions.

An earlier tradition associated with the British Empiricists views belief as a kind of pale imitation of perceptual experience. But recent work on belief largely takes for granted a sharp distinction between belief and the various mental images that may or may not accompany it.

1   Beliefs as sentences in mentalese: the language of thought
2   Two problems for LOTH
3   Belief as a map by which we steer

1   Beliefs as sentences in mentalese: the language of thought

Fred's belief in the Devil cannot literally be a relation between Fred and the Devil. Otherwise he could not have the belief, unless the Devil existed. One response is to treat belief as a relation to sentences. To believe is to 'believe-true' a sentence: Fred believes-true 'The Devil exists'. But animals that lack a language have beliefs. My dog may believe that his master is home, or that it is time for a walk. Moreover, monolingual French speakers and monolingual English speakers may agree in what they believe, say, that it would be good if they knew more than one language, and yet they may not agree on which sentences they believe true. Finally, you might believe-true the sentence 'The Devil exists' and yet not believe that the Devil exists because you wrongly think that the word 'Devil' means 'God'. In this case what you believe is that God exists while wrongly thinking that the sentence 'The Devil exists' is a good sentence to use to express this belief. For these reasons, and others, belief is usually thought of as a relation to a proposition. A proposition is what is expressed by a sentence; it is what is in common between sentences in French and English that mean the same; the proposition expressed is what is grasped when you understand a sentence. Monolingual speakers believe alike by believing the same propositions; dogs have beliefs by virtue of believing propositions despite not having a language to express them; someone who believes that the sentence 'The Devil exists' is true while thinking that 'Devil' means 'God' does not thereby believe that the Devil exists because they are wrong about what proposition 'The Devil exists' expresses. These remarks slide over a lively controversy concerning the ontological status of propositions (see PROPOSITIONS, SENTENCES AND STATEMENTS). Our immediate concern will be with a popular view that gives sentences a prominent role in the account of belief, but in a way which avoids the problems just rehearsed.

According to the language of thought hypothesis (LOTH), not only do certain sentences serve to provide the propositional objects of beliefs (and thoughts in general) but, in addition, the beliefs are themselves sentence-like. A sentence may be viewed as made up of significant parts put together according to certain rules. In the same general way, according to LOTH, beliefs have parts put together in certain ways (see LANGUAGE OF THOUGHT).

How does LOTH mesh with the idea that beliefs are relations to propositions? The idea is that a belief's propositional object is determined by how it is made up from parts which have representational or semantic properties – that is, the parts stand for things, properties and relations much as the parts of a natural-language sentence do (see SEMANTICS). In English 'biscuit' represents certain things, and 'crisp' represents a certain property, and when we combine them together to form the sentence 'Biscuits are crisp' we get a sentence that makes a claim that is true or false according to whether or not the things have the property. This is how the sentence expresses the proposition that biscuits are crisp (see COMPOSITIONALITY). In the same way, there are brain structures that represent things and properties, and when these brain structures are put together in the right way we get, says LOTH, a more complex structure, a sentence in mentalese, that represents the things as having the properties – as it might be, the sentence of mentalese that says that biscuits are crisp, that expresses that proposition, and that thereby provides us with a token of the belief that biscuits are crisp.

This theory can allow that dogs have beliefs. Dogs might have a language of thought even though they do not have a public language. It can explain how monolingual speakers of different language can agree in belief – their sentences of mentalese may express the same propositions. It also provides an explanation of a number of phenomena associated with belief. First, it explains how what a person believes can be causally relevant to what else they believe and what they do. If you believe that Mary is at the party and then learn that Mary is always accompanied at parties by Tom, you will typically come to believe that Tom is at the party. What you believe combines with what you learn to produce a new belief. LOTH explains these causal transactions as transactions between the structures that are the various beliefs. Much as a computer processes information by manipulating electronically coded structures so we arrive at new beliefs by virtue of our brains manipulating the symbols of mentalese. Similarly, what we believe contributes to explanations of what we do. My belief that there is coffee over there together with suitable desires may lead me to move over there by virtue of its being a belief that there is coffee over there. LOTH accounts for this fact in terms of the causal influence of the sentences of mentalese on the causal path to bodily movement.

Second, LOTH explains the fact that typically one who can believe that Jill loves Mary can believe that Mary loves Jill, and in general if you can believe that aRb, then you can believe that bRa (the phenomenon known as systematicity). The fact that if you can believe that aRb, then you can believe that bRa is explained by the fact that the state that encodes the former is a re-arrangement of the parts of the state that encodes the latter. And, of course, this explanation generalizes to explain more complex cases.

Finally, LOTH can explain our ability to form quite new beliefs (the property known as productivity). Just as we can form new sentences by novel combinations of the relevant words of a public language, so the brain can form new beliefs by means of novel combinations of the relevant words of mentalese.

LOTH thus explains a lot of what needs to be explained. Nevertheless, there are two serious problems for this view as applied to belief.

2 Two problems for LOTH

First, unless the claim that mentalese exists is trivialized – no matter what neuroscience reveals about how the brain processes information, what it reveals will count as the brain containing mentalese – LOTH involves risky speculation about how our brains work. The theory gives a hostage to fortune. Some are happy to accept this. If neuroscience reveals that there is no mentalese and that we do not process information in a sentential manner, we should say that we do not have beliefs and so embrace eliminativism about belief (see ELIMINATIVISM). This is, however, very much a minority view.

Second, LOTH leaves the intimate connection between belief and behaviour obscure. On the face of it predictions about the behaviour of highly complex organisms like ourselves should be enormously difficult. Trees bend in the wind whereas we put on jumpers, go inside houses, lean into the wind, cancel our games of tennis, or whatever. Unlike trees and simple machines, we respond to stimuli in enormously varied ways. Nevertheless we are quite good at predicting human behaviour. We all make many successful predictions of the following kind: someone who has uttered the word 'Yes' on hearing the sentence 'Would you like to come to dinner at 19.30 on the 21st?' will arrive around 19.30 at the house of the person the sentence came from. What we do, of course, is use hypotheses about what people believe and desire and predict in terms of the rule that subjects will tend to behave in such a way that they achieve what they desire if what they believe is true. Our subject's 'Yes' tells us what they desire, and what we predict – their turning up at the named time – is behaviour that will achieve their desire for dinner.

Now we noted above how LOTH explains the way belief contributes to causing behaviour. In the same general way it explains how belief together with desire explains behaviour. For LOTH treats desires as like beliefs in being internal sentences of mentalese. The difference is that, as it is often put, the desires are stored in the 'desire' box, and the beliefs are stored in the 'belief' box. The metaphor of different locations marks the fact that beliefs and desires differ in how they relate to the world. Belief is a state that seeks to conform to how things are – the sight of coffee tends to extinguish my belief that there is no coffee near; whereas desire is a state that seeks to conform things to how it is – desire for coffee tends to bring one near coffee. The stored sentences that do the first job count as being in the belief box; the stored sentences of mentalese that do the second job count as being in the desire box. So the way belief and desire combine to produce behaviour is not a problem for the LOTH. The two 'differently located' stored sentences get together to produce the behaviour.

The problem, rather, arises from the fact that the connection between behaviour and what subjects believe and desire is most immediately one between behaviour and a rich system of belief and desire. Individual beliefs and desires grossly underdetermine behaviour. There is no behaviour that the belief that there is a mine near the tree, together with the desire to live, as such points to. It is, rather, a rich system of belief – to the effect, say, that there is a mine near the tree, that the mine is likely to be triggered by going near it, that moving one's legs in such and such a way will not bring one near the tree, that there is not a bigger mine that can only be avoided by going close to the tree, that triggering mines tends to cause death, and so on and so forth, along with the desire to live being greater than the desire to test out the trigger system of the mines – that points to behaviour. When we give little illustrations of connections between subjects' beliefs and desires and what they do, we take for granted a great deal about what they believe and desire. This is fine. It is by and large common knowledge. But the point remains that only rich systems of belief and desire have the intimate connection with behaviour. The same point could be made with the dinner invitation story. The prediction of our subject's behaviour assumed a great deal by way of belief and desire. We assumed beliefs about what the words mean, about who uttered them, about which month was intended, ..., and we assumed that there were no countervailing desires that outweighed the desire to go to dinner.

The problem for LOTH is that it takes as its starting point individual beliefs and desires. This leaves it seriously unclear what the theory has to say about the connection between a rich story about belief and desire, on the one hand, and behaviour, on the other. There is no behaviour that the individual belief that p and desire that q point to. *It is rich systems of both belief and desire that point in some reasonably determinate way to behaviour.* The challenge for LOTH is to find some kind of guarantee that the account of individual beliefs and desires it offers is such that if subjects have rich enough sets of these individual beliefs and desires, these rich enough sets of beliefs and desires will cause the reasonably determinate behaviour that tends to satisfy their desires if their beliefs are true.

3 Belief as a map by which we steer

One obvious fact about belief is the way we use sentences to state what we believe. An equally obvious fact is the connection between belief and behaviour via desire discussed above. F.P. Ramsey (1931) famously captured this idea by describing belief as a map by which we steer. The alternative to LOTH is an account of belief that sees belief as map like.

For LOTH, individual beliefs are fundamental; while on the map view systems of belief are fundamental. Inside us is a hugely complex structure that richly represents how things around us are in an essentially holistic way. When you believe the bank is bigger than the post office, there is no individual structure, no sentence of mentalese in your head, that represents your belief that the bank is bigger than the post office. Rather you believe that the bank is bigger than the post office by having a belief system according to which, among a great many other things, the bank is bigger than the post office. The key point can be made in terms of maps. A map of the Earth might represent the fact that the taller mountains are mostly near the deeper oceans, but there is no part of the map that says just that in the way that there may be a sentence that says just that – for instance the very sentence 'The taller mountains are mostly near the deeper oceans'. Or consider holograms. Holograms are 'laser photographs'. When light from the laser is projected through the negative, the well known, three dimensional, coloured array is produced. The negative can be thought of as representing things as being the way the coloured array depicts them. However, no part of the negative has special responsibility for some part of the array. Each part contains information about the whole array. In consequence, what happens if you damage part of the hologram is a loss of detail, a blurring, of the three dimensional array, not a loss in any particular part of it.

Many of the phenomena explained by LOTH can equally be explained by the map theory. We noted how LOTH can explain the evolution of belief over time in terms of the causal interactions of the internal sentences with each other, and how beliefs cause behaviour in terms of how the stored sentences figure in the causal path to behaviour. But internal maps guide rockets to their targets and evolve over time. The same goes for the maps we use every day – they guide our behaviour and evolve over time. We noted that LOTH can explain the fact that those with the capacity to believe that the bookshop is bigger than the post office are also able to believe that the post office is bigger than the bookshop. But maps (and holograms) that can represent that the bookshop is bigger than the post office can equally represent that the post office is bigger than the bookshop.

It has recently been argued that there is empirical evidence that our brains represent how things are around us in something like the way an internal map or hologram might. This has led to a renewed interest in the map theory of belief (see CONNECTIONISM).

The major question for the map theory concerns whether believing is closed under entailment. On the map theory to believe that p is to have a system of belief according to which p; that is, to have a system that could not be true unless p. But if p entails q, then a system that could not be true unless p must also be a system that could not be true unless q. This means that the map view must accept closure under entailment, the principle that if p entails q, anyone who believes p believes q. But is it not possible to believe that a triangle is equiangular without believing that it is equilateral – as many beginning geometry students know only too well? The usual reply by map theorists is to insist that one who believes that a triangle is equiangular does believe that it is equilateral; what they may lack is knowledge about the right words to capture what they believe. But this is a matter of lively debate.

See also: BEHAVIOURISM, ANALYTIC; BELIEF AND KNOWLEDGE; DE RE/DE DICTO; FUNCTIONALISM; INTENTIONALITY; PROBABILITY; PROPOSITIONAL ATTITUDES

References and further reading

Armstrong, D. M. (1973) *Belief, Truth and Knowledge*, Cambridge: Cambridge University Press. (Detailed development of the map theory that takes off from F. P. Ramsey's idea.)

Fodor, J. (1987) *Psychosemantics*, Cambridge, MA: MIT Press. (The appendix contains a very readable defence of LOTH by one of its major proponents.)

Hume, D. (1739–40) *A Treatise of Human Nature*, ed. L.A. Selby-Bigge, Oxford: Oxford University Press, 1888. (The Treatise is a classic widely available in many editions and is the standard source for the 'pale imitation of experience' view of belief, pretty much passed over in this entry.)

Lewis, D. (1994) 'Reduction of Mind', in S. Guttenplan (ed.) *A Companion to Philosophy of Mind*, Oxford: Blackwell. (Compares the map view to the language of thought view in detail.)

Quine, W.V. (1960) *Word and Object*, Cambridge, MA: MIT Press. (Detailed, sympathetic discussion of whether belief should be thought of as 'believing-true' some linguistic item. Relates the discussion to the distinction between belief *de dicto* and belief *de re* not touched on in this entry.)

* Ramsey, F.P. (1931) *The Foundations of Mathematics*, London: Kegan Paul. (Classic source of the view of belief as a map by which we steer, and of treatments of degree of belief in terms of betting behaviour.)

Ryle, G. (1949) *The Concept of Mind*, London: Hutchinson. (Classic exposition of behaviourism about belief.)

Stalnaker, R.C. (1984) *Inquiry*, Cambridge, MA: MIT Press. (One of the most detailed discussions of whether belief is closed under entailment, along with two matters not touched on in this entry: treatments of what a subject believes in terms of where in the set of possibilities believers take themselves to be located, and the relation between belief and acceptance.)

DAVID BRADDON-MITCHELL
FRANK JACKSON

BELIEF AND KNOWLEDGE

It is often said that for people to know that such and such is the case, they must have something like a belief that such and such is the case. Call this the 'entailment thesis'. It is usually added that the converse (call it the 'converse entailment thesis') is false: it is false that my belief-like attitude that such and such is the case always counts as knowledge. This standard view, combining the entailment thesis with the denial of the converse thesis, has been challenged in a number of ways.

The 'identity thesis' would retain the entailment thesis but would also endorse the converse entailment thesis. Knowledge and belief entail each other. (While no one has defended precisely this claim, Donald Davidson has come close.) The 'incompatibility thesis' rejects the entailment thesis as well as the converse entailment thesis, and says that knowledge and belief are mutually incompatible. Similarly, the 'separability thesis' also rejects the entailment thesis and the converse entailment thesis, but adds that knowledge and belief are mutually compatible. Those who defend the 'eliminativism thesis' hold that belief, like other elements of 'folk' or popular psychology, is an outmoded notion, and what is 'in our heads' when we know about the world is something other than beliefs.

1 Standard view
2 Identity thesis
3 Incompatibility thesis
4 Separability thesis
5 Eliminativism thesis

1 Standard view

Perhaps the most common version of this view is that while some beliefs count as knowledge, not all do. And while epistemologists need to identify the conditions beliefs must meet if they are to acquire the status of knowledge, it is obvious that we cannot know that something is the case if we do not even believe it (see KNOWLEDGE, CONCEPT OF). The common version of the standard view deals specifically with belief states. But some philosophers would claim that while knowledge entails belief-*like* states (but not vice versa), it is not precisely belief states that are entailed. Some of the substitutes that have been defended are psychological certainty, conviction, and acceptance.

A.J. Ayer is among those who say that knowledge entails psychological certainty, where I am psychologically certain that something is the case when I am not at all disposed to doubt it. Psychological certainty is not the same thing as infallibility, and it is only the former that Ayer links to knowledge (see CERTAINTY). His view is based on an analysis of the meaning of the term 'know': according to him, 'to say of oneself that one knew that such and such a statement was true but that one was not altogether sure of it would be self-contradictory' (Ayer 1956: 16).

Keith Lehrer (1974) argued that, given common usage, knowledge need not entail conviction, but that philosophers ought none the less to restrict the use of 'know' so that knowledge does entail conviction. His grounds are that philosophers want to explain how it is possible for people to know what they *claim* to know: if I claim to know something, then I must be convinced that I do know it, but more importantly, I must be convinced that it is the case.

Later (1989) Lehrer retracted. He suggested that we need only to *accept* that something is the case in order to know that it is the case. There are two advantages to this. First, when we accept that something is the case, we do so for a purpose, and the relevant purpose for epistemic agents is the pursuit of truth. When we believe (or harbour a conviction) we need not have any such purpose. So the use of 'acceptance' rather than 'conviction' helps us keep in sight the goal-oriented nature of epistemic agents. Second, a belief (and conviction) can be the product of entirely irrational factors, such as wishful thinking, and one can believe things against one's better judgment. Acceptance, on the other hand, is governed by epistemic norms.

2 Identity thesis

While no one defends the claim that knowledge entails belief and vice versa, Donald Davidson (1983) comes close. He assumes the entailment thesis (that knowledge entails belief), but he also argues that belief is veridical, so that it is impossible for many of our beliefs to be false. Since belief is veridical, most beliefs constitute knowledge. Davidson bases his view that belief is veridical on theories of meaning and belief that appeal to a principle of charity and to a type of verificationism (see CHARITY, PRINCIPLE OF §4; DAVIDSON, D. §5).

First, Davidson assumes that when others interpret what we say, and attempt to figure out what we mean and what we believe, they must do their best to ensure that what we say is intelligible, and that requires that they avoid ascribing to us very many false beliefs. So it is largely their own beliefs which they must attribute to us. Any interpreter must be *charitable*, and attribute to us beliefs that they consider to be largely true.

Next, Davidson adopts a form of verificationism. He claims that what interpreters of our discourse who are fully knowledgeable of our circumstances and speech behaviour would *say* we mean and believe *is* what we mean and believe. Combining his principle of charity with his verificationism, Davidson reasons as follows: The beliefs of ideally situated interpreters are by hypothesis true. Given their charitableness, when they interpret our discourse it will be largely these accurate views which they will attribute to us. But given verificationism, what they say goes: when they say that what we believe is largely true, they are right. 'Most of the sentences a speaker holds to be true... are true'; 'Belief is in its nature veridical' (Davidson 1983: 434, 432). If I wonder whether my beliefs are true, I have only to run through the above reasoning to see that 'beliefs are by nature generally true' (Davidson 1983: 437). This is not to say that it is impossible for me to believe a falsehood, however, for the ideal interpreter may be forced to attribute to me some false views.

There is plenty of room for doubt about Davidson's argument, however. One challenge made by Luper-Foy (1987) and others is that ensuring that a speaker's discourse is intelligible (which, according to Davidson, is the point of the principle of charity) need not involve attributing to the speaker what in the main we believe. What charitable interpreters, who are out to secure intelligibility, should attribute to speakers is what those interpreters would believe (and mean by what they say) if they were in the speaker's circumstances. Yet this policy might require attributing to speakers mostly false beliefs. For example, people who are in circumstances described by sceptics would be unintelligible to us if their views were not as mistaken as ours would be if *we* were there (see LePore 1986).

3 Incompatibility thesis

Arguments for the thesis that knowledge and belief are incompatible are not very strong. This thesis has been attributed to Plato, who suggested that belief (or opinion) was fallible while knowledge was not, but this suggestion does not imply the incompatibility thesis. People with a (fallible) belief state might also be related to the world in such a way that, given that relationship, their belief could not be false. For example, their (fallible) belief that *p* might be produced by a mechanism that infallibly detects the fact that *p*.

As developed by A. Duncan-Jones (1938), the incompatibility thesis is based on the claim that linguistic evidence precludes our saying that people know something once we have said that they believe it. People say things like 'I do not believe that Clinton is president, I *know* he is', which might suggest that only when we hold an opinion on weak or nonexistent grounds is the opinion a belief, so that belief is incompatible with knowledge. But the linguistic evidence need not suggest this. The evidence is consistent with the possibility that knowledge requires belief and something else, such as strong evidence. To say 'I believe that Clinton is president' when I have overwhelming evidence would be misleading to my listeners, who would assume that if I had overwhelming evidence I would say I *knew* that Clinton was president, not merely that I believed he was president (Grice 1989). Compare: 'I do not *grasp* the theory, I devised it' (see IMPLICATURE).

H.A. Prichard (1950) argued that knowledge entails psychological certainty, while mere belief always falls short of certainty. So the confident attitude we have when we know that something is the case rules out (merely) believing that it is the case. However, belief involves some degree of confidence, and surely I can increase my confidence indefinitely without ceasing to believe what I am so confident about.

4 Separability thesis

Perhaps the most prominent defence of the claim that knowledge and belief are separable is given by Colin Radford (1966). A.D. Woozley (1953) had argued that knowledge is compatible with the absence of confidence about what is known, for people who can pass a test prove themselves to know the material even if they are not confident about their responses. Radford uses a similar argument to suggest that knowledge is consistent with a complete absence of belief. Consider the diffident people just mentioned who pass the test. Suppose that they give the correct response 'Washington' to a particular question such as 'Who was the first president of the USA?' If they are sufficiently unconfident about their response, they might be prepared to *deny* that they believe that the first president was Washington, which is strong evidence that they do *not* believe it. Yet their accurate performance on the test suggests that they knew the truth of their response. (Perhaps it would be inappropriate for them to *claim* that they knew, but that is not because they fail to know; rather, it is because they do not meet the conditions under which it is appropriate to claim knowledge, which would require that they believe that they have the knowledge they claim.)

Radford's argument can be challenged on various grounds. First, we might point out that we are not infallible authorities about which beliefs we have. Perhaps we think we do not have a belief (say because we cannot detect it through introspection) when in fact we do (say because beliefs are behavioural dispositions such as the tendency to assent when asked the appropriate question) (see INTROSPECTION, EPISTEMOLOGY OF §§1-2). Second, we might deny that the people in Radford's cases really do know what he claims that they know. After all, they have no evidence for the truth of their test responses; indeed, they have reason to think that their responses are incorrect. So, from their own subjective view, the truth of their responses would be an accident at best.

5 Eliminativism thesis

Patricia Churchland (1986), Paul Churchland (1979) and Stephen Stich (1983) offer a final, and somewhat oblique, challenge to the standard view. They suggest that the notion of belief is scientifically outmoded and ought to go the way of notions like phlogiston and ether. Moreover, theories of knowledge ought to focus on elements of cognition that are more primitive than any belief-like states could be.

Paul Churchland supports the latter point by attacking the common idea that the cognitive apparatus of epistemic agents functions essentially by manipulating sentences, and that rational agents are ones whose apparatus manipulates sentences in accordance with given logical and quasi-logical relations among those sentences. A problem with this common view is that it cannot possibly be true of infants. It is no more tempting to explain the behaviour of infants in terms of propositional attitudes than it is to explain the behaviour of protozoa or plants that way. Their development must be explained in terms of something more primitive than propositional attitudes. But if the rational development of adults is continuous with that of infants, then the rationality of adults must be explained in terms of the same primitives as that of infants.

Eliminativism is sketchy and hence hard to assess as a challenge to the standard view of knowledge. It is not clear what a less 'folksy', more scientific psychology would use in place of the notion of belief. It might still need a notion that is very much like the notion of belief, in which case a version of the standard view might survive (see ELIMINATIVISM; FOLK PSYCHOLOGY).

See also: BELIEF

References and further reading

All the following works are nontechnical, although demanding.

* Ayer, A.J. (1956) *The Problem of Knowledge*, Harmondsworth: Penguin. (Referred to in §1. Analyses knowledge; discusses scepticism and certainty.)
* Churchland, P.M. (1979) *Scientific Realism and the Plasticity of Mind*, Cambridge: Cambridge University Press. (Clear presentation of scientific realism which challenges the idea that knowledge should be understood in terms of belief. Referred to in §5.)
* Churchland, P.S. (1986) *Neurophilosophy*, Cambridge, MA: Bradford Books/MIT Press. (Referred to in §5. Develops a view concerning the relationship between philosophy of mind and the scientific study of the central nervous system.)
* Davidson, D. (1983) 'A Coherence Theory of Truth and Knowledge', in *Kant Oder Hegel*, Stuttgart: Klett-Cotta Buchhandlung, 423–38. (Referred to in §2. Attempts to refute scepticism by showing that belief is by its nature veridical.)
* Duncan-Jones, A. (1938) 'Further Questions about "Know" and "Think"', *Analysis* 5 (5): 96–106; repr. in M. MacDonald (ed.) *Philosophy and Analysis*, Oxford: Blackwell, 1966. (Develops the incompatibility thesis. Referred to in §3.)
* Grice, H.P. (1989) *Studies in the Ways of Words*, Harvard, MA: Harvard University Press. (Referred to in §3. Develops an account of the conversational implications of 'believe' and 'know'.)
* Lehrer, K. (1974) *Knowledge*, Oxford: Oxford University Press. (Referred to in §1. Provides an analysis of knowledge and justification.)
* —— (1989) 'Knowledge Reconsidered', in M. Clay and K. Lehrer (eds) *Knowledge and Skepticism*, Boulder, CO: Westview Press. (Revises Lehrer's theory of knowledge. Referred to in §1.)
* LePore, E. (ed.) (1986) *Truth and Interpretation: Perspectives on the Philosophy of Donald Davidson*, Oxford: Blackwell. (Collection of essays about the views of Donald Davidson. Referred to in §2.)
* Luper-Foy, S. (1987) 'Doxastic Skepticism', *The Southern Journal of Philosophy* 25 (4): 529–38. (Referred to in §2. Critically discusses Davidson's view that belief is by nature veridical.)
* Prichard, H.A. (1950) *Knowing and Perception*, Oxford: Clarendon Press. (Analyses knowledge and perception. Referred to in §3.)
* Radford, C. (1966) 'Knowledge – By Examples', *Analysis* 27 (1): 1–11. (Defends the separability thesis. Referred to in §4.)
* Stich, S. (1983) *From Folk Psychology to Cognitive Science: The Case against Belief*, Cambridge, MA: Bradford Books/MIT Press. (Referred to in §5. Develops a philosophy of mind according to which common-sense psychological terms are not suited to cognitive science.)
* Woozley, A.D. (1953) 'Knowing and Not Knowing', *Proceedings of the Aristotelian Society* 53 (1952–3): 151–72. (Discusses the relationship between knowledge and confidence. Referred to in §4.)

STEVEN LUPER

BELINSKII, VISSARION GRIGORIEVICH (1811–48)

Belinskii was considered by his followers in the nineteenth century, and by the official ideology of the Soviet period, to be not only Russia's greatest literary critic, but also a leading Russian thinker. Soviet encyclopedias label him 'critic, publicist and philosopher'. His role in Russian cultural life has been given positive as well as negative assessments, but there can be no doubt as to his huge influence. He is largely responsible for the fact that Russian literature and art, for a century and a half now, have been considered an organ of society, a mirror of the Russian nation's destiny and a vehicle of its historical progress. It is largely his merit – or fault – that in Russia, art and literature have been accorded a lofty status of leadership and authority, and also that 'art for art's sake' never became respectable in Russia. The influence of Belinskii's philosophy of art extended through the entire political spectrum, far beyond his political legacy which was limited to the revolutionary left. The idea that art and literature are organic functions of society, nationhood and historical progress, which Belinskii took for granted, was passed on even to the Slavophile right and the liberal Westernizing centre. It was still an integral part of the doctrine of Socialist Realism.

1 Life and critical career
2 Evolution of Belinskii's aesthetics
3 Art and socio-historical reality
4 Legacy to Russian aesthetic thought

1 Life and critical career

Belinskii was born in 1811 in Sveaborg, Finland, the son of a naval surgeon. He attended Moscow University from 1829 to 1832, but was dismissed 'for reasons of health and limited ability'. He was an active member of a discussion group led by Nikolai Stankevich and inspired by the philosophy of J.G. FICHTE and F.W.J. SCHELLING. Among its members were Mikhail Bakunin, Timofei Granovskii and Konstantin Aksakov (see SCHELLINGIANISM, RUSSIAN §1). In 1833 Nikolai Nadezhdin, Belinskii's professor, engaged him as a collaborator of *Teleskop* (Telescope), a literary journal he had founded in 1831. Belinskii's first major essay, 'Literary Reveries', appeared there in 1834. It was the first of his many surveys of Russian literature and very much under the sway of Schellingian ideas. After the suppression of *Teleskop* in 1836, Belinskii worked, in succession, for *The Moscow Observer* (1838–9), *National Annals* (1839–46) and *The Contemporary* (1846–8). During his only trip abroad in 1847, Belinskii wrote his celebrated 'Letter to Gogol''. He died of consumption in 1848.

During his brief career, Belinskii published a series of annual surveys of Russian literature, scores of major essays and many hundreds of reviews of books on any conceivable subject. Many of his reviews were essays in their own right, for instance, when he would use a book for children as an occasion to expound his views on education. Belinskii correctly recognized every major poet and writer of his age (Pushkin, Gogol', Lermontov, Herzen, Turgenev, Dostoevskii) and dismissed minor lights, even if they were ephemerally successful. He established an approach to literature that saw it as an organic whole of which individual works were a living part.

Belinskii read French, but no other foreign language. However, his friends kept him well informed on recent developments in the West and all the major classics were by then available in Russian translation. Belinskii was reasonably well read in the major authors of the West and regularly responded to recent works of French, English and German literature as they were translated into Russian (Hugo, Janin, Sue, George Sand, Hoffmann, Heine, Walter Scott, Dickens, J.F. Cooper and many others).

2 Evolution of Belinskii's aesthetics

Belinskii's philosophy of art developed under the influence of a series of Western authors, yet always in direct connection with Russian life and the development of Russian literature. Specifically, he experienced, in succession, the stimulating influence of Romantic theories of art and poetry (Fichte, Schelling, the Schlegel brothers); Hegel (after 1837); and the Left Hegelians and French Utopian Socialists (in the 1840s) (see ROMANTICISM, GERMAN §§1–3; HEGEL, G.W.F; HEGELIANISM §§1–3).

Belinskii's conception of the organic nature of the work of art (its idea being to its form as soul to body); his notion of the symbolic nature of all true art (along with a dismissal of allegory and schematism as 'nonart'); and his belief in the cognitive power of art and the prophetic powers of genius were derived from Schelling's *System des transcendentalen Idealismus* (*System of Transcendental Idealism*) (1800). Given in 'The Idea of Art' (1841), Belinskii's famous definition of art as 'the *immediate* contemplation of truth, or thinking in *images*' (1952–9: 584; original emphases), squares with Schelling's: 'Art may be defined as the real representation of the forms of things as they are in themselves – their proper, native forms, then'. Even more closely, it tallies with A.W. Schlegel's definition of poetry as 'expression of thought in sense images'.

In 1837, Belinskii, along with Stankevich and Bakunin (later his collaborator on *The Moscow Observer*), were converted to a Hegelian philosophy of art and history (see HEGELIANISM, RUSSIAN §§2–3). Specifically, Belinskii used a conspectus of Hegel's lectures on aesthetics, which M.N. Katkov had translated for him. The list of Belinskii's positions that may be derived from Hegel is a long one. As early as 1838, in a major essay on Shakespeare's *Hamlet*, Belinskii wrote of works of art as 'a manifestation of the Spirit, [as] a given stage of its consciousness'. Soon enough he developed a thoroughly historicist approach to literature, following the evolution of the Spirit in concrete historical developments. Concretely, Pushkin's verse epic 'Poltava' (1828) he considered anachronistic and hence a failure, because the age of epic poetry belongs to the past. Also quite concretely, Belinskii observed progress in literature, as Lermontov's Pechorin (in *A Hero of Our Time* (1841)) is perceived as an advance from Pushkin's Onegin (in *Evgenii Onegin* (1830)), while Gogol''s prose represents an advance from the poetry of his predecessors.

During his Schellingian period, Belinskii had been inclined towards Romantic ideas. Under Hegel's influence, his critical thought took a decisive turn to realism. (He called it 'poetry of reality'.) Belinskii's Hegelian historicism caused him to place Russia in the position of an emerging nation, which actually caused him to downgrade the achievement of his contemporaries Pushkin and Gogol', crediting the former with having created the formal tools for a literature of the future, the latter with being the first to deal with Russian life in a constructive way, and denying both international stature. He confidently predicted that Russia would make original contributions to world literature in the future. At the same time, Belinskii overestimated the importance of some Western writers, Walter Scott and J.F. Cooper in particular.

Up to 1840, Belinskii interpreted – or misinterpreted – Hegel's dictum, 'All that is rational is real, and all that is real is rational', to mean that Russians had to reconcile themselves to Russia's all too real backwardness, because it was a necessary stage in the nation's rational development. Later he rejected this notion, realizing instead that it was a Russian's moral duty to work for what was perceived as the rational advancement of Russian nationhood. Belinskii followed Hegel in assuming that the World Spirit realized itself in national spirits. In 1846 he polemicized with the critic Valerian Maikov, who had suggested that progress was proportional to an increase of independence from national ties. A Westernizer, Belinskii was also a Russian patriot.

Hegel's influence shows in some specific details, such as the meaning given to the word 'pathos' ('the rich, powerful individual quality in which the substantial movements of the Spirit are brought to life, achieving reality and expression', as defined in Hegel's *Aesthetics*), as it appears in Russian criticism to this day. Belinskii's conception of an ideal expressed through its negation is clearly Hegelian, for example, when he interprets Gogol''s comedy *The Inspector-General* as the presentation of a 'phantom reality' flowing from the irrational, chaotic principle of life and struggling against the emergence of a positive, rational reality ('Woe from Wit' 1840). Hegelian, too, is Belinskii's resolute rejection of both formalism and naturalism in art.

After 1842 Belinskii began to lean towards a Left-Hegelian or Utopian Socialist position, with an emphasis on socialité (*sotsial'nost'*), an overriding concern with social ills and their correction. He now developed the notion that true art is necessarily in step with social progress, in the same sense as he had always taken for granted that art is true to life. Induced by his social and political concerns, Belinskii departed from his previous, Hegelian position that art should be objective and dispassionate. He now suggested that in a 'critical epoch' (a Saint-Simonian term!), such as his own, works with a subjective tendency could play a useful role as catalysts of correct ideas, even if they were not artistically flawless. The practical consequence of this attitude was that Belinskii would now respond approvingly to works he admitted were 'unartistic', but were instrumental in leading the public in the right direction. Such was, for example, Aleksandr Herzen's novel *Whose Is To Blame?* (1847) (see HERZEN, A.I. §1).

3 Art and socio-historical reality

Belinskii thus opened the door to didacticism, moralism and political propaganda in Russian literature (art was to follow soon enough, in the *Itinerant* movement). However, he was himself able to discriminate between the aesthetic merits of a given work and its moral and political virtues. In a way, Belinskii would – and did – eat his cake and have it, too, for he could demonstrate, at least to his own satisfaction, that the works which he loved and respected were, by and large, morally and politically on the right track. When his beloved Gogol' turned reactionary, Belinskii could say, with some justification, that he was no longer the great artist he once was.

Belinskii considered a nation's world of letters (*pis'mennost'*) to be an organic whole, consisting of hierarchically layered, but independent parts: *poesy* (*poèziia*, German *Dichtung*), whose creations of genius reveal the truth of historical progress; *belles-lettres* (*belletristika*) which reduce the insights of poesy to terms readily understood by a broad reading public; and *journalism* (*zhurnalizm*) which applies these insights to the nation's day-to-day concerns.

Belinskii's aesthetic was, like that of his Western influences, an aesthetic of content (German *Gehaltsaesthetik*), meaning that the merits of a work of art were explored proceeding from an analysis of its social, moral, political and historical content, rather than from an analysis of its formal traits (composition, style, language, poetic devices). From the viewpoint of a Kantian aesthetic of form (German *Formaesthetik*), a Belinskiian approach ignores the very essence of art: the expression of aesthetic intuitions through appropriate artistic devices. In 'On the Poet's Calling' (1921), the poet Aleksandr Blok said that Belinskii had done more damage to poesy than Benckendorff, chief of gendarmes under Nicholas I, for the latter's censorship had only temporarily stopped the publication of some works, while Belinskii had induced Russian poets to betray their calling. A negative opinion of Belinskii's role in Russian letters was consistently expressed in the works of the Russian Formalist school of the 1920s (see RUSSIAN LITERARY FORMALISM).

The most telling criticism of Belinskii's method

came from a radical critic who declared himself to be the master's faithful disciple: Dmitrii Pisarev (1840–68) correctly charged that Belinskii had projected his own humane and progressive ideas into works of 'pure art', such as Pushkin's *Evgenii Onegin*, because he wished to make his own progressive ideas agree with his love of Pushkin.

4 Legacy to Russian aesthetic thought

The generation of 'progressive' critics who claimed to be Belinskii's heirs, like Nikolai CHERNYSHEVSKII (1828–89), Nikolai Dobroliubov (1836–61) and Mikhail Saltykov (1826–89), developed the habit of using works of literature as texts for their political sermons (see RUSSIAN MATERIALISM: 'THE 1860S' §3). Belinskii was to some extent responsible for this practice. He interpreted Gogol''s *Dead Souls* or Dostoevskii's *Poor Folk* as indictments of the ills of Russian society and not as works of art, and therefore failed to see their whole depth, but he did base his observations on the text referred to. Later Chernyshevskii would assert that, inasmuch as all literature was inherently 'propaganda', the only thing that mattered was that it propagate the right ideas; Dobroliubov would often simply ignore the text under review; and Saltykov would merely dismiss as irrelevant works that did not clearly state their ideological position.

From a theoretical viewpoint, the right-wing followers of Belinskii's organic aesthetics, such as Apollon Grigor'ev (1822–64) and Fëdor DOSTOEVSKII (1821–81), were closer to his position. They postulated, like Belinskii, that a true artist who would honestly follow the demands of his craft would *eo ipso* find the right content for his creations. But more unequivocally than Belinskii, they would insist that this agreement between art and the truth of life should be reached on art's terms – not those of ideology.

Belinskii was canonized by Chernyshevskii and Dobroliubov as the first of Russia's revolutionary democrats and as a precursor of the revolutionary movement of the 1860s. This happened largely on the strength of his 'Letter to Gogol'', his correspondence, and oral tradition, for his published writings were of course heavily censored. On balance, Belinskii was less radical than his disciples of the 1860s. He did claim, in his 'Letter to Gogol'', that the Russian people were at bottom atheist and anti-Church, but it is also quite clear from his correspondence and his essays on Russian folklore that he was less inclined to fall prey to a populist mystique than the radicals of the 1860s. He was of course passionately opposed to serfdom, but so were even some officials close to the Tsar. He considered the imperial bureaucracy to be a corporation of embezzlers and extortionists, but this was really an open secret: the Tsar himself had heartily guffawed at the first night of *The Inspector-General*. It appears that Belinskii's involvement with Utopian Socialism was a passing one and that his political vistas were rather down-to-earth. He mentions 'enforcement of existing laws' as a reasonable target in 'Letter to Gogol''.

List of works

Belinskii, V.G. (1952–9) *Polnoe sobranie sochinenii* (Collected Works), Moscow: AN SSSR, 13 vols. (Academy edition, with notes and indices.)

—— (1956) *Selected Philosophical Works*, Moscow: Progress. (Contains most of Belinskii's programmatic articles.)

References and further reading

* Blok, A. (1921) 'O naznachenii poèta' (On the Poet's Calling), in *Stikhotvoreniya* (Poems), Leningrad, 1936, 483–6.
Bowman, H. (1954) *Vissarion Belinski, 1811–1848: A Study in the Origins of Social Criticism in Russia*, Cambridge, MA: Harvard University Press. (A solid study of the social aspect of Belinskii's criticism.)
Fasting, S. (1972) *V.G. Belinskij: Die Entwicklung Seiner Literaturtheorie* (V.G. Belinksii: The Evolution of his Theory of Literature), Bergen: Universitetsforlaget. (A meticulous analysis of the development of Belinskii's literary theory; combines attention to Belinskii's Western sources with careful attention to his critical practice.)
Terras, V. (1974) *Belinskij and Russian Literary Criticism: The Heritage of Organic Aesthetics*, Madison, WI: University of Wisconsin Press. (Concentrates on Belinskii's sources and the legacy of his criticism in the nineteenth and twentieth centuries.)

VICTOR TERRAS

BELL'S THEOREM

Bell's theorem is concerned with the outcomes of a special type of 'correlation experiment' in quantum mechanics. It shows that under certain conditions these outcomes would be restricted by a system of inequalities (the 'Bell inequalities') that contradict the predictions of quantum mechanics. Various experimental tests confirm the quantum predictions to a high degree and hence violate the Bell inequalities. Although these tests contain loopholes due to experimental inefficiencies, they do suggest that the assumptions behind the Bell inequalities are incompatible not only with quantum theory but also with nature.

A central assumption used to derive the Bell inequalities is a species of no-action-at-a-distance, called 'locality': roughly, that the outcomes in one wing of the experiment cannot immediately be affected by measurements performed in another wing (spatially distant from the first). For this reason the Bell theorem is sometimes cited as showing that locality is incompatible with the quantum theory, and the experimental tests as demonstrating that nature is nonlocal. These claims have been contested.

1 **Survey**
2 **The Bell inequalities**
3 **Behind the inequalities**
4 **Without the inequalities**

1 Survey

'Bell's theorem' is the generic name for a family of results that restrict the statistics for a certain type of quantum mechanical 'correlation experiment'. This is the sort of arrangement proposed by Einstein, Podolsky and Rosen ('EPR') (1935), where they argue that either quantum mechanics violates a condition of local causality or it is incomplete (see EINSTEIN, A. §5; BOHR, N.). In the experiment a uniform source emits pairs of 'particles' in a special state. The particles then separate, each moving to a distant wing of the experimental apparatus. The separate wings contain devices that can perform any one of several different 'yes/no' measurements; that is, measurements with just two possible outcomes. For the most economical case suppose that in the 'A-wing' there are two possible measurements A or A' and similarly measurements B or B' in the 'B-wing'.

It is important for the analysis that in a given wing no two measurements can be performed simultaneously (technically, that the quantities being measured are incompatible – like position and linear momentum, or spin components in skew directions). A particular run of the experiment then corresponds to a choice of a single A-wing measurement and a single B-wing measurement, allowing four possible runs: AB, AB', $A'B$ and $A'B'$. From the frequencies of outcomes we can gather statistics that govern these runs. For an AB-run, for example, we can calculate the probability $P(A)$ that the A-measurement turns up 'yes', the probability $P(B)$ that the B-measurement turns up 'yes' and the probability $P(AB)$ that both the A and the B measurements turn up 'yes'. (These probabilities suffice to fix the probabilities for 'no' outcomes as well.) In the same way, for other runs we can determine $P(A')$, $P(B')$, $P(AB')$, $P(A'B)$, and $P(A'B')$. The experiment is so designed that $P(A)$, from an AB-run, is the same as $P(A)$ from an AB'-run, and similarly for the other single probabilities. By using sufficiently long runs, we should be able to approximate the probabilities experimentally to any desired degree of accuracy. We can also calculate them from the quantum mechanical state function that governs the pairs emitted from the source (see QUANTUM MECHANICS, INTERPRETATION OF §§1–2).

Bell's theorem shows that under certain assumed conditions these probabilities satisfy a restrictive system of inequalities (the 'Bell inequalities') which, for special states of the pairs, are violated by the probabilities of quantum mechanics. The quantum probabilities have been verified to a high degree in various experimental tests and hence the Bell inequalities are violated. There are loopholes in the tests due to inefficiencies in the detection and pairing of results, but the experiments do suggest that the assumptions behind the Bell inequalities are not only incompatible with quantum theory but also with nature. One of the central conditions on which the derivation of the Bell inequalities depends is a species of no-action-at-a-distance, called 'locality': roughly, the condition that the outcomes in one wing are not immediately affected by measurements performed in the other wing. For this reason, the Bell theorem is sometimes cited as showing that locality is incompatible with the quantum theory, or that nature is nonlocal. These claims have been contested (Fine 1997).

2 The Bell inequalities

For the correlation experiment described above the strongest set of Bell inequalities are these:

$$P(A) + P(B) - 1$$
$$\leq P(AB) + P(AB') + P(A'B) - P(A'B'),$$
$$\leq P(A) + P(B)$$

together with the three permutations of this obtained by interchanging A with A', B with B' and both together. This system has the following purely probabilistic significance. If we are given any four joint probabilities, $P(AB)$, $P(AB')$, $P(A'B)$, $P(A'B')$, and four 'compatible' singles, $P(A)$, $P(A')$, $P(B)$ and $P(B')$, (where 'compatibility' here means that, for instance, the probability for A-values derived from $P(AB)$ is the same as the probability for A-values derived from $P(A)$), then the system of Bell inequalities above are the necessary and sufficient conditions for all of the given probabilities to be derivable from one distribution, $P(AA'BB')$, for all four variables. Put differently, the Bell inequalities are the conditions that the given probabilities can be represented on a classical probability space where all outcomes (even for incompatible measurements) are defined.

These inequalities fail maximally in the case most studied experimentally (for example, by the Aspect experiment that is often cited as decisive (Aspect *et al.* 1982)). Here quantum mechanics assigns 0.5 to all the single probabilities and assigns $P(AB) = P(AB') = P(A'B) = 0.4268$ and $P(A'B') = 0.0732$. The inequality becomes $0 \leq 1.2072 \leq 1$; and so it fails.

There are also cases where several correlations (represented by the joint probabilities) are strict (that is, 0 or 1); for example, where $P(AB') = P(A'B) = 0$, $P(A'B') \neq 0$ and $P(A \text{ or } B) = 1$. Although strict correlations are difficult to acheive in practice, Hardy (1993) has shown how to realize these probabilities, in principle, by means of a simple experimental design. Since $P(A \text{ or } B) = P(A) + P(B) - P(AB)$, we have that $P(AB) = P(A) + P(B) - 1$ and the left side of the Bell inequality reduces to $0 \leq -P(A'B')$. Since probabilities are non-negative, this implies that $P(A'B') = 0$, which contradicts the value assigned.

It is easy to construct a rationale for why a contradiction arises here. Because $P(A'B') \neq 0$, there are runs where B' yields 'yes'. In these runs if A were measured, then, because $P(AB') = 0$, A would show 'no'. But if A were 'no' and B were measured, then B would be 'yes', since $P(A \text{ or } B) = 1$. Hence where B' yields 'yes', if B were measured instead, then B would yield 'yes'. But where B yields 'yes', A' would show 'no' because $P(A'B) = 0$. So, where B' yields 'yes', A' yields 'no'; contradicting $P(A'B') \neq 0$.

Clearly this rationale requires strong assumptions to make the counterfactuals along the sequence $B'A \rightarrow BA \rightarrow BA' \rightarrow B'A'$ mesh just right. Each arrow marks a use of locality, but in addition we need further assumptions that allow for transitivity so that we can transfer the B' value from the far left to the far right. Assumptions of 'counterfactual definiteness' (that for each measurement there is an outcome such that if the measurement were made that outcome would result) and of pre-existing values (that each particle in a wing already possess the value – 'yes' or 'no' – that any measurement in that wing would reveal) have been considered. If locality forbids a measurement in one wing from altering the counterfactually definite or the pre-existing values in the other wing, then the stated rationale goes through. Speaking roughly, we can say the Bell theorem rules out the combination of locality plus determinism. If the result of a measurement is not predetermined, however, but is a matter of chance, corresponding to a random choice of 'yes' or 'no', then it is difficult to vindicate the claim that the assigned probabilities alone conflict with locality.

3 Behind the inequalities

In the general case, a standard rationale for the Bell inequalities involves two assumptions. One is an assumption that forbids a distant change in local probabilities. We can call it 'locality'. The other assumption is not related to locality so clearly; it is that there are no basic correlations between the measurement outcomes in the wings. This is 'factorizability' (other names are 'outcome independence' and 'completeness'). A simple framework for these is to consider an elementary sort of hidden variables ('noncontextual') model for a correlation experiment. In such a model, we introduce a set of parameters 'x' (the hidden variables) that do not depend on any measurements or their results, and let $p(A, x)$ be the probability at x that a measurement of A in the A-wing would produce a 'yes' (similarly for the other single measurements), and let $p(AB, x)$ be the probability at x that both A and B would yield 'yes' (similarly, again, for the other products). The overall probabilities above (the $P(A)$, $P(AB)$, and so on) are to be realized by averaging over the parameters x.

Locality is automatically satisfied in this framework since the situation in one wing (that is, the single probabilities assigned at x) depend only on the measurement to be performed in that wing and on the particular parameter x, which is measurement-independent. (If x is measurement-independent violations of locality require that probabilities at x in one wing depend on measurements made in the other wing, so give rise to a representation like $p(S, x, T)$, where S represents the result of a measurement in one wing and T represents a measurement performed in the other wing. This would be a 'contextual' hidden variables' theory.) *Factorizability* is just the requirement that the joint probabilities factor; that is, that $p(AB, x) = P(A, x)P(B, x)$, which is the condition for stochastic independence at x (similarly for the other products). This condition is equivalent to requiring for each parameter x that measurement outcomes in the two wings are uncorrelated.

It is straightforward to prove the Bell inequality of §2 from these assumptions provided a third condition is satisfied: namely, that each measurement produces, or is likely to produce, a result. Local, factorizable models can be constructed where this condition fails ('prism' models) and these models can accommodate the quantum probabilities and, so far, the statistics of all the experiments. (This is connected with the efficiency loophole mentioned in §1.) Finally, notice that these hidden variables' models are stochastic so that measurement outcomes are governed by probabilities and need not correspond to predetermined values (whether actual or counterfactual). Thus the Bell theorem here does not depend on determinism. On the other hand, it does not rule out locality alone but only the combination of locality and factorizability (given that the third condition holds).

Locality is an intuitively plausible constraint whose violation would in principle allow one to signal between the distant wings instantaneously, provided one could control the parameters x. If those parameters are not controllable, however, and instantaneous signalling is still ruled out, then locality may seem less compelling. (This is the situation in Bohmian mechanics, which is nonlocal but where instantaneous signalling does not occur. See QUANTUM MECHANICS, INTERPRETATIONS OF §3). The rationale for factorizability is much less clear. It seems to represent a feeling that stable correlations need to be explained and that the only acceptable explanation traces correlations to statistically uncorrelated events. A contrasting point of view might accept some correlations as basic, not themselves in need of explanation, and try to account for others on that foundation.

Considerations about correlations are more pointed when the correlations are strict. Where the probabilities are 0 or 1 the stochastic case become deterministic. Locality then is not about affecting probabilities at-a-distance but about affecting values. So if $P(AB' = 0$ (as in §2)) then there are not just statistics to account for but, arguably, the fact that when a measurement in one wing produces a 'yes' the distant measurement always comes out 'no'. Factorizability becomes the requirement that the value at x assigned to the product of physical quantities just be the product of the values at x assigned to each quantity separately; using an obvious notation, that $\mathrm{val}(AB') = \mathrm{val}(A)\mathrm{val}(B)'$. This 'product rule' is studied in another theorem (the Bell–Kochen–Specker theorem) where it is shown to contradict quantum mechanics for certain systems, regardless of the state of the system, if the only values assigned are those allowed by the quantum theory. The product rule has been challenged on the grounds that the quantum theory only requires it in certain very special cases (technically, only in eigenstates of the quantities) and that these alone are not sufficient to produce a contradiction. Bohmian mechanics violates the product rule, as do a host of hidden variables' models, and each of these produce the very same statistical predictions as the quantum theory itself.

4 Without the inequalities

Although the Hardy example of §2 violates the Bell inequality, the rationale for why it gives rise to a contradiction does not involve all the machinery that lies behind deriving the Bell inequalities in general. There are other such 'Bell theorems without inequalities'. One set-up, due to Greenberger, Horne, Shimony and Zeilinger (GHSZ) (1990), involves three systems (labelled 1, 2 and 3) in a certain special state. Imagine these as moving away from a common centre along three straight lines in the same plane. For each system we are interested in yes/no quantities that relate to the vertical (x) and horizontal (y) directions (where z is the direction of motion of the system). So, for example, Q_{x1} is the quantity relating to the x-direction for system 1, Q_{y3} the quantity relating to the y-direction for system 3, and so on. Consider an assignment of values to the various quantities where $x_1 = \mathrm{val}(Q_{x1})$, $y_3 = \mathrm{val}(Q_{y3})\ldots$, then if 'yes' is assigned 1 and 'no' assigned 0, the following system of equations hold

$$x_1 x_2 x_3 = -1$$
$$x_1 y_2 y_3 = 1$$
$$y_1 x_2 y_3 = 1$$
$$y_1 y_2 x_3 = 1$$

since if we add Q to the xs and ys these four equations give the values prescribed by quantum mechanics for the respective product operators. Since $(x_1)^2 = (y_1)^2 = 1$, if we multiply the first two equations we get $x_2 x_3 y_2 y_3 = -1$. If we now multiply the second two we get a contradiction; namely, $x_2 x_3 y_2 y_3 = 1$.

It is clear that the GHSZ example relies heavily on the product rule discussed in §3, extended here to the product of three quantities. Locality enters in the supposition that the same x_1 occurs in the first two equations; for example, that if x_1 were determined by distant measurements of Q_{x2} and Q_{x3}, and if instead we had measured Q_{y2} and Q_{y3}, then the value of Q_{x1} would not be altered. Similar uses of locality underlie the occurrence of the other terms shared between equations. As in the Hardy example, here too locality needs to be supported by further assumptions in order to justify the manipulations that lead to a contradiction.

In all the cases covered by the Bell theorem, simple-looking arguments that seem to overthrow locality are deceptive. Without question, however, the Bell theorem challenges certain features that one might desire, such as the picture of an observer-independent reality that measurement simply reveals (see SCIENTIFIC REALISM AND ANTIREALISM); it challenges them, that is, provided locality too is assumed.

See also: PROBABILITY, INTERPRETATIONS OF; QUANTUM MEASUREMENT PROBLEM

References and further reading

* Aspect, A., Dalibard, J. and Roger, G. (1982) 'Experimental Test of Bell's Inequalities Using Time-varying Analyzers', *Physical Review Letters* 49: 1,804–7. (Frequently cited experimental test of the Bell inequalities, §2.)
* Ballentine, L. and Jarrett, J. (1987) 'Bell's Theorem: Does Quantum Mechanics Contradict Relativity?', *American Journal of Physics* 55: 696–701. (Locality and no-signalling treated for contextual hidden variables; §3.)
* Bell, J. (1987) *Speakable and Unspeakable in Quantum Mechanics*, Cambridge, Cambridge University Press. (Contains most of Bell's important papers, including his version of the Kochen–Specker theorem mentioned in §3.)
* Branning, D. (1997) 'Does Nature Violate Realism?', *American Scientist* 85: 160–7. (Readable account of an optical experiment attempting to realize the Hardy example of §2.)
* Cushing, J.T. and McMullin, E. (eds) (1989) *Philosophical Consequences of Quantum Theory*, South Bend, IN: University of Notre Dame Press. (Readable collection of articles on the Bell theorem representing many different philosophical points of view.)
* * Einstein, A., Podolsky, B. and Rosen, N. (1935) 'Can Quantum-Mechanical Description of Physical Reality be Considered Complete?', *Physical Review* 17: 777–80. (The famous EPR paper referred to in §1.)
* Fine, A. (1982) 'Hidden Variables, Joint Probability and the Bell Inequalities', *Physical Review Letters* 48: 291–5. (Elementary calculations showing the probabilistic content of the Bell inequalities; §2.)
* —— (1996) *The Shaky Game: Einstein, Realism and the Quantum Theory*, Chicago, IL: University of Chicago Press, 2nd edn. (Chapter 4 contrasts Bell with Einstein on locality, and discusses the prism models mentioned in §3. Chapter 9 considers the impact of the Bell theorem on quantum realism.)
* * —— (1997) 'Contextualism, Locality and the No-Go Theorems', in M. Ferrero and A. van der Merwe (eds) *New Developments on Fundamental Problems in Quantum Physics*, Dordrecht: Kluwer, ch. 16. (Contests the claim that nature is nonlocal, §1.)
* * Greenberger, D.M., Horne, M.A., Shimony, A. and Zeilinger, Z. (1990) 'Bell's Theorem without Inequalities', *American Journal of Physics* 58: 1,131–43. (Elementary exposition of the GHSZ theorem of §4.)
* * Hardy, L. (1993) 'Nonlocality for Two Particles Without Inequalities for Almost All Entangled States', *Physical Review Letters* 71: 1,665–8. (The source of the strict correlation example in §2.)
* Kochen, S. and Specker, E.P. (1967) 'The Problem of Hidden Variables in Quantum Mechanics', *Journal of Mathematics and Mechanics* 17: 59–87. (The original of the Kochen–Specker theorem, §3.)
* Mermin, N.D. (1990a) *Boojum's All the Way Through*, Cambridge, Cambridge University Press. (Chapter 12 is an informative elementary account of the Bell theorem.)
* —— (1990b) 'Quantum Mysteries Revisited', *American Journal of Physics* 58: 731–4. (Elementary account of the GHSZ theorem of §4.)
* —— (1993) 'Hidden Variables and the Two Theorems of John Bell', *Reviews of Modern Physics* 65: 803–15. (Comprehensive review of the Bell–Kochen–Specker theorem and recent simplifications, §3.)
* —— (1994) 'Quantum Mysteries Refined', *American Journal of Physics* 62: 880–7. (Elementary account of the Hardy example of §2.)
* Redhead, M. (1987) *Incompleteness, Nonlocality and Realism*, Oxford: Clarendon Press. (Background and details on issues surrounding the Bell theorem.)

ARTHUR FINE

BENEFICENCE *see* HELP AND BENEFICENCE

BENJAMIN, WALTER (1892–1940)

Walter Benjamin was one of the most influential twentieth-century philosophers of culture. His work combines formal analysis of art works with social theory to generate an approach which is historical, but is far more subtle than either materialism or conventional Geistesgeschichte *(cultural and stylistic chronology). The ambiguous alignment of his work between Marxism and theology has made him a challenging and often controversial figure.*

1   Life and works
2   Art: Nietzsche and Marx
3   Symbolism, melancholy and politics
4   Technology
5   History

1 Life and works

Benjamin was born into an affluent family of assimilated Berlin Jews. He wrote his doctorate on *Der Begriff der Kunstkritik in der deutschen Romantik* (The Concept of Art Criticism in German Romanticism), and, in 1925 submitted *Ursprung des deutschen Trauerspiels* (*The Origin of German Tragic Drama*) for the degree of habilitated doctor at the University of Frankfurt. This book is now considered a classic. The application failed, however, and Benjamin abandoned his plans for a university career. After some years as a *feuilleton* journalist in Berlin, during which he met and worked with Bertolt Brecht, Theodor ADORNO and other left-wing intellectuals, Benjamin was forced to flee to Paris in 1933. Under commission from the 'Institute for Social Research' (that is, the 'Frankfurt School' then in emigration in New York), he devoted himself to a major theoretical and historical project on nineteenth-century Paris (the 'Arcades Project'). After a financially and personally precarious decade, he was again forced to flee from the Nazis, and eventually took his own life after crossing the Pyrenees in a vain attempt to reach safety in Spain. Benjamin was little known during his lifetime; since 1955, however, under the stewardship of such erstwhile associates as Adorno, his work has been widely published and translated.

2 Art: Nietzsche and Marx

The agenda for modern aesthetic theory was set by Friedrich NIETZSCHE (§2), who believed that art expressed a realm more fundamental and constitutive than that accessible to the natural sciences. His many followers were happy to invoke such a superior legitimation for the human sciences. They were resisted by Marxists who, while assigning art a place in history, none the less insisted that this history was exclusively political, and that the nature of art was exhausted by determining the side it joined in the political struggle. Art, in other words, was not constitutive even of its own reality, but was merely a 'superstructural' reflection of the political 'base'.

Benjamin inclined by temperament and association towards the Marxists, not least because the most interesting art of the first third of the twentieth century was Marxist, at least by declaration (for example, Soviet Constructivism, Sergei Eisenstein, Brecht and the Bauhaus). It was clear, however, that 'base–superstructure' model of orthodox Marxism could scarcely account for such creativity.

Benjamin's project may be understood as an attempt to uncover the manner in which art engages in spheres describable in the terms of political economy, but autonomously and without adhering to simplistic criteria, such as 'progressive'. By abandoning the Marxist categorization of art as mere epiphenomenal superstructure, then, Benjamin accepts elements of Nietzsche's metaphysics.

3 Symbolism, melancholy and politics

Benjamin's thought runs through two phases. In his earlier work, which included the important essay 'Goethes Wahlverwandtschaften' (Goethe's *Elective Affinities*) (1922) and culminated in *The Origin of German Tragic Drama*, Benjamin is concerned to explore the manner in which art adopts pragmatic stances. His initial target is what he calls the 'symbolist' approach to art: the view, whether asserted by critics or implied by art works themselves, that art makes magical contact with essential structures of reality. It may issue (as it did with GOETHE) in a superstitious fatalism, or (as in certain seventeenth-century dramas) in a naive faith in the capacity of art mimetically to capture God's creation.

Diametrically opposed to this stance is what Benjamin terms 'melancholy', a scepticism about the claims of science and empirical knowledge. The melancholic artist devises allegories and conceits to emphasize their despair at the inaccessibility of God's reality; the Baroque *Trauerspiel* is a typical example of this attitude. However, this is a rash response to the problems of mimetic realism, or 'symbolism', for there is a third possibility available to artists: an interventionist pragmatism. This depends on their ability to perceive their own activities within a wider, political frame. In Benjamin's view, if they can do this, they will 'awaken under the open sky of history'; but the precise nature of interventionist art is something that, in the early work, still remains obscure.

4 Technology

The latter part of Benjamin's work – from the late 1920s onwards – was concerned to delineate with more precision how art assumes a political identity. This was a matter of describing how art manifested itself in the public arena at all, and how it assimilated itself, deliberately or not, to the conflicts dominating that arena. This discussion has two aspects: the theory of technology and the theory of history.

Benjamin's most important essay on art and technology is 'Das Kunstwerk im Zeitalter seiner technischen Reproduzierbarkeit' (The Work of Art in the Age of its Mechanical Reproducibility) (1935). He argues that there is a general tendency away from the 'auratic'. Under more primitive social conditions, art primarily performs a ritual function, for example, a symbolization of the divinity. It has a high 'cultic' value. This, however, goes hand in hand with low public availability; cultic or auratic works of art retain or increase their power by being confined to inaccessible ritual spaces. In the modern era, despite a decline of express ritual, aura is mimicked by high culture, which favours works that can be restricted to an elite (in museums, concert halls and opera houses).

Because this 'auratic' approach evades the issues of contemporary history, however, it scarcely deserves the designation of culture. Proper art has – indeed, has always had – its vehicles for engaging people in general. These are, nowadays, the instruments of mass dissemination. They have two aspects. In the first place, modern art dispenses with the notion of the unique object, invested with auratic magic. Modern art may be reproduced without losing its identity – as one sees in the case of film and photography and in all electronically storable works. In the second place, art loses its finality; it becomes part of a process of revision, testing and provisional application. Brecht's collaborative and plagiarizing treatment of art is one example; the collective contribution necessary for any movie is another. Because of its provisionality, art becomes subject to the interventions of many; and because of that, in turn, it becomes integrated into wider structures of social dynamics, such as politics.

5 History

The theory of history is the topic of Benjamin's last work, 'Über den Begriff der Geschichte' (On the Concept of History) (1940). Just as his aesthetics break with representationalism of orthodox Marxism, so his notion of history turns away from its characteristic faith in progress. The course of history becomes radically disrupted: that is to say, history is understood as being in a permanent state of emergency, where identities emerge only through isolated and contingent acts of struggle. The 'meaning' of history ceases to be theoretically recoverable, and yields only to redemptive recollection. From this perspective, the task of the historian is to cite those struggles for freedom which, by example or analogy, cast light on the conflicts of the present.

Benjamin represents this view as Messianism and thus as a form of theology. It should be noted, however, that the basic model applies also to common-law notions of legal precedent; this important work is not confined to religious realms, but, as with all of Benjamin's writings, has wide and continuing secular relevance.

See also: FRANKFURT SCHOOL §3

List of works

Benjamin, W. (1974–88) *Gesammelte Schriften*, ed. R. Tiedemann and H. Schweppenhäuser, Frankfurt am Main: Suhrkamp.
—— (1922) 'Goethes *Wahlverwandschaften*' (Goethe's *Elective Affinities*), in *Gesammelte Schriften*, vol. 1, 123–202. (A riposte to the conventional hagiographies of Goethe.)
—— (1935) 'Das Kunstwerk im Zeitalter seiner technischen Reproduzierbarkeit' (The Work of Art in the Age of its Mechanical Reproducibility), in *Gesammelte Schriften*, vol. 1, 431–508. (Benjamin's most famous work, and the source of his 'aura' theory. A translation is available in Benjamin (1968).)
—— (1940) 'Über den Begriff der Geschichte' (On the Concept of History), in *Gesammelte Schriften*, vol. 1, 691. (The 'Theses on History' which allegedly document Benjamin's turn from Marxism.)
—— (1968) *Illuminations*, ed. H. Arendt, New York: Fontana. (Contains works useful for a first encounter; the selection is tendentious, however, and the translation unreliable.)
—— (1973) *Understanding Brecht*, London: Verso. (An accessible exploration of Marxist cultural theory.)
—— (1977) *The Origin of German Tragic Drama*, London: Verso. (Benjamin's most challenging work.)

References and further reading

Buck-Morss, S. (1990) *The Dialectics of Seeing. Walter Benjamin and the Arcades Project*, Cambridge, MA: MIT Press. (A useful discussion of Benjamin's major project.)
Marcus, L. and Nead, L. (eds) (1993) 'The actuality of Walter Benjamin', special issue of *New Formations* Summer 20.
Bartram, G. (ed.) (1994) 'Walter Benjamin in the Postmodern', special issue of *New Comparison* Autumn 18.
Roberts, J. (1982) *Walter Benjamin*, London: Macmillan. (An intellectual and personal biography.)

JULIAN ROBERTS

BENTHAM, JEREMY (1748–1832)

Jeremy Bentham held that all human and political action could be analysed in terms of pleasure and pain, and so made comprehensible. One such analysis is how people actually do behave; according to Bentham, seeking pleasure and avoiding pain. Another such analysis is of how they ought to behave. For Bentham, this is that they should maximize utility, which for him is the same as producing the greatest happiness of the greatest number, which, again, is the same for him as maximizing pleasure and minimizing pain. His chief study was planning how there could be a good system of government and law; that is, how laws could be created so that people being as they actually are (seeking their own pleasure) might nevertheless do what they ought (seek the greatest pleasure of all). The instruments which government use in this task are punishment and reward, inducing action by threats and offers. For Bentham, punishment is done not for the sake of the offender, but to deter other people from doing the same kind of thing. Hence on his theory it is the apparent punishment which does all the good, the real punishment which does all the harm.

Bentham thought that the primary unit of significance was the sentence, not the word. He used this idea to produce profound analyses of the nature of law and legal terms, such as 'right', 'duty' or 'property'. These are what he calls names of fictions – terms which do not directly correspond to real entities. However, this does not mean that they are meaningless. Instead, meaning can be given to them by translating sentences in which they occur into sentences in which they do not occur. Thus legal rights are understood in terms of legal duties, because sentences involving the former can be understood in terms of sentences involving the latter; these in turn can be analysed in terms of threats of punishment or, again, pleasure and pain. This gives sense to legal rights, but sense cannot be given in the same way to natural rights. For Bentham, we have no natural rights and the rights that we do have, such as property rights, are created by government, whose chief task is to protect them. Bentham also worked out how people could be protected from government itself, designing an elaborate system of constitutional law in which representative democracy was a central element.

Bentham invented the word 'international', and when he died he had an international legal and political influence. His chief influence in philosophy has been as the most important historical exponent of a pure form of utilitarianism.

1 Life and writing
2 The principle of utility
3 Duty and interest
4 Public reason
5 Fiction and paraphrase
6 Government

1 Life and writing

Writing was the centre of Bentham's life. He shut himself away in remote cottages and even when in London described himself as a 'hermit'. Increasingly, the hermit merely produced large sheets of manuscript, and the task of selecting from these and turning them into books was left to others, such as the young John Stuart MILL, who produced five large volumes of Bentham's thought on evidence from a much larger mass of nearly illegible manuscript. When Bentham died he left 70,000 sheets of foolscap manuscript behind him – theoretical work, but also highly detailed designs for states, prisons, banknotes, and much else. His principal writings on language, ontology and the philosophy of law were only published posthumously.

Jeremy Bentham was born in London on 15 February 1748. He was the son and grandson of lawyers and was educated to follow them making money from the practice of law. However he soon became revolted at the current condition of the law and so, instead of making money from it, devoted the rest of his life to a study of how it could be improved. He started to design a perfect penal code; then diverted to write a criticism of the leading current legal thinker, William BLACKSTONE; then diverted again from the main body of this criticism to write a lengthy refutation of one of Blackstone's digressions. This was published as *A Fragment on Government* (1776). He returned to working on the principles of penal legislation and printed the main part of his introduction to them in 1780. However, seeking to work out the identity conditions for a single law, he became entangled in a 'metaphysical maze' which meant that he had to lay the uncompleted book aside. He buried himself away and produced his main work on the philosophy of law, only published a century after his death. The work laid aside was finally published in 1789 as *An Introduction to the Principles of Morals and Legislation*. It had a new preface, but it was neither complete in itself nor accompanied by the worked-out penal code to which it was meant merely to be the introduction.

Since the *Introduction* and the *Fragment* are Bentham's two best known works, it is worth noting that they are both parts of much larger uncompleted works. The *Fragment* is a fragment, the *Introduction* an introduction, and much of his most profound thought of the time, if it gets in at all, only makes the footnotes. They are also both relatively early works. However they do have the advantage, unlike most of what followed, that they were published by Bentham himself rather than by one of his disciples.

While the *Introduction* lay fallow, printed but not

published, Bentham switched into writing in French with the hope of interesting Catherine the Great of Russia in his proposals for legal reform. He visited Russia, where his brother was living, and found a suitably remote cottage. He wrote on the principles of a civil code and of reward. Yet even when Catherine was near, he remained in his seclusion and failed to exert any influence. On his return to England he finally published the *Introduction*. However, it was the year of the French Revolution; public attention was elsewhere; and the work was half consumed by rats. Bentham bombarded the new French revolutionary government with proposals which had no effect beyond his being created an honorary citizen of their new republic. Then, in the chief diversion of his life from writing, he turned his attention to pushing the British government for a contract to build and manage a panopticon prison.

The idea of the panopticon, a circular building in which the unseen overseer in the centre would observe the inmates, derived from Bentham's brother in Russia. At first Bentham wrote about it relatively light-heartedly as a 'simple idea in architecture' which would solve all manners of different problems (such as allowing Turkish seraglios to be run with fewer eunuchs) (Bentham 1791). Editions of the work were printed in Dublin and Paris. A circular prison was built in Edinburgh. However, when Bentham tried to obtain a contract from the British government to manage the country's prisoners, matters became much more serious. He bought the iron and other materials, nearly ruined himself, and energetically lobbied the government for permission to build his 'mill for grinding rogues honest'. Several times in the 1790s it looked as if he would succeed; but the project was effectively over by 1803 (although not completely killed until 1813).

While Bentham was trying to get his panopticon contract, Etienne Dumont was working on his manuscripts. In 1802 Dumont produced the three volumes which first made Bentham's name, the *Traités de législation civile et pénale* (1802). Dumont moved on to editing other Bentham manuscripts, while Bentham returned to full-time production of the supply. In the 1800s Bentham wrote on economics, evidence and judicial organization. In the next decade he expanded into logic, language, ontology, and criticisms of the religious and legal establishment. His central concern became constitutional law. He offered to draft constitutional codes for all nations, and worked hard on the ideal code. This and pamphleteering for a more democratic government were his chief concerns in the 1820s. His reputation was now established. Newly created countries consulted him. Dumont's work was translated into English. A team of disciples produced other work from the manuscript. The *Fragment* and the *Introduction* were republished in second editions. A Benthamite journal was founded. His place in philosophy was secured, his influence being transmitted most of all by J.S. Mill, who was as a young man a great admirer and Bentham editor, and who arranged meetings of the younger utilitarians in Bentham's house. Bentham died in London on 6 June 1832.

2 The principle of utility

Both in the *Fragment* and the *Introduction* Bentham calls his central normative principle the 'principle of utility'. Utility provides the 'standard of right and wrong'. 'By the principle of utility', he says in the *Introduction* (I 2), 'is meant that principle which approves or disapproves of every action whatsoever, according to the tendency which it appears to have to augment or diminish the happiness of the party whose interest is in question'. Utility is therefore to be understood in terms of happiness; and the *Fragment* starts with the famous formula, declared as an 'axiom', that 'it is the greatest happiness of the greatest number that is the measure of right and wrong'. This formula reappears in his late work, and is stated in the *Constitutional Code* (1830), as the proper end of government. In this later work Bentham came to prefer 'the greatest happiness principle' as the best description of his central principle. However, in spite of Bentham's preference, the term 'utility' has stuck, and Bentham is normally thought of as a utilitarian. Indeed the prescient young Bentham dreamed once that he founded a 'sect of utilitarians'.

He founded a sect, but neither utility nor happiness originate with Bentham. They were plucked from the surrounding Enlightenment air. Bentham says that he used 'utility' because of Hume, and the famous 'greatest happiness' formula appears in the Italian legal theorist Cesare Bonesana Beccaria, whom Bentham much admired. Originality was not the point; indeed the more agreed, or hackneyed, the statement of the final goal was, the better. Bentham's purpose was to work out in detail the means by which this goal could be achieved.

The greatest happiness is therefore the appropriate end of action. The next question is whose happiness. The famous formula says 'of the greatest number'; but this could render the formula indeterminate between recommending that the greatest happiness be achieved and recommending that the greatest number get happiness. In fact Bentham makes it clear that he always means the former: happiness is to be maximized whomever it may belong to. He therefore occasionally recommends omitting the 'of the greatest number' part of the formula, noting that otherwise the slight pleasures of a majority would count more than the severe pains of a minority.

'Pleasure' and 'pain' seem to introduce yet more alternative sources of value. However this promiscuous use of terms does not for Bentham indicate any diversity or conflict of values. For him these terms are all convertible. He says in the *Introduction* (I 3) that 'benefit, advantage, pleasure, good, or happiness' all 'come to the same thing' as also do their opposites, 'mischief, pain, evil, or unhappiness'. 'Interest' is also to be understood in these terms; something is in someone's interest when it tends to increase their pleasure. Bentham's is a monistic and consequentialist system of value. There is only one ultimate value, although it may have different descriptions, and actions should be done so as to bring about those states of affairs which have most of this value.

Bentham usually takes the proper aim of government to be concern with the greatest happiness of the people composing the country for which it is the government. This is less than all the people there are, which is the standard universalistic sense given to the ground principle of utilitarianism. This might be taken as a merely practical recommendation, so that Bentham is still supposed to have universal happiness as his end but is taken to be claiming that this is best achieved if every government restricts itself to maximizing the happiness of its own people. Or it could be taken, as David Lyons (1973) holds, to be explicitly intended by Bentham as a necessary feature of his brand of utilitarianism.

Another claim of Bentham's would, conversely, give his principle a wider scope than the standard utilitarianism. For, as he puts it in the *Introduction* (XVII 4.n), 'the question is not, Can they *reason*? nor, Can they *talk*? but, Can they *suffer*?' So Bentham's utilitarianism goes beyond people and extends to all sentient creatures; animals also count.

In these statements of Bentham's ground principle there is constant use of the word 'tend'. Hence application of them inevitably has a generalizing effect. The precise utilities which follow on a single occasion of action are not as important as the general tendencies of that kind of action.

3 Duty and interest

At the start of chapter one of the *Introduction* (I 1), Bentham says that we are under the 'governance of two sovereign masters, *pain* and *pleasure*', and adds, 'it is for them alone to point out what we ought to do, as well as to determine what we shall do'. Two different things are involved here. On the one hand there is a standard of right and wrong determining what people ought to do. On the other hand there is a psychology of human action determining what they will actually do. Bentham is writing for legislators who have the task of bringing about the goal of maximizing happiness while working with people as they actually are. The legislator needs therefore to understand both the goal and also how people are; both value theory and psychology. These are both treated in the *Introduction*, but much more space is devoted to psychology than to value theory. Its central idea is that people seek their own happiness. Preventing pain and providing pleasure are the ways in which people, as they actually are, can be influenced in their actions.

'The state', says Bentham, 'has two great engines, *punishment* and *reward*' (*Introduction*: XVI 18). This does not mean that they have to be used. Follower of Adam SMITH, Bentham realized that the desired end could often be achieved by leaving people alone to get on with their lives. So his chief economic prescription to the legislator is 'be quiet'. He even out-Smithed Smith in an early work, *The Defence of Usury* (1787), arguing against Smith's claim that interest rates should be controlled. However, interference is not ruled out in principle. It all depends upon what is needed to maximize happiness. Bentham was prepared, for example, to allow the control of corn prices in times of starvation; and he believed that relief of extreme poverty should be the concern of the state rather than being left to private charity.

People are moved in many ways. Bentham (1776, 1789) lists the 'sanctions', as he calls them, which operate on them. The central one he is concerned with, the great engines of punishment and reward, he calls the 'political' (sometimes 'legal') sanction. There is also the 'moral or popular' sanction, which is Bentham's name for public opinion. Then there is the religious sanction, the force exerted by God's displeasure. These are the only ones mentioned in the *Fragment*, but Bentham brings it up to four in the *Introduction* by adding the 'physical' sanction: purely natural processes which influence behaviour (such as the pain of falling out of a window). Later he added the 'sympathetic' sanction, where people are moved merely by the pleasures and pains of others, but which he thinks is much weaker than the others.

If people are going to do the right thing under the operation of one of these other sanctions, the legislator does not need to interfere with them by use of the political sanction. The legislator may, however, seek to strengthen the other sanctions by what Bentham calls 'indirect legislation' – for example, by education. Sometimes, however, more direct action is required. In spite of the non-political sanctions, people seeking their own pleasure sometimes cause greater unhappiness to others and so diminish overall happiness. Then the legislator has to interfere, deploying the political sanction, and threatening punishment. By having a code of criminal law, which announces in advance the kinds of penalties that are attached to particular kinds of behaviour, the legislator changes the payoffs. Self-interested people who might otherwise have done these things are now deterred by the threat of punishment.

For Bentham all punishment is a pain. It is therefore, for him, an evil. Its justification is therefore indirect: it is a present harm done so that good may come (rather like drilling a tooth to prevent future toothache). In fact, as Bentham points out, it is the apparent pain which does all the good, the real pain which does all the harm. So if people could only appear to be punished, this would be even better. Punishment is not done for the sake of the offender, as in retributive theories, but for the future benefit of others. The amount of punishment is accordingly fixed as the minimum amount which is necessary to deter a sufficient number of similar actions by others; it does not depend directly on the seriousness of the offence.

The legislator can only calculate this amount with knowledge of psychology – that is, of how a typical individual calculates the value to themselves of a portion of pain or pleasure. Bentham thinks that the chief factors involved are, in his words, intensity, duration, certainty (or probability), and propinquity. That is, as well as obvious facts like the length or unpleasantness of punishment, the deterrent effect also depends on how imminent the threatened punishment is and how likely someone is to be caught.

Bentham developed this psychology in his *Civil Code* writings (1802), where he laid down what he calls 'axioms of mental pathology' (this is part of the material that was first published by Dumont in the *Traités*). Crucial among these is that equal increments of a good do not produce equal increments of happiness. In other words, the utility produced by goods diminishes at the margin. Therefore, other things being equal, happiness is maximized by an equal distribution of goods.

When Bentham moved on to design of prisons and poorhouses, and eventually to constitutional law, the root idea was similarly to distinguish between the *is* and the *ought* of human action, and then make them work together. The idea is, as he puts it in his work *Pauper Management Improved* 'to make it each man's interest to observe on every occasion that conduct which it is his duty to observe' (II iv. 2), which Bentham calls the 'duty and interest junction principle'. Similarly, the ground idea of the *Constitutional Code* is to construct a system of political offices, such that each office can be occupied by purely self-interested people who will nevertheless be led to behave as they ought to behave if the system as a whole is to deliver good government (that is, promote the greatest happiness).

4 Public reason

Both the prisoners in the panopticon and the guard in the centre will be led to behave well by the force of publicity. Publicity solves the old problem of who is to guard the guards. The same applies in the *Constitutional Code*, where a central role is given to what Bentham calls the 'public opinion tribunal'. Similarly, judges are to be forced to give public reasons for their decisions. This, he thinks, leads to better law.

So far, this is deployment of the 'popular' sanction. 'The eye of the public', as Bentham puts it, 'makes the statesman virtuous' (1843, vol. 10: 145). But it is also centrally connected with Bentham's espousal of his chief evaluative principle. For he thinks that only utility (and its cognates) are appropriate for use in such public justification. In the utility chapter of the *Introduction* (I 2) Bentham allows that 'that which is used to prove everything else, cannot itself be proved'; but he does add some considerations designed to make people 'relish' the principle of utility. Chief among these is that there would not otherwise be any public standards of justification; anyone's opinions would be worth just as much or as little as anyone else's; and this would be 'despotical' if someone imposed them, 'anarchical' if not. In other words, unless all argument is to be 'at an end', utility must be taken as the standard. Only utility can be used in public reasoning.

Bentham puts this as a way of giving a 'meaning' to 'the words *ought*, and *right* and *wrong*, and others of that stamp' (I 10). His concern, here and elsewhere, is to give meaning; to clarify; to make things comprehensible. The chief justification of his foundational evaluative principle is that, by connecting *right* and *wrong* with pleasure and pain, it gives them public meaning.

5 Fiction and paraphrasis

Bentham carries his clarificatory mission into the centre of the law. His aim is that the central legal terms, such as 'right', 'duty', or 'property', should be understood. To make something clear for Bentham is to connect it with perception. These legal terms are names of what he calls fictional entities; and fictional entities are understood by connecting them with perceivable real entities like pleasure and pain.

For terms like 'duty' or 'obligation' Bentham invented the technique he called paraphrasis, most fully described in his *Essay on Logic*. For Bentham the primary unit of meaning is the sentence rather than the word, and he uses this insight to relate the tricky legal terms to perception. They do not themselves refer to things that can either be perceived or directly inferred from perception. However, Bentham's proposal is that if the difficult term is placed in a sentence, the whole sentence may then be given meaning by being translatable into another sentence the words of which can be more easily understood.

Armed with his technique of paraphrasis, Bentham accordingly analyses fundamental legal terms. Rights, for example, are analysed in terms of duties. That is, a sentence about rights, such as 'John has a right to wear his coat', can be translated into a sentence about duties, such as 'Everyone has a duty not to prevent John wearing his coat'. We are now still in the realm of fiction. But Bentham proceeds to the analysis of duty. Someone is said to be under a duty when they are threatened by punishment for non-performance. But the threat of punishment is the threat of pain. So, at last, we reach pain, an immediate object of experience; the law has been clarified and made comprehensible to all. As he puts it in the Preface to the *Fragment*, '*pain* and *pleasure*, at least, are words which a man has no need, we may hope, to go to a Lawyer to know the meaning of'.

For Bentham, rights are the benefits created by the imposition of duties. He analyses the varying kinds of rights according to the different kinds of duties, and in an embryonic deontic logic brings out the different connections between obligation and permission. Thus analysis of fictions (such as Bentham conducts in his *Of Laws in General* (1970)) gives clarification. The point of calling them 'fictions' is not to designate them as merely imaginary items which can be disregarded. Such things (ghosts; the pagan gods) Bentham calls, by contrast, 'fabulous' entities. Legal rights and obligations have what he calls a 'verbal' reality, and the paraphrastic analysis shows what this consists in: if I disobey a (verbally real) obligation, then I am liable to real pain.

Bentham holds that fictions are necessary for the use of language, yet he also sometimes uses 'fiction' in a merely pejorative way to stigmatize something as merely imaginary; so care has to be taken as to which use he intends on a particular occasion. He is being merely pejorative in the *Fragment* when he talks of the supposed original contract, which was meant to justify political obligation, as the 'sandy foundation of a fiction', or when he talks of 'pestilential breath of Fiction' poisoning the operations of law. In these cases he is talking about what he calls the lies of lawyers – of justification on the basis of purely imaginary happenings.

Bentham's account of natural rights illustrates both his techniques of analysis and this problem. 'From *real* laws come *real* rights', he says, 'from *imaginary* laws come imaginary ones' (1973 – *Anarchical Fallacies* conclusion). Natural rights are just fictions. But, it might be objected, since all rights are fictions for Bentham, why can natural rights not also be given a meaning by paraphrastic analysis? The answer is as follows. Since (sentences about) rights can be analysed in terms of (sentences about) duties, the problem is not with natural rights, as such. They can be analysed in terms of natural duties. The problem is with the next step, where duties are analysed in terms of threats of pain (punishment). With the supposed natural duties there is, for Bentham, no such threat. There is no legislator. As he puts it in *Supply without Burthen* (1795), 'a natural right is a son that never had a father' (1952, vol.1: 334).

For Bentham, people talking of natural rights are really saying that they wished that there were (real, political) rights. But, as he says, 'want is not supply; hunger is not bread'. Even worse, for him, is when people suppose, as did the framers of the French *Declaration of the Rights of Man and of the Citizen*, that such rights are unalterable (imprescriptible). As Bentham famously puts it, 'natural rights is simple nonsense, natural and imprescriptible rights, rhetorical nonsense, nonsense upon stilts' (1973 – *Anarchical Fallacies* art. II).

6 Government

So, in Bentham, for real rights we need real laws. We need government. The argument for the states and for government is therefore straightforward: they confer the benefits we gain from the possession of rights. Of these benefits the chief, for Bentham, is security; and hence the principal task of government is to provide for the security of individuals. Possessing security, they can plan ahead in confidence, realize their plans, and increase their happiness. Bentham's main concern is to protect areas in which individuals may maximize their own utilities rather than having a government that constantly interferes to promote happiness. In this sense he is on the side of liberty – although this is a liberty which is only produced by government and does not predate it in the way that supposed natural liberty would.

Property is included by Bentham under security. Again, it is the creation of law and does not predate it. This means that Bentham avoids the problems about taxation or obedience to the state which philosophers run into when they start with natural rights to property. With John LOCKE we get an original contract argument for government, whereby people antecedently having property contract into government. Bentham mocks such arguments in the *Fragment*. For him justification of obedience is a matter of utilitarian calculation, of whether the 'probable mischiefs of obedience are less than the probable mischiefs of resistance' (I 43). Analogously, there are no problems about taxation. Government creates property and it can remove the property it creates.

As well as security, Bentham lists three other 'subordinate ends' of government in the *Civil Code*: subsistence, abundance, and equality. The utilitarian argument for equality was noted above; and both subsistence and abundance are naturally positively correlated with utility. They are therefore appropriate goals for the legislator, although it should be noted that this emphasis upon subordinate ends shows Bentham's indirect utilitarian aspect: the legislator protects security or provides subsistence rather than directly promoting utility. Security easily outranks the others, being thought by Bentham a necessary condition for their achievement.

When Bentham was writing the *Civil Code* he was happy to appeal to enlightened dictators to get his legal proposals put into effect. However he came to realize that the chief power against which people need security is the power of government itself. Hence his turn in his later writings to the construction of a constitutional code; and hence also his turn to democracy.

The argument for democracy follows simply from the central principles outlined above. Since, by the principle guiding human action, people tend to act in their own interest, so also do governors. Kings look after the interests of kings; oligarchs after the interests of the oligarchy; and so on. Yet the proper end of government is not just a sectional but a general interest. It is general happiness. The solution is to make the governors as far as possible the people themselves. The greatest happiness of the greatest number is safest in the hands of the greatest number. Merely by following their own interest, in accordance with the chief factual principle, they will also promote the general interest, in accordance with the chief evaluative principle.

The kind of democracy promoted is representative democracy. Bentham distinguishes between 'constitutive' and 'operative' powers. The people as a whole are to be the supreme constitutive power, electing governments and having final authority. But they elect, and can dismiss, the operatives. The operatives have to be controlled. Hence the *Constitutional Code*.

As before, the guards are to be guarded. Politicians are to be forced by all the available sanctions so that, acting merely selfishly, they in fact promote general happiness.

See also: DEMOCRACY; HAPPINESS; LAW, PHILOSOPHY OF; MILL, J.S.; UTILITARIANISM

List of works

Bentham, J. (1843) *The Works of Jeremy Bentham*, ed. J. Bowring, Edinburgh, 10 vols. (The original collected edition, gradually being replaced, but still the source for *Essay on Logic* and *Essay on Language*, both in volume 8.)
—— (1776) *A Fragment on Government*, Cambridge: Cambridge University Press, 1988.
—— (1789) *An Introduction to the Principles of Morals and Legislation*, London: Athlone Press, 1970.
—— (1791) *The Panopticon Writings* London: Verso, 1995. (A selection which also contains *Fragment on Ontology*; the complete *Panopticon* writings are only in Bentham (1843).)
—— (1802) *Traités de législation civile et pénale*, Paris; greater part translated in J. Bentham, *The Theory of Legislation*, London: Kegan Paul, 1932.
—— (1817) *Chrestomathia*, Oxford: Oxford University Press, 1983. (Appendix 4 contains considerable material on language and fictions.)
—— (1830) *Constitutional Code, Vol. 1*, Oxford: Oxford University Press, 1983.
—— (1952) *Jeremy Bentham's Economic Writings*, ed. W. Stark, London: Allen & Unwin. (Contains *Defence of Usury* and *Supply without Burthen*, mentioned in the main text, as well as other economic writings.)
—— (1970) *Of Laws in General*, London: Athlone Press.
—— (1973) *Bentham's Political Thought*, ed. B. Parekh, New York: Barnes & Noble. (Wide selection of useful extracts edited from the original manuscript, including the *Anarchical Fallacies*.)

References and further reading

Harrison, R. (1983) *Bentham*, London: Routledge. (General introduction to all the philosophical aspects of Bentham.)
Hart, H.L.A. (1982) *Essays on Bentham*, Oxford: Oxford University Press. (Essays on Bentham's philosophy of law; moderately difficult.)
Kelly, P.J. (1990) *Utilitarianism and Distributive Justice*, Oxford: Oxford University Press. (Uses the *Civil Code* material to argue for an indirect utilitarianism account of Bentham.)

Long D. (1977) *Bentham on Liberty*, Toronto Ont.: University of Toronto Press. (Particularly full on the not yet published early manuscript material.)
* Lyons, D. (1973) *In the Interest of the Governed*, Oxford: Oxford University Press, revised 1991. (Innovative reading of Bentham claiming that he held that people should seek particular rather than the universal interest.)
Postema, G. (1989) *Bentham and the Common Law Tradition*, Oxford: Oxford University Press. (A fuller account than the title suggests. A central problem considered is Bentham's thought about legal adjudication.)
Rosen, F. (1983) *Jeremy Bentham and Representative Democracy*, Oxford: Oxford University Press. (Accessible description of Bentham's later political thought, including the *Constitutional Code*.)

ROSS HARRISON

BENTLEY, RICHARD (1662–1742)

A towering figure in the history of textual criticism, Bentley's importance in the development of English philosophical thought rests on both public and private achievements. His great public contribution was made in the first Boyle lectures of 1692. In private, his correspondence with Newton sought the great man's blessing on the arguments and opinions advanced in these lectures, persistently questioning him on the possibility of a natural origin for the universe and on the role and nature of gravity in physics in general. Bentley's influence helped to establish the Newtonian consensus dominant in Europe until the end of the nineteenth century.

Richard Bentley was born into an English family of modest means in Oulton, Yorkshire. He entered St John's College, Cambridge in 1676. He later came under the patronage of Bishop Stillingfleet and served as tutor to his family. He took holy orders, his scholarly eminence resulting in a rapid rise to the post of Keeper of the Royal Libraries and election to the Royal Society in 1694. For an advocate of religion as a source of peace and concord, Bentley managed to provoke a great deal of acrimony. A famous dispute with Oxford scholars regarding the relative merits of the Ancients and the Moderns led to his great work of textual criticism – *Dissertation on the Epistles of Phalaris* – demolishing the claims to authenticity of the epistles of 'Phalaris'. In 1699 he became Master of Trinity College, Cambridge, a post he retained until his death. His despotic rule was not to the liking of the Fellows, whose unsuccessful efforts to remove him involved two trials before the Bishop of Ely.

The annual courses of lectures endowed by Robert BOYLE became the main public forum for the exposition and defence of the Newtonian world picture as a basis for latitudinarian natural religion (see LATITUDINARIANISM). Bentley gave the first series in 1692. The picture of a rationally ordered universe, in which the designing and maintaining hand of God could be discerned, was presented as a model for a rationally ordered social universe, providentially arranged for our delight and wellbeing. This happy state of affairs would be much facilitated, Bentley implied, if we followed the teachings of the Anglican 'broad church' party. According to Bentley (1692 vol. 3: 13), 'Religion itself gives us the greatest delights and advantages even in this life also, though there should prove in the event to be no resurrection to another'. It is significant that Bentley entitled his lectures *The folly and unreasonableness of atheism* (1692).

Bentley singled out gravity as peculiar evidence of the direct and arbitrary action of a wise creator. In an exchange of letters he pressed NEWTON on the role of gravity in the origin of the universe as we now observe it, and the possibility of a purely mechanical explanation of the origin of the material world. In his response of 10 December 1692 to Bentley's first letter Newton expresses a firm commitment to the principles of natural religion: 'I had an eye,' he says, 'upon such Principles as might work with discerning men for the belief of a Deity' (Turnbull 1961). Bentley realized that the clumping of matter into discrete material bodies out of a primeval atomic chaos by any natural force, such as universal gravity, was implausible when the extremely low density of such a state was considered. Newton's first response was to distinguish between the general problem of the condensation of matter and particular difficulty of the separation of 'shining' matter into stars and 'opaque' matter into planets, without, as he says, the work of 'a voluntary Agent'. Bentley expressed his general point as follows: 'No Quantity of common Motion could ever cause those straggling Atoms to convene into great masses' (Letter of 18 February 1692); so there could be no natural explanation for the origin of the solar system. This provoked Newton's famous reply: 'Gravity must be Caused by an Agent acting constantly according to certain laws, but whether that agent be material or immaterial I leave to the consideration of my readers' (Letter of 25 February 1692). We can hardly doubt what he expected their opinion to be!

Of all Newton's followers it was above all Bentley

and Samuel CLARKE who made the Newtonian point of view available to an extensive lay audience, and, indeed created the Newtonian consensus which dominated English and later Continental thought for more than a century.

See also: COLLINS, A. §2

List of works

Bentley, R. (1838) *The works of Richard Bentley*, ed. A. Dyce, London. (These volumes are mainly concerned with his scholarly controversies. *The Dissertation on the Epistles of Phalaris* is found in volume 1, pages 75–430 and volume 2, pages 1–181.)

—— (1692) *The folly and unreasonableness of atheism*, London. (A comprehensive survey of the evidence for God's existence from human psychology and biology and from physics.)

References and further reading

Jacob, M.C. (1976) *The Newtonians and the English Revolution: 1689–1720*, Hassocks: Harvester Wheatsheaf. (A detailed account of the interactions between religious controversy, social theory and science in the seventeenth century.)

Turnbull, H.W. (1961) *The correspondence of Isaac Newton*, vol. 3, Cambridge: Cambridge University Press. (In this volume are collected letters to Locke, Huyghens, Leibniz as well Bentley and others, 1684–93.)

ROM HARRÉ

BERDIAEV, NIKOLAI ALEKSANDROVICH (1874–1948)

Nikolai Berdiaev, Russian religious idealist, was one of many non-Marxist thinkers expelled from Russia by communist authorities in 1922. Although attracted to Marxism in his youth, even then he tempered it with a Neo-Kantian ethical theory. Well before the Bolshevik Revolution, he became seriously disenchanted with Marxist philosophy (though not with the idea of socialism) and embarked on the career of elaborating a personalistic Christian philosophy that occupied him for the rest of his life.

Dubbed 'the philosopher of freedom', Berdiaev wrote prolifically on that subject and on related topics in metaphysics, philosophy of history, ethics, social philosophy and other fields (but not epistemology, which he rejected as a fruitless exercise in scepticism). Because his approach to philosophy was admittedly anthropocentric and subjective, he accepted the label 'existentialist' and acknowledged his kinship with Dostoevskii, Nietzsche and (to a lesser degree) Jaspers. Like them, he constructed no philosophical system, though he did expound views that were coherently interrelated in the main, if impressionistically and sometimes obscurely expressed. Among his more prominent ideas were his conception of freedom (for which he was indebted to the mystical philosophy of Jakob Boehme), his distinction between spirit and nature, his theory of 'objectification', his doctrine of creativity and his conception of time.

The most frequently translated of twentieth-century Russian thinkers, Berdiaev has been widely studied in the West since the 1930s, particularly in schools of religion and theology and by philosophers in the existentialist and personalist traditions. Although many Western readers considered him the voice of Russian Orthodox Christianity, his independent views drew fire from some Orthodox philosophers and theologians and also from strongly anti-Soviet Russian émigrés. His writings in emigration were eagerly embraced in his homeland once they could be published there, beginning in the late 1980s.

1 Life and works
2 Metaphysics
3 Philosophy of history
4 Ethics
5 Social and political philosophy

1 Life and works

Nikolai Aleksandrovich Berdiaev was born into an aristocratic family in 1874 near Kiev. A student of law at the University of Kiev, he was expelled in 1898 for his activity in radical student circles; this marked the end of his formal education, except for a semester of study with Wilhelm Windelband at Heidelberg in 1903. In 1900 Berdiaev, along with other members of the Social Democratic Party in Kiev, was banished to the northern province of Vologda. Philosophically, like many Russian thinkers of his generation, the young Berdiaev sought to complement Marxist socioeconomic views with Kantian transcendental idealism, and this effort is evident in his first philosophical book, *Sub"ektivizm i individualizm v obshchestvennoi filosofii* (Subjectivism and Individualism in Social Philosophy) (1901).

Allowed to return to Kiev in 1903, Berdiaev moved in the following year to St Petersburg and in 1908 to Moscow, where he became prominent in the lively cultural world of Russia's 'Silver Age'. The first decade of the century was a period of intense spiritual searching for Berdiaev as for many others; under the influence of a great range of thinkers, including Schopenhauer, Nietzsche, Vladimir Solov'ëv, Vasilii Rozanov, Fëdor Dostoevskii, Lev Tolstoi and Dmitrii Merezhkovskii (see RUSSIAN RELIGIOUS-PHILOSOPHICAL RENAISSANCE), he moved from Neo-Kantian Marxism (though without abandoning his socialist convictions, as we shall see in §5) to the religiously oriented, mystically coloured personalism that he would continue to elaborate throughout his life. His writings of the period 1907–11 may be considered transitional. It was not until 1916, in *Smysl tvorchestva* (The Meaning of Creativity) (his last philosophical book published in Russia), that Berdiaev provided a comprehensive account of the chief principles of his new worldview. This work, which Berdiaev in his autobiography called his most significant book, exhibits the impact of a major influence on his mature outlook – the mysticism of Jakob Boehme.

Berdiaev welcomed the Russian Revolution of February 1917, but he was opposed to the policies of the Bolsheviks, who seized power in October. Despite that opposition, he was able to take an active part in the cultural life of Moscow during the first years of communist rule. In 1919 he founded the Free Academy of Spiritual Culture, and in 1920 was named Professor of Philosophy at Moscow University. In 1922, however, Berdiaev and more than 100 other prominent non-Marxist intellectuals were abruptly stripped of their positions and required to leave the country, prohibited from returning on pain of death.

After a stay in Berlin, in 1924 Berdiaev with his family joined the growing Russian émigré community in Paris. He taught at the Russian Religious-Philosophical Academy there, an institution he had first organized in Berlin with the assistance of the Young Men's Christian Association (YMCA) of North America; he founded and edited (1925–40) the religious-philosophical journal *Put'* (The Way); and he served as editor-in-chief (1924–48) of the YMCA-Press in Paris, the principal publishing outlet for émigré Russian religious philosophers.

Berdiaev won worldwide fame with his book *Novoe srednevekov'e* (The New Middle Ages) (1924), which was translated into a dozen languages. He continued to develop various aspects of his philosophical outlook in many subsequent books, also widely translated, until his death in 1948 at his home in Clamart, a suburb of Paris.

2 Metaphysics

In keeping with his existentialist orientation, Berdiaev defines 'metaphysics' not as the study of reality in general but as 'the philosophy of human existence', and he contends that this philosophy is not 'objective' but 'subjective'. In calling it subjective he means to indicate both that its focus is the subject and that it is not a sphere of demonstrable, impersonal truth. 'Truth and reality', he writes, 'are not identical with objectivity' ([1937b] 1952: 17). Yet, as this statement itself indicates, he does not reject truth or reality, and his worldview, however subjectively conceived, is in fact phrased as a general theory of reality for which truth is implicitly claimed. This theory was set forth most fully in his 1947 book, *Opyt ėskhatologicheskoi metafiziki* (An Essay in Eschatological Metaphysics).

Berdiaev was willing to call his doctrine a form of dualism, but not a dualism of idea versus matter or divine versus human. Rather, he opposes *dukh* ('spirit', both divine and human) to *priroda* ('nature') or *byt'ë* ('being'), although he also frequently uses the latter word to signify reality in general. Spirit is the realm of freedom, personality and creative activity; nature is the realm of necessity, objects, routine and passivity. Berdiaev likens this dualism to the Kantian distinction between noumena and phenomena: the spiritual (noumenal) realm has primacy over the realm of nature (the phenomenal realm), in that it alone is truly 'real' and fully independent of the other (see KANT, I. §3). Unlike Kant, however, Berdiaev did not regard the world of spirit as unknowable (except for the ultimate mystery of the one perfect spirit, God); he considered it accessible through intuitive – essentially, spiritual and mystical – experience, which is the only true foundation for a philosophical system. Rational knowledge of the world of 'nature', on the other hand, is 'objective' knowledge, which has no philosophical value.

Berdiaev links God, human spirits and the objectified world of nature in a philosophical cosmology based on a controversial interpretation of the Christian idea of divine creation *ex nihilo*. Drawing on Boehme's mystical doctrine of the primitive Ungrund ('the groundless') that underlies all reality (see BOEHME, J.), Berdiaev contends that the 'nothing' out of which God creates the world is not sheer emptiness but a positive potentiality, which he also calls 'meonic freedom' – a volitional, irrational, formless, creative potency or energy that is metaphysically prior not only to the world but to God the creator. God creates himself out of this irrational freedom, overcoming it in his own nature through his perfection. But in proceeding to create human beings out of the *Ungrund* as well, he produces creatures whose irrational freedom is neither generated nor controlled by him. Thus when humans misuse their freedom by choosing evil, God is not implicated in the choice; indeed he does not even have foreknowledge of it. Berdiaev valued this doctrine as providing an explanation of evil within a theistic philosophy; but for abandoning the metaphysical primacy and the omnipotence and omniscience of God, he was severely criticized by Russian philosophers who adhered more closely to traditional Orthodox theological doctrine.

The ability of the free human spirit to choose evil is also invoked by Berdiaev in his idealist account of the genesis of nature. The realm of objects is produced not by God but by the fallen human subject: 'the subject is the creation of God while the object is the creation of the subject' ([1947] 1952: 17). The proud individual subject, intoxicated by freedom, creates the world of exteriority by separating itself from God and other spirits. The subject engages in what Berdiaev calls 'objectification' (*ob"ektivatsiia*) – a process of self-alienation in which a spirit gives itself and others an objectified form as part of a system of external substances and relations. Characterized by division, disintegration, materiality and necessity, this system functions to enslave the very subject that created it. Although Berdiaev frequently speaks of this objectified world of nature as phenomenal – a realm of 'appearances' – he also calls it ontologically real, albeit of a lower order of reality. By this he apparently means that nature, once created by the objectification of spirit, is truly 'objective' as an independently subsisting force, not simply an imaginary one. He regards the overcoming of objectification in the name of freedom as the daunting but imperative task of the human spirit.

3 Philosophy of history

Human history, as Berdiaev explains it (primarily in *Opyt èskhatologicheskoi metafiziki* and in his 1923 *Smysl istorii* (*The Meaning of History*)), is a temporal process connected with the creation and conquest of objectification. History begins with the Fall. The dividedness or exteriority of the objective world that is generated by the sinful use of human freedom is manifested not only spatially but temporally, in the separation of past, present and future. The flow of time in the objective world may be viewed in two ways, according to Berdiaev: either cyclically, as an endless repetition of natural processes operating independently of human thought or action (he calls this *cosmic* time, symbolized by a circle), or linearly, as an unrepeatable succession of events involving human agency (this is *historical* time, symbolized by a line).

Berdiaev argues eloquently against interpreting the historical process as progressive, for 'progress' as he understands it signifies that existing generations of people are regarded simply as means for improving the lot of those to come. Berdiaev used this moralistic, Kantian condemnation of the idea of progress (anticipated by his Russian predecessor Nikolai FËDOROV) to great effect in his attack on Russian communism as a quintessential case of treating existing human beings as raw material for the production of a better future. At the same time, Berdiaev's philosophy is strongly eschatological, and he argues that history would be meaningless if it had no termination and if objectification were not overcome. In his eyes the ultimate horror, adding moral crime to meaninglessness, would be a conception of history as *endless progress* – the perpetual instrumentalization of one generation after another with none ever becoming an end in itself.

The 'end of history', or conquest of objectification, postulated by Berdiaev takes place not in historical time but in time of still a third type, which he calls *existential*. This is the time of the free, creative act, and he symbolizes it by a point; it is durationless and integral. The creative act in existential time manifests itself as essentially an irruption of 'meta-history' into history, of the spiritual plane of eternity into the objectified world of historical time. One such irruption of great significance was the Incarnation, but in fact every creative act at any historical moment in the 'divine–human' process of redemption is a victory of spirit over nature and freedom over necessity. Berdiaev incorporates in his eschatology such traditional Christian concepts as the Kingdom of God, paradise, hell, universal resurrection (it must be universal, or some persons would not be valued as ends in themselves) and immortality, but in keeping with his notion of existential time he interprets these concepts as referring not to future events or conditions but to timeless and purely spiritual presences. Paradise and immortality are accessible to the creative spirit at any (historical) moment.

Berdiaev's reasoning concerning the overcoming of objectification through creativity appears to be that since the succession of events in historical time is itself a product of objectification, the annulment of the latter cannot be considered an event in that succession but must occur in another temporal dimension – the extrahistorical dimension he calls 'existential'. But this conception raises further questions that Berdiaev does not answer unequivocally. Commentators on his philosophy are divided as to whether the 'overcoming' of objectification requires that historical time literally come to an end or simply that it be rendered insignificant. In either case, if the 'end of history' is located outside historical time, that would appear once again to deprive history *per se* of meaning.

4 Ethics

The issue of the impact of creativity on the world is encountered once again in Berdiaev's personalistic ethics, which ascribes supreme value to the individual spirit and identifies moral action with the creativity that combats and ultimately defeats the objectification produced by the Fall. His mature ethical views were first suggested in *Smysl tvorchestva* and were developed most fully in his widely read book *O naznachenii cheloveka* (On the Destiny of Man) (1931).

Berdiaev distinguishes three stages in the development of moral consciousness, each of which gives rise to a corresponding type of ethics. Earliest and lowest but still most widespread is the ethics of *law*, which subjects individuals to abstract norms of behaviour in the name of social order. Morality at this pre-Christian level is negative and impersonal, and it is based on the distinction between good and evil – a distinction that is itself part of the objectification created by the Fall. Berdiaev concedes that the ethics of law is a social necessity in a fallen world, but argues that it is far from adequate to the developed moral consciousness.

A higher, Christian stage is marked by what Berdiaev calls the ethics of *redemption*, which speaks to the individual rather than the group and offers as its standard of value not an abstract law but the figure of a loving, all-forgiving saviour. This ethics of Christian love correctly acknowledges the Incarnation and redemption as elements in divine creation and in the transfiguration of the objectified world. But it, too, is flawed, according to Berdiaev: it can degenerate into 'transcendental egoism', an exclusive concern for one's own salvation.

The highest stage of the moral consciousness is reflected in the more advanced Christian ethics of *creativity*, in which human beings, as free spirits, transcend the good–evil distinction through unique and unrepeatable acts that bring novelty into the world. In responding freely in this way to God's command to overcome evil, the individual person becomes a co-creator of the universe. Human creators are 'beyond good and evil' in the sense that they, undetermined by social standards or any other form of objectification, define the moral sphere through personal decisions. At this highest level, morality and creativity are effectively coextensive for Berdiaev: 'the moral act is a creative act [and]…all creation has moral significance, even if it is the creation of cognitive or aesthetic values' ([1937b] 1952: 20–1). 'The creator is justified by his creative achievement' ([1931] 1935: 130).

To the critic who would charge Berdiaev with Nietzschean egoism here, he responds that it is precisely in creative acts that individuals are the most selfless, since all energies are focused on the acts and their products. Berdiaev denies, too, that the genuine creator would seek to wound or dominate other people: the free person recognizes that no one should be treated as a mere means. This continued appeal to the Kantian principle, however, suggests that Berdiaev is, after all, admitting a universal moral law to which individuals must conform – a suspicion furthered by his acceptance of 'conscience' as 'the organ of perception of the religious revelation, of goodness, righteousness and truth in its entirety' ([1931] 1935: 167). Berdiaev is also criticized for 'deifying' human beings; Sergei Levitskii (1975) and Piama Gaidenko (1994) argue that in glorifying human powers Berdiaev is forgetting the gulf that separates flawed and finite humanity from divine perfection.

The most widely debated feature of Berdiaev's philosophical outlook is the redemptive value he attributes to creativity in its dual capacity of giving meaning to history and expressing the highest morality. In both contexts, the value of creativity hinges on its effectiveness in overcoming objectification. But inasmuch as human creators are concerned with their 'products' and must operate in the external world (Berdiaev acknowledges that, unlike God, they require material other than 'meonic freedom'), they cannot escape the dead hand of objectification: 'every expression of creative action in the external [world] falls into the power of that [objectified] world' ([1939] 1943: 127). Thus, in the 'irruption' of existential time into historical time, creativity participates in the succession of historical events and is enmeshed in the very objectification it sets out to avoid. Berdiaev himself calls this situation 'tragic': 'It is the tragedy of creativeness that it wants eternity and the eternal, but produces the temporal and builds up culture which is in time and a part of history' ([1931] 1935: 136). V.V. Zenkovsky (1948–50) and some other critics contend that on Berdiaev's principles the creative act is not merely tragic but meaningless and futile; Fuad Nucho (1966) and others reply that creativity retains spiritual value despite its tragic character.

5 Social and political philosophy

Berdiaev's first book (1901) was devoted to social and political philosophy, and the subject figures prominently in virtually everything he wrote, including his last, posthumously published book, *Tsarstvo dukha i tsarstvo kesaria* (*The Realm of Spirit and the Realm of Caesar*) (1949b). In most of his mature works dedicated to the subject, such as *Filosofiia neravenstva* (The Philosophy of Inequality) (1923a), the critique of

Russian communism is a principal concern. Two works – *The Origin of Russian Communism* (1937a) and *Russkaia ideia* (The Russian Idea) (1946) – include extensive critical discussion of the history of Russian social and political thought.

In using the term 'nature' for the world of objectification opposed to spirit, Berdiaev does not mean to exclude *social* factors from the objectifying forces that enslave personality; indeed, it is the objectifying power of society above all that he sees as a threat to freedom. He protests against the depersonalizing processes in which the self is moulded by objectified social relationships and comes to be considered a part of society rather than an independent bearer of value. The great error of Marxist communism and all forms of collectivism is that they view humanity as simply a product of society, determined by social laws, and consequently have no regard for personal freedom. As early as 1906, Berdiaev predicted that the Bolshevik Party in Russia would produce a society united by force, ruled by an unlimited and 'deified' state (1906: 536).

At the same time, Berdiaev believed that individualism is as much a threat to personality as collectivism is, since setting the person *apart* from others is no less a form of objectification. In this regard Berdiaev retained what he called 'a soft spot' for Marxism; he shared Marx's abhorrence of 'bourgeois', capitalist society as alienating and dehumanizing. A critic of the free market economy and of claims to an absolute right of private ownership, Berdiaev at times found points of agreement with Soviet ideology; in entertaining (especially during and immediately after the Second World War) the possibility that Soviet rule might become more benign, he incurred the wrath of much of the Russian émigré community.

In opposition to both collectivism and individualism, Berdiaev offered his own 'personalistic socialism' – a form of free sociality having much in common with the older Russian ideal of *sobornost'* (see SLAVOPHILISM §3). Personality, as a spiritual category, he argues, is not only free but universal, and as such is inherently social in the sense of requiring others for its fulfilment. To achieve the fullness of personal being, the individual must be in communion with other individuals, where 'communion' signifies a complete but fully voluntary union based on love. It is in this essentially spiritual sense of 'socialism' that Berdiaev can affirm that a Christian not only may but must be a socialist.

Berdiaev's hostility towards all established ('objectified') social arrangements – whether totalitarian or democratic – prevented him from spelling out 'personalistic socialism' beyond such broad descriptions of its aim as 'a synthesis of the aristocratic, qualitative principle of personality with the democratic, socialist principle of justice and brotherly cooperation' ([1937b] 1952: 20). The state as such appears to have no role in effecting such a synthesis, for Berdiaev views every political structure as an impediment to the realization of personality; he expresses no preference, for example, for a constitutional state based on the rule of law over a totalitarian state. Because he regards the state and law as essentially parts of the objectified world that must be vanquished, his political philosophy amounts to a form of anarchism.

See also: EXISTENTIALISM; EXISTENTIALIST THEOLOGY; NEO-KANTIANISM, RUSSIAN §5; NIETZSCHE: IMPACT ON RUSSIAN THOUGHT §2

List of works

Berdiaev's principal works are listed here in order of their initial publication; since 1988 most of them have been reprinted in Russia, many with new editorial commentary and some in more than one edition.

Berdiaev, N. [Berdyaev] (1901) *Sub"ektivizm i individualizm v obshchestvennoi filosofii. Kriticheskii étiud o N.K. Mikhailovskom* (Subjectivism and Individualism in Social Philosophy: A Critical Study of N.K. Mikhailovskii), St Petersburg: Popova. (Berdiaev's first book, in which he sought to complement Marxist socioeconomic views with Kantian transcendental idealism.)

—— (1906) 'Sotsializm, kak religiia' (Socialism as Religion), in *Voprosy filosofii i psikhologii* (Problems of Philosophy and Psychology) 85: 508–45; trans. M. Schwartz, in B.G. Rosenthal and M. Bohachevsky-Chomiak (eds), *A Revolution of the Spirit: Crisis of Value in Russia, 1890–1924*, New York: Fordham University, 1990, 107–33.

—— (1907) *Novoe religioznoe soznanie i obshchestvennost'* (The New Religious Consciousness and Society), St Petersburg: Pirozhkov.

—— (1911) *Filosofiia svobody* (Philosophy of Freedom), Moscow: Put'.

—— (1916) *Smysl tvorchestva. Opyt opravdaniia cheloveka* (The Meaning of Creativity: An Essay in the Justification of Man), Moscow: Leman & Sakharov; trans. D.A. Lowrie, *The Meaning of the Creative Act*, New York: Harper & Bros, 1955. (Berdiaev's last philosophical book in Russia.)

—— (1923a) *Filosofiia neravenstva. Pis'ma k nedrugam po sotsial'noi filosofii* (The Philosophy of Inequality: Letters to Opponents on Social Philosophy), Berlin: Obelisk; trans. C. and A. Andronikof, *De l'inégalité*, Lausanne: Éditions l'Age d'Homme, 1976. (A critique of Russian communism.)

—— (1923b) *Smysl istorii. Opyt filosofii chelovecheskoi sud'by* (The Meaning of History: An Essay in the Philosophy of Human Destiny), Berlin: Obelisk; trans. G. Reavey, *The Meaning of History*, London: Geoffrey Bles, 1936.

—— (1924) *Novoe srednevekov'e. Razmyshlenie o sud'be Rossii i Evropy* (The New Middle Ages: Reflections on the Destinies of Russia and Europe), Berlin: Obelisk; trans. D. Attwater, *The End of Our Time*, New York: Sheed & Ward, 1933. (The book which won Berdiaev worldwide fame.)

—— (1927–8) *Filosofiia svobodnogo dukha. Problematika i apologiia khristianstva* (Philosophy of the Free Spirit: Christianity's Problems and Apologia), Paris: YMCA-Press, 2 vols; trans. O. Clarke, *Freedom and the Spirit*, London: Geoffrey Bles, 1935.

—— (1931) *O naznachenii cheloveka. Opyt paradoksal'noi ėtiki* (On the Destiny of Man: An Essay in Paradoxical Ethics), Paris: Sovremennye zapiski; trans. N. Duddington, *The Destiny of Man*, London: Geoffrey Bles, 1935. (Here Berdiaev's mature ethical views are developed most fully.)

—— (1934) *Ia i mir ob"ektov. Opyt filosofii odinochestva i obshcheniia* (The Self and the World of Objects: An Essay in the Philosophy of Solitude and Community), Paris: YMCA-Press; trans. G. Reavey, *Solitude and Society*, London: Geoffrey Bles, 1938.

—— (1937a) *The Origin of Russian Communism*, trans. R.M. French, London: Geoffrey Bles. (Originally published in translation; the Russian text was first published in 1955 as *Istoki i smysl russkogo kommunizma* (The Sources and Meaning of Russian Communism), Paris: YMCA-Press.)

—— (1937b) 'Die Philosophische Weltanschauung N.A. Berdiaeffs (Selbstdarstellung)' (The Philosophical Worldview of N.A. Berdiaev (Self-Exposition)), in *Philosophen-Lexicon: Handwörterbuch der philosophie nach personen*, Berlin: Walter de Gruyter; repr. in *'Berdiaeff, Nicolei'* (1949) 1: 102–8, ed. W. Ziegenfuss; 1st Russian edn, 'Filosofskoe mirosozertsanie N.A. Berdiaeva (Avtoizlozhenie)' in *Vestnik Russkogo studencheskogo khristiankogo dvizheniia* (1952) 4/5: 15–21. (A text, first published as a German translation, in which Berdiaev summarized his own views in an unusually systematic fashion.)

—— (1939) *O rabstve i svobode cheloveka. Opyt personalisticheskoi filosofii* (On Slavery and the Freedom of Man: An Essay in Personalist Philosophy), Paris: YMCA-Press; trans. R.M. French, *Slavery and Freedom*, London: Geoffrey Bles, 1943.

—— (1946) *Russkaia ideia. Osnovnye problemy russkoi mysli XIX veka i nachala XX veka* (The Russian Idea: Basic Problems of Russian Thought of the Nineteenth and Early Twentieth Centuries), Paris: YMCA-Press; trans. R.M. French, *The Russian Idea*, London: Geoffrey Bles, 1947. (Includes extensive critical discussion of the history of Russian social and political thought.)

—— (1947) *Opyt (skhatologicheskoi metafiziki. Tvorchestvo i ob"ektivatsiia* (An Essay in Eschatological Metaphysics: Creativity and Objectification), Paris: YMCA-Press; trans. R.M. French, *The Beginning and the End*, London: Geoffrey Bles, 1952. (Sets forth a general theory of reality.)

—— (1949a) *Samopoznanie. Opyt filosofskoi avtobiografii* (Self-Knowledge: An Essay in Philosophical Autobiography), Paris: YMCA-Press; trans. K. Lampert, *Dream and Reality*, London: Geoffrey Bles, 1950. (Because of abridgment and other editorial changes, the English translation is untrustworthy; translations into many other languages exist.)

—— (1949b) *Tsarstvo dukha i tsarstvo kesaria*, Paris: YMCA-Press; trans. D.A. Lowrie, *The Realm of Spirit and the Realm of Caesar*, London: Gollancz, 1952. (Social and political philosophy figures prominently in Berdiaev's last, posthumously published book.)

References and further reading

Ermichev, A.A. (1994) *N.A. Berdiaev: Pro et contra. Antologiia* (N.A. Berdiaev: Pro and Contra: An Anthology), book 1, St Petersburg: Russkii khristianskii gumanitarnyi institut. (A collection of memoirs and critical studies by a long list of distinguished Russian contemporaries; includes reprints of Berdiaev [1937b] 1952 and Levitskii 1975; contains bibliography.)

* Gaidenko, P.P. (1994) 'The Philosophy of Freedom of Nikolai Berdiaev', in J.P. Scanlan (ed.), *Russian Thought after Communism: The Recovery of a Philosophical Heritage*, Armonk, NY: M.E. Sharpe, 104–20. (Referred to in §4. A post-Soviet Russian critique of Berdiaev's philosophy with special reference to social and political questions.)

Klépinine, T. (1978) *Bibliographie des oeuvres de Nicolas Berdiaev*, Paris: YMCA-Press. (A well-organized bibliography of almost 500 works by Berdiaev; contains a detailed chronology of his life.)

* Levitskii, S.A. (1975) *'Berdiaev: prorok ili eretik?'* (Berdiaev: Prophet or Heretic?), in *Novyi zhurnal* (New Journal) 119: 230–53. (Referred to in §4. A

critical assessment of Berdiaev's philosophy, field by field.)

Lowrie, D.A. (1960) *Rebellious Prophet: A Life of Nicolai Berdyaev*, New York: Harper & Bros. (A general biography by a long-time associate; contains bibliographies.)

* Nucho, F. (1966) *Berdyaev's Philosophy: The Existential Paradox of Freedom and Necessity*, Garden City, NY: Doubleday. (Referred to in §4. A sympathetic analysis of Berdiaev's philosophy of freedom; contains bibliographies, including an annotated bibliography of the philosopher's principal writings.)

* Zenkovsky, V.V. (1948–50) *Istoriia russkoi filosofii*, Paris: YMCA-Press, 2 vols; 2nd edn 1989; trans. G.L. Kline, A History of Russian Philosophy, vol. 2, London: Routledge & Kegan Paul and New York: Columbia University Press, 1953, 760–80. (Referred to in §4. Exposition and critique of the philosophy of Berdiaev by the authoritative historian of Russian philosophy.)

JAMES P. SCANLAN

BERGSON, HENRI-LOUIS (1859–1941)

So far as he can be classified, Bergson would be called a 'process philosopher', emphasizing the primacy of process and change rather than of the conventional solid objects which undergo those changes. His central claim is that time, properly speaking and as we experience it (which he calls 'duration'), cannot be analysed as a set of moments, but is essentially unitary. The same applies to movement, which must be distinguished from the trajectory it covers. This distinction, he claims, solves Zeno of Elea's paradoxes of motion, and analogues of it apply elsewhere, for instance, in biology and ethics.

Bergson makes an important distinction between sensation and perception. He repudiates idealism, but claims that matter differs only in degree from our perceptions, which are always perfused by our memories. Perception free from all memory, or 'pure' perception, is an ideal limit and not really perception at all, but matter. Real perception is pragmatic: we perceive what is necessary for us to act, assisted by the brain which functions as a filter to ensure that we remember only what we need to remember. Humans differ from animals by developing intelligence rather than instinct, but our highest faculty is 'intuition', which fuses both. Bergson is not anti-intellectualist, though, for intuition (in one of its two senses) presupposes intelligence. He achieved popularity partly by developing a theory of evolution, using his élan vital, *which seemed to allow a role for religion. In ethics he contrasted a 'closed' with a (more desirable) 'open' morality, and similarly contrasted 'static' with 'dynamic' religion, which culminates in mysticism.*

1 Life
2 Time and duration
3 Bergson and Zeno
4 Process philosophy
5 Metaphysics and philosophy of mind
6 Humour
7 Science and metaphysics: the *élan vital*
8 Morality and religion

1 Life

Bergson was born in Paris on 18 October 1859 with a musician as father and a mother from Yorkshire. He married Louise Neuberger, a relative of Proust, and had one daughter. After teaching in Angers, Clermont-Ferrand and Paris, he held a chair at the Collège de France from 1900 to 1921, where his lectures before the First World War attracted so many people that it was seriously proposed to move them to the Opéra. After the war, interest in his lectures declined and he turned from academic teaching (though only partly from writing) to promoting international understanding as a prophylactic against war. Fiercely patriotic, he died at France's darkest hour on 3 January or 4 January 1941, after seventeen years of crippling arthritis, and after supporting his fellow Jews by refusing an offer of exemption from anti-Semitic regulations; the same sympathy may have stopped him officially adopting the Catholic religion, to which in later life he became spiritually close (despite having his books placed on the Index in 1914).

Bergson was a man of wide intellectual attainments. At seventeen he won first prize in an open mathematical competition and also solved a problem left unsolved by Pascal. His subsidiary degree thesis (written in Latin) dealt with Aristotle on place, and he lectured on Lucretius. He devoted several years to a detailed study of the literature on aphasia, in connection with memory, and similarly used detailed scientific evidence to support his views on evolution. He was also a great stylist and his books can stand beside those of Berkeley, Russell and the early Plato as among the more readable works of philosophy.

2 Time and duration

The core of Bergson's philosophy, which, as he

pointed out in a letter of 1915 (1972: 1148), every account of his philosophy must start from and constantly return to, on pain of distortion, is the 'intuition of duration'. Time, for Bergson, is of two fundamentally different kinds, or better, especially for his later philosophy, appears in two fundamentally different guises. For science, time is essentially particulate. It consists of an infinite, dense set of instants, and science uses the calculus to study the world as it is at these instants. Change is nothing over and above the world's being in different states at different instants, and the transition from one state to another is something science can take no account of except by using the calculus in this way. (This interpretation of the role of the calculus for Bergson has been disputed: see Milet 1974.) For experience, however, this transition is the very essence of time, now called duration (*durée*). We do not live from moment to moment, but in a continuous stream of experience (the similarity to William James' 'stream of consciousness' is unsurprising, given the close personal and professional friendship between Bergson and James, who reached their views independently).

One might wonder why change should not consist simply in being in different states at different instants, provided the instants form a dense set, so that no two are adjacent (a feature Bergson unfortunately ignores in his favourite image of time as cinematographic). Bergson's reply, that this overlooks the phenomenology of experience, surely has merit, and helps to solve several problems. We experience the immediate past, and possibly the immediate future, along with the present, as actual, and we can perhaps avoid objections that have confronted James' independently developed 'specious present' if (with Bergson) we avoid treating the act of experiencing as itself separate and momentary. But be that as it may, Bergson can avoid Augustine's problem that time vanishes because only the present is actual and the present does not last long enough to be real at all. He also need not worry about how we acquire a concept of the past when experience only ever presents us with the present.

However, problems do arise. Duration is introduced as essentially linked to consciousness; but does duration exist in the outer world? Bergson's first major book *Essai sur les données immédiates de la conscience* (Time and Free Will) (1889) states unambiguously that it does not, but his next book *Matière et mémoire: Essai sur les relations du corps avec l'esprit* (Matter and Memory) (1896) does allow duration to the outer world, as do his later works. The change of view was well motivated, for how could a consciousness embedded in duration live in a world devoid of it? Science still treats the world as cinematographic, and so now falsifies it, but inevitably and harmlessly, so long as we do not expect from science more than it can give; it is for metaphysics, using 'intuition', to describe the world philosophically, but only science can give us our indispensable practical understanding of the world. Bergson, however, never seemed conscious of a real change of view, and in his much later *La pensée et le mouvant: essais et conférences* (The Creative Mind) (1934) talks simply of *Matter and Memory* as getting nearer to what he wanted to say. Nor did he ever satisfactorily explain the extent to which duration is bound up with consciousness.

Bergson's treatment of time and duration invites comparison with McTaggart's B-series and A-series respectively. McTaggart wrote in 1908, after Bergson's main treatments, but Bergson's later writings show no knowledge of him. In McTaggart's terms Bergson would be a thoroughgoing A-theorist, especially from *Matter and Memory* onwards (see McTaggart, J.M.E. §2).

Discrete plurality for Bergson is essentially spatial, and time with its multiplicity of moments is duration spatialized. This contrast between space and genuine time (duration) introduces an asymmetry between space and time which puts Bergson at odds with recent philosophy (which tends to treat them alike), and assimilates him in this respect to older philosophers such as the Greeks. One of his favourite examples for illustrating duration is a melody, which we can only hear as a melody if we hear it as a whole. Critics have pointed out that, similarly, we can only see a circle by seeing it as a whole (Boudot 1980: 349), and have claimed that in order to distinguish space and time Bergson uses a distinction between the psychological and the mathematical that applies within space and time equally (Berthelot 1913: 354–5). The critics are somewhat justified, though Bergson does in a lower key distinguish space from extensity, and could perhaps thereby deal with the circle. But the critics do scant justice to the real asymmetries between space and time in terms of directions and 'flow' which support Bergson's general approach (see Time §1).

3 Bergson and Zeno

The ideas so far outlined provide Bergson with a tool which he uses first to deal with Zeno's paradoxes of motion, but then goes on to apply in other spheres, such as biology and ethics. This tool is the distinction between a movement and its trajectory. The reason that Zeno's Achilles never overtakes his tortoise is that Zeno insists on applying to the movement, which occurs in time, the infinite process of division that really only applies to the trajectory, which is spatial (see ZENO OF ELEA §7). The movement is essentially unitary and indivisible. This gives the spirit of Bergson's views, though only as a rough approximation: evidently Achilles' movement does have parts – his steps – and it is these that have no parts. But Bergson never seems to succeed in giving adequate criteria for deciding just when a movement is unitary and so has no parts.

The use of this tool in other spheres begins with the treatment of free will in *Time and Free Will*, where it joins a sort of dialectical device that Bergson repeatedly employs: the insistence that two antagonistic approaches that together dominate a philosophical topic share a common error, though he often admits that his own view lies nearer to one pole than to the other. On free will, the poles are determinism and libertarianism, and the error, as so often, amounts to replacing a movement by its trajectory. Bergson's own view, that a free act will proceed from the self alone and 'express the whole of the self' ([1889] 1990: 165–6), is nearer to libertarianism, but the libertarian, insisting that the agent 'could have done otherwise', shares with the determinist the view that the trajectory is already there before the action and that it makes sense to imagine a replay, stopping the action halfway through, as it were, and sending it off on a different course. His point seems to be that there is no 'halfway through' at which the action could be stopped; the process flowing from deliberation to completed action (the doing, as opposed to the things done) is unitary and indivisible (see FREE WILL §1–2).

4 Process philosophy

Process philosophy is a philosophical tradition which goes back as far as Heraclitus, and if Bergson can be placed in any tradition, it is in this, despite his repudiation of allegiance to Heraclitus. Process philosophy stands in opposition to the tradition stemming from Aristotle's scheme of categories, where the world consists of substances which have properties and undergo change. For process philosophy the world consists of processes, and Bergson often says things like, 'There are changes, but there are underneath the change no things which change... movement does not imply a mobile' ([1934] 1946: 173). Objects are like 'snapshots' of a flux, which is duration. This echo of the cinematographic approach of science illustrates another feature of Bergson: his pragmatism. He does not deny that language (itself a pragmatic device for dealing with the world) uses the Aristotelian apparatus of subject and predicate, but we see the world in terms of objects which change because that is the only way we can act in it, just as science gives us our only way of manipulating it.

5 Metaphysics and philosophy of mind

This pragmatism appears again in Bergson's philosophy of mind, which, as we might expect from the way in which he links duration to consciousness, is itself closely linked to his metaphysics. He repudiates idealism, and begins the introduction to the 1911 edition of *Matter and Memory* by calling himself a dualist, 'affirming the reality of spirit and the reality of matter'. But his dualism is not 'vulgar'. It can be called a dualism of time and space (it is tempting to call it one of movement and trajectory), but from another point of view it could be called one of perception and memory, terms which he constantly contrasts as differing in kind, not in degree.

But though matter and spirit are both real, they differ only in degree, and here we reach a central part of Bergson's metaphysics, and also his epistemology, for our knowledge of the world is essentially bound up with the nature of the world itself. Bergson is one of the few philosophers to distinguish clearly between sensation and perception. We cannot start with sensations, treated as unextended and inside ourselves, and somehow turn them into perceptions telling us of an extended outer world, just as we cannot get a concept of the past by starting from a momentary present, and treating memories simply as weaker ('fainter', as Hume would say) sensations or perceptions. Bergson's target here is the associationism that underlies so much of eighteenth- and nineteenth-century empiricism, and his criticisms are of fundamental importance, whether or not his own view also faces difficulties.

Although officially dualist, Bergson's view is somewhat akin to the 'neutral monism' of William James and others (see JAMES, W. §6; NEUTRAL MONISM). Though perception differs in kind from memory, it essentially involves it in varying degrees. Our perceptions are always affected by our experience, and if we had no memories we would have no real perceptions – another important criticism of Humean empiricism. Perception takes place not inside us but where its object is, and a perception unmediated by memory, and in that sense a 'pure' perception, is an ideal limit, and not really perception at all; it 'is really part of matter'. In effect it is the object itself, or rather, since it now lacks duration, it is what we might now describe as a momentary time-slice of the object.

Bergson's pragmatism reappears here: we perceive what we need to perceive in order to act (we might think this more obviously true in the case of animals), and the function of the brain is to filter memories so that only those enter consciousness which are of practical use, notably in perceiving; he used his study of aphasia to argue that the brain cannot be used as a storehouse for memories. Superficially, his treatment of memory involves an excessively crude dichotomy between picture-memory and habit-memory, but he was not concerned with many of the problems that interest later thinkers.

6 Humour

Le rire: essai sur la signification du comique (Laughter: An Essay on the Meaning of the Comic) (1900), probably Bergson's most popular book, can be seen as an appendix to his philosophy of mind and body. For him, a human being is a creature who is both body and spirit (to avoid too intellectual a term: see §7) and uses its body for practical purposes. But sometimes the body takes over and we act as though we were simply a body, either obeying only physical laws – when we slip on a banana-skin, for instance – or when our actions become wooden, mechanical, automatic or stereotyped. It is then that others laugh at us and we have the makings of comedy, low or high. Bergson also gives laughter a function, as a social corrective (his target has something in common with Sartre's 'bad faith'). 'A humorist is a moralist disguised as a scientist' (1900: 128).

7 Science and metaphysics: the *élan vital*

Bergson distinguishes three cognitive faculties: intelligence, instinct and intuition. As evolution has advanced, animals and humans have diverged and developed instinct and intelligence respectively as their tools for confronting the world. These are equally suited for their tasks, intelligence being extensible but hazardous, while intuition is limited but safe. Bergson uses detailed scientific evidence to illustrate the remarkable achievements of which instinct is capable. Intuition is a development of instinct, mediated by intelligence, which occurs only in humans but takes them to their highest level, and is the faculty used by metaphysics to say what reality is really like, while science uses intelligence to study reality in a manner inevitably distorted – but essential for practical living. But 'intuition' is ambiguous in Bergson. In one sense it turns quantity into quality, and, for example, enables us to see trillions of vibrations as the colour red, and experience duration; metaphysics uses it to study life and spirit. But in another sense it is insight, the getting of bright ideas, which both presupposes and is essential for the development of intelligence.

On evolution, Bergson again claims that two antagonistic theories, Darwinian mechanism and finalism or teleology, share a common presupposition, that the path or trajectory of evolution is somehow already laid out. His own view involves his famous *élan vital* ('vital impetus', usually left untranslated) which drives evolution on, though not towards any pre-ordained goal. It drives rather than draws, and to that extent resembles mechanism, but it also overcomes obstacles – a puzzling idea if it has no goals. Perhaps Bergson is here taking up a stance nearer to one extreme (teleology) than to the other, evolution having intermediate goals but no overall goal.

8 Morality and religion

Bergson turned to morality, and to an explicit discussion of religion, late in life in his last major work, *Les deux sources de la morale et de la religion* (The Two Sources of Morality and Religion) (1932). On both topics he uses a dualistic framework, but not, as in previous works, to show how two antagonistic approaches share a common premise. He contrasts closed morality with open morality and static religion with dynamic religion, and in each case his preference for the second term is unambiguous. The open morality is one of aspiration rather than impulsion and is universal in scope. Dynamic religion is somewhat similar, culminating in mysticism, of whose nature and development he gives an extended account. Obligation he sees as the pull of instinct against the waywardness introduced by intelligence, and he rightly emphasizes that we perform the great majority of our obligations as a matter of course and without any heroic Kantian struggle. The contrast between trajectory and movement is used twice here. Just as we can never build up a movement out of elements of its trajectory, but must treat it as something distinct and unitary, we can never construct a motive for moral action from individual intellectual considerations: the motive must already be there, given by instinct (there are echoes of Hume here). The second point is that we can never pass from ever-expanding group loyalties, which always require some out-group as a foil, to the universal love of mankind that open morality demands and that only the mystic can provide.

See also: COMEDY §2; HUMOUR §§2, 4

List of works

Bergson, H.-L. (1889) *Essai sur les données immédiates de la conscience*, Paris: Alcan; trans. F.L. Pogson, *Time and Free Will*, New York: Swan Sonnenschein, and London: Allen & Unwin, 1990.

(Introduces contrasts between time and duration and between movement and trajectory.)

—— (1896) *Matière et mémoire: Essai sur les relations du corps avec l'esprit*, Paris: Alcan; trans. N.M. Paul and W. Scott Palmer, *Matter and Memory*, New York: Swan Sonnenschein, and London: Allen & Unwin, 1911. (Translation contains a new introduction by Bergson.)

—— (1900) *Le Rire: Essai sur la signification du comique*, Paris: Alcan; trans. C. Brereton and F. Rothwell, *Laughter: An Essay on the Meaning of the Comic*, London and New York: Macmillan, 1911. (Applies his general ideas to the sphere of humour.)

—— (1903) 'Introduction à la métaphysique', *Revue de Métaphysique et de Morale* 29: 1–36; trans. T.E. Hulme, *Introduction to Metaphysics*, New York: Putnam, 1912; and in *The Creative Mind*, 1934. (More on epistemology than on metaphysics, this is where Bergson introduces his notion of 'intuition'.)

—— (1907) *L'evolution créatrice*, Paris: Alcan; trans. A. Mitchell, *Creative Evolution*, New York: Holt, 1911. (Important for Bergson's treatment not only of biology but of intuition, and also of different types of order and disorder and their relations, and of the concept of nothing.)

—— (1919) *L'energie spirituelle*, Paris: Alcan; trans. H. Wildon Carr, *Mind-Energy: Lectures and Essays*, New York: Holt, and London: Macmillan, 1920. (Collected essays, mainly on mind and body.)

—— (1922) *Durée et simultanéité: a propos de la théorie d'Einstein*, Paris: Alcan; trans. L. Jacobson, with introduction by H. Dingle, *Duration and Simultaneity*, Indianapolis, IN: Bobbs-Merrill, 1965. (The second edition in 1923 adds three appendices replying to criticisms. Bergson tries to defuse some paradoxical consequences of relativity theory, writing before these were empirically confirmed. It is now agreed he was wrong in the letter, though some say he was right in the spirit and anticipated later developments; see Čapek and Heidsieck.)

—— (1932) *Les deux sources de la morale et de la religion*, Paris: Alcan; trans. R.A. Audra, C. Brereton and W.H. Carter, *The Two Sources of Morality and Religion*, New York: Holt, 1935. (Distinguishes two levels, higher and lower, in each of these spheres.)

—— (1934) *La pensée et le mouvant: essais et conférences*, Paris: Alcan; trans. M.L. Andison, *The Creative Mind*, New York: Philosophical Library, 1946. (Essays, historical and on method, including 'Introduction à la métaphysique' and two new introductions which form perhaps the best entrance-point for newcomers to Bergson.)

—— (1959) *Oeuvres*, Paris: Presses Universitaires de France. (Centennial edition containing all the above except *Durée et simultaneité*, with an introduction by H. Gouhier and critical and historical notes by A. Robinet.)

—— (1972) *Mélanges*, Paris: Presses Universitaires de France. (Edited with notes by A. Robinet and with foreword by H. Gouhier, this contains virtually all Bergson's writings whose publication he allowed (except those in *Oeuvres* 1959), including his early thesis on place in Aristotle and *Durée et simultanéité*.)

References and further reading

Barlow, M. (1966) *Henri Bergson*, Paris: Presses Universitaires de France. (Brief French biography which succeeds in integrating Bergson's life and works.)

Barreau, H. (1973) 'Bergson et Einstein: A propos de *Durée et simultaneité*', *Les Études bersoniennes* 10: 73–134. (Extended but accessible discussion, critical of Bergson.)

* Berthelot, R. (1913) *Un Romantisme utilitaire: étude sur le mouvement pragmatiste. Troisième partie. Un Pragmatisme psychologique; le pragmatisme partial de Bergson* (A Utilitarian Romanticism: A Study of the Pragmatist Movement. Part 3: A Psychological Pragmatism; The Partial Pragmatism of Bergson), Paris: Alcan. (Full and scholarly, though rather unsympathetic, treatment of Bergson and influences on him.)

* Boudot, M. (1980) 'L'Espace selon Bergson' (Space According to Bergson), *Revue de Métaphysique et de Morale* 85 (3): 332–56. (Mentioned in §2. Very hostile discussion, claiming, among other things, that the asymmetry Bergson sees between space and time is illusory.)

* Čapek, M. (1971) *Bergson and Modern Physics*, Dordrecht: Reidel. (Full and scholarly treatment of Bergson, going well beyond its title, but accessible. Much more sympathetic to Bergson than Berthelot.)

—— (1980) 'Ce qui est vivant et ce qui est mort dans la critique bergsonienne de la rélativité' ('What is living and what is dead in Bergson's critique of relativity'), *Revue de synthèse* 101 (99–100): 313–44. (Sympathetic and accessible.)

Gale, R.M. (1973–4) 'Bergson's analysis of the concept of nothing', *The Modern Schoolman* 51: 269–300. (On a topic on which Bergson says some important things in chap. 4 of *Creative Evolution*, though not covered in this entry.)

Gunter, P.A.Y. (1974, 1986) *Henri Bergson: A Bibliography*, Bowling Green, OH: Philosophy Documentation Centre. (Massive work with over

6,000 entries by and on Bergson, many with summaries, extensive in the case of Bergson's main works.)
* Heidsieck, F. (1957) *Henri Bergson et la notion d'espace* (Henri Bergson and the Notion of Space), Paris: Le Cercle du Livre. (Influential in the rehabilitation of Bergson after the Second World War. See especially the discussion, with some technicalities, of *Durée et simultanéité*, claiming that Bergson was right in spirit, though not in letter.)
  Husson, L. (1947) *L'intellectualisme de Bergson*, Paris: Presses Universitaires de France. (Emphasizes that Bergson's use of intuition does not imply that he was anti-intellectualist.)
  Kolakowski, L. (1985) *Bergson*, Oxford: Oxford University Press. (Brief elementary overview.)
  Lacey, A.R. (1989) *Bergson*, London: Routledge. (The book on which this entry is based. Confined to philosophy, not the history of ideas.)
* Milet, J. (1974) *Bergson et le calcul infinitésimal* (Bergson and the Infinitesimal Calculus), Paris: Presses Universitaires de France. (Referred to in §2. Nontechnical discussion claiming Bergson saw the calculus as a means of dealing with duration, not as something limited to the 'cinematographic' method. See English résumé of his views in Papanicolaou and Gunter 1987.)
  Moore, F.C.T. (1996) *Bergson: Thinking Backwards*, Cambridge: Cambridge University Press. (Good attempt to give brief and accessible expression to some of Bergson's more difficult doctrines, and to bring out their significance.)
  Mullarkey, J. (ed.) (1998) *The New Bergson*, Manchester, Manchester University Press. (Essays aimed at bringing out the contemporary relevance of Bergson in a wide variety of spheres.)
  Papanicolaou, A.C. and Gunter, P.A.Y. (eds) (1987) *Bergson and Modern Thought*, Chur, Switzerland: Harvard Academic Publishers. (Essays, sometimes technical, claiming Bergson anticipated elements of various modern scientific developments, which confirm many of his ideas.)

A.R. LACEY

BERKELEY, GEORGE (1685–1753)

George Berkeley, who was born in Ireland and who eventually became Bishop of Cloyne, is best known for three works that he published while still very young: An Essay towards a New Theory of Vision *(1709),* Three Dialogues between Hylas and Philonous *(1713), and in particular for* A Treatise concerning the Principles of Human Knowledge *(1710). In the* Principles *he argues for the striking claim that there is no external, material world; that houses, trees and the like are simply collections of 'ideas'; and that it is God who produces 'ideas' or 'sensations' in our minds. The* New Theory of Vision *had gone some way towards preparing the ground for this claim (although that work has interest and value in its own right), and the* Dialogues *represent Berkeley's second attempt to defend it. Other works were to follow, including* De Motu *(1721),* Alciphron *(1732) and* Siris *(1744), but the three early works established Berkeley as one of the major figures in the history of modern philosophy.*

The basic thesis was certainly striking, and from the start many were tempted to dismiss it outright as so outrageous that even Berkeley himself could not have taken it seriously. In fact, however, Berkeley was very serious, and certainly a very able philosopher. Writing at a time when rapid developments in science appeared to be offering the key to understanding the true nature of the material world and its operations, but when scepticism about the very existence of the material world was also on the philosophical agenda, Berkeley believed that 'immaterialism' offered the only hope of defeating scepticism and of understanding the status of scientific explanations. Nor would he accept that his denial of 'matter' was outrageous. Indeed, he held that, if properly understood, he would be seen as defending the views of 'the vulgar' or 'the Mob' against other philosophers, including Locke, whose views posed a threat to much that we would ordinarily take to be common sense. His metaphysics cannot be understood unless we see clearly how he could put this interpretation on it; and neither will we do it justice if we simply dismiss the role he gives to God as emerging from the piety of a future bishop. Religion was under threat; Berkeley can probably be judged prescient in seeing how attractive atheism could become, given the scientific revolution of which we are the heirs; and though it could hardly be claimed that his attempts to ward off the challenge were successful, they merit respectful attention. Whether, however, we see him as the proponent of a fascinating metaphysics about which we must make up our own minds, or as representing merely one stage in the philosophical debate that takes us from Descartes to Locke and then to Hume, Kant and beyond, we must recognize Berkeley as a powerful intellect who had an important contribution to make.

1 Life
2 Influences
3 Berkeley's metaphysics
4 The *New Theory of Vision*

5   The Introduction to the *Principles*
6–8 The *Principles*
9   *Three Dialogues between Hylas and Philonous*
10 *De Motu*
11 *Alciphron* and *The Analyst*
12 *Siris*
13 Concluding Remarks

1 Life

George Berkeley was born in (or near) the town of Kilkenny, Ireland, and educated at Kilkenny College and at Trinity College, Dublin, where he took the degree of B.A. in 1704, and that of M.A. in 1707, becoming a Junior Fellow in the latter year. Before long he published the books for which he is now most renowned. However, mention must first be made of two notebooks, now known as the *Philosophical Commentaries*, which he filled during the years 1707–8. Since their first publication in 1871 (but more particularly since it was established that they had at some stage been bound together in the wrong order, thus giving a distorted picture of the development of Berkeley's thought) these have proved an invaluable resource for scholars seeking to understand the evolution of his thinking during this crucial period. The major fruits of that thinking were *An Essay towards a New Theory of Vision* (1709), *A Treatise concerning the Principles of Human Knowledge* (1710) – which was originally intended to be merely Part I of a three- or four-part work– and the *Three Dialogues between Hylas and Philonous* (1713), which Berkeley published after he had moved to London. In between the *Principles* and *Dialogue* he published a slighter work, *Passive Obedience* (1712), which gives the main insight into his thinking on ethics, and on the basis of which he has been described as a theological rule-utilitarian. Also dating from about this time there are essays published in Richard Steele's *Guardian* during the year 1713, which evidence his disdain for the antireligious sentiments of the 'free-thinkers'.

From this time onwards, Berkeley's life was active and interesting. He made two continental tours, the first (1713–14) as chaplain to Lord Peterborough, during which he apparently met Malebranche, and the second (1716–20) as tutor to George Ashe, son of the Bishop of Clogher. Towards the end of the second tour he wrote the Latin tract *De Motu* for submission to the Royal Academy of Sciences at Paris, which had offered a prize for an essay on the cause of motion. He published this in 1721, returned to Ireland in the same year, and was appointed Dean of Derry in 1724. Already, however, he had conceived a remarkable project that was to dominate his life for ten years.

During the spring of 1722 he resolved to found a college on the island of Bermuda, and before long he set about soliciting support for and gaining a charter for St Paul's College, which would, had it come into existence, have educated a number of young Native Americans, as well as the sons of English planters.

In fact he never reached Bermuda but, newly married, he set sail for Rhode Island in 1728, where he stayed for over two years awaiting a promised government grant, and where his house is preserved as a monument to him. The grant never materialized, so there was to be no college, either in Bermuda or, as he had come to think would be preferable, on the mainland. His time in Rhode Island was not, however, wasted. While there he wrote *Alciphron: or the Minute Philosopher*, an attack on atheism and deism in dialogue form, which was published in 1732, the year after his return to London. He also became a friend of Samuel JOHNSON, later the first president of King's College, New York. Johnson's *Elementa Philosophica* (1752) is dedicated to Berkeley, and two letters from Johnson written in 1729 and 1730 (published with Berkeley's replies in volume two of the standard edition of Berkeley's *Works*) reveal that he was basically sympathetic to, but also an acute critic of, Berkeley's main metaphysical doctrines.

Certainly the same could not be said of Andrew Baxter, who in 1733 included as part of his *Enquiry into the Nature of the Human Soul* what was, in fact, the first extended critique of Berkeley's *Principles*. Baxter's tone was hostile throughout. Berkeley chose not to respond, though in the same year he did answer an anonymous critic of the *New Theory of Vision* – a third edition of which had been annexed to *Alciphron* – by publishing *The Theory of Vision, Vindicated and Explained*. He also published a revised edition of the *Principles* and *Dialogues* in 1734. *The Analyst* (1734), which criticizes Newton's doctrine of fluxions, also relates to his earlier work in that Berkeley refers back to his observations on mathematics in the *Principles*, and it may be that remarks Baxter had made on his treatment of the mathematicians there played at least a minor role in encouraging him to publish it. Berkeley does not name the critic who, he says, had challenged him to 'make good' what he had said in the *Principles*, but if it was Baxter he treats him dismissively as someone who 'doth not appear to think maturely enough to understand either those metaphysics which he would refute, or mathematics which he would patronize' (*The Analyst* §50).

However, Berkeley also had to think about securing his and his family's future, and his efforts to gain preferment in the church were rewarded in 1734 when he was appointed Bishop of Cloyne in Ireland. There, he thoroughly earned the reputation he has had ever since as 'the good Bishop'. The tangible legacy includes *The Querist* (1735–7), which evidences his concern for the economic wellbeing of Ireland, and *Siris* (1744), so successful at the time that it went through six editions in the year of publication but which is now regarded as little more than a curiosity. However, this was to be his last original publication of any substance. He remained in Cloyne almost to the end of his life, moving to Oxford, where one of his sons was to study, in the summer of 1752. He died there in the following year.

2 Influences

The primary influence on Berkeley is unquestionably John Locke, whose *Essay concerning Human Understanding* Berkeley had studied as an undergraduate and continued to dwell on afterwards. The long introduction to Berkeley's *Principles* is for the most part a sustained attack on the view that we can frame abstract ideas, focusing on Locke's account of abstraction. Illegitimate abstraction is ultimately blamed for the supposedly untenable distinction between primary and secondary qualities, the belief in 'material substance', and the view that objects have an existence distinct from 'ideas', all of which are features of Locke's position (see LOCKE, J. §§2–5). Yet Berkeley also owed a great deal to Locke whom he likened in the notebooks to 'a Gyant' and who should be seen as his mentor as well as one of his philosophical targets. It is therefore understandable that Berkeley has most often been seen as the second of the three great British Empiricists, as successor to Locke and precursor of HUME, these three being placed in opposition to the three great Rationalist philosophers, DESCARTES, SPINOZA and LEIBNIZ. Certainly, it would be tempting to say that the importance of Locke's influence on Berkeley could hardly be overestimated, were it not for the fact that it sometimes has been.

If only as a corrective, then, it is important to stress that while it is evident that Locke was often in Berkeley's mind as he formulated his own position, and while there is no doubt that none of Berkeley's major works would have existed in their present form had Locke never published the *Essay*, Berkeley would have insisted that much more was at stake than whether Locke got things right. He targeted certain views and assumptions that were very widely held. Thus Locke is the only philosopher he actually identifies and quotes from in the attack on abstract ideas, but even there he sees himself as opposing, not simply some quirky view of Locke's, but one which, as he put it in a letter, 'Mr. Locke held in common with the Schoolmen, and I think all other philosophers' (*Works*, vol. 2: 293). These certainly included Malebranche, for example, who, Berkeley elsewhere complained, 'builds on the most abstract general ideas' (*Works*, vol. 2: 214). Again, when he says that 'Some there are who make a distinction betwixt *primary* and *secondary* qualities' (*Principles* §9), he really does mean 'some', and not just Locke; and the same could be said of his opposition to the notion of 'material substance'. In short, Berkeley often had his eye on other thinkers too, and some of these must also count as influences. As is now widely recognized, these included writers in the Cartesian tradition, most notably Malebranche but also probably Pierre Bayle.

The relationship between Berkeley and Descartes is interesting – after all, it was Descartes who had introduced a radical dualism of 'matter' and 'mind', and although Berkeley rejected matter, he adhered to a broadly Cartesian view of the mind (see DUALISM). However, MALEBRANCHE is particularly important in the story, both because Berkeley had studied his *De la recherche de la vérité* at an early stage, and because Berkeley's position struck many as remarkably close to that of Malebranche. In particular, Berkeley positively denies the existence of bodies 'without the mind', but Malebranche had already argued that it was impossible to prove their existence conclusively, thus paving the way for their dismissal. Again, Malebranche had insisted that there are no corporeal *causes*, and that, strictly speaking, God is the only cause, and Berkeley certainly holds that only spirits can act. Moreover, Malebranche held, and Berkeley at least suggested, that in perception, God's ideas are revealed to us. It is significant, then, that in his own day, despite his protestations, Berkeley was often seen as essentially a follower of Malebranche. We might note, finally, that while Malebranche had concluded that neither sense nor reason could conclusively establish the existence of bodies, he also held that faith in the Scriptures did require this belief. When in the *Principles* Berkeley considers a number of possible objections to his positive rejection of 'matter', this argument from the Scriptures is the last that he chooses to tackle. As he says, 'I do not think, that either what philosophers call *matter*, or the existence of objects without the mind, is any where mentioned in Scripture' (*Principles* §82).

There is evidence that BAYLE too was an early influence, and when, as in the preface to the *Principles*, Berkeley refers to 'those who are tainted with scepticism', arguments he found in Bayle's *Dictionnaire historique et critique* were probably towards the front of his mind. Bayle had offered arguments against regarding extension and motion as any more objective than colour or smell (which the Cartesians recognized as mere 'sensations'), and for the view that the notion of real extension (for Cartesians the essence of matter) involved contradictions. Strict reasoning, Bayle argued, would thus lead us to deny the existence of bodies, in the face of our (fortunately) ineradicable beliefs. Berkeley could welcome and adapt these arguments to the extent that he was concerned to reject bodies 'without the mind', and while, unlike Bayle, Berkeley firmly denied that they lead to scepticism or to any conflict with common sense, it is hardly surprising if many of his contemporaries took a different view. As Andrew Baxter saw it, Berkeley was committed to the conclusion that 'he has neither *country* nor *parents*, nor any *material body* (but that all these things are mere *illusions*, and have no existence but in the fancy' (Baxter [1733] 1737, vol. 2: 260).

3 Berkeley's metaphysics

Berkeley is understandably best known for his (at first sight outrageous) claim that mind or spirit is the only substance, and that it is God who produces 'sensations' or 'ideas' in our minds. From the beginning, many regarded this view as sceptical at best or insane at worst, and Berkeley recognized that this might be the initial reaction. It is, then, an important feature of his position that, if rightly understood, his standpoint will be seen as common sense, and in accord with the views of the unsophisticated 'vulgar'. The purpose of the present section is to sketch in very general terms how Berkeley could see things in this way.

To begin with, we can hardly make sense of Berkeley's position unless we see him as starting from an assumption that he took both to be obviously true and to be shared by other philosophers, which was that each of us is aware only of the 'ideas', 'sensations' or 'perceptions' that are somehow or other produced in our minds. On the most common view – that taken by Descartes and Locke for example – these are produced in us by external objects, which objects we do not perceive 'immediately' because, as Locke put it (whatever precisely he meant by it), 'the Mind...perceives nothing but its own *Ideas*' (Locke, *Essay* IV 4: §3). Berkeley's first insight, and it is one that his reading of Malebranche and Bayle must have encouraged, was that if we set things up in this way – distinguishing between the 'ideas' we perceive and the 'real' objects which lie hidden beyond them – scepticism becomes inevitable. At best we can hypothesize the existence of 'real' objects as the *most likely* causes of our ideas, but then we are vulnerable to the suggestion that there could be other causes, including, most plausibly, God. There are other difficulties too. Berkeley found it widely admitted that it is quite unclear how inert 'matter' could act on minds so as to produce ideas or perceptions in them (and Malebranche and other 'occasionalists' had denied that it in fact does) (see OCCASIONALISM); moreover, Berkeley found only obscurities and incoherencies in the prevalent conceptions of 'material substance'. Yet the most fundamental insight was to follow.

This insight was that when we – ordinary men and women – talk of houses, mountains, rivers and so on, we are talking about what we experience or are aware of, not of occult objects that we are not directly aware of at all. It follows, or at least it seemed to Berkeley to follow, that if when we refer to houses, mountains and rivers we are referring to things we are aware of, and if (as other philosophers agreed) we are aware only of ideas, houses, mountains and rivers must *be* 'ideas' or appearances or, better, 'collections' of such ideas. Certainly – and this was one thing that his readers found most difficult to handle, but which Berkeley himself was most insistent on – there is no need to deny that houses, mountains and rivers exist, but only to stress (common-sensibly) that they are the very things we perceive, which is to say that they are mind-dependent ideas. Their *esse* (being) is *percipi* (to be perceived); they exist only in the mind.

Berkeley's major philosophical works, and in particular the *Principles* and *Dialogues*, are, in the main, a sustained defence of these insights and doctrines, together with a working out of their implications. For Berkeley, the implications, including those for religion and the sciences, are as important as the basic metaphysics. Yet the fundamental case for that metaphysics is supposed to be very simple indeed. Even by the end of section six of the *Principles* (under three pages in most editions) that case has supposedly been established.

4 The *New Theory of Vision*

Although Berkeley's *An Essay towards a New Theory of Vision* (1709) was published just one year before the *Principles*, and Berkeley was already convinced that there was no such thing as 'matter', or bodies 'without the mind', this, his first major work, stopped short of making that claim. As he said in the *Principles*, although the earlier book had shown that 'the proper objects *of sight* neither exist without the mind, nor are the images of external things (*Principles* §44; emphasis added), it had done nothing to disabuse readers of the view that tangible objects are external. At one level, then, the work can be seen as a sort of halfway house on the route to presenting his full case for immaterialism, but it is undoubtedly also true that he was fascinated by problems concerning vision in their own right. He was clearly very well read in optical theory, he had his own highly distinctive contribution to make, and for many years that contribution was esteemed by many who had little interest in, or were possibly quite blind to, any wider implications it may have had.

Ostensibly, then, the *New Theory of Vision* is merely an attempt to 'shew the manner wherein we perceive by sight the distance, magnitude, and situation of objects', though, still in the opening section, Berkeley also announces that he will be considering 'the difference there is betwixt the ideas of sight and touch, and whether there be any idea common to both senses' (*New Theory of Vision* §1). Broadly, the issue concerning 'situation', which others had recognized, is that of how we see things the 'right' way up (so to speak) when their images are inverted on the retina; that concerning 'magnitude' is how we judge objects at a distance to be small or large (one particular problem was why the moon on the horizon looks larger than the moon in the zenith, although they are virtually the same distance from us); and that concerning 'outness' or distance is that of how we come to see things as being at various distances, given that, as Berkeley observes, it was accepted that 'distance being a line directed end-wise to the eye, it projects only one point in the fund of the eye, which point remains invariably the same, whether the distance be longer or shorter' (*New Theory of Vision* §2). Berkeley's solution is similar in each case. In the case of distance, for example, even when an object is relatively close, we do not, as others had supposed, make our judgments on the basis of what Descartes had described as a sort of 'natural geometry', and on facts such as that lines drawn from the two eyes to the object form a greater angle the closer the object is: the supposed lines and angles are only theoretical entities, and are not at any rate perceived. Rather, we *learn* to make these judgments solely on the strength of certain sensory cues including, for example, the sensations accompanying the turn of the eyes, and the increasingly confused appearance of an object as it comes closer to us. An explanation in terms of geometry is thus replaced by a psychology of vision in which, crucially, the connection between the cues and the distance discoverable by touch turns out to be purely contingent. '[I]f it had been the ordinary course of Nature that the farther off an object were placed, the more confused it should appear, it is certain the very same perception that now makes us think an object approaches would then have made us to imagine it went farther off' (*New Theory of Vision* §26).

Though often regarded as controversial, Berkeley's work on the psychology of vision was also highly influential even though, and indeed partly because, Berkeley's ultimate metaphysical commitments are not apparent, and certainly not necessarily required for an acceptance, for example, that 'a man born blind, being made to see, would at first have no idea of distance by sight'. Admittedly Berkeley's account of our judgments is in terms of 'sensations', 'appearances' and 'ideas', as all we have to go on, and we are told, for example, not only that the man just cured of blindness would take the 'objects intromitted by sight' to be 'no other than a new set of thoughts or sensations, each whereof is as near to him as the perceptions of pain or pleasure, or the most inward passions of his soul', but that he would be right to do so (*New Theory of Vision* §41). Yet nothing is said to disabuse the reader of the thought that there is, for example, a distant moon, which is not at all dependent on the mind. There is a sense, therefore, in which the *New Theory of Vision* offers us some of the fruits of idealism without explicitly announcing the immaterialism, and one of those fruits is an indication of the existence of God (see IDEALISM). By the end of the work, Berkeley has concluded that there are no ideas common to sight and touch: the extension perceived by touch, for example, is quite distinct from, and has no likeness to, any visual idea. Here he considers a problem first raised by William MOLYNEUX and discussed by Locke, agreeing with them that a man just cured of blindness who saw a cube and a globe for the first time would not know just by looking which was which, but seeing this answer as confirming his own view that visual ideas are merely 'signs'. These we learn to correlate with tangible ideas in much the same way as we learn a language. Berkeley takes this analogy very seriously. His conclusion in the first edition is thus that 'the proper objects of vision constitute the universal language of nature, whereby we are instructed how to regulate our actions', but by the third edition 'nature' has become 'the Author of nature', or God (*New Theory of Vision* §147).

5 The Introduction to the *Principles*

Berkeley prefaces *A Treatise concerning the Principles of Human Knowledge* (1710) with an important introduction which is for the most part devoted to an attack on abstract ideas, and in particular abstract general ideas. In it he quotes freely from Locke. Yet, as already stated, his target was wider, including philosophers generally and, ultimately, a variety of philosophical confusions. One needs to look outside the introduction to discover what these alleged confusions are. Sometimes this is fairly straightforward. Even in the *New Theory of Vision* the notion that there is an idea of extension common to both sight and touch is ascribed to the supposition that we can abstract it from all other visible and tangible qualities; while, in the *Principles*, the notion that the supposed 'primary' qualities exist in the outward object, although colours and the like are 'in the mind alone', is undermined by the observation that 'extension, figure, and motion, abstracted from all other qualities, are inconceivable'. Similarly, the idea of 'pure' or 'absolute' space is ruled out, it being 'a most abstract idea'. In one important case the connection is perhaps less obvious: Berkeley claims that holding that sensible objects can exist unperceived depends on illegitimate abstraction, but commentators have often found it difficult to see precisely how this is supposed to work. In yet other cases, the supposed connections have been less frequently explored in the literature, as for example when Berkeley has it that the Schoolmen were 'masters of abstraction' and, in the *Dialogues*, that Malebranche 'builds on the most abstract general ideas'. These matters can probably be sorted out. Malebranche had attacked the 'disordered abstractions' of the Schoolmen, who posited occult qualities and powers, and who supposed that matter is something distinct from its known attributes, and in particular from extension, and Berkeley had probably learned from that. Yet Malebranche himself fell foul of Berkeley's anti-abstractionism by talking of 'absolute' and 'intelligible' extension, by supposing that extension was the essence of matter, and by assuming an idea of 'being in general'. The connection between abstraction and the denial of the '*esse* is *percipi*' principle is trickier.

Berkeley's introduction attacks the view that, although the qualities of objects are always 'blended together' in them, we can frame a separate idea of each quality; that we can form, for example, an abstract idea of colour or extension in general; and that we can frame an idea corresponding to the word 'man' or 'triangle', as distinct from the ideas of particular men or particular triangles, as Locke had suggested. This in turn requires from Berkeley an alternative account of language to Locke's, which will not require that each general term stands for an idea. This alternative account is not worked out very fully, but Berkeley does insist that 'a word becomes general by being made the sign, not of an abstract general idea but, of several particular ideas, any one of which it indifferently suggests to the mind' (*Principles*, Intro. §11). Moreover, suggestions towards the end of the introduction that words have other uses than to mark out ideas, including the production of appropriate emotions – 'May we not, for example, be affected with the promise of a *good thing*, though we have not an idea of what it is?' (*Principles*, Intro. §20) – have rightly been seen as significant, and further developments along these lines, in particular in the seventh dialogue of *Alciphron*, have even been seen as making him a precursor of WITTGENSTEIN in this area.

6 The *Principles*

Berkeley's basic metaphysical position is usually known as 'idealism' or, because of what it denies, as 'immaterialism', and the classic defence of this position is offered in *A Treatise Concerning the Principles of Human Knowledge*. Like all Berkeley's works, this is well structured, with just 156 short sections: sections 1–33 argue the case for his idealism, sections 34–84 anticipate and answer possible objections, and the remaining sections take 'a view of our tenets in their consequences'.

As already indicated, Berkeley takes even his opponents to accept that, whatever else there may turn out to be in the world, we perceive only ideas. This assumption emerges in the opening section of the *Principles* (which is clearly modelled on the opening sections of the first chapter of Book II of Locke's *Essay*). Here Berkeley writes, or at least suggests, that 'the objects of human knowledge' are all 'ideas', adding that when certain ideas, for example a certain colour, smell and so on, are found going together they are 'reputed as one thing'. On the face of it, this blurs Locke's distinction between 'qualities' and 'ideas', and ignores Locke's supposition of a 'substratum' for the qualities. Yet Berkeley knows what he is doing, and clearly found encouragement in Locke's own preparedness not only to use 'idea' where he means 'quality', but also to assert that we have no other ideas of particular sorts of substances 'than that which is framed by a collection of those simple *ideas* which are to be found in them'. Certainly, we are supposed to start with 'ideas', although – as Berkeley points out in the second section – there are also the minds or spirits that perceive them. However, he soon insists that there can be no substance apart from mind. Given that sensible objects are ideas, and that ideas exist only when perceived, it becomes simply absurd to suppose that these objects could have any existence apart from perception; a fact that is confirmed, in Berkeley's view, simply by attending to 'what is meant by the term *exist* when applied to sensible things'. When I say that a table 'exists', I am referring to something that I perceive, or at least that I might perceive, and certainly not applying 'exists' to some object which, because it is not an idea, is not perceived at all.

This argument, like most of Berkeley's arguments, is tricky and needs careful handling. Ostensibly, it seems to have very little to do with the word 'exists' because, as Andrew Baxter observed, neither philosophers nor ordinary people seem to mean 'is perceived' by 'exists' in sentences such as 'the table exists'. That point is a fair one, and Berkeley's actual argument does seem to depend heavily on the underlying assumption that the only perceivable objects are mind-dependent items, which must consequently be actually perceived. The stress put on the word 'exists' remains puzzling, however, and one relevant fact seems to be that Locke had held that 'existence' was a simple idea 'suggested to the Understanding, by every Object without, and every *Idea* within' (Locke, *Essay*, II 7: §7). Berkeley had convinced himself both that the idea thus described was abstract (and hence impossible), and that this idea is involved when people suppose things to exist quite independently of perception. To perceive a table as existing and to simply perceive it are one and the same experience, and the existence cannot be separated from the perception so that we can attribute an 'absolute existence' to the thing.

That is at any rate what Berkeley concludes on the basis of the first few sections. But of course he expected resistance. His tactic now becomes, therefore, to seize on supposedly unsatisfactory features of his opponents' position and, by exposing them, to further his own case. If it is suggested, for example, that our ideas are merely the *likenesses* of external qualities, the counter is that an idea (or perceived thing) can be *like* nothing but an idea (or another perceivable thing). To those who argue that the supposed 'primary' qualities exist in outward objects but that colours and the like do not, his response is twofold: first, we cannot even conceive of an object having merely extension, figure and motion, but lacking any of the qualities these other philosophers recognize as mind-dependent; second, the basic argument deployed to prove that secondary qualities are mind-dependent (that is, that the appearance varies in varying circumstances) would prove the same of any quality whatsoever. Furthermore, those who posit a material substratum as the *support* of qualities find that they can attach no clear meaning in this context even to the term 'support'. There are other arguments, including a particularly tricky and much discussed one in which he proudly claims that it is impossible to conceive that there even *might* be a mind-independent object, for to conceive it would be to frame the idea of it, which would mean that it was an object of thought or perception after all. However, Berkeley is at his rumbustious best in sections 18–20, arguing that neither sense nor reason can establish that there are external bodies, and that they cannot even be posited as an hypothesis to account for our receiving the ideas we do. Even if we suppose, arbitrarily, that there are external bodies, the materialists 'by their own confession are never the nearer knowing how our ideas are produced: since they own themselves unable to comprehend in what manner body can act upon spirit, or how it is possible it should imprint any idea in the mind' (*Principles* §19). What emerges, predictably, is that the only possible cause of our ideas is another, superior spirit, who presents our ideas to us in orderly ways which in fact *constitute* the Laws of Nature, and which Berkeley also sees as constituting the *language* of God himself.

7 The *Principles* (cont.)

While the first thirty-three sections of the *Principles* are in an obvious sense basic, the sections in which Berkeley deals with possible objections to his thesis are important too. Here most readers new to Berkeley are likely to find that the first objections that spring to their minds have been anticipated, while the answers Berkeley gives help to clarify his basic thesis. The objections he envisages include, for example, that, given his idealism, everything becomes illusory or unreal; that we see things at a distance from us, so they are not 'in the mind'; that, if the *esse* of sensible things is *percipi*, they will disappear when we stop perceiving them, which is absurd; and that, if objects are only ideas, or collections of ideas, there can be no causal interaction between them, so we will have to deny that fire heats and that water cools. Whether Berkeley's answers to such objections satisfy us is another matter, but the objections are at least confronted, and the answers are always interesting. On the third objection mentioned above, for example, it is eventually suggested that for an object to exist it is necessary only for some mind to perceive it, with the implication that God's perception may guarantee the continued existence of objects. The answer to the fourth objection above is that, just as we continue to say that the sun 'rises' despite scientific knowledge that it is the earth that moves, so this is another area where 'we ought to *think with the learned, and speak with the vulgar*' (*Principles* §51), recognizing that, strictly, the regularities in nature we describe as causal are ultimately down to God. In answering both these objections, Berkeley is typically quick to point out that his philosophical opponents are insecurely placed to make them. Even those who hold that there are external and material bodies are committed to the view that light and colours, or visible objects, are 'mere sensations', and thus to holding that these disappear when I shut my eyes; while, when it comes to causal relationships between objects, many other philosophers, both among the Schoolmen and modern philosophers, have held that God is the 'immediate efficient cause of all things'.

In answering the second of the above objections,

Berkeley predictably refers the reader back to the *New Theory of Vision*; but his answer to the first objection is more complex. There are, he stresses, decisive differences between the 'faint, weak, and unsteady' ideas of the imagination and those imprinted on the senses by God, and though he calls both 'ideas' to emphasize that they are equally in the mind, he would not object to simply calling the latter 'things'. Nor does he deny even that there are corporeal substances, if 'substance' is taken 'in the vulgar sense, for a combination of sensible qualities'. It is, he suggests, only other *philosophers* he opposes, for they take corporeal substance to be 'the support of accidents or qualities without the mind'. We may well feel that this point glosses over the one big difference between Berkeley and the vulgar, which is that the vulgar do not recognize sensible qualities to be mind-dependent ideas, but it is one that Berkeley insists on. 'The only thing whose existence we deny, is that which philosophers call matter or corporeal substance. And in doing of this, there is no damage done to the rest of mankind, who, I dare say, will never miss it' (*Principles* §35).

8   The *Principles* (cont.)

The full title of the *Principles* describes it as a work 'Wherein the chief causes of error and difficulty in the Sciences, with the grounds of Scepticism, Atheism, and Irreligion, are inquired into'. While Berkeley believes idealism to be true, he is as interested in the benefits that flow from accepting it. These include establishing the existence of God and attaining a proper understanding of God's role in the world; the banishment of scepticism concerning the nature and the very existence of 'real' things, both of which result from distinguishing the 'real' from what we perceive; and the resolution of certain philosophical, scientific and mathematical perplexities. From section 85 onwards, therefore, Berkeley takes 'a view of our tenets in their consequences'.

Some of the supposed advantages are obvious once stated, and they include the resolution of three issues Berkeley mentions at the outset: 'Whether corporeal substance can think?' (a possibility mooted by Locke, which threatened belief in the natural immortality of the soul); 'Whether matter be infinitely divisible?' (a long-standing issue, with Bayle in particular having exposed the paradoxes that arise whether we suppose that it is or it is not); and 'how [matter] operates on spirit?' (a problem that had exercised the Cartesians). None of these questions arises once it has been proved that there is no 'matter'; that the soul is immaterial, or 'one simple, undivided, active being' which is therefore 'indissoluble by the force of Nature'; and that, just as we can produce ideas in our own minds when exercising our fancies, so God (the superior spirit) can produce in our minds those ideas which constitute sensible things. In addition, however, Berkeley explores at some length the implications for natural philosophy and mathematics.

These, it must be stressed, were not simply casual interests for Berkeley. His very first publication – a compilation of two titles, *Arithmetica* and *Miscellanea Mathematica*, (1707) – evidences his early proficiency in mathematics, and the philosophically more significant manuscript *Of Infinites* was written at about the same time. The latter concentrates on the 'disputes and scruples' which infect modern analytical geometry, all arising from 'the use that is made of quantitys infinitely small'. Moreover *De Motu* (1721) includes an examination of the role that such concepts as force, gravitation and attraction play in Newtonian mechanics. There would have been more on these topics in the additional parts of the *Principles* which Berkeley intended to write, as indeed there would have been on persons, perceivers or spirits. What he does say on the latter subject in the *Principles* as we have it is thin, and it is perhaps necessary only to note that Berkeley's view is indeed broadly Cartesian, though the Berkeleian dualism is between 'indivisible, incorporeal, unextended' minds and ideas, not minds and 'matter'; that he even convinces himself that the soul always thinks; and that the stress is on Berkeley's claim that we do not know ourselves, or other spirits, by way of *idea*. This insistence underlies our earlier observation that in the opening section of the *Principles* Berkeley writes, or at least *suggests*, that all the objects of knowledge are ideas; for the truth is that, though Berkeley was prepared to give this impression at the outset (presumably so as not to raise an unnecessary complication early on), his own use of 'idea' for 'any sensible or imaginable thing', as he put it in the *Philosophical Commentaries*, rules out any 'idea' of spirit, or of the operations of the mind. Certainly, though, this is not supposed to be worrying, and Berkeley is not suggesting that the word 'mind' is insignificant. When he started penning the entries in the *Commentaries* he had indeed accepted the Lockian view that all significant words stand for ideas, but he had soon rejected that principle, partly as a result of deciding that the essentially active mind must be carefully distinguished from its passive objects or 'ideas'.

9   *Three Dialogues between Hylas and Philonous*

The *Principles of Human Knowledge* is the most important book in the Berkeleian corpus and, had its reception not been so disappointing to Berkeley, the

Three Dialogues between Hylas and Philonous (1713) would probably not have been written. People were readier to ridicule than to read a treatise that denied the existence of 'matter', while those who did read it usually misunderstood it. The *Dialogues*, therefore, were written, as Berkeley says in the preface, 'to treat more clearly and fully of certain principles laid down in the First [Part of the *Principles*], and to place them in a new light', and the dialogue form proved an admirable way of allowing likely objections to be dealt with at each stage (as well as making the book still perhaps the most attractive introduction to Berkeley). The protagonists are Hylas (the name derives from the Greek word for 'matter') and Philonous (the 'lover of mind', representing Berkeley himself). At the outset Hylas assumes that the Berkeleian is the proponent of 'the most extravagant opinion that ever entered into the mind of man' (*Works*, vol. 2: 172), but, as the discussion progresses, Philonous is able to demonstrate that, although he accepts with other philosophers that 'the things immediately perceived, are ideas which exist only in the mind', his additional acceptance of the view of ordinary men and women that 'those things they immediately perceive are the real things' allies him with common sense (*Works*, vol. 2: 262).

Doctrinally there are no substantial innovations here, although Berkeley has Philonous take pains early on to convince Hylas that 'sensible qualities', or the things *immediately* perceived, are mind-dependent, making great play of how appearances vary for different perceivers, and for the same perceiver in different circumstances. Other features include a striking passage, expanded in the third edition, which contains an anticipation of, and an attempt to answer, what is normally taken to be the Humean point that material and spiritual substance are on a par, so that if one is rejected, so too should the other. It is indeed a particularly attractive feature of the work that Hylas is allowed to be a quite pugnacious opponent who really does test the idealist's position. To give just one other instance, it is likely to occur to us that, if the things we perceive are identified with 'ideas' or 'sensations', surely each idea will be dependent on the particular mind that has or perceives it, with the apparently far from common-sense consequence that 'no two can see the same thing'. Berkeley's answer may or (more likely) may not satisfy us, but there is a deeper issue underlying Hylas' challenge which Berkeley himself may not have adequately explored. This concerns the relationship between particular ideas – whether described as 'sensations' or 'appearances' – and the 'collections' of ideas which, for Berkeley, constitute publicly observable objects. There are no more than hints that Berkeley may be prepared to countenance the notion that the permanently existent table is an archetypal idea in God's mind, and that we can be said to perceive it when we perceive any of the 'fleeting...and changeable ideas' which, to some degree, correspond to it.

10 *De Motu*

Berkeley intended to publish additional parts of the *Principles* and apparently made some progress on the second part, telling Samuel Johnson in 1729 that 'the manuscript was lost about fourteen years ago, during my travels in Italy, and I never had leisure since to do so disagreeable a thing as writing twice on the same subject', but that was as far as he got. Remarks in the *Philosophical Commentaries* suggest that one part would have been 'our Principles of Natural Philosophy', and we can assume that it would have included the sort of material covered in a work he did publish, *De Motu* (1721). This work reiterates and develops certain points already made in the *Principles* when Berkeley was taking 'a view of our tenets in their consequences', but although it is indeed assumed that minds are not corporeal, it would not have been apparent to the reader that Berkeley holds that the *esse* of sensible things is *percipi*. Rather, what is insisted on is that 'it is idle to adduce things which are neither evident to the senses, nor intelligible to reason' (*De Motu* §21), and that when we attribute gravity and force to bodies we are improperly positing occult qualities which take us beyond anything we can experience or conceive. 'Abstract terms (however useful they may be in argument) should be discarded in meditation, and the mind should be fixed on the particular and the concrete, that is, on the things themselves' (*De Motu* §4).

It is, therefore, idle to look to the qualities of bodies themselves in order to discover a cause of motion, for 'what we know in body is agreed not to be the principle of motion' (*De Motu* §24). Relying as we should on what we can conceive, we must look to mind for that principle, for we know from our ability to move our limbs that minds can act. On this basis we should conclude that 'all the bodies of this mundane system are moved by Almighty Mind according to certain and constant reason' (*De Motu* §32).

It is clear, then, that *De Motu* fits in with Berkeley's ultimate aim in all his philosophical writings, which is to bring out the dependence of the world upon God. Yet here, as in the case of everything he was to publish later, the elements of his metaphysics that had most perplexed the readers of the *Principles* and the *Dialogues* are either absent or in the background. Indeed, it is a feature of *De Motu* that Berkeley is anxious to present himself as representing a tradition going back to the ancient Greeks, but including the Schoolmen and the Cartesians, which recognizes the ultimate dependence of motion on God. Indeed, 'Newton everywhere frankly intimates that not only did motion originate from God, but that still the mundane system is moved by the same actus' (*De Motu* §32). It must be stressed, however, that it is not this supposed consensus that makes Berkeley's philosophy of science interesting, but his understanding of the proper role of the natural scientist as contrasted with that of the metaphysician. Terms such as 'gravity' and 'force', for example, have a legitimate use, in facilitating calculations on the basis of certain observable regularities in the behaviour of objects. We go wrong only if we confuse the discovery of regularities with genuine explanations of them. By contrast, absolute space and absolute motion, which were posited in Newtonian mechanics, are rejected outright, as indeed they were in the *Principles*. We should 'consider motion as something sensible, or at least imaginable,' and 'be content with relative measures' (*De Motu* §66). If there were but one body in the universe, it would make no sense to suppose that it moved (see NEWTON, I.).

11 *Alciphron* and *The Analyst*

Berkeley published *De Motu* in 1721 and nothing of any philosophical significance for over ten years thereafter. Indeed none of his later writings matched in importance what had already appeared. Yet all were controversial, and some were taken very seriously at the time. These included *Alciphron* (1732) and *The Analyst* (1734) which represent, if in very different ways, Berkeley's commitment to defending religion against those seeking to undermine it.

Alciphron is composed of seven lively dialogues in which two Christian gentlemen, Euphranor and Crito, defend the religious and Christian standpoint against two 'free-thinkers', Alciphron and Lysicles. These are, of course, fictitious characters, but are allowed on occasion to present (or misrepresent, as many have claimed) the views of such actual, though unnamed, figures as the third Earl of SHAFTESBURY and Bernard MANDEVILLE. Mandeville complained bitterly that his thesis that private vices are public benefits had been totally distorted in *Alciphron*; others have said the same of Berkeley's treatment of Shaftesbury's ethical theory. For all that, the book remains very readable. It contains, moreover, the only account of free-will published by Berkeley, and also the first explicit linking of the doctrine concerning the heterogeneity of the objects of sight and touch to a proof of the existence of God. Additionally there is a discussion in the Seventh Dialogue of particular interest in that it returns us to the topic of language.

The context is still the acceptability of religion, but at this point the objection from the free-thinker Alciphron is that the Christian religion is ultimately unacceptable, not because it can be shown to be false, but because it is straightforwardly unintelligible, involving, as it does, such meaningless notions as that of 'grace'. Here Alciphron appeals to the principle that 'words that suggest no ideas are insignificant'. Consequently this principle, which Berkeley had himself assumed in a demonstration of immaterialism nearly half way through the *Commentaries*, now becomes his explicit target. He reiterates his objection to abstract ideas, but also stresses the role of words in directing our practices, whether in mathematics and natural science, or in the religious sphere. It has been debated whether or not what we find here marks any decided shift from the line he had taken in the introduction to the *Principles*, and it is certainly true that Berkeley had long since moved towards the position he adopts here, but the discussion in *Alciphron* does reflect his mature consideration of the topic. It stresses the use of words as signs which, as he had put it to Samuel Johnson, 'as often terminate in the will as in the understanding, being employed rather to excite, influence, and direct action, than to produce clear and distinct ideas' (*Works*, vol. 2: 293).

By contrast with *Alciphron*, the *Analyst* is a technical work in the philosophy of mathematics, containing criticisms of Newton's calculus. The adequacy of these criticisms is still debated, but they were sufficiently acute to generate considerable controversy among the mathematicians. To this controversy Berkeley contributed two further works in 1735, *A Defence of Free-thinking in Mathematics*, and *Reasons for not replying to Mr. Walton's Full Answer*. Berkeley's theological preoccupations are again relevant in this area, for *The Analyst* was addressed to an unnamed 'infidel mathematician', who has generally been identified with Edmund Halley (of Halley's Comet fame). Halley had been reported as claiming that Christian doctrines were 'incomprehensible', and the religion an 'imposture'. Berkeley is able to take delight in answering that the objection comes ill from a mathematician. He targets what he saw as obscurities and contradictions in the calculus. Some of these result from assuming an increment of infinitesimal value which, without reaching zero, proceeds towards a limit of zero, allowing the analyst to predict the system's value at a conceptual point at which the increment becomes nothing. A consequence is that these 'ghosts of departed qualities' are both used and disregarded in one and the same proof. As already mentioned, Berkeley's interest in mathematics was of long standing, as was his opposition to infinitesimal quantities. He was able to show how these lead to absurdities in the calculus, and to argue against those who 'though they shrink at all other mysteries, make no difficulty of their own'. Moreover, he was able to do this without mentioning his own idealist view that, because *esse* is *percipi*, the smallest quantity must be what he had earlier called the *minimum sensibile*, which cannot be divided into parts.

12 Siris

Siris (1744), the last of Berkeley's writings of any substance, is also in many ways the strangest. His championship of tar-water as a useful remedy against many diseases (and as a possible panacea) is likely to strike us as foolish, though it was to some extent understandable given his apparently successful use of it in his diocese. Moreover, although it was practical experience that had led him to his belief in the virtues of tar-water, Berkeley does go deeply into the explanation of its effectiveness, relying on theories which gave prominence to the role of 'aether', or 'pure invisible fire', as the vital principle of the corporeal world. Here again we can now see that Berkeley was wrong, although he was able to appeal to authorities, both ancient and modern. Indeed, this readiness to appeal to authorities, or to seek for maximum consensus, extends to the final sections in which his chain of philosophical reflections leads him to focus on God as 'the First Mover, invisible, incorporeal, unextended, intellectual source of life and being' (*Siris* §296). Here themes familiar from the early works re-emerge – including the view that 'all phenomena are, to speak truly, appearances in the soul or mind' (*Siris* §251) and that there are, strictly, no corporeal causes. Yet these are now tied in with what appear to be alien elements. There is a tendency to disparage the senses, and Berkeley's fascination with the philosophies of the ancients extends to a degree of sympathy for the Platonic Theory of Forms. That said, Berkeley's eclectic and somewhat hesitant approach in *Siris* is such that it would be wrong to look to it for evidence of a substantially new philosophical position. Though fascinating in its way, *Siris* now seems very dated indeed.

13 Concluding Remarks

Inevitably, Berkeley is famed for the metaphysics of the *Principles*, and *Dialogues*. It would be easy to multiply quotations from people who treated that metaphysics as absurd, but very wrong to suggest that all the reactions have been hostile, or that the more hostile responses have not frequently been based on misunderstandings. At the other extreme, John Stuart Mill was to refer to Plato, Locke and Kant among others when describing Berkeley as 'the one of greatest philosophic genius' (Mill [1871] 1978: 451), while A.A. Luce, the most prominent Berkeley scholar of the twentieth century, held Berkeley's views to be fundamentally correct, and to coincide with the common-sense view of the world. Even many who would be less effusive have at least seen Berkeley as playing an important role in the history of philosophy, if only as marking one important stage on the route from Locke to Hume, and then to Kant and modern idealism. Certainly, no serious commentators would judge that his views can be easily or simply dismissed, though they would often give very different accounts of what makes him important and interesting. Luce, for example, found the role God has to play in Berkeley's system attractive; Mill thought it an embarrassment. Phenomenalism, the theory of perception which Mill himself espoused, could indeed be described as 'Berkeley without God' (see MILL, J.S. §6; PHENOMENALISM).

The fact is that Berkeley was grappling with problems that are perennial in philosophy, including that of the relationship between appearance and reality, or between our experiences and what we take them to be experiences of. Their treatments of these issues have very often led philosophers to say things that would strike the 'vulgar' as strange, and if Locke's position, for example, seems initially more congenial (in that Locke never doubts the existence of a world corresponding to, but distinct from, our 'ideas', and treats scepticism in that area as absurd), Berkeley was neither the first nor the last to see him as, in effect, making knowledge of that world impossible. Berkeley did not invent the sceptical challenge that arises from insisting on a distinction between what we 'immediately' perceive and an external 'material' world; if his way of dealing with it is radical, one must recognize that 'idealism' in one form or another was to have quite a history – even now there are philosophers who are happy to use the label to describe their own philosophical positions.

Certainly Berkeley does sometimes exaggerate the extent to which he is at one with the 'vulgar', or with our ordinary views about the world. He may be quite right that he is at one with those who believe that '*those things they immediately perceive are the real things*'. Yet, as we saw in §9 above, it is only by combining this with the claim that '*the things immediately perceived, are ideas which exist only in the mind*', which he attributes to 'the philosophers', that he arrives at a theory concerning the nature of reality that is very much his own. Consequently, although he can chide his opponents for their commitment to such views as that 'the Wall is not white, the fire is not hot', remarking in the *Commentaries* (entry 392) that 'We Irish men cannot attain to these truths', many of his own claims, such as that 'Strictly speaking...we do not see the same object that we feel; neither is the same object perceived by the microscope, which was by the naked eye' (*Works*, vol. 2: 245), would strike the vulgar as equally odd. Berkeley's beliefs about what it is that we 'immediately' perceive may or may not be true, but clearly they are not vulgar views.

To be fair, Berkeley was not unaware that this was the position. For example, his comment that on the issue of causal relationships between objects we should *'think with the learned, and speak with the vulgar'* (*Principles* §51) suggests that the vulgar have not appreciated the truth of the matter; while claims that he opposes only other philosophers contrast with passages such as that in the *Principles* in which he actually refers to the 'mistake' of the vulgar who believe that the 'objects of perception [have] an existence independent of, and without the mind' (*Principles* §56). To be sure, in the same discussion he suggests that they cannot *really* believe this, because the supposed belief involves a contradiction, and 'Strictly speaking, to believe that which involves a contradiction, or has no meaning in it, is impossible' (*Principles* §54), but the whole passage rests on the equation of the objects of perception with 'ideas', which is what *makes* the supposed belief contradictory.

The truth is, therefore, that for all his resolve in the *Commentaries* (entry 751)'To be eternally banishing Metaphisics &c & recalling Men to Common Sense' (and what he seems to have in mind there is the arid metaphysics of the Schools), Berkeley does offer us what we would naturally describe as a metaphysics, and one that cannot be refuted simply on the ground that it might strike the average person as outrageous. His arguments must be examined on their merits, together with any underlying assumptions; attention has to be paid to the notion of 'immediate' perception which he works with; and account must be taken of possible problems generated by his metaphysical conclusions. These may include, as has often been claimed, an unrecognized tendency towards solipsism. Not that it is necessary to reject or accept his philosophy in total, for there may be insights alongside what we believe are mistakes. As with any philosopher of Berkeley's stature, doing justice to Berkeley's philosophy turns out to be a very complex, but also a rewarding exercise, which is why his philosophy still exercises the commentators today.

See also: MEANING AND UNDERSTANDING; VISION

List of works

Berkeley, G. (1948–57) *The Works of George Berkeley, Bishop of Cloyne*, ed. A.A. Luce and T.E. Jessop, Edinburgh: Thomas Nelson, 9 vols. (The standard edition, containing Berkeley's published and unpublished writings, both philosophical and non-philosophical. The philosophical correspondence between Berkeley and Samuel Johnson is in vol. 2.)

—— (1707) *Arithmetica* and *Miscellanea Mathematica*, in *Works*, vol. 4, Edinburgh: Thomas Nelson. (Published anonymously in one volume, these slight pieces are of relatively little interest today, even to mathematicians.)

—— (1707) *Of Infinites*, in *Works*, vol. 4, Edinburgh: Thomas Nelson. (Although Berkeley never published it, this essay is of some interest, both because of its anticipation of attacks on assumptions underlying the infinitesimal calculus that Berkeley developed in later works and for the use he makes of the Lockian principle – which he was to soon reject – that all words stand for ideas.)

—— (1707–8) *Philosophical Commentaries*, in *Works*, vol. 1, Edinburgh: Thomas Nelson. (Berkeley's notebooks, filled as he prepared to publish the *New Theory of Vision* and the *Principles*. They are of inestimable value to scholars. The dates given represent Luce's reasoned speculation; the title is that given to them by Luce.)

—— (1709) *An Essay towards a New Theory of Vision*, in *Works*, vol. 1, Edinburgh: Thomas Nelson. (The first of Berkeley's major works, and for long influential as a work on the psychology underlying our visual perception of the distance from us and the size and situation of objects. Although Berkeley's ultimate metaphysical commitments were not made manifest here, awaiting the publication of the *Principles* in the following year, this work prepared the ground for them.)

—— (1710) *A Treatise concerning the Principles of Human Knowledge*, in *Works*, vol. 2, Edinburgh: Thomas Nelson. (Undoubtedly Berkeley's most important work, in which he attacks 'material substance' and the notion that sensible objects exist 'without the mind'. Originally published as 'Part I', no further parts appeared.)

—— (1712) *Passive Obedience*, in *Works*, vol. 6, Edinburgh: Thomas Nelson. (An interesting little work in that it represents a rare excursion into political philosophy and ethics, and suggests a basically utilitarian position. Berkeley denies the legitimacy of resisting even a manifestly unjust ruler.)

—— (1713) *Three Dialogues between Hylas and Philonous*, in *Works*, vol. 2, Edinburgh: Thomas Nelson. (A lively exposition of the metaphysics argued for in the *Principles of Human Knowledge*, with an emphasis on its supposed conformity with common sense. Highly recommended to those reading Berkeley for the first time.)

—— (1713) Essays in the *Guardian*, in *Works*, vol. 7, Edinburgh: Thomas Nelson. (Short essays published in Richard Steele's short-lived periodical, evidencing Berkeley's opposition to any form of irreligion. Essays in the *Guardian* were published anonymously. Those included in *Works*, vol. 7, are the ones Luce judged were by Berkeley.)

—— (1721) *De Motu*, in *Works*, vol. 4, Edinburgh: Thomas Nelson. (Berkeley abandoned his plans to publish further parts of the *Principles*, including one on natural philosophy. This essay on the cause of motion covers some of the ground that might have been dealt with there.)

—— (1732) *Alciphron: or the Minute Philosopher*, in *Works*, vol. 3, Edinburgh: Thomas Nelson. (A defence of religion, and Christianity in particular, against 'free-thinkers'. Observations on the uses of language contained in the last of the seven dialogues into which the work is divided give insights into how Berkeley's thinking in this area developed.)

—— (1733) *The Theory of Vision, Vindicated and Explained*, in *Works*, vol. 1, Edinburgh: Thomas Nelson. (A third edition of the *New Theory of Vision* had been annexed to the first edition of *Alciphron*. In *The Theory of Vision, Vindicated and Explained*, Berkeley responded to an anonymous critic.)

—— (1734) *The Analyst*, in *Works*, vol. 4, Edinburgh: Thomas Nelson. (A technical work on mathematics, revealing alleged obscurities and contradictions lying at the root of the infinitesimal calculus. The work, which was addressed to 'an infidel mathematician', argued that mathematicians were poorly placed to object to obscurities in Christian doctrine.)

—— (1735) *A Defence of Free-thinking in Mathematics* and *Reasons for not replying to Mr. Walton's Full Answer*, in *Works*, vol. 4, Edinburgh: Thomas Nelson. (Two tracts, published in the same year, responding to two critics of *The Analyst*.)

—— (1735–7) *The Querist*, in *Works*, vol. 6, Edinburgh: Thomas Nelson. (A series of short rhetorical questions, motivated by Berkeley's deep concern with the economic state of Ireland and the poverty of the Irish people. By now little more than a curiosity, the work was deservedly popular at the time.)

—— (1744) *Siris: a Chain of Philosophical Reflexions and Inquiries* (etc.), in *Works*, vol. 5, Edinburgh: Thomas Nelson. (A work in which Berkeley moves from a consideration of the supposed virtues of tar-water as a medicine, through reflections on natural science, to observations on God and the Trinity. Although popular at the time, this work is of little interest now, except to specialist scholars.)

References and further reading

Atherton, M. (1990) *Berkeley's Revolution in Vision*, Ithaca, NY: Cornell University Press. (Argues that, far from being a mere halfway house on the route to the philosophy of the *Principles* and *Dialogues*, Berkeley's New Theory of Vision has value in its own right, and provides a key to a more adequate understanding of those works.)

* Baxter, A. (1733), *An Enquiry into the Nature of the Human Soul*, London: G. Strahan; 2nd edn, London: A. Millar, 1737; repr. Bristol: Thoemmes Press, 1990. (The section in volume two entitled 'Dean Berkeley's scheme against the existence of matter, and a material world examined, and shewn inconclusive' contains the first extended critique of Berkeley's *Principles*.)

Berman, D. ed. (1989) *George Berkeley: Eighteenth-Century Responses*, 2 vols, New York: Garland Publishing. (Contains many of the early responses to various of Berkeley's works. These include some from important or influential figures such as James Beattie and Thomas Reid, the first reviews of the *Principles* and *Dialogues*, and materials not easily accessible elsewhere.)

—— (1994) *George Berkeley: Idealism and the Man*, Oxford: Clarendon Press. (A lively introduction to Berkeley's life and writings which is particularly interesting on works such as *Passive Obedience*, *Alciphron*, and *Siris*, and which throws light on the Irish context of Berkeley's thought.)

Brook, R.J. (1973) *Berkeley's Philosophy of Science*, The Hague: Martinus Nijhoff. (A thorough examination of Berkeley's writings on optics, physics and mathematics, against the background of his theory of meaning and signification.)

Grayling, A.C. (1986) *Berkeley: The Central Arguments*, London: Duckworth. (Argues that 'Berkeley's views are, in some important respects, more defensible than has in general been allowed', and – against Pitcher, Tipton and others – that Berkeley's 'theistic' realism can be plausibly presented as a defence of common sense.)

Johnston, G.A. (1923) *The Development of Berkeley's Philosophy*, London: Macmillan; repr. New York: Garland Publishing, 1988. (Originally published early in the twentieth century, Johnston's judicious and scholarly introduction to the Berkeleian corpus contains much that is still of value.)

* Locke, J. (1689) *An Essay concerning Human Understanding*, ed. P.H. Nidditch, Oxford: Clarendon Press, 1974. (Listed here because Locke has been mentioned frequently in the article, but also because Locke was undoubtedly the most important influence on Berkeley.)

Luce, A.A. (1934) *Berkeley and Malebranche*, Oxford: Oxford University Press, 1934; 2nd edn, Oxford: Clarendon Press, 1967. (While not underestimating the importance of Locke's influence on Berkeley, Luce's important monograph showed that Berkeley's reading of Malebranche's *Search After Truth* made a very deep impression on him. Luce also argued for the likely influence of Bayle.)

—— (1949) *The Life of George Berkeley, Bishop of Cloyne*, Edinburgh: Thomas Nelson; repr. Bristol: Thoemmes Press, 1992. (The standard biography of Berkeley.)

—— (1963) *The Dialectic of Immaterialism*, London: Hodder & Stoughton. (A study of the *Philosophical Commentaries* published when Luce was in his eighties, this book rested on more than thirty years of devoted research.)

* Mill, J.S. (1871) 'Berkeley's Life and Writings', *Fortnightly Review*, n.s. X (Nov.) repr. in *Collected Works of John Start Mill*, ed. J.M. Robson, Toronto: University of Toronto Press and London: Routledge & Kegan Paul, 1978, vol. 11. (Fascinating observations on Berkeley's philosophy from an important nineteenth-century philosopher.)

Muehlmann, R.G. (1992) *Berkeley's Ontology*, Indianapolis, IN: Hackett Publishing Company. (A fairly demanding but rewarding study, revealing an indepth knowledge of the recent literature on Berkeley, as well as a sensitivity towards the intellectual background against which Berkeley wrote.)

Pitcher, G. (1977) *Berkeley*, London: Routledge & Kegan Paul. (Although he tends to write as if Berkeley was reacting solely against Locke, Pitcher's philosophical acuity and clarity of style make this a stimulating introduction to Berkeley.)

Tipton, I.C. (1974) *Berkeley: The Philosophy of Immaterialism*, London: Methuen; repr. Bristol: Thoemmes Press, 1994. (A careful examination of Berkeley's arguments in the *Principles* and *Dialogues*, this book aims to be of value to scholars and other philosophers as well as to those requiring a comprehensible introduction to Berkeley.)

Winkler, K.P. (1989) *Berkeley: An Interpretation*, Oxford: Clarendon Press. (This sympathetic exposition of Berkeley's metaphysics will appeal to the more advanced student. Concentrates on topics such as representation, abstraction, and cause and effect, in an attempt to deepen our understanding of Berkeley's central arguments.)

IAN TIPTON

BERLIN, ISAIAH (1909–97)

Berlin said that he decided about 1945 to give up philosophy, in which he had worked up to that time, in favour of the history of ideas. Some of his best-known work certainly belongs to the history of ideas, but he continued in fact both to write philosophy and to pursue philosophical questions in his historical work.

His main philosophical contributions are to political philosophy and specifically to the theory of liberalism. He emphasizes a distinction between 'negative' and 'positive' concepts of liberty: the former is a Hobbesian idea of absence of constraint or obstacle, while the latter is identified with a notion of moral self-government, expressed for instance in Rousseau, which Berlin finds politically threatening. His anti-utopian approach to politics is expressed also in his view that values necessarily conflict; this irreducible 'value pluralism' may be his most original contribution to philosophy, though he advances it through example and historical illustration rather than in semantic or epistemological terms. He also expresses himself against necessitarian interpretations of history, and in favour of an anti-determinist conception of free will.

1 Against reductionism
2 Value pluralism
3 Liberty

1 Against reductionism

Isaiah Berlin was born in Riga, Latvia, of Jewish parents; the family emigrated in 1919 to Britain, where he was educated and spent his life. He worked first in general philosophy, and in the 1930s took part, with A.J. Ayer, J.L. Austin and others, in discussions of questions about knowledge and meaning which were raised by the logical positivist agenda of the time. (Papers related to these interests, mostly published rather later, are collected in Berlin 1978a.) Berlin was never tempted by positivism. Besides pressing realist objections against such proposals as the dispositional analysis of statements about the unobserved, he rejected its scientific paradigm of knowledge and its lack of interest in historical understanding. Paradoxically, the most positivist element to survive in Berlin's thought is his definition of philosophy, as concerned with questions that defy solution by the a priori and the empirical sciences. It may also have been a positivist influence that encouraged him to draw a sharp distinction, in his formulations though not in his practice, between his philosophical and his historical interests (see LOGICAL POSITIVISM).

In his work in the history of ideas, Berlin paid particular and sympathetic attention to thinkers such as VICO and HERDER who have emphasized cultural difference across time, have stressed the need to understand other ways of life 'from the inside', and have resisted the impulse of the more rationalistic strains of the Enlightenment to reduce the range of human concerns to some limited set of motivations which are met more or less efficiently by different social formations. He denied that there is a 'fixed and unalterable' human nature. At the same time, however, he firmly resisted relativism of any type.

At the level of interpreting other societies, he accepts that there are universal human potentialities, limitations, and indeed sentiments, and believes in fact that we would not be able to understand those societies except on this assumption. The denial of a fixed human nature comes to saying first, that there are many different and no canonically correct expressions of these potentialities; second, that what expressions these potentialities might receive cannot be recognized in advance of historical experience; third, that these two points hold good for the future, so that there can be no Hegelian (or – more particularly for Berlin's concerns – Marxist) total realization of human possibilities (see HEGEL, G.W.F.; MARX, K.).

How far, in Berlin's view, we might go in forming a definite picture of human potentialities is unclear. On the one hand, Berlin, sharing with his favoured authors a keen sense of cultural particularity, is impressed by the unpredictable distinctiveness of different forms of life, as of artistic styles. On the other hand, we understand these forms of life, in part, through values that are expressed in them, and there is nothing in Berlin's work to rule out the idea that, although the cultural forms are manifold, the values expressed in them might be limited, and indeed quite few, in number. If so, there may be room for an account of human nature which would explain why, at a general level, only a certain range of values are candidates for expression in recognizably human cultures (see HUMAN NATURE).

2 Value pluralism

These values, Berlin repeatedly urged, make conflicting claims and cannot be totally reconciled with one another without loss. Political schemes, moral theories, and religious aspirations have repeatedly tried to deny this truth and to claim that, properly understood, values do not ultimately conflict: 'true' liberty, for instance, will not conflict with 'true' equality. Berlin rejects such outlooks, for several reasons. Politically, attempts to put them into practice have always been a disaster, in terms which only their most fanatical adherents can deny. Ethically, they are an evasion, and pretend that an intellectual construction can make life easier than it is. Philosophically, they are a mistake.

Not being concerned with meta-ethical analysis, Berlin does not try to counter the objection made by some critics that the status of this last claim is obscure, but concentrates on substantiating the first two claims. Berlin himself, because of his views on the nature of philosophy, is disposed to agree that the philosophical claim is distinct from political and ethical claims, but the best interpretation of his outlook may well be that the philosophical claim is to be understood through the others. Whatever theory of values we accept, our conclusions about their structure can be sensibly constrained, protected against being an arbitrary fantasy, only by serious reflection on political and ethical experience, and for Berlin this essentially depends on our best historical understanding.

Berlin's claim of ultimate value pluralism encounters philosophical problems about its content, as well as about its status. In practice, policies do have to be adopted, some ways of life favoured over others. Berlin's pluralism insists that such choices often involve value loss, denies that there is one currency in which the gains and losses can be calculated, but claims that the choices are not therefore irrational. Questions of how these views can be consistently interpreted are important to the theory of practical and evaluative reasoning: they are sometimes expressed as questions about the incommensurability of values.

Questions about the status and the content of value pluralism are important to Berlin's defence of liberalism. He clearly regards liberalism as a political order which in some sense particularly respects value pluralism. It would be untrue to Berlin's outlook to take this in a metaphysical sense, as implying that the liberal state best expresses the real structure of values. Rather, the arguments for liberalism use the same historical and political materials as the arguments for pluralism. To this extent, Berlin's liberalism, with its emphasis on the human costs of non-liberal, 'totalizing', political visions, is close to what Judith Shklar (1989) called 'the liberalism of fear', an outlook which owes much to MONTESQUIEU, CONSTANT, DE TOCQUEVILLE and a strong sense of modern historical experience.

Another line of interpretation suggests that, for Berlin, value pluralism is specially honoured by liberalism because liberal states emphasize the individual's freedom to choose, in particular between different values and forms of life. This makes such freedom – freedom as autonomy – a privileged value in Berlin's outlook, and associates him rather with VON HUMBOLDT and J.S. MILL. But it is doubtful whether autonomy is privileged by Berlin in this way. It would be barely consistent with his own treatment of liberty (see §3), and it is questionable whether value pluralism can be coherently used to promote one value over others. In any case, Berlin is notably ambivalent about the more defiantly individualist aspect of liberal societies. Above all because of his Zionist sympathies, he is at least as much interested in the individual's 'need to belong' to a community, and in cultural rather than individual self-determination. To some extent, these sympathies stand in tension with his liberalism, but they also condition it, in such a way that radical autonomy and individual self-expression should not be seen as its most central values (see MORAL PLURALISM).

3 Liberty

Berlin discussed more than one question related to liberty: he opposed ideas of historical inevitability, and resisted compatibilist theories of free will. He is best known, however, for his views on liberty as a distinctively political value, in particular for a distinction between 'negative' and 'positive' conceptions of liberty. Negative liberty is defined in traditionally Hobbesian or empiricist terms, as the absence of external constraint or interference. Positive liberty is understood, rather, as self-mastery or self-realization, two aspects which are themselves not very strongly distinguished from one another.

It is important that this is not only a distinction between two political conceptions, but a political distinction, which gets its content from its relation to two different styles of political thought. It is not, for instance, a distinction between 'freedom from' and 'freedom to'. Though negative liberty centrally covers freedom from intentional interference, it does not cover the famous freedoms of post-war liberal politics, such as the freedoms from want, disease and unemployment. Berlin is not opposed to the objectives that are expressed in this way, but in the general spirit of pluralism finds it more helpful to place them under values other than freedom, such as welfare or equality. Again, negative liberty does not cover freedom from internal compulsions. This freedom might be said in any case to represent an ethical or psychological aspiration, rather than a political conception. However, Berlin does associate it with positive liberty, and this precisely illustrates the point that on his view positive liberty is a political conception that aspires to have too much ethical content (it is, in John Rawls' terminology, 'perfectionist' (Rawls 1971: 25)). Negative liberty can extend to freedom from political manipulation, but seemingly only in gross forms which would be described even by everyday conceptions as restricting agents' freedom to act. It would not extend to freedom from ideological determination or false consciousness, which again would be associated with positive liberty.

The thread that holds together these various associations and exclusions seems to be that negative liberty is meant to be minimally normative in its definition. It is, of course, a value and brings with it a norm or positive evaluation, but in giving an account of its content, Berlin tries as far as possible to exclude other normative and evaluative ideas. This same point comes out in Berlin's treatment of the traditional difficulty that if liberty is measured by the ratio of actual desires to the capacity to fulfil them, it will follow that one can increase liberty just as much by reducing agents' desires as by increasing their capacities. Berlin answers this simply by appealing to possible as well as actual desires. This line involves the difficulty that if no limits are put on what an agent could possibly desire, everyone will be equally unfree; it seems that Berlin would rather face this problem than appeal to measures of liberty that bring in further normative elements, such as the idea of desires that agents might reasonably be expected to have, or of those that agents in society might reasonably expect to satisfy.

Berlin's treatment of liberty seems have three different sources. One is his pluralistic aim of keeping liberty as far as possible distinct from other political values. Another is that he is suspicious of accounts of political values which tie them too closely to non-political values, in particular to perfectionist ethical aspirations for the individual. Third, and relatedly, he is impressed by the fact that political programmes which advance such values have been historically associated with the actions of an elite trying to impose an interpretation of people's supposed real interests. Berlin's favoured negative concept of liberty, like other aspects of his thought, is not a purely analytical proposal, but is defined by conceptions of liberalism and of the political which are consciously shaped by responses to actual historical developments, above all the Russian Revolution (see LIBERALISM).

See also: ENLIGHTENMENT, CONTINENTAL; FREEDOM AND LIBERTY; INCOMMENSURABILITY; HISTORICISM; PLURALISM; VALUES

List of works

Berlin, I. (1939) *Karl Marx: His Life and Environment*, London: Thornton Butterworth; repr. with a new introduction by A. Ryan, London: Fontana, 1955. (A vivid representation of Marx as well as of his ideas; some modifications in later editions.)

—— (1969) *Four Essays on Liberty*, Oxford: Oxford University Press. (A central text. In his long introduction Berlin discusses the two central essays, 'Historical Inevitability' and 'Two Concepts of Liberty'.)

—— (1976) *Vico and Herder*, London: Hogarth Press. (Basic to the work on the history of ideas.)

—— (1978a) *Concepts and Categories*, ed. H. Hardy, London: Hogarth Press. (Contains some early contributions to general philosophy; and, among other essays, 'From Hope and Fear Set Free', which complements the essays on liberty, and 'Does Political Theory Still Exist?'.)

—— (1978b) *Russian Thinkers*, ed. H. Hardy and A. Kelly, London: Hogarth Press. (Includes 'The Hedgehog and the Fox', 'On Tolstoy' and 'Fathers and Children', important for the understanding of liberalism.)

—— (1979) *Against the Current*, ed. H. Hardy, London: Hogarth Press. (Essays in the history of ideas. Contains a complete bibliography of Berlin's writings, updated in a later edition 1991, Oxford: Clarendon Press, and further in 1997, London: Pimlico Press.)

—— (1980) *Personal Impressions*, ed. H. Hardy, London: Hogarth Press. (Vivid and often moving biographical essays.)

—— (1990) *The Crooked Timber of Humanity*, ed. H. Hardy, London: Murray. (Starts with Berlin's retrospective summary of his views, and includes a long essay on de Maistre.)

—— (1993) *The Magus of the North: J.G. Hamann and the Origins of Modern Irrationalism*, ed. H. Hardy, London: Murray. (Short monograph on the obscure Prussian thinker regarded by Berlin as one of the fathers of romanticism.)

—— (1996) *The Sense of Reality: Studies in Ideas and their History*, ed. H. Hardy, London: Chatto & Windus. (Mostly historical essays written in the 1950s and 1960s, with one exception published for the first time.)

—— (1997) *The Proper Study of Mankind*, ed. H. Hardy and R. Hausheer, London: Chatto & Windus. (An anthology of Berlin's best-known essays.)

References and further reading

Galipeau, C.J. (1994) *Isaiah Berlin's Liberalism*, Oxford: Oxford University Press. (Careful and well-documented discussion.)

Gray, J. (1995) *Isaiah Berlin*, London: HarperCollins. (Interpretation in terms of 'agonistic liberalism', emphasizing radical choice.)

Margalit, E. and Margalit, A. (eds) (1991) *Isaiah Berlin, A Celebration*, London: Hogarth Press. (Essays by various writers, about half of them on philosophical subjects.)

* Rawls, J. (1971) *A Theory of Justice*, Cambridge, MA: Harvard University Press. (A classic modern statement of liberal political philosophy.)

Ryan, A. (ed.) (1979) *The Idea of Freedom: Essays in Honour of Isaiah Berlin*, Oxford: Oxford University Press. (Essays by various writers, most on philosophical topics.)

* Shklar, J. (1989) 'The Liberalism of Fear', in N.L. Rosenblum (ed.) *Liberalism and the Moral Life*, Cambridge, MA: Harvard University Press. (See §2.)

BERNARD WILLIAMS

BERNARD OF CLAIRVAUX (1090–1153)

Bernard was recognized by his contemporaries as the spiritual leader of western Europe. He was an indefatigable advocate of the monastic life and occasionally criticized the schools on moral grounds, but he was by no means an anti-intellectual. He encouraged a number of early scholastic philosopher-theologians in their work. Although he devoted the better part of his efforts to his wide-ranging pastoral duties, Bernard's own sermons and treatises make a significant contribution to twelfth-century theology and philosophy.

Bernard was born into a noble family in 1090 near Dijon in Burgundy, and studied grammar, rhetoric and logic at Châtillon. Abandoning plans for further study, he joined the Cistercian Order at Cîteaux in 1113. Only two years later, he became the first abbot of the new Cistercian foundation at Clairvaux, a position he held until his death in 1153. During his abbacy of almost forty years, Bernard exerted a profound influence over the intellectual and religious life of western Europe. The extent of his influence may be measured by the sixty-five daughter monasteries established by Clairvaux during Bernard's lifetime, his nearly single-handed resolution of the papal schism of 1130, and the fact that one of his own monks assumed the papacy as Eugenius III (1145–53).

Bernard was actively interested in the schools of his day (the precursors of the medieval universities) and was reasonably well-informed about academic discussions in theology. In his controversies, first with Peter ABELARD in 1140 and then with GILBERT OF POITIERS in 1148, Bernard wished to expose and correct what he saw as heretical opinions. Concerning atonement, for example, Bernard opposed Abelard's claim that Christ redeemed humanity simply by inspiring love for God and providing a perfect pattern of life. Regarding the trinity, Bernard maintained, also against Abelard, that the relation of the second person to the first was not a relation of species to genus, and that certain divine properties, such as power or wisdom, were not specific to just one or another person of the trinity (see TRINITY). In the case of Gilbert, Bernard also disputed some of his assertions about the trinity, the incarnation and the divine essence.

In attacking certain of Abelard's and Gilbert's conclusions, Bernard also showed a distrust of their method, but he did not condemn outright their application of logic to doctrine. Bernard considered all knowledge good in itself, but he believed the pursuit of knowledge should be governed by practical concerns, especially salvation, and not by a desire to know simply for the sake of knowing.

Bernard's feuds with Abelard and Gilbert were more than counterbalanced by his support for other philosopher-theologians. He was, for example, a protector of Peter LOMBARD and a friend to JOHN OF SALISBURY. He praised the English scholastic Robert Pullen for his 'sound doctrine' and endeavoured to keep him in Paris. Bernard responded to some inquiries of HUGH OF ST VICTOR with a long letter (*circa* 1127) on baptism, salvation before Christ's death and resurrection, and other disputed matters, which clearly influenced Hugh's massive work, *De sacramentis christianae fidei* (On the Sacraments of the Christian Faith). More than once, Bernard admitted the practical value, even necessity, of scholastic theology in refuting heresy, clarifying obscure points of doctrine and guiding church leaders.

Bernard was an accomplished theologian in his own right, and his writings are characterized by strict adherence to scriptural and patristic sources rather than by philosophical development of doctrine. Most of his sermons and treatises are concerned with the exposition of Scripture and doctrine along moral and contemplative lines. *De gradibus humilitatis et superbiae* (Steps of Humility and Pride), for example, describes the pursuit of truth through three kinds of knowledge: humility (self-knowledge), compassion (knowledge of one's neighbour) and contemplation (knowledge of God). *De diligendo Deo* (On Loving God) takes up the nature of disinterested love and describes the steps by which one attains it. His longest work, *Sermones super Cantica canticorum* (Sermons on the Song of Songs), begun in 1135 and left unfinished at his death in 1153, combines scriptural commentary with an examination of the moral and contemplative aspects of religious life.

Bernard sometimes wrote works of theology that were more philosophical than scriptural. His treatise *De gratia et libero arbitrio* (Grace and Free Choice) is a substantial work of philosophical theology, markedly influenced by Augustine, in which he attempts to reconcile human freedom with God's grace. Bernard thinks that the will is necessarily free; in consenting to the good, the will cooperates with grace. His treatise is notable for its definition of free choice as 'a spontaneous inclination of the will,' and for its innovative distinction among three types of human freedom: freedom from necessity, freedom from sin and freedom from sorrow (see FREE WILL; GRACE). This was the most influential of Bernard's works among scholastic thinkers, and elements of it appear in Peter Lombard's *Sentences* and, in the next century, in the works of ALEXANDER OF HALES and ALBERT THE GREAT.

See also: ABELARD, P.; HUGH OF ST VICTOR; RELIGION, HISTORY OF PHILOSOPHY OF

List of works

Bernard of Clairvaux (1090–1153) *Sancti Bernardi Opera*, ed. J. Leclerq *et al.*, Rome: Editiones Cisterciensis, 1957–77, 8 vols; trans. as *The Works of Bernard of Clairvaux*, Cistercian Fathers Series, Kalamazoo, MI: Cistercian Publications, 1973–80. (The English translation series includes most of Bernard's treatises and many of his sermons.)

—— (c.1125) *De gradibus humilitatis et superbiae* (Steps of Humility and Pride), in J. Leclerq *et al.* (eds) *Sancti Bernardi Opera*, Rome: Editiones Cisterciensis, vol. 3, 1963; trans. M. Ambrose Conway, *The Steps of Humility and Pride*, Cistercian Fathers Series, Kalamazoo, MI: Cistercian Publications, 1973; repr. 1989. (A profound study of the nature of humility – as reflected in twelve manifestations of pride – and its importance in the attainment of truth; an important source for later medieval ethics.)

—— (1126–41) *De diligendo Deo* (On Loving God), in J. Leclerq *et al.* (eds) *Sancti Bernardi Opera*, Rome: Editiones Cisterciensis, vol. 3, 1963; trans. E. Stiegman, Cistercian Fathers Series, Kalamazoo, MI: Cistercian Publications, 1973; repr. 1985. (The best introduction to several overarching themes in Bernard's life and thought.)

—— (*c.*1127) *De gratia et libero arbitrio* (Grace and Free Choice), in J. Leclerq *et al.* (eds) *Sancti Bernardi Opera*, Rome: Editiones Cisterciensis, vol. 3, 1963; trans. D. O'Donovan, Cistercian Fathers Series, Kalamazoo, MI: Cistercian Publications, 1977; repr. 1988. (Takes a moderate, sometimes novel approach to one of the most complex and divisive issues in Christian thought.)

—— (1135–53) *Sermones super Cantica canticorum* (Sermons on the Song of Songs), in J. Leclerq *et al.* (eds) *Sancti Bernardi Opera*, Rome: Editiones Cisterciensis, vols 1–2, 1957–8; trans. K. Walsh and I.M. Edmonds, Cistercian Fathers Series, Kalamazoo, MI: Cistercian Publications, 1971–80, 4 vols. (A model of allegorical exegesis, this detailed commentary should be read more for its sustained analysis of Christian life and doctrine than for its nominal subject matter.)

References and further reading

Saint Bernard Théologien: Actes Du Congrès De Dijon, 15–19 Septembre 1953 (Saint Bernard the Theologian: Proceedings of the Dijon Conference, 15–19 September 1953) (1953), 2nd edn in Analecta Sacri Ordinis Cisterciensis IX, foreword and introduction by J. Leclercq, Rome: Editiones Cistercienses. (An unsurpassed collection of essays, all in French, on various aspects of Bernard's theology.)

Evans, G.R. (1983) *The Mind of St. Bernard of Clairvaux*, Oxford: Clarendon Press. (A very helpful introduction to Bernard's writings and his place in the intellectual life of the twelfth century, but sometimes weak in its exposition of his ideas.)

Gilson, E. (1940) *The Mystical Theology of St. Bernard*, trans. A.H.C. Downes, London and New York: Sheed & Ward; repr. Kalamazoo, MI: Cistercian Publications, 1990. (First published in 1934, this still indispensable classic reconstructs the theological system underlying Bernard's contemplative writings.)

SEAN MURPHY

BERNARD OF TOURS
(*fl.* 1147, d. before 1178)

Bernard of Tours, better known as Bernardus Silvestris, was closely acquainted with the major developments in science and theology which took place in the mid-twelfth century. His major work, the Cosmographia, *an allegorical account of the creation of the universe and humankind, is dedicated to the philosopher-theologian Thierry of Chartres, who was probably also his teacher. However, Bernard himself was best known as a poet, and he seems to have made his living primarily as a teacher of grammar and rhetoric. His career perhaps reflects the fragmentation of the liberal arts curriculum in his day, including the segregation of literary studies from the increasingly specialized pursuit of the sciences.*

Little is known of Bernard's career beyond his attachment to Tours. The city is recalled affectionately in the *Cosmographia*; Bernard is praised by his pupil Matthew of Vendôme, author of one of the earliest medieval treatises on the art of poetry, as 'the master of Tours', and we know that a nephew inherited his house in the city at some time prior to 1178. The *Cosmographia* also contains a fulsome compliment to Pope Eugenius III, and a manuscript gloss reports that the work was read before Eugenius, to the latter's great satisfaction. This was presumably in 1147, when Eugenius came to France to attend the trial of GILBERT OF POITIERS.

No more is known of Bernard's life. Matthew notes his mastery of *dictamen*, the arts of composition, and later writers cite his poems almost exclusively as examples of literary style, so we may assume that this was the main focus of his teaching. Commentaries on Vergil and Martianus Capella, which use mythographic analysis to raise philosophical and religious questions and often closely echo the commentaries of WILLIAM OF CONCHES, have been attributed to Bernard, but despite suggestive thematic correspondences with the *Cosmographia*, they cannot be assigned to him with certainty.

The *Cosmographia* consists of alternating chapters of prose and verse, in emulation of Boethius' *De consolatione philosophiae* and the *De nuptiis Philologiae et Mercurii* of Martianus Capella, and its narrative of the cosmogony is based broadly on Plato's *Timaeus* (Wetherbee 1972: 152–86) (see BOETHIUS, A.M.S.; ENCYCLOPEDISTS; PLATO). Its theme is the process of creation, the realization of the 'seminal virtues' that come to fruition through the union of matter and form. The work begins with the noble and impassioned appeal of Nature to Noys, the agent of divine Wisdom, to order the formless existence of primal matter, which longs for 'the shaping influence of number and bonds of harmony'. The flowering of created life which results has important implications for man, the lesser universe, whose creation will be the culmination of the adaptation of Nature's vitality to the shaping influence of divine Wisdom. Man will find his fulfilment in recognition of the completeness with which his nature corresponds to the pattern and activity of the macrocosm. For man to comprehend this great affinity will be to simultaneously recognize his own lordship and destiny, a realization that mirrors the ordering activity of Noys, confirming that man's mind is created in the image of the Divine Wisdom.

Bernard's vision of the human condition is darkened by a strong sense of the precariousness of material existence and the uncertain power of reason to govern the aberrant tendencies of human nature. Like the visions vouchsafed to Adam in the last books of Milton's *Paradise Lost*, Bernard's foreshadowings of world history offer clear evidence of human guilt and folly. But they also celebrate the fruits of human genius in art, science and technology. The final vision of the *Cosmographia* is heroic, the stoic dignity with which man labours to resist his own instability and order and perpetuate his existence in the face of seemingly insuperable necessity. The work conveys the anxiety as well as the excitement of an age newly engaged with the study of nature and the tenuous linkage of cosmic order and physical law.

At times the pessimistic strain in the *Cosmographia* becomes a kind of determinism, and a similar note is struck in Bernard's other known works. The *Mathematicus* (The Astrologer), a narrative in Latin elegiacs, tells of a young man confronted by a prophecy that he will slay his father, who resolves instead to take his own life, affirming that such a death will be a release from the prison of material existence (Dronke 1974: 131–41). Bernard's introduction to the *Experimentarius*, a Latin adaptation of an Arab manual of geomancy, affirms the power of God but acknowledges that the planets have a 'natural' power to affect 'the destinies of all mortal things'.

See also: BOETHIUS, A.M.S.; CHARTRES, SCHOOL OF; COSMOLOGY; NATURAL PHILOSOPHY, MEDIEVAL; PLATONISM, MEDIEVAL

List of works

Bernard of Tours (c.1147) *Cosmographia*, ed. P. Dronke, Textus Minores 53, Leiden: Brill, 1978. (This work has been published in an edition translated by W. Wetherbee, Records of Civilization: Sources and Studies 89, New York: Columbia University Press, 1973.)

—— (c.1147) *Mathematicus* (The Astrologer), ed. B. Hauréau, Paris: C. Klincksieck, 1895. (This work also appears in *Patrologia Latina* 171, cols. 1365–80, where it is attributed to Hildebert of Lavardin.)

—— (c.1147) *Experimentarius*, ed. M. Brina-Savorelli, *Rivista critica di storia della filosofia* 14, 1959: 283–342. (Latin adaptation of Arab work with introduction by Bernard.)

References and further reading

* Dronke, P. (1974) *Fabula: Explorations into the Uses of Myth in Medieval Platonism*, Mittellateinische Studien und Texte 9, Leiden: Brill. (Places Bernard in a tradition of philosophical and religious interpretation of ancient myth.)

Edwards, R.R. (1993) 'Poetic Invention and the Medieval *Causae*', *Mediaeval Studies* 55: 183–217. (On the *Mathematicus* and other Latin poems attributed to Bernard.)

Stock, B. (1972) *Myth and Science in the Twelfth Century: A Study of Bernard Silvester*, Princeton, NJ: Princeton University Press. (A detailed reading of the *Cosmographia* as a document in the history of ideas.)

* Wetherbee, W. (1972) *Platonism and Poetry in the Twelfth Century*, Princeton, NJ: Princeton University Press. (Considers the *Cosmographia* as synthesizing the concerns of earlier twelfth-century philosophy.)

WINTHROP WETHERBEE

BERNARDUS SILVESTRIS *see* BERNARD OF TOURS

BERNIER, FRANÇOIS (1620–88)

Bernier was a minor figure who influenced the history of philosophy out of all proportion to his own strictly philosophical abilities. He was effective as a propagandist in the debates over the analysis of matter, and especially as a popularizer of the views of Pierre Gassendi, whose nominalism he sought to apply with greater consistency.

Bernier was and remains the best-known disciple of GASSENDI, whose eyes he is supposed to have closed at his death. In the seventeenth and for at least the next two centuries, Bernier was rather less known as a philosopher than as a traveller, especially for his *Memoirs...of the Grand Mogul's Empire* (1670–1), a classic that detailed his ten-year visit to the Indian subcontinent. Dryden based his *Aureng-Zebe* on this work, and LOCKE, a physician like Bernier, was interested in it, particularly as a source for his investigation of religious psychology under the rubric of 'enthusiasm'.

In philosophy Bernier was a minor figure who none the less played an important role as a polemicist, as a popularizer and as a philosopher in his own right. As a polemicist, he wrote at greatest length in *Anatomia* (1651) and *Favilla* (1653) on Gassendi's behalf against the imprecations of the astrologer J.-B. Morin. More effectively, he turned his satirical pen in common cause with the Cartesians against the political machinations of the Jesuit Aristotelians in his *Requeste des maistres* (1671). Finally, he joined the debates over matter and transubstantiation and, as Pierre BAYLE (who published his work) commented on Eclaircissement (1684), strongly opposed the Cartesians in order better to make his peace with the Jesuit La Ville.

By far the most influential of Bernier's works was his *Abrégé* of Gassendi's philosophy (1674–8). This abridgement, consisting of paraphrase and some translation, and written in straightforward, non-technical French, became for many their only access to the views expressed in the obscure, late scholastic Latin of Gassendi's lengthy tomes. Bayle's hope that it would remove the need to work through those tomes proved idle, however, for Bernier was an original thinker whose own views influenced the choice, ordering, emphasis and evaluation of the material.

Bernier's independence of Gassendi emerged explicitly in his *Doutes de M. Bernier sur quelques uns des principaux chapitres de son Abrégé de Gassendi* (1682). His eleven doubts raise questions about Gassendi's views on space, time, motion, collision and other important topics. However, in the preface to the second edition published with the second and last edition of the *Abrégé*, Bernier says that he 'doubts no longer, having despaired of being able ever to understand any of [these questions]'.

Beyond this negative or academic scepticism, however, the Doutes contains a more consistent application of Gassendi's own empiricism and nominalism than anything found in Gassendi himself (see NOMINALISM). A good example is the treatment of space, which for Gassendi was an uncreated, incorporeal tridimensionality, a third kind of being that was neither substance nor accident. In addition to the ubiquitous theological objection that such a space would be independent even of God, and thus pose a rival divinity, Bernier argued that it would not have parts and that it would be imperceptible. His deepest argument was that space is nothing at all: for there to be space between two things, there need not be a third thing between them, any more than for two things to be equal there need be a thing – equality – to make them so. Equality and distance are 'abstract terms, which like all others of this sort, lead us into error if we conceive something abstract or separated from the concrete' (1684 II: 387–8).

Explicitly exempted from Bernier's critique is Gassendi's atomism, for he does not think that one can reasonably philosophize on any system other than that of atoms and the void. Yet even here Bernier gives arguments that extend Gassendi's position beyond physical theory in an adumbration of the metaphysical atomism of HUME.

See also: ATOMISM, ANCIENT

List of works

Bernier, F. (1651) *Anatomia, ridiculi muris, hoc est dissertatiunculae I.B. Morini astrologi adversus expositam a P. Gassendo Epicuri Philosophiam...* (An analysis of an absurdity, that is, of the short dissertation of the astrologer I.B. Morin against the Epicurean philosophy of P. Gassendi), Paris. (A defence of Gassendi against the outré attacks of the astrologer Jean-Baptiste Morin.)

—— (1653) *Favilla ridiculi muris, hoc est dissertatiunculae ridicule defensae a Ioan. Bapt. Morino astrologo adversus expositam a Petro Gassendo Epicuri philosophiam* (The remains of an absurdity, that is, of the little dissertation defended by the astrologer J.-B. Morin against Gassendi's exposition of the philosophy of Epicurus), Paris. (A continuation of the polemic with Morin.)

—— (1670–1) *Memoires du sieur Bernier sur l'empire du grand Mogul*, Paris; trans. T. Brock as *Travels in the Mogul Empire AD 1656–1668*, New Delhi: Schand, 1968. (Earning its author the nickname of "Mogul", this account of his ten-year stay in the Indian subcontinent was a standard reference work well into the nineteenth century.)

—— (1671) *Requeste des maistres ès-arts, professeurs et regents de l'Université de Paris, presénte à la Cour souveraine du Parnasse, ensemble L'arrest intervenue sur ladite requeste contre tous ceux qui pretendent faire enseigner ou croire de nouvelles découvertes qui ne soient pas dans Aristotle* (Request of the authorities at the university of Paris, presented to the sovereign court of Parnasse, to intervene against all those who claim to teach or believe the new discoveries which are actually not in Aristotle), in G. Gueret, *La guerre des auteurs anciens et modernes*, The Hague. (A propaganda tract directed against the Sorbonne's attempt to re-establish Aristotelianism in the schools.)

—— (1678) *Abrégé de la philosophie de Gassendi* (Abridgement of the philosophy of Gassendi), Lyons, 7 vols, 2nd edn, 1684; repr. Paris: Fayard, 1992. (First published in proto-editions beginning 1674. Although it has been regarded as a principal source for the views of Gassendi, this translation, paraphrase, summary and interpolation of Gassendi's main work sometimes evidences Bernier's own, different views.)

—— (1682) *Doutes de M. Bernier sur quelques uns des principaux chapitres de son Abrégé de Gassendi* (Doubts of M. Bernier about some of the main chapters of his *Abrégé*), Paris. (A set of sceptical doubts about Gassendi's views on such topics as space, time, motion and collision; published in a second edition in volume two of the second edition of the *Abrégé*.)

—— (1684) *Eclaircissement sur le livre de M. de la Ville intitulé: Sentiments de M. Descartes touchant l'essence et les propriétés des corps* (Clarification of the work by M. de la Ville entitled 'Thoughts of Descartes regarding the essence and properties of bodies'), in P. Bayle *Recueil de quelques pièces concernant la philosophie de M. Descartes*, Amsterdam. (A reply to the Jesuit Le Valois, who pseudonymously had attacked Bernier's views as incompatible with the doctrine of transubstantiation.)

References and further reading

Lennon, T.M. (1993) *The Battle of The Gods And Giants: The Legacies of Descartes And Gassendi, 1655–1715*, Princeton, NJ: Princeton University Press. (Sections 5–9 discuss Bernier as participant in the seventeenth-century contest between Cartesian Platonism and materialism.)

Murr, S. (1992) 'Bernier et les Gassendistes', *Corpus* special double issue 20–1. (The most extensive treatment ever accorded Bernier, comprising thirteen articles on topics related to him, and ten brief, rare texts either about or by him, including the Requeste des maistres.)

THOMAS M. LENNON

BERNSTEIN, EDUARD (1850–1932)

Eduard Bernstein, an eminent German social democrat, is now noted as 'the father of revisionism'. He made a reputation as the radical editor of the German Social Democratic Party organ, Der Sozialdemokrat, *and became a close associate of Friedrich Engels. However, after the death of Engels he abandoned revolutionary Marxism and argued that socialism could be achieved by legal means and piecemeal reform. In doing this, he raised fundamental questions concerning the validity of Marxism and the direction of socialist political strategy, thus provoking what is now known as the 'revisionist debate'.*

Eduard Bernstein was born in Berlin. In 1872, a year after the fall of the Paris Commune, he joined the *Eisenach* wing of the German socialist movement and soon became known as an activist. He attended the Gotha Conference in 1875, at which the *Eisenachers* joined with the *Lassalleans* to form what was to become the German Social Democratic Party (SPD). However, in 1878 the Reichstag passed legislation effectively making the SPD illegal, and Bernstein fled to Switzerland. Here, upon reading ENGELS' recently published *Anti-Dühring*, he became a Marxist. He made contact with MARX and Engels and laid the basis for a long and fruitful collaboration (particularly with Engels). Around the same time, he met Karl KAUTSKY, with whom he collaborated for many years. In 1881 he became editor of the official party organ, *Der Sozialdemokrat*, in which capacity he established a reputation as a Marxist of impeccable orthodoxy and the guardian of the party's radical conscience.

In 1887 Bernstein moved to London where he continued editing *Der Sozialdemokrat* and consolidated his relationship with Engels. But by this time Bernstein had begun to nourish doubts about revolutionary Marxism as a basis for party policy. The terminal crisis of capitalism, predicted by Marx and Engels, had not occurred and, as far as Bernstein could see, it was not going to occur. There was no evidence that the means of production were being concentrated in fewer and fewer hands, or that cutthroat competition was wiping out large sections of the middle classes, or that the proletariat was being relentlessly reduced to abject poverty. Capitalism seemed to be in robust good health and likely to remain so for the foreseeable future. It was, therefore, idle for socialists to pin their hopes on an imminent collapse of bourgeois society. On the other hand, the advance of democracy in most industrialized countries had enabled working–class parties to enter the political arena, and there was a real prospect that significant reforms could be achieved by parliamentary means. Indeed, Bernstein argued, the victory of socialism might well be accomplished by the steady implementation of socialist principles by democratic and constitutional means. In his view, it was not a matter of pursuing utopian visions. It was a matter of hard political work guided by basic socialist principles. 'The final goal of socialism' was, as he put it, 'nothing to me, the movement is everything' (Tudor and Tudor 1988: 168–9).

From these observations Bernstein drew two general conclusions. First, that Marx's doctrines would have to be re-evaluated and, where necessary, 'revised'. Second, the SPD should abandon its revolutionary aspirations and acknowledge that it was now a democratic socialist party of reform.

Bernstein developed these views, in part in a series of articles published in *Die Neue Zeit* under the title 'Problems of Socialism' and in part in a polemical exchange with the English socialist Ernest Belfort Bax (Tudor and Tudor 1988: 168–9). The consequent uproar within the party culminated in the rejection of Bernstein's 'revisionism' at the party conference at Stuttgart in 1898. Early in the following year Bernstein published his *Die Voraussetzungen des Sozialismus und die Aufgaben der Sozialdemokratie* (*The Preconditions of Socialism*). In it, he commended Marx and Engels for their open-ended, scientific approach. Their own investigations had, he argued, quite rightly led them to revise and qualify the initial formulations of their theories. They had, for instance, been the first to recognize the abstract nature (and therefore limited usefulness) of the theory of surplus value. They had, in their later years, amplified the materialist conception of history to allow political and ideological factors greater autonomy in effecting historical change. And they had modified their analysis of capitalist development in ways that made it less deterministic.

In Bernstein's view, these scientific advances pointed towards an evolutionary interpretation of the transition from capitalism to socialism. However, it was undeniable that Marx and Engels had drawn a different conclusion. They had never abandoned their revolutionary expectations. The reason for this, according to Bernstein, was that, to the very end, their thinking had been confined within the straightjacket of Hegelian dialectics. It was Hegelian dialectics, not their painstaking scientific work, that ultimately dictated their conclusions. Scientific socialists should, Bernstein argued, emulate Marx the scientist, not Marx the dialectician.

Bernstein's own philosophical predilections were ill-defined. His view of science and knowledge was vaguely positivist in character, and in ethics he was much influenced by the neo-Kantians, particularly Friedrich Albert LANGE (see NEO-KANTIANISM). However, he was not a professional philosopher. Apart from the opening chapters of *Preconditions*, the nearest he came to stating his philosophical position was in his 1901 lecture, 'How is Scientific Socialism Possible?' (1976). Here he argued that science, by its nature, is disinterested; it is mere cognition and cannot move men to action. Socialism, however, is a movement with aims and objectives, and these embody, not the results of scientific investigation, but the interests of the working class. In short, socialism does move men to action, it is not disinterested, and it therefore cannot be scientific.

The controversy provoked by Bernstein's views lasted for many years. His opponents included luminaries such as Georgii Plekhanov, Rosa LUXEMBURG and, above all, his old friend Karl Kautsky (see PLEKHANOV, G. §2). The party conferences at Hanover (1899) and Dresden (1903) were devoted mainly to Bernstein and the 'revisionist' question. Bernstein himself returned to Germany in 1901 where he continued his literary activity and, for most of the rest of his life, served as Reichstag deputy. After various political vicissitudes, he died in 1932.

See also: SOCIALISM; MARXISM, WESTERN

List of works

Bernstein, E. (1899) *Die Voraussetzungen des Sozialismus und die Aufgaben der Sozialdemokratie*, Stuttgart: Dietz; trans. and ed. H. Tudor, *The Preconditions of Socialism*, Cambridge: Cambridge University Press, 1993. (Bernstein's main theoretical work.)

—— (1901) *Zur Geschichte und Theorie des Sozialismus* (Towards the History and Theory of Socialism), Berlin and Bern: J. Edelheim. (A collection of Bernstein's most significant articles.)

—— (1976) *Ein revisionistisches Sozialismusbild* (*A Revisionist Picture of Socialism*), trans. and ed. H. Hirsch, Berlin and Bonn: Dietz. (Three lectures, including 'How is Scientific Socialism Possible?' together with other materials from the revisionist debate.)

References and further reading

Gay, P. (1962) *The Dilemma of Democratic Socialism*, New York: Columbia University Press. (The only book-length study of Bernstein in English.)

Gustafsson, B. (1972) *Marxismus und Revisionismus* (Marxism and Revisionism), Frankfurt: Europaische Verlagsanstalt. (A historical account of the development of Bernstein's ideas.)

Meyer, T. (1977) *Bernsteins konstruktiver Sozialismus* (Bernstein's Constructive Socialism), Berlin and Bonn: Dietz. (On Bernstein's contribution to socialist theory.)

* Tudor, H. and Tudor, J.M. (eds and trans) (1988) *Marxism and Social Democracy: The Revisionist Debate 1896–1898*, with intro. by H. Tudor, Cambridge: Cambridge University Press. (Contains all but two of the articles entitled 'The Problems of Socialism'.)

H. TUDOR

BETH'S THEOREM AND CRAIG'S THEOREM

Beth's theorem is a central result about definability of non-logical symbols in classical first-order theories. It states that a symbol P is implicitly defined by a theory T if and only if an explicit definition of P in terms of some other expressions of the theory T can be deduced from the theory T. Intuitively, the symbol P is implicitly defined by T if, given the extension of these other symbols, T fixes the extension of the symbol P uniquely. In a precise statement of Beth's theorem this will be replaced by a condition on the models of T. An explicit definition of a predicate symbol states necessary and sufficient conditions: for example, if P is a one-place predicate symbol, an explicit definition is a sentence of the form $(x)(Px \equiv \phi(x))$, where $\phi(x)$ is a formula with free variable x in which P does not occur. Thus, Beth's theorem says something about the expressive power of first-order logic: there is a balance between the syntax (the deducibility of an explicit definition) and the semantics (across models of T the extension of P is uniquely determined by the extension of other symbols).

Beth's definability theorem follows immediately from Craig's interpolation theorem. For first-order logic with identity, Craig's theorem says that if ϕ is deducible from ψ, there is an interpolant θ, a sentence whose non-logical symbols are common to ϕ and ψ, such that θ is deducible from ψ, while ϕ is deducible from θ. Craig's theorem and Beth's theorem also hold for a number of non-classical logics, such as intuitionistic first-order logic and classical second-order logic, but fail for other logics, such as logics with expressions of infinite length.

1 The axiomatic method
2 Beth's theorem and Craig's interpolation theorem
3 Further developments and applications

1 The axiomatic method

Questions concerning the definability of concepts arose within the development of the formal axiomatic method by late nineteenth- and twentieth-century mathematicians such as Moritz Pasch, Giuseppe Peano, David Hilbert and Alfred Tarski. What sets apart the formal axiomatic method from the earlier axiomatic thinking of, say, Euclid's geometry is that the primitive terms occurring in the axioms are uninterpreted and the axioms devoid of any meaning; and that the rules of reasoning have been made completely explicit and formal. The axioms state purely formal relationships between the terms. This suffices for the purpose of deducing theorems from the axioms by rigorous reasoning. The development of the formal axiomatic method is the culmination of the movement to rigorize mathematics started in the early nineteenth century by mathematicians such as Cauchy and Bolzano. But these earlier efforts were directed chiefly towards ontology, for example, cleansing the language of analysis of visual images and reference to movement – and a mathematical theory still had subject matter, albeit abstract. In the formal axiomatic method the subject matter is provided from the outside by an interpretation of the primitive terms of the theory. One and the same theory may be open to radically diverse interpretations.

A perspicuous system of axioms requires under the formal axiomatic method the independence of each axiom from the others: a dependent axiom can be dropped without loss of content. Peano developed a method to prove independence: give an interpretation of the primitive terms which makes the one axiom false and the others true. This now common method is the formalization of an earlier idea of Eugenio Beltrami who felt that the so-called non-Euclidean geometry of Lobachevskii lacked a 'real foundation', that is a foundation in actual physical space. In 1868 Beltrami offered an interpretation of this geometry in terms of the acceptable Euclidean geometry: Lobachevskian 'geometry' could be understood as being about a special kind of line (a geodesic) in a special kind of plane (a surface with constant negative curvature) in Euclidean space. But Beltrami's project was one of meaning and he did not have the consistency of non-Euclidean geometry in mind nor was he concerned with the independence of Euclid's parallel axiom. In fact, only two years later, the French mathematician Guillaume Hoüel pointed out that Beltrami's construction showed the independence of the parallel axiom: while the other axioms are true for all planes, the parallel axiom holds only in planes of zero curvature (see Scanlan 1988).

Another idea from the pre-formal period was

absorbed by the formal axiomatic method through the work of the Italian mathematician Alessandro Padoa, a close collaborator of Peano. Padoa was concerned with the definability of concepts. He pointed out that there exists a parallel between, on the one hand, the methodological concepts of being an axiom and being derivable as a theorem and, on the other hand, concepts from the theory of definition: the notion of primitive term corresponds to the notion of being an axiom, and the notion of definability corresponds to the notion of deducibility. A perspicuous system of axioms therefore also requires the independence of the primitive concepts used in the axioms. Padoa was thus led to ask in 1900 whether there could be a method to prove independence of concepts, just as Peano's method had shown independence of axioms.

Early in the nineteenth century the French mathematician Jose Diez Gergonne had suggested the contrasting terms 'explicit' and 'implicit' as regards definition (Gergonne 1918–19). Gergonne's distinction was suggested by the difference, in algebra, between a set of solved equations, which gives as it were explicit definitions of the unknowns, and a set of unsolved equations which is strong enough to determine a unique solution for the unknowns. Gergonne characterizes implicit definitions as 'phrases that make us understand one of the words that occur in it through the known meaning of the other words'. Analogously to the algebraic case, Gergonne requires that the number of unknown words should be equal to the number of phrases that together implicitly define them. Completely forgotten by the end of the nineteenth century it was Giovanni Vacca, an assistant of Peano, who around 1896 gave a short account of Gergonne's paper on definitions. Padoa's paper (1901), read at the First International Congress of Philosophy in Paris, is clearly motivated by Gergonne's work. To prove the independence of a concept from the other concepts occurring in a theory Padoa proposed a new method: find a true interpretation of the theory, considered as an abstract system, that remains a true interpretation when solely the meaning of that concept is changed. Thus, though Padoa did not refer to Gergonne or use the term 'implicit definition', his so-called 'two-model method' establishes that a term is not implicitly defined by a theory in the sense of Gergonne.

Since Padoa did not indicate how to construct the two models it may be better to speak of the 'Padoa criterion' for undefinability. Padoa claimed without further proof that his criterion was both necessary and sufficient for the explicit undefinability of a given concept by means of the other concepts in a given theory. Sufficiency is clear: if an explicit definition were to be implied by the theory two such models could not exist since the truth of the explicit definition would force the uniqueness of the interpretation of the explicitly defined term given an interpretation of the other terms. But necessity is not obvious. Does the absence of two such models guarantee that an explicit definition exists and is derivable? With hindsight this question could not have been answered at that time for it requires a more careful specification of the underlying logical system than was available to Padoa.

Alfred Tarski (1935) answered the question affirmatively for a modification of the ramified theory of types of Whitehead and Russell's *Principia Mathematica* (see THEORY OF TYPES). His proof was a rather straightforward derivation within the system, since the meta-claim that Padoa's two models do not exist can be expressed in the language of type theory.

2 Beth's theorem and Craig's interpolation theorem

In 1953 the Dutch philosopher and logician Evert Beth proved the necessity of Padoa's criterion for first-order or elementary logic. Beth showed that if no explicit definition of a term can be deduced from a theory, two models of the theory exist that differ only in the interpretation of the term in question. Moreover, in his so-called semantic tableau method, Beth found the means to construct systematically, in the absence of definability, the two models required by Padoa's criterion, albeit often through an infinite process, while a closed tableau makes it possible to find an explicit definition of the term in question (see NATURAL DEDUCTION, TABLEAU AND SEQUENT SYSTEMS §4). Beth thus took away some of the concerns of the American mathematician Oswald Veblen who had remarked in 1902 that what Padoa proposed 'seems hardly adequate' when the issue was to replace an axiomatic system by one with independent axioms and independent terms, since he gave no method to find the two models and thus prove independence, or to construct the explicit definition, in the case of dependency.

Let L be a first-order language and P an arbitrary non-logical constant not in L. Let $L(P)$ denote the language obtained by adding P to L. To simplify our notation we will assume that P is a one-place predicate symbol. If T is an arbitrary theory in the language L, then $T(P)$ will be a theory in the language $L(P)$. Deducibility in first-order logic will be denoted by '$\vdash$'. An interpretation or model M for L specifies extensions in a domain D for all the non-logical constants of L (see MODEL THEORY). If M is a model of L, a model of $L(P)$ will be denoted by (M, X), where X is a subset of the domain D of M. Thus P is here interpreted as the subset X.

We will now define the notions of explicit and implicit definability. $T(P)$ is said to *define P explicitly* if there is a formula $\phi(x)$ of L such that $T(P) \vdash (x)(Px \equiv \phi(x))$. If P is not a one-place predicate symbol, this definition can be modified in the obvious way. Furthermore, let T be the set of first-order consequences of $T(P)$ in the language L, in which P does not occur. Then $T(P)$ is said to *define P implicitly* when, for every model M of T, there is exactly one expansion (M, X) of M which is a model of $T(P)$.

'Beth's definability theorem' for first-order logic states that a theory $T(P)$ defines a term P implicitly if and only if $T(P)$ defines P explicitly. Beth's original proof of 1956 uses a modification of Gentzen's 'extended *Hauptsatz*', which shows that, in first-order logic, every proof can be carried out without any detours. Nowadays Beth's theorem is usually proved to be a direct implication of Craig's interpolation theorem.

'Craig's interpolation theorem' for first-order logic with identity says that if a sentence ψ of first-order logic entails a sentence θ there is an 'interpolant', a sentence ϕ in the vocabulary common to θ and ψ, that entails θ and is entailed by ψ. William Craig originally proved this theorem as a lemma to be used in obtaining a simpler proof of Beth's theorem (Craig 1957). Since then, however, the result has come to stand on its own.

We will now sketch a proof that Craig's theorem implies Beth's theorem. Since first-order logic is complete, implicit definability, a model-theoretic condition, is equivalent to the following deducibility condition, which is in fact Beth's original definition of (implicit) definability. Let P' be a one-place predicate not in L and distinct from P, and let $T(P')$ be the theory in $L(P')$ obtained by replacing P by P' in $T(P)$ wherever it occurs. Then P is implicitly defined by $T(P)$ if and only if $T(P) \cup T(P') \vdash (x)(Px \equiv P'x)$. Assume now that this condition holds, and that $T(P)$ is a finite set of sentences, or, rather, one big conjunction of axioms, and similarly for $T(P')$. So we can write $T(P) \& T(P') \vdash (x)(Px \equiv P'x)$. But then also $T(P) \& Pc \vdash (T(P') \to P'c)$, where c is a new individual constant not in L. By Craig's theorem there is an interpolant $\phi(c)$ such that $T(P) \& Pc \vdash \phi(c)$ and $\phi(c) \vdash (T(P') \to P'c)$. Since P' does not occur in $\phi(c)$ it is also true that $\phi(c) \vdash (T(P) \to Pc)$. Thus $T(P) \vdash (Pc \equiv \phi(c))$. Since c does not occur in $T(P)$, we also have $T(P) \vdash (x)(Px \equiv \phi(x))$. This completes the proof that if $T(P)$ defines P implicitly, then $T(P)$ defines P explicitly. The other direction of Beth's theorem follows independently of Craig's theorem.

3 Further developments and applications

Again, let T be the set of first-order consequences of $T(P)$ in the language L. We said that $T(P)$ defines P implicitly when for every model M of T there is exactly one expansion (M, X) which is a model of $T(P)$. In Padoa's method two models (M, X) and (M, X') of $T(P)$ are exhibited. Another way in which implicit definability can be violated is if there is a model of T that cannot in any way be expanded to a model of the full $T(P)$. Karel de Bouvère (1959) studied this so-called one-model method to show undefinability of addition and multiplication in number theory. In the philosophy of science literature this is called a failure of Ramsey eliminability of the term.

Not to be confused with the above concept of definability of a term in a theory is the concept of definability of a set in a model which, for Tarski, belongs to semantic definability rather than to the formal definability involved in Padoa's question since now we have a fixed model for an interpreted language. Given a model M of L, a subset X of its domain D is *definable in the model M* if there is a formula of L with one free variable $\phi(x)$ such that $(x)(Px \equiv \phi(x))$ is true in (M, X), where P is interpreted as X. Obviously, if P is explicitly definable in $T(P)$ and if (M, X) is a model of $T(P)$, then X is definable in M. Moreover, the concept of definability in a model can be iterated, whereas definability of a term in a theory cannot since a set of terms is not itself a term of the language.

We say that the predicate P is definable in a model (M, X) of $T(P)$ if an explicit definition of P holds in (M, X). Different models of $T(P)$ may satisfy different, non-equivalent definitions. But a theorem proven by Lars Svenonius in 1959 shows that if P is definable in every model (M, X) of $T(P)$ then each model (M, X) of $T(P)$ satisfies one of a finite list of definitions. That is, $T(P)$ implies a (finite) disjunction of explicit definitions of P. This property is called 'explicit definability up to disjunction' or 'piecewise definability'.

In model theory the concept of 'a logic' is defined and logics for which Craig's interpolation theorem hold are said to have the Craig or interpolation property; similarly for the Beth property. Any usual logic with the Craig property has the Beth property, but the latter has been shown to be weaker.

See also: DEFINITION; GEOMETRY, PHILOSOPHICAL ISSUES IN; LOGICAL AND MATHEMATICAL TERMS, GLOSSARY OF

References and further reading

Barwise, J. and Feferman, S. (eds) (1985) *Model-Theoretic Logics*, New York: Springer. (The papers by Ebbinghaus and by Makowsky give details about the relation between the Beth property and the Craig property in abstract model theory.)

Benthem, J.F. van (1978) 'Ramsey Eliminability', *Studia Logica* 37: 321–36. (A detailed exposition of Ramsey eliminability with a discussion of its relevance for the philosophy of the empirical sciences.)

* Beth, E.W. (1953) 'On Padoa's Method in the Theory of Definition', *Indagationes Mathematica* 15: 330–9. (Gives Beth's result that for first-order logic implicit definability implies explicit definability in Beth's original proof-theoretic formulation.)

—— (1956) *L'Existence en Mathématiques*, Paris: Gauthier-Villars. (Includes an example of the one-model method to show undefinability. This involves constructing a model of the consequences of the theory without the terms whose undefinability has to be demonstrated, a model which cannot be extended to a model of the full theory.)

—— (1962) *Formal Methods: An Introduction to Symbolic Logic and to the Study of Effective Operations in Arithmetic and Logic*, Dordrecht: Reidel. (Shows how Beth's semantic tableau gives a method for constructing a Craig interpolant, and how this leads to the construction of an explicit definition in case Padoa's method fails.)

* Bouvère, K.L. de (1959) *A Method in Proofs of Undefinability, With Applications to Functions in the Arithmetic of Natural Numbers*, Amsterdam: North Holland. (De Bouvère's dissertation with the one-model method, which shows that, under certain conditions, a term is essentially undefinable, that is, undefinable in any consistent extension.)

Chang, C.C. and Keisler, H.J. (1973) *Model Theory*, Amsterdam: North Holland. (Gives a complete account of interpolation and definition results for classical logic.)

* Craig, W. (1957) 'Three Uses of the Herbrand–Gentzen Theorem in Relating Model Theory and Proof Theory', *Journal of Symbolic Logic* 22: 269–85. (Derives Craig's theorem about the existence of an 'intermediate' formula or interpolant from a consequence of Gentzen's extended *Hauptsatz*, and applies it in a proof of Beth's definability theorem, formulating it as a result relating model theory and proof theory.)

Ebbinghaus, H.-D. (ed.) (1987) *Bibliography of Mathematical Logic*, vol. 3, *Model Theory*, Berlin: Springer. (§C40 gives an extensive bibliography on interpolation and definability.)

* Gergonne, J.D. (1918–19) 'Essai sur la théorie des definitions', *Annales de Mathématiques Pures et Appliquées* 9: 1–35. (Referred to in §1. Defines the concept of implicit definition before the advent of the formal axiomatic method.)

Kleene, S.C. (1967) *Mathematical Logic*, New York: Wiley. (A good account of the formal axiomatic method.)

* Padoa, A. (1901) 'Essai d'une théorie algébrique des nombres entiers, précédé d'une introduction logique à une théorie déductive quelconque', in *Premier Congrès International de Philosophie*, vol. 3, *Logique et Histoire des Sciences*, Paris: Armand Colin, 309–65; partial trans. 'Logical Introduction to any Deductive Theory', in J. van Heijenoort (ed.) *From Frege to Gödel: A Source Book in Mathematical Logic, 1879–1931*, Cambridge, MA: Harvard University Press, 1967, 118–23. (Referred to in §1. The 'Logical Introduction on Deductive Theories in General' has the first statement of Padoa's criterion for the undefinability of a symbol on the basis of a theory.)

* Scanlan, M.J. (1988) 'Beltrami's Model and the Independence of the Parallel Postulate', *History and Philosophy of Logic* 9: 13–34. (Referred to in §1. Compares the work of Beltrami and Hoüel with the treatment of Euclidean and non-Euclidean geometry after the development of the formal axiomatic method by Pasch, Peano and others.)

* Tarski, A. (1935) 'Einige methodologische Untersuchungen über die Definierbarkeit der Begriffe', *Erkenntnis* 5: 80–100; trans. 'Some Methodological Investigations on the Definability of Concepts', in *Logic, Semantics, Metamathematics: Papers from 1923 to 1938*, trans. and ed. J.H. Woodger, Oxford: Clarendon Press, 1956, 296–319. (Referred to in §1. Includes the proof that in the logical system of *Principia Mathematica* the two extensions required by Padoa's method do exist if a term cannot be explicitly defined.)

Tarski, A. and Kuratowski, C. (1931) 'Les opérations logiques et les ensembles projectifs' (Logical Operations and Projective Sets), *Fundamenta Mathematicae* 17: 240–8. (The first occurrence of the expression 'implicit definition' in the sense of Gergonne in the modern literature. The authors point out that definitions by induction are a type of implicit definition.)

Tuomela, R. (1973) *Theoretical Concepts*, Vienna: Springer. (An accessible discussion of definability and Ramsey eliminability in the empirical sciences.)

* Vacca, G. (1896–9) 'Sui precursori della logica mathematica. II. J.D. Gergonne' (On Precursors of Mathematical Logic. II. J.D. Gergonne), *Rivista di matematica* 6: 183–6. (Referred to in §1. Brings

the work of Gergonne on definition to the attention of the new logic.)

ZENO SWIJTINK

BHARTṚHARI (c. 5th century)

Bhartṛhari is the Indian philosopher of grammar par excellence. *Drawing on practically all the schools of thought of his time – religious, philosophical, linguistic and ritual – he uses elements from them to create a philosophy. This philosophy, while claiming to be grammatical, goes far beyond traditional grammar, constituting a new and remarkably original system of thought.*

1 Life, works and influence
2 Philosophical outline
3 Role of grammar

1 Life, works and influence

Bhartṛhari is the author of the *Vākyapadīya* or *Trikāṇḍī* and probably the *Mahābhāṣyaṭīkā* or *Mahābhāṣyadīpikā*, perhaps the earliest commentary on the *Mahābhāṣya* of Patañjali, which survives only in part. The Indian tradition also ascribes to Bhartṛhari the *Vākyapadīyavṛtti*, the earliest surviving commentary on the first two books of the *Vākyapadīya*, but this is doubtful.

Bhartṛhari was long believed to have lived in the seventh century AD, according to the testimony of the Chinese pilgrim Yijing (eighth century AD). However, as his *Vākyapadīya* was known to the Buddhist philosopher DIGNĀGA, this has pushed his date back to the fifth century AD. It is unlikely that Bhartṛhari was active any earlier than Kālidāsa, a famous Sanskrit poet and playwright, who is widely believed to allude to the Gupta emperor Candragupta II (375–413 AD).

The philosophy of Bhartṛhari is expressed in the *Vākyapadīya*, a difficult work whose serious scholarly study remains in its infancy. Later grammarians claim Bhartṛhari's philosophy to be inseparable from the grammatical tradition and cite from the *Vākyapadīya* selectively. However, other thinkers, such as Abhinavagupta and Dharmapāla found aspects of his text with which they concur. The Buddhist Dharmapāla is known to have written a commentary (now lost) on part of the *Vākyapadīya* and the Chinese pilgrim Yijing mistook Bhartṛhari for a Buddhist. Hindu Tantric thinkers (especially ABHINAVAGUPTA) took a deep interest in Bhartṛhari's work. His philosophy is also often looked upon as a form of Vedānta (see VEDĀNTA). All these links and claims are justified by certain aspects of Bhartṛhari's thought, but they do not provide an integrated picture of his philosophy.

2 Philosophical outline

In order to understand Bhartṛhari on his own terms, he must be read in the context of his time. The *Vākyapadīya* must be understood against the background of the philosophical and religious currents with which Bhartṛhari was acquainted and to which he refers, although often implicitly. These references show that Bhartṛhari was a Vedic *brāhmaṇa* (most probably belonging to the Maitrāyaṇīya branch of the black Yajurveda), who was strongly influenced by the Vaiśeṣika philosophy and especially by Mādhyamika Buddhism (see NYĀYA-VAIŚEṢIKA; BUDDHISM, MĀDHYAMIKA: INDIA AND TIBET). He was first and foremost a grammarian who claimed allegiance to Patañjali and tried to elevate grammatical studies to the rank of a philosophy with the further implication that its study would provide access to liberation. Bhartṛhari combined these and other ideas to produce a philosophy of his own for which he claimed no originality. However, his work stands apart from all that preceded and followed him, including the philosophy of the later grammarians who present themselves as his inheritors.

Modern scholarship has not yet reached agreement on the precise nature of Bhartṛhari's philosophy. His philosophy distinguishes between two levels of reality, a higher and a lower. Only the higher reality can be considered to be real; lower reality is not real in an absolute sense. Language cannot describe higher reality. Indeed, language plays a major role in bringing about the lower reality, which is the reality of everyday experience. The resemblance between these ideas and those current among the Buddhists of the time is striking. There are, however, a number of major differences. First, for Bhartṛhari language is not just any language: it is Sanskrit, the sacred language of the Brahmans, which took form in the Veda, the corpus of canonical texts believed to be eternal. The world of everyday experience is in this way created, or organized by the Veda. At this point, Bhartṛhari turns an essentially Buddhist argument into a confirmation of the pre-eminence of the Veda.

A second major difference concerns the nature of the higher, absolute reality. Variant schools of Buddhism had various ideas about this, depending on the school to which they belonged: consciousness, emptiness, the fundamental elements of existence (*dharma*). Bhartṛhari accepts none of these positions.

For him the absolute is the totality of all there is, has been and will be. He used this idea, borrowed from earlier Brahmanical thinkers, as an element in his own philosophy.

Lower reality is the result of a division of the absolute. The precise nature of this division is determined, among other things, by language. Sometimes Bhartṛhari also mentions analytical imagination (*vikalpa*), but there is reason to believe that he looked upon these different factors as amounting to the same thing. The 'parts' resulting from this division undergo the influence of a number of powers (*śakti*) of the absolute, foremost among them time and space. These operations bring about the objects of everyday experience, which are accordingly looked upon as consisting of 'real' and 'unreal' parts. Bhartṛhari is not categorical as to what constitutes the 'real' parts of familiar objects. Among the various possibilities he proposes are that the substance of, or the universal inhering in the object is its 'real' part. He does not choose between these alternatives. This is due to what J.E.M. Houben (1995) has called Bhartṛhari's perspectivism: reality is different from different points of view. This perspectivism is a pervading characteristic of Bhartṛhari's thought. It applies to lower reality, but not to the absolute.

Bhartṛhari's vision of the absolute as the totality of all that exists, has existed and will exist, has repercussions in the realm of ordinary reality. For Bhartṛhari, any totality or whole is more real than its constituents. A vase, for example, is more real than its parts. Again we see how Bhartṛhari uses a Buddhist position for his own purposes, by turning it into its opposite. For the Buddhists wholes do not exist: only their ultimate parts (*dharma*) (see BUDDHIST PHILOSOPHY, INDIAN). To Bhartṛhari, a whole is more real than its parts and the absolute whole is absolutely real.

3 Role of grammar

Bhartṛhari considers himself a grammarian. Generally, grammar deals with the analysis of language and produces words from stems and suffixes. Language also obeys the general rule that totalities are more real than their constituents. This is particularly clear in the case of words which convey meaning, whereas their constituents do not. Grammatical analysis, Bhartṛhari argues, is artificial as stems and suffixes are the inventions of grammarians. In this respect his position appears to be very close to that of Patañjali. Words, too, are merely the result of an artificial analysis of sentences which, in their turn, are parts of more encompassing and therefore more real, linguistic units.

Once again, Bhartṛhari uses ideas which he borrowed from Buddhism. The Sarvāstivādins postulated long before Bhartṛhari the existence of three entities (*dharma*), corresponding to individual phonemes, words and sentences. Bhartṛhari accepts these entities, but orders them in an hierarchical ontology in agreement with his overall vision of reality.

Grammar allows its practitioner to 'ascend' from the smallest elements isolated by grammatical analysis, such as phonemes, stems and suffixes, to 'higher' units of speech. This way he will learn about the world, which is largely determined by the linguistic analysis that is imposed upon it. He will also learn to appreciate the unreality of the everyday world. In the end, the realization that the highest reality is beyond language and concerns the totality of things can be attained. Insight into the all leads to liberation, as it does in a number of classical texts of Mahāyāna Buddhism. It is in this sense that Bhartṛhari states at the beginning of his *Vākyapadīya* that grammar is the door to liberation.

Bhartṛhari's remarks concerning the nature of language should be understood in the light of the above. There has been much confusion among recent scholars about Bhartṛhari's concept of the absolute, which is often depicted as being of the nature of speech. The *Vākyapadīya* does not support this point of view. Bhartṛhari does discuss the distinction between the real word, sometimes called *sphoṭa* and the sounds which manifest it. The real word, he believes, has no sequence. It is only the sounds that manifest it which are sequential. Among the manifesting sounds, he makes a distinction between primary (*prākṛta*) and secondary (*vaikṛta*) sounds. The former have the duration attributed to the real word, the latter are responsible for the differences of pronunciation between different speakers. Bhartṛhari's perspectivism in the *Vākyapadīya* is pertinent here, implying that a different explanation of the same fact may be presented elsewhere in the same text without clear indication to that effect. As well as this explanation of the duration of a word in terms of primary sounds (*Vākyapadīya* 1.77) there are verses in the text (1.105–6), which speak of the *sphoṭa* as the first sound produced, whose duration is not affected by the sounds produced subsequently.

See also: LANGUAGE, INDIAN THEORIES OF; PATAÑJALI

List of works

Bhartṛhari (*c*.5th century AD) *Vākyapadīya* (Bhartṛhari's Vākyapadīya), ed. W. Rau, Wiesbaden: Franz Steiner, 1977. (A difficult work whose serious scholarly study remains in its infancy.)

—— (c.5th century AD) *Mahābhāṣyaṭīkā (Mahābhāṣyadīpikā)*, ed. and trans. by V.B. Bhagavat, S. Bhate, J. Bronkhorst, G.V. Devasthali, V.P. Limaye, G.B. Palsule, Poona: Bhandarkar Oriental Research Institute, 1985–91, 8 vols. (Perhaps the earliest commentary on the *Mahābhāṣya* of Patañjali, which survives only in part.)

References and further reading

Bronkhorst, J. (1991) 'Studies on Bhartṛhari 3: Bhartṛhari on *sphoṭa* and universals', *Asiatische Studien/Études Asiatiques* 45 (1): 5–18. (A discussion of Bhartṛhari's notion of *sphoṭa* – the distinction between the real word and the sounds which manifest it.)

—— (1992) 'Études sur Bhartṛhari 4: l'Absolu dans le *Vākyapadīya* et son lien avec le Madhyamaka', *Asiatische Studien/Études Asiatiques* 46 (1): 56–80. (A discussion of the Absolute in Bhartṛhari's work and its link with the 'middle' school of Buddhism.)

—— (1996a) 'Sanskrit and reality: the Buddhist contribution', *Ideology and Status of Sanskrit: Contributions to the history of the Sanskrit language*, ed. J.E.M. Houben, Leiden: E.J. Brill, 109–35. (A discussion of the Sanskrit language.)

—— (1996b) 'Studies on Bhartṛhari 7: Grammar as the door to liberation', *Annals of the Bhandarkar Oriental Research Institute* 76: 97–106. (A discussion of Bhartṛhari's system of grammar.)

* Houben, J.E.M. (1995) *The Saṃbandhasamuddeśa (Chapter on Relation) and Bhartṛhari's Philosophy of Language: a Study of Bhartṛhari* Saṃbandhasamuddeśa *in the context of the Vākyapadīya*, with a translation of Helārāja's commentary Prakīrṇaprakāśa, Groningen: Egbert Forsten. (Important study of Bhartṛhari's thought, taking as a point of departure a chapter of the third book of the *Vākyapadīya*.)

Iyer, K.A. Subramania (1969) *Bhartṛhari*, Poona: Deccan College. (The most comprehensive study of Bhartṛhari, his works and thought.)

Ramseier, Y. (1993) 'Bibliography on Bhartṛhari', *Asiatische Studien/Études Asiatiques* 47 (1): 235–267. (A complete bibliography of Bhartṛhari's work. Contains translations of the *Vākyapadīya* and the *Mahābhāṣyaṭīkā*.)

JOHANNES BRONKHORST

BHĀVAVIVEKA *see* BUDDHISM, MĀDHYAMIKA: INDIA AND TIBET

BIBLE, HEBREW

Although the Bible is not a work of systematic philosophy, it none the less contains a wide variety of philosophical and theological ideas which have served as the framework for rabbinic speculation through the centuries. Although these views about the nature and activity of God are not presented systematically, they do provide an overview of the ancient Israelite understanding of the Godhead, creation, divine providence and human destiny. Throughout rabbinic literature these notions served as the bedrock for theological speculation, and with the emergence of systematic Jewish philosophy in the Middle Ages, they came to preoccupy a variety of thinkers. Similarly, in the post-Enlightenment period until the present, scriptural teaching has served as the starting point for philosophical and theological reflection.

Foremost among scriptural beliefs is the conviction that one God has created the cosmos. As the transcendent creator of the universe, he reigns supreme throughout nature and is intimately involved in earthly life. God is both omnipotent and omniscient and exercises divine providence over all creatures – from on high he oversees all the inhabitants of the earth. In exercising his providential care, Scripture repeatedly asserts, God is a benevolent ruler who shows compassion and mercy to all. Furthermore, as lord of history, he has chosen Israel to be his special people and has revealed the Torah to them on Mount Sinai. The Jewish people are to be a light to the nations, and from their midst will come a Messianic redeemer who will inaugurate a period of divine deliverance and eventually usher in the world to come. Israel thus plays a central role in the unfolding of God's plan for all human beings.

1   **Divine unity**
2   **Transcendence and immanence**
3   **Omnipotence and omniscience**
4   **Creation and providence**
5   **Goodness, revelation and sin**
6   **The chosen people**
7   **The Messiah**

1   Divine unity

Pre-eminent among scriptural ideas is belief in the existence of one God. In the Hebrew Bible, the Israelites experienced God as the lord of history. The most uncompromising expression of his unity is the *Shema* prayer: 'Hear, O Israel, the Lord, our God, is one Lord' (Deuteronomy 6: 4). According to Scripture, the universe owes its existence to the one God, the creator of heaven and earth, and since all human beings are created in his image, all men and women are brothers and sisters. Hence the belief in one God implies that there is one humanity and one world (see GOD, CONCEPTS OF).

Jewish biblical teaching therefore emphasizes that God alone is to be worshipped. As the prophet Isaiah declared, 'I am the Lord, and there is no other, besides me there is no God; ... I form light and create darkness, I make weal and create woe, I am the Lord, who do all these things' (Isaiah 45: 5, 7).

2 Transcendence and immanence

For the biblical writers, God is conceived as the transcendent creator of the universe. Thus in Genesis 1: 1–2, he is depicted as forming heaven and earth: 'In the beginning God created the heavens and the earth. The earth was without form and void, and darkness was upon the face of the deep; and the Spirit of God was moving over the face of the waters'. Throughout Scripture this theme of divine transcendence is repeatedly affirmed. Thus Isaiah proclaims:

> Have you not known? Have you not heard? Has it not been told you from the beginning? Have you not understood from the foundations of the earth? It is he who sits above the circle of the earth, and its inhabitants are like grasshoppers; who stretches out the heavens like a curtain and spreads them like a tent to dwell in.
>
> (Isaiah 40: 21–2)

Later in the same book Isaiah declares that God is beyond human comprehension: 'For my thoughts are not your thoughts neither are your ways my ways, says the Lord. For as heavens are higher than the earth, so are my ways higher than your ways and my thoughts than your thoughts' (Isaiah 55: 8–9).

In the book of Job the same idea is repeated – God's purposes transcend human understanding:

> Can you find out the deep things of God? Can you find out the limit of the Almighty? It is higher than heaven – what can you do? Deeper than Sheol – what can you know? Its measure is longer than the earth, and broader than the sea.
>
> (Job 11: 7–9)

According to the author of Ecclesiastes, God is in heaven whereas human beings are confined to the earth. Thus the wise should recognize the limitations of human knowledge: 'Be not rash with your mouth, nor let your heart be hasty to utter a word before God, for God is in heaven, and you upon earth; therefore let your words be few' (Ecclesiastes 5: 2). Despite this view of God's remoteness from his creation, he is also viewed as actively involved in the cosmos. In the Bible, his omnipresence is stressed repeatedly. Thus the Psalmist rhetorically asks:

> Whither shall I go from thy Spirit? Or whither shall I flee from thy presence? If I ascend to Heaven, thou art there! If I take the wings of the morning and dwell in the uttermost parts of the sea, even there thy hand shall lead me.
>
> (Psalms 139: 7–12)

Throughout Scripture, God is also described as having neither beginning nor end. Thus the Psalmist stated, 'Before the mountains were brought forth, or ever thou hadst formed the earth and the world, from everlasting to everlasting thou art God. (Psalms 90: 2).

In the Bible, the term *olam* is most frequently used to denote the concept of God's eternity. In Genesis 21: 33 he is described as the Eternal God; he lives for ever (Deuteronomy 32: 40) and reigns forever (Exodus 15: 18; Psalms 10: 16). He is the living God and everlasting King (Jeremiah 10: 10); his counsel endures for ever (Psalms 33: 11) as does his mercy (Psalms 106: 1). For the biblical writers, God's eternal existence is different from the rest of creation – he exists permanently without beginning or end (see God, concepts of).

3 Omnipotence and omniscience

Concerning God's power, the belief in his omnipotence has been a central feature from biblical times. Thus in Genesis when Sarah expressed astonishment at the suggestion that she should have a child at the age of ninety, she was criticized: 'The Lord said to Abraham, "Why did Sarah laugh, and say 'Shall I indeed bear a child now that I am old?' Is anything too hard for the Lord?"' (Genesis 18: 13–14). Similarly, in the book of Jeremiah when the city of Jerusalem was threatened by the Chaldeans, God declared: 'Behold, I am the Lord the God of all flesh: is anything too hard for me?' (Jeremiah 32: 27). On such a view there is nothing God cannot do: what appears impossible is within his power (see OMNIPOTENCE).

Similarly, Scripture affirms that God is all-knowing (see OMNISCIENCE). As the Psalmist states, 'The Lord looks down from heaven, he sees all the sons of men ... he who fashions the hearts of them all, and observes all their deeds' (Psalms 33: 13, 15).

4 Creation and providence

Turning from God's attributes to his acts, Scripture declares that he created the universe:

> In the beginning God created the Heaven and the Earth. The Earth was without form and void, and darkness was upon the face of the deep; and the Spirit of God was brooding over the face of the waters. And God said, 'Let there be light': and there was light. And God saw that the light was good.
>
> (Genesis 1: 1–4)

That God controls and guides the universe is an essential belief. The Hebrew term for such divine action is *hashgahah*, derived from Psalm 33: 14: 'From where He sits enthroned He looks forth (*hishgiah*) on all the inhabitants of the earth'. Such a view implies that the dispensation of a wise and benevolent providence is found everywhere – all events are ultimately foreordained by God. According to tradition, there are two types of providence: (1) general providence, God's provision for the world in general, and (2) special providence, God's care for each individual. In Scripture God's general providence was manifest in his freeing the ancient Israelites from Egyptian bondage and guiding them to the Promised Land. The belief in the unfolding of his plan for salvation is a further illustration of such providential care for his creatures. Linked to this concern for all is God's providential concern for every person. In the words of the prophet Jeremiah: 'I know, O Lord, that the way of man is not in himself, that it is not in man who walks to direct his steps' (Jeremiah 10: 23) (see CREATION AND CONSERVATION, RELIGIOUS DOCTRINE OF; PROVIDENCE).

5 Goodness, revelation and sin

In exercising divine providential care for creation, Scripture repeatedly asserts that God is the all-good ruler of the universe. Thus in the Psalms, he is depicted as good and upright (25: 8); his name is good (52: 11; 54: 8); he is good and ready to forgive (86: 5); he is good and does good (118: 68); he is good to all (145: 9). Throughout the biblical narrative God is viewed as the supremely beneficent creator who guides all things to their ultimate destiny. In the unfolding of his plan, he chose Israel as his messenger to all peoples. As creator and redeemer, he is the father to all. Such affirmations about God's goodness have given rise to intense speculation about the mystery of evil. In Scripture the authors of Job and Ecclesiastes explored the question why the righteous suffer, and this quest continued into the rabbinic period (see GOODNESS, PERFECT; EVIL, PROBLEM OF).

The Hebrew Bible also asserts that God revealed himself in history. According to tradition, God revealed 613 commandments to Moses on Mount Sinai: they are recorded in the Five Books of Moses (Genesis, Exodus, Leviticus, Numbers and Deuteronomy). These prescriptions, which are to be observed as part of God's covenant with Israel, are classified in two major categories: (l) statutes concerned with ritual performances characterized as obligations between human beings and God; and (2) judgments consisting of laws that would have been adopted by society even if they had not been decreed by God (such as laws regarding murder and theft). These 613 commandments consist of 365 negative prescriptions (prohibited) and 248 positive prescriptions (duties to be performed) (see REVELATION).

For the biblical writers, sin is understood as a violation of these divine decrees. In Scripture the word *chet* (sin) means 'to miss' or 'to fail'. Here sin is understood as a failing, a lack of perfection in carrying out one's duty. The term *peshah* means a 'breach'; it indicates a broken relationship between human beings and God. The word *avon* expresses the idea of crookedness. Thus according to biblical terminology, sin is characterized by failure, waywardness and illicit action. A sinner is one who has not fulfilled his obligations to God.

6 The chosen people

A central feature of biblical Judaism is the belief that God chose the Jews as his special people. In the Bible the Hebrew root *b-h-r* (to choose) denotes the conviction that God selected the Jewish nation from all other peoples. As the book of Deuteronomy declares, 'For you are a people holy to the Lord your God: the Lord your God has chosen you to be a people for his own possession out of all the peoples that are on the face of the earth' (Deuteronomy 7: 6). According to Scripture, this act was motivated by divine love: 'It was not because you were more in number than any other people that the Lord set his love upon you and chose you, for you were the fewest of all peoples; but it is because the Lord loves you' (Deuteronomy 7: 7–8). Through its election Israel has been given an historic mission to convey divine truth to humanity. Thus, before God proclaimed the Ten Commandments on Mount Sinai, He admonished the people to carry out this appointed task:

> You have seen what I did to the Egyptians, and how I bore you on eagles' wings, and brought you to myself. Now therefore, if you will obey my voice,

and keep my covenant, you shall be my own possession among all peoples; for all the earth is mine, and you shall be to me a kingdom of priests and a holy nation.

(Exodus 19: 4–6)

God's choice of Israel thus carries with it numerous responsibilities. As God declares regarding Abraham in Genesis, 'For I have chosen him, that he may charge his children and his household after him to keep the way of the Lord by doing righteousness and justice' (Genesis 18: 19).

Divine choice demands reciprocal response. Israel is obliged to keep God's statutes and observe his laws. In doing so, the nation will be able to persuade the peoples of the world that there is only one universal God. Israel is to be a prophet to the nations, in that it will bring them to salvation. Yet despite this obligation, the Bible asserts that God will not abandon his chosen people even if they violate his covenant. The wayward nation will be punished, but God will not reject them: 'Yet for all that, when they are in the land of their enemies, I will not spurn them, neither will I abhor them so as to destroy them utterly and break My covenant with them: for I am the Lord their God' (Leviticus 26: 44).

As God's chosen people, Israel is to inherit a land of its own. Thus, in Genesis, God calls Abraham to travel to Canaan, where he promises to make him a great nation: 'Go from your country and your kindred and your father's house to the land that will show you. And I will make of you a great nation' (Genesis 12: 1–2). This same declaration was repeated to Abraham's grandson Jacob who, after wrestling with God's messenger, was renamed Israel. After Jacob's son Joseph became vizier in Egypt, the Israelite clan settled in Egypt for several hundred years. Eventually Moses led them out of Egyptian bondage and the people settled in the land that was promised to their ancestors.

7 The Messiah

In the unfolding of God's providential plan for Israel and humanity, the Messiah is to play a pivotal role. The term 'Messiah' is an adaptation of the Hebrew *Ha-Mashiach* (the Anointed), a term used frequently in Scripture. Initially, in the Book of Samuel, the view was expressed that the Lord had chosen David and his descendants to reign over Israel to the end of time (2 Samuel 7; 23: 1, 3, 5). Eventually there arose the belief that the house of David would return in time to rule over the two divided kingdoms as well as neighbouring peoples. Such an expectation paved the way for the vision of a transformation of earthly life through a universal Messianic redemption.

See also: ENLIGHTENMENT, JEWISH; GOD, CONCEPTS OF; HALAKHAH; MIDRASH; MAIMONIDES, M.; THEOLOGY, RABBINIC

References and further reading

Anderson, G.W. (1972) *The History and Religion of Israel*, London: Oxford University Press. (Authoritative and well-written history of ancient Israel.)

Bright, J. (1996) *A History of Israel*, Philadelphia, PA: Westminster Press. (Excellent survey of biblical history.)

Cohn-Sherbok, D. (1996) *The Hebrew Bible*, London: Cassell. (Outline and brief description of the books of the Bible.)

Franfort, H., Frankfort H.A., Wilson, J.A. and Jacobsen, T. (1951) *Before Philosophy*, Baltimore, MD: Penguin. (Stimulating exploration of the relationship between the Bible and the ancient Near East.)

Jacobs, L. (1973) *A Jewish Theology*, London: Darton, Longman & Todd. (Definitive survey of the history of Jewish theology from biblical times.)

DAN COHN-SHERBOK

BIEL, GABRIEL (before 1425–95)

Biel was the last great systematizer of scholastic theology and philosophy. Not noted for originality, he sought to produce a synthesis of the work of his predecessors. His thought is pervasively religious; a profound sense of the freedom of God's will is basic to his perspective. He followed Ockham and Duns Scotus in emphasizing the sheer contingency of things. Nature, morality and salvation depend entirely on God's will, and God could have determined otherwise. Such a view places sharp limits on the ability of reason to discover the truth about the nature and will of God; Biel subordinates reason to faith (although he is a master in the use of reason to defend revealed truth). The radical freedom of God coexists with significant moral freedom in humanity, since it is decreed by God that humans should be free to play an active role in determining their own destiny. Implied in this view of the human situation is an activist, pragmatic tendency, an interest in concrete applications of theoretical insights rather than in abstract speculation for its own sake.

BIEL, GABRIEL

1 Life
2 Practical concerns
3 Human nature and justification
4 Nominalism, voluntarism and fideism
5 Influence

1 Life

Gabriel Biel was born sometime before 1425 at Speyer, and died on 7 December 1495, at Einsiedel in Schönbuch. He was the last and arguably the ablest champion of 'the modern way' in late medieval theology (that is, a nominalism based on the system of WILLIAM OF OCKHAM). He studied at Heidelberg (BA 1435; MA 1438), Erfurt (1442–3, 1451–3) and Cologne (from 1453). At Erfurt he was exposed to Ockham's thought, at Cologne to that of ALBERT THE GREAT and Thomas AQUINAS. Biel assumed the chair in theology at Tübingen in 1484; he was invested as rector in 1485 and again in 1489.

Pragmatic and spiritual concerns are interwoven into Biel's intellectual enterprise. His perspective is more pervasively pastoral and religious than is Ockham's. The deeply religious tone of Biel's thought reflects his role as a cathedral-preacher in Mainz and as a proponent of the 'modern devotion' (*devotio moderna*) throughout southern and central Germany. His concerns for spiritual guidance and moral growth find abundant expression in his *De communi vita clericorum* (On the Common Life of Clerics) (1468–77), *Canonis misse expositio* (Exposition of the Canon of the Mass) (1488) and *Collectorium circa quattuor libros Sententiarum* (Commentary on the Four Books of Sentences) (1501).

2 Practical concerns

The coherence of Biel's thought is derived from his commitment to Ockhamism. Although he consults other theologians on subjects that OCKHAM fails to treat in depth, Ockham's perspective provides the framework within which he appropriates their work. Yet Biel is no narrow partisan. He is eager to synthesize the best elements from the competing traditions of late medieval thought – the 'ancient way' (*via antiqua*) of AQUINAS and DUNS SCOTUS and the 'modern way' (*via moderna*) of Ockham and his disciples. Biel's thought is eclectic in the best sense: emphatic about his loyalty to Ockham's perspective, he does not hesitate to draw on the wisdom of BONAVENTURE, Aquinas and above all Duns Scotus. A wide-ranging dialogue with various philosophers and theologians makes Biel's work valuable as an encyclopedic overview of the diversity in Western thought at the end of the Middle Ages.

Biel seeks an integration not only of the ancient and modern 'ways' but also of knowledge and piety. His *Canonis misse expositio* (1488) is a remarkable example of the symbiosis between late medieval theology and spirituality.

The pragmatic tendency of Biel's thought can be seen in the attention he pays to social ethics, and the practical consequences of theological conclusions. This is seen most clearly in the fourth book of his *Collectorium circa quattuor libros sententiarum* (1501), where Biel explores the sources of legitimate political authority, the mutual obligations of rulers and citizens, the morality of usury and the place of money in a just economy. Biel's contributions to a modern economic perspective include his vindication of the role of money in economic transactions and of supply and demand (rather than abstract theoretical considerations) as determining a just price.

3 Human nature and justification

This practical emphasis is reflected in an activist impulse that is linked with Biel's optimism about the moral potentialities latent in human nature: 'To those who do what in them lies, God does not deny his grace' (*Canonis misse expositio*, lect.59(D); II Sent. d.27 q.1 a.3 dub.3 (N)). Oberman (1963) regarded Biel's doctrine of justification as 'essentially Pelagian', since Biel exalts the sinner's ability to take certain crucial steps towards repairing the effects of sin by utilizing purely human moral resources, quite apart from any special enablement by God's grace (see PELAGIANISM; JUSTIFICATION, RELIGIOUS §3). Others (Clark 1965; Ernst 1972; McGrath 1981) have contested that verdict. The themes of covenant and divine generosity make it clear that for Biel the ultimate basis of salvation is God's mercy rather than human achievement. Furthermore, Biel teaches that the preparation for grace and the infusion of grace are simultaneous: even though the preparation of the soul for justification is accomplished without the assistance of grace, still there is never a moment when the required disposition for grace (sorrow for sin based on love for God above all things) exists in one who is not a recipient of grace (see GRACE §2). Yet Biel's doctrine seems at least quasi-Pelagian: a rhetoric of grace cloaks a spirituality of self-reliance. What Biel's theology arouses is not a sense of dependence on the enablement of grace but rather an imperative to do what one can and must do for oneself. To be sure, Biel insists that sinners cannot save themselves or take the first step towards reconciliation with God; the process leading to justification begins with a covenant whose source is sovereign mercy, preceding every human act of goodness or merit. It is gracious that

God established a covenant at all, gave the Law as a guide to its fulfilment, sent Jesus as Teacher/Example, created humanity with the moral endowment of conscience, reason, synderesis (an innate tendency of the will to prefer the good over the evil) and freedom, which make it possible (in some limited sense, at least) for sinners to merit the first grace. Once God has taken the initiative, however, Biel interprets the actual economy of salvation in such a way that the decisive issue is what the sinner's free response will be. Technically, Biel's doctrine may not be Pelagian, but for all practical purposes (psychologically and morally), it might as well be.

4 Nominalism, voluntarism and fideism

On the hotly-debated question of the ontological status of universals, Biel articulates a nominalist position, reflecting and reinforcing the inclination of his thought towards the concrete rather than the abstract (see NOMINALISM). Universals are merely names, applied arbitrarily to categories of entities; only individuals are actual existents. Other philosophical themes emerge from Biel's doctrine of God, which follows Duns Scotus' voluntarism in emphasizing God's absolute freedom from any external necessity. The realm of what God could do, if God so willed, is limited only by the law of non-contradiction. Anything that is logically possible is a real possibility for omnipotence. From the infinite possibilities available, God freely chose a finite number to be actualized, but might have chosen differently (see OMNIPOTENCE §5). In the ultimate freedom of the divine will, God could have decided to create a vastly different physical, moral or salvific order; everything is utterly contingent on God's absolutely free decision. This implies a radical contingency in the actual order of things. Right and wrong are defined by the arbitrary act of the divine will, for which no prior reason may be sought. 'It is right because God wills it' (CANONIS MISSE EXPOSITIO, lect.23 (E)), not vice versa. Biel is a master of dialectics in the service of revealed truth, but his voluntarism motivates a radical critique of the scope of reason's competence. Reason can manipulate logical possibilities, but in the actual order of morality and piety, reason is powerless to discern the content of the divine will, which must be communicated through authority and accepted by a faith that is submissive to God's revelation (in Scripture and tradition), interpreted according to the determination of the Church and, above all, the Pope. Biel seeks to be faithful, not original. His personal modesty combines with an emphasis on the primacy of faith over reason to foster an attitude of submission to the Church and a high view of papal supremacy.

5 Influence

Biel's writings underwent numerous editions. His admirers included Johannes Altenstaig, Johann Eck and Wendelin Steinbach. Influential at the Council of Trent, Biel's ideas continued over several centuries to be an important resource for a wide range of Roman Catholic thinkers.

The young LUTHER (§1) was a diligent student of the *Expositio* and *Collectorium*, but Biel's relation to Luther is complex. Luther's doctrine of justification is a massive assault on Biel's synergism. Yet on several key issues, Luther's theology betrays a basic continuity with Biel's thought. Luther's high view of the sacraments is faithful to much of what he learned from Biel. Biel's voluntarism sets the stage for Luther's radical view of divine sovereignty: God's will is the sole basis for human salvation. When Luther stresses God's hiddenness and calls reason 'the devil's whore', echoes of Biel's fideism are unmistakable. Yet Luther's dialectical skills were moulded by his early exposure to the clarity and rigour of Biel's logic.

See also: GRACE; NOMINALISM §§1–2; OMNIPOTENCE; PELAGIANISM

List of works

For works by Biel that are only available in Renaissance editions, see Oberman 1963 (in references and further reading).

Biel, G. (1468–77) *Tractatus magistri gabrielis Byell de communi vita clericorum* (Treatise by Master Gabriel Biel on the Common Life of Clerics), ed. W. Landeen, *Research Studies* 28: 79–95. (An account of the spiritual disciplines of the *devotio moderna* as practised by the Brethren of the Common Life.)

—— (1488) *Canonis misse expositio* (Exposition of the Canon of the Mass), Wiesbaden: Franz Steiner, 1963–76. (A commentary on the liturgy of the mass, outlining Biel's position on moral and religious questions in dialogue with a variety of medieval intellectual traditions.)

—— (1501) *Epithoma pariter et collectorium circa quattuor libros Sententiarum* (Synopsis and Commentary on the Four Books of Sentences), Mohr: Paul Siebeck, 1973–84. (Biel's most thorough exposition of his position on a wide range of philosophical and theological issues.)

—— (1516) *Tractatus de potestate et utilitate monetarum*, trans. R.B. Burke, *Treatise on the Power and Utility of Moneys*, Philadelphia, PA: University of Pennsylvania Press, 1930. (An extract from the

References and further reading

Burkard, F. (1974) *Philosophische Lehrgehalte in Gabriel Biels Sentenzenkommentar unter besonderer Berücksichtigung seiner Erkenntnislehre* (The Content of the Philosophical Teaching in Gabriel Biel's Commentary on the Sentences, with Special Attention to his Theory of Knowledge), Meisenheim am Glan: Hain. (An exploration of the epistemology of Biel's *Collectorium*.)

* Clark, F. (1965) 'A new appraisal of late-medieval theology', *Gregorianum* 46: 733–65. (Referred to in §3. A defence of Biel's teachings against the charge that his view of the human situation before God is Pelagian or at least semi-Pelagian.)

* Ernst, W. (1972) *Gott und Mensch am Vorabend der Reformation* (God and Man on the Eve of the Reformation), Leipzig: St Benno. (Referred to in §3. A defence of the orthodoxy of Biel's teaching about justification.)

Farthing, J. (1988) *Thomas Aquinas and Gabriel Biel*, Durham, NC: Duke University Press. (An analysis of Biel's citations and interpretations of materials drawn from Aquinas' theology.)

Feckes, C. (1925) *Die Rechtfertigungslehre des Gabriel Biel und ihre Stellung innerhalb der nominalistischen Schule* (Gabriel Biel's Doctrine of Justification and its Place Within the Nominalist School), Münster: Aschendorff. (A critique of Biel's doctrine of justification from a Thomistic point of view.)

—— (1927) 'Gabriel Biel, der erste grosse Dogmatiker der Universität Tübingen in seiner wissenschaftlichen Bedeutung' (Gabriel Biel, the scholarly significance of the first great dogmatician of the University of Tübingen), *Theologische Quartalschrift* 108: 50–76. (An examination of Biel's place in the early history of the University of Tübingen.)

* McGrath, A. (1981) 'The anti-Pelagian structure of "Nominalist" doctrines of justification', *Ephemerides Theologicae Lovanienses* 57 (1): 107–19. (Referred to in §3. A vindication of the orthodoxy of Biel's doctrine of justification.)

* Oberman, H. (1963) *The Harvest of Medieval Theology*, Cambridge, MA: Harvard University Press. (Referred to in §3. The most important comprehensive study of Biel's thought, including invaluable notes, a helpful glossary and a very thorough bibliography, listing works by Biel available only in Renaissance editions.)

Ruch, C. (1932) 'Biel, Gabriel', *Dictionnaire de théologie catholique*, vol. 2, 814–25. (A thorough yet concise overview of religious themes in Biel's writings.)

JOHN L. FARTHING

BIOETHICS

While bioethics, a part of applied ethics, is usually identified with medical ethics, in its broadest sense it is the study of the moral, social and political problems that arise out of biology and the life sciences generally and involve, either directly or indirectly, human well-being. Thus, environmental and animal ethics are sometimes included within it. In this regard, bioethics can be of broader concern than is either medical/biomedical ethics or the study of the moral problems that arise out of new developments in medical technology.

The interrelated issues of who or what has moral status, of what justifies a certain kind of treatment of one creature as opposed to another, and whether, if a creature has moral status, it can lose it, have proved especially important issues in this broadest sense of bioethics. The philosophical task of probing arguments for soundness appears essential to deciding these issues.

As a part of applied ethics, bioethics is exposed to the difficulty that (1) we do not agree in our moral convictions and principles about many of the cases that feature in bioethics, (2) we do not agree in the moral theories in which our moral principles find their home and by which we try to justify them, and (3) we do not agree in the test(s) of adequacy by which to resolve the disagreements at the level of moral theory. We seem left with no way of deciding between contending principles and theories.

1 Conceptions of bioethics
2 The role of the philosopher
3 Moral status and justification of treatment
4 The problem of disagreement

1 Conceptions of bioethics

In contemporary discussions of applied ethics, the term 'bioethics' is used generally in three ways.

Narrowly, it refers to a number of moral problems that attend recent developments in biotechnology, especially developments in four overlapping areas. These areas concern life-saving technologies at the beginning and end of life, life-enhancing technologies to improve the quality of life, reproductive technologies, the technologies to do with genetic engineering and gene therapy, and the implications for humans of the recently announced technology for cloning sheep. It is morally difficult to decide when and how to use these various technologies. For example, advances in our ability to correlate diseases and illnesses with particular genes and advances in gene therapy/gene replacement obviously raise important moral issues about how we are to use and control this ability and the information about individuals that genetic testing increasingly yields us. Again, even rather small developments in reproductive technology raise the spectre in some countries, for example, of aborting foetuses of the 'wrong' sex (see GENETICS AND ETHICS).

More broadly, and much more commonly, 'bioethics' refers to medical ethics generally and to all the various problems – moral, social, political, economic – that arise therein, including those moral issues to do with the development of biotechnologies encompassed by the narrower view. Resource allocation, informed consent, abortion, euthanasia, physician-assisted suicide, surrogate motherhood, the doctor/patient relationship, genetic engineering/genetic enhancement: on this broader usage, all form part of bioethics (see SUICIDE, ETHICS OF; LIFE AND DEATH; REPRODUCTION AND ETHICS). Since medical ethics has been perhaps the major growth area of applied ethics, this broader usage of the term 'bioethics' has become dominant in the Anglo-American world (see MEDICAL ETHICS).

More broadly still, and in keeping with V.R. Potter's introduction of the term (1971), 'bioethics' refers to the moral, social and political problems that arise from biology and the life sciences generally and that involve, directly or indirectly, human wellbeing. On this broadest usage, environmental ethics and animal ethics are parts of bioethics, though it should also be noted that Anglo-American medical ethicists increasingly include concerns to do with animals within their brief and so seek, at least in part, to incorporate these concerns into medical ethics (see ANIMALS AND ETHICS; ENVIRONMENTAL ETHICS; AGRICULTURAL ETHICS).

Accordingly, there is no specific discipline that is bioethics. Rather, there are sets or series of moral problems that arise out of biotechnologies, medicine, and human interaction with animals and the environment and that, directly or indirectly, affect human wellbeing. Which set of problems is emphasized can vary among philosophers and ethicists generally, and some sets have come to be so widely discussed that they have taken on a life of their own. Thus, some issues in environmental ethics (such as whether and how an ecosystem has value) and a great many issues in animal ethics (including the moral status of animals and their use as experimental subjects) flourish in their own right, whatever their relationship to human medicine and biotechnology. Again, so prominent have the problems of medical ethics become that medical ethicists, including those who speak of 'biomedical ethics', rarely engage directly with environmental issues. As indicated, the case of animal ethics is more complicated here, since the moral problems that surround medical experimentation upon animals for human benefit are increasingly regarded as important issues of medical ethics.

2 The role of the philosopher

Bioethics is a part of applied ethics (see APPLIED ETHICS). Since the mid-1960s, the application of ethical theory to moral, social and political issues has been one of the major growth areas of philosophy. To some extent, of course, philosophers had always been concerned with normative issues except, perhaps, in the very heyday of ordinary language philosophy. On the whole, however, they did little more than sketch some implications or draw some provisional conclusions based upon distant familiarity with a few empirical facts. All this has now changed, as philosophers have come to immerse themselves in the subject-matter of the areas and issues of normative concern to them, whether these come from medicine and biotechnology or from business, law and the affairs of social and political life (see BUSINESS ETHICS). Not only do they apply their theories in the midst of a much broader and deeper understanding of the empirical settings within which these issues arise but their works have also changed in other respects. Real-life examples abound; normative claims that are a part of ordinary life are legion; and attempts to justify such claims, as well as to unravel the concepts in terms of which they are expressed, are common. Expressed in more or less nontechnical language, these works in the main address the educated and not merely the philosophical public, and they have had the effect of taking philosophy to some extent into the public arena.

One must distinguish here between philosophers approaching an empirical discipline and members of such disciplines approaching philosophy, a distinction usually marked in the case of medical ethics as that between philosophical and clinical medical ethicists. The latter find that their practices raise certain moral issues that need to be resolved in order for them to act, or to advise others about how to act, and to act in what they think can be shown to be a justified manner; they turn to philosophy to help them achieve these ends. The task of the former, however, even when they are ethical consultants in hospitals, remains what the philosopher's task has always been:

to test arguments for soundness. To this end, they deploy the tools and canons of logic on behalf of accuracy in argument; they explore questions of meaning, implication, presupposition, derivation, relation, compatibility; they pry into and generate examples and counter-examples, both realistic and hypothetical; and so on. One important tool they use is the analysis of those concepts employed in the arguments being tested; analysis is not, however, an alternative view of what philosophers should be about, in some way competing with their assessment of arguments. Thus, while philosophers can immerse themselves in the factual material pertaining to the arguments they are assessing, increases in this material and in the knowledge pertaining thereto are not their concern. Applied ethics at its best, when done by philosophers, does not involve the philosopher as an agent of empirical discovery – therefore, complaints based upon lack of expertise or professional qualifications in the relevant empirical disciplines do not automatically succeed – but as the agent of sound and, therefore, probed or tested argument.

3 Moral status and justification of treatment

To consider only the very broad usage of 'bioethics', it is easy to see how this picture of what the philosopher is about inserts itself into the moral discussion. In the case of environmental ethics, for example, issues to do with the value, integrity and treatment of the environment, including whole ecosystems, are of fundamental concern, and the theoretical stances within which these notions are addressed become important. To focus upon value, traditional ethical theorists, such as utilitarians and Kantians, embrace value theories that are typically human-centred; environmental concerns figure in them through their effect upon and implications for human interests (see KANTIAN ETHICS; UTILITARIANISM). Nor will it matter that an essentially human-centred value theory is extended to some animals, since such a theory typically favours humans (and animals) on the strength of criteria (such as sentience and desire-satisfaction) that exclude inanimate nature. Many environmentalists claim to want a nature-centred, truly ecological ethic, in which the environment, viewed either holistically, as a well-functioning biotic community, or as separate parts of such a community, parts with a good of their own, counts for something quite apart from its service to human (and animal) interests, purposes and goals.

Traditional ethical theories incorporate a distinction between instrumental and intrinsic value (see VALUES). Nature is viewed as instrumentally valuable, and some facet of persons (or, more narrowly, agents) is viewed as intrinsically valuable, valuable in its own right. To the extent that some animals share in these facets, to that extent they can be viewed as intrinsically valuable. It seems clear, however, that little of inanimate nature can be so viewed. Numerous environmentalists want to break out from these person- or agent-centred value theories and to extend the notion of intrinsic value into nature. Talk of 'intrinsic value', of course, is ambiguous, so we might characterize the matter this way: what some environmentalists appear to claim is that an ecosystem or nature is valuable independently of any reference to human (or animal) interests, states of mind or desires. Unless we can extend this concept of independent value to nature, we have no real case for regarding rocks, forests and dirt as part of an expanded moral community, in circumstances in which only those things within that community enjoy the moral protections that, for example, affect how they are treated. Of course, someone might think that we are under some duty not to pollute rivers, and so hold rivers as a result to enjoy moral protection, but this duty would not obviously make rivers count for anything in their own right. So the case for a wider view of the moral community seems in large measure to depend upon our agreeing that there are independent values in nature. The philosopher enters this discussion easily; for if we sever talk of value from any connection with humans (and their conative and cognitive states), so that there could in essence be values without valuers, we need to go on to provide an account of the generation of the whole notion of value. For this severance from humans has deprived us of what the traditional theories have seen as the origin of value. Thus, the generation and source(s) of value become important issues, ones that fall within the domain of the philosopher (see VALUE, ONTOLOGICAL STATUS OF).

The issue of who or what is a part of the moral community has been an important one in bioethics with regard to foetuses, those in permanently vegetative states, members of future generations, and inanimate nature and animals. A related issue has been the matter of justification of treatment. If, for example, (some) animals are not members of the moral community, then the case for medical and scientific experimentation upon them seems relatively easy to make; if they are members of the moral community, then why do they not enjoy the protections accorded human members? Can we treat different members of that community differently? Why, if a heart transplant is required to save a child, should we use the heart of a healthy baboon instead of the heart of, say, an anencephalic infant?

A further issue is of obvious importance here: can, for example, a person or an agent, who has been a member of the moral community, cease to be a member? If membership is determined by some specific characteristic, then loss of that characteristic could remove one from the moral community, and the whole issue of how those outside the moral community can be treated arises. It seems important, then, to be able to retain membership. But how is this to be achieved? The integrative personality that we associate with human persons can come apart, and those in the advanced stages of Alzheimer's disease, unless they can be included by means of the interests of others in having them protected, can fall at risk. Yet, if they are included within the moral community through others, do they continue to count for anything in their own right? They remain alive, but they have lost, arguably, that which ensured their inclusion within the moral community; their inclusion now seems to depend upon the contingent fact of whether other people's interests encompass them.

Much of contemporary bioethics, then, is concerned with these interlocking questions of moral standing, justification of treatment, and loss of moral considerability in one's own right. The human cases of the brain dead, anencephalic infants, and those in a permanently vegetative state seem cases in point. May one permissibly use the organs of these individuals? If so, then the case for xenotransplantation, or the transplanting of animal organs into humans, is surely affected, even if not perhaps extinguished (see MORAL STANDING).

4 The problem of disagreement

As a part of applied ethics, bioethics in its broad usages is subject to a difficulty that seems fundamental. The standard conception of applied ethics is one of the application of principles to practice, and the various subject areas of bioethics appear to share in this conception. Thus, much of recent medical ethics appears to be the working out in practice of the implications of those moral principles that one takes to be relevant to the cases at hand, and environmental and animal ethics are usually portrayed in the same light. Now this standard conception of applied ethics is thought by some to leave out such things as personal relations and emotions, as integral parts of how we view cases morally, but others think that it can be made to include these things (see MORALITY AND IDENTITY §4). What seems quite clear, however, is that there is a deeper difficulty with this standard conception.

The fact is that we do not agree in our moral principles and do not agree, moreover, if several of them seem to apply to a particular case, on the measures or principles by which we weigh and balance the contending principles in order to decide which predominate in that case (see MORAL JUDGMENT). This much is clear to all parties to the debate, who stress different moral principles applicable to the situation or different weights to those principles. Nor can we be said to be moving towards a consensus in principles: in the cases of abortion, euthanasia, physician-assisted suicide, and homosexuality, for example, there is widespread, deep disagreement both over the permissibility of such acts and over the moral principles which are supposed to make them permissible or impermissible.

Moreover, we do not agree in the moral theories in which our moral principles find a home and by which we try to justify them. Utilitarianism, Kantianism, contractualism, virtue theory and more remain at odds with each other as philosophical accounts of morality. Those, for example, who use a broadly consequentialist theory continue to find themselves at odds with Kantians and others.

Yet the difficulty runs deeper still. For we do not even agree upon the test(s) of adequacy of the moral theories in which moral principles find their home. Indeed, this whole issue of the earmarks of adequacy in ethical theory is hotly disputed today, and resolution of it is hostage to our inability to agree on a number of things. One is how appropriate the model of the physical sciences and its determination of theoretical adequacy is for ethics. Another is the meanings and logical properties of the moral concepts and whether, say, the terms 'right' and 'good' are identical with and to be understood exhaustively in terms of natural properties, empirical properties occurring in the natural world (see NATURALISM IN ETHICS). Still another is the role of our moral intuitions in the assessment of theoretical adequacy in ethics (see INTUITIONISM IN ETHICS). As for this last, any direct reliance upon intuitions is rejected by many, whereas indirect reliance through some form of 'reflective equilibrium', whether narrowly or broadly construed, has also proved contentious (see MORAL JUSTIFICATION §2). Of course, the overwhelming temptation may well be to think that moral intuitions have probative force, because the model of science can seem virtually to compel us to regard them as the data of ethics. But why should we think that that model is appropriate to ethics in the first place?

To many, then, bioethics suffers from a complaint that infects applied ethics generally, a complaint the resolution of which awaits further work in ethical theory rather than in applied ethics itself. The problem is not that people disagree over the moral principles (or the weight of such principles) by which they set out and discuss cases; it is that there is no obvious way at the moment of resolving this disagreement at the level of ethical theory wherein we seek to justify our principles. The result is that much of bioethics, and applied ethics generally, takes the form of setting out cases in terms of different moral principles and theories, without providing us with any way of deciding between them. One can pick and choose among those items on offer, but all the interesting philosophical work lies outside the scope of any such view of bioethics and applied ethics. This is one of the reasons why some challenge the view that applied ethics is, as it were, a separate branch of ethics.

See also: BIOETHICS, JEWISH; RESPONSIBILITIES OF SCIENTISTS AND INTELLECTUALS; TECHNOLOGY AND ETHICS

References and further reading

Beauchamp, T.L. and Childress, J.F. (1979) *Principles of Biomedical Ethics*, New York: Oxford University Press; 4th edn, 1994. (A major text in contemporary medical ethics.)

Brody, H. (1976) *Ethical Decisions in Medicine*, Boston, MA: Little, Brown; revised and extended 2nd edn, 1984. (A survey of a mix of issues in medical ethics from the standpoint of different theoretical positions.)

Culver, C.M. and Gert, B. (1982) *Philosophy in Medicine*, New York: Oxford University Press. (A general statement of theoretical positions in approaches to medicine and medical decision-making.)

Englehardt, H.T., Jr (1986) *The Foundations of Bioethics*, New York: Oxford University Press; revised and extended 2nd edn, 1995. (A defence of one important, philosophical position in medical ethics.)

Frey, R.G. (1996) 'Medicine, Animal Experimentation, and The Moral Problem of Unfortunate Humans', *Social Philosophy and Policy* 13: 181–211. (An attempt to show how views about animals affect certain cases involving humans in medical ethics.)

Gillon, R. (ed.) (1993) *Principles of Health Care Ethics*, Chichester: John Wiley & Sons. (A major survey of issues and debates in medical ethics and in bioethics, broadly considered.)

Harris, J. (1985) *The Value of Life: An Introduction to Medical Ethics*, London: Routledge & Kegan Paul. (An introduction to life and death decisions in medicine.)

Mepham, T.B., Tucker, G.A. and Wiseman, J. (eds) (1995) *Issues in Agricultural Bioethics*, Nottingham: University of Nottingham Press. (Essays in the area of bioethics, broadly understood.)

Pence, G. (1990) *Classic Cases in Medical Ethics*, New York, McGraw-Hill; revised and extended 2nd edn, 1995. (A survey of cases in medical ethics, including cases involving animal ethics.)

* Potter, V.R. (1971) *Bioethics: Bridge to the Future*, Englewood Cliffs, NJ: Prentice Hall. (Considered to be the first text to introduce the term 'bioethics', where it is understood to include environmental concerns.)

Reich, W.T. (ed.) (1978) *Encyclopedia of Bioethics*, New York: Free Press, revised and extended 2nd edn, 1995. (Major compendium of discussions on issues in medical and animal ethics.)

Singer, P. (1994) *Rethinking Life and Death*, New York: St Martin's Griffin. (A challenge to the Judaeo-Christian ethic that has been traditionally understood to underlie Anglo-American medical animal ethics.)

VanDeVeer, D. and Regan, T. (eds) (1987) *Health Care Ethics*, Philadelphia, PA: Temple University Press. (Articles on important issues in medical and animal ethics.)

Veatch, R.M. (ed.) (1989) *Medical Ethics*, Boston, MA: Jones & Bartlett Publishers. (Major compendium on a number of important and lasting issues in medical ethics.)

R.G. FREY

BIOETHICS, JEWISH

Jewish bioethics seeks to apply Jewish modes of normative discourse in bioethics. For some moral issues in medicine, explicit guidance may be found in the traditional sources of halakhah; *but many others require creative application of ancient or medieval precedents and norms. Much of the contemporary writing in this area takes the classical form of rabbinic Responsa to specific queries from adherents of the halakhah. But the field also includes contributions from thinkers who offer not rulings on religious law but the fruits of moral inspiration by the tradition.*

In the Judaic tradition the idea that each human being is created in God's image fosters a powerful commitment to saving and prolonging life. Murder and suicide are terrible sacrileges. Procreation is highly valued. Contraception is not easily countenanced, and still less is abortion. But abortion is clearly distinguished from homicide.

The symbolic preciousness of the divine image disallows disfigurement of human corpses. The implica-

tions of this prohibition for pathology and for the study of anatomy are hotly disputed. The prohibition is overridden, however, in cases of immediate life-saving.

Regarding triage and resource allocation, the universal egalitarianism implied by the idea of God's image fosters a powerful reluctance against bringing about any person's death, even to save a number of lives. Some tension arises between this egalitarianism and traditional structures of social and religious hierarchy.

1 Problems of method
2 Basic attitudes towards medicine
3 At the deathbed
4 Triage
5 Procreation and abortion
6 The human body as resource

1 Problems of method

Jewish bioethics, like other areas of applied Jewish ethics, faces foundational problems of method and disciplinary presuppositions. These problems arise from the conjunction of reasoned ethical discourse with a tradition whose core teachings are deemed to be divinely revealed.

Jewish religious law (see HALAKHAH) is a central aspect of the Jewish normative tradition, but when Jewish bioethics focuses on this aspect, it can become a discourse of authority, taking the form of commandments and injunctions addressed to those bound by that law. Such teachings, it has been forcefully argued, cannot validly claim relevance to non-Jews or even to secular Jews.

Certain writers, however, find in *halakhic* discourse a more universal aspect, whose norms do not draw their authority from the particular commitments of the Jewish covenant. Some locate this aspect of *halakhah* in the seven 'Noahide Laws', which are seen to represent a sort of natural law. Others find the universal aspects in specific broadly humanistic themes. But in either case, the challenge of imbuing Jewish bioethics with general relevance consists in identifying the appropriate strands within *halakhah*. Since *halakhah* is not only a positive legal system but an articulated code of values, the significance of its teachings need not depend on accepting the legal system's authority *en bloc*. The fact is that *halakhic* discourse often appeals to reasons that are intelligible independently of religious authority. It can thus be seen as constituting a language of moral discourse that is widely accessible and relevant and that bears its own distinctive emphases and valuations.

2 Basic attitudes towards medicine

Because Judaism attaches great value to human life, not only is homicide viewed as sacrilege, but there is a positive duty to rescue any person from mortal danger: 'Anyone who saves a single life – it is as though he had saved an entire world' (Mishnah Sanhedrin 4: 5). Yet according to one strand of Jewish tradition, this duty, particularly in the context of medical practice, may conflict with an ideal of utter acceptance of God's providence. Thus the rabbis found it necessary to deduce from Scripture an explicit divine dispensation for medical intervention: 'a physician is granted permission to heal' (Berakhot 60a).

Several medieval thinkers, most prominently NAHMANIDES (himself also a physician), retained some uneasiness about human self-reliance and depicted medicine as compromising perfect piety. MAIMONIDES, by contrast, emphasized the divine origin of our capacities for healing and treated medicine as a most valuable art and profession that can secure the years human beings need to attain spiritual fulfilment. Mainstream *halakhic* policy follows Maimonides in accepting medical interventions and regards a physician's duty to heal as but one instance of the general religious obligations to forestall dangers and to relieve human suffering. This duty is antecedent to any contractual relation between doctor and patient and, needless to say, holds even where the patient is unable to pay the costs of medical services.

In *halakhah* the obligation to forestall even a small risk to human life takes precedence over all other injunctions save three: the prohibitions against bloodshed, idolatry and incest. In practice, this confers great authority upon physicians. For it is they who can proclaim a state of emergency concerning the endangerment of human life. This authority does not extend, however, to the formulation of normative judgments. Thus 'Medical Halakhah' could not in principle be a set of special norms adopted by physicians. Rather, it takes the form of guidance for medical practice, derived from the *halakhic* tradition (see MEDICAL ETHICS).

3 At the deathbed

In the classic sixteenth-century code of Jewish law and ritual, Joseph Karo's *Shulkhan "Arukh*, the sections on caring for the sick are followed by a special section on 'laws pertaining to gosses [that is, a dying person]' (Yoreh De'ah 339). The sacredness of human life is conveyed by a Talmudic metaphor: the life of a *gosses* is like a flickering candle – 'anyone who touches him is a shedder of blood'. When a person reaches this final phase, the soul's departure must be neither hindered nor hastened, even where a quicker release is requested by the dying person. *Halakhic* writers place this rule in the context of the prohibition on suicide (see Genesis 9: 5–6 as interpreted at *Genesis Rabbah* 34: 13). The underlying principle, once again, is the exalted value of the life of the human being, created in God's image.

Contemporary writers commonly ground the prohibition of suicide in affirmations of God's sovereignty over life and death. Arguing against secular assertions of human autonomy, they condemn active euthanasia even at the patient's explicit behest. 'Passive' euthanasia is cautiously accepted – extending, on some views, even to the removal of artificial life-support. This acceptance applies, however, only to a patient in the phase of *gosses* – a term traditionally limited to patients who could not be expected to live more than three days. In the context of modern medical capabilities, the proper scope of the term seems uncertain, but it is clearly narrower than that of 'terminal'. In practice, determination of the point beyond which efforts to prolong life should be foregone is commonly left to the patient (and patient's family), especially where further treatment itself involves some risk of death.

Against the main contemporary trend of opposition to active euthanasia and assisted suicide, stands the rabbinic endorsement of King Saul's act in falling on his sword to avoid capture and torture. This biblical precedent, alongside the self-sacrifice of martyrs, is cited as an express qualification to the original prohibition on suicide. The precise circumstances justifying Saul's suicide are variously defined. Some commentators, at least, find them simply in the expectation of inescapable death accompanied by great suffering.

It has also been argued that, under Jewish law, killing a terminal patient is less severe than murder, since capital punishment – the normative penalty for murder – does not apply to one who kills a terminally ill individual. It is not clear what moral significance the distinction carries, however, since it is but one among a host of instances in which the rabbis renounce capital punishment. In all these instances, the rabbis' hesitation is arguably directed at the punishment, rather than at the culpability of the act.

4 Triage

Grounding the value of human life in the belief that human beings are created in God's image implies a basic equality regarding life itself, transcending cultural boundaries and social hierarchy. No (innocent) person may be killed in order to save the life of another. But does the same standard point towards an absolute prohibition of killing, even to save a great many persons? An early rabbinic text reads:

> If a group is told by heathens: 'Hand over one of your number and we shall kill him; otherwise, we shall kill all of you!' they should all be killed, rather than surrender one individual of Israel.
>
> (Tosefta Terumot 7: 20)

The emphasis on 'one individual of Israel' has prompted an interpretation in terms of group solidarity in the face of 'heathen' persecution. But a prevalent alternative reading sees here a more general principle which would clearly preclude, say, killing one person in order to provide transplant organs for the saving of several lives. Rabbinic debates are recorded regarding some exceptions to the rule, for instance, where the said individual is sure to perish anyway.

When the choice involves not killing but deciding whom to save, there is broad agreement that the numbers should count. This quantitative angle appears to extend to triage as well: the 'one bed' or 'one kidney' should go to the patient who is expected to gain a full lifespan, not to one whose death will only be somewhat postponed. According to some writers, there is room also for traditional considerations of personal status or merit: one learned in Torah might be given precedence over an ignoramus, one of priestly descent (a *kohen*) over an ordinary Jew, a man over a woman, or a Jew over a Gentile. Other writers reject any such distinctions; some strongly advocating 'first come, first served' (see NURSING ETHICS).

5 Procreation and abortion

Rabbinic traditions regarding abortion are far from consistent. Two oft-quoted passages (Mishnah Niddah 3: 7 and Babylonian Talmud Yevamot 69b) refer to pregnancy up to forty days as 'mere fluid'. Beyond this point, some mandate abortion for the sake of a moderate interest of the woman, arguing that the embryo is simply 'her body' ('Arakhin 7a). Others denounce it as 'bloodshed' (Sanhedrin 57b). But all draw a sharp boundary between a foetus, even at full term, which must be killed to save the woman, and a newborn, who may not be harmed (Mishnah Ohalot 7.6).

Contemporary views reflect this early diversity, differing greatly about the gravity of the prohibition of abortion at various stages of a pregnancy. The issue is not exhausted here, however, since the tradition emphasizes a positive duty of procreation. This is illustrated by the fact that infertility (of either spouse) has traditionally served as sufficient grounds for divorce. Contraception is in general not easily countenanced, and abortion is commonly viewed as slighting the value inherent in each new human life, created in God's image.

Yet *halakhic* rulings on the morality of either contraception or abortion reflect also the force of the reasons weighing against pregnancy. These may include concerns about birth defects, the woman's health, food supplies (in times of famine), or even the pursuits of one or both of the prospective parents. The weight assigned to such factors in modern rabbinic opinions can reflect in turn the extent to which patriarchal attitudes are replaced by more egalitarian ethical concerns.

The view of procreation as an important mitzvah (divinely commanded obligation) entails a generally positive attitude towards medical interventions against infertility. Artificial insemination and in-vitro fertilization are widely condoned, as long as they use no 'third party' gametes. But donor insemination is condemned by several *halakhists* as 'artificial adultery'. The view that a woman may be fertilized only by her husband's sperm is not accepted by all, however. Some argue that adultery means only sexual infidelity.

6 The human body as resource

The obligation to preserve one's own life leads to some debate regarding the risks assumed in donating an organ such as a kidney. But most *halakhic* discussion regarding medical use of human bodies focuses on the bodies of the dead. First, it is necessary to determine when a person may be considered dead. Traditional *halakhic* teachings focus on breathing, and some contemporary scholars still adhere to this criterion, rejecting any notion of 'brain death'. This rules out transplantation of a heart, liver or other vital organ. To remove the heart of one who has not ceased to breathe is viewed as outright murder. Others, including the Chief Rabbinate of Israel, have adopted innovative interpretations that permit such transplantations. According to one argument, the traditional criterion of ceasing to breathe is met upon complete death of the brain stem, since that precludes *autonomous* breathing.

The *halakhic* requirement of respect for the dead and the concomitant prohibition against disfiguring the dead raise serious problems regarding the use of corpses. Most interpreters understand the normative concern not in terms of the interests of the deceased but as a matter of reverence for God's image. The prohibition is outweighed, however, by the duty of saving life. Thus transplants of kidneys, corneas and the like, which do not depend on endorsing brain death, are widely condoned.

But less immediate medical uses, such as dissections for the study and teaching of anatomy or surgery, post-mortem examinations, and research using cadaveric organs or tissues, are hotly contended. Do such pursuits come under the overarching concept of *life-saving*, a duty that overrides virtually any prohibition? Or should that rubric be confined to immediate emergencies? The view adopted by many *halakhists* opposes post-mortem pathological practices, and poses a serious obstacle to the study of medicine. Those who follow such teachings yet avail themselves of modern medicine have consequently been criticized as free riders.

See also: LIFE AND DEATH; HALAKHAH; MEDICAL ETHICS; MEDICINE, PHILOSOPHY OF

References and further reading

Bleich, J.D. and Rosner, F. (1983) *Jewish Bioethics*, New York: Hebrew Publishing Company, 2nd edn. (Wide-ranging collection of essays offering a detailed introduction to the field from an Orthodox perspective.)

Feldman, D.M. (1974) *Marital Relations, Birth Control and Abortion in Jewish Law*, New York: Schocken. (Well-rounded presentation and analysis of the major sources and opinions.)

Green, R.M. (1985) 'Contemporary Jewish Bioethics: A Critical Assessment', in E.E. Shelp (ed.) *Theology and Bioethics*, Dordrecht: Reidel, 245–66. (An illuminating critique of what the author sees as a prevalent, unnecessarily rigid tendency in modern Jewish bioethics. Examples cover several important issues, with useful references.)

Jakobovits, I. (1975) *Jewish Medical Ethics*, New York: Bloch. (Revised text by the former Chief Rabbi of Great Britain, widely considered the founder of this academic subdiscipline.)

Newman, L.A. (1993) 'Talking Ethics with Strangers: A View from the Jewish Tradition', *Journal of Medicine and Philosophy* 18: 549–67. (Engaging the basic problem of particularism versus universalism in Jewish bioethics, including discussions of 'Noahide Law' and natural law.)

The Journal of Medicine and Philosophy (1983) 8 (3). (Issue devoted to Jewish bioethics.)

Steinberg, A. (1988–) *Encyclopedia of Medicine and Jewish Law*, Jerusalem: Schlesinger Institute, 5 vols. (In Hebrew; these are the first five volumes of the planned six. An English translation of the complete work by F. Rosner is in progress, and its publication is expected in 1998/9. The encyclopedia is a comprehensive and reliable reference work which presents virtually all issues addressed in *halakhic* bioethics. Its citations lead mainly to primary sources and are therefore most useful for those capable of reading rabbinic discourse in the original texts and languages.)

Zohar, N. (1997) *Alternatives in Jewish Bioethics*, Albany, NY: State University of New York Press. (A non-authoritarian presentation and analysis of various traditional voices in dialogue with contemporary philosophical bioethics.)

NOAM J. ZOHAR

BIOLOGY, PHILOSOPHY OF

see EVOLUTION, THEORY OF; GENETICS; MOLECULAR BIOLOGY; SPECIES; TAXONOMY; VITALISM

BION OF BORYSTHENES *see* CYNICS

BLACKSTONE, WILLIAM (1723–80)

Blackstone produced the first systematic exposition of English law as a body of principles. His enterprise was founded upon the assumption that the detailed rules of English law embodied and enforced natural law. Blackstone's invocation of natural law has frequently been regarded as ornamental rather than substantial, but there is no good reason for taking this view. Blackstone is now remembered as much for Bentham's attacks upon him as for his own contribution.

Sir William Blackstone was the first Vinerian Professor of English Law in the University of Oxford; he subsequently became a judge of the King's Bench, and then of Common Pleas. He is most famous for his four-volume *Commentaries on the Laws of England*, which was published between 1765 and 1769.

Among philosophers, Blackstone is probably principally remembered for the attacks mounted upon his work by Jeremy BENTHAM (§1). This greatly underestimates his true significance, however, for the *Commentaries* constituted the first systematic treatment of English law as a body of orderly rights and principles. English law-books prior to Blackstone were unsystematic in arrangement: they were huge compendia of legal information arranged alphabetically, or collections of writs and pleadings with associated commentary. Blackstone introduced into English legal writing a tradition of exposition and analysis which related more specific rules to general principles, the latter forming an integrated structure of rights. This was not simply a matter of giving well-organized expression to traditional legal ideas: in order to express the common law in systematic form it was necessary to reconceptualize it fundamentally, and this Blackstone did by relating his account to what he conceived to be the law's foundations in natural law (see NATURAL LAW).

Blackstone begins his masterwork (1765–9: vol. 1, section 2) by embarking upon a general discussion of natural law. Anyone seeking to present Blackstone as a serious contributor to natural law theory is bound to be discouraged by this opening discussion: the points are loosely structured and ambiguous, and are asserted rather than argued for; the game of spotting contradictions has proved easy, if unrewarding. The insubstantial nature of the discussion has led many to conclude that Blackstone's invocation of natural law serves purely ornamental purposes. It is certainly true that such discussions were conventional among institutional writers of the period. Yet what does such a convention signify? We have not explained the presence of the discussion simply by pointing to its conventional nature; and an explanation of the convention itself requires an understanding of the deep assumptions underpinning the emergence of systematic legal writing.

Why should it be assumed that laws will form an orderly system? In so far as law is a product of authority, identified by its source, laws might well be expected to form a haphazard list, incapable of reduction to any limited set of general principles. For Blackstone, the relevant grounding perspective was provided by the assumption that English law was concerned to enforce natural rights. It was this perspective which enabled him to abandon the traditional framework of legal thought, within which the common law was thought of as a body of remedies, and to systematize the law in terms of substantive rights. Even though English law might not reflect natural law with perfect accuracy, it was capable of systematic study to the extent that it did so reflect natural law. Thus he endeavours to expound English law in terms of a system of natural rights, and he draws on the writings of natural lawyers throughout the *Commentaries* (and not simply in the opening section).

The tendency of Blackstone's work (in common with that of other treatise writers) to expound the extant legal rules in terms of the moral values which (in his view) served to justify them formed the focus for Bentham's attack upon him. Bentham argued that

Blackstone conflated the law as it *is* with the law as it *ought to be*. Intellectual clarity required, in Bentham's view, a clearer separation between the roles of *expositor* and *censor*.

Those who deny the substantial nature of Blackstone's reliance upon a theory of natural law are unduly influenced by the *ad hoc* and broadly utilitarian character of many of his arguments. This does not seem to correspond to the conventional image of a natural law theory. In fact it is very much in line with what we might expect from a natural law writer in the mid eighteenth century. The theories of GROTIUS and PUFENDORF, which were influential in the preceding century, had separated the mode in which we ascertain the *content* of natural law (in considerations of the requirements of social life) from the basis of its obligatory force (in the divine will). This meant that, behind the deontological façade provided by the notion of the divine will, natural law developed a somewhat utilitarian and empirical character which is clearly reflected in Blackstone's work.

It is also suggested that Blackstone's defence of Parliamentary sovereignty involves a commitment to the legal positivist belief that legal validity is a matter of source alone, and not of content (see LEGAL POSITIVISM §1). The error here lies in the assumption that natural law theories must deny the source-based view of legal validity: the point of such theories, however, is to emphasize the extent to which the content of law reflects the requirements of natural law, rather than to offer any particular account of the criteria of legal validity.

Finally, Blackstone's extensive use of history is sometimes thought to be inconsistent with a commitment to timeless principles of natural law. There is indeed a tension between Blackstone's deployment of history and his invocations of natural law. He seeks to address this problem only on a rhetorical plane: he claims that the rights conferred by natural law are, in other countries, so debased that they may now fairly be called 'the rights of the people of England'. This enables him to use the language of one ideology, within which rights are an inheritance of the English, while not abandoning natural law theory, within which such rights are universal.

See also: COMMON LAW; LAW, PHILOSOPHY OF; LEGAL HERMENEUTICS

List of works

Blackstone, W. (1765–9) *Commentaries on the Laws of England*, 4 vols, Chicago, IL: Chicago University Press, 1979. (The 1979 edition contains valuable editorial introductions to each volume.)

References and further reading

Bentham, J. (1776) *A Comment on the Commentaries* and *A Fragment on Government*, ed. J.H. Burns and H.L.A. Hart, London: Athlone Press, 1977. (The two works, the former unpublished in the author's lifetime, which set forth Bentham's – frequently unfair – critique of Blackstone.)

Boorstin, D.J. (1996) *The Mysterious Science of the Law: An Essay on Blackstone's Commentaries*, 2nd edn, Chicago, IL: University of Chicago Press. (A valuable if idiosyncratic survey.)

Lobban, M. (1991) *The Common Law and English Jurisprudence 1760–1850*, Oxford: Clarendon Press. (Chapter 2 concentrates on Blackstone.)

Simmonds, N.E. (1988) 'Reason, History and Privilege: Blackstone's Debt to Natural Law', *Zeitschrift der Savigny-Stiftung fur Rechtsgeschichte: Germanistische Abteilung* 118: 200–13. (Examines Blackstone's invocation of natural law.)

N.E. SIMMONDS

BLAIR, HUGH (1718–1800)

Blair was the foremost literary critic and preacher of the Scottish Enlightenment. He participated in the thriving cultural life of eighteenth-century Edinburgh, and along with William Robertson, Adam Ferguson and other enlightened Moderate party clergymen was a close friend of that city's greatest philosopher, David Hume.

As minister of the High Kirk in St Giles Church, Edinburgh, from 1758 until his death, and Regius Professor of Rhetoric and Belles-Lettres at the University of Edinburgh from 1762 to 1784, Hugh Blair occupied Scotland's most prestigious platforms for literary and religious oratory. His phenomenally successful publications were direct outgrowths of his preaching and teaching. In 1807 the Critical Review declared Blair's *Sermons* (1777–1801) to be, excepting the Spectator, 'the most popular work in the English language'. His *Lectures on Rhetoric and Belles-Lettres* (1783), the first comprehensive guide to the rules of written and spoken English in the various branches of polite discourse, enjoyed comparable popularity in the literary world. One of his early academic lectures, revised and published in 1763 as *A Critical Dissertation on the Poems of Ossian*, did much to encourage the subsequent Ossianic vogue. These works by Blair were frequently reprinted and translated; along with his professorship and church living, they brought him international fame and considerable income.

Blair contributed to the philosophy of the Scottish Enlightenment (see ENLIGHTENMENT, SCOTTISH) in two major ways. First, his Lectures included influential discussions of the principles of literary taste and philosophical discourse. At their core is the idea that clarity, simplicity and perspicuity constitute the proper foundation of all forms of communication. In regard to philosophical writing specifically, Blair's thirty-seventh lecture states that 'beyond mere perspicuity, strict accuracy and precision are required in a Philosophical Writer', in addition to 'embellishment' attained through 'illustrations' and 'a polished, a neat, and elegant Style' that avoids 'too much ornament'. Plato and Cicero among the ancients, and John Locke among the moderns, are held up as the models of clear and elegant philosophical discourse, whereas Seneca and the Earl of Shaftesbury are censured for their excessively ornamental styles.

Second, Blair's *Sermons* popularized the ideal of Christian Stoicism, or the belief that happiness is to be found within – in resignation to the will of God – rather than in worldly matters. Blair repeatedly asserts 'that mind is superior to fortune; that what one feels within is of much greater importance than all that befalls him without'; that 'the happiness of every man depends more upon the state of his own mind, than ... upon all external things put together', and that awareness of the nature of the human condition points out 'how submissive ought we to be to the disposal of Providence'. Such preaching represented a comforting, polite form of Presbyterianism, which complemented Stoic elements in the philosophy of other thinkers of the Scottish Enlightenment.

See also: COMMON SENSE SCHOOL; FERGUSON, A.; HUME, D.; STOICISM

List of works

Blair, H. (1763) *A Critical Dissertation on the Poems of Ossian.* (Laudatory introduction to James Macpherson's Ossianic poetry, revised in the second edition of 1765 to answer doubts raised by David Hume.)

—— (1777–1801) *Sermons*, 5 vols. (Most popular sermons of the late eighteenth and early nineteenth centuries.)

—— (1783) *Lectures on Rhetoric and Belles-lettres*, ed. H.F. Harding, Carbondale, Il: Southern Illinois University Press, 1965, 2 vols. (Facsimile of first edition, with a useful introduction and bibliography.)

References and further reading

Bevilacqua, V. (1967) 'Philosophical Assumptions Underlying Hugh Blair's Lectures on Rhetoric and Belles-Lettres', *Western Speech* 31: 150–64. (Emphasizes Blair's ties with the Scottish common sense tradition.)

Daiches, D. (1990) 'Style Périodique and Style Coup: Hugh Blair and the Scottish Rhetoric of Independence', in R.B. Sher and J.R. Smitten (eds) *Scotland and America in the Age of the Enlightenment*, Edinburgh: Edinburgh University Press, 209–26. (A suggestive reading of the influence of Blair's rhetorical theory on the American Founding Fathers.)

Hill, J. (1807) *An Account of the Life and Writing of Hugh Blair*, Edinburgh. (The standard contemporary life.)

Miller, T.P. (1990) 'Witherspoon, Blair and the Rhetoric of Civic Humanism', in R.B. Sher and J.R. Smitten (eds) *Scotland and America in the Age of the Enlightenment*, Edinburgh: Edinburgh University Press, 100–14. (Contrasts Blair's belletristic approach to rhetoric with Witherspoon's civic one.)

Schmitz, R.M. (1948) *Hugh Blair*, New York. (Still the standard modern biography, though dated and flawed.)

Sher, R.B. (1985) *Church and University in the Scottish Enlightenment: The Moderate Literati of Edinburgh*, Edinburgh: Edinburgh University Press. (A study of Blair's circle of Presbyterian clergymen of letters, with a lengthy bibliography.)

Warnick, B. (1993) *The Sixth Canon: Belletristic Rhetorical Theory and Its French Antecedents*, Columbia, SC: University of South Carolina Press. (Relates Blair's theory of rhetoric to earlier French theorists.)

RICHARD SHER

BLAISE OF PARMA *see* BLASIUS OF PARMA

BLAME *see* PRAISE AND BLAME

BLANCHOT, MAURICE (1907–)

Maurice Blanchot, has since the 1940s been a dominant voice in French philosophy and letters, initiating a postmodern discourse which has had a profound impact

on Bataille, Levinas, Foucault and Derrida. His early writings, between 1930 and 1940, consisted of cultural and political criticism. The experience of the Second World War led him to disengage from politics and he became an essayist and novelist. His works have included novels, narratives, and criticism, notably. Since the 1970s he has produced a series of fragmentary writings in which the line between literature and philosophy is shattered and, since the 1980s, meditations on language, death, the 'disaster' and community.

Basing himself on Mallarmé, Blanchot distinguishes two kinds of language, or speech. Crude speech is utilitarian, descriptive, and representational; it puts us in touch with the object-world. Essential speech is poetic, what Blanchot designates as the 'pure language' through which, as he asserts in *L'Éspace littéraire* (1955) (*The Space of Literature*, 1982: 41) 'it is being that tends to speak and speech that wants to be'. Essential language can reveal what is normally concealed, something which still is when everything has disappeared: being. 'The essence of being is to be there still where it lacks, to be inasmuch as it is hidden' (1982: 253). As with Heidegger, this poetic language has ontological priority for Blanchot. For him, the poem, literature, is an act of transgression; it reaches beyond all limits. As he says in *L'Entretien infini* (1969) (*The Infinite Conversation*, 1993: 453), following Bataille, 'Transgression designates what is radically out of reach: assailment of the inaccessible, a surpassing of what cannot be surpassed.'

Writing as transgression, literature as an expression of essential speech, occurs under the spectre of human finitude, and so as a confrontation with death. This link between writing and death is particularly clear in the novel *Le Très-Haut* (1948) (*The Most High*, 1996), in the last line of which, the hero, Henri Sorge, at the very moment of his death, cries out: 'Now, now I'm speaking' (1996: 254). Death is the primordial experience for Blanchot, and it is through their encounter with it that humans make themselves mortal. Hence, as he says in *The Space of Literature*: 'Death, in the human perspective, is not a given, it must be achieved' (1982: 96). Blanchot distinguishes between two kinds of death: death as the disappearing of consciousness, the biological extinction which humans flee, the dying which does not permit us to complete our death; and death as consciousness of disappearing, the death which the poet wants to shape, and through which humans seek to achieve their mortality. It is because death as consciousness of disappearing is so elusive, indeed even self-contradictory, that Blanchot is driven beyond the limits of discursive language in his effort to grapple with it.

For Blanchot, modernity's quest for community is haunted by totalitarianism, and by what he designates as the disaster. While his image of totalitarianism as an omnipresent feature of the political topography of the twentieth century has been shaped by the experiences of Nazism and Stalinism, it is not exhausted by them. For Blanchot, the danger of totalitarianism is that all negativity or independent action will be appropriated by the state, all opposition recuperated, all criticism absorbed. His fear, expressed in *L'Écriture du désastre* (1980) (*The Writing of the Disaster*, 1986: 45), is that the totalization of the state in modernity will lead to a world in which 'the prisoners construct their prison themselves'. The disaster, as Blanchot conceives it, is encapsulated by the totalitarian state, with its camps, in which what takes place is 'dying, as forgetfulness of death' (1986:17). So powerful is the presence of the Holocaust, and its death camps, that Blanchot designates it 'the *absolute* event of history' (1986: 47).

Yet in the face of the disaster, Blanchot sees humankind's search for community. Community appears in two forms in Blanchot's thinking. In the 1930s, in his earliest writings, his views were shaped by the extreme right-wing *Action Française*, to which he was then linked. At that time 'community' meant an organic community, based on rootedness in a common place, a native soil, and ethnicity. The experience of Nazi barbarism and occupation led him to reject any conception of a traditional community, opening the way to his thematization of *l'autrui*, the other, as a basis of his thinking. Here, we can see the profound influence of his friend Emmanuel LEVINAS. As the antithesis of totality, and identity, as the embodiment of *l'autrui*, the Jew becomes the point of departure for a different vision of community. This Blanchotian vision, articulated in *La Communauté inavouable* (1983b) (*The Unavowable Community*, 1988) is an elective community based on friendship and open to alterity, in which the other is no longer despised, and execrated; a community in which *l'autrui* is an irreducible element. In contrast to the traditional communities imposed on humans by virtue of blood or race, such an elective community would gather its members around a choice, 'that gave permission to everyone, without distinction of class, age, sex or culture, to mix with the first comer as if with an already loved being, precisely because he was the unknown-familiar' (1988: 30).

Blanchot's daring linkage of the dangers of the totalizing state, and the disaster which confronts humankind, as well as the need for a community in which *l'autrui* is at home, to the experience of the Holocaust, and its death camps, make his a seminal voice in postmodern thinking.

See also: HOLOCAUST, THE; TOTALITARIANISM; ALTERITY AND IDENTITY, POSTMODERN THEORIES OF

List of works

Blanchot, M. (1948) *Le Très-Haut*, Paris: Gallimard; trans. A. Stoekl, *The Most High*, Lincoln, NE: University of Nebraska Press, 1996. (A dystopian novel, in which the totalization of the state and the prospects for revolt are thematized.)
—— (1955) *L'Éspace littéraire*, Paris: Gallimard; trans. A. Smock, *The Space of Literature*, Lincoln, NE: University of Nebraska Press, 1982. (Explorations of the relation of literature to artistic creation, time and death.)
—— (1969) *L'Entretien infini*, Paris: Gallimard; trans. S. Hanson, *The Infinite Conversation*, Minneapolis, MN: University of Minnesota Press, 1993. (Blanchot's dialogues with Pascal, Kafka and Nietzsche, and his meditations on language, nihilism and what it is to be Jewish.)
—— (1980) *L'Écriture du désastre*, Paris: Gallimard; trans. A. Smock, *The Writing of the Disaster*, Lincoln, NE: University of Nebraska Press, 1986. (An inquiry, in fragments, which seeks to write about the disasters of the twentieth century: total war, concentration camps and the Holocaust.)
—— (1983a) *Après coup*, Paris: Éditions de Minuit; trans. P. Auster, *Vicious Circles: Two Fictions and 'After the Fact'*, Barrytown, NY: Station Hill Press, 1985. (Two pre-war narratives and a 1983 addendum which look forward to, and back from, the Holocaust, and raise the question of the difficulty of bearing witness.)
—— (1983b) *La Communauté inavouable*, Paris: Éditions de Minuit; trans. P. Joris, *The Unavowable Community*, Barrytown, NY: Station Hill Press, 1988. (A meditation on the meaning and possibility of community, through reflections on the writings of Georges Bataille and Marguerite Duras.)

References and further reading

Foucault, M. (1986) *La Pensée du dehors*, Paris: Fata Morgana; trans. B. Massumi, 'Maurice Blanchot: The Thought From Outside', in *Foucault/Blanchot*, New York: Zone Books, 1987. (A particularly insightful treatment of Blanchot's understanding of writing and language as a thought that stands outside subjectivity.)
Gregg, J. (1994) *Maurice Blanchot and the Literature of Transgression*, Princeton, NJ: Princeton University Press. (A comprehensive overview of Blanchot, which includes an excellent bibliography of both primary and secondary sources.)
Levinas, E. (1975) *Sur Maurice Blanchot*, Paris: Fata Morgana. (An important contribution by a thinker both influenced by Blanchot, and an important influence on him.)
Mehlman, J. (1983) 'Blanchot at Combat: Of Literature and Terror', in *Legacies of Anti-Semitism in France*, Minneapolis, MN: University of Minnesota Press. (An analysis of Blanchot's early right-wing political journalism, and its intellectual sources.)
Ungar, S. (1995) *Scandal and Aftereffect: Blanchot and France since 1930*, Minneapolis, MN: University of Minnesota Press. (A significant contribution to elucidating Blanchot's origins as a theorist of the Young Right, and possible links to the themes of his mature writings; this work includes a comprehensive bibliography of the early writings.)

ALAN MILCHMAN
ALAN ROSENBERG

BLASIUS DE PELACANIS
see BLASIUS OF PARMA

BLASIUS OF PARMA (d. 1416)

Blasius of Parma was an important Italian philosopher, mathematician and astrologer who popularized the achievements of Oxford logic and Parisian physics in Italy. He questioned the Aristotelian foundations of medieval physical science, mechanics, astronomy and optics, thus helping to open the way to the mathematics, optics and statics of modern times. His teaching influenced the artists of the Florentine Renaissance in their rediscovery of linear perspective, and his discussion of proportions influenced the Paduan mathematicians up to the time of Galileo. He presented an atomist and quantitative account of physical reality, and a materialist account of the human intellect. His consequent denial of the immortality of the soul won him the title of 'diabolical doctor' (doctor diabolicus). His position on the human ability to avoid astrological determinism was equivocal. Though his work was scholastic in style, he enjoyed good relations with such Italian humanists as Vittorino da Feltre, whose request for lessons in mathematics he refused. In Florence, he took part in conversations between humanists and scholastics.

1 Life
2 Metaphysics
3 Human beings
4 Epistemology and science

1 Life

Blasius of Parma (Blasius de Pelacanis or Biagio Pelacani da Parma) was born on an uncertain date in Costamezana (Parma), but is known to have received his doctorate at Pavia in about 1374. He died in Parma and was buried there on 23 April 1416. He visited Paris during his youth, sometime before 1388, but spent most of his life in Italy. At various times he taught logic, natural and moral philosophy, medicine, mathematics, and astrology (which included natural philosophy or physics) at the Universities of Bologna, Padua, Pavia and Florence. He was forced to retire from the University of Padua in 1411 on the grounds that he had no students, and was no longer fit to teach. He wrote a large number of works, including commentaries on Aristotle's *On the Soul* (*Conclusiones de anima* in 1382; *Quaestiones de anima*, copying finished in 1385) and *Physics* (*Quaestiones physicorum*, two manuscript versions, 1382–8 and 1397), *Quaestiones de motuum proportionibus* (Questions on the Proportions of Motions) (two manuscript versions, 1389 and 1407) and *Quaestiones perspectivae* (Questions on Perspective) (two versions, before 1390 and 1403). Many of his works are available only in manuscript (for details, see Federici Vescovini 1979: 413–52). His writings show the strong influence of English and French authors, including WILLIAM OF OCKHAM, William HEYTESBURY, the OXFORD CALCULATORS, John BURIDAN and ALBERT OF SAXONY, as well as of Arabic science, astrology and optics.

2 Metaphysics

In the context of the fourteenth century, Blasius' metaphysics is strongly original, for he was a materialist. He worked out a doctrine of substance as prime matter, an indeterminate substratum common to all beings. This metaphysical conception of reality as prime matter resulted in its being conceived as ungenerable, incorruptible and eternal. The forms of particular beings originate from prime matter in so far as it is constituted internally by qualities which are dispositions to become this or that individual form, such as human being or horse. With the death of the individual, these forms disappear by returning to prime matter. Prime matter, however, is only a conjoint cause of the generation of forms. The other universal cause of generation is the universal movement of the heavens which, through the influence of their motion, activate the dispositions of prime matter, and bring individual forms to birth.

3 Human beings

A corollary of Blasius' metaphysical views and his desire to unify all observable phenomena is his inclusion of humans among those natural beings whose generation is accounted for in terms of prime matter, individual dispositions and heavenly influences. For Blasius, even the intellective soul of human beings is a naturally generated form, a material power which results from prime matter disposed to receive it by the movement of the stars. In this Blasius shows himself not a follower of Averroes (see IBN RUSHD §3), but rather of ALEXANDER OF APHRODISIAS (§2). This materialist account was reinforced by Blasius' epistemology, which led him to argue that the existence of the intellect could be known only through inference from observation of the intellect's operations, and that such observable operations could not be independent of the body and matter in general. As a result Blasius denied the immortality of the human intellective soul. He was reprimanded by the Bishop of Pavia in 1396, but the reprimand was a mild one, without financial consequences or any effect on his teaching, which he pursued without hindrance until his retirement. Nonetheless he showed greater caution in his later writings, and made reference to the priority of faith.

Blasius' materialist metaphysics raised obvious difficulties for human freedom, since the doctrine that humans can make free choices seems incompatible with astrological causality. Blasius resolved this problem of individual freedom by arguing that the human contains dispositions to act in one way or another, even when confronted with two objects which are equally attractive to reason, and that in providing these dispositions the stars incline but do not necessitate. As a result the individual is always confronted with freedom of choice (*libertas differentiae contradictionis*), though it is the impulse and not rationality that is impartial in the face of a decision. Blasius added in his later writings that the stars are only secondary instrumental causes. God is the true first cause, though his activity is only known through the activity of his instrument, the heavens.

4 Epistemology and science

Blasius adopted the English empiricism of WILLIAM OF OCKHAM (§§4–5) and his followers as filtered through the French teaching of John BURIDAN (§3) and ALBERT OF SAXONY. He thus held that we know only the singular, present individual (Peter, for example) whom we perceive in visual cognition (*intuitio*) by means of a repeated sensible experience. Through this sensible experience, a general image is formed in the memory, and this is the universal concept of some individual (Peter viewed as this man). Thus the difference between the intuitive cognition of the singular (Peter) and the abstractive cognition (the concept of the man Peter) does not depend on the thing cognized, which will always be a singular thing (*res*), but on the psychological and epistemological processes of our mind. Since Blasius is a materialist, he appeals to the doctrine of the agent sense (see JOHN OF JANDUN and John Buridan) which plays a role analogous to the one the agent intellect was held to play in intellection. Blasius also assigned a role to species in perception, interpreting them as sensible impressions which are material signs of the external objects, while concepts are representational signs of the cause of the impressions. Blasius owed this doctrine of signs to Buridan and Albert of Saxony.

Given the centrality of visual experience in the elaboration of his empiricist epistemology, it is not surprising that Blasius devoted an important treatise, *Quaestiones perspectivae*, to the problems of optics, including the geometric laws of direct vision, reflection and refraction. The work consists of questions on the earlier work of John PECHAM, and owes a great deal to the influence of the Arab Alhazen (see IBN HAZM; OPTICS §1). He was critical of the perspectivists of the thirteenth century (the *antiqui*) in his discussion of the problem of the appearance of visual magnitudes which, he claimed, depended on distance and not only on the angle of vision. This view was important for the construction of the visual pyramid which, in connection with the geometrical approach to the perception of the distance of visual objects, was to generate the pictorial representation of perspective.

In accordance with his generally rationalist formulations, Blasius offered explanations of interesting superstitions of his time, as did Pietro POMPONAZZI (§3) in his work *De incantationibus* (On Incantations) (1556). Blasius explained many phenomena held to be miraculous or diabolical as products of optical illusion, due to the laws of refraction. For instance he showed that some apparently miraculous apparitions in the sky of Busseto, near Milan, were phenomena brought about by the refraction of light on clouds during a thunderstorm.

His treatises on statics (*De ponderibus*) and on mathematical physics, *De motuum proportionibus* (On the Proportions of Motions) are also of great importance, for in them he established for the first time the concept of the quantitative measure of an extended physical substratum, understood as an atom (*quantum*) which is indivisible, limited and finite. These *quanta* could be both material and spiritual, for the human intellect can be regarded as an indivisible quantum. Blasius' atomism places him firmly in the anti-Aristotelian tradition. It is also important for the rise of mathematical physics through its emphasis on what is measurable and quantifiable as opposed to the Aristotelian doctrine of qualities. In this context he used the notion of latitude, or a range of degrees, which he took from Nicole ORESME (§2), to explain qualitative variations in a material subject, but he also followed the tradition of the Italian school of Simone di Castello, Giovanni da Casale and Jacopo da Napoli (see Clagett 1968: 66–107). He reduced the so-called intension of forms to extension and mathematical measure.

Blasius' logic is related to his science in that he applies terminist analysis, particularly with respect to supposition theory, to physical doctrines. He wrote a commentary on PETER OF SPAIN which shows the influence of William Heytesbury and of Henry Hopton's treatise (formerly attributed to Heytesbury) on the significate of true propositions, as well as of Albert of Saxony.

Through his scientific reflection on the world of nature and a philosophy freed of any subordination to theology, Blasius opened the way to a formulation of a mathematical method which would come to fruition in the modern science of Galileo GALILEI (§2).

See also: ARISTOTELIANISM, RENAISSANCE; LOGIC, MEDIEVAL; NATURAL PHILOSOPHY, MEDIEVAL

List of works

Blasius of Parma wrote a large number of works, many of which are available only in manuscript. Details of these can be found in Federici Vescovini 1979: 413–52 (see references and further reading).

Blasius of Parma (1382–5) commentaries on Aristotle's *On the Soul*, in G. Federici Vescovini (ed.) *Le Quaestiones de anima di Biagio Pelacani da Parma*, Florence: Olschki, 1974; Italian trans. by V. Sorge, Naples: Morano, 1994. (Editions of the manuscripts *Conclusiones de anima* (1382) and *Quaestiones de anima* (copying finished in 1385).)

—— (1386) *In quodam iudicio anno currente [13]86* (Prognostication of the Year 1386), in G. Federici Vescovini (ed.) *Rinascimento* 22 (1971): 90–3.

—— (before 1390–1403) *Quaestiones perspectivae libri tres* (Three Books of Questions on Perspective), in G. Federici Vescovini and V. Sorge (eds) *Quaderni di 'Physis'*, Florence: Olschki, forthcoming; G. Federici Vescovini (ed.) 'Le questioni di "Perspectiva" di Biagio Pelacani da Parma', *Rinascimento* 12:

163–243. (Devoted to problems of optics, Blasius' *Quaestiones perspectivae* appeared in two versions, the first before 1390 and the second in 1403.)

—— (before 1416) *Tractatus de ponderibus* (Treatise on Statics), in E.A. Moody and M. Clagett (eds) *The Medieval Science of Weights*, Madison and Milwaukee, WI, and London: University of Wisconsin Press, 1952, 238–78.

—— (before 1416) *Le Quaestiones dialecticae di Biagio Pelacani da Parma* (Dialectical Questions by Blasius of Parma), ed. G. Federici Vescovini, J. Biard and V. Sorge, Florence, forthcoming.

—— (before 1416) *La 'quaestio de intensione et remissione formarum' di Biagio Pelacani da Parma* (The 'Question of the Intension and Remission of Forms' by Blasius of Parma), ed. G. Federici Vescovini, *Physis: Rivista internazionale di storia della scienza* 31 (1994): 433–535. (Federici Vescovini gives an introduction and notes.)

—— (before 1416) 'Questioni inediti di ottica' (Unpublished Questions on Optics), in F. Alessio (ed.) *Rivista critica di storia della filosofia* 16 (1961): 79–110, 188–221.

References and further reading

Barocelli, F. (1992) 'Per Biagio Pelacani, un Convegno e un "Centro Studi"' (A Convention and 'Core Study' for Blasius of Parma), in G. Federici Vescovini (ed.) *Filosofia, scienza e astrologia nel Trecento Europeo*, Padua: il Poligrafo, 21–38. (Bibliography of manuscripts and editions on pages 183–216; includes an interview with Raymond Klibansky.)

* Clagett, M. (ed.) (1968) *Nicole Oresme and the Medieval Geometry of Qualities and Motions: A Treatise on the Uniformity and Difformity of Intensities known as Tractatus de configurationibus qualitatum et motuum*, Madison, WI: University of Wisconsin Press. (Referred to in §3. Contains Latin text and English translation of Oresme's principal work on his doctrine of configurations. Clagett also provides a chronological ordering of Oresme's writings.)

* Federici Vescovini, G. (1979) *Astrologia e scienza: La crisi dell'aristotelismo sul cadere del Trecento e Biagio Pelacani da Parma* (Astrology and Science: Blasius of Parma and the Crisis of Aristotelianism at the End of the 14th Century), Florence: Vallecchi. (Referred to in §1. Detailed analysis of Blasius' thought.)

—— (1983) '*Arti' e filosofia nel secolo XIV* ('Arts' and Philosophy in the 14th Century), Florence: Vallecchi. (Contains several papers on Blasius.)

Lindberg, D.C. (1975) *A Catalogue of Medieval and Renaissance Optical Manuscripts*, Toronto: Pontifical Institute of Mediaeval Studies. (Very useful on Blasius' manuscripts on optics.)

Maier, A. (1949) *Die Vorlaüfer Galileis im 14. Jahrhundert* (Galileo's 14th-Century Predecessor), Rome: Storia e Letteratura. (Discusses the probable causes of the episcopal condemnation.)

Murdoch, J.E. (1976) 'Music and Natural Philosophy: Hitherto Unnoticed *Questiones* by Blasius of Parma', *Manuscripta* 20: 119–36. (A well-founded attribution of work on music to Blasius.)

Translated E.J. Ashworth

GRAZIELLA FEDERICI VESCOVINI

BLOCH, ERNST SIMON (1885–1977)

Bloch was one of the most innovative Marxist philosophers of the twentieth century. His metaphysical and ontological concerns, combined with a self-conscious utopianism, distanced him from much mainstream Marxist thought. He was sympathetic to the classical philosophical search for fundamental categories, but distinguished earlier static, fixed and closed systems from his own open system, in which he characterized the universe as a changing and unfinished process. Furthermore, his distinctive materialism entailed the rejection of a radical separation of the human and the natural, unlike much twentieth-century Western Marxism. His validation of utopianism was grounded in a distinctive epistemology centred on the processes whereby 'new' material emerges in consciousness. The resulting social theory was sensitive to the many and varied ways in which the utopian impulse emerges, as, for example, in its analysis of the utopian dimension in religion.

1 Life and works
2 Metaphysics and ontology
3 Epistemology
4 Utopianism

1 Life and works

Ernst Simon Bloch was born in Ludwigshafen, Germany. He studied at the Universities of Munich and Würzburg, and had associations with Simmel's private colloquium in Berlin and Weber's circle in Heidelberg. For much of his adult life he lived as a freelance writer and critic. Like many left-wing Jewish intellectuals he left Germany on Hitler's accession to power in 1933, and eventually moved to the USA. In 1948 he received his first university post, as Professor of Philosophy at Leipzig, East Germany. Although initially sympathetic to East German regime, he eventually came into conflict with it, and in 1961 did not return from a visit to West Germany. Subsequently he became Professor of Philosophy in Tübingen, where he died. His most notable works are *Geist der Utopie* (Spirit of Utopia) (1918) and *Das Prinzip Hoffnung* (The Principle of Hope) (1954–9).

2 Metaphysics and ontology

Throughout his working life, Bloch attempted to refurbish the ancient category of 'matter' to provide a dynamic materialist theory of the universe (see MATERIALISM). Matter, the substance of the universe, is not inert, but rather, in nature and humanity, capable of movement and development. In this respect Bloch distances himself from much twentieth-century Western Marxism, which seeks to prioritize the social over the natural (see MARXISM, WESTERN §§2–3). He credits the 'Aristotelian Left' (notably Avicenna and Averroes) with the earliest formulation of this radical materialism (see AVERROISM). The universe is open-ended and rich with 'possibility', allowing development, novelty, intervention and alternative outcomes to occur. From a human perspective, this open-endedness is both an opportunity and a constraint, for the possibility of choice is beset by the hazards of uncertainty; human life is therefore experimental. Bloch attempts to resolve the Marxist conundrum of the relationship between freedom and necessity. He is at pains to avoid ultra-subjectivity or hyper-voluntarism: possibility can take the form of the nonsensical and the impractical, but rational movement will take the form of the 'objectively-real possible' – the possibility grounded in existing social tendencies. Aspiration is thus combined with a non-positivist empiricism, which he terms 'process empiricism'. It is thus to be distinguished from a determinist teleology, which, following the analogy of the acorn and the oak, envisages humanity in terms of a fixed, inevitable future growing out of iron historical trends.

A fundamental way in which Bloch conceptualizes the dynamic tension at work within matter is by building up composite concepts around the category of 'not'. 'Not' is meant to register the absent and unfinished dimensions of reality, as in his logical proposition that 'S is not yet P'. In the human world the 'not' is present in the form of need. Absence, initially of food, drives the individual on to more and more sophisticated forms of interaction with nature and society. Humans are thus 'not-yet'; the completion of their being lies in the future, they constantly hunger for themselves. 'Not' is the negative aspect of the historical process, 'Hope' is the positive. 'Subjective' hope is to be distinguished from 'objective'; the former involves the perpetual and ubiquitous representation of that which is deemed to be absent. Bloch's massive *Das Prinzip Hoffnung* (1954–9) contains an encyclopedic account of the many manifestations of hope in human history, from simple daydreams to complex visions of perfection. Objective hope is the concrete possibility present in each successive age, which enables subjective hope actively to develop the world (see HOPE).

3 Epistemology

Bloch conceives of consciousness as a narrow field or band. Beyond the lower boundary lies the 'no-longer-conscious', the realm of the forgotten and the repressed, explored by FREUD. The upper boundary delimits the 'not-yet-conscious', the place where new material enters consciousness, 'the psychological birthplace of the New'. It is the unexplored territory that Bloch sought to map, and which makes up his central epistemological category. The production of new material occurs through the stages of incubation, inspiration and explication. Incubation is the period of active fermentation of the new, much of it below the surface of consciousness, to a point where it bursts into the conscious world. This is the moment of inspiration, a sudden lucid moment of illumination. Bloch is keen to anchor the epistemological in the social. The newness, which he terms the 'Novum', emerges with the confluence of subjective and objective conditions. The historical timetable generates the material which is incubated in the individual, and the inspiration is as much historical as individual. A Marxist sense of history informs this interpretation; progressive classes are the fundamental fact in the emergence of the Novum. The initial entry, however, occurs through immensely gifted individuals, such as Marx. The realization of newness requires the third stage in the process – explication. This is the immensely difficult task of adequately representing the new, such that it re-enters the historical timetable as immanent potentiality. It also involves overcoming the resistances of the existing world to novelty. Bloch calls the site at which present and future meet the 'Front'. Like the military use of this word, it is meant to suggest an advancing, although not necessarily straight, line into as yet unconquered territory.

4 Utopianism

Nowhere is Bloch more untypically Marxist than in his self-conscious utopianism. He distinguishes 'abstract utopia' from 'concrete utopia'. The former manifests the utopian function in its weakest form; it is mere dreaming, unanchored in the real tendencies of the age. Concrete utopia, in contrast, is rooted in objective possibility; it is grounded in the ascending forces of the age, and is the most pregnant form of the utopian function (see UTOPIANISM). Bloch's unorthodox Marxism is also apparent in his attempt to harness aspects of religion to his revolutionary project. In *Atheismus im Christentum* (*Atheism in Christianity*), he argues that religious consciousness has been a potent vehicle for utopian longings and asserts the paradoxical claim that 'only an atheist can be a good Christian; only a Christian can be a good atheist' ([1968] 1972: 9) (see ATHEISM). He is sensitive to the temporal aspects of the utopian impulse, and maintains that individuals may be contemporaries in a physical sense but not necessarily in terms of forms of consciousness – 'not all people exist in the same Now'. In the 1930s he deployed the term 'non-contemporaneity' to designate this experience, and cited the peasantry as an example. Marxism had been blind to the subversive and utopian elements in non-contemporaneity, and had left these strata to be co-opted and distorted by fascism.

Also out of joint with much twentieth-century Marxism is Bloch's radical materialist concept of a 'natural subject'. Given that matter is active and dynamic, and that developed consciousness has emerged out of it in the shape of humanity, is it not possible to conceive of further creative development in the realm of nature? Furthermore, since the human cannot be radically separated from the natural, Bloch conceives of a creative interaction of the two in the future. Nature too has its 'not-yet'. The complexity of such a universe, Bloch argues, requires the abandonment of classical conceptions of time and space. He is attracted to the non-Euclidian conception of space developed by Riemann, in which space is altered by local variables. He proposes, by analogy, 'a kind of "Riemannian" time' which is neither universal nor unilinear, but rather contains a plurality of differing time scales. Only in a future, interactive reconciliation between humanity and nature might convergences of time occur.

Bloch's work tends to be known about rather than known. His writing is forbidding: structural complexity and formal eclecticism are combined with a style studded with opaque metaphor, untranslatable puns, obscure neologisms and overblown rhetoric. Furthermore, the political cast of much of the work is a deeply unattractive, unreconstructed Marxism-Leninism. Apart from his youthful dialogue with the young LUKÁCS, he has had little influence on other major figures in twentieth-century Marxism, and none at all on the pre-eminent philosophical currents of the century. There is, however, growing interest in his work. Radical theologians have long valued his insightful analyses of the utopian dimension in religion; literary theorists are increasingly using his work in their studies of utopias and science fiction; whilst social and political theorists have found his utopian socialism deeply stimulating.

List of works

Bloch, E. (1918) *Geist der Utopie* (Spirit of Utopia), Frankfurt: Suhrkamp Verlag, 1971. (Bloch's first important published work combines messianic utopianism with wide-ranging cultural criticism.)

—— (1935) *Erbschaft dieser Zeit*, Frankfurt: Suhrkamp Verlag, 1962; trans. N. Plaice and S. Plaice, *Heritage of Our Times*, Oxford: Polity Press, 1971. (Contains a highly distinctive analysis of national socialism, focusing on the dreams and fantasies of Weimar Germany.)

—— (1954–9) *Das Prinzip Hoffnung*, Frankfurt: Suhrkamp Verlag, 2 vols; trans. N. Plaice, S. Plaice and P. Knight, *The Principle of Hope*, Oxford: Blackwell, 3 vols, 1986. (Bloch's undoubted *magnum opus*, containing an encyclopedic presentation of the manifold forms of the utopian.)

—— (1961) *Naturrecht und menschliche Würde*, Frankfurt: Suhrkamp Verlag; trans. D.J. Schmidt, *Natural Law and Human Dignity*, Cambridge, MA: MIT Press, 1986. (An analysis of the positive and negative dimensions of the European natural law tradition.)

—— (1963–4) *Tübinger Einleitung in die Philosophie*, Frankfurt: Suhrkamp Verlag, 2 vols; vol. 1, trans. J. Cumming, *A Philosophy of the Future*, New York: Herder & Herder, 1970. (A succint presentation of many of the major components of Bloch's philosophy.)

—— (1968) *Atheismus im Christentum*, Frankfurt: Suhrkamp Verlag; trans. J.T. Swann, *Atheism in Christianity*, New York: Herder & Herder, 1972. (The most sustained presentation of Bloch's attempt to combine atheism and Christianity.)

References and further reading

Geoghegan, V. (1996) *Ernst Bloch*, London: Routledge. (A basic introduction to the main ideas and themes.)

Harper, C. (1991) 'Ernst Bloch: A Bibliography of

Primary Sources in English', *Bloch-Almanach*, vol. 12, 167–80. (A valuable guide to the English translations of Bloch.)

Hudson, W. (1982) *The Marxist Philosophy of Ernst Bloch*, London: Macmillan. (The best study to date of Bloch's thought.)

Jones, J.M. (1995) *Assembling (Post)modernism: The Utopian Philosophy of Ernst Bloch*, New York: Peter Lang. (Interesting attempt to relate Bloch's work to post-modern theory.)

Roberts, R.H. (1990) *Hope and its Hieroglyph: A Critical Decipherment of Ernst Bloch's Principle of Hope*, Atlanta, GA: Scholars Press. (Concentrated study of *The Principle of Hope*, focusing on the religious dimensions.)

West, T.H. (1991) *Ultimate Hope Without God: The Atheistic Eschatology of Ernst Bloch*, New York: Peter Lang. (General discussion of Bloch's work, ultimately concentrating on Bloch's 'religious' vision.)

VINCENT GEOGHEGAN

BOBBIO, NORBERTO (1909–)

The foremost legal and political theorist in Italy today, Norberto Bobbio founded in the 1940s Italian analytical legal positivism, trying to merge logical positivism and Kelsen's legal positivism. As a political thinker, he defends a synthesis of liberalism and socialism, focusing in particular on the defence of human and civil rights in democratic societies.

Norberto Bobbio taught Jurisprudence and Political Philosophy at the universities of Camerino, Siena, Padua and Turin for over forty years. After the Second World War, he founded the school of Italian analytical legal positivism. Bobbio took part in the Resistance. After the Liberation he withdrew from direct political involvement, still, however, taking an active part in Italian political debate. He defends a tolerant, secular point of view and a synthesis of liberalism and socialism. In 1984 he was made a Life Member of the Italian Senate.

Bobbio's original outlook was largely formed by Croce's historicism in philosophy, and Gobetti's radical liberalism in politics (see CROCE, B.). Yet, while Bobbio's political thought has always been inspired by Gobetti's project of reconciling social justice with individual civil and political liberty, Crocean idealism he soon rejected. He examined the phenomenology of Husserl and Scheler as well as the existentialism of Heidegger and Jaspers. In the mid 1940s he finally abandoned these philosophies to embrace a very different approach, influenced by logical positivism, which he saw as simultaneously rigorous, rationalistic, empirical, and ethically and politically committed (see VIENNA CIRCLE §2) – and for these reasons suitable to his own epistemological preferences, which have always been against the trends of what he has called the 'Italian ideology', that is congenitally speculative and idealistic in bias.

These developments culminated in Bobbio's founding of Italian analytical legal positivism. It is worth emphasizing what kind of legal positivism it was, because Italian analytical legal positivism has been an eclectic but fruitful attempt to graft a philosophical outlook – logical positivism – on to the legal positivism of Hans Kelsen's *Pure Theory of Law* (see KELSEN, H.; LOGICAL POSITIVISM §2).

The first phase of Bobbio's theory of law (1949–65) was marked by his acceptance of Kelsen's interpretation of legal theory as a scientific, value-free form of legal study not concerned with the moral or political evaluation of law, nor with the sociological description of legal phenomena, but with the analysis of fundamental legal concepts and with the structure and logical interrelation of the elements of a legal system. As a consequence, Bobbio's main concern was to clarify fundamental legal notions such as 'legal rule' and 'legal system' as well as to give an account of the structure of legal orders.

Bobbio defended a version of normativism (the opinion that law is made up of rules), but answered many of the criticisms raised against this approach by elaborating a theory of legal systems, which successfully addressed many problems that could not be solved analysing single legal rules. So, in his *Teoria dell'ordinamento giuridico* (A Theory of Legal System) (1958), Bobbio contended that the definition of law, as well as the distinction of law from other normative phenomena such as morals and customs, is possible only if the legal system is taken into consideration. There are no special features belonging to all legal rules and only to legal rules. In fact, it is the legal system as a whole that has identifying features such as effectiveness or coerciveness. A rule is legal because it belongs to a legal system; a system is legal because of the specific characteristics it has as a system (see NORMS, LEGAL).

This account of legal systems allowed Bobbio to acknowledge the existence of different types of legal rules. He refused Kelsen's reduction of all legal norms to duty- or sanction-imposing rules, taking into consideration the wide class of second-level rules (meta-rules), such as power-conferring rules, constitutive rules and so on. The classification of different kinds of legal rules and the description of their interrelationship within legal systems has been one of Bobbio's main contributions to legal theory.

Towards the mid 1960s, Bobbio came to a turning point in his interpretation of legal theory. It became clear that the two basic neo-positivistic philosophical assumptions at the root of Bobbio's outlook, namely the theory of discourse levels and the distinction between 'is' and 'ought' statements, were not consistent with Kelsen's interpretation of legal theory as a scientific endeavour. First, Bobbio distinguished between legal theory (jurisprudence) and the discussion of the method of legal theory (meta-jurisprudence). Second, he criticized Kelsen's meta-jurisprudence as prescriptive – thus not scientific at all, as it did not aim at describing what jurists actually do but at prescribing what they should do. Third, Bobbio argued that Kelsen's doctrine of the basic norm, which gives unity and validity to a legal order, must rely on an ideological rather than a logical ground and so cannot be the basis for a value-free science of law.

In this second phase (from 1965 onwards) Bobbio thus acknowledged the prescriptive nature of the legal positivist's approach to law. Such an approach is not based on the desire to elaborate a scientific, value-free legal theory. Rather, the idea of a scientific description of the law is maintained by legal positivists because such an idea is logically required by the very notion of applying the law, which is central to the working of legal and political institutions based on the rule of law. Thus, the legal positivists' argument in favour of an objective description of the law simply shows their choice of the values of the rule of law (see LEGAL POSITIVISM §2).

Since the 1970s, Bobbio has on the one hand developed a sociological theory aimed at describing the social functions of law; on the other hand he has increasingly devoted his studies to political theory. In his functional analysis of law, Bobbio has focused on the 'promotional' function played by legal orders of developed countries, by stimulating desirable behaviour, mainly in economic and business activity, through positive sanctions such as subsidies, tax exemptions and so on. This function is one of the characteristic features of the welfare state, defended by Bobbio, as opposed to the liberal minimal state.

In fact, Bobbio's liberalism is basically a doctrine of constitutional guarantees for individual freedom and civil rights, not an economic theory of the free market. Bobbio sees no contradiction between liberalism and democracy. The basic rights – freedom of opinion, speech, association, and so on – on which the liberal state has been founded since its inception are the premises of the democratic state: if liberalism provides those liberties necessary for the proper exercise of democratic power, democracy guarantees the existence and persistence of fundamental liberties.

Bobbio's main concern in political theory has always been that of reconciling this understanding of liberal democracy with the demands of socialists for greater equality. He suggests that socialists must rethink their goals of social equality in ways compatible with the institutional framework of liberal democracies. Representative democracy has to be seen as a set of rules that cannot be given up if the risk of despotic regimes is to be avoided. Social rights, as the extension of civil and political rights, will be granted through the extension of representative democracy to the level of social life – to bureaucracies, to health and educational authorities, to the workplace and so on.

Bobbio has consistently played a part in active political debate in many fields: politics and culture, the defence of human and civil rights, the problem of peace in the nuclear age. A major contribution to political theory has been to show the strict link between human rights, peace and democracy.

See also: DEMOCRACY; LAW AND MORALITY; LAW, PHILOSOPHY OF; LIBERALISM

List of works

Bobbio, N. (1938) *L'analogia nella logica del diritto* (Analogy and Legal Logic), Turin: Istituto Giuridico della Reale Università. (The first important contribution by Bobbio to the analysis of legal reasoning.)

—— (1950) *Teoria della scienza giuridica* (A Theory of Legal Science), Turin: Giappichelli. (States that legal theory is a value-free form of legal study, on the basis of a neo-positivistic account of science.)

—— (1955a) *Studi sulla teoria generale del diritto* (Studies of General Theory of Law), Turin: Giappichelli. (Through a critical examination of the main positions in legal theory, Bobbio comes to accept Kelsen's interpretation of normativism.)

—— (1955b) *Politica e cultura* (Politics and Culture), Turin: Einaudi. (Contains many important writings in defence of a synthesis of liberalism and socialism and about the political role of culture.)

—— (1958) *Teoria della norma giuridica* (A Theory of Legal Norm), Turin: Giappichelli; *Teoria dell'ordinamento giuridico* (A Theory of Legal System), Turin: Giappichelli, 1960; new edn of the two books together, *Teoria generale del diritto* (General Theory of Law), Turin: Giappichelli, 1993. (A wide and uncommonly clear examination of the main problems of the philosophy of law, from the point of view of Kelsen's critically revised normativism.)

—— (1965) *Giusnaturalismo e positivismo giuridico*

(Natural Law Theory and Legal Positivism), Milan: Comunità. (Develops and defends a normativist version of legal positivism and criticizes the natural law theory.)

—— (1976) *Quale socialismo?*, Turin: Einaudi; *Which Socialism?*, Oxford: Polity Press, 1987. (An examination of Marxist writings on the state and democracy, and the rethinking of socialism in liberal-democratic terms.)

—— (1977) *Dalla struttura alla funzione* (From Structure to Function), Milan: Comunità. (The major contributions of Bobbio to a sociological theory aimed at describing the social functions of law.)

—— (1984) *Il futuro della democrazia*, Turin: Einaudi; *The Future of Democracy*, Oxford: Polity Press, 1987. (Defends the liberal idea of representative democracy, trying to extend it beyond parliamentary politics to many domains of social life.)

References and further reading

Borsellino, P. (1991) *Norberto Bobbio metateorico del diritto* (Norberto Bobbio as a Meta-theorist of Law), Milan: Giuffrè. (A critical examination of Bobbio's contribution to methodology and general theory of law.)

Jori, M. (1987) *Il giuspositivismo analitico italiano prima e dopo la crisi* (Italian Analytical Legal Positivism before and after its Crisis), Milan: Giuffrè. (A critical examination of Italian analytical legal positivism.)

Lanfranchi, E. (1989) *Un filosofo militante* (A Committed Philosopher), Turin: Bollati Boringhieri. (An account of Bobbio's opinions about the relationship between politics and culture.)

Ruiz-Miguel, A. (1983) *Filosofía y derecho en Norberto Bobbio* (Philosophy and Law in Bobbio's Thinking), Madrid: Centro de estudios constitucionales. (A wide account of Bobbio's legal and political philosophy.)

Violi, C. and Maiorca, B. (1984) *Norberto Bobbio: 50 anni di studi* (Norberto Bobbio: 50 Years of Studies), Milan: Angeli. (A general bibliography of writings by and about Bobbio.)

PATRIZIA BORSELLINO

BODILY SENSATIONS

Bodily sensations are those feelings, or sensory experiences, most intimately associated with one's body: aches, tickles; feelings of pain and pleasure, of warmth, of fatigue. Many philosophers contrast bodily sensations with perceptions of the external world, claiming that sensations provide one with awareness of nothing independent of them. An alternative approach is to take sensations to be a form of awareness of one's body – on one view sensations are simply the perception of the state and properties of one's body. Bodily sensations have been seen as a major problem for any attempt to give an account of the mind that takes it to be part of the material world as investigated by the physical sciences.

1   **Bodily sensations and the body**
2   **Sensations as subjective**
3   **Awareness of one's body and sensations as perceptions**

1   Bodily sensations and the body

The most intimate causes of bodily sensation are changes or states within one's body: dental decay leads to toothache; general exhaustion to a feeling of fatigue. Bodily sensations are distinctive in acting as signs for the bodily changes that cause them. Pains are signs of damage to or disorder in one's body; an agent will react to feelings of warmth or cold in a way appropriate to the change in temperature of their body; feelings of hunger or satiation will control someone's feeding. Yet sensations are not invariably correlated with their typical bodily causes: someone can feel hunger when they are satiated; pains in parts of the body that are not damaged. This is most commonly the case with referred pain, where damage to one part of the body leads to feelings of pain in some other part.

One typically feels bodily sensations to have locations within one's body. One may feel a pain in one's ankle or a ticklish sensation behind one's knee. Sensations can also fill or suffuse body parts, such as a burning sensation throughout one's upper arm, or a feeling of being bloated in one's abdomen. Location in the body may be more or less determinate – a pin prick may be felt at a particular point on one's finger, while an erotic sensation may lack a precise location. Some sensations are associated with the body without having a location, such as feelings of fatigue or depression. Even sensations which normally have a location may sometimes lack one: certain patients who have lost general feeling in a limb can be brought to have 'deep pain' without knowledge of where it is.

With some sensations we can draw a distinction between the sensation and what it is a sensation of. One's body may actually be warm when one does not feel it to be so – while one's body may feel cold even when it is not, as when one has a fever. The same is true of hunger, satiation and exhaustion. For other sensations there is no such separation between a feeling and what is felt. It may seem obvious that there cannot be a pain without a feeling of pain, and that there is no such thing as false pain, the feeling of pain without actually being in pain. In the former kind of case, we talk of sensations of warmth, but not warm sensations; the term 'sensation' is used to pick out the state of feeling rather than any object of that feeling. In the latter kind of case, we use the term 'sensation' not only for the feeling, as in the phrase 'a sensation of pain', but also for the object of that feeling, as when we say that pain is a sensation.

However, some philosophers think that even in the latter case, a feeling and its object are distinct. It has been claimed that one can have pains without feelings of pain, since there can be unconscious pains, as when one only gradually comes to notice a pain in one's thumb. And conversely, it has been claimed that one can have feelings of pain without the accompanying pain: someone in a confused state might come to mistake a feeling of intense cold for a sharp pain. Neither example offers a conclusive counterexample. At best, they demonstrate the gap between having a feeling and making a judgment about it. In the former example, unless it is supposed that one can be conscious only of what one notices, all that has been described is someone who does not notice the pain in their thumb; this is not pain without consciousness, only pain without attention to it. The latter example can be interpreted as one in which someone mistakes a feeling of extreme cold for a feeling of pain. This may challenge a claim about the epistemology of sensations – that one has incorrigible knowledge of them – but not the link between feeling and its object.

2 Sensations as subjective

The close link between feeling and its object lends itself to one account of the nature of bodily sensation, which may be labelled 'subjectivist'. On this view, sensations are to be contrasted with sensory states such as perceptions, or intentional states such as beliefs that can take external objects, as in beliefs about the sun. One can have a perception of an object that exists whether one perceives it or not – the table I see will still be there when I turn my back. I can also have a sensory experience when there is no appropriate object for me to perceive: I may hallucinate a table. By contrast, bodily sensations may be claimed to be purely subjective states of mind, which are directed on no object at all, or none that is external or independent of them. This view of sensation may, but need not, be associated with a more general account of sense perception, on which all perception of the world involves the subject's having a purely subjective state, a sensation (see PERCEPTION). On such a view of perception, bodily sensations will just be one special case of sensation in general. The view does not so obviously apply to bodily sensations such as feelings of warmth or fatigue where what is felt does have a nature independent of the feeling. But for these, subjectivists may appeal to a distinction between felt warmth or fatigue, which will be taken to be a subjective quality, and the objective qualities of heat or exhaustion associated with those felt qualities. In support of this, they may point out how it is imaginable that different objective qualities could have been typically responsible for feelings with those felt qualities – for example, that the feeling of warmth could have been typically brought about by tickling the skin.

Subjectivism can take different forms. One approach, often labelled 'the act – object' view of sensation, retains the idea that there is a genuine object of awareness in having bodily sensations, even if that object depends for its existence on the subject's awareness of it. Others repudiate the idea that there are any such objects of awareness and insist that to feel a pain is to be in pain, denying that there is any distinction to be made between the feeling of pain and the pain felt. For one may be suspicious of the idea that genuine objects could be dependent on our awareness of them, and doubtful that such things could have a location in the world. In place of a feeling of pain and a pain felt, this 'no-object' view talks of feeling in a painful manner, or being in a painful state. This is rather like insisting that there are not such things as individual dances: when we say that Mary danced a polka, we do not mean that there was a certain thing, a polka, which she danced, but rather that she danced in a certain manner. So, too, one may insist that to say that Mary felt a pain is not to talk of some thing of which she was aware, but to talk of the manner in which she felt, or to talk of the character of her feeling (see MENTAL STATES, ADVERBIAL THEORY OF).

Much of our ordinary talk about sensations, in particular the way in which we can locate them in the body, is resistant to these ways of eliminating the objects of awareness. If states of feeling are to be located anywhere, it is plausible to locate them only in the brain and central nervous system, but one can feel a pain in one's ankle, or a crick in one's neck. Since it is not the feeling that is located in one's ankle, the 'no-object' view must deny that we speak literally when we say that the ankle hurts. What then does it mean to talk of a pain in one's ankle? One answer would be to suppose that there are certain non-spatial qualities of one's sensations which one associates with spatial vocabulary. This idea is not particularly plausible: for there seems to be no prior limit to the exact positions on or in one's body where one could feel a sensation to be located; and one can feel a sensation to be located in a place where one has never had a sensation before. In addition, the felt location of a sensation has a different status to the non-spatial qualities of a sensation. Take any feeling in your left hand that you like – an itch, a tingle or whatever – and now imagine a qualitatively identical sensation in your right hand. You need imagine no difference in the character of the sensation other than its location in one hand rather than the other. The felt location of sensation seems to play a similar role to spatiotemporal location for physical things: qualitatively identical but distinct objects can exist at the same time if they are in different locations; qualitatively identical but distinct sensations can be had at the same time if they are felt to be in different parts of one's body.

An alternative is to suppose that the attributed location of a sensation does not report any quality of the sensation at all. Perhaps talk of location reflects the subject's dispositions to act towards or talk about the location to which the sensation is referred. Someone who feels pain in an ankle may be inclined to rub that ankle, or say that that is the part of them which hurts – on this view, what it is for one to feel a pain to be located in one's ankle rather than anywhere else just is for one to be disposed to rub that ankle or say that that is where the pain is. But are there really any such definitional connections between felt location of pains and dispositions to behaviour? Someone who is paralysed will have no disposition to rub their ankle; and someone might be unbothered by pain and not inclined to answer any questions about whether they have a pain. Furthermore, we can explain why someone feels concerned about their ankle by reference to the fact that they feel pain and the pain they feel is in their ankle – both the quality and the location of sensation explain the subject's attitude. So it is implausible that we could simply explain away the location of sensations in terms of the non-linguistic and linguistic behaviour for which they give reasons.

3 Awareness of one's body and sensations as perceptions

If we have to take seriously the felt location of sensations, then we also have to take seriously things being felt at those locations, and the elimination of an act – object approach to bodily sensations will consequently seem unattractive. This need not, however, mean a return to the idea of pains and itches as inner objects of mind. One may instead claim that in having a sensation one comes to be aware of one's body. When I feel a pain in my ankle, what I feel is that my ankle hurts in some way: the felt location of sensation is the body part that one is aware of in having the sensation. When we count pains, we count the number of parts of the body which hurt. One's ankles, toes or teeth are no less part of the objective world than are tables and chairs, so bodily sensations cannot be purely subjective states of mind which give one awareness of nothing independent of them. Rather, having sensations gives one an awareness of an item in the objective world: one's body.

What is it to say that sensations give one an awareness of one's body? Some philosophers have claimed that sensations are just a form of perception of one's body. This view is difficult to defend. For other kinds of perception, there is a contrast between the qualities perceived and the perceiving of them. A book may be square without looking square; and it may look square without actually being so. One can also have visual or tactual hallucinations, as when Macbeth 'sees' a dagger; or a disturbed individual may feel insects on their arm when nothing is there. It is more difficult to establish this separation in the case of sensations. Phantom-limb sensations are the best candidates for the example of bodily illusions or hallucinations, since the amputee feels hurt in a body part which no longer exists. But one cannot take feeling pain simply to be the perception or apparent perception of damage or disorder to one's body: a body part does not have to be damaged in order to hurt. Referred pain is not a form of illusion: we do not suppose that the pain is somehow illusory, and lose concern for the part of our anatomy which hurts; rather we distinguish between where we feel pain and the cause of that pain. Nor do we suppose that a damaged but anaesthetized limb is really hurting – hurt has to go with the feeling of hurt.

Second, even if some aspects of sensation can be treated as perceptual, there are other aspects of what our sensations are like which are not plausibly ascribed to any aspect of the state of our bodies: when I feel a nagging toothache, or a burning sensation, there does not seem to be any objective feature of my tooth or my arm of which I am aware in having that sensation. In both cases the characteristic seems to belong to my state of awareness and not my body as an object of awareness. Of course the fact that I have a burning sensation may tell a medic much about the state of my body, but that is not to say that I am aware of the change in state of my body through having the sensation.

The implausibility of a purely perceptual model of bodily sensation need not lead us to reject entirely the idea that sensation is a form of primitive awareness of one's body that gives one an intimate link to it and through which one knows it and has feelings about it in a way that one has for no other object in the world. Supposing that sensation is a form of awareness of one's body fits very well the physiological and psychological links between sensation and kinaesthesia and proprioception – the sense we all ordinarily have of the movement and position of our limbs. It also fits another feature of sensations: that, primarily, we feel the location of sensations to be locations within the body, and not within other parts of space. This is true even for persons having a phantom-limb pain – they do not feel the pain to be located out in empty space, but feel it to be in an apparent limb which extends beyond the point of amputation.

See also: BEHAVIOURISM, ANALYTIC; MIND, IDENTITY THEORY OF; INTENTIONALITY; PRIVATE LANGUAGE ARGUMENT; QUALIA; SENSE-DATA

References and further reading

Anscombe, G.E.M. (1957) *Intention*, Oxford: Blackwell, esp. 13–14, 49–51.
—— (1962) 'On sensations of position', *Analysis* 22: 55–8. (Anscombe rejects the view that we observe our sensations, and suggests a dispositional account of sensation location.)
Armstrong, D.M. (1962) *Bodily Sensations*, London: Routledge & Kegan Paul. (This is a detailed defence of the view that sensations are perceptions of one's body.)
Descartes, R. (1641) *Meditations on First Philosophy*, in *The Philosophical Writings of René Descartes*, J. Cottingham, R. Stoothoff, D. Murdoch (eds), Cambridge: Cambridge University Press, 1984. (The sixth meditation contains an important discussion of the function of sensations, and the intimate awareness each of us has of our own body.)
Jackson, F. (1977) *Perception*, Cambridge: Cambridge University Press, ch. 3. (A defence of the view that there are inner objects of awareness.)
O'Shaughnessy, B. (1980) *The Will*, Cambridge: Cambridge University Press, vol. 1, chaps 5–7. (A detailed account of the need to attribute bodily locations to sensations, and of the special kind of awareness we have of our own bodies.)
Pitcher, G. (1970) 'Pain Perception', *Philosophical Review* 79: 368–93. (Another defence of the view that bodily sensations are perceptions.)
Reid, Thomas, (1764) *An Inquiry into the Human Mind on the Principles of Common Sense*, repr. Indianapolis, IN: Hackett Publishing Company, 1983, ch. 5. (An account of the role of bodily sensations in outer perception.)
Wittgenstein, L. (1952) *Philosophical Investigations*, Oxford: Blackwell, §242–315. (The famous private language argument, which some philosophers take to be an attack on the idea of sensations as inner or private objects.)
—— (1969) *Blue and Brown Books*, Oxford: Blackwell, 2nd edn, 49–55. (A discussion of the location and ownership of sensations.)

M.G.F. MARTIN

BODIN, JEAN (1529/30–96)

Jean Bodin was one of the great universal scholars of the later Renaissance. Despite political distractions, he made major contributions to historiography and the philosophy of history, economic theory, public law and comparative public policy, the sociology of institutions, as well as to religious philosophy, comparative religion and natural philosophy. Among his most celebrated achievements are his theory of sovereignty, which introduced a new dimension to the study of public law, and his Neoplatonist religion, which opened new perspectives on universalism and religious toleration.

Many of these intellectual positions, moreover, were responses, at least in part, to great political issues of the time. Against doctrines of popular sovereignty and the right of resistance put forward in the course of the religious wars, Bodin sought to show that the king of France was absolute. Against the widespread corruption and laxity that weakened and undermined the monarchy, he argued for administrative reform. And against the party that pressed the king to impose religious uniformity, he cautiously supported religious toleration. In all these respects Bodin's thought helped to inform the policies of the early Bourbon dynasty esatblished by Henry IV.

1 Life
2 Public law – the theory of sovereignty
3 Public law – the French monarchy and absolution
4 Other contributions to social theory
5 Religious thought

1 Life

Bodin was born in Angers, France, into a modestly successful middle-class family. Obtaining an excellent humanist education in his youth, he was to become in the course of his career one of the most outstanding humanist scholars of his age. His erudition was formidable in scope as well as depth, and his many publications include important contributions to almost every field of learning pursued by his contemporaries.

Bodin's professional training was in law which he studied at the University of Toulouse during the 1550s. Unable to secure a regular faculty position, he embarked on a public career as a barrister in the *Parlement* of Paris. However, at no point in his career did he retreat from the encyclopedic programme of research and writing that he had projected in his early years. The success of his earlier publications on history (1566), public finance (1568), and public law and policy (1576) gave him access as adviser and confidant to high political circles in and around the royal court. In the 1570s he was often a dinner companion of Henry III, and he became counsellor to Henry's ambitious younger brother, the Duke d'Alençon. But in 1576, as a deputy to the Estates General of Blois, Bodin took a public-spirited if impolitic stand against requests for new taxation. He was thus at odds with Henry's policy and no longer enjoyed royal favour. The death of d'Alençon in 1584, marked the end of Bodin's involvement in high politics. He moved from Paris to Laon where he was a royal magistrate from 1587 until his death in 1596.

These last years were a time of trouble for Bodin. The French Religious Wars, which had gone on intermittently since 1562, were now entering a climactic phase. With the assassination of Henry III in 1589, a savage struggle had broken out over the claims to succession of the Protestant Henry of Navarre (King Henry IV). Large parts of France, including Laon, came under the control of the militantly revolutionary Catholic League, whose programme and doctrine contradicted Bodin's long-standing principles of legitimacy, non-resistance and religious tolerance. Yet Bodin, like many other royalist magistrates of the time, openly collaborated with the League. He sought to justify his course by mystical reflections on the preordained doom of the ruling dynasty. But he seems to have been driven by fears not only for his office and his property, but perhaps for his life as well; now, as in the past, he was under suspicion of heresy. He stood publicly for Navarre only in 1594 when the forces of the latter were victorious.

These troubles notwithstanding, Bodin never ceased to pursue his vast programme of scholarly and philosophic research. Between 1588 and his death he produced two short works on ethics, a major treatise on religion and a system of natural philosophy. His writings make it clear that Bodin's religion was a Judaizing Neoplatonism. But outwardly at least he remained within the church, and on his death he was buried as a Catholic in accordance with his will.

2 Public law – the theory of sovereignty

Bodin's most celebrated work is his *Les six livres de la république* (The Six Books of a Commonwealth) (1576), an encyclopedic treatise of public law and policy that appeared in 1576. The theory of sovereignty, which provides its framework, was a major event in the development of European political thought. Bodin's precise definition of supreme authority, his determination of its scope and his analysis of the functions it logically entailed helped to turn public law into a scientific discipline. With Bodin and his followers (especially in Germany), the various jurisdictions of a state could be systematically ordered with respect to an ultimate centre of authority. And his elaboration of the implications of sovereignty through a vast synthesis of comparative public law helped to launch a whole new literary genre.

Bodin's doctrine of sovereignty, however, was seriously flawed by his erroneous views on the indivisibility of sovereignty. He believed that all the powers of the state had ultimately to be concentrated in a single individual or group. This was presented not only as a recommendation of political prudence but as the analytic condition of a coherent and coordinated legal system. Bodin could thus conclude that a mixed constitution, in which the prerogatives of sovereignty were shared or separated, was logically impossible. He therefore failed to see that shared or separated powers produced a compound sovereign, the components of which were coordinated by an underlying basic norm, or rule of recognition, accepted by the general community. Sovereignty, for Bodin, was always that of a ruler. What he needed, but could not imagine, was some notion of constituent authority distinct from the ordinary power of a government. (see CONSTITUTIONALISM §1; SOVEREIGNTY §§1, 3)

3 Public law – the French monarchy and absolutism

Bodin's rejection of the mixed constitution would ultimately lead him to an absolutist interpretation of the French and other monarchies of Western Europe. (see ABSOLUTISM §§2–3). This was not his original intention, and in his *Methodus ad facilem historiarum cognitionem* (Method for the Easy Comprehension of History) (1566), he worked with a notion of limited supremacy. Ten years later, however, he had come to the conclusion that sovereign authority was absolute as well as indivisible. This seems to have resulted in part from further reflections on the logic of undivided power and in part from his deep fears of imminent anarchy arising from challenges to royal authority in the renewed religious wars. In the *République* Bodin developed an absolutist interpretation of the French kingship as well as of the Spanish and the English, which supplied a conservative reply to existing doctrines of resistance. Yet it must be emphasized that Bodin was no friend of arbitrary governance. Although a proper king was absolute juridically, prudence and decency required that he seek the advice of the Estates and respect the judgments of the *Parlements*. The king, moreover, was limited, morally at least, by the law of nature as well as by certain fundamental laws on the organization of the crown and its domain (see NATURAL LAW). The law of nature, furthermore, was rigorously interpreted, and it even prohibited, at least in Bodin's reasoning, the imposition of new taxes without consent. The critical point for him politically was that a king's obligation to the law of nature was owed to God alone. Resistance by subjects was thus excluded, for according to contemporary notions, resistance to an authority that was absolute in the sense of not responsible to human agents was forbidden by the law of God.

4 Other contributions to social theory

Bodin's account of sovereignty and public law was only one of many pioneering contributions to social theory. His *Methodus* of 1566, which was a guide to the profitable study of universal history, included a critical method for evaluating historical statements, a system of universal chronology and a theory of progress in the arts and sciences, as well as an extensive preliminary exposition of his theory of public law. And both the *République* and the *Methodus* contain a long chapter, clearly anticipating Montesquieu, on how climate and geography shape the social and political temperament of nations. In *La response de Jean Bodin à M. de Malestroit* (The Response of Jean Bodin to the Paradoxes of M. Malestroit) (1568), Bodin explained the price revolution of the sixteenth century as the result of the sudden influx of precious metals from America. Although anticipated somewhat by Copernicus, he was the first to arrive at a clear explanation of the quantity theory of money. His thesis, furthermore, was illustrated and proven by a reconstruction of the historical movement of French prices, which was a model of sophisticated economic historiography. And his findings on the movements of bullion and goods across national boundaries led him to shrewd observations on the international division of labour.

5 Religious thought

Bodin's religious thought was also strikingly bold and highly influential. His main work on religion, the *Colloquium heptaplomeres de rerum sublimium arcanis abditis* (Colloquium of the Seven about Secrets of the Sublime), was to seem scandalously freethinking to contemporaries. Probably written around 1593, Bodin left it in manuscript form and wanted it burned upon his death. It survived in manuscript and obtained underground circulation among scholars until it was finally published in the nineteenth century.

Bodin seems to have resolved his lifelong search for religious truth with a theistic form of Neoplatonism (see NEOPLATONISM §5). Neoplatonic religiosity had strong appeal to Renaissance intellectuals. But Bodin's version is distinctive, however, in that it is Judaized and very strictly unitarian. Speculative reason teaches us that God exists, that he orders the cosmos by his angels and demons, and that he reveals his will for humankind and his purposes in history by inspiring his prophets. Thus disciplined, speculative reason conducts humans to their highest good, which consists of a kind of mystic unity with God. As Bodin describes it in the *Paradoxon* (The Paradox of Jean Bodin) (1596a), this unity is not, and cannot be, a participation in divinity, or even an active form of contemplation. It is rather a passive opening to God, by way of contemplation, that allows God's light to enter and illuminate the soul. Properly ordered, all aspects of life, both intellectual and moral, are subordinated to this goal. The science of nature, which Bodin treats in his *Universae naturae theatrum* (Theatre of Nature in its Entirety) (1596b), teaches the wonders and beauties of God's creation. Contemplative wisdom, however, leads beyond science in bringing us closer to God and culminates in illumination, the content of which, for those chosen to receive it, is the gift of prophetic powers.

Although this approach to God is possible in all religions, Judaism is held to be the oldest and truest, and the revelations of its prophets and sages are said to be the best. Christianity is portrayed as flawed, not only for its trinitarianism but also for its doctrine of original sin and the need for a saviour. Nevertheless, it is not the purpose of the *Colloquium heptaplomeres* to prove the claims of any one of the revealed religions. All the interlocutors – each representing a different theological position – agree that the differences among them cannot be resolved by argument, that sincere worship in any of the positive religions is pleasing to God, and that they will agree to disagree in the tolerant spirit of Venice, which is the imagined locale of the colloquium.

With respect to public policy, Bodin's recommendations, although still liberal for the time, are more cautious and politically aware. Where religious uniformity existed, it was to be preserved no matter what its form, since politico-religious factionalism was among the worst of evils. Since a state religion would not be unacceptable to God, the philosopher could observe it outwardly, while cultivating truth in private. But forced conversions are always to be shunned, and where a religious minority has become numerous, limited toleration is the prudent course.

Bodin's religious mysticism also had its darker side. He believed in astrology and numerology and attempted to apply both to political science. Darker still was his all too influential book, *De la démonomanie des sorciers* (On The Demon-mania of Witches) (1580), on the detection and punishment of witches. Nevertheless, these deviations into superstition were not uncommon in the Renaissance and ought not to obscure the fact that Bodin's religious thought was a significant moment in the development of universalism and religious toleration. This body of thought, together with his contributions to political and social theory, entitle him to be regarded as one of the foremost thinkers of his time.

See also: TOLERATION

List of works

For an extended bibliography containing all known editions of each work and editions of Bodin's letters, see Denzer (1973: 492–500).

Bodin, J. (1566) *Methodus ad facilem historiarum cognitionem*; in P. Mesnard (ed.) *Œuvres philosophiques de Jean Bodin*, Paris: Presses Universitaires de France, 1951, 107–269; trans. B. Reynolds, *Method for the Easy Comprehension of History*; New York: Columbia University Press, 1945; repr. 1969. (A collection of essays on various topics designed to supply the reader with the information and critical tools needed to read historians with profit.)

—— (1568) *La vie chère au XVIe siècle. La response de Jean Bodin à M. de Malestroit*; ed. H. Hauser, Paris: A. Colin, 1932; trans. of 1578 edn, G.A. Moore, *The Response of Jean Bodin to the Paradoxes of M Malestroit*, Washington, DC: Country Dollar Press, 1946. (An early statement of the quantity theory of money designed to show that the great price inflation of the time was caused by the importation of precious metals, mostly from America.)

—— (1576) *Les six livres de la république*, Paris: Jacques du Puy, 1583; repr. Aalen: Scientia, 1961; trans. J. Bodin, *De republica libri sex*, Paris: Jacques du Puy, 1586; trans. R. Knolles, *The Six Books of a Commonwealth*, London: B. Bishop, 1606; repr. with apparatus by K.D. McRae, Cambridge, MA: Harvard University Press, 1962; ed. and partial trans. into modern English, J.H. Franklin, *Bodin: On Sovereignty*, Cambridge: Cambridge University Press, 1992. (Bodin's grand synthesis of comparative public law and policy centring around his investigation of the nature of sovereignty.)

—— (1580) *De la démonomanie des sorciers*, Hildesheim and New York: G. Olms, 1988; trans. R.A. Scott, abridged J.L. Pearl, *On The Demonomania of Sorcerers*, Toronto, Ont: Centre for Reformation and Renaissance Studies, Victoria University in the University of Toronto, 1995. (A study of the satanic practices of witches and how to detect and convict them.)

—— (c.1593) *Colloquium heptaplomeres de rerum sublimium arcanis abditis*, ed. L. Noack, Schwerin: F.G. Baereusprung, 1st complete edn, 1857; repr. Hildesheim and New York: G. Olms, 1970; trans. L. Daniels Kuntz, *Colloquium of the Seven about Secrets of the Sublime*, Princeton, NJ: Princeton University Press, 1975. (The text consists of a friendly debate among representatives of seven religions/religious positions as to which religion is the truest and best, ending in an agreement to disagree.)

—— (1596a) *Paradoxon, quod nec virtus ulle in mediocritate, nec summum hominis bonum in virtutis actione consistere possit* (The Paradox of Jean Bodin... that there is no virtue in mediocrity or in the mean between two vices), Paris; trans. J. Bodin, *Le Paradoxe de J. Bodin... qu'il n'y a pas une seule vertu en médiocrité, ny euy milieu de deux vices*, Paris, 1598; repr. P.L. Rose (ed.) *Jean Bodin, Selected Writings on Philosophy, Religion and Politics*, Geneva: Librairie Droz, 1980, 43–75. (Rejects the Aristotelian idea idea of the mean as the decisive criterion of virtue in favour of the pure love of divine truth.)

—— (1596b) *Universae naturae theatrum* (Theatre of Nature in its Entirety), Lyon and Paris: Jacob Roussoon; trans. Fr. de Fougerolles, *Le theatre de la nature universelle*, Lyon: Jean Pillehotte, 1597. (A systematic account, broadly Platonic in inspiration, of the natural order of the cosmos.)

References and further reading

Chauviré, R. (1914) *Jean Bodin, auteur de la République* (Jean Bodin, Author of the République), La Flèche: E. Besnier; repr. Geneva: Slatkine, 1969. (Although now outdated in some aspects, still a useful treatment in one volume of Bodin's political thought as a whole.)

Denzer, H. (ed.) (1973) *Verhandlungen der internationalen Bodin Tagung in Munchen* (Proceedings of the International Conference on Bodin held in

Munich), Munich: C.H. Beck. (Contains a very extensive bibliography of secondary works as well as a number of important scholarly articles, some in English, on diverse aspects of Bodin's life and thought.)

Franklin, J.H. (1973) *Jean Bodin and the Rise of Absolutist theory*, Cambridge: Cambridge University Press. (A critical analysis of the genesis, structure and ideological impact of Bodin's theory of sovereignty.)

Goyard-Fabre, S. (1989) *Jean Bodin et le droit de la république* (Jean Bodin's and the Law of the Commonwealth), Paris: Presses Universitaires de France. (A useful running commentary on the overall system of the *République*; includes an extensive bibliography of secondary works.)

Mesnard, P. (1929) 'La pensée religieuse de Bodin', *Revue du seizième siècle* 16: 77–121. (A judicious treatment of Bodin's religious thought by the most eminent of Bodin's commentators. There is no book-length study by Mesnard, but for listings of his numerous articles on many aspects of Bodin's thought and biography, see the bibliographies in Denzer 1973, and in Goyard-Fabre 1989.)

Rose, P.L. (1980) *Bodin and the Great God of Nature, The Moral and Religious Universe of a Judaizer*, Geneva: Librairie Droz. (An extensive study of the development and character of Bodin's religious thought, with heavy emphasis on its Judaizing element.)

JULIAN H. FRANKLIN

BOEHME, JAKOB (1575–1624)

Boehme was a Lutheran mystic and pantheist. He held that God is the Abyss that is the ground of all things. The will of the Abyss to know itself generates a process that gives rise to nature, which is thus the image of God. Life is characterized by a dualistic struggle between good and evil; only by embracing Christ's love can unity be regained. Boehme was highly regarded by such diverse writers as Law, Newton, Goethe and Hegel.

A Lutheran theosopher, with a predilection for both mysticism and philosophy of nature, Jakob Boehme was a Silesian, a native of Alt Seidelberg near Görlitz. Situated between Catholic Poland and Lutheran Saxony, Silesia was a haven for heterodoxies in the late sixteenth century, although its tradition of hospitality ended abruptly with the Thirty Years War. Boehme spent most of his life in Görlitz, as a member of the Cobblers' Guild. He was an astute businessman, who had no formal training in the liberal arts but read voraciously and wrote inspiringly. His first mystical experience was in 1600, when he contemplated the 'Being of all beings, the Byss and the Abyss' in the sunlight reflected in a pewter dish.

Published in 1612, *Morgenröthe im Anfang* (The Red Light at Dawn) was Boehme's first attempt at solving the problem of theodicy. It immediately incurred the condemnation of Görlitz's Lutheran church. He was forbidden to write further, but his reputation was established. Boehme kept silent for seven years and then released the *Beschreibung der drey Principien Göttliches Wesen* (Concerning the Three Principles of the Divine Essence) in 1619, and *Hohe und tieffe Grund von dem drey fachen Leben des Menschen* (The High and Deep Searching Out of the Threefold Life of Man), *De incarnatione verbi* (On the Incarnation of the Word), *Sechs theosophischen Puncten* (Six Theosophic Points) and *Kurtze Erklärung von Sechs mystischen Puncten* (Short Exposition of Six Mystical Points) in 1620. A large commentary on Genesis, *Mysterium magnum* (The Great Mystery), came out in 1623, followed in 1624 by a collection of small treatises, *Der Weg zu Christo* (The Way to Christ). Written in 1622, *De signatura rerum* (The Signature of All Things) was posthumously published in 1635.

Like Valentin Weigel (1533–88), a subjective pantheist, Boehme began with the self, but he emphasized its will. The self, the source of all knowledge, is derived from the universal feeling for life (*Lebensgefühl*). Boehme saw himself as an agent of the Spirit, which, in his worldview, began the process of self-understanding that culminated in the inner vision of a universally present and active Christ. What is God? He is the Abyss (*Ungrund*), the ground of all things, the undifferentiated absolute, the eternal, natureless, unconscious Nothing that lies at the foundation of everything. At the core of the Abyss lies a will to self-intuition. This will initiates the process of self-knowledge, and its outgoing dynamic activity creates the inner world, which is the prototype of the outer world. In the self-noetic process, the will of the Nothing searches for something and discovers it within itself. Eternal nature finds its being in this process. With differentiation emerge evil, dualism and conflict. Boehme's voluntarism, which bears Luther's mark, is coupled with the doctrine of the Trinity and flavoured with the Manichean dualism of light and darkness, good and evil, love and hatred, grace and wrath.

For Boehme, nature is the image of God; he thus formulated the identity of God with nature half a century before SPINOZA (§2). He also framed a theory of seven natural properties. In a letter dating from 11 November 1623, which furnishes a clear compendium of his metaphysics, Boehme defines these seven properties as desire, sensation, anxiety, fire, light, sound and being. The Trinity arises from the unfathomable will of the Father, which creates for all eternity the unfathomable will of the Son; from both emanates the Spirit, the 'moving life' that mirrors both the Father and the Son. History is where the struggle for life unfolds, which Boehme describes as a fight between good and evil, where the decision for or against God is made. Meaning is to be found in Christ. The purpose of life is to retrieve the lost unity by allowing the fire of love, Christ's heart, to embrace everything. Life should therefore be an imitation of Christ's suffering and triumph.

Boehme's theosophy, which can be characterized as a preparation for the mystical acknowledgement of Christ, shows the influence of Neoplatonism, Gnosticism, kabbalism, Paracelsian pansophism, Caspar Schwenckfeld's spiritualism, and Sebastian Franck's humanistic illuminism. Boehme's influence has been considerable. He was the most often translated German author of the seventeenth century. Descartes, Spinoza, the Cambridge Platonists and Newton read his works. His cosmic, metaphysical and ethical dualism enchanted the Romantics Novalis, Tieck and Goethe. Hegel celebrated him as the first true German philosopher, and Schelling owed to him his philosophy of identity. Besides a crucial influence on the devotional writer William Law, the quietist Antoinette Bourignon and the poet William Blake, Boehme had an ecclesiastical following in the Low Countries (The Invisible Church of the Angel's Brothers) and in England (The Philadelphians).

List of works

Boehme, J. (1955–61) *Sämmtliche Schriften*, ed. W.-E. Peuckert, Stuttgart: Frommanns, 11 vols. (The standard edition of Boehme's works.)

—— (1612) *Morgenröthe im Anfang* (The Red Light at Dawn), trans. J. Sparrow, ed. C.J. Barker and D.S. Hehner, *The Aurora*, London: J.M. Watkins, 1960. (Written to preserve the memory of his mystical experience, and to probe God's relation to the world and its evils.)

—— (1619) *Beschreibung der drey Principien Göttliches Wesen*, trans. J. Sparrow, ed. C.J. Barker, *Concerning the Three Principles of the Divine Essence*, London: J.M. Watkins, 1910. (A secretly composed and very opaque work in which Boehme dips into alchemy and astrology to 'clarify' his previous book.)

—— (1620a) *Hohe und tieffe Grund von dem drey fachen Leben des Menschen*, trans. J. Sparrow, ed. C.J. Barker, *The High and Deep Searching Out of the Threefold Life of Man*, London: J.M. Watkins, 1909. (Boehme's system deepens: God is the absolute person who reveals himself by creating the world which is known by human thought.)

—— (1620b) *De incarnatione verbi, Von der menschwerdung Jesu Christi*, trans. J.R. Earle and S.R. Webster, *De incarnatione verbi: Of the Incarnation of Jesus Christ*, London: Constable, 1934. (Sections on the Incarnation and Mary, the Christian's union with Christ's cross, and the way to being one in Spirit with God.)

—— (1620c) *Sechs theosophischen Puncten*, trans. J.R. Earle, in *Six Theosophic Points and Other Writings*, Ann Arbor, MI: University of Michigan Press, 1958. (English edition printed with 1620d and other works. Further expansions and descriptions of Boehme's complete scheme.)

—— (1620d) *Kurtze Erklärung von Sechs mystischen Puncten* (Short Exposition of Six Mystical Points), trans. J.R. Earle, in *Six Theosophic Points and Other Writings*, Ann Arbor, MI: University of Michigan Press, 1958. (See 1620c for further details.)

—— (1620e) *Viertzig Fragen von der Seele*, trans. J. Sparrow, *Forty Questions on the Soul and The Clavis*, London: J.M. Watkins, 1911. (Further complexification of the system: Boehme treats God as the Ungrounded One who objectifies himself.)

—— (1623) *Mysterium magnum* (The Great Mystery), trans. J. Sparrow, ed. C.J. Barker, London: J.M. Watkins, 2 vols, 1941. (A substantial commentary on the book of Genesis; the English translation leaves some material out.)

—— (1624) *Der Weg zu Christo*, trans. P.C. Erb, *The Way to Christ*, New York: Paulist Press, 1978. (Nine mystical treatises: the best introduction to Boehme's spirituality.)

—— (1635) *De signatura rerum*, trans. J. Ellistone, *The Signature of All Things, With Other Writings*, London and Cambridge: J.M. Clarke, 1969. (The original subtitle in English (1651) shows the ambition of Boehme's system: 'shewing the sign and signification of the severall forms and shapes in the creation, and what the beginning, ruin, and cure of every thing is'.)

—— (1763–81) *The Works of Jacob Behmen, the Teutonic Theosopher*, trans. J. Sparrow and J. Ellistone, London: M. Richardson; microfilm, New Haven, CT: Research Publications, 1973. (This English edition contains a sketch of Boehme's life by William Law.)

—— (1963–6) *Die Urschriften* (The Original Manuscripts), ed. W. Buddecke, Stuttgart: Frommanns, 2

vols. (A critical edition of previously unpublished materials.)
—— (1989) *Jacob Boehme: Essential Readings*, ed. R. Waterfield, Wellingborough: Crucible. (Some obscure texts, fragments and letters which together provide an overview of Boehme's thought.)

References and further reading

Brown, R.F. (1977) *The Later Philosophy of Schelling: The Influence of Boehme on the Works of 1809–1815*, London and New York: Associated University Presses. (A long first section on Boehme treats several of his works in depth, and presents a systematic outline of his mature system.)

Buddecke, W. (1937–57) *Die Jakob Böhme-Ausgaben*, Göttingen: Ludwig Häntschel, 2 vols. (A complete bibliography of Boehme's works.)

Koyré, A. (1929) *La Philosophie de Jacob Boehme*, Paris: J. Vrin. (Remains the best book on Boehme.)

Peuckert, W.-E. (1924) *Das Leben Jakob Böhmes*, Jena: Eugen Diederichs. (The first critical biography, and still the benchmark.)

Stoudt, J.J. (1957) *Sunrise to Eternity: A Study in Jacob Boehme's Life and Thought*, Philadelphia, PA: University of Pennsylvania Press. (A reliable and thorough biography.)

Walsh, D. (1983) *The Mysticism of Innerworldly Fulfillment: A Study of Jacob Boehme*, Gainesville, FL: University of Florida Press. (An exploration of Boehme's significance in the context of late-Renaissance magico-mystical movements.)

Weeks, A. (1991) *Boehme: An Intellectual Biography of the Seventeenth-Century Philosopher and Mystic*, Albany, NY: State University of New York Press. (Places Boehme firmly in his social and historical context.)

JEAN-LOUP SEBAN

BOETHIUS, ANICIUS MANLIUS SEVERINUS (*c*.480–525/6)

Boethius was a principal transmitter of classical Greek logic from Aristotle, the Stoics and the Neoplatonists to the schoolmen of the medieval Latin West. His contemporaries were largely unimpressed by his learned activities, and his writings show him to have been a lonely, rather isolated figure in a world where the old Roman aristocrats were struggling to maintain high literary culture in an Italy controlled by barbarous and bibulous Goths, whose taste in music and hairgrease Boethius found painful.

Boethius himself was born into a patrician family in Rome, but was orphaned and raised instead by Q. Aurelius Memmius Symmachus, a rich Christian heir to a distinguished pagan line; Boethius later married the latter's daughter, Rusticiana. As well as Symmachus, Boethius had a small circle of educated friends, including the Roman deacon John (who probably became Pope John I, 523–6), who shared his enthusiasm for logical problems. The Gothic king of Italy at Ravenna, Theoderic, had met high culture during his education at Constantinople and made use of experienced Roman aristocrats as administrators. He employed Boethius to design a sundial for the Burgundian king and also a waterclock, specimens of advanced technology intended to impress a barbarian; he also sent a harpist to Clovis, the Frankish king, no doubt intended to soften the latter's bellicose spirit.

By 507 Boethius had gained the title 'patrician' and received letters addressed to 'your magnitude'. Symmachus was in a position to promote his public career. He was nominated consul for the year 510, a position without political power but of high standing and requiring large disbursements of private wealth; it also carried the perquisite that the consul's name stood on all dated documents for that year. In 522 his two sons were installed as consuls, a promotion that gave their father intense pride and pleasure, and he took up seriously the political post of Master of the Offices. In this capacity, his determination to eliminate corruption earned him numerous enemies among both Goths and his fellow Roman aristocrats. His relations with the courtiers at Ravenna became disastrous.

Boethius' fall came when he rashly defended a senator who had been delated to King Theoderic for conducting treasonable correspondence with persons high in the court of the emperor at Constantinople. There is no improbability in the notion that, along with other Roman aristocrats, Boethius would have preferred to be rid of the crude Goths and to see Theoderic replaced by a ruler congenial to the emperor. His great erudition had aroused fears that he was engaged in occult practices dangerous to the Ravenna dynasty. In 524 or early 525, Boethius was imprisoned at Pavia (Ticinum). Here, while awaiting the execution already decreed against him, he composed his masterpiece, De consolatione philosophiae (*The Consolation of Philosophy*).

De consolatione philosophiae, a bitterly hostile attack on Theoderic prefacing a philosophical discussion of innocent suffering and the problem of evil, must have been smuggled out of prison, no doubt with the aid of gold coins from Rusticiana or Symmachus. In the ninth century, the work captured the imagination of

Alcuin at the court of Charlemagne, became a standard textbook in schools and was set on the way to being one of the greatest books of medieval culture, especially popular among laymen.

Boethius' earlier works have been the preserve of more specialized readers, especially concerned with the history of ancient philosophy. His stated original intention was to educate the West by translating all of Plato and Aristotle into Latin and to supply explanatory commentaries on many of their writings. That was too ambitious. He did not proceed beyond some of the logical works (*Organon*) of Aristotle, prefaced by a commentary on a Latin translation of Porphyry's *Isagōgē* (*Introduction*) made in the fourth century by Marius Victorinus, an African teaching in Rome, and then by a second commentary on a translation of the same text made by himself. This commentary underlay the medieval debates on universals. He also wrote a commentary on Aristotle's *Categories* and two commentaries on Aristotle's *De interpretatione*. In addition, Boethius adapted Nicomachus of Gerasa's *Arithmetic* for Latin readers, Nicomachus' introduction to music as a liberal art, a commentary on Cicero's *Topics*, a short treatise 'On Division', important treatises on categorical and hypothetical syllogisms and a further tract on different kinds of 'topic'.

Intricate theological debates between Rome and Constantinople convinced him that a trained logician could contribute clarification, and he composed four theological tractates on the doctrines of the Trinity and the person of Christ, concentrating on logical problems. In addition, a fifth tract became a statement of orthodox belief without much reference to logical implications. The five pieces, or *Opuscula sacra*, became hardly less influential than *De consolatione philosophiae*, especially from the twelfth century onwards. We hear of critics who thought contemporary theologians knew more about Boethius than about the Bible.

1 Life
2 Works
3 Logic
4 *Opuscula sacra*
5 *De consolatione philosophiae*
6 Influence

1 Life

Boethius was born in Rome into a wealthy Christian family of senatorial standing, in an age when barbarian soldiers ruled and the old aristocratic families had yielded power to them, yet remained indispensable to their Gothic masters for the good order of civil administration. Under the rule of the Ostrogoth king Theoderic, the old Roman families continued to assert their Roman-ness by the study and re-editing of classics of Latin literature – Livy, Cicero, Virgil, Seneca and so on – but also by retaining a politically hazardous contact with the eastern Roman emperor in Constantinople. Boethius' father died when Boethius himself was young, and he was taken in by Q. Aurelius Memmius Symmachus, whose daughter Rusticiana he later married.

The best-educated person of his time in the West, he could read Greek, even if not quite fluently, and his works are rich in literary allusions and reminiscences. He was well read in the Neoplatonic commentators on the logical and other writings of Aristotle, especially PORPHYRY and PROCLUS. He was also familiar with at least some of the major writings of AUGUSTINE of Hippo, and wrote five theological tractates (*Opuscula sacra*), four of which are devoted to clarifying logical problems in orthodox Catholic doctrine, especially in regard to the doctrines of the person of Christ and the divine Trinity. The quest for acceptable language to express Christian belief on these themes had a bearing on the break in communion between the papacy and the patriarchate of Constantinople from 484 to 518. Boethius and his circle of aristocratic friends in Italy were concerned to heal this breach, and this aspiration led him to attempt to use his dialectical skills to define the terms more closely than had been done previously. The set of five tracts on theology provided influential themes for exegesis by commentators in medieval times, especially during the twelfth and thirteenth centuries, including Thomas AQUINAS. However, the contacts with Constantinople and the religious disagreements between the Arian Theoderic and the Orthodox Emperor Justin also played a part in bringing about Boethius' death. To Dante, he was a martyr and hero, and on 23 October 1883 his veneration as a saint was authorized at Pavia.

In his twenties, Boethius embarked on a programme of translation, commentary and adaptation to make available to the Latin West the logic of Aristotle and the standard Greek texts on the four mathematical 'arts', arithmetic, geometry, music and astronomy, for which he coined the term 'quadrivium', parallel to the 'trivium' of grammar (that is, literature), rhetoric and dialectic. Soon, King Theoderic was inviting him to revise the coinage system, to design a waterclock and sundial to send to the Burgundian king Gundobald and to review the system of weights and measures. He was asked to select a harpist to send to Clovis the Frankish king. His intellectual powers and the patronage of his powerful father-in-law Symmachus launched him on a meteoric career in the civil administration. He was nominated consul for 510; his young sons were consuls for 522, when he also delivered a panegyric on Theoderic (a text now lost but known to Cassiodorus). In the same year he became Master of the Offices, a post of considerable power, from which he tried to root out bribery and corruption in the bureaucracy, thereby ensuring that he made many enemies. He understood himself to be following Plato's principle that philosophers must accept government posts since, if they do not do so, wicked gangsters take over.

In 519 Theoderic's heir presumptive died, and speculation about his successor was rife. Boethius rashly defended another senator suspected of a correspondence with Constantinople, an act regarded by King Theoderic as treasonable. In the Eastern empire the new emperor Justin, guided by his nephew Justinian, had a programme of suppressing heresy to give social cohesion, and the sects being harassed included the Arians. However, Theoderic and his Gothic soldiers had received their faith from Arian missionaries. The eastern Roman imperial policy of intolerance therefore appeared to Theoderic at Ravenna as an ambition to eliminate both heresy and Goths in Italy. Tension became high, and Boethius was accused by other Roman aristocrats, keen perhaps to dissociate themselves from someone suspected of dangerously pro-Byzantine sentiment, and was imprisoned at Pavia (Ticinum) and sentenced to death. During his many months awaiting execution he wrote *De consolatione philosophiae* (The Consolation of Philosophy). The scorn and hatred for Theoderic and other powerful Goths shown in the first book of this work, which was probably smuggled out of prison by his wife and other influential friends, proves that he was not writing an ingratiating work to submit to Theoderic in hope of a reprieve.

In effect, Boethius in his prison was a hostage under deteriorating conditions, being used by Theoderic in an unsuccessful attempt to restrain Byzantine political and religious aspirations. Late in 525 or possibly early in 526 he was subjected to vile tortures and battered to death. Under Theoderic's anger his father-in-law Symmachus and his intimate friend Pope John I also lost their lives. A Ravenna chronicler, the so-called Anonymus Valesianus, thought that Arian heresy had addled the king's brain and deprived him of his wits. The Byzantine historian Procopius reports a story that Theoderic was haunted by guilt and died in bitter remorse (on 30 August 526). The king may well have come to perceive that the killing of Boethius and others had played into Constantinople's hands, enabling the Byzantine emperor to undermine the general admiration hitherto felt in Italy for Gothic government in cooperation with the old Roman families. Boethius' tomb is in the church of Ciel d'Oro at Pavia.

2 Works

De consolatione philosophiae (in late Latin *consolatio* came to mean help or support) owes its survival to being discovered in the ninth century, probably by Alcuin (see CAROLINGIAN RENAISSANCE), and was to become Boethius' most widely read work. Pervaded by passionate feeling, composed in a sophisticated Latin in alternating passages of verse and prose and in the last two books handling complex philosophical ideas such as, for example, divine providence, human freedom, eternity and time, the work became a major classic of western literature. The emergence of the *De consolatione philosophiae* and of the *Opuscula sacra* in the ninth century, followed soon after by the logical works, made Boethius' writings important in medieval education. Boethius taught good morality and fine Latinity in an age when both were hard to get. From this time onwards there survive a number of commentaries on the *De consolatione philosophiae*, as much concerned with style and metre as with the content of the argument. That initially the primary function of the work was educational is illustrated by manuscripts of the Latin text with marginal notes in vernacular languages. *De consolatione* also attracted vernacular translators; in England these included King Alfred in the ninth century and Geoffrey Chaucer in the fourteenth. The earliest of several German translations is by Notker of St Gallen circa 1010; Jean de Meun translated the work into medieval French in the late thirteenth century, and Jacob Vilt of Bruges translated it into Dutch in 1462. Queen Elizabeth I was among the later translators in England. In the Byzantine world, a Greek translation of *De consolatione philosophiae* was produced by Maximos Planudes (1260–1310), the humanist and monk who also produced a Greek version of Augustine on the Trinity. His translations reflected his support for the contemporary effort by Emperor Michael VIII to avert further military aggression from the West by ending the schism between Constantinople and Rome.

De consolatione philosophiae's first book protests that its author was innocent of the charges brought against him based on forged letters. Then, in contemplation of his hopeless position, the work moves on to a philosophical vindication of the goodness of providence, even in a world where the just are not rewarded with prosperity and the wicked are allowed power. *De consolatione* is a clearly religious work written by a Christian, and yet it is not a Christian work in the sense that it contains nothing about the forgiveness of sins or redemption. Nevertheless, while turns of phrase are much more Neoplatonic than Christian, there is one clear quotation from the Bible (III pr.12. 23–4). There Boethius expresses special pleasure at the fact that the lady Philosophy uses some words from the Wisdom of Solomon, admittedly to reinforce a truth of natural, not revealed, theology. As the title indicates, the work sets out to present the philosophical arguments for a Platonic theodicy, a subject to which all Platonists needed to give some attention and which in late antiquity was specially studied not only by PROCLUS but also by Hierocles of Alexandria (see NEOPLATONISM).

The *Opuscula sacra* regard faith and reason as independent but parallel and compatible ways of attaining to higher metaphysical truths, and the independent validity of logical reasoning is also an underlying presupposition throughout *De consolatione*. The apparently conscious reticence of *De consolatione* about Christianity led to conjectures, beginning in the eighteenth century, that perhaps the *Opuscula sacra* were by a different author. More recently it has been proposed that, under the stress of his misfortunes and perhaps in disappointment that the Pope and bishops were impotent to help him, Boethius abandoned Christianity and in his last work wrote as a pagan apostate. The manner of the citation from the Wisdom of Solomon makes the last conjecture inherently unlikely, and the old assumption that *De consolatione* presents Neoplatonic philosophy while the *Opuscula sacra* do not fails to withstand critical examination. In any event a fragment of Cassiodorus records subjects on which Boethius had written, and these include 'a book on the Holy Spirit and some dogmatic chapters and a book against Nestorius'. Cassiodorus, who succeeded Boethius immediately as Master of the Offices, clearly understood him to be a believer. The intention of the *De consolatione philosophiae* is to explore the philosophical arguments in defence of belief in providence, where, if there is authority, it is located in Plato. Boethius had certainly read the three studies of providence written by Proclus, and in *De consolatione* I pr.4.30 cites loosely from Proclus' commentary on Plato's *Parmenides*: 'If there is a god, whence comes evil? Whence comes good, if there is not?' There are also themes from Proclus in the *Opuscula sacra*. In writing on the Trinity, Boethius uses the analysis of the relation between identity and difference discussed by PLATO (§§15–16) in the *Sophist* and the *Parmenides* and thereafter by Proclus in his commentary on the *Parmenides*. The face that meets us in the *Consolatione* is identical with that of the *Opuscula sacra*.

Of the five *opuscula* on Christian theology, the fourth 'on Catholic Faith' stands apart and, as early as Reginbert of Reichenau in the ninth century, has been thought by some to belong to a different author. However, the manuscript tradition shows that it formed part of the corpus from a very early stage, and its diction is demonstrably Boethian. It states what believers accept on authority, succinctly summarizing Augustinian doctrine, and contains no allusion to the logical problems which mark the other four *opuscula*. The tractate 'Against Eutyches and Nestorius' is among Boethius' most original pieces, addressed to the confusions of thought and language in the debate about the unity of the person of Christ which, since the council of Chalcedon in 451, had split the Greek churches. Successive attempts at formulas of reconciliation angered the popes by implications that the controversy had not been fully settled by Pope Leo the Great. Boethius discerned confusion over the terms 'nature' and 'person', defining the latter as 'the individual substance of a rational nature'. In his second commentary on Aristotle's *De interpretatione*, 'person' is the incommunicable quality of a human individual. The third tractate answers questions put by John (probably the future Pope John I) arising out of another paper entitled Hebdomads (Groups of Seven). A highly Neoplatonic piece, without theology, it inquires 'how substances are good in that they exist, yet are not substantial goods'. The influence of Proclus is pervasive. The second tractate on the Trinity illuminates the belief that God is one, yet three (in a way that Augustine thought hard to define in the traditional terms such as person or substance) by using the observation that to say two entities are 'the same' implies some distinction between them. Identity and difference are mutually related concepts.

De consolatione philosophiae reflects a mind soaked not only in classical Latin poetry but also in the arguments and philosophical methods of ARISTOTLE and his Neoplatonic commentators. Boethius' declared programme was to translate all the works of Plato and Aristotle. He was persuaded by the contention of PORPHYRY (mirrored also in Augustine's *Contra academicos* (Against the Academicians)) that in the basic essentials Plato and Aristotle were not in disagreement. Dialectic had long shared with grammar (that is, the study of literature) and rhetoric an important place in the trivium of elementary education. However, dialectic could claim more, even that it was an indispensable instrument in all mental skills. The 'liberal arts' (the skills necessary for the education of a gentleman) included not only the trivium but also the four mathematical 'arts', arithmetic, music, geometry and (theoretical) astronomy. For these four, Boethius coined the term 'quadrivium'. In Platonic and Pythagorean education these were skills which trained the mind to cope with immaterial realities.

Boethius' intention to translate Plato came to nothing, but from 504 onwards he did serious work on Aristotelian logic. Porphyry's *Isagōgē* (Introduction) to this subject had been translated into Latin by MARIUS VICTORINUS, an African who taught in Rome in the middle years of the fourth century and who had also translated Aristotle's *Categories* and some other works of Porphyry and Plotinus. The *Isagōgē*, written in the late third century (see PORPHYRY), was the standard preface to the study of Aristotelian logic and was generally used in the Neoplatonic schools; Greek Neoplatonists wrote commentaries on it. Boethius used Victorinus' version as his basis for a commentary but, as he wrote, became increasingly and justifiably critical of it; so, for a second commentary, he produced his own version. He also produced his own translations of Aristotle's *Categories* and *De interpretatione*, and provided them with commentaries. In the case of *De interpretatione* there were two commentaries, one short and simple and the other full-length. He also translated the *Prior* and *Posterior Analytics*, *Topics* and *Sophistical Refutations*, and his notes on the *Prior Analytics* have been preserved. Porphyry's first commentary on the *Categories* largely served as his model for this; Boethius does not appear to have known Porphyry's second exposition, but he had access to the commentary by his own contemporary SIMPLICIUS. Much labour has been expended on the determination of Boethius' sources, and here it must suffice to say that numerous parallels of thought and language show his intellectual milieu to be identical with that of the eastern Neoplatonists and their commentaries on the logical works of Porphyry and Aristotle. A constant feature of his translations was the desire to be meticulously accurate.

Boethius' treatises on logic overlapped in some degree with his commentaries. He wrote *De divisione* (On Division) (that is, on the classification of ideas), *De syllogismo categorico* (On Categorical Syllogisms) expounding the *Prior Analytics*, *De hypotheticis syllogismis* (On Hypothetical Syllogisms) harmonizing Aristotle and the Stoics, *De topicis differentiis* (On Topical Differences) and a commentary on Cicero's *Topics*, transmitted incomplete. Boethius also mentions some scholia of his on Aristotle's *Physics*, which have not survived. In these he probably drew on Simplicius' huge commentary.

Boethius' commentaries amass the opinions of numerous previous exegetes of Aristotle, often borrowing such matter from Porphyry who, as far as the earlier authors are concerned, had done most of the work already. One cannot assume that Boethius had himself read every author he cites, but it is probable that he had access to manuscripts of others beside Porphyry and Proclus. J. Shiel (1958) ingeniously but controversially suggested that he may have worked from a single codex of Aristotle's Organon with wide margins filled with summaries of the opinions of commentators, in the manner of the contemporary biblical *catenae*. It is in any event non-controversial that as a logician, Boethius did not set out to be original or independent of the Greek authorities, whose work he was 'sweating' to make available to the Latin world. At the same time he was something more than a simple transcriber of others, and wrote as a man personally engaged by the logical problems on which he was writing. The historian of ancient logic has good reason to be grateful for all that he preserves of which otherwise there would be insufficient or even no record. The treatise *De hypotheticis syllogismis* is more informative than any other ancient source about this part of Aristotelian dialectic. His contemporaries did not manifest much gratitude for his educational labours, and he often had occasion to refer to unkind critics. In his commentary on the *Categories*, he remarked candidly that with the general neglect of the liberal arts, much of the knowledge acquired by past generations would soon be lost. Nevertheless, we hear also of a small circle of influential admirers.

The curriculum of Neoplatonic education influenced him to produce adaptations of the *Arithmetic* of the second-century Pythagorean Nicomachus of Geras (Iamblichus' exegesis of which is extant), and of Nicomachus' treatise on music, the latter with some additional dependence on the *Harmonics* of PTOLEMY (extant also). In both cases, Boethius' Greek models survive. The Neoplatonists accepted the traditional view that the study of the mathematical arts prepares the mind for the contemplation of immaterial realities. They followed Plato's *Timaeus* in seeing harmonic ratios and exact proportionality located in the very structure of the cosmos: for them, the distance of the planets from the earth was determined by musical theory (see PLATO §16). One does not go to Boethius' work on music to learn anything of the practice of making ordered sound. His latent theme is the providential harmony of the heavens and the seasons, the mathematical principles that operate in music and hold the diverse elements together in the grand consonance of the world-soul, and that are therefore a clue to the secret concord of God and nature in a world where the only source of discord is the evil in the human heart.

Cassiodorus records an introduction to geometry by Boethius, but the work has not survived. Medieval writers filled the gap in his name. The early sections of

De consolatione philosophiae imply some serious study of astronomy, perhaps even that his expert knowledge in this field had been brought into the accusations against him, as if he had been using astrological almanacs to predict the future succession after Theoderic. A sentence in a letter drafted by Cassiodorus may mean that Boethius had made some adaptation of Ptolemy on astronomy, but there is no trace of the work surviving.

3 Logic

In presenting Aristotelian logic to the Latin world, Boethius' first task was to explicate the *Isagōgē* of PORPHYRY, who was interested in showing the compatibility of Aristotle's dialectic with Platonic metaphysics. The book Porphyry wrote on that agreement is lost, but its influence is apparent in AUGUSTINE and in the Greek Neoplatonic commentators (see NEOPLATONISM). He was concerned to rebut Christian polemic against the disagreements of the philosophical schools and to establish agreement among his own authorities. A subject on which Platonists and Aristotelians differed was that of universals. Are they prior to particulars, or is it the other way round? If nothing exists beyond particulars, must not the mind find knowledge impossible? At least the mind needs to have the capacity to see together things that are somehow linked, and to hold related particulars together under a common species or genus (see PARTICULARS; UNIVERSALS). The issue required some treatment, especially in Boethius' second commentary on Porphyry; but he declined to give any verdict between Plato and Aristotle, saying that this question was one for more advanced inquiries. At least he was able to follow the Peripatetic ALEXANDER OF APHRODISIAS, who was ready to grant that if the universal has no existence, there can be no particulars.

Boethius' commentary on the *Categories* has a preface to Book II which firmly dates the work in 510, Boethius' consular year. He expresses regret that his public social duties have interfered with his educational task. He takes Aristotle's intention to be the examination of verbal distinctions and the provision of an elementary introduction to lead on to the higher truths of his metaphysics. Here and throughout, dependence on the extant but incompletely transmitted commentary by Porphyry is evident. There is also, however, an explicit use of material taken directly or indirectly from the lost commentary by IAMBLICHUS, whose work was also drawn upon in the surviving exegesis by Proclus' pupil SIMPLICIUS.

Aristotle's *De interpretatione* was regarded in antiquity as an exceptionally opaque work. From a mass of ancient commentaries, the two by Boethius and that of AMMONIUS of Alexandria are the principal survivors. The work of Porphyry is once again a dominant guide. A substantial part of Boethius' second commentary concerns the tracing of interconnections between an object (*res*), thinking about that object (*intellectus*), talking about it (*vox*) and then putting the spoken thought into writing (*litterae*). The second commentary also discusses a range of questions that had long presented difficulty. For instance, people can have the same general conceptions of justice and goodness; but if they then differ on what in particular is just and good, does that establish moral relativism or merely human fallibility? Aristotle's ninth chapter (the sea-fight tomorrow) provoked a large debate on future contingents and modal logic. In using the terms '*contingens*' and '*contingentia*', Boethius was anticipated by MARIUS VICTORINUS. The words were needed for matters which might be other than they are, especially where the chances are even either way.

Boethius shared the Peripetatic aversion to the Stoics' surrender to determinism (see STOICISM). Necessity controls the heavenly bodies; but in this world, human wills are capable of acting after rational deliberation. In Aristotle's vocabulary, 'necessity' is a term to use for what is invariably the case, and therefore not for individual historical events. The debate about determinism, partly paralleled in ALEXANDER OF APHRODISIAS (in *On Fate*), has a theological bearing, partly because of belief in oracles and prophecy. Do inspired prophets make predictions of future events, or do they foresee trouble coming and, like a physician's prognosis or a weather forecast, utter sage warnings advising on actions to avoid? And if what they foresee is correctly discerned, is it their inspired knowing which in any sense makes the event fated to occur, or can it be said that the gods' knowledge of contingent things is itself contingent? Boethius' second commentary on *De interpretatione* therefore anticipates some of the material in the last book of the *De consolatione philosophiae*, where divine foreknowledge is a sign of future things but not in itself a cause, just as human beings can see what is going to happen without making it occur.

The treatise *De hypotheticis syllogismis* has attracted much attention, in part because of Boethius' awareness of the ambiguity surrounding conditional statements of the form 'If..., then...'. The characteristic account distinguishes hypothetical syllogisms which are affirmative (in the form, 'if A is, B is; if A is not, B is') from those which are negative (in the form, 'if A is, B is not; if A is not, B is not'). The consequent is the decider whether the hypothetical syllogism is affirmative or negative. Porphyry wrote on this subject, and perhaps Boethius made use of his work, which is not extant. The detail with which the subject is treated is significant of the strength of his commitment to the labour of convincing a society in cultural decline of the necessity of logic for clear statement: 'Those who reject logic are bound to make mistakes.' His Greek Neoplatonic masters had already taught him that in this field Aristotle was the supreme guide: '*Aristotelica auctoritas*', he writes in the second commentary on *De interpretatione* (218.26). This could readily be fitted into a Neoplatonic conception of the cosmos or even more readily into a Platonism from which Christian convictions had purged away some of the more mythological elements, such as reincarnation (see LOGIC, MEDIEVAL).

4 *Opuscula sacra*

Debate in the Church from about AD 370 had revolved around the correct and adequate way to express (a) that Christ is both divine and human, and therefore combines 'two natures', and (b) that nevertheless Christ is one person and the union of divine and human in him is necessary to his work of redemption. How could the singleness of person be affirmed if a determination to safeguard the reality and spontaneity of Christ's humanity imposed an inextinguishable duality of natures? Boethius was not the first writer to try the use of Porphyry's logical terminology in the attempt to alleviate this formidable conundrum. Cyril of Alexandria, a prominent fifth-century critic of those who held an unmitigated duality of natures, had already employed Porphyrian terms. However, there was still much defining and clarifying to be done. There remained thorny problems of inconsistency, for example between the meaning of terms expressing the doctrine of the Trinity and the meaning of the same terms of Christology. In both, the words 'nature' and 'hypostasis' were current, but not always in the same sense in the two contexts. Pietistic fideists who liked to pride themselves on the supernatural faith of Galilean fishermen could look down on the clever logicians who seemed to think Aristotle could better express their religious beliefs. In the West, the stress on the use of papal authority to determine controversies produced a comparable insistence both on submissive adherence to what had been canonically defined by the ecumenical council of Chalcedon (451) and confirmed (after some hesitations) by Pope Leo I, and on resistance to any further explanations or compromises made to placate the Monophysite critics of Chalcedon's language. However, the logicians saw correctly that the methods and terms of the Neoplatonic commentators on Aristotle could do a little to clarify some obscurities and muddles (see PATRISTIC PHILOSOPHY).

AUGUSTINE (§3) had proclaimed that theologians could not safely neglect dialectic. The fifth tract in Boethius' *Opuscula*, dedicated to John, a Roman deacon (probably the future Pope John I), was evoked by a critical moment in the debate at Rome with an immediate bearing on East–West relations in the Church and society. The then Pope, Symmachus (498–514), had execrable relations with the Byzantine emperor Anastasius, who found papal insults hard to bear, and with the patriarchs of Constantinople. Probably in 513 a Greek bishop, no doubt in the name of a group of bishops, had written to Symmachus affirming acceptance of Chalcedon's language and approval of Pope Leo I, but in the qualified formula 'in two natures *and of* two natures', and rejecting the dissenting Monophysite formula 'one nature after the union'. The Greek letter provoked consternation and a storm at Rome in a meeting attended by Boethius and other senators. Reflection on the incapacity of those present to define their terms led him to write the fifth tractate, entitled 'Against Eutyches and Nestorius' (Eutyches being for one nature, Nestorius for two, both in extreme and radical forms). The 'in and of' formula had been used by Pope Gelasius (492–6), but in 512–13 was unwelcome to the advisers of Pope Symmachus.

It is instructive that Boethius unreservedly welcomed the two prepositions. Close parallels to his language and method appear in Greek writers a few years after his time. Four definitions of 'nature' are given:

(a) 'Nature consists of those things which, since in some way they exist, can be grasped by the mind'. (This language is found in Ammonius' exegesis of Porphyry's *Isagōgē*, 2.22.)

(b) 'Nature is either that which can act or that which can be acted upon'. (Plato, *Phaedrus* 270d; *Sophist* 247d–e; Aristotle, *Topics* VI 10.148a18.)

(c) 'Nature is the principle of motion per se and not as an accident'. (Aristotle, *Physics* II 1.192b20; VIII 4.255a32–; Proclus, *Commentary on Plato's Timaeus* I 2.20.)

(d) 'Nature is the specific difference imparting form to each individual thing'. (Aristotle, *Physics* II 1.193a28–31; Alexander of Aphrodisias, *Commentary on Aristotle's Metaphysics* p.357. 25–.)

A definition of 'person' is more difficult. Person is subordinate to nature, as particular to general. 'Person' can be used only of a substance, and then only of a being endowed with mind and reason. Christian usage applies the term *persona* to God, human beings and angels. Therefore the definition of person is 'the individual substance of rational nature'. This is the equivalent of the Greek term *hypostasis*. The Greek *ousia* (being), on the other hand, is used of the universal, with *hypostasis* used of the particular. The main thrust of Boethius' argument is to show that 'nature' and 'person' are very distinct terms, and therefore that 'two natures' does not imply two persons and 'one person' does not imply one nature (in other words, denying the propositions associated with Nestorius and Eutyches, respectively). In connection with the Incarnation, it is impious absurdity to think either that the immutable God can be transformed into humanity or that the reverse is possible (see INCARNATION AND CHRISTOLOGY §1). Change is possible only to entities which share a common substrate of matter (Aristotle, *On Generation and Corruption* 226a10). Nothing corporeal in genus can fall under an incorporeal species. Nevertheless, Boethius concedes a place to some of the language of devotion invoked by the critics of Chalcedon's 'two natures', who wanted to proclaim the worship of the one person of Christ; so, he can say Christ is 'one of the Trinity', 'God suffered', and therefore it is acceptable to say 'both in and of two natures'. The effect of Boethius' argument, (which must have been unwelcome to Pope Symmachus and perhaps to his successor Hormisdas (514–523)), is to justify a middle path between the extremes, defending Chalcedon's preposition *in*, yet also conceding the *of* designed to reconcile its more moderate critics. Thus, Boethius was advocating a position congenial to a powerful group at Constantinople and anticipating the policies of Justinian, who became Byzantine emperor a year or two after Boethius' death but who was highly influential before his accession.

The first of the *Opuscula*, 'How the Trinity is one God not three', juxtaposes Catholic orthodoxy with Aristotle's map of ascending human knowledge (*Metaphysics* 1026a18), also set out early in Boethius' first commentary on Porphyry's *Isagōgē*. The study of nature deals with concrete physical entities. Mathematics is a half-way house towards the immaterial abstract realm of theology, where God is form without matter, one substance, indeed Being itself. In God there is no number, no multiplicity; and if 'substance' is a term applied to God, that must imply no substrate to accidents. Following MARIUS VICTORINUS, Boethius affirms God, Father, Son and Spirit to be *et ipse et idem* (the same, not identical). The sameness does not exclude differentiation in terms. The ten categories of Aristotle apply only to the realm of sense, not to that of divine forms. God transcends time and space; the everlastingness of the cosmos is other than the eternity of God. The one category which helps the speculative theologian is relation, since 'father' and 'son' are relational terms. The conventional term 'person' is in this context a source of confusion (as Augustine had already said). However, the language about sameness and differentiation within identity found in the *Parmenides* and in Proclus' commentary on it can offer more illumination. Sentences about the contrast between divine eternality and the everlasting temporal duration of the cosmos anticipate the section on the same subject in the *De consolatione* (V pr.6) and are closely related to the propositions in Plotinus III 7.

5 *De consolatione philosophiae*

By using the form of alternate verse and prose, Boethius was able to deploy all his intellectual resources, literary and philosophical. The work takes the form of a dialogue between Boethius, in a prison which is symbolic of his spiritual condition, and a visionary lady who is a personification of Philosophy and addresses her sick patient in discourse designed to give him fortitude in the indignity and injustice that have befallen him. The setting owes a conscious debt to the *Phaedo* of Plato, where Socrates' prison discourse (I pr.3) contrasts the immortality of the soul with the trivialities of life in a mortal material body and enables him to face the death sentence with total serenity. The dank cell and chains are symbolic of Boethius' all too earthbound mind. The lady Philosophy has a robe embroidered with a ladder connecting the initials Ξ and Π (for 'practical' and 'theoretical', or contemplative), and she will lead him upwards on a gradual ascent. The Π is also the letter on his prison dress standing for Thanatos: he is to die. Gradualism is essential to good medical treatment, and she cannot apply all her remedies at once. The verse passages ease the reader's path but are not presented as light entertainment; the Muses of amusement and love (in his youth Boethius wrote some erotic poems) are sharply dismissed. The poetic sections are in content integrated with the prose argument. In the first four books all the verse is uttered by Boethius; from V.3, Philosophy becomes the poetic speaker, adopting this form of address as a concession to his still weak and frail spiritual condition. However, the verses given to Boethius are also an ascent of the soul. At the central hinge-point of the whole work the famous poem *O qui perpetua* ('You who govern the world by perpetual reason...') – versifies the cosmology of Plato's *Timaeus* interpreted with the help of Proclus' commentary on that dialogue (III m.9).

Book I states Boethius' problem; an innocent person is suffering gross injustice. He complains of the way in which, as in the case of Seneca, a brilliantly successful career at the summit of the administration of government has been shattered by treacherous colleagues among his fellow Roman aristocrats and by the cruel tyranny of Theoderic. However, as the work proceeds Boethius himself fades to become a secondary and background figure, while the real exposition is that of Philosophy. She has to remind him of what he has forgotten, namely that power, wealth and honour are secondary matters at best, useful if they enable the possessor to do good to others but otherwise irrelevant to spiritual wisdom.

The second book uses mainly Stoic themes which had already been domesticated with the Neoplatonic scheme of things in writers such as Hierocles and Proclus. The pain of loss is made endurable by a psychological process of adjusting oneself to accept with resignation what cannot be changed. Those in exile must tell themselves that the wretched place to which they have been sent is home to the people who normally live there. To brood nostalgically for a lost past happiness is a peculiarly awful form of misery. Worldly secular honours are precarious and transient, dependent on others and wholly relative to the limited society in which they happen to be held. A holder of high office becomes a nobody beyond the imperial frontier. A philosopher when insulted should remain silent and not answer back. A wise person knows that in death all human beings are equal. Book 2 ends with a poem in praise of the love which binds together the diverse elements in the cosmos and averts disintegration. Human beings would be happy if only the love by which the stars are ruled could reign in their minds. The poem is a bridge to the third book, which moves from Stoic to Platonic vindications of providence.

The third book, after *O qui perpetua*, seeks to establish the identity of the supreme Good with Good 'than whom nothing better can be thought', employing an Aristotelian argument from the imperfection of every individual good. The ladder of goods, which cannot have an infinite number of steps, has its end in the perfect Good which is also complete happiness. A good person participates in that goodness, which justifies the language of a deification synonymous with salvation. Individual goods give happiness not piecemeal but as a single totality. Boethius sees this principle as pointing to the truth that the supreme good is the One, and from this derives the universal experience of all living things seeking to avert disintegration and to survive by maintaining unity. In the cosmos the forces for disintegration are kept in check by providence; 'whatever holds everything together is what I mean by God' (III 12.25). God is Being itself (*esse*), and evil is a deficiency of being, a nothingness, a privation belonging to an inferiority in the hierarchy of being (see GOD, CONCEPTS OF).

The fourth book depends on Plato's *Gorgias* (470–6): the wicked are the most miserable, and punishment benefits them by purification. Goodness is an essential element in true happiness. To the question as to why providence does not reward the virtuous with good and the wicked with evil, the classic Platonic answer is that virtue is the only really good fortune and is its own reward (see GOOD, THEORIES OF THE §1). That presupposes some freedom of choice, and that in turn raises the question of providence and fate. From Plotinus onwards, the Neoplatonists held that providence controls the higher celestial order of things, while fate is the inexorable chain of cause and effect in this lower world. Like Proclus, Boethius thinks this fate may be controlled by 'angels' (a term as much as home in pagan Neoplatonists as in Christian writers) or by the world-soul or by the stars. The lower one's position in the great chain of being, the more tightly one is bound by fate. Providence is like the unmoved centre of a great wheel or sphere (a simile also in Plotinus and Proclus). Behind all change is the unmoved mover.

The fifth and last book takes Boethius to higher flights in the discussion of providence (see PROVIDENCE). He begins from Aristotle's description of chance (*Physics* II 4–5) as an event with a traceable cause, yet an event falling outside the intention of human wills whose purposes are otherwise. As in the unexpected discovery of buried treasure, the action of digging had different intentions but another chain of causation intervened. For the Neoplatonists and for Boethius, such meetings of independent lines of causation are ultimately under the care of divine providence, not of a blind determinism. 'Luck' or 'fortune' is a way of talking about this hidden power of providence to surprise us. But if that were to mean that every event occurs within a closed system of causes, where is there room for determination by free choice and deliberation? Nature does nothing in vain, and human beings are not for nothing endowed with powers of deliberation enabling them to make choices between different options. This is inherent in being a rational being. Admittedly, Boethius does not think all members of the human race possess equal powers of exercising free choice. Moreover, a Platonist who had also read some Augustine, as Boethius demonstrably had, would not think freedom of choice neutral between truth and error, right and wrong; real freedom is to be liberated from the body's downward pull into error and mistaken judgements. So there are degrees of freedom, higher to those who are contemplating the divine mind, lower to those who slide down to the world of physical senses, reaching complete loss of freedom when vice has damaged the power of reason.

Free choice implies that not all events are wholly predictable. Some are contingent; they might turn out otherwise, and that is difficult to reconcile with perfect foreknowledge. At the initial stage of discussion it seems to Boethius more implausible than it appears to the lady Philosophy to hold that human wills do not make their choices because divine foreknowledge has foreseen them and cannot err, but rather that an omniscient divine foreknowledge foresees what choices human beings will make. After all, to know somebody's character intimately is to predict very accurately how they will react to a situation. *A fortiori* this must be true of the divine being who knows all hearts. Nevertheless, if there is contingency in the choices made, divine foreknowledge will, unthinkably, be in error if the choices are taken to be certain when they are inherently uncertain. To maintain that divine foreknowledge, which by definition cannot err, excludes indeterminacy seems to abolish distinctions of moral value between virtue and vice and undermines any sense in either hope or prayer for the avoidance of disaster. (The reference here to prayer does not step outside the conventions of Neoplatonic language, and does not have to be Christian.) The problem, long ago discussed by Cicero in his book on divination, is declared to be one on which Boethius has bestowed much study. The difficulty is alleviated by recalling that to foresee an event is not causative of its occurrence, that the finite mind is out of its depth when the foreknowledge in question is divine and, crucially, that everything which is known is grasped not according to its inherent nature or power but relative to the capacity of the knowing mind (V 4.25). Foreknowledge of an event is not a sign that an event is absolutely necessary unless there are other causes that bring it about, and to say God knows contingent events to be contingent does not have to mean that because many outcomes are possible even God cannot really know which is will be (see DETERMINISM AND INDETERMINISM; OMNISCIENCE; FREE WILL).

On fate and destiny, Boethius had probably read the tract by ALEXANDER OF APHRODISIAS where the correctness of divine foreknowledge is safeguarded by the proposition that the divine knows the contingent to be contingent and this knowing does not make the uncertain certain. Boethius, however, preferred the argument found in IAMBLICHUS and PROCLUS that divine knowledge is qualitatively quite distinct from human. Events in the temporal process are indeed known to God, but divine knowledge transcends all the successiveness of past, present, and future. Divine knowing is eternal in its mode, and embraces all things and events in simultaneity without the transience inherent in this realm of sense and becoming. To speak of a divine foreknowledge suggests to our finite minds knowing beforehand, in advance. The temporal word 'before' is inapplicable in the case of a time-transcending divine perfection. What is before or after for limited minds is an absolute present (but not a frozen instant) for an eternal knower whose duration is paradoxically both infinite and atemporal. Both in his *De trinitate* and in the last section of the *De consolatione philosophiae*, Boethius stresses that eternity is more than mere perpetuity or everlastingness, but is 'the simultaneous and complete possession of life without limits' (*Interminabilis vitae tota simul et perfecta possessio*). The definition, as Boethius himself says, derives its force from contrast with temporal and finite life. It is not presented as an original reflection, and in fact closely echoes Plotinus and Augustine (see ETERNITY).

Aristotle, therefore, was not mistaken to think that the world had no beginning or end (*On the Heavens* I 12.283b 26), but that does not mean it is eternal. The cosmos can be dependent for its existence on the Creator without thereby being transcendent in relation to the temporal process. This created world is not coeternal with the Creator, as Plato observed in the *Timaeus* (37d). Accordingly, God's knowledge is 'in the simplicity of his present' and imposes no necessity on choices and events in time. Moreover, as Aristotle pointed out in the *Physics* (II 9), 'necessity' is a term with more than one meaning. There is absolute necessity, for example, that all human beings are mortal, or that the sun rises, and there is also conditional necessity: it is necessary that if a man is walking, then he are walking. For Boethius, the kind of necessity attaching to events in the foreknowledge of God is conditional, not absolute. Certain future events which are to occur by the free choice of human wills and which might occur otherwise are, in divine foreknowledge, conditionally necessary. If you change your mind and intention, you do not empty providence; divine prescience knew that that was what you were going to do. (AUGUSTINE in *De civitate Dei* (The City of God) makes the same point: our human wills are included in the causes known to God (V 9)).

6 Influence

Boethius was born into an aristocratic senatorial society concerned to see that the past achievements of Roman culture would not be lost now that the West was controlled by barbarians. He was not the only author to speak the language of Neoplatonism in a way that the medieval world would absorb; that he shared with Calcidius, Martianus Capella, and

Macrobius (see ENCYCLOPEDISTS, MEDIEVAL). Among that company, however, he was distinctive in belonging to a Christian family and in writing influential tractates on controverted theological questions. His masterpiece, *De consolatione philosophiae*, presented the theodicy of Proclus as a flying buttress to a religious statement compatible with Christian belief. This work, taken together with his translations and commentaries, taught the medieval West its first steps in logic and the meaning of inference.

In the ninth century, the Carolingian educational programme gave special prominence to *De consolatione philosophiae* as a medium for the teaching of prose and poetry, and this drew attention to the *Opuscula sacra* as well. The surviving manuscripts of Boethius written in the Carolingian age are reasonably numerous (see CAROLINGIAN RENAISSANCE). Remigius of Auxerre was first to write a commentary on the tract on the Trinity, the first of the five *Opuscula*. However, it was in the twelfth century that these theological tractates rose to a rank of authority. They also came to stimulate controversy. This was largely because of Gilbert de la Porrée, who became bishop of Poitiers and caused alarm both by his catechetical teaching and his commentaries on four of the *Opuscula* (omitting *De fide catholica*) (see GILBERT OF POITIERS). Conservatively minded critics were frightened when a clever logician began applying Boethian methods of argument to such transcendent subjects as the Trinity and the person of Christ. It made them anxious to be told that without qualification the divine essence is not to be called God, or that it was muddled to say that the divine nature was made flesh and assumed our human nature.

In the same century, THIERRY OF CHARTRES more cautiously commented only on the first of the *Opuscula* (*De trinitate*) and on the highly Neoplatonic third which the medievals called *De hebdomadibus*. CLAREMBALD OF ARRAS joined the critics of Gilbert, also commenting on the two tractates chosen by Thierry. The consequence of these debates, in which Thomas AQUINAS was to participate in the next century, was to insert into the consciousness of the Latin West a sharper awareness of some problems inherent in the logic of traditional Christian language about God, and at the same time to arouse among the less dialectical faithful a sense of disapprobation of theologians who knew more about Boethius than about the apostles.

See also: ENCYCLOPEDISTS, MEDIEVAL §5; GOD, CONCEPTS OF; LOGIC, MEDIEVAL; MEDIEVAL PHILOSOPHY; NATURAL PHILOSOPHY, MEDIEVAL §1; NEOPLATONISM; PATRISTIC PHILOSOPHY; PLATONISM, MEDIEVAL; PLOTINUS; PORPHYRY

List of works

Boethius, Anicius Manlius Severinus (*c.*480–525/6) translations of Aristotle, ed. L. Minio-Paluello, *Aristotles Latinus*, vols I–VI (vol. VI ed. B. Dod), Bruges: Desclée de Brouwer, 1966–75. (Collected editions of Boethius' translations of Aristotle's works.)

—— (*c.*480–525/6) *In Isagogen Porphyrii commenta* (Commentaries on Porphyry's *Isagōgē*), ed. S. Brandt, Corpus Scriptorum Ecclesiasticorum Latinorum 48, Vienna: Tempsky, 1906. (Includes the commentaries based on the translation by Marius Victorinus and that of Boethius himself.)

—— (*c.*480–525/6) Commentary on Aristotle's *Categories*, in J.-P. Migne (ed.) *Patrologia Latina*, vol. 64, Paris, 1860. (Boethius' commentary uses the translation of Marius Victorinus as its base; he also produced his own translation.)

—— (*c.*480–525/6) Two Commentaries on Aristotle's *De interpretatione*, ed. R. Meiser, *Anicii Manlii Severini Boetii in librum Aristotelis Peri hermeneias*, Leipzig: Teubner, 1877–80, 2 vols. (One commentary is full-length, the other is shorter and simpler.)

—— (*c.*480–525/6) Notes on *Prior Analytics*, in L. Minio-Paluello (ed.) *Aristoteles Latinus*, vol. III, Bruges: Desclée de Brouwer, 1965. (Notes which accompanied Boethius' translation of the *Prior Analytics*.)

—— (*c.*480–525/6) *In Ciceronis Topica* (Commentary on Cicero's *Topics*), in J.C. Orelli and J.G. Baiter (eds) *Ciceronis Opera*, Vol. V, part 1, Zurich: Fuesslini, 1833; trans. E. Stump, *Boethius's In Ciceronis Topica*, Ithaca, NY: Cornell University Press, 1988. (This commentary has been transmitted incomplete.)

—— (*c.*480–525/6) *De hypotheticis syllogismis* (On Hypothetical Syllogisms), ed. L. Obertello, Brescia: Paideia, 1969. (A Greek paraphrase by Maximos Holobolos (*fl.* 1261–80) is edited by D.Z. Nikitas in *Eine byzantinische Übersetzung von Boethius' 'De hypotheticis syllogismis'*, Göttingen: Vandenhoeck & Rupprecht, 1982.)

—— (*c.*480–525/6) *De divisione* (On Division), in J.-P. Migne (ed.), *Patrologia Latina*, vol. 64, Paris, 1860; trans. E. Stump and N. Kretzmann in *The Cambridge Translations of Medieval Philosophical Texts* I, Cambridge: Cambridge University Press, 1988. (On the classification of ideas.)

—— (*c.*480–525/6) *De syllogismo categorico* (On Categorical Syllogism), in J.-P. Migne (ed.) *Patrologia Latina*, vol. 64, Paris, 1860. (Expounds on the *Prior Analytics*.)

—— (*c.*480–525/6) *Introductio ad syllogismos categoricos* (Introduction to Categorical Syllogisms), in J.-

P. Migne (ed.) *Patrologia Latina*, vol. 64, Paris, 1860. (Shorter work on categorical syllogisms.)

—— (c.480–525/6) *De topicis differentiis* (On Topical Differences), in J.-P. Migne (ed.) *Patrologia Latina*, vol. 64, Paris, 1860; trans. E. Stump, *Boethius's De topicis differentiis*, Ithaca, NY: Cornell University Press, 1978. (Boethius' own writings on topical differences.)

—— (c.480–525/6) *Opuscula sacra* (Theological Tractates), ed. and trans. H.F. Stewart, E.K. Rand and S.J. Tester, *Boethius: Theological Tractates, Consolation of Philosophy*, Cambridge, MA: Harvard University Press, 1973; ed. and trans. M. Elsässer, *Die Theologischen Traktate*, Hamburg: Felix Meiner, 1988; trans. H. Merle, *Court traités de theologie*, Paris: Éditions du Cerf, 1991. (Elsässer's German translation has good notes. Merle's French translation is annotated, without the Latin text.)

—— (c.480–525/6) *De consolatione philosophiae* (The Consolation of Philosophy), ed. and trans. H.F. Stewart, E.K. Rand and S.J. Tester, *Boethius: Theological Tractates, Consolation of Philosophy*, Cambridge, MA: Harvard University Press, 1973; ed. L. Bieler, Corpus Christianorum, Series Latina 94, Turnhout: Brepols, 1957; ed. J.J. O'Donnell, *Boethius Consolatio Philosophiae*, Bryn Mawr Latin Commentaries, Bryn Mawr, PA: Bryn Mawr College, 1984. (Part of Books IV and V are edited with English translation and good commentary by R.W. Sharples in *Cicero: On Fate (De Fato) & Boethius: The Consolation of Philosophy (Philosophiae consolationis) IV 5–7, V*, Warminster: Aris & Phillips, 1991. For an English translation only, see V.E. Watts, *The Consolation of Philosophy*, Baltimore, MD: Penguin, 1969.)

—— (c.480–525/6) Introductions to *Arithmetic* and *Music*, ed. G. Friedlein, *De institutione arithmetica libri duo, De institutione musica libri quinque*, Leipzig: Teubner, 1867. (Boethius' works are adaptations of earlier works by Nicomachus of Geras; see §2.)

References and further reading

Chadwick, H. (1981) *Boethius, the Consolations of Music, Logic, Theology and Philosophy*, Oxford: Clarendon Press; Italian translation, Bologna: Mulino, 1986. (Describes Boethius' works in relation to the historical context of his life and to the intellectual background of his philosophical writings, with bibliography.)

Courcelle, P. (1967) *La Consolation du philosophie dans la tradition littéraire, antécédents et posterité de Boèce* (The Consolation of Philosophy in Literary Tradition, Antecedents and Influence of Boethius), Paris: Études Augustiniennes. (Demonstrates the neoplatonic character of the *Consolatio*, and traces some of its later influence; a work of great erudition.)

Daley, B.E. (1984) 'Boethius' Theological Tractates and Early Byzantine Scholasticism', *Medieval Studies* 46: 158–91. (On the relation between the Tractates and the arguments of Byzantine schoolmen.)

Ebbesen, S. (1990) 'Boethius as an Aristotelian commentator', in R. Sorabji (ed.) *Aristotle Transformed*, London: Duckworth, 373–92. (Clear analysis by a logician.)

Fuhrmann, M. and Gruber, J. (eds) (1984) *Boethius*, Wege der Forschung 483, Darmstadt: Wissenschaftliche Buchgesellschaft. (Gathers twenty-three papers of major importance from journals.)

Gibson, M.T. (ed.) (1981) *Boethius, His Life, Thought and Influence*, Oxford: Blackwell. (A symposium of different authors, more on Boethius' influence than on his contemporary setting.)

Gibson, M.T. and Smith, L. (eds) (1995) *Codices Boethiani: A Conspectus of Manuscripts of the Work of Boethius*, London: University of London, The Warburg Institute. (Illuminating on Boethius' influence on medieval culture.)

Gruber, J. (1978) *Kommentar zu Boethius de Consolatione Philosophiae* (Commentary on Boethius' Consolation of Philosophy), Berlin: de Gruyter. (Masterly on the literary side, indispensable on the detail of its structure.)

Kneale, W.C. and Kneale, M. (1981) *The Development of Logic*, Oxford: Clarendon Press, 1981. (Boethius' place in the history of logic.)

Kretzmann, N. (1987) 'Boethius and the Truth about Tomorrow's Sea Battle', in *Logos and Pragma, Essays on the Philosophy of Language in Honour of Gabriel Nuchelmans*, Nijmegen, *Aristarium* suppl. 3, 53–87. (On the exposition of Aristotle's *De interpretatione* IX.)

Lerer, S. (1985) *Boethius and Dialogue: Literary Method in the Consolation of Philosophy*, Princeton, NJ: Princeton University Press. (Applies modern techniques of literary criticism.)

Magee, J. (1989) *Boethius on Signification and Mind*, Philosophia Antiqua 52, Leiden: Brill. (Detailed examination of the commentaries on Aristotle's *De interpretatione*.)

Marenbon, J. (1983) *Early Medieval Philosophy (480–1150), An Introduction*, London: Routledge & Kegan Paul. (Clear and short.)

Masi, M. (ed.) (1981) *Boethius and the Liberal Arts*, Berne: Peter Lang. (A valuable symposium.)

Minnis, A.J. (ed.) (1987) *The Medieval Boethius*,

Cambridge: D.S. Brewer. (Important studies of the versions of the *Consolatio*.)

Obertello, L. (1974) *Severino Boezio*, Genoa: Accademia Ligure di scienze e lettere, 2 vols. (Authoritative general study with full bibliography.)

O'Daly, G.P.D. (1991) *The Poetry of Boethius*, London: Duckworth. (A major study of the verse sections of *De consolatione philosophiae*.)

Patch, H.R. (1935) *The Tradition of Boethius*, New York: Oxford University Press. (On the influence of Boethius.)

Reiss, E. (1982) *Boethius*, Boston: Twayne. (Reliable biography.)

Rijk, L.M. de (1964) 'On the Chronology of Boethius' Works on Logic', *Vivarium* 2: 1–49. (Gives the chronology of Boethius' logical works.)

Schurr, V. (1935) *Die Trinitätslehre des Boethius im Lichte der Skythischen Kontroversen* (The Trinitarian Doctrine of Boethius in the Light of the Scythian Controversies), Paderborn, 1935. (A pioneer exploration of the Aristotelian and Neoplatonic background of the *Opuscula sacra*.)

* Shiel, J. (1958) 'Boethius' Commentaries on Aristotle', *Medieval and Renaissance Studies* 4: 217–44; repr. in M. Fuhrmann and J. Gruber (eds) *Boethius*, Wege der Forschung 483, Darmstadt: Wissenschaftliche Buchgesellschaft, 1984; repr. in R. Sorabji, (ed.) *Aristotle Transformed*, London: Duckworth, 1990. (Acute conjectures about Boethius' philosophical works.)

Sorabji, R. (1980) *Necessity, Cause and Blame*, London: Duckworth. (Analysis of questions basic to Boethius' writings on *De interpretatione*.)

—— (ed.) (1990) *Aristotle Transformed*, London: Duckworth. (On the Neoplatonic commentaries.)

Stump, E. and Kretzmann, N. (1981) 'Eternity', *The Journal of Philosophy* 78: 429–57. (Careful philosophical analysis of the idea.)

HENRY CHADWICK

BOETHIUS OF DACIA
(*fl. c.*1275)

Boethius developed an original theory of scientific knowledge designed to reconcile science with Christian doctrine without allowing one to determine the contents of the other. His main strategy was to consider each science as an independent system of axioms and theorems while also operating with a hierarchy of causes, the highest of which (God) is fundamentally unpredictable as to its operations. Boethius did, however, stress the powers of the human intellect and the possibility of reaching happiness through rational understanding; he vigorously objected to demands that natural science should adapt its axioms to the demands of Christian faith. This laid him open to suspicions of heresy. Boethius' work on grammar is the most complete application of his ideas of how to construct a science.

1 Life and works
2 Ethics, theory of knowledge and science
3 Grammar

1 Life and works

All information about Boethius' life before 1277 is contained in the number and nature of his extant or attested writings, and in the title and the epithet accompanying his name in medieval sources, 'Magister Boethius de Dacia' or 'Dacus', which identifies him as a Dane. All his works, whether preserved or only attested, are such as a medieval master of arts would produce. Their number and quality suggest a rather long career, starting perhaps about 1265. If he was a master of arts by then, he cannot have been born much later than 1240.

Among his surviving works, the best known are the treatises *De summo bono* (On the Highest Good) and *De aeternitate mundi* (On the Eternity of the World). However, there are a number of extant works in other fields, including logic (a sophisma on meaning, truth and knowledge, and *Quaestiones super librum Topicorum* (Questions on Aristotle's *Topics*), natural philosophy (questions on Aristotle's *Physics* and *On Generation and Corruption* – the extant version of the questions is a reworking by someone else of Boethian material) and grammar (a sophisma, *Quaestiones super Priscianum maiorem* (Questions on Priscian)). His questions on Aristotle's *Metaphysics* has been lost, but passages borrowed from it seem to be preserved in a near-contemporary anonymous work. Boethius also wrote one of the very first Latin commentaries on Aristotle's *Rhetoric*, which appears to be irretrievably lost.

During the 1270s, Boethius taught at the University of Paris. In 1277, Etienne Tempier, Bishop of Paris, accused unnamed masters in the faculty of arts of propagating un-Christian doctrines and specifically prohibited the teaching of any of 219 theses (see ARISTOTELIANISM, MEDIEVAL). Many of these theses were extracted from Boethius' works. It is the general, but unproven, assumption that he was still at Paris at the time of the condemnation of 1277, and that this event halted his university career. He may have sought a new life among the Dominican Order, for although he was almost certainly a secular during his regency (active professorship) in arts, his works occur in a medieval catalogue of books composed by Dominicans. Some of his books and ideas lived on, but Boethius himself was soon forgotten; only in the twentieth century has he re-emerged as an important figure in the history of philosophy.

2 Ethics, theory of knowledge and science

Boethius was an epistemological optimist. Real knowledge, even some knowledge about the First Cause, he thought, is within human grasp. The full realization of human nature, happiness, is the philosopher's life in which all lower powers are directed towards the supreme activity, the contemplation of truth, and of the First Truth in particular. By contrast, the layman's uncontemplative life is only quasi-human. As was common in his day, Boethius assumed a hierarchical structure of reality in which beings can be arranged on a scale according to their proximity to the First Cause. His philosopher first achieves an insight into the causal structures of the material (sublunary) world and thence proceeds to an understanding of higher forms of being, which are causes in relation to the lower ones. Eventually he arrives at the contemplation of the First Object of Knowledge, the First Cause.

Such intellectualism was not unusual for the time. Boethius' peculiar contribution was the way he connected it with a theory of science, based on Aristotle (in particular on his *Posterior Analytics*) but also inspired by the stylized disputations of thirteenth-century university life. To Boethius, the objects of knowledge are 'things with regard to their causes', not simply individual things nor hypostasized quiddities (or essences), for he would accept no uninstantiated quiddities. The proposition 'every human being is an animate being' expresses a piece of knowledge about the (formal) cause of human beings, but since the existence of humans is contingent, Boethius claimed that the proposition is false unless taken to mean 'supposing there exists at least one human being, it is true that every human being is an animate being'. Scientific propositions are only conditionally true, on the presupposition that their subject terms have referents, and in the natural sciences this presupposition could fail to be satisfied.

Each science has its own primitive terms and propositions, and each science incorporates insight into one causal network. However, one thing may enter into more than one network and one type of cause may annihilate the effect of another. To Boethius, scientific activity was similar to participation in a rule-governed university disputation in which a proposition should be granted or denied according to whether it cohered or not with certain other propositions, rather than on the basis of correspondence with external facts. He held that as long as one works within some particular science, A, one should grant any theorem properly derived from the axioms of A and deny any proposition inconsistent with them. The tacit presupposition is that there are such things as the objects of science A, and that only the causal mechanisms known through A are at work. In actual fact foreign causal mechanisms, known perhaps to science B, may prevent the predictions of A from corresponding to reality. Boethius may be said to have held a coherence theory of truth within a science, and a correspondence theory of truth simpliciter (see TRUTH, COHERENCE THEORY OF; TRUTH, CORRESPONDENCE THEORY OF).

The hierarchy of entities and causes provides an explanation of why the work of lower causes can be frustrated by higher ones, and why the assumption of a divine free will makes the First Cause not totally transparent. Consequently, it is not possible to unify all sciences into one science of the First Cause (see CAUSATION).

In Boethius' view, it follows that the same person can consistently hold that it is a truth of natural science that every human being had a father and mother, and a revealed truth that there was a first couple of humans with no parents. The revealed truths are truths simpliciter, but truths knowable only thanks to revelation cannot be incorporated into scientific theories on pain of inconsistency. In this way Boethius tried to solve one of the burning questions of his day, how to reconcile faith and natural science, which seemed to clash over the question whether there can have been a beginning of the world as a whole and of natural species. Standard theology took the doctrine of creation to imply that the world is not infinitely old; standard science implied the contrary (see CREATION AND CONSERVATION, RELIGIOUS DOCTRINE OF; ETERNITY OF THE WORLD, MEDIEVAL VIEWS OF; NATURAL PHILOSOPHY, MEDIEVAL).

3 Grammar

We see Boethius' theory of science at work in his grammar. Grammar, he held, deals with the ways humans can express what their minds have grasped. Concepts have a core corresponding to the core, or 'common nature', of real entities, attended by 'modes of understanding' corresponding to 'modes of being' of the common nature, that is, ways in which it can manifest itself. The linguistic expression of a concept has a core, the significate (what is signified) attended by modes of signifying. For example, if someone's back is aching, the pain is in one way something static like a substance and can carry accidental properties: thus it can be more or less acute. In another way, the pain is an accidental entity in the process of actualization. Pain 'is' in both ways, and is conceptualized in both ways; it is also signified in both ways, statically by the noun 'a pain', processively by the verb 'to ache'.

It is none of the grammarian's business to investigate what things there are or what properties they have; grammaticality is not measured by correspondence with the external world, so a grammatical explanation must never appeal to properties of the significate of a word. Nor can grammar establish the inventory of modes of signifying; they are a function of the modes of understanding which in turn are a function of the modal structure of extramental reality. To the grammarian, the modes of signifying are primitive terms. Neither can the grammarian predict what sounds will embody the significates and the modes of signifying. Any sound may conventionally represent any significate or mode of signifying, and languages may vary considerably; thus Greek (Boethius mistakenly thought) uses separate words (articles) to express what in Latin is expressed by the inflexion of nouns (case, number). What a Boethian grammarian can do is formulate the rules governing which combinations of modes of signifying yield well-formed sentences if instantiated. The rules of grammar are independent of the existence of any sentence of any language, but no actual sentence in any language can be fully intelligible if it breaks the rules (see LANGUAGE, MEDIEVAL THEORIES OF; LANGUAGE, PHILOSOPHY OF §15). By strictly separating grammar from metaphysics, psychology and other sciences, Boethius tried to transform it into a formal discipline like geometry or logic, unshakeable by any contingent fact but also unable to support deductions about the extralinguistic world.

See also: ARISTOTELIANISM, MEDIEVAL; AVERROISM; LANGUAGE, MEDIEVAL THEORIES OF; NATURAL PHILOSOPHY, MEDIEVAL §7; SIGER OF BRABANT

List of works

Boethius of Dacia [Boethius Dacus] (*c.*1275) *Opera*, ed. J. Pinborg, H. Roos, N.J. Green-Pedersen, S. Ebbesen and I. Rosier, Corpus Philosophorum Danicorum Medii Aevi vols IV–IX, Copenhagen: DSL/Gad, 1969–. (Vol. IX, *Sophismata*, has not yet appeared.)
—— (*c.*1275) *De summo bono* (On the Supreme Good), ed. N.J. Green-Pedersen in *Opera*, vol. VI, Copenhagen: DSL/Gad, 1976; trans. J.F. Wippel, *On the Supreme Good. On the Eternity of the World. On Dreams*, Mediaeval Sources in Translation 30, Toronto, Ont.: Pontifical Institute of Mediaeval Studies, 1987. (Boethius' major work on the good.)
—— (*c.*1275) *De aeternitate mundi* (On the Eternity of the World), ed. N.J. Green-Pedersen in *Opera*, vol. VI, Copenhagen: DSL/Gad, 1976; trans. J.F. Wippel, *On the Supreme Good. On the Eternity of the world. On Dreams*, Mediaeval Sources in Translation 30, Toronto, Ont.: Pontifical Institute of Mediaeval Studies, 1987. (Boethius' important work on eternity.)
—— (*c.*1275) *Quaestiones super librum Topicorum* (Questions on Aristotle's *Topics*), ed. N.J. Green-Pedersen and J. Pinborg in *Opera*, vol. VI, Copenhagen: DSL/Gad, 1976. (Boethius' major logical work.)
—— (*c.*1275) *De somniis* (On Dreams), ed. N.J. Green-Pedersen in *Opera*, vol. VI, Copenhagen: DSL/Gad, 1976; trans. J.F. Wippel, *On the Supreme Good. On the Eternity of the World. On Dreams*, Mediaeval Sources in Translation 30, Toronto, Ont.: Pontifical Institute of Mediaeval Studies, 1987. (Boethius on natural philosophy.)
—— (*c.*1275) *Quaestiones super libros Physicorum* (Questions on Aristotle's *Physics*), ed. G. Sajó in *Opera*, vol. V.2, Copenhagen: DSL/Gad, 1974. (Boethius on natural philosophy.)
—— (*c.*1275) *Quaestiones de generatione et corruptione* (Questions on *Generation and Corruption*), ed. G. Sajó in *Opera*, vol. V.1, Copenhagen: DSL/Gad, 1972. (Boethius on natural philosophy.)
—— (*c.*1275) *Quaestiones super Priscianum maiorem* (Questions on Priscian Major), ed. J. Pinborg and H. Roos in *Opera*, vol. IV, Copenhagen: DSL/Gad, 1969; trans. A.C. Senape McDermott, *Godfrey of Fontaine's Abridgement of Boethius of Dacia's Modi Significandi sive Quaestiones super Priscianum Majorem*, Amsterdam Studies in the Theory and History of Linguistic Science, Series III, Studies in the History of Linguistics vol. 22, Amsterdam: Benjamins, 1980. (Work on grammar which shows Boethius' philosophy of science at work.)

References and further reading

Kretzmann, N. and Stump, E. (1988) *Logic and the Philosophy of Language*, Cambridge Translations of Medieval Philosophical Texts 1, Cambridge: Cambridge University Press. (Contains translation of a part of *Sophisma* I.)
Marmo, C. (1994) *Semiotica e linguaggio nella scolastica: Parigi, Bologna, Erfurt 1270–1330* (Semiotics and Language in Scholasticism: Paris, Bologna, Erfurt 1270–1330), Rome: Istituto Storico

Italiano per il Medio Evo. (A large-scale study of modism, drawing on both grammatical and logical sources.)

Pinborg, J. (1967) *Die Entwicklung der Sprachtheorie im Mittelalter* (The Development of Theory of Language in the Middle Ages), Beiträge zur Geschichte der Philosophie und Theologie des Mittelalters, Texte und Untersuchungen 42.2, Münster: Ashendorff, and Copenhagen: Frost-Hansen. (A pioneering and authoritative study of modistic grammar.)

—— (1972) *Logik und Semantik im Mittelalter. Ein Überblick* (Logic and Semantics in the Middle Ages: A Survey), Stuttgart: Frommann-Holzboog. (Discusses Boethius' views on several matters.)

—— (1984) *Medieval Semantics, Selected Studies on Medieval Logic and Grammar*, ed. S. Ebbesen, London: Variorum. (Several relevant papers, including 'Zur Philosophie des Boethius de Dacia, Ein Überblick'.)

STEN EBBESEN

BOGDANOV, ALEKSANDR ALEKSANDROVICH (1873–1928)

Aleksandr Aleksandrovich Bogdanov, né Malinovskii, was a Russian thinker who helped Lenin create the Bolshevik or Communist Party, broke with Lenin over a mixture of philosophical and political issues, yet would not quit the Revolution. His life and thought illuminate the interaction of philosophy and politics within the tumultuous context of a 'developing' country, which calls in question political philosophies that take for granted the conditions of 'developed' countries.

Bogdanov never won such widespread interest as those dissident communists – Georg Lukács, most notably – who turned Marxism away from claims of science towards theories of consciousness and wilful action. Bogdanov sought a positivist basis for his philosophy of action or practice. He offered 'empiriomonism' and 'organizational science' to creators of a 'free collectivism', but the creators of the Soviet system brushed him aside. He has been studied by scholars who wonder why the Russian Revolution – or twentieth-century revolutions in many developing countries – have failed to realize dreams of justice and freedom, and by a different cluster of scholars who conceive of a metascience that might unify the fragmented world of knowledge. Less known is Bogdanov's sense of tragic contradictions in revolutionary pragmatism, as we may call active belief in Marx's famous declaration that the point of philosophizing is not merely to interpret the world but to change it.

1, 2 Life and thought
3   Reception and significance

1 Life and thought

'Spiteful stupid administrators', who ran a provincial boarding school as a 'barracks, a jailhouse', taught young Bogdanov to 'fear and hate those who rule, to reject authorities', he reports in his 'Avtobiografiia' (Autobiography) (1926). Pragmatism – in the mundane sense of adapting to things as they are – must have tempered his fearful hatred, for he won a gold medal from those administrators, and then a degree in natural science at Moscow University, though revolutionary activity caused his student career to be interrupted by arrest and banishment from the capital. He also earned a medical degree, and intermittently worked as a physician for the rest of his life. Constant involvement in revolutionary propaganda brought repeated periods in jail and banishment, which gave him leisure to study and write. At the outset he was a populist of the 'People's Will' persuasion, believing in heroic action as the way to a just and prosperous Russia, but he soon turned to the Marxist or positivist belief that science reveals the way forward. He began a lifelong outpouring of publications with *Kratkii kurs ekonomicheskoi nauki* (*A Short Course of Economic Science*) (1897), which won high praise from the young Lenin and became a widely used textbook in Marxist circles.

Acting as a propagandist among provincial workers, Bogdanov discovered their need for a worldview, and responded with *Osnovnye elementy istoricheskogo vzgliada na prirodu* (Basic Elements of the Historical View of Nature) (1899). The most basic 'element' in this view was energy, Ostwald's substitute for the matter-and-force of mechanical or vulgar materialism. This book also won the admiration of LENIN, who failed to perceive the difference from the materialism, dialectical and historical, which he admired in the works of PLEKHANOV, 'the father of Russian Marxism'. By the time that Lenin learned the difference – talking with Plekhanov in Swiss exile – Bogdanov and he had become leaders of the emergent Bolshevik faction within the Russian Social Democratic Party. Though Plekhanov was a major figure in the rival Menshevik faction, Lenin still considered him the greatest teacher of orthodox Marxist philosophy. Bogdanov sneered at such orthodoxy as a fetish, not the philosophy of science that it claimed to be. That he found in a wide array of thinkers, including Nietzsche, and especially MACH, whose empiriocriticism he refashioned as empiriomonism, to unify all types of knowledge and action (see RUSSIAN EMPIRIOCRITICISM §2).

This disarray in political and philosophical commitments did not prevent Lenin and Bogdanov from joint action through the first Russian revolution in 1905–6. Their Bolshevik faction pressed the Russian Social Democratic Party towards more aggressive policies than the Mensheviks favoured, and thereby pushed towards a formal split into separate parties. When the Tsar's government had succeeded in putting down the first Russian Revolution, and Russian Marxists retreated from the politics of mass action to the quarrels of underground cells and exile circles, Lenin wrote *Materializm i ėmpiriokrititsizm* (Materialism and Empiriocriticism) (1909). It was a vituperative attack on Bogdanov and the other Marxists who had been drawing on Mach to remedy the movement's lack of proper philosophical grounding. Bogdanov responded with a counterattack on Lenin, *Padenie velikogo fetishizma; Vera i nauka* (The Fall of a Great Fetishism; Faith and Science) (1910), as he had earlier responded to Menshevik attacks with *Prikliucheniia odnoi filosofskoi shkoly* (The Adventures of a Philosophical School) (1908a). Efforts to draw German notables into these disputes provoked illuminating refusals. In a private letter Mach declared his 'social democratic' sympathies to be separate from the philosophizing that he did in public, while KAUTSKY, the chief theorist of German Marxism, saw things the other way round: not politics but philosophy was a matter of individual taste – separate from the 'public sphere', he might have said, had he known a buzzword that German Marxism would generate later on.

One common way to sort out political from philosophical issues in the polemics of Russian Marxists is to blame Lenin's fanaticism for entangling two realms of discourse that would otherwise have been as civilly separated in Russia as in the West. This interpretation ignores the pattern of entanglement that preceded Lenin's outburst, and caused it. Empiriocriticism was linked with Bolshevik theorists, materialist orthodoxy with Mensheviks, and the correlation seemed logical. To ground Marxism in historical materialism, pointing to long-term social processes that determine human thought and action, seemed to support the go-slow politics of the Mensheviks, while emphasis on the active role of collective mentalities in ordering experience seemed to favour the urgent push to revolt that the Bolsheviks advocated. That scheme, presented to Western comrades by Bogdanov's article, 'Ernst Mach und die Revolution' (Ernst Mach and the Revolution) (1908b), in the major journal of German Social Democracy, was becoming conventional wisdom in Marxist circles. Lenin's outburst was designed to prove that his party was *not* revisionist but orthodox, as all true Marxists must be.

At a showdown meeting of Bolshevik leaders in 1909 Bogdanov and Lunacharskii mocked the push to establish a party line in philosophy. Lenin denied that he was doing any such thing, while pressing for expulsion of the unorthodox. Bogdanov tried to gain acknowledgement of the inconsistency, in vain. He was expelled from the Bolshevik organization, and intensified his warning against 'fetishism' – formulaic idolatry in place of creative theory – and against 'vampirism' – the desiccation of revolutionary thought by worship of formulas. His polemics against Lenin and Plekhanov declared them to be victims of 'the Vampire', which appeared in a novel of Bogdanov's as a hectoring monster within the revolutionary hero's mind, in a melodramatic imitation of the Devil appearing to Ivan Karamazov.

'Dilettantism' was Trotsky's diagnostic label for superficial pretensions of unifying knowledge and action, when knowledge is actually fragmented in professional disciplines apart from the Marxists' realm of political action. Trotsky himself was hardly immune. He wrote on almost as many topics as Bogdanov, from a supposedly Marxist viewpoint, and accepted an invitation to lecture at a school for revolutionaries that Bogdanov's group established on Capri, where the famous writer Gor'kii provided a haven. Bogdanov soon found there the same 'authoritarianism' that he opposed in the party high command. In a letter of resignation he noted his lifelong struggle 'against two enemies, authoritarianism and individualism, and the former is the more hateful to me'. By 1911 he announced his withdrawal from politics altogether, in favour of 'cultural' and 'scientific' work. He meant separation from any political party; his understanding of culture was thoroughly politicized in the broad sense of both terms.

2 Life and thought (cont.)

Brooding over the revolutionary passions of the lower classes, which promised imminent overthrow of the existing system, while their cultural backwardness portended their inability to use power effectively, Bogdanov began preaching the need to develop 'proletarian culture'. He was thinking by analogy with the flowering of bourgeois culture *before* the French Revolution brought the bourgeoisie to power. Lenin expressed a more wilful belief in practice as the criterion of truth. He asked why the Party might not mobilize lower-class anger to overthrow the rule of landlords and capitalists, and *then* have the 'cultural revolution' that would enable any cook to manage public affairs. Both men perceived the lower-class nature of the imminent revolution, and both took it for granted that a vanguard party must guide the masses, but Bogdanov was concerned to foster a 'free collectivism' at every level. Hence his paradoxical efforts to combine a sceptical epistemology with a totalizing worldview.

That dream was central both to his philosophy of 'empiriomonism' and to his 'organizational science' or 'tektology'. He emphasized the philosophy in publications of 1903–9, the science afterward, as he 'moved to a decisive recognition of "the decline of philosophy"', of transition to construction of a purely scientific monism' ([1913] 1923: 328). The 'purely scientific monism', expounded in three volumes of *Tektologiia: Vseobshchaia organizatsionnaia nauka* (Tektology: The Universal Organizational Science), (1913–25), drew its title from Haeckel, and its central thesis from Le Chatelier. Assuming 'equilibrium' to be inherent in all systems, mental and social as well as biological and mechanical, Bogdanov offered rules of 'organization' that could serve for scientific management in all spheres.

In 1917 mass revolt broke up the tsarist system and opened the way for Lenin's establishment of a Soviet state ruled by the Communist Party. The quarrels of émigré intellectuals shrank in significance and dissidents rejoined the Party to serve the victorious revolution, but Bogdanov declined to do so. He published gloomy criticisms of Lenin's policies in 1917–18, which he never retracted, though he stayed in Russia to help the cause. In a letter to Lunacharskii, declining the offer of a post in the Commissariat of Enlightenment, Bogdanov explained why he could neither join the new regime nor work against it. He found a repulsive distortion of socialism 'in the often absurd but almost always *compulsory* things that are done in your regime. I not only see, but think that *you* see the tragic quality [*tragizm*] of your situation' (1990: 352; original emphases). He summed up the tragedy with an aphorism: 'A situation is often stronger than logic' (1990: 355) – which implicitly challenged his lifelong faith in pragmatic reason fused with collective action, but he left the implication unexamined. He simply chose to stay in 'the wearisome isolation of a sighted person among the blind', doing 'cultural and scholarly' preparation for revival of a genuinely socialist party. One may call that a tragic version of revolutionary pragmatism, with only a trace of the usual reassurance that present defeat must surely turn into future triumph since scientific revolutionaries know what the future must bring.

Bogdanov's philosophizing about knowing and acting usually emphasized some version of that reassurance – most melodramatically through the mouth of a novelistic heroine: 'In order to wage the struggle one must know the future', which Bogdanov's *Krasnaia zvezda* (*Red Star*) (1908) laid out in utopian detail. But he could also express dark suggestions that the struggle for justice and freedom may be a losing gamble.

For a time, 1918–20, he was a leader of 'Proletarian Culture' or Proletcult – a network of study circles, art studios and theatre companies, bringing traditional knowledge and skills to the masses while also developing their capacities to overcome the hegemony of bourgeois culture. Lenin was initially sympathetic, but he insisted that the movement must accept subordination to the new regime. Proletcult refused, and was shut down. Bogdanov thereafter confined his activities to the newly established Communist Academy, which published his works in philosophy and social science, and to experiments in blood transfusion at a new institute directed by himself. An official campaign against his philosophy during the drive to suppress Proletcult had put 'Bogdanovism' out of bounds for Soviet Marxists even in the relatively free 1920s. Logically, his views should have been central to the debate between neo-Hegelian and neo-positivist interpretations of Marxist philosophy, but the neo-positivists' affinity with an outright critic of Lenin had become a political smear, to be hurled or dodged without serious discussion of the critic's arguments. Thus his warnings against philosophy desiccated by idolatry fell against a wall of silence, erected by an ideological bureaucracy seeking formulas for a confessional Marxism.

The most poignant irony of this situation was the pragmatism that all these Marxists shared but could not openly acknowledge or freely debate. They all agreed that practice is the criterion of truth, that the way forward is through collective action based on 'the lessons of practice'. As the ideological establishment read the lessons, an obvious inference emerged: since Lenin was the supremely practical leader of the successful revolution, he must also be considered the supreme philosopher. The next step, the extension of that pragmatic logic to Stalin worship, would be taken in 1929–30, but Bogdanov did not live to see it. In 1928 he submitted his body to an exchange of all its blood for that of a man suffering from malaria and consumption, and died. No direct evidence of suicidal intent has come to light, though one notes that suicide was a debatable issue, not a taboo, in Bogdanov's philosophizing. The official eulogies described his experiment as heroic self-sacrifice for the advancement of science, but that did not rescue his philosophy from the limbo of enemy doctrines, recalled only to be reviled.

3 Reception and significance

Khrushchev's reforms of the 1950s and early 1960s revived a vision of socialism as a freely self-regulating system, but the most practical visionaries drew on mathematical economics rather than Bogdanov's legacy. Memory of Bogdanov's tektology, as a precursor of cybernetics and systems theory, cropped up in talk of improving the Soviet system by a 'scientific technological revolution' – fuzzy talk that served to evade serious engagement with the mounting problems of a command economy and an ideology that stifled thought. Bogdanov's mockery of 'fetishism' and 'vampirism', and his insistence on free collectivism, were not recalled until the late 1980s, during Gorbachev's push for 'openness' in thought and 'restructuring' in social organization. But that push turned so quickly into systemic collapse, with total revulsion against Marxist thought in any form, that Bogdanov's period of respect in his native land was very brief. Whether Russian thinkers will ever have a sustained revival of interest in his thought depends still, as it has all along, on the stand they take between extremes of total revulsion and total passivity, between wild attempts to leap out of the system they are born into and fatalistic adaptation to it. If they attempt careful thought about ways to make effective use of their historic experience, the part that Bogdanov played will take on a new significance.

It seems unlikely that Bogdanov's thought ever will be considered of major significance apart from the life that gave it meaning within the Russian revolution. Few of his works have been translated into Western languages, though some historians and some believers in systems theory have called attention to him. Tektology may be 'a kind of metascience' (Gorelik 1980), comparable to Wiener's cybernetics or Bertalanffy's general system theory, but it has attracted less interest. The most searching studies of Bogdanov's thought have set it in an historical context that it does not transcend. Such studies emphasize either the logical inconsistencies of his efforts to combine epistemological scepticism with a monistic faith (see Kolakowski 1978), or the derivative quality of his popularized knowledge and overabundant theorizing (see Grille 1966), or the utopian faith that he struggled to keep creatively alive while the victorious revolutionaries were turning utopia into ritualized worship of a dream deferred (see Sochor 1988). Sympathy abounds, but it does not save the thought. Sochor dwells on Bogdanov's creative utopianism as evidence that the Russian Revolution might have developed less tyrannically than it actually did, and Grille pictures Bogdanov as a 'red Hamlet', whose balancing between the demands of action and of thought reflects honour on him. Both authors, and Kolakowski even more, avoid the hardest philosophical question posed by the history of political thought and action in Third World countries. They fail to ask whether practice as the criterion of truth in Russia – or China, or Angola, or Iran – is compatible with pragmatism as a philosophy of comfortable thinkers in advanced countries.

See also: RUSSIAN EMPIRIOCRITICISM; MARXIST PHILOSOPHY, RUSSIAN AND SOVIET

List of works

Bogdanov, A.A. (1897) *Kratkii kurs ekonomicheskoi nauki*; trans. *A Short Course of Economic Science*, London: Communist Party of Great Britain. (Bogdanov's first publication, which became a widely used textbook in Marxist circles.)

—— (1899) *Osnovnye elementy istoricheskogo vzgliada na prirodu* (Basic Elements of the Historical View of Nature), St Petersburg: Izdatel'. (An energeticist foundation for Marxism.)

—— (1904) *Iz psikhologii obshchestva; stat'i 1901–04* (From the Psychology of Society; Articles 1901-4), St Petersburg: Delo; 2nd edn, enlarged, 1906. (Much on ideology, little on psychology, in the sense of an academic discipline.)

—— (1905–7) *Ėmpiriomonizm; stat'i po filosofii* (Empiriomonism: Articles on Philosophy), 3 vols, Moscow: Dorovatovskii & Charushkinov; 2nd and 3rd edn, 1906–8. (An assemblage of articles, rather than the unified treatise that this work is often assumed to be.)

—— (1908a) *Prikliucheniia odnoi filosofskoi shkoly* (The Adventures of a Philosophical School), St Petersburg: Znanie. (Response to criticisms by orthodox Mensheviks.)

—— (1908b) 'Ernst Mach und die Revolution' (Ernst Mach and the Revolution), in Neue Zeit XXVI (1): 695–700. (Abridged translation of his preface to Russian translation of Mach's *Analyse der Empfindungen*.)

—— (1908/1911) *Krasnaia zvezda/Inzhener Menni*, trans. C. Rougle, ed. L. Graham and R. Stites, *Red Star and Engineer Menni*, Bloomington, IN: Indiana University Press. (Translation of Bogdanov's two works of science fiction, with commentary.)

—— (1910) *Padenie velikogo fetishizma (sovremennyi krizis ideologii); Vera i nauka* (The Fall of a Great Fetishism; Faith and Science), Moscow: Dorova-

tovskii & Charushkinov. (The response to Lenin's *Materializm i èmpiriokrititsizm*.)
—— (1913) *Filosofiia zhivogo opyta: populiarnye ocherki; materializm, empiriokrititsizm, dialekticheskii materializm, èmpiriomonizm, i nauka budushchego* (A Philosophy of Living Experience: Popular Essays; Materialism, Empiriocriticism, Dialectical Materialism, Empiriomonism and the Science of the Future), St Petersburg: Semenov; 2nd and 3rd edn, enlarged 1920, 1923. (See analysis by Jensen.)
—— (1913–25) *Tektologiia: Vseobshchaia organizatsionnaia nauka* (Tektology: The Universal Organizational Science), St Petersburg, Moscow, Berlin: various publishers; trans. and ed. G. Gorelik, *Essays in Tektology*, Seaside, CA: Intersystems, 1980. (Three editions of his major work on systems theory; for bibliographic specifics see Susiluoto. Note also a German translation of 1926–8; and a two-volume Russian edition, Moscow, 1990.)
—— (1924) *O proletarskoi kul'ture, 1904–24* (On Proletarian Culture, 1904–24), Moscow: Kniga. (Collection of articles with prefatory explanation.)
—— (1926) 'Avtobiografiia' (Autobiography), in *Èntsiklopedicheskii slovar' Granat* XLI (1): 29–33. (Includes Bogdanov's own list of his most important publications. German translation in Grille.)
—— (1990) *Voprosy sotsializma: raboty raznykh let* (Problems of Socialism: Works of Various Years), Moscow: Politizdat. (Includes criticisms of the Bolshevik Revolution originally published in 1917–18, the letter to Lunacharskii and so on.)

References and further reading

Bailes, K.E. (1967) 'Lenin and Bogdanov: The End of an Alliance', in *Columbia Essays in International Affairs* II: 107–33, New York: Columbia University Press. (Contains valuable archival material, including Trotsky's and Bogdanov's letters to the school on Capri.)
* Grille, D. (1966) *Lenins Rivale: Bogdanov und sein Philosophie*, Köln: Wissenschaft und Politik. (The most detailed intellectual biography, emphasizing the derivative nature of his thought and his character as 'the red Hamlet'.)
Jensen, K. (1982) *Beyond Marx and Mach: Aleksandr Bogdanov's Philosophy of Living Experience*, Dordrecht: Reidel. (Analysis focused on Bogdanov's *Filosofiia zhivogo opyta*.)
Joravsky, D. (1961) *Soviet Marxism and Natural Science, 1917–1932*, New York: Columbia University Press. (Analyses the conflict between Bogdanov and Lenin before 1917, and sets Bogdanov in context of the 1920s.)
* Kolakowski, L. (1978) *Main Currents of Marxism II: The Golden Age*, Oxford: Clarendon Press. (Bogdanov is analysed on 432–45.)
Rossiiskaia Akademiia Nauk, Institut Ekonomiki, Kommissiia po nauchnomu naslediiu A.A. Bogdanova (1992) *Trudy*. (Articles about Bogdanov and some items by him.)
* Sochor, Z.A. (1988) *Revolution and Culture: The Bogdanov–Lenin Controversy*, Ithaca, NY: Cornell University Press. (A detailed analysis with emphasis on the role of utopian faith.)
Susiluoto, I. (1982) *The Origins and Development of Systems Thinking in the Soviet Union: Political and Philosophical Controversies from Bogdanov and Bukharin to Present-Day Reevaluations*, Helsinki. (A careful analysis of tektology and its reception.)
Vucinich, A. (1976) *Social Thought in Tsarist Russia: The Quest for a General Science of Society, 1861–1917*, Chicago: University of Chicago Press. (The last chapter credits Bogdanov with significant innovation.)

DAVID JORAVSKY

BOHR, NIELS (1885–1962)

One of the most influential scientists of the twentieth century, the Danish physicist Niels Bohr founded atomic quantum theory and the Copenhagen interpretation of quantum physics. This radical interpretation renounced the possibility of a unified, observer-independent, deterministic description in the microdomain. Bohr's principle of complementarity – the heart of the Copenhagen philosophy – implies that quantum phenomena can only be described by pairs of partial, mutually exclusive, or 'complementary' perspectives. Though simultaneously inapplicable, both perspectives are necessary for the exhaustive description of phenomena. Bohr aspired to generalize complementarity into all fields of knowledge, maintaining that new epistemological insights are obtained by adjoining contrary, seemingly incompatible, viewpoints.

Bohr's elaborations of complementarity can be divided into two distinct periods marked by the challenge of the Einstein–Podolsky–Rosen (EPR) paper in 1935 (see EINSTEIN, A. §5). The first period explores the compatibility of the quantum formalism with experiments through Heisenberg's uncertainty principle, which implies that in the quantum domain spacetime and energy–momentum (or causal) descriptions are not simultaneously applicable (see HEISENBERG, W.). In Bohr's terminology, spacetime and causality are complementary. Similar complementarity relations hold between wave and particle attributes of atomic objects, which are exhibited in mutually exclusive experimental arrangements.

Bohr's initial formulations of complementarity relied on the idea of an 'uncontrollable' physical disturbance of the microscopic object by the measuring device, due to the 'indivisibility' of the quantum of action and necessitating the 'inseparability' of atomic phenomena from their means of observation. This disturbance is the source of the 'final renunciation' of causality and objective reality in the atomic domain. According to Bohr, realistic causal descriptions presuppose the possibility of the definition of a system's state, excluding in principle all disturbances.

The EPR paper undercut Bohr's notion of disturbance. Einstein and his co-workers devised a thought experiment where for two previously interacting particles one is free to predict either the position or the momentum of the first particle on the basis of observations made on the spatially separated second particle. Since the measurement on the second particle cannot immediately 'disturb' the state of the first one, they concluded that both position and momentum can be attributed to the first particle simultaneously, contrary to the uncertainty, complementarity and 'completeness' of the quantum theory.

Bohr countered this challenge by resorting to operational and relational definitions of concepts, replacing his idea of physical disturbance by a 'semantic' one. In the EPR experiment, measuring the position of the first particle precludes the prediction, or meaningful assignment, of momentum to the second one. Scientific concepts are to be defined only relative to the 'whole' experimental arrangement. After EPR, such positivistic statements are frequent in Bohr's writings.

The central claim of Bohr's philosophy after EPR is the indispensability of classical concepts, supplemented by ordinary language, for unambiguous communication of experimental results. Unambiguous description presupposes a strict separation between the observed object and the observing subject. This is possible only at the classical level, where the quantum of action can be neglected. Classical concepts, guided by complementarity in different experimental arrangements, are therefore the fundamental descriptive concepts in the quantum domain. There are no 'quantum concepts' and no 'quantum reality', only an abstract formalism for the calculation and prediction of measurement results. Progress in science consists in 'rational generalizations' of the old frameworks, not in their replacement by genuinely new conceptual schemes. This claim, placing a priori limits on scientific theorizing, was contested by Bohr's opponents and sympathizers alike.

Bohr's doctrine of the indispensability of classical concepts is rooted in his correspondence principle, which, by relying on classical analogies, guided the search for a consistent quantum theory before its creation in 1925. Yet the difference between correspondence and complementarity is striking. The former was a heuristic principle leading to many new discoveries, culminating in Heisenberg's quantum formalism. The latter had no new empirical import, being aimed at the philosophical legitimization of the quantum theory.

Bohr supports his view that the classical realm is privileged by arguments stressing direct accessibility of classical reality to immediate sense perception. These arguments, together with Bohr's preoccupation with the conditions and limits of the applicability of concepts, have strong Kantian roots. In this respect there is a substantial similarity between Bohr and the philosophy of his teacher, the Neo-Kantian philosopher Harald Høffding.

In his later years, Bohr aspired to extend the 'epistemological lesson' of complementarity to biology, psychology and anthropology, maintaining that in these fields, as in quantum physics, observational interaction can be neither neglected nor precisely determined. These generalizations are rarely developed, by Bohr or others, into more than suggestive analogies.

The value of Bohr's philosophy for the advancement of physics is controversial. His followers consider complementarity a profound insight into the nature of the quantum realm. Others consider complementarity an illuminating but superfluous addendum to quantum theory. More severe is the opinion that Bohr's philosophy is an obscure 'web of words' and mute on crucial foundational issues.

Opinions are also divided about the status of Bohr's philosophy after Bell's results (see BELL'S THEOREM). Some scholars consider Bell's proof that rules out local deterministic realistic theories a vindication of Bohr's philosophy of indeterminism and inseparability. Others hold that Bohr's positivistic prohibitions are irrelevant to the contemporary quest for an adequate quantum ontology. Once a ruling 'dogma', Bohr's philosophy is no longer considered the final word about the nature of the quantum world.

See also: LOGICAL POSITIVISM §4; OPERATIONALISM; QUANTUM MECHANICS, INTERPRETATION OF

List of works

(The first three collections contain Bohr's main body of philosophical essays on quantum theory.)

Bohr, N. (1934) *Atomic Theory and the Description of Nature*, Cambridge: Cambridge University Press.
—— (1963a) *Atomic Physics and Human Knowledge*, New York: Wiley.
—— (1963b) *Essays 1958–1962 on Atomic Physics and Human Knowledge*, New York: Wiley.
—— (1972–86) *Collected Works, Volumes 1–9*, Amsterdam: North Holland. (Contains Bohr's major scientific and philosophical papers on quantum theory until 1932, and those on nuclear physics until 1952.)

References and further reading

Beller, M. and Fine, A. (1994) 'Bohr's Response to EPR', in J. Faye and H. Folse (eds) *Niels Bohr and Contemporary Philosophy*, Amsterdam: North Holland, 1–31. (A close reading of Bohr's response to the Einstein–Podolsky–Rosen challenge with an emphasis on a positivistic shift in Bohr's thought.)
Chevalley, C. (1991) 'Le dessin et la couleur' ('The drawing and the colour'), in *Introduction to Niels Bohr, Physique Atomique et Connaissance Humaine* (Atomic Physics and Human Knowledge), Paris: Gallimard, 19–140, 307–641. (A presentation of Bohr's philosophy in the Neo-Kantian tradition.)
Darrigol, O. (1992) *From c-Numbers to q-Numbers. The Classical Analogy in the History of Quantum Theory*, Berkeley, CA: University of California Press. (Analysis of the origins and the applications of Bohr's correspondence principle.)
Faye, J. (1991) *Niels Bohr: His Heritage and Legacy. An Antirealist View of Quantum Mechanics*, Dordrecht: Kluwer. (Analysis of the impact of Høffding's philosophy on Bohr's interpretation of quantum physics.)
Faye, J. and Folse, H.J. (eds) (1994) *Niels Bohr and Contemporary Philosophy*, Amsterdam: North Holland. (A collection of essays on Bohr's philosophy, with an emphasis on realism and positivism.)
Folse, H.J. (1985) *The Philosophy of Niels Bohr: The Framework of Complementarity*, Amsterdam: North Holland. (Analysis of Bohr's extension of complementarity into domains beyond physics.)
Honner, J. (1987) *The Description of Nature: Niels Bohr and the Philosophy of Quantum Mechanics*, New York: Oxford University Press. (Argues that Bohr's philosophy is best understood as a transcendental inquiry into the very preconditions of the possibility of experience.)
Hooker, C.A. (1972) 'The Nature of Quantum Mechanical Reality: Einstein vs. Bohr', in R.G. Colodny (ed.) *Paradigms and Paradoxes*, Pittsburgh, PA: University of Pittsburgh Press. (Treats conceptual intricacies of the Bohr–Einstein debate.)
Murdoch, D. (1987) *Niels Bohr's Philosophy of Physics*, Cambridge: Cambridge University Press. (Analysis of different meanings of Bohr's complementarity, with an emphasis on the measurement problem.)
Pais, A. (1991) *Niels Bohr's Times: In Physics, Philosophy and Polity*, New York: Oxford University Press. (Description of Bohr's life and thought by a physicist who adheres to Bohr's complementarity.)

MARA BELLER

BOLD, SAMUEL (1649–1737)

Samuel Bold (or Bolde) was a Latitudinarian minister who defended John Locke's Reasonableness of Christianity *and his* Essay Concerning Human Understanding. *Bold published a series of pamphlets and short books which argued a theological position substantially identical to that of Locke. He also mounted a philosophical defence of Locke's definition of knowledge and his supposition that it was possible that God could, if he so wished, superadd to matter the power of thought. In a book on the theological issue of the resurrection of the same body he defended Locke's account of personal identity.*

Samuel Bold entered English public controversy in his Dorset ministries with a published sermon in defence of moderation for dissenters, followed by other controversial publications, including pamphlets in the late 1690s supporting Locke's *Reasonableness of Christianity* (Bold later surmised that Locke was the author of this anonymous work) (see LOCKE, J. §§1, 7). He was also much impressed with Locke's *Essay Concerning Human Understanding* and, when this was attacked by John Edwards, he defended it in a further pamphlet, *Some Considerations on the Principal Objections and Arguments Which have been Publish'd against Mr Lock's Essay of Humane Understanding* (1699).

Bold's defence of Locke was centred on two issues: Locke's definition of knowledge and his conjecture that God could add to matter a power of thinking, issues which were also central in Locke's controversy with Stillingfleet. On the first of these, Locke had defined knowledge in terms of seeing an agreement or disagreement between ideas. As Bold explained it, propositions are known to be true 'by perceiving that the Ideas, signified by the words of which the proposition doth consist, have such a connection or agreement, repugnancy, or disagreement, as the Proposition doth express' (1699: 6). He claimed that Locke was correct in holding that there was no way to truth except via ideas. He underlined that this was no threat to the Christian religion as long as we clearly distinguished knowledge (which is certain) from faith on evidence (which, although reasonable, is not).

With regard to the possibility of thinking matter Bold fully appreciated what Locke's detractors generally did not, that Locke's claim was an epistemic one: *for all we know* God might add the power of thinking to matter (because there was no inconsistency between the ideas of matter and thinking). It was not a disguised attempt to argue for the truth of the claim. As such, Bold held, it could not be faulted. The power of thinking could in principle be added by God to any substance, mental or physical, for we cannot understand in either case how that power actually produces its effect. All we know is that it does.

Bold shows himself to be an able, if unoriginal, philosopher. His next work, the book *A Discourse Concerning the Resurrection of the Same Body* (1705), is again a defence of Locke's philosophy, this time focusing on his account of personal identity and its implications for theology, especially as it relates to the necessary articles of the Christian faith. Although Bold's argument does not advance beyond Locke's position, it brings out clearly the close relationship between the epistemic issues which Locke raises and contemporary Christian theology. This is further confirmed by the subsequent section of the work, separately titled *A Discourse concerning the Immateriality of the Soul*, in which once again it is Locke's epistemology that is defended.

Bold is rarely more than a clear-headed commentator on Locke, but he is undoubtedly a superior philosopher to many of those who sought to attack the *Essay Concerning Human Understanding* for its supposedly unacceptable theological implications.

See also: LATITUDINARIANISM; SOCINIANISM

List of works

Bold, S. (1706) *A Collection of Tracts, Publish'd in Vindication of Mr Lock's Reasonableness of Chrsitianity, as deliver'd in the Scriptures; and of his Essay Concerning Humane Understanding*, London. (This contains many of Bold's writings, including those listed here.)
—— (1699) *Some Considerations on the Principal Objections and Arguments Which have been Publish'd against Mr. Lock's Essay of Humane Understanding*, London. (A strong defence of Locke's epistemology, including his definition of knowledge, especially against those critics who read it as a threat to established religion.)
—— (1705) *A Discourse Concerning the Resurrection of the Same Body: with two Letters Concerning the Necessary Immateriality of Created Thinking Substance*, London. (Defends Lockean positions on identity of personhood and on the logical possibility of God superadding to matter the power of thought without claiming that God has actually done that in the case of human beings.)

References and further reading

Bayne, R. (1886) 'Samuel Bold' in *Dictionary of National Biography*, vol. 5, London, 317–8. (A brief account of Bold's life and works.)
Locke, J. (1689) *An Essay Concerning Human Understanding*, ed. P.H. Nidditch, London and Oxford: Oxford University Press, 1975. (The work that Bold saw as expressing the philosophy to which he was committed.)
—— (1695) *The Reasonableness of Christianity, as Delivered in the Scriptures*, ed. J. Higgins-Biddle, Oxford: Oxford University Press, 1998. (Anonymous, but identified by Bold as by Locke's. It expressed Bold's own understanding of Christianity.)
Edwards, J. (1695) *Some Thoughts Concerning the Several Causes and Occasions of Atheism, Especially in the Present Age. With some Brief Reflections on Socinianism: And on a Late Book Entitled The Reasonableness of Christianity as deliver'd in the Scriptures*, London; repr. New York: Garland, 1984. (The work to which Bold's writings were, in a large part, a response.)

G.A.J. ROGERS

BOLZANO, BERNARD (1781–1848)

Bernard Bolzano was a lone forerunner both of analytical philosophy and phenomenology. Born in Prague in the year when Kant's first Critique *appeared, he became one of the most acute critics both of Kant and of German Idealism. He died in Prague in the same year in which Frege was born; Frege is philosophically closer to him than any other thinker of the nineteenth or twentieth century. Bolzano was the only outstanding* proponent of utilitarianism among German-speaking philosophers, and was a creative mathematician whose name is duly remembered in the annals of this discipline. His *Wissenschaftslehre* (Theory of Science) of 1837 makes him the greatest logician in the period between Leibniz and Frege. The book was sadly neglected by Bolzano's contemporaries, but rediscovered by Brentano's pupils: Its ontology of propositions and ideas provided Husserl with much of his ammunition in his fight against psychologism and in support of phenomenology, and through Twardowski it also had an impact on the development of logical semantics in the Lwæw-Warsaw School.

1 Life and main works
2 Basic ontological categories
3 Truth and degrees of validity
4 Analyticity, deducibility and consequentiality

1 Life and main works

Bolzano was son of a German mother and an Italian father. As a young man he became keenly interested in the foundations of mathematics (his first mathematical paper appeared in 1804), yet he decided to study theology. In his native city, Prague, he graduated with a Ph.D. and was ordained a priest in 1805. In the same year he was appointed professor of the philosophy of religion to a newly-founded chair at the Charles-Ferdinand University. Nevertheless his first book was *Beyträge zu einer begründeteren Darstellung der Mathematik* (Contributions to a More Well-founded Presentation of Mathematics) (1810) in which he attacked Kant's views on geometry and arithmetic. Bolzano's university lectures are preserved in his monumental *Lehrbuch der Religionswissenschaft* (Textbook of the Science of Religion) (1834). His philosophy of religion is based on his ethics. He criticizes Kant's categorical imperative and his doctrine of postulates, and advocates a version of utilitarianism. Bolzano's logical notion of a manifold (*Inbegriff*) is the conceptual core of his version of a cosmological argument for the existence of God (see GOD, ARGUMENTS FOR THE EXISTENCE OF §1). Only the conclusion of this argument is the possible content of a religious belief. Bolzano maintains that a religious belief is, or strengthens the motivational power of, a moral belief. He takes beliefs to be indirectly under the control of our will and presents a lucid account of self-deception. Someone's religious belief may be due to self-deception, he argues, and yet the steps taken to acquire it may be justifiable by utilitarian principles. Taking divine revelation to be an attempt at communicating, he gives a very subtle analysis of this concept. He rejects the Humean definition of a miracle and tries to defend the possibility of miracles with the help of his theory of probability.

Owing to his public lectures, many of which are collected in his *Erbauungsreden* (Sermons) (1813, 1849–52), Bolzano became the protagonist of the 'Bohemian Enlightenment'. He pleaded for social reforms, attacked militarism and strongly criticized both the discrimination against Czech Bohemians by their German compatriots and the anti-Semitism on both sides. The Austrian Emperor Francis was infuriated by much of this and dismissed Bolzano from his chair in 1820.

Bolzano withdrew to a small village in southern Bohemia where he composed some of his most important works. His metaphysical treatise *Athanasia* (Immortality) (1827) is inspired by Leibniz's *Monadology*. The four volumes of his *Theory of Science* contain a highly original (philosophy of) logic (vols 1–2), an empiricist epistemology and a theory of scientific discovery (vol. 3), and a methodology for writing useful textbooks (vol. 4). His *Größenlehre* (Theory of Magnitudes) comprising Zahlenlehre (Theory of Numbers), Functionenlehre (Theory of Functions) and Raumwissenschaft (Theory of Space) remained unfinished (and will eventually be published in the complete edition of his works (1969–)). Bolzano spent the last seven years of his life back in Prague, where he frequently delivered papers (mainly on aesthetics and mathematics) to the Bohemian Academy of the Sciences. Among his most outstanding mathematical contributions are the following: he defined convergence and indicated convergence criteria (several years before Cauchy), and described a function continuous but not differentiable in an interval (several decades before Weierstrass). He realized that any infinite set contains a subset that stands in bi-univocal correspondence to it, and he realized that this is not a contradiction. This is a central topic in his *Paradoxien des Unendlichen* (Paradoxes of the Infinite) (1851). Cantor thought very highly of this book, and Peirce praised its author as conferring 'a singular benefit upon humanity' (1909).

2 Basic ontological categories

Bolzano's universe is a universe of objects (*Gegenstände*). Objects are either actual (*wirklich*, effectual) or non-actual. Something is actual iff it is an element of the causal order. (Bolzano outlines his ontology of actual objects at the beginning of his *Athanasia*.) Actual objects are either substances or adherences. An object is an 'adherence' iff it is actual and a feature of another actual object on whose existence and identity it depends. (Your last headache would be an example.) An object is a 'substance' iff it is actual and not an adherence. (Sometimes Bolzano takes substances to be non-composite as well.) Some adherences are mental: volitions, wishes, sensations and, most importantly for the *Theory of Science*, subjective ideas (*subjektive Vorstellungen*) and acts of judgment (*Urteile*). Properties as shareable by many objects are non-actual objects, and so are numbers. Seen against the background of earlier metaphysics *Sätze an sich* ('sentences-as-such': henceforth, 'propositions') and their constituents are the most remarkable non-actual objects in Bolzano's ontology as developed in his *Theory of Science*. In his use of '*Satz*' Bolzano can appeal to one prominent use of this term in German. A definite description such as '*der Satz des Pythagoras*' (Pythagoras' theorem) refers to something purportedly discovered by a Greek philosopher-mathematician which can be expressed by many sentences in many languages. In Bolzano's usage, the epithet '*an sich*' amounts to something like the gloss 'in the strict sense of this term'.

Propositions are not true or false in a language or in a context, but simply true or false, full-stop. They differ from true or false utterances or judgments in that they are non-actual. Thus something is a proposition iff it is both *simpliciter* true or false and non-actual. An utterance is true iff the proposition expressed by it is true. The proposition expressed by an utterance is the sense (*Sinn*) of this utterance. Bolzanian sense is not to be identified with the linguistic meaning of the sentence uttered. (Sentences with the same linguistic meaning might be used to express different propositions: your utterance of 'I have blood-type A' might express a true proposition, while my utterance of '*Ich habe Blutgruppe A*' expresses a false one.) Propositions also play a psychological role in being the potential contents (*Stoff* (matter)) of judgments. A judgment is true iff the proposition which is its content is true. Propositions are composite, structured entities. P is the same proposition as Q iff P is built in the same way from the same components as Q.

A component of a proposition which is not itself a proposition is a *Vorstellung an sich* ('idea-as-such': henceforth, 'idea'). The idea expressed by a non-sentential component of a sentential utterance is the sense of this component. (Not all words in an utterance express ideas: the phrase 'really sad' expresses the same idea as 'sad'. Not all ideas which are components of the proposition expressed by an utterance are expressed by components of the utterance: if you now say, 'It is snowing', the proposition expressed must contain an idea which represents a place, otherwise it would not be *simpliciter* true or false.) One and the same idea can be the content of many subjective ideas, that is, of many non-judgmental components of judgments. An idea is objectual (*gegenständlich*) iff there is at least one object to which it refers. An idea which refers to exactly one object and is not composed of other ideas is an 'intuition' (*Anschauung an sich*). An intuition is expressed by an indexical use of 'this'. An idea which neither is nor contains an intuition is a pure 'concept' (*reiner Begriff*). Equivalent ideas (*Wechselvorstellungen*) are objectual ideas which refer to the same objects. Bolzanian ideas are very fine-grained: 'trilateral' and 'triangular', for example, in spite of being analytically coextensive, do not express the same idea.

3 Truth and degrees of validity

A proposition P attributing property y to object x is true, Bolzano explains, iff x has y. Here 'P attributes y to x' is meant to characterize not a linguistic or mental activity, but the internal structure of a proposition. The copula 'has' could be paraphrased by 'exemplifies' or 'instantiates'. Bolzano's conception of truth is thoroughly non-epistemic. Some truths may never be known (by any finite mind): 'The number of blossoms that were on a certain tree last spring is a statable, if unknown figure. Thus, the proposition which states this figure I call an objective truth, even if nobody knows it.' Nor is there any allusion in the definiens to what could be known under ideal conditions.

Bolzano's explication of truth presupposes that every proposition has the structure 'x has y'. But we can say something true or false by sentences such as 'It is snowing' or 'Nobody is perfect', although *prima facie*, at least, they do not seem to ascribe a property to an object. In his philosophical grammar Bolzano offers reformulations with the appropriate structure: 'The idea of a snowfall occurring here and now has objectuality' and 'The idea of a perfect person has lack of objectuality'. (Bolzano anticipates Frege's and Russell's conception of existence as a second-order notion.) But of course, the search for such a canonical paraphrase threatens to become rather tedious when we have to deal with sentences of the form 'If P then either Q or R', for example. Bolzano himself was by no means sure that his programme of paraphrase could always be carried out.

The basic procedure in Bolzano's logic is that of considering 'variants' of a given proposition with respect to one or more ideas contained in it. Let us take the idea expressed by the numeral '6' to be the variandum in the proposition P_1 that Beethoven's *Symphony No. 6* is in F major. (I shall refer to this idea as [6] and to variants of P_1 with respect to it as

[6]-variants of P_1.) Let us only consider objectual [6]-variants of P_1, that is, only those variants the subject-idea of which is objectual. Some of these variants are true, some are false. If we want to determine the ratio between true variants and all variants we must forbid the replacement of [6] by any equivalent idea. Otherwise the floodgates would be opened for infinitely many ideas: [7–1], [8–2], [9–3], etc. Using '$P[i/j]$' to denote the proposition which differs from P by containing the idea j at all places where P contains the idea i, we can introduce the following abbreviation: Q is a 'relevant' variant of P with respect to the idea i contained in P iff ($Q = P$) or ($Q = P[i/j]$, the ideas i and j are not equivalent, and Q is objectual). Bolzano defines the 'degree of validity' (*Grad der Gültigkeit*) of a proposition with respect to its component i as the ratio between the number of all its relevant true i-variants and the number of *all* its relevant i-variants. This degree of validity can be represented by a fraction the numerator of which is the first of those numbers and the denominator of which is the second. Thus the degree of validity of P_1 with respect to [6] is ⅔. (Bolzano makes important use of this machinery in his theory of probability.) With respect to [6], the degree of validity of the proposition P_2 that Beethoven's *Symphony No. 6* contains more than one note is one, since all relevant variants of P_2 are true. Such propositions are universally valid (*allgemeingültig*) with respect to a component idea. With respect to [6] the degree of validity of the proposition P_3 that Beethoven's *Symphony No. 6* consists of a single note is zero, since all relevant variants of P_3 are false. Such propositions are universally invalid (*allgemein ungültig*) with respect to a component idea.

4 Analyticity, deducibility and consequentiality

A proposition is 'analytic' (in the broader sense), Bolzano explains, iff it contains at least one idea i such that it is either universally valid or universally invalid with respect to i. All other propositions are synthetic. Hence propositions P_2 and P_3 above are both analytic, whereas P_1 is synthetic. A proposition is 'logically analytic' iff it is either universally valid or universally invalid with respect to all the nonlogical ideas contained in it. Hence 'Whatever is square is square' expresses a logically analytic truth, since presumably the concept of a square is the only nonlogical idea in this proposition. Bolzano, like TARSKI (§1) (1936), takes the borderline between logical and nonlogical ideas not to be sharp. Using a convenient terminology introduced by QUINE we can say: a logically analytic truth contains only logical ideas essentially; any other idea occurring in it can be varied at will without engendering falsity. (Quine acknowledges the affinity of his view of logical truth to Bolzano's conception.) A truth which is analytic in the broader sense contains at least one idea nonessentially. (There is no counterpart to broad analyticity in Quine.) Bolzano explains analyticity as a property of propositions, not of sentences. This explanation is, like his account of truth, strictly non-epistemic, and it is vastly different from the Kantian one (see KANT, I. §4): for Bolzano, to illustrate just one of the many differences, your utterance of 'This cup which was taken from my cupboard is broken', expresses an analytic truth with respect to the intuition expressed by the demonstrative in your utterance if all the cups in your cupboard happen to be broken.

P and Q are 'compatible' (*verträglich*) with respect to idea i iff there is an idea x such that both $P[i/x]$ and $Q[i/x]$ are true. Q is 'deducible' (in the broader sense) from P with respect to idea i iff P and Q are compatible with respect to i and for all ideas x, if $P[i/x]$ is true then $Q[i/x]$ is true. Hence nothing is deducible (*ableitbar*) from a contradiction. As deducibility with respect to an idea is a relation between propositions, it is neither a syntactic nor a semantic relation in the modern sense. The proposition P_4 that in Prague it was warmer in August 1830 than it was in July 1830 is deducible from the proposition P_5 that in Prague the thermometer registered higher in August 1830 than it did in July 1830, and vice versa, with regard to the chronological and geographical ideas they contain, since every variation on any of these components that transforms P_4 into a true proposition also makes P_5 true, and vice versa. Q is 'logically deducible' from P iff Q is deducible from P with respect to all nonlogical ideas contained in them. This conception, or rather its generalization as found in Bolzano, has often been described as a forerunner of Tarski's notion of logical consequence, and that is what Tarski himself took it to be.

Bolzano contrasts deducibility with 'consequentiality' (*Abfolge*) which only obtains between true propositions and which is never reciprocal. When a truth is deducible from and explained by another truth it is its consequence. Suppose propositions P_4 and P_5 above are true. Obviously P_4 is not a consequence of P_5: It is not the case that there was a rise in temperature *because* the thermometer registered higher. Rather, P_5 is a consequence of P_4. Bolzano also maintains that for all truths P, the proposition that it is true that P is a consequence of the proposition that P, while admitting that such propositions are always reciprocally deducible. Since nothing is its own consequence, Bolzano (as opposed to Frege and F.P. RAMSEY (§4)) takes 'It is true that P' and 'P' to express *different* propositions.

See also: ANALYTICAL PHILOSOPHY

List of works

Bolzano, B. (1969–) *Gesamtausgabe* (Collected Works), ed. J. Berg *et al.*, Stuttgart: Frommann/Holzboog. (The standard collected works. Vols E 2/1 (1972), E 2/1, Supp. 1 (1982) and E 2/1, Supp. 2 (1988) contain the first instalments of an invaluable bibliography.)

—— (1810) *Beyträge zu einer begründeteren Darstellung der Mathematik* (Contributions to a More Well-founded Presentation of Mathematics), Prague, repr. Darmstadt: Wissenschaftliche Buchgesellschaft, 1974. (A sketch of an anti-Kantian philosophy of mathematics, insisting on logical rigour.)

—— (1813, 1849–52) *Erbauungsreden* (Sermons), Prague, Vienna and Leipzig, 5 vols. (Public lectures on religious, moral and political topics.)

—— (1827) *Athanasia oder Gründe für die Unsterblichkeit der Seele* (Grounds for the Immortality of the Soul), Sulzbach: Seidel, 2nd edn, 1838; reprinted Frankfurt am Main, Minerva, 1970. (Metaphysics of simple substances and accidents.)

—— (1834) *Lehrbuch der Religionswissenschaft* (Textbook of the Science of Religion), Sulzbach: Seidel, 4 vols. (Rationalist philosophy of religion and utilitarian ethics.)

—— (1837) *Wissenschaftslehre*, Sulzbach: Seidel, 4 vols; selections, trans. and ed. R. George, in *Theory of Science*, Oxford: Blackwell, 1972; selections, trans. B. Terrell, ed. J. Berg, in *Theory of Science*, Dordrecht: Reidel, 1973. (A highly original philosophy of logic followed by treatises on empiricist epistemology, heuristics and textbook methodology.)

—— (1851) *Paradoxien des Unendlichen*, Leipzig: Reclam; repr. Hamburg, Meiner, 1975; trans. and with intro. by D.A. Steele, *Paradoxes of the Infinite*, London and New Haven, CT, Routledge, 1950. (A theory of infinite manifolds and metaphysics of simple substances and forces.)

References and further reading

Bolzano's Wissenschaftslehre 1837–1987, International Workshop (1992) Biblioteca di Storia della Scienza 31, Florence. (Useful collection of articles on vols 1–2 of Bolzano (1837), all in English.)

Berg, J. (1962) *Bolzano's Logic*, Stockholm: Almqvist & Wiksell. (Pioneering study of all the topics covered in §§3–4.)

—— (1992) *Ontology Without Ultrafilters And Possible Worlds, An Examination of Bolzano's Ontology*, Salzburg: Academia Verlag. (Resolutely technical reconstruction, also covering Bolzano's mathematical work.)

Buhl, G. (1961) *Ableitbarkeit und Abfolge in der Wissenschaftstheorie Bolzanos* (Deducibility and Consequentiality in Bolzano's Theory of Science), Köln: Universitätsverlag. (Lucid discussion of topics covered in §4.)

Cantor, G. (1883) 'Über unendliche, lineare Punktmannichfaltigkeiten' ('On Infinite Linear Point-Manifolds'), in *Gesammelte Abhandlungen*, Berlin, 1932, esp. 179–, 194, 212. (Important for assessing Bolzano's role in the history of set theory.)

Coffa, J.A. (1991) 'Bolzano and the Birth of Semantics', in *The Semantic Tradition from Kant to Carnap*, Cambridge: University Press, chap. 2, (22–40). (Useful overview with an interesting historical perspective.)

Dummett, M. (1993) *Origins of Analytical Philosophy*, London: Duckworth. (Places Bolzano in the pre-history of analytic philosophy and phenomenology.)

George, R. (1983) 'Bolzano's Consequence, Relevance and Enthymemes', *Journal of Philosophical Logic* 12: 299–325. (Points out significant differences between Bolzano's logic and that of the Frege–Russell tradition.)

Künne, W. (forthcoming) *Bernard Bolzano – Ein analytischer Philosoph im Schatten des deutschen Idealismus* (Bernard Bolzano – An Analytic Philosopher in the Shadow of German Idealism). (Expands on all material in this entry.)

Morscher, E. (1973) *Das logische An-sich bei Bernard Bolzano* (Logical Objects in Bolzano), Salzburg: Pustet. (Extremely well-documented and penetrating study of the topics covered in §2.)

—— (ed.) (1987) 'Bolzano-Studien', *Philosophia Naturalis* 24, 4. (Useful collection of articles, some of them in English, on various parts of Bolzano's philosophy, including a biographical sketch.)

* Peirce, C.S. (1909) 'Meaning (Pragmatism)', in *The New Elements of Mathematics*, The Hague and Paris: Humanities Press, 1976, vol. 4, esp. 117. (Interesting remarks on Bolzano as mathematician and logician.)

* Quine, W.V. (1954) 'Carnap and Logical Truth', *The Ways of Paradox*, Cambridge, MA: Harvard University Press, 1976, esp. §2, 109–. (Key text for comparing Bolzano's conception of logically analytic truth with modern notions of logical truth.)

* Tarski, A. (1936) 'On the Concept of Logical Consequence', *Logic, Semantics, Metamathematics*, Oxford: Clarendon Press, 1956, 408–20. (Key text

for comparing Bolzano's conception of deducibility with modern notions of logical consequence.)

WOLFGANG KÜNNE

BONAVENTURE (c.1217–74)

Bonaventure (John of Fidanza) developed a synthesis of philosophy and theology in which Neoplatonic doctrines are transformed by a Christian framework. Though often remembered for his denunciations of Aristotle, Bonaventure's thought includes some Aristotelian elements. His criticisms of Aristotle were motivated chiefly by his concern that various colleagues, more impressed by Aristotle's work than they had reason to be, were philosophizing with the blindness of pagans instead of the wisdom of Christians.

To Bonaventure, the ultimate goal of human life is happiness, and happiness comes from union with God in the afterlife. If one forgets this goal when philosophizing, the higher purpose of the discipline is frustrated. Philosophical studies can indeed help in attaining happiness, but only if pursued with humility and as part of a morally upright life. In the grander scheme of things, the ascent of the heart is more important than the ascent of the mind.

Bonaventure's later works consistently emphasize that all creation emanates from, reflects and returns to its source. Because the meaning of human life can be understood only from this wider perspective, the general aim is to show an integrated whole hierarchically ordered to God. The structure and symbolism favoured by Bonaventure reflect mystical elements as well. The world, no less than a book, reveals its creator: all visible things represent a higher reality. The theologian must use symbols to reveal this deeper meaning. He must teach especially of Christ, through whom God creates everything that exists and who is the sole medium by which we can return to our creator.

Bonaventure's theory of illumination aims to account for the certitude of human knowledge. He argues that there can be no certain knowledge unless the knower is infallible and what is known cannot change. Because the human mind cannot be entirely infallible through its own power, it needs the cooperation of God, even as it needs God as the source of immutable truths. Sense experience does not suffice, for it cannot reveal that what is true could not possibly be otherwise; so, in Bonaventure's view, the human mind attains certainty about the world only when it understands it in light of the 'eternal reasons' or divine ideas. This illumination from God, while necessary for certainty, ordinarily proceeds without a person's being conscious of it.

1 **Life and works**
2 **Neoplatonism and mysticism**
3 **Happiness and the limits of philosophy**
4 **Knowledge of God's existence**
5 **The question of an eternal world**
6 **Metaphysics**
7 **The illumination of the intellect**
8 **Virtue**

1 Life and works

The scholastic philosopher and theologian John of Fidanza, honoured as the 'Seraphic Doctor' but better known as Bonaventure, was born in Bagnoregio, a small town in Tuscany. After preparatory education in his home town, he completed a master's degree in arts at the University of Paris. There he joined the Franciscan order (*circa* 1243), taking the name Bonaventure probably to mark his entry into religious life. Bonaventure went on to study theology under the leading Franciscan masters at Paris during the years 1243–8, first with ALEXANDER OF HALES, a famous theologian whose influence is evident in Bonaventure's works, then with JOHN OF LA ROCHELLE and Odo Rigaud. As an advanced theology student, he lectured on the Bible (1248–50) and the *Sentences* of Peter LOMBARD (1250–2). From 1253 to 1257, when he resigned his position to serve as minister general of the Franciscan Order, Bonaventure was regent master of the Franciscan school at Paris. Works composed during this period include the disputed questions *De scientia Christi* (Concerning Christ's Knowledge) and *De mysterio Trinitatis* (On the Mystery of the Trinity). The *Breviloquium*, a highly condensed summary of theology for beginners, probably dates from around 1257.

The Franciscans were badly divided when Bonaventure became the Order's head. Many believed that the prophecies of JOACHIM OF FIORE concerning a new, spiritual age of history were to be fulfilled by drastic institutional changes and commitment to the life of wandering mendicancy exemplified by St Francis. Though Joachim's teachings influenced Bonaventure's view of history, he himself thought that only a chosen few were suited to live as St Francis did: the time had not yet come for the transformation of the world. Bonaventure did his best to control the extremists, give the order a firmer institutional structure and articulate an understanding of Franciscan poverty compatible with university study and teaching.

Bonaventure's struggles as minister general often receive only passing mention in philosophical accounts of his work, and his conflicts with heterodox masters of arts at Paris naturally appear to have greater philosophical import. However, the emphasis on the latter tends to conceal one of the most serious dilemmas Bonaventure faced. As he opposed the cult of Aristotle at Paris, so he opposed the cult of apocalyptic asceticism in his own order. The same thinker now sometimes regarded as an anti-intellectual theologian was regarded by some of his own confrères as a creature of the universities who had betrayed the spirit of St Francis. When viewed in context, Bonaventure's writings are remarkable less for the occasional polemics than for the balanced vision he consistently worked to communicate.

After two years of governing the Franciscan Order, Bonaventure retreated to Mount Alverno in Italy, where he wrote the *Itinerarium mentis in Deum* (Journey of the Mind to God). The intellectual ascent described in this work suggests a solution to the problem of learning within the Franciscan Order (see Brown 1993). Bonaventure does not urge his readers to repudiate the world; he tells us how we may see there the power, wisdom and goodness of its creator. Beginning with contemplation of sensible things, we may rise by stages to contemplation of the soul as the image of God, God's presence within the soul and the attributes of God himself. Philosophical studies aid in the ascent, but only if pursued with humility and as part of a morally upright life: the external world has little use as a mirror 'unless the mirror of our soul has been cleansed and polished.' Bonaventure explains the relations between philosophy and other divisions of human knowledge in *De reductione artium ad theologiam* (On Retracing the Arts to Theology), a highly condensed treatise of unknown date, possibly based on a sermon preached towards the end of his regency at Paris.

Bonaventure's 'collations' – *Collationes de decem praeceptis* (On the Ten Commandments), *Collationes de septem donis Spiritus Sancti* (On the Seven Gifts of the Holy Spirit) and *Collationes in Hexaemeron* (On the Six Days of Creation) – represent three series of sermons given during Lent to Franciscans studying and teaching theology at the University of Paris. The third series was cut short in May of 1273, when Pope Gregory X appointed Bonaventure cardinal bishop of Albano. He left Paris to meet with the pope, to be consecrated as bishop (November 1273) and to help with preparations for the Second Council of Lyons. He died unexpectedly in July 1274, shortly before the Council ended, and was buried in the Franciscan church at Lyons.

The three series of Lenten sermons mentioned above bear witness to growing tensions at Paris. Some members of the arts faculty at the University of Paris had taken to defending views contrary to Christian doctrine – defending them, if not as true in the absolute sense, at least as positions that human reason, unaided by faith, seemed legitimately to reach. They tended to see Aristotle as the pinnacle of human reason, and Averroes, who advocated the separation of philosophy from theology, as Aristotle's foremost interpreter (see ARISTOTELIANISM, MEDIEVAL; AVERROISM). Scandalized by the trend toward neo-pagan philosophizing, Bonaventure in his sermons cites various doctrines popular in the arts faculty as examples of the errors philosophers inevitably make when their reasoning is unillumined by faith. Some of the same views he attacked in 1267 and 1268 were formally condemned by the Bishop of Paris in 1270, but apparently with little effect. Bonaventure's sermons of 1273 accordingly display an even greater sense of urgency. The crisis culminated, three years after his death, in the most extensive doctrinal condemnation of the Middle Ages.

Bonaventure's works fall into different genres, related to the two stages of his career: the period when he was studying and teaching at Paris and the period beginning in 1257, when he resigned his university position to become minister general of the Franciscans. Most works from the first period are academic exercises with a conventional form. In his commentary on the *Sentences* and disputed questions, for example, Bonaventure cites authorities and marshals arguments on both sides of an issue before presenting his own resolution and answering objections to it. His later works differ strikingly from these academic compositions. The *collationes*, it should be remembered, are university sermons, and even the *Itinerarium* has some of the hallmarks of a sermon. The genre should be kept in mind when comparing Bonaventure's later works with academic productions by contemporaries, such as the *Summa theologiae* of Thomas AQUINAS.

2 Neoplatonism and mysticism

In the second stage of his career Bonaventure's writing becomes rich in metaphor and heavily reliant on symbolic modes of expression. An elaborate hierarchical structure, itself of symbolic significance, replaces the pro-and-con method characteristic of scholastic compositions. Here we see a writer who, though eloquent, operates within a carefully controlled structure. Unfortunately, even the best translations cannot preserve the many layers of meaning in Bonaventure's language. Today's readers are likely to recognize that the metaphysics of participation and exemplarism, like the themes of light and illumination, emanation and return, have older philosophical roots in Plato and the ancient Neoplatonists. At the same time, they may be tempted to dismiss all the complicated divisions and subdivisions in Bonaventure's writings as so much stylistic embellishment. The temptation should be resisted, for what looks like ornament turns out to be more substantial.

Works like the *Itinerarium* and the *collationes* draw on a Christian tradition well known to Bonaventure's contemporaries but now generally neglected. Perhaps the most basic idea is that all creation emanates from, mirrors and returns to its source – a fundamentally Plotinian doctrine prominent in the writings of AUGUSTINE (see PLOTINUS). Because the meaning of human life can be understood only from this broader perspective, the overarching aim is to show an interrelated totality hierarchically ordered to God. The structure of Bonaventure's later works reflects this ordering. As the structure is significant, so too is the symbolism, derived partly from mystical writings by the twelfth-century school of St Victor. Building on the thought of Augustine and the PSEUDO-DIONYSIUS, HUGH OF ST VICTOR taught that God communicates his plans everywhere, in a symbolic language we must learn to recognize and decipher. The world is like a book, revealing its author no less than Scripture does (see Zinn 1973). All creation reflects the triune character of God; all visible things represent an invisible, transcendent reality. The theologian must accordingly use symbols to show what cannot be expressed more directly. He must demonstrate the deeper meaning and order of the world, helping us to rise above the confusing multiplicity presented by our senses. To do so, he must teach especially of Christ, the Word through whom all things are created, the source of all true wisdom and the medium enabling us to return to God (see MYSTICISM, HISTORY OF).

This sketch of the intellectual background may help to explain not only the hierarchical structure of Bonaventure's later works but also the significance he attached to numbers: threefold divisions symbolize the Trinity, sixfold divisions symbolize the six days of creation and so on (see NEOPLATONISM). Of course, Neoplatonic and mystical writings are hardly Bonaventure's only sources. Like all masters schooled at Paris in the mid-thirteenth century, he studied Aristotle closely and often appealed to Aristotle's teachings. Stoic doctrines, derived from CICERO and patristic writers, are equally present in his thought (see PATRISTIC PHILOSOPHY; STOICISM). The philosophical eclecticism displayed by the earliest Christian thinkers is even greater among the scholastics, so that scholarly debates about whether a given master is Aristotelian, Neoplatonic or something else – debates extremely common in the literature on Bonaventure – are fundamentally disagreements about the dominant strains in a mixed breed.

3 Happiness and the limits of philosophy

What Bonaventure considers to be the place and function of philosophy becomes easier to understand if one reflects upon happiness, the end of human life. By nature we strive for happiness, and we can never be fulfilled unless we attain it. This ultimate goal has both practical and speculative implications. As Bonaventure explains in Chapter 1 of the *Itinerarium*, 'Since happiness is nothing else than the enjoyment of the Supreme Good, and the Supreme Good is above us, no one can enjoy happiness unless he rise above himself – not, of course, by a bodily ascent, but by an ascent of the heart.'

The ascent of the heart involves the ascent of the mind, and yet the mind takes us only so far. The complete happiness experienced through union with God comes more from love than from knowledge, more from will than from intellect. Small wonder, then, that Bonaventure consistently emphasizes the higher purpose of speculation. Anyone who remains ignorant of this purpose, or who knows it but loses sight of it, is doomed not only to frustrated desire but also to intellectual confusion. A good philosopher must therefore understand the place of philosophy within the wider context of human life. As no one can perceive the beauty of a poem unless he sees the whole, Bonaventure argues, so no one can grasp the beauty of the order regulating reality unless he views it in its totality (see FAITH).

Bonaventure's conviction that union with God constitutes the ultimate goal of all learning might well lead one to wonder whether philosophy has any genuine place in his thought. Why devote time to studying logic, much less the writings of pagan philosophers, when the example of St Francis proves such studies unnecessary for attaining the goal of eternal happiness? The title of one of Bonaventure's best-known treatises, *De reductione artium ad theologiam*, can reinforce the impression that he values the art of philosophy only insofar as philosophy can be 'reduced' to theology. This impression is misleading not only because the title, like the titles of many scholastic works, was invented by later editors rather than the author himself, but also because the term *reductio* is properly translated as 'retracing' rather than 'reducing'.

For Bonaventure, *reductio* signifies both a process and a method of analysis (Bougerol 1964, 1988). As a process, it is the return to God, in whom all rational beings find their fulfilment. While individuals may or may not choose the path that leads them home, the process of humanity's return to its source continues to operate. God's grace, working ever to draw us back to himself, governs the historical process and gives it meaning. Hence, *reductio* can also serve as a method of analysis. Humans, as rational beings, find the path home more easily when someone shows them how the various areas of human knowledge are so many rungs of a ladder, all leading in the same direction. As a method of analysis, *reductio* accordingly seeks to demonstrate how the many lead to the one, the composite to the simple, even as the many and the composite are based on and derive a deeper meaning from the one and the simple. The aim is to articulate an intelligible order and direction by bringing out fundamental organizing principles; it is not to boil away everything else, as cooks do in 'reducing' a sauce. While philosophy should point in the right direction and understand its place in the wider context, it need not be distilled into theology to become valuable. Logic is well worth studying, even though it teaches us nothing about the meaning of life.

The culinary interpretation of Bonaventure's *reductio* of the arts to theology arises partly from his claim that all divisions of human knowledge are 'handmaids of theology'. They surely are 'handmaids' in the sense that they have a higher purpose. Anyone who pursues philosophy or any other art strictly as an end in itself, as if there were nothing more exalted or fulfilling, is making a disastrous mistake. On the other hand, to say that philosophy is not the pinnacle of human life is not to say that it has value only insofar as it can be distilled into theology. As Bonaventure makes philosophy a handmaid of theology, so he also makes agriculture and navigation handmaids of theology. Is he arguing that farmers are worthless unless they sow their crops in threes, or that sailors cannot chart a course to Rome without fixing on God? Not at all. To argue that an art has a higher purpose is not to insist that it has no legitimacy or value in its own domain.

Bonaventure's attitude towards Aristotle's philosophy should be understood within the context of his views on philosophy in general. In the *Collationes in Hexaemeron*, where he traces the most serious errors of philosophy to Aristotle's rejection of exemplar ideas and his affirmation that God knows only himself, Bonaventure's preference for a broadly Platonic metaphysics is evident. His diatribe, however, is much less against Aristotle than against members of the Paris arts faculty who defended as philosophically sound virtually every position they believed Aristotle had held. In Bonaventure's view, even the best philosophers of antiquity were ignorant of original sin and the need for God's grace. Knowing nothing of Christ, and having to rely exclusively on their own powers of reason, the ancients could not help but make grave mistakes. Bonaventure accordingly urges the arts masters to philosophize as Christians, with the illumination of faith to guide them (see ARISTOTELIANISM, MEDIEVAL; PLATONISM, MEDIEVAL).

4 Knowledge of God's existence

Though Bonaventure offered proofs for the existence of God in other works, the twenty-nine arguments in his disputed questions *De mysterio Trinitatis* represent his most developed treatment of the topic (see Doyle 1974). The arguments go on to prove three conclusions: that every truth impressed on all minds is an indubitable truth, that every truth which all creatures proclaim is an indubitable truth and that every truth that is in itself most certain and evident is an indubitable truth. Bonaventure's position combines these three conclusions into a single master conclusion: that the existence of God is an indubitable truth in its own right and can be doubted only because of some defect in the knower. A human being might doubt God's existence from failing to understand correctly what the term 'God' signifies. Doubt might likewise spring from failing to carry one's thinking far enough, or from having only a partial view of the evidence. In all cases, Bonaventure argues, doubt arises from failures of the human intellect, not from God's existence as a truth considered in itself.

In arguing that God's existence is self-evident, Bonaventure repeatedly appeals to Anselm's *Proslogion* (see ANSELM OF CANTERBURY). He argues, for example, that God is 'a being than which nothing greater can be thought'; but that which exists only in thought does not meet this description, for something existing in reality would be greater, and hence God cannot be thought not to exist in reality. Anselmian arguments are supplemented by Augustinian arguments for the existence of truth (see AUGUSTINIANISM). To Bonaventure, each particular truth implies the existence of an absolute truth that is its cause. To affirm any particular truth is thus to affirm, even though one might fail to recognize it, the existence of God (see GOD, ARGUMENTS FOR THE EXISTENCE OF).

Bonaventure's arguments reflect his belief that all human souls belong to a hierarchically ordered intelligible realm that is more real and more knowable than the world of the senses. Belonging to the same realm as God, the soul can know God's existence directly, through thought. This position stands in sharp contrast to the views of Bonaventure's contemporary, AQUINAS. Sharing Aristotle's belief that we obtain knowledge from the initial data of sense experience, Aquinas taught that we can know God's existence by considering creatures and reasoning from effect to cause, but that God's existence is not self-evident to us.

5 The question of an eternal world

Bonaventure again differs from Aquinas on whether the world could have been created from eternity, a topic of heated debate in the thirteenth century. The problem, as he formulates it in his commentary on the *Sentences*, is 'Whether the world has been produced from eternity or in time.' The idea that the world was indeed produced is crucial to the question. To Bonaventure, there is nothing incoherent in believing that the world is eternal, only in believing that the world is both created and eternal (see Bonansea 1974).

Bonaventure's principal argument rests on the very notion of creation. Whatever is created in the truest sense – that is, produced from nothing rather than from pre-existing material – must come to have 'being after non-being': it must have a *beginning*. To say that something with a beginning is eternal, meaning that it has no beginning, is an obvious contradiction. Thus the thesis that the world was created from eternity is not merely false but unintelligible. In offering this argument, Bonaventure does not mean to imply that creation took place at some point within time, for he accepts the prevailing view that time began with creation. His challenge is to those who conceive of the world as both beginningless and created *ex nihilo*.

Another argument points to a problem with positing an actual, as opposed to merely potential, infinity. Bonaventure reasons that it is impossible to make the actually infinite greater, for this would be contrary to its nature, so that if the world existed from eternity, it would admit of no additional duration. In effect, extra days could not add to the number of days preceding the present, since the number preceding the present would already be infinite, and all actual infinites, Bonaventure assumes, must be equal. How could we even have reached the present day if infinitely many days had to elapse before today? One need not review all of Bonaventure's arguments to see how the notion of a world created from eternity raised issues, such as the problem of unequal infinites, that were of more than theological interest (see ETERNITY OF THE WORLD, MEDIEVAL VIEWS OF).

6 Metaphysics

Bonaventure's metaphysics, by his own description, is a doctrine of emanation, exemplarism and consummation or return. To his mind, anyone who denies the existence of exemplar ideas might reasonably draw the kind of conclusions drawn by Aristotle: that the first cause knows only itself and 'moves' the world only as a final cause, as an object of desire rather than as an agent and efficient cause. Even though his teachings recall Plotinian doctrine on emanation from the One, Bonaventure's metaphysics owes much more to the distinctively Christian Neoplatonism of AUGUSTINE. In place of the One we find God; in place of a world emanating necessarily from the very nature of the One we find a world God created freely, out of nothing. The world comes from God as its efficient cause, mirrors God, the exemplar cause, and is destined to return to God as its end or final cause (see CREATION AND CONSERVATION, RELIGIOUS DOCTRINE OF).

As archetypes of all actual and possible creatures, exemplar ideas help to explain both how God made what exists and how he knows everything that could be. The plurality of ideas does, however, raise questions about the unity of God. Bonaventure explains that there is no real plurality of ideas in God. As they are not distinct from God himself, so they are not distinct from each other. Properly understood, the exemplar ideas are distinct only from the standpoint of reason. What 'idea' actually signifies is a creature's relation to God.

Bonaventure's 'universal hylomorphism' – the doctrine that all creatures are composed of matter and form – turns out to be less bizarre than it seems at first glance. For him, 'matter' is a principle of potentiality that may or may not be corporeal. Because all beings other than God are susceptible to change, and change is the actualization of potential, all beings other than God must have an element of potentiality. Thus the 'spiritual matter' of angels is matter understood on an analogy with the corporeal matter of human beings, similar only in its status as a principle of potentiality and necessary complement to form.

7 The illumination of the intellect

Bonaventure's theory of knowledge roughly conforms to that of Aristotle as regards knowledge of the sensible world. Declaring the human mind a *tabula rasa* (blank slate) at birth, he teaches that we cannot acquire concepts of material objects, much less a knowledge of biology, without abstracting from sense experience. Aristotle's empiricism nonetheless has limitations: it fails to account for our idea of God, and fails even more miserably in accounting for certitude.

Bonaventure does not claim that the idea of God is innate in the sense that it is present at birth or will inevitably develop as the child matures. The idea might nonetheless be considered innate insofar as it is does not depend on abstraction from sense experience. To acquire the idea of God, the soul need only turn inward and reflect on its own nature, or on its natural desire for complete happiness, which God alone can provide. In arguing that the idea of God does not come from presentations of the senses, Bonaventure's purpose is mainly to emphasize that the human soul, made in God's image and belonging to the intelligible realm, need not have recourse to the material world to know its creator.

The theory of illumination, well presented in question 4 of Bonaventure's disputed questions *De scientia Christi*, aims above all to account for the certitude of human knowledge. In his view, there can be no certain knowledge without both infallibility on the part of the knower and immutability on the part of the object of knowledge. Because the mind of a creature cannot be entirely infallible through its own power, it needs the cooperation of God, even as it needs God as the source of immutable truths. Sense experience does not suffice, for it cannot reveal that what is true could not possibly be otherwise. The human mind attains certitude about the world only when it understands it in light of the 'eternal reasons' or divine ideas. In doing so, the mind will ordinarily be unconscious of divine illumination. Certitude, however, would be impossible if God did not provide an immutable object of knowledge and move the mind to assent (see ILLUMINATION).

In arguing for his theory of illumination, Bonaventure expressly denies that God is the sole source of human certainty. Such a view would fail to distinguish earthly knowledge from heavenly knowledge, knowledge of nature from knowledge of grace, and knowledge by reason from knowledge by revelation. On the other hand, Bonaventure thinks it insufficient for the knower to benefit from the eternal reasons without attaining to them. The human mind could not acquire certain knowledge if it did not in some way rise above the created order. According to Bonaventure, this is possible because, and insofar as, the soul is the image of God. Sense experience remains necessary as a source of our ideas about the world, but what certainty we attain comes from the cooperation of God.

8 Virtue

Bonaventure's doctrine of virtue, as presented in his *Collationes in Hexaemeron*, clearly reflects his metaphysics and theology (see Synan 1973). Since the end of virtue is happiness, which comes from the enjoyment of God in the afterlife, virtues must be ordered to that end. They must help us return to our creator. Return, however, is possible only through Christ; without Christ, human beings remain infected with original sin and doomed to remain forever separated from God. Indeed, at their fourth, highest level of reality, the virtues exist in Christ as exemplar ideas.

Virtues in human beings participate in these divine exemplars to various degrees. The cardinal virtues of prudence, justice, temperance and fortitude may accordingly be possessed at any of three levels. At the lowest level they are 'political' and belong to us insofar as we are social animals; at the next they are 'cleansing' and belong to us insofar as we are fit for God; and at the next they belong to those already completely cleansed. At all levels of the hierarchy human virtues depend for their reality on the exemplars. The cardinal virtues likewise also depend on the theological virtues of faith, hope and charity to attain their perfection and achieve their ends.

The four-level hierarchy of virtue comes from Macrobius' commentary on Cicero's *Dream of Scipio*, a work that explains the teachings of Plotinus. This Neoplatonic material is nevertheless transformed, not only by the addition of the theological virtues but also by Bonaventure's recasting of the cardinal virtues as products of grace and the foundation of that 'merit' which makes us deserving in the eyes of God. In his commentary on the *Sentences*, he explains that merit is rooted in free decision (*liberum arbitrium*). Thus the cardinal virtues can belong only to the intellect and the will, those powers of the soul that share in free decision. Bonaventure even argues that *all* virtues, insofar as they are virtues, must belong to the rational part of the soul. Virtues are attributed to the lower, emotional part of the soul only because habituation makes it more submissive to reason; they cannot exist principally in the seat of the passions because they would then be beyond the scope of free decision. One would be attributing virtues to the part of the soul we have in common with animals instead of to the part we have in common with angels (see Kent 1995).

For Bonaventure, then, a virtue such as fortitude has less to do with our emotional responses to danger than with what we freely decide. The appropriate emotional responses are not essential to virtue; at most they are 'annexed' to it. While this view would seem to have distant origins in the Stoic restriction of virtue to what lies within the agent's control, the emphasis on virtue as the basis of merit is of no small significance. It is one thing to see virtues as traits of character that make us happy in this life, another to see them as traits of character that make us deserving of happiness in the afterlife.

The influence of theology in Bonaventure's thought appears to have two results that some of today's moral philosophers – especially those sympathetic to KANT – would find appealing. First, virtue comes to depend on the freedom that all rational creatures have in common, even as the moral significance of emotions declines sharply. Second, it becomes quite reasonable to say that someone is both virtuous and unhappy, for virtue is now what makes someone deserving of happiness, even though internal emotional conflict, illness and misfortune may in fact cause the person great suffering (see VIRTUE ETHICS; VIRTUES AND VICES).

See also: AQUINAS, T.; ARISTOTELIANISM, MEDIEVAL; AUGUSTINIANISM; AVERROISM; MYSTICISM, HISTORY OF; PLATONISM, MEDIEVAL

List of works

Bonaventure (1250–73) *Opera omnia* (Complete Works), Quaracchi: Collegium S. Bonaventurae, 1882–1902, 10 vols. (For English translations, see *The Works of Bonaventure*, 5 vols, trans. J. de Vinck, Paterson, NJ: St Anthony Guild, 1960–70.)

—— (1253–7) *De scientia Christi* (Concerning Christ's Knowledge), Q.4 published in E. Fairweather (ed.) *A Scholastic Miscellany*, Philadelphia, PA: Westminster, 1956. (Argues that divine illumination is necessary to account for the certitude of human knowledge.)

—— (1253–7) *De mysterio Trinitatis* (On The Mystery of the Trinity), trans Z. Hayes, *Disputed Questions on the Mystery of the Trinity*, St Bonaventure, NY: Franciscan Institute, 1979. (Includes detailed analysis of arguments for God's existence.)

—— (c.1257) *Breviloquium*, in *Opera omnia*, Quaracchi: Collegium S. Bonaventurae, 1882–1902, vol. 5; trans. J. de Vinck, *The Works of Bonaventure*, Paterson, NJ: St Anthony Guild, 1960–70, vol. 2. (A brief handbook of theology for beginners.)

—— (1259) *Itinerarium mentis in Deum* (Journey of the Mind to God), trans. P. Boehner, *The Journey of the Mind to God*, ed. S. Brown, Indianapolis, IN: Hackett, 1993. (The mind's ascent from the contemplation of the sensible world to the contemplation of God.)

—— (1267) *Collationes de decem praeceptis* (On the Ten Commandments), in *Opera omnia*, Quaracchi: Collegium S. Bonaventurae, 1882–1902, vol. 5. (Christian teachings with the ethics of the pagan philosophers.)

—— (1268) *Collationes de septem donis Spiritus Sancti* (On the Seven Gifts of the Holy Spirit), in *Opera omnia*, Quaracchi: Collegium S. Bonaventurae, 1882–1902, vol. 5. (Discusses piety, understanding, wisdom and other dispositions attributed by the theologian to God's grace.)

—— (1273) *Collationes in Hexaemeron* (On the Six Days of Creation), ed. F. Delorme, *Collationes in Hexaemeron*, Quaracchi: Collegium S. Bonaventurae, 1934. (This edition is preferred by some scholars to that published in the *Opera omnia*.)

—— (before 1274) *De reductione artium ad theologiam* (Retracing the Arts to Theology), in *Opera omnia*, Quaracchi: Collegium S. Bonaventurae, 1882–1902, vol. 5; trans. J. de Vinck, *The Works of Bonaventure*, Paterson, NJ: St Anthony Guild, 1960–70, vol. 3. (The divisions, order and unity of human knowledge.)

—— (1250–2) *Commentarius in quattuor libros Sententiarum Petri Lombardi* (Commentary on the *Sentences* of Peter Lombard), in *Opera omnia*, Quaracchi: Collegium S. Bonaventurae, 1882–1902, vols 1–4. (A selection, specifically *Sent.* II, d.1, p.1, a.1, q.2, is translated by P.M. Byrne in C.Vollert *et al.*, *On the Eternity of the World (Thomas Aquinas, Siger of Brabant, St Bonaventure)*, Milwaukee, WI: Marquette University Press, 1964.)

References and further reading

* Bonansea, B. (1974) 'The Question of an Eternal World in the Teaching of St Bonaventure', *Franciscan Studies* 34: 7–33. (More complete and detailed presentation of Bonaventure on the eternity of the world.)
* Bougerol, J.G. (1964) Introduction to the Works of Bonaventure, trans. J. de Vinck, Paterson, NJ: St Anthony Guild. (Expanded discussion of Bonaventure's life and works.)
* —— (1988) *Introduction à Saint Bonaventure*, Paris: Vrin. (A revised edition of Bougerol (1964), in French.)
* Brown, S. (1993) *The Journey of the Mind to God*, Indianapolis, IN: Hackett. (Brown's introduction and notes to this translation of *Itinerarium mentis in Deum*, written with elegant simplicity, provide valuable guidance not only to this particular treatise but to Bonaventure's thought as a whole.)
* Doyle, J.P. (1974) 'Saint Bonaventure and the Ontological Argument', *Modern Schoolman* 52: 27–48. (A clear exposition of Bonaventure's arguments on the knowledge of God's existence and their Platonic background.)
  Gilson, E. (1965) *The Philosophy of St Bonaventure*, trans. I. Trethowan and F. Sheed, Paterson, NJ: St Anthony Guild. (The standard exegesis of Bonaventure's philosophy, tendentious in places but probably still unrivalled.)
* Kent, B. (1995) *Virtues of the Will: The Transformation of Ethics in the Late Thirteenth Century*, Washington, DC: Catholic University of America. (Discusses virtue and Bonaventure's *Sentences* commentary.)
  Quinn, J.F. (1973) *The Historical Constitution of St*

Bonaventure's Philosophy, Toronto, Ont.: Pontifical Institute of Mediaeval Studies. (Provides a wealth of information about Bonaventure's thought while differing sharply from Gilson's interpretation.)

* Synan, E. (1973) 'Cardinal Virtues in the Cosmos of Saint Bonaventure', in J.G. Bougerol *et al.* (eds) *S. Bonaventura, 1274–1974*, Grottaferrata: Collegium S. Bonaventurae, vol. 3: 21–38. (A brief but clear account of the moral doctrine of the *Hexaemeron* and its connection with exemplarism.)

Vollert, C. *et al.* (trans.) (1964) *On the Eternity of the World (Thomas Aquinas, Siger of Brabant, St Bonaventure)*, Milwaukee, WI: Marquette University Press. (Includes a translation of a section from Bonaventure's commentary on the Sentences.)

* Zinn, G. (1973) 'Book and Word: The Victorine Background of Bonaventure's Use of Symbols', in J.G. Bougerol *et al.* (eds) *S. Bonaventura, 1274–1974*, Grottaferrata: Collegium S. Bonaventurae, vol. 2: 143–69. (Detailed look at mysticism in Bonaventure's philosophy.)

BONNIE KENT

BONHOEFFER, DIETRICH (1906–45)

Dietrich Bonhoeffer was a twentieth-century Lutheran theologian who associated Christian belief and political action in an exemplary fashion. His part in the struggle of the Confessing Church and of the German resistance against the National-Socialist dictatorship cost him his life. Christocentric and ecclesiocentric, he stressed personal and collective piety and revived the idea of the imitation of Christ; the concepts of obedience and of the suffering God are central to his view. His Ethik *(1949) was widely influential; in it, he argued that Christians should not retreat from the world, but have a duty to act within it. His answer to the secularization of the modern world was a 'religionless Christianity', a communocentric, pietistic, personal discipline.*

1 Life and theological background
2 Ethics
3 Nonreligious interpretation of Christianity

1 Life and theological background

Born in Breslau, Bonhoeffer was raised in Berlin in an intellectual milieu. Early in his life he felt a vocation to be a theologian and studied at Tübingen in 1923 and Berlin from 1924 to 1927. His dissertation was a theological reflection on the sociology of the Church, which critically examined Hegel, Max Weber and Ernst Troeltsch. Bonhoeffer had just discovered Karl Barth's dialectical theology and was anxious to relate Christology to ecclesiology (see BARTH §§1–2). In opposition to liberal and sociological views, he asserted that the Church is the body of Christ concretely. His other early writings show the influence of Kant, Heidegger, Barth and Luther.

Following the rise of Hitler, Bonhoeffer helped to organize the Pastor's Emergency League, and took a stand against the racist policies of National Socialism, publishing 'Die Kirche vor der Judenfrage' (The Church and the Jewish Question) (1933a) and 'Der Arierparagraph in der Kirche' (The Aryan Paragraph in the Church) (1933b). His involvement with the Confessing Church, which Karl Barth had helped organize, led to his being banned from teaching and publishing. In 1938, he came into contact with the political resistance against National Socialism. He worked with the resistance until 1944, when, in the wake of the failed attempt on Hitler's life, he was arrested, imprisoned and later hanged.

Bonhoeffer's original contribution to Christian theology was prompted by historical circumstances, particularly the National Socialist dictatorship. However, a number of quite varied influences can be detected in his work, notably dialectical theology, which he discovered in the early 1930s, Moravian Pietism, Lutheranism, Roman Catholicism, and the neo-Protestantism of Wilhelm Herrmann, Adolf von Harnack, Ernst Troeltsch, Max Weber, Martin Kähler, Rudolf Otto, Karl Holl and Wilhelm Dilthey. Bonhoeffer's critical stance towards the phenomenon of religion was inspired by Barth's distinction between faith and religion, and his assertion that revelation abolished religion.

Bonhoeffer understood Christian faith as a combination of Old Testament legalism and New Testament Christocentrism. It seems that he experienced a conversion in 1931, while studying the Sermon on the Mount and Psalm 119, the famous love poem to the Law. To him, the central issue was that of obedience, and the concept of discipleship grew into a major theological theme. It culminated in *Nachfolge* (Following After) (1937), a study of the imitation of Christ in the Gospels, in which Bonhoeffer argues that 'only the believer is obedient, and only the obedient believes'. He believed that faith consists in following in Jesus Christ's footsteps by accepting God's messianic suffering. Two elements are constitutive of faith: the implementation of justice and the acceptance of divine suffering. Jesus' agony only ends with the end of the world. In Bonhoeffer's theology of the cross, God is not the triumphant and enthroned God of Isaiah 6, but a God of suffering, suffering in the world and for the world. Discipleship, then, is following Christ at Gethsemane.

2 Ethics

Begun in 1940, Bonhoeffer's *Ethik* was published as fragments in 1949 by Eberhard Bethge. It is Bonhoeffer's *magnum opus*, and must be understood against the background of his political involvement. In June 1939, he had refused to move to the USA, even though staying in Germany meant accepting a double life, simultaneously this-worldly and other-worldly. For Europe was in a such a predicament that, in his view, Christians were not morally allowed to retreat from the world. On the contrary, it behoved Christians to be involved in worldly affairs and to collaborate with non-Christians. Consequently, Christian theology had to address the question of the possibility of acknowledging the world from a Christocentric perspective. Bonhoeffer propounded five major ideas. First, though distinct, the Christian community and the world should not be kept apart. Christian action always is action in the world. Faith is not an escape from the world, but is existentially this-worldly. Second, the world is the world accepted by Christ, who is the uniting principle of Western civilization. Third, a Christian's participation in the reality of Jesus Christ and in the reality of the world, even a Godless world, is possible because in Christ God enabled us to participate concomitantly in a dual reality, that of God and that of the world. Fourth, only in the reality of the world can one truly be a Christian. But there is no real worldliness except in the reality of Jesus Christ. Christ's sovereignty is the focal concept of Christian ethics. Finally, penitence clears the path for the imitation of Christ or discipleship.

3 Nonreligious interpretation of Christianity

In a letter from prison, dated 30 April 1944, Bonhoeffer introduces and discusses the concept of religionless Christianity. He often referred to this idea as the nonreligious interpretation of Christianity. As early as his dissertation, *Sanctorum communio* (1930), Bonhoeffer had argued for a nonreligious Christianity. His diagnosis of the 'churchliness of the modern bourgeoisie' led him to call the Church back to a more sincere and genuine community modelled on Christ. He was dismayed by the empty religiosity of the Church and further outraged by its passive enslavement to National Socialism. Under the joint influences of Dilthey, Kant and Barth, he developed a negative concept of religion. According to Bonhoeffer, Christian religion is 'a historically conditioned and transient form of human self expression'.

Religion is a human answer to anxiety. In the human quest for security, God is the ultimate refuge. Towards the close of the Middle Ages, people ceased to believe in the authority of the Church. European thought turned away from other-worldliness towards this-worldliness, intellectual autonomy was established and personal emancipation encouraged. The Enlightenment and the subsequent nineteenth-century revolutions anticipated 'the world come of age' of the twentieth century. Progressive secularization transformed the Christian world into a world without God. The religious interpretation of life and history has ended, and religion is ending as well. This process is irreversible. The end of religion also implies the end of traditional Christianity. In a world beyond Christendom, a world come to adulthood and further progressing towards a religionless time, the only suitable apologetics consists in providing a nonreligious interpretation of Scripture. The Bible is not a religious book, but the story of a people progressing through suffering towards justice and God's kingdom.

Bonhoeffer's response to the demise of Christianity was both pietistic and ethical; it was a theological extrapolation of the piety of his home life. His call for a nonreligious Christianity was a call for a sincere Christocentric and communocentric Christianity. It was an attempt to bring Christian life into harmony with Christian discourse. In our secular world, Christianity can recover its identity only as a personal and secret discipline. In his most widely read book, *Gemeinsames Leben* (Life Together) (1939), he argued for the renewal of some forms of monastic life in order to serve the world. Bonhoeffer's courageous death at the hands of the National Socialists testified to his belief that 'before God and with God we live without God'.

List of works

Bonhoeffer, D. (1986–1996) *Dietrich Bonhoeffer Werke*, ed. E. Bethge *et al.*, Munich: Chr. Kaiser Verlag, 16 vols; various translators, ed. W.W. Floyd, Jr, *Dietrich Bonhoeffer's Works*, Minneapolis, MN: Fortress Press, 1995–. (The new critical edition, with extensive introductions, notes and bibliographies; the English version is still appearing at the time of writing.)

—— (1965–7) *Gesammelte Schriften* (Collected Writings), ed. E. Bethge, Munich: Chr. Kaiser Verlag, 5 vols; selections trans. E.H. Robertson and J. Bowden, ed. E. Robertson, *No Rusty Swords: Letters, Lectures and Notes 1928–1936*; *The Way to Freedom: Letters, Lectures and Notes 1935–1939*; *True Patriotism: Letters, Lectures and Notes 1939–1945*, London: Collins, 1965–7. (The English volumes selected from this earlier complete edition contain much that is still not available elsewhere, as well as a detailed chronology of Bonhoeffer's life.)

—— (1930) *Sanctorum communio: eine Untersuchung zur Sociologie der Kirche*, Berlin and Frankfurt-an-der-Oder: Trowitzsch & Sohn; trans. R. Gregor Smith, *Sanctorum Communio: A Dogmatic Inquiry into the Sociology of the Church* [in the USA: *The Communion of Saints:* ...], London: Collins, 1963. (Bonhoeffer's 1927 Berlin doctoral dissertation, a somewhat technical sociological and theological discussion of personhood, community, sin and the Church.)

—— (1931) *Akt und Sein: Transzendentalphilosophie und Ontologie in der systematischen Theologie* (Act and Being: Transcendental Philosophy and Ontology in Systematic Theology), Gütersloh: C. Bertelsman; trans. B. Noble, *Act and Being*, London: Collins, 1964. (Bonhoeffer's *Habilitationsschrift*, a highly technical piece in which he claims that theology can mediate between an act-based philosophy associated with Kant – and Barth in theology – and a being-based philosophy associated with Heidegger, among others.)

—— (1933a) 'Die Kirche vor der Judenfrage', in *Gesammelte Schriften*, ed. E. Bethge, vol. 2, Munich: Chr. Kaiser Verlag, 1965–7; trans. E.H. Robinson and J. Bowden, 'The Church and the Jewish Question', in *No Rusty Swords: Letters, Lectures and Notes 1928–1936*, ed. E.H. Robertson, London: Collins, 1965–7. (After the boycott of Jewish businesses was declared on 1 April 1933 and the German Church banned Jews from positions of authority on 7 April, Bonhoeffer delivered this lecture against anti-Semitism, trying to reclaim pro-Semitic emphases in Luther.)

—— (1933b) 'Der Arierparagraph in der Kirche' (The Aryan Paragraph in the Church), in *Gesammelte Schriften*, ed. E. Bethge, vol. 2, Munich: Chr. Kaiser Verlag, 1965–7. (In this leaflet, Bonhoeffer presented a set of theses and antitheses, arguing against the anti-Semitic stance of the German Christians.)

—— (1933c) *Schöpfung und Fall: theologische Auslegung von Genesis 1–3*, Munich: Chr. Kaiser Verlag; trans. J.C. Fletcher, *Creation and Fall: A Theological Interpretation of Genesis 1–3*, London: SCM, 1959. (In a very different mode, Bonhoeffer interprets Genesis in a way reminiscent of Karl Barth on Romans: treating it as a book of the Church, to be interpreted in and for the Church.)

—— (1933d) 'Christologie', in *Gesammelte Schriften*, ed. E. Bethge, vol. 3, Munich: Chr. Kaiser Verlag, 1965–7; trans. J. Bowden, *Christology* [*Christ the Center* in the USA], London: Collins, 1961. (An unfinished lecture course, which treats of 'the present Christ' and 'the historical Christ', and presents Christ as the boundary and hidden centre of reality.)

—— (1937) *Nachfolge* (Following After), Munich: Chr. Kaiser Verlag; trans. R.H. Fuller, *The Cost of Discipleship*, London: SCM, enlarged edn, 1959. (A very influential nontechnical condemnation of 'cheap grace' – a reminder of the way of the Cross, and the harsh calls of Jesus' Sermon on the Mount.)

—— (1939) *Gemeinsames Leben*, Munich: Chr. Kaiser Verlag; trans. J.W. Doberstein, *Life Together*, New York: Harper, 1954. (A description of Christian community, based, like *The Cost of Discipleship*, on Bonhoeffer's experience of common life in an irregular seminary in Finkenwalde, closed by the Gestapo in 1937.)

—— (1949) *Ethik*, ed. E. Bethge, Munich: Chr. Kaiser Verlag; trans. N. Horton Smith, *Ethics*, London: SCM, 1955. (An incomplete and fragmentary work, *Ethik* was written secretly by Bonhoeffer in the years before his arrest, and deals very practically with Christian citizenship and conformity to Christ.)

—— (1951) *Widerstand und Ergebung: Briefe und Aufzeichnungen aus der Haft* (Resistance and Humility: Letters and Notes from Prison), Munich: Chr. Kaiser Verlag; trans. R. Fuller *et al.*, *Letters and Papers from Prison*, London: SCM, enlarged edn, 1971. (Now a religious classic, this collection casts much light on the directions Bonhoeffer's thought was taking when he died. Includes 'After Ten Years', Bonhoeffer's own assessment of the 1930s and early 1940s.)

—— (1990) *Testament to Freedom: The Essential Writings of Dietrich Bonhoeffer*, ed. G.B. Kelly and F.B. Nelson, New York: Harper. (A useful introductory reader with a long introductory essay, and a selection of letters, poems and essays, each with a short introduction.)

References and further reading

Barth, K. (1919) *Der Römerbrief*, Bern: Bäschlin; 2nd edn, much changed, Munich: Chr. Kaiser Verlag, 1922; 6th edn trans. E.C. Hoskyns, *The Epistle to the Romans*, Oxford: Oxford University Press, 1968. (Barth was a strong influence on Bonhoeffer, whose *Creation and Fall* resembles this book.)

Bethge, E. (1967) *Dietrich Bonhoeffer*, Munich: Chr. Kaiser Verlag; trans. E. Mossbacker *et al.*, *Dietrich Bonhoeffer: Theologian, Christian, Contemporary*, London: Collins, 1970. (A massively detailed and absolutely essential biography from one of Bonhoeffer's closest friends.)

Dumas, A. (1968) *Une théologie de la réalité: Dietrich*

Bonhoeffer, Geneva: Éditions Labor et Fides; trans. R. McAfee Brown, *Dietrich Bonhoeffer: Theologian of Reality*, London: SCM, 1971. (Something of a classic interpretation of Bonhoeffer's thought, stressing the continuities of the corpus, and Bonhoeffer's relationship to Hegel.)

Feil, E. (1971) *Die Theologie Dietrich Bonhoeffers*, Munich: Kaiser & Grumwald; trans. M. Rumscheidt, *The Theology of Dietrich Bonhoeffer*, Philadelphia, PA: Fortress Press, 1985. (A good, solid investigation of Bonhoeffer's theology.)

Floyd, W.W. and Marsh, C. (eds.) (1994) *Theology and the Practice of Responsibility: Essays on Dietrich Bonhoeffer*, Valley Forge, PA: Trinity Press International. (A collection of recent scholarship: Bonhoeffer and modernity, and social analysis, and postmodernism, and so on.)

Kelly, G.B. (1984) *Liberating Faith: Bonhoeffer's Message for Today*, Minneapolis, MN: Augsburg. (An accessible, nontechnical introduction to Bonhoeffer's life and work.)

Marsh, C. (1994) *Reclaiming Dietrich Bonhoeffer: The Promise of His Theology*, Oxford: Oxford University Press. (Marsh reads Bonhoeffer as in pursuit of a Christologically redescribed philosophy within a roughly Barthian theology. Technical but clear; includes material on Bonhoeffer's relationship to Hegel and Heidegger.)

Ott, H. (1966) *Wirklichkeit und Glaube*, vol. 1: *Zum theologischen Erbe Dietrich Bonhoeffers*, Zurich: Vandenhoeck & Ruprecht; trans. A.A. Morrison, *Reality and Faith: The Theological Legacy of Dietrich Bonhoeffer*, London: Lutterworth, 1971. (A lengthy and detailed examination of Bonhoeffer's work in the context of German theology and philosophy.)

Peck, W.J. (ed.) (1987) *New Studies in Bonhoeffer's Ethics*, Lewiston and Queenstown: Edwin Mellen. (Useful, detailed essays on the text, context and content of Bonhoeffer's *Ethik*.)

Zimmerman, W.D. and Smith, R.G. (eds.) (1964) *Begegnungen mit Dietrich Bonhoeffer: Ein Almanach* (Encounters with Dietrich Bonhoeffer), Munich: Chr. Kaiser Verlag; trans. K.G. Smith, *I Knew Dietrich Bonhoeffer*, London: Collins, 1966. (Chronologically arranged reminiscences, from childhood acquaintances to those who knew him in prison.)

JEAN-LOUP SEBAN

BONNET, CHARLES (1720–93)

In his youth, Bonnet made a meticulous and creative study of insects, which won him international fame for his discoveries, as well as his methods. He turned to psychology and offered a detailed, but speculative, account of the physiology of mental states. His empirical work was overtaken by speculative ambition. In later life, he developed (from elements already present in his early studies) a comprehensive view of the universe, of its history and its natural history, of theology and of moral philosophy. Christianity was proved, the great chain of being was mapped over time towards an ultimate perfection, and human morality, based on self-love, formed part of the Creator's scheme. The Creator, at the moment of creation, brought into being all the elements from which this vast unfolding would occur, without further intervention.

1 Life and works
2 Thought

1 Life and works

Charles Bonnet, Swiss naturalist and philosopher, was born in Geneva and belonged to a family which had left France during the period of persecution of Protestants in the mid-sixteenth century. A youthful interest in natural history, and in insects in particular, led to his discovery, as a result of painstaking experimentation and observation, of the parthenogenesis of aphids. He was only 18 at the time of this important discovery, but received recognition from the Académie des Sciences in Paris to which his correspondent and mentor Réaumur presented his results in 1740. He then turned his attention to the regeneration of worms cut into parts, and to the respiratory mechanism of caterpillars. At the age of 23, he was elected fellow of the Royal Society in London, and his work *Traité d'insectologie* (Treatise on Entomology) was also published in 1745.

His vision deteriorated seriously, something which Bonnet attributed to overwork at the microscope. He did not at once abandon his empirical studies, but turned to the study of leaves. He investigated their movement and anatomy, maintaining that plants displayed a form of sensibility. Though lacking some of the essential theoretical concepts, he was in effect the first to investigate photosynthesis. He published his *Recherches sur l'usage des feuilles dans les plantes* (Investigations into the Function of Leaves in Plants) in 1754.

But his interests had already turned towards psychology and philosophy. His poor eyesight made it difficult for him to read or write, so that books were read to him. LEIBNIZ made a special impression. His subsequent writings were dictated, including the *Essai de psychologie* (Essay on Psychology) (1754b), the *Essai analytique sur les facultés de l'âme* (Analytical Essay on Mental Faculties) (1760), the *Considérations sur les corps organisés* (Considerations on Organic Bodies) (1762–8), the *Contemplation de la nature (The Contemplation of Nature)* (1764), *La Palingénésie philosophique* (Philosophical Palingenesis) (1769), as well as a collected edition of his writings which he supervised, *Œuvres d'histoire naturelle et de philosophie* (1779–83).

2 Thought

Bonnet's thought has two organizing principles, potentially in conflict, both of which stemmed from his work as an entomologist. One is the importance of classification. The second is the idea that there are no gaps in nature. Between any two differently classified items, an intermediary item can be found.

In the *Essai de psychologie* and the *Essai analytique sur les facultés de l'âme*, Bonnet put forward a sensualist psychology, like, for instance, HARTLEY and CONDILLAC. Sensations consisted in the vibration of nerve fibres in the brain. Once a 'virgin fibre' had first been caused to vibrate by an external stimulus, it could subsequently vibrate for internal reasons, giving rise to other types of mental phenomena. We pass smoothly from sensations to ideas. In developing this conception, Bonnet used the same model as Condillac: that of a statue successively presented with simple sensations of smell.

In spite of his speculative physiological account of sensation and other mental operations, Bonnet was not a materialist. On the contrary, he held that sensation required the activity of the soul, which, though linked to the body at a certain point in the nervous system, was an eternally existing 'germ'. (Bonnet did not have a fixed view about where this point was situated.)

Thus, Bonnet's psychology included an application of his general doctrine of 'preformation', already envisaged in his entomological work. He considered that the parthenogenesis of aphids demonstrated the existence of preformed germs of organisms in the female germ cell. In his *Considérations sur les corps organisés*, he argued against epigenesis, the view that ontogenesis could be explained in some mechanical or developmental fashion, and maintained that from the time of creation, the universe contained a multitude of preformed 'germs', whose future development was already built into them. These ideas were brought together in an even more elaborate synthesis in the *La Palingénésie philosophique*. Here we see the 'great chain of being' presented in dynamic form. We see an eschatological cosmology spread over time: the history of the earth consists of a series of cataclysms in which all organic life is destroyed, except the germs themselves. Over time, at each moment of rebirth, the germs produce a new and more perfect instantiation of what was already built into them at the moment of creation, until the final state is reached through the resurrection (or 'palingenesis') announced in the Christian gospel.

Bonnet also produced an apologetic work, *Recherches philosophiques sur les preuves du christianisme* (Philosophical Investigations into the Proofs of Christianity) (1770) in which, apart from reproducing some of the traditional proofs, he explained miracles, not as divine interventions in the natural order, but as apparently anomalous events which were already provided for at the moment of creation. His moral philosophy, developed in *Philalèthe* (before 1783), goes from the avoidance of pain and the search for pleasure, through self-love, but claims that this preutilitarian conception has its place in a divinely planned order. The 'invisible hand' of Adam SMITH is the hand of God.

The grandiose system which Bonnet developed was widely influential in his day. But perhaps his more lasting philosophical impact arose from his detailed physiological theory of sensation, which influenced CABANIS and MAINE DE BIRAN.

See also: EVOLUTION, THEORY OF

List of works

Bonnet, C. (1745) *Traité d'insectologie ou observations sur les pucerons* (Treatise on Entomology; or Observations on Aphids), Paris: Durand. (Describes Bonnet's famous discovery of the parthenogenesis of aphids.)

—— (1754a) *Recherches sur l'usage des feuilles dans les plantes* (Investigations into the Functions of Leaves in Plants), Leiden: Luzac; repr. Hildesheim and New York: Olms, 1978. (Prefigures much later studies of photosynthesis.)

—— (1754b) *Essai de psychologie* (Essay on Psychology), Leiden: Luzac; repr. Hildesheim and New York: Olms, 1978. (Attempts a materialist account of mental processes.)

—— (1760) *Essai analytique sur les facultés de l'âme* (Analytical Essay on mental faculties), Copenhagen: C. & A. Philibert; repr. Hildesheim and New York: Olms, 1973. (Further development of associationist/materialist views of the mind, including the 'hypothesis of the statue' which also occurs in Condillac.)

—— (1762) *Considérations sur les corps organisés: où l'on traite de leur origine, de leur développement, de leur reproduction etc., et où l'on a rassemblé en abrégé tout ce que l'histoire naturelle offre de plus certain et de plus intéressant sur ce sujet* (Considerations on Organic Bodies; treating of their origin, development, reproduction etc., with a summary of the most certain and interesting findings of natural history on this subject), Amsterdam: Marc-Michel Rey. (The first of a series of works in which Bonnet argues that the epigenetic view of biological development, whch assumes that it can be explained mechanically, must be rejected in favour of 'preformation'.)

—— (1764) *Contemplation de la nature*, Amsterdam: Marc-Michel Rey; trans. anon. as *The Contemplation of Nature*, London: Longman, Becket, de Hondt, 1766. (Further development of ideas in Bonnet 1762.)

—— (1769) *La Palingénésie philosophique, ou Idées sur l'état passé et sur l'état futur des êtres vivants* (Philosophical Palingensis; or Ideas on the Past and Future State of Living Beings), Amsterdam: Marc-Michel Rey. (A major, and somewhat mystical, synthesis of previous biological theories.)

—— (1770) *Recherches philosophiques sur les preuves du christianisme*, Geneva: C. Philibert & B. Chirol; trans. J.L. Boissier, *Philosophical and Critical Inquiries concerning Christianity*, London: Stockdale, 1787. (Reproduces some traditional theistic proofs, and adds the claim that miracles were prefigured.)

—— (1779–83) *Œuvres d'histoire naturelle et de philosophie* (Works in Natural History and Philosophy), Neuchâtel: Fauche. (This edition additionally contains the following philosophical opuscula in vol. 18: Principes Philosophiques; Vue de leibnitzianisme; Hypothèse sur l'âme des bêtes et leur industrie; Philalèthe ou Essai d'une méthode pour établir quelques vérités de philosophie rationnelle.)

—— (1788) *Précis de la doctrine de Kant sur l'entendement pur et remarques sur cette doctrine* (Summary of Kant's Doctrine on Pure Understanding and Remarks on this Doctrine) and *Remarques sur quelques endroits du livre de M. Kant intitulé 'Critique de l'entendement pur'*. (Comments on Kant.)

—— (1971) *Bonnet, Charles: Lettres à M. l'abbé Spallanzani*, ed. Castellani, C., Milan: Episteme. (Letters to Spallanzani.)

—— (1986) *Science against the Unbelievers: The Correspondence of Bonnet and Needham, 1760–1780*, ed. Mazzolini, R. and Roe, S.A., Oxford: Voltaire Foundation at the Taylor Institution. (Correspondence.)

—— (1948) *Mémoires autobiographiques de Charles Bonnet de Genève* (Autobiographical Memoirs of Charles Bonnet of Geneva), ed. Savioz, R. Paris: Vrin.

References and further reading

Anderson, L. (1982) *Charles Bonnet and the Order of the Known*, Dordrecht: Reidel. (A thorough and interesting survey of Bonnet's work, influenced by the approach of Foucault.)

Bonnet, G. (1929) *Charles Bonnet*, Paris: M. Lac. (A thorough study.)

Claparède, E. (1909) *La Psychologie animale de Charles Bonnet* (The Animal Psychology of Charles Bonnet), Geneva: Georg. (A specialized study.)

Marx, J. (1976) 'Charles Bonnet contre les Lumières', *Studies on Voltaire and the Eighteenth Century*, Oxford: Voltaire Foundation at the Taylor Institute, 156–7. (A scholarly work which helps to place Bonnet in his intellectual environment, and which includes a thorough bibliography.)

Müller, G.H. and Pozzo, R. (eds) (1988) 'Bonnet, critico di Kant : due cahiers ginevrini del 1788', *Rivista di storia della filosofia*, 131–64. (Discussion of Kant's ideas.)

Offner, M. (1893) *Die Psychologie Charles Bonnets*, Leipzig. (Still a standard work.)

Rocci, G. (1975) *Charles Bonnet: filosofia e scienza*, Florence: Sansoni. (Should not be neglected.)

Roger, J. (1971) *Les Sciences de la vie dans la pensée française du XVIII siècle* (Life Sciences in French Thought of the Eighteenth Century), Paris: A. Colin, 2nd edn. (A helpful historical study from a particular point of view.)

Rostand, J. (1945) *Esquisse d'une histoire de la biologie: Un préformationniste – Ch. Bonnet* (Sketch of a History of Biology: A Prereformationist – C. Bonnet), Paris: Gallimard. (Important for those interested in the history and philosophy of biology, and Bonnet's relevance to it.)

Savioz, R. (1948) *La Philosophie de Charles Bonnet de Genève* (The Philosophy of Charles Bonnet of Geneva), Paris: Vrin. (A helpful review.)

F.C.T. MOORE

BOOK OF CAUSES *see* LIBER DE CAUSIS

BOOK OF CHANGES see Yijing

BOOLE, GEORGE (1815–64)

George Boole, a British mathematician, is credited with making a fundamental contribution to modern logic. If Leibniz's manuscript essays on logic, effectively unknown until the end of the nineteenth century, are excluded, then Boole's algebra of logic (1847, 1854) was the first successful mathematical treatment of one part of logic. The treatment was mathematical in the broad sense of using a formal language expressed in symbols with definite rules. It was also mathematical in a narrow sense of being closely modelled after numerical algebra, from which it differed by an additional axiom, $x^2 = x$. Letter symbols of this algebra were conceived as representing classes, 1 standing for a 'universe' of objects and 0 for the empty class. By identifying logical terms with their extensions, that is, with classes, inferences of a much more general character than those of the traditional syllogistic could be carried out. Boole also showed how this algebra could be used in propositional logic, presenting its earliest systematic general formulation.

1 Beginnings
2 *The Laws of Thought*

1 Beginnings

Boole, eldest child of a Lincolnshire shoemaker, had no formal secondary or higher education, though he was recognized early on as a gifted child. He taught himself Latin, Greek and the major European languages, reading widely in many subjects. At the age of 16, impelled by his family's financial hardship, he became assistant to a schoolmaster. At that time he also began the serious study of higher mathematics by reading works of the masters. At the age of 19 he opened his own school. While still teaching he managed to do mathematical research, attaining considerable prominence when he was awarded a Royal Society gold medal for a paper printed in the Society's *Philosophical Transactions*. In 1849, although without a university degree, he was appointed Professor of Mathematics at the newly opened Queen's College in Cork (now University College, Cork).

Boole's innovative ideas first appeared in a pamphlet, *The Mathematical Analysis of Logic* (1847). Boole was evidently a newcomer to the subject, as his exposition of the traditional syllogism paraphrased that contained in Richard Whately's popular treatise *Elements of Logic* (1844). Whately's conception of the subject as a formal, abstract discipline marked a sharp break with the view, prevalent through the eighteenth century, of logic as a language art, or as an epistemological tool in the search for truth. Moreover, Whately's explanations of logical principles were couched extensionally, logical terms being taken as representing classes of objects, not intensionally as representing combinations of attributes. To this extensional setting Boole adjoined a mathematical feature, adapting notions from operator algebra for this purpose. With each class (term) X he associated a selection operator, x, which selects from a universe of objects those which are X. In operator algebra, successive operation is indicated by 'multiplication' (of operators). Hence yx selects the Y from what x selects, that is, from the X. As selection in either order results in the same class, he has the 'law',

$$xy = yx$$

Similarly, since a repeated selection of the same class results in nothing new, he has

$$xx \,(\text{or } x^2) = x$$

Propositions are represented by equations. The universal affirmative 'All X are Y', for example, is represented by '$x = xy$' (selection of the Xs from the Ys yields just the Xs if and only if all X are Y). The universal negative 'No X are Y' is represented by '$xy = 0$' (0 representing 'nothing'). Inferences are performed by the substitution and replacement of equals. Thus from '$x = xy$' and '$y = yz$', on replacing y in the first equation by yz and then the combination xy by x, one obtains

$$x = x(yz) = (xy)z = xz$$

justifying the validity of the AAA syllogism.

2 *The Laws of Thought*

These few items suffice to illustrate the nature of Boole's initial venture. Seven years later it was supplanted by his more carefully constructed and elaborated *The Laws of Thought* (1854). In a significant change from the earlier work, the symbols $x, y, z, \ldots$ are no longer operations selecting classes but stand directly for the classes themselves. The common understanding of the term class is extended so as to include 'universe' and 'nothing', these being denoted by 1 and 0 respectively. Unlike 'xy', defined for any two classes, the combinations '$x + y$' and '$x - y$' are only partially defined: '$x + y$' has meaning only if x and y have nothing in common, and '$x - y$' has meaning only if y is part of x. Citing examples from ordinary language for justification, he states a number of laws which hold for classes, such as the two mentioned above, and others such as '$z(x+y) = zx + zy$', for which he gives as an example 'European men and women' is the same as 'European men and European women'.

He contends that for purposes of logical deduction the only verb needed is 'is', or 'are', symbolically expressed by '='. Logical deductions are accomplished by algebraic operations on equations, such as substituting equals for equals. What is new here is a more sophisticated justification for the use of algebra in doing logic, one based on the idea (at that time quite novel) of an algebra different from standard numerical algebra. Commenting on the analogy of his laws of class symbols with those of 'Number', all but '$x^2 = x$' being true of numbers, and that also if x is restricted to being either 0 or 1, he says:

> Let us conceive, then, of an Algebra in which the symbols $x, y, z, \ldots$ admit indifferently of the values 0 and 1, and of these values alone. The laws, the axioms, and the processes, of such an Algebra will be identical in their whole extent with the laws, the axioms, and the processes of an Algebra of Logic. Difference of interpretation will alone divide them.
> (1854: 37–8)

With the adoption of this principle Boole vastly extended the range and applicability of traditional term logic. For – as in numerical algebra – terms of any size or complexity are constructible, resulting in new inference forms unlimited in number. Moreover, as in algebra, transformations on such complex terms can be carried out mechanically by rule, that is, 'computationally'.

But there were difficulties associated with the principle. According to it one may freely use algebraic expressions constructible by use of the binary operators $+$, $-$, $\times$, the (class) variables $x, y, z, \ldots$ and the constants 0 and 1. But then Boole had the problem of what to do with expressions such as '$1+1$' and '$0-1$' to which no meaning was attached. He argued that if the initial algebraic formulas were interpretable in terms of class notions, and if the end result was also so interpretable then the result was valid even if some of the intermediary steps were not. He likened this to the use of the imaginary $\sqrt{-1}$ in trigonometry. With considerable ingenuity Boole introduced procedures which enabled him to obtain correct results.

All this ingenuity became needless when Boole's partially defined addition was replaced by one based on non-exclusive 'or' (as suggested by W.S. Jevons (1864), C.S. Peirce (1867)), so that '$x + x = x$', resulting in what is now called 'Boolean Algebra'. An alternative simplification appeared in the twentieth century. This produced an algebra ('Boolean ring with unit') even closer to Boole's conceptions in having a meaningful subtraction. Here addition is taken to be 'symmetric difference' – what Boole would have written as '$x(1-y) + y(1-x)$' – resulting in the law '$x + x = 0$' for this interpretation of addition.

The same algebra that Boole used for the logic of terms he also employed for propositional logic. Now, instead of $x, y, z, \ldots$ standing for classes $X, Y, Z, \ldots$ they stand for 'portions of time' for which propositions $X, Y, Z, \ldots$ are true. Then, for example, '$x = 1$' stands for X being true (for all time), and '$y = 0$' for Y not true and '$x(1-y) = 0$' for 'If X is true, then Y is true' (since for no time is X true and Y not true). In this application, without explicitly realizing it, Boole was adjoining '$x = 1$ or $x = 0$', a property not necessarily holding for classes and, in effect, reducing his algebra to a special kind of algebra in which there are only two classes.

It will be no denigration of Boole's remarkable achievement in logic if its inadequacies are cited. As already noted, his choice of an addition, incompletely defined for classes, required excessively complicated methods to recover logical content. On the other hand, some of his devices (for example, expansion of a logical function into normal form) became valuable techniques. His treatment of the particular proposition (those involving 'some') was defective, as would be expected since his algebra had no formal means of expressing non-emptiness of a class. He thought his propositional logic had to be based on his logic of terms via the notion of 'portions of time'. Currently the logic of terms is treated as part of the predicate calculus, the development of which *presupposes* propositional logic. Finally, despite Boole's belief that his treatment was fully adequate for all of logic, it did not have the ability to express quantifiers.

See also: BOOLEAN ALGEBRA; LOGIC IN THE 19TH CENTURY §3

List of works

Boole, G. (1847) *The Mathematical Analysis of Logic, Being an Essay Towards a Calculus of Deductive Reasoning*, Cambridge: Macmillan, Barclay & Macmillan; London: George Bell; repr. Oxford, Blackwell, 1948, and in Boole, 1952, 49–124. (Written in haste, Boole wished it to be replaced by his more maturely considered *Laws of Thought*.)

—— (1854) *An Investigation of the Laws of Thought, on Which are Founded the Mathematical Theories of Logic and Probabilities*, London: Walton & Maberly; repr. as *George Boole's Collected Logical Works*, Chicago, IL, and New York: Open Court,

1916, vol. 2; repr. New York: Dover, 1951. (This work is also notable for its contribution to the origins of modern algebra and, less so, for its extensive discussions, from an unconventional viewpoint, of probability matters.)

—— (1952) *Studies in Logic and Probability*, ed. R. Rhees, London: Watts & Co. (The most extensive commentary on Boole's ideas on logic and probability. Somewhat mathematical in parts, but much of it accessible to the general reader.)

References and further reading

Hailperin, T. (1976) *Boole's Logic and Probability: A Critical Exposition from the Standpoint of Contemporary Algebra, Logic and Probability Theory*, Amsterdam: North Holland; 2nd edn, 1986. (The second edition has been revised and enlarged, and contains an extensive bibliography.)

* Jevons, W.S. (1864) *Pure Logic or the Logic of Quality apart from Quantity. With Remarks on Boole's System and on the Relation of Logic and Mathematics*, London: E. Stanford. (Of significance only for its introduction of the non-exclusive 'or'.)

MacHale, D. (1985) *George Boole: His Life and Work*, Dublin: Boole Press. (A highly recommended biography. Contains an extended bibliography.)

* Peirce, C.S. (1867) 'On an Improvement in Boole's Calculus of Logic', *Proceedings of the American Academy of Arts and Sciences* 7: 250–61; repr. in *Collected Papers*, Cambridge, MA: Harvard University Press, vol. 3, 1933; also in *Writings of Charles S. Peirce*, Bloomington, IN: Indiana University Press, 1984, vol. 2. (Peirce's first paper on logic, the beginning of a long sequence of his distinguished contributions to the subject.)

* Whately, R. (1844) *Elements of Logic: Comprising the Substance of the Article in the Encyclopedia Metropolitana: with additions, etc.*, 8th edn, revised, London: B. Fellowes. (This work, dating from 1827, appeared in many printings, editions, and by various publishers.)

THEODORE HAILPERIN

BOOLEAN ALGEBRA

Boolean algebra, or the algebra of logic, was devised by the English mathematician George Boole (1815–64) and embodies the first successful application of algebraic methods to logic.

Boole seems to have had several interpretations for his system in mind. In his earlier work he thinks of each of the basic symbols of his 'algebra' as standing for the mental operation of selecting just the objects possessing some given attribute or included in some given class; later he conceives of these symbols as standing for the attributes or classes themselves. In each of these interpretations the basic symbols are conceived as being capable of combination under certain operations: 'multiplication', corresponding to conjunction of attributes or intersection of classes; 'addition', corresponding to (exclusive) disjunction or (disjoint) union; and 'subtraction', corresponding to 'excepting' or difference. He also recognizes that the algebraic laws he proposes are satisfied if the basic symbols are interpreted as taking just the number values 0 and 1.

Boole's ideas have since undergone extensive development, and the resulting concept of Boolean algebra now plays a central role in mathematical logic, probability theory and computer design.

1 Basic facts
2 Important types of Boolean algebra
3 Boolean algebras as algebras of truth-values

1 Basic facts

Boolean algebra, devised by the English mathematician George Boole, embodies the first successful application of algebraic methods to logic (see Boole 1847, 1854).

The algebraic structures implicit in Boole's analysis were first explicitly presented by Huntington (1904), and termed 'Boolean algebras' by Sheffer (1913). As Huntington recognized, there are various equivalent ways of characterizing Boolean algebras. One of the most convenient definitions is as follows. A 'Boolean algebra' is a structure $(B, +_B, *_B, -_B, 0_B, 1_B)$, with B a non-empty set, $+_B$ and $*_B$ binary operations on B, $-_B$ a unary operation on B, and $0_B, 1_B$ distinct elements of B such that the following are true for all x, y, z in B.

$$x + (y+z) = (x+y) + z$$
$$x * (y*z) = (x*y) * z$$
(associativity)

$$x + y = y + x$$
$$x * y = y * x$$
(commutativity)

$$x + (x*y) = x$$
$$x * (x+y) = x$$
(absorption)

$$x + (y*z) = (x+y) * (x+z)$$
$$x * (y+z) = (x*y) + (x*z)$$
(distributivity)

$$x + (-x) = 1$$
$$x * (-x) = 0$$
(complementation)

(We omit the subscript when confusion is unlikely.) The operations '+' (Boolean 'addition' – here corresponding to *inclusive* disjunction), '*' (Boolean 'multiplication' – intersection) and '–' (taking the complement) are called Boolean operations. Note that the operation sending x, y to $x * (-y)$ corresponds to Boole's 'subtraction'. The elements 0 and 1 are called the 'zero element' and 'unit element' of B, respectively. We shall usually identify somewhat loosely a Boolean algebra by its underlying set; thus, for example, the Boolean algebra just introduced will be denoted simply by 'B'.

The following basic identities can be readily shown to hold in any Boolean algebra.

$-(x+y) = (-x) * (-y)$ (De Morgan's laws)
$-(x*y) = (-x) + (-y)$

$-(-x) = x$ (double complement law)

We observe that in the axioms characterizing Boolean algebras the roles played by + and *, and by 0 and 1, are entirely symmetrical. This observation leads to the important 'principle of duality' for Boolean algebras which may be formulated as follows. Let P be any statement about Boolean algebras which involves just the Boolean operations +, * and – and the elements 0, 1. The 'dual' of P is obtained from P by interchanging + with * and 0 with 1. If P holds in all Boolean algebras, then so does the dual of P. Thus, for example, once we have established one of De Morgan's laws above, the principle of duality leads automatically to the other one.

We define a 'subalgebra' of a Boolean algebra B to be a non-empty subset of B which is closed under the Boolean operations in B.

2   Important types of Boolean algebra

Boole seems to have had several interpretations for his algebraic system in mind. In his original pamphlet (1847) he thinks of each of the basic symbols of his 'algebra' as standing for the mental operation of selecting just the objects possessing some given attribute or included in some given class. Later (1854) he conceives of these symbols as standing for the attributes or classes themselves.

Two standard types of Boolean algebra arise in set theory and logic, corresponding to these two interpretations. To obtain the first of these, consider any non-empty set X and let $\wp(X)$ be its power set, that is, the set of all its subsets. Then the structure $(\wp(X), \cup, \cap, -, \emptyset, X)$ is a Boolean algebra – the power set algebra of X – in which $\cup, \cap, -$ are the operations of set-theoretic union, intersection and complementation with respect to X, respectively.

A subalgebra of a power set algebra is called an algebra of sets. As an example, for any set X, let $Z(X)$ be the set of all finite and cofinite subsets of X (a 'cofinite' set being the complement of a finite set). Then $(Z(X), \cup, \cap, -, \emptyset, X)$ is an algebra of sets called the finite–cofinite algebra of X.

When X is a singleton $\{a\}$, $\wp(X)$ reduces to the set $\{0, 1\}$, with $0 = \emptyset$ and $1 = X$. This algebra is called the 'two-element Boolean algebra' and is denoted by '2'. Its operations are displayed in the table below.

x	y	$x+y$	$x*y$	$-x$
0	0	0	0	1
0	1	1	0	1
1	0	1	0	0
1	1	1	1	0

The standard types of Boolean algebra arising in logic are the so-called Lindenbaum–Tarski algebras. To obtain these, we start with a theory T in a propositional or first-order language L. Define the equivalence relation $\approx$ on the set of formulas of L by $\phi \approx \psi$ if $T \vdash \phi \leftrightarrow \psi$. For each formula ϕ let $[\phi]$ be its $\approx$-equivalence class. On the set $A(T)$ of such equivalence classes define the operations +, *, – and the elements 1, 0 by:

$$[\phi] + [\psi] = [\phi \vee \psi]$$
$$[\phi] * [\psi] = [\phi \wedge \psi]$$
$$-[\phi] = [\neg \phi]$$
$$1 = [\alpha_0 \vee \neg \alpha_0]$$
$$0 = [\alpha_0 \wedge \neg \alpha_0],$$

where α_0 is a fixed but arbitrary formula. Then the structure $(A(T), +, *, -, 0, 1)$ is a Boolean algebra, called the Lindenbaum–Tarski algebra of T. The Boolean algebra $A(\emptyset)$ (which depends solely on the language L) is denoted by $Alg(L)$ and is called the Lindenbaum–Tarski algebra of L.

Algebras of sets and Lindenbaum–Tarski algebras are typical Boolean algebras in the following sense. Call two Boolean algebras $(B, +_B, *_B, -_B, 0_B, 1_B)$ and $(C, +_C, *_C, -_C, 0_C, 1_C)$ 'isomorphic' if there is a one-one, onto map (that is, an 'isomorphism') $f: B \to C$ such that $f(0_B) = 0_C, f(1_B) = 1_C$ and, for any x, y in B,

$$f(x +_B y) = f(x) +_C f(y)$$
$$f(x *_B y) = f(x) *_C f(y)$$
$$f(-_B x) = -_C f(x).$$

Then it can be shown that any Boolean algebra is isomorphic both to an algebra of sets and to the Lindenbaum–Tarski algebra of some propositional theory. (Isomorphic Boolean algebras are structurally indistinguishable.) These facts (the first of which is the famous 'Stone representation theorem' of 1936) together show that Boolean algebras embody just the common structural features of set theory and logic.

Since, as is readily shown, there are Boolean algebras (for example, the finite–cofinite algebra of the set of natural numbers) which are *not* isomorphic to any power set algebra, nor to the Lindenbaum–Tarski algebra of a propositional language, it is of interest to try to determine the additional characteristic features of these two latter types of algebra.

For power set algebras, we need the following concepts. Given a Boolean algebra B, we define the relation $\leqslant$ on B by $x \leqslant y$ if and only if $x*y = x$. It is easily shown that $\leqslant$ is reflexive ($x \leqslant x$ for all x), transitive (if $x \leqslant y$ and $y \leqslant z$ then $x \leqslant z$) and antisymmetric (if $x \leqslant y$ and $y \leqslant x$ then $y = x$); in other words, $\leqslant$ is a 'partial ordering' on B. B is then said to be 'complete' if every subset X of B has both a greatest lower bound and a least upper bound with respect to $\leqslant$. (It is not hard to see that a *finite* subset $\{x_1,\ldots,x_n\}$ of any Boolean algebra has greatest lower bound $x_1*\ldots*x_n$ and least upper bound $x_1+\ldots+x_n$.) An element $a \neq 0$ of a Boolean algebra B is called an 'atom' if, for any x in B, if $x \leqslant a$, then $x = 0$ or $x = a$. B is said to be 'atomic' if for any $x \neq 0$ in B there is an atom a such that $a \leqslant x$. Then we have the fundamental result of Lindenbaum and Tarski (1935) characterizing power set algebras: a Boolean algebra is isomorphic to a power set algebra if and only if it is complete and atomic (see Halmos 1963: §16, theorem 5).

Turning to Lindenbaum–Tarski algebras of propositional languages, we define a subset X of a Boolean algebra B to be 'free' if for any finite subset $\{x_1,\ldots,x_n\}$ of X we have $y_1*\ldots*y_n \neq 0$, where each y_i is either x_i or $-x_i$. X is said to 'generate' B if the only subalgebra of B containing X is B itself, that is, if every element b of B can be expressed in the form $b = y_1 + \ldots + y_n$, where each y_i is of the form $z_1*\ldots*z_m$ with either z_i or $-z_i$ in X. Finally X is said to be 'freely generated' if it has a free set of generators. It can then be shown that, for any propositional language L, the algebra $Alg(L)$ is freely generated (with the equivalence classes of the proposition letters constituting a free set of generators) and, moreover, that any (infinite) freely generated Boolean algebra is isomorphic to some $Alg(L)$.

3 Boolean algebras as algebras of truth-values

The simplest Boolean algebra is the algebra $2 = \{0,1\}$, which it is customary to think of as the algebra of two 'truth-values'; 0 standing for False and 1 for True. More generally, we may conceive of an arbitrary Boolean algebra as an algebra of 'generalized truth-values' – that is, containing elements corresponding to 'truth-values' different from True and False. In that case, it becomes natural to extend the usual idea of truth-valuations of (propositional) formulas (that is, in the algebra 2) to valuations in arbitrary Boolean algebras. Thus we define a 'valuation' of a propositional language L in a Boolean algebra B to be a map v from the set of formulas of L to B such that, for arbitrary formulas ϕ, ψ we have

$$v(\phi \vee \psi) = v(\phi) + v(\psi)$$
$$v(\phi \wedge \psi) = v(\phi) * v(\psi)$$
$$v(\neg \phi) = -v(\phi).$$

It can then be shown that, for any formula ϕ, the following assertions are equivalent:

(1) ϕ is a propositional theorem.

(2) $v(\phi) = 1$ for every valuation v in 2.

(3) $v(\phi) = 1$ for any valuation v in any Boolean algebra.

(The equivalence between (1) and (2) is the completeness theorem for propositional logic.) A similar result may be established for predicate logic (extending the relevant completeness theorem), this time using the idea of a valuation in a complete Boolean algebra to enable quantified formulas to receive 'truth-values'.

The idea of using Boolean algebras as algebras of truth-values scored what is regarded by logicians as its most spectacular success in the 1960s when it was shown by Robert Solovay and Dana Scott, and independently by Petr Vopenka, that Paul Cohen's celebrated proofs of independence in set theory could be formulated in terms of what has come to be known as the method of 'Boolean-valued models' (see Bell 1985). Briefly, the method runs as follows. Let L be the language of Zermelo–Fraenkel set theory (ZF; see SET THEORY, DIFFERENT SYSTEMS OF), and suppose that σ is a sentence of L whose formal independence of ZF we wish to establish – the continuum hypothesis, for example (see CONTINUUM HYPOTHESIS). A complete Boolean algebra B is chosen and a class $V^{(B)}$ of sets – the Boolean universe induced by B – constructed. Let $L^{(B)}$ be the language obtained by adding to L a name for each element of $V^{(B)}$. Now one can construct a 'valuation' v of the (sentences of) the language $L^{(B)}$ in B: for each sentence ϕ of $L^{(B)}$, $v(\phi)$ is the element of B representing the 'Boolean truth-value' of ϕ in $V^{(B)}$. This map v is defined so as to map all the theorems of ZF to the unit element 1 of B: accordingly the 'structure' $(V^{(B)}, v)$ is called a Boolean-valued model of set theory. If the Boolean algebra B is chosen with finesse, it is possible to arrange things so that $v(\sigma) = 0_B$. That is, for a suitable choice of B, $V^{(B)}$ is a Boolean-valued model of set theory in which the given statement σ is false. This amounts to a proof of the independence of σ from the axioms of set theory. It follows that the problem of establishing the independence of a particular set-theoretic statement boils down in principle to demonstrating the existence of a complete Boolean algebra with specified properties. This method has been exploited with great success in recent years.

See also: BOOLE, G.; LOGICAL AND MATHEMATICAL TERMS, GLOSSARY OF

References and further reading

* Bell, J.L. (1985) *Boolean Valued Models and Independence Proofs in Set Theory*, Oxford Logic Guides 12, Oxford: Clarendon Press. (A detailed technical account of the subject.)
* Boole, G. (1847) *The Mathematical Analysis of Logic, Being an Essay Towards a Calculus of Deductive Reasoning*, London: G. Bell & Sons; repr. in *Studies in Logic and Probability*, London: Watts, and LaSalle, IL: Open Court, 1952; also repr. in *An Investigation of the Laws of Thought*, New York: Dover, 1973. (The first appearance of Boole's system.)
* —— (1854) *An Investigation of the Laws of Thought, on which are Founded the Mathematical Theories of Logic and Probabilities*, London: Walton & Maberley; repr. in *An Investigation of the Laws of Thought*, New York: Dover, 1973. (Further elaboration.)
   Hailperin, T. (1976) *Boole's Logic and Probability*, Amsterdam: North Holland; 2nd edn, 1986. (An illuminating critical exposition of Boole's achievement from a modern standpoint.)
* Halmos, P.R. (1963) *Lectures on Boolean Algebras*, Princeton, NJ: Van Nostrand. (An attractively written exposition of the basic theory of Boolean algebras.)
* Huntington, E.V. (1904) 'Sets of Independent Postulates for the Algebra of Logic', *Transactions of the American Mathematical Society* 5: 288–309. (The first explicit postulate systems for Boolean algebra.)
   Monk, J.D. (ed.) (1989) *Handbook of Boolean Algebras*, Amsterdam: Elsevier Science, 3 vols. (This set includes a series of articles on all mathematical aspects of Boolean algebras. Volume 1 is an excellent introduction to the subject.)
   Rasiowa, H. and Sikorski, R. (1963) *The Mathematics of Metamathematics*, Warsaw: PWN. (A systematic technical account of the algebraic approach to logic.)
* Sheffer, H.M. (1913) 'A Set of Five Independent Postulates for Boolean Algebras, With Application to Logical Constants', *Transactions of the American Mathematical Society* 14: 481–8. (Here it is shown that Boolean algebras can be axiomatized in terms of the single primitive operation corresponding to 'not both' – a fact apparently already known to Peirce.)

J.L. BELL

BOSANQUET, BERNARD (1848–1923)

One of the most prominent and prolific of the British Idealists of the late nineteenth and early twentieth centuries, Bosanquet ranged across most fields of philosophy, making his main contributions in epistemology, metaphysics, aesthetics and especially political philosophy. He was deeply influenced by Plato and by Hegel. Bosanquet and F.H. Bradley were close on many matters, and each regarded the other as a co-worker; however, Bosanquet was always more Hegelian, less rigorous in argument than Bradley and lacking his sceptical approach. Bosanquet treats knowledge and reality as a single whole, working out the implications in the concrete 'modes of experience' of philosophy, science, morality, art, religion, and social and political life. He is at his best in explaining and developing the thoughts of others, particularly of Hegel, Bradley, Rousseau and T.H. Green.

Bernard Bosanquet was educated at Harrow and Balliol College, Oxford. He was much influenced by Green's philosophy, and by his example of active citizenship (see GREEN, T.H. §3). Elected a fellow of University College in 1870 (beating F.H. BRADLEY), Bosanquet taught philosophy and Greek history. He resigned in 1881 in order to have time to write and to engage in social work with the Charity Organisation Society in London; he was also a frequent adult education lecturer and organizer. He was professor of moral philosophy at St Andrews University in the years 1903–8.

Bosanquet propounds a version of absolute or objective idealism derived principally from HEGEL. The key to Bosanquet's general metaphysics is 'the whole'. Our knowledge is always of particular parts of experience conceived in a particular way (scientific, aesthetic, religious, etc.); hence our judgments may conflict (for instance, the findings of science and religion). But what we experience as parts are in reality interrelated and constitute a whole, which reveals its different aspects in the different concrete forms of our experience. So all our knowledge is partial, inconsistent, incomplete and not fully true; we strive to unify it. Complete knowledge, or truth, would be comprehensive and systematic knowledge of the all-inclusive and self-consistent and coherent whole (or Absolute), and thus of every part in all its relations to every other part. The Absolute is not transcendent, in 'another' world, but immanent here in ours. Our knowledge rests on experience of appearances of reality.

Correspondingly, individual parts of the whole, for example, an animal, a work of art, or a person, are not completely real; only the whole of which they are part is real. Ultimately there is but one true, real, individual: namely, the whole. It follows that persons, for example, are 'finite individuals', incomplete and not as real as the communities to which they belong (which in turn are not fully real, relative to the whole). Reality and value are not found to the full in individual persons. Bosanquet drew the controversial conclusions, for example, that the traditional belief in an immortal soul peculiar to each person is groundless, a symptom of our mistaken religious individualism. He is not denying the separateness and uniqueness of persons: each is a particular 'modification' of the social whole. But each becomes more real by drawing on the ideas and institutions of their society. True individuality is judged not by the atomic and exclusive self, nor by what persons are, but by what they can become, and that is shown in their society and its cultural achievements.

Bosanquet's approach shows to advantage in his political philosophy. It arms him against the atomic individualism he finds in the 'theories of the first look' of Bentham, Spencer and J.S. Mill. Instead, combining Rousseau and Hegel, Bosanquet argues that the individual members of a state are linked together by their common ideas and through their participation in its institutions. Taken as a whole, they each have a 'general will', aiming at the common good, which is more real than their particular wills; and their freedom lies in acting according to the general will, as expressed in the law and practices of the state. Bosanquet also takes account of the various levels and kinds of groups (finite wholes) in a state: families, professions, trade unions, churches, local communities, for instance. He shows how these interact, how they express different and sometimes conflicting interests, and how the sovereign state harmonizes their demands. He is thus able, in later editions of *The Philosophical Theory of the State*, to incorporate the arguments of the Pluralists. He explains how change is effected in the state and in its component parts as ideas clash and are reconciled through a 'social logic'. This analysis works particularly well in the case of a parliamentary democracy. Bosanquet is no conservative. Because the Absolute is immanent, improvement is not postponable to another world: 'here or nowhere is your America', 'the Kingdom of God is on earth'. Not everything is as it should be; and the state should sometimes be used confidently to widen persons' opportunities. The state is justified in restricting its members' narrow freedom from interference because its laws are in the interest of all, and bring greater freedom, the freedom to develop oneself. The state is more real than the person, the whole in which the person can enrich their life (but Bosanquet in no way considered the value of persons to be instrumental to the state). The state too is finite, in relation to other states. Bosanquet did not think the political conditions for international federations or world government existed yet, but there is space for it in his theory. The state is also finite relative to the deeper experience of religion, art and philosophy, which enable persons to enlarge their individuality.

Bosanquet suffered severely from Hobhouse's not altogether fair but very effective attacks on him as being politically authoritarian, confusing the state with society and idealizing actual states. Generally Bosanquet's style of philosophizing became unfashionable: Russell, for example, found it vague, loose, shallow, evasive, dogmatic and claiming more for philosophy than it could deliver. For most of the twentieth century Bosanquet has been ignored. It remains to be seen whether his ties to Hegel will benefit him as Hegel's reputation rises again.

See also: ABSOLUTE, THE; HEGELIANISM §5; STATE, THE

List of works

Bosanquet, B. (1888) *Logic, or the Morphology of Knowledge*, Oxford: Clarendon Press, 2nd edn, 1911. (The systematic and fullest statement of his theory of truth.)

—— (1892) *A History of Aesthetic*, London: Swan Sonnenschein. (The aesthetic consciousness traced from the Greeks to the nineteenth century.)

—— (1899) *The Philosophical Theory of the State*, London & New York: Macmillan, 4th edn, 1923. (Bosanquet's major contribution to political philosophy.)

—— (1912) *The Principle of Individuality and Value; The Gifford Lectures for 1911*, London: Macmillan. (Outlines Bosanquet's metaphysics.)

—— (1913) *The Value and Destiny of the Individual;*

The Gifford Lectures for 1912, London: Macmillan. (Further details of Bosanquet's metaphysics.)

—— (1924) 'Life and Philosophy', in J.H. Muirhead (ed.) *Contemporary British Philosophy, Personal Statements, First Series*, London: Allen & Unwin, 51–74. (Bosanquet's philosophical autobiography, stating the main principles of his philosophy in its typical language.)

Muirhead, J.H. and R.C. Bosanquet (eds) (1927) *Science and Philosophy and Other Essays by the Late Bernard Bosanquet*, London: Allen & Unwin. (Good selection of previously published papers in logic, metaphysics, ethics, politics and aesthetics.)

Muirhead, J.H. (ed.) (1935) *Bernard Bosanquet and His Friends. Letters Illustrating the Sources and the Development of his Philosophical Opinions*, London: Allen & Unwin. (Correspondence with other philosophers, particularly in his later years.)

References and further reading

Bosanquet, H. (1924) *Bernard Bosanquet. A Short Account of his Life*, London: Macmillan. (By his wife; the main biographical source.)

Gaus, G.F. (1994) 'T.H. Green, Bernard Bosanquet and the Philosophy of Coherence', in C.L. Ten (ed.) *The Routledge History of Philosophy, vol. 7: The Nineteenth Century*. (Treats complex issues of how Bosanquet's philosophy connects with his politics; he is helpfully compared with Green.)

* Hobhouse, L.T. (1918) *The Metaphysical Theory of the State*, London: Allen & Unwin. (Famous attack on Bosanquet's political philosophy.)

Hoernlé, R.F.A. (1927) *Idealism as a Philosophy*, New York: George H. Doran, chaps 8–10. (Very clear and sympathetic account of the basics of Bosanquet's metaphysics and political philosophy.)

Lang, B. (1968) 'Bosanquet's Aesthetic: A History and Philosophy of the Symbol', *Journal of Aesthetics and Art Criticism* 26: 377–87. (Overview of Bosanquet's philosophy of art.)

Nicholson, P.P. (1978) 'A Bibliography of the Writings of Bernard Bosanquet (1848–1923)', *Idealistic Studies* 8: 261–80. (Full listing of the published and unpublished writings.)

—— (1990) *The Political Philosophy of the British Idealists: Selected Studies*, Cambridge: Cambridge University Press, Study 6. (Examines Bosanquet on the General Will. Extensive bibliography.)

Primoratz, I. (1994) 'The Word "Liberty" on the Chains of Galley-Slaves: Bosanquet's Theory of the General Will', in *History of Political Thought* 15: 249–67. (Argues that the theory fails to solve the problem of political obligation.)

* Russell, B. (1992) Reviews of Bosanquet's Gifford Lectures, in *Collected Papers, vol. 6: Logical and Philosophical Papers 1909–13*, ed. J.G. Slater, London & New York: Routledge, 368–70, 372–3. (Challenges Bosanquet's Hegelian conception of philosophy.)

Sweet, W. (1996) *Idealism and Rights: The Social Ontology of Rights in the Political Thought of Bernard Bosanquet*, Lanham, MD: University Press of America. (Clear, careful and detailed appraisal, basically sympathetic, of the main features of Bosanquet's political philosophy. Fullest bibliography.)

PETER P. NICHOLSON

BOURDIEU, PIERRE (1930–)

Critically assessing both hermeneutic and structuralist approaches, Pierre Bourdieu's social theory aims at transcending the opposition between the individual and society. On the one hand, people exhibit practical skills which are adjusted to the constraints of the environment. On the other hand, society does not determine people's actions: the very same practical skills allow them to improvise and deal with an infinite number of situations. Although Bourdieu takes into account the individual, he does not succumb to the Cartesian notion of a self-sufficient subject. Also, his view is very much in opposition to rational choice theory. His theoretical framework has emerged out of his empirical research and vice versa. In his research Bourdieu applies his reflexive sociology: a critical reflection on the part of the social scientist towards their own practices.

Initially educated at the École normale supérieure and eventually Professor of Sociology at the Collège de France, Bourdieu is known for his contributions to the theory of society. The label 'social theorist' is, however, not entirely appropriate. First, his writings cover various fields in the social sciences, ranging from the abstract to the ethnographic. Second, rather than providing a theory that is independent of empirical research, Bourdieu aims at a method derived from and directed towards social research. Rather than embarking upon a grand theory, Bourdieu invites the reader to ask certain questions.

Pierre Bourdieu spent most of his academic life in France, apart from a short spell in Algeria. It is thus not surprising that many of his writings deal with French society. Neither is it far-fetched to read some of his writings as a dialogue with Sartre and Lévi-Strauss – the two leading French intellectuals at the time of Bourdieu's formative academic years (see

SARTRE, J.-P.; LÉVI-STRAUSS, C.). Always sceptical of existentialist philosophy, Bourdieu was initially attracted to structuralism but soon also distanced himself from the latter (see STRUCTURALISM IN SOCIAL SCIENCE §5). Where existentialism lacks objectivity, structuralism erroneously dismisses the relevance of hermeneutics (see HERMENEUTICS). Related to his critique of both philosophies, Bourdieu's project has been to transcend the opposition between the individual and society. However, Bourdieu's attention to the agent does not mean that he succumbs to a Cartesian notion of a self-sufficient subject; instead Bourdieu adopts some of the phenomenological and Wittgensteinian insights vis-à-vis shared, tacit knowledge (see PHENOMENOLOGICAL MOVEMENT; PHENOMENOLOGY, EPISTEMIC ISSUES IN; WITTGENSTEIN, L.). Likewise, his focus upon social structure does not entail the 'economism' of French Marxism. Indeed, Bourdieu pays much attention to power struggles in society, not merely at the economic level, but also in the symbolic sphere (see MARXIST PHILOSOPHY OF SCIENCE).

In spite of his reluctance to build a consistent theoretical system, Bourdieu's writings exhibit a particular philosophical outlook. He describes his own work as an attempt to transcend the alleged dualism between what he calls 'objectivism' and 'subjectivism'. Characteristic of structuralist perspectives, objectivism searches for underlying structures independent of people's knowledge or strategies. Central to humanist approaches, subjectivism attributes a pivotal role to people's experiences, strategies and improvisations. Focusing on one side only, each perspective inevitably distorts reality. Subjectivist accounts tend to conceive of social life as created *de novo* by individuals, failing to acknowledge the internalization of societal constraints within the individual. Objectivism tends to adopt a mechanistic model of human action, and fails to recognize that social life is a practical achievement of competent individuals. It mistakenly reduces the complexity of practices to a coherent and simplified cultural logic. Hence Bourdieu's argument for 'objectifying the act of objectification' implies that the researcher, while observing and objectifying, takes a similar critical distance towards the objectification itself. Bourdieu's proposal for 'participant objectivation' attempts to objectify the object of research, examine the validity and presuppositions of that objectification, and finally to take into account people's skilful achievements. Relatedly, the practices of the social scientist in general are embedded in structural conditions and power struggles themselves. Hence Bourdieu's 'reflexive sociology' aims at a critical distance regarding its own practice.

Central to Bourdieu's view is people's practical mastery of the logic of everyday life. Most of the time people know how to go on in their daily activities, without needing to formulate that knowledge discursively. This practical knowledge is thus not part of the realm of consciousness, nor is it, strictly speaking, unconscious. People's practical logic relies upon *doxa* or 'doxic experience', that is, the taken-for-granted nature of people's daily existence. Both practical logic and *doxa* are central to Bourdieu's concepts of 'habitus', 'strategy' and 'field'. *Habitus* refers to an acquired generative scheme of dispositions. These dispositions are tacitly acquired in early childhood, and, once inculcated, they endure. Dispositions generate practices, perceptions or bodily '*hexis*', adjusted to the constraints of the social world in which the *habitus* has emerged. Hence different social backgrounds will produce a different *habitus*. The *habitus* provides a 'feeling for the game'. It makes it possible for people to develop any number of strategies attuned to an infinite number of situations. The external social world consists of 'fields': that is, areas where, through strategies, struggles take place over goods or resources (capital). Fields are not restricted to struggles over economic capital: they might also deal with social capital (contacts and acquaintances), cultural capital (education, culture and related skills) or symbolic capital (distinction and prestige). Although Bourdieu's use of 'capital' suggests that interests are at stake, these are not necessarily material, nor do individuals normally adopt a conscious calculative orientation towards them.

Bourdieu has been criticized mainly for his alleged lack of analytical precision and for his tendency to read too much into his empirical material. Although there is some truth in both criticisms, neither affects the core of Bourdieu's frame of reference. In this context, his strengths reveal his weaknesses. Bourdieu's incisiveness lies in accounting for the reproduction of society, as becomes apparent in his notion of skilful, unquestioned reproduction of structures or in the presupposition that the *habitus* tends to be adjusted to social constraints. One of the upshots of this is that Bourdieu pays less attention to the ability of individuals to distance themselves from the facticity of daily existence – the ability to turn tacit knowledge into theoretical knowledge. Bourdieu tends to do so only in so far as people's distancing towards everyday life is a result of social scientific intervention. He thereby fails to acknowledge fully that people may also exhibit that ability for distancing in the absence of scientific interference. If people's theoretical knowledge enters the public-collective realm, it might become an important source of change or deliberate maintenance of structures.

See also: ANTHROPOLOGY, PHILOSOPHY OF; SOCIOLOGY OF KNOWLEDGE; SOCIOLOGY, THEORIES OF; SOCIAL SCIENCE, METHODOLOGY OF

List of works

Bourdieu, P. (1972) *Esquisse d'une théorie de la pratique: précédée de trois études d'ethnologie kabyle*, Geneva: Droz; trans. R. Nice *Outline of a Theory of Practice*, Cambridge: Cambridge University Press, 1977. (Bourdieu discusses the main outline of his social theory. Complex. The English version differs substantially from the original *Esquisse*.)

—— (1980) *Le sens pratique*, Paris: Les Editions de Minuit; trans. R. Nice, *The Logic of Practice*, Cambridge: Polity Press, 1990. (Bourdieu explains very clearly some of the themes introduced in *Esquisse*. He uses his framework to analyse kinship and other social phenomena. More accessible than *Esquisse*.)

Bourdieu, P. and Wacquant, L. (1992) *An Invitation to Reflexive Sociology*, Cambridge: Polity Press. (Has an excellent introduction by Wacquant to Bourdieu's sociology. Also contains a useful interview by Wacquant with Bourdieu.)

References and further reading

Calhoun, C., LiPuma, E. and Postone, M. (eds) (1993) *Bourdieu: Critical Perspectives*, Cambridge: Polity Press. (An inspiring collection of articles. Reaches a high level while remaining remarkably lucid.)

Jenkins, R. (1992) *Pierre Bourdieu*, London: Routledge. (An elementary introduction, but Jenkins' criticisms are sometimes unclear.)

Harker, R., Mahar, C. and Wilkes, C. (eds) (1990) *An Introduction to the Work of Pierre Bourdieu: The Practice of Theory*, Basingstoke: Macmillan. (A lively reconstruction of the major themes in Bourdieu's work, while taking into account the French academic context. One chapter is an interview with the man himself.)

Robbins, D. (1991) *The Work of Pierre Bourdieu: Recognising Society*, Milton Keynes: Open University Press. (A comprehensive and chronological account of Bourdieu's writings.)

PATRICK BAERT

BOUTROUX, ÉMILE (1845–1921)

The French philosopher Émile Boutroux wanted to reestablish metaphysics in the face of a growing tendency towards materialism, but without rejecting the natural sciences. He hoped to achieve this by showing that only an immaterial mind that is a free and final cause of everything that is determined can give an absolute foundation to the sciences and to nature. Scientific determinism, according to which all phenomena are governed by mathematical necessities, is not incompatible with freedom. Indeed, the contingency of things and of human reason, which one sees in scientific experience, shows that the mind is free; it is therefore only mind which can give a determined existence to things and necessity to scientific explanations. In trying to reconcile metaphysics and science through a philosophy of nature, Boutroux represents a major turning point in French spiritualism, foreshadowing not only Bergson but also Bachelard.

Boutroux defended his thesis *De la contingence des lois de la nature* (On the contingency of the laws of nature) in 1874. Having taught at the École Normale Supérieure, among other places, he moved to the Sorbonne, where he became Professor of the History of Modern Philosophy in 1888. As a member of the Academy of Moral and Political Sciences and of the Académie Française, he was one of the important thinkers of his time. He was a former pupil of Jules LACHELIER and participated in a brilliant and original way in the growing renewal of spiritualist thought brought about by RAVAISSON from the end of the Second Empire. As free from the declining eclecticism as he was hostile to scientific materialism, Boutroux upheld a rationalism influenced by LEIBNIZ that tried to include elements of British empiricism and the positivism of COMTE. He studied Aristotle, Descartes and Kant, but concentrated on German philosophy of the seventeenth century, and above all on Leibniz, whose *Monadology* and *New Essays on Human Understanding* (First book) he translated into French. His lecture courses on natural law, given in 1892–3, contain a critique of scientific rationalism through which he returned to the metaphysical position put forward in his thesis of 1874.

As a historian of philosophy, Boutroux denounced the Hegelian philosophy of history and its introduction into France by Victor COUSIN (see HEGELIANISM §4). He did not want to judge works dogmatically in looking for a successive development of an immanent spirit in history. As history is not a system in which the historian is required to uncover a teleological regularity under the particularities, Boutroux practised a critical study of philosophies taken in themselves as individual. Without neglecting the historical context, he attempted to make clear the acts of free creativity that throughout history have led philosophers to return time and again to the great problems of metaphysics.

Boutroux's philosophy of nature gives meaning to this conception of history. In it he criticizes the modern idea of natural law and its regulating principle of determinism, according to which everything is governed by necessary mathematical relations. According to Boutroux, laws are contingent because the relations they establish are never entirely a priori, and because reality is incommensurable and irreducible to mathematical necessity. As mathematics is applied to experience, the laws become more determinate and particular, and thereby less necessitating. It is an error of scientism to confuse determinism with necessitarianism. Science, in its effort to reduce experience to the mathematical, loses its sense of the radical contingency at work in nature; it generalizes and takes things to extremes in transforming its useful regulative idea into a constitutive principle of nature.

This philosophy of science foreshadows certain ideas that are present both in Bergson's metaphysics and Bachelard's epistemology (see BACHELARD, G. §2; BERGSON, H.-L. §5). For example, there is the empiricist idea, taken from Ravaisson and developed by Bergson, according to which scientific laws are habits of reproduction that assimilate reality to our minds so that we may act on it, but which only partially correspond to how things are. There is also the idea that scientific rationalism proceeds by using an artificial construction of experience without which it would never be able to apply itself; and that the specialization of the sciences results in an irreducible pluralism of local determinisms; ideas which Bachelard developed in more radical and unforeseen ways. Nevertheless, it is metaphysics that he wants to save, as much from being dissolved by science as from being divorced from it. Boutroux wanted to retain rationalism without falling either into scientism, or into the illusion denounced by Kant as the transcendental use of the laws of nature, or into the dangerous error of separating the deterministic natural world from the intelligible world of freedom, as Kant did (see KANT, I. §§8, 9). It is in his reading of Aristotle, and still more of Leibniz, that Boutroux tries to reconcile determinism and freedom, in showing that mechanism presupposes finality. Contingency – which is not chance but determination through a *telos* (life), and, from the human point of view, determination by the idea of progress – is presupposed by determinism, because it is incapable of giving an account of it.

This movement that reaches above science to metaphysics is completed in a moral reflection on the relation between science and faith. Boutroux shows that, as human beings are conscious living things irreducible to mechanism, there is no contradiction between science and religion. Science presupposes not only a reality that extends beyond what it can assimilate, but also that the human mind goes beyond the intellectual faculties it employs. Both outside and inside us, it presupposes a creative vital force that, in human beings, implies faith, the ideal and love, the three principles of all religions. Religious works, dogmas and rites are neither adventitious for religion nor unjustifiable for reason, even if religion is a matter of feeling and if its truth, as it would be developed by Bergson, is a mystical sentiment. Thus it is once again a matter of demonstrating the possibility of a spiritualism that goes beyond the scientific outlook without opposing it.

List of works

Boutroux, É. (1879) *De la contingence des lois de la nature*, Paris: Alcan; trans. F. Rothwell, *The Contingency of the Laws of Nature*, Chicago, IL and London: Open Court, 1916. (Contains Boutroux's first discussion of necessity and contingency.)

—— (1889) *La philosophie allemande au XVIIe siècle* (German philosophy of the seventeenth century), Paris: Vrin. (Mainly contains material on Leibniz.)

—— (1895) *De l'idée de loi naturelle dans la science et la philosophie contemporaine*, Paris: Vrin; trans. F. Rothwell, *Natural Law in Science and Philosophy*, London: Macmillan, 1914. (Lectures of 1892–3, further developing Boutroux's views on necessity and contingency.)

—— (1908a) *Science et religion dans la philosophie contemporaine*, Paris: Flammarion; trans. as *Science and Religion in Contemporary Philosophy*, Associated Faculty Press Ltd, 1970. (Attempts a reconciliation between scientific rationalism and religious thought.)

—— (1908b) 'Rapport sur la philosophie en France depuis 1867' (Report on philosophy in France since 1867), in *Nouvelles études d'histoire de la philosophie*, Paris: Alcan, 1927. (Account of the state of contemporary French philosophy.)

—— (1926) *Nature et esprit* (Nature and mind), Paris: Vrin. (Posthumously published work.)

References and further reading

Brunschvicg, L. (1922) 'La philosophie d'Émile Boutroux' (The philosophy of Émile Boutroux), *Revue de Métaphysique et de Morale* 1922. (A summary of Boutroux's position.)

Archambault, P. (1928) *Émile Boutroux*, Paris: Vald. Rasmussen. (General study.)

Gil, D. (1996) 'La philosophie de la nature d'É. Boutroux' (Boutroux's philosophy of nature), in *Les philosophies de la nature*, Paris: Presses Universitaires de France. (Discussion of Boutroux's philosophy of nature.)

Translated from the French by Robert Stern

DIDIER GIL

BOWNE, BORDEN PARKER (1847–1910)

Bowne was one of the most influential thinkers and writers of the American personalist school of philosophy. His position is theistic and idealistic, and finds in human persons the key to meaning in the world. Knowledge comes only through personal experience, through which we understand ourselves to be enduring thinking entities with a certain degree of freedom. The uniformity of God's activity is such as to make nature intelligible to us, but our minds are nevertheless independent of God's.

Borden Parker Bowne was born in a New Jersey manse and educated at Pennington Seminary, New York University and in Europe (chiefly Paris, Halle and Göttingen). He taught at Boston University from 1876 to 1910, serving as the first dean of the graduate school. His views were strongly influenced by the ideas of Kant, Lotze (with whom he studied) and Bergson. He was ordained in the Methodist Episcopal Church as a local preacher in 1872 and an elder in 1882. During a long career of teaching and publishing he became the most influential exponent of American personalism, a philosophical school of which he was arguably the founder.

Bowne held that the basis for knowledge is personal experience: 'For each person, his own self is known in immediate experience and all others are known through their effects' (1902: 269). If the world is intelligible, there is continuity that underlies the flux of human experience; in self-consciousness, one is aware of various sensory and introspective phenomena that are unified in that they are objects of a single awareness. In memory, one recognizes the identity of one's current centre of awareness with prior centres. Thus one finds in oneself the continuity of a mental substance; one knows oneself as an enduring, thinking thing. One also experiences a measure of self-control, so that purposive action is possible, feelings can be controlled, and competing ends assessed; we find that we have a relative independence of our environment and of others. But we also experience a degree of dependence on our environment and on others that makes it clear that our independence is only relative. Bowne held that these facts are incontrovertible, and that no philosophy can be adequate that denies or ignores them.

One thing Bowne believed these facts to rule out is any view in which the thoughts and feelings that some or all human beings experience are really the thoughts and feelings that God has in or through them. Such a view is incompatible with both our relative independence (we are self-directing agents, not mere passive receivers or conduits) and our relative dependence (God cannot be dependent). These facts, even without further appeal to such things as our having false beliefs and our performing wrong actions, make it clear that no notion that our consciousness is really part of God's consciousness is defensible. Thus God is not to be thought of along the lines of 'the collection of all finite minds'; rather God possesses an independence and freedom on which our relative independence and freedom is modelled.

Bowne's view was that the sort of absolute idealism for which each human mind is somehow part of a cosmic mind, and the deterministic materialism for which mind reduces to matter, while at opposite ends of the metaphysical spectrum, are alike in certain of their most important consequences. Leaving no room for free human agency, both are incompatible with human responsibility. Both make evil action impossible: the former by making God the only agent, and the latter by allowing for no agents at all but only mechanistically produced effects.

Bowne had no difficulty in accepting evolutionary theory, and viewed the evolutionary process as directed by God so as to produce human beings. As a metaphysical idealist, he held that one's body at any particular time is simply a collection of one's sensory images, and over time is but a series of such collections. The bodies of persons are images that they do not create, and the laws of nature are descriptions of the uniformity of God's activity in causing our perceptual images. Since God's willing is rational, what we call 'nature' is intelligible. This makes science and planned practical activity possible. One consequence of this sort of view is that 'existing in this world' is a matter of having perceptual and introspective experiences of a familiar, if not easily characterized, form and type. Thus 'existing in another world' would be a matter of having perceptual and introspective images of a significantly different form and type. A complete world will be composed of various such 'worlds' and will exist within a single divine purpose, being unified in that each 'world' occurs within the framework of a single coherent divine plan that assures 'fit' between them.

See also: PERSONALISM

List of works

Bowne, B.P. (1887) *Philosophy of Theism*, New York: Harper & Brothers. (Presents theism as the fundamental postulate of our total life.)

—— (1897) *The Theory of Thought and Knowledge*, New York: Harper & Brothers. (Detailed account of Bowne's idealistic epistemology.)

—— (1902) *Theism*, New York: American Book Company. (Revision and expansion of *Philosophy of Theism*.)

—— (1908) *Personalism*, Boston, MA: Houghton Mifflin. (A more popular presentation of the personalist viewpoint, based on the N.W. Harris Lectures of 1907 at Northwestern University.)

—— (1910) *Metaphysics*, New York: American Book Company. (Detailed argument for Bowne's personalist metaphysic.)

References and further reading

Cunningham, G.W. (1953) *The Idealistic Argument in Recent British and American Philosophy*, Westport, CT: Greenwood Press, 1969. (Discusses a century of Anglo-American idealist thought (1808–1910) in expository and critical terms; includes a chapter on Bowne.)

McConnell, F.J. (1929) *Borden Parker Bowne*, New York: Abington Press. (Biography of Bowne by close friend who was a Methodist bishop.)

KEITH E. YANDELL

BOYLE, ROBERT (1627–91)

Boyle is often remembered for the contributions that he made to the sciences of chemistry and pneumatics. Like other natural philosophers in seventeenth-century England, however, he was a synthetic thinker who sought to advance knowledge in all areas of human concern. An early advocate of experimental methods, he argued that experimentation would not only reveal the hidden processes operative in the world but would also advance the cause of religion. Through the study of nature, experimentalists would come to understand that the intricacy of design manifest in the world must be the result of an omniscient and omnipotent creator.

Boyle's experimental investigations and theological beliefs led him to a conception of the world as a 'cosmic mechanism' comprised of a harmonious set of interrelated processes. He agreed with the leading mechanical philosophers of his day that the corpuscular hypothesis, which explains the causal powers of bodies by reference to the motions of the least parts (corpuscles) of matter, provided the best means for understanding nature. He insisted, however, that these motions and powers could not be known by reasoning alone, but would have to be discovered experimentally.

1 Life and works
2 Experimental philosophy
3 Theology
4 Corpuscular hypothesis

1 Life and works

Robert Boyle, born 1627 at Lismore Castle, Ireland, was the youngest son of the first Earl of Cork, one of the wealthiest members of the English aristocracy. Boyle's formal schooling was limited to four years at Eton (1635–9) after which he embarked upon a tour of Europe. He read the works of Galileo while visiting Florence, and studied the classics, languages, Calvinist theology and Epicurean philosophy during an extended stay in Geneva. Upon the death of his father in 1644 he returned to England and resided in London with his sister Katherine, Lady Ranelagh, through whom he met a number of leading educational theorists, mechanical philosophers and chemists such as Samuel Hartlib, John Milton, Kenelm DIGBY and Benjamin Worseley.

In 1646 Boyle retired to his inherited estate at Stalbridge where he wrote moral and theological essays, compiled catalogues of medicinal remedies, and began experimental studies in chemistry and anatomy. He moved to Oxford in 1655 in order to work with an informal group of experimentalists meeting there that included Robert Hooke, John Locke and Christopher Wren. While at Oxford he also associated with theologians and linguists such as Thomas Hyde, Samuel CLARKE and Thomas Barlow, and he became involved in a number of business ventures including the Hudson's Bay Company and the East India Trading Company. In 1665 he received an honorary medical degree from Oxford. In 1668 he returned to London and lived there with his sister until both of them died, a week apart, in December 1691.

Boyle gained international recognition with the

publication of his first major scientific work, *New Experiments Physico-Mechanical, Touching the Spring of the Air* (1660), in which he reported a series of experiments performed with an air-pump designed to support the notion of the weight of the air developed by Pascal and Torricelli and his own conception of the spring (elasticity) of the air. His work was seen by many as a significant improvement upon earlier Aristotelian speculations, yet it was also severely criticized, by Henry More and Thomas Hobbes among others. In 1662 he published responses to his critics in a second edition of *New Experiments* that also contained the first formulation of Boyle's law, which describes the inverse proportion between the pressure and volume of a gas.

Boyle's interests were broad and eclectic and his inherited wealth provided him with the leisure to pursue many areas of study. During his lifetime he published over forty works ranging from comprehensive experimental histories to defences of the Christian religion and the new corpuscular philosophy. In one of his last books, *The Christian Virtuoso* (1690), he explained that such eclecticism was warranted because 'true philosophy' is 'of greater extent, than the hypothesis of any one sect of philosophers, being indeed a comprehension of all the sciences, arts, disciplines, and other considerable parts of useful knowledge'.

2 Experimental philosophy

Boyle first became acquainted with the Baconian concept of useful knowledge through his association with the Hartlib group in London, and his own laboratory investigations, particularly in chemistry, increased his conviction that experimental practices would be required to improve upon what he perceived to be the 'barrenness' of the natural philosophy taught in the schools. He agreed with Bacon that the Aristotelian distinction between natural and artificial processes was not tenable and that the experimental manipulation of natural bodies could yield more than immediate utilitarian benefits (see BACON, F.). As Boyle explained in his *Usefulness of Experimental Philosophy* (1670), the production of effects under the controlled conditions of a laboratory may 'either hint to us the causes of them, or at least acquaint us with some of the properties or qualities of things concurring to the production of such effects'.

Although he designed his experimental method as a way by which to learn about the causal processes operative in nature, he opposed what he found to be the premature theoretical systems of many of his contemporaries. In *The Sceptical Chymist* (1661), for example, he produced experimental refutations of the prevalent Aristotelian and alchemical theories of elements, but he offered no theoretical account of his own with which to replace them (see ALCHEMY; NATURAL PHILOSOPHY, MEDIEVAL §1). In other works where he did speculate about the causal powers of bodies, his discussions were tentative and hesitant. Boyle's caution was in part a result of the many practical problems that he encountered in his laboratory. His reflection upon the epistemological significance of these 'contingencies of experiment' led him to write one of the earliest and most complete accounts of the systematic errors associated with experimental practice.

In his *Certain Physiological Essays* (1661), Boyle discussed how the use of impure ingredients, imperfect instruments or inappropriate techniques could lead to experimental failure. To mitigate the effects of systematic error, he designed a number of methodological strategies. Some were meant for specific areas of investigation, such as the indicator tests that he developed for the identification of acids and alkalies. Others, such as repetition and variation, were offered as general strategies to be used for all areas of investigation. In order to establish that an experimental result provides reliable evidence about a natural process, one has to ensure that it is not an artefact of the particular materials or instruments used in its production. Not only is it necessary to repeat experimental trials and vary their circumstances, it is also necessary to publish complete accounts of experiments so that others will be able to repeat the trials for themselves or at least judge the appropriateness of the experimental conditions and the soundness of any inferences drawn from them. Boyle's practical implementation of his programmatic methodological statements can be seen in the experimental histories that he wrote on *Colours* (1664), *Cold* (1665), *Blood* (1684) and *Air* (1692).

Unlike the stress upon individual reasoning found in the Scholastic and Cartesian philosophical traditions, Boyle insisted that collaboration and cooperation among naturalists were necessary for the advancement of knowledge. This belief was a product of his methodological dictates as well as a consequence of his view concerning the justification of theoretical speculations. According to Boyle, a theory is acceptable only after a 'concurrence of probabilities' has been produced whereby all of the relevant and available evidence supports a particular conclusion.

Experimentation should 'beget a confederacy, and an union between parts of learning', because often more than one area of investigation would be required to learn about a natural process. A full understanding of the circulation of the blood, for example, had required the efforts of workers whose areas of expertise were in physiology, anatomy, chemistry and mechanics. As he explained in his *Usefulness of Natural Philosophy* (1664), there is a 'dependency, continuation, and confederacy of causes' in nature that results from the 'secret correspondencies and alliances' between things. This ontological conception was supported by his experimental work as well as by his theological worldview.

3 Theology

In addition to being an experimentalist, Boyle was also a lay theologian who emphasized the importance of revealed religion. In *The Excellency of Theology* (1674) he argued for the intellectual superiority of scriptural studies over natural philosophy and early in his career he published a work on what we would today call biblical hermeneutics, *The Style of the Holy Scriptures* (1661), that is significant for understanding his views on interpretation. According to Boyle, the 'seeming contradictions' identified by critics of the Bible are the product not of its divine author but 'of our ignorance'. The Bible is a complex interrelated whole that must be 'coherent' because God would not require humans to believe inconsistencies. The proper method of interpretation, therefore, would require that readers attempt to eliminate apparent contradictions by a gradual process of reconciliation.

In *A Free Inquiry into the Received Notion of Nature* (1686), Boyle discussed how nature could also be described as a divine text because it is composed of a complex set of interrelated parts all of which were designed by God to produce one coherent whole. The relations that obtain in nature are the 'result of the universal matter, or corporeal substance of the universe, considered as it is contrived in the present structure and constitution of the world, whereby all bodies, that compose it, are enabled to act upon, and fitted to suffer from one another'. In anticipation of LEIBNIZ, Boyle discussed the perfection of the world and maintained that there is an 'intercourse and harmony between truths'. Naturalists must attempt to discover the 'connection of physical truths, and the relations that material bodies have to one another' and thus the interpretation of nature would require the same type of reconciliation process that he had recommended for the Scriptures.

Boyle criticized the Cartesians and atomists who excluded considerations of final causality from their philosophical systems because he believed that the investigation of nature provided one of the best means for learning about its creator. In his *Disquisition about the Final Causes of Natural Things* (1688), he argued that God may 'declare truths to men, and instruct them, by his creatures and his actions, as well as by his words'. The study of nature could thus lead an experimentalist to the 'acknowledgement of the divine Architect's power, wisdom and beneficence'. He did agree with his contemporaries' criticisms of Aristotelian teleology, however, and he maintained that it was not legitimate to refer to God's purposes when explaining physical processes. Yet some appeal to God's initial act of creation could provide a valuable heuristic for natural investigations. Indeed, his conception of the coherence of the world guided his specific formulation of the corpuscular hypothesis and his belief in the omniscience of the creator led him to insist that corpuscular explanations could not be justified by a priori reasoning, but would require experimental proof.

4 Corpuscular hypothesis

In his 'Excellency and Grounds of the Mechanical or Corpuscular Hypothesis' (1674) Boyle argued that corpuscularianism was simpler and more intelligible than the alternative Aristotelian doctrine that appealed to the occult qualities and substantial forms of bodies. In his *Origin of Forms and Qualities* (1666) he also defended a mechanical account of nature by which physical phenomena were to be explained by considering 'only the size, shape, motion (or want of it), texture, and the resulting qualities and attributes of the small particles of matter'. These arguments were similar to those of other mechanical philosophers. Boyle's extensive experimental practice and his interest in the chemical composition of bodies led him to reject what he saw to be the purely quantitative and mathematical analysis of Descartes, however, and to advocate a more qualitative approach to the study of nature. According to Boyle, it is the set of qualities possessed by a body that defines its essence and gives it the causal power to produce changes in other bodies. He developed an account of the primary and secondary qualities of bodies, which would receive further elaboration and refinement in the philosophical writings of John Locke, in order to describe how corpuscular explanations would allow for a qualitative understanding of physical phenomena (see LOCKE, J. §4; PRIMARY–SECONDARY DISTINCTION §1).

Primary qualities are those 'affections', such as size and shape, that must belong to all parts of matter. Secondary qualities, on the other hand, are those properties of bodies such as colour and temperature that result from the internal configuration of the parts of matter of which they are composed as well as the external relations that they have to other bodies. Boyle maintained that these secondary qualities 'do as well seem to belong to natural bodies generally considered, as place, time, motion and those other things...treated of in the general part of natural philosophy'. Although the secondary qualities of bodies are causally responsible for human sensations, they are not 'like to the ideas they occasion in us'. Heat, for example, is a product of the rapid motion of the particles composing a body, such as the sun. The sun has the secondary quality of heat that gives it the power to produce the sensation of heat in a human, but even if all 'sensitive beings in the world were annihilated' the sun would retain its secondary quality and thus continue to have the power to affect other bodies such as ice and wax.

In *The Mechanical Origin or Production of Divers Particular Qualities* (1675), Boyle reported experiments that he had performed to show how secondary qualities could be added to or taken away from bodies simply by a mechanical alteration of their structure. Repeatedly striking a metallic body with a hammer will cause it to become hot, for example, whereas a piece of glass operated upon in the same way will lose its transparent quality and be reduced to a white powder. Although this work helped to establish the feasibility and intelligibility of mechanical explanations, Boyle was never able to specify the ultimate causal mechanisms responsible for the effects that he produced in his laboratory. His lack of theoretical success may be attributed to his overly cautious attitude that resulted from his appreciation of the fallibility of experimental practice and the complexity of natural processes, as well as to his eclectic and comprehensive approach whereby he sought to combine researches in physics, chemistry and biology. His works are of lasting historical significance not so much because of the specific theories that he developed but because of his successful promotion of a new way of thinking about nature and a new method for investigating physical processes. A self-proclaimed 'underbuilder', he provided the materials and methods that later thinkers such as Newton and Lavoisier would use to great advantage (see NEWTON, I.; CHEMISTRY, PHILOSOPHICAL ASPECTS OF §3).

See also: ATOMISM, ANCIENT; EXPERIMENT; MATTER; SCIENTIFIC METHOD

List of works

Boyle, R. (1744) *The Works of the Honourable Robert Boyle*, ed. T. Birch, London, 5 vols. Available on microfilm in the *Landmarks of Science* series, eds Sir H. Hartley and D.H.D. Roller, New York: Readex Microprint, 1967–76. (Contains all of the works published by Boyle during his lifetime as well as some posthumous works, an autobiographical account of his youth, Birch's life of Boyle and correspondence between Boyle and a number of the leading figures of his day.)

—— (1772) *The Works of the Honourable Robert Boyle*, ed. T. Birch, London, 6 vols; repr. Hildesheim: Georg Olms, 1965–6. (Contents the same as the 1744 edition. The reprint has an introduction by Douglas McKie.)

—— (1991) *The Early Essays and Ethics of Robert Boyle*, ed. J. Harwood, Carbondale, IL: Illinois University Press. (Contains selections from Boyle's early ethical and theological manuscripts. Harwood's introduction provides helpful information concerning the historical context in which these papers were composed.)

—— (1992) *The Letters and Papers of Robert Boyle*, Bethesda, MD: University Press of America. (A microfilm collection of all of Boyle's surviving manuscripts, notebooks and correspondence housed at the Royal Society of London. A separate introduction and guide to the manuscript material by Michael Hunter is also available.)

References and further reading

Alexander, P. (1985) *Ideas, Qualities and Corpuscles: Locke and Boyle on the External World*, Cambridge: Cambridge University Press. (An interesting and thorough examination of Boyle's views on the experimental investigation of the corpuscular constitution of matter and how his work influenced John Locke.)

Conant, J.B. (1970) 'Robert Boyle's Experiments in Pneumatics', in *Harvard Case Histories in Experimental Science*, vol. 1, Cambridge, MA: Harvard University Press. (Contains an edited version of Boyle's New Experiments Physico-Mechanical and a discussion of the methodological aspects of this work.)

Fulton, J. (1961) *A Bibliography of Robert Boyle*, London: Oxford University Press. (Contains the most complete bibliography of Boyle's works as well as secondary works published about Boyle up to 1940.)

Hall, M.B. (1958) *Robert Boyle and Seventeenth-Century Chemistry*, Cambridge: Cambridge University Press. (A detailed examination of Boyle's role in the chemical revolution of the seventeenth century.)

—— (1965) *Robert Boyle on Natural Philosophy: An Essay with Selections from His Writings*, Bloomington, IN: Indiana University Press. (Contains a brief account of Boyle's life followed by a discussion of his work. A detailed and well-documented study that contains substantial excerpts from Boyle's published works.)

Hunter, M. (ed.) (1994) *Robert Boyle Reconsidered*, Cambridge: Cambridge University Press. (Contains a helpful introductory essay by Hunter that discusses scholarship on Boyle prior to 1994. The individual essays cover Boyle's experimental, philosophical and theological works as well as his intellectual and social context. Contains a complete bibliography of all works published on Boyle between 1940 and 1993.)

Jacob, J.R. (1977) *Robert Boyle and the English Revolution*, New York: Franklin. (Speculates about the political motivations behind Boyle's scientific and religious views based upon early manuscript material and the known political ambitions of some of Boyle's associates.)

Maddison, R.E.W. (1969) *The Life of the Honourable Robert Boyle*, New York: Barnes & Noble. (The most definitive life of Boyle, corrects some errors contained in Birch's account as well as supplementing it with material from the private papers of Boyle's relations.)

Sargent, R.-M. (1995) *The Diffident Naturalist: Robert Boyle and the Philosophy of Experiment*, Chicago, IL: University of Chicago Press. (An analysis of Boyle's development and practice of experimental methodology from a philosophical perspective.)

Shapin, S. and Schaffer, S. (1985) *Leviathan and the Air-pump: Hobbes, Boyle, and the Experimental Life*, Princeton, NJ: Princeton University Press. (Discusses the controversy surrounding Boyle's pneumatic experiments primarily from the point of view of his critics, and focuses upon the political implications of the debates.)

Wojcik, J.W. (1997) *Robert Boyle and the Limits of Reason*, Cambridge: Cambridge University Press. (Examines Boyle's theological and philosophical works in the historical context of the religious debates in seventeenth-century England.)

ROSE-MARY SARGENT

BRACKETING

see PHENOMENOLOGY, EPISTEMIC ISSUES IN

BRADLEY, FRANCIS HERBERT (1846–1924)

Bradley was the most famous and philosophically the most influential of the British Idealists, who had a marked impact on British philosophy in the later nineteenth and earlier twentieth centuries. They looked for inspiration less to their British predecessors than to Kant and Hegel, though Bradley owed as much to lesser German philosophers such as R.H. Lotze, J.F. Herbart and C. Sigwart.

Bradley is most famous for his metaphysics. He argued that our ordinary conceptions of the world conceal contradictions. His radical alternative can be summarized as a combination of monism (that is, reality is one, there are no real separate things) and absolute idealism (that is, reality is idea, or consists of experience – but not the experience of any one individual, for this is forbidden by the monism). This metaphysics is said to have influenced the poetry of T.S. Eliot. But he also made notable contributions to philosophy of history, to ethics and to the philosophy of logic, especially of a critical kind. His critique of hedonism – the view that the goal of morality is the maximization of pleasure – is still one of the best available. Some of his views on logic, for instance, that the grammatical subject of a sentence may not be what the sentence is really about, became standard through their acceptance by Bertrand Russell, an acceptance which survived Russell's repudiation of idealist logic and metaphysics around the turn of the century. Russell's and G.E. Moore's subsequent disparaging attacks on Bradley's views signalled the return to dominance in England of pluralist (that is, non-monist) doctrines in the tradition of Hume and J.S. Mill, and, perhaps even more significantly, the replacement in philosophy of Bradley's richly metaphorical literary style and of his confidence in the metaphysician's right to adjudicate on the ultimate truth with something more like plain speaking and a renewed deference to science and mathematics.

Bradley's contemporary reputation was that of the greatest English philosopher of his generation. This status did not long survive his death, and the relative dearth of serious discussion of his work until more general interest revived in the 1970s has meant that the incidental textbook references to some of his most characteristic and significant views, for example, on relations and on truth, are often based on hostile and misleading caricatures.

1 Life and works
2 Philosophy of history
3 Ethics

4 Logic
5 Metaphysics

1 Life and works

Bradley was born in Clapham, England, on 30 January 1846. The literary critic A.C. Bradley was a younger brother. Educated at fee-paying schools and University College, Oxford (where he studied classical languages and literature, and ancient history and philosophy), he began the study of German, and is recorded to have read some at least of Kant's *Critique*, while still at school. In 1870 he was elected to a fellowship requiring no teaching and terminable only on marriage, at Merton College, Oxford. Six months later he suffered a severe inflammation of the kidneys: he had little public life thereafter, for cold, fatigue or stress was apt to make him ill. He occupied his fellowship until his death from blood poisoning on 18 September 1924. His major works are *Ethical Studies* (1876), *The Principles of Logic* (1883), *Appearance and Reality* (1893), *Essays on Truth and Reality* (1914) and the posthumously published *Collected Essays* (1935). He was awarded honours both foreign and domestic, including the Order of Merit. Though a freethinker, he was said to be politically conservative. His writings reveal a character far from narrowly intellectual.

2 Philosophy of history

Bradley's first publication was the pamphlet 'The Presuppositions of Critical History' (1874). Though perhaps the earliest major theoretical study in English of the notion of historical fact, it had little impact at the time, but the kind of position it takes has been subsequently influential, especially in religious studies. Bradley's acknowledged sources were German historians of the origins of Christianity, but his position resembles that of Hume on miracles in its scepticism concerning astonishing historical reports. The question raised by Bradley's argument – by what criterion should the credibility of historical testimony be judged? – stimulated the reflections of such philosophers as R.G. Collingwood. This essay provides a good introductory sample of Bradley's writing: characteristic in its highly-charged style, frequent obscurity and disdain of example, it also anticipates some of his later holistic themes, for example, the fallibility of any individual judgment and the rejection of correspondence notions of truth.

3 Ethics

Greater recognition came with *Ethical Studies*, a work which more than any of his others reveals Hegel's influence in both its ideas and its dialectical construction. This construction means that Bradley's prefatory remark that the essays 'must be read in the order in which they stand' should be taken seriously. Although the third essay is a *locus classicus* of arguments against hedonistic utilitarianism (see HEDONISM; PLEASURE §5; UTILITARIANISM) and the fifth presents with some passion a social conception of the moral life, the common idea that these two can be read in isolation as representing Bradley's own final views is mistaken. What *Ethical Studies* aimed at was a gradual working-out of an account of morality which, unlike the prevalent utilitarianism, did full justice to ordinary moral ideas and did not rely on a deficient notion of the self. (One of the book's governing notions is that ordinary moral thinking is not to be displaced by the fruits of moral philosophy.) This development originates in an examination of the 'vulgar' notion of moral responsibility, and a rejection of both determinism and indeterminism as one-sided views obtained by concentrating on different aspects of human action which coexist unproblematically but are made to appear as conflicting by abstraction from the whole (see FREE WILL §§1–2, 4). It continues in the second essay by asking 'Why should I be moral?' His answer is that the moral end for each of us is self-realization, but as he holds all action to be self-realization whether the action be wicked or otherwise, he has to explain the kind of self-realization which is morality's goal: it is to realize oneself as an infinite whole (see SELF-REALIZATION). One thing this may mean is that the fully moral self is not to be limited by any other self: that is, one aim of morality is the resolution of conflict between one's good and bad selves in favour of the former. Another is that self-realization can be accomplished only through the mutual dependence of self and society. But what it amounts to is meant to be revealed through consideration of representative philosophical theories, each of which, through its one-sidedness, is more or less unsatisfactory as it stands. One is hedonistic utilitarianism, from which, roughly speaking, Bradley drops the hedonism and individualism but retains the utilitarianism (being prepared to regard happiness as the goal of morality (see HAPPINESS) provided it is not thought of as some independently identifiable state which could just as well be attained by some more convenient means, that is, as externally related to morality itself). Next comes a Kantian ethics of duty, from which he retains the idea that the performance of *duties* is essential to morality, while dropping the notion that duty should be done for duty's sake rather than because of the particular content of the individual duty (see DUTY;

KANTIAN ETHICS). Both these theories come to grief because of erroneous views about the nature of the self, which, Bradley thinks, is a concrete universal and essentially social. In the fifth essay he develops a Hegelian account of morality according to which the self is fully realized by playing its role in the social organism. While Bradley recognizes this account to be inadequate, because, for example, communities themselves can have moral imperfections, it nevertheless differs in status from the views he considered previously, for he regards it as merely requiring supplementation (undertaken in the next essay on ideal morality). But he does not make clear how self-realization as a part of the social organism can be an intelligible moral demand, for Bradley's argument against social contract theories – that they presuppose an impossible metaphysics of persons, in that the parties to the contract are only contingently social – requires him to hold that the self is already and necessarily social. Yet perhaps this does not matter, for the book closes by condemning morality itself as ultimately a self-contradictory enterprise, depending for its existence on the existence of the evil it seeks to overcome, and thus rendering impossible the ultimate realization of the ideal self, a realization obtainable only in religion.

Some of Bradley's metaphysical apparatus is deployed in his moral philosophy, along with anticipations of his idealism and hostility to external relations. One example is the concrete universal, a notion which arises from his rejection of the standard universal–particular distinction, on the grounds that this distinction abstracts unreal elements (that is, those incapable of independent existence) from actual things. Thus when we attribute greenness to a leaf, both the particular (the leaf without its greenness) to which the greenness is attributed and the universal (the greenness without the leaf) are figments of the intellect; any impression of their independent existence arises from the mechanisms of thought. Thought has to divide reality up like this in order to function at all, but thereby distorts its nature. The concrete universal and the concrete particular are both the one individual thing: a leaf is universal in collecting together diverse abstract particulars, such as its various stages over time, and particular in its being distinct from other leaves. Communities and individual persons are likewise concrete universals, the former retaining their identities over many generations, the latter through many actions, and Bradley thought moral philosophy had to recognize this. Although the expression 'concrete universal' rarely figures in Bradley's work subsequent to *The Principles of Logic*, the idea involved is fundamental to his thought in both logic and metaphysics in its encapsulation of the idea that abstraction is falsification (see HEGEL, G.W.F. §6; UNIVERSALS).

4 Logic

The Principles of Logic looks strange to anyone whose conception of logic has been shaped by the formalism of Frege and Russell. Devoid of mathematically inspired methods, of axioms and rules of inference, it proves no theorems and employs no calculi. Often the text seems contaminated with discussion of psychological matters. Familiar terms, such as 'identity of indiscernibles', are used in ways unfamiliar enough to make one unsure whether they have much to do with what other people mean by them, and the terminology is often bewilderingly loose. Nevertheless, and despite its idealist vocabulary and florid metaphor, its title is apposite, for the book is devoted to issues fundamental to logic. It brought the notion of meaning, for instance, to the centre of the philosophical stage; and the absence of calculi is at least partly the result of a principled opposition to formal logic and the mathematicization of reasoning on the grounds that inference was thereby detached from the practice of science and the acquisition of knowledge. Some of its doctrines have been greatly influential, often via their impact on Russell, such as the suggestion that the logical form of universal sentences is hypothetical (a prototypical instance of the distinction between logical and grammatical form). It is a transitional work, expressing in the vocabulary of ideas and judgments views which were to usher in the era of meanings, sentences and propositions.

Much of the book is polemical, and, as in *Ethical Studies*, Bradley develops his own views gradually through criticism of others. It is divided into three, the first dealing with judgment and the remainder with inference. He begins by arguing that atomists such as Hume, who thought of judgments in terms of ideas, failed to distinguish the sense of 'idea' in which ideas are important to logic: they are not datable occurrences like mental images but abstract universals. He is thus often portrayed as rejecting psychologism in logic, but this is an exaggeration, for he thinks of logic's subject matter as mental acts, not as sentences, or propositions in the sense of Russell or of Moore. He then rejects some standard accounts of judgment. He complains that a subject–predicate account cannot do justice to relational judgments, and that thinking of judgment as the coupling of two ideas makes it impossible to see how judgment can be about anything real, since all the ingredients of judgments are universal and belong to the realm of idea, whereas reality is stubbornly particular and actual. As Bradley also argued that there could be no unique designation of individuals, even grammatical names and demonstratives being disguised general terms, he may have planted the seed of Russell's elimination of grammatically proper names by application of the Theory of Definite Descriptions (see RUSSELL, B.A.W.). Bradley's own account of judgment is 'the act which refers an ideal content...to a reality beyond the act'. (By 'ideal content' he means a universal abstracted from a mental image; later he realized that this overestimates the role of mental imagery in judgment.)

When Bradley turns to inference, his targets remain the same. He complains that the mathematical logics of his time cannot represent valid relational inferences. He rejects Hume's account of inference in terms of the association of ideas on the grounds that Hume's ideas, as datable particulars, are fleeting entities which cannot be revived by association (see HUME, D. §2). Association is possible between ideas only if they are universals. (He calls this process 'redintegration'.) He rejects both syllogistic and Mill's methods of induction for failing to recognize that reasoning can proceed only on the basis of the generality implicit in the universals essential to inference (see INDUCTIVE INFERENCE). His own account of inference is that it is 'ideal experiment': ideal in that it belongs to thought, experiment in that its results are not guaranteed in advance by a complete set of logical laws which infallibly determine their own application.

Underlying much of Bradley's criticism of previous accounts of judgment and inference is hostility to psychological atomism, whose particulars he regarded not as concrete universals, realities in their own right, but as abstractions from the continuous whole which is psychological life. But likewise he regarded judgments themselves as infected with abstraction, since their subject matter is necessarily selected from a background and accordingly falsifies reality. Thus the objections which destroy misleading accounts of logic start to threaten logic itself, and, consistently, the book ends by suggesting that no inference is ever really valid and no judgment ever really true. Here it spills over into the metaphysics it had ostensibly tried to avoid. Bradley's view is that logic presupposes a 'copy' (correspondence) theory of truth, but it is clear that he thinks this theory metaphysically inadequate, a view he develops in *Essays on Truth and Reality*, where he argues for 'the identity of truth knowledge and reality'. Thus the claim that Bradley held a coherence theory of truth (endlessly repeated in textbooks) is mistaken. (Because he held reality to be a unified whole, he thought the *test* of truth to be 'system', which includes what is commonly meant by coherence (see TRUTH, COHERENCE THEORY OF §1).)

This identity theory of truth, that for a thought to be true is for it to be identical with the logical subject of which it is predicated – reality itself – has led to his being unfairly accused of confusing predication with identity. His relation to the correspondence theory exemplifies a constant difficulty in trying to understand Bradley: he adopts various theories and suggestions temporarily only to abandon them as ultimately unsatisfactory, so that it can be hard to work out his commitments.

5 Metaphysics

Bradley's metaphysics gets its fullest exposition in *Appearance and Reality*, though this needs to be considered in the light of subsequent essays. It is divided into two books. The first, 'Appearance', is brief and destructive. It argues that 'the ideas by which we try to understand the universe' all involve us ultimately in contradiction. Some of these are philosophical, such as the suggestion that only primary qualities are real, while others belong to common sense, such as motion, space, time, relation, thing and self. The second, 'Reality', concerns the Absolute, the ultimate, unconditioned reality, undistorted by human conceptualization (see ABSOLUTE, THE).

Many of the arguments in Book I are not unique to Bradley and make only part of his case: for example, primary qualities are inconceivable without secondary, motion involves paradoxes. But the arguments of the chapter 'Relation and Quality', which in generalized form allege that relations are unintelligible either with or without their terms, and terms unintelligible with or without their relations, are of a different order. Bradley himself said that a grasp of these arguments would lead the reader to condemn 'the great mass of phenomena', and it is clear that his views on relations are central to his thought. Thus it is unfortunate that the arguments are so sketchily and unconvincingly presented that even sympathetic commentators have found it hard to defend him. In part this is because the arguments are often read as designed to prove the doctrine of the internality of all relations (that is, their reducibility to qualities or their holding necessarily, depending on the sense of 'internal'). This is a misreading, but it is understandable, for Bradley flirted with the doctrine of internality in *Appearance and Reality*, only repudiating it in later works less frequently read, like the unfinished essay 'Relations'. Also he rejected the reality of external relations, and it is natural to interpret this as adherence to the doctrine of internality. But his considered view was that neither external nor internal relations are real. One of his main arguments for this conclusion was that if relations were another kind of real thing along with their terms, then a further relation would be required to relate them to the terms (and so on, *ad infinitum*). It is clear from this and from his own explanation that to be real is to be a substantial individual, that the denial of the reality of relations is the denial that they are independent existents (see SUBSTANCE). But some have thought he meant that all relational judgments are false, for instance, that it is false that Galileo preceded Newton. And Bradley's theory of truth gives credence to such suggestions, for by that theory no ordinary judgment is perfectly true, so that to someone who assumes that truth is two-valued, his claim looks to be that such judgments are all false. But Bradley thought truth admitted of degrees, and that, provided we confine ourselves to everyday purposes and do not try to meet the exacting demands of metaphysics, it is true that Galileo preceded Newton. The imperfection of this truth is nothing to do with the judgment's being relational as opposed to predicative. A perfect truth would be one which did not abstract from reality at all. Such a complete description would have to be identical with reality itself and thus would no longer be a *judgment*. On Bradley's view, then, the final truth about reality is literally and in principle inexpressible.

An outline, though, is possible. When Bradley comes to ask what reality is, his answer is that it is experience, in a wide sense of that term: 'Feeling, thought and volition (any groups under which we class psychological phenomena) are all the material of existence, and there is no other material, actual or even possible' ([1897] 1930: 127) (see IDEALISM). His insouciantly brief argument for this challenges the reader to think otherwise without self-contradiction; he is more concerned to make clear that reality is not the experience of his individual mind, and that his doctrine is not solipsistic.

Bradley's criterion of reality is the absence of contradiction, and as he argues that the distinctions necessarily employed in judgment introduce contradiction, it follows that thought cannot capture reality. Nor can anything involving relatedness. Thus reality must be a non-relational unity, one which contains diversity because room must be found for appearances themselves. How? For illustration, Bradley appeals to a pre-conceptual state of immediate experience in which there are differences but no separations and from which the cognitive consciousness arises by imposing distinctions upon the differences. Reality, he thinks, is like this, except in transcending rather than falling short of thought, including everything in one comprehensive and harmonious whole (see MONISM). Wollheim suggests that the best analogy for the relation of appearances to the Absolute is that of a painting (another might be an ecosystem): particular segments of the canvas would be falsified, even made ugly, by abstraction from the whole to which they contribute, yet that character which makes for ugliness in isolation may nevertheless be itself beautiful in its surroundings and essential to the beauty of the whole. Bradley rejects the demand for detailed explanations of how phenomena like error are reconcilable with the Absolute, trying to shift the burden of proof to those who profess confidence in their incompatibility. His general answer is that anything that exists, even evil, is somehow real and thus belongs to the Absolute, which comprehends and transcends both good and evil (as well as religion): it is neither, but is further from the latter than the former.

Few philosophers have found Bradley's positive metaphysics persuasive. But it stands as a permanent challenge to the capacity of discursive thought to represent the world as it is in itself, a challenge posed by turning the mechanisms of thought upon themselves and demanding that they meet their own standards.

See also: BOSANQUET, B.; GREEN, T.H.; HEGELIANISM §5; HERBART, J.F.; JAMES, W.; LOTZE, R.H.; MOORE, G.E. §§1–2

List of works

Bradley's works are best consulted in the latest of the editions mentioned. These are the ones usually cited in recent discussion; they are also the most useful in that, while the earlier text is usually left intact, Bradley's later thoughts are added in the form of notes, appendices and essays. The library of Merton College, Oxford, holds Bradley's unpublished papers, notebooks and letters received. The Russell Archives at McMaster University contain letters from Bradley to Russell (some interesting extracts appear in *The Collected Papers of Bertrand Russell*, vol. 6, 349–53), and the John Rylands Library of the University of Manchester has letters from Bradley to Samuel Alexander.

Bradley, F.H. (1876, 1927) *Ethical Studies*, Oxford: Clarendon Press. (The second edition, published posthumously, contains unfinished notes by Bradley; the text is otherwise that of the first.)

—— (1883, 1922) *The Principles of Logic*, London: Oxford University Press. (The second, revised edition adds extensive commentary and terminal essays to the text of the first. Out of print at the time of writing.)

—— (1893, 1897) *Appearance and Reality*, London: Swan Sonnenschein. (The second edition contains a substantial and important Appendix. The most commonly encountered version now is the so-called 'ninth impression' of 1930, on which all subsequent printings have been based. This was published in Oxford at the Clarendon Press after the rights were secured from George Allen & Unwin, which as George Allen had taken over Swan Sonnenschein. This ninth impression is a textually corrected version of the second edition, but has a completely different pagination. Out of print at the time of writing.)

—— (1914) *Essays on Truth and Reality*, Oxford: Clarendon Press. (Mostly published in *Mind* from 1899 onwards, these are major essays containing developments of Bradley's logic and metaphysics, incisive criticism of William James and Bertrand Russell, and reflections on religion. Out of print at the time of writing.)

—— (1930) *Aphorisms*, Oxford: privately printed at the Clarendon press; Bristol: Thoemmes Press, 1993, facsimile edn. (The modern edition is bound together with 'The Presuppositions of Critical History' and contains an introduction to the latter by Guy Stock.)

—— (1935) *Collected Essays*, Oxford: Clarendon Press. (Contains the two pamphlets 'The Presuppositions of Critical History' (1874) and 'Mr Sidgwick's Hedonism' (1877) as well as the valuable unfinished essay 'Relations' and a good bibliography of Bradley's published works. Out of print at the time of writing.)

—— (1994) *Writings on Logic and Metaphysics*, ed. and with intros by J.W. Allard and G. Stock, Oxford: Oxford University Press. (Contains well-chosen extracts from the *Logic*, *Appearance and Reality* and *Essays on Truth and Reality*. The helpful introductions are both general and topic-specific; this is a very useful edition for undergraduates.)

References and further reading

Bradley Studies (1995–), Harris Manchester College, Oxford. (This journal 'aims to publish critical and scholarly articles on philosophical issues arising from Bradley's writings and from those of related authors' and 'to include each year an ongoing list of what has been published on Bradley and related themes'.)

Campbell, C.A. (1931) *Scepticism and Construction: Bradley's Sceptical Principle as the Basis of Constructive Philosophy*, London: George Allen & Unwin. (One of the clearest pictures of Bradley's metaphysics from within his own tradition. Critical but sympathetic. Out of print.)

Candlish, S. (1978) 'Bradley on My Station and Its Duties', *Australasian Journal of Philosophy* 56 (2): 155–70. (A critical exposition of the place of Bradley's most famous essay in his moral thought, relating it also to his metaphysics. Suitable for undergraduates.)

—— (1989) 'The Truth about F.H. Bradley', *Mind*, 98 (391): 331–48. (On analytic philosophy's distorted picture of Bradley, and his theory of truth; intelligible to advanced undergraduates.)

Horstmann, R.-P. (1984) *Ontologie und Relationen*, Königstein: Athenäum. (A thorough discussion, in German, of the treatment of relations by Bradley, Hegel and Russell, concluding in favour of Hegel. A work for scholars.)

Ingardia, R. (ed.) (1991) *Bradley: A Research Bibliography*, Bowling Green, OH: Philosophy Documentation Center. (Indexes primary sources, books, articles, dissertations, book reviews. Littered with trivial errors, but very comprehensive. Many of the articles attributed to Cresswell are by Crossley.)

Mander, W.J. (1994) *An Introduction to Bradley's Metaphysics*, Oxford: Clarendon Press. (Intended for serious beginners, but also of scholarly interest. Draws on such reassessments of Bradley as those in Manser and Stock (below) and covers Bradley's best known ideas and arguments.)

—— (ed.) (1996) *Perspectives on the Logic and Metaphysics of F.H. Bradley*, Bristol: Thoemmes Press. (Papers from the 1993 F.H. Bradley Colloquium, accessible to advanced undergraduates.)

Manser, A. (1983) *Bradley's Logic*, Oxford: Blackwell. (A study of *The Principles of Logic* with particular attention to its historical background, which argues that the original text of 1883 is free of the later metaphysics and unfairly neglected. Not difficult, but presupposes knowledge of twentieth century analytic philosophy. Out of print.)

Manser, A. and Stock, G. (eds) (1984) *The Philosophy of F.H. Bradley*, Oxford: Clarendon Press. (A well-reviewed collection of essays, covering the full range of Bradley's work, with a useful scene-setting editorial introduction. Suitable for advanced undergraduates. Reprinted in paperback in 1986.)

Nicholson, P. (1990) *The Political Philosophy of the British Idealists: Selected Studies*, Cambridge: Cambridge University Press. (Study I is an accurate and sympathetic but somewhat uncritical account of *Ethical Studies*, readable by beginners. There is an extensive bibliography.)

Passmore, J. (1969) 'Russell and Bradley', in R. Brown and C.D. Rollins (eds), *Contemporary Philosophy in Australia*, London: George Allen & Unwin.

(One of the most perceptive comparisons of the two philosophers, straightforwardly written and free of technicality. Out of print.)

Sprigge, T.L.S. (1993) *James and Bradley: American Truth and British Reality*, Chicago and La Salle, IL: Open Court. (A substantial critical comparison of the work of Bradley and William James, which pays more than usual attention to Bradley's views on religion, has a detailed summary of the philosophers' correspondence and gives chronologies listing their works by year of appearance. Clearly written but very long.)

Stock, G. (ed.) (1997) *Appearance versus Reality*, Oxford: Clarendon Press. (Originating in the F.H. Bradley Colloquium 1993, a collection of major articles on the metaphysics and logic, plus other material, accessible to advanced undergraduates.)

Taylor, A.E. (1924–5) 'Francis Herbert Bradley, 1846–1924', *Proceedings of the British Academy* 11 (2): 458–68. (The standard source for biographical information, some of which was obtained with family help.)

Wollheim, R. (1956) 'F.H. Bradley', in Ayer, A.J. *et al.*, *The Revolution in Philosophy*, London: Macmillan, 12–25. (Perhaps the best short depiction of central themes in Bradley's logic and metaphysics, written with great clarity and insight; accessible to complete beginners. Out of print.)

—— (1969) *F.H. Bradley*, Harmondsworth: Penguin, 2nd edn. (For many years the standard text on Bradley. Accessible to undergraduates. Admirably clear and free of jargon, but should not be regarded as reliable. Out of print.)

STEWART CANDLISH

BRADWARDINE, THOMAS (*c.*1300–49)

Thomas Bradwardine was a leading figure in fourteenth-century philosophy and theology from 1328, when he completed De proportionibus velocitatum in motibus *(On the Ratios of Velocities in Motions), until his death in 1349, shortly after becoming Archbishop of Canterbury. His theory of ratios of velocities in motions was an important reinterpretation of Aristotle and was influential throughout Europe. The author of numerous mathematical and logical works, Bradwardine helped to initiate a style of natural philosophical analysis using a standard set of logical and mathematical tools. On the Continent, Nicole Oresme, Albert of Saxony and many others wrote works on the ratios of velocities in motions following Bradwardine's lead. In his* De futura contingentibus *(On Future Contingents) and* De causa Dei contra Pelagium *(On the Cause of God Against the Pelagians), Bradwardine staked positions emphasizing the symmetry of God's omniscience with respect to past, present and future.*

1 Life and works
2 Theory of ratios in motions
3 Other works

1 Life and works

Born around 1300, Bradwardine is known for his association with Merton College, Oxford, and it was probably while he was at Merton that he composed the treatises *De insolubilibus* (On Insolubles) *De incipit et desinit* (On 'It Begins' and 'It Ceases'), *De proportionibus velocitatum in motibus* (On the Ratios of Velocities in Motions), *De continuo* (On the Continuum), *Arithmetica speculativa* (Speculative Arithmetic), *Geometria speculativa* (Speculative Geometry) and possibly other logical works. In approximately 1332–3 Bradwardine, as a bachelor of theology, lectured on Peter Lombard's *Sentences*. Only fragments of these lectures remain, probably including what is known separately as *De futuribus contingentibus* (On Future Contingents). In 1335 Bradwardine became a member of the group of scholars surrounding Richard de Bury, Bishop of Durham. He became a Master of Theology in the late 1330s, was named chancellor of Saint Paul's Cathedral in London in 1337, chaplain to Edward III in 1339 and Archbishop of Canterbury in June 1349. The *De causa Dei contra Pelagium et de virtute causarum ad suos Mertonenses* (In Defence of God Against the Pelagians and On the Power of Causes), begun at Oxford, was completed in London probably in 1344 (see AUGUSTINIANISM).

2 Theory of ratios in motions

Within the arts faculty at Oxford, Bradwardine's greatest impact undoubtedly came from his *De proportionibus velocitatum in motibus*. Aristotle, in the *Physics*, had supposed that the velocities of motions are related to their causes in such a way that when the force causing a motion is multiplied, the velocity will be similarly multiplied. Likewise, Aristotle had supposed that when resistance to motion is multiplied, the velocity is, inversely, reduced in a like ratio. Aristotle's discussion of the relationships of forces, resistances and velocities served his purposes in arguing that a vacuum is impossible. If there were a vacuum, Aristotle argued, then an elemental heavy body falling in the vacuum would have no resistance, and hence an infinite velocity would result. Since an infinite velocity is a self-contradiction, a vacuum is impossible.

In *De proportionibus*, Bradwardine first laid out the theory of ratios familiar from the theory of musical ratios as found in BOETHIUS. He used this understanding of operations on ratios to reinterpret Aristotle's theory. Velocities vary, he said, as the ratio of force to resistance. When the ratio of force to resistance is 'doubled' the velocity is doubled, when the ratio is 'tripled' the velocity is tripled and so on, with the understanding that 'double' the ratio 3:1 is the ratio 9:1 (its square), and that 'triple' the ratio 2:1 is the ratio 8:1 (its cube). This new understanding of Aristotle's theory had the advantage of being expressed in similar words while avoiding a serious weakness of the theory itself, namely that it could not explain the mathematical relationships of forces and resistances in very slow motions. Everyone agreed that for motion to occur at all the force must be greater than the resistance. Suppose, then, that the ratio 2:1 produces a certain velocity. It follows on Aristotle's theory that the ratio of 1:1 should produce half that velocity, but in fact it produces no velocity at all, since the force is not greater than the resistance. Thus Aristotle's theory cannot account for any velocity smaller than half the velocity produced by the ratio 2:1. By contrast, Bradwardine's function provided values of the ratio of force to resistance greater than 1:1 for any velocity down to zero, since any root of a ratio greater than 1:1 is always a ratio greater than 1:1.

Bradwardine's proposed new function won immediate acceptance in universities all over Europe, beginning at Oxford where the so-called OXFORD CALCULATORS took it up. It also inspired people to quantify motions in every way possible. Bradwardine's function was assumed to hold for rotations as well as rectilinear motions, and for alterations, augmentations and diminutions as well as local motions. In Paris, Nicole ORESME and ALBERT OF SAXONY wrote treatises on ratios, building on Bradwardine's rule. Oresme used the theory to argue that since most ratios are incommensurable with one another, when ratios of ratios are understood in the Bradwardinian sense, the velocities of motion of the planets caused by ratios of force to resistance will also likely be incommensurable, meaning that planets will never return to exact conjunctions in the same location in the sky. Astrological predictions based on such repetitions of positions will therefore be impossible.

Taking the ratio of force to resistance as the measure of motion 'as if with respect to cause' (*tanquam penes causam*), philosophers then asked about the measure 'as if with respect to effect' (*tanquam penes effectum*). For instance, should a rotation be measured by the average velocity of the points of the rotating body or by the distance traversed by the fastest moved point, as Bradwardine had argued in the last book of *De proportionibus*? Learning how to operate with ratios as Bradwardine did became a standard part of the arts curriculum in many later medieval universities, and subsequently became part of the theology curriculum as well.

3 Other works

In contrast to the novelty of Bradwardine's *De proportionibus*, his *De continuo* argued for what were at the time well-established conclusions. As Aristotle had argued, no continuum is composed of indivisibles. Moreover, indivisibles such as points, lines, planes and instants, despite their use by mathematicians, do not exist in the real world (a position also taken by Ockham, Buridan and other fourteenth-century nominalists). However, although most scholastics believed that the composition of continua from indivisibles was inconsistent with both Euclidean geometry and Aristotelian physics, in the period just before Bradwardine no less a scholar than HENRY OF HARCLAY, Chancellor of Oxford, had been persuaded by theoretical considerations of God's knowledge that the points in a line must be immediate to each other. Harclay's defense of immediate indivisibles derived from the view proposed by Robert GROSSETESTE that God measures a line by intuiting the infinitely many mediate points contained within it. In Harclay's opinion, Grosseteste's view implied his own: if God intuits all the points in a line, Harclay argued, they must be immediate to each other.

Perhaps the most original aspect of Bradwardine's *De continuo* was his strategy for combatting indivisibilists (or 'atomists') of every kind. Instead of arguing in turn against each of the theories that posited the composition of continua from indivisibles, Bradwardine began in an axiomatic format and then argued against key theses combined in different ways by the different theories. Thus he argued first against immediately conjoined indivisibles, a thesis common to the Pythagoreans (see PYTHAGOREANISM), Harclay and Walter CHATTON. Then he argued against the composition of a continuum from finitely many indivisibles, a thesis maintained by the Pythagoreans and Chatton but not by Grosseteste or Harclay, proving his point by running through every known discipline or science. Turning next to the theory that a continuum is composed of infinitely many indivisibles, a view common to Harclay and Grosseteste, Bradwardine used both natural philosophical and mathematical arguments. A key conclusion in the axiomatic part of *De continuo* was that if one continuum has (infinitely or finitely many) immediate atoms, any continuum has them. This enabled Bradwardine to argue that if a line has immediate atoms, so do bodies, motion and time, and vice versa.

Despite the supposed reciprocity between conclusions in the different disciplines, natural philosophical arguments were fundamental to Bradwardine's project. What would happen to indivisible surfaces if a single body of water were divided in two or if two bodies of water were joined together? Would the division create new surfaces and the joining destroy them and, if so, what would cause such creation or destruction of indivisibles? It was in light of such physical considerations that Bradwardine in Part VIII of *De continuo* finally denied the existence of indivisibles altogether. Thus despite the prominence of mathematics in his work, Bradwardine remained an Aristotelian, implicitly assuming that natural philosophy gives a truer description of reality than mathematics.

Bradwardine's other mathematical and logical works do not seem to have been particularly notable. In *De insolubilibus*, Bradwardine may have been the first to suppose that insoluble propositions – for example, the liar paradox – imply not only their own falsity but also their own truth. In *De incipit et desinit*, Bradwardine not only restated standard views concerning first and last instants of permanent and successive things, but also raised questions about the relations of successive continua such as motion and time to future contingency. If, for instance, no motion has a last instant of being, then if a body is in motion at an instant, it will necessarily be true that it must continue in motion in the future, since the instant at which it is in motion cannot be the last instant. However, the continuation of its motion is, presumably, contingent. How then can the continuation of the motion after the present instant of motion be both necessary and contingent?

Bradwardine's *De futuris contingentibus* and *De causa Dei contra Pelagium* were directed against contemporaries who had argued that there are real future contingents despite God's omniscience and who had adopted a Pelagian position with regard to human action, admitting the possibility that human merit and willpower could lead to salvation without God's freely given grace (see PELAGIANISM). WILLIAM OF OCKHAM was the most prominent target of Bradwardine's arguments in *De futuris contingentibus*, and his major opponent in *De causa Dei contra Pelagium* was most likely Thomas Buckingham, who modified his own position as a result of Bradwardine's views.

Like *De continuo*, *De causa Dei contra Pelagium*, a work of 876 printed folio pages, has an unusual format, combining strings of conclusions with prolific quotations from authoritative authors. Admitting that earlier in his life the Pelagian position had seemed more reasonable to him, Bradwardine emphasized instead the necessity of grace. The revival of a Pelagian position among Bradwardine's contemporaries seems to have arisen in part from considerations of God's freedom. Could God choose to allow some individuals to lead meritorious lives without divine grace? To say no would seem to limit God's liberty.

In response to such a line of thought, Bradwardine reaffirmed God's power, goodness and immutability. God is the first and most immediate cause of everything that happens, including the choices humans make by their free wills. Being the cause of everything that happens, God causes evil as well as good, but this is only relative evil and contributes to the overall good (see EVIL, PROBLEM OF). Absolutely central to Bradwardine's argument was the assertion that God is eternal and therefore immutable: God is not in time, and any implication that he might 'change his mind' or be affected by human choices after they occur is mistaken (see GOD, CONCEPTS OF).

In *De consolatione philosophiae*, written in the early sixth century, BOETHIUS had attempted to address questions of God's foreknowledge and human free will by arguing that God's timeless knowledge of the future does not determine the future any more than human observation determines what is seen. Using the ideas of logical possibility introduced into the discussion of free will by DUNS SCOTUS – who had argued that for an act to be freely chosen it is not necessary that the individual making the choice ever actually make a different choice, only that it not be logically contradictory to have made a different choice – Bradwardine argued that God's relations to past, present and future are identical. God freely chooses how he designs the cosmos, though he does so only once. It is not logically contradictory that God could make a different choice, but he will not in fact do so since he is not in time. In a way beyond human comprehension, human free will and divine determination are said to be not inconsistent, but rather compatible with each other (see ETERNITY; FREE WILL; OMNIPOTENCE).

See also: AUGUSTINIANISM; NATURAL PHILOSOPHY, MEDIEVAL; OXFORD CALCULATORS

List of works

Bradwardine, Thomas (*c.*1322–5?) *De insolubilibus* (On Insolubles), ed. M.L. Roure in 'La problématique des propositions insolubles du XIIIe siècle et du début du XIVe, suivie de l'édition des traités de William Shyreswood, Walter Burleigh et Thomas Bradwardine', *Archives d'histoire doctrinale et littéraire du moyen âge* 37, 1970: 205–326. (Covers solutions to the problem of propositions that seem to falsify themselves, such as 'I am telling a lie.')

—— (c.1323–5) *De incipit et desinit* (On 'It Begins' and 'It Ceases'), ed. L.O. Nielsen, *Cahiers de l'Institut du moyen âge grec et latin* 42, 1982: 1–83. (Bradwardine's contribution to the common fourteenth-century problem of assigning intrinsic or extrinsic temporal limits to entities and/or processes.)

—— (c.1323–5) *Geometria speculativa* (Speculative Geometry), ed. and trans. A.G. Molland, *Thomas Bradwardine, Geometria Speculativa*, Wiesbaden: Franz Steiner Verlag, 1989. (For an analysis of the significance of this work, see A.G. Molland (1978) 'An Examination of Bradwardine's Geometry', *Archive for History of Exact Sciences* 19: 113–175.)

—— (c.1323–5) *Arithmetica speculativa* (Speculative Arithmetic), Paris, 1495. (Following this edition the work was reprinted many times.)

—— (1328) *De proportionibus velocitatum in motibus* (On the Ratios of Velocities in Motions), ed. and trans. H.L. Crosby, Jr in *Thomas of Bradwardine: His Tractatus de Proportionibus*, Madison, WI: University of Wisconsin Press, 1955. (Bradwardine's extremely influential exposition of one traditional interpretation of the Euclidean theory of operations on ratios, along with its application to the Aristotelian problem of the relations of forces, resistances and velocities in motions.)

—— (c.1328–35) *De continuo* (On the Continuum), ed. J.E. Murdoch in 'Geometry and the Continuum in the Fourteenth Century: A Philosophical Analysis of Thomas Bradwardine's *Tractatus de continuo*', Ph.D. thesis, University of Wisconsin, 1957. (For a description of this work, with Latin text of the conclusions, see J.E. Murdoch , 'Thomas Bradwardine: Mathematics and Continuity in the Fourteenth Century', in E. Grant and J.E. Murdoch (eds) *Mathematics and its Applications to Science and Natural Philosophy in the Middle Ages*, Cambridge: Cambridge University Press, 1984, 103–37.)

—— (c.1332–3) *De futuris contingentibus* (On Future Contingents), ed. J.-F. Genest, *Recherches augustiniennes* 14, 1979: 249–336. (See Genest (1992) for a description of what the issues were, with regard to future contingents, for Bradwardine and other fourteenth-century thinkers.)

—— (c.1332–3) Commentary on the *Sentences* of Peter Lombard. (Previously thought to be lost, but some questions in MS Paris Bibl. Nat. lat. 15805, f. 40-49v, identified as coming from Bradwardine, are discussed in J.-F. Genest and K. Tachau, 'La lecture de Thomas Bradwardine sur les Sentences', *Archives d'histoire doctrinale et littéraire du moyen âge* 57, 1990: 301–6. The *De futuris contingentibus* may have been derived from this commentary.)

—— (1344) *De causa Dei contra Pelagium et de virtute causarum ad suos Mertonenses, libri tres* (In Defense of God Against the Pelagians and On the Power of Causes), ed. H. Savile, London: ex officina Nortoniana apud Ioannem Billium, 1618; repr. Frankfurt: Minerva, 1964.

References and further reading

Dolnikowski, E.W. (1995) *Thomas Bradwardine: A View of Time and a Vision of Eternity in Fourteenth-Century Thought*, Leiden: Brill. (Links Bradwardine's mathematics, logic, natural philosophy and theology through his concept of time.)

Genest, J.-F. (1992) *Prédétermination et Liberté Crée à Oxford au XIVe Siècle. Buckingham contra Bradwardine* (Predetermination and Created Liberty at Oxford in the Fourteenth Century: Buckingham against Bradwardine), Paris: Vrin. (Unravels existing confusions concerning Bradwardine's position on the controverted issues of God's predetermination and free will and edits questions of his main opponent, Thomas Buckingham.)

Knuuttila, S. (1982) 'Modal Logic', in N. Kretzmann, A. Kenny and J. Pinborg (eds) *The Cambridge History of Later Medieval Philosophy*, Cambridge: Cambridge University Press, 342–57. (For understanding concepts of necessity, contingency and possibility presupposed by Bradwardine's *De causa Dei*.)

Molland, A.G. (1996) 'Addressing Ancient Authority: Thomas Bradwardine and Prisca Sapientia', *Annals of Science* 53: 213–33. (Considers Bradwardine's attitudes about authority and the relations of science and religion on the basis of *De causa Dei*.)

Murdoch, J.E. (1970) 'Bradwardine, Thomas', in *Dictionary of Scientific Biography*, vol. 2, New York: Charles Scribner's Sons, 390–7. (A description of Bradwardine's mathematical and scientific work, with references to the standard earlier books and articles on Bradwardine.)

Normore, C. (1982) 'Future Contingents', in N. Kretzmann, A. Kenny and J. Pinborg (eds) *The Cambridge History of Later Medieval Philosophy*, Cambridge: Cambridge University Press, 358–81. (Essential contextual background for understanding Bradwardine on future contingents and on human free will.)

Oberman, H. and Weisheipl, J.A. (1958) 'The 'Sermo Epinicius' ascribed to Thomas Bradwardine

(1346)', *Archives d'histoire doctrinale et littéraire du moyen âge* 26: 295–329. (Contains Weisheipl's reconstruction of the time line of Bradwardine's works, as well as the text of Bradwardine's sermon.)

Sbrozi, M. (1990) 'Metodo matematico e pensiero teologico nel "De causa Dei" di Thomas Bradwardine' (Mathematical Method and Theological Thinking in *De causa Dei* of Thomas Bradwardine), *Studi Medievali*, serie terza, XXXI: 143–91. (Argues that the axiomatic form (*more geometrico*) of *De causa Dei* reflects Bradwardine's view that God's knowledge is atemporal, or in other words that God's knowledge of future contingents does not differ in kind from God's knowledge of past and present.)

EDITH DUDLEY SYLLA